Coleman

INSPIRED BY NATURE™

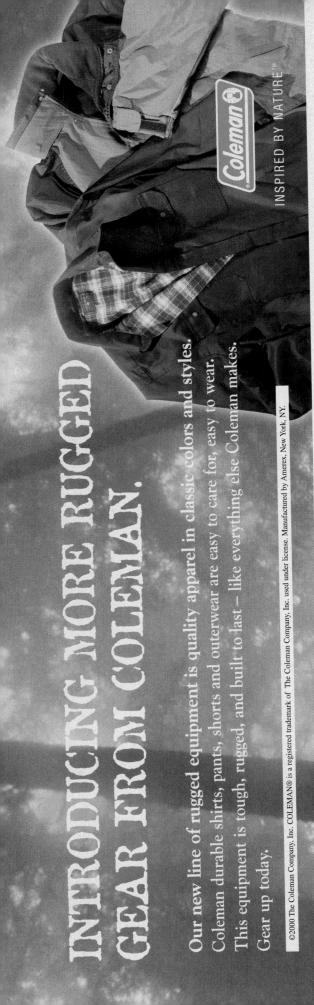

UPDATES AND SUGGESTIONS FOR FUTURE EDITIONS OF THE DIRECTORY

Please include your name and contact information with your submissions.

by mail: Our Forests, Inc.
                  P.O. Box 1344
                  Whitefish, Montana 59937

by e-mail: mail@ournationalforests.com

Index

Using this directory

There are over 4,300 National Forest campgrounds across the United States—tucked in remote canyons, among dense forests, alongside lakes and streams or on mountaintops. While some are popular and well-known, many of these campgrounds are obscure gems, seldom visited. This directory will help you find National Forest campgrounds that best fit your needs and help you discover some great places and experiences.

The book is organized by state first. In each state National Forests are listed in alphabetical order with a highlight summary from that forest. After each forest summary, a listing of campgrounds follows.

Maps for each forest provide navigation to the general location of campgrounds. Many city and town names are included on the maps to help you approximate the locations of campgrounds in relation to surrounding landmarks. The maps are not intended to direct you to a campground's exact location. Driving directions to each campground are provided in the campground listings, with directions from the nearest town. A state highway map may be useful to use in conjunction with the directory for finding some campgrounds.

On pages two and three of this directory you will find a national map with National Forest names and locator pins. This is to assist you in locating names of National Forests in the area you are traveling as well as find the page with the specific map and campground listings in this directory.

Additional Content

NATIONAL FOREST LOCATOR MAP
Pages 2 & 3

FINDING A CAMPGROUND
Page 4

READING THE LISTINGS
Page 4

MAKING RESERVATIONS
Page 4

NATIONAL FOREST CAMPGROUND RULES
Page 5

A special thanks to the great people at the US Forest Service as well as to the hundreds of individuals across the country who helped contribute information for this directory, and to the people at The Coleman Company for their vision and support in making this book a reality.

Project Manager
John Frandsen

Information Manager
Joel Stevenson

Information Specialists
Sarah Goebel
Tina Bruni
Barbara Simon
Sheila Parker

Design and Production
John Bonner
Brandon Goodin
Deborah Schatz
Rich Kurth
Joli Christensen

The National Forest Campground and Recreation Directory is produced by Our Forests, Inc. in cooperation with The Coleman Company and The Globe Pequot Press. Every effort was made to present accurate information at the time of printing. Price and use information is subject to change at any time. Our Forests, Inc, The Coleman Company, Inc. and The Globe Pequot Press, and the authors of this book assume no liability for accidents happening to, or injuries sustained by readers who engage in any of the activities described in this book.

Cover: Redfish Lake, Sawtooth National Forest, Idaho
Michael Sedam Photo

ID #   Forest Name — Page #

National

Forest Finder

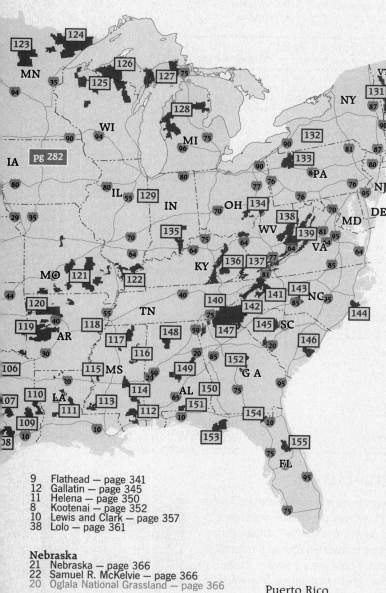

National Forest sites are found on pages 6 - 620 marked with green tabs.

Army Corps Recreation Lakes facilities are found on pages 621 - 641 marked with red tabs.

Puerto Rico

Finding Campgrounds

The maps in this directory provide the general locations of National Forest campgrounds and nearby towns. Often you will notice a number of campgrounds clustered in a small area. On the maps, this area is indicated by a white square with a line linking the square to a list of numbers. These numbers correspond to the numbers on each campground listing on the pages following the maps.

Each campground has a description as well as driving directions from a near town. Usually, you will be able to find a campground using the map in the book and the driving directions on the campground's listing. In other instances you may need to refer to a state highway map or travel atlas to help you find a campground.

Many National Forest campgrounds are in remote locations and require high-clearance vehicles to access them. Some of the campgrounds listed in this directory require that you hike, take a boat, or even ride an airplane to access them! Please read the campground descriptions and directions carefully. Don't hesitate to inquire locally at a forest ranger office (telephone numbers are indicated on the maps) or with locals before driving far into the backcountry to find a campground.

However, don't let the rugged, remote and obscure locations of some of these campgrounds keep you away. Some of the best camping experiences in America are in these places—and they will become great memories for you. This book is your launching point to adventure and discovery!

⊙ Making Reservations

While most National Forest campgrounds have space available for drive-up visits, you can ensure there will be a space for you by making a reservation. Reservations are available at many, but not all of the 4,300 National Forest campgrounds nationwide. In this directory, those campgrounds with sites that may be reserved are marked with the icon indicated above. Some campgrounds do not participate in the national reservation system. For these, reservations may be made by calling the local forest office (telephone numbers are listed on the maps). The nationwide number is:

1-877-444-6777
8:00 a.m. to midnight, Eastern Standard Time
7 days each week
Single-site reservation charge: $8.65

How to Read the Listings

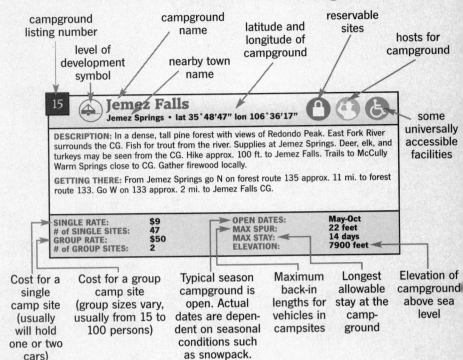

campground listing number

level of development symbol

campground name

nearby town name

latitude and longitude of campground

reservable sites

hosts for campground

some universally accessible facilities

15	⊙ **Jemez Falls**				🔒 🌐 ♿

Jemez Springs • lat 35°48'47" lon 106°36'17"

DESCRIPTION: In a dense, tall pine forest with views of Redondo Peak. East Fork River surrounds the CG. Fish for trout from the river. Supplies at Jemez Springs. Deer, elk, and turkeys may be seen from the CG. Hike approx. 100 ft. to Jemez Falls. Trails to McCully Warm Springs close to CG. Gather firewood locally.

GETTING THERE: From Jemez Springs go N on forest route 135 approx. 11 mi. to forest route 133. Go W on 133 approx. 2 mi. to Jemez Falls CG.

SINGLE RATE:	$9	OPEN DATES:	May-Oct
# of SINGLE SITES:	47	MAX SPUR:	22 feet
GROUP RATE:	$50	MAX STAY:	14 days
# of GROUP SITES:	2	ELEVATION:	7900 feet

Cost for a single camp site (usually will hold one or two cars)

Cost for a group camp site (group sizes vary, usually from 15 to 100 persons)

Typical season campground is open. Actual dates are dependent on seasonal conditions such as snowpack.

Maximum back-in lengths for vehicles in campsites

Longest allowable stay at the campground

Elevation of campground above sea level

Abbreviations

N	North
S	South
E	East
W	West
mi.	Miles
CG	Campground

Facilities symbols

 Rustic— No paved roads, pit-style toilets (if any), No potable water (carry own)

 Semi-developed—Paved or well maintained gravel roads, pit, vault or flush toilets. May or may not have potable water

 Developed—Paved roads suitable for large RVs or trailers, flush toilets and shower, potable water

⊙ Camp Hosts

Many campgrounds are staffed with hosts that help maintain the facilities, provide assistance to campers, and collect fees. Some campgrounds have at least one committed host to the facilities; others will share a host among several campground facilities. Those campgrounds marked with the host icon will have a host during primary operating season.

♿ Accessible Facilities

The campgrounds marked with the accessible symbol offer some facilities that are universally accessible. This symbol does not mean that every facility of campsite is universally accessible.

Forest routes are numbered and identified by small brown signs with white lettering.

Campground Rules

- As a visitor to the National Forests, you are asked to follow certain rules designed to ensure a quality experience for all forest visitors.
- You are primarily responsible for your own safety. Recreation in the outdoors has inherent risks. Many forest locations are remote and emergency assistance may not be readily available.

Camping

- Use picnic sites, swimming beaches and other day-use areas only between the hours of 6 a.m. and 10 p.m.
- Campgrounds and other recreation sites can be used only for recreation purposes. Permanent use, or use as a principal residence without authorization is not allowed.
- In campgrounds, camp only in those places specifically marked or provided.
- At least one person must occupy a camping area during the first night after camping equipment has been set up, unless permission has otherwise been granted by the Forest Ranger.
- Do not leave camping equipment unattended for more than 24 hours without permission from the Forest Ranger. The federal government is not responsible for any loss or damage to personal property.
- Remove all personal property and trash when leaving.

Campfires

- Obey restrictions on fires. Open fires may be limited or prohibited at certain times.
- Within campgrounds and other recreation sites, build fires only in fire rings, stoves, grills or fireplaces provided for that purpose.
- Be sure your fire is completely extinguished before leaving. You are responsible for keeping fires under control.

Property

- Do not carve, chop, cut, or damage any live trees.
- Preserve and protect your National Forests. Leave natural areas the way you found them.
- Enter buildings, structures, or enclosed areas in National Forests only when they are expressly opened to the public.
- Native American sites, old cabins, and other structures, along with objects and artifacts associated with them, have historical or archaeological value. Do not damage or remove any such historic or archaeological resource.

Sanitation

- Throw all garbage and litter in containers provided for this purpose, or take it with you.
- Garbage containers, when provided, are reserved for use by visitors to the National Forest. They are not provided for use by visitors to, or owners of private lands or lands under permit.
- Wash food and personal items away from drinking water supplies. Use water facilities only for drawing water.
- Prevent pollution by keeping garbage, litter, and foreign substances out of lakes, streams and other water.
- Use toilets properly. Do not throw garbage, litter, fish cleanings, or other foreign substances in toilets and plumbing fixtures.

Operation of Vehicles

- Obey all traffic signs. State traffic laws apply to National Forests unless otherwise specified.
- When operating vehicles of any kind, do not damage the land or vegetation or disturb wildlife. Avoid driving on unpaved roads or trails when they are wet or muddy, causing deep ruts.
- Within campgrounds and other recreation sites, use cars, motorbikes, motorcycles, or other motor vehicles only for entering or leaving, unless areas or trails are specifically marked for them. Park only in marked parking areas.
- Do not block, restrict, or interfere with the use of roads or trails.
- Obey area and trail restrictions on the use of trail bikes and other off-the-road vehicles.

Pets and Animals

- Pets must always be restrained or on a leash while in developed recreation sites.
- Pets (except guide dogs) are not allowed in swimming areas.
- Saddle and pack animals are allowed in recreation sites only where authorized by posted instructions.

Firearms and Explosives

- Fireworks and explosives are prohibited in the National Forests. Only persons with a permit from the Forest Service may engage in these types of activities.
- Firing a gun is not allowed: a) in or within 150 yards of a residence, building, campsite, developed recreation site or occupied area; b) across or on a road or body of water; c) in any circumstance whereby any person may be injured or property damaged.

Fee Areas

- You must pay a fee to use certain developed sites and facilities. Such areas are clearly signed or posted as requiring a fee.
- Where fees are required, you must pay them before using the site, facility, equipment, or service furnished.

Public Behavior

- No fighting or boisterous behavior.
- Keep noise to a reasonable level. Please be considerate of fellow visitors.

Business Activities

- Permits are required for any commercial activity on National Forest lands.

Audio Devices

- Operate any audio device, such as a radio or musical instrument, so it does not disturb other visitors.
- A permit is required for a public address system used in or near a campsite, developed recreation site, or over a body of water.

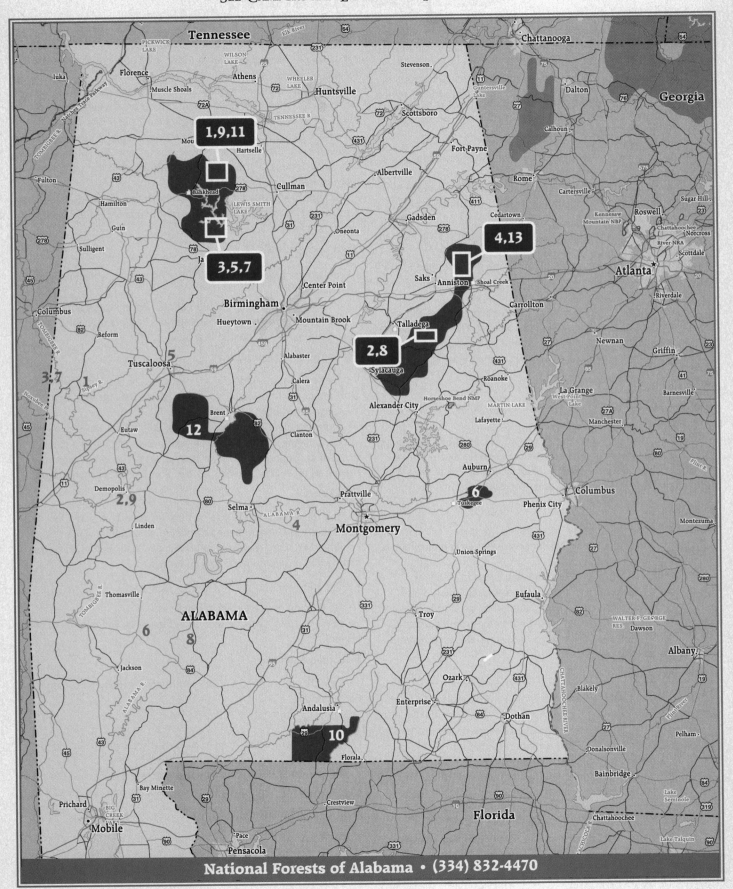

BARTRAM'S TRAIL

William Bartram, America's first native born artist - naturalist, passed through Macon County during the Revolutionary era, making the first scientific notations of its flora, fauna and inhabitants. As the appointed botanist of Britain's King George III, he traveled 2,400 miles in three journeys into the southern colonies in 1775-1776, collecting rare plants and specimens and making detailed drawings of plants and animals.

USFS Photo

NATIONAL FORESTS OF ALABAMA

Called "Alabama's Largest Natural Treasure", the Bankhead, Conecuh, Talladega, and Tuskegee National Forests encompass 664,000 acres of public land.

High overlooks, rolling hills, and tree-studded flat land makeup the contrasting terrain in the forests. Hikers, bikers and horseback riders enjoy an extensive network of trails. There are roads for quiet drives with far-reaching scenic views and special walk-in areas designed for seeing wildlife. Boaters and waterskiers can enjoy large, clean lakes. The quiet coves on these lakes will satisfy anglers as well.

The forests contain two wilderness areas. The 25,002-acre Sipsey Wilderness in the Bankhead National Forest, is the second largest wilderness area east of the Mississippi while the 7,245-acre Cheaha Wilderness in the Talladega National Forests offers high elevations, with numerous overlooks for panoramic views of east-central Alabama.

The four forests also provide habitats for some 900 species of birds, mammals, reptiles, amphibians, fish, either as residents or seasonal migrants. Game animals include white-tailed deer, bob-white quail, gray and fox squirrels, turkeys, rabbits, raccoons, and various waterfowl. The four forests are also home to a number of threatened and endangered species, such as, the gopher tortoise, flattened musk turtle and the red-cockaded woodpecker.

1 Brushy Lake

Double Springs • lat 34°18'00" lon 087°15'00"

DESCRIPTION: In a hardwood forest setting on Brushy Lake. Fish for bass and bream on the lake. Boat ramp available for electric motors only on lake. Supplies at Double Springs. Deer, birds and squirrels are common to the area. Campers may gather firewood. Trails near lake and an OHV trail nearby. Tent camping preferred.

GETTING THERE: From Double Springs go N 8 mi. on state HWY 33 to the Hurricane Creek Shooting Range. Go RT 1 mi. on forest route 234 to county route 63. Go N 2 mi. to Grayson. Take forest route 245 to Brushy Lake CG.

SINGLE RATE:	$5	OPEN DATES:	Yearlong
# of SINGLE SITES:	13		
		MAX STAY:	14 days
		ELEVATION:	700 feet

2 Cheaha Shelter
Talladega • lat 33°26'00" lon 085°49'00"

DESCRIPTION: Located in a mixed forest setting. This is a primative CG for people using the Chinnabee Trail. Numerous animals can be viewed in the surrounding areas. Campers may gather firewood.

GETTING THERE: This is a hike in and tent only camp area. CG is located on the Chinnabee Trail.

SINGLE RATE:	No fee	OPEN DATES:	Yearlong
		MAX STAY:	14 days
		ELEVATION:	1500 feet

3 Clear Creek

Poplar Springs • lat 34°01'17" lon 087°16'09"

DESCRIPTION: In an oak, hickory and pine forest setting on Lake Lewis Smith. Fish for bass or bream in the lake. Boat ramp and playground at lake. Supplies at Poplar Springs. Deer, birds, wild turkey and squirrels are common to the area. Campers may gather firewood. A 1.5 mi. bike trail and a 2 mi. hiking trail start at the CG.

GETTING THERE: From Poplar Springs go S on state HWY 195 approx. 4 mi. to county route 27. Follow county route 27 approx. 4 mi. to the Clear Creek CG

SINGLE RATE:	Varies	OPEN DATES:	Mar-Oct
# of SINGLE SITES:	104	MAX SPUR:	99 feet
GROUP RATE:	$30	MAX STAY:	14 days
# of GROUP SITES:	2	ELEVATION:	530 feet

4 Coleman Lake

Heflin • lat 33°47'03" lon 085°33'28"

DESCRIPTION: This large and secluded CG is peacefully nestled into the Talladega mountains. Fish for bass, bream, catfish on the lake. A boat ramp is located nearby. Access to Pinhoti Trail for hiking and horseback riding starts from the CG. An interpretive trail at CG. RV dump station.

GETTING THERE: From Heflin take US HWY 78 NE approx. 7 mi. to forest route 553. Follow 553 approx. 3.5 mi. to forest route 548. Follow 548 approx. 5 mi. to Coleman Lake CG.

SINGLE RATE:	$12	OPEN DATES:	Apr-Nov
# of SINGLE SITES:	39	MAX SPUR:	35 feet
		MAX STAY:	14 days
		ELEVATION:	1153 feet

5 Corinth
Double Springs • lat 34°06'18" lon 087°19'12"

DESCRIPTION: In an oak, hickory and pine forest setting on Lake Lewis Smith. Fish for bass or bream and swim in the lake. Supplies at Double Springs. Deer, birds and squirrels are common to the area. Campers may gather firewood. No designated trails in the CG area. Sanitary station in CG.

GETTING THERE: From Double Springs go E on US HWY 278 approx. 4 mi. to county route 57. Go S on 57 approx. 3 mi. to the Corinth CG.

SINGLE RATE:	$20	OPEN DATES:	Mar-Oct
# of SINGLE SITES:	52	MAX SPUR:	90 feet
		MAX STAY:	14 days
		ELEVATION:	530 feet

 Campground has hosts   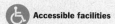 **Reservable sites**   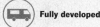 **Accessible facilities**   **Fully developed**   **Semi-developed**   **Rustic facilities**

NOTE: Open dates listed are typical. Actual dates are dependent on conditions such as snow pack.

6 Dispersed Primitive Sites
Tuskegee • lat ˚'" lon ˚'"

DESCRIPTION: There are 10 dispersed camp sites on the Tuskegee NF. These CG's are located near many interesting sites that range from a wildlife viewing area, the Bartram Trail, a circular horse trail that is 14 mi. in length or 2 fishing ponds. Please contact the Tuskegee Ranger District Office at (334) 727-2652 for further information.

GETTING THERE: Go NE on US HWY 29 out of Tuskegee approx. 2 mi. to county route 53. Go left on 53 3/4 mi. to the Bartram Trail trailhead parking area.

SINGLE RATE:	No fee	OPEN DATES:	Yearlong
		MAX STAY:	14 days
		ELEVATION:	400 feet

7 Houston
Double Springs • lat 34˚07'28" lon 087˚17'53"

DESCRIPTION: In an oak, hickory and pine forest setting on Lake Lewis Smith. Fish for bass or bream and swim in the lake. Boat ramp and beach at lake. Supplies at Double Springs. Deer, birds, wild turkeys and squirrels are common to the area. Campers may gather firewood. No designated trails in the CG area. Trailer dump station nearby.

GETTING THERE: From Double Springs take US HWY 278 approx. 7 mi. to county route 63. Go S to the town of Houston. Take county route 67 W to forest route 118. Follow 118 approx. 2 mi. to the Houston CG

SINGLE RATE:	$10	OPEN DATES:	May-Sept
# of SINGLE SITES:	86	MAX SPUR:	30 feet
GROUP RATE:	$15	MAX STAY:	14 days
# of GROUP SITES:	1	ELEVATION:	530 feet

8 Lake Chinnabee
Talladega • lat 33˚27'47" lon 085˚52'41"

DESCRIPTION: In a mixed forest setting on Lake Chinnabee. Fish for bass and bream from the lake. Boat ramp located at CG, electric motors only on lake. Supplies available at Talladega. Deer, raccoons, turkeys, rabbits and birds are common to the area. This is a starting point for the Chinnabee Trail and a 2 mi. lakeshore trail.

GETTING THERE: From Talladega take state route 21 NE to Munford. Take county route 42 S from Munford approx. 7 mi. to forest route 646. Follow 646 approx. 2 mi. to Lake Chinnabee CG.

SINGLE RATE:	$10	OPEN DATES:	Yearlong
# of SINGLE SITES:	8	MAX SPUR:	22 feet
		MAX STAY:	14 days
		ELEVATION:	950 feet

9 McDougle Camp
Double Springs • lat 34˚19'00" lon 087˚22'00"

DESCRIPTION: A primative CG in a hardwood forest setting. Supplies available at Devil Springs. Deer, birds and squirrels are common to the area. Campers may gather firewood. Trails in the area. Primarily a hunting camp.

GETTING THERE: From Double Springs go N on state HWY 33 approx. 15 mi. to McDougle Camp CG.

SINGLE RATE:	No fee	OPEN DATES:	Yearlong*
# of SINGLE SITES:	10	MAX SPUR:	28 feet
		MAX STAY:	14 days
		ELEVATION:	700 feet

10 Open Pond
Andalusia • lat 31˚05'19" lon 086˚33'03"

DESCRIPTION: In a mixed hardwood, park-like setting on Open Pond. There is wonderful fishing at Open Pond, Ditch Pond and Buck Pond. Supplies at Andalusia. Deer, turkeys, squirrels, rabbits and woodpeckers are common to the area. Campers may gather firewood. There is a trail system that loops near the CG.

GETTING THERE: From Andalusia go S on US Hwy 29 approx. 11 mi. to state HWY 137. Go S on 137 approx. 5 mi. to county route 24. Go W on 24 approx. 2.5 mi. to forest route 337. Go S on 337 approx. 1.5 mi. to forest route 348. Follow 348 2.5 mi. to CG

SINGLE RATE:	Varies	OPEN DATES:	Yearlong
# of SINGLE SITES:	55	MAX SPUR:	40 feet
		MAX STAY:	14 days
		ELEVATION:	118 feet

11 Owl Creek
Double Springs • lat 34˚19'24" lon 087˚14'21"

DESCRIPTION: A primitive CG in a mixed forest setting on Owl Creek. Creek is more for looks and sound rather than fishing. Supplies at Double Springs. Deer, birds, wild turkeys and squirrels are common to the area. Campers may gather firewood. The National Forest Wolf Creek Horse Trail System is a 30 mi. trail and originates nearby the CG.

GETTING THERE: From Double Springs go N approx. 8 mi. on state HWY 33 to forest route 234. Go E on 234 approx. 1 mi. to county route 63. Go N approx. 2 mi. on 63 to Grayson. Take forest route 245 to Owl Creek CG.

SINGLE RATE:	$3	OPEN DATES:	Yearlong
# of SINGLE SITES:	15	MAX SPUR:	28 feet
		MAX STAY:	14 days
		ELEVATION:	950 feet

12 Payne Lake
Harrisburg • lat 32˚53'01" lon 087˚26'24"

DESCRIPTION: In a pine, dogwood and oak mixed forest setting on the Payne Lake. Fish for trout, bream and bass from the lake. Boat launch at CG. Supplies available at Harrisburg. Deer, squirrels, turkeys and birds are common to the area. No designated trails in the area, just hike around the lake. RV dump station at CG.

GETTING THERE: From Harrisburg take state HWY 25 approx. 15 mi. W to the Payne Lake CG.

SINGLE RATE:	Varies	OPEN DATES:	Yearlong
# of SINGLE SITES:	76	MAX SPUR:	22 feet
		MAX STAY:	14 days
		ELEVATION:	235 feet

13 Pine Glen
Heflin • lat 33˚43'28" lon 085˚36'12"

DESCRIPTION: This primitive CG is in a large old pine forest setting on Shoal Creek. Fish for Red-eye Bass from the creek. Supplies can be found at Heflin. Deer, turkeys, raccoon and squirrels are common to the area. Access to the Pinhoti Trail from the CG area. In the Choccolocco Wildlife Manangement Area.

GETTING THERE: From Heflin take US HWY 78 N approx. 3 mi. to forest route 548. Follow 548 approx. 2 mi. to forest route 531. Follow 531 approx. 3 mi. to Pine Glen CG.

SINGLE RATE:	$3	OPEN DATES:	Yearlong
# of SINGLE SITES:	31	MAX SPUR:	22 feet
		MAX STAY:	14 days

 Campground has hosts   🔒 Reservable sites   Accessible facilities   Fully developed    Semi-developed    Rustic facilities

NOTE: Open dates listed are typical. Actual dates are dependent on conditions such as snow pack.

Tom Iraci Photo, USDA Forest Service

CHUGACH NATIONAL FOREST

The Chugach National Forest, second largest in the United States (after the Tongass National Forest in southeast Alaska), encompasses some of the most breathtakingly beautiful country in North America. The Chugach is perhaps best known as a great place for fun—a place to fish, hunt, hike, camp, ski, snowshoe, or just enjoy the marvelous scenery.

The name Chugach (CHEW-gatch) was adapted by the Russians and evolved from "Chugatz" or "Tchougatskoe". This is what the Chugach natives, the first human inhabitants of the area, called themselves. They were once dispersed throughout much of Prince William Sound, and were among the most southerly of the widespread, sea-oriented cultural groups who dominated the Alaskan arctic.

Fly a floatplane, paddle a canoe, or hike to some great fishing. The lakes and streams in the Cordova area provide some of the best sportfishing in Alaska. On the Kenai Peninsula, hike your own backcountry route or walk some of the more than 200 miles of maintained trails. Roaring rivers, tranquil alpine lakes, winding fjords and hidden coves beckon the kayaker and sailboater. Visit Columbia Glacier, one of the largest tidewater glaciers in North America.

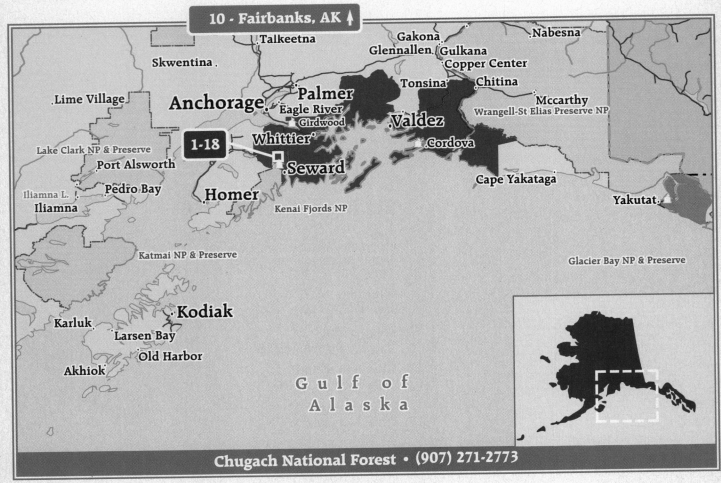

Chugach National Forest • (907) 271-2773

1 Bertha Creek
Portage • lat 60°45'02" lon 149°15'03"

DESCRIPTION: In a mixed forest setting located near Granite Creek. Fish for trout and salmon at the nearby creek. Supplies available at Portage. Moose, bears, black-tail deer, caribou, sheep, mountain goat, red fox, squirrel and bald eagles can be seen in the area. Campers may gather firewood. No designated trails in the area.

GETTING THERE: Take state HWY 1 W approx. 15 mi. out of Portage to the Bertha Creek CG.

SINGLE RATE: # of SINGLE SITES:	Varies 12	OPEN DATES: MAX SPUR: MAX STAY: ELEVATION:	May-Sept 22 feet 14 days 750 feet

2 Black Bears
Portage • lat 60°47'30" lon 148°53'50"

DESCRIPTION: In a mixed forest setting located near Beich Boggs. Supplies available at Portage. Moose, bears, black-tail deer, caribou, sheep, mountain goats, red foxes, squirrels and bald eagles can be seen in the area. Campers may gather firewood. No designated trails in the area. Beich Boggs visitor center is nearby.

GETTING THERE: From Portage go SE approx. 3 mi. on forest highway 35 to the Black Bears CG.

SINGLE RATE: # of SINGLE SITES:	Varies 12	OPEN DATES: MAX SPUR: MAX STAY: ELEVATION:	May-Sept 22 feet 14 days 125 feet

3 Coeur d'Alene
Hope • lat 60°51'05" lon 149°31'55"

DESCRIPTION: This tent only CG is in a mixed forest setting on Palmer Creek. Boat and fish from the creek. Supplies available at Hope. Moose, bears, deer, caribou, red foxes, coyotes, squirrels and birds are common in the area. Campers may gather firewood. Many trails in the area.

GETTING THERE: From Hope go S on Hope Hwy approx. 1/2 mi. to Palmer Creek Road. Go E on Palmer Creek Road approx. 7 mi. to the Coeur d'Alene CG. High clearance required.

SINGLE RATE: # of SINGLE SITES:	Varies 6	OPEN DATES: MAX STAY: ELEVATION:	May-Sept 14 days 1750 feet

4 Cooper Creek
Cooper Landing • lat 60°29'13" lon 149°53'26"

DESCRIPTION: Along the Kenai River with views of forested mountain sides. Rain, wind and cooler temperatures are possible. Fly fishing on Kenai River (designated areas, special regs apply). Supplies in Cooper Landing. CG fills during salmon run. Gather deadwood for firewood. Prepare for mosquitos all summer. Bears area.

GETTING THERE: From Seward go N on state HWY 9 to state HWY 1. Go S on state HWY 1 approx.11 mi. to Cooper Landing. Cooper Creek CG is located 1/2mi. S on Cooper Creek road. Camping on both mtn and stream sides.

SINGLE RATE: # of SINGLE SITES:	$10 26	OPEN DATES: MAX STAY: ELEVATION:	May-Sept 14 days 500 feet

5 Crescent Creek
Seward • lat 60°29'59" lon 149°40'47"

DESCRIPTION: In a mixed forest setting on Crescent Creek. Fish or swim from the creek. Supplies available at Seward. Moose, deer, bears, red, foxes, squirrels and birds are some of the many animals that can be seen in the area. Campers may gather firewood. Many trails are in the area.

GETTING THERE: From Seward go N on state HWY 9 (Seward HWY) to state HWY 1 (Sterling HWY). Go W on 1 approx. 4 mi. to Crescent Creek CG.

SINGLE RATE: # of SINGLE SITES:	No fee 9	OPEN DATES: MAX STAY: ELEVATION:	May-Sept 14 days 750 feet

6 Granite Creek
Portage • lat 60°43'31" lon 149°17'44"

DESCRIPTION: In a mixed forest setting located near Granite Creek. Fish for trout and salmon at the creek. Supplies available at Portage. Moose, bears, black-tail deer, caribou, sheep, mountain goats, red foxes, squirrels and bald eagles can be seen in the area. Campers may gather firewood. No designated trails in the area.

GETTING THERE: Take state HWY 1 W approx. 15 mi. out of Portage to the Bertha Creek CG.

SINGLE RATE: # of SINGLE SITES:	Varies 18	OPEN DATES: MAX SPUR: MAX STAY: ELEVATION:	May-Sept 22 feet 14 days 750 feet

7 Meadow Creek
Seward • lat 60°23'45" lon 149°25'18"

DESCRIPTION: In a mixed forest setting by Kenai Lake. Fish or swim from the lake. Supplies available at Seward. Moose, bears, deer, red foxes, squirrels and birds are a few of the many animals that can be seen in the area. Campers may gather firewood. Many trails in the area.

GETTING THERE: Go N of Seward approx. 20 mi. on state HWY 9 to boat launch. Boat into Meadow Creek CG.

SINGLE RATE: # of SINGLE SITES:	No fee 2	OPEN DATES: MAX STAY: ELEVATION:	May-Sept 14 days 450 feet

8 Porcupine
Hope • lat 60°55'50" lon 149°39'32"

DESCRIPTION: In a mixed forest setting on the Turnagain Arm. Boat and fish from the arm. Supplies available at Hope. Moose, bears, deer, caribou, red foxes, coyotes, squirrels and birds are common in the area. Campers may gather firewood. Many trails in the area.

GETTING THERE: From Hope go NW approx. 5 mi. on the Hope HWY to Porcupine CG.

SINGLE RATE: # of SINGLE SITES:	$10 24	OPEN DATES: MAX SPUR: MAX STAY: ELEVATION:	May-Sept 22 feet 14 days 100 feet

9 Porcupine Island
Seward • lat 60°24'25" lon 149°37'15"

DESCRIPTION: In a mixed forest setting on Kenai Lake. This is a canoe-in only CG. Fish and swim from the lake. Supplies are located at Seward. Moose, deer, bears, red foxes, squirrels and birds are just some of the many wildlife that can be seen in the area. Campers may gather firewood. Many trails can be found nearby.

GETTING THERE: From Seward go N on state HWY 9 approx. 15 mi. to boat launch area. Canoe up the lake to Porcupine Island CG.

SINGLE RATE: # of SINGLE SITES:	No fee 3	OPEN DATES: MAX STAY: ELEVATION:	May-Sept 14 days 450 feet

10 Primrose
Seward • lat 60°20'27" lon 149°22'08"

DESCRIPTION: In a mixed forest setting located on Kenai Lake. Boat ramp at the CG. Fish for trout and salmon on the lake. Supplies available at Seward. Moose, bears, black-tail deer, caribou, sheep, mountain goats, red foxes, squirrels and bald eagles can be seen in the area. Campers may gather firewood. No designated trails in the area.

GETTING THERE: From Seward go N approx. 15 mi. on state HWY 9 to the Primrose CG.

SINGLE RATE: # of SINGLE SITES:	Varies 10	OPEN DATES: MAX SPUR: MAX STAY: ELEVATION:	May-Sept 22 feet 14 days 450 feet

 Campground has hosts   🔒 **Reservable sites**   ♿ **Accessible facilities**   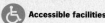 **Fully developed**   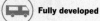 **Semi-developed**   **Rustic facilities**

NOTE: Open dates listed are typical. Actual dates are dependent on conditions such as snow pack.

11 Ptarmigan Creek
Seward • lat 60°24'15" lon 149°21'40"

DESCRIPTION: In a mixed forest setting located near Kenai Lake. Fish for trout and salmon on the lake. Supplies available at Seward. Moose, bears, black-tail deer, caribou, sheep, mountain goats, red foxes, squirrels and bald eagles can be seen in the area. Campers may gather firewood. No designated trails in the area.

GETTING THERE: From Seward go approx 23.5 mi. N on state HWY 9 (Seward HWY) to the Ptarmigan Creek CG.

SINGLE RATE:	No fee	OPEN DATES:	Sept-May
# of SINGLE SITES:	16		
		MAX STAY:	14 days
		ELEVATION:	460 feet

12 Quartz Creek
Seward • lat 60°28'45" lon 149°43'32"

DESCRIPTION: In a mixed forest setting on Kenai Lake. A boat ramp is located at the CG. Boat, fish or swim from the lake. Supplies available at Seward. Moose, bears, deer, red foxes, squirrels and birds are a few of the many animals that can be seen in the area. Campers may gather firewood. Many trails in the area.

GETTING THERE: From Seward go N on Seward Hwy to the junction with Sterling HWY. Go S on Sterling Hwy approx. 7 mi. to Quartz Creek CG.

SINGLE RATE:	Varies	OPEN DATES:	May-Sept
# of SINGLE SITES:	32	MAX SPUR:	22 feet
		MAX STAY:	14 days
		ELEVATION:	300 feet

13 Russian River
Cooper Landing • lat 60°29'09" lon 149°58'07"

DESCRIPTION: Along the Kenai River with views of forested mountain sides. Rain, wind and cooler temperatures are possible. Fly fishing on Kenai River (designated areas, special regs apply). Supplies in Cooper Landing. CG fills during salmon run. Gather deadwood for firewood. Prepare for mosquitos all summer. Bears area.

GETTING THERE: From Seward go N on state HWY 9 (Seward HWY) to the junction with state HWY 1 (Sterling HWY). Go W on 1 approx. 13 mi. to the Russian River CG.

SINGLE RATE:	$13	OPEN DATES:	May-Sept
# of SINGLE SITES:	83		
		MAX STAY:	3 days
		ELEVATION:	500 feet

14 Ship Creek
Seward • lat 60°23'25" lon 149°30'40"

DESCRIPTION: In a mixed forest setting by Kenai Lake. Fish or swim from the lake. Supplies available at Seward. Moose, bears, deer, red foxes, squirrels and birds are a few of the many animals that can be seen in the area. Campers may gather firewood. Many trails in the area. No drinking water available.

GETTING THERE: Go N of Seward approx. 20 mi. on state HWY 9 to boat launch. Boat into Meadow Creek CG.

SINGLE RATE:	No fee	OPEN DATES:	May-Sept
# of SINGLE SITES:	2		
		MAX STAY:	14 days
		ELEVATION:	450 feet

15 Tenderfoot Creek
Seward • lat 60°38'08" lon 149°29'45"

DESCRIPTION: In mixed forest setting on Summitt Lake. Fish, boat or swim from the lake. Boat ramp located at CG. Supplies located at Seward. Moose, bears, black-tail deer, coyotes, red foxes, squirrels and bald eagle can be seen in the area. Campers may gather firewood. No designated trails in the area.

GETTING THERE: From Seward go N on Seward Hwy approx. 46 mi. to Tenderfoot CG.

SINGLE RATE:	$10	OPEN DATES:	May-Sept
# of SINGLE SITES:	28	MAX SPUR:	22 feet
		MAX STAY:	14 days
		ELEVATION:	1400 feet

16 Tern Lake
Seward • lat 60°31'48" lon 149°33'03"

DESCRIPTION: In a mixed forest setting on Tern Lake. Fish or swim from the lake. Supplies available at Seward. Moose, deer, bears, red, foxes, squirrels and birds are some of the many animals that can be seen in the area. Campers may gather firewood. Many trails are in the area.

GETTING THERE: From Seward go N on state HWY 9 to the junction of state HWY 1. Tern Lake CG is located at this junction.

SINGLE RATE:	No fee	OPEN DATES:	May-Sept
# of SINGLE SITES:	25		
		MAX STAY:	14 days
		ELEVATION:	750 feet

17 Trail River
Seward • lat 60°24'46" lon 149°22'45"

DESCRIPTION: In a mixed forest setting located on Kenai Lake. Fish for trout and salmon on the lake. Supplies available at Seward. Moose, bears, black-tail deer, caribou, sheep, mountain goats, red foxes, squirrels and bald eagles can be seen in the area. Campers may gather firewood. No designated trails in the area.

GETTING THERE: From Seward go approx. 17 mi. N on Seward Hwy to the Trail River CG.

SINGLE RATE:	$10	OPEN DATES:	May-Sept
# of SINGLE SITES:	63		
GROUP RATE:	$100	MAX STAY:	14 days
# of GROUP SITES:	1	ELEVATION:	450 feet

18 Williwaw
Portage • lat 60°47'08" lon 148°52'48"

DESCRIPTION: In a mixed forest setting located near Beich Boggs. Supplies available at Portage. Moose, bears, black-tail deer, caribou, sheep, mountain goats, red foxes, squirrels and bald eagles can be seen in the area. Campers may gather firewood. No designated trails in the area. Beich Boggs visitor center is nearby.

GETTING THERE: From Portage go SE approx. 2.5 mi. on forest highway 35 to the Black Bears CG.

SINGLE RATE:	Varies	OPEN DATES:	May-Sept
# of SINGLE SITES:	39	MAX SPUR:	22 feet
		MAX STAY:	14 days
		ELEVATION:	100 feet

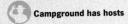 **Campground has hosts**   🔒 **Reservable sites**   ♿ **Accessible facilities**   **Fully developed**   **Semi-developed**   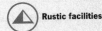 **Rustic facilities**

NOTE: Open dates listed are typical. Actual dates are dependent on conditions such as snow pack.

USFS Photo

TONGASS NATIONAL FOREST

The Tongass National Forest is a glimmering rain forest the size of New Jersey, full of glaciers, spectacular scenery, mountains, waterways, and thousands of islands separated by straits and channels. This landscape is home to over four hundred species of terrestrial and marine wildlife, fish, and shellfish. Species, such as the bald eagle and the brown bear, endangered in other parts of the United States, have plenty of room to roam in the forest's nearly 17 million acres.

With about one-third designated as wilderness, the Tongass offers outstanding recreation opportunities, some very different from anything you'll experience in National Forests in the lower 48 states. Camp in a campground—or in a cabin. Hike through dense forest, alpine meadow, or on a wooden trail through marshland called muskeg. Explore world-class caves. Enjoy salt water fjords and unending waterways by canoe or kayak, your own motor or sail boat, charter boat, ferry, or cruise ship. Watch bears, eagles, whales, and countless other critters in their natural settings. Visit glaciers by land or sea. And of course, fish—fresh or salt water, everything from herring to trout to salmon to halibut. Each area is unique in its terrain, scenic beauty and opportunities for recreation and solitude.

TONGASS NATIONAL FOREST • ALASKA

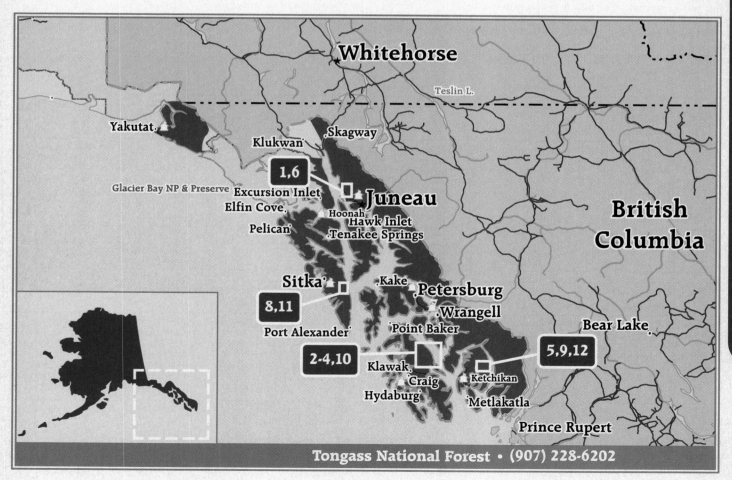

Tongass National Forest • (907) 228-6202

1 Auke Village
Juneau • lat 58°22'44" lon 134°43'34"

DESCRIPTION: In a heavily forested setting of spruce, hemlock and cedar. Fish for salmon and halibut from the area. Supplies available at Juneau. Black and brown bear can be seen in the area along with beaver, lynx, red fox and bald eagles. Campers may gather firewood. No designated trails in the area.

GETTING THERE: From Juneau go NW approx. 15 mi. on the Glacier HWY to Auke Village CG.

SINGLE RATE:	$8	OPEN DATES:	May-Sept
# of SINGLE SITES:	12	MAX SPUR:	20 feet
		MAX STAY:	14 days
		ELEVATION:	50 feet

2 Eagle's Nest
Thorne Bay • lat 55°40'00" lon 132°40'00"

DESCRIPTION: In a heavily forested setting of spruce, hemlock and cedar. Fish for salmon and from the area. Supplies available at Thorne Bay. Black and brown bear can be seen in the area along with beaver, lynx, red fox and bald eagles. Campers may gather firewood. Hike on the nearby trails. No drinking water available.

GETTING THERE: From Thorne Bay go NW approx. 10 mi. to Eagle's Nest CG.

SINGLE RATE:	$5	OPEN DATES:	May-Sept
# of SINGLE SITES:	9	MAX SPUR:	25 feet
		MAX STAY:	14 days
		ELEVATION:	400 feet

3 Horseshoe Hole
Thorne Bay • lat 55°48'30" lon 133°07'23"

DESCRIPTION: In a heavily forested setting of spruce, hemlock and cedar. Fish for salmon and from the area. Supplies available at Thorne Bay. Black and brown bear can be seen in the area along with beaver, lynx, red fox and bald eagles. Campers may gather firewood. Hike on the nearby trails. No drinking water available.

GETTING THERE: From Thorne Bay go W on 2054000 approx. 10 mi. to forest route 2054305. Go S on 2054305 approx. 2 mi. to Horseshoe Hole CG. Hike-in last portion.

SINGLE RATE:	No fee	OPEN DATES:	May-Sept
# of SINGLE SITES:	2		
		MAX STAY:	14 days
		ELEVATION:	60 feet

4 Lake No. 3
Thorne Bay • lat 55°40'00" lon 132°40'00"

DESCRIPTION: In a heavily forested setting of spruce, hemlock and cedar on hill overlooking Lake #3. Fish for salmon and halibut from the area. Supplies available at Thorne Bay. Black and brown bear can be seen in the area along with beaver, lynx, red fox and bald eagles. Campers may gather firewood. Hike on the nearby trails.

GETTING THERE: From Thorne Bay go S on forest route 2030 approx. 5.5 mi. to Lake No. 3 CG.

SINGLE RATE:	No fee	OPEN DATES:	May-Sept
# of SINGLE SITES:	2		
		MAX STAY:	14 days
		ELEVATION:	200 feet

5 Last Chance
Ketchikan • lat 55°13'00" lon 131°50'00"

DESCRIPTION: In a heavily forested setting of spruce, hemlock and cedar. Fish for salmon and halibut from the area. Supplies available at Ketchikan. Black and brown bear can be seen in the area along with beaver, lynx, red fox and bald eagles. Campers may gather firewood. Hike on the nearby trails.

GETTING THERE: From Ketchikan go N approx. 10 mi. on Revilla Road to Last Chance CG.

SINGLE RATE:	$10	OPEN DATES:	May-Sept
# of SINGLE SITES:	24	MAX SPUR:	25 feet
		MAX STAY:	14 days
		ELEVATION:	100 feet

6 Mendenhall Lake
Juneau • lat 58°25'24" lon 134°34'10"

DESCRIPTION: In a heavily forested setting of spruce, hemlock and cedar. Fish for salmon and halibut from the area. Supplies available at Juneau. Black and brown bear can be seen in the area along with beaver, lynx, red fox and bald eagles. Campers may gather firewood. No designated trails in the area.

GETTING THERE: From Juneau go NW approx. 10 mi. to Mendenhall Lake.

SINGLE RATE:	Varies	OPEN DATES:	May-Sept
# of SINGLE SITES:	68	MAX SPUR:	25 feet
		MAX STAY:	14 days
		ELEVATION:	100 feet

7 Ohmer Creek
Petersburg • lat 56°34'48" lon 132°44'23"

DESCRIPTION: This tent only CG is located in a heavily forested setting of spruce, hemlock and cedar. Fish for salmon and halibut from the area. Supplies available at Petersburg. Black and brown bear can be seen in the area along with beaver, lynx, red fox and bald eagles. Campers may gather firewood. Hike on the nearby trails.

GETTING THERE: From Petersburg go SW approx. 20 mi. to the Ohmer Creek CG.

SINGLE RATE:	Varies	OPEN DATES:	May-Sept
# of SINGLE SITES:	10	MAX SPUR:	35 feet
		MAX STAY:	14 days
		ELEVATION:	5 feet

8 Sawmill Creek
Sitka • lat 57°10'00" lon 135°10'00"

DESCRIPTION: In a heavily forested setting of spruce, hemlock and cedar. Fish for salmon and halibut from the area. Supplies available at Sitka. Black and brown bear can be seen in the area along with beaver, lynx, red fox and bald eagles. Campers may gather firewood. Hike on the nearby trails.

GETTING THERE: From Sitka go E approx. 5 mi. to Sawmill Creek CG.

SINGLE RATE:	No fee	OPEN DATES:	May-Sept
# of SINGLE SITES:	10		
		MAX STAY:	14 days
		ELEVATION:	75 feet

9 Signal Creek
Ketchikan • lat 55°13'00" lon 131°50'00"

DESCRIPTION: In a heavily forested setting of spruce, hemlock and cedar. Fish for salmon and halibut from the area. Supplies available at Ketchikan. Black and brown bear can be seen in the area along with beaver, lynx, red fox and bald eagles. Campers may gather firewood. Hike on the nearby trails.

GETTING THERE: From Ketchikan go NW approx. 10 mi. to Signal Creek CG.

SINGLE RATE:	$10	OPEN DATES:	May-Sept
# of SINGLE SITES:	24	MAX SPUR:	25 feet
		MAX STAY:	14 days
		ELEVATION:	100 feet

10 Staney Creek Bridge
Thorne Bay • lat 55°47'45" lon 133°07'03"

DESCRIPTION: This hik-in, tent only CG is in a heavily forested setting of spruce, hemlock and cedar. Fish for salmon and from the area. Supplies available at Thorne Bay. Black and brown bear can be seen in the area along with beaver, lynx, red fox and bald eagles. Campers may gather firewood. Hike on the nearby trails. No drinking water available.

GETTING THERE: From Thorne Bay go W on 2054000 approx. 10 mi. to forest route 2054305. Go S on 2054305 approx. 5 mi. to forest route 2050000. Go SW on 2050000 approx. 2 mi. to Staney Bridge CG.

SINGLE RATE:	No fee	OPEN DATES:	May-Sept
# of SINGLE SITES:	2		
		MAX STAY:	14 days
		ELEVATION:	100 feet

 Campground has hosts   🔒 **Reservable sites**   ♿ **Accessible facilities**   **Fully developed**   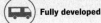 **Semi-developed**   **Rustic facilities**

NOTE: Open dates listed are typical. Actual dates are dependent on conditions such as snow pack.

11 Starrigavan

Sitka • lat 57˚07'59" lon 135˚21'56"

DESCRIPTION: In a heavily forested setting of spruce, hemlock and cedar. Fish for salmon and halibut from the area. Supplies available at Sitka. Black and brown bear can be seen in the area along with beaver, lynx, red fox and bald eagles. Campers may gather firewood. Hike on the nearby trails.

GETTING THERE: From Sitka go N approx. 10 mi. to Starrigavan CG.

SINGLE RATE:	$8	OPEN DATES:	May-Sept
# of SINGLE SITES:	31	MAX SPUR:	25 feet
		MAX STAY:	14 days
		ELEVATION:	12 feet

12 Three C's

Ketchikan • lat 55˚13'00" lon 131˚50'00"

DESCRIPTION: In a heavily forested setting of spruce, hemlock and cedar. Fish for salmon and halibut from the area. Supplies available at Ketchikan. Black and brown bear can be seen in the area along with beaver, lynx, red fox and bald eagles. Campers may gather firewood. Hike on the nearby trails.

GETTING THERE: From Ketchikan go NW approx. 10 mi. to the Three C's CG.

SINGLE RATE:	$10	OPEN DATES:	May-Sept
# of SINGLE SITES:	4	MAX SPUR:	25 feet
		MAX STAY:	14 days
		ELEVATION:	100 feet

Camping in Bear Country

Keep a clean camp– don't be careless with food or garbage when camping.

Properly store food–keep all food and food-related items inside a closed, hard-sided vehicle or special bear-resistant container.

Keep pets on a leash– pets may harass wildlife and can led predators to your camp. Don't leave pets unattended in bear country.

 Campground has hosts   **Reservable sites**   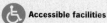 **Accessible facilities**    **Fully developed**   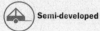 **Semi-developed**   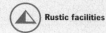 **Rustic facilities**

NOTE: Open dates listed are typical. Actual dates are dependent on conditions such as snow pack.

USFS Photo

APACHE-SITGREAVES NATIONAL FOREST

The Apache and the Sitgreaves National Forests were administratively combined in 1974. The two million-acre forest encompasses magnificent mountain country in east central Arizona along the Mogollon Rim and the White Mountains.

What makes this forest so special is the water, which runs off the high mountains forming numerous lakes and streams. It's a fisherman's paradise in the arid Southwest.

The Apache-Sitgreaves has 24 lakes and reservoirs and more than 450 miles of rivers and streams—more than can be found in any other southwestern national forest. The White Mountains contain the headwaters of several Arizona rivers including the Black, the Little Colorado, and the San Francisco.

The Sitgreaves was named after Captain Lorenzo Sitgreaves, a government topographical engineer who conducted the first scientific expedition across Arizona in the early 1850s. The major attractions for visitors from the hot valleys of Phoenix or Tucson are the Mogollon Rim and the string of man-made lakes. From the Rim's 7600-foot elevation, vista points provide inspiring views of the low country to the south and west.

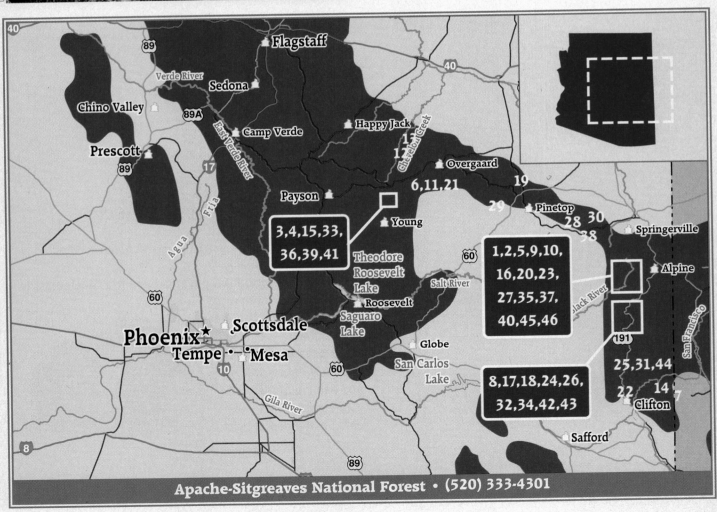

Apache-Sitgreaves National Forest • (520) 333-4301

1 Alpine Divide
Alpine • lat 33°53'36" lon 109°09'10"

DESCRIPTION: CG is tucked away in a picturesque setting; at the base of the Escudilla Mountains, in a cool, quiet grove of ponderosa pine. Its convenient location makes it a good base for travel throughout the area. Supplies and groceries are available in Alpine. Various wildlife in area.

GETTING THERE: From Alpine go N on US HWY 180/191 4 mi. to Alpine Divide CG.

SINGLE RATE:	$6	OPEN DATES:	May-Sept
# of SINGLE SITES:	12	MAX SPUR:	12 feet
		MAX STAY:	14 days
		ELEVATION:	8480 feet

2 Aspen
Alpine • lat 33°48'27" lon 109°18'56"

DESCRIPTION: The CG is set in ponderosa pine, oak, aspen, and douglas fir. Woods Canyon Lake offers boating (boat ramp and launch) and fishing. Trail at N end of lake. Supplies and groceries are available at Woods Canyon Store or 10 miles E at Forest Lakes. RV sanitary station is nearby.

GETTING THERE: From Alpine go N on US HWY 180/191 approx. 1 mi. to forest route 249. Go W on 249 approx. 5 mi. to forest route 276. Go S on 276 approx. 7 mi. to Aspen CG.

SINGLE RATE:	$12	OPEN DATES:	May-Sept*
# of SINGLE SITES:	136	MAX SPUR:	32 feet
GROUP RATE:	$70	MAX STAY:	14 days
# of GROUP SITES:	1	ELEVATION:	7780 feet

3 Aspen
Heber • lat 34°19'57" lon 110°56'30"

DESCRIPTION: The CG is situated in ponderosa pine, oak, aspen, and douglas fir. Woods Canyon Lake offers boating and fishing opportunities. Interpretative nature trail at the N end of lake. Gas, phone, and groceries are available 10 mi. E at Forest Lakes. RV sanitary station is nearby. Boat ramp and launch.

GETTING THERE: From Heber go W on state HWY 260 approx. 11 mi. to forest route 300. Go W on 300 approx. 3 mi. to forest route 105. Go N on 105 approx. 1 mi. to Aspen CG.

SINGLE RATE:	$12	OPEN DATES:	May-Oct
# of SINGLE SITES:	136	MAX SPUR:	32 feet
GROUP RATE:	$70	MAX STAY:	14 days
# of GROUP SITES:	70	ELEVATION:	7610 feet

4 Bear Canyon Lake
Heber • lat 34°24'22" lon 111°00'12"

DESCRIPTION: Semi-primitive and rustic CG is set among mixed conifer, oak, and aspen. This peaceful CG is located .25 mi. from the lake and trails. Popular fishing and hiking spot. Artificial lures are required for fishing. Supplies are available 20 mi. E at Forest Lakes.

GETTING THERE: From Heber go W on state HWY 260 approx. 11 mi. to forest route 300. Go W on 300 approx. 11 mi. to forest route 89. Go N on 89 approx. 2 mi. to Bear Canyon Lake CG.

SINGLE RATE:	No fee	OPEN DATES:	May-Oct
		MAX STAY:	14 days
		ELEVATION:	7600 feet

5 Benny Creek
Springerville • lat 34°02'39" lon 109°26'55"

DESCRIPTION: CG set in the open, under a canopy of ponderosa pine, situated on a bench above Benny Creek, within walking distance of Bunch Reservoir. Abert squirrels and chipmunks are common CG residents. Expect heavy rain through July and August. Supplies at Greer. Firewood is sold by concessionaire.

GETTING THERE: From Springerville go W on state HWY 260 approx. 11 mi. to state HWY 373. Go S on 373 approx. 2 mi. to Benny Creek CG.

SINGLE RATE:	$6	OPEN DATES:	Yearlong
# of SINGLE SITES:	24	MAX SPUR:	24 feet
		MAX STAY:	14 days
		ELEVATION:	8250 feet

6 Black Canyon Rim
Heber • lat 34°18'19" lon 110°44'31"

DESCRIPTION: The CG is set among ponderosa pine. Fishing and boating opportunities are popular at Black Canyon Lake. Please check fishing regulations. An historical grave site is located within walking distance of the CG. Supplies are available 8 mi. W at Forest Lakes.

GETTING THERE: From Heber go W on state HWY 260 approx. 11 mi. to forest route 300. Go S on 300 approx. 2 mi. to Black Canyon Rim CG.

SINGLE RATE:	$8	OPEN DATES:	May-Nov
# of SINGLE SITES:	21	MAX SPUR:	16 feet
		MAX STAY:	14 days
		ELEVATION:	7600 feet

7 Black Jack
Clifton • lat 33°03'00" lon 109°05'30"

DESCRIPTION: This CG is located in a park-like setting among ponderosa pine and oak trees. There are beautiful views of the rocky bluffs above Blackjack Cave. Supplies and groceries are available in Clifton. Wildlife in the area includes raptors, deer, wild turkeys, and javelinas.

GETTING THERE: From Clifton go S on US 191 to state HWY 781. Go N on 781 approx. 11 mi. to Black Jack CG.

SINGLE RATE:	No fee	OPEN DATES:	Yearlong*
# of SINGLE SITES:	10	MAX SPUR:	16 feet
		MAX STAY:	14 days
		ELEVATION:	6300 feet

8 Blue Crossing
Alpine • lat 33°37'44" lon 109°05'49"

DESCRIPTION: This CG is situated among cottonwoods along the Blue River. Beautiful rock art can be found near the CG. Wildlife in the area includes raptors, deer, javelinas, and wild turkeys. CG is located near the Blue Range Primitive Area. Tutt Creek Trail is accessable from CG.

GETTING THERE: From Alpine go S on US HWY 191 approx. 11 mi. to forest route 58. Go S on 58 approx. 3 mi. to forest route 567. Go S on 567 approx. 7 mi. to Blue Crossing CG.

SINGLE RATE:	No fee	OPEN DATES:	May-Oct
# of SINGLE SITES:	4	MAX SPUR:	16 feet
		MAX STAY:	14 days
		ELEVATION:	5800 feet

9 Brook Char
Springerville • lat 33°52'41" lon 109°24'30"

DESCRIPTION: CG with walk-in sites in a mixed setting of confier and aspen. This campground is the nearest to the lake shore. Expect rain, often heavy, through July and August. Full service store at the lake. Firewood sold by concessionaire. Bears can sometimes be a problem. Tent camping only.

GETTING THERE: From Springerville go W on state HWY 260 3 mi. to state HWY 261. Go S 17 mi. to forest route 113. Go S on 113 3 mi. to forest route 115. Go W on 115 1 mi. to forest route 115B and Brook Char CG.

SINGLE RATE:	$8	OPEN DATES:	May-Sept
# of SINGLE SITES:	13		
		MAX STAY:	14 days
		ELEVATION:	9040 feet

10 Buffalo Crossing
Alpine • lat 33°46'04" lon 109°21'16"

DESCRIPTION: CG sits on the East Fork. The river meanders through a forested valley shaded by tall ponderosa pine. CG is bordered by grasses, alder, and streamside hardwoods. Hiking, and fishing near CG. This is the largest CG along the river, and can accomodate larger recreation vehicles.

GETTING THERE: From Alpine go N on US HWY 180/191 approx. 2 mi. to forest route 249. Go E on 249 approx. 5 mi. to forest route 276. Go S on 276 approx. 6 mi. to Buffalo Crossing CG.

SINGLE RATE:	No fee	OPEN DATES:	May-Oct
# of SINGLE SITES:	16	MAX SPUR:	20 feet
		MAX STAY:	14 days
		ELEVATION:	7540 feet

 Campground has hosts   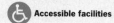 **Reservable sites**   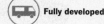 **Accessible facilities**

 Fully developed   **Semi-developed**   **Rustic facilities**

NOTE: Open dates listed are typical. Actual dates are dependent on conditions such as snow pack.

11 Canyon Point

Heber • lat 34°19'05" lon 110°49'29"

DESCRIPTION: CG located in a ponderosa pine forest. Be prepared for rain, often heavy, through July and August. CG is approx. 5 mi. from Willow Springs Lake with boating and fishing. Supplies are 2 mi. E at Forest Lakes. Hiking trails to Sinkhole and edge of the Mogollon Rim are nearby. RV sanitary station.

GETTING THERE: From Heber go W on state HWY 260 approx. 15 mi. to forest route 238. Go S on 238 approx. 1/2 mi. to Canyon Point CG.

SINGLE RATE:	Varies	OPEN DATES:	May-Oct
# of SINGLE SITES:	88	MAX SPUR:	75 feet
GROUP RATE:	Varies	MAX STAY:	14 days
# of GROUP SITES:	2	ELEVATION:	7680 feet

12 Chevelon Canyon Lake
Heber • lat 34°30'30" lon 110°50'00"

DESCRIPTION: The CG is situated in a mixture of ponderosa pine, juniper, and pinyon pine. Modestly developed. CG offers spectacular views and opportunities for hiking and fishing. The 3/4 mile trail down to the lake is a steady descent. Supplies and groceries can be found in Heber.

GETTING THERE: From Heber go W on state HWY 260 1 mi. to forest route 504. Go N on 504 16 mi. to Chevelon Crossing. Go S on forest route 169 7 mi. to forest route 169B. Go E 2 mi. to Chevelon Canyon Lake CG.

SINGLE RATE:	No fee	OPEN DATES:	May-Oct
# of SINGLE SITES:	8		
		MAX STAY:	14 days
		ELEVATION:	6800 feet

13 Chevelon Crossing
Heber • lat 34°35'30" lon 110°46'00"

DESCRIPTION: This CG was originally built by the Civilian Conservation Corps in the 1930's. Chevelon Crossing is a scenic and historic canyon area with the CG situated along Chevelon Creek. Supplies are available in Heber. Campers may gather dead and down firewood.

GETTING THERE: From Heber go W on state HWY 260 approx. 1 mi. to forest route 504. Go N on 504 approx. 16 mi. to Chevelon Crossing CG.

SINGLE RATE:	No fee	OPEN DATES:	Yearlong
# of SINGLE SITES:	7	MAX SPUR:	16 feet
		MAX STAY:	14 days
		ELEVATION:	6300 feet

14 Coal Creek
Clifton • lat 33°06'00" lon 109°04'00"

DESCRIPTION: This small CG is situated under large ponderosa pine and oak trees. The seasonal Coal Creek flows nearby. Campers may enjoy fishing in the area but please check fishing regulations. Wildlife in the area includes raptors, deer, wild turkeys, and javelinas. Supplies are available in Clifton.

GETTING THERE: From Clifton go S on US 191 to state HWY 781. Go N on 781 approx. 14 mi. to Coal Creek CG.

SINGLE RATE:	No fee	OPEN DATES:	Yearlong*
# of SINGLE SITES:	5	MAX SPUR:	16 feet
		MAX STAY:	14 days
		ELEVATION:	5900 feet

15 Crook

Heber • lat 34°23'00" lon 110°54'00"

DESCRIPTION: This CG is situated among ponderosa pine. CG is approx. .75 mi. from Woods Canyon Lake which offers boating, fishing, and supplies. Supplies also available 9 mi. E at Forest Lakes. 3 mi. away is the Rim Lakes Vista Trail, which provides spectacular views of the Mogollon Rim.

GETTING THERE: From Heber go W on state HWY 260 approx. 11 mi. to forest route 300. Go W on 300 approx. 3 mi. to forest route 105. Go N on 105 approx. 1/2 mi. to Crook CG.

SINGLE RATE:	$8	OPEN DATES:	May-Oct
# of SINGLE SITES:	26	MAX SPUR:	32 feet
		MAX STAY:	14 days
		ELEVATION:	7540 feet

16 Cutthroat Campground

Springerville • lat 33°52'41" lon 109°24'30"

DESCRIPTION: CG has many large ponderosa pine trees and stands of spruce and aspen. Tent camping only. Fishing, boating, hiking, bicycling, horseback riding, and bird watching are available nearby. Full service store at the lake. Dump station available on site. Bears can sometimes be a problem.

GETTING THERE: From Springerville go W on state HWY 260 3 mi. to state HWY 261. Go S on 261 17 mi. to forest route 113. Go S on 113 3 mi. to forest route 115. Go W on 115 approx. 1 mi. to Cutthroat CG.

SINGLE RATE:	$8	OPEN DATES:	May-Sept
# of SINGLE SITES:	18		
		MAX STAY:	14 days
		ELEVATION:	9040 feet

17 Deer Creek
Alpine • lat 33°48'27" lon 109°18'56"

DESCRIPTION: This CG is situated in a park-like setting and is the most rustic area along the East Fork of the Black River. Enjoy fishing in the area but please check for fishing regulations. Supplies are located in Alpine. Campers may gather dead and down firewood.

GETTING THERE: From Alpine go N on US HWY 180/191 approx. 1 mi. to forest route 249. Go W on 249 approx. 5 mi. to forest route 276. Go S on 276 approx. 6 mi. to Deer Creek CG.

SINGLE RATE:	No fee	OPEN DATES:	May-Oct
# of SINGLE SITES:	6	MAX SPUR:	45 feet
		MAX STAY:	14 days
		ELEVATION:	7645 feet

18 Diamond Rock
Alpine • lat 33°49'07" lon 109°17'58"

DESCRIPTION: This CG is shaded by tall ponderosa pine and bordered by grasses, alder, and streamside hardwoods. Situated along side the East Fork. Historical three-sided adirondack style shelters that were built by the CCC on site. Supplies and groceries can be found in Alpine.

GETTING THERE: From Alpine go N on US HWY 180/191 approx. 1 mi. to forest route 249. Go W on 249 approx. 5 mi. to forest route 276. Go S on 276 approx. 6 mi. to Diamond Rock CG.

SINGLE RATE:	No fee	OPEN DATES:	May-Oct
# of SINGLE SITES:	12	MAX SPUR:	10 feet
		MAX STAY:	14 days
		ELEVATION:	7890 feet

19 Fool Hollow Lake
Show Low • lat 34°16'00" lon 110°04'00"

DESCRIPTION: CG is located in ponderosa pine with juniper and pinyon pine scattered about. Many campsites have a view of the 150 acre lake and wildlife islands. A newly constructed day use area offers five large group picnic ramadas and two playgrounds. Supplies are available in Show Low.

GETTING THERE: From Show Low go N on forest route 331 approx. 2 mi. to Fool Hollow Lake CG.

SINGLE RATE:	Varies	OPEN DATES:	Yearlong
# of SINGLE SITES:	123	MAX SPUR:	45 feet
		MAX STAY:	15 days
		ELEVATION:	6280 feet

20 Gabaldon
Springerville • lat 33°53'00" lon 109°30'00"

DESCRIPTION: Gabaldon CG is situated amid spruce trees at the foot of the Mount Baldy. Trails connect the CG to the wilderness via the East Baldy Trail. Horse back riding, hiking, and fishing, are available in the surrounding area. CG is limited to campers with horses or stock animals.

GETTING THERE: From Springerville go W on state HWY 260 approx. 3 mi. to state HWY 261. Go S on 261 approx. 14 mi. to forest route 113. Go NW on 113 approx. 4 mi. to Gabaldon CG.

SINGLE RATE:	No fee	OPEN DATES:	June-Sept
# of SINGLE SITES:	5	MAX SPUR:	16 feet
		MAX STAY:	14 days
		ELEVATION:	9400 feet

 Campground has hosts   **Reservable sites**   **Accessible facilities**   **Fully developed**   **Semi-developed**   **Rustic facilities**

NOTE: Open dates listed are typical. Actual dates are dependent on conditions such as snow pack.

21 Gentry
Heber • lat 34°18'03" lon 110°42'36"

DESCRIPTION: This CG is set among ponderosa pine. Fishing and boating are popular at Black Canyon Lake which is located 4.5 mi. NE of CG. Please check fishing regulations. Enjoy a visit to Gentry Lookout which is located nearby. Supplies are available 10.5 mi. W at Forest Lakes.

GETTING THERE: From Heber go W on state HWY 260 approx. 11 mi. to forest route 300. Go S on 300 approx. 5 mi. to Gentry CG.

SINGLE RATE: # of SINGLE SITES:	No fee 6	OPEN DATES: MAX SPUR: MAX STAY: ELEVATION:	May-Nov 16 feet 14 days 7725 feet

26 Horse Springs
Alpine • lat 33°47'00" lon 109°21'30"

DESCRIPTION: This CG is situated in a forested valley. The site is shaded by tall ponderosa pine and bordered by grasses, alder, and streamside hardwoods. Adjacent to the East Fork of the Black River. Hiking and fishing available in the area. Supplies and groceries can be found in Alpine.

GETTING THERE: From Alpine go N on US HWY 180/191 approx. 1 mi. to forest route 249. Go W on 249 approx. 5 mi. to forest route 276. Go S on 276 approx. 6 mi. to Horse Springs CG.

SINGLE RATE: # of SINGLE SITES:	$10 27	OPEN DATES: MAX SPUR: MAX STAY: ELEVATION:	May-Oct 32 feet 14 days 7610 feet

22 Granville
Clifton • lat 33°11'15" lon 109°22'57"

DESCRIPTION: This pleasant CG offers plenty of shade from Arizona cypress, quaking aspen and gambel oak trees. The CG offers wildlife viewing opportunities. Wildlife in the area includes raptors, deer, wild turkeys, and javelinas. Supplies are available in Clifton.

GETTING THERE: From Clifton go N on US HWY 191 approx. 16 mi. to Granville CG.

SINGLE RATE: # of SINGLE SITES:	No fee 11	OPEN DATES: MAX SPUR: MAX STAY: ELEVATION:	Apr-Nov 16 feet 14 days 6604 feet

27 KP Cienega
Alpine • lat 33°34'34" lon 109°21'19"

DESCRIPTION: CG set in a green mountain meadow surrounded by fir and spruce trees. A network of hiking trails that wander all through the forest from CG. Only a few miles to Bear Wallow Wilderness area. The best mushroom hunting in Arizona is said to be in this area. Supplies at nearby Hannagan Meadow.

GETTING THERE: From Alpine go S on US HWY 191 approx. 27 mi. to KP Cienega CG.

SINGLE RATE: # of SINGLE SITES:	No fee 5	OPEN DATES: MAX SPUR: MAX STAY: ELEVATION:	May-Sept 16 feet 14 days 8960 feet

23 Grayling
Springerville • lat 33°52'41" lon 109°24'30"

DESCRIPTION: CG is set in a grove conifer and aspen, offers perhaps the most secluded sites in the Big Lake complex. Fishing, hiking, mountain biking, and horseback riding, are available nearby, as is the Mt. Baldy Wilderness Area. Dump station available on site. Bears may pose a problem.

GETTING THERE: From Springerville go W on state HWY 260 3 mi. to state HWY 261. Go S 17 mi. to forest route 113. Go S on 113 3 mi. to forest route 115. Go W on 115 1 mi. to forest route 115B & Grayling CG.

SINGLE RATE: # of SINGLE SITES:	$10 23	OPEN DATES: MAX SPUR: MAX STAY: ELEVATION:	May-Sept 22 feet 14 days 9040 feet

28 Lakeside
Lakeside • lat 34°09'27" lon 109°58'43"

DESCRIPTION: This CG is situated near Rainbow Lake and in the midst of beautiful ponderosa pine. The CG is one of the oldest National Forest campgrounds in the state of Arizona. This CG is very popular and can be busy weekends and holidays. There is a RV dump station on site.

GETTING THERE: Lakeside CG is located on Rainbow Lake at Lakeside, AZ on state HWY 173.

SINGLE RATE: # of SINGLE SITES:	Varies 82	OPEN DATES: MAX SPUR: MAX STAY: ELEVATION:	May-Sept 32 feet 14 days 6950 feet

24 Hannagan
Alpine • lat 33°38'09" lon 109°19'34"

DESCRIPTION: This CG is located in a mature forest setting. Elk, mule deer, and wild turkeys are abundant. CG accesses wonderful hiking trails that wander through the forest. Only a few mi. to the Bear Wallow Wilderness area. Supplies and groceries can be found in nearby Hannagan Meadow.

GETTING THERE: From Alpine go S on US HWY 91 approx. 21 mi. to Hannagan CG.

SINGLE RATE: # of SINGLE SITES:	No fee 8	OPEN DATES: MAX SPUR: MAX STAY: ELEVATION:	Apr-Nov 16 feet 14 days 9120 feet

29 Lewis Canyon Group Site
Pinedale • lat 34°17'11" lon 110°14'16"

DESCRIPTION: CG is located in a beautiful ponderosa pine setting with a large open field nearby. Wild turkeys, elk, and deer are often seen nearby. The trailhead to the Juniper Ridge Trail #640 is located at the group campground. This trail is open to non-motorized vehicles, hikers, horses, and mountain bicycles.

GETTING THERE: From Pinedale go S on forest route 130 approx. 2 mi. to Lewis Canyon Group Site CG.

GROUP RATE: # of GROUP SITES:	Varies 1	OPEN DATES: MAX SPUR: MAX STAY: ELEVATION:	May-Sept 45 feet 14 days 6540 feet

25 Honeymoon
Morenci • lat 33°28'31" lon 109°28'50"

DESCRIPTION: This CG is a quiet, remote site with lots of shade provided by sycamore and cottonwood trees along with pinyon and juniper trees. The CG is next to Eagle Creek. Wildlife in the area includes raptors, deer, wild turkeys, and javelinas. Supplies are available in Morenci.

GETTING THERE: From Morenci go N on US HWY 191 approx. 17 mi. to forest route 217. Go N on 217 approx. 18 mi. to Honeymoon CG.

SINGLE RATE: # of SINGLE SITES:	No fee 4	OPEN DATES: MAX SPUR: MAX STAY: ELEVATION:	May-Sept 16 feet 14 days 5440 feet

30 Los Burros
McNary • lat 34°08'27" lon 109°46'36"

DESCRIPTION: This CG is located in aspen at the edge of a large meadow. No drinking water available on site. There is also no garbage service. The CG is near a historic ranger station. Supplies and groceries are available 6 mi. S at McNary. Los Burros Trail is nearby.

GETTING THERE: From McNary go N on forest route 224 approx. 6 mi. to Los Burros CG.

SINGLE RATE: # of SINGLE SITES:	Varies 10	OPEN DATES: MAX SPUR: MAX STAY: ELEVATION:	May-Oct 30 feet 14 days 7820 feet

 Campground has hosts   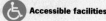 **Reservable sites**   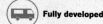 **Accessible facilities**   **Fully developed**   **Semi-developed**   **Rustic facilities**

NOTE: Open dates listed are typical. Actual dates are dependent on conditions such as snow pack.

APACHE-SITGREAVES NATIONAL FOREST • ARIZONA • 21 — 30

31 Lower Juan Miller
Morenci • lat 33°16'02" lon 109°20'24"

DESCRIPTION: This quiet CG is shaded by large gambel oak and sycamore trees. An old, hand dug cistern well can be seen north of the CG. This CG is seldom full. No drinking water is available on site. Supplies are available in Morenci. Campers may gather dead and down firewood.

GETTING THERE: From Morenci go N on US HWY 191 approx. 18 mi. to forest route 475. Go E on 475 approx. 2 mi. to Lower Juan Miller CG.

SINGLE RATE:	No fee	OPEN DATES:	Yearlong*
# of SINGLE SITES:	4	MAX SPUR:	16 feet
		MAX STAY:	14 days
		ELEVATION:	5740 feet

32 Luna Lake
Alpine • lat 33°50'10" lon 109°04'32"

DESCRIPTION: CG is located in a relatively open stand of ponderosa pine and is the largest CG on the Alpine District. CG is within walking distance of Luna Lake which has good rainbow trout fishing. Numerous wildlife in area. A system of trails are close to the camp. Supplies can be found in Alpine.

GETTING THERE: From Alpine go E on US HWY 180 approx. 5 mi. to forest route 570. Go N on 570 approx. 1 mi. to Luna Lake CG.

SINGLE RATE:	$8	OPEN DATES:	May-Sept
# of SINGLE SITES:	50	MAX SPUR:	32 feet
GROUP RATE:	Varies	MAX STAY:	14 days
# of GROUP SITES:	1	ELEVATION:	7960 feet

33 Mogollon
Heber • lat 34°23'00" lon 110°56'30"

DESCRIPTION: This CG is located among ponderosa pine. Woods Canyon Lake, which offers boating and fishing, is nearby. Supplies are available 9 mi. E at Forest Lakes; also available at Woods Canyon Store. Rim Lakes Vista Trail which provides spectacular views of the Mogollon Rim is 3 mi. away.

GETTING THERE: From Heber go W on state HWY 260 approx. 11 mi. to forest route 300. Go W on 300 approx. 3 mi. to Mogollon CG.

SINGLE RATE:	$8	OPEN DATES:	May-Oct
# of SINGLE SITES:	26	MAX SPUR:	32 feet
		MAX STAY:	14 days
		ELEVATION:	7515 feet

34 Racoon
Alpine • lat 33°48'27" lon 109°18'56"

DESCRIPTION: This CG is located in a forested valley and is shaded by tall ponderosa pine. The CG is bordered by grasses, alder, and streamside hardwoods. Campers may enjoy fishing in the area but please check for fishing regulations. Supplies and groceries are available in Alpine.

GETTING THERE: From Alpine go N on US HWY 180/191 approx. 1 mi. to forest route 249. Go E on 249 approx. 5 mi. to forest route 276. Go S on 276 approx. 6 mi. to Raccon CG.

SINGLE RATE:	No fee	OPEN DATES:	May-Oct
# of SINGLE SITES:	10	MAX SPUR:	40 feet
		MAX STAY:	14 days
		ELEVATION:	7600 feet

35 Rainbow
Springerville • lat 33°52'41" lon 109°24'30"

DESCRIPTION: This CG is in mixed conifer and aspen. It is the largest CG in the Big Lake complex. Deer, skunks, and bears are common CG visitors. A spur trail connects the campground with the Indian Springs hiking and biking trail. A RV dump station is available on site. Supplies are available in Springerville.

GETTING THERE: From Springerville go W on state HWY 260 3 mi. to state HWY 261. Go S on 261 17 mi. to forest route 113. Go S on 113 3 mi. to forest route 115. Go W on 115 1 mi. to forest route 559 and Rainbow CG

SINGLE RATE:	$10	OPEN DATES:	May-Sept
# of SINGLE SITES:	152	MAX SPUR:	32 feet
		MAX STAY:	14 days
		ELEVATION:	9100 feet

36 Rim
Heber • lat 34°17'00" lon 110°44'30"

DESCRIPTION: The CG is in the ponderosa pine. Willow Springs Lake and Woods Canyon Lake are nearby. Supplies are available 7 mi. E at Forest Lakes. Rim Lakes Vista Trail provides spectacular views of the Mogollon Rim. The General Crook National Recreation Trail is approx. 1 mi. from the CG.

GETTING THERE: Rim CG is located approx. 19 mi. W of Heber on state HWY 260.

SINGLE RATE:	$8	OPEN DATES:	May-Oct
# of SINGLE SITES:	26	MAX SPUR:	32 feet
		MAX STAY:	14 days
		ELEVATION:	7540 feet

37 Rolfe C. Hoyer
Springerville • lat 34°03'00" lon 109°28'30"

DESCRIPTION: CG situated among ponderosa pine. The Greer Lakes and the Little Colorado River are within walking distance for avid anglers. Interpretative programs are offered at the amphitheater and hosted nature walks occur throughout the summer. Supplies are available in Greer. Dump station available on site.

GETTING THERE: From Springerville go W on state HWY 260 approx. 11 mi. to state HWY 373. Go S on 373 approx. 3 mi. to Rolfe C. Hoyer CG.

SINGLE RATE:	$12	OPEN DATES:	May-Sept
# of SINGLE SITES:	100	MAX SPUR:	32 feet
		MAX STAY:	14 days
		ELEVATION:	8300 feet

38 Scott Reservoir
Lakeside • lat 34°10'23" lon 109°58'00"

DESCRIPTION: CG has only modest developments but is very popular throughout the summer. CG is near Scott's Reservoir. Many types of fish in Scott's Reservoir; rainbow trout, brown trout, channel cat, large mouth bass, green sunfish, blue gill, black bull head, and carp. Supplies at Pinetop-Lakeside, approx. 2 mi. away.

GETTING THERE: Scott Reservoir CG is located N of Lakeside on forest route 45.

SINGLE RATE:	No fee	OPEN DATES:	Yearlong*
# of SINGLE SITES:	12	MAX SPUR:	25 feet
		MAX STAY:	14 days
		ELEVATION:	6800 feet

39 Sink Hole
Heber • lat 34°22'00" lon 110°53'00"

DESCRIPTION: This CG is located in a ponderosa pine forest, and within walking distance of Willow Springs Lake. Supplies are available at Forest Lakes, 6 mi. E. Hiking and mountain bike trails are nearby. The General Crook National Recreation Trail is also within a mile of the CG.

GETTING THERE: From Heber go W on state HWY 260 approx. 18 mi. to Sink Hole CG.

SINGLE RATE:	$8	OPEN DATES:	May-Oct
# of SINGLE SITES:	26	MAX SPUR:	32 feet
		MAX STAY:	14 days
		ELEVATION:	7560 feet

40 South Fork
Springerville • lat 34°04'44" lon 109°24'43"

DESCRIPTION: CG set among ponderosa pine, with views of the 400-acre human caused forest fire of May 1989. Set along the South Fork of the Little Colorado River. Site of historic fish hatchery, converted into a CG in 1940. The South Fork trail (97) begins here, going S to Mexican Hay Lake, 7 mi. SE.

GETTING THERE: From Springerville go W on state HWY 260 approx. 5.5 mi. to forest route 560. Go S on 560 approx. 3 mi. to South Fork CG.

SINGLE RATE:	$6	OPEN DATES:	Yearlong*
# of SINGLE SITES:	8	MAX SPUR:	32 feet
		MAX STAY:	14 days
		ELEVATION:	7520 feet

 Campground has hosts   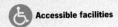 **Reservable sites**   **Accessible facilities**   **Fully developed**   **Semi-developed**   **Rustic facilities**

NOTE: Open dates listed are typical. Actual dates are dependent on conditions such as snow pack.

41 Spillway
Heber • lat 34°19'57" lon 110°56'30"

DESCRIPTION: This CG is situated in a forest setting of ponderosa pine, oak, and douglas fir. Woods Canyon Lake, which offers boating and fishing, is nearby. Supplies are available 10 mi. E at Forest Lakes. Interpretative nature trail at the north end of lake. RV sanitary station.

GETTING THERE: From Heber go W on state HWY 260 approx. 11 mi. to forest route 300. Go W on 300 approx. 3 mi. to forest route 105. Go N on 105 approx. 2 mi. to Spillway CG.

SINGLE RATE:	$14	OPEN DATES:	May-Sept
# of SINGLE SITES:	26	MAX SPUR:	16 feet
GROUP RATE:	$50	MAX STAY:	14 days
# of GROUP SITES:	1	ELEVATION:	7500 feet

42 Stray Horse
Alpine • lat 33°33'01" lon 109°19'03"

DESCRIPTION: The rustic CG is set among large pine and oak. Located six miles below the Mogollon Rim, the CG provides a cool shady site for camping. Strayhorse is the head for two major trails: Highline Trail #47 and Raspberry Trail #35. Horse are corrals available on site.

GETTING THERE: From Alpine go S on US HWY 191 approx. 26 mi. to Stray Horse CG.

SINGLE RATE:	No fee	OPEN DATES:	Apr-Nov
# of SINGLE SITES:	7	MAX SPUR:	16 feet
		MAX STAY:	14 days
		ELEVATION:	7780 feet

43 Upper Blue
Alpine • lat 33°41'42" lon 109°04'17"

DESCRIPTION: This CG is situated among pine along the Blue River. Campers may enjoy fishing in the area but please check fishing regulations. Wildlife in the area includes raptors, deer, wild turkeys, and javelinas. Supplies are available in Alpine.

GETTING THERE: From Alpine go E on US HWY 180 approx. 2 mi. to forest route 281. Go S on 281 approx. 12 mi. to Upper Blue CG.

SINGLE RATE:	No fee	OPEN DATES:	Yearlong
# of SINGLE SITES:	3	MAX SPUR:	16 feet
		MAX STAY:	14 days
		ELEVATION:	6200 feet

44 Upper Juan Miller
Morenci • lat 33°16'08" lon 109°20'50"

DESCRIPTION: This quiet CG is shaded by large gambel oak and sycamore trees. The CG is seldom full. The area provides camping, water play and wildlife viewing. No drinking water is available on site. Campers may gather dead and down firewood. Supplies are available in Morenci.

GETTING THERE: From Morenci go N on US HWY 191 approx. 18 mi. to forest route 475. Go E on 475 approx. 1 mi. to Upper Juan Miller CG. Not suitable for trailers. Tent camping only.

SINGLE RATE:	No fee	OPEN DATES:	Yearlong*
# of SINGLE SITES:	4	MAX SPUR:	16 feet
		MAX STAY:	14 days
		ELEVATION:	5780 feet

45 West Fork
Alpine • lat 33°46'37" lon 109°24'52"

DESCRIPTION: This CG has upstream sites that have more of a deep forest character, while downstream sites tend to be open and grassy. Three-sided Adirondack shelters built by the CCC give this area a quaint historic atmosphere. Supplies and groceries can be found Alpine. Trails in nearby area.

GETTING THERE: From Alpine go N 1 mi. on US HWY 180/191 to forest route 249. Go W 5 mi. to forest route 276. Go S 12 mi. to forest route 25. Go W 4 mi. to forest route 68. Go N 2 mi. to West Fork CG.

SINGLE RATE:	No fee	OPEN DATES:	May-Oct
# of SINGLE SITES:	70		
		MAX STAY:	14 days
		ELEVATION:	7740 feet

46 Winn
Springerville • lat 33°58'04" lon 109°29'03"

DESCRIPTION: This CG situated among mixed conifer and aspen. Near the Mount Baldy trailheads and East Colorado River. Some sites border a large meadow where elk are often seen at twilight. Activities such as horse back riding, hiking, and fishing, are available in the surrounding area.

GETTING THERE: From Springerville go W on state HWY 260 3 mi. to state HWY 261. Go S on 261 14 mi. to forest route 113. Go NW on 113 5 mi. to forest route 554. Go N on 554 approx. 2 mi. to Winn CG.

SINGLE RATE:	$10	OPEN DATES:	May-Oct
# of SINGLE SITES:	63	MAX SPUR:	45 feet
GROUP RATE:	$50	MAX STAY:	14 days
# of GROUP SITES:	2	ELEVATION:	9320 feet

 Campground has hosts   **Reservable sites**   **Accessible facilities**   **Fully developed**   **Semi-developed**   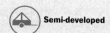 **Rustic facilities**

NOTE: Open dates listed are typical. Actual dates are dependent on conditions such as snow pack.

USFS Photo

COCONINO NATIONAL FOREST

Located near Flagstaff, the Coconino National Forest contains 1.8 million acres, which vary from semi-arid desert through ponderosa pine forests to alpine tundra. Elevation ranges from 2,600 feet in canyon bottoms to 12,643 feet at the top of the San Francisco Peaks.

The Coconino is made up of a number of distinct environments, each with their own unique flavor. The Volcanic Highlands is an area of high-country mountain forests and meadows where views from the summit of the San Francisco Peaks stretch to the Grand Canyon's North Rim over eighty miles away. Plateau Country provides wide-open spaces, dotted with lakes and abundant wildlife. You will find lush forests on the edge of the Mogollon Rim, a rugged escarpment that forms the southern limit of the Colorado Plateau. Deep wilderness canyons await the visitor to Desert Canyon Country, and in the Red Rocks region, see the colorful collection of buttes, pinnacles, mesas and canyons, the subject of countless paintings, photographs and other works of art.

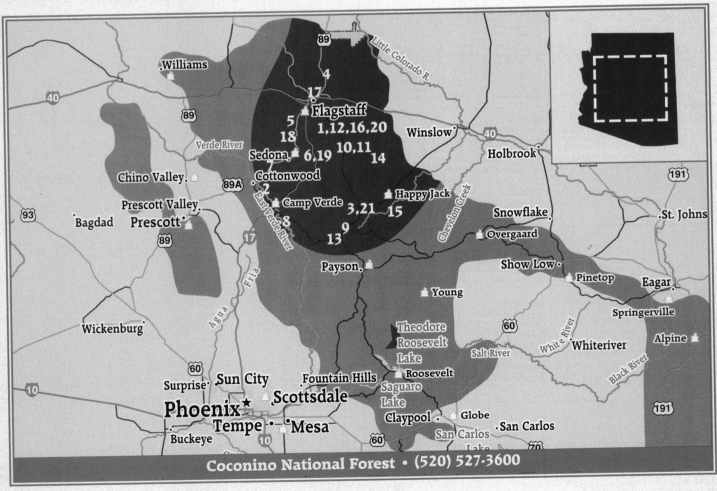

Coconino National Forest • (520) 527-3600

1. Ashurst Lake
Flagstaff • lat 35°01'09" lon 111°24'25"

DESCRIPTION: A lakeside CG in a gnarly stand of old juniper trees and pinyon pines. Warm to hot days, sometimes windy. Fish and sail-board Lake Ashurst even in drought years. Gather firewood locally. Supplies in Flagstaff. Birdwatching for Ibis, teal, pintails, bald eagles, osprey, hawks, and song birds.

GETTING THERE: From Flagstaff go S on US HWY 66 approx. 3 mi. to forest HWY 3. Go SE on 3 approx. 17 mi. to forest route 82E. Go E on 82E approx. 3 mi. to Ashurst Lake CG.

SINGLE RATE:	$8	OPEN DATES:	May-Sept
# of SINGLE SITES:	25	MAX SPUR:	35 feet
		MAX STAY:	14 days
		ELEVATION:	7000 feet

2. Beaver Creek
Camp Verde • lat 34°40'11" lon 111°42'49"

DESCRIPTION: Set in a desert of sycamores, Arizona Cypress, cottonwood, juniper, cacti, & sandstone rock formations on Beaver Creek. Hot summers, cold winters. Fish for rainbow & bass. Prehistoric Rock Art site, V-V. Beaver Creek Wilderness, Bell, Walker Basin, & Long Canyon Trails nearby. Racoon, javalinas, & snakes.

GETTING THERE: From Camp Verde go N on I-17 approx. 12 mi. to Sedona interchange. Go E on forest route 618 approx. 2 mi. to Beaver Creek CG.

SINGLE RATE:	$8	OPEN DATES:	Yearlong
# of SINGLE SITES:	13	MAX SPUR:	32 feet
GROUP RATE:	Varies	MAX STAY:	14 days
# of GROUP SITES:	1	ELEVATION:	3800 feet

3. Blue Ridge
Pine • lat 34°35'29" lon 111°12'01"

DESCRIPTION: CG is an open, park-like setting within a ponderosa pine forest. Fishing and boating 5 mi. at Blue Ridge Lake. Supplies are 10 mi. SE of CG at Clints Well. Great for photography of wildlife and scenery. Arizona Trail passes right by the CG. This CG is especially nice for families with small children.

GETTING THERE: From Pine go NE on state HWY 87 approx. 29 mi. to forest route 138. Go S on 138 approx. 1 mi. to Blue Ridge CG.

SINGLE RATE:	$5	OPEN DATES:	May-Sept*
# of SINGLE SITES:	10	MAX SPUR:	32 feet
		MAX STAY:	14 days
		ELEVATION:	7300 feet

4. Bonito
Flagstaff • lat 35°22'09" lon 111°32'30"

DESCRIPTION: Open CG set in the high desert plans. Views of cinder cones and lava rock. Hot days with cool nights. Nearby Sunset Crater and Wupatki National Monument for native history. Supplies available in Flagstaff. Firewood is scarce. One accessible site. Interpretive programs and hiking.

GETTING THERE: From Flagstaff go N on US HWY 89 approx. 12 mi. to forest route 545. Go E on 545 approx. 2 mi. to Bonito CG.

SINGLE RATE:	$10	OPEN DATES:	May-Sept *
# of SINGLE SITES:	44	MAX SPUR:	22 feet
		MAX STAY:	14 days
		ELEVATION:	6900 feet

5. Bootlegger
Sedona • lat 34°57'30" lon 111°45'00"

DESCRIPTION: A small creekside CG with fishing and swimming holes on site. Arizona ash, gravel beaches, and streambed boulders. Colorful songbirds. Popular site, fills fast. Superb scenery, clear water, excellent wildlife, picturesque hiking trails. Supplies in Sedona. Firewood may be scarce. No drinking water.

GETTING THERE: Bootlegger CG is located approx. 9 mi. N of Sedona on US HWY 89A. Not suitable for trailers or RVs.

SINGLE RATE:	$15	OPEN DATES:	Mar-Oct
# of SINGLE SITES:	10		
		MAX STAY:	10 days
		ELEVATION:	5200 feet

6. Cave Spring
Sedona • lat 34°59'47" lon 111°44'19"

DESCRIPTION: CG set in shady stand of pine, ash, and maple trees in the upper canyon on Oak Creek. Fish for stocked rainbow trout from the creek. See the cave in the meadow by CG, where early settlers lived. Supplies in Sedona. Firewood sold at CG. Trails into canyon offer great birdwatching.

GETTING THERE: Cave Spring CG is located approx. 12 mi. N of Sedona on US HWY 89A.

SINGLE RATE:	$15	OPEN DATES:	Apr-Oct
# of SINGLE SITES:	78	MAX SPUR:	32 feet
		MAX STAY:	7 days
		ELEVATION:	5400 feet

7. Chavez Crossing Group
Sedona • lat 34°50'36" lon 111°46'34"

DESCRIPTION: This CG is situated at the edge of Sedona in a sycamore and cypress grove. Offers a country and creekside setting known for red rock scenery. Firewood may be scarce, best to bring your own. Fishing in Oak Creek, check for local regulations. Swimming and hiking opportunities are nearby.

GETTING THERE: Chavez Crossing is located approx. 2 mi. S of Sedona on state HWY 179. Not suitable for trailers.

GROUP RATE:	Varies	OPEN DATES:	Yearlong
		MAX SPUR:	35 feet
# of GROUP SITES:	3	MAX STAY:	14 days
		ELEVATION:	4100 feet

8. Clear Creek Group Site
Camp Verde • lat 34°30'55" lon 111°45'52"

DESCRIPTION: A desert canyon country camp on West Clear Creek. Cool water. Stream fishing on creek. Wildlife watching in adjacent oasis for songbirds and raptors. Cactus may be seen on nearby hiking treks. Supplies in are available at Camp Verde. $8-$30 depending on group size (15-80 persons).

GETTING THERE: From Camp Verde go E on state HWY 9 approx. 5 mi. to forest route 626. Go N on 626 to Clear Creek CG.

SINGLE RATE:	Varies	OPEN DATES:	Yearlong
# of SINGLE SITES:	18	MAX SPUR:	32 feet
		MAX STAY:	7 days
# of GROUP SITES:	1	ELEVATION:	3200 feet

9. Clints Well
Happy Jack • lat 34°33'00" lon 111°19'00"

DESCRIPTION: This CG is situated in shady stand of tall, old growth ponderosa pine. Easy access makes this a popular CG, fills quickly. Mogollon rim, a 2,000' drop off marking Colorado Plateau is nearby. Easy driving to a number of forest lakes known for fishing. Numerous hiking trails in area.

GETTING THERE: Clints Well CG is located approx. 13 mi. S of Happy Jack on forest HWY 3.

SINGLE RATE:	No fee	OPEN DATES:	Yearlong*
# of SINGLE SITES:	7	MAX SPUR:	22 feet
		MAX STAY:	14 days
		ELEVATION:	7000 feet

10. Dairy Springs
Mormon Lake • lat 34°57'24" lon 111°29'04"

DESCRIPTION: CG in a park like grove of pine and fir with scenic mountain views. Boat and shore fishing, along with swimming, on Mormon Lake. Excellent bird watching. Elk and deer frequent area. Supplies and gas at resort village on lake. Gather firewood locally. Horse, hiking, and mountain bike trails nearby.

GETTING THERE: From Mormon Lake go N on forest route 90 approx. 3.5 mi. to Dairy Springs CG.

SINGLE RATE:	$8	OPEN DATES:	May-Sept*
# of SINGLE SITES:	27	MAX SPUR:	35 feet
GROUP RATE:	Varies	MAX STAY:	14 days
# of GROUP SITES:	2	ELEVATION:	7000 feet

 Campground has hosts   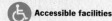 **Reservable sites**   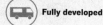 **Accessible facilities**   **Fully developed**   **Semi-developed**   Rustic facilities

NOTE: Open dates listed are typical. Actual dates are dependent on conditions such as snow pack.

11 Double Springs
Mormon Lake • lat 34°56'34" lon 111°29'30"

DESCRIPTION: This CG is situated In park like groves of pine and fir. Scenic mountain views. Boat and shore fishing on Mormon Lake. Excellent bird watching. Elk, deer, and small wildlife in area. Supplies and gas at resort village on lake. Horse, hiking, and mountain bike trails.

GETTING THERE: From Mormon Lake go N on forest route 90 approx. 3.5 mi. to Double Springs CG.

SINGLE RATE:	$8	OPEN DATES:	May-Sept
# of SINGLE SITES:	16	MAX SPUR:	35 feet
		MAX STAY:	14 days
		ELEVATION:	7000 feet

16 Lakeview
Flagstaff • lat 35°03'00" lon 111°30'00"

DESCRIPTION: CG in a cool stand of pine bordered by high country meadows on Upper Lake Mary. Fishin and swiming on the lake. Many stocked trout lakes are in the area. Boat ramp nearby. Supplies available at Lakeview. Elk, mule deer, bald eagles, and osprey, can be seen in the area. Hiking trails nearby.

GETTING THERE: From Lakeview go S on US HWY 66 approx. 3 mi. to forest HWY 3. Go SE on 3 approx. 13 mi. to Lakeview CG.

SINGLE RATE:	$8	OPEN DATES:	May-Oct*
# of SINGLE SITES:	30	MAX SPUR:	26 feet
		MAX STAY:	14 days
		ELEVATION:	6900 feet

12 Forked Pine
Flagstaff • lat 35°01'16" lon 111°23'54"

DESCRIPTION: A lakeside CG in a gnarly stand of old juniper trees and pinyon pine. Warm to hot days, may be windy. Fish and sail board Lake Ashurst even in drought years. Gather firewood locally. Supplies in Flagstaff. Birdwatching for Ibis, teals, pintails, bald eagles, osprey, hawks, and song birds.

GETTING THERE: From Flagstaff go S on US HWY 66 approx. 3 mi. to forest HWY 3. Go SE on 3 approx. 17 mi. to forest route 82E. Go E on 82E approx. 4 mi. to Forked Pine CG.

SINGLE RATE:	$8	OPEN DATES:	May-Sept
# of SINGLE SITES:	33	MAX SPUR:	26 feet
		MAX STAY:	14 days
		ELEVATION:	7100 feet

17 Little Eldon Springs
Flagstaff • lat 35°16'00" lon 111°35'00"

DESCRIPTION: CG is located at the base of Mt. Elden in a grove of ponderosa pine and gamble oak. Supplies available at Flagstaff. Desert and mountain wildlife can be seen in the area. Campers may gather firewood. A horse trail system that leads into the mountain areas is located nearby.

GETTING THERE: From Flagstaff go N on US HWY 89 approx. 5 mi. to forest route 556. Go W on 556 approx. 2.5 mi. to Little Eldon Springs CG.

SINGLE RATE:	$8	OPEN DATES:	Apr-Sept
# of SINGLE SITES:	44	MAX SPUR:	35 feet
		MAX STAY:	14 days
		ELEVATION:	7200 feet

13 Kehl Spring
Pine • lat 34°26'00" lon 111°19'00"

DESCRIPTION: In shady ponderosa pine stand at brink of Mogolon Rim. Super views of Four Peaks, Sierra Anchas and Mazatzals. Fishing and boating nearby. The rim marks the end of the Colorado Plateau with a drop-off plunging 2,000' from forested highland to Sonoran desert. Nearby hiking, mountain biking trails.

GETTING THERE: From Pine go N on state HWY 87 approx. 13 mi. to forest route 300. Go E on 300 approx. 7 mi. to Kehl Springs CG.

SINGLE RATE:	No fee	OPEN DATES:	May-Sept
# of SINGLE SITES:	8	MAX SPUR:	22 feet
		MAX STAY:	14 days
		ELEVATION:	7500 feet

18 Manzanita
Sedona • lat 34°56'11" lon 111°44'39"

DESCRIPTION: A small creekside CG with fishing and swimming holes on site. Arizona ash, gravel beaches, and streambed boulders. Colorful songbirds. Popular site, fills fast. Superb scenery, clear water, excellent wildlife, picturesque hiking trails. Supplies in Sedona. Firewood may be scarce, best to bring your own.

GETTING THERE: Manzanita CG is located approx. 6 mi. N of Sedona on US HWY 89A. Trailers and RVs are not permitted.

SINGLE RATE:	$12	OPEN DATES:	Yearlong
# of SINGLE SITES:	19		
		MAX STAY:	10 days
		ELEVATION:	4800 feet

14 Kinnikinnick
Mormon Lake • lat 34°53'47" lon 111°18'42"

DESCRIPTION: CG near cold water lakes of Kinnikinick and Morton. Views of San Francisco Peaks, prairies and lake. Rainbow, brown, and brook trout are stocked in lake (boats up to 8 hp). Elk, antelope, bald eagles, and small wildlife in area. Canoe and hiking popular. No drinking water available.

GETTING THERE: From Flagstaff go S on forest route 3 approx. 30 mi. to forest route 125. Go E on 125 approx. 4 mi. to forest route 82. Go SE on 82 approx. 5.5 mi. to Kinnikinick CG.

SINGLE RATE:	$6	OPEN DATES:	May-Sept*
# of SINGLE SITES:	18	MAX SPUR:	22 feet
		MAX STAY:	14 days
		ELEVATION:	7000 feet

19   Pine Flat
Sedona • lat 35°00'42" lon 111°44'13"

DESCRIPTION: CG located in shady a stand of pine on Oak Creek. Very popular swimming holes and fishing on the creek. Hot days with cold nights. Supplies in Sedona or Flagstaff. Fills fast, weekdays are best. Campers may gather firewood. Trails into canyon offer great birdwatching. Photographer's heaven.

GETTING THERE: Pine Flat CG is located approx. 13 mi. N of Sedona on US HWY 89A.

SINGLE RATE:	$12	OPEN DATES:	Mar-Oct
# of SINGLE SITES:	58	MAX SPUR:	30 feet
		MAX STAY:	7 days
		ELEVATION:	5500 feet

15 Knoll Lake
Pine • lat 34°25'39" lon 111°05'31"

DESCRIPTION: Located near the spectacular Mogollon Rim, a 2,000' escarpment marking the edge of the Colorado Plateau. Shore and small boat fishing on Knoll lake. Warm days, cool nights. Supplies in Pine or 50 mi. in Flagstaff. Scenic panoramic setting for photography, hiking, mountain biking, and horseback riding.

GETTING THERE: From Pine go N on state HWY 87 approx. 13 mi. to forest route 300. Go E on 300 approx. 29 mi. to forest route 295E. Go NE on 295E approx. 3.5 mi. to Knoll Lake CG.

SINGLE RATE:	$6	OPEN DATES:	May-Sept
# of SINGLE SITES:	33	MAX SPUR:	32 feet
		MAX STAY:	14 days
		ELEVATION:	7400 feet

20   Pine Grove
Flagstaff • lat 35°01'43" lon 111°27'12"

DESCRIPTION: CG in a cool stand of pine bordered by high country meadows on Upper Lake Mary. Fishing and swiming on the lake. Many stocked trout lakes are in the area. Boat ramp nearby. Supplies available at Lakeview. Elk, mule deer, bald eagles, and osprey can be seen in the area. Hiking trails nearby.

GETTING THERE: From Flagstaff go S on US HWY 66 approx. 3 mi. to forest HWY 3. Go SE on 3 approx. 17 mi. to forest route 651. Go W on 651 approx. 1/2 mi. to Pine Grove CG.

SINGLE RATE:	$10	OPEN DATES:	May-Sept*
# of SINGLE SITES:	46	MAX SPUR:	46 feet
		MAX STAY:	14 days
		ELEVATION:	6900 feet

 Campground has hosts   **Reservable sites** 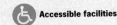 **Accessible facilities** 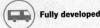 **Fully developed**   **Semi-developed**   **Rustic facilities**

NOTE: Open dates listed are typical. Actual dates are dependent on conditions such as snow pack.

21 · Rock Crossing
Pine • lat 34°33'45" lon 111°12'56"

DESCRIPTION: Near Blue Ridge Reservoir, which is within forested canyon walls in secluded wooded setting. Warm days with cool nights. Shore or boat fish for trout species on lake. Supplies in Pine or in Flagstaff. Hiking, and mountain biking opportunities available in canyon uplands.

GETTING THERE: From Pine go NE on state HWY 87 approx. 26 mi. to forest route 751. Go SE on 751 approx. 3 mi. to Rock Crossing CG.

SINGLE RATE:	**$5**	**OPEN DATES:**	**May-Sept***
# of SINGLE SITES:	**35**	**MAX SPUR:**	**32 feet**
		MAX STAY:	**14 days**
		ELEVATION:	**7500 feet**

The Lighthouses of the West...

Fire-looks outs were used in days gone by as vantage points to watch for distant signs of smoke. Lookouts are less critical today given modern satellite and infrared technologies. The views, however, have not become obsolete! You can rent many of these lookouts on a nightly basis, from $20 to $40 on average.

 Campground has hosts   **Reservable sites**   **Accessible facilities**   **Fully developed**   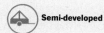 **Semi-developed**   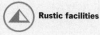 **Rustic facilities**

NOTE: Open dates listed are typical. Actual dates are dependent on conditions such as snow pack.

USFS Photo

CORONADO NATIONAL FOREST

The Spanish explorer Don Francisco Vasques de Coronado and his expedition entered southern Arizona from Mexico in 1540 in search of gold. But instead of the Seven Golden Cities of Cibola, which legend said existed somewhere to the north, the trailblazers found nothing but a vast country of grassy hills, cactus, lizards, and scattered, rugged mountain ranges. They rise like islands in a sea of desert. Their heights pierce the clouds, capturing the snow and rain that are the lifeblood of cities, industry, and agriculture. In the arid Southwest, water from the highlands makes possible a wide range of activities in a land that would otherwise be barren.

That area today is part of the Coronado National Forest, which consists of twelve mountain ranges totaling 1.7 million acres in southern Arizona and New Mexico. The area offers an unusual range of vegetation types and climates and in only one hour, a visitor can drive from the hot, arid desert to the cool pines. From the rolling grasslands to the high mountain conifer forests, there is an exceptionally diverse selection of flora and fauna.

The elevations of the twelve mountain ranges span from 2,400 feet up to 10,500 feet.

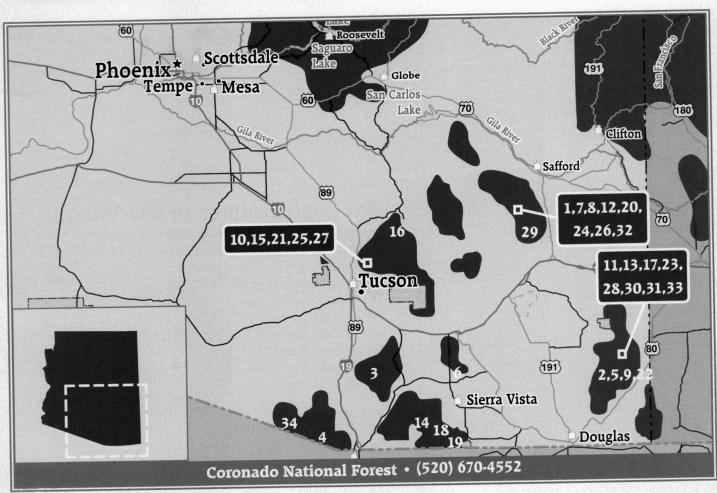

Coronado National Forest • (520) 670-4552

1 Arcadia
Safford • lat 32°38'55" lon 109°49'08"

DESCRIPTION: This CG is situated in a dense oak and pine forest with the only views being those of the forest. Supplies are available at Safford. Deer, bears, skunks, squirrels, and chipmunks are common to the area. The National Recreation Trail runs near CG and goes to Shanon CG.

GETTING THERE: From Safford go S on US HWY 191 approx. 8 mi. to state HWY 366. Go SW on 366 approx. 12 mi. to Arcadia CG.

SINGLE RATE:	$10	OPEN DATES:	May-Oct*
# of SINGLE SITES:	19	MAX SPUR:	22 feet
		MAX STAY:	14 days
		ELEVATION:	6700 feet

2 Bathtub
Elfrida • lat 31°46'46" lon 109°18'35"

DESCRIPTION: This CG is situated on a forested bench overlooking Rucker Lake. Enjoy fishing for rainbow trout in the lake. Supplies are available at Elfrida. There is numerous wildlife to view in the area. Campers may gather their firewood (dead and down) locally. Several trails are in the area.

GETTING THERE: From Elfrida go N on US HWY 191 approx. 6 mi. to forest route 74. Go E on 74 approx. 23 mi. to forest route 74E. Go NE on 74E approx. 5 mi. to Bathtub CG. Not suitable for trailers.

SINGLE RATE:	$7	OPEN DATES:	Yearlong
# of SINGLE SITES:	11	MAX SPUR:	16 feet
		MAX STAY:	14 days
		ELEVATION:	6300 feet

3 Bog Springs
Green Valley • lat 31°43'36" lon 110°52'28"

DESCRIPTION: CG set in a douglas fir and alpine forest with shaded sites. Views of the Santa Rita Mountains. The only sites within the Madera Canyon Rec. Area. Supplies are available in Green Valley. CG is known for its world famous birdwatching. Bring your own firewood. Numerous trails in the area.

GETTING THERE: From Green Valley go S on I-19 approx. 2 mi. to forest route 62. Go S on 62 approx. 7 mi. to forest route 70. Go S on 70 approx. 6 mi. to Bog Springs CG.

SINGLE RATE:	$10	OPEN DATES:	Yearlong
# of SINGLE SITES:	13	MAX SPUR:	22 feet
		MAX STAY:	14 days
		ELEVATION:	5200 feet

4 Calabasas Group Site
Nogales • lat 31°23'05" lon 111°03'05"

DESCRIPTION: In a quiet area near PeÒa Blanca Lake. The lake is a popular area for fishing, boating, and birdwatching. Supplies at Nogales. Deer, bears, and elk in area. Pathways lead to tops of low hills in area where you will find good views of the surrounding hills, valleys, and mountains. Bring your own firewood.

GETTING THERE: From Nogales go N on I-19 approx. 5 mi. to state HWY 289 (Ruby Interchange). Go W on state HWY 289 approx. 6 mi. to Calabasas CG.

		OPEN DATES:	Yearlong
		MAX SPUR:	22 feet
GROUP RATE:	Varies	MAX STAY:	14 days
# of GROUP SITES:	1	ELEVATION:	4000 feet

5 Camp Rucker
Elfrida • lat 31°45'37" lon 109°22'00"

DESCRIPTION: CG situated in a mixture of oak, juniper, and walnut trees with grassy open areas. Views of Monte Vista Peak nearby. Rucker Creek is close to CG. Fish for trout from the creek. Historical Rucker Military Camp and Ranch nearby. RV dump station. Rucker Canyon Trail nearby.

GETTING THERE: From Elfrida go N on US HWY 191 approx. 6 mi. to forest route 74. Go E on 74 approx. 23 mi. to Camp Rucker CG.

SINGLE RATE:	$7	OPEN DATES:	Yearlong
		MAX SPUR:	16 feet
GROUP RATE:	Varies	MAX STAY:	14 days
# of GROUP SITES:	1	ELEVATION:	5600 feet

6 Cochise Stronghold
Pearce • lat 31°55'30" lon 109°49'00"

DESCRIPTION: This CG is situated in a beautiful, dense stand of oak and juniper. Supplies are available in Pearce. There is numerous wildlife to view in the area. The CG is a trailhead to the Cochise Trail. Nature and historic trails also start at this CG.

GETTING THERE: From Pearce go N on US HWY 191 approx. 3 mi. to county route 84. Go W on 84 approx. 8 mi. to Cochise Stronghold CG.

SINGLE RATE:	$10	OPEN DATES:	Yearlong
# of SINGLE SITES:	18	MAX SPUR:	22 feet
		MAX STAY:	14 days
		ELEVATION:	5000 feet

7 Columbine Corrals
Safford • lat 32°40'00" lon 109°54'00"

DESCRIPTION: In a primarily spruce and fir forest setting with Rigs Lake and Ash Creek nearby. Fish from Rigs Lake for stocked rainbow trout and from Ash Creek for trout. Supplies available at Safford. Deer, bears, skunks, squirrels and chipmunks are common to this area. Ash Creek Trail leads you to Ash Creek.

GETTING THERE: From Safford go S on US HWY 191 approx. 8 mi. to state HWY 366. Go SW on 366 approx. 28 mi. to Columbine Corrals CG.

SINGLE RATE:	$10	OPEN DATES:	May-Oct*
# of SINGLE SITES:	6	MAX SPUR:	16 feet
		MAX STAY:	14 days
		ELEVATION:	9600 feet

8 Cunningham
Safford • lat 32°39'00" lon 109°53'00"

DESCRIPTION: In a primarily spruce and fir forest setting with an open meadow. Supplies available at Safford. Deer, bears, skunks, squirrels and chipmunks are common to this area. Campers may gather firewood. A trail from CG leads you to Grant Creek where you can fish for trout.

GETTING THERE: From Safford go S on US HWY 191 approx. 8 mi. to state HWY 366. Go SW on 366 approx. 25 mi. to Cunningham CG.

SINGLE RATE:	No fee	OPEN DATES:	May-Oct
# of SINGLE SITES:	10	MAX SPUR:	22 feet
		MAX STAY:	14 days
		ELEVATION:	9000 feet

9 Cypress
Elfrida • lat 31°46'30" lon 109°19'00"

DESCRIPTION: CG in a setting of exceptionally large Arizona cypress nestled on the banks of Rucker Creek. Rucker Lake is nearby with stocked trout fishing. Supplies available at Elfrida. Numerous wildlife in the area. Campers may gather their firewood locally. A number of forest trails are in the area.

GETTING THERE: From Elfrida go N on US HWY 191 approx. 6 mi. to forest route 74. Go E on 74 approx. 23 mi. to forest route 74E. Go NE on 74E approx. 4 mi. to Cypress Park CG.

SINGLE RATE:	$5	OPEN DATES:	Mar-Oct
# of SINGLE SITES:	7	MAX SPUR:	16 feet
		MAX STAY:	14 days
		ELEVATION:	6000 feet

10 General Hitchcock
Tucson • lat 32°22'41" lon 110°40'53"

DESCRIPTION: Small CG in a canopy of ponderosa pine, juniper and oak near the rocky streambed of upper Bears Canyon. The nearby granite strata have weathered into outlandish shapes, a number of which can be seen through breaks in the tree cover that shades the CG. Supplies available at Tucson.

GETTING THERE: General Hitchcock CG is located approx. 29 mi. NE of Tucson on the Catalina HWY. Not suitable for trailers.

SINGLE RATE:	$5	OPEN DATES:	Yearlong
# of SINGLE SITES:	11	MAX SPUR:	22 feet
		MAX STAY:	11 days
		ELEVATION:	6000 feet

 Campground has hosts   **Reservable sites**   **Accessible facilities**   **Fully developed**   **Semi-developed** **Rustic facilities**

NOTE: Open dates listed are typical. Actual dates are dependent on conditions such as snow pack.

11 Herb Martyr
Portal • lat 31°52'15" lon 109°14'00"

DESCRIPTION: CG in a mixed forest on Cave Creek with great views of the waterfall. Fish and swim from the creek. Supplies available at Portal. Numerous wildlife in the area. Crystal Cave nearby. Historical Herb Martyr Dam next to the CG. Hiking trails and Chiricahua Wilderness in the area. No drinking water available.

GETTING THERE: From Portal go S on forest route 42 approx. 5 mi. to forest route 42A. Go W on 42A approx. 2 mi. to Herb Martyr CG. Not suitable for trailers.

SINGLE RATE:	No fee	OPEN DATES:	Yearlong
# of SINGLE SITES:	5		
		MAX STAY:	14 days
		ELEVATION:	5800 feet

12 Hospital Flat
Safford • lat 32°39'56" lon 109°52'27"

DESCRIPTION: This CG is tent camping only. There is a central parking area with a short hike to CG. In a primarily spruce and fir forest with a meadow in the middle of CG. A small creek runs through CG where you can fish and play. Supplies at Safford. Deer, bears, skunks, squirrels, and chipmunks are common to the area.

GETTING THERE: From Safford go S on US HWY 191 approx. 8 mi. to state HWY 366. Go SW on 366 approx. 23 mi. to Hospital Flat CG. Not suitable for trailers.

SINGLE RATE:	$10	OPEN DATES:	May-Sep
		MAX STAY:	14 days
		ELEVATION:	9000 feet

13 Idlewilde
Portal • lat 31°53'30" lon 109°09'57"

DESCRIPTION: This CG is situated in a mixed forest setting adjacent to Cave Creek. Fish and swim from the creek. Supplies are available at Portal. Numerous wildlife in the area. Crystal Cave nearby. Gather firewood locally or bring your own. Trails to the Chiricahua Wilderness are close by the CG.

GETTING THERE: From Portal go W on forest route 42 approx. 1.5 mi. to Idlewilde CG. Not suitable for trailers.

SINGLE RATE:	$10	OPEN DATES:	Apr-Oct
# of SINGLE SITES:	10	MAX SPUR:	16 feet
		MAX STAY:	14 days
		ELEVATION:	5000 feet

14 Lakeview
Sonoita • lat 31°26'07" lon 110°27'14"

DESCRIPTION: CG in a stand of oak and juniper above Parker Canyon Lake. A short walk to the lakeshore to go fishing for rainbow trout, bass, sunfish, and catfish. Boat launch at lake. A 5-mile trail goes around the lake. Trail has viewing areas with benches and signs. Bald eagles and osprey also frequent the area.

GETTING THERE: From Sonoita go S on state HWY 83 approx. 30 mi. to Lakeview CG.

SINGLE RATE:	$10	OPEN DATES:	Yearlong
# of SINGLE SITES:	65	MAX SPUR:	32 feet
		MAX STAY:	14 days
		ELEVATION:	5400 feet

15 Molino Basin
Tucson • lat 32°20'18" lon 110°41'30"

DESCRIPTION: CG in an oak studded grassland, surrounded by steep, rugged cliffs and granite peaks with Molino Creek flowing nearby. Supplies are available at Tucson. The Arizona Trail passes through, providing access to the extensive trail system that criss crosses the Santa Catalina Mountains.

GETTING THERE: Molino Basin CG is located approx. 22 mi. NE of Tucson on the Catalina HWY.

SINGLE RATE:	$5	OPEN DATES:	Oct-Apr
# of SINGLE SITES:	37	MAX SPUR:	22 feet
		MAX STAY:	14 days
		ELEVATION:	4500 feet

16 Peppersauce
Oracle • lat 32°32'27" lon 110°42'32"

DESCRIPTION: This CG is situated in a shallow, tree-filled canyon at the foot of Mount Lemmon. Peppersauce Creek runs through the CG and offers trout fishing. Supplies are available at Oracle. Deer, elk, and the usual "camp robbers" may be viewed in the area. Peppersauce Cave is nearby.

GETTING THERE: From Oracle go SE on forest route 38 approx. 15 mi. to Peppersauce CG. Trailers not recommended.

SINGLE RATE:	$8	OPEN DATES:	Yearlong
# of SINGLE SITES:	19	MAX SPUR:	22 feet
GROUP RATE:	$35	MAX STAY:	14 days
# of GROUP SITES:	7	ELEVATION:	4700 feet

17 Pinery Canyon
Portal • lat 31°55'59" lon 109°16'14"

DESCRIPTION: This is a small CG with dispersed sites. It is situated in a rustic setting among ponderosa pine. There is numerous wildlife to view in the area. Supplies can be found in Portal. There are several trails nearby. No drinking water available on site. Crystal Cave is nearby.

GETTING THERE: From Portal go S on forest route 42 approx. 18 mi. to Pinery Canyon CG.

SINGLE RATE:	No fee	OPEN DATES:	Apr-Nov
# of SINGLE SITES:	4	MAX SPUR:	16 feet
		MAX STAY:	14 days
		ELEVATION:	7000 feet

18 Ramsey Vista
Sierra Vista • lat 31°25'38" lon 110°18'17"

DESCRIPTION: This CG is situated in a stand of ponderosa pine. Beautiful views of Ramsey Peak, famous for its wedding cake stack of sheer white cliffs. Supplies are available at Sierra Vista. Numerous trails around CG area. Campers may gather their firewood locally. Horse corral are available.

GETTING THERE: From Sierra Vista go S on state HWY 92 approx. 7 mi. to forest route 368. Go W on 368 approx. 6 mi. to Ramsey Vista CG. Trailers longer than 12' can't negotiate the switchbacks on Carr Canyon Road.

SINGLE RATE:	$10	OPEN DATES:	Yearlong
# of SINGLE SITES:	8	MAX SPUR:	12 feet
		MAX STAY:	14 days
		ELEVATION:	7200 feet

19 Reef
Sierra Vista • lat 31°25'57" lon 110°17'11"

DESCRIPTION: This high mountain CG is located on a site that was once occupied by the old Reef Townsite. Picnic tables and tent pads were placed within the visible outlines of old cabin foundations. Supplies in Sierra Vista. Interpretive history trail and hiking and horseback trails nearby.

GETTING THERE: From Sierra Vista go S on state HWY 92 approx. 7 mi. to forest route 368. Go W on 368 approx. 4.5 mi. to Reef CG. Trailers longer than 12' can't negotiate the switchbacks on Carr Canyon Rd.

SINGLE RATE:	$10	OPEN DATES:	Yearlong
# of SINGLE SITES:	14	MAX SPUR:	16 feet
		MAX STAY:	14 days
		ELEVATION:	7200 feet

20 Riggs Flat
Safford • lat 32°42'29" lon 109°57'42"

DESCRIPTION: CG in a mature stand of ponderosa pine with great views of Riggs Lake. Fish for stocked rainbow trout from the lake. Supplies at Safford. Deer, bears, skunks, squirrels, and chipmunks are common to the area. Trails around lake start from the CG. This is the most popular CG and is full most of the time.

GETTING THERE: From Safford go S on US HWY 191 approx. 8 mi. to state HWY 366. Go SW on 366 approx. 32 mi. to forest route 287. Go S on 287 approx. 1 mi. to Riggs Flat CG.

SINGLE RATE:	$10	OPEN DATES:	May-Oct*
# of SINGLE SITES:	26	MAX SPUR:	22 feet
		MAX STAY:	14 days
		ELEVATION:	8500 feet

 Campground has hosts   **Reservable sites** **Accessible facilities**   **Fully developed**   **Semi-developed**   **Rustic facilities**

NOTE: Open dates listed are typical. Actual dates are dependent on conditions such as snow pack.

21 Rose Canyon
Tucson • lat 32°23'35" lon 110°42'14"

DESCRIPTION: This CG has campsites that are open and spacious, spread among stands of large pine and oak. Rose Creek runs through the area. Enjoy fishing for stocked rainbow trout from the lake. Supplies are available at Catalina. There is a one-mile trail that runs around the lake.

GETTING THERE: Rose Canyon CG is located approx. 33 mi. NE of Tucson on the Catalina HWY.

SINGLE RATE:	$9	OPEN DATES:	Apr-Oct
# of SINGLE SITES:	74	MAX SPUR:	22 feet
		MAX STAY:	14 days
		ELEVATION:	7000 feet

22 Rucker Forest Camp
Elfrida • lat 31°47'00" lon 109°18'00"

DESCRIPTION: CG situated in a mixed stand of pine and cypress next to a clear mountain stream. Rucker Lake is nearby for rainbow trout fishing. Supplies are available at Elfrida. Numerous wildlife in the area. A number of forest trails are in the area of the CG. Rucker Canyon Trail nearby.

GETTING THERE: From Elfrida go N on US HWY 191 approx. 6 mi. to forest route 74. Go E in 74 approx. 23 mi. to forest route 74E. Go NE on 74E approx. 6 mi. to Rucker Forest Camp CG.

SINGLE RATE:	$7	OPEN DATES:	Mar-Oct
# of SINGLE SITES:	13	MAX SPUR:	16 feet
		MAX STAY:	14 days
		ELEVATION:	6500 feet

23 Rustler Park
Portal • lat 31°54'20" lon 109°16'45"

DESCRIPTION: CG is in a shady, cool, high mountain meadow and pine forest. Rustler Spring is nearby. Historic log cabins constructed by the CCC close by. Supplies at Portal. Deer, bears, and birds in area. Access to hiking trails and Chiricahua Wilderness. Crystal Cave nearby. Bears boxes available.

GETTING THERE: From Portal go S on forest route 42 approx. 18 mi. to forest route 42D. Go S on 42D approx. 2 mi. to Rustler Park CG. Forty foot length limit on forest route 42.

SINGLE RATE:	$10	OPEN DATES:	Yearlong
# of SINGLE SITES:	22	MAX SPUR:	41 feet
		MAX STAY:	14 days
		ELEVATION:	8500 feet

24 Shannon
Safford • lat 32°39'26" lon 109°51'28"

DESCRIPTION: CG in a spruce and fir forest with the only views being those of the forest. A small stream runs nearby. Supplies are available at Safford. Deer, bears, skunks, squirrels, and chipmunks are common to the area. Trails from CG to Arcadia CG. This is the most shaded and coolest of all CGs in the area.

GETTING THERE: From Safford go S on US HWY 191 approx. 8 mi. to state HWY 366. Go SW on 366 approx. 22 mi. to Shannon CG.

SINGLE RATE:	$10	OPEN DATES:	May-Oct
# of SINGLE SITES:	11	MAX SPUR:	16 feet
		MAX STAY:	14 days
		ELEVATION:	9100 feet

25 Showers Point
Tucson • lat 31°25'30" lon 110°43'00"

DESCRIPTION: This CG is situated in a cool, forested area of ponderosa pine with an overlook of Palisade Canyon (located at the CG's edge). Views are of the pyramid-shaped Mount Wrightson. Supplies are available at Tuscon. A nearby trailhead links to the Palisade Trail.

GETTING THERE: Showers Point CG is located approx. 36 mi. NE of Tuscon on the Catalina HWY. Not suitable for trailers.

GROUP RATE:	$50	OPEN DATES:	Apr-Oct
# of GROUP SITES:	3	MAX STAY:	14 days
		ELEVATION:	7700 feet

26 Soldier Creek
Safford • lat 32°41'56" lon 109°55'11"

DESCRIPTION: This CG is situated in a primarily spruce and fir forest with Soldier Creek running nearby. Enjoy fishing from creek for native trout. Supplies are available at Safford. Deer, bears, skunks, squirrels, and chipmunks are common to this area. Soldier Creek Trail begins on site.

GETTING THERE: From Safford go S on US HWY 191 approx. 8 mi. to state HWY 366. Go SW on 366 approx. 30 mi. to Soldier Creek CG.

SINGLE RATE:	$10	OPEN DATES:	May-Sept
# of SINGLE SITES:	12	MAX SPUR:	22 feet
		MAX STAY:	14 days
		ELEVATION:	9300 feet

27 Spencer Canyon
Tucson • lat 32°25'00" lon 110°44'24"

DESCRIPTION: This CG is located at the head of a shallow, forested canyon a short distance off the Catalina HWY. Overlooks Tucson and the Santa Cruz Valley, provides a dazzling night show of city lights below and stars above. Days and nights are cool. Supplies are available at Tuscon. Trails in the area.

GETTING THERE: Spencer Canyon CG is located approx. 37 mi. NE of Tuscon on the Catalina HWY.

SINGLE RATE:	$8	OPEN DATES:	Apr-Oct
# of SINGLE SITES:	60	MAX SPUR:	22 feet
		MAX STAY:	14 days
		ELEVATION:	7800 feet

28 Stewart
Portal • lat 31°53'10" lon 109°10'15"

DESCRIPTION: This CG is a cool, shady streamside camp located in a cypress and sycamore forest. CG is adjacent to Cave Creek. Fish and play in the creek. Supplies are available at Portal. Birdwatching is good in the CG. Crystal Cave nearby. Vista Point Trail and Silver Peak Trail are nearby.

GETTING THERE: From Portal go S on forest route 42 approx. 2 mi. to Stewart CG.

SINGLE RATE:	$10	OPEN DATES:	Yearlong
# of SINGLE SITES:	6	MAX SPUR:	16 feet
		MAX STAY:	14 days
		ELEVATION:	5100 feet

29 Stockton Pass
Safford • lat 32°35'31" lon 109°51'09"

DESCRIPTION: This CG is situated in a primarily oak and juniper grassland. Supplies are available at Safford. Gather firewood locally or bring your own. Deer, bears, skunks, squirrels, and chipmunks are common to this area. Numerous trails can be found in the area.

GETTING THERE: From Safford go S on US HWY 191 approx. 17 mi. to state HWY 266. Go W on 266 approx. 12 mi. to forest route 198. Go E on 198 approx. 1/2 mi. to Stockton Pass CG.

SINGLE RATE:	No fee	OPEN DATES:	Yearlong
# of SINGLE SITES:	7	MAX SPUR:	16 feet
		MAX STAY:	14 days
		ELEVATION:	5600 feet

30 Sunny Flat
Portal • lat 31°52'53" lon 109°10'30"

DESCRIPTION: In an open park-like setting of sycamore and oak with a grassy meadow in middle. CG sits on Cave Creek with fishing and swimming. Supplies at Portal. A diverse community of birds and other wildlife in the area. A number of hiking trails in the area. Bears proof containers provided. Crystal Cave nearby.

GETTING THERE: From Portal go S on forest route 42 approx. 3 mi. to Sunny Flat CG.

SINGLE RATE:	$10	OPEN DATES:	Yearlong
# of SINGLE SITES:	12	MAX SPUR:	23 feet
		MAX STAY:	14 days
		ELEVATION:	5200 feet

 Campground has hosts   Reservable sites   Accessible facilities   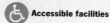 Fully developed    Semi-developed   Rustic facilities

NOTE: Open dates listed are typical. Actual dates are dependent on conditions such as snow pack.

31 Sycamore
Elfrida • lat 31˚52'00" lon 109˚21'00"

DESCRIPTION: CG set in sycamore and oak with the West Turkey Creek running through it. Fish and swim in the creek. Dispersed sites. Supplies at Elfrida. A diverse community of birds and other wildlife in the area. Turkey Creek Road is a jump off into the Chiricahua Wilderness. Bears proof containers provided.

GETTING THERE: From Elfrida go N on US HWY 191 approx. 15 mi. to state HWY 181. Go E on 181 approx. 12 mi. to forest route 41. Go E on 41 approx. 10 mi. to Sycamore CG.

SINGLE RATE:	**No fee**	**OPEN DATES:**	**Yearlong**
# of SINGLE SITES:	**5**	**MAX SPUR:**	**16 feet**
		MAX STAY:	**14 days**
		ELEVATION:	**6200 feet**

32 Upper Arcadia
Safford • lat 32˚37'30" lon 109˚48'00"

DESCRIPTION: In a dense oak and pine forest setting with the only views being of the forest. Supplies available at Safford. Deer, bears, skunks, squirrels and chipmunks are common to the area. The National Recreation Trail runs near the CG and goes to Shanon CG.

GETTING THERE: From Safford go S on US HWY 191 approx. 8 mi. to state HWY 366. Go SW on 366 approx. 12 mi. to Upper Arcadia CG.

		OPEN DATES:	**May-Oct***
		MAX SPUR:	**22 feet**
GROUP RATE:	**Varies**	**MAX STAY:**	**14 days**
# of GROUP SITES:	**1**	**ELEVATION:**	**6700 feet**

33 West Turkey Creek
Elfrida • lat 31˚51'52" lon 109˚21'31"

DESCRIPTION: CG in silver barked Arizona sycamore, on the banks of the West Turkey Creek. Fish and swim in the creek. Dispersed sites. Supplies at Elfrida. A diverse community of birds areside in the area. Trails that follow the sides of the canyon start in the area. Bears proof containers provided. No drinking water.

GETTING THERE: From Elfrida go N on US HWY 191 approx. 15 mi. to state HWY 181. Go E on 181 approx. 12 mi. to forest route 41. Go E on 41 approx. 8 mi. to West Turkey Creek CG. No trailers.

SINGLE RATE:	**No fee**	**OPEN DATES:**	**Yearlong**
# of SINGLE SITES:	**4**		
		MAX STAY:	**14 days**
		ELEVATION:	**5900 feet**

34 White Rock
Nogales • lat 31˚23'53" lon 111˚05'19"

DESCRIPTION: Sites are on the banks of PeÒa Blanca Creek, in the shadow of a rocky cliff. Good fishing for bass, catfish, crappie, and bluegill. Supplies are in Nogales. CG fills quickly. Bring your own firewood. Trails are nearby. A paved boat ramp at the lake and a trail that leads most of the way around the lake.

GETTING THERE: From Nogales go N on I-19 approx. 5 mi. to state HWY 289 (Ruby Interchange). Go W on state HWY 289 approx. 9 mi. to White Rock CG.

SINGLE RATE:	**$5**	**OPEN DATES:**	**Yearlong**
# of SINGLE SITES:	**15**	**MAX SPUR:**	**22 feet**
		MAX STAY:	**14 days**
		ELEVATION:	**4000 feet**

 Campground has hosts   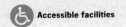 Reservable sites   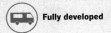 Accessible facilities   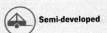 Fully developed   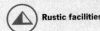 Semi-developed   Rustic facilities

NOTE: Open dates listed are typical. Actual dates are dependent on conditions such as snow pack.

KAIBAB NATIONAL FOREST

The Kaibab National Forest is part of the largest contiguous ponderosa pine forest in the United States. Bordering both the north and south rims of the Grand Canyon, the 1.6 million acres of the Kaibab have the distinction of being divided by one of nature's greatest attractions. Elevations range from 5,500 feet to 10,418 feet at the summit of Kendrick Peak.

Large wild animals commonly seen are elk, mule deer, antelope, turkey and coyote. The most commonly encountered small animals on the Kaibab are Abert's squirrels, chipmunks, and ground squirrels.

The climate in the Kaibab varies. During the summer, the thermometer may reach 90 degrees during the day but dip to the 50s at night. The sunny weather can be deceptive, be it summer or winter, and visitors who hike, bike, or ride the forest roads should always be prepared for inclement weather. The rainy season brings brief but often violent thunderstorms across the forest which make wildfires a serious threat.

Whether you seek the challenges of rugged terrain, the solitude of nature, or the nostalgia of Old Route 66, you'll find nothing short of a once-in-a-lifetime experience on the Kaibab National Forest.

KAIBAB NATIONAL FOREST • ARIZONA • LOCATOR MAP

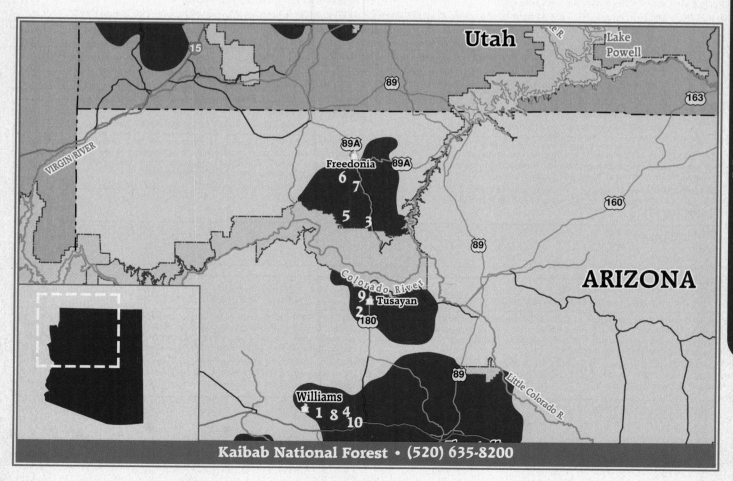

Kaibab National Forest • (520) 635-8200

1 Cataract Lake
Williams • lat 35°15'09" lon 112°12'38"

DESCRIPTION: CG in ponderosa pine on Cataract Lake. Lake is stocked with rainbow & brown trout for fishing. Boats with up to 1 hp on lake; boat ramp. Supplies in Williams. Elk & deer in area. Firewood sold by host. Bill Williams Mountain Trail for hiking, Historic Route 66 at Devil Dog RD for mountain biking.

GETTING THERE: In Williams turn N onto 7th St., cross RR tracks, turning W at first road. Go 1 mi. to Cataract CG.

SINGLE RATE:	No fee	OPEN DATES:	May-Oct
# of SINGLE SITES:	18	MAX SPUR:	16 feet
		MAX STAY:	14 days
		ELEVATION:	6800 feet

6 Jacob Lake
Fredonia • lat 34°42'59" lon 112°12'49"

DESCRIPTION: This CG is situated on the main access route to the Grand Canyon's North Rim. Several hiking opportunities in area. Look for wildlife including mule deer and the rare Kaibab Squirrel. Naturalist programs in season and a self-guided trail. Horse riding and chuckwagon meals from nearby source.

GETTING THERE: From Fredonia go SE approx. 30 mi. to intersection of US HWY 89A and state HWY 67. Jacob Lake CG is located approx. 1/2 mi. N of Jacob Lake on US HWY 89A.

SINGLE RATE:	$10	OPEN DATES:	May-Nov*
# of SINGLE SITES:	53	MAX SPUR:	32 feet
GROUP RATE:	Varies	MAX STAY:	14 days
# of GROUP SITES:	2	ELEVATION:	6800 feet

2 Charlie Tank Group
Grand Canyon • lat 35°56'13" lon 112°07'20"

DESCRIPTION: CG is an open area located in a ponderosa pine and gambel oak forest. Entrance to Grand Canyon National Park is 4.3 mi. away. Supplies can be found 10 mi. N at Grand Canyon. CG recieves moderate use. Firewood is sold by host. Self guided nature trails and outdoor amphitheater available.

GETTING THERE: From Grand Canyon go S on US HWY 180 approx. 10.5 mi. to entrance for Ten-X CG and Charlie Tank Group.

SINGLE RATE:	$10	OPEN DATES:	May-Oct
# of SINGLE SITES:	70		
GROUP RATE:	Varies	MAX STAY:	14 days
# of GROUP SITES:	2	ELEVATION:	6650 feet

7 Jacob Lake Group
Fredonia • lat 36°42'59" lon 112°12'49"

DESCRIPTION: Located on main access route to the Grand Canyon Norht Rim. Supplies available at Fredonia. Horse riding and chuckwagon meals from nearby sources. Wildlife viewing, including rare Kaibab Squirrel can be done nearby. Naturalist programs, while in season, are at the CG. Hiking trails nearby.

GETTING THERE: Jacob Lake Group CG is located at the juction of US HWY 89A and state HWY 67.

SINGLE RATE:	$10	OPEN DATES:	May-Nov*
# of SINGLE SITES:	53	MAX SPUR:	32 feet
GROUP RATE:	Varies	MAX STAY:	14 days
# of GROUP SITES:	2	ELEVATION:	7900 feet

3 DeMotte
Jacob Lake • lat 36°25'25" lon 112°07'49"

DESCRIPTION: Located 7 mi. from Grand Canyon Nat'l Park's North rim. Excellent scenery and wildlife viewing, including mule deer and the rare Kaibab Squirrel. Guided hikes and horse riding available at nearby sources. Numerous trails and roads provide unique views of Grand Canyon from the forest perspective.

GETTING THERE: From Jacob Lake CG go S on state HWY 67 approx. 25 mi. to DeMotte CG.

SINGLE RATE:	$10	OPEN DATES:	May-Nov*
# of SINGLE SITES:	23	MAX SPUR:	22 feet
		MAX STAY:	14 days
		ELEVATION:	9000 feet

8 Kaibab Lake
Williams • lat 35°17'10" lon 112°08'41"

DESCRIPTION: CG among ponderosa pine, set on Kaibab Lake (8 hp limit) with trout fishing . Boat ramp and amphitheater on site. Supplies 4 miles in historic Williams. Elk and deer frequent the area. Firewood may be purchased from camp hosts. Trails on Bill Williams Mountain. No drinking water Oct-May.

GETTING THERE: From Williams go E on I-40 approx. 2 mi. to state HWY 64. Go N on 64 approx. 1 mi. to forest route 47. Go W on 47 approx. 1 mi. to Kaibab Lake CG.

SINGLE RATE:	$10	OPEN DATES:	May-Oct
# of SINGLE SITES:	72	MAX SPUR:	22 feet
GROUP RATE:	Varies	MAX STAY:	14 days
# of GROUP SITES:	2	ELEVATION:	6800 feet

4 Dogtown Lake
Williams • lat 35°12'30" lon 112°07'30"

DESCRIPTION: This CG is located on the trout fishing Dogtown Lake among ponderosa pine. Up to 1 hp motors allowed on lake. Supplies are available in Williams 7 Mi. North. Elk and deer are known to frequent the area. Firewood may be gathered by campers or purchased from camp hosts. Hiking trails nearby.

GETTING THERE: From Williams go S on county route 73 approx. 3 mi. to forest route 140. Go E on 140 approx. 2.5 mi. to forest route 132. Go N on 132 approx. 1 mi. to Dogtown Lake CG.

SINGLE RATE:	$8	OPEN DATES:	May-Oct*
# of SINGLE SITES:	51	MAX SPUR:	25 feet
GROUP RATE:	Varies	MAX STAY:	14 days
# of GROUP SITES:	1	ELEVATION:	7000 feet

9 Ten-X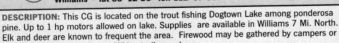
Grand Canyon • lat 35°56'13" lon 112°07'20"

DESCRIPTION: This CG is situated in a ponderosa pine forest. Wildlife in the area includes elk, deer, and occasional mountain lions. Supplies can be found 10 mi. N at Grand Canyon. Firewood is available to be purchased from host. Grand Canyon National Park is close to CG for numerous hiking opportunities.

GETTING THERE: From Grand Canyon go S on US HWY 180 approx. 10.5 mi. to entrance of Ten-X CG.

SINGLE RATE:	$10	OPEN DATES:	May-Oct
# of SINGLE SITES:	70	MAX SPUR:	22 feet
GROUP RATE:	Varies	MAX STAY:	14 days
# of GROUP SITES:	1	ELEVATION:	6600 feet

5 Indian Hollow
Fredonia • lat 36°27'45" lon 112°29'03"

DESCRIPTION: Amid spectacular scenery near Grand Canyon rim. No fishing in nearby vicinity. Remote site, no water, firewood may be scarce. Hiking trails access Thunder River Trail in Grand Canyon Nat'l Park and Kanab Creek Wilderness. Bighorn sheep can be seen regularly. 4WD recommended.

GETTING THERE: From Fredonia go S 2 mi. on US HWY 89A to primary forest route 22. Go S 33 mi. on 22 to forest route 425. Go SW 9 mi. on 425 to forest route 232. Go W 5 mi. on 232 to Indian Hollow CG.

SINGLE RATE:	No fee	OPEN DATES:	May-Nov*
# of SINGLE SITES:	3	MAX SPUR:	32 feet
		MAX STAY:	14 days
		ELEVATION:	6000 feet

10 White Horse Lake
Williams • lat 35°06'45" lon 112°00'30"

DESCRIPTION: Located in pine on Whitehorse Lake with trout fishing (1 hp electric motors); boat ramp. Picturesque Sycamore Canyon & Mogollon Rim nearby. Deer & elk sometimes seen. Overland Road Historic Trail is nearby. Supplies in Williams. Moderate use. Buy firewood from host or gather own. No drinking water Oct-May.

GETTING THERE: From Williams go S on forest route 173 (Perkinsville Road) approx. 9 mi. to forest route 110 (White Horse Road). Go E approx. 7 mi. to forest route 109. Go E approx. 3 mi. to White Horse Lake CG.

SINGLE RATE:	$10	OPEN DATES:	Yearlong*
# of SINGLE SITES:	105	MAX SPUR:	32 feet
GROUP RATE:	Varies	MAX STAY:	14 days
# of GROUP SITES:	1	ELEVATION:	6600 feet

 Campground has hosts   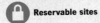 **Reservable sites**   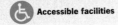 **Accessible facilities**   **Fully developed**   **Semi-developed**   **Rustic facilities**

NOTE: Open dates listed are typical. Actual dates are dependent on conditions such as snow pack.

USFS Photo

PRESCOTT NATIONAL FOREST

Prescott National Forest lies in a mountainous section of central Arizona between forested plateaus to the north and arid desert to the south. The natural beauty of mountaintops, clear lakes and rivers, great varieties of fish, unique wildlife, and remnants of cultural heritage provide settings for a diversity of outdoor recreation activities.

Comprised of about 1.25 million acres, the Prescott borders three other national forests in Arizona: Kaibab, Coconino, and Tonto. Roughly half of the forest lies west of the city of Prescott, Arizona, in the Juniper, Santa Maria, Sierra Prieta, and Bradshaw mountains. The other half of the forest lies east of Prescott and takes in the Black Hills, Mingus Mountain, Black Mesa, and the headwaters of the Verde River.

Portions of the Prescott National Forest today are much the same are they were when Sam Miller panned for gold in Lynx Creek and was wounded by a cougar, or when General Crook's flag fluttered over Palace Station.

At the lowest elevation, the primary vegetation is of the Sonoran Desert type. As the elevation rises, chaparral becomes common, followed by pinion pine and juniper. Above that, Ponderosa pine dominate the landscape.

PRESCOTT NATIONAL FOREST • ARIZONA • LOCATOR MAP

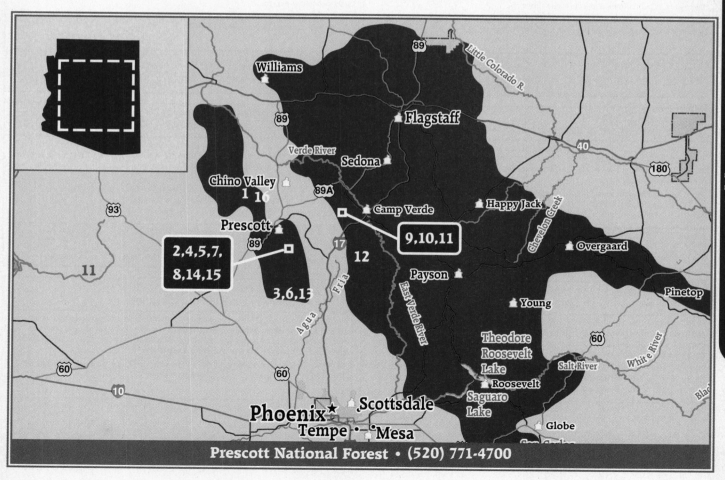

Prescott National Forest • (520) 771-4700

1 Granite Basin Group

Prescott • lat 34°36'40" lon 112°32'45"

DESCRIPTION: In rugged, boulder strewn cliffs of Granite Mountain Wilderness. Short walk to shore of Granite Basin Lake for the patient angler (no swimming). Elec. motors only on lake. No drinking water. Hike trails into Granite Mountain Wilderness. Fee depends on number of persons, 100 person, 30 vehicle max. $25-$100.

GETTING THERE: From Prescott go W on county route 10 approx. 4 mi. to forest route 374. Go N on 374 approx. 4 mi. to Granite Group CG. Parking for RVs and camping trailers is difficult.

		OPEN DATES:	Yearlong
		MAX SPUR:	40 feet
		MAX STAY:	14 days
GROUP RATE:	Varies	ELEVATION:	5600 feet
# of GROUP SITES:	14		

2 Groom Creek Horse Camp

Prescott • lat 34°28'30" lon 112°26'47"

DESCRIPTION: This CG is expressly for equestrian campers located in beautiful pine forest. Spacious, open site. Redeveloped under cooperative venture with Saddlebag Club of Phoenix. Large RV and trailer spurs. Supplies in Prescott. Reservations available for 7 sites. Access to Groom Creek loop trail #307.

GETTING THERE: From Prescott go S on county route 56 approx. 6 mi. to Groom Creek Horse Camp CG.

SINGLE RATE:	$10	OPEN DATES:	May-Oct
# of SINGLE SITES:	37	MAX SPUR:	50 feet
		MAX STAY:	14 days
		ELEVATION:	6000 feet

3 Hazlett Hollow

Bumblebee • lat 34°10'10" lon 112°17'04"

DESCRIPTION: Small rustic CG in pine. Most of CG was built by CCC's in 1930's. Well developed and attractive site, in Horsethief Basin. Some wooden camping shelters with concrete floors. Gather firewood locally. Supplies in Bumblebee or Preston. Day hikes or trailheads for Castle Creek and Twin Peaks Trails.

GETTING THERE: From Bumblebee go N and W on county route 59 approx. 22 mi. to forest route 52. Go E on 52 approx. 6 mi. to Hazlett Hollow CG.

SINGLE RATE:	$6	OPEN DATES:	May-Nov
# of SINGLE SITES:	15	MAX SPUR:	32 feet
		MAX STAY:	14 days
		ELEVATION:	6000 feet

4 Hilltop

Prescott • lat 34°30'38" lon 112°22'54"

DESCRIPTION: This CG is situated among ponderosa pine on Lynx Lake. Fish for stocked trout on lake. Electric motors are allowed, no swimming. Boats may be rented from nearby marina. Limited supplies at marina. Other supplies in Prescott. Recreational gold panning is popular.

GETTING THERE: From Prescott go E on state HWY 69 approx. 3 mi. to county route 57. Go S on 57 approx. 3 mi. to forest route 623. Go E on 623 approx. 1/2 mi. to Hilltop CG.

SINGLE RATE:	$10	OPEN DATES:	May-Sept
# of SINGLE SITES:	38	MAX SPUR:	32 feet
		MAX STAY:	7 days
		ELEVATION:	5700 feet

5 Indian Creek

Prescott • lat 34°28'57" lon 112°30'02"

DESCRIPTION: This CG is situated in rolling hills among ponderosa pine, oak, and walnut trees. Expect warm days with cold nights. Easy and convenient access to city of Prescott. Large and spacious sites. Numerous hiking opportunities available nearby. No drinking water available on site.

GETTING THERE: Indian Creek CG is located approx. 6.4 mi. S of Prescott on state HWY 89. Go S on US HWY 89 (Montezuma St) approx. 5.7 mi. to forest route 97. Go on 97 approx. 1 mi. to CG. Follow signs.

SINGLE RATE:	$6	OPEN DATES:	May-Sept
# of SINGLE SITES:	27	MAX SPUR:	32 feet
		MAX STAY:	14 days
		ELEVATION:	5800 feet

6 Kentuck Springs

Bumblebee • lat 34°10'31" lon 112°16'35"

DESCRIPTION: Small, rustic site among ponderosa pine. In Bradshaw Mountains Horsethief Basin Rec Area. During wet season, a stream comes through the CG. Supplies in Bumblebee, Crown King, or Prescott. Pack it in, pack it out. No trash collection, no drinking water. Hiking trails nearby.

GETTING THERE: From Bumblebee go N and W on county route 59 approx. 22 mi. to forest route 52. Go E on 52 approx. 7 mi. to Kentuck Springs CG.

SINGLE RATE:	No fee	OPEN DATES:	May-Nov
# of SINGLE SITES:	15	MAX SPUR:	32 feet
		MAX STAY:	14 days
		ELEVATION:	6000 feet

7 Lower Wolf Creek

Prescott • lat 34°27'14" lon 112°27'34"

DESCRIPTION: This CG is situated among Arizona walnut and oak trees. Beautiful open rock formations to investigate. No drinking water available on site. Firewood may be scarce, best to bring your own. Supplies can be found in Prescott. No services are offered October through May 14. Few hiking trails.

GETTING THERE: From Prescott go S on state HWY 89 approx. 6 mi. to county route 97. Go E on 97 approx. 5 mi. to Lower Wolf Creek CG.

SINGLE RATE:	$6	OPEN DATES:	Yearlong*
# of SINGLE SITES:	20	MAX SPUR:	32 feet
		MAX STAY:	14 days
		ELEVATION:	6000 feet

8 Lynx Lake

Prescott • lat 34°31'00" lon 112°23'00"

DESCRIPTION: This CG is situated among ponderosa pine on Lynx Lake. Fish for stocked trout on man-made lake. Boats with electric motors are allowed, no swimming. Rental boats and limited supplies at nearby marina. Other supplies in Prescott. Recreational gold panning is popular.

GETTING THERE: From Prescott go E on state HWY 69 approx. 3 mi. to county route 57. Go S on 57 approx. 2 mi. to Lynx Lake CG.

SINGLE RATE:	$10	OPEN DATES:	Apr-Nov
# of SINGLE SITES:	39	MAX SPUR:	40 feet
		MAX STAY:	7 days
		ELEVATION:	5600 feet

9 Mingus Mountain

Jerome • lat 34°41'34" lon 112°07'08"

DESCRIPTION: CG set in pine atop Mingus Mountain, with panoramic views of Verde Valley. Relatively cool summer days. No drinking water, no services. Supplies in Jerome. Hiking access to Norh Mingus, View Point, Coleman, and Gaddes Trails. CG will be upgraded in the near future; no fee until that time.

GETTING THERE: From Jerome go SW on state HWY 89A approx. 6 mi. to forest route 104. Go E on 104 approx. 2 mi. to Mingus Mountain CG.

SINGLE RATE:	$6	OPEN DATES:	May-Nov*
# of SINGLE SITES:	24	MAX SPUR:	22 feet
		MAX STAY:	14 days
		ELEVATION:	7600 feet

10 Playground Group

Jerome • lat 34°41'54" lon 112°08'10"

DESCRIPTION: This CG is situated among ponderosa pine. Hiking accessible nearby. Beautiful scenic views. Supplies can be found in Jerome. Reservations required. Fee varies depending upon group size; $25-$100. Maximum capacity: 100 people, 30 vehicles. Busy all summer. No drinking water available on site.

GETTING THERE: From Jerome go SW on state HWY 89A approx. 6 mi. to forest route 104. Go E on 104 approx. 2 mi. to Playground Group CG.

		OPEN DATES:	Seasonal
# of SINGLE SITES:	9	MAX SPUR:	22 feet
GROUP RATE:	Varies	MAX STAY:	14 days
		ELEVATION:	7500 feet

 Campground has hosts   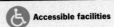 **Reservable sites**   **Accessible facilities**   **Fully developed**   **Semi-developed**   **Rustic facilities**

NOTE: Open dates listed are typical. Actual dates are dependent on conditions such as snow pack.

11 Potato Patch
Jerome • lat 34˚41'54" lon 112˚07'47"

DESCRIPTION: This CG is set in a pine forest atop Mingus Mountain. Cooler temperatures in the summer. Supplies can be found in Jerome. Historic mining town of Jerome 8 mi. NE. Hiking access to Woodchute Wilderness. Campers may gather their firewood locally. No drinking water available on site.

GETTING THERE: From Jerome go SW on state HWY 89A approx. 6 mi. to Potato Patch CG.

SINGLE RATE:	$8	OPEN DATES:	May-Nov*
# of SINGLE SITES:	30	MAX SPUR:	40 feet
		MAX STAY:	14 days
		ELEVATION:	7000 feet

16 Yavapai
Prescott • lat 34˚36'40" lon 112˚32'45"

DESCRIPTION: This CG is near Granite Basin Lake with views of boulder strewn cliffs of Granite Mountain Wilderness. Patient anglers may catch bluegill, bass, or catfish. The lake allows electric motors only, no swimming. Firewood may be scarce. Supplies in Prescott. Hiking access into the wilderness nearby.

GETTING THERE: From Prescott go NW on county route 10 approx. 5 mi. to forest route 374. Go N on 374 approx. 2 mi. to Yavapai CG.

SINGLE RATE:	$10	OPEN DATES:	Yearlong
# of SINGLE SITES:	25	MAX SPUR:	40 feet
		MAX STAY:	14 days
		ELEVATION:	5600 feet

12 Powell Springs
Dewey • lat 34˚34'41" lon 112˚04'11"

DESCRIPTION: This CG is situated among high desert chapparal. Limited supplies are available in Deway. No drinking water available on site. CG remains busy all summer.

GETTING THERE: From Deway go E on state HWY 169 approx. 8 mi. to county route 75. Go N on 75 approx. 5 mi. to Powell Springs CG.

SINGLE RATE:	$6	OPEN DATES:	Yearlong
# of SINGLE SITES:	10	MAX SPUR:	16 feet
		MAX STAY:	14 days
		ELEVATION:	5300 feet

13 Turney Gulch Group
Bumblebee • lat 34˚10'24" lon 112˚17'18"

DESCRIPTION: This CG is situated on the shores of Horsethief Lake. Fishing from shore or boat (electric motor). Please check for local fishing regulations. Supplies can be found in Crown King. Access into Castle Creek Wilderness for numerous hiking and horseback riding opportunities.

GETTING THERE: From Bumblebee go N and W on county route 59 approx. 22 mi. to forest route 52. Go E on 52 approx. 6.5 mi. to Turney Gulch Group CG.

		OPEN DATES:	Apr-Sept
		MAX SPUR:	35 feet
GROUP RATE:	Varies	MAX STAY:	14 days
# of GROUP SITES:	1	ELEVATION:	6000 feet

14 Upper Wolf Creek Group
Prescott • lat 34˚27'18" lon 112˚27'12"

DESCRIPTION: In boulder strewn park like area of ponderosa pine. Warm days, cold nights. Supplies in Prescott. 100 person, 30 vehicle max. 1 accessible site. Walker Mining District. No drinking water; no services. Hiking trails and Goldwater Lake nearby. From $25 to $100 fees, depending on group size. Reservations required.

GETTING THERE: From Prescott go S on state HWY 89 approx. 5 mi. to county route 101. Go E on 101 approx. 5 mi. to Upper Wolf Creek Group CG.

		OPEN DATES:	Yearlong
		MAX SPUR:	32 feet
GROUP RATE:	Varies	MAX STAY:	14 days
# of GROUP SITES:	21	ELEVATION:	6000 feet

15 White Spar
Prescott • lat 34˚30'33" lon 112˚28'33"

DESCRIPTION: This CG is situated in an old growth ponderosa pine forest. A convenient and easy drive from the city of Prescott. Expect warm days with cold nights. Large and spacious sites. Scenic drive to nearby Sharlot Hall Museum. Numerous hiking trails can be found in the vicinity.

GETTING THERE: White Spar CG is located approx. 3 mi. S of Prescott on state HWY 89. (In Prescott go S on Montezuma St. approx. 3 m. to forest route 62.)

SINGLE RATE:	$10	OPEN DATES:	May-Sept
# of SINGLE SITES:	62	MAX SPUR:	40 feet
		MAX STAY:	14 days
		ELEVATION:	5700 feet

 Campground has hosts   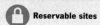 Reservable sites   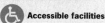 Accessible facilities   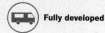 Fully developed   Semi-developed   Rustic facilities

NOTE: Open dates listed are typical. Actual dates are dependent on conditions such as snow pack.

TONTO NATIONAL FOREST

The Tonto embraces nearly three million acres of rugged, scenic landscapes ranging from cactus-studded desert to pine-clad mountains. This variety, coupled with outstanding year-round recreational opportunities, make the Tonto one of the most heavily visited forests in the nation.

The forest was created in 1905 to protect the watersheds of the Salt and Verde Rivers. This continues to be a central focus of the Tonto National Forest while the six reservoirs built along these rivers have created outstanding recreational opportunities for thousands of Arizonans. During winter months, mild weather attracts residents and tourists to beautiful lakes along multi-hued desert canyons. Seeking refuge from the summer heat, visitors flock to the forest's rivers and lakes as well as to alluring trout streams and the cool shade of tall pines in the Mogollon Rim country.

Hikers, all-terrain cyclists, and horseback riders have over 1000 miles of trails to explore. Power-boating, sailing, water-skiing, swimming, rafting, and tubing are some of the more popular recreation activities on the forest's lakes and waterways, while world-class whitewater can be experienced on the upper stretches of the Salt River.

USFS Photo

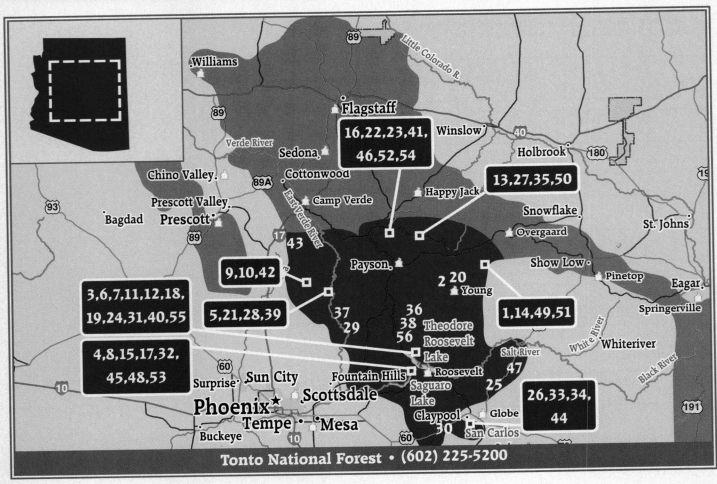

Tonto National Forest • (602) 225-5200

1 Airplane Flat
Young • lat 34°16'56" lon 110°48'30"

DESCRIPTION: Dispersed campsites rest in an open stand of ponderosa pine with forest and meadow views. Fish for trout in nearby Canyon Creek. Wildlife in area includes black bears, mountain lions, deer, elk, turkeys, hawks, and eagles. Hiking and horse trails in area. Visit nearby fish hatchery. No drinking water.

GETTING THERE: From Young go N on forest route 512 approx. 19 mi. to forest route 33. Go E on 33 approx. 4 mi. to Airplane Flat CG.

SINGLE RATE:	No fee	OPEN DATES:	Apr-Nov
		MAX STAY:	14 days
		ELEVATION:	6600 feet

2 Alderwood
Young • lat 34°13'00" lon 111°00'00"

DESCRIPTION: Dispersed sites rest in a well shaded, water-chiseled canyon. Fish for rainbow trout in adjacent Haigler Creek. Wildlife in area includes black bear, mountain lion, coyote, javelina, deer, elk, turkey, hawks, and eagles. CG can be busy weekends and holidays. Hiking and horse trails in area. No drinking water.

GETTING THERE: From Young go N on forest route 512 approx. 3 mi. to forest route 200. Go W on 200 approx. 6 mi. to forest route 249. Go W on 249 approx. 1/2 mi. to Alderwood CG.

SINGLE RATE:	No fee	OPEN DATES:	Apr-Nov
		MAX STAY:	14 days
		ELEVATION:	5200 feet

3 Bachelors Cove
Payson • lat 33°42'50" lon 111°12'14"

DESCRIPTION: Dispersed sites on Roosevelt Lake with Sonoran Desert plants. Beautiful lake and Sierra Ancha Mountain views. Shore or boat fish for crappie and bass. Supplies at Roosevelt Marina. Deer and javelina in area. Buy or bring own firewood. Hike, ATV, & bike trails nearby. Gnats until July. No drinking water.

GETTING THERE: From Payson go S on HWY 87 approx. 14 mi. to state HWY 188. Go E on 188 approx. 28 mi. to Bachelors Cove CG. Additional $2 fee per boat.

SINGLE RATE:	$4	OPEN DATES:	Yearlong
		MAX SPUR:	16 feet
		MAX STAY:	14 days
		ELEVATION:	2100 feet

4 Bagley Flat
Apache Junction • lat 33°34'10" lon 111°29'21"

DESCRIPTION: Dispersed campsites are located in mesquite shade trees on Saguaro Lake. Fish for largemouth and yellow bass, walleye, trout, catfish, and sunfish in lake. Supplies available in Apache Junction. Black bears, mountain lions, bobcats, coyotes, great blue herons, eagles, and lizards in area. Busy in winter. No drinking water.

GETTING THERE: Bagley Flat CG is located on the S shore of Saguaro Lake and is accessible by boat only.

SINGLE RATE:	No fee	OPEN DATES:	Yearlong
		MAX STAY:	14 days
		ELEVATION:	1500 feet

5 Bartlett Flat
Carefree • lat 34°51'45" lon 111°36'30"

DESCRIPTION: CG is on the shore of Bartlett Lake with dispersed sites among cactus and mesquite. Spectacular views of desert vistas with a mountain backdrop. Fish for crappie, catfish, and bass in reservoir. Supplies 20 mi.. Coyotes, hawks, and bald eagles in area. Boat ramp. Hiking trails. No drinking water.

GETTING THERE: From Carefree go E on Cave Creek Road approx. 5 mi. to Bartlett Dam Road. Go E on Bartlett Dam Road approx. 11 mi. to forest route 459. Go N on 459 approx. 3 mi. to Bartlett Flat CG.

SINGLE RATE:	$4	OPEN DATES:	Yearlong
		MAX STAY:	14 days
		ELEVATION:	1800 feet

6 Bermuda Flat
Apache Junction • lat 33°44'44" lon 111°13'32"

DESCRIPTION: CG in open grassy expanse on Arizona's largest lake, Roosevelt Lake. Boat ramp. Site size varies depending on water level of lake, no spaces in high water times. Bring firewood. Supplies at Roosevelt or Globe. Deer, coyotes, snakes, and javelinas in area. Lake trails for hiking. No drinking water.

GETTING THERE: From Apache Junction go NE on state HWY 88 approx. 38 mi. to state HWY 188. Go N on 188 approx. 9 mi. to Bermuda Flat CG.

SINGLE RATE:	$11	OPEN DATES:	Feb-Nov
		MAX SPUR:	32 feet
		MAX STAY:	14 days
		ELEVATION:	2100 feet

7 Burnt Corral
Apache Junction • lat 33°37'35" lon 111°12'15"

DESCRIPTION: This CG is set in a lush mesquite grove on Apache Lake. Boat and shore fish or swim from the lake. Bring your own firewood. Supplies are available at Apache Lake Marina or in Globe. Deer and javelinas can be seen in the area. There are hiking trails surrounding the lake. A scenic drive overlooks the painted bluffs of the lake.

GETTING THERE: Burnt Corral CG is located approx. 33 mi. NE of Apache Junction on state HWY 88. Road is narrow and winding - not recommended for trailers or RVs.

SINGLE RATE:	$8	OPEN DATES:	Yearlong
# of SINGLE SITES:	79	MAX SPUR:	22 feet
		MAX STAY:	14 days
		ELEVATION:	1900 feet

8 Canyon Lake Marina
Apache Junction • lat 33°32'09" lon 111°25'13"

DESCRIPTION: RV camping only with beautiful views of adjacent Canyon Lake and bluffs. Flora includes mesquite, paloverde, ironwoods, and saguaro cactus. Black bears, mountain lions, coyotes, and great blue herons in area. On site trailhead leads to Superstition Wilderness. No drinking water available. Boat ramp.

GETTING THERE: Canyon Lake Marina CG is located approx. 14 mi. NE of Apache Junction on state HWY 88 (The Apache Trail).

SINGLE RATE:	$8	OPEN DATES:	Yearlong
		MAX SPUR:	16 feet
		MAX STAY:	14 days
		ELEVATION:	1700 feet

9 Cave Creek Group
Carefree • lat 33°58'31" lon 111°51'57"

DESCRIPTION: This CG was constructed in 1934 by the Civilian Conservation Corps. CG is located in sycamore, juniper, and cottonwood near Cave Creek. Minimal wildlife includes deer and small rodents. CG is near the Cave Creek Trail System. Volleyball and horseshoes facilities. No drinking water.

GETTING THERE: From Carefree go NE on Cave Creek Road approx. 17 mi. to Cave Creek Group CG.

SINGLE RATE:		OPEN DATES:	Yearlong
# of SINGLE SITES:	16	MAX SPUR:	16 feet
GROUP RATE:	Varies	MAX STAY:	14 days
# of GROUP SITES:	1	ELEVATION:	3400 feet

10 CCC
Carefree • lat 33°58'11" lon 111°51'54"

DESCRIPTION: This CG is situated on the former site of a Civilian Conservation Camp. CG is located among sycamore and cottonwood near Cave Creek and natural springs. Forested views. This area is a good spot for birdwatching. CG is near the Cave Creek Trail System. No drinking water available on site.

GETTING THERE: From Carefree go NE on Cave Creek Road approx. 16 mi. to CCC CG.

SINGLE RATE:	$4	OPEN DATES:	Yearlong
# of SINGLE SITES:	16	MAX SPUR:	16 feet
		MAX STAY:	14 days
		ELEVATION:	3300 feet

 Campground has hosts   **Reservable sites**   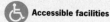 **Accessible facilities**   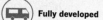 **Fully developed**   **Semi-developed**   **Rustic facilities**

NOTE: Open dates listed are typical. Actual dates are dependent on conditions such as snow pack.

11 Cholla
Apache Junction • lat 33°43'06" lon 111°12'12"

DESCRIPTION: CG set on Roosevelt Lake, Arizona's largest lake. Fish for bass, crappie, catfish, and bluegill. Shade shelters, playground, and showers provided. Bring your own firewood. Supplies are available at Rosevelt or Punkin Center or Globe. Deer, javelinas, snakes, and skunks in area. Lake trails in the area.

GETTING THERE: From Apache Junction go NE on state HWY 88 approx. 38 mi. to state HWY 188. Go N on 188 approx. 7 mi. to Cholla CG.

SINGLE RATE:	Varies	OPEN DATES:	Yearlong
# of SINGLE SITES	206	MAX SPUR:	32 feet
		MAX STAY:	14 days
		ELEVATION:	2100 feet

12 Cholla Bay
Apache Junction • lat 33°43'06" lon 111°12'12"

DESCRIPTION: CG on the shoreline of Roosevelt Lake, Arizona's largest lake. These dispersed sites change with the water level. Playground and showers. Bring your own firewood. Supplies at Roosevelt, Punkin Center, or Globe. Deer, javelinas, snakes, & skunks in area. Lake trails in the area. No drinking water available.

GETTING THERE: From Apache Junction go NE on state HWY 88 approx. 38 mi. to state HWY 188. Go N on 188 approx. 7 mi. to Cholla Bay CG.

SINGLE RATE:	No fee	OPEN DATES:	Yearlong
		MAX SPUR:	16 feet
		MAX STAY:	14 days
		ELEVATION:	2100 feet

13 Christopher Creek
Payson • lat 34°18'29" lon 111°02'05"

DESCRIPTION: CG set among tall pine trees near Christopher Creek. Fish for trout in the creek. Group site max is 25 persons and 8 vehicles. Amphitheatre on site with campfire programs. RV dump station 15 mi. away. Basic supplies on site or in Payson. Access to Highline National Recreation Trail aprox. 7 mi. E.

GETTING THERE: From Payson go E on state HWY 260 approx. 21 mi. to forest route 159. Go S on 159 approx. 1/2 mi. to Christopher Creek CG.

SINGLE RATE:	$11	OPEN DATES:	May-Oct
# of SINGLE SITES:	43	MAX SPUR:	22 feet
GROUP RATE:	$30	MAX STAY:	14 days
# of GROUP SITES:	1	ELEVATION:	5800 feet

14 Colcord Ridge
Young • lat 34°15'45" lon 110°50'32"

DESCRIPTION: Dispersed campsites rest in ponderosa pine and fir with panoramic views. Fish for trout in nearby Canyon Creek. Wildlife in area includes mountian lions, black bears, deer, elk, turkeys, hawks, and eagles. Hiking and horse trails in area. Visit nearby fish hatchery. No drinking water.

GETTING THERE: Colcoroute Ridge CG is located approx. 19 mi. N of Young on forest route 512.

SINGLE RATE:	No fee	OPEN DATES:	Apr-Nov
		MAX STAY:	14 days
		ELEVATION:	7600 feet

15 Coon Bluff
Apache Junction • lat 33°32'52" lon 111°38'16"

DESCRIPTION: Dispersed campsites are located in the Salt River Canyon. Flora includes mesquite, paloverde, ironwood, and cactus. Fish for bass, trout, and catfish in adjacent Lower Salt River. Bears, mountain lions, coyotes, great blue herons, big horn sheep, and eagles in the area. No drinking water.

GETTING THERE: From Apache Junction go W 5 mi. on US HWY 89 to Ellsworth Usery Pass RD. Go N 8 mi. to Bush HWY. Go W 1 mi. to forest route 204E. Go N 1/2 mi. to Coon Bluff CG. Not suitable for trailers.

SINGLE RATE:	No fee	OPEN DATES:	Yearlong
		MAX STAY:	14 days
		ELEVATION:	1300 feet

16 Flowing Spring
Payson • lat 34°18'10" lon 111°21'06"

DESCRIPTION: Located on the East Verde River with views of rock formations and pastoral scenes. No drinking water available on site. No services. Trout fishing on river. Bears frequent the area, so bear regulations are in effect. Use caution during rainy seasons as all Arizona creeks are prone to flash flooding.

GETTING THERE: Flowing Spring CG is located approx. 6 mi. N of Payson on state HWY 87.

SINGLE RATE:	No fee	OPEN DATES:	May-Sept
		MAX STAY:	14 days
		ELEVATION:	4600 feet

17 Goldfield
Apache Junction • lat 33°33'15" lon 111°37'13"

DESCRIPTION: Dispersed sites are located in the Salt River Canyon. Flora includes mesquite, paloverde, ironwood, and cactus. Fish for bass, trout, and catfish in adjacent Lower Salt River. Bears, mountain lions, coyotes, great blue herons, big horn sheep, and eagles frequent the area. No drinking water.

GETTING THERE: From Apache Junction go W on US HWY 89 approx. 5 mi. to Ellsworth Usery Pass Road. Go N approx. 8 mi. to Bush HWY. Continue N on 204A approx. 1 mi. to Goldfield CG. Not suitable for trailers.

SINGLE RATE:	No fee	OPEN DATES:	Yearlong
		MAX STAY:	14 days
		ELEVATION:	1400 feet

18 Grapevine Bay
Apache Junction • lat 33°38'30" lon 111°03'00"

DESCRIPTION: CG set on the shoreline of Roosevelt Lake which produces trophy bass. Boat launch at Windy Hill 5 mi. N. Hot summer days. Supplies are available in Mesa or Globe. Gather firewood. Deer, coyotes, javelinas, and occasional black bears in the area. No drinking water available on site. No services.

GETTING THERE: From Apache Junction go NE on state HWY 88 approx. 43 mi. to forest route 84. Go N on 84 approx. 2.5 mi. to Grapevine Bay CG.

SINGLE RATE:	$8	OPEN DATES:	Yearlong
		MAX SPUR:	16 feet
		MAX STAY:	14 days
		ELEVATION:	2100 feet

19 Grapevine Group
Apache Junction • lat 33°38'30" lon 111°03'00"

DESCRIPTION: Adjacent to Roosevelt Lake which produces trophy bass. Boat launch at Windy Hill 5 mi. N. Hot summer days. Showers, sports field, playground, shade ramadas, & amphitheatre. Supplies in Mesa or Globe. Gather firewood. Deer, coyotes, javelinas, snakes, & occasional black bears in area. No drinking water.

GETTING THERE: From Apache Junction go NE on state HWY 88 approx. 43 mi. to forest route 84. Go N on 84 approx. 2.5 mi. to Grapevine Group CG.

SINGLE RATE:		OPEN DATES:	Yearlong
		MAX SPUR:	32 feet
GROUP RATE:	Varies	MAX STAY:	14 days
# of GROUP SITES:	2	ELEVATION:	2200 feet

20 Haigler Canyon
Young • lat 34°13'00" lon 110°58'00"

DESCRIPTION: Dispersed sites rest in a well shaded, water-chiseled canyon. Fish for rainbow trout in adjacent Haigler Creek. Wildlife in area includes black bears, mountain lions, coyotes, javelinas, deer, elk, turkeys, hawks, and eagles. CG marks the end of a 6 mi. horse trail. No drinking water available.

GETTING THERE: From Young go N on forest route 512 approx. 3 mi. to forest route 200. Go NE on 200 approx. 7 mi. to Haigler Canyon CG.

SINGLE RATE:	No fee	OPEN DATES:	Apr-Nov
		MAX STAY:	14 days
		ELEVATION:	5300 feet

 Campground has hosts   **Reservable sites**   **Accessible facilities**   **Fully developed**   **Semi-developed**   **Rustic facilities**

NOTE: Open dates listed are typical. Actual dates are dependent on conditions such as snow pack.

21 Horseshoe
Carefree • lat 33°58'38" lon 111°43'01"

DESCRIPTION: CG is located in large mesquite along the Verde River. Good fishing opportunities for catfish, crappie, blue gill, and bass in nearby Horseshoe Reservoir. Area is a good spot for birdwatching bald eagles and great blue herons. There are hiking trails in the area. No drinking water available.

GETTING THERE: From Carefree go E on Cave Creek Road approx. 5 mi. to Horseshoe Dam Road. Go NE on Horseshoe Dam Road approx. 14 mi. to Horseshoe CG.

SINGLE RATE:	$4	OPEN DATES:	Yearlong
# of SINGLE SITES:	12	MAX SPUR:	16 feet
		MAX STAY:	14 days
		ELEVATION:	1900 feet

26 Kellner
Globe • lat 33°20'06" lon 110°49'42"

DESCRIPTION: CG in open area of scrub oak and pinyon pine trees. No drinking water, no services. No nearby fishing. Supplies in Globe. Bring your own firewood. Open area is good for group use. Deer, coyotes, javelinas, and occasional black bears in area.

GETTING THERE: From Globe go S on forest route 112 approx. 2 mi. to forest route 55. Go S on 55 approx. 3 mi. to Kellner CG.

SINGLE RATE:	No fee	OPEN DATES:	Yearlong
# of SINGLE SITES:	4		
GROUP RATE:	Varies	MAX STAY:	14 days
# of GROUP SITES:	1	ELEVATION:	4500 feet

22 Houston Mesa
Payson • lat 34°17'00" lon 111°18'00"

DESCRIPTION: This CG is situated in an open park-like area. Supplies are available in Payson. Houston Mesa Interpretive Trail (1/2 mi. long), begins on site. Various other trails nearby. An amphitheater is available where interpretive programs are offered. Showers and an RV dump station are provided.

GETTING THERE: Houston Mesa CG is located on the N end of Payson on state HWY 87.

SINGLE RATE:	$12	OPEN DATES:	Yearlong
# of SINGLE SITES:	75	MAX SPUR:	30 feet
		MAX STAY:	14 days
		ELEVATION:	5100 feet

27 Lower Tonto Creek
Payson • lat 34°19'45" lon 111°05'31"

DESCRIPTION: This dispersed CG is on the East Verde River set in ponderosa pine, aspen and pinyons. Fish for stocked rainbow on river. Supplies available in Payson. Bears, coyotes, elk, deer, skunks, racoons, and javelinas in area. Campers may gather firewood on site. No drinking water or services at this CG.

GETTING THERE: Lower Tonto Creek CG is located approx. 17 mi. E of Payson on state HWY 260.

SINGLE RATE:	No fee	OPEN DATES:	Apr-Nov
# of SINGLE SITES:	17	MAX SPUR:	22 feet
		MAX STAY:	14 days
		ELEVATION:	5600 feet

23 Houston Mesa Equestrian
Payson • lat 34°17'00" lon 111°18'00"

DESCRIPTION: This CG is used primarily as a horse camp facility. Showers and an RV dump station are available on site. Interpretive programs available. No more than 10 persons and 2 vehicles per unit. Supplies are available in Payson. Houston Mesa Interpretive Trail can be found nearby.

GETTING THERE: Houston Mesa Equestrian CG is located on the N end of Payson on state HWY 87.

SINGLE RATE:	$12	OPEN DATES:	Yearlong
# of SINGLE SITES:	75	MAX SPUR:	30 feet
GROUP RATE:	Varies	MAX STAY:	14 days
# of GROUP SITES:	2	ELEVATION:	5100 feet

28 Mesquite
Carefree • lat 33°57'55" lon 111°43'05"

DESCRIPTION: CG is located in large mesquite along the Verde River. Good fishing opportunities for catfish, crappie, blue gill, and bass in nearby Horseshoe Reservoir. Area is a good spot for birdwatching bald eagles and great blue herons. There are hiking trails in the area. No drinking water available.

GETTING THERE: From Carefree go E on Cave Creek Road approx. 5 mi. to Bartlett Dam Road. Go E on Bartlett Dam Road approx. 5 mi. to Horseshoe Dam Road. Go NE on Horseshoe Dam Road approx. 13 mi. to Mesquite CG.

SINGLE RATE:	$4	OPEN DATES:	Yearlong
# of SINGLE SITES:	12	MAX SPUR:	16 feet
		MAX STAY:	14 days
		ELEVATION:	1900 feet

24 Indian Point
Apache Junction • lat 33°46'30" lon 111°13'00"

DESCRIPTION: This CG is situated in an open area, quiet and more isolated. No water frontage or fishing nearby. Good place to get away. Hot days with cool nights. Supplies are available at Apache Junction. Bring your own firewood. Deer, javelinas, snakes, and small wildlife in area.

GETTING THERE: From Apache Junction go NE on state HWY 88 (Apache Trail) 38 mi. to state HWY 188. Go NW approx. 13 mi. to forest route 60. Go E 2 mi. to forest route 661. Go S 2 mi. to Indian Point CG.

SINGLE RATE:	$8	OPEN DATES:	Yearlong
# of SINGLE SITES:	90	MAX SPUR:	16 feet
		MAX STAY:	14 days
		ELEVATION:	2200 feet

29 Needle Rock
Carefree • lat 33°46'30" lon 111°38'30"

DESCRIPTION: CG is located near a rocky beach on the Verde River. Views of unusual rock formations. Good fishing opportunities in nearby Bartlett Reservoir. Area is a good spot for birdwatching bald eagles and great blue herons. Mesquite Bosque, a natural riparian area with hiking paths, is nearby. No drinking water.

GETTING THERE: From Carefree go S on Scottsdale Road approx. 6 mi. to Dynamite Road/Rio Verde Drive. Go E approx. 16 mi. to forest route 20. Go N approx. 3 mi. to Needle Rock CG. Not suitable for trailers.

SINGLE RATE:	$4	OPEN DATES:	Yearlong
# of SINGLE SITES:	10	MAX SPUR:	20 feet
		MAX STAY:	14 days
		ELEVATION:	1550 feet

25 Jones Water
Globe • lat 33°35'31" lon 110°38'32"

DESCRIPTION: CG in open area of scrub oak and pinyon pine trees. No nearby fishing. Supplies available in Globe. Indian Ruins near Roosevelt. Bring your own firewood. Open area is good for group use. Deer, coyotes, javelinas, and occasional black bears in area. Hiking trail (6 shooter) nearby. No drinking water or services at this CG.

GETTING THERE: Jones Water CG is located approx. 18 mi. N of Globe on US HWY 60.

SINGLE RATE:	No fee	OPEN DATES:	Yearlong
# of SINGLE SITES:	12	MAX SPUR:	16 feet
		MAX STAY:	14 days
		ELEVATION:	4500 feet

30 Oak Flat
Superior • lat 33°18'27" lon 111°02'34"

DESCRIPTION: CG set in open area of scrub oak and pinyon pine trees. No nearby fishing. Supplies available in Globe. Bring your own firewood. Open area is good for group use. Deer, coyotes, javelinas, and occasional black bears in area. Indian Ruins near Roosevelt. Arboretum between Globe and Superior. No drinking water on site.

GETTING THERE: Oak Flat CG is located 3 mi. E of Superior on US HWY 60.

SINGLE RATE:	No fee	OPEN DATES:	Yearlong
# of SINGLE SITES:	16	MAX SPUR:	16 feet
		MAX STAY:	14 days
		ELEVATION:	4200 feet

 Campground has hosts   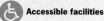 **Reservable sites**   **Accessible facilities**   **Fully developed**   **Semi-developed**   **Rustic facilities**

NOTE: Open dates listed are typical. Actual dates are dependent on conditions such as snow pack.

Page 39

TONTO NATIONAL FOREST • ARIZONA • 21 — 30

31 Orange Peel
Apache Junction • lat 33°45'43" lon 111°15'09"

DESCRIPTION: CG on Roosevelt Lake, with trophy bass fishing. Number of sites is affected by level of lake water; call 602-236-5929 for information. No large boat may be launched. No drinking water. Hot days with cool nights. Supplies at Apache Junction. Deer, elk, javelinas, and black bears in area. Lake trails.

GETTING THERE: From Apache Junction go NE on state HWY 88 approx. 38 mi. to state HWY 188. Go N on 188 approx. 10 mi. to Orange Peel CG. Not recommended for trailers over 16'.

SINGLE RATE:	No fee	OPEN DATES:	Yearlong
		MAX SPUR:	16 feet
		MAX STAY:	14 days
		ELEVATION:	2100 feet

32 Phon D. Sutton
Apache Junction • lat 33°36'00" lon 111°39'30"

DESCRIPTION: Dispersed campsites are located in the Salt River Canyon. Flora includes mesquite, paloverde, ironwood, and cactus. Fish for bass, trout, and catfish in adjacent Lower Salt River. Bears, mountain lions, coyotes, great blue herons, big horn sheep, and eagles in the area. No drinking water.

GETTING THERE: From Apache Junction go W on US HWY 89 5 mi. to Ellsworth Usery Pass Road. Go N 8 mi. to Bush HWY. Go W 2 mi. to forest route 169. Go N 1 mi. to Phon D. Sutton CG. Not suitable for trailers.

SINGLE RATE:	No fee	OPEN DATES:	Yearlong
		MAX STAY:	14 days
		ELEVATION:	1300 feet

33 Pinal & Upper Pinal
Globe • lat 33°17'00" lon 110°49'45"

DESCRIPTION: In open area of scrub oak and pinyon trees. No services, drinking water only in summer. No nearby fishing. Supplies in Globe. Bring own firewood. Open area is good for group use. Deer, coyotes, javelinas, and occasional black bears in area. Rarely fills. Hike to Pinal Peak. Indian Ruins near Roosevelt.

GETTING THERE: From Globe go S on forest route 112 approx. 2 mi. to forest route 55. Go S on 55 approx. 3 mi. to forest route 651. Go S on 651 approx. 8 mi. to Pinal and Upper Pinal CGs.

SINGLE RATE:	No fee	OPEN DATES:	May-Nov
# of SINGLE SITES:	19	MAX SPUR:	16 feet
		MAX STAY:	14 days
		ELEVATION:	7500 feet

34 Pioneer Pass
Globe • lat 33°16'50" lon 110°47'46"

DESCRIPTION: In open area of scrub oak and pinyon trees. No services, drinking water in summer only. No nearby fishing. Supplies in Globe. Bring own firewood. Open area is good for group use. Deer, coyotes, javelinas, and occasional black bears in area. Indian Ruins near Roosevelt. Arboretum near Globe.

GETTING THERE: From Globe go S on forest route 112 approx. 7.5 mi. to Pioneer Pass CG.

SINGLE RATE:	No fee	OPEN DATES:	Yearlong
# of SINGLE SITES:	25	MAX SPUR:	16 feet
		MAX STAY:	14 days
		ELEVATION:	6000 feet

35 Ponderosa
Payson • lat 34°17'56" lon 111°06'50"

DESCRIPTION: This CG is in a cool setting among majestic ponderosa pine. An amphitheater and sewage dump can be found close by. Supplies are available in Payson. Two group sites for up to 50 persons each must be reserved and are open May through December. Hike Abert Nature Trail nearby.

GETTING THERE: Ponderosa CG is located approx. 15 mi. E of Payson on state HWY 260. Not recommended for trailers over 22'.

SINGLE RATE:	$11	OPEN DATES:	Yearlong
# of SINGLE SITES:	61	MAX SPUR:	22 feet
GROUP RATE:	$50	MAX STAY:	14 days
# of GROUP SITES:	2	ELEVATION:	5600 feet

36 Reynolds Creek
Young • lat 33°52'30" lon 110°59'00"

DESCRIPTION: This CG is situated in an open meadow with some ponderosa pine and sycamore. Views are of the beautiful Sierra Ancha mountains. Fish for trout in adjacent Reynolds Creek. This CG is within walking distance to the Sierra Ancha and Salome Wilderness areas. Black bears, mountain lions, and hawks.

GETTING THERE: Reynolds Creek CG is located approx. 18 mi. S of Young on state HWY 288.

SINGLE RATE:	$8	OPEN DATES:	Apr-Nov
		MAX SPUR:	32 feet
GROUP RATE:	Varies	MAX STAY:	14 days
# of GROUP SITES:	1	ELEVATION:	5200 feet

37 Riverside
Carefree • lat 33°48'51" lon 111°38'40"

DESCRIPTION: CG is located on the Verde River just south of Bartlett Reservoir. Cactus and mesquite in area. Spectacular views of desert vistas with a mountain backdrop. Fish for crappie, catfish, and bass in reservoir. Coyotes, hawks, and bald eagles in area. Hiking trails. No drinking water available.

GETTING THERE: From Carefree go NE on Cave Creek Road approx. 5 mi. to Bartlett Dam Road. Go E on Bartlett Dam Road approx. 13 mi. to forest route 162. Go S on 162 approx. 3 mi. to Riverside CG.

SINGLE RATE:	$4	OPEN DATES:	Yearlong
# of SINGLE SITES:	12	MAX SPUR:	20 feet
		MAX STAY:	14 days
		ELEVATION:	1600 feet

38 Rose Creek
Young • lat 33°49'46" lon 110°58'44"

DESCRIPTION: This CG is located in between the Salome and Sierra Ancha Wilderness Areas. Rose Creek runs adjacent to CG. Wildlife in area includes black bears, mountain lions, coyotes, deer, elk, javelinas, hawks, and eagles. Several hiking and horse trails in area. CG can be busy weekends and holidays.

GETTING THERE: From Young go S on state HWY 288 approx. 21 mi. to Rose Creek CG.

SINGLE RATE:	No fee	OPEN DATES:	Apr-Nov
# of SINGLE SITES:	5	MAX SPUR:	16 feet
		MAX STAY:	14 days
		ELEVATION:	5400 feet

39 S.B. Cove
Carefree • lat 33°52'06" lon 111°37'00"

DESCRIPTION: CG is on Bartlett Reservoir with dispersed on-shore sites. Cactus and mesquite in area. Spectacular views of desert vistas with a mountain backdrop. Fish for crappie, catfish, and bass in reservoir. Wildlife includes coyotes, hawks, and bald eagles. Hiking trails in area. No drinking water available.

GETTING THERE: From Carefree go E on Cave Creek Road approx. 5 mi. to Bartlett Dam Road. Go E on Bartlett Dam Road approx. 11 mi. to forest route 459. Go N on 459 approx. 2 mi. to S.B. Cove CG.

SINGLE RATE:	$4	OPEN DATES:	Yearlong
		MAX STAY:	14 days
		ELEVATION:	1800 feet

40 Schoolhouse Point
Apache Junction • lat 33°39'00" lon 111°00'34"

DESCRIPTION: CG set on the southern shores of Salt River arm of Roosevelt Lake. Excellent catfishing area. Shoreline boat launch. Hot days with cool nights. Supplies in Spring Creek or Globe. Deer, coyotes, javelinas, and occasional bears in the area. Lake trails. No drinking water available on site.

GETTING THERE: From Apache Junction go NE on state HWY 88 approx. 45 mi. to forest route 447. Go N on 447 approx. 3 mi. to Schoolhouse Point CG.

SINGLE RATE:	$8	OPEN DATES:	Yearlong
# of SINGLE SITES:	200	MAX SPUR:	32 feet
		MAX STAY:	14 days
		ELEVATION:	2100 feet

 Campground has hosts   **Reservable sites**   **Accessible facilities**   **Fully developed**   **Semi-developed**   **Rustic facilities**

NOTE: Open dates listed are typical. Actual dates are dependent on conditions such as snow pack.

Page 40

41 Second Crossing
Payson • lat 34°21'17" lon 111°16'58"

DESCRIPTION: This rustic CG is surrounded by beautiful pine on the East Verde River. Enjoy fishing for trout on the river but please check for fishing regulations. There is no drinking water on site. Supplies are available in Payson. Campers may gather firewood. Numerous wildlife in the area. There are no designated trails nearby.

GETTING THERE: From Payson go N on state HWY 87 approx. 2 mi. to forest route 199. Go N on 199 approx. 7 mi. to Second Crossing CG.

SINGLE RATE:	No fee	OPEN DATES:	May-Sept
		MAX STAY:	14 days
		ELEVATION:	5100 feet

42 Seven Springs
Carefree • lat 33°57'58" lon 111°51'45"

DESCRIPTION: This CG is located in sycamore and cottonwood with views of the surrounding forest area. Fish or swim in nearby Cave Creek. Minimal wildlife includes deer and small rodents. This is a good spot for birdwatching. CG is located near the Cave Creek Trail System. No drinking water available on site.

GETTING THERE: From Carefree go NE on Cave Creek Road approx. 15 mi. to Seven Springs CG. Not suitable for trailers.

SINGLE RATE:	$4	OPEN DATES:	Yearlong
# of SINGLE SITES:	23	MAX SPUR:	16 feet
		MAX STAY:	14 days
		ELEVATION:	3300 feet

43 Sheep Bridge
Carefree • lat 34°04'37" lon 111°42'34"

DESCRIPTION: This CG is located among sycamore, cottonwood, and willows with dispersed campsites. This CG is situated along the Upper Verde River. There is a historic bridge on site. Also, an on site trailhead leads to the majestic Mazatzal Wilderness. No drinking water available on site.

GETTING THERE: From Carefree go E and N on forest route 24 approx. 33 mi. to forest route 269. Go E on 269 approx. 11 mi. to Sheep Bridge CG. Not suitable for trailers.

SINGLE RATE:	No fee	OPEN DATES:	Yearlong
		MAX STAY:	14 days
		ELEVATION:	2100 feet

44 Sulphide Del Ray
Globe • lat 33°17'37" lon 110°52'00"

DESCRIPTION: CG in open area of scrub oak and pinyon trees. No drinking water, no services. No nearby fishing. Supplies in Globe. Bring own firewood. Open area is good for group use. Deer, coyotes, javelinas, and occasional black bears in area. Hike trail to Pinal Peak nearby. Indian Ruins near Roosevelt.

GETTING THERE: From Globe go S on forest route 112 2 mi. to forest route 55. Go S 3 mi. to forest route 651. Go S 5 mi. to Sulphide Del Ray CG. Not recommended for trailers or RVs, tight turn around.

SINGLE RATE:	No fee	OPEN DATES:	Apr-Nov
# of SINGLE SITES:	10	MAX SPUR:	16 feet
		MAX STAY:	14 days
		ELEVATION:	6000 feet

45 The Point
Apache Junction • lat 33°33'25" lon 111°24'38"

DESCRIPTION: CG is on Canyon Lake. Flora includes mesquite, paloverde, ironwood, and saguaro cactus. Fish for bass, walleye, trout, and catfish. Wildlife in area includes black bears, mountain lions, bobcats, coyotes, great blue herons, eagles, and hawks. No drinking water. Hike adjacent Superstition Wilderness.

GETTING THERE: The Point CG is located on the N shore of Canyon Lake and is accessible only by boat.

SINGLE RATE:	$8	OPEN DATES:	Yearlong
# of SINGLE SITES:	3	MAX SPUR:	16 feet
		MAX STAY:	14 days
		ELEVATION:	1700 feet

46 Third Crossing
Payson • lat 34°21'51" lon 111°16'47"

DESCRIPTION: This dispersed CG is surrounded by beautiful pine trees on the East Verde River. Fish or swim from the river. Supplies available at Payson. Bears frequent the area, take bear precautions while in the area. No services or drinking water available on site. No designated trails nearby.

GETTING THERE: From Payson go N on state HWY 87 approx. 2 mi. to forest route 199. Go N on 199 approx. 8 mi. to Third Crossing CG. 4WD or chains advised after heavy rains or snows.

SINGLE RATE:	No fee	OPEN DATES:	May-Sept
		MAX STAY:	14 days
		ELEVATION:	5100 feet

47 Timber Camp
Globe • lat 33°40'00" lon 110°35'00"

DESCRIPTION: CG set in an open area of scrub oak and pinyon trees. No drinking water, no services. No nearby fishing. Supplies in Globe. Bring own firewood. Open area is good for group use. Deer, coyotes, javelinas, and occasional black bears in the area. Rarely fills. 2 tables, dispersed sites, good for groups.

GETTING THERE: Timber Camp CG is located approx. 25 mi. N of Globe on US HWY 60.

SINGLE RATE:	No fee	OPEN DATES:	Apr-Nov
# of SINGLE SITES:	2	MAX SPUR:	32 feet
		MAX STAY:	14 days
		ELEVATION:	5500 feet

48   Tortilla
Apache Junction • lat 33°32'00" lon 111°24'00"

DESCRIPTION: Near Canyon Lake adjacent to historic Tortilla Flat(town) with views of Tortilla Creek & wilderness. Closed in summer for heat. Gather firewood. Fish for bass, walleye, trout, & catfish. Black bear, mountain lion, coyote, great blue heron, eagles. Hike nearby Superstition Wilderness. Dump station.

GETTING THERE: From Apache Junction go NE on state HWY 88 approx. 15 mi. to Tortilla CG.

SINGLE RATE:	$8	OPEN DATES:	Oct-Apr
# of SINGLE SITES:	77	MAX SPUR:	22 feet
		MAX STAY:	14 days
		ELEVATION:	1800 feet

49 Upper Canyon Creek
Young • lat 34°17'30" lon 110°47'30"

DESCRIPTION: CG with dispersed campsites rest in ponderosa pine and fir with forest and meadow views. Fish for rainbow trout in nearby Canyon Creek. Wildlife in area includes black bears, mountain lions, deer, elk, turkeys, hawks, and eagles. Hiking and horse trails in area. Visit nearby fish hatchery. No drinking water.

GETTING THERE: From Young go N on forest route 512 approx. 19 mi. to forest route 33. Go E on 33 approx. 5 mi. to Upper Canyon Creek CG.

SINGLE RATE:	No fee	OPEN DATES:	Apr-Nov
		MAX STAY:	14 days
		ELEVATION:	6600 feet

50 Upper Tonto Creek
Payson • lat 34°19'45" lon 111°05'31"

DESCRIPTION: CG sits at the confluence of Tonto and Horton Creeks. Fish for trout from either of the creeks. Supplies available at Payson or Christopher Creek. Wildlife can be seen in the area. The Tonto Hatchery is approx. 4 mi. from the CG. Hiking trails #285-Horton Creek, and #33-Derrick, access Highline National Recreation Trail.

GETTING THERE: From Payson go E on state HWY 260 approx. 18 mi. to forest route 289. Take 289 approx. 1 mi. to Upper Tonto Creek CG. Trailers over 16' not recommended.

SINGLE RATE:	$7	OPEN DATES:	Apr-Nov
# of SINGLE SITES:	9	MAX SPUR:	16 feet
		MAX STAY:	14 days
		ELEVATION:	5600 feet

 Campground has hosts   Reservable sites   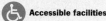 Accessible facilities   Fully developed   Semi-developed   Rustic facilities

NOTE: Open dates listed are typical. Actual dates are dependent on conditions such as snow pack.

51 Valentine Ridge
Young • lat 34°15'00" lon 110°48'00"

DESCRIPTION: CG rests in an open stand of ponderosa pine near Canyon Creek. Fish for rainbow trout in the nearby creek. Supplies available at Young. Wildlife in the area include mountain lions, deer, elk, turkeys, hawks, and eagles. Visit nearby fish hatchery. Frequented by black bears. There is an on site mountain biking trail.

GETTING THERE: From Young go N on forest route 512 approx. 16 mi. to forest route 188. Go E on 188 approx. 2 mi. to Valentine Ridge CG.

SINGLE RATE:	No fee	OPEN DATES:	Apr-Nov
# of SINGLE SITES:	9	MAX SPUR:	16 feet
		MAX STAY:	14 days
		ELEVATION:	6700 feet

52 Verde Glen
Payson • lat 34°24'00" lon 111°16'00"

DESCRIPTION: This CG is situated along the green banks of the East Verde River. Dispersed sites. Trout fishing opportunities on the river. Check for local fishing regulations. No drinking water available on site. Supplies can be found in Payson. No services are offered.

GETTING THERE: From Payson go N on state HWY 87 approx. 2 mi. to forest route 199. Go N approx. 10.5 mi. to Verde Glen CG. 4WD or chains advised after heavy rains or snows. Not recommended for trailers over 16'.

SINGLE RATE:	No fee	OPEN DATES:	May-Sept
		MAX STAY:	14 days
		ELEVATION:	5600 feet

53 Water Users
Apache Junction • lat 33°33'20" lon 111°32'18"

DESCRIPTION: Dispersed campsites are located in the Salt River Canyon. Flora includes mesquite, paloverde, ironwood, and cactus. Fish for bass, trout, and catfish in adjacent Lower Salt River. Bears, mountain lions, coyotes, great blue herons, big horn sheep, and eagles in area. No drinking water available.

GETTING THERE: From Apache Junction go W on US HWY 89 approx. 5 mi. to Ellsworth Usery Pass Road. Go N on Ellsworth Usery to Bush HWY. Go E on Bush HWY approx. 4 mi. to Water Users CG.

SINGLE RATE:	No fee	OPEN DATES:	Yearlong
		MAX STAY:	14 days
		ELEVATION:	1400 feet

54 Waterwheel
Payson • lat 34°20'30" lon 111°17'00"

DESCRIPTION: CG on the East Verde River set in pine, aspen, pinyon, and hardwoods. No drinking water, no services. Hot days, cold nights. Fish for stocked rainbow on river. Gather firewood locally. Supplies in Payson. Bears, coyotes, elk, deer, skunks, racoons, and javelinas in area. Dispersed sites.

GETTING THERE: From Payson go N on state HWY 87 approx. 2 mi. to forest route 199. Go N on 199 approx. 6 mi. to Waterwheel CG.

SINGLE RATE:	No fee	OPEN DATES:	May-Sept
		MAX STAY:	14 days
		ELEVATION:	5000 feet

55 Windy Hill
Apache Junction • lat 33°40'13" lon 111°05'12"

DESCRIPTION: CG in and open area on peninsula of Roosevelt lake. Hot days with cool nights. Great lake fishing. Shade ramadas, amphitheater, playgrounds, showers, boat ramps, and phones provided. Bring own firewood. Supplies at Roosevelt or Punkin Center. Several miles of hiking and lake access trails.

GETTING THERE: From Apache Junction go SE on US HWY 60 approx. 40 mi. to Globe. Go N on state HWY 88 approx. 24 mi. to forest route 82. E on 82 approx. 2 mi. to Windy Hill CG.

SINGLE RATE:	Varies	OPEN DATES:	Yearlong
# of SINGLE SITES:	347	MAX SPUR:	32 feet
		MAX STAY:	14 days
		ELEVATION:	2100 feet

56 Workman Creek Area
Globe • lat 33°49'05" lon 110°55'50"

DESCRIPTION: These campsites are situated in ponderosa pine, douglas fir, and white fir. Views are of the adjacent riparian area of Workman Creek. Fish for rainbow trout in the creek. Black bears, mountain lions, coyotes, javelinas, deer, hawks, and eagles in area. No drinking water. Several trails nearby.

GETTING THERE: From Globe go N on state HWY 88 approx. 15 mi. to state HWY 288. Go N 288 approx. 26 mi. to forest route 487. Go SE on 487 approx. 3 mi. to Workman Creek Area CG.

SINGLE RATE:	No fee	OPEN DATES:	Apr-Nov
GROUP RATE:	Varies	MAX SPUR:	20 feet
# of GROUP SITES:	3	MAX STAY:	14 days
		ELEVATION:	5900 feet

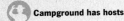 Campground has hosts   Reservable sites   Accessible facilities 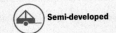 Fully developed 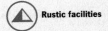 Semi-developed Rustic facilities

NOTE: Open dates listed are typical. Actual dates are dependent on conditions such as snow pack.

Page 42

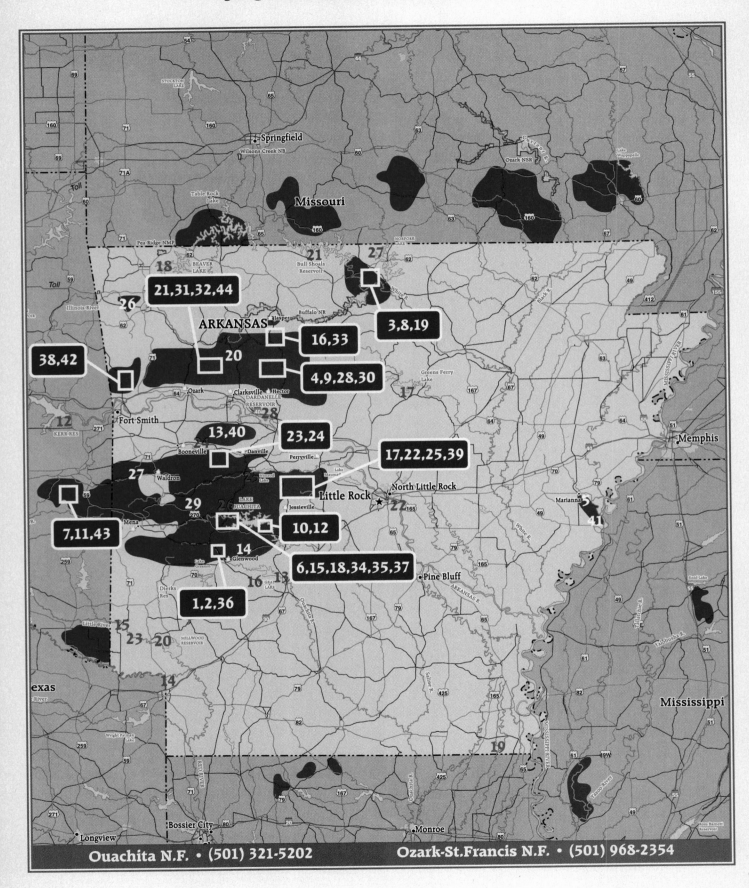

USFS Photo

NATIONAL FORESTS OF ARKANSAS

The forests of Arkansas include the Ouachita National Forest, the oldest National Forest in the South, and the 1.5 million acre Ozark-St. Francis National Forests. As one of America's most scenic and picturesque areas, the forests of Arkansas provide a lot of the "natural" in the natural state of Arkansas.

Recreation opportunities abound on the forests of Arkansas. There are over 900 miles of trails, eight scenic byways and many campgrounds and picnic areas. Natural scenery and solitude are found in the eleven wilderness areas. Numerous rivers, lakes and streams provide excellent fishing and floating. Some of the most popular float streams are the Ouachita River, the Cossatot and Little Missouri. The spectacular cave formations at Blanchard Springs Caverns offer the visitor a view of the subterranean world below. Rustic mountain cabins have provided a peaceful getaway for people since the 1930s at Lake Wedington and White Rock Mountain.

1 Albert Pike
Glenwood • lat 34°22'20" lon 093°52'46"

DESCRIPTION: In a mixed hardwood setting on the Little Missouri River. Fish for bass, trout and bream or swim in river. Supplies available at Glenwood. Deer, bear, squirrels and birds are common to the area. Campers may gather firewood. The Little Missouri Trail and the Winding Stairs Scenic Area are nearby.

GETTING THERE: From Glenwood go W US HWY 70 approx. 4.5 mi. to state HWY 84. Go W on 84 approx. 12.5 mi. to state HWY 369. Go N on 369 approx. 6 mi. to Albert Pike CG.

SINGLE RATE:	$10	OPEN DATES:	Yearlong*
# of SINGLE SITES:	46	MAX SPUR:	22 feet
		MAX STAY:	14 days
		ELEVATION:	950 feet

2 Bard Spring
Glenwood • lat 34°23'29" lon 094°00'38"

DESCRIPTION: This primitive tent only CG is in a mixed hardwood forest setting on Blalock Creek. Fish and swim in the creek. Supplies available at Glenwood. Deer, bears, squirrels and birds are common in the area. Campers may gather firewood. The Caney Creek Wilderness Trail is in the area. NO RV's.

GETTING THERE: From Glenwood go 4.5 mi. W on state HWY 27 to state HWY 84. Go W 20.5 mi. on 84 to state HWY 246. Go NW 2 mi. on 246 to county route 38. Go N 7 mi. on 38 to forest route 106. Go E 1/2 mi. on 106 to Bard Springs CG.

SINGLE RATE:	$5	OPEN DATES:	Yearlong*
# of SINGLE SITES:	17		
		MAX STAY:	14 days
		ELEVATION:	1230 feet

3 Barkshed
Mountain View • lat 36°01'07" lon 092°15'00"

DESCRIPTION: CG set in an oak and hickory forest with views of bluffs and clear creeks. Warm water fishing in North Sylamore Creek. Site of Barkshed Forest Camp from the 1930's. Supplies available at Mountain View. Deer, snakes, and bears are common to the area. Gather firewood. Hike rugged North Sylamore trail.

GETTING THERE: From Mountain View go NW on state HWY 14 approx. 19 mi. to forest route 11120. Go NE on 11120 approx. 3 mi. to Barkshed CG. Steep, rugged road; not recommended for large RVs. 4WD recommended.

SINGLE RATE:	$3	OPEN DATES:	Yearlong
# of SINGLE SITES:	1	MAX SPUR:	32 feet
		MAX STAY:	14 days
		ELEVATION:	450 feet

4 Bayou Bluff
Hector • lat 35°31'28" lon 092°56'39"

DESCRIPTION: In a mixed forest setting near the Illinois Bayou River. Excellent views of the picturesque bluffs in area. Fish and swim in the river. Supplies available at Hector. Many animals can be seen in the area. Campers may gather firewood. Many trails in the area.

GETTING THERE: Bayou Bluff CG is located approx. 4 mi. NE of Hector on state HWY 27.

SINGLE RATE:	$4	OPEN DATES:	Dec-Apr
# of SINGLE SITES:	7		
		MAX STAY:	14 days
		ELEVATION:	500 feet

5 Bears Creek Lake
Marianna • lat 34°42'32" lon 090°41'50"

DESCRIPTION: In a mixed forest setting on Bears Creek Lake which sits atop Crowley's Ridge. Boating (max 10 hp), boat ramp at CG. Fish, boat and swim in the lake. Supplies available at Marianna. Many animals can be seen in the area. Campers may gather firewood. The Bears Creek Lake Nature Trail is nearby.

GETTING THERE: From Marianna go SE approx. 7 mi. on state HWY 44 to Bears Creek Lake CG.

SINGLE RATE:	No fee	OPEN DATES:	Yearlong
# of SINGLE SITES:	31	MAX SPUR:	28 feet
		MAX STAY:	14 days
		ELEVATION:	289 feet

 Campground has hosts   **Reservable sites**   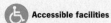 **Accessible facilities**   **Fully developed**   **Semi-developed**   **Rustic facilities**

NOTE: Open dates listed are typical. Actual dates are dependent on conditions such as snow pack.

6 Big Brushy
Mount Ida • lat 34°41'06" lon 093°48'41"

DESCRIPTION: An attractive wooded setting on Mill Creek. Fish and swim in Creek. Supplies available at Mount Ida. Many animals can be seen in the area. Campers may gather firewood. Playground and a loop trail at the CG. Access to the Ouachita National Recreation Trail from the CG area.

GETTING THERE: Big Brushy CG is located approx. 13 mi. NW of Mount Ida on US HWY 270.

SINGLE RATE:	$7	OPEN DATES:	Yearlong
# of SINGLE SITES:	9	MAX SPUR:	32 feet
		MAX STAY:	14 days
		ELEVATION:	1000 feet

11 Cedar Lake
Heavener • lat 34°47'30" lon 094°41'30"

DESCRIPTION: In a mixed forest setting on the shores of Cedar Lake. Fish, boat and swim in the lake. Fishing pier, playground volleyball court and picnic shelter at CG. Supplies available at Heavener. Campers may gather firewood. Many animals can be seen in the area. Many trails in the area.

GETTING THERE: From Heavener go S on US HWY 270-59 approx. 10 mi. to Holson Valley Road. Go W on road approx. 3 mi. to forest route 7269. Go N on 7269 approx. 1 mi. to Cedar Lake CG.

SINGLE RATE:	Varies	OPEN DATES:	June-Nov
# of SINGLE SITES:	87	MAX SPUR:	82 feet
		MAX STAY:	14 days
		ELEVATION:	860 feet

7 Billy Creek
Big Cedar • lat 34°41'23" lon 094°43'58"

DESCRIPTION: In a hardwood setting on Billy Creek with a natural pool nearby. Fish and swim in the creek. Supplies available at Heavoner. Many animals can be seen in the area. Campers may gather firewood. A hiking trail begins at the CG, climbs the mountain and loops back to the CG.

GETTING THERE: From Big Cedar go W on state HWY 63 approx. 6 mi. to forest route 6022. Go N on 6022 approx. 2 mi. to Billy Creek CG.

SINGLE RATE:	No fee	OPEN DATES:	Apr-Sept
# of SINGLE SITES:	11		
		MAX STAY:	14 days
		ELEVATION:	868 feet

12 Charlton
Hot Springs • lat 34°31'03" lon 093°23'00"

DESCRIPTION: In a mixed forest setting along banks of a picturesque stream. Fish and swim in the stream. Supplies available at Hot Springs. Deer, bears, squirrels and birds are common to the area. Campers may gather firewood. A 4-mi. hiking trail. RV dump station, amphitheater, playground and an interpretive trail at CG.

GETTING THERE: Charlton CG is located approx. 20 mi. W of Hot Springs on US HWY 270.

SINGLE RATE:	Varies	OPEN DATES:	Yearlong*
# of SINGLE SITES:	57	MAX SPUR:	22 feet
		MAX STAY:	14 days
		ELEVATION:	500 feet

8 Blanchard
Blanchard • lat 35°57'50" lon 092°10'45"

DESCRIPTION: CG in a mixed forest setting on North Sylamore Creek with views of nearby bluffs. Fish and swim from creek or nearby Mirror Lake. Supplies available at Mountain View. Deer, snakes, and bears are common to the area. Campers may gather firewood. An amphitheater with summer programs is on site.

GETTING THERE: Blanchard CG is located just past Blanchard Springs Caverns Visitor Center.

SINGLE RATE:	$10	OPEN DATES:	Yearlong
# of SINGLE SITES:	32	MAX SPUR:	32 feet
GROUP RATE:	Varies	MAX STAY:	5 days
# of GROUP SITES:	3	ELEVATION:	450 feet

13 Cove Lake
Paris • lat 35°13'31" lon 093°37'28"

DESCRIPTION: A high mountain CG set on the shores of Cove Lake. Spectacular views of Magazine Mountain. Fish, swim, and boat from the lake. Boat ramp available in CG. Supplies available at Paris. Numerous animals can be seen in the area. Campers may gather firewood. Hike and horse trails nearby.

GETTING THERE: From Paris go S on state HWY 109 to state HWY 309. Go SW on 309 approx. 9 mi. to Cove Lake CG.

SINGLE RATE:	$7	OPEN DATES:	Yearlong
# of SINGLE SITES:	28	MAX SPUR:	36 feet
		MAX STAY:	14 days
		ELEVATION:	1080 feet

9 Brock Creek Lake
Jerusalem • lat 35°29'06" lon 092°48'06"

DESCRIPTION: This primitive CG is located in a mixed forest setting on Brock Creek Lake. Fish and swim in the lake. Supplies available at Jerusalem. Many animals can be seen in the area. Campers may gather firewood. Trail opportunities are in the area.

GETTING THERE: From Jerusalem go N on forest route 1305 approx. 5 mi. to forest route 1309. Go E on 1309 approx. .1 mi. to forest route 133. Go W on 133 approx. 1 mi. to Brock Creek Lake CG.

SINGLE RATE:	No fee	OPEN DATES:	Dec-Apr
# of SINGLE SITES:	6		
		MAX STAY:	14 days
		ELEVATION:	760 feet

14 Crystal
Norman • lat 34°28'46" lon 093°38'17"

DESCRIPTION: An attractive wooded site on a stream with Collier Springs nearby. Fish and swim in stream and springs. Supplies are available at Norman. Numerous wildlife can be seen in the area. Campers may gather firewood. A shelter is located at the CG. Many trails in the CG area.

GETTING THERE: From Norman go N on state HWY 27 approx. 1 mi. to forest route 177. Go E on 177 approx. 3 mi. to Crystal CG.

		OPEN DATES:	Yearlong*
# of SINGLE SITES:	9	MAX SPUR:	36 feet
		MAX STAY:	14 days
		ELEVATION:	970 feet

10 Camp Clearfork
Hot Springs • lat 34°30'32" lon 093°23'29"

DESCRIPTION: This rustic group CG is in a mixed forest setting on a small scenic lake. Fish and swim in lake. Deer, bears, squirrels and birds are common in the area. Campers may gather firewood. Facilities include a dining hall, recreation building, cabins and a softball field. Trails in the area.

GETTING THERE: From Hot Springs go W on US HWY 270 approx. 20 mi. to forest route 513. Go S on 513 approx. 1 mi. to Camp Clearfork CG.

		OPEN DATES:	May-Oct
		MAX SPUR:	99 feet
GROUP RATE:	$330	MAX STAY:	14 days
# of GROUP SITES:	9	ELEVATION:	500 feet

15 Dragover
Mount Ida • lat 34°38'33" lon 093°37'50"

DESCRIPTION: On the Ouachita River in a mixed hardwood forest setting. Fish for bass, bream, catfish and walleye from the river. Supplies available at Mount Ida. Many types of animals can be seen in the area. Campers may gather firewood. No designated trails in the area.

GETTING THERE: From Mount Ida go NW on US HWY 270 approx. 11.5 mi. to forest route 138. Go S on 138 approx. 1 mi. to Dragover CG.

SINGLE RATE:	$7	OPEN DATES:	Yearlong
# of SINGLE SITES:	7	MAX SPUR:	32 feet
		MAX STAY:	14 days
		ELEVATION:	700 feet

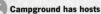 **Campground has hosts**　　 **Reservable sites**　　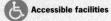 **Accessible facilities**　　 **Fully developed**　　 **Semi-developed**　　 **Rustic facilities**

16 Fairview
Jasper • lat 35˚44'15" lon 093˚05'39"

DESCRIPTION: In a mixed hardwood forest setting. Supplies available at Jasper. Deer, turkey, squirrels and birds can be seen in the area. Campers may gather firewood locally. Access to the Ozark Highlands Trail can be made from this CG.

GETTING THERE: Fairview CG is located approx. 28 mi. S of Jasper on state HWY 7.

SINGLE RATE:	No fee	OPEN DATES:	Yearlong
# of SINGLE SITES:	11	MAX SPUR:	28 feet
GROUP RATE:	No fee	MAX STAY:	14 days
# of GROUP SITES:	1	ELEVATION:	2180 feet

17 Fourche Mountain
Rover • lat 34˚53'42" lon 093˚23'34"

DESCRIPTION: This small rustic CG sits on Fourche Mountain with scenic views. Supplies can be found at Rover. Numerous wildlife can be viewed in the area. Campers may gather firewood. Many trails in the area.

GETTING THERE: Fourche Mountain CG is located approx. 5 mi. S of Rover on state HWY 27.

SINGLE RATE:	No fee	OPEN DATES:	Yearlong
# of SINGLE SITES:	5		
		MAX STAY:	14 days
		ELEVATION:	110 feet

18 Fulton Branch
Mount Ida • lat 34˚37'33" lon 933˚93'4"

DESCRIPTION: On the Ouachita River in a mixed hardwood setting. Fish for bass, bream, catfish and walleye from the CG. Boat and canoe in this river. Supplies are available at Mount Ida. Deer, bears, squirrels and birds may be seen in the area. Campers may gather firewood. Many trails in the area.

GETTING THERE: From Mount Ida go NW on US HWY 270 approx. 5.5 mi. to forest route 568. Go E on 568 approx. 2 mi. to Fulton Branch CG.

SINGLE RATE:	No fee	OPEN DATES:	Yearlong*
# of SINGLE SITES:	7		
		MAX STAY:	14 days
		ELEVATION:	740 feet

19 Gunner Pool
Mountain View • lat 35˚59'32" lon 092˚12'39"

DESCRIPTION: CG set in a mixed oak and hickory forest on pool and creek with views of bluffs. Stream fish the North Sylamore Creek. Supplies available in Mountain View. Deer, armadillo, snakes, and bears are common to the area. Gather firewood. Hike and horse trails are nearby. Check out the nearby caverns.

GETTING THERE: From Mountain View go NW on state HWY 14 approx. 16 mi. to forest route 1102. Go N on 1102 approx. 3 mi. to Gunner Pool CG. Not recommed for large vehicles.

SINGLE RATE:	$7	OPEN DATES:	Yearlong
# of SINGLE SITES:	27	MAX SPUR:	32 feet
		MAX STAY:	14 days
		ELEVATION:	450 feet

20 Haw Creek Falls
Hagarville • lat 35˚40'35" lon 093˚15'19"

DESCRIPTION: Located on a small mountain stream with picturesque falls, rocks, and bluff; beautiful mature hardwood forest. Big Piney Wild and Scenic River nearby. Accessible trail to the Haw Creek Falls.

GETTING THERE: Haw Creek Falls CG is located approx. 14 mi. N of Hagarville on state HWY 123.

SINGLE RATE:	$6	OPEN DATES:	Apr-Nov
# of SINGLE SITES:	9		
		MAX STAY:	14 days
		ELEVATION:	1720 feet

21 Horsehead Lake
Clarksville • lat 35˚33'57" lon 093˚38'23"

DESCRIPTION: In a mixed forest setting on Horsehead Lake. Boat ramp, boats are limited to 10 hp motors. Swimming beach in the CG. Supplies available at Clarksville. Numerous animals can be seen in the area. Campers may gather firewood. Horsehead Lake Trail leaves from the CG.

GETTING THERE: From Clarksville go NW on state HWY 103 approx. 8 mi. to state HWY 164. Go W on 164 approx. 4 mi. to forest route 1408. Go NW on 1408 approx. 3 mi. to Horsehead Lake CG.

SINGLE RATE:	$7	OPEN DATES:	Apr-Oct
# of SINGLE SITES:	10	MAX SPUR:	28 feet
		MAX STAY:	14 days
		ELEVATION:	695 feet

22 Iron Springs
Jessieville • lat 34˚45'30" lon 093˚03'00"

DESCRIPTION: In a wooded roadside setting on a stream near historic springs. Fish and wade in the stream. Supplies available at Jessieville. Numerous wildlife can be seen in the area. Campers may gather firewood. Many trails in the area.

GETTING THERE: Iron Springs CG is located approx. 4.5 mi. N of Jessieville on state HWY 7.

SINGLE RATE:	$7	OPEN DATES:	Yearlong
# of SINGLE SITES:	6	MAX SPUR:	22 feet
		MAX STAY:	14 days
		ELEVATION:	650 feet

23 Jack Creek
Booneville • lat 35˚02'04" lon 093˚50'50"

DESCRIPTION: CG sits on Sugar Creek in a mixed forest setting with scenic overlooks and rugged rock bluffs. Fish and swim from the creek. Supplies available at Booneville. Deer, bears, squirrels and birds are common in the area. A 1/2 mi. scenic loop trail and a 4 mi. trail connects to Dry Creek Wilderness.

GETTING THERE: From Booneville go S 2 mi. on HWY 23 to HWY 116. Go E 1 mi. on 116 to county route. Go S 4 mi. on county route to forest route 19. Go S 1 mi. on 19 to forest route 141. Go E 1 mi. on 141 to Jack Creek CG.

SINGLE RATE:	No fee	OPEN DATES:	Yearlong
# of SINGLE SITES:	5		
		MAX STAY:	14 days
		ELEVATION:	737 feet

24 Knoppers Ford
Booneville • lat 35˚01'10" lon 093˚51'48"

DESCRIPTION: This small CG is in a mixed forest setting on Sugar Creek with natural pools for swimming. Fish for bass and trout from the creek. Supplies available at Booneville. Numerous wildlife can be seen in the area. Campers may gather firewood. A 3.5 mi. trail connects CG to Jack Creek.

GETTING THERE: From Booneville go S on state HWY approx. 2 mi. to state HWY 116. Go E on 116 approx. 1 mi. to county route. Go S on county route approx. 4 mi. to forest route 19. Go S on 19 approx. 3 mi. to Knoppers Ford CG.

SINGLE RATE:	No fee	OPEN DATES:	Yearlong
# of SINGLE SITES:	6		
		MAX STAY:	14 days
		ELEVATION:	700 feet

25 Lake Sylvia
Perryville • lat 34˚51'59" lon 092˚49'09"

DESCRIPTION: This beautiful scenic CG is set on Sylvia Lake in a pine forest setting. Non-motorized boats only on lake. Fish and swim in lake. Supplies available at Perryville. Numerous wildlife can be seen in the area. Two interpretive trails nearby. RV dump station, amphitheater and play areas at the CG.

GETTING THERE: From Perryville go S on state HWY 9 approx. 9mi. to state HWY 324. Go SW on 324 approx. 4 mi. to Lake Sylvia CG.

SINGLE RATE:	Varies	OPEN DATES:	May-Oct
# of SINGLE SITES:	27	MAX SPUR:	22 feet
GROUP RATE:	$25	MAX STAY:	14 days
# of GROUP SITES:	1	ELEVATION:	720 feet

 Campground has hosts   **Reservable sites**   **Accessible facilities**   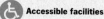 **Fully developed**   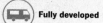 **Semi-developed**   **Rustic facilities**

NOTE: Open dates listed are typical. Actual dates are dependent on conditions such as snow pack.

26 Lake Wedington

Fayetteville • lat 36°05'21" lon 094°22'23"

DESCRIPTION: Located in a mixed forest setting on Lake Wedington. Fish and swim in lake. A boat launch is available at the CG-10 hp maximum allowed on the lake. Supplies available in Fayetteville. Numerous wildlife can be seen in the area. Campers may gather firewood. A seven mile hiking trail is in the area.

GETTING THERE: From Fayetteville go W on state HWY 16 approx. 13 mi. to Lake Wedington CG.

SINGLE RATE:	Varies	OPEN DATES:	Yearlong
# of SINGLE SITES:	18	MAX SPUR:	32 feet
		MAX STAY:	14 days
		ELEVATION:	1150 feet

27 Little Pine

Waldron • lat 34°50'00" lon 094°16'00"

DESCRIPTION: In a peaceful forest setting on Lake Hinkle. Boat ramp and fishing pier at the CG. Fish, boat and swim in lake. No water skiing allowed. Supplies located at Waldron. Numerous wildlife located in the area. Campers may gather firewood. Many trails located in area. RV dump station nearby.

GETTING THERE: From Waldron go W on state HWY 248 approx. 11.5 mi. to Little Pine CG.

SINGLE RATE:	Varies	OPEN DATES:	Apr-Sept*
# of SINGLE SITES:	21	MAX SPUR:	25 feet
		MAX STAY:	14 days
		ELEVATION:	800 feet

28 Long Pool

Dover • lat 35°32'55" lon 093°09'35"

DESCRIPTION: This CG is in a mature pine forest setting across from a large natural pool. Views of high picturesque bluffs from the CG. Fish and swim in the pool. Supplies available at Dover. Numerous wildlife can be seen in the area. Trails in the area.

GETTING THERE: From Dover go N on state HWY 7 6 mi. to state HWY 164. Go W on 164 3 mi. to county route 15. Go NE on 15 approx. 3 mi. to forest route 1804. Go NW on 1804 approx. 2 mi. to Long Pool CG.

SINGLE RATE:	$7	OPEN DATES:	Mar-Nov
# of SINGLE SITES:	20	MAX SPUR:	28 feet
		MAX STAY:	14 days
		ELEVATION:	560 feet

29 Mill Creek

Y City • lat 34°43'53" lon 093°59'45"

DESCRIPTION: In a mixed forest setting with a natural pool on a scenic portion of Mill Creek. Fish and swim in the creek. Supplies available at "Y" City. Deer, bears, squirrels and birds are common in the area. Hitching posts in the CG area. A hiking trail and an interpretive trail lead from CG.

GETTING THERE: Mill Creek CG is located approx. 4.5 mi. E of "Y" City on US HWY 270.

SINGLE RATE:	$5	OPEN DATES:	Apr-Sept*
# of SINGLE SITES:	27	MAX SPUR:	40 feet
		MAX STAY:	14 days
		ELEVATION:	890 feet

30 Moccasin Gap Horse Camp

Russellville • lat 35°34'30" lon 093°06'00"

DESCRIPTION: This horse camp is in a mix of hardwoods and pine with many streams and small waterfalls in the area. Fish and swim in the streams. Check for local regulations. Supplies available at Russellville. Campers may gather firewood. Moccasin Gap Horse Trail leaves from the CG.

GETTING THERE: From Russellville go N on state HWY 7 approx. 25 mi. to Moccasin Gap Horse Camp CG.

SINGLE RATE:	No fee	OPEN DATES:	Yearlong
# of SINGLE SITES:	17	MAX SPUR:	99 feet
		MAX STAY:	14 days
		ELEVATION:	1600 feet

31 Ozone

Clarksville • lat 35°40'13" lon 093°26'58"

DESCRIPTION: This primitive CG is situated in tall pine timber and is the site of old Civilian Conservation Corps Camp. Supplies available at Ozark. Campers may gather firewood. Many types of animals can be seen in the area. No drinking water. This CG is an access point to the Ozark Highlands Trail.

GETTING THERE: Ozone CG is located approx. 18 mi. N of Clarksville on state HWY 21.

SINGLE RATE:	$3	OPEN DATES:	Yearlong
# of SINGLE SITES:	8	MAX STAY:	14 days
		ELEVATION:	1860 feet

32 Redding

Ozark • lat 35°40'55" lon 093°47'08"

DESCRIPTION: This primitive CG is in a bottomland mixture of vegetation. Supplies available at Ozark. Campers may gather firewood. Many types of animals can be seen in the area. No designated trails in the area.

GETTING THERE: From Ozark go N on state HWY 23 approx. 18 mi. to forest route 1003. Go E on 1003 approx. 3 mi. to Redding CG.

SINGLE RATE:	$10	OPEN DATES:	Yearlong
# of SINGLE SITES:	27	MAX STAY:	14 days
		ELEVATION:	960 feet

33 Richland Creek

Witts Springs • lat 35°52'26" lon 092°53'47"

DESCRIPTION: In a mixed forest setting on the edge of Richland Creek, a small picturesque mountain stream. Fish for bass and bream or swim and play in the creek. Supplies available at Witts Springs. Deer, squirrels, turkey and birds are common to the area. Campers may gather firewood. Hiking trails in the area. No water.

GETTING THERE: From Witts Springs go SW on state HWY 16 approx. 1 mi. to county route 265. Go W on 265 approx. 3 mi. to county route 1. Go N on 1 approx. 3 mi. to Richland Creek CG. No trailers.

SINGLE RATE:	No fee	OPEN DATES:	Yearlong
# of SINGLE SITES:	11	MAX STAY:	14 days
		ELEVATION:	1000 feet

34 River Bluff

Mount Ida • lat 34°38'23" lon 093°37'33"

DESCRIPTION: On the Ouachita River in a mixed hardwood setting. Fish for bass, bream, catfish and walleye from the CG. Boat and canoe from this river. Supplies are available at Mount Ida. Deer, bears, squirrels and birds may be seen in the area. Campers may gather firewood. Many trails in the area.

GETTING THERE: From Mount Ida go N on state HWY 27 approx. 1/2 mi. to county route 59. Go NW on 59 approx. 3.5 mi. to forest route 138. Go N on 138 approx. 2.5 mi. to River Bluff CG.

SINGLE RATE:	No fee	OPEN DATES:	Yearlong
# of SINGLE SITES:	7	MAX STAY:	14 days
		ELEVATION:	650 feet

35 Rocky Shoals

Mount Ida • lat 34°36'43" lon 093°41'49"

DESCRIPTION: On the Ouachita River in a mixed hardwood setting. Fish for bass, bream, catfish and walleye from the CG. Boat and canoe from this river. Supplies are available at Mount Ida. Deer, bears, squirrels and birds may be seen in the area. Campers may gather firewood. Many trails in the area.

GETTING THERE: From Mount Ida go NW on US HWY 270 approx. 6 mi. to Rocky Shoals CG.

SINGLE RATE:	No fee	OPEN DATES:	Yearlong
# of SINGLE SITES:	7	MAX STAY:	14 days
		ELEVATION:	690 feet

 Campground has hosts   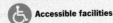 Reservable sites   Accessible facilities   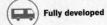 Fully developed   Semi-developed   Rustic facilities

NOTE: Open dates listed are typical. Actual dates are dependent on conditions such as snow pack.

36 Shady Lake
Athens • lat 34°21'45" lon 094°01'55"

DESCRIPTION: This CG is situated in a mixed forest. Fishing possibilities nearby. Supplies are available in Athens. A trail is offered on site. Numerous roads and trails in the area provide for hiking and mountan bike opportunities. An Amphitheater and playground area are provided at the CG.

GETTING THERE: From Athens go NW on state HWY 246 approx. 2 mi. to county route 38. Go NW on 38 approx. 5 mi. to Shady Lake CG.

# of SINGLE SITES:	96	OPEN DATES:	Yearlong
		MAX STAY:	14 days
		ELEVATION:	1000 feet

37 Shirley Creek
Mount Ida • lat 34°36'30" lon 093°49'33"

DESCRIPTION: On the Ouachita River in a mixed hardwood setting. Fish for bass, bream, catfish and walleye from the CG. Boat and canoe from this river. Supplies are available at Mount Ida. Deer, bears, squirrels and birds may be seen in the area. Campers may gather firewood. Many trails in the area.

GETTING THERE: From Mount Ida go NW on US HWY 270 approx. 9 mi. to state HWY 88. Go W on 88 approx. 5.5 mi. to county route 7991. Go S on 7991 approx. 1/2 mi. to Shirley Creek CG.

SINGLE RATE:	$7	OPEN DATES:	Yearlong
# of SINGLE SITES:	6		
		MAX STAY:	14 days
		ELEVATION:	800 feet

38 Shores Lake
Mulberry • lat 35°38'36" lon 093°57'36"

DESCRIPTION: This CG is located in a mountain setting on Shores Lake. Shores Lake is an 82-acre lake with great fishing. Boat ramp available at CG-limit to 10 hp motor size on the lake. Supplies available at Mulberry. Numerous wildlife can be seen in the area. Trails are in the area.

GETTING THERE: From Mulberry go N on state HWY 215 approx. 15 mi. to forest route 1505. Continue on 1505 approx. 1/2 mi. to Shores Lake CG.

SINGLE RATE:	$8	OPEN DATES:	Apr-Oct
# of SINGLE SITES:	19	MAX SPUR:	22 feet
		MAX STAY:	14 days
		ELEVATION:	700 feet

39 South Fourche
Hollis • lat 34°52'12" lon 093°06'28"

DESCRIPTION: In a mixed forest setting located on the picturesque South Fourche Stream. Fish the stream. CG has a canoe access for stream. Supplies available at Hollis. Deer, squirrels and birds are common in the area. Campers may gather firewood. Hunt's Loop Trail is accessible from the CG and is 4.2 mi. long.

GETTING THERE: South Fourche CG is located approx. 1 mi. S of Hollis on state HWY 7.

SINGLE RATE:	$7	OPEN DATES:	Yearlong
# of SINGLE SITES:	6	MAX SPUR:	22 feet
		MAX STAY:	14 days
		ELEVATION:	490 feet

40 Spring Lake
Dardanelle • lat 35°09'02" lon 093°25'27"

DESCRIPTION: A high mountain CG set on the shores of Cove Lake. Fish, boat, and swim from the lake. Boat ramp provided at the CG. Beach and bathhouse available on site. Watch for deer and small wildlife in the area. Supplies can be found in Dardanelle. Campers may gather firewood. No designated trails in the area.

GETTING THERE: From Dardanelle go SW on state HWY 27 approx. 9 mi. to state HWY 307. Go W on 307 approx. 3 mi. to forest route 1602. Continue on 1602 approx. 4 mi. to Spring Lake CG.

SINGLE RATE:	$7	OPEN DATES:	May-Sept
# of SINGLE SITES:	13	MAX SPUR:	36 feet
		MAX STAY:	14 days
		ELEVATION:	520 feet

41 Storm Creek Lake
West Helena • lat 34°35'58" lon 090°36'46"

DESCRIPTION: In a mixed forest setting on Storm Creek Lake which sits atop Crowley's Ridge. Boating (max 10 hp), boat ramp at CG. Fish, boat and swim from the lake. Supplies available at West Helena. Many animals can be seen in the area. Campers may gather firewood. No designated trails in the area.

GETTING THERE: From West Helena go NW on state HWY 242 approx. 1 mi. to forest route 1900. Go E on 1900 approx. 3 mi. to Storm Creek Lake CG.

SINGLE RATE:	$4	OPEN DATES:	Apr-Sept
# of SINGLE SITES:	13	MAX SPUR:	28 feet
		MAX STAY:	14 days
		ELEVATION:	300 feet

42 White Rock
Mulberry • lat 35°41'26" lon 093°57'23"

DESCRIPTION: CG is located in a rugged mountain setting with view of spectacular bluffs nearby. Supplies available in Mulberry. Numerous wildlife can be seen in the area. Cool climate in the summer. Campers may gather firewood. This CG is a major access point to the Ozark Highlands Trail.

GETTING THERE: From Mulberry go N on state HWY 215 approx. 15 mi. to forest route 1505. Continue on 1505 approx. 8 mi. to forest route 1003. Continue on 1003 approx. 2.5 mi. to White Rock CG.

SINGLE RATE:	$5	OPEN DATES:	Yearlong
# of SINGLE SITES:	8	MAX SPUR:	22 feet
		MAX STAY:	14 days
		ELEVATION:	2300 feet

43 Winding Stair
Big Cedar • lat 34°44'52" lon 094°47'10"

DESCRIPTION: Mountain-top camping area adjacent to Talimena Scenic Byway. Supplies available in Big Cedar. Many animals can be seen in the area. Campers may gather firewood. A 2.2 mi. hiking loop from the CG and an access to Ouachita National Recreation Trail.

GETTING THERE: From Big Cedar go N on US HWY 259 approx. 5 mi. to state HWY 1. Go W on 1 approx. 1.5 mi. to Winding Stair CG.

# of SINGLE SITES:	26	OPEN DATES:	June-Nov
GROUP RATE:	Varies		
		MAX STAY:	14 days
		ELEVATION:	1900 feet

44 Wolf Pen
Ozark • lat 35°40'33" lon 093°37'50"

DESCRIPTION: This primitive CG is in a bottomland mixture of vegetation with pine. Mulberry River is next to CG where you may fish for bass and swim. A canoe launch area is close by. Supplies available at Ozark. Campers may gather firewood. Many types of animals can be seen in the area. No drinking water.

GETTING THERE: From Ozark go W on state HWY 215 approx. 3.5 mi. to Wolf Pen CG.

SINGLE RATE:	$3	OPEN DATES:	Apr-Oct
# of SINGLE SITES:	6		
		MAX STAY:	14 days
		ELEVATION:	960 feet

Campground has hosts   Reservable sites   Accessible facilities   Fully developed   Semi-developed   Rustic facilities

NOTE: Open dates listed are typical. Actual dates are dependent on conditions such as snow pack.

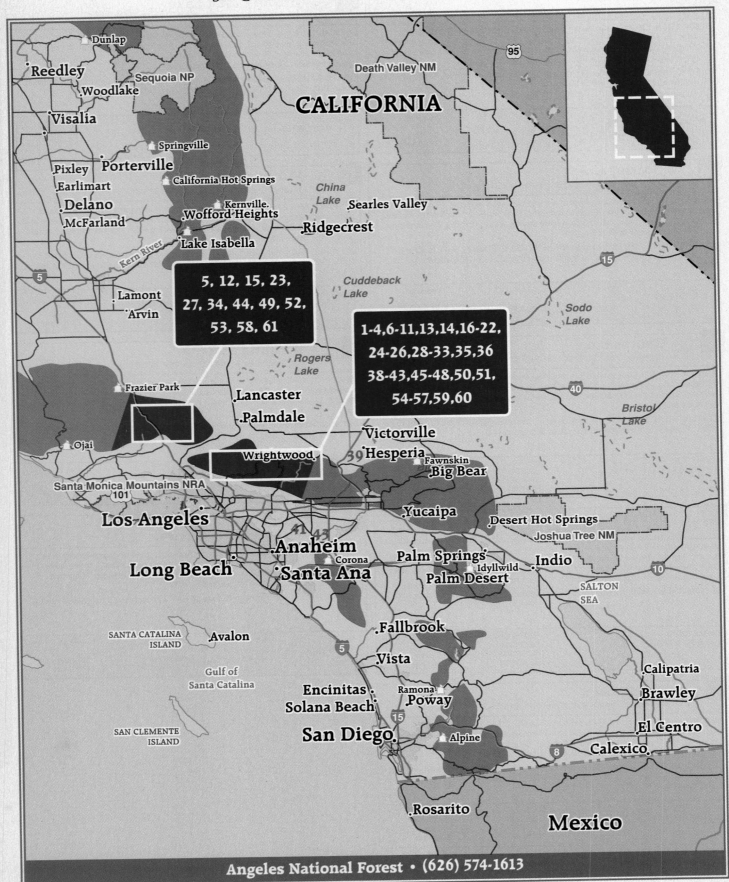

CALIFORNIA

5, 12, 15, 23, 27, 34, 44, 49, 52, 53, 58, 61

1-4,6-11,13,14,16-22, 24-26,28-33,35,36 38-43,45-48,50,51, 54-57,59,60

Angeles National Forest • (626) 574-1613

USFS Photo

ANGELES NATIONAL FOREST

The Angeles National Forest is the backyard playground to the metropolitan area of Los Angeles. It covers over 650,000 acres and is one of 18 national forests in California. Established in December, 1892, the watersheds within its boundaries are managed to provide valuable water to Southern California and to protect surrounding communities from catastrophic floods.

The land within the forest is diverse in appearance and terrain. Elevations range from 1,200 to 10,064 feet. Much of the forest is covered with dense chaparral which changes to pine and fir-covered slopes in the higher elevations. Beautiful wildflowers and a variety of wildlife are abundant throughout the forest.

The Angeles National Forest not only serves as a valuable watershed, but also provides a place for recreation. Here, you may hike more than 500 miles of trails. Follow a portion of the Pacific Crest Trail to the top of Mt. Baden-Powell which overlooks the rugged canyons of the Sheep Mountain Wilderness. Cast your line into a beautiful stream. Take a dip at Pyramid Lake or enjoy the winter activities at one of the four ski areas located on the forest. Explore the 364 miles of designated off-highway vehicle routes or just enjoy the beautiful scenery at one of the camping and picnicking sites. The choices range from sunny streamsides under cottonwood and native live oak trees to stands of tall pines at the higher elevations.

1 Appletree
Wrightwood • lat 34°23'10" lon 117°42'47"

DESCRIPTION: This CG is in a chaparral setting. Supplies available in Wrightwood. Bighorn sheep, black bears and migratory birds can be seen in the area. Can be busy on the weekends. No designated trails in the area.

GETTING THERE: From Wrightwood go W on primary forest route 61 (state HWY 2) 3.6 mi. to Appletree CG.

SINGLE RATE:	$8	OPEN DATES:	Apr-Nov
# of SINGLE SITES:	8		
GROUP RATE:	Varies	MAX STAY:	14 days
# of GROUP SITES:	1	ELEVATION:	6200 feet

2 Bandido Group
La Canada • lat 34°20'45" lon 118°00'10"

DESCRIPTION: In a jeffrey pine and scrub oak forest setting. Supplies available at La Canada. Deer, bears and birds are common to the area. Many trails in the area. Water faucets, 20 horse corrals, and 3 water troughs.

GETTING THERE: From La Canada go NE on state HWY 2 approx. 25 mi. to forest route going N. Go W on forest route approx. 1.5 mi. to Bandido Group CG.

		OPEN DATES:	Apr-Nov
		MAX SPUR:	16 feet
GROUP RATE:	Varies	MAX STAY:	14 days
# of GROUP SITES:	2	ELEVATION:	5700 feet

3 Basin
Four Points • lat 34°27'28" lon 118°01'05"

DESCRIPTION: In a chaparral setting with no drinking water available. Supplies available at Four Points. Bighorn sheep, black bears and migratory birds are just some of the animals you can see in this area. No designated trails in the area.

GETTING THERE: From Four Points go S on forest route 5N04 (Cheeseboro route) approx. 6 mi. to Basin CG. 4 WD recommended.

SINGLE RATE:	$10	OPEN DATES:	Yearlong
# of SINGLE SITES:	15	MAX SPUR:	28 feet
		MAX STAY:	14 days
		ELEVATION:	3400 feet

4 Bears Canyon Trail
La Canada • lat 34°14'41" lon 118°08'22"

DESCRIPTION: In an oak and pine forest setting with Bears Canyon stream and Arroyo Seco stream nearby. Fish for trout on Arroyo Seco. Waterfalls upstream from CG. Supplies available at La Canada. Deer, bears, raccoon and a wide variety of birds in the area. Trails in the area.

GETTING THERE: From La Canada go N on state HWY 2 7 mi. to Clear Creek work station. From Clear Creek work station hike S 3 mi. to Bears Canyon Trail CG. Hike in only.

SINGLE RATE:	No fee	OPEN DATES:	Yearlong
# of SINGLE SITES:	3		
		MAX STAY:	14 days
		ELEVATION:	3400 feet

5 Bears Trail
Lake Hughes • lat 34°40'00" lon 118°38'00"

DESCRIPTION: In a desert setting with streams running nearby. Fish or swim from the streams. Supplies located at Lake Hughes. Bighorn sheep, black bears and migratory birds are just some of the animals you can see in this area. Campers may gather firewood. Trails can be found in the area.

GETTING THERE: From Lake Hughes go NW on state HWY 138 (Pine Canyon route) approx. 1.5 mi. to forest route 7N23. Go on 7N23 SW approx. 7 mi. to Bears Trail CG.

SINGLE RATE:	No fee	OPEN DATES:	May-Dec
# of SINGLE SITES:	6		
		MAX STAY:	14 days
		ELEVATION:	3400 feet

 **Campground has hosts** **Reservable sites** 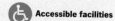 **Accessible facilities** **Fully developed** **Semi-developed** **Rustic facilities**

NOTE: Open dates listed are typical. Actual dates are dependent on conditions such as snow pack.

6 — Big Buck Trail
Acton • lat 34°23'08" lon 118°08'26"

DESCRIPTION: A small CG in a pine plantation forest setting. Supplies available at Acton. Deer, bears, mountain lions, raccoon and birds can be viewed in the area. The Pacific Crest Trail is in the area. Walk-in.

GETTING THERE: From Acton go E on Canyon route 2 mi. to Aliso Canyon route. Go SE on Aliso Canyon route approx. 11 mi. to forest route 3N17. Go on 3N17 5.5 mi. to Big Buck Trail CG.

SINGLE RATE: # of SINGLE SITES:	No fee 3	OPEN DATES: MAX STAY: ELEVATION:	Mar-Nov 14 days 5500 feet

7 — Big Rock
Valyermo • lat 34°23'16" lon 117°46'33"

DESCRIPTION: This tent only CG is in a chaparral setting with no drinking water available. Supplies available at Valyermo. Bighorn sheep, black bears and migratory birds are some of the animals you can see in this area. Campers may gather firewood. Many backcountry roads and trails in the area.

GETTING THERE: From Valyermo go SE approx. 1 mi. on Big Pines HWY to forest route 4N11 (Big Rock route). Go SE on 4N11 approx. 5 mi. to Big Rock CG. 4WD recommended.

SINGLE RATE: # of SINGLE SITES:	$5 8	OPEN DATES: MAX STAY: ELEVATION:	June-Oct 14 days 4500 feet

8 — Blue Ridge
Mountain Top Junction • lat 34°21'34" lon 117°41'09"

DESCRIPTION: In a mixed forest setting with no drinking water available. Supplies available at Mountain Top Junction. Bighorn sheep, black bears and migratory birds are just some of the animals you can see in this area. Campers may gather firewood. The Pacific Crest Trail runs next to the CG.

GETTING THERE: From Mountain Top Junction go SW on state HWY 2 approx. 12 mi. to forest route 3N06. Go SE on 3N06 approx. 2 mi. to Blue Ridge CG.

SINGLE RATE: # of SINGLE SITES:	$5 8	OPEN DATES: MAX SPUR: MAX STAY: ELEVATION:	June-Oct 16 feet 14 days 7200 feet

9 — Buckhorn
La Canada • lat 34°20'00" lon 117°54'00"

DESCRIPTION: This is the most beautiful of the CG's, located in a douglas fir and spruce forest setting with a stream most of the year. Supplies at La Canada. Deer, bears and birds are common in the area. High Desert National Recreation Trail runs through CG. Archeological sites in the CG.

GETTING THERE: From La Canada go NE on state HWY 2 approx. 30 mi. to Buckhorn CG.

SINGLE RATE: # of SINGLE SITES:	Varies 38	OPEN DATES: MAX SPUR: MAX STAY: ELEVATION:	May-Nov 20 feet 14 days 6300 feet

10 — Cabin Flat
Mountain Top Junction • lat 34°20'31" lon 117°41'49"

DESCRIPTION: In a chaparral setting with no drinking water available. Supplies available at Mountain Top Junction. Bighorn sheep, black bears and migratory birds are just some of the animals you can see in this area. Campers may gather firewood. Many backcountry roads and trails in the area.

GETTING THERE: From Mountain Top Junction go SW on state HWY 2 approx. 12 mi. to forest route 3N06. Go SE on 3N06 approx. 4 mi. to Cabin Flat CG.

SINGLE RATE: # of SINGLE SITES:	$5 11	OPEN DATES: MAX SPUR: MAX STAY: ELEVATION:	June-Oct 16 feet 14 days 5300 feet

11 — Chilao Recreation Area
La Canada • lat 34°19'26" lon 118°01'06"

DESCRIPTION: In a combination pine and open manzanita forest area. A small stream runs through CG. Supplies available at La Canada. Deer, raccoon and birds in the area. Bears warnings are in force for this CG. The Pacific Crest Trail is north of the CG. The Silver Mocassin National Recreation Trail runs through the CG.

GETTING THERE: From La Canada go NE on state HWY 2 approx. 22 mi. to Chilao Recreation Area CG.

SINGLE RATE: # of SINGLE SITES:	$12 210	OPEN DATES: MAX SPUR: MAX STAY: ELEVATION:	Yearlong 35 feet 14 days 5300 feet

12 — Cienega
Castaic • lat 34°37'09" lon 118°38'08"

DESCRIPTION: This rustic CG is in a desert setting. Tents or pickup campers only. Supplies available at Castaic. Bighorn sheep, black bears and migratory birds are just some of the animals you can see in this area. Campers may gather firewood. CG is near a trail that is routed into the backcountry around Redrock Mountain.

GETTING THERE: From Castaic go N on US HWY 5 approx. 16 mi. to Smokey Bears route interchange, taking forest route 7N32. Go S then N on 7N32 approx. 6 mi. to Cienega CG.

SINGLE RATE: # of SINGLE SITES:	No fee 12	OPEN DATES: MAX STAY: ELEVATION:	Apr-Nov 14 days 2100 feet

13 — Coldbrook
Azusa • lat 34°17'30" lon 117°50'17"

DESCRIPTION: In a mixed conifer forest setting situated on the North Fork of the San Gabriel River. Fish for stocked rainbow trout during summer. Supplies located at Azusa. CG is very busy on weekends. Campers may gather firewood. Trailhead to nearby wilderness 1/4 mile from CG. CG is frequented by bears.

GETTING THERE: From Azusa go N on state HWY 39 approx. 15 mi. to Coldbrook CG.

SINGLE RATE: # of SINGLE SITES:	$8 22	OPEN DATES: MAX SPUR: MAX STAY: ELEVATION:	Yearlong 22 feet 14 days 3350 feet

14 — Cooper Canyon Trail
La Canada • lat 34°21'37" lon 117°55'12"

DESCRIPTION: In a mix of douglas fir, white fir and pine forest setting. Cooper Canyon stream runs through the CG. Fish or play in the stream. Supplies at La Canada. Deer, bears, raccoon and birds can be seen near the CG. The CG is on the Pacific Crest Trail. An amphitheater is in the CG.

GETTING THERE: From La Canada go NE on state HWY 2 approx. 27 mi. to trailhead. From trailhead go N approx. 2 mi. to Cooper Canyon Trail CG.

SINGLE RATE: # of SINGLE SITES:	No fee 8	OPEN DATES: MAX STAY: ELEVATION:	Mar-Nov 14 days 6600 feet

15 — Cottonwood
Lake Hughes • lat 34°38'25" lon 118°30'14"

DESCRIPTION: This CG is in a desert setting with streams running nearby. Supplies available at Lake Hughes. Bighorn sheep, black bears and migratory birds are just some of the animals you can see in this area. Campers may gather firewood. No designated trails in the area.

GETTING THERE: From Lake Hughes go SW on forest route 7N09 approx. 3.5 mi. to Cottonwood CG.

SINGLE RATE: # of SINGLE SITES:	No fee 22	OPEN DATES: MAX SPUR: MAX STAY: ELEVATION:	Yearlong 22 feet 14 days 2100 feet

 Campground has hosts   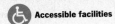 **Reservable sites**   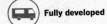 **Accessible facilities**   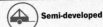 **Fully developed**   Semi-developed   Rustic facilities

NOTE: Open dates listed are typical. Actual dates are dependent on conditions such as snow pack.

Page 52

16 Coulter Group
La Canada • lat 34˚18'30" lon 118˚01'30"

DESCRIPTION: In a combination pine and open manzanita forest area. A small stream runs through CG. Supplies available at La Canada. Deer, raccoon and birds in the area. Bears warnings are in force for this CG. The Pacific Crest Trail is north of the CG. The Silver Mocassin National Recreation Trail runs through the CG.

GETTING THERE: From La Canada go NE on state HWY 2 approx. 21 mi. to Coulter Group CG.

		OPEN DATES:	**Apr-Nov**
		MAX SPUR:	**35 feet**
GROUP RATE:	**$100**	**MAX STAY:**	**14 days**
# of GROUP SITES:	**1**	**ELEVATION:**	**5300 feet**

17 Crystal Lake Recreation Area
Azusa • lat 34˚19'32" lon 117˚50'14"

DESCRIPTION: Located near the lake. The climate is nice. Non-motorized boats only on the lake. Fish for trout from the lake. Firewood is sold at the CG. Many trails in and out of the CG area. CG is very busy on weekends. Amphitheater located at CG. Bears are in this area and can be a problem, take precautions.

GETTING THERE: From Azusa go N on state HWY 39 approx. 18 mi. to Crystal Lake CG.

		OPEN DATES:	**Yearlong**
SINGLE RATE:	**$10**	**MAX SPUR:**	**22 feet**
# of SINGLE SITES:	**176**	**MAX STAY:**	**14 days**
		ELEVATION:	**5800 feet**

18 Deer Flat Group
Azusa • lat 34˚19'58" lon 117˚50'17"

DESCRIPTION: Located near the lake. The climate is nice. Non-motorized boats only on lake. Fish for trout from the lake. Firewood is sold at the CG. Many trails in and out of the CG area. CG is very busy on weekends. Amphitheater located at CG. Bears are in this area and can be a problem, take precautions.

GETTING THERE: From Azusa go N on state HWY 39 approx. 21 mi. to Deer Flat Group CG. Road is narrow with sharp curves. Large vehicles should use caution.

		OPEN DATES:	**May-Oct**
		MAX SPUR:	**30 feet**
GROUP RATE:	**Varies**	**MAX STAY:**	**14 days**
# of GROUP SITES:	**9**	**ELEVATION:**	**6300 feet**

19 DeVore Trail
La Canada • lat 34˚12'59" lon 117˚24'02"

DESCRIPTION: In a very dense oak and sycamore forest setting. CG is on the West Fork of San Gabriel. Fish for trout from the river. Supplies available in La Canada. Deer, bears and birds are common in the area. An OHV trail and a trail to Mount Wilson are nearby.

GETTING THERE: From La Canada go N on state HWY 2 approx. 7 mi. to forest route 2N24. Go S on 2N24 approx. 5 mi. to DeVore Trail CG.

		OPEN DATES:	**Yearlong**
SINGLE RATE:	**No fee**		
# of SINGLE SITES:	**6**	**MAX STAY:**	**14 days**
		ELEVATION:	**3000 feet**

20 Fall Creek Trail
Tujunga • lat 34˚18'20" lon 118˚09'29"

DESCRIPTION: In a pine plantation and oak forest setting on the Big Tujunga Creek. Fish for native trout from the creek. Beautiful waterfalls on the creek nearby. Supplies at Tujunga. Deer, bears and birds are common in the area. Hike the roads in the area. Walk-in only.

GETTING THERE: From Tujunga go N on primary forest route 12 (Mount Gleason Ave.) approx. 12 mi. to Fall Creek Trail CG.

		OPEN DATES:	**Yearlong**
SINGLE RATE:	**No fee**		
# of SINGLE SITES:	**10**	**MAX STAY:**	**14 days**
		ELEVATION:	**2500 feet**

21 Glenn Trail
Azusa • lat 34˚15'00" lon 117˚75'00"

DESCRIPTION: This hike-in, tent only CG is in a mixed forest setting near the West Fork River. Fish for trout from the river. Supplies available at Azusa. CG is very busy on weekends. Campers may gather firewood. A bicycle trail runs along the West Fork. OHV area is located approx. 2 mi. S on SR 2. CG is frequented by bears.

GETTING THERE: From Azusa go N on state HWY 39 approx. 10 mi. to forest route 2N25. Park here and hike 6.5 mi. to Glenn Trail CG. Physically challenged may drive in, call Ranger Station at (626) 335-1251.

		OPEN DATES:	**Yearlong**
SINGLE RATE:	**No fee**		
# of SINGLE SITES:	**10**	**MAX STAY:**	**14 days**
		ELEVATION:	**2000 feet**

22 Gould Mesa Trail
La Canada • lat 34˚13'23" lon 118˚10'39"

DESCRIPTION: In an oak and alder forest setting with Bears Canyon stream and Arroyo Seco stream nearby. Fish for trout on Arroyo Seco. Supplies available at La Canada. Deer, bears, raccoon and a wide variety of birds in the area. Trails in the area. Hike in only. Corral at CG.

GETTING THERE: From La Canada go N on state HWY 2 approx. 1 mi. to Gould Mesa Trail CG.

		OPEN DATES:	**Yearlong**
SINGLE RATE:	**No fee**		
# of SINGLE SITES:	**8**	**MAX STAY:**	**14 days**
		ELEVATION:	**1500 feet**

23 Green Valley Trail
Green Valley • lat 34˚40'00" lon 118˚24'00"

DESCRIPTION: This primitive trail camp is in a desert setting. Supplies available at Green Valley. Bighorn sheep, black bears and migratory birds can be seen in the area. Many trails in the area.

GETTING THERE: From Green Valley go NE on Seco Canyon route to Green Valley CG.

		OPEN DATES:	**Yearlong**
SINGLE RATE:	**No fee**		
# of SINGLE SITES:	**1**	**MAX STAY:**	**14 days**
		ELEVATION:	**3300 feet**

24 Guffy
Wrightwood • lat 34˚20'29" lon 117˚39'13"

DESCRIPTION: This tent only CG is in a high mountain timber setting with no drinking water available. Supplies available at Wrightwood. Bighorn sheep, black bears and migratory birds are just some of the animals you can see in this area. The Pacific Crest Trail runs nearby the CG.

GETTING THERE: From Wrightwood go NW on state HWY 2 approx. 4 mi. to forest route 3N06. Go SE on 3N06 approx. 4 mi. to Guffy CG. 4WD recommended.

		OPEN DATES:	**May-Nov**
SINGLE RATE:	**$5**		
# of SINGLE SITES:	**6**	**MAX STAY:**	**14 days**
		ELEVATION:	**8300 feet**

25 Hoegees Trail
Sierra Madre • lat 34˚12'28" lon 118˚01'57"

DESCRIPTION: In a high elevation wooded area with Sana Anita Creek nearby. Swimming and fishing from the creek. Supplies at Sierra Madre. Deer, bears and birds are common in the area. Winter Creek Trail system to Mount Wilson nearby the CG. Walk-in.

GETTING THERE: From Sierra Madre go N on Santa Anita Ave. approx. 2.5 mi. to trailhead. From trailhead go NW approx. 2 mi. to Hoegees Trail CG.

		OPEN DATES:	**Yearlong**
SINGLE RATE:	**No fee**		
# of SINGLE SITES:	**15**	**MAX STAY:**	**14 days**
		ELEVATION:	**2500 feet**

 ANGELES NATIONAL FOREST • CALIFORNIA • 16 — 25

 Campground has hosts   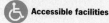 **Reservable sites**   **Accessible facilities**   **Fully developed**   **Semi-developed**   **Rustic facilities**

NOTE: Open dates listed are typical. Actual dates are dependent on conditions such as snow pack.

26 Horse Flats
La Canada • lat 34°17'44" lon 118°33'02"

DESCRIPTION: In an open pine forest setting with a stream approx. 1 mi. from CG. Supplies at La Canada. Deer, bears and birds are common in the area. Trails to the Pacific Crest Trail. Corrals for horses in the CG.

GETTING THERE: From La Canada go NE on state HWY 2 approx. 24 mi. to forest route 3N17. Go W on 3N17 approx. 1.5 mi. to Horse Flats CG.

SINGLE RATE:	$10	OPEN DATES:	Apr-Nov
# of SINGLE SITES:	25	MAX SPUR:	32 feet
		MAX STAY:	14 days
		ELEVATION:	5700 feet

31 Lightning Point Group
 Acton • lat 34°22'06" lon 118°11'09"

DESCRIPTION: In a pine forest setting on a knob with beautiful views. Supplies at Acton. Deer, bears and birds are common in the area. The Pacific Crest Trail and Trail Canyon Trail are near CG. There is a 1 mile interpretive trail in the CG. There are 25 single horse corrals and large gathering areas.

GETTING THERE: From Acton go E on Canyon route 2 mi. to Aliso Canyon route. Go SE on Aliso Canyon route approx. 11 mi. to forest route 3N17. Go on 3N17 10 mi. to Lightning Point Group CG.

		OPEN DATES:	Apr-Oct*
GROUP RATE:	Varies	MAX STAY:	14 days
# of GROUP SITES:	6	ELEVATION:	6200 feet

27 Horse Trail
Three Points • lat 34°44'20" lon 118°39'14"

DESCRIPTION: This primitive, hike-in, trail camp is in a desert setting. Supplies available at Green Valley. Bighorn sheep, black bears and migratory birds can be seen in the area. Many trails in the area.

GETTING THERE: From Three Points go W on Oakdale Canyon route approx. 3 mi. to trailhead. Go S on trail 1 mi. to Horse Trail CG.

SINGLE RATE:	No fee	OPEN DATES:	Yearlong
# of SINGLE SITES:	1		
		MAX STAY:	14 days
		ELEVATION:	4000 feet

32 Little Jimmy Trail
La Canada • lat 34°20'51" lon 117°49'45"

DESCRIPTION: This hike-in, tent only CG is located in a mixed forest setting near Crystal Lake. Fish or swim from nearby springs. Supplies available in La Canada. CG is very busy on weekends. Campers may gather firewood. No designated trails nearby.

GETTING THERE: From La Canada go NE on state HWY 2 approx. 38 mi. to Little Jimmy CG.

SINGLE RATE:	No fee	OPEN DATES:	May-Nov
# of SINGLE SITES:	8		
		MAX STAY:	14 days
		ELEVATION:	7500 feet

28 Idlehour Trail
Sierra Madre • lat 34°12'28" lon 118°04'58"

DESCRIPTION: In a high elevation wooded area with Sana Anita Creek nearby. Swimming and fishing from the creek. Supplies at Sierra Madre. Deer, bears and birds are common in the area. Winter Creek Trail system to Mount Wilson nearby the CG. Walk-in.

GETTING THERE: From Sierra Madre go N on forest route 2N45 1 mi. to trailhead. Go N on trailhead approx. 1 mi. to Idlehour Trail CG.

SINGLE RATE:	No fee	OPEN DATES:	Yearlong
# of SINGLE SITES:	4		
		MAX STAY:	14 days
		ELEVATION:	2500 feet

33 Live Oak
Sand • lat 34°22'44" lon 118°24'07"

DESCRIPTION: Located in a desert setting. Supplies available at Green Valley. Bighorn sheep, black bears and migratory birds can be seen in the area. CG's are usually busy on weekends. Many trails can be found in the area.

GETTING THERE: From Sand go S on Bears Canyon route approx. 1/2 mi. to Live Oak CG.

SINGLE RATE:	$8	OPEN DATES:	Yearlong
# of SINGLE SITES:	7	MAX SPUR:	30 feet
		MAX STAY:	14 days
		ELEVATION:	2000 feet

29 Jackson Flat Group
Wrightwood • lat 34°22'51" lon 117°44'11"

DESCRIPTION: This walk-in, tent only CG is in a high mountain timber setting. Supplies available at Wrightwood. Bighorn sheep, black bears and migratory birds are just some of the animals you can see in this area. Campers may gather firewood. No designated trails available nearby.

GETTING THERE: From Wrightwood go W on primary forest route 61 (state HWY 2) approx. 3 mi. to forest route turnoff at Grassy Hollow CG. Go W on forest route approx. 2 mi. to Jackson Flat CG.

		OPEN DATES:	May-Nov
GROUP RATE:	Varies	MAX STAY:	14 days
# of GROUP SITES:	5	ELEVATION:	7500 feet

34 Los Alamos
Gorman • lat 34°42'02" lon 118°48'20"

DESCRIPTION: In a desert setting near Pyramid Lake. Tents or pickup campers only at this CG. Supplies available at Castaic. Bighorn sheep, black bears and migratory birds are just some of the animals you can see in this area. Campers may gather firewood. A nearby trail is routed into the backcountry around Redrock Mountain.

GETTING THERE: From Gorman go SE on US HWY 5 for 9 mi. to forest route 7N32. Go 2 mi. S, then 2 mi. N on 7N32 to Los Alamos CG.

SINGLE RATE:	$10	OPEN DATES:	Yearlong
# of SINGLE SITES:	93	MAX SPUR:	26 feet
GROUP RATE:	$50	MAX STAY:	14 days
# of GROUP SITES:	3	ELEVATION:	2600 feet

30 Lake
Mountain Top Jct • lat 34°23'28" lon 117°43'19"

DESCRIPTION: In a chaparral setting with wonderful views of Jackson Lake. Fish or swim from the CG area. Supplies available at Mountain Top Junction. Bighorn sheep, black bears and migratory birds are just some of the animals you can see in this area. No designated trails in the area.

GETTING THERE: From Mountain Top Junction go SW on state HWY 2 approx. 9 mi. to forest route 4N47. Go W on 4N47 approx. 3 mi. to Lake CG.

SINGLE RATE:	$10	OPEN DATES:	May-Nov
# of SINGLE SITES:	8	MAX SPUR:	18 feet
		MAX STAY:	14 days
		ELEVATION:	6100 feet

35 Lupine
Wrightwood • lat 34°19'00" lon 117°41'00"

DESCRIPTION: In a chaparral setting with no drinking water available. Supplies available at Wrightwood. Bighorn sheep, black bears and migratory birds are just some of the animals you can see in this area. This CG gives access to many trail in the area, one leads to the Devil's Punchbowl County Park.

GETTING THERE: From Wrightwood go NW on state HWY 2 approx. 4 mi. to forest route 3N06. Go SE on 3N06 approx. 6 mi. to Lupine CG.

SINGLE RATE:	$5	OPEN DATES:	June-Oct
# of SINGLE SITES:	11	MAX SPUR:	16 feet
		MAX STAY:	14 days
		ELEVATION:	6500 feet

 Campground has hosts   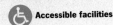 Reservable sites   Accessible facilities   Fully developed   Semi-developed   Rustic facilities

NOTE: Open dates listed are typical. Actual dates are dependent on conditions such as snow pack.

36 Manker Flats

Claremont • lat 34°15'54" lon 117°37'43"

DESCRIPTION: In a mixed conifer forest setting. Supplies available at Claremont. CG is very busy on weekends. Campers may gather firewood. No designated trails in the area. CG is frequented by bears.

GETTING THERE: From Claremont go N on Mount Baldy route approx. 9 mi. to Manker Flats CG. Road is narrow with sharp curves. Large vehicles should use caution.

SINGLE RATE:	$8	OPEN DATES:	May-Oct
# of SINGLE SITES:	21	MAX SPUR:	22 feet
		MAX STAY:	14 days
		ELEVATION:	6300 feet

37 Maxwell Trail

Three Points • lat 34°41'00" lon 118°31'00"

DESCRIPTION: This primitive, hike-in, trail camp is in a desert setting. Supplies available at Green Valley. Bighorn sheep, black bears and migratory birds can be seen in the area. Many trails in the area.

GETTING THERE: From Lake Hughs go S on forest route 7N09 approx. 1/2 mi. Go W on 7N08 approx. 5 mi. to Maxwell CG.

SINGLE RATE:	No fee	OPEN DATES:	Yearlong
# of SINGLE SITES:	1		
		MAX STAY:	14 days
		ELEVATION:	4400 feet

38 Messenger Flats

Acton • lat 34°22'49" lon 118°11'19"

DESCRIPTION: CG is located in a pine stand on hillside with the Pacific Crest Trail running through the CG. Supplies at Acton. A lot of deer and bears are in the area. Trails to streams and river nearby. CG has two corrals.

GETTING THERE: From Acton go E on Cyn route 2 mi. to Aliso Cyn route. Go SE on Aliso Cyn route 8 mi. to forest route 4N18. Go on 4N18 SE 3 mi. to forest route 3N17. Go on 3N17 5.5 mi. to Messenger Flats CG.

SINGLE RATE:	$5	OPEN DATES:	Yearlong
# of SINGLE SITES:	10		
		MAX STAY:	14 days
		ELEVATION:	5500 feet

39 Millard

Millard • lat 34°12'16" lon 118°09'57"

DESCRIPTION: CG is located in an alder, pine and oak forest setting. Stream and waterfall within .5 mi. from CG. Supplies available in Millard. Deer, bears and birds are common to the area. CG is with-in the city limits. Walk-in site.

GETTING THERE: From Millard go N 1/8 mi. to Millard CG.

SINGLE RATE:	No fee	OPEN DATES:	Yearlong
# of SINGLE SITES:	10		
		MAX STAY:	14 days
		ELEVATION:	1900 feet

40 Monte Cristo

La Canada • lat 34°19'00" lon 118°06'00"

DESCRIPTION: In a large old growth sycamore stand with Mill Creek running through the CG. No fishing from the creek. Supplies at La Canada. Deer, bears and birds are common to the area. Trails in the area. This CG is popular with artist and painters because of the beautiful trees in the area.

GETTING THERE: From La Canada go N on state HWY 2 approx. 15 mi. to forest route 3N19 (Shortcut Work Station). Go NW on 3N19 approx. 9 mi. to Monte Cristo CG.

SINGLE RATE:	$8	OPEN DATES:	Yearlong
# of SINGLE SITES:	10	MAX SPUR:	30 feet
		MAX STAY:	14 days
		ELEVATION:	3600 feet

41 Mount Lowe Trail

Millard • lat 34°13'35" lon 118°06'34"

DESCRIPTION: In a pine plantation forest setting. Supplies available at Millard. Deer, bears, raccoon and a wide variety of birds in the area. National Historic Echo Mountain RR in the area. Trails or fire road for hiking in the area. CG is popular with mountain bikers. Walk-in only.

GETTING THERE: From Millard go N on 2N50 approx. 3 mi. to Mount Lowe CG.

SINGLE RATE:	No fee	OPEN DATES:	Yearlong
# of SINGLE SITES:	6		
		MAX STAY:	14 days
		ELEVATION:	4500 feet

42 Mount Pacifico

La Canada • lat 34°22'32" lon 118°06'30"

DESCRIPTION: On mountain of pine with rock outcrops with views of the desert. Supplies at Vincent. Deer, bears and birds are common in the area. OHV trail next to CG. Large boulder for climbing in the CG. CG popular with rock climbers. Walk-in.

GETTING THERE: From Vincent go S on Kennedy Springs route (FH59) approx. 10 mi. to forest route 3N17. Go E on 3N17 approx. 4 mi. to Mount Pacifico CG.

SINGLE RATE:	No fee	OPEN DATES:	May-Nov
# of SINGLE SITES:	6		
		MAX STAY:	14 days
		ELEVATION:	7100 feet

43 Mountain Oak

Mountain Top Juntion • lat 34°24'00" lon 117°43'30"

DESCRIPTION: This CG is located in a chaparral setting. Supplies available at Mountain Top Junction. Bighorn sheep, black bears and migratory birds are just some of the animals you can see in this area. No designated trails in the area.

GETTING THERE: From Mountain Top Junction go SW on state HWY 2 approx. 9 mi. to Big Pines HWY. Go W on Big Pines HWY approx. 3 mi. to Mountain Oak CG.

SINGLE RATE:	$10	OPEN DATES:	May-Nov
# of SINGLE SITES:	17	MAX SPUR:	18 feet
		MAX STAY:	14 days
		ELEVATION:	6100 feet

44 Oak Flat

Castaic • lat 34°35'55" lon 118°43'22"

DESCRIPTION: In a desert setting with no water. Supplies available at Castaic. Bighorn sheep, black bears and migratory birds are just some of the animals you can see in this area. Campers may gather firewood. No designated trails in the area.

GETTING THERE: From Castaic go NW on US HWY 5 approx. 6 mi. to forest route 6N32 (exit provided). Go on 6N32 NW approx. 3 mi. to Oak Flat CG.

SINGLE RATE:	No fee	OPEN DATES:	Yearlong
# of SINGLE SITES:	21	MAX SPUR:	32 feet
		MAX STAY:	14 days
		ELEVATION:	2800 feet

45 Oakwilde Trail

La Canada • lat 34°14'30" lon 118°11'00"

DESCRIPTION: In an oak and pine forest setting with Bears Canyon stream and Arroyo Seco stream nearby. Fish for trout on Arroyo Seco. Waterfalls upstream from CG. Supplies available at La Canada. Deer, bears, raccoon and a wide variety of birds in the area. Trails in the area. Walk-in.

GETTING THERE: From La Canada go N on state HWY 2 approx. 2 mi. to Oakwilde CG.

SINGLE RATE:	No fee	OPEN DATES:	Yearlong
# of SINGLE SITES:	5		
		MAX STAY:	14 days
		ELEVATION:	1800 feet

 Campground has hosts   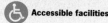 Reservable sites   Accessible facilities   Fully developed   Semi-developed   Rustic facilities

NOTE: Open dates listed are typical. Actual dates are dependent on conditions such as snow pack.

46 Peavine
Wrightwood • lat 34°23'18" lon 117°42'58"

DESCRIPTION: This tent only CG is located in a chaparral setting. Supplies located at Wrightwood. Bighorn sheep, black bears and migratory birds are just some of the animals you can see in this area. No designated trails in the area.

GETTING THERE: From Wrightwood go W on primary forest route 61 (state HWY 2) 3.6 mi. to Peavine CG.

SINGLE RATE:	$8	OPEN DATES:	May-Nov
# of SINGLE SITES:	4	MAX STAY:	14 days
		ELEVATION:	6100 feet

47 Rocky Point
Four Points • lat 34°32'00" lon 118°01'30"

DESCRIPTION: In a chaparral setting with no drinking water available. Supplies available at Four Points. Bighorn sheep, black bears and migratory birds are just some of the animals you can see in this area. No designated trails in the area.

GETTING THERE: From Four Points go S on Cheseboro route approx. 5 mi. to Rocky Point CG.

SINGLE RATE:	$10	OPEN DATES:	Yearlong
# of SINGLE SITES:	3	MAX STAY:	14 days
		ELEVATION:	3500 feet

48 Sage
Four Points • lat 34°28'00" lon 118°01'30"

DESCRIPTION: This walk-in, tent only CG is in a chaparral setting with no drinking water available. Supplies available at Four Points. Bighorn sheep, black bears and migratory birds are just some of the animals you can see in this area. No designated trails in the area.

GETTING THERE: From Four Points go S on Cheseboro route 3 mi. to forest route 5N04. Go S on 5N04 approx. 2.5 mi. to Sage CG.

SINGLE RATE:	$10	OPEN DATES:	Yearlong
# of SINGLE SITES:	5	MAX STAY:	14 days
		ELEVATION:	3400 feet

49 Sawmill
Three Points • lat 34°42'04" lon 118°34'16"

DESCRIPTION: This CG is in a high forest setting with no drinking water available. Supplies are located at Three Points. Campers may gather firewood. CG is on the Pacific Crest Trail and approx. 1 mi. from the Burnt Peak Trailhead which leads to the backcountry.

GETTING THERE: From Three Points go S on Pine Canyon Route approx. 1 mi. to forest route 7N14. Go S on 7N14 approx. 2 mi. to 7N23. Go E on 7N23 approx. 2.5 mi. to Sawmill CG.

SINGLE RATE:	No fee	OPEN DATES:	May-Oct
# of SINGLE SITES:	8	MAX SPUR:	16 feet
		MAX STAY:	14 days
		ELEVATION:	5200 feet

50 Soledad
Lange • lat 34°26'28" lon 118°18'25"

DESCRIPTION: This group site is located in a desert setting. Supplies available at Lange. Bighorn sheep, black bears and migratory birds can be seen in the area. Many trails are in the area.

GETTING THERE: From Lange to E on Soledad Canyon route 3.5 mi. to Soledad CG.

		OPEN DATES:	Yearlong
		MAX SPUR:	25 feet
GROUP RATE:	Varies	MAX STAY:	14 days
# of GROUP SITES:	1	ELEVATION:	2500 feet

51 South Fork
Valyermo • lat 34°23'40" lon 117°49'10"

DESCRIPTION: This tent only CG is located in a chapparrel setting with no drinking water. Supplies available at Valyermo. Bighorn sheep, black bears and migratory birds are just some of the animals you can see in this area. No designated trails in the area.

GETTING THERE: From Valyermo go SE on state HWY 2 (Big Pines Highway) 1 mi. to forest route 4N11. Go SE on 4N11 1.5 mi. to forest route 4N11A. Go S on 4N11A 1 mi. to South Fork CG.

SINGLE RATE:	No fee	OPEN DATES:	May-Nov
# of SINGLE SITES:	21	MAX STAY:	14 days
		ELEVATION:	4550 feet

52 Spunky
Green Valley • lat 34°36'36" lon 118°23'25"

DESCRIPTION: This rustic CG is in a chaparral setting. Supplies available at Green Valley. Bighorn sheep, black bears and migratory birds are just some of the animals you can see in this area. Campers may gather firewood. The Pacific Crest Trail passes within a mile of the CG.

GETTING THERE: From Green Valley go SE approx. 1/2 mi. to Spunky CG.

SINGLE RATE:	No fee	OPEN DATES:	May-Nov
# of SINGLE SITES:	10	MAX STAY:	14 days
		ELEVATION:	3300 feet

53 Streamside
Saugus • lat 34°32'58" lon 118°25'49"

DESCRIPTION: This tent only CG is in a desert setting with no drinking water available. Supplies available at Saugus. Bighorn sheep, black bears and migratory birds are just some of the animals you can see in this area. No designated trails in the area.

GETTING THERE: From Saugus go N on Bouquet Canyon route approx. 8 mi. to Streamside CG.

SINGLE RATE:	No fee	OPEN DATES:	Yearlong
# of SINGLE SITES:	9	MAX STAY:	14 days
		ELEVATION:	2500 feet

54 Sulphur Springs
La Canada • lat 34°21'30" lon 117°92'00"

DESCRIPTION: In a pine stand in the Little Rock Drainage area. Supplies available in La Canada. Deer, bears and birds are common in the area. Campers may gather firewood. Many trails in the area.

GETTING THERE: From La Canada go NE on state HWY 2 approx. 25 mi. to forest route going N. Go W on forest route approx. 6 mi. to Sulphur Springs Group CG.

		OPEN DATES:	Apr-Nov
		MAX SPUR:	16 feet
GROUP RATE:	$100	MAX STAY:	14 days
# of GROUP SITES:	12	ELEVATION:	5400 feet

55 Sycamore Flats
Valyermo • lat 34°24'47" lon 117°49'25"

DESCRIPTION: This walk-in CG is in a chaparral setting with no drinking water available. Supplies available at Valyermo. Bighorn sheep, black bears and migratory birds are just some of the animals you can see in this area. No designated trails in this area.

GETTING THERE: From Valyermo go SE on Big Pines HWY approx. 1 mi. to forest route 4N11 (Big Rock Creek). Go S on 4N22 approx. 2 mi. to Sycamore Flats CG.

SINGLE RATE:	$8	OPEN DATES:	Yearlong
# of SINGLE SITES:	11	MAX SPUR:	22 feet
		MAX STAY:	14 days
		ELEVATION:	4250 feet

 Campground has hosts **Reservable sites**   **Accessible facilities** 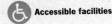 **Fully developed**   **Semi-developed**   **Rustic facilities**

NOTE: Open dates listed are typical. Actual dates are dependent on conditions such as snow pack.

56 Table Mountain
Mountain Top Junction • lat 34°23'14" lon 117°41'21"

DESCRIPTION: In a chaparral setting. Supplies available at Mountain Top Junction. Bighorn sheep, black bears and migratory birds are just some of the animals you can see in this area. No designated trails in the area.

GETTING THERE: From Mountain Top Junction go SW on state HWY 2 approx. 9 mi. to forest route 4N04. Go N on 4N04 1/2 mi. to Table Mountain CG.

SINGLE RATE:	$12	OPEN DATES:	May-Nov
# of SINGLE SITES:	115	MAX SPUR:	32 feet
		MAX STAY:	14 days
		ELEVATION:	7000 feet

57 Tom Lucas Trail
Tujunga • lat 34°19'52" lon 118°14'31"

DESCRIPTION: In an alder and oak tree forest setting. CG has a stream running most of the year nearby. Waterfalls are down stream from the CG. Supplies available in Tujunga. This is an equestrian use CG. There is a hitching rail in the CG. Trails in the area. Hike-in only. No water.

GETTING THERE: From Tujunga go N on MT Gleason Ave. approx. 4 mi. to Trail Canyon trailhead. Go N on Trail Canyon trail approx. 4 mi. to Tom Lucas CG.

SINGLE RATE:	No fee	OPEN DATES:	Yearlong
# of SINGLE SITES:	2		
		MAX STAY:	14 days
		ELEVATION:	2900 feet

58 Upper Shake
Lake Hughs • lat 34°41'29" lon 118°31'44"

DESCRIPTION: In an chaparral setting with no drinking water. Supplies available at Lake Hughs. Bighorn sheep, black bears and migratory birds are just some of the animals you can see in this area. No designated trails in the area.

GETTING THERE: From Lake Hughs go NW on Pine Canyon route approx. 2 mi. to forest route 7N23. Go S on 7N23 approx. 1/2 mi. to forest route 7N38. Go E on 7N38 approx. 1 mi. to Upper Shake CG.

SINGLE RATE:	No fee	OPEN DATES:	May-Dec
# of SINGLE SITES:	13	MAX SPUR:	22 feet
		MAX STAY:	14 days
		ELEVATION:	4400 feet

59 Valley Forge
La Canada • lat 34°14'46" lon 118°04'54"

DESCRIPTION: In a high elevation dense forest setting. Supplies at La Canada. Deer, bears and birds are common in the area. Trails are nearby the CG. Walk-in. Closed to motor vehicles. Campfire permit required. Hike/bike/horse only.

GETTING THERE: From La Canada go N on state HWY 2 aprox. 7 mi. to forest route 2N24. Go S on 2N24 approx. 2 mi. to Valley Forge CG.

SINGLE RATE:	No fee	OPEN DATES:	Yearlong
# of SINGLE SITES:	12		
		MAX STAY:	14 days
		ELEVATION:	3500 feet

60 West Fork
La Canada • lat 34°14'43" lon 118°02'52"

DESCRIPTION: In a high elevation dense forest setting. Supplies at La Canada. Deer, bears and birds are common in the area. Trails are nearby the CG. Walk-in. Closed to motor vehicles. Campfire permit required. Hike/bike/horse only.

GETTING THERE: From La Canada go N on state HWY 2 aprox. 7 mi. to forest route 2N24. Go S on 2N24 approx. 3 mi. to West Fork CG.

SINGLE RATE:	No fee	OPEN DATES:	May-Nov
# of SINGLE SITES:	7		
		MAX STAY:	14 days
		ELEVATION:	3100 feet

61 Zuni
Saugus • lat 34°30'34" lon 118°27'09"

DESCRIPTION: In a desert setting with no drinking water available. Supplies available at Saugus. Bighorn sheep, black bears and migratory birds are just some of the animals you can see in this area. No designated trails in the area.

GETTING THERE: From Saugus go NE on Bouquet Canyon route approx. 6 mi. to Zuni CG.

SINGLE RATE:	No fee	OPEN DATES:	Yearlong
# of SINGLE SITES:	9		
		MAX STAY:	14 days
		ELEVATION:	1700 feet

 Campground has hosts   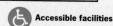 **Reservable sites**   **Accessible facilities**   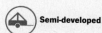 **Fully developed**    **Semi-developed**    **Rustic facilities**

NOTE: Open dates listed are typical. Actual dates are dependent on conditions such as snow pack.

USFS Photo

CLEVELAND NATIONAL FOREST

The Cleveland National Forest is the southernmost national forests in California. Its 567,000 acres are located in Orange, Riverside and San Diego counties, at elevations ranging from 460 to 6,271 feet.

Each year more than two million people visit the Cleveland. Until the arrival of Juan Rodriguez Cabrillo in 1542, these lands were known only to desert and coastal Indian tribes. Many trails today follow the routes first used by these early dwellers.

A warm dry Mediterranean climate prevails over the forest - hot in the summer, mild in the winter. Most of the vegetation is chaparral and coastal sage. Magnificent oaks are found in meadows and along streams, with pine forests at the higher elevations.

The Cleveland's ecosystems are unique, irreplaceable habitats. It's a place where biodiversity is preserved and threatened and endangered plants and animals are protected.

Camping, picnicking, hiking, equestrian use and sight-seeing are popular activities in the forest. There is plenty of open space where you can escape from a busy life. If you really want to "get away from it all," the forest has four officially designated wilderness areas.

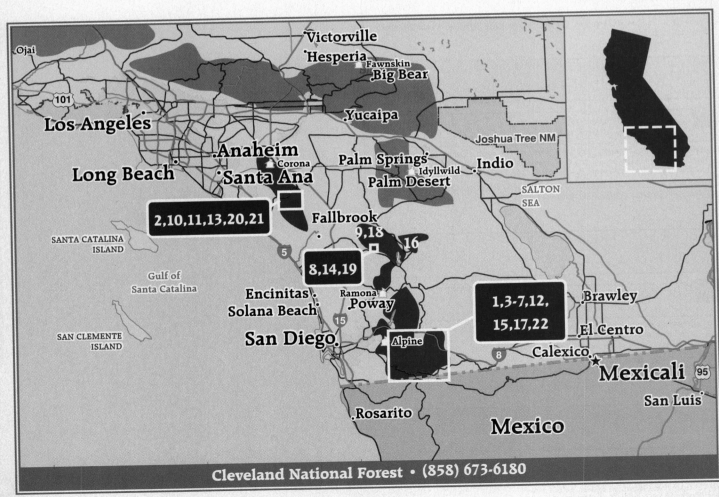

Cleveland National Forest • (858) 673-6180

1 Aqua Dulce
Pine Valley • lat 32°51'12" lon 116°26'01"

DESCRIPTION: This walk-in CG is located in an open grove of oak. Wildlife in this area includes the infrequent mountain lions, as well as coyotes, deer, turkeys, and redtail hawks. CG is busy holidays. Enjoy hiking the nearby Laguna Meadow trail system which includes horse and mountain bike trails. Supplies in Pine Valley.

GETTING THERE: From Pine Valley go S on forest route 16S06 approx. 1 mi. to Sunrise Scenic Byway. Go NE on Byway approx. 8.5 mi. to Aqua Dulce CG.

SINGLE RATE: # of SINGLE SITES:	Varies 5	OPEN DATES: MAX SPUR: MAX STAY: ELEVATION:	May-Sept 20 feet 14 days 5900 feet

6 Cibbets Flat
Pine Valley • lat 32°46'41" lon 116°26'42"

DESCRIPTION: This CG is situated in an open grove of oak. Enjoy the adjacent Kitchen Creek. Wildlife in this area includes the infrequent mountain lions, as well as coyotes, deer, turkeys, and redtail hawks. CG is a short walk to the Pacific Crest Trail. Supplies in Pine Valley.

GETTING THERE: From Pine Valley go S approx. 7 mi. on state HWY 1 to forest route 15S17. Go N on 15S17 approx. 4 mi. to Cibbets Flat CG.

SINGLE RATE: # of SINGLE SITES:	$13 24	OPEN DATES: MAX SPUR: MAX STAY: ELEVATION:	Yearlong 27 feet 14 days 4200 feet

2 Blue Jay
Morrell Potrero • lat 33°39'06" lon 117°26'59"

DESCRIPTION: This CG is located in an open grove of mixed conifers. Enjoy nearby creek. Wildlife in the area includes mountain lions, coyotes, deer, hawks, and reptiles. Hike the San Juan Trail which runs along San Juan Creek and offers panoramic mountain views. Supplies in Morrel Potrero. Visit waterfalls in area.

GETTING THERE: From Morrell Potrero go NW on forest route 6S07 approx. 4.5 mi. to forest route 3S04. Go NW on 3S04 approx. 3.5 mi. to Blue Jay CG.

SINGLE RATE: # of SINGLE SITES: # of GROUP SITES:	$15 50 5	OPEN DATES: MAX SPUR: MAX STAY: ELEVATION:	Yearlong 40 feet 14 days 3400 feet

7 Corral Canyon
Morena Village • lat 32°42'47" lon 116°34'16"

DESCRIPTION: This CG is situated in an open grove of oak. Wildlife in this area includes the infrequent mountain lions, as well as coyotes, deer, turkeys, and redtail hawks. CG is busy holidays. Enjoy riding in the nearby Corral Canyon OHV trail system. Supplies in Morena Village.

GETTING THERE: From Morena Village go N on county route S1 approx. 2 mi. to forest route 17S04. Go W on 17S04 approx. 6.5 mi. to Corral Canyon CG.

SINGLE RATE: # of SINGLE SITES:	No fee 28	OPEN DATES: MAX SPUR: MAX STAY: ELEVATION:	Yearlong 27 feet 14 days 3500 feet

3 Bobcat Meadow
Morena Village • lat 32°42'30" lon 116°34'30"

DESCRIPTION: This CG is situated in an open grove of oak. Wildlife in this area includes the infrequent mountain lions, as well as coyotes, deer, turkeys, and redtail hawks. CG is busy holidays. Enjoy riding in the nearby Corral Canyon OHV trail system. Supplies in Morena Village. No drinking water.

GETTING THERE: From Morena Village go N on county route 1 approx. 2 mi. to forest route 17S04. Go W on 17S04 approx. 2 mi. to the Bobcat Meadow CG turnoff, continue approx. 1 mi. to Bobcat Meadow CG.

SINGLE RATE: # of SINGLE SITES:	No fee 20	OPEN DATES: MAX SPUR: MAX STAY: ELEVATION:	Yearlong 27 feet 14 days 3800 feet

8 Crestline
Pauma Valley • lat 33°18'52" lon 116°51'44"

DESCRIPTION: Dispersed group site is in an open meadow with some shade trees. There is a nearby visitor information center and small, seasonal creek. Wildlife in the area includes black bear, mtn lions, bobcat, lynx, coyotes, deer, hawks and eagles. CG is busy holidays. Hike in nearby Barker Valley. Bring firewood.

GETTING THERE: From Pauma Valley go SE approx. 6 mi. to county route S6. Go NE on S6 approx. 5.5 mi. to Crestline CG.

		OPEN DATES:	May-Nov*
GROUP RATE: # of GROUP SITES:	$75 1	MAX STAY: ELEVATION:	14 days 4800 feet

4 Boulder Oaks
Pine Valley • lat 32°43'54" lon 116°29'02"

DESCRIPTION: This CG is situated in an open grove of oak with sagebrush understory. Wildlife in this area includes the infrequent mountain lions, as well as coyotes, deer, turkeys, and redtail hawk. CG is busy holidays. Hike the Pacific Crest Trail (trailhead on site). This CG offers horse facilities.

GETTING THERE: From Pine Valley go S on country route S1 approximately 6 miles to Boulder Oaks CG.

SINGLE RATE: # of SINGLE SITES:	Varies 30	OPEN DATES: MAX SPUR: MAX STAY: ELEVATION:	Yearlong 27 feet 14 days 3300 feet

9 Dripping Springs
Temecula • lat 33°28'21" lon 116°59'16"

DESCRIPTION: This CG is in scattered oak trees next to seasonal Dripping Spring Creek. Hike the Agua Tibia Wilderness. Wildlife in the area includes black bear, mtn lions, bobcat, lynx, coyotes, deer, hawks and eagles. In fire season, the adjacent fire station provides information and permits. Bring your own firewood.

GETTING THERE: From Temecula go E on state HWY 79 approx. 9.5 mi. to Dripping Springs CG.

SINGLE RATE: # of SINGLE SITES:	$12 34	OPEN DATES: MAX SPUR: MAX STAY: ELEVATION:	Yearlong 22 feet 14 days 1600 feet

5 Burnt Rancheria
Pine Valley • lat 32°51'41" lon 116°24'58"

DESCRIPTION: This CG rests in an open grove of oak with spectacular views of the desert below. Wildlife includes the infrequent mountain lions, as well as coyotes, deer, turkeys, and redtail hawks. Enjoy hiking the nearby Laguna Meadow Trail system, on site interpretive trail or Pacific Crest Trail.

GETTING THERE: From Pine Valley go S on forest route 16S06 approx. 1 mi. to Sunrise Scenic Byway. Go NE on Byway approx. 9 mi. to Burnt Rancheria CG.

SINGLE RATE: # of SINGLE SITES:	$13 110	OPEN DATES: MAX SPUR: MAX STAY: ELEVATION:	May-Oct 50 feet 14 days 6000 feet

10 El Cariso North
Morrell Potrero • lat 33°39'32" lon 117°24'35"

DESCRIPTION: This CG is located in an open grove of mixed conifers. Enjoy nearby creek. Wildlife in the area includes mountain lions, coyotes, fox, deer, hawks, and reptiles. Hike and mountain bike on nearby trails. Supplies in Morrel Potrero. Visit waterfalls in area and Holy Jim Historic Trail.

GETTING THERE: From Morrell Potrero go NW on forest route 6S07 approx. 4.5 mi. to forest route 3S04. Go NW on 3S04 approx. .5 mi. to El Cariso North CG.

SINGLE RATE: # of SINGLE SITES:	$15 24	OPEN DATES: MAX SPUR: MAX STAY: ELEVATION:	Yearlong 22 feet 14 days 2600 feet

 Campground has hosts   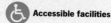 **Reservable sites**   **Accessible facilities**   **Fully developed**   **Semi-developed**   Rustic facilities

NOTE: Open dates listed are typical. Actual dates are dependent on conditions such as snow pack.

11 El Cariso South
Morrell Potrero • lat 33°39'32" lon 117°24'35"

DESCRIPTION: This CG is located in an open grove of mixed conifers. Enjoy nearby creek. Wildlife in the area includes mountain lions, coyotes, fox, deer, hawks, and reptiles. Hike and mountain bike on nearby trails. Supplies in Morrel Potrero. Visit waterfalls in area and Holy Jim Historic Trail.

GETTING THERE: From Morrell Potrero go NW on forest route 6S07 approx. 4.5 mi. to forest route 3S04. Go NW on 3S04 approx. .5 mi. to El Cariso South CG.

SINGLE RATE:	$15	OPEN DATES:	Yearlong
# of SINGLE SITES:	11	MAX SPUR:	17 feet
		MAX STAY:	14 days
		ELEVATION:	2600 feet

16 Indian Flats
Agape Village • lat 33°20'57" lon 116°39'39"

DESCRIPTION: This CG will be closed April 3, 2000 for ecological study. Please contact the Palomar Ranger District at (760) 788-0250 for open date. This remote, tent only CG is situated in an open oak grove near small, seasonal creeks. Numerous wildlife. Bring firewood. Hike the nearby Pacific Crest Trail.

GETTING THERE: From Agape Village go S on state HWY 79 approx. 6.5 mi. to forest route 9S05. Go N on 9S05 approx. 5 mi. to Indian Flats CG.

SINGLE RATE:	$10	OPEN DATES:	Yearlong
# of SINGLE SITES:	17	MAX SPUR:	15 feet
		MAX STAY:	14 days
		ELEVATION:	3600 feet

12 El Prado
Pine Valley • lat 32°53'18" lon 116°26'59"

DESCRIPTION: This CG is located in an open grove of oak and pine with views of the seasonal Little Laguna Lake. Wildlife includes the infrequent mtn lions, as well as coyotes, deer, turkeys, and redtail hawks. CG is busy holidays. Enjoy hiking the nearby Laguna Meadow trail system which includes horse and mtn bike trails.

GETTING THERE: From Pine Valley go S on forest route 16S06 approx. 1 mi. to Sunrise Scenic Byway. Go NE on Byway approx. 11.5 mi. to El Prado CG.

SINGLE RATE:	Varies	OPEN DATES:	May-Sept*
		MAX SPUR:	30 feet
GROUP RATE:	Varies	MAX STAY:	14 days
# of GROUP SITES:	5	ELEVATION:	5600 feet

17 Laguna
Pine Valley • lat 32°53'14" lon 116°26'47"

DESCRIPTION: This CG is located in an open grove of oak and pine with views of the seasonal Little Laguna Lake. Wildlife includes the infrequent mountain lions, as well as coyotes, deer, turkeys, and redtail hawks. CG is busy holidays. Enjoy hiking the extensive Laguna Meadow trail system which includes horse and mountain bike trails.

GETTING THERE: From Pine Valley go S on forest route 16S06 approx. 1 mi. to Sunrise Scenic Byway. Go NE on Byway approx. 10 mi. to Laguna CG.

SINGLE RATE:	$12	OPEN DATES:	Yearlong
# of SINGLE SITES:	104	MAX SPUR:	27 feet
		MAX STAY:	14 days
		ELEVATION:	5600 feet

13 Falcon
Morrell Potrero • lat 33°39'23" lon 117°27'11"

DESCRIPTION: This CG is located in an open grove of mixed conifers. Enjoy nearby creek. Wildlife in the area includes mountain lions, coyotes, fox, deer, hawks, and reptiles. Hike and mountain bike on nearby trails. Supplies in Morrel Potrero. Hike nearby San Juan Trail. Visit waterfalls in area and Holy Jim Historic Trail.

GETTING THERE: From Morrell Potrero go NW on forest route 6S07 approx. 4.5 mi. to forest route 3S04. Go NW on 3S04 approx. 3 mi. to Falcon CG.

		OPEN DATES:	Yearlong
		MAX SPUR:	20 feet
GROUP RATE:	Varies	MAX STAY:	14 days
# of GROUP SITES:	3	ELEVATION:	3300 feet

18 Oak Grove
Agape Village • lat 40°50'53" lon 122°21'10"

DESCRIPTION: This CG rests in a quiet grove of red shank trees with some undergrowth between sites. Wildlife in the area includes black bear, mountain lions, bobcat, lynx, coyotes, deer, hawks and eagles. CG is busy holidays. Hike in nearby Barker Valley. Bring your own firewood. Supplies in Agape Village.

GETTING THERE: From Agape Village go NW on state HWY 79 approx. 5 miles to Oak Grove CG.

SINGLE RATE:	$15	OPEN DATES:	Yearlong
# of SINGLE SITES:	81	MAX SPUR:	27 feet
		MAX STAY:	14 days
		ELEVATION:	2800 feet

14 Fry Creek
Pauma Valley • lat 33°20'43" lon 116°52'56"

DESCRIPTION: CG rests in dense conifer and oak. Hike on adjacent loop trail. Visit nearby Palomar Observatory. Wildlife in the area includes black bear, mountain lions, bobcat, lynx, coyotes, deer, hawks and eagles. CG is busy holidays. Trailers are not recommended in this CG. Bring your own firewood.

GETTING THERE: From Pauma Valley go SE approx. 6 mi. to county route S6. Go NE on S6 approx. 8 mi. to Fry Creek CG.

SINGLE RATE:	$12	OPEN DATES:	May-Nov
# of SINGLE SITES:	20	MAX SPUR:	15 feet
		MAX STAY:	14 days
		ELEVATION:	4900 feet

19 Observatory
Pauma Valley • lat 33°20'30" lon 116°52'30"

DESCRIPTION: Dispersed group site is near an open meadow with stands of conifer and oak. Enjoy hiking the Observatory Trail which offers beautiful valley views and ends at Palomar Observatory. Wildlife in the area includes black bear, mountain lions, coyotes, deer, hawks and eagles. CG is busy holidays. Bring firewood.

GETTING THERE: From Pauma Valley go SE approx. 6 mi. to county route S6. Go NE on S6 approx. 8 mi. to Observatory CG.

SINGLE RATE:	$12	OPEN DATES:	May-Nov
# of SINGLE SITES:	42	MAX SPUR:	27 feet
		MAX STAY:	14 days
		ELEVATION:	4800 feet

15 Horse Heaven
Pine Valley • lat 32°53'07" lon 116°26'23"

DESCRIPTION: This CG rests in an open grove of oak and pine with views of the surrounding forest. Wildlife includes the infrequent mountain lions, as well as coyotes, deer, turkeys, and redtail hawks. CG is busy holidays. Hike to nearby Laguna CG and access its extensive Laguna Meadow trail system.

GETTING THERE: From Pine Valley go S on forest route 16S06 approx. 1 mi. to Sunrise Scenic Byway. Go NE on Byway approx. 10.5 mi. to Horse Heaven CG.

SINGLE RATE:	Varies	OPEN DATES:	May-Sept
		MAX SPUR:	45 feet
GROUP RATE:	Varies	MAX STAY:	14 days
# of GROUP SITES:	3	ELEVATION:	5600 feet

20 Upper San Juan
Morrell Potrero • lat 33°36'23" lon 117°25'56"

DESCRIPTION: This CG is located in an open grove of mixed conifers. Enjoy nearby creek. Wildlife in the area includes mountain lions, coyotes, fox, deer, hawks, and reptiles. Hike and mountain bike on nearby trails. Supplies in Morrel Potrero. Hike nearby San Juan Trail. Visit waterfalls in area and Holy Jim Historic Trail.

GETTING THERE: From Morrell Potrero go NW on forest route 6S07 approx. 7.5 mi. to Upper San Juan CG.

SINGLE RATE:	$15	OPEN DATES:	Yearlong
# of SINGLE SITES:	18	MAX SPUR:	32 feet
		MAX STAY:	14 days
		ELEVATION:	1800 feet

 Campground has hosts   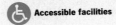 **Reservable sites**   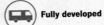 **Accessible facilities**   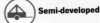 **Fully developed**   **Semi-developed**   **Rustic facilities**

NOTE: Open dates listed are typical. Actual dates are dependent on conditions such as snow pack.

21 Wildomar

Morrell Potrero • lat 33°35'56" lon 117°16'45"

DESCRIPTION: This CG is located in an open grove of mixed conifers. Enjoy nearby creek. Wildlife in the area includes mountain lions, coyotes, fox, deer, hawks, and reptiles. Ride this CGs many OHV trails. Supplies in Morrel Potrero. Visit waterfalls in area and Holy Jim Historic Trail.

GETTING THERE: From Morrell Potrero go S on forest route 6S07 approx. 3.5 miles to Wildomar CG.

SINGLE RATE:	$15	OPEN DATES:	Yearlong
# of SINGLE SITES:	12	MAX SPUR:	22 feet
		MAX STAY:	14 days
		ELEVATION:	2400 feet

22 Wooded Hill

Pine Valley • lat 32°51'05" lon 116°26'01"

DESCRIPTION: This trailer and RV CG is located in an open grove of oak. Wildlife in this area includes the infrequent mountain lions, as well as coyotes, deer, turkeys, and redtail hawks. CG is busy holidays. Enjoy hiking the nearby Laguna Meadow trail system or on-site interpretive trail. Supplies in Pine Valley.

GETTING THERE: From Pine Valley go S on forest route 16S06 approx. 1 mi. to Sunrise Scenic Byway. Go NE on Byway approx. 8 mi. to Wooded Hill CG.

SINGLE RATE:	Varies	OPEN DATES:	May-Sept
		MAX SPUR:	45 feet
GROUP RATE:	Varies	MAX STAY:	14 days
# of GROUP SITES:	1	ELEVATION:	6000 feet

Texas Big

If all the Forest Service lands were puzzled together in one piece, it would equal an area of land the size of the State of Texas—roughly 191 million acres of forests and grasslands in all.

 Campground has hosts   **Reservable sites**   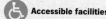 **Accessible facilities**   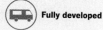 **Fully developed**   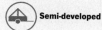 **Semi-developed**    **Rustic facilities**

NOTE: Open dates listed are typical. Actual dates are dependent on conditions such as snow pack.

USFS Photo

Eldorado National Forest

The miners who came to California in the gold rush of 1849 called this land "el dorado," for the fabled Spanish "land of gold." Today, thousands of visitors are drawn each year to the Eldorado National Forest's rivers, lakes and streams. Four hundred miles of hiking trails pass through all kinds of terrain, from gentle oak foothills on the west to the 10,000-foot crest of the Sierra Nevada. Two major highways-Highway 50 and Highway 88-run through the forest, making it an easy drive from Sacramento and the San Franscisco Bay Area.

The Eldorado offers many outdoor recreation opportunities. In the winter, you will find excellent cross-country skiing at Strawberry Canyon and Loon Lake in the Crystal Basin. Two alpine ski resorts operate in the Eldorado: Kirkwood Ski Resort and Sierra-at-Tahoe. Fishing in the forest is exceptional. Most reservoirs and rivers are planted seasonally and many lakes are home to resident trout. Lake fishing is open year-round while stream fishing season is open from the last Saturday in April through mid-November. Choose from more than 50 developed campgrounds, with camping season generally from late May through mid October.

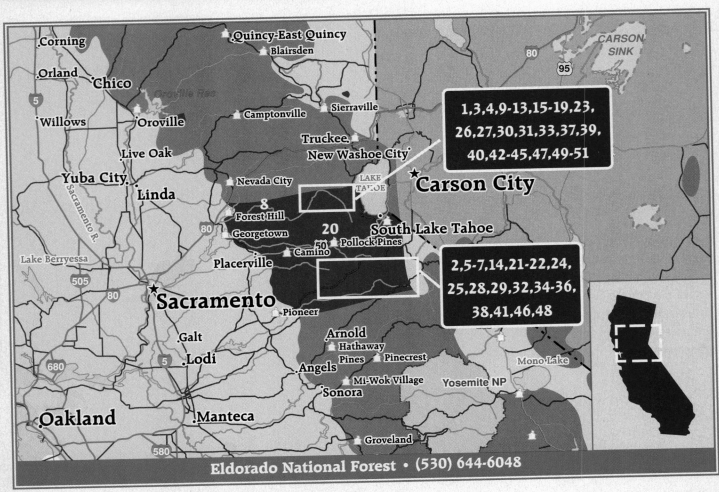

Eldorado National Forest • (530) 644-6048

1 Airport Flat
Riverton • lat 38°59'00" lon 120°22'30"

DESCRIPTION: This CG is situated on the banks of Gerle Creek, set in the Crystal Basin. Primary vegetation for the area is pine. Fishing in creek. Please check for local fishing regulations. Watch for deer and bears in the area. Supplies are available 28 mi. away at Riverton. No drinking water.

GETTING THERE: From Riverton go N on primary forest route 3 (Ice House Road) approx. 25 mi. to primary forest route 33. Continue N on 33 approx. 3 mi. to Airport Flat CG.

SINGLE RATE:	No fee	OPEN DATES:	June-Oct
# of SINGLE SITES:	16		
		MAX STAY:	14 days
		ELEVATION:	5300 feet

6 Capps Crossing
Pollock Pines • lat 38°39'04" lon 120°24'22"

DESCRIPTION: This CG is set on the banks of the North Fork Cosumnes River, situated in a pine forest. Views of the river. Fishing opportunities in river. Please check for local fishing regulations. Hiking trails are available nearby. Watch for deer, various birds, small wildlife, and bears in the area.

GETTING THERE: From Pollock Pines go S then E on primary forest route 5 to primary forest route 51 (Bonetti Road). Go SE on 51 approx. 13 mi. to Capps Crossing CG.

SINGLE RATE:	$11	OPEN DATES:	June-Oct
# of SINGLE SITES:	12	MAX SPUR:	50 feet
		MAX STAY:	14 days
		ELEVATION:	5200 feet

2 Bears River Group
Allen Camp • lat 38°32'03" lon 120°13'47"

DESCRIPTION: This CG is situated in a mixed conifer forest, not far from Lower Bears River Reservoir. Good fishing opportunities in lake and nearby streams. Watch for deer and bears in the area. Receives heavy use. Numerous trails can be found nearby. Supplies are at a store located at the north end of the lake.

GETTING THERE: From Allen Camp go SW on state HWY 88 approx. 6 mi. to primary forest route 08. Go SE on 08 approx. 4 mi. to Bears River Group CG.

SINGLE RATE:	Varies	OPEN DATES:	June-Sept
		MAX SPUR:	50 feet
		MAX STAY:	14 days
# of GROUP SITES:	3	ELEVATION:	6000 feet

7 China Flat
Kyburz • lat 38°45'16" lon 120°16'01"

DESCRIPTION: This CG is set on the banks of the Silver Fork American River, situated in a pine forest. Views of the river. Fishing opportunities in river. Please check for local fishing regulations. Watch for deer and bears in the area. Supplies are available 2 mi. away at Kyburz.

GETTING THERE: China Flat CG is located approx. 2 mi. S of Kyburz on primary forest route 71 (Silver Fork Road).

SINGLE RATE:	$11	OPEN DATES:	Apr-Nov
# of SINGLE SITES:	18	MAX SPUR:	60 feet
		MAX STAY:	14 days
		ELEVATION:	4800 feet

3 Big Meadows
Foresthill • lat 39°04'29" lon 120°25'39"

DESCRIPTION: This CG is situated on the banks of South For Long Canyon Creek, situated in a mixed conifer forest. Fishing opportunities in creek. Check for local fishing regulations. Watch for deer and bears in the area. Supplies are available 41 mi. away at Foresthill. Trails in area.

GETTING THERE: From Foresthill go E on primary forest route 96 approx. 30 mi. to primary forest route 22. Go S then NE on 22 approx. 11 mi. to Big Meadows CG.

SINGLE RATE:	$8	OPEN DATES:	May-Nov
# of SINGLE SITES:	54	MAX SPUR:	60 feet
		MAX STAY:	14 days
		ELEVATION:	5300 feet

8 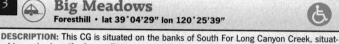 Dru Barner
Georgetown • lat 38°56'15" lon 120°46'00"

DESCRIPTION: This CG is situated in a pine forest. Watch for deer, various birds, small wildlife, and bears in the area. There are Numerous hiking, mountain biking, and horse trails are accessible nearby. No motorcycles permitted at CG. Various supplies are available 7 mi. away at Georgetown.

GETTING THERE: From Georgetown go E on county route 63 approx. 6 mi. to forest route 13N58. Go NW on 13N58 approx. 1 mi. to Dru Barner CG.

SINGLE RATE:	$6	OPEN DATES:	Yearlong
# of SINGLE SITES:	47	MAX SPUR:	100 feet
		MAX STAY:	14 days
		ELEVATION:	3000 feet

4 Black Oak
Georgetown • lat 38°54'10" lon 120°35'02"

DESCRIPTION: This CG is set on the shores of Stumpy Meadows lake, situated in a mixed conifer forest. Fishing opportunities in lake. Please check for local fishing regulations. Watch for deer, birds, and bears in the area. Self-contained vehicles only. No drinking water available on site.

GETTING THERE: Black Oak CG is located approx. 18 mi. E of Georgetown on county route 63.

		OPEN DATES:	Apr-Oct
GROUP RATE:	$50	MAX STAY:	14 days
# of GROUP SITES:	4	ELEVATION:	4400 feet

9 Fashoda
Riverton • lat 38°52'09" lon 120°23'46"

DESCRIPTION: This CG is set on the east side of Union Valley Reservoir, situated in a pine forest. Fishing opportunities in lake. Please check for local fishing regulations. Watch for deer, birds, and bears in the area. Supplies are available 15 mi. away at Riverton. Tent camping only.

GETTING THERE: From Riverton go N on primary forest route 3 (Ice House Road) approx. 14 mi. to forest route 12N35. Go W on 12N35 approx. 1.5 mi. to Fashoda CG.

SINGLE RATE:	$13	OPEN DATES:	June-Oct
# of SINGLE SITES:	30		
		MAX STAY:	14 days
		ELEVATION:	4900 feet

5 Caples Lake
Woodfords • lat 38°42'20" lon 120°03'14"

DESCRIPTION: This CG is set on the shores of Caples Lake, situated in a mixed conifer forest. Good fishing opportunities in lake. Please check for local fishing regulations. Popular hiking area. Watch for deer and bears in the area. Supplies are available at a store located nearby.

GETTING THERE: Caples Lake CG is located approx. 17 mi. W of Woodford on state HWY 89 (Carson Pass National Scenic Byway).

SINGLE RATE:	$11	OPEN DATES:	June-Oct
# of SINGLE SITES:	35	MAX SPUR:	50 feet
		MAX STAY:	14 days
		ELEVATION:	7800 feet

10 Gerle Creek
Riverton • lat 38°58'32" lon 120°23'35"

DESCRIPTION: This CG is set on the banks of the Gerle Creek Fork of Gerle Creek Divide Reservoir, situated in a pine forest. Possible fishing in Reservoir, check for local regulations. Watch for deer and bears in the area. No motorboats permitted. Numerous hiking opportunities in the area.

GETTING THERE: From Riverton go N on primary forest route 3 (Ice House Road) 25 mi. to primary forest route 33. Continue N 3 mi. to forest route 13N26. Go S 1 mi. to Gerle Creek CG.

SINGLE RATE:	$13	OPEN DATES:	May-Oct
# of SINGLE SITES:	50	MAX SPUR:	45 feet
		MAX STAY:	14 days
		ELEVATION:	5300 feet

 Campground has hosts   **Reservable sites**   **Accessible facilities**   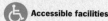 **Fully developed**   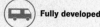 **Semi-developed**   **Rustic facilities**

NOTE: Open dates listed are typical. Actual dates are dependent on conditions such as snow pack.

11 Hell Hole
Foresthill • lat 39°03'57" lon 120°25'03"

DESCRIPTION: This CG is set approx. 1 mi. NW of Hell Hole Reservoir, situated in a pine forest. Fishing opportunities in reservoir. Please check for local fishing regulations. Watch for deer and bears in the area. Walk-in sites. Tent camping only. Several hiking trails nearby.

GETTING THERE: From Foresthill go E on primary forest route 96 approx. 30 mi. to primary forest route 22. Go S then NE on 22 approx. 11 mi. to Hell Hole CG.

SINGLE RATE:	$8	OPEN DATES:	May-Nov
# of SINGLE SITES:	10	MAX STAY:	14 days
		ELEVATION:	5200 feet

12 Ice House
Riverton • lat 38°49'43" lon 120°21'47"

DESCRIPTION: This CG is set on the shores of Ice House Reservoir, situated in a pine forest. Fishing opportunities in lake. Please check for local fishing regulations. Watch for numerous deer and bears in the area. Several hiking and mountain biking trails are accessible nearby.

GETTING THERE: From Riverton go NE on the Ice House Road (primary forest route 3) approx. 10 mi. to forest route 32. E on 32 1.5 mi. to Ice House CG.

SINGLE RATE:	$13	OPEN DATES:	May-Oct
# of SINGLE SITES:	83	MAX SPUR:	50 feet
GROUP RATE:	$20	MAX STAY:	14 days
		ELEVATION:	5500 feet

13 Jones Fork
Riverton • lat 38°51'00" lon 120°22'45"

DESCRIPTION: This CG is set at the south end of the Union Valley Bike Trail, situated in a pine forest. Fishing opportunities in area lakes. Check for local regulations. Watch for deer and bears in the area. Popular mountain biking area. Several hiking and horse trails are also accessible nearby.

GETTING THERE: Jones Fork CG is located approx. 13 mi. N of Riverton on primary forest route 3.

SINGLE RATE:	$5	OPEN DATES:	May-Nov
# of SINGLE SITES:	10	MAX SPUR:	50 feet
		MAX STAY:	14 days
		ELEVATION:	4900 feet

14 Kirkwood
Woodfords • lat 38°42'00" lon 120°05'00"

DESCRIPTION: This CG is set on the shores of Kirkwood Lake, situated in a mixed conifer forest. Fishing opportunities in lake. Check for local regulations. Watch for deer and bears in the area. Numerous trails nearby. Short spurs. No trailers allowed. Narrow, winding road; use caution.

GETTING THERE: Kirkwood CG is located approx. 19 mi. W of Woodfords on state HWY 89 (Carson Pass National Scenic Byway). No trailers or motorboats.

SINGLE RATE:	$10	OPEN DATES:	June-Oct
# of SINGLE SITES:	12	MAX SPUR:	50 feet
		MAX STAY:	14 days
		ELEVATION:	7600 feet

15 Loon Lake
Riverton • lat 38°58'53" lon 120°19'17"

DESCRIPTION: This CG is set on the shores of Loon Lake in the Crystal Basin, situated in a mixed pine forest. Fishing opportunities in lake. Check for local regulations. Watch for deer and bears in the area. Adjacent access into the Desolation Wilderness Area. Numerous trails available nearby.

GETTING THERE: From Riverton go N on primary forest route 3 (Ice House Road) approx. 30 mi. to Loon Lake CG.

SINGLE RATE:	$13	OPEN DATES:	May-Oct
# of SINGLE SITES:	77	MAX SPUR:	50 feet
GROUP RATE:	Varies	MAX STAY:	14 days
# of GROUP SITES:	21	ELEVATION:	6378 feet

16 Loon Lake Boat Ramp
Riverton • lat 38°58'53" lon 120°19'17"

DESCRIPTION: CG is located in pines on Loon Lake in the Crystal Basin. Fishing in lake. Deer and bears in area. Adjacent to the Desolation Wilderness Area. Trails in area.

GETTING THERE: From Riverton go N on primary forest route 3 (Ice House Road) approx. 30 mi. to Loon Lake Boat Ramp CG.

SINGLE RATE:	$13	OPEN DATES:	May-Oct
# of SINGLE SITES:	15	MAX SPUR:	30 feet
		MAX STAY:	14 days
		ELEVATION:	6378 feet

17 Loon Lake Equestrian
Riverton • lat 38°58'53" lon 120°19'17"

DESCRIPTION: CG is located in pines on Loon Lake in the Crystal Basin. Fishing in lake. Deer and bears in area. Adjacent to the Desolation Wilderness Area. Trails in area.

GETTING THERE: From Riverton go N on primary forest route 3 (Ice House Road) approx. 30 mi. to Loon Lake Equestrian CG.

SINGLE RATE:	$13	OPEN DATES:	May-Oct
# of SINGLE SITES:	9	MAX SPUR:	50 feet
GROUP RATE:	$50	MAX STAY:	14 days
# of GROUP SITES:	5	ELEVATION:	6378 feet

18 Loon Lake Group #1
Riverton • lat 38°59'00" lon 120°20'00"

DESCRIPTION: This CG is set on the shores of Loon Lake in the Crystal Basin, situated in a mixed pine forest. Fishing opportunities in lake. Check for local regulations. Watch for deer and bears in the area. Adjacent access into the Desolation Wilderness Area. Numerous trails available nearby.

GETTING THERE: From Riverton go N on primary forest route 3 (Ice House Road) approx. 30 mi. to forest route 13N18. Go NE on 13N18 approx. 1 mi. to Loon Lake Group #1 CG.

		OPEN DATES:	Yearlong
		MAX SPUR:	20 feet
GROUP RATE:	$75	MAX STAY:	14 days
# of GROUP SITES:	1	ELEVATION:	6500 feet

19 Loon Lake Group #2
Riverton • lat 38°59'00" lon 120°20'00"

DESCRIPTION: CG is located in pines on Loon Lake in the Crystal Basin. Fishing in lake. Deer and bears in area. Adjacent to the Desolation Wilderness Area. Trails in area.

GETTING THERE: From Riverton go N on primary forest route 3 (Ice House Road) approx. 30 mi. to Loon Lake Group #2 CG.

		OPEN DATES:	Yearlong
		MAX SPUR:	40 feet
GROUP RATE:	$50	MAX STAY:	14 days
# of GROUP SITES:	1	ELEVATION:	6500 feet

20 Lovers Leap
Twin Bridges • lat 38°47'59" lon 120°08'22"

DESCRIPTION: All walk-in sites at this CG, no RV or trailer camping. A primitive setting, with no services and no drinking water on site. Campers may gather dead and down firewood. Groceries and a cafe are available at Strawberry Lodge. Picnic areas offered. Historic Lincoln Highway is nearby.

GETTING THERE: Lovers Leap CG is located approx. 2 mi. W of Twin Bridges on I-50. Not suitable for trailers.

SINGLE RATE:	No fee	OPEN DATES:	May-Oct
# of SINGLE SITES:	21	MAX SPUR:	50 feet
		MAX STAY:	14 days
		ELEVATION:	5800 feet

 Campground has hosts   **Reservable sites**   **Accessible facilities**   **Fully developed**   **Semi-developed**   **Rustic facilities**

NOTE: Open dates listed are typical. Actual dates are dependent on conditions such as snow pack.

21 Lumberyard
Allen Camp • lat 38°32'54" lon 120°18'25"

DESCRIPTION: This CG is set on the banks of upper East Panther Creek, situated in a beautiful mixed conifer forest. Wildlife in the area includes deer, birds, and bears. No drinking water available on site. Various hiking trails nearby. Supplies are available 8 mi. away at Allen Camp.

GETTING THERE: Lumberyard CG is located approx. 8 mi. S of Allen Camp on state HWY 88.

SINGLE RATE:	No fee	OPEN DATES:	Yearlong
# of SINGLE SITES:	5	MAX SPUR:	25 feet
		MAX STAY:	14 days
		ELEVATION:	6200 feet

22 Middle Fork Cosumnes
Allen Camp • lat 38°34'30" lon 120°17'30"

DESCRIPTION: This CG is set on the banks of the Middle Fork Cosumnes Creek, situated in a mixed conifer forest. Fishing opportunities in creek. Check for local regulations. Numerous hiking trails nearby. Watch for deer and bears in the area. Supplies are available 11 mi. away at Allen Camp.

GETTING THERE: From Allen Camp go S on state HWY 88 approx. 7 mi. to forest route 8N23. Go N on 8N23 approx. 4 mi. to Middle Fork Cosumnes CG.

SINGLE RATE:	$13	OPEN DATES:	June-Nov
# of SINGLE SITES:	5	MAX SPUR:	50 feet
		MAX STAY:	14 days
		ELEVATION:	6780 feet

23 Middle Meadows
Foresthill • lat 39°03'04" lon 120°27'58"

DESCRIPTION: This CG is set on the banks of the South Fork Long Canyon Creek, situated in a mixed pine forest. Fishing opportunities in creek. Check for local regulations. Numerous hiking trails available nearby. Watch for deer and bears in the area. Supplies are available 38 mi. away at Foresthill.

GETTING THERE: From Foresthill go E on primary forest route 96 approx. 30 mi. to primary forest route 22. Go S then NE on 22 approx. 8 mi. to Middle Meadows CG.

		OPEN DATES:	May-Sept
GROUP RATE:	Varies	MAX STAY:	14 days
# of GROUP SITES:	2	ELEVATION:	5000 feet

24 Mokelumne River
Allen Camp • lat 38°28'41" lon 120°16'10"

DESCRIPTION: This CG is set along the banks of the Mokelumne River, situated in a mixed conifer forest. Fishing opportunities in river. Please check for local regulations. Good swimming holes nearby. Watch for deer and bears in the area. Numerous hiking trails are available nearby.

GETTING THERE: From Allen Camp go S on state HWY 88 8 mi. to primary forest route 92 (Ellis Road). Go S on 92 7 mi. to forest route 8N50. Go SE on 8N50 3 mi. to Mokelumne River CG.

SINGLE RATE:	No fee	OPEN DATES:	Yearlong
# of SINGLE SITES:	8	MAX SPUR:	50 feet
		MAX STAY:	14 days
		ELEVATION:	3200 feet

25 Moore Creek
Allen Camp • lat 38°28'47" lon 120°15'57"

DESCRIPTION: This CG is set along the banks of the Mokelumne River, situated in a mixed conifer forest. Fishing opportunities in river. Please check for local regulations. Good swimming holes nearby. Watch for deer and bears in the area. Numerous hiking trails are available nearby.

GETTING THERE: From Allen Camp go S on state HWY 88 8 mi. to primary forest route 92 (Ellis Road). Go S on 92 7 mi. to forest route 8N50. Go SE on 8N50 3.5 mi. to Moore Creek CG.

SINGLE RATE:	No fee	OPEN DATES:	Yearlong
# of SINGLE SITES:	8	MAX SPUR:	50 feet
		MAX STAY:	14 days
		ELEVATION:	3200 feet

26 Northshore RV
Riverton • lat 39°00'00" lon 120°18'15"

DESCRIPTION: This CG is situated on the shores of Loon Lake in the Crystal Basin, situated in mixed pine forest. Fishing opportunities in lake. Watch for deer and bears in the area. Adjacent access into the Desolation Wilderness Area. Trails in area. No drinking water available on site.

GETTING THERE: From Riverton go N on primary forest route 3 (Ice House Road) approx. 30 mi. to forest route 13N18. Go NE on 13N18 approx. 3 mi. to Northshore RV CG.

SINGLE RATE:	$5	OPEN DATES:	June-Sept
# of SINGLE SITES:	15	MAX SPUR:	50 feet
		MAX STAY:	14 days
		ELEVATION:	6378 feet

27 Northwind
Twin Bridges • lat 38°49'00" lon 120°21'00"

DESCRIPTION: This CG is set on the north shore of Ice House Reservoir, situated in a mixed pine forest. Watch for deer, various birds, and bears in the area. Supplies are available 17 mi. away at Twin Bridges. Access to numerous mountain bike trails. No drinking water available on site.

GETTING THERE: From Twin Bridges go W on I-50 approx. 6 mi. to primary forest route 4. Go N on 4 approx. 6 mi. to primary forest route 32. Go NW on 32 approx. 7 mi. to Northwind CG.

SINGLE RATE:	$5	OPEN DATES:	May-Nov
# of SINGLE SITES:	10	MAX SPUR:	50 feet
		MAX STAY:	14 days
		ELEVATION:	5500 feet

28 Pardoes Point
Allen Camp • lat 38°32'30" lon 120°14'45"

DESCRIPTION: This CG is situated among mixed conifer on Lower Bears River Reservoir. Good fishing opportunities in lake. Check for local regulations. Supplies are available at a store located on the north side of reservoir. Watch for deer and bears in the area. Numerous trails can be found nearby.

GETTING THERE: From Allen Camp go S on state HWY 88 approx. 6 mi. to primary forest route 08. Go SE on 08 approx. 3.5 mi. to Pardoes Point CG.

SINGLE RATE:	$8	OPEN DATES:	June-Nov
# of SINGLE SITES:	10	MAX SPUR:	50 feet
		MAX STAY:	14 days
		ELEVATION:	6000 feet

29 PiPi
Pollock Pines • lat 38°34'00" lon 120°26'00"

DESCRIPTION: This CG is set on the banks of Middle Fork Cosumnes Creek, situated in a mixed conifer forest. Fishing opportunities in creek. Please check for local fishing regulations. Barrier free interpretive trail and fishing dock available on site. Watch for deer and bears in the area.

GETTING THERE: From Pollock Pines go S then E on forest route 5 to forest route 51 (Bonetti Road). Go SE 13 mi. to primary forest route 6 (North South Road). Go S 11 mi. to PiPi CG.

SINGLE RATE:	$10	OPEN DATES:	Apr-Nov
# of SINGLE SITES:	51	MAX SPUR:	50 feet
		MAX STAY:	14 days
		ELEVATION:	4100 feet

30 Pleasant
Riverton • lat 39°00'52" lon 120°17'31"

DESCRIPTION: This CG is set on the shores of Loon Lake, situated in a mixed conifer forest. Accessible by boat or trail only. Pack it in/pack it out. Fishing opportunities in lake. Check for local regulations. Watch for deer and bears in the area. Numerous trails can be found nearby.

GETTING THERE: Pleasant CG is located on the N shore of Loon Lake and is accessible by boat or trail only.

SINGLE RATE:	No fee	OPEN DATES:	May-Sept
# of SINGLE SITES:	10		
		MAX STAY:	14 days
		ELEVATION:	6500 feet

 Campground has hosts   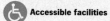 **Reservable sites**   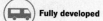 **Accessible facilities**   **Fully developed**   **Semi-developed**   **Rustic facilities**

NOTE: Open dates listed are typical. Actual dates are dependent on conditions such as snow pack.

ELDORADO NATIONAL FOREST • CALIFORNIA • 21 — 30

31 Red Fir
Riverton • lat 39°00'00" lon 120°18'15"

DESCRIPTION: This CG is set on the shores of Loon Lake in the Crystal Basin, situated in a mixed conifer forst. Fishing opportunities in lake. Check for local regulations. Watch for deer and bears in the area. Adjacent access into the Desolation Wilderness Area. Numerous trails nearby.

GETTING THERE: From Riverton go N on primary forest route 3 (Ice House Road) approx. 30 mi. to forest route 13N18. Go NE on 13N18 approx. 3 mi. to Red Fir CG.

		OPEN DATES:	June-Sept
GROUP RATE:	$35	MAX STAY:	14 days
# of GROUP SITES:	1	ELEVATION:	6500 feet

32 Sand Flat
Kyburz • lat 38°45'45" lon 120°19'38"

DESCRIPTION: This CG is set on the banks of the South Fork American river, situated in a mixed pine forest. Fishing in river. Check for local regulations. Watch for deer and bears in the area. Supplies are available approx. 2 mi. away at Kyburz. Numerous hiking trails can be found nearby.

GETTING THERE: Sand Flat CG is located approx. 2 mi. W of Kyburz on I-50.

		OPEN DATES:	Apr-Nov
SINGLE RATE:	$11	MAX SPUR:	80 feet
# of SINGLE SITES:	29	MAX STAY:	14 days
		ELEVATION:	3900 feet

33 Silver Creek
Riverton • lat 38°48'58" lon 120°22'47"

DESCRIPTION: This CG is set on the banks of Silver Creek, situated in a mixed pine forest. Good fishing opportunities in creek. Please check for local fishing regulations. No drinking water available on site. Watch for deer and bears in the area. Numerous hiking trails can be found nearby.

GETTING THERE: From Riverton go N on primary forest route 3 (Ice House Road) approx. 7.5 mi. to Silver Creek CG. No trailers.

		OPEN DATES:	May-Oct
SINGLE RATE:	$6	MAX SPUR:	25 feet
# of SINGLE SITES:	11	MAX STAY:	14 days
		ELEVATION:	5200 feet

34 Silver Fork
Kyburz • lat 38°42'01" lon 120°12'24"

DESCRIPTION: This CG is set on the banks of the South Fork American River, situated in a mixed pine forest. Fishing opportunities in river. Check for local regulations. Watch for deer and bears in the area. Supplies are available approx. 8 mi. away at Kyburz. Several trails can be found nearby.

GETTING THERE: Silver Fork CG is located approx. 8 mi. S of Kyburz on Silver Fork Road.

		OPEN DATES:	May-Nov
SINGLE RATE:	$11	MAX SPUR:	65 feet
# of SINGLE SITES:	35	MAX STAY:	14 days
		ELEVATION:	5600 feet

35 Silver Lake East
Woodfords • lat 38°40'18" lon 120°07'03"

DESCRIPTION: This CG is set on the shore of Silver Lake, situated in a mixed conifer forest. Fishing opportunities in lake. Please check for local regulations. Watch for deer and bears in the area. Supplies are available at a store located nearby. Several trails can be found nearby.

GETTING THERE: Silver Lake East CG is located approx. 24 mi. W of Woodfords on state HWY 89 (Carson Pass National Scenic Byway).

		OPEN DATES:	June-Oct
SINGLE RATE:	$11	MAX SPUR:	50 feet
# of SINGLE SITES:	62	MAX STAY:	14 days
		ELEVATION:	7200 feet

36 Silver Lake West
Woodford • lat 38°40'18" lon 120°07'03"

DESCRIPTION: CG is located in conifer on Silver Lake. Fishing in lake. Deer and bears in area. Store located nearby. Trails in area.

GETTING THERE: From Woodford go W on state HWY 89 (Carson Pass National Scenic Byway) approximately 24 miles to Silver Lake West CG.

		OPEN DATES:	June-Oct
SINGLE RATE:	$15	MAX SPUR:	50 feet
# of SINGLE SITES:	35	MAX STAY:	14 days
		ELEVATION:	7200 feet

37 South Fork
Riverton • lat 38°56'56" lon 120°24'00"

DESCRIPTION: This CG is set on the banks of South Fork Rubicon Creek, situated in a mixed pine forest. Fishing opportunities in creek. Please check for local regulations. Watch for deer and bears in the area. Supplies are available 25 mi. away at Riverton. No drinking water available on site.

GETTING THERE: From Riverton go N on primary forest route 3 (Ice House Road) approx. 24 mi. to forest route 13N28. Go NW on 13N28 approx. 1 mi. to South Fork CG.

		OPEN DATES:	June-Oct
SINGLE RATE:	No fee	MAX SPUR:	45 feet
# of SINGLE SITES:	17	MAX STAY:	14 days
		ELEVATION:	5200 feet

38 South Shore
Allen Camp • lat 38°32'02" lon 120°14'33"

DESCRIPTION: This CG is set on the south side of Lower Bears River Reservoir, situated in a mixed conifer forest. Fishing opportunities in lake. Please check for local regulations. Watch for deer and bears. Supplies are available at a store on the north side of reservoir. Several trails nearby.

GETTING THERE: From Allen Camp go S on state HWY 88 approx. 6 mi. to primary forest route 08. Go SE on 08 approx. 4 mi. to South Shore CG.

		OPEN DATES:	June-Nov
SINGLE RATE:	$11	MAX SPUR:	50 feet
# of SINGLE SITES:	22	MAX STAY:	14 days
		ELEVATION:	5900 feet

39 Strawberry Point
Twin Bridges • lat 38°49'30" lon 120°20'30"

DESCRIPTION: This CG is set on the north shore of Ice House Reservoir, situated in a mixed pine forest. Fishing opportunities in lake. Please check for local regulations. Watch for deer and bears. Supplies are available 17 mi. away at Twin Bridges. Access to bike trails. No drinking water.

GETTING THERE: From Twin Bridges go W on I-50 approx. 6 mi. to primary forest route 4. Go N on 4 approx. 6 mi. to primary forest route 32. Go NW on 32 approx. 7 mi. to Strawberry Point CG.

		OPEN DATES:	May-Nov
SINGLE RATE:	$5	MAX SPUR:	50 feet
# of SINGLE SITES:	10	MAX STAY:	14 days
		ELEVATION:	5500 feet

40 Stumpy Meadows
Georgetown • lat 38°54'13" lon 120°35'27"

DESCRIPTION: This CG is set on Stumpy Meadows Lake, situated in a mixed conifer forest. Fishing opportunities in lake. Please check for local regulations. Watch for deer and bears. Some space for self-contained vehicles provided. Supplies are available at Georgetown. Access to bike trails. No drinking water.

GETTING THERE: Stumpy Meadows CG is located approx. 18 mi. E of Georgetown on county route 63.

		OPEN DATES:	Apr-Nov
SINGLE RATE:	$10	MAX SPUR:	50 feet
# of SINGLE SITES:	40	MAX STAY:	14 days
GROUP RATE:	$20	ELEVATION:	4400 feet

 Campground has hosts   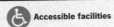 **Reservable sites**   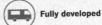 **Accessible facilities**   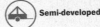 **Fully developed**   **Semi-developed**   **Rustic facilities**

NOTE: Open dates listed are typical. Actual dates are dependent on conditions such as snow pack.

41 Sugar Pine Point
Allen Camp • lat 38°32'30" lon 120°14'45"

DESCRIPTION: This CG is set on the noth side of Lower Bears River Reservoir, situated in a mixed conifer forest. Fishing in lake. Please check for local regulations. Watch for deer and bears. Supplies are available at a store located to the west on north side of reservoir. Access to various trails.

GETTING THERE: From Allen Camp go S on state HWY 88 approx. 4.5 mi. to forest route 8N18. Go E approx. 3 mi. to 8N21. Go S approx. 1 mi. to 8N20. Go S approx. 1.5 mi. to Sugar Pine Point CG.

SINGLE RATE:	$8	OPEN DATES:	June-Nov
# of SINGLE SITES:	10	MAX SPUR:	25 feet
		MAX STAY:	14 days
		ELEVATION:	6000 feet

42 Sunset
Riverton • lat 38°51'57" lon 120°24'14"

DESCRIPTION: This CG is set on the Union Valley Reservoir, situated in a mixed conifer forest. Fishing opportunities in lake. Please check for local regulations. Watch for deer and bears. Supplies are available 5 mi. away at a nearby store/cafe. Access to mountain bike and hiking trails nearby.

GETTING THERE: From Riverton go N on primary forest route 3 (Ice House Road) approx. 14 mi. to forest route 12N35. Go W on 12N35 approx. 1.5 mi. to Sunset CG.

SINGLE RATE:	$13	OPEN DATES:	May-Oct
# of SINGLE SITES:	131	MAX SPUR:	50 feet
GROUP RATE:	$26	MAX STAY:	14 days
		ELEVATION:	4900 feet

43 Upper Hell Hole
Foresthill • lat 39°03'57" lon 120°25'03"

DESCRIPTION: This CG is set on Upper Hell Hole Reservoir, situated in a mixed pine forest. Accessible by boat or trail only. Pack it in, pack it out. Watch for deer and bears in the area. Stream or lake water only; no drinking water available on site. Campfire permits required.

GETTING THERE: Upper Hell Hole CG is located on the E side of Hell Hole Reservoir and is accessible by boat or trail only.

SINGLE RATE:	No fee	OPEN DATES:	May-Sept
# of SINGLE SITES:	15		
		MAX STAY:	14 days
		ELEVATION:	4600 feet

44 Wench Creek
Riverton • lat 38°53'25" lon 120°22'38"

DESCRIPTION: This CG is set on the east shore of Union Valley Reservoir in the Crystal Basin, situated in a mixed pine forest. Fishing in lake. Please check for local regulations. Watch for deer and bears in the area. Supplies are available at a nearby store. Access to mountain bike trails nearby.

GETTING THERE: From Riverton go N on primary forest route 3 (Ice House Road) approx. 16 mi. to Wench Creek CG.

SINGLE RATE:	$13	OPEN DATES:	May-Oct
# of SINGLE SITES:	100	MAX SPUR:	55 feet
GROUP RATE:	$60	MAX STAY:	14 days
# of GROUP SITES:	2	ELEVATION:	4900 feet

45 Wentworth Springs
Riverton • lat 39°00'44" lon 120°19'28"

DESCRIPTION: This CG is situated in a mixed pine forest, located approx. 1 mi. north of Loon Lake in the Crystal Basin. Fishing opportunities in Wentworth Creek and Loon Lake. Check for local regulations. Watch for deer and bears in the area. Supplies are available 35 mi. away at Riverton.

GETTING THERE: From Riverton go N on primary forest route 3 (Ice House Road) 25 mi. to primary forest route 33 (Wentworth Springs Road). Continue N 10 mi. to Wentworth Springs CG. 4WD recommended.

SINGLE RATE:	No fee	OPEN DATES:	June-Nov
# of SINGLE SITES:	8	MAX SPUR:	50 feet
		MAX STAY:	14 days
		ELEVATION:	6000 feet

46 White Azalea
Allen Camp • lat 38°29'08" lon 120°15'38"

DESCRIPTION: This CG is set on the Mokelumne River, situated in a mixed conifer forest. Fishing opportunities in river. Please check for local regulations. Good swimming holes nearby. Watch for deer and bears in the area. Supplies are available at Allen Camp. No drinking water available.

GETTING THERE: From Allen Camp go S on state HWY 88 8 mi. to primary forest route 92 (Ellis Road). Go S 7 mi. to forest route 8N50. Go SE 4 mi. to White Azalea CG.

SINGLE RATE:	No fee	OPEN DATES:	Yearlong
# of SINGLE SITES:	6	MAX SPUR:	50 feet
		MAX STAY:	14 days
		ELEVATION:	3500 feet

47 Wolf Creek
Riverton • lat 38°53'00" lon 120°24'00"

DESCRIPTION: This CG is set on the north shore of Union Valley Reservoir in the Crystal Basin, situated in a mixed pine forest. Good fishing opportunities in lake. Please check for local regulations. Watch for deer and bears in the area. Supplies are available at a nearby store/cafe.

GETTING THERE: From Riverton go N on primary forest route 3 (Ice House Road) approx. 21 mi. to forest route 12N78. Go SW on 12N78 approx. 2 mi. to Wolf Creek CG.

SINGLE RATE:	$13	OPEN DATES:	May-Oct
# of SINGLE SITES:	42	MAX SPUR:	50 feet
GROUP RATE:	$26	MAX STAY:	14 days
		ELEVATION:	4900 feet

48 Woods Lake
Woodfords • lat 38°41'10" lon 120°00'36"

DESCRIPTION: This CG is set on Woods Lake, situated in a mixed conifer forest. Good fishing opportunities in lake. Check for local regulations. No motorboats allowed. Watch for deer and bears in the area. Supplies are available at Woodfords. Numerous hiking and mountain bike trails can be accessed nearby.

GETTING THERE: Woods Lake CG is located approx. 13 mi. W of Woodfords on state HWY 88.

SINGLE RATE:	$10	OPEN DATES:	July-Oct
# of SINGLE SITES:	25	MAX SPUR:	50 feet
		MAX STAY:	14 days
		ELEVATION:	8200 feet

49 Wrights Lake
Twin Bridges • lat 38°50'34" lon 120°13'54"

DESCRIPTION: This CG is set on Wrights Lake in the Crystal Basin, situated in a mixed pine forest. Good fishing opportunities in lake. Check for local regulations. Watch for deer and bears in the area. Supplies are available 14 mi. away at Twin Bridges. Numerous hiking trails can be accessed nearby.

GETTING THERE: From Twin Bridges go W on I-50 approx. 6 mi. to primary forest route 4. Go N on 4 approx. 8 mi. to Wrights Lake CG.

SINGLE RATE:	$12	OPEN DATES:	June-Oct
# of SINGLE SITES:	82	MAX SPUR:	50 feet
		MAX STAY:	14 days
		ELEVATION:	7000 feet

50 Wrights Lake Equestrian
Twin Bridges • lat 38°50'34" lon 120°13'54"

DESCRIPTION: CG is located in pines on Wrights Lake in the Crystal Basin. Fishing in lake. Deer and bears in area. 14 mi. to Twin Bridges for supplies.

GETTING THERE: From Twin Bridges go W on I-50 approx. 6 mi. to primary forest route 4. Go N on 4 approx. 8 mi. to Wrights Lake Equestrian CG.

SINGLE RATE:	$12	OPEN DATES:	June-Oct
# of SINGLE SITES:	15	MAX SPUR:	20 feet
		MAX STAY:	14 days
		ELEVATION:	7000 feet

 Campground has hosts   **Reservable sites**   **Accessible facilities**   **Fully developed**   **Semi-developed** **Rustic facilities**

NOTE: Open dates listed are typical. Actual dates are dependent on conditions such as snow pack.

51 **Yellowjacket**
Riverton • lat 38°54'00" lon 120°23'00"

DESCRIPTION: This CG is set on the north shore of Union Valley Reservoir in the Crystal Basin, situated in a mixed pine forest. Good fishing opportunities in lake. Check for local regulations. Watch for deer and bears in the area. Supplies are available at a nearby store and cafe. Mountain bike trails nearby.

GETTING THERE: From Riverton go N on primary forest route 3 (Ice House Road) approx. 21 mi. to forest route 12N78. Go SW on 12N78 approx. 1 mi. to Yellowjacket CG.

SINGLE RATE:	$13	**OPEN DATES:**	**May-Oct**
# of SINGLE SITES:	40	**MAX SPUR:**	**45 feet**
		MAX STAY:	**14 days**
		ELEVATION:	**4900 feet**

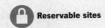 **Campground has hosts**   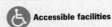 **Reservable sites**   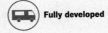 **Accessible facilities**   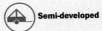 **Fully developed**   **Semi-developed**   **Rustic facilities**

NOTE: Open dates listed are typical. Actual dates are dependent on conditions such as snow pack.

Page 68

USFS Photo

INYO NATIONAL FOREST

The Inyo National Forest is a unique and special area of public land located along the eastern edge of California and the Sierra Nevada. Extending 165 miles along the California/Nevada border between Los Angeles and Reno, the Inyo National Forest includes 1.9 million acres of pristine lakes, fragile meadows, winding streams, rugged Sierra Nevada peaks, and arid Great Basin Mountains. With elevations ranging from 4,000 to 14,495 feet, the Inyo is home to the tallest peak in the lower 48 states, Mt. Whitney (14,495 feet) and is adjacent to the lowest point in North America (Death Valley National Park).

The Inyo provides a variety of recreational opportunities. Camping and fishing attracts thousands of visitors during the summer months. Anglers can try their luck fishing at more than 400 lakes and 1,100 miles of streams that provide habitat for several species of trout.

Mammoth Mountain Ski Area becomes a summer mecca for mountain bike enthusiasts as they ride the challenging Kamakazi trail from the top of Mammoth Mountain. Thirty-one trailheads provide access to wilderness for hikers seeking to escape into the forest's pristine areas.

INYO NATIONAL FOREST • CALIFORNIA • LOCATOR MAP

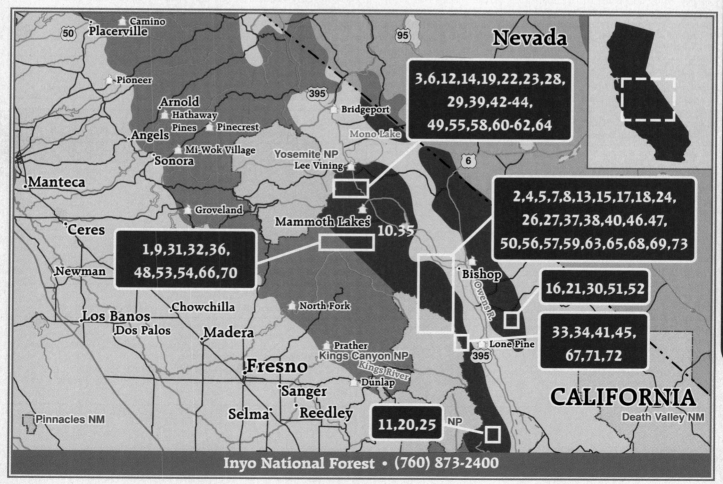

Inyo National Forest • (760) 873-2400

1 Agnew Meadow
Mammoth Lakes • lat 37°40′56″ lon 119°05′22″

DESCRIPTION: This CG rests in mixed pine and hemlock near the Middle Fork of San Joaquin River. Enjoy fishing for trout. Wildlife in this area includes black bears, mtn lion, coyotes, deer, redtail hawks, and bald eagle. CG is busy fall summer. Visit nearby Rainbow Falls and Devils Postpile National Monument.

GETTING THERE: From Mammoth Lakes go NW on state HWY 203 approx. 6.5 mi. to forest route 3S11. Go W on 3S11 approx. 3 mi. to Agnew Meadow CG.

SINGLE RATE:	$12	OPEN DATES:	June-Sept
# of SINGLE SITES:	21	MAX SPUR:	55 feet
GROUP RATE:	Varies	MAX STAY:	14 days
# of GROUP SITES:	4	ELEVATION:	8400 feet

2 Aspen Group
Bishop • lat 37°31′21″ lon 118°42′36″

DESCRIPTION: This open CG rests in a lodgepole pine and aspen forest. Rock Creek runs next to the CG with trout fishing. Supplies are 3-6 mi. away. Campers may gather firewood or purchase nearby. Enjoy hiking in nearby John Muir Wilderness. This CG is frequented by bears.

GETTING THERE: From Bishop go NW on US HWY 395 approx. 23.5 mi. to primary forest route 12. Go S on 12 approx. 3 mi. to Aspen CG. Road is narrow with sharp curves. Large vehicles should use caution.

		OPEN DATES:	May-Oct
		MAX SPUR:	30 feet
GROUP RATE:	$40	MAX STAY:	7 days
# of GROUP SITES:	1	ELEVATION:	8100 feet

3 Big Bend
Lee Vining • lat 37°56′44″ lon 119°12′08″

DESCRIPTION: In a mixed forest setting off of Lee Vining Creek. Fish and swim from the creek. Supplies are available at Lee Vining, approx. 5 mi. from CG. This is a wildlife viewing area, look for black bears, mtn lion, coyotes, deer, and birds. Campers may gather firewood. No designated trails nearby.

GETTING THERE: From Lee Vining go W on state HWY 120 (Vining Canyon Nat'l Scenic Byway). Go W on 120 approx. 4 mi. to forest route 1N21. Go W on 1N21 approx. 1.5 mi. to Big Bend CG.

SINGLE RATE:	$11	OPEN DATES:	Apr-Oct
# of SINGLE SITES:	17	MAX SPUR:	20 feet
		MAX STAY:	14 days
		ELEVATION:	7800 feet

4 Big Meadow
Mammoth Lakes • lat 37°30′37″ lon 118°42′47″

DESCRIPTION: CG is in a park-like setting with a creek running along the CG. Supplies are 3-5 mi. away. CG may be frequented by bears.

GETTING THERE: From Mammoth Lakes go NW on HWY 203 approx. 6.5 mi. to forest route 3S11. Go W on 3S11 approx. 4 mi. to Big Meadow CG. Road is narrow with sharp curves. Large RVs may have problems.

SINGLE RATE:	$13	OPEN DATES:	May-Sept
# of SINGLE SITES:	11	MAX SPUR:	28 feet
		MAX STAY:	7 days
		ELEVATION:	8600 feet

5 Big Pine Creek
Big Pine • lat 37°07′20″ lon 118°26′15″

DESCRIPTION: This CG is situated in a mixed forest set in a narrow canyon. A stream runs through the CG. Firewood is for sale on site. Fish for trout from the stream. Glacier Lodge and Store is outside the CG. Hike to glacier and lakes in nearby John Muir Wilderness. Frequented by bears.

GETTING THERE: Big Pine Creek CG is located approx. 10 mi. from Big Pine on forest route 9S21. Road is narrow with sharp curves. Large vehicles should use caution.

SINGLE RATE:	$11	OPEN DATES:	May-Oct
# of SINGLE SITES:	36	MAX SPUR:	25 feet
		MAX STAY:	14 days
		ELEVATION:	7874 feet

6 Big Springs
Mammoth Lakes • lat 37°45′00″ lon 118°56′00″

DESCRIPTION: In a mixed forest setting with Deadman Creek nearby. Fish and swim from the creek. Visit nearby Inyo Crater Lakes. Supplies are available at Mammoth Lakes. Wildlife in the area includes black bears, mountain lion, coyotes, deer, and birds. Campers may gather firewood. Hike nearby to Glass Creek Meadow.

GETTING THERE: From Mammoth Lakes go N on forest route 3S23 (Mammoth Scenic Loop) approx. 5.5 mi. to US HWY 395. Go N on 395 approx. 1 mi. to forest route 2S07. Go NE on 2S07 approx. 2 mi. to Big Springs CG.

SINGLE RATE:	No fee	OPEN DATES:	Apr-Nov
# of SINGLE SITES:	26	MAX SPUR:	20 feet
		MAX STAY:	21 days
		ELEVATION:	7300 feet

7 Big Trees
Bishop • lat 37°15′53″ lon 118°34′38″

DESCRIPTION: This CG is located in large Jeffery Pine with open areas along the creek. Historical Cardinal Mine is nearby. Supplies are in Bishop. CG is frequented by bears.

GETTING THERE: From Bishop go SW on HWY 168 approx. 11 mi. to the forest route. Go S on forest route approx. 1 mi. to Big Trees CG. Road is narrow with sharp curves. Large vehicles should use caution.

SINGLE RATE:	$12	OPEN DATES:	Apr-Sept
# of SINGLE SITES:	9	MAX SPUR:	28 feet
		MAX STAY:	7 days
		ELEVATION:	7500 feet

8 Bishop Park
Bishop • lat 37°14′42″ lon 118°35′31″

DESCRIPTION: CG is in a forested setting adjacent to Bishop Creek. Fish in a stocked trout stream. Supplies at Bishop. Firewood for sale at the site. Deer and birds are in the area. This CG is frequented by bears. Enjoy hiking in nearby John Muir Wilderness.

GETTING THERE: From Bishop go SW on state HWY 168 approx. 13 mi. to Bishop Park CG. Road is narrow with sharp curves. Large vehicles should use caution.

SINGLE RATE:	$12	OPEN DATES:	Apr-Oct
# of SINGLE SITES:	21	MAX SPUR:	22 feet
GROUP RATE:	$42	MAX STAY:	7 days
# of GROUP SITES:	1	ELEVATION:	8400 feet

9 Coldwater
Mammoth Lakes • lat 37°35′30″ lon 118°58′00″

DESCRIPTION: This CG is situated in mixed pine and hemlock with mountain crest and lake views. Enjoy fishing in nearby Lake Mary. Wildlife includes black bears, mountain lion, coyotes, deer, redtail hawks, and baldeagles. CG is busy all summer. Visit nearby Rainbow Falls and Devils Postpile National Monument.

GETTING THERE: From Mammoth Lakes go S on primary forest route 10 (Lake Mary route) approx. 2 mi. to forest route 4S09. Go S on 4S09 1/2 mi. to forest route 4S25. Go S on 4S25 1/4 mi. to Coldwater CG.

SINGLE RATE:	$13	OPEN DATES:	June-Sept
# of SINGLE SITES:	77	MAX SPUR:	45 feet
		MAX STAY:	14 days
		ELEVATION:	8900 feet

10 Convict Lake
Mammoth Lakes • lat 37°35′19″ lon 118°51′28″

DESCRIPTION: This CG is located in mixed pine and hemlock near Convict Lake. Boat launch available. Wildlife in this area includes black bears, mountain lion, coyotes, deer, redtail hawks, and baldeagles. CG is busy all summer. Hike the Convict Lake Trail which leads to high alpine lakes. RV dump station on site.

GETTING THERE: From Mammoth Lakes, go E on HWY 203 approx. 2.5 mi. to US HWY 395. Go E on 395 approx. 4 mi. to primary forest route 7. Go S on 7 approx. 2 mi. to Convict Lake CG.

SINGLE RATE:	$10	OPEN DATES:	Apr-Nov
# of SINGLE SITES:	88	MAX SPUR:	55 feet
		MAX STAY:	7 days
		ELEVATION:	7600 feet

 Campground has hosts   **Reservable sites**   **Accessible facilities**   **Fully developed**   Semi-developed   Rustic facilities

NOTE: Open dates listed are typical. Actual dates are dependent on conditions such as snow pack.

11 Cottonwood Lakes Backpacker
Lone Pine Indian Reservation • lat 36˚27'30" lon 118˚10'00"

DESCRIPTION: CG is situated in a mixed forest near Cottonwood Creek with views of Horseshow Meadow. Fish or swim in the creek. Supplies available at Lone Pine Indian Reservation. Deer and birds in the area. Campers may gather firewood. The Cottonwood Pass Trail is nearby. Walk-in sites.

GETTING THERE: From the Lone Pine Indian Reservation go W approx. 3 mi. on the Whitney Portal route to state HWY 190. Go S on 190 approx. 17 mi. to Cottonwood Lakes Backpacker CG.

SINGLE RATE:	$6	OPEN DATES:	May-Oct
# of SINGLE SITES:	12		
		MAX STAY:	14 days
		ELEVATION:	10000 feet

16 Fossil Group
Big Pine • lat 37˚16'45" lon 118˚08'39"

DESCRIPTION: This remote, tent only CG is in a forested setting with a creek nearby. Fish or play in the creek. Historic Toll House Site is within 5 mi. of CG. Supplies available at Big Pine. Deer, bears and birds are common. Campers may gather firewood. No running water or garbage service.

GETTING THERE: From Big Pine go NE on state HWY 168 approx. 11 mi. to Fossil CG. Road is narrow with sharp curves. Large vehicles should use caution.

		MAX SPUR:	28 feet
		OPEN DATES:	Yearlong
GROUP RATE:	$20	MAX STAY:	14 days
# of GROUP SITES:	1	ELEVATION:	7200 feet

12 Deadman
Mammoth Lakes • lat 37˚42'00" lon 119˚01'00"

DESCRIPTION: In a mixed forest setting on Deadman Creek. Fish and swim from the creek. Visit nearby Inyo Crater Lakes. Supplies are available at Mammoth Lakes. Wildlife in the area includes black bears, mountain lion, coyotes, deer, and birds. Campers may gather firewood. Hike nearby to Glass Creek Meadow. No water.

GETTING THERE: From Mammoth Lakes go N on HWY 203 approx. 1 mi. to forest route 3S23. Go N on 3S23 (Mammoth Scenic Loop) approx. 4 mi. to forest route 2S29. Go NW on forest route 2S29 3 mi. to Deadman CG.

SINGLE RATE:	No fee	OPEN DATES:	Apr-Nov
# of SINGLE SITES:	26	MAX SPUR:	20 feet
		MAX STAY:	21 days
		ELEVATION:	7800 feet

17 Four Jeffrey
Bishop • lat 37˚14'55" lon 118˚34'10"

DESCRIPTION: This CG is in a forested setting adjacent to Bishop Creek with views of Table Mountain. Fish from a stocked trout stream and swim in the creek. Supplies at Bishop. Firewood for sale on site. Enjoy hiking in nearby John Muir Wilderness. This CG is frequented by bears. Other wildlife includes deer.

GETTING THERE: From Bishop go SW on state HWY 168 approx. 11.5 mi. to Four Jeffrey CG. Road is narrow with sharp curves. Large vehicles should use caution.

SINGLE RATE:	$12	OPEN DATES:	Apr-Oct
# of SINGLE SITES:	106	MAX SPUR:	28 feet
		MAX STAY:	14 days
		ELEVATION:	8100 feet

13 East Fork
Bishop • lat 37˚29'01" lon 118˚43'03"

DESCRIPTION: CG is in a lodgepole pine and aspen forest setting on Rock Creek and near Crowley Lake. Trout fishing from the creek. Supplies are available at Bishop. Campers may gather firewood or purchase close by. Enjoy hiking in nearby John Muir Wilderness. CG is frequented by bears.

GETTING THERE: From Bishop go NW on US HWY 395 approx. 23.5 mi. to primary forest route 12. Go S on 12 approx. 7 mi. to East Fork CG. Road is narrow with sharp curves. Large vehicles should use caution.

SINGLE RATE:	$12	OPEN DATES:	May-Oct
# of SINGLE SITES:	133	MAX SPUR:	40 feet
		MAX STAY:	14 days
		ELEVATION:	9000 feet

18 French Camp
Bishop • lat 37˚33'00" lon 118˚42'00"

DESCRIPTION: CG is in a forested setting on Rock Creek and close to Lake Crowley. Fish and swim in the creek or lake. Supplies are available at Bishop. Deer and birds are common to the area. Campers may gather firewood. There are hiking and horseback riding trails in the area. This CG is frequented by bears.

GETTING THERE: From Bishop go NW on US HWY 395 approx. 24 mi. to primary forest route 12. Go S on 12 approx. 1/2 mi. to French Camp CG. Road is narrow with sharp curves. Large vehicles should use caution.

SINGLE RATE:	$12	OPEN DATES:	Apr-Oct
# of SINGLE SITES:	86	MAX SPUR:	40 feet
		MAX STAY:	21 days
		ELEVATION:	7500 feet

14 Ellery Lake
Lee Vining • lat 37˚56'15" lon 119˚14'19"

DESCRIPTION: In a mixed forest setting on Ellery Lake. Fish for trout and swim from the lake. Supplies are available at Lee Vining. Wildlife in the area includes black bears, mountain lion, coyotes, and deer. Campers may gather firewood. Near Mono Lake, Ansel Adams Wilderness and Harvey Monroe Hall Research Natural Area.

GETTING THERE: From Lee Vining go E on state HWY 120 (Vining Canyon Nat'l Scenic Byway) 8 mi. to Ellery Lake CG.

SINGLE RATE:	$11	OPEN DATES:	June-Oct
# of SINGLE SITES:	12	MAX SPUR:	20 feet
		MAX STAY:	14 days
		ELEVATION:	9500 feet

19 Glass Creek
Lee Vining • lat 37˚45'13" lon 118˚59'49"

DESCRIPTION: In a mixed forest setting near Glass Creek. Fish for trout and swim from the creek. Supplies are available at Lee Vining. Wildlife in the area includes black bears, mountain lion, coyotes, and deer. Campers may gather firewood. Hike to trailhead to Glass Creek Meadow nearby. Visit nearby Obsidian Dome. No water.

GETTING THERE: From Lee Vining to S on US HWY 395 approx. 16 mi. to Glass Creek CG.

SINGLE RATE:	No fee	OPEN DATES:	May-Nov
# of SINGLE SITES:	50	MAX SPUR:	20 feet
		MAX STAY:	21 days
		ELEVATION:	7600 feet

15 Forks
Bishop • lat 37˚15'23" lon 118˚34'39"

DESCRIPTION: This CG is in a forested setting adjacent to Bishop Creek with views of Table Mountain. Fish from a stocked trout stream and swim in the creek. Supplies at Bishop. Firewood for sale on site. Deer and birds are common. Enjoy hiking in John Muir Wilderness. CG is frequented by bears.

GETTING THERE: From Bishop go SW on state HWY 168 approx. 11 mi. to Forks CG. Road is narrow with sharp curves. Large vehicles should use caution.

SINGLE RATE:	$12	OPEN DATES:	Apr-Sept
# of SINGLE SITES:	8	MAX SPUR:	28 feet
		MAX STAY:	7 days
		ELEVATION:	7800 feet

20 Golden Trout
Lone Pine Indian Reservation • lat 36˚27'30" lon 118˚10'30"

DESCRIPTION: CG situated in a mixed forest near Cottonwood Creek with views of Horseshow Meadow. Fish or swim in the creek. Supplies available at Lone Pine Indian Reservation. Deer and birds in the area. Campers may gather firewood. The Cottonwood Pass Trail is nearby. Walk-in sites. Corrals at CG.

GETTING THERE: From the Lone Pine Indian Res. go W approx. 3 mi. on the Whitney Portal route to state HWY 190. Go S on 190 approx. 18 mi. to Golden Trout CG.

SINGLE RATE:	$6	OPEN DATES:	May-Oct*
# of SINGLE SITES:	18	MAX SPUR:	28 feet
		MAX STAY:	14 days
		ELEVATION:	10000 feet

 Campground has hosts **Reservable sites** **Accessible facilities** **Fully developed** **Semi-developed** **Rustic facilities**

NOTE: Open dates listed are typical. Actual dates are dependent on conditions such as snow pack.

21 Grandview
Big Pine • lat 37°20'00" lon 118°11'20"

DESCRIPTION: This remote CG is in a forested setting with a creek nearby. Fish or play in the creek. Historic Toll House Site is within 5 mi. of CG. Supplies available at Big Pine. Deer and birds are common. Campers may gather firewood. There is a trail to Grandview Mine/Quarry. No water or garbage removal.

GETTING THERE: From Big Pine go NE on HWY 168 approx. 11 mi. to primary forest route 01. Go N on 01 approx. 4 mi. to Grandview CG. Road is narrow with sharp curves. Large vehicles should use caution.

SINGLE RATE:	No fee	OPEN DATES:	Yearlong
# of SINGLE SITES:	26	MAX SPUR:	28 feet
		MAX STAY:	14 days
		ELEVATION:	8600 feet

26 Intake 2
Bishop • lat 37°14'43" lon 118°35'17"

DESCRIPTION: This CG is in a forested setting on a lake with views of Table Mountain. Fish for trout or swim in the lake. Supplies at Bishop. Firewood for sale at the site. Deer and birds are common. Enjoy hiking in nearby John Muir Wilderness. This CG is frequented by bears.

GETTING THERE: From Bishop go SW on state HWY 168 approx. 12.5 mi. to Intake 2 CG.

SINGLE RATE:	$12	OPEN DATES:	Apr-Oct
# of SINGLE SITES:	15	MAX SPUR:	28 feet
		MAX STAY:	7 days
		ELEVATION:	8200 feet

22 Gull Lake
Lee Vining • lat 37°46'23" lon 119°04'51"

DESCRIPTION: In a mixed forest setting near Gull Lake. Fish for trout and swim from the lake. Supplies are available at Lee Vining. Wildlife in the area includes black bears, mountain lion, coyotes, deer, and birds. Campers may gather firewood. Trailhead to Reversed Peak.

GETTING THERE: From Lee Vining go SE on US HWY 395 approx. 10 mi. to state HWY 158. Go S on 158 approx. 4 mi. to Gull Lake CG.

SINGLE RATE:	$12	OPEN DATES:	Apr-Nov
# of SINGLE SITES:	11	MAX SPUR:	20 feet
		MAX STAY:	14 days
		ELEVATION:	7600 feet

27 Iris Meadow
Bishop • lat 37°31'03" lon 118°42'41"

DESCRIPTION: This open CG is surrounded with lodgepole pine and aspen trees. Rock Creek runs next to the CG and offers trout fishing. Supplies are 3-6 mi. away. Campers may gather firewood or purchase it nearby. Enjoy a hike in nearby John Muir Wilderness. This CG is frequented by bears.

GETTING THERE: From Bishop go NW on US HWY 395 approx. 24 mi. to primary forest route 12. Go S on 12 approx. 4 mi. to Iris CG. Road is narrow with sharp curves. Large vehicles should use caution.

SINGLE RATE:	$12	OPEN DATES:	May-Sept
# of SINGLE SITES:	14	MAX SPUR:	28 feet
		MAX STAY:	7 days
		ELEVATION:	8300 feet

23 Hartley Springs
Lee Vining • lat 37°45'57" lon 119°02'26"

DESCRIPTION: In a mixed forest setting near springs. Supplies are available at Lee Vining. Wildlife in the area includes black bears, mountain lion, coyotes, deer, and birds. Campers may gather firewood. No designated trails in the area. Visit nearby Obsidian Dome. No water.

GETTING THERE: From Lee Vining go SE on US HWY 395 approx. 13 mi. to forest route 2S10. Go SW on 2S10 1 mi. to forest route 2S48. Go W on 2S48 approx. 1/2 mi. to Hartley Springs CG.

SINGLE RATE:	No fee	OPEN DATES:	June-Oct
# of SINGLE SITES:	20	MAX SPUR:	20 feet
		MAX STAY:	14 days
		ELEVATION:	8400 feet

28 Junction
Lee Vining • lat 37°56'19" lon 119°14'55"

DESCRIPTION: In a mixed forest setting near Ellery Lake. Fish for trout and swim from the lake. Supplies are available at Lee Vining. Wildlife in the area includes black bears, mountain lion, coyotes, deer, and birds. Campers may gather firewood. Lee Vining Mine nearby. CG is the trailhead to Bennettville.

GETTING THERE: From Lee Vining go E on state HWY 120 (Vining Canyon Nat'l Scenic Byway) 8 mi. to Junction CG.

SINGLE RATE:	$6	OPEN DATES:	June-Oct
# of SINGLE SITES:	13	MAX SPUR:	20 feet
		MAX STAY:	14 days
		ELEVATION:	9600 feet

24 Holiday
Bishop • lat 37°33'09" lon 118°40'30"

DESCRIPTION: This CG is in a forested setting on Rock Creek and close to Lake Crowley. Fish and swim in the creek or lake. Supplies available at Bishop. Deer and birds are common to the area. Campers may gather firewood. There are hiking and horseback riding trails in the area. CG is frequented by bears.

GETTING THERE: From Bishop go NW on US HWY 395 approx. 24 mi. to primary forest route 12. Go S on 12 for 1/2 mi. to Holiday CG. Road is narrow with sharp curves. Large vehicles should use caution.

SINGLE RATE:	$12	OPEN DATES:	Yearlong
# of SINGLE SITES:	35	MAX SPUR:	28 feet
		MAX STAY:	14 days
		ELEVATION:	7500 feet

29 June Lake
Lee Vining • lat 37°47'19" lon 119°04'25"

DESCRIPTION: In a mixed forest setting near June Lake. Fish for trout and swim from the lake. Boat ramp at the CG. Supplies are available at Lee Vining. Wildlife in the area includes black bears, mountain lion, coyotes, deer, and birds. Campers may gather firewood. Trailhead to Yost Meadow and lake.

GETTING THERE: From Lee Vining go SE on US HWY 395 approx. 10 mi. to state HWY 158. Go S on 158 approx. 3 mi. to June Lake CG.

SINGLE RATE:	$12	OPEN DATES:	Apr-Nov
# of SINGLE SITES:	28	MAX SPUR:	35 feet
		MAX STAY:	14 days
		ELEVATION:	7600 feet

25 Horseshoe Meadow Equestrian
Lone Pine Indian Reservation • lat 36°27'30" lon 118°10'30"

DESCRIPTION: CG situated in a mixed forest near Cottonwood Creek with views of Horseshow Meadow. Fish or swim in the creek. Supplies available at Lone Pine Indian Reservation. Deer and birds in the area. Campers may gather firewood. The Cottonwood Pass Trail is nearby. Walk-in sites.

GETTING THERE: From the Lone Pine Indian Res. go W approx. 3 mi. on the Whitney Portal route to state HWY 190. Go S on 190 approx. 17.5 mi. to Horseshoe Meadow Equestrian CG.

SINGLE RATE:	$12	OPEN DATES:	May-Oct
# of SINGLE SITES:	10	MAX SPUR:	28 feet
		MAX STAY:	1 days
		ELEVATION:	10000 feet

30 Juniper Group
Big Pine • lat 40°27'12" lon 121°18'25"

DESCRIPTION: This remote campsite is set in a beautiful forested setting. Historic Toll House Site is within 5 mi. of the CG. Supplies are available at Big Pine. Deer, bears and birds are common in the area. Campers may gather firewood. There are many trails in the area. No running water or garbage removal.

GETTING THERE: From Big Pine go NE on state HWY 168 approx. 12 mi. to Juniper CG.

GROUP RATE:	$20	OPEN DATES:	Yearlong
# of GROUP SITES:	1	MAX SPUR:	25 feet
		MAX STAY:	14 days
		ELEVATION:	7200 feet

 Campground has hosts   **Reservable sites**   **Accessible facilities**   **Fully developed**   **Semi-developed**   Rustic facilities

NOTE: Open dates listed are typical. Actual dates are dependent on conditions such as snow pack.

31 Lake George
Mammoth Lakes • lat 37˚35'00" lon 119˚01'00"

DESCRIPTION: This CG is situated in mixed pine and hemlock with mountain crest and lake views. Enjoy fishing in nearby Lake George. Wildlife includes black bears, mountain lion, coyotes, deer, redtail hawks, and baldeagles. CG is busy all summer. Visit nearby Rainbow Falls and Devils Postpile National Monument.

GETTING THERE: From Mammoth Lakes go S on primary forest route 10 (Lake Mary route) 2 mi. to forest route 4S09 (loop). Go S on 4S09 approx. 1 mi. to Lake George CG.

SINGLE RATE:	$13	OPEN DATES:	June-Sept
# of SINGLE SITES:	16	MAX SPUR:	20 feet
		MAX STAY:	7 days
		ELEVATION:	9000 feet

32 Lake Mary
Mammoth Lakes • lat 37˚36'00" lon 119˚00'01"

DESCRIPTION: This CG rests in mixed pine and hemlock with mountain crest and lake views. Enjoy fishing in nearby Lake Mary. Wildlife includes black bears, mountain lion, coyotes, deer, redtail hawks, and baldeagles. CG is busy all summer. Visit nearby Rainbow Falls and Devils Postpile National Monument.

GETTING THERE: From Mammoth Lakes go S on primary forest route 10 (Lake Mary route) 2 mi. to forest route 4S09 (loop). Go S on 4S09 approx. 1 mi. to Lake Mary CG.

SINGLE RATE:	$13	OPEN DATES:	June-Sept
# of SINGLE SITES:	48	MAX SPUR:	25 feet
		MAX STAY:	14 days
		ELEVATION:	8900 feet

33 Lone Pine 🔒
Lone Pine Indian • lat 36˚35'30" lon 118˚10'30"

DESCRIPTION: CG situated in a mixed forest on the banks of a small creek. Fish for trout or swim in the creek. Supplies available at Lone Pine Indian Reservation. Deer and birds are common in the area. Firewood for sale at CG. CG is seven miles from Whitney Portal National Scenic Trailhead.

GETTING THERE: Lone Pine CG is located approx. 7 mi. W of Lone Pine Indian Res. on forest route 15S07.

SINGLE RATE:	$11	OPEN DATES:	Apr-Oct
# of SINGLE SITES:	43	MAX SPUR:	40 feet
GROUP RATE:	$30	MAX STAY:	14 days
# of GROUP SITES:	1	ELEVATION:	6000 feet

34 Lower Grays Meadow 🔒
Independence • lat 36˚46'30" lon 118˚16'30"

DESCRIPTION: CG situated in a mixed forest on the banks of Independence Creek and near Baron Springs. Fish for trout or swim in the creek. Supplies available at Independence. Deer and birds are common to the area. Campers may gather firewood. Trails nearby. Several mines within 5 mi. of the CG.

GETTING THERE: Lower Grays Meadow CG is located approx. 6 mi. W of Independence on forest route 13S17.

SINGLE RATE:	$11	OPEN DATES:	Mar-Oct
# of SINGLE SITES:	17	MAX SPUR:	28 feet
		MAX STAY:	14 days
		ELEVATION:	6000 feet

35 McGee Creek 🔒 ♿
Bishop • lat 37˚23'51" lon 118˚29'28"

DESCRIPTION: In an open area with sagebrush and some aspen near a meadow. CG is adjacent to Bishop Creek. Fish in the creek. Firewood is for sale at the site. Trails in the area for hiking, wildlife viewing, horseback riding, photography and geology study. Inyo Creek Equestrian Center.

GETTING THERE: From Bishop go NW 28 mi. to South Landing. Then go S on the county road 1 mi. to the county jct. Go E on the county route 3 mi. to forest route 4S06. Go S on 4S06 1.5 mi. to McGee Creek CG.

SINGLE RATE:	$12	OPEN DATES:	May-Oct
# of SINGLE SITES:	28	MAX SPUR:	35 feet
		MAX STAY:	14 days
		ELEVATION:	7600 feet

36 Minaret Falls
Mammoth Lakes • lat 37˚38'27" lon 119˚05'38"

DESCRIPTION: This CG is located in mixed pine and hemlock near the Middle Fork of San Joaquin River. Enjoy fishing for trout. Wildlife in this area includes black bears, mountain lion, coyotes, deer, redtail hawks, and baldeagles. CG is busy all summer. Visit nearby Rainbow Falls and Devils Postpile National Monument.

GETTING THERE: From Mammoth Lakes go NW on S HWY 203 approx. 6.5 mi. to forest route 3S11. Go W on 3S11 approx. 6 mi. to Minaret Falls CG.

SINGLE RATE:	$12	OPEN DATES:	June-Sept
# of SINGLE SITES:	27	MAX SPUR:	55 feet
		MAX STAY:	14 days
		ELEVATION:	7600 feet

37 Mosquito Flat Trailhead
Bishop • lat 37˚26'04" lon 118˚44'45"

DESCRIPTION: Open camp with lodgepole pine and aspen surrounding. Serene Lake nearby with trout fishing. Supplies at Bishop. Camper may gather firewood or purchase close by. CG is close to John Muir Wilderness. Trails to high country lakes. Bears can be a problem. Walk-in sites. No water.

GETTING THERE: From Bishop go NW on US HWY 395 approx. 23.5 mi. to primary forest route 12. Go S on 12 for 7.5 mi. to forest route 6S05. Go S on 6S05 approx. 2 mi. to Mosquito Flat Trailhead CG.

SINGLE RATE:	No fee	OPEN DATES:	May-Oct
# of SINGLE SITES:	10		
		MAX STAY:	1 days
		ELEVATION:	10230 feet

38 Mountain Glen
Bishop • lat 37˚13'26" lon 118˚33'55"

DESCRIPTION: In a dense pine forest setting near high mountain lakes. Fish for trout from lakes. Supplies at Bishop. Deer, bears, raccoon, squirrel and birds are common in the area. Campers may gather firewood. Trails in the area. No water.

GETTING THERE: From Bishop go W on HWY 168 approx. 14 mi. to South Lake Road. Go S on South Lake Road approx. 4 mi. to Mountain Glen CG.

SINGLE RATE:	$11	OPEN DATES:	May-Oct*
# of SINGLE SITES:	5	MAX SPUR:	28 feet
		MAX STAY:	7 days
		ELEVATION:	8200 feet

39 New Shady Rest
Mammoth Lakes • lat 37˚39'01" lon 118˚57'33"

DESCRIPTION: This CG is situated in mixed conifer. Enjoy a drive on the nearby Mammoth Scenic Loop. Wildlife includes black bears, mountain lion, coyotes, deer, redtail hawks, and baldeagles. CG is busy all summer. Trails in area include hikes to Mammoth Rock and Valentine Lake, and a 5 mi. mountain biking loop. RV dump station.

GETTING THERE: From Mammoth Lakes go N 1/2 mi. on forest route 3S08 to New Shady Rest CG.

SINGLE RATE:	$12	OPEN DATES:	May-Oct
# of SINGLE SITES:	94	MAX SPUR:	55 feet
		MAX STAY:	14 days
		ELEVATION:	7800 feet

40 North Lake
Bishop • lat 37˚13'39" lon 118˚37'35"

DESCRIPTION: In a forested setting on North Lake with views of Table Mountain. Fish for trout or swim in the lake. Supplies at Bishop. Firewood for sale at the site. Deer, bears and birds are in the area. Trails to mountain lakes are in the area. CG is located near John Muir Wilderness.

GETTING THERE: From Bishop to SW on state HWY 168 approx. 15 mi. to forest route 8S02. Go W on 8S02 approx. 1.5 mi. to North Lake CG. No trailers or RVs.

SINGLE RATE:	$12	OPEN DATES:	June-Sept
# of SINGLE SITES:	11	MAX SPUR:	28 feet
		MAX STAY:	7 days
		ELEVATION:	9500 feet

 Campground has hosts   **Reservable sites**   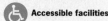 **Accessible facilities**   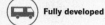 **Fully developed**   **Semi-developed**   **Rustic facilities**

NOTE: Open dates listed are typical. Actual dates are dependent on conditions such as snow pack.

41 Oak Creek
Independence • lat 36°51'00" lon 118°15'30"

DESCRIPTION: This CG is situated in a mixed forest on the banks of Oak Creek. Fish or swim in the creek. Supplies are available at Independence. Deer and birds are common to the area. Campers may gather their firewood localy. Located a short distance away from Independence and Baxter Pass Trailheads.

GETTING THERE: From Independece go N on US HWY 395 approx. 22 mi. for forest route 13S04. Go NW on 13S04 approx. 1 mi. to forest route 13S04A. Go W on 13S04A approx. 1 mi. to Oak Creek CG.

SINGLE RATE:	$11	OPEN DATES:	Apr-Oct
# of SINGLE SITES:	22	MAX SPUR:	25 feet
		MAX STAY:	14 days
		ELEVATION:	5000 feet

46 Palisade
Mammoth Lakes • lat 37°29'40" lon 118°43'06"

DESCRIPTION: Open camp with lodgepole pine and aspen surrounding. Rock Creek runs next to CG with trout fishing. Supplies at Mammoth Lakes. Camper may gather firewood or purchase nearby. CG is close to John Muir Wilderness. Bears can be a problem.

GETTING THERE: From Mammoth Lakes go NW on state HWY 203 approx. 6.5 mi. to forest route 3S11. Go W on 3S11 approx. 5 mi. to Palisade CG.

SINGLE RATE:	$12	OPEN DATES:	May-Sept
# of SINGLE SITES:	5	MAX SPUR:	28 feet
		MAX STAY:	7 days
		ELEVATION:	8600 feet

42 Obsidian Flat Group
Mammoth Lakes • lat 37°45'33" lon 119°01'10"

DESCRIPTION: In a mixed forest setting with Deadman Creek nearby. Fish and swim from the creek. Visit nearby Inyo Crater Lakes. Supplies are available at Mammoth Lakes. Wildlife in the area includes black bears, mountain lions, coyotes, deer, and birds. Campers may gather firewood. Hike nearby to Glass Creek Meadow.

GETTING THERE: From Mammoth Lakes go N on state HWY 203 approx. 1 mi. to forest route 3S23. Go N on 3S23 (Mammoth Scenic Loop) approx. 4 mi. to forest route 2S29. Go NW on forest route 2S29 approx. 3 mi. to Obsidian Flat Group CG.

		OPEN DATES:	June-Oct
		MAX SPUR:	99 feet
GROUP RATE:	$20	MAX STAY:	14 days
# of GROUP SITES:	1	ELEVATION:	7800 feet

47 Palisade/Clyde
Big Pine • lat 37°08'00" lon 118°24'30"

DESCRIPTION: CG situated in a mixed forest set in a narrow canyon. A stream runs full length of camp with views of the mountains. Fish for trout from the stream. Firewood for sale at site. Supplies nearby. There is wilderness hiking to glacier and lakes in John Muir Wilderness. Corrals for equestrian use.

GETTING THERE: Palisade/Clyde CG is located approx. 9.2 mi. W on forest route 9S21.

		OPEN DATES:	Apr-Oct
		MAX SPUR:	28 feet
GROUP RATE:	$32	MAX STAY:	14 days
# of GROUP SITES:	2	ELEVATION:	7600 feet

43 Oh! Ridge
Lee Vining • lat 37°48'02" lon 119°04'13"

DESCRIPTION: In eastern high Sierras of California near June Lake. Day use area has a swimming beach located adjacent to the CG. Fish for trout and swim from the lake. Supplies are available at Lee Vining. Wildlife in the area includes black bears, mountain lion, coyotes, deer, and birds. Campers may gather firewood. No designated trails.

GETTING THERE: From Lee Vining go SE on US HWY 395 approx. 10 mi. to state HWY 158. Go S on 158 approx. 1 mi. to forest route. Go W on forest route approx. 1/2 mi. to Oh! Ridge CG.

SINGLE RATE:	$12	OPEN DATES:	Apr-Nov
# of SINGLE SITES:	148	MAX SPUR:	40 feet
		MAX STAY:	14 days
		ELEVATION:	7600 feet

48 Pine City
Mammoth Lakes • lat 37°36'00" lon 119°00'01"

DESCRIPTION: This CG is situated in mixed pine and hemlock with mountain crest and lake views. Enjoy fishing in nearby Lake Mary. Wildlife includes black bears, mountain lion, coyotes, deer, redtail hawks, and baldeagles. CG is busy all summer. Visit nearby Rainbow Falls and Devils Postpile National Monument.

GETTING THERE: From Mammoth Lakes go S on primary forest route 10 (Lake Mary route) 2 mi. to forest route 4S09. Go S on 4S09 approx. 1/2 mi. to forest route 4S25. Go S on 4S25 1/4 mi. to Pine City CG.

SINGLE RATE:	$13	OPEN DATES:	June-Sept
# of SINGLE SITES:	10	MAX SPUR:	50 feet
		MAX STAY:	14 days
		ELEVATION:	8900 feet

44 Old Shady Rest
Mammoth Lakes • lat 37°38'56" lon 118°57'52"

DESCRIPTION: This CG is located in mixed conifer. Enjoy a drive on the nearby Mammoth Scenic Loop. Wildlife includes black bears, mountain lion, coyotes, deer, red-tail hawks, and baldeagles. CG is busy all summer. Trails in area include hikes to Mammoth Rock and Valentine Lake, and a 5 mi. mountain biking loop.

GETTING THERE: From Mammoth Lakes go N 1/2 mi. on forest route 3S08 to Old Shady Rest CG.

SINGLE RATE:	$12	OPEN DATES:	June-Sept
# of SINGLE SITES:	51	MAX SPUR:	50 feet
		MAX STAY:	14 days
		ELEVATION:	7800 feet

49 Pine Glen
Mammoth Lakes • lat 37°38'57" lon 118°57'19"

DESCRIPTION: This CG is located in mixed conifer within the city of Mammoth Lakes. Enjoy a drive on the nearby Mammoth Scenic Loop. CG is busy all summer. Trails in area include hikes to Mammoth Rock and Valentine Lake, and a 5 mi. mountain biking loop. There are interpretive programs available at this CG.

GETTING THERE: From Mammoth Lakes go N 1/2 mi. on forest route 3S08 to Pine Glen CG.

SINGLE RATE:	$12	OPEN DATES:	May-Sept
# of SINGLE SITES:	11	MAX SPUR:	55 feet
GROUP RATE:	Varies	MAX STAY:	14 days
# of GROUP SITES:	6	ELEVATION:	7800 feet

45 Onion Valley
Independence • lat 36°46'30" lon 118°20'30"

DESCRIPTION: This CG is situated in a mixed forest a shore distance away from Robinson Lake. Fish for trout or swim in the lake. Supplies are available at Lone Pine Indian Reservation. Deer and birds are common to the area. Firewood is for sale on site. Keursarge Pass and Golden Trout Lakes Trailhead nearby.

GETTING THERE: Onion Valley CG is located approx. 12 mi. W of Independence on forest route 13S17. Trailers are not recommended.

SINGLE RATE:	$11	OPEN DATES:	June-Oct
# of SINGLE SITES:	29	MAX SPUR:	30 feet
		MAX STAY:	14 days
		ELEVATION:	9200 feet

50 Pine Grove
Mammoth Lakes • lat 37°28'16" lon 118°43'23"

DESCRIPTION: In a lodgepole pine and aspen forest setting with Rock Creek running next to CG. Trout fishing from creek. Supplies at Mammoth Lakes. Camper may gather firewood or purchase nearby. CG is close to John Muir Wilderness. Trails in the area. Bears can be a problem.

GETTING THERE: From Mammoth Lakes go NW on state HWY 203 approx. 6.5 mi. to forest route 3S11. Go W on 3S11 approx. 7 mi. to Pine Grove CG.

SINGLE RATE:	$12	OPEN DATES:	May-Oct
# of SINGLE SITES:	11	MAX SPUR:	28 feet
		MAX STAY:	7 days
		ELEVATION:	9300 feet

 Campground has hosts   **Reservable sites**   **Accessible facilities**   **Fully developed**   **Semi-developed**   **Rustic facilities**

NOTE: Open dates listed are typical. Actual dates are dependent on conditions such as snow pack.

51 Pinyon Group
Big Pine • lat 37°16'26" lon 118°08'50"

DESCRIPTION: This remote campsite is in a forested setting with a creek nearby. Historical Toll House Site is with in 5 mi. of CG. Supplies available at Big Pine. Deer, bears and birds area common in the area. Campers may gather firewood. Many trails in the area. There is no running water or garbage removal.

GETTING THERE: From Big Pine go NE on state HWY 168 approx. 11 mi. to Pinon Group CG.

		OPEN DATES:	**Yearlong**
GROUP RATE:	$20	**MAX SPUR:**	**28 feet**
# of GROUP SITES:	2	**MAX STAY:**	**14 days**
		ELEVATION:	**7200 feet**

52 Poleta Group
Big Pine • lat 37°16'33" lon 118°08'43"

DESCRIPTION: This remote campsite is in a forested setting with a creek nearby. Historical Toll House Site is with in 5 mi. of CG. Supplies available at Big Pine. Deer, bears and birds area common in the area. Campers may gather firewood. Many trails in the area. There is no running water or garbage removal.

GETTING THERE: From Big Pine go NE on state HWY 168 approx. 12 mi. to Poleta Group CG.

		OPEN DATES:	**Yearlong**
GROUP RATE:	$20	**MAX SPUR:**	**28 feet**
# of GROUP SITES:	1	**MAX STAY:**	**14 days**
		ELEVATION:	**7200 feet**

53 Pumice Flat
Mammoth Lakes • lat 37°38'56" lon 119°04'25"

DESCRIPTION: This CG rests in mixed pine and hemlock near the Middle Fork of San Joaquin River. Enjoy fishing for trout. Wildlife in this area includes black bears, mountain lion, coyotes, deer, and baldeagles. CG is busy all summer. Visit nearby Rainbow Falls and Devils Postpile National Monument.

GETTING THERE: From Mammoth Lakes go NW on state HWY 203 approx. 6.5 mi. to forest route 3S11. Go W on 3S11 approx. 5 mi. to Pumice Flat CG.

SINGLE RATE:	$12	**OPEN DATES:**	**June-Sept**
# of SINGLE SITES:	17	**MAX SPUR:**	**55 feet**
GROUP RATE:	Varies	**MAX STAY:**	**14 days**
# of GROUP SITES:	4	**ELEVATION:**	**7700 feet**

54 Reds Meadow
Mammoth Lakes • lat 37°37'10" lon 119°04'24"

DESCRIPTION: This CG is located in mixed pine and hemlock near Sotcher Lake. Wildlife in this area includes black bears, mountain lion, coyotes, deer, redtail hawks, and baldeagles. CG is busy all summer. Several trails in the area. Visit nearby Rainbow Falls and Devils Postpile National Monument.

GETTING THERE: From Mammoth Lakes go NW on state HWY 203 approx. 6.5 mi. to forest route 3S11. Go W on 3S11 approx. 7.5 mi. to Reds Meadow CG.

SINGLE RATE:	$12	**OPEN DATES:**	**June-Oct**
# of SINGLE SITES:	56	**MAX SPUR:**	**50 feet**
		MAX STAY:	**14 days**
		ELEVATION:	**7600 feet**

55 Reversed Creek
Lee Vining • lat 37°46'00" lon 119°07'15"

DESCRIPTION: In a mixed forest setting on Reversed Creek. Fish for trout and swim from the creek. Supplies are available at Lee Vining. Wildlife in the area includes black bears, mountain lion, coyotes, deer, and birds. Campers may gather firewood. Near trailhead to Yost Meadow and lake.

GETTING THERE: From Lee Vining go SE on US HWY 395 approx. 10 mi. to state HWY 158. Go S on 158 approx. 4 mi. to Reversed Creek CG.

SINGLE RATE:	$12	**OPEN DATES:**	**May-Oct**
# of SINGLE SITES:	17	**MAX SPUR:**	**20 feet**
		MAX STAY:	**14 days**
		ELEVATION:	**7600 feet**

56 Rock Creek Lake
Bishop • lat 37°27'14" lon 118°44'17"

DESCRIPTION: CG is situated in a pine forest setting on the shores of Rock Creek Lake. Fish for trout on the lake. Interpretive programs are provided. Supplies at Bishop. Deer and birds are common to the area. Campers may gather firewood. Many trails are near the CG.

GETTING THERE: From Bishop go NW on US HWY 395 approx. 23.5 mi. to primary forest route 12. Go S on 12 approx. 8 mi. to Rock Creek Lake CG.

SINGLE RATE:	$12	**OPEN DATES:**	**May-Oct**
# of SINGLE SITES:	28	**MAX SPUR:**	**25 feet**
GROUP RATE:	$40	**MAX STAY:**	**7 days**
# of GROUP SITES:	1	**ELEVATION:**	**9600 feet**

57 Sabrina
Bishop • lat 37°13'15" lon 118°36'14"

DESCRIPTION: In a forested setting near Lake Sabrina. Fish for trout or swim in the lake. Boat launch at the lake. Supplies at Bishop. Firewood for sale at the site. Deer, bears and birds are in the area. Trails to mountain lakes are in the area. Campground is located near John Muir Wilderness.

GETTING THERE: From Bishop go SW on state HWY 168 approx. 15 mi. to Sabrina CG.

SINGLE RATE:	$12	**OPEN DATES:**	**May-Oct**
# of SINGLE SITES:	18	**MAX SPUR:**	**28 feet**
		MAX STAY:	**7 days**
		ELEVATION:	**9000 feet**

58 Saddlebag Lake
Lee Vining • lat 37°58'24" lon 119°16'25"

DESCRIPTION: In a mixed forest setting near Saddlebag Lake. Fish for trout and swim from the lake. Supplies are available at Lee Vining. Wildlife in the area includes black bears, mountain lion, coyotes, deer, and birds. Campers may gather firewood. Trailhead around the lake. Lee Vining Mine in area.

GETTING THERE: From Lee Vining go E on state HWY 120 (Vining Canyon Nat'l Scenic Byway) 10.5 mi. to Saddlebag Lake CG. Small trailers and RVs only.

SINGLE RATE:	$11	**OPEN DATES:**	**June-Oct**
# of SINGLE SITES:	20	**MAX SPUR:**	**20 feet**
GROUP RATE:	Varies	**MAX STAY:**	**14 days**
# of GROUP SITES:	1	**ELEVATION:**	**10000 feet**

59 Sage Flat
Independence • lat 37°07'30" lon 118°24'30"

DESCRIPTION: CG set in a mixed forest in a narrow canyon. A stream runs full length of camp with views of the mountains sorrounding CG. Firewood for sale at site. Fish for trout from the stream. Glacier Lodge and Store outside the CG. There is wilderness hiking to glacier and lakes in John Muir Wilderness.

GETTING THERE: Sage Flat CG is located approx. 8.5 mi. W on forest route 9S21.

SINGLE RATE:	$11	**OPEN DATES:**	**Apr-Oct**
# of SINGLE SITES:	28	**MAX SPUR:**	**28 feet**
		MAX STAY:	**14 days**
		ELEVATION:	**7400 feet**

60 Sawmill
Lee Vining • lat 37°57'29" lon 119°16'07"

DESCRIPTION: In a mixed forest setting near Lee Vining Creek. Fish for trout and swim from the creek. Supplies are available at Lee Vining. Wildlife in the area includes black bears, mountain lion, coyotes, deer, and birds. Campers may gather firewood. Trailhead around the Saddlebag Lake nearby. Lee Vining Mine in area. Walk-in sites. No water.

GETTING THERE: From Lee Vining go E on state HWY 120 (Vining Canyon Nat'l Scenic Byway) 8 mi. to Sawmill CG.

SINGLE RATE:	$6	**OPEN DATES:**	**June-Oct**
# of SINGLE SITES:	12	**MAX SPUR:**	**20 feet**
		MAX STAY:	**14 days**
		ELEVATION:	**9800 feet**

 Campground has hosts   **Reservable sites**   **Accessible facilities**   **Fully developed**   **Semi-developed**   **Rustic facilities**

NOTE: Open dates listed are typical. Actual dates are dependent on conditions such as snow pack.

61 Sherwin Creek
Mammoth Lakes • lat 37°37'48" lon 118°56'06"

DESCRIPTION: This CG rests in mixed conifer on Sherwin Creek. Enjoy a drive on the nearby Mammoth Scenic Loop. Wildlife includes black bears, mountain lion, coyotes, deer, hawks, and baldeagles. CG is busy all summer. Trails in area include hikes to Mammoth Rock and Valentine Lake. Interpretive programs here.

GETTING THERE: From Mammoth Lakes go SE on forest route 4S08 2.5 mi. to Sherwin Creek CG.

SINGLE RATE:	$12	OPEN DATES:	May-Sept
# of SINGLE SITES:	87	MAX SPUR:	55 feet
		MAX STAY:	21 days
		ELEVATION:	7600 feet

66 Twin Lakes
Mammoth Lakes • lat 38°10'11" lon 119°19'21"

DESCRIPTION: This CG is situated in mixed pine and hemlock with mountain crest and lake views. Enjoy fishing in nearby Twin Lakes. Wildlife includes black bears, mountain lion, coyotes, deer, redtail hawks, and baldeagles. CG is busy all summer. Visit nearby Rainbow Falls and Devils Postpile National Monument.

GETTING THERE: From Mammoth Lakes go S on primary forest route 10 (Lake Mary route) 1.5 mi. to Twin Lakes CG.

SINGLE RATE:	$13	OPEN DATES:	June-Nov
# of SINGLE SITES:	95	MAX SPUR:	55 feet
		MAX STAY:	7 days
		ELEVATION:	8700 feet

62 Silver Lake
Lee Vining • lat 37°46'58" lon 119°07'30"

DESCRIPTION: In a mixed forest setting on Silver Lake. Fish for trout and swim in the lake. Boat ramp at the CG. Supplies are available at Lee Vining. Wildlife in the area includes black bears, mountain lion, coyotes, deer, and birds. Campers may gather firewood. Trails to Ansel Adams Wilderness. Horse facilities at CG.

GETTING THERE: From Lee Vining go SE on US HWY 395 approx. 10 mi. to state HWY 158. Go S on 158 approx. 7.5 mi. to Silver Lake CG.

SINGLE RATE:	$12	OPEN DATES:	Apr-Nov
# of SINGLE SITES:	63	MAX SPUR:	20 feet
		MAX STAY:	14 days
		ELEVATION:	7200 feet

67 Upper Grays Meadow
Independence • lat 36°46'30" lon 118°16'30"

DESCRIPTION: CG situated in a mixed forest on the banks of Independence Creek and near Baron Springs. Fish for trout or swim in the creek. Supplies available at Independence. Deer and birds are common to the area. Campers may gather firewood locally. Trails nearby. Several mines with in 5 mi. of the CG.

GETTING THERE: Upper Grays Meadow CG is located approx. 6.2 mi. W of Independence on forest route 13S17.

SINGLE RATE:	Varies	OPEN DATES:	Apr-Oct
# of SINGLE SITES:	35	MAX SPUR:	28 feet
		MAX STAY:	14 days
		ELEVATION:	6200 feet

63 Table Mountain
Bishop • lat 37°12'30" lon 118°34'06"

DESCRIPTION: Firewood is for sale on site. Stores, marinas, restaurants and pack stations available in the canyon area. South Fork Bishop Creek is located adjacent to the campground. This is a stocked trout stream. Popular activities include fishing, hiking, horseback riding and wildlife viewing. Located near the John Muir Wilderness trailheads.

GETTING THERE: From Highway 395 in center of Bishop, turn west on Line Street (Highway 158) and continue west for 13 miles, then south for 5 miles up South Fork Road.

		OPEN DATES:	May-Oct
		MAX SPUR:	22 feet
GROUP RATE:	$42	MAX STAY:	14 days
# of GROUP SITES:	1	ELEVATION:	8500 feet

68 Upper Pine Grove
Mammoth Lakes • lat 37°28'16" lon 118°43'23"

DESCRIPTION: In a forested setting on Rock Creek. Fish for trout or swim from the creek. Supplies available at Mammoth Lakes. Numerous wildlife in the area. Campers may gather firewood. Many trails in the area.

GETTING THERE: From Mammoth Lakes go NW on state HWY 203 approx. 6.5 mi. to forest route 3S11. Go W on 3S11 approx. 3 mi. to Upper Pine Grove CG.

SINGLE RATE:	$12	OPEN DATES:	May-Sept
# of SINGLE SITES:	8	MAX SPUR:	28 feet
		MAX STAY:	7 days
		ELEVATION:	9400 feet

64 Tioga Lake
Lee Vining • lat 37°55'30" lon 119°15'07"

DESCRIPTION: In a mixed forest setting near Tioga Lake. Fish for trout and swim from the lake. Wildlife in the area includes black bears, mountain lion, coyotes, deer, and birds. Campers may gather firewood. Trailhead to Bennettville. CG is near Mono Lake, Ansel Adams Wilderness and Harvey Monroe Hall.

GETTING THERE: From Lee Vining go E on state HWY 120 (Vining Canyon Nat'l Scenic Byway) approx. 9 mi. to Tioga Lake CG. Small trailers and RV's only.

SINGLE RATE:	$11	OPEN DATES:	June-Oct
# of SINGLE SITES:	13	MAX SPUR:	20 feet
		MAX STAY:	14 days
		ELEVATION:	9700 feet

69 Upper Sage Flat
Big Pine • lat 37°08'00" lon 118°24'30"

DESCRIPTION: CG situated in a mixed forest set in a narrow canyon. A stream runs full length of camp with views of the mountains sorrounding CG. Firewood for sale at site. Fish for trout from the stream. Glacier Lodge and Store outside the campground. There is hiking to glaciers and lakes in John Muir Wilderness.

GETTING THERE: Upper Sage Flat CG is located approx. 9 mi. W on forest route 9S21.

SINGLE RATE:	$11	OPEN DATES:	Apr-Oct
# of SINGLE SITES:	21	MAX SPUR:	28 feet
		MAX STAY:	14 days
		ELEVATION:	7600 feet

65 Tuff
Bishop • lat 37°33'45" lon 118°39'51"

DESCRIPTION: In a mixed forested setting on Lower Rock Creek and close to Lake Crowley. Fish and swim from the creek or lake. Supplies available at Bishop. Deer, bears and birds are common to the area. Campers may gather firewood. Hiking and horseback riding trails in the area

GETTING THERE: From Bishop go NW on US HWY 395 approx. 24 mi. to forest route 4S02. Go N on 4S02 approx. 1 mi. to 4S38. Go SE on 4S38 approx. 1 mi. to Tuff CG.

SINGLE RATE:	$12	OPEN DATES:	Apr-Oct
# of SINGLE SITES:	34	MAX SPUR:	45 feet
		MAX STAY:	21 days
		ELEVATION:	7000 feet

70 Upper Soda Springs
Mammoth Lakes • lat 37°38'56" lon 119°04'25"

DESCRIPTION: This CG is located in mixed pine and hemlock near the Middle Fork of San Joaquin River. Enjoy fishing for trout. Wildlife in this area includes black bears, mountain lion, coyotes, deer, redtail hawks, and baldeagles. CG is busy all summer. Visit nearby Rainbow Falls and Devils Postpile National Monument.

GETTING THERE: From Mammoth Lakes go NW on state HWY 203 approx. 6.5 mi. to forest route 3S11. Go W on 3S11 approx. 4.5 mi. to Upper Soda Springs CG.

SINGLE RATE:	$12	OPEN DATES:	June-Sept
# of SINGLE SITES:	29	MAX SPUR:	55 feet
		MAX STAY:	14 days
		ELEVATION:	7700 feet

 Campground has hosts   **Reservable sites**   **Accessible facilities**   **Fully developed**   **Semi-developed**   **Rustic facilities**

NOTE: Open dates listed are typical. Actual dates are dependent on conditions such as snow pack.

71 Whitney Portal
Lone Pine • lat 36°35'00" lon 118°13'30"

DESCRIPTION: Campground is adjacent to Whitney Creek. Roads are paved. Restrooms are provided. Firewood is available for sale. Small store with showers nearby. Popular activities are hiking and fishing. Campground is 1/2 mile from Mt. Whitney, Meysan Lake and National Recreation trailheads.

GETTING THERE: Whitney Portal CG is located approx. 11 mi. W of Lone Pine on the Whitney Portal route.

SINGLE RATE:	$13	OPEN DATES:	May-Oct
# of SINGLE SITES:	44	MAX SPUR:	30 feet
GROUP RATE:	$35	MAX STAY:	7 days
# of GROUP SITES:	1	ELEVATION:	8000 feet

72 Whitney Trailhead
Lone Pine • lat 36°34'30" lon 118°15'00"

DESCRIPTION: Campground is adjacent to Whitney Creek. Roads are paved. Restrooms are provided. Firewood is available for sale. Small store with showers nearby. Popular activities are hiking and fishing. Campground is 1/2 mile from Mt. Whitney, Meysan Lake and National Recreation trailheads. Walk-in sites.

GETTING THERE: Whitney Trailhead walk-in CG is located approx. 11 mi. W of Lone Pine on the Whitney Portal route.

SINGLE RATE:	$6	OPEN DATES:	May-Oct
# of SINGLE SITES:	10	MAX SPUR:	28 feet
		MAX STAY:	1 days
		ELEVATION:	8300 feet

73 Willow
Bishop • lat 37°12'30" lon 118°35'30"

DESCRIPTION: In a forest setting used for equestrian trail to Tyee Lakes. Fish from the lakes. Supplies available at Bishop. Deer, bears and birds in the area. Linder Mine nearby. Many trails in the area. No water.

GETTING THERE: Willows CG is located approx. 18.5 mi. SW of Bishop on state HWY 168.

SINGLE RATE:	$11	OPEN DATES:	May-Oct
# of SINGLE SITES:	7	MAX SPUR:	28 feet
		MAX STAY:	7 days
		ELEVATION:	9000 feet

 Campground has hosts    **Reservable sites**   **Accessible facilities**   **Fully developed**   **Semi-developed**   **Rustic facilities**

NOTE: Open dates listed are typical. Actual dates are dependent on conditions such as snow pack.

USFS Photo

KLAMATH NATIONAL FOREST

The Klamath National Forest is one of America's most biologically-diverse regions. Its trees, plant life, rivers and streams, fish, birds, reptiles, and mammals, combined with its climate and terrain, form a number of interrelated and complex ecosystems. The beautiful forest that results is a haven for campers, hikers, wildlife watchers, hunters, fishermen, mountain bikers, rafters, kayakers, and naturalists.

The 1.7 million-acre Klamath is home to the goshawk, great grey owl, willow flycatcher, several furbearers, and Chinook salmon.

The wilderness areas offer the greatest views and solitude you'll ever find. You often won't see a single soul, even on a weekend! For breathtaking panoramic views (including Mt. Shasta) take the time to climb to the top of any ridge. Pristine alpine and glacial lakes with granite backdrops make peaceful, quiet camping places after long hikes. A visitor permit is required in the Trinity Alps, and there are no quotas in any of the wildernesses.

With more than 4,000 miles of roads and trails, the Klamath is also a mountain biking paradise. And the 200 miles of whitewater river make the Salmon, Scott and Klamath rivers popular with rafters and kayakers.

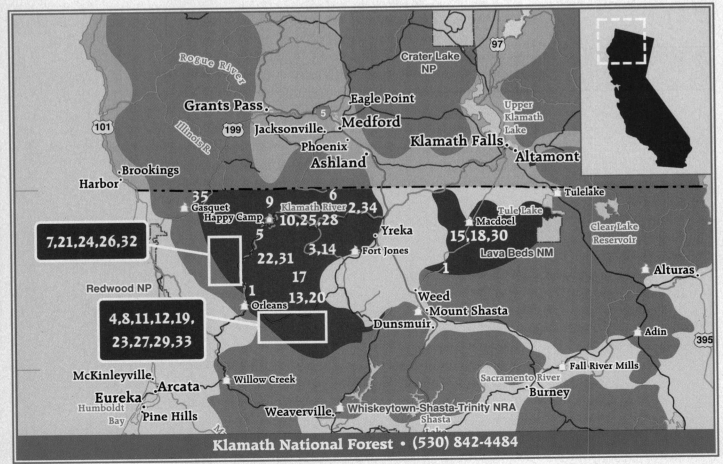

Klamath National Forest • (530) 842-4484

1 Beans Camp
Orleans • lat 41°26'39" lon 123°36'41"

DESCRIPTION: CG is a high elevation camp originally built by hunters. Cool in summer. Supplies at Orleans Ranger District Office or in town of Orleans. Various wildlife. Busy during hunting season. Gather firewood locally. Campfire permit required. No drinking water.

GETTING THERE: From Orleans go N on forest route 15N01 (Eyesee Road and locally known as the GO ROAD) approx. 17 mi. to forest route 12N22. Go N on 12N22 approx. 1/2 mi. to Beans Camp CG.

SINGLE RATE:	No fee	OPEN DATES:	May-Oct
# of SINGLE SITES:	6	MAX STAY:	14 days
		ELEVATION:	4000 feet

6 Deer Mountain Snowmobile Park
Weed • lat 41°34'00" lon 122°07'30"

DESCRIPTION: CG situated in a pine, fir, juniper, and manzanita forest with views of Mount Shasta. Supplies available at Weed. Firewood may be scarce. Horse facilities offered during summer. Snowmobiling, cross country skiing, and log cabin style warming hut available during winter. No drinking water.

GETTING THERE: From Weed go N on state HWY 97 approx. 16 mi. to forest route 19. Go E on 19 approx. 4 mi. to Deer Mountain Snowmobile Park CG.

SINGLE RATE:	No fee	OPEN DATES:	Yearlong
# of SINGLE SITES:	8	MAX SPUR:	30 feet
		MAX STAY:	14 days
		ELEVATION:	5600 feet

2 Beaver Creek
Klamath River • lat 41°55'38" lon 122°49'48"

DESCRIPTION: Open timber setting along stream. Beaver Creek has good trout fishing. Historical mining sites nearby. Supplies are 4 mi. away at Quigley's general store and RV park. Campers may gather firewood. CG is generally quiet and not busy.

GETTING THERE: From Klamath River go E on state HWY 96 approx. .5 mi. to primary forest route 11. Go N on 11 approx. 4 mi. to Beaver Creek CG.

SINGLE RATE:	No fee	OPEN DATES:	May-Oct
# of SINGLE SITES:	8	MAX SPUR:	30 feet
		MAX STAY:	14 days
		ELEVATION:	2400 feet

7 Dillon
Clear Creek • lat 41°32'24" lon 123°38'55"

DESCRIPTION: CG is carved into the mountain slopes and is sheltered, shaded, and offers privacy with a fresh spring cascading down the towering mountain nearby. A natural swimming hole and trails near CG. Fish the Klamath River adjacent to CG. "Bears proof" garbage containers at CG.

GETTING THERE: From Clear Creek go S on state HWY 96 approx. 11 mi. to Dillon CG.

SINGLE RATE:	$8	OPEN DATES:	May-Oct
# of SINGLE SITES:	21		
GROUP RATE:	$15	MAX STAY:	14 days
		ELEVATION:	800 feet

3 Bridge Flat
Fort Jones • lat 41°39'01" lon 123°06'43"

DESCRIPTION: Open timber setting with river nearby. Fish for steelhead and trout in river. Fishing is available throughout the season. Historical Kelsey Creek Trail by CG. Supplies are 21 mi. at Fort Jones. CG is never full. Campers may gather own firewood.

GETTING THERE: From Fort Jones go W on county route 7F01 approx. 21 mi. to Bridge Flat CG.

SINGLE RATE:	No fee	OPEN DATES:	May-Oct
# of SINGLE SITES:	4	MAX SPUR:	30 feet
		MAX STAY:	14 days
		ELEVATION:	2000 feet

8 East Fork
Cecilville • lat 41°09'15" lon 123°06'27"

DESCRIPTION: In a mixed conifer forest setting on the East Fork of the Salmon River. Trout, salmon and steelhead in river. Supplies at the historical town of Cecilville. Deer, bears and birds are common in area. Campers may gather firewood. Old mining areas nearby. No designated trails in the area.

GETTING THERE: East Fork CG is located approx. 2 mi. NE of Cecilville on primary forest route 93.

SINGLE RATE:	No fee	OPEN DATES:	May-Oct
# of SINGLE SITES:	9		
		MAX STAY:	14 days
		ELEVATION:	2600 feet

4 Carter Meadows
Callahan • lat 41°13'00" lon 122°55'00"

DESCRIPTION: Old growth timber and open meadow setting with lots of shade. Many lakes close to CG. Supplies are 13 mi. from CG. Campers may gather firewood. Many foot trails nearby. CG accomodates horses. Reservation only, call 530-468-5351.

GETTING THERE: Carter Meadows Group Horse Camp CG is located approx. 13 mi. SW of Callahan on primary forest route 93.

		OPEN DATES:	June-Oct*
		MAX SPUR:	40 feet
GROUP RATE:	$30	MAX STAY:	14 days
# of GROUP SITES:	1	ELEVATION:	5700 feet

9 Fort Goff
Seiad Valley • lat 41°51'55" lon 123°15'23"

DESCRIPTION: CG is located in old growth douglas fir and is adjacent to the Klamath River. There are excellent swimming, rafting and fishing (trout, salmon, and steelhead)opportunities. Various wildlife in area includes deer, otters, and osprey. Campsites are walk-in only.

GETTING THERE: Fort Goff CG is located approx. 5 mi. W of Seiad Valley on state HWY 96.

SINGLE RATE:	No fee	OPEN DATES:	Yearlong*
# of SINGLE SITES:	5		
		MAX STAY:	14 days
		ELEVATION:	1300 feet

5 Curley Jack
Happy Camp • lat 41°47'08" lon 123°23'25"

DESCRIPTION: CG is located in white oak, ponderosa pine, and madrone with semi-shaded sites. Good trout, salmon, and steelhead fishing in adjacent Klamath River. Excellent swimming and rafting opportunities. Various wildlife in area includes deer, otters, and osprey. Can be busy holiday weekends.

GETTING THERE: Curley Jack CG is located approx. 1 mi. S of Happy Camp on county route 7C001.

SINGLE RATE:	Varies	OPEN DATES:	Yearlong*
# of SINGLE SITES:	17	MAX SPUR:	50 feet
GROUP RATE:	Varies	MAX STAY:	14 days
# of GROUP SITES:	2	ELEVATION:	1000 feet

10 Grider Creek
Seiad Valley • lat 41°48'00" lon 123°13'00"

DESCRIPTION: CG is located in shady area of maple, pacific yew, and old growth douglas fir. Grider Creek runs along CG. Good trout, salmon, and steelhead fishing in area. Various wildlife includes deer, black bears, and mtn lion.

GETTING THERE: Grider Creek CG is located approx. 2.5 mi. S of Seiad Valley on forest route 46N66.

SINGLE RATE:	No fee	OPEN DATES:	Yearlong*
# of SINGLE SITES:	10	MAX SPUR:	40 feet
		MAX STAY:	14 days
		ELEVATION:	1400 feet

 Campground has hosts   **Reservable sites**   **Accessible facilities**   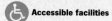 **Fully developed**   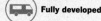 **Semi-developed**   **Rustic facilities**

NOTE: Open dates listed are typical. Actual dates are dependent on conditions such as snow pack.

11 Hidden Horse
Callahan • lat 41°12'45" lon 122°55'00"

DESCRIPTION: Old growth timber, alpine setting with trails to back country lakes. Supplies are 13 mi. from CG. CG is seldom full. Campers may gather firewood. Hiking and horse trails near CG. Corral for horses in each campsite.

GETTING THERE: Hidden Horse CG is located approx. 13 mi. SW of Callahan on primary forest route 93.

SINGLE RATE:	$10	OPEN DATES:	May-Oct
# of SINGLE SITES:	6	MAX SPUR:	40 feet
		MAX STAY:	14 days
		ELEVATION:	5700 feet

12 Hotelling
Forks of Salmon • lat 41°14'23" lon 123°16'27"

DESCRIPTION: In a dense pine forest setting adjacent to the south fork of the Salmon River. Fish for trout and salmon in the river. Supplies available at Forks of Salmon. Deer, bears and birds are common in the area. Campers may gather firewood. No designated trails in the area.

GETTING THERE: Hotelling CG is located approx. 3 mi. S of Forks of Salmon on primary forest route 93.

SINGLE RATE:	No fee	OPEN DATES:	May-Oct
# of SINGLE SITES:	5	MAX SPUR:	16 feet
		MAX STAY:	14 days
		ELEVATION:	1760 feet

13 Idlewild
Sawyers Bar • lat 41°19'50" lon 123°03'34"

DESCRIPTION: In medium dense forest setting next to the North Fork of the Salmon River. Fish for trout and salmon from the river. Supplies at Sawyers Bar. Deer, bears and birds are common to the area. Campers may gather firewood. Mulebridge trailhead is within 2 mi. of the CG.

GETTING THERE: Idlewild CG is located approx. 6 mi. E of Sawyers Bar on county route 1C01.

SINGLE RATE:	$6	OPEN DATES:	May-Oct
# of SINGLE SITES:	18	MAX SPUR:	24 feet
		MAX STAY:	14 days
		ELEVATION:	2600 feet

14 Indian Scotty
Fort Jones • lat 41°38'03" lon 123°04'42"

DESCRIPTION: Located in fir trees on the Scott River. Summers are hot. Deer, bears and birds with fishing on nearby river and lakes. Light use, quiet. Firewood sold locally by Boy Scouts. Several trailheads to Marble Mtn Wilderness. Bears in area. Reservations required for group site.

GETTING THERE: From Fort Jones go W on county route 7F01 approx. 18 mi. to forest route 44N45. Go SW on 44N45 approx. 1/2 mi. to Indian Scotty CG.

SINGLE RATE:	$6	OPEN DATES:	May-Oct
# of SINGLE SITES:	28	MAX SPUR:	65 feet
GROUP RATE:	$30	MAX STAY:	14 days
# of GROUP SITES:	1	ELEVATION:	2400 feet

15 Juanita Lake
Macdoel • lat 41°49'03" lon 122°07'23"

DESCRIPTION: On Jaunita Lake among fir with lake and mtn views. Mild days, expect PM winds. Fish for trout, bass and bullheads on no motor lake. Historic Meiss Lake (wildlife refuge) and mill sites nearby. Supplies at Mt. Hebron, 8 mi. Deer, bobcats in area. Hike/horse trails nearby. Prepare for ticks and mosquitos.

GETTING THERE: From Macdoel go S on US HWY 97 approx. 4 mi. to Ball Mountain Road. Go W on Ball Mountain Road approx. 3 mi. to forest route 46N04. Go N on 46N04 approx. 4 mi. to Juanita Lake CG.

SINGLE RATE:	Varies	OPEN DATES:	May-Oct
# of SINGLE SITES:	23	MAX SPUR:	30 feet
GROUP RATE:	$15	MAX STAY:	14 days
# of GROUP SITES:	1	ELEVATION:	5100 feet

16 Kangaroo Lake
Callahan • lat 41°20'04" lon 122°38'16"

DESCRIPTION: High mountain area with views of lake and valleys below. Mild summers. Boating, no motors allowed. Accessible fishing dock. Supplies at Callahan. Deer, bears and birds. Light use. Firewood sold by Boy Scouts. Pacific Crest Trail and botanical trail on site. Terrific CG. Bears in area.

GETTING THERE: From Callahan go E on state HWY 3 approx. 2 mi. to county route 2H01. Go N on 2H01 approx. 9 mi. to forest route 41N08. Go SE on 41N08 approx. 6 mi. to Kangaroo Lake CG.

SINGLE RATE:	$10	OPEN DATES:	May-Oct
# of SINGLE SITES:	18	MAX SPUR:	40 feet
		MAX STAY:	14 days
		ELEVATION:	6000 feet

17 Lovers Camp
Fort Jones • lat 41°35'20" lon 123°08'45"

DESCRIPTION: Among timber with views of Marble Mtn Wilderness, summers are mild. Fishing at wilderness lakes with trails nearby for hiking or horses. Supplies in Ft. Jones 20 mi. Deer, bears and birds at this lightly used CG. Gather firewood locally. Tent use only.

GETTING THERE: From Fort Jones go W on county route 7F01 approx. 14 mi. to forest route 44N45. Go SW on 44N45 approx. 4.5 mi. to forest route 43N45. Go S on 43N45 approx. 1.5 mi. to Lovers Camp CG.

SINGLE RATE:	No fee	OPEN DATES:	May-Oct
# of SINGLE SITES:	8	MAX SPUR:	15 feet
		MAX STAY:	14 days
		ELEVATION:	4300 feet

18 Martins Dairy
Macdoel • lat 41°48'00" lon 122°12'30"

DESCRIPTION: Alpine forest on Little Shasta River, which may be fished for rainbow trout. View volcanic Goosenest mountain Mild days, cold nights. Historic milk dairy. Supplies at Mt. Hebron, 15 mi. large birds, deer, bobcats in area. Moderate use, heavy for fall hunt. Gather dead wood. Horse, bike, hike trails. Bears area.

GETTING THERE: From Macdoel go S on US HWY 97 approx. 12 mi. to primary forest route 70. Go NW on 70 approx. 12 mi. to forest route 46N09. Go SW on 46N09 approx. 1.5 mi. to Martins Dairy CG.

SINGLE RATE:	Varies	OPEN DATES:	June-Oct
# of SINGLE SITES:	8	MAX SPUR:	30 feet
GROUP RATE:	Varies	MAX STAY:	14 days
# of GROUP SITES:	1	ELEVATION:	6000 feet

19 Matthews Creek
Cecilville • lat 41°11'13" lon 123°12'46"

DESCRIPTION: In an oak, madrone and ponderosa pine forest setting. CG sits next to the south fork of the Salmon River. Nice swimming hole at CG. Fish for trout and in the river. Supplies at Cecilville. Deer, bears and birds in area. Campers may gather firewood. No designated trails in the area.

GETTING THERE: Matthews Creek is located approx. 7 mi. NW of Cecilville on county route 1C02.

SINGLE RATE:	$6	OPEN DATES:	May-Oct
# of SINGLE SITES:	12	MAX SPUR:	24 feet
		MAX STAY:	14 days
		ELEVATION:	1760 feet

20 Mule Bridge
Sawyers Bar • lat 41°21'24" lon 123°04'26"

DESCRIPTION: Small CG in a pine and fir setting on the north fork of the Salmon River. Fish for trout in the river. Supplies at Sawyers Bar. Campers may gather firewood. CG is the trailhead for the North Fork Trail into the Marble Mountain Wilderness. There are public corrals with stock water.

GETTING THERE: From Sawyers Bar go E on county route 1C01 approx. 6 mi. to forest route 41N37.

SINGLE RATE:	No fee	OPEN DATES:	May-Oct
# of SINGLE SITES:	5	MAX SPUR:	24 feet
		MAX STAY:	14 days
		ELEVATION:	2800 feet

 Campground has hosts 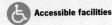 **Reservable sites**   **Accessible facilities** 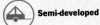 **Fully developed** **Semi-developed**   **Rustic facilities**

NOTE: Open dates listed are typical. Actual dates are dependent on conditions such as snow pack.

21 No Mans Trailhead
Clear Creek • lat 41°43'49" lon 123°31'59"

DESCRIPTION: CG is located in old growth douglas fir and is adjacent to No Man's Creek. CG has a large parking area. CG is 1/2 mi. from the Siskiyou Wilderness Area which has scenic lakes and the best swimming holes in area.

GETTING THERE: From Clear Creek go N approx. 1 mi. to forest route 15N35. Go w on 15N35 6 mi. to No Mans River Trailhead CG. Road has tight turns and is not recommended for large RVs or trailers.

SINGLE RATE:	No fee	OPEN DATES:	Yearlong*
# of SINGLE SITES:	2	MAX SPUR:	30 feet
		MAX STAY:	14 days
		ELEVATION:	1600 feet

22 Norcross
Happy Camp • lat 41°38'51" lon 123°18'37"

DESCRIPTION: CG is located in old growth forest with some chinquipin, madrone, and tan oak. There is also an open meadow on site. CG has horse facilities including corrals and trails. Good fishing in area. Can be busy holiday weekends. CG trail leads into magnificent Marble Mtn Wilderness. No drinking water.

GETTING THERE: From Happy Camp go S on county route 7C001 approx. 12 mi. to Norcross CG.

SINGLE RATE:	No fee	OPEN DATES:	Yearlong
# of SINGLE SITES:	6	MAX SPUR:	40 feet
		MAX STAY:	14 days
		ELEVATION:	2400 feet

23 Nordheimer Flat
Somes Bar • lat 41°17'58" lon 123°21'39"

DESCRIPTION: CG is located in mixed conifer and hardwoods including oak and madrone. Some sites have creek views. Good salmon fishing in Nordheimer Creek and Salmon River. Visit historical mining sites. Supplies 4 mi. to Forks of Salmon. Deer, foxes, raccoons, and squirrels. Busy holidays.

GETTING THERE: Nordheimer Flat CG is located approx. 12 mi. E of Somes Bar on primary forest route 93 (Salmon River Road).

SINGLE RATE:	$8	OPEN DATES:	May-Oct
# of SINGLE SITES:	8		
GROUP RATE:	$40	MAX STAY:	14 days
# of GROUP SITES:	4	ELEVATION:	1200 feet

24 Oak Bottom
Somes Bar • lat 41°22'39" lon 123°27'01"

DESCRIPTION: CG is in conifer and hardwood forest across Salmon River Road from the Salmon River. Supplies 2 mi. to Somes Bar. Deer, foxes, squirrel, and raccoons in area. Busy holidays. Gather firewood locally.

GETTING THERE: Oak Bottom CG is located approx. 2 mi. E of Somes Bar on primary forest route 93 (Salmon River Road).

SINGLE RATE:	$8	OPEN DATES:	May-Oct
# of SINGLE SITES:	26		
		MAX STAY:	14 days
		ELEVATION:	700 feet

25 O'Neil Creek
Seiad Valley • lat 41°48'34" lon 123°06'58"

DESCRIPTION: CG is located in a heavily forested area with big leaf maples. O'Neil Creek runs along CG. Good salmon, steelhead, and trout fishing area. Various wildlife includes deer, black bears and mtn lions. CG can be busy holiday weekends.

GETTING THERE: O'Neil Creek CG is located approx. 5 mi. E of Seiad Valley on state HWY 96.

SINGLE RATE:	Varies	OPEN DATES:	Yearlong*
# of SINGLE SITES:	18	MAX SPUR:	25 feet
		MAX STAY:	14 days
		ELEVATION:	1500 feet

26 Oogaromtok (Frog Pond)
Somes Bar • lat 41°28'00" lon 123°31'30"

DESCRIPTION: CG is in a mixed conifer and hardwood forest setting on Oogaromtok Lake. This lake is stocked with trout for good fishing. Very scenic drive to CG with views of river corridor below. Supplies at Somes Bar. Deer, bears, elk, foxes, raccoons, bald eagles and squirrels. No designated trails in the area.

GETTING THERE: From Somes Bar go N on state HWY 96 15.5 mi. to forest route 14N69. Go S on 14N69 2 mi. to forest route 14N21. Go S on 14N21 to forest route 13N13. Go S on 13N13 10 mi. to Oogaromtok CG.

SINGLE RATE:	No fee	OPEN DATES:	May-Oct
# of SINGLE SITES:	3		
		MAX STAY:	14 days
		ELEVATION:	1900 feet

27 Red Bank
Forks of Salmon • lat 41°17'53" lon 123°13'45"

DESCRIPTION: This is an often missed CG, situated in a dense stand of pine, madrone and fir. CG sits adjacent to the North Fork of the Salmon River. Fish for trout from the banks. Supplies at Forks of Salmon. Deer, bears and birds can be seen in the area. No designated trails in the area.

GETTING THERE: Red Bank CG is located approx. 7 mi. NE of Forks of Salmon on county route 1C01.

SINGLE RATE:	No fee	OPEN DATES:	May-Oct
# of SINGLE SITES:	5		
		MAX STAY:	14 days
		ELEVATION:	2900 feet

28 Sarah Totten
Seiad Valley • lat 41°47'15" lon 123°03'06"

DESCRIPTION: CG is located in oak and ponderosa pine along the Klamath River. Good steelhead, trout and salmon fishing in river. Various wildlife in area includes deer, black bears, otters, osprey and mtn lions. Can be busy holiday weekends.

GETTING THERE: Sarah Totten CG is located approx. 9 mi. E of Seiad Valley on state HWY 96.

SINGLE RATE:	Varies	OPEN DATES:	Yearlong*
# of SINGLE SITES:	8	MAX SPUR:	40 feet
GROUP RATE:	Varies	MAX STAY:	14 days
# of GROUP SITES:	2	ELEVATION:	1400 feet

29 Shadow Creek
Cecilville • lat 41°12'07" lon 123°04'05"

DESCRIPTION: CG is in a mixed conifer setting with shady camping units. CG sits at the confluence of Salmon Creek and east fork of the Salmon River. Fish for trout and salmon in the river. Supplies at Cecilville. Deer, bears and birds are common in the area. Campers may gather firewood.

GETTING THERE: Shadow Creek CG is located approx. 7 mi. NE of Cecilville on primary forest route 93.

SINGLE RATE:	No fee	OPEN DATES:	May-Oct
# of SINGLE SITES:	5	MAX SPUR:	16 feet
		MAX STAY:	14 days
		ELEVATION:	2900 feet

30 Shafter
Mount Hebron • lat 41°42'38" lon 121°58'47"

DESCRIPTION: Park like setting on Butte Cr. with views of Mt. Shasta and Orr mountain Heavy snow, no services in winter. Trout in nearby creeks. Historic mill sites and logging towns. S. Pacific RR route for train fans. Supplies at Mt. Hebron. Deer, predator birds among wildlife. Gather firewood. Excellent mountain bike roads.

GETTING THERE: From Mount Hebron go S on state HWY 8Q01 approx. 6 mi. to Shafter CG.

SINGLE RATE:	Varies	OPEN DATES:	Yearlong
# of SINGLE SITES:	10	MAX SPUR:	30 feet
		MAX STAY:	14 days
		ELEVATION:	4300 feet

 Campground has hosts   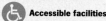 **Reservable sites**   **Accessible facilities**   **Fully developed**   **Semi-developed**   **Rustic facilities**

NOTE: Open dates listed are typical. Actual dates are dependent on conditions such as snow pack.

31 Sulphur Springs
Happy Camp • lat 41°39'33" lon 123°19'09"

DESCRIPTION: CG is located in old growth douglas fir. Fifty yard walk from parking to sites. Good fishing in area. Wildlife includs deer and black bears. Busy holiday weekends. Elk Creek Trail leads into magnificent Marble Mtn Wilderness. Hot spring pool in adjacent Elk Creek.

GETTING THERE: From Happy Camp go S on county route 7C001 approx. 11 mi. to Sulpher Springs CG.

SINGLE RATE:	No fee	OPEN DATES:	Yearlong*
# of SINGLE SITES:	7		
		MAX STAY:	14 days
		ELEVATION:	3100 feet

32 Ti Bar Flat
Somes Bar • lat 41°31'00" lon 123°31'30"

DESCRIPTION: CG is located on a large river bar on the Klamath River with some open and some shaded sites. Good salmon fishing on the Klamath River. Campers may gather firewood. Campfire permit required. Native boat launch.

GETTING THERE: Ti Bar CG is located approx. 13 mi. N of Somes Bar on state HWY 96.

SINGLE RATE:	No fee	OPEN DATES:	May-Oct
# of SINGLE SITES:	5		
		MAX STAY:	14 days
		ELEVATION:	700 feet

33 Trail Creek
Cecilville • lat 41°13'45" lon 122°58'20"

DESCRIPTION: In a mixed conifer setting, medium developed CG. Supplies at Cecilville. Deer, bears and birds are viewed in the area. Nearby Trail Creek and East Fork offer stream fishing. CG offers great day hiking into several lakes in the Trinity Alps Wilderness. Access to the Pacific Crest Trail is nearby.

GETTING THERE: Trail Creek CG is located approx. 13 mi. NE of Cecilville on primary forest route 93.

SINGLE RATE:	$6	OPEN DATES:	May-Oct
# of SINGLE SITES:	12	MAX SPUR:	20 feet
		MAX STAY:	14 days
		ELEVATION:	4700 feet

34 Tree of Heaven
Swiss Bar • lat 41°49'56" lon 122°39'30"

DESCRIPTION: In an open setting on the banks of the Klamath River with boat launch. There is a Birding Nature Trail at CG. The Klamath River has year round trout and seasonal steelhead and salmon fishing. Supplies are at Swiss Bar. Trails in the area. The day use area has horseshoe pits and volleyball area.

GETTING THERE: Tree of Heaven CG is located approx. 4 mi. E of Swiss Bar on state HWY 96.

SINGLE RATE:	$10	OPEN DATES:	Yearlong
# of SINGLE SITES:	20	MAX SPUR:	34 feet
		MAX STAY:	14 days
		ELEVATION:	2100 feet

35 West Branch
Happy Camp • lat 41°55'54" lon 123°28'26"

DESCRIPTION: CG is located in old growth douglas fir with some white fir, madrone and oak. Sites are semi-shaded and reside between Indian Creek and the West Branch of Indian Creek. Good trout, salmon, and steelhead fishing in area. Various wildlife include deer and black bears. Can be busy holiday weekends.

GETTING THERE: West Branch CG is located approx. 11 mi. N of Happy Camp on county route 7C01.

SINGLE RATE:	Varies	OPEN DATES:	Yearlong*
# of SINGLE SITES:	15	MAX SPUR:	12 feet
		MAX STAY:	14 days
		ELEVATION:	2200 feet

 Campground has hosts   🔒 Reservable sites   ♿ Accessible facilities   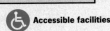 Fully developed   Semi-developed   Rustic facilities

NOTE: Open dates listed are typical. Actual dates are dependent on conditions such as snow pack.

USFS Photo

LAKE TAHOE BASIN MANAGEMENT UNIT

Majestic scenery and diverse recreation opportunities draw millions of visitors to the Lake Tahoe Basin annually. Changing colors throughout the year afford a brilliant backdrop to the many available activities. The Basin is home to a rich diversity of plants and animals that can be viewed during guided walks at interpretive sites and on the many forest trails. Seasonal activities include skiing, snowshoeing, camping, fishing, hiking, music and cultural festivals, art and craft exhibits, and many other sports and events.

Lake Tahoe has a rich and diverse cultural heritage spanning thousands of years. At the time of first European contact, the Washoe Indians and their ancestors had been calling the resource-rich Lake Tahoe their home for at least 2000 years. Many different people have left their mark on the land during and since that time. Basque sheepherders left their carvings on aspen trees in groves around the lake. Chinese laborers left evidence of their campsites on the wooded slopes surrounding the lake and European-operated lumber mill sites have been recorded as having extensive historic road systems, railroad alignments, trails, and flumes.

Lake Tahoe is now a destination for visitors worldwide, and it is also still home to the Washoe Tribe.

LAKE TAHOE BASIN MANAGEMENT UNIT • CALIFORNIA • LOCATOR MAP

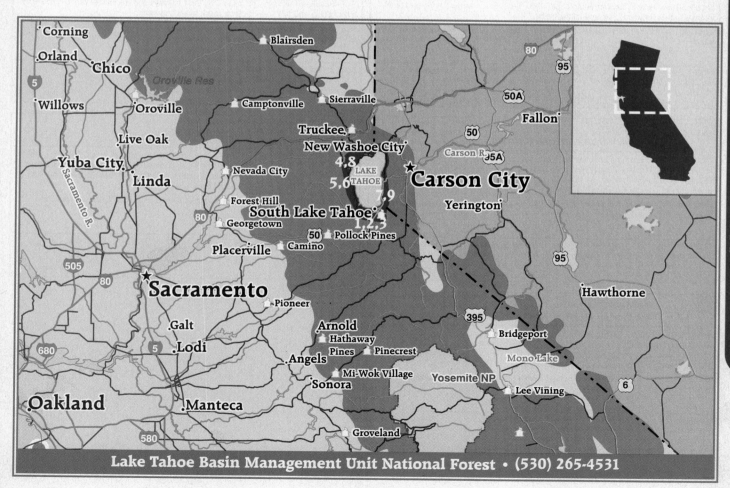

Lake Tahoe Basin Management Unit National Forest • (530) 265-4531

1 Bayview
Emerald Bay • lat 38°56'41" lon 120°05'58"

DESCRIPTION: CG above Emerald Bay with exceptional views of Lake Tahoe and wild-flowers. Fish for trout on area lakes. Coyotes, raccoons, and various birds in area. Fills daily by August. Gather firewood. Horse and hiking trails. Wilderness permits required. Be cautious of bears, ticks, and poison oak.

GETTING THERE: Bayview CG is located approx. 3 mi. S of Emerald Bay on state HWY 89.

SINGLE RATE:	$5	OPEN DATES:	May-Oct*
# of SINGLE SITES:	10	MAX SPUR:	20 feet
		MAX STAY:	7 days
		ELEVATION:	6300 feet

6 Meeks Bay
Tahoma • lat 39°02'09" lon 120°07'20"

DESCRIPTION: This CG is situated in a mixed pine, fir, and juniper forest with some manzanita brush. Views of Lake Tahoe and a lovely beach. Historic damn at Tahoe City. Supplies are available 3 mi. away at Tahoma. Firewood can be purchased on site. Numerous recreation trails nearby.

GETTING THERE: Meeks Bay Resort and Marina CG is located approx. 3 mi. S of Tahoma on state HWY 89.

SINGLE RATE:	Varies	OPEN DATES:	May-Oct
# of SINGLE SITES:	28	MAX SPUR:	45 feet
		MAX STAY:	14 days
		ELEVATION:	6250 feet

2 Camp Richardson
Camp Richardson • lat 38°55'55" lon 120°02'30"

DESCRIPTION: CG set among tall pine, fir, and cedar on Lake Take Tahoe. Beaches, marina, and restaurant on site. Noon rain until Aug.. Trout in area lakes and Taylor Creek. CG is historic 1900's site. Supplies on site. Watch for bears and coyotes. Gather or buy firewood or buy locally. Multiple trails.

GETTING THERE: Camp Richardson CG is located approx. 3 mi. N of South Lake Tahoe on HWY 89.

SINGLE RATE:	Varies	OPEN DATES:	May-Oct
# of SINGLE SITES:	320	MAX SPUR:	35 feet
		MAX STAY:	14 days
		ELEVATION:	6250 feet

7 Nevada Beach
Lakeridge • lat 38°58'47" lon 119°57'08"

DESCRIPTION: CG situated on Lake Tahoe's east shore, in a park-like area. Trout fishing opportunities, average size 4-8 lbs.. Historic Zephyr Cove is nearby. Supplies are available at Round Hill. Firewood can be purchased in Round Hill. Numerous hiking and mountain bike trails available in the area.

GETTING THERE: Nevada Beach CG is located approx. 5 mi. S of Lakeridge on I-50.

SINGLE RATE:	Varies	OPEN DATES:	May-Oct
# of SINGLE SITES:	54	MAX SPUR:	45 feet
		MAX STAY:	14 days
		ELEVATION:	6250 feet

3 Fallen Leaf Lake
Camp Richardson • lat 38°56'00" lon 120°02'30"

DESCRIPTION: In mixed thick fir forest near Fallen Leaf Lake and Taylor Creek. Trout fishing. Expect rain until July. Mild days. 1 mi. to Historic Tallac and Camp Richardson. Supplies 1 mi. away at store or South Lake Tahoe. Raccoons, coyotes, bears, and birds in area. Gather firewood. Bike and hiking trails.

GETTING THERE: Fallen Leaf Lake CG is located approx. 3 mi. N of Lake Tahoe on HWY 89.

SINGLE RATE:	$15	OPEN DATES:	May-Oct
# of SINGLE SITES:	205	MAX SPUR:	40 feet
		MAX STAY:	14 days
		ELEVATION:	6250 feet

8 William Kent
Idlewild • lat 39°08'23" lon 120°09'26"

DESCRIPTION: CG set in a grove of pine and fir with some rock and brush between sites. Thundershowers are common. Good fishing in adjacent Lake Tahoe. Visit historic dam. Supplies 4 mi. away at Tahoe City. Busy holidays and weekends. Various mountain bike, hiking, and ATV trails in area. Black bears common.

GETTING THERE: William Kent CG is located approx. 2 mi. N of Idlewild on state HWY 89.

SINGLE RATE:	$14	OPEN DATES:	May-Oct*
# of SINGLE SITES:	91	MAX SPUR:	57 feet
		MAX STAY:	7 days
		ELEVATION:	6250 feet

4 Kaspian
Tahoe City • lat 39°06'51" lon 120°09'27"

DESCRIPTION: CG set in a pine and fir forest. Boat and shore fish for large lake trout. T-storms in early summer. Donner Memorial State Park and Tallac Historic Site are nearby. Supplies in Homewood. Watch for bears and coyotes. Busy through summer. Gather fire-wood. Hiking, mountain bike, and ATV trails.

GETTING THERE: From Tahoe City go S on HWY 89 approx. 6 mi. to Kaspian CG on Lake Tahoe's W shore.

SINGLE RATE:	$12	OPEN DATES:	May-Oct
# of SINGLE SITES:	10	MAX SPUR:	20 feet
		MAX STAY:	14 days
		ELEVATION:	6250 feet

9 Zephyr Cove
Lakeridge • lat 39°00'30" lon 119°57'00"

DESCRIPTION: CG set among semi-dense pine and fir with lake views. T-showers are common. Good fishing on adjacent Lake Tahoe. Limited supplies on site. Busy holidays, weekends, and late summer. Firewood on site. Various trails in area. Horse stable with rentals on site. Be cautious of black bears.

GETTING THERE: Zephyr Cove CG is located approx. 3 mi. S of Lakeridge on I-50.

SINGLE RATE:	Varies	OPEN DATES:	May-Oct*
# of SINGLE SITES:	175	MAX SPUR:	40 feet
GROUP RATE:	Varies	MAX STAY:	14 days
		ELEVATION:	6250 feet

5 Meeks Bay
Tahoe City • lat 39°02'09" lon 120°07'20"

DESCRIPTION: CG set among fir and juniper with manzanita brush. Some sites have views Beach provided. Abundant wildflowers. Fish for trout at lake or Meeks Creek. Historic Tallac Site and Donner Memorial Park nearby. Heavy use. Be cautious of bears. Hiking, mountain bike, jeep, and ATV trails.

GETTING THERE: Meeks Bay CG is located approx. 10 mi. S of Tahoe City on state HWY 89.

SINGLE RATE:	$15	OPEN DATES:	May-Sept
# of SINGLE SITES:	40	MAX SPUR:	20 feet
		MAX STAY:	14 days
		ELEVATION:	6250 feet

 Campground has hosts   **Reservable sites**   **Accessible facilities**    **Fully developed**   **Semi-developed**   **Rustic facilities**

NOTE: Open dates listed are typical. Actual dates are dependent on conditions such as snow pack.

Page 84

USFS Photo

LASSEN NATIONAL FOREST

Lassen National Forest lies at the heart of a fascinating region of California—a crossroads of people and nature. This is where the granite of the Sierra Nevada, the lava of the Cascades and the Modoc Plateau and the sagebrush of Great Basin meet and blend.

It is an area of great variety, greeting visitors with a diversity of recreational opportunities and adventures. Within Lassen National Forest, you can explore a lava tube or the land of Ishi, the last survivor of the Yahi Yana Native American tribe; drive four-wheel trails into high granite country appointed with sapphire lakes, or discover spring wildflowers on foot. Bask in the spectacular scenery of Crater Lake, a 27-acre deep blue lake nestled in the crater of an old volcano, or spend a quiet day angling for trout, Chinook salmon or small mouth bass at one of the forest's hundreds of lakes and streams. Winter means sledding, tobogganing and tubing. Lassen has extensive snowmobiling areas, cross-country trail systems, and a small private downhill area, Stover Mountain.

Over 360 species of fish and wildlife call Lassen National Forest home. A little luck, persistence, and patience can result in an unforgettable wildlife experience. Bald eagles, deer, pronghorns, and coyotes are all waiting to be seen.

LASSEN NATIONAL FOREST • CALIFORNIA • LOCATOR MAP

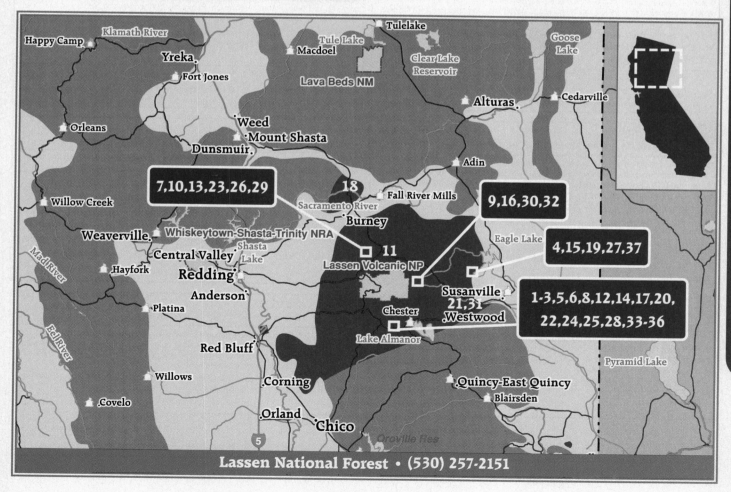

Lassen National Forest • (530) 257-2151

1 Alder
Chester • lat 40°12'37" lon 121°29'42"

DESCRIPTION: Located in mixed pine and oak forest along scenic Deer Creek. Cooler than valley w/mild days, cool nights. Stream fish the creek (special regs apply). Supplies in Chester. Numerous birds and black tailed deer in area. Gather firewood locally.

GETTING THERE: From Chester go W on state HWY 36/89 approx. 12 mi. to state HWY 32. Go SW on 32 approx. 7 mi. to Alder CG. Not recommended for trailers.

SINGLE RATE:	$9	OPEN DATES:	Mar-Nov*
# of SINGLE SITES:	6	MAX STAY:	14 days
		ELEVATION:	3900 feet

2 Almanor
Chester • lat 40°13'07" lon 121°10'37"

DESCRIPTION: Among mixed pine and fir forest on Lake Almanor. Warm days, cool mornings. Fish for trout, bass, salmon & catfish. Deer, bear, raptors and small wildlife. Gather firewood locally. Access paved Lake Almanor Rec Trail (9.6 mi. long), for hiking, biking & roller blading (no motorized use).

GETTING THERE: From Chester go SW on state HWY 36/89 approx. 2 mi. to state HWY 89. Go SE 89 approx. 6 mi. to county route 310. Go E on 310 approx. 1 mi. to Almanor CG.

SINGLE RATE:	$15	OPEN DATES:	May-Nov*
# of SINGLE SITES:	103	MAX SPUR:	32 feet
GROUP RATE:	$25	MAX STAY:	14 days
# of GROUP SITES:	1	ELEVATION:	4550 feet

3 Almanor Group
Chester • lat 40°13'07" lon 121°10'37"

DESCRIPTION: In open pine stand surrounded by forest. Lake Almanor has fishing. Historic Lassen Emigrant Trail passes nearby. Supplies in Chester. Deer and small wildlife in area. Gather firewood locally. Access to paved Lake Almanor Rec Trail for hiking, biking and roller blading. (Non motorized use only).

GETTING THERE: From Chester go SW on state HWY 36/89 approx. 2 mi. to state HWY 89. Go SE 89 approx. 6 mi. to county route 310. Go E (right) on 310 approx. 1 mi. to Almanor Group CG. Located next to rest area.

		OPEN DATES:	May-Nov*
GROUP RATE:	$85	MAX STAY:	14 days
# of GROUP SITES:	20	ELEVATION:	4500 feet

4 Aspen
Susanville • lat 40°33'20" lon 120°46'16"

DESCRIPTION: Located in pines w/little grass, mostly sand on Eagle Lake. Warm days, cool mornings. Shady site, frequent noon winds. Fish Eagle Lake for trout from boat or shore. Historic Gallatin House nearby. Basic supplies 1/4 mi.. Osprey and waterfowl in area. Boat ramp. Many multi-use trails nearby. Walk-in only.

GETTING THERE: From Susanville go W on state HWY 36 2 mi. to county route A-1. Go NW on A-1 12 mi. to county route 231. Go E on 231 2 mi. to Aspen CG. Road is narrow with sharp curves.

SINGLE RATE:	$12	OPEN DATES:	May-Oct*
# of SINGLE SITES:	26	MAX SPUR:	20 feet
		MAX STAY:	14 days
		ELEVATION:	5100 feet

5 Battle Creek
Mineral • lat 40°21'15" lon 121°37'30"

DESCRIPTION: In open park like pine forest on Battle Creek. Stream fishing on creek (special regs may apply). Basic supplies in Mineral, or go to Red Bluff, 35 mi. W. Deer and small wildlife. Gather firewood locally. Hiking access to Spencer Meadows, Heart Lake and Pacific Crest Trails nearby.

GETTING THERE: Battle Creek CG is located approx. 1.5 mi. W of Mineral on state HWY 36.

SINGLE RATE:	$14	OPEN DATES:	Apr-Nov*
# of SINGLE SITES:	50	MAX SPUR:	20 feet
		MAX STAY:	14 days
		ELEVATION:	4800 feet

6 Benner
Chester • lat 40°23'44" lon 121°16'03"

DESCRIPTION: Located in pine & fir forest on Benner Creek. Stream fish the creek. Supplies in Chester, 7 mi. Deer, bear and small wildlife. Gather firewood locally. Hiking access to Pacific Crest Trail, Caribou Wilderness and Lassen Volcanic Nat'l Park nearby.

GETTING THERE: Benner CG is located approx. 7 mi. N of Chester on county route 318.

SINGLE RATE:	$9	OPEN DATES:	May-Nov*
# of SINGLE SITES:	9	MAX SPUR:	20 feet
		MAX STAY:	14 days
		ELEVATION:	5500 feet

7 Big Pine
Burney • lat 40°37'59" lon 121°27'58"

DESCRIPTION: CG is located in ponderosa and jeffery pine on Hat Creek. Hat Creek is world renowned for fly fishing for trout. Trails in area. Busy on holiday weekends in summer. Deer, chipmunks and birds in area. CG has water. Due to swift current in creek swimming is discouraged. Near Lassen NP.

GETTING THERE: From Burney go NE on state HWY 299 approx. 5 mi. to state HWY 89. Go SE on 89 approx. 27 mi. to forest route 32N13. Go S on 32N13 approx. 1 mi. to Big Pine CG.

SINGLE RATE:	$10	OPEN DATES:	Apr-Oct
# of SINGLE SITES:	19	MAX SPUR:	20 feet
		MAX STAY:	14 days
		ELEVATION:	4500 feet

8 Black Rock
Paynes Creek • lat 40°11'02" lon 121°42'44"

DESCRIPTION: Located in low elevation oak woods mixed w/pine on Mill Creek. Stream fish creek, special regs apply. Hot days. Basic supplies in Paynes Creek. Deer, turkeys, wild pigs and bear in area on occasion. Rarely fills. Gather firewood. Access to Ishi Wilderness and Ponderosa Way. Ticks are a problem.

GETTING THERE: From Paynes Creek go SE on county route 202 approx. 8 mi. to county route 707B. Go S on 707B approx. 18 mi. to Black Rock CG.

SINGLE RATE:	$9	OPEN DATES:	Yearlong*
# of SINGLE SITES:	6	MAX SPUR:	20 feet
		MAX STAY:	14 days
		ELEVATION:	2100 feet

9 Bogard
Susanville • lat 40°34'34" lon 121°05'54"

DESCRIPTION: Surrounded by tall pine forest. Hot summer days, noon t-storms. Trout fish Eagle Lake or McCoy Reservoir or stream fish Hat Creek. Supplies in Susanville. Deer, antelope, bobcats & small wildlife. Low use. Gather firewood. Hike Caribou Wilderness nearby. Dirt roads for ATV & mountain bikes.

GETTING THERE: From Susanville go E on state HWY 36 approx. 5 mi. to state HWY 44. Go NW on 44 approx. 21 mi. to forest route 31N26. Go W on 31N26 approx. 2 mi. to Bogard CG.

SINGLE RATE:	$9	OPEN DATES:	May-Oct
# of SINGLE SITES:	22	MAX SPUR:	25 feet
		MAX STAY:	14 days
		ELEVATION:	5600 feet

10 Bridge
Burney • lat 40°43'50" lon 121°26'01"

DESCRIPTION: CG is located in ponderosa and jeffery pine on Hat Creek. Hat Creek is world renowned for fly fishing for trout. Trails in area. Busy on holiday weekends in summer. Deer, chipmunks and birds in area. CG has water. Due to swift current in creek swimming is discouraged. Near Lassen NP.

GETTING THERE: From Burney go NE on state HWY 299 approx. 5 mi. to state HWY 89. Go SE on 89 approx. 19 mi. to Bridge CG.

SINGLE RATE:	$11	OPEN DATES:	Apr-Oct
# of SINGLE SITES:	25	MAX SPUR:	20 feet
		MAX STAY:	14 days
		ELEVATION:	4000 feet

 Campground has hosts   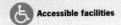 **Reservable sites**   **Accessible facilities**   **Fully developed**   **Semi-developed**   **Rustic facilities**

NOTE: Open dates listed are typical. Actual dates are dependent on conditions such as snow pack.

11 Butte Creek
Burney • lat 40°36'40" lon 121°17'42"

DESCRIPTION: In cleared area of tall pines & aspen on seasonal creek. Hot summers with frequent t-storms. Trout fish Butte Lake, 3 mi. or Hat Cr, 20 mi. Basic supplies 10 mi. Some bear, deer, bobcats & small wildlife. Fills hunt season. Gather firewood. Hiking at Lassen Nat'l Park. Horse, mountain bike & ATV use nearby.

GETTING THERE: From Burney go NE on state HWY 299 5 mi. to state HWY 89. Go SE on 89 23 to state HWY 44. Go E on 44 10 mi. to forest route 32N21. Go S on 32N21 2.5 mi. to Butte Creek CG.

SINGLE RATE:	No fee	OPEN DATES:	May-Oct
# of SINGLE SITES:	20	MAX SPUR:	20 feet
		MAX STAY:	14 days
		ELEVATION:	5600 feet

12 Butte Meadows
Butte Meadows • lat 40°04'48" lon 121°30'57"

DESCRIPTION: Set in pine forest on Butte Creek. Stream fishing in creek. Basic supplies in Butte Meadows or go to Chico. Deer and small wildlife. Fills holiday weekends. Gather firewood locally.

GETTING THERE: Butte Meadows CG is located approx. 1 mi. W of Butte Meadows on county route 91422 (Humboldt Road).

SINGLE RATE:	$10	OPEN DATES:	Apr-Nov*
# of SINGLE SITES:	12	MAX SPUR:	20 feet
		MAX STAY:	14 days
		ELEVATION:	4600 feet

13 Cave
Burney • lat 40°41'06" lon 121°25'13"

DESCRIPTION: CG is located in ponderosa and jeffery pine on Hat Creek. Hat Creek is a world renowned fly fishing stream. Trails in area. Busy on holiday weekends in summer. Deer, chipmunks and birds in area. CG has water. Swimming is discouraged. Near Lassen NP. Barrier free fishing access.

GETTING THERE: From Burney go NE on state HWY 299 approx. 5 mi. to state HWY 89. Go SE on 89 approx. 23 mi. to Cave CG.

SINGLE RATE:	$13	OPEN DATES:	Apr-Oct
# of SINGLE SITES:	46	MAX SPUR:	20 feet
		MAX STAY:	14 days
		ELEVATION:	4300 feet

14 Cherry Hill
Butte Meadows • lat 40°05'54" lon 121°29'35"

DESCRIPTION: This CG is situated in a mixed pine and fir forest on the banks of Butte Creek. Stream fishing on creek. Limited supplies are available in Butte Meadows, or go to Chico. Deer and small wildlife in the area. Campers may gather their firewood locally. There are 13 walk-in tent only campsites.

GETTING THERE: Cherry Hill CG is located approx. 3 mi. NE of Butte Meadows on county route 91422 (Humboldt Road).

SINGLE RATE:	$11	OPEN DATES:	Apr-Nov*
# of SINGLE SITES:	26	MAX SPUR:	20 feet
GROUP RATE:	$18	MAX STAY:	14 days
# of GROUP SITES:	1	ELEVATION:	4700 feet

15 Christie
Susanville • lat 40°34'05" lon 120°50'11"

DESCRIPTION: CG is located in tall pine with scattered underbrush. Fish for trout on adjacent Eagle Lake. Visit historic Gallatin House and Spalding Cabin. Supplies 3 mi. away at marina. Wildlife includes ospreys, pelicans, egrets, coyotes, and foxes. Firewood on site. Numerous multi-use trails in area.

GETTING THERE: From Susanville go W on state HWY 36 approx. 3 mi. to county route A-1. Go N on A-1 approx. 15.5 mi. to Christie CG. Road is narrow with sharp curves. Large vehicles should use caution.

SINGLE RATE:	$2	OPEN DATES:	May-Oct
# of SINGLE SITES:	69	MAX SPUR:	50 feet
		MAX STAY:	14 days
		ELEVATION:	5100 feet

16 Crater Lake
Susanville • lat 40°37'37" lon 121°02'30"

DESCRIPTION: CG set in a ponderosa pine and aspen forest among lava rocks on the shores of Crater Lake (which is actually inside of a small volcano crater). Warm days with cool nights. Boat and shore fish for rainbows. Supplies in Susanville. Gather firewood locally. Hike dirt logging roads.

GETTING THERE: From Susanville go W on state HWY 36 5 mi. to state HWY 44. NW 22 mi. to forest route 32N08. NE 7 mi. to Crater Lake CG. Not recommended for large RVs; road is steep with sharp curves and washboard.

SINGLE RATE:	$11	OPEN DATES:	June-Oct
# of SINGLE SITES:	17	MAX SPUR:	20 feet
		MAX STAY:	14 days
		ELEVATION:	6800 feet

17 Domingo Springs
Chester • lat 40°21'00" lon 121°20'00"

DESCRIPTION: CG set in a mixed pine and fir forest on Domingo Springs. Views of the springs and streams (natural spring with wild watercress), which feed the Feather River. Supplies in Chester. Deer and small wildlife in area. Gather firewood locally. Pacific Crest Trail is nearby. Prepare for mosquitos in early summer.

GETTING THERE: From Chester go NW on county route 312 approx. 5.5 mi. to county route 311. Go NW on 311 approx. 2 mi. to Domingo Springs CG. Not recommended for trailers.

SINGLE RATE:	$11	OPEN DATES:	May-Nov*
# of SINGLE SITES:	18	MAX SPUR:	20 feet
		MAX STAY:	14 days
		ELEVATION:	5060 feet

18 Dusty
Burney • lat 41°00'57" lon 121°36'37"

DESCRIPTION: CG is set among ponderosa and jeffery pine on the banks of Hat Creek. Hat Creek is world renowned for fly fishing for trout. Several trails in area. Busy on holiday weekends in summer. Water and services available. Due to swift current in creek swimming is discouraged. Near Lassen Volcanic National Park.

GETTING THERE: From Burney go NE on state HWY 299 approx. 5 mi. to state HWY 89. Go NW on 89 approx. 6.5 mi. to forest route 37N59Y. Go E on 37N59Y approx. 1/2 mi. to Dusty CG.

SINGLE RATE:	Varies	OPEN DATES:	May-Oct
# of SINGLE SITES:	5	MAX SPUR:	20 feet
		MAX STAY:	14 days
# of GROUP SITES:	2	ELEVATION:	3000 feet

19 Eagle
Susanville • lat 40°32'55" lon 120°46'44"

DESCRIPTION: CG is located in an open grove of tall pine. P.M. t-showers and winds. Good trout fishing at nearby Eagle Lake. Visit historic Galatin House and Spalding Cabin. Supplies 1 mi. at marina. Wildlife includes foxes, coyotes, pelicans, and egrets. Busy holidays. Trails in area. Reservations only.

GETTING THERE: From Susanville go W on state HWY 36 3 mi. to county route A-1. Go N 12 mi. to county route 231. Go E 1.5 mi. to Eagle CG. Road is narrow with sharp curves. Large vehicles should use caution.

SINGLE RATE:	$14	OPEN DATES:	May-Oct
# of SINGLE SITES:	50	MAX SPUR:	38 feet
		MAX STAY:	14 days
		ELEVATION:	5100 feet

20 Elam
Chester • lat 40°14'43" lon 121°26'51"

DESCRIPTION: CG situated in a mixed pine and fir forest on the banks of Elam Creek. Views of creek and surrounding forest. Stream fish the creek. Supplies are available in Chester. Watch for deer, squirrels, and various birds in the area. Fills opening weekend of fishing season. Gather firewood locally.

GETTING THERE: From Chester go W on state HWY 36/89 approx. 12 mi. to state HWY 32. Go SW on 32 approx. 3 mi. to Elam CG.

SINGLE RATE:	$12	OPEN DATES:	Apr-Nov*
# of SINGLE SITES:	15	MAX SPUR:	20 feet
		MAX STAY:	14 days
		ELEVATION:	4400 feet

 Campground has hosts 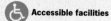 **Reservable sites**   **Accessible facilities**   **Fully developed**   **Semi-developed**   **Rustic facilities**

NOTE: Open dates listed are typical. Actual dates are dependent on conditions such as snow pack.

21 Goumaz
Susanville • lat 40°24'30" lon 120°52'30"

DESCRIPTION: CG situated in a ponderosa pine forest with Susan River running through it. Bank fish for rainbow trout from river. Historical Bizz Johnston trail is 9 mi. E at Devil's Corral. Supplies are available at Susanville. Campers may gather their firewood locally. No drinking water available on site.

GETTING THERE: From Susanville go W on state HWY 36 approx. 7 mi. to forest route 30N03. Go W on 30N03 approx. 6 mi. to Goumaz CG.

SINGLE RATE:	$6	OPEN DATES:	May-Oct*
# of SINGLE SITES:	5	MAX SPUR:	20 feet
		MAX STAY:	14 days
		ELEVATION:	5200 feet

22 Gurnsey Creek
Chester • lat 40°18'29" lon 121°25'27"

DESCRIPTION: CG set on the banks of Gurnsey Creek in a mixed pine and fir forest. Views of the creek and surrounding forest. Stream fish in creek. Supplies are available in Chester. Deer and small wildlife in area. Gather firewood locally. Within driving distance of Lassen Volcanic National Park for day trips.

GETTING THERE: Gurnsey Creek CG is located approx. 14 mi. W of Chester on state HWY 36.

SINGLE RATE:	$11	OPEN DATES:	May-Nov*
# of SINGLE SITES:	32	MAX SPUR:	20 feet
GROUP RATE:	$110	MAX STAY:	14 days
# of GROUP SITES:	20	ELEVATION:	4700 feet

23 Hat Creek
Burney • lat 40°40'04" lon 121°26'44"

DESCRIPTION: CG set among ponderosa and jeffery pine on the banks of Hat Creek. Hat Creek is world renowned for fly fishing for trout. Trails in area. Busy on holiday weekends in summer. Due to swift current in creek swimming is discouraged. Near Lassen Volcanic National Park. Barrier free fishing access.

GETTING THERE: From Burney go NE on state HWY 299 approx. 5 mi. to state HWY 89. Go SE on 89 approx. 25 mi. to Hat Creek CG.

SINGLE RATE:	$13	OPEN DATES:	Apr-Oct
# of SINGLE SITES:	72	MAX SPUR:	20 feet
		MAX STAY:	14 days
# of GROUP SITES:	3	ELEVATION:	4300 feet

24 High Bridge
Chester • lat 40°20'16" lon 121°18'19"

DESCRIPTION: This CG is situated in a mixed pine and fir forest overlooking Warner Creek and the surrounding woods. Stream fishing in creek. Check for local regulations. Supplies are available in Chester. Watch for deer, elk, various birds, and small wildlife in the area. Campers may gather their firewood locally.

GETTING THERE: High Bridge CG is located approx. 5 mi. NW of Chester on county route 312. No turn around space; not recommended for trailers or RVs.

SINGLE RATE:	$11	OPEN DATES:	May-Nov
# of SINGLE SITES:	12	MAX SPUR:	20 feet
		MAX STAY:	14 days
		ELEVATION:	5200 feet

25 Hole in the Ground
Mineral • lat 40°18'35" lon 121°33'32"

DESCRIPTION: CG set in a mixed pine and fir forest with views of Mill Creek and surrounding woods. Stream fishing in Mill Creek, special regulations apply. Supplies are available in Mineral. Campers may gather their firewood locally. Hiking on Mill Creek Trail which accesses the Ishi Wilderness after 13 mi..

GETTING THERE: From Mineral go SE on county route 172 approx. 4 mi. to forest route 28N06. Go SW on 28N06 approx. 2 mi. to Hole in the Ground CG.

SINGLE RATE:	$11	OPEN DATES:	Apr-Nov*
# of SINGLE SITES:	13	MAX SPUR:	20 feet
		MAX STAY:	14 days
		ELEVATION:	4300 feet

26   Honn
Burney • lat 40°46'45" lon 121°30'05"

DESCRIPTION: CG set among ponderosa and jeffery pine on the banks of Hat Creek. Hat Creek is world renowned for fly fishing for trout. Trails in area. Busy on holiday weekends in summer. Due to swift current in creek, swimming is discouraged. Near Lassen Volcanic National Park. No drinking water available.

GETTING THERE: From Burney go NE on state HWY 299 approx. 5 mi. to state HWY 89. Go SE on 89 approx. 13 mi. to Honn CG. Not recommended for trailers.

SINGLE RATE:	$8	OPEN DATES:	Apr-Oct
# of SINGLE SITES:	9	MAX SPUR:	20 feet
		MAX STAY:	14 days
		ELEVATION:	3400 feet

27 Merrill
Susanville • lat 40°32'59" lon 120°48'39"

DESCRIPTION: CG is in an open grove of pine next to Eagle Lake (good trout fishing). P.M. t-showers and winds are common. Visit historic Gallatin House and Spalding Cabin. Supplies at nearby marina. Foxes, coyotes, egrets, and pelicans reside in the area. Busy holidays. Firewood on site. Trails in area. Amphitheater.

GETTING THERE: From Susanville go W on state HWY 36 approx. 3 mi. to county route A-1. Go N on A-1 approx. 13 mi. to Merrill CG. Road is narrow. Large vehicles should take caution.

SINGLE RATE:	$14	OPEN DATES:	May-Oct
# of SINGLE SITES:	181	MAX SPUR:	38 feet
		MAX STAY:	14 days
		ELEVATION:	5100 feet

28 Potato Patch
Chester • lat 40°11'17" lon 121°31'55"

DESCRIPTION: CG situated in a mixed pine, fir, and oak forest on the banks of Deer Creek. Fishing for trout in creek. 22 mi. to Chester for supplies. Watch for elk, deer, squirrels, and various birds in the area. Gather firewood locally. Deer Creek trail provides for hiking opportunities.

GETTING THERE: From Chester go W on state HWY 36 approx. 11.5 mi. to state HWY 32. Go SW on 32 approx. 10 mi. to Potato Patch CG.

SINGLE RATE:	$11	OPEN DATES:	Apr-Nov
# of SINGLE SITES:	32	MAX SPUR:	20 feet
		MAX STAY:	14 days
		ELEVATION:	3400 feet

29 Rocky
Burney • lat 40°43'34" lon 121°25'36"

DESCRIPTION: CG is located in ponderosa and jeffrey pine on Hat Creek. Hat Creek is world renowned for fly fishing for trout. Trails in area. Busy on holiday weekends in summer. Deer, chipmunks and birds in area. Due to swift current in creek swimming is discouraged. Near Lassen National Park. No water. Not recommended for trailers.

GETTING THERE: From Burney go NE on state HWY 299 approx. 5 mi. to state HWY 89. Go SE on 89 approx. 19 mi. to Rocky CG.

SINGLE RATE:	$8	OPEN DATES:	Apr-Oct
# of SINGLE SITES:	9	MAX SPUR:	20 feet
		MAX STAY:	14 days
		ELEVATION:	4000 feet

30 Rocky Knoll
Westwood • lat 40°29'57" lon 121°09'19"

DESCRIPTION: CG situated in a mixed pine and fir forest. Walking distance to Silver Lake for boat or shore fishing. Check local regulations. Warm days with cold nights. Supplies are available in Westwood. Gather firewood locally. Caribou Wilderness access within one mi. of CG. Prepare for mosquitos all summer.

GETTING THERE: From Westwood go N on county route A21 approx. 15 mi. to county route 110. Go W on 110 approx. 5 mi. to Rocky Knoll CG.

SINGLE RATE:	$11	OPEN DATES:	May-Nov*
# of SINGLE SITES:	18	MAX SPUR:	27 feet
		MAX STAY:	14 days
		ELEVATION:	6000 feet

 Campground has hosts   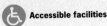 Reservable sites   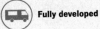 Accessible facilities   Fully developed   Semi-developed   Rustic facilities

NOTE: Open dates listed are typical. Actual dates are dependent on conditions such as snow pack.

31 Roxie Peconom
Susanville • lat 40°21'15" lon 120°48'00"

DESCRIPTION: This CG is set in a pine forest with Willard Creek running nearby. Bank fish from the creek for rainbow and brown trout. Supplies are availabe at Susanville. Campers may gather their firewood locally. Bizz Johnson Trailhead is nearby. Short walk to sites from parking lot.

GETTING THERE: From Susanville go W on state HWY 36 approx. 8 mi. to forest route 29N03. Go S on 29N03 approx. 2 mi. to Roxie Peconom CG.

SINGLE RATE:	No fee	OPEN DATES:	May-Oct*
# of SINGLE SITES:	10		
		MAX STAY:	14 days
		ELEVATION:	4800 feet

32 Silver Bowl
Westwood • lat 40°29'58" lon 121°09'47"

DESCRIPTION: CG situated in a mixed pine and fir forest within walking distance of Silver Lake. Cold nights. Boat or shore fishing on lake. Supplies are available in Westwood. Watch for deer and small wildlife in the area. Gather firewood locally. Hiking access into Caribou Wilderness within one mile of CG.

GETTING THERE: From Westwood go N on county route A21 approx. 15 mi. to county route 110. Go W on 110 approx. 5.5 mi. to Silver Bowl CG.

SINGLE RATE:	$11	OPEN DATES:	May-Nov*
# of SINGLE SITES:	18	MAX SPUR:	20 feet
		MAX STAY:	14 days
		ELEVATION:	6000 feet

33 Soldier Creek
Butte Meadows • lat 40°11'00" lon 121°15'30"

DESCRIPTION: This CG is set on the banks of Soldier Creek, situated in a meadow in a mixed pine and fir forest. Views of meadows and creek. Stream fish on the creek. Supplies are available in Chester. Campers may gather their firewood locally. Prepare for mosquitos in spring.

GETTING THERE: From Chester go S on state HWY 89 6 mi. to county route 308 (Humbug/Humboldt Road). Go W on 308 5 mi. to forest route 28N36. Go N on 28N36 approx. 1.5 mi. to Soldier Creek CG.

SINGLE RATE:	$9	OPEN DATES:	May-Nov*
# of SINGLE SITES:	15	MAX SPUR:	20 feet
		MAX STAY:	14 days
		ELEVATION:	4890 feet

34 South Antelope
Paynes Creek • lat 40°15'13" lon 121°45'27"

DESCRIPTION: CG set in a mixed pine and fir forest on the banks of Antelope Creek. Stream fishing in creek (special regulations apply). Historic Ishi Wilderness nearby. Supplies in Paynes Creek. Watch for deer, wild pigs, and wild turkeys in the area. Gather firwood locally. Hiking access into Ishi Wilderness. Tents only.

GETTING THERE: From Paynes Creek go SE on county route 202 approx. 8 mi. to county route 707B. Go S on 707B approx. 8 mi. to South Antelope CG. 4X4 necessary

SINGLE RATE:	No fee	OPEN DATES:	Yearlong
		MAX SPUR:	20 feet
		MAX STAY:	14 days
		ELEVATION:	2700 feet

35 Warner Creek
Chester • lat 40°21'44" lon 121°18'25"

DESCRIPTION: CG situated in a mixed pine and fir forest on the banks of Warner Creek. Supplies are available in Chester. Watch for deer, small wildlife, and occasional bear in the area. Gather firewood locally. Trails lead into Lassen Volcanic National Park and Drakesbad Guest Ranch (6 mi.).

GETTING THERE: From Chester go NW on county route 312 approx. 7 mi. to Warner Creek CG.

SINGLE RATE:	$9	OPEN DATES:	May-Nov*
# of SINGLE SITES:	15	MAX SPUR:	20 feet
		MAX STAY:	14 days
		ELEVATION:	5040 feet

36 West Branch
Butte Meadows • lat 40°02'04" lon 121°30'24"

DESCRIPTION: CG set in a mixed pine and fir forest on the West Branch of the Feather River. Stream fishing in river. Basic supplies in Butte Meadows or go to Chico. Deer, squirrels, and birds in area. Gather firewood locally. High Lakes area is approx. 8 mi. away, providing trails for hiking, horse, and ATV use.

GETTING THERE: From Butte Meadows go S on county route 51262 approx. 5 mi. to county route 91513. Go NE on 91513 approx. 1.5 mi. to forest route 25N27. Go S on 25N27 approx. 1/2 mi. to West Branch CG.

SINGLE RATE:	$10	OPEN DATES:	May-Nov*
# of SINGLE SITES:	15	MAX SPUR:	20 feet
		MAX STAY:	14 days
		ELEVATION:	5000 feet

37 West Eagle Group
Susanville • lat 40°32'49" lon 120°47'14"

DESCRIPTION: CG set among tall pine with scattered underbrush. Afternoon winds and thunder showers. Fish for trout on adjacent Eagle Lake. Visit historic Gallatin House and Spalding Cabin. Supplies 3/4 mi. at marina. Busy all summer. Reservation only. Wildlife includes ospreys, egrets, and pelicans.

GETTING THERE: From Susanville go W on state HWY 36 approx. 3 mi. to county route A-1. Go N on A-1 approx. 12 mi. to county route 231. Go E on 231 approx. 1 mi. to West Eagle Group CG.

GROUP RATE:	Varies	OPEN DATES:	May-Oct
		MAX SPUR:	50 feet
# of GROUP SITES:	2	MAX STAY:	14 days
		ELEVATION:	5100 feet

38 Willow Springs
Chester • lat 40°18'21" lon 121°22'30"

DESCRIPTION: This CG is situated in a mixed pine and fir forest on the banks of Willow Creek. Stream fishing on creek. Check for local regulations. Supplies are available at Chester. Wildlife in the area includes deer, squirrels, and a variety of birds. Gather firewood locally. Hike the Pacific Crest Trail, a short drive away.

GETTING THERE: From Chester go SW on state HWY 36/89 approx. 8 mi. to forest route 29N19. Go N on 29N19 approx. 4 mi. to Willow Springs CG.

SINGLE RATE:	$9	OPEN DATES:	May-Nov*
# of SINGLE SITES:	14	MAX SPUR:	20 feet
		MAX STAY:	14 days
		ELEVATION:	5100 feet

 Campground has hosts   **Reservable sites**   **Accessible facilities**   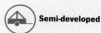 **Fully developed**    **Semi-developed**   **Rustic facilities**

NOTE: Open dates listed are typical. Actual dates are dependent on conditions such as snow pack.

Carey Given Photo, USDA Forest Service

LOS PADRES NATIONAL FOREST

Los Padres National Forest encompasses nearly two million acres in the beautiful coastal mountains of central California. Stretching almost 220 miles from the Carmel Valley area to the western edge of Los Angeles County, it provides the scenic backdrop for many communities including Big Sur, San Luis Obispo, Santa Barbara and Ojai.

Los Padres National Forest was established before the turn of the century as several separate forest reserves for the purpose of protecting vital watersheds and ensuring a continuous flow of water for developing communities. While watershed protection remains the principal mission, the Los Padres has become an "urban forest," providing recreation opportunities for the millions of people who live within a day's drive.

Los Padres is often thought of as "brush country," but in fact it consists of an amazing variety of landscapes. It sustains thousands of fascinating plant and animal species.

While many of its campgrounds and picnic areas are easily reached by vehicle, much of the forest is remote and unroaded, with excellent opportunities for primitive backcountry recreation.

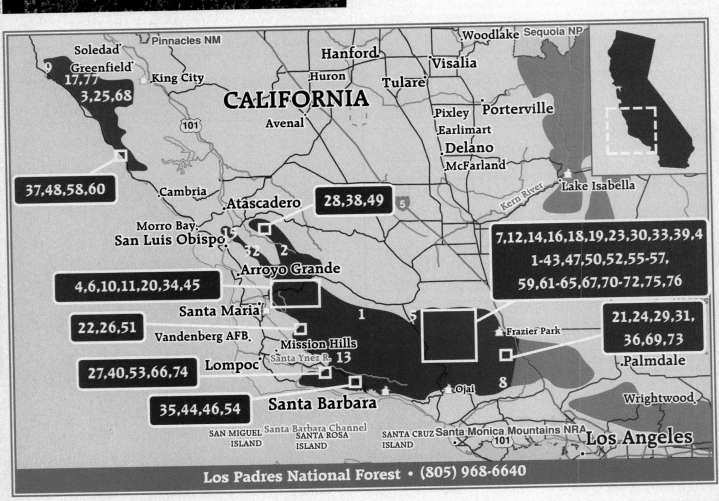

Los Padres National Forest • (805) 968-6640

1 — Alsio Park

South Cuyama • lat 34°56'00" lon 119°45'30"

DESCRIPTION: In shaded oak setting. No nearby fishing. No water. Bring firewood. Deer, mountain lion, bears and small wildlife in area. Horse or hiking use on Alsio Trail.

GETTING THERE: From South Cuyama go W on forest route 10N04 approximately 1.5 miles to Alsio Park CG.

SINGLE RATE:	No fee	OPEN DATES:	Yearlong
# of SINGLE SITES:	10	MAX SPUR:	20 feet
		MAX STAY:	14 days
		ELEVATION:	3200 feet

2 — American Canyon

Pozo • lat 35°17'01" lon 120°15'55"

DESCRIPTION: Grassy open area among oaks and sycamore. Supplies approx. 40 mi. Road open to general public only during deer hunting season. Gather firewood for camp use only. Horse TH to Machesna mountain Wilderness. Prepare for ticks, mosquitos and gnats. Large game, rattlesnakes in summer and bears in area. Adventure Pass required.

GETTING THERE: From Pozo go E on state HWY 58 1 mi. to forest route 29S01. Go SE on 29S01 7.5 mi. to forest route 30S04. Go NE on 30S04 2 mi. to American Canyon CG. High clearance required.

SINGLE RATE:	No fee	OPEN DATES:	Aug-Sept
# of SINGLE SITES:	14	MAX SPUR:	20 feet
GROUP RATE:		MAX STAY:	14 days
		ELEVATION:	1700 feet

3 — Arroyo Seco

Sycamore Flat • lat 36°14'27" lon 121°28'55"

DESCRIPTION: CG is located along the Arroyo Seco River and The Lakes. Buy or gather firewood on site. Busy May-Sept. Hiking and horse trails in area. New state of the art CG.

GETTING THERE: From Sycamore Flat go SW on county route G16 approx. 2 mi. to forest route 19S09. Go SW on 19S09 approx. 3.5 mi. to Arroyo Seco CG.

SINGLE RATE:	$16	OPEN DATES:	Yearlong
# of SINGLE SITES:	50	MAX SPUR:	20 feet
GROUP RATE:	Varies	MAX STAY:	14 days
# of GROUP SITES:	1	ELEVATION:	900 feet

4 — Baja

Santa Maria • lat 35°09'30" lon 120°07'30"

DESCRIPTION: Set among oak with rock formation views. Hot and windy days in summer, rain and cold days in winter. Supplies approx. 30 mi. Large cats, various birds and occasional bears frequent area. Full during hunt season, spring has light use. Gather firewood, do not remove from forest. Hunting, mountain bike OHV routes.

GETTING THERE: From Santa Maria go E on HWY 166 approx. 25 mi. to Branch Creek Road (30S02). Go NW on Branch Cr. Road approx. 3 mi. to Baja CG. Adventure Pass required to park.

SINGLE RATE:	No fee	OPEN DATES:	Yearlong
# of SINGLE SITES:	1	MAX SPUR:	18 feet
		MAX STAY:	14 days
		ELEVATION:	1400 feet

5 — Ballinger

South Cuyama • lat 34°53'02" lon 119°26'35"

DESCRIPTION: Primitive site in badlands terrain. Primarily a motorcycle use area, using designated trail system. No nearby fishing. No water. Bring firewood. Deer, mountain lion, bears and small wildlife in area. Ballinger Canyon Trail for OHV use.

GETTING THERE: From South Cuyama go N on forest route 10N04 3 mi. to state HWY 166. Go E on 166 11 mi. to state HWY 33. Go S on 33 4 mi. to county route. Go E on county route 2.5 mi. to Ballinger CG.

SINGLE RATE:	No fee	OPEN DATES:	Yearlong
# of SINGLE SITES:	15	MAX SPUR:	20 feet
		MAX STAY:	14 days
		ELEVATION:	3000 feet

6 — Bates Canyon

Santa Lucia • lat 34°57'14" lon 119°54'24"

DESCRIPTION: Located among oak, sycamore and bay laurel. Hot summers bring ticks and flies, cold and rainy winters. Supplies 20 mi. Large cats, foxes, deer, small wildlife and bears in area. Full during deer hunt. Gather but do not remove firewood. Hunt and hiking access to Sierra Madre Ridge and San Rafael Wilderness.

GETTING THERE: From Santa Maria go E on HWY 166 approx. 50 mi. to Cottonwood Canyon Road. Go SW on Cottonwood approx. 7.5 mi. to Bates Canyon CG. Adventure pass required to park.

SINGLE RATE:	No fee	OPEN DATES:	Yearlong
# of SINGLE SITES:	6	MAX SPUR:	18 feet
		MAX STAY:	14 days
		ELEVATION:	2900 feet

7 — Beaver

Ojala • lat 34°35'55" lon 119°14'30"

DESCRIPTION: In canyon setting among some cottonwoods on Sespe Creek near Sespe Gorge. No water. Gather firewood locally. Hike or mountain bike on Middle Sespe Trail (to Lion CG). May be closed for overnight use in 2000 season during ecological study; check with Ranger District.

GETTING THERE: From Ojala, go north on state HWY 33 approx. 10 miles to Beaver CG. Park and hike-in.

SINGLE RATE:	No fee	OPEN DATES:	Yearlong
# of SINGLE SITES:	12		
		MAX STAY:	14 days
		ELEVATION:	3200 feet

8 — Blue Point

Santa Paula • lat 34°31'47" lon 118°45'25"

DESCRIPTION: In oak and chaparell setting on the Piru River near Lake Piru. Hike-in sites. Fish for trout. Access Pothole Tr. 1 mi. and Agua Blanca Cr. Tr. No drinking water. Deer, mountain lion, black bears and small wildlife. May be closed for 2000 season during ecological study; check with Ranger District.

GETTING THERE: From Santa Paula go NE approx. 15.5 mi. on state HWY 126 to forest route 4N13. Go N on 4N13 approx. 12 mi. to Blue Point CG. Park and hike in.

SINGLE RATE:	No fee	OPEN DATES:	Seasonal
# of SINGLE SITES:	42		
		MAX STAY:	14 days
		ELEVATION:	1200 feet

9 — Bottchers Gap

Big Sur • lat 36°21'16" lon 121°48'46"

DESCRIPTION: CG is located in oak trees. Limited supplies on site. Firewood may be gathered locally. Woods offer handsome display of fall colors. Hiking and horse trails nearby. No ATV roads.

GETTING THERE: From Big Sur go NW on state HWY 1 approx. 12.5 mi. to Palo Colorado. Go SE approx. 6.5 mi. to Bottchers Gap CG.

SINGLE RATE:	$12	OPEN DATES:	Yearlong
# of SINGLE SITES:	9	MAX SPUR:	20 feet
		MAX STAY:	14 days
		ELEVATION:	2100 feet

10 — Brookshire Spring

Santa Maria • lat 35°01'16" lon 120°06'50"

DESCRIPTION: CG is in a canyon among oak and sycamore on a creek. Hot summer, cold and rainy winters. Supplies at Santa Maria. Bears, large cats, foxes and other wildlife. Gather firewood for camp use. Hunting, hike, OHV opportunites nearby. Flies, ticks, yellow jackets active in summer. Adventure pass required.

GETTING THERE: From Santa Maria go NE on HWY 166 25 mi. to forest route 32S13. Go SE on 32S13 10 mi. to forest route 11N04. Go 3 mi. to forest route 11N04A. Go NE on 11N04A 2 mi. to Brookshire Spring CG.

SINGLE RATE:	No fee	OPEN DATES:	Yearlong
# of SINGLE SITES:	2		
		MAX STAY:	14 days
		ELEVATION:	1500 feet

 Campground has hosts   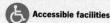 **Reservable sites**   **Accessible facilities**   **Fully developed**   **Semi-developed**   **Rustic facilities**

NOTE: Open dates listed are typical. Actual dates are dependent on conditions such as snow pack.

11 Buck Spring
Santa Maria • lat 35°08'30" lon 120°06'30"

DESCRIPTION: Among oak and chaparral with rock formation views. Hot summer, windy noons; cold and rainy winters. Supplies approx. 30 mi. at Santa Maria. Bears, large cats, foxes, snakes. Gather wood for CG use only. Hunt, mountain bike and OHV opportunities nearby. Ticks, flies, gnats and bees in summer. Adventure Pass required.

GETTING THERE: From Santa Maria go E on HWY 166 25 mi. to forest route 30S02. Go NW on forest route 30S02 2 mi. to forest route 32S25. Turn right on 32S25 and go 3/4 mi. to Buck Spring CG. High clearance.

SINGLE RATE:	No fee	OPEN DATES:	Yearlong
# of SINGLE SITES:	2		
		MAX STAY:	14 days
		ELEVATION:	1400 feet

12 Caballo
Apache Potrero • lat 34°52'09" lon 119°13'31"

DESCRIPTION: Campground is located in shaded setting in pinons. No nearby fishing. No water. Bring your own firewood. Deer, mountain lion, bears and small wildlife in area. No nearby trails.

GETTING THERE: From Apache Potrero go approx. 5 mi. E on county route FH95 to forest route 9N27. Go N on 9N27 approx. 1/2 mi. to Caballo CG. Dirt road, 4WD may be needed.

SINGLE RATE:	No fee	OPEN DATES:	Seasonal
# of SINGLE SITES:	5	MAX SPUR:	20 feet
		MAX STAY:	14 days
		ELEVATION:	5800 feet

13 Cachuma
Santa Barbara • lat 34°41'52" lon 119°54'44"

DESCRIPTION: Mountain and tree views with Cachuma Creek nearby. Fish the creek. Supplies at County Park, 10 mi. S, Lake Cachuma or Santa Ynez 10 mi. N. Mod to heavy use. Gather firewood locally. Hiking trails to Figueroa mountain nearby. Prepare for ticks and mosquitos in summer.

GETTING THERE: From W. Santa Barbara go NW on state HWY 154 20 mi. to county route 246 (Armour Ranch Rd). Go N then E on 246 2 mi. to county route 3350 (Happy Canyon Rd). Go NE on 3350 8 mi to Cachuma CG.

SINGLE RATE:	No fee	OPEN DATES:	Yearlong
# of SINGLE SITES:	6		
		MAX STAY:	14 days
		ELEVATION:	2100 feet

14 Campo Alto
Apache Potrero • lat 34°49'54" lon 119°12'37"

DESCRIPTION: Set among jeffrey pines on top of Mount Able. No nearby fishing. No water. Bring firewood. Deer, mountain lion, bears and small wildlife in area. Horseback riding and hiking trails into Chumach Wilderness.

GETTING THERE: From Apache Potrero go approx. 6 mi. E on county route FH95 to forest route 9N07. Go S on 9N07 approx. 6 mi. to Campo Alto CG.

SINGLE RATE:	No fee	OPEN DATES:	Seasonal
# of SINGLE SITES:	17	MAX SPUR:	20 feet
		MAX STAY:	14 days
# of GROUP SITES:	2	ELEVATION:	8300 feet

15 Cerro Alto

Atascadero • lat 35°25'29" lon 120°44'21"

DESCRIPTION: Among oaks, sycamore, willows with beautiful vegetation and a stream. Hot summers make ticks and mosquitos active, cool breezes off ocean; rainy and cold winters. Supplies 10 mi. Wildlife include deer, foxes, bobcats, bats and bears. Buy firewood from PMC. Hiking, horse and mountain bike trails nearby.

GETTING THERE: From Atascadero go SW on HWY 41 approx. 8 mi. to forest route 29S11. Go E on 29S11 approx. 1 mi. to Cerro Alto CG.

SINGLE RATE:	$16	OPEN DATES:	Yearlong
# of SINGLE SITES:	21	MAX SPUR:	30 feet
		MAX STAY:	14 days
		ELEVATION:	1000 feet

16 Cherry Creek
St. Nicolas • lat 34°51'12" lon 119°02'15"

DESCRIPTION: CG is set among mixed oak and conifer offering shade. Located on a designated 4WD trail. No nearby fishing. No water. Bring firewood. Deer, mountain lion, bears and small wildlife in area.

GETTING THERE: From St. Nicolas go E on county route approx. 1 mi. to forest route 9N53. Go NE on 9N53 approx. 1.5 mi. to Cherry Creek CG. 4WD access only.

SINGLE RATE:	No fee	OPEN DATES:	Yearlong
# of SINGLE SITES:	2	MAX SPUR:	20 feet
		MAX STAY:	14 days
		ELEVATION:	5200 feet

17 China Camp
Carmel Valley • lat 36°17'46" lon 121°34'00"

DESCRIPTION: Among madrone and oak with poison oak. Hot summers, cold winters. Frequent wind and fog. Fish in the nearby stream. Supplies in Carmel Valley. Wild cats and small wildlife. Moderate use. Bring own firewood. Horse and hike trails nearby. Prepare for bugs in spring and summer. Adventure Pass required.

GETTING THERE: From Carmel Valley go S on county route G16 (Carmel Valley Rd) 20 mi. to county route 5007 (Cachagua Rd). Go W on 5007 1 mi. to Tassajara Rd. Go S on Tassajara Rd. 10 mi. to China Camp CG.

SINGLE RATE:	$5	OPEN DATES:	Yearlong
# of SINGLE SITES:	6	MAX SPUR:	20 feet
		MAX STAY:	14 days
		ELEVATION:	4300 feet

18 Chuchupate
Apache Potrero • lat 34°47'14" lon 119°00'03"

DESCRIPTION: Set in open area of pinyon pines. No nearby fishing. No water. Bring firewood. Deer, mountain lion, bears and small wildlife in area. No nearby trails. May be closed, please call Mount Pinos Ranger District (805)245-3731.

GETTING THERE: From Apache Potrero go approx. 16.5 mi. E on county route FH95 to forest route 9N03. Go SW on 9N03 approx. 1 mi. to forest route 8N01. Go SE on 8N01 approx. 1.5 mi. to Chuchupate CG.

SINGLE RATE:	No fee	OPEN DATES:	Seasonal
# of SINGLE SITES:	24	MAX SPUR:	20 feet
		MAX STAY:	14 days
		ELEVATION:	6200 feet

19 Chula Vista
Apache Potrero • lat 34°48'57" lon 119°07'37"

DESCRIPTION: In a shaded Jeffery Pine site with walk-in sites (500' to parking lot) on top of Mount Pinos. No nearby fishing. No water. Bring firewood. Deer, mountain lion, bears and small wildlife in area. Hike trail system to summit. Cross country skiing in winter.

GETTING THERE: From Apache Potrero go approx. 13 mi. E on county route FH95 to forest route 9N24. Go S on 9N24 approx. 7 mi. to Chula Vista CG.

SINGLE RATE:	No fee	OPEN DATES:	Yearlong
# of SINGLE SITES:	12	MAX SPUR:	20 feet
		MAX STAY:	14 days
		ELEVATION:	8300 feet

20 Colson
Santa Lucia • lat 34°56'24" lon 120°10'08"

DESCRIPTION: Among oak, brush and chaparral with views of wooded hills. Supplies approx. 35 mi. Bears, large cats, foxes, bats, deer and small wildlife. Full during deer hunt season. Gather firewood for camp use only. Hike, horse, OHV and mountain bike opportunities. Ticks, bees in summer. Adventure Pass required.

GETTING THERE: From Santa Maria go E on Betteravia Rd 7 mi. to Mesa Rd. Go E on Mesa Rd. 4.5 mi. to Tepusquet Cyn Rd. Go N on Tepusquet Cyn Rd approx. 4.5 mi. to Colson Cyn Rd. Go E on Colson 4.2 mi. to Colson CG.

SINGLE RATE:	No fee	OPEN DATES:	Yearlong
# of SINGLE SITES:	5		
		MAX STAY:	14 days
		ELEVATION:	2000 feet

 Campground has hosts **Reservable sites** 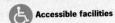 **Accessible facilities** 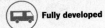 **Fully developed** 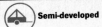 **Semi-developed**  **Rustic facilities**

NOTE: Open dates listed are typical. Actual dates are dependent on conditions such as snow pack.

21 Cottonwood
Stauffer • lat 34°43'06" lon 119°01'13"

DESCRIPTION: Set along a stream, accessible from the Lockwood Trail via a spur trail. No nearby fishing. No water. Bring firewood. Deer, mountain lion, bears and small wildlife in area. OHV trails/roads.

GETTING THERE: From Stauffer go SE on forest route 9N03 approx. 2.5 mi. to forest route 8N12 (Lockwood RTE). Go SE on 8N12 approx. 1 mi. to Cottonwood CG. 4WD access only.

SINGLE RATE:	No fee	OPEN DATES:	Yearlong
# of SINGLE SITES:	1	MAX SPUR:	20 feet
		MAX STAY:	14 days
		ELEVATION:	4600 feet

22 Davy Brown
Los Olivos • lat 34°45'28" lon 119°57'03"

DESCRIPTION: Among oak, sycamore, chaparral and poison oak on a creek. Hot windy summers bring bees and flies, cold rainy winters. Creek stocked with trout in spring. 25 mi. to supplies. Bears, large cats, foxes, bats. Full weekends and hunt season. Gather firewood for CG use only. Many hiking trails. Adventure Pass required.

GETTING THERE: From Los Olivos go S on state HWY 154 4 mi. to Armor Ranch Rd/Happy Cyn Rd. Go NE on Happy Cyn Rd 11 mi. to Cachuma Saddle/Sunset Valley Rd. Go N on Sunset Valley Rd. 4 mi. to Davy Brown CG.

SINGLE RATE:	No fee	OPEN DATES:	Yearlong
# of SINGLE SITES:	13	MAX SPUR:	30 feet
		MAX STAY:	14 days
		ELEVATION:	2100 feet

23 Dome Springs
Stauffer Landing • lat 34°45'23" lon 119°14'03"

DESCRIPTION: Located near the road among cottonwood with badlands terrain. No nearby fishing. No water. Bring firewood. Deer, mountain lion, bears and small wildlife in area. OHV access and OHV roads.

GETTING THERE: From Stauffer Landing go SW on forest route 7N03 3 mi. to forest route 9N03. Go W on 9N03 8 mi. to forest route 8N40. Go N on 8N40 2.5 mi. to Dome Springs CG. Sandy roads, 4WD may be needed.

SINGLE RATE:	No fee	OPEN DATES:	Yearlong
# of SINGLE SITES:	4	MAX SPUR:	20 feet
		MAX STAY:	14 days
		ELEVATION:	4800 feet

24 Dutchman
Stauffer Landing • lat 34°40'18" lon 118°58'35"

DESCRIPTION: In open grove of jeffery pines offering shade. No nearby fishing. No water. Bring firewood. Deer, mountain lion, bears and small wildlife in area. OHV roads available.

GETTING THERE: From Stauffer Landing go SE on forest route 8N12 approximately 7 miles to Dutchman CG.

SINGLE RATE:	No fee	OPEN DATES:	Yearlong
# of SINGLE SITES:	8	MAX SPUR:	20 feet
		MAX STAY:	14 days
		ELEVATION:	6800 feet

25 Escondido
King City • lat 36°08'25" lon 121°29'38"

DESCRIPTION: In oak forest with chaparral and poison oak, surrounded by rock formations. Stream fish the Arroyo Seco River nearby. Supplies 1 1/2 hrs. Large cats and small wildlife. Fills during summer. Small wood to gather for fires. Horse and hike trails nearby. Prepare for bugs all summer. Horse facilities.

GETTING THERE: From King City go SW on Jolon Rd 21 mi. to Sulphur Spring Rd. Go W on Sulphur Spring Road 2 mi. to Fort Hunter Liggett and Del Venturi Rd. Go NW on Del Venturi 20 mi. to Escondido CG.

SINGLE RATE:	$9	OPEN DATES:	May-Oct
# of SINGLE SITES:	9	MAX SPUR:	20 feet
		MAX STAY:	14 days
		ELEVATION:	2200 feet

26 Figueroa
Los Olivos • lat 34°44'08" lon 119°59'19"

DESCRIPTION: Among oak, fir and manzanita with beautiful views of wooded hills. Hot breezy summers, cold rainy winters. Supplies 13 mi. Bears, bob cat, deer, racoons, opossums, snakes and lizards. CA condor. Gather wood for CG use only. Numerous hiking trails, mountain biking, scenic views. Flies and bees in summer.

GETTING THERE: From HWY 154 at Los Olivos go NE on forest route 7N07 approx. 10 mi. to Figueroa CG. Adventure pass required.

SINGLE RATE:	No fee	OPEN DATES:	Yearlong
# of SINGLE SITES:	33		
		MAX STAY:	14 days
		ELEVATION:	3500 feet

27 Fremont
Santa Barbara • lat 34°32'35" lon 119°49'13"

DESCRIPTION: Among scrub oak, expect some poison oak bushes. Mountain views with Santa Ynez river nearby for fishing. Hot summer days, cold winter nights. Supplies at store W 1.5 mi. Occasional deer, turkeys and bobcats. Mod-heavy summer use, light in winter. Gather or buy firewood. Horse, hike or bike trails nearby. Ticks early.

GETTING THERE: From Santa Barbara go NW approx. 10 mi. on state HWY 154 to forest route 5N18. Go E on 5N18 approx. 1.5 mi. to Fremont CG.

SINGLE RATE:	$12	OPEN DATES:	Yearlong
# of SINGLE SITES:	15		
		MAX STAY:	14 days
		ELEVATION:	1000 feet

28 Friis
Santa Margarita • lat 35°22'53" lon 120°19'40"

DESCRIPTION: Among oak, chaparral, sycamores with hill views. Hot summers, cold rainy winters. Supplies 25 mi. Bears, mountain lion, bobcats, deer, wild boars, CA condor, wild horses. Gather wood for CG use only. Hunting, horse trails, OHV opportunities. Flies, ticks and yellow jackets very active in spring and summer.

GETTING THERE: From Santa Margarita go E on Pozo county road 22.5 mi. to forest route 29S02. Go NE on 29S02 4 mi. to undesignated route. Go N approx. 1 mi. to Friis CG. Adventure Pass required.

SINGLE RATE:	No fee	OPEN DATES:	Yearlong
# of SINGLE SITES:	3		
		MAX STAY:	14 days
		ELEVATION:	2200 feet

29 Gold Hill
Bakersfield • lat 34°42'13" lon 118°56'05"

DESCRIPTION: Located adjacent to Piru Creek among pinyon and chaparral vegetation in mostly open area. Hot summer days. Dispersed sites. Primarily for motorcycle use. No nearby fishing. No water. Bring firewood. Deer, mountain lion, bears and small wildlife in area. OHV road/trail near Piru Cr.

GETTING THERE: From Bakersfield go S approx. 42.5 mi. on US HWY 5 to forest route 8N01. Go S on 8N01 approx. 10.5 mi. to Goldhill CG.

SINGLE RATE:	No fee	OPEN DATES:	Yearlong
# of SINGLE SITES:	17	MAX SPUR:	20 feet
		MAX STAY:	14 days
		ELEVATION:	3800 feet

30 Halfmoon
Stauffer Landing • lat 34°38'00" lon 118°75'30"

DESCRIPTION: At roads end among shady jeffery pine and pinyon pine on Piru Creek. No nearby fishing. No water. Bring firewood. Deer, mountain lion, bears and small wildlife in area. Access to OHV roads/trails.

GETTING THERE: From Stauffer Landing go SW approx. 11.5 mi. on forest route 7N03 to Halfmoon CG.

SINGLE RATE:	No fee	OPEN DATES:	Seasonal
# of SINGLE SITES:	10	MAX SPUR:	20 feet
		MAX STAY:	14 days
		ELEVATION:	4700 feet

 Campground has hosts Reservable sites   Accessible facilities   Fully developed Semi-developed Rustic facilities

NOTE: Open dates listed are typical. Actual dates are dependent on conditions such as snow pack.

31 Hardluck
Bakersfield • lat 34°41'16" lon 118°50'44"

DESCRIPTION: Located along Piru Creek in open area of cottonwoods, north of Pyramid Lake with streamside sites. No nearby fishing. No water. Bring firewood. Deer, mountain lion, bears and small wildlife in area. Buck Cr. Trail accesses the wilderness for horse or foot use. May be closed, contact Mt. Pinos Ranger District (805)245-3731.

GETTING THERE: From Bakersfield go S approx. 51 mi. on US HWY 5 to the Emigrant Landing turn off. Go SW on forest route approx. 7 mi. to Hardluck CG.

SINGLE RATE:	No fee	OPEN DATES:	Yearlong
# of SINGLE SITES:	26	MAX SPUR:	20 feet
		MAX STAY:	14 days
		ELEVATION:	2800 feet

36 Kings Camp
Bakersfield • lat 34°43'02" lon 118°55'41"

DESCRIPTION: Set in open area off the Gold Hill Road. Primarily used for motorcyclists. Hot summer days. No nearby fishing. No water. Bring firewood. Deer, mountain lion, bears and small wildlife in area. OHV trails/roads near Piru Creek.

GETTING THERE: From Bakersfield go S approx. 42.5 mi. on US HWY 5 to forest route 8N01. Go S on 8N01 approx. 10 mi. to Kings Camp CG.

SINGLE RATE:	No fee	OPEN DATES:	Yearlong
# of SINGLE SITES:	7	MAX SPUR:	20 feet
		MAX STAY:	14 days
		ELEVATION:	4200 feet

32 Hi Mountain
San Luis Obispo • lat 35°15'41" lon 120°24'46"

DESCRIPTION: Set among oak and chaparral with Rocky Mountain views. Hot summers, cold rainy winters. Supplies 30 mi. Bears, large cats, foxes, CA condor, rattlesnakes, birds. Gather wood for CG use only. Hunt, hike access to Santa Lucia and Garcia Wilderness. OHV opportunities. Flies, ticks and bees active during summer.

GETTING THERE: From San Luis Obispo go N on HWY 101 8 mi. to HWY 58. Go E on HWY 58 3 mi. to Pozo Rd. Go SE on Pozo 16 mi. to forest route 30S05. Go SW on 30S05 4 mi. to Hi Mountain CG. Adventure Pass required.

SINGLE RATE:	No fee	OPEN DATES:	Yearlong
# of SINGLE SITES:	11	MAX SPUR:	12 feet
		MAX STAY:	14 days
		ELEVATION:	2400 feet

37 Kirk Creek
San Antonio Mission • lat 35°59'20" lon 121°29'41"

DESCRIPTION: On Otter Bay of ocean with trail to oceanside and small beach area. Open area with pampass grass and some pines. A small creek runs past the site. Basic supplies at San Antonio Mission. Multiple hiking trails into the mountains.

GETTING THERE: From San Antonio Mission go SW on county route 4004 approx. 19 mi. to Kirk Creek CG.

SINGLE RATE:	$16	OPEN DATES:	Yearlong
# of SINGLE SITES:	33	MAX SPUR:	20 feet
		MAX STAY:	14 days
		ELEVATION:	100 feet

33 Holiday Group
Ojala • lat 34°31'02" lon 119°16'37"

DESCRIPTION: Set in oak and chapparal. Hike-in site. Firewood may be scarce. Deer, mountain lion, black bears, rattlesnakes and small wildlife in area. No drinking water. Access to Ortega Trail for OHV use. Up to 100 persons.

GETTING THERE: From Ojala go N on state HWY 33 approx. 5 miles to Holiday Group CG. Park and hike-in.

SINGLE RATE:	No fee	OPEN DATES:	Yearlong
# of SINGLE SITES:	8		
		MAX STAY:	14 days
# of GROUP SITES:	1	ELEVATION:	2090 feet

38 La Panza
Santa Margarita • lat 35°21'15" lon 120°15'42"

DESCRIPTION: CG is among oak and chaparral. Hot summers, cold winter days. Supplies 40 mi. Bears, deer, large cats, CA condors, turkeys, boars. Full during deer hunt season. Gather wood for CG use only. Hunt, horse, OHV opportunities. Access to Machesna mountain Wilderness. Summer brings insects. Adventure Pass required.

GETTING THERE: From Santa Margarita go E on HWY 58 3 mi. to Pozo Rd. Go E on Pozo Rd 26 mi. to forest route 29S18. Go E on 29S18 1.5 mi. to La Panza CG. High clearance necessary.

SINGLE RATE:	No fee	OPEN DATES:	Yearlong
# of SINGLE SITES:	16		
		MAX STAY:	14 days
		ELEVATION:	2400 feet

34 Horseshoe Spring
Santa Maria • lat 34°59'49" lon 120°07'31"

DESCRIPTION: Among oak, sycamore and poison oak on small creek. 1940 CCC site. Supplies at Santa Maria. Bears, large. cat, foxes, rattlesnakes, turkeys and small wildlife in area. Fills during hunt season. Gather firewood for CG use only. Flies, ticks and yellow jackets active in summer. Adventure Pass required.

GETTING THERE: From Santa Maria go NE on HWY 166 25 mi. to forest route 32S13 (Sierra Madre Ridge). Go SE on 32S13 10 mi. to forest road 11N04 (La Brea Jct). Go SE on forest route 11N04 3 mi. to Horseshoe Spring CG.

SINGLE RATE:	No fee	OPEN DATES:	Yearlong
# of SINGLE SITES:	3		
		MAX STAY:	14 days
		ELEVATION:	1600 feet

39 Lion
Ojai • lat 34°33'40" lon 119°09'47"

DESCRIPTION: Near Sespe Creek in open pine forest. No water. Gather firewood locally, may be scarce. Deer, mountain lion, black bears, rattlesnakes and small wildlife. Access Middle Sespe, Sespe River and Gene Marshall Piedra Blanca Nat'l Rec. Trail. May be closed for 2000 season during ecological study; check withRanger Dist.

GETTING THERE: From Ojai go N on state HWY 33 approx. 13.5 mi. to forest route 6N313. Go E on 6N313 approx. 4.5 mi. to Lion CG. Park and hike-in.

SINGLE RATE:	No fee	OPEN DATES:	Yearlong
# of SINGLE SITES:	30		
		MAX STAY:	14 days
		ELEVATION:	3065 feet

35 Juncal
Santa Barbara • lat 34°29'19" lon 119°32'18"

DESCRIPTION: Grassy site among oak withmountain views on the Santa Ynez River. Trout, bass fish the river. Supplies 15 mi. at Santa Barbara. Deer, coyotes, and occasional large cats in area. Mod-heavy use all summer, temp closed in winter, call for info. Collect firewood locally. Prepare for mosquitos and ticks.

GETTING THERE: From Santa Barbara go NW approx. 8 mi. on state HWY 154 to forest route 5N12. Go E on 5N12 approx. 13 mi. to forest route 5N15. Continue on 5N15 approx. 4.5 mi. to Juncal CG.

SINGLE RATE:	No fee	OPEN DATES:	Yearlong
# of SINGLE SITES:	6		
		MAX STAY:	14 days
		ELEVATION:	1800 feet

40 Los Prietos
Santa Barbara • lat 34°32'25" lon 119°47'52"

DESCRIPTION: Thick oak grove withmountain views adjacent to Santa Ynez river. Shore fish for 7 bass. hot summers, cold winter mornings. Limited supplies at store. Deer, foxes, turkeys, bobcats, raccoons. Best in spring and fall. Buy firewood or gather own. Hike, bike, horse trails and OHV roads nearby. Ticks and flies in summer.

GETTING THERE: From Santa Barbara go SE approx. 10 mi. on state HWY 154 to forest route 5N18. Go E on 5N18 approx. 3 mi. to Los Prietos CG.

SINGLE RATE:	$12	OPEN DATES:	Yearlong
# of SINGLE SITES:	38		
		MAX STAY:	14 days
		ELEVATION:	1000 feet

 Campground has hosts   **Reservable sites**   **Accessible facilities**   **Fully developed**   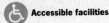 **Semi-developed**   **Rustic facilities**

NOTE: Open dates listed are typical. Actual dates are dependent on conditions such as snow pack.

41 Marian
Apache Potrero • lat 34°52'50" lon 119°12'56"

DESCRIPTION: In open shady area of jeffrey pines. Supplies in Pine Mountain Club. No nearby fishing. No water. Bring firewood. Deer, mountain lion, bears and small wildlife in area. OHV roads, Blue Ridge Trail, Brush Mountain and Doc Williams Canyon access.

GETTING THERE: From Apache Potrero go E on county route FH95 approx. 4.5 mi. to forest route 9N27. Go N on 9N27 approx. 1.5 mi. to Marian CG. 4WD may be needed.

SINGLE RATE:	No fee	OPEN DATES:	Seasonal
# of SINGLE SITES:	5	MAX SPUR:	20 feet
		MAX STAY:	14 days
		ELEVATION:	6600 feet

42 McGill
St. Nicolas • lat 34°48'56" lon 119°05'54"

DESCRIPTION: In shaded jeffrey pines. Supplies in St. Nicolas. No nearby fishing. No water. Bring firewood. Deer, mountain lion, bears and small wildlife in area. Mount Pines trails, includes skiing in winter.

GETTING THERE: From St. Nicolas go S on forest route 9N24 approximately 4 mi. to McGill CG.

SINGLE RATE:	$8	OPEN DATES:	May-Sept*
# of SINGLE SITES:	73	MAX SPUR:	20 feet
GROUP RATE:	$75	MAX STAY:	14 days
# of GROUP SITES:	2	ELEVATION:	6600 feet

43 Middle Lion
Ojai • lat 34°32'59" lon 119°09'53"

DESCRIPTION: In pine forest setting. Gather firewood locally. No water. Lion Cyn. Trail to Rose Valley Lake and E Fork Lion Camp and W Fork Lion Camps. Deer, mountain lion, black bears, rattlesnakes and small wildlife. Access to Sespe Wilderness. May be closed for 2000 season during ecological study; check with Ranger District.

GETTING THERE: From Ojai go N on state HWY 33 approx. 13.5 mi. to forest route 6N313. Go E on 6N313 approx. 4.5 mi. to Middle Lion CG. Park and hike in.

SINGLE RATE:	No fee	OPEN DATES:	Yearlong
# of SINGLE SITES:	8		
		MAX STAY:	14 days
		ELEVATION:	3250 feet

44 Middle Santa Ynez
Santa Barbara • lat 34°30'39" lon 119°34'43"

DESCRIPTION: Among oak with mountain views. On fishing Santa Ynez River, no boats, shore catch trout, bass and catfish. Supplies 17 mi. CG fills quickly. Gather firewood. Hiking, horse and biking trails to Mono-Alamar and Indian Cr. Prepare for mosquitoes and ticks in summer.

GETTING THERE: From Santa Barbara go SE 8 mi. on state HWY 154 to forest route 5N12. Go E on 5N12 17 mi. to forest route 5N15. Continue on 5N15 approx. 7 mi. to Middle Santa Ynez CG. Parking pass required.

SINGLE RATE:	No fee	OPEN DATES:	Yearlong*
# of SINGLE SITES:	13		
		MAX STAY:	14 days
		ELEVATION:	1500 feet

45 Miranda Pine
Santa Maria • lat 35°02'07" lon 120°02'11"

DESCRIPTION: Set in pine, oak and chaparral with views of beautiful San Rafael Wilderness. Access to wilderness nearby. Hot, windy summers, cold rain winters with snow at times. Bears, deer, large. cats, CA condor, bats. Gather firewood for CG use only. Hike, mountain bike. Summer ticks, flies, bees.

GETTING THERE: From Santa Maria go NE on HWY 166 25 mi. to Sierra Madre Ridge. Go SE on Sierra Madre Ridge 10 mi. to Miranda Pine CG. High clearance necessary. Adventure Pass required to park.

SINGLE RATE:	No fee	OPEN DATES:	Yearlong
# of SINGLE SITES:	3		
		MAX STAY:	14 days
		ELEVATION:	4000 feet

46 Mono
Santa Barbara • lat 34°31'44" lon 119°37'41"

DESCRIPTION: CG is located among oak with river and mountain views. On Santa Ynez River, fish for trout, bass and catfish. Supplies 22 mi. Deer, coyotes, foxes, large. cats in area. Fills in summer, come early. Gather firewood. Trails to Mono-Alamar, Indian Cr. Prepare for mosquitoes and ticks in summer.

GETTING THERE: From Santa Barbara go SE 20 mi. on state HWY 154 to forest route 5N12. Go E on 5N12 17 mi. to forest route 5N15. Continue on 5N15 10 mi. to Mono CG. Adventure Pass for parking required.

SINGLE RATE:	No fee	OPEN DATES:	Yearlong*
# of SINGLE SITES:	5		
		MAX STAY:	14 days
		ELEVATION:	1400 feet

47 Mt. Pinos
St. Nicolas • lat 34°48'36" lon 119°06'27"

DESCRIPTION: Located among shady jeffrey pines. No nearby fishing. No water. Bring firewood. Deer, mountain lion, bears and small wildlife in area. A large network of trails and open terrain includes cross country skiing in winter.

GETTING THERE: From St. Nicolas go S on forest route 9N24 approximately 5.5 miles to Mt. Pinos CG.

SINGLE RATE:	No fee	OPEN DATES:	Seasonal
# of SINGLE SITES:	19	MAX SPUR:	20 feet
		MAX STAY:	14 days
		ELEVATION:	8000 feet

48 Nacimiento
Jolon • lat 36°00'00" lon 121°23'30"

DESCRIPTION: Set in oak and madrone trees in open area along the Nacimiento River. Poison oak in area. Hot summers with fog and t-showers. Trout fishing on river. Supplies 35 mi. Bobcats and birds. Buy or gather (sparse) firewood. Coastal hiking trails in vicinity. Flies get thick on hot days.

GETTING THERE: From Jolon go W on Milpitas Rd approx. 2.5 mi. to Nacimiento Rd (county route 4004). Go W on 4004 approx. 9 mi. to Nacimiento CG.

SINGLE RATE:	$5	OPEN DATES:	Yearlong
# of SINGLE SITES:	8	MAX SPUR:	20 feet
		MAX STAY:	14 days
		ELEVATION:	1600 feet

49 Navajo
Santa Margarita • lat 35°22'08" lon 120°18'38"

DESCRIPTION: View the hills from CG set in oak and chaparral. Expect hot summers, cold and rainy winters. Fills holidays and hunt season. Bears, deer, large cats, boars, turkeys, various birds. Gather firewood for CG use only. Hunting, OHV opportunities. Summer bring ticks, flies, gnats and yellow jackets.

GETTING THERE: From Santa Margaita go E on state HWY 58 3 mi. to Pozo Rd. Go SE on Pozo Rd 21 mi. to forest route 29S02. Go NE on 29S02 4 mi. to Navajo CG. High clearance necessary. Adventure Pass required.

SINGLE RATE:	No fee	OPEN DATES:	Yearlong
# of SINGLE SITES:	2		
		MAX STAY:	14 days
		ELEVATION:	1900 feet

50 Nettle Springs
Ojala • lat 34°48'11" lon 119°17'22"

DESCRIPTION: Set among pinyon and chapparel trees, providing shade. No nearby fishing. No water. Bring firewood. Deer, mountain lion, bears and small wildlife in area. Access to OHV roads/trails.

GETTING THERE: From Ojala go N on state HWY 33 approx. 30 mi. to forest route 8N06. Go NE on 8N06 approx. 8 mi. to Nettle Springs CG.

SINGLE RATE:	No fee	OPEN DATES:	Yearlong
# of SINGLE SITES:	11	MAX SPUR:	20 feet
		MAX STAY:	14 days
		ELEVATION:	4400 feet

 Campground has hosts 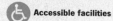 Reservable sites 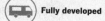 Accessible facilities   Fully developed Semi-developed   Rustic facilities

NOTE: Open dates listed are typical. Actual dates are dependent on conditions such as snow pack.

51 Nira
Los Olivos • lat 34°46'14" lon 119°56'12"

DESCRIPTION: Among oak, sycamore, some poison oak, views of hills and creek. Hot summers, cold and rainy winters. Trout fish the creek. Supplies 20 mi. Bears, large. cat, foxes, opposum, racoons. Fills holidays and deer hunt season. Gather wood for CG use only. Horse, hike trails, major TH into San Rafael Wilderness. Summer ticks, flies, bees.

GETTING THERE: From Los Olivos go S on state HWY 154 4 mi. to Armor Ranch Rd/Happy Cyn Rd. Go NE on Happy Cyn Rd 11 mi. to Cachuma Saddle/Sunset Valley Road. Go N on Sunset Valley Rd. 5 mi. to Nira CG. Adventure Pass required.

SINGLE RATE:	No fee	OPEN DATES:	Yearlong
# of SINGLE SITES	11		
		MAX STAY:	14 days
		ELEVATION:	1800 feet

52 Ozena
Ojala • lat 34°41'35" lon 119°19'45"

DESCRIPTION: Campground is located among scattered cottonwoods. No nearby fishing. No water. Bring firewood. Deer, mountain lion, bears and small wildlife in area. Heavy fall use during hunting season. No nearby trails.

GETTING THERE: From Ojala go N on state HWY 33 approx. 25 mi. to forest route 9N03. Go E on 9N03 approx. 1.5 mi. to Ozena CG.

SINGLE RATE:	No fee	OPEN DATES:	Yearlong
# of SINGLE SITES:	10	MAX SPUR:	20 feet
		MAX STAY:	14 days
		ELEVATION:	3600 feet

53 Paradise
Los Olivos • lat 34°32'32" lon 119°48'46"

DESCRIPTION: CG has open sites located in scrub oak. Santa Ynez River is a short walk from CG. Excellent fishing and swimming opportunities in river. Deer, foxes, wild turkeys, wild pigs, bobcats, and bears in area. CG is busy Memorial Day-Labor Day. Reservation only in summer. Numerous hiking, horse, and mountain biking trails.

GETTING THERE: From Los Olivos go SE approx. 16.5 mi. on state HWY 154 to forest route 5N18. Go E on 5N18 approx. 2 mi. to Paradise CG.

SINGLE RATE:	$12	OPEN DATES:	Yearlong
# of SINGLE SITES:	15	MAX SPUR:	72 feet
		MAX STAY:	14 days
		ELEVATION:	1000 feet

54 P-Bar Flat
Santa Barbara • lat 34°30'54" lon 119°35'24"

DESCRIPTION: Set among oak on Santa Ynez River. Shore fish for trout, bass and catfish. Fills quickly in summer, come early. Gather firewood. Hike Mono-Alamar, Indian Creek trails. Cameusa OHV road. Summer brings mosquitos and many ticks.

GETTING THERE: From Santa Barbara go SE 10 mi. on state HWY 154 to forest route 5N12. Go E on 5N12 17 mi. to forest route 5N15. Continue on 5N15 7.5 mi. to P-Bar Flat CG. Adventure pass required for parking.

SINGLE RATE:	No fee	OPEN DATES:	Yearlong*
# of SINGLE SITES:	4		
		MAX STAY:	14 days
		ELEVATION:	1500 feet

55 Piedra Blanca Group
Ojai • lat 34°35'06" lon 119°09'51"

DESCRIPTION: Set among pine trees. Gather firewood, may be sparse. No water. Horse corral. Gene Marshall Piedra Blanca Nat'l Rec. Trail, Sespe and Middle Sespe trails nearby. Deer, black bears, rattlesnakes. Access to Sespe Wilderness nearby. May be closed for 2000 season during ecological study; check withRanger Dist.

GETTING THERE: From Ojai go N on state HWY 33 approx. 13.5 mi. to forest route 6N313. Go E on 6N313 approx. 4.5 mi. to Piedra Blanca Group CG.

		OPEN DATES:	Yearlong
GROUP RATE:	$50	MAX STAY:	14 days
# of GROUP SITES:	1	ELEVATION:	3100 feet

56 Pine Mountain
Ojala • lat 34°38'17" lon 119°19'33"

DESCRIPTION: In pine trees in small valley along top of Pine Mountain. No water. Gather firewood, may be sparse. Deer, mountain lion, black bears, rattlesnakes and small wildlife. Access to Boulder Mountain Trail and McGuire Trail in Mount Pinos District begins here. XC ski area, closed to camping in winter.

GETTING THERE: From Ojala go N on state HWY 33 approx. 22 mi. to forest route 6N06. Go E on 6N06 approx. 3.5 mi. to Pine Mountain CG.

SINGLE RATE:	No fee	OPEN DATES:	Seasonal
# of SINGLE SITES:	6	MAX SPUR:	20 feet
		MAX STAY:	14 days
		ELEVATION:	6650 feet

57 Pine Springs
Stauffer Landing • lat 34°41'23" lon 119°08'01"

DESCRIPTION: Campground is located in shaded setting in pinyons along Grande Valley Road. No nearby fishing. No water. Bring firewood. Deer, mountain lion, bears and small wildlife in area. No trails, open hiking, no OHV use.

GETTING THERE: From Stauffer Landing go SW approx. 5.5 mi. on forest route 7N03 to forest route 7N03A. Go W on 7N03A approx. 1 mi. to Pine Springs CG.

SINGLE RATE:	No fee	OPEN DATES:	Seasonal
# of SINGLE SITES:	12	MAX SPUR:	20 feet
		MAX STAY:	14 days
		ELEVATION:	5800 feet

58 Plaskett Creek
San Antonio Mission • lat 35°55'14" lon 121°27'52"

DESCRIPTION: In pine trees and grass on State Bay off the ocean. Sand dollar beach is across the highway. Basic supplies at San Antonio Mission. Occasional otter sightings in bay. Some short trails for hiking.

GETTING THERE: From San Antonio Mission go SW on county route 4004 approx. 19 mi. to state HWY 1. Go S on HWY 1 approx. 4 mi. to Plaskett Creek CG.

SINGLE RATE:	$16	OPEN DATES:	Yearlong
# of SINGLE SITES:	44	MAX SPUR:	20 feet
		MAX STAY:	14 days
# of GROUP SITES:	3	ELEVATION:	200 feet

59 Pleito
St. Nicolas • lat 34°52'00" lon 119°06'30"

DESCRIPTION: In mixed oak and jeffrey pine site providing shade. Located on designated 4WD trail. No nearby fishing. No water. Bring firewood. Deer, mountain lion, bears and small wildlife in area. Nearby Cherry Creek fault has steep drainage drop for OHV use.

GETTING THERE: From St. Nicolas go E on county route approx. 1 mi. to Pleito RTE. Go NW on Pleito RTE approx. 4.5 mi. to Pleito Creek CG. 4WD access only.

SINGLE RATE:	No fee	OPEN DATES:	Yearlong
# of SINGLE SITES:	2	MAX SPUR:	20 feet
		MAX STAY:	14 days
		ELEVATION:	5000 feet

60 Ponderosa
San Antonio Mission • lat 40°09'59" lon 121°11'03"

DESCRIPTION: Set in oak and madrone trees in open area along the Nacimiento River. Poison oak in area. Hot summers with fog and t-showers. Trout fishing on river. Supplies 35 mi. Bobcats and birds. Buy or gather (sparse) firewood. Coastal hiking trails in vicinity. Flies get thick on hot days.

GETTING THERE: From San Antonio Mission go SW on county route 4004 approx. 10.5 mi. to Ponderosa CG.

SINGLE RATE:	$9	OPEN DATES:	Yearlong
# of SINGLE SITES:	22	MAX SPUR:	20 feet
		MAX STAY:	14 days
		ELEVATION:	1500 feet

 Campground has hosts   Reservable sites 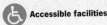 Accessible facilities   Fully developed   Semi-developed Rustic facilities

NOTE: Open dates listed are typical. Actual dates are dependent on conditions such as snow pack.

61 Potrero Seco
Ojala • lat 34°38'16" lon 119°25'37"

DESCRIPTION: Located on Sespe Creek in oak and chaparral setting. Gather local firewood. Deer, mountain lion, black bears, rattlesnakes and small wildlife. No nearby trails.

GETTING THERE: From Ojala go N on state HWY 33 approx. 22 mi. to forest route 6N03. Go W on 6N03 approx. 2.5 mi. to Potrero Seco CG. Park and hike in.

SINGLE RATE:	No fee	OPEN DATES:	Seasonal
# of SINGLE SITES:	4		
		MAX STAY:	14 days
		ELEVATION:	4850 feet

62 Rancho Nuevo
Ojala • lat 34°41'39" lon 119°23'49"

DESCRIPTION: In open grassy canyon bottom on small creek. Walk in approximately 1/2 mile. No nearby fishing. No water. Bring firewood. Deer, mountain lion, bears and small wildlife in area. Hike Dear Trail and Rancho Nuevo Trail.

GETTING THERE: From Ojala go N on state HWY 33 approx. 27 mi. to forest route 7N04. Go W on 7N04 approx. 1.5 mi. to Rancho Nuevo CG. 4WD access only, sandy river crossing.

SINGLE RATE:	No fee	OPEN DATES:	Seasonal*
# of SINGLE SITES:	2	MAX SPUR:	20 feet
		MAX STAY:	14 days
		ELEVATION:	3600 feet

63 Reyes Creek
Ojala • lat 34°40'45" lon 119°18'26"

DESCRIPTION: A shady site set in mixed oak, pinyon and cottonwood on a stream. Fish for trout in stream. Horse corral available. Barrier free fishing pier. No nearby fishing. No water. Bring firewood. Deer, mountain lion, bears and small wildlife in area. Hiking trail access.

GETTING THERE: From Ojala go N on state HWY 33 approx. 25 mi. to forest route 9N03. Go E on 9N03 approx. 3 mi. to forest route 7N11. Go S on 7N11 approx. 1 mi. to Reyes Creek CG.

SINGLE RATE:	No fee	OPEN DATES:	Yearlong
# of SINGLE SITES:	30	MAX SPUR:	20 feet
		MAX STAY:	14 days
		ELEVATION:	4000 feet

64 Reyes Peak
Ojala • lat 34°38'13" lon 119°18'49"

DESCRIPTION: Set on Sespe Creek along a ridge with views of the ocean and Cuyama Badlands. No water. Gather firewood, may be sparse. Supplies in Ojala. Deer, mountain lion, black bears, rattlesnakes and small wildlife. Access to Choro Grande Canyon, Reyes Peak and Raspberry Spring Trails.

GETTING THERE: From Ojala go N on state HWY 33 approximately 17 miles to Reyes CG.

SINGLE RATE:	No fee	OPEN DATES:	Seasonal
# of SINGLE SITES:	6	MAX SPUR:	20 feet
		MAX STAY:	14 days
		ELEVATION:	7000 feet

65 Rose Valley
Ojala • lat 34°31'57" lon 119°10'53"

DESCRIPTION: On Upper Rose Lake with some cottonwood tree shaded sites. No water. Fish 3 small nearby lakes for native rainbow, steelhead is endangered, check regs. Firewood may be sparse. Deer, mountain lion, rattlesnakes, black bears and small wildlife. Trail to Rose Valley Falls and gated access to 4WD Nordoff Ridge Road.

GETTING THERE: From Ojala go N on state HWY 33 approx. 8.5 mi. to 6N313. Go E on 6N313 approx. 2 mi. to 5N42. Go S on 5N42 approx. 1 mi. to Rose Valley CG. Park and hike in.

SINGLE RATE:	No fee	OPEN DATES:	Yearlong
# of SINGLE SITES:	9		
		MAX STAY:	14 days
		ELEVATION:	3450 feet

66 Sage Hill
Santa Barbara • lat 34°32'21" lon 119°47'28"

DESCRIPTION: In open park like setting with mountain views. On the Santa Ynez River, fishing for trout, bass and other species. Hot summers, cold winters. Limited supplies nearby. Deer, large, cats, coyotes in area. CG fills frequently. Buy or gather firewood. Hike, bike, horse trails nearby. Ticks in brush during summer.

GETTING THERE: From Santa Barbara go SE approx. 10 mi. on state HWY 154 to forest route 5N18. Go E on 5N18 approx. 5 mi. to Sage Hill CG. Horse corrals available.

		OPEN DATES:	Yearlong
GROUP RATE:	Varies	MAX STAY:	14 days
# of GROUP SITES:	6	ELEVATION:	1100 feet

67 Salt Creek
St. Nicolas • lat 34°50'30" lon 119°03'00"

DESCRIPTION: CG is located in a shady site set in mixed oak, jeffery pine and cottonwood. No nearby fishing. No water. Bring firewood. Deer, mountain lion, bears and small wildlife in area. OHV trail/road access.

GETTING THERE: From St. Nicolas go E on county route approx. 1 mi. to forest route 9N53. Go NE on 9N53 approx. 1.5 mi. to Salt Creek CG. 4WD access only.

SINGLE RATE:	No fee	OPEN DATES:	Yearlong
# of SINGLE SITES:	2	MAX SPUR:	20 feet
		MAX STAY:	14 days
		ELEVATION:	3000 feet

68 Santa Lucia Memorial Park
Sycamore Flat • lat 36°07'08" lon 121°27'51"

DESCRIPTION: Set in pines on the Arroyo Seco River. View of large rock formations. Fish for trout in river. Basic supplies at Sycamore Flat. Bobcats, deer, wild pigs, snakes and small wildlife in area. Hike the Arroyo Seco Trail into Ventana Wilderness.

GETTING THERE: From Sycamore Flat go SW on county route G16 approx. 2 mi. to forest route 19S09. Go SW on 19S09 approx. 12.5 mi. to Santa Lucia Memorial Park CG.

SINGLE RATE:	$9	OPEN DATES:	Yearlong
# of SINGLE SITES:	12	MAX SPUR:	20 feet
		MAX STAY:	14 days
		ELEVATION:	2000 feet

69 Sunset
Stauffer • lat 34°41'56" lon 118°59'51"

DESCRIPTION: A canyon setting among scrub oak and scattered pine. This camp is located on a designated 4WD trail. No nearby fishing. No water. Bring firewood. Deer, mountain lion, bears and small wildlife in area.

GETTING THERE: From Stauffer go SE on forest route 9N03 approx. 2.5 mi. to forest route 8N12 (Lockwood RTE). Go SE on 8N12 approx. 2 mi. to Sunset CG. 4WD access only.

SINGLE RATE:	No fee	OPEN DATES:	Yearlong
# of SINGLE SITES:	1	MAX SPUR:	20 feet
		MAX STAY:	14 days
		ELEVATION:	4300 feet

70 Thorn Meadows
Stauffer Landing • lat 34°37'34" lon 119°06'48"

DESCRIPTION: Set in the open among jeffrey pine offering shade. Horse corral. No nearby fishing. No water. Bring firewood. Deer, mountain lion, bears and small wildlife in area. Horse and hiking trail access into Sespe Wilderness.

GETTING THERE: From Stauffer Landing go SW approx. 9.5 mi. on forest route 7N03 to forest route 7N03A. Go SW approx. 1.5 mi. to Thorn Meadows CG. 4WD recommended.

SINGLE RATE:	No fee	OPEN DATES:	Seasonal
# of SINGLE SITES:	5	MAX SPUR:	20 feet
		MAX STAY:	14 days
		ELEVATION:	5000 feet

 Campground has hosts   **Reservable sites**   **Accessible facilities**   **Fully developed**   **Semi-developed**   **Rustic facilities**

NOTE: Open dates listed are typical. Actual dates are dependent on conditions such as snow pack.

71 Tinta
Ojala • lat 34°42'55" lon 119°24'54"

DESCRIPTION: Located on a small flat in the canyon under a pinyon pine stand. Spring and fall are nice, hot summers. Primarily used for motorcyclists. Designated roads and trails for MC use. No nearby fishing. No water. Bring firewood. Deer, mountain lion, bears and small wildlife in area.

GETTING THERE: From Ojala go N on state HWY 33 approx. 27 mi. to forest route 7N04. Go W on 7N04 approx. 2 mi. to Tinta CG. Road not recommended for cars.

SINGLE RATE:	No fee	OPEN DATES:	Seasonal
# of SINGLE SITES:	3	MAX SPUR:	20 feet
		MAX STAY:	14 days
		ELEVATION:	3600 feet

72 Toad Springs
Apache Potrero • lat 34°51'40" lon 119°13'35"

DESCRIPTION: CG is located in an open area with some willows. No nearby fishing. No water. Bring firewood. Deer, mountain lion, bears and small wildlife in area. OHV trails closed due to landslide.

GETTING THERE: From Apache Potrero go E on county route FH95 approx. 5 mi. to forest route 22W01. Go S on 22W01 approx. 1/2 mi. to Toad Springs CG.

SINGLE RATE:	No fee	OPEN DATES:	Yearlong
# of SINGLE SITES:	5	MAX SPUR:	20 feet
		MAX STAY:	14 days
		ELEVATION:	5700 feet

73 Twin Pines
Stauffer • lat 34°40'08" lon 118°57'03"

DESCRIPTION: In jeffrey pine, shaded camp off a graded dirt road. No nearby fishing. No water. Bring firewood. Deer, mountain lion, bears and small wildlife in area. Alamo Mountain is nearby, no trails, open hiking.

GETTING THERE: From Stauffer go SE on forest route 8N12 approx. 7 mi. to forest route 7N01. Go SE on 7N01 approx. 2 mi. to Twin Pines CG.

SINGLE RATE:	No fee	OPEN DATES:	Yearlong
# of SINGLE SITES:	5	MAX SPUR:	20 feet
		MAX STAY:	14 days
		ELEVATION:	6600 feet

74 Upper Oso
Santa Barbara • lat 34°33'25" lon 119°46'13"

DESCRIPTION: Among oak with mountain and trail views. Hot summer days, cold nights. Fish trout, bass, catfish 1 mi. away. Supplies at Santa Barbara. Deer, foxes, mountain lions, many birds. Heavy weekend use. Gather or buy firewood. Hike Santa Cruz trail. OHV roads. Ticks, black flies and mosquitos in summer. Some horse sites.

GETTING THERE: From Santa Barbara go NW approx. 10 mi. on state HWY 154 to forest route 5N18. Go E on 5N18 approx. 5.5 mi. to Upper Oso CG.

SINGLE RATE:	$12	OPEN DATES:	Yearlong
# of SINGLE SITES:	24		
		MAX STAY:	14 days
		ELEVATION:	1200 feet

75 Valle Vista
Apache Potrero • lat 34°52'40" lon 119°20'25"

DESCRIPTION: Located in a shady area of pinyon and oak off a paved road. Great views of valley. No nearby fishing. No water. Bring firewood. Deer, mountain lions, bears and small wildlife in area. No nearby trails.

GETTING THERE: From Apache Potrero go N on county route FH95 approximately 2.5 miles to Valle Vista.

SINGLE RATE:	No fee	OPEN DATES:	Yearlong
# of SINGLE SITES:	7	MAX SPUR:	20 feet
		MAX STAY:	14 days
		ELEVATION:	4800 feet

76 Wheeler Gorge
Ojala • lat 34°30'43" lon 119°16'25"

DESCRIPTION: In pine forest setting on Matilija Creek. Gather firewood, may be sparse. Deer, mountain lions, black bears, rattlesnakes and small wildlife in area. Supplies in Ojala. Access to OHV use on Ortega Trail. One-mile self guided trail is nearby.

GETTING THERE: From Ojala go N on state HWY 33 approximately 4 miles to Wheeler Gorge CG.

SINGLE RATE:	Varies	OPEN DATES:	Yearlong
# of SINGLE SITES:	70	MAX SPUR:	20 feet
		MAX STAY:	14 days
		ELEVATION:	1850 feet

77 White Oaks
Carmel Valley • lat 34°31'55" lon 119°45'01"

DESCRIPTION: Amid madrone and oak trees with chaparral and poison oak. Hot summers, chilly winters with fog, wind, rain and possible snow. Supplies in Carmel Valley. Wild cats and birds in area. Rarely fills. Bring own firewood. Hiking trails within driving distance. Prepare for bugs spring and summer. Adventure pass required.

GETTING THERE: From Carmel Valley go S on county route G16 (Carmel Valley Rd) approx. 20 mi. to county route 5007 (Cachagua Rd). Go W on 5007 approx. 1 mi. to Tassajara Rd. Go S on Tassajara Rd. approx. 8 mi. to White Oaks CG.

SINGLE RATE:	$5	OPEN DATES:	Yearlong
# of SINGLE SITES:	8	MAX SPUR:	20 feet
		MAX STAY:	14 days
		ELEVATION:	4200 feet

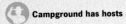 Campground has hosts 🔒 Reservable sites ♿ Accessible facilities   Fully developed 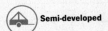 Semi-developed  Rustic facilities

MENDOCINO NATIONAL FOREST

The Mendocino National Forest was set aside by President Roosevelt in 1907. Straddling the eastern spur of the Coastal Mountain Range in northwestern California, it is just a three hour drive north of San Francisco and Sacramento. Some 65 miles long and 35 miles across, the forest's one million acres of mountains and canyons offer a variety of recreational opportunities that include camping, hiking, backpacking, boating, fishing, hunting, nature study, photography, and off-highway vehicle travel.

Take a day or overnight hike along one of the forest's crest trails and you'll be treated to a series of dramatic vistas as views open out over forested mountains or down into rugged river canyons. In the spring and early summer, blue lupine, bright orange poppies, red bud, bush lilac, and an array of other wildflowers enliven meadows, grasslands, and just about any open space with swatches of brilliant color.

Venture into the forest's more remote areas and it's likely you will have the trail to yourself, surrounded by the quiet of the woodlands and clean mountain air. The only one of California's 18 national forests not crossed by a paved road or highway, the Mendocino Forest is a place for people seeking an outdoor experience of tranquility and solitude.

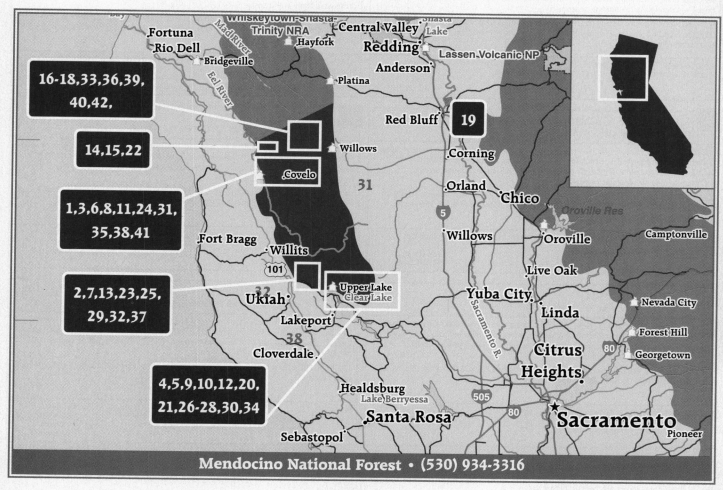

Mendocino National Forest • (530) 934-3316

1 Atchison
Covelo • lat 39°45'02" lon 122°55'29"

DESCRIPTION: This CG is situated in a fir, pine, and cedar forest with many creeks running through the area. Fish for trout on the creeks. Check for local regulations Supplies are available at Covelo. Deer, bears, turkeys, and grouse are common to the area. Gather firewood locally. Several trails nearby.

GETTING THERE: From Covelo go E on primary forest route 7 approx. 19 mi. to forest route. Go S approx. 4 mi. to Atchison CG.

SINGLE RATE:	No fee	OPEN DATES:	May-Oct
# of SINGLE SITES:	3	MAX SPUR:	22 feet
		MAX STAY:	14 days
		ELEVATION:	3900 feet

2 Bears Creek
Potter Valley • lat 39°19'22" lon 122°50'09"

DESCRIPTION: CG situated in a mixed hardwood forest with Bears Creek running nearby. Fish for rainbow trout from Bears Creek. Supplies are at Potter Valley. Deer, bears, turkeys, grouse, and squirrels are common to the area. Campers may gather their firewood locally. Numerous trails nearby.

GETTING THERE: From Potter Valley go S on county route 249 2 mi. to forest route 18N01. Go E 8 mi. to county route 301. Go S 1 mi. to county route 301C. Continue 6 mi. to Bears Creek CG.

SINGLE RATE:	No fee	OPEN DATES:	May-Oct
# of SINGLE SITES:	16	MAX SPUR:	22 feet
		MAX STAY:	14 days
		ELEVATION:	2000 feet

3 Boardman Ridge
Covelo • lat 39°51'01" lon 123°00'37"

DESCRIPTION: CG set in a primative oak, fir, and pine forest, situated on a cliff with spectacular views. Fishing opportunities with-in 8 mi. of the CG. Deer, raccoons, squirrels, mountain lions, and snakes reside in the area. No designated trails nearby. Receives heavy use during the fall hunting season.

GETTING THERE: From Covelo go E on state HWY 162 approx. 2.5 mi. to county route 338. Go E on 338 approx. 8 mi. to primary forest route M1. Go E on M1 approx. 7 mi. to Boardman Ridge CG.

SINGLE RATE:	No fee	OPEN DATES:	May-Oct
# of SINGLE SITES:	2	MAX SPUR:	22 feet
		MAX STAY:	14 days
		ELEVATION:	4500 feet

4 Cedar Camp
Stonyford • lat 39°15'52" lon 122°41'56"

DESCRIPTION: CG set in a fir, pine, and cedar forest with many creeks running nearby. Fish for trout on the creeks. Check for local regulations. Supplies at Stonyford. Deer, bears, turkeys, grouse and squirrels reside in the area. Gather firewood locally. Numerous trails are available nearby.

GETTING THERE: From Stonyford go W on primary forest route M10 approx. 5.5 mi. to primary forest route M5. Go S on M5 approx. 10 mi. to Cedar Camp CG. Not recommended for trailers.

SINGLE RATE:	No fee	OPEN DATES:	June-Oct
# of SINGLE SITES:	5		
		MAX STAY:	14 days
		ELEVATION:	4300 feet

5 Davis Flat
Stonyford • lat 39°13'44" lon 122°30'07"

DESCRIPTION: CG set in a fir, pine, and cedar forest with many creeks running nearby. Fish for trout on the creeks. Check for local regulations. Supplies at Stonyford. Deer, bears, turkeys, grouse, and squirrels reside in the area. Gather firewood locally. Numerous trails are available nearby.

GETTING THERE: From Stonyford go W on primary forest route M10 approx. 5.5 mi. to forest route 18N06. Go S on 18N06 approx. 2.5 mi. to Davis Flat CG.

SINGLE RATE:	No fee	OPEN DATES:	Yearlong
# of SINGLE SITES:	70	MAX SPUR:	22 feet
		MAX STAY:	14 days
		ELEVATION:	1700 feet

6 Dead Mule
Covelo • lat 39°50'49" lon 122°49'34"

DESCRIPTION: This CG is situated in a mixed conifer forest. No drinking water available on site. Supplies can be found in Covelo. Wildlife in the area includes deer, bears, birds, squirrells, and mountain lions. Campers may gather their firewood locally. No designated hiking trails available.

GETTING THERE: From Covelo go E on primary forest route 7 approx. 19 mi. to primary forest route M4. Go E on M4 approx. 12.5 mi. to Dead Mule CG.

SINGLE RATE:	No fee	OPEN DATES:	June-Oct
# of SINGLE SITES:	2	MAX SPUR:	22 feet
		MAX STAY:	14 days
		ELEVATION:	5000 feet

7 Deer Valley
Potter Valley • lat 39°15'58" lon 122°53'00"

DESCRIPTION: CG situated in a fir, pine, and cedar forest with many creeks running nearby. Fish for trout on the creeks. Chceck for local regulations Supplies at Potter Valley. Deer, bears, turkeys, and grouse are common to the area. Campers may gather their firewood locally. Numerous trails available for use.

GETTING THERE: From Potter Valley go S on county route 249 2 mi. to forest route 18N01. Go E on 18N01 8 mi. to county route 301. Go S 2 mi. to forest route 16N01. Go SE 3.5 mi. to Deer Valley CG.

SINGLE RATE:	No fee	OPEN DATES:	Apr-Nov
# of SINGLE SITES:	13		
		MAX STAY:	14 days
		ELEVATION:	3700 feet

8 Del Harleson
Paskenta • lat 39°47'15" lon 122°41'08"

DESCRIPTION: This CG is situated in a mixed conifer forest. Dispersed sites. Supplies are available at Covelo. No drinking water on site. Wildlife in the area includes deer, bears, various birds, and mountain lions. Campers may gather their firewood locally. No designated trails in the area.

GETTING THERE: From Paskenta go SE on county route 55 approx. 6.5 mi. to forest route 23N69. Go SE approx. 6 mi. to primary forest route M9. Go S on M9 approx. 1.5 mi. to Del Harleson CG.

SINGLE RATE:	No fee	OPEN DATES:	Apr-Nov
# of SINGLE SITES:	2	MAX SPUR:	22 feet
		MAX STAY:	14 days
		ELEVATION:	4200 feet

9 Digger Pine
Stonyford • lat 39°17'10" lon 122°34'35"

DESCRIPTION: CG set in a fir, pine, and cedar forest with many creeks running nearby. Fish for trout on the creeks. Check for local regulations. Supplies at Stonyford. Deer, bears, turkeys, grouse, and squirrels reside in the area. Gather firewood locally. Numerous trails are available nearby.

GETTING THERE: From Stonyford go S on primary forest route M10 approx. 5 mi. to forest route. Go SW approx. 3 mi. to Digger Pine CG.

SINGLE RATE:	No fee	OPEN DATES:	Oct-June
# of SINGLE SITES:	7	MAX SPUR:	22 feet
		MAX STAY:	14 days
		ELEVATION:	1500 feet

10 Dixie Glade
Stonyford • lat 39°20'30" lon 112°41'30"

DESCRIPTION: CG situated in a mixed hardwood forest. Fish for trout on the creeks or lake nearby. Check for local regulations Supplies are available at Stonyford. Deer, bears, turkeys, grouse, and squirrels reside in the area. Campers may gather their firewood locally. Numerous trails available for use.

GETTING THERE: From Stonyford go W on primary forest route M10 approx. 10 mi. to Dixie Glade CG.

SINGLE RATE:	No fee	OPEN DATES:	Apr-Oct
# of SINGLE SITES:	5	MAX SPUR:	22 feet
		MAX STAY:	14 days
		ELEVATION:	3700 feet

 Campground has hosts   Reservable sites   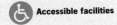 Accessible facilities   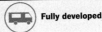 Fully developed    Semi-developed   Rustic facilities

NOTE: Open dates listed are typical. Actual dates are dependent on conditions such as snow pack.

11 Eel River
Covelo • lat 39°49'28" lon 123°05'04"

DESCRIPTION: CG set in a fir, pine, and cedar forest with many creeks running nearby. Fish for trout on the creeks. Check for local regulations. Supplies at Covelo. Deer, bears, turkeys, grouse and squirrels reside in the area. Gather firewood locally. Numerous trails are available nearby.

GETTING THERE: Eel River CG is located approx. 8.5 mi. fom Covelo on county route 338.

SINGLE RATE:	$6	OPEN DATES:	May-Oct
# of SINGLE SITES:	16	MAX SPUR:	22 feet
		MAX STAY:	14 days
		ELEVATION:	1500 feet

12 Fouts
Stonyford • lat 39°21'40" lon 122°39'09"

DESCRIPTION: CG set in a fir, pine, and cedar forest with views of Stony Creek. Fish for trout on Stony Creek. Check for local regulations. Supplies at Stonyford. Deer, bears, turkeys, grouse and squirrels reside in the area. Gather firewood locally. Numerous trails are available nearby.

GETTING THERE: Fouts CG is located approx. 6.5 mi. SW of Stonyford on primary forest route M10.

SINGLE RATE:	$6	OPEN DATES:	Yearlong
# of SINGLE SITES:	9	MAX SPUR:	16 feet
		MAX STAY:	14 days
		ELEVATION:	3700 feet

13 Fuller Grove
Potter Valley • lat 39°20'57" lon 120°39'14"

DESCRIPTION: CG set in a fir, pine, and cedar forest on Lake Pillsbury. Fish for rainbow trout, largemouth bass, and sunfish. Supplies at Potter Valley. Deer, bears, turkeys, and grouse in area. Gather firewood locally. Many trails nearby. Boat ramp available. Food storage lockers offered.

GETTING THERE: From Potter Valley go N on county route 249 approx. 3.5 mi. to primary forest route M8. Go NE approx. 11 mi. to primary forest route M1. Go N approx. 1 mi. to Fuller Grove CG.

SINGLE RATE:	$10	OPEN DATES:	Yearlong
# of SINGLE SITES:	20	MAX SPUR:	40 feet
GROUP RATE:	$100	MAX STAY:	14 days
# of GROUP SITES:	1	ELEVATION:	1900 feet

14 Green Springs
Covelo • lat 39°58'21" lon 122°55'58"

DESCRIPTION: CG set in a fir, pine, and cedar forest with Green Springs nearby. Fish and play from the springs. Supplies at Covelo. Deer, bears, turkeys, and grouse reside in the area. CG is used primarily as a trailhead camp and popular jumping off spot into the Yolla Bolly-Middle Eel Wilderness.

GETTING THERE: From Covelo go E on state HWY 162 approx. 1.5 mi. to county route 338. Go E on 338 approx. 19 mi. to primary forest route M2. Go N on M2 approx. 12 mi. to Green Springs CG.

SINGLE RATE:	No fee	OPEN DATES:	May-Oct
# of SINGLE SITES:	4	MAX SPUR:	22 feet
		MAX STAY:	14 days
		ELEVATION:	6000 feet

15 Hammerhorn
Covelo • lat 39°56'54" lon 122°59'21"

DESCRIPTION: CG set in a lush forest with views of Hammerhorn Lake. Fish for trout from the lake. Supplies at Covelo. Deer, bears, and grouse reside in the area. Gather firewood locally. Hammerhorn Trail (1/4 mi.) leads along the lake shore from the campground to two fully accessible fishing piers.

GETTING THERE: From Covelo go E on state HWY 162 1.5 mi. to county route 338. Go E 19 mi. to forest route M2. Go N 11 mi. to forest route M21. Go W on M21 approx. 6.5 mi. to Hammerhorn CG.

SINGLE RATE:	$6	OPEN DATES:	Apr-Nov
# of SINGLE SITES:	9	MAX SPUR:	20 feet
		MAX STAY:	14 days
		ELEVATION:	3500 feet

16 Ides Cove Backpacker
Paskenta • lat 40°02'30" lon 122°50'30"

DESCRIPTION: This CG is situated in a mixed conifer forest with creeks running nearby. Fish and swim from the creeks. Supplies are at Paskenta. Deer, bears, and various birds reside in the area. Campers may gather their firewood locally. The Ides Cove National Recreational Trail begins on site.

GETTING THERE: From Paskenta go W on county route 122 12.5 mi. to forest route 24N04. Go NW 2 mi. to forest route 24N38. Go NW 5 mi. to forest route M22. Go N 8 mi. to Ides Cove Backpacker CG.

SINGLE RATE:	No fee	OPEN DATES:	May-Oct
# of SINGLE SITES:	4		
		MAX STAY:	14 days
		ELEVATION:	6300 feet

17 Ides Cove Equestrian
Paskenta • lat 40°02'27" lon 122°50'30"

DESCRIPTION: This CG is situated in a mixed conifer forest with creeks running nearby. Fish and swim from the creeks. Supplies are at Paskenta. Deer, bears, and various birds reside in the area. Campers may gather their firewood locally. The Ides Cove National Recreational Trail begins on site.

GETTING THERE: From Paskenta go W on county route 122 12.5 mi. to forest route 24N04. Go NW 2 mi. to forest route 24N38. Go NW 5 mi. to forest route M22. Go N 8 mi. to Ides Cove Equestrian CG.

SINGLE RATE:	No fee	OPEN DATES:	May-Oct
# of SINGLE SITES:	2		
		MAX STAY:	14 days
		ELEVATION:	6200 feet

18 Kingsley Glade
Paskenta • lat 40°11'26" lon 122°44'07"

DESCRIPTION: This CG is situated in a mixed conifer forest, with springs flowing nearby. Fish and swim in the creeks. Check for local regulations. Supplies available at Paskenta. Deer, bears, and mountain lions reside in the area. Campers may gather their firewood locally. No designated trails available.

GETTING THERE: From Paskenta go W on primary forest route M2 approx. 16 mi. to forest route 24N01. Go W on 24N01 approx. 3.5 mi. to Kingsley Glade CG.

SINGLE RATE:	No fee	OPEN DATES:	May-Nov
# of SINGLE SITES:	4	MAX SPUR:	22 feet
		MAX STAY:	14 days
		ELEVATION:	4500 feet

19 Lake Red Bluff
Red Bluff • lat 40°09'33" lon 122°12'21"

DESCRIPTION: This CG is situated in a fir, pine, and cedar forest with views of Lake Red Bluff. Fish for salmon and steelhead from the lake. Supplies are at Red Bluff. Deer, bears, and turkeys are common to the area. The Lake Red Bluff Trail originates on site. A boat ramp is available.

GETTING THERE: From Red Bluff and I-5 go E on state HWY 36 to the first turnoff (about 100 yards) which is Sale Lane. Go S approx. .5 mi. to Lake Red Bluff CG.

SINGLE RATE:	$10	OPEN DATES:	Mar-Nov
# of SINGLE SITES:	30	MAX SPUR:	22 feet
GROUP RATE:	Varies	MAX STAY:	14 days
# of GROUP SITES:	1	ELEVATION:	3000 feet

20 Lakeview
Clearlake Oaks • lat 39°05'30" lon 112°45'00"

DESCRIPTION: This CG is situated in a fir, pine, and cedar forest, a short distance away from Clear Lake. Fish for rainbow trout on the lake. Supplies at Clearlake Oaks. Deer, bears, turkeys, and grouse are common to the area. Campers may gather their firewood locally. Numerous trails are available nearby.

GETTING THERE: Lakeview CG is located approx. 8.5 mi. N of Clearlake Oaks on forest route 15N09.

SINGLE RATE:	No fee	OPEN DATES:	May-Oct
# of SINGLE SITES:	8		
		MAX STAY:	14 days
		ELEVATION:	3400 feet

MENDOCINO NATIONAL FOREST • CALIFORNIA • 11 — 20

 Campground has hosts　 **Reservable sites**　 **Accessible facilities**　 **Fully developed**　 **Semi-developed**　 **Rustic facilities**

NOTE: Open dates listed are typical. Actual dates are dependent on conditions such as snow pack.

21   Letts Lake
Stonyford • lat 39°18'11" lon 122°42'26"

DESCRIPTION: CG set in a fir, pine, and cedar forest on Letts Lake. Fish for rainbow trout, largemouth bass, and channel catfish from the lake. Supplies at Stonyford. Deer, bears, grouse, and eagles are common to the area. Trail meanders along the lake shore with a fully-accessible fishing pier.

GETTING THERE: Letts Lake is located approx. 16 mi. W of Stonyford on forest route 17N02.

SINGLE RATE:	$8	OPEN DATES:	Apr-Nov
# of SINGLE SITES:	40	MAX SPUR:	16 feet
		MAX STAY:	14 days
		ELEVATION:	4500 feet

22 Little Doe
Covelo • lat 39°53'41" lon 122°59'13"

DESCRIPTION: CG set in a fir, pine, and cedar forest with many creeks running nearby. Fish for trout on the creeks. Check for local regulations. Supplies are at Covelo. Deer, bears, turkeys, grouse, and squirrels reside in the area. Gather firewood locally. Numerous trails are available nearby.

GETTING THERE: From Covelo go E on state HWY 162 approx. 2.5 mi. to county route 338. Go E on 338 approx. 8 mi. to primary forest route M1. Go E on M1 approx. 12 mi. to Little Doe CG.

SINGLE RATE:	No fee	OPEN DATES:	June-Oct
# of SINGLE SITES:	13		
		MAX STAY:	14 days
		ELEVATION:	3600 feet

23 Lower Nye
Potter Valley • lat 39°26'36" lon 122°49'28"

DESCRIPTION: CG set in a fir, pine, and cedar forest with Skeleton Creek. Fish for trout on Skeleton Creek. Check for local fishing regulations. Supplies at Potter Valley. Deer, bears, turkeys, grouse, and squirrels reside in the area. Gather firewood locally. Numerous trails are available nearby.

GETTING THERE: From Potter Valley go S 2 mi. on county route 249 to forest route 18N01. E 8 mi. to county route 301. S 1 mi. to county route 301C. S 4.5 mi. to forest route 18N04. N 10.5 mi. to Lower Nye CG.

SINGLE RATE:	No fee	OPEN DATES:	May-Sept
# of SINGLE SITES:	6		
		MAX STAY:	14 days
		ELEVATION:	3300 feet

24 Masterson Group
Covelo • lat 39°44'05" lon 122°50'31"

DESCRIPTION: CG set in a fir and pine forest 1/2 mi. away from Plaskett Lakes. Fish for rainbow trout. No motorized boats allowed. Lake not recommended for swimming. Supplies at Covelo. Deer, bears, grouse, and eagles are common to the area. Gather firewood locally. Numerous trails nearby.

GETTING THERE: From Covelo go E on primary forest route 7 approx. 19 mi. to primary forest route FH7. Go SE on FH7 approx. 8 mi. to Masterson Group CG.

		OPEN DATES:	May-Oct
		MAX SPUR:	22 feet
		MAX STAY:	14 days
GROUP RATE:	$35	ELEVATION:	6000 feet
# of GROUP SITES:	1		

25 Middle Creek
Upper Lake • lat 39°15'11" lon 122°57'00"

DESCRIPTION: This CG is set in a fir, pine, and cedar forest a short distance away from Middle Creek. Fish for rainbow trout on the creek. Supplies at Upper Lake. Deer, bears, turkeys, and grouse reside in the area. Gather firewood locally. Many trails nearby. One equestrian staging area (no camping).

GETTING THERE: From Upper Lake go N on county route 301 approx. 9 mi. to Middle Creek CG.

SINGLE RATE:	$4	OPEN DATES:	Yearlong
# of SINGLE SITES:	23	MAX SPUR:	22 feet
		MAX STAY:	14 days
		ELEVATION:	2000 feet

26 Mill Creek
Stonyford • lat 39°21'12" lon 122°39'20"

DESCRIPTION: CG set in a fir, pine, and cedar forest with views of Mill Creek. Fish for trout on the creek. Check for local fishing regulations. Supplies are at Stonyford. Deer, bears, turkeys, grouse, and squirrels reside in the area. Gather firewood locally. Numerous trails are available nearby.

GETTING THERE: Mill Creek CG is located approx. 7 mi. SW of Stonyford on primary forest route M10.

SINGLE RATE:	$6	OPEN DATES:	Yearlong
# of SINGLE SITES:	5	MAX SPUR:	16 feet
		MAX STAY:	14 days
		ELEVATION:	1640 feet

27 Mill Valley
Stonyford • lat 39°19'03" lon 122°42'26"

DESCRIPTION: CG set in a fir, pine, and cedar forest with Letts Lake 1 mi. away. Fish for trout on the lake. Check for local regulations. Supplies at Stonyford. Deer, bears, turkeys, grouse, and squirrels reside in the area. Gather firewood locally. Numerous trails are available nearby.

GETTING THERE: From Stonyford go W on primary forest route M10 approx. 12 mi. to forest route 17N80. Go E on 17N80 approx. 2 mi. to Mill Valley CG.

SINGLE RATE:	$5	OPEN DATES:	Apr-Nov
# of SINGLE SITES:	16	MAX SPUR:	22 feet
		MAX STAY:	14 days
		ELEVATION:	200 feet

28 North Fork
Stonyford • lat 39°22'45" lon 122°38'51"

DESCRIPTION: CG situated in an open grove of oak trees with many creeks running nearby. Fish for trout on the creeks. Check for local fishing regulations. Supplies at Stonyford. Deer, bears, turkeys, grouse, and squirrels reside in the area. Gather firewood locally. Numerous trails are available nearby.

GETTING THERE: From Stonyford go SE approx. 7 mi. on primary forest route M10 to forest route 18N06. Go N on 18N06 approx. 3 mi. to North Fork CG.

SINGLE RATE:	No fee	OPEN DATES:	Yearlong
# of SINGLE SITES:	6	MAX SPUR:	22 feet
		MAX STAY:	14 days
		ELEVATION:	1700 feet

29 Oak Flat
Potter Valley • lat 39°26'35" lon 122°57'08"

DESCRIPTION: CG set in a fir, pine, and cedar forest on the shores of Lake Pillsbury. Fish for rainbow trout, largemouth bass, and sunfish. Check for local regulations Supplies at Stonyford. Deer, bears, turkeys, grouse, and squirrels reside in the area. Gather firewood locally. Numerous trails are available.

GETTING THERE: From Potter Valley go N on county route 249 approx. 3.5 mi. to primary forest route M8. Go NE approx. 11 mi. to forest route M1. Go N on M1 approx. 4 mi. to Oak Flat CG.

SINGLE RATE:	No fee	OPEN DATES:	Yearlong
# of SINGLE SITES:	12	MAX SPUR:	40 feet
		MAX STAY:	14 days
		ELEVATION:	1810 feet

30 Old Mill
Stonyford • lat 39°18'38" lon 122°38'29"

DESCRIPTION: This CG is situated in a fir, pine, and cedar forest. Supplies are available at Stonyford. Wildlife in the area includes deer, bears, turkeys, grouse, and squirrels. Campers may gather their firewood locally. Numerous hiking, horse, and mountain bike trails are available nearby.

GETTING THERE: From Stonyford go W on primary forest route M10 approx. 5.5 mi. to primary forest route M5. Go S on M5 approx. 4.5 mi. to Old Mill CG.

SINGLE RATE:	No fee	OPEN DATES:	May-Nov
# of SINGLE SITES:	10	MAX SPUR:	22 feet
		MAX STAY:	14 days
		ELEVATION:	3700 feet

 Campground has hosts   Reservable sites   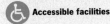 Accessible facilities   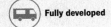 Fully developed   Semi-developed   Rustic facilities

NOTE: Open dates listed are typical. Actual dates are dependent on conditions such as snow pack.

31 Plaskett Meadows
Covelo • lat 39°43'37" lon 122°50'30"

DESCRIPTION: CG set in a fir and pine forest on the shores of Plaskett Lake. Fish for rainbow trout. No motorized boats. Lake not recommended for swimming. Supplies at Covelo. Deer, bears, turkeys, grouse, and eagles reside in the area. Gather firewood locally. Numerous trails are available nearby.

GETTING THERE: From Covelo go E on primary forest route 7 approx. 28 mi. to Plaskett Meadows CG.

SINGLE RATE:	$5	OPEN DATES:	June-Oct
# of SINGLE SITES:	32	MAX SPUR:	16 feet
		MAX STAY:	14 days
		ELEVATION:	6000 feet

32 Pogie Point
Potter Valley • lat 39°26'34" lon 122°58'04"

DESCRIPTION: CG set in a fir, pine, and cedar forest on the shores of Lake Pillsbury. Fish for rainbow trout, largemouth bass, and sunfish. Check for local regulations Supplies at Stonyford. Deer, bears, turkeys, grouse, and squirrels reside in the area. Gather firewood locally. Numerous trails are available.

GETTING THERE: From Potter Valley go N on county route 249 approx. 3.5 mi. to primary forest route M8. Go NE on M8 approx. 11 mi. to primary forest route M1. Go N on M1 2 mi. to Pogie Point CG.

SINGLE RATE:	$10	OPEN DATES:	Yearlong
# of SINGLE SITES:	49	MAX SPUR:	40 feet
		MAX STAY:	14 days
		ELEVATION:	1900 feet

33 Rock Cabin
Paskenta • lat 39°57'09" lon 122°44'10"

DESCRIPTION: This CG is situated in a fir, pine, and cedar forest. Supplies are available at Paskenta. Wildlife in the area includes deer, bears, turkeys, grouse, and squirrels. This CG is used primarily as a trailhead camp and popular jumping off spot to the Yolla Bolly-Middle Eel Wilderness.

GETTING THERE: From Paskenta go W on county route 122 approx. 12.5 mi. to forest route 24N04. Go NW on 24N04 approx. 2 mi. to forest route 24N38. Go NW on 24N38 approx. 5 mi. to Rocky Cabin CG.

SINGLE RATE:	No fee	OPEN DATES:	May-Nov
# of SINGLE SITES:	3	MAX SPUR:	22 feet
		MAX STAY:	14 days
		ELEVATION:	6250 feet

34 South Fork
Stoneyford • lat 39°22'30" lon 122°38'30"

DESCRIPTION: CG set in a fir, pine, and cedar forest with views of a creek. Fish for trout on the creek. Check for local fishing regulations. Supplies at Stonyford. Deer, bears, turkeys, grouse, and squirrels reside in the area. Gather firewood locally. Numerous trails are available nearby.

GETTING THERE: South Fork CG is located approx. 6 mi. SW of Stonyford on primary forest route M10.

SINGLE RATE:	No fee	OPEN DATES:	Yearlong
# of SINGLE SITES:	5		
		MAX STAY:	14 days
		ELEVATION:	1900 feet

35 Sugar Springs
Covelo • lat 39°51'30" lon 122°54'00"

DESCRIPTION: This CG is situated in a mixed conifer forest. Supplies are available at Covelo. Wildlife in the area includes deer, bears, birds, squirrels, and mountain lions. Campers may gather their firewood locally. No drinking water available on site. No designated trails in the area.

GETTING THERE: From Covelo go E on primary forest route H7 approx. 19 mi. to forest route 24N02. Go N on 24N02 approx. 4.5 mi. to forest route 23N69. Go E on 23N69 approx. 2 mi. to Sugar Springs CG.

SINGLE RATE:	No fee	OPEN DATES:	May-Nov
# of SINGLE SITES:	2	MAX SPUR:	22 feet
		MAX STAY:	14 days
		ELEVATION:	5400 feet

36 Sugarfoot Glade
Paskenta • lat 39°52'53" lon 122°46'41"

DESCRIPTION: This CG is situated in a mixed oak and conifer forest. A small creek runs through the CG early on in the season. Supplies are available at Paskenta. Deer, bears, birds, and squirrels are common to the area. Campers may gather their firewood locally. No designated trails in the area.

GETTING THERE: From Paskenta go W on primary forest route M2 approx. 16 mi. to forest route 24N01. Go W on 24N01 approx. 7.5 mi. to Sugarfoot Glade CG.

SINGLE RATE:	No fee	OPEN DATES:	May-Nov
# of SINGLE SITES:	6	MAX SPUR:	20 feet
		MAX STAY:	14 days
		ELEVATION:	4200 feet

37 Sunset
Potter Valley • lat 39°27'30" lon 122°56'00"

DESCRIPTION: CG set in a fir, pine, and cedar forest on the shores of Lake Pillsbury. Fish for rainbow trout, largemouth bass, and sunfish. Check for local regulations Supplies at Stonyford. Deer, bears, turkeys, grouse, and squirrels reside in the area. Gather firewood locally. Numerous trails are available.

GETTING THERE: From Potter Valley go N on county route 249 approx. 3.5 mi. to primary forest route M8. Go NE on M8 approx. 11 mi. to primary forest route M1. Go N on M1 approx. 5 mi. to Sunset CG.

SINGLE RATE:	$10	OPEN DATES:	Yearlong
# of SINGLE SITES:	54	MAX SPUR:	40 feet
		MAX STAY:	14 days
		ELEVATION:	1800 feet

38 Surveyor Camp
Covelo • lat 39°49'09" lon 122°58'26"

DESCRIPTION: CG set in a fir, pine, and cedar forest with many creeks in the area. Dispersed sites. Fish for trout on the creeks. Check for local regulations. Supplies at Covelo. Deer, bears, turkeys, grouse, and squirrels reside in the area. Gather firewood locally. Numerous trails are available.

GETTING THERE: Surveyor Camp CG is located approx. 16 mi. E of Covelo on primary forest route FH7.

SINGLE RATE:	No fee	OPEN DATES:	May-Oct
# of SINGLE SITES:	3	MAX SPUR:	22 feet
		MAX STAY:	14 days
		ELEVATION:	3900 feet

39 Three Prong
Paskenta • lat 39°55'14" lon 122°47'24"

DESCRIPTION: This CG is situated in a mixed conifer forest, adjacent to a large meadow. Springs flow nearby. Supplies are available at Paskenta. Wildlife in the area includes deer, bears, and mountain lions. Campers may gather their firewood locally. No designated trails in the area.

GETTING THERE: From Paskenta go W on county route 122/primary forest route N2 approx. 19 mi. to forest route 24N25. Go W on 24N25 approx. 3 mi. to Three Prong CG.

SINGLE RATE:	No fee	OPEN DATES:	May-Nov
# of SINGLE SITES:	4	MAX SPUR:	20 feet
		MAX STAY:	14 days
		ELEVATION:	4800 feet

40 Toomes
Paskenta • lat 40°00'12" lon 122°45'28"

DESCRIPTION: This CG is situated in a mixed conifer forest. No drinking water available on site. No fishing opportunities in the area. Supplies are available at Paskenta. Watch for deer, bears, and various birds. Campers may gather their firewood locally. No designated trails in the area.

GETTING THERE: From Paskenta go W on county route 122 12.5 mi. to forest route 24N04. NW 2 mi. to forest route 24N38. NW 5 mi. to forest route M22. N 3 mi. to county route 693. E .2 mi. to Toomes CG.

SINGLE RATE:	No fee	OPEN DATES:	June-Oct
# of SINGLE SITES:	2	MAX SPUR:	22 feet
		MAX STAY:	14 days
		ELEVATION:	6000 feet

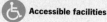 **Campground has hosts**   🔒 **Reservable sites**   ♿ **Accessible facilities**   **Fully developed**   **Semi-developed**   **Rustic facilities**

NOTE: Open dates listed are typical. Actual dates are dependent on conditions such as snow pack.

41 Wells Cabin
Covelo • lat 39°50'16" lon 122°56'54"

DESCRIPTION: This CG is situated in a red and white fir forest with spectacular views of the surrounding mountains. Supplies are available at Covelo. Wildlife in the area includes deer, bears, birds, and occasional mountain lions. Anthony Peak Lookout can be found approx. 1 mi. away from the CG.

GETTING THERE: From Covelo go E approx. 19 mi. on primary forest route FH7 to primary forest route M2. Go N on M2 approx. 3 mi. to Wells Cabin CG.

SINGLE RATE:	No fee	OPEN DATES:	May-Nov
# of SINGLE SITES:	25		
		MAX STAY:	14 days
		ELEVATION:	6300 feet

42 Whitlock
Paskenta • lat 39°55'13" lon 122°41'07"

DESCRIPTION: This CG is situated in a mixed conifer forest. No drinking water available on site. No fishing opportunities in the area. Supplies are available at Paskenta. Watch for deer, bears, and various birds. Campers may gather their firewood locally. No designated trails in the area.

GETTING THERE: From Paskenta go NW on county route 122 approx. 10 mi. to forest route 24N19. Go N on 24N19 approx. .5 mi. to Whitlock CG.

SINGLE RATE:	No fee	OPEN DATES:	May-Nov
# of SINGLE SITES:	3	MAX SPUR:	22 feet
		MAX STAY:	14 days
		ELEVATION:	4300 feet

Make Your Voice Heard

The National Environmental Policy Act of 1969 requires the Forest Service to involve the public in policy decisions made about National Forest Lands. The NFS routinely proposes timber sales, restoration projects, and even ski area expansions. Your comments helps the FS learn about issues of public concern. The NFS will present findings of environmental effects to the public in **environmental impact statements.**

Watch for notices of FS proposals in the legal notice section of local newspapers, or call a FS office for information about upcoming projects.

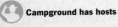 Campground has hosts
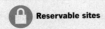 Reservable sites
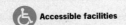 Accessible facilities
 Fully developed
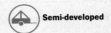 Semi-developed
 Rustic facilities

NOTE: Open dates listed are typical. Actual dates are dependent on conditions such as snow pack.

USFS Photo

MODOC NATIONAL FOREST

The Modoc National Forest is a land of rugged beauty and "burnt out fires" according to its original Indian occupants. Nestled in the extreme northeastern corner of California, the Modoc is 140 miles east of Redding.

The Modoc features several mountain areas: The Warner Mountains, to the east, the western edge of the Great Basin Province; the Medicine Lake highlands, and to the northwest is a southern spur of the Cascade Range. Bordered by Oregon to the north and Nevada to the east, the Modoc has the best of many landscapes—mountains, pine forests and meadows, lakes, streams and rugged canyons, and wetlands, lava beds and high desert plateaus.

The Modoc has many visitor attractions and outdoor opportunities. Fort Bidwell in Surprise Valley, is the site of a cavalry unit established in the 1860s to protect settlers against Indian attack. Abandoned homesteads dot the forest and represent the first pioneers to the area. Evidence of the forest's early inhabitants can be found in the forms of petroglyphs (rock carvings) and pictographs. The Modoc's South Warner Wilderness Area offers the backpacker peace and solitude. The forest is also home to an abundant array of plant and wildlife species, including beautiful wild horses.

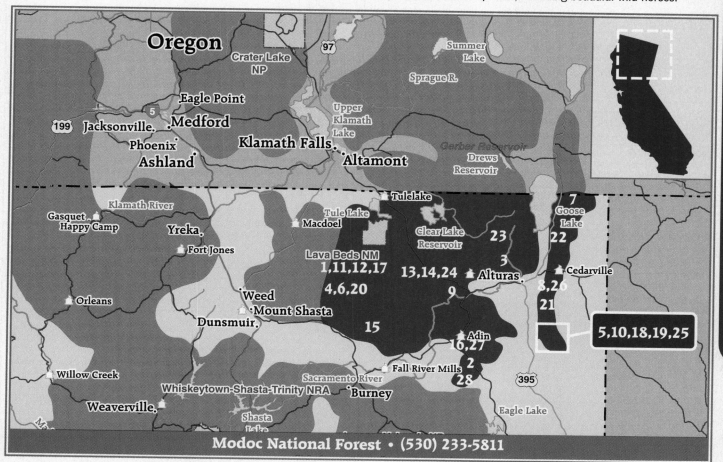

Modoc National Forest • (530) 233-5811

1 A.H. Hogue
Newell • lat 41°35'00" lon 121°35'00"

DESCRIPTION: CG is in the Medicine Lake Highlands and is one of several small CG's on the shores of Medicine Lake. CG is located adjacent to the Modoc Volcanic Scenic Byway. Fishing good in Medicine Lake. Boating is available. California Backcountry Discovery Trail is nearby. Supplies are located in Tionesta.

GETTING THERE: From Newell go SE approx. 14.5 mi. on state HWY 139 to primary forest route 97. Go W on 97 approx. 21 mi. to forest route 43N48. Go W on 43N48 approx. 1 mi. to A.H. Hogue CG.

SINGLE RATE:	$7	
# of SINGLE SITES:	24	
	OPEN DATES:	July-Oct
	MAX SPUR:	30 feet
	MAX STAY:	14 days
	ELEVATION:	6700 feet

2 Ash Creek
Addin • lat 41°09'40" lon 120°49'46"

DESCRIPTION: CG is in an open park-like setting with views of meadow. Good trout fishing from creek through out most of the year. Supplies at Adin. Deer can often be seen in the meadow. No designated trails in area, venture off on old roads or wildlife trails for quiet walks. No water.

GETTING THERE: From Addin go SE approx. 8.5 mi. on county route 88 to forest route. Go N on forest route, follow signs approx. .5 mi. to Ash Creek CG.

SINGLE RATE:	No fee	
# of SINGLE SITES:	7	
	OPEN DATES:	May-Oct
	MAX SPUR:	22 feet
	MAX STAY:	14 days
	ELEVATION:	4800 feet

3 Big Sage
Alturas • lat 41°34'48" lon 120°37'41"

DESCRIPTION: CG is located on Big Sage reservoir surrounded by juniper woodland and sagebrush. A new boat ramp at CG. Birds find safe refuge for nesting on the reservoir. California Back Country Trail is nearby. Wild horse herds. Supplies are located in Alturas.

GETTING THERE: From Alturas go W on state HWY 299 approx. 2 mi. to primary forest route 73. Go N on 73 approx. 6 mi. to forest route 44N03. Go NE on 44N03 approx. 3.5 mi. to Big Sage CG.

SINGLE RATE:	No fee	
# of SINGLE SITES:	6	
	OPEN DATES:	May-Oct
	MAX SPUR:	22 feet
	MAX STAY:	14 days
	ELEVATION:	5100 feet

4 Blanche Lake
Newell • lat 41°33'23" lon 121°34'13"

DESCRIPTION: CG has dispersed camping in a dense forest setting on Blanche Lake. Fishing from the lake is good. Many trails close to the CG. Supplies at Tooly Lake. Mosquitos can be a problem.

GETTING THERE: From Newell go SE on state HWY 139 14.5 mi. to primary forest route 97. Go W on 97 19.5 mi. to forest route 44N75. Go S on 444N75 .5 mi. to forest route 43N17. Go E on 43N17 .5 mi. to Blanche Lake CG.

SINGLE RATE:	No fee	
	OPEN DATES:	May-Oct*
	MAX STAY:	14 days
	ELEVATION:	6500 feet

5 Blue Lake
Likely • lat 41°08'42" lon 120°16'55"

DESCRIPTION: In a high desert setting with views of lake and rock formations surrounding area. Fish for trout in the lake. Trails, old roads and wildlife paths for quiet adventures. Supplies at Likely.

GETTING THERE: From Likely go E on primary forest route 64 approx. 14 mi. to forest route 39N30. Go S on 39N30 approx. 1.5 mi. to Blue Lake CG.

SINGLE RATE:	$7	
# of SINGLE SITES:	24	
	OPEN DATES:	June-Oct
	MAX STAY:	14 days
	ELEVATION:	6000 feet

6 Bullseye Lake
Newell • lat 41°33'18" lon 121°34'28"

DESCRIPTION: CG has dispersed camping in a dense forest setting on Blanche Lake. Fishing from the lake is good. Many trails close to the CG. Supplies at Tooly Lake. Mosquitos can be a problem.

GETTING THERE: From Newell go SE on state HWY 139 14.5 mi. to primary forest route 97. Go W on 97 19.5 mi. to forest route 44N75. Go S on 444N75 .5 mi. to forest route 43N17. Go E on 43N17 .5 mi. to Bullseye Lake CG.

SINGLE RATE:	No fee	
	OPEN DATES:	May-Oct*
	MAX STAY:	14 days
	ELEVATION:	6500 feet

7 Cave Lake
Fort Bidwell • lat 41°58'42" lon 120°12'17"

DESCRIPTION: CG is in a forest setting with caves nearby. Great place to rest and gather your thoughts. Fishing is good in Cave Lake. A short hike to Lily Lake. The Highgrade Trail and California Back Country Trail is nearby. Supplies can be purchased in New Pine Creek, OR, Ft. Bidwell or Davis Creek, CA.

GETTING THERE: Cave Lake CG is located approx. 9 mi. N of Fort Bidwell on primary forest route 2. Not recommended for trailers.

SINGLE RATE:	No fee	
# of SINGLE SITES:	6	
	OPEN DATES:	July-Oct
	MAX SPUR:	16 feet
	MAX STAY:	14 days
	ELEVATION:	6600 feet

8 Cedar Pass
Cedarville • lat 41°33'34" lon 120°17'34"

DESCRIPTION: CG is in the West Warner Mountains with a small sparkling stream to splash in and the greenest trees surrounding it. It is the perfect spot for rest and relaxation. Supplies are located in the town of Cedarville.

GETTING THERE: Cedar Pass CG is located approx. 6.5 mi. W of Cedarville on state HWY 299.

SINGLE RATE:	No fee	
# of SINGLE SITES:	17	
	OPEN DATES:	May-Oct
	MAX SPUR:	17 feet
	MAX STAY:	14 days
	ELEVATION:	5900 feet

9 Cottonwood Flat
Canby • lat 41°25'48" lon 121°03'45"

DESCRIPTION: CG is in a forest setting with a stream running through it. Hiking and biking trails are nearby. Supplies are located in the town of Canby.

GETTING THERE: From Canby go SW approx. 3.5 mi. on state HWY 299 to primary forest route 84. Go NW on 84 approx. 7 mi. to forest route 42N95. Go N on 42N95 approx. .5 mi. to Cottonwood Flat CG.

SINGLE RATE:	No fee	
# of SINGLE SITES:	10	
	OPEN DATES:	June-Oct
	MAX SPUR:	22 feet
	MAX STAY:	14 days
	ELEVATION:	4700 feet

10 Emerson
Eagleville • lat 41°15'48" lon 120°08'17"

DESCRIPTION: In a high desert setting close to Emerson Lake. Great fishing for trout at lake, which is a 3.5 mi. hike away from CG. Swimming is allowed at Emerson Lake. North and South Emerson Trails to the South Warner Wilderness are located here. Supplies in Eagleville and Cedarville. Horses allowed at CG.

GETTING THERE: From Eagleville go S on county route 1 approx. 1 mi. to county route 40. Go SW on 40 approx. 2.5 mi. to Emerson CG.

SINGLE RATE:	No fee	
# of SINGLE SITES:	4	
	OPEN DATES:	July-Oct
	MAX SPUR:	16 feet
	MAX STAY:	14 days
	ELEVATION:	6000 feet

 Campground has hosts   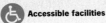 Reservable sites   Accessible facilities   Fully developed   Semi-developed   Rustic facilities

NOTE: Open dates listed are typical. Actual dates are dependent on conditions such as snow pack.

Page 106

11 Headquarters
Newell • lat 41˚35'00" lon 121˚37'30"

DESCRIPTION: In the Medicine Lake Highlands is one of several small CG's located on the shores of Medicine Lake. CG is adjacent to the Modoc Volcanic Scenic Byway. Fishing is very good in Medicine Lake. Boating is available. California Backcountry Discovery Trail is nearby. Supplies are at Tionesta.

GETTING THERE: From Newell go SE approx. 14.5 mi. on state HWY 139 to primary forest route 97. Go W on 97 approx. 21 mi. to forest route 43N48. Go W on 43N48 approx. 2 mi. to Headquarters CG.

SINGLE RATE:	$7	OPEN DATES:	July-Oct
# of SINGLE SITES:	9	MAX SPUR:	16 feet
		MAX STAY:	14 days
		ELEVATION:	6700 feet

12 Hemlock
Newell • lat 41˚34'00" lon 121˚35'00"

DESCRIPTION: In the Medicine Lake Highlands this is one of several small CG's located on the shores of Medicine Lake. CG is adjacent to the Modoc Volcanic Scenic Byway. California Backcountry Discovery Trail is nearby. Fishing is very good in Medicine Lake. Boating is available. Supplies is located in Tionesta.

GETTING THERE: From Newell go SE approx. 14.5 mi. on state HWY 139 to primary forest route 97. Go W on 97 approx. 21 mi. to forest route 43N48. Go W on 43N48 approx. 1 mi. to Hemlock CG.

SINGLE RATE:	$7	OPEN DATES:	July-Oct
# of SINGLE SITES:	19	MAX SPUR:	22 feet
		MAX STAY:	14 days
		ELEVATION:	6700 feet

13 Howards Gulch
Canby • lat 41˚29'08" lon 120˚58'06"

DESCRIPTION: CG is in a forested setting with a stream running through it (dries up during late summer). Pitt River and reservoir in area for fishing. A short hiking trail provides a wonderful overview of the areas east of the campground. Supplies are located in the town of Canby.

GETTING THERE: Howards Gulch CG is located approx. 4.5 mi. N of Canby on forest route 42N14.

SINGLE RATE:	$6	OPEN DATES:	May-Oct
# of SINGLE SITES:	11	MAX SPUR:	22 feet
		MAX STAY:	14 days
		ELEVATION:	4700 feet

14 James Reservoir
Alturas • lat 41˚26'00" lon 120˚50'00"

DESCRIPTION: In a remote high desert setting of scrub brush, rocks and dirt. Views of reservoir with some deer, mountain lions and birds in area. Fish for trout in reservoir. Campers may gather firewood. Trails, old roads and wildlife paths in area for quiet adventures.

GETTING THERE: From Alturas go W on state HWY 299 approx. 10 mi. to Devils Garden turn off. Follow signs to James Reservoir CG.

SINGLE RATE:	No fee	OPEN DATES:	June-Oct
		MAX STAY:	14 days
		ELEVATION:	5100 feet

15 Lava Camp
Canby • lat 41˚24'08" lon 121˚20'15"

DESCRIPTION: This is an isolated, rocky, and dry area for camping, located in lava bed, juniper and sage brush. This CG is mostly used for a hunting camp and has large sites. A lot of deer and antelope seen from CG. Supplies are located in the town of Bieber. No water.

GETTING THERE: From Canby go N on state HWY 139 15 mi. to county route 91. Go S on 91 4.5 mi. to primary forest route 56. Go W on 56 11.5 mi. to forest route 42N23. Go S on 42N23 6 mi. to Lava Camp CG.

SINGLE RATE:	No fee	OPEN DATES:	May-Oct
# of SINGLE SITES:	12	MAX SPUR:	32 feet
		MAX STAY:	14 days
		ELEVATION:	4400 feet

16 Lower Rush Creek
Adin • lat 41˚17'34" lon 120˚52'40"

DESCRIPTION: CG sites are surrounded by mixed conifer providing welcome shade for the hot summer days. Rush Creek runs along the edge of the campground providing a relaxing atmosphere. Fishing in Rush Creek. Supplies are located in the town of Adin approx. 7 mi. SW of the CG.

GETTING THERE: From Adin go approx. 6 mi. N on state HWY 299 to forest route. Follow signs forest route approx. 1 mi. NE to Lower Rush Creek CG.

SINGLE RATE:	$6	OPEN DATES:	May-Oct
# of SINGLE SITES:	10	MAX SPUR:	22 feet
		MAX STAY:	14 days
		ELEVATION:	4200 feet

17 Medicine Camp
Newell • lat 41˚34'54" lon 121˚35'52"

DESCRIPTION: In the Medicine Lake Highlands this is one of several small CG's located on the shores of Medicine Lake. CG is adjacent to the Modoc Volcanic Scenic Byway. California Backcountry Discovery Trail is nearby. Fishing is very good in Medicine Lake. Boating is available. Supplies are located in Tionesta.

GETTING THERE: From Newell go SE approx. 14.5 mi. on state HWY 139 to primary forest route 97. Go W on 97 approx. 21 mi. to forest route 43N48. Go W on 43N48 approx. 1.5 mi. to Medicine Camp CG.

SINGLE RATE:	$7	OPEN DATES:	July-Oct
# of SINGLE SITES:	22	MAX SPUR:	30 feet
		MAX STAY:	14 days
		ELEVATION:	6700 feet

18 Mill Creek Falls
Likely • lat 41˚16'36" lon 120˚17'17"

DESCRIPTION: CG is set in the Warner Mountains with the perfect view of all the trees. Mill Creek Falls is approximately a half mile hike from CG. Fishing is good in both Mill Creek and Clear Lake. Supplies are located in the town of Likely. Many trails in the area.

GETTING THERE: Mill Creek Falls CG is located approx. 11.5 mi. E of Likely on county route 64.

SINGLE RATE:	$6	OPEN DATES:	June-Oct
# of SINGLE SITES:	19		
		MAX STAY:	14 days
		ELEVATION:	5700 feet

19 Patterson
Eagleville • lat 41˚11'46" lon 120˚11'33"

DESCRIPTION: CG serves as a major equestrian trailhead to the South Warner Wilderness. CG is at the South End of the Summit Trail which traverses the South Warner Wilderness which has many trails. Supplies are located in the town of Eagleville or Likely.

GETTING THERE: From Eagleville go S on county route 1 approx. 3 mi. to primary forest route 64. Go SW on 64 approx. 10.5 mi. to Patterson CG.

SINGLE RATE:	No fee	OPEN DATES:	July-Oct
# of SINGLE SITES:	5	MAX SPUR:	16 feet
		MAX STAY:	14 days
		ELEVATION:	7200 feet

20 Paynes Spring
Newell • lat 41˚33'23" lon 121˚33'43"

DESCRIPTION: CG is located adjacent to the Modoc Volcanic Scenic Byway in the Medicine Lake Highlands. California Backcountry Discovery Trail and Lava Beds National Monument are nearby. Supplies are located in Tionesta.

GETTING THERE: From Newell go S on state HWY 139 15 mi. to county route 97. Go W on 97 15.5 mi. to forest route 43N42. Go SW on 43N42 2 mi. to 43N17. Go N on 43N17 1 mi. to Payne Springs CG.

SINGLE RATE:	No fee	OPEN DATES:	July-Oct
# of SINGLE SITES:	6	MAX SPUR:	20 feet
		MAX STAY:	14 days
		ELEVATION:	6500 feet

 Campground has hosts　 **Reservable sites**　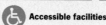 **Accessible facilities**　 **Fully developed**　 **Semi-developed**　 **Rustic facilities**

NOTE: Open dates listed are typical. Actual dates are dependent on conditions such as snow pack.

21 Pepperdine
Alturas • lat 41°27'12" lon 120°14'43"

DESCRIPTION: In a high desert setting. Trailhead facilities for the South Warner Wilderness with horse stalls. Supplies located in the town of Alturas.

GETTING THERE: From Alturas go E on county route 56 approx. 12 mi. to primary forest route 31. Continue E on 31 approx. 6.5 mi. to Pepperdine CG.

SINGLE RATE:	No fee	OPEN DATES:	July-Oct
# of SINGLE SITES:	5	MAX SPUR:	22 feet
		MAX STAY:	14 days
		ELEVATION:	5680 feet

22 Plum Valley
Davis Creek • lat 41°42'43" lon 120°19'29"

DESCRIPTION: CG is in the perfect setting for a mid-day picnic or splash in the stream. The plants and animals surrounding the site are very pretty and calming. Historic Highgrade Mining District. Numerous abandon mines are located in the area. the California Back Country Supplies are located in the Davis Creek.

GETTING THERE: From Davis Creek go E on county route 11 approx. 2 mi. to forest route 45N35. Plum Valley CG is located just off of 45N35.

SINGLE RATE:	No fee	OPEN DATES:	June-Oct
# of SINGLE SITES:	7	MAX SPUR:	16 feet
		MAX STAY:	14 days
		ELEVATION:	5600 feet

23 Reservoir C
Alturas • lat 41°39'37" lon 120°46'29"

DESCRIPTION: In a remote high desert setting of scrub brush, rocks and dirt. Views of reservoir with some deer, mountain lions and birds in area. Fish for trout in reservoir. Supplies in Alturas. Campers may gather firewood. Trails, old roads and wildlife paths in area for quiet adventures.

GETTING THERE: From Alturas go W on state HWY 299 approx. 2 mi. to primary forest route 73. Go N on 73 approx. 9 mi. to forest route 43N18. Go NW on 43N18 approx. 6 mi. to forest route 44N32. Go N on 44N32 approx. 1 mi. to Reservoir C CG.

SINGLE RATE:	No fee	OPEN DATES:	May-Oct
# of SINGLE SITES:	6	MAX SPUR:	22 feet
		MAX STAY:	14 days
		ELEVATION:	4900 feet

24 Reservoir F
Alturas • lat 41°35'00" lon 120°52'30"

DESCRIPTION: In a remote high desert setting of scrub brush, rocks and dirt. Views of reservoir with some deer, mountain lions and birds in area. Fish for trout in reservoir. Supplies in Alturas. Campers may gather firewood. Trails, old roads and wildlife paths in area for quiet adventures.

GETTING THERE: From Alturas go W on state HWY 299 approx. 10 mi. to Devils Garden turn off. Follow signs to Reservior F CG.

SINGLE RATE:	No fee	OPEN DATES:	June-Oct
		MAX STAY:	14 days
		ELEVATION:	5100 feet

25 Soup Springs
Likely • lat 41°18'33" lon 120°16'35"

DESCRIPTION: In a high desert setting. Horse corrals and parking for horse trailers are located within the CG area for use by campers and trailhead users. Major trailhead to the South Warner Wilderness. Supplies are located in the town of Likely.

GETTING THERE: From Likely go E on county route 64 approx. 8.5 mi. to primary forest route 5. Go N on 5 approx. 4 mi. to forest route 40N24. Go E on 40N24 approx. 4.5 mi. to Soup Springs CG.

SINGLE RATE:	$6	OPEN DATES:	June-Oct
# of SINGLE SITES:	14	MAX SPUR:	22 feet
		MAX STAY:	14 days
		ELEVATION:	6800 feet

26 Stowe Reservoir
Cedarville • lat 41°33'46" lon 120°15'15"

DESCRIPTION: CG is located in a high desert setting. Fishing and hiking close by. Supplies are located in the town of Cedarville.

GETTING THERE: Stowe CG is located approx. 4.5 mi. NW of Cedarville on state HWY 299.

SINGLE RATE:	No fee	OPEN DATES:	May-Oct
# of SINGLE SITES:	14	MAX SPUR:	22 feet
		MAX STAY:	14 days
		ELEVATION:	6200 feet

27 Upper Rush Creek
Adin • lat 41°18'06" lon 120°50'58"

DESCRIPTION: CG sites are surrounded by mixed conifer providing welcome shade for the hot summer days. Rush Creek runs along the edge of the campground providing a relaxing atmosphere. Fishing from Rush Creek. Supplies are located in the town of Adin approx. 9 mi. SW of the CG.

GETTING THERE: From Adin go approx. 6 mi. N on state HWY 299 to forest route. Follow signs on forest route approx. 1 mi. NE to Upper Rush Creek CG. Not recommended for vehicles pulling trailers.

SINGLE RATE:	$6	OPEN DATES:	May-Oct
# of SINGLE SITES:	13	MAX SPUR:	22 feet
		MAX STAY:	14 days
		ELEVATION:	5200 feet

28 Willow Creek
Adin • lat 41°00'54" lon 120°49'39"

DESCRIPTION: In a forested setting, next to HWY on Willow Creek. No fishing from creek due to endangered species, the Modoc Sucker, living in the stream. Supplies are located in the town of Adin, 14 mi. N of the CG. Deer and antelope found in area. No designated trails, venture off onto old roads in area.

GETTING THERE: Willow Creek CG is located approx. 13.5 mi. S of Adin on state HWY 139.

SINGLE RATE:	$6	OPEN DATES:	May-Oct
# of SINGLE SITES:	8	MAX SPUR:	22 feet
		MAX STAY:	14 days
		ELEVATION:	5200 feet

 Campground has hosts   **Reservable sites**   **Accessible facilities**   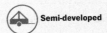 **Fully developed**    **Semi-developed**   **Rustic facilities**

NOTE: Open dates listed are typical. Actual dates are dependent on conditions such as snow pack.

USFS Photo

PLUMAS NATIONAL FOREST

The Plumas National Forest covers over a million acres of tree covered mountains, filled with hundreds of high alpine lakes and thousands of miles of clear running streams. Situated in the Sierra Nevada, just south of the Cascade Range, the Plumas is versatile in its land features as well as uncrowded and enhanced by a pleasant climate.

Beginning in the foothill country near Lake Oroville, the Plumas extends through heavily timbered slopes and into the rugged high country near U.S. Highway 395. State Highway 70 provides year-round access, and State Highway 89 provides convenient connections through the Tahoe, Plumas, and Lassen forests.

A few of the area's attractions are Oroville's Chinese Temple, built in 1863, which shows the role that chinese labor played in the development of California. The 67-mile Maidu Indian World Maker Route links Quincy to Susanville and follows the ancient trail through the land of the Mountain Maidu Indians.

Some of the most popular activities on the Plumas include camping, fishing, boating, swimming, hiking, winter sports, seasonal hunting, waterskiing, wildlife-watching and sight-seeing. For the more adventurous, rock climbing, kayaking, snow camping, and whitewater rafting opportunities are available.

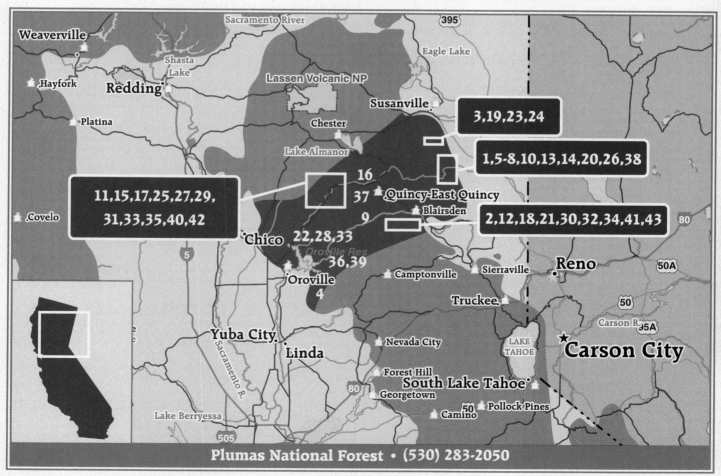

Plumas National Forest • (530) 283-2050

1. Big Cove

Chilcoot • lat 39°54'07" lon 120°10'21"

DESCRIPTION: CG set in a mixed forest on Frenchman Lake. Fishing for trout, boating, and water skiing are popular activities at Frenchman Lake Recreation Area. Supplies are at Chilcoot. Little Last Chance Canyon Scenic Area is nearby. Gather firewood. Deer, bears, and waterfowl in area. RV dump station nearby.

GETTING THERE: From Chilcoot go N on primary forest route 176 approx. 8 mi. to forest route 24N01. Go E on 24N01 approx. 2 mi. to Big Cove CG.

SINGLE RATE:	Varies	OPEN DATES:	May-Sept
# of SINGLE SITES:	38	MAX SPUR:	48 feet
		MAX STAY:	14 days
		ELEVATION:	5800 feet

2. Black Rock

La Porte • lat 39°43'46" lon 121°00'34"

DESCRIPTION: CG set in a mixed forest on the Little Grass Valley Reservoir. Fish for trout, boat, and swim from the reservoir. Boat ramps available in area. Supplies are at Strawberry. Deer, bears, and waterfowl are common to the area. Gather firewood locally. Many hiking and sightseeing trails nearby.

GETTING THERE: From La Porte go NE on county route 512 approx. 1.5 mi. to county route 514. Go NW on 514 approx. 7 mi. to Black Rock CG.

SINGLE RATE:	$12	OPEN DATES:	May-Oct
# of SINGLE SITES:	10	MAX SPUR:	35 feet
		MAX STAY:	14 days
		ELEVATION:	5000 feet

3. Boulder Creek

Taylorsville • lat 40°11'30" lon 120°36'43"

DESCRIPTION: This CG is situated on the shores of Antelope Lake. Excellent fishing, swiming, and limited boating on this remote and quiet lake. Watch for deer, a variety of bids, and various small wildlife. Boat ramp available nearby. Gather firewood locally. Kid's programs offered. Interpretive trail on site.

GETTING THERE: From Taylorsville go E on county route 112 approx. 6 mi. to county route 111 (primary forest route 43). Go N on 111 approx. 16.5 mi. to Boulder Creek CG.

SINGLE RATE:	Varies	OPEN DATES:	May-Oct
# of SINGLE SITES:	70	MAX SPUR:	35 feet
		MAX STAY:	14 days
		ELEVATION:	5000 feet

4. Burnt Bridge

Challenge • lat 39°25'16" lon 121°10'02"

DESCRIPTION: This CG is situated in a mixed forest near New Bullards Bar Reservoir. Fish for trout from shoreline or use the boat ramp on the south side of the reservoir. Wildlife in the area includes deer, occasional black bears, and various waterfowl. Numerous trails can be found in the vicinity.

GETTING THERE: Burnt Bridge CG is located approx. 6 mi. SE of Challenge on county route 129.

SINGLE RATE:	No fee	OPEN DATES:	May-Oct
# of SINGLE SITES:	30	MAX SPUR:	35 feet
		MAX STAY:	14 days
		ELEVATION:	2200 feet

5. Chilcoot

Chilcoot • lat 39°51'56" lon 120°09'58"

DESCRIPTION: This CG is situated in a mixed fir and pine forest near Frenchman Lake. Fish for trout from the lake nearby. Check for localy regulations. Supplies are available at Chilcoot. Deer, bears, and waterfowl are common to the area. Little Last Chance Canyon Scenic Trail is nearby. Gather firewood locally.

GETTING THERE: Chilcoot CG is located approx. 4 mi. N of Chilcoot on primary forest route 176.

SINGLE RATE:	$12	OPEN DATES:	Apr-Oct
# of SINGLE SITES:	40	MAX SPUR:	35 feet
		MAX STAY:	14 days
		ELEVATION:	5400 feet

6. Conklin Park

Milford • lat 40°02'50" lon 120°21'59"

DESCRIPTION: CG set in a mixed fir and pine forest on the banks of Willow Creek. Fish for trout from the creek. Supplies are available at Milford. Deer, bears, and waterfowl are common to the area. Squaw Valley Peak is in the area along with the Snake Tree. Gather firewood. No drinking water available.

GETTING THERE: Conklin Park CG is located approx. 10 mi. S of Milford on county route 336/primary forest route 70.

SINGLE RATE:	No fee	OPEN DATES:	Yearlong
# of SINGLE SITES:	9	MAX SPUR:	15 feet
		MAX STAY:	14 days
		ELEVATION:	5900 feet

7. Cottonwood Spring

Chilcoot • lat 39°53'26" lon 120°12'28"

DESCRIPTION: CG set in a mixed forest on Frenchman Lake. Fishing for trout, boating, and water skiing are popular activities at Frenchman Lake Recreation Area. Supplies are at Chilcoot. Little Last Chance Canyon Scenic Area is nearby. Gather firewood locally. Deer, waterfowl, and bears in area. RV dump station nearby.

GETTING THERE: Cottonwood Spring CG is located approx. 8 mi. N of Chilcoot on primary forest route 176.

SINGLE RATE:	$12	OPEN DATES:	Apr-Oct
# of SINGLE SITES:	20	MAX SPUR:	35 feet
GROUP RATE:	Varies	MAX STAY:	14 days
# of GROUP SITES:	2	ELEVATION:	5700 feet

8. Crocker

Beckwourth • lat 39°53'36" lon 120°25'21"

DESCRIPTION: CG set in a mixed fir and pine forest on the banks of Crocker Creek. Fish for trout on the creek. Supplies are available at Beckwourth. Deer, bears, and waterfowl are common to the area. Gather firewood locally. No drinking water available on site. Primarily used as a fall hunting camp. No services.

GETTING THERE: Crocker CG is located approx. 6 mi. N of Beckwourth on county route 111/primary forest route 177.

SINGLE RATE:	No fee	OPEN DATES:	May-Nov
# of SINGLE SITES:	10	MAX SPUR:	15 feet
		MAX STAY:	14 days
		ELEVATION:	5800 feet

9. Deanes Valley

Quincy • lat 39°53'15" lon 121°01'00"

DESCRIPTION: This CG is situated on the banks of a high mountain stream. Set in Deanes Valley on South Fork Rock Creek. Supplies are available in Quincy. Wildlife in the area includes black bears, deer, and waterfowl. The Pacific Crest Trail runs nearby. No drinking water available on site.

GETTING THERE: From Quincy go W on forest route 119 approx. 3.5 mi. to forest route 24N28. Go S on 24N28 approx. 5 mi. to Deanes Valley CG.

SINGLE RATE:	No fee	OPEN DATES:	Apr-Oct
# of SINGLE SITES:	7	MAX SPUR:	20 feet
		MAX STAY:	14 days
		ELEVATION:	4400 feet

10. Frenchman

Chilcoot • lat 39°53'59" lon 120°11'12"

DESCRIPTION: CG set in a mixed forest on Frenchman Lake. Fishing for trout, hiking, boating, and water skiing are popular activities in the recreation area. There is a boat ramp adjacent to the CG. An accessible fishing trail starts in this campground. Supplies are available at Chilcoot. Firewood for sale on site.

GETTING THERE: From Chilcoot go N on primary forest route 176 approx. 8 mi. to forest route 24N01. Go E on 24N01 approx. 1 mi. to Frenchman CG.

SINGLE RATE:	$12	OPEN DATES:	Apr-Oct
# of SINGLE SITES:	38	MAX SPUR:	45 feet
		MAX STAY:	14 days
		ELEVATION:	5800 feet

 Campground has hosts   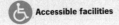 **Reservable sites**   **Accessible facilities**   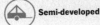 **Fully developed**   **Semi-developed**   **Rustic facilities**

NOTE: Open dates listed are typical. Actual dates are dependent on conditions such as snow pack.

11 Gansner Bar

Belden • lat 40˚01'12" lon 121˚13'17"

DESCRIPTION: CG rests among mixed firs and pines on North Fork Feather River. Enjoy good fishing opportunities in the river. Hike the Pacific Crest Trail which runs along Chips Creek. This steep stream canyon is filled with ancient firs and pines. Supplies are available in Belden. Watch for bears and deer in the area.

GETTING THERE: From Belden go E on state HWY 70 approx. 1.5 mi. to forest route 27N26. Go N on 27N26 approx. 1 mi. to Gansner Bar CG.

SINGLE RATE:	$12	OPEN DATES:	Apr-Oct
# of SINGLE SITES:	14	MAX SPUR:	15 feet
		MAX STAY:	14 days
		ELEVATION:	2300 feet

16 Hallsted

Twain • lat 40˚01'03" lon 121˚04'23"

DESCRIPTION: CG rests among mixed firs and pines on East Branch North Fork Feather River. Enjoy a drive on adjacent Feather River National Scenic Byway. Visit Butterfly Valley Botanical Area or Soda Rock, a rare limestone rock formation. Supplies in Twain. Wildlife includes black bears and deer. RV dump station nearby.

GETTING THERE: Hallsted CG is located approx. 1/2 mi. W of Twain on state HWY 70.

SINGLE RATE:	$14	OPEN DATES:	Apr-Sept
# of SINGLE SITES:	20	MAX SPUR:	35 feet
		MAX STAY:	14 days
		ELEVATION:	2800 feet

12 Gold Lake

Graeagle • lat 39˚40'00" lon 120˚38'00"

DESCRIPTION: In a mixed fir and pine forest setting along the shores of Gold Lake. Fish for trout and boat from the lake. Supplies available at Milford. Deer, bears and waterfowl are common to the area. Campers may gather firewood. No piped water. Four wheel drive vehicles required.

GETTING THERE: From Graeagle go SE on state HWY 89 approx. 2 mi. to county route 519/forest route 24. Go SW on 519 approx. 9 mi. to Gold Lake CG.

SINGLE RATE:	No fee	OPEN DATES:	Yearlong
# of SINGLE SITES:	6	MAX SPUR:	15 feet
		MAX STAY:	14 days
		ELEVATION:	6250 feet

17 Hutchins Group

Quincy • lat 39˚54'12" lon 121˚11'57"

DESCRIPTION: This CG is set among mixed pines and firs on Bucks Lake. There is a boat ramp available nearby. Enjoy fishing, boating, and water skiing on lake. The Pacific Crest Trail runs nearby. Wildlife in the area includes black bears, deer, and waterfowl. Supplies in Quincy. Gather dead and down firewood.

GETTING THERE: From Quincy go SW on county route 414 approx. 19 mi. to primary forest route 33. Go N on 33 approx. 3.5 mi. to Hutchins Group CG.

SINGLE RATE:	$45	OPEN DATES:	May-Sept
		MAX SPUR:	27 feet
		MAX STAY:	14 days
# of GROUP SITES:	3	ELEVATION:	5200 feet

13 Grasshopper Flat

Portola • lat 39˚53'26" lon 120˚28'37"

DESCRIPTION: CG set in a mixed forest on Davis Lake with views of mountains and valleys. Within the Lake Davis Recreation Area. Fish for trout, boat, and swim from the lake. Boat ramps, docks, an RV dump station, numerous fishing access points, and a convenience store. Many trails in the area. Gather firewood locally.

GETTING THERE: From Portola go N on county route 126 approx. 8 mi. to county route 112. Go N on 112 approx. 1/2 mi. to Grasshopper Flat CG. No services.

SINGLE RATE:	$13	OPEN DATES:	May-Oct
# of SINGLE SITES:	70	MAX SPUR:	15 feet
		MAX STAY:	14 days
		ELEVATION:	5900 feet

18 Lakes Basin

Graeagle • lat 39˚42'03" lon 120˚39'28"

DESCRIPTION: CG set in a mixed forest with scenic geological features of granitic ridges & glacially serrated rock outcroppings. Crystal lakes in area for trout fishing. Supplies at Graeagle. Deer, bears, & waterfowl in the area. Many trails nearby. Snowmobiling & cross-country skiing are popular winter activities.

GETTING THERE: From Graeagle go SE on state HWY 89 approx. 2 mi. to county route 519/primary forest route 24. Go SW on 519 approx. 7 mi. to Lakes Basin CG.

SINGLE RATE:	Varies	OPEN DATES:	June-Oct
# of SINGLE SITES:	23	MAX SPUR:	15 feet
GROUP RATE:	$45	MAX STAY:	14 days
# of GROUP SITES:	1	ELEVATION:	6400 feet

14 Grizzly

Portola • lat 39˚53'14" lon 120˚28'21"

DESCRIPTION: CG set in a mixed forest on Davis Lake with views of mountains and valleys. Within the Lake Davis Recreation Area. Fish for trout, boat, and swim from the lake. Boat ramps, docks, an RV dump station, numerous fishing access points, and a convenience store. Many trails in the area. Gather firewood locally.

GETTING THERE: From Portola go N on county route 126 approx. 8 mi. to county route 112. Go N on 112 approx. 1 mi. to Grizzly CG.

SINGLE RATE:	$13	OPEN DATES:	May-Oct
# of SINGLE SITES:	55	MAX SPUR:	35 feet
		MAX STAY:	14 days
		ELEVATION:	5900 feet

19 Laufman

Milford • lat 40˚08'06" lon 120˚20'50"

DESCRIPTION: CG in a mixed fir and pine forest in East Canyon, set on a small creek. Fish for trout from the creek. Supplies available at Milford. Deer, bears, and waterfowl are common to the area. Many trails are available for hiking and mountain biking. Gather firewood locally. No drinking water on site.

GETTING THERE: Laufman CG is located approx. 3 mi. S of Milford on county route 336.

SINGLE RATE:	No fee	OPEN DATES:	Yearlong
# of SINGLE SITES:	6	MAX SPUR:	15 feet
		MAX STAY:	14 days
		ELEVATION:	5100 feet

15 Grizzly Creek

Quincy • lat 39˚52'02" lon 121˚12'22"

DESCRIPTION: This CG is situated in a mixed fir and pine forest near Bucks Lake. Fishing, boating, and waterskiing are popular activities on the lake. The Pacific Crest Trail runs nearby. Wildlife in the area includes black bears, deer, and waterfowl. Supplies are available in Quincy. Gather dead and down firewood.

GETTING THERE: Grizzly Creek CG is located approx. 20 mi. SW of Quincy on county route 414.

SINGLE RATE:	$12	OPEN DATES:	Apr-Oct
# of SINGLE SITES:	8	MAX SPUR:	15 feet
		MAX STAY:	14 days
		ELEVATION:	5400 feet

20 Lightning Tree

Portola • lat 39˚55'45" lon 120˚30'30"

DESCRIPTION: CG set in a mixed forest on Davis Lake with views of mountains and valleys. Within the Lake Davis Recreation Area. Fish for trout, boat, and swim from the lake. Boat ramps, docks, an RV dump station, numerous fishing access points, and a convenience store. Many trails in the area. Gather firewood locally.

GETTING THERE: From Portola go N on county route 126 approx. 8 mi. to county route 112. Go N on 112 approx. 5.5 mi. to Lightning Tree CG.

SINGLE RATE:	Varies	OPEN DATES:	May-Oct
# of SINGLE SITES:	40	MAX SPUR:	35 feet
		MAX STAY:	14 days
		ELEVATION:	5800 feet

Campground has hosts • **Reservable sites** • **Accessible facilities** • **Fully developed** • **Semi-developed** • **Rustic facilities**

NOTE: Open dates listed are typical. Actual dates are dependent on conditions such as snow pack.

Page 111

PLUMAS NATIONAL FOREST • CALIFORNIA • 11 — 20

21 Little Beaver
La Porte • lat 39°43'14" lon 120°58'00"

DESCRIPTION: CG set in a mixed forest on the Little Grass Valley Reservoir. Fish for trout, boat, and swim from the reservoir. Boat ramps available. Supplies are at Strawberry. Deer, bears, and waterfowl reside in the area. RV dump station nearby. Gather firewood locally. Many hiking and sightseeing trails nearby.

GETTING THERE: From La Porte go NE on county route 512 approx. 1.5 mi. to county route 514. Go NW on 514 approx. 1 mi. to forest route 22N57. Go N on 22N57 approx. 2.5 mi. to Little Beaver CG.

SINGLE RATE:	$12	OPEN DATES:	May-Oct
# of SINGLE SITES:	120	MAX SPUR:	35 feet
		MAX STAY:	14 days
		ELEVATION:	5060 feet

22 Little North Fork
Berry Creek • lat 39°46'55" lon 121°15'32"

DESCRIPTION: CG in a mixed forest on the Little North Fork of the Feather River. Fish for trout from the river. CG is near Historical Buck's Powerhouse. Supplies are at Berry Creek. Deer, bears, and waterfowl are common to the area. Gather firewood locally. Harman Bar Trail is nearby. No drinking water.

GETTING THERE: From Berry Creek go NE on primary forest route 119 approx. 14 mi. to primary forest route 60. Go N on 60 approx. 5 mi. to Little North Fork CG.

SINGLE RATE:	No fee	OPEN DATES:	May-Oct
# of SINGLE SITES:	8	MAX SPUR:	35 feet
		MAX STAY:	14 days
		ELEVATION:	4000 feet

23  Lone Rock
Taylorsville • lat 40°11'43" lon 120°37'02"

DESCRIPTION: This CG is set on the shores of Antelope Lake. Excellent fishing opportunities. Popular activities on the lake include swimming, water skiing, and boating. Lake is remote and quite. Boat ramp available for use. Gather firewood locally. Kid's programs offered. Interpretive trail begins on site.

GETTING THERE: From Taylorsville go E on county route 112 approx. 6 mi. to county route 111 (primary forest route 43). Go N on 111 approx. 16.5 mi. to Lone Rock CG.

SINGLE RATE:	Varies	OPEN DATES:	Apr-Sept
# of SINGLE SITES:	86	MAX SPUR:	45 feet
		MAX STAY:	14 days
		ELEVATION:	5000 feet

24 Long Point
Taylorsville • lat 40°10'42" lon 120°34'42"

DESCRIPTION: This CG is set on the shores of Antelope Lake. Excellent fishing opportunities. Popular activities on the lake include swimming, water skiing, and boating. A remote and quite atmosphere. Boat ramp available for use. Campers may gather their firewood locally. Barrier free trail and fishing dock.

GETTING THERE: From Taylorsville go E on county route 112 approx. 6 mi. to county route 111 (primary forest route 43). Go N approx. 15.5 mi. primary forest route 03. Go E on 03 approx. 4 mi. to Long Point CG.

SINGLE RATE:	Varies	OPEN DATES:	Apr-Sept
# of SINGLE SITES:	38	MAX SPUR:	99 feet
GROUP RATE:	Varies	MAX STAY:	14 days
# of GROUP SITES:	4	ELEVATION:	5000 feet

25 Lower Bucks
Quincy • lat 39°54'00" lon 121°12'30"

DESCRIPTION: This CG rests among mixed pines and firs on Lower Bucks Lake. Popular activities on the lake include fishing, boating and water skiing. Black bears, deer, and waterfowl frequent the area. Multi-use trails in the vicinity, and the Pacific Crest Trail runs nearby. Supplies are at Quincy. Gather firewood locally.

GETTING THERE: From Quincy go SW on county route 414 approx. 19 mi. to primary forest route 33. Go N on 33 approx. 3 mi. to Lower Bucks CG.

SINGLE RATE:	$8	OPEN DATES:	May-Oct
# of SINGLE SITES:	6	MAX SPUR:	35 feet
		MAX STAY:	14 days
		ELEVATION:	5200 feet

26 Meadow View
Doyle • lat 40°02'15" lon 120°13'30"

DESCRIPTION: CG set in a mixed fir and pine forest on the banks of a small creek. Fish for trout from the creek. Supplies are available at Doyle. Deer, bears, and waterfowl are common to the area. Visit Meadow View Peak nearby. Campers may gather their firewood locally. No drinking water, no services.

GETTING THERE: From Doyle go W on county route 331 approx. 7 mi. to county route 101. Continue W on 101 approx. 1 mi. to Meadow View CG.

SINGLE RATE:	No fee	OPEN DATES:	Yearlong
# of SINGLE SITES:	6	MAX SPUR:	15 feet
		MAX STAY:	14 days
		ELEVATION:	6100 feet

27 Mill Creek
Quincy • lat 39°54'50" lon 121°11'13"

DESCRIPTION: This CG is situated among mixed pines and firs on Bucks Lake. A boat ramp is available for use. Enjoy fishing, boating and water skiing on lake. The Pacific Crest Trail runs nearby. Wildlife in the area includes black bears, deer, and waterfowl. Supplies in Quincy. Gather dead and down firewood.

GETTING THERE: From Quincy go SW on county route 414 approx. 19 mi. to primary forest route 33. Go N on 33 approx. 5 mi. to Mill Creek CG.

SINGLE RATE:	Varies	OPEN DATES:	May-Oct
# of SINGLE SITES:	10	MAX SPUR:	35 feet
		MAX STAY:	14 days
		ELEVATION:	5200 feet

28 Milsap Bar
Berry Creek • lat 39°42'30" lon 121°16'15"

DESCRIPTION: This CG is situated in a mixed forest on the Little North Fork of the Feather River. Fish for trout from the river. Supplies are at Berry Creek. Deer, bears, and waterfowl are common to the area. Campers may gather their firewood locally. Hartman Bar Trail runs nearby. No drinking water.

GETTING THERE: From Berry Creek go NE on primary forest route 119 approx. 5.5 mi. to Brush Creek Work Center. Follow signs approx. 8 mi. to Milsap Bar CG.

SINGLE RATE:	No fee	OPEN DATES:	May-Oct
# of SINGLE SITES:	20	MAX SPUR:	15 feet
		MAX STAY:	14 days
		ELEVATION:	1600 feet

29 North Fork
Belden • lat 40°02'24" lon 121°13'08"

DESCRIPTION: This CG rests among mixed firs and pines on North Fork Feather River. Enjoy good fishing opportunities in river. Hike the Pacific Crest Trail which runs along Chips Creek. This steep stream canyon is filled with ancient firs and pines. Supplies in Belden. Wildlife in the area includes black bears and deer.

GETTING THERE: From Belden go E on state HWY 70 approx. 1.5 mi. to forest route 27N26. Go N on 27N26 approx. 2.5 mi. to North Fork CG.

SINGLE RATE:	$12	OPEN DATES:	May-Oct
# of SINGLE SITES:	20	MAX SPUR:	35 feet
		MAX STAY:	14 days
		ELEVATION:	2600 feet

30 Peninsula
La Porte • lat 39°43'00" lon 120°58'00"

DESCRIPTION: CG set in a mixed forest on the Little Grass Valley Reservoir. Fish for trout, boat, and swim from the reservoir. Boat ramps available for use. Supplies are at Strawberry. Deer, bears, and waterfowl are common to the area. Campers may gather their firewood locally. Many hiking and sightseeing trails nearby.

GETTING THERE: From La Porte go NE on county route 512 approx. 1.5 mi. to county route 514. Go NW on 514 approx. 1 mi. to forest route 22N57. Go N on 22N57 approx. 2.5 mi. to Peninsula CG.

SINGLE RATE:	$12	OPEN DATES:	May-Oct
# of SINGLE SITES:	25	MAX SPUR:	35 feet
		MAX STAY:	14 days
		ELEVATION:	5060 feet

 Campground has hosts   **Reservable sites**   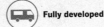 **Accessible facilities**   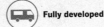 **Fully developed**   **Semi-developed**   **Rustic facilities**

NOTE: Open dates listed are typical. Actual dates are dependent on conditions such as snow pack.

31 Queen Lily
Belden • lat 40°02'45" lon 121°13'01"

DESCRIPTION: This CG rests among mixed firs and pines on North Fork Feather River. Enjoy good fishing opportunities in river. Hike the Pacific Crest Trail which runs along Chips Creek. This steep stream canyon is filled with ancient firs and pines. Supplies in Belden. Wildlife in the area includes black bears and deer.

GETTING THERE: From Belden go E on state HWY 70 approx. 1.5 mi. to forest route 27N26. Go N on 27N26 approx. 3.5 mi. to Queen Lily CG.

SINGLE RATE:	$12	OPEN DATES:	Apr-Oct
# of SINGLE SITES:	12	MAX SPUR:	35 feet
		MAX STAY:	14 days
		ELEVATION:	2600 feet

36 Sly Creek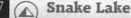
Strawberry Valley • lat 39°35'05" lon 121°06'59"

DESCRIPTION: CG set in a mixed fores on the Sly Creek Reservoir. Fish for trout, boat, and swim from the reservoir. Boat ramps available for use. Supplies are at Strawberry Valley. Deer, bears, and waterfowl are common to the area. Gather firewood locally. Many hiking and sightseeing trails in the area.

GETTING THERE: From Strawberry Valley go SW on primary forest route 120 approx. 1 mi. to primary forest route 16. Go N on 16 approx. 4 mi. to Sly Creek CG.

SINGLE RATE:	$14	OPEN DATES:	Apr-Oct
# of SINGLE SITES:	26	MAX SPUR:	15 feet
		MAX STAY:	14 days
		ELEVATION:	3530 feet

32 Red Feather
La Porte • lat 39°43'45" lon 120°58'00"

DESCRIPTION: CG set in a mixed forest on the Little Grass Valley Reservoir. Fish for trout, boat, and swim from the reservoir. Boat ramps available. Supplies at La Porte. Deer, bears, and waterfowl reside in the area. Campers may gather their firewood locally. Many hiking and sightseeing trails nearby. RV dump station nearby.

GETTING THERE: From La Porte go NE on county route 512 approx. 1.5 mi. to county route 514. Go NW on 514 approx. 1 mi. to forest route 22N57. Go N on 22N57 approx. 3 mi. to Red Feather CG.

SINGLE RATE:	Varies	OPEN DATES:	May-Oct
# of SINGLE SITES:	60	MAX SPUR:	40 feet
		MAX STAY:	14 days
		ELEVATION:	5060 feet

37 Snake Lake
Quincy • lat 39°58'38" lon 121°00'19"

DESCRIPTION: CG set in a mixed pine and fir forest on Snake Lake. Popular fishing lake. Visit the Butterfly Valley Botanical Area or Soda Rock, a rare limestone rock formation. There are multi-use trails nearby. Wildlife in vicinity includes black bears, deer, and waterfowl. No drinking water available.

GETTING THERE: From Quincy go W on primary forest route 119 approx. 5 mi. to county route 422. Go N on 422 approx. 3 mi. to Snake Lake CG.

SINGLE RATE:	No fee	OPEN DATES:	Apr-Oct
		MAX SPUR:	15 feet
		MAX STAY:	14 days
		ELEVATION:	5800 feet

33 Rogers Cow Camp
Berry Creek • lat 39°46'03" lon 121°18'41"

DESCRIPTION: CG set in a mixed forest on the Little North Fork of the Feather River. Fish for trout from the river. CG is near Historical Buck's Powerhouse. Supplies are at Berry Creek. Deer, bears, and waterfowl are common to the area. Gather firewood locally. Hartman Bar Trail is nearby. No drinking water on site.

GETTING THERE: From Berry Creek go NE on primary forest route 119 approx. 16.5 mi. to Rogers Cow Camp CG.

SINGLE RATE:	No fee	OPEN DATES:	May-Oct
# of SINGLE SITES:	5	MAX SPUR:	35 feet
		MAX STAY:	14 days
		ELEVATION:	4000 feet

38 Spring Creek
Chilcoot • lat 39°53'45" lon 120°10'35"

DESCRIPTION: CG set in a mixed forest on Frenchman Lake. Spectacular views. Trout fish, boat, and water ski at Frenchman Lake Recreation Area. Little Last Chance Canyon Scenic Area is nearby. Gather firewood. Deer, bears, and waterfowl. Hiking trails nearby. Fills most weekends all summer. RV dump station.

GETTING THERE: From Chilcoot go N on primary forest route 176 approx. 8 mi. to forest route 24N01. Go E on 24N01 approx. 1.5 mi. to Spring Creek CG.

SINGLE RATE:	$12	OPEN DATES:	Apr-Oct
# of SINGLE SITES:	35	MAX SPUR:	35 feet
		MAX STAY:	14 days
		ELEVATION:	5800 feet

34 Running Deer
La Porte • lat 39°44'00" lon 120°58'00"

DESCRIPTION: CG set in a mixed forest on the Little Grass Valley Reservoir. Fish for trout, boat, and swim from the reservoir. Boat ramps available for use. Supplies are at Strawberry. Watch for deer, bears, and waterfowl. RV dump station nearby. Gather firewood locally. Many hiking and sightseeing trails in the area.

GETTING THERE: From La Porte go NE on county route 512 approx. 1.5 mi. to county route 514. Go NW on 514 approx. 1 mi. to forest route 22N57. Go N on 22N57 approx. 3.5 mi. to Running Deer CG.

SINGLE RATE:	Varies	OPEN DATES:	May-Oct
# of SINGLE SITES:	40	MAX SPUR:	35 feet
		MAX STAY:	14 days
		ELEVATION:	5060 feet

39 Strawberry
Strawberry Valley • lat 39°35'19" lon 121°05'21"

DESCRIPTION: CG set in a mixed forest on the Sly Creek Reservoir. Fish for trout, boat, and swim from the reservoir. Boat ramps available for use. Supplies are at Strawberry Valley. Deer, bears, and waterfowl are common to the area. Gather firewood locally. Many hiking and sightseeing trails nearby.

GETTING THERE: From Strawberry Valley go NE on primary forest route 120 approx. 1.5 mi. to forest route 21N20. Go W on 21N20 approx. 1 mi. to Strawberry CG.

SINGLE RATE:	$12	OPEN DATES:	Apr-Nov
# of SINGLE SITES:	17	MAX SPUR:	15 feet
		MAX STAY:	14 days
		ELEVATION:	3530 feet

35 Silver Lake
Meadow Valley • lat 39°57'33" lon 121°08'04"

DESCRIPTION: CG set in a mixed fir and pine forest on the shores of Silver Lake. Excellent fishing opportunities. Wildlife in the area includes black bears, deer, and waterfowl. The Pacific Crest Trail runs nearby. Gather dead and down firewood. Supplies are available in Meadow Valley. No drinking water on site.

GETTING THERE: Silver Lake CG is located approx. 6 mi. NW of Meadow Valley on forest route 24N29X.

SINGLE RATE:	No fee	OPEN DATES:	May-Oct
		MAX SPUR:	15 feet
		MAX STAY:	14 days
		ELEVATION:	5760 feet

40 Sundew
Quincy • lat 39°54'03" lon 121°12'02"

DESCRIPTION: This CG is set among mixed pines and firs on Bucks Lake. There is a boat ramp available for use. Enjoy fishing, boating, and water skiing on lake. The Pacific Crest Trail runs nearby. Wildlife in the area includes black bears, deer, and waterfowl. Supplies in Quincy. Gather dead and down firewood.

GETTING THERE: From Quincy go SW on county route 414 approx. 19 mi. to primary forest route 33. Go N on 33 approx. 3 mi. to Sundew CG.

SINGLE RATE:	Varies	OPEN DATES:	May-Oct
# of SINGLE SITES:	19	MAX SPUR:	35 feet
		MAX STAY:	14 days
		ELEVATION:	5200 feet

 Campground has hosts   **Reservable sites**   **Accessible facilities**   **Fully developed**   **Semi-developed**   **Rustic facilities**

NOTE: Open dates listed are typical. Actual dates are dependent on conditions such as snow pack.

PLUMAS NATIONAL FOREST • CALIFORNIA • 31 — 40

41 Tooms Boat Ramp
La Porte • lat 39°43'00" lon 120°59'00"

DESCRIPTION: CG set in a mixed forest on the Little Grass Valley Reservoir. Fish for trout, boat, and swim from the reservoir. Boat ramps available for use. Supplies are at Strawberry Valley. Deer, bears, and waterfowl are common to see. RV dump station nearby. Gather firewood. Many hiking and sightseeing trails nearby.

GETTING THERE: From La Porte go NE on county route 512 approx. 1.5 mi. to county route 514. Go NW on 514 approx. 1 mi. to forest route 22N57. Go N on 22N57 approx. 3 mi. to Tooms Boat Ramp CG.

SINGLE RATE:	$12	OPEN DATES:	May-Oct
# of SINGLE SITES:	20	MAX SPUR:	35 feet
		MAX STAY:	14 days
		ELEVATION:	5060 feet

42 Whitehorse
Meadow Valley • lat 39°53'30" lon 121°08'30"

DESCRIPTION: This CG is situated among mixed pines and firs on Bucks Creek. Enjoy fishing, boating, and water skiing on nearby Bucks Lake. Wildlife in the area includes black bears, deer, and waterfowl. Supplies in Meadow Valley. There are multi-use trails in the vicinity. Gather firewood locally.

GETTING THERE: Whitehorse CG is located approx. 6 mi. SW of Meadow Valley on county route 414.

SINGLE RATE:	$12	OPEN DATES:	Apr-Oct
# of SINGLE SITES:	20	MAX SPUR:	35 feet
		MAX STAY:	14 days
		ELEVATION:	5200 feet

43 Wyandotte
La Porte • lat 39°43'00" lon 120°59'00"

DESCRIPTION: CG set in a mixed forest on the Little Grass Valley Reservoir. Fish for trout, boat, and swim from the reservoir. Boat ramps available for use. Supplies are at Strawberry Valley. Deer, bears, and waterfowl in area. RV dump station nearby. Gather firewood locally. Many hiking and sightseeing trails nearby.

GETTING THERE: From La Porte go NE on county route 512 approx. 1.5 mi. to county route 514. Go NW on 514 approx. 1 mi. to forest route 22N57. Go N on 22N57 approx. 3 mi. to Wyandotte CG.

SINGLE RATE:	Varies	OPEN DATES:	May-Oct
# of SINGLE SITES:	28	MAX SPUR:	35 feet
		MAX STAY:	14 days
		ELEVATION:	5100 feet

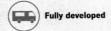 **Fully developed**    **Semi-developed**    **Rustic facilities**

Campground has hosts   Reservable sites   Accessible facilities

SAN BERNARDINO NATIONAL FOREST

The San Bernardino National Forest is situated in the San Gabriel, San Bernardino, San Jacinto, and Santa Rosa mountains about 60 miles east of Los Angeles. The forest is a rich and diverse biological resource of trees, rivers and streams, fish, birds, reptiles, mammals, and a myriad of interrelated life forms and natural resources.

Points of interest include the Rim of the World Scenic Byway which takes you through some of the most beautiful areas in Southern California. Spectacular views are everywhere along the route as well as areas of biological and historical significance. Along the way, take a dip or go waterskiing at Big Bears Lake or visit the Baldwin Lake Preserve where you will see rare and endangered plants that grow nowhere else on earth. Wildflowers bloom during spring and a variety of waterfowl visit the lake during the winter, including bald eagles. At Heaps Peak Arboretum, walk the 45-minute self-guided trail which tells you the story of the forest and its environment.

Another scenic drive on the forest is located on the San Jacinto Ranger District. Commonly called the "Palms to Pine" drive, the scenery changes from desert to high mountain wilderness.

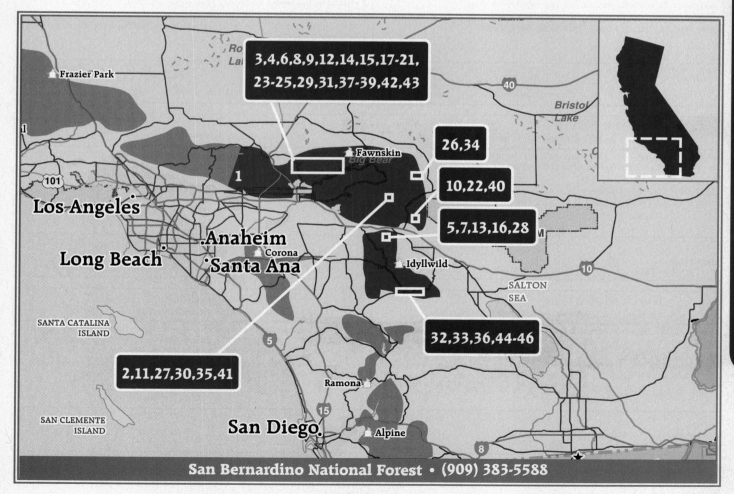

San Bernardino National Forest • (909) 383-5588

San Bernardino National Forest • California • Locator Map

1. Applewhite
Scotland • lat 34˚15'40" lon 117˚29'38"

DESCRIPTION: The CG is located in a flat grassy area of pine, oak and sycamore trees. Stream fish for trout or drive 7 miles to Lost Lake. Bring your own firewood. Horse and hiking trails nearby.

GETTING THERE: From Scotland go N on forest route 3N06 approximately 1.5 miles to Applewhite CG.

SINGLE RATE:	$10	OPEN DATES:	Yearlong
# of SINGLE SITES:	44	MAX SPUR:	30 feet
		MAX STAY:	14 days
		ELEVATION:	3300 feet

2. Barton Flats
Angelus Oaks • lat 34˚10'20" lon 116˚52'28"

DESCRIPTION: The CG is located in a fir forest with some oak trees. Bring your own firewood. No nearby fishing. Deer, bears, coyotes and occasional bobcat or big horn sheep in area. Horse and hiking trails nearby.

GETTING THERE: From Angelus Oaks go E on state HWY 38 approximately 6 miles to Barton Flats CG.

SINGLE RATE:	Varies	OPEN DATES:	May-Sept*
# of SINGLE SITES:	52	MAX SPUR:	30 feet
		MAX STAY:	14 days
		ELEVATION:	6500 feet

3. Big Pine Flats
Fawnskin • lat 34˚19'30" lon 117˚01'00"

DESCRIPTION: The CG is located in a pine and fir forest. No nearby fishing. Bring your own firewood. Deer, black bears, coyotes and small wildlife are common in the area. OHV road nearby. Access to Pacific Crest Trail approximately two miles.

GETTING THERE: From Fawnskin go N on forest route 2N80 approx. 2.5 mi. to forest route 3N14. Go N on 3N14 approx. 2 mi. to Big Pine Flat CG.

SINGLE RATE:	$10	OPEN DATES:	May-Nov*
# of SINGLE SITES:	17	MAX SPUR:	30 feet
		MAX STAY:	14 days
		ELEVATION:	6800 feet

4. Big Pine Horse
Fawnskin • lat 34˚19'30" lon 117˚01'00"

DESCRIPTION: Up to 60 persons in this group site. Set in pine and fir forest. Bring your own firewood. Deer, black bears, coyotes and small wildlife are common in the area. OHV roads nearby.

GETTING THERE: From Fawnskin go N on forest route 2N80 approx. 2.5 mi. to forest route 3N14. Go N on 3N14 approx. 2 mi. to Big Pine Horse CG. Parking for 15 vehicles.

GROUP RATE:	$50	OPEN DATES:	May-Sept*
# of GROUP SITES:	1	MAX SPUR:	25 feet
		MAX STAY:	14 days
		ELEVATION:	6800 feet

5. Black Mountain
Pine Cove • lat 33˚49'59" lon 116˚44'21"

DESCRIPTION: 100 person maximum. Located in a park-like setting. Supplies are 10 miles away in Pine Cove. Many nearby trails for hiking and mountain biking. Tent camping only.

GETTING THERE: From Pine Cove go N on state HWY 243 approx. 3.5 mi. to forest route 4S01. Go N on 4S01 approx. 3.5 mi. to Black Mountain CG.

GROUP RATE:	Varies	OPEN DATES:	May-Oct
# of GROUP SITES:	1	MAX STAY:	14 days
		ELEVATION:	7280 feet

6. Bluff Mesa Group
Camp Osito • lat 34˚12'30" lon 117˚00'00"

DESCRIPTION: The CG is located in a pine and fir forest setting. Big Bears Lake approximately 1 mile. Trout fish the lake. No drinking water. Up to 40 persons, 8 vehicle spaces. Bring your own firewood. Deer, black bears, coyotes and small wildlife are common in the area.

GETTING THERE: From Camp Osito go W on forest route 2N86 approximately 3.5 miles to Bluff Mesa Group CG.

GROUP RATE:	$50	OPEN DATES:	May-Sept*
# of GROUP SITES:	1	MAX SPUR:	25 feet
		MAX STAY:	14 days
		ELEVATION:	6800 feet

7. Boulder Basin
Pine Cove • lat 33˚49'35" lon 116˚45'14"

DESCRIPTION: No RVs. Set in the pines with valley views. Bring your own firewood. Supplies are 10 mi. S on HWY 243 at Pine Cove. CG is close to Black Mountain fire tower. Deer and small wildlife are common in the area. Bears can be a problem.

GETTING THERE: From Pine Cove go N on state HWY 243 approx. 3.5 mi. to forest route 4S01. Go N on 4S01 approx. 2.5 mi. to Boulder Basin CG.

SINGLE RATE:	$10	OPEN DATES:	May-Oct
# of SINGLE SITES:	34	MAX SPUR:	24 feet
		MAX STAY:	14 days
		ELEVATION:	7550 feet

8. Boulder Group
Camp Osito • lat 33˚49'35" lon 116˚45'14"

DESCRIPTION: A group site in a pine and fir forest setting. No drinking water. Up to 40 persons. Approx. 2 miles to Big Bears Lake. Fish for trout on lake. Bring your own firewood. Deer, black bears, coyotes and small wildlife are common in the area. Snow Forest winter sport area approximately 2 miles.

GETTING THERE: From Camp Osito go W on forest route 2N86 approximately 1.5 miles to Boulder Group CG.

GROUP RATE:	$50	OPEN DATES:	May-Sept*
# of GROUP SITES:	8	MAX SPUR:	25 feet
		MAX STAY:	14 days
		ELEVATION:	6500 feet

9. Buttercup Group
Moonridge • lat 34˚14'08" lon 116˚52'39"

DESCRIPTION: Up to 40 persons in this group site. Parking for 8 vehicles. Set in pine and fir forest. Approx. 2 miles to Big Bears Lake. Trout fishing on lake. Bring your own firewood. Deer, black bears, coyotes and small wildlife are common in the area.

GETTING THERE: From Moonridge go W approximately 1 mile to Buttercup Group CG.

GROUP RATE:	$75	OPEN DATES:	May-Sept*
# of GROUP SITES:	1	MAX SPUR:	25 feet
		MAX STAY:	14 days
		ELEVATION:	6500 feet

10. Coon Creek Cabin
Heart Bar • lat 34˚09'00" lon 116˚46'15"

DESCRIPTION: A group use cabin set in pine and fir forest. No drinking water, 40 person maximum. Water may be obtained on road driving into site. Bring your own firewood. Deer, bears, coyotes and occasional Big Horn Sheep in area. Reservations a must.

GETTING THERE: From Heart Bar go E on forest route 2E03 approx. 2 mi. to forest route 1N02. Go E on 1N02 approx. 3.5 mi. to Coon Creek Cabin CG. No RVs.

GROUP RATE:	$50	OPEN DATES:	May-Sept*
# of GROUP SITES:	1	MAX STAY:	14 days
		ELEVATION:	5500 feet

 Campground has hosts   **Reservable sites**   **Accessible facilities**   **Fully developed**   **Semi-developed** **Rustic facilities**

NOTE: Open dates listed are typical. Actual dates are dependent on conditions such as snow pack.

Page 116

11 Council
Angelus Oaks • lat 34°10'17" lon 116°52'54"

DESCRIPTION: On the Santa Anna River in pine and fir trees. Trout fish the river. 50 person maximum in group site. Frequently used by scouts. Deer, bears, coyotes and small wildlife are common in the area. Bring your own firewood. Trail in vicinity.

GETTING THERE: From Angelus Oaks go E on state HWY 38 approximately 6 miles to Council CG. 10 parking spaces, no RVs.

SINGLE RATE:		OPEN DATES:	May-Sept*
# of SINGLE SITES:	50	MAX SPUR:	10 feet
GROUP RATE:	$100	MAX STAY:	14 days
# of GROUP SITES:	10	ELEVATION:	6500 feet

12 Crab Flats
Green Valley Lake • lat 34°15'48" lon 117°05'08"

DESCRIPTION: The CG is located in a pine and fir forest setting. No nearby fishing. Bring your own firewood. Deer, black bears, coyotes and small wildlife are common in the area. Hiking access to Pacific Crest Trail.

GETTING THERE: From Green Valley Lake go N on forest route 3N16 approx. 3 mi. to forest route 3N34. Go W on 3N34 approx. 1/2 mi. to Crab Flats CG.

SINGLE RATE:	$10	OPEN DATES:	May-Sept*
# of SINGLE SITES:	29	MAX SPUR:	15 feet
		MAX STAY:	14 days
		ELEVATION:	6200 feet

13 Dark Canyon
Pine Cove • lat 33°48'13" lon 116°43'52"

DESCRIPTION: CG is under pines and cedars, close to creek with fishing during seasons of good rain fall. Bring your own firewood. Supplies are 4 miles to Pine Cove. Bears can be a problem. Deer and small wildlife are common in the area.

GETTING THERE: From Pine Cove go N on state HWY 243 approx. 2 mi. to forest route 4S02. Go E on 4S02 approx. 2.5 mi. to Dark Canyon CG.

SINGLE RATE:	$12	OPEN DATES:	May-Oct
# of SINGLE SITES:	21	MAX SPUR:	22 feet
		MAX STAY:	14 days
		ELEVATION:	5800 feet

14 Deer Group
Camp Osito • lat 34°13'10" lon 116°54'57"

DESCRIPTION: A group site in pine and fir forest. No drinking water. Up to 40 persons and 8 vehicles. Approximately 2 miles to Big Bears Lake. Trout fish on lake. Snow Forest winter sports area. Bring your own firewood. Deer, black bears, coyotes and small wildlife are common in the area.

GETTING THERE: From Camp Osito go E on forest route 2N10 approximately 1 mile to Deer Group CG.

		OPEN DATES:	May-Sept*
		MAX SPUR:	25 feet
GROUP RATE:	$50	MAX STAY:	14 days
# of GROUP SITES:	8	ELEVATION:	6000 feet

15 Dogwood
Blue Jay • lat 34°14'07" lon 117°12'33"

DESCRIPTION: The CG is located in a fir and pine forest setting. Lake Arrowhead is approximately one mile away. Fish for trout on the lake. Bring your own firewood. Deer, black bears, coyotes and small wildlife are common in the area. Hike to Strawberry Peak lookout.

GETTING THERE: From Blue Jay go S approx. 1/2 mi. on state HWY 173 to forest route. Go W on forest route approx. 1/2 mi. to Dogwood CG.

SINGLE RATE:	$15	OPEN DATES:	May-Sept*
# of SINGLE SITES:	93	MAX SPUR:	22 feet
		MAX STAY:	14 days
		ELEVATION:	5600 feet

16 Fern Basin
Pine Cove • lat 33°47'19" lon 116°44'16"

DESCRIPTION: CG is located in a forest setting. Supplies are 4 miles to Pine Cove. Bring your own firewood. Deer, occasional bears and small wildlife are common in the area.

GETTING THERE: From Pine Cove go N on state HWY 243 approx. 2 mi. to forest route 4S02. Go E on 4S02 approx. 1/2 mi. to Fern Basin CG.

SINGLE RATE:	$10	OPEN DATES:	May-Oct
# of SINGLE SITES:	22	MAX SPUR:	20 feet
		MAX STAY:	14 days
		ELEVATION:	6300 feet

17 Fishermans
Green Valley Lake • lat 34°14'49" lon 117°06'35"

DESCRIPTION: The CG is located in a pine and fir forest setting on Deep Creek. Up to 40 persons, hike-in only. Supplies at Green Valley Lake, approx. 2 mi. No drinking water. Bring your own firewood. Deer, black bears, coyotes and small wildlife are common in the area. OHV roads nearby.

GETTING THERE: From Green Valley Lake go N on forest route 3N16 approx. 3 mi. to forest route 3N34. Go W on 3N34 approx. 1 mi. to Tent Peg CG, continue S on 2W07 to Fishermans CG. Walk-in only.

		OPEN DATES:	May-Sept*
GROUP RATE:	$10	MAX STAY:	14 days
# of GROUP SITES:	1	ELEVATION:	6500 feet

18 Grays Peak Group
Fawnskin • lat 34°15'39" lon 116°58'12"

DESCRIPTION: The CG is located in a pine and fir forest setting. No drinking water. Up to 40 persons and 8 vehicles. Bring your own firewood. Deer, black bears, coyotes and small wildlife are common in the area. Hike to Gray's Peak or access the Pacific Crest Trail nearby.

GETTING THERE: GFrom Fawnskin go NW on forest route 2N80 approximately 1.5 miles to Grays Peak Group CG.

		OPEN DATES:	May-Sept*
		MAX SPUR:	25 feet
GROUP RATE:	$50	MAX STAY:	14 days
# of GROUP SITES:	1	ELEVATION:	7000 feet

19 Green Spot Group
Big Bears City • lat 34°13'25" lon 116°48'18"

DESCRIPTION: A group site in a pine and fir forest setting. Maximum 25 persons, 8 vehicles. Bring your own firewood. Deer, black bears, coyotes and small wildlife are common in the area. Access to Green Canyon Trail and Sugarloaf National Recreation Trail.

GETTING THERE: From Big Bears City go S on state HWY 38 approximately 2 miles to Green Spot Group CG.

		OPEN DATES:	May-Sept*
GROUP RATE:	$50	MAX STAY:	14 days
# of GROUP SITES:	1	ELEVATION:	6800 feet

20 Green Valley
Green Valley Lake • lat 34°14'41" lon 117°03'43"

DESCRIPTION: The CG is located in a pine and fir forest near Green Valley Lake. Fish for trout on the lake. Bring your own firewood. Basic supplies in Running Springs. Deer, black bears, coyotes and small wildlife are common in the area. No nearby trails.

GETTING THERE: From Green Valley Lake go NE approximately 1 mile on county route to Green Valley CG.

SINGLE RATE:	$12	OPEN DATES:	May-Sept*
# of SINGLE SITES:	36	MAX SPUR:	22 feet
		MAX STAY:	14 days
		ELEVATION:	7000 feet

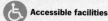 **Campground has hosts**   **Reservable sites**   **Accessible facilities**   **Fully developed**   **Semi-developed**   **Rustic facilities**

NOTE: Open dates listed are typical. Actual dates are dependent on conditions such as snow pack.

21 Hanna Flats
Fawnskin • lat 34°17'17" lon 116°58'29"

DESCRIPTION: The CG is located in a pine and fir forest setting. Fish for trout in Big Bears Lake, approx. 3 mi. away. Bring your own firewood. Deer, bears, coyotes and small wildlife are common in the area. Many roads in the area for mountain biking. Access to Pacific Crest Trail.

GETTING THERE: From Fawnskin go N on forest route 2N80 approximately 2.5 miles to Hanna Flats CG.

SINGLE RATE:	$15	OPEN DATES:	May-Sept*
# of SINGLE SITES:	88	MAX SPUR:	40 feet
		MAX STAY:	14 days
		ELEVATION:	7000 feet

22 Heart Bar Equestrian
Heart Bar • lat 34°09'31" lon 116°47'09"

DESCRIPTION: In pine and fir setting with horse facilities. Group site has 21 parkings spots with 65 person maximum. No nearby fishing. Bring your own firewood. Deer, bears, coyotes and occasional bobcats or big horn sheep in area. Horse and hiking access to Santa Anna River Trail, Pacific Crest Trail and San Gorgonio Wilderness.

GETTING THERE: From Heart Bar go E on forest route approximately 2 miles to Heart Bar Equestrian and Group CG.

SINGLE RATE:	Varies	OPEN DATES:	May-Sept*
# of SINGLE SITES:	95	MAX SPUR:	21 feet
GROUP RATE:	$200	MAX STAY:	14 days
# of GROUP SITES:	1	ELEVATION:	6900 feet

23 Holcomb Valley
Fawnskin • lat 34°18'10" lon 116°53'47"

DESCRIPTION: The CG is located in a pine and fir forest. Near Caribou Creek, 5 miles to Big Bears Lake for trout fishing. No drinking water. Bring your own firewood. Deer, black bears, coyotes and small wildlife are common in the area. Pacific Crest Trail access approximately 2 miles.

GETTING THERE: From Fawnskin go NE on forest route 2N09 approximately 4.5 miles to Holcomb Valley CG.

SINGLE RATE:	$10	OPEN DATES:	Yearlong*
# of SINGLE SITES:	19	MAX SPUR:	25 feet
		MAX STAY:	14 days
		ELEVATION:	7400 feet

24 Horse Springs
Northshore • lat 41°20'32" lon 120°52'53"

DESCRIPTION: The CG is located in a pine and fir setting Near Chuker Spring. Rattlesnake Mountain approx. 1 mi. Bring your own firewood. No drinking water. Deer, black bears, coyotes and small wildlife are common in the area. Forest roads for mountain biking.

GETTING THERE: From Fawnskin go NW on forest route 3N14 approx. 12 mi. to Horse Springs CG.

SINGLE RATE:	No fee	OPEN DATES:	Yearlong*
# of SINGLE SITES:	17	MAX SPUR:	25 feet
		MAX STAY:	14 days
		ELEVATION:	5800 feet

25 Ironwood Group
Fawnskin • lat 34°18'14" lon 117°00'40"

DESCRIPTION: The CG is located in a pine and fir forest. No drinking water. 25 person maximum, 5 vehicles. Bring your own firewood. Deer, black bears, coyotes and small wildlife are common in the area. Access the Pacific Crest Trail.

GETTING THERE: From Fawnskin go N on forest route 2N80 2.5 mi. to forest route 3N14. Go N on 3N14 2 mi. to forest route 3N16. Go S on 3N16 1.5 mi. to forest route 3N97. Go E on 3N97 1 mi. to Ironwood Group CG. No RVs.

		OPEN DATES:	May-Sept*
GROUP RATE:	$50	MAX STAY:	14 days
# of GROUP SITES:	1	ELEVATION:	7000 feet

26 Juniper Springs Group
Big Bears City • lat 33°45'58" lon 117°05'00"

DESCRIPTION: CG is set in a pine and fir forest. 40 person maximum, 8 vehicles. Bring your own firewood. Deer, black bears, coyotes and small wildlife are common in the area. OHV roads approximately 2 miles north. Broom Springs nearby. Access to Pacific Crest Trail approximately 1.5 miles.

GETTING THERE: From Big Bears City go S on state HWY 38 approx. 6 mi. to forest route 2N04. Go E on 2N04 approx. 4 mi. to Juniper Springs Group CG.

		OPEN DATES:	May-Sept*
		MAX SPUR:	25 feet
GROUP RATE:	$50	MAX STAY:	14 days
# of GROUP SITES:	1	ELEVATION:	6500 feet

27 Lobo Group
Angelus Oaks • lat 34°10'33" lon 116°51'38"

DESCRIPTION: The CG is located in a fir forest with scenic overlook. Fish nearby Jenks Lake for trout. Bring your own firewood. Deer, bears and coyotes are common in the area. Amphitheatre and visitor center nearby. 75 person maximum, 15 vehicles.

GETTING THERE: From Angelus Oaks go E on state HWY 38 approximately 7.5 miles to Lobo Group CG. 15 spaces for vehicle parking.

		OPEN DATES:	May-Sept*
		MAX SPUR:	15 feet
GROUP RATE:	$150	MAX STAY:	14 days
# of GROUP SITES:	1	ELEVATION:	5500 feet

28 Marion Mountain
Pine Cove • lat 33°47'30" lon 116°43'55"

DESCRIPTION: CG is located on a terrace and has many valley and mountain views. Supplies are 5 mi. to Pine Cove. Tent camping only. Bring own firewood. Deer and small wildlife are common in the area. Bears can be a problem.

GETTING THERE: From Pine Cove go N on state HWY 243 approx. 2 mi. to forest route 4S02. Go E on 4S02 approx. 1.5 mi. to Marion Mountain CG.

SINGLE RATE:	$10	OPEN DATES:	May-Oct*
# of SINGLE SITES:	24	MAX SPUR:	20 feet
		MAX STAY:	14 days
		ELEVATION:	6420 feet

29 North Shore
North Shore • lat 34°16'02" lon 117°09'48"

DESCRIPTION: The CG is located in a pine and fir forest adjacent to Lake Arrowhead. Fish for trout on the lake. Bring your own firewood. Basic supplies in vicinity. Deer, black bears, coyotes & small wildlife in area. OHV roads nearby.

GETTING THERE: From North Shore go E on state HWY 173 approximately 1 mile to North Shore CG.

SINGLE RATE:	$12	OPEN DATES:	May-Sept*
# of SINGLE SITES:	27	MAX SPUR:	22 feet
		MAX STAY:	14 days
		ELEVATION:	5300 feet

30 Oso
Angelus Oaks • lat 34°10'33" lon 116°51'38"

DESCRIPTION: The CG is located in a pine and fir forest with scenic overlook. Fish nearby Jenks Lake for trout. Bring your own firewood. Deer, bears and coyotes are common in the area. Amphitheatre and visitor center nearby. Maximum 100 persons, 20 vehicles.

GETTING THERE: From Angelus Oaks go E on state HWY 38 approximately 7.5 miles to Oso CG. 20 parking spaces.

		OPEN DATES:	May-Sept*
		MAX SPUR:	15 feet
GROUP RATE:	$200	MAX STAY:	14 days
# of GROUP SITES:	1	ELEVATION:	5500 feet

 Campground has hosts   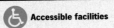 **Reservable sites**   **Accessible facilities**   **Fully developed**   **Semi-developed**   **Rustic facilities**

31 Pineknot
Big Bears City • lat 34°14'07" lon 116°52'59"

DESCRIPTION: The CG is located in a pine and fir forest setting approx. 1 mile from Big Bears Lake. Nearby winter sports area has cross country skiing. Bring your own firewood. Deer, black bears, coyotes and small animals are common in the area.

GETTING THERE: From Big Bears City go SW on state HWY 18 approx. 4 mi. to Pineknot CG.

SINGLE RATE:	$15	OPEN DATES:	May-Sept*
# of SINGLE SITES:	48	MAX SPUR:	45 feet
		MAX STAY:	14 days
		ELEVATION:	7000 feet

32 Pinyon Flat
Cahuilla Hills • lat 33°35'07" lon 116°27'15"

DESCRIPTION: CG is in a desert type vegetation setting with views of the mountains. Supplies are 20 miles to Palm Desert. Bring your own firewood. Hiking and mountain bike trails are nearby.

GETTING THERE: From Cahuilla Hills go S on state HWY 74 approximately 10 miles to Pinyon Flat CG.

SINGLE RATE:	$7	OPEN DATES:	Yearlong
# of SINGLE SITES:	18	MAX SPUR:	15 feet
		MAX STAY:	14 days
		ELEVATION:	4000 feet

33 Ribbonwood Equestrian
Palm Desert • lat 33°34'00" lon 116°25'00"

DESCRIPTION: CG is in a desert setting with views of mountains. Supplies are 20 miles away. Bring own firewood. Rattle snakes are in area. CG is seldom full. Santa Rosa Wilderness is nearby. CG accommodates horses.

GETTING THERE: From Palm Desert go S on state HWY 74 approx. 19 mi. to Pinyon Pines. Turn left on Pinyon Pines Rd to Ribbonwood Equestrian CG. Look for Sawmill Trailhead sign.

SINGLE RATE:	$15	OPEN DATES:	Yearlong
# of SINGLE SITES:	8	MAX SPUR:	25 feet
GROUP RATE:	Varies	MAX STAY:	14 days
# of GROUP SITES:	70	ELEVATION:	4020 feet

34 Round Valley Group
Big Bears City • lat 40°06'39" lon 120°57'08"

DESCRIPTION: The CG is set in a pine and fir forest. 15 person maximum, 3 vehicles. Bring your own firewood. Deer, black bears, coyotes and small wildlife are common in the area. OHV roads approximately 2 miles north. Broom Springs nearby. Access to the Pacific Crest Trail approximately 1.5 miles.

GETTING THERE: From Big Bears City go S on state HWY 38 approx. 6 mi. to forest route 2N04. Go E on 2N04 approx. 3.5 mi. to forest route 2N01. Go N on 2N01 2.5 mi. to Round Valley Group CG. No RVs.

		OPEN DATES:	May-Sept*
GROUP RATE:	$35	MAX STAY:	14 days
# of GROUP SITES:	1	ELEVATION:	6500 feet

35 San Gorgonio Group
Angelus Oaks • lat 34°10'28" lon 116°51'59"

DESCRIPTION: The CG is set in a pine and fir forest. No nearby fishing. Showers and phone available. Bring your own firewood. Deer, bears, coyotes and small wildlife are common in the area. Horse and hiking access to Jenks Lake area and San Gorgonio Wilderness.

GETTING THERE: From Angelus Oaks go E on state HWY 38 approximately 7 miles to San Gorgonio CG.

SINGLE RATE:	Varies	OPEN DATES:	May-Sept*
# of SINGLE SITES:	52	MAX SPUR:	55 feet
		MAX STAY:	14 days
		ELEVATION:	6500 feet

36 Santa Rosa Springs
Cahuilla Hills • lat 33°32'30" lon 116°27'57"

DESCRIPTION: Desert setting under tall cedars with fantastic valley and desert views. Mild days, may snow in winter, rain in summers. Piped water. Supplies at Anza, 20 miles. Tent camping only. Moderate use. Hike/bike Sawmill Trail nearby.

GETTING THERE: From Cahuilla Hills go S on state HWY 74 approx. 13 mi. to forest route 7S02. Go S on 7S02 approx. 5 mi. to Santa Rosa Springs CG. 4WD recommended. Parking is limited. Winter snow may make site inaccessible.

SINGLE RATE:	No fee	OPEN DATES:	Yearlong
# of SINGLE SITES:	3		
		MAX STAY:	14 days
		ELEVATION:	7300 feet

37 Serrano
Fawnskin • lat 34°15'40" lon 116°54'53"

DESCRIPTION: The CG is located on Big Bears Lake set among pine and fir trees. Boat or shore fish the lake for trout. Bring your own firewood. Shower, electric hook-ups. Deer, black bears and small wildlife are common in the area. Access to Pacific Crest Trail approximately 2 miles.

GETTING THERE: From Fawnskin go E on state HWY 18 approximately 1.5 miles to Serrano CG.

SINGLE RATE:	Varies	OPEN DATES:	May-Nov
# of SINGLE SITES:	132	MAX SPUR:	55 feet
		MAX STAY:	14 days
		ELEVATION:	6800 feet

38 Shady Cove Group
Running Springs • lat 34°12'24" lon 117°02'37"

DESCRIPTION: Group sites 100 person max. In pine and fir forest. Bring your own firewood. Deer, black bears, coyotes and small wildlife are common in the area. Hike to Keller Peak Lookout. Pacific Crest Trail approx. 6 miles.

GETTING THERE: From Running Springs go E on state HWY 18 approx. 1 mi. to forest route 1N96. Go E on 1N96 approx. 2.5 mi. to Shady Cove Group CG. No RVs.

		OPEN DATES:	May-Sept*
GROUP RATE:	Varies	MAX STAY:	14 days
# of GROUP SITES:	1	ELEVATION:	7000 feet

39 Siberia Creek Group
Running Springs • lat 34°12'33" lon 117°00'40"

DESCRIPTION: Walk-in, 40 person maximum. The CG is set in a pine and fir forest. Bring your own firewood. Deer, black bears, coyotes and small wildlife are common in the area. Hike to Lookout Point and access Siberia Creek Trail.

GETTING THERE: From Running Springs go NE on state HWY 18 3.5 mi. to Lake View Point parking area. Follow the Camp Creek National Recreation Trail 1.5 mi. to Siberia Creek Group CG. Walk-in only.

SINGLE RATE:	No fee	OPEN DATES:	May-Sept*
		MAX STAY:	14 days
# of GROUP SITES:	1	ELEVATION:	6500 feet

40 Skyline
Heart Bar • lat 34°09'31" lon 116°47'09"

DESCRIPTION: The CG is located in a pine and fir setting with horse facilities. 25 person max. with 9 parking spaces. No nearby fishing. Bring your own firewood. Deer, bears, coyotes and occasional bobcats or big horn sheep in area. Horse and hiking access to Santa Anna River Trail, Pacific Crest Trail and San Gorgonio Wilderness.

GETTING THERE: From Heart Bar go E on forest route approximately 2 miles to Skyline CG. Part of Heart Bar CG.

		OPEN DATES:	May-Sept*
		MAX SPUR:	25 feet
GROUP RATE:	$25	MAX STAY:	14 days
# of GROUP SITES:	1	ELEVATION:	6900 feet

 Campground has hosts   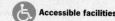 Reservable sites   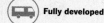 Accessible facilities   Fully developed   Semi-developed   Rustic facilities

NOTE: Open dates listed are typical. Actual dates are dependent on conditions such as snow pack.

41 South Fork Group
Angelus Oaks • lat 34°10'08" lon 116°49'30"

DESCRIPTION: The CG is set among pine and fir trees. Group sites need reservations. Fish for trout in the river. Bring your own firewood. Deer, black bears, coyotes and small wildlife are common in the area.

GETTING THERE: From Angelus Oaks go E on state HWY 38 approximately 8 miles to South Fork Group CG.

SINGLE RATE:		OPEN DATES:	May-Sept*
		MAX SPUR:	30 feet
GROUP RATE:	$15	MAX STAY:	14 days
# of GROUP SITES:	24	ELEVATION:	6400 feet

42 Tanglewood Group
Big Bears City • lat 34°17'43" lon 116°51'30"

DESCRIPTION: The CG is located in a pine and fir forest. No drinking water. 40 person maximum, 8 vehicles spaces. Bring your own firewood. Deer, black bears, coyotes and small wildlife are common in the area. Access to the Pacific Crest Trail nearby.

GETTING THERE: From Big Bears City go W on forest route 3N09 approx. 3 mi. to forest route 3N16. Go E on 3N16 approx. 2 mi. to Tanglewood Group CG.

		OPEN DATES:	May-Sept*
		MAX SPUR:	25 feet
GROUP RATE:	$50	MAX STAY:	14 days
# of GROUP SITES:	1	ELEVATION:	6500 feet

43 Tent Peg Group
Green Valley Lake • lat 34°15'41" lon 117°05'46"

DESCRIPTION: Group sites up to 30 persons, parking for 5 vehicles. Set in pine and fir forest. No drinking water. Bring your own firewood. Deer, black bears, coyotes and small wildlife are common in the area. OHV roads.

GETTING THERE: From Green Valley Lake go N on forest route 3N16 approx. 1.5 mi. to 2N12X. Go N on 2N12X approx. 2 mi. to Tent Peg Group CG.

		OPEN DATES:	May-Sept*
		MAX SPUR:	25 feet
GROUP RATE:	$50	MAX STAY:	14 days
# of GROUP SITES:	1	ELEVATION:	6200 feet

44 Thomas Mountain
Thomas Mountain • lat 33°37'22" lon 116°40'51"

DESCRIPTION: Adventure Pass required at this dispersed site located under tall pines. Views of Mt. San Jacinto, Garner Valley. Hot summer days, may be cold and snowy in winters. Bring own firewood. Supplies at Lake Hemet Market. Deer, occasional bears and small wildlife in area.

GETTING THERE: From Lake Hemet go S on state HWY 74 1 mi. to forest route 6S13. Go SW on 6S13 5 mi. to intersection w/5S15. Continue on 6S13, going SW 2.5 mi. to Thomas Mountain CG. No RV's; OHV's must be licensed.

SINGLE RATE:	No fee	OPEN DATES:	Yearlong
		MAX STAY:	14 days
		ELEVATION:	6640 feet

45 Tool Box Spring
Thomas Mountain • lat 33°36'45" lon 116°39'34"

DESCRIPTION: Among tall pine with chaparral and open grass areas. Views of Garner and Anza Valleys. Hot summer days, may snow in winter. Bring own firewood. Moderate usage. Supplies at Lake Hemet Market. Horse, mountain bike Ramona Trail is nearby. Adventure pass required.

GETTING THERE: From Thomas Mountain go S on state HWY 74 approx. 1 mi. to forest route 6S13. Go NW on 6S13 approx. 5 mi. to Tool Box Springs CG. No RVs.

SINGLE RATE:	No fee	OPEN DATES:	Yearlong
# of SINGLE SITES:	6		
		MAX STAY:	14 days
		ELEVATION:	6120 feet

46 Toro
Palm Desert • lat 33°30'05" lon 116°26'30"

DESCRIPTION: Among sparsely scattered tall pine with northern views. Mild summer days; rain frequent. May snow in winter. Supplies at Anza. No drinking water. Deer, coyotes and mountain lions possible. Mod. use turning heavy during hunting season. Bring own firewood. Very few hiking or horse trails. Adventure Pass required.

GETTING THERE: From Pinyon Pines go approx. 3 mi. W on state HWY 74 to forest route 7S02 (Santa Rose mountain Road). Go S on 7S02 approx. 12 mi. to Toro CG. High clearance required. No RVs.

SINGLE RATE:	No fee	OPEN DATES:	Yearlong
# of SINGLE SITES:	5		
		MAX STAY:	14 days
		ELEVATION:	7600 feet

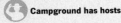 Campground has hosts   Reservable sites   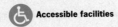 Accessible facilities   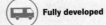 Fully developed   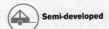 Semi-developed    Rustic facilities

NOTE: Open dates listed are typical. Actual dates are dependent on conditions such as snow pack.

USFS Photo

SEQUOIA NATIONAL FOREST

The Sequoia National Forest takes its name from the giant sequoia, the world's largest tree, which grows in more than 30 groves on the forest's lower slopes. The Sequoia's landscape is as spectacular as its trees. Located at the Sierra Nevada's southern end, elevations in the forest range from around 1,000 to 12,000 feet creating precipitous canyon and mountain streams with spectacular mountain waterfalls.

You can find both the past and the present in the Sequoia National Forest. If the land could speak, it would tell of a varied history of Native American villages, settlers' cabins, mining towns, cattle ranches, gold prospecting, lumber camps, redwood logging, early day resorts, mineral springs, and much more.

Hikers, bikers, off-highway vehicle users and horseback riders have over 1500 miles of maintained roads, 1000 miles of abandoned roads and 850 miles of trails in the forest available for their use and enjoyment. The Pacific Crest National Scenic Trail crosses the Sequoia for approximately 78 miles. Four designated wild and scenic rivers flow through the forest's wilderness areas and trout can be found in nearly every stream and lake. Shirley Meadows offers downhill skiing just south of Greenhorn Summit.

SEQUOIA NATIONAL FOREST • CALIFORNIA • LOCATOR MAP

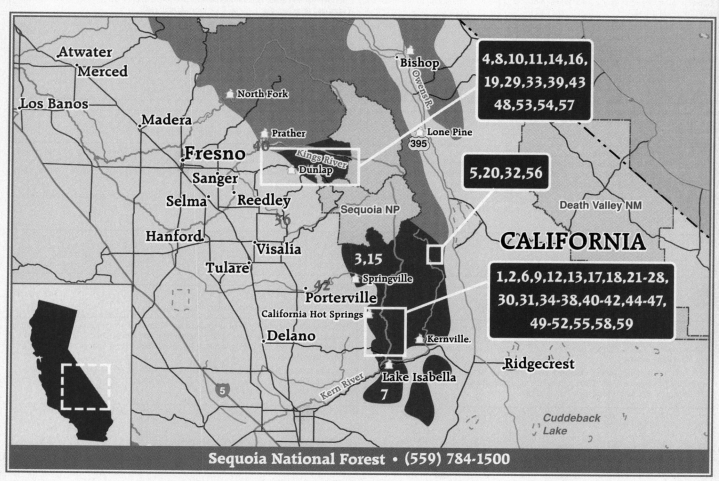

Sequoia National Forest • (559) 784-1500

1 Alder Creek
Glennville • lat 35°43'07" lon 118°36'39"

DESCRIPTION: This CG is located in pine and cedar on Cedar Creek. Fish for trout. Wildlife in this area includes black bears, mountain lion, coyotes, deer, osprey, herons, and eagles. CG is busy weekends and holidays. The on site trailhead leads to Cedar Creek CG. Supplies in Glennville. Poison oak in area.

GETTING THERE: From Glennville go E approx. 5.5 mi. on state HWY 155 to forest route 25S04. Go S on 25S04 approx. 2.5 mi. to Alder Creek CG.

SINGLE RATE:	No fee	OPEN DATES:	May-Oct
# of SINGLE SITES:	12	MAX SPUR:	20 feet
		MAX STAY:	14 days
		ELEVATION:	3900 feet

2 Auxiliary Dam Recreation Area
Lake Isabella • lat 35°38'00" lon 118°28'00"

DESCRIPTION: This dispersed CG is located in California live oak and grey pine on Lake Isabella. Fish for trophy bass, trout, silver salmon, and crappie. Wildlife includes osprey, blue herons, and bald eagles. RV dump station on site. A nearby trail leads to Cook Peak. CG is busy weekends and holidays.

GETTING THERE: From Lake Isabella go NE on state HWY 178 approx. 2 mi. to Auxiliary Dam Recreation Area CG.

SINGLE RATE:	No fee	OPEN DATES:	Yearlong
		MAX SPUR:	75 feet
		MAX STAY:	14 days
		ELEVATION:	2500 feet

3 Belknap
Camp Nelson • lat 36°08'29" lon 118°35'50"

DESCRIPTION: In a grove of giant sequoia on S. Fork of Middle Fork of Tule River. Fish for trout species. Deer, bears and mountain lions in area. Basic supplies at Camp Nelson. Gather firewood locally. Hike Wheel Meadow Grove Trail connecting to Summit Nat'l Recreation Trail.

GETTING THERE: Belknap CG is located approx. 1 mi. E of Camp Nelson on forest route 30E29. No trailers or RVs.

SINGLE RATE:	$12	OPEN DATES:	Apr-Nov
# of SINGLE SITES:	15		
		MAX STAY:	14 days
		ELEVATION:	5000 feet

4 Big Meadows
Hume • lat 36°43'03" lon 118°49'50"

DESCRIPTION: Among giant sequoia on small creek. Horse corrals. Fish for trout in the creek. Gather firewood locally. Basic supplies at Grant Grove or Stony Cr. Village. Deer, black bears and mountain lions in area. Multiple horse and hike trails, some leading into the Jennie Lake Wilderness or Sequoia National Park (permit required).

GETTING THERE: From Hume go S on forest route 13S09 approx. 8.5 mi. to forest route 14S57. Go SE on 14S57 approx. 2.5 mi. to forest route 14S11. Go NE on 14S11 approx. 5 mi. to Big Meadows CG.

SINGLE RATE:	No fee	OPEN DATES:	June-Oct
# of SINGLE SITES:	25	MAX SPUR:	30 feet
		MAX STAY:	14 days
		ELEVATION:	7600 feet

5 Blackrock Trailhead
Johnsondale • lat 36°11'30" lon 118°16'30"

DESCRIPTION: Set in Jeffery and lodgepole pine forest Fish for trout on trails entering wilderness. Deer, black bears, coyotes, mountain lions, snakes and lizards in area. Gather firewood locally. Primary use is to access Golden Trout Wilderness. Blackrock mountain Peak nearby.

GETTING THERE: From Johnsondale go E on county route SM99 approx. 3 mi. to forest route 22S05. Continue E on 22S05 approx. 22 mi. to forest route 21S03. Continue on 21S03 approx. 8.5 mi. to Blackrock Trailhead CG.

SINGLE RATE:	No fee	OPEN DATES:	May-Sept*
# of SINGLE SITES:	16		
		MAX STAY:	1 days
		ELEVATION:	9000 feet

6 Boulder Gulch
Wofford Heights • lat 35°39'30" lon 118°28'10"

DESCRIPTION: This CG is located in California live oak and grey pine on Lake Isabella. Fish for trophy bass, trout, silver salmon, and crappie. Wildlife includes osprey, blue herons, and bald eagles. Playground and fish cleaning station on site. A nearby trail leads to Cook Peak. CG is busy weekends and holidays.

GETTING THERE: From Wofford Heights go S on state HWY 155 approximately 2.5 miles to Boulder Gulch CG.

SINGLE RATE:	$14	OPEN DATES:	Apr-Sept
# of SINGLE SITES:	78	MAX SPUR:	45 feet
		MAX STAY:	14 days
		ELEVATION:	2500 feet

7 Breckenridge
Havilah • lat 35°28'03" lon 118°34'55"

DESCRIPTION: This CG is located in pine and cedar on Mill Creek. Fish for trout in creek. Wildlife in this area includes black bears, mountain lions, coyotes, deer, osprey, herons, and eagles. CG is busy weekends and holidays. Enjoy a drive to the Breckenridge Mountain lookout or hike the nearby trail. Poison oak in area.

GETTING THERE: From Havilah go S on primary forest route 83 approx. 2 mi. to forest route 28S06. Go W on 28S06 approx. 7 mi. to Breckenridge CG.

SINGLE RATE:	No fee	OPEN DATES:	May-Oct
# of SINGLE SITES:	8	MAX SPUR:	20 feet
		MAX STAY:	14 days
		ELEVATION:	6600 feet

8 Buck Rock
Hume • lat 36°43'09" lon 118°50'49"

DESCRIPTION: Among giant sequoia on small creek. Fish for trout in the creek. Gather firewood locally. Basic supplies at Grant Grove or Stony Cr. Village. Deer, black bears and mountain lions in area. Multiple horse and hike trails, some leading into the Jennie Lake Wilderness and Sequoia National Park (permit required).

GETTING THERE: From Hume go S on forest route 13S09 approx. 8.5 mi. to forest route 14S57. Go SE on 14S57 approx. 2.5 mi. to forest route 14S11. Go NE on 14S11 approx. 3 mi. to Buck Rock CG.

# of SINGLE SITES:	5	OPEN DATES:	May-Sept
GROUP RATE:	$112.50	MAX SPUR:	30 feet
# of GROUP SITES:	1	MAX STAY:	14 days
		ELEVATION:	7600 feet

9 Camp 3
Kernville • lat 35°49'30" lon 118°36'00"

DESCRIPTION: In gray pine and alder on east side of Kern River. Fish for planted golden and rainbow trout. Gather firewood. Deer, black bears, coyotes, lizards and snakes in area. Cyn trail on W side of river accessed near Fairview CG or at Kernville. Whiskey Flat trail is a short hiking trail. Poison oak in area.

GETTING THERE: Camp 3 CG is located approx. 4 mi. N of Kernville on county route SM99.

SINGLE RATE:	$12	OPEN DATES:	May-Sept
# of SINGLE SITES:	52	MAX SPUR:	30 feet
GROUP RATE:	$60	MAX STAY:	14 days
# of GROUP SITES:	2	ELEVATION:	2800 feet

10 Camp 4
Dunlap • lat 36°50'30" lon 119°06'30"

DESCRIPTION: Set among giant sequoia on the Kings River. No drinking water. Fish for trout in the river or Hume River nearby. Gather firewood locally. Deer, black bears and mountain lions in area. Horse and hike trails access Kings River Special Management Area. Poison oak in area.

GETTING THERE: From Dunlap go E on state HWY 180 approx. 4.5 mi. to forest route 13S97. Go E on 13S97 approx. 1 mi. to forest route 12S01. Go N on 12S01 approx. 8 mi. to Camp 4 CG. Not for trailer or RV use.

SINGLE RATE:	No fee	OPEN DATES:	Yearlong
# of SINGLE SITES:	5		
		MAX STAY:	14 days
		ELEVATION:	1000 feet

Campground has hosts   **Reservable sites**   **Accessible facilities**   **Fully developed**   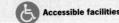 **Semi-developed**   **Rustic facilities**

NOTE: Open dates listed are typical. Actual dates are dependent on conditions such as snow pack.

11 Camp 4.5
Dunlap • lat 36°51'30" lon 119°07'30"

DESCRIPTION: Set among giant sequoia on the Kings River. No drinking water. Fish for trout in the river or Hume River nearby. Gather firewood locally. Deer, black bears and mountain lions in area. Horse and hike trails access Kings River Special Management Area. Poison oak in area.

GETTING THERE: From Dunlap go E on state HWY 180 4.5 mi. to forest route 13S97. Go E on 13S97 approx. 1 mi. to forest route 12S01. Go N on 12S01 approx. 8.5 mi. to Camp 4.5 CG. Not suitable for trailers or RVs.

SINGLE RATE:	No fee	OPEN DATES:	Yearlong
# of SINGLE SITES:	5		
		MAX STAY:	14 days
		ELEVATION:	1000 feet

16 Eshom Creek
Hartland • lat 36°41'21" lon 118°56'58"

DESCRIPTION: Located in sequoia near Eshom Creek. Fish for trout species. Gather firewood locally. Supplies 3-10 mi. Deer, black bears, mountain lions and small wildlife in area. Horse and hike access to Sequoia National Park (secure permit).

GETTING THERE: From Hartland go N on county route 469 approximately 3 miles to Eshorn Creek CG.

SINGLE RATE:	Varies	OPEN DATES:	May-Nov
# of SINGLE SITES:	24	MAX SPUR:	20 feet
		MAX STAY:	14 days
		ELEVATION:	4800 feet

12 Camp 9
Kernville • lat 35°41'00" lon 118°24'00"

DESCRIPTION: This CG is located in California live oak and grey pine near Lake Isabella. Fish for trophy bass, trout, silver salmon, and crappie. Wildlife includes osprey, blue herons, and bald eagles. RV dump station and fish cleaning station on site. A nearby trail leads to Cook Peak. CG is busy weekends and holidays.

GETTING THERE: From Kernville go S on county route 521 approximately 5 miles to Camp 9 CG.

SINGLE RATE:	$6	OPEN DATES:	Yearlong
# of SINGLE SITES:	109	MAX SPUR:	75 feet
GROUP RATE:	Varies	MAX STAY:	14 days
# of GROUP SITES:	2	ELEVATION:	2500 feet

17 Evans Flat
Wofford Heights • lat 35°38'39" lon 118°35'16"

DESCRIPTION: This CG is situated in pine and cedar on Ranger Spring. Fish for trout. Wildlife in this area includes black bears, mountain lion, coyotes, deer, osprey, herons, and eagles. CG is busy weekends and holidays. Poison oak in area. Visit scenic Woodward Peak. Supplies in Wofford Heights.

GETTING THERE: From Wofforoute Heights go S approx. 2.5 mi. on state HWY 55 to forest route 26S03. Go W on 26S03 approx. 8 mi. to Evans Flat CG.

SINGLE RATE:	No fee	OPEN DATES:	May-Oct
# of SINGLE SITES:	16	MAX SPUR:	20 feet
		MAX STAY:	14 days
		ELEVATION:	6100 feet

13 Cedar Creek
Glennville • lat 35°44'55" lon 118°34'54"

DESCRIPTION: This CG is located in pine and cedar on Cedar Creek. Fish for trout. Wildlife in this area includes black bears, mountain lions, coyotes, deer, osprey, heron, and eagles. CG is busy weekends and holidays. The on site trailhead leads to Alder Creek CG. Supplies in Glennville. Poison oak in area.

GETTING THERE: Cedar Creek CG is located approx. 8.5 mi. from Glennville on state HWY 155.

SINGLE RATE:	No fee	OPEN DATES:	Yearlong
# of SINGLE SITES:	10	MAX SPUR:	20 feet
		MAX STAY:	14 days
		ELEVATION:	4800 feet

18 Fairview
Kernville • lat 35°55'44" lon 118°29'32"

DESCRIPTION: In gray pine and alder on east side of Kern River. Fish for planted golden and rainbow trout. Gather firewood. Deer, black bears, coyotes, lizards and snakes in area. Cyn trail on W side of river accessed near Fairview CG or at Kernville. Poison oak. Packsaddle Cyn Trail and river trails to hike.

GETTING THERE: Fairview CG is located approx. 13 mi. N of Kernville on county route SM99.

SINGLE RATE:	$12	OPEN DATES:	Apr-Nov
# of SINGLE SITES:	55	MAX SPUR:	45 feet
GROUP RATE:	$60	MAX STAY:	14 days
# of GROUP SITES:	1	ELEVATION:	3500 feet

14 Cove Group
Hume • lat 36°39'59" lon 118°50'22"

DESCRIPTION: In giant sequoia setting near Stony Creek. Gather own firewood locally. Deer, black bears, mountain lions and small wildlife in area. Horse and hike trails into Jennie Lakes Wilderness or Sequoia National Park (obtain permit). Max. 50 persons.

GETTING THERE: From Hume go S on forest route 13S09 approx. 8.5 mi. to forest route 14S57. Go SE on 14S57 approx. 5.5 mi. to Cove Group CG.

		OPEN DATES:	May-Sept
		MAX SPUR:	35 feet
GROUP RATE:	Varies	MAX STAY:	14 days
# of GROUP SITES:	1	ELEVATION:	6400 feet

19 Fir Group
Hume • lat 36°39'57" lon 118°50'33"

DESCRIPTION: In giant sequoia setting near Stony Creek. Gather own firewood locally. Deer, black bears, mountain lions and small wildlife in area. Horse and hike trails into Jennie Lakes Wilderness or Sequoia National Park (obtain permit). Max. 100 persons.

GETTING THERE: From Hume go S on forest route 13S09 approx. 8.5 mi. to forest route 14S57. Go SE on 14S57 approx. 6 mi. to Fir Group CG.

		OPEN DATES:	May-Sept
		MAX SPUR:	35 feet
GROUP RATE:	$75	MAX STAY:	14 days
# of GROUP SITES:	1	ELEVATION:	6500 feet

15 Coy Flat
Camp Nelson • lat 36°07'37" lon 118°37'06"

DESCRIPTION: Set among giant sequoia on the South Fork of Middle Fork of the Tule River. Fish for trout species in river. Deer, black bears and mountain lions in area. Gather own firewood locally. Basic Supplies in Camp Nelson. Hike Belknap Camp Grove Trail connecting to Summit Nat'l Recreation Trail.

GETTING THERE: Coy Flat CG is located approx. 1.5 mi. S of Camp Nelson on forest route 21S94.

SINGLE RATE:	$10	OPEN DATES:	Apr-Nov
# of SINGLE SITES:	20	MAX SPUR:	24 feet
		MAX STAY:	14 days
		ELEVATION:	5000 feet

20 Fish Creek
Johnsondale • lat 36°03'32" lon 118°13'03"

DESCRIPTION: Set among Jeffery, Ponderosa and lodgepole pine. Fish nearby on S. Fork of Kern for Golden or Rainbow Trout. Gather firewood. Deer, black bears, coyotes, lizards and snakes in area. Access to Jackass National Recreation Trail for hiking.

GETTING THERE: From Johnsondale go E on county route SM99 approx. 3 mi. to forest route 22S05. Continue E on 22S05 approx. 27 mi. to Fish Creek CG.

SINGLE RATE:	$5	OPEN DATES:	May-Nov
# of SINGLE SITES:	36	MAX SPUR:	27 feet
		MAX STAY:	14 days
		ELEVATION:	7400 feet

 Campground has hosts   **Reservable sites**   **Accessible facilities**   **Fully developed**   **Semi-developed**   **Rustic facilities**

NOTE: Open dates listed are typical. Actual dates are dependent on conditions such as snow pack.

Sequoia National Forest • California • 11 — 20

21 French Gulch Group Area
Lake Isabella • lat 35°38'30" lon 118°28'30"

DESCRIPTION: This group CG is located in California live oak and grey pine on Lake Isabella. Fish for trophy bass, trout, silver salmon, and crappie. Wildlife includes osprey, blue herons, and bald eagles. A nearby trail leads to Cook Peak. CG is busy weekends and holidays. Supplies in Lake Isabella.

GETTING THERE: From Lake Isabella go N on state HWY 155 approximately 2.5 miles to French Gulch Group Area CG.

		OPEN DATES:	Yearlong
		MAX SPUR:	75 feet
GROUP RATE:	$185	MAX STAY:	14 days
# of GROUP SITES:	1	ELEVATION:	2500 feet

26 Holey Meadow Group
Johnsondale • lat 35°57'12" lon 118°37'08"

DESCRIPTION: A group site in giant sequoia near Double Bun and Starvation creeks. Fishing for trout species may be seasonal. Supplies at Ponderosa Lodge. Gather own firewood locally. Deer, black bears, mountain lions and small wildlife in area. No trails in immediate vicinity. Max 60 persons.

GETTING THERE: Holey Meadow is located approx. 4.5 mi. SW of Johnsondale on forest route 23S15. Suitable for RVs up to 16'.

		OPEN DATES:	May-Nov
		MAX SPUR:	20 feet
GROUP RATE:	$75	MAX STAY:	14 days
# of GROUP SITES:	1	ELEVATION:	6400 feet

22 Frog Meadow
Johnsondale • lat 35°52'22" lon 118°34'33"

DESCRIPTION: A rustic CG in giant sequoia forest. Dispersed sites for approx. 10 units. No drinking water. Nearby Tobias Creek for trout fishing. Gather own firewood locally. Deer, black bears, mountain lions and small wildlife in area. Supplies at Glennville. Trail to Tobias Meadow or Deer Mill Creek area.

GETTING THERE: From Johnsondale go W 2 mi. on forest route 23S15 to forest route 23S16. Go S on 23S16 15.5 mi. to forest route 24S50. Go N on 24S50 1 mi. to Frog Meadow CG. Unsuitable for trailers and RVs.

SINGLE RATE:	No fee	OPEN DATES:	June-Nov
# of SINGLE SITES:	10		
		MAX STAY:	14 days
		ELEVATION:	7500 feet

27 Horse Meadow
Johnsondale • lat 35°54'06" lon 118°22'18"

DESCRIPTION: A beautiful site in Jeffery and pinyon pine with sage. Adjacent to S. Fork of Kern River. Fish for stocked golden and rainbow trout. Gather firewood. Black bears, deer, lizards and snakes in area. Pacific Crest Trail passes through CG. Access to Sierra Wilderness or Dome Land Wilderness.

GETTING THERE: From Johnsondale go E on county route SM99 approx. 4 mi. to forest route 22S05. Go E on 22S05 approx. 3.5 mi. to forest route 22S12. Go S on 22S12 approx. 7.5 mi. to Horse Meadow CG.

SINGLE RATE:	$5	OPEN DATES:	May-Nov
# of SINGLE SITES:	41	MAX SPUR:	22 feet
		MAX STAY:	14 days
		ELEVATION:	7400 feet

23 Gold Ledge
Kernville • lat 35°52'40" lon 118°27'23"

DESCRIPTION: In gray pine and alder on east side of Kern River. Fish for planted golden and rainbow trout. Gather firewood. Deer, black bears, coyotes, lizards and snakes in area. Cyn trail on W side of river accessed near Fairview CG or at Kernville. Poison oak in area.

GETTING THERE: Gold Ledge CG is located approx. 9.5 mi. N of Kernville on county route SM99.

SINGLE RATE:	$12	OPEN DATES:	May-Sept
# of SINGLE SITES:	37	MAX SPUR:	30 feet
		MAX STAY:	14 days
		ELEVATION:	3200 feet

28 Hospital Flat
Kernville • lat 35°49'43" lon 118°27'28"

DESCRIPTION: In gray pine and alder on east side of Kern River. Fish for planted golden and rainbow trout. Gather firewood. Deer, black bears, coyotes, lizards and snakes in area. Canyon trail on W side of river accessed near Fairview CG or at Kernville. Poison oak in area.

GETTING THERE: Hospital Flat CG is located approx. 5.5 mi. N of Kernville on county route SM99.

SINGLE RATE:	$12	OPEN DATES:	May-Sept
# of SINGLE SITES:	40	MAX SPUR:	30 feet
GROUP RATE:	$60	MAX STAY:	14 days
# of GROUP SITES:	1	ELEVATION:	3000 feet

24 Headquarters
Kearnville • lat 35°47'45" lon 118°27'04"

DESCRIPTION: In gray pine and alder on east side of Kern River. Fish for planted golden and rainbow trout. Gather firewood. Deer, black bears, coyotes, lizards and snakes in area. Cyn trail on W side of river accessed near Fairview CG or at Kernville. Poison oak in area.

GETTING THERE: Headquarters CG is located approx. 3.5 mi. N of Kernville on county route SM99.

SINGLE RATE:	$12	OPEN DATES:	Yearlong
# of SINGLE SITES:	44	MAX SPUR:	27 feet
		MAX STAY:	14 days
		ELEVATION:	2800 feet

29 Hume Lake
Hume • lat 36°47'33" lon 118°54'30"

DESCRIPTION: Situated on Hume Lake among giant sequoia. Fish for trout from shore or boat. Campers may gather firewood. Supplies at Hume Lake or Grant Grove. Beautiful Grizzly Falls is nearby. Deer, black bears, mountain lions and small wildlife in area. Bears boxes. Hike to Huckleberry Meadow.

GETTING THERE: From Hume go E on forest route 13S09 approximately 1/2 mile to Hume Lake CG.

SINGLE RATE:	$14	OPEN DATES:	May-Sept
# of SINGLE SITES:	75	MAX SPUR:	35 feet
		MAX STAY:	14 days
		ELEVATION:	5200 feet

25 Hobo
Bodfish • lat 35°34'28" lon 118°31'32"

DESCRIPTION: This CG rests in grey pine at the confluence of Kern River and Clear Creek. Wildlife includes black bears, mountain lions, coyotes, deer, osprey, herons, and eagles. CG is busy weekends and holidays. Hike the nearby trail to Lightner Peak or try your hand at rafting the swift and cold Kern River.

GETTING THERE: Hobo CG is located approx. 3.5 mi. SW of Bodfish on county route 214.

SINGLE RATE:	$13	OPEN DATES:	Yearlong
# of SINGLE SITES:	35	MAX SPUR:	24 feet
		MAX STAY:	14 days
		ELEVATION:	2300 feet

30 Hungry Gulch
Wofford Heights • lat 35°39'00" lon 118°29'00"

DESCRIPTION: This CG is located in California live oak and grey pine near Lake Isabella. Fish for trophy bass, trout, silver salmon, and crappie. Wildlife includes osprey, blue herons, and bald eagles. Playground on site. Nearby trail leads to Cook Peak. CG is busy weekends and holidays. Supplies in Wofford Heights.

GETTING THERE: From Wofford Heights go S on state HWY 155 approximately 2.5 miles to Hungry Gulch CG.

SINGLE RATE:	$14	OPEN DATES:	Apr-Sept
# of SINGLE SITES:	78	MAX SPUR:	30 feet
		MAX STAY:	14 days
		ELEVATION:	2500 feet

 Campground has hosts   **Reservable sites**   **Accessible facilities**   **Fully developed**   **Semi-developed**   **Rustic facilities**

NOTE: Open dates listed are typical. Actual dates are dependent on conditions such as snow pack.

31 Jerkey Trailhead
Johnsondale • lat 36°11'06" lon 118°29'13"

DESCRIPTION: A 1 night stopover site for horse/hike trail users. Set in sequoia forest, with water and corral. Deer, black bears and mountain lions in area. Gather firewood. Pull-thru parking. Spring runoff may limit uses. Call Ranger District for permit prior to camping. Horse/hike access to Golden Trout Wilderness.

GETTING THERE: Jerkey Trailhead CG is located approx. 16.5 mi. N of Johnsondale on forest route 22S82.

SINGLE RATE:	No fee	OPEN DATES:	Varies*
# of SINGLE SITES:	12	MAX SPUR:	30 feet
		MAX STAY:	1 days
		ELEVATION:	6400 feet

32 Kennedy Meadow
Johnsondale • lat 36°03'10" lon 118°07'49"

DESCRIPTION: A beautiful site in Jeffery and pinyon pine sage. Adjacent to S. Fork of Kern River. Fish for stocked golden and rainbow trout. Gather firewood. Black bears, deer, lizards and snakes in area. Pacific Crest Trail passes through CG. Multiple horse and hike trails to Dome Land Wilderness and Manter Meadow.

GETTING THERE: From Johnsondale go E on county route SM99 approx. 3 mi. to forest route 22S05. Continue E on 22S05 approx. 34 mi. to county route 152B. Go N on 152B approx. 3.5 mi. to Kennedy Meadows CG.

SINGLE RATE:	$5	OPEN DATES:	Yearlong
# of SINGLE SITES:	38	MAX SPUR:	30 feet
		MAX STAY:	14 days
		ELEVATION:	6100 feet

33 Landslide
Hume • lat 36°45'49" lon 118°52'52"

DESCRIPTION: Overlooking Hume Lake set in giant sequoia forest. Fish for trout on lake by shore or boat. Gather firewood locally. Supplies at Hume Lake or Grant Grove. Deer, black bears, mountain lions and small wildlife in area. Trail to Huckleberry Meadows.

GETTING THERE: From Hume go SE on forest route 13S09 approximately 3 miles to Landslide CG.

SINGLE RATE:	Varies	OPEN DATES:	May-Oct
# of SINGLE SITES:	6	MAX SPUR:	40 feet
		MAX STAY:	14 days
		ELEVATION:	5800 feet

34 Leavis Flat
California HS • lat 35°52'46" lon 118°40'32"

DESCRIPTION: In California Hot Springs near Deer Creek. Fish for trout in season. Gather own firewood locally. Deer, black bears, mountain lion and small wildlife in area. Poison oak may be present. Supplies in Pine Flat. No trails in vicinity.

GETTING THERE: Leavis Flat CG is located approx. 1/2 mi. W of California Hot Springs.

SINGLE RATE:	$10	OPEN DATES:	Yearlong
# of SINGLE SITES:	9	MAX SPUR:	30 feet
		MAX STAY:	14 days
		ELEVATION:	3000 feet

35 Limestone
Kernville • lat 35°57'46" lon 118°28'48"

DESCRIPTION: A popular, pretty, small site in gray and Jeffery pine and alder on east side of Kern River. No drinking water. Fish for golden and rainbow trout. Gather firewood. Deer, black bears, lizards and snakes. Cyn trail on W side of river accessed near Fairview CG or at Kernville. Poison oak. Heavy use. 2 mi to Rincon Fault Trail.

GETTING THERE: Limestone CG is located approx. 15 mi. N of Kernville on county route SM99.

SINGLE RATE:	$10	OPEN DATES:	Apr-Nov
# of SINGLE SITES:	22	MAX SPUR:	30 feet
		MAX STAY:	14 days
		ELEVATION:	3800 feet

36 Live Oak Group
Wofford Heights • lat 35°40'00" lon 118°28'00"

DESCRIPTION: This CG is located in California live oak and grey pine near Lake Isabella. Fish for trophy bass, trout, silver salmon, and crappie. Wildlife includes osprey, blue herons, and bald eagles. A nearby trail leads to Cook Peak. CG is busy weekends and holidays. Supplies in Wofford Heights.

GETTING THERE: From Wofford Heights go S on state HWY 155 approximately 1/2 mile to Live Oak Group CG.

GROUP RATE:	$150	OPEN DATES:	May-Sept
# of GROUP SITES:	1	MAX SPUR:	30 feet
		MAX STAY:	14 days
		ELEVATION:	2500 feet

37 Live Oak North
Wofford Heights • lat 35°40'00" lon 118°28'00"

DESCRIPTION: This CG is located in California live oak and grey pine close to Lake Isabella. Fish for trophy bass, trout, silver salmon, and crappie. Wildlife includes osprey, blue herons, and bald eagles. A nearby trail leads to Cook Peak. CG is busy weekends and holidays.

GETTING THERE: From Wofford Heights go S on state HWY 155 approximately 1/2 mile to Live Oak North CG.

SINGLE RATE:	$14	OPEN DATES:	Yearlong
# of SINGLE SITES:	60	MAX SPUR:	30 feet
GROUP RATE:	$150	MAX STAY:	14 days
# of GROUP SITES:	1	ELEVATION:	2500 feet

38 Live Oak South
Wofford Heights • lat 35°40'00" lon 118°28'00"

DESCRIPTION: This CG is located in California live oak and grey pine on Lake Isabella. Fish for trophy bass, trout, silver salmon, and crappie. Wildlife includes osprey, blue herons, and bald eagles. Supplies in Wofford Heights. A nearby trail leads to Cook Peak. CG is busy weekends and holidays.

GETTING THERE: From Wofford Heights go S on state HWY 155 approximately 1/2 mile to Live Oak South CG.

SINGLE RATE:	$14	OPEN DATES:	Yearlong
# of SINGLE SITES:	90	MAX SPUR:	30 feet
		MAX STAY:	14 days
		ELEVATION:	2500 feet

39 Logger Flat Group
Hume • lat 36°46'25" lon 118°53'38"

DESCRIPTION: A group site adjacent to small creek set in giant sequoia forest. Fish nearby Hume Lake for trout species from shore or boat. Gather firewood locally. Supplies at Hume Lake or Grant Grove. Deer, black bears, mountain lions and small wildlife in area. No nearby trails.

GETTING THERE: From Hume go SE on forest route 13S09 approximately 1.5 miles to Logger Flat CG.

GROUP RATE:	$75	OPEN DATES:	May-Sept
# of GROUP SITES:	1	MAX SPUR:	40 feet
		MAX STAY:	14 days
		ELEVATION:	5300 feet

40 Long Meadow
Johnsondale • lat 35°58'51" lon 118°34'55"

DESCRIPTION: A group site in giant sequoia forest near Long Meadow Cr. No drinking water. Fish for trout in season. Deer, black bears, mountain lions in area. A loop trail is available at nearby Redwood Meadow CG. Max 36 persons. Access to Long Meadow Giant Sequoia Grove and Trail of a Hundred Giants.

GETTING THERE: From Johnsondale go SW approx. 4 mi. on forest route 23S15 to county route SM107. Go NE on SM107 approx. 2.5 mi. to Long Meadow CG.

GROUP RATE:	$24	OPEN DATES:	May-Nov
# of GROUP SITES:	1	MAX SPUR:	35 feet
		MAX STAY:	14 days
		ELEVATION:	6000 feet

 Campground has hosts 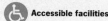 **Reservable sites**   **Accessible facilities**   **Fully developed** Semi-developed   **Rustic facilities**

NOTE: Open dates listed are typical. Actual dates are dependent on conditions such as snow pack.

Sequoia National Forest • California • 31 — 40

41 Lower Peppermint
Johnsondale • lat 36°03'59" lon 118°29'25"

DESCRIPTION: Set in giant sequoia forest on Peppermint Creek. Fish for trout species in season. Gather own firewood locally. Deer, black bears, mountain lions and small wildlife in area. Supplies at Ponderosa. Trails in vicinity include Peppermint Meadows. Fee demo site.

GETTING THERE: Lower Peppermint CG is located approx. 8 mi. N of Johnsondale on forest route 22S82.

SINGLE RATE:	$12	OPEN DATES:	May-Oct
# of SINGLE SITES:	17	MAX SPUR:	18 feet
		MAX STAY:	14 days
		ELEVATION:	5300 feet

46 Peppermint
Camp Nelson • lat 36°05'04" lon 118°31'05"

DESCRIPTION: A dispersed camping site set in sequoia trees. No drinking water, no services. Campfire permit required. Basic supplies at Ponderosa Lodge. Seasonal Creek nearby. Deer, black bears and mountain lions in area. Gather firewood locally. Peppermint Cr nearby. Horse/hike trails in vicinity.

GETTING THERE: From Camp Nelson go SE approx. 9 mi. on state HWY 190 to forest route 21S07. Go E on 21S07 approx. 1 mi. to Peppermint CG.

SINGLE RATE:	No fee	OPEN DATES:	Yearlong*
		MAX STAY:	14 days
		ELEVATION:	7100 feet

42 Main Dam
Lake Isabella • lat 35°38'00" lon 118°29'00"

DESCRIPTION: This CG is situated in California live oak and grey pine close to Lake Isabella. Fish for trophy bass, trout, silver salmon, and crappie. Wildlife includes osprey, blue herons, and bald eagles. RV dump station on site. A nearby trail leads to Cook Peak. CG is busy weekends and holidays.

GETTING THERE: From Lake Isabella go N on state HWY 155 approx. 2 mi. to Main Dam CG.

SINGLE RATE:	$12	OPEN DATES:	May-Sept
# of SINGLE SITES:	82	MAX SPUR:	45 feet
		MAX STAY:	14 days
		ELEVATION:	2500 feet

47 Pioneer Point
Lake Isabella • lat 35°38'00" lon 118°30'00"

DESCRIPTION: This CG is located in California live oak and grey pine on Lake Isabella. Fish for trophy bass, trout, silver salmon, and crappie. Wildlife includes osprey, blue herons, and bald eagles. Playground and fish cleaning station on site. A nearby trail leads to Cook Peak. CG is busy weekends and holidays.

GETTING THERE: From Lake Isabella go N on state HWY 155 approximately 2 miles to Pioneer Point CG.

SINGLE RATE:	$14	OPEN DATES:	Yearlong
# of SINGLE SITES:	78	MAX SPUR:	30 feet
		MAX STAY:	14 days
		ELEVATION:	2500 feet

43 Mill Flat
Dunlap • lat 36°51'34" lon 119°05'49"

DESCRIPTION: Situated among giant sequoia along the Kings River. Fish river for trout species. Supplies in Piedra or Dunlap. Poison oak may be present. Gather firewood locally. Deer, black bears, mountain lions and small wildlife in area. Trails access Kings River Special Management Area.

GETTING THERE: From Dunlap go E approx. 4.5 mi. on state HWY 180 to forest route 13S97. Go E on 13S97 aprpox. 1 mi. to forest route 12S01. Go N on 12S01 approx. 7.5 mi. to Mill Flat Creek CG. Not suitable for trailers.

SINGLE RATE:	No fee	OPEN DATES:	Yearlong
# of SINGLE SITES:	5		
		MAX STAY:	14 days
		ELEVATION:	1100 feet

48 Princess
Hume • lat 36°48'14" lon 118°56'33"

DESCRIPTION: A special CG, quiet, secluded yet close to events located on Indian Creek among giant sequoia. Fish creek or travel approx. 4 mi. to Hume Lake for trout species. Supplies at Grant Grove. Gather firewood locally. Deer, black bears, mountain lions and small wildlife in area. Short trails in vicinity. Fills holidays.

GETTING THERE: From Hume go N on forest route 13S09 approx. 3 mi. to primary forest route 30. Go W on primary forest route 30 approx. 1/2 mi. to Princess CG.

SINGLE RATE:	Varies	OPEN DATES:	May-Sept
# of SINGLE SITES:	90	MAX SPUR:	30 feet
		MAX STAY:	14 days
		ELEVATION:	5900 feet

44 Panorama
Johnsondale • lat 35°48'33" lon 118°34'11"

DESCRIPTION: Located in giant sequoia forest near Deep Creek. Dispersed sites. No drinking water. Supplies at Glennville. Fish for trout species in season. Deer, black bears, mountain lion and small wildlife in area. Gather firewood locally. No trails in immediate vicinity.

GETTING THERE: Panorama CG is located approx. 18 mi. S of Johnsondale on forest route 23S16. Dirt narrow road. Site is unsuitable for trailers and RVs.

SINGLE RATE:	No fee	OPEN DATES:	Yearlong
# of SINGLE SITES:	10	MAX SPUR:	18 feet
		MAX STAY:	14 days
		ELEVATION:	7400 feet

49 Quaking Aspen
Camp Nelson • lat 36°07'14" lon 118°32'39"

DESCRIPTION: Located in aspen grove near Freeman Creek. Super fall colors. Fish for trout species nearby. Deer, black bears and mountain lions in area. Gather firewood locally. Basic supplies at Camp Nelson. Summit Nat'l Recreation Trail and many other horse or hike trails nearby.

GETTING THERE: Quaking Aspen CG is located approx. 6.5 mi. SE of Camp Nelson on state HWY 190.

SINGLE RATE:	$12	OPEN DATES:	May-Nov
# of SINGLE SITES:	32	MAX SPUR:	24 feet
		MAX STAY:	14 days
		ELEVATION:	7000 feet

45 Paradise Cove
Mountain Mesa • lat 35°38'00" lon 118°24'00"

DESCRIPTION: This CG is located in California live oak and grey pine on Lake Isabella. Fish for trophy bass, trout, silver salmon, and crappie. Wildlife includes osprey, blue herons, and bald eagles. RV dump station and fish cleaning station on site. A nearby trail leads to Cook Peak. CG is busy weekends and holidays.

GETTING THERE: From Mountain Mesa go W on state HWY 178 approximately 1/5 mile to Paradise Cove CG.

SINGLE RATE:	Varies	OPEN DATES:	Yearlong
# of SINGLE SITES:	138	MAX SPUR:	75 feet
		MAX STAY:	14 days
		ELEVATION:	2500 feet

50 Quaking Aspen Group
Camp Nelson • lat 36°07'09" lon 118°32'50"

DESCRIPTION: Located in aspen grove near Freeman Creek. Super fall colors. Fish for trout species nearby. Deer, black bears and mountain lions in area. Gather firewood locally. Basic supplies at Camp Nelson. Summit Nat'l Recreation Trail and many other horse or hike trails nearby.

GETTING THERE: Quaking Aspen Group CG is located approx. 6.5 mi. SE of Camp Nelson on state HWY 190. No trailers.

		OPEN DATES:	May-Nov
GROUP RATE:	Varies	MAX STAY:	14 days
# of GROUP SITES:	3	ELEVATION:	7000 feet

 Campground has hosts   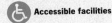 Reservable sites   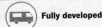 Accessible facilities   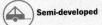 Fully developed   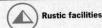 Semi-developed   Rustic facilities

NOTE: Open dates listed are typical. Actual dates are dependent on conditions such as snow pack.

51 Redwood Meadow
Johnsondale • lat 35°58'35" lon 118°35'27"

DESCRIPTION: In giant sequoia and redwood forest near Long Meadow Cr. Fish for trout species in season. Gather own firewood locally. Supplies at Ponderosa Lodge. Deer, black bears, mountain lions and small wildlife in area. A loop trail is available from CG. Adacent to Long Meadow Giant Sequoia Grove and Trail of a Hundred Giants.

GETTING THERE: From Johnsondale go SW approx. 4 mi. on forest route 23S15 to county route SM107. Go NE on SM107 approx. 2 mi. to Redwood Meadow CG.

SINGLE RATE:	$12	OPEN DATES:	May-Nov
# of SINGLE SITES:	15	MAX SPUR:	16 feet
		MAX STAY:	14 days
		ELEVATION:	6100 feet

56 Troy Meadow
Johnsondale • lat 36°04'04" lon 118°14'09"

DESCRIPTION: Set among Jeffery, Ponderosa and lodgepole pine. Fish nearby on S. Fork of Kern for golden or rainbow trout. Gather firewood. Deer, black bears, coyotes, lizards and snakes in area. Access to Jackass National Recreation Trail for hiking. Under rehab construction 2001-2002 seasons.

GETTING THERE: From Johnsondale go E on county route SM99 approx. 3 mi. to forest route 22S05. Continue E on 22S05 approx. 27 mi. to forest route 22S05. Go N on 22S05 approx. 1 mi. to Troy Meadows CG.

SINGLE RATE:	$5	OPEN DATES:	Apr-Nov
# of SINGLE SITES:	73	MAX SPUR:	20 feet
		MAX STAY:	14 days
		ELEVATION:	7800 feet

52 Stine Cove Recreation Area
Kernville • lat 35°38'00" lon 118°24'00"

DESCRIPTION: This dispersed CG is located in California live oak and grey pine on Lake Isabella. Fish for trophy bass, trout, silver salmon, and crappie. Wildlife includes osprey, blue herons, and bald eagles. A nearby trail leads to Cook Peak. CG is busy weekends and holidays. Supplies at Kernville.

GETTING THERE: From Kernville go S on county route 521 approximately 6 miles to Stine Cove Recreation Area.

SINGLE RATE:	No fee	OPEN DATES:	Yearlong
		MAX SPUR:	75 feet
		MAX STAY:	14 days
		ELEVATION:	2500 feet

57 Upper Stoney
Hume • lat 36°39'52" lon 118°49'56"

DESCRIPTION: In giant sequoia setting near Stony Creek. Gather own firewood locally. Deer, black bears, mountain lions and small wildlife in area. Horse and hike trails into Jennie Lakes Wilderness and Sequoia National Park (obtain permit). Bears boxes available. Creek in summer is very swift and dangerous for children and pets.

GETTING THERE: From Hume go S on forest route 13S09 approx. 8.5 mi. to forest route 14S57. Go SE on 14S57 approx. 6.5 mi. to Upper Stony Creek CG.

SINGLE RATE:	$12	OPEN DATES:	May-Oct
# of SINGLE SITES:	20	MAX SPUR:	18 feet
		MAX STAY:	14 days
		ELEVATION:	6400 feet

53 Stony Creek
Hume • lat 36°39'52" lon 118°49'56"

DESCRIPTION: In giant sequoia setting near Stony Creek. Gather own firewood locally. Deer, black bears, mountain lions and small wildlife in area. Horse and hike trails into Jennie Lakes Wilderness or Sequoia National Park (obtain permit). Bears boxes available.

GETTING THERE: From Hume go S on forest route 13S09 approx. 8.5 mi. to forest route 14S57. Go SE on 14S57 approx. 6.5 mi. to Stony Creek CG.

SINGLE RATE:	$14	OPEN DATES:	May-Oct
# of SINGLE SITES:	49	MAX SPUR:	30 feet
		MAX STAY:	14 days
		ELEVATION:	6400 feet

58 White River
Pine Flat • lat 35°50'40" lon 118°38'06"

DESCRIPTION: Part of Hot Springs Complex on the White River set among giant sequoia. Fish for trout species in season. Gather firewood locally. Supplies at Pine Flat. Deer, black bears, mountain lions and small wildlife in area. Trails into Dark Cyn and Ames Hole.

GETTING THERE: From Pine Flat go S on county route SM56 approx. 2 mi. to White River CG.

SINGLE RATE:	$10	OPEN DATES:	May-Oct
# of SINGLE SITES:	12	MAX SPUR:	16 feet
		MAX STAY:	14 days
		ELEVATION:	4000 feet

54 Tenmile
Hume • lat 36°50'23" lon 118°52'47"

DESCRIPTION: Set on Tenmile Creek in giant sequoia forest. Fish creek or travel approx. 4 mi. to Hume Lake for trout species. Supplies at Grant Grove or Hume Lake. Gather own firewood locally. Deer, black bears, mountian lions and small wildlife in area. No nearby trails.

GETTING THERE: From Hume go SE on forest route 13S09 approximately 4.5 miles to Tenmile CG.

SINGLE RATE:	No fee	OPEN DATES:	May-Oct
# of SINGLE SITES:	13	MAX SPUR:	18 feet
		MAX STAY:	14 days
		ELEVATION:	5800 feet

59 Wishon
Camp Nelson • lat 37°17'50" lon 119°32'02"

DESCRIPTION: Among giant sequoia on the North Fork of the Middle Fork of Tule River. Fish for golden and rainbow trout. Basic supplies at Camp Nelson or Springville. Gather firewood. Deer, black bears and mountain lions in area. Trails North include access (approx. 8 mi. hike, permits required) to Sequoia Nat'l Park.

GETTING THERE: From Camp Nelson go NW approx. 5 mi. on state HWY 190 to county route 208. Go NE on 208 approx. 2.5 mi. to Camp Wishon CG.

SINGLE RATE:	$12	OPEN DATES:	Yearlong*
# of SINGLE SITES:	33	MAX SPUR:	24 feet
		MAX STAY:	14 days
		ELEVATION:	4000 feet

55 Tillie Creek
Wofford Heights • lat 35°41'00" lon 118°28'30"

DESCRIPTION: This CG is located in California live oak and grey pine on Lake Isabella. Fish for trophy bass, trout, silver salmon, and crappie. Wildlife includes osprey, blue herons, and bald eagles. Playground, amphitheater, RV dump station, and fish cleaning station on site. CG is busy weekends and holidays.

GETTING THERE: From Wofford Heights go S on state HWY 155 to Tillie Creek CG.

SINGLE RATE:	$14	OPEN DATES:	Yearlong
# of SINGLE SITES:	159	MAX SPUR:	45 feet
GROUP RATE:	Varies	MAX STAY:	14 days
# of GROUP SITES:	4	ELEVATION:	2500 feet

 Campground has hosts   **Reservable sites**   **Accessible facilities**   **Fully developed**   **Semi-developed**   **Rustic facilities**

NOTE: Open dates listed are typical. Actual dates are dependent on conditions such as snow pack.

SEQUOIA NATIONAL FOREST • CALIFORNIA • 51 — 59

SHASTA-TRINITY NATIONAL FOREST

The Shasta-Trinity is home to picturesque Mt. Shasta and the Trinity Alps, as well as Shasta Lake and Clair Engle Lake. At Shasta Lake you'll find Shasta Dam, the second largest dam in the United States. The dam contains enough concrete to build a sidewalk three feet wide and four inches thick around the world.

Developed recreation facilities such as campgrounds, picnic areas, wildlife viewing areas, trails, boat ramps, and resorts and marinas can all be found in the Shasta-Trinity Forest. More than 105 miles of rivers within the forests are designated wild and scenic. These rivers are preserved in a free flowing condition to maintain water quality and protect the rivers' environments.

The forests also contain five wilderness areas for the experienced trekker who wishes to escape to more remote and undisturbed areas. Another point of interest is the Trinity Scenic Byway which follows State Highway 299W between Old Shasta and Blue Lake. Throughout the ages, the route has seen travelers of all kinds, from Indians, miners, and pack trains, to kayakers and logging trucks.

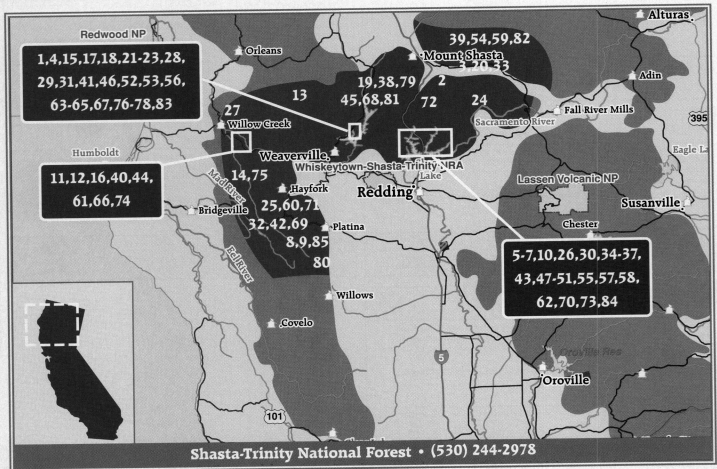

Shasta-Trinity National Forest • (530) 244-2978

1 Ackerman
Lewiston • lat 40°47'09" lon 122°46'14"

DESCRIPTION: Set in scattered oak, walnut, and pine on Lewiston Lake. Hot summers, cool winters. Excellent fly fishing on nearby Trinity River. Supplies at South Pine Cove Marina. Deer, foxes, coyotes, eagles, and small wildlife in area. Busy in spring and fall. Gather firewood. Hiking curls in area.

GETTING THERE: Ackerman CG is located approx. 8 mi. N of Lewiston on county route 105.

SINGLE RATE:	Varies	OPEN DATES:	Yearlong
# of SINGLE SITES:	66	MAX SPUR:	40 feet
		MAX STAY:	14 days
		ELEVATION:	2000 feet

2 AH-DI-NA
McCloud • lat 41°06'36" lon 122°05'50"

DESCRIPTION: In a dense forest setting on the lower McCloud River. Fish for rainbow and brook trout from the river. Historic trail just off of the CG. Supplies at McCloud. Deer, bears, turkeys and squirrels are common in the area. The Pacific Crest Trail is 1.5 mi. from the CG.

GETTING THERE: From McCloud go S on primary forest route 11 approx. 10.5 mi. to forest route 38N53. Go S on 38N53 approx. 3.5 mi. to AH-DI-NA CG.

SINGLE RATE:	$8	OPEN DATES:	May-Nov
# of SINGLE SITES:	16	MAX SPUR:	17 feet
		MAX STAY:	14 days
		ELEVATION:	2300 feet

3 Algoma
McCloud • lat 41°15'24" lon 121°52'56"

DESCRIPTION: In a dense forest setting on the upper McCloud River. Fish for rainbow and brook trout in the river. Supplies at McCloud. Deer, bears, turkeys and squirrels are common in the area. A trail starts at the CG and runs approx. 14 mi. to Lower Falls.

GETTING THERE: From McCloud go E on state HWY 89 approx. 13.5 mi. to forest route 39N06. Go S on 39N06 approx. 1/2 mi. to Algoma CG.

SINGLE RATE:	No fee	OPEN DATES:	May-Oct
# of SINGLE SITES:	8	MAX STAY:	14 days
		ELEVATION:	3800 feet

4 Alpine View
Trinity Center • lat 40°53'14" lon 122°45'57"

DESCRIPTION: In an open park-like setting with well developed trails and campsites for children, elderly and handicapped. Close to Trinity Lake where there is good fishing and swimming. Bowerman boat ramp is nearby. Bowerman Barn, an historic landmark is close to CG. Supplies at Trinity Center.

GETTING THERE: From Trinity Center go S on state HWY 3 approx. 7 mi. to county route 160. Go S on 160 approx. 3 mi. to Alpine View CG.

SINGLE RATE:	$12	OPEN DATES:	May-Sept
# of SINGLE SITES:	66	MAX SPUR:	32 feet
		MAX STAY:	14 days
		ELEVATION:	2400 feet

5 Antlers
Redding • lat 40°53'15" lon 122°22'39"

DESCRIPTION: CG is in a dense forest of pines and manzanita on the Sacramento arm of Lake Shasta. Fishing in lake. Supplies at the nearby marina resort. Deer and small wildlife in area. Campers may gather firewood. Trails in the area. The nearest public boat ramp is located adjacent to the CG.

GETTING THERE: Antlers CG is located approx. 23 mi. N of Redding on I-5.

SINGLE RATE:	$15	OPEN DATES:	Yearlong
# of SINGLE SITES:	41	MAX SPUR:	30 feet
GROUP RATE:	$25	MAX STAY:	14 days
# of GROUP SITES:	18	ELEVATION:	1100 feet

6 Arbuckle Flat
Redding • lat 40°45'54" lon 122°07'10"

DESCRIPTION: This CG is situated in a dense forest on the shores of Shasta Lake. Fish for bass and trout in the lake. Check for local regulations. Supplies at Redding. Deer, bears, osprey, and bald eagles are common to the area. Gather firewood locally. No designated trails in the area. No drinking water.

GETTING THERE: Arbuckle Flat CG is located on the Pit River Arm of Shasta Lake and is accessible by boat only.

SINGLE RATE:	No fee	OPEN DATES:	Yearlong
		MAX STAY:	14 days
		ELEVATION:	1085 feet

7 Bailey Cove
Redding • lat 40°48'06" lon 122°16'55"

DESCRIPTION: CG is on a forested knoll overlooking water in the O'Brien Area on the McCloud arm of Shasta Lake. Bailey Cove boat ramp is located adjacent to CG. Fishing on the lake. Supplies are 5 mi. N of CG. Abundant wildlife and osprey nests are nearby and in easy view. A 3 mi. hiking trail along the shoreline.

GETTING THERE: From Redding go N on I-5 approximately 16 mi. to Bailey Cove/Holiday Harbor Resort exit. Follow road E to Bailey Cove CG.

SINGLE RATE:	$15	OPEN DATES:	Yearlong
# of SINGLE SITES:	5	MAX SPUR:	30 feet
GROUP RATE:	$25	MAX STAY:	14 days
# of GROUP SITES:	2	ELEVATION:	1085 feet

8 Basin Gulch
Beegum • lat 40°21'13" lon 122°57'36"

DESCRIPTION: In an open stand of pine, fir and oak on Cottonwood Creek. Fish for trout and swim in the creek. Supplies available at Beegum. Campers may gather firewood. Deer, bears and birds are common to the area. An historical CCC camp is nearby. Take bears precautions. No water.

GETTING THERE: From Beegum go W on state HWY 36 approx. 8 mi. to forest route 28N10. Go S on 28N10 approx. 1 mi. to Basin Gulch CG.

SINGLE RATE:	No fee	OPEN DATES:	May-Oct
# of SINGLE SITES:	13	MAX SPUR:	20 feet
		MAX STAY:	14 days
		ELEVATION:	2700 feet

9 Beegum Gorge
Beegum • lat 40°18'50" lon 122°56'00"

DESCRIPTION: This CG is primarily in an oak stand with thick underbrush on Beegum Creek. Fish for trout and swim in the creek. Supplies available at Beegum. Deer, bears and birds are common to the area. Campers may gather firewood. Trails are in the area of the CG. No water. 4WD recommended.

GETTING THERE: From Beegum go W on state HWY 36 approx. 3.5 mi. to forest route 29N06. Go S on 29N06 approx. 6 mi. to Beegum Gorge CG. Not recommended for trailers.

SINGLE RATE:	No fee	OPEN DATES:	May-Oct
# of SINGLE SITES:	2	MAX STAY:	14 days
		ELEVATION:	2200 feet

10 Beehive Beach
Lakehead • lat 40°50'00" lon 122°23'00"

DESCRIPTION: On the shoreline below oaks and manzanita with beautiful views of Shasta Lake. Fish for bass and trout on the lake. Supplies approx. 4 mi. from CG. Deer and osprey are common to the area. Campers may gather firewood. Several trails are located nearby.

GETTING THERE: From Lakehead go S on Lakeshore Drive approximately 4 miles to Beehive Beach CG.

SINGLE RATE:	$6	OPEN DATES:	May-Sept
		MAX SPUR:	30 feet
		MAX STAY:	14 days
		ELEVATION:	1100 feet

 Campground has hosts 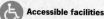 **Reservable sites**   **Accessible facilities**   **Fully developed** **Semi-developed** **Rustic facilities**

NOTE: Open dates listed are typical. Actual dates are dependent on conditions such as snow pack.

11 Big Bar
Weaverville • lat 40˚44'23" lon 123˚14'37"

DESCRIPTION: In an open fir forest setting with Price Creek next to CG. Fish for trout from neaby Trinity River. Supplies at Weaverville. Deer, foxes, bears, coyotes, mountain lion and squirrels can be found around CG area. Campers may gather firewood. No designated trails in the area.

GETTING THERE: From Weaverville go E on state HWY 299 approx. 20 mi. to Big Bar CG.

SINGLE RATE:	No fee	OPEN DATES:	Yearlong
# of SINGLE SITES:	3		
		MAX STAY:	14 days
		ELEVATION:	1250 feet

12 Big Flat
Weaverville • lat 40˚44'22" lon 123˚12'17"

DESCRIPTION: In an open fir forest setting with Price Creek next to CG. Fish for trout from neaby Trinity River. Supplies at Weaverville. Deer, foxes, bears, coyotes, mountain lion and squirrels can be found around CG area. Campers may gather firewood. No designated trails in the area.

GETTING THERE: Big Flat CG is located approx. 17 mi. E of Weaverville on state HWY 299.

SINGLE RATE:	$8	OPEN DATES:	Yearlong
# of SINGLE SITES:	10	MAX SPUR:	25 feet
		MAX STAY:	14 days
		ELEVATION:	1300 feet

13 Big Flat
Coffee Creek • lat 41˚04'05" lon 122˚56'01"

DESCRIPTION: In a dense ponderosa and sugar pine forest setting. Deer, snakes, bears, mountain lion and birds. Supplies at Coffee Creek. Big Flat Trailhead begins at CG and goes to Caribou Lake. No water.

GETTING THERE: From Coffee Creek go W on county route 104 approx. 18 mi. to Big Flat CG.

SINGLE RATE:	No fee	OPEN DATES:	Yearlong
# of SINGLE SITES:	5	MAX SPUR:	16 feet
		MAX STAY:	14 days
		ELEVATION:	5000 feet

14 Big Slide
Hyampom • lat 40˚39'50" lon 123˚29'41"

DESCRIPTION: This rustic CG is in an open pine, fir and oak forest setting. The South Fork Trinity River runs next to the CG. Supplies are available at Hyampom. Campers may gather firewood. Deer, bears and birds are common in the area. Trails in the area. No water.

GETTING THERE: Big Slide CG is located approx. 3 mi. N of Hyampom on county route 311.

SINGLE RATE:	No fee	OPEN DATES:	May-Oct
# of SINGLE SITES:	8	MAX SPUR:	16 feet
		MAX STAY:	14 days
		ELEVATION:	1250 feet

15 Bridge Camp
Weaverville • lat 40˚52'30" lon 122˚54'00"

DESCRIPTION: In a tall fir forest setting situated on the Stuart's Fork of the Trinity River. Fishing on the river. CG lies at the trailhead leading to the Shasta-Trinity WIlderness area. Many hiking trails in the area. Horse corral at end of CG. Gold panning in area. Supplies at Weaverville.

GETTING THERE: From Weaverville go NE on state HWY 3 approx. 14 mi. to county route 112. Go NW on 112 approx. 1.5 mi. to forest route 35N33Y. Continue NW on 35N33Y approx. 2 mi. to Bridge Camp CG.

SINGLE RATE:	$8	OPEN DATES:	Yearlong
# of SINGLE SITES:	11	MAX SPUR:	12 feet
		MAX STAY:	14 days
		ELEVATION:	2700 feet

16 Burnt Ranch
Weaverville • lat 40˚49'40" lon 123˚28'51"

DESCRIPTION: In an open fir forest setting with Price Creek next to CG. Fish for trout from neaby Trinity River. Supplies at Weaverville. Deer, foxes, bears, coyotes, mountain lion and squirrels can be found around CG area. Campers may gather firewood. Trail from CG leading to the river approx. 1.5 mi. away.

GETTING THERE: Burnt Ranch is located approx. 36 mi. W of Weaverville on state HWY 299.

SINGLE RATE:	$8	OPEN DATES:	Yearlong
# of SINGLE SITES:	16	MAX SPUR:	25 feet
		MAX STAY:	14 days
		ELEVATION:	1000 feet

17 Bushytail Group
Weaverville • lat 40˚51'15" lon 122˚49'00"

DESCRIPTION: This CG is situated in a mixed forest setting about 1/4 mi. off of Trinity Lake. Fish in the lake. Boat ramps are nearby. Bushytail is ideal for groups with a desire to go boating, but don't want to be lakeside. Supplies and groceries can be found in Weaverville. Many trails in the area.

GETTING THERE: From Weaverville go NE on state HWY 3 approx. 17 mi. to Bushytail Group CG.

		OPEN DATES:	May-Sept
		MAX SPUR:	40 feet
GROUP RATE:	$60	MAX STAY:	14 days
# of GROUP SITES:	1	ELEVATION:	2600 feet

18 Captains Point
Weaverville • lat 40˚51'47" lon 122˚43'28"

DESCRIPTION: In a heavily forested setting of pines, cedar and douglas fir. Fish for trout and bass from lake. Deer, bears and birds are common in the area. No designated trails in the area.

GETTING THERE: Captains Point CG is located on the W shore of Clair Engle Lake and is accessible by boat only.

SINGLE RATE:	No fee	OPEN DATES:	Yearlong
# of SINGLE SITES:	3		
		MAX STAY:	14 days
		ELEVATION:	2400 feet

19 Castle Lake
Mount Shasta • lat 41˚14'07" lon 122˚22'44"

DESCRIPTION: In a mixed forest setting with views of Mt. Shasta. Fish for rainbow and brook trout at Castle Lake just up the road. Supplies available at Mount Shasta. Deer, bears, skunk and squirrels are common in the area. Trails to other lakes and the Castle Crag Wilderness in area.

GETTING THERE: From Mount Shasta go SW on county route 2M020 approx. 7 mi. to Castle Lake CG.

SINGLE RATE:	No fee	OPEN DATES:	May-Oct*
# of SINGLE SITES:	8	MAX SPUR:	16 feet
		MAX STAY:	14 days
		ELEVATION:	5280 feet

20 Cattle Camp
McCloud • lat 41˚16'30" lon 121˚55'30"

DESCRIPTION: In a dense forest setting on the upper McCloud River. Fish for rainbow and brook trout in the river. Supplies at McCloud. Deer, bears and squirrels are common in the area. A trail starts at the CG and runs approx. 14 mi. to Lower Falls.

GETTING THERE: From McCloud go E on state HWY 89 approx. 10 mi. to Cattle Camp CG.

SINGLE RATE:	No fee	OPEN DATES:	May-Oct
# of SINGLE SITES:	25		
		MAX STAY:	14 days
		ELEVATION:	3700 feet

 Campground has hosts   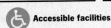 **Reservable sites**   **Accessible facilities**   **Fully developed**   **Semi-developed**   **Rustic facilities**

21 Clark Springs
Weaverville • lat 40°51'24" lon 122°48'46"

DESCRIPTION: A unique CG in a mixed forest setting on Trinity Lake. This CG is smaller and less developed than most in area. A set of springs run through the CG. Fishing at the lake. Supplies available at Weaverville. A boat ramp and a swimming beach just below the CG.

GETTING THERE: From Weaverville via state HWY 299W and HWY 3, CG is located on Trinity Lake.

SINGLE RATE:	$20	OPEN DATES:	May-Sept
# of SINGLE SITES:	8	MAX SPUR:	20 feet
		MAX STAY:	14 days
		ELEVATION:	2400 feet

22 Clear Creek
Coffee Creek • lat 40°55'57" lon 122°35'08"

DESCRIPTION: In a heavily forested setting of pines, cedar and douglas fir. Fish for small fish from the creek running by CG. Supplies at Coffee Creek. Deer, bears and birds are common in the area. No designated trails in the area. No water.

GETTING THERE: From Coffee Creek go S on state HWY 3 approx. 2.5 mi. to county route 106. Go S on 106 approx. 12 mi. to forest route 8G012. Go E on 8G012 approx. 2 mi. to Clear Creek CG.

SINGLE RATE:	No fee	OPEN DATES:	Yearlong
# of SINGLE SITES:	22	MAX SPUR:	22 feet
		MAX STAY:	14 days
		ELEVATION:	3400 feet

23 Cooper Gulch
Lewiston • lat 40°44'45" lon 122°48'21"

DESCRIPTION: In an oak, walnut and pine forest setting on the lake. Fish in Trinity Lake. Boat launch and supplies at Pinecove Marina. Visit the fish hatchery below Lewiston Dam. This campground will accommodate motor homes and trailers.

GETTING THERE: Cooper Gulch CG is located approx. 3 mi. N of Lewiston on county route 105.

SINGLE RATE:	$10	OPEN DATES:	Apr-Oct
# of SINGLE SITES:	5	MAX SPUR:	16 feet
		MAX STAY:	14 days
		ELEVATION:	2000 feet

24 Deadlun
Redding • lat 41°03'41" lon 121°58'27"

DESCRIPTION: In a dense forest setting on Iron Canyon Reservoir. Fishing for bass and trout in the reservoir. Supplies at Redding. Deer, bears, osprey and bald eagles are common in the area. Campers may gather firewood. No designated trails in the area. No water.

GETTING THERE: From Redding go NE on state HWY 299 approximately 30 mi. to county route 7M01. Go N on 7M01 approximately 22 mi. to Deadlun CG.

SINGLE RATE:	No fee	OPEN DATES:	Yearlong
# of SINGLE SITES:		MAX STAY:	14 days
		ELEVATION:	2680 feet

25 Deerlick Springs
Beegum • lat 40°27'00" lon 122°54'00"

DESCRIPTION: A primitive CG in a dense pine and fir forest setting on Browns Creek. Fish for trout in the creek. Deer, bears and birds are common to the area. Campers may gather firewood. The Chanchalulla Wilderness trail is accessible from the CG. Take bears precautions. No water.

GETTING THERE: From Beegum go W on state HWY 36 approx. 12 mi. to primary forest route 1. Go NE on 1 approx. 10 mi. to Deerlick Springs CG.

SINGLE RATE:	No fee	OPEN DATES:	May-Oct
# of SINGLE SITES:	10		
		MAX STAY:	14 days
		ELEVATION:	3100 feet

26 Dekkas Rock Group
Redding • lat 40°52'26" lon 122°14'07"

DESCRIPTION: In a variety of oak and pine with views of the lake. Fish for bass and trout from shoreline. Historical Samwell Caves nearby. Supplies approx. 20 mi. from CG. Deer, bears, osprey and bald eagles can be seen in the area. Campers may gather firewood. Hirz Bay Hiking Trail is nearby.

GETTING THERE: From Redding go N on I-5 approx. 19 mi. to county route 7H009. Go E on 7H009 approximately 9 mi. to Dekkas Rock Group CG.

GROUP RATE:	$90	OPEN DATES:	Apr-Oct
# of GROUP SITES:	1	MAX SPUR:	20 feet
		MAX STAY:	14 days
		ELEVATION:	1085 feet

27 Denny
Denny • lat 40°55'59" lon 123°23'36"

DESCRIPTION: In an open fir forest setting on the New River. Catch and release fishing only on the river. Supplies at Dailey. Deer, foxes, bears, coyotes, mountain lion and squirrels can be found around CG area. Campers may gather firewood. No designated trails in the area.

GETTING THERE: Denny CG is located approx. 1/2 mi. SW of Denny on county route 402.

SINGLE RATE:	No fee	OPEN DATES:	Yearlong
# of SINGLE SITES:	16	MAX SPUR:	22 feet
		MAX STAY:	14 days
		ELEVATION:	1400 feet

28 Eagles Creek
Coffee Creek • lat 41°09'07" lon 122°40'08"

DESCRIPTION: CG sits between Eagles Creek and the Trinity River. Excellent stream fishing, or travel a short distance to Trinity Lake for trout and bass fishing. Supplies at Coffee Creek. Deer, bears and birds are common to the area. Campers may gather firewood. Trails in the area.

GETTING THERE: From Coffee Creek go N on state HWY 3 approx. 2.5 mi. to county route 140. Go N on 140 approx. 4 mi. to Eagles Creek CG.

SINGLE RATE:	$8	OPEN DATES:	May-Oct
# of SINGLE SITES:	3	MAX SPUR:	30 feet
		MAX STAY:	14 days
		ELEVATION:	2800 feet

29 East Weaver
Weaverville • lat 40°46'23" lon 122°55'15"

DESCRIPTION: A rustic CG in a densly forest setting on the East Weaver Creek. Fish for trout from the creek. Supplies at Weaverville. Joss House State Historic park located at Weaverville. Many hiking trails in the area.

GETTING THERE: From Weaverville go approx. 2 mi. on state HWY 3 to county route 228. Go N on 228 approx. 1.5 mi. to forest route 34N34. Go NW on 34N34 approx. .5 mi. to East Weaver CG.

SINGLE RATE:	$8	OPEN DATES:	Yearlong
# of SINGLE SITES:	11	MAX SPUR:	16 feet
		MAX STAY:	14 days
		ELEVATION:	2700 feet

30 Ellery Creek
Redding • lat 40°54'57" lon 122°14'27"

DESCRIPTION: In a mixture of oak and pine with berry bushes. CG has great views of Shasta Lake with shoreline fishing for trout and bass. Historical Samwell Caves nearby. Supplies at Redding. Deer, bears, osprey and bald eagles can be seen in the CG area. Campers may gather firewood.

GETTING THERE: From Redding go N on I-5 approximately 19 mi. to county route 7H009. Go E on 7H009 approximately 12.5 mi. to Ellery Creek CG.

SINGLE RATE:	$12	OPEN DATES:	May-Sept
# of SINGLE SITES:	19	MAX SPUR:	30 feet
		MAX STAY:	14 days
		ELEVATION:	1085 feet

 Campground has hosts   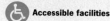 **Reservable sites**   **Accessible facilities**   **Fully developed**   **Semi-developed**   **Rustic facilities**

NOTE: Open dates listed are typical. Actual dates are dependent on conditions such as snow pack.

31 Fawn Group

Weaverville • lat 40°50'40" lon 122°50'30"

DESCRIPTION: Located in an oak, walnut and pine forest setting on the Stuart's Fork arm of Trinity Lake. Fishing and water sports on the lake. Supplies at Weaverville. All sites have room for a tent and have tables and firepits. Many hiking trails in the area.

GETTING THERE: Fawn Group CG is located approx. 12 mi. NW of Weaverville on state HWY 3.

		OPEN DATES:	May-Sept
		MAX SPUR:	40 feet
GROUP RATE:	$60	MAX STAY:	14 days
# of GROUP SITES:	3	ELEVATION:	2500 feet

32 Forest Glen

Hayfork • lat 40°22'35" lon 123°19'35"

DESCRIPTION: In an open stand of pine, fir and oak with views of the South Fork Trinity River. Fish and swim in the river. Supplies available at Hayfork. Campers may gather firewood. The South Fork National Recreation Trail is in the area.

GETTING THERE: From Hayfork go S on state HWY 3 approx. 9 mi. to state HWY 36. Go SW on 36 approx. 19 mi. to Forest Glen CG.

		OPEN DATES:	May-Oct
SINGLE RATE:	$4	MAX SPUR:	16 feet
# of SINGLE SITES:	15	MAX STAY:	14 days
		ELEVATION:	2300 feet

33 Fowlers Camp

McCloud • lat 41°14'44" lon 122°01'19"

DESCRIPTION: In a mixed forest setting on the McCloud River. Fish for rainbow and brook trout in the river. Supplies at McCloud. Deer, bears, turkeys and squirrels are common in the area. A trail starts at the CG and runs approx. 14 mi. to Lower Falls. Trails go up and down river to falls either direction.

GETTING THERE: From McCloud go E on state HWY 89 approx. 5.5 mi. to forest route 40N44. Go S on 40N44 approx. 1 mi. to Fowlers Camp CG.

		OPEN DATES:	May-Oct
SINGLE RATE:	$12	MAX SPUR:	26 feet
# of SINGLE SITES:	39	MAX STAY:	14 days
		ELEVATION:	3400 feet

34 Gooseneck Cove
Lakehead • lat 40°49'34" lon 122°25'23"

DESCRIPTION: In a dense forest setting on Shasta Lake. Fish for bass and trout in the lake. Supplies at Lakehead. Deer, bears, osprey and bald eagles are common in the area. Campers may gather firewood. No designated trails in the area. No water

GETTING THERE: Gooseneck Cove CG is located on the Sacramento River Arm of Shasta Lake and is accessible by boat only.

		OPEN DATES:	Yearlong
SINGLE RATE:	No fee		
		MAX STAY:	14 days
		ELEVATION:	1050 feet

35 Greens Creek
Redding • lat 40°49'34" lon 122°15'18"

DESCRIPTION: In a dense forest setting on the Shasta Lake. Fish for bass and trout in the lake. Supplies at Redding. Deer, bears, osprey and bald eagles are common in the area. Campers may gather firewood. No designated trails in the area. No water.

GETTING THERE: Greens Creek CG is located on the McCloud River Arm of Shasta Lake and is accessible by boat only.

		OPEN DATES:	Yearlong
SINGLE RATE:	No fee		
# of SINGLE SITES:	11		
		MAX STAY:	14 days
		ELEVATION:	1085 feet

36 Gregory Beach

Redding • lat 40°53'07" lon 122°22'07"

DESCRIPTION: Dispersed CG is located on shoreline below oaks and manzanita with views of Shasta Lake. Fish for bass and trout from the shore. Supplies approx. 4 mi. from CG. Deer and osprey are common in the area. Campers may gather firewood.

GETTING THERE: Gregory Beach CG is located approx. 21 mi. N of Redding off of I-5.

		OPEN DATES:	Yearlong
SINGLE RATE:	$6	MAX SPUR:	30 feet
		MAX STAY:	14 days
		ELEVATION:	1067 feet

37 Gregory Creek
Redding • lat 40°53'15" lon 122°22'03"

DESCRIPTION: In mostly an oak and manzanita forest setting with views of Shasta Lake. Fish from the shore for bass and trout. Supplies about 7 mi. from CG. Deer and osprey are common to the area. Early summer is the best time to visit CG. Campers may gather firewood.

GETTING THERE: Gregory Creek CG is located approx. 21 mi. N of Redding off of I-5.

		OPEN DATES:	May-Sept
SINGLE RATE:	$12	MAX SPUR:	20 feet
# of SINGLE SITES:	18	MAX STAY:	14 days
		ELEVATION:	1085 feet

38 Gumboot
Mount Shasta • lat 41°12'42" lon 122°30'33"

DESCRIPTION: In a mixed forest setting on Gumboot Lake with views of Mt. Shasta. Fish for trout in the lake. Supplies available at Mount Shasta. Deer, skunk, squirrels and birds are common in the area. Campers may gather firewood. An equestrian trail to the Pacific Crest Trail from the CG.

GETTING THERE: From Mount Shasta go SW on county route 2M020 approx. 2 mi. to forest route 26. Go W on 26 approx. 13 mi. to Gumboot CG.

		OPEN DATES:	May-Oct
SINGLE RATE:	No fee		
# of SINGLE SITES:	10		
		MAX STAY:	14 days
		ELEVATION:	6080 feet

39 Harris Springs
McCloud • lat 41°27'00" lon 121°47'30"

DESCRIPTION: In a high elevation, white fir, white and lodgepole pine setting. Supplies at McCloud. Deer, bears and birds are common in the area. Campers may gather firewood. Many trails in the area.

GETTING THERE: From McCloud go E on state HWY 89 approx. 2 mi. to primary forest route 13. Go NE on 13 approx. 19.5 mi. to forest route 43N15. Go N on 43N15 approx. 1.5 mi. to Harris Springs CG.

		OPEN DATES:	Aug-Oct
SINGLE RATE:	No fee	MAX SPUR:	32 feet
# of SINGLE SITES:	15	MAX STAY:	14 days
		ELEVATION:	4800 feet

40 Hayden Flat

Trinity Village • lat 40°47'03" lon 123°20'32"

DESCRIPTION: In an open fir forest setting with Price Creek next to CG. Fish for trout in nearby Trinity River. Supplies at Trinity Village. Deer, foxes, bears, coyotes, mountain lion and squirrels can be found around CG area. Campers may gather firewood. No designated trails in the area.

GETTING THERE: Hayden Flat CG is located approx. 14 mi. SE of Trinity Village on state HWY 299.

		OPEN DATES:	Yearlong
SINGLE RATE:	Varies	MAX SPUR:	30 feet
# of SINGLE SITES:	35	MAX STAY:	14 days
		ELEVATION:	1200 feet

 Campground has hosts   🔒 **Reservable sites**   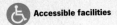 **Accessible facilities**   **Fully developed**    **Semi-developed**   **Rustic facilities**

NOTE: Open dates listed are typical. Actual dates are dependent on conditions such as snow pack.

Page 132

41 Hayward Flat
Weaverville • lat 40°52'25" lon 122°46'03"

DESCRIPTION: This CG is one of the most popular on the lake in a dense stand of pines. Fish for trout on the lake. Supplies at Weaverville. Hayward Flat is the favorite among the watersports crowd at Trinity. Many hiking trails in the area. CG hosts the weekly Jr. Ranger programsand amphitheatre presentations.

GETTING THERE: From Weaverville go approx. 16 mi. on state HWY 3 to forest route 35N26Y. Go SE on 35N26Y approx. 2 mi. to Hayward Flat CG.

SINGLE RATE:	Varies	OPEN DATES:	May-Sept
# of SINGLE SITES:	98	MAX SPUR:	40 feet
		MAX STAY:	14 days
		ELEVATION:	2400 feet

42 Hell Gate
Hayfork • lat 40°22'13" lon 123°18'50"

DESCRIPTION: In an open pine, fir and oak forest setting on the South Fork Trinity River. Fish and swim in the river. Deer, bears and birds are common in the area. Supplies are available at Hayfork. Campers may gather firewood. The South Fork National Recreation Trail is close by the CG.

GETTING THERE: From Hayfork go S on state HWY 3 approx. 9 mi. to state HWY 36. Go SW on 36 approx. 18 mi. to Hell Gate CG.

SINGLE RATE:	Varies	OPEN DATES:	May-Oct
# of SINGLE SITES:	15	MAX SPUR:	16 feet
		MAX STAY:	14 days
		ELEVATION:	2300 feet

43 Hirz Bay
Lakehead • lat 40°52'00" lon 122°15'11"

DESCRIPTION: The campground is well forested mix of oak and pines sitting on the McCloud Arm of Shasta Lake. Fish for bass and trout from the lake. Supplies at Lakehead. Deer, bears, bald eagles and osprey are common in the area. Campers may gather firewood. Hirz Bay Trail is nearby.

GETTING THERE: From Lakehead go S on I-5 approx. 4.5 mi. to county route 7H009. Go W on 7H009 approx. 8 mi. to Hirz Bay CG.

SINGLE RATE:	Varies	OPEN DATES:	Apr-Oct
# of SINGLE SITES:	48	MAX SPUR:	30 feet
		MAX STAY:	14 days
		ELEVATION:	1100 feet

44 Hobo Gulch
Junction City • lat 40°55'32" lon 123°09'10"

DESCRIPTION: In a dense fir and pine forest setting with a small creek running through the CG. Supplies at Junction City. Deer, bears, coyotes, foxes, mountain lion and squirrels can be found in the CG area. Campers may gather firewood. Hobo Gulch trailhead starts at CG. No piped water.

GETTING THERE: From Junction City go W on state HWY 299 approx. 2 mi. to county route 421. Go N on 421 approx. 15 mi. to Hobo Gulch CG.

SINGLE RATE:	No fee	OPEN DATES:	Yearlong
# of SINGLE SITES:	10	MAX SPUR:	16 feet
		MAX STAY:	14 days
		ELEVATION:	3000 feet

45 Horse Flat
Stewart Springs • lat 41°09'59" lon 122°41'29"

DESCRIPTION: Dispersed CG in a heavily forested setting of pines, cedar and douglas fir. CG is near Eagles Creek and close to the North Fork of the Trinity River. Fish for trout and bass from the river. Supplies at Stewart Springs. Deer, bears and birds are common in the area. Trails in the area. No water. Horse corral in CG.

GETTING THERE: From Stewart Springs go S on primary forest route 17 18 mi. to state HWY 3. Go S on 3 6 mi. to county route 140. Go N on 140 1 mi. to the Eagles Creek CG turnoff and continue NW 1.5 mi. to Horse Flat CG.

SINGLE RATE:	No fee	OPEN DATES:	May-Oct
# of SINGLE SITES:	16	MAX SPUR:	16 feet
		MAX STAY:	14 days
		ELEVATION:	3200 feet

46 Jackass Springs
Trinity Center • lat 40°57'42" lon 122°38'39"

DESCRIPTION: In a heavily forested setting of pines, cedar and douglas fir. CG is .25 mi. from Trinity Lake. Fish for trout and bass in lake. Supplies at Trinity Center. Deer, bears and birds are common in the area. No designated trails in the area. Hike on the old logging roads in the area. No water.

GETTING THERE: From Trinity Center go N on state HWY 3 approx. 5.8 mi. to county route 106. Go SE on 106 approx. 12.9 mi. to county route 119. Go W on 119 approx. 4.5 mi. to Jackass Springs CG.

SINGLE RATE:	No fee	OPEN DATES:	Yearlong
# of SINGLE SITES:	21	MAX SPUR:	32 feet
		MAX STAY:	14 days
		ELEVATION:	2600 feet

47 Jones Inlet
Redding • lat 40°43'46" lon 122°13'49"

DESCRIPTION: Dispersed CG located on the shoreline below oaks and pines with views of Shasta Lake. Fish for bass, trout and catfish in lake. Supplies nearby. Deer and osprey are common to the area. Early summer visit are best. Campers may gather firewood. Several nice trails are located in the area.

GETTING THERE: From Redding go N on I-5 approx. 2.5 mi. to county route 3H02. Go NE on 3H02 approx. 3.5 mi. to county route 5H02. Go NE on 5H02 approx. 8 mi. to Jones Inlet CG.

SINGLE RATE:	$6	OPEN DATES:	Mar-Oct
		MAX SPUR:	30 feet
		MAX STAY:	14 days
		ELEVATION:	1067 feet

48 Lakeshore East
Lakehead • lat 40°52'34" lon 122°23'17"

DESCRIPTION: In a well forested setting on the edge of the Sacramento Arm of Shasta Lake. Fish for trout in the lake. Supplies available at Lakehead. There is abundant wildlife in the area. Campers may gather firewood. Trails in the area.

GETTING THERE: Lakeshore East CG is located approx. 2.5 mi. S of Lakehead off of I-5.

SINGLE RATE:	$15	OPEN DATES:	Apr-Oct
# of SINGLE SITES:	20	MAX SPUR:	30 feet
GROUP RATE:	$25	MAX STAY:	14 days
# of GROUP SITES:	6	ELEVATION:	1100 feet

49 Lower Jones Valley
Redding • lat 40°43'39" lon 122°13'41"

DESCRIPTION: CG is located in oaks with some underbrush. Campsites have great views of Shasta Lake. Fish for bass and trout. Supplies about 1 mi. from the CG. Deer and osprey are common to the area. Late spring and early summer are best times to visit CG. Gather firewood. Several nice trails near CG.

GETTING THERE: From Redding go N on I-5 approx. 2.5 mi. to county route 3H02. Go NE on 3H02 approx. 3.5 mi. to county route 5H02. Go NE on 5H02 approx. 8 mi. to Lower Jones Valley CG.

SINGLE RATE:	$15	OPEN DATES:	Yearlong
# of SINGLE SITES:	11	MAX SPUR:	30 feet
GROUP RATE:	$25	MAX STAY:	14 days
# of GROUP SITES:	3	ELEVATION:	1085 feet

50 Madrone
Redding • lat 40°55'28" lon 122°05'39"

DESCRIPTION: In a dense forest setting with Squaw Creek running through the CG. Fish for trout in the creek. Supplies at Redding. Deer, bears, osprey and bald eagles are common in the area. Campers may gather firewood. No designated trails in the area. No water.

GETTING THERE: From Redding go NE on state HWY 299 25 mi. to forest route 34N17. Go NW on 34N17 5.5 mi. to forest route 27. NW on 27 10 mi. to forest route 35N07. Go N on 35N07 1/2 mi. to Madrone CG.

SINGLE RATE:	No fee	OPEN DATES:	Yearlong
# of SINGLE SITES:	10	MAX SPUR:	16 feet
		MAX STAY:	14 days
		ELEVATION:	1500 feet

 Campground has hosts   **Reservable sites**   **Accessible facilities**   **Fully developed**   **Semi-developed** **Rustic facilities**

NOTE: Open dates listed are typical. Actual dates are dependent on conditions such as snow pack.

51 Mariners Point
Redding • lat 40˚45'11" lon 122˚15'04"

DESCRIPTION: In a mixture of oaks and pines with nice views of the lake. Fish for bass and trout on the lake. Supplies at Redding. Deer, osprey and bald eagles common in the area. This is a Bald Eagles nesting area. Campers may gather firewood. Several trails are located within 5 mi. of CG.

GETTING THERE: From Redding go NE on I-5 approx. 6.5 mi. to county route 4J02. Go N on 4J02 approx. 10.5 mi. to Mariners Point CG.

SINGLE RATE:	$8	OPEN DATES:	Aug-Jan
		MAX SPUR:	20 feet
		MAX STAY:	14 days
		ELEVATION:	1085 feet

56 Minersville
Weaverville • lat 40˚50'56" lon 122˚48'38"

DESCRIPTION: In a mixed forest setting on the Stuart's Fork of Trinity Lake. One of the more popular CG's on the lake. Fish from the lake. Minersville is one of the few places to launch when water levels drop. Excellent waterskiing is available just N of CG. Lake trail goes through CG is an enjoyable hike.

GETTING THERE: From Weaverville go NE on state HWY 3 approx. 16.9 mi. to forest route 35N28. Go SE on 35N28 approx. .9 mi. to minersville CG.

SINGLE RATE:	Varies	OPEN DATES:	Apr-Oct
# of SINGLE SITES:	21	MAX SPUR:	18 feet
		MAX STAY:	14 days
		ELEVATION:	2600 feet

52 Mariners Roost
Weaverville • lat 40˚50'22" lon 122˚46'13"

DESCRIPTION: In a heavily forested setting of pines, cedar and douglas fir. Fish for trout and bass from Trinity Lake. Supplies at Weaverville. Deer, bears and birds are common in the area. No designated trails in the area.

GETTING THERE: From Weaverville go N on state HWY 3 approx. 13.3 mi. Travel by boat only 5.2 mi. E to Mariners Roost CG.

SINGLE RATE:	No fee	OPEN DATES:	Yearlong
# of SINGLE SITES:	7		
		MAX STAY:	14 days
		ELEVATION:	2400 feet

57 Moore Creek
Lakehead • lat 40˚53'20" lon 122˚13'25"

DESCRIPTION: In a mostly oak forest setting with views of the lake. Fish for bass and trout from the lake. Deer, bears, osprey and bald eagles are common in the area. Campers may gather firewood. No designated trails in the area.

GETTING THERE: From Lakehead go S on I-5 approx. 4.5 mi. to county route 7H009. Go NE on 7H009 approx. 10 mi. to Moore Creek CG.

SINGLE RATE:	$12	OPEN DATES:	May-Sept
# of SINGLE SITES:	12	MAX SPUR:	16 feet
GROUP RATE:	$90	MAX STAY:	14 days
# of GROUP SITES:	1	ELEVATION:	1085 feet

53 Mary Smith
Lewistown • lat 40˚43'54" lon 122˚48'27"

DESCRIPTION: In an open oak, walnut and pine forest setting on the water's edge of Lewiston Lake and is tent camping only. Fishing from the lake. Historic towns, Lewiston and Weaverville are nearby. Boat launch and supplies at Pinecove Marina. Just below Lewiston Dam is a fish hatchery.

GETTING THERE: From Lewistown go N on county route 105 approx. 2.1 mi. to forest route 33N79. Go N on 33N79 approx. .2 mi. to Mary Smith CG.

SINGLE RATE:	$9	OPEN DATES:	May-Oct
# of SINGLE SITES:	18		
		MAX STAY:	14 days
		ELEVATION:	2000 feet

58 Nelson Point
Lakeside • lat 40˚50'54" lon 122˚20'36"

DESCRIPTION: In a mixture of oaks and pines on the Sacramento Arm of Shasta Lake. Fish for bass and trout in the lake. Supplies are in Lakehead. Deer and osprey are common to this area. Campers may gather firewood. Many trails.

GETTING THERE: From Lakeside go S on I-5 approx. 4.5 mi. to Nelson Point CG.

SINGLE RATE:	$8	OPEN DATES:	Apr-Sept
# of SINGLE SITES:	8	MAX SPUR:	30 feet
GROUP RATE:	$65	MAX STAY:	14 days
# of GROUP SITES:	1	ELEVATION:	1085 feet

54 McBride Springs
Mount Shasta • lat 41˚21'10" lon 122˚17'00"

DESCRIPTION: In a white fir and cedar forest setting with views of Mt. Shasta. A small spring runs by CG. Supplies at Mount Shasta. Deer, bears and birds are common in the area. No designated trails in the area. Hikers and climbers use this CG primarily.

GETTING THERE: From Mount Shasta go NE on county route A10 approx. 5 mi. to McBride Springs CG.

SINGLE RATE:	$10	OPEN DATES:	May-Nov
# of SINGLE SITES:	11	MAX SPUR:	16 feet
		MAX STAY:	7 days
		ELEVATION:	4880 feet

59 Panther Meadows
Mount Shasta • lat 41˚21'13" lon 122˚12'06"

DESCRIPTION: In a mixed forest setting with views of Mt. Shasta and Panther Meadow. Panther Springs runs through the nearby meadow. Supplies at Mount Shasta. Deer, bears and birds are common in the area. Trails to Mt. Shasta Wilderness leave the CG. Used primarily by climbers and hikers.

GETTING THERE: From Mount Shasta go NE on county route A10 approx. 12 mi. to Panther Meadows CG.

SINGLE RATE:	No fee	OPEN DATES:	July-Oct
# of SINGLE SITES:	12		
		MAX STAY:	14 days
		ELEVATION:	7450 feet

55 McCloud Bridge
Lakehead • lat 40˚56'09" lon 122˚14'38"

DESCRIPTION: In a mixture of pines, oaks and fruit trees with nice views of the lake. Fish for bass and trout. Historical Samwell Caves and Ellery Homestead in the area. Supplies at Lakehead. Deer, bears and bald eagles are common in the area. Campers may gather firewood. Hike or bike on old logging roads nearby.

GETTING THERE: From Lakehead go S on I-5 approx. 4.5 mi. to county route 7H009. Go NE on 7H009 approx. 14 mi. to McCloud Bridge CG.

SINGLE RATE:	$15	OPEN DATES:	May-Sept
# of SINGLE SITES:	11	MAX SPUR:	30 feet
GROUP RATE:	$25	MAX STAY:	14 days
# of GROUP SITES:	3	ELEVATION:	1085 feet

60 Philpot
Hayfork • lat 40˚27'53" lon 123˚11'25"

DESCRIPTION: This rustic CG is in an open stand of pine, fir and oak on Philpot Creek. Supplies available at Hayfork. Numerous wildlife can be seen in the area. Historic town site of Peanut is nearby. Campers may gather firewood. The Philpot interpretive trail is located at the CG. This CG is a tent only site.

GETTING THERE: Philpot CG is located approx. 5.5 mi. S of Hayfork on state HWY 3.

SINGLE RATE:	No fee	OPEN DATES:	May-Oct
# of SINGLE SITES:	6		
		MAX STAY:	14 days
		ELEVATION:	2500 feet

 Campground has hosts   Reservable sites 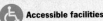 Accessible facilities   Fully developed   Semi-developed Rustic facilities

NOTE: Open dates listed are typical. Actual dates are dependent on conditions such as snow pack.

Page 134

61 Pigeon Point
Junction City • lat 40°46'02" lon 123°07'51"

DESCRIPTION: In an open fir forest setting with Price Creek next to CG. Fish for trout in nearby Trinity River. Supplies at Weaverville. Deer, foxes, bears, coyotes, mountain lion and squirrels can be found around CG area. Campers may gather firewood. No designated trails in the area. No piped water.

GETTING THERE: Pigeon Point CG is located approx. 3 mi. W of Junction City on state HWY 299.

SINGLE RATE:	$6	**OPEN DATES:**	**May-Nov**
# of SINGLE SITES:	10	**MAX SPUR:**	**22 feet**
		MAX STAY:	**14 days**
		ELEVATION:	**1100 feet**

62 Pine Point
Lakehead • lat 40°55'40" lon 122°14'44"

DESCRIPTION: CG is in a densely forested pine setting on the upper McCloud Arm of Shasta Lake. Fish for bass and trout from the shorline. Historical Samwell Caves are nearby. Supplies are located at Lakehad. Deer, bears, osprey and bald eagles are common to the area. Campers may gather firewood.

GETTING THERE: From Lakehead go S on I-5 approx. 4.5 mi. to county route 7H009. Go NE on 7H009 approx. 13.5 mi. to Pine Point CG.

SINGLE RATE:	$12	**OPEN DATES:**	**May-Sept**
# of SINGLE SITES:	14	**MAX SPUR:**	**30 feet**
GROUP RATE:	$90	**MAX STAY:**	**14 days**
# of GROUP SITES:	1	**ELEVATION:**	**1090 feet**

63 Preacher Meadow
Trinity Center • lat 40°57'53" lon 122°43'39"

DESCRIPTION: In a park-like setting just off of Trinity Lake. Fishing for trout from the lake. Swift Creek is a short walk from CG. Supplies at Trinity Center. Many trails in the area.

GETTING THERE: From Trinity Center go SW on state HWY 3 approx. 1.7 mi. to forest route 36N98. Go SW on 36N98 approx. .3 mi. to Preacher Meadow CG.

SINGLE RATE:	$8	**OPEN DATES:**	**May-Oct**
# of SINGLE SITES:	63	**MAX SPUR:**	**40 feet**
		MAX STAY:	**14 days**
		ELEVATION:	**2900 feet**

64 Ridgeville
Weaverville • lat 40°50'48" lon 122°47'54"

DESCRIPTION: In a heavily forested setting of pines, cedar and douglas fir. Fish for trout and bass in Trinity Lake. Supplies at Weaverville. Deer, bears and birds are common in the area. No designated trails in the area.

GETTING THERE: From Weaverville go NE on state HWY 3 approx. 13.3 mi. to Ridgeville CG. Ridgeville CG is accessible only by boat.

SINGLE RATE:	No fee	**OPEN DATES:**	**Yearlong**
# of SINGLE SITES:	21		
		MAX STAY:	**14 days**
		ELEVATION:	**2400 feet**

65 Ridgeville Island
Weaverville • lat 40°50'50" lon 122°47'17"

DESCRIPTION: In a more open forested setting of pines, cedar and douglas fir. Fish for trout and bass in Trinity Lake. Supplies at Weaverville. Deer, bears and birds are common in the area. No designated trails in the area.

GETTING THERE: From Weaverville go NE on state HWY 3 approx. 13.3 mi. to Ridgeville Island CG. Ridgeville Island CG is accessible only by boat.

SINGLE RATE:	No fee	**OPEN DATES:**	**Yearlong**
# of SINGLE SITES:	3		
		MAX STAY:	**14 days**
		ELEVATION:	**2400 feet**

66 Ripstein
Junction City • lat 40°52'37" lon 123°01'41"

DESCRIPTION: In an open fir forest setting with Canyon Creek next to CG. Supplies at Junction City. Deer, foxes, bears, coyotes, mountain lion and squirrels can be found around CG area. Campers may gather firewood. Canyon Creek Trailhead is within 1 mi. of the CG. No piped water.

GETTING THERE: Ripstein CG is located approx. 12 mi. N of Junction City on county route 401.

SINGLE RATE:	No fee	**OPEN DATES:**	**Yearlong**
# of SINGLE SITES:	10	**MAX SPUR:**	**22 feet**
		MAX STAY:	**14 days**
		ELEVATION:	**2600 feet**

67 Rush Creek
Weaverville • lat 40°48'57" lon 122°53'37"

DESCRIPTION: A rustic CG with lots of trees on Rush Creek. Fish, swim, and gold pan in the creek. Supplies can be found in Weaverville. Many hiking trails in the area. No water.

GETTING THERE: Rush Creek CG is located approx. 8 mi. N of Weaverville on state HWY 3.

SINGLE RATE:	$5	**OPEN DATES:**	**May-Sept**
# of SINGLE SITES:	11	**MAX SPUR:**	**16 feet**
		MAX STAY:	**14 days**
		ELEVATION:	**3850 feet**

68 Scott Mountain
Stewart Springs • lat 41°16'36" lon 122°41'50"

DESCRIPTION: In a heavily forested setting of pines, cedar and douglas fir. Fish for trout and bass in Trinity Lake. Supplies at Stewart Springs. Deer, bears and birds are common in the area. Trailhead for the Pacific Crest Trail. This CG is used mostly by hikers.

GETTING THERE: From Stewart Springs go S on primary forest route 17 approx. 18 mi. to forest route 40N03. Go NW on 40N03 approx. 4.5 mi. to Scott Mountain CG.

SINGLE RATE:	No fee	**OPEN DATES:**	**Yearlong**
# of SINGLE SITES:	7	**MAX SPUR:**	**15 feet**
		MAX STAY:	**14 days**
		ELEVATION:	**5400 feet**

69 Scotts Flat
Hayfork • lat 40°22'30" lon 123°22'30"

DESCRIPTION: This rustic CG is in an open stand of pine, oak and fir on the South Fork Trinity River. Supplies at Hayfork. Deer, bears and birds are common to the area. The South Fork Trinity River NRT is next to CG. Campers may gather firewood. Take bears precations.

GETTING THERE: From Hayfork go S on state HWY 3 approx. 9 mi. to state HWY 36. Go SW on 36 approx. 22 mi. to Scotts Flat CG.

SINGLE RATE:	No fee	**OPEN DATES:**	**May-Oct**
# of SINGLE SITES:	7	**MAX SPUR:**	**30 feet**
		MAX STAY:	**14 days**
		ELEVATION:	**2300 feet**

70 Shasta
Redding • lat 40°43'00" lon 122°25'30"

DESCRIPTION: Open sites with some young trees and nice views of Shasta Dam and the Sacramento River. Fish for trout from the river. Supplies at Redding. Deer and osprey are common to the area. Campers may gather firewood.

GETTING THERE: From Redding go N on I-5 approx. 5 mi. to state HWY 151. Go W on 151 approx. 7 mi. to Shasta CG.

SINGLE RATE:	$10	**OPEN DATES:**	**Yearlong**
# of SINGLE SITES:	22	**MAX SPUR:**	**30 feet**
		MAX STAY:	**14 days**
		ELEVATION:	**620 feet**

 Campground has hosts   **Reservable sites**   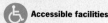 **Accessible facilities**   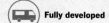 **Fully developed**   **Semi-developed**   **Rustic facilities**

NOTE: Open dates listed are typical. Actual dates are dependent on conditions such as snow pack.

71 Shiell Gulch
Wildwood • lat 40°27'25" lon 123°03'13"

DESCRIPTION: This primitive, tent only CG is in a pine forest setting on Hayfork Creek. Supplies available at Wildwood. Deer, bears and birds are common to the area. Historical natural bridge massacre site is nearby. Campers may gather firewood. No designated trails in the area. No water.

GETTING THERE: Shiell Gulch CG is located approx. 8 mi. N of Wildwood on county route 302.

SINGLE RATE:	No fee	OPEN DATES:	July-Oct
# of SINGLE SITES:	5		
		MAX STAY:	14 days
		ELEVATION:	2600 feet

72 Sims Flat
Lakehead • lat 41°03'40" lon 122°21'31"

DESCRIPTION: In a ponderosa pine and cedar forest setting on the Sacramento River. Catch and release only on this river. Supplies at Lakehead. This CG was a CCC camp. Historic trail nearby that goes through an old mill and CCC camp. Deer, bears and birds are common to the area.

GETTING THERE: Sims Flat CG is located approx. 15 mi. N of Lakehead off of I-5.

SINGLE RATE:	$12	OPEN DATES:	Apr-Nov
# of SINGLE SITES:	17	MAX SPUR:	20 feet
		MAX STAY:	14 days
		ELEVATION:	1600 feet

73 Ski Island
Redding • lat 40°45'38" lon 122°15'23"

DESCRIPTION: In a dense forested setting on Shasta Lake. Fish for bass and trout in the lake. Supplies at Redding. Deer, bears, osprey and bald eagles are common in the area. Campers may gather firewood. No designated trails in the area. No water.

GETTING THERE: Ski Island CG is located on the Pit River Arm of Shasta Lake and is accessible by boat only.

SINGLE RATE:	No fee	OPEN DATES:	Yearlong
		MAX STAY:	14 days
		ELEVATION:	1085 feet

74 Skunk Point Group
Junction City • lat 40°44'00" lon 123°13'45"

DESCRIPTION: In an open fir forest setting with Price Creek next to CG. Fish for trout in nearby Trinity River. Supplies at Weaverville. Deer, foxes, bears, coyotes, mountain lion and squirrels can be found around CG area. Campers may gather firewood. No designated trails in the area.

GETTING THERE: Skunk Point Group CG is located approx. 10 mi. W of Junction City on state HWY 299.

		OPEN DATES:	Yearlong
GROUP RATE:	Varies	MAX STAY:	14 days
# of GROUP SITES:	2	ELEVATION:	1200 feet

75 Slide Creek
Hyampom • lat 40°40'06" lon 123°30'06"

DESCRIPTION: This rustic, primitive CG is in an open stand of pine, fir and oak. CG is on the South Fork Trinity River where you can fish for trout. Supplies available at Hyampom. Campers may gather firewood. Deer, bears and birds are common to the area. No water. Tent only.

GETTING THERE: Big Slide CG is located approx. 3.5 mi. N of Hyampom on county route 311.

SINGLE RATE:	No fee	OPEN DATES:	May-Oct
# of SINGLE SITES:	4		
		MAX STAY:	14 days
		ELEVATION:	1250 feet

76 Stoney Creek Group
Weaverville • lat 40°50'54" lon 122°51'30"

DESCRIPTION: CG is nestled in a mixed forest setting across from the Stoney Creek swim area. Fish in the Trinity Lake nearby. Supplies at Weaverville. Swimming at beach at CG or at swim area. Many hiking trails in the area. Just relax and enjoy the beautiful scenery.

GETTING THERE: Stoney Creek Group CG is located approx. 13 mi. NE of Weaverville on state HWY 3.

		OPEN DATES:	May-Sept
		MAX SPUR:	40 feet
GROUP RATE:	$50	MAX STAY:	14 days
# of GROUP SITES:	1	ELEVATION:	2400 feet

77 Stoney Point
Weaverville • lat 40°50'54" lon 122°51'30"

DESCRIPTION: In an oak, walnut and pine forest setting with views of Trinity Lake. Excellent fishing for bass, trout, and catfish in the lake or on the Stuart's Fork of the Trinity river. Less crowded then most campgrounds in the area. Tent camping only.

GETTING THERE: Stoney Point CG is located approx. 12.5 mi. NE of Weaverville on state HWY 3.

SINGLE RATE:	Varies	OPEN DATES:	Apr-Oct
# of SINGLE SITES:	21		
		MAX STAY:	14 days
		ELEVATION:	2400 feet

78 Tannery Gulch
Weaverville • lat 40°50'06" lon 122°50'41"

DESCRIPTION: In a park-like setting of oak, walnut and pine with views of Trinity Lake. Fishing, swimming, water skiing, and boating in the lake. Gold panning in the area. Supplies at Weaverville. Joss House Historic Park nearby. Many trails in the area.

GETTING THERE: From Weaverville go N on state HWY 3 approx. 11 mi. to county route. Go E on county route approx. 1.5 mi. to Tannery Gulch CG.

SINGLE RATE:	Varies	OPEN DATES:	Apr-Sept
# of SINGLE SITES:	83	MAX SPUR:	40 feet
		MAX STAY:	14 days
# of GROUP SITES:	4	ELEVATION:	2400 feet

79 Toad Lake
Mount Shasta • lat 41°16'57" lon 122°30'03"

DESCRIPTION: In a primitive forest setting on edge of lake. Fish for brook and rainbow trout on the lake. Deer, bears and birds are common to the area. Pacific Crest Trail is approx. .25 mi. from the CG. This is used as an equestrian stop over camp.

GETTING THERE: Toad Lake CG is located on the Pacific Crest National Scenic Trail due W of Lake Siskiyou. Get to CG by unimproved roads with a 1/4 mi. hike to CG. Please call (530)926-4511 for directions.

SINGLE RATE:	No fee	OPEN DATES:	May-Oct
# of SINGLE SITES:	4		
		MAX STAY:	14 days
		ELEVATION:	6940 feet

80 Tomhead Saddle
Red Bluff • lat 40°08'25" lon 122°49'45"

DESCRIPTION: This rustic CG is in an open stand of pine and fir. Supplies are available at Red Bluff. Deer, birds and squirrels are common to the area. Campers may gather firewood. The Yolla Bolla Wilderness is nearby with many trails. The Old Humbolt Trail goes through the CG. No water.

GETTING THERE: From Red Bluff go W on state HWY 36 13 mi. to county route 181. Go SW on 181 5 mi. to county route 146. Go W on 146 19 mi. to forest route 27N06. Go SW on 27N06 5 mi. to Tomhead Saddle CG.

SINGLE RATE:	No fee	OPEN DATES:	May-Oct
		MAX STAY:	14 days
		ELEVATION:	5600 feet

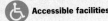 **Campground has hosts**   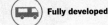 **Reservable sites**   **Accessible facilities**   **Fully developed**   **Semi-developed**   **Rustic facilities**

NOTE: Open dates listed are typical. Actual dates are dependent on conditions such as snow pack.

Page 136

81 Trinity River
Stewart Springs • lat 41°06'46" lon 122°42'22"

DESCRIPTION: In an open park-like setting on Trinity River. Fishing on the river. Supplies at Coffee Creek. Early spring offers kayaking and rafting. It is a good stopping off point for hikes to mountain lakes and other hiking trails. Ask the host about gold panning.

GETTING THERE: From Stewart Springs go S on primary forest route 17 approx. 18 mi. to state HWY 3. Go S on 3 approx. 9.5 mi. to Trinity River CG.

SINGLE RATE:	$8	OPEN DATES:	Yearlong
# of SINGLE SITES:	7	MAX SPUR:	40 feet
		MAX STAY:	14 days
		ELEVATION:	2500 feet

82 Trout Creek
McCloud • lat 41°25'05" lon 121°55'37"

DESCRIPTION: In a dense forest setting with Trout Creek running through the middle of the CG. Fish for rainbow and brook trout from the creek. Red Band Trout fishery nearby. Supplies at McCloud. Deer, bears, turkeys and squirrels are common in the area. A wildlife nature trail runs through the CG.

GETTING THERE: From McCloud go E on state HWY 89 approx. 2 mi. to primary forest route 13. Go NE on 13 approx. 14 mi. to Trout Creek CG.

SINGLE RATE:	No fee	OPEN DATES:	June-Oct
# of SINGLE SITES:	10		
		MAX STAY:	14 days
		ELEVATION:	5100 feet

83 Tunnel Rock
Lewistown • lat 40°46'27" lon 122°46'40"

DESCRIPTION: In a beautiful oak, walnut and pine forest setting with views of the lake. CG is near a popular fishing spot. Boat launch and supplies at Pinecove Marina. Tunnel Rock offers easy access to both Lewiston and Trinity Lake. Many trails in the area. Visit the fish hatchery below Lewiston Dam. No water.

GETTING THERE: From Lewistown go N on county route 105 approx. 6.5 mi. to Tunnel Rock CG.

SINGLE RATE:	$5	OPEN DATES:	Yearlong
# of SINGLE SITES:	6	MAX SPUR:	15 feet
		MAX STAY:	14 days
		ELEVATION:	2000 feet

84 Upper Jones Valley
Redding • lat 40°43'39" lon 122°13'41"

DESCRIPTION: In a mostly oak forested setting about .5 mi. from the lake. Fish for bass, trout and catfish in the lake. Supplies at Redding. Deer, bears and bald eagles can be seen in the area. Campers may gather firewood. Several hiking, biking and horse trails nearby.

GETTING THERE: From Redding go N on I-5 approx. 2.5 mi. to county route 3H02. Go NE on 3H02 approx. 3.5 mi. to county route 5H02. Go NE on 5H02 approx. 8 mi. to Upper Jones Valley CG.

SINGLE RATE:	$12	OPEN DATES:	May-Sept
# of SINGLE SITES:	8	MAX SPUR:	20 feet
		MAX STAY:	14 days
		ELEVATION:	1100 feet

85 White Rock
Wildwood • lat 40°15'10" lon 123°01'23"

DESCRIPTION: A primitive CG in a mixed forest setting on Small Creek. Supplies available at Wildwood. Historical White Rock Guard Station site is nearby. Deer, bears, snakes, birds and squirrels are common to the area. Campers may gather firewood. Near the Yolla Bolla Wilderness. No water.

GETTING THERE: From Wildwood go S on primary forest route 30 approx. 8 mi. to primary forest route 35. Go SE on 35 approx. 4 mi. to forest route 28N10. Go SE on 28N10 approx. 1.5 mi. to White Rock CG.

SINGLE RATE:	No fee	OPEN DATES:	May-Oct
# of SINGLE SITES:	3		
		MAX STAY:	14 days
		ELEVATION:	4800 feet

 Campground has hosts   **Reservable sites**   **Accessible facilities**   **Fully developed**  **Semi-developed**  **Rustic facilities**

NOTE: Open dates listed are typical. Actual dates are dependent on conditions such as snow pack.

SIERRA NATIONAL FOREST

The Sierra National Forest, located on the western slope of the central Sierra Nevada, is known for spectacular mountain scenery and abundant natural resources. Placed under federal management in 1893, these lands have met public needs for wood, water, and outdoor recreation for more than a century. Today, the forest's recreation areas and its rugged wilderness make it one of the most popular national forests in the United States.

The forest encompasses more than 1.3 million acres between 900 feet and 13,157 feet in elevation. The terrain includes rolling, oak-covered foothills, heavily forested middle elevation slopes, and the starkly beautiful alpine landscape of the high Sierra. The forest is home to more than 315 different animal species and 31 different species of fish.

Weather conditions in the Sierra vary with elevation and exposure. Summer weather is generally hot and dry, with lower elevation high temperatures ranging from 90 degrees to more than 100 degrees. At higher elevations, temperatures are cooler, and short, but dramatic, afternoon thundershowers are common. Snow may fall at any time of the year in the high country.

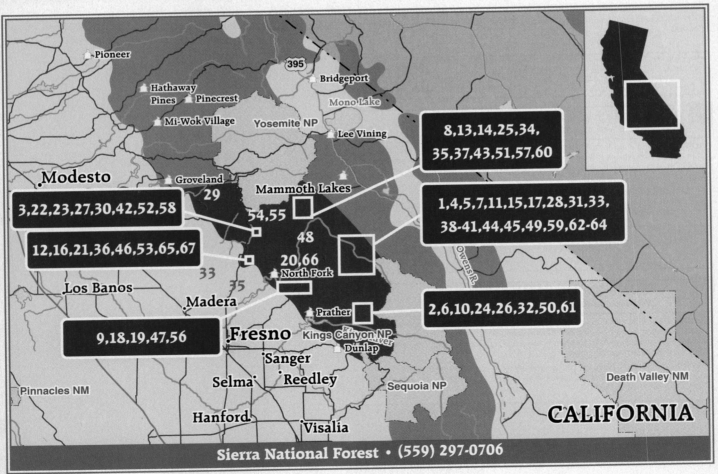

Sierra National Forest • (559) 297-0706

1 Badger Flat
Cedar Crest • lat 37°16'09" lon 119°06'55"

DESCRIPTION: This CG is situated in a mixed forest. Trout fishing nearby at Huntington and in surrounding lakes. Check for local regulations. Supplies 3 mi. away to the head of Huntington Lake at Rancheria Enterprises. Gather firewood locally. Kaiser Wilderness hiking trail nearby. Horses accomodated.

GETTING THERE: Badger Flat CG is located approx. 7 mi. NE of Cedar Crest on primary forest route 80 (Huntington Road).

SINGLE RATE:	$8	OPEN DATES:	June-Oct
# of SINGLE SITES:	15		
GROUP RATE:	$75	MAX STAY:	14 days
# of GROUP SITES:	1	ELEVATION:	8200 feet

6 Black Rock
Balch Camp • lat 36°55'17" lon 119°01'27"

DESCRIPTION: This CG is situated in a pine forest a short distance away from Black Rock Reservoir. Mild summers, snow in winter. Fish Kings River or Black Rock Lake (no boats). Supplies are 30 mi. away in Piedra. Watch for bears and deer in the area. Mod. use. Gather firewood locally. Drinking water in summer only.

GETTING THERE: From Balch Camp go E on forest route 11S12 (Black Rock Road) approx. 8 mi. to forest route 11S50. Go E on 11S50 approx. 1 mi. to Black Rock CG.

SINGLE RATE:	$10	OPEN DATES:	Yearlong
# of SINGLE SITES:	10		
		MAX STAY:	14 days
		ELEVATION:	4200 feet

2 Bears Wallow
Balch Camp • lat 36°52'43" lon 119°04'23"

DESCRIPTION: CG is set along side Kings River. Two trout fly fishing limit. Supplies 20 mi. in Piedra. Very hot and dry summers. No drinking water. Gather dead and downed wood for fires. Bears Wallow and Kings River National Recreation Trails nearby. Moderate use. Tent only. Reservations required from Trimmer Ranger District.

GETTING THERE: From Balch Camp go S on forest route 11S12 approx. 3 mi. to forest route 12S01. Go E on 12S01 approx. 2 mi. to Bears Wallow CG. 4WD recommended.

		OPEN DATES:	Yearlong
GROUP RATE:	No fee	MAX STAY:	14 days
# of GROUP SITES:	1	ELEVATION:	1100 feet

7 Bolsillo
Cedar Crest • lat 37°18'53" lon 119°02'29"

DESCRIPTION: This CG is situated in a mixed forest with views of the Sierras. Expect afternoon rain in the summer. Fish nearby Portal Forebay, Edison Lake, or Florence. Supplies 3 mi. at Mono Hot Springs Resort. Light use. Gather firewood locally. Hiking and horse trails close by. Frequented by bears.

GETTING THERE: Bolsillo CG is located approx. 15.5 mi. NE of Cedar Crest on primary forest route 80 (Kaiser Pass Road).

SINGLE RATE:	No fee	OPEN DATES:	June-Oct
# of SINGLE SITES:	3		
		MAX STAY:	14 days
		ELEVATION:	7400 feet

3 Big Sandy
Oakhurst • lat 37°28'00" lon 119°34'52"

DESCRIPTION: CG set in fir, cedar, and pine. No drinking water. Near Big White Chief Branch with great fishing nearby. Supplies in Oakhurst. Deer, black bears, mountain lions, bobcats, foxes, coyotes, and skunks in area. Hike the Lewis Creek National Recreation Trail nearby. Near Nelder Grove Giant Sequoias.

GETTING THERE: From Oakhurst go N on state HWY 41 approx. 5 mi. to primary forest route 10 (Ranch Road). Go NE 8 mi. to forest route 6S07. Go NW 4 mi. to Big Sandy CG. Dirt road.

SINGLE RATE:	Varies	OPEN DATES:	May-Sept*
# of SINGLE SITES:	18	MAX SPUR:	30 feet
		MAX STAY:	14 days
		ELEVATION:	5800 feet

8 Bowler Group
Bass Lake • lat 37°30'30" lon 119°19'38"

DESCRIPTION: CG situated in a fir and pine forest on a seasonal creek. Deer, black bears, mountain lions, bobcats, foxes, coyotes, and skunks in area. Gather firewood. Horse facilites and amphitheater. The French Trail system and access to Ansel Adams Wilderness are the primary attractions to this CG.

GETTING THERE: Bowler CG is located approx. 23 mi. NE of Bass Lake on primary forest route 7 (Beasore Road). Dirt road.

SINGLE RATE:	No fee	OPEN DATES:	June-Oct*
		MAX SPUR:	50 feet
		MAX STAY:	14 days
# of GROUP SITES:	12	ELEVATION:	7000 feet

4 Billy Creek Lower
Huntington Lake • lat 37°14'17" lon 119°13'40"

DESCRIPTION: This CG is situated in a park-like area with views of Huntington Lake. Winds and thundershowers are common. Supplies are available at several places around the lake. Campers may gather or buy firewood on site. Numerous foot trails in the Kaiser Wilderness area. Bears frequent the area.

GETTING THERE: Billy Creek Lower CG is located approx. 1/2 mi. E of Huntington Lake on primary forest route 80 (Huntington Road).

SINGLE RATE:	Varies	OPEN DATES:	May-Oct
# of SINGLE SITES:	13	MAX SPUR:	25 feet
		MAX STAY:	14 days
		ELEVATION:	7000 feet

9 Bretz Mill
Dinkey Creek • lat 37°02'15" lon 119°14'20"

DESCRIPTION: This CG is situated in a park-like area with views of a small stream. Brook trout fishing from stream. Check for local regulations. Supplies are at Dinkey Creek. CG receives light use, never filling. Campers may gather their firewood locally. No drinking water available on site.

GETTING THERE: Bretz Mill CG is approx. II mi. N of the Blue Canyon Work Center.

SINGLE RATE:	No fee	OPEN DATES:	Apr-Oct
# of SINGLE SITES:	10		
		MAX STAY:	14 days
		ELEVATION:	3300 feet

5 Billy Creek Upper
Huntington Lake • lat 37°14'17" lon 119°13'40"

DESCRIPTION: This CG is situated in a park-like area with views of Huntington Lake. Winds and thundershowers are common. Supplies are available at several places around the lake. Campers may gather or buy firewood locally. Numerous foot trails in the Kaiser Wilderness area. Bears frequent the area.

GETTING THERE: Billy Creek Upper CG is located approx. 1/2 mi. E of Huntington Lake on primary forest route 80 (Huntington Road).

SINGLE RATE:	Varies	OPEN DATES:	May-Sept
# of SINGLE SITES:	44	MAX SPUR:	25 feet
		MAX STAY:	14 days
		ELEVATION:	7000 feet

10 Buck Meadow
Dinkey Creek • lat 37°00'44" lon 119°03'53"

DESCRIPTION: This CG is set along the banks of Deer Creek, situated in a mixed conifer forest. Supplies are available 22 mi. away at Shaver Lake. Possible fishing opportunities nearby. Campers may gather their firewood locally. Swamp Lake OHV route is nearby. No drinking water available on site.

GETTING THERE: Buck Meadow CG is located approx. 9 mi. E of Dinkey Creek on primary forest route 40 (McKinley Grove Road).

SINGLE RATE:	No fee	OPEN DATES:	May-Nov
# of SINGLE SITES:	10		
		MAX STAY:	14 days
		ELEVATION:	6800 feet

 Campground has hosts   **Reservable sites**   **Accessible facilities**   **Fully developed**   **Semi-developed** **Rustic facilities**

NOTE: Open dates listed are typical. Actual dates are dependent on conditions such as snow pack.

11 Catavee
Cedar Crest • lat 37°15'09" lon 119°10'37"

DESCRIPTION: This CG is situated in a heavily wooded area adjacent to a lake. Possible fishing opportunities nearby. Check for local reguloitons. Supplies are available at Lakeshore Resort. Campers may gather dead and downed wood or buy it at various locations in the area. Bears can sometimes be a problem.

GETTING THERE: Catavee CG is located approx. 2 mi. NE of Cedar Crest on primary forest route 80 (Huntington Road).

SINGLE RATE:	Varies	OPEN DATES:	May-Sept
# of SINGLE SITES:	23	MAX SPUR:	30 feet
		MAX STAY:	14 days
		ELEVATION:	7000 feet

12 Chilkoot
Bass Lake • lat 37°21'46" lon 119°32'19"

DESCRIPTION: CG set among spring flowers, situated in a hardwood, aspen, and dogwood forest. Close canopy makes filtered shade. Exceptionally beautiful autumn colors. No drinking water. Deer, black bears, mountain lions, bobcats, foxes, and coyotes. Small waterfalls on Chilkoot Creek and N Fork Willow nearby.

GETTING THERE: Chilkoot CG is located approx. 4 mi. NE of Bass Lake on primary forest route 7 (Beasore Road).

SINGLE RATE:	$11	OPEN DATES:	May-Sept
# of SINGLE SITES:	14	MAX SPUR:	30 feet
		MAX STAY:	14 days
		ELEVATION:	4600 feet

13 China Bar
South Fork • lat 37°22'14" lon 119°18'04"

DESCRIPTION: CG in an exposed area on Mammoth Pool Reservoir. No drinking water. Closed to boats 5/1-6/16 during deer migration. Water level may drop making boat-in difficult. Fish for trout. Deer, black bears, mountain lions, bobcats, foxes, coyotes, and skunks. Gather firewood. Near French Trail System.

GETTING THERE: China Bar CG is located on the W shore of Mammoth Pool Reservoir and is accesible by boat or hike-in only. Parking is at Mammoth Pool CG.

SINGLE RATE:	No fee	OPEN DATES:	Apr-Sept*
# of SINGLE SITES:	6		
		MAX STAY:	14 days
		ELEVATION:	3300 feet

14 Clover Meadow
Bass Lake • lat 37°31'43" lon 119°16'47"

DESCRIPTION: This CG is situated in a pine and fir forest. Hike to Granite Creek for fishing. Watch for deer, black bears, mountain lions, bobcats, foxes, coyotes, and skunks. Gather firewood. Nearby French Trail system and access to Ansel Adams Wilderness. Mosquitos are thick from snow melt until mid-Aug.

GETTING THERE: From Bass Lake go NE on primary forest route 7 (Beasore Road)to forest route 5S30. Go N on 5S30 approx. 2 mi. to Clover Meadow CG.

SINGLE RATE:	No fee	OPEN DATES:	June-Oct*
# of SINGLE SITES:	7	MAX SPUR:	30 feet
		MAX STAY:	14 days
		ELEVATION:	7000 feet

15 College
Cedar Crest • lat 37°15'07" lon 119°10'08"

DESCRIPTION: This CG is situated in a heavily wooded area set on the edge of Huntington Lake. Possible fishing in lake, please check for local fishing regulations. Supplies are available at Lakeshore Resort. Campers can gather firewood on site, or buy it at various locations nearby. Bears can be a problem.

GETTING THERE: College CG is located approx. 2 mi. E of Cedar Crest on primary forest route 80 (Huntington Road).

SINGLE RATE:	Varies	OPEN DATES:	June-Sept
# of SINGLE SITES:	11	MAX SPUR:	30 feet
		MAX STAY:	14 days
		ELEVATION:	7000 feet

16 Crane Valley
Bass Lake • lat 37°20'00" lon 119°35'07"

DESCRIPTION: A more exposed CG, with hot dusty summer days. Nearby Bass Lake has fishing for bass, rainbow trout, catfish, sunfish, and kokanee. Watch for deer, black bears, mountain lions, bobcats, foxes, coyotes, and skunks in the area. Gather firewood in nearby areas. Max 30 person, 12 vehicles.

GETTING THERE: Crane Valley CG is located approx. 1 mi. NW of Bass Lake on county route 222. Unpaved road and facilities.

		OPEN DATES:	June-Sept*
		MAX SPUR:	50 feet
GROUP RATE:	Varies	MAX STAY:	14 days
# of GROUP SITES:	7	ELEVATION:	3500 feet

17 Deer Creek
Cedar Crest • lat 37°15'07" lon 119°10'37"

DESCRIPTION: This CG is situated in a heavily wooded area set on the edge of Huntington Lake. Possible fishing in lake, please check for local fishing reguloitons. Supplies are available at Lakeshore Resort. Campers can gather firewood on site, or buy it at various locations nearby. Bears can be a problem.

GETTING THERE: Deer Creek CG is located approx. 2.5 mi. E of Cedar Crest on primary forest route 80 (Huntington Road).

SINGLE RATE:	Varies	OPEN DATES:	June-Oct
# of SINGLE SITES:	28	MAX SPUR:	30 feet
		MAX STAY:	14 days
		ELEVATION:	7000 feet

18 Dinkey Creek
Dinkey Creek • lat 37°03'57" lon 119°09'20"

DESCRIPTION: This CG is set along the banks of Dinkey Creek, situated in a mixed conifer forest. Supplies are available 13 mi. away at Shaver Lake. Campers may gather firewood on site, or purchase it at the Dinkey Creek Store. Numerous trails nearby. CG has an amphitheater. Bears due frequent the area.

GETTING THERE: Dinkey Creek CG is located approx. 1/2 mi. S of Dinkey Creek on primary forest route 40 (McKinley Grove Road).

SINGLE RATE:	$15	OPEN DATES:	May-Sept
# of SINGLE SITES:	128		
GROUP RATE:	$50	MAX STAY:	14 days
# of GROUP SITES:	1	ELEVATION:	5700 feet

19 Dorabelle
Shaver Lake • lat 37°06'50" lon 119°18'35"

DESCRIPTION: This CG is situated in a heavily wooded area with views of Shaver Lake. Possible fishing in Shaver Lake, please check for local fishing reguloitons. Campers may gather firewood on site or purchase it locally. Horseback riding opportunities nearby along with numerous hiking trails.

GETTING THERE: Dorabelle CG is located approx. 1/2 mi. E of Shaver Lake on the SW shore of Shaver Lake.

SINGLE RATE:	$12	OPEN DATES:	May-Sept
# of SINGLE SITES:	68	MAX SPUR:	30 feet
		MAX STAY:	14 days
		ELEVATION:	5400 feet

20 Fish Creek
South Fork • lat 37°15'37" lon 119°21'10"

DESCRIPTION: A charming shady CG situated in a cedar and pine forest on a seasonal creek (stocked with trout). No drinking water. Watch for deer, black bears, mountain lions, bobcats, foxes, coyotes, and skunks. Gather firewood. Hiking on nearby French Trail System. Fees and services are less off season.

GETTING THERE: From South Fork go E on county route 233 1/2 mi. to county route 225. Go SE 3 mi. to forest route 81 (Minarets Road). Go E then N 12 mi. to Fish Creek CG. Tight curves, not recommended for large RVs.

SINGLE RATE:	$12	OPEN DATES:	May-Sept*
# of SINGLE SITES:	7	MAX SPUR:	28 feet
		MAX STAY:	14 days
		ELEVATION:	4600 feet

 Campground has hosts   **Reservable sites**   **Accessible facilities**   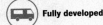 **Fully developed**   **Semi-developed**   **Rustic facilities**

21 Forks
Oakhurst • lat 37°18'47" lon 119°34'12"

DESCRIPTION: CG situated in a mature conifer and oak forest set on Bass Lake. Fish for bass, rainbow trout, catfish, sunfish, and kokanee. No drinking water. Deer, black bears, bald eagles, osprey, mountain lions, bobcats, foxes, coyotes, and skunks. Bring your own firewood. Basic supplies and burgers at resort.

GETTING THERE: From Oakhurst go E on county route 426 approx. 6.5 mi. to county route 222. Go E on 222 approx. 3/4 mi. to Forks CG.

SINGLE RATE:	$16	OPEN DATES:	Apr-Sept*
# of SINGLE SITES:	31	MAX SPUR:	40 feet
		MAX STAY:	14 days
		ELEVATION:	3400 feet

22 Fresno Dome
Oakhurst • lat 37°27'22" lon 119°32'54"

DESCRIPTION: CG situated in a mixed conifer and pine forest. Fish nearby creek for rainbow and german brown trout. No drinking water. Watch for deer, black bears, mountain lions, bobcats, foxes, coyotes, and skunks. Gather firewood. Nearby Nelder Grove Giant Sequoias. Hiking on Lewis Creek National Recreation Trail.

GETTING THERE: From Oakhurst go N on state HWY 41 approx. 5 mi. to primary forest route 10 (Ranch Road). Go NE approx. 8 mi. to forest route 6S07. Go NW approx. 1.5 mi. to Fresno Dome CG.

SINGLE RATE:	$11	OPEN DATES:	June-Oct*
# of SINGLE SITES:	15	MAX SPUR:	40 feet
		MAX STAY:	14 days
		ELEVATION:	6400 feet

23 Gaggs Camp
Bass Lake • lat 37°21'40" lon 119°27'59"

DESCRIPTION: CG on a shady SW slope of cedar, pine, and oak. Warm summer days. Best to go downstream fishing. No drinking water. Watch for deer, black bears, mountain lions, bobcats, foxes, and coyotes. Gather firewood. Mountain biking, hunting, and motor cycling on 007 Trail. Big ride 4/15 weekend to Shuteye Mountain.

GETTING THERE: From Bass Lake go S on county route 274 approx. 4 mi. to forest route 6S42 (Central Camp Road). Go N approx. 8.5 mi. to Gaggs Camp CG. Rough dirt road, not recommended for RVs.

SINGLE RATE:	$11	OPEN DATES:	May-Oct*
# of SINGLE SITES:	12	MAX SPUR:	28 feet
		MAX STAY:	14 days
		ELEVATION:	5700 feet

24 Gigantea
Dinkey Creek • lat 37°00'53" lon 119°06'21"

DESCRIPTION: CG situated in a mixed conifer forest near Wishon Courtright Reservoir. Stream fish in Dinkey Creek or boat fish the reservoir. Warm days with cool nights. Supplies at Shaver Lake. Fills holiday weekends. Gather firewood. Hike McKinley Grove Interpretive Trail. Swamp Lake OHV route nearby. No drinking water.

GETTING THERE: Gigantea CG is located approx. 5.5 mi. E of Dinkey Creek on primary forest route 40 (McKinley Grove Road).

SINGLE RATE:	No fee	OPEN DATES:	May-Nov
# of SINGLE SITES:	10		
		MAX STAY:	14 days
		ELEVATION:	6500 feet

25 Granite Creek
Bass Lake • lat 37°32'32" lon 119°15'58"

DESCRIPTION: This CG is situated in a mixed conifer and oak forest on Granite Creek. Horse facilities, some dispersed sites. No drinking water. Deer, black bears, mountain lions, bobcats, foxes, coyotes, and skunks in area. Gather firewood. French Trail system and access to Ansel Adams Wilderness nearby.

GETTING THERE: From Bass Lake go NE on primary forest route 7 (Beasore Road) to forest route 5S30. Go N 2.5 mi. to forest route 4S60. Go NE 1 mi. to Granite Creek CG. Rough dirt road, not RV recommended.

SINGLE RATE:	No fee	OPEN DATES:	June-Oct*
# of SINGLE SITES:	20	MAX SPUR:	40 feet
		MAX STAY:	14 days
		ELEVATION:	7000 feet

26 Gravel Flat
Balch Camp • lat 36°51'47" lon 119°07'00"

DESCRIPTION: CG situated in an oak woodland with grassy areas and views of Kings River. Fly or stream fish from the river. Check for local regulations. Supplies are available at Fresno. Campers may gather their firewood locally. Bears Wallow and Kings river National Recreation Trails are nearby.

GETTING THERE: From Balch Camp go S on forest route 11S12 approx. 3 mi. to forest route 12S01. Go E on 12S01 approx. 1 mi. to Bears Wallow CG.

		OPEN DATES:	Yearlong
GROUP RATE:	No fee	MAX STAY:	14 days
# of GROUP SITES:	1	ELEVATION:	1200 feet

27 Greys Mountain
Oakhurst • lat 37°23'48" lon 119°33'51"

DESCRIPTION: This CG is situated in a mixed cedar, pine, fir, and hardwood forest on the North Fork of Willow Creek. Fish for native rainbow and brown trout. No drinking water. Deer, black bears, mountain lions, bobcats, foxes, coyotes, and skunks in area. Gather firewood. Approx. 1.5 mi. to hiking trailhead.

GETTING THERE: From Oakhurst go N on state HWY 41 5 mi. to primary forest route 10 (Ranch Road). Go NE 5.5 mi. to forest route 6S40. Go S 2 mi. to Greys Mountain CG. Rough road, not recommended for RVs.

SINGLE RATE:	$11	OPEN DATES:	June-Oct*
# of SINGLE SITES:	26	MAX SPUR:	28 feet
		MAX STAY:	14 days
		ELEVATION:	5400 feet

28 Jackass Meadow
Cedar Crest • lat 37°16'59" lon 118°57'40"

DESCRIPTION: This CG is situated in a park-like rea within walking distance of the San Joaquin River. Check for local fishing regulations. Supplies are available at Florence. Campers may gather their firewood locally. Numerous trails nearby. Bears do frequent the area. No drinking water available on site.

GETTING THERE: From Cedar Crest go NE on primary forest route 80 (Huntington Road) approx. 16.5 mi. to Florence Lake Road. Go SE approx. 6 mi. to Jackass Meadow CG.

SINGLE RATE:	$12	OPEN DATES:	May-Sept
# of SINGLE SITES:	44	MAX SPUR:	20 feet
		MAX STAY:	14 days
		ELEVATION:	7200 feet

29 Jerseydale
Mariposa • lat 37°33'49" lon 119°51'23"

DESCRIPTION: In open grassy oak stand near Jerseydale Guard Station. Nearby Skelton Creek is seasonal, drying up frequently. Cooler days. Close to the south entrance of Yosemite National Park. Deer, rattlesnakes amd small wildlife. No nearby trails.

GETTING THERE: From Mariposa go N on state route 140 3 mi. to Triangle Road. Go E on Triangle Road 6 mi. turning N at Jct with E Westfall Road. Continue N on Triangle Road approx. 2 mi. to Jerseydale CG.

SINGLE RATE:	No fee	OPEN DATES:	May-Oct*
# of SINGLE SITES:	8	MAX SPUR:	40 feet
		MAX STAY:	14 days
		ELEVATION:	3600 feet

30 Kelty Meadow
Oakhurst • lat 37°26'25" lon 119°32'38"

DESCRIPTION: This CG is a horse camp situated in a pine and fir forest. No nearby fishing. No drinking water. Watch for deer, black bears, mountain lions, bobcats, foxes, coyotes, and skunks in the area. Gather firewood. Horse and hiking trail leads to Fresno Dome. Nearby Nelder Grove Giant Sequoias.

GETTING THERE: From Oakhurst go N on state HWY 41 approx. 5 mi. to primary forest route 10 (Ranch Road). Go NE on 10 approx. 8 mi. to Kelty Meadow CG. Good paved road.

SINGLE RATE:	Varies	OPEN DATES:	June-Oct*
# of SINGLE SITES:	11	MAX SPUR:	40 feet
		MAX STAY:	14 days
		ELEVATION:	5800 feet

 Campground has hosts 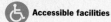 Reservable sites  Accessible facilities Fully developed Semi-developed Rustic facilities

NOTE: Open dates listed are typical. Actual dates are dependent on conditions such as snow pack.

31 Kinnikinnick
Cedar Crest • lat 37°15'10" lon 119°10'40"

DESCRIPTION: CG situated in a heavily wooded area, views of nearby lake with boat or shore fishing for trout and Kokanee. Moderate use. Firewood may be sold nearby or gathered by campers. Horse and hiking trails, D&F Pack Station nearby. Area is frequented by deer, squirrels, birds, and bears.

GETTING THERE: Kinnikinnick CG is located approx. 2 mi. NE of Cedar Crest on primary forest route 80 (Huntington Road).

SINGLE RATE:	Varies	OPEN DATES:	June-Sept
# of SINGLE SITES:	27	MAX SPUR:	40 feet
		MAX STAY:	14 days
		ELEVATION:	7000 feet

36 Lupine/Cedar Bluff
Oakhurst • lat 37°18'28" lon 119°32'39"

DESCRIPTION: CG set on the shores of Bass Lake among tall conifer and oak trees. Fish for bass, rainbow trout, catfish, sunfish, and kokanee. Watch for deer, black bears, bald eagles, osprey, mountain lions, bobcats, foxes, coyotes, and skunks. Bring your own firewood. Fills weekends and holidays.

GETTING THERE: From Oakhurst go E on county route 426 approx. 6.5 mi. to county route 222. Go E on 222 approx. 3 mi. to Lupine/Cedar Bluff CG.

SINGLE RATE:	$16	OPEN DATES:	Yearlong
# of SINGLE SITES:	113	MAX SPUR:	40 feet
		MAX STAY:	14 days
		ELEVATION:	3400 feet

32 Kirch Flat
Balch Camp • lat 36°52'47" lon 119°08'56"

DESCRIPTION: This CG is situated in an oak woodland with grassy areas and views of Kings River. Fly or stream fish from the river. Supplies are available at Fresno. Campers may gather their firewood locally. Bears Wallow and Kings river National Recreation Trails are nearby. No drinking water on site.

GETTING THERE: From Balch Camp go S on forest route 11S12 approx. 3 mi. to forest route 12S01. Go NW on 12S01 approx. 2 mi. to Kirch Flat CG.

SINGLE RATE:	No fee	OPEN DATES:	Yearlong
# of SINGLE SITES:	17		
GROUP RATE:	$50	MAX STAY:	14 days
# of GROUP SITES:	1	ELEVATION:	1100 feet

37 Mammoth Pool
South Fork • lat 37°20'37" lon 119°19'52"

DESCRIPTION: CG situated in a pine and fir forest on a large reservoir. Fishing closed May 1 through June 16 for deer migration. Deer, black bears, bald eagles. osprey, crawdads, mountain lions, bobcats, foxes, coyotes, and skunks. Gather firewood. Hike the French Trail system nearby. Fills after June 16.

GETTING THERE: From South Fork go E on county route 233 1/2 mi. to county route 225. Go SE on 225 3 mi. to forest route 81. Go E then N 28 mi. to Mammoth Pool route. Go SE 4 mi. to Mammoth Pool CG.

SINGLE RATE:	$11	OPEN DATES:	Apr-Sept*
# of SINGLE SITES:	47	MAX SPUR:	30 feet
		MAX STAY:	14 days
		ELEVATION:	3500 feet

33 Lily Pad
Dinkey Creek • lat 37°00'26" lon 118°58'31"

DESCRIPTION: This CG is situated an open forest a short distance away from Wishon Reservoir. Boat fish at reservoir. Please check for local fishing regulations. Suplies are available at Wishon village. Campers may gather their firewood localy. Hiking and OHV trails nearby.

GETTING THERE: Lily Pad CG is located approx. 14 mi. E of Dinkey Creek on primary forest route 40 (McKinley Grove Road).

SINGLE RATE:	$15	OPEN DATES:	May-Nov
# of SINGLE SITES:	15		
		MAX STAY:	14 days
		ELEVATION:	6500 feet

38 Marmot Rock
Dinkey Creek • lat 37°04'39" lon 118°58'32"

DESCRIPTION: CG set in an open fir forest with views of Courtright Reservoir and Maxon Dome. Frequent afternoon thundershowers. Fish from the reservoir. Supplies at Wishon Village. Gather firewood. Nearby trails are Dusy/Ershim OHV route, Maxon Trailhead, and Dinkey Lakes TH. Boat ramp. Tent camping only.

GETTING THERE: From Dinkey Creek go E on primary forest route 40 (McKinley Grove Road) approx. 12 mi. to forest route 10S16 (Courtright Road). Go N on 10S16 approx. 7 mi. to Marmot Rock CG.

SINGLE RATE:	$15	OPEN DATES:	June-Oct
# of SINGLE SITES:	15		
		MAX STAY:	14 days
		ELEVATION:	8200 feet

34 Little Jackass
South Fork • lat 37°23'57" lon 119°20'10"

DESCRIPTION: This CG is situated in a pine and fir forest. Fish Chiquto Creek or go to Mamoth Pool. No drinking water. Watch for deer, black bears, mountain lions, bobcats, foxes, coyotes, and skunks in the area. Gather firewood locally. Off the Scenic Byway near the French Trail System for hiking.

GETTING THERE: From South Fork go E on county route 233 1/2 mi. to county route 225. Go SE 3 mi. to forest route 81. Go E then N 30 mi. to forest route 6S22. Go E 1 mi. to Little Jackass CG.

SINGLE RATE:	No fee	OPEN DATES:	June-Oct*
# of SINGLE SITES:	5	MAX SPUR:	40 feet
		MAX STAY:	14 days
		ELEVATION:	4800 feet

39 Midge Creek
Huntington • lat 37°15'27" lon 119°08'26"

DESCRIPTION: Among pine with pretty views. Warm days with few showers and cool nights. Boat and shore fish nearby Huntington Lake. Supplies at Lakeshore. CG receives light use. Firewood may be gathered or purchased at Huntington. Hiking at nearby Kaiser Wilderness. Deer and bears frequent area. Group sites only.

GETTING THERE: From Huntington go E on forest route 80 (Kaiser Pass Road) 4 miles to Midge Creek CG.

		OPEN DATES:	June-Sept
GROUP RATE:	$75	MAX STAY:	14 days
# of GROUP SITES:	2	ELEVATION:	7400 feet

35 Lower Chiquito
South Fork • lat 37°24'49" lon 119°23'05"

DESCRIPTION: CG situated in a pine and fir forest on creek. Fish for native rainbow and brown trout. No drinking water. Deer, black bears, mountain lions, bobcats, foxes, coyotes, and skunks. Close short hiking trails or hike nearby French Trail system. Paved road with sharp drop-off and tight turn arounds; use caution.

GETTING THERE: From South Fork go E on county route 233 1/2 mi. to county route 225. Go SE 3 mi. to forest route 81. Go E then N 27 mi. to forest route 6S01. Go N 3 mi. to Lower Chiquito CG.

SINGLE RATE:	$11	OPEN DATES:	June-Oct*
# of SINGLE SITES:	7	MAX SPUR:	28 feet
		MAX STAY:	14 days
		ELEVATION:	4900 feet

40 Mono Creek
Huntington Lake • lat 37°21'31" lon 118°59'51"

DESCRIPTION: This CG is situated among pine near a trout creek. Warm days with cool nights, expect rain. Supplies at Mono Hot Springs and Vermilion. Moderate to heavy use. Gather firewood. Horse riding nearby, Hike Ansel Adams or John Muir Wilderness. No drinking water. Watch for deer and bears in the area.

GETTING THERE: From Huntington Lake go N approx. 20 mi. on primary forest route 80 (Edison Road) to Mono Creek CG. Not recommended for trailers over 18' due to narrow pass.

SINGLE RATE:	Varies	OPEN DATES:	June-Sept
# of SINGLE SITES:	14	MAX SPUR:	20 feet
		MAX STAY:	14 days
		ELEVATION:	7400 feet

 Campground has hosts   **Reservable sites**   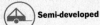 **Accessible facilities**   **Fully developed**   **Semi-developed**   **Rustic facilities**

NOTE: Open dates listed are typical. Actual dates are dependent on conditions such as snow pack.

41 Mono Hot Springs
Cedar Crest • lat 37°19'35" lon 119°01'04"

DESCRIPTION: CG situated near the San Joaquin River in a thick pine forest. Warm days with cool nights, frequent rain. Shore fish the river. Supplies at Mono Hot Springs Resort. Watch for bears and deer in the area. Gather firewood locally. Multiple horse and hiking trails nearby. No drinking water availble.

GETTING THERE: Mono Hot Springs CG is located approx. 18 mi. NE of Cedar Crest on primary forest route 80 (Kaiser Pass Road).

SINGLE RATE:	$12	OPEN DATES:	June-Sept
# of SINGLE SITES:	26		
		MAX STAY:	14 days
		ELEVATION:	6500 feet

46 Recreation Point
Oakhurst • lat 37°19'43" lon 119°34'40"

DESCRIPTION: On Bass Lake among tall mixed conifer and oak. Fish lake for bass, rainbow, catfish, sunfish, kokanee. Baseball, volleyball areas and amphitheater. Deer, black bears, mountain lion, bobcats, foxes, coyotes, skunk and small wildlife in area. Gather firewood. Max. 30 persons, 8 vehicles per site.

GETTING THERE: From Oakhurst go N on state HWY 41 approx. 2.5 mi. to county route 222. Go SE on 222 approx. 4 mi. to Recreation Point CG.

# of SINGLE SITES:	4	OPEN DATES:	Yearlong
GROUP RATE:	Varies	MAX SPUR:	40 feet
		MAX STAY:	14 days
		ELEVATION:	3413 feet

42 Nelder Grove
Oakhurst • lat 37°25'52" lon 119°34'57"

DESCRIPTION: This CG is situated in a mixed forest with an interpretive trail on site. No drinking water. Historic logging site and Giant Sequoia Grove; including Bull Buck, the 2nd largest Sequoia. Watch for deer, black bears, mountain lions, bobcats, foxes, coyotes, and skunks. Gather firewood locally.

GETTING THERE: From Oakhurst go N on state HWY 41 5 mi. to forest route 10 (Ranch Road). Go NE 6 mi. to forest route 6S90. Go N 2 mi. to Nelder Grove CG. Road is narrow with steep drop-offs.

SINGLE RATE:	No fee	OPEN DATES:	May-Sept*
# of SINGLE SITES:	7	MAX SPUR:	30 feet
		MAX STAY:	14 days
		ELEVATION:	5500 feet

47 Redinger Lake
South Fork • lat 37°08'42" lon 119°27'02"

DESCRIPTION: In an open setting on Redinger Lake. Hot days, paved campsites. Boat launch for recreational boating. No drinking water. No open fires. Deer, rattlesnakes and small wildlife in area. Popular for party groups, filling weekends and some weekdays.

GETTING THERE: From South Fork go SE on county route 225 approx. 6 mi. to county route 235. Go SW on 235 approx. 3 mi. to Redinger Lake CG.

SINGLE RATE:	No fee	OPEN DATES:	May-Oct*
# of SINGLE SITES:	5		
		MAX STAY:	14 days
		ELEVATION:	1400 feet

43 Placer
South Fork • lat 37°22'24" lon 119°21'48"

DESCRIPTION: This CG is situated in a young pine forest, set on the banks of Ciguito Creek. Near Placer Guard Station. Fish for trout in creek. Watch for deer, black bears, mountain lions, bobcats, foxes, coyotes, and skunks in the area. Gather firewood locally. Hike nearby French Trail system.

GETTING THERE: From South Fork go E on county route 233 1/2 mi. to county route 225. Go SE 3 mi. to forest route 81. Go E then N 28 mi. to Mammoth Pool route. Go SE 4 mi. to Placer CG. No recommended for RVs.

SINGLE RATE:	$11	OPEN DATES:	June-Oct*
# of SINGLE SITES:	8	MAX SPUR:	28 feet
		MAX STAY:	14 days
		ELEVATION:	4100 feet

48 Rock Creek
South Fork • lat 37°17'28" lon 119°21'34"

DESCRIPTION: CG set on the shores of Bass Lake among tall conifer and oak trees. Fish for bass, rainbow trout, catfish, sunfish, and kokanee. Fills weekends and holidays. Deer, black bears, mountain lions, bobcats, foxes, coyotes, and skunks. Bring your own firewood. Nearby hiking on French Trail System.

GETTING THERE: From South Fork go E on county route 233 approx. 1/2 mi. to county route 225. Go SE approx. 3 mi. to primary forest route 81 (Minarets Road). Go E then N approx. 15 mi. to Rock Creek CG.

SINGLE RATE:	Varies	OPEN DATES:	Apr-Oct*
# of SINGLE SITES:	18	MAX SPUR:	30 feet
		MAX STAY:	14 days
		ELEVATION:	4300 feet

44 Portal Forebay
Cedar Crest • lat 37°19'13" lon 119°04'01"

DESCRIPTION: This CG is situated in an open sandy area with pine nearby. Scenic views. Expect frequent noon rains. Warm days with cool nights, breezy. Shore and small boat fish nearby Forebay. Suplies at Mono Hot Springs Reort. Gather firewood locally. Many horse and hiking trails. No drinking water.

GETTING THERE: Portal Forebay CG is located approx. 12 mi. NE of Cedar Crest on primary forest route 80 (Kaiser Pass Road).

SINGLE RATE:	$8	OPEN DATES:	June-Sept
# of SINGLE SITES:	11		
		MAX STAY:	14 days
		ELEVATION:	7200 feet

49 Sample Meadow
Cedar Crest • lat 37°20'11" lon 119°09'19"

DESCRIPTION: CG situated in a dense pine forest on Kaiser Creek. Warm days with cool nights, frequent noon rains. Fish Kaiser Creek. Supplies at Hungtinton Lake. Watch for bears and deer. Moderate use. Gather firewood locally. Hike Kaiser Wilderness trails. Mountain bike opportunities nearby. No drinking water.

GETTING THERE: From Cedar Crest go NE on primary forest route 80 (Huntington Road) approx. 10 mi. to primary forest route 5. Go NW on 5 approx. 3 mi. to Sample Meadow CG.

SINGLE RATE:	No fee	OPEN DATES:	June-Sept
# of SINGLE SITES:	16		
		MAX STAY:	14 days
		ELEVATION:	7800 feet

45 Rancheria
Cedar Crest • lat 37°14'52" lon 119°09'40"

DESCRIPTION: This CG is situated in a dense pine forest with views of Huntington Lake. Warm days with cool evenings, breezy. Shore or boat fish the Lake. Supplies at Rancheria or Lakeshore Resort. Watch for bears and deer in the area. Buy or gather firewood. Muliple horse and hiking trails in Kaiser Wilderness.

GETTING THERE: From Cedar Crest go NE on primary forest route 80 (Huntington Road) approx. 3 mi. to state HWY 168 (intersection of Huntington RD and Kaiser Pass RD). Go S approx. 1/4 mi. to Rancheria CG.

SINGLE RATE:	Varies	OPEN DATES:	May-Oct*
# of SINGLE SITES:	149	MAX SPUR:	30 feet
		MAX STAY:	14 days
		ELEVATION:	7000 feet

50 Sawmill Flat
Dinkey Creek • lat 36°58'11" lon 119°00'58"

DESCRIPTION: This CG is situated in a dense fir forest. Expect mild days with cool nights. Supplies are available at Wishon Village. CG receives light use. Campers may gather their firewood locally. No designated trails, but a myriad of primitive trails meander through the woods.

GETTING THERE: From Dinkey Creek go E on primary forest route 40 (McKinley Grove Road) approx. 11 mi. to forest route 11S12. Go S on 11S12 approx. 2 mi. to Sawmill Flat CG.

SINGLE RATE:	No fee	OPEN DATES:	May-Nov
# of SINGLE SITES:	15		
		MAX STAY:	14 days
		ELEVATION:	6700 feet

 Campground has hosts **Reservable sites** 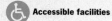 **Accessible facilities** **Fully developed** **Semi-developed** **Rustic facilities**

NOTE: Open dates listed are typical. Actual dates are dependent on conditions such as snow pack.

51 Soda Springs
South Fork • lat 37°22'52" lon 119°23'13"

DESCRIPTION: This CG is situated in a dense pine forest. No nearby fishing - go to Mammoth Pool for day trips. No drinking water available on site. Watch for deer, black bears, mountain lions, bobcats, foxes, coyotes, and skunks in the area. Gather firewood locally. No hiking trails in the vicinity.

GETTING THERE: From South Fork go E on county route 233 1/2 mi. to county route 225. Go SE 3 mi. to primary forest route 81 (Minarets Road). Go E then N 26 mi. to Soda Springs CG.

SINGLE RATE:	$11	OPEN DATES:	May-Oct*
# of SINGLE SITES:	18	MAX SPUR:	40 feet
		MAX STAY:	14 days
		ELEVATION:	4300 feet

56 Swanson Meadow
Shaver Lake • lat 37°05'43" lon 119°16'35"

DESCRIPTION: CG set in heavily wooded area, near some meadows. Warm days with cool evenings. Shore or boat fish Shaver Lake, 2 mi. away. Supplies at Shaver Lake. Moderate use, fills weekends August-September. Gather firewood locally. Hike nearby trails. Horse trails available 4-6 mi. away. Snow may change dates.

GETTING THERE: Swanson Meadow CG is located approx. 2 mi. E of Shaver Lake on Dinkey Creek Road.

SINGLE RATE:	$8	OPEN DATES:	May-Oct
# of SINGLE SITES:	8	MAX SPUR:	25 feet
		MAX STAY:	14 days
		ELEVATION:	5600 feet

52 Soquel
Oakhurst • lat 37°24'18" lon 119°33'38"

DESCRIPTION: This CG is situated in a mixed cedar, pine, fir, and hardwood forest on the North Fork of Willow creek. Fish for native rainbow and brown trout. No drinking water. Watch for deer, black bears, mountain lions, bobcats, foxes, coyotes, and skunks. Gather firewood. Hiking and horse trails nearby.

GETTING THERE: From Oakhurst go N on state HWY 41 5 mi. to primary forest route 10 (Ranch Road). Go NE 5.5 mi. to forest route 6S40. Go S 1 mi. to Soquel CG. Rough road, no recommended for RVs.

SINGLE RATE:	$11	OPEN DATES:	June-Oct*
# of SINGLE SITES:	11		
		MAX STAY:	14 days
		ELEVATION:	5400 feet

57 Sweet Water
South Fork • lat 37°21'54" lon 119°21'08"

DESCRIPTION: CG situated among mixed conifer and oak. Approx. 2 mi. to Mammoth Pool for fishing (closed 5/1-6/16 to boating). Watch for deer, black bears, mountain lions, bobcats, foxes, coyotes, and skunks. Gather firewood. Nearby French Trail system for hiking. Fills holidays and weekends, reservations required.

GETTING THERE: From South Fork go E on county route 233 1/2 mi. to county route 225. Go SE 3 mi. to forest route 81. Go E then N 28 mi. to Mammoth Pool route. Go SE 2 mi. to Sweet Water CG. RVs not recommended.

SINGLE RATE:	$11	OPEN DATES:	May-Oct*
# of SINGLE SITES:	10		
		MAX STAY:	14 days
		ELEVATION:	3800 feet

53 Spring Cove
Oakhurst • lat 37°18'02" lon 119°32'29"

DESCRIPTION: This CG is set on the shores of Bass Lake, situated among tall pine and oak trees. Fish lake for bass, rainbow trout, catfish, sunfish, and kokanee. Watch for deer, bald eagle, osprey, black bears, mountain lions, bobcats, foxes, coyotes, skunks. Bring your own firewood. Fills weekends and holidays.

GETTING THERE: From Oakhurst go E on county route 426 approx. 6.5 mi. to county route 222. Go E on 222 approx. 4 mi. to Spring Cove CG.

SINGLE RATE:	$16	OPEN DATES:	Apr-Sept*
# of SINGLE SITES:	63	MAX SPUR:	40 feet
		MAX STAY:	14 days
		ELEVATION:	3400 feet

58 Texas Flat Group
Oakhurst • lat 37°23'34" lon 119°34'54"

DESCRIPTION: Located in mixed conifer. No drinking water. Stream fish nearby. Deer, black bears, mountain lion, bobcats, foxes, coyotes, skunk and small wildlife in area. Gather firewood. Nearby Nelder Grove giant sequoias have the second largest sequoia. Horse facilites. Horse and hiking trails nearby.

GETTING THERE: From Oakhurst go N on state HWY 41 3.5 mi. to primary forest route 10. Continue on 10 5.5 mi. to forest route 6S40. Go S on 6S40 1.5 mi. to forest route 6S38. Go N on 6S38 3 mi. to Texas Flat Group CG.

SINGLE RATE:	$12	OPEN DATES:	June-Oct*
		MAX SPUR:	40 feet
		MAX STAY:	14 days
# of GROUP SITES:	4	ELEVATION:	5500 feet

54 Summerdale
Fish Camp • lat 37°29'31" lon 119°37'57"

DESCRIPTION: CG situated in a pine and fir forest on a small creek. Fish for trout. Deer, black bears, mountain lions, bobcats, foxes, coyotes, and skunks. Gather firewood. Some Campground programs. Hike Lewis Creek Nat'l Rec. Trail. Close access to S entrance of Yosemite NP. Goat Meadow Winter Sports area nearby.

GETTING THERE: Summerdale CG is located approx. 1 mi. N of Fish Camp on state HWY 41.

SINGLE RATE:	$13	OPEN DATES:	Apr-Oct*
# of SINGLE SITES:	30	MAX SPUR:	40 feet
		MAX STAY:	14 days
		ELEVATION:	5000 feet

59 Trapper Springs
Dinkey Creek • lat 37°06'01" lon 118°59'04"

DESCRIPTION: This CG is situated in a dense fir forest a short distance away from Courtright Reservoir. Fish from the reservoir. Check for local fishing regulations. Supplies are available at Wishon Reservoir. Campers may gather their firewood locally. Several trails in the area.

GETTING THERE: From Dinkey Creek go E on forest route 40 (McKinley Grove Road) 12 mi. to forest route 10S16 (Courtright Road). Go N 7 mi. to forest route 8S07. Go N 2 mi. to Trapper Springs CG.

SINGLE RATE:	$15	OPEN DATES:	June-Oct
# of SINGLE SITES:	75		
		MAX STAY:	14 days
		ELEVATION:	8200 feet

55 Summit Camp
Fish Camp • lat 37°30'32" lon 119°41'37"

DESCRIPTION: This CG will unfortunately be closed for repairs through the 2000 season. Contact Mariposa/Minarets RD at 559-877-2218 for further information and opening dates.

GETTING THERE: Summit Camp CG is located approx. 5 mi. NW of Fish Camp on forest route 5S09X.

		OPEN DATES:	Temporarily C
# of SINGLE SITES:	6		
		MAX STAY:	14 days
		ELEVATION:	5800 feet

60 Upper Chiquito
Bass Lake • lat 37°30'08" lon 119°24'35"

DESCRIPTION: This CG is situated in a mixed fir, lodgepole, and cedar forest on the East Fork of Chiquito Creek. Good fishing. Cooler days. No drinking water. Watch for deer, black bears, mountain lions, bobcats, foxes, coyotes, and skunks. Gather firewood locally. Horse and hiking trails in Ansel Adams Wilderness.

GETTING THERE: Upper Chiquito CG is located approx. 18 mi. NE of Bass Lake on primary forest route 7 (Beasore Road).

SINGLE RATE:	No fee	OPEN DATES:	June-Oct*
# of SINGLE SITES:	20	MAX SPUR:	28 feet
		MAX STAY:	14 days
		ELEVATION:	6800 feet

 Campground has hosts   **Reservable sites**   **Accessible facilities**   **Fully developed**   **Semi-developed**   **Rustic facilities**

NOTE: Open dates listed are typical. Actual dates are dependent on conditions such as snow pack.

61 Upper Kings
Dinkey Creek • lat 36°51'54" lon 119°01'24"

DESCRIPTION: This CG is situated in a dense mixed conifer forest, surrounded by granite rock. Fish on the Upper Kings River or Wishon Reservoir. Please check for local fishing regulations. Supplies are available at Wishon Village. Campers may gather or buy firewood at Wishon Village. CG may be frequented by bears.

GETTING THERE: Upper Kings CG is located approx. 14 mi. E of Dinkey Creek on primary forest route 40 (McKinley Grove Road).

		OPEN DATES:	May-Sept
GROUP RATE:	$125	MAX STAY:	14 days
# of GROUP SITES:	1	ELEVATION:	6000 feet

62 Vermillion
Cedar Crest • lat 37°22'37" lon 119°00'41"

DESCRIPTION: CG set in a rocky area with trees on Thomas A. Edison Lake. Warm, windy days. Shore or boat fish the lake. Limited supplies at Lake Edison or Vermilion Valley Resort. Watch for deer and bears in the area. Fills weekends July-August. Gather firewood. Muliple hiking and horse trails to wilderness.

GETTING THERE: Vermillion CG is located approx. 24 mi. NE of Cedar Crest on primary forest route 80 (Kaiser Pass Road). Not recommended for trailers over 18' due to narrow pass.

		OPEN DATES:	June-Sept
SINGLE RATE:	$12	MAX STAY:	14 days
# of SINGLE SITES:	31	ELEVATION:	7700 feet

63 Voyager Rock
Dinkey Creek • lat 37°06'13" lon 118°57'39"

DESCRIPTION: CG situated in a dense fir forest with views of Courtright Reservoir. Fish from the reservoir. Supplies are at Wishon Village. Gather firewood localy. A few trails nearby. Mosquitos can be a problem early in the summer. Tent camping only. No drinking water. CG accessible by boat or 4WD only.

GETTING THERE: From Dinkey Creek go E on forest route 40 12 mi. to forest route 10S16 (Courtright Road). Go N 7 mi. to Dusty Ershim Route (OHV). Go N 3 mi. to Voyager Rock CG. 4WD required.

		OPEN DATES:	June-Nov
SINGLE RATE:	No fee	MAX STAY:	14 days
# of SINGLE SITES:	13	ELEVATION:	8200 feet

64 Ward Lake
Cedar Crest • lat 37°18'06" lon 118°59'05"

DESCRIPTION: This CG is situated in a pine and fir forest a short distance away from Ward Lake. Fish for trout on lake. Check for local regulations. Watch for deer and bears in the area. No drinking water available on site. Numerous trails in area for horse and hiking use. Access into John Muir Wilderness nearby.

GETTING THERE: From Cedar Crest go NE on forest route 80 (Huntington Road) 16.5 mi. to Florence Lake Road. Go SE 3 mi. to Ward Lake CG. Not recommended for trailers over 18' due to narrow pass.

		OPEN DATES:	June-Oct
SINGLE RATE:	$8	MAX STAY:	14 days
# of SINGLE SITES:	17	ELEVATION:	7300 feet

65 Whiskers
Bass Lake • lat 37°20'02" lon 119°29'29"

DESCRIPTION: CG set in an exposed area on the banks of Sand Creek. Hot summer days. No drinking water. Watch for deer, black bears, mountain lions, bobcats, foxes, coyotes, and skunks. Gather firewood locally. Mountain biking, motor cycle trails, hunting, 007 Trail to Shuteye Mountain (big ride April 15 weekend).

GETTING THERE: From Bass Lake go S on county route 274 approx. 4 mi. to forest route 6S42 (Central Camp Road). Go N on 6S42 approx. 6.5 mi. to Whiskers CG. Very rough road, not recommended for RVs.

		OPEN DATES:	May-Nov*
SINGLE RATE:	$11	MAX STAY:	14 days
# of SINGLE SITES:	8	ELEVATION:	5300 feet

66 Whiskey Falls
South Fork • lat 37°17'08" lon 119°26'23"

DESCRIPTION: A shady CG set among black oak, pine, and cedar. Light fishing on scenic Whiskey Creek. No drinking water. Watch for deer, black bears, mountain lions, bobcats, foxes, coyotes, and skunks in the area. Bring your own firewood. Known as a relaxing, peaceful area. Mosquitos are thick until mid-August.

GETTING THERE: From South Fork go E on county route 233 2 mi. to forest route 8S09. Go N 6 mi. to forest route 8S70. Go NE 1 mi. to Whiskey Falls CG. No recommended for RVs.

		OPEN DATES:	May-Oct*
SINGLE RATE:	No fee	MAX STAY:	14 days
# of SINGLE SITES:	14	ELEVATION:	5800 feet

67 Wishon Bass Lake
Oakhurst • lat 37°17'50" lon 119°32'02"

DESCRIPTION: CG situated in a mature conifer and oak forest a Bass Lake. Fish for bass and trout. Deer, black bears, bald eagles, osprey, mountain lions, bobcats, foxes, coyotes, and skunks in the area. Bring your own firewood. Hiking on the Goat Mountain or Willow Creek Trails. Fills weekends and holidays.

GETTING THERE: From Oakhurst go E on county route 426 approx. 6.5 mi. to county route 222. Go E on 222 approx. 5 mi. to Wishon Bass Lake CG.

		OPEN DATES:	May-Sept
SINGLE RATE:	Varies	MAX SPUR:	40 feet
# of SINGLE SITES:	47	MAX STAY:	14 days
		ELEVATION:	3400 feet

 Campground has hosts **Reservable sites** **Accessible facilities** 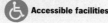 **Fully developed** 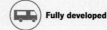 **Semi-developed**  **Rustic facilities**

NOTE: Open dates listed are typical. Actual dates are dependent on conditions such as snow pack.

SIX RIVERS NATIONAL FOREST

"Can you name the six rivers?" is one of the commonly asked questions on the North Coast. The rivers, which are the Smith, Klamath, Trinity, Eel, Mad, and Van Duzen, flow through the more than 1,500 square miles of the Six Rivers National Forest. Native Americans, trappers, gold miners, settlers, loggers, the Civilian Conservation Corps, the Forest Service, recreation visitors and even the legendary "Bigfoot" have all contributed to the rich history of these lands.

The forest is as biologically and geologically diverse as the tapestry of people who have called this land home or relied on its bounty for their livelihood. As you travel the forest, which ranges from 1,500 feet to 7,000 feet in elevation, you'll see evidence of times past and experience continuing traditions. Discover what makes the forest a special place to relax, explore, and enjoy.

Visit the Smith River National Recreation Area which encompasses the largest wild and scenic river system in the nation. Hike to a lookout tower for a 360-degree view of mountains as far as you can see. Raft emerald green waters. There's something here for everyone, from the solitude of remote areas or to comfortable, developed recreation sites.

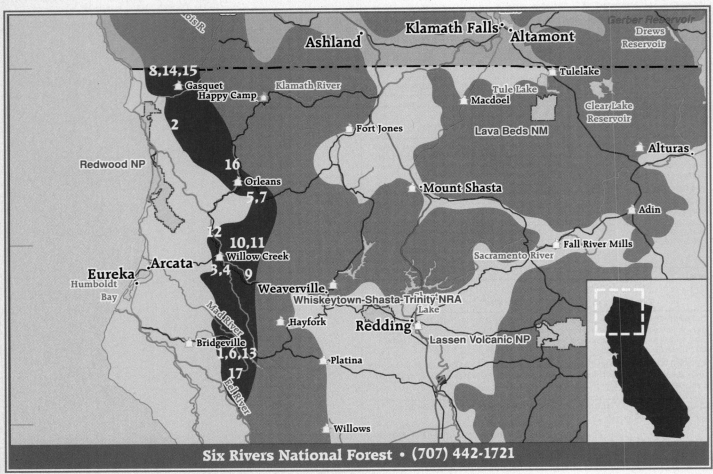

Six Rivers National Forest • (707) 442-1721

1 Bailey Canyon
Sportshaven • lat 40°20'26" lon 123°23'55"

DESCRIPTION: This CG is situated in ponderosa pine and douglas fir on Ruth Reservoir. Enjoy fishing for bass and trout. Wildlife in this area includes black bears, mountain lions, coyotes, deer, osprey, and falcons. CG is busy holidays. Visit nearby Lassics Botanical Area which offers unique geological sites.

GETTING THERE: From Sportshaven go S on county route 501 approx. 13 mi. to Bailey Canyon CG.

SINGLE RATE:	$12	OPEN DATES:	May-Sept*
# of SINGLE SITES:	25	MAX SPUR:	22 feet
		MAX STAY:	14 days
		ELEVATION:	2600 feet

2 Big Flat
Gasquet • lat 41°41'16" lon 123°54'31"

DESCRIPTION: This CG rests in fir, madrone, and some cedar near South Fork Smith River. Enjoy fishing for salmon and steelhead. Wildlife includes black bears, mountain lions, deer, redtail hawks, songbirds and otters. CG is busy holiday weekends. Hike the South Kelsey Trail to the Siskiyou Wilderness. No drinking water.

GETTING THERE: From Gasquet go W on US HWY 199 approx. 8 mi. to county route 427. Go SE on 427 approx. 17 mi. to county route 405. Go N on 405 approx. 1/2 mi. to Big Flat CG.

SINGLE RATE:	$6	OPEN DATES:	May-Sept
# of SINGLE SITES:	28	MAX SPUR:	22 feet
		MAX STAY:	14 days
		ELEVATION:	660 feet

3 Boise Creek
Willow Creek • lat 40°56'42" lon 123°39'26"

DESCRIPTION: This CG is situated in oak and madrone on Willow Creek. Fishing is not allowed in this creek but is allowed in other areas. Please check fishing regulations. Wildlife in this area includes black bears, mountain lions, deer, otters, and raptors. There is a short trail that leads to the Creek and swimming hole.

GETTING THERE: Boise Creek CG is located approx. 2 mi. W of Willow Creek on state HWY 299.

SINGLE RATE:	Varies	OPEN DATES:	Yearlong
# of SINGLE SITES:	17	MAX SPUR:	35 feet
		MAX STAY:	14 days
		ELEVATION:	1680 feet

4 East Fork
Willow Creek • lat 40°54'30" lon 123°42'20"

DESCRIPTION: This CG rests in alder, cedar and fir on East Fork Willow Creek. Fishing is not allowed in this creek but is allowed in other areas. Please check fishing regulations. Wildlife in this area includes black bears, mountain lions, deer, otters, and raptors. No drinking water. Hiking/mountain biking opportunities nearby.

GETTING THERE: East Fork CG is located approx. 6 mi. W of Willow Creek off of state HWY 299.

SINGLE RATE:	$6	OPEN DATES:	May-Oct
# of SINGLE SITES:	9	MAX SPUR:	20 feet
		MAX STAY:	14 days
		ELEVATION:	1600 feet

5 E-Ne-Nuck
Orleans • lat 41°14'00" lon 123°39'30"

DESCRIPTION: This CG is situated in lodgepole pine and douglas fir on Bluff Creek. Enjoy fishing for salmon and steelhead. Wildlife in this area includes black bears, mountain lions, coyotes, deer, osprey, bald eagles, and otters. Hike in nearby Trinity Alps and Marble Mountain Wilderness areas.

GETTING THERE: E-Ne-Nuck CG is located approx. 9 mi. SW of Orleans on state HWY 96.

SINGLE RATE:	$8	OPEN DATES:	May-Nov
# of SINGLE SITES:	11	MAX SPUR:	30 feet
		MAX STAY:	14 days
		ELEVATION:	400 feet

6 Fir Cove
Sportshaven • lat 40°20'35" lon 123°24'12"

DESCRIPTION: This CG is located in ponderosa pine and douglas fir on Ruth Reservoir. Enjoy fishing for bass and trout. Wildlife in this area includes black bears, mountain lions, coyotes, deer, opsprey, and falcons. CG is busy holidays. Visit nearby Lassics Botanical Area which offers unique geological sites.

GETTING THERE: Fir Cove is located approx. 13 mi. S of Sportshaven on county route 501.

SINGLE RATE:	Varies	OPEN DATES:	May-Sept
# of SINGLE SITES:	19	MAX SPUR:	22 feet
GROUP RATE:	Varies	MAX STAY:	14 days
# of GROUP SITES:	1	ELEVATION:	2600 feet

7 Fish Lake
Orleans • lat 41°15'54" lon 123°41'04"

DESCRIPTION: This CG is located in lodgepole pine, douglas fir, and some Port Orford cedar on Fish Lake. Enjoy fishing for trout. Wildlife in this area includes black bears, mountain lions, coyotes, deer, osprey, bald eagles, and otters. Hike in nearby Trinity Alps and Marble Mountain Wilderness areas.

GETTING THERE: From Orleans go SW on state HWY 96 approx. 10 mi. to primary forest route 13. Go NW on 13 approx. 4.5 mi. to forest route 10N12. Go N on 10N12 approx. 2.5 mi. to Fish Lake CG.

SINGLE RATE:	$8	OPEN DATES:	May-Sept*
# of SINGLE SITES:	24	MAX SPUR:	20 feet
		MAX STAY:	14 days
		ELEVATION:	1750 feet

8 Grassy Flat
Gasquet • lat 41°51'24" lon 123°53'16"

DESCRIPTION: This open CG rests in fir, madrone, and some cedar on Middle Fork Smith River. Enjoy fishing for salmon and steelhead. Wildlife includes black bears, mountain lions, deer, redtail hawks, songbirds and otters. Hike the Darlingtonia Trail and view the extraordinary California Pitcher Plant, an insect digesting plant.

GETTING THERE: Grassy Flat CG is located approx. 5 mi. E of Gasquet on US HWY 199.

SINGLE RATE:	$10	OPEN DATES:	May-Sept
# of SINGLE SITES:	19	MAX SPUR:	30 feet
		MAX STAY:	14 days
		ELEVATION:	500 feet

9 Grays Falls
Trinity Village • lat 40°51'26" lon 123°29'26"

DESCRIPTION: This CG is currently closed for updates. Please contact the Lower Trinity Ranger District at (530) 629-2118 for open date.

GETTING THERE: Grays Falls CG is located approx. 2 mi. SE of Trinity Village on state HWY 299.

SINGLE RATE:	$10	OPEN DATES:	May-Sept
# of SINGLE SITES:	33	MAX SPUR:	35 feet
		MAX STAY:	14 days
		ELEVATION:	220 feet

10 Groves Prairie
Trinity Village • lat 40°57'00" lon 123°29'00"

DESCRIPTION: This rustic CG rests in a large prairie with fir and hardwood. Fishing is not allowed in this creek but is allowed in other areas. Please check fishing regulations. Wildlife in this area includes black bears, mountain lions, deer, otters, and many birds. The nearby Grizzly Camp Trail leads to Trinity Alps summit area.

GETTING THERE: From Trinity Village go NE on route 402 4 mi. to forest route 7N26. Go N on 7N26 9 mi. to forest route 7N10. Go NW on 7N10 3 mi. to forest route 7N04. Go S on 7N04 2 mi. to Groves Prairie CG.

SINGLE RATE:	No fee	OPEN DATES:	Yearlong
# of SINGLE SITES:	10	MAX SPUR:	20 feet
		MAX STAY:	14 days
		ELEVATION:	1140 feet

 Campground has hosts 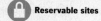 **Reservable sites** 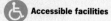 **Accessible facilities** 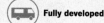 **Fully developed**   **Semi-developed** **Rustic facilities**

NOTE: Open dates listed are typical. Actual dates are dependent on conditions such as snow pack.

11 Happy Camp
Trinity Village • lat 40°55'11" lon 123°29'24"

DESCRIPTION: This rustic CG is situated in fir and hardwood. Fishing is not allowed in this creek but is allowed in other areas. Please check fishing regulations. Wildlife in this area includes black bears, mountain lions, deer, otters, and many birds. The nearby Grizzly Camp Trail leads to Trinity Alps summit area.

GETTING THERE: From Trinity Village go NE on co route 402 4 mi. to forest route 7N26. Go N on 7N26 3 mi. to forest route 6N10. Go NW on 6N10 1 mi. to forest route 8N02. Go N on 8N02 1 mi. to Happy Camp CG.

SINGLE RATE:	No fee	OPEN DATES:	Yearlong
# of SINGLE SITES:	2	MAX SPUR:	20 feet
		MAX STAY:	14 days
		ELEVATION:	1220 feet

12 Horse Linto
Willow Creek • lat 41°00'15" lon 123°36'30"

DESCRIPTION: This CG is located in oak, fir and alder at the confluence of Horse Linto and Cedar Creeks. Fishing is not allowed in these creeks but is allowed in other areas. Please check fishing regulations. Wildlife includes black bears, mountain lions, deer, otters, and many birds. Interpretive trail on site. No drinking water.

GETTING THERE: From Willow Creek go N on county route approx. 1 mi. to forest route 8N03. Go N on 8N03 approx. 3.5 mi. to Horse Linto CG.

SINGLE RATE:	No fee	OPEN DATES:	Yearlong
# of SINGLE SITES:	3	MAX SPUR:	20 feet
		MAX STAY:	14 days
		ELEVATION:	480 feet

13 Mad River
Sportshaven • lat 40°24'12" lon 123°27'56"

DESCRIPTION: This CG rests in ponderosa pine and douglas fir on Mad River. Enjoy catch and release fishing for trout. Wildlife in this area includes black bears, mountain lions, coyotes, deer, and peregrine falcons. CG is busy holidays. Visit nearby Lassics Botanical Area which offers unique geological sites.

GETTING THERE: Mad River is located approx. 4 mi. S of Sportshaven on county route 501.

SINGLE RATE:	$12	OPEN DATES:	Yearlong
# of SINGLE SITES:	40	MAX SPUR:	30 feet
		MAX STAY:	14 days
		ELEVATION:	2500 feet

14 Panther Flat
Gasquet • lat 41°50'33" lon 123°55'47"

DESCRIPTION: This open CG rests in fir, madrone, and some cedar on Middle Fork Smith River. Enjoy fishing for salmon and steelhead. Wildlife includes black bears, mountain lions, deer, redtail hawks, songbirds and otters. Hike the Darlingtonia Trail and view the extraordinary California Pitcher Plant, an insect digesting plant.

GETTING THERE: Panther Flat CG is located approx. 3 mi. E of Gasquet on US HWY 199.

SINGLE RATE:	$14	OPEN DATES:	Yearlong
# of SINGLE SITES:	39	MAX SPUR:	40 feet
		MAX STAY:	14 days
		ELEVATION:	500 feet

15 Patrick Creek
Gasquet • lat 41°52'19" lon 123°50'40"

DESCRIPTION: This open CG rests in fir, madrone, and some cedar at the confluence of Patrick Creek and Middle Fork Smith River. Enjoy fishing for salmon and steelhead. Wildlife includes black bears, mountain lions, deer, redtail hawks, songbirds and otters. Visit historic Patrick Creek Lodge and watch for a future interpretive trail.

GETTING THERE: Patrick Creek CG is located approx. 8 mi. E of Gasquet on US HWY 199.

SINGLE RATE:	$12	OPEN DATES:	May-Sept
# of SINGLE SITES:	13	MAX SPUR:	35 feet
		MAX STAY:	14 days
		ELEVATION:	800 feet

16 Pearch Creek
Orleans • lat 41°18'33" lon 123°31'11"

DESCRIPTION: This shady CG rests in lodgepole pine and douglas fir on Pearch Creek. Enjoy the quiet solitude and bubbling creek of this beautiful CG. Wildlife in this area includes black bears, mountain lions, coyotes, deer, osprey, bald eagles, and otters. Hike in nearby Trinity Alps and Marble Mountain Wilderness areas.

GETTING THERE: Pearch Creek CG is located approx. 1.5 mi. NE of Orleans on state HWY 96.

SINGLE RATE:	$8	OPEN DATES:	May-Nov
# of SINGLE SITES:	10	MAX SPUR:	22 feet
		MAX STAY:	14 days
		ELEVATION:	650 feet

17 Watts Lake
Zenia • lat 40°15'02" lon 123°29'45"

DESCRIPTION: This dispersed CG sits in ponderosa pine and douglas fir on Watts Lake. Wildlife in this area includes black bears, mountain lions, coyotes, deer, and peregrine falcons. CG is busy during hunting season. Visit nearby Lassics Botanical Area which offers unique geological sites. No drinking water.

GETTING THERE: From Zenia go SE on county route 503 approx. 1/2 mi. to county route 502. Go NE on 502 approx. 1.5 mi. to forest route 2S08. Go N on 2S08 approx. 3.5 mi. to Watts Lake CG.

SINGLE RATE:	No fee	OPEN DATES:	Yearlong
		MAX STAY:	14 days
		ELEVATION:	5000 feet

 Campground has hosts   **Reservable sites**   **Accessible facilities**   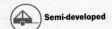 **Fully developed**   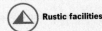 **Semi-developed**   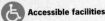 **Rustic facilities**

NOTE: Open dates listed are typical. Actual dates are dependent on conditions such as snow pack.

Page 148

Kathleen Burnett Photo, USDS Forest Service

STANISLAUS NATIONAL FOREST

You can fish in over 800 miles of rivers and streams, stay in a campground, or hike into the backcountry seeking pristine solitude on the Stanislaus National Forest.

The Stanislaus, created on February 22, 1897, is among the oldest of the national forests. It is named for the Stanislaus River whose headwaters rise within forest boundaries. The Spanish explorer Gabriel Moraga named the river "Our Lady of Guadulupe" during an 1806 expedition. Later, the river was renamed in honor of Estanislao, an Indian leader. During the gold rush, the area became a busy place, occupied by miners and other immigrants, homesteaders and ranchers, dam builders and loggers. Ditches were built, providing water to the mines. Several railroads were constructed to haul logs out of the woods. Evidence of these early activities still exist.

Within its diverse landscapes, the Stanislaus provides habitat for 325 wildlife species and 18 fish species. It also offers a variety of recreational opportunities. You can swim near a sandy beach or wade into cold clear streams cooling your feet while lost in the beauty of nature. Raft the exciting and breathtaking Tuolumne River, or canoe one of the many gorgeous lakes. You can ride a horse, a mountain bike or a snowmobile.

STANISLAUS NATIONAL FOREST • CALIFORNIA • LOCATOR MAP

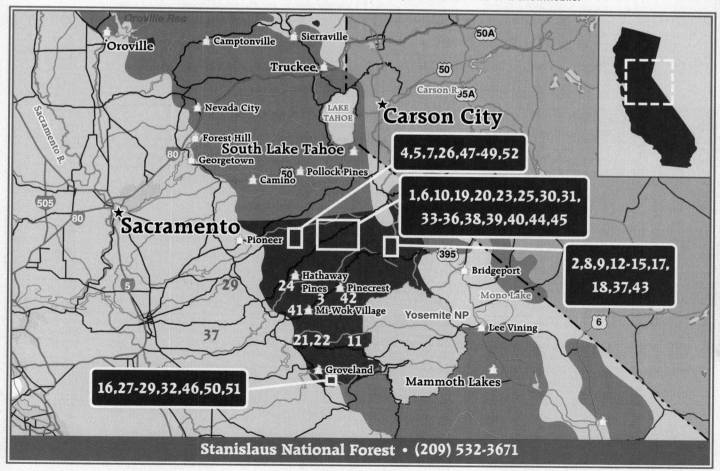

Stanislaus National Forest • (209) 532-3671

1 Backpackers
Murphys • lat 38°28'56" lon 119°59'14"

DESCRIPTION: CG set in a dense lodgepole pine and fir forest with views of Lake Alpine. Backpack in only. Supplies are available in Bears Valley or at Lake Alpine Lodge. Fish for trout. Walk-in sites. No parking. Paved bike/hike trail from Bears Valley to Lake Alpine. Silver Valley TH accesses Carson-Iceberg Wilderness.

GETTING THERE: From Murphys go NE approx. 45 mi. on state HWY 4 to Backpackers CG. No parking, hike-in only.

SINGLE RATE:	$14.50	OPEN DATES:	June-Oct*
# of SINGLE SITES:	10	MAX STAY:	1 days
		ELEVATION:	7300 feet

2 Baker
Sonora • lat 38°19'27" lon 119°45'07"

DESCRIPTION: CG set on the banks of the Middle Fork Stanislaus River within the Brightman Rec. Area. Fish for rainbow, brook, or german brown trout. Supplies at Kennedy Meadows Resort. Gather firewood. Watch for bears, deer, and wildcats. Kennedy Trails access Emigrant Wilderness. Be cautious of poison oak in area.

GETTING THERE: From Sonora go NE on state HWY 108 approx. 48.5 mi. to Baker CG.

SINGLE RATE:	$9.50	OPEN DATES:	May-Oct
# of SINGLE SITES:	44	MAX SPUR:	22 feet
		MAX STAY:	14 days
		ELEVATION:	6200 feet

3 Beardsley
Sonora • lat 38°14'00" lon 120°05'30"

DESCRIPTION: CG set in an open area along the shores of Beardsley Reservoir. No drinking water. Boat ramp, picnic area, swimming, and nature trail nearby. Fish reservoir or Middle Fork Stanislaus River for trout. Watch for bears, deer, and wildcats in the area. Short downstream trail to afterbay. Poison oak in area.

GETTING THERE: From Sonora go NE on HWY 108 approx. 15 mi. to Beardsley Road. Go W on Beardsley Road approx. 7 miles to Beardsley CG.

SINGLE RATE:	No fee	OPEN DATES:	May-Oct
# of SINGLE SITES:	26	MAX SPUR:	22 feet
		MAX STAY:	14 days
		ELEVATION:	3400 feet

4 Big Meadow
Murphys • lat 38°24'59" lon 120°06'18"

DESCRIPTION: CG set in a mature forest with views of natural granitic rock outcropings. Fishing for brown and rainbow trout on the North Fork Stanislaus River, via a 3/4 mi. unmaintained trail. Supplies in Arnold and Lake Alpine. Gather firewood locally. Watch for deer, black bears, mountain lions, and bobcats.

GETTING THERE: Big Meadow CG is located approx. 28 mi. NE of Murphys on state HWY 4.

SINGLE RATE:	$11	OPEN DATES:	June-Oct*
# of SINGLE SITES:	65	MAX SPUR:	27 feet
		MAX STAY:	14 days
		ELEVATION:	6460 feet

5 Big Meadow Group
Murphys • lat 38°24'59" lon 120°06'18"

DESCRIPTION: CG set in a mature forest with views of natural granitic rock outcropings. Fishing for brown and rainbow trout on the North Fork Stanislaus River, via a 3/4 mi. unmaintained trail. Supplies in Arnold and Lake Alpine. Gather firewood locally. Watch for deer, black bears, mountain lions, and bobcats.

GETTING THERE: Big Meadow CG is located approx. 28 mi. NE of Murphys on state HWY 4.

		OPEN DATES:	May-Sept*
		MAX SPUR:	21 feet
GROUP RATE:	Varies	MAX STAY:	14 days
# of GROUP SITES:	10	ELEVATION:	6460 feet

6 Bloomfield
Murphys • lat 38°32'17" lon 119°49'29"

DESCRIPTION: CG in a timbered setting on the banks of North Fork Mokelumne River. Trout fish the river. Warm days with frequent noon t-storms. Gather firewood locally. Supplies in Bears Valley, Lake Alpine, or Markleville. Watch for black bears, mountain lions, and bobcats. 3 mi. to Carson-Iceberg Wilderness access.

GETTING THERE: From Murphys go NE approx. 47.5 mi. on state HWY 4 to forest route. Go SE on forest route approx. 1.5 mi. to Bloomfield CG. Not recommended for trailers or RVs.

SINGLE RATE:	$8	OPEN DATES:	June-Oct*
# of SINGLE SITES:	20	MAX SPUR:	15 feet
		MAX STAY:	14 days
		ELEVATION:	7800 feet

7 Boards Crossing
Murphys • lat 38°18'16" lon 120°13'59"

DESCRIPTION: CG in a mature grove of ponderosa pine and black oak. Dispersed sites. No drinking water, no services. Fire permit required. Supplies available at Arnold and Camp Connell. Fishing for brown and rainbow trout in North Fork Stanislaus River. Watch for deer, black bears, and bobcats. No nearby trails.

GETTING THERE: From Murphys go 14 mi. on state HWY 4 to primary forest route 52. Go E 1.5 mi. to forest route 5N75. Go S on 5N75 1 mi. to Boards Crossing CG. Not recommended for trailers.

SINGLE RATE:	No fee	OPEN DATES:	June-Oct*
# of SINGLE SITES:	5		
		MAX STAY:	14 days
		ELEVATION:	6800 feet

8 Boulder Flat
Sonora • lat 38°21'18" lon 119°51'40"

DESCRIPTION: CG set on the banks of the Middle Fork Stanislaus River within the Brightman Rec. Area. Fish for rainbow, brook, or german brown trout. Supplies at Kennedy Meadows Resort. Gather firewood. Watch for deer, black bears, mountain lions, and bobcats in the area. Be cautious of poison oak. No nearby trails.

GETTING THERE: From Sonora go NE on state HWY 108 approx. 42.5 mi. to Boulder Flat CG.

SINGLE RATE:	Varies	OPEN DATES:	May-Oct
# of SINGLE SITES:	20	MAX SPUR:	22 feet
		MAX STAY:	14 days
		ELEVATION:	5600 feet

9 Brightman Flat
Sonora • lat 38°21'09" lon 119°50'57"

DESCRIPTION: CG set on the banks of the Middle Fork Stanislaus River within the Brightman Rec. Area. Fish for rainbow, brook, or german brown trout. Supplies at Kennedy Meadows Resort. Gather firewood. Watch for deer, black bears, mountain lions, and bobcats in the area. Be cautious of poison oak.

GETTING THERE: From Sonora go NE on state HWY 108 approx. 43 mi. to Brightman Flat CG.

SINGLE RATE:	$8	OPEN DATES:	May-Oct
# of SINGLE SITES:	33	MAX SPUR:	22 feet
		MAX STAY:	14 days
		ELEVATION:	5700 feet

10 Cascade Creek
Sonora • lat 38°17'30" lon 119°95'00"

DESCRIPTION: This CG is situated in a mixed conifer forest, a rustic site with no drinking water. A creek runs through seasonally, no fish. Gather firewood locally. Watch for black bears, deer, mountain lions, and bobcats. Busy CG, filling most weekends. Used primarily for OHV use with roads nearby.

GETTING THERE: From Sonora go NE on state HWY 108 approx. 33 mi. to Cascade Creek CG.

SINGLE RATE:	$5	OPEN DATES:	May-Oct
# of SINGLE SITES:	12	MAX SPUR:	22 feet
		MAX STAY:	14 days
		ELEVATION:	6000 feet

 Campground has hosts   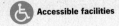 **Reservable sites**   **Accessible facilities**   **Fully developed**   **Semi-developed**   **Rustic facilities**

NOTE: Open dates listed are typical. Actual dates are dependent on conditions such as snow pack.

11 Cherry Valley
Groveland • lat 37°59'08" lon 119°54'57"

DESCRIPTION: This CG is situated in a mixed conifer forest, a short distance from Cherry Lake. Boat launch available. Fish for planted rainbow trout and salmon. Gather firewood locally. Moderate use. Lake Eleanor Trail and Kibbie Lake Trail access into Yosemite (requires permit). Be cautious of poison oak.

GETTING THERE: From Groveland go E on state HWY 120 approx. 11 mi. to primary forest route 17. Go NE on 17 approx. 23.5 mi. to Cherry Valley CG.

SINGLE RATE: # of SINGLE SITES:	Varies 46	OPEN DATES: MAX SPUR: MAX STAY: ELEVATION:	Apr-Nov* 22 feet 14 days 4700 feet

16 Diamond O
Groveland • lat 37°51'54" lon 119°51'57"

DESCRIPTION: This CG is set on the banks of Middle Fork Tuolumne River, situated in a mixed conifer forest. Gather firewood locally. Watch for deer, black bears, mountain lions, and bobcats in the area. Busy CG, filling most weekends. Hiking trails nearby. Be cautious of poison oak.

GETTING THERE: From Groveland go E on state HWY 120 approx. 18.5 mi. to primary forest route 12. Go N on 12 approx. 6 mi. to Diamond O CG.

SINGLE RATE: # of SINGLE SITES:	$11 38	OPEN DATES: MAX SPUR: MAX STAY: ELEVATION:	Apr-Nov 22 feet 14 days 4400 feet

12 Clark Fork
Sonora • lat 38°23'47" lon 119°48'00"

DESCRIPTION: CG set on the banks of the Clark Fork River, within the Clark Fork Rec. Area. Fish for rainbow, brook, and german brown trout. Supplies at resort. RV dump station at entrance to CG. Gather firewood. Watch for black bears and mountain lions. Trailhead accesses into Carson-Iceberg Wilderness.

GETTING THERE: From Sonora go NE on state HWY 108 approx. 41.5 mi. to forest route 7N83. Go NE on 7N83 approx. 6.5 mi. to Clark Fork CG.

SINGLE RATE: # of SINGLE SITES:	Varies 88	OPEN DATES: MAX SPUR: MAX STAY: ELEVATION:	May-Oct 22 feet 14 days 6200 feet

17 Eureka Valley
Sonora • lat 37°45'37" lon 122°26'06"

DESCRIPTION: CG set on the banks of the Middle Fork Stanislaus River within the Brightman Recreation Area. Fish for rainbow, brook, or german brown trout. Supplies at nearby Kennedy Meadows Resort. Gather firewood. Watch for black bears, mountain lions, and bobcats. Be cautious of poison oak.

GETTING THERE: From Sonora go NE on state HWY 108 approx. 47 mi. to Eureka Valley CG.

SINGLE RATE: # of SINGLE SITES:	$11 28	OPEN DATES: MAX SPUR: MAX STAY: ELEVATION:	May-Oct 22 feet 14 days 6100 feet

13 Clark Fork Horse Camp
Sonora • lat 38°23'47" lon 119°48'00"

DESCRIPTION: CG set on the Clark Fork River, within the Clark Fork Rec. Area. Suitable for camping with stock. Fish for rainbow, brook, and german brown trout. Supplies at resort. RV dump station at entrance to nearby Clark Fork CG. Watch for black bears and mountain lions. Access into Carson-Iceberg Wilderness.

GETTING THERE: From Sonora go NE on state HWY 108 approx. 41.5 mi. to forest route 7N83. Go NE on 7N83 approx. 7 mi. to Clark Fork Horse Camp CG.

SINGLE RATE: # of SINGLE SITES:	$5 14	OPEN DATES: MAX SPUR: MAX STAY: ELEVATION:	May-Oct 22 feet 14 days 6200 feet

18 Fence Creek
Sonora • lat 38°21'51" lon 119°52'30"

DESCRIPTION: This CG is set along the banks of Fence Creek, situated in a mixed conifer forest. Within the Clark Fork Recreation Area. Fish for rainbow, brook, or german brown trout. Supplies nearby at Dardanelle Resort. Gather firewood locally. Watch for black bears, mountain lions, and bobcats.

GETTING THERE: From Sonora go NE on state HWY 108 approx. 41.5 mi. to forest route 7N83. Go NE on 7N83 approx. 1 mi. to Fence Creek CG.

SINGLE RATE: # of SINGLE SITES:	$5 34	OPEN DATES: MAX SPUR: MAX STAY: ELEVATION:	May-Oct 22 feet 14 days 6100 feet

14 Dardanelle
Sonora • lat 38°20'31" lon 119°49'56"

DESCRIPTION: CG set on the banks of the Middle Fork Stanislaus River within the Brightman Recreation Area. Fish for rainbow, brook, or german brown trout. Supplies at Dardanelles Resort and Kennedy Meadows Resort. Gather firewood. Watch for black bears, mountain lions, and bobcats. Be cautious of poison oak.

GETTING THERE: From Sonora go NE on state HWY 108 approx. 44.5 mi. to Dardanelle CG.

SINGLE RATE: # of SINGLE SITES:	Varies 28	OPEN DATES: MAX SPUR: MAX STAY: ELEVATION:	May-Oct 22 feet 14 days 5000 feet

19 Fraser Flat
Sonora • lat 38°10'09" lon 120°04'02"

DESCRIPTION: CG is in a forested setting on the South Fork Stanislaus River. Rainbow, brook, and german brown trout fishing opportunities. Barrier free fishing dock available. Gather firewood locally. Watch for deer, black bears, mountain lions, and bobcats. Numerous hiking trails nearby.

GETTING THERE: From Sonora go NE on state HWY 108 approx. 21 mi. to forest route 4N01. Go N on 4N01 approx. 2 mi. to Fraser Flat CG.

SINGLE RATE: # of SINGLE SITES:	$9 38	OPEN DATES: MAX SPUR: MAX STAY: ELEVATION:	May-Oct 22 feet 14 days 4800 feet

15 Deadman
Sonora • lat 38°19'02" lon 119°44'56"

DESCRIPTION: CG set on the banks of the Middle Fork Stanislaus River within the Brightman Recreation Area. Fish for rainbow, brook, or german brown trout. Supplies at nearby Kennedy Meadows Resort. Gather firewood. Watch for black bears, mountain lions, and bobcats. Be cautious of poison oak.

GETTING THERE: From Sonora go NE on state HWY 108 approx. 49 mi. to Deadman CG.

SINGLE RATE: # of SINGLE SITES:	$9.50 17	OPEN DATES: MAX SPUR: MAX STAY: ELEVATION:	May-Oct 22 feet 14 days 6200 feet

20 Hermit Valley
Murphys • lat 38°32'36" lon 119°53'03"

DESCRIPTION: CG set in a large, open, park-like area of timber and rock outcroppings. Fish the nearby North Fork Mokelumne River. Supplies in Bears Valley, Lake Alpine, or Markleville. Gather firewood. Dispersed sites. No drinking water. Fire permit required. Black bears, deer, bobcats, and mountain lions

GETTING THERE: From Murphys go NE approx. 44 mi. on state HWY 4 to Hermit Valley CG.

SINGLE RATE: # of SINGLE SITES:	No fee 8	OPEN DATES: MAX SPUR: MAX STAY: ELEVATION:	June-Oct* 50 feet 14 days 7100 feet

 Campground has hosts   **Reservable sites**   **Accessible facilities**   **Fully developed**   **Semi-developed**   **Rustic facilities**

NOTE: Open dates listed are typical. Actual dates are dependent on conditions such as snow pack.

21 Herring Creek
Sonora • lat 38°14'40" lon 119°55'55"

DESCRIPTION: This CG is situated in a high elevation forest. Fishing opportunities for rainbow, brook, and brown trout on Herring Creek or at Herring Reservoir. Please check for local fishing regulations. Campers may gather dead and down firewood. No drinking water available on site.

GETTING THERE: Herring Creek CG is located 7 mi. from HWY 108 on Herring Creek Road.

SINGLE RATE:	No fee	OPEN DATES:	May-Oct
# of SINGLE SITES:	8	MAX SPUR:	22 feet
		MAX STAY:	14 days
		ELEVATION:	7300 feet

22 Herring Reservoir Road
Sonora • lat 39°14'19" lon 121°00'15"

DESCRIPTION: This CG is situated in a high elevation forest. Fishing opportunities for rainbow, brook, and brown trout on Herring Creek or at Herring Reservoir. Please check for local fishing regulations. Campers may gather dead and down firewood. No drinking water available on site.

GETTING THERE: Herring Reservoir Road CG is located 7 mi. from HWY 108 on Herring Creek Road.

SINGLE RATE:	No fee	OPEN DATES:	May-Oct
# of SINGLE SITES:	42	MAX SPUR:	22 feet
		MAX STAY:	14 days
		ELEVATION:	7300 feet

23 Highland Lakes
Murphys • lat 38°29'19" lon 119°48'21"

DESCRIPTION: In alpine forest saddle surrounded by high peaks. Adjacent to Highland Lakes for fishing. Some horse facilities. Supplies in Markleville or Murphys. Deer, black bears, mountain lion, bobcats and small wildlife in area. Access for horse and hike trails into Carson Iceberg Wilderness. Superb Fall wildflowers.

GETTING THERE: From Murphys go NE approx. 47.5 mi. on state HWY 4 to forest route. Go SE on forest route approx. 5.5 mi. to Highland Lakes CG. Not recommended for trailers or RVs.

SINGLE RATE:	$8	OPEN DATES:	June-Oct*
# of SINGLE SITES:	35		
		MAX STAY:	14 days
		ELEVATION:	8600 feet

24 Hull Creek
Sonora • lat 38°05'38" lon 120°02'28"

DESCRIPTION: In a secluded area of mixed conifer near several small streams. Gather firewood locally. Deer, black bears, mountain lion, bobcats and small wildlife in area. Supplies in Sonora.

GETTING THERE: From Sonora go NE on state HWY 120 approx. 14 mi. to primary forest route 31. Go E on 31 approx. 8 mi. to Hull Creek CG.

SINGLE RATE:	$5	OPEN DATES:	Yearlong
# of SINGLE SITES:	16	MAX SPUR:	22 feet
		MAX STAY:	14 days
		ELEVATION:	5600 feet

25 Lake Alpine
Murphys • lat 38°28'39" lon 120°00'17"

DESCRIPTION: In mature conifer forest on the shore of Lake Alpine. Fishing from shore or boat (launch available)for trout. Mild days, frequent noon t-storms. Supplies in Bears Valley or Lake Alpine Lodge. Interpretive programs in summer. Bike/hike/accessible paved trail, Bears Valley to L. Alpine and Doug Lake Trail.

GETTING THERE: From Murphys go NE approx. 37 mi. on state HWY 4 to Lake Alpine CG.

SINGLE RATE:	$14.50	OPEN DATES:	June-Oct*
# of SINGLE SITES:	25	MAX SPUR:	27 feet
		MAX STAY:	14 days
		ELEVATION:	7303 feet

26 Lodgepole Group
Dorrington • lat 38°30'00" lon 120°02'00"

DESCRIPTION: In open, flat meadow setting near Bears Valley Ski area. Walk-in sites. No nearby fishing or trails. Black bears, deer, mountain lion, bobcats and small wildlife in area. Gather firewood on forest. Fills most weekends.

GETTING THERE: From Murphys go NE approx. 36 mi. on state HWY 4 to forest route 207. Go W on 207 approx. 1.5 mi. to Lodgepole Group CG.

		OPEN DATES:	May-Oct*
# of SINGLE SITES:	1		
GROUP RATE:	$60	MAX STAY:	14 days
		ELEVATION:	7300 feet

27 Lost Claim
Groveland • lat 37°49'16" lon 120°02'51"

DESCRIPTION: In mixed conifer forest. No fishing or trails in nearby vicinity. A remote site, out of the way and quiet. Receives light use. Gather firewood locally. Black bears, deer, mountain lion, bobcats and small wildlife in area. Poison oak in area.

GETTING THERE: Lost Claim CG is located approx. 10 mi. E of Groveland on state HWY 120.

SINGLE RATE:	$8	OPEN DATES:	May-Sept
# of SINGLE SITES:	10		
		MAX STAY:	14 days
		ELEVATION:	3100 feet

28 Lumsden
Groveland • lat 37°50'18" lon 120°03'02"

DESCRIPTION: CG is in a pine and oak forest setting on the Tuolumne River. Fish the river for planted salmon, rainbow and brown trout. Gather firewood locally. Black bears, deer, mountain lion, bobcats and small wildlife in area. Busy CG, filling most weekends. Poison oak.

GETTING THERE: From Groveland go E on state HWY 120 approx. 6 mi. to forest route 1N10. Go approx. 4 mi. on 1N10 to Lumsden CG. Not recommended for trailers.

SINGLE RATE:	No fee	OPEN DATES:	Yearlong
# of SINGLE SITES:	11	MAX SPUR:	22 feet
		MAX STAY:	14 days
		ELEVATION:	1500 feet

29 Lumsden Bridge
Groveland • lat 37°50'52" lon 120°01'43"

DESCRIPTION: CG is in a pine and oak forest setting on the Tuolumne River. Fish the river for planted salmon, rainbow and brown trout. Gather firewood locally. Black bears, deer, mountain lion, bobcats and small wildlife in area. Busy CG, filling most weekends. Poison oak in area.

GETTING THERE: From Groveland go E on state HWY 120 approx. 6 mi. to forest route 1N10. Go approx. 5 mi. on 1N10 to Lumsden Bridge CG

SINGLE RATE:	No fee	OPEN DATES:	Apr-Oct
# of SINGLE SITES:	9	MAX SPUR:	22 feet
		MAX STAY:	14 days
		ELEVATION:	1500 feet

30 Meadowview
Sonora • lat 38°11'07" lon 120°00'16"

DESCRIPTION: CG is in a forested and open setting with views of Pinecrest Lake. Fish for planted rainbow, brook and german brown trout. Supplies nearby at Pinecrest Lake Resort. Boat ramp, picnic, swimming and trails nearby at Pinecrest Day Use Area.

GETTING THERE: Meadowview CG is located approx. 23.5 mi. NE of Sonora.

SINGLE RATE:	$12.50	OPEN DATES:	May-Sept
# of SINGLE SITES:	100	MAX SPUR:	22 feet
		MAX STAY:	14 days
		ELEVATION:	5600 feet

 Campground has hosts   **Reservable sites**   **Accessible facilities**   **Fully developed**   **Semi-developed**   **Rustic facilities**

NOTE: Open dates listed are typical. Actual dates are dependent on conditions such as snow pack.

31 Mill Creek
Sonora • lat 38°19'30" lon 119°56'30"

DESCRIPTION: CG is located in a forested setting on Mill Creek. Deer and bears in area. Good fishing in area. Go to Strawberry for supplies.

GETTING THERE: From Sonora go NE on state HWY 108 approx. 36 mi. to mill Creek CG.

SINGLE RATE:	$5	OPEN DATES:	May-Oct
# of SINGLE SITES:	17	MAX SPUR:	22 feet
		MAX STAY:	14 days
		ELEVATION:	6200 feet

32 Moore Creek Group
Groveland • lat 37°47'25" lon 120°03'47"

DESCRIPTION: In a mixed conifer forest setting along Moore Creek. Poison Oak in area. Fishing on creek for trout is seasonal. Gather firewood locally. Black bears, deer, mountain lion, bobcats and small wildlife in area. Busy CG, filling most weekends. No nearby trails.

GETTING THERE: From Groveland go E on state HWY 120 approx. 9 mi. to primary forest route 20. Go S on 20 approx. 2 mi. to Moore Crrek Group CG.

		OPEN DATES:	Yearlong
		MAX SPUR:	22 feet
GROUP RATE:	No fee	MAX STAY:	14 days
# of GROUP SITES:	1	ELEVATION:	2800 feet

33 Mosquito Lakes
Murphys • lat 38°30'58" lon 119°54'47"

DESCRIPTION: High alpine area surrounded by mature conifer forest across from Mosquito Lake. Fish for trout. No drinking water. Gather firewood. Supplies at Lake Alpine Lodge or Murphys. Black bears, deer, mountain lion, bobcats and small wildlife. Mosquito Lakes Trailhead accesses Carson-Iceberg Wilderness.

GETTING THERE: From Murphys go NE approx. 42 mi. on state HWY 4 to Mosquito CG.

SINGLE RATE:	$5	OPEN DATES:	June-Oct*
# of SINGLE SITES:	8	MAX SPUR:	40 feet
		MAX STAY:	14 days
		ELEVATION:	8260 feet

34 Niagara Creek
Sonora • lat 38°19'54" lon 119°56'22"

DESCRIPTION: CG is situated in a mixed conifer forest, a rustic site with no drinking water. A creek runs through seasonally, no fish. Gather firewood locally. Watch for black bears, deer, mountain lions, and bobcats. Busy CG, filling most weekends. Used primarily for OHV use with roads nearby.

GETTING THERE: From Sonora go NE on state HWY 108 approx. 37 mi. to forest route 6N24. Continue NE on 6N24 approx. 5 mi. to Niagra Creek CG.

SINGLE RATE:	$5	OPEN DATES:	May-Oct
# of SINGLE SITES:	10	MAX SPUR:	22 feet
		MAX STAY:	14 days
		ELEVATION:	6600 feet

35 Niagara OHV
Sonora • lat 38°20'00" lon 119°53'00"

DESCRIPTION: CG is in a forested and open area along Niagara Creek. A creek runs through seasonally, no fish. Gather firewood locally. Watch for black bears, deer, mountain lions, and bobcats. Busy CG, filling most weekends. Used primarily for OHV use with roads nearby.

GETTING THERE: From Sonora go NE on state HWY 108 approx. 37 mi. to forest route 6N24. Continue NE on 6N24 approx. 5.25 mi. to forest route 5N01. Go approx. 3 mi. E on 5N01 to Niagra OHV CG

SINGLE RATE:	$5	OPEN DATES:	May-Oct
# of SINGLE SITES:	10	MAX SPUR:	22 feet
		MAX STAY:	14 days
		ELEVATION:	6600 feet

36 Pacific Valley
Pacific Valley • lat 38°31'03" lon 119°54'05"

DESCRIPTION: CG set in a park-like area adjacent to Mokelumne River. Dispersed sites. No drinking water. Campfire permit required. Supplies at Bears Valley and Lake Alpine. Horse camp at south end, near the trailhead. Fish Mosquito Lakes for planted trout. Trail access to Carson-Iceberg Wilderness.

GETTING THERE: Pacific Valley CG is approx. 1/4 mi. S of HWY 4 at Pacific Valley, midway between Lake Alpine and Ebbetts Pass. Not recommended for trailers.

SINGLE RATE:	No fee	OPEN DATES:	June-Oct*
# of SINGLE SITES:	9		
		MAX STAY:	14 days
		ELEVATION:	7600 feet

37 Pigeon Flat
Sonora • lat 38°20'24" lon 119°48'17"

DESCRIPTION: GC is in mixed forested and open area along the Middle Fork Stanislaus River within the Brightman Recreation Area. Fish for trout. Supplies at nearby at Dardanelles Resort and Kennedy Meadows Resort. Column of the Giants interpretive walk nearby. No water. Walk-in sites.

GETTING THERE: From Sonora go NE on state HWY 108 approx. 46 mi. to Pigeon Flat CG.

SINGLE RATE:	$8	OPEN DATES:	May-Oct
# of SINGLE SITES:	7		
		MAX STAY:	14 days
		ELEVATION:	7000 feet

38 Pine Marten
Murphys • lat 38°28'52" lon 119°59'19"

DESCRIPTION: Located in mature conifer on the shores of Lake Alpine. Warm days, frequent noon t-storms. Lake offers fishing, low-speed boating. Interpretive programs in summer. Gather firewood. Supplies at L. Alpine Lodge or Murphys. Fee Showers at Lodge. Hike and bike trails nearby. No nearby Trailheads.

GETTING THERE: From Murphys go NE approx. 45 mi. on state HWY 4 to Pine Marten CG.

SINGLE RATE:	$14.50	OPEN DATES:	June-Oct*
# of SINGLE SITES:	32	MAX SPUR:	27 feet
		MAX STAY:	14 days
		ELEVATION:	7400 feet

39 Pinecrest
Sonora • lat 38°11'23" lon 119°59'40"

DESCRIPTION: CG is in a forested and open setting near the shore of Pinecrest Lake. Supplies at nearby Pinecrest Lake Resort. Lake has boat ramp, picnic, swimming and trails. Fish for trout varieties. RV dump station at CG. Dogs are discouraged, strict rules apply.

GETTING THERE: Pinecrest CG is located approx. 24.5 mi. NE of Sonora.

SINGLE RATE:	$15.50	OPEN DATES:	May-Oct*
# of SINGLE SITES:	200	MAX SPUR:	40 feet
		MAX STAY:	14 days
		ELEVATION:	5600 feet

40 Pioneer Trail Group
Sonora • lat 38°11'15" lon 119°59'15"

DESCRIPTION: This CG is situated in a mixed forest setting a short distance away from Pinecrest Lake. A restaurant, showers, and supplies are available less than 2 mi. away from CG at Pinecrest Lake Resort. Fish for trout varieties. Lake offers a boat ramp, picnic area, and swimming. Trails nearby.

GETTING THERE: Pioneer Trail Group CG is located approx. 24.5 mi. NE of Sonora.

		OPEN DATES:	May-Oct*
		MAX SPUR:	40 feet
GROUP RATE:	Varies	MAX STAY:	14 days
# of GROUP SITES:	3	ELEVATION:	5700 feet

 Campground has hosts   Reservable sites   Accessible facilities   Fully developed   Semi-developed   Rustic facilities

NOTE: Open dates listed are typical. Actual dates are dependent on conditions such as snow pack.

41 River Ranch
Sonora • lat 37°59'37" lon 120°10'41"

DESCRIPTION: This CG is situated in a meadow near the confluence of Basin Creek and the North Fork Tuolumne River. Fish for trout species on river. Check for local fishing regulations. Campers may gather their firewood locally. Watch for deer, black bears, mountain lions, bobcats in the area.

GETTING THERE: From Sonora go E approx. 9 mi. on county route to primary forest route 14. Continue E on 14 2.5 mi. to River Ranch CG.

SINGLE RATE:	$14	OPEN DATES:	May-Oct*
# of SINGLE SITES:	38	MAX SPUR:	22 feet
		MAX STAY:	14 days
		ELEVATION:	2500 feet

42 Sand Bar Flat
Sonora • lat 38°11'02" lon 120°09'17"

DESCRIPTION: This CG is situated in a mixed forest setting on the Middle Fork Stanislaus River. Check for local fishing regulations. Swimming and fishing for trout on river. Campers may gather their firewood locally. Watch for deer, black bears, mountain lions, bobcats, and small wildlife in the area.

GETTING THERE: From Sonora go NE on state HWY 108 21 mi. to forest route 4N01. Go N 5 mi. to forest route 4N88. Go N 2 mi. to 4N85. Go W 2.5 mi. to Sand Bar Flat CG. Not recommended for trailers or RVs.

SINGLE RATE:	$7	OPEN DATES:	May-Nov
# of SINGLE SITES:	10	MAX SPUR:	22 feet
		MAX STAY:	14 days
		ELEVATION:	3000 feet

43 Sand Flat
Dorrington • lat 37°30'00" lon 120°06'00"

DESCRIPTION: CG in a mature forest with views of natural granitic rock outcrops. No driking water. Fish for wild brown and rainbow trout on the N Fork Stanislaus River. Supplies in Arnold and Lake Alpine. Gather firewood locally. Deer, black bears, mountain lions, and bobcats in area. Trail to Spicer Reservoir.

GETTING THERE: Sand Flat CG is located approx. 28 mi. NE of Murphys on state HWY 4. On SE side of HWY across from Big Meadow CG. 4WD road approx. 1/2 mi. to Sand Flat CG. Steep rough road, no trailers or RVs.

SINGLE RATE:	No fee	OPEN DATES:	May-Oct
# of SINGLE SITES:	68	MAX SPUR:	40 feet
		MAX STAY:	14 days
		ELEVATION:	5900 feet

44 Silver Valley
Sonora • lat 38°28'48" lon 119°59'09"

DESCRIPTION: CG set on the shores of Lake Alpine, situated among conifer. Boat launch on lake for low-speed boating and fishing access. Fish for planted trout. Busy, fills weekends. Summer interpretive programs. Lake Alpine hiking and bike trails accessible nearby. Deer, black bears, and wildcats in area.

GETTING THERE: Silver Valley CG is located approx. 24.5 mi. NE of Sonora.

SINGLE RATE:	$14.50	OPEN DATES:	June-Oct*
# of SINGLE SITES:	21	MAX SPUR:	27 feet
		MAX STAY:	14 days
		ELEVATION:	7400 feet

45 Silvertip
Murphys • lat 38°28'50" lon 120°01'01"

DESCRIPTION: CG set on the shores of Lake Alpine, situated among conifer. Boat launch on lake for low-speed boating and fishing access. Fish for planted trout. Busy, fills weekends. Summer interpretive programs. Lake Alpine hiking and bike trails accessible nearby. Deer, black bears, and wildcats in area.

GETTING THERE: From Murphys go NE approx. 36 mi. on state HWY 4 to Silvertip CG.

SINGLE RATE:	$14.50	OPEN DATES:	June-Oct*
# of SINGLE SITES:	23	MAX SPUR:	27 feet
		MAX STAY:	14 days
		ELEVATION:	7300 feet

46 South Fork
Groveland • lat 37°50'17" lon 120°02'44"

DESCRIPTION: This CG is situated in a pine and oak forest on the banks of the Tuolumne River. Fish the river for planted salmon, rainbow, and brown trout. Gather firewood locally. Watch for black bears, deer, mountain lions, and bobcats in the area. CG receives moderate-heavy use, filling most weekends.

GETTING THERE: From Groveland go E on state HWY 120 approx. 6 mi. to forest route 1N10. Go approx. 4 mi. on 1N10 to South Fork CG. Not recommended for trailers.

SINGLE RATE:	No fee	OPEN DATES:	Apr-Oct
# of SINGLE SITES:	8	MAX SPUR:	22 feet
		MAX STAY:	14 days
		ELEVATION:	1500 feet

47 Spicer
Sherman Acres • lat 38°23'36" lon 119°59'45"

DESCRIPTION: CG set on the shores of Spicer Reservoir. Boat launch available on lake for low-speed boating and fishing access. Fish for planted rainbow and brown trout, and catfish. North arm of lake is reserved for non-motorized recreation. Supplies in Arnold. Hiking and horse trails nearby.

GETTING THERE: From Sherman Acres go SW on state HWY 4 approx. 1 mi. to forest route 7N01. Go E on 7N01 approx. 8 mi. to Spicer CG.

SINGLE RATE:	$12	OPEN DATES:	June-Oct*
# of SINGLE SITES:	60	MAX SPUR:	50 feet
		MAX STAY:	14 days
		ELEVATION:	6200 feet

48 Spicer Group
Sherman Acres • lat 38°23'36" lon 119°59'45"

DESCRIPTION: Set on the shores of Spicer Reservoir. Boat launch on lake for low-speed boating and fishing access. Fish for planted rainbow and brown trout, and catfish. North arm of lake is reserved for non-motorized recreation. Supplies in Arnold. Hiking and horse trails. Reservations required. 60 person max..

GETTING THERE: From Sherman Acres go SW on state HWY 4 approx. 1 mi. to forest route 7N01. Go E on 7N01 approx. 8 mi. to Spicer Group CG

		OPEN DATES:	June-Oct*
		MAX SPUR:	25 feet
GROUP RATE:	Varies	MAX STAY:	14 days
# of GROUP SITES:	10	ELEVATION:	6300 feet

49 Stanislaus River
Sherman Acres • lat 38°25'20" lon 120°02'45"

DESCRIPTION: CG situated in a mature conifer forest on the North Fork Stanislaus River. Fish on the river or nearby Spicer Reservoir for planted rainbow and brown trout, and catfish. Union and Utica Reservoirs also nearby. Sandy beach on site. Supplies in Arnold, Camp Connell, or Bears Valley. No nearby hiking trails.

GETTING THERE: From Sherman Acres go SW on state HWY 4 approx. 1 mi. to forest route 7N01. Go E on 7N01 approx. 10.5 mi. to Stanislaus River CG.

SINGLE RATE:	$8	OPEN DATES:	June-Oct*
# of SINGLE SITES:	25	MAX SPUR:	35 feet
		MAX STAY:	14 days
		ELEVATION:	6200 feet

50 Sweetwater
Groveland • lat 37°49'30" lon 119°59'57"

DESCRIPTION: This CG is situated in a mixed conifer forest. A peaceful and serene CG receiving light use. Be cautious of poison oak in area. Gather firewood locally. Watch for black bears, deer, mountain lions, and bobcats in the area. No nearby trails.

GETTING THERE: Sweetwater CG is located approx. 13 mi. E of Groveland on state HWY 120

SINGLE RATE:	$10	OPEN DATES:	Apr-Nov
# of SINGLE SITES:	13	MAX SPUR:	22 feet
		MAX STAY:	14 days
		ELEVATION:	3000 feet

 Campground has hosts   **Reservable sites**   **Accessible facilities**   **Fully developed**   **Semi-developed** **Rustic facilities**

NOTE: Open dates listed are typical. Actual dates are dependent on conditions such as snow pack.

51 The Pine

Groveland • lat 37°49'04" lon 120°05'36"

DESCRIPTION: CG is set in a mixed conifer forest. Ranger Station nearby. Group site requires reservations. Popular site for rafters. Gather firewood. Black bears, deer, mountain lions, and bobcats in the area. Busy CG, filling most weekends. Short interpreive trail (Little Children's Forest). Poison oak in area.

GETTING THERE: The Pine CG is located approx. 20.5 mi. E of Groveland on state HWY 120.

SINGLE RATE:	$9	OPEN DATES:	Yearlong
# of SINGLE SITES:	12	MAX SPUR:	22 feet
GROUP RATE:	$50	MAX STAY:	14 days
# of GROUP SITES:	1	ELEVATION:	3200 feet

52 Wa Ka Luu Hep Yoo

Dorington • lat 38°19'19" lon 120°12'55"

DESCRIPTION: CG set in the Sourgrass Recreation Complex near the North Fork Stanislaus River. Planted and native trout fishing. CG has recently been remodeled. Popular rafting stretch of river. Interpretive programs. Supplies in Dorington. Gather firewood. Deer, black bears, and wildcats in area. Hiking trails nearby.

GETTING THERE: From Dorington go NE on primary forest route 52 approx. 4.5 mi. to Wa Ka Luu Hep Yoo (Wild River) CG.

SINGLE RATE:	$13	OPEN DATES:	June-Oct
# of SINGLE SITES:	50		
		MAX STAY:	14 days
		ELEVATION:	3900 feet

Hiking Bear Country

Inquire about recent bear activity.

Make your presence know to bears. Call out, clap your hands, or sing.

Look for signs of bear activity: tracks, scat, diggins, tornup logs, and turned over rocks.

Keep children close to you and within your sight.

Carry items to drop to distract approaching bear, such as a hat.

Avoid taking pets.

 Campground has hosts   Reservable sites   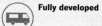 Accessible facilities   Fully developed   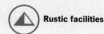 Semi-developed   Rustic facilities

NOTE: Open dates listed are typical. Actual dates are dependent on conditions such as snow pack.

TAHOE NATIONAL FOREST

The Tahoe National Forest, covering 800,000 acres, offers an abundance of natural beauty and historic charm. Visitors can choose from a wide range of activities, including exploring beautiful high mountain lakes, the fascinating geology of the Sierras, or the rugged Granite Chief Wilderness. The 1,500 to 9,400 foot elevation range of the Tahoe provides a wide variety of year-round recreational activities. There are also wonderful opportunities for discovering the rich history of the area.

There are over 800 miles of trails for use by hikers, backpackers, mountain bikers and equestrians. Many of the forest trails used today were begun by Native Americans and early pioneers. The Tahoe's granite peaks also offer challenging routes for rock climbers.

Other attractions are the Washington Overlook, a turnout on Highway 20 that offers a panoramic view of the forest, the Big Trees Grove, the northernmost grove of giant Sequoias, and the Donner Camp Picnic Area, the last campsite for the George and Jacob Donner families on their trip west. While walking the interpretive trail, imagine what it was like to be stranded in the mountains during that fateful harsh winter of 1846.

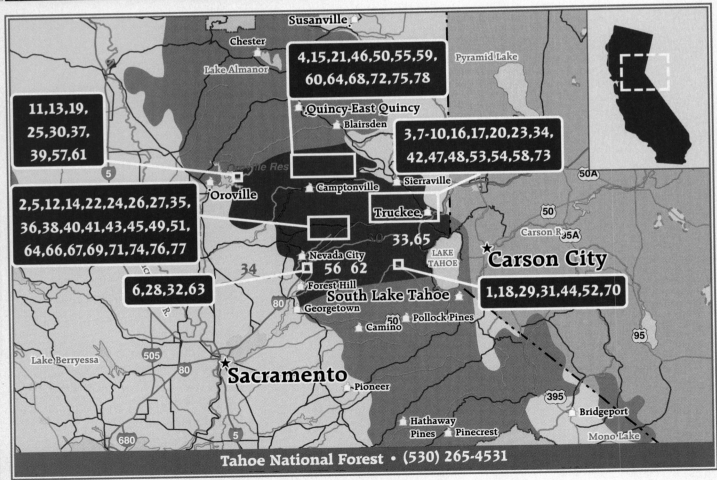

Tahoe National Forest • (530) 265-4531

1 Ahart
Foresthill • lat 39°08'45" lon 120°24'23"

DESCRIPTION: CG set among red fir and pine stands overlooking the American River. Fish for trout in river and nearby reservoir. Supplies in Foresthill. Busy weekends. Gather firewood locally. Hike Granite Chief Wilderness access 4 mi. away. Some trails on site. CG is frequented by bears. No drinking water available.

GETTING THERE: Located at French Meadows Recreation Complex. From Foresthill go E 3 mi. on Mosquito Ridge Road 96. Go 1 mi. above French Meadows reservoir to Ahart CG. Narrow road. Large vehicles use caution.

SINGLE RATE:	$8	OPEN DATES:	May-Oct
# of SINGLE SITES:	12	MAX SPUR:	47 feet
		MAX STAY:	14 days
		ELEVATION:	5300 feet

2 Aspen Group
Truckee • lat 39°30'19" lon 120°32'17"

DESCRIPTION: CG in a mixed conifer forest on Jackson Meadows Reservoir. Dry, hot summers. Fish for trout planted in lake. Swim beach and boat ramp nearby. Supplies at Truckee. Fills holiday weekends. Gather firewood locally. Multiple hiking trails including Mount Lola, highest peak in the forest.

GETTING THERE: From Truckee go N on HWY 80 17 mi. to forest route 07 (Fibreboard Rd.). Go W 16 mi. to Jackson Meadow Reservoir. Aspen Group CG is on the NE side of the reservoir.

GROUP RATE:	Varies	OPEN DATES:	June-Oct
# of GROUP SITES:	3	MAX SPUR:	26 feet
		MAX STAY:	14 days
		ELEVATION:	6100 feet

3 Bears Valley
Sierraville • lat 39°33'27" lon 120°14'06"

DESCRIPTION: CG was burned over in 1994 (Cottonwood Fire) so it has open views of mountains. Low thick vegetation has grown, and trees remain in CG. Fish Bears Valley Creek for brown trout. Deer, black bears, and upland game birds. Fills holiday weekends. Gather firewood. Heavy OHV use area; trailhead with parking.

GETTING THERE: From Sierraville go S on state HWY 89 approx. 8 mi. to forest route 451 (Cottonwood Cr Rd). Go NE on 451 approx. 6 mi. to Bears Valley CG.

SINGLE RATE:	No fee	OPEN DATES:	June-Oct*
# of SINGLE SITES:	10	MAX SPUR:	26 feet
		MAX STAY:	14 days
		ELEVATION:	6700 feet

4 Berger
Sierra City • lat 39°37'40" lon 120°38'37"

DESCRIPTION: CG set in a mixed forest with lakes nearby. Fish for trout and swim from those lakes. Supplies are available at Bassetts Station. Deer, bears, coyotes, woodpeckers, and squirrels are common to the area. Gather firewood locally. Hiking opportunities on the nearby Sierra Buttes Lookout Trail.

GETTING THERE: From Sierra City go NE on state HWY 49 approx. 4 mi. to county route S620. Go NW on S620 approx. 1 mi. to county route S621. Go NW on 621 approx. 2 mi. to Berger CG.

SINGLE RATE:	No fee	OPEN DATES:	May-Oct
# of SINGLE SITES:	10	MAX SPUR:	26 feet
		MAX STAY:	14 days
		ELEVATION:	5900 feet

5 Big Bend
Truckee • lat 39°18'23" lon 120°31'06"

DESCRIPTION: CG set among mixed conifer on the South Yuba River. Fish lakes and streams for stocked trout nearby. Historical Overland Emigrant Trail. Supplies in Truckee. Gather firewood. Loch Leven Trail leads to a series of alpine lakes. Bridge to CG was washed out by flooding in 1997. Closed through the 2000 season.

GETTING THERE: From Truckee go E on I-80 approx. 19 mi. to Raindbow Road exit. G W 1.5 mi. to Big Bend CG, adjacent to visitor center.

SINGLE RATE:	No fee	OPEN DATES:	Closed for 20
# of SINGLE SITES:	15		
		MAX STAY:	14 days
		ELEVATION:	5900 feet

6 Big Reservoir
Foresthill • lat 39°08'35" lon 120°45'17"

DESCRIPTION: CG set among red fir and pine stands on Big Reservoir. Warm days with cool nights. Native trout fishing in nearby streams, no motors on lake. Supplies are at Foresthill. Bears country. Fills weekends. Gather firewood, may be scarce. OHV trail nearby on FR24/FR10. Hiking trails within a few miles.

GETTING THERE: From Foresthill go NE on Foresthill Divide Road approx. 8.5 mi. to primary forest route 26. Go W on 26 approx. 4 mi. to primary forest route 24. Go S on 26 approx. 1 mi. to Big Reservoir CG.

SINGLE RATE:	$15	OPEN DATES:	May-Oct
# of SINGLE SITES:	100	MAX SPUR:	26 feet
		MAX STAY:	14 days
		ELEVATION:	4000 feet

7 Boca
Truckee • lat 39°23'12" lon 120°06'09"

DESCRIPTION: This CG is situated among yellow pine and sage with spectacular views of lakes and hills. Fish for trout in the Boca Reservoir. Historical Boca Townsite is approx. 1 mi. away. Campers may gather their firewood locally. Boca Interpretive Trail can be found approx. 1 mi. away from CG.

GETTING THERE: From Truckee go E on I-80 approx. 7 mi. to primary route 73. Go N on 73 approx. 1 mi. to Boca CG.

SINGLE RATE:	$8	OPEN DATES:	June-Oct
# of SINGLE SITES:	20	MAX SPUR:	26 feet
		MAX STAY:	14 days
		ELEVATION:	5600 feet

8 Boca Rest
Truckee • lat 39°25'09" lon 120°05'10"

DESCRIPTION: CG in a mountain setting with sparse vegetation. Views of Boca Reservoir. Fish for trout from the Little Truckee River. Historical Boca Townsite neaby. Supplies in Truckee. Watch for deer and coyotes. CG is full on holidays. Bring your own firewood. Interpretive trail at Boca Townsite.

GETTING THERE: From Truckee go E on I-80 approx. 7 mi. to county route 894. Go N on 894 approx. 4 mi. to Boca Rest CG.

SINGLE RATE:	$8	OPEN DATES:	June-Oct
# of SINGLE SITES:	25	MAX SPUR:	26 feet
		MAX STAY:	14 days
		ELEVATION:	5700 feet

9 Boca Spring
Truckee • lat 39°25'45" lon 120°04'30"

DESCRIPTION: This CG is situated among yellow pine and sage with spectacular views of lakes and hills. Fish for trout on the Boca Reservoir. Historical Boca Townsite is just N on I-80. Campers may gather their firewood locally. Boca Interpretive Trail can be found approx. 1 mi. away from CG.

GETTING THERE: From Truckee go E on I-80 approx. 7 mi. to county route 894. Go N on 894 approx. 4 mi. to Boca Spring CG.

SINGLE RATE:	$10	OPEN DATES:	June-Oct
# of SINGLE SITES:	16	MAX SPUR:	26 feet
GROUP RATE:	$55	MAX STAY:	14 days
# of GROUP SITES:	1	ELEVATION:	5800 feet

10 Boyington Mill
Truckee • lat 39°26'15" lon 120°05'26"

DESCRIPTION: This CG is situated among sparse vegetation with spectacular views of rivers and mountains. Fishing for trout on the Little Truckee River. Historical Boca townsite nearby (get information at the Truckee RD). Supplies are 11 mi. away at Truckee. Little or no firewood available at CG.

GETTING THERE: From Truckee go E on I-80 approx. 7 mi. to county route 2258. Go N on 2258 approx. 5.5 mi. to Boyington Mill CG.

SINGLE RATE:	$10	OPEN DATES:	June-Oct
# of SINGLE SITES:	12	MAX SPUR:	26 feet
		MAX STAY:	14 days
		ELEVATION:	5700 feet

 Campground has hosts 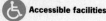 **Reservable sites**   **Accessible facilities**   **Fully developed**   **Semi-developed** **Rustic facilities**

NOTE: Open dates listed are typical. Actual dates are dependent on conditions such as snow pack.

11 Cal-Ida
Downieville • lat 39°31'34" lon 121°00'53"

DESCRIPTION: CG sits within a pine and oak forest on the edge of Fiddle Creek. Fish for trout or swim from the creek. Supplies available at Downieville. Deer, bears, coyotes chipmunks and squirrels can be seen in the area. Campers may gather firewood. CG is a trailhead to Halls Ranch.

GETTING THERE: From Downieville go W on state HWY 49 approx. 11 mi. to Cal-Ida CG.

SINGLE RATE:	$12	OPEN DATES:	Apr-Nov
# of SINGLE SITES:	20	MAX SPUR:	26 feet
		MAX STAY:	14 days
		ELEVATION:	2200 feet

16 Cold Creek
Sierraville • lat 39°32'34" lon 120°18'53"

DESCRIPTION: CG sits on Cold Creek in a meadow situated in a fairly dense forest. Fish for trout on the creek. Supplies at Randolph. Deer and raccoons can be seen in the area. Gather firewood locally. An interpretive trail and a couple of trailheads are located across the street at Cottonwood CG.

GETTING THERE: From Sierraville go S on HWY 89 approx. 4.5 mi. to Cold Creek CG.

SINGLE RATE:	$11	OPEN DATES:	June-Oct
# of SINGLE SITES:	13	MAX SPUR:	26 feet
		MAX STAY:	14 days
		ELEVATION:	5600 feet

12 Canyon Creek
Nevada City • lat 39°26'13" lon 120°34'44"

DESCRIPTION: This CG is situated among mixed conifer on the banks of Canyon Creek. Mild days with cool nights. Rainbow and brown trout fishing on creek or Faucherie and Bowman Lakes. Check for local fishing regulations. Supplies are available in Nevada City. Campers may gather their firewood locally.

GETTING THERE: From Nevada City go E 23.2 mi. on state HWY 20 to forest route 18. Go N 13.2 mi. to county route 843. Go SE 4 mi. to forest route. Go SE 2.3 mi. to Canyon Creek CG. High clearance required.

SINGLE RATE:	No fee	OPEN DATES:	May-Sept
# of SINGLE SITES:	20	MAX SPUR:	26 feet
		MAX STAY:	14 days
		ELEVATION:	6000 feet

17 Cottonwood
Randolph • lat 39°32'58" lon 120°18'59"

DESCRIPTION: CG set in a mixed forest with Cold Creek running nearby. Fish from the creek for trout. Supplies are available at Randolph. Deer and raccoons can be seen in the area. An interpretive trail and a couple trailheads start on site. Receives low use. Campers may gather their firewood locally.

GETTING THERE: Cottonwood CG is located approx. 5.2 mi. SE of Randolph.

SINGLE RATE:	$11	OPEN DATES:	June-Oct
# of SINGLE SITES:	49	MAX SPUR:	26 feet
GROUP RATE:	Varies	MAX STAY:	14 days
# of GROUP SITES:	1	ELEVATION:	5600 feet

13 Carlton
Downieville • lat 39°30'30" lon 121°00'00"

DESCRIPTION: This CG is situated on the banks of the Yuba River with spectacular river and mountain views. Trout fishing opportunities on the river. Check for local regulations. Limited supplies at a store 1 mi. away, or 11 mi. at Downieville. Gather firewood locally. Numerous trailheads nearby.

GETTING THERE: From Downieville go W on state HWY 49 approx. 11 mi. to Carlton CG.

SINGLE RATE:	$12	OPEN DATES:	June-Oct
# of SINGLE SITES:	30	MAX SPUR:	26 feet
		MAX STAY:	14 days
		ELEVATION:	2200 feet

18 Coyotes
Foresthill • lat 39°08'08" lon 120°24'38"

DESCRIPTION: CG set in red fir and pine stands on the French Meadows Reservoir. Mild days with cool nights. Trout fish the reservoir and nearby creeks. Supplies are in Foresthill. Bears frequent the area. Fills weekends. Buy or gather firewood on site. Fees are $45-$60 depending on group size.

GETTING THERE: From Foresthill go NE on primary forest route 96 (Mosquito Ridge Road) approx. 36 mi. to French Meadows Reservoir. Coyotes CG is located on the east side of the reservoir.

		OPEN DATES:	May-Oct
		MAX SPUR:	26 feet
GROUP RATE:	Varies	MAX STAY:	14 days
# of GROUP SITES:	4	ELEVATION:	5300 feet

14 Carr Lake
Nevada City • lat 39°24'00" lon 120°38'25"

DESCRIPTION: This CG is situated among mixed conifer with mountain and lake views. Warm summer days with cool nights. Enjoy rainbow and brook trout fishing in adjacent Carr Lake. Supplies 35 mi. away at Nevada City. Gather firewood locally. Hike the on site Round Lake Trail to several scenic lakes.

GETTING THERE: From Nevada City go E on state HWY 20 21 mi. to Bowman Road (county route 18). Go N 9 mi. to forest route 17. NE 5 mi. to Carr Lake CG. Narrow with sharp curves. Large vehicles should use caution.

SINGLE RATE:	No fee	OPEN DATES:	May-Sept
# of SINGLE SITES:	5	MAX SPUR:	26 feet
		MAX STAY:	14 days
		ELEVATION:	5565 feet

19 Dark Day
Camptonville • lat 39°25'54" lon 121°06'19"

DESCRIPTION: Among huge ponderosa pine and fir with mountain and lake views. Wildflowers are beautiful when in season. Boat or shore fish for trout and salmon in Bullards Bar Reservoir. Supplies available at the marina. Gather dead and down firewood locally. Easy hikes are nearby.

GETTING THERE: Dark Day CG is located approx. 5 mi. W of Camptonville on Marysville Road.

SINGLE RATE:	$14	OPEN DATES:	Apr-Oct
# of SINGLE SITES:	16	MAX SPUR:	26 feet
		MAX STAY:	14 days
		ELEVATION:	1900 feet

15 Chapman Creek
Randolph • lat 39°37'50" lon 120°32'34"

DESCRIPTION: CG set in the Sierras among mixed fir trees on the banks of Chapman Creek. Mild in summer with heavy snow by winter. Fish Chapman Creek and nearby N Yuba River for trout. Historic Kentucky mine and museum 7 mi. W at Sierra City. Supplies are 3 mi. W at Bassetts Station. Gather firewood locally.

GETTING THERE: From Randolph go W approx. 12 mi. to Chapman Creek CG.

SINGLE RATE:	$12	OPEN DATES:	May-Oct
# of SINGLE SITES:	29	MAX SPUR:	26 feet
		MAX STAY:	14 days
		ELEVATION:	6000 feet

20 Davies Creek
Truckee • lat 39°30'19" lon 120°05'55"

DESCRIPTION: This CG is situated among jeffrey pine and white fir stands overlooking Stampede Reservoir and mountains. Mild days with cool nights. Boat fish the lake; boat ramp available at S end of lake. Supplies in Truckee. Gather dead or down firewood. Surrounding area is open for OHV use. No drinking water.

GETTING THERE: From Truckee go E on I-80 approx. 7 mi. to county route 894 (Hirschdale exit). Go N 7 mi. to county route 270 (N side of reservoir). Go N 4 mi. to Davies Creek CG.

SINGLE RATE:	No fee	OPEN DATES:	June-Oct
# of SINGLE SITES:	7	MAX SPUR:	26 feet
		MAX STAY:	14 days
		ELEVATION:	6000 feet

 Campground has hosts　　 **Reservable sites**　　 **Accessible facilities**　　 **Fully developed**　　 **Semi-developed**　　 **Rustic facilities**

NOTE: Open dates listed are typical. Actual dates are dependent on conditions such as snow pack.

21 Diablo
Sierra City • lat 39°37'59" lon 120°38'12"

DESCRIPTION: This CG is situated among mixed fir near Packer Creek. Expect mild temperatures. Fish for trout on Packer and Sardine Lakes. Historic Kentucky Mine and museum at Sierra City. Supplies are available 2 mi. away at Bassetts Station. Receives moderate use. Campers may gather their firewood locally.

GETTING THERE: From Sierra City go NE on state HWY 49 approx. 4 mi. to county route S620. Go NW on S620 approx. 1 mi. to county route S621. Go NW on S621 approx. 1.8 mi. to Diablo CG.

SINGLE RATE:	No fee	OPEN DATES:	June-Oct
# of SINGLE SITES:	15	MAX SPUR:	26 feet
		MAX STAY:	14 days
		ELEVATION:	5800 feet

22 East Meadow
Truckee • lat 39°29'41" lon 120°31'51"

DESCRIPTION: CG set among mixed conifer and aspen on a high isolated mountain lake. Warm days with cool nights. Fish for planted trout in Jackson Meadows Reservoir and Milton Reservoir. Supplies are available at Truckee or Sierraville. Campers may gather deadwood for firewood. Numerous hiking trails nearby.

GETTING THERE: From Truckee go N on HWY 89 approx. 17 mi. to forest route 07. Go W on 07 approx. 16 mi. to Jackson Meadow Resevoir. East Meadow CG is located on the NE shore.

SINGLE RATE:	$13	OPEN DATES:	June-Oct
# of SINGLE SITES:	46	MAX SPUR:	26 feet
		MAX STAY:	14 days
		ELEVATION:	6100 feet

23 Emigrant Group
Truckee • lat 39°28'14" lon 120°06'59"

DESCRIPTION: CG set in a stand of pine and fir. Adjacent Stampede Reservoir has good trout fishing. Historical sites in area. Supplies are 15 mi. away at Truckee. Wildlife includes mule deer and coyotes. Busy summer weekends. Gather firewood locally. Many trails nearby. Boat ramp available.

GETTING THERE: From Truckee go E on I-80 approx. 6 mi. to county route S270 (Hirschdale exit). Go N on S270 approx. 7 mi. to county route 261. Go W on 261 approx. 2 mi. to Emigrant Group CG.

		OPEN DATES:	June-Oct
		MAX SPUR:	26 feet
GROUP RATE:	Varies	MAX STAY:	14 days
# of GROUP SITES:	4	ELEVATION:	6000 feet

24 Faucherie
Nevada City • lat 39°25'41" lon 120°34'11"

DESCRIPTION: This quiet CG is situated in a mixed conifer forest. Warm summer days with cool evenings. Enjoy fishing for brown and rainbow trout in adjacent Faucherie Lake. Supplies are available 40 mi. away at Nevada City. Busy weekends and holidays. Gather firewood locally. Hiking trails nearby.

GETTING THERE: From Nevada City go E on state HWY 20 23 mi. to forest route 18 (Bowman Lake Road). N 13 mi. (pass Bowman Lake) to route 122-80. N 6 mi. to Faucherie CG. High clearance required.

		OPEN DATES:	June-Oct
		MAX SPUR:	26 feet
GROUP RATE:	$50	MAX STAY:	14 days
# of GROUP SITES:	1	ELEVATION:	6100 feet

25 Fiddle Creek
Downieville • lat 39°31'08" lon 120°59'48"

DESCRIPTION: CG situated on the banks of the Yuba River among mixed fir. Expect mild temperatures with cold nights. Fish for trout on river. Supplies are available 3/4 mi. away at a store or 10 mi. at Downieville. Moderate use. Gather firewood locally. Several trailheads nearby. One site wheelchair accessible.

GETTING THERE: From Downieville go W on state HWY 49 approx. 10.8 mi. to Fiddle Creek CG.

SINGLE RATE:	$12	OPEN DATES:	Apr-Nov
# of SINGLE SITES:	16	MAX SPUR:	26 feet
		MAX STAY:	14 days
		ELEVATION:	2200 feet

26 Findley
Truckee • lat 39°29'05" lon 120°33'11"

DESCRIPTION: This CG is situated in a mixed confier and aspen forest. Warm days with cool nights. Fish for planted trout in Jackson Meadows Reservoir and Milton Reservoir. Supplies are available at Truckee or Sierraville. Campers may gather deadwood for firewood. Hiking trail a few miles away.

GETTING THERE: From Truckee go N on HWY 89 approx. 16 mi. to forest route 07 (Jackson Meadow Road). Go W on 07 approx. 16 mi. to Jackson Meadows Reservoir. Findley CG is located on the W side of reservoir.

SINGLE RATE:	$13	OPEN DATES:	June-Oct
# of SINGLE SITES:	14	MAX SPUR:	26 feet
		MAX STAY:	14 days
		ELEVATION:	6200 feet

27 Fir Top
Truckee • lat 39°29'08" lon 120°33'01"

DESCRIPTION: CG set on Jackson Meadow Reservoir among mixed conifer and aspen. Warm days with cool nights. Fish for planted trout on reservoir or Milton Reservoir. Supplies in Truckee or Sierraville. Campers may gather deadwood for fires. A hiking trail to Mount Lola can be found a few miles away.

GETTING THERE: From Truckee go N on HWY 89 approx. 17 mi. to forest route 07 (Jackson Meadow Rd). Go W on 07 approx. 16 mi. to Jackson Meadow Reservoir. Fir Top CG is on W side of reservoir.

SINGLE RATE:	$13	OPEN DATES:	June-Oct
# of SINGLE SITES:	12	MAX SPUR:	26 feet
		MAX STAY:	14 days
		ELEVATION:	6200 feet

28   Forbes
Foresthill • lat 39°07'58" lon 120°47'11"

DESCRIPTION: CG situated among pine and cedar stands overlooking Sugar Pine Reservoir. Warm days with cool evenings. Trout and bass fish on lake. Supplies in Forestill. Bears frequent the area. Fills summer weekends. Buy or gather firewood on site. Horse and hiking trails nearby. By reservation only.

GETTING THERE: From Foresthill go NE on Foresthill Divide RD 8.5 mi. to forest route 26 (Sugar Pine/Lowa Hill Road). W 5.5 mi. to Sugar Pine Rec. Complex. Forbes CG is on SE side of reservoir.

		OPEN DATES:	May-Oct
		MAX SPUR:	26 feet
GROUP RATE:	$60	MAX STAY:	14 days
# of GROUP SITES:	2	ELEVATION:	3800 feet

29   French Meadows
Foresthill • lat 39°06'47" lon 120°25'35"

DESCRIPTION: CG situated among stands of red fir and pine on French Meadows Reservoir. Warm days with cool nights. Lake is planted with trout for fishing. Supplies are available in Foresthill. Watch for deer, bears, and small wildlife in area. Buy or gather firewood (may be scarce). Numerous trails to hike.

GETTING THERE: From Foresthill go NE on primary forest route 96 (Mosquito Ridge Road) approx. 33 mi. to French Meadows CG. The CG is on the S shore of the reservoir.

SINGLE RATE:	$11	OPEN DATES:	June-Oct
# of SINGLE SITES:	75	MAX SPUR:	26 feet
		MAX STAY:	14 days
		ELEVATION:	5300 feet

30   Garden Point
Comptonville • lat 39°25'57" lon 121°07'27"

DESCRIPTION: This boat-in CG rests in an open, park-like area on Bullards Bar Reservoir with views of the surrounding hills. Enjoy boat fishing for kokanee, trout and other species. Moderate use. Campers ma gather dead and down firewood locally. Supplies nearby marina. Reservations are required.

GETTING THERE: From Comptonville go S on HWY 49 approx. 2.5 mi. to county route 8. Go W on 8 approx. 3.5 mi. to Dark Day CG. From Dark Day CG, canoe or boat-in approx. 1 mi. to Garden Point CG.

SINGLE RATE:	$14	OPEN DATES:	Apr-Oct
		MAX STAY:	14 days
		ELEVATION:	2000 feet

 Campground has hosts   **Reservable sites**   **Accessible facilities**   **Fully developed**   **Semi-developed**   **Rustic facilities**

NOTE: Open dates listed are typical. Actual dates are dependent on conditions such as snow pack.

31 Gates
Foresthill • lat 39°08'29" lon 120°24'33"

DESCRIPTION: CG in fir and pine stands overlooking French Meadows Reservoir. Warm days. Fish for planted trout in reservoir and below dam. Supplies in Foresthill. Bears frequent the area. Purchase or gather firewood. Several hiking trails nearby (Mosquito Ridge Road). Fees $45-$60; by reservation only.

GETTING THERE: From Foresthill go NE on primary forest route 96 (Mosquito Ridge Road) approx. 36 mi. to French Meadows Recretion Complex. Gates CG is on the east side of the reservoir.

		OPEN DATES:	May-Oct
		MAX SPUR:	26 feet
		MAX STAY:	14 days
GROUP RATE:	Varies	ELEVATION:	5300 feet
# of GROUP SITES:	3		

32 Giant Gap
Foresthill • lat 39°08'14" lon 120°47'36"

DESCRIPTION: CG set in cedar, jeffrey pine, and ponderosa pine overlooking Sugar Pine Reservoir. Warm days with cool evenings. Fish for planted trout and bass. Supplies are available 15 mi. away. Full weekends and holidays. Buy or gather firewood locally. Trails at Sugar Pine Rec Complex. OHV use Trailhead nearby.

GETTING THERE: From Foresthill go NE on Foresthill Divide Road approx. 8.5 mi. to primary forest route 26. Go W on 26 approx. 7 mi. to Sugar Pine Reservoir. Giant Gap CG is on the NW shore.

		OPEN DATES:	May-Oct
SINGLE RATE:	$11	MAX SPUR:	30 feet
# of SINGLE SITES:	30	MAX STAY:	14 days
		ELEVATION:	3700 feet

33 Goose Meadow
Truckee • lat 39°15'27" lon 120°12'33"

DESCRIPTION: CG set among yellow pine and lodgepoles with shruberies overlooking Truckee River. Mild days with cool nights. Trout fish the river and creeks. Supplies in Truckee. Fills weekends and holidays. Gather deadwood for fires. Trailheads at Squaw Valley Fire Station including Granite Chief and Pacific Crest Trails.

GETTING THERE: From Truckee go W approx. 1 mi. on I-80 to state HWY 89. Go S on 89 approx. 4.5 mi. to Goose Meadow CG.

		OPEN DATES:	June-Oct
SINGLE RATE:	$10		
# of SINGLE SITES:	25		
		MAX STAY:	14 days
		ELEVATION:	5800 feet

34 Granite Flat
Truckee • lat 39°17'57" lon 120°12'13"

DESCRIPTION: CG set among yellow and lodgepole pine on Truckee River. Mild days with cool nights. Fish for planted rainbow trout on river. Truckee Donner State Park and museum nearby. Fills some weekends. Gather firewood locally. Nearby Squaw Valley hiking trails provide access to Pacific Crest Trail. OHV roads nearby.

GETTING THERE: From Truckee go W approx. 1 mi. on I-80 to state HWY 89. Go S on 89 approx. 1.5 mi. to Granite Flat CG. Parking is limited.

		OPEN DATES:	June-Oct
SINGLE RATE:	$12	MAX SPUR:	26 feet
# of SINGLE SITES:	74	MAX STAY:	14 days
		ELEVATION:	5800 feet

35 Grouse Ridge
Nevada City • lat 39°23'23" lon 120°36'28"

DESCRIPTION: This quiet CG is situated among mixed conifer with mountain views. Warm summer days with cool evenings. Enjoy trout fishing in the area's many lakes. Supplies are available 35 mi. away at Nevada City. Gather firewood locally. Several major hiking trails can be found in the area.

GETTING THERE: From Nevada City go E on state HWY 20 23 mi. to Bowman Road (county route 18). Go N 5 mi. to Grouse Ridge turnoff (forest route 14). Go N 5 mi. to Grouse Ridge CG. High clearance vehicles required.

		OPEN DATES:	June-Oct
SINGLE RATE:	No fee	MAX SPUR:	26 feet
# of SINGLE SITES:	9	MAX STAY:	14 days
		ELEVATION:	7400 feet

36 Hampshire Rocks
Truckee • lat 39°18'38" lon 120°29'48"

DESCRIPTION: CG set among lodgepole pine and cottonwoods with moderate undergrowth. Views are of adjacent South Yuba River and mountains. Warm summer days with cool nights. Enjoy fishing the area's many lakes. Supplies are 3 mi. away at Cisco Grove. Adjacent swimming hole makes CG busy. Frequented by bears.

GETTING THERE: Hampshire Rocks CG is located approx. 22 mi. W of Truckee on I-80 at the Rainbow Road exit.

		OPEN DATES:	May-Sept
SINGLE RATE:	$12	MAX SPUR:	26 feet
# of SINGLE SITES:	31	MAX STAY:	14 days
		ELEVATION:	5800 feet

37 Hornswoggle Group
Nevada City • lat 39°24'27" lon 121°06'12"

DESCRIPTION: CG situated in a mixed conifer forest. Warm days with cool nights. Fish for kokanee and sockeye salmon, trout, bass, and crappie. Steep shoreline, boats recommended. Gather firewood locally. Supplies at marina, Camptonville, N San Juan, or Dobbins. Reservation required; please call 530-692-3200.

GETTING THERE: From Nevada City go NW on state HWY 49 approx. 16 mi. to county route 8. Go W on 8 approx. 3.5 mi. to Hornswoggle Group CG.

		OPEN DATES:	June-Oct
		MAX SPUR:	26 feet
		MAX STAY:	14 days
GROUP RATE:	Varies	ELEVATION:	2200 feet
# of GROUP SITES:	5		

38 Indian Springs
Truckee • lat 39°19'42" lon 120°34'03"

DESCRIPTION: CG rests among lodgepole pine and cottonwoods with moderate undergrowth. Views are of the adjacent Yuba River and surrounding mountains. Enjoy fishing the area's many lakes. Supplies are 3 mi. away at Cisco Grove. Wildlife includes bears and deer. Adjacent swimming hole makes this a busy CG. Hiking in area.

GETTING THERE: Indian Springs CG is located approx. 22 mi. W of Truckee on I-80 at the Rainbow Road exit.

		OPEN DATES:	June-Oct
SINGLE RATE:	$12	MAX SPUR:	26 feet
# of SINGLE SITES:	35	MAX STAY:	14 days
		ELEVATION:	5600 feet

39 Indian Valley
Downieville • lat 39°30'47" lon 120°58'43"

DESCRIPTION: CG situated among mixed fir on the North Yuba River. Good trout fishing opportunities. Expect mild temperatures with cool nights. Supplies are at an adjacent store. Moderate use. Gather firewood locally. Devils Postpile, North Yuba, Fiddle Creek Ridge, and Halls Ranch Trailheads nearby.

GETTING THERE: From Downieville go W on state HWY 49 approx. 10 mi. to Indian Valley CG.

		OPEN DATES:	Apr-Nov
SINGLE RATE:	$14	MAX SPUR:	26 feet
# of SINGLE SITES:	17	MAX STAY:	14 days
		ELEVATION:	2200 feet

40 Jackson Creek
Nevada City • lat 39°27'28" lon 120°36'00"

DESCRIPTION: This CG is situated among mixed conifer with mountain views. Warm summer days with cool evenings. Enjoy fishing for rainbow and brown trout in this area's many lakes. Supplies are available 40 mi. away at Nevada City. Gather firewood locally. Several hiking trails nearby. No drinking water on site.

GETTING THERE: From Nevada City go E 23 mi. on state HWY 20 to forest route 18 (Bowman Road). N 13 mi. to county route 843. SE 4 mi. (passing Bowman Lake) to Jackson Creek CG. High clearance vehicles required.

		OPEN DATES:	May-Sept
SINGLE RATE:	No fee	MAX SPUR:	26 feet
# of SINGLE SITES:	14	MAX STAY:	14 days
		ELEVATION:	5600 feet

 Campground has hosts   **Reservable sites**   **Accessible facilities**   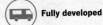 **Fully developed**   **Semi-developed**   **Rustic facilities**

41 Jackson Point
Truckee • lat 39°29'58" lon 120°32'35"

DESCRIPTION: CG set on Jackson Meadow Reservoir among mixed conifer and aspen. Fish the reservoir or Milton Reservoir for stocked trout. Check for local regulations. Warm days with cool nights. Supplies in Truckee or Sierraville. Gather dead firewood. Mount Lola hiking trail can be found a few miles away.

GETTING THERE: From Truckee go N on HWY 89 17 mi. to forest route 07 (Jackson Meadow Rd). Go W 16 mi. to Jackson Meadow Reservoir. Jackson Point CG is at the SE end of the reservoir. Accessible by boat only.

SINGLE RATE:	No fee	OPEN DATES:	June-Oct
# of SINGLE SITES:	10	MAX SPUR:	26 feet
		MAX STAY:	14 days
		ELEVATION:	6100 feet

42 Lakeside
Truckee • lat 39°23'05" lon 120°10'17"

DESCRIPTION: CG set among yellow pine, brush, and sage. Boat and shore fish for rainbow trout on Prosser Reservoir. Historical Donner Camp Site is approx. 2.5 mi. N of I-80 on HWY 89. Supplies are available at Truckee. Gather firewood locally. Bird watching is popular. Donner Camp Interpretive Trail and OHV route nearby.

GETTING THERE: From Truckee go N on state HWY 89 approx. 3.5 mi. to the Prosser Recreation Area sign. Lakeside CG is located on the NW shore of Prosser Reservoir.

SINGLE RATE:	$8	OPEN DATES:	June-Oct
# of SINGLE SITES:	30	MAX SPUR:	26 feet
		MAX STAY:	14 days
		ELEVATION:	5700 feet

43 Lasier Meadow Horse Camp
Truckee • lat 39°28'00" lon 120°30'00"

DESCRIPTION: CG set among mixed conifer with forest views. Warm days with cool nights. Fish Jackson Meadows Reservoir or Milton Reservoir for planted trout. Supplies are available in Truckee or Sierraville. Gather dead firewood. Horse corrals. Preference given to horse camping. By reservation only.

GETTING THERE: From Truckee go N on HWY 89 approx. 17 mi. to forest route 07 (Jackson Meadow Road). Go W on 07 approx. 14 mi. to forest route 70. Go approx. 1.5 mi. on 70 to Lasier Meadow Horse Camp CG.

SINGLE RATE:	$13	OPEN DATES:	June-Oct
# of SINGLE SITES:	6	MAX SPUR:	26 feet
		MAX STAY:	14 days
		ELEVATION:	6200 feet

44 Lewis
Foresthill • lat 39°08'19" lon 120°24'28"

DESCRIPTION: This CG is situated among ponderosa and fir on the shores of the French Meadows Reservoir. Good fishing opportunities in lake. Busy in July and August. Bears frequent the area, and occasionally create problems for campers. Nice secluded CG that many people overlook. Numerous trails in the area.

GETTING THERE: From Foresthill go NE on primary forest route 96 (Mosquito Ridge Road) approx. 35 mi. to Lewis CG.

SINGLE RATE:	$10	OPEN DATES:	June-Oct
# of SINGLE SITES:	40	MAX SPUR:	26 feet
		MAX STAY:	14 days
		ELEVATION:	5300 feet

45 Lindsey Lake
Nevada City • lat 39°24'52" lon 120°37'56"

DESCRIPTION: This CG is set among mixed conifer with views of adjacent Lindsey Lake. Warm summer days with cool nights. Fish for rainbow, brown, and bullhead trout in Lindsey Lake. Supplies are 35 mi. away at Nevada City. Busy weekends and holidays. Gather firewood. No drinking water. High clearance required.

GETTING THERE: From Nevada City go E on state HWY 20 23 mi. to forest route 18 (Bowman Road). N 8 mi. to forest route 17 (Grouse Ridge Road). NE 2 mi. to fork in road, take left fork 2 mi. to Lindsey Lake CG.

SINGLE RATE:	No fee	OPEN DATES:	June-Oct
# of SINGLE SITES:	7	MAX SPUR:	26 feet
		MAX STAY:	14 days
		ELEVATION:	6200 feet

46 Loganville
Sierra City • lat 39°33'53" lon 120°39'36"

DESCRIPTION: CG set among pine in the Yuba River canyon. Trout fish in the river. Hot days with cold nights. Gather firewood locally. Fills holiday weekends. Watch for deer, raccoons, and occasional bears in the area. No nearby hiking - trailhead's 5 mi. W at Rocky Rest CG. Prepare for mosquitos all summer.

GETTING THERE: Loganville CG is located approx. 1 mi. W of Sierra City on state HWY 49.

SINGLE RATE:	$12	OPEN DATES:	Apr-Oct*
# of SINGLE SITES:	19	MAX SPUR:	26 feet
		MAX STAY:	14 days
		ELEVATION:	3800 feet

47 Logger
Truckee • lat 39°27'59" lon 120°07'43"

DESCRIPTION: CG is set in a stand of pine and fir on Stampede Reservoir. Boat ramp provided. Good trout fishing on reservoir and nearby lakes, rivers, and streams. Historical sites and trails in the area. Watch for mule deer and coyotes. Supplies in Truckee. Busy summer weekends. Gather firewood locally.

GETTING THERE: From Truckee go E on I-80 approx. 6 mi. to county route S270 (Hirschdale exit). Go N on S270 approx. 7 mi. to county route 261. Go W on 261 approx. 2 mi. to Logger CG.

SINGLE RATE:	$13	OPEN DATES:	June-Oct
# of SINGLE SITES:	252	MAX SPUR:	26 feet
		MAX STAY:	14 days
		ELEVATION:	6000 feet

48 Lower Little Truckee
Sierraville • lat 39°28'15" lon 120°07'58"

DESCRIPTION: CG set in an open park like area among mixed conifer. Fish stocked trout in Little Truckee River. Warm days with cool nights. Supplies in Sierraville. 2.5 mi. N to Donner Historical site. Numerous bird species at nearby Kyburz Marsh. Deer common. Wildflowers May-June. Gather dead firewood.

GETTING THERE: Lower Little Truckee CG is located approx. 12 mi. S of Sierraville on state HWY 89.

SINGLE RATE:	$11	OPEN DATES:	June-Oct
# of SINGLE SITES:	15	MAX SPUR:	26 feet
		MAX STAY:	14 days
		ELEVATION:	6000 feet

49 North Fork
Cisco Grove • lat 39°16'14" lon 120°39'28"

DESCRIPTION: CG situated in a stand of large cedar, pine, and fir with views of the North Fork American River. Fish for rainbow trout from the river. Supplies at Emigrant Gap. Bears, deer, coyotes, and squirrels are common to the area. Campers may gather their firewood locally. Take bears precautions.

GETTING THERE: From Cisco Grove go W on I-80 approx. 5 mi. to primary forest route 19. Go SE on 19 approx. 14 mi. to North Fork CG.

SINGLE RATE:	$12	OPEN DATES:	May-Sept
# of SINGLE SITES:	17	MAX SPUR:	26 feet
		MAX STAY:	14 days
		ELEVATION:	4400 feet

50 Pack Saddle
Randolph • lat 39°37'00" lon 120°38'30"

DESCRIPTION: CG set among fir with views of Sierra Buttes. Mild days with cool nights. Trout fishing in the many area lakes and Packer Creek. Supplies at Bassetts Station 4 mi. away. Heavy use during fall hunting season. Gather firewood locally. Deer Lake, Tamarack Lake(OHV), and Sierra Buttes Lookout Trails nearby.

GETTING THERE: From Sierra City go N on state HWY 49 4.5 mi. to state route S620 (Gold Lake HWY). Go N on S620 approx. 2 mi. to state route S621 (Packer Lake Rd) approx. 4 mi. to Pack Saddle CG.

SINGLE RATE:	$12	OPEN DATES:	May-Oct
# of SINGLE SITES:	16	MAX SPUR:	26 feet
		MAX STAY:	14 days
		ELEVATION:	5900 feet

 Campground has hosts   **Reservable sites**   **Accessible facilities**   **Fully developed**   **Semi-developed**   **Rustic facilities**

NOTE: Open dates listed are typical. Actual dates are dependent on conditions such as snow pack.

51 Pass Creek

Sierraville • lat 39°30'15" lon 120°32'00"

DESCRIPTION: CG set among mixed conifer and aspen on Jackson Meadow Reservoir. Trout fish here and on Milton Reservoir. Boat ramp available. Supplies in Sierraville or Truckee. Numerous bird species, raptors, and mule deer in area. Fills weekends. Gather dead firewood. Hiking access to Mount Lola nearby.

GETTING THERE: From Truckee go N on HWY 89 approx. 17 mi. to forest route 07 (Jackson Meadow Road). Go W on 07 approx. 16 mi. to Jackson Meadow Reservoir. Pass Creek CG is on the NE shore.

SINGLE RATE:	$13	OPEN DATES:	June-Oct
# of SINGLE SITES:	30	MAX SPUR:	26 feet
		MAX STAY:	14 days
		ELEVATION:	6100 feet

56 Robinson Flat

Foresthill • lat 39°08'00" lon 120°30'00"

DESCRIPTION: In a mixed conifer setting with forest views. Fish for trout in the American River nearby. Supplies are available at Foresthill. Bears, deer, coyotes, squirrels and chipmunks are common to the area. Campers may gather firewood. The Sailor Flat Trail is nearby. Tent camping only. Take bears precautions.

GETTING THERE: From Foresthill go NE on the Foresthill Divide Road approx. 27 mi. to Robinson Flat CG.

SINGLE RATE:	No fee	OPEN DATES:	June-Oct
# of SINGLE SITES:	2	MAX SPUR:	26 feet
		MAX STAY:	14 days
		ELEVATION:	5400 feet

52 Poppy

Foresthill • lat 39°07'13" lon 120°26'10"

DESCRIPTION: Boat or hike-in to CG of red fir and pine stands on French Meadows Reservoir. Trout fish lake and below dam. Boat ramps available. Supplies 35 mi. away. Be cautious of bears. Fills summer weekends. Gather firewood. Hike McGuire Trail. No drinking water, pack it in/pack it out.

GETTING THERE: Poppy CG is located on the N shore of French Meadows Reservoir and is accessible by boat or trail only.

SINGLE RATE:	No fee	OPEN DATES:	June-Oct
# of SINGLE SITES:	12	MAX SPUR:	26 feet
		MAX STAY:	14 days
		ELEVATION:	5300 feet

57 Rocky Rest

Downieville • lat 39°30'50" lon 120°58'24"

DESCRIPTION: This CG is situated in a mixed forest on the banks of the North Yuba River. Fish for rainbow trout planted in the river. Check for local regulations. Supplies are available .25 mi. away at Indian Valley Outpost. Campers may gather their firewood locally. Numerous hiking opportunities in the area.

GETTING THERE: From Downieville go W on state HWY 49 approx. 10 mi. to Rocky Rest CG.

SINGLE RATE:	$12	OPEN DATES:	Apr-Nov
# of SINGLE SITES:	10	MAX SPUR:	26 feet
		MAX STAY:	14 days
		ELEVATION:	2200 feet

53 Prosser
Truckee • lat 39°22'40" lon 120°09'38"

DESCRIPTION: CG set among yellow pine overlooking Prosser Reservoir and hillsides. Boat fish for rainbow and brown trout on lake or native trout in Alder and Prosser Creeks. Historic Donner Camp nearby. Gather firewood. Fills weekends and holidays. OHV trails nearby. Commemorative Emigrant Trail 3 mi. away.

GETTING THERE: From Truckee go N on state HWY 89 approx. 3.5 mi. to Prosser Recreation Area Road. Go W approx. 1 mi. to Prosser CG.

SINGLE RATE:	$10	OPEN DATES:	June-Oct
# of SINGLE SITES:	29	MAX SPUR:	26 feet
		MAX STAY:	14 days
		ELEVATION:	5800 feet

58 Sagehen Creek

Truckee • lat 39°26'04" lon 120°14'50"

DESCRIPTION: CG set on Sagehen Creek among mixed conifer, yellow pine, and sage. Hot dusty days with cool nights. Stream fish the creek for trout. Supplies in Truckee. Watch for deer, bears, and coyotes. Light use. OHV dirt roads. Mosquitos thick in June and July. No drinking water, no services.

GETTING THERE: From Truckee go N on state HWY 89 approx. 9 mi. to primary forest route 11 (may be gated). Go W on 11 approx. 2.5 mi. to forest route. Go 1.5 mi. to Sagehen Creek CG. Road is rough.

SINGLE RATE:	No fee	OPEN DATES:	June-Oct
# of SINGLE SITES:	10	MAX SPUR:	26 feet
		MAX STAY:	14 days
		ELEVATION:	6500 feet

54 Prosser Ranch
Truckee • lat 39°22'44" lon 120°09'15"

DESCRIPTION: CG set on Prosser Reservoir among yellow pine and sage. Views of lake and hillsides. Boat fish for rainbow and brown trout. Boat ramp. 2.5 mi. N to Donner Camp Historic Site. Supplies in Truckee. OHV trails 1 mi. at Lakewide CG. Commemorative Emigrant Trail access from Alder Creek Trail Road.

GETTING THERE: From Truckee go N on state HWY 89 approx. 3.5 mi. to Prosser Recreation Area Road, then E approx. 1.5 mi. to Prosser Ranch CG.

		OPEN DATES:	June-Oct
		MAX SPUR:	26 feet
GROUP RATE:	$75	MAX STAY:	14 days
# of GROUP SITES:	1	ELEVATION:	5800 feet

59 Salmon Creek

Sierra City • lat 39°37'37" lon 120°36'52"

DESCRIPTION: CG set among mixed fir with views of Sierra Buttes. Mild days with cool nights. Trout fish on nearby Packer and Salmon Creeks. Supplies are 2 mi. away at Bassetts Station. Gather firewood. Heavy use during the fall hunting season. Trailheads for hiking and OHV use are available in the area.

GETTING THERE: From Sierra City go NE on state HWY 49 approx. 4.5 mi. to primary forest route S620 (at Bassetts Station). Go NW on S620 (Gold Lake HWY) approx. 2 mi. to Salmon Creek CG.

SINGLE RATE:	$12	OPEN DATES:	May-Oct*
# of SINGLE SITES:	31	MAX SPUR:	26 feet
		MAX STAY:	14 days
		ELEVATION:	5800 feet

55 Ramshorn

Downieville • lat 39°32'21" lon 120°54'30"

DESCRIPTION: CG set among pine and oak with forest views. Stream fishing accesses for planted trout nearby. Supplies at Downieville. Receives moderate use. Gather firewood locally. Many hiking trails including North Yuba, Goodyears Bar, Rocky Rest, Halls Ranch, Fiddle Creek Ridge, and Devils Postpile.

GETTING THERE: From Downieville go W on state HWY 49 approx. 6 mi. to Ramshorn CG.

SINGLE RATE:	$12	OPEN DATES:	Apr-Oct
# of SINGLE SITES:	16	MAX SPUR:	26 feet
		MAX STAY:	14 days
		ELEVATION:	2600 feet

60 Sardine

Sierra City • lat 39°37'08" lon 120°36'59"

DESCRIPTION: CG situated close to a warm shallow lake with views of Sierra Buttes. Trout fishing in Sardine Lakes. Boat ramp available. Gather firewood. 6 mi. to historic Kentucky Mine and Museum. Supplies are at Bassetts Station 2 mi. away. Hiking trails available. Snow lingers late into the season.

GETTING THERE: From Sierra City go NE on state HWY 49 approx. 4 mi. to primary forest route S620. Go NW on S620 approx. 2 mi. to Sardine CG.

SINGLE RATE:	$12	OPEN DATES:	May-Oct
# of SINGLE SITES:	28	MAX SPUR:	26 feet
		MAX STAY:	14 days
		ELEVATION:	5800 feet

 Campground has hosts   **Reservable sites**   **Accessible facilities**   **Fully developed**   **Semi-developed**   **Rustic facilities**

NOTE: Open dates listed are typical. Actual dates are dependent on conditions such as snow pack.

61 Schoolhouse

Camptonville • lat 39°25'02" lon 121°07'18"

DESCRIPTION: Among pine and fir on Bullards Bar Reservoir. Wildflowers are beautiful when in season. Mild to hot days. Boat fish for kokanee, trout and other species. Supplies are at the marina, 1 mi. away. Gather firewood locally. Enjoy hiking the trails around the reservoir. Reservations required.

GETTING THERE: From Camptonville go S on HWY 49 approx. 2.5 mi. to county route 8 (Marysville Rd). Go W on 8 approx. 3.5 mi. to Schoolhouse CG.

		OPEN DATES:	Apr-Oct
		MAX SPUR:	26 feet
GROUP RATE:	$14	MAX STAY:	14 days
# of GROUP SITES:	12	ELEVATION:	2280 feet

66 Silver Tip

Truckee • lat 39°29'13" lon 120°32'40"

DESCRIPTION: This CG is situated in a dense forest with views of Jackson Meadow Reservoir. Fish for stocked rainbow and brown trout in reservoir. Supplies at Truckee. Deer, bears, and various birds are common to the area. Campers may gather their firewood locally. No designated trails available.

GETTING THERE: From Truckee go N on HWY 89 approx. 17 mi. to forest route 07. Go W on 07 approx. 16 mi. to Silver Tip CG.

		OPEN DATES:	June-Oct
		MAX SPUR:	26 feet
GROUP RATE:	$60	MAX STAY:	14 days
# of GROUP SITES:	2	ELEVATION:	6000 feet

62 Secret House

Foresthill • lat 39°11'14" lon 120°35'06"

DESCRIPTION: Tent only CG in heavily forested stands of red fir and pine. Stream fish for wild trout. Supplies are 19 mi. away. Be cautious of bears. Gather deadwood for fires. 5 mi. W to China Wall OHV Staging Area. Numerous other OHV and hiking opportunities in area. No drinking water. Pack it in, pack it out.

GETTING THERE: Secret House CG is located approx. 17.5 mi. NE of Foresthill on the Foresthill Divide Road. Trailers and RVs not recommended.

		OPEN DATES:	May-Oct
SINGLE RATE:	No fee	MAX SPUR:	15 feet
# of SINGLE SITES:	2	MAX STAY:	14 days
		ELEVATION:	5400 feet

67 Skillman

Nevada City • lat 39°19'06" lon 120°47'21"

DESCRIPTION: CG set in a mature stand of mixed conifer with mountain views. Fish for trout on the South Fork fo the Yuba River. Supplies at Nevada City. Bears, deer, coyotes, and band-tailed pigeons are common to the area. Gather fiewood locally. Pioneer Trail runs through the CG. Take bears precations.

GETTING THERE: Skillman CG is located approx. 11.5 mi. E of Nevada City on state HWY 20.

		OPEN DATES:	June-Oct
		MAX SPUR:	26 feet
GROUP RATE:	Varies	MAX STAY:	14 days
# of GROUP SITES:	15	ELEVATION:	4400 feet

63 Shirttail Creek

Foresthill • lat 39°08'40" lon 120°47'05"

DESCRIPTION: This CG is situated among ponderosa pine and manzanitas on the banks of Sugar Pine Creek. Dry climate. OK fishing in lake. Check for local fishing regulations. Busy on weekends in summer. Watch for deer and bears. Numerous trails in the area, including a trail that wraps around the lake.

GETTING THERE: From Foresthill go NE on Foresthill Divide Road approx. 8.5 mi. to primary forest route 26. Go W on 26 approx. 6.5 mi. to Shirttail Creek CG

		OPEN DATES:	June-Oct
SINGLE RATE:	$10	MAX SPUR:	30 feet
# of SINGLE SITES:	30	MAX STAY:	14 days
		ELEVATION:	3700 feet

68 Snag Lake

Sierra City • lat 39°40'09" lon 120°37'35"

DESCRIPTION: This CG is situated among mixed fir set on Snag Lake which is stocked with brook trout. Mild days with cool nights. Bassetts Station, 5 mi. away, has supplies. Receives moderate use. Gather firewood locally. Trail ends at Salmon Lake 2 mi. away. Snow may delay opening.

GETTING THERE: From Sierra Ctiy go N approx. 4 mi. on state HWY 49 to county route S620. Go NW on S620 approx. 4.5 mi. to Snag Lake CG.

		OPEN DATES:	May-Oct
SINGLE RATE:	No fee	MAX SPUR:	26 feet
# of SINGLE SITES:	10	MAX STAY:	14 days
		ELEVATION:	6600 feet

64 Sierra

Sierra City • lat 39°37'51" lon 120°33'27"

DESCRIPTION: CG set on the banks of the Yuba River, situated among fir trees. Nearby downstream Bassetts is stocked. Mild days with cool nights. Gather firewood locally. Historic Bassetts Station, 2 mi. away, has supplies. Pacific Crest, Wild Plum Loop, Loves Falls, and South Bound Trailheads nearby.

GETTING THERE: Sierra CG is located approx. 7 mi. E of Sierra City on state HWY 49.

		OPEN DATES:	May-Oct
SINGLE RATE:	$10	MAX SPUR:	26 feet
# of SINGLE SITES:	16	MAX STAY:	14 days
		ELEVATION:	5600 feet

69 Sterling Lake

Cisco Grove • lat 39°21'12" lon 120°29'35"

DESCRIPTION: CG set in a mixed conifer forest with views of Lake Sterling. Fish for brook or rainbow trout from the lake. Supplies at Cisco Grove. Bears, deer, coyotes, squirrels, and blue grouse are common to the area. Gather firewood. Trails within 5 mi. of CG. Trailers not recommended, tent camping only.

GETTING THERE: From Cisco Grove go N on primary forest route 85 approx. 3 mi. to forest route. Go N on forest route approx. 2 mi. to Sterling Lake CG. 4WD recommended.

		OPEN DATES:	June-Oct
SINGLE RATE:	No fee		
# of SINGLE SITES:	6		
		MAX STAY:	14 days
		ELEVATION:	7000 feet

65 Silver Creek

Truckee • lat 39°13'23" lon 120°12'03"

DESCRIPTION: CG set on the Truckee River among yellow pine and lodgepoles. Seven walk-in tent sites. Fish planted rainbow trout on the river. Several other creeks nearby for native trout fishing. Fills weekends and holidays. Gather firewood. Squaw Valley area offers many hiking trails including Pacific Crest.

GETTING THERE: From Truckee go approx. 1 mi. W on I-80 to state HWY 89. Go S on 89 approx. 7 mi. to Silver Creek CG.

		OPEN DATES:	May-Oct*
SINGLE RATE:	$10	MAX SPUR:	26 feet
# of SINGLE SITES:	27	MAX STAY:	14 days
		ELEVATION:	6070 feet

70 Talbot

Foresthill • lat 39°11'14" lon 120°22'22"

DESCRIPTION: CG is set in a dense forest on the Middle Fork of the American River. Warm days with cool nights. Good trout fishing in river, nearby French Meadows Reservoir, and creeks. Supplies 41 mi. to Foresthill. Busy weekends. Gather firewood locally. Numerous trails in area. CG may be frequented by bears.

GETTING THERE: From Foresthill go NE on primary forest route 96 (Mosquito Ridge Road) approx. 38.5 mi. to Talbot CG.

		OPEN DATES:	June-Oct
SINGLE RATE:	No fee	MAX SPUR:	26 feet
# of SINGLE SITES:	5	MAX STAY:	14 days
		ELEVATION:	5600 feet

 Campground has hosts   **Reservable sites**   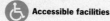 **Accessible facilities**   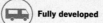 **Fully developed**   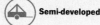 **Semi-developed**   **Rustic facilities**

NOTE: Open dates listed are typical. Actual dates are dependent on conditions such as snow pack.

71 Tunnel Mills
Cisco Grove • lat 39°15'10" lon 120°39'06"

DESCRIPTION: CG set in a stand of large pine and fir on the East Fork of the North Fork American River. Fish for trout from the river. Supplies are at Emigrant Gap. Bears, deer, coyotes, squirrels, and red-tailed hawks are common in the area. Gather firewood locally. Take bears precautions.

GETTING THERE: From Cisco Grove go W on I-80 approx. 5 mi. to primary forest route 19. Go SE on 19 approx. 15 mi. to Tunnel Mills CG.

		OPEN DATES:	June-Oct
		MAX SPUR:	26 feet
GROUP RATE:	$70	MAX STAY:	14 days
# of GROUP SITES:	2	ELEVATION:	4000 feet

72 Union Flat
Downieville • lat 39°34'03" lon 120°44'37"

DESCRIPTION: This CG is situated in a mixed forest with views of the North Yuba River. Rainbow trout fishing from river. Supplies are available 6 mi. away at Downieville. Gather firewood locally. Gold panning and digging along the banks of the river is a popular activity in the early fall.

GETTING THERE: Union Flat CG is located approx. 6 mi. E of Downieville on state HWY 49.

		OPEN DATES:	Apr-Nov
SINGLE RATE:	$12	MAX SPUR:	26 feet
# of SINGLE SITES:	11	MAX STAY:	14 days
		ELEVATION:	3400 feet

73 Upper Little Truckee
Truckee • lat 39°29'27" lon 120°14'38"

DESCRIPTION: CG set among mixed confier in an open park like setting on Little Truckee River. Heavy fishing on stocked river. Historic Donner Camp nearby. Supplies in Sierraville. Gather dead firewood. Numerous bird species to see at Kyburz Marsh 10 mi. S. Profuse wildflowers May-June. Walk interpretive trail on site.

GETTING THERE: Upper Little Truckee CG is located approx. 11.5 mi. S of Sierraville on state HWY 89 along the Little Truckee River.

		OPEN DATES:	May-Oct
SINGLE RATE:	$11	MAX SPUR:	26 feet
# of SINGLE SITES:	17	MAX STAY:	14 days
GROUP RATE:	Varies	ELEVATION:	6100 feet
# of GROUP SITES:	1		

74 White Cloud
Nevada City • lat 39°19'14" lon 120°50'43"

DESCRIPTION: CG set in a mature mixed conifer forest with mountain views. Fish for trout on the South Fork of the Yuba River nearby. Supplies are in Nevada City. Bears, deer, coyotes, and red-tailed hawks. Gather firewood. The Pioneer Trail is accessible at the back of the CG. Take bears precautions.

GETTING THERE: White Cloud CG is located approx. 11 mi. E of Nevada City on state HWY 20.

		OPEN DATES:	June-Oct
SINGLE RATE:	$12	MAX SPUR:	26 feet
# of SINGLE SITES:	46	MAX STAY:	14 days
		ELEVATION:	4200 feet

75 Wild Plum
Sierra City • lat 39°33'59" lon 120°35'53"

DESCRIPTION: This CG is situated in a mixed forest with views of Haypress Creek. Rainbow trout fishing from the creek. Supplies in Sierra City. Gather firewood locally. Hiking on Wild Plum Loop; a short 2.5 mi. loop from east end of upper CG, with excellent views of towering Sierra Buttes.

GETTING THERE: Wild Plum CG is located approx. 1 mi. E of Sierra City.

		OPEN DATES:	Apr-Oct
SINGLE RATE:	$12	MAX SPUR:	26 feet
# of SINGLE SITES:	44	MAX STAY:	14 days
		ELEVATION:	4400 feet

76 Woodcamp
Randolph • lat 39°29'08" lon 120°32'52"

DESCRIPTION: CG set among mixed conifers and aspen. Fish for planted trout in Jackson Meadows Reservoir and Milton Reservoir. Supplies are in Truckee or Sierraville. Numerous bird species, deer, bald eagles, and small wildlife in area. Campers may gather deadwood. Hiking trails nearby.

GETTING THERE: From Truckee go N on HWY 89 approx. 17 mi. to forest route 7. Go E on 7 16 mi. to Jackson Meadow Reservoir. Woodcamp CG is on the SW shore.

		OPEN DATES:	June-Oct
SINGLE RATE:	$13	MAX SPUR:	26 feet
# of SINGLE SITES:	20	MAX STAY:	14 days
		ELEVATION:	6100 feet

77 Woodchuck
Cisco Grove • lat 39°19'59" lon 120°31'06"

DESCRIPTION: This CG is situated in a mixed conifer forest with forest views. Fish for brook and rainbow trout at nearby Lake Sterling. Supplies are available at Cisco Grove. Bears, deer, coyotes, and squirrels are common to the area. Campers may gather their firewood locally.

GETTING THERE: Woodchuck CG is located approx. 3 mi. NE of Cisco Grove on primary forest route 85. Not recommended for trailers.

		OPEN DATES:	June-Oct
SINGLE RATE:	No fee		
# of SINGLE SITES:	6	MAX STAY:	14 days
		ELEVATION:	6300 feet

78 Yuba Pass
Sierra City • lat 39°37'03" lon 120°29'20"

DESCRIPTION: This CG is situated in a stand of large red fir set on a meadow at the headwaters of the North Yuba River. Fishing opportunities in river, check for local regulations. Gather firewood locally. Supplies are available 4 mi. away at Bassetts Station. Several trails are nearby.

GETTING THERE: Yuba Pass CG is located approx. 9 mi. E of Sierra Ctiy on state HWY 49.

		OPEN DATES:	June-Oct
SINGLE RATE:	$11	MAX SPUR:	26 feet
# of SINGLE SITES:	20	MAX STAY:	14 days
		ELEVATION:	6700 feet

 Campground has hosts   **Reservable sites**   **Accessible facilities**   **Fully developed**   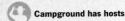 **Semi-developed**   **Rustic facilities**

NOTE: Open dates listed are typical. Actual dates are dependent on conditions such as snow pack.

Grinding Rock Indian Historical Site
Los Padres National Forest, California
Kathleen Burnett Photo

USFS Photo

ARAPAHO-ROOSEVELT NATIONAL FOREST

The Arapaho and Roosevelt National Forests include 1.3 million acres of public land in the Rocky Mountains and foothills of north central Colorado. The Arapaho National Forest includes lands on both sides of the Continental Divide, while the Roosevelt National Forest is confined to the eastern side of the Divide.

The forests are rich in cultural history. Native tribes occupied the forests and plains through the 19th century until mining prospectors and ranchers homesteaded in the area. Signs of early uses are old mines, pack trails, wagon roads, narrow and standard gauge railroad routes and prospector, trapper and homestead cabins.

Fun and adventure for the whole family are less than an hour's drive from Denver. Enjoy the breathtaking mountain scenery along the world's highest paved highway to the summit of Mt. Evans, at 14,258 feet, or along the Peak to Peak or Guanella Pass National Scenic Byways.

Make a splash at Arapaho National Recreation Area. The area has five lakes, four campgrounds and plenty of fishing, boating, hiking, and horseback riding. Whitewater rafters and kayakers can shoot the rapids on the Cache la Poudre River.

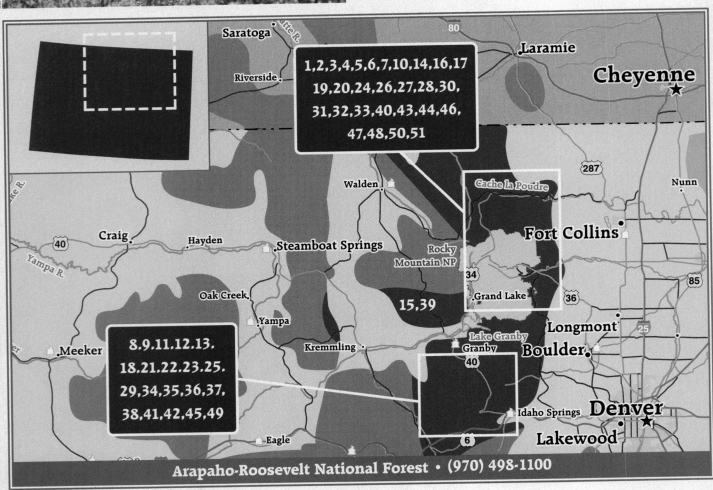

Arapaho-Roosevelt National Forest • (970) 498-1100

1 Ansel Watrous
Fort Collins • lat 40°41'22" lon 105°20'58"

DESCRIPTION: This CG is set in short grass and shrubs with cottonwood trees, willows, and prickly pear cactus. There is fishing in the area. Look for burrowing owls, chestnut collared longspur badgers, antelope, and deer. Hiking, mountain biking, and scenic drives are all close to the CG.

GETTING THERE: From Fort Collins go W on state HWY 14 approx. 16 mi. to Ansel Watrous CG.

SINGLE RATE:	$9	OPEN DATES:	Yearlong
# of SINGLE SITES:	19	MAX SPUR:	30 feet
		MAX STAY:	14 days
		ELEVATION:	5800 feet

2 Arapaho Bay
Granby • lat 40°07'20" lon 105°45'38"

DESCRIPTION: This CG is adjacent to Granby Lake. Campers should prepare for typical afternoon thunderstorm weather pattern. There is a boat launch ramp nearby. Campers may gather dead and down firewood locally. There are several hiking trails in the area.

GETTING THERE: From Granby go N on US HWY 34 approx. 5 mi. to forest route 125. Go E on 125 approx. 8 mi. to Arapaho Bay CG.

SINGLE RATE:	$12	OPEN DATES:	May-Sept
# of SINGLE SITES:	84	MAX SPUR:	45 feet
		MAX STAY:	14 days
		ELEVATION:	8320 feet

3 Aspen Glen
Fort Collins • lat 40°37'07" lon 105°49'09"

DESCRIPTION: CG in a pine, fir, and juniper forest with a variety of vegetation. Fishing in the area. Look for great horned owls, mountain chickadees, deer, cougars, bighorn sheep, and cottontail rabbits. Scenic 4 Wheel and OHV trails in the area. Hiking and mountain biking (near a wilderness area)close to CG.

GETTING THERE: From Fort Collins go W on state HWY 14 approx. 47 mi. to Aspen Glen CG.

SINGLE RATE:	$8	OPEN DATES:	May-Nov
# of SINGLE SITES:	8	MAX SPUR:	30 feet
		MAX STAY:	14 days
		ELEVATION:	8660 feet

4 Bellaire Lake
Fort Collins • lat 40°46'15" lon 105°37'03"

DESCRIPTION: CG in a pine, fir, and juniper forest with a variety of vegetation. Fishing in the lake. Look for great horned owls, mountain chickadees, deer, cougars, bighorn sheep, and cottontail rabbits. Scenic 4 Wheel and OHV trails in the area. Hiking and mountain biking (near a wilderness area)close to CG.

GETTING THERE: From Fort Collins go W on state HWY 14 approx. 32 mi. to county route 69. Go N on 69 approx. 3 mi. to county route 162. Go W on 162 approx. 5 mi. to Bellaire Lake CG.

SINGLE RATE:	$12	OPEN DATES:	May-Sept
# of SINGLE SITES:	26	MAX SPUR:	60 feet
		MAX STAY:	14 days
		ELEVATION:	8650 feet

5 Big Bend
Fort Collins • lat 40°42'27" lon 105°43'27"

DESCRIPTION: In a pine, fir, and juniper forest with a variety of vegetation. Fishing in the area. Look for great horned owls, mountain chickadees, deer, cougars, bighorn sheep, and cottontail rabbits. Scenic 4 Wheel and OHV trails in the area. Hiking and mountain biking (near a wilderness area)close to CG.

GETTING THERE: From Fort Collins go W on state HWY 14 approx. 39 mi. to Big Bend CG. Walk-in sites.

SINGLE RATE:	$9	OPEN DATES:	Yearlong
# of SINGLE SITES:	9	MAX SPUR:	20 feet
		MAX STAY:	14 days
		ELEVATION:	7700 feet

6 Big South
Fort Collins • lat 40°37'58" lon 105°48'17"

DESCRIPTION: In a pine, fir and juniper, forest with a variety of vegetation. Fishing in the area. Look for great horned owls, mountain chickadees, deer, cougars, bighorn sheep, and cottontail rabbits. Scenic 4 Wheel and OHV trails in the area. Hiking and mountain biking (near a wilderness area)close to CG.

GETTING THERE: From Fort Collins go W on state HWY 14 approx. 46 mi. to Big South CG.

SINGLE RATE:	$7	OPEN DATES:	June-Nov
# of SINGLE SITES:	4	MAX SPUR:	25 feet
		MAX STAY:	14 days
		ELEVATION:	8440 feet

7 Browns Park
Fort Collins • lat 40°47'46" lon 105°55'36"

DESCRIPTION: In a pine, fir and juniper, forest with a variety of vegetation. Fishing in the area. Look for great horned owls, mountain chickadees, deer, cougars, bighorn sheep, and cottontail rabbits. Scenic 4 Wheel and OHV trails in the area. Hiking and mountain biking (near a wilderness area)close to CG.

GETTING THERE: From Fort Collins go W on state HWY 14 approx. 49 mi. to county route 103. Go N on 103 approx. 12 mi. to county route 80C. Go W on 80C approx. 2 mi. to Browns Park CG.

SINGLE RATE:	$8	OPEN DATES:	June-Nov
# of SINGLE SITES:	28	MAX SPUR:	30 feet
		MAX STAY:	14 days
		ELEVATION:	8440 feet

8 Byers Creek
Fraser • lat 39°52'35" lon 105°53'51"

DESCRIPTION: This CG is situated in a pine, fir, and juniper forest. Wide variety of vegetation and flowers to be viewed. Fishing and boating in area. Look for deer, cougars, bighorn sheep, coyotes, rabbits, bluebirds, great horned owls, and magpies in the area. Trails in area.

GETTING THERE: From Fraser go S on county route 73 (St. Louis Creek Road) approx. 6 mi. to Byers Creek CG.

SINGLE RATE:	$10	OPEN DATES:	May-Sept
# of SINGLE SITES:	6	MAX SPUR:	32 feet
		MAX STAY:	14 days
		ELEVATION:	9400 feet

9 Camp Dick
Ward • lat 40°07'46" lon 105°31'08"

DESCRIPTION: CG is in a mixed conifer forest and is adjacent to the Middle St. Vrain River. Fish for trout. Afternoon t-showers. Supplies 5 mi. Busy weekends. Good hiking, mountain biking, and horse trails in area. Firewood sold on site. Horse facilities nearby. The Indian Peaks Wilderness is 4 mi. W.

GETTING THERE: From Ward go N on state HWY 72 approx. 5 mi. to forest route 114. Go W on 114 approx. 1 mi. to Camp Dick CG.

SINGLE RATE:	$12	OPEN DATES:	May-Oct*
# of SINGLE SITES:	41	MAX SPUR:	55 feet
		MAX STAY:	14 days
		ELEVATION:	8650 feet

10 Chambers Lake
Fort Collins • lat 40°35'51" lon 105°51'05"

DESCRIPTION: CG situated in a rustic, mountainous, lodgepole pine forest. Popular activities include fishing and boating on Chambers Lake. Boat ramp located on lake. Look for a variety of animals in area. Scenic 4 Wheel, mountain biking, hiking, and OHV trails in the area. A playground area is available on site.

GETTING THERE: From Fort Collins go W on state HWY 14 approx. 50 mi. to Chambers Lake CG.

SINGLE RATE:	Varies	OPEN DATES:	June-Sept
# of SINGLE SITES:	51	MAX SPUR:	35 feet
		MAX STAY:	14 days
		ELEVATION:	9200 feet

 Campground has hosts   **Reservable sites**   **Accessible facilities**   **Fully developed**   **Semi-developed**   **Rustic facilities**

NOTE: Open dates listed are typical. Actual dates are dependent on conditions such as snow pack.

ARAPAHO-ROOSEVELT NATIONAL FOREST • COLORADO • 1 — 10

11 Clear Lake
Georgetown • lat 39°39'07" lon 105°42'29"

DESCRIPTION: CG is located in pine, spruce, and aspen with mountain views. Afternoon thundershowers are common. Trout fishing in area. Visit historical mining sites. Supplies 6 mi. to Georgetown. Can be busy on weekends. Gather firewood locally. Hiking, mountain biking, and 4WD trails in area.

GETTING THERE: From Georgetown go S on county route 381 approx. 6 mi. to Clear Lake CG.

SINGLE RATE:	$9	OPEN DATES:	May-Sept
# of SINGLE SITES:	8	MAX SPUR:	15 feet
		MAX STAY:	7 days
		ELEVATION:	10000 feet

16 Dowdy Lake
Fort Collins • lat 40°47'30" lon 105°33'24"

DESCRIPTION: CG is situated adjacent to Dowdy Lake in a mountainous, ponderosa pine forest. Fishing and boat ramp at the lake. Mountain lions and black bears are common to area. Supplies at Fort Collins. Hiking, horse, and mountain bike trails in area. Four wheel drive roads are within 5 miles of the CG.

GETTING THERE: From Fort Collins go N on US HWY 267 to Livermore. Go W on county route 74E approx. 18 mi. to Dowdy Lake CG.

SINGLE RATE:	$10	OPEN DATES:	Yearlong*
# of SINGLE SITES:	62	MAX SPUR:	40 feet
		MAX STAY:	14 days
		ELEVATION:	8140 feet

12 Cold Springs
Golden • lat 39°50'29" lon 105°29'15"

DESCRIPTION: In the foothills among lodgepole pine and aspen. No fishing in area. Historic Central City, Black Hawk, and abandoned mine sites. Supplies at Nederland, 14 mi. Deer, bears, mountain lions, and various birds in area. Gather deadwood or buy firewood. Mountain bike, ATV, and 4X4 routes nearby. Mosquitos early on.

GETTING THERE: From Golden go W on US HWY 6 approx. 9 mi. to state HWY 119. Go N on 119 approx. 10 mi. to Cold Springs CG.

SINGLE RATE:	$11	OPEN DATES:	May-Sept
# of SINGLE SITES:	38	MAX SPUR:	50 feet
		MAX STAY:	14 days
		ELEVATION:	9200 feet

17 Dutch George Flats
Fort Collins • lat 40°44'00" lon 105°26'30"

DESCRIPTION: This CG is situated in a rustic, mountainous, lodgepole pine forest. Popular activities include fishing and boating on Chambers Lake. Boat ramp located on lake. Moose and black bears are common to the area. Scenic 4 Wheel, mountain biking, hiking, and OHV trails in the area.

GETTING THERE: From Fort Collins go W on state HWY 14 approx. 23 mi. to Dutch George CG.

SINGLE RATE:	$10	OPEN DATES:	May-Oct
# of SINGLE SITES:	20	MAX SPUR:	33 feet
		MAX STAY:	14 days
		ELEVATION:	6500 feet

13 Columbine
Golden • lat 39°49'01" lon 105°32'55"

DESCRIPTION: This CG in a park like setting among pine and aspen with views of peaks and valleys. Warm days with cool nights. No fishing. Historic cemeteries and mining sites in area. Supplies at Central City. Collect dead wood or buy firewood. 4X4 routes nearby. Prepare for mosquitos and ticks until mid-June.

GETTING THERE: From Golden go W on US HWY 6 approx. 9 mi. to state HWY 119. Go N on 119 approx. 7 mi. to state HWY 279. Go W on 279 approx. 4 mi. to Columbine CG.

SINGLE RATE:	$10	OPEN DATES:	May-Sept
# of SINGLE SITES:	47	MAX SPUR:	20 feet
		MAX STAY:	14 days
		ELEVATION:	9020 feet

18 Echo Lake
Idaho Springs • lat 39°39'25" lon 105°35'37"

DESCRIPTION: Park like setting among spruce and firs with views of lakes and Mount Evans Wilderness. Cool days, cold nights; possible snow. Fly and bait fish on Echo and Summit Lakes for trout; no boats. Supplies at Echo Lake. Deer, elk, and bears in area. Horse and hiking trails nearby. Ticks and mosquitos early on.

GETTING THERE: From Idaho Springs go S on state HWY 103 approx. 14 mi. to Echo Lake CG.

SINGLE RATE:	$10	OPEN DATES:	June-Sept
# of SINGLE SITES:	18	MAX SPUR:	20 feet
		MAX STAY:	14 days
		ELEVATION:	10600 feet

14 Cutthroat Bay
Granby • lat 40°11'26" lon 105°52'25"

DESCRIPTION: CG in a pine, fir, and juniper forest. Wide variety of vegetation and flowers to be viewed. Fishing and boating in area. Look for deer, cougars, bighorn sheep, coyotes, rabbits, bluebirds, great horned owls, and magpies in the area. Trails in area. Horseshoe and volleyball pits, covered pavilion.

GETTING THERE: Cutthroat Bay CG is located on the N shore of Lake Granby off of US HWY 34.

		OPEN DATES:	May-Sept
		MAX SPUR:	32 feet
GROUP RATE:	$60	MAX STAY:	14 days
# of GROUP SITES:	2	ELEVATION:	8400 feet

19 Grand View
Fort Collins • lat 40°29'38" lon 105°48'06"

DESCRIPTION: CG situated in a rustic, mountainous, lodgepole pine forest. Popular activities include fishing and boating on Chambers Lake. Boat ramp located on lake. Look for a variety of animals in area. Scenic 4 Wheel, mountain biking, hiking, and OHV trails in the area. A playground area is available on site.

GETTING THERE: From Fort Collins go W approx. 51 mi. on state HWY 14 to forest route 156. Go E on 156 approx. 9 mi. to Grand View CG. Tent camping only.

SINGLE RATE:	$8	OPEN DATES:	July-Nov
# of SINGLE SITES:	8		
		MAX STAY:	14 days
		ELEVATION:	10220 feet

15 Denver Creek
Granby • lat 40°15'17" lon 106°04'44"

DESCRIPTION: This CG is in a pine, fir, and juniper forest. Wide variety of vegetation and flowers to be viewed. Fishing and boating in area. Supplies available at Granby. Look for deer, cougars, bighorn sheep, coyotes, rabbits, bluebirds, great horned owls, and magpies in the area. Trails in area.

GETTING THERE: From Granby go W on US HWY 40 approx. 3 mi. to state HWY 125. Go N on 125 approx. 11 mi. to Denver Creek CG.

SINGLE RATE:	$10	OPEN DATES:	May-Sept
# of SINGLE SITES:	22	MAX SPUR:	25 feet
		MAX STAY:	14 days
		ELEVATION:	8600 feet

20 Green Ridge
Granby • lat 40°12'30" lon 105°51'30"

DESCRIPTION: CG is in a pine, fir, and juniper forest adjacent to Shadow Mountain Reservoir. Boat ramp and fish at Res.(National Fishing Week is popular here). Supplies at Granby. Look for deer, cougars, bighorn sheep, coyotes, rabbits, bluebirds, great horned owls, and magpies in the area. Trails in area.

GETTING THERE: Green Ridge CG is located on the S shore of Shadow Mountain Lake approx. 10 mi. N of Grandby off of US HWY 34.

SINGLE RATE:	$12	OPEN DATES:	May-Sept
# of SINGLE SITES:	77	MAX SPUR:	35 feet
		MAX STAY:	14 days
		ELEVATION:	8400 feet

 Campground has hosts   Reservable sites 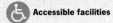 Accessible facilities 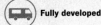 Fully developed   Semi-developed   Rustic facilities

NOTE: Open dates listed are typical. Actual dates are dependent on conditions such as snow pack.

21 Guanella Pass

Georgetown • lat 39°36'46" lon 105°42'58"

DESCRIPTION: CG is in a dense pine forest with views of peaks and pass. Cool days, frequent rain. Fly or bait stream fish for trout on S Clear Creek. Historic mining area. Supplies at Georgetown. Deer and elk in area. Moderate use. Gather firewood. Hike Guanella Pass and Silver Dollar trails nearby. Mosquitos early on.

GETTING THERE: From Georgetown go S on county route 62 approx. 9 mi. to Guanella Pass CG.

SINGLE RATE:	$11	OPEN DATES:	May-Sept
# of SINGLE SITES:	18	MAX SPUR:	35 feet
		MAX STAY:	14 days
		ELEVATION:	10900 feet

22 Horseshoe
Hot Sulphur Springs • lat 39°54'01" lon 106°05'44"

DESCRIPTION: This CG is in a pine, fir, and juniper forest. Wide variety of vegetation and flowers to be viewed. Fishing and boating in area. Look for deer, cougars, bighorn sheep, coyotes, rabbits, bluebirds, great horned owls, and magpies in the area. Trails in area.

GETTING THERE: From Hot Sulphur Springs go W on US HWY 40 approx. 5 mi. to county route 3. Go S on 3 approx. 14 mi. to Horseshoe CG.

SINGLE RATE:	$9	OPEN DATES:	May-Sept
# of SINGLE SITES:	7	MAX SPUR:	23 feet
		MAX STAY:	14 days
		ELEVATION:	8540 feet

23 Idlewild

Winter Park • lat 39°54'15" lon 105°46'41"

DESCRIPTION: In a pine, fir and juniper, forest. Wide variety of vegetation and flowers to be viewed. Fishing and boating in area. Look for deer, cougars, bighorn sheep, coyotes, rabbits, bluebirds, great horned owls, and magpies in the area. Trails in area: Rollins Pass and Fraser Valley Trail.

GETTING THERE: Idlewild CG is located approx. 1 mi. S of Winter Park on US HWY 40.

SINGLE RATE:	$10	OPEN DATES:	May-Sept
# of SINGLE SITES:	24	MAX SPUR:	32 feet
		MAX STAY:	14 days
		ELEVATION:	9000 feet

24 Jacks Gulch

Fort Collins • lat 40°38'00" lon 105°31'30"

DESCRIPTION: CG situated in a rustic, mountainous, lodgepole pine forest. Popular activities include fishing and boating on Chambers Lake. Boat ramp located on lake. Look for a variety of animals in area. Scenic 4 Wheel, mountain biking, hiking, and OHV trails in the area. A playground area is available on site.

GETTING THERE: From Fort Collins go W on state HWY 14 approx. 27 mi. to county route 63E. Go S on 63E approx. 5 mi. to Jacks Gulch CG.

SINGLE RATE:	$12	OPEN DATES:	May-Oct
# of SINGLE SITES:	70	MAX SPUR:	50 feet
GROUP RATE:	$100	MAX STAY:	14 days
# of GROUP SITES:	1	ELEVATION:	8000 feet

25 Kelly Dahl

Nederland • lat 39°55'57" lon 105°29'50"

DESCRIPTION: CG is in an open meadow with some mixed conifer stands. Afternoon t-showers. Good fishing in Barker Reservoir 4 mi. N of CG. Visit historic gold mining towns of Blackhawk and Central City. Supplies 2 mi. away. Firewood sold on site. Horse facilities nearby. Excellent hiking trails in area.

GETTING THERE: Kelly Dahl CG is located approx. 3 mi. S of Nederland on state HWY 119.

SINGLE RATE:	$12	OPEN DATES:	May-Oct
# of SINGLE SITES:	46	MAX SPUR:	40 feet
		MAX STAY:	14 days
		ELEVATION:	8600 feet

26 Kelly Flats

Fort Collins • lat 40°40'57" lon 105°29'00"

DESCRIPTION: CG situated in a rustic, mountainous, lodgepole pine forest. Popular activities include fishing and boating on Chambers Lake. Boat ramp located on lake. Look for a variety of animals in area. Scenic 4 Wheel, mountain biking, hiking, and OHV trails in the area. A playground area is available on site.

GETTING THERE: From Fort Collins go W on state HWY 14 approx. 26 mi. to Kelly Flats CG.

SINGLE RATE:	$9	OPEN DATES:	July-Nov
# of SINGLE SITES:	23	MAX SPUR:	40 feet
		MAX STAY:	14 days
		ELEVATION:	6750 feet

27 Long Draw
Fort Collins • lat 40°30'45" lon 105°45'55"

DESCRIPTION: CG situated in a rustic, mountainous, lodgepole pine forest. Popular activities include fishing and boating on Chambers Lake. Look for a variety of animals in area. Moose and black bears common to the area. Scenic 4 Wheel, mountain biking, hiking, and OHV trails in the area.

GETTING THERE: From Fort Collins go W approx. 51 mi. on state HWY 14 to forest route 156. Go E on 156 approx. 6 mi. to Long Draw CG.

SINGLE RATE:	$8	OPEN DATES:	July-Nov
# of SINGLE SITES:	25	MAX SPUR:	30 feet
		MAX STAY:	14 days
		ELEVATION:	10030 feet

28 Meeker Park
Estes Park • lat 40°14'36" lon 105°31'57"

DESCRIPTION: CG is located in an open, mixed conifer forest. Many small lakes and streams nearby. Expect afternoon thunder showers. Supplies 1 mi. away. Busy holidays. Summer is the best season. Firewood sold on site. Numerous trails in area including trail heads leading into Rocky Mountain National Park.

GETTING THERE: Meeker Park CG is located approx. 13 mi. S of Estes Park on state HWY 72.

SINGLE RATE:	$6	OPEN DATES:	May-Sept
# of SINGLE SITES:	29	MAX SPUR:	30 feet
		MAX STAY:	14 days
		ELEVATION:	8600 feet

29 Mizpah

Empire • lat 39°46'28" lon 105°47'33"

DESCRIPTION: Dense fir forest with views of Clear Creek Bethoud Pass. Cool days on W fork of Clear Creek. Fly and bait fish for trout. Old mining sites. Supplies at Empire. Deer and elk. Moderate use. Collect dead wood or buy from LandL. Trail above Henderson Mine and ATV 4X4 road to Jones Pass. Mosquitos through June.

GETTING THERE: Mizpah CG is located approx. 6 mi. W of Empire on US HWY 40.

SINGLE RATE:	$10	OPEN DATES:	May-Sept
# of SINGLE SITES:	10	MAX SPUR:	20 feet
		MAX STAY:	14 days
		ELEVATION:	9600 feet

30 Mountain Park

Fort Collins • lat 40°40'57" lon 105°28'01"

DESCRIPTION: CG is adjacent to Cache La Poudre River. Area varies from heavily forested to open meadow and is surrounded by steep mountains. Electric hook-up sites available. Popular activities include fishing, white water rafting, hiking, volleyball, and basketball. Playground area on site.

GETTING THERE: Mountain Park CG is located approx. 25 mi. W of Fort Collins on state HWY 14.

SINGLE RATE:	$12	OPEN DATES:	May-Sept
# of SINGLE SITES:	55	MAX SPUR:	50 feet
GROUP RATE:	$75	MAX STAY:	14 days
# of GROUP SITES:	1	ELEVATION:	6650 feet

 Campground has hosts   **Reservable sites**    **Accessible facilities**   **Fully developed**    **Semi-developed**   **Rustic facilities**

NOTE: Open dates listed are typical. Actual dates are dependent on conditions such as snow pack.

31 Narrows
Fort Collins • lat 40°41'28" lon 105°25'53"

DESCRIPTION: This CG is situated in a rustic, mountainous, lodgepole pine forest. Popular activities include fishing and boating on Chambers Lake. Please check for fishing regulations. Look for a variety of animals in area. Scenic ATV, mountain biking, hiking, and OHV trails are in the area.

GETTING THERE: From Fort Collings go W on state HWY 14 approx. 22 mi. to Narrows CG. Walk-in sites.

SINGLE RATE:	**$7**	**OPEN DATES:**	**May-Sept**
# of SINGLE SITES:	**9**	**MAX SPUR:**	**30 feet**
		MAX STAY:	**14 days**
		ELEVATION:	**6500 feet**

36  Pickle Gulch
Golden • lat 39°50'31" lon 105°31'29"

DESCRIPTION: Group use only with views of high peaks. No fishing nearby. Historic mining area. Supplies at Central City. Deer, elk, and occasional bears. Playground and horseshoe pit. Gather firewood or buy from LandL. Short hiking trail; ATV 4X4 drive nearby. Mosquitos until early June.

GETTING THERE: From Golden go W on US HWY 6 approx. 6 mi. to state HWY 119. Go N on 119 approx. 9 mi. to county route 15. Go W on 15 approx. 1 mi. to Pickle Gulch CG.

		OPEN DATES:	**May-Sept**
GROUP RATE:	**Varies**	**MAX STAY:**	**14 days**
# of GROUP SITES:	**6**	**ELEVATION:**	**9100 feet**

32 North Fork Poudre
Red Feather Lakes • lat 40°48'50" lon 105°42'34"

DESCRIPTION: CG situated in a rustic, mountainous, lodgepole pine forest. Popular activities include fishing and boating on Chambers Lake. Look for a variety of animals in area. Mountain lions and black bears are common to area. Scenic 4 Wheel, mountain biking, hiking, and OHV trails in the area.

GETTING THERE: North Fork Poudre CG is located approx. 7 mi. W of Red Feather Lakes on county route 162.

SINGLE RATE:	**$7**	**OPEN DATES:**	**June-Nov**
# of SINGLE SITES:	**9**	**MAX SPUR:**	**30 feet**
		MAX STAY:	**14 days**
		ELEVATION:	**9150 feet**

37 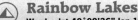 Rainbow Lakes
Ward • lat 40°00'36" lon 105°34'14"

DESCRIPTION: CG is located in open, park-like area with a small stream nearby. Several small lakes in area with good fishing opportunities. Afternoon t-showers. Suppplies are available 10 mi. away. Busy weekends and holidays. Firewood sold on site. Excellent trails in area with access to Indian Peaks Wilderness.

GETTING THERE: From Ward go S on state HWY 72 approx. 3 mi. to forest route 298 (county route 116). Go W then S on 298 approx. 4 mi. to Rainbow Lakes CG. High clearance vehicles recommended.

SINGLE RATE:	**$6**	**OPEN DATES:**	**July-Oct**
# of SINGLE SITES:	**16**	**MAX SPUR:**	**20 feet**
		MAX STAY:	**14 days**
		ELEVATION:	**10000 feet**

33 Olive Ridge
Estes Park • lat 40°12'28" lon 105°31'24"

DESCRIPTION: This CG is situated in a generally flat, mixed conifer and aspen forest. Sites are in mixed sun and shade. Fishing is within 5 mi. of the CG. Supplies are less than 3 mi. away. Firewood is sold on site. Mountain climbing is in the area. Playground and amphitheater are available on site.

GETTING THERE: From Estes Park go S on state HWY 7 approx. 10 mi. to Olive Ridge CG.

SINGLE RATE:	**$12**	**OPEN DATES:**	**May-Sept**
# of SINGLE SITES:	**56**	**MAX SPUR:**	**40 feet**
		MAX STAY:	**14 days**
		ELEVATION:	**8350 feet**

38 Robbers Roost
Winter Park • lat 39°50'01" lon 105°45'20"

DESCRIPTION: CG set in sub-alpine firs, spruce and aspen. Pick huckleberries from CG. A variety of vegetation is in this area. Fishing close to CG. Supplies at Winter Park. Look for bobcats, elk, pine squirrels, and black bears. Midland picnic ground nearby. Rollins Pass and hiking/biking trails close to CG.

GETTING THERE: Robbers Roost CG is located approx. 6 mi. S of Winter Park on US HWY 40.

SINGLE RATE:	**$10**	**OPEN DATES:**	**May-Sept**
# of SINGLE SITES:	**11**	**MAX SPUR:**	**25 feet**
		MAX STAY:	**14 days**
		ELEVATION:	**9826 feet**

34 Pawnee
Ward • lat 40°04'43" lon 105°34'08"

DESCRIPTION: CG is located in mixed conifer forest with lake and Continental Divide views. Can snow in summer. Many lakes and streams nearby. Check fishing Visit historic town of Ward. Supplies 5 mi. away. Firewood sold on site. Excellent hiking trails in adjacent Indian Peaks Wilderness.

GETTING THERE: From Ward go W on county route 102 approx. 5 mi. to Pawnee CG.

SINGLE RATE:	**$12**	**OPEN DATES:**	**July-Sept**
# of SINGLE SITES:	**55**	**MAX SPUR:**	**45 feet**
		MAX STAY:	**14 days**
		ELEVATION:	**10350 feet**

39 Sawmill Gulch
Granby • lat 40°13'42" lon 106°03'25"

DESCRIPTION: This CG is situated in a pine, fir, and juniper forest. Wide variety of vegetation and flowers to be viewed. Fishing and boating in area. Look for deer, cougars, bighorn sheep, coyotes, rabbits, bluebirds, great horned owls, and magpies in the area. Trails available in the area.

GETTING THERE: From Granby go W on US HWY 40 approx. 3 mi. to state HWY 125. Go N on 125 approx. 9 mi. to Sawmill Gulch CG.

SINGLE RATE:	**$9**	**OPEN DATES:**	**May-Sept**
# of SINGLE SITES:	**6**	**MAX SPUR:**	**32 feet**
		MAX STAY:	**14 days**
		ELEVATION:	**8780 feet**

35 Peaceful Valley
Ward • lat 40°07'35" lon 105°30'00"

DESCRIPTION: CG is in open, mixed conifer forest and is adjacentto Middle St. Vrain Creek. Good fishing in creek. Afternoon t-showers. Supplies 4 mi.away. Numerous mountain wildlife. Busy weekends and holidays. Firewood sold on site. Excellent trail system in area with access to Indian Peaks Wilderness.

GETTING THERE: Peaceful Valley is located approx. 6 mi. N of Ward just W of state HWY 72.

SINGLE RATE:	**$12**	**OPEN DATES:**	**May-Oct**
# of SINGLE SITES:	**17**	**MAX SPUR:**	**55 feet**
		MAX STAY:	**14 days**
		ELEVATION:	**8650 feet**

40 Sleeping Elephant
Fort Collins • lat 40°41'00" lon 105°46'00"

DESCRIPTION: CG situated in a rustic, mountainous, lodgepole pine forest. Popular activities include fishing and boating on Chambers Lake. Look for a variety of animals in area. Moose and black bears common to the area. Scenic 4 Wheel, mountain biking, hiking, and OHV trails in the area.

GETTING THERE: From Fort Collins go W on state HWY 14 approx. 42 mi. to Sleeping Elephant CG.

SINGLE RATE:	**$9**	**OPEN DATES:**	**May-Nov**
# of SINGLE SITES:	**15**	**MAX SPUR:**	**20 feet**
		MAX STAY:	**14 days**
		ELEVATION:	**7850 feet**

 Campground has hosts   Reservable sites   Accessible facilities   Fully developed   Semi-developed   Rustic facilities

NOTE: Open dates listed are typical. Actual dates are dependent on conditions such as snow pack.

41 South Fork
Hot Sulphur Springs • lat 39˚47'44" lon 106˚01'44"

DESCRIPTION: This CG is set in a pine, fir, and juniper forest. Wide variety of vegetation and flowers to be viewed. Fishing and boating in area. Look for deer, cougars, bighorn sheep, coyotes, rabbits, bluebirds, great horned owls, and magpies in the area. Trails in area. Horse corral at CG.

GETTING THERE: From Hot Sulphur Springs go W on US HWY 40 approx. 5 mi. to county route 3. Go S on 3 approx. 22 mi. to South Fork CG.

SINGLE RATE:	$10	
# of SINGLE SITES:	21	
	OPEN DATES:	May-Sept
	MAX SPUR:	23 feet
	MAX STAY:	14 days
	ELEVATION:	8940 feet

46 Sunset Point
Granby • lat 40˚09'17" lon 105˚52'24"

DESCRIPTION: In a pine, fir and juniper setting on Lake Granby. Wide variety of vegetation and flowers to be viewed. Fishing and boating on the lake. Look for deer, cougar, bighorn sheep, coyote, rabbit, bluebird, great horned owl, magpie in the area. Trails in area.

GETTING THERE: From Granby go NW on US HWY 34 approx. 6 mi. to county route 6. Go E on 6 approx. 1.5 mi. to Sunset Point CG.

SINGLE RATE:	$15	
# of SINGLE SITES:	25	
	OPEN DATES:	May-Sept
	MAX SPUR:	50 feet
	MAX STAY:	14 days
	ELEVATION:	8970 feet

42 St. Louis Creek
Fraser • lat 39˚55'00" lon 105˚51'30"

DESCRIPTION: CG in a pine, fir, and juniper forest. Wide variety of vegetation and flowers to be viewed. Fishing and boating in area. Look for deer, cougars, bighorn sheep, coyotes, rabbits, bluebirds, great horned owls, and magpies in area. Trails in area. Byers Peak and Vasquez Peak Wilderness in area.

GETTING THERE: From Fraser go S on county route 73 (St. Louis Creek Road) approx. 3 mi. to St. Louis Creek CG.

SINGLE RATE:	$10	
# of SINGLE SITES:	16	
	OPEN DATES:	May-Sept
	MAX SPUR:	32 feet
	MAX STAY:	14 days
	ELEVATION:	9000 feet

47 Tom Bennett
Fort Collins • lat 40˚36'00" lon 105˚36'00"

DESCRIPTION: In a pine, fir and juniper setting with a variety of vegetation. Fishing in the area. Hiking, mountain biking in area (near a wilderness area and trails that enter Rocky Mountain National Park). Scenic and 4 wheel driving nearby. Wildlife watching (moose and black bear common to area).

GETTING THERE: From Fort Collins go N on US HWY 287 approx. 11 mi. to state HWY 14. Go W on 14 approx. 22 mi. to Pingree Park Road turnoff. Go S approx. 17 mi. to Tom Bennett CG.

SINGLE RATE:	$7	
# of SINGLE SITES:	12	
	OPEN DATES:	May-Oct*
	MAX SPUR:	20 feet
	MAX STAY:	14 days
	ELEVATION:	9000 feet

43 Stillwater
Granby • lat 40˚02'43" lon 107˚04'10"

DESCRIPTION: CG in a pine, fir, and juniper forest. Wide variety of vegetation and flowers to be viewed. Fishing and boating in area. Boat ramp nearby. Look for deer, cougars, bighorn sheep, coyotes, rabbits, bluebirds, great horned owls, and magpies in area. Trails in area. RV dump station, amphitheater, and showers.

GETTING THERE: Stillwater CG is located on the W shore of Lake Granby approx. 8 mi. N of Granby off of US HWY 34.

SINGLE RATE:	Varies	
# of SINGLE SITES:	129	
	OPEN DATES:	May-Sept
	MAX SPUR:	32 feet
	MAX STAY:	14 days
	ELEVATION:	8350 feet

48 Tunnel
Fort Collins • lat 40˚40'25" lon 105˚51'28"

DESCRIPTION: This CG is situated in a rustic, mountainous, lodgepole pine forest. Popular activities include fishing and boating on Chambers Lake. Please check for fishing regulations. There are a variety of animals in this area. Scenic ATV, mountain biking, hiking, and OHV trails are in the area.

GETTING THERE: From Fort Collins go W on state HWY 14 approx. 49 mi. to county route 103. Go N on 103 approx. 4 mi. to Tunnel CG.

SINGLE RATE:	$10	
# of SINGLE SITES:	49	
	OPEN DATES:	May-Sept
	MAX SPUR:	40 feet
	MAX STAY:	14 days
	ELEVATION:	8600 feet

44 Stove Prairie
Fort Collins • lat 40˚41'02" lon 105˚23'47"

DESCRIPTION: This CG is situated in a rustic, mountainous, lodgepole pine forest. Popular activities include fishing and boating on Chambers Lake. Please check for fishing regulations. Look for a variety of animals in area. Scenic ATV, mountain biking, hiking, and OHV trails are in the area.

GETTING THERE: From Fort Collins go W on state HWY 14 approx. 19 mi. to Stove Prairie Landing CG. Walk-in sites.

SINGLE RATE:	$10	
# of SINGLE SITES:	9	
	OPEN DATES:	Yearlong
	MAX SPUR:	30 feet
	MAX STAY:	14 days
	ELEVATION:	6000 feet

49 West Chicago Creek
Idaho Springs • lat 39˚40'37" lon 105˚39'34"

DESCRIPTION: Park like sites among lodgepole and aspen with views of higher peaks and Mount Evans Wilderness. Fly and boat fish for trout on W Chicago Creek. Old mining sites in area. Supplies at Idaho Springs. LandL sells firewood or gather deadwood. Hike Hell's Hole trail. Prepare for ticks. Heavy weekend use.

GETTING THERE: From Idaho Springs go S on state HWY 103 approx. 6 mi. to forest route 188. Go W on 188 approx. 2 mi. to West Chicago Creek CG.

SINGLE RATE:	$9	
# of SINGLE SITES:	16	
	OPEN DATES:	May-Sept
	MAX SPUR:	30 feet
	MAX STAY:	14 days
	ELEVATION:	9600 feet

45 Sugar Loaf
Hot Sulphur Springs • lat 39˚47'44" lon 106˚01'44"

DESCRIPTION: CG in a pine, fir, and juniper forest. Variety of vegetation and flowers to be viewed. Fishing and boating in area. Look for deer, cougars, bighorn sheep, coyotes, rabbits, bluebirds, great horned owls, and magpie in area. Universally accessible boardwalk. Byers Peak Wilderness and Williams Fork nearby.

GETTING THERE: From Hot Sulphur Springs go W on US HWY 40 approx. 5 mi. to county route 3. Go S on 3 approx. 23 mi. to Sugar Loaf CG.

SINGLE RATE:	$10	
# of SINGLE SITES:	11	
	OPEN DATES:	May-Sept
	MAX SPUR:	23 feet
	MAX STAY:	14 days
	ELEVATION:	8970 feet

50 West Lake
Fort Collins • lat 40˚47'23" lon 105˚34'06"

DESCRIPTION: This CG is adjacent to West Lake in a mountainous, ponderosa pine forest. Supplies and groceries can be found in Fort Collins. Popular activities include fishing, boating on the lake, and hiking in the woods around the campground. Mountain lions and black bears are common to the area.

GETTING THERE: From Fort Collins go N on US HWY 267 to Livermore. Go W on county route 74E approx. 18 mi. to West Lake CG.

SINGLE RATE:	$10	
# of SINGLE SITES:	29	
	OPEN DATES:	May-Sept
	MAX SPUR:	50 feet
	MAX STAY:	14 days
	ELEVATION:	8200 feet

 Campground has hosts   **Reservable sites**   **Accessible facilities**   **Fully developed**   **Semi-developed**   **Rustic facilities**

NOTE: Open dates listed are typical. Actual dates are dependent on conditions such as snow pack.

ARAPAHO-ROOSEVELT NATIONAL FOREST • COLORADO • 41 — 50

51 **Willow Creek**
Granby • lat 40°08'37" lon 105°57'03"

DESCRIPTION: This CG is situated in a pine, fir, and juniper forest. Wide variety of vegetation and flowers to be viewed. Fishing and boating in area. Look for deer, cougars, bighorn sheep, coyotes, rabbits, bluebirds, great horned owls, and magpies in the area. Trails in area.

GETTING THERE: From Granby go N on US HWY 34 approx. 4 mi. to county route 90. Go W on 90 approx. 3 mi. to Willow Creek CG.

SINGLE RATE:	$10	**OPEN DATES:**	**May-Sept**
# of SINGLE SITES:	35	**MAX SPUR:**	**25 feet**
		MAX STAY:	**14 days**
		ELEVATION:	**8130 feet**

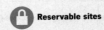 **Campground has hosts**   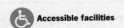 **Reservable sites**   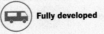 **Accessible facilities**   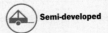 **Fully developed**   **Semi-developed**   **Rustic facilities**

GRAND MESA, UNCOMPAHGRE AND GUNNISON NATIONAL FOREST

The Grand Mesa, Uncompahgre and Gunnison National Forests unit is a combination of three separate national forests located in the Colorado Rockies. These forests cover 3,161,912 acres of land in the Rocky Mountains in an area that lies south of the Colorado River and west of the Continental Divide. The forests vary in elevation from 5,800 feet above sea level in Roubideau Creek Canyon to 14,309 feet on Uncompahgre Peak.

Providing some of the most spectacular scenery in the Rockies, forest attractions include the 355 foot-high Bridal Vail falls, the tallest waterfall in Colorado; the Grand Mesa, the world's largest flat top mountain; Alpine Tunnel, the highest railroad tunnel in North America; and Dry Mesa Dinosaur quarry, where the world's largest dinosaur fossils were found.

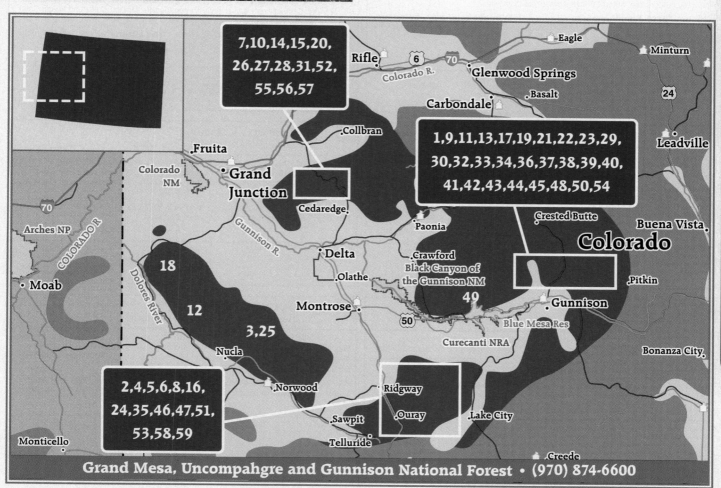

Grand Mesa, Uncompahgre and Gunnison National Forest • (970) 874-6600

1 Almont
Gunnison • lat 38°39'21" lon 106°51'17"

DESCRIPTION: Among shady cottonwood with cool mornings and mild days. Expect noon rain June and July. Trout and Kokanee Salmon found in nearby Gunnison River. Supplies 1 mi. at Almont or 10 mi. S at Gunnison. Moderateerate use. Gather firewood. Prepare for ticks during May and June. Open til Dec 1 with reduced services.

GETTING THERE: From Gunninson go N on state HWY 135 approx. 9.5 mi. to Almont CG.

SINGLE RATE:	$8	OPEN DATES:	May-Sept
# of SINGLE SITES:	10	MAX SPUR:	28 feet
		MAX STAY:	14 days
		ELEVATION:	8000 feet

2 Amphitheatre
Ouray • lat 38°01'22" lon 107°40'15"

DESCRIPTION: This CG has a large white fir overstory with heavy choke cherry and oak brush underneath. Campers can enjoy fishing in the area but please check for fishing regulations. The historical mining town of Ouray (2 mi. away) has supplies. Firewood is sold by concessionaire on site.

GETTING THERE: From Ouray go S on US HWY 550 approx. 1 mi. to Amphitheatre CG. Road is narrow with sharp curves. Large vehicles should use caution.

SINGLE RATE:	$14	OPEN DATES:	May-Sept
# of SINGLE SITES:	33	MAX SPUR:	20 feet
		MAX STAY:	7 days
		ELEVATION:	8400 feet

3 Antone Spring
Montrose • lat 38°19'23" lon 108°10'57"

DESCRIPTION: Primative CG with forest views. Supplies and groceries are available 20 mi. away in Montrose. Anton CG sign is no longer displayed.

GETTING THERE: From Montrose go SW on state HWY 90 approx. 24 mi. to forest route 402. Go NW on 402 approx. 1 mi. to Antone Springs CG. (Anton CG sign is no longer displayed.)

SINGLE RATE:	No fee	OPEN DATES:	June-Sept
# of SINGLE SITES:	3	MAX SPUR:	25 feet
GROUP RATE:	No fee	MAX STAY:	14 days
# of GROUP SITES:	1	ELEVATION:	9700 feet

4 Beaver Lake
Montrose • lat 38°14'58" lon 107°32'37"

DESCRIPTION: This rustic CG is situated in a forest of spruce and fir. A small 4 acre lake stocked with rainbow trout is near the CG. Campers may enjoy fishing in the area but please check fishing regulations. Supplies and groceries are available in Montrose. Gather dead and down firewood locally.

GETTING THERE: From Montrose go S on US HWY 550 18 mi. to forest route 858/859. Go E 13 mi. to forest route 860. Go N on 860 approx. 6 mi. to forest route 863. Go N on 863 approx. 3.5 mi. to Beaver Lake CG.

SINGLE RATE:	$8	OPEN DATES:	May-Sept
# of SINGLE SITES:	11	MAX SPUR:	20 feet
		MAX STAY:	14 days
		ELEVATION:	8800 feet

5 Big Blue
Lake City • lat 38°13'02" lon 107°23'06"

DESCRIPTION: CG is set among fir on open creek drainage. Views of Uncompagre Wilderness. Expect rain June/July. Mild days, cold nights. Brook trout fishing at Big Blue Creek 1/2 mi away. Supplies at Lake City. Light use. Elk and deer frequent the area. Gather firewood. Big Blue Trailhead nearby.

GETTING THERE: From Lake City go N on state HWY 149 approx. 11 mi. to forest route 868. Go W on 868 approx. 8 mi. to Big Blue CG.

SINGLE RATE:	$6	OPEN DATES:	May-Sept
# of SINGLE SITES:	11	MAX SPUR:	25 feet
		MAX STAY:	14 days
# of GROUP SITES:	11	ELEVATION:	9600 feet

6 Big Cimarron
Montrose • lat 38°15'27" lon 107°32'40"

DESCRIPTION: This rustic CG is situated in a spruce and fir forest. The CG is located along Big Cimarron River. Campers may enjoy fishing in the area but please check fishing regulations. Supplies and groceries are available in Montrose. Gather dead and down firewood locally.

GETTING THERE: From Montrose go S on US HWY 50 approx. 18 mi. to forest route 858. Go N on 858 approx. 16 mi. to Big Cimarron CG.

SINGLE RATE:	$4	OPEN DATES:	May-Sept
# of SINGLE SITES:	10	MAX SPUR:	20 feet
		MAX STAY:	14 days
# of GROUP SITES:	2	ELEVATION:	8600 feet

7 Big Creek
Collbran • lat 40°56'07" lon 106°36'27"

DESCRIPTION: This CG is located high in the mountains on Big Creek. Enjoy fishing from the creek. Supplies are at Collbran, approx. 15 mi. from the CG. Campers may gather their firewood locally. Crag Crest National Recreation Trail is nearby for hiking and biking. There is a RV dump station in the area.

GETTING THERE: From Collbran go S on county HWY 58.5/59 approx. 7 mi. to primary forest route 121. Go S on 121 approx. 8 mi. to Big Creek CG.

SINGLE RATE:	$6	OPEN DATES:	July-Sept
# of SINGLE SITES:	26	MAX SPUR:	30 feet
		MAX STAY:	14 days
		ELEVATION:	10000 feet

8 Cebolla
Lake City • lat 38°02'40" lon 107°05'58"

DESCRIPTION: CG is set in a stand of mature spruce and fir timber. Views of Cebolla Creek. Brook, rainbow, and brown trout fishing in Cebolla Creek. Supplies are available at Lake City. Campers may gather their firewood locally. Mineral Creek and Rough Creek trails are nearby. Tent camping is recommended.

GETTING THERE: From Lake City go SE on state HWY 149 approx. 9 mi. to forest route 788. Go NE on 788 approx. 9 mi. to Cebolla CG.

SINGLE RATE:	$8	OPEN DATES:	May-Sept
# of SINGLE SITES:	4	MAX SPUR:	20 feet
		MAX STAY:	14 days
		ELEVATION:	9200 feet

9 Cement Creek
Gunnison • lat 38°49'31" lon 106°50'15"

DESCRIPTION: This CG is in a forest setting with thick vegetation and underbrush. Views of Crested Butte ski area. Supplies and groceries are available at Crested Butte or Gunnison. Campers may gather firewood or pick some up at concessionaire. Mountain biking trails nearby.

GETTING THERE: From Gunninson go N on state HWY 135 approx. 18 mi. to forest route 740. Go NE on 740 approx. 4 mi. to Cement Creek CG.

SINGLE RATE:	$10	OPEN DATES:	May-Sept
# of SINGLE SITES:	13	MAX SPUR:	28 feet
		MAX STAY:	14 days
		ELEVATION:	9000 feet

10 Cobbett Lake
Cedaredge • lat 39°02'27" lon 107°59'06"

DESCRIPTION: CG located in a high mountain area on Cobbett Lake. Fish from the lake. Supplies at Cedaredge. Grand Mesa Visitor Center at CG. Campers may gather firewood. Many trails in this area, The Discovery Trail (.5 mi. loop) starts at the visitor center. RV dump station in area.

GETTING THERE: From Cedaredge go N on state HWY 65 (Grand Mesa Scenic Byway) approx. 15 mi. to forest route 116. Go E on 116 approx. 1/2 mi. to Cobbett Lake CG.

SINGLE RATE:	$8	OPEN DATES:	July-Sept
# of SINGLE SITES:	20	MAX SPUR:	30 feet
		MAX STAY:	14 days
		ELEVATION:	10300 feet

 Campground has hosts   **Reservable sites**   **Accessible facilities**   **Fully developed**   **Semi-developed**   **Rustic facilities**

NOTE: Open dates listed are typical. Actual dates are dependent on conditions such as snow pack.

11 Cold Spring
Almont • lat 38°46'02" lon 106°38'33"

DESCRIPTION: This rustic CG is in a setting of lodgepole pines. Enjoy fly and lure fishing for trout in the nearby Taylor River. Please check fishing regulations. Supplies and groceries can be found at the Three Rivers Resort at Almont. Campers may gather their firewood (dead and down) locally.

GETTING THERE: From Almont go NE on forest route 742 approx. 16 mi. to Cold Spring CG.

SINGLE RATE:	$8	OPEN DATES:	May-Sept
# of SINGLE SITES:	6	MAX SPUR:	10 feet
		MAX STAY:	14 days
		ELEVATION:	9000 feet

12 Columbine
Delta • lat 38°25'29" lon 108°22'49"

DESCRIPTION: This CG is located among spruce and firs. Fising opportunities close by. Deer and elk frequent the area. Nearest supplies can be found in Delta. Firewood may be gathered locally. The Tabegauache Mountain Bike trail is nearby. Weather is moderateer-aterate. Tends to be busy during the hunting season.

GETTING THERE: From Delta go S on Delta-Nucla Road approx. 28 mi. to Columbine CG.

SINGLE RATE:	$4	OPEN DATES:	June-Sept
# of SINGLE SITES:	6	MAX SPUR:	30 feet
		MAX STAY:	14 days
		ELEVATION:	9000 feet

13 Comanche
Ohio • lat 38°35'56" lon 106°36'10"

DESCRIPTION: CG in park-like oak, willow, and grass. Mild days and cool nights. Trout fish at nearby Gold Creek. Supplies at Ohio City, Gunnison, or Pitkin. Deer and beavers in area. Light use, fall is best. Gather firewood locally or purchase at Pitkin CG. Horse, hiking, and ATV on road to Gold Creek.

GETTING THERE: From Ohio City go N on forest route 771 approx. 2 mi. to Comanche CG.

SINGLE RATE:	$6	OPEN DATES:	May-Sept
# of SINGLE SITES:	4	MAX SPUR:	25 feet
		MAX STAY:	14 days
		ELEVATION:	8900 feet

14 Cottonwood
Collbran • lat 39°04'00" lon 107°58'00"

DESCRIPTION: This CG is located high in the mountains. Due to high elevation, there are rapid weather changes. Fish close to CG. Supplies are at Collbran. Campers may gather their firewood locally. Crag Crest National Recreation Trail is nearby for hiking and biking. There is RV dump station in the area.

GETTING THERE: From Collbran go S on county HWY 58.5/59 approx. 7 mi. to primary forest route 121. Go S on 121 approx. 6 mi. to forest route 257. Go W on 257 approx. 5 mi. to Cottonwood CG.

SINGLE RATE:	$8	OPEN DATES:	July-Sept
# of SINGLE SITES:	42	MAX SPUR:	30 feet
		MAX STAY:	14 days
		ELEVATION:	10000 feet

15 Crag Crest
Cedaredge • lat 39°02'30" lon 107°56'30"

DESCRIPTION: This CG is located in a high mountain area. Fishing close to the CG. Supplies at Cedaredge. Campers may gather their firewood locally. Many trails are nearby for hiking and biking. RV dump station in area.

GETTING THERE: From Cedaredge go N on state HWY 65 (Grand Mesa Scenic Byway) approx. 14.5 mi. to primary forest route 121. Go E on 121 approx. 4 mi. to Crag Crest CG.

SINGLE RATE:	$8	OPEN DATES:	July-Sept
# of SINGLE SITES:	11	MAX SPUR:	30 feet
		MAX STAY:	14 days
		ELEVATION:	10100 feet

16 Deer Lakes
Lake City • lat 38°01'20" lon 107°11'09"

DESCRIPTION: This CG is in a forest setting with views of mountains. Fish in nearby mountain streams. Supplies and groceries are available in Lake City, approx. 18 mi. away. Campers may gather their firewood locally. Mountain biking trails are nearby. Bears may be a problem.

GETTING THERE: From Lake City go SE on state HWY 149 approx. 9 mi. to forest route 788. Go NE on 788 approx. 4 mi. to Deer Lakes CG.

SINGLE RATE:	$10	OPEN DATES:	May-Sept
# of SINGLE SITES:	12	MAX SPUR:	30 feet
		MAX STAY:	14 days
		ELEVATION:	10400 feet

17 Dinner Station
Almont • lat 38°54'19" lon 106°35'10"

DESCRIPTION: CG is located in Upper Taylor Park area, sheltered by lodgepole pine trees and adjacent to the Taylor River. Fishing from the river. Dinner Station was a stop on an old stage coach route from Aspen. Supplies are at Almont. Mountian biking, hiking, and off road vehicle trails in the area.

GETTING THERE: From Almont go NE on forest route 742 approx. 32 mi. to Dinner Station CG.

SINGLE RATE:	$10	OPEN DATES:	June-Sept
# of SINGLE SITES:	22	MAX SPUR:	99 feet
		MAX STAY:	14 days
		ELEVATION:	9600 feet

18 Divide Fork
Whitewater • lat 38°41'04" lon 108°41'20"

DESCRIPTION: CG in an open and park-like setting of aspen with views of a meadow. This CG is primarily used as a hunting camp during season. CG is never full. Supplies available at Whitewater. Campers may gather firewood. No designated trails in area, just venture off in woods to explore.

GETTING THERE: From Whitewater go SW on state HWY 141 approx. 13 mi. to forest route 402. Go SW on 402 approx. 15 mi. to Divide Fork CG.

SINGLE RATE:	No fee	OPEN DATES:	July-Sept
# of SINGLE SITES:	11	MAX SPUR:	22 feet
		MAX STAY:	14 days
		ELEVATION:	9200 feet

19 Dorchester
Almont • lat 38°57'54" lon 106°39'45"

DESCRIPTION: This CG is very quiet in a park-like setting. There are views of surrounding mountains. Historical Dorchester Guard Station is nearby. Supplies and groceries can be found at Taylor Canyon Trading Post in Almont. Campers may gather their firewood (dead and down) locally.

GETTING THERE: From Almont go NE on forest route 742 approx. 40 mi. to Dorchester CG.

SINGLE RATE:	$10	OPEN DATES:	May-Sept
# of SINGLE SITES:	10	MAX SPUR:	28 feet
		MAX STAY:	14 days
		ELEVATION:	9800 feet

20 Eggelston
Cedaredge • lat 39°02'52" lon 107°56'45"

DESCRIPTION: This CG is situated in a forested setting adjacent to Eggelston Lake. A boat ramp is provided at the CG. Fishing from the lake. Supplies are available at Cedaredge approx. 18 mi. from CG. Campers may gather their firewood locally. Many hiking opportunities in the area.

GETTING THERE: From Cedaredge go N on state HWY 65 (Grand Mesa Scenic Byway) approx. 14.5 mi. to primary forest route 121. Go E on 121 approx. 3.5 mi. to Eggelston CG.

SINGLE RATE:	$8	OPEN DATES:	June-Sept
# of SINGLE SITES:	6	MAX SPUR:	30 feet
GROUP RATE:	$60	MAX STAY:	14 days
# of GROUP SITES:	1	ELEVATION:	10100 feet

 Campground has hosts   **Reservable sites** 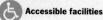 **Accessible facilities** 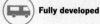 **Fully developed**   **Semi-developed**   **Rustic facilities**

NOTE: Open dates listed are typical. Actual dates are dependent on conditions such as snow pack.

21 Erickson Springs
Paonia • lat 38°57'10" lon 107°16'25"

DESCRIPTION: CG under cottonwood near a stream at mouth of Dark Canyon. Hot days with frequent noon rains. Trout fly fish on stream. Supplies at Paonia. Deer, elk, mountain goats, and occasional bears frequent the area. Moderateerateerate use. Horse and hiking trail up Dark Canyon. Prepare for ticks until mid-June.

GETTING THERE: From Paonia go NE on state HWY 133 approx. 15 mi. to county route 12. Go E on 12 approx. 6 mi. to Erickson Springs CG.

SINGLE RATE:	Varies	OPEN DATES:	May-Nov
# of SINGLE SITES:	18	MAX SPUR:	35 feet
		MAX STAY:	14 days
		ELEVATION:	6800 feet

26 Island Lake
Cedaredge • lat 39°01'55" lon 108°00'36"

DESCRIPTION: This CG is located in a high mountain area on Island Lake. Fish from the lake. Supplies and groceries can be found in Cedaredge. Campers may gather their firewood locally. Many trails nearby for hiking and biking. RV dump station in area. Fish cleaning station available at CG.

GETTING THERE: From Cedaredge go N on state HWY 65 (Grand Mesa Scenic Byway) approx. 15 mi. to forest route 116. Go SW on 116 approx. 2 mi. to Island Lake CG.

SINGLE RATE:	$8	OPEN DATES:	July-Sept
# of SINGLE SITES:	41	MAX SPUR:	45 feet
		MAX STAY:	14 days
		ELEVATION:	10300 feet

22 Gold Creek
Ohio • lat 38°39'17" lon 106°34'26"

DESCRIPTION: This CG is quiet and peaceful in a forest setting with views of the mountains. Historical gold mines nearby. Campers may gather firewood or buy from the Pitkin CG. Horseback, hiking, and ATV trails nearby.

GETTING THERE: From Ohio go N on forest route 771 approx. 6 mi. to Gold Creek CG.

SINGLE RATE:	$6	OPEN DATES:	May-Sept
		MAX STAY:	14 days
		ELEVATION:	10000 feet

27 Jumbo
Mesa • lat 39°03'17" lon 108°05'40"

DESCRIPTION: In a primarily forested area of spruce and fir on Jumbo Lake. Fish for native rainbow trout in the lake. Supplies are available at Mesa. Watch local wildlife in area. CG is usually full on the 4th of July. Many trails in the area, some leading to one or more of the other lakes in the area.

GETTING THERE: From Mesa go S on state HWY 65 approx. 13 mi. to Jumbo CG.

SINGLE RATE:	$10	OPEN DATES:	July-Sept
# of SINGLE SITES:	26	MAX SPUR:	22 feet
		MAX STAY:	14 days
		ELEVATION:	9800 feet

23 Gothic
Crested Butte • lat 39°58'53" lon 107°00'19"

DESCRIPTION: CG is in a park-like setting with little underbrush and views of mountains. CG is near a stream, with good fly fishing for trout. Historical Gothic Botony School is nearby. Supplies and groceries are available in Crested Butte. Campers may gather their firewood locally.

GETTING THERE: From Crested Butte go N on county route 3 approx. 7.5 mi. to forest route 317. Go N on 317 approx. 2 mi. to Gothic CG. 4WD recommended.

SINGLE RATE:	$8	OPEN DATES:	May-Sept
		MAX STAY:	14 days
		ELEVATION:	9600 feet

28 Kiser Creek
Cedaredge • lat 39°02'15" lon 107°56'50"

DESCRIPTION: This CG is located in a high mountain area on Kiser Creek. Fish from the creek. Supplies at Cedaredge, approx. 19 mi. from CG. Campers may gather their firewood locally. Crag Crest National Recreation Trail and other trails are nearby for hiking and biking. RV dump station in area.

GETTING THERE: From Cedaredge go N on state HWY 65 approx. 16 mi. to primary forest route 121. Go E on 121 approx. 3 mi. to forest route 123. Go S on 123 approx. 1 mi. to Kiser Creek CG.

SINGLE RATE:	$8	OPEN DATES:	July-Sept
# of SINGLE SITES:	12	MAX SPUR:	16 feet
		MAX STAY:	14 days
		ELEVATION:	10200 feet

24 Hidden Valley
Lake City • lat 38°02'27" lon 107°07'57"

DESCRIPTION: This tent only CG is set in a forest setting, rustic and private. Cebolla Creek is nearby. Campers may enjoy fishing in the area but please check fishing regulations. Supplies and groceries are available at Lake City. Campers may gather dead and down firewood locally. Hiking trails nearby.

GETTING THERE: From Lake City go SE on state HWY 149 approx. 9 mi. to forest route 788. Go NE on 788 approx. 7 mi. to Hidden Valley CG. Tent camping only.

SINGLE RATE:	$8	OPEN DATES:	May-Sept
		MAX STAY:	14 days
		ELEVATION:	9700 feet

29 Lake Irwin
Crested Butte • lat 38°52'52" lon 107°06'25"

DESCRIPTION: CG adjacent to Lake Irwin, most sites are shaded by mature spruce and subalpine fir trees. High in the Colorado Rockies, evenings are cool to cold, days being cool with frequent noon showers. Fishing and canoeing from the lake. Supplies at Crested Butte. Biking and hiking trails nearby.

GETTING THERE: From Crested Butte go W on county route 12 approx. 6 mi. to forest route 826. Go N on 826 approx. 2 mi. to Lake Irwin CG.

SINGLE RATE:	$10	OPEN DATES:	July-Sept
# of SINGLE SITES:	32	MAX SPUR:	35 feet
		MAX STAY:	14 days
		ELEVATION:	10200 feet

25 Iron Spring
Montrose • lat 38°19'00" lon 108°09'50"

DESCRIPTION: This CG is situated among dense spruce and fir trees. Due to high elevation, campers should prepare for rapid weather changes. Elk and deer frequent the area. The nearest supplies can be found in Montrose. Campers may gather dead and down firewood locally. Tabeguache Mountain Bike Trail is nearby.

GETTING THERE: From Montrose go SW on state HWY 90 approx. 24 mi. to Iron Spring CG.

SINGLE RATE:	$4	OPEN DATES:	June-Sept
# of SINGLE SITES:	7	MAX SPUR:	20 feet
		MAX STAY:	14 days
# of GROUP SITES:	1	ELEVATION:	9500 feet

30 Lake View
Almont • lat 39°05'53" lon 106°21'54"

DESCRIPTION: CG on Taylor Lake Reservoir among fir with mountain views. Mild days, cool nights. Several creeks nearby or boat on lake to fish trout. Historic Tincup area. Supplies at Almont, Taylor, or Gunnison. Frequented by deer, elk, beavers, and black bears. Firewood sold by RRM. Hiking and mountain bike trails.

GETTING THERE: From Almont go NE on forest route 742 approx. 23 mi. to Lake View CG.

SINGLE RATE:	$12	OPEN DATES:	May-Sept
# of SINGLE SITES:	46	MAX SPUR:	35 feet
		MAX STAY:	14 days
		ELEVATION:	9400 feet

 Campground has hosts   **Reservable sites**   **Accessible facilities**   **Fully developed**   **Semi-developed**   **Rustic facilities**

NOTE: Open dates listed are typical. Actual dates are dependent on conditions such as snow pack.

Page 176

31   **Little Bear**
Cedaredge • lat 39°02'01" lon 107°59'50"

DESCRIPTION: In a primarily forested area of spruce and fir on Highland Lake. Fish for native rainbow trout in the lake. Supplies and groceries are available at Cedaredge. Watch local wildlife in area. Many trails in the area, some leading to one or more of the other lakes in the area.

GETTING THERE: From Cedaredge go N on state HWY 65 (Grand Mesa Scenic Byway) approx. 15 mi. to forest route 116. Go SW on 116 approx. 1 mi. to Little Bear CG.

SINGLE RATE:	$8	OPEN DATES:	July-Sept
# of SINGLE SITES:	36	MAX SPUR:	22 feet
		MAX STAY:	14 days
		ELEVATION:	10200 feet

36 **McClure**
Redstone • lat 38°03'34" lon 107°52'16"

DESCRIPTION: Among Aspen near small a stream with beaver activity. Frequent noon rains. Historic marble quarry town and Redstone Castle 9 mi. away from CG. Supplies and groceries are available 9 mi. away at Redstone. Deer, elk, and beavers can be seen in the area. Moderateerateerate use.

GETTING THERE: From Redstone go S on state HWY 133 approx. 9 mi. to McClure CG.

SINGLE RATE:	Varies	OPEN DATES:	May-Nov
# of SINGLE SITES:	19	MAX SPUR:	35 feet
		MAX STAY:	14 days
		ELEVATION:	8200 feet

32 **Lodgepole**
Almont • lat 38°45'40" lon 106°39'40"

DESCRIPTION: Heavily shaded by fir with mild days and cool nights. On Taylor River with trout fishing. Supplies at Taylor, Almont, or Gunnison. Frequented by deer and black Bears. Moderateerate use. Firewood sold by RRM or may be gathered. Mountain biking and hiking trails nearby. Prepare for ticks early in season.

GETTING THERE: From Almont go NE on forest route 742 approx. 15 mi. to Lodgepole CG.

SINGLE RATE:	$10	OPEN DATES:	May-Sept
# of SINGLE SITES:	16	MAX SPUR:	35 feet
		MAX STAY:	14 days
		ELEVATION:	8800 feet

37 **Middle Quartz**
Pitkin • lat 38°37'23" lon 106°25'28"

DESCRIPTION: Park-like area withfirs on Middle Quartz Creek with trout fishing. Mild days, cool nights, expect noon rains. Historic Alpine Tunnel nearby. Supplies at Pitkin, Ohio City, or Gunnison. Deer, beavers, moose, and elk in area. Firewood may be gathered locally. Hiking, horse, and mountain bike trails.

GETTING THERE: From Pitkin go E on forest route 767 approx. 4 mi. to middle Quartz CG. Road is rough and slow.

SINGLE RATE:	$4	OPEN DATES:	June-sept
		MAX STAY:	14 days
		ELEVATION:	10200 feet

33 **Lost Lake**
Crested Butte • lat 38°52'12" lon 107°12'28"

DESCRIPTION: Overlooking Lost Lake under spruce and fir. Cold am, frequent afternoon rain, cool days. Boat or bank fish for trout; no motors allowed. Historic mining towns nearby. Supplies at Crested Butte. Deer, elk, coyotes, and occasional bears in area. Heavy use. Horse and hike trails nearby. Snow may change open dates.

GETTING THERE: From Crested Butte go W on county route 12 approx. 14 mi. to forest route 706. Go S on 706 approx. 2.5 mi. to Lost Lake CG.

SINGLE RATE:	Varies	OPEN DATES:	June-Nov
# of SINGLE SITES:	11	MAX SPUR:	21 feet
		MAX STAY:	14 days
		ELEVATION:	9600 feet

38 **Mirror Lake**
Almont • lat 38°44'9" lon 106°25'48"

DESCRIPTION: Open park-like site on lake. Trout fishing in lake. Views of mountains. Expect mild days with cool nights. Historic Tincup area. Supplies at Tincup, Taylor, Almont, or Gunnison. Moderateerate use. Firewood sold by RRM or may be gathered. Hiking, ATV trails nearby. Deer and black bears frequent the area.

GETTING THERE: From Almont go NE on forest route 742 approx. 27 mi. to forest route 765. Go SE on 765 approx. 8 mi. to forest route 267. Go E on 267 approx. 3 mi. to mirror Lake CG. Road is rough and slow going for 3 mi.

SINGLE RATE:	$6	OPEN DATES:	June-Sept
# of SINGLE SITES:	10	MAX SPUR:	16 feet
		MAX STAY:	14 days
		ELEVATION:	11000 feet

34 **Lottis Creek**
Almont • lat 38°46'33" lon 106°37'37"

DESCRIPTION: CG shaded by fir with mountain views. Set on Taylor River and Lottis Creek. Expect mild days with cool nights. Supplies are available at Taylor, Almont, or Gunnison. Frequented by deer and mountain goatss. Moderateerate use. Firewood sold by RRM or may be gathered. Hiking and mountain biking trails.

GETTING THERE: From Almont go NE on forest route 742 approx. 17 mi. to Lottis Creek CG.

SINGLE RATE:	$12	OPEN DATES:	May-Sept
# of SINGLE SITES:	27	MAX SPUR:	35 feet
GROUP RATE:	$60	MAX STAY:	14 days
# of GROUP SITES:	8	ELEVATION:	9000 feet

39 **Mosca**
Almont • lat 38°51'36" lon 105°52'24"

DESCRIPTION: CG in park-like area on Spring Creek Reservoir. Trout fishing and non-motorized boating. Expect mild days, cool nights. Supplies at Taylor, Almont, or Gunnison. Moderateerate use. Deer, beavers, and elk in area. Firewood sold by RRM or may be gathered. Hiking, mountain biking, and ATV trails.

GETTING THERE: From Almont go NE on forest route 742 approx. 7 mi. to forest route 744. Go N on 744 approx. 12 mi. to Mosca CG. Last 15 mi. of road is rough but very scenic.

SINGLE RATE:	$10	OPEN DATES:	June-Sept
# of SINGLE SITES:	16	MAX SPUR:	35 feet
		MAX STAY:	14 days
		ELEVATION:	10000 feet

35 **Matterhorn**
Telluride • lat 37°50'43" lon 107°52'52"

DESCRIPTION: Among mixed pine and aspen on a trout fishing creek or nearby Alta Lake and San Miguel River. Mild days, cool nights. Rain July-Aug. Histoic Lizard Head Pass and mining town of Rico in area. Supplies at Telluride. Moderateerate-heavy use. Firewood sold by RRM. Hiking trails nearby. Deer, elk, and occasional bears.

GETTING THERE: From Telluride go W on state HWY 145 approx. 3 mi. Go S on 145 approx. 9 mi. to Matterhorn CG.

SINGLE RATE:	Varies	OPEN DATES:	May-Sept
# of SINGLE SITES:	28	MAX SPUR:	35 feet
		MAX STAY:	7 days
		ELEVATION:	9500 feet

40 **North Bank**
Almont • lat 38°43'53" lon 106°45'28"

DESCRIPTION: Park-like CG on pleasant Taylor River, close to reservoir with trout fishing. Expect mild days with cool nights. Supplies in Almont or Gunnison. Moderateerate use. Firewood sold by RRM or may be gathered. Hiking and ATV trails nearby. Frequented by deer, fox, and black bears. Expect ticks in early season.

GETTING THERE: From Almont go NE on forest route 742 approx. 8 mi. to North Bank CG.

SINGLE RATE:	$10	OPEN DATES:	May-Sept
# of SINGLE SITES:	17	MAX SPUR:	35 feet
		MAX STAY:	14 days
		ELEVATION:	8600 feet

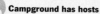 Campground has hosts   Reservable sites   Accessible facilities   Fully developed   Semi-developed   Rustic facilities

NOTE: Open dates listed are typical. Actual dates are dependent on conditions such as snow pack.

41 Onemile
Almont • lat 38°43'38" lon 106°45'34"

DESCRIPTION: CG in park-like area with river and moutain views. Expect mild days and cool nights. Fish for trout on Taylor River and Reservoir. Supplies at Almont or Gunnison. Deer, fox, and black bears can be seen in the area. CG receives moderateerateerate use. Firewood sold by RRM. Hike nearby trails.

GETTING THERE: From Almont go NE on forest route 742 approx. 8 mi. to Onemile CG.

SINGLE RATE:	$14	OPEN DATES:	May-Sept
# of SINGLE SITES:	25	MAX SPUR:	35 feet
		MAX STAY:	14 days
		ELEVATION:	8600 feet

46 Silver Jack
Montrose • lat 38°14'42" lon 107°32'36"

DESCRIPTION: Among aspen and tall grass with mesa and mountain views. Expect rain in July. Big Cimarron River is nearby. Wildlife includes deer and elk. Light use except July 4. Firewood may be gathered or purchased on site. Hiking and horse Trailheads to Uncompahgre Wilderness are close. Bears frequent the area.

GETTING THERE: From Montrose go E on US HWY 50 approx. 18 mi. to forest route 858 (Big Cimmaron RD). Go N on 858 20 mi. to Silver Jack CG.

SINGLE RATE:	$10	OPEN DATES:	June-Sept
# of SINGLE SITES:	60	MAX SPUR:	30 feet
		MAX STAY:	14 days
		ELEVATION:	8900 feet

42 Pitkin
Pitkin • lat 38°36'38" lon 106°30'02"

DESCRIPTION: CG among lodgepoles on Quartz Creek. Fishing at Alpine Tunnel. Mild days, cool mornings. Closest supplies at Pitkin or 28 mi. to Gunnison. Wildlife includes deer, beavers, and fox. Moderateerate use. Firewood may be purchased from host or gathered locally. ATV trails nearby. Prepare for ticks in June and July.

GETTING THERE: From Pitkin go E approx. 1 mi. to Pitkin CG.

SINGLE RATE:	$12	OPEN DATES:	May-Sept
# of SINGLE SITES:	22	MAX SPUR:	35 feet
		MAX STAY:	14 days
		ELEVATION:	9300 feet

47 Slumgullion
Lake City • lat 37°59'11" lon 107°13'24"

DESCRIPTION: CG among fir with mountain views and trout fishing in nearby streams. Mild days, cold nights. This site receives moderateerateerate use. Deer are in the area. Supplies are available at Lake City. Firewood may be gathered by campers. Hiking and ATV trails/roads nearby. Bears frequent this area.

GETTING THERE: From Lake City go SE on state HWY 149 approx. 9.5 mi. to Slumgullion CG.

SINGLE RATE:	$8	OPEN DATES:	June-Sept
# of SINGLE SITES:	21		
		MAX STAY:	14 days
		ELEVATION:	11200 feet

43 Quartz
Pitkin • lat 38°38'17" lon 106°28'07"

DESCRIPTION: CG in a spruce and pine setting with a creek running through. Great fishing for brown trout from creek. Historical Alpine Tunnel nearby. Look for moose and beavers in the area. Busy on 4th of July and Labor Day. Many trails nearby. Cumberland Pass and Williams Pass nearby.

GETTING THERE: From Pitkin go NE on forest route 765 approx. 3 mi. to Quartz CG.

SINGLE RATE:	$6	OPEN DATES:	May-Sept
# of SINGLE SITES:	10		
		MAX STAY:	14 days
		ELEVATION:	9800 feet

48 Snowblind
Sargents • lat 38°31'17" lon 106°24'52"

DESCRIPTION: CG set among pines on river frontage. Trout fish the river. Hike, bike, or ATV the trails. Historic Waunita Hot Springs is nearby. Cooler days, cold nights. Deer, elk, beavers, and fox frequent the area. Moderateerateerate use. Supplies at Sargents or Gunnison. Firewood may be gathered locally.

GETTING THERE: From Sargents go NE on US HWY 50 approx. 1 mi. to forest route 888. Go N on 888 approx. 7 mi. to Snowblind CG.

SINGLE RATE:	$10	OPEN DATES:	May-Sept
# of SINGLE SITES:	232		
		MAX STAY:	14 days
		ELEVATION:	9300 feet

44 Rivers End
Almont • lat 38°51'27" lon 106°34'07"

DESCRIPTION: This CG is set in and open grassy area with lake and mountain views. Boat and fly fish Taylor Lake, river, and Texas Creek. Historic Tincup area. Supplies at Taylor, Almont, and Gunnison. Deer and black bears frequent the area. Firewood sold by RRM. Hiking, biking, and ATV trails/roads.

GETTING THERE: From Almont go NE on forest route 742 approx. 28 mi. to Rivers End CG.

SINGLE RATE:	$10	OPEN DATES:	May-Sept
# of SINGLE SITES:	15	MAX SPUR:	35 feet
		MAX STAY:	14 days
		ELEVATION:	9400 feet

49 Soap Creek
Gunnison • lat 38°32'46" lon 107°18'57"

DESCRIPTION: This CG is set among pines near Blue Mesa Lake and several trout fishing streams. Expect mild days with cool nights. Firewood sold by RRM. Supplies at Blue Mesa, Lake City, or Gunnison. Hiking, biking , and ATV trails/roads nearby. Deer and black bears frequent the area.

GETTING THERE: From Gunninson go W on US HWY 50 26 mi. to state HWY 92. Go NW on 92 approx. 1 mi. to forest route 721. Go N on 721 7 mi. to Soap Creek CG. Road is rough and dusty over last 7 mi.

SINGLE RATE:	$10	OPEN DATES:	May-Sept
# of SINGLE SITES:	21	MAX SPUR:	35 feet
		MAX STAY:	14 days
		ELEVATION:	7700 feet

45 Rosy Lane
Almont • lat 38°43'50" lon 106°44'48"

DESCRIPTION: CG in an open grassy area with mountain and river views. Fishing on Taylor River or by boat on reservoir. Mild days, cool nights. Supplies at Almont or Gunnison. Frequented by deer, fox, and black bears. Firewood sold by RRM. Hiking and mountain bike trails nearby. Expect ticks in the early season.

GETTING THERE: From Almont go NE on forest route 742 approx. 9 mi. to Rosy Lane CG.

SINGLE RATE:	$12	OPEN DATES:	May-Sept
# of SINGLE SITES:	20	MAX SPUR:	35 feet
		MAX STAY:	14 days
		ELEVATION:	8600 feet

50  Spring Creek
Almont • lat 38°44'57" lon 106°45'58"

DESCRIPTION: CG is among pine and aspen on Spring Creek and Reservoir. Mountain views and trout fishing in the area. Supplies at Almont or Gunnison. Frequented by deer, big horn sheep, and black bears. Moderateerateerate use. Firewood is sold by RRM. Hiking, biking, and ATV trails nearby. Expect mosquitos and ticks in early season.

GETTING THERE: From Almont go NE on forest route 742 approx. 7 mi. to forest route 744. Go N on 744 approx. 2 mi. to Spring Creek CG.

SINGLE RATE:	$8	OPEN DATES:	May-Sept
# of SINGLE SITES:	12	MAX SPUR:	35 feet
		MAX STAY:	14 days
		ELEVATION:	10900 feet

 Campground has hosts   **Reservable sites**   **Accessible facilities**   **Fully developed**   **Semi-developed**   **Rustic facilities**

NOTE: Open dates listed are typical. Actual dates are dependent on conditions such as snow pack.

51 Spruce
Lake City • lat 38°02'49" lon 107°06'59"

DESCRIPTION: This CG rests in a forest setting with a stream nearby. Campers may enjoy fishing in the area but please check fishing regulations. Supplies and groceries are available at Lake City. Campers may gather their firewood (dead and down) locally. There are many trails nearby.

GETTING THERE: From Lake City go SE on state HWY 149 approx. 9 mi. to forest route 788. Go NE on 788 approx. 8 mi. to Spruce CG.

SINGLE RATE:	$8	OPEN DATES:	May-Sept
# of SINGLE SITES:	9	MAX STAY:	14 days
		ELEVATION:	9300 feet

52 Spruce Grove
Mesa • lat 39°02'57" lon 108°04'41"

DESCRIPTION: This CG is situated in a primarily forested area of spruce and fir on Jumbo Lake. Fish for native rainbow trout in the lake. Supplies and groceries are available at Mesa. Watch local wildlife in area. Many trails in the area, some leading to one or more of the other lakes in the area.

GETTING THERE: From Mesa go S on state HWY 65 approx. 14 mi. to Spruce Grove CG.

SINGLE RATE:	$8	OPEN DATES:	July-Sept
# of SINGLE SITES:	16	MAX SPUR:	22 feet
		MAX STAY:	14 days
		ELEVATION:	9900 feet

53 Sunshine
Telluride • lat 37°53'22" lon 107°53'22"

DESCRIPTION: CG among thick pine and aspen. Cool nights. Expect rain July-Aug. Trout fish nearby. Historic Lizard Head Pass and mining towns of Rico and Alta. Supplies at Telluride. Moderateerate-heavy use. Firewood sold by RRM. Hiking nearby. Deer, elk, occasional bears, and small wildlife. Closed for renovations summer of 2000.

GETTING THERE: From Telluride go W on state HWY 145 approx. 3 mi. Go S on 145 approx. 5 mi. to Sunshine CG.

SINGLE RATE:	$12	OPEN DATES:	May-Sept
# of SINGLE SITES:	14	MAX SPUR:	18 feet
		MAX STAY:	7 days
		ELEVATION:	9500 feet

54 Taylor Canyon
Almont • lat 38°43'37" lon 106°45'58"

DESCRIPTION: CG is set among pine trees with little vegetation on the bank of the Taylor River. Trout fishing by fly or lure in the Taylor River. Supplies are available in Almont or Gunnison. Firewood at Northbank CG. This CG is tent camping only. Bears can sometimes be a problem.

GETTING THERE: From Almont go NE on forest route 742 approx. 7 mi. to Taylor Canyon CG. Tent camping only.

SINGLE RATE:	$6	OPEN DATES:	May-Sept
		MAX SPUR:	6 feet
		MAX STAY:	14 days
		ELEVATION:	8600 feet

55 Twin Lake
Collbran • lat 39°03'53" lon 107°50'29"

DESCRIPTION: This CG is located in a high mountain area on Twin Lake. Fish from the lake. Supplies are available at Collbran, approx. 18 mi. from CG. Campers may gather their firewood locally. Crag Crest National Recreation Trail and other trails are nearby for hiking and biking. RV dump station in area.

GETTING THERE: From Collbran go S on county HWY 58.5/59 approx. 7 mi. to primary forest route 121. Go S on 121 approx. 9 mi. to forest route 126. Go E on 126 approx. 2 mi. to Twin Lake CG.

SINGLE RATE:	$6	OPEN DATES:	July-Sept
# of SINGLE SITES:	13	MAX SPUR:	22 feet
		MAX STAY:	14 days
		ELEVATION:	10300 feet

56 Ward Lake
Cedaredge • lat 39°02'27" lon 107°58'35"

DESCRIPTION: This CG is located in a high mountain area on Ward Lake. Fish from the lake. Supplies and groceries are available at Cedaredge. Campers may gather their firewood locally. Crag Crest National Recreation Trail and other trails are nearby for hiking and biking. RV dump station in area.

GETTING THERE: From Cedaredge go N on state HWY 65 (Grand Mesa Scenic Byway) approx. 14.5 mi. to primary forest route 121. Go E on 121 approx. 1/2 mi. to Ward Lake CG.

SINGLE RATE:	$10	OPEN DATES:	July-Sept
# of SINGLE SITES:	27	MAX SPUR:	20 feet
		MAX STAY:	14 days
		ELEVATION:	10200 feet

57 Weir and Johnson
Collbran • lat 39°03'58" lon 107°49'52"

DESCRIPTION: CG in a primarily forested area of spruce and fir with a view of the surrounding lakes. This is a more primitive CG but one of the busiest of all. Fish for native rainbow trout in the lakes. Supplies at Collbran. Many trails in the area, some leading to one or more of the other lakes in the area.

GETTING THERE: From Collbran go S on county HWY 58.5/59 approx. 7 mi. to primary forest route 121. Go S on 121 approx. 9 mi. to forest route 126. Go E on 126 approx. 3 mi. to Weir and Johnson CG.

SINGLE RATE:	$6	OPEN DATES:	July-Sept
# of SINGLE SITES:	12	MAX SPUR:	22 feet
		MAX STAY:	14 days
		ELEVATION:	10500 feet

58 Williams Creek
Lake City • lat 38°53'00" lon 107°20'00"

DESCRIPTION: This CG is situated in a park-like setting with a stream nearby. Historical Alpine Loop close to CG. Supplies and groceries are available at Lake City. Firewood can be purchased from concessionaire. Trails nearby for ATV and mountain bikes. Bears can be a problem.

GETTING THERE: From Lake City go S on state HWY 149 approx. 3 mi. to BLM route 3306. Go S on 3306 approx. 7 mi. to Williams Creek CG.

SINGLE RATE:	$10	OPEN DATES:	May-Sept
# of SINGLE SITES:	23	MAX SPUR:	20 feet
		MAX STAY:	14 days
		ELEVATION:	9200 feet

59 Woods Lake
Telluride • lat 37°53'03" lon 108°03'16"

DESCRIPTION: CG in a thick pine and aspen forest. Cool nights with rain July-Aug. Fly fish lake, bait fish Fall Creek. Supplies at Telluride, 18 mi. Moderateerate-heavy use. Firewood may be scarce. Hiking nearby. Horse facilities. Deer, elk, and occasional bears in area. Closed for renovations during summer 2000.

GETTING THERE: From Telluride go W on state HWY 145 approx. 13 mi. to forest route 618. Go S on 618 approx. 8 mi. to Woods Lake CG.

SINGLE RATE:	Varies	OPEN DATES:	May-Sept
# of SINGLE SITES:	41	MAX SPUR:	30 feet
		MAX STAY:	7 days
		ELEVATION:	9400 feet

 Campground has hosts 🔒 **Reservable sites** ♿ **Accessible facilities** **Fully developed**  **Semi-developed** △ **Rustic facilities**

NOTE: Open dates listed are typical. Actual dates are dependent on conditions such as snow pack.

USFS Photo

MEDICINE BOW-ROUTT NATIONAL FOREST

The Medicine Bow-Routt National Forests (MBR) and Thunder Basin National Grasslands (TBNG) encompass nearly three million acres from the north and eastern borders of Wyoming, south to the I-70 corridor that traverses north central Colorado. The forests provide a variety of uses and outdoor opportunities. The Colorado front range communities are located within three hours of much of the forest. Nearly three million residents from these areas have discovered the solitude of the Medicine Bow and Routt National Forests.

The origin of the "Medicine Bow" is legendary. Native American tribes which inhabited southeastern Wyoming found mountain mahogany in one of the valleys, from which bows of exceptional quality were made. Friendly tribes assembled there annually to construct their weapons and hold ceremonial powwows for the cure of disease, which was known as "making medicine." Eventually settlers associated the terms "making medicine" and "making bows", and Medicine Bow resulted as the name of the locality.

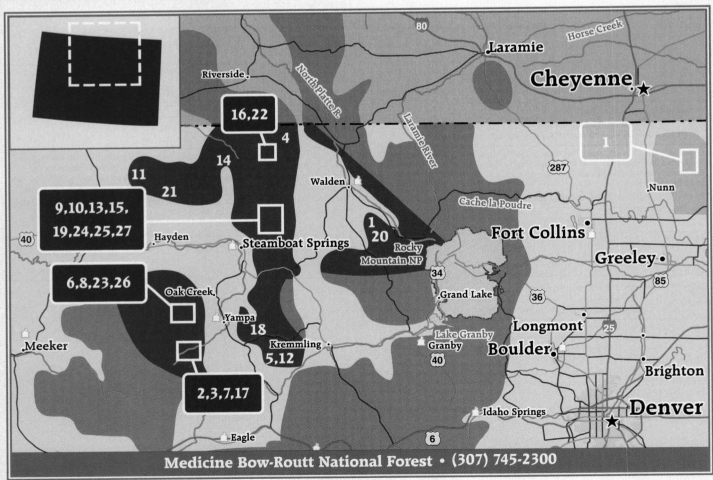

Medicine Bow-Routt National Forest • (307) 745-2300

1 — Aspen

Walden • lat 40°31'02" lon 106°01'55"

DESCRIPTION: CG in a park-like setting of lodgepole and aspen next to a stream lined with willows. Afternoon showers and cooler temperatures are possible. Fly fishing in the South Fork of the Michigan River. Supplies can be found 3 mi. N at KOA. Because of high bear frequency store food in correct containers.

GETTING THERE: From Walden go S on state HWY 14 approx. 17 mi. to forest route 740. S on 740 1 mi. to Aspen CG.

SINGLE RATE:	$10	OPEN DATES:	May-Sept
# of SINGLE SITES:	7	MAX SPUR:	20 feet
		MAX STAY:	14 days
		ELEVATION:	9052 feet

2 — Bear Lake

Yampa • lat 40°02'36" lon 107°04'18"

DESCRIPTION: CG with views spectacular of the Flat Tops Wilderness, set in a mixture of spruce and firs. Located next to Bear Lake with good fishing. Expect warm days with cold nights. Limited supplies located in Yampa, 12 mi. away from CG. Gather firewood locally. Hiking and horse trails in area.

GETTING THERE: From Yampa go S on county route 7 to Yampa Reservoir and the Bear Lake CG.

SINGLE RATE:	$10	OPEN DATES:	June-Oct
# of SINGLE SITES:	29	MAX SPUR:	40 feet
		MAX STAY:	14 days
		ELEVATION:	9600 feet

3 — Bear River

Yampa • lat 40°02'30" lon 107°00'00"

DESCRIPTION: CG situated in a high mountain setting. Rustic camping with dispersed sites. Limited services. No drinking water available on site. Fish Yampa reservoir nearby. Warm to hot days with cold nights. Windy at times. Limited supplies in Yampa. Flat Tops Wilderness hiking, horse access approx. 1 mi.

GETTING THERE: From Yampa go S on county route 7 approx. 7 mi. to Bear River CG.

SINGLE RATE:	$5	OPEN DATES:	June-Oct
# of SINGLE SITES:	32	MAX SPUR:	40 feet
		MAX STAY:	14 days
		ELEVATION:	9800 feet

4 — Big Creek Lakes

Walden • lat 40°56'11" lon 106°36'42"

DESCRIPTION: CG is in a park-like area with pines. Lake & mountain views. Summer showers & possible snow. Great fishing on nearby lake with boat ramp. Visit historic cabins nearby. Supplies in Walden. Numerous wildlife. Gather firewood locally. Interpretive trail on site. Many multi-use trails. Horse facilities.

GETTING THERE: From Walden go N on state HWY 125 to county route 6W. Go W on 6W approx. 18 mi. to forest route 600. Go W on 600 approx. 5 mi. to Big Creek Lakes CG.

SINGLE RATE:	$10	OPEN DATES:	June-Sept
# of SINGLE SITES:	54	MAX SPUR:	45 feet
		MAX STAY:	14 days
		ELEVATION:	9136 feet

5 — Blacktail Creek

Kremmling • lat 40°04'02" lon 106°34'48"

DESCRIPTION: This CG is situated in a high mountain pass near Blacktail Creek. Fish for trout in creek. Expect warm to hot days with cold nights. Weather may change rapidly. Limited supplies and groceries can be found in Kremmling. Gather firewood locally. Hiking trailhead nearby.

GETTING THERE: From Kremmling go N on US HWY 40 approx. 5 mi. to state HWY 134. W on 134 12 mi. to Blacktail Creek CG.

SINGLE RATE:	$10	OPEN DATES:	June-Nov
# of SINGLE SITES:	8	MAX SPUR:	40 feet
		MAX STAY:	14 days
		ELEVATION:	9100 feet

6 — Chapman Reservoir

Yampa • lat 40°11'11" lon 107°05'26"

DESCRIPTION: This CG is located on Chapman Reservoir in a mountainous valley. Fishing for trout in reservoir. Expectency warm to hot days with cold nights. Campers may gather their firewood locally. Limited supplies and groceries can be found in Yampa. Approx. 5 mi. from Flat Tops Wilderness access.

GETTING THERE: From Yampa go N on county route 17 5 mi. to county route 132. Go W approx. 4 mi. to forest route 16. Go W on 16 approx. 4 mi. to forest route 940. Go S approx. 1 mi. to Chapman Reservoir CG.

SINGLE RATE:	$5	OPEN DATES:	June-Nov
# of SINGLE SITES:	12	MAX SPUR:	35 feet
		MAX STAY:	14 days
		ELEVATION:	9400 feet

7 — Cold Springs
Yampa • lat 40°01'49" lon 107°07'08"

DESCRIPTION: This CG located on the Stillwater Reservoir. High elevation brings warm to hot days with cold nights. Prepare for quick weather changes. Fish the reservoir for trout. Gather firewood locally. Limited supplies are available in Yampa. Horse and hiking access to Flat Tops Wilderness.

GETTING THERE: From Yampa go S on county route 7 approx. 11 mi. to Cold Springs CG.

SINGLE RATE:	$10	OPEN DATES:	June-Oct
# of SINGLE SITES:	5	MAX SPUR:	30 feet
		MAX STAY:	14 days
		ELEVATION:	10400 feet

8 — Crosho Lake
Yampa • lat 40°10'23" lon 107°03'22"

DESCRIPTION: This high elevation CG is located on Crosho Lake with Allen Basin Reservoir nearby. Campers may enjoy fishing in the area but please check for fishing regulations. Expect warm to hot days with cold nights. Limited supplies and groceries can be found in Yampa. Some hiking trails are available nearby.

GETTING THERE: From Yampa go W on county route 17 approx. 4 mi. to county route 15. Go W on 15 approx. 4 mi. to Crosho Lake CG.

SINGLE RATE:	$3	OPEN DATES:	June-Oct
# of SINGLE SITES:	10	MAX SPUR:	25 feet
		MAX STAY:	14 days
		ELEVATION:	9000 feet

9 — Dry Lake
Steamboat Springs • lat 40°32'11" lon 106°46'53"

DESCRIPTION: This CG is a small but popular site. The CG offers access to great hiking and biking (on roadway). There is no fishing in immediate vicinity. Supplies and groceries can be found in Steamboat Springs. This CG is close to a ski area. Campers may gather dead and down firewood.

GETTING THERE: From Steamboat Springs go N on county route 36 approx. 2 mi. to forest route 60. Go E and N on 60 approx. 3 mi. To Dry Lake CG. Not recommended for trailers over 16'.

SINGLE RATE:	$10	OPEN DATES:	July-Nov
# of SINGLE SITES:	8	MAX SPUR:	16 feet
		MAX STAY:	14 days
		ELEVATION:	8000 feet

10 — Dumont Lake

Steamboat Springs • lat 40°24'06" lon 106°37'41"

DESCRIPTION: CG was reconstructed in 1987. Set on Continental Divide with spectacular views of the Colorado Mountains. Fishing on Dumont Lake, boats must be electric or hand-powered. Boat ramp on site. Fly fish lakes and streams. Bird watching and profuse wild flowers. Hiking and mountain biking trails/roads.

GETTING THERE: From Steamboat Springs go S on US HWY 40 approx. 19 mi. to forest route 315. Go N on 315 approx. 1 mi. to Dumont Lake CG.

SINGLE RATE:	$10	OPEN DATES:	July-Oct
# of SINGLE SITES:	22	MAX SPUR:	40 feet
		MAX STAY:	14 days
		ELEVATION:	9500 feet

 **Campground has hosts**   **Reservable sites** 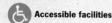 **Accessible facilities**  **Fully developed**   **Semi-developed**   **Rustic facilities**

NOTE: Open dates listed are typical. Actual dates are dependent on conditions such as snow pack.

11 Freeman

Craig • lat 40°45'43" lon 107°25'08"

DESCRIPTION: This high elevation CG offers shore fishing and boat fishing on a nearby reservoir. Please check for fishing regulations. No electric motors are permitted at the CG. Campers may gather dead and down wood for campfires. Supplies and groceries are available in Craig.

GETTING THERE: From Craig go N on state HWY 13 approx. 12 mi. to county route 11. Go N on 11 approx. 9 mi. to Freeman CG.

SINGLE RATE:	$10	**OPEN DATES:**	June-Nov
# of SINGLE SITES:	17	**MAX SPUR:**	22 feet
		MAX STAY:	14 days
		ELEVATION:	8800 feet

12 Gore Pass
Kremmling • lat 40°04'28" lon 106°33'35"

DESCRIPTION: This CG is located high in the Colorado mountains. Campers should prepare for warm to hot days with cold nights. Weather may change rapidly. Campers may gather their firewood locally. Limited supplies and groceries can be found in Kremmling. There is a hiking trailhead nearby.

GETTING THERE: From Kremmling go N on US HWY 40 approx. 5 mi. to state HWY 134. Go W on 134 approx. 11 mi. to Gore Pass CG.

SINGLE RATE:	$10	**OPEN DATES:**	June-Oct
# of SINGLE SITES:	12	**MAX SPUR:**	40 feet
		MAX STAY:	14 days
		ELEVATION:	9500 feet

13 Grizzly Creek
Walden • lat 40°33'30" lon 106°36'15"

DESCRIPTION: Located among aspen and grass with an abundance of wildflowers in July. Mountain view of Rabbit Ears Pass. Hot with noon showers. Rainbow Trout fishing at local lakes. Supplies in Walden. Light use except holiday weekends. Gather firewood locally. Trailhead to Mount Zirkel Wilderness.

GETTING THERE: From Walden go S on State HWY 14 approx. 12 mi. to county route 24 at Hebron. Go W on 24 11 mi. to Grizzly Creek CG.

SINGLE RATE:	$10	**OPEN DATES:**	May-Sept
# of SINGLE SITES:	12	**MAX SPUR:**	20 feet
		MAX STAY:	14 days
		ELEVATION:	8612 feet

14 Hahns Peak Lake

Hahns Peak • lat 40°50'23" lon 106°59'45"

DESCRIPTION: This CG is situated in a spruce and fir forest. Some pull though spaces (under 40'). Fish for stocked rainbow and brook trout on Hahns Peak Lake by shore or boat (using electric motor or hand-powered boats). Gather firewood locally. Moderateerate use, fills up on most holidays. Hiking trails nearby.

GETTING THERE: From Steamboat Spring go N on Routt County road 129 approx 30 mi. to forest route 486. Go W on 486 approx. 2.5 mi. to Hahns Peak Lake CG.

SINGLE RATE:	$10	**OPEN DATES:**	June-Oct
# of SINGLE SITES:	25	**MAX SPUR:**	40 feet
		MAX STAY:	14 days
		ELEVATION:	8500 feet

15 Hidden Lakes
Walden • lat 40°30'24" lon 106°36'29"

DESCRIPTION: This CG is situated among lodgepole pines. CG is cooler and shaded. Expect noon showers. Walk to lake for rainbow or native trout; non-motorized equipment on lake. Supplies at Walden. Elk and deer frequent the area. Gather firewood locally. Trailheads to Mount Zirkel Wilderness.

GETTING THERE: From Walden go S on State HWY 14 approx. 12 mi. to county route 24. Go W on 24 12 mi. to forest route 20. Go S on 20 3.5 mi. to Hidden Lakes CG.

SINGLE RATE:	$10	**OPEN DATES:**	June-Sept
# of SINGLE SITES:	9	**MAX SPUR:**	20 feet
		MAX STAY:	14 days
		ELEVATION:	9066 feet

16 Hinman
Steamboat Springs • lat 40°44'55" lon 106°50'01"

DESCRIPTION: This CG is located in a scenic area with a lower elevation. Some pull through spaces (under 22'). Supplies and groceries can be found in Steamboat Springs. Campers may gather their firewood locally. Fishing in a nearby stream. Hiking and mountain biking trails and roads nearby.

GETTING THERE: From Steamboat Springs go N on forest route 129 20 mi. to forest route 400 (at Glen Eden). Go E approx. 6 mi. to forest route 440 (Reed Creek Road). Go S on 440 approx. 1/2 mi. to Hinman CG.

SINGLE RATE:	$10	**OPEN DATES:**	June-Nov
# of SINGLE SITES:	13	**MAX SPUR:**	22 feet
		MAX STAY:	14 days
		ELEVATION:	7600 feet

17 Horseshoe
Yampa • lat 40°02'05" lon 107°06'45"

DESCRIPTION: This CG is in a mountain setting approx. 2 mi. from the Stillwater Reservoir. Fish and canoe in the reservoir. High elevation brings warm to hot days with cold nights. Limited supplies can be found in Yampa. Nearby hiking and horse trail access into the Flat Top Wilderness.

GETTING THERE: From Yampa go S on county route 7 approx. 10 mi. to Horseshoe CG.

SINGLE RATE:	$10	**OPEN DATES:**	June-Nov
# of SINGLE SITES:	7	**MAX SPUR:**	40 feet
		MAX STAY:	14 days
		ELEVATION:	10000 feet

18 Lynx Pass
Oak Creek • lat 40°06'19" lon 106°40'57"

DESCRIPTION: This CG is set high in the mountains near Lagunita Lake. Fish for trout on the small lake. Please check for fishing regulations. Expect warm days with cold nights. The weather may change quickly. Limited supplies can be found in Oak Creek or in Kremmling. There is a hiking trailhead nearby.

GETTING THERE: From Oak Creek go S on HWY 131 approx. 2 mi. to county route 14. Go E on 14 approx. 3 mi. to county route 16/270. Go S on 16/270 approx. 16 mi. to Lynx Pass CG.

SINGLE RATE:	$10	**OPEN DATES:**	June-Nov
# of SINGLE SITES:	11	**MAX SPUR:**	40 feet
		MAX STAY:	14 days
		ELEVATION:	8900 feet

19 Meadows
Steamboat Springs • lat 40°22'24" lon 106°43'28"

DESCRIPTION: This CG is situated in Rabbit Ears Pass surrounded by tall evergreens. A quiet and serene site. Some pull through spaces (up to 40'). Supplies and groceries can be found in Streamboat Springs. Gather firewood locally. Water in season only. Hiking and mountain biking on trails and roads nearby.

GETTING THERE: From Steamboat Springs go E on US HWY 40 approx. 14 mi. to Meadows CG.

SINGLE RATE:	$10	**OPEN DATES:**	July-Oct
# of SINGLE SITES:	30	**MAX SPUR:**	40 feet
		MAX STAY:	14 days
		ELEVATION:	9300 feet

20 Pines
Walden • lat 40°29'30" lon 106°00'28"

DESCRIPTION: Among lodgepole on Michigan River with brook trout. A lake is nearby. Expect noon showers. Cool and shady with possible snow. Historic Teller City 4 mi. away. Supplies at KOA CG 7 mi. or Walden. Gather firewood locally. Trailheads to Never Summer Wilderness. Frequented by bears.

GETTING THERE: From Walden go S on state HWY 14 approx. 17 mi. to forest route 740. Go S on 740 3.5 mi. to Pines CG.

SINGLE RATE:	$10	**OPEN DATES:**	June-Sept
# of SINGLE SITES:	11	**MAX SPUR:**	20 feet
		MAX STAY:	14 days
		ELEVATION:	9200 feet

 Campground has hosts   **Reservable sites**   **Accessible facilities** 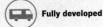 **Fully developed** 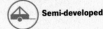 **Semi-developed**   **Rustic facilities**

NOTE: Open dates listed are typical. Actual dates are dependent on conditions such as snow pack.

21 Sawmill Creek
Craig • lat 40°45'28" lon 107°19'52"

DESCRIPTION: This high elevation CG is rustic and undeveloped. There is no drinking water available on site. Campers should prepare for rapid weather changes. Supplies and groceries can be found in Craig. Campers may gather dead and down wood for campfires.

GETTING THERE: From Craig go N on state HWY 13 approx. 11 mi. to county route 27(forest route 110). Go E on 27 14 mi. to Sawmill Creek CG.

SINGLE RATE:	$10	OPEN DATES:	July-Oct
# of SINGLE SITES:	6	MAX SPUR:	6 feet
		MAX STAY:	14 days
		ELEVATION:	9000 feet

22 Seedhouse
Steamboat Springs • lat 40°46'21" lon 106°53'44"

DESCRIPTION: This CG is just W of the Mount Zirkel Wilderness. A severe wind storm on October 25, 1997 has impacted the area with a temporary closure. Set to re-open 1999 season. Please contact Ranger District at 970-879-1870 for an opening date. Gather firewood locally. Hiking into wilderness nearby.

GETTING THERE: From Steamboat Springs go N on forest route 129 approx. 20 mi. forest route 400. Go E on 400 approx. 9.5 mi. to Seedhouse CG.

SINGLE RATE:	$10	OPEN DATES:	June-Oct
# of SINGLE SITES:	24	MAX SPUR:	25 feet
		MAX STAY:	14 days
		ELEVATION:	8000 feet

23 Sheriff Reservoir
Yampa • lat 40°08'55" lon 107°08'02"

DESCRIPTION: This CG is situated in high mountains near small reservoir. Fish for trout in reservoir and stream. Expect warm days with cold nights. Windy at times. Gather firewood locally. Limited supplies can be found in Yampa. Horse and hiking access into the Flat Top Wilderness.

GETTING THERE: From Yampa go N on county route 17 approx. 5 mi. to county route 132. W on 132 3 mi. to forest route 16. W on 16 5 mi. to forest route 959. S on 959 3 mi. to Sheriff Reservoir CG.

SINGLE RATE:	$5	OPEN DATES:	June-Nov
# of SINGLE SITES:	5	MAX SPUR:	30 feet
		MAX STAY:	14 days
		ELEVATION:	9800 feet

24 Summit Lake
Steamboat Springs • lat 40°32'47" lon 106°40'59"

DESCRIPTION: This CG is located in a spruce and fir forest setting on Summit Lake. There is good fishing in the lake and also on other lakes in the area. Campers should prepare for rapid weather changes. Deer, elk, bears, porcupines, and grouse are common. There are nice hiking trails nearby.

GETTING THERE: From Steamboat Springs go N on county route 36 approx. 2 mi. to forest route 60. Go E on 60 9 mi. to Summit Lake CG.

SINGLE RATE:	$10	OPEN DATES:	May-Oct
# of SINGLE SITES:	16	MAX SPUR:	18 feet
		MAX STAY:	14 days
		ELEVATION:	10300 feet

25 Teal Lake
Walden • lat 40°35'00" lon 106°36'00"

DESCRIPTION: This CG is set among evergreens on a small lake (electric motors only) with rainbow trout. Cold mornings with noon showers, getting hot in August. Supplies at Walden. Moderate use, growing in popularity. Gather firewood locally. 30 multi-use vehicle trails plus trailheads to Mount Zirkel Wilderness.

GETTING THERE: From Walden go S on State HWY 14 approx. 12 mi. to county route 24 at Hebron. Go W on 24 approx. 11 mi. to forest route 615. Go N on 615 approx. 3 mi. to Teal Lake CG.

SINGLE RATE:	$10	OPEN DATES:	June-Sept
# of SINGLE SITES:	17	MAX SPUR:	25 feet
GROUP RATE:	Varies	MAX STAY:	14 days
# of GROUP SITES:	1	ELEVATION:	8905 feet

26 Vaughn Lake
Yampa • lat 40°07'30" lon 107°15'30"

DESCRIPTION: This CG is situated high in the Colorado mountains. Campers should prepare for rapid weather changes. There is fishing nearby. Campers may gather dead and down firewood locally. Limited supplies are available in Yampa. Access to Flat Top Wilderness is approximately three miles away.

GETTING THERE: From Yampa go W on county route 17 approx. 5 mi. to county route 132. W on 132 3 mi. to forest route 16. Go W on 16 19 mi. to Vaughn Lake CG.

SINGLE RATE:	$10	OPEN DATES:	June-Nov
# of SINGLE SITES:	6	MAX SPUR:	36 feet
		MAX STAY:	14 days
		ELEVATION:	9500 feet

27 Walton Creek
Steamboat Springs • lat 40°22'53" lon 106°41'02"

DESCRIPTION: This CG is located in a spruce and fir forest on Walton Creek. Due to high elevation, campers should prepare for rapid weather changes. Deer, elk, bears, porcupines, grouse and (if you're lucky) pine martens can be seen in the area. This CG tends to be busy on holidays.

GETTING THERE: From Steamboat Springs go E on US HWY 40 approx. 16 mi. to Walton Creek CG.

SINGLE RATE:	$10	OPEN DATES:	June-Sept
# of SINGLE SITES:	16	MAX SPUR:	22 feet
		MAX STAY:	14 days
		ELEVATION:	9400 feet

1 Crow Valley Rec. Area
Briggsdale • lat 40°38'00" lon 104°20'00"

DESCRIPTION: CG is located in a grove of elm and cottonwood trees on the open prairie. A ball diamond, group camping area, the Steward J. Adams Education Site, group picnic area, and a ten-unit family CG provide opportunities for bird-watching, team sports and games, camping, picnicking or just relaxing.

GETTING THERE: Briggsdale CG is located on forest route 702 just NW of the junction of state route 14 and county route 77 in Briggsdale.

SINGLE RATE:	Varies	OPEN DATES:	Yearlong
# of SINGLE SITES:	10	MAX SPUR:	25 feet
GROUP RATE:	Varies	MAX STAY:	14 days
# of GROUP SITES:	4	ELEVATION:	4820 feet

 Campground has hosts   **Reservable sites**   **Accessible facilities**   **Fully developed**   **Semi-developed**   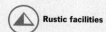 **Rustic facilities**

NOTE: Open dates listed are typical. Actual dates are dependent on conditions such as snow pack.

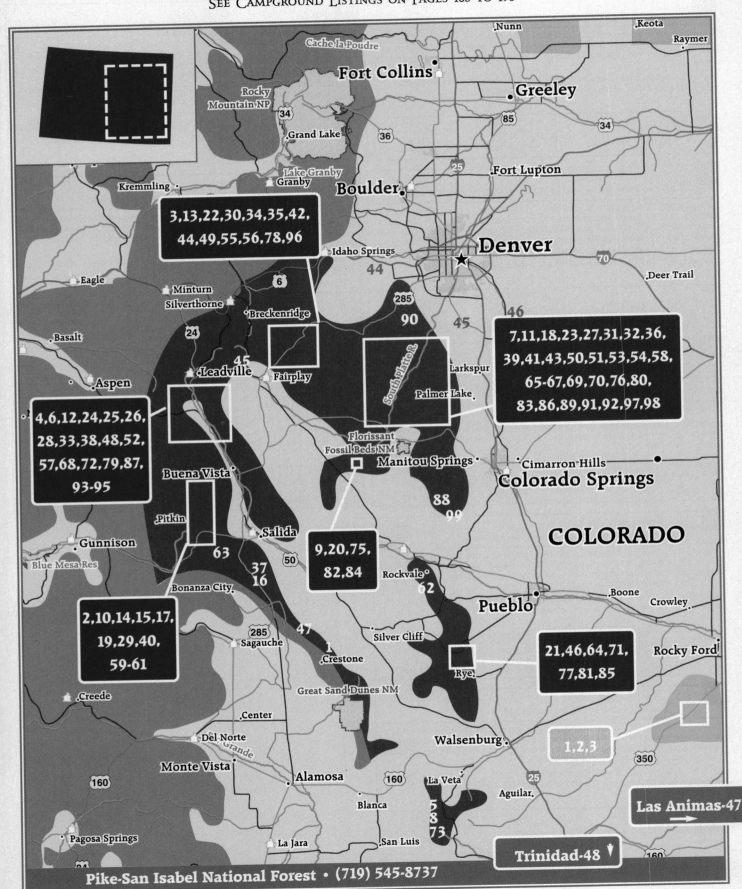

Cache la Poudre

Nunn
Keota
Raymer

Fort Collins

Greeley

Rocky
Mountain NP

34

85

34

Grand Lake

36

Kremmling

Lake Granby
Granby

Boulder

Fort Lupton

25

**3,13,22,30,34,35,42,
44,49,55,56,78,96**

Idaho Springs

Denver

70

Deer Trail

Eagle

6

44

285

46

Minturn
Silverthorne

90

45

**7,11,18,23,27,31,32,36,
39,41,43,50,51,53,54,58,
65-67,69,70,76,80,
83,86,89,91,92,97,98**

Breckenridge

24

Basalt

South Platte R.

Larkspur

45

Leadville

Aspen

Fairplay

Palmer Lake

**4,6,12,24,25,26,
28,33,38,48,52,
57,68,72,79,87,
93-95**

Florissant
Fossil Beds NM

Cimarron Hills

Manitou Springs

Colorado Springs

Buena Vista

88
99

Pitkin

COLORADO

Gunnison

63

Salida

**9,20,75,
82,84**

Blue Mesa Res

37
16

50

Rockvale

Boone

Crowley

Bonanza City

62

**2,10,14,15,17,
19,29,40,
59-61**

285

47

Pueblo

Sagauche

Silver Cliff

**21,46,64,71,
77,81,85**

Rocky Ford

Creede

Crestone

Center

Great Sand Dunes NM

Rye

Del Norte

Rio Grande

Walsenburg

1,2,3

350

Monte Vista

160

La Veta

25

160

Alamosa

Aguilar

Las Animas-47
→

Pagosa Springs

La Jara

Blanca

5
8
73

San Luis

Trinidad-48 ↓

160

Pike-San Isabel National Forest • (719) 545-8737

USFS Photo

PIKE-SAN ISABEL NATIONAL FOREST

The Pike and San Isabel National Forests provide opportunities for everyone. This forest and grassland grouping offers nearly three million acres of public lands which spans from the southeast corner of Colorado and into western Kansas. Part or all of seven different wilderness areas are included: Mount Evans, Lost Creek, Sangre De Cristo, Collegiate Peaks, Buffalo Peaks, Mount Massive and Holy Cross. The 1890 discovery of gold at Cripple Creek brought prospectors here, but now magnificent scenery and recreational opportunities draw visitors.

Hike Colorado Trail through Waterton Canyon, enjoy the gold-medal waters of the South Platte River, or "bag a peak" in the Collegiate Mountain Range, famous for its 14,000-foot peaks. Hundreds of miles of trails will challenge any hiker or rider. Sightseers can explore the forest on self-guided car tours. Photography and wildlife-watching are popular activities. Big game species include elk, deer, bighorn sheep, and bears.

Among the forest's most majestic mountains are 14,433 Mt. Elbert, Colorado's highest, and Pikes Peak, Colorado's most famous. Turquoise Lake Recreation Area and Twin Lakes Reservoir are open for water skiing, boating, fishing and camping.

1 Alvarado
Westcliff • lat 38°04'44" lon 105°33'48"

DESCRIPTION: This CG is situated in a dense stand of fir and spruce. Enjoy fishing the nearby lakes and creeks that are within 5 mi. of this CG. Please check fishing regulations. Supplies and groceries can be found in Westcliff approx. 10 mi. from CG. Rainbow Trail is next to CG.

GETTING THERE: From Westcliff go S on state HWY 69 approx. 3.5 mi. to county route 140. Go W on 140 approx. 7 mi. to Alvarado CG.

SINGLE RATE:	$9	OPEN DATES:	May-Sept
# of SINGLE SITES:	47	MAX SPUR:	35 feet
		MAX STAY:	14 days
		ELEVATION:	9000 feet

2 Angel of Shavano
Maysville • lat 38°34'58" lon 106°13'12"

DESCRIPTION: This CG is situated in ponderosa pine, douglas fir, and aspen near the North Fork of the South Arkansas River. Fishing is available in the river and nearby North Fork Reservoir. Afternoon t-showers are common. Busy weekends and holidays. Frequented by bearss. Hiking in area. Watch for bald eagles.

GETTING THERE: From Maysville go N on county route 240 approx. 4 mi. to Angel of Shavano CG.

SINGLE RATE:	$10	OPEN DATES:	May-Sept
# of SINGLE SITES:	20	MAX SPUR:	45 feet
GROUP RATE:	Varies	MAX STAY:	14 days
# of GROUP SITES:	1	ELEVATION:	9200 feet

3 Aspen
Jefferson • lat 39°25'31" lon 105°50'27"

DESCRIPTION: CG is located in a park-like stand of aspen, ponderosa pine, and lodgepole pine. Boat and fish for rainbow, brown, and lake trout in nearby Jefferson Lake. Deer, elk, and coyotes in area. The Colorado Trail runs through the area. Busy weekends and holidays. May be frequented by bears.

GETTING THERE: From Jefferson go NW on county route 35 approx. 3 mi. to county route 54. Go NW on 54 1.5 mi. Go NE on forest route 37 approx. 2 mi. to forest route 37. Go NW on 37 approx. 1/2 mi. to Aspen CG.

SINGLE RATE:	$10	OPEN DATES:	Yearlong
# of SINGLE SITES:	12	MAX SPUR:	30 feet
		MAX STAY:	14 days
		ELEVATION:	9900 feet

4 Baby Doe
Leadville • lat 39°16'11" lon 106°21'02"

DESCRIPTION: CG located in a shaded lodgepole forest, along Turquoise Lake. Seldom gets over 80' during summer. Restrooms and trash service are provided. Firewood is for sale at the CG. Full most weekends. Nature trails nearby. RV dump stations near Molly Brown or Printer Boy CG's. Recycling center.

GETTING THERE: Baby Doe CG is located in the Turquoise Lake Recreation Area on the E shore of Torquoise Lake.

SINGLE RATE:	$11	OPEN DATES:	May-Sept
# of SINGLE SITES:	50	MAX SPUR:	45 feet
		MAX STAY:	14 days
		ELEVATION:	9900 feet

5 Bears Lake
Cuchara • lat 37°19'34" lon 105°08'34"

DESCRIPTION: In a dense stand of douglas fir and engelmann spruce with views of Blue Lake. Trout fishing in Bears and Blue Lakes. The Spanish Peaks Area is a National Natural Landmark and considered a Wilderness Study Area. Bears, deer, elk, turkeys, and grouse in area. Supplies at Cuchara. Trails in area.

GETTING THERE: From Cuchara go S on state HWY 12 approx. 3 mi. to forest route 422. Go W on 422 approx. 4 mi. to Bears Lake CG.

SINGLE RATE:	$9	OPEN DATES:	May-Sept
# of SINGLE SITES:	14	MAX SPUR:	40 feet
		MAX STAY:	14 days
		ELEVATION:	10500 feet

 Campground has hosts 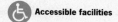 **Reservable sites**   **Accessible facilities**   **Fully developed**   **Semi-developed** △ **Rustic facilities**

NOTE: Open dates listed are typical. Actual dates are dependent on conditions such as snow pack.

6 Belle of Colorado
Leadville • lat 39°16'00" lon 106°22'00"

DESCRIPTION: CG located in a high mountain valley surrounded by snow capped peaks on Turquoise Lake. Fish from the lake. Boat ramp at CG. Summers seldom over 80'. Supplies available at Leadville. RV dump station by Molly Brown or Printer Boy CG's. Firewood is sold for $4 a bundle at CG.

GETTING THERE: Belle of Colorado CG is located in the Turquoise Lake Recreation Area on the E shore of Torquoise Lake. Tent camping only.

SINGLE RATE:	$12	OPEN DATES:	May-Sept
# of SINGLE SITES:	19		
		MAX STAY:	14 days
		ELEVATION:	9900 feet

7 Big Turkey
Florissant • lat 39°07'11" lon 105°13'36"

DESCRIPTION: CG set in a douglas fir and pine forest on Turkey Creek. Fish for brook trout. Bring firewood. Mountain lionss, deer, foxeses, eagles, coyotes, and occasional black bears. Light use, rarely fills. Popular area to climb on turkey rocks. 4WD in gulches. Motorized vehicles restricted to established routes.

GETTING THERE: From Florissant go N on county route 3 approx. 8 mi. to county route 33. Go W on 33 approx. 1.5 mi. to county route 330. Go NE on 330 approx. 4 mi. to Big Turkey CG. No trailers or RVs.

SINGLE RATE:	$10	OPEN DATES:	Apr-Oct*
# of SINGLE SITES:	10	MAX SPUR:	16 feet
		MAX STAY:	14 days
		ELEVATION:	8000 feet

8 Blue Lake
Cuchara • lat 37°18'48" lon 105°08'17"

DESCRIPTION: In a dense stand of douglas fir and engelmann spruce with views of Blue Lake. Trout fishing in Bears and Blue Lakes. The Spanish Peaks Area is a National Natural Landmark and considered a Wilderness Study Area. Bears, deer, elk, turkeys, and grouse in area. Supplies at Cuchara. Trails in area.

GETTING THERE: From Cuchara go S on state HWY 12 approx. 3 mi. to forest route 422. Go W on 422 approx. 3 mi. to Blue Lake CG.

SINGLE RATE:	$9	OPEN DATES:	May-Sept
# of SINGLE SITES:	15	MAX SPUR:	40 feet
		MAX STAY:	14 days
		ELEVATION:	10500 feet

9 Blue Mountain
Lake George • lat 38°57'41" lon 105°21'41"

DESCRIPTION: This CG is located in a mature, park-like stand of ponderosa pine and spruce. Fish for rainbow and brown trout in nearby South Platte River. Wildlife includes coyotes, deer, and elk. On site trailhead leads to Eleven Mile Canyon. CG may be frequented by bears.

GETTING THERE: From Lake George go S on county route 96 approx. 1 mi. to county route 61. Go SE on 61 approx. 1/4 mi. to forest route 61B. Go SE on 61B approx. 1/4 mi. to Blue Mountain CG.

SINGLE RATE:	$9	OPEN DATES:	Yearlong
# of SINGLE SITES:	21	MAX SPUR:	40 feet
		MAX STAY:	14 days
		ELEVATION:	8200 feet

10 Boot Leg
Buena Vista • lat 38°43'00" lon 106°11'00"

DESCRIPTION: This walk-in only CG is located in the Chalk Creek Canyon with mountain views. Fishing is available in the lower canyon. There are several hiking trails and OHV roads in this area. Afternoon t-showers are common. CG may be frequented by bears. Visit the historic mining town of St. Elmo.

GETTING THERE: From Buena Vista go S on county route 321 approx. 8 mi. to county route 162. Go W on 162 approx. 2 mi. to Boot Leg CG.

SINGLE RATE:	Varies	OPEN DATES:	Apr-Sept
# of SINGLE SITES:	6		
		MAX STAY:	14 days
		ELEVATION:	8400 feet

11 Buffalo
Buffalo Creek • lat 39°21'03" lon 105°19'09"

DESCRIPTION: This CG is situated in a fir and pine forest. Bring your own firewood. Mountain lionss, deer, foxeses, eagles, coyotes, and occasional black bears frequent the area. No nearby fishing. Rarely fills. Hiking and biking access to Colorado Trail, check regulations for uses.

GETTING THERE: From Buffalo Creek go S on state HWY 126 approx. 4 mi. to forest route 550. Go W on 550 approx. 4 mi. to Buffalo CG.

SINGLE RATE:	$10	OPEN DATES:	Apr-Oct*
# of SINGLE SITES:	41	MAX SPUR:	20 feet
		MAX STAY:	14 days
		ELEVATION:	7400 feet

12 Buffalo Springs
Fairplay • lat 39°02'02" lon 105°59'21"

DESCRIPTION: CG is located in mature, park-like stand of pine and aspen. Boating and fishing at nearby Antero Reservoir. Wildlife includes deer, elk, and coyotes. Numerous hiking, horse, mountain biking and OHV trails in area. Busy holidays and weekends. CG may be frequented by bears.

GETTING THERE: From Fairplay go S on US HWY 285 approx. 13 mi. to forest route 431. Go W on 431 approx. 1/2 mi. to Buffalo Springs CG.

SINGLE RATE:	$9	OPEN DATES:	Yearlong
# of SINGLE SITES:	18	MAX SPUR:	40 feet
		MAX STAY:	14 days
		ELEVATION:	9000 feet

13 Burning Bears
Grant • lat 39°30'49" lon 105°42'35"

DESCRIPTION: This CG is situated in a lodgepole pine forest. No nearby fishing. CG tends to fill up quickly on weekends and holidays. Bring your own firewood. Mountain lionss, deer, elk, foxeses, eagles, coyotes, and occasional black bears in area. Horse and hiking trails into the Mount Evans Wilderness.

GETTING THERE: From Grant go NW on county route 62 approx. 5 mi. to Burning Bears CG.

SINGLE RATE:	$10	OPEN DATES:	Yearlong*
# of SINGLE SITES:	13	MAX SPUR:	20 feet
		MAX STAY:	14 days
		ELEVATION:	9500 feet

14 Cascade
Buena Vista • lat 38°42'38" lon 106°14'39"

DESCRIPTION: CG sits along Chalk Creek, near the Chalk Cliffs in pine, fir, and aspen. Very busy in summer. Fishing is available in lower canyon. Several hiking trails and OHV roads in this area. Afternoon t-showers are common. CG may be frequented by bears. Visit the historic mining town of St. Elmo.

GETTING THERE: From Buena Vista go S on county route 321 approx. 8 mi. to county route 162. Go W on 162 approx. 4 mi. to Cascade CG.

SINGLE RATE:	$10	OPEN DATES:	May-Sept
# of SINGLE SITES:	23	MAX SPUR:	60 feet
		MAX STAY:	14 days
		ELEVATION:	9000 feet

15 Chalk Lake
Buena Vista • lat 38°42'32" lon 106°13'56"

DESCRIPTION: CG sits along Chalk Creek, near the Chalk Cliffs in some pine, cedar, and aspen. Very busy in summer. Fishing is available in lower canyon. Several hiking trails and OHV roads in this area. Afternoon t-showers are common. CG may be frequented by bears. Visit the historic mining town of St. Elmo.

GETTING THERE: From Buena Vista go S on county route 321 approx. 8 mi. to county route 162. Go W on 162 approx. 4 mi. to Chalk Lake CG.

SINGLE RATE:	$10	OPEN DATES:	May-Sept
# of SINGLE SITES:	21	MAX SPUR:	35 feet
		MAX STAY:	14 days
		ELEVATION:	8700 feet

 Campground has hosts   **Reservable sites**   **Accessible facilities**   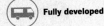 **Fully developed**   **Semi-developed**   **Rustic facilities**

NOTE: Open dates listed are typical. Actual dates are dependent on conditions such as snow pack.

16 Coaldale

Coaldale • lat 38°20'30" lon 105°48'00"

DESCRIPTION: This CG is located in oak, cottonwood, pine, and cedar near Hayden Creek. Enjoy fishing in creek or hiking in adjacent Sangre de Cristo Wilderness. No drinking water on site. Afternoon t-showers are common. CG may be frequented by bears. Hike the nearby Rainbow Trail to high elevation lakes.

GETTING THERE: From Coaldale go SW on county route 6 approx. 4 mi. to Coaldale CG.

SINGLE RATE:	$6	OPEN DATES:	May-Sept
# of SINGLE SITES:	11	MAX SPUR:	30 feet
		MAX STAY:	14 days
		ELEVATION:	8500 feet

17 Collegiate Peaks

Buena Vista • lat 38°48'47" lon 106°18'55"

DESCRIPTION: CG is situated along the Middle Cottonwood Creek, near the top of Cottonwood Pass. Enjoy fishing in the creek or nearby lakes. Heavily wooded area with aspen, douglas fir, and ponderosa pine. Busy weekends and holidays. Afternoon t-showers are common. CG may be frequented by bears.

GETTING THERE: From Buena Vista go W on county route 306 approx. 10 mi. to Collegiate Peaks CG.

SINGLE RATE:	$10	OPEN DATES:	May-Sept
# of SINGLE SITES:	56	MAX SPUR:	35 feet
		MAX STAY:	14 days
		ELEVATION:	9800 feet

18 Colorado

Woodland Park • lat 39°04'47" lon 105°05'36"

DESCRIPTION: CG set in a shady ponderosa pine forest. In Monitor Park Rec. Area. Fish for rainbow and brook trout. Supplies in Woodland park. Black bearss, deer, elk, turkeys, beavers, in area. Bike popular Centennial Bike Trail; other hiking trails and interpretive programs offered.

GETTING THERE: From Woodland Park go N on state HWY 67 approx. 5.5 mi. to Colorado CG.

SINGLE RATE:	$12	OPEN DATES:	May-Sept
# of SINGLE SITES:	81	MAX SPUR:	30 feet
		MAX STAY:	14 days
		ELEVATION:	7800 feet

19 Cottonwood Lake

Buena Vista • lat 38°46'51" lon 106°17'30"

DESCRIPTION: This CG is near Cottonwood Lake among aspen. Enjoy fishing in lake or nearby South Cottonwood Creek. Hike the Poplar Gulch trail and view beaver ponds at its trailhead. CG tends to be busy on weekends and holidays. Afternoon t-showers are common. CG may be frequented by bears.

GETTING THERE: From Buena Vista go W on county route 306 approx. 6 mi. to county route 344. Go S on 344 approx. 4 mi. to Cottonwood Lake CG.

SINGLE RATE:	$10	OPEN DATES:	May-Sept
# of SINGLE SITES:	28	MAX SPUR:	40 feet
		MAX STAY:	14 days
		ELEVATION:	9600 feet

20 Cove

Lake George • lat 38°54'33" lon 105°27'37"

DESCRIPTION: CG sits in a mature, park-like stand of pine, spruce, and aspen. Fish for rainbow and brown trout in adjacent South Platte River. Wildlife includes deer, elk, and coyotes. Can be busy weekends and holidays. Numerous hiking, horse, mountain biking, and OHV trails in area. CG may be frequented by bears.

GETTING THERE: Cove CG is located is Eleven mile Canyon. From Lake George go S on county route 96 approx. 9 mi. to Cove CG.

SINGLE RATE:	$10	OPEN DATES:	Yearlong
# of SINGLE SITES:	4	MAX SPUR:	30 feet
		MAX STAY:	14 days
		ELEVATION:	8400 feet

21 Davenport

San Isabel • lat 38°03'20" lon 105°04'17"

DESCRIPTION: This CG is situated in a dense forest of spruce and fir. Creek nearby for fishing and fun. Supplies and groceries can be found in San Isabel. Deer, bears, and elk can be seen in the area. Trails are available nearby. Look for Biships Castle close to CG.

GETTING THERE: From San Isabel go N on state HWY 165 approx. 5 mi. to forest route 382. Go E on 382 approx. 1.5 mi. to Davenport CG.

SINGLE RATE:	$9	OPEN DATES:	May-Sept
# of SINGLE SITES:	12	MAX SPUR:	25 feet
		MAX STAY:	14 days
		ELEVATION:	8500 feet

22 Deer Creek

Highland Park • lat 39°33'21" lon 105°09'43"

DESCRIPTION: This CG is situated in a fir and pine forest on Deer Creek. Fish for small brook trout. Bring your own firewood. Mountain lionss, deer, foxeses, eagles, coyotes, and occasional black bears can be seen in the area. Fills holidays. Horse and hiking trails nearby. Wilderness access.

GETTING THERE: From Highland Park go W on forest route 100 approx. 1.5 mi. to Deer Creek CG. 4WD recommended.

SINGLE RATE:	$10	OPEN DATES:	Yearlong*
# of SINGLE SITES:	13	MAX SPUR:	20 feet
		MAX STAY:	14 days
		ELEVATION:	9000 feet

23 Devils Head
Sedalia • lat 39°16'17" lon 105°06'10"

DESCRIPTION: CG is set in a forest of douglas fir and ponderosa pine. Fire lookout 1 mi. has great forest views. No nearby fishing. Bring your own firewood. Mountain lionss, deer, foxeses, eagles, coyotes, and occasional black bears in area. Fills holidays. Horse and hiking trails to Devils Head Mountain.

GETTING THERE: From Sedalia go SW on state HWY 67 approx. 10 mi. to forest route 300. Go S on 300 approx. 9 mi. to forest route 180. Go SE on 180 approx. 1/2 mi. to Devils Head CG.

SINGLE RATE:	$10	OPEN DATES:	Apr-Oct*
# of SINGLE SITES:	21	MAX SPUR:	20 feet
		MAX STAY:	14 days
		ELEVATION:	8800 feet

24 Dexter Point

Balltown • lat 39°16'30" lon 106°22'00"

DESCRIPTION: This CG is situated in a ponderosa pine and sage habitat on Twin Lakes. Fish from the lake. Supplies and groceries are available at Balltown. Nature trails are nearby. Aluminum can recycling is provided. Firewood is available for sale at the CG. RV dump station at White Star CG.

GETTING THERE: Dexter Point CG is located in the Twin Lakes Recreation Area on the N shore of Twin Lakes Reservoir.

SINGLE RATE:	$9	OPEN DATES:	May-Sept
# of SINGLE SITES:	24	MAX SPUR:	37 feet
		MAX STAY:	14 days
		ELEVATION:	9300 feet

25 Elbert Creek

Leadville • lat 39°09'10" lon 106°24'47"

DESCRIPTION: A quiet CG located in a forested setting of lodgepole pine just off of Halfmoon Creek. Fish for trout from creek. Supplies are available at Leadville. Numerous wildlife in area including squirrels, eagles, bears, and the occasional cougar. Trails in the area.

GETTING THERE: From Leadville go S on US HWY 24 approx. 3 mi. to Malta. Go W from Malta approx. 1 mi. to forest route 110. Go S on 110 approx. 6 mi. to Elbert Creek CG.

SINGLE RATE:	$9	OPEN DATES:	May-Sept
# of SINGLE SITES:	17	MAX SPUR:	16 feet
		MAX STAY:	14 days
		ELEVATION:	10000 feet

 Campground has hosts   **Reservable sites**   **Accessible facilities**   **Fully developed**   **Semi-developed**   **Rustic facilities**

NOTE: Open dates listed are typical. Actual dates are dependent on conditions such as snow pack.

26 Father Dyer
Leadville • lat 39°16'30" lon 106°22'00"

DESCRIPTION: CG located in a shaded lodgepole pine forest area. Afternoon thunderstorms are possible. Seldom gets over 80' during summer. There is a foot trail to the lake. Pressurized water hydrants are located throughout the campground. RV dump station by Molly Brown or Printer Boy CGs.

GETTING THERE: Father Dyer CG is located in the Turquoise Lake Recreation Area on the E shore of Torquoise Lake.

SINGLE RATE:	$12	OPEN DATES:	May-Sept
# of SINGLE SITES:	26	MAX SPUR:	35 feet
		MAX STAY:	14 days
		ELEVATION:	9900 feet

27 Flat Rocks
Sedalia • lat 39°18'30" lon 105°06'00"

DESCRIPTION: This CG is set in a high forest of douglas fir and ponderosa pine. No nearby water or fishing. Mountain lionss, coyotes, foxeses, eagles, deer, and occasional black bears in area. Fills most holidays. Mountain bike trails nearby. Motorcycling (dirt bikes) routes available.

GETTING THERE: Flat Rocks CG is located in the Rampart Range. From Sedalia go SW on state HWY 67 approx. 10 mi. to forest route 300. Go S on 300 approx. 5 mi. to Flat Rocks CG.

SINGLE RATE:	$10	OPEN DATES:	Apr-Oct*
# of SINGLE SITES:	19	MAX SPUR:	20 feet
		MAX STAY:	14 days
		ELEVATION:	8200 feet

28 Fourmile
Fairplay • lat 39°14'00" lon 106°05'00"

DESCRIPTION: CG is located in a mature, park-like stand of pine and aspen. Boating and fishing at nearby Antero Reservoir. Wildlife includes deer, elk, and coyotes. Numerous hiking, horse, mountain biking, and OHV trails in area. Busy holidays and weekends. CG may be frequented by bears.

GETTING THERE: From Fairplay go S on US HWY 285 approx. 1.5 mi. to county route 18. Go W on 18 approx. 8 mi. to Fourmile CG.

SINGLE RATE:	$9	OPEN DATES:	Yearlong
# of SINGLE SITES:	14	MAX SPUR:	25 feet
		MAX STAY:	14 days
		ELEVATION:	10762 feet

29 Garfield
Poncha Springs • lat 38°32'50" lon 106°18'11"

DESCRIPTION: This CG is among ponderosa pine and douglas fir along the South Arkansas River. Hike the Colorado Trail and the Continental Divide Trail. Afternoon t-showers are common. Frequented by bears. Other wildlife in area includes mountain lionss, deer, elk, and bald eagles. Supplies in Poncha Springs.

GETTING THERE: From Poncha Springs go W on US HWY 50 approx. 13 mi. to Garfield CG.

SINGLE RATE:	$9	OPEN DATES:	June-Sept
# of SINGLE SITES:	11	MAX SPUR:	35 feet
		MAX STAY:	14 days
		ELEVATION:	10000 feet

30 Geneva Park
Grant • lat 39°31'56" lon 105°44'14"

DESCRIPTION: CG set in a lodgepole pine forest with views of the forest and peaks. No nearby fishing. Bring your own firewood. Mountain lionss, deer, foxeses, eagles, coyotes, and occasional black bears can be seen in the area. Fills holidays. Horse and hiking access to Burning Bears and wilderness areas.

GETTING THERE: From Grant go NW on county route 62 approx. 6 mi. to Geneva Park CG.

SINGLE RATE:	$10	OPEN DATES:	Apr-Oct*
# of SINGLE SITES:	26	MAX SPUR:	20 feet
		MAX STAY:	14 days
		ELEVATION:	9800 feet

31 Goose Creek
Woodland Park • lat 39°10'29" lon 105°22'33"

DESCRIPTION: CG set in a douglas fir and ponerosa pine forest with forest and wilderness peaks in view. Set right on Goose Creek where brook and rainbow trout may be fished. Bring own firewood. Mountain lionss, deer, foxeses, coyotes, and occasional black bears. Horse and hiking access to Lost Creek Wilderness.

GETTING THERE: From Woodland Park go NW on state HWY 67 approx. 24 mi. to state HWY 126. Go SW on 126 approx. 3 mi. to county route 211. Go S on 211 approx. 12 mi. to Goose Creek CG.

SINGLE RATE:	$10	OPEN DATES:	Apr-Oct*
# of SINGLE SITES:	10	MAX SPUR:	20 feet
		MAX STAY:	14 days
		ELEVATION:	8100 feet

32 Green Mountain
Buffalo Creek • lat 39°19'00" lon 105°21'30"

DESCRIPTION: CG with tent sites located in a fir and pine forest on a small creek. 3 nearby creeks offer brook trout fishing. Fills most weekends. Bring own firewood. Mountain lionss, deer, foxeses, eagles, coyotes, and occasional black bears. Hike and mountain bike access to Colorado Trail.

GETTING THERE: From Buffalo Creek go S on state HWY 126 approx. 4 mi. to forest route 550. Go W on 550 approx. 4 mi. to forest route 543. Go SW on 543 approx. 2 mi. to Green Mountain CG. Tent camping only.

SINGLE RATE:	$10	OPEN DATES:	Apr-Oct*
# of SINGLE SITES:	6	MAX SPUR:	20 feet
		MAX STAY:	14 days
		ELEVATION:	7600 feet

33 Halfmoon
Leadville • lat 39°09'34" lon 106°23'45"

DESCRIPTION: A quiet CG located in a more open forested setting of lodgepole pine just off of Halfmoon Creek. Fish for trout from creek. Supplies are available at Leadville. Numerous wildlife in area including squirrels, eagles, bears, and the occasional cougar. Trails in the area.

GETTING THERE: From Leadville go S on US HWY 24 approx. 3 mi. to Malta. Go W from Malta approx. 1 mi. to forest route 110. Go S on 110 approx. 5 mi. to Halfmoon CG.

SINGLE RATE:	$9	OPEN DATES:	May-Sept
# of SINGLE SITES:	22	MAX SPUR:	16 feet
		MAX STAY:	14 days
		ELEVATION:	9900 feet

34 Hall Valley
Grant • lat 39°28'55" lon 105°48'07"

DESCRIPTION: This CG set in a pine and fir forest on a small creek. No nearby fishing. Historic mining area. Bring own firewood. Mountain lionss, deer, foxeses, eagles, coyotes, and occasional black bears can be seen in the area. Red Cone and Webster are ATV or 4WD roads. Dirt motorcycle riding on roads.

GETTING THERE: From Grant go W on US HWY 285 approx. 3 mi. to county route 60. Go W on 60 approx. 5 mi. to Hall Valley CG.

SINGLE RATE:	$10	OPEN DATES:	Apr-Oct*
# of SINGLE SITES:	9	MAX SPUR:	20 feet
		MAX STAY:	14 days
		ELEVATION:	9900 feet

35 Handcart
Grant • lat 39°29'00" lon 105°47'00"

DESCRIPTION: CG has tent only sites in this pine and fir forest on a small creek. No nearby fishing. Historic mining area. Bring own firewood. Mountain lionss, deer, foxeses, eagles, coyotes, and occasional black bears. Fills holidays. Red Cone and Webster for ATV or 4WD use. Motorcylce dirt bikes may use roads.

GETTING THERE: From Grant go W on US HWY 285 approx. 3 mi. to county route 60. Go W on 60 approx. 5 mi. to Handcart CG. Tent camping only.

SINGLE RATE:	$10	OPEN DATES:	Apr-Oct*
# of SINGLE SITES:	11		
		MAX STAY:	14 days
		ELEVATION:	9800 feet

 Campground has hosts   **Reservable sites**   **Accessible facilities**   **Fully developed**   **Semi-developed**   **Rustic facilities**

NOTE: Open dates listed are typical. Actual dates are dependent on conditions such as snow pack.

36 Happy Meadows
Lake George • lat 39°01'00" lon 105°21'45"

DESCRIPTION: This newly renovated CG sits in a park-like stand of cottonwood along the South Platte River. Fish for rainbow and brown trout. Wildlife includes deer, elk, and coyotes. Numerous hiking, horse, mountain biking, and OHV trails in area. CG can be busy weekends and holidays. Frequented by bears.

GETTING THERE: From Lake George go N on US HWY 24 approx. 1/2 mi. to county route 77. Go N on 77 approx. 1.5 mi. to county route 112. Go E on 112 approx. 1 mi. to Happy Meadows CG.

SINGLE RATE:	$9	OPEN DATES:	Yearlong
# of SINGLE SITES:	10	MAX SPUR:	25 feet
		MAX STAY:	14 days
		ELEVATION:	7900 feet

37 Hayden Creek
Coaldale • lat 38°19'48" lon 105°49'09"

DESCRIPTION: This CG is adjacent to the Sangre de Cristo Wilderness along the Middle Prong of Hayden Creek. Enjoy fishing in the creek. Oak, cottonwood, pine and cedar provide shade. Afternoon t-showers are common. Wildlife includes mountain lionss, deer, bears, and elk. Hike the Rainbow Trail.

GETTING THERE: From Coaldale go SW on county route 6 approx. 5 mi. to Hayden Creek CG.

SINGLE RATE:	$8	OPEN DATES:	May-Sept
# of SINGLE SITES:	11	MAX SPUR:	30 feet
		MAX STAY:	14 days
		ELEVATION:	8000 feet

38 Horseshoe
Fairplay • lat 39°12'06" lon 106°05'10"

DESCRIPTION: CG is located in a mature, park-like stand of pine and aspen. Boating and fishing at nearby Antero Reservoir. Wildlife includes deer, elk, and coyotes. Numerous hiking, horse, mountain biking, and OHV trails in area. Busy holidays and weekends. CG may be frequented by bears.

GETTING THERE: From Fairplay go S on US HWY 285 approx. 1.5 mi. to county route 18. Go W on 18 approx. 7 mi. to Horseshoe CG.

SINGLE RATE:	$9	OPEN DATES:	Yearlong
# of SINGLE SITES:	19	MAX SPUR:	30 feet
		MAX STAY:	14 days
		ELEVATION:	10560 feet

39 Indian Creek
Sedalia • lat 39°22'52" lon 105°05'55"

DESCRIPTION: This CG is located in a high pine forest. Bring your own firewood. Mountain lionss, deer, foxeses, eagles, coyotes, and occasional black bears can be seen in the area. No nearby fishing. Fills holidays and some weekends. Mountain bike and motorcylce dirt bike trails nearby.

GETTING THERE: From Sedalia go SW on state HWY 67 approx. 10 mi. to Indian Creek CG.

SINGLE RATE:	$10	OPEN DATES:	Apr-Oct*
# of SINGLE SITES:	11	MAX SPUR:	20 feet
		MAX STAY:	14 days
		ELEVATION:	7500 feet

40 Iron City
Buena Vista • lat 39°43'00" lon 106°21'30"

DESCRIPTION: CG sits along Chalk Creek, near the Chalk Cliffs among pine, fir, and aspen. Very busy in summer. Fishing is available in lower canyon. Several hiking trails and OHV roads in this area. Afternoon t-showers are common. CG may be frequented by bears. Visit the historic mining town of St. Elmo.

GETTING THERE: From Buena Vista go S on county route 321 approx. 8 mi. to county route 162. Go W on 162 approx. 9.5 mi. to Iron City CG.

SINGLE RATE:	$10	OPEN DATES:	June-Sept
# of SINGLE SITES:	15	MAX SPUR:	35 feet
		MAX STAY:	14 days
		ELEVATION:	9900 feet

41 Jackson Creek
Sedalia • lat 39°15'00" lon 105°05'00"

DESCRIPTION: This CG is set in ponderosa pine and douglas fir forest with great views of Devils Head Mountain. Fish for brook trout on nearby Jackson Creek. Bring your own firewood. Mountain lionss, deer, foxeses, eagles, coyotes, and occasional black bears. Fills holidays. Access to OHV trails nearby.

GETTING THERE: From Sedalia go S on state HWY 67 1 mi. to state HWY 105. Go SE on 105 approx. 7 mi. to county route 38. Go W on 38 approx. 7 mi. to forest route 507. Go S approx. 5 mi. to Jackson Creek CG.

SINGLE RATE:	$10	OPEN DATES:	Apr-Oct*
# of SINGLE SITES:	9	MAX SPUR:	20 feet
		MAX STAY:	14 days
		ELEVATION:	8100 feet

42   Jefferson Creek
Jefferson • lat 39°26'13" lon 105°51'39"

DESCRIPTION: CG is located in a park-like stand of ponderosa pine, lodgepole pine, and aspen. Boat and fish for rainbow, brown, and lake trout in nearby Jefferson Lake. Wildlife includes deer, elk, and coyotes. The Colorado Trail runs through the area. Busy weekends and holidays. Frequented by bears.

GETTING THERE: From Jefferson go NW on county route 35 approx. 3 mi. to county route 54. Go NW on 54 1.5 mi. Go NE on forest route 37 approx. 2 mi. to forest route 37. Go NW on 37 2 mi. to Jefferson Creek CG.

SINGLE RATE:	$10	OPEN DATES:	Yearlong
# of SINGLE SITES:	17	MAX SPUR:	30 feet
		MAX STAY:	14 days
		ELEVATION:	10100 feet

43 Kelsey
Buffalo Creek • lat 39°17'00" lon 105°15'30"

DESCRIPTION: Level, quiet, shady sites in a pine and fir forest. Forest and mountain peak views. No nearby fishing. Firewood for sale on site. Mountain lionss, deer, foxeses, eagles, coyotes, and occasional black bears. "Bike to Nature" mountain bike ride on Labor Day. Hike and mountain bike the Colorado Trail.

GETTING THERE: From Buffalo Creek go S on state HWY 126 approx. 8 mi. to Kelsey CG.

SINGLE RATE:	$10	OPEN DATES:	May-Sept
# of SINGLE SITES:	17	MAX SPUR:	20 feet
		MAX STAY:	14 days
		ELEVATION:	8000 feet

44 Kenosha Pass
Grant • lat 39°24'00" lon 105°45'30"

DESCRIPTION: CG set in a pine, fir, and aspen forest with views of the forest and mountain peaks. No nearby fishing. In the fall the colors are spectacular. Fills holidays. Bring own firewood. Mountain lionss, deer, foxeses, eagles, coyotes, and occasional black bears. Hiking and biking access to Colorado Trail.

GETTING THERE: From Grant go SW on US HWY 285 approx. 8 mi. to Kenosha Pass CG.

SINGLE RATE:	$10	OPEN DATES:	Apr-Oct*
# of SINGLE SITES:	25	MAX SPUR:	20 feet
		MAX STAY:	14 days
		ELEVATION:	10000 feet

45 Kite Lake
Fairplay • lat 39°19'45" lon 106°07'40"

DESCRIPTION: This CG is the highest national forest CG in the United States. Sites are located in a rocky area next to Kite Lake. Fish in lake for brook trout. Minimal wildlife. Numerous hiking and mountain biking opportunities in area. Tent camping only. No drinking water available on site.

GETTING THERE: From Fairplay go NW o state HWY 9 approx. 5 mi. to county route 8. Go NW on 8 approx. 5 mi. to Kite Lake CG. No trailers.

SINGLE RATE:	$7	OPEN DATES:	Yearlong
# of SINGLE SITES:	7	MAX SPUR:	15 feet
		MAX STAY:	14 days
		ELEVATION:	12000 feet

 Campground has hosts   **Reservable sites**   **Accessible facilities**   **Fully developed**   **Semi-developed**   **Rustic facilities**

NOTE: Open dates listed are typical. Actual dates are dependent on conditions such as snow pack.

46 La Vista
San Isabel • lat 37°59'00" lon 105°04'00"

DESCRIPTION: This CG is situated in a forest setting with views of the lake and mountains. Enjoy boating and fishing in the lake. Supplies and groceries can be found in San Isabel. Firewood is sold on site. There are many trails in the area. There is no dump station on site. Tents must be on pads.

GETTING THERE: La Vista CG is located in the San Isabel Recreation Area just SW of San Isabel.

SINGLE RATE:	$14	OPEN DATES:	May-Sept
# of SINGLE SITES:	29	MAX SPUR:	50 feet
		MAX STAY:	14 days
		ELEVATION:	8600 feet

51 Lost Park
Jefferson • lat 39°17'03" lon 105°30'16"

DESCRIPTION: This CG is located in ponderosa, lodgepole, and aspen. Boat and fish for rainbow, brown, and lake trout in nearby Jefferson Lake. Wildlife includes deer, elk, and coyotes. CG may be frequented by bears. Numerous hiking, horse, mountain biking, and OHV trails available in the area.

GETTING THERE: From Jefferson go NW on US HWY 285 approx. 1 mi. to county route 56 (Lost Park Road). Go E on 56 approx. 18 mi. to Lost Park CG.

SINGLE RATE:	$7	OPEN DATES:	Yearlong
# of SINGLE SITES:	12	MAX SPUR:	22 feet
		MAX STAY:	14 days
		ELEVATION:	10000 feet

47 Lake Creek
Westcliffe • lat 38°15'53" lon 105°39'43"

DESCRIPTION: This CG is situated in a dense stand of douglas fir and spruce with views Lake Creek. Fish for rainbow trout from creek. Well water available at CG. Deer and bears can be seen in the area. Supplies and groceries can be found in Westcliffe. Rainbow Trail is 1 mi. from CG.

GETTING THERE: From Westcliffe go NE on state HWY 69 approx. 11 mi. to county route 198. Go W on 198 approx. 3 mi. to Lake Creek CG.

SINGLE RATE:	$9	OPEN DATES:	May-Sept
# of SINGLE SITES:	12	MAX SPUR:	30 feet
		MAX STAY:	14 days
		ELEVATION:	8200 feet

52 May Queen
Leadville • lat 39°16'30" lon 106°25'00"

DESCRIPTION: Campground is situated in a shaded lodgepole pine forest, adjacent to Turquoise Lake. Seldom does the weather get over 80° during summer. Supplies at Leadville. CG is full most weekends. Firewood is available for sale at the campground. RV dump station at Molly Brown or Printer Boy CG's.

GETTING THERE: May Queen CG is located in the Turquoise Lake Recreation Area on the E shore of Torquoise Lake.

SINGLE RATE:	$12	OPEN DATES:	May-Sept
# of SINGLE SITES:	27	MAX SPUR:	32 feet
		MAX STAY:	14 days
		ELEVATION:	9900 feet

48 Lakeview
Balltown • lat 39°05'30" lon 106°22'30"

DESCRIPTION: This CG is situated in a ponderosa pine and sage habitat on Twin Lakes. Enjoy fishing in the lake. Please check fishing regulations. Supplies and groceries can be found in Balltown. Nature trails are nearby. Aluminum can recycling is provided. Firewood is available for sale at the CG.

GETTING THERE: Lakeview CG is located in the Twin Lakes Recreation Area on the N shore of Twin Lakes Reservoir.

SINGLE RATE:	$10	OPEN DATES:	May-Sept
# of SINGLE SITES:	59	MAX SPUR:	32 feet
		MAX STAY:	14 days
		ELEVATION:	9500 feet
# of GROUP SITES:	4		

53 Meadow Ridge
Woodland Park • lat 38°58'39" lon 104°59'05"

DESCRIPTION: This CG is situated in a shady ponderosa pine forest near Rampart Reservoir. Boat fishing on the lake. Dump station. Buy firewood locally. Black bears, deer, elk, turkeys, beavers, and small wildlife can be seen in the area. Hiking and mountain biking trails nearby.

GETTING THERE: From Woodland Park go N on county route 22 approx. 7 mi. to forest route 306. Go NE on 306 approx. 1 mi. to forest route 306A. Go N on 306A approx. 1/2 mi. to Meadow Ridge CG.

SINGLE RATE:	$10	OPEN DATES:	May-Dec
# of SINGLE SITES:	19	MAX SPUR:	21 feet
		MAX STAY:	14 days
		ELEVATION:	9200 feet

49 Lodgepole
Jefferson • lat 39°25'18" lon 105°50'33"

DESCRIPTION: CG is located in a park-like stand of ponderosa, lodgepole, and aspen. Boat and fish for rainbow, brown, and lake trout in nearby Jefferson Lake. Wildlife includes deer, elk, and coyotes. The Colorado Trail runs through the area. Busy weekends and holidays. May be frequented by bears.

GETTING THERE: From Jefferson go NW on county route 35 approx. 3 mi. to county route 54. Go NW on 54 approx. 1.5 mi. to forest route 37. Go NE on 37 approx. 2 mi. to forest route 37. Go NW on 37 approx. 1/2 mi. to Lodgepole CG.

SINGLE RATE:	$10	OPEN DATES:	Yearlong
# of SINGLE SITES:	35	MAX SPUR:	40 feet
		MAX STAY:	14 days
		ELEVATION:	9900 feet

54 Meadows Group
Buffalo Creek • lat 39°20'30" lon 105°20'30"

DESCRIPTION: CG situated in a pine and fir forest. Mild days. Fishing dock nearby. Rarely fills. Buffalo Creek Mountain Biking Area and Lost Creek Wilderness access via Colorado Trail. "Bike to Nature" mountain bike ride over Labor Day. Rates from $30 to $155, 25 to 150 persons.

GETTING THERE: From Buffalo Creek go S on state HWY 126 approx. 4 mi. to forest route 550. Go W on 550 approx. 4 mi. to forest route 543. Go SW on 543 approx. 1 mi. to Meadows CG.

		OPEN DATES:	Apr-Oct*
		MAX SPUR:	28 feet
GROUP RATE:	Varies	MAX STAY:	14 days
# of GROUP SITES:	2	ELEVATION:	7000 feet

50 Lone Rock
South Platte • lat 39°15'06" lon 105°14'03"

DESCRIPTION: CG set among ponderosa pine and douglas fir with paved roads. Fish for brook and rainbow trout on South Platte River. Fills weekends and holidays. Bring own firewood. Mountain lionss, deer, foxeses, eagles, coyotes, and occasional black bears. No nearby trails. Tubing, rafting, and boating are popular.

GETTING THERE: From South Platte go S on county route 97 approx. 10 mi. to state HWY 126. Go W on 126 approx. 1 mi. to Lone Rock CG.

SINGLE RATE:	$10	OPEN DATES:	Yearlong*
# of SINGLE SITES:	19	MAX SPUR:	20 feet
		MAX STAY:	14 days
		ELEVATION:	6400 feet

55 Meridian
Highland Park • lat 39°32'19" lon 105°31'23"

DESCRIPTION: This CG is set in a ponderosa pine and douglas fir forest. Fills quickly on holidays. Bring your own firewood. Mountain lionss, deer, foxeses, eagles, coyotes, and occasional black bears can be seen in the area. Horse riding and hiking on the Meridian Trail to Mount Evans Wilderness.

GETTING THERE: From Highland Park go N on county route 47 approx. 1 mi. to Meridian CG.

SINGLE RATE:	$10	OPEN DATES:	Apr-Oct*
# of SINGLE SITES:	18	MAX SPUR:	20 feet
		MAX STAY:	14 days
		ELEVATION:	9000 feet

 Campground has hosts   **Reservable sites**   **Accessible facilities**   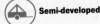 **Fully developed**   **Semi-developed**   **Rustic facilities**

NOTE: Open dates listed are typical. Actual dates are dependent on conditions such as snow pack.

56 Michigan Creek
Jefferson • lat 39°24'41" lon 105°53'01"

DESCRIPTION: CG is located in a park-like stand of ponderosa, lodgepole, and aspen. Boat and fish for trout in nearby Jefferson Lake. Wildlife includes deer, elk, and coyotes. May be frequented by bears. Numerous hiking, horse, mountain biking, and OHV trails in area. Visit scenic Georgia Pass.

GETTING THERE: From Jefferson go NW on county route 35 approx. 3 mi. to county route 54. Go NW on 54 approx. 2 mi. to forest route 54. Go W on 54 approx. 1/2 mi. to Michigan Creek CG.

SINGLE RATE:	$7	OPEN DATES:	Yearlong
# of SINGLE SITES:	13	MAX SPUR:	30 feet
		MAX STAY:	14 days
		ELEVATION:	10000 feet

57 Molly Brown
Leadville • lat 39°16'00" lon 106°22'00"

DESCRIPTION: CG Located in shaded a lodgepole pine forest, situated next to the lake. Fish from lake. Seldom gets over 80' during summer. Supplies are available at Leadville. Full most weekends. Firewood is for sale at the site. The nature trail is a popular attraction. A dump station is provided.

GETTING THERE: Molly Brown CG is located in the Turquoise Lake Recreation Area on the E shore of Torquoise Lake.

SINGLE RATE:	$12	OPEN DATES:	May-Sept
# of SINGLE SITES:	49	MAX SPUR:	32 feet
		MAX STAY:	14 days
		ELEVATION:	9900 feet

58 Molly Gulch
Woodland Park • lat 39°11'39" lon 105°20'36"

DESCRIPTION: Located in pine and fir forest with views of forest and wilderness mountain peaks. Nearby Goose Creek has brook and rainbow trout for fishing. Fills holidays. Bring your own firewood. Mountain lionss, deer, foxeses, eagles, coyotes, and occasional black bears. Horse riding and hiking access to Lost Creek Wilderness.

GETTING THERE: From Woodland Park go NW on state HWY 67 approx. 24 mi. to state HWY 126. Go SW on 126 approx. 3 mi. to county route 211. Go S on 211 approx. 10 mi. to Molly Gulch CG.

SINGLE RATE:	$10	OPEN DATES:	Apr-Oct*
# of SINGLE SITES:	15	MAX SPUR:	20 feet
		MAX STAY:	14 days
		ELEVATION:	7500 feet

59 Monarch Park
Poncha Springs • lat 38°30'56" lon 106°19'27"

DESCRIPTION: CG rests in a ponderosa pine and douglas fir near Monarch Pass and South Fork Arkansas River. Enjoy fishing in the river. Popular activities include hiking the Colorado Trail and the Continental Divide Trail, and 4-wheel driving. Afternoon t-showers are common. CG may be frequented by bears.

GETTING THERE: From Poncha Springs go W on US HWY 50 approx. 16 mi. to Monarch Park CG.

SINGLE RATE:	$10	OPEN DATES:	June-Sept
# of SINGLE SITES:	38	MAX SPUR:	40 feet
		MAX STAY:	14 days
		ELEVATION:	10500 feet

60 Mt. Princeton
Buena Vista • lat 38°42'51" lon 106°13'22"

DESCRIPTION: CG sits along Chalk Creek, near the Chalk Cliffs among pine, aspen, and cedar. Very busy in summer. Fishing is available in lower canyon. Several hiking trails and OHV roads in this area. Afternoon t-showers are common. CG may be frequented by bears. Visit the historic mining town of St. Elmo.

GETTING THERE: From Buena Vista go S on county route 321 approx. 8 mi. to county route 162. Go W on 162 approx. 2 mi. to Boot Leg CG.

SINGLE RATE:	$10	OPEN DATES:	May-Sept
# of SINGLE SITES:	17	MAX SPUR:	40 feet
		MAX STAY:	14 days
		ELEVATION:	8000 feet

61 North Fork
Maysville • lat 38°36'43" lon 106°19'10"

DESCRIPTION: This CG is located next to the North Fork Reservoir among pine, fir, and aspen. The North Fork South Arkansas River flows from the reservoir. Enjoy fishing in reservoir and river. Hike the Colorado Trail or use OHV roads in area. Afternoon t-showers are common. CG may be frequented by bears.

GETTING THERE: From Maysville go N on county route 240 approx. 10 mi. to North Fork Reservoir CG.

SINGLE RATE:	$6	OPEN DATES:	June-Sept
# of SINGLE SITES:	8	MAX SPUR:	20 feet
		MAX STAY:	14 days
		ELEVATION:	11000 feet

62 Oak Creek
Canon City • lat 38°17'47" lon 105°15'59"

DESCRIPTION: This primitive CG is situated in a dense forest of douglas fir and spruce. Enjoy fishing at the nearby creek. Deer and bears can be seen in the area. Supplies and groceries can be found in Canon City. Trails start from this CG and lead to Locke Mountain.

GETTING THERE: From Canon City go S on county route 143 approx. 10 mi. to Oak Creek CG.

SINGLE RATE:	No fee	OPEN DATES:	May-Sept
# of SINGLE SITES:	15	MAX SPUR:	25 feet
		MAX STAY:	14 days
		ELEVATION:	7600 feet

63 O'Haver Lake
Poncha Springs • lat 38°25'30" lon 106°08'40"

DESCRIPTION: This CG is located on the shore of O'Haver Lake surrounded by tall pine. Barrier free fishing pier available. Easy shoreline trail for fishing access. Interpretive programs on some weekends. Hike the Rainbow Trail. Afternoon thunder-showers are common. CG may be frequented by bears.

GETTING THERE: From Poncha Springs go S on US HWY 285 approx. 5 mi. to county route 200. Go SW on 200 approx. 3 mi. to O'Haver Lake CG.

SINGLE RATE:	$10	OPEN DATES:	May-Sept
# of SINGLE SITES:	29	MAX SPUR:	30 feet
		MAX STAY:	14 days
		ELEVATION:	9200 feet

64 Ophir
San Isabel • lat 38°03'36" lon 105°06'25"

DESCRIPTION: This CG is situated in a dense forest of douglas fir and spruce with views of Ophir Creek. Fish from the creek for trout. Deer, bears, and mountain lionss can be seen ocassionally at CG. Supplies can be found in San Isabel. Trails at Davenport CG. Look for Bishops Castle nearby.

GETTING THERE: From San Isabel go N on state HWY 165 approx. 6 mi. to Ophir CG.

SINGLE RATE:	$9	OPEN DATES:	May-Sept
# of SINGLE SITES:	31	MAX SPUR:	40 feet
		MAX STAY:	14 days
		ELEVATION:	8900 feet

65 Osprey
Sedalia • lat 39°21'00" lon 105°09'00"

DESCRIPTION: In open area on South Platte River. Good fishing for trout. Open views. Tubing, rafts, boats on river. Occasional deer, coyote, eagles in area. Fills most weekends and holidays. No nearby trails. No drinking water. Walk-in sites. Reduced fee and services off season.

GETTING THERE: From Sedalia go SW on state route 67 approx. 18 mi. to county route 97. Go N on 97 approx. 3 mi. to Osprey CG. Note: Nighthawk Hill is shorter, however, it is very steep and rocky. Park and walk in.

SINGLE RATE:	$9	OPEN DATES:	Yearlong
# of SINGLE SITES:	13		
		MAX STAY:	14 days
		ELEVATION:	7000 feet

 Campground has hosts   **Reservable sites**    **Accessible facilities**   **Fully developed**   **Semi-developed**   **Rustic facilities**

NOTE: Open dates listed are typical. Actual dates are dependent on conditions such as snow pack.

66 Ouzel

Sedalia • lat 39°18'00" lon 105°09'00"

DESCRIPTION: In open area on South Platte River. Good fishing for trout. Open views. Tubing, rafts, boats on river. Occasional deer, coyote, eagles in area. Fills most weekends and holidays. No nearby trails. No drinking water. Walk in sites. Reduced fee and services off season.

GETTING THERE: From Sedalia go SW on state route 67 approx. 18 mi. to county route 97. Go N on 97 approx. 5 mi. to Ouzel CG. Note: Nighthawk Hill is shorter, however, it is very steep and rocky. Park and walk in.

SINGLE RATE:	$9	OPEN DATES:	Yearlong
# of SINGLE SITES:	13	MAX STAY:	14 days
		ELEVATION:	7000 feet

67 Painted Rocks

Woodland Park • lat 39°05'04" lon 105°06'19"

DESCRIPTION: CG set in a shady ponderosa pine forest. In Monitor Park Rec. Area. Fish for rainbow and brook trout. Black bears, deer, elk, turkeys, beavers, and small wildlife in area. Gather firewood locally. Bike popular Centennial Bike Trail; other hike trails and interpretive programs on weekends.

GETTING THERE: From Woodland Park go N on state HWY 67 approx. 6 mi. to county route 78. Go NW on 78 approx. 1 mi. to Painted Rocks CG.

SINGLE RATE:	$10	OPEN DATES:	May-Sept
# of SINGLE SITES:	18	MAX SPUR:	30 feet
		MAX STAY:	14 days
		ELEVATION:	7900 feet

68 Parry Peak

Balltown • lat 39°04'30" lon 106°24'30"

DESCRIPTION: This CG is situated in a ponderosa pine and sage habitat on Twin Lakes. Fish from the lake. Supplies and groceries are available at Balltown. Nature trails are nearby. Aluminum can recycling is provided. Firewood is available for sale at the CG. RV dump station at White Star CG.

GETTING THERE: Parry Peak CG is located in the Twin Lakes Recreation Area on the W side of Twin Lakes Reservoir.

SINGLE RATE:	$10	OPEN DATES:	May-Sept
# of SINGLE SITES:	26	MAX SPUR:	32 feet
		MAX STAY:	14 days
		ELEVATION:	9500 feet

69 Pike Community Group

Woodland Park • lat 39°04'07" lon 105°05'20"

DESCRIPTION: Warm days, cool nights, frequent noon t-storms. Group sites only. Playground, sand volleyball court, softball field, and horseshoe pits. RV dump station. Black bears, deer, elk, turkeys, and beavers. Fee is per vehicle; max of 150 persons. $9/vehicle, $4/extra vehicle. Centennial Trail nearby.

GETTING THERE: From Woodland Park go N on state HWY 67 approx. 2.5 mi. to Pike Community Group CG.

		OPEN DATES:	May-Sept
		MAX SPUR:	30 feet
GROUP RATE:	Varies	MAX STAY:	14 days
# of GROUP SITES:	53	ELEVATION:	7700 feet

70 Platte River

Buffalo Creek • lat 39°17'38" lon 105°12'14"

DESCRIPTION: CG set among fir and pine along the river. Tent sites only. Fish for brook and rainbow trout. Fills weekends and holidays. Bring own firewood. Mountain lionss, deer, foxeses, eagles, coyotes, and occasional black bears. No nearby trails. Tubing, rafting, and boating on the river are popular.

GETTING THERE: From Buffalo Creek go NE on county route 96 approx. 8 mi. to county route 97. Go S on 97 approx. 8 mi. to Platte River CG.

SINGLE RATE:	$10	OPEN DATES:	Yearlong*
# of SINGLE SITES:	10		
		MAX STAY:	14 days
		ELEVATION:	6300 feet

71 Ponderosa Group

San Isabel • lat 37°59'00" lon 105°04'00"

DESCRIPTION: CG set in a dense forest of douglas fir and spruce with views of St. Charles River running through the middle of CG. Fish from river for trout. Deer, bears, and the occasional mountain lions can be seen in the area. CG full on holidays. Numerous trails in the area. Supplies at San Isabel. Well water at CG.

GETTING THERE: Ponderosa CG is located in the San Isabel Recreation Area just SW of San Isabel.

		OPEN DATES:	May-Sept
		MAX SPUR:	20 feet
GROUP RATE:	$35	MAX STAY:	14 days
# of GROUP SITES:	1	ELEVATION:	8800 feet

72 Printer Boy
Leadville • lat 39°16'00" lon 106°22'00"

DESCRIPTION: CG in a high mountain valley surrounded by snow capped peaks. Near Turquoise Lake. Summers seldom get over 80'. Full most weekends. RV dump station available at CG. There is a centrally located cooking shelter available on a firt come, firt serve basis. Firewood is sold on site.

GETTING THERE: Printer Boy CG is located in the Turquoise Lake Recreation Area on the E shore of Torquoise Lake.

		OPEN DATES:	May-Sept
		MAX SPUR:	99 feet
GROUP RATE:	Varies	MAX STAY:	14 days
# of GROUP SITES:	4	ELEVATION:	9900 feet

73 Purgatoire
Cuchara • lat 37°15'00" lon 105°07'00"

DESCRIPTION: This CG is situated in a dense forest of douglas fir and spruce with a stream nearby. Deer and bears can be seen occasionally around CG. No designated trails around CG, just venture off into the forest to explore. Supplies and groceries can be found in Cuchara.

GETTING THERE: From Cuchara go S on state HWY 12 approx. 13.5 mi. to forest route 34. Go W on 34 approx. 5.5 mi. to Purgatoire CG.

SINGLE RATE:	$9	OPEN DATES:	May-Sept
# of SINGLE SITES:	23	MAX SPUR:	40 feet
		MAX STAY:	14 days
		ELEVATION:	9800 feet

74 Redrocks Group
Woodland Park • lat 39°02'39" lon 105°04'47"

DESCRIPTION: Mild days and cool nights. Frequent noon t-storms. Hike Red Rocks Trail #612. Asphalt bike trail #669 connects to CGs in Manitou Park Rec Area. Fishing in Manitou Park Lakes. Black bears, deer, elk, turkeys, and beavers. Reservations required. Max of 125 persons. Fee: $30-$130, depending on number of persons.

GETTING THERE: From Woodland Park go N on state HWY 67 approx. 3 mi. to Redrocks CG.

		OPEN DATES:	Apr-Oct
		MAX SPUR:	30 feet
GROUP RATE:	Varies	MAX STAY:	14 days
# of GROUP SITES:	90	ELEVATION:	8200 feet

75 Riverside

Lake George • lat 38°57'37" lon 105°22'24"

DESCRIPTION: CG resides in a mature, park-like stand of pine, spruce, and aspen. Fish for rainbow and brown trout in adjacent South Platte River. Wildlife includes deer, elk, and coyotes in area. Can be busy weekends and holidays. Numerous hiking, horse, mountain biking, and OHV trails in area. Frequented by bears.

GETTING THERE: Riverside CG is located in Eleven Mile Canyon. From Lake George go S on county route 96 approx. 2 mi. to Riverside CG.

SINGLE RATE:	$10	OPEN DATES:	Yearlong
# of SINGLE SITES:	13	MAX SPUR:	30 feet
		MAX STAY:	14 days
		ELEVATION:	8000 feet

 Campground has hosts   **Reservable sites**   **Accessible facilities**   **Fully developed**   **Semi-developed**   **Rustic facilities**

NOTE: Open dates listed are typical. Actual dates are dependent on conditions such as snow pack.

76 Round Mountain
Lake George • lat 39°00'13" lon 105°25'00"

DESCRIPTION: CG is located in a mature, park-like stand of ponderosa pine and spruce. Fish for rainbow and brown trout in nearby South Platte River. Wildlife includes coyotes, deer, and elk. Numerous hiking, horse, mountain biking, and OHV trails in area. CG may be frequented by bears.

GETTING THERE: From Lake George go NW on US HWY 24 approx. 5 mi. to Round Mountain CG.

SINGLE RATE:	$9	OPEN DATES:	Yearlong
# of SINGLE SITES:	16	MAX SPUR:	35 feet
		MAX STAY:	14 days
		ELEVATION:	8500 feet

81 Southside
San Isabel • lat 37°59'00" lon 105°04'00"

DESCRIPTION: CG is in a mountain setting with lakes and streams. Sites are close to the lake, but not very private. Boating and fishing on lakes and streams. Numerous wildlife in the area. Firewood is for sale at the CG. Hiking trails in the area for recreation. This CG is not desirable for tents. No RV hook-ups.

GETTING THERE: Southside CG is located in the San Isabel Recreation Area just SW of San Isabel.

SINGLE RATE:	$9	OPEN DATES:	May-Sept
# of SINGLE SITES:	8	MAX SPUR:	40 feet
		MAX STAY:	14 days
		ELEVATION:	8800 feet

77 Saint Charles
San Isabel • lat 37°59'00" lon 105°04'00"

DESCRIPTION: This CG is situated in a mountain setting with lakes and streams. Enjoy boating and fishing on lakes and streams. There is numerous wildlife in the CG area. Firewood is for sale at the campsite. There are no RV hook-ups. There are hiking trails in the area for recreation.

GETTING THERE: Saint Charles CG is located in the San Isabel Recreation Area just SW of San Isabel.

SINGLE RATE:	$9	OPEN DATES:	May-Sept
# of SINGLE SITES:	15	MAX SPUR:	45 feet
		MAX STAY:	14 days
		ELEVATION:	8800 feet

82 Spillway
Lake George • lat 38°55'00" lon 105°29'00"

DESCRIPTION: CG sits in a mature, park-like stand of pine, spruce, and aspen. Fish for rainbow and brown trout in adjacent South Platte River. Wildlife includes deer, elk, and coyotes. Can be busy weekends and holidays. On site trailhead leads to scenic canyon overlook. Frequented by bears.

GETTING THERE: Spillway CG is located is Eleven Mile Canyon. From Lake George go S on county route 96 approx. 10 mi. to Spillway CG.

SINGLE RATE:	$10	OPEN DATES:	Yearlong
# of SINGLE SITES:	23	MAX SPUR:	30 feet
		MAX STAY:	14 days
		ELEVATION:	8500 feet

78 Selkirk
Como • lat 39°22'21" lon 105°57'05"

DESCRIPTION: CG is located in a mature, park-like stand of lodgepole pine. This small, quiet CG is a great place to relax. Wildlife includes coyotes, deer, and elk. CG may be frequented by bears. Numerous trails in area. Visit scenic Boreas Pass. No drinking water available on site.

GETTING THERE: From Como go NW on county route 50 approx. 3.5 mi. to forest route 801 and Selkirk CG. 4WD recommended.

SINGLE RATE:	$7	OPEN DATES:	Yearlong
# of SINGLE SITES:	15	MAX SPUR:	25 feet
		MAX STAY:	14 days
		ELEVATION:	10500 feet

83 Springdale
Woodland Park • lat 39°01'15" lon 105°00'58"

DESCRIPTION: CG is located 3.5 mi. from Rampart Reservoir Rec area. Mild days, cool nights, frequent noon t-storms. No drinking water available on site. Supplies in Woodland Park. Gather firewood locally. Black bears, deer, elk, turkeys, beavers, and small wildlife in area.

GETTING THERE: From Woodland Park go NW on county route 22 approx. 3.5 mi. to Springdale CG.

SINGLE RATE:	$9	OPEN DATES:	May-Sept
		MAX SPUR:	30 feet
GROUP RATE:	$13	MAX STAY:	14 days
# of GROUP SITES:	30	ELEVATION:	9200 feet

79 Silver Dollar
Leadville • lat 39°15'30" lon 106°22'00"

DESCRIPTION: Located in a shaded lodgepole pine forest with views of snow capped peaks and Turquise Lake. Summers seldom over 80'. Full most weekends. A boat ramp is provided. Firewood is available for sale at the CG. There is a trail to the lake. RV dump station by Molly Brown or Printer Boy CGs.

GETTING THERE: Silver Dollar CG is located in the Turquoise Lake Recreation Area on the E shore of Torquoise Lake.

SINGLE RATE:	$12	OPEN DATES:	May-Sept
# of SINGLE SITES:	43	MAX SPUR:	22 feet
		MAX STAY:	14 days
		ELEVATION:	9900 feet

84 Springer Gulch
Lake George • lat 38°55'30" lon 105°25'30"

DESCRIPTION: CG sits in a mature, park-like stand of pine, spruce, and aspen. Fish for rainbow and brown trout in adjacent South Platte River. Wildlife includes deer, elk, and coyotes. Can be busy weekends and holidays. Numerous hiking, horse, mountain biking, and OHV trails in area. CG may be frequented by bears.

GETTING THERE: Springer Gulch CG is located is Eleven Mile Canyon. From Lake George go S on county route 96 approx. 5 mi. to forest route 96E. Go W on 96E approx. 1/4 mi. to Springer Gulch CG.

SINGLE RATE:	$10	OPEN DATES:	Yearlong
# of SINGLE SITES:	15	MAX SPUR:	30 feet
		MAX STAY:	14 days
		ELEVATION:	8300 feet

80 South Meadows
Woodland Park • lat 39°03'53" lon 105°05'32"

DESCRIPTION: CG set in a ponderosa pine forest. In Monitor Park Rec. Area. Fish for rainbow and brook trout. Buy firewood and basic supplies at small store. Black bears, deer, elk, turkeys, beavers, and small wildlife. Bike popular Centennial Bike Trail; other hiking trails and interpretive programs on weekends.

GETTING THERE: From Woodland Park go N on state HWY 67 approx. 2.5 mi. to South Meadows CG.

SINGLE RATE:	$12	OPEN DATES:	Yearlong
# of SINGLE SITES:	64	MAX SPUR:	30 feet
		MAX STAY:	14 days
		ELEVATION:	8000 feet

85 Spruce Group
San Isabel • lat 37°59'00" lon 105°04'00"

DESCRIPTION: CG in a dense forest of douglas fir and spruce with views of St. Charles River running through middle of CG. Fish from river for trout. Deer, bears, and the occasional mountain lions can be seen in the area. CG full on holidays. Numerous trails in the area. Supplies at San Isabel. Well water available at CG.

GETTING THERE: Spruce CG is located in the San Isabel Recreation Area just SW of San Isabel.

		OPEN DATES:	May-Sept
		MAX SPUR:	20 feet
GROUP RATE:	$35	MAX STAY:	14 days
# of GROUP SITES:	1	ELEVATION:	8800 feet

 Campground has hosts   **Reservable sites**   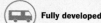 **Accessible facilities**   **Fully developed**   **Semi-developed**   **Rustic facilities**

NOTE: Open dates listed are typical. Actual dates are dependent on conditions such as snow pack.

86 Spruce Grove
Lake George • lat 39°14'33" lon 105°18'19"

DESCRIPTION: CG sits in an area with pine, spruce, and large rock outcroppings. The Tarryall River runs adjacent to CG. Wildlife includes coyotes, bighorn sheep, deer, and elk. Numerous hiking, horse, mountain biking and OHV trails in area including one on site TH. CG may be frequented by bears.

GETTING THERE: From Lake George go NW on US HWY 24 approx. 6 mi. to county route 31. Go N on 31 approx. 9 mi. to Spruce Grove CG.

SINGLE RATE:	$9	OPEN DATES:	Yearlong
# of SINGLE SITES:	27	MAX SPUR:	35 feet
		MAX STAY:	14 days
		ELEVATION:	8600 feet

87 Tabor
Leadville • lat 39°16'00" lon 106°21'30"

DESCRIPTION: This CG is set in a high mountain valley surrounded by snow capped peaks with views of Turquoise Lake. Fishing from the lake. Supplies are available at Leadville. Summers seldom get over 80'. Full most weekends. RV dump stations at Molly Brown or Printer Boy CGs. Many trails in area.

GETTING THERE: Tabor CG is located in the Turquoise Lake Recreation Area on the E shore of Torquoise Lake.

SINGLE RATE:	$10	OPEN DATES:	May-Sept
# of SINGLE SITES:	44	MAX SPUR:	37 feet
		MAX STAY:	14 days
		ELEVATION:	9900 feet

88 The Crags
Woodland Park • lat 38°52'16" lon 105°07'16"

DESCRIPTION: Secluded site with common noon t-storms. Heavy use all summer. The Crags Trail #664, and access to Mueller State Park nearby. Black bears, deer, elk, turkeys, and beavers in area. Historic Cripple Creek and Victor 15 miles S. Winter activities include x-country skiing. Bears-proof trash receptacles.

GETTING THERE: From Woodland Park go SW on US HWY 24 approx. 7 mi. to state HWY 67. Go S approx. 4.5 mi. to forest route 1094. Go E approx. 3.5 mi. to The Crags CG. Road is narrow with sharp curves.

SINGLE RATE:	$9	OPEN DATES:	Yearlong
# of SINGLE SITES:	17	MAX SPUR:	22 feet
		MAX STAY:	14 days
		ELEVATION:	10100 feet

89 Thunder Ridge
Woodland Park • lat 38°58'40" lon 104°58'54"

DESCRIPTION: This CG is situated in a high and shady pine forest. Boating and fishing on nearby Rampart Reservoir. Gather firewood locally. Supplies can be found in Woodland Park. Black bears, deer, elk, turkeys, beavers, and small wildlife in the area. Hiking trails available from site.

GETTING THERE: From Woodland Park go N on county route 22 approx. 7 mi. to forest route 306. Go NE on 306 approx. 1.5 mi. to forest route 306B. Go N on 306B approx. 1/2 mi. to Thunder Ridge CG.

SINGLE RATE:	$10	OPEN DATES:	May-Sept
# of SINGLE SITES:	21	MAX SPUR:	30 feet
		MAX STAY:	14 days
		ELEVATION:	9200 feet

90 Timberline
Grant • lat 39°26'00" lon 105°45'15"

DESCRIPTION: This CG is situated among ponderosa pine and douglas fir. Nearby Hoosier River affords trout fishing. CG tends to fill up quickly on holidays. Bring your own firewood. Mountain lionss, deer, foxeses, eagles, coyotes, and occasional black bears in the area. No nearby trails.

GETTING THERE: From Grant go W on US HWY 285 approx. 6 mi. to Timberline CG.

		OPEN DATES:	Apr-Oct*
		MAX SPUR:	28 feet
GROUP RATE:	Varies	MAX STAY:	14 days
# of GROUP SITES:	2	ELEVATION:	9800 feet

91 Trail Creek
Florissant • lat 39°07'10" lon 105°10'45"

DESCRIPTION: Located between Westcreek and Florissant offering quiet and solitude. Gather firewood locally. Heavy summer use, light during winter and spring. Supplies in Florissant. Black bears, deer, elk, turkeys, and beavers. 4WD, ATV, and motorcycle roads and trails network through area. No drinking water.

GETTING THERE: From Florissant go N on county route 3 approx. 14 mi. to Trail Creek CG.

SINGLE RATE:	$5	OPEN DATES:	May-Oct
# of SINGLE SITES:	5	MAX SPUR:	30 feet
		MAX STAY:	14 days
		ELEVATION:	7800 feet

92 Twin Eagles Trailhead
Lake George • lat 39°09'09" lon 105°26'46"

DESCRIPTION: CG sits in an area with pine and spruce. The Tarryall River runs near CG. Wildlife include coyote, bighorn sheep, deer, and elk. Numerous hiking, horse, mountain biking and OHV trails in area including on-site trailhead. CG may be frequented by bears. No drinking water. CG has some walk-in sites.

GETTING THERE: From Lake George go NW on US HWY 24 approx. 1/2 mi. to county route 77. Go N on 77 approx. 14 mi. to Twin Eagles Trailhead CG.

SINGLE RATE:	$7	OPEN DATES:	Yearlong
# of SINGLE SITES:	9	MAX SPUR:	25 feet
		MAX STAY:	14 days
		ELEVATION:	8600 feet

93 Twin Peaks
Balltown • lat 39°04'30" lon 106°24'30"

DESCRIPTION: This CG is situated in a ponderosa pine and sage habitat on Twin Lakes. Fish from the lake. Supplies and groceries are available at Balltown. Nature trails are nearby. Aluminum can recycling is provided. Firewood is available for sale at the CG. RV dump station at White Star CG.

GETTING THERE: Twin Peaks CG is located in the Twin Lakes Recreation Area on the W side of Twin Lakes Reservoir.

SINGLE RATE:	$10	OPEN DATES:	May-Sept
# of SINGLE SITES:	39	MAX SPUR:	32 feet
		MAX STAY:	14 days
		ELEVATION:	9600 feet

94 Weston
Fairplay • lat 39°04'44" lon 106°08'10"

DESCRIPTION: CG is located in mature, park-like stand of pine and aspen. A small stream with brook trout runs adjacent to CG. Boating and fishing at nearby Antero Reservoir. Wildlife includes deer, elk, and coyotes. Numerous hiking, horse, mountain biking, and OHV trails in area. Frequented by bears.

GETTING THERE: From Fairplay go S on US HWY 285 approx. 4.5 mi. to county route 5. Go SW on 5 approx. 6 mi. to county route 22. Go SW on 22 approx. 4 mi. to Weston CG.

SINGLE RATE:	$9	OPEN DATES:	Yearlong
# of SINGLE SITES:	14	MAX SPUR:	30 feet
		MAX STAY:	14 days
		ELEVATION:	10200 feet

95 White Star
Balltown • lat 39°05'30" lon 106°22'30"

DESCRIPTION: This CG is located in a ponderosa pine and sage habitat on Twin Lake. This CG tends to fill up quickly on weekends and holidays. A dump station for RVs is available on site. Summer days seldom get over eighty degrees. Firewood is available nearby. There are several trails in the area.

GETTING THERE: White Star CG is located in the Twin Lakes Recreation Area on the N shore of Twin Lakes Reservoir.

SINGLE RATE:	$10	OPEN DATES:	May-Sept
# of SINGLE SITES:	68	MAX SPUR:	32 feet
		MAX STAY:	14 days
		ELEVATION:	9300 feet

 Campground has hosts   **Reservable sites**   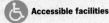 **Accessible facilities**   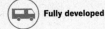 **Fully developed**   **Semi-developed**   **Rustic facilities**

96 Whiteside
Grant • lat 39˚29'00" lon 105˚42'00"

DESCRIPTION: CG is now in an open area due to a burn over fire in 1999. Tent sites only. Geneva Creek is nearby offering quiet but no fish. Fills holidays. Bring own firewood. Mountain lionss, deer, foxeses, eagles, coyotes, and occasional black bears. Approx. 3 mi. to TH for access to Mount Evans Wilderness.

GETTING THERE: From Grant go NW on county route 62 approx. 2 mi. to Whiteside CG. Tent sites only.

SINGLE RATE:	$10	OPEN DATES:	Apr-Oct*
# of SINGLE SITES:	5		
		MAX STAY:	14 days
		ELEVATION:	8900 feet

97 Wigwam
Buffalo Creek • lat 39˚14'30" lon 105˚15'57"

DESCRIPTION: On the South Platte River among ponderosa pine and douglas fir with walk-in sites. Fish for brook and rainbow trout on river. Fills holidays. Bring your own firewood. Mountain lionss, deer, foxeses, eagles, coyotes, and occasional black bears. No trails nearby.

GETTING THERE: From Buffalo Creek go S on state HWY 126 approx. 12 mi. to Wigwam CG.

SINGLE RATE:	$10	OPEN DATES:	Apr-Oct*
# of SINGLE SITES:	10	MAX SPUR:	20 feet
		MAX STAY:	14 days
		ELEVATION:	6600 feet

98 Wildhorn
Florissant • lat 39˚03'00" lon 105˚15'15"

DESCRIPTION: CG set between Westcreek and Florissant offering quiet and solitude. Gather firewood locally. Heavy summer use, light during winter and spring. Supplies in Florissant. Black bears, deer, elk, turkeys, and beavers. 4WD, ATV, and motorcycle roads and trails network through area. Pack it in/pack it out.

GETTING THERE: From Florissant go N on county route 3 approx. 8 mi. to county route 33. Go W on 33 approx. 1 mi. to Wildhorn CG. Road is narrow and winding; not well suited for large trailers or RVs.

SINGLE RATE:	$9	OPEN DATES:	May-Oct
# of SINGLE SITES:	9	MAX SPUR:	16 feet
		MAX STAY:	14 days
		ELEVATION:	9100 feet

99 Wye
Colorado Springs • lat 38˚44'14" lon 104˚56'31"

DESCRIPTION: Located approx. 1.5 mi. E of Penrose - Rosemont Reservoir. Mild summer days, cool nights with noon t-storms common. Fishing on Reservoir. Black bears, deer, elk, turkeys, and beavers in area. No drinking water, no services. Supplies in Broadmoor. Gather firewood locally. Cross-country skiing in winter.

GETTING THERE: From Colorado Springs/Broadmoor go W Gold Camp Road approx. 5 miles. Go right on FDR 381 1/2 mi. to Wye CG.

SINGLE RATE:	$9	OPEN DATES:	May-Oct
# of SINGLE SITES:	21	MAX SPUR:	22 feet
		MAX STAY:	14 days
		ELEVATION:	10300 feet

1 Carrizo Canyon
Springfield • lat 37˚07'50" lon 103˚00'50"

DESCRIPTION: CG is located in junipers on the East Fork of Carrizo Creek. An easy 1/2 mi. hiking trail takes you along the creek and back to the picnic area. Fish and swim in the creek. Birds, quail, big horn sheep, and antelope can be found in the area. Supplies available in Springfield.

GETTING THERE: From Springfield go S on US HWY 287 approx. 17 mi. to county road M. Go W on M approx. 22 mi. to forest route 539. Go S on 539 approx. 2 mi. to Carrizo Canyon CG.

SINGLE RATE:	No fee	OPEN DATES:	Yearlong
# of SINGLE SITES:	1	MAX SPUR:	25 feet
		MAX STAY:	14 days
		ELEVATION:	4720 feet

2 Picture Canyon
Springfield • lat 37˚00'50" lon 102˚44'30"

DESCRIPTION: Camping is permitted only, in parking area of the Picture Canyon Picnic Area. Several springs in area support a variety of plants and wildlife. Homestead ruins from the Dust Bowl era remain. Supplies available at Springfield. Many animals can be seen in the area.

GETTING THERE: From Springfield go S on US HWY 287 approx. 20 mi. to county route J. Go W on J approx. 10 mi. to county route 18. Go S on 18 approx. 5 mi. to the Picture Canyon CG.

SINGLE RATE:	No fee	OPEN DATES:	Yearlong
# of SINGLE SITES:	1	MAX SPUR:	25 feet
		MAX STAY:	14 days
		ELEVATION:	4300 feet

3 Vogel Canyon
La Junta • lat 37˚45'20" lon 103˚30'00"

DESCRIPTION: Camping is permited in parking area only, of picnic ground located in juniper trees and shortgrass prairie in geologically scenic Vogel Canyon. View rock art, left on the canyon walls, by Native Americans 300-800 years ago. Also view sections of the historic Santa Fe Trail and station ruins. Four hiking trails in area.

GETTING THERE: From La Junta go S on state HWY 109 approx. 13 mi. to county route 802. Go W on 802 approx. 1 mi. to forest route 505A. Go S on 505A approx. 1/2 mi. to Vogel Canyon CG.

SINGLE RATE:	No fee	OPEN DATES:	Yearlong
# of SINGLE SITES:	1	MAX SPUR:	25 feet
		MAX STAY:	14 days
		ELEVATION:	4375 feet

 Campground has hosts   **Reservable sites**   **Accessible facilities**   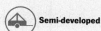 **Fully developed**    **Semi-developed**   **Rustic facilities**

NOTE: Open dates listed are typical. Actual dates are dependent on conditions such as snow pack.

USFS Photo

RIO GRANDE NATIONAL FOREST

Established in 1908 by President Theodore Roosevelt, the Rio Grande National Forest includes almost two million acres of land on the eastern slope of the Continental Divide. Parts of two spectacular mountain ranges, the San Juan and the Sangre de Cristo, are within the forest.

Also included are the headwaters of the third longest river in the United States–the Rio Grande del Norte, or "Great river of the North," as it was known by the early Spanish and Indian inhabitants of the Southwest.

From the floor of the San Luis Valley, visitors to the Rio Grande have a view to the east of the pristine Sangre de Cristo Range, with 14,300 foot Mt. Blanca. To the west, the San Juan Mountains dominate the skyline.

Fishing in the Conejos and Rio Grande Rivers or on one of the forest's many lakes and streams promises hours of enjoyment and great fare for the table back at camp. Hikers, horseback riders, and mountain bikers will all find numerous trails. The forest also has a variety of motorcycle and all-terrain vehicle roads.

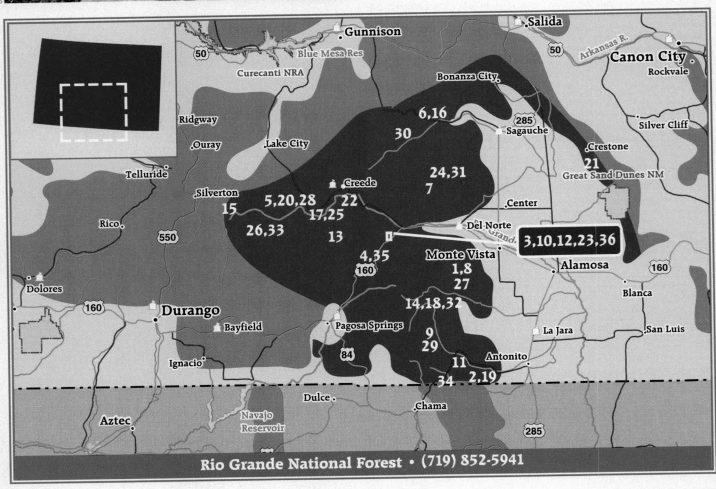

Rio Grande National Forest • (719) 852-5941

1 Alamosa
Monte Vista • lat 37°22'46" lon 106°20'41"

DESCRIPTION: This CG is situated on the Alamosa River in a spruce and cottonwood forest. Cool summer temperatures, steep canyon walls provide shade. Supplies and groceries are available at Monte Vista. Birds, elk, deer, and occasional bighorn sheep can be seen in the area. This CG is rarely full.

GETTING THERE: From Monte Vista go S on state HWY 15 approx. 12 mi. to primary forest route 250. Go W on 250 approx. 13 mi. to Alamosa CG.

SINGLE RATE:	No fee	OPEN DATES:	Yearlong*
# of SINGLE SITES:	10	MAX SPUR:	60 feet
		MAX STAY:	14 days
		ELEVATION:	8500 feet

2 Aspen Glade
Canon • lat 37°04'23" lon 106°16'27"

DESCRIPTION: CG in spruce forest setting with open areas on Conejos River. Scenic views of Conejos River Valley. Trout fishery on Conejos River. Supplies at Fox Creek Store. Elk, deer, and various birds in area. CG usually full on weekends. Buy firewood from ALandL. No close hiking trails; see forest map for trails.

GETTING THERE: From Canon go W on state HWY 17 approx. 16 mi. to Aspen Glade CG.

SINGLE RATE:	$11	OPEN DATES:	May-Sept
# of SINGLE SITES:	34	MAX SPUR:	90 feet
		MAX STAY:	14 days
		ELEVATION:	8500 feet

3 Beaver Creek
South Fork • lat 37°36'58" lon 106°40'32"

DESCRIPTION: In overstory of large pine and grass near Beaver Creek. Mild days, t-storms June-Aug. Stream or lake fish creek and reservoir for trout. Deer and elk in area. Fills July 4. Buy firewood from LandL. Horse, hiking, and ATV trails nearby on Trout Creek and Cross Creek Trails. Ticks and mosquitos are light.

GETTING THERE: From South Fork go S on US HWY 160 approx. 1 mi. to primary forest route 20. Go S on 20 approx. 2.5 mi. to Beaver Creek CG.

SINGLE RATE:	$10	OPEN DATES:	May-Sept
# of SINGLE SITES:	19	MAX SPUR:	35 feet
		MAX STAY:	14 days
		ELEVATION:	8400 feet

4 Big Meadows
South Fork • lat 37°32'17" lon 106°47'46"

DESCRIPTION: CG in a shady spruce forest near a meadow and reservoir. Views of lake and Weminuche Wilderness. Mild days, frequent afternoon t-storms. Fish for stocked trout on creek and lake; boat ramp. Elk and deer in area. Fills July 4. Buy firewood from LandL. Supplies 11 mi. away. Horse, hiking, and ATV trails.

GETTING THERE: From South Fork go S on US HWY 160 approx. 11 mi. to forest route 410. Go SW on 410 approx. 1.5 mi. to Big Meadows CG.

SINGLE RATE:	$11	OPEN DATES:	May-Sept
# of SINGLE SITES:	56	MAX SPUR:	35 feet
		MAX STAY:	14 days
		ELEVATION:	9500 feet

5 Bristol Head
Creede • lat 37°49'00" lon 107°09'45"

DESCRIPTION: CG in park like grass meadow on South Clear Creek. Views of Bristol Head Peak. Warm days, cool nights with noon t-storms June-Aug. Supplies in Creede or Lake City. Stream fish for trout. Elk, deer, moose, beavers and waterfowl. Rarely full. Buy firewood from LandL. Hike 1/4 mi. along creek to waterfall.

GETTING THERE: From Creede go W on state HWY 149 approx. 21 mi. to Bristol Head CG.

SINGLE RATE:	$9	OPEN DATES:	May-Sept
# of SINGLE SITES:	16	MAX SPUR:	30 feet
		MAX STAY:	14 days
		ELEVATION:	9500 feet

6 Buffalo Pass
Saguache • lat 38°11'05" lon 106°30'59"

DESCRIPTION: CG is located in park-like grove of ponderosa pine and douglas fir. Frequent afternoon thundershowers. Trout fishing nearby at East Pass Creek. Historical stage route. Supplies 25 mi. to Saguache. Mountain sheep, deer, and elk. Seldom full. Gather firewood locally. Ticks in early spring.

GETTING THERE: From Saguache go W on state HWY 114 approx. 25 mi. to Buffalo Pass CG.

SINGLE RATE:	$5	OPEN DATES:	May-Dec
# of SINGLE SITES:	23	MAX SPUR:	25 feet
		MAX STAY:	14 days
		ELEVATION:	9000 feet

7 Cathedral
Alpine • lat 37°49'20" lon 106°36'16"

DESCRIPTION: In aspen grove with grass near meadow and creek. Views of rock bluffs and forest slopes. Cool nights, noon t-storms July-Aug. Supplies in South Fork. 1848 Expedition camp 3 mi. hike. Stream fish for trout on Embargo Creek. Gather firewood. Deer and elk in area. Never fills. Horse, hiking, and ATV trails.

GETTING THERE: From Alpine go N on forest route 650 approx. 3.5 mi. to forest route 640. Go N on 640 approx. 7 mi. to Cathedral CG. 4WD recommended; road rough and rocky.

SINGLE RATE:	No fee	OPEN DATES:	May-Sept
# of SINGLE SITES:	33	MAX SPUR:	35 feet
		MAX STAY:	14 days
		ELEVATION:	9400 feet

8 Comstock
Monte Vista • lat 37°26'43" lon 106°21'44"

DESCRIPTION: In spruce forest with meadows nearby on Rock Creek. Views of high peaks and wooded slopes. Cool nights, noon t-storms July-Aug. Supplies in Monte Vista. Trout fish the stream. Never fills. Gather firewood. Horse ride or hike Alamosa River #703 from site or Rock Creek Trail #702.

GETTING THERE: From Monte Vista go S on state HWY 15 approx. 3 mi. to forest route 28. Go W on 28 approx. 16 mi. to Comstock CG. Narrow road w/sharp curves, large vehicles should use caution.

SINGLE RATE:	No fee	OPEN DATES:	May-Sept
# of SINGLE SITES:	8	MAX SPUR:	30 feet
		MAX STAY:	14 days
		ELEVATION:	9700 feet

9 Conejos
Canon • lat 37°10'17" lon 106°01'09"

DESCRIPTION: In an open stand of spruce and fir next to the Conejos River with views of the Conejos Canyon. Trout fish on river. Supplies 1 mi. at Rocky Mountain Lodge. Elk, deer, and bird watching. Full on holidays and weekends. Buy firewood from ALandL. Hike Notch and Ruybalid trails to South San Juan Wilderness.

GETTING THERE: From Canon go W on state HWY 17 approx. 23 mi. to primary forest route 250. Go NW on 250 approx. 7 mi. to Conejos CG.

SINGLE RATE:	$9	OPEN DATES:	May-Dec*
# of SINGLE SITES:	16	MAX SPUR:	62 feet
		MAX STAY:	14 days
		ELEVATION:	8700 feet

10 Cross Creek
South Fork • lat 37°34'48" lon 106°38'58"

DESCRIPTION: CG in an aspen and spruce stand near open grass meadows looking on Beaver Reservoir. Lake and stream fish for trout on lake. Warm days, noon t-storms June-Aug. Supplies 7 mi. away. Deer and elk in area. Fills holiday weekends. Buy firewood from LandL. Trailheads for Cross Creek and Big Tree adjacent to CG.

GETTING THERE: From South Fork go S on US HWY 160 approx. 1 mi. to forest route 20. Go S on 20 approx. 6 mi. to Cross Creek CG. RD is narrow with sharp curves, large vehicles should use caution.

SINGLE RATE:	$9	OPEN DATES:	May-Sept
# of SINGLE SITES:	12	MAX SPUR:	25 feet
		MAX STAY:	14 days
		ELEVATION:	8800 feet

 Campground has hosts   **Reservable sites**   **Accessible facilities**   **Fully developed**   **Semi-developed**   **Rustic facilities**

NOTE: Open dates listed are typical. Actual dates are dependent on conditions such as snow pack.

11 Elk Creek
Canon • lat 37˚07'33" lon 106˚22'03"

DESCRIPTION: CG located in an open blue spruce stand on Elk Creek with views of the Conejos Canyon. Cool summer days with cold nights. Fish Elk Creek or Conejos River. Supplies 1 mi. away at Horca store. Elk, deer, and various birds in area. Moderate use, full most weekends. Buy firewood from ALandL.

GETTING THERE: From Canon go W on state HWY 17 approx. 24 mi. to FDR 128, then 1/2 mi. to Elk Creek CG.

SINGLE RATE:	$11	OPEN DATES:	May-Dec
# of SINGLE SITES:	45	MAX SPUR:	62 feet
		MAX STAY:	14 days
		ELEVATION:	8500 feet

16 Luders Creek
Saguache • lat 38˚10'53" lon 106˚35'01"

DESCRIPTION: CG is in park-like grove of ponderosa and lodgepole pine with open views. Frequent afternoon thundershowers. Trout fishing nearby. Historical stage route in area. Supplies 28 mi. to Saguache. Various wildlife. Seldom full. Fall is good time to visit. Gather firewood locally.

GETTING THERE: From Saguache go W on state HWY 114 approx. 20 mi. to primary forest route NN14. Go W on NN14 appprox. 8 mi. to Luders Creek CG.

SINGLE RATE:	No fee	OPEN DATES:	May-Dec
# of SINGLE SITES:	6	MAX SPUR:	25 feet
		MAX STAY:	14 days
		ELEVATION:	9900 feet

12 Highway Springs
South Fork • lat 37˚36'58" lon 106˚40'32"

DESCRIPTION: CG in an open meadow with pine trees. A primitive site frequented by overnight travelers. No drinking water on site. Warms days with cool nights. Supplies in South Fork. Trout fishing in Rio Grande River. Deer and elk in area. Rarely full. Buy firewood from LandL. Hike Trout Creek TH 1 mi. away.

GETTING THERE: From South Fork go S on US HWY 160 approx. 3.5 mi. to Highway Springs CG.

SINGLE RATE:	$5	OPEN DATES:	May-Sept
# of SINGLE SITES:	11	MAX SPUR:	35 feet
		MAX STAY:	14 days
		ELEVATION:	8400 feet

17 Marshall Park
Creede • lat 37˚47'20" lon 106˚59'07"

DESCRIPTION: In an open meadow along the Rio Grande River with views of Bristol Head Peak and LaGarita Mountains. Cool nights, noon t-storms July-Aug. Supplies in Creede. Fish river for trout. Dear, elk, and bighorn sheep in area. Fills July 4. Buy firewood from LandL. No nearby hiking. Some ticks and mosquitos.

GETTING THERE: From Creede go SW on state HWY 149 approx. 6.5 mi. to Marshall Park CG.

SINGLE RATE:	$10	OPEN DATES:	May-Sept
# of SINGLE SITES:	15	MAX SPUR:	30 feet
		MAX STAY:	14 days
		ELEVATION:	8800 feet

13 Ivy Creek
Creede • lat 37˚41'00" lon 107˚00'10"

DESCRIPTION: On the edge of a large meadow with Ivy and Red Mountain Creeks nearby. Warm days, cool nights. Noon t-storms. Stream fish trout on the river. Supplies in Creede. Deer, elk, and moose in area. Rarely fills. Gather firewood locally. Ivy Creek Trail #805 leads into Weminuche Wilderness.

GETTING THERE: From Creede go S on state HWY 149 6.5 mi. to forest route 523. Go S 4 mi. to forest route 528. Go S 3 mi. to forest route 526. Go S 2 mi. to Ivy Creek CG. Road is narrow with sharp curves.

SINGLE RATE:	No fee	OPEN DATES:	May-Sept
# of SINGLE SITES:	4	MAX SPUR:	25 feet
		MAX STAY:	14 days
		ELEVATION:	9500 feet

18 Mix Lake
Canon • lat 37˚21'30" lon 106˚32'15"

DESCRIPTION: CG set in an open spruce location above Conegjos River drainage and Mix Lake. Mild days with cool nights. Moderate use, full July 4. Fishing on river, Mix lake and Platoro Reservoir. Supplies 1 mi. away in Platoro. Deer, elk, and birds in area. Hike to Mix Lake - trail is very steep.

GETTING THERE: From Canon go W on state HWY 17 approx. 23 mi. to forest route 250. Go NW on 250 approx. 22 mi. to FDR 250b, then 1 mi. to Mix Lake CG. Washboard RD can be hard on RVs and trailers.

SINGLE RATE:	$9	OPEN DATES:	May-Sept*
# of SINGLE SITES:	22	MAX SPUR:	60 feet
		MAX STAY:	14 days
		ELEVATION:	10000 feet

14 Lake Fork
Cannon • lat 37˚18'33" lon 106˚28'36"

DESCRIPTION: This CG is situated in a spruce stand on the Conejos River. Cool days with cold nights. Trout fishing on the river. Supplies in Platoro, 6 mi. away. Elk, deer, and bird watching. Moderate use, fills July 4. Buy firewood from ALandL. Hiking trails to Lake Fork and Big Lake 1 mi. away.

GETTING THERE: From Canon go W on state HWY 17 approx. 23 mi. to primary forest route 250. Go NW on 250 approx. 16 mi. to Lake Fork CG. Road may be rough.

SINGLE RATE:	$9	OPEN DATES:	May-Oct*
# of SINGLE SITES:	19	MAX SPUR:	76 feet
		MAX STAY:	14 days
		ELEVATION:	9500 feet

19 Mogote
Canon • lat 37˚03'53" lon 106˚14'04"

DESCRIPTION: This CG is situated on the Conejos River in pine and cottonwood. Views of scenic Conejos Canyon. Pleasant cool summer temperatures. Fish for trout on river. Supplies are available at Fox Creek Store, 1 mi. away. Birds, deer, and elk in area. Fills July 4. Buy firewood from ALandL.

GETTING THERE: From Canon go W on state HWY 17 approx. 15 mi. to Mogote CG.

SINGLE RATE:	$11	OPEN DATES:	May-Sept
# of SINGLE SITES:	41	MAX SPUR:	90 feet
GROUP RATE:	Varies	MAX STAY:	14 days
# of GROUP SITES:	2	ELEVATION:	8400 feet

15 Lost Trail
Creede • lat 37˚46'06" lon 107˚20'57"

DESCRIPTION: CG set in a meadow along West Lost Trail Creek. Views of high snow covered peaks. Stream fish for trout. Deer, elk, and moose in the area. Rarely full. Supplies available in Creede or Lake City (48 mi.). Gather firewood locally. Nearby trails are West Lost #821 and Ute Creek #819.

GETTING THERE: From Creede go W on state HWY 149 approx. 18 mi. to forest route 520. Go W on 520 approx. 16 mi. to Lost Trail CG. Road is narrow w/sharp curves. Large vehicles should use caution.

SINGLE RATE:	No fee	OPEN DATES:	May-Sept
# of SINGLE SITES:	7	MAX SPUR:	25 feet
		MAX STAY:	14 days
		ELEVATION:	9500 feet

20 North Clear Creek
Creede • lat 37˚50'54" lon 107˚08'57"

DESCRIPTION: CG in meadows with scattered young aspen on North Clear Creek. View of forest slopes and Bristol Head Mountain. Stream fish for trout. Deer, elk, moose, beavers, and waterfowl in area. Rarely full. Buy firewood from LandL. No nearby hiking, North Clear Creek Falls approx. 2 mi. away.

GETTING THERE: From Creede go W on state HWY 149 approx. 26 mi. to forest route 510. Go E on 510 3 mi. to North Clear Creek CG. Road is narrow with sharp curves. Large vehicles should use caution.

SINGLE RATE:	$9	OPEN DATES:	May-Sept
# of SINGLE SITES:	25	MAX SPUR:	30 feet
		MAX STAY:	14 days
		ELEVATION:	9900 feet

 Campground has hosts   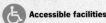 **Reservable sites**   **Accessible facilities**   **Fully developed**   **Semi-developed**   **Rustic facilities**

NOTE: Open dates listed are typical. Actual dates are dependent on conditions such as snow pack.

21 North Crestone Creek
Crestone • lat 38˚02'00" lon 105˚39'00"

DESCRIPTION: CG is in a narrow,wooded mountain canyon with spectacular mountain and valley views. Afternoon showers. Trout fishing in North Crestone Creek. Supplies 2.5 mi. to Crestone. Mountain sheep and deer. Frequented by black bears. Gather firewood locally. Horse and hiking trails. Ticks May and June.

GETTING THERE: From Crestone go N on forest route 950 approx. 2.5 mi. to North Crestone Creek CG. 4WD recommended.

SINGLE RATE:	$7	OPEN DATES:	May-Dec
# of SINGLE SITES:	13	MAX SPUR:	25 feet
		MAX STAY:	14 days
		ELEVATION:	8800 feet

26 River Hill
Creede • lat 37˚43'47" lon 107˚13'47"

DESCRIPTION: Set in a meadow surrounded by willow on the Rio Grande River. Views of forest hills and rock bluffs. Stream fish for trout. Supplies in Creede or Lake City 42 mi. away. Deer, elk, and moose can be seen in the area. Fills July 4. Buy firewood from LandL. No nearby trails.

GETTING THERE: From Creede go W on state HWY 149 approx. 18 mi. to forest route 520. Go W on 520 approx. 9 mi. to River Hill CG. Narrow road with sharp curves. Large vehicles should use caution.

SINGLE RATE:	$10	OPEN DATES:	May-Sept
# of SINGLE SITES:	20	MAX SPUR:	30 feet
		MAX STAY:	14 days
		ELEVATION:	9200 feet

22 Palisade
South Fork • lat 37˚45'03" lon 106˚45'51"

DESCRIPTION: CG along Rio Grande River with mixed shady and open meadow sites. River is dangerously fast and high Apr-June. Old mining town of Creede 13 mi. N. Fish river for trout. Supplies in South Fork. Deer, elk, and bighorn sheep in area. Fills holiday weekends. Buy firewood from LandL. No nearby trails.

GETTING THERE: From South Fork go NW on state HWY 149 approx. 8 mi. to Palisade CG.

SINGLE RATE:	$10	OPEN DATES:	May-Sept
# of SINGLE SITES:	12	MAX SPUR:	30 feet
		MAX STAY:	14 days
		ELEVATION:	8300 feet

27 Rock Creek
Monte Vista • lat 37˚28'07" lon 106˚19'54"

DESCRIPTION: In forested area on Rock Creek. Some shady willow and some meadow sites. Warm days, noon t-storms Jul-Aug. Supplies in Monte Vista. Trout fishing on Rock Creek. Deer, elk, and beaver in area. Fills July 4. Gather firewood. Horse, hike Rock Creek #701 trail (no ATV or MC use). Few ticks and mosquitos present.

GETTING THERE: From Monte Vista go S on state HWY 15 approx. 3 mi. to primary forest route 28. Go W on 28 approx. 13 mi. to Rock Creek CG. Narrow road w/sharp curves. Large vehicles should use caution.

SINGLE RATE:	No fee	OPEN DATES:	May-Sept
# of SINGLE SITES:	23	MAX SPUR:	30 feet
		MAX STAY:	14 days
		ELEVATION:	9200 feet

23 Park Creek
South Fork • lat 37˚35'30" lon 106˚43'43"

DESCRIPTION: Among cottonwood and willow on the South Fork of the Rio Grande. Trout fish in river. Shady with cool mornings and warm days. Noon t-storms June-Aug. River is high and dangerous in June. Supplies 8 mi. away. Deer and elk in area. Fills July 4. Buy firewood. Horse and hike Lake Fork Trail, 3 mi. E.

GETTING THERE: From South Fork go S on US HWY 160 approx. 8 mi. to Park Creek CG.

SINGLE RATE:	$10	OPEN DATES:	May-Sept
# of SINGLE SITES:	16	MAX SPUR:	35 feet
		MAX STAY:	14 days
		ELEVATION:	8500 feet

28 Silver Thread
Creede • lat 37˚49'30" lon 107˚09'45"

DESCRIPTION: Located in open meadow edged in aspen forest on South Clear Creek with falls close. Trout fish the stream. Warm days, cool nights. Noon t-storms June-Aug. Supplies in Creede or Lake City (28 mi. W). Deer, elk, moose, and beaver in area. Rarely full. Buy firewood from LandL. Trail to South Clear Creek Falls.

GETTING THERE: From Creede go W on state HWY 149 approx. 22 mi. to Silver Thread CG.

SINGLE RATE:	$9	OPEN DATES:	May-Sept
# of SINGLE SITES:	11	MAX SPUR:	30 feet
		MAX STAY:	14 days
		ELEVATION:	9500 feet

24 Poso
La Garita • lat 37˚54'29" lon 106˚25'37"

DESCRIPTION: CG sits on bench above South Fork Carnero Creek in fir with mountain stream views. Trout fishing. Historical John C. Fremont's expedition site. Supplies 12 mi. to Saguache. Mountain sheep, deer, and elk in the area. Seldom full. Fall is good time to visit. Gather firewood locally.

GETTING THERE: From La Garita go NW on primary forest route 41G approx. 10 mi. to forest route 675. Go W on 675 approx. 2 mi. to Poso CG.

SINGLE RATE:	$5	OPEN DATES:	May-Dec
# of SINGLE SITES:	11	MAX SPUR:	16 feet
		MAX STAY:	14 days
		ELEVATION:	9100 feet

29 Spectacle Lake
Canon • lat 37˚10'03" lon 106˚26'18"

DESCRIPTION: CG in an open setting of blue spruce on the Conejos River with views of the Scenic Conejos Canyon. Fish for trout on river or Spectacle Lake. Supplies 2 mi. away at Rocky Mountain Lodge. Deer, elk, and bird watching. Receives moderate use, filling on July 4. Buy firewood on site from ALandL.

GETTING THERE: From Canon go W on state HWY 17 approx. 23 mi. to primary forest route 250. Go NW on 250 approx. 7 mi. to Spectacle Lake CG.

SINGLE RATE:	$9	OPEN DATES:	May-Sept
# of SINGLE SITES:	24	MAX SPUR:	60 feet
		MAX STAY:	14 days
		ELEVATION:	8700 feet

25 Rio Grande
Creede • lat 37˚45'41" lon 107˚00'43"

DESCRIPTION: In a meadow with willow on edge of the Rio Grande River. Warm days, cool nights, noon t-storms June-Aug. Supplies in Creede. Historic Creede Mining District. Trout fish in River. Deer and elk can be seen in the area. Rarely fills. Gather driftwood for fires. No nearby hiking.

GETTING THERE: From Creede go SW on state HWY 149 11 mi. to forest route 529. Go S approx. 1 mi. to Rio Grande CG. 4WD recommended. Narrow road with sharp curves. Large vehicles should use caution.

SINGLE RATE:	No fee	OPEN DATES:	May-Sept
# of SINGLE SITES:	4	MAX SPUR:	25 feet
		MAX STAY:	14 days
		ELEVATION:	9300 feet

30 Stone Cellar
Gunnison • lat 38˚01'08" lon 106˚40'35"

DESCRIPTION: CG is located along Saguache Creek on the edge of a meadow. Open valley views of La Garita Wilderness. Frequent afternoon showers. Trout fishing. Historical battle, grave site nearby. Supplies 45 mi. away. Deer and elk in vicinity. Full July and August weekends. Gather firewood locally.

GETTING THERE: From Gunnison go E on US HWY 50 7 mi. to state HWY 114. Go S 19 mi. to BLM route 3083. Go S 9 mi. to BLM route 3088. Go S on 3088 (becomes forest route 787) 12 mi. to Stone Cellar CG.

SINGLE RATE:	No fee	OPEN DATES:	May-Nov
# of SINGLE SITES:	2	MAX SPUR:	25 feet
		MAX STAY:	14 days
		ELEVATION:	9500 feet

 Campground has hosts   **Reservable sites**   **Accessible facilities**   **Fully developed**   **Semi-developed**   **Rustic facilities**

NOTE: Open dates listed are typical. Actual dates are dependent on conditions such as snow pack.

RIO GRANDE NATIONAL FOREST • COLORADO • 21 — 30

31 Storm King

La Garita • lat 37˚57'33" lon 106˚25'50"

DESCRIPTION: This CG is located in aspen and fir with open views. Frequent afternoon showers. Trout fishing in Middle Fork of Carnero Creek at CG. Supplies are available 20 mi. away. Deer and elk in vicinity. Fall is good time to visit. Campers may gather their firewood locally.

GETTING THERE: From La Garita go NW on primary forest route 41G approx. 15 mi. to Storm King CG.

SINGLE RATE:	$5	OPEN DATES:	May-Dec
# of SINGLE SITES:	11	MAX SPUR:	25 feet
		MAX STAY:	14 days
		ELEVATION:	9400 feet

 Campground has hosts   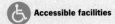 Reservable sites   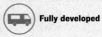 Accessible facilities    Fully developed   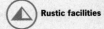 Semi-developed   Rustic facilities

NOTE: Open dates listed are typical. Actual dates are dependent on conditions such as snow pack.

SAN JUAN NATIONAL FOREST

Located in southwestern Colorado on the western slope on the Continental Divide, the San Juan National Forest covers an area from east to west of more than 120 miles and from north to south more than 60 miles, encompassing an area of 1,869,931 acres.

Alpine lakes, canyons, cataracts, waterfalls, unusual geological formations, historic mines, and broad variations in elevations characterize this area. Archeological ruins of the Anasazi are preserved at Chimney Rock. The Durango and Silverton Narrow Gauge Railroad takes passengers on a historic ride through the deep, gorgeous canyon of the Animas River. The Needle Mountains, a paradise for mountain climbers and one of the roughest ranges in the United States, lies within the Weminuche Wilderness. Three of these peaks rise to more than 14,000 feet above sea level. Within the Lizard Head Wilderness are three more peaks greater than 14,000 feet in elevation. These areas are accessible only by trail for foot and horseback only.

Numerous campgrounds and picnic sites are scattered throughout the forest. Skiers are attracted to the Purgatory Ski Area north of Durango. Fishing for trout in high mountain lakes, swift streams or reservoirs offer the angler many challenges.

USFS Photo

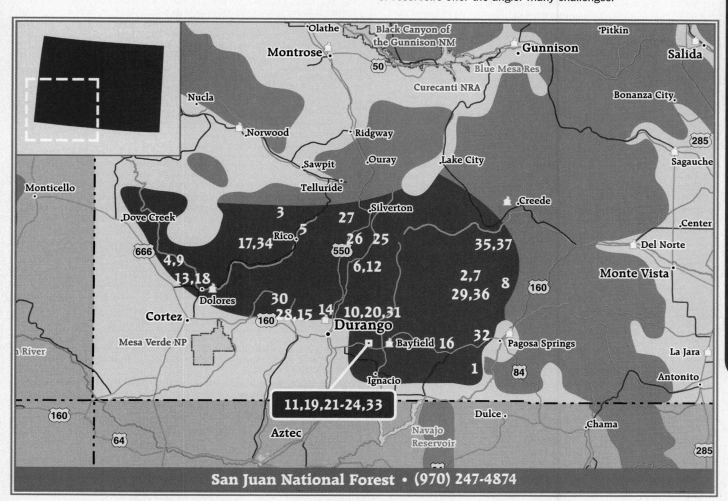

San Juan National Forest • (970) 247-4874

1 Blanco River
Pagosa Springs • lat 37°08'43" lon 106°52'57"

DESCRIPTION: CG has large ponderosa pine providing shade and is a convenient stopping point between Chama, NM and Pagosa Springs, CO. Sites are usually available. The Blanco River is stocked with trout but lightly fished, so fishing may be good. Three nearby trails access the unroaded country to the east.

GETTING THERE: From Pagosa Springs go S on Hwy 84 approx. 13 mi. and turn E on forest route 656 for approx. 1.75 mi. to Blanco River CG.

SINGLE RATE:	$8	OPEN DATES:	May-Nov
# of SINGLE SITES:	6	MAX SPUR:	16 feet
		MAX STAY:	14 days
		ELEVATION:	7200 feet

2 Bridge
Pagosa Springs • lat 37°27'53" lon 107°11'53"

DESCRIPTION: Open park like CG in pine stands with views of Colorado Mountains. Williams Creek runs through CG. Fly and boat fishing for trout. Mild days, frequent noon rains. Supplies 1 mi. away. Mule deer, elk, and turkeys in area. Gather firewood. Piedra River trail is open to horses and hiking, 2 mi. from CG.

GETTING THERE: From Pagosa Springs go W on US HWY 160 approx. 2 mi. to county route 600/primary forest route 631. Go NW on 600/631 approx. 18 mi. to Bridge CG.

SINGLE RATE:	$8.5	OPEN DATES:	May-Nov
# of SINGLE SITES:	19	MAX SPUR:	50 feet
		MAX STAY:	14 days
		ELEVATION:	7800 feet

3 Burro Bridge
Dolores • lat 37°47'14" lon 108°03'50"

DESCRIPTION: CG is located in a grove of spruce, fir, and aspen. Frequent thundershowers. Trout fishing in West Dolores River nearby. Supplies 35 mi. to Dolores. Deer and elk in area. Rarely full. July and August good times to visit. Navaho Lake hiking trail 2 mi. from CG. Horse facilities.

GETTING THERE: From Dolores go E on state HWY 145 approx. 12 mi. to primary forest route 535. Go N on 535 approx. 23 mi. to Burro Bridge CG.

SINGLE RATE:	$8	OPEN DATES:	May-Sept
# of SINGLE SITES:	15	MAX SPUR:	35 feet
		MAX STAY:	30 days
		ELEVATION:	9100 feet

4 Cabin Canyon
Cortez • lat 37°37'46" lon 108°41'34"

DESCRIPTION: CG is in tall cottonwood with canyon views. Dolores River borders entire CG with barrier free sidewalk. Trout fishing in Dolores River and nearby dam. Supplies 15 mi. to Dove Creek. Various wildlife including songbirds. Rarely full. Spring and fall are good times to visit. Dry RV dump station.

GETTING THERE: From Cortez go N on US HWY 191 approx. 18 mi. to forest route 505. Go E then N on 505 approx. 5.5 mi. to primary forest route 504. Go SE on 504 approx. 4 mi. to Cabin Canyon CG.

SINGLE RATE:	$8	OPEN DATES:	May-Sept
# of SINGLE SITES:	11	MAX SPUR:	45 feet
		MAX STAY:	30 days
		ELEVATION:	6500 feet

5 Cayton
Dolores • lat 37°46'16" lon 107°58'37"

DESCRIPTION: CG is located in spruce and fir with canyon side views. Frequent thunder showers. Trout fishing in Dolores River which runs along one loop of CG. Supplies 6 mi. to historical mining town of Rico. Deer and elk in area. Rarely full. Numerous hiking trails in vicinity. Dry RV dump station.

GETTING THERE: From Dolores go E on state HWY 145 approx. 12 mi. to forest route 578 and Cayton CG.

SINGLE RATE:	$10	OPEN DATES:	May-Sept
# of SINGLE SITES:	27	MAX SPUR:	35 feet
		MAX STAY:	30 days
		ELEVATION:	9400 feet

6 Chris Park
Durango • lat 37°31'09" lon 107°48'18"

DESCRIPTION: This CG is situated in an open and flat area, partly shaded by a few large ponderosa pine. Haviland Lake and Forebay Lake and Creek are nearby. Campers may enjoy fishing in the area but please check fishing regulations. This CG is reservation only.

GETTING THERE: From Durango go N on US HWY 550 approx. 16 mi. to Chris Park CG.

		OPEN DATES:	May-Sept
GROUP RATE:	$30	MAX STAY:	14 days
# of GROUP SITES:	3	ELEVATION:	8000 feet

7 Cimarona
Pagosa Springs • lat 37°32'21" lon 107°12'32"

DESCRIPTION: CG set in a shady spruce stand with views of the Colorado Mountains. Nice days, frequent noon t-storms. Fly and boat fish for trout nearby. Mule deer, elk, turkeys, and black bears frequent area. Moderate use. Gather firewood locally. Hike and horse ride nearby Cimarrona and Williams Creek Trails.

GETTING THERE: From Pagosa Springs go W on US HWY 160 approx. 2 mi. to county route 600/primary forest route 631. Go NW approx. 22 mi. to forest route 640. Go N on 640 approx. 4 mi. to Cimaronna CG.

SINGLE RATE:	$8.5	OPEN DATES:	May-Sept
# of SINGLE SITES:	21	MAX SPUR:	35 feet
		MAX STAY:	14 days
		ELEVATION:	8400 feet

8 East Fork
Pagosa Springs • lat 37°22'37" lon 106°53'20"

DESCRIPTION: CG located in pine on shady ridge with views of the Colorado Mountains. Mild days, frequent t-showers. Fly fishing for trout E Fork of San Juan. Supplies in Pagosa Springs. Mule deer, elk, turkeys, and black bears in area. Gather firewood locally. Hiking trailheads 2 mi. away. 4X4 road to Elwood Pass.

GETTING THERE: From Pagosa Springs go N on US HWY 160 approx. 9.5 mi. to forest route 667. Go E on 667 approx. 1 mi. to East Fork CG.

SINGLE RATE:	$8	OPEN DATES:	May-Nov
# of SINGLE SITES:	26	MAX SPUR:	35 feet
		MAX STAY:	30 days
		ELEVATION:	7600 feet

9 Ferris Canyon
Cortez • lat 37°37'30" lon 108°38'00"

DESCRIPTION: This CG is in box elder trees with views of sandstone bluffs. Trout fishing in Dolores River which runs along entire CG. Supplies are available 15 mi. away in Dove Creek. Various wildlife including songbirds. Rarely full. Spring and fall good times to visit. Dry RV dumpstation 3 mi. away.

GETTING THERE: From Cortez go N on US HWY 666 approx. 18 mi. to forest route 505. Go E then N on 505 approx. 5.5 mi. to primary forest route 504. Go SE on 504 approx. 6 mi. to Ferris Canyon CG.

SINGLE RATE:	$8	OPEN DATES:	May-Sept
# of SINGLE SITES:	6	MAX SPUR:	45 feet
		MAX STAY:	30 days
		ELEVATION:	6500 feet

10 Florida
Durango • lat 37°27'09" lon 107°40'54"

DESCRIPTION: CG is 4 mi. N of Miller Creek above the reservoir. Colorado blue spruce, douglas fir, and aspen dominate the area. This is a low use CG. Popular activities include hiking, hunting, stream fishing, bicycling and the Colorado Free Fishing Days. Supplies can be found 7.5 mi. away.

GETTING THERE: From Durango go NE on county route 240 approx. 12 mi. to county route 243. Go N on 243 approx. 6.5 mi. to Florida CG.

SINGLE RATE:	$10	OPEN DATES:	Apr-Sept
# of SINGLE SITES:	20	MAX SPUR:	26 feet
GROUP RATE:	Varies	MAX STAY:	14 days
# of GROUP SITES:	1	ELEVATION:	8500 feet

 Campground has hosts   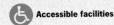 Reservable sites   Accessible facilities   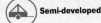 Fully developed   Semi-developed   Rustic facilities

NOTE: Open dates listed are typical. Actual dates are dependent on conditions such as snow pack.

11 Graham Creek
Bayfield • lat 37°23'26" lon 107°32'21"

DESCRIPTION: Some sites in CG are surrounded by large trees while others are more open. Willows separate CG from lake but paths provide access to the shoreline. Sites are available for large RVs, although entrance and exit roads are steep. Stables close by. Natural-surface boat ramp available.

GETTING THERE: Graham Creek CG is located on the E shore of the Vallecito Reservoir. From Bayfield go N on county route 501 approx. 4 mi. to forest route 603. Go NE approx. 3.5 mi. to Graham Creek CG.

SINGLE RATE:	$10	OPEN DATES:	May-Sept*
# of SINGLE SITES:	25	MAX SPUR:	26 feet
		MAX STAY:	14 days
		ELEVATION:	7900 feet

16 Lower Piedra
Pagosa Springs • lat 37°14'31" lon 107°20'32"

DESCRIPTION: Large, level sites in shady pine stands with views of Piedra River. Warm days, frequent noon t-showers. Fly fishing for trout on river. Limited supplies 1 mi. away. Mule deer and turkeys in area. Moderate use. Gather firewood locally. No immediate hiking trails. No drinking water available on site.

GETTING THERE: From Pagosa Springs go W on U.S. HWY 160 approx. 25 mi. to forest route 621. Go N on 621 (Behind Chimney Rock Store) approx. 1 mi. to Lower Piedra CG.

SINGLE RATE:	$6	OPEN DATES:	May-Sept
# of SINGLE SITES:	17	MAX SPUR:	35 feet
		MAX STAY:	14 days
		ELEVATION:	7200 feet

12 Haviland Lake
Durango • lat 37°32'01" lon 107°48'25"

DESCRIPTION: CG with ponderosa pine shading the scenic campsites with the Hermosa Cliffs in the background. Fishing at Forebay or Haviland Lake. There is a good selection of sites for RVs and tents, some are near the shore of Haviland Lake. Roads and trails can be found near the Hermosa Cliffs.

GETTING THERE: From Durango go N on US HWY 550 approx. 16 mi. to Haviland Lake CG.

SINGLE RATE:	No fee	OPEN DATES:	May-July
# of SINGLE SITES:	45	MAX SPUR:	66 feet
		MAX STAY:	14 days
		ELEVATION:	8705 feet

17 Mavreeso
Dolores • lat 37°39'03" lon 108°17'47"

DESCRIPTION: This CG is located along the West Dolores River. Several sites have shady tent areas beneath spruce and fir. Campers can enjoy fishing in the area but please check fishing regulations. There are pull-thrus for RVs. A RV dump station is near one of the toilets. Supplies are in Dolores.

GETTING THERE: From Dolores go E on state HWY 145 approx. 12 mi. to primary forest route 535. Go N on 535 approx. 5.5 mi. to Mavreeso CG.

SINGLE RATE:	$10	OPEN DATES:	May-Sept
# of SINGLE SITES:	14	MAX SPUR:	35 feet
		MAX STAY:	14 days
		ELEVATION:	7600 feet

13 House Creek
Dolores • lat 37°31'00" lon 108°32'00"

DESCRIPTION: This CG is located in a gently sloping, grassy area near the McPhee Reservoir's high-water line. CG has a dump station. Hiking and walking roads and trails are scattered around McPhee Reservoir. Boating at McPhee Reservoir. Four-lane boat ramp available at reservoir. Open play area at CG.

GETTING THERE: From Dolores go N on primary forest route 526 approx. 7 mi. to primary forest route 528. Go SE on 528 approx. 5 mi. to House Creek CG.

SINGLE RATE:	$12	OPEN DATES:	May-Sept
# of SINGLE SITES:	72	MAX SPUR:	50 feet
GROUP RATE:	$40	MAX STAY:	14 days
# of GROUP SITES:	2	ELEVATION:	6900 feet

18 McPhee
Dolores • lat 37°30'01" lon 108°33'10"

DESCRIPTION: This CG is situated on the south side of McPhee Reservoir and offers the most modern camping facilities in the forest. Campers can enjoy fishing in the area but please check fishing regulations. There are scenic overlooks near this CG. Supplies are available in Dolores.

GETTING THERE: From Dolores go W on state HWY 145 approx. 2 mi. to state HWY 184. Go N on 184 approx. 4 mi. to county route 25. Go N approx. 1/2 mi. to forest route 271. Go E on 271 approx. 2 mi. to McPhee CG.

SINGLE RATE:	$12	OPEN DATES:	May-Sept
# of SINGLE SITES:	73	MAX SPUR:	50 feet
GROUP RATE:	$40	MAX STAY:	30 days
# of GROUP SITES:	2	ELEVATION:	7100 feet

14 Junction Creek
Durango • lat 37°20'20" lon 107°55'00"

DESCRIPTION: This CG is situated on a south-facing hillside a small distance above Junction Creek. Many sites are level and well shaded by ponderosa pine. Skilled fishermen may have good luck near the campground, but chances improve upstream. Hiking and walking on nearby Colorado Trail.

GETTING THERE: From Durango go N on county route 204 approx. 4 mi. to Junction Creek CG.

SINGLE RATE:	$10	OPEN DATES:	May-Sept
# of SINGLE SITES:	34	MAX SPUR:	50 feet
		MAX STAY:	14 days
		ELEVATION:	7300 feet

19 Middle Mountain
Bayfield • lat 37°24'26" lon 107°32'06"

DESCRIPTION: CG is adjacent to the mouth of the Pine River where it enters Vallecito Reservoir. S exposure and easy access to the water. CG very open and sunny with a grassy shoreline. Shade is provided by ponderosa pine and small aspen. A few sites can accommodate large RVs. Trails and fishing nearby.

GETTING THERE: Middle Mountain CG is located on the E shore of the Vallecito Reservoir. From Bayfield go N on county route 501 approx. 4 mi. to forest route 603. Go NE approx. 5 mi. to Middle Mountain CG.

SINGLE RATE:	$10	OPEN DATES:	May-Sept
# of SINGLE SITES:	24	MAX SPUR:	35 feet
		MAX STAY:	14 days
		ELEVATION:	7900 feet

15 Kroeger
Durango • lat 37°22'33" lon 108°04'40"

DESCRIPTION: This CG is shaded by a mixture of spruce, fir, aspen, and cottonwood near the La Plata River. Due to high elevation, campers should prepare for rapid weather changes. The river is close to the road, so fishing is popular. Please check fishing regulations. Supplies are in Durango.

GETTING THERE: From Durango go W on US HWY 160 approx. 11 mi. to county route 124. Go N on 124 approx. 5 mi. to Kroeger CG.

SINGLE RATE:	$8	OPEN DATES:	May-Sept
# of SINGLE SITES:	11	MAX SPUR:	35 feet
		MAX STAY:	14 days
		ELEVATION:	9000 feet

20 Miller Creek
Durango • lat 37°24'00" lon 107°40'30"

DESCRIPTION: This CG is located about 2 mi. N of the dam on Lemon Reservoir. The CG offers a choice of sunny or shady campsites. A concrete boat ramp is available at the N end of the CG. Campers may enjoy fishing in the area but please check for fishing regulations. Supplies are located in Durango.

GETTING THERE: From Durango go NE on county route 240 approx. 12 mi. to county route 243. Go N on 243 approx. 3.5 mi. to miller Creek CG.

SINGLE RATE:	$10	OPEN DATES:	May-Sept*
# of SINGLE SITES:	12	MAX SPUR:	35 feet
		MAX STAY:	14 days
		ELEVATION:	8000 feet

 Campground has hosts   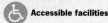 **Reservable sites**   **Accessible facilities**   **Fully developed**   **Semi-developed**   **Rustic facilities**

NOTE: Open dates listed are typical. Actual dates are dependent on conditions such as snow pack.

21 North Canyon
Bayfield • lat 37°23'38" lon 107°32'18"

DESCRIPTION: This CG has large ponderosa pine scattered throughout. Willows separate the campground from the Vallecito Reservoir, and underbrush separates campsites for privacy. Numberous paths provide access to the water. Trails and fishing are activities available in the area.

GETTING THERE: North Canyon CG is located on the E shore of the Vallecito Reservoir. From Bayfield go N on county route 501 approx. 4 mi. to forest route 603. Go NE on 603 approx. 4 mi. to North Canyon CG.

SINGLE RATE:	$10	OPEN DATES:	May-Sept
# of SINGLE SITES:	21	MAX SPUR:	26 feet
		MAX STAY:	14 days
		ELEVATION:	7900 feet

22 Old Timers
Bayfield • lat 37°22'30" lon 107°34'00"

DESCRIPTION: This CG is in a fir and spruce forest on Vellecito Lake. Great views of the lake which has salmon and pike fishing. Supplies in Bayfield or basics and boat rentals at marina. Deer, elk, and black bears in area. Horse, hiking, mountain biking, and ATV trails nearby, see forest map. Water skiing on lake.

GETTING THERE: Old Timers CG is located on the E shore of the Vallecito Reservoir. From Bayfield go N on county route 501 approx. 4 mi. to forest route 603. Go NE on 603 approx. 2 mi. to Old Timers CG.

SINGLE RATE:	$10	OPEN DATES:	May-Sept*
# of SINGLE SITES:	10	MAX SPUR:	25 feet
		MAX STAY:	14 days
		ELEVATION:	7900 feet

23 Pine Point
Bayfield • lat 37°24'02" lon 107°32'05"

DESCRIPTION: This CG is situated on the upper end of the Vallecito Reservoir. The CG offers good views of high, snowcapped peaks. Campers may enjoy fishing in the area but please check for fishing regulations. A sheltered area for boats and an open play area are located just south of the CG.

GETTING THERE: Pine Point CG is located on the E shore of the Vallecito Reservoir. From Bayfield go N on county route 501 approx. 4 mi. to forest route 603. Go NE on 603 approx. 4.5 mi. to Pine Point CG.

SINGLE RATE:	$10	OPEN DATES:	May-Sept*
# of SINGLE SITES:	30	MAX SPUR:	35 feet
		MAX STAY:	14 days
		ELEVATION:	7900 feet

24 Pine River
Bayfield • lat 37°26'50" lon 107°30'16"

DESCRIPTION: CG and Trailhead are often used as a temporary base camp and parking area for hikers and backpackers entering the wilderness. All six campsites have outstanding views up the Pine River Valley. Although RVs easily fit in the parking area, the campsites accommodate only tents or small RVs.

GETTING THERE: Pine River CG is on the E shore of the Vallecito Reservoir. From Bayfield go N on county route 501 approx. 4 mi. to forest route 603. Go NE 5 mi. to forest route 602. Go N 4 mi. to Pine River CG.

SINGLE RATE:	$6	OPEN DATES:	May-Sept
# of SINGLE SITES:	6	MAX SPUR:	20 feet
		MAX STAY:	14 days
		ELEVATION:	8100 feet

25 Purgatory
Durango • lat 37°37'41" lon 107°48'29"

DESCRIPTION: This CG is well shaded by spruce and fir. Campers may enjoy fishing in the area but please check for fishing regulations. Gas, groceries, and a RV dump station can be found approx. 2.5 mi. S on U.S. HWY 550. There are hiking and walking trails that lead to the Animas River.

GETTING THERE: From Durango go N on US HWY 550 approx. 24 mi. to Purgatory CG.

SINGLE RATE:	$10	OPEN DATES:	May-Sept
# of SINGLE SITES:	14	MAX SPUR:	30 feet
		MAX STAY:	14 days
		ELEVATION:	8800 feet

26 Sig Creek
Durango • lat 37°37'58" lon 107°52'57"

DESCRIPTION: CG sits on a south-facing hillside about .25 mi. from the East Fork of Hermosa Creek. Many streams and lakes in area for fishing. Much of the gravel road leading to Sig Creek CG follows the route of the Pinkerton Trail and Scotch Creek Toll Road. Several trails are in the area.

GETTING THERE: From Durango go N on US HWY 550 approx. 24 mi. to forest route 578. Go W on 578 approx. 7 mi. to Sig Creek CG.

SINGLE RATE:	$8	OPEN DATES:	May-Sept
# of SINGLE SITES:	9	MAX SPUR:	30 feet
		MAX STAY:	14 days
		ELEVATION:	9400 feet

27 South Mineral
Silverton • lat 37°48'21" lon 107°46'24"

DESCRIPTION: This CG rests in spruce and fir which provide abundant shade. There are some sunny sites as well. A few sites are set along the creek. Views of nearby peaks and a waterfall on the creek are just upstream from the CG. Many lakes can be found in area with good fishing. Please check fishing regulations.

GETTING THERE: From Silverton go NW on US HWY 550 approx. 2.5 mi. to forest route 585. Go W on 585 approx. 4 mi. to South Mineral CG.

SINGLE RATE:	$10	OPEN DATES:	May-Sept
# of SINGLE SITES:	26	MAX SPUR:	45 feet
		MAX STAY:	14 days
		ELEVATION:	9800 feet

28 Target Tree
Mancos • lat 37°20'22" lon 108°10'59"

DESCRIPTION: Many sites are shady, but still heat up on sunny summer days. CG is dominated by 12-acres of large pine and is known for its variety of birds. The Narrow Gauge Trail begins near campsite #37 and leads gradually uphill .75 mi. to the old railroad grade. Has an interpretive trail and plenty of shade.

GETTING THERE: From Mancos go E on US HWY 160 approx. 8 mi. to Target Tree CG.

SINGLE RATE:	$10	OPEN DATES:	May-Nov
# of SINGLE SITES:	25	MAX SPUR:	45 feet
		MAX STAY:	14 days
		ELEVATION:	7800 feet

29 Teal
Pagosa Springs • lat 37°30'36" lon 107°13'43"

DESCRIPTION: CG in open park like setting with pine. Views of Williams Creek Reservoir and Colorado Mountains. Frequent noon t-showers. Fish for trout on reservoir; light weight boat launching. Supplies 4 mi.. Mule deer, elk, turkeys, and bears in area. Williams Creek and Cimarrona Trails nearby for horse use and hiking.

GETTING THERE: From Pagosa Springs go W on US HWY 160 approx. 2 mi. to county route 600/primary forest route 631. Go NW approx. 22 mi. to forest route 640. Go N on 640 approx. 1 mi. to Teal CG.

SINGLE RATE:	$9.50	OPEN DATES:	May-Nov
# of SINGLE SITES:	16	MAX SPUR:	35 feet
		MAX STAY:	14 days
		ELEVATION:	8300 feet

30 Transfer
Mancos • lat 37°28'02" lon 108°12'34"

DESCRIPTION: In shady & cool aspen grove. Views of LaPlata Mtns. Quiet mild days. No nearby fishing. Deer, elk, turkeys, & grouse in area. Light use, fills July 4. Numerous trails for horse & hike use. Mtn bike or ATV roads. Access West Mancos River Cyn.. Big Al trail is fully accessible. Volleyball court & group use area.

GETTING THERE: From Mancos go N on county route 42 approx. 9 mi. to Transfer CG.

SINGLE RATE:	$10	OPEN DATES:	June-Sept
# of SINGLE SITES:	12	MAX SPUR:	45 feet
GROUP RATE:	Varies	MAX STAY:	14 days
# of GROUP SITES:	1	ELEVATION:	8500 feet

 Campground has hosts   **Reservable sites**   **Accessible facilities**   **Fully developed**   **Semi-developed**   **Rustic facilities**

31 Transfer Park
Durango • lat 37°27'45" lon 107°40'49"

DESCRIPTION: CG is 11 acres and offers cool settings under mixed conifer and small aspen. There are large open play areas. This is a low use campground. The history of Transfer Park can be traced back to the mining era. The Park was used for transferring ore and supplies between pack mules and wagons.

GETTING THERE: From Durango go NE on county route 240 approx. 12 mi. to county route 243. Go N on 243 approx. 6.5 mi. to Transfer Park CG.

SINGLE RATE:	$10	OPEN DATES:	May-Sept*
# of SINGLE SITES:	25	MAX SPUR:	35 feet
		MAX STAY:	14 days
		ELEVATION:	8600 feet

32 Ute
Pagosa Springs • lat 37°13'00" lon 107°15'00"

DESCRIPTION: The CG is on a gentle, south-facing slope just off the highway. Ponderosa pine provide shade, but the area gets warm on sunny summer days. The hillside above the CG offers excellent vantage points with views of Chimney Rock to the south.

GETTING THERE: From Pagosa Springs go W on US HWY 160 for 18 mi. and campground is on N side of the highway.

SINGLE RATE:	$8	OPEN DATES:	May-Sept
# of SINGLE SITES:	24	MAX SPUR:	35 feet
GROUP RATE:	$25	MAX STAY:	14 days
# of GROUP SITES:	32	ELEVATION:	6900 feet

33 Vallecito
Bayfield • lat 37°28'35" lon 107°32'47"

DESCRIPTION: This CG is one of the largest and most popular in the Forest. The CG is adjacent to Vallecito Creek and the Weminuche Wilderness. There is limited parking for the heavily used Vallecito Creek Trail, a major access point for the wilderness, at the north end of the CG.

GETTING THERE: Vallecito CG is located on the E shore of the Vallecito Reservoir. From Bayfield go N on county route 501 approx. 8 mi. to forest route 600. Go N on 600 approx. 3 mi. to Vallecito CG.

SINGLE RATE:	$10	OPEN DATES:	May-Sept
# of SINGLE SITES:	80	MAX SPUR:	35 feet
		MAX STAY:	14 days
		ELEVATION:	8000 feet

34 West Dolores
Dolores • lat 37°39'35" lon 108°16'30"

DESCRIPTION: This CG is located near the Dolores River. Most sites are shady and level, and several are suitable for large RVs. There is a RV dump station available on site. Campers can enjoy cold water fishing in the Dolores River but please check for fishing regulations. Supplies area in Dolores.

GETTING THERE: From Dolores go E on state HWY 145 approx. 12 mi. to primary forest route 535. Go N on 535 approx. 6.5 mi. to West Dolores CG.

SINGLE RATE:	$10	OPEN DATES:	May-Sept
# of SINGLE SITES:	13	MAX SPUR:	35 feet
		MAX STAY:	14 days
		ELEVATION:	7800 feet

35 West Fork
Pagosa Springs • lat 37°26'46" lon 106°54'28"

DESCRIPTION: Shady spruce setting with Colorado Mountain views. West Fork of San Juan River runs by CG. West Fork Hot Springs nearby. Frequent noon t-showers. Supplies 16 mi.. Mule deer, elk, and bears in ara. Moderate use. Gather firewood. Horse and hiking TH to Weminuche Wilderness.

GETTING THERE: From Pagosa Springs go N on US HWY 160 approx. 14 mi. to forest route 648. Go W on 648 approx. 2 mi. to West Fork CG.

SINGLE RATE:	$8	OPEN DATES:	May-Nov
# of SINGLE SITES:	28	MAX SPUR:	35 feet
		MAX STAY:	30 days
		ELEVATION:	8000 feet

36 Williams Creek
Pagosa Springs • lat 37°29'41" lon 107°13'24"

DESCRIPTION: Shaded and open sites among spruce and fir with views of Colorado Mountains. Frequent noon t-showers. Willams Creek runs through CG. Fly and boat fishing, canoeing on reservoir. Limited supplies 4 mi.. Deer, elk, turkeys, and black bears in area. Moderate use. Horse and hike trails available.

GETTING THERE: From Pagosa Springs go W on US HWY 160 approx. 2 mi. to county route 600/forest route 631. Go NW on 600/631 approx. 22 mi. to forest route 640. Go NW on 640 approx. 1/2 mi. to Williams Creek CG.

SINGLE RATE:	$9.50	OPEN DATES:	May-Sept
# of SINGLE SITES:	65	MAX SPUR:	45 feet
		MAX STAY:	14 days
		ELEVATION:	8300 feet

37 Wolf Creek
Pagosa Springs • lat 37°26'27" lon 106°53'12"

DESCRIPTION: Well shaded spruce setting with views of Colorado Mountains. Frequent noon t-showers. Fly fish for trout on Wolf Creek which runs beside CG. Supplies 16 mi.. Deer, elk, turkeys, and black bears in area. Moderate use. Gather own firewood. Horse and hiking West Fork Trail 1 mi. Mountain bike trail nearby.

GETTING THERE: From Pagosa Springs go N on US HWY 160 approx. 14 mi. to forest route 648. Go W on 648 approx. 1/2 mi. to Wolf Creek CG. Some RV pull throughs; level sites.

SINGLE RATE:	$8	OPEN DATES:	May-Nov
# of SINGLE SITES:	26	MAX SPUR:	22 feet
		MAX STAY:	14 days
		ELEVATION:	8000 feet

SAN JUAN NATIONAL FOREST • COLORADO • 31 — 37

 Campground has hosts   Reservable sites   Accessible facilities   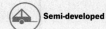 Fully developed   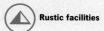 Semi-developed   Rustic facilities

NOTE: Open dates listed are typical. Actual dates are dependent on conditions such as snow pack.

WHITE RIVER NATIONAL FOREST

The two and one-quarter million acre White River National Forest is located in the heart of the Colorado Rocky Mountains, approximately two to four hours west of Denver on Interstate 70. The scenic beauty of the area, along with ample recreation opportunities on the forest, accounts for the White River being consistently ranked as one of the top five forests nationwide for total recreation use.

The forest provides an excellent variety of opportunities for outdoor enthusiasts in all seasons with eleven ski areas, eight designated wildernesses, several national trails, approximately 70 developed sites and over one and one-half million acres for general motorized and non-motorized backcountry enjoyment. Popular activities on the forest include downhill and cross-country skiing, camping, sightseeing, hunting, fishing, hiking, and boating.

Warm days and cool to freezing nights can be expected in the mountains during the summer. July and August are usually the warmest months, and afternoon thunderstorms are common. Fall in the forest is brief but spectacular, as changing aspen cloak the mountains in gold. Peak color time is normally the last part of September. Crisp, sunny days mingle with early snowstorms in what many consider the premier seasons of the year.

Dave Steinke Photo, USDA Forest Service

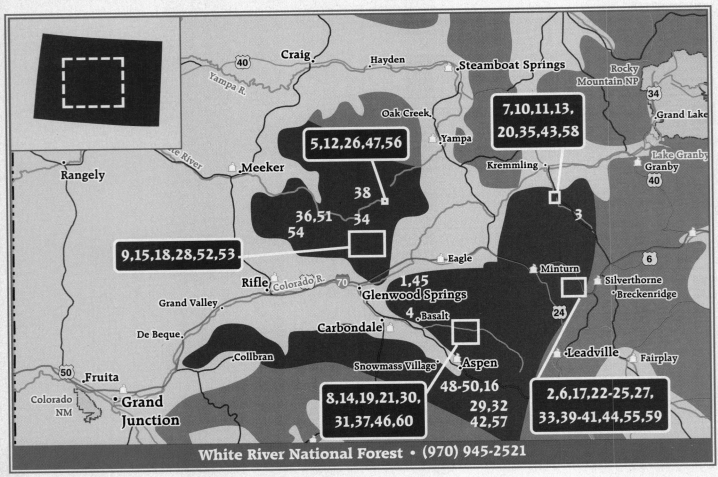

White River National Forest • (970) 945-2521

1 Avalanche
Carbondale • lat 39°14'10" lon 107°12'13"

DESCRIPTION: CG is located on Avalanche Creek. This site provides easy access to the Maroon Bells and Snowmass Wilderness for back country recreation. Fish the creek. Supplies are available 2.5 mi. and 11 mi. North. Buy or gather firewood. Horse and hiking trails accessed from SE part of CG.

GETTING THERE: From Carbondale go S on state HWY 133 approx. 11 mi. to forest route 310. Go E on 310 approx. 2.5 mi. to Avalanche CG.

SINGLE RATE:	$10	OPEN DATES:	May-Nov
# of SINGLE SITES:	13	MAX SPUR:	16 feet
		MAX STAY:	14 days
		ELEVATION:	7400 feet

2 Blodgett
Dowds Junction • lat 39°28'19" lon 106°21'58"

DESCRIPTION: Small CG within walking distance of Homestake Creek and Reservoir for fishing. Supplies and groceries are available in Minturn. Gather firewood locally. Homestake Road leads to excellent multiple hiking and mountain biking trailheads. Large and small game can be found in the area.

GETTING THERE: Blodgett CG is located approx. 12 mi. S of Dowds Junction (I-70) on US HWY 24.

SINGLE RATE:	$10	OPEN DATES:	May-Sept*
# of SINGLE SITES:	6	MAX SPUR:	30 feet
		MAX STAY:	10 days
		ELEVATION:	8900 feet

3 Blue River
Silverthorne • lat 39°43'33" lon 106°07'51"

DESCRIPTION: This CG is located among cottonwoods, fir, and aspen on the Blue River. Fish and float the river. Supplies can be found in Silverthorne. Gather or bring firewood. Deer, and large birds frequent area. Hike Rock Creek TH to Eagles Nest Wilderness and the Gore Range Trail.

GETTING THERE: Blue River CG is located approx. 6 mi. N of Silverthorne on state HWY 9.

SINGLE RATE:	$10	OPEN DATES:	May-Nov*
# of SINGLE SITES:	29	MAX SPUR:	21 feet
		MAX STAY:	10 days
		ELEVATION:	8400 feet

4 Bogan Flats
Carbondale • lat 39°05'59" lon 107°15'40"

DESCRIPTION: This CG is adjacent to Crystal River, one of the most scenic and popular CGs on District. Group site is 1/4 mi. E of CG. Fishing on the river. Yule creek marble quarry nearby. Buy firewood from host. Supplies can be found at Carbondale. Numerous hiking trails within a few miles of CG.

GETTING THERE: From Carbondale go S on state HWY 133 approx. 18 mi. to forest route 314. Go S on 314 approx. 1 mi. to Bogan Flats CG.

SINGLE RATE:	$11	OPEN DATES:	May-Nov
# of SINGLE SITES:	37	MAX SPUR:	30 feet
GROUP RATE:	$50	MAX STAY:	14 days
# of GROUP SITES:	1	ELEVATION:	7600 feet

5 Bucks
Meeker • lat 39°59'39" lon 107°14'21"

DESCRIPTION: CG is located in a park-like grove of pine, spruce, and willow with mountain views. Frequent afternoon showers. Fly fishing nearby. Historical Trappers Lake in area. Supplies 1/4 mi. from CG. CG tends to fill up quickly on holidays. Firewood sold on site. Several trails nearby.

GETTING THERE: From Meeker go E on state HWY 13 approx. 1 mi. to county route 8. Go S on 8 approx. 39 mi. to Trappers Lake Road. Go W on Trappers Lake Road approx. 11 mi. to Bucks CG.

SINGLE RATE:	$11	OPEN DATES:	May-Nov
# of SINGLE SITES:	10	MAX SPUR:	36 feet
		MAX STAY:	14 days
		ELEVATION:	9800 feet

6 Camp Hale
Dowds Junction • lat 39°26'35" lon 106°19'20"

DESCRIPTION: CG is located in thin pine stands. Once a military training ground during WWII. On historic register as site used to start Vail and Beaver Creek ski areas. Moderate use. Supplies in Minturn. Gather firewood locally. Large game in area. Numerous horse, hiking, and mountain biking trails nearby.

GETTING THERE: Camp Hale CG is located approx. 17 mi. S of Dowds Junction (I-70) on US HWY 24.

SINGLE RATE:	$10	OPEN DATES:	May-Sept*
# of SINGLE SITES:	21	MAX SPUR:	60 feet
		MAX STAY:	10 days
		ELEVATION:	9200 feet

7 Cataract Creek
Silverthorne • lat 39°49'00" lon 106°18'30"

DESCRIPTION: West of Green Mountain Reservoir near Cataract Lake. Fishing access with boat launch on site. Popular area for sailing and hunting. Supplies in silverthorne. Firewood may be gathered. Deer and elk frequent area. Horse and hiking trails nearby. Fee Demo area, fee charged to enter CG.

GETTING THERE: From Silverthorne go N on state HWY 9 approx. 14 mi. to forest route 30. Go N on 30 approx. 3 mi. to forest route 1725. Go W on 1725 approx. 2 mi. to Cataract Creek CG.

SINGLE RATE:	$5	OPEN DATES:	May-Sept*
# of SINGLE SITES:	4	MAX SPUR:	21 feet
		MAX STAY:	14 days
		ELEVATION:	8600 feet

8 Chapman
Basalt • lat 39°18'31" lon 106°38'11"

DESCRIPTION: Adjacent to Fryingpan River in beautiful wide valley of pine forest. Anglers note Lower Fringpany is "gold medal water". Canoeing, swimming, and ball field. Buy firewood or gather locally. Supplies in Thomasville, 4 mi. W. Hiking trails from CG with interpretative signs.

GETTING THERE: From Basalt go E on county route 104 approx. 6 mi. past Ruedi Reservoir to Chapman CG.

SINGLE RATE:	$11	OPEN DATES:	May-Sept
# of SINGLE SITES:	84	MAX SPUR:	50 feet
GROUP RATE:	$75	MAX STAY:	14 days
# of GROUP SITES:	1	ELEVATION:	8800 feet

9 Coffee Pot Spring
Dotsero • lat 39°40'33" lon 107°12'11"

DESCRIPTION: CG on the edge of an aspen and fir forest overlooking an open meadow with views of mountain peaks. Wildflowers are abundant in season. 4X4 roads in area. Sub-alpine growth is fragile. Connections to horse and hiking trails. Supplies are available in Gypsum. Firewood may be scarce.

GETTING THERE: From Dotsero (exit 133 on I-70) go N on county route 40 approx. 2 mi. to forest route 600. Go W on 600 approx. 13 mi. to Coffee Pot Spring CG.

SINGLE RATE:	$6	OPEN DATES:	June-Oct
# of SINGLE SITES:	8	MAX SPUR:	20 feet
		MAX STAY:	14 days
		ELEVATION:	10160 feet

10 Cow Creek North
Silverthorne • lat 39°52'45" lon 106°17'19"

DESCRIPTION: In open sagebrush set on Green Mountain Reservoir. Boating and fishing access on site. Windsurfing, sailing, and canoeing are popular on lake. Supplies in Silverthorne. Bring your firewood or gather locally. Hiking and mountain biking trails in area. Undeveloped CG with no drinking water.

GETTING THERE: Cow Creek North CG is located approx. 19 mi. N of Silverthorne on state HWY 9.

SINGLE RATE:	No fee	OPEN DATES:	May-Nov*
# of SINGLE SITES:	32		
		MAX STAY:	14 days
		ELEVATION:	8000 feet

 Campground has hosts 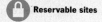 **Reservable sites**   **Accessible facilities**   **Fully developed**   **Semi-developed**   **Rustic facilities**

NOTE: Open dates listed are typical. Actual dates are dependent on conditions such as snow pack.

11 Cow Creek South
Silverthorne • lat 39˚52'45" lon 106˚17'19"

DESCRIPTION: CG set in open sagebrush on the shores of Green Mountain Reservoir. Boating and fishing access on site. Windsurfing, sailing, and canoeing are popular on lake. Supplies in Silverthorne. Firewood may be scarce. Hiking and mountain biking trails nearby. Undeveloped CG, no drinking water.

GETTING THERE: Cow Creek South CG is located approx. 19 mi. N of Silverthorne on state HWY 9.

SINGLE RATE:	No fee	OPEN DATES:	May-Nov*
# of SINGLE SITES:	10	MAX SPUR:	40 feet
		MAX STAY:	14 days
		ELEVATION:	8000 feet

16 Difficult
Aspen • lat 39˚08'29" lon 106˚46'24"

DESCRIPTION: This CG is located in pine forest. Fishing on nearby Roaring Fork River. Supplies available in Aspen. Gather firewood locally. Deer and elk frequent the area. Interpretative talks on Saturdays. Hike Difficult Trail from CG or mountain bike Independence Pass Road 14 mi. E.

GETTING THERE: Difficult CG is located approx. 5 mi. S of Aspen on state HWY 82.

SINGLE RATE:	$12	OPEN DATES:	May-Sept
# of SINGLE SITES:	47	MAX SPUR:	40 feet
GROUP RATE:	$45	MAX STAY:	5 days
# of GROUP SITES:	1	ELEVATION:	8180 feet

12 Cutthroat
Meeker • lat 39˚59'35" lon 107˚14'29"

DESCRIPTION: CG is in a pine, spruce, and willow grove with spectacular mountain views. Frequent afternoon showers. Fly fishing nearby. Historical Trappers Lake. Supplies are available only 1/4 mi. away. CG tends to fill up quickly on holidays. Firewood sold on site. Numerous foot and horse trails in area.

GETTING THERE: From Meeker go E on state HWY 13 approx. 1 mi. to county route 8. Go S on 8 approx. 39 mi. to Trappers Lake Road. Go W on Trappers Lake Road approx. 11 mi. to Cutthroat CG.

SINGLE RATE:	$11	OPEN DATES:	May-Nov
# of SINGLE SITES:	14	MAX SPUR:	36 feet
		MAX STAY:	14 days
		ELEVATION:	9800 feet

17 East Fork
Dowds Junction • lat 39˚26'00" lon 106˚17'30"

DESCRIPTION: Group site is open and park-like located within Camp Hale, site of military camp during WWII. Fish Eagle Fork River. Hike trails from CG. Horse and mountain bike trail nearby at Kokomo Pass and Tennessee Pass. Roads for 4X4 use. Up to 200 people at CG. Fee based on number of people.

GETTING THERE: From Dowds Junction (I-70) go S on US HWY 24 approx. 17 mi. to forest route 714. Go E on 714 approx. 2 mi. to East Fork CG.

		OPEN DATES:	May-Sept*
GROUP RATE:	Varies	MAX STAY:	10 days
# of GROUP SITES:	1	ELEVATION:	9200 feet

13 Davis Springs
Silverthorne • lat 39˚50'16" lon 106˚13'50"

DESCRIPTION: CG set in park like aspen and grassy areas. Near upper end (west side) of Green Mountain Reservoir. Pit toilets, with no water. Good foot access for fishing. Boating, sailing, and canoeing are popular. Supplies in Silverthorne. Horse and mountain biking trails in area.

GETTING THERE: Davis Springs CG is located approx. 15 mi. N of Silverthorne on state HWY 9.

SINGLE RATE:	No fee	OPEN DATES:	May-Nov*
# of SINGLE SITES:	6		
		MAX STAY:	14 days
		ELEVATION:	8000 feet

18 East Marvine
Meeker • lat 40˚00'38" lon 107˚25'34"

DESCRIPTION: CG is in grove of pine with spectacular mountain views. Frequent afternoon showers. Stream fishing in area. Supplies and groceries are available 10 mi. at Buford store. Deer and Elk in vicinity. Full on weekends. Firewood sold on site. Horse and foot trails nearby. Horse corral.

GETTING THERE: From Meeker go E on state HWY 13 approx. 1 mi. to county route 8. Go S on 8 approx. 28 mi. to county route 12 (Marvine Road). Go W on 12 approx. 6 mi. to East Marvine CG.

SINGLE RATE:	$10	OPEN DATES:	May-Nov
# of SINGLE SITES:	7	MAX SPUR:	50 feet
		MAX STAY:	14 days
		ELEVATION:	8200 feet

14 Dearhamer
Basalt • lat 39˚21'40" lon 106˚44'14"

DESCRIPTION: This CG is situated on Fryingpan River east of Reudi Reservoir. There is a boat launch to Reudi Reservoir on site. Enjoy fishing in both the reservoir and river. Supplies and groceries are available at Meredith (1/2 mi. E) or Basalt. Firewood is sold on site. No designated trails are nearby.

GETTING THERE: Dearhamer CG is located approx. 19 mi. E of Basalt on county route 104.

SINGLE RATE:	$11	OPEN DATES:	May-Sept
# of SINGLE SITES:	13	MAX SPUR:	32 feet
		MAX STAY:	14 days
		ELEVATION:	7800 feet

19 Elk Wallow
Basalt • lat 39˚20'38" lon 106˚36'43"

DESCRIPTION: This CG is situated adjacent to the N Fork of the Fryingpan River. Fishing on river. A quiet and relatively primitive setting. No drinking water available on site. Supplies are 7 mi. W in Meredith. Light use, heavier during the hunting season. Hiking trail 1 mi. E on forest road 501. Donations accepted.

GETTING THERE: From Basalt go E on county route 104 approx. 27 mi. to forest route 501. Go E on 501 approx. 3 mi. to Elk Wallow CG.

SINGLE RATE:	No fee	OPEN DATES:	May-Nov*
# of SINGLE SITES:	7	MAX SPUR:	22 feet
		MAX STAY:	14 days
		ELEVATION:	8800 feet

15 Deep Lake
Dotsero • lat 39˚46'18" lon 107˚18'05"

DESCRIPTION: This CG is set among subalpine growth of spruce and fir on the lake shore. Popular fishing area for rainbow and brook trout. Ramp for electric motored boats or canoes. Historic Ute and pioneer area. Firewood may be scarce. Supplies and groceries are available in Gypsum.

GETTING THERE: From Dotsero (exit 133 on I-70) go N on county route 40 approx. 2 mi. to forest route 600. Go W on 600 approx. 25 mi. to Deep Lake CG.

SINGLE RATE:	$6	OPEN DATES:	July-Sept
# of SINGLE SITES:	35	MAX SPUR:	35 feet
		MAX STAY:	14 days
		ELEVATION:	10460 feet

20 Elliot Creek
Silverthorne • lat 39˚52'30" lon 106˚20'30"

DESCRIPTION: This CG is situated among fir and aspen. Fairly open and set on a creek near the N side of Green Mountain Reservoir. No drinking water available on site. Boating and fishing nearby. Supplies can be found in Silverthorne. Firewood may be scarce. Hiking trails in area.

GETTING THERE: From Silverthorne go N on state HWY 9 approx. 14 mi. to forest route 30. Go N on 30 approx. 6 mi. to Elliot Creek CG.

SINGLE RATE:	No fee	OPEN DATES:	May-Nov*
# of SINGLE SITES:	28		
		MAX STAY:	14 days
		ELEVATION:	8000 feet

 Campground has hosts   Reservable sites   Accessible facilities   Fully developed   Semi-developed   Rustic facilities

NOTE: Open dates listed are typical. Actual dates are dependent on conditions such as snow pack.

21 — Fulford Cave

Eagle • lat 39°29'30" lon 106°39'30"

DESCRIPTION: This CG is a cluster of small, partially shaded sites near East Brush Creek with an active beaver pond. Brook and rainbow trout in Brush Creek. Historic mining area and caves nearby. Firewood may be scarce. Supplies in Eagle. Many trails for hiking begin nearby, but not on site.

GETTING THERE: From Eagle go S on county route 307 (forest route 400) approx. 8 mi. to forest route 415. Go E on 415 approx. 6 mi. to Fulford Cave CG.

SINGLE RATE:	$8	OPEN DATES:	June-Oct
# of SINGLE SITES:	7	MAX SPUR:	20 feet
		MAX STAY:	14 days
		ELEVATION:	9600 feet

22 — Gold Pan
Frisco • lat 40°47'14" lon 106°53'22"

DESCRIPTION: This CG is situated in the Peninsula Recreation Area on Dillon Reservoir. There is a boat launch nearby. Expect warm days with cool nights. Prepare for rapid weather changes. There are nearby trails for hiking and mountain biking. Supplies and groceries can be found at Fisco or Silverthorne.

GETTING THERE: Gold Pan CG is located on Frisco Bay of Dillon Reservoir outside of Frisco, CO. Reservations required.

SINGLE RATE:	$8	OPEN DATES:	May-Sept*
# of SINGLE SITES:	1		
		MAX STAY:	10 days
		ELEVATION:	9100 feet

23 — Gold Park

Dowds Junction • lat 39°24'12" lon 106°26'06"

DESCRIPTION: This is a small CG located in Homestake Valley. Supplies and groceries can be found in Minturn. Fishing in area, canoeing on Homestake Reservoir. Campers may gather their firewood locally. CG receives moderate use. Horse, mountain biking, and many hiking trails in area.

GETTING THERE: From Dowds Junction (I-70) go S on US HWY 24 approx. 12 mi. to forest route 703. Go S on 703 approx. 6 mi. to Gold Park CG.

SINGLE RATE:	$10	OPEN DATES:	May-Sept*
# of SINGLE SITES:	11	MAX SPUR:	40 feet
		MAX STAY:	10 days
		ELEVATION:	9300 feet

24 — Gore Creek

Vail • lat 39°37'39" lon 106°16'21"

DESCRIPTION: This CG is located in a forested area close to Vail and Eagle's Nest Wilderness. There is fishing access at the CG. This CG receives heavy use. Supplies and groceries can be found in Vail. There is a road for mountain biking nearby. A hiking trailhead to the wilderness area stems from this CG.

GETTING THERE: Gore Creek CG is located approx. 4 mi. E of Vail off of I-70 to frontage road. Follow frontage road approx. 2 mi. to closure gate. CG is adjacent to gate.

SINGLE RATE:	$12	OPEN DATES:	May-Oct*
# of SINGLE SITES:	25	MAX SPUR:	60 feet
		MAX STAY:	10 days
		ELEVATION:	8700 feet

25 — Heaton Bay
Dillon • lat 39°35'30" lon 106°05'30"

DESCRIPTION: This CG is located on Dillon Reservoir and offers fishing access. Expect mild to hot days with cold nights. The high elevation may bring rapid weather changes. Supplies and groceries can be found in Dillon. Firewood may be scarce, it is best to bring your own. Multiple hiking trails are nearby.

GETTING THERE: Heaton Bay CG is located on Dillon Reservoir between Dillon and Silverthorne on US HWY 6.

SINGLE RATE:	$11	OPEN DATES:	May-Oct*
# of SINGLE SITES:	72	MAX SPUR:	90 feet
		MAX STAY:	8 days
		ELEVATION:	9100 feet

26 — Himes Peak
Meeker • lat 40°01'42" lon 107°16'18"

DESCRIPTION: This CG is situated in a grove of pine with mountain views. There are frequent afternoon showers. Stream and fly fishing is nearby. Supplies and groceries are available 4 mi. away. CG tends to fill up quickly on weekends. Firewood is sold on site. Hiking and horse trails are in the area.

GETTING THERE: From Meeker go E on state HWY 13 approx. 1 mi. to county route 8. Go S on 8 approx. 39 mi. to Trappers Lake Road. Go W on Trappers Lake Road approx. 6 mi. to Himes Peak CG.

SINGLE RATE:	$10	OPEN DATES:	June-Nov
# of SINGLE SITES:	11	MAX SPUR:	36 feet
		MAX STAY:	14 days
		ELEVATION:	8800 feet

27 — Hornsilver
Dowds Junction • lat 39°29'20" lon 106°22'02"

DESCRIPTION: Small forested CG adjacent to Highway 24 and Hornsilver Creek. Supplies and groceries can be found in Minturn. Campers may gather their firewood locally. CG receives moderate use. Holy Cross Wilderness may be accessed from Homestake Road, south of the CG.

GETTING THERE: Hornsilver CG is located approx. 11 mi. S of Dowds Junction (I-70) on US HWY 24.

SINGLE RATE:	$10	OPEN DATES:	May-Oct*
# of SINGLE SITES:	12	MAX SPUR:	30 feet
		MAX STAY:	10 days
		ELEVATION:	8800 feet

28 — Klines Folly
Dotsero • lat 39°45'34" lon 107°18'39"

DESCRIPTION: CG located in an open subalpine meadow on the edge of a small lake. No drinking water available on site. Shore or non-motorized boat fishing on Heart Lake. 4X4 roads nearby. No trails. Subalpine meadows are fragile and closed. Firewood may be scarce. Supplies are available in Gypsum.

GETTING THERE: From Dotsero (exit 133 on I-70) go N on county route 40 approx. 2 mi. to forest route 600. Go W on 600 approx. 28 mi. to forest route 645. Go W on 645 approx. 1 mi. to Klines Folly CG.

SINGLE RATE:	$6	OPEN DATES:	July-Sept
# of SINGLE SITES:	4		
		MAX STAY:	14 days
		ELEVATION:	10750 feet

29 — Lincoln Gulch
Aspen • lat 39°07'02" lon 106°41'43"

DESCRIPTION: This CG is situated in a pine forest. Fishing on nearby Roaring Fork and Lincoln Creeks. Supplies in Aspen approx. 7 mi. N of CG. Deer, elk, and small wildlife can be seen in the area. Gather firewood locally. Mountain biking and hiking trails on Lincoln Creek RD. OHV to Grizzly Reservoir.

GETTING THERE: Lincoln Gulch CG is located approx. 7 mi. S of Aspen on state HWY 82.

SINGLE RATE:	$9	OPEN DATES:	June-Sept
# of SINGLE SITES:	6	MAX SPUR:	30 feet
		MAX STAY:	5 days
		ELEVATION:	9700 feet

30 — Little Mattie
Basalt • lat 39°22'30" lon 106°47'30"

DESCRIPTION: This CG is set on Ruedi Reservoir. Sailing, boating (1/4 mi. to boat ramp), wind surfing, (3 mi. E on county Rd 104), and fishing on the reservoir. Dump station on site. Buy firewood from host. Supplies can be found in Meredith (8 mi. E) or Basalt. Hiking trails 1/2 mi. from CG.

GETTING THERE: Little Mattie CG is located approx. 16 mi. E of Basalt on county route 104.

SINGLE RATE:	$10	OPEN DATES:	May-Sept
# of SINGLE SITES:	20	MAX SPUR:	22 feet
		MAX STAY:	14 days
		ELEVATION:	7800 feet

 Campground has hosts   **Reservable sites**   **Accessible facilities**   **Fully developed**   **Semi-developed**   **Rustic facilities**

NOTE: Open dates listed are typical. Actual dates are dependent on conditions such as snow pack.

WHITE RIVER NATIONAL FOREST • COLORADO • 21—30

31 Little Maud
Basalt • lat 39°22'30" lon 106°47'30"

DESCRIPTION: This CG is located on Ruedi Reservoir. Fishing, boating, (ramp 1/4 mi.) wind surfing, (3 mi. E), and canoeing on the reservoir. Dump station on site. Buy firewood from host. Limited supplies can be found 8 mi. away at local stores. Hiking trails 1/2 mi. E on county RD 104.

GETTING THERE: Little Maud CG is located approx. 13 mi. E of Basalt on county route 104.

SINGLE RATE:	$14	OPEN DATES:	May-Sept
# of SINGLE SITES:	22	MAX SPUR:	32 feet
		MAX STAY:	14 days
		ELEVATION:	7800 feet

36 Meadow Lake
Buford • lat 39°49'30" lon 107°31'30"

DESCRIPTION: This CG offers boating and fishing access to Meadow Lake. Electric motors allowed on the lake. A boat ramp and accessible fishing pier are on site. Please check fishing regulations for the area. There are mountain biking trails in the area. High elevation brings rapid weather changes.

GETTING THERE: From Buford go S on county route 59 approx. 11 mi. to forest route 823. Go E on 823 approx. 4.5 mi. to Meadow Lake CG.

SINGLE RATE:	No fee	OPEN DATES:	June-Oct
# of SINGLE SITES:	10	MAX SPUR:	16 feet
		MAX STAY:	14 days
		ELEVATION:	9600 feet

32 Lost Man
Aspen • lat 39°07'18" lon 106°37'28"

DESCRIPTION: This CG is situated in a pine forest with fishing nearby. Expect mild days with frequent afternoon rains. Supplies can be found in Aspen approx. 14.5 mi. N of CG. Campers may gather their firewood locally. Hike Midway and Lost Man Trails. Mountain bike on Independence RD.

GETTING THERE: Lost Man CG is located approx. 14.5 mi. S of Aspen on state HWY 82.

SINGLE RATE:	$9	OPEN DATES:	June-Sept
# of SINGLE SITES:	10	MAX SPUR:	30 feet
		MAX STAY:	5 days
		ELEVATION:	10700 feet

37 Mollie B.
Basalt • lat 39°22'30" lon 106°47'30"

DESCRIPTION: This CG is situated on Ruedi Reservoir. Fishing, sailing, boating (boat launch 1/4 mi.), and wind surfing (3 mi. E on County Rd 104) on the reservoir. Supplies and groceries can be found 8 mi. E at local store or at Basalt. Buy firewood from host. Hiking trail 1/2 mi. E on county route 104.

GETTING THERE: Mollie B. CG is located on the Reudi Reservoir approx. 14 mi. E of Basalt on county route 104.

SINGLE RATE:	$14	OPEN DATES:	May-Sept
# of SINGLE SITES:	26	MAX SPUR:	32 feet
		MAX STAY:	14 days
		ELEVATION:	7800 feet

33 Lowry
Silverthorne • lat 39°32'30" lon 105°90'30"

DESCRIPTION: This CG is situated in a dense fir and pine forest. No immediate fishing opportunities in the vicinity. A dump station and some electric hookups (for an additional fee) are offered at the CG. Campers may gather dead and down firewood. Supplies are available at Silverthorne.

GETTING THERE: From Silverthorne go E on HWY 6 approx. 4 mi. to Swan Mtn. Road. Go S on Swan Mtn. Rd. approx. 3 mi. to Lowry CG.

SINGLE RATE:	Varies	OPEN DATES:	May-Sept*
# of SINGLE SITES:	29	MAX SPUR:	28 feet
		MAX STAY:	14 days
		ELEVATION:	9320 feet

38 North Fork
Meeker • lat 40°03'30" lon 107°25'30"

DESCRIPTION: CG is located in aspen with underbrush and plentiful flowers. Mountain views. Cold mornings, warm summers, afternoon T-showers. 14 mi. to Buford Store for grocs. Flyfishing in nearby streams. Deer, elk, birds, chipmunks, and marmots in area. Rarely full, nice all Summer. Hiking and horse trails.

GETTING THERE: From Meeker go E on state HWY 13 1 mi. to county route 8. Go S on 8 34 mi. to North Fork CG.

SINGLE RATE:	$11	OPEN DATES:	June-Nov
# of SINGLE SITES:	39	MAX SPUR:	60 feet
GROUP RATE:	$45	MAX STAY:	14 days
# of GROUP SITES:	1	ELEVATION:	7750 feet

34 Marvine
Blanco • lat 40°00'43" lon 107°25'41"

DESCRIPTION: This CG is in a park-like grove of pine with spectacular mountain views. Frequent afternoon showers. Stream and fly fishing nearby. Supplies 8 mi. to Buford store. Elk and deer in vicinity. Full weekends. Firewood sold on site. Hiking and horse trails in area. Horse corral.

GETTING THERE: From Blanco go E on county route 8 approx. 24 mi. to forest/county route 12. Go S on 12 approx. 4 mi. to Marvine CG.

SINGLE RATE:	$10	OPEN DATES:	June-Nov
# of SINGLE SITES:	18	MAX SPUR:	60 feet
		MAX STAY:	14 days
		ELEVATION:	8200 feet

39 Peak One
Silverthorne • lat 39°35'01" lon 106°04'12"

DESCRIPTION: This CG is situated in a mixed forest on the shores of Dillon Reservoir. Fish the reservoir by shore or boat. Check for local regulations. Warm days with cold nights. Supplies are available at Frisco or Silverthorne. Campers may gather dead and down firewood. Hiking and walking trails from site.

GETTING THERE: From Silverthorne go W on I-70 approx. 6 mi. to Frisco Exit 203 for HWY 9. Go S on 9 to Peninsular Recreation Area. Go N approx. 2 mi. to Peak One CG on west side of road.

SINGLE RATE:	$11	OPEN DATES:	May-Sept*
# of SINGLE SITES:	79	MAX SPUR:	35 feet
		MAX STAY:	8 days
		ELEVATION:	9040 feet

35 McDonald Flats
Silverthorne • lat 39°51'02" lon 106°14'14"

DESCRIPTION: This CG is in an open area on shore of Green Mountain Reservoir. Power boat fishing access nearby. Canoeing, sailboating, and wind surfing access on site. Firewood is scarce, best to bring your own. Supplies and groceries can be found in Silverthorne. Light hiking trails nearby.

GETTING THERE: From Silverthorne go N on state HWY 9 approx. 15 mi. to McDonald Flats CG.

SINGLE RATE:	$4	OPEN DATES:	May-Oct*
# of SINGLE SITES:	13	MAX SPUR:	21 feet
		MAX STAY:	10 days
		ELEVATION:	8000 feet

40 Peninsula
Frisco • lat 39°35'08" lon 106°30'34"

DESCRIPTION: This CG is set in the Peninsula Recreational Area on Dillon Reservoir. There is a boat launch nearby. Expect warm days with cool nights. High elevation may bring rapid weather changes. There are nearby trails for hiking and mountain biking. Supplies can be found in Frisco or Silverthorne.

GETTING THERE: Peninsula CG is located approx. 2 mi. E of Frisco on Dillon Reservoir.

SINGLE RATE:	$8	OPEN DATES:	May-Sept*
# of SINGLE SITES:	129	MAX SPUR:	50 feet
		MAX STAY:	10 days
		ELEVATION:	9100 feet

 Campground has hosts   🔒 **Reservable sites**   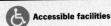 **Accessible facilities**   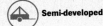 **Fully developed**   **Semi-developed**   **Rustic facilities**

41 Pine Cove
Silverthorne • lat 39°35'18" lon 106°04'05"

DESCRIPTION: This CG is situated in the Peninsula Recreation Area on the shores of Dillon Reservoir. Fish from reservoir. Boat launch provided on lake. Expect warm days with cool nights. Numerous trails for hiking and mountain biking can be found nearby. Supplies are available at Fisco or Silverthorne.

GETTING THERE: From Silverthorne go W on I-70 6 mi. the Frisco Exit 203 for HWY 9. Go S on 9 3 mi. to the Peninsula Recreation Area. Turn N (left) and go 2 mi. to Pine Cove CG.

SINGLE RATE:	$8	OPEN DATES:	May-Sept*
# of SINGLE SITES:	55	MAX SPUR:	40 feet
		MAX STAY:	10 days
		ELEVATION:	9040 feet

42 Portal
Aspen • lat 39°04'35" lon 106°36'43"

DESCRIPTION: This CG is situated in a pine forest with fishing access on Grizzly Reservoir. Supplies can be found in Aspen approx. 18 mi. N of CG. Deer, elk, and small wildlife can be seen in the area. Gather firewood locally. Hiking and mountain biking on nearby trails. OHV opportunities.

GETTING THERE: From Aspen go S on state HWY 82 approx. 11 mi. to forest route 106. Go S on 106 approx. 7 mi. to Portal CG.

SINGLE RATE:	$7	OPEN DATES:	June-Sept
# of SINGLE SITES:	7	MAX SPUR:	30 feet
		MAX STAY:	5 days
		ELEVATION:	10700 feet

43 Prairie Point
Silverthorne • lat 39°50'34" lon 106°13'49"

DESCRIPTION: This CG is set in an open area near Green Mountain Reservoir. Fish shore or power boat on the reservoir. Canoes, sail boats, and sail boards are popular on the lake. Supplies and groceries can be found in Silverthorne. Firewood may be scarce, best to bring your own. Hiking trails in the area.

GETTING THERE: Prairie Point CG is located approx. 14 mi. N of Silverthorne on state HWY 9.

SINGLE RATE:	$4	OPEN DATES:	May-Nov*
# of SINGLE SITES:	33	MAX SPUR:	20 feet
		MAX STAY:	14 days
		ELEVATION:	8000 feet

44 Prospector
Silverthorne • lat 39°35'59" lon 106°02'31"

DESCRIPTION: This CG is set high in the mountains near Dillon Reservoir. Power boats are allowed on the reservoir. Hiking and mountain biking is available in the surrounding area. Firewood is also available. Supplies and groceries can be found in Silverthorne.

GETTING THERE: From Silverthorne go E on US HWY 6 approx. 4 mi. to forest route 95 (Swan Mtn. Road). Go N on 95 approx. 1 mi. to Prospector CG.

SINGLE RATE:	$10	OPEN DATES:	May-Sept*
# of SINGLE SITES:	107	MAX SPUR:	32 feet
		MAX STAY:	8 days
		ELEVATION:	9100 feet

45 Redstone
Carbondale • lat 39°12'00" lon 107°13'50"

DESCRIPTION: CG set next to the Crystal River. Fishing on river. Modern CG designed for use by large RVs. Showers. Some electrical hookup sites. Playground, basketball court, horseshoe pits. Supplies in Redstone 1 mi. S. Hiking trail 1/2 mi. S on road to Redstone. Climbing 1/2 mi. N on HWY 133.

GETTING THERE: Redstone CG is located approx. 17 mi. S of Carbondale on state HWY 133.

SINGLE RATE:	Varies	OPEN DATES:	May-Sept
# of SINGLE SITES:	35	MAX SPUR:	40 feet
		MAX STAY:	14 days
		ELEVATION:	7200 feet

46 Ruedi Marina
Basalt • lat 39°22'23" lon 106°48'48"

DESCRIPTION: Providing access to water sports and mountain recreation. No trailer size limits. Reservoir is open to fishing, boating and water skiing (launch on site), sailing and wind surfing. Hiking trails 1/2 mi. Supplies at Basalt.

GETTING THERE: From Basalt go E approx. 16 mi. on Fryingpan Rd (County Rd 104) to Reudi Marina CG.

SINGLE RATE:	$10	OPEN DATES:	May-Sept*
# of SINGLE SITES:	5	MAX SPUR:	20 feet
		MAX STAY:	14 days
		ELEVATION:	7800 feet

47 Shepherds Rim
Meeker • lat 39°59'43" lon 107°14'33"

DESCRIPTION: CG is located in pine, spruce, and willow; with underbrush. Cold mornings, warm summers, afternoon T-showers. Flyfishing for cutthroats. Deer, elk, birds, chipmunks, and marmots. Busy weekends and holidays, nice mid-July through August. Several trails nearby. Mosquitos.

GETTING THERE: From Meeker go E on state HWY 13 approx. 1 mi. to county route 8. Go RT on 8 39 mi. to Trappers Lake Road. Go 11 mi. to Shepherds Rim CG.

SINGLE RATE:	$11	OPEN DATES:	June-Nov
# of SINGLE SITES:	20	MAX SPUR:	36 feet
		MAX STAY:	14 days
		ELEVATION:	9750 feet

48 Silver Bar
Aspen • lat 39°08'30" lon 106°53'00"

DESCRIPTION: This CG is located in pine forest setting. Fishing within walking distance to Maroon Creek. Supplies in Aspen approx. 5 mi. N of CG. Campers may gather firewood locally. Elk, deer, and small wildlife in area. Hike 5 mi. to Maroon Lake for interpretative talks. Mountain biking opportunities.

GETTING THERE: From Aspen go S on forest route 125 approx. 5 mi. to Silver Bar CG.

SINGLE RATE:	$12	OPEN DATES:	May-Sept
# of SINGLE SITES:	4	MAX SPUR:	30 feet
		MAX STAY:	5 days
		ELEVATION:	8300 feet

49 Silver Bell
Aspen • lat 39°08'00" lon 106°53'00"

DESCRIPTION: This CG is located in a park-like setting of pine and aspen with open meadows nearby. Fishing access at Maroon Creek. Trails to hike and mountain bike within 5 mi. of CG. Supplies in Aspen approx. 4 mi. N of CG. Campers may gather firewood. Elk, deer, and small wildlife in area.

GETTING THERE: From Aspen go S on forest route 125 approx. 4 mi. to Silver Bell CG. No trailers or RV's permitted.

SINGLE RATE:	$12	OPEN DATES:	May-Sept
# of SINGLE SITES:	4	MAX SPUR:	30 feet
		MAX STAY:	5 days
		ELEVATION:	8400 feet

50 Silver Queen
Aspen • lat 39°08'00" lon 106°53'30"

DESCRIPTION: CG is in a park-like setting situated along a small creek. Fishing on Maroon Creek. Wildflowers are especially nice. Supplies in Aspen approx. 6.5 mi. N of CG. Campers may gather firewood locally. Elk, deer, moose, and small wildlife in area. Trails nearby to hike and mountain bike to Maroon Lake.

GETTING THERE: From Aspen go S on HWY 82 approx. 1 mi. to forest route 125. Go S on 125 approx. 5.5 mi. to Silver Queen CG. No trailers or RVs permitted.

SINGLE RATE:	$12	OPEN DATES:	May-Sept
# of SINGLE SITES:	6	MAX SPUR:	30 feet
		MAX STAY:	5 days
		ELEVATION:	9100 feet

 Campground has hosts   Reservable sites   Accessible facilities   Fully developed   Semi-developed   Rustic facilities

NOTE: Open dates listed are typical. Actual dates are dependent on conditions such as snow pack.

51 South Fork
Buford • lat 39°52'00" lon 107°32'00"

DESCRIPTION: This CG is set in a valley with views of pass. The South Fork of White River offers fishing. Limited supplies 10 mi. away. Expect mild days with frequent noon rains. Gather firewood locally. Deer and elk in area. S Fork TH is adjacent to the CG accessing multiple trails.

GETTING THERE: Go E on Highway 13 from Meeker approx. 1 mile to county road 8. Go E on 8 approx. 18 miles to county route 10 (S Fork RD). Go S on 10 approx. 12 mi. to South Fork CG.

		OPEN DATES:	May-Nov*
SINGLE RATE:	$10	MAX SPUR:	60 feet
# of SINGLE SITES:	17	MAX STAY:	14 days
		ELEVATION:	7600 feet

52 Supply Basin
Dotsero • lat 39°45'35" lon 107°19'10"

DESCRIPTION: This CG is on a small lake set in a spruce and fir forest. Some shady sites, most sites too small for RVs. Fish for trout on nearby Heart Lake; no gas motors. Supplies in Gypsum. Firewood may be scarce, best to bring your own. Multiple 4X4 roads in area. No drinking water available on site.

GETTING THERE: From Dotsero (exit 133 on I-70) go N on county route 40 approx. 2 mi. to forest route 600. Go W on 600 approx. 24 mi. to forest route 645. Go W on 645 approx. 1 mi. to Supply Basin CG.

		OPEN DATES:	July-Sept
SINGLE RATE:	$6	MAX SPUR:	20 feet
# of SINGLE SITES:	7	MAX STAY:	14 days
		ELEVATION:	10750 feet

53 Sweetwater Lake
Dotsero • lat 39°47'48" lon 107°09'37"

DESCRIPTION: This CG is located in an open setting of scrub oak on Sweetwater Lake. Canoe or small electric motors are allowed for fishing. Supplies and groceries are available in Gypsum. Firewood may be scarce, it is best to bring your own. Numerous horse and hiking trails are nearby.

GETTING THERE: From Dotsero (exit 133 on I-70) go N on state HWY 37 approx. 7 mi. to county route 40. Go N on 40 approx. 9 mi. to Sweetwater Lake CG.

		OPEN DATES:	May-Nov
SINGLE RATE:	$8	MAX SPUR:	30 feet
# of SINGLE SITES:	10	MAX STAY:	14 days
		ELEVATION:	7700 feet

54 Three Forks
Rifle • lat 39°45'49" lon 107°41'37"

DESCRIPTION: This CG is set along side of East Rifle Creek, which offers stream fishing. Supplies in Rifle. Hike, horse, and mountain bike Three Forks Trail. No horses allowed in CG. Rock Climb nearby Rifle Mountain Park. Firewood is scarce. No drinking water. Open beyond dates with limited services.

GETTING THERE: From Rifle go N on state HWY 13 approx. 1 mi. to state HWY 325. Go N on 325 approx. 11 mi. to forest route 832. Go N on 832 aprox. 3 mi. to Three Forks CG.

		OPEN DATES:	May-Nov*
SINGLE RATE:	$11	MAX SPUR:	16 feet
# of SINGLE SITES:	3	MAX STAY:	7 days
		ELEVATION:	7600 feet

55 Tigiwon
Dowds Junction • lat 39°31'24" lon 106°25'11"

DESCRIPTION: This CG is situated in a forested setting with views of Gore Range. Fish at Cross Creek and Lake Constantine close to CG. No drinking water available on site. Supplies and groceries can be found in Minturn. Campers may gather their firewood locally. Hiking trailheads on site.

GETTING THERE: From Dowds Junction (I-70) go S on US HWY 24 approx. 4 mi. to county route 100. Go S on 100 approx. 5 mi. to Tigiwon CG. Not recommended for trailers or RVs. 4WD necessary.

		OPEN DATES:	July-Sept
SINGLE RATE:	$8	MAX SPUR:	25 feet
# of SINGLE SITES:	9	MAX STAY:	10 days
		ELEVATION:	9900 feet

56 Trapline
Meeker • lat 39°59'38" lon 107°14'25"

DESCRIPTION: CG is a part of the Trappers Lake area CGs. Forested area with multiple fishing lakes and creeks nearby. Dump station. Limited supplies 2 mi. or at Meeker. Gather firewood locally. Flat Tops Wilderness hiking, mechanized vehicles prohibited. Weather allowing, may be open beyond posted dates.

GETTING THERE: From Meeker go E on county route 8 approx. 39 mi. to forest route 205. Go S on 205 approx. 8 mi. to Trapline CG.

		OPEN DATES:	May-Oct
SINGLE RATE:	$11	MAX SPUR:	36 feet
# of SINGLE SITES:	13	MAX STAY:	10 days
		ELEVATION:	9750 feet

57 Weller
Aspen • lat 39°07'30" lon 106°44'30"

DESCRIPTION: This CG is set in an aspen grove on Independence Pass. Fishing on nearby Roaring Fork River. Expect mild days with frequent afternoon rains. Supplies in Aspen approx. 9 mi. NW of CG. Deer and moose in area. Campers may gather their firewood locally. Hiking on Weller Trail, across road.

GETTING THERE: Weller CG is located approx. 9 mi. SE of Aspen on state HWY 82. WARNING - No vehicles over 35 feet are allowed on Hwy. 82 to access this campground.

		OPEN DATES:	May-Sept*
SINGLE RATE:	$11	MAX SPUR:	40 feet
# of SINGLE SITES:	11	MAX STAY:	5 days
		ELEVATION:	9200 feet

58 Willow
Silverthorne • lat 39°53'21" lon 106°18'30"

DESCRIPTION: This CG is located on Green Mountain Reservoir. Power boat launch available. Canoeing, sailboating, and sail boarding are popular on the lake. Firewood may be scarce, best to bring your own. CG is undeveloped except for vault toilets, no drinking water available on site.

GETTING THERE: From Silverthorne go N on state HWY 9 approx. 21 mi. to forest route 30. Go W on 30 approx. 1 mi. to Willow CG. Located on the N shore of Green Mountain Reservoir.

		OPEN DATES:	May-Nov*
SINGLE RATE:	No fee	MAX SPUR:	25 feet
# of SINGLE SITES:	24	MAX STAY:	14 days
		ELEVATION:	7950 feet

59 Windy Point Group Site
Silverthorne • lat 39°36'30" lon 106°03'00"

DESCRIPTION: CG in an open area located on Swan Mtn. RD on the shore of Dillon Reservoir. Power boating, canoeing, sailboating, and fishing on the reservoir. Supplies at Frisco. Firewood may be scarce. Reservations required. Fee based on # of persons, 15-200 capacity. Hiking and mountain biking trails.

GETTING THERE: From Silverthorne go E on US HWY 6 approx. 3 mi. to forest route 95. Go N on 95 approx. 2 mi. to Windy Point CG. Parking lot will hold 40 vehicles.

		OPEN DATES:	May-Sept
		MAX SPUR:	99 feet
GROUP RATE:	Varies	MAX STAY:	10 days
# of GROUP SITES:	1	ELEVATION:	9100 feet

60 Yeoman Park
Eagle • lat 39°30'06" lon 106°40'35"

DESCRIPTION: In partial forest on edge of wetland meadow, near Brush Creek. Mountain views. Some tent platforms. Fish for brook trout. Large game and small wildlife can be seen in the area. Supplies are available in Eagle. Campers may gather their firewood locally. Horse and hiking trails nearby.

GETTING THERE: From Eagle go S on county route 307 (forest route 400) approx. 8 mi. to forest route 415. Go E on 415 approx. 5 mi. to Yeoman Park CG.

		OPEN DATES:	June-Oct
SINGLE RATE:	$8	MAX SPUR:	30 feet
# of SINGLE SITES:	23	MAX STAY:	14 days
		ELEVATION:	9000 feet

 Campground has hosts   **Reservable sites**   **Accessible facilities**   **Fully developed**   **Semi-developed**   **Rustic facilities**

NOTE: Open dates listed are typical. Actual dates are dependent on conditions such as snow pack.

Woodsy's New Look

"Give a Hoot-Don't Pollute," was the message Woodsy Owl appeared with on America's first Earth Day in 1970. The original keep-it-clean owl was a chubby, mid-ddle-aged cartoon caricature that children seemed to lose interest in by the 1990s. It was then that Woodsy adopt-ed the look that you see here—a slimmer more teenage image. Be on the lookout for an even more modern Woodsy. In the near future, he will likely be sporting cargo pants!

NATIONAL FORESTS OF FLORIDA

The National Forests of Florida are comprised of the Apalachico Ocala, and Osceola National Forests. Each forest offers a myria of year round recreation activities. Leon Sinks is an unusual geo logical area in the Apalachicola. At Leon Sinks take a walk dow nearly six miles of well-maintained trails to see sinkholes, swale caverns, natural bridges, circular depressions and a disappearing stream. On the Ocala, the Florida National Scenic Trail opens th way to the forest. Many of this forest's natural lakes are the hab of trophy bass. Canoeing is also a good way to see the vast sub tropical areas of towering palms, buttressed cypress and sprea maples. Horseback riding on the Osceola provides the opportu to journey quietly through open pine flatwoods and wet, scenic bays. History buffs will enjoy the reenactment of the Battle of Olustee, which pays tribute to the largest Civil War battle in Flo and has become one of the largest reenactments in the nation.

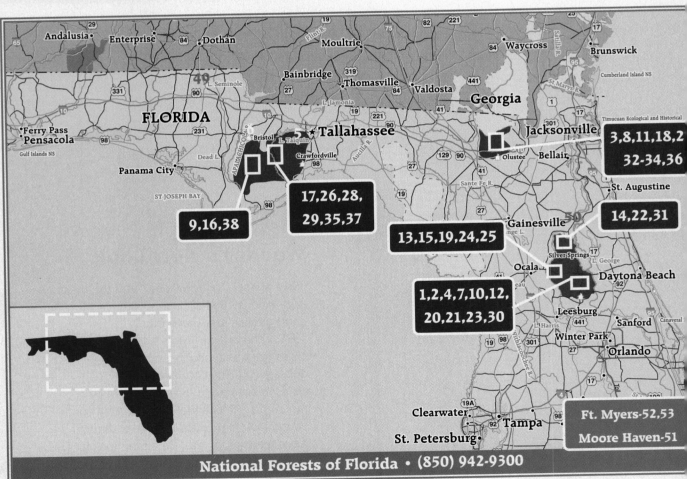

National Forests of Florida • (850) 942-9300

1 Alexander Springs
Umatilla • lat 29°04'44" lon 081°34'48"

DESCRIPTION: In a mixed hardwood and pine forest setting on Alexander Springs. Boat, fish and swim in the springs. Boat launch, for canoe only, at the CG. Supplies available at Umatilla. Deer, bears and birds are common to the area. Many hiking trails in the area. RV dump station at the CG.

GETTING THERE: From Umatilla go N on state HWY 19 approx. 7.5 mi. to county route S 445. Go NE on S 445 approx. 5 mi. to forest route 570. Go N on 570 approx. 1/2 mi. to Alexander Springs CG.

SINGLE RATE:	$13	OPEN DATES:	Yearlong
# of SINGLE SITES:	67	MAX SPUR:	45 feet
		MAX STAY:	14 days
		ELEVATION:	50 feet

2 Big Bass Lake
Umatilla • lat 28°59'08" lon 081°47'03"

DESCRIPTION: In a mixed hardwood and pine forest setting on Big Bass Lake. Boat, fish and swim from the lake. Supplies available at Umatilla. Deer, bears and birds are common to the area. Campers may gather firewood. Many hiking trails in the area. RV dump station at the CG.

GETTING THERE: From Umatilla go NW on state HWY 450 approx. 6 mi. to state HWY 42. Go W on 42 approx. 2 mi. to Big Bass Lake CG.

SINGLE RATE:	$6	OPEN DATES:	Oct-Apr
# of SINGLE SITES:	35	MAX SPUR:	99 feet
		MAX STAY:	14 days
		ELEVATION:	73 feet

3 Big Camp Hunt Camp
Sanderson • lat 30°23'43" lon 082°26'15"

DESCRIPTION: No drinking water. This primitive CG is located in a mixed forest setting adjacent to the Big Gum Swamp Wilderness area. No water supply in the CG area. Supplies available at Sanderson. Deer, raccoons, squirrels and birds are common in the area. Many trails in the area.

GETTING THERE: From Sanderson go NW on state HWY S-229 4 mi. to state HWY S-250. Go W on S-250 3 mi. to forest route 235. Go N on 235 6 mi. to forest route 212. Go W on 212 approx. 1 mi. to Big Camp Hunt CG.

SINGLE RATE:	No fee	OPEN DATES:	Yearlong
		MAX STAY:	14 days
		ELEVATION:	137 feet

4 Buck Lake
Umatilla • lat 29°05'54" lon 081°39'07"

DESCRIPTION: In a mixed hardwood and pine forest setting on Buck Lake. Boat, fish and swim in the lake. Boat launch at the CG. Supplies available at Umatilla. Deer, bears and birds are common to the area. Campers may gather firewood. Many hiking trails in the area.

GETTING THERE: From Umatilla go NE on state HWY 19 12 mi. to forest route 535. Go W on 535 1 mi. to forest route 595-2. Go E on 595-2 1/2 mi. to forest route. Go S on forest route 1/2 mi. to Buck Lake CG.

SINGLE RATE:	$4	OPEN DATES:	Yearlong
		MAX SPUR:	35 feet
		MAX STAY:	14 days
		ELEVATION:	57 feet

5 Buckhorn Hunt Camp
Hilliardville • lat 30°18'00" lon 084°31'30"

DESCRIPTION: This primitive hunt camp is in a mixed forest setting. Drinking water at the CG. Supplies available at Hilliardville. Numerous wildlife can be viewed in the area. Campers may gather firewood. Many trails are nearby.

GETTING THERE: From Hilliardville go NW on state HWY 267 approx. 9 mi. to forest route 360. Go S on 360 approx. 2 mi. to Buckhorn Hunt CG.

SINGLE RATE:	$2	OPEN DATES:	Yearlong
# of SINGLE SITES:	20	MAX STAY:	14 days
		ELEVATION:	110 feet

6 Camel Lake
Woods • lat 30°16'33" lon 084°59'27"

DESCRIPTION: This developed CG is in a mixed forest setting on Camel Lake. Fish, boat and swim from the lake. Boat ramp is at the CG. Supplies available at Woods. Campers may gather firewood. Numerous wildlife can be seen in the area. Hiking trails located in the area.

GETTING THERE: From Woods go S on state HWY 12 approx. 5.5 mi. to forest route 105. Go E on 105 approx. 2 mi. to Camel Lake CG.

SINGLE RATE:	$5	OPEN DATES:	Yearlong
# of SINGLE SITES:	6	MAX SPUR:	99 feet
		MAX STAY:	14 days
		ELEVATION:	55 feet

7 Clearwater Lake
Umatilla • lat 28°58'30" lon 081°33'00"

DESCRIPTION: Located in a tall, longleaf pine forest setting on Clearwater Lake. Fish, canoe and swim in the lake. Supplies available at Umatilla. Deer, turkey, black bears and birds are common in the area. Firewood is provided in the CG area. A 1-mile trail surrounds the lake and many other trails are in the area.

GETTING THERE: From Umatilla go NE on state HWY 19 approx. 2.5 mi. to state HWY 42. Go E on 42 approx. 6 mi. to forest route 536. Go N on 536 approx. .5 mi. to Clearwater Lake CG.

SINGLE RATE:	$8	OPEN DATES:	Yearlong
# of SINGLE SITES:	42	MAX SPUR:	35 feet
		MAX STAY:	14 days
		ELEVATION:	86 feet

8 Cobb Hunt Camp
Olustee • lat 30°14'53" lon 082°24'33"

DESCRIPTION: No drinking water. This primitive CG is located in a mixed forest setting on Ocean Pond. Fish and swim in the pond. Supplies available at Olustee. Deer, raccoons, squirrels and birds are common in the area. Many trails in the area. The Florida National Scenic Hiking Trail is nearby.

GETTING THERE: From Olustee go E on state HWY 10 approx. 1 mi. to state HWY 250-A. Go N on 250-A approx. 2 mi. to forest route 235. Go NE on 235 approx. 1/2 mi. to Cobb Hunt CG.

SINGLE RATE:	No fee	OPEN DATES:	Yearlong
		MAX STAY:	14 days
		ELEVATION:	150 feet

9 Cotton Landing
Sumatra • lat 30°03'08" lon 085°04'18"

DESCRIPTION: This tent only CG is in a mixed forest setting with streams nearby. Fish, boat and swim in nearby streams. Boat launch at the CG. Supplies available at Sumatra. Numerous wildlife can be seen in the area. Campers may gather firewood. No designated trails in the area.

GETTING THERE: From Sumatra go NW on state HWY 379 approx. 2.5 mi. to forest route 123. Go W on 123 approx. 2.5 mi. to forest route 193. Go S on 193 approx. 1.5 mi. to Cotton Landing CG.

SINGLE RATE:	No fee	OPEN DATES:	Yearlong
		MAX STAY:	14 days
		ELEVATION:	21 feet

10 Doe Lake
Umatilla • lat 29°02'17" lon 081°49'34"

DESCRIPTION: In a mixed hardwood and pine forest setting on Lake Catherine. Boat, fish and swim in the lake. Boat launch at the CG. Supplies available at Umatilla. Deer, bears and birds are common to the area. Campers may gather firewood. Many hiking trails in the area.

GETTING THERE: From Umatilla go NW on state HWY 450 6 mi. to state HWY 42. Go W on 42 1.5 mi. to county route 210AV. Go NW on 210AV 4 mi. to forest route 573. Go NE on 573 approx. 1.5 mi. to Doe Lake CG.

SINGLE RATE:	No fee	OPEN DATES:	Yearlong
		MAX SPUR:	35 feet
		MAX STAY:	14 days
		ELEVATION:	63 feet

 Campground has hosts    Reservable sites   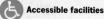 Accessible facilities   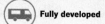 Fully developed   Semi-developed   Rustic facilities

NOTE: Open dates listed are typical. Actual dates are dependent on conditions such as snow pack.

11 East Tower Hunt Camp
Sanderson • lat 30˚23'01" lon 082˚19'52"

DESCRIPTION: This primitive CG is located in a mixed forest setting on the Saint Mary's River. Fish and swim in the river. Supplies available at Sanderson. Deer, raccoons, squirrels and birds are common in the area. Many trails in the area.

GETTING THERE: From Sanderson go NW on state Hwy S-229 approx. 4 mi. to state HWY S-250. Go NE on S-250 approx. 2 mi. to forest route 202. Go E on 202 to East Tower Hunt CG.

SINGLE RATE:	No fee	OPEN DATES:	Yearlong
		MAX STAY:	14 days
		ELEVATION:	128 feet

12 Farles Prairie
Umatilla • lat 29˚06'13" lon 081˚40'28"

DESCRIPTION: In a mixed hardwood and pine forest setting on Farles Lake. Boat, fish and swim in the lake. Boat launch at the CG. Supplies available at Umatilla. Deer, bears and birds are common to the area. Campers may gather firewood. Many hiking trails in the area.

GETTING THERE: From Umatilla go NE on state HWY 19 approx. 12 mi. to forest route 535. Go W on 535 approx. 1 mi. to forest route 595-2. Go E on 595-2 approx. 1 mi. to Farles Lake CG.

SINGLE RATE:	$4	OPEN DATES:	Yearlong
		MAX SPUR:	35 feet
		MAX STAY:	14 days
		ELEVATION:	55 feet

13 Fore Lake
Ocala • lat 29˚16'13" lon 081˚55'05"

DESCRIPTION: In a mixed forest setting of hardwood and pine on Fore Lake. Fish, canoe and swim in the lake. Canoe launch only at CG. Supplies available at Ocala. Black bears, bald eagles and cranes are common to the area. Campers may gather firewood. RV dump station at the CG area. No designated trails near CG.

GETTING THERE: From Ocala go E on state HWY 40 for 11 mi. to state HWY 314. Go NE on 314 approx. 5.5 mi. to Fore Lake CG.

SINGLE RATE:	$5	OPEN DATES:	Yearlong
# of SINGLE SITES:	31	MAX SPUR:	35 feet
		MAX STAY:	14 days
		ELEVATION:	75 feet

14 Grassy Pond
Ocala • lat 29˚22'41" lon 081˚48'29"

DESCRIPTION: In a mixed forest setting of hardwood and pine on Grassy Pond. Fish, canoe and swim in the pond. Supplies available at Ocala. Black bears, bald eagles and cranes are common to the area. Campers may gather firewood. RV dump station at the CG area. Hiking trails located near the CG area.

GETTING THERE: From Ocala go E on state HWY 40 for 9 mi. to state HWY 315. Go N on 315 for 10 mi. to state route 316. Go E on 316 for 9 mi. to forest route 88-4. Go N 1 mi. on 88-4 to forest route 88-C. Go E .5 mi. on 88-C to Grassy Pond CG.

SINGLE RATE:	$4	OPEN DATES:	Yearlong
# of SINGLE SITES:	6	MAX SPUR:	35 feet
		MAX STAY:	14 days
		ELEVATION:	50 feet

15 Halfmoon Lake
Ocala • lat 29˚09'33" lon 081˚49'14"

DESCRIPTION: In a mixed hardwood and pine forest setting on Halfmoon Lake. Boat, fish and swim in the lake. Boat launch at the CG. Supplies available at Ocala. Deer, bears and birds are common to the area. Campers may gather firewood. Many hiking trails in the area.

GETTING THERE: From Ocala go E on state HWY 40 for 21 mi. to forest route 579. Go S on 579 .5 mi. to forest route 579-D. Go S on 579-D .5 mi. to Halfmoon Lake CG.

SINGLE RATE:	No fee	OPEN DATES:	Yearlong
		MAX SPUR:	35 feet
		MAX STAY:	14 days
		ELEVATION:	75 feet

16 Hickory Landing
Sumatra • lat 30˚03'08" lon 085˚04'18"

DESCRIPTION: In a mixed forest setting surrounded by streams. Fish, boat and swim in nearby streams. Boat launch at CG. Supplies available at Sumatra. Numerous wildlife can be seen in the area. Campers may gather firewood. Designated trails in the area. Drinking water available.

GETTING THERE: From Sumatra go S approx. 3.5 mi. on state HWY 65 to forest route 101. Go W approx. 1 mi. on 101 to forest route 101-B. Go SW approx. 1 mi. on 101-B to Hickory Landing CG.

SINGLE RATE:	$3	OPEN DATES:	Yearlong
# of SINGLE SITES:	10	MAX SPUR:	20 feet
		MAX STAY:	14 days
		ELEVATION:	21 feet

17 Hitchcock Lake
Telogia • lat 30˚04'49" lon 084˚39'02"

DESCRIPTION: CG is in a mixed forest setting on Hitchcock Lake. Fish, boat and swim in the lake. Boat launch located at the CG. Supplies available at Telogia. Campers may gather firewood. Numerous wildlife can be seen in the area. no designated trails in the area.

GETTING THERE: Hitchcock Lake CG is located approx. 21 mi. SE of Telogia on state HWY 67.

SINGLE RATE:	$3	OPEN DATES:	Yearlong
# of SINGLE SITES:	10		
		MAX STAY:	14 days
		ELEVATION:	10 feet

18 Hog Pen Hunt Camp
Olustee • lat 30˚14'30" lon 082˚26'00"

DESCRIPTION: No drinking water. This primitive CG is located in a mixed forest setting on Ocean Pond. Fish and swim in the pond. Supplies available at Olustee. Deer, raccoons, squirrels and birds are common in the area. Many trails in the area. The Florida National Scenic Hiking Trail is nearby.

GETTING THERE: From Olustee go E on state HWY 10 1 mi. to state HWY 250-A. Go N on 250-A 4 mi. to forest route 241. Go S on 241 1.5 mi. to forest route 241-A. Go SE on 241-A approx. 1/2 mi. to Hog Pen Hunt CG.

SINGLE RATE:	$2	OPEN DATES:	Yearlong
		MAX STAY:	14 days
		ELEVATION:	150 feet

19 Hopkins Prairie
Ocala • lat 29˚16'35" lon 081˚42'41"

DESCRIPTION: In a hardwood and pine forest setting on Hopkins Prairie Lake. Boat ramp at CG. Fish and swim in the lake. Supplies available at Ocala. Black bears, bald eagles and cranes are common in the area. Campers may gather firewood. The Florida National Scenic Trail runs through the CG area.

GETTING THERE: From Ocala go E on state HWY 40 approx. 13 mi. to forest route 88. Go N on 88 for 6.5 mi. to forest route 86. Go E on 86 approx. 5 mi. to forest route 86-F. Go N on 86-F approx. 1 mi. to Hopkins Prairie CG.

SINGLE RATE:	$4	OPEN DATES:	Yearlong
# of SINGLE SITES:	21	MAX SPUR:	35 feet
		MAX STAY:	14 days
		ELEVATION:	50 feet

20 Juniper Springs
Ocala • lat 29˚10'55" lon 081˚42'33"

DESCRIPTION: In a mixed forest setting of hardwood and pine on Juniper Springs. Supplies available at Ocala. Black bears, bald eagles and cranes are common to the area. Campers may gather firewood. RV dump station at the CG area. Hiking trails located near the CG area.

GETTING THERE: Juniper Springs CG is located approx. 27 mi. E of Ocala on state HWY 40.

SINGLE RATE:	Varies	OPEN DATES:	Yearlong
# of SINGLE SITES:	79	MAX SPUR:	35 feet
		MAX STAY:	14 days
		ELEVATION:	45 feet

 Campground has hosts   🔒 **Reservable sites**   **Accessible facilities**   **Fully developed**   **Semi-developed**   **Rustic facilities**

21 Lake Catherine
Umatilla • lat 29°04'03" lon 081°49'59"

DESCRIPTION: In a mixed hardwood and pine forest setting on Lake Catherine. Boat, fish and swim in the lake. Boat launch at the CG. Supplies available at Umatilla. Deer, bears and birds are common to the area. Campers may gather firewood. Many hiking trails in the area.

GETTING THERE: From Umatilla go NW on state HWY 450 6 mi. to state HWY 42. Go W on 42 1.5 mi. to county route 210AV. Go NW on 210AV approx. 6 mi. to Lake Catherine exit. Follow sign 1 mi. to Lake Catherine CG.

SINGLE RATE:	No fee	OPEN DATES:	Yearlong
		MAX SPUR:	35 feet
		MAX STAY:	14 days
		ELEVATION:	68 feet

22 Lake Delancy
Ocala • lat 29°25'51" lon 081°47'09"

DESCRIPTION: In a mixed forest setting of hardwood and pine on Lake Delancy. Fish and swim in the lake. Supplies available at Ocala. Black bears, bald eagles and cranes are common to the area. Campers may gather firewood. Hiking trails located near the CG area.

GETTING THERE: From Ocala go E 11 mi. on HWY 40 to HWY 314. Go NE 16 mi. on 314 to HWY 19. Go N 1 mi. on 19 to HWY 316. Go W 6 mi. on 316 to forest route 88-4. Go N 4 mi. on 88-4 to forest route 75-2. Go E 1 mi. on 75-2 to Lake Delancy CG.

SINGLE RATE:	$4	OPEN DATES:	Yearlong
# of SINGLE SITES:	59	MAX SPUR:	35 feet
		MAX STAY:	14 days
		ELEVATION:	50 feet

23 Lake Dorr
Umatilla • lat 29°00'47" lon 081°38'09"

DESCRIPTION: In a mixed hardwood and pine forest setting on Lake Dorr. Boat, fish and swim in the lake. Boat launch at the CG. Supplies available at Umatilla. Deer, bears and birds are common to the area. Campers may gather firewood. Many hiking trails in the area.

GETTING THERE: Lake Dorr CG is located approx. 5.5 mi. N of Umatilla on state HWY 19.

SINGLE RATE:	$7	OPEN DATES:	Yearlong
# of SINGLE SITES:	34	MAX SPUR:	35 feet
		MAX STAY:	14 days
		ELEVATION:	50 feet

24 Lake Eaton
Ocala • lat 29°15'14" lon 081°51'53"

DESCRIPTION: In a hardwood and pine setting on Lake Eaton. Fish, boat and swim in the lake. Supplies are located in Ocala. Many animals can be seen in the area. Campers may gather firewood. The Sinkhole Trail and an observation platform, viewing area are nearby.

GETTING THERE: From Ocala go E on state HWY 40 for 11 mi. to state HWY 314. Go NE on 314 approx. 6.5 mi. to state HWY 314-A. Go S on 314-A 2 mi. to forest route 96. Go E on 96 .5 mi. to FR 96A. Go N on 96A 1 mi. to Lake Eaton CG.

SINGLE RATE:	Varies	OPEN DATES:	Yearlong
# of SINGLE SITES:	14	MAX SPUR:	35 feet
		MAX STAY:	14 days
		ELEVATION:	40 feet

25 Lake Shore Organizational Camp
Ocala • lat 29°16'28" lon 081°55'02"

DESCRIPTION: In a mixture of hardwood and pine on Lake Shore. Fish, boat and swim in the lake. Supplies available at Ocala. Black bears, bald eagles and cranes are common to the area. Campers may gather firewood. No designated trails in the area.

GETTING THERE: From Ocala go E on state HWY 40 for 11 mi. to state HWY 314. Go NE on 314 approx. 6 mi. to Lake Shore Organizational CG.

GROUP RATE:	$25	OPEN DATES:	Yearlong
# of GROUP SITES:	1	MAX SPUR:	99 feet
		MAX STAY:	14 days
		ELEVATION:	70 feet

26 Mack Landing
Sopchoppy • lat 30°05'35" lon 084°38'42"

DESCRIPTION: This CG is tent camping only in a mixed forest setting on the Ochlockonee River. Fish, boat and swim in the river. Boat ramp at the CG. Supplies available at Sopchoppy. Campers may gather firewood. Numerous animals can be seen in the area. No designated trails nearby.

GETTING THERE: From Sopchoppy go NW on state HWY 375 approx. 10.5 mi. to forest route 336. Go W on 336 approx. 1 mi. to Mack Landing CG.

SINGLE RATE:	No fee	OPEN DATES:	Yearlong
		MAX STAY:	14 days
		ELEVATION:	32 feet

27 Ocean Pond
Olustee • lat 30°14'24" lon 082°25'58"

DESCRIPTION: This CG is located in a mixed forest setting on Ocean Pond. Fish and swim in the pond. Supplies available at Olustee. Deer, raccoons, squirrels and birds are common in the area. Many trails in the area. The Florida National Scenic Hiking Trail is nearby. Showers and RV dump station at CG.

GETTING THERE: From Olustee go E on state HWY 10 approx. 1 mi. to state HWY 250-A. Go N on 250-A approx. 3.5 mi. to forest route 268. Go S on 268 approx. 1 mi. to Ocean Pond CG.

SINGLE RATE:	$8	OPEN DATES:	Yearlong
# of SINGLE SITES:	50		
		MAX STAY:	14 days
		ELEVATION:	161 feet

28 Pine Creek Landing
Sopchoppy • lat 30°14'46" lon 084°41'48"

DESCRIPTION: This primitive CG is in a mixed forest setting on Pine Creek. Fish and swim in the creek. Boat ramp at the CG. Supplies available at Sopchoppy. Many animals can be seen in the area. Campers may gather firewood. No designated trails nearby.

GETTING THERE: From Sopchoppy go NW on state HWY 375 approx. 21 mi. to forest route 335. Go W on 335 approx. 1 mi. to Pine Creek Landing CG.

SINGLE RATE:	No fee	OPEN DATES:	Yearlong
		MAX STAY:	14 days
		ELEVATION:	24 feet

29 Porter Lake
Telogia • lat 30°09'45" lon 084°40'30"

DESCRIPTION: CG is in a mixed forest setting on Porter Lake. Fish, boat, canoe and swim in lake. Supplies available at Telogia. Campers may gather firewood. Numerous wildlife can be seen in the area. Many designated trails in the area.

GETTING THERE: From Telogia go SW approx. 15.5 mi. to forest route FH13. Go E on FH13 approx. 1.5 mi. to forest route 186. Go SE on 186 approx. 1.5 mi. to Porter Lake CG.

SINGLE RATE:	$2	OPEN DATES:	Yearlong
# of SINGLE SITES:	4		
		MAX STAY:	14 days
		ELEVATION:	20 feet

30 River Forest
Umatilla • lat 29°00'22" lon 081°23'09"

DESCRIPTION: In a mixed hardwood and pine forest setting adjacent to the Lake Woodruff Wilderness. Supplies available at Umatilla. Deer, bears and birds are common to the area. Campers may gather firewood. The St. Francis Interpretive Trail is near the CG.

GETTING THERE: From Umatilla go N on state HWY 19 approx. 2.5 mi. to state HWY 42. Go E on 42 approx. 17 mi. to River Forest CG.

GROUP RATE:	$100	OPEN DATES:	Yearlong
# of GROUP SITES:	1	MAX SPUR:	99 feet
		MAX STAY:	14 days
		ELEVATION:	10 feet

 Campground has hosts   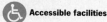 **Reservable sites**   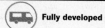 **Accessible facilities**   **Fully developed**   **Semi-developed**   **Rustic facilities**

NOTE: Open dates listed are typical. Actual dates are dependent on conditions such as snow pack.

31 Salt Springs
Ocala • lat 29°21'24" lon 081°43'56"

DESCRIPTION: Located in a lush semi-tropical setting on Salt Springs. Boat, fish and swim in the springs. Supplies available at Ocala. Black bears, bald eagles and cranes are common in the area. Florida National Scenic Trail and the Salt Springs Trail are nearby. RV dump station at CG.

GETTING THERE: From Ocala go E 11 mi. on state HWY 40 to state HWY 314. Go NE 16 mi. on 314 to state HWY 19. Go N 1 mi. on 19 to Salt Springs CG.

SINGLE RATE: # of SINGLE SITES:	Varies 162	OPEN DATES: MAX SPUR: MAX STAY: ELEVATION:	Yearlong 99 feet 14 days 45 feet

32 Sandhill Hunt Camp
Deep Creek • lat 30°22'53" lon 082°30'37"

DESCRIPTION: No drinking water. This primitive CG is located in a mixed forest setting with many small streams in the area. Fish and swim in the streams. Supplies available at Deep Creek. Deer, raccoons, squirrels and birds are common in the area. Many trails in the area. A designated horse trail leaves from the CG area.

GETTING THERE: From Deep Creek go N 1 mi. on state HWY 47 to forest route 285. Go E 2.5 mi. on 285 to forest route 237. Go N 1 mi. on 237 to forest route 234. Go E 2.5 mi. on 234 to forest route 272. Go NE 1.5 mi. on 272 to Sandhill Hunt CG.

SINGLE RATE:	No fee	OPEN DATES: MAX STAY: ELEVATION:	Yearlong 14 days 136 feet

33 Seventeenmile Camp
Sanderson • lat 30°20'10" lon 082°22'56"

DESCRIPTION: No drinking water. This primitive CG is located in a mixed forest setting on Ocean Pond. Fish and swim from the pond. Supplies available at Sanderson. Deer, raccoons, squirrels and birds are common in the area. Many trails in the area. The Florida National Scenic Hiking Trail is nearby.

GETTING THERE: From Sanderson go NE on state HWY S-229 approx. 3.5 mi. to state HWY S-250. Go SW on S-250 approx. 2 mi. to forest route 286. Go NW on 285 approx. 1/2 mi. to Seventeenmile CG.

SINGLE RATE:	No fee	OPEN DATES: MAX STAY: ELEVATION:	Yearlong 14 days 150 feet

34 West Tower Hunt Camp
Deep Creek • lat 30°18'25" lon 082°33'27"

DESCRIPTION: No drinking water. This primitive CG is located in a mixed forest setting with many streams in the area. Fish and swim in the streams. Supplies available at Deep Creek. Deer, raccoons, squirrels and birds are common in the area. A horse and a scenic trail are in the CG area. The Gum Swamp Wilderness Area is nearby.

GETTING THERE: From Deep Creek go S on state HWY 47 approx. 2.5 mi. to forest route 236. Go E on 236 approx. 4 mi. to forest route 233. Go NE on 233 approx. 1/2 mi. to West Tower Hunt CG.

SINGLE RATE:	No fee	OPEN DATES: MAX STAY: ELEVATION:	Yearlong 14 days 135 feet

35 Whitehead Lake
Telogia • lat 30°10'35" lon 084°40'35"

DESCRIPTION: This CG is in a mixed forest setting on Whitehead Lake. Fish, boat and swim from the lake. Boat launch at the CG. Supplies available at Telogia. Campers may gather firewood. Many animals can be seen in the area. No designated trails in the area.

GETTING THERE: From Telogia go SW approx. 15.5 mi. to forest route FH13. Go E on FH13 approx. 1.5 mi. to forest route 186. Go SE on 186 approx. 1.5 mi. to Whitehead Lake CG.

SINGLE RATE: # of SINGLE SITES:	$3 10	OPEN DATES: MAX STAY: ELEVATION:	Yearlong 14 days 20 feet

36 Wiggins Hunt Camp
Lake City • lat 30°14'41" lon 082°30'30"

DESCRIPTION: No drinking water. This primitive CG is located in a mixed forest setting. Supplies available at Lake City. Deer, raccoons, squirrels and birds are common in the area. Campers may gather firewood. No designated trails in the area. A woodpecker colony is located near CG area for viewing.

GETTING THERE: From Lake City go N on state HWY 47 approx. 1 mi. to state HWY S-250. Go NE on S-250 approx. 7 mi. to Wiggins Hunt CG.

SINGLE RATE:	No fee	OPEN DATES: MAX STAY: ELEVATION:	Yearlong 14 days 150 feet

37 Wood Lake
Sopchoppy • lat 30°01'26" lon 084°33'55"

DESCRIPTION: In a mixed forest setting on Wood Lake. Boat ramp is located at the CG. Fish and swim from the lake. Supplies available at Sopchoppy. Turkeys, wild frogs and other animals can be seen in the area. Campers may gather firewood. No designated trails in the area.

GETTING THERE: From Sopchoppy go W on state HWY 22 approx. 1.5 mi. to state HWY 399. Go S on 399 approx. 3 mi. to forest route 338. Go W on 338 approx. 1.5 mi. to Wood Lake CG.

SINGLE RATE:	No fee	OPEN DATES: MAX STAY: ELEVATION:	Yearlong 14 days 8 feet

38 Wright Lake
Sumatra • lat 30°00'06" lon 085°00'10"

DESCRIPTION: This CG is in a mixed forest setting on Wright Lake. Fish, boat and swim in lake. Boat launch at the CG. Supplies available at Telogia. Many animals can be seen in the area. Designated trails can be found in the area and an interpretive trail is at CG. RV dump station available in the CG.

GETTING THERE: From Sumatra go S 3.5 mi. on state HWY 65 to forest route 101. Go W 2 mi. on 101 to forest route 101-C. Go N 1/2 mi. on 101-C to Hickory Landing CG.

SINGLE RATE: # of SINGLE SITES:	$8 20	OPEN DATES: MAX SPUR: MAX STAY: ELEVATION:	Yearlong 50 feet 14 days 18 feet

---

 Campground has hosts   🔒 **Reservable sites**   **Accessible facilities**   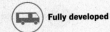 **Fully developed**   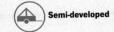 **Semi-developed**    **Rustic facilities**

NOTE: Open dates listed are typical. Actual dates are dependent on conditions such as snow pack.

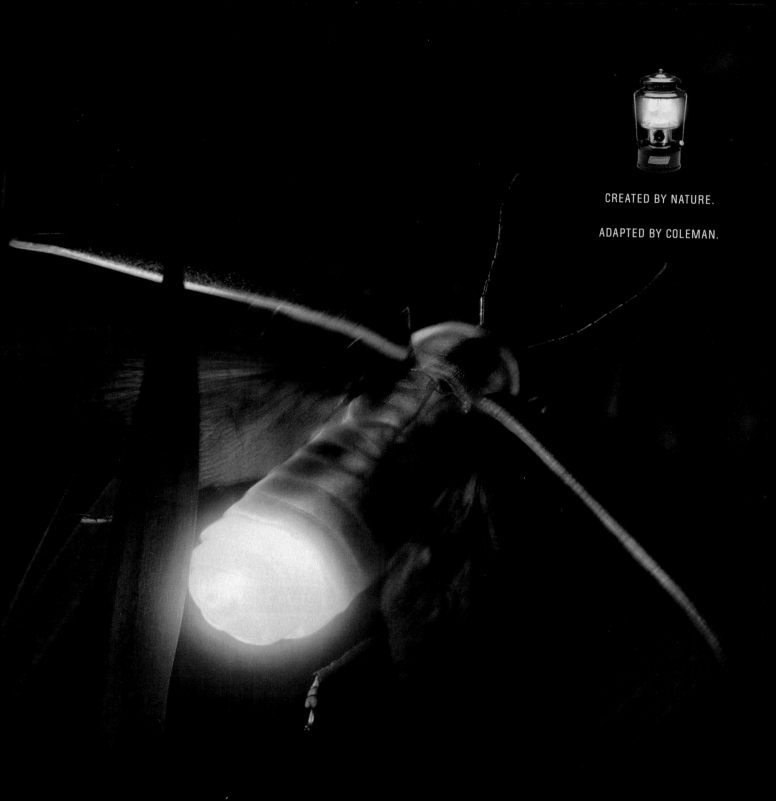

CREATED BY NATURE.

ADAPTED BY COLEMAN.

INSPIRED BY NATURE™

www.coleman.com Visit. Explore. Discover.

USFS Photo

NATIONAL FORESTS OF GEORGIA

Georgia's national forests are said to be a hiker's paradise. Winding trails lead visitors through scenic mountains and rolling hills, past wild rushing rivers and cascading waterfalls. They also lead visitors through the history books: Spanish conquistador Hernando de Soto's futile search for gold, the Cherokee Indians' struggle to hold on to their lands, and major battles of the Civil War.

Drive along the Ridge and Valley Scenic Byway, which tours the Armuchee Ridges of the Appalachian Mountains, the site of several major Civil War battles. Across from the Armuchee Ridges lie the Blue Ridge Mountains. Here visitors will find Lake Conasauga, the state's highest lake and Brasstown Bald, Georgia's highest peak which offers breathtaking panoramic views of mountains and valleys.

Unlike the tall peaks of the Chattahoochee, the Oconee National Forest is relatively flat with small hills. Visit Lake Sinclair, popular for swimming, fishing, boating, and camping. If a wealth of trails is the hallmark of the Chattahoochee, bountiful game is the signature of the Oconee. There are also plenty of excellent fishing opportunities.

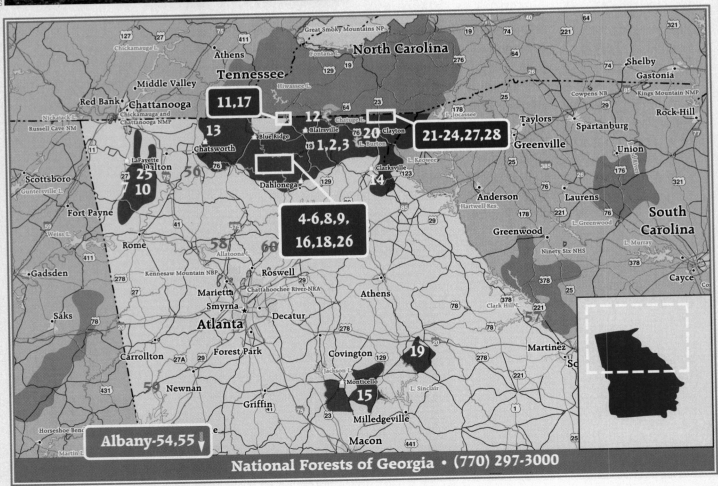

National Forests of Georgia • (770) 297-3000

1 Andrews Cove
Cleveland • lat 34°46'38" lon 083°44'22"

DESCRIPTION: This CG is located on Andrews Creek, a cool mountain stream that offers a quiet atmosphere. Enjoy fishing for trout in the stream. 2 mi. Andrews Cove Foot Trail accesses the Appalachian Trail. High Shoals Scenic Area, and Anna Ruby Falls are nearby. Drinking water is not available at this time.

GETTING THERE: Andrews Cove CG is located approx. 14 mi. N of Cleveland on state HWY 75.

SINGLE RATE:	$8	OPEN DATES:	May-Nov
# of SINGLE SITES:	10	MAX SPUR:	30 feet
		MAX STAY:	14 days
		ELEVATION:	2085 feet

2 Boggs Creek
Helen • lat 34°46'38" lon 083°45'00"

DESCRIPTION: This CG is located high in the mountains. Enjoy fishing along the headwaters of the Chattahoochee River. Supplies available in Helen. Anna Ruby Falls is nearby and offers two hiking trails. The Lion's Eye Trail is accessible to people with disabilities. No drinking water on site.

GETTING THERE: From Helen go N on HWY 75 aprx. 8 mi. to Chattahoochee River RD. Go W on Chattahoochee River RD aprx. 1 mi. to Martin Branch RD. Go S on Martin Branch RD aprx. 1/2 mi. to CG. Road is narrow.

SINGLE RATE:	$2	OPEN DATES:	Yearlong
# of SINGLE SITES:	12	MAX SPUR:	25 feet
		MAX STAY:	14 days
		ELEVATION:	2100 feet

3 Chattahoochee River
Helen • lat 34°48'15" lon 083°45'00"

DESCRIPTION: This CG is located high in the mountains. Enjoy fishing along the headwaters of the Chattahoochee River. Anna Ruby Falls is also nearby and offers two hiking trails. The Lion's Eye Trail is accessible to people with disabilities. Horse Trough Falls Foot Trail, 0.2 mi. is nearby.

GETTING THERE: From Helen go N on state HWY 75 approx. 8 mi. to Chattahoochee River Road. Go W on Chattahoochee River Road approx. 5 mi. to CG. Expect narrow, curving and steep roads to and from the area.

SINGLE RATE:	$8	OPEN DATES:	Mar-Dec
# of SINGLE SITES:	34	MAX SPUR:	25 feet
GROUP RATE:	$25	MAX STAY:	14 days
# of GROUP SITES:	1	ELEVATION:	2100 feet

4 Cooper Creek
Blue Ridge • lat 34°45'45" lon 084°04'05"

DESCRIPTION: Located along the banks of Cooper Creek next to Cooper Creek Scenic Area. Fish in Cooper and Mulky Creeks for stocked and wild trout. Enjoy a hike on the Yellow Mountain Trail through forests of hemlock, pine and hardwood or on several other trails in area. Spring and fall are good times to visit.

GETTING THERE: From Blue Ridge go E on US HWY 76 approx. 5 mi. to state HWY 60. Go S on 60 approx. 16 mi. to forest route 4. Go E on 4 approx. 6 mi. to Cooper Creek CG. Road is narrow with sharp curves.

SINGLE RATE:	$8	OPEN DATES:	Mar-Oct
# of SINGLE SITES:	17	MAX SPUR:	20 feet
		MAX STAY:	14 days
		ELEVATION:	2200 feet

5 Deep Hole
Blue Ridge • lat 34°44'25" lon 084°08'26"

DESCRIPTION: This CG is located along the banks of the Toccoa River. Enjoy a float down the river or fish for bass and trout. Cooper Creek Scenic Area is nearby. The path to the canoe launch and fishing deck is barrier free. There are hiking trails nearby. Spring through Fall is a good time to visit this CG.

GETTING THERE: From Blue Ridge go E on US HWY 76 approx. 5 mi. to state HWY 60. Go S on 60 approx. 16 mi. to Deep Hole CG.

SINGLE RATE:	Varies	OPEN DATES:	Yearlong
# of SINGLE SITES:	8	MAX SPUR:	20 feet
		MAX STAY:	14 days
		ELEVATION:	1980 feet

6 DeSoto Falls
Cleveland • lat 34°42'31" lon 083°54'51"

DESCRIPTION: CG is located in the mountains along beautiful Frogtown Creek. Enjoy fishing for trout in creek but please check fishing regulations Desoto Falls Scenic Area is adjacent to the campground. Hike along the 2-mile Desoto Falls Trail, first mi. is fairly easy and leads to two waterfalls.

GETTING THERE: From Cleveland go N on US HWY 129 approx. 15 mi. to DeSoto Falls CG.

SINGLE RATE:	Varies	OPEN DATES:	Apr-Nov
# of SINGLE SITES:	24	MAX SPUR:	25 feet
		MAX STAY:	14 days
		ELEVATION:	2150 feet

7 Dispersed Camping Areas
Crandall • lat °'" lon °'"

DESCRIPTION: The Cohutta Ranger district offers several rustic, dispersed camping areas. These campgrounds offer minimal facilities. Please contact the Cohutta Ranger district at (706)695-6736 for directions.

GETTING THERE: Please contact the Cohutta Ranger district at (706)695-6736 for directions.

| SINGLE RATE: | No fee | OPEN DATES: | Yearlong |
| | | MAX STAY: | 14 days |

8 Dockery Lake
Dahlonega • lat 34°40'26" lon 083°58'32"

DESCRIPTION: CG overlooks Dockery Lake and is nestled deep off the side of a mountain. Lakeshore Trail, a 1/2 mile loop around lake leads to an accessible fishing pier. Visit nearby Dockery Gap Scenic Overlook and Woody Gap which offer spectacular. The Appalachian Trail is accessible at Woody Gap.

GETTING THERE: From Dahlonega go N on US HWY 19 approx. 8 mi. to state HWY 60. Go NW on 60 approx. 3.5 mi. to forest route 654. Go NE on 654 approx. 1 mi. to Dockery Lake CG.

SINGLE RATE:	$8	OPEN DATES:	Apr-Oct
# of SINGLE SITES:	11	MAX SPUR:	25 feet
		MAX STAY:	14 days
		ELEVATION:	2410 feet

9 Frank Gross
Blue Ridge • lat 34°42'04" lon 084°08'54"

DESCRIPTION: This CG is located along the banks of Rock Creek and far from civilization. Enjoy fishing in Rock Creek and Mill Creek for trout. The Chattahoochee National Fish Hatchery is located on Rock Creek. The Appalachian Trail and Benton MacKaye Trail are nearby.

GETTING THERE: From Blue Ridge go E on US HWY 76 approx. 5 mi. to state HWY 60. Go S on 60 approx. 15 mi. to forest route 69. Go SE approx. 5 mi. to Frank Gross CG. Road is narrow with sharp curves.

SINGLE RATE:	$8	OPEN DATES:	Mar-Oct
# of SINGLE SITES:	9	MAX SPUR:	20 feet
		MAX STAY:	14 days
		ELEVATION:	2236 feet

10 Hidden Creek
Calhoun • lat 34°30'52" lon 085°04'21"

DESCRIPTION: This CG is located next to Hidden Creek, which appears and runs for a day or two and then disappears. The CG rests in the Johns Mountain. Wildlife Management Area. Wildlife includes deer, turkeys, quail, and coyotes. Johns Mountain Overlook and Keown Falls Scenic Area is located nearby.

GETTING THERE: From Calhoun go SW on HWY 156 approx. 7.5 mi. to Everett Springs RD. Go NW approx. 2 mi. to Rock House RD. Go N approx. 3 mi. to forest route 955. Go N on 955 approx. 2 mi. to Hidden Creek CG.

SINGLE RATE:	No fee	OPEN DATES:	May-Oct
# of SINGLE SITES:	16	MAX SPUR:	40 feet
		MAX STAY:	14 days
		ELEVATION:	800 feet

 Campground has hosts   Reservable sites   Accessible facilities   Fully developed   Semi-developed   Rustic facilities

NOTE: Open dates listed are typical. Actual dates are dependent on conditions such as snow pack.

11 Lake Blue Ridge
Blue Ridge • lat 34°50'46" lon 084°17'28"

DESCRIPTION: This CG is surrounded by mountains on Blue Ridge Lake. This 3,290-acre lake is home to bass, bream, catfish, perch and crappie. Please check fishing regulations. Enjoy a hike on a 0.6-mile loop trail that follows the shoreline of Lake Blue Ridge and offers a beautiful view of the lake.

GETTING THERE: From Blue Ridge go E on US HWY 76 approx. 1.5 mi. to Dry Branch Road. Go S on Dry Branch Road approx. 3 mi. to Lake Blue Ridge CG.

SINGLE RATE:	Varies	OPEN DATES:	Apr-Oct
# of SINGLE SITES:	58	MAX SPUR:	30 feet
		MAX STAY:	14 days
		ELEVATION:	1810 feet

16 Lake Winfield Scott
Blairsville • lat 34°44'21" lon 083°53'17"

DESCRIPTION: This CG is situated in mixed hardwoods next to beautiful Lake Winfield Scott in the mountains. Enjoy swimming or fishing with electric motorboats only. A paved boat launch is located near the head of the lake and an accessible fishing deck is nearby. Hike the many trails in this area.

GETTING THERE: From Blairsville go S on US HWY 19/129 approx. 10 mi. to state HWY 180. Go W on 180 approx. 7 mi. to Lake Winfield Scott CG.

# of SINGLE SITES:	Varies	OPEN DATES:	Yearlong*
# of SINGLE SITES:	36	MAX SPUR:	25 feet
GROUP RATE:	Varies	MAX STAY:	14 days
# of GROUP SITES:	1	ELEVATION:	2720 feet

12 Lake Chatuge
Hiawassee • lat 34°57'16" lon 083°46'47"

DESCRIPTION: This CG is situated on Lake Chatuge in the mountains. Enjoy fishing for bass, bream and catfish. Georgia's highest mountain, Brasstown Bald, is a nearby attraction. Hike the Lake Chatuge Foot Trail, 1.2 miles loop from the CG. Wildlife in this area includes deer, turkeys, quail, and coyotes.

GETTING THERE: From Hiawassee go NW on US HWY 76 approx. 2 mi. to state HWY 288. Go S on 288 approx. 1 mi. to Lake Chatuge CG.

SINGLE RATE:	$8	OPEN DATES:	Apr-Oct
# of SINGLE SITES:	30	MAX SPUR:	25 feet
		MAX STAY:	14 days
		ELEVATION:	2000 feet

17 Morganton Point
Blue Ridge • lat 34°52'05" lon 084°14'37"

DESCRIPTION: This CG overlooks beautiful Lake Blue Ridge in the mountains. Fishing and swimming in this clear 3,290-acre lake are popular. A paved boat launch is located near the campground. Hikers can enjoy a scenic trail that runs along the lake shore.

GETTING THERE: From Blue Ridge go S on US HWY 515 approx. 4 mi. to state HWY 60. Go SW on 60 approx. 3 mi. to county route 616. Go W on 616 approx. 1 mi. to Morganton Point CG.

# of SINGLE SITES:	Varies	OPEN DATES:	Apr-Sept
# of SINGLE SITES:	44	MAX SPUR:	30 feet
GROUP RATE:	$25	MAX STAY:	14 days
# of GROUP SITES:	1	ELEVATION:	1730 feet

13 Lake Conasauga
Charsworth • lat 34°17'14" lon 085°14'07"

DESCRIPTION: This CG is located on beautiful, 19-acre, Conasauga Lake, the highest in Georgia. Enjoy fishing for bass, bream, and trout (electric motors only). Hike the Grassy Mountain Tower Trail, Lake Conasauga Trail(lake loop), or access the adjacent Cohutta Wilderness. Visit nearby For Mountain State Park.

GETTING THERE: From Chatsworth go N on US HWY 411 approx. 4 mi. to forest route 18. Go E on 18 approx. 10 mi. to forest route 68. Go NE on 68 approx. 10 mi. to Lake Conasauga CG.

SINGLE RATE:	$8	OPEN DATES:	Apr-Oct
# of SINGLE SITES:	35	MAX SPUR:	40 feet
		MAX STAY:	14 days
		ELEVATION:	1000 feet

18 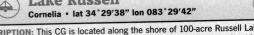 Mulky
Blue Ridge • lat 34°45'30" lon 084°05'13"

DESCRIPTION: This CG is situated along beautiful Cooper Creek. Enjoy fishing in Cooper Creek and in Mulky Creek for stocked and wild trout. Cooper Creek Scenic Area is nearby. Hike the Yellow Mountain Trail, the 2.4-mile Mill Shoals Trail, and the Cooper Creek Trail, a .4-mile connecting trail.

GETTING THERE: From Blue Ridge go E on US HWY 76 approx. 5 mi. to state HWY 60. Go S on 60 approx. 16 mi. to forest route 4. Go E on 4 approx. 5 mi. to Mulky CG. Road is narrow with sharp curves.

SINGLE RATE:	$8	OPEN DATES:	Mar-Oct
# of SINGLE SITES:	11	MAX SPUR:	20 feet
		MAX STAY:	14 days
		ELEVATION:	2190 feet

14 Lake Russell
Cornelia • lat 34°29'38" lon 083°29'42"

DESCRIPTION: This CG is located along the shore of 100-acre Russell Lake with a grassy beach. Enjoy fishing for bass, bream, perch and catfish. There is a boat launch for electric motorboats only. Hike the Rhododendron Trail, 1.5 mi. to Chenocetah Mountain. Locust Stake ORV Area is nearby. RV dump station on site.

GETTING THERE: From Cornelia go NE on US HWY 123 approx. 2 mi. to forest route 59. Go S on 59 approx. 1.5 mi. to forest route 92. Go W on 92 approx. 1.5 mi. to Russell Lake CG.

SINGLE RATE:	Varies	OPEN DATES:	May-Oct
# of SINGLE SITES:	42	MAX SPUR:	40 feet
GROUP RATE:	Varies	MAX STAY:	14 days
# of GROUP SITES:	9	ELEVATION:	1100 feet

19 Oconee River
Greensboro • lat 33°43'16" lon 083°17'24"

DESCRIPTION: CG is located along the bank of the Oconee river, fish for bass, bream and catfish here. Boat launch located at end of main area road. Supplies in Greensboro. The Scull Shoals Historic Area is nearby. The 1 mi. Scull Shoals Trail originates at CG. The Dyar Pasture Waterfowl Conservation Area is near CG.

GETTING THERE: From Greensboro go N on state HWY 15 approx. 13 mi. to Oconee River CG.

SINGLE RATE:	$5	OPEN DATES:	Yearlong
# of SINGLE SITES:	6		
		MAX STAY:	14 days
		ELEVATION:	450 feet

15 Lake Sinclair
Eatonton • lat 33°12'00" lon 083°22'45"

DESCRIPTION: Located along the shore of beautiful Lake Sinclair. Fish for bass, crappie, and catfish from the lake. A boat launch is also located at CG. Hikers can enjoy the Twin Bridges Trail, which is 1.8 miles and originates in area. The Scull Shoals Historic Area is nearby. RV dump station at CG.

GETTING THERE: From Eatonton go S on US HWY 129 approx. 10 mi. to state HWY 212. Go SE on 212 approx. 1 mi. to county route. Go E on county route approx. 1.5 mi. to Lake Sinclair CG.

SINGLE RATE:	$7	OPEN DATES:	Apr-Dec
# of SINGLE SITES:	44	MAX SPUR:	28 feet
GROUP RATE:	$30	MAX STAY:	14 days
# of GROUP SITES:	1	ELEVATION:	340 feet

20 Rabun Beach
Clayton • lat 34°45'25" lon 083°28'55"

DESCRIPTION: This CG overlooks Lake Rabun. Enjoy fishing for bass, bream, perch, trout and catfish. Boat launch, water skiing, and fishing pier on site. The Tallulah Gorge Overlook offers spectacular views of the Tallulah River and the surrounding mountains. Hook-ups, RV dump station, and showers on site.

GETTING THERE: From Clayton go S 7 mi. on US HWY 441/23 to county route. Go W 1/8 mi. on county route to state HWY 15. Go S 2 mi. on 15 to county route 10. Go W 5 mi. on 10 to Rabun Beach CG.

# of SINGLE SITES:	Varies	OPEN DATES:	May-Nov
# of SINGLE SITES:	80	MAX SPUR:	40 feet
GROUP RATE:	Varies	MAX STAY:	14 days
# of GROUP SITES:	1	ELEVATION:	1680 feet

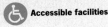

Campground has hosts   **Reservable sites**   **Accessible facilities**   **Fully developed**   **Semi-developed**   **Rustic facilities**

NOTE: Open dates listed are typical. Actual dates are dependent on conditions such as snow pack.

21 Sandy Bottom
Clayton • lat 34°57'20" lon 083°33'00"

DESCRIPTION: This CG rests on Tallulah River with rugged mountain views. The Tallulah River offers good trout fishing. The Coleman River Trail runs along the river through stands of old-growth timber. The Southern Nantahala Wilderness, Chattooga Wild and Scenic River and Appalachian Trail are nearby.

GETTING THERE: From Clayton go W on US HWY 76 approx. 8 mi. to county route. Go N on county route. approx. 4 mi. to forest route 70. Go NW on 70 approx. 5 mi. to Sandy Bottom CG. Road is narrow with sharp curves.

SINGLE RATE:	$8	OPEN DATES:	June-Oct
# of SINGLE SITES:	12	MAX SPUR:	20 feet
		MAX STAY:	14 days
		ELEVATION:	2300 feet

22 Sarah's Creek
Clayton • lat 34°56'30" lon 083°16'00"

DESCRIPTION: This rustic CG is located on Sarah's Creek with views of the surrounding mountains. Fish and swim from the creek. Supplies located in Clayton. Numerous wildlife can be seen in the area. Hike and horseback ride the Rocky Gap Trail and Willis Knob Trail. No drinking water.

GETTING THERE: From Clayton go E on Warwoman Road approx. 9 mi. to forest route 156. Go N on 156 approx. 3 mi. to Sarah's Creek CG.

SINGLE RATE:	$3	OPEN DATES:	Yearlong
# of SINGLE SITES:	28	MAX SPUR:	20 feet
		MAX STAY:	14 days
		ELEVATION:	2300 feet

23 Tallulah River
Clayton • lat 34°55'39" lon 083°32'36"

DESCRIPTION: This CG rests on Tallulah River with rugged mountain views. The Tallulah and Coleman Rivers offer good trout fishing. The Coleman River Trail runs along the river through stands of old-growth timber. The Southern Nantahala Wilderness, Chattooga Wild and Scenic River and Appalachian Trail are nearby.

GETTING THERE: From Clayton go W approx. 8 mi. to county route. Go N on county route approx. 4 mi. to forest route 70. Go NW on 70 approx. 1 mi. to Tallulah River CG. Road is narrow with sharp curves.

SINGLE RATE:	$12	OPEN DATES:	Mar-Nov
# of SINGLE SITES:	17	MAX SPUR:	20 feet
		MAX STAY:	14 days
		ELEVATION:	2000 feet

24 Tate Branch
Clayton • lat 34°57'18" lon 083°33'08"

DESCRIPTION: This remote CG rests at the junction of the Tallulah River and Tate Branch. Trout fishing is good. The Coleman River Trail runs along the river through stands of old-growth timber. The Southern Nantahala Wilderness, Chattooga Wild and Scenic River and Appalachian Trail are nearby.

GETTING THERE: From Clayton go W on US HWY 76 approx. 8 mi. to county route. Go N on county route. approx. 4 mi. to forest route 70. Go NW on 70 approx. 4 mi. to Tate Branch CG. Road is narrow with sharp curves.

SINGLE RATE:	$10	OPEN DATES:	Yearlong
# of SINGLE SITES:	19	MAX SPUR:	20 feet
		MAX STAY:	14 days
		ELEVATION:	2286 feet

25 The Pocket
LaFayette • lat 34°35'08" lon 085°04'54"

DESCRIPTION: This CG is located in a mixed hardwood glen surrounding a large spring and small stream. Johns Mountain Overlook is located nearby, as well as the Keown Falls Scenic Area. Nature trails and a large picnic shelter are nearby. Wildlife in this area includes deer, turkeys, quail, and coyotes.

GETTING THERE: From LaFayette go E on state HWY 136 approx. 13.5 mi. to county route (Pocket Road). Go S on county route (Pocket Road) approx. 7 mi. to The Pocket CG.

SINGLE RATE:	$8	OPEN DATES:	May-Nov
# of SINGLE SITES:	27	MAX SPUR:	40 feet
		MAX STAY:	14 days
		ELEVATION:	800 feet

26 Waters Creek
Dahlonega • lat 34°40'45" lon 083°56'13"

DESCRIPTION: This CG is located along Waters Creek, one of Georgia's trophy trout streams. Please check fishing regulations. Dockery Lake, Woody Gap, the Appalachian Trail, and Lake Winfield Scott are all close by. Wildlife in this area includes deer, turkeys, quail, and coyotes.

GETTING THERE: From Dahlonega go N on US HWY 19 approx. 12 mi. to forest route. Go W on forest route approx. 1 mi. to Waters Creek CG.

SINGLE RATE:	$6	OPEN DATES:	Mar-Oct
# of SINGLE SITES:	8	MAX SPUR:	25 feet
		MAX STAY:	14 days
		ELEVATION:	2200 feet

27 Wildcat Creek
Clayton • lat 34°49'30" lon 083°37'30"

DESCRIPTION: This rustic CG is situated on Wildcat Creek and has two separate camping areas. Fish in the creek or nearby Lake Burton but please check fishing regulations Supplies available in Clayton. Many animals can be seen in the area. The Tray Mountain Wilderness is adjacent to this CG. No drinking water available.

GETTING THERE: From Clayton go W on US HWY 76 approx. 11 mi. to state HWY 197. Go S on 197 approx. 4 mi. to forest route 26. Go W on 26 approx. 3 mi. to Wildcat Creek CG.

SINGLE RATE:	$6	OPEN DATES:	Yearlong
# of SINGLE SITES:	32	MAX SPUR:	20 feet
		MAX STAY:	14 days
		ELEVATION:	1900 feet

28 Willis Knob
Clayton • lat 34°53'49" lon 083°12'56"

DESCRIPTION: This reservation only CG is ideal for horseback riders. This area offers a spring-fed watering trough, riding and hiking trails, and fishing in the nearby Chattooga Wild and Scenic River. Hike and horseback ride the Rocky Gap Trail and Willis Knob Trail. Visit the wilderness areas.

GETTING THERE: From Clayton go E on Warwoman Road approx. 11.5 mi. to forest route 157. Go S on 157 approx. 2 mi. to Willis Knob CG.

SINGLE RATE:	Varies	OPEN DATES:	Yearlong
# of SINGLE SITES:	8	MAX SPUR:	20 feet
		MAX STAY:	14 days
		ELEVATION:	2300 feet

 Campground has hosts   **Reservable sites**    **Accessible facilities**    **Fully developed**   **Semi-developed**   **Rustic facilities**

NOTE: Open dates listed are typical. Actual dates are dependent on conditions such as snow pack.

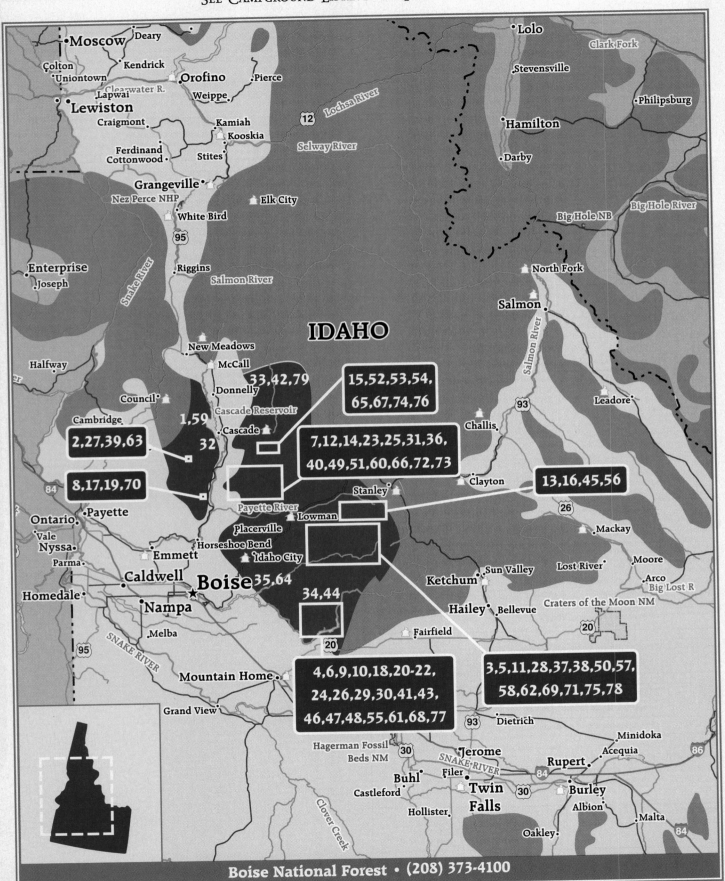

Moscow
Deary
Colton
Kendrick
Uniontown
Orofino
Pierce
Lapwai
Weippe
Clearwater R.
Lewiston
Craigmont
Kamiah
Kooskia
Ferdinand
Cottonwood
Stites
Grangeville
Nez Perce NHP
Elk City
White Bird
Riggins
Salmon River
Enterprise
Joseph
Halfway
Council
Cambridge

Lolo
Clark Fork
Stevensville
Philipsburg
Hamilton
Darby
Lochsa River
Selway River
Big Hole River
Big Hole NB
North Fork
Salmon
Salmon River
Leadore
Challis
Clayton
Mackay
Lost River
Moore
Arco
Big Lost R

IDAHO

New Meadows
McCall
Donnelly
Cascade Reservoir
Cascade
Payette River
Placerville
Idaho City
Horseshoe Bend
Lowman
Stanley
Ketchum
Sun Valley
Hailey
Bellevue
Craters of the Moon NM
Fairfield

Ontario
Payette
Vale
Nyssa
Parma
Emmett
Caldwell
Boise
Nampa
Melba
Homedale

33,42,79

**15,52,53,54,
65,67,74,76**

2,27,39,63

1,59

32

8,17,19,70

**7,12,14,23,25,31,36,
40,49,51,60,66,72,73**

13,16,45,56

35,64

34,44

**4,6,9,10,18,20-22,
24,26,29,30,41,43,
46,47,48,55,61,68,77**

**3,5,11,28,37,38,50,57,
58,62,69,71,75,78**

Mountain Home
Grand View
Dietrich
Hagerman Fossil
Beds NM
Jerome
Minidoka
Acequia
Rupert
SNAKE RIVER
Buhl
Filer
Castleford
Twin
Falls
Burley
Albion
Hollister
Oakley
Malta
Clover Creek
SNAKE RIVER

Terril Stevenson Photo

BOISE NATIONAL FOREST

Comprising the seventh largest national forest in the United States, Boise National Forest's 2.6 million acres provide a variety of recreational opportunities throughout the seasons. With 300,000 people living within an hour's drive, the forest is fast becoming southwest Idaho's big backyard.

The predominantly Ponderosa pine and Douglas fir ecosystem provides homes for fish and wildlife. Large expanses of summer range provide habitat for big game species, such as mule deer and Rocky Mountain elk. Trout are native to most streams and lakes, while ocean-going salmon and steelhead inhabit the many tributaries of the Salmon River. The forest is also home to the Giant Helleborine, a threatened orchid which only grows in certain parts of the western U.S. and Canada.

In the spring, hikers, mountain bikers and equestrians will enjoy spotting migrating birds along the Hulls Gulch National Recreation Trail. World-class whitewater and floating opportunities on the forks of the Payette and Boise rivers attract summer visitors. The Pondersa Pine Scenic Byway offers spectacular vistas of the Sawtooth Range cloaked in fall foliage. Hot springs across the forest can be enjoyed year-round, but offer especially pleasant respite from cooler days. In winter, downhill ski at Bogus Basin, near Boise, or enjoy the many groomed snowmobile routes across the forest.

---

1 Amanita
Donnelly • lat 44°42'06" lon 116°07'48"

DESCRIPTION: CG set on the shores of Lake Cascade in a medium, dense growth conifer forest. Filtered views of lake and mountains. Boat ramp at Rainbow Point CG. Boat and shore fish for trout or perch. Warm days, cold nights. Deer, elk, moose, and eagles are common in area. CG is full most weekends. Gather or buy firewood.

GETTING THERE: Amanita CG is located approx. 5 mi. SW of Donnelly on the NW shore of Cascade Reservoir.

SINGLE RATE:	$10	OPEN DATES:	May-Sept
# of SINGLE SITES:	10	MAX SPUR:	40 feet
		MAX STAY:	14 days
		ELEVATION:	5000 feet

2 Antelope
Cascade • lat 44°20'07" lon 116°11'06"

DESCRIPTION: High mountain CG set in a conifer forest on Sagehen Reservoir and Creek. Limited boat and fly fishing for trout. Warm days with cool nights. Supplies at Emmett. Buy or gather firewood locally. Deer, elk, bears, and birds in area. Mushroom picking and hunting available. Numerous trails nearby.

GETTING THERE: From Cascade go S on state HWY 55 approx. 17 mi. to forest route 644. Go W on 644 approx. 2 mi. to forest route 626. Go NW on 626 approx. 7 mi. to Antelope CG.

SINGLE RATE:	$10	OPEN DATES:	May-Sept
# of SINGLE SITES:	28	MAX SPUR:	30 feet
		MAX STAY:	14 days
		ELEVATION:	4800 feet

3 Bad Bears
Idaho City • lat 43°54'03" lon 115°42'27"

DESCRIPTION: This CG is situated in a pine and fir forest with an open understory. Warm days, cold mornings. Supplies 10 mi. away. No fishing nearby. Deer, elk, and bears in area. Fills holidays and some weekends. Fall is nice. Gather firewood locally. No nearby trails. Mosquitos all summer.

GETTING THERE: Bad Bears CG is located approx. 9.5 mi. NE of Idaho City on state HWY 21.

SINGLE RATE:	$10	OPEN DATES:	May-Oct
# of SINGLE SITES:	8		
		MAX STAY:	14 days
		ELEVATION:	5200 feet

4 Badger Creek
Boise • lat 43°39'44" lon 115°42'39"

DESCRIPTION: This CG is situated in an open area at the confluence of Badger Creek and the Middle Fork Boise River. Mild days with cold nights. Fish for trout, bass, and kokanee, check for regulations. Elk, deer, and occasional bears in the area. Fills weekends. Supplies in Boise. No hiking trails in immediate vicinity.

GETTING THERE: From Boise go E on state HWY 21 approx. 16 mi. to forest route 268. Go E on 268 approx. 26 mi. to Badger Creek CG. Narrow and winding road; not recommended for RVs.

SINGLE RATE:	No fee	OPEN DATES:	Apr-Oct
# of SINGLE SITES:	5	MAX SPUR:	20 feet
		MAX STAY:	14 days
		ELEVATION:	3200 feet

5 Bald Mountain
Idaho City • lat 43°44'57" lon 115°44'37"

DESCRIPTION: CG in a douglas fir forest with an open understory. Views of mountains to the east. Cold mornings. Supplies 10 mi. away. Historic Idaho City and Thorn Creek Butte lookout. No fishing nearby. Deer, elk, and bears. Rarely full. Gather firewood locally. Horse and ATV trails available. Mosquitos all summer.

GETTING THERE: From Idaho City go S on forest route 304 approx. 8 mi. to forest route 203. Go S on 203 approx. 1 mi. to Bald Mountain CG. 4WD recommended.

SINGLE RATE:	No fee	OPEN DATES:	July-Sept
# of SINGLE SITES:	4		
		MAX STAY:	14 days
		ELEVATION:	6000 feet

 Campground has hosts   **Reservable sites**   **Accessible facilities**   **Fully developed**   **Semi-developed**   **Rustic facilities**

NOTE: Open dates listed are typical. Actual dates are dependent on conditions such as snow pack.

Page 225

6 Barneys
Grimes Pass • lat 44°19'34" lon 115°38'49"

DESCRIPTION: CG rests in a dense grove of lodgepole pine and douglas fir on Deadwood Reservoir. Fish for atlantic salmon, kokanee, and trout. Wildlife includes black bears, coyotes, mountain lions, mule deer, and raptors. There is a hiking trail along the West side of the Reservoir. No drinking water.

GETTING THERE: From Grimes Pass go E on primary forest route 24 approx. 7 mi. to forest route 555. Go N on 555 approx. 24 mi. to Barneys CG.

SINGLE RATE:	No fee	OPEN DATES:	July-Sept
# of SINGLE SITES:	6	MAX SPUR:	40 feet
		MAX STAY:	14 days
		ELEVATION:	5300 feet

7 Bears Valley
Stanley • lat 44°24'40" lon 115°22'08"

DESCRIPTION: This CG is located in an open grove of pine and fir on Bears Valley Creek. Catch and release fishing for trout. Black bears, coyotes, mountain lions, mule deer, and raptors. Hike the Wyoming-Fir Trail or access the bordering Frank Church River of No Return Wilderness Area. No drinking water on site.

GETTING THERE: From Stanley go NW on state HWY 21 approx. 22 mi. to forest route 579. Go NW on 579 approx. 13 mi. to Bears Valley CG.

SINGLE RATE:	No fee	OPEN DATES:	July-Sept
# of SINGLE SITES:	10	MAX SPUR:	40 feet
		MAX STAY:	14 days
		ELEVATION:	6400 feet

8 Big Eddy
Banks • lat 44°13'14" lon 116°06'21"

DESCRIPTION: CG on a high forested mountain along the fast flowing North Fork Payette River. Mild days with cool nights. Fish for whitefish and rainbow trout. Historic steam engine site. Supplies in Banks. Deer, elk, and bears reside in the area. Full most weekends. Bring your own firewood. No nearby trails.

GETTING THERE: From Banks go N on state HWY 55 approx. 11 mi. to Big Eddy CG.

SINGLE RATE:	$8	OPEN DATES:	May-Sept
# of SINGLE SITES:	4	MAX SPUR:	30 feet
		MAX STAY:	14 days
		ELEVATION:	3600 feet

9 Big Roaring
Mountain Home • lat 43°37'08" lon 115°26'34"

DESCRIPTION: CG set in a lodgepole pine and spruce forest near Big Roaring Lake. Fish for rainbow and brook trout on the lake. Historical Trinity Guard Station nearby. Warm days with cool nights. Supplies are available at Mountain Home. Gather firewood locally. Numerous hiking trails in the vicinity.

GETTING THERE: From Mountain Home go NE on US HWY 20 approx. 24 mi. to forest route 134. Go N 6 mi. to forest route 113. Go NE approx. 9 mi. to forest route 123. Go N on 123 approx. 19 mi. to Big Roaring CG.

SINGLE RATE:	$5	OPEN DATES:	July-Oct*
# of SINGLE SITES:	12	MAX SPUR:	20 feet
		MAX STAY:	14 days
		ELEVATION:	8200 feet

10 Big Trinity
Mountain Home • lat 43°37'26" lon 115°25'29"

DESCRIPTION: CG is set in a lodgepole pine and spruce forest with views of rocky outcrops and large fields of granite bolders. Big Trinity Lake is nearby for rainbow and brook trout fishing. Historical Trinity Guard Station nearby. Supplies are available at Pine. Gather firewood locally. Numerous trails nearby.

GETTING THERE: From Mountain Home go NE on US HWY 20 approx. 24 mi. to forest route 134. Go N approx. 6 mi. to forest route 113. Go NE approx. 9 mi. to forest route 123. Go N approx. 19 mi. to Big Trinity CG.

SINGLE RATE:	$5	OPEN DATES:	July-Oct*
# of SINGLE SITES:	17	MAX SPUR:	20 feet
		MAX STAY:	14 days
		ELEVATION:	7900 feet

11 Black Rock
Idaho City • lat 43°47'43" lon 115°35'14"

DESCRIPTION: CG overlooking the North Fork Boise River, among ponderosa pine. Hot days, cold mornings. Supplies 20 mi. away. Fly or bait fish stocked and wild trout. Deer, elk, bald eagles, osprey, and bears in area. Moderate use, full July 4. Gather firewood locally. No nearby hiking. Mosquitos all summer.

GETTING THERE: From Idaho City go NE on state HWY 21 approx. 2.5 mi. to forest route 327. Go E on 327 approx. 16 mi. to Black Rock CG.

SINGLE RATE:	$8	OPEN DATES:	June-Oct
# of SINGLE SITES:	10		
GROUP RATE:	$16	MAX STAY:	14 days
# of GROUP SITES:	1	ELEVATION:	4000 feet

12 Boiling Springs
Garden Valley • lat 44°21'35" lon 115°51'30"

DESCRIPTION: CG is situated in a heavily forested narrow mountain valley next to Middle Fork Payette River. Summers are warm. Stream fishing for whitefish and rainbow trout. Supplies in Crouch, 25 mi. away. Bring your own firewood. Hot springs nearby. Hike Middle Fork Trail. ATV use on other trails.

GETTING THERE: From Garden Valley go W on primary forest route 24 approx. 2.5 mi. to forest route 698. Go N on 698 approx. 22 mi. to Boiling Springs CG.

SINGLE RATE:	$6	OPEN DATES:	May-Sept
# of SINGLE SITES:	7	MAX SPUR:	30 feet
		MAX STAY:	14 days
		ELEVATION:	4000 feet

13 Bonneville
Lowman • lat 44°09'25" lon 115°18'48"

DESCRIPTION: This CG is situated among pine and fir on Warm Spring Creek near South Fork Payette River. Enjoy a soak in the local hot springs or fish for rainbow trout in the river. Wildlife includes black bears, coyotes, mountain lions, mule deer, and raptors. Hike the nearby Warm Springs Trail system.

GETTING THERE: Bonneville CG is located approx. 18 mi. E of Lowman on state HWY 21.

SINGLE RATE:	$10	OPEN DATES:	May-Sept
# of SINGLE SITES:	22	MAX SPUR:	60 feet
		MAX STAY:	14 days
		ELEVATION:	4700 feet

14 Bruce Meadows Rest Area
Stanley • lat 44°25'36" lon 115°19'51"

DESCRIPTION: This CG rests in an open grove of pine and fir near Bears Valley Creek. Catch and release fishing for trout. Black bears, coyotes, mountain lions, mule deer, and raptors. Hike the Wyoming-Fir Trail or access the bordering Frank Church River of No Return Wilderness Area. No drinking water available.

GETTING THERE: From Stanley go NW on state HWY 21 approx. 22 mi. to forest route 579. Go NW on 579 approx. 10 mi. to Bruce Meadows Rest Area CG.

SINGLE RATE:	No fee	OPEN DATES:	July-Sept
# of SINGLE SITES:	2	MAX SPUR:	100 feet
		MAX STAY:	14 days
		ELEVATION:	6400 feet

15 Buck Mountain
Cascade • lat 44°40'55" lon 115°32'20"

DESCRIPTION: CG situated in a fir and pine forest near Johnson Creek. Fish for trout and perch from the creek. Supplies available at Warm Lake Lodge. Deer, elk, bears, raptors, and water fowl can be seen in area. Gather firewood locally. Numerous hiking, mountain bike, and ATV trails in the area.

GETTING THERE: From Cascade go N on state HWY 55 approx. 1 mi. to primary forest route 22. Go NE on 22 approx. 32 mi. to forest route 413. Go N on 413 approx. 2.5 mi. to Buck Mountain CG.

SINGLE RATE:	No fee	OPEN DATES:	June-Oct
# of SINGLE SITES:	4	MAX SPUR:	20 feet
		MAX STAY:	14 days
		ELEVATION:	6500 feet

 Campground has hosts   Reservable sites   Accessible facilities   Fully developed   Semi-developed Rustic facilities

NOTE: Open dates listed are typical. Actual dates are dependent on conditions such as snow pack.

16 Bull Trout
Stanley • lat 44°17'49" lon 115°15'17"

DESCRIPTION: This CG is set among ponderosa pine on Bull Trout Lake. Fish for rainbow trout in lake. Black bears, coyotes, mountain lions, mule deer, osprey, and bald eagles. This CG accomodates horses and accesses the Warm Spring Trail System. Supplies in Stanley. Mild days with cool nights. Busy holiday weekends.

GETTING THERE: From Stanley go NW on state HWY 21 approx. 25 mi. to forest route 520. Go SW on 520 approx. 2 mi. to Bull Trout CG.

SINGLE RATE:	Varies	OPEN DATES:	June-Sept
# of SINGLE SITES:	19	MAX SPUR:	60 feet
		MAX STAY:	14 days
		ELEVATION:	6900 feet

17 Canyon
Banks • lat 44°11'17" lon 116°06'52"

DESCRIPTION: CG in a sheltered forest along the fast flowing North Fork Payette River. Mild days with cool nights. Fish for whitefish and rainbow trout. Historic steam engine site. Supplies 9 mi. away in Banks. Deer, elk, and bears reside in the area. Full most weekends. Bring your own firewood. No nearby trails.

GETTING THERE: Canyon CG is located approx. 8.5 mi. N of Banks on state HWY 55.

SINGLE RATE:	$8	OPEN DATES:	May-Sept
# of SINGLE SITES:	6	MAX SPUR:	30 feet
		MAX STAY:	14 days
		ELEVATION:	3800 feet

18 Castle Creek
Mountain Home • lat 43°22'00" lon 115°23'00"

DESCRIPTION: CG set on Anderson Ranch Reservoir in an open area with some pine and fir. Use drift wood for firewood. Water ski on lake. Fish for trout, bass, and kokanee. Supplies in Mountain Home. Deer, elk, mountain lions, black bears, lizards, and osprey. Horse, hiking, and mountain bike trails. No drinking water on site.

GETTING THERE: From Mountain Home go NE on US HWY 20 approx. 24 mi. to forest route 134. Go N on 134 approx. 6 mi. to forest route 113. Go NE on 113 approx. 8 mi. to Castle Creek CG.

SINGLE RATE:	No fee	OPEN DATES:	May-Oct
# of SINGLE SITES:	2	MAX SPUR:	20 feet
		MAX STAY:	14 days
		ELEVATION:	4300 feet

19 Cold Springs
Banks • lat 44°11'37" lon 116°06'44"

DESCRIPTION: CG on a high forested mountain along the fast flowing North Fork Payette River. Mild days with cool nights. Fish for whitefish and rainbow trout. Historic steam engine site. Supplies in Banks. Deer, elk, and bears reside in the area. Full most weekends. Bring your own firewood. No nearby trails.

GETTING THERE: Cold Springs CG is located approx. 9 mi. N of Banks on state HWY 55.

SINGLE RATE:	$8	OPEN DATES:	May-Sept
# of SINGLE SITES:	6	MAX SPUR:	30 feet
		MAX STAY:	14 days
		ELEVATION:	3600 feet

20 Cottonwood
Boise • lat 43°37'57" lon 115°49'27"

DESCRIPTION: CG situated in an open area on a creek, 1/2 mi. N of Arrowrock Reservoir. Fish for trout, bass, and kokanee. Mild days, cool nights. Supplies in Boise. Deer, elk, and occasional black bears frequent the area. Fills weekends. Horse and hiking trails can be found in the vicinity. No RVs.

GETTING THERE: From Boise go E on state HWY 21 approx. 16 mi. to forest route 268. Go E on 268 approx. 12 mi. to forest route 377. Go N on 377 approx. 1 mi. to Cottonwood CG. No RVs.

SINGLE RATE:	No fee	OPEN DATES:	Apr-Oct
# of SINGLE SITES:	3	MAX SPUR:	20 feet
		MAX STAY:	14 days
		ELEVATION:	3300 feet

21 Cozy Cove
Grimes Pass • lat 44°17'28" lon 115°39'04"

DESCRIPTION: CG rests in a dense grove of lodgepole pine and douglas fir on Deadwood Reservoir. Fish for atlantic salmon, kokanee, and trout. Black bears, coyotes, mountain lions, mule deer, osprey, and bald eagles in area. There is a hiking trail along the West side of the Reservoir. No drinking water.

GETTING THERE: From Grimes Pass go E on primary forest route 24 approx. 7 mi. to forest route 555. Go N on 555 approx. 20 mi. to Cozy Cove CG.

SINGLE RATE:	No fee	OPEN DATES:	July-Sept
# of SINGLE SITES:	9	MAX SPUR:	40 feet
		MAX STAY:	14 days
		ELEVATION:	5300 feet

22 Curlew Creek
Mountain Home • lat 43°26'41" lon 115°17'12"

DESCRIPTION: CG set on Anderson Ranch Reservoir in an open area with some pine and fir. Use drift wood for firewood. Water ski on lake. Boat or shore fish for trout, bass, and kokanee. Supplies in Mountain Home. Deer, elk, mountain lions, black bears, lizards, and osprey. Horse, hiking, and mountain bike trails.

GETTING THERE: From Mountain Home go NE on US HWY 20 approx. 35 mi. to primary forest route 61. Go N on 61 approx. 13.5 mi. to Curlew Creek CG.

SINGLE RATE:	$4	OPEN DATES:	May-Oct
# of SINGLE SITES:	12	MAX SPUR:	20 feet
		MAX STAY:	14 days
		ELEVATION:	4300 feet

23 Deadwood
Lowman • lat 44°04'52" lon 115°39'28"

DESCRIPTION: This CG rests among ponderosa pine on Deadwood River (not Deadwood Reservoir). Fish for trout in river. Enjoy a hike on the adjacent trail. Wildlife includes black bears, coyotes, mountain lions, mule deer, osprey, and bald eagles. Enjoy a drive on the Ponderosa Pine National Scenic Byway.

GETTING THERE: Deadwood CG is located approx. 3.5 mi. W of Lowman on primary forest route 24.

SINGLE RATE:	$6	OPEN DATES:	May-Sept
# of SINGLE SITES:	6	MAX SPUR:	40 feet
		MAX STAY:	14 days
		ELEVATION:	3700 feet

24 Deer Creek
Mountain Home • lat 43°27'00" lon 115°17'00"

DESCRIPTION: This CG is typically used as a boat launch area with overnight parking and camping available. Vegetation consists of pine and fir trees. Set on Anderson Ranch Reservoir. Fish for trout, bass, and kokanee. Supplies at Pine. Watch for deer and osprey in the area. No designated trail systems in area.

GETTING THERE: From Mountain Home go NE on US HWY 20 approx. 35 mi. to primary forest route 61. Go N on 61 approx. 15 mi. to Deer Creek CG.

SINGLE RATE:	No fee	OPEN DATES:	May-Oct
# of SINGLE SITES:		MAX SPUR:	20 feet
		MAX STAY:	14 days
		ELEVATION:	4300 feet

25 Deer Flat
Stanley • lat 44°24'32" lon 115°33'10"

DESCRIPTION: This CG is situated among ponderosa pine at the confluence of the North and South Forks of Deer Creek. Fish for trout in the creeks. Wildlife includes black bears, coyotes, mountain lions, mule deer, osprey, and bald eagles. Mild days with cool nights. Supplies in Stanley. No drinking water available.

GETTING THERE: From Stanley go NW on state HWY 21 approx. 22 mi. to forest route 579. Go NW on 579 approx. 22 mi. to Deer Flat CG.

SINGLE RATE:	No fee	OPEN DATES:	July-Sept
# of SINGLE SITES:	5	MAX SPUR:	30 feet
		MAX STAY:	14 days
		ELEVATION:	6300 feet

 Campground has hosts   **Reservable sites**   **Accessible facilities**   **Fully developed**   **Semi-developed**   **Rustic facilities**

NOTE: Open dates listed are typical. Actual dates are dependent on conditions such as snow pack.

26 Dog Creek
Mountain Home • lat 43°31'39" lon 115°18'21"

DESCRIPTION: CG is shaded and quiet, situated along the banks of Dog Creek across the highway from South Fork Boise River. Fish on either the creek or river. Mild days, cool nights. Supplies available at Mountain Home. Deer, osprey and a variety of birds are common to the area. Campers may gather firewood. Green Creek Trail is nearby.

GETTING THERE: From Mountain Home go NE on US HWY 20 approx. 35 mi. to primary forest route 61. Go N on 61 approx. 20 mi. to Dog Creek CG.

SINGLE RATE:	$6	OPEN DATES:	May-Oct
# of SINGLE SITES:	13	MAX SPUR:	35 feet
		MAX STAY:	14 days
		ELEVATION:	4400 feet

31 Fir Creek
Stanley • lat 44°25'42" lon 115°17'03"

DESCRIPTION: This CG rests in an open grove of lodgepole pine and douglas fir on Bears Valley Creek. Catch and release fishing for trout. Black bears, coyotes, mountain lions, mule deer, and raptors in area. Hike to Blue Mountain or access the bordering Frank Church River of No Return Wilderness. No drinking water.

GETTING THERE: From Stanley go NW on state HWY 21 approx. 22 mi. to forest route 579. Go NW on 579 approx. 8 mi. to Fir Creek CG.

SINGLE RATE:	No fee	OPEN DATES:	July-Sept
# of SINGLE SITES:	5	MAX SPUR:	40 feet
		MAX STAY:	14 days
		ELEVATION:	6400 feet

27 Eastside
Cascade • lat 44°19'56" lon 116°10'25"

DESCRIPTION: CG set in a thick pine forest adjacent to Sagehen Reservoir. Warm days with cool nights. Limited boat fishing for trout. Bears, elk, deer, and birds in area. Full most weekends. Supplies in Emmett or Ola. Motorcycle trails and non-motorized trails available.

GETTING THERE: From Cascade go S on state HWY 55 approx. 17 mi. to forest route 644. Go W on 644 approx. 2 mi. to forest route 626. Go NW on 626 approx. 6 mi. to Eastside CG.

SINGLE RATE:	$10	OPEN DATES:	May-Sept
# of SINGLE SITES:	6	MAX SPUR:	30 feet
GROUP RATE:	$75	MAX STAY:	14 days
# of GROUP SITES:	1	ELEVATION:	5200 feet

32 French Creek
Cascade • lat 44°32'00" lon 116°06'30"

DESCRIPTION: This CG is situated in an open and park-like forest with French Creek running through. Cascade Lake is nearby for fishing, boating, and swimming. Supplies available at West Mountain Lodge. Deer and elk reside in the area. Gather firewood locally. The Van Wyck ATV trail is nearby.

GETTING THERE: From Cascade travel S and W (around S shore of Cascade Reservoir) approx. 4 mi. on Lakeshore Drive to forest route 422. Go W and N on 422 approx. 5 mi. to French Creek CG.

SINGLE RATE:	$10	OPEN DATES:	May-Nov
# of SINGLE SITES:	21	MAX SPUR:	40 feet
		MAX STAY:	14 days
		ELEVATION:	4850 feet

28 Edna Creek
Lowman • lat 43°57'45" lon 115°37'17"

DESCRIPTION: CG in an open area of pine and fir with an open understory. Warm days, cold mornings. Supplies 17 mi. away. Historic Idaho City 17 mi.. Fly and bait fish for trout on nearby stream. Deer, elk, and bears in area. Full Holiday weekends. Gather firewood locally. Hiking and bike trails nearby. Mosquitos all summer.

GETTING THERE: Edna Creek CG is located approx. 11 mi. S of Lowman on state HWY 21.

SINGLE RATE:	$10	OPEN DATES:	June-Oct
# of SINGLE SITES:	9		
		MAX STAY:	14 days
		ELEVATION:	5200 feet

33 Golden Gate
Yellow Pine • lat 44°56'08" lon 115°29'04"

DESCRIPTION: CG situated in a fir and pine forest set on Johnson Creek. Fish for trout and perch or swim on the creek. Supplies available at Yellow Pine. Deer, elk, bears, raptors, and water fowl are common to the area. Gather firewood locally. Many hiking trails in the area. No drinking water available on site.

GETTING THERE: Golden Gate CG is located approx. 2 mi. S of Yellow Pine on forest route 413.

SINGLE RATE:	No fee	OPEN DATES:	June-Oct
# of SINGLE SITES:	9		
		MAX STAY:	14 days
		ELEVATION:	4800 feet

29 Elks Flat
Mountain Home • lat 43°33'00" lon 115°17'30"

DESCRIPTION: This CG is situated along the banks of Dog Creek, across the Hwy from South Fork Boise River. Sites are quite and shaded. Mild days with cool nights. Supplies in mountain Home. Deer, elk, humming birds, and occasional black bears are common to the area. Newly renovated, opening July 2000.

GETTING THERE: From Mountain Home go NE on US HWY 20 approx. 35 mi. to primary forest route 61. Go N on 61 approx. 21 mi. to Elks Flat CG.

SINGLE RATE:	Varies	OPEN DATES:	May-Sept
# of SINGLE SITES:	23	MAX SPUR:	50 feet
GROUP RATE:	Varies	MAX STAY:	14 days
# of GROUP SITES:	2	ELEVATION:	4400 feet

34 Graham Bridge
Lowman • lat 43°57'49" lon 115°16'25"

DESCRIPTION: CG in a pine forest, recently burned (1994). Views of Sawtooth Mountains (E). Cold mornings, warm days. Historic Graham Town site. Fish for trout in nearby small streams. Deer, elk, moose, and occasional bears. Receives light use. Gather firewood locally. Hiking access into Sawtooth Wilderness.

GETTING THERE: From Lowman go S on state HWY 21 11 mi. to forest route 384. Go E 3.5 mi. to forest route 385. Go NE 1.5 mi. to forest route 312. Go E 23 mi. to Graham Bridge CG. 4X4 required all summer.

SINGLE RATE:	No fee	OPEN DATES:	July-Sept
# of SINGLE SITES:	4		
		MAX STAY:	14 days
		ELEVATION:	5700 feet

30 Evans Creek
Mountain Home • lat 43°24'01" lon 115°24'48"

DESCRIPTION: CG set on Anderson Ranch Reservoir in an open area with some pine and fir. Use drift wood for firewood. Water ski on lake. Boat or shore fish for trout, bass, and kokanee. Supplies in Mountain Home. Deer, elk, mountain lions, black bears, lizards, and osprey. Little Wilson trail system is nearby.

GETTING THERE: From Mountain Home go NE on US HWY 20 approx. 24 mi. to forest route 134. Go N on 134 approx. 6 mi. to forest route 113. Go NE on 113 approx. 6 mi. to Evans Creek CG.

SINGLE RATE:	No fee	OPEN DATES:	May-Oct
# of SINGLE SITES:	12	MAX SPUR:	20 feet
		MAX STAY:	14 days
		ELEVATION:	4300 feet

35 Grayback
Idaho City • lat 43°48'26" lon 115°51'39"

DESCRIPTION: CG set in a pine forest with some shady sites, on a hillside. Level parking sites. Historic mining town 2 mi.. Dump Station and supplies 3 mi. away. Hot days, cold mornings. Historic Idaho City. No fishing nearby. Deer, elk, and bears. Fills most weekends. Buy or gather firewood. ATV trails nearby.

GETTING THERE: Grayback CG is located approx. 2 mi. SW of Idaho City on state HWY 21.

SINGLE RATE:	$10	OPEN DATES:	May-Oct
# of SINGLE SITES:	18	MAX SPUR:	55 feet
GROUP RATE:	$20	MAX STAY:	14 days
# of GROUP SITES:	2	ELEVATION:	4000 feet

 Campground has hosts   **Reservable sites**   **Accessible facilities**   **Fully developed**   **Semi-developed**   Rustic facilities

NOTE: Open dates listed are typical. Actual dates are dependent on conditions such as snow pack.

36 Hardscrabble
Garden Valley • lat 44°14'23" lon 115°53'54"

DESCRIPTION: CG set in a shady forest with thick undergrowth overlooking the Middle Fork Payette River. Mild days, cool nights. Supplies in Crouch, 13 mi. away. Bank fish for whitefish and rainbow trout. Deer, elk, and bears. Fills holiday weekends. Bring your own firewood. Numerous hiking and ATV trails.

GETTING THERE: From Garden Valley go W on primary forest route 24 approx. 2.5 mi. to forest route 698. Go N on 698 approx. 11 mi. to Hardscrabble CG.

SINGLE RATE:	$7	OPEN DATES:	May-Sept
# of SINGLE SITES:	6	MAX SPUR:	30 feet
		MAX STAY:	14 days
		ELEVATION:	3300 feet

37 Hayfork Group
Idaho City • lat 43°54'31" lon 115°41'49"

DESCRIPTION: CG set among fir and subalpine fir with an open understory. Hayfork and Mores Creek are nearby. Warm days, cold mornings. Supplies 11 mi. away. Historic Idaho city nearby. Deer, elk, and bears in area. Fills holiday weekends. Gather firewood locally. No nearby trails. Mosquitos all summer.

GETTING THERE: Hayfork Group CG is located approx. 10 mi. NE of Idaho City on state HWY 21.

		OPEN DATES:	June-Oct
GROUP RATE:	$50	MAX STAY:	14 days
# of GROUP SITES:	1	ELEVATION:	5100 feet

38 Helende
Lowman • lat 44°05'52" lon 115°28'11"

DESCRIPTION: This CG rests among ponderosa pine on South Fork Payette River. Fish for trout in river. Wildlife includes black bears, coyotes, mountain lions, mule deer, raptors. Enjoy a drive on the Ponderosa Pine National Scenic Byway. Busy holiday weekends. Supplies in Lowman. Frisbee golf is a popular activity.

GETTING THERE: Helende CG is located approx. 10 mi. E of Lowman on state HWY 21.

SINGLE RATE:	$8	OPEN DATES:	May-Sept
# of SINGLE SITES:	10	MAX SPUR:	30 feet
		MAX STAY:	14 days
		ELEVATION:	4100 feet

39 Hollywood
Cascade • lat 44°19'36" lon 116°10'39"

DESCRIPTION: CG situated in a tall pine forest with thick vegetation. Overlooking Sagehen Reservoir and mountains. Limited boat fishing for trout. Bears, elk, deer, and birds in area. Fills most weekends. Supplies in Emmett or Ola. Buy or gather firewood. Both motorcycle and non-motorized trails nearby.

GETTING THERE: From Cascade go S on state HWY 55 approx. 17 mi. to forest route 644. Go W on 644 approx. 2 mi. to forest route 626. Go NW on 626 approx. 6 mi. to Hollywood CG.

SINGLE RATE:	$10	OPEN DATES:	May-Sept
# of SINGLE SITES:	6	MAX SPUR:	30 feet
		MAX STAY:	14 days
		ELEVATION:	5200 feet

40 Hot Springs
Garden Valley • lat 44°03'42" lon 115°55'04"

DESCRIPTION: CG in an open ponderosa pine stand on South Fork Payette River. Great bank fishing for whitefish and trout. Fills most weekends. Supplies in Crouch or Garden Valley. Deer, elk, and bears in area. Bring your own firewood. Station Creek Trail nearby. Group rates depend on number of persons; reservable.

GETTING THERE: Hot Springs CG is located approx. 3.5 mi. SE of Garden Valley on primary forest route 24.

SINGLE RATE:	$10	OPEN DATES:	Apr-Oct
# of SINGLE SITES:	8	MAX SPUR:	45 feet
GROUP RATE:	Varies	MAX STAY:	14 days
# of GROUP SITES:	3	ELEVATION:	3200 feet

41 Howers
Grimes Pass • lat 44°18'30" lon 115°38'30"

DESCRIPTION: CG rests in a dense grove of lodgepole pine and douglas fir on Deadwood Reservoir. Fish for atlantic salmon, kokanee, and trout. Black bears, coyotes, mountain lions, mule deer, osprey, and bald eagles in area. There is a hiking trail along the West side of the Reservoir. No drinking water.

GETTING THERE: From Grimes Pass go E on primary forest route 24 approx. 7 mi. to forest route 555. Go N on 555 approx. 24 mi. to Howers CG.

SINGLE RATE:	No fee	OPEN DATES:	July-Sept
# of SINGLE SITES:	5	MAX SPUR:	40 feet
		MAX STAY:	14 days
		ELEVATION:	5300 feet

42 Ice Hole
Yellow Pine • lat 44°53'17" lon 115°29'55"

DESCRIPTION: CG in a fir and pine forest set on Johnson Creek. Fish for trout and perch or swim on the creek. Supplies at Yellow Pine. Deer, elk, bears, raptors, and water fowl are common to the area. Gather firewood locally. No designated trails in the area. Deadhorse Rapids is approx. 1/4 mi. N. No drinking water.

GETTING THERE: Ice Hole CG is located approx. 5.5 mi. S of Yellow Pine on forest route 413.

SINGLE RATE:	No fee	OPEN DATES:	June-Oct
# of SINGLE SITES:	10		
		MAX STAY:	14 days
		ELEVATION:	4800 feet

43 Ice Springs
Mountain Home • lat 43°28'59" lon 115°23'46"

DESCRIPTION: CG situated in a mature ponderosa pine forest on the banks of Fall Creek. Fish for trout, bass, and kokanee from the creek. Supplies available at Mountain Home. Deer, osprey, squirrels, and chipmunks reside in the area. Campers may gather their firewood locally. Numerous trails in the vicinity.

GETTING THERE: From Mountain Home go NE on US HWY 20 approx. 24 mi. to forest route 134. Go N 6 mi. to forest route 113. Go NE approx. 9 mi. to forest route 123. Go N approx. 4 mi. to Ice Springs CG.

SINGLE RATE:	No fee	OPEN DATES:	May-Sept
# of SINGLE SITES:	3	MAX SPUR:	20 feet
		MAX STAY:	14 days
		ELEVATION:	5000 feet

44 Johnson Creek
Lowman • lat 43°56'23" lon 115°16'59"

DESCRIPTION: CG set among lodgepole pine, which burned over in 1994. Johnson Creek fronts the CG with Sawtooth Mountains to the east. Supplies 47 mi.. Bait or fly fish nearby streams or Alpine lakes in Sawtooth Wilderness. Deer, elk, moose, bears, and mountain goats in area. Gather firewood. Hiking access into Wilderness.

GETTING THERE: From Lowman go S on state HWY 21 11 mi. to forest route 384. Go E 3.5 mi. to forest route 385. Go NE 1.5 mi. to forest route 312. Go E 25 mi. to Johnson Creek CG. July-Oct a small river forms.

SINGLE RATE:	No fee	OPEN DATES:	July-Sept
# of SINGLE SITES:	3		
		MAX STAY:	14 days
		ELEVATION:	5600 feet

45 Kirkham
Lowman • lat 44°04'21" lon 115°32'31"

DESCRIPTION: This CG rests among ponderosa pine on South Fork Payette River. Fish for trout in river. Wildlife includes black bears, coyotes, mountain lions, mule deer, and raptors. Enjoy a drive on the Ponderosa Pine National Scenic Byway. Busy holiday weekends. Supplies in Lowman. Try a soak in the local hot spring.

GETTING THERE: Kirkham CG is located approx. 3.5 mi. E of Lowman on state HWY 21.

SINGLE RATE:	$10	OPEN DATES:	May-Sept
# of SINGLE SITES:	16	MAX SPUR:	60 feet
		MAX STAY:	14 days
		ELEVATION:	4000 feet

 Campground has hosts   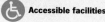 **Reservable sites**   **Accessible facilities**   **Fully developed**   **Semi-developed**   **Rustic facilities**

NOTE: Open dates listed are typical. Actual dates are dependent on conditions such as snow pack.

46 Little Camas
Mountain Home • lat 43°21'05" lon 115°23'30"

DESCRIPTION: CG in an open sagebrush flat with vegetation consisting primarily of choke cherry trees and grasses. Fish for trout and bass on Little Camas Reservoir. Hot summer days with cool nights. Supplies at Mountain Home. Boat ramp. Bring your own firewood. No drinking water. No developed trail system in area.

GETTING THERE: From Mountain Home go NE on US HWY 20 approx. 26.5 mi. to forest route 160. Go N on 160 approx. 3 mi. to Little Camas CG.

SINGLE RATE:	No fee	OPEN DATES:	June-Sept
# of SINGLE SITES:	16	MAX SPUR:	20 feet
		MAX STAY:	14 days
		ELEVATION:	5000 feet

47 Little Roaring
Mountain Home • lat 43°37'45" lon 115°26'35"

DESCRIPTION: This CG is situated in an open alpine setting near Little Roaring River Lake. Fish for rainbow and brook trout from the lake. Warm days, cool nights. Historical Trinity Guard Station is nearby. Supplies at Mountain Home. Gather firewood locally. Hiking trailheads on site, no horses.

GETTING THERE: From Mountain Home go NE on US HWY 20 approx. 24 mi. to forest route 134. Go N approx. 6 mi. to forest route 113. Go NE approx. 9 mi. to forest route 123. Go N approx. 19 mi. to Little Roaring CG.

SINGLE RATE:	No fee	OPEN DATES:	July-Oct*
# of SINGLE SITES:	4	MAX SPUR:	20 feet
		MAX STAY:	14 days
		ELEVATION:	7900 feet

48 Little Wilson
Mountain Home • lat 43°22'40" lon 115°26'03"

DESCRIPTION: CG set on Anderson Ranch Reservoir in an open area with some pine and fir. Use drift wood for firewood. Water ski on lake. Boat or shore fish for trout, bass, and kokanee. Supplies in Mountain Home. Deer, elk, mountain lions, black bears, lizards, and osprey. Little Wilson trail system is nearby.

GETTING THERE: From Mountain Home go NE on US HWY 20 approx. 24 mi. to forest route 134. Go N on 134 approx. 6 mi. to forest route 113. Go NE on 113 approx. 2 mi. to Little Wilson CG.

SINGLE RATE:	No fee	OPEN DATES:	May-Oct
# of SINGLE SITES:	2	MAX SPUR:	20 feet
		MAX STAY:	14 days
		ELEVATION:	4600 feet

49 Mountain View
Lowman • lat 44°04'44" lon 115°36'11"

DESCRIPTION: This CG rests among ponderosa pine on South Fork Payette River. Fish for trout in river. Wildlife includes black bears, coyotes, mountain lions, mule deer, and raptors. Enjoy a drive on the Ponderosa Pine National Scenic Byway. Busy holiday weekends. Supplies in Lowman. Be sure to visit the scenic overlook nearby.

GETTING THERE: Mountain View CG is located approx. .5 mi. E of Lowman on state HWY 21.

SINGLE RATE:	$10	OPEN DATES:	May-Sept
# of SINGLE SITES:	14	MAX SPUR:	50 feet
		MAX STAY:	14 days
		ELEVATION:	3900 feet

50 Neinmeyer
Atlanta • lat 43°45'30" lon 115°34'30"

DESCRIPTION: CG set in the Middle Fork Boise River canyon among ponderosa pine. Views of canyon walls and river. Check fishing regulations. Hot days, cold nights. Fly or bait fish for trout. Deer, elk, bald eagles, osprey, and bears in area. Full July 4. Gather firewood locally. No nearby trails. Mosquitos all summer.

GETTING THERE: Neinmeyer CG is located approx. 27 mi. W of Atlanta on forest route 268.

SINGLE RATE:	No fee	OPEN DATES:	June-Oct
# of SINGLE SITES:	8		
		MAX STAY:	14 days
		ELEVATION:	3700 feet

51 Park Creek
Lowman • lat 44°07'01" lon 115°34'49"

DESCRIPTION: This CG is situated in ponderosa pine at the confluence of Park and Clear Creeks. Fish for rainbow trout. Wildlife includes black bears, coyotes, mountain lions, mule deer, osprey, and bald eagles. Hike the Kirkham Ridge Trail. Supplies in Lowman. Busy holiday weekends. Mild days with cool nights.

GETTING THERE: Park Creek CG is located approx. 4 mi. N of Lowman on forest route 582.

SINGLE RATE:	$7	OPEN DATES:	May-Sept
# of SINGLE SITES:	26	MAX SPUR:	60 feet
GROUP RATE:	Varies	MAX STAY:	14 days
# of GROUP SITES:	1	ELEVATION:	4200 feet

52 Pen Basin
Cascade • lat 44°37'54" lon 115°31'24"

DESCRIPTION: CG situated in a fir and pine forest set near Johnson Creek. Fish for trout at the creek, check for local regulations. Warm days with cool nights. Supplies are available at Warm Lake Lodge. Deer, elk, bears, raptors, and water fowl reside in the area. Gather firewood locally. Numerous trails in area.

GETTING THERE: From Cascade go N on state HWY 55 approx. 1 mi. to primary forest route 22. Go NE on 22 approx. 35 mi. to Pen Basin CG.

SINGLE RATE:	No fee	OPEN DATES:	June-Oct
# of SINGLE SITES:	6	MAX SPUR:	35 feet
		MAX STAY:	14 days
		ELEVATION:	6700 feet

53 Penny Springs
Cascade • lat 44°41'00" lon 115°40'00"

DESCRIPTION: In a dense mixed pine forest setting with huckleberry and grouse berry brush in area. Fish for trout from the South Fork Salmon River nearby. Historical Knox townsite is 4 mi. from CG. Supplies available at Warm Lake Lodge. Deer, elk, bears and small wildlife are common to the area. Campers may gather firewood. Trails nearby.

GETTING THERE: From Cascade go NE on forest route 22 approx. 24 mi. to forest route 474. Go N on 474 approx. 4 mi. to Penny Springs CG.

SINGLE RATE:	No fee	OPEN DATES:	June-Oct
# of SINGLE SITES:	4	MAX SPUR:	20 feet
		MAX STAY:	14 days
		ELEVATION:	5200 feet

54 Picnic Point
Cascade • lat 44°39'16" lon 115°40'17"

DESCRIPTION: This primitive tent only CG is in open ponderosa on a rocky point overlooking Warm Lake. Boat or shore fish for trout. Historic Knox townsite and Kline's Grave are nearby. Supplies available at North Shore Lodge. Deer, elk, bears, moose, raptors, and waterfowl. Full most weekends. Gather or buy firewood.

GETTING THERE: From Cascade go NE on primary forest route 22 approx. 25 mi. to forest route 489. Go SW on 489 approx. 1.5 mi. to Picnic Point CG. Park and walk-in.

SINGLE RATE:	$6	OPEN DATES:	May-Oct
# of SINGLE SITES:	8		
		MAX STAY:	14 days
		ELEVATION:	5300 feet

55 Pine
Mountain Home • lat 43°27'30" lon 115°18'40"

DESCRIPTION: CG set on Anderson Ranch Reservoir in an open area with some pine and fir. Water ski on lake. Boat or shore fish for trout, bass, and kokanee. Warm days, cool nights. Supplies in Mountain Home. Deer, elk, mountain lions, occasional black bears. Horse, hiking and mountain bike trails. ATV on roads if licensed.

GETTING THERE: From Mountain Home go NE on US HWY 20 approx. 35 mi. to primary forest route 61. Go N on 61 approx. 17 mi. to forest route 128. Go S on 128 approx. 2 mi. to Pine CG.

SINGLE RATE:	No fee	OPEN DATES:	May-Oct
# of SINGLE SITES:	8	MAX SPUR:	20 feet
		MAX STAY:	14 days
		ELEVATION:	4300 feet

 Campground has hosts   **Reservable sites**   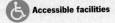 **Accessible facilities**   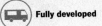 **Fully developed**   **Semi-developed**    **Rustic facilities**

NOTE: Open dates listed are typical. Actual dates are dependent on conditions such as snow pack.

56 Pine Flats

Lowman • lat 44°03'47" lon 115°40'52"

DESCRIPTION: This CG is set among ponderosa pine on the South Fork Payette River. Fish for rainbow trout. Wildlife in this area includes black bears, coyotes, mountain lions, mule deer, osprey, and bald eagles. Supplies in Lowman. Enjoy a soak in the local hot spring. Mild days with cool nights. Busy holiday weekends.

GETTING THERE: Pine Flats CG is located approx. 4 mi. W of Lowman on primary forest route 24.

SINGLE RATE:	$10	OPEN DATES:	May-Sept
# of SINGLE SITES:	27	MAX SPUR:	60 feet
		MAX STAY:	14 days
		ELEVATION:	4400 feet

57 Power Plant

Atlanta • lat 43°48'54" lon 115°06'15"

DESCRIPTION: CG on the Middle Fork Boise River among pine and fir. Views of Greylock Mountain and Sawtooth Peaks. Expect cold mornings. Supplies 50 mi. away. Historic Atlanta townsite. Trout fish the river. Deer, elk, bald eagles, osprey, and bears. Fills July 4. Gather firewood. Trails into Sawtooth Wilderness.

GETTING THERE: Power Plant CG is located approx. 1.5 mi. NE of Atlanta on forest route 268.

SINGLE RATE:	No fee	OPEN DATES:	June-Sept
# of SINGLE SITES:	24		
GROUP RATE:	No fee	MAX STAY:	14 days
# of GROUP SITES:	1	ELEVATION:	5500 feet

58 Queens River

Atlanta • lat 43°49'16" lon 115°12'33"

DESCRIPTION: CG on the banks of Queens River in a pine and fir forest with an open understory. Fly fish for trout on Queens or Middle Fork Boise River. Supplies 50 mi. away. Gather firewood. Fills July 4. Deer, elk, bald eagles, osprey, and bears. Horse and hiking trails into Sawtooth Wilderness. Mosquitos.

GETTING THERE: Queens River CG is located approx. 5 mi. W of Atlanta on forest route 268.

SINGLE RATE:	No fee	OPEN DATES:	June-Sept
# of SINGLE SITES:	4		
		MAX STAY:	14 days
		ELEVATION:	5000 feet

59 Rainbow Point

Donnelly • lat 44°42'12" lon 116°07'52"

DESCRIPTION: CG set on the shores of Lake Cascade in a pine forest. Filtered views of lake and mountains. Boat or shore fish for trout and perch. Boat ramp available. Supplies at Tamarack Falls Store. Deer, elk, bears, raptors, and waterfowl are common to the area. Gather or buy firewood. Wasps July-August.

GETTING THERE: Rainbow Point CG is located approx. 6 mi. SW of Donnelly on the NW shore of Cascade Reservoir.

SINGLE RATE:	$10	OPEN DATES:	May-Nov
# of SINGLE SITES:	12	MAX SPUR:	45 feet
		MAX STAY:	14 days
		ELEVATION:	5000 feet

60 Rattlesnake

Garden Valley • lat 44°15'58" lon 115°52'44"

DESCRIPTION: CG in an open park-like area of fir and pine on Middle Fork Payette River. Bank fish for whitefish and rainbow trout. Supplies in Crouch, 17 mi. away. Bring your own firewood. Fills holiday weekends. Deer, elk, and bears in area. Numerous ATV, hiking, mountain bike, and horse trails in area.

GETTING THERE: From Garden Valley go W on primary forest route 24 approx. 2.5 mi. to forest route 698. Go N on 698 approx. 14 mi. to Rattlesnake CG.

SINGLE RATE:	$10	OPEN DATES:	May-Sept
# of SINGLE SITES:	10	MAX SPUR:	30 feet
		MAX STAY:	14 days
		ELEVATION:	3300 feet

61 Riverside

Grimes Pass • lat 44°20'00" lon 115°38'00"

DESCRIPTION: CG rests in a dense grove of lodgepole pine and douglas fir on Deadwood Reservoir. Fish for atlantic salmon, kokanee, and trout. Black bears, coyotes, mountain lions, mule deer, osprey, and bald eagles in area. There is a hiking trail along the West side of the Reservoir. No drinking water.

GETTING THERE: From Grimes Pass go E on primary forest route 24 approx. 7 mi. to forest route 555. Go N on 555 approx. 25 mi. to Riverside CG.

SINGLE RATE:	No fee	OPEN DATES:	July-Sept
# of SINGLE SITES:	9	MAX SPUR:	35 feet
		MAX STAY:	14 days
		ELEVATION:	5300 feet

62 Riverside

Atlanta • lat 43°48'32" lon 115°07'47"

DESCRIPTION: CG on the Middle Fork Boise River among pine and fir. Views of Greylock Mountain and Sawtooth Peaks. Cold mornings. Supplies 50 mi. away. Historic Atlanta townsite. Trout fish the river. Elk, bald eagles, osprey, and bears. Fills July 4. Trails into Sawtooth Wilderness. 4X4 and ATV roads nearby.

GETTING THERE: From Atlanta go W on forest route 268 approx. 1/2 mi. to forest route 205. Go N on 205 approx. 1/2 mi. to Riverside CG.

SINGLE RATE:	No fee	OPEN DATES:	June-Sept
# of SINGLE SITES:	10		
		MAX STAY:	14 days
		ELEVATION:	5600 feet

63 Sagehen Creek

Cascade • lat 43°01'15" lon 111°49'33"

DESCRIPTION: High mountain CG set in a thick conifer forest at Sagehen Reservoir and Creek. Warm days with cool nights. Boat launch on site. Mushroom picking, fishing (stocked trout), and hunting. Buy or gather firewood. Supplies are available in Emmet or Ola. Fills weekends. Numerous hiking and ATV trails in area.

GETTING THERE: From Cascade go S on state HWY 55 approx. 17 mi. to forest route 644. Go W on 644 approx. 2 mi. to forest route 626. Go NW on 626 approx. 7 mi. to Sagehen Creek CG.

SINGLE RATE:	$10	OPEN DATES:	May-Sept
# of SINGLE SITES:	15	MAX SPUR:	30 feet
		MAX STAY:	14 days
		ELEVATION:	4800 feet

64 Shafer Butte

Idaho City • lat 43°47'00" lon 116°05'03"

DESCRIPTION: CG in a high open meadow with views of high mountain peaks. No nearby fishing. Warm days with cool nights. Supplies in Idaho City. Elk, deer, mountain lions, coyotes, and occasional black bears in area. Moderate to heavy use. 3 mi. to Nature Trail. Easy loop to lookout and Moore's Mountain.

GETTING THERE: From Idaho City go SW on state HWY 21 approx. 9 mi. to forest route 364. Go NW on 364 approx. 3 mi. to forest route 366. Go W on 366 approx. 7 mi. to Shafer Butte CG. 4WD recommended.

SINGLE RATE:	$6	OPEN DATES:	July-Sept
# of SINGLE SITES:	5	MAX SPUR:	20 feet
GROUP RATE:	$30	MAX STAY:	14 days
		ELEVATION:	7000 feet

65 Shoreline

Cascade • lat 44°39'25" lon 115°40'07"

DESCRIPTION: CG set on the shores of Warm Lake in a medium dense growth pine forest. Views of lake. Boat ramp nearby. Boat or shore fish for trout. Historic Knox Townsite and Kline's Grave nearby. Supplies at North Shore Lodge. Deer, elk, moose, bears, and raptors in area. Full most weekends. Gather or buy firewood.

GETTING THERE: From Cascade go NE on forest route 22 approx. 25 mi. to forest route 489. Go approx. 1 mi. on 489 to Shoreline CG.

SINGLE RATE:	$10	OPEN DATES:	May-Nov
# of SINGLE SITES:	25	MAX SPUR:	45 feet
GROUP RATE:	$50	MAX STAY:	14 days
# of GROUP SITES:	1	ELEVATION:	5300 feet

 Campground has hosts   **Reservable sites**   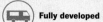 **Accessible facilities**   **Fully developed**   **Semi-developed**   **Rustic facilities**

NOTE: Open dates listed are typical. Actual dates are dependent on conditions such as snow pack.

66 Silver Creek
Garden Valley • lat 44°21'14" lon 115°48'48"

DESCRIPTION: CG is partially shaded by a lodgepole pine stand. Views of Peace Rock. Mild days with cool nights. Trout fishing opportunities nearby, check regulations. Supplies in Crouch, 28 mi. away. Deer, elk, moose, and bears in area. Rarely fills. Bring your own firewood. Several marked trails in area.

GETTING THERE: From Garden Valley go W on primary forest route 24 approx. 2.5 mi. to forest route 698. Go N on 698 approx. 15 mi. to forest route 671. Go NE on 671 approx. 10 mi. to Silver Creek CG.

SINGLE RATE:	No fee	OPEN DATES:	May-Sept
# of SINGLE SITES:	5	MAX SPUR:	30 feet
		MAX STAY:	14 days
		ELEVATION:	4600 feet

67 South Fork Salmon River
Cascade • lat 44°39'11" lon 115°42'03"

DESCRIPTION: CG in a medium dense pine and fir forest set on the Salmon River. Views of river and mountians. Shore fish for trout on river, check regulations Historic Knox and Kline's Grave are nearby. Supplies available at Warm Lake Lodge. Deer, elk, bears, and hawks. Full on holiday weekends. Gather or buy firewood.

GETTING THERE: From Cascade go NE on primary forest route 22 approx. 23 mi. to South Fork Salmon River CG.

SINGLE RATE:	$10	OPEN DATES:	May-Oct
# of SINGLE SITES:	14	MAX SPUR:	45 feet
		MAX STAY:	14 days
		ELEVATION:	5200 feet

68 Spillway
Mountain Home • lat 43°21'00" lon 115°27'30"

DESCRIPTION: CG set on Anderson Ranch Reservoir in an open meadow. Use drift wood for firewood. Water ski on lake. Boat or shore fish for trout, bass, and kokanee. Supplies in Mountain Home. Deer, elk, mountain lions, black bears, lizards, and osprey in area. Little Wilson trail system is within 1 mi. of CG.

GETTING THERE: From Mountain Home go NE on US HWY 20 approx. 24 mi. to forest route 134. Go N on 134 approx. 6 mi. Spillway CG.

SINGLE RATE:	No fee	OPEN DATES:	May-Oct
# of SINGLE SITES:	3	MAX SPUR:	20 feet
		MAX STAY:	14 days
		ELEVATION:	4200 feet

69 Summit Lake
Cascade • lat 44°38'42" lon 115°35'08"

DESCRIPTION: CG set on the shores of Summit Lake in a fir and pine forest. Shore or boat fish for trout from Summit and Warm Lakes, check for local regulations. Supplies located at Warm Lake Lodge. Deer, elk, bears, raptors, and water fowl can be seen in area. Gather firewood locally. Numerous trails nearby.

GETTING THERE: From Cascade go NE on forest route 22 approx. 32 mi. to Summit Lake CG.

SINGLE RATE:	No fee	OPEN DATES:	June-Oct
# of SINGLE SITES:	3	MAX SPUR:	20 feet
		MAX STAY:	14 days
		ELEVATION:	7000 feet

70 Swinging Bridge
Banks • lat 44°10'18" lon 116°07'12"

DESCRIPTION: CG set among shady surrounded by mountains along the North Fork Payette River. River canyon views. Fish for rainbow trout and whitefish. Warm summer days, cool nights. Supplies in Banks, 4 mi.. Bring own firewood. Events include a free fishing day in June, and White Water Roundup. No nearby trails.

GETTING THERE: Swinging Bridge CG is located approx. 7 mi. N of Banks on state HWY 55.

SINGLE RATE:	$8	OPEN DATES:	May-Sept
# of SINGLE SITES:	11	MAX SPUR:	30 feet
		MAX STAY:	14 days
		ELEVATION:	3700 feet

71 Tenmile
Idaho City • lat 43°53'52" lon 115°42'32"

DESCRIPTION: CG situated in a pine and fir forest with an open understory on Mores and Tenmile Creek. Warm days, cold mornings. Supplies 10 mi. away. Historic Idaho City nearby. Deer, elk, and bears in area. Fills holidays and most weekends. Buy or gather firewood. No nearby trails. Mosquitos all summer.

GETTING THERE: Tenmile CG is located approx. 9 mi. NE of Idaho City on state HWY 21.

SINGLE RATE:	$10	OPEN DATES:	May-Oct
# of SINGLE SITES:	14		
GROUP RATE:	$20	MAX STAY:	14 days
# of GROUP SITES:	2	ELEVATION:	5000 feet

72 Tie Creek
Garden Valley • lat 44°12'32" lon 115°55'30"

DESCRIPTION: CG set in a shady forest with thick undergrowth overlooking the Middle Fork Payette River. Mild days, cool nights. Supplies in Crouch, 11 mi. away. Bank fish for whitefish and rainbow trout. Deer, elk, and bears. Fills holiday weekends. Bring your own firewood. Numerous hiking and ATV trails.

GETTING THERE: From Garden Valley go W on primary forest route 24 approx. 2.5 mi. to forest route 698. Go N on 698 approx. 8 mi. to Tie Creek CG.

SINGLE RATE:	$8	OPEN DATES:	May-Sept
# of SINGLE SITES:	8	MAX SPUR:	30 feet
		MAX STAY:	14 days
		ELEVATION:	3200 feet

73 Trail Creek
Garden Valley • lat 44°16'37" lon 115°52'26"

DESCRIPTION: CG among douglas fir and ponderosa pine overlooking the middle Fork Payette River. Bank fish for whitefish and rainbow trout. Mild days, cool nights. Supplies in Crouch. Fills holiday weekends. Deer, elk, and bears in area. Bring your own firewood. Horse or hike Middle Fork trail. ATV trails also available.

GETTING THERE: From Garden Valley go W on primary forest route 24 approx. 2.5 mi. to forest route 698. Go N on 698 approx. 15 mi. to Trail Creek CG.

SINGLE RATE:	$8	OPEN DATES:	May-Sept
# of SINGLE SITES:	11	MAX SPUR:	30 feet
		MAX STAY:	14 days
		ELEVATION:	3700 feet

74 Trout Creek
Yellow Pine • lat 44°44'50" lon 115°33'15"

DESCRIPTION: CG situated in a pine and fir forest set near both Trout and Johnson Creeks. Fish for trout from either creek, check for local regulations. Supplies are available at Yellow Pine. Deer, elk, bears, and water fowl can be seen in the area. Gather firewood locally. Numerous trails in the area.

GETTING THERE: Trout Creek CG is located approx. 17 mi. S of Yellow Pine on forest route 413.

SINGLE RATE:	No fee	OPEN DATES:	July-Oct
# of SINGLE SITES:	6	MAX SPUR:	30 feet
		MAX STAY:	14 days
		ELEVATION:	6300 feet

75 Troutdale
Atlanta • lat 43°42'59" lon 115°37'27"

DESCRIPTION: This CG is situated in an open area at the confluence of Badger Creek and the Middle Fork Boise River. Mild days with cold nights. Fish for trout, bass, and kokanee, check for regulations. Elk, deer, and occasional bears in the area. Fills weekends. Supplies in Boise. No hiking trails in immediate vicinity.

GETTING THERE: Troutdale is located approx. 31 mi. W of Atlanta on forest route 268.

SINGLE RATE:	No fee	OPEN DATES:	Apr-Oct
# of SINGLE SITES:	4	MAX SPUR:	20 feet
		MAX STAY:	14 days
		ELEVATION:	3600 feet

 Campground has hosts   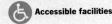 **Reservable sites**   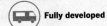 **Accessible facilities**   **Fully developed**   **Semi-developed**   **Rustic facilities**

NOTE: Open dates listed are typical. Actual dates are dependent on conditions such as snow pack.

76 Warm Lake
Cascade • lat 44°39'08" lon 115°39'20"

DESCRIPTION: This CG is situated in an old growth ponderosa pine forest along Chipmunk Creek. Fish for trout and perch, check for local regulations. Warm days with cold nights. Deer, elk, bears, raptors, and water fowl in area. Gather firewood locally. ATV, mountain bike, hiking, and horse trails nearby.

GETTING THERE: From Cascade go N on state HWY 55 approx. 1 mi. to primary forest route 22. Go NE on 22 approx. 22 mi. to Warm Lake CG.

SINGLE RATE:	$10	OPEN DATES:	Yearlong
# of SINGLE SITES:	10	MAX SPUR:	35 feet
		MAX STAY:	14 days
		ELEVATION:	5300 feet

77 Willow Creek
Lowman • lat 43°57'00" lon 115°31'00"

DESCRIPTION: This CG is situated in a pine and fir forest on Willow Creek. Cold mornings. Fly or bait fish for trout on creek. Deer, elk, and occasional bears frequent the area. Full July 4. Gather firewood locally. Supplies are available 21 mi. away. Horse trails nearby. Mosquitos all summer.

GETTING THERE: From Lowman go S on state HWY 21 approx. 11 mi. to forest route 384. Go E on 384 approx. 5 mi. to Willow Creek CG.

SINGLE RATE:	No fee	OPEN DATES:	June-Oct
# of SINGLE SITES:	4		
		MAX STAY:	14 days
		ELEVATION:	5400 feet

78 Willow Creek
Boise • lat 43°38'39" lon 115°45'48"

DESCRIPTION: This CG is situated in an open area at the confluence of Badger Creek and the Middle Fork Boise River. Mild days with cold nights. Fish for trout, bass, and kokanee, check for regulations. Elk, deer, and occasional bears in the area. Fills weekends. Supplies in Boise. No hiking trails in immediate vicinity.

GETTING THERE: From Boise go E on state HWY 21 approx. 16 mi. to forest route 268. Go E on 268 approx. 16 mi. to Willow Creek CG.

SINGLE RATE:	No fee	OPEN DATES:	Apr-Oct
# of SINGLE SITES:	10	MAX SPUR:	20 feet
		MAX STAY:	14 days
		ELEVATION:	3200 feet

79 Yellow Pine
Yellow Pine • lat 44°57'17" lon 115°29'44"

DESCRIPTION: CG situated in a pine and fir forest set on Johnson Creek. Fish for trout and perch on creek or the East Fork of the South Fork Salmon River. Supplies available at Yello Pine. Deer, elk, bears, raptors, and water fowl in area. Gather firewood locally. Numerous trails in the area.

GETTING THERE: Yellow Pine CG is located approx. 1 mi. S of Yellow Pine on forest route 413.

SINGLE RATE:	No fee	OPEN DATES:	June-Oct
# of SINGLE SITES:	14	MAX SPUR:	35 feet
		MAX STAY:	14 days
		ELEVATION:	4800 feet

Campground has hosts   **Reservable sites**   **Accessible facilities**   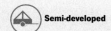 **Fully developed**    **Semi-developed**   **Rustic facilities**

CARIBOU NATIONAL FOREST

Established in 1903 by President Theodore Roosevelt, the Caribou National Forest is located primarily in southeastern Idaho. The forest is comprised of just over one million acres, which includes the 47,000-acre Curlew National Grassland, and has approximately 250 miles of streams and 8,100 acres of lakes and reservoirs.

The forest was named for an early miner nicknamed Caribou Jack who, along with two friends, discovered the first gold in 1870 near what is now called Caribou Mountain. After the first discovery, the gold rush lasted nearly 20 years and produced $50 million worth of placer gold. Two of Idaho's largest "gold" cities were Keenan City (900 population) and Iowa Bar (1,500 population), later called Caribou City. Both sites are now abandoned.

A multitude of special recreation opportunities such as fishing, hunting, horseriding and biking exist in the Caribou, Elkhorn and Deep Creek mountain ranges.

The Curlew National Grasslands provide a diversity of activities different from forested lands. Of special interest is the Sweeten Pond area developed especially for waterfowl and shorebirds.

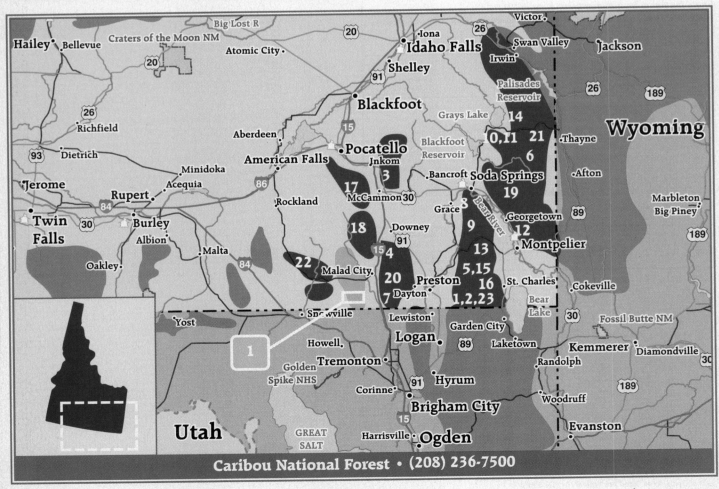

Caribou National Forest • (208) 236-7500

1 Allred Flat
Afton • lat 42°29'17" lon 110°57'43"

DESCRIPTION: CG situated in a pine and fir forest on the banks of Little White Creek. Stream fish in creek for trout. Warm days with cold nights. Supplies in Afton. Gather firewood locally. Watch for moose, elk, deer, and bears in the area. Horse and hiking trails available in vicinity. Prepare for mosquitos in the evening.

GETTING THERE: From Afton go S on US HWY 89 approx. 19 mi. to Allred Flat CG.

SINGLE RATE:	$5	OPEN DATES:	May-Oct
# of SINGLE SITES:	32	MAX SPUR:	99 feet
GROUP RATE:	Varies	MAX STAY:	16 days
# of GROUP SITES:	2	ELEVATION:	6800 feet

2 Angles
Jackson • lat 43°50'30" lon 110°10'00"

DESCRIPTION: In thick forest of pine, aspen and fir. No services, no water. Mild days, cold nights. Supplies in Jackson. Gather firewood locally. Elk, deer, moose and bears in area. Bear boxes available. Trailhead for horse or hiking into Teton Wilderness. Horse corral.

GETTING THERE: From Jackson go N on US HWY 191 approx. 30 mi. to Moran Jct. Go E at the Jct on US HWY 26/287 approx. 16 mi. to forest route 30041. Go N on 30041 approx. 1/2 mi. to Angles CG.

SINGLE RATE:	$5	OPEN DATES:	June-Sept*
# of SINGLE SITES:	4		
		MAX STAY:	10 days
		ELEVATION:	7000 feet

3 Atherton Creek
Kelly • lat 43°38'13" lon 110°31'21"

DESCRIPTION: CG set in an open area overlooking the Gros Ventre River and a geologic slide. Trout fish river or Lower Slide Lake. Warm days with cold nights. Supplies in Jackson. Gather firewood locally. Watch for deer, elk, moose, and occasional bears. Hiking and horse trails nearby. Access into the Gros Ventre Wilderness.

GETTING THERE: Atherton Creek CG is located approx. 7.5 mi. E of Kelly on forest route 30400 (Gros Ventre Road).

SINGLE RATE:	$5	OPEN DATES:	June-Oct
# of SINGLE SITES:	13	MAX SPUR:	45 feet
		MAX STAY:	14 days
		ELEVATION:	7200 feet

4 Big Sandy
Boulder • lat 42°41'13" lon 109°16'16"

DESCRIPTION: A rustic CG in high mountain pine forest. No drinking water, no services. Rain common in June. Supplies 60 mi.. Elk, moose, deer, and bears in area. Gather firewood. Horse/hike access into Bridger Wilderness. Corrals on site. Nearest access from West side to Cirque of Towers. ATV use on forest roads.

GETTING THERE: From Boulder go SE on state HWY 353 15 mi. to county route. Continue SE 9 mi. to Emigrant Trail Road (Lander Cutoff). Go E 6.5 mi. to forest route 850. Go N 11 mi. to Big Sandy CG. Rough road.

SINGLE RATE:	$4	OPEN DATES:	June-Sept
# of SINGLE SITES:	12	MAX SPUR:	22 feet
		MAX STAY:	10 days
		ELEVATION:	9100 feet

5 Blackrock Bike Camp
Jackson • lat 43°50'00" lon 110°18'00"

DESCRIPTION: Off highway in stand of old growth pine and fir. Bike-in stopover only. Rustic, no services, no drinking water. Bear boxes. Mild days, cold nights. Supplies in Jackson. Gather local firewood. Moose, elk, deer and small wildlife. Bear country!

GETTING THERE: From Jackson go N on US HWY 191 approx. 30 mi. to US HWY 26/187. Go E on 26/187 approx. 11.5 mi. to Blackrock Bike Camp.

SINGLE RATE:	No fee	OPEN DATES:	June-Sept*
# of SINGLE SITES:	9		
		MAX STAY:	14 days
		ELEVATION:	7500 feet

6 Boulder Lake
Boulder • lat 42°51'20" lon 109°37'13"

DESCRIPTION: Rustic CG set on the shore of Boulder Lake in a pine forest. Views of creek and lake. Mild days, cold nights. Trout and kokanee fishing. Supplies in Pinedale. Gather firewood. Moose, elk, deer, raptors, and bears in area. No services, no drinking water. Horse and hiking access into wilderness.

GETTING THERE: From Boulder go E on state HWY 353 approx. 2.5 mi. to forest route 780. Go N on 780 approx. 10 mi. to Boulder Lake CG. Rough road.

SINGLE RATE:	No fee	OPEN DATES:	June-Oct
# of SINGLE SITES:	20	MAX SPUR:	45 feet
		MAX STAY:	14 days
		ELEVATION:	7315 feet

7 Box Creek
Moran • lat 44°51'00" lon 110°18'00"

DESCRIPTION: CG situated in a thick lodgepole pine forest. A popular hunting camp with horse corrals. No drinking water or services. Stream fish for trout on Box Creek. Warm days with cold nights. Deer, moose, elk, and grizzly bears in area. Gather firewood. Supplies in Jackson. Access into Teton Wilderness nearby.

GETTING THERE: From Moran go E on US HWY 26/287 approx. 4 mi. to forest route 30050. Go NE on 30050 approx. 8 mi. to Box Creek CG.

SINGLE RATE:	$5	OPEN DATES:	June-Sept
# of SINGLE SITES:	6		
		MAX STAY:	10 days
		ELEVATION:	7300 feet

8 Bridge
Alpine • lat 43°08'36" lon 110°58'36"

DESCRIPTION: CG set on the banks of the Greys River, situated in an old growth pine and aspen forest. Blue ribbon trout fishing on river. No drinking water or services. Warm days with cold nights. Limited supplies in Alpine. Gather firewood. CG is at the beginning of long canyon with several hiking and horse trails nearby.

GETTING THERE: From Alpine go SE on forest route 10138 approx. 3 mi. to Bridge CG. Not suitable for trailers.

SINGLE RATE:	$3	OPEN DATES:	May-Oct
# of SINGLE SITES:	5	MAX SPUR:	36 feet
		MAX STAY:	16 days
		ELEVATION:	5600 feet

9 Cabin Creek
Alpine • lat 43°15'06" lon 110°46'33"

DESCRIPTION: CG set on the banks of the Snake River. Canyon views. River is swift and high with spring runoff, making it well-known for rafting. Mild days with cold nights. Astoria Hot Springs are 4 mi. away. Supplies are available in Hoback or Jackson. Gather firewood locally. Hiking and horse trails nearby.

GETTING THERE: Cabin Creek CG is located approx. 19 mi. S of Jackson on US HWY 26/89.

SINGLE RATE:	$10	OPEN DATES:	May-Sept
# of SINGLE SITES:	10	MAX SPUR:	30 feet
		MAX STAY:	10 days
		ELEVATION:	5800 feet

10 Cottonwood Lake
Afton • lat 42°38'27" lon 110°48'57"

DESCRIPTION: CG set on the shores on Cottonwood Lake in an old growth pine and aspen forest. Fishing and boating on lake. Warm days with cold nights. Supplies in Afton. Gather firewood locally. Watch for elk, moose, deer, and occasional bears in the area. Horse corrals available. Hiking and horse trail head nearby.

GETTING THERE: From Afton go S on US HWY 89 approx. 10 mi. to forest route 10208. Go E on 10208 approx. 5.5 mi. to Cottonwood Lake CG.

SINGLE RATE:	$5	OPEN DATES:	May-Oct
# of SINGLE SITES:	18	MAX SPUR:	75 feet
GROUP RATE:	Varies	MAX STAY:	16 days
# of GROUP SITES:	2	ELEVATION:	7000 feet

 Campground has hosts   Reservable sites   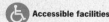 Accessible facilities   Fully developed   Semi-developed   Rustic facilities

NOTE: Open dates listed are typical. Actual dates are dependent on conditions such as snow pack.

11 Crystal Creek
Kelly • lat 43°36'39" lon 110°25'50"

DESCRIPTION: CG set among aspen on Crystal Creek. Views of colorful Gros Ventre Moutains. Stream fish for trout in creek or Soda Lake. Warm days, cold nights. Watch for elk, moose, deer, and occasional bears. Supplies in Jackson. Gather firewood locally. Hiking and horse trails access into Gros Ventre Wilderness.

GETTING THERE: Crystal Creek CG is located approx. 13 mi. E of Kelly on forest route 30400 (Gros Ventre Road).

SINGLE RATE:	$10	OPEN DATES:	June-Oct
# of SINGLE SITES:	6	MAX SPUR:	45 feet
		MAX STAY:	14 days
		ELEVATION:	7300 feet

16 Granite Creek
Bondurant • lat 43°21'32" lon 110°26'39"

DESCRIPTION: CG set among thick old growth pine on the banks of Granite Creek. Fish for trout. Granite Hot Springs swimming pool (fee area) built by CCCs is approx. 2 mi. away. Warm days with cold nights. Supplies in Jackson. Gather firewood locally. Horse and hiking trails access into Gros Ventre Wilderness nearby.

GETTING THERE: From Bondurant go W on US HWY 189/191 approx. 10 mi. to forest route 30500. Go NE on 30500 approx. 9 mi. to Granite Creek CG.

SINGLE RATE:	$12	OPEN DATES:	June-Sept
# of SINGLE SITES:	52	MAX SPUR:	45 feet
		MAX STAY:	14 days
		ELEVATION:	7100 feet

12 Curtis Canyon
Jackson • lat 43°30'45" lon 110°39'38"

DESCRIPTION: CG set in a park like area of pine and aspen. Spectacular views of Jackson Hole Valley. Warm days with cold nights. Gather firewood locally. Supplies in Jackson. Watch for elk, deer, and occasional bears. Mountain biking on roads. Hiking and horse access into Gros Ventre Wilderness nearby.

GETTING THERE: From Jackson go NE on Flat Creek Road approx. 6 mi. to forest route 30440. Continue on 30440 approx. 1 mi. to Curtis Canyon CG.

SINGLE RATE:	$10	OPEN DATES:	June-Sept
# of SINGLE SITES:	12	MAX SPUR:	45 feet
		MAX STAY:	10 days
		ELEVATION:	7600 feet

17   Green River Lake
Pinedale • lat 43°18'43" lon 109°51'35"

DESCRIPTION: CG set in a pine & fir forest. Short walk to Green River Lake for shore or boat trout fishing. Spectacular views of Square Top Mountain. Mild days with cold nights. Supplies in Pinedale. Moose, elk, deer, and occasional bears in area. Gather firewood locally. Horse and hiking access into Bridger Wilderness.

GETTING THERE: From Pinedale go W on US HWY 191 10 mi. to state HWY 352. Go N approx. 24 mi. to forest route 600. Go N 3 mi. to forest route 650. Go NE 15 mi. to Green River Lake CG. Rough road, slick when wet.

SINGLE RATE:	$7	OPEN DATES:	June-Sept
# of SINGLE SITES:	37	MAX SPUR:	30 feet
GROUP RATE:	$25	MAX STAY:	10 days
# of GROUP SITES:	3	ELEVATION:	8000 feet

13 East Table
Jackson • lat 43°12'42" lon 110°48'24"

DESCRIPTION: CG in a mixed conifer and cottonwood forest set in the Snake River Canyon. Mild days with cold nights. Fish the river upstream. Popular white water rafting (Class 3) launch spot. Astoria Hot Springs are 6 mi. away. Gather firewood. Supplies in Hoback or Jackson. Horse and hiking trails nearby.

GETTING THERE: East Table CG is located approx. 24 mi. S of Jackson on US HWY 26/89.

SINGLE RATE:	$15	OPEN DATES:	June-Sept
# of SINGLE SITES:	18	MAX SPUR:	30 feet
		MAX STAY:	10 days
		ELEVATION:	5800 feet

18 Half Moon Lake
Pinedale • lat 42°55'54" lon 109°45'21"

DESCRIPTION: CG set on Half Moon Lake among old growth pine and fir. Mild days with cold nights. Shore or boat fishing for trout. Gather firewood locally. Supplies in Pinedale. Deer, elk, moose, raptors, and bears in area. Receives moderate use. Horse and hiking access to wilderness nearby. No drinking water.

GETTING THERE: From Pinedale go NE on county route 740. 3 mi. to forest route 740. N on 740 approx. 3 mi. to forest route 743. E on 743 approx. 2 mi. to Half Moon Bay CG.

SINGLE RATE:	$3	OPEN DATES:	June-Sept
# of SINGLE SITES:	18	MAX SPUR:	45 feet
		MAX STAY:	14 days
		ELEVATION:	7600 feet

14 Forest Park
Alpine • lat 42°49'53" lon 110°41'21"

DESCRIPTION: CG set on the banks of the Greys River among old growth lodgepole pine. Blue ribbon trout fishing on river. Warm days with cold nights. Weather changes quickly. Limited supplies in Alpine. Gather firewood locally. Watch for elk, deer, moose, and occasional bears in the area. Hiking and mountain bike trails.

GETTING THERE: Forest Park CG is located approx. 34 mi. SE of Alpine on forest route 10138.

SINGLE RATE:	$5	OPEN DATES:	May-Oct
# of SINGLE SITES:	13	MAX SPUR:	75 feet
		MAX STAY:	16 days
		ELEVATION:	7000 feet

19 Hams Fork
Cokeville • lat 42°15'03" lon 110°43'47"

DESCRIPTION: CG set in a pine and fir forest on the Ham's Fork. Stream fish for trout. Mild to hot days with cold nights. Supplies in Cokeville. Watch for moose, elk, deer, and occasional bears in the area. Fills during the fall hunting season. Gather firewood locally. Horse, mountain bike, and hiking trails nearby.

GETTING THERE: From Cokeville go N on state HWY 232 approx. 7 mi. to forest route 10069. Go NE on 10069 approx. 11 mi. to forest route 10062. Go E on 10062 approx. 2 mi. to Hams Fork CG.

SINGLE RATE:	$5	OPEN DATES:	May-Oct
# of SINGLE SITES:	13	MAX SPUR:	45 feet
		MAX STAY:	14 days
		ELEVATION:	8000 feet

15 Fremont Lake
Pinedale • lat 42°54'23" lon 109°50'14"

DESCRIPTION: This CG is set on the shores of Fremont Lake, among pine and fir. Boat launch on site or shore fish for a variety of trout and kokanee. Mild days with cold nights. Supplies in Pinedale. Gather firewood locally. Fills holidays. Deer and moose reside in the in area. Mosquitos all summer.

GETTING THERE: From Pinedale go NE on county route approx. 3 mi. to forest route 741. N on 741 approx. 3 mi. to Fremont Lake CG.

SINGLE RATE:	$7	OPEN DATES:	May-Sept
# of SINGLE SITES:	53	MAX SPUR:	45 feet
		MAX STAY:	10 days
		ELEVATION:	7600 feet

20 Hatchet
Moran • lat 43°49'27" lon 110°21'10"

DESCRIPTION: CG set in a lodgepole pine forest with spectacular views of the Grand Tetons. Stream fish Buffalo River in the spring. Supplies are available in Jackson. Gather firewood locally. Watch for elk, moose, deer, and grizzly bears. Bear resistant storage boxes. Access into Teton Wilderness nearby.

GETTING THERE: From Moran go E on US HWY 26/287 approx. 8 mi. to forest route 30160. Go SW on forest route 30160 approx. 1/2 mi. to Hatchet CG.

SINGLE RATE:	$10	OPEN DATES:	June-Sept
# of SINGLE SITES:	9		
		MAX STAY:	14 days
		ELEVATION:	8000 feet

  Campground has hosts   Reservable sites   Accessible facilities   Fully developed   Semi-developed   Rustic facilities

NOTE: Open dates listed are typical. Actual dates are dependent on conditions such as snow pack.

21 Hoback
Jackson • lat 43°16'47" lon 110°35'37"

DESCRIPTION: CG set on the banks of the Hoback River in old growth pine and aspen. Scenic canyon setting. River is high and swift in spring, settling into good fishing by July 4. Mild days with cold nights. Limited supplies are available at Hoback Junction. Hiking trails available in Cliff Creek area (approx. 6 mi. E).

GETTING THERE: From Jackson go S on US HWY 89 approx. 13 mi. to Hoback Jct. and HWY 189/161. Go E on 189/161 approx. 12 mi. to Hoback CG.

SINGLE RATE:	$12	OPEN DATES:	June-Sept
# of SINGLE SITES:	14	MAX SPUR:	45 feet
		MAX STAY:	14 days
		ELEVATION:	6225 feet

22 Hobble Creek
Cokeville • lat 42°23'54" lon 110°46'56"

DESCRIPTION: CG set in a pine and fir forest on the banks of Hobble Creek. Stream fish for trout on creek or Lake Alice (1.5 mi.). Mild to hot days, cold nights. Supplies in Cokeville. Watch for moose, elk, deer, and occasional bears. Fills during the fall hunting season. Gather firewood locally. Horse and hiking trails nearby.

GETTING THERE: From Cokeville go N on state HWY 232 13 mi. to forest route 10062. NE 9 mi. to forest route 10066. Go N 5 mi. to forest route 10193. Go N 10 mi. to Hobble Creek CG. Roads not suitable for trailers.

SINGLE RATE:	$5	OPEN DATES:	July-Oct
# of SINGLE SITES:	18	MAX SPUR:	35 feet
		MAX STAY:	14 days
		ELEVATION:	7300 feet

23 Kozy
Jackson • lat 43°16'13" lon 110°30'47"

DESCRIPTION: This CG is situated in the Hoback River Canyon among tall pine. Views of river and canyon. River runs high and fast with spring runoff, settling down for good trout fishing by July 4. Popular kayaking river. Limited supplies at Hoback Junction or go to Jackson. Gather firewood locally. Hiking trails nearby.

GETTING THERE: From Jackson go S on US HWY 189/191 approx. 12 mi. to Hoback Jct. Go E at the Jct on HWY 189/191 approx. 12 mi. to Kozy CG.

SINGLE RATE:	$5	OPEN DATES:	June-Sept
# of SINGLE SITES:	8	MAX SPUR:	25 feet
		MAX STAY:	16 days
		ELEVATION:	6400 feet

24 Little Cottonwood Group
Jackson • lat 45°02'25" lon 108°48'01"

DESCRIPTION: Set among cottonwoods on the Snake River with canyon views. Fishing upstream. White water rafting is popular. Astoria Hot Springs in canyon. Basic supplies in Hoback or go to Jackson. Moose, elk and deer in area. Fills quickly until fall. Gather firewood nearby. Horse and hiking trails nearby.

GETTING THERE: From Jackson go S on US HWY 89 approximately 30 miles to Little Cottonwood Group CG.

		OPEN DATES:	June-Sept
		MAX SPUR:	20 feet
GROUP RATE:	$60	MAX STAY:	10 days
# of GROUP SITES:	5	ELEVATION:	6500 feet

25 Lynx Creek
Alpine • lat 43°05'53" lon 110°50'44"

DESCRIPTION: CG set on the banks of the Greys River, situated in an old growth pine and aspen forest. Blue ribbon trout fishing on river. No drinking water or services. Warm days with cold nights. Weather changes quickly. Limited supplies in Alpine. Gather firewood. Numerous hiking and horse trails nearby.

GETTING THERE: Lynx Creek CG is located approx. 12.5 mi. SE of Alpine on forest route 10138.

SINGLE RATE:	$3	OPEN DATES:	May-Oct
# of SINGLE SITES:	14	MAX SPUR:	36 feet
		MAX STAY:	16 days
		ELEVATION:	6200 feet

26 Middle Piney Lake
Big Piney • lat 42°36'10" lon 110°33'46"

DESCRIPTION: CG set on Middle Piney Lake among tall pine. Fishing for trout and boating on lake, electric motors permitted. Warm days with cold nights. Gather firewood locally. Supplies in Big Piney. Watch for deer, elk, moose, and occasional bears in area. Hiking trails nearby. Snow lingers late at this elevation.

GETTING THERE: From Big Piney go W on state HWY 350 (Middle Piney Road) approx. 22 mi. to forest route 10024. Go SW on 10024 approx. 3 mi. to Middle Piney Lake CG. Not recommended for trailers.

SINGLE RATE:	$5	OPEN DATES:	July-Sept*
# of SINGLE SITES:	5		
		MAX STAY:	16 days
		ELEVATION:	8600 feet

27 Moose Flat
Alpine • lat 42°58'20" lon 110°45'56"

DESCRIPTION: CG set on the banks of the Greys River among old growth lodgepole pine. Blue ribbon trout fishing on river. Warm days with cold nights. Weather changes quickly. Limited supplies in Alpine. Gather firewood locally. Watch for elk, deer, moose, and occasional bears in the area. Hiking trails nearby.

GETTING THERE: Moose Flat CG is located approx. 22 mi. SE of Alpine on forest route 10138.

SINGLE RATE:	$10	OPEN DATES:	May-Oct
# of SINGLE SITES:	10	MAX SPUR:	75 feet
		MAX STAY:	16 days
		ELEVATION:	6400 feet

28 Murphy Creek
Alpine • lat 43°04'20" lon 110°50'07"

DESCRIPTION: This CG is situated at confluence of Murphy Creek and Greys River. Blue ribbon trout fishing on river. No drinking water or services. Warm days with cold nights. Limited supplies in Alpine. Gather firewood locally. Various hiking, mountain bike, and horse trails available nearby.

GETTING THERE: Murphy Creek CG is located approx. 14 mi. SE of Alpine on forest route 10138.

SINGLE RATE:	$5	OPEN DATES:	May-Oct
# of SINGLE SITES:	12	MAX SPUR:	75 feet
		MAX STAY:	16 days
		ELEVATION:	6300 feet

1 Curlew
Holbrook • lat 42°04'19" lon 112°41'26"

DESCRIPTION: Group site may be under construction during the summer of 2000. Open sagebrush area in Curlew Grassland. Hot days with frequent winds. Supplies available at Malad. Boat ramp on Stone Reservoir for fishing access. Water fowl viewing. Campers should bring firewood.

GETTING THERE: From Holbrook go S on forest route 080 approx. 9.5 mi. to forest route 020. Go N on 020 approx. 1 mi. to Curlew CG.

SINGLE RATE:	$6	OPEN DATES:	Apr-Nov
# of SINGLE SITES:	20	MAX SPUR:	55 feet
GROUP RATE:	Varies	MAX STAY:	14 days
# of GROUP SITES:	1	ELEVATION:	4700 feet

 Campground has hosts   Reservable sites   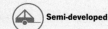 Accessible facilities   Fully developed   Semi-developed   Rustic facilities

NOTE: Open dates listed are typical. Actual dates are dependent on conditions such as snow pack.

USFS Photo

CLEARWATER NATIONAL FOREST

The Clearwater National Forest is nestled on the west side of the Bitterroot Mountains in north central Idaho. The forest stretches from the high mountains in the east to the fertile Palouse prairie to the west.

Several major tributaries to the Columbia River flow through the forest including the North Fork of the Clearwater, the Lochsa, the Potlatch and the Palouse rivers. The Clearwater River runs through deep canyons, dramatic "slashes" cut through the mountains. The North Fork of the Clearwater and the Lochsa rivers provide miles of tumbling whitewater interspersed with quiet pools for migratory and resident fish.

The excellent wildlife habitat of these mountains provides for large herds of elk, moose and other big game. The ridges between the deep canyons have provided travel corridors across the mountains for centuries of mankind, including Nez Perce Indians and, in 1805-1806, the Lewis and Clark Expedition. Today the main travel route is U.S. Highway 12 following the dramatic canyon of the Middle Fork of the Clearwater River and its tributary, the Lochsa River.

IDAHO
Clearwater National Forest • (208) 476-8279

1 Apgar
Kooskia • lat 46°12'50" lon 115°32'09"

DESCRIPTION: This CG is located in cedar and douglas fir with some underbrush and open areas on the Lochsa River. Fly and spin fishing in river for trout. Wildlife in the area includes deer, elk, moose, and an occasional bear or two. Busy on weekends from July 4th through mid-August. Trails in area.

GETTING THERE: From Kooskia go E on US HWY 12 approx. 27 mi. to Apgar CG.

SINGLE RATE:	$6	OPEN DATES:	May-Sept
# of SINGLE SITES:	7	MAX SPUR:	22 feet
		MAX STAY:	14 days
		ELEVATION:	1800 feet

2 Aquarius
Pierce • lat 46°52'00" lon 115°37'30"

DESCRIPTION: CG is in a park-like stand of tall cedar, fir, and pine alongside the North Fork Clearwater River. Warm temps but can be rainy in summer. Great fishing. Supplies 50 mi. to Pierce. Various wildlife dusk and dawn. Busy weekends and holidays. Gather firewood locally. Several hiking trails in area.

GETTING THERE: From Pierce go N on state HWY 11 to Headquarters. At Headquarters take forest route 247 N approx. 23 mi. to Aquarius CG.

SINGLE RATE:	$5	OPEN DATES:	May-Sept
# of SINGLE SITES:	7	MAX SPUR:	60 feet
		MAX STAY:	14 days
		ELEVATION:	1700 feet

3 Cedar
Superior • lat 46°52'07" lon 115°04'26"

DESCRIPTION: CG is in park-like grove of large old red cedar. Pleasant weather, some thundershowers. Good fishing on nearby North Fork Clearwater River and Kelly Creek. Historic Moose City is nearby. Groceries 45 mi. E in Superior. Various wildlife dawn and dusk. Full weekends and holidays. Several trails in area.

GETTING THERE: From Superior take forest route 250 approx. 45 mi. to junction with forest route 720. Turn RT on 720 and go approx. 1 mi. to bridge. Stay LT after bridge and follow signs to Cedar CG.

SINGLE RATE:	No fee	OPEN DATES:	Yearlong*
# of SINGLE SITES:	5	MAX SPUR:	60 feet
		MAX STAY:	14 days
		ELEVATION:	3700 feet

4 Elk Summit
Kooskia • lat 46°19'19" lon 114°39'04"

DESCRIPTION: Elk Summit CG is situated in subalpine fir on Hoodoo Lake. Fish for trout on the lake. Wildlife in area includes deer, elk, moose, and an occasional bear or two. Hunting when in season. Campers may gather their firewood locally. Several trails in surrounding area.

GETTING THERE: From Kooskia go E on US HWY 12 approx. 83 mi. to Powell. At Powell take forest route 102 2 mi. to forest route 111. Take 111 3.5 mi. to forest route 360. Take 360 12 mi. to Hoodoo Lake CG.

SINGLE RATE:	No fee	OPEN DATES:	July-Fall
# of SINGLE SITES:	15		
		MAX STAY:	14 days
		ELEVATION:	5700 feet

5 Giant White Pine
Potlatch • lat 47°00'33" lon 116°40'22"

DESCRIPTION: This CG is located in an older growth forest setting with significant underbrush. Mannering creek runs adjacent to CG. Fishing in creek. Gather firewood locally. A historical wagon road, Sampson Trail is nearby. Supplies and groceries are located S on HWY 6 in Potlatch.

GETTING THERE: From Potlatch go approx. 16 mi. E then N on state HWY 6 to Giant White Pine CG.

SINGLE RATE:	$7	OPEN DATES:	May-Sept
# of SINGLE SITES:	14	MAX SPUR:	45 feet
		MAX STAY:	14 days
		ELEVATION:	3046 feet

6 Hidden Creek
Superior • lat 46°49'56" lon 115°10'43"

DESCRIPTION: Located in grove of large red cedar. Pleasant weather, some thundershowers in summer. Good fishing on North Fork Clearwater River and Kelly Creek. Special fishing regulations. Visit historical cabins and Moose City mining area. Supplies 50 mi. to Superior. Various wildlife dawn and dusk. CG seldom full. Trails in area.

GETTING THERE: From Superior follow forest route 250 approx. 50 mi. to Hidden Creek CG.

SINGLE RATE:	$5	OPEN DATES:	Yearlong*
# of SINGLE SITES:	12	MAX SPUR:	60 feet
		MAX STAY:	14 days
		ELEVATION:	3400 feet

7 Jerry Johnson
Kooskia • lat 46°28'34" lon 114°54'30"

DESCRIPTION: This CG is located in cedar and douglas fir with some underbrush and open areas on the Lochsa River. Fly and spin fishing for trout on the river. Deer, elk, and moose in area. Bears have been seen on occasion. Busy on weekends from July 4th through mid-August. Several trails in area.

GETTING THERE: From Kooskia go E on US HWY 12 approx. 73 mi. to Jerry Johnson CG.

SINGLE RATE:	$8	OPEN DATES:	May-Sept*
# of SINGLE SITES:	15	MAX SPUR:	22 feet
		MAX STAY:	14 days
		ELEVATION:	3000 feet

8 Kelly Forks
Pierce • lat 46°44'00" lon 115°15'00"

DESCRIPTION: Set in tall willow and birch shrubs along Kelly Creek. Moderate temps.. Great fishing with special regulations. Historical cabins and Moose City mining area nearby. Supplies 43 mi. W to Pierce. Various wildlife dawn and dusk. Busy weekends and holidays. Gather firewood locally. Hiking/horse trails in area.

GETTING THERE: From Pierce take forest route 250 E approx. 43 mi. to Kelly Forks CG.

SINGLE RATE:	$5	OPEN DATES:	Yearlong
# of SINGLE SITES:	19	MAX SPUR:	60 feet
		MAX STAY:	14 days
# of GROUP SITES:	1	ELEVATION:	2737 feet

9 Laird Park
Potlatch • lat 46°56'35" lon 116°38'56"

DESCRIPTION: Located in park-like setting on Palouse River where trout may be fished. Deer frequent the area. Moderate. use, area is cool in June turning hot by July, with cool nights. Laird Park Monument is nearby, as is a playground. Potlatch and Moscow have supplies. No fee firewood is available at host site.

GETTING THERE: From Potlatch go 12 mi. E on state HWY 6 to forest route 447. Take 447 E 1 mi. to Laird Park CG.

SINGLE RATE:	$7	OPEN DATES:	May-Sept
# of SINGLE SITES:	31	MAX SPUR:	50 feet
GROUP RATE:	$25	MAX STAY:	14 days
# of GROUP SITES:	2	ELEVATION:	2700 feet

10 Little Boulder Creek
Moscow • lat 46°46'30" lon 116°28'00"

DESCRIPTION: CG is located in a coniferous forest setting with an open meadow. CG is adjacent to the Potlatch River where bank fishing from river is popular. In the early 1900's, this CG was a RR logging camp. Supplies in Deary, 8 mi. from CG. Firewood available at host's site. Many trails in the area.

GETTING THERE: From Moscow go E approx. 28 mi. on state HWY 8 to Helmer. At Helmer take forest route 1963 S 3 mi. to Little Boulder Creek CG.

SINGLE RATE:	$7	OPEN DATES:	May-Sept
# of SINGLE SITES:	16	MAX SPUR:	50 feet
GROUP RATE:	$25	MAX STAY:	14 days
# of GROUP SITES:	1	ELEVATION:	2700 feet

 Campground has hosts   **Reservable sites** 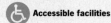 **Accessible facilities** 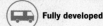 **Fully developed**   **Semi-developed**   **Rustic facilities**

NOTE: Open dates listed are typical. Actual dates are dependent on conditions such as snow pack.

11 Noe Creek
Pierce • lat 46°41'00" lon 115°25'00"

DESCRIPTION: CG is located in park-like grove of larch/fir with views of mountains and N Fork Clearwater River. Moderate temps. Good fishing. Supplies 36 mi. W to Pierce. Various wildlife dusk and dawn. Busy weekends and holidays. Gather firewood locally. Several hiking/horse/ATV trails nearby.

GETTING THERE: From Pierce take forest route 250 E approx. 36 mi. to Noe Creek CG.

SINGLE RATE:	$5	OPEN DATES:	Yearlong
# of SINGLE SITES:	7	MAX SPUR:	60 feet
		MAX STAY:	14 days
		ELEVATION:	2700 feet

12 Powell
Kooskia • lat 46°30'44" lon 114°43'18"

DESCRIPTION: CG is located in cedar and douglas fir with some underbrush and open areas on the Lochsa River. Fly and spin fishing for trout on the river. Wildlife in area includes deer, elk, moose, and an occasional bear or two. Busy on weekends from July 4th through mid-August. Trails in area.

GETTING THERE: From Kooskia go E on US HWY 12 approx. 83 mi. to Powell CG.

SINGLE RATE:	Varies	OPEN DATES:	May-Sept
# of SINGLE SITES:	39	MAX SPUR:	40 feet
		MAX STAY:	14 days
# of GROUP SITES:	1	ELEVATION:	3300 feet

13 Washington Creek
Pierce • lat 46°42'16" lon 115°33'18"

DESCRIPTION: This CG is located in park-like grove of fir, cedar, and pine with views of North Fork Clearwater River. Moderate temperatures. Great fishing. Supplies 34 mi. W to Pierce. Various wildlife dawn and dusk. Busy on holidays. Several trails in area. No ATV trails. Gather firewood locally.

GETTING THERE: From Pierce take forest route 250 E approx. 28 mi. to forest route 247. Take 247 approx. 6 mi. to Washington Creek CG.

SINGLE RATE:	$5	OPEN DATES:	May-Sept
# of SINGLE SITES:	25	MAX SPUR:	60 feet
		MAX STAY:	14 days
		ELEVATION:	2200 feet

14 Weitas
Pierce • lat 46°26'07" lon 115°28'52"

DESCRIPTION: CG is in a park-like grove of Grand Fir with mountain and river views. Pleasant weather. Some T-storms. Good fishing on North Fork Clearwater river and Weitas Creek. Supplies 31 mi. W to Pierce. Various wildlife dawn and dusk. CG is seldom full. Gather firewood locally. Several trails in area.

GETTING THERE: From Pierce take forest route 250 E approx. 31 mi. to Weitas CG.

SINGLE RATE:	No fee	OPEN DATES:	Yearlong*
# of SINGLE SITES:	6	MAX SPUR:	50 feet
		MAX STAY:	14 days
		ELEVATION:	2400 feet

15 Wendover
Kooskia • lat 46°30'36" lon 114°47'01"

DESCRIPTION: CG is located in cedar and douglas fir with some underbrush and open areas on the Lochsa River. Fly and spin fishing for trout on the river. Wildlife in area includes deer, elk, moose, and an occasional bear or two. Busy on weekends from July 4th through mid-August. Trails in area.

GETTING THERE: From Kooskia go E on US HWY 12 approx. 80 mi. to Wendover CG.

SINGLE RATE:	$8	OPEN DATES:	May-Sept
# of SINGLE SITES:	26	MAX SPUR:	35 feet
		MAX STAY:	14 days
		ELEVATION:	3180 feet

16 Whitehouse
Kooskia • lat 46°30'23" lon 114°46'25"

DESCRIPTION: CG is located in cedar and douglas fir with some underbrush and open areas on the Lochsa River. Fly and spin fishing in river for trout. Wildlife in area includes deer, elk, moose, and an occasional bear or two. Busy on weekends from July 4th through mid-August. Trails in area.

GETTING THERE: From Kooskia go E on US HWY 12 approx. 84 mi. to Whitehouse CG.

SINGLE RATE:	$8	OPEN DATES:	May-Sept
# of SINGLE SITES:	13	MAX SPUR:	32 feet
		MAX STAY:	14 days
		ELEVATION:	3190 feet

17 Whitesand
Kooskia • lat 46°30'44" lon 114°41'00"

DESCRIPTION: CG is located in cedar and douglas fir with some underbrush and open areas on the Lochsa River. Fly and spin fishing for trout on the river. Wildlife in area includes deer, elk, moose, and an occasional bear or two. Busy on weekends from July 4th through mid-August. Trails in area.

GETTING THERE: From Kooskia go E on US HWY 12 approx. 83 mi. to Powell. At Powell take forest route 102 2 mi. to Whitesand CG.

SINGLE RATE:	$8	OPEN DATES:	May-Sept
# of SINGLE SITES:	6	MAX SPUR:	32 feet
		MAX STAY:	14 days
		ELEVATION:	3350 feet

18 Wild Goose
Kooskia • lat 46°08'09" lon 115°37'31"

DESCRIPTION: CG is located in cedar and douglas fir with some underbrush and open areas on the Middle Fork Clearwater River. Fly and spin fishing for trout on river. Deer, elk, moose, and an occasional bear or two in the area. Busy on weekends from July 4th through mid-August. Trails in area.

GETTING THERE: From Kooskia go E on US HWY 12 approx. 19 mi. to Wild Goose CG.

SINGLE RATE:	$6	OPEN DATES:	May-Sept
# of SINGLE SITES:	6	MAX SPUR:	22 feet
		MAX STAY:	14 days
		ELEVATION:	1750 feet

19 Wilderness Gateway
Kooskia • lat 46°20'00" lon 115°18'43"

DESCRIPTION: Set in cedar and douglas fir with some underbrush and open areas on the Lochsa River. Fly and spin fishing in river for trout. Deer, elk, moose and maybe a bear or two in area. Busy on weekends from July 4th through mid-August. Trails in area. Playground and pavillion. Reserve pavillion and group sites through NRRS.

GETTING THERE: From Kooskia go E on US HWY 12 approx. 49 mi. to Wilderness Gateway CG.

SINGLE RATE:	$8	OPEN DATES:	May-Sept
# of SINGLE SITES:	89	MAX SPUR:	40 feet
		MAX STAY:	14 days
# of GROUP SITES:	26	ELEVATION:	2120 feet

 Campground has hosts   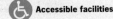 Reservable sites   Accessible facilities    Fully developed    Semi-developed   Rustic facilities

NOTE: Open dates listed are typical. Actual dates are dependent on conditions such as snow pack.

Idaho Panhandle National Forest

The Idaho Panhandle National Forests lie in "the panhandle" of beautiful north Idaho and extend into eastern Washington and western Montana. An aggregation of the Coeur d'Alene and portions of the Kaniksu and St. Joe's National Forests, the Panhandle is comprised of around 2.5 million acres of public lands. Some 300 miles from the Pacific Ocean, the forest is in the east-central part of the Columbia Plateau, snuggled in between the spectacular Cascade Mountains to the west and the rugged Bitterroot Mountains to the east.

It's a nature lover's paradise where quaint villages snuggle up against soaring peaks or hug the shores of deep blue lakes. Over 4,000 miles of rivers are home to world-class sport fisheries. Foam-flecked rapids challenge the whitewater rafter. Glassy, quiet runs beckon the canoeist to travel where steamboats once carried miners with dreams of riches gouged from the earth. Backcountry trails guide the traveler through evergreen forests to remote lakes and spectacular views like Lookout Mountain located above the thoroughfare between Priest Lake and Upper Priest Lake. A land rich with history, quiet country lanes take the motorist by abandoned mining towns, and trace Civil War era military wagon roads.

Idaho Panhandle National Forest • (208) 765-7223

1 Beauty Creek
Coeur d'Alene • lat 47°36'24" lon 116°40'04"

DESCRIPTION: This CG contains a mix of open and shady sites. A group site for up to 50 people is reservable. CG is fully accessible. Lake Coeur d'Alene is located near the CG for activities such as fishing and swimming. Supplies and groceries can be found at Coeur d'Alene.

GETTING THERE: From Coeur d'Alene go E on I-90 6 mi. to state HWY 97. Take 97 S approx. 2 mi. to primary forest route 438. Take 438 E approx. 1 mi. to Beauty Creek GC.

SINGLE RATE:	Varies	OPEN DATES:	May-Sept
# of SINGLE SITES:	15	MAX SPUR:	32 feet
		MAX STAY:	14 days
		ELEVATION:	2150 feet

2 Beaver Creek
Nordman • lat 44°24'54" lon 112°11'34"

DESCRIPTION: This CG located in a forested area on Priest Lake. Scenic views of river from CG. Swimming area. Gather firewood locally. Limited supplies along HWY 57 or at town of Priest River. Deer and small wildlife in area. Trailhead and portage to Thorofare nearby. Easily accessible sites.

GETTING THERE: From Priest River go N approx. 39 mi. on HWY 57 to forest route 1339 (Nordman). Go E on 1339 approx. 12 mi. to Beaver Creek CG.

SINGLE RATE:	Varies	OPEN DATES:	May-Oct
# of SINGLE SITES:	40	MAX SPUR:	35 feet
GROUP RATE:	Varies	MAX STAY:	14 days
# of GROUP SITES:	1	ELEVATION:	2500 feet

3 Beaver Creek
Avery • lat 47°04'55" lon 115°21'14"

DESCRIPTION: Set among large cedar, fir and spruce on the St. Joe Wild and Scenic River Corridor. Catch and release fishing for trout from the river. Historical Red Ives Ranger Station nearby. Supplies approx. 37 mi. to Avery. Deer, elk, and bears in the area. Gather firewood locally. Many hiking trails nearby.

GETTING THERE: From Avery go E on forest route 50 (St. Joe River Rd) approx. 29 mi. to forest route 218 (Red Ives Rd). Go S on 218 approx. 7 mi. to Beaver Creek CG.

SINGLE RATE:	No fee	OPEN DATES:	May-Oct
# of SINGLE SITES:	2	MAX SPUR:	35 feet
		MAX STAY:	14 days
		ELEVATION:	3618 feet

4 Bell Bay
Coeur d'Alene • lat 47°28'36" lon 116°50'26"

DESCRIPTION: This CG has mixed open and shady sites on Lake Coeur d'Alene. Available activities include fishing and swimming in the lake. Fishing and boat dock available. Supplies and groceries can be found at Coeur d'Alene. Trail system for hiking around CG. Gather firewood locally or bring your own.

GETTING THERE: From Coeur d'Alene go E on I-90 6 mi. to state HWY 97. Take 97 21 mi. to county route 314. Take 314 3 mi. to Bell Bay GC.

SINGLE RATE:	Varies	OPEN DATES:	May-Sept
# of SINGLE SITES:	26	MAX SPUR:	22 feet
		MAX STAY:	14 days
		ELEVATION:	2561 feet

5 Berlin Flats
Kellogg • lat 47°47'35" lon 115°57'10"

DESCRIPTION: This CG is situated in a thick forest on the North Fork of the Coeur d'Alene River. Shore fishing and floating are popular activities on the river. Deer and small wildlife in area. Supplies and groceries can be found at Kellogg. Gather firewood locally or bring your own.

GETTING THERE: From Kellogg go W on I-90 approx. 6.5 mi. to forest route FH9. Take FH9 21 mi. to forest route 208. Take 208 6 mi. to forest route 412. Go N on 412 approx. 7 mi. to Berlin Flats CG.

SINGLE RATE:	Varies	OPEN DATES:	May-Sept
# of SINGLE SITES:	9	MAX SPUR:	22 feet
		MAX STAY:	14 days
		ELEVATION:	2800 feet

6 Big Creek
St. Maries • lat 47°18'00" lon 116°07'30"

DESCRIPTION: This CG is situated in a pine and fir setting on Big Creek. Views of Big Creek River Corridor. Fish and play from Big Creek. Historical Marble Creek Interpretive Site is 7 mi. from CG. Supplies at Calder. Elk, deer, and bears can be seen from CG. Gather firewood locally.

GETTING THERE: From St. Maries go E on forest route 50 21 mi. to Calder, cross the river to Northside Road. Go E on Northside Road approx. 5 mi. to forest route 537. Go N on 537 approx. 3 mi. to Big Creek CG.

SINGLE RATE:	No fee	OPEN DATES:	May-Oct
# of SINGLE SITES:	9	MAX SPUR:	45 feet
		MAX STAY:	14 days
		ELEVATION:	2380 feet

7 Big Hank
Kellogg • lat 47°49'27" lon 116°06'00"

DESCRIPTION: This CG is located in tall lodgepole pines in a park like setting. Beautiful views of the river. Shore fish and float the Coeur d'Alene River. Supplies and groceries available at Kellogg. Cool days, cold nights at Big Hank CG. Hiking trails near CG. Gather firewood locally or bring your own.

GETTING THERE: From Kellogg go W on I-90 approx. 6.5 mi. to primary forest route FH9. Take FH9 approx. 20 mi. to Primary forest route 208. Take 208 approx. 18 mi. to Big Hank CG.

SINGLE RATE:	Varies	OPEN DATES:	May-Oct
# of SINGLE SITES:	30	MAX SPUR:	22 feet
		MAX STAY:	14 days
		ELEVATION:	2707 feet

8 Bumblebee
Kellogg • lat 47°38'01" lon 116°16'43"

DESCRIPTION: This CG is situated in thick Idaho forest. Accessible camp units. Fishing and floating on North Fork of Coeur d'alene River. Large game and small wildlife in area. Hunting when in season. Supplies and groceries available at Kingston. Gather firewood locally or bring your own.

GETTING THERE: From Kingston go E on primary forest route 9 for approx. 6 mi. to forest route 209. Go NW on 209 aprrox. 3 mi. to Bumblebee CG.

SINGLE RATE:	Varies	OPEN DATES:	May-Sept
# of SINGLE SITES:	25	MAX SPUR:	16 feet
		MAX STAY:	14 days
		ELEVATION:	2240 feet

9 CCC Stock Camp
Calder • lat 47°17'30" lon 116°07'30"

DESCRIPTION: Located in pines with large, open grassy area with views of Big Creek River Corridor. Historical Marble Creek Interpretive Site is 6 mi. from CG. Supplies at Calder. Elk, deer and bears in the area. Campers may gather firewood. Many trails in the area.

GETTING THERE: From St. Maries go E on forest HWY 50 approx. 21 mi. to Calder. Cross the river to Northside Road. Go E on RD approx. 5 mi. to forest route 537. Go N on 537 approx. 2 mi. to CCC Stock Camp.

SINGLE RATE:	No fee	OPEN DATES:	May-Oct
# of SINGLE SITES:	7		
		MAX STAY:	14 days
		ELEVATION:	2300 feet

10 Cedar Creek
Clarkia • lat 47°03'04" lon 116°17'17"

DESCRIPTION: Situated on St.Maries River among lodgepole pines with views of the forest. Fishing on the river. Historical Clarkia Ranger Station approx. 3 mi. from CG. Gather firewood locally. No drinking water available. CG will be closed for reconstruction Summer 2000.

GETTING THERE: From Clarkia go N on state HWY 3 approx. 3 mi. to Cedar Creek CG.

SINGLE RATE:	No fee	OPEN DATES:	May-Oct
# of SINGLE SITES:	3	MAX SPUR:	50 feet
		MAX STAY:	14 days
		ELEVATION:	2760 feet

 Campground has hosts   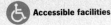 **Reservable sites**   **Accessible facilities**   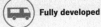 **Fully developed**   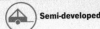 **Semi-developed**    **Rustic facilities**

11 Conrad Crossing
Avery • lat 47°09'31" lon 115°24'57"

DESCRIPTION: This CG is in a large, old growth setting on the St. Joe Wild & Scenic Rivers. Fish for trout & float the rivers. Historical Red Ives Ranger Station is nearby. Gather firewood locally. Wildlife includes elk, deer, & bears. Many trails in the area. Drinking water June-Oct only.

GETTING THERE: From Avery go E on forest route 50 (St. Joe River Rd) approx. 28 mi. to Conrad Crossing CG.

SINGLE RATE:	No fee	OPEN DATES:	May-Oct
# of SINGLE SITES:	8	MAX SPUR:	50 feet
		MAX STAY:	14 days
		ELEVATION:	3350 feet

12 Copper Creek
Bonners Ferry • lat 48°59'07" lon 116°09'07"

DESCRIPTION: This CG is situated in Idaho forest. Copper Creek CG contains 3 accessible sites. Enjoy Hikes to beautiful Copper Falls, and other activities such as hiking or fishing along the Moyie River. Supplies and groceries can be found at Bonners Ferry. Gather firewood locally.

GETTING THERE: From Bonners Ferry go N on US HWY 95 approx. 29 mi. to forest route 2517. Go S on 2517 1 mi. Copper Creek CG.

SINGLE RATE:	Varies	OPEN DATES:	May-Oct
# of SINGLE SITES:	16	MAX SPUR:	32 feet
		MAX STAY:	14 days
		ELEVATION:	2630 feet

13 Devils Elbow
Kellogg • lat 47°46'16" lon 116°01'53"

DESCRIPTION: This CG located among mixed lodgepole and has mostly open sites. Enjoy activities such as fishing or floating the North Fork of the Coeur d'Alene River. Gather firewood locally or bring your own. Deer and small wildlife in area. Supplies and groceries available at Kellogg.

GETTING THERE: From Kellogg go W on I-90 approx. 6.5 mi. to primary forest route FH9. Take FH9 approx. 21 mi. to Primary forest route 208. Take 208 approx. 12 mi. to Devils Elbow CG.

SINGLE RATE:	Varies	OPEN DATES:	May-Sept
# of SINGLE SITES:	20	MAX SPUR:	22 feet
		MAX STAY:	14 days
# of GROUP SITES:	1	ELEVATION:	2603 feet

14 Emerald Creek
Clarkia • lat 47°00'22" lon 116°19'35"

DESCRIPTION: In forested area set on Emerald Creek with views of Cedar Butte. Stream fishing in creek. Historical Clarkia Work Center is 12 mi. from CG. Good area for rockhounding for garnets. Supplies at Clarkia. Deer and small wildlife in area. Gather local firewood. Hiking trails nearby.

GETTING THERE: From Clarkia go N on state HWY 3 approx. 6 mi. to primary forest route 447. Go S on 447 6 mi. to Emerald Creek CG.

SINGLE RATE:	$6	OPEN DATES:	May-Sept
# of SINGLE SITES:	18	MAX SPUR:	50 feet
		MAX STAY:	14 days
		ELEVATION:	3000 feet

15 Fly Flat
Avery • lat 47°06'46" lon 115°23'24"

DESCRIPTION: This CG situated in a dense stand of pines, larch and firs on Packsaddle Recreation River. Catch and release fishing on the St. Joe Wild and Scenic River. Historical Red Ives Ranger Station near CG. Supplies available at Avery. Gather firewood locally. Many trails nearby.

GETTING THERE: From Avery go E on primary forest route 50 approx. 29 mi. to primary forest route 218. Go S on 218 approx. 4 mi. to Fly Flat CG.

SINGLE RATE:	No fee	OPEN DATES:	May-Oct
# of SINGLE SITES:	14	MAX SPUR:	50 feet
		MAX STAY:	14 days
		ELEVATION:	3491 feet

16 Heller Creek
Avery • lat 47°03'54" lon 115°13'04"

DESCRIPTION: This CG is located in an open setting of tall lodgepole pines with beautiful views of Heller Creek. Fish in trout waters of St. Joe Wild and Scenic River nearby. Historic Heller gravesite close to CG. Pack it in, pack it out. No drinking water available. Gather firewood locally.

GETTING THERE: From Avery go E 21 mi. on forest route 50 to forest route 218. Take 218 S 8 mi. to forest route 320. Take 320 13 mi. to Heller Creek CG. High clearance vehicles required.

SINGLE RATE:	No fee	OPEN DATES:	June-Oct
# of SINGLE SITES:	4	MAX SPUR:	20 feet
		MAX STAY:	14 days
		ELEVATION:	4693 feet

17 Honeysuckle
Coeur d'Alene • lat 47°44'23" lon 116°28'27"

DESCRIPTION: This CG located in a beautiful grassy park like area with tall lodgepole pines. Fishing on the Little North Fork Coeur d'Alene River. Moderate use turning heavy during hunting season. Large game and small wildlife in area. Supplies and groceries available at Coeur d'Alene.

GETTING THERE: From Coeur d'Alene go E on Fernan Lake Road 268 for approx. 11 mi. to forest route 612. Go N on 612 approx. 10 mi. to Huneysuckle CG.

SINGLE RATE:	Varies	OPEN DATES:	May-Sept
# of SINGLE SITES:	7	MAX SPUR:	16 feet
		MAX STAY:	14 days
		ELEVATION:	2800 feet

18 Kit Price
Kellogg • lat 47°44'27" lon 116°00'20"

DESCRIPTION: This CG is situated in a park like forested area with beautiful views of Coeur d'Alene River. Activities such as fishing and floating are popular on the river. Supplies and groceries are available at Kellogg. Deer and small wildlife in area. Gather firewood locally or bring your own.

GETTING THERE: From Kellogg go W on I-90 6.5 mi. to primary forest route FH9. Take FH9 approx. 21 mi. to primary forest route 208. Take 208 9 mi. to Kit Price CG.

SINGLE RATE:	Varies	OPEN DATES:	May-Sept
# of SINGLE SITES:	52	MAX SPUR:	22 feet
		MAX STAY:	14 days
		ELEVATION:	2560 feet

19 Line Creek Stock Camp
Avery • lat 47°02'16" lon 115°20'48"

DESCRIPTION: In large old spruce and fir forest setting with views of St. Joe Wild and Scenic River. Catch and release fish from the river. Historical Red Ives Ranger Station is nearby. Supplies at Avery. Elk, deer and bears can be seen from the CG. Campers may gather firewood. Many trails in the area.

GETTING THERE: From Avery go E on forest route 50 approx. 29 mi. to forest route 218. Go S on 218 approx. 11 mi. to Line Creek Stock Camp.

SINGLE RATE:	No fee	OPEN DATES:	May-Oct
# of SINGLE SITES:	9		
		MAX STAY:	14 days
		ELEVATION:	3800 feet

20 Luby Bay
Priest River • lat 48°32'59" lon 116°55'25"

DESCRIPTION: This CG is located in thick forest on Priest Lake. Fish by shore or boat on the lake. CG complete with swimming area. Supplies available at Vans Corner or town of Priest Lake. Gather firewood locally. RV dump station and amphitheater. Beautiful shoreline hiking trails.

GETTING THERE: From Priest River take state HWY 57 N approx. 28 mi. to Vans Corner. Go N on forest route 1337 2 mi. to Luby Bay CG.

SINGLE RATE:	Varies	OPEN DATES:	May-Oct
# of SINGLE SITES:	52	MAX SPUR:	55 feet
		MAX STAY:	14 days
		ELEVATION:	2400 feet

 Campground has hosts   **Reservable sites** 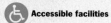 **Accessible facilities**   **Fully developed**   **Semi-developed**   **Rustic facilities**

NOTE: Open dates listed are typical. Actual dates are dependent on conditions such as snow pack.

IDAHO PANHANDLE NATIONAL FOREST • IDAHO • 11 — 20

21 Mammoth Springs
Avery • lat 47°05'52" lon 115°35'51"

DESCRIPTION: This CG is situated in a lodgepole pine forest, 1 mile from Dismal Lake. Fish from the lake. Historical Red Ives Ranger Station close by. Supplies and groceries available at Avery. Wildlife in area includes elk, deer, and bears. Gather firewood locally. Hiking trails nearby.

GETTING THERE: From Avery go E on forest route 50 (St. Joe River Rd) 22 mi. to forest route 509. Take 509 S 14 mi. to forest route 201 (Avery Timber Cr. Rd). Take 201 S 2.5 mi. to Mammoth Springs CG.

SINGLE RATE:	No fee	OPEN DATES:	June-Oct
# of SINGLE SITES	8	MAX SPUR:	40 feet
		MAX STAY:	14 days
		ELEVATION:	5700 feet

22 Meadow Creek
Bonners Ferry • lat 48°49'10" lon 116°08'47"

DESCRIPTION: This CG situated in Idaho forest of pine and fir. Fishing on the nearby Moyie River. Supplies and groceries can be found at Bonner's Ferry. Campers may gather their firewood locally. August is great for huckleberry picking. Various wildlife in area dusk and dawn. Deer frequent the area.

GETTING THERE: From Bonners Ferry go N 2 mi. on US HWY 95. Go E on US HWY 2 2 mi. to county route 34. Take 34 N approx. 11 mi. to Meadow Creek CG.

SINGLE RATE:	Varies	OPEN DATES:	May-Oct
# of SINGLE SITES	22	MAX SPUR:	22 feet
		MAX STAY:	14 days
		ELEVATION:	2400 feet

23 Mokins Bay
Hayden Lake • lat 47°47'04" lon 116°39'52"

DESCRIPTION: This CG is located among tall lodgepole pines, and set on Hayden Lake. Available activities include fishing and swimming in the lake. Deer and small wildlife in area. Supplies and groceries are available at Coeur d'Alene. Forest access for hiking a few miles away. Gather firewood locally.

GETTING THERE: From Coeur d'Alene go N 6 mi. on HWY 95 to Lancaster Road. Go E 16 mi. around Hayden Lake to Mokins Bay. Turn E at "Public Camp" sign and go 200' to Mokins Bay CG.

SINGLE RATE:	Varies	OPEN DATES:	May-Sept
# of SINGLE SITES	16	MAX SPUR:	22 feet
		MAX STAY:	14 days
		ELEVATION:	2300 feet

24 Navigation
Priest River • lat 48°47'41" lon 116°54'34"

DESCRIPTION: This CG is situated in a heavily timbered forest with views of Priest Lake and Lookout Mountain. Enjoy boating and fishing in Priest Lake and Upper Priest Lake Thorofare. Pack it in/pack it out. No drinking water available on site. Gather firewood locally.

GETTING THERE: Navigation CG is located on Upper Priest Lake and is accessible only by boat or trail.

SINGLE RATE:	No fee	OPEN DATES:	May-Oct
# of SINGLE SITES	5		
		MAX STAY:	14 days
		ELEVATION:	3000 feet

25 North Cove
Priest Lake • lat 48°34'26" lon 116°53'43"

DESCRIPTION: This CG is located on Kalispell Island with scenic views of Priest Lake. CG is secluded and quiet. Fishing in the lake. No hiking trails near CG, and no drinking water or water facets. Firewood may be scarce on island. Pack it in/pack it out. Enjoy a rustic experience at North Cove CG.

GETTING THERE: North Cove CG is located on the north end of Kalispell Island in Priest Lake and is accessible only by boat.

SINGLE RATE:	No fee	OPEN DATES:	May-Oct
# of SINGLE SITES	4		
		MAX STAY:	14 days
		ELEVATION:	2400 feet

26 Osprey
Priest Lake • lat 48°30'22" lon 116°53'15"

DESCRIPTION: This CG is situated on Priest Lake, some sites have lake views or lake frontage. Activities available include swimming and fishing in the lake. Limited supplies and groceries along HWY 57 or at town of Priest Lake. Gather firewood locally. Deer and small wildlife in area.

GETTING THERE: From Priest River take state HWY 57 N approx. 25 mi. to forest route 237. Take 237 E and N 2 mi. to Osprey CG.

SINGLE RATE:	Varies	OPEN DATES:	June-Sept
# of SINGLE SITES	17	MAX SPUR:	20 feet
		MAX STAY:	14 days
		ELEVATION:	2400 feet

27 Outlet
Priest River • lat 48°29'56" lon 116°53'32"

DESCRIPTION: This CG is located in a forested area on Priest River. Small swimming beach available at the CG. Fishing in the lake and river. Enjoy scenic views of Priest Lake. Gather firewood locally. Supplies and groceries can be found in the town of Priest River. Deer and small wildlife in area. A popular CG.

GETTING THERE: From Priest River take state HWY 57 N approx. 25 mi. to forest route 237. Take 237 E 1 mi. to Outlet CG.

SINGLE RATE:	Varies	OPEN DATES:	May-Sept
# of SINGLE SITES	31	MAX SPUR:	22 feet
		MAX STAY:	14 days
		ELEVATION:	2400 feet

28 Packsaddle
Avery • lat 47°13'55" lon 115°43'42"

DESCRIPTION: CG is situated in open park like area of mixed conifers on the St. Joe Wild and Scenic River. Fishing and floating can be done on the river. Historical Marble Creek Site is 12 mi. from CG. Deer, elk, and small wildlife in area. Gather firewood locally. Trails in the area.

GETTING THERE: From Avery go E approx. 5 mi. on primary forest route 50 (St. Joe River Road) to Packsaddle CG.

SINGLE RATE:	No fee	OPEN DATES:	May-Oct
# of SINGLE SITES	2	MAX SPUR:	25 feet
		MAX STAY:	14 days
		ELEVATION:	2800 feet

29 Plowboy
Priest River • lat 48°46'11" lon 116°52'47"

DESCRIPTION: This CG is located in Idaho forest on Upper Priest Lake. Beautiful views of Priest Lake and surrounding mountains. Available activities include fishing in the lake, and hiking on the many trails around the CG. Pack it in/pack it out. Gather firewood locally. No drinking water available.

GETTING THERE: Navigation CG is located on Upper Priest Lake and is accessible only by boat or trail.

SINGLE RATE:	No fee	OPEN DATES:	May-Oct
# of SINGLE SITES	5		
		MAX STAY:	14 days
		ELEVATION:	2400 feet

30 Reeder Bay
Priest River • lat 48°37'31" lon 116°53'27"

DESCRIPTION: This CG is located in a park like area on Priest Lake with open views of the lake. Enjoy shore or boat fishing on the 25,000 acre lake. Gather firewood locally. Supplies and groceries at stores on HWY 57 or in the town of Priest River. Deer and small wildlife in area. Shore hiking.

GETTING THERE: From Priest River take state HWY 57 N to Norouteman. At Norouteman take forest route 1339 E 3 mi. to Reeder Bay CG.

SINGLE RATE:	Varies	OPEN DATES:	May-Oct
# of SINGLE SITES	24	MAX SPUR:	50 feet
		MAX STAY:	14 days
		ELEVATION:	2400 feet

 Campground has hosts   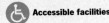 **Reservable sites**   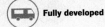 **Accessible facilities**    **Fully developed**   **Semi-developed**   Rustic facilities

NOTE: Open dates listed are typical. Actual dates are dependent on conditions such as snow pack.

Page 244

31 ## Robinson Lake
Bonners Ferry • lat 48°58'11" lon 116°12'57"

DESCRIPTION: This CG is located in Idaho forest on 60-acre Robinson Lake. Activities include fishing and swimming in the lake; boat ramp available. Hiking trails around the lake. CG contains 3 accessible sites. Supplies and groceries at Eastport or Bonners Ferry. Warm days, cold nights.

GETTING THERE: From Bonners Ferry go N on US HWY 95 approx. 25 mi. to Robinson Lake CG.

SINGLE RATE:	Varies	OPEN DATES:	May-Oct
# of SINGLE SITES:	10	MAX SPUR:	32 feet
		MAX STAY:	14 days
		ELEVATION:	2800 feet

36 ## Spruce Tree
Avery • lat 47°02'16" lon 115°20'48"

DESCRIPTION: Thick forest with lodgepole, fir & larch. Nice area in fall. Fish & float the St. Joe Wild & Scenic River (beginning of wild portion). Historical Red Ives Ranger Station nearby. Elk, deer, & bears in area. Supplies at Avery. Potable water June-Oct. St. Joe River Trail Head nearby.

GETTING THERE: From Avery go E on forest route 50 (St. Joe River Rd) approx. 29 mi. to forest route 218 (Red Ives Rd). Take 218 S approx. 12 mi. to Spruce Tree CG.

SINGLE RATE:	No fee	OPEN DATES:	May-Oct
# of SINGLE SITES:	9	MAX SPUR:	50 feet
		MAX STAY:	14 days
		ELEVATION:	3800 feet

32 ## Rocky Point
Priest River • lat 48°34'20" lon 116°53'35"

DESCRIPTION: This CG is located on E shore of Kalispell Island on Priest Lake. Superior views. Available activities include fishing and swimming from the shore of the island. Quiet, and rustic. Firewood may be scarce. Pack it in/pack it out. No hiking trails, no drinking water available.

GETTING THERE: Rocky Point CG is located on the northeast end of Kalispell Island in Priest Lake and is accessible only by boat.

SINGLE RATE:	No fee	OPEN DATES:	May-Oct
# of SINGLE SITES:	6		
		MAX STAY:	14 days
		ELEVATION:	2500 feet

37 ## Squaw Creek
Avery • lat 47°17'46" lon 115°46'28"

DESCRIPTION: CG in a park-like setting of tall pines with views of the North Fork St. Joe River. Catch and release fishing from the river. Historical Hiawatha Bike Trail 1 mi. from CG. No drinkable water. Deer, elk, bears, and small wildlife in area. Gather firewood locally. Trails in the area.

GETTING THERE: From Avery go N on county route 456 approx. 6 mi. to Moon Pass Road. Go S on Moon Pass approx. 1 mi. to Squaw Creek CG. Not recommended for trailers.

SINGLE RATE:	No fee	OPEN DATES:	May-Oct
# of SINGLE SITES:	5	MAX SPUR:	20 feet
		MAX STAY:	14 days
		ELEVATION:	2700 feet

33 ## Samowen
Clark Fork • lat 48°13'08" lon 116°17'16"

DESCRIPTION: Samowen is a large CG situated in heavily forested area on point of Lake Pend Oreille. Beach available for swimming. CG equipped with RV dump station and a boat ramp. Fishing in lake. Deer and small wildlife in area. No hiking trails. Adjacent to David Thompson Game Preserve.

GETTING THERE: From Clark Fork go NW on state HWY 200 approx. 7 mi. to forest route 1002. Take 2001 approx. 1 mi. to Sam Owen CG.

SINGLE RATE:	Varies	OPEN DATES:	May-Oct
# of SINGLE SITES:	80	MAX SPUR:	30 feet
		MAX STAY:	14 days
# of GROUP SITES:	1	ELEVATION:	2105 feet

38 ## Stagger Inn
Priest River • lat 48°44'00" lon 117°03'00"

DESCRIPTION: Set in thick forest near Granite Creek. Granite Falls is nearby. Historic Roosevelt Grove of Ancient Cedars also near the CG. Gather firewood locally. Supplies several miles S along HWY 57 or at town of Priest Lake. Large game and small wildlife in area. Hiking trails close by.

GETTING THERE: From Priest River go N on state HWY 57 to Norouteman. At Norouteman go N on forest route 302 approx. 13 mi. to Stagger Inn CG.

SINGLE RATE:	No fee	OPEN DATES:	May-Oct
# of SINGLE SITES:	4	MAX SPUR:	15 feet
		MAX STAY:	14 days
		ELEVATION:	3200 feet

34 ## Shadowy St. Joe
St. Maries • lat 47°18'13" lon 116°22'08"

DESCRIPTION: CG in an open and grassy setting with views of the St. Joe Wild and Scenic River Corridor. Fishing, boating, and floating on the St. Joe Wild and Scenic River. Historical Marble Creek Interpretive Site is 29 mi. from CG. Supplies at St. Maries. Boat dock at CG. Gather firewood locally.

GETTING THERE: From St. Maries go E on forest HWY 50 approx. 10 mi. to Shadowy St. Joe CG.

SINGLE RATE:	$6	OPEN DATES:	May-Sept
# of SINGLE SITES:	14	MAX SPUR:	50 feet
		MAX STAY:	14 days
		ELEVATION:	2100 feet

39 ## Three Pines
Priest Lake • lat 48°33'52" lon 116°53'37"

DESCRIPTION: This CG is located on the E shore of Kalispell Island on Priest Lake. Superior views of the lake. Available activities include fishing and swimming from the shore of the island. Quiet and rustic CG. Firewood may be scarce. Pack it in/pack it out. No hiking trails, no drinking water.

GETTING THERE: Three Pines CG is located on the SE end of Kalispell Island in Priest Lake and is accessible only by boat.

SINGLE RATE:	No fee	OPEN DATES:	May-Oct
# of SINGLE SITES:	8		
		MAX STAY:	14 days
		ELEVATION:	2500 feet

35 ## Smith Lake
Bonners Ferry • lat 48°46'37" lon 116°15'46"

DESCRIPTION: This CG is located on Smith Lake. Beautiful scenic views of lake. Available activities include swimming, shore fishing, and boat fishing on Smith Lake. Boat ramp at CG. Deer and small wildlife in area. Gather firewood locally. Supplies and groceries available at Bonners Ferry.

GETTING THERE: From Bonners Ferry go N on US HWY 95 4 mi. to 1005. Take 1005 2 mi. to Smi.th Lake CG.

SINGLE RATE:	No fee	OPEN DATES:	May-Oct
# of SINGLE SITES:	7		
		MAX STAY:	14 days
		ELEVATION:	3010 feet

40 ## Tin Can Flat
Avery • lat 47°13'48" lon 115°37'12"

DESCRIPTION: This CG is shaded by tall lodgepole pine on the St. Joe Wild and Scenic River. Fishing and floating on river until mid-July. Historical Hiawatha Bike Trail is 18 mi. from CG. Supplies at Avery. Deer and bears in the area. Gather firewood locally. Trails in the area.

GETTING THERE: From Avery go E on forest route 50 (St. Joe River Road) approx. 10 mi. to Tin Can Flat CG.

SINGLE RATE:	$6	OPEN DATES:	May-Oct
# of SINGLE SITES:	11	MAX SPUR:	50 feet
		MAX STAY:	14 days
		ELEVATION:	2900 feet

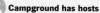 **Campground has hosts**   **Reservable sites**   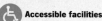 **Accessible facilities**   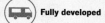 **Fully developed**   **Semi-developed**   **Rustic facilities**

NOTE: Open dates listed are typical. Actual dates are dependent on conditions such as snow pack.

41 **Turner Flat**
Avery • lat 47°14'13" lon 115°39'12"

DESCRIPTION: CG in an open park like area on St. Joe Wild and Scenic River. Views of the St. Joe Wild and Scenic Corridor. Fishing and floating on the St. Joe Wild and Scenic River. Historical Avery Ranger Station nearby. Supplies at Avery. Deer and small wildlife in area. Gather firewood locally.

GETTING THERE: From Avery go E on primary forest route 50 (St. Joe River Rd) approx. 8 mi. to Turner Flat CG.

SINGLE RATE:	$6	OPEN DATES:	May-Oct
# of SINGLE SITES:	10	MAX SPUR:	50 feet
GROUP RATE:	Varies	MAX STAY:	14 days
# of GROUP SITES:	1	ELEVATION:	2850 feet

42 **Whiskey Rock**
Clark Fork • lat 48°03'03" lon 116°27'16"

DESCRIPTION: CG situated in a forested area with 3 sites on Lake Pend Oreille. Shore and boat fishing in the lake; dock available. Open areas onto the lake provide for swimming. Deer and small wildlife in area. Gather firewood locally. Supplies and groceries can be found at Clark Fork.

GETTING THERE: From Clark Fork go S on forest route 278 approx. 23 mi. to Whiskey Rock CG.

SINGLE RATE:	No fee	OPEN DATES:	May-Oct
# of SINGLE SITES:	9	MAX SPUR:	16 feet
		MAX STAY:	14 days
		ELEVATION:	2080 feet

Equal Access

The Forest Service and Recreational management concessionaires are working to provide better access to National Forest opportunities. Many facilities built today meet the standards of the Americans with Disabilities Act(ADA). Throughout the National Forest System today, you'll find many universally accessible campsites, wahrooms, nature trails, boating facilities, picnic sites and visitor centers. Talk to your local National Forest office to learn about accessibility in your area.

 Campground has hosts 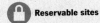 **Reservable sites** 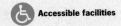 **Accessible facilities** 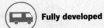 **Fully developed** 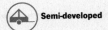 **Semi-developed**  **Rustic facilities**

NEZ PERCE NATIONAL FOREST

Welcome to the Nez Perce National Forest–2.2 million acres of beautiful and diverse land located in the heart of north central Idaho. Created in 1908 by President Theodore Roosevelt, the Forest has a rich cultural heritage and was the traditional home of the Ni Mii Pu (The People), who were later named the Nez Perce Indians by the Lewis and Clark expeditions.

From the dry, rugged canyons of the Salmon River to the moist cedar forests of the Selway drainage, the forest offers something for everyone.

This vast and diverse area is managed to provide a variety of goods and services including breathtaking scenery, wilderness, wildlife, fisheries, timber harvests, livestock grazing, mining, pristine water quality and a wide array of recreation opportunities.

The forest is best known for its wild character. Nearly half of the forest is designated wilderness. It also sports two rivers popular with thrill-seeking floaters–the Selway and the Salmon.

NEZ PERCE NATIONAL FOREST • IDAHO • LOCATOR MAP

Nez Perce National Forest • (208) 983-1950

1 American River
Elk City • lat 45˚53'50" lon 115˚27'30"

DESCRIPTION: CG is situated among lodgepole pine on the American River. Fishing on the river. Hunting when in season. Wildlife in the area includes deer, elk, moose, and bears. 6.5 mi. to Elk City for groceries and supplies. Seldom full except holiday weekends. No drinking water available.

GETTING THERE: From Elk City go N on primary forest route 443 approx. 6.5 mi. to the American River CG.

SINGLE RATE:	No fee	OPEN DATES:	Yearlong
# of SINGLE SITES:	2	MAX SPUR:	20 feet
		MAX STAY:	14 days
		ELEVATION:	4500 feet

2 Boyd Creek
Kooskia • lat 46˚04'52" lon 115˚26'30"

DESCRIPTION: CG is in cedar and fir on the Selway River. Cool mornings and hot afternoons in summer. Fly fishing on river. Supplies and groceries 10 mi. at Lowell. Deer, elk, moose, and bears in area. Bald eagles in fall. Busy on holidays. East Boyd Glover Roundtop National Recreation Trailhead near CG.

GETTING THERE: From Kooskia take US HWY 12 to the Lochsa/Selway confluence. Go SE on primary forest route 223 approx. 10 mi. to the Boyd Creek CG.

SINGLE RATE:	No fee	OPEN DATES:	Yearlong
# of SINGLE SITES:	5	MAX SPUR:	20 feet
		MAX STAY:	14 days
		ELEVATION:	1700 feet

3 Bridge Creek
Elk City • lat 45˚46'58" lon 115˚12'44"

DESCRIPTION: CG is located in lodgepole pine stand on Bridge Creek. Trout fishing in creek. Other available activiies include hunting and picnicking. Wildlife in area includes deer, moose, elk, and bears. 24 mi. to Elk City for supplies and grocs.. Busy on holidays in summer. No drinking water.

GETTING THERE: From Elk City go W on State HWY 14 2 mi. to primary forest route 222. Take 222 SE approx. 13 mi. to primary forest route 234. Go E on 234 approx. 9 mi. to Bridge Creek CG.

SINGLE RATE:	No fee	OPEN DATES:	Yearlong
# of SINGLE SITES:	5	MAX SPUR:	20 feet
		MAX STAY:	14 days
		ELEVATION:	4900 feet

4 Castle Creek
Grangeville • lat 45˚49'41" lon 115˚58'03"

DESCRIPTION: This CG is situated in a forested canyon on the South Fork Clearwater River. Deer and various small wildlife occupy the area. Steelhead and trout fishing in the river. CG tends to be busy on summer weekends. Be aware of logging trucks passing through on the HWY.

GETTING THERE: From the E side of Grangeville go S on Primary forest route 221 1 mi. to state HWY 14. Take 14 approx. 11 mi. to Castle Creek CG.

SINGLE RATE:	$8	OPEN DATES:	Yearlong
# of SINGLE SITES:	8	MAX SPUR:	30 feet
		MAX STAY:	14 days
		ELEVATION:	2200 feet

5 CCC Camp
Kooskia • lat 46˚05'30" lon 115˚31'00"

DESCRIPTION: CG is in cedar and fir on Selway River. Cool mornings and hot in summer. Fly fishing on river. Available activities include paddling, hunting, and picnicking. Supplies and grocs. 10 mi. to Lowell. Deer, elk, moose, and bears in area. Bald eagles in fall. Busy on holidays. Trails in area.

GETTING THERE: From Kooskia take US HWY 12 to the Lochsa/Selway confluence. Go SE on primary forest route 223 approx. 5 mi. to the CCC Camp CG.

SINGLE RATE:	No fee	OPEN DATES:	Yearlong
# of SINGLE SITES:	3	MAX SPUR:	20 feet
		MAX STAY:	14 days
		ELEVATION:	1620 feet

6 Crooked River 2
Elk City • lat 45˚47'37" lon 115˚31'48"

DESCRIPTION: CG is located in lodgepole pine on the Crooked River. Trout fishing in river. Hunting when in season. Wildlife in area includes deer, elk, and moose. Bears have been seen on occasion. 8 mi. to Elk City for supplies and grocs.. Gather firewood locally. No drinking water available.

GETTING THERE: From Elk City Go W on state HWY 14 approx. 6 mi. to primary forest route 233. Go south on 233 2 mi. to Crooked River 2 CG.

SINGLE RATE:	No fee	OPEN DATES:	Yearlong
# of SINGLE SITES:	4	MAX SPUR:	20 feet
		MAX STAY:	14 days
		ELEVATION:	4100 feet

7 Crooked River 3
Elk City • lat 45˚47'48" lon 115˚31'44"

DESCRIPTION: This CG is located in lodgepole pine on the Crooked River. Trout fishing in river. Other activities at Crooked River 3 CG include hunting and picnicking. Wildlife in the area includes deer, elk, and moose. 8 mi. to Elk City for supplies and grocs.. No drinking water available.

GETTING THERE: From Elk City Go W on state HWY 14 approx. 6 mi. to primary forest route 233. Go south on 233 2 mi. to Crooked River 3 CG.

SINGLE RATE:	No fee	OPEN DATES:	Yearlong
# of SINGLE SITES:	4	MAX SPUR:	20 feet
		MAX STAY:	14 days
		ELEVATION:	4170 feet

8 Ditch Creek
Elk City • lat 45˚44'50" lon 115˚17'47"

DESCRIPTION: This CG is located in pine at the confluence of Ditch Creek and the Red River. Fishing on the creek and river. Hunting when in season. Supplies and groceries can be found 19 mi. away in Elk City. Wildlife in area includes deer, elk, and bears. CG tends to be busy on holidays in summer.

GETTING THERE: From Elk City go W on State HWY 14 2 mi. to primary forest route 222. Take 222 SE approx. 13 mi. to primary forest route 234. Go E on 234 approx. 3.5 mi. to Ditch Creek CG.

SINGLE RATE:	No fee	OPEN DATES:	Yearlong
# of SINGLE SITES:	4	MAX SPUR:	20 feet
		MAX STAY:	14 days
		ELEVATION:	4528 feet

9 Dixie Meadows
Elk City • lat 45˚32'00" lon 115˚31'30"

DESCRIPTION: CG is located in pine. Deer, elk, bears, moose and wolves in area. 36 mi. to Elk City for supplies.

GETTING THERE: From Elk City go W on state HWY 14 approx. 6 mi. to primary forest route 233. Go S on 233 approx. 30 mi. to Dixie Meadows CG.

SINGLE RATE:	No fee	OPEN DATES:	Yearlong
# of SINGLE SITES:	2	MAX SPUR:	20 feet
		MAX STAY:	14 days
		ELEVATION:	5500 feet

10 Dry Saddle
Elk City • lat 45˚39'00" lon 115˚00'00"

DESCRIPTION: CG is located in pine on the Montana Road. 38 mi. to Elk City for supplies. Deer, elk, moose, bears and wolves in area. The Montana Road is a world renowned drive, but often very difficult to drive owing to lingering snow drifts (often into July) or fire traffic in the high fire season.

GETTING THERE: From Elk City go W on state HWY 14 approx. 2 mi. to primary forest route 222. Take 222 SE approx. 14 mi. to forest route 486. Go E on 468 approx. 29 mi. to Dry Saddle CG.

SINGLE RATE:	No fee	OPEN DATES:	Yearlong
# of SINGLE SITES:	2	MAX SPUR:	15 feet
		MAX STAY:	14 days
		ELEVATION:	6650 feet

 Campground has hosts   **Reservable sites**   **Accessible facilities**   **Fully developed**   **Semi-developed**   **Rustic facilities**

NOTE: Open dates listed are typical. Actual dates are dependent on conditions such as snow pack.

11 Fish Creek Meadows

Grangeville • lat 45°50'30" lon 116°05'00"

DESCRIPTION: This CG is located among pine and fir. Set against the edge of a meadow, Fish Creek runs nearby. Fishing in creek. Wildlife in area includes deer and elk. Summer temperatures are nice and cool. A pleasant weekend getaway for locals in the heat of July and August.

GETTING THERE: From Grangeville go 7 mi. S on primary forest route 221 to Fish Creek Meadows CG.

SINGLE RATE:	$6	OPEN DATES:	Yearlong
# of SINGLE SITES:	84	MAX SPUR:	30 feet
		MAX STAY:	14 days
		ELEVATION:	4800 feet

16 Granite Spring

Elk City • lat 45°43'30" lon 115°07'42"

DESCRIPTION: This CG is situated among pine on the Montana Road. Wildlife in the area includes deer, elk, bears, moose, and wolves. Hunting when in season. Fishing nearby. Supplies and groceries can be found 31 mi. away in Elk City. CG tends to be busy on holiday weekends in summer.

GETTING THERE: From Elk City go W on State HWY 14 2 mi. to primary forest route 222. Take 222 SE approx. 14 mi. to forest route 486. Go E on 468 approx. 15 mi. to Granite Spring CG.

SINGLE RATE:	No fee	OPEN DATES:	Yearlong
# of SINGLE SITES:	4	MAX SPUR:	20 feet
		MAX STAY:	14 days
		ELEVATION:	6654 feet

12 Five Mile

Elk City • lat 45°43'00" lon 115°32'43"

DESCRIPTION: CG is situated among pine on Five Mile Creek. Trout fishing in creek. Supplies and groceries can be found 15 mi. away in Elk City. Various wildlife in area includes deer and elk. Hunting when in season. Campers my gather their firewood locally. CG tends to be busy on holiday weekends.

GETTING THERE: From Elk City Go W on state HWY 14 approx. 6 mi. to primary forest route 233. Go south on 233 9 mi. to Five Mile CG.

SINGLE RATE:	No fee	OPEN DATES:	Yearlong
# of SINGLE SITES:	4	MAX SPUR:	20 feet
		MAX STAY:	14 days
		ELEVATION:	4700 feet

17 Halfway House

Elk City • lat 45°30'34" lon 115°31'36"

DESCRIPTION: CG is located in lodgepole pine. Tends to be busy on holiday weekends in summer. Wildlife in area includes deer, elk, moose, bears, and wolves. Hunting when in season. Fishing nearby. Supplies and groceries can be found 38 mi. away in Elk City. No drinking water available on site.

GETTING THERE: From Elk City Go W on state HWY 14 approx. 6 mi. to primary forest route 233. Go south on 233 approx. 30 mi. to forest route 311A. Take 311A 1.5 mi. to Halfway House CG.

SINGLE RATE:	No fee	OPEN DATES:	Yearlong
# of SINGLE SITES:	4	MAX SPUR:	20 feet
		MAX STAY:	14 days
		ELEVATION:	5500 feet

13 French Gulch

Elk City • lat 45°47'00" lon 115°23'10"

DESCRIPTION: This CG is located in lodgepole pine on the Red River. Deer, elk, bears, and moose in the area. Hunting when in season. Fishing for trout in the river. Supplies and groceries can be found 8 mi. away in Elk City. Enjoy nearby historical sites. CG tends to be busy on holiday weekends in summer.

GETTING THERE: From Elk City go W on State HWY 14 2 mi. to primary forest route 222. Take 222 SE approx. 6 mi. to French Gulch CG.

SINGLE RATE:	No fee	OPEN DATES:	Yearlong
# of SINGLE SITES:	3	MAX SPUR:	20 feet
		MAX STAY:	14 days
		ELEVATION:	4500 feet

18 Johnson Bar

Kooskia • lat 46°06'29" lon 115°33'32"

DESCRIPTION: CG is in cedar and fir on the Selway River. Cool mornings and hot in summer. Fly fishing on river. Paddling is popular on the river. Supplies and groceries can be found 10 mi. away in Lowell. Hunting when in season. Deer, elk, moose, and bears in area. Bald eagles in fall. Busy on holidays.

GETTING THERE: From Kooskia take US HWY 12 to the Lochsa/Selway confluence. Go SE on primary forest route 223 approx. 3 mi. to Johnson Bar CG.

SINGLE RATE:	No fee	OPEN DATES:	Yearlong
# of SINGLE SITES:	8	MAX SPUR:	20 feet
		MAX STAY:	14 days
# of GROUP SITES:	1	ELEVATION:	1960 feet

14 Gedney Creek

Kooskia • lat 46°03'26" lon 115°18'44"

DESCRIPTION: This CG is set in cedar and fir on the Selway River. Cool mornings and hot in summer. Fly fishing on the river. Supplies 10 mi. to Lowell. Hunting when in season. Deer, elk, moose, and bears in area. Bald eagles in fall. Paddling is popular on the river. Busy on holidays. Trails in area.

GETTING THERE: From Kooskia take US HWY 12 to the Lochsa/Selway confluence. Go SE on primary forest route 223 approx.15 mi. to Gedney Creek CG.

SINGLE RATE:	No fee	OPEN DATES:	Yearlong
# of SINGLE SITES:	1	MAX SPUR:	40 feet
		MAX STAY:	14 days
		ELEVATION:	1698 feet

19 Leggett Creek

Elk City • lat 45°49'37" lon 115°37'34"

DESCRIPTION: This CG is situated among spruce and fir on the South Fork Clearwater River. Fishing in river. Wildlife in the area includes deer, elk, moose, and bears. Hunting when in season. Groceries and supplies can be found 13 mi. away in Elk City. CG tends to be busy on holiday weekends.

GETTING THERE: From Elk City go W on state HWY 14 approx. 13 mi. to Leggett Creek CG.

SINGLE RATE:	No fee	OPEN DATES:	Yearlong
# of SINGLE SITES:	6	MAX SPUR:	20 feet
		MAX STAY:	14 days
		ELEVATION:	4200 feet

15 Glover Creek

Kooskia • lat 46°04'07" lon 115°21'42"

DESCRIPTION: CG is set in cedar and fir on the Selway River. Fly fishing on river. Cool mornings and hot in summer. Supplies 10 mi. to Lowell. Deer, elk, moose, and bears in area. Bald eagles in fall. Busy on holidays. East Boyd Glover Roundtop National Recreation Trailhead near CG.

GETTING THERE: From Kooskia take US HWY 12 to the Lochsa/Selway confluence. Go SE on primary forest route 223 approx. 13 mi. to Glover Creek CG.

SINGLE RATE:	No fee	OPEN DATES:	Yearlong
# of SINGLE SITES:	7	MAX SPUR:	20 feet
		MAX STAY:	14 days
		ELEVATION:	1780 feet

20 Limber Luke

Elk City • lat 45°56'48" lon 115°26'55"

DESCRIPTION: This CG is located in lodgepole pine on Limber Luke Creek. Fishing in creek. Wildlife in area includes deer, elk, moose, wolves, and bears. Hunting when in season. 13 mi. to Elk City for supplies and groceries. Tends to be busy on holiday weekends. No drinking water available on site.

GETTING THERE: From Elk City go N on forest route 443 approx. 13 mi. to Limber Luke CG.

SINGLE RATE:	No fee	OPEN DATES:	Yearlong
# of SINGLE SITES:	1	MAX SPUR:	20 feet
		MAX STAY:	14 days
		ELEVATION:	5400 feet

 Campground has hosts   **Reservable sites**   **Accessible facilities**   **Fully developed**   **Semi-developed**   **Rustic facilities**

NOTE: Open dates listed are typical. Actual dates are dependent on conditions such as snow pack.

21 Mackay Bar
Elk City • lat 45°23'33" lon 115°29'35"

DESCRIPTION: This CG is situated among fir and spruce on the Salmon River. Fishing for trout and steelhead in river. Deer, elk, bears, moose, and wolves in area. Hunting when in season. Supplies and groceries can be found 51 mi. away in Elk Creek. No drinking water available on site.

GETTING THERE: From Elk City Go W on state HWY 14 approx. 6 mi. to primary forest route 233. Go south on 233 approx. 45 mi. to Mackay Bar CG.

SINGLE RATE:	No fee	OPEN DATES:	Yearlong
# of SINGLE SITES:	3	MAX SPUR:	15 feet
		MAX STAY:	14 days
		ELEVATION:	2280 feet

22 Mallard Creek
Elk City • lat 45°35'30" lon 115°18'50"

DESCRIPTION: CG is located in pine on Mallard Creek. Deer, elk, bears, moose and wolves in area. 24 mi. to Elk City for supplies. Busy on holiday weekends in summer.

GETTING THERE: From Elk City go W on state HWY 14 approx. 3 mi. to forest route 222. Go S on 222 approx. 18 mi. to forest route 421. Go S on 421 approx. 7 mi. to Mallard Creek CG.

SINGLE RATE:	No fee	OPEN DATES:	Yearlong
# of SINGLE SITES:	3	MAX SPUR:	10 feet
		MAX STAY:	14 days
		ELEVATION:	5170 feet

23 Meadow Creek
Grangeville • lat 45°49'46" lon 115°55'36"

DESCRIPTION: This CG is situated in a forested canyon on the South Fork Clearwater River. Deer frequent the area. Steelhead and trout fishing in river. Campers may gather their firewood locally. CG tends to be busy on summer weekends. Be aware of log trucks passing through on the HWY.

GETTING THERE: From the E side of Grangeville go S on Primary forest route 221 1 mi. to state HWY 14. Take 14 approx. 14 mi. to Meadow Creek CG.

SINGLE RATE:	No fee	OPEN DATES:	Yearlong
# of SINGLE SITES:	2	MAX SPUR:	10 feet
		MAX STAY:	14 days
		ELEVATION:	2200 feet

24 Newsome
Elk City • lat 45°53'42" lon 115°37'41"

DESCRIPTION: This CG is located among lodgepole pine on Newsome Creek. Fishing in creek. Supplies and groceries can be found 17 mi. away in Elk City. Historic Newsome Townsite is nearby. Wildlife in the area includes deer, elk, moose, and bears. Hunting when in season. No drinking water available.

GETTING THERE: From Elk City go W on state HWY 14 approx. 11 mi. to forest route 1858. Go N on 1858 approx. 6 mi. to Newsome CG.

SINGLE RATE:	No fee	OPEN DATES:	Yearlong
# of SINGLE SITES:	6	MAX SPUR:	20 feet
		MAX STAY:	14 days
		ELEVATION:	4084 feet

25 North Fork Slate Creek
Riggins • lat 45°38'24" lon 116°07'06"

DESCRIPTION: This CG is located in fir on Slate Creek. Trout fishing in creek. Wildlife in the area includes deer, elk, bears, and moose. Hunting when in season. CG tends to be busy on holiday weekends in summer. North Fork Slate Creek trailhead nearby. Access road not suitable for trailers.

GETTING THERE: From Riggins go N on US HWY 95 17 mi. to Slate Creek. From Slate Creek go E on primary forest route 354 8 mi. to North Fork Slate Creek CG.

SINGLE RATE:	No fee	OPEN DATES:	Yearlong
# of SINGLE SITES:	5	MAX SPUR:	20 feet
		MAX STAY:	14 days
		ELEVATION:	5500 feet

26 O'Hara Bar
Kooskia • lat 46°05'06" lon 115°31'00"

DESCRIPTION: CG is set among cedar and fir on Selway River. Cool mornings and hot days in the summer. Fly fishing on river. Supplies and groceries can be found 10 mi. away in Lowell. Hunting when in season. Deer, elk, moose, and bears in area. Bald eagles in fall. Busy on holidays. Trailhead near CG.

GETTING THERE: From Kooskia take US HWY 12 to the Lochsa/Selway confluence. Go SE on primary forest route 223 approx. 6 mi. to O'Hara Bar CG.

SINGLE RATE:	$10	OPEN DATES:	May-Sept
# of SINGLE SITES:	32	MAX SPUR:	35 feet
		MAX STAY:	14 days
		ELEVATION:	1680 feet

27 O'Hara Saddle
Elk City • lat 45°58'00" lon 115°25'00"

DESCRIPTION: CG is located in lodgepole pine. Deer, elk, wolves, bear and moose in area. Busy on holiday weekends. 17 mi. to Elk City for supplies.

GETTING THERE: From Elk City go N on forest route 443 approx. 17 mi. to O'Hara Saddle CG.

SINGLE RATE:	No fee	OPEN DATES:	Yearlong
# of SINGLE SITES:	2	MAX SPUR:	20 feet
		MAX STAY:	14 days
		ELEVATION:	5910 feet

28 Orogrande
Elk City • lat 45°41'51" lon 115°32'43"

DESCRIPTION: This CG is situated among lodgepole pine on Mulcahy Creek. Fishing in creek. Supplies and groceries can be found 17 mi. away in Elk City. Wildlife in the area includes deer, elk, moose, bears, and wolves. Hunting when in season. Historic Orogrande Townsite is nearby.

GETTING THERE: From Elk City Go W on state HWY 14 approx. 6 mi. to primary forest route 233. Go south on 233 11 mi. to Orogrande CG.

SINGLE RATE:	No fee	OPEN DATES:	Yearlong
# of SINGLE SITES:	11	MAX SPUR:	20 feet
		MAX STAY:	14 days
		ELEVATION:	4760 feet

29 Orogrande Summit
Elk City • lat 45°38'24" lon 115°36'49"

DESCRIPTION: This CG is situated among pine. Supplies and groceries can be found 22 mi. away in Elk City. Wildlife in the area includes deer, elk, bears, and moose. Hunting when in season. CG tends to be busy in the summer on holiday weekends. Enjoy historical sites in the area.

GETTING THERE: From Elk City Go W on state HWY 14 approx. 6 mi. to primary forest route 233. Go south on 233 16 mi. to Orogrande Summit CG.

SINGLE RATE:	No fee	OPEN DATES:	Yearlong
# of SINGLE SITES:	5		
		MAX STAY:	14 days
		ELEVATION:	7250 feet

30 Ox Bow
Elk City • lat 45°40'50" lon 115°37'20"

DESCRIPTION: CG is situated among spruce and fir on Newsome Creek. Trout fishing in the creek. Supplies and groceries can be found 15 mi. away in Elk City. Wildlife in area includes deer, elk, moose, and wolves. Hunting when in season. CG tends to be busy on holiday weekends in the summer.

GETTING THERE: From Elk City go W on state HWY 14 approx. 11 mi. to forest route 1858. Go N on 1858 approx. 3.5 mi. to Ox Bow CG.

SINGLE RATE:	No fee	OPEN DATES:	Yearlong
# of SINGLE SITES:	1	MAX SPUR:	15 feet
		MAX STAY:	14 days
		ELEVATION:	3900 feet

 **Campground has hosts**   **Reservable sites**   **Accessible facilities**   **Fully developed**   **Semi-developed**   **Rustic facilities**

NOTE: Open dates listed are typical. Actual dates are dependent on conditions such as snow pack.

31 Poet Creek
Elk City • lat 45°43'23" lon 115°01'59"

DESCRIPTION: CG rests in pine on Poet Creek & Montana Road. Trout in creek. Deer, elk, bears, moose, & wolves in area. 30 mi. to Elk City for groceries. The Montana Road is world renowned, but often difficult to drive owing to lingering snow drifts(often into July)or fire traffic in the high fire season.

GETTING THERE: From Elk City go W on State HWY 14 2 mi. to primary forest route 222. Take 222 SE approx. 14 mi. to forest route 486. Go E on 468 approx. 21 mi. to Poet Creek CG.

SINGLE RATE:	No fee	OPEN DATES:	Yearlong
# of SINGLE SITES:	4	MAX SPUR:	15 feet
		MAX STAY:	14 days
		ELEVATION:	7500 feet

36 Rocky Bluff
Riggins • lat 45°37'57" lon 116°00'36"

DESCRIPTION: This CG is located in spruce and fir on upper Slate Creek. Fishing on the creek. Wildlife in the area includes deer, elk, bears, and moose. Hunting when in season. Gather firewood locally. Access road is not suitable for trailers. Cool place to get away from summer heat.

GETTING THERE: From Riggins go N on US HWY 95 17 mi. to Slate Creek. From Slate Creek go E on primary forest route 354 14 mi. to forest route 221. Take 221 E 1 mi. to Rocky Bluff CG.

SINGLE RATE:	No fee	OPEN DATES:	Yearlong
# of SINGLE SITES:	4	MAX SPUR:	20 feet
		MAX STAY:	14 days
		ELEVATION:	6100 feet

32 Race Creek
Kooskia • lat 46°02'39" lon 115°16'59"

DESCRIPTION: CG is in cedar and fir on Selway River. Cool mornings and hot days in the summer. Fly fishing on river. Supplies and groceries can be found 10 mi. in Lowell. Hunting when in season. Deer, elk, moose, and bears in area. Bald eagles in fall. CG tends to be busy on holidays. Trailhead near CG.

GETTING THERE: From Kooskia take US HWY 12 to the Lochsa/Selway confluence. Go SE on primary forest route 223 approx. 17 mi. to Race Creek CG.

SINGLE RATE:	No fee	OPEN DATES:	Yearlong
# of SINGLE SITES:	3	MAX SPUR:	20 feet
		MAX STAY:	14 days
		ELEVATION:	1830 feet

37 Sams Creek
Elk City • lat 45°32'10" lon 115°29'45"

DESCRIPTION: This CG is situated among pine at the confluence of Sams Creek and Crooked Creek. Trout fishing in creeks. Wildlife in area includes deer, elk, bears, wolves, and moose. Hunting when in season. Gather firewood locally. Supplies and groceries can be found 35 mi. away in Elk City.

GETTING THERE: From Elk City Go W on state HWY 14 approx. 6 mi. to primary forest route 233. Go south on 233 approx. 29 mi. to Sams Creek CG.

SINGLE RATE:	No fee	OPEN DATES:	Yearlong
# of SINGLE SITES:	3	MAX SPUR:	20 feet
		MAX STAY:	14 days
		ELEVATION:	5595 feet

33 Rackliff
Kooskia • lat 46°05'06" lon 115°31'00"

DESCRIPTION: CG is in cedar and fir on Selway River. Cool mornings and hot in summer. Fly fishing on river. Supplies 10 mi. to Lowell. Deer, elk, moose and bears in area. Bald eagles in fall. Busy on holidays. Recreation trailhead near CG.

GETTING THERE: From Kooskia take US HWY 12 to the Lochsa/Selway confluence. Go SE on primary forest route 223 approx. 6 mi. to Rackliff CG.

SINGLE RATE:	No fee	OPEN DATES:	Yearlong
# of SINGLE SITES:	6	MAX SPUR:	20 feet
		MAX STAY:	14 days
		ELEVATION:	1650 feet

38 Selway Falls
Kooskia • lat 46°02'23" lon 115°17'39"

DESCRIPTION: CG is in cedar and fir on the Selway River. Cool mornings and hot days in summer. Fly fishing on river. Supplies and groceries can be found 10 mi. away in Lowell. Hunting when in season. Deer, elk, moose, and bears in area. Bald eagles in fall. CG tends to be busy on holidays.

GETTING THERE: From Kooskia take US HWY 12 to the Lochsa/Selway confluence. Go SE on primary forest route 223 approx. 17 mi. to Selway Falls CG.

SINGLE RATE:	No fee	OPEN DATES:	Yearlong
# of SINGLE SITES:	7	MAX SPUR:	20 feet
		MAX STAY:	14 days
		ELEVATION:	1840 feet

34 Rainy Day Point
Elk City • lat 45°45'48" lon 115°42'01"

DESCRIPTION: This CG is situated among lodgepole pine on Rainy Day Creek. Fishing in creek. Deer, elk, moose, bears, and wolves in area. Hunting when in season. Supplies and groceries can be found 26 mi. away in Elk City. CG tends to be busy on holiday weekends. No drinking water available on site.

GETTING THERE: From Elk City go W on state HWY 14 approx. 13.5 mi. to forest route 492. Go S on 492 approx. 12 mi. to Rainy Day Point CG.

SINGLE RATE:	No fee	OPEN DATES:	Yearlong
# of SINGLE SITES:	2	MAX SPUR:	15 feet
		MAX STAY:	14 days
		ELEVATION:	5959 feet

39 Sing Lee
Elk City • lat 45°53'07" lon 115°37'24"

DESCRIPTION: CG is located in fir and spruce on Sing Lee Creek. Fishing in creek. Deer, elk, moose, bears, and wolves in area. Hunting when in season. Supplies and groceries can be found 16 mi. away in Elk City. Tends to be busy on holiday weekends in summer. Enjoy historical settings which are in the area.

GETTING THERE: From Elk City go W on state HWY 14 approx. 11 mi. to forest route 1858. Go N on 1858 approx.5 mi. to Sing Lee CG.

SINGLE RATE:	No fee	OPEN DATES:	Yearlong
# of SINGLE SITES:	5	MAX SPUR:	20 feet
		MAX STAY:	14 days
		ELEVATION:	3980 feet

35 Red River
Elk City • lat 45°44'55" lon 115°16'16"

DESCRIPTION: This CG is located in lodgepole pine on the Red River. Trout fishing in river. Deer, elk, moose, bears, and wolves in area. Hunting when in season. Busy on holidays and weekends in the summer. Groceries and supplies area available 20 mi. away in Elk City. RV facilities.

GETTING THERE: From Elk City go W on State HWY 14 2 mi. to primary forest route 222. Take 222 SE approx. 13 mi. to primary forest route 234. Go E on 234 approx. 5 mi. to Red River CG.

SINGLE RATE:	$6	OPEN DATES:	May-Sept
# of SINGLE SITES:	16	MAX SPUR:	40 feet
		MAX STAY:	14 days
		ELEVATION:	4732 feet

40 Six Mile
Elk City • lat 45°45'48" lon 115°38'00"

DESCRIPTION: This CG is located among pine on Six Mile Creek. Fish for trout in the creek. Wildlife in the area includes deer, elk, moose, wolves, and bears. Hunting when in season. Supplies and groceries can be found 24 mi. away in Elk City. Campers may gather their firewood locally.

GETTING THERE: From Elk City go W on state HWY 14 approx. 13.5 mi. to forest route 492. Go S on 492 approx. 8 mi. to Six mile CG.

SINGLE RATE:	No fee	OPEN DATES:	Yearlong
# of SINGLE SITES:	2	MAX SPUR:	20 feet
		MAX STAY:	14 days
		ELEVATION:	6200 feet

 **Campground has hosts**   **Reservable sites**   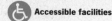 **Accessible facilities**   **Fully developed**   **Semi-developed**   **Rustic facilities**

NOTE: Open dates listed are typical. Actual dates are dependent on conditions such as snow pack.

41 Slide Creek
Kooskia • lat 46°05'06" lon 115°27'06"

DESCRIPTION: CG is set in cedar and fir on the Selway River. Cool mornings and hot days in the summer. Fly fishing on river. Supplies and groceries are available 10 mi. away in Lowell. Hunting when in season. Deer, elk, moose, and bears in area. Bald eagles in fall. Tends to be busy on holidays.

GETTING THERE: From Kooskia take US HWY 12 to the Lochsa/Selway confluence. Go SE on primary forest route 223 approx. 9 mi. to Slide Creek CG.

SINGLE RATE:	No fee	OPEN DATES:	Yearlong
# of SINGLE SITES:	2		
		MAX STAY:	14 days
		ELEVATION:	1620 feet

42 Slims Camp
Kooskia • lat 46°01'48" lon 115°17'21"

DESCRIPTION: CG is in cedar and fir on the Selway River. Cool mornings and hot days in the summer. Fly fishing on river. Supplies and groceries. 10 mi. to Lowell. Hunting when in season. Deer, elk, moose, and bears in area. Bald eagles in fall. Busy on holidays. Recreation Trailhead near CG.

GETTING THERE: From Kooskia take US HWY 12 to the Lochsa/Selway confluence. Go SE on primary forest route 223 approx. 18 mi. to Slims CG.

SINGLE RATE:	No fee	OPEN DATES:	Yearlong
# of SINGLE SITES:	2	MAX SPUR:	20 feet
		MAX STAY:	14 days
		ELEVATION:	1845 feet

43 Sourdough Saddle
Wisdom • lat 45°43'18" lon 115°48'20"

DESCRIPTION: This CG is located among pine. Wildlife in area includes deer, elk, moose, bears, and wolves. Hunting when in season. Campers may gather their firewood locally. CG tends to be busy on holiday weekends in the summer. Supplies and groceries are available 34 mi. away in Elk City.

GETTING THERE: From Elk City go W on state HWY 14 approx. 13.5 mi. to forest route 492. Go S on 492 approx. 20 mi. to Sourdough Saddle CG.

SINGLE RATE:	No fee	OPEN DATES:	Yearlong
# of SINGLE SITES:	4	MAX SPUR:	20 feet
		MAX STAY:	14 days
		ELEVATION:	6080 feet

44 South Fork
Grangeville • lat 45°49'30" lon 115°57'44"

DESCRIPTION: This CG is situated in a forested canyon on the South Fork Clearwater River. Deer frequent the area. Steelhead and trout fishing in the river. CG tends to be busy on summer weekends. Gather firewood locally. Be aware of log trucks passing through on the HWY.

GETTING THERE: From the E side of Grangeville go S on Primary forest route 221 1 mi. to state HWY 14. Take 14 approx. 12 mi. to South Fork CG.

SINGLE RATE:	$8	OPEN DATES:	Yearlong
# of SINGLE SITES:	6	MAX SPUR:	30 feet
		MAX STAY:	14 days
# of GROUP SITES:	1	ELEVATION:	2100 feet

45 Spring Bar
Riggins • lat 45°25'37" lon 116°09'04"

DESCRIPTION: This CG is located in a desert canyon setting with some scattered ponderosa pine on the Salmon River. Climate is dry and hot in the summer. Old historic homestead orchard provides shade trees. Wildlife in area includes deer. Fishing in river. Popular boating use area in spring.

GETTING THERE: From Riggins go E on primary forest route 1614 10 mi. to Spring Bar CG.

SINGLE RATE:	$10	OPEN DATES:	Yearlong
# of SINGLE SITES:	18	MAX SPUR:	40 feet
		MAX STAY:	14 days
		ELEVATION:	1844 feet

46 Table Meadows
Elk City • lat 45°56'08" lon 115°30'43"

DESCRIPTION: This CG is situated among lodgepole pine on the West Fork American River. Trout fishing in creek. Deer, elk, bears, and wolves in area. Hunting when in season. Supplies and groceries are available 9 mi. away in Elk City. CG tends to be busy on holiday weekends in summer.

GETTING THERE: From Elk City go N on primary forest route 443 aprox. 4 mi. to forest route 420. Go N on 420 5 mi. to Table Meadows CG.

SINGLE RATE:	No fee	OPEN DATES:	Yearlong
# of SINGLE SITES:	6	MAX SPUR:	20 feet
		MAX STAY:	14 days
		ELEVATION:	4835 feet

47 Twenty Five Mile Bar
Kooskia • lat 46°04'24" lon 115°22'27"

DESCRIPTION: CG is in cedar and fir on Selway River. Cool mornings and hot days in the summer. Fly fishing on river. Supplies and groceries can be found 10 mi. away in Lowell. Hunting when in season. Deer, elk, moose, and bears in area. Bald eagles in fall. CG tends to be busy on holidays.

GETTING THERE: From Kooskia take US HWY 12 to the Lochsa/Selway confluence. Go SE on primary forest route 223 approx. 14 mi. to Twenty Five mile Bar CG.

SINGLE RATE:	No fee	OPEN DATES:	Yearlong
# of SINGLE SITES:	3		
		MAX STAY:	14 days
		ELEVATION:	1760 feet

48 Twenty Mile Bar
Kooskia • lat 46°05'12" lon 115°28'09"

DESCRIPTION: CG is set among cedar and fir on the Selway River. Cool mornings and hot days in the summer. Fly fishing on river. Supplies and groceries can be found 10 mi. away in Lowell. Hunting when in season. Deer, elk, moose, and bears in area. Bald eagles in fall. Busy on holidays.

GETTING THERE: From Kooskia take US HWY 12 to the Lochsa/Selway confluence. Go SE on primary forest route 223 approx. 8 mi. to Twenty mile Bar CG.

SINGLE RATE:	No fee	OPEN DATES:	Yearlong
# of SINGLE SITES:	2	MAX SPUR:	20 feet
		MAX STAY:	14 days
		ELEVATION:	1960 feet

49 Whitewater
Elk City • lat 45°31'00" lon 115°18'00"

DESCRIPTION: CG is located in lodgepole pine on the Salmon River. Deer, elk, moose, bears and wolves in area. 42 mi to Elk City for supplies. Busiest place on the forest in September because of hunts. Deer, elk, bears, moose and wolves in area.

GETTING THERE: From Elk City go W on state HWY 14 approx. 3 mi. to forest route 222. Go S on 222 approx. 18 mi. to forest route 421. Go S on 421 approx. 20 mi. to Whitewater CG.

SINGLE RATE:	No fee	OPEN DATES:	Yearlong
# of SINGLE SITES:	2		
		MAX STAY:	14 days
		ELEVATION:	3500 feet

50 Wild Horse
Elk City • lat 45°38'30" lon 115°38'00"

DESCRIPTION: This CG is located among pine on Wildhorse Lake. Trout fishing in lake and creek. Wildlife in the area includes deer, elk, moose, wolves, and bears. Hunting when in season. Supplies and groceries can be found 24 mi. away in Elk City. No drinking water available on site.

GETTING THERE: From Elk City Go W on state HWY 14 approx. 6 mi. to forest route 233. Go south on 233 16 mi. to Orogrande Summit. From the summit take forest route 2331 NE 2 mi. to Wild Horse CG.

SINGLE RATE:	No fee	OPEN DATES:	Yearlong
# of SINGLE SITES:	6	MAX SPUR:	15 feet
		MAX STAY:	14 days
		ELEVATION:	7300 feet

 Campground has hosts   **Reservable sites**   **Accessible facilities**   **Fully developed**   **Semi-developed**   **Rustic facilities**

NOTE: Open dates listed are typical. Actual dates are dependent on conditions such as snow pack.

PAYETTE
NATIONAL FOREST

The Payette National Forest encompasses some of Idaho's most beautiful and diverse country. Located in west-central Idaho north of Boise, the 2.3–million acre forest extends 100 miles west to east from Hells Canyon to the Middle Fork Salmon River. It stretches 70 miles north to south, from the Salmon River to the Weiser River. Nature has carved rough, granite mountains, high lakes, lush meadows, and deep river canyons. In one day you can travel from hot desert grasslands through cool conifer forests to snow-capped peaks. Elevations range from 1,500 feet on the west side to over 9,500 feet on the east side.

Tour the forest on 2,000 miles of roads, hike 2,100 miles of trails, and camp at 30 campgrounds. Numerous reservoirs, lakes, and streams offer a myriad of camping and fishing opportunities. The Salmon River and Middle Fork Salmon River offer world-class river rafting. The Frank Church-River of No Return Wilderness, the largest in the lower 48 states, offers world-class backcountry hiking, fishing, and hunting. In winter, downhill skiing is excellent at Brundage Mountain ski area, and backcountry skiing and snowmobiling trails are unlimited.

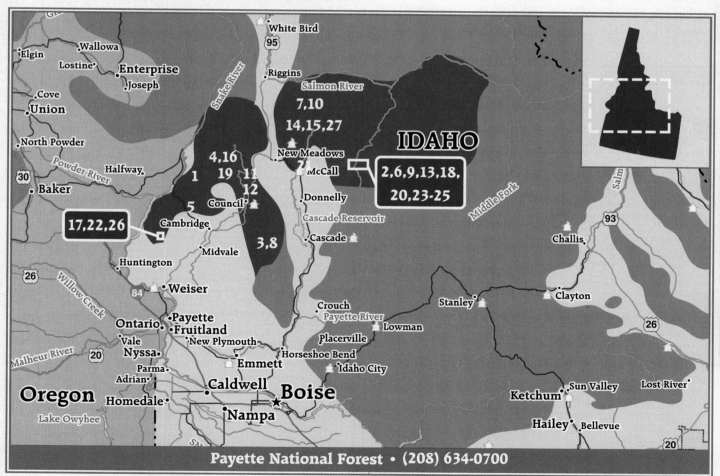

Payette National Forest • (208) 634-0700

1 Big Bar
Oxbow • lat 45°07'30" lon 116°45'45"

DESCRIPTION: Dispersed sites are situated among scattered fruit trees on the shores of Hells Canyon Reservoir, the deepest canyon in the US. Enjoy boating, rafting, and fishing for trout and bass. Boat dock/ramp. Hiking trails. No drinking water. Bears, mountain lions, elk, bighorn sheep, and bald eagles.

GETTING THERE: From Oxbow go N on forest route 454 approx. 13 mi. to Big Bar CG.

SINGLE RATE:	No fee	OPEN DATES:	Apr-Nov
		MAX STAY:	14 days
		ELEVATION:	1720 feet

2 Big Creek Airstrip
Edwardsburg • lat 45°07'30" lon 115°20'30"

DESCRIPTION: This walk-in CG is set underneath a closed canopy of mixed conifer near a small creek. CG adjacent to the airstrip. Venture into the nearby Frank Church River of No Return Wilderness Area. Wildlife in this area includes bears, mountain lions, coyotes, deer, elk, osprey, and bald eagles.

GETTING THERE: Big Creek Airstrip CG is located approx. 1 mi NE of Edwardsburg. Road can be narrow with sharp curves. Large vehicles should use caution.

SINGLE RATE:	Varies	OPEN DATES:	July-Oct
# of SINGLE SITES:	4	MAX SPUR:	20 feet
		MAX STAY:	14 days
		ELEVATION:	5743 feet

3 Big Flat
Indian Valley • lat 44°30'00" lon 116°15'00"

DESCRIPTION: CG is in a pine, fir, larch, and spruce forest on the Little Weiser River. Good trout fishing opportunities in the river. Wildlife in the area includes black bears, mountain lions, wolves, coyotes, deer, elk, bighorn sheep, bald eagles, and peregrine falcons. CG may be busy during hunting season.

GETTING THERE: From Indian Valley go S on county route approx. 3.5 mi. to forest route 206. Go E on 206 approx. 13 mi. to Big Flat CG.

SINGLE RATE:	$5	OPEN DATES:	May-Nov
# of SINGLE SITES:	16	MAX SPUR:	50 feet
		MAX STAY:	14 days
		ELEVATION:	4500 feet

4 Black Lake
Bear • lat 45°11'22" lon 116°33'40"

DESCRIPTION: This quiet CG is set among subalpine fir in the crags of the surrounding peaks. Enjoy beautiful panoramic views. Fish for trout in adjacent Black Lake. On site hiking trails lead to other high, alpine lakes. Wildlife in area includes black bears, coyotes, bighorn sheep, mountain goats, deer, and elk.

GETTING THERE: From Bear go N on forest route 105 approx. 6.5 mi. to forest route 112. Go N on 112 approx. 12 mi. to Black Lake CG. High clearance vehicles only.

SINGLE RATE:	$5	OPEN DATES:	July-Sept
# of SINGLE SITES:	4	MAX SPUR:	25 feet
		MAX STAY:	14 days
		ELEVATION:	7200 feet

5 Brownlee
Cambridge • lat 44°44'00" lon 116°48'45"

DESCRIPTION: This CG is nestled in an open grove of ponderosa pine and douglas fir. Visit the nearby Brownlee Reservoir, and fish for crappie, bass, trout, and catfish. Wildlife includes black bears, mountain lions, deer, elk, turkeys, and bald eagles. CG is busy weekends and holidays. Hiking and OHV trails nearby.

GETTING THERE: Brownlee CG is located approx. 16.5 mi. NW of Cambridge on state HWY 71.

SINGLE RATE:	$5	OPEN DATES:	June-Sept
# of SINGLE SITES:	11	MAX SPUR:	40 feet
		MAX STAY:	14 days
		ELEVATION:	4400 feet

6 Buckhorn
McCall • lat 44°56'19" lon 115°44'14"

DESCRIPTION: This CG is set underneath a closed canopy of mixed conifer on the South Fork of the Salmon River. Enjoy fishing for trout, whitefish, and chinook salmon. Wildlife includes black bears, mountain lions, coyotes, deer, elk, osprey, and bald eagles. CG does not fill but may be busy summer weekends.

GETTING THERE: From McCall go NE on primary forest route 48 approx. 36 mi. to forest route 674. Go S approx. 7 mi. to Buckhorn CG. Road can be narrow with sharp curves. Large vehicles should use caution.

SINGLE RATE:	Varies	OPEN DATES:	May-Nov
# of SINGLE SITES:	10	MAX SPUR:	30 feet
		MAX STAY:	14 days
		ELEVATION:	3800 feet

7 Burgdorf
Burgdorf • lat 45°16'30" lon 115°54'26"

DESCRIPTION: This CG is situated in a dense forest. Historical Burgdorf Site, an old mining town, is nearby. Supplies are available at McCall. Early in the summer elk herds come into the meadows nearby. Moose and deer also hang out in the area. Numerous hiking trails can be found in the vicinity.

GETTING THERE: Burgdorf CG is located approx. .2 mi. N of Burgdorf on forest route 246.

SINGLE RATE:	Varies	OPEN DATES:	June-Sept
# of SINGLE SITES:	6	MAX STAY:	14 days
		ELEVATION:	6115 feet

8 Cabin Creek
Council • lat 44°39'28" lon 116°16'20"

DESCRIPTION: CG among tall, mature ponderosa pine set on Cabin Creek. Good trout fishing opportunities in adjacent Middle Fork of Weiser River. Wildlife includes black bears, coyotes, deer, elk, bighorn sheep, bald eagles, and falcons. Hike the on-site trail to Council Mountain which offers spectacular views.

GETTING THERE: From Council go S on US HWY 95 approx. 5 mi. to forest route 186. Go E on 186 approx. 10 mi. to Cabin Creek CG.

SINGLE RATE:	$5	OPEN DATES:	May-Nov
# of SINGLE SITES:	12	MAX SPUR:	30 feet
		MAX STAY:	14 days
		ELEVATION:	4200 feet

9 Camp Creek
Yellow Pine • lat 44°53'30" lon 115°42'00"

DESCRIPTION: CG rests in a open grove of pine on the South Fork Salmon River. Fish for trout, chinook salmon, and whitefish. Black bears, coyotes, elk, osprey, and bald eagles in area. Busy summer weekends. An on-site trailhead offers horse, hiking, and mountain biking opportunities. Horse facilities. No drinking water on site.

GETTING THERE: From Yellowpine go W on primary forest route 48 approx. 14 mi. to forest route 674. Go S approx. 8 mi. to Camp Creek CG. Road is narrow with sharp curves. Large vehicles should use caution.

SINGLE RATE:	Varies	OPEN DATES:	May-Nov
# of SINGLE SITES:	4	MAX SPUR:	30 feet
		MAX STAY:	14 days
		ELEVATION:	4062 feet

10 Chinook
Warren Guard Station • lat 45°12'45" lon 115°48'32"

DESCRIPTION: This CG rests in a grove of mixed conifer along the Secesh River with views of surrounding mountains. Enjoy good fishing for trout, chinook salmon, and whitefish. Venture onto on-site trail which leads to the Loon Lake area. This CG offers a horse loading ramp and hitching rails. No drinking water.

GETTING THERE: From Warren Guard Station go SW on primary forest route 21 approx. 8 mi. to Chinook CG.

SINGLE RATE:	Varies	OPEN DATES:	June-Sept
# of SINGLE SITES:	9	MAX SPUR:	20 feet
		MAX STAY:	14 days
		ELEVATION:	5700 feet

 Campground has hosts   Reservable sites   Accessible facilities   Fully developed   Semi-developed   Rustic facilities

NOTE: Open dates listed are typical. Actual dates are dependent on conditions such as snow pack.

11 Cold Springs
Pine Ridge • lat 44°56'58" lon 116°26'24"

DESCRIPTION: CG is situated in a pine, fir, and larch forest, next to a large meadow. 1/4 mi. to Lost Valley Reservoir, where you can fish for trout. Black bears, mountain lions, wolves, coyotes, deer, and bald eagles reside in the area. Busy July weekends. Hike in nearby Frank Church River of No Return Wilderness.

GETTING THERE: Cold Springs CG is located approx. 3 mi. W of Pine Ridge on forest route 089.

SINGLE RATE:	Varies	OPEN DATES:	June-Sept
# of SINGLE SITES:	33	MAX SPUR:	45 feet
		MAX STAY:	14 days
# of GROUP SITES:	2	ELEVATION:	4800 feet

16 Huckleberry
Bear • lat 45°05'00" lon 116°37'00"

DESCRIPTION: CG is situated among mixed conifer near Bear Creek. Beautiful views of Smith Mountain. Bears, mountain lions, coyotes, bighorn sheep, bald eagles, and peregrine falcons. Busy during hunting season. Hike in nearby Hells Canyon and Seven Devils Wilderness Areas. Visit Sheep Rock Scenic Overlook.

GETTING THERE: From Bear go N on forest route 105 approx. 5 mi. to forest route 110. Go E on 110 approx. .5 mi. to Huckleberry CG.

SINGLE RATE:	$5	OPEN DATES:	June-Nov
# of SINGLE SITES:	8	MAX SPUR:	30 feet
		MAX STAY:	14 days
		ELEVATION:	4800 feet

12 Evergreen
Pine Ridge • lat 44°53'36" lon 116°23'17"

DESCRIPTION: CG situated in a pine, fir, larch, and spruce forest set in a river canyon. Good trout fishing opportunities in the East Fork of Weiser River. Wildlife in the area includes black bears, mountain lions, wolves, coyotes, deer, elk, bighorn sheep, bald eagles, and peregrine falcons.

GETTING THERE: Evergreen CG is located approx. 4 mi. S of Pine Ridge on US HWY 95.

SINGLE RATE:	$5	OPEN DATES:	June-Sept
# of SINGLE SITES:	12	MAX SPUR:	30 feet
		MAX STAY:	14 days
		ELEVATION:	3800 feet

17 Justrite
Weiser • lat 44°33'00" lon 116°54'00"

DESCRIPTION: This rustic CG is situated in cottonwood, pine and fir on Mann Creek. Enjoy fishing for rainbow trout in the creek. Wildlife in the area includes black bear, mountain lion, deer, elk, turkey, bald eagle, and golden eagle. CG can be busy weekends and holidays. Numerous trails in vicinity.

GETTING THERE: From Weiser go N on US HWY 95 approx. 9 mi. to forest route 600. Go N on 600 approx. 12 mi. to Justrite CG.

SINGLE RATE:	No fee	OPEN DATES:	June-Sept
# of SINGLE SITES:	4	MAX SPUR:	35 feet
		MAX STAY:	14 days
		ELEVATION:	4200 feet

13 Fourmile
Yellow Pine • lat 44°51'47" lon 115°41'31"

DESCRIPTION: CG rests in a open grove of pine on the South Fork Salmon River. Fish for trout, chinook salmon, and whitefish. Black bears, coyotes, elk, osprey, and bald eagles in area. Busy summer weekends. An on-site trailhead offers horse, hiking, and mountain biking opportunities. Horse facilities. No drinking water on site.

GETTING THERE: From Yellowpine go W on primary forest route 48 approx. 14 mi. to forest route 674. Go S approx. 11 mi. to Fourmile CG. Road can be narrow with sharp curves. Large vehicles should use caution.

SINGLE RATE:	Varies	OPEN DATES:	May-Nov
# of SINGLE SITES:	4	MAX SPUR:	30 feet
		MAX STAY:	14 days
		ELEVATION:	3900 feet

18 Kennally Creek
Donnelly • lat 44°46'57" lon 115°52'29"

DESCRIPTION: This CG is situated in a mixed forest setting a short distance away from South Fork East Fork Kenally Creek and North Fork Kennally Creek. Fish and swim in either creek. Please check for local fishing regulations. Supplies are available in Donnelly. Popular equestrian area.

GETTING THERE: From Donnelly go N on state HWY 55 approx. 3 mi. to forest route 388. Go E approx. 5 mi. to forest route 389. Go E 6 mi. to forest route 388. Go E on 388 approx. 3 mi. to Kennally Creek CG.

# of SINGLE SITES:	10	OPEN DATES:	June-Sept
		MAX STAY:	14 days
		ELEVATION:	6000 feet

14 Grouse
New Meadows • lat 45°04'06" lon 116°10'01"

DESCRIPTION: This quiet CG is located among spruce and pine on Goose Lake. Enjoy fishing for rainbow and cutthroat trout, check regulations. Wildlife includes black bears, mountain lions, wolves, coyotes, deer, elk, moose, and bald eagles. CG is busy July weekends. An on-site trailhead offers hiking along Six Mile Creek.

GETTING THERE: From New Meadows go E on state HWY 55 approx. 6 mi. to forest route 257. Go N on 257 approx. 11 mi. to Grouse CG.

SINGLE RATE:	$4	OPEN DATES:	July-Oct
# of SINGLE SITES:	6	MAX SPUR:	30 feet
		MAX STAY:	14 days
		ELEVATION:	6500 feet

19 Lafferty
Bear • lat 44°56'24" lon 116°39'15"

DESCRIPTION: A centrally located CG set in a fir, pine, spruce, and larch forest. The Crooked River runs nearby. Black bears, mountain lions, wolves, coyotes, deer, elk, bighorn sheep, bald eagles, and peregrine falcons. There are hiking, horse, and OHV trails in the area. May be busy during hunting season.

GETTING THERE: Lafferty CG is located approx. 6 mi. S of Bear on forest route 002.

SINGLE RATE:	$4	OPEN DATES:	May-Nov
# of SINGLE SITES:	8	MAX SPUR:	24 feet
		MAX STAY:	14 days
		ELEVATION:	4300 feet

15 Hazard Lake
New Meadows • lat 45°12'13" lon 116°08'23"

DESCRIPTION: This CG is situated among subalpine fir and spruce on Hazard Lake. Enjoy fishing for rainbow and cutthroat trout, check regulations. Wildlife includes black bears, mountain lions, wolves, coyotes, deer, elk, moose, and bald eagles. CG is busy July weekends. Hike the Upper Hazard Lake Trail (on-site trailhead).

GETTING THERE: From New Meadows go E on state HWY 55 approx. 6 mi. to forest route 257. Go N on 257 approx. 19 mi. to Hazard Lake CG.

SINGLE RATE:	$4	OPEN DATES:	July-Sept
# of SINGLE SITES:	12	MAX SPUR:	30 feet
		MAX STAY:	14 days
		ELEVATION:	7100 feet

20 Lake Fork
McCall • lat 44°55'23" lon 115°56'42"

DESCRIPTION: This CG is situated underneath a canopy of large trees with little ground covering. Spectacular views of the North Fork of Lake Fork River. Fishing opportunities in the river, check for local regulations. Supplies at McCall. Rarely fills. Several trails in area. Mosquitos can be a problem.

GETTING THERE: Lake Fork CG is located approx. 9.5 mi. E of McCall on primary forest route 48.

SINGLE RATE:	Varies	OPEN DATES:	June-Sept
# of SINGLE SITES:	9		
		MAX STAY:	14 days
		ELEVATION:	5360 feet

 Campground has hosts 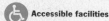 Reservable sites 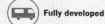 Accessible facilities   Fully developed   Semi-developed   Rustic facilities

NOTE: Open dates listed are typical. Actual dates are dependent on conditions such as snow pack.

PAYETTE NATIONAL FOREST • IDAHO • 11 — 20

21 Last Chance
New Meadows • lat 44˚59'22" lon 116˚11'23"

DESCRIPTION: This CG is situated among mixed conifer on Goose Creek. Enjoy fishing for rainbow and cutthroat trout, check regulations. Wildlife includes black bears, mountain lions, wolves, coyotes, deer, elk, moose, and bald eagles. CG is busy July weekends. An on-site trailhead offers hiking along Goose Creek.

GETTING THERE: From New Meadows go E on state HWY 55 approx. 3.5 mi. to forest route 453. Go N on 453 approx. 2 mi. to Last Chance CG.

SINGLE RATE:	Varies	OPEN DATES:	May-Sept
# of SINGLE SITES:	23	MAX SPUR:	45 feet
GROUP RATE:	Varies	MAX STAY:	14 days
# of GROUP SITES:	1	ELEVATION:	4600 feet

26 Spring Creek
Weiser • lat 44˚34'13" lon 116˚56'45"

DESCRIPTION: This CG is situated at the confluence of Spring and Mann Creeks. Sites rest under a dense overstory of pine and fir. Enjoy fishing in Mann Creek for rainbow trout. Wildlife includes black bears, mountain lions, deer, elk, turkeys, and eagles. The CG's interpretive trail has one barrier free loop.

GETTING THERE: From Weiser go N on US HWY 95 approx. 13 mi. to forest route 009. Go N on 009 approx. 17 mi. to Spring Creek CG.

SINGLE RATE:	$5	OPEN DATES:	June-Sept
# of SINGLE SITES:	14	MAX SPUR:	50 feet
		MAX STAY:	14 days
		ELEVATION:	4800 feet

22 Paradise
Weiser • lat 44˚33'00" lon 116˚54'00"

DESCRIPTION: This rustic CG is situated in cottonwood, pine and fir on Mann Creek. Enjoy fishing for rainbow trout in the creek. Wildlife in the area includes black bear, mountain lion, deer, elk, turkey, bald eagle, and golden eagle. CG can be busy weekends and holidays.

GETTING THERE: From Weiser go N on US HWY 95 approx. 9 mi. to forest route 600. Go N on 600 approx. 12 mi. to Paradise CG.

SINGLE RATE:	No fee	OPEN DATES:	June-Sept
# of SINGLE SITES:	3	MAX SPUR:	35 feet
		MAX STAY:	14 days
		ELEVATION:	4200 feet

27 Upper Payette Lake
McCall • lat 45˚07'22" lon 116˚01'41"

DESCRIPTION: This CG is situated in the high mountains with views of Upper Payette lake. Fish for rainbow trout from the lake, check regulations. Supplies are available at McCall approx. 16 mi. away. Watch for deer, geese, and moose in the area. CG fills up fast. Numerous trails can be found in the vicinity.

GETTING THERE: From McCall go N on primary forest route 21 approx. 19 mi. to forest route 495. Go N on 495 approx. 1 mi. to Upper Payette Lake CG.

SINGLE RATE:	Varies	OPEN DATES:	June-Sept
# of SINGLE SITES:	25		
GROUP RATE:	Varies	MAX STAY:	14 days
# of GROUP SITES:	3	ELEVATION:	5600 feet

23 Ponderosa
McCall • lat 45˚03'44" lon 115˚45'31"

DESCRIPTION: This CG is set in a grove of mixed conifer on the Secesh River. Fish for trout, chinook salmon, and whitefish. Black bears, coyotes, elk, osprey, and bald eagles in area. CG may be busy summer weekends. An on-site trailhead offers horse, hiking, and mountain biking opportunities. No drinking water.

GETTING THERE: Ponderosa CG is located approx. 31 mi. NE of McCall on primary forest route 48. Road can be narrow with sharp curves. Large vehicles should use caution.

SINGLE RATE:	Varies	OPEN DATES:	June-Oct
# of SINGLE SITES:	14	MAX SPUR:	20 feet
		MAX STAY:	14 days
		ELEVATION:	4000 feet

24 Poverty Flat
Krassel Work Center • lat 44˚49'23" lon 115˚42'10"

DESCRIPTION: CG is situated in a open grove of pine on the South Fork Salmon River. Fish for trout, chinook salmon, and whitefish. Wildlife includes bears, coyotes, elk, osprey, and bald eagles. Busy during fishing season. An on-site trailhead offers horse, hiking, and mountain biking opportunities. Horse facilities.

GETTING THERE: From Krassel Work Center go S on forest route 674 approx. 13.5 mi. to Poverty Flat CG. Road can be narrow with sharp curves. Large vehicles should use caution.

SINGLE RATE:	Varies	OPEN DATES:	Mar-Nov
# of SINGLE SITES:	10	MAX SPUR:	30 feet
		MAX STAY:	14 days
		ELEVATION:	4225 feet

25 Secesh River
Yellow Pine • lat 45˚01'15" lon 115˚40'30"

DESCRIPTION: This CG is situated in a grove of mixed conifer on the Secesh River. Fish for trout, chinook salmon, and whitefish. Black bears, coyotes, elk, osprey, and bald eagles in area. CG may be busy summer weekends. An on-site trailhead offers horse, hiking, and mountain biking opportunities. Horse facilities.

GETTING THERE: Secesh River CG is located approx. 15 mi. W of Yellow Pine on primary forest route 48. Road can be narrow with sharp curves. Large vehicles should use caution.

SINGLE RATE:	Varies	OPEN DATES:	June-Oct
# of SINGLE SITES:	5	MAX SPUR:	30 feet
		MAX STAY:	14 days
		ELEVATION:	4000 feet

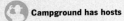 **Campground has hosts**   **Reservable sites**   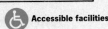 **Accessible facilities**   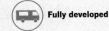 **Fully developed**   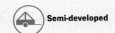 **Semi-developed**    **Rustic facilities**

USFS Photo

SALMON-CHALLIS NATIONAL FOREST

The Salmon and Challis National Forests cover over 4.3 million acres, over 130,000 acres of which are located within the Frank Church-River of No Return Wilderness.

Congress established the River of No Return Wilderness on July 23, 1980. After the death of Frank Church, a former Idaho senator, the area was renamed the Frank Church-River of No Return Wilderness. Over 2.3 million acres in size, it is the largest wilderness area outside of Alaska.

Rugged and remote, this country offers adventure, solitude, and breathtaking scenery. Panoramic vistas highlight travel atop the Continental Divide; northwest-southeast trending mountain ranges culminate in the jagged heights of Mt. Borah, Idaho's tallest peak. The Wild and Scenic Middle Fork and Salmon Rivers plunge through the shadowy depths of immense canyons; and sagebrush slopes are blanketed with colorful displays of wildflowers in spring.

Other points of interest include the Copper Basin area, where glaciation has produced the alpine lakes and sharp, narrow ridges of the Pioneer Mountains and the Yankee Fork of the Salmon River. Here the ghost towns of Custer and Bonanza can be found.

Salmon-Challis National Forest • Idaho • Locator Map

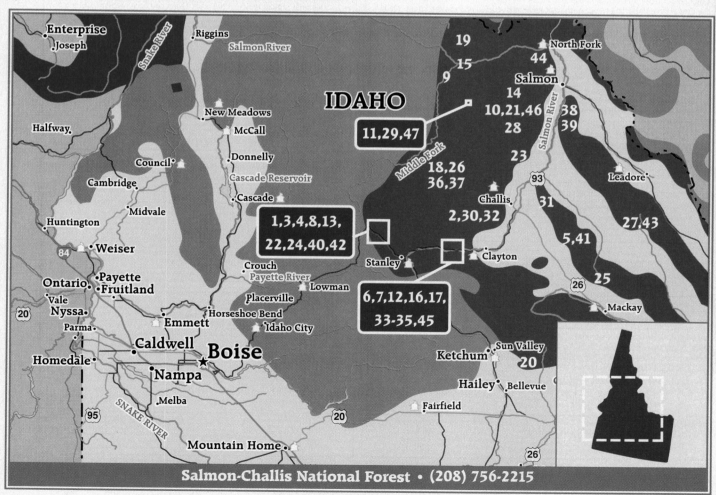

Salmon-Challis National Forest • (208) 756-2215

1 Banner Creek
Stanley • lat 44°21'00" lon 115°13'30"

DESCRIPTION: This CG is situated in a dense lodgepole pine forest on the banks of Cape Horn Creek. Fishing on creek, please check for local fishing regulations. Supplies are avaiable at Stanley. Elk, wolves, and sandhill cranes can be seen in the area. Gather firewood locally. Several trails in the area.

GETTING THERE: Banner Creek CG is located approx. 19 mi. NW of Stanley on state HWY 21 (Ponderosa Pine Scenic Route).

SINGLE RATE:	No fee	OPEN DATES:	July-Sept
# of SINGLE SITES:	3	MAX SPUR:	22 feet
		MAX STAY:	14 days
		ELEVATION:	6800 feet

2 Bayhorse Lake
Bayhorse • lat 44°24'43" lon 114°24'09"

DESCRIPTION: CG situated above Bayhorse Lake in a mixed conifer forest. Fish for rainbow and cuthroat trout from the lake. Supplies are available at Bayhorse. Elk, moose, deer, goats, and bears seen in the area. Hiking trails nearby. ATV trailhead starts at CG. Full weekends and July 4th. No drinking water.

GETTING THERE: Bayhorse Lake CG is located approx. 4.5 mi. W of Bayhorse on forest route 051.

SINGLE RATE:	No fee	OPEN DATES:	July-Sept
# of SINGLE SITES:	7	MAX SPUR:	21 feet
		MAX STAY:	14 days
		ELEVATION:	8600 feet

3 Beaver Creek
Stanley • lat 44°24'51" lon 115°08'45"

DESCRIPTION: CG situated in an open park-like forest on the banks of Beaver Creek. Catch and release only in creek. Supplies at Stanley. Elk, deer, and bears can be seen in the area. Horse unloading ramp, hitch rack and stalls located accross the street. Many trails in the area take you to high mountain lakes.

GETTING THERE: From Stanley go NW on state HWY 21 (Ponderosa Pine Scenic Route) approx. 16 mi. to forest route 008. Go NE on 008 approx. 2 mi. to Beaver Creek CG.

SINGLE RATE:	$5	OPEN DATES:	July-Sept
# of SINGLE SITES:	12	MAX SPUR:	32 feet
		MAX STAY:	14 days
		ELEVATION:	6400 feet

4 Bench Creek
Stanley • lat 44°19'00" lon 115°14'30"

DESCRIPTION: This CG is situated in a dense lodgepole pine forest with an open meadow nearby. Fish at Banner Creek is nearby. Supplies are available at Stanley. Elk, deer, and bears can be seen in the area. Bench Creek Trail (next to CG) leads into numerous high mountain lakes. Gather firewood locally.

GETTING THERE: Bench Creek CG is located approx. 21 mi. NW of Stanley on state HWY 21 (Ponderosa Pine Scenic Route).

SINGLE RATE:	No fee	OPEN DATES:	July-Sept
# of SINGLE SITES:	5	MAX SPUR:	16 feet
		MAX STAY:	14 days
		ELEVATION:	6800 feet

5 Big Creek
Goldburg • lat 44°27'30" lon 113°37'00"

DESCRIPTION: This CG is situated in a douglas fir and willow forest set on Big Creek. Fish for cuthroat from creek. Supplies are available at Goldburg. Deer, elk, moose, and bears reside in the area. CG is a trail head for 2 major trails: South Fork Big Creek Trail and North Fork Big Creek Trail.

GETTING THERE: From Goldburg go N on county route approx. 4 mi. to forest route 097. Go E on 097 approx. 3 mi. to Big Creek CG.

SINGLE RATE:	No fee	OPEN DATES:	June-Sept
# of SINGLE SITES:	3	MAX SPUR:	16 feet
		MAX STAY:	14 days
		ELEVATION:	6600 feet

6 Blind Creek
Stanley • lat 44°16'51" lon 114°43'55"

DESCRIPTION: CG set in a constricted canyon on the Yankee Fork River. Fish for trout from the river, or from the stocked ponds nearby. Historical Custer Ghost Town within 8 mi. of CG. Supplies available at Stanley. Deer, bears, goats, and elk may be seen in area. Many trails near CG. Gather firewood locally.

GETTING THERE: From Stanley go E on state HWY 75 (Sawtooth Scenic Route) approx. 12 mi. to forest route 013. Go N on 013 approx. 1 mi. to Blind Creek CG.

SINGLE RATE:	$5	OPEN DATES:	June-Sept
# of SINGLE SITES:	5	MAX SPUR:	32 feet
		MAX STAY:	14 days
		ELEVATION:	6100 feet

7 Bonanza CCC Group
Sunbeam • lat 44°22'20" lon 114°43'42"

DESCRIPTION: In a lodgepole pine stand right above the West Fork of the Yankee Fork River. Fish from the river for trout. CG is an historical CCC camp from the 30's. Supplies at Sunbeam. Deer, moose, elk and goat in the area. West Fork Trailhead has stock facilities approx. .5 mi. from CG. Great hiking in the area.

GETTING THERE: From Sunbeam go N on forest route 013 approx. 8 mi. to Bonanza Guard Station. Go .25 miles behind the guard station to Bonanza CCC Group CG.

		OPEN DATES:	Yearlong
		MAX SPUR:	30 feet
GROUP RATE:	Varies	MAX STAY:	14 days
# of GROUP SITES:	1	ELEVATION:	5800 feet

8 Boundary Creek
Lowman • lat 44°31'30" lon 115°17'30"

DESCRIPTION: CG in a dense lodgepole pine forest on the Middle Fork of Salmon River. Catch and release fishing only from the river. Supplies at Lowman. Grey wolves, deer, elk, wolverines, and raptors reside in the area. Bears can be a problem. CG is a busy launch point for float trips. Several trails in the area.

GETTING THERE: From Lowman go NE on forest route 582 approx. 32 mi. to forest route 668. Go N on 668 approx. 13 mi. to Boundary Creek CG.

SINGLE RATE:	$5	OPEN DATES:	June-Sept
# of SINGLE SITES:	14	MAX SPUR:	22 feet
		MAX STAY:	14 days
		ELEVATION:	5800 feet

9 Corn Creek
Salmon • lat 45°30'00" lon 114°41'00"

DESCRIPTION: CG in an open park-like forest of pine with views of The Wild and Scenic Salmon River. Supplies at Salmon. Deer, moose, bears, and osprey. This CG is the major launch point for rafters and jet boaters. Gather firewood. Rattle snakes and yellowjackets could be a problem. Trailhead to Frank Church Wilderness.

GETTING THERE: From Salmon go N on US HWY 93 approx. 20 mi. to forest route 030. Go W on 030 approx. 39 mi. to Corn Creek CG.

SINGLE RATE:	$5	OPEN DATES:	Mar-Nov
# of SINGLE SITES:	30	MAX SPUR:	22 feet
		MAX STAY:	14 days
		ELEVATION:	2800 feet

10 Cougar Point
Salmon • lat 45°04'51" lon 114°03'17"

DESCRIPTION: CG set in a mixed forest with Williams Creek running nearby. Fish and swim in the creek. Check for local fishing regulations. Supplies are available at Salmon. Deer, bears, and birds are common to the area. Williams Summit is within 1 mi. of the CG. Several trails in the area.

GETTING THERE: From Salmon go S on US HWY 93 approx. 6 mi. to forest route 021. Go W on 021 approx. 9.5 mi. to Cougar Point CG.

SINGLE RATE:	$4	OPEN DATES:	June-Sept
# of SINGLE SITES:	18	MAX SPUR:	20 feet
		MAX STAY:	14 days
		ELEVATION:	6600 feet

 Campground has hosts   **Reservable sites**   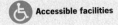 **Accessible facilities**   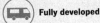 **Fully developed**   **Semi-developed**   **Rustic facilities**

NOTE: Open dates listed are typical. Actual dates are dependent on conditions such as snow pack.

11 Crags
Deep Creek • lat 45°06'10" lon 114°31'21"

DESCRIPTION: CG situated among mixed conifer with Golden Trout Lake nearby. Fish for trout or swim from the lake. Supplies are available at Deep Creek. Deer, bears, and birds are common to the area. Many trails in the area, some leading to Clear Creek Trail and into high mountain lakes. Gather firewood locally.

GETTING THERE: From Deep Creek go S on forest route 055 approx. 11 mi. to forest route 112. Go W on 112 approx. 6.5 mi. to forest route 113. Go N approx. 7 mi. to forest route 114. Go N approx. 2.5 mi. to Crags CG.

SINGLE RATE:	$4	OPEN DATES:	July-Oct
# of SINGLE SITES:	24		
		MAX STAY:	14 days
		ELEVATION:	8400 feet

12 Custer
Stanley • lat 44°23'58" lon 114°39'46"

DESCRIPTION: CG in a lodgepole and fir forest on the Yankee Fork River. Fish for trout from the river or stocked ponds close to CG. Supplies at Stanley. The 5 Mile Creek Trail starts at CG and leads to a lookout tower built in the 40's. Historical Custer Ghost Town within 8 mi. of CG. No drinking water on site.

GETTING THERE: From Stanley go E on state HWY 75 (Sawtooth Scenic Route) approx. 12 mi. to forest route 013. Go N on 013 approx. 8 mi. to forest route 070. Go NE on 070 approx. 3 mi. to Custer CG.

SINGLE RATE:	No fee	OPEN DATES:	July-Sept
# of SINGLE SITES:	6	MAX SPUR:	32 feet
		MAX STAY:	14 days
		ELEVATION:	6600 feet

13 Dagger Falls
Lowman • lat 44°31'30" lon 115°17'30"

DESCRIPTION: This CG is situated in a dense lodgepole pine forest adjacent to Dagger Falls. Supplies are available at Lowman. Wildlife in the area includres grey wolves, deer, elk, wolverines, and raptors. Bears can be a problem. Numerous trails can be found in the vicinity.

GETTING THERE: From Lowman go NE on forest route 582 approx. 32 mi. to forest route 668. Go N on 668 approx. 13 mi. to Dagger Falls CG.

SINGLE RATE:	$5	OPEN DATES:	June-Sept
# of SINGLE SITES:	10	MAX SPUR:	22 feet
		MAX STAY:	14 days
		ELEVATION:	5800 feet

14 Deep Creek
Salmon • lat 45°07'30" lon 114°14'00"

DESCRIPTION: This CG is set on the banks of Deep Creek in a mixed conifer forest. Fish for trout and swim in the creek. Check for local regulations. Supplies are available at Salmon. Deer, bears, and birds are common to the area. Napias Creek Falls is within 1 mi. of the CG. No designated trails in the area.

GETTING THERE: From Salmon go S on US HWY 93 approx. 6 mi. to forest route 021. Go W on 021 approx. 19 mi. to Deep Creek CG.

SINGLE RATE:	No fee	OPEN DATES:	May-Oct
# of SINGLE SITES:	6	MAX SPUR:	15 feet
		MAX STAY:	14 days
		ELEVATION:	4800 feet

15 Ebenezer Bar
Salmon • lat 45°18'18" lon 114°30'53"

DESCRIPTION: CG in an open park-like setting of pine, sitting above Salmon River. Fish for rainbow trout on Salmon River or Corn Creek nearby. Supplies at Salmon. Deer, moose, and bears reside in the area. Rattle snakes could be a problem. Trailhead to Frank Church River of No Return Wilderness is nearby.

GETTING THERE: From Salmon go N on US HWY 93 approx. 20 mi. to forest route 030. Go W on 030 approx. 29 mi. to Ebenezer Bar CG.

SINGLE RATE:	$5	OPEN DATES:	Mar-Oct
# of SINGLE SITES:	33	MAX SPUR:	30 feet
		MAX STAY:	14 days
		ELEVATION:	3100 feet

16 Eightmile
Stanley • lat 44°25'35" lon 114°37'13"

DESCRIPTION: A secluded CG situated in an open lodgepole forest set on the Yankee Fork River. Fish for trout on the river. Check for local fishing regulations. Supplies available at Stanley. Historical Custer Ghost Town is within 8 mi. of CG. No designated trails in the area. Gather firewood locally.

GETTING THERE: From Stanley go E on state HWY 75 (Sawtooth Scenic Route) approx. 12 mi. to forest route 013. Go N on 013 approx. 8 mi. to forest route 070. Go NE on 070 approx. 7 mi. to Eightmile CG.

SINGLE RATE:	No fee	OPEN DATES:	July-Sept
# of SINGLE SITES:	2	MAX SPUR:	16 feet
		MAX STAY:	14 days
		ELEVATION:	7000 feet

17 Flat Rock
Stanley • lat 44°17'27" lon 114°43'01"

DESCRIPTION: This CG is situated in a dense douglas fir forest, set in a canyon with views of cliffs. Fish from the Yankee Fork River flowing nearby. Check for local fishing regulations. Supplies are available at Stanley. Deer, elk, and bears, and goats can be seen in the area. Gather firewood locally.

GETTING THERE: From Stanley go E on state HWY 75 (Sawtooth Scenic Route) approx. 12 mi. to forest route 013. Go N on 013 approx. 2 mi. to Flat Rock CG.

SINGLE RATE:	$5	OPEN DATES:	June-Sept
# of SINGLE SITES:	9	MAX SPUR:	32 feet
		MAX STAY:	14 days
		ELEVATION:	6200 feet

18 Fly Creek
Challis • lat 44°40'17" lon 114°33'15"

DESCRIPTION: This CG is situated in a douglas fir, spruce, and willow forest with views of Fly Creek. Fish for trout from the creek. Check for local regulations. Dispersed sites. Supplies are available at Challis. Deer, elk, moose, and bears reside in the area. Gather firewood locally. Trails nearby the CG.

GETTING THERE: From Challis go N and W on county route approx. 8.5 mi. to forest route 086. Continue NW on 086 approx. 16 mi. to Fly Creek CG.

SINGLE RATE:	No fee	OPEN DATES:	July-Sept
		MAX STAY:	14 days
		ELEVATION:	9000 feet

19 Horse Creek Hot Springs
Salmon • lat 45°30'15" lon 114°27'34"

DESCRIPTION: CG in a subalpine forest with views of Salmon National Forest lands. Fish for rainbow trout on Horse Creek. Supplies at Salmon. Deer, elk, bighorn sheep, and bears reside in the area. Gather firewood locally. Several trails in the area. There is a natural hot springs at CG with a historical bath house.

GETTING THERE: From Salmon go N on US HWY 93 20 mi. to forest route 030. W 14.5 mi. to forest route 038. Go N 7 mi. to forest route 044. NW 11 mi. to forest route 065. Go S 3 mi. to Horse Creek Hot Springs CG.

SINGLE RATE:	No fee	OPEN DATES:	July-Oct
# of SINGLE SITES:	12	MAX SPUR:	22 feet
		MAX STAY:	14 days
		ELEVATION:	6200 feet

20 Iron Bog
Moore • lat 43°36'30" lon 113°45'00"

DESCRIPTION: This CG is situated in an open sage desert on Antelope Creek, with views of the surrounding mountains. Supplies are available at Moore. Elk, deer, mountain lions, bears, and grouse reside in the area. CG is never full. Several non-motorized trails in the area. Hitching rail for horses available.

GETTING THERE: From Moore go NE approx. 3 mi. to forest route 135 (Antelope Road). Go SW on 135 approx. 21 mi. to Iron Bog CG.

SINGLE RATE:	$4	OPEN DATES:	June-Sept
# of SINGLE SITES:	21	MAX SPUR:	32 feet
		MAX STAY:	14 days
		ELEVATION:	7600 feet

 Campground has hosts   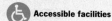 **Reservable sites**   **Accessible facilities**   **Fully developed**   **Semi-developed**   **Rustic facilities**

NOTE: Open dates listed are typical. Actual dates are dependent on conditions such as snow pack.

SALMON-CHALLIS NATIONAL FOREST • IDAHO • 11 — 20

21 Iron Lake
Salmon • lat 44°54'20" lon 114°11'35"

DESCRIPTION: CG set on the shores of Iron Lake, situated in a mixed conifer forest. Fish and swim in the lake. Check for local fishing regulations. Supplies are available at Salmon. Deer, bears, and birds are common to the area. Trail to Hat Creek Lakes provides for excellent hiking opportunities.

GETTING THERE: From Salmon go S on US HWY 93 approx. 6 mi. to forest route 021. Go W on 021 approx. 13 mi. to forest route 020. Go S on 020 approx. 18 mi. to Iron Lake CG.

SINGLE RATE:	$4	OPEN DATES:	June-Sept
# of SINGLE SITES:	6	MAX SPUR:	20 feet
		MAX STAY:	14 days
		ELEVATION:	8800 feet

22 Josephus Lake
Stanley • lat 44°32'30" lon 115°08'00"

DESCRIPTION: This CG is situated in a primitive pine forest with views of Josephus Lake. Josephus Lake is a small, shallow lake where you can fish for trout. Please check for local fishing regulations. Supplies are available at Stanley. Numerous hiking trails can be found in the vicinity.

GETTING THERE: From Stanley go NW on state HWY 21 (Ponderosa Pine Scenic Route) approx. 16 mi. to forest route 008. Go NE on 008 approx. 18 mi. to Josephus Lake CG.

SINGLE RATE:	No fee	OPEN DATES:	July-Sept
# of SINGLE SITES:	3		
		MAX STAY:	14 days
		ELEVATION:	7200 feet

23 Little West Fork
Challis • lat 44°42'08" lon 114°18'54"

DESCRIPTION: This CG is situated in a douglas fir and willow forest on the banks of the West Fork of Morgan Creek. Fish for cuthroat from creek. Check for local fishing regulations. Supplies are available at Challis. Deer, elk, wolves, and bears reside in the area. Trail head for 2 major trails is with in a mile of CG.

GETTING THERE: From Challis go N on US HWY 93 approx. 8 mi. to county route. Go NW approx. 6.5 mi. to forest route 057. Go W on 057 approx. 4 mi. to Little West Fork CG.

SINGLE RATE:	No fee	OPEN DATES:	June-Sept
# of SINGLE SITES:	2		
		MAX STAY:	14 days
		ELEVATION:	6600 feet

24 Lola Creek
Stanley • lat 44°24'28" lon 115°10'47"

DESCRIPTION: This CG is situated in a dense lodgepole forest on the banks of Marsh Creek. Fish from the creek. Largest CG in the district area. Supplies are available at Stanley. Marsh Creek Trail starts on site. Stock use facility is approx. .5 mi. away from CG. Numerous hiking trails in the area.

GETTING THERE: From Stanley go NW on state HWY 21 (Ponderosa Pine Scenic Route) approx. 16 mi. to forest route 083. Go N on 083 approx. 1 mi. to Lola Creek CG.

SINGLE RATE:	$5	OPEN DATES:	June-Sept
# of SINGLE SITES:	27	MAX SPUR:	32 feet
		MAX STAY:	14 days
		ELEVATION:	6400 feet

25 Loristica Group
Makee • lat 44°01'00" lon 113°29'00"

DESCRIPTION: In a big meadow surrounded by pine and fir forest with views of the mountain. Pond on each side of the CG with no fish. Supplies at Makee. Gather firewood locally. Hitching rail for horses at CG. Many trails in the area.

GETTING THERE: From Makee go SE on HWY 93 approx. 7 mi. to county route 122. Go N on 122 approx. 11 mi. to forest route 539. Go W on 539 approx. 1.5 mi. to Loristica Group CG.

		OPEN DATES:	May-Sept
GROUP RATE:	$30	MAX STAY:	14 days
# of GROUP SITES:	1	ELEVATION:	8000 feet

26 Mahoney Creek
Challis • lat 44°39'00" lon 114°31'30"

DESCRIPTION: This CG is situated in a douglas fir, spruce, and willow forest with views of Fly Creek. Fish for trout from the creek. Check for local regulations. Dispersed sites. Supplies are available at Challis. Deer, elk, moose, and bears reside in the area. Gather firewood locally. Trails nearby the CG.

GETTING THERE: From Challis go N and W on county route approx. 8.5 mi. to forest route 086. Continue NW on 086 approx. 15 mi. to Mahoney Creek CG.

SINGLE RATE:	No fee	OPEN DATES:	July-Sept
# of SINGLE SITES:	2		
		MAX STAY:	14 days
		ELEVATION:	9100 feet

27 Meadow Lake
Leadore • lat 44°26'02" lon 113°19'00"

DESCRIPTION: This CG is situated in an open alpine forest with views of Meadow Lake. Fish for stocked trout from the lake. Check for local fishing regulations. Supplies are available at Leadore. Deer, bears, and elk are common to the area. Trail to Lemhi Divide and a 1 mile oval hiking trail start from the CG.

GETTING THERE: From Leadore go S on state HWY 28 approx. 15.5 mi. to forest route 002. Go W on 002 approx. 6 mi. to Meadow Lake CG.

SINGLE RATE:	$5	OPEN DATES:	July-Sept
# of SINGLE SITES:	16	MAX SPUR:	24 feet
		MAX STAY:	14 days
		ELEVATION:	9100 feet

28 Meyers Cove
Salmon • lat 44°51'00" lon 114°30'00"

DESCRIPTION: This CG is situated in a mixed pine and fir forest. Several creeks in the area for fishing and swimming opportunities. Check for local fishing regulations Supplies available at Salmon. Deer, bears, mountain lions, squirrels, and birds are common to the area. Gather firewood locally. Trails in area.

GETTING THERE: From Salmon go S on US HWY 93 approx. 6 mi. to forest route 021. Go W approx. 19 mi. to forest route 055. Go SW approx. 15 mi. to forest route 108. Go SW on 108 approx. 11 mi. to Meyers Cove CG.

SINGLE RATE:	$4	OPEN DATES:	July-Sept
# of SINGLE SITES:	8	MAX SPUR:	20 feet
		MAX STAY:	14 days
		ELEVATION:	8200 feet

29 Middle Fork Peak
Salmon • lat 44°57'45" lon 114°38'36"

DESCRIPTION: This CG is situated in a mixed conifer forest with Camp Creek flowing nearby. Fish and swim in the creek. Check for local fishing regulations. Supplies are available at Salmon. Deer, bears, and birds are common to the area. Campers may gather their firewood locally. Several trails in the area.

GETTING THERE: From Salmon go S on US HWY 93 approx. 6 mi. to forest route 021. Go W approx. 19 mi. to forest route 055. Go S approx. 12 mi. to forest route 112. Go W approx. 24.5 mi. to Middle Fork Peak CG.

SINGLE RATE:	No fee	OPEN DATES:	July-Nov
# of SINGLE SITES:	3		
		MAX STAY:	14 days
		ELEVATION:	8000 feet

30 Mill Creek
Challis • lat 44°28'21" lon 114°26'25"

DESCRIPTION: This CG is situated in a dense douglas fir, spruce, and willow forest. Fish for trout from Mill Creek. Check for local regulations. Supplies available at Challis. Elk and deer reside in the area. There are no designated trails in the area, just venture off into the forest to explore.

GETTING THERE: From Challis go W on county route approx. 4 mi. to forest route 070. Continue NW on 070 approx. 8 mi. to Mill Creek CG.

SINGLE RATE:	$4	OPEN DATES:	June-Sept
# of SINGLE SITES:	15	MAX SPUR:	35 feet
		MAX STAY:	14 days
		ELEVATION:	7600 feet

 Campground has hosts   **Reservable sites**   **Accessible facilities**   **Fully developed**   **Semi-developed**   **Rustic facilities**

NOTE: Open dates listed are typical. Actual dates are dependent on conditions such as snow pack.

Page 260

31 Morse Creek
Ellis • lat 44°37'30" lon 113°46'30"

DESCRIPTION: This CG is situated on the banks of Morse Creek in a dense douglas fir, spruce, and willow forest. Fish for trout from the creek, please check for localy fishing regulations. Watch for deer, moose, and elk in the area. Supplies are available at Ellis. Morse Creek Trailhead starts on site.

GETTING THERE: From Ellis go SE on county route approx. 10.5 mi. to forest route 094. Go E on 094 approx. 7 mi. to Morse Creek CG.

SINGLE RATE:	No fee	OPEN DATES:	June-Sept
# of SINGLE SITES:	2	MAX SPUR:	16 feet
		MAX STAY:	14 days
		ELEVATION:	6500 feet

32 Mosquito Flat
Challis • lat 44°31'19" lon 114°26'00"

DESCRIPTION: In an open and park-like setting of douglas fir and lodgepole. Fish for rainbow trout from Mosquito Flat Reservoir. Supplies at Challis. Boat ramp at CG. Deer, elk and bear can be found around CG area. Campers may gather firewood. Many trails in the area.

GETTING THERE: From Challis go W on forest route 080 (Challis Creek RD) approx. 20 mi. to Mosquito Flat CG.

SINGLE RATE:	No fee	OPEN DATES:	Yearlong*
# of SINGLE SITES:	12		
		MAX STAY:	14 days
		ELEVATION:	6931 feet

33 Park Creek
Sun Valley • lat 43°50'09" lon 114°15'28"

DESCRIPTION: A secluded and rarely used CG, heavily wooded with sub alpine firs and spruce. Summit Creek is across the road and a nice sized pond is on site for fishing. Supplies at Sun Valley. Deer, elk, and grouse can be seen in the area. Beavers are common at CG pond. Gather firewood. Many trails in the area.

GETTING THERE: From Sun Valley go NE on forest route 408 (Trail Creek Road) approx. 11 mi. to Park Creek CG.

SINGLE RATE:	$4	OPEN DATES:	July-Sept
# of SINGLE SITES:	11	MAX SPUR:	32 feet
GROUP RATE:	$4	MAX STAY:	14 days
# of GROUP SITES:	1	ELEVATION:	7700 feet

34 Phi Kappa
Sun Valley • lat 43°51'31" lon 114°13'05"

DESCRIPTION: CG in a heavily wooded lodgepole forest setting. Summit Creek is nearby for trout fishing. Supplies at Sun Valley. Deer, elk, bears, and grouse in area. Gather firewood locally. Many trails nearby. Good CG for family reunions or larger get togethers. Water is tested drinkable but could be a rusty color.

GETTING THERE: From Sun Valley go NE on forest route 408 (Trail Creek Road) approx. 11 mi. to forest route 208. Continue NE on 208 approx. 3 mi. to Phi Kappa CG.

SINGLE RATE:	$4	OPEN DATES:	July-Sept
# of SINGLE SITES:	21	MAX SPUR:	32 feet
		MAX STAY:	14 days
		ELEVATION:	7100 feet

35  Pole Flat
Stanley • lat 44°17'00" lon 114°43'00"

DESCRIPTION: This CG is situated in an open lodgepole pine forest, with Yankee Fork River nearby. Fish from the river for trout. Check for local regulations. Supplies available at Stanley. Historical Custer Ghost Town within 8 mi. of CG. Deer, elk, goats, and bears are common to the area.

GETTING THERE: From Stanley go E on state HWY 75 (Sawtooth Scenic Route) approx. 12 mi. to forest route 013. Go N on 013 approx. 3 mi. to Pole Flat CG.

SINGLE RATE:	$5	OPEN DATES:	June-Sept
# of SINGLE SITES:	12	MAX SPUR:	32 feet
		MAX STAY:	14 days
		ELEVATION:	6200 feet

36 Sleeping Deer
Challis • lat 44°45'00" lon 114°39'30"

DESCRIPTION: This CG is situated in a douglas fir, spruce, and willow forest. Fish for trout from Rock Lakes nearby. Please check for local fishing regulations. Supplies are available at Challis. Deer, elk, moose, and bears are common to the area. Campers may gather their firewood locally. Several hiking trails in area.

GETTING THERE: From Challis go N and W on county route approx. 8.5 mi. to forest route 086. Continue NW on 086 approx. 26 mi. to Sleeping Deer CG.

SINGLE RATE:	No fee	OPEN DATES:	July-Sept
# of SINGLE SITES:	4		
		MAX STAY:	14 days
		ELEVATION:	9400 feet

37 South Fork Camas
Challis • lat 44°44'00" lon 114°38'00"

DESCRIPTION: This CG is situated in a douglas fir, spruce, and willow forest with views of South Fork Camas Creek. Fish for trout from the creek. Check for local fishing regulations. Supplies at Challis. Deer, elk, moose, and bears can be seen in the area. Gather firewood locally. Trails start at the CG.

GETTING THERE: From Challis go N and W on county route approx. 8.5 mi. to forest route 086. Continue NW on 086 approx. 22 mi. to South Fork Camas CG.

SINGLE RATE:	No fee	OPEN DATES:	July-Sept
# of SINGLE SITES:	3		
		MAX STAY:	14 days
		ELEVATION:	9200 feet

38 Spring Creek
Salmon • lat 43°27'00" lon 111°23'58"

DESCRIPTION: CG is in an open park-like forest setting on the Salmon River. Fish for trout from the banks. Close to the Gold Hill Mine and the town of Shoup. Supplies in Salmon. Deer, bear, and birds are seen. Gather firewood. No designated trails. CG has boat ramp and is a launch point for day raft trips. Rattlesnakes can be a problem.

GETTING THERE: From Salmon go N on US HWY 93 approx. 20 mi. to forest route 030. Go W on 030 approx. 15 mi. to Spring Creek CG.

SINGLE RATE:	No fee	OPEN DATES:	Yearlong*
# of SINGLE SITES:	19	MAX SPUR:	32 feet
		MAX STAY:	14 days
		ELEVATION:	3200 feet

39 Starhope
Sun Valley • lat 43°45'00" lon 114°55'00"

DESCRIPTION: CG in a dense forest of firs, spruce and lodgepoles close to Starhope Creek. Fish for rainbow and brook trout from creek. Supplies at Sun Valley. Elk, deer, bears, and grouse in area. Gather firewood locally. Many trails in the area. CG has central horse corral and hitching rail. This is a busy CG.

GETTING THERE: From Sun Valley go NE on forest route 408 11 mi. to forest route 208. Continue NE on 208 approx. 9 mi. to forest route 135. Go S approx. 11 mi. to forest route 138. Go S on 138 9 mi. to Starhope CG.

SINGLE RATE:	No fee	OPEN DATES:	June-Oct*
# of SINGLE SITES:	21	MAX SPUR:	32 feet
		MAX STAY:	14 days
		ELEVATION:	8000 feet

40 Thatcher Creek
Stanley • lat 44°22'04" lon 115°08'40"

DESCRIPTION: This CG is situated in a lodgepole pine forest with a meadow nearby. Thatcher Creek runs nearby (very small). Supplies are available at Stanley. Several trails in the area lead into high mountain lakes. Check for local fishing regulations. Fly fisherman are attracted to this area.

GETTING THERE: Thatcher Creek CG is located approx. 14 mi. NW of Stanley on state HWY 21 (Ponderosa Pine Scenic Route).

SINGLE RATE:	$5	OPEN DATES:	July-Sept
# of SINGLE SITES:	5	MAX SPUR:	32 feet
		MAX STAY:	14 days
		ELEVATION:	6400 feet

 Campground has hosts   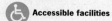 **Reservable sites**   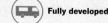 **Accessible facilities**   **Fully developed**   **Semi-developed**   **Rustic facilities**

NOTE: Open dates listed are typical. Actual dates are dependent on conditions such as snow pack.

41 Timber Creek

Goldburg • lat 44°25'00" lon 113°23'30"

DESCRIPTION: CG in a heavily forested setting of lodgepole and spruce bordered by Timber Creek on one side and Little Lost River on the other. Fish for trout from either place. Catch and release only on bull trout. Supplies at Goldburg. Stock loading ramp at CG. Numerous trails cab be found in the vicinity.

GETTING THERE: From Goldburg go S on Pahsimeroi Road approx. 16 mi. to Sawmill Canyon Road. Go NE on Sawmill Canyon Road approx. 5 mi. to forest route 101. Go N on 101 approx. 6.5 mi. to Timber Creek CG.

SINGLE RATE:	$5	OPEN DATES:	June-Oct*
# of SINGLE SITES:	12	MAX SPUR:	32 feet
		MAX STAY:	14 days
		ELEVATION:	8000 feet

42 Tin Cup

Stanley • lat 44°36'30" lon 114°47'30"

DESCRIPTION: This CG is situated in a lodgepole pine forest with Loon Creek running nearby. Fishing and wading in the creek. Please check for local fishing regulations. Supplies are available at Stanley. Campers may gather their firewood locally. Numerous hiking trails can be found in the area.

GETTING THERE: From Stanley go E on state HWY 75 (Sawtooth Scenic Route) approx. 12 mi. to forest route 013. Go N 9 mi. to forest route 172. Go N 18 mi. to forest route 007. Go NE 2 mi. to Tin Cup CG.

SINGLE RATE:	No fee	OPEN DATES:	July-Sept
# of SINGLE SITES:	13	MAX SPUR:	22 feet
		MAX STAY:	14 days
		ELEVATION:	5600 feet

43 Twin Creek

Salmon • lat 45°36'30" lon 113°58'08"

DESCRIPTION: CG in a dense, cool and shady pine forest with Twin Creek running nearby. Fish for small trout from creek. Historical Lewis and Clark route nearby. Supplies available at Salmon. Deer, moose, and bears are common to the area. Campers may gather firewood locally. Day use area within the CG.

GETTING THERE: Twin Creek CG is located approx. 35.5 mi. N of Salmon on US HWY 93.

SINGLE RATE:	$5	OPEN DATES:	June-Oct
# of SINGLE SITES:	40	MAX SPUR:	32 feet
		MAX STAY:	14 days
		ELEVATION:	5100 feet

44 Wallace Lake

Salmon • lat 45°14'51" lon 114°00'18"

DESCRIPTION: This CG is situated in a mixed conifer forest with breath taking views of Wallace Lake. Fish and swim in the lake. Check for local fishing regulations. Supplies are available at Salmon. Deer, bears, and birds are common to the area. Gather firewood locally. Several trails in the area.

GETTING THERE: From Salmon go N on US HWY 93 approx. 4 mi. to forest route 023. Go W on 023 approx. 10 mi. to forest route 020. Go S on 020 approx. 4 mi. to Wallace Lake CG.

SINGLE RATE:	$4	OPEN DATES:	June-Sept
# of SINGLE SITES:	12	MAX SPUR:	20 feet
		MAX STAY:	14 days
		ELEVATION:	8800 feet

45 Wildhorse

Sun Valley • lat 43°49'21" lon 114°05'42"

DESCRIPTION: The most popular CG in the district. Set in a heavily timbered, primarily lodgepole forest with spectacular views. Wildhorse Creek runs adjacent to CG. Fish for trout from the creek. Supplies are available at Sun Valley. Numerous trails for hiking in the area. Gather firewood locally.

GETTING THERE: From Sun Valley go NE on forest route 408 11 mi. to forest route 208. Continue NE on 208 approx. 9 mi. to forest route 135. Go S approx. 1.5 mi. to forest route 136. Go S 5.5 mi. to Wildhorse CG.

SINGLE RATE:	$5	OPEN DATES:	June-Oct
# of SINGLE SITES:	12	MAX SPUR:	22 feet
GROUP RATE:	$5	MAX STAY:	14 days
# of GROUP SITES:	1	ELEVATION:	7400 feet

46 Williams Lake

Salmon • lat 45°01'04" lon 113°58'53"

DESCRIPTION: CG in a mixed conifer forest with views of Williams Lake. Fish for trout, swim, and boat at the lake. Williams Lake Resort is at the SE end of the lake. Supplies at Salmon. Deer, bears, and birds in the area. Thunder Mountain Historical Trail is within a few miles (W) of CG off of forest rout 028.

GETTING THERE: From Salmon go S on US HWY 93 approx. 11.5 mi. to Williams Lake exit. Go W approx. 1.5 mi. to Williams Lake CG.

SINGLE RATE:	No fee	OPEN DATES:	June-Sept
# of SINGLE SITES:	15	MAX STAY:	14 days
		ELEVATION:	4500 feet

47 Yellowjacket Lake

Deep Creek • lat 45°04'00" lon 114°34'00"

DESCRIPTION: CG in a conifer forest on the shores of Yellowjacket Lake, with views of Frog Meadow. Fish for trout or swim from the lake. Supplies at Deep Creek. Deer, bears, and birds are common to the area. Trails in the area, some leading to Clear Creek Trail and into high mountain lakes. Gather firewood locally.

GETTING THERE: From Deep Creek go S on forest route 055 approx. 11 mi. to forest route 112. Go W on 112 approx. 6.5 mi. to forest route 113. Go N on 113 approx. 11 mi. to Yellowjacket Lake CG.

SINGLE RATE:	No fee	OPEN DATES:	June-Sept
# of SINGLE SITES:	6	MAX STAY:	14 days
		ELEVATION:	8000 feet

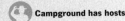 Campground has hosts Reservable sites 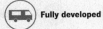 Accessible facilities  Fully developed  Semi-developed Rustic facilities

NOTE: Open dates listed are typical. Actual dates are dependent on conditions such as snow pack.

USFS Photo

SAWTOOTH NATIONAL FOREST

The Sawtooth National Forest encompasses 2.1 million acres of some of the nation's most magnificent country.

Recreational opportunities on the Sawtooth National Forest are unlimited no matter the season. Wintertime offers outstanding experiences for cross-country skiing on both groomed and ungroomed trails. Downhill skiing is offered at four developed winter sports areas that provide some of the finest terrain and snow conditions found anywhere. Snowmobiling is popular with marked and groomed trails and warming huts are available.

Springtime visitors are rewarded with snow-capped mountain peaks, rushing streams and meadows carpeted with hundreds of varieties of wildflowers.

Summer visitors will enjoy swimming, fishing, scenic driving, camping, picnicking, backpacking, photography, and horseback riding. Visitor activities such as guided hikes, campfire programs, auto tours and exhibits are provided throughout the forest.

Fall brings a very pleasant change to the Sawtooth. Spectacular color displays occur in areas where aspen, cottonwood, and willow trees abound.

SAWTOOTH NATIONAL FOREST • IDAHO • LOCATOR MAP

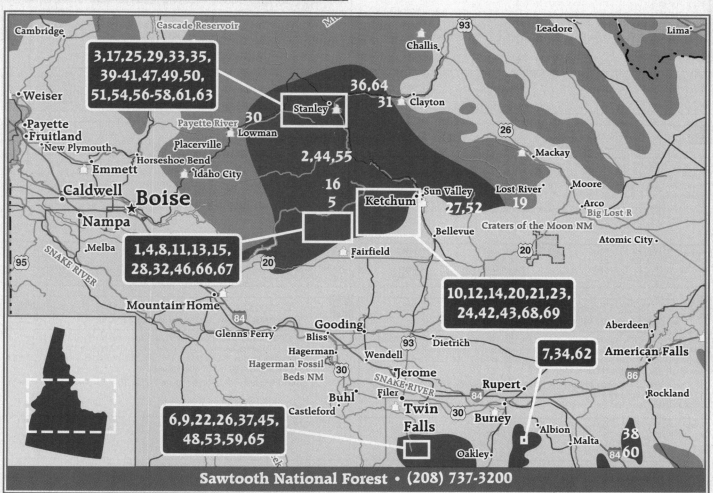

Sawtooth National Forest • (208) 737-3200

1 Abbot
Featherville • lat 43°36'29" lon 115°13'01"

DESCRIPTION: CG set in a pine and fir forest on the banks of the South Fork Boise. Trout fish the river, check for local fishing regulations. Rustic camping with no drinking water on site. Gather firewood locally. Supplies are available in Featherville. Deer and elk reside in the area. No nearby trails.

GETTING THERE: Abbot CG is located approx. 2.5 mi. E of Featherville on forest route 227.

SINGLE RATE:	$2	OPEN DATES:	May-Sept
# of SINGLE SITES:	7	MAX SPUR:	38 feet
		MAX STAY:	14 days
		ELEVATION:	4400 feet

2 Alturas Inlet
Stanley • lat 43°54'24" lon 114°52'39"

DESCRIPTION: CG set on the shores of Alturas Lake, among mixed conifer. Sunny days common. Fish for trout, waterski, sail, boat, and swim on lake. Canoe and fish nearby Perkins Lake. Deer and elk. Amphitheater for interpretive programs. Biking trails nearby. Access to Sawtooth Wilderness at the end of Forest Road 205.

GETTING THERE: From Stanley go S approx. 21 mi. on state route 75 to forest route 205. Go W on 205 approx. 5 mi. to Alturas Inlet CG.

SINGLE RATE:	Varies	OPEN DATES:	June-Sept
# of SINGLE SITES:	55	MAX SPUR:	30 feet
		MAX STAY:	14 days
		ELEVATION:	7032 feet

3 Basin Creek
Stanley • lat 44°15'48" lon 114°49'07"

DESCRIPTION: CG situated in an open marshlike meadow at the confluence of Salmon River and Basin Creek. Fish for trout and steelhead, check local regulations. Deer, elk, and coyotes reside in the area. Access to Frank Church River of No Return Wilderness (N) or White Cloud Peaks (S). Bike and OHV use areas.

GETTING THERE: Basin Creek CG is located approx. 9 mi. NE of Stanley on state HWY 75.

SINGLE RATE:	Varies	OPEN DATES:	May-Sept
# of SINGLE SITES:	15	MAX SPUR:	20 feet
		MAX STAY:	10 days
		ELEVATION:	6100 feet

4 Baumgartner
Featherville • lat 43°36'21" lon 115°04'31"

DESCRIPTION: CG set in pine and fir forest on the South Fork Boise. Trout fish the river. Gather firewood locally. Supplies are available in Featherville. Deer and elk reside in the area. Short interpretive trail on site. Access to a popular motorized trail to Iron Mountain Lookout. Some pull-through sites.

GETTING THERE: Baumgartner CG is located approx. 11 mi. E of Featherville on forest route 227.

SINGLE RATE:	$10	OPEN DATES:	May-Sept
# of SINGLE SITES:	31	MAX SPUR:	27 feet
GROUP RATE:	$40	MAX STAY:	14 days
# of GROUP SITES:	1	ELEVATION:	5100 feet

5 Bear Creek Transfer Camp
Fairfield • lat 43°43'30" lon 115°63'30"

DESCRIPTION: CG is a rustic horse camp in an open setting, used primarily for horse transfer. Corrals, mangers, a barrier free stock loading ramp, and toilets are available. Dispersed sites. Gather firewood locally. Deer and elk reside in the area. Busy hunting season. Horse trails accessible nearby.

GETTING THERE: From Fairfield go N on forest route 094 approx. 18 mi. to forest route 227. Go N 6 mi. to forest route 012. Go NE approx. 10 mi., taking the left fork at end of road, to Bear Creek Transfer Camp CG.

SINGLE RATE:	No fee	OPEN DATES:	June-Sept
# of SINGLE SITES:	5	MAX SPUR:	38 feet
		MAX STAY:	14 days
		ELEVATION:	5300 feet

6 Bear Gulch
Hansen • lat 42°13'41" lon 114°22'46"

DESCRIPTION: This CG is situated in high desert among pine, aspen, and sagebrush. Set on Shoshone Creek. Good trout fishing in creek. Gather firewood locally. Supplies in Hansen. Deer and elk in area. Horse facilities available. Horse, hiking, and mountain bike trails. ATV roads available, check with map.

GETTING THERE: From Hansen go S on forest route 515 approx. 28 mi. to forest route 500. Go W on 500 approx. 8.5 mi. to forest route 513. Go N on 513 approx. 1 mi. to Bear Gulch CG. 4WD recommended.

SINGLE RATE:	Varies	OPEN DATES:	June-Sept
# of SINGLE SITES:	10	MAX STAY:	14 days
GROUP RATE:	Varies	ELEVATION:	5960 feet
# of GROUP SITES:	1		

7 Bennett Springs
Albion • lat 42°09'57" lon 114°10'05"

DESCRIPTION: CG set on a small stream among pine and fir. Limited trout fishing on the stream, check local regulations No drinking water available on site. Gather firewood locally. Light use, filling during fall hunting season. Deer and elk in area. Access to Howell Canyon Trails. Hiking, mountain bike, and nordic trails.

GETTING THERE: From Albion go SE on state HWY 77 approx. 5.5 mi. to forest route 549. Go W on 549 approx. 5 mi. to Bennett Springs CG.

SINGLE RATE:	No fee	OPEN DATES:	June-Oct
# of SINGLE SITES:	6	MAX SPUR:	40 feet
		MAX STAY:	14 days
		ELEVATION:	7000 feet

8 Bird Creek
Featherville • lat 43°37'14" lon 115°10'29"

DESCRIPTION: CG set in a fir and pine forest on the banks of the South Fork Boise. Trout fish the river, please check for local fishing regulations. Rustic camping with no drinking water on site. Gather firewood locally. Supplies are available in Featherville. Deer and elk reside in the area. No nearby trails.

GETTING THERE: Bird Creek CG is located approx. 5 mi. E of Featherville on forest route 227.

SINGLE RATE:	$2	OPEN DATES:	May-Sept
# of SINGLE SITES:	5	MAX SPUR:	38 feet
		MAX STAY:	14 days
		ELEVATION:	4680 feet

9 Bostetter
Oakley • lat 42°09'57" lon 114°10'05"

DESCRIPTION: This CG is situated in a high elevation pine forest. Trout fishing oppotunities nearby, check for localy regulations. Supplies in Oakley. Gather firewood locally. Deer and elk reside in the area. Horse, hiking, and mountain bike trails can be found nearby. ATV roads available, see FS map for use.

GETTING THERE: From Oakley go W on forest route 500 approx. 21 mi. to Bostetter CG.

SINGLE RATE:	Varies	OPEN DATES:	June-Sept
# of SINGLE SITES:	18	MAX SPUR:	20 feet
GROUP RATE:	Varies	MAX STAY:	14 days
# of GROUP SITES:	1	ELEVATION:	7160 feet

10 Boundary
Sun Valley • lat 43°43'18" lon 114°19'29"

DESCRIPTION: CG situated among cottonwoods has been newly remodeled. Fish for trout nearby, check local regulations. Close to Sun Valley. Gather firewood locally. Deer, elk, and small wildlife in area. Horse, hiking and mountain bike trails accessible nearby. ATV roads and trails available, see FS map for use.

GETTING THERE: Boundary CG is located approx. 2 mi. NE of Sun Valley on forest route 408.

SINGLE RATE:	$9	OPEN DATES:	June-Nov
# of SINGLE SITES:	6	MAX SPUR:	30 feet
		MAX STAY:	3 days
		ELEVATION:	6100 feet

 Campground has hosts   **Reservable sites**   **Accessible facilities**   **Fully developed**   **Semi-developed**   **Rustic facilities**

NOTE: Open dates listed are typical. Actual dates are dependent on conditions such as snow pack.

Page 264

11 Bounds
Featherville • lat 43°36'00" lon 115°52'30"

DESCRIPTION: This CG is situated in a pine and fir forest on the banks of the Big Smokey River and South Fork Boise River. Trout fish the rivers, check for local fishing regulations. Gather firewood locally. Supplies are available in Featherville. Deer and elk reside in the area. No nearby trails.

GETTING THERE: Bounds CG is located approx. 23 mi. E of Featherville on forest route 227.

SINGLE RATE:	$6	OPEN DATES:	May-Sept
# of SINGLE SITES:	12	MAX SPUR:	38 feet
		MAX STAY:	14 days
		ELEVATION:	5500 feet

12 Bridge
Hailey • lat 43°31'34" lon 114°28'48"

DESCRIPTION: CG set among cottonwoods on the banks of a small creek. Trout fishing, please check for local regulations. Supplies are available in Hiley. Gather firewood locally. Deer and elk reside in the area. Horse, hiking and mountain bike trails nearby. ATV roads and trails available, see FS map for use.

GETTING THERE: From Hiley go N on state HWY 75 approx. 2 mi. to forest route 097. Go W on 097 approx. 10 mi. to Bridge CG.

SINGLE RATE:	No fee	OPEN DATES:	June-Oct
# of SINGLE SITES:	3		
		MAX STAY:	14 days
		ELEVATION:	5600 feet

13 Canyon
Fairfield • lat 43°37'41" lon 114°51'29"

DESCRIPTION: CG is set in a pine and fir forest on the Big Smokey River. Trout fish the river, check for local regulations. Gather firewood locally. Supplies in Featherville. Deer and elk reside in the area. Access to Big Smokey Trail system for motorized and non-motorized trails (consult Ranger District).

GETTING THERE: From Fairfield go N on forest route 094 approx. 18 mi. to forest route 227. Go N on 227 approx. 6 mi. to forest route 085. Go NE on 085 approx. 3 mi. to Canyon CG.

SINGLE RATE:	$4	OPEN DATES:	May-Sept
# of SINGLE SITES:	6	MAX SPUR:	38 feet
		MAX STAY:	14 days
		ELEVATION:	5500 feet

14 Caribou
Ketchum • lat 43°48'30" lon 114°25'30"

DESCRIPTION: CG in a pine overstory in Northfork Canyon. Fishing in Murdock Creek or hike to Amber Lakes and over the Boulder Mountains. SNRA visitor center nearby. Deer, elk, and coyotes in area. Gather firewood locally. Supplies in Ketchum. Dump station, drinking water, and interpretive programs 2 mi. away.

GETTING THERE: From Ketchum go N on state route 75 approx. 8 mi. to forest route 146. Go N on 146 approx. 3 mi., staying left, to Caribou CG.

SINGLE RATE:	Varies	OPEN DATES:	May-Sept
# of SINGLE SITES:	7		
		MAX STAY:	14 days
		ELEVATION:	6560 feet

15 Chapparal
Featherville • lat 43°36'52" lon 115°12'09"

DESCRIPTION: CG set in a pine and fir forest on the banks of the South Fork Boise. Trout fish the river, check local regulations. Rustic camping with no drinking water on site. Gather firewood locally. Supplies are available in Featherville. Deer and elk reside in the area. A trailhead begins approx. 1 mi. from CG.

GETTING THERE: Chapparal CG is located approx. 3.5 mi. E of Featherville on forest route 227.

SINGLE RATE:	$2	OPEN DATES:	May-Sept
# of SINGLE SITES:	7	MAX SPUR:	38 feet
		MAX STAY:	14 days
		ELEVATION:	4600 feet

16 Chemeketen Group
Ketchum • lat 43°49'30" lon 114°44'30"

DESCRIPTION: CG set in a secluded, remote area with a lodgepole pine overstory. Fish for trout and steelhead in nearby Salmon River. Pack in/out. Deer, elk, and coyotes. Supplies in Ketchum. Hike the Idaho Centennial Trail. Biking or winter sports use also. If no group events, may be used by other campers.

GETTING THERE: From Ketchum go N approx. 34 mi. on state route 75 to Galena Summit. From Galena Summit go S on Forest route 215 approx. 3 mi. to Chemeketan Group CG.

GROUP RATE:	Varies	OPEN DATES:	June-Sept
# of GROUP SITES:	1	MAX SPUR:	30 feet
		MAX STAY:	14 days
		ELEVATION:	6500 feet

17 Chinook Bay
Stanley • lat 44°09'32" lon 114°54'43"

DESCRIPTION: CG in a lodgepole pine overstory on Redfish Lake Creek near Little Redfish Lake. Fish for rainbows. Non-motorized boating and floating; boat ramp. Horse stables, boat rentals, and dump station at visitor's center. Deer, elk, and coyotes. Winter XC ski trails. Hiking, biking, and horse trails nearby.

GETTING THERE: From Stanley go S on state HWY 75 approx. 4.5 mi. to forest route 214. Go SW on 214 approx. 1/2 mi. to Chinook Bay CG. (Located on the N shore of Little Redfish Lake.)

SINGLE RATE:	Varies	OPEN DATES:	May-Sept
# of SINGLE SITES:	13	MAX SPUR:	20 feet
		MAX STAY:	10 days
		ELEVATION:	6500 feet

18 Clear Creek
Strevell • lat 41°57'17" lon 113°19'02"

DESCRIPTION: CG set on the banks of Clear Creek, among pine and fir. Trout fishing in creek. No drinking water available on site. Gather firewood locally. Deer and elk reside in the area. Fills most weekends. Supplies in Strevell. Both hiking and ATV trails to Raft River Mountain, a 12 mile loop.

GETTING THERE: From Strevell go W on county route approx. 3.5 mi. to county route. Go S on county route approx. 3 mi. to forest route 001. Go W on 001 approx. 3 mi. to Clear Creek CG.

SINGLE RATE:	No fee	OPEN DATES:	June-Oct
# of SINGLE SITES:	12	MAX SPUR:	45 feet
		MAX STAY:	14 days
		ELEVATION:	5500 feet

19 Copper Creek
Bellevue • lat 43°36'00" lon 113°54'00"

DESCRIPTION: This CG is situated among aspen. Trout fishing nearby, check for local fishing regulations. Supplies are available in Bellevue. Gather firewood locally. Deer and elk reside in the area. Horse, hiking, and mountain bike trails nearby. Designated ATV roads and trails available, see FS map for use.

GETTING THERE: Copper Creek CG is located approx. 24 mi. E of Bellevue on forest route 134.

SINGLE RATE:	No fee	OPEN DATES:	May-Oct*
# of SINGLE SITES:	5		
		MAX STAY:	16 days
		ELEVATION:	6400 feet

20 Cottonwood
Ketchum • lat 43°39'27" lon 114°27'28"

DESCRIPTION: This CG is situated on the banks of a small stream in a forested area. No drinking water, no services. Fish the stream. Fills most days all summer. Gather firewood locally. Deer and elk in area. Horse, hiking, and mountain bike trails. Designated ATV roads and trails available, see FS map for use.

GETTING THERE: Cottonwood CG is located approx. 6 mi. W of Ketchum on forest route 227.

SINGLE RATE:	No fee	OPEN DATES:	May-Oct
# of SINGLE SITES:	1		
		MAX STAY:	3 days
		ELEVATION:	6000 feet

 Campground has hosts   **Reservable sites**   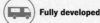 **Accessible facilities**   **Fully developed**   **Semi-developed**   **Rustic facilities**

NOTE: Open dates listed are typical. Actual dates are dependent on conditions such as snow pack.

21 Deer Creek
Hailey • lat 43˚31'44" lon 114˚30'07"

DESCRIPTION: This CG is situated in a pine forest. Trout fishing opportunities nearby, check for local regulations. Supplies are available in Hailey. Gather firewood locally. Deer and elk reside in the area. Horse, hiking, and mountain bike trails. Designated ATV roads available, see FS map for use.

GETTING THERE: From Hailey go N on state HWY 75 approx. 2.5 mi. to forest route 097. Go W on 097 approx. 9 mi. to Deer Creek CG.

SINGLE RATE:	No fee	OPEN DATES:	June-Oct
# of SINGLE SITES:	3		
		MAX STAY:	16 days
		ELEVATION:	6020 feet

22 Diamondfield Jack
Hansen • lat 42˚10'30" lon 114˚17'15"

DESCRIPTION: This CG's purpose is primarily for winter sports. Set in a pine forest, with no nearby fishing. A large enclosed warming hut is available. Gather firewood locally. Supplies in Hansen. Deer and elk reside in the area. Horse, hiking, and mountain bike trails. ATV roads available, see FS map for use.

GETTING THERE: From Hansen go S on forest route 515 approx. 26.5 mi. to Diamondfield Jack CG.

SINGLE RATE:	Varies	OPEN DATES:	Yearlong
# of SINGLE SITES:	8	MAX SPUR:	25 feet
GROUP RATE:	Varies	MAX STAY:	14 days
# of GROUP SITES:	1	ELEVATION:	7000 feet

23 Easley
Ketchum • lat 43˚46'44" lon 114˚32'06"

DESCRIPTION: CG straddles the Big Wood River. Vegetation primarily aspen and cotton-woods. Fish the river, check for local regulations Supplies in Ketchum. Hot springs swimming pool at adjacent Easley Resort. Deer, elk, and coyotes reside in the area. Access to Harrimon Trail. Several hiking and bike trails nearby.

GETTING THERE: From Ketchum go N on state route 75 approx. 14 mi. to turnoff (signs). Go S approx 1/2 mi. further on 75 to Easley CG.

SINGLE RATE:	Varies	OPEN DATES:	June-Sept
# of SINGLE SITES:	20	MAX SPUR:	20 feet
GROUP RATE:	Varies	MAX STAY:	14 days
# of GROUP SITES:	2	ELEVATION:	6800 feet

24 East Fork Baker Creek
Ketchum • lat 43˚44'50" lon 114˚33'49"

DESCRIPTION: This CG is situated in a pine forest. Trout fishing opportunities nearby. Supplies can be found in Ketchum. Gather firewood locally. Deer, elk, and small wildlife in area. Adjacent horse, hiking, and mountain bike trails. Designated ATV roads and trails available, see FS map for use.

GETTING THERE: From Ketchum go N on state HWY 75 (Sawtooth Scenic Route) approx. 15 mi. to forest route 162. Go S on 162 approx. 3 mi. to East Fork Baker Creek CG.

SINGLE RATE:	No fee	OPEN DATES:	June-Nov
# of SINGLE SITES:	2		
		MAX STAY:	16 days
		ELEVATION:	6920 feet

25 Elk Creek
Stanley • lat 44˚24'55" lon 115˚28'09"

DESCRIPTION: CG set in a lodgepole pine overstory. Short walk in. Fly fishing for trout on nearby Valley Creek, check local regulations. Watch for birds, moose, and elk in the meadow. The 3 individual sites may be combined to make 1 group site. Supplies are available in Stanley. Hiking and biking trails nearby.

GETTING THERE: Elk Creek CG is located approx. 8 mi. NW of Stanley on state HWY 21.

SINGLE RATE:	Varies	OPEN DATES:	May-Sept
# of SINGLE SITES:	3		
GROUP RATE:	Varies	MAX STAY:	14 days
# of GROUP SITES:	1	ELEVATION:	7000 feet

26 Father and Sons
Oakley • lat 42˚09'47" lon 114˚11'05"

DESCRIPTION: This CG is situated in a high elevation pine forest. Trout fishing opportunities nearby, check for localy regulations. Supplies in Oakley. Gather firewood locally. Deer and elk reside in the area. Horse, hiking, and mountain bike trails can be found nearby. ATV roads available, see FS map for use.

GETTING THERE: From Oakley go W on forest route 500 approx. 21 mi. to Father and Sons CG.

SINGLE RATE:	Varies	OPEN DATES:	June-Sept
# of SINGLE SITES:	19	MAX SPUR:	25 feet
GROUP RATE:	Varies	MAX STAY:	14 days
# of GROUP SITES:	1	ELEVATION:	7320 feet

27 Federal Gulch
Gimlet • lat 43˚40'08" lon 114˚09'08"

DESCRIPTION: This CG is set in a pine forest with limited fishing nearby. Horse facilities available. Supplies are available in Gimlet. Gather firewood locally. Deer and elk reside in the area. Horse and hiking trailhead on site. Designated ATV and mountain bike roads and trails available, see FS map for use.

GETTING THERE: From Gimlet go E on forest route 124 approx. 8 mi. to forest route 118. Go NE on 118 approx. 4 mi. to Federal Gulch CG.

SINGLE RATE:	No fee	OPEN DATES:	May-Oct
# of SINGLE SITES:	3		
		MAX STAY:	16 days
		ELEVATION:	6800 feet

28 Five Points
Fairfield • lat 43˚32'32" lon 114˚49'03"

DESCRIPTION: This CG is situated in a pine and fir forest. Set near the little Smokey River (1/2 mi.). Trout fish the river, check for local regulations. Rustic camping with no drinking water on site. Gather firewood locally. Supplies are available in Fairfield. Deer and elk reside in the area. No nearby trails.

GETTING THERE: Five Points CG is located approx. 17.5 mi. NW of Fairfield on forest route 094.

SINGLE RATE:	No fee	OPEN DATES:	May-Sept
# of SINGLE SITES:	3	MAX SPUR:	38 feet
		MAX STAY:	14 days
		ELEVATION:	5880 feet

29 Glacier View
Stanley • lat 44˚08'52" lon 114˚54'40"

DESCRIPTION: CG set among lodgepole pine on Redfish Lake. Boat ramp at Sandy Beach. Ski, sail, swim, canoe, motorboat, and trout fish the lake. Deer, elk, and coyotes in area. Idaho Centennial Trail and access to Sawtooth Wilderness nearby. Horse stables, dump station, boat rentals, and play ground available.

GETTING THERE: From Stanley go S on state HWY 75 approx. 4.5 mi. to forest route 214. Go SW on 214 approx. 2.5 mi. to Glacier View CG. (Located on the N shore of Little Redfish Lake.)

SINGLE RATE:	Varies	OPEN DATES:	June-Sept
# of SINGLE SITES:	65	MAX SPUR:	20 feet
		MAX STAY:	14 days
# of GROUP SITES:	8	ELEVATION:	6500 feet

30 Grandjean
Stanley • lat 44˚08'55" lon 115˚09'04"

DESCRIPTION: CG set among old growth ponderosa pine. Fish the South Fork of the Payette River. Deer, elk, and coyotes in area. Hot Springs 1.5 mi. away at Sawtooth Lodge. Swimming 1 mi. away. Provides ten horse sites. Several horse and hiking trails meander along Payette River, with access to Sawtooth Wilderness.

GETTING THERE: From Stanley go NW-then-S on state route 21 approx. 36 mi. to forest route 524. Go E on 524 approx. 7 mi to forest route 824 (Sawtooth Lodge, left) to Grandjean CG.

SINGLE RATE:	$10	OPEN DATES:	May-Sept
# of SINGLE SITES:	31		
		MAX STAY:	14 days
		ELEVATION:	5200 feet

 **Campground has hosts**   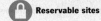 **Reservable sites**   **Accessible facilities**   **Fully developed**   **Semi-developed**   **Rustic facilities**

31 Holman Creek
Stanley • lat 44°14'57" lon 114°31'44"

DESCRIPTION: This CG is divided by a creek at the base of a tree covered rock slope. Excellent trout and steelhead fishing on nearby Salmon River. Please check local fishing regulations. Supplies are available in Stanley. Deer, elk, and coyotes reside in the area. Trail leads S on Holman Creek.

GETTING THERE: From Stanley go approx. 28 mi. NE on state route 75 to Holman Creek CG.

SINGLE RATE:	$11	**OPEN DATES:**	**May-Sept**
# of SINGLE SITES:	10	**MAX SPUR:**	**20 feet**
		MAX STAY:	**10 days**
		ELEVATION:	**5600 feet**

36 Lower O'Brien
Stanley • lat 44°15'27" lon 114°41'39"

DESCRIPTION: CG set among lodgepole pine on the Salmon River. Nearby Indian Riffles Overlook with fantastic views of Salmon River. Fish for steelhead and trout on river. Historic mining area. Deer, elk, and coyotes in area. Nearby Warm Springs Creek Trail leads to Garland Lakes. Closes August 15, for revegetation.

GETTING THERE: From Stanley go NE approx. 14 mi on state route 75 to forest route 454. Go S on 454 (Robinson Bar Road) to Lower O'Brien CG. RVs not recommended.

SINGLE RATE:	$11	**OPEN DATES:**	**May-Sept**
# of SINGLE SITES:	10		
		MAX STAY:	**10 days**
		ELEVATION:	**5800 feet**

32 Hunter Creek Transfer Camp
Fairfield • lat 43°26'30" lon 115°07'30"

DESCRIPTION: CG is a rustic horse camp in an open setting, used primarily for horse transfer. Corrals, mangers, a barrier free stock loading ramp, and toilets are available. Dispersed sites. Gather firewood locally. Deer and elk reside in the area. Busy hunting season. Horse trails accessible nearby.

GETTING THERE: From Fairfield go W on state HWY 20 approx. 8 mi. to the forest route 055. Go W approx. 6 mi. to Cow Creek Reservoir. Continue NW on 055 approx. 6 mi. to Hunter Creek Transfer Camp CG.

SINGLE RATE:	No fee	**OPEN DATES:**	**May-Nov**
# of SINGLE SITES:	3	**MAX SPUR:**	**38 feet**
GROUP RATE:	No fee	**MAX STAY:**	**14 days**
# of GROUP SITES:	1	**ELEVATION:**	**5600 feet**

37 Lower Penstemon
Hansen • lat 42°11'48" lon 114°16'57"

DESCRIPTION: CG set on the banks of a small stream. Situated in a high desert of aspen, willows, birch, and junipers. Fish for trout in stream. Gather firewood locally. Supplies in Hansen. Deer and elk reside in the area. Horse, hiking, and mountain bike trails. ATV roads available, see FS map for use.

GETTING THERE: From Hansen go S on forest route 515 approx. 24 mi. to Lower Penstemon CG.

SINGLE RATE:	Varies	**OPEN DATES:**	**Yearlong**
# of SINGLE SITES:	10	**MAX SPUR:**	**20 feet**
GROUP RATE:	Varies	**MAX STAY:**	**14 days**
# of GROUP SITES:	2	**ELEVATION:**	**6600 feet**

33 Iron Creek
Stanley • lat 44°11'56" lon 115°00'32"

DESCRIPTION: CG set in an overstory of lodgepole pine on Iron Creek. Fish creek for cutthroat, check regulations. Supplies in Stanley. Deer, elk, and coyotes in area. Easy hike to Sawtooth Lake at base of Mount Regan. Trail loops around Grandjean CG branching S and E for more alpine lakes. May be wet in late spring.

GETTING THERE: From Stanley go NW on state HWY 21 approx. 2.5 mi. to forest route 619. Go S on 619 approx. 4 mi. to Iron Creek CG.

SINGLE RATE:	$11	**OPEN DATES:**	**May-Sept**
# of SINGLE SITES:	9	**MAX SPUR:**	**20 feet**
		MAX STAY:	**14 days**
		ELEVATION:	**6704 feet**

38 Mill Flat
Rockland • lat 42°26'00" lon 113°00'15"

DESCRIPTION: CG situated in a pine and fir forest. No nearby fishing. No drinking water. Gather firewood locally. Supplies in Rockland. Fills most weekends. Deer and elk in area. Trailhead facilities for both motorized and non-motorized use. Networked trails, contact the Ranger District for info. and maps.

GETTING THERE: From Rockland go W and S on Houtz Canyon Road approx. 10 mi. to forest route 577. Continue S on 577 approx. 5.5 mi. to forest route 565. Go N on 565 approx. 1/2 mi. to Mill Flat CG.

SINGLE RATE:	No fee	**OPEN DATES:**	**June-Oct**
# of SINGLE SITES:	6	**MAX SPUR:**	**50 feet**
		MAX STAY:	**14 days**
		ELEVATION:	**5500 feet**

34 Lake Cleveland
Albion • lat 42°19'30" lon 113°38'30"

DESCRIPTION: CG set on a lake surrounded by fir and pine. Fish for planted trout. Supplies are available in Albion. Gather firewood locally. Fills most weekends. Deer and elk reside in the area. Hiking, mountain bike, and nordic trails. A barrier free trail around the lake and self-guided trails nearby.

GETTING THERE: From Albion go SE on state HWY 77 approx. 5.5 mi. to forest route 549. Go W on 549 approx. 8.5 mi. to Lake Cleveland CG.

SINGLE RATE:	$5	**OPEN DATES:**	**June-Oct**
# of SINGLE SITES:	15	**MAX SPUR:**	**50 feet**
		MAX STAY:	**14 days**
		ELEVATION:	**8200 feet**

39 Mormon Bend
Stanley • lat 44°15'42" lon 114°50'28"

DESCRIPTION: This CG is situated in a meadow among lodgepole pine and sagebrush. Set on the Salmon River with trout and steelhead fishing, check local regulations. A designated put-in for the Salmon River. Deer, elk, and coyotes reside in the area. Supplies are available in Stanley. No nearby trails.

GETTING THERE: Mormon Bend CG is located approx. 8 mi. NE of Stanley on state HWY 75.

SINGLE RATE:	$11	**OPEN DATES:**	**May-Oct**
# of SINGLE SITES:	15	**MAX SPUR:**	**20 feet**
		MAX STAY:	**10 days**
		ELEVATION:	**6200 feet**

35 Lakeview
Stanley • lat 30°15'00" lon 115°02'30"

DESCRIPTION: CG set on the shores of Stanley Lake with a lodgepole pine overstory. Fish for rainbow and lake trout. Sail, motorboat, or swim in the lake. Deer, elk, and coyotes in area. Trailhead for Idaho Centennial Trail nearby leads through a lake-filled region of Sawtooth Wilderness. Gather firewood locally.

GETTING THERE: From Stanley go NW on state HWY 21 approx. 5 mi. to forest route 455. Go W on 455 approx. 3.5 mi. to Lakeview CG. (Located on the N shore of Stanley Lake.)

SINGLE RATE:	Varies	**OPEN DATES:**	**May-Sept**
# of SINGLE SITES:	6	**MAX SPUR:**	**20 feet**
		MAX STAY:	**14 days**
		ELEVATION:	**6537 feet**

40 Mount Heyburn
Stanley • lat 44°07'54" lon 114°55'19"

DESCRIPTION: CG in overstory of lodgepole pine near Redfish Lake. Trout fish the lake or walk W into Sawtooth Wilderness for wild cutthroat. Deer & elk in area. Swim, sail, ski, canoe, & motorboat (boat ramp available). Horse stables, boat rentals, & dump station at Redfish Lodge. Horse & hike nearby Idaho Centennial Trail.

GETTING THERE: From Stanley go S on state HWY 75 approx. 4.5 mi. to forest route 214. Go SW on 214 approx. 3 mi. to Mount Heyburn CG. (Located on the N shore of Little Redfish Lake.)

SINGLE RATE:	Varies	**OPEN DATES:**	**June-Sept**
# of SINGLE SITES:	20	**MAX SPUR:**	**20 feet**
		MAX STAY:	**10 days**
		ELEVATION:	**6500 feet**

 Campground has hosts　 **Reservable sites**　 **Accessible facilities**　 **Fully developed**　 **Semi-developed**　 **Rustic facilities**

NOTE: Open dates listed are typical. Actual dates are dependent on conditions such as snow pack.

SAWTOOTH NATIONAL FOREST • IDAHO • 31 — 40

41 Mountain View
Stanley • lat 44°09'25" lon 114°54'40"

DESCRIPTION: CG in a lodgepole pine overstory on Redfish Lake Creek near Little Redfish Lake. Fish for rainbows. Non-motorized boating and floating; boat ramp. Horse stables, boat rentals, and dump station at visitor's center. Deer, elk, and coyotes. Winter XC ski trails. Hiking, biking, and horse trails nearby.

GETTING THERE: From Stanley go S on state HWY 75 approx. 4.5 mi. to forest route 214. Go SW on 214 approx. 1 mi. to Mountain View CG. (Located on the E shore of Little Redfish Lake.)

SINGLE RATE:	$13	OPEN DATES:	June-Sept
# of SINGLE SITES:	7	MAX SPUR:	20 feet
		MAX STAY:	10 days
		ELEVATION:	6500 feet

42 Murdock
Ketchum • lat 43°48'13" lon 114°25'10"

DESCRIPTION: Set in pine overstory in Northfork Canyon. Fish Murdock Creek. Moose frequent marshy areas of canyon. Deer, elk and small wildlife. Hiking and biking trails nearby. Scenic area. Gather firewood locally. Supplies in Ketchum.

GETTING THERE: From Ketchum go N on state route 75 approx. 8 mi. to forest road 146 (right at SNRA HQ office). Go N on 146 approx. 2 mi. to Murdock CG.

SINGLE RATE:	$11	OPEN DATES:	May-Sept
# of SINGLE SITES:	5	MAX SPUR:	20 feet
		MAX STAY:	14 days
		ELEVATION:	6200 feet

43 North Fork
Ketchum • lat 43°47'16" lon 114°25'29"

DESCRIPTION: On edge of Big Wood River in aspen and cottonwood setting. Fishing the river. Buy firewood. Basic supplies at nearby store. Elk, deer, moose and small wildlife in area. Trails in Northfork Canyon to Amber Lakes and Boulder Mountains. Nearby visitor center has dump station, exhibits and programs.

GETTING THERE: From Ketchum go N on state route 75 approx. 8 mi. to North Fork CG. (CG is first CG on S side of HWY past the SNRA HQs.)

SINGLE RATE:	Varies	OPEN DATES:	May-Sept
# of SINGLE SITES:	29	MAX SPUR:	20 feet
		MAX STAY:	14 days
		ELEVATION:	6280 feet

44 North Shore
Stanley • lat 43°55'08" lon 114°51'57"

DESCRIPTION: A quiet CG overlooking Alturas Lake, situated among mixed conifer. Trout fish, ski, sail, motorboat, and swim on the lake. Canoe and fish nearby Perkins Lake. Deer and elk in area. Amphitheater complete with programs. Horse and hiking trails available at the end of FS road 205 lead into Sawtooth Wilderness.

GETTING THERE: From Stanley go S approx. 21 mi. on state route 75 to forest route 205. Go W on 205 approx. 3 mi. to North Shore CG.

SINGLE RATE:	Varies	OPEN DATES:	June-Sept
# of SINGLE SITES:	15	MAX SPUR:	20 feet
		MAX STAY:	14 days
		ELEVATION:	7044 feet

45 Pettit
Hansen • lat 42°10'58" lon 114°16'53"

DESCRIPTION: This CG is situated among lodgepole pine in a high desert. Stream fish for trout nearby. Supplies are available in Hansen. Gather firewood locally. Deer and elk reside in the area. Horse, hiking, and mountain bike trails can be found nearby. ATV roads available, see FS map for use.

GETTING THERE: From Hansen go S on forest route 515 approx. 25.5 mi. to Pettit CG.

SINGLE RATE:	Varies	OPEN DATES:	June-Sept
# of SINGLE SITES:	7		
		MAX STAY:	14 days
		ELEVATION:	6800 feet

46 Pioneer
Fairfield • lat 43°29'30" lon 114°48'30"

DESCRIPTION: This CG is situated in a pine and fir forest on the banks of Solider Creel. No nearby fishing. Potable water is available on site. Supplies can be found in Fairfield. Campers may gather their firewood locally. Hiking, mountain bike, and horse trails, as well as a ski area, are accessible nearby.

GETTING THERE: From Fairfield go N on forest route 094 approx. 10 mi. to forest route 093. Go NW on 093 approx. 2 mi. to Pioneer CG.

SINGLE RATE:	No fee	OPEN DATES:	May-Sept
# of SINGLE SITES:	4	MAX SPUR:	38 feet
		MAX STAY:	14 days
		ELEVATION:	6500 feet

47 Point
Stanley • lat 44°08'08" lon 114°55'54"

DESCRIPTION: CG set in a pine forest on Redfish Lake. Trout fish the lake; boat ramp at Sandy Beach. Sail, ski, swim, canoe, & motorboat the lake. Horse stables & boat rentals at Redfish Lake Lodge. 8 walk-in tent sites; carts available for gear transportation. Deer and elk reside in the area. Closed Mondays after July 4.

GETTING THERE: From Stanley go S on state HWY 75 approx. 1.5 mi. to forest route 214. Go SW on 214 approx. 2.5 mi. to Point CG. (Located on the N shore of Little Redfish Lake.)

SINGLE RATE:	$13	OPEN DATES:	June-Sept
# of SINGLE SITES:	17	MAX SPUR:	20 feet
		MAX STAY:	14 days
		ELEVATION:	6500 feet

48   Porcupine Springs
Hansen • lat 42°05'43" lon 111°31'03"

DESCRIPTION: CG situated among lodgepole pine, used primarily as a horse camp. Trout fishing opportunities nearby. Supplies in Hansen. Gather firewood locally. Deer and elk can be seen in the area. Horse, hiking, and mountain bike trails. ATV roads available, see FS map for use. Group site for up to 240 persons.

GETTING THERE: From Hansen go S on forest route 515 approx. 26.5 mi. to forest route 500. Go E on 500 approx. 1 mi. to Porcupine Springs CG.

SINGLE RATE:	Varies	OPEN DATES:	June-Sept
# of SINGLE SITES:	5	MAX SPUR:	20 feet
GROUP RATE:	Varies	MAX STAY:	14 days
# of GROUP SITES:	1	ELEVATION:	6950 feet

49 Redfish Outlet
Stanley • lat 44°08'21" lon 114°55'03"

DESCRIPTION: CG set in lodgepole pine on Redfish Lake. Trout fish the lake. Access into Sawtooth Wilderness for cutthroat in alpine lakes. Idaho Centennial Trail nearby. Short walk on fishhok Nature Trail. Deer and elk. Swim, sail, ski, canoe, and motorboat. Closed Sundays after July 4 for irrigation.

GETTING THERE: From Stanley go S on state HWY 75 approx. 4.5 mi. to forest route 214. Go SW on 214 approx. 2.5 mi. to Redfish Outlet CG. (Located on the N shore of Little Redfish Lake.)

SINGLE RATE:	Varies	OPEN DATES:	June-Sept
# of SINGLE SITES:	19	MAX SPUR:	20 feet
		MAX STAY:	14 days
		ELEVATION:	6500 feet

50 Riverside
Stanley • lat 44°16'01" lon 114°50'57"

DESCRIPTION: CG set among lodgepole pine on roaring Salmon river. Fish for steelhead (check regs.). Deer, elk, and coyotes reside in the area. Horse and hiking trails to isolated and pristine Casino Lakes and on into jagged White Cloud Peaks. Sites 10-18 closed 8/15-5/1, and sites 1-8 are reservable as group site.

GETTING THERE: Riverside CG is located approx. 6 mi. NE of Stanley on state HWY 75. Not recommended for RVs over 25 feet long.

SINGLE RATE:	$11	OPEN DATES:	May-Sept
# of SINGLE SITES:	17	MAX SPUR:	34 feet
GROUP RATE:	$85	MAX STAY:	10 days
# of GROUP SITES:	1	ELEVATION:	6100 feet

 Campground has hosts   **Reservable sites**   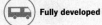 **Accessible facilities**   **Fully developed**   **Semi-developed**   **Rustic facilities**

NOTE: Open dates listed are typical. Actual dates are dependent on conditions such as snow pack.

51 Salmon River
Stanley • lat 44°15'02" lon 114°52'07"

DESCRIPTION: This CG is situated in a meadow among mixed lodgepole pine and sage-brush. Set on the banks of turbulent Salmon River. Fantastic steelhead fishing, check for local regulations. Historic Stanley Museum at Stanley. Deer, elk, and coyotes reside in the area. Gather firewood locally.

GETTING THERE: Salmon River CG is located approx. 5 mi. NE of Stanley on state HWY 75.

SINGLE RATE: # of SINGLE SITES:	Varies 30	OPEN DATES: MAX SPUR: MAX STAY: ELEVATION:	May-Sept 30 feet 10 days 6135 feet

52 Sawmill
Gimlet • lat 43°40'00" lon 114°09'45"

DESCRIPTION: CG set in sparse cottonwood stands with limited trout fishing nearby. Supplies are available in Gimlet. Gather firewood locally. Deer and elk reside in the area. Adjacent horse, hiking, and mountain bike trails. Designated ATV roads and trails available, see FS map for use.

GETTING THERE: From Gimlet go E on forest route 124 approx. 8 mi. to forest route 118. Go NE on 118 approx. 4 mi. to Sawmill CG.

SINGLE RATE: # of SINGLE SITES:	No fee 3	OPEN DATES: MAX STAY: ELEVATION:	May-Oct 16 days 6700 feet

53 Schipper
Hansen • lat 42°19'22" lon 114°16'02"

DESCRIPTION: CG is set on the banks of a small stream, situated in a high desert environment of pine. Fish for trout on the stream. Supplies are available in Hansen. Gather firewood locally. Deer and elk reside in the area. Horse, hiking, and bike trails. ATV roads available, see FS map for use.

GETTING THERE: From Hansen go S on forest route 515 approx. 16 mi. to Schipper CG.

SINGLE RATE: # of SINGLE SITES:	Varies 7	OPEN DATES: MAX SPUR: MAX STAY: ELEVATION:	June-Sept 20 feet 14 days 4600 feet

54 Sheep Trail
Stanley • lat 44°18'22" lon 115°03'19"

DESCRIPTION: CG set in a lodgepole pine overstory. Multiple creeks in vicinity for fishing. CG may be reserved as 1 group site for up to 40 persons. Deer, elk, and coyotes in area. Gather firewood locally. Horse-back ride or hike the Idaho Centennial Trail which passes nearby. Pack it in/pack it out.

GETTING THERE: Sheep Trail CG is located approx. 9 mi. NW of Stanley on state HWY 21.

SINGLE RATE: # of SINGLE SITES: GROUP RATE: # of GROUP SITES:	Varies 4 $35 1	OPEN DATES: MAX SPUR: MAX STAY: ELEVATION:	May-Sept 20 feet 14 days 6600 feet

55 Smoky Bear
Stanley • lat 43°55'13" lon 114°51'40"

DESCRIPTION: CG set on the shores of Alturas Lake among lodgepoles. Boat ramp, trailer parking, amphitheater, & group picnic area. Trout fish, ski, sail, motorboat, & swim on lake. Canoe & fish nearby Perkins Lake. Deer, elk, & coyotes. Gather firewood. Access Sawtooth Wilderness at end of FS road 205.

GETTING THERE: From Stanley go S on state route 75 approx. 21 mi. to forest route 205. Go W on 205 approx. 2.5 mi. to Smoky Bear CG.

SINGLE RATE: # of SINGLE SITES:	Varies 12	OPEN DATES: MAX SPUR: MAX STAY: ELEVATION:	May-Sept 20 feet 14 days 7034 feet

56 Sockeye
Stanley • lat 44°07'52" lon 114°55'00"

DESCRIPTION: CG set on the shores of Redfish lake in a lodgepole pine overstory. Great trout fishing on lake or trek W into Sawtooth Wilderness for wild cutthroat in alpine lakes. Nearby Sandy Beach has boat ramp. Swim, sail, ski, canoe, and motorboat on lake. Deer, elk, and coyotes in area. Idaho Centennial Trail nearby.

GETTING THERE: From Stanley go S on state HWY 75 approx. 4.5 mi. to forest route 214. Go SW on 214 approx. 3 mi. to Sockeye CG. (Located on the N shore of Little Redfish Lake.)

SINGLE RATE: # of SINGLE SITES:	Varies 23	OPEN DATES: MAX SPUR: MAX STAY: ELEVATION:	June-Sept 20 feet 10 days 6500 feet

57 Stanley Lake
Stanley • lat 44°14'55" lon 115°03'09"

DESCRIPTION: CG set on the shores of Stanley Lake with a lodgepole pine overstory. Fish for rainbow and lake trout. Sail, motorboat, or swim in the lake. Deer, elk, and coyotes in area. Trailhead for Idaho Centennial Trail nearby leads through a lake-filled region of Sawtooth Wilderness. Gather firewood locally.

GETTING THERE: From Stanley go NW on state HWY 21 approx. 5 mi. to forest route 455. Go W on 455 approx. 3.5 mi. to Stanley Lake CG. (Located on the N shore of Stanley Lake.)

SINGLE RATE: # of SINGLE SITES:	Varies 19	OPEN DATES: MAX SPUR: MAX STAY: ELEVATION:	May-Sept 20 feet 14 days 6400 feet

58 Stanley Lake Inlet
Stanley • lat 44°14'55" lon 115°03'09"

DESCRIPTION: CG set on the shores of Stanley Lake with a lodgepole pine overstory. Fish for rainbow and lake trout. Boat ramp. Sail, motorboat, or swim in the lake. Deer, elk, and coyotes in area. Trailhead for Idaho Centennial Trail leads through a lake-filled region of Sawtooth Wilderness. Gather firewood.

GETTING THERE: From Stanley go NW on state HWY 21 approx. 5 mi. to forest route 455. Go W on 455 approx. 3. mi. to Stanley Lake Inlet CG. (Located on the NW shore of Stanley Lake.)

SINGLE RATE: # of SINGLE SITES:	Varies 14	OPEN DATES: MAX SPUR: MAX STAY: ELEVATION:	May-Sept 20 feet 14 days 6537 feet

59 Steer Basin
Hansen • lat 42°16'47" lon 114°15'34"

DESCRIPTION: This CG is situated among pine in a very high desert terrain. Fish the nearby sream for trout, check for local regulations. Supplies are available in Hansen. Gather firewood locally. Deer and elk reside in the area. Horse, hiking, and mountain bike trails. ATV roads available, see FS map for use.

GETTING THERE: From Hansen go S on forest route 515 approx. 20 mi. to Steer Basin CG.

SINGLE RATE: # of SINGLE SITES:	Varies 5	OPEN DATES: MAX SPUR: MAX STAY: ELEVATION:	June-Sept 20 feet 14 days 5000 feet

60 Sublett
Rockland • lat 42°19'40" lon 113°00'09"

DESCRIPTION: This CG is set on the banks of Sublette Creek, among pine and fir. Reservoir nearby. Trout fishing on the creek and reservoir, check for local regulations. Fills most weekends. Gather firewood locally. Supplies are available in Rockland. Deer and elk reside in the area. No nearby trails.

GETTING THERE: From Rockland go W and S on Houtz Canyon Road approx. 10 mi. to forest route 577. Continue S on 577 approx. 5.5 mi. to forest route 565. Go S on 565 approx. 9 mi. to Sublett CG.

SINGLE RATE: # of SINGLE SITES:	No fee 6	OPEN DATES: MAX SPUR: MAX STAY: ELEVATION:	June-Oct 32 feet 14 days 5000 feet

 Campground has hosts   **Reservable sites**   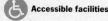 **Accessible facilities**   **Fully developed**   **Semi-developed**   **Rustic facilities**

NOTE: Open dates listed are typical. Actual dates are dependent on conditions such as snow pack.

Sawtooth National Forest • Idaho • 51 — 60

61 Sunny Gulch
Stanley • lat 44°10'35" lon 114°54'33"

DESCRIPTION: CG located 3 mi. from Redfish Lake among lodgepole pine on Salmon River. Great fishing in river with access near entrance, check regulations. Deer, elk, and coyotes in area. Supplies in Stanley. Gather firewood locally. Visitor Center and horse rides at Redfish Lake. Dump station 1 mi. away.

GETTING THERE: Sunny Gulch CG is located approx. 4 mi. S of Stanley on state HWY 75. Watch for signs.

SINGLE RATE:	$11	OPEN DATES:	May-Oct
# of SINGLE SITES:	19	MAX SPUR:	20 feet
		MAX STAY:	10 days
		ELEVATION:	6560 feet

66 Willow Creek
Featherville • lat 43°36'24" lon 115°08'33"

DESCRIPTION: This CG is situated in a pine and fir forest on Willow Creek. Limited fishing for trout on the creek, please check for local fishing regulations. Supplies are available in Featherville. Gather firewood locally. Deer and elk reside in the area. Willow Creek Trail System access.

GETTING THERE: Willow Creek CG is located approx. 7 mi. E of Featherville on forest route 227.

SINGLE RATE:	$2	OPEN DATES:	May-Sept
# of SINGLE SITES:	5	MAX SPUR:	38 feet
		MAX STAY:	14 days
		ELEVATION:	5100 feet

62 Thompson Flat
Albion • lat 42°19'30" lon 113°37'23"

DESCRIPTION: CG set on a lake surrounded by fir and pine. Fish for planted trout on the lake. Supplies are available in Albion. Gather firewood locally. Fills most weekends. Deer and elk reside in the area. Hiking, mountain bike, and nordic trails nearby. Horse facilities and self-guided trail nearby.

GETTING THERE: From Albion go SE on state HWY 77 approx. 5.5 mi. to forest route 549. Go W on 549 approx. 7.5 mi. to Thompson Flat CG.

SINGLE RATE:	$3	OPEN DATES:	June-Oct
# of SINGLE SITES:	20	MAX SPUR:	60 feet
		MAX STAY:	14 days
# of GROUP SITES:	2	ELEVATION:	8000 feet

67 Willow Creek Transfer Camp
Fairfield • lat 43°36'24" lon 115°08'33"

DESCRIPTION: CG is a rustic horse camp in an open setting, used primarily for horse transfer. Corrals, mangers, a barrier free stock loading ramp, and toilets are available. Dispersed sites. Gather firewood locally. Deer and elk reside in the area. Busy hunting season. Horse trails accessible nearby.

GETTING THERE: From Featherville go E approx. 7 mi. to Willow Creek CG. Go N of Willow Creek CG approx. 1 mi. to Willow Creek Transfer Camp CG.

SINGLE RATE:	$2	OPEN DATES:	May-Sept
		MAX SPUR:	38 feet
		MAX STAY:	14 days
		ELEVATION:	6000 feet

63 Trap Creek
Stanley • lat 44°18'59" lon 115°05'18"

DESCRIPTION: CG set in a pine overstory. Walk in to sites from general parking area. The 3 sites may be used as one reservable group camp. Many nearby creeks for fishing. Deer, elk, and coyotes in area. Gather firewood locally. The Idaho Centennial Trail passes through, paralleling the byway.

GETTING THERE: Trap Creek CG is located approx. 15 mi. NW of Stanley on state HWY 21.

SINGLE RATE:	$13	OPEN DATES:	July-Sept
# of SINGLE SITES:	3		
GROUP RATE:	$35	MAX STAY:	14 days
# of GROUP SITES:	1	ELEVATION:	6670 feet

68 Wolftone
Hailey • lat 43°31'58" lon 114°27'57"

DESCRIPTION: This CG is set in a cottonwood, pine, and aspen forest. Trout fishing nearby, check for local regulations. Supplies are available in Hiley. Gather firewood locally. Deer and elk reside in the area. Horse, hiking, and mountain bike trails nearby. Designated ATV roads and trails available, see FS map for use.

GETTING THERE: From Hiley go N on state HWY 75 approx. 2 mi. to forest route 097. Go W on 097 approx. 8 mi. to Wolftone CG.

SINGLE RATE:	No fee	OPEN DATES:	May-Oct
# of SINGLE SITES:	1		
		MAX STAY:	16 days
		ELEVATION:	5500 feet

64 Upper O'Brien
Stanley • lat 44°15'34" lon 114°41'51"

DESCRIPTION: CG in a lodgepole pine overstory on Salmon River where Class III and IV rapids are located. Fish for steelhead and trout. Boat ramp at Yankee Fork for floating (rafts, canoes, and kayaks only). Soak in Sunbeam Hot Springs. Historic mining and dam area. Deer, elk, and coyotes in area. Gather firewood.

GETTING THERE: From Stanley go NE on state route 75 approx. 14 mi. to forest route 454. Go S on 454 to Robinson Bar Road, following to Upper O'Brien CG. Narrow bridge crossing, not for large RVs.

SINGLE RATE:	$11	OPEN DATES:	May-Sept
# of SINGLE SITES:	9		
		MAX STAY:	10 days
		ELEVATION:	5730 feet

69 Wood River
Ketchum • lat 43°47'35" lon 114°27'31"

DESCRIPTION: CG divided by the Big Wood River, set in a dense forest. Fish the Big Wood River. Self-guided nature trail & other trails in canyon lead to Amber Lakes & over the Boulder Mountains. Amphitheater & group picnic area for a max of 150 persons (fee use, reservations needed). Buy firewood on site. Dump Station nearby.

GETTING THERE: From Ketchum go NW approx. 10 mi. on state HWY 75 to Wood River CG. (2nd CG past SNRA HQ office.)

SINGLE RATE:	$11	OPEN DATES:	May-Sept
# of SINGLE SITES:	30	MAX SPUR:	20 feet
		MAX STAY:	14 days
		ELEVATION:	6366 feet

65 Upper Penstemon
Hansen • lat 42°11'40" lon 114°17'06"

DESCRIPTION: CG situated in a pine forest. Trout fishing opportunities nearby, check for local regulations Winter use of X-country skiing, and sledding. Supplies in Hansen. Gather firewood locally. Deer and elk reside in the area. Horse, hiking, and mountain bike trails. ATV roads available, see FS map for use.

GETTING THERE: From Hansen go S on forest route 515 approx. 24.5 mi. to Upper Penstemon CG.

SINGLE RATE:	Varies	OPEN DATES:	Yearlong
# of SINGLE SITES:	6		
		MAX STAY:	14 days
		ELEVATION:	6680 feet

 Campground has hosts   Reservable sites   Accessible facilities   Fully developed   Semi-developed   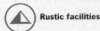 Rustic facilities

NOTE: Open dates listed are typical. Actual dates are dependent on conditions such as snow pack.

TARGHEE NATIONAL FOREST

USFS Photo

Encompassing 1.8 million acres, the Targhee National Forest is named in honor of a Bannock Indian warrior. Established by President Theodore Roosevelt in 1908, the majority of the forest lies in eastern Idaho and the remainder in western Wyoming. Situated next to Yellowstone and Grand Teton National Parks, the forest is home to a diverse number of wildlife and fish, including threatened and endangered species, wilderness areas, and scenic panoramas.

The Targhee provides numerous opportunities for recreation. Over 1200 trails exist on the Targhee, accessible by horse or foot. Streams, reservoirs and natural lakes provide excellent fishing for rainbow, eastern brook, brown and cutthroat trout, kokanee salmon and whitefish.

Visitors will also enjoy the many sight-seeing opportunities. In the Lemhi/Medicine Lodge area, visitors will find remnants of old mining sites. Located in the Birch Creek Valley are four preserved brick adobe charcoal kilns which were originally built to furnish charcoal to the Nicholia Mine. The Upper and Lower Mesa Falls, the last major undisturbed falls on the Columbia River System, can be accessed via the The Mesa Falls Scenic Byway, established in 1989.

TARGHEE NATIONAL FOREST • IDAHO • LOCATOR MAP

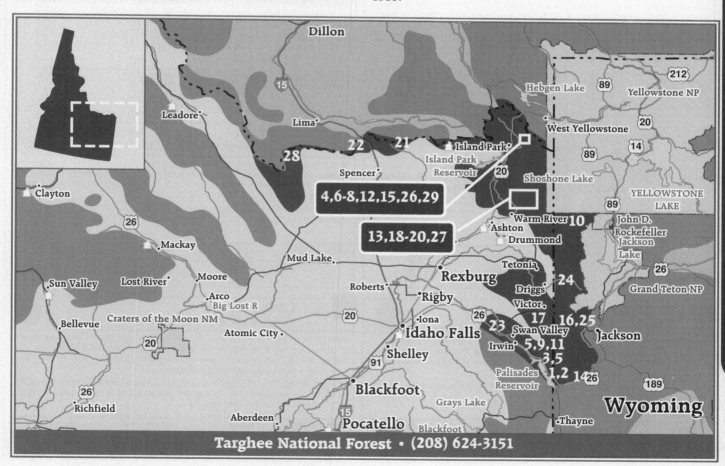

Targhee National Forest • (208) 624-3151

1. Alpine

Alpine • lat 43°11'47" lon 111°02'33"

DESCRIPTION: CG set a dense aspen grove a short walk away from Palisades Reservoir. Fish for cutthroat, lake, and rainbow trout. Boating is popular on the lake. Dispersed sites. Otters, black bears, elk, deer, hawks, waterfowl, and songbirds in area. Busy holiday weekends. Numerous trails nearby.

GETTING THERE: Alpine CG is located approx. 2 mi. N of Alpine on US HWY 26.

SINGLE RATE:		OPEN DATES:	June-Sept
# of SINGLE SITES:	22	MAX SPUR:	45 feet
		MAX STAY:	16 days
		ELEVATION:	5800 feet

2. Bear Creek
Palisades • lat 43°16'30" lon 111°14'00"

DESCRIPTION: CG set a dense aspen grove adjacent to Palisades Reservoir. Fish for cutthroat, lake, and rainbow trout. Boating is popular on the lake. Dispersed sites. No drinking water available. Otters, black bears, elk, deer, hawks, waterfowl, and songbirds in area. Busy holiday weekends. Numerous trails nearby.

GETTING THERE: From Palisades go S on US HWY 26 approx. 1.5 mi. to forest route 058. Go SW on 058 approx. 6 mi. to Bear Creek CG.

SINGLE RATE:		OPEN DATES:	June-Oct
# of SINGLE SITES:	8		
		MAX STAY:	16 days
		ELEVATION:	5800 feet

3. Big Elk Creek

Palisades • lat 43°19'33" lon 111°07'02"

DESCRIPTION: This CG is set in an aspen grove adjacent to Palisades Reservoir. Group sites are situated in an open area. Boating is popular. Fish for cutthroat, lake, and rainbow trout. Otters, waterfowl, deer, elk, black bears, and hawks reside in the area. Busy holiday weekends. Numerous trails in area.

GETTING THERE: From Palisades go S on US HWY 26 approx. 4 mi. to forest route. Go W approx. 2 mi. to Big Elk Creek CG.

SINGLE RATE:		OPEN DATES:	May-Sept
# of SINGLE SITES:	21	MAX SPUR:	22 feet
GROUP RATE:	Varies	MAX STAY:	16 days
# of GROUP SITES:	2	ELEVATION:	5800 feet

4. Big Springs

Macks Inn • lat 44°30'00" lon 111°15'00"

DESCRIPTION: CG is in a lodgepole pine forest with thick underbrush, near the headwaters of the Henry's Fork of the Snake River. Wildlife includes moose, deer, elk, antelope, fox, wolves, coyotes, and bears. Several hiking trails in area including Continental Divide Trail and on site interpretive trail.

GETTING THERE: From Macks Inn go E on forest route 59 approx. 5 mi. to Big Springs CG.

SINGLE RATE:		OPEN DATES:	June-Sept
# of SINGLE SITES:	17	MAX SPUR:	45 feet
		MAX STAY:	16 days
# of GROUP SITES:	1	ELEVATION:	6400 feet

5. Blowout Ramp

Alpine • lat 43°16'30" lon 111°07'15"

DESCRIPTION: This CG is the second largest boating facility on the Plisades Reservoir. Popular activities include swimming, fishing, and water skiing. Excellent area for RVs, large boats, and trailers. Not suitable for tents due to a gravel parking lot. Watch for elk, black bears, mountain lions, and redtail hawks.

GETTING THERE: Blowout Ramp CG is located along Palisades Reservoir approx. 8 mi. N of Alpine on US HWY 26.

SINGLE RATE:		OPEN DATES:	May-Sept
# of SINGLE SITES:	19	MAX SPUR:	35 feet
		MAX STAY:	16 days
		ELEVATION:	5800 feet

6. Box Canyon

West Yellowstone • lat 44°24'30" lon 111°23'30"

DESCRIPTION: CG is situated in a lodgepole pine and douglas fir forest. An open, park-like setting; near the Henry's Fork of the Snake River. Wildlife in the area includes moose, deer, elk, antelope, fox, wolves, coyotes, and bears. Several hiking trails in area including Continental Divide Trail.

GETTING THERE: From West Yellowstone go W and S on US HWY 20 approx. 30 mi. to forest route 134. Go .5 mi. to forest route 284. Go W on 284 approx. 1 mi. to Box Canyon CG.

SINGLE RATE:		OPEN DATES:	June-Sept
# of SINGLE SITES:	18	MAX SPUR:	35 feet
		MAX STAY:	16 days
		ELEVATION:	6200 feet

7. Buffalo

West Yellowstone • lat 44°25'28" lon 111°22'06"

DESCRIPTION: This CG is situated among pine and aspen, which provide some shade. There is a lodge and a grocery store nearby for supplies. Good trout fishing and canoeing on the Buffalo River. Fishing dock is barrier free. Remains busy all year. The Island Park Rodeo is the first Saturday in August.

GETTING THERE: From West Yellowstone go W and S on US HWY 20 approx. 28.5 mi. Buffalo CG.

SINGLE RATE:		OPEN DATES:	May-Sept
# of SINGLE SITES:	127	MAX SPUR:	45 feet
		MAX STAY:	16 days
		ELEVATION:	6200 feet

8. Buttermilk

West Yellowstone • lat 44°26'01" lon 111°25'27"

DESCRIPTION: CG set on the shore of Island Park Reservoir, situated among lodgepole pine. Good fishing for brown, rainbow, and cutthroat trout. Wildlife includes moose, deer, elk, antelope, fox, wolves, coyotes, and bears. Several hiking trails in area including Continental Divide Trail. Boat ramp on site.

GETTING THERE: From West Yellowstone go W and S on US HWY 20 approx. 23.5 mi. to forest route 030. Go W on 030 approx. 1 mi. to forest route 126. Go S on 126 approx. 3.5 mi. to Buttermilk CG.

SINGLE RATE:		OPEN DATES:	June-Sept
# of SINGLE SITES:	54	MAX SPUR:	35 feet
		MAX STAY:	16 days
		ELEVATION:	6200 feet

9. Calamity

Palisades • lat 43°19'46" lon 111°12'30"

DESCRIPTION: This CG is situated in a mixed conifer and lodgepole pine forest with northern exposure. Set along the Snake River drainage at the north end of Palisades Reservoir. Fishing in reservoir. A large boat ramp and parking facilities are available. Boating on the lake is a popular activity in the area.

GETTING THERE: From Palisades go S on US HWY 26 approx. 1.5 mi. to forest route 058. Go SW on 058 approx. 1 mi. to Calamity CG.

SINGLE RATE:	$10	OPEN DATES:	May-Sept
# of SINGLE SITES:	42	MAX SPUR:	99 feet
		MAX STAY:	16 days
		ELEVATION:	5800 feet

10. Cave Falls

Warm River • lat 44°07'45" lon 111°00'15"

DESCRIPTION: This CG is situated in an open park like area, set in a pine forest. Views of nearby Cave Falls River. Fish the fast moving river for trout. Warm days, weather changes quickly. Deer, moose, elk, and occasional grizzly and black bears reside in the area. Several hiking trails are nearby. Heavy mosquitos.

GETTING THERE: From Warm River go N 1/2 mi. on state HWY 47 to forest route 082. Go NE 4 mi. to forest route 241. Go S on 241 approx. 3.5 mi. to forest route 582. Go E on 582 approx. 10.5 mi. to Cave Falls CG.

SINGLE RATE:		OPEN DATES:	June-Sept
# of SINGLE SITES:	16	MAX SPUR:	30 feet
		MAX STAY:	16 days
		ELEVATION:	6200 feet

 Campground has hosts   Reservable sites   Accessible facilities   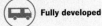 Fully developed   Semi-developed   Rustic facilities

NOTE: Open dates listed are typical. Actual dates are dependent on conditions such as snow pack.

11 Falls
Swan Valley • lat 43°26'13" lon 111°21'41"

DESCRIPTION: This CG is situated on the banks of the Snake River, among old and new growth cottonwoods. Fishing for cutthroat and boating are popular activities on the river. Watch for various wildlife in this flat-bottom environment. Numerous hiking opportunities can be found in the vicinity. Gather firewood locally.

GETTING THERE: From Swan Valley go W on US HWY 26 approx. 3 mi. to forest route 058. Go SE on 058 approx. 3 mi. to Falls CG.

SINGLE RATE:	Varies	OPEN DATES:	May-Sept
# of SINGLE SITES:	23	MAX SPUR:	45 feet
		MAX STAY:	16 days
		ELEVATION:	5400 feet

16 Mike Harris
Victor • lat 43°33'24" lon 111°04'09"

DESCRIPTION: CG situated in an open area of lodgepole with moderate undergrowth. Stream fish for brook trout in nearby Trail Creek. Check for local fishing regulations. Supplies are available in Victor. Deer, moose, hawks, and ducks are common to the area. Gather firewood locally. No drinking water on site.

GETTING THERE: Mike Harris is located approx. 4 mi. SE of Victor off of state HWY 33.

SINGLE RATE:	Varies	OPEN DATES:	June-Sept
# of SINGLE SITES:	12	MAX SPUR:	25 feet
		MAX STAY:	16 days
		ELEVATION:	6200 feet

12 Flat Rock
West Yellowstone • lat 44°17'27" lon 114°43'01"

DESCRIPTION: Shady CG situated adjacent to the Snake River. Popular activities include fishing and canoeing. Supplies are available on site. Interpretive hikes at nearby Coffee Pot CG. Grey water dump station provided. The Island Park Rodeo is the first Saturday in August and is a popular event.

GETTING THERE: Flat Rock CG is located approx. 22 mi. W of West Yellowstone on US HWY 20.

SINGLE RATE:	Varies	OPEN DATES:	June-Sept
# of SINGLE SITES:	40	MAX SPUR:	45 feet
		MAX STAY:	16 days
		ELEVATION:	6400 feet

17 Palisades
Swan Valley • lat 43°23'53" lon 111°13'12"

DESCRIPTION: CG set in a mixed conifer forest across the road from Palisades Reservoir. Good cutthroat, lake, and rainbow trout fishing in reservoir. Various wildlife in the area includes otters, waterfowl, elk, deer, and black bears. Busy weekends. Numerous hiking, horse, and mountain biking trails in area.

GETTING THERE: From Swan Valley go SE on US HWY 26 approx. 7 mi. to forest route 255. Go NE on 255 approx. 2 mi. to Palisades CG.

SINGLE RATE:	Varies	OPEN DATES:	June-Sept
# of SINGLE SITES:	8	MAX SPUR:	40 feet
		MAX STAY:	16 days
		ELEVATION:	5600 feet

13 Grandview
Ashton • lat 44°10'00" lon 111°20'00"

DESCRIPTION: CG situated in a lightly wooded lodgepole pine forest on rim above Henry's Fork of the Snake River. Scenic views of Lower Mesa Falls. Fish for trout in Henry's Fork. Deer, moose, and elk, and occasional grizzly and black bears in the area. Hiking trails nearby. No drinking water, dispersed sites.

GETTING THERE: From Ashton to N on US HWY 20 approx. 18 mi. to forest route 294. Go S on 294 approx. 13 mi. to Grandview CG.

SINGLE RATE:	Varies	OPEN DATES:	June-Oct
# of SINGLE SITES:	5		
		MAX STAY:	16 days
		ELEVATION:	6200 feet

18 Pine Creek
Victor • lat 43°34'25" lon 111°12'22"

DESCRIPTION: CG situated in an open area of lodgepole with moderate undergrowth. Stream fish for brook trout in nearby Pine Creek. Check for local fishing regulations. Supplies are available in Victor. Deer, moose, hawks, and ducks are common to the area. Gather firewood locally. No drinking water available.

GETTING THERE: Pine Creek CG is located approx. 6 mi. W of Victor on state HWY 31. Not recommended for RVs or trailers.

SINGLE RATE:	Varies	OPEN DATES:	June-Sept
# of SINGLE SITES:	11	MAX SPUR:	25 feet
		MAX STAY:	16 days
		ELEVATION:	6600 feet

14 McCoy Creek
Alpine • lat 43°10'30" lon 111°06'00"

DESCRIPTION: CG is set in a dense forest of lodgepole pine, douglas fir, and alpine fir. Various wildlife in the area includes deer, elk, black bears, mountain lions, redtail hawks, and song birds. CG can be busy holiday weekends. Numerous hiking, horse, and mountain biking opportunities are available.

GETTING THERE: From Alpine go S on US HWY 89 approx. 3.5 mi. to forest route 087. Go NW on 087 approx. 6 mi. to McCoy Creek CG.

SINGLE RATE:	Varies	OPEN DATES:	June-Sept
# of SINGLE SITES:	19	MAX SPUR:	20 feet
		MAX STAY:	16 days
		ELEVATION:	5800 feet

19 Pole Bridge
Ashton • lat 44°15'30" lon 111°16'45"

DESCRIPTION: This CG offers dispersed camping in a lightly woooded lodgepole pine forest. Fishing in Warm River which flows past the CG. Check for local fishing regulations. Wildlife includes deer, moose, grizzly and black bears, and elk. Numerous hiking trails in area. Mosquitos can be a nuisance in spring.

GETTING THERE: From Ashton to N on US HWY 20 approx. 18 mi. to forest route 294. Go S on 294 approx. 11 mi. to forest route 150. Go N on 150 approx. 7.5 mi. to Pole Bridge CG.

SINGLE RATE:	Varies	OPEN DATES:	June-Oct
# of SINGLE SITES:	20	MAX SPUR:	30 feet
		MAX STAY:	16 days
		ELEVATION:	6300 feet

15 McCrea Bridge
West Yellowstone • lat 44°27'45" lon 111°23'57"

DESCRIPTION: CG is located at the backwaters of Island Park Reservoir, receiving slight shade. Power boat launch available on site. Popular activities include bridge fishing, trout fishing, power boating, and water skiing. No reservoir access from site during August due to low water levels.

GETTING THERE: From West Yellowstone go W and S on US HWY 20 approx. 23.5 mi. to forest route 030. Go W on 030 approx. 2 mi. to McCrea Bridge CG.

SINGLE RATE:	Varies	OPEN DATES:	May-Sept
# of SINGLE SITES:	25	MAX SPUR:	45 feet
		MAX STAY:	16 days
		ELEVATION:	6200 feet

20 Riverside
Ashton • lat 44°16'01" lon 111°28'00"

DESCRIPTION: This CG is set on the banks of the Henry's Fork Snake River. CG rests in a quiet area with lodgepole pine trees to provide shade. Popular activities include hiking and fishing. Check for local fishing regulations. Supllies are available 8 mi. away. Various hiking opportunities in the area.

GETTING THERE: From Ashton go N on US HWY 20 approx. 14 mi. to forest route 304. Go E on 304 approx. 1 mi. to Riverside CG.

SINGLE RATE:	Varies	OPEN DATES:	May-Sept
# of SINGLE SITES:	57	MAX SPUR:	40 feet
		MAX STAY:	16 days
		ELEVATION:	6200 feet

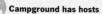 **Campground has hosts**   **Reservable sites**   **Accessible facilities**   **Fully developed**   **Semi-developed**   **Rustic facilities**

NOTE: Open dates listed are typical. Actual dates are dependent on conditions such as snow pack.

TARGHEE NATIONAL FOREST • IDAHO • 11 — 20

21 Steel Creek
Spencer • lat 44°27'56" lon 112°01'17"

DESCRIPTION: CG is a reservation only group site and is located in a mixed conifer forest with douglas fir, lodgepole pine, and snowberry bushes. Good fishing in area. Wildlife in the area includes whitetail and mule deer, moose, elk, bears, mountain lions, golden eagles, and osprey. Busy weekends and holidays.

GETTING THERE: From Spencer go N on county route approx. 4 mi. to forest route 002. Go E on 002 approx. 1 mi. to forest route 006. Go E on 006 approx. 13 mi. to Steel Creek CG.

		OPEN DATES:	June-Sept
GROUP RATE:	Varies	MAX STAY:	14 days
# of GROUP SITES:	1	ELEVATION:	6600 feet

26 Upper Coffee Pot
West Yellowstone • lat 44°29'28" lon 111°21'54"

DESCRIPTION: CG is set among lodgepole pine with thick underbrush, on the banks of the Henry's Fork of the Snake River. Wildlife includes moose, deer, elk, antelope, fox, wolves, coyotes, and bears. Busy all summer. Several hiking trails in area including Continental Divide Trail and on site river trail.

GETTING THERE: From West Yellowstone go W and S on US HWY 20 approx. 24 mi. to forest route 130. Go E on 130 approx. 1.5 mi. to Upper Coffee Pot CG.

SINGLE RATE:	Varies	OPEN DATES:	June-Sept
# of SINGLE SITES:	15	MAX SPUR:	35 feet
		MAX STAY:	16 days
		ELEVATION:	6300 feet

22 Stoddard Creek
Spencer • lat 44°25'05" lon 112°12'58"

DESCRIPTION: This CG is situated in a mixed conifer forest with douglas fir, lodgepole pine, and snowberry bushes. Good fishing in area. Wildlife in the area includes whitetail and mule deer, moose, elk, bears, mountain lions, golden eagles, and osprey. CG can be busy weekends and holidays.

GETTING THERE: From Spencer go N on county route approx. 4 mi. to forest route 002. Go W on 002 approx. 1 mi. to Stoddard Creek CG.

SINGLE RATE:	Varies	OPEN DATES:	June-Sept
# of SINGLE SITES:	13	MAX SPUR:	80 feet
		MAX STAY:	14 days
		ELEVATION:	6200 feet

27 Warm River
Ashton • lat 44°07'14" lon 111°18'39"

DESCRIPTION: This CG is set on the banks of the slow moving Warm River, situated in a willow and pine forest. Supplies are available nine miles away. Hiking, fishing, tubing, mountain biking, and visiting the National Parks nearby are popular activities. Please check for local fishing regulations.

GETTING THERE: Warm River CG is located approx. 9 mi. NE of Ashton on state HWY 47.

SINGLE RATE:	Varies	OPEN DATES:	May-Sept
# of SINGLE SITES:	15	MAX SPUR:	40 feet
		MAX STAY:	16 days
		ELEVATION:	5200 feet

23  Table Rock
Ririe • lat 43°38'00" lon 111°36'00"

DESCRIPTION: This CG is set in densely wooded area of mixed conifers. A small creek runs adjacent to CG. Wildlife includes elk, deer, black bears, mountain lions, redtail hawks, and songbirds. CG can be busy on holiday weekends. Numerous hiking, mountain biking, and horse trails in area.

GETTING THERE: Table Rock CG is located approx. 2 mi. E of Kelly Canyon Ski Area on Kelly Canyon Road.

SINGLE RATE:	Varies	OPEN DATES:	May-Sept
# of SINGLE SITES:	9	MAX SPUR:	22 feet
GROUP RATE:	Varies	MAX STAY:	16 days
# of GROUP SITES:	1	ELEVATION:	5800 feet

28 Webber Creek
Dubois • lat 44°21'30" lon 112°41'00"

DESCRIPTION: CG is situated in a mixed conifer forest with douglas fir, lodgepole pine, and snowberry bushes. Good fishing in adjacent Webber Creek. Wildlife in the area includes whitetail and mule deer, moose, elk, bears, mountain lions, golden eagles, and osprey. CG can be busy weekends and holidays.

GETTING THERE: From Dubois go W on state HWY approx. 6 mi. to county route. Go NE approx. 16 mi. to forest route 196. Go W on 196 approx. 4.5 mi. to Webber Creek CG. Not recommended for large vehicles/trailers.

SINGLE RATE:	Varies	OPEN DATES:	June-Sept
# of SINGLE SITES:	4		
		MAX STAY:	14 days
		ELEVATION:	7000 feet

24 Teton Canyon
Driggs • lat 43°45'00" lon 110°54'30"

DESCRIPTION: This CG is situated among aspen and pine trees, set along Teton Creek. Days are mild and evenings are cool. Activities in the area include hiking, horseback riding, backpacking, and fishing. Trailheads and a horse transfer station are nearby. Firewood is scarce, please bring your own.

GETTING THERE: Teton Canyon CG is located approx. 10 mi. NE of Driggs on forest route 009.

SINGLE RATE:	Varies	OPEN DATES:	May-Sept
# of SINGLE SITES:	20	MAX SPUR:	99 feet
		MAX STAY:	16 days
		ELEVATION:	7200 feet

29 West End
Ashton • lat 44°22'30" lon 111°31'00"

DESCRIPTION: CG is set on the shore of Island Park Reservoir, situated among lodgepole pine. Good fishing for brown, rainbow, and cutthroat trout. Wildlife includes moose, deer, elk, antelope, fox, wolves, coyotes, and bears. Several hiking trails in area including Continental Divide Trail. Boat ramp available.

GETTING THERE: From Ashton go N on US HWY 20 approx. 14 mi. to forest route 167. Go W on 167 approx. 9 mi. to forest route 465. Go N on 465 approx. 1.5 mi. to West End CG.

SINGLE RATE:	Varies	OPEN DATES:	June-Oct
# of SINGLE SITES:	19	MAX SPUR:	35 feet
		MAX STAY:	16 days
		ELEVATION:	6200 feet

25 Trail Creek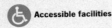
Victor • lat 43°34'00" lon 111°02'00"

DESCRIPTION: This CG is situated in an open area of lodgepole with moderate undergrowth. Stream fish for brook trout in nearby Trail Creek. Check for local fishing regulations. Supplies are available in Victor. Deer, moose, hawks, and ducks are common to the area. Gather firewood locally. No drinking water on site.

GETTING THERE: Trail Creek CG is located approx. 5.5 mi. SE of Victor off of state HWY 33.

SINGLE RATE:	Varies	OPEN DATES:	June-Sept
# of SINGLE SITES:	11	MAX SPUR:	25 feet
		MAX STAY:	16 days
		ELEVATION:	6600 feet

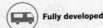 Campground has hosts  Reservable sites 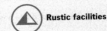 Accessible facilities Fully developed Semi-developed Rustic facilities

NOTE: Open dates listed are typical. Actual dates are dependent on conditions such as snow pack.

Page 274

Henry's Fork River from Sheep Falls
Targhee National Forest, Idaho
USFS Photo

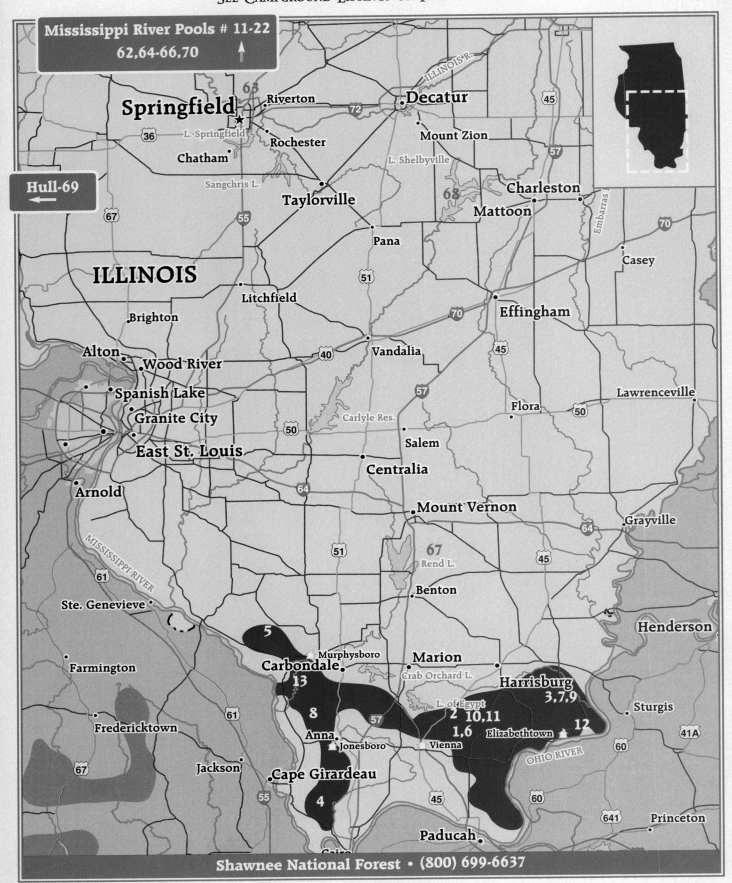

Mississippi River Pools # 11-22
62,64-66,70

Hull-69

Springfield

Riverton

Decatur

Mount Zion

L. Shelbyville

Charleston

Mattoon

Rochester

Chatham

L. Springfield

Sangchris L.

Taylorville

Pana

ILLINOIS

Litchfield

Casey

Brighton

Effingham

Alton

Vandalia

Wood River

Spanish Lake

Flora

Lawrenceville

Granite City

Carlyle Res.

East St. Louis

Salem

Arnold

Centralia

Mount Vernon

Grayville

Mississippi River

Rend L.

Ste. Genevieve

Benton

Henderson

Farmington

5

Murphysboro

Marion

Carbondale

Crab Orchard L.

Harrisburg
3,7,9

Sturgis

13

8

L. of Egypt

2 10,11

Anna

1,6

Elizabethtown

12

Fredericktown

Jonesboro

Vienna

Jackson

Cape Girardeau

Ohio River

4

Paducah

Princeton

SHAWNEE NATIONAL FOREST

The Shawnee National Forest embraces nearly 250,000 acres of forested, rolling hills, lakes and spectacular rock outcroppings, which stretch across southern Illinois from the Mississippi River to the Ohio.

The Shawnee offers a variety of recreation activities. Hikers, bikers and equestrians can enjoy miles of maintained trails including the River to River Trail which stretches from the Ohio to the Mississippi. Three swimming beaches and numerous lakes, ponds, streams and rivers offer boating, fishing and canoeing for water lovers. Backpackers have seven wilderness areas to explore and rock climbers will find several areas throughout the forest to test their scaling skills.

Hunters and photographers will appreciate the many wildlife species who call the forest home. The LaRune Pine Hills area, known for its habitat diversity, is an excellent place to view neotropical migratory birds, deer, turkey, waterfowl, beaver and others. The forest is also a winter roosting area for bald eagles.

Other unique and historical attractions include the Garden of the God's area, formed about 200 million years ago from geological uplifting. There you'll find rock formations with names like Camel Rock and Devil's Smokestack. The Trail of Tears National Historic Trail, which commemorates the tragic march of the Cherokee Nation from Georgia to Oklahoma is another must-see. American history buffs will also want to visit the Jonesboro Ranger District which boasts the site of one of the famous Lincoln-Douglas debates.

1 Bailey Place
Vienna • lat °'" lon °'"

DESCRIPTION: In a pine and hardwood forest setting on Lake Glendale. Fish and swim from the lake. Boat ramp for non-gasoline motors only. Supplies are available at Vienna. Numerous wildlife can be seen in the area. Campers may gather firewood. A hiking trail circles the lake. This CG is reservation only.

GETTING THERE: From Vienna go E on state route 146 approx. 12 mi. to Lake Glendale Recreation Area Complex turnoff. Go N on turnoff approx. 3 mi. to Bailey Place CG which is inside of complex.

		OPEN DATES:	Yearlong
		MAX SPUR:	99 feet
GROUP RATE:	$10	MAX STAY:	14 days
# of GROUP SITES:	1	ELEVATION:	300 feet

2 Buck Ridge
Marion • lat 37°34'50" lon 088°53'03"

DESCRIPTION: In a hardwood and pine forest setting on Lake of Egypt. Some sites overlook the lake. Fish for sunfish, catfish, bass and walleye in the lake. Boat landing at Hickory Point. Supplies available at Marion. Many animals can be viewed in the area. No designated hiking trails in the CG area.

GETTING THERE: From Marion go E on state HWY 13 approx. 6 mi. to state route 166. Go S on 166 approx. 6 mi. to secondary route. Go S approx. 4 mi. to Lake of Egypt Recreation Area and Buck Ridge CG.

SINGLE RATE:	$5	OPEN DATES:	Mar-Dec
# of SINGLE SITES:	31	MAX SPUR:	76 feet
		MAX STAY:	14 days
		ELEVATION:	480 feet

3 Camp Cadiz
Harrisburg • lat 37°34'42" lon 088°14'41"

DESCRIPTION: This CG rests in a forest setting. There are hitching rails at the CG. This CG is the site of a CCC camp. Old foundations and fireplace chimneys remain. ATV usage is popular at this CG. Supplies are available at Harrisburg. Many animals can be seen in the area. Several trails nearby.

GETTING THERE: From Harrisburg go E on state HWY 13 approx. 8 mi. to state HWY 1. Go S on 1 approx. 12 mi. to West turnoff. Go W on turnoff approx. 3 mi. to Camp Cadiz CG.

SINGLE RATE:	$5	OPEN DATES:	Apr-Dec
# of SINGLE SITES:	11	MAX SPUR:	42 feet
		MAX STAY:	14 days
		ELEVATION:	320 feet

4 Grapevine Trail
Mound City • lat °'" lon °'"

DESCRIPTION: In an eastern hardwood forest setting. Supplies are available at Mound City. Deer, raccoons, bobcats, frogs and birds are common in the area. Campers may gather firewood. Warm and humid in summer months. CG is a trailhead to many other trails in the area. Ticks and mosquitos are abundant.

GETTING THERE: From Mound City go NW on state HWY 3 approx. 10 mi. to secondary HWY. Go N on secondary HWY approx. 12 mi. to Grapevine Trail CG.

SINGLE RATE:	No fee	OPEN DATES:	Yearlong
# of SINGLE SITES:	6	MAX SPUR:	30 feet
		MAX STAY:	14 days
		ELEVATION:	300 feet

5 Johnson Creek
Murphysboro • lat 37°50'03" lon 089°31'15"

DESCRIPTION: CG rests in a young hardwood forest setting on Kinkaid Lake. Boat ramp available at the CG. Fish for a variety of species in the lake. Supplies are available at Murphysboro. Numerous wildlife can be seen in this area. Many hiking trails are accessible from CG. RV dump station located at the CG.

GETTING THERE: From Murphysboro go W on state HWY 140 approx. 4 mi. to state HWY 3. Go NW on 3 approx. 10 mi. to Johnson Creek Recreation Area and Johnson Creek CG.

SINGLE RATE:	Varies	OPEN DATES:	Yearlong
# of SINGLE SITES:	75	MAX SPUR:	72 feet
		MAX STAY:	14 days
		ELEVATION:	680 feet

 Campground has hosts   **Reservable sites**   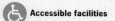 **Accessible facilities**   **Fully developed**   **Semi-developed**   **Rustic facilities**

NOTE: Open dates listed are typical. Actual dates are dependent on conditions such as snow pack.

6 Oak Point
Vienna • lat 37°24'34" lon 088°39'44"

DESCRIPTION: In a forest setting on Lake Glendale. Fish for a variety of fish from the lake. Boat ramp, volleyball court and swimming beach located at the CG. Electric motors only on lake. Supplies available at Vienna. Numerous wildlife can be seen in the area. Many trails are nearby.

GETTING THERE: From Vienna go E on state route 146 approx. 12 mi. to Lake Glendale Recreation Area Complex turnoff. Go N on turnoff approx. 3 mi. to Oak Point CG which is inside of the complex.

SINGLE RATE:	Varies	OPEN DATES:	Yearlong
# of SINGLE SITES:	57	MAX SPUR:	72 feet
		MAX STAY:	14 days
		ELEVATION:	340 feet

7 Pharaoh
Harrisburg • lat 37°36'07" lon 088°22'47"

DESCRIPTION: This CG rests in a eastern hardwood setting with panoramic views of the valley. Summer months can be warm and humid. Supplies are available at Harrisburg. Numerous animals can be seen in this area. Campers may gather dead and down firewood. There are several trails in the area.

GETTING THERE: From Harrisburg go S on state HWY 34 approx. 14 mi. to East turnoff. Go E approx. 4 mi. to Garden of the Gods Recreation Area turnoff. Go N approx. 4 mi. to Pharaoh CG.

SINGLE RATE:	$5	OPEN DATES:	Yearlong
# of SINGLE SITES:	12	MAX SPUR:	56 feet
		MAX STAY:	14 days
		ELEVATION:	620 feet

8 Pine Hills
Jonesboro • lat 37°30'55" lon 089°25'21"

DESCRIPTION: This rustic CG is in hardwoods and conifer (similar to the Blue Ridge Mountain Area). CG is within 2 mi. of Hutchins Creek where campers may fish and swim. Supplies are available at Jonesboro. A 300' limestone bluff is nearby with a hiking trail that looks out over the surrounding swamp land.

GETTING THERE: From Jonesboro go E on state HWY 46 approx. 5 mi. to state route 127. Go N on 127 approx. 2 mi. to forest route 345. Go NE on 345 approx. 10 mi. to Pine Hills CG.

SINGLE RATE:	$5	OPEN DATES:	Yearlong
# of SINGLE SITES:	13	MAX SPUR:	42 feet
		MAX STAY:	14 days
		ELEVATION:	300 feet

9 Pine Ridge
Rosiclare • lat 37°36'53" lon 088°16'04"

DESCRIPTION: This CG is located on Pounds Hollow Lake in a dense stand of mature red pine and hardwood. Enjoy fishing for bass, catfish and sunfish. Electric motorboats only. Trails in the area include a hiking trail around the lake and an interpretive trail. Wildlife includes water moccasin, deer and birds.

GETTING THERE: From Rosiclare go N on state HWY 146 approx. 12 mi. to state HWY 1. Go N on 1 approx. 12 mi. to Pounds Hollow Recreation Area and Pine Ridge CG.

SINGLE RATE:	$5	OPEN DATES:	Apr-Dec
# of SINGLE SITES:	76	MAX SPUR:	51 feet
		MAX STAY:	14 days
		ELEVATION:	642 feet

10 Redbud
Harrisburg • lat 37°31'11" lon 088°39'28"

DESCRIPTION: This CG is heavily wooded with red pines and hardwoods. It offers nice, secluded sites. Supplies are available at Harrisburg. Numerous wildlife can be seen in the area. Campers may gather dead and down firewood. There are no designated trails in the area.

GETTING THERE: From Harrisburg go S on state HWY 34/145 approx. 6 mi. to forest route 402. Go W on 402 approx. 4 mi. to Bell Smith Spring Recreation Area and Redbud CG.

SINGLE RATE:	$5	OPEN DATES:	Mar-Dec
# of SINGLE SITES:	21	MAX SPUR:	73 feet
		MAX STAY:	14 days
		ELEVATION:	420 feet

11 Teal Pond
Harrisburg • lat 37°32'28" lon 088°38'34"

DESCRIPTION: This CG is located in a dense stand of red pines and hardwoods. The sites are secluded. Enjoy fishing for channel catfish and bass at the nearby lake. Supplies are available at Harrisburg. Many animals can be seen in the area. Campers may gather firewood. There are no designated trails in the area.

GETTING THERE: From Harrisburg go S on state HWY 34/145 approx. 6 mi. to forest route 402. Go W on 402 approx. 4 mi. to Bell Smith Spring Recreation Area and Teal Pond CG.

SINGLE RATE:	$5	OPEN DATES:	Yearlong
# of SINGLE SITES:	10	MAX SPUR:	63 feet
		MAX STAY:	14 days
		ELEVATION:	500 feet

12 Tower Rock
Rosiclare • lat 37°27'33" lon 088°13'46"

DESCRIPTION: The CG is located adjacent to the Ohio River. Fish for a variety of species in the river. Boat ramp at CG. Electric motors only on this river. Supplies available at Rosiclare. Numerous animals can be seen in the area. Campers may gather firewood. Tower Rock Trail is near the CG.

GETTING THERE: From Rosiclare go N on state HWY 146 approx. 2 mi. to turnoff. Go E on turnoff approx. 4 mi. to Tower Rock CG.

SINGLE RATE:	$5	OPEN DATES:	May-Dec
# of SINGLE SITES:	25	MAX SPUR:	57 feet
		MAX STAY:	14 days
		ELEVATION:	80 feet

13 Turkey Bayou
Murphysboro • lat 37°40'59" lon 089°24'45"

DESCRIPTION: This CG is in an open setting adjacent to the Big Muddy River. Boat ramp at CG, electric motorboats only. Enjoy fishing for crappie and channel catfish in the river. Supplies available at Murphysboro. Many animals can be seen in the area. Campers may gather dead and down firewood. Trails are nearby.

GETTING THERE: From Murphysboro go E on state HWY 149 approx. 3 mi. to state HWY 3. Go S on 3 approx. 10 mi. to forest route 786. Go E on 786 approx. 5 mi. to Turkey Bayou CG.

SINGLE RATE:	$3	OPEN DATES:	Yearlong
# of SINGLE SITES:	17	MAX SPUR:	59 feet
		MAX STAY:	14 days
		ELEVATION:	540 feet

Notes:

 Campground has hosts   Reservable sites   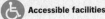 Accessible facilities   Fully developed    Semi-developed   Rustic facilities

NOTE: Open dates listed are typical. Actual dates are dependent on conditions such as snow pack.

CREATED BY NATURE.

ADAPTED BY COLEMAN.

INSPIRED BY NATURE™

www.coleman.com Visit. Explore. Discover.

USFS Photo

HOOSIER NATIONAL FOREST

Tucked away in the foothills of southern Indiana, the 196,000-acre Hoosier has many unique and interesting areas waiting to be discovered. Rolling hills, back-country trails, and rural crossroad communities make this small but beautiful forest a favorite in Indiana.

The area was used and inhabited continuously from as early as 12,000 years ago, first by Native Americans, and later by European and African Americans. Each group of people had an influence on the land leaving remnants such as cabins and house sites, abandoned charcoal pits, and rows of rocks piled up as fences by farmers a century ago.

The forest is also a collage of ecosystems which are home to over 381 species of mammals, birds, reptiles and amphibians, and fish. Each season holds its own special beauty; the white dogwoods and pink redbuds of spring, summer's emerald hills reflected in quiet lakes, the colorful pallet of autumn, and the shimmering beauty of a new snowfall. Approximately 239 miles of trails are available for your hiking, biking, or horse riding pleasure. Campgrounds sheltered under towering trees and thousands of acres open to hunting and nature study wait your visit.

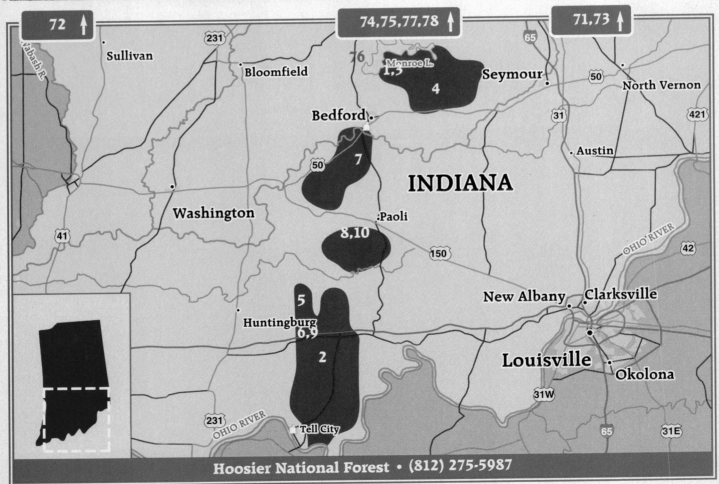

Hoosier National Forest • (812) 275-5987

1 Blackwell Trailhead
Bedford • lat 39°00'51" lon 086°23'52"

DESCRIPTION: This CG is located in an open meadow surrounded by hardwoods. Wildlife in the area includes deer, grouse, quail, hawks and eagle. This CG accesses approx. 31 mi. of horse and hiking trails in the Charles C. Deem Wilderness. No drinking water. Supplies in Bedford. Gather firewood locally.

GETTING THERE: From Bedford go NE on state HWY 58 approx. 8 mi. to state HWY 446. Go N on 446 approx. 8 mi. to forest route turnoff going east. Go E approx. 3/4 mi. to Blackwell Trailhead CG.

SINGLE RATE:	No fee	OPEN DATES:	Yearlong
# of SINGLE SITES:	100	MAX SPUR:	30 feet
		MAX STAY:	14 days
		ELEVATION:	760 feet

2 German Ridge
Cannelton • lat 37°57'06" lon 086°35'20"

DESCRIPTION: This CG is located in mixed hardwoods near German Ridge and a small lake. Enjoy the many hiking, mountain biking, and horse trails in the area. There are fishing and swimming opportunities 1 mi. away. Horses are allowed in the CG. Wildlife in this area includes deer, turkeys, quail, and songbirds.

GETTING THERE: From Cannelton go NE on state HWY 66 approx. 14 mi. to county route going N. Go N on the county route approx. 1 mi. to German Ridge CG.

SINGLE RATE:	$4	OPEN DATES:	Yearlong
# of SINGLE SITES:	20		
		MAX STAY:	14 days
		ELEVATION:	755 feet

3 Hardin Ridge
Bedford • lat 39°01'08" lon 086°27'05"

DESCRIPTION: This CG is located in maple and oak on Lake Monroe. Enjoy fishing for bass, bluegill, walleye, pike, and catfish. Wildlife includes deer, grouse, quail, eagle, and hawks. Busy weekends and holidays. Showers are provided. Playground, ampitheatre, boat ramp, and nature walks available on site.

GETTING THERE: From Bedford go NE on state HWY 58 approx. 8 mi. to state HWY 446. Go N on 446 approx. 8 mi. to Hardin Ridge Road. Go E on Hardin Ridge Rd. approx. 2.5 mi. to Hardin Ridge CG.

SINGLE RATE:	Varies	OPEN DATES:	Apr-Oct
# of SINGLE SITES:	198	MAX SPUR:	30 feet
		MAX STAY:	14 days
		ELEVATION:	800 feet

4 Hickory Ridge Trailhead
Norman • lat 38°95'00" lon 086°17'00"

DESCRIPTION: This CG is located in mixed hardwoods with forest views. Wildlife in the area includes deer, grouse, quail, eagle and hawks. Enjoy the many horse, hiking, and mountain biking trails nearby. Supplies in Norman. Gather firewood locally. This CG offers no drinking water but does have a water tank for horses.

GETTING THERE: From Norman go N approximately 2 miles to Hickory Ridge Trailhead CG.

SINGLE RATE:	$4	OPEN DATES:	Yearlong
# of SINGLE SITES:	20	MAX SPUR:	30 feet
		MAX STAY:	14 days
		ELEVATION:	750 feet

5 Indian-Celina Lake
Tell City • lat 38°11'27" lon 086°39'20"

DESCRIPTION: In an open park-like setting of oak and hickory. Indian and Celina Lakes are nearby. Pan fish in the lakes. Historic Rickenbaugh House and Cemetery nearby. Supplies approx. 5 mi. Deer, turkeys, quail, osprey and raptors in the area. Two Lakes Loop National Recreation Trail encircles the lakes. Busy weekends.

GETTING THERE: From Tell City go NE on state HWY 37 approx. 19 mi. to forest route 501. Go E on 501 approx. 1/2 mi. to Lake Celina CG and 3 mi. to Indian Lake CG.

SINGLE RATE:	Varies	OPEN DATES:	Apr-Oct
# of SINGLE SITES:	63	MAX SPUR:	50 feet
		MAX STAY:	14 days
		ELEVATION:	480 feet

6 Saddle Lake
Tell City • lat 38°03'50" lon 086°39'57"

DESCRIPTION: This CG is situated in mixed hardwoods on Saddle Lake. Enjoy fishing and boating on the lake. A boat ramp is provided at this CG. There is also a hiking trail nearby. Wildlife in this area includes deer, turkeys, quail, and songbirds. Campers may also catch a glimpse of hawks, bald eagle and osprey.

GETTING THERE: From Tell City go N on state HWY 37 approx. 9 mi. to forest route 443. Go W on 443 approx. 1.5 mi. to Saddle Lake CG.

SINGLE RATE:	No fee	OPEN DATES:	Yearlong
# of SINGLE SITES:	10	MAX SPUR:	20 feet
		MAX STAY:	14 days
		ELEVATION:	570 feet

7 Shirley Creek Trailhead
Prospect • lat 38°38'58" lon 086°35'51"

DESCRIPTION: This CG is located in mixed hardwoods with a nearby spring for watering horses. No drinking water. Wildlife in the area includes deer, grouse, quail, eagle, and hawks. Enjoy the many horse, hiking, and mountain biking trails nearby. Supplies in Prospect. Gather firewood locally.

GETTING THERE: From Prospect go N on county route approx. 4.5 mi. to Shirley Creek Trailhead CG.

SINGLE RATE:	Varies	OPEN DATES:	Apr-Oct
# of SINGLE SITES:	40	MAX SPUR:	30 feet
		MAX STAY:	14 days
		ELEVATION:	695 feet

8 Springs Valley
Paoli • lat 38°30'00" lon 086°43'30"

DESCRIPTION: This primitive CG is located in mixed hardwoods on Tucker Lake. There are horse and hiking trails, and a boat ramp nearby. Wildlife in this area includes deer, turkeys, quail, and songbirds. The route of Vincennes (Buffalo) Trace runs close to this CG. Supplies in Paoli.

GETTING THERE: From Paoli go SW on county route approx. 8 mi. to Springs Valley Recreation Area and CG.

SINGLE RATE:	No fee	OPEN DATES:	Yearlong
		MAX STAY:	14 days
		ELEVATION:	600 feet

9 Tipsaw Lake
Tell City • lat 38°07'28" lon 086°38'57"

DESCRIPTION: In open park like setting of mixed hickory, oak and pine. Some sites with power. Hot humid summers. Fish by boat (electric motors allowed) for bass, crappie, bluegill and catfish. Boat ramp, fishing pier. Supplies 5 mi. Deer, turkeys and small wildlife. Fills weekends. Hiking trail around lake.

GETTING THERE: From Tell City go N on state HWY 37 approx. 17 mi. (Tipsaw sign) to forest route 503. Go W on 503 approx. 3 mi. to Tipsaw CG. (OR approx. 6 mi. S of HWY 64 off state HWY 37 to Tipsaw sign.)

SINGLE RATE:	Varies	OPEN DATES:	May-Oct
# of SINGLE SITES:	41	MAX SPUR:	60 feet
GROUP RATE:	Varies	MAX STAY:	14 days
# of GROUP SITES:	3	ELEVATION:	450 feet

10 Youngs Creek Horse Camp
Paoli • lat 38°30'00" lon 086°28'00"

DESCRIPTION: This primitive CG is situated in mixed hardwoods near a small creek. This CG is ideal for horse trail riding with several miles of trails nearby. The horse, hiking, and mountain biking trails may require permits for use. Wildlife in this area includes deer, turkeys, quail, and songbirds.

GETTING THERE: From Paoli go SW on county roads approx. 3 mi. to Youngs Creek Horse Camp.

SINGLE RATE:	No fee	OPEN DATES:	Yearlong
# of SINGLE SITES:	50	MAX SPUR:	30 feet
		MAX STAY:	14 days
		ELEVATION:	600 feet

 Campground has hosts   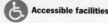 **Reservable sites**   **Accessible facilities**   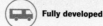 **Fully developed**   **Semi-developed**   **Rustic facilities**

NOTE: Open dates listed are typical. Actual dates are dependent on conditions such as snow pack.

Iowa Recreation Lakes site listings: page 626

Kansas Recreation Lakes site listings: page 626-627

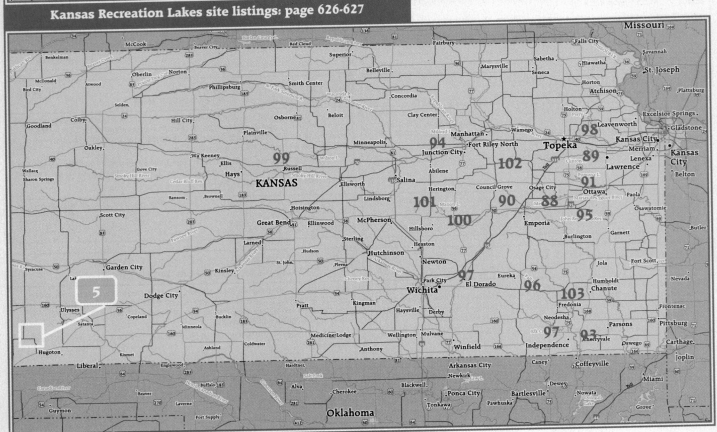

Wild Fire Expense

In 1999, the federal government spent $591 million to fight fires that burned 605,000 acres in the USA. Many of these fires were started by careless people, some of whom were billed for the expenses of putting out the fires they started. These bills can reach into the hundreds of thousands of dollars. Ouch! That burns!

Daniel Boone National Forest

Located in the mountains of eastern Kentucky, the Daniel Boone National Forest encompasses over 693,043 acres of land. This land is generally rugged and characterized by steep forested ridges, narrow valleys, and over 3,400 miles of cliff lines. The forest contains two large lakes (Cave Run Lake and Laurel River Lake), many rivers and streams, two wilderness areas, and the 269-mile Sheltowee Trace National Recreation Trail that extends across the length of the forest. Abundant wildlife, lush vegetation, magnificent scenery, and numerous recreation opportunities offer visitors much to enjoy.

Named in the honor of the explorer who came to know and love the forested land and waterways, the Daniel Boone National Forest is one of the most heavily used forests in the South, with over 5 million visitors annually. People come here to backpack, camp, picnic, rock climb, boat, hunt, fish, and relax.

Much of the forest is quiet and primitive. It is rich in cultural resources, containing the highest concentration of rock shelters in the U.S. and the oldest archeological site in the Southeast. There are many geological wonders such as the Red River Gorge Geological Area and Natural Arch Scenic Area.

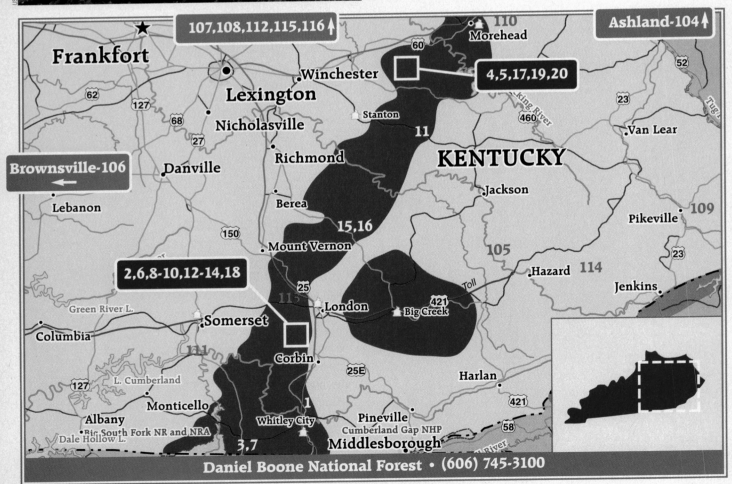

1 Barren Fork
Whitley City • lat 36°46'30" lon 084°27'30"

DESCRIPTION: Among hardwood & pine, with some shady sites. Hot summer, frequent t-storms. Stream fish for bass & panfish. Historic site of a coal mining town nearby. Deer, turkeys & birds in area. Hiking, horse & mountain biking trails nearby. Gnats, flies & ticks in summer.

GETTING THERE: From Whitley City go N on US HWY 27 approx. 3 mi. to forest route 684. Go E on 684 approx. 1/2 mi. to Barren Fork CG.

SINGLE RATE:	$8	OPEN DATES:	Yearlong
# of SINGLE SITES:	41	MAX SPUR:	60 feet
		MAX STAY:	14 days
		ELEVATION:	1240 feet

2 Bee Rock
London • lat 37°01'37" lon 084°19'19"

DESCRIPTION: This CG sits along the Rockcastle River and offers a beautiful view of the dramatic rocks and cliffs. Be aware: Swift currents and undertows on this river can make swimming and wading very dangerous. No swimming within 100 feet of boat ramp. Visit Old Sublimity Bridge, a historical CCC structure.

GETTING THERE: From London go W on state HWY 192 approx. 18 mi. to Bee Rock CG.

SINGLE RATE:	Varies	OPEN DATES:	Apr-Oct
# of SINGLE SITES:	28	MAX SPUR:	35 feet
		MAX STAY:	14 days
		ELEVATION:	800 feet

3 Bell Farm
Whitley City • lat 36°40'10" lon 084°40'06"

DESCRIPTION: In a sparse overstory of walnut trees on Rock Creek, a Wild & Scenic river. Hot days, frequent t-storms. Trout fish the creek. Supplies 2 mi. away. Deer, turkeys, raccoons and birds in area. Historic logging and mining town nearby. Fills weekends May-Sept. Horse, hike & mtn bike trails nearby.

GETTING THERE: From Whitley City go S on US HWY 27 approx. 4.7 mi. to state HWY 92. Go W approx. 6.5 mi. to state HWY 1363. Go SW on 1363 approx. 11.4 mi. to Bell Farm CG.

SINGLE RATE:	No fee	OPEN DATES:	Yearlong
# of SINGLE SITES:	5	MAX SPUR:	45 feet
GROUP RATE:	No fee	MAX STAY:	14 days
# of GROUP SITES:	5	ELEVATION:	941 feet

4 Claylick Boat-in
Morehead • lat 38°03'32" lon 083°28'20"

DESCRIPTION: CG is located on Cave Run Lake and is accessible by boat or foot (weather permitting) only. Some sites are on lakeshore and some are in hardwood forest. Fish for muskie, bass, crappie, and catfish. Visit historic iron furnace and fire tower. Busy summer weekends. Trails in area. Boat ramp.

GETTING THERE: From Morehead go S on US HWY 60 approx. 1 mi. to HWY 519. Go S on 519 approx. 2.5 mi. to HWY 1274. Go W then S on 1274 approx. 5 mi. to forest route 968. Go W on 968 approx. 1 mi. to CG.

SINGLE RATE:	$5	OPEN DATES:	Apr-Nov
# of SINGLE SITES:	19		
		MAX STAY:	14 days
		ELEVATION:	778 feet

5 Clear Creek
Salt Lick • lat 38°02'30" lon 083°35'30"

DESCRIPTION: CG is located in dense hardwoods with Clear Creek running through it. Good fishing in nearby Clear Creek Lake. Near the remains of an old iron furnace and a restored fire tower. Supplies 2 mi. to Clear Creek Market. Deer, turkeys and waterfowl in area. Busy holiday weekends. Numerous trails in area.

GETTING THERE: From Salt Lick go S on state HWY 211 approx. 4 mi. to forest route 129. Go S and E on 129 approx. 2.5 to Clear Creek CG.

SINGLE RATE:	$8	OPEN DATES:	Mar-Nov
# of SINGLE SITES:	18	MAX SPUR:	45 feet
GROUP RATE:	$12	MAX STAY:	14 days
# of GROUP SITES:	3	ELEVATION:	750 feet

6 Craigs Creek
London • lat 37°36'30" lon 084°15'30"

DESCRIPTION: This CG is in an open park-like setting on Laurel River Lake. Fish for trout and bass from the lake. Historical site and supplies in London. Deer, birds, small mammals and reptiles in the area. Campers may gather firewood. Craigs Creek Trail #420 connects to the CG. Boat ramp 1/2 mi. away.

GETTING THERE: From London go W on state HWY 192 approx. 12.2 miles to forest route 62. Go S on 62 approx. 2 mi. to Craigs Creek CG.

		OPEN DATES:	Apr-Oct
		MAX SPUR:	45 feet
GROUP RATE:	Varies	MAX STAY:	14 days
# of GROUP SITES:	3	ELEVATION:	1050 feet

7 Great Meadow
Whitley City • lat 36°37'57" lon 084°43'40"

DESCRIPTION: This CG is located in an open, park like setting of pine and hardwoods on Rock Creek. Summer days are hot with frequent thunder storms. Enjoy fishing for trout in the creek. Supplies are approximately 8 mi. away. Deer, turkeys, raccoons are common in this area. Horses are not allowed in CG.

GETTING THERE: From Whitley City go S 5 mi. on US HWY 27 to HWY 92. Go W 7 mi. on 92 to HWY 1363. Go SW 11 mi. on 1363 to forest route 564. Go SW 1 mi. on 564 to forest route 137. Go SW 4 mi. on 137 to CG.

SINGLE RATE:	No fee	OPEN DATES:	Yearlong
# of SINGLE SITES:	18	MAX SPUR:	45 feet
GROUP RATE:	No fee	MAX STAY:	14 days
# of GROUP SITES:	2	ELEVATION:	1100 feet

8 Grove
Corbin • lat 36°56'00" lon 084°13'30"

DESCRIPTION: In a mixed hardwood forest setting on a ridge above Laurel River Lake. Fish for bass, trout and catfish from the river. Supplies at Grove Marina approx. 1/2 mi. from CG. Deer, bird, small mammals and reptiles are common to the area. Firewood is sold by concessionaire. Many trails in the area.

GETTING THERE: From Corbin go S on US HWY 25W approx. 3 mi. to state HWY 1193. Go N on 1193 approx. 2 mi. to forest route 558. Go NE on 558 approx. 3 mi. to Grove CG.

SINGLE RATE:	Varies	OPEN DATES:	Apr-Oct
# of SINGLE SITES:	56	MAX SPUR:	45 feet
		MAX STAY:	14 days
		ELEVATION:	1140 feet

9 Grove Boat-in
Corbin • lat 36°57'00" lon 084°13'30"

DESCRIPTION: CG is accessible by boat or by trail from Grove CG. It rests in a mixed forest setting on Laurel River Lake. Fish for trout, bass and catfish. Supplies at Grove Marina. Deer and reptiles are common to area. Firewood is sold by concessionaire. There are many trails in the area.

GETTING THERE: From Corbin go S on US HWY 25W approx. 3 mi. to state HWY 1193. Go N on 1193 approx. 2 mi. to forest route 558. Go NE on 558 approx. 3 mi. to Grove CG. Then boat or hike 1 mi. N to CG.

SINGLE RATE:	Varies	OPEN DATES:	Yearlong
# of SINGLE SITES:	32		
		MAX STAY:	14 days
		ELEVATION:	1050 feet

10 Holly Bay
London • lat 36°58'56" lon 084°16'00"

DESCRIPTION: In a mixed hardwood forest setting just above Laurel River Lake. Fish for bass, trout & catfish from the lake. Supplies available at Holly Bay Marina. Firewood is sold by concessionaire. Boat ramp, RV dump station, amphitheater, & interpretive programs on site. Deer, amphibians & reptiles are common.

GETTING THERE: From London go W on state HWY 192 approx. 14 miles to state HWY 1193. Go S on 1193 approx. 3 mi. to Holly Bay CG.

SINGLE RATE:	Varies	OPEN DATES:	Apr-Oct
# of SINGLE SITES:	94	MAX SPUR:	45 feet
		MAX STAY:	14 days
		ELEVATION:	1085 feet

 Campground has hosts   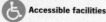 **Reservable sites**   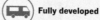 **Accessible facilities**   **Fully developed**   Semi-developed   **Rustic facilities**

NOTE: Open dates listed are typical. Actual dates are dependent on conditions such as snow pack.

11 Koomer Ridge
Stanton • lat 37°47'06" lon 083°37'45"

DESCRIPTION: Tent only camping in hardwood-pine forest. Nearby overlooks feature 100' cliffs. Mild days. Stream fish for bass and catfish. Historic Gladie Creek Site is along a 30-mi loop in the Red River Gorge Geological Area. Basic supplies are 3 mi. away. Deer, raccoons & small wildlife are common to this area.

GETTING THERE: From Stanton go SE on state HWY 15 approx. 15 mi. to Koomer Ridge CG.

SINGLE RATE:	$10	OPEN DATES:	Yearlong
# of SINGLE SITES:	54		
		MAX STAY:	14 days
		ELEVATION:	1200 feet

16 Turkeys Foot
Richmond • lat 37°28'00" lon 083°53'00"

DESCRIPTION: This CG is located near War Fork Creek. Hiking, OHV, mountain biking and horseback riding are allowed on portions of the nearby Sheltowee Trace. Deer, amphibians and reptiles are common to the area. No drinking water is available at this CG. There is a playing field nearby.

GETTING THERE: From Richmond go S on US HWY 421 approx. 30 mi. to state HWY 89. Go N on 89 approx. 3 mi. to forest route 4. Go E on 4 approx. 3 mi. to Turkeys Foot CG.

SINGLE RATE:	No fee	OPEN DATES:	Apr-Nov
# of SINGLE SITES:	15		
		MAX STAY:	14 days
		ELEVATION:	1000 feet

12 Little Lick
Somerset • lat 36°57'52" lon 084°23'52"

DESCRIPTION: This CG sits on a long ridgetop at the end of the Nathan McClure Trail. The CG sits north of the Cumberland River and west of the Rockcastle River which both offer good fishing. The CG is designed for horses with trailer parking, stock watering pond, corral, and a hitching rail. No drinking water on site.

GETTING THERE: From Somerset go E on state HWY 192 aprx. 21 mi. to forest route 122. Go S on 122 aprx. 4 mi. to forest route 816. Go W on 816 aprx. 2 mi. to forest route 816B. Go S on 816B aprx. 2 mi. to CG.

SINGLE RATE:	No fee	OPEN DATES:	Yearlong
# of SINGLE SITES:	8	MAX SPUR:	20 feet
		MAX STAY:	14 days
		ELEVATION:	1050 feet

17 Twin Knobs
Owingsville • lat 38°05'41" lon 083°31'01"

DESCRIPTION: CG is located on a peninsula and offers open and forested sites with views of Cave Run Lake. Fish for muskie, bass, crappie, and catfish. Supplies are on site. Deer, turkeys, and geese in area. Busy summer weekends. There are a variety of trails nearby. Boat ramp, RV dump station, & beach on site.

GETTING THERE: From Owingsville go E on US HW 60 approx. 12 mi. to state HWY 801. Go SE on 801 approx. 6.5 mi. to Twin Knobs CG.

SINGLE RATE:	Varies	OPEN DATES:	Mar-Oct
# of SINGLE SITES:	216	MAX SPUR:	50 feet
GROUP RATE:	Varies	MAX STAY:	14 days
# of GROUP SITES:	3	ELEVATION:	795 feet

13 Rockcastle
London • lat 36°57'42" lon 084°20'48"

DESCRIPTION: In a hardwood forested area with views of Cumberland Lake. Fish for bass, trout and catfish from the lake. Supplies available at London Dock Marina. Deer, amphibians and reptiles are common to the area. Campers may gather firewood. Several hiking trails are accessible from the CG.

GETTING THERE: From London go W on state HWY 192 approx. 14 mi. to state HWY 1193. Go S on 1193 approx. 1 mi. to state HWY 3497. Go W on 3497 approx. 6 mi. to Rockcastle CG. Small RVs only.

SINGLE RATE:	$8	OPEN DATES:	May-Oct
# of SINGLE SITES:	24	MAX SPUR:	25 feet
		MAX STAY:	14 days
		ELEVATION:	840 feet

18 White Oak Boat-In
London • lat 37°59'30" lon 084°13'30"

DESCRIPTION: This boat or hike-in CG is in mixed hardwoods with views of Laurel River Lake. Fish for bass, trout, crappie and catfish from the lake. Supplies are available at London. Deer, amphibians, small mammals, birds and reptiles are common to the area. Firewood sold at CG. Many trails in the area.

GETTING THERE: From London go W on state HWY 192 approx. 12 mi. to forest route 774. Go S on 774 approx. 2 mi. to Marsh Branch boat launch. Boat or hike 1 mi. S to White Oak CG. CG is on W side of lake.

SINGLE RATE:	Varies	OPEN DATES:	Yearlong
# of SINGLE SITES:	51		
		MAX STAY:	14 days
		ELEVATION:	1040 feet

14 Sawyer
Cumberland Falls • lat 36°56'13" lon 084°20'38"

DESCRIPTION: This quiet CG rests on Upper Lake Cumberland. The CG offers scenic views of the Cumberland River, cliff formations, and fishing opportunities. Enjoy a hike on the Cliffside Trail. This trail is an easy hike for most and offers fishing spots made by previous fishermen. No drinking water on site.

GETTING THERE: From Cumberland Falls go W on state HWY 90 approx. 2 mi. to state HWY 896. Go N on 896 approx. 6 mi. to state HWY 1609. Go N on 1609 approx. 1.5 mi. to Sawyer CG.

SINGLE RATE:	No fee	OPEN DATES:	Apr-Oct
# of SINGLE SITES:	6	MAX SPUR:	35 feet
		MAX STAY:	14 days
		ELEVATION:	960 feet

19 White Sulphur
Salt Lick • lat 38°05'30" lon 083°34'30"

DESCRIPTION: This is a rustic, wooded, and dispersed CG. Good fishing is nearby. Visit the historic iron furnace & fire tower. Supplies 2 mi. at Clear Creek store. There are almost 100 miles of trails. Horse trailer parking, corrals. Trail riders must use extra caution during hunting season, especially Oct & Nov..

GETTING THERE: From Salt Lick go S on state HWY 211 approx. 4 mi. to forest route 129. Go SE on 129 approx. 1.5 mi. to forest route 105. Go NE on 105 approx. 2 mi. to White Sulphur CG.

SINGLE RATE:	$10	OPEN DATES:	Yearlong
		MAX SPUR:	70 feet
		MAX STAY:	14 days
		ELEVATION:	800 feet

15 S-Tree
Mount Vernon • lat 37°22'30" lon 084°03'30"

DESCRIPTION: This CG is located in a remote forest setting. No drinking water is available on site. Hiking, OHV, mtn. biking and horseback riding are allowed on portions of the Sheltowee Trace National Recreation Trail and the Renfro Loop Trail. There is a picnic shelter on site.

GETTING THERE: From Mount Vernon go E on US HWY 25 approx. 2 mi. to state HWY 89. Go E on 89 approx. 18 mi. to forest route 20. Go N on 20 approx. 2 mi. to S-Tree CG.

SINGLE RATE:	No fee	OPEN DATES:	Apr-Nov
# of SINGLE SITES:	20		
		MAX STAY:	14 days
		ELEVATION:	1000 feet

20 Zilpo Recreation Area
Salt Lick • lat 38°03'00" lon 083°29'00"

DESCRIPTION: CG is located on a peninsula and has both open & shady sites with dense underbrush. Scenic views are of Cave Run Lake. Deer, turkeys, & geese are common in the area. Busy summer weekends. Firewood on site. There are almost 100 trails in area. Boat ramp, amphitheater, & RV dump station on site.

GETTING THERE: From Salt Lick go S on state HWY 211 approx. 4 mi. to forest route 129. Go S and E on 129 approx. 12 mi. to Zilpo Recreation Area.

SINGLE RATE:	Varies	OPEN DATES:	Apr-Oct
# of SINGLE SITES:	174	MAX SPUR:	50 feet
		MAX STAY:	14 days
		ELEVATION:	800 feet

 Campground has hosts   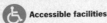 **Reservable sites**   **Accessible facilities**   **Fully developed**   **Semi-developed**   **Rustic facilities**

NOTE: Open dates listed are typical. Actual dates are dependent on conditions such as snow pack.

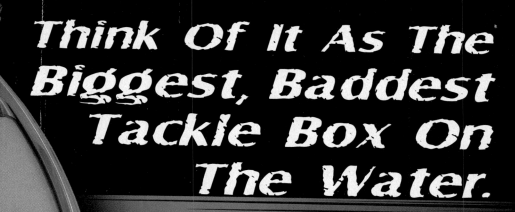

Think Of It As The Biggest, Baddest Tackle Box On The Water.

VX SERIES Comanche

Out here, seconds and ounces rule. And coming unprepared is not an option. We couldn't have asked for a better arena to introduce the extreme performance of the all-new VX series. Designed with more deck space, lockable storage, and fuel capacity, as well as even greater stability, responsivness, and comfort... VX engineering is setting the standards for the next millennium. VX. It's where you go for confidence and where you find the leaders.

See Your Authorized Ranger Dealer or Call:
1·800·373·BOAT(2628)

©Copyright 1999 Ranger® Boats

Ranger BOATS
rangerboats.com

Model Shown:
522VX Comanche

Nowhere near actual size!

EVINRUDE

USFS Photo

KISATCHIE NATIONAL FOREST

The Kisatchie National Forest encompasses over a million acres of lush undulating hills, lakes and bayous. With over 342 miles of trails and 8,700 acres of remote wilderness, the Kisatchie provides a special place to relax and savor your leisure time.

The forest supports a variety of wildlife, including more than 280 species. The bald eagle, black bear, red-cockaded woodpecker and the American alligator are animals found in the Kisatchie who are federally listed as threatened. The presence of at least 92 species of fish has been documented on the Kisatchie's reservoirs, lakes, streams and ponds.

The Kisatchie is a great place to recreate no matter what the season. Float along the bottomland hardwood forest of the Saline Bayou National Scenic and Wild River. Escape the summer heat at one of the forest's many lakes, or kick up rustling leaves along one of the many hiking trails in the fall. Gather around the campfire during a mild Louisiana winter or discover the first flush of wildflowers in early spring. One scenic byway, the 17-mile Longleaf Trail, traverses the forest, which allows visitors to see the forest by car.

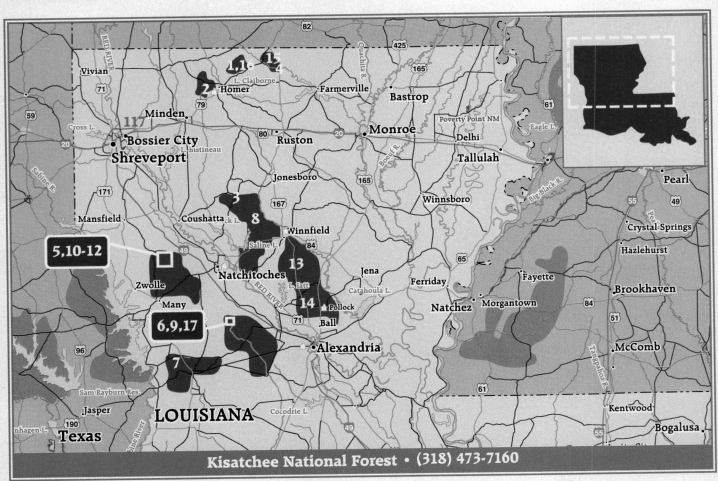

Kisatchee National Forest • (318) 473-7160

1 Bucktail Camp
Homer • lat 32°53'30" lon 093°00'00"

DESCRIPTION: This primitive CG is located in a pine-hardwood forest setting near the Middle Fork of the Bayou D'Arbonne River. Fish and swim in the river. Supplies available at Homer. Deer, raccoons, squirrels and birds are common to the area. No designated trails in the area.

GETTING THERE: From Homer go N on US HWY 79 approx. 6 mi. to country route 937. Go E on 937 approx. 4.5 mi. to Bucktail Camp CG.

SINGLE RATE:	No fee	OPEN DATES:	Yearlong
# of SINGLE SITES:	25		
		MAX STAY:	14 days
		ELEVATION:	200 feet

2 Caney Lakes
Minden • lat 32°41'00" lon 091°80'00"

DESCRIPTION: CG is surrounded by wooded hills on the Caney Lakes shores. Boat ramps at the CG. Fish and swim the lakes in the area. Supplies available at Minden. Deer, raccoons and birds are common to the area. Campers may gather firewood. Many trails in the area. RV dump station at the CG.

GETTING THERE: From Minden go N on state HWY 159 approx. 3 mi. to forest route 929. Go W on 929 approx. 2 mi. to Caney Lakes CG.

SINGLE RATE:	Varies	OPEN DATES:	Yearlong
# of SINGLE SITES:	51	MAX SPUR:	36 feet
		MAX STAY:	14 days
		ELEVATION:	200 feet

3 Cloud Crossing
Goldonna • lat 32°05'00" lon 092°54'24"

DESCRIPTION: In a mixed forest setting on the Faline Bayou. Fish or boat on the Bayou, no swimming here. Supplies available at Goldonna. Many animals can be seen in the area. Campers may gather firewood. A 2.3 mi. hiking trail is near the CG area.

GETTING THERE: From Goldonna go N on parish route 585 approx. 3 mi. to forest route 570. Go NW on 570 approx. 1 mi. to forest route 513. Go E on 513 approx. 2 mi. to Cloud Crossing CG.

SINGLE RATE:	No fee	OPEN DATES:	Yearlong
# of SINGLE SITES:	15	MAX SPUR:	42 feet
		MAX STAY:	14 days
		ELEVATION:	145 feet

4 Corney Lake
Summerfield • lat 32°54'30" lon 092°44'00"

DESCRIPTION: In a mixed forest setting on Corney Lake. Excellent area for fishing. Boat ramp at CG. Supplies available at Summerfield. Deer, raccoons and waterfowl can be seen in the area. Campers may gather firewood. Many trails in the area. Picnic area nearby.

GETTING THERE: From Summerfield go N on state HWY 9 approx. 2.5 mi. to forest route 900. Go SE on 900 approx. 3 mi. to Corney Lakes CG.

SINGLE RATE:	No fee	OPEN DATES:	Yearlong
		MAX STAY:	14 days
		ELEVATION:	200 feet

5 Dogwood
Provencal • lat 31°29'24" lon 093°11'42"

DESCRIPTION: In an attractive forest setting of pines and dogwood with the Kisatchie Bayou nearby. Supplies available at Provencal. Numerous wildlife can be seen in the area. Campers may gather firewood. An interpretive display about the national forest is near the CG area.

GETTING THERE: From Provencal go S on state HWY 117 approx. 11 mi. to Dogwood CG.

SINGLE RATE:	No fee	OPEN DATES:	Yearlong
# of SINGLE SITES:	12	MAX SPUR:	42 feet
		MAX STAY:	14 days
		ELEVATION:	201 feet

6 Evangeline Camp
Alexandria • lat 31°13'55" lon 092°36'37"

DESCRIPTION: This semi-primitive dispersed CG near Kincaid Lake. Fish and swim in the lake. Boat ramp in the area. Supplies available at Alexandria. Deer, raccoons and birds are common in the area. Campers may gather firewood. A network of hiking trails in the area connecting with the Wild Azalea NRT.

GETTING THERE: From Alexandria go SW on state HWY 488 approx. 8.5 mi. to forest route 273. Go N on 273 approx. 1 mi. to Evangeline Camp CG.

SINGLE RATE:	No fee	OPEN DATES:	Yearlong
# of SINGLE SITES:	30		
		MAX STAY:	14 days
		ELEVATION:	195 feet

7 Fullerton Lake
Pitkin • lat 31°00'40" lon 092°59'15"

DESCRIPTION: In a mixed hardwood forest setting on Fullerton Lake. Fish for bass and swim in lake. Boat ramp at CG, non-motorized boats only. Supplies available at Pitkin. Deer, raccoons and birds are common in the area. Campers may gather firewood. Many trails in area.

GETTING THERE: From Pitkin go N on Parish route 41 approx. 3.5 mi. to forest route 449. Go W on 449 approx. 2 mi. to Fullerton Lake CG.

SINGLE RATE:	$2	OPEN DATES:	Yearlong
		MAX STAY:	14 days
		ELEVATION:	215 feet

8 Gum Springs
Winnfield • lat 31°53'49" lon 092°46'43"

DESCRIPTION: In a bottomland hardwood forest setting on the Saline Bayou. Bank or boat fish for bass, bluegill, dollar sunfish and catfish. Supplies available at Winnfield. Deer, rabbit, wood ducks, mink and many other animals can be seen in the area. Many trails nearby.

GETTING THERE: From Winnfield go SW on US HWY 84 approx. 7.5 mi. to Gum Springs CG.

SINGLE RATE:	$3	OPEN DATES:	Yearlong
# of SINGLE SITES:	16	MAX SPUR:	42 feet
		MAX STAY:	14 days
		ELEVATION:	307 feet

9 Kincaid
Alexandria • lat 31°15'40" lon 092°37'40"

DESCRIPTION: In a mixed hardwood setting on Kincaid Lake. Fish and swim in lake. Boat ramp in the area. Supplies available at Alexandria. Deer, raccoons and birds are common in the area. Campers may gather firewood. A network of hiking trails in the area connecting with the Wild Azalea National Recreation Trail.

GETTING THERE: From Alexandria go SW on state HWY 488 approx. 10 mi. to Parish Road 279. Go N on 279 approx. 2 mi. to forest route 205. Go NE on 205 approx. 2.5 mi. to Kincaid CG.

SINGLE RATE:	Varies	OPEN DATES:	Yearlong
# of SINGLE SITES:	50		
		MAX STAY:	14 days
		ELEVATION:	174 feet

10 Kisatchie Bayou Camp
Provencal • lat 31°26'29" lon 093°05'21"

DESCRIPTION: This hike-in tent only CG is situated on the banks of the Kisatchie Bayou. Fishing and canoeing can be done on the bayou. Supplies available at Provencal. Numerous animals can be seen in the area. The Backbone Trail is nearby for hiking and horseback riding.

GETTING THERE: From Provencal go S on state HWY 117 to state HWY 118. Go SE 7 mi. on 118 to FS 360. Go N 2 mi. on 360 to FS 321. Go N 1.5 mi. on 321 to FS 366. Go NW 2 mi. on 366 to Kisatchie Bayou Camp.

SINGLE RATE:	$2	OPEN DATES:	Yearlong
		MAX STAY:	14 days
		ELEVATION:	235 feet

KISATCHIE NATIONAL FOREST • LOUISIANA • 1 — 10

 Campground has hosts   **Reservable sites**   **Accessible facilities**   **Fully developed**   **Semi-developed**   **Rustic facilities**

NOTE: Open dates listed are typical. Actual dates are dependent on conditions such as snow pack.

11 Lotus
Provencal • lat 31˚29'09" lon 093˚07'58"

DESCRIPTION: This primitive CG is located in a hardwood and pine forest setting adjacent to the National Red Dirt Wildlife Management Preserve. Supplies available at Provencal. Deer, turkeys, squirrels and birds are common to the area. Campers may gather firewood. Trails in the area.

GETTING THERE: From Provencal go S on state HWY 117 approx. 11 mi. to state HWY 119. Go E on 119 approx. 4.5 mi. to Lotus CG.

SINGLE RATE:	No fee	OPEN DATES:	Yearlong
		MAX STAY:	14 days
		ELEVATION:	24 feet

12 Red Bluff
Provencal • lat 31˚29'52" lon 093˚08'32"

DESCRIPTION: This primitive tent only CG is in a mixed forest setting on the banks of the Kisatchie Bayou. Supplies available at Provencal. Numerous wildlife can be seen in the area. Campers may gather firewood. Many trails in the area.

GETTING THERE: From Provencal go S on state HWY 117 approx. 11 mi. to state HWY 119. Go E on 119 approx. 5 mi. to forest route 342. Go NW on 342 approx. 2.5 mi. to Red Bluff CG.

SINGLE RATE:	No fee	OPEN DATES:	Yearlong
		MAX STAY:	14 days
		ELEVATION:	224 feet

13 Saddle Bayou Hunter Camp
Dry Prong • lat 31˚42'10" lon 092˚36'11"

DESCRIPTION: This tent only, primitive CG is in a mixed forest setting. No drinking water. Supplies available at Dry Prong. Deer, squirrels and birds are common to the area. Campers may gather firewood. Trails in the area.

GETTING THERE: From Dry Prong go N on US HWY 167 approx. 5.5 mi. to parish route 155. Go NW on 155 approx. 3 mi. to Saddle Bayou CG.

SINGLE RATE:	No fee	OPEN DATES:	Yearlong
		MAX STAY:	14 days
		ELEVATION:	115 feet

14 Stuart Lake
Dry Prong • lat 31˚30'33" lon 092˚26'38"

DESCRIPTION: In an attractive wooded setting on peaceful Stuart Lake. Fish or swim in lake, non-motorized boats only. Supplies available at Dry Prong. Deer, squirrels and birds are common to area. Hike and bike trails nearby. An interpretive trail leads around CG area. RV dump station and amphitheater at CG.

GETTING THERE: From Dry Prong go SE on US HWY 167 approx. 4.5 mi. to state HWY 8. Go E on 8 approx. 4 mi. to forest route 144. Go S on 144 approx. 1 mi. to Stuart Lake CG.

SINGLE RATE:	$5	OPEN DATES:	Yearlong
# of SINGLE SITES:	8	MAX SPUR:	32 feet
		MAX STAY:	14 days
		ELEVATION:	160 feet

15 Sugar Creek Camp
Summerfield • lat 32˚58'30" lon 092˚47'00"

DESCRIPTION: This primitive CG is located in a pine-hardwood forest setting on Sugar Creek. Fish or swim in the creek. Supplies available at Summerfield. Deer, raccoons, squirrels and birds are common to the area. Campers may gather firewood. Trails in the area. No drinking water.

GETTING THERE: From Summerfield go NE on state HWY 9 approx. 6 mi. to forest route 904. Go W on 904 approx. 2 mi. to Sugar Creek Camp CG.

SINGLE RATE:	No fee	OPEN DATES:	Yearlong
# of SINGLE SITES:	10	MAX STAY:	14 days
		ELEVATION:	200 feet

16 Turkeys Trot Camp
Antioch • lat 33˚53'00" lon 092˚75'30"

DESCRIPTION: This tent only, primitive CG is set in a mixed forest setting. Supplies available at Antioch. Deer, raccoons, squirrels and birds are common to the area. Campers may gather firewood. No designated trails in the area.

GETTING THERE: Turkeys Trot Camp is located approx. 2 mi. N on Antioch on forest route 940.

SINGLE RATE:	No fee	OPEN DATES:	Yearlong
# of SINGLE SITES:	20	MAX STAY:	14 days
		ELEVATION:	200 feet

17 Valentine Lake
Alexandria • lat 31˚14'30" lon 092˚40'47"

DESCRIPTION: In a mixed hardwood setting with views of Valentine Lake. Fish and swim in the lake. Boat ramp in area, non-motorized boats only. Supplies available at Alexandria. Deer, raccoons and birds are common in the area. Campers may gather firewood. The Wild Azalea National Recreation Trail is nearby.

GETTING THERE: From Alexandria go W on state HWY 28 approx. 30 mi. to state HWY 121. Go S on 121 approx. 2 mi. to forest route 217. Go E on 217 approx. 3 mi. to Valentine Lake CG.

SINGLE RATE:	$7	OPEN DATES:	Yearlong
# of SINGLE SITES:	34	MAX STAY:	14 days
		ELEVATION:	136 feet

 Campground has hosts   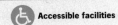 Reservable sites   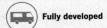 Accessible facilities    Fully developed    Semi-developed   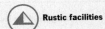 Rustic facilities

NOTE: Open dates listed are typical. Actual dates are dependent on conditions such as snow pack.

The Costs of Getting Lost

If you are lost in the woods-keep track of your wallet! You may be sent a bill for helicopter or on-the-ground searches, especially if you've been reckless or irresponsible. However, most routine searches involve voluneers who do not charge for time or equipment. Packing a cell phone and GPS unit may help to minimize your risk.

USFS Photo

Hiawatha National Forest

The Hiawatha National Forest is located in the central and eastern Upper Peninsula of Michigan. The forest encompasses approximately 880,000 acres and receives over 1.5 million recreational visits per year. Many of these visits are directly attributed to the use of Grand Island National Recreation Area, national wild and scenic rivers, winter recreation, trails, a scenic byway, wilderness areas and many camping, hunting, and fishing opportunities.

Recreation on the forest spans all seasons. Every spring and fall, anglers come to enjoy fishing. With over 80 inland lakes, and 400 miles of rivers and streams, the Hiawatha is truly a fisherman's paradise. Some of the species found in the lakes of the Hiawatha are yellow perch, bluegill, pumkinseed, bass, black crappie, walleye, and several types of trout. The summer season attracts hikers, mountain bikers, campers, and sightseers. During the fall, hunters flock to the forest seeking white-tailed deer, bears, and other wildlife. Autumn's spectacular foliage also draws many visitors annually.

Other areas of interest are the historic lighthouses along the Great Lakes shoreline, and the Isle Royale National Park, which provides habitat for moose, and wolves as well as loons, ducks and other waterfowl.

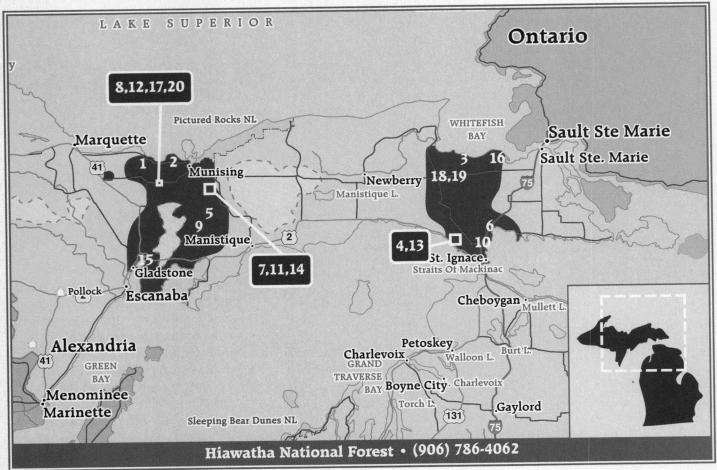

Hiawatha National Forest • (906) 786-4062

1 Au Train Lake
Munising • lat 46°23'45" lon 086°50'30"

DESCRIPTION: Located on Au Train Lake in wooded area. A boat ramp, sandy beach and swim area on site. Fish for walleye, perch and northern pike. Canoeing available. Supplies in Au Train or Munising.

GETTING THERE: From Munising go NW on state HWY 28 10 mi. to county route H-03. Go S on H-03 5 mi. to forest route 2276. Go E on 2276 1.5 mi. to forest route 2596. Go N on 2596 1.5 mi. to Au Train Lake CG.

SINGLE RATE:	$7	OPEN DATES:	May-Oct
# of SINGLE SITES:	37	MAX SPUR:	22 feet
		MAX STAY:	14 days
		ELEVATION:	640 feet

2 Bay Furnace
Munising • lat 46°26'31" lon 086°42'29"

DESCRIPTION: Located on Lake Superior near Pictured Rocks National Lakeshore. Many waterfalls nearby. Fish for trout and salmon. Diving is popular. Historic site of Onota. Basic supplies and firewood to buy on site. Dump station.

GETTING THERE: From Munising go NW on state HWY 28 approx. 3.5 mi. to Bay Furnace CG.

SINGLE RATE:	$8	OPEN DATES:	May-Oct
# of SINGLE SITES:	50	MAX SPUR:	28 feet
		MAX STAY:	14 days
		ELEVATION:	610 feet

3 Bay View
Strongs Corner • lat 46°26'30" lon 084°46'00"

DESCRIPTION: This CG is located on Lake Superior among red and white pine. There is swimming and a sandy beach on site. Campers may enjoy fishing in this area but please check fishing regulations. It is a popular CG, filling most weekends. Deer and small wildlife frequent this area.

GETTING THERE: From Strongs Corner go N on forest route 3159 approx. 9 mi. to forest route 3150. Go E on 3150 approx. 6 mi. to Bayview CG.

SINGLE RATE:	$9	OPEN DATES:	May-Oct
# of SINGLE SITES:	24	MAX SPUR:	55 feet
		MAX STAY:	14 days
		ELEVATION:	649 feet

4 Brevoort Lake
Allenville • lat 46°00'41" lon 084°58'10"

DESCRIPTION: CG is set among hemlock, birch and oak trees on Brevoort Lake. Boat launch on site. Popular fishing spot for walleye, northern pike, muskie and panfish. Supplies are in Allenville. Busy most weekends and holidays. Deer, raccoons, foxes and an occasional black bear or wolf are in the area. Ridge Trail is nearby.

GETTING THERE: From Allenville go NW 3 mi. on HWY 123 to county route 520. Go W 6 mi. on 520 to forest route 3108. Go S 1.5 mi. on 3108 to forest route 3473. Go NE 1 mi. on 3473 to CG.

SINGLE RATE:	$12	OPEN DATES:	May-Oct
# of SINGLE SITES:	70	MAX SPUR:	55 feet
GROUP RATE:	$14	MAX STAY:	14 days
# of GROUP SITES:	2	ELEVATION:	629 feet

5 Camp 7 Lake
Manistique • lat 46°03'28" lon 086°32'59"

DESCRIPTION: Set among paper birch and maple on Camp 7 Lake. Fish for bluegill, perch and bass. Fills most weekends. Accessible fishing pier. Annual kids fish day first weekend in June. Supplies in Manistique. Hike Van Winkle Trail, a 3 mi. trail.

GETTING THERE: From Manistique go SW on US HWY 2 10.5 mi. to county route 442. Go N on 442 1.5 mi. to county route 437. Go N on 437 10 mi. to county route 443. Go W on 443 1.5 mi. to county route 442. Continue W 1.5 mi. on 442 to forest route 2218. Go N .5 mi. on 2218 to Camp 7 Lake CG.

SINGLE RATE:	Varies	OPEN DATES:	May-Oct
# of SINGLE SITES:	41	MAX SPUR:	50 feet
		MAX STAY:	14 days
		ELEVATION:	769 feet

6 Carp River
Evergreen Shores • lat 46°01'51" lon 084°43'23"

DESCRIPTION: This CG is set among red and white pine on the Carp River. Fish for brookies, steelhead and in spring for smelt. Deer, bald eagles, foxes and occasionally a black bear or wolf can be seen in the area. Busy holidays. There is a canoe route on the river. Supplies are available in Evergreen Shores.

GETTING THERE: From Evergreen Shores go N on county route H63 approx. 9.5 mi. to Carp River CG.

SINGLE RATE:	$10	OPEN DATES:	May-Nov
# of SINGLE SITES:	44	MAX SPUR:	55 feet
		MAX STAY:	14 days
		ELEVATION:	630 feet

7 Colwell Lake
Manistique • lat 46°13'18" lon 086°26'15"

DESCRIPTION: Located on Colwell Lake among sugar maple, beech and yellow birch trees. Great fall colors. Fish the lake for perch, bluegill or bass. Supplies in Manistique. Deer, small wildlife and occasional bears in area. CG fills most weekends. There is a 1.6 mile barrier free trail.

GETTING THERE: From Manistique go N on state HWY 94 approx. 24 mi. to Colwell Lake CG.

SINGLE RATE:	$9	OPEN DATES:	May-Oct
# of SINGLE SITES:	35	MAX SPUR:	50 feet
		MAX STAY:	14 days
		ELEVATION:	748 feet

8 Corner Lake
Munising • lat 46°09'12" lon 086°36'28"

DESCRIPTION: Located on Corner Lake among birch and maple hardwoods. Fish for bluegill, bass and perch. Supplies in Munising. Fills most weekends. Deer, raccoons, skunk, porpupine and occasional black bears in area. Full July 4. Hike trails within 10 mile radius. Biking on roads.

GETTING THERE: From Munising go SE on HWY 28 2 mi. to state HWY 94. Go SW on 94 6.5 mi. to forest route 2254. Go SE on 2254 8 mi. to county route(cr) H-13. Go S on H-13 7 mi. to cr 440. Go E on 440 1.5 mi. to Corner Lake CG.

SINGLE RATE:	$7	OPEN DATES:	May-Sept
# of SINGLE SITES:	9	MAX SPUR:	50 feet
		MAX STAY:	14 days
		ELEVATION:	787 feet

9 Flowing Well
Rapid River • lat 45°56'15" lon 086°42'25"

DESCRIPTION: In spruce forest on Sturgeon River with some pull through sites. Fish the Sturgeon River for brown trout. Deer, raccoons, skunk, porpupine and occasional black bears in area. Fills July 4. No nearby trails, primarily the CG is used for single overnight stops.

GETTING THERE: From Rapid River go W on US HWY 2 approx. 13.5 mi. to county route H-13. Go N on H-13 approx. 3 mi. to Flowing Well CG.

SINGLE RATE:	$7	OPEN DATES:	May-Dec
# of SINGLE SITES:	10	MAX SPUR:	50 feet
		MAX STAY:	14 days
		ELEVATION:	618 feet

10 Foley Creek
Evergreen Shores • lat 45°56'01" lon 084°44'5"

DESCRIPTION: This CG is located on Foley Creek among red and white pine trees. Fish the creek for brookies and steelhead. CG fills most weekends and holidays. Supplies are in Evergreen Shores. Deer, racoons, foxes and an occasional black bear or wolf can be seen in the area. Enjoy a hike on the North Country Scenic Trail.

GETTING THERE: From Evergreen Shores go N on county route H63 approx. 3 mi. to Foley Creek CG.

SINGLE RATE:	$10	OPEN DATES:	May-Sept
# of SINGLE SITES:	54	MAX SPUR:	55 feet
		MAX STAY:	14 days
		ELEVATION:	630 feet

HIAWATHA NATIONAL FOREST • MICHIGAN • 1 — 10

 Campground has hosts   **Reservable sites** 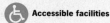 **Accessible facilities**   **Fully developed**   **Semi-developed** **Rustic facilities**

NOTE: Open dates listed are typical. Actual dates are dependent on conditions such as snow pack.

11 Indian River
Hiawatha • lat 46°09'21" lon 086°24'15"

DESCRIPTION: In forest of huge red pine on the Indian River. Fish for brook and brown trout. Deer, raccoons, skunk, porcupine and occasional black bears in area. CG receives light use, rarely filling. Hiking trails along the river.

GETTING THERE: From Hiawatha go NW on state HWY 94 approximately 8 miles to Indian River CG.

SINGLE RATE:	$6	OPEN DATES:	May-Sept
# of SINGLE SITES:	5	MAX SPUR:	50 feet
		MAX STAY:	14 days
		ELEVATION:	715 feet

12 Island Lake
Munising • lat 46°16'15" lon 086°38'00"

DESCRIPTION: In wooded setting on Island Lake. Canoe and boat fishing for panfish and black bass. Many other lakes nearby. Supplies in Wetmore. Access to Brunos Run Trail is five miles south.

GETTING THERE: From Munising go SE on state HWY 28 2 mi. to state HWY 94. Go SW on 94 6.5 mi. to forest route 2254. Go SE on 2254 5.5 mi. to forest route 2268. Go W on 2268 1 mi. to Island Lake CG.

SINGLE RATE:	Varies	OPEN DATES:	May-Oct
# of SINGLE SITES:	45	MAX SPUR:	22 feet
		MAX STAY:	14 days
		ELEVATION:	859 feet

13 Lake Michigan
Gros Cap • lat 45°59'01" lon 084°58'07"

DESCRIPTION: CG is set in an oak forest on Lake Michigan. This CG is popular for its 5 mile stretch of sandy beach. Campers should use caution when swimming due to heavy currents. Deer, bald eagles, foxes, raccoons and small wildllife are common in this area. There are no designated trails but beach walking is popular.

GETTING THERE: From Gros Cap go NW on US HWY 2 approx. 10 mi. to Lake Michigan CG.

SINGLE RATE:	$12	OPEN DATES:	May-Oct
# of SINGLE SITES:	35	MAX SPUR:	55 feet
		MAX STAY:	14 days
		ELEVATION:	630 feet

14 Little Bass Lake
Hiawatha • lat 46°09'50" lon 086°27'00"

DESCRIPTION: A remote site in white and red pine forest on Little Bass Lake. Bass, bluegill and northern pike fishing on the lake. Low use, rarely filling. Used primarily as a hunting and fishing camp. Supplies in Hiawatha. Deer, skunks, porcupines and occasional black bears in area. No nearby trails.

GETTING THERE: From Hiawatha go NW on state HWY 94 approx. 10 mi. to county route 437. Go W on 437 approx. 2 mi. to forest route 2213. Go S on 2213 approx. 2 mi. to Little Bass Lake CG.

SINGLE RATE:	$6	OPEN DATES:	May-Sept
# of SINGLE SITES:	12	MAX SPUR:	50 feet
		MAX STAY:	14 days
		ELEVATION:	761 feet

15 Little Bay de Noc
Rapid River • lat 45°46'22" lon 086°59'27"

DESCRIPTION: Located on Little Bay de Noc in spruce forest. Fish for walleye, salmon and perch. A popular CG, filling most weekends. Deer, small wildlife and occasional black bears in area. Three hiking trails, including Maywood History Trail, a 1/2 mi. accessible trail, nearby.

GETTING THERE: From Rapid River go SW on US HWY 2 approx. 2 mi. to county route 513. Go S on 513 approx. 6.5 mi. to Little Bay De Noc CG.

SINGLE RATE:	$7	OPEN DATES:	May-Sept
# of SINGLE SITES:	38	MAX SPUR:	50 feet
GROUP RATE:	$25	MAX STAY:	14 days
# of GROUP SITES:	2	ELEVATION:	580 feet

16 Monocle Lake
Brimley • lat 46°28'27" lon 084°38'45"

DESCRIPTION: This CG is located in a red and white pine forest on Monocle Lake. Beach and boat launch available. Fish for walleye and bass. Point Iroquois Lighthouse is nearby. Supplies are in Brimley. A two mile trail includes barrier free gravel paths and pier. A beaver dam can be viewed along the trail.

GETTING THERE: From Brimley go NW on forest route 3150 approx. 5.5 mi to forest route 3699. Go W on 3699 approx. 1 mi. to Monocle Lake CG.

SINGLE RATE:	$9	OPEN DATES:	May-Oct
# of SINGLE SITES:	30	MAX SPUR:	55 feet
		MAX STAY:	14 days
		ELEVATION:	639 feet

17 Petes Lake
Munising • lat 46°13'45" lon 086°35'57"

DESCRIPTION: Located on Petes Lake among large shade trees and surrounded by many lakes. Boat ramp, swimming and fishing for northern pike, small mouth bass and panfish. Nice sandy beach on site. Basic supplies at small store. Access to Brunos Run Trail, a 7-mile loop.

GETTING THERE: From Munising go SE on state HWY 28 2 mi. to state HWY 94. Go SW on 94 6.5 mi. to forest route(fr) 2254. Go SE on 2254 8 mi. to county route H-13. Go S on H-13 2 mi. to fr 2173. Go E on 2173 .5 mi. to Petes Lake CG.

SINGLE RATE:	Varies	OPEN DATES:	May-Oct
# of SINGLE SITES:	41	MAX SPUR:	22 feet
		MAX STAY:	14 days
		ELEVATION:	804 feet

18 Soldier Lake
Strongs Corner • lat 46°20'57" lon 084°52'10"

DESCRIPTION: This CG is set among pine and jack pine on Soldier Lake. Fish for perch or bluegill in this lake. Non-motorized boating only. CG is busy on weekends. Supplies are in Strongs Corner. Deer, raccoons, foxes and an occasional black bear or wolves can be seen in the area. There is a hiking trail nearby.

GETTING THERE: From Strongs Corner go E on state HWY 28 approx. 4.5 mi. to forest route 3602. Go S on 3602 approx. 1 mi. to Soldier Lake CG.

SINGLE RATE:	$9	OPEN DATES:	May-Oct
# of SINGLE SITES:	44	MAX SPUR:	55 feet
		MAX STAY:	14 days
		ELEVATION:	922 feet

19 Three Lakes
Strongs Corner • lat 46°19'10" lon 084°58'39"

DESCRIPTION: This is a remote CG on Walker Lake, near West Lake and Brown Lake. Fish in nearby Whitemarsh Lake for trout. Supplies are in Strongs Corner. Deer, raccoons, foxes, and an occasional black bear or wolf may be seen in this area. There is a one mile hiking trail around the lake.

GETTING THERE: From Strongs Corner go S on forest route 3142 approx. 2 mi. to Three Lakes CG.

SINGLE RATE:	$9	OPEN DATES:	May-Oct
# of SINGLE SITES:	28	MAX SPUR:	55 feet
		MAX STAY:	14 days
		ELEVATION:	875 feet

20 Widewater
Munising • lat 46°12'30" lon 086°39'30"

DESCRIPTION: On the Indian River in forested area. Canoe and fish for brook trout. Small store nearby has basic supplies. Deer, small wildlife and the occasional black bear or wolf may be seen. Hiking on Bruno's Run Trail, a 7 mile loop.

GETTING THERE: From Munising go SE on state HWY 28 2 mi. to state HWY 94. Go SW on 94 6.5 mi. to forest route(fr) 2254. Go SE on 2254 8 mi. to county H-13. Go S on H-13 3.5 mi. to fr 2262. Go NW on 2262 1.5 mi. to Widewater CG.

SINGLE RATE:	$7	OPEN DATES:	May-Oct
# of SINGLE SITES:	34	MAX SPUR:	22 feet
		MAX STAY:	14 days
		ELEVATION:	680 feet

 Campground has hosts　　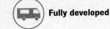 **Reservable sites**　　**Accessible facilities**　　**Fully developed**　　 **Semi-developed**　　**Rustic facilities**

NOTE: Open dates listed are typical. Actual dates are dependent on conditions such as snow pack.

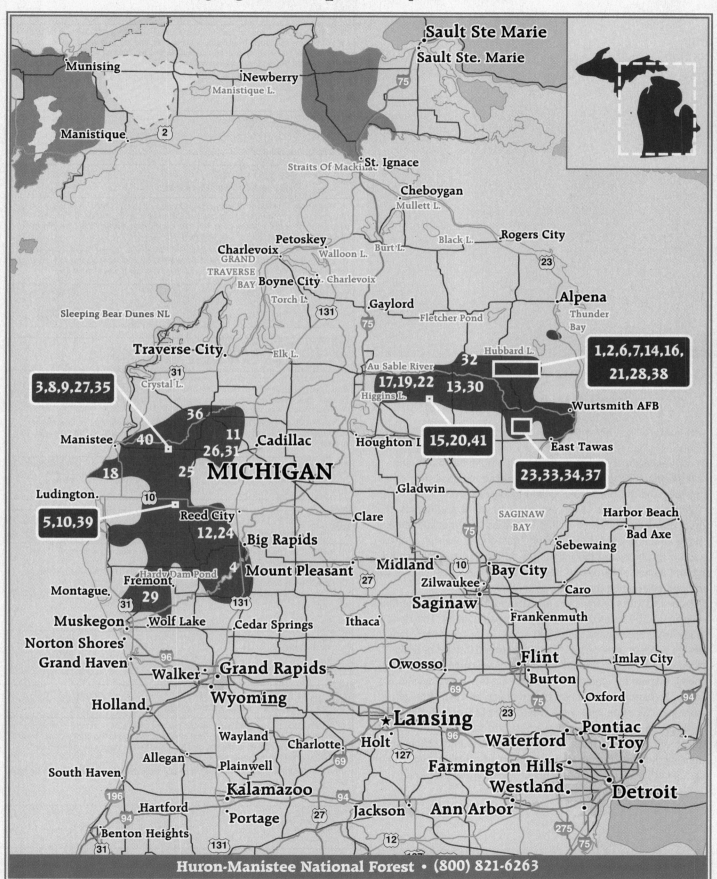

Sault Ste Marie
Sault Ste. Marie

Munising

Newberry
Manistique L.

Manistique

2

Straits Of Mackinac
St. Ignace

Cheboygan
Mullett L.

Petoskey
Charlevoix
GRAND
TRAVERSE
BAY
Walloon L.
Burt L.
Black L.
Rogers City

23

Boyne City
Charlevoix
Torch L.

Gaylord

Alpena
Thunder
Bay

Sleeping Bear Dunes NL

131

Fletcher Pond

75

Traverse City

31

Elk L.

Crystal L.

3,8,9,27,35

Au Sable River

Hubbard L.

32

**1,2,6,7,14,16,
21,28,38**

17,19,22

13,30

Higgins L.

Wurtsmith AFB

36

40

11

26,31

Manistee

MICHIGAN

25

Cadillac

Houghton L.

15,20,41

East Tawas

23,33,34,37

18

Ludington

10

Gladwin

5,10,39

Reed City

12,24

Clare

SAGINAW
BAY

Harbor Beach

Bad Axe

Sebewaing

Big Rapids

Midland

10

Bay City

Caro

Montague

Hardy Dam Pond

4

Mount Pleasant

27

Zilwaukee

Frankenmuth

Fremont

29

31

Wolf Lake

Cedar Springs

Ithaca

Saginaw

Muskegon

Norton Shores

Grand Haven

96

Owosso

Flint

Burton

Imlay City

Walker

Grand Rapids

69

75

Oxford

94

Holland

Wyoming

★**Lansing**

23

**Pontiac
Troy**

Wayland

Charlotte

Holt

96

Waterford

Allegan

Plainwell

69

127

Farmington Hills

South Haven

Kalamazoo

Jackson

Westland

Detroit

196

94

Hartford

Portage

27

Ann Arbor

275

Benton Heights

31

131

12

75

HURON-MANISTEE NATIONAL FOREST • MICHIGAN • LOCATOR MAP

USFS Photo

HURON-MANISTEE NATIONAL FOREST

Nearly a million acres of sandy, rolling hills make up the Huron-Manistee National Forest, which is the only national forest in the Lower Peninsula of Michigan. Spreading across the state from Lake Michigan on the west to Lake Huron on the east, the Manistee and the Huron are "united by rivers."

Within a day's drive of Chicago, Detroit, and Grand Rapids, the forest draws thousands of visitors from these metropolitan cities during all four seasons. Along quiet forest trails, colorful wildflowers and shrubs bloom throughout the spring and summer, and in autumn stands of hardwood trees burn in brilliant shades of yellow and red, celebrating the climax of another season.

Over 330 miles of trails are available for hiking while nine rivers offer about 550 miles of canoeing and small boating. The Hoist Lakes Area, encompassing 10,600 acres, is for the visitor who desires a longer walk or ski. Containing over 20 miles of trails which wind their way through forests of pine, aspen and hardwoods, this area is ideal for a backpacking trip of two days to a week. The Nordhouse Dunes situated along the Lake Michigan shoreline offer stunning sunset views. The 5000-acre Tuttle Marsh Wildlife Area provides some of the best bird watching in the state. Mushroom gathering, mountain biking, cross-country skiing, snowmobiling, hunting, horseback riding, off-road vehicle riding, camping, and other recreation opportunities keep visitors returning.

1 Au Sable Loop
Mio • lat 44°38'00" lon 084°07'30"

DESCRIPTION: This canoe or walk-in CG is situated near the Au Sable River. Enjoy fishing for rainbow and brown trout, bass, walleye, pike, and crappie. Wildlife in this area includes black bears, coyotes, deer, and bald eagles. No drinking water. The Michigan Shore to Shore Horse/Hiking Trail runs nearby.

GETTING THERE: From Mio go N on state HWY 33 approx. 1.5 mi. to county route 600. Go E on 600 approx. 2 mi. to forest route 4366. Go S on 4366 approx. 1 mi. to Au Sable Loop CG.

SINGLE RATE:	No fee	OPEN DATES:	May-Sept
# of SINGLE SITES:	5	MAX STAY:	14 days
		ELEVATION:	1100 feet

2 Bear Island
Mio • lat 44°37'30" lon 083°53'00"

DESCRIPTION: This canoe or walk-in CG is located on the Au Sable River. Enjoy fishing for rainbow and brown trout, bass, walleye, pike, and crappie. Wildlife in this area includes black bears, coyotes, deer, and bald eagles. No drinking water. The Michigan Shore to Shore Horse/Hiking Trail runs nearby.

GETTING THERE: From Mio go N on state HWY 33 approx. 1.5 mi. to county route 600. Go E on 600 approx. 10.5 mi. to forest route 4061. Go E on 4061 approx. 1.5 mi. to forest route 4836. Go SE on 4836 approx. 2.5 mi. to access to Bear Island CG.

SINGLE RATE:	No fee	OPEN DATES:	May-Sept
# of SINGLE SITES:	6	MAX STAY:	14 days
		ELEVATION:	1100 feet

3 Bear Track
Freesoil • lat 44°08'30" lon 086°01'30"

DESCRIPTION: This rustic CG is in a hardwood forest setting on the Little Manistee River. The river is lined with cedar trees. Fish or canoe from the river. Supplies at Freesoil. Bears, racoons and birds are seen in area. Campers may gather firewood. Access the North Country National Scenic Trail from the CG.

GETTING THERE: From Freesoil go E on Freesoil Road approx. 9 mi. to forest route 5203. Go N on 5203 approx. 2.5 mi. to forest route 5331. Go NE on 5331 approx. 1 mi. to Bear Track CG.

SINGLE RATE:	$4	OPEN DATES:	May-Sept
# of SINGLE SITES:	16	MAX SPUR:	25 feet
		MAX STAY:	14 days
		ELEVATION:	800 feet

4 Benton Lake
Brohman • lat 43°40'07" lon 085°53'21"

DESCRIPTION: This CG is located in oak and white pine with views of Benton Lake. Enjoy fishing for blue gill and bass. Wildlife includes bears, deer, coyotes, bald eagles, goshawks, and turkeys. CG is busy weekends and holidays. Hike the nearby North Country National Scenic Trail. Barrier free fishing pier.

GETTING THERE: From Brohman go SW on forest route 5308 approx. 3.5 mi. to Benton Lake CG.

SINGLE RATE:	Varies	OPEN DATES:	Apr-Oct
# of SINGLE SITES:	24	MAX SPUR:	65 feet
		MAX STAY:	14 days
		ELEVATION:	827 feet

5 Bowman Bridge
Baldwin • lat 43°52'30" lon 085°75'30"

DESCRIPTION: This quiet CG is situated in oak and white pine along the Pere Marquette River. Enjoy fishing for trout, salmon, and steelhead. Wildlife in this area includes bears, coyotes, deer, bald eagles, goshawks, and turkeys. There is an on-site trailhead for the North Country National Scenic Hiking Trail.

GETTING THERE: From Baldwin go W on county route approx. 5 mi. to Bowman Bridge CG.

SINGLE RATE:	$10	OPEN DATES:	Apr-Oct
# of SINGLE SITES:	24	MAX SPUR:	30 feet
GROUP RATE:	$40	MAX STAY:	14 days
# of GROUP SITES:	4	ELEVATION:	640 feet

 Campground has hosts   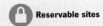 Reservable sites   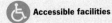 Accessible facilities   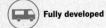 Fully developed   Semi-developed   Rustic facilities

NOTE: Open dates listed are typical. Actual dates are dependent on conditions such as snow pack.

6 Buttercup Rest Stop

Mio • lat 44°37'30" lon 083°55'00"

DESCRIPTION: This canoe or walk-in CG is located on the Au Sable River. Enjoy fishing for rainbow and brown trout, bass, walleye, pike, and crappie. Wildlife in this area includes black bear, coyotes, deer, and bald eagles. No drinking water. The Michigan Shore to Shore Horse/Hiking Trail runs nearby.

GETTING THERE: From Mio go N on state HWY 33 approx. 1.5 mi. to county route 600. Go E on 600 approx. 10.5 mi. to forest route 4061. Go E on 4061 approx. 1.5 mi. to access to Buttercup Rest Stop CG.

SINGLE RATE:	No fee	OPEN DATES:	May-Sept
# of SINGLE SITES:	3		
		MAX STAY:	14 days
		ELEVATION:	1100 feet

7 Cathedral Pines
Mio • lat 44°38'00" lon 084°02'00"

DESCRIPTION: This canoe or walk-in CG is located on the Au Sable River. Enjoy fishing for rainbow and brown trout, bass, walleye, pike, and crappie. Wildlife in this area includes black bears, coyotes, deer, and bald eagles. No drinking water. The Michigan Shore to Shore Horse/Hiking Trail runs nearby.

GETTING THERE: From Mio go N on state HWY 33 approx. 1.5 mi. to county route 600. Go E on 600 approx. 5 mi. to Comins Flat Boat Ramp. From there go E on the river approx. 3 mi. to Cathedral Pines CG.

SINGLE RATE:	No fee	OPEN DATES:	May-Sept
# of SINGLE SITES:	1		
		MAX STAY:	14 days
		ELEVATION:	1100 feet

8 Dorner Lake

Dublin • lat 44°12'10" lon 085°56'00"

DESCRIPTION: This rustic CG is in a hardwood forest setting on Dorner Lake. Excellent fishing for pan fish from the lake. Boat or swim on lake. Supplies available at Dublin. Bears, racoons and birds are common to the area. Campers may gather firewood. Trails in the area.

GETTING THERE: From Dublin go N on county route approx. 1.5 mi. to Dorner Lake CG.

SINGLE RATE:	$4	OPEN DATES:	May-Sept
# of SINGLE SITES:	8	MAX SPUR:	25 feet
		MAX STAY:	14 days
		ELEVATION:	787 feet

9 Driftwood Valley

Luke Corners • lat 44°08'30" lon 086°00'00"

DESCRIPTION: Rustic camping in a hardwood forest setting on the Little Manistee River. Fish for trout or canoe on the river. Supplies are available at Irons. Bears, racoons, squirrels and birds are common to the area. Campers may gather firewood. Trails in the area.

GETTING THERE: From Luke Corners go N on county route approx. 2 mi. to county route. Go W on county route approx. 1 mi. to Driftwood Valley CG.

SINGLE RATE:	$4	OPEN DATES:	May-Sept
# of SINGLE SITES:	19	MAX SPUR:	25 feet
		MAX STAY:	14 days
		ELEVATION:	800 feet

10 Gleasons Landing

Baldwin • lat 43°52'16" lon 085°55'13"

DESCRIPTION: This walk-in CG is situated in oak, hemlock, and white pine along the Pere Marquette River. Enjoy fishing for trout, salmon, and steelhead. Wildlife in this area includes bears, coyotes, deer, bald eagles, goshawks, and turkeys. There several hiking, horse, mountain biking, and OHV trails in the area.

GETTING THERE: From Baldwin go W on county route approx. 3.5 mi. to county route. Go SE on county route approx. 1 mi. to Gleasons Landing CG.

SINGLE RATE:	$8	OPEN DATES:	May-Oct
# of SINGLE SITES:	8		
		MAX STAY:	14 days
		ELEVATION:	740 feet

11 Hemlock

Cadillac • lat 44°13'53" lon 085°30'42"

DESCRIPTION: In a mixed forest setting of hardwoods with marshy area on the W end of Lake Mitchell. Fish for trout on the lake. Boat launch at CG. Supplies available at Cadillac. Bears, racoons, squirrels and birds are common in the area. Campers may gather firewood. Trails in the area.

GETTING THERE: From Cadillac go W on state HWY 55 approx. 4 mi. to county route. Go W on county route approx. 1.5 mi. to Hemlock CG.

SINGLE RATE:	$4	OPEN DATES:	May-Sept
# of SINGLE SITES:	19	MAX SPUR:	25 feet
		MAX STAY:	14 days
		ELEVATION:	1292 feet

12 Highbank Lake
Lilley • lat 43°46'14" lon 085°53'16"

DESCRIPTION: This CG is in an open grove of oak and white pine along Highbank Lake. Enjoy fishing for bass and bluegill. Supplies 3 mi. at Lilley. Wildlife in this area includes bears, coyotes, deer, bald eagles, goshawks, and turkeys. Busy weekends and holidays. Hike the nearby North Country National Scenic Hiking Trail.

GETTING THERE: From Lilley go W on county route approx. 1 mi. to forest route 5396. Go NW on 5396 approx. 2 mi. to Highbank Lake CG.

SINGLE RATE:	Varies	OPEN DATES:	Apr-Oct
# of SINGLE SITES:	9	MAX SPUR:	50 feet
		MAX STAY:	14 days
		ELEVATION:	900 feet

13 Hoist Lakes Area
Mio • lat °'" lon °'"

DESCRIPTION: CG is located in mixed hardwoods, pine, and aspen. Fish in North and South Hoist Lakes. Wildlife in this area includes black bears, coyotes, deer, and bald eagles. This area offers over 20 mi. of trails and is ideal for a backpacking trip of 2-5 days. Drinking water may not be available-bring purifier.

GETTING THERE: Hoist Lakes Area CG is a walk-in only CG off of forest route 3993.

SINGLE RATE:	No fee	OPEN DATES:	Yearlong
# of SINGLE SITES:	3		
		MAX STAY:	14 days
		ELEVATION:	1100 feet

14 Horseshoe Lake
Glennie • lat 44°36'02" lon 083°45'56"

DESCRIPTION: CG is situated in an open grove of mixed hardwoods and pine adjacent to Horseshoe Lake. Enjoy fishing for bluegill and bass. Wildlife includes black bears, coyotes, foxes, badgers, whitetail deer, turkeys, hawks, and bald eagles. CG is busy weekends, holidays, and hunting season. Nature trail around lake.

GETTING THERE: From Glennie go N on state HWY 65 approx. 3.5 mi. to forest route 4124. Go W on 4124 approx. 1 mi. to Horseshoe Lake CG.

SINGLE RATE:	$3	OPEN DATES:	May-Dec
# of SINGLE SITES:	9	MAX SPUR:	30 feet
		MAX STAY:	14 days
		ELEVATION:	900 feet

15 Island Lake

Rose City • lat 44°31'00" lon 084°07'30"

DESCRIPTION: This CG rests in mixed hardwoods on Island Lake. Enjoy fishing for perch, bass, and sunfish. Wildlife in this area includes black bears, coyotes, deer, and bald eagles. CG is busy weekends and holidays. Gather firewood locally. There are OHV and snowmobile trails nearby.

GETTING THERE: Island Lake CG is located 6.5 mi. N of Rose City on HWY 33.

SINGLE RATE:	$9	OPEN DATES:	May-Sept
# of SINGLE SITES:	17	MAX SPUR:	20 feet
		MAX STAY:	14 days
		ELEVATION:	859 feet

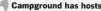 **Campground has hosts**   **Reservable sites** 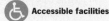 **Accessible facilities** 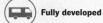 **Fully developed**   **Semi-developed**   **Rustic facilities**

NOTE: Open dates listed are typical. Actual dates are dependent on conditions such as snow pack.

16 Jewell Lake
Barton City • lat 44°40'50" lon 083°36'24"

DESCRIPTION: CG rests in an open grove of mixed hardwoods and pine adjacent to Jewell Lake. Enjoy fishing for pike, walleye, bass and pike. Wildlife includes black bears, coyotes, foxes, badgers, whitetail deer, turkeys, hawks and bald eagles. Busy weekends and holidays. There is a boat ramp and nature trail at the lake.

GETTING THERE: From Barton City go S on the SE shore of Jewell Lake 1/2 mi. to Jewell Lake CG.

SINGLE RATE:	$3	OPEN DATES:	May-Sept
# of SINGLE SITES:	32	MAX SPUR:	30 feet
		MAX STAY:	14 days
		ELEVATION:	822 feet

21 McKinley Trail
Mio • lat 44°37'30" lon 083°59'00"

DESCRIPTION: This canoe or walk-in CG is situated near the Au Sable River. Enjoy fishing for rainbow and brown trout, bass, walleye, pike, and crappie. Wildlife in this area includes black bears, coyotes, deer, and bald eagles. No drinking water. The Michigan Shore to Shore Horse/Hiking Trail runs nearby.

GETTING THERE: From Mio go E on county route 602 approx. 8 mi to forest route 4004. Go N on 4004 approx. 1 mi. to McKinley Trail CG.

SINGLE RATE:	No fee	OPEN DATES:	May-Sept
# of SINGLE SITES:	100		
		MAX STAY:	14 days
		ELEVATION:	1100 feet

17 Kneff Lake
Grayling • lat 44°38'16" lon 084°34'37"

DESCRIPTION: CG is located in mixed hardwoods on Kneff Lake. Fish for perch and trout. Wildlife in this area includes black bears, coyotes, deer and bald eagles. CG is busy weekends and holidays. Visit nearby Wakeley Lake Semi-primitive Non-motorized Area. Supplies in Grayling. Gather firewood locally.

GETTING THERE: From Grayling go W on state HWY 72 approx. 5.5 mi. to county route. Go S on county route approx. 1 mi. to forest route 4003. Go E on 4003 approx. 1 mi. to Kneff Lakes CG.

SINGLE RATE:	$9	OPEN DATES:	July-Sept
# of SINGLE SITES:	26	MAX SPUR:	20 feet
		MAX STAY:	14 days
		ELEVATION:	1180 feet

22 Meadow Springs Rest Stop
Mio • lat 44°38'00" lon 084°04'00"

DESCRIPTION: This canoe or walk-in CG is located on the Au Sable River. Enjoy fishing for rainbow and brown trout, bass, walleye, pike, and crappie. Wildlife in this area includes black bears, coyotes, deer, and bald eagles. No drinking water. The Michigan Shore to Shore Horse/Hiking Trail runs nearby.

GETTING THERE: From Mio go N on state HWY 33 approx. 1.5 mi. to county route 600. Go E on 600 approx. 3 mi. to forest route 4971. Go S on 4971 approx. .5 mi. to access to Meadow Springs Rest Stop CG.

SINGLE RATE:	No fee	OPEN DATES:	May-Sept
# of SINGLE SITES:	2		
		MAX STAY:	14 days
		ELEVATION:	1100 feet

18 Lake Michigan Recreation Area
Freesoil • lat 44°07'15" lon 862°50'0"

DESCRIPTION: In a hardwood forest setting on Lake Michigan. Fish for trout on the lake. Supplies available at Manistee. Bears, racoons, snake and birds are common to the area. Campers may gather firewood. Trails in the area, a 3 mi. bike trail around CG. Beach and playground at CG.

GETTING THERE: From Freesoil go W 3 mi. on county route to US HWY 31. Go N 1 mi. on 31 to forest route 5629. Go W 8 mi. on 5629 to forest route 5972. Go W 1.5 mi. on 5972 to Lake Michigan Recreation Area CG.

SINGLE RATE:	$10	OPEN DATES:	May-Oct
# of SINGLE SITES:	99	MAX SPUR:	25 feet
GROUP RATE:	Varies	MAX STAY:	14 days
# of GROUP SITES:	3	ELEVATION:	634 feet

23 Monument
Wicker Hills • lat 44°26'03" lon 083°37'13"

DESCRIPTION: CG is located in pines near the Au Sable River and local visitor center. Enjoy fishing for trout, pike, and bass. Wildlife in this area includes black bears, coyotes, foxes, badgers, whitetail deer, turkeys, hawks, and bald eagles. Busy weekends and holidays. An interpretive trail is on site.

GETTING THERE: From Wicker Hills go E on River Road National Scenic Byway approx. 9.5 mi. to Monument CG.

SINGLE RATE:	$6	OPEN DATES:	May-Oct
# of SINGLE SITES:	20	MAX SPUR:	30 feet
		MAX STAY:	7 days
		ELEVATION:	832 feet

19 Luzerne Trail
Luzerne • lat 44°35'06" lon 084°17'17"

DESCRIPTION: This CG is located in mixed hardwoods and is a trailhead for the Michigan Shore to Shore Hiking/Horse Trail. There is also an OHV trail nearby. Wildlife in this area includes black bears, coyotes, deer and bald eagles. CG is busy weekends and holidays. Gather firewood locally.

GETTING THERE: From Luzerne go S on county route 490 approx. 2 mi. to forest route. Go S on forest route approx. 1 mi. to Luzerne Trail CG.

SINGLE RATE:	No fee	OPEN DATES:	Yearlong
# of SINGLE SITES:	10	MAX SPUR:	20 feet
		MAX STAY:	14 days
		ELEVATION:	1250 feet

24 Nichols Lake
Woodland Park • lat 43°43'55" lon 085°54'32"

DESCRIPTION: This CG is in an open grove of oak and white pine along Nichols Lake. Enjoy fishing for walleye, bass and bluegill. Wildlife in this area includes bears, coyotes, deer, bald eagles, goshawks, loon, and turkeys. Barrier free fishing and boardwalk. Numerous hiking, horse, mountain biking, and OHV trails in the area.

GETTING THERE: From Woodland Park go W on county route approx. 3.5 mi. to Nichols Lake CG.

SINGLE RATE:	$9	OPEN DATES:	Apr-Oct
# of SINGLE SITES:	28	MAX SPUR:	65 feet
		MAX STAY:	14 days
		ELEVATION:	853 feet

20 Mack Lake
Mio • lat 44°34'44" lon 084°03'53"

DESCRIPTION: This CG is located in jack pine on Mack Lake. Fish for sunfish, perch and pike. Wildlife in this area includes black bears, coyotes, deer and bald eagles. CG is busy weekends and holidays. An OHV trailhead is at this CG and the trail runs throughout the forest. Gather firewood locally.

GETTING THERE: From Mio go S on state HWY 33 approx. 3 mi. to county route 489. Go E on 489 approx. 3 mi. to forest route 4146. Go S on 4146 approx. 1 mi. to Mack Lake CG.

SINGLE RATE:	$9	OPEN DATES:	May-Nov
# of SINGLE SITES:	42	MAX SPUR:	20 feet
		MAX STAY:	14 days
		ELEVATION:	1190 feet

25 Old Grade
Peacock • lat 44°03'40" lon 085°50'57"

DESCRIPTION: This CG is nestled in trees near Little Manistee River. Enjoy fishing for rainbow and brown trout. Supplies available at Peacock. Wildlife in this area includes bears, coyotes, deer, bald eagles, goshawks and turkeys. Several hiking, horse, OHV and mountain biking trails in this area.

GETTING THERE: From Peacock go E on county route approx. 2 mi. to state HWY 37. Go N on 37 approx. 1 mi. to Old Grade CG.

SINGLE RATE:	Varies	OPEN DATES:	Apr-Oct
# of SINGLE SITES:	20	MAX SPUR:	65 feet
		MAX STAY:	14 days
		ELEVATION:	902 feet

 Campground has hosts　　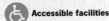 **Reservable sites**　　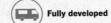 **Accessible facilities**　　 **Fully developed**　　 **Semi-developed**　　 **Rustic facilities**

NOTE: Open dates listed are typical. Actual dates are dependent on conditions such as snow pack.

26 Peterson Bridge
Peacock • lat 44°12'07" lon 085°47'53"

DESCRIPTION: In a hardwood forest setting on the Pine River, one of the best canoeing and trout fishing rivers in the midwest. Bears, racoons and birds are common to the area. Supplies available at Peacock. Campers may gather firewood. No designated trails in the area.

GETTING THERE: From Peacock go E on county route approx. 2 mi. to state HWY 37. Go N on 37 approx. 10.5 mi. to Peterson Bridge CG.

SINGLE RATE:	$5	OPEN DATES:	Apr-Sept
# of SINGLE SITES:	20	MAX SPUR:	25 feet
		MAX STAY:	14 days
		ELEVATION:	840 feet

27 Pine Lake
Wellston • lat 44°09'30" lon 086°00'30"

DESCRIPTION: In a hardwood forest setting on Pine Lake. Excellent fishing for pan fish on the lake. Supplies available at Wellston. Wetland frogs, toads, bears, and birds are common in the area. Loons and eagles may be sighted. Gather firewood. Trails in area. Boat launch.

GETTING THERE: From Wellston go W on forest route 5172 approx. 3.5 mi. to Pine Lake CG.

SINGLE RATE:	$4	OPEN DATES:	May-Sept
# of SINGLE SITES:	12	MAX SPUR:	25 feet
		MAX STAY:	14 days
		ELEVATION:	746 feet

28 Pine River
Glennie • lat 46°13'44" lon 084°52'37"

DESCRIPTION: CG is situated in an open grove of mixed hardwoods and pines adjacent to Pine River. Enjoy fishing for trout. Wildlife in this area includes black bears, foxes, badgers, whitetail deer, turkeys, hawks and bald eagles. CG is busy weekends, holidays and hunting season. A short trail accesses the river.

GETTING THERE: From Glennie go E on county route F30 approx. 8 mi. to forest route 4121. Go S on 4121 approx. 2 mi. to Pine River CG.

SINGLE RATE:	$3	OPEN DATES:	May-Dec
# of SINGLE SITES:	11	MAX SPUR:	30 feet
		MAX STAY:	14 days
		ELEVATION:	797 feet

29 Pines Point
Hesperia • lat 43°31'40" lon 086°07'10"

DESCRIPTION: This CG is in an open grove of oak near White River. Enjoy fishing for trout, salmon, and steelhead. Supplies at Hesperia. Wildlife in this area includes bears, coyotes, deer, bald eagles, goshawks and turkeys. Busy weekends and holidays. Several hiking, horse, OHV, and mountain biking trails in the area.

GETTING THERE: From Hesperia go W on state HWY 20 2 mi. to county route. Go S on CR 1 mi. to CR. Go W on CR 3 mi. to CR. Go S on CR 1.5 mi. to forest route 5637. Go E on 5637 1 mi. to Pines Point CG.

SINGLE RATE:	Varies	OPEN DATES:	Apr-Oct
# of SINGLE SITES:	33	MAX SPUR:	65 feet
		MAX STAY:	14 days
		ELEVATION:	663 feet

30 Primitive Camps
Mio • lat °'" lon °'"

DESCRIPTION: This canoe or walk-in CG is situated near the Au Sable River. Enjoy fishing for rainbow and brown trout, bass, walleye, pike, and crappie. Wildlife in this area includes black bears, coyotes, deer, and bald eagles. No drinking water. The Michigan Shore to Shore Horse/Hiking Trail runs nearby.

GETTING THERE: There are several primitive camps located along the Au sable River. Inquire at the ranger station in Mio for directions to specific camps.

SINGLE RATE:	No fee	OPEN DATES:	May-Sept
# of SINGLE SITES:	5		
		MAX STAY:	14 days
		ELEVATION:	1100 feet

31 Ravine
Cadillac • lat 44°10'51" lon 085°39'27"

DESCRIPTION: A rustic CG in a hardwood forest setting adjacent to Poplar Creek. CG offers peace and solitude. Fish and swim in the creek. Supplies are available in Cadillac. Bears, racoons and owls are common in the area. No designated trails in the area.

GETTING THERE: From Cadillac go W on state HWY 55 approx. 12 mi. to forest route 5406. Go S on 5406 approx. 2 mi. to forest route 5334. Go S on 5334 approx. 1 mi. to Ravine CG.

SINGLE RATE:	No fee	OPEN DATES:	Yearlong*
# of SINGLE SITES:	6	MAX SPUR:	25 feet
		MAX STAY:	14 days
		ELEVATION:	1076 feet

32 River Dune Rest Stop
Mio • lat 44°38'00" lon 084°07'30"

DESCRIPTION: This canoe or walk-in CG is located on the Au Sable River. Enjoy fishing for rainbow and brown trout, bass, walleye, pike. Wildlife in this area includes black bears, coyotes, deer, and bald eagles. No drinking water. The Michigan Shore to Shore Horse/Hiking Trail runs nearby.

GETTING THERE: From Mio go N on state HWY 33 approx. 1.5 mi. to county route 600. Go E on 600 approx. 2 mi. to forest route 4366. Go S on 4366 approx. 1 mi. to access to River Dune Rest Stop CG.

SINGLE RATE:	No fee	OPEN DATES:	May-Sept
# of SINGLE SITES:	1		
		MAX STAY:	14 days
		ELEVATION:	1100 feet

33 Rollways
Long Lake • lat 44°27'43" lon 083°46'24"

DESCRIPTION: CG rests in an open grove of hardwoods and overlooks the scenic Au Sable River and Loud Dam Pond. A short, steep walk leads to the river. Enjoy fishing for trout, pike and bass. Wildlife includes black bears, coyotes, foxes, badgers, deer, turkeys, hawks and bald eagles. Busy weekends and holidays.

GETTING THERE: From Long Lake go N on forest roue 4435 approx. 1 mi. to forest route 4423. Go NE on 4423 approx. 7 mi. to Rollways CG.

SINGLE RATE:	$6	OPEN DATES:	May-Sept
# of SINGLE SITES:	19	MAX SPUR:	30 feet
		MAX STAY:	7 days
		ELEVATION:	860 feet

34 Round Lake
Sand Lake • lat 44°20'37" lon 083°39'40"

DESCRIPTION: CG rests in an open grove of hardwoods on Round Lake. There is a beach and boat ramp. Enjoy fishing for bluegill, pike and bass. Wildlife in the area includes black bears, coyotes, foxes, badgers, whitetail deer, turkeys, hawks and bald eagles. CG is busy weekends and holidays.

GETTING THERE: From Sand Lake go NE on county route approx. 2 mi. to Round Lake CG. CG is located on the NW shore of Indian Lake.

SINGLE RATE:	$9	OPEN DATES:	May-Sept
# of SINGLE SITES:	33	MAX SPUR:	30 feet
		MAX STAY:	14 days
		ELEVATION:	800 feet

35 Sand Lake
Dublin • lat 44°10'05" lon 085°55'46"

DESCRIPTION: In a mixed hardwood forest setting on Sand Lake. Swim and fish from the lake. Supplies available at Dublin. Bears, racoons and owls are common in the area. Campers may gather firewood. Trails are in the area.

GETTING THERE: From Dublin go S on county route approx. 1/2 mi. to forest route 5728. Go SW on 5278 approx. 1 mi. to Sand Lake CG.

SINGLE RATE:	$12	OPEN DATES:	May-Sept
# of SINGLE SITES:	45	MAX SPUR:	30 feet
GROUP RATE:	$15	MAX STAY:	14 days
# of GROUP SITES:	1	ELEVATION:	861 feet

 Campground has hosts 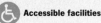 **Reservable sites**   **Accessible facilities**   **Fully developed**   **Semi-developed**   **Rustic facilities**

NOTE: Open dates listed are typical. Actual dates are dependent on conditions such as snow pack.

36 Seaton Creek
Mesick • lat 44˚21'28" lon 085˚48'33"

DESCRIPTION: In a mixed forest setting on Seaton Creek, offering a very rustic setting. Fish and canoe from surrounding waters. Supplies at Mesick. Bears, racoon, porcupine, bobcats and birds are common to the area. Campers may gather firewood. Trailhead for the Manistee River Trail in CG and access to Hodenphyl Backwater.

GETTING THERE: From Mesick go W on state HWY 115 approx. 2.5 mi. to Beers Road. Go SW on Beers Road approx. 4.5 mi. to county route. Go S on county route approx. 1.5 mi. to Seaton Creek CG.

SINGLE RATE:	$4	OPEN DATES:	May-Sept
# of SINGLE SITES:	17	MAX SPUR:	25 feet
		MAX STAY:	14 days
		ELEVATION:	869 feet

37 South Branch Trail
Long Lake • lat 44˚29'13" lon 083˚47'47"

DESCRIPTION: CG rests in an open grove of hardwoods with forest views. This horse camp offers hitching posts and a trailhead for hiking and horseback riding. Wildlife in the area includes black bears, coyotes, foxes, badgers, whitetail deer, turkeys, hawks and bald eagles. Busy weekends and holidays.

GETTING THERE: From Long Lake go N on forest route 4435 approx. 1 mi. to forest route 4423. Go NE on 4423 approx. 5.5 mi. to South Branch Trail CG.

SINGLE RATE:	$6	OPEN DATES:	Apr-Nov
# of SINGLE SITES:	15	MAX SPUR:	30 feet
		MAX STAY:	14 days
		ELEVATION:	840 feet

38 The Gabions
Mio • lat 44˚36'00" lon 083˚50'00"

DESCRIPTION: This CG is located on the Au Sable River. Enjoy fishing for rainbow and brown trout, bass, walleye, pike, and crappie. Wildlife in this area includes black bears, coyotes, deer, and bald eagles. No drinking water. The Michigan Shore to Shore Horse/Hiking Trail runs nearby.

GETTING THERE: From Mio Go N on state HWY 33 approx. 1 mi. to county route 600 (McKinley Road). Go E on 600 approx. 18 mi. to forest route 4001. Go W on 4001 approx. 1/2 mi. to forest route 4143. Go N on 4143 approx. 3/4 mi. to The Gabions CG.

SINGLE RATE:	No fee	OPEN DATES:	May-Sept
# of SINGLE SITES:	7		
		MAX STAY:	14 days
		ELEVATION:	1100 feet

39 Timber Creek
Branch • lat 43˚62'30" lon 085˚95'30"

DESCRIPTION: This CG is in an open field with surrounding red and white pine. Timber Creek runs adjacent to the CG. Supplies 2 mi. at Branch. Wildlife in this area includes bears, coyotes, deer, bald eagles, goshawks, and turkeys. There is an on-site trailhead for the North Country National Scenic Hiking Trail.

GETTING THERE: From Branch go E on US HWY 10 approx. 2 mi. to Timber Creek CG.

SINGLE RATE:	No fee	OPEN DATES:	Apr-Nov
# of SINGLE SITES:	9		
		MAX STAY:	14 days
		ELEVATION:	640 feet

40 Udell Rollways
Udell • lat 44˚15'25" lon 086˚04'46"

DESCRIPTION: In a mixed forest setting overlooking the Manistee River. Steep banks make river unaccessible. Supplies at Wellston. Bears, racoons and owls are common in the area. CG was named in 1900's, when logs were rolled down to the river. Gather firewood. No designated trails in area.

GETTING THERE: From Udell go N on forest route 5238 approx. 1.5 mi. to Udell Rollways CG.

SINGLE RATE:	$4	OPEN DATES:	Yearlong*
# of SINGLE SITES:	23	MAX SPUR:	25 feet
		MAX STAY:	14 days
		ELEVATION:	719 feet

41 Wagner Lake
Mio • lat 44˚33'12" lon 084˚08'51"

DESCRIPTION: This CG rests in mixed hardwoods on Wagner Lake. Enjoy fishing for perch, bass, and sunfish. There are snowmobile and OHV trails nearby as well as the Michigan Shore to Shore Horse/Hiking Trail. Wildlife includes black bears, coyotes, deer, and bald eagles. CG is busy weekends and holidays.

GETTING THERE: From Mio go S on state HWY 33 approx. 6 mi. to forest route. Go W on forest route approx. 1 mi. to Wagner Lake CG.

SINGLE RATE:	$9	OPEN DATES:	May-Sept
# of SINGLE SITES:	12	MAX SPUR:	20 feet
		MAX STAY:	14 days
		ELEVATION:	1150 feet

 Campground has hosts   **Reservable sites**   **Accessible facilities**   **Fully developed**    **Semi-developed**   **Rustic facilities**

NOTE: Open dates listed are typical. Actual dates are dependent on conditions such as snow pack.

USFS Photo

OTTAWA NATIONAL FOREST

The one million acres of the Ottawa National Forest are located in the western upper peninsula of Michigan. It extends from the south shore of Lake Superior down to Wisconsin and the Nicolet National Forest. The area is rich in wildlife viewing opportunities and topography in the northern region is the most dramatic with breathtaking views of rolling hills dotted with lakes, rivers and spectacular waterfalls.

Water plays an important role in the natural appeal of the Ottawa National Forest. In addition to many miles of Lake Superior shoreline, the forest contains over 500 lakes, both large and small, and 2,000 miles of rivers and streams that provide canoeing and kayaking opportunities and prime trout fishing.

The area is rich in wildlife. There are numerous opportunities to see deer, fox, snowshoe hare, bald eagles, loons, and songbirds. Bear and coyotes are plentiful but may require more patience to see.

Another way to see the forest is via the Black River National Scenic Byway, a popular 12-mile travel route which passes by scenic waterfalls, old growth forests and the historic Black River Harbor Village.

OTTAWA NATIONAL FOREST • LOCATOR MAP

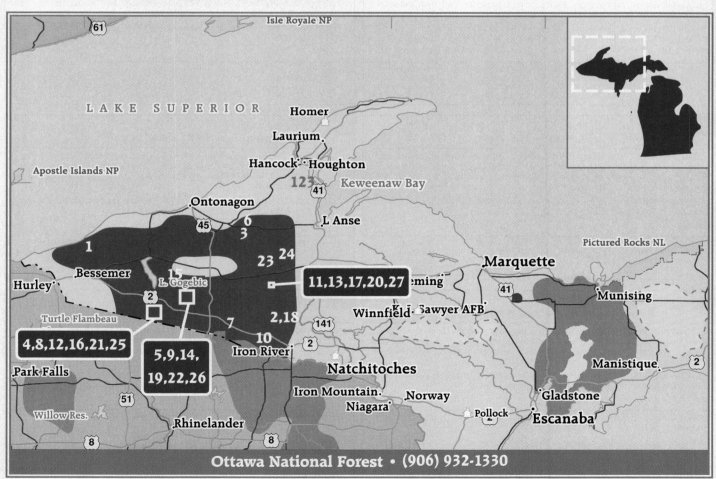

Ottawa National Forest • (906) 932-1330

OTTAWA NATIONAL FOREST • MICHIGAN

1. Black River Harbor
Bessemer • lat 46°39'30" lon 090°03'00"

DESCRIPTION: CG is situated in large pine and hemlock trees on the shore of Lake Superior. Scenic views of the lake and the Apostle Islands. RV dump station and firewood for sale on site. Enjoy hiking the North Country National Scenic Hiking Trail, boating, biking, fishing, and nature trails in this area.

GETTING THERE: From Bessemer go N on county route 513 approx. 16 mi. to Black River Harbor CG.

SINGLE RATE:	$10	OPEN DATES:	May-Sept
# of SINGLE SITES:	40	MAX SPUR:	45 feet
		MAX STAY:	14 days
		ELEVATION:	600 feet

2. Block House
Mineral Hills • lat 46°15'00" lon 088°37'00"

DESCRIPTION: This CG rests in northern hardwoods on the Paint River. Enjoy fishing for bass & trout in the river. This CG offers excellent canoeing opportunities. There is also a nearby snowmobile trail. Visit historic Camp Gibbs. Wildlife includes black bears, deer, and grouse. No drinking water on site.

GETTING THERE: From Mineral Hills go N on forest route 3480 approx. 6 mi. to forest route 3485. Go N on 3485 approx. 3 mi. to Block House CG.

SINGLE RATE:	No fee	OPEN DATES:	May-Dec*
# of SINGLE SITES:	2	MAX SPUR:	45 feet
		MAX STAY:	14 days
		ELEVATION:	1475 feet

3. Bob Lake
Greenland • lat 46°39'43" lon 088°54'50"

DESCRIPTION: Among northern maples w/underbrush on Bob Lake. Some sites overlook the lake. Fish for walleye, bass or panfish by boat or trout. Also fish nearby stream. Historic Old Victoria Townsite 20 mi. Basic supplies in Mass City. Deer, birds and small wildlife. Rarely full. Gather firewood. Hiking trails nearby.

GETTING THERE: From Greenland go E 8 mi. on HWY 38 to forest HWY 16. Go S 6 mi. on 16 to Pori RD. Go W 2 mi. on Pori RD to forest rte 1470. Go S 1 mi. on 1470 to forest rte 1478. Go SE 1 mi. on 1478 CG.

SINGLE RATE:	$5	OPEN DATES:	May-Nov*
# of SINGLE SITES:	17	MAX SPUR:	60 feet
		MAX STAY:	14 days
		ELEVATION:	1196 feet

4. Bobcat Lake
Marenisco • lat 46°21'30" lon 089°40'27"

DESCRIPTION: This CG is set in a mixed hardwood and conifer forest on Bobcat Lake. Warm summer days with cool lake breezes. Fish for bass, pike, crappie and blue gill. Boat ramp on site. Supplies in Marenisco. Whitetail deer and small wildlife in area. Fills occasionally. No firewood. Mtn. bike trails in area.

GETTING THERE: From Marenisco go S on forest route 8500 approx. 1.5 mi. to Bobcat Lake CG.

SINGLE RATE:	$5	OPEN DATES:	May-Oct
# of SINGLE SITES:	12	MAX SPUR:	45 feet
		MAX STAY:	14 days
		ELEVATION:	1565 feet

5. Burned Dam
Watersmeet • lat 46°18'51" lon 089°03'14"

DESCRIPTION: This CG is situated in northern hardwoods near the Middle Ontonogan River. Enjoy fishing in the river for bass, muskellunge, trout, and panfish. There are excellent canoeing opportunites and the beautiful Mex-i-min-e Falls at this CG. Wildlife includes black bears, deer, and grouse.

GETTING THERE: From Watersmeet go NE on county route 208 approx. 6 mi. to forest route 4500. Go N on 4500 approx. 1.5 mi. to Burned Dam CG.

SINGLE RATE:	No fee	OPEN DATES:	May-Oct
# of SINGLE SITES:	6	MAX SPUR:	45 feet
		MAX STAY:	14 days
		ELEVATION:	1574 feet

6. Courtney Lake
Greenland • lat 46°45'07" lon 088°56'22"

DESCRIPTION: In northern hardwood and red pine forest on Courtney Lake. Views of lake. Fish for stocked trout in lake/streams. Nearby 6-mile Lake has walleye & pike. Old Victoria & Pori CCC Camp site. Supplies in Mass City. Deer, upland birds and small wildlife in area. Rarely full. Hike/horse trails nearby.

GETTING THERE: From Greenland go E on state HWY 38 approx. 7 mi. to forest route 1960. Go S on 1960 approx. 1 mi. to Courtney Lake CG.

SINGLE RATE:	$6	OPEN DATES:	May-Oct.
# of SINGLE SITES:	21	MAX SPUR:	45 feet
		MAX STAY:	14 days
		ELEVATION:	1171 feet

7. Golden Lake
Beechwood • lat 46°10'15" lon 088°53'00"

DESCRIPTION: This CG is located in northern hardwoods on Golden Lake. Enjoy fishing for bass, trout, and panfish. This CG offers canoeing opportunities, a boat ramp, and RV dump station. There is a nearby snowmobile trail. Hike to nearby Silver and Timber Lakes. Wildlife includes black bears, deer, and loons.

GETTING THERE: From Beechwood go W on US HWY 2 approx. 5 mi. to forest HWY 16. Go N on 16 approx. 1 mi. to Golden Lake CG.

SINGLE RATE:	$6	OPEN DATES:	May-Nov
# of SINGLE SITES:	22	MAX SPUR:	45 feet
		MAX STAY:	14 days
		ELEVATION:	1649 feet

8. Henry Lake
Marenisco • lat 46°19'50" lon 089°47'31"

DESCRIPTION: Set in hardwood forest on Henry Lake. Some views of lake. Warm summer days. Fish for bass & blue gill on this lake. Supplies in Marenisco. Whitetail deer, upland birds and small wildlife in area. Fills some weekends. No firewood. Mtn bike trail system. Black flies until July, mosquitos in summer.

GETTING THERE: From Marenisco go S on state HWY M-64 approx. 6 mi. to forest route 8100. Go W on 8100 approx. 4.5 mi. to Henry Lake CG.

SINGLE RATE:	$5	OPEN DATES:	May-Oct
# of SINGLE SITES:	11	MAX SPUR:	55 feet
		MAX STAY:	14 days
		ELEVATION:	1585 feet

9. Imp Lake
Watersmeet • lat 46°13'10" lon 089°04'17"

DESCRIPTION: This CG is located in northern hardwoods near Imp Lake. Enjoy fishing for bass, trout, and panfish in area lakes and creeks. The CG offers a boat ramp, picnic area, and hiking trail. Wildlife includes black bears, deer, grouse, and loons. Supplies at Watersmeet. Summer days are mild.

GETTING THERE: From Watersmeet go SE on US HWY 2 approx. 5 mi. to forest route 3978. Go S on 3978 approx. 1 mi. to Imp Lake CG.

SINGLE RATE:	$5	OPEN DATES:	May-Dec
# of SINGLE SITES:	22	MAX SPUR:	45 feet
		MAX STAY:	14 days
		ELEVATION:	1731 feet

10. Lake Ottawa
Iron River • lat 46°04'49" lon 088°45'42"

DESCRIPTION: This CG is situated in northern hardwoods on Lake Ottawa. Enjoy fishing in the lake for walleye, bass, pike, trout, and panfish. This CG offers a boat ramp, RV dump station, picnic area, hiking and cross country ski trails. Wildlife in this area includes black bears, deer, grouse, and loons.

GETTING THERE: From Iron River go SW on state HWY 73 approx. 1 mi. to Lake Ottawa Road. Go W on Lake Ottawa Road approx. 3.5 mi. to Lake Ottawa CG.

SINGLE RATE:	Varies	OPEN DATES:	May-Sept
# of SINGLE SITES:	32	MAX SPUR:	45 feet
		MAX STAY:	14 days
		ELEVATION:	1599 feet

 Campground has hosts   Reservable sites   Accessible facilities   Fully developed Semi-developed   Rustic facilities

NOTE: Open dates listed are typical. Actual dates are dependent on conditions such as snow pack.

11 Lake Sainte Kathryn
Kenton • lat 46°23'10" lon 088°43'35"

DESCRIPTION: This CG is situated in northern hardwoods on Lake Sainte Kathryn. Enjoy fishing in the lake for walleye, pike, bass, and panfish. This CG offers a boat ramp, as well as a hiking and snowmobile trail. Wildlife in this area includes black bears, deer, grouse, and loons. Supplies are available in Kenton.

GETTING THERE: From Kenton go S 2.5 mi. on forest HWY 16 to forest route 3660. Go SE 6 mi. on 3660 to forest route 3500. Go S 1.5 mi. on 3500 to forest route 2127. Go E 3.5 mi. on 2127 to CG.

SINGLE RATE:	Varies	OPEN DATES:	May-Dec
# of SINGLE SITES:	25	MAX SPUR:	45 feet
		MAX STAY:	14 days
		ELEVATION:	1556 feet

16 Moosehead Lake
Marenisco • lat 46°14'28" lon 089°36'15"

DESCRIPTION: CG rests in a forested setting on Moosehead Lake. Some lake views. Warm summer days. Fishing for bass, pike, muskie & blue gill. Boat ramp on site. Supplies in Marenisco. Whitetail deer, upland birds and bald eagles in area. Firewood may be scarce. Mountain bike trails nearby.

GETTING THERE: From Marenisco go E 6 mi. on US HWY 2 to forest route 7300. Go S 8 mi. on 7300 to forest route 6860. Go S 2 mi. on 6860 to forest route 6862. Go SE 2 mi. on 6862 to CG.

SINGLE RATE:	$5	OPEN DATES:	May-Oct
# of SINGLE SITES:	13	MAX SPUR:	45 feet
		MAX STAY:	14 days
		ELEVATION:	1680 feet

12 Langford Lake
Marenisco • lat 46°16'25" lon 089°29'30"

DESCRIPTION: Among mixed hardwood and conifer forest on Langford Lake. Several lakeside sites. Warm summer days. Fish for bass, pike, walleye, crappie, blue gill. Supplies in Marenisco. Whitetail deer, upland birds, bald eagles in area. Fills some weekends. Firewood may be scarce. Black flies May-June.

GETTING THERE: From Marenisco go E on US HWY 2 approx. 10 mi. to forest route 7100. Go S on 7100 approx. 6 mi. to county route 527. Go E on 527 to county route 531. Go approx. 3 mi. on 531 to CG.

SINGLE RATE:	$5	OPEN DATES:	May-Oct
# of SINGLE SITES:	11	MAX SPUR:	45 feet
		MAX STAY:	14 days
		ELEVATION:	1686 feet

17 Norway Lake
Sidnaw • lat 46°25'06" lon 088°41'08"

DESCRIPTION: This CG rests in hardwoods on Norway Lake. Enjoy fishing in the lake for walleye and panfish. This CG offers a boat ramp and hiking trail. There is a snowmobile trail nearby. Wildlife in this area includes black bears, deer and grouse. Supplies are available in Kenton. Summer days are mild.

GETTING THERE: From Sidnaw go S on Sidnaw Road approx. 5.5 mi. to forest route 2400. Go E on 2400 approx. 2 mi. to Norway Lake CG.

SINGLE RATE:	Varies	OPEN DATES:	May-Dec
# of SINGLE SITES:	28	MAX SPUR:	45 feet
		MAX STAY:	14 days
		ELEVATION:	1525 feet

13 Lower Dam Lake
Kenton • lat 46°27'12" lon 088°46'49"

DESCRIPTION: This CG is located in northern hardwoods on Lower Dam Lake. Enjoy fishing for trout in the nearby Ontanogan River. There is a snowmobile trail nearby. Wildlife in this area includes black bears, deer, and grouse. Supplies are available in Kenton. Summer days are usually mild.

GETTING THERE: From Kenton go S on forest HWY 16 approx. 2.5 mi. to forest route 3660. Go SE on 3660 approx. 6 mi. to forest route 3500. Go N on 3500 approx. 2.5 mi. to Lower Dam Lake CG.

SINGLE RATE:	$5	OPEN DATES:	May-Dec
# of SINGLE SITES:	7	MAX SPUR:	45 feet
		MAX STAY:	14 days
		ELEVATION:	1384 feet

18 Paint River Forks
Gibbs City • lat 46°14'09" lon 088°43'10"

DESCRIPTION: This CG is located in hardwoods at the fork of the Paint River. Enjoy fishing for bass and trout in the river. This CG offers excellent canoeing. There is also a nearby snowmobile trail. Visit historic Camp Gibbs. Wildlife in this area includes black bears, deer and grouse. No drinking water on site.

GETTING THERE: From Gibbs City go W on county route 657 approx. 1 mi. to Paint River Forks CG.

SINGLE RATE:	No fee	OPEN DATES:	May-Dec*
# of SINGLE SITES:	4	MAX SPUR:	45 feet
		MAX STAY:	14 days
		ELEVATION:	1475 feet

14 Marion Lake
Watersmeet • lat 46°16'02" lon 089°05'01"

DESCRIPTION: This CG rests in northern hardwoods on Marion Lake. Enjoy fishing in the lake for walleye, bass, muskellunge, and panfish. This CG offers a boat ramp and picnic site. There are also snowmobile and canoe routes in the vicinity. Wildlife in the area includes black bears, deer, grouse, and loons.

GETTING THERE: From Watersmeet go SE on US HWY 2 approx. 3.5 mi. to forest route 3980. Go N on 3980 approx. 1.5 mi. to forest route 3985. Go E on 3985 approx. 1.5 mi. to Marion Lake CG.

SINGLE RATE:	$6	OPEN DATES:	May-Dec
# of SINGLE SITES:	39	MAX SPUR:	45 feet
GROUP RATE:	Varies	MAX STAY:	14 days
		ELEVATION:	1659 feet

19 Paulding Pond
Watersmeet • lat 46°23'28" lon 089°08'12"

DESCRIPTION: This CG is situated in northern hardwoods on Paulding Pond. Enjoy fishing for trout in the lake or nearby Paulding Creek. Visit the beautiful Bond Falls nearby. Wildlife in this area includes black bear, deer, grouse and loons. Supplies are available in Watersmeet. Summer days are mild.

GETTING THERE: From Watersmeet go N on US HWY 45 approx. 9 mi. to Paulding Pond CG.

SINGLE RATE:	$5	OPEN DATES:	May-Dec
# of SINGLE SITES:	4	MAX SPUR:	45 feet
		MAX STAY:	14 days
		ELEVATION:	1360 feet

15 Matchwood
Bergland • lat 46°29'48" lon 089°25'40"

DESCRIPTION: Near farm fields among mixed hardwoods and conifers. Expect snow from Oct-May. Mild summers. Historic Norwich Mine nearby. Popular hunt camp, fills during deer season (Nov 15-30). Beautiful fall colors. Firewood may be scarce. Gravel roads for mtn. biking. May-June black flies are bothersome.

GETTING THERE: From Bergland go E o M28 approx. 5 mi. to forest route 6930 (Topas). Go S on 6930 approx. 7 mi. to Matchwood CG.

SINGLE RATE:	No fee	OPEN DATES:	May-Dec
# of SINGLE SITES:	5	MAX SPUR:	45 feet
		MAX STAY:	14 days
		ELEVATION:	1312 feet

20 Perch Lake
Kenton • lat 46°21'47" lon 088°40'26"

DESCRIPTION: This CG is located in northern hardwoods on Perch Lake. Enjoy fishing in the lake for walleye, pike, bass, and panfish. This CG offers a boat ramp. There is also a snowmobile trail nearby. Wildlife in this area includes black bears, deer, grouse and loons. Supplies are available in Kenton.

GETTING THERE: From Kenton go S 2.5 mi. on forest HWY 16 to forest route 3660. Go SE 6 mi. on 3660 to forest route 3500. Go S 1.5 mi. on 3500 to forest route 2127. Go E 6.5 mi. on 2127 to Perch Lake CG.

SINGLE RATE:	Varies	OPEN DATES:	May-Dec
# of SINGLE SITES:	20	MAX SPUR:	45 feet
		MAX STAY:	14 days
		ELEVATION:	1555 feet

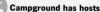 Campground has hosts   Reservable sites 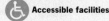 Accessible facilities 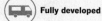 Fully developed   Semi-developed   Rustic facilities

NOTE: Open dates listed are typical. Actual dates are dependent on conditions such as snow pack.

21 **Pomeroy Lake**
Marenisco • lat 46°16'54" lon 089°34'25"

DESCRIPTION: In hardwood forest on Pomeroy Lake. Warm days. Fish for bass, pike, walleye, muskie, crappie & blue gill. Boat ramp. Supplies in Marenisco. Deer, upland birds and bald eagles in area. Firewood supply is scarce. Mountain bike trails in area. Black flies in May & June. Mosquitos until Aug.

GETTING THERE: From Marenisco go E on US HWY 2 approx. 5 mi. to forest route 7300. Go S on 7300 approx. 8 mi. to county route 525. Go E on 525 approx. 1.5 mi. to forest route 6828. Go S on 6828 to CG.

SINGLE RATE:	$5	OPEN DATES:	May-Oct
# of SINGLE SITES:	17	MAX SPUR:	50 feet
		MAX STAY:	14 days
		ELEVATION:	1637 feet

22 **Robbins Pond**
Paulding • lat 46°22'36" lon 089°13'43"

DESCRIPTION: This CG is situated in northern hardwoods on Sucker Creek. Enjoy fishing for trout in the creek or visit the beautiful Rock Bluff Falls nearby. There is also a scenic viewpoint approx. 2 mi. N of the CG. Wildlife in this area includes black bears, deer and grouse. Supplies in Paulding.

GETTING THERE: From Paulding go S on county route approx. 4 mi. to county route 5230. Go NW on 5230 approx. 3.5 mi. to Robbins Pond CG.

SINGLE RATE:	No fee	OPEN DATES:	May-Dec
# of SINGLE SITES:	3	MAX SPUR:	45 feet
		MAX STAY:	14 days
		ELEVATION:	1286 feet

23 **Sparrow Rapids**
Kenton • lat 46°30'15" lon 088°56'48"

DESCRIPTION: This CG is situated in northern hardwoods on the Ontonagan River at Sparrow Rapids. Enjoy fishing in the river for trout. There are hiking trails in the area. Wildlife in the vicinity includes black bears, deer and grouse. Summer days are mild. Supplies are available in Kenton.

GETTING THERE: From Kenton go N on forest HWY 16 approx. 1/2 mi. to forest route 1100. Go NW on 1100 approx. 3 mi. to Sparrow Rapids CG.

SINGLE RATE:	$5	OPEN DATES:	May-Dec
# of SINGLE SITES:	6	MAX SPUR:	45 feet
		MAX STAY:	14 days
		ELEVATION:	1154 feet

24 **Sturgeon River**
Sidnaw • lat 43°34'14" lon 088°39'22"

DESCRIPTION: This CG is situated in northern hardwoods on the Sturgeon River. Enjoy fishing for trout in the river. The North Country National Scenic Trial runs close to this CG and offers excellent hiking opportunities. Wildlife in the vicinity includes black bears, deer, and grouse.

GETTING THERE: From Sidnaw go N on forest route 2200 approx. 5.5 mi. to Sturgeon River CG.

SINGLE RATE:	$5	OPEN DATES:	May-Dec
# of SINGLE SITES:	9	MAX SPUR:	45 feet
		MAX STAY:	14 days
		ELEVATION:	1033 feet

25 **Sylvania**
Watersmeet • lat 46°14'27" lon 089°20'24"

DESCRIPTION: This CG rests in northern hardwoods near Clark Lake. Enjoy fishing in the lake for walleye, bass, and trout. This CG offers a boat ramp, hiking trail, and there are snowmobile trails in the vicinity. Summers are mild. Wildlife includes black bears, deer, grouse and loons. Supplies in Watersmeet.

GETTING THERE: From Watersmeet go W on US HWY 2 approx. 4 mi. to county route 535. Go SW on 535 approx. 4 mi. to Sylvania CG.

SINGLE RATE:	$8	OPEN DATES:	May-Sept
# of SINGLE SITES:	35	MAX SPUR:	45 feet
		MAX STAY:	14 days
		ELEVATION:	1710 feet

26 **Taylor Lake**
Fuller • lat 46°14'52" lon 089°02'53"

DESCRIPTION: This CG is located in northern hardwoods on Taylor Lake. Enjoy fishing in the lake for walleye, bass, and trout. Black bears, deer, grouse and loons frequent this area. There is a boat ramp on site. Summer days are mild. Supplies are available in Watersmeet, approx. 10 mi. away.

GETTING THERE: From Fuller go E on county route 208 approx. 2 mi. to forest route 3960. Go S on 3960 approx. 3 mi. to Taylor Lake CG.

SINGLE RATE:	$5	OPEN DATES:	May-Dec
# of SINGLE SITES:	6	MAX SPUR:	45 feet
		MAX STAY:	14 days
		ELEVATION:	1688 feet

27 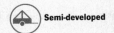 **Teepee Lake**
Kenton • lat 46°22'30" lon 088°52'30"

DESCRIPTION: This CG rests in northern hardwoods on Teepee Lake. Enjoy fishing in the lake for walleye, bass, pike, and panfish. This CG offers a boat ramp and hiking trail. Wildlife in this area includes black bears, deer and grouse. Supplies are available in Kenton. Summer days are usually mild.

GETTING THERE: From Kenton go S on forest HWY 16 approx. 7 mi. to forest route 3630. Go E on 3630 approx. 1/2 mi. to Teepee Lake CG.

SINGLE RATE:	$5	OPEN DATES:	May-Dec
# of SINGLE SITES:	17	MAX SPUR:	45 feet
		MAX STAY:	14 days
		ELEVATION:	1300 feet

 Campground has hosts   **Reservable sites**   **Accessible facilities**   **Fully developed**   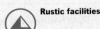 **Semi-developed**   **Rustic facilities**

ROUGHING IT ISN'T WHAT IT USED TO BE...

IT'S BETTER!

WELCOME TO CAMPING COUNTRY

Remember those childhood camping experiences with your family and friends catching a glimpse of a wild animal studying the night sky, making s'mores over the fire? It was those experiences that shaped your love of the outdoors and created some of your best memories. Why not create new traditions and cherished memories with your family?

Coleman® Folding Trailers by Fleetwood® offers the absolute best value in construction, comfort, convenience and safety. Exclusive features, unparalleled designs, towability and exciting new floor plans make this the best selling trailer in the industry.

Visit your local Coleman Folding Trailer dealer today and see the full line of America's best-selling folding trailers. There's one just right for your family in a price range you can afford.

For more information check out our website at
www.colemantrailers.com
or call this toll free number today!
1-800-444-4905

Ontario

L. of the Woods

Agassiz Pool

Clearwater R.

Upper Red L.

Lower Red L.

RAINY RIVER

South International Falls

International Falls

Seine River

Namakan L.

Lac la Croix

Kabetogama L.

Voyageurs NP

Crane Lake

Pelican L.

Trout L.

MINNESOTA

Little Fork R.

71

Big Fork R.

Blackduck

10

23

11

3

Bowstring L.

Marcell

53

Cook

Vermilion L.

Birch L.

Ely

Babbitt

Aurora

4-6,9,14,15,18,21,22

20

L. Winnibigoshish

Mountain Iron

Virginia

Eveleth

2

Bemidji

Cass Lake

Cass L.

130

Deer River

169

Hibbing

Whiteface Res.

Leech L.

Mississippi R.

128

Grand Rapids

129

1,2,7,12,13,16,19

59

Walker

17

8

Island L. Res.

Park Rapids

169

Big Sandy L.

124

Cloquet

Duluth

Superior

10

Detroit Lakes

Big Pine L.

Fish L. Res.

2

Perham

L. Lida

Rush L.

Wadena

Pelican L.

Crosby

125

Gull L.

127

Brainerd

35

53

Staples

10

Mille Lacs L.

Saint Croix NSR

71

Little Falls

Alexandria

L. Osakis

Long Prairie

Mora

Pine City

Spooner

Sauk Centre

Princeton

8

Barron

Glenwood

L. Minnewaska

94

St. Cloud

Milaca

East Bethel

Amery

5

Cold Spring

MISSISSIPPI R.

Big Lake

Ramsey

Big Marine L.

59

Benson

Paynesville

Monticello

Buffalo

North Oaks

63

12

Willmar

Litchfield

12

Cokato

Fridley

Maplewood

Lower Saint Croix NSR

Montevideo

Plymouth

Mississippi NRA

Granite Falls

Olivia

212

Hutchinson

Glencoe

Minneapolis

St. Paul

Bloomington

Ellsworth

126

Durand

Minnesota River

71

Belle Plaine

169

Jordan

Lakeville

61

10

USFS Photo

CHIPPEWA NATIONAL FOREST

The first national forest in the eastern United States, The Chippewa forest boundary encompasses about 1.6 million acres of rolling uplands blanketed with aspen, birch, pines, balsam fir, and maples.

Visitors can explore over 700 lakes and 920 miles of rivers. The Chippewa is recognized for its quality walleye and muskie fishing lakes. Camp along the shores of some of Minnesota's largest lakes and share a golden sunset, or venture into the backcountry to enjoy the solitude of the north woods. You will find family campgrounds, located across the forest's 666,000 acres, offering access to hiking or biking trails, fishing piers, scenic byways, and of course, some of the best fishing in the state.

Winter enthusiasts discover excellent snowshoeing, cross-country skiing, ice fishing and snowmobiling opportunities. Watch for winter celebrations throughout the forest communities, and take in a slightly colder but uniquely exciting season on the Chippewa.

Today, the Chippewa National Forest boasts the highest breeding density of bald eagles in the lower 48 United States. From the smallest of orchids to towering pine trees, the forest offers a wonderful discover zone of plants and animals.

1 Cass Lake

Cass Lake • lat 47˚26'22" lon 094˚38'08"

DESCRIPTION: CG is nestled among red pines on Cass Lake. Fish for bass, perch, northern pike, and panfish. Interpretive trails, paved biking trail, and visitor center are close to CG. Wildlife in area includes bears, wolves, deer, eagles, loons, and herons. Firewood on site. Boat ramp.

GETTING THERE: Cass Lake CG is located approx. 4 mi. E of Cass Lake on US HWY 2.

SINGLE RATE:	$14	OPEN DATES:	May-Sept
# of SINGLE SITES:	23	MAX SPUR:	50 feet
		MAX STAY:	14 days
		ELEVATION:	1337 feet

2 Chippewa

Cass Lake • lat 48˚03'37" lon 092˚50'59"

DESCRIPTION: CG is nestled among red pine on Cass Lake. Fish for bass, perch, northern pike, and panfish. Interpretive trails, paved biking trail, and visitor center are close to CG. Wildlife in area includes bears, wolves, deer, eagles, loons, and herons. Firewood on site. Boat ramp.

GETTING THERE: Chippewa CG is located approx. 4 mi. E of Cass Lake on US HWY 2.

SINGLE RATE:	$16	OPEN DATES:	May-Sept
# of SINGLE SITES:	46	MAX SPUR:	50 feet
		MAX STAY:	14 days
		ELEVATION:	1350 feet

3 Clubhouse

Marcell • lat 47˚36'15" lon 093˚34'16"

DESCRIPTION: This CG is situated in mixed pine and hardwoods on Clubhouse Lake which is 90 feet deep. Great fishing for northern pike, bass and panfish. Smaller boats & canoes can access several lakes. Wildlife in this area includes bears, wolves, eagles, loons, and herons. There is a barrier free fishing dock on site.

GETTING THERE: From Marcell go E on county route 45 approx. 7 mi. to forest route 2181. Go N on 2181 approx. 1 mi. to forest route 3758. Go NE on 3758 approx. 1.5 mi. to Clubhouse CG.

SINGLE RATE:	$12	OPEN DATES:	May-Oct
# of SINGLE SITES:	47	MAX SPUR:	20 feet
		MAX STAY:	14 days
		ELEVATION:	1341 feet

4 Cut Foot Horse Camp

Deer River • lat 47˚33'00" lon 094˚05'00"

DESCRIPTION: This CG is situated in a mixed pine and hardwood forest near Cut Foot Sioux Lake. Fish for walley, northern pike, muskie, and perch. The 26 mi. Cut Foot Sioux National Recreation hiking and horse trail runs near this CG. A picket line is provided for tying your horse and there are manure pits at the campsites.

GETTING THERE: Drive 3.5 mi. past the Cut Foot Sioux Visitor Center along Highway 46, turn left on Forest Road 2171 and go three miles to Cut Foot Horse Camp.

SINGLE RATE:	$12	OPEN DATES:	Apr-Nov
# of SINGLE SITES:	23	MAX SPUR:	50 feet
		MAX STAY:	14 days
		ELEVATION:	1350 feet

5 Deer Lake

Deer River • lat 47˚30'54" lon 094˚06'18"

DESCRIPTION: This CG is located in mixed pine & hardwoods. A boat ramp provides access to Deer Lake via Biauswah Creek. Fish for walley, pike, muskie, and perch. The 26 mi. Cut Foot Sioux National Recreation Trail runs through the CG. Wildlife includes bears, wolves, and eagles.

GETTING THERE: From Deer River go NW on state HWY 46 approx. 20 mi. to forest route 2198. Go W on 2198 approx. 4 mi. to Deer Lake CG. CG is located on the W shore of Cut Foot Sioux Lake.

SINGLE RATE:	$14	OPEN DATES:	May-Nov
# of SINGLE SITES:	48	MAX SPUR:	50 feet
		MAX STAY:	14 days
		ELEVATION:	1322 feet

 Campground has hosts   Reservable sites   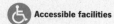 Accessible facilities   Fully developed   Semi-developed   Rustic facilities

NOTE: Open dates listed are typical. Actual dates are dependent on conditions such as snow pack.

6 East Seelye Bay
Deer River • lat 47°31'18" lon 094°05'10"

DESCRIPTION: This CG rests in mixed pine & hardwood. A boat ramp provides access to Cutfoot Sioux Lake. Fish for walley, pike, muskie, and perch. The 26 mi. Cut Foot Sioux National Recreation Trail runs past the CG to Seelye Point. Wildlife includes bears, wolves, loons, and eagles.

GETTING THERE: From Deer River go N on state HWY 46 approx. 20 mi. to forest route 2198. Go W on 2198 approx. 2.5 mi. to East Seelye Bay CG.

SINGLE RATE:	$14	OPEN DATES:	May-Oct
# of SINGLE SITES:	13	MAX SPUR:	40 feet
		MAX STAY:	14 days
		ELEVATION:	1350 feet

11 North Star
Marcell • lat 47°33'25" lon 093°39'13"

DESCRIPTION: This CG is situated in mixed pine and hardwoods on North Star Lake. The lake has many sheltered bays and inlets that provide calm water for fishing. Species include walley, pike, muskie, bass, and panfish. Other wildlife in the area includes bears, wolves, deer, eagles, loons, and herons.

GETTING THERE: North Star CG is located approx. 4 mi. S of Marcell on county route 262.

SINGLE RATE:	$12	OPEN DATES:	May-Oct
# of SINGLE SITES:	38	MAX SPUR:	20 feet
		MAX STAY:	14 days
		ELEVATION:	1401 feet

7 Knutson Dam
Cass Lake • lat 47°27'00" lon 094°29'04"

DESCRIPTION: This CG is nestled in red pine on Cass Lake. This CG is known for its canoe access to the Mississippi River. Interpretive trails, paved bike trail, and visitor center are close to CG. Bears, wolves, deer, eagles, loons, and herons are in the area. Firewood on site.

GETTING THERE: From Cass Lake go E on US HWY 2 approx. 6 mi. to county route 10. Go N on 10 approx. 5 mi. to Knutson Dam CG.

SINGLE RATE:	$12	OPEN DATES:	May-Oct
# of SINGLE SITES:	14	MAX SPUR:	50 feet
		MAX STAY:	14 days
		ELEVATION:	1305 feet

12 Norway Beach
Cass Lake • lat 47°22'48" lon 094°31'20"

DESCRIPTION: CG rests in red pine on Cass Lake. Good fishing for bass, perch, northern pike, and panfish. Interpretive trails, paved biking trail, and visitor center are close to CG. Wildlife in area includes bears, wolves, deer, eagles, loons, and herons. Firewood on site. Boat ramp.

GETTING THERE: Norway Beach CG is located approx. 4 mi. E of Cass Lake on US HWY 2.

SINGLE RATE:	$14	OPEN DATES:	May-Sept
# of SINGLE SITES:	55	MAX SPUR:	50 feet
		MAX STAY:	14 days
		ELEVATION:	1305 feet

8 Mabel Lake
Walker • lat 47°02'59" lon 094°04'18"

DESCRIPTION: This is a secluded CG that rests in a hardwood and pine forest setting. There are good fishing opportunities on adjacent Mable Lake. The nearby Boy River is an excellent river to paddle and view eagles, osprey and waterfowl. There is a boat ramp on site.

GETTING THERE: Mabel Lake CG is located 26 mi. E of Walker on state HWY 200.

SINGLE RATE:	$12	OPEN DATES:	May-Oct
# of SINGLE SITES:	22	MAX SPUR:	30 feet
		MAX STAY:	14 days
		ELEVATION:	1350 feet

13 Nushka Group Camp
Cass Lake • lat 47°26'22" lon 094°29'55"

DESCRIPTION: Dispersed sites rest in red pine near Cass Lake. There is good fishing in this lake for bass, perch, northern pike, and panfish. Interpretive trails, paved biking trail, and visitor center are close to CG. Wildlife includes bears, wolves, deer, eagles, loons, and herons.

GETTING THERE: From Cass Lake go E on US HWY 2 approx. 6 mi. to county route 10. Go N on 10 to Nushka Group CG.

SINGLE RATE:	Varies	OPEN DATES:	May-Oct
# of SINGLE SITES:	20		
GROUP RATE:	$40	MAX STAY:	14 days
# of GROUP SITES:	2	ELEVATION:	1325 feet

9 Mosomo Point
Deer River • lat 47°31'03" lon 094°02'52"

DESCRIPTION: This CG is located in mixed pine & hardwoods. A boat ramp provides access to Cutfoot Sioux Lake. Fish for walley, pike, muskie, and perch. The 26 mi. Cut Foot Sioux National Recreation Trail runs near this CG. Wildlife in the area includes bears, wolves, coyote, deer, loons, and eagles.

GETTING THERE: From Deer River go N on state HWY 46 approx. 19 mi. to forest route 2190. Go W on 2190 approx. 1/2 mi. to Mosomo Point CG.

SINGLE RATE:	$14	OPEN DATES:	May-Nov
# of SINGLE SITES:	23	MAX SPUR:	40 feet
		MAX STAY:	14 days
		ELEVATION:	1350 feet

14 O-Ne-Gum-E
Deer River • lat 47°30'00" lon 094°05'30"

DESCRIPTION: This CG is situated in mixed pine & hardwoods on Little Cutfoot Sioux Lake. Fish for walley, northern pike, muskie, and perch. The 26 mi. Cut Foot Sioux National Recreation Trail runs near this CG. Wildlife in this area includes bears, wolves, deer, loons, and eagles. The CG is busy during fishing season.

GETTING THERE: O-Ne-Gum-E is located approx. 18 mi. NW of Deer River on state HWY 46.

SINGLE RATE:	$14	OPEN DATES:	May-Oct
# of SINGLE SITES:	48	MAX SPUR:	50 feet
		MAX STAY:	14 days
		ELEVATION:	1350 feet

10 Noma Lake
Wirt • lat 47°45'15" lon 093°58'05"

DESCRIPTION: CG is surrounded by a beautiful stand of paper birch. Noma Lake offers good fishing for bass, northern pike, and panfish. A boat ramp is on the south end of Noma Lake. A fish cleaning station & firewood on site. Wildlife in the area includes bears, wolves, deer, eagles, goshawks, loons, & herons.

GETTING THERE: Noma CG is located approx. 2 mi. NW of Wirt on county route 31.

SINGLE RATE:	$10	OPEN DATES:	May-Oct
# of SINGLE SITES:	14	MAX SPUR:	20 feet
		MAX STAY:	14 days
		ELEVATION:	1365 feet

15 Plug Hat Point
Deer River • lat 47°26'00" lon 094°04'00"

DESCRIPTION: This CG rests in a mixed pine and hardwood forest on Lake Winnibigoshish. Fish for walley, northern pike, muskie, and perch. The 26 mi. Cut Foot Sioux National Recreation hiking and horse trail runs near this CG. Wildlife in area includes bears, wolves, deer, loons, and eagles. Open during fishing season.

GETTING THERE: From Deer River go N on state HWY 46 to county route 9. Go W on 9 approx. 2 mi. to forest route 2160. Go N on 2160 to Plug Hat Point CG.

SINGLE RATE:	$10	OPEN DATES:	May-Memorial
# of SINGLE SITES:	13	MAX SPUR:	20 feet
		MAX STAY:	14 days
		ELEVATION:	1350 feet

 Campground has hosts   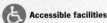 **Reservable sites**   **Accessible facilities**   **Fully developed**   **Semi-developed**   **Rustic facilities**

NOTE: Open dates listed are typical. Actual dates are dependent on conditions such as snow pack.

16 South Pike Bay
Cass Lake • lat 47˚19'44" lon 094˚34'46"

DESCRIPTION: This CG is nestled in mixed pine and hardwoods on Pike Bay. The CG is known for its clear, secluded waters. Fish for bass, perch, northern pike and panfish. Bears, wolves, deer, eagles, loons, and herons frequent the area. Enjoy a visit to the Lost Forty virgin pine forest.

GETTING THERE: From Cass Lake go S on state HWY 371 approx. 3 mi. to forest route 2137. Go E on 2137 approx. 2 mi. to South Pike Bay CG.

SINGLE RATE:	$14	OPEN DATES:	May-Oct
# of SINGLE SITES:	24	MAX SPUR:	50 feet
		MAX STAY:	14 days
		ELEVATION:	1350 feet

17 Stony Point
Walker • lat 47˚08'17" lon 094˚27'20"

DESCRIPTION: This is an open, grassy CG surrounded by old growth forest that includes oak, elm, maple and ash. There are good fishing opportunities in adjacent Leech Lake. Electricity, showers, an RV dump station and fish cleaning station are all on site. There is boat access to the lake with 2 boat harbors at the CG.

GETTING THERE: Stony Point CG is located approx. 14 mi. E of Walker on Leech Lake.

SINGLE RATE:	$18	OPEN DATES:	May-Oct
# of SINGLE SITES:	44	MAX SPUR:	50 feet
		MAX STAY:	14 days
		ELEVATION:	1311 feet

18 Tamarack Point
Deer River • lat 47˚26'52" lon 094˚06'33"

DESCRIPTION: This CG is is situated in mixed pine & hardwoods on Lake Winnibigoshish. Fish for walley, northern pike, muskie, and perch. The 26 mi. Cut Foot Sioux National Recreation Trail runs near this CG. Wildlife in the area includes bears, wolves, deer, loons, and eagles. The CG is busy during fishing season.

GETTING THERE: From Deer River go NW on state HWY 46 approx. 13 mi. to county route 9. Go SW on 9 approx. 6 mi. to forest route 2163. Go NW on 2163 approx. 5 mi. to Tamarack Point CG.

SINGLE RATE:	$12	OPEN DATES:	May-Nov
# of SINGLE SITES:	35	MAX SPUR:	50 feet
		MAX STAY:	14 days
		ELEVATION:	1350 feet

19 Wanaki
Cass Lake • lat 47˚23'13" lon 094˚30'28"

DESCRIPTION: CG rests in red pine on Cass Lake. Good fishing in this lake for bass, perch, northern pike, and panfish. Interpretive trails, paved biking trail, and visitor center are close to CG. Wildlife includes bears, wolves, deer, eagles, loons, and herons. Firewood on site. Boat ramp.

GETTING THERE: Wanaki CG is located approx. 4 mi. E of Cass Lake on US HWY 2.

SINGLE RATE:	$14	OPEN DATES:	May-Sept
# of SINGLE SITES:	46	MAX SPUR:	50 feet
		MAX STAY:	14 days
		ELEVATION:	1350 feet

20 Webster Lake
Blackduck • lat 47˚36'18" lon 094˚30'24"

DESCRIPTION: This CG is located in mixed pine and hardwoods on Webster Lake. Enjoy fishing for bass, panfish, and northern pike. There is a boat launch on site. This CG is near the Bogwash Hiking Trail. Wildlife in the area includes bears, wolves, eagles, goshawks, loons, and herons.

GETTING THERE: From Blackduck go S on county route 39 approx. 7 mi. to forest route 2207. Go E on 2207 approx. 1 mi. to forest route 2236. Go S on 2236 approx. 2 mi. to Webster Lake CG.

SINGLE RATE:	$10	OPEN DATES:	May-Oct
# of SINGLE SITES:	24	MAX SPUR:	30 feet
		MAX STAY:	14 days
		ELEVATION:	1363 feet

21 West Seelye Bay
Deer River • lat 47˚31'21" lon 094˚05'54"

DESCRIPTION: This CG rests in mixed pine & hardwoods on Cutfoot Sioux Lake. Fish for walley, northern pike, muskie and perch. The 26 mi. Cut Foot Sioux National Recreation Trail runs near this CG. Wildlife in the area includes bears, wolves, deer, loons, and eagles. The CG is busy during fishing season.

GETTING THERE: From Deer River go N on state HWY 46 approx. 20 mi. to forest route 2198. Go W on 2198 approx. 3 mi. to West Seelye Bay CG.

SINGLE RATE:	$12	OPEN DATES:	May-Sept
# of SINGLE SITES:	22	MAX SPUR:	40 feet
		MAX STAY:	14 days
		ELEVATION:	1350 feet

22 Williams Narrows
Deer River • lat 47˚30'12" lon 094˚04'37"

DESCRIPTION: This CG is situated in mixed pine & hardwoods on Little Cutfoot Sioux Lake. Enjoy fishing for walley, and northern pike. This CG is busy during fishing season. The 26 mi. Cut Foot Sioux National Recreation Trail runs near this CG. Wildlife in the area includes bears, wolves, deer, loons, and eagles.

GETTING THERE: From Deer River go N on state HWY 46 approx. 15 mi. to county route 148. Go W on 148 approx. 3 mi. to Williams Narrows CG.

SINGLE RATE:	$14	OPEN DATES:	May-Oct
# of SINGLE SITES:	17	MAX SPUR:	40 feet
		MAX STAY:	14 days
		ELEVATION:	1320 feet

23 Winnie
Cass Lake • lat 47˚25'32" lon 094˚19'02"

DESCRIPTION: This CG is surrounded by red and white pine near Cass Lake. Fish in this lake for bass, perch, northern pike, and panfish. Interpretive trails, paved bike trail, and visitor center are close to CG. Wildlife in the area includes bears, wolves, deer, eagles, loons, and herons.

GETTING THERE: From Cass Lake go E 6 mi. on US HWY 2 to county route 10. Go N 2 mi. on 10 to forest route 2171. Go NE 6 mi. on 2171 to forest route 2168. Go S 4 mi. on 2168 to Winnie CG.

SINGLE RATE:	$12	OPEN DATES:	May-Nov
# of SINGLE SITES:	35	MAX SPUR:	50 feet
		MAX STAY:	14 days
		ELEVATION:	1350 feet

 Campground has hosts 🔒 **Reservable sites** ♿ **Accessible facilities** **Fully developed** **Semi-developed**  **Rustic facilities**

NOTE: Open dates listed are typical. Actual dates are dependent on conditions such as snow pack.

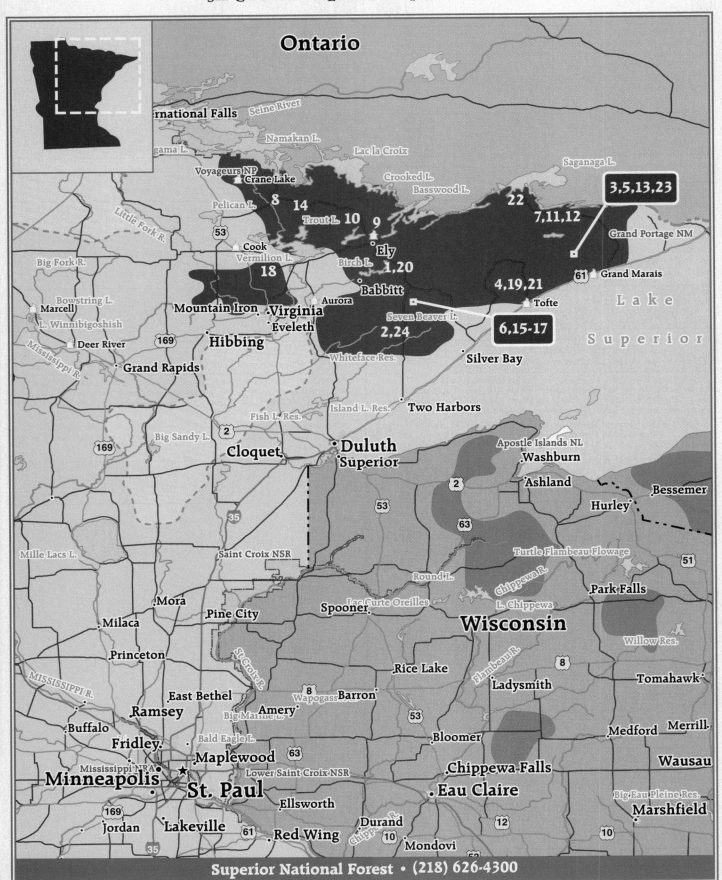

Ontario

International Falls
Seine River
Namakan L.
Lac la Croix
Saganaga L.
gama L.
Voyageurs NP
Crane Lake
Pelican L.
8
14
Trout L.
10
9
Crooked L.
Basswood L.
22
7,11,12
3,5,13,23
Grand Portage NM
Little Fork R.
53
Cook
Vermilion L.
Ely
Birch L.
1,20
4,19,21
61
Grand Marais
Big Fork R.
18
Babbitt
Lake
Marcell
Mountain Iron
Virginia
Aurora
Seven Beaver L.
6,15-17
Tofte
Superior
Bowstring L.
L. Winnibigoshish
Eveleth
2,24
Deer River
169
Hibbing
Whiteface Res.
Silver Bay
Mississippi R.
Grand Rapids
Island L. Res.
Two Harbors
Fish L. Res.
Apostle Islands NL
Big Sandy L.
2
Washburn
169
Cloquet
Duluth
Superior
Ashland
Bessemer
35
2
Hurley
63
51
Saint Croix NSR
Turtle Flambeau Flowage
Park Falls
Mille Lacs L.
Round L.
Chippewa R.
L. Chippewa
Mora
Lac Courte Oreilles
Spooner
Wisconsin
Willow Res.
Milaca
Pine City
Rice Lake
Tomahawk
Princeton
Flambeau R.
Ladysmith
Medford
Merrill
MISSISSIPPI R.
8
East Bethel
Wapogass
Barron
Bloomer
Wausau
Ramsey
Amery
53
Buffalo
Big Marine L.
St. Croix R.
63
Chippewa Falls
Big Eau Pleine Res.
Fridley
Bald Eagle L.
Maplewood
Lower Saint Croix NSR
Eau Claire
Marshfield
Minneapolis
Mississippi NRA
St. Paul
Ellsworth
Jordan
Lakeville
169
61
Red Wing
Durand
10
35
Mondovi
12
10

USFS Photo

SUPERIOR NATIONAL FOREST

The Superior National Forest in northeastern Minnesota spans 150 miles along the United States-Canadian border. Established as a national forest in 1909 by President Teddy Roosevelt, this 3 million-acre forest is a rich and varied resource.

The Superior offers numerous recreation opportunities year-round. Camping opportunities range from fully developed campgrounds to secluded wilderness as well as backcountry sites that have few or no facilities. Boating, canoeing, and fishing opportunities are nearly endless on the more than 2,000 lakes and streams found within the forest. Many of these lakes and streams boast some of the country's finest fishing for walleye, northern pike, and smallmouth bass. If you are interested in hiking, the Superior offers trails varying in length and difficulty to provide an adventure of just a few hours or an extended trip of a week or more.

The Boundary Waters Canoe Area Wilderness, a true American wilderness, has changed little since the glaciers melted. With 1,500 miles of canoe routes, nearly 2,200 designated campsites, and more than 1,000 lakes and streams waiting, the Boundary Waters draws thousands of visitors each year.

The northern forest community is home to numerous wildlife species including deer, moose, and black bears. Northern Minnesota is also the last stronghold of the gray wolf in the lower 48 states. Approximately 300-400 wolves continue to roam within Superior National Forest today.

1 Birch Lake

Ely • lat 47°45'30" lon 091°47'01"

DESCRIPTION: This CG is located in an open stand of white birch, aspen and some pines with views of Birch Lake. Fish for walleye and northern pike in the lake. Supplies are approx. 13 mi. from the CG. Local wildlife includes whitetailed deer, raccoons, eagles and loons. June brings mosquitoes and black flies.

GETTING THERE: From Ely go S on state HWY 1 approx. 7 mi. to forest route 429. Go S on 429 approx. 3 mi. to Birch Lake CG.

SINGLE RATE:	Varies	OPEN DATES:	May-Sept
# of SINGLE SITES:	28	MAX SPUR:	22 feet
		MAX STAY:	14 days
		ELEVATION:	1600 feet

2 Cadotte Lake

Aurora • lat 47°22'50" lon 091°55'00"

DESCRIPTION: This CG is nestled among aspen, spruce and balsam on Cadotte Lake. Enjoy fishing for walley and northern pike in the lake. Limited supplies are available at a small store 2 mi. away. Whitetailed deer, raccoons, and bald eagles frequent the area. June brings mosquitos and black flies.

GETTING THERE: From Aurora go S on county route 100 approx. 1 mi. to county route 110. Go E on 110 approx. 22 mi. to Cadotte Lake CG.

SINGLE RATE:	$8	OPEN DATES:	May-Sept
# of SINGLE SITES:	27	MAX SPUR:	22 feet
		MAX STAY:	14 days
		ELEVATION:	1630 feet

3 Cascade River

Tofte • lat 47°50'01" lon 090°31'49"

DESCRIPTION: This CG rests in birch, aspen and pines with views of Cascade River, which is wonderful for trout fishing. Supplies are approx. 16 mi. at Grand Marais. Wildlife includes deer, raccoons and eagles. Campers may gather firewood. Mountain bike roads are nearby. June brings mosquitos and black flies.

GETTING THERE: From Tofte go NE on US HWY 61 approx. 18 mi. to county route 7. Go NE on 7 approx. 5 mi. to forest route 158. Go NW on 158 approx. 9 mi. to Cascade River CG.

SINGLE RATE:	No fee	OPEN DATES:	May-Oct
# of SINGLE SITES:	4	MAX SPUR:	22 feet
		MAX STAY:	14 days
		ELEVATION:	1600 feet

4 Crescent Lake

Tofte • lat 47°49'30" lon 090°46'25"

DESCRIPTION: This CG is set among aspen, birch, hardwood and firs on Crescent Lake. Boat fish in the lake for northern and walleye pike. Deer, bear and ruffed grouse are in the area. There is a barrier free fishing pier on site. June brings mosquitos and black flies. This CG offers one backcountry campsite.

GETTING THERE: From Tofte go N on county route 2 approx. 14 mi. to forest route 170. Go NE on 170 approx. 3 mi. to Crescent lake CG.

SINGLE RATE:	$9.30	OPEN DATES:	May-Sept
# of SINGLE SITES:	33	MAX SPUR:	22 feet
		MAX STAY:	14 days
		ELEVATION:	1889 feet

5 Devil Track Lake

Tofte • lat 47°49'20" lon 090°25'30"

DESCRIPTION: This CG is located in a open forest setting of aspen, balsam fir and conifers. CG has wibderfyk views of Devils Track Lake. Boat and shore fishing are popular at this CG. Supplies are approx. 12 mi. away at Grand Marais. Wildlife in this area includes deer, raccoons and eagles.

GETTING THERE: From Tofte go NE 18 mi. on US HWY 61 to county route 7. Go NE 5 mi. on 7 to forest route 158. Go NW 8 mi. on 158 to county route 57. Go E 3 mi. on 57 to Devil Track Lake CG.

SINGLE RATE:	$8	OPEN DATES:	May-Oct
# of SINGLE SITES:	16	MAX SPUR:	22 feet
		MAX STAY:	14 days
		ELEVATION:	1635 feet

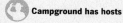 **Campground has hosts** **Reservable sites** **Accessible facilities** **Fully developed** **Semi-developed** **Rustic facilities**

NOTE: Open dates listed are typical. Actual dates are dependent on conditions such as snow pack.

6 Divide Lake
Isabella • lat 47°36'37" lon 091°15'22"

DESCRIPTION: This CG is in a dense cover of aspen, balsam fir and spruce on Divide Lake. Boat fish for rainbow trout. CG is on historic Laurentian Divide. Deer and ruffed grouse are in the area. There is a hiking trail around the lake. Black flies and mosquitos are thick in June. This CG offers one backcountry campsite.

GETTING THERE: From Isabella go E on forest route 172 approx. 3 mi. to Divide Lake CG. Road is narrow with sharp curves. Large vehicles should use caution.

SINGLE RATE: $6	OPEN DATES: May-Sept
# of SINGLE SITES: 3	MAX SPUR: 22 feet
	MAX STAY: 14 days
	ELEVATION: 1957 feet

11 Flour Lake
Grand Marais • lat 48°03'09" lon 090°24'30"

DESCRIPTION: This CG is located on Flour Lake and offers boat fishing for bass, walleye and lake trout. Supplies are available in Grand Marais. Deer, bear, moose, loons, and bald eagles can be seen in the area. Hike nearby Honeymoon Bluff trail 1/2 mi. to Hungry Jack Lake. June brings mosquitos and black flies.

GETTING THERE: From Grand Marias go N on county route 12 approx. 24 mi. to Flour Lake CG.

SINGLE RATE: Varies	OPEN DATES: May-Sept
# of SINGLE SITES: 37	MAX SPUR: 22 feet
	MAX STAY: 14 days
	ELEVATION: 1735 feet

7 East Bearskin Lake
Grand Marais • lat 48°02'34" lon 090°21'54"

DESCRIPTION: This CG is situated in aspen, balsam fir, spruce and white pine on East Bearskin Lake. Boat fish for walleye and northern pike. Supplies are available in Grand Marais. Local wildlife includes deer, eagles, black bear and racoon. Campers may gather dead and down firewood. June brings mosquitos and black flies.

GETTING THERE: From Grand Marais go N on county route 12 approx. 21 mi. to East Bearskin Lake CG.

SINGLE RATE: $10	OPEN DATES: May-Oct
# of SINGLE SITES: 33	MAX SPUR: 22 feet
	MAX STAY: 14 days
	ELEVATION: 1702 feet

12 Iron Lake
Grand Marais • lat 48°04'04" lon 090°36'53"

DESCRIPTION: This small, quiet CG is located in an open stand of aspen and red pine with views of the adjacent Iron Lake. The CG offers non-motorized boating and fishing for walley and nothern pike on Iron Lake. Supplies available at Grand Marias. Wildlife includes black bear, deer, moose and grouse.

GETTING THERE: From Grand Marias go N then W on county route 12 approx. 29 mi. to Iron Lake CG. Road is narrow. Large vehicles should use caution.

SINGLE RATE: $10	OPEN DATES: May-Sept
# of SINGLE SITES: 7	MAX SPUR: 22 feet
	MAX STAY: 14 days
	ELEVATION: 1860 feet

8 Echo Lake
Cook • lat 48°10'14" lon 092°29'28"

DESCRIPTION: This CG rests in an open, park-like area of aspens on Echo Lake. Supplies are available in Cook. Deer, bear, racoon, and eagles are common to the area. A series of trails loop from the CG. Good grouse hunting in area. This CG is adjacent to Echo Lake "back country" CG which offers 3 campsites.

GETTING THERE: From Cook go N on US HWY 53 approx. 18 mi. to county route 23. Go NE on 23 approx. 15 mi. to county route 24. Go NE on 24 approx. 5 mi. to Echo Lake CG.

SINGLE RATE: $8	OPEN DATES: May-Sept
# of SINGLE SITES: 24	MAX SPUR: 22 feet
GROUP RATE: $16	MAX STAY: 14 days
# of GROUP SITES: 1	ELEVATION: 1283 feet

13 Kimball Lake
Grand Marais • lat 47°51'45" lon 090°13'34"

DESCRIPTION: This CG is located in a dense canopy of aspen, balsam fir and pine on Kimball Lake. Boat fish for trout. Summer days are mild. Supplies are in Grand Marais. Local wildlife includes whitetailed deer, racoon, black bear, bald eagles. Gather firewood. Prepare for mosquitos and black flies in June.

GETTING THERE: From Grand Marais go N on Gunflint Trail (county road 12) approx. 11 mi. to forest route 140. Go right on 140 approx. 2 mi. to Kimball Lake CG. Road is narrow with sharp curves.

SINGLE RATE: $10	OPEN DATES: May-Sept
# of SINGLE SITES: 10	MAX SPUR: 22 feet
	MAX STAY: 14 days
	ELEVATION: 1690 feet

9 Fall Lake
Ely • lat 47°57'09" lon 091°42'59"

DESCRIPTION: This CG is set in open canopy of aspen, birch and red pine with views of Fall Lake. Boat, swim and fish for walleye, northern pike, bass and crappie in the lake. Supplies available at Ely. Deer, loons, ruffed grouse, bald eagles and racoons can be seen in the area. No nearby trails.

GETTING THERE: From Ely go NE on state HWY 169 approx. 6 mi. to forest route 551. Go NE on 551 approx. 2 mi. to Fall Lake CG.

SINGLE RATE: Varies	OPEN DATES: May-Sept
# of SINGLE SITES: 66	MAX SPUR: 22 feet
	MAX STAY: 14 days
	ELEVATION: 1340 feet

14 Lake Jeanette
Cook • lat 48°07'56" lon 092°17'45"

DESCRIPTION: CG rests in an open area of pine and aspen overlooking Jeanette Lake. Supplies available at Cook. Deer, racoons, black bear and bald eagles are common to the area. CG is full most of the summer. June brings mosquitos and black flies. This CG offers three backcountry sites (boat access only).

GETTING THERE: From Cook go N on US HWY 53 apprx. 18 mi. to county route 23. Go NE on 23 apprx. 15 mi. to county route 24. Go NE on 24 apprx. 5 mi. to county route 116. Go E on 116 apprx. 15 mi. to CG.

SINGLE RATE: $8	OPEN DATES: May-Sept
# of SINGLE SITES: 12	MAX SPUR: 22 feet
	MAX STAY: 14 days
	ELEVATION: 1200 feet

10 Fenske Lake
Ely • lat 47°59'42" lon 091°54'55"

DESCRIPTION: CG rests in a fairly dense forest of pine, birch and aspen. Views are of adjacent Fenske Lake. Fish for bass, northern and walleye. Wildlife includes deer, raccoons, eagles, loons, foxes and bear. CG offers a pavillion, barrier free fishing pier and nature/hiking trail. June brings biting bugs.

GETTING THERE: From Ely go NW on county route 116 approx. 7 mi. to Fenske Lake CG. Road is narrow with sharp curves. Large vehicles should use caution.

SINGLE RATE: $10	OPEN DATES: May-Sept
# of SINGLE SITES: 16	MAX SPUR: 22 feet
GROUP RATE: $24	MAX STAY: 14 days
# of GROUP SITES: 1	ELEVATION: 1450 feet

15 Little Isabella River
Illgen City • lat 47°38'51" lon 091°25'28"

DESCRIPTION: This CG rests in a forest of norway pines with some aspen. The CG is close to the Little Isabella River. Enjoy trout fishing in the river from a nearby trail. Supplies are available at Illgen City. Deer and red squirrels frequent this area. Campers may gather dead and down firewood. June brings biting bugs.

GETTING THERE: From Illgen City go NW on state HWY 1 approx. 22 mi. to Little Isabella River CG. Road is narrow with sharp curves. Large vehicles should use caution.

SINGLE RATE: $7	OPEN DATES: May-Sept
# of SINGLE SITES: 11	MAX SPUR: 22 feet
	MAX STAY: 14 days
	ELEVATION: 1831 feet

 Campground has hosts　　 **Reservable sites**　　 **Accessible facilities**　　 **Fully developed**　　 **Semi-developed**　　 **Rustic facilities**

NOTE: Open dates listed are typical. Actual dates are dependent on conditions such as snow pack.

16  McDougal Lake
Illgen City • lat 47°38'21" lon 091°32'06"

DESCRIPTION: This CG is located in an open mixture of pines, spruce and balsam fir with some aspen and white birch. CG is close to McDougal Lake. Fish for walleye, northern pike and bass. Supplies are at Illgen City. Numerous wildlife in the area. A short loop hiking trail leads to scenic overlooks with benches.

GETTING THERE: From Illgen City go NW on state HWY 1 approx. 26 mi. to McDougal Lake CG.

SINGLE RATE:	$7	OPEN DATES:	May-Sept
# of SINGLE SITES:	21	MAX SPUR:	22 feet
		MAX STAY:	14 days
		ELEVATION:	1791 feet

21 Temperance River
Tofte • lat 47°43'05" lon 090°52'47"

DESCRIPTION: This CG is located in mixed conifers next to the Temperance River. This river supports a cold water trout fishery. Please check fishing regulations. Nearby there are several mountain bike routes. Supplies are available in Tofte. Wildlife in this area includes deer and small mammals.

GETTING THERE: From Tofte go N on county route 2 approx. 10 mi. to Temperance River CG.

SINGLE RATE:	$9	OPEN DATES:	Apr-Nov
# of SINGLE SITES:	9	MAX SPUR:	22 feet
GROUP RATE:		MAX STAY:	14 days
		ELEVATION:	1515 feet

17 Ninemile Lake
Tofte • lat 47°34'40" lon 091°05'00"

DESCRIPTION: This CG is set in mixed conifers and offers several campsites that overlook Ninemile Lake. Enjoy fishing, boating and canoeing in the lake. There is a boat ramp with parking on site. A 5-mile hiking trail is located a short distance from the CG. Wildlife includes deer, birds and small mammals.

GETTING THERE: From Tofte go N on county route 2 approx. 5 mi. to forest route 166. Go W on 166 approx. 12 mi. to county route 7. Go S on 7 approx. 4 mi. to Ninemile CG.

SINGLE RATE:	Varies	OPEN DATES:	Apr-Nov
# of SINGLE SITES:	24	MAX SPUR:	22 feet
		MAX STAY:	14 days
		ELEVATION:	1630 feet

22  Trails End
Grand Marais • lat 34°27'28" lon 095°11'13"

DESCRIPTION: This CG rests under a canopy of aspen, pine and spruce trees fronting Seagull and Gull Lakes. Boat fish for walleye, lake trout, northern pike and small mouth bass. Bald eagles, osprey, hawks, and moose in area. There is a nature trail near Seagull Lake landing. Mosquitos and black flies in June.

GETTING THERE: From Grand Marias go NW on county route 12 approx. 43 mi. to Trails End CG.

SINGLE RATE:	Varies	OPEN DATES:	May-Sept
# of SINGLE SITES:	32	MAX SPUR:	22 feet
		MAX STAY:	14 days
		ELEVATION:	1200 feet

18 Pfeiffer Lake
Virginia • lat 47°44'56" lon 092°28'41"

DESCRIPTION: This CG is located in an open grove of aspen and birch. The CG overlooks Pfeiffer Lake. Boat fish in the lake for pike and panfish. Summer days are mild. Supplies are in Virginia. Deer, bald eagles, loons and raccoons are common. There is an interpretive trail and playground on site.

GETTING THERE: From Virginia go N on HWY 53/19 4 mi. to Hwy 169. Go N on 169 16 mi. to HWY 1. Go W on HWY 1 5 mi. to forest route 256. Go S on 256 2 mi. to Pfeiffer Lake CG. Road is narrow.

SINGLE RATE:	$9	OPEN DATES:	May-Sept
# of SINGLE SITES:	16	MAX SPUR:	22 feet
		MAX STAY:	14 days
		ELEVATION:	1431 feet

23 Two Island Lake
Grand Marais • lat 47°52'44" lon 090°26'47"

DESCRIPTION: This CG rests among pine, spruce and hardwoods in a fairly open area on Two Island Lake. Boat fish for walleye and northern pike. Supplies are available in Grand Marais. White tailed deer, black bear, ruffed grouse, red foxes, loons and bald eagles are common to the area. Mosquitos and black flies in June.

GETTING THERE: From Grand Marais go N on county route 12 approx. 3 mi. to county route 8. Go NW on 8 approx. 2 mi. to county route 27. Go N on 27 approx. 10 mi. to Two Island Lake CG.

SINGLE RATE:	$10	OPEN DATES:	May-Sept
# of SINGLE SITES:	38	MAX SPUR:	22 feet
		MAX STAY:	14 days
		ELEVATION:	1783 feet

19 Sawbill Lake
Tofte • lat 47°48'00" lon 090°52'00"

DESCRIPTION: This CG rests in aspen and conifers with views of adjacent Sawbill Lake. Fish for walleye, northern and bass. CG offers limited supplies, a barrier free fishing pier, a nature trail, and entrance to BWCA Wilderness. Wildlife includes deer, eagles, moose, and grouse. June brings biting bugs.

GETTING THERE: From Tofte go N on county route 2 approx. 18 mi. to Sawbill Lake CG. Road is narrow with sharp curves. Large vehicles should use caution.

SINGLE RATE:	$9.30	OPEN DATES:	May-Sept
# of SINGLE SITES:	50	MAX SPUR:	22 feet
		MAX STAY:	14 days
		ELEVATION:	1640 feet

24 Whiteface Reservoir
Virginia • lat 47°19'58" lon 092°08'38"

DESCRIPTION: Among mixed pine and aspen on Whiteface Reservoir. Boat fish for northern, pike, and walleye. Limited supplies on site. Whitetailed deer, grouse, bald eagles and raccoons are in the area. CG is busy weekends and holidays. There are walking trails in vicinity. June brings mosquitos and black flies.

GETTING THERE: From Virginia go S on US HWY 53 approx. 9 mi. to county route 16. Go E on 16 approx. 16 mi. to forest route 417. Go S on 417 approx. 5 mi. to Whiteface Reservoir CG. Road is narrow.

SINGLE RATE:	Varies	OPEN DATES:	May-Sept
# of SINGLE SITES:	53	MAX SPUR:	22 feet
GROUP RATE:	$30	MAX STAY:	14 days
# of GROUP SITES:	1	ELEVATION:	1472 feet

20 South Kawishiwi River
Ely • lat 47°46'00" lon 091°42'00"

DESCRIPTION: This CG is located in a mix of aspen, balsam fir, and conifers near the South Kawishiwi River. Boat fish on the river for walleye and northern pike. Supplies are located approx. 9 mi. away at Ely. Deer, bear, eagles, red foxes, and ruffed grouse in area. Nature trail nearby. June brings mosquitoes and black flies.

GETTING THERE: From Ely go SE on state HWY 1 approx. 9 mi. to South Kawishiwi River CG. Road is narrow with sharp curves. Large vehicles should use caution.

SINGLE RATE:	Varies	OPEN DATES:	May-Sept
# of SINGLE SITES:	32	MAX SPUR:	22 feet
		MAX STAY:	14 days
		ELEVATION:	1600 feet

 Campground has hosts **Reservable sites** **Accessible facilities** **Fully developed**  **Semi-developed** **Rustic facilities**

NOTE: Open dates listed are typical. Actual dates are dependent on conditions such as snow pack.

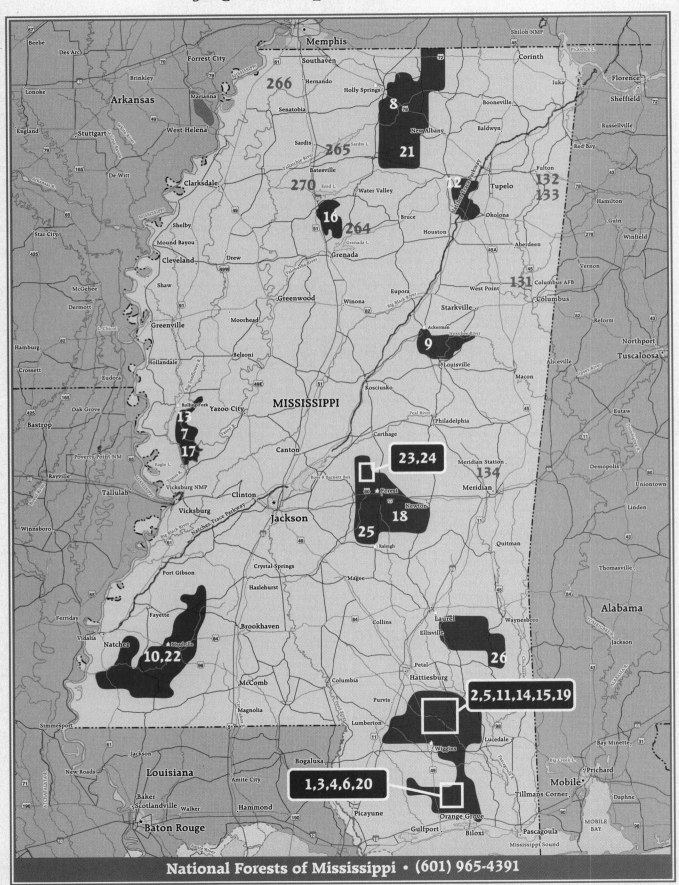

USFS Photo

NATIONAL FORESTS OF MISSISSIPPI

Diversity and beauty best describe the national forests in Mississippi. Six forests are dispersed over the entire state, each with its own special features. The Bienville National Forest is filled with towering pines and spacious grass prairies. The DeSoto National Forest, located just north of the Gulf Coast, provides two national recreation trails, two wilderness areas, and the Black Creek Wild and Scenic River. Shaded lakeshore camping areas are found on the Tombigbee National Forest. One of its units, bisected by the Natchez Trace Parkway, is popular for its historical sites and dogwood-filled forests. The Holly Springs National Forest, near Tennessee, contains rolling hills and hardwoods that splash the landscape with bright colors in the fall. The Homochitto National Forest, with its small lakes nestled in the very steep Tunica Hills, provides settings comparable to mountainous states. Lush cypress swamps and reservoirs fill the Delta National Forest—the only bottomland hardwood national forest in the nation.

Float down one of the forests' winding streams in canoe, raft or jon-boat. Numerous hiking trails provide the nature lover, history buff or hiker with the chance to view nature at its best. Camping, fishing and picnicking are also available on the forests' tranquil creeks and rivers. All year round, the forest visitor will find a paradise of things to see or do in the national forests in Mississippi.

1 ▲ Airey Lake
Saucier • lat 30°41'25" lon 089°03'31"

DESCRIPTION: This CG rests in a semi-open mixed forest with views of Airey Lake. This small lake can be fished for bass, bream, and catfish. Frequent PM T-showers. Visit historic CCC Camp nearby. Supplies at Saucier. Deer, squirrels and birds are common. The Tuxachanie Hiking Trail runs through the camp.

GETTING THERE: From Saucier go E on state HWY 67 approx. 4.5 mi. to county route 412. Go N on 412 approx. 3 mi. to Airey Lake CG.

SINGLE RATE:	No fee	OPEN DATES:	Yearlong
# of SINGLE SITES:	3	MAX SPUR:	30 feet
		MAX STAY:	14 days
		ELEVATION:	170 feet

2 ▲ Ashe Lake
Wiggins • lat 31°01'46" lon 089°10'07"

DESCRIPTION: This dispersed CG rests in a mixed forest setting on Ashe Lake. Fish for bass and brim. A boat ramp and fishing pier are on site. Supplies 2 mi. at Brooklyn. Deer, possum and birds are common. Campers may gather firewood. A trail runs around the lake. CG is busy weekends and during hunting season.

GETTING THERE: From Wiggins go N on US HWY 49 11 mi. to county 316. Go E on 316 1/2 mi. to county 313. Go N on 313 1/4 mi. to county 319 (New York Road) to county 308 (Ashe Nursery Road). Go S on 308 1/8 mi. to Ashe Lake CG.

SINGLE RATE:	$7	OPEN DATES:	Yearlong
		MAX SPUR:	30 feet
		MAX STAY:	14 days
		ELEVATION:	270 feet

3 ▲ Bethel ATV Trail
Saucier • lat 30°39'00" lon 088°57'00"

DESCRIPTION: In a pine forest setting with no water nearby. Historical Bethel Cemetery and Ramsey Cemetery nearby. Supplies located at Saucier. Deer, turkeys, raccoons and birds are common in the area. Campers may gather firewood. The Bethel ATV Trail, the Tuxachanie Hiking Trail and the Bigfoot Horse Trail are nearby.

GETTING THERE: From Saucier go approx. 4.5 mi. on state HWY 67 to county route 402. Go E on 402 approx. 5 mi. to county route 417. Go N on 417 approx. 2 mi. to 417A. Go E on 417A to Bethel ATV Trail CG.

SINGLE RATE:	$7	OPEN DATES:	Yearlong
		MAX SPUR:	30 feet
		MAX STAY:	14 days
		ELEVATION:	100 feet

4 ▲ Big Biloxi
McHenry • lat 30°34'10" lon 089°07'50"

DESCRIPTION: In a park-like setting of pines and hardwoods, with beautiful views of the Biloxi River. Fish for bass and catfish or swim in river. Supplies available at McHenry. Deer, red foxes, squirrels and birds are common to the area. Campers may gather firewood. An interpretive trail is in the CG.

GETTING THERE: Big Biloxi CG is located approx. 9.5 mi. S of McHenry on US HWY 49.

SINGLE RATE:	Varies	OPEN DATES:	Yearlong
# of SINGLE SITES:	25	MAX SPUR:	30 feet
		MAX STAY:	14 days
		ELEVATION:	50 feet

5 ▲ Big Creek Landing
Brooklyn • lat 31°04'00" lon 089°15'00"

DESCRIPTION: In an open, park-like setting on Black Creek. Fish for bass, bream and catfish from the creek. Historical Simmons Cemetery and Granny Bound Cemetery are nearby. Supplies available at Brooklyn. Deer, raccoons, squirrels and birds are common to the area. Campers may gather firewood. Many trails in the area.

GETTING THERE: From Brooklyn go W approx. 1 mi. on county route 334 to county route 335. Go W approx. 3 mi. on 335 to Big Creek Landing CG.

SINGLE RATE:	No fee	OPEN DATES:	Yearlong
		MAX SPUR:	30 feet
		MAX STAY:	14 days
		ELEVATION:	165 feet

 Campground has hosts   🔒 **Reservable sites**   ♿ **Accessible facilities**   **Fully developed**   **Semi-developed**   **Rustic facilities**

NOTE: Open dates listed are typical. Actual dates are dependent on conditions such as snow pack.

6 Bigfoot Horse Trail
Saucier • lat 30°40'00" lon 089°03'00"

DESCRIPTION: In a semi-open pine forest setting. CG is hot and humid during summer months. Historical WWII German POW camp nearby. Supplies available at Saucier. Deer, turkeys, squirrels and birds are common to the area. Campers may gather firewood. The Bigfoot Horse Trail starts at CG and the Tuxachanie Hiking Trail is nearby.

GETTING THERE: From Saucier go approx. 4.5 mi. on state HWY 67 to county route 412. Go N on 412 approx. 3 mi. to forest route 440. Go E on 440 approx. 1 mi. to Bigfoot Horse Trail CG.

SINGLE RATE:	$7	OPEN DATES:	Yearlong
		MAX SPUR:	30 feet
		MAX STAY:	14 days
		ELEVATION:	150 feet

11 Cypress Creek
Janice • lat 30°57'55" lon 089°00'17"

DESCRIPTION: This CG rests in a semi-open pine and hardwood forest overlooking the Black Creek Nat'l Scenic River. Enjoy fishing for catfish and bass. Boat ramp on site. Visit historic Breland Cemetery. Deer, bobcats and turkeys are common. Campers may gather firewood. Hike the Black Creek Nat'l Hiking Trail. Busy weekends.

GETTING THERE: From Janice go SE on county route 305 approx. 3 mi. to forest route 305B. Go S on 305B approx. 1.5 mi. to Cypress Creek CG.

SINGLE RATE:	$7	OPEN DATES:	Yearlong
# of SINGLE SITES:	14	MAX SPUR:	30 feet
		MAX STAY:	14 days
		ELEVATION:	100 feet

7 Blue Lake
Rolling Fork • lat 32°49'15" lon 090°48'32"

DESCRIPTION: This CG rests in mature bottomland hardwood forest with views of Cypress trees. Summers are hot. This CG is near a small slough with alligator and beaver. Bank fish for catfish and crappie. Visit various historical sites. Busy during hunting season. Hike Blue Lake interpretive trail.

GETTING THERE: From Rolling Fork go SE on state HWY 16 approx. 10.5 mi. to forest route 715. Go W on 715 approx. 3.5 mi. to Blue Lake CG.

SINGLE RATE:	$10	OPEN DATES:	Yearlong
# of SINGLE SITES:	4		
		MAX STAY:	14 days
		ELEVATION:	85 feet

12 Davis Lake
Houston • lat 34°02'50" lon 088°56'20"

DESCRIPTION: In a quiet park-like setting of mature hardwood pine with views of Davis Lake. No fishing on this lake at current time. Historical Natchez Trace Parkway within 4 mi. of CG. Deer, turkeys and bald eagles are seen from CG. The Witch Dance Horse Trail is nearby. RV dump station available.

GETTING THERE: From Houston go N on state HWY 15 approx. 9 mi. to county route 903. Go E on 903 approx. 5 mi. to Davis Lake CG.

SINGLE RATE:	Varies	OPEN DATES:	Apr-Oct
# of SINGLE SITES:	25	MAX SPUR:	24 feet
GROUP RATE:	Varies	MAX STAY:	14 days
# of GROUP SITES:	1	ELEVATION:	350 feet

8 Chewalla
Holly Springs • lat 34°44'00" lon 089°20'30"

DESCRIPTION: In an open hardwood forest setting with views of Chewalla Lake. Boat ramp at CG, 5 mi. per hour limit on lake. No fishing on lake until 2001. Supplies available at Holly Springs. Deer, turkeys, quail and squirrels are common to the area. This CG has a 1/2 mi. trail from boat ramp to the beach area.

GETTING THERE: From Holly Springs go SE on county route 634 approx. 6 mi. to forest route 611. Go E on 611 approx. 1.5 mi. to Chewalla CG.

SINGLE RATE:	Varies	OPEN DATES:	Apr-Nov
# of SINGLE SITES:	35	MAX SPUR:	30 feet
		MAX STAY:	14 days
		ELEVATION:	450 feet

13 Dispersed Primitive Sites
Rolling Fork • lat °'" lon °'"

DESCRIPTION: There are several "Jamboree Style" CGs in the Delta NF. These CGs are located in mature bottomland hardwood forest and accommodate horses. CGs are dispersed along forest roads, district-wide. Most CGs will accommodate two small trailers. Please call the Delta Ranger Office at (662) 873-6256 for maps and reservations.

GETTING THERE: Several CGs require 4WD vehicles Dec-Mar. Please call the Delta Ranger Office at (662) 873-6256 for maps and directions.

SINGLE RATE:	$7	OPEN DATES:	Yearlong
# of SINGLE SITES:	75		
		MAX STAY:	14 days
		ELEVATION:	85 feet

9 Choctaw Lake
Ackerman • lat 33°18'00" lon 089°09'30"

DESCRIPTION: In a park-like setting of mature pine and hardwood forest with views of the lake. Fish for bass, bream, crappie and catfish from boat or piers. Deer, turkeys and small wildlife. Full most holidays. Chatta Hiking Trail nearby. Natchez Trace Parkway, 14 mi. Some ticks and mosquitoes.

GETTING THERE: From Ackerman go S on state HWY 15 approx. 2 mi. to forest route 967. Go E on 967 approx. 1.5 mi. to Choctaw Lake CG.

SINGLE RATE:	$13	OPEN DATES:	Apr-Oct
# of SINGLE SITES:	20	MAX SPUR:	24 feet
		MAX STAY:	14 days
		ELEVATION:	500 feet

14 Fairley Bridge Landing
Wiggins • lat 30°55'05" lon 088°57'59"

DESCRIPTION: This small, park-like CG rests in a mixed forest on Black Creek National Scenic River. Fish for bass, bream and catfish. Boat ramp on site. Supplies at Wiggins. Deer, possums, raccoons and birds are common. Campers may gather firewood. Hike the nearby Black Creek Hiking Trail. Summer brings biting bugs.

GETTING THERE: From Wiggins go NE on state HWY 29 7 mi. to county route 318 (Fairley Bridge Road). Go E on 318 approx. 6 mi. to 374. Go S on 374 approx. 1/2 mi. to Fairley Bridge Landing CG.

SINGLE RATE:	$7	OPEN DATES:	Yearlong
# of SINGLE SITES:	3	MAX SPUR:	30 feet
		MAX STAY:	14 days
		ELEVATION:	90 feet

10 Clear Springs
Bude • lat 31°25'30" lon 090°59'10"

DESCRIPTION: In a mixed forest setting on Clear Spring Lake. Fish, boat and swim in the lake. Non-motorized boats only on lake. Supplies available at Bude. Deer, raccoons and armadillo are common to the area. Amphitheater and pavilion in CG. Many trails in the area. RV dump station at CG.

GETTING THERE: From Bude go NW on US HWY 84/98 approx. 7.5 mi. to county route 104. Go S on 104 approx. 3.5 mi. to forest route 104-A. Go SW on 104-A approx. 1/2 mi. to Clear Springs CG.

SINGLE RATE:	$13	OPEN DATES:	Yearlong
# of SINGLE SITES:	22	MAX SPUR:	35 feet
GROUP RATE:	$40	MAX STAY:	14 days
# of GROUP SITES:	1	ELEVATION:	447 feet

15 Janice Landing
Janice • lat 30°59'40" lon 089°03'01"

DESCRIPTION: This CG is located in an open grove of mixed hardwoods and pines on Black Creek National Scenic River. Enjoy fishing for bass and bream. Boat ramp and swimming area at the CG. Deer, small mammals, and birds are common. Campers may gather firewood. Hiking and interpretive trails nearby. Biting bugs common in summer.

GETTING THERE: From Janice go S on state HWY 29 approx. 2 mi. to Janice Landing CG. Road is narrow with sharp curves. Large vehicles should use caution.

SINGLE RATE:	$7	OPEN DATES:	Yearlong
# of SINGLE SITES:	5	MAX SPUR:	30 feet
		MAX STAY:	14 days
		ELEVATION:	100 feet

 Campground has hosts   Reservable sites   Accessible facilities   Fully developed   Semi-developed   Rustic facilities

NOTE: Open dates listed are typical. Actual dates are dependent on conditions such as snow pack.

16 Lake Tillatoba
Scobey • lat 33°58'00" lon 089°49'00"

DESCRIPTION: In an open hardwood forest setting with views of Lake Tillatoba. Boat ramp at CG. Fish from the lake. Supplies available at Scobey. Deer, turkeys, quail and squirrels are common to the area. Campers may gather firewood. No designated trails in the area. No RV hook-ups.

GETTING THERE: From Scobey go NE on county route 801 approx. 4.5 mi. to Lake Tillatoba CG.

SINGLE RATE:	No fee	OPEN DATES:	Yearlong
# of SINGLE SITES:	10		
		MAX STAY:	14 days
		ELEVATION:	350 feet

17 Little Sunflower Boat
Rolling Fork • lat 32°40'00" lon 090°50'00"

DESCRIPTION: This dispersed, primitive CG rests in mature bottomland hardwood forest near a slow-flowing delta river. Boat ramp on site. Visit various historical sites. Summers are hot. Numerous wildlife in area including hogs. Busy during hunting season. Hike the many trails in this area. Gather firewood locally.

GETTING THERE: From Rolling Fork go S on US HWY 61 approx. 1 mi. to Omega Road. Go E on Omega Road approx. 1 mi. to Dummyline Road. Go S on Dummyline Road approx. 3.5 mi. to Little Sunflower Boat Ramp CG.

SINGLE RATE:	$10	OPEN DATES:	Yearlong
# of SINGLE SITES:	4		
		MAX STAY:	14 days
		ELEVATION:	85 feet

18 Marathon
Forest • lat 32°12'03" lon 089°21'37"

DESCRIPTION: This CG is rests in pines on Marathon Lake. Fish for bass, bream and catfish or enjoy swimming in the lake. Boat ramp at the lake. Wildlife such as deer and turkeys can be viewed in the area. Supplies 15 mi. at Forest. Busy holiday weekends. A hiking trail leads around the lake. Picnic pavilions on site.

GETTING THERE: From Forest go S on state HWY 35 9 mi. to Morton-Marathon Road (county route 506). Go E on Morton-Marathon Road 9 mi. to forest route 520. Go S on 520 approx. 1 mi. to Marathon CG.

SINGLE RATE:	$13	OPEN DATES:	Yearlong*
# of SINGLE SITES:	34		
		MAX STAY:	14 days
		ELEVATION:	420 feet

19 Moody's Landing
Brooklyn • lat 31°03'23" lon 089°07'03"

DESCRIPTION: This CG rests in an open, mixed forest on Black Creek Nat'l Scenic River. Fish for bass, bream, and catfish. A boat ramp and beautiful beach are located at the CG. Deer, possums, and birds are common. Campers may gather firewood. Hike the nearby Black Creek Nat'l Hiking Trail. Ticks, flies and mosquitoes in summer.

GETTING THERE: From Brooklyn go E on county route 301 approx. 3.5 mi. to Moody's Landing CG. Road is narrow with sharp curves. Large vehicles should use caution.

SINGLE RATE:	$7	OPEN DATES:	Yearlong
# of SINGLE SITES:	4	MAX SPUR:	30 feet
		MAX STAY:	14 days
		ELEVATION:	130 feet

20 POW Lake
Saucier • lat 30°38'00" lon 089°00'00"

DESCRIPTION: In an open, park-like setting on POW Lake. Fish for bass, bream and catfish from the lake. This CG is an historical WWII German officer POW camp. Supplies are available at Saucier. Deer, turkeys and birds are common in the area. Campers may gather firewood. The Tuxachanie Hiking Trail adn the Bigfoot Horse Trail are near the CG.

GETTING THERE: From Saucier go E on state HWY 67 approx. 4.5 mi. to county route 402. Follow 402 approx. 4.5 mi. to POW Lake CG.

SINGLE RATE:	No fee	OPEN DATES:	Yearlong
		MAX SPUR:	30 feet
		MAX STAY:	14 days
		ELEVATION:	100 feet

21 Puskus
Darden • lat 34°26'18" lon 089°20'53"

DESCRIPTION: In an open hardwood forest setting with views of Chewalla Lake. Boat ramp at CG. Fish on lake. Supplies available at Darden. Deer, turkeys, quail and squirrels are common to the area. Campers may gather firewood. A 2 mi. trail near the CG.

GETTING THERE: From Darden go S on county route 14 1.5 mi. to county route 130. Go W on 130 approx. 1 mi. to state HWY 30. Go SW on 30 9 mi. to forest route 2089. Go N on 2089 approx. 3 mi. to Puskus CG.

SINGLE RATE:	Varies	OPEN DATES:	Yearlong
# of SINGLE SITES:	15		
		MAX STAY:	14 days
		ELEVATION:	400 feet

22 Richardson Creek
Bude • lat 31°25'30" lon 090°59'10"

DESCRIPTION: This primitive CG is in a mixed forest setting near Clear Springs Lake. Fish, boat (non-motorized boats only) and swim on the lake. Supplies available at Bude. Deer, raccoons and armadillos are common to the area. Many trails in the area. RV dump station at Clear Springs CG.

GETTING THERE: From Bude go NW on US HWY 84/98 approx. 7.5 mi. to county route 104. Go S on 104 approx. 3.5 mi. to forest route 104-A. Go SW on 104-A approx. 5/8 mi. to Clear Springs CG.

SINGLE RATE:	No fee	OPEN DATES:	Yearlong
		MAX STAY:	14 days
		ELEVATION:	447 feet

23 Schokaloe Base Camp #2
Forest • lat 32°21'56" lon 089°33'44"

DESCRIPTION: In a pine and oak forest setting with forest views. Supplies available at Forest. Deer, turkeys and squirrels are common to the area. Campers may gather firewood. A 23-mi. trail is located within the CG. Tent camping only. CG accommodates horses.

GETTING THERE: From Forest go W on US HWY 80 approx. 5 mi. to forest route 513. go N on 513 approx. 5 mi. to Shockaloe Base Camp #2.

SINGLE RATE:	$7	OPEN DATES:	Yearlong
		MAX STAY:	14 days
		ELEVATION:	500 feet

24 Shockaloe Base Camp #1
Forest • lat 32°21'56" lon 089°33'44"

DESCRIPTION: In a pine and oak forest setting with forest views. Supplies available at Forest. Deer, turkeys and squirrels are common to the area. Campers may gather firewood. A 23-mi. trail is located within the CG. Tent camping only. CG accommodates horses.

GETTING THERE: From Forest go W on US HWY 80 approx. 5 mi. to forest route 513. go N on 513 approx. .5 mi. to Shockaloe Base Camp #1.

SINGLE RATE:	$7	OPEN DATES:	Apr-Oct
# of SINGLE SITES:	10		
		MAX STAY:	14 days
		ELEVATION:	500 feet

25 Shongelo
Forest • lat 32°06'10" lon 089°30'47"

DESCRIPTION: This is a primitive CG in a pine hardwood forest setting on Shongelo Lake. This beautiful spring fed lake is a popular place for swimmers. No fishing right now due to work being done at the lake. Many animals in the area. A trail around the lake leads to a deck overlooking the area.

GETTING THERE: Shongelo CG is located approx. 18.5 mi. S of Forest on state HWY 35.

SINGLE RATE:	$7	OPEN DATES:	Apr-Sept
# of SINGLE SITES:	6		
		MAX STAY:	14 days
		ELEVATION:	600 feet

 Campground has hosts   **Reservable sites**   **Accessible facilities**   **Fully developed**   Semi-developed   Rustic facilities

NOTE: Open dates listed are typical. Actual dates are dependent on conditions such as snow pack.

26 **Turkeys Fork**
Sand Hill • lat 31°20'18" lon 088°42'10"

DESCRIPTION: In a pine and hardwood forest setting on Turkeys Fork Lake. Fish for bass, catfish and bream from the shore or boat. Swim beach and boat ramp at CG. Supplies at Sand Hill. Deer, raccoons, eagles and water fowl are common to the area. A nature trail is close to the CG. A pavilion is at the day use area of CG.

GETTING THERE: From Sand Hill go NE on state HWY 63 1 mi. to state HWY 42. Go E n 42 3 mi. to county route 230. Go SE on 230 3 mi. to Turkeys Forks Reservoir boat ramp. CG is located on the E bank of reservoir.

SINGLE RATE:	**$13**	**OPEN DATES:**	**Yearlong**
# of SINGLE SITES:	**20**		
		MAX STAY:	**14 days**
		ELEVATION:	**195 feet**

 Campground has hosts   **Reservable sites**   ♿ **Accessible facilities**   **Fully developed**   **Semi-developed**   **Rustic facilities**

NOTE: Open dates listed are typical. Actual dates are dependent on conditions such as snow pack.

REWARDS

for Campers

Save Money
- No Annual Fee
- 3.9% Introductory Annual Percentage Rate (APR) for cash advance checks and balance transfers†
- Credit line up to $100,000

Save Time
- Credit line increase decisions in 15 minutes
- *Platinum Plus*℠ Registry for card and document registry, emergency cash, and more*
- 24-Hour Customer Satisfaction

Earn Rewards
- Earn Coleman Rewards points every time you use your account to make a purchase, use a cash advance check or make a balance transfer transaction**
- Use your points to save 10%-40% off selected Coleman products offered in a special catalog.

Request Yours Today!
Call 1-800-523-7666
or complete and return the form below. Use priority code ZQ4T when calling.

Priority Code
ZQ4T
JR-727
HT

No-Annual-Fee Coleman *Platinum Plus*℠ MasterCard® credit card.

Print your name as you would like it to appear on card. *Please print clearly in black or blue ink.*

Name _____

Social Security # ___ - ___ - ___   Birth date ___ / ___ / ___ (must be 18 to apply)

Address _____

Mother's maiden name (for security purposes) _____

City _____ State ____ ZIP _____

Monthly housing payment $ ____ , ____

Are you: ☐ Homeowner ☐ Renter ☐ Other
Years at residence: _____

Home phone (___) ___ - _____   Business phone (___) ___ - _____

Employer _____
(If self-employed, please state the nature of your business.)

Position‡‡ _____
‡‡If student, please specify the name of your school and year of graduation.

Years there ____

Your yearly salary $ ____ , ____
Other income‡ + $ ____ , ____

Please send an additional card at no extra cost for: _____

Relationship: _____

Total yearly household income $ ____ , ____

X _____   Date ___ / ___

Source of other income‡

MY SIGNATURE MEANS THAT I AGREE TO THE CONDITIONS APPEARING ON THIS FORM AND TO BE BOUND BY EACH OF THE TERMS OF THE CREDIT CARD AGREEMENT, INCLUDING ARBITRATION.

‡Alimony, child support, or separate maintenance income need not be revealed if you do not wish it considered as a basis for repayment.

Please return form to: MBNA *Platinum Plus* New Account Acceptance Center, P.O. Box 981054, El Paso, TX 79998-9937.

Annual fee	None.
†p Annual Percentage Rate (APR)	*Platinum Plus* or Preferred account: 15.99% APR for purchases.
Grace period for repayment of balance for purchases	At least 25 days, if each month, we receive payment in full of your New Balance Total by the Payment Due Date.
Method of computing the balance for purchases	Average Daily Balance (including new transactions).
Transaction fees for cash advances and fees for paying late or exceeding the credit limit	Transaction fee for Bank and ATM cash advances: 3% of each cash advance (minimum $5). Transaction fee for credit card cash advance checks and balance transfers: 3% of each cash advance (minimum $5, maximum $30). Late-payment fee: $29. Over-the-credit-limit fee: $29.
Transaction fee for purchases	Transaction fee for the purchase of wire transfers, money orders, bets, lottery tickets, and casino gaming chips: 3% of each such purchase (minimum $5).

* Certain restrictions apply to this benefit and others described in the materials sent soon after your account is opened. Preferred Card benefits differ from *Platinum Plus* card benefits: year End Summary of Charges is available upon request and there are additional costs for Registry benefits.

**Earn 5 Points for every dollar in new net purchase, cash advance check and balance transfer transactions made with the account. 500 Points=10% discount on selected Coleman merchandise purchases. Coupons may not be used to pay taxes, shipping and handling costs, or any other additional fees or service charges. Other conditions apply. Details are provided with the card. The terms of this offer are subject to change. This program is void where prohibited. The information in this application was accurate as of 9/00. The information may have changed after that date. For more current information, please call MBNA at 1-800-523-7666. TTY users, please call 1-800-833-6262.

MBNA America Bank, N.A., is the exclusive issuer and administrator of the *Platinum Plus* credit card program. MBNA America, MBNA, and *Platinum Plus* are service marks of MBNA America Bank, N.A. MasterCard and Visa are federally registered service marks of MasterCard International Inc. and Visa U.S.A. Inc., respectively; each is used pursuant to license. ©2000 MBNA America Bank, N.A.   1AVO 9/00

†– MORE APR INFORMATION –
The current promotional Annual Percentage Rate (APR) offer for cash advance check and balance transfer transactions made with either account is 3.9% through your first four statement closing dates, commencing the month after your account is opened. When your minimum monthly payment is late (that is, not received by its Payment Due Date), or when the promotional offer expires, the APR that will be applied to all new and outstanding cash advance balances (consisting of cash advance check and balance transfer transactions) will be 15.99% for both the *Platinum Plus* and Preferred accounts. Should your payment be late, the non-promotional APR will be applied to all new and outstanding cash advance check and balance transfer balances as of the first day of the billing cycle in which the payment was late (or never received). MBNA will allocate your payments to balances (including new transactions) with lower APRs before balances with higher APRs.

– CONDITIONS –
I have read this application and everything I have stated in it is true. I authorize MBNA America Bank, N.A. (MBNA) to check my credit, employment history, or any other information and to report to others such information and credit experience with me. I understand that the acceptance or use of any card issued will be subject to the terms of this application and the Credit Card Agreement that will be sent with the card, and I agree to be responsible for all charges incurred according to such terms. I am at least 18 years of age and a United States citizen or permanent resident of the U.S. or Puerto Rico. I consent to and authorize MBNA, any of its affiliates, or its marketing associates to monitor and/or record any of my telephone conversations with their representatives or the representatives of any of those companies. **I understand that if this credit card application is approved for an account with a credit line of less than $5,000, I will receive a Preferred account.** I accept that MBNA may, at its discretion, periodically consider any account for an automatic upgrade. **Information about me or my account may be shared among MBNA and its related companies for marketing or administrative purposes. I may prohibit such sharing of information, other than information pertaining solely to transactions or experiences between me and MBNA (or an MBNA-related company), by writing to MBNA at PO Box 15342, Wilmington, DE 19850 and including my name, address, home phone number, and the applicable MBNA account number(s).**

USFS Photo

MARK TWAIN NATIONAL FOREST

The 1.5-million-acre Mark Twain National Forest extends from the St. Francis Mountains in the southeast to glades in the southwest, and from the prairie lands along the Missouri River to the nation's most ancient mountains in the south. Clear spring fed rivers and streams, rocky bluffs, pastoral views and shaded trails all welcome visitors to explore and enjoy the beauty of the renowned Ozarks.

Named after the famous writer, the Mark Twain National Forest has seven wilderness areas totaling more than 63,000 acres, which hikers and horseback riders escape to for peace and solitude. More than 350 miles of streams suitable for floating offers spectacular views of rocky bluffs, caves, springs, vegetation, birds and animals. Hikers will enjoy the hundreds of miles of trails which includes three national recreation trails and part of the 500-mile Ozark Trail which winds from near St. Louis to the Arkansas border. Over 40 campgrounds and picnic areas await you. Several scenic drives wind through ridgetops and cedar groves. The scenery is especially attractive in mid-April to early May when redbud and dogwood bloom and in mid-October to early November when leaves change color.

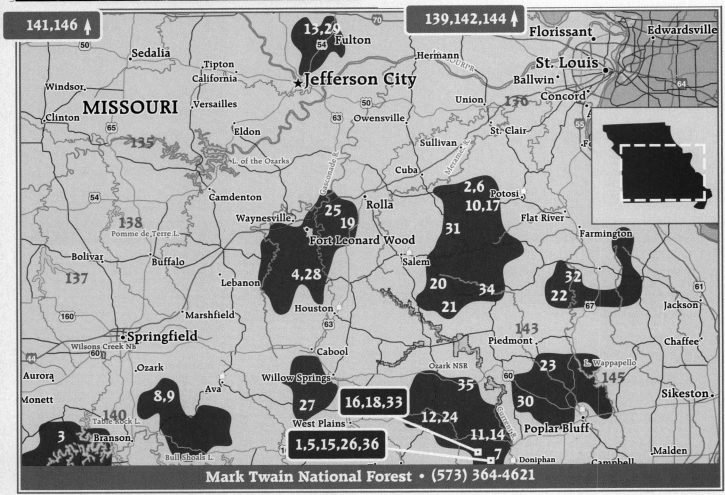

Mark Twain National Forest • (573) 364-4621

1 Barn Hollow
Greer • lat 36°44'44" lon 091°13'53"

DESCRIPTION: This dispersed CG is located in mixed hardwood and pine on the Eleven Point National Scenic River. Fish for rainbow trout, catfish, bass, walley and perch. Wildlife includes coyote, foxes, osprey, herons, turkeys, otters and armadillos. Horse and hiking trails in area. No drinking water.

GETTING THERE: From Greer go N 4.5 mi. on state HWY 19 to forest route 3152. Go E 5.5 mi. on 3152 to forest route 3190. Go S 1.5 mi. on 3190 to the Turner Mill boat launch. Boat-in 2.5 mi. to Barn Hollow CG.

SINGLE RATE:	Varies	OPEN DATES:	Yearlong
# of SINGLE SITES:	4		
		MAX STAY:	14 days
		ELEVATION:	500 feet

2 Berryman
Steelville • lat 37°55'49" lon 091°03'47"

DESCRIPTION: This CG is located in oak and hickory forest with some pine. This CG accomodates horses and accesses the 24 mi. Berryman Loop Trail as well as the Ozark National Scenic Trail. Wildlife in this area includes infrequent black bears, bobcat, foxes, deer and turkeys. No drinking water.

GETTING THERE: From Steelville go E on statae HWY 8 approx. 18.5 mi. to forest route 2266. Go N on 2266 approx. 3 mi. to Berryman CG.

SINGLE RATE:	No fee	OPEN DATES:	Yearlong
# of SINGLE SITES:	8	MAX SPUR:	25 feet
		MAX STAY:	14 days
		ELEVATION:	1500 feet

3 Big Bay
Cassville • lat 36°37'06" lon 093°34'02"

DESCRIPTION: This CG is in eastern red cedar on Table Rock Lake. Fish for bass, crappie, bluegill and catfish in the lake. Boat ramp on site. Wildlife includes whitetailed deer, wild turkeys, foxes, coyotes and occasional black bears. Campers may gather firewood. Hike in nearby Piney Creek Wilderness.

GETTING THERE: From Cassville go S on state HWY 112 approx. 2 mi. to state HWY 76. Go E on 76 approx. 10 mi. to state HWY 39. Go SE on 39 approx. 6 mi. to state HWY YY. Go E on YY approx. 3 mi. to Big Bay CG.

SINGLE RATE:	Varies	OPEN DATES:	Yearlong
# of SINGLE SITES:	35	MAX SPUR:	25 feet
		MAX STAY:	14 days
		ELEVATION:	1300 feet

4 Big Piney Trail Camp
Rolla • lat 37°33'57" lon 092°02'36"

DESCRIPTION: This CG is located in hardwoods near Paddy Creek. Wildlife in this area includes deer, turkeys, coyotes, foxes, bald eagle, and small mammals. Campers may gather dead and down firewood. This CG offers horse facilities and an on site trail (ride only when dry) that leads to the Paddy Creek Wilderness.

GETTING THERE: From Rolla go S on US HWY 63 approx. 32 mi. to state HWY 32. Go NW on 32 approx. 4 mi. to state HWY N. Continue on N approx. 2 mi. to state HWY AF. Go W on AF approx. 8 mi. to Big Piney CG.

SINGLE RATE:	No fee	OPEN DATES:	Yearlong
# of SINGLE SITES:	4	MAX SPUR:	20 feet
		MAX STAY:	14 days
		ELEVATION:	1200 feet

5 Boze Mill
Greer • lat 36°39'55" lon 091°11'50"

DESCRIPTION: This dispersed CG is situated in mixed hardwood and pine on the Eleven Point National Scenic River. Fish for rainbow trout, catfish, bass, walley and perch. Wildlife includes coyotes, foxes, osprey, herons, turkeys, otters and armadillos. Supplies available in Greer.Horse and hiking trails in area. No drinking water.

GETTING THERE: From Greer go N 4.5 mi. on state HWY 19 to forest route 3152. Go E 5.5 mi. on 3152 to forest route 3190. Go S 1.5 mi. on 3190 to the Turner Mill boat launch and boat-in 8.5 mi. to Boze Mill CG.

SINGLE RATE:	Varies	OPEN DATES:	Yearlong
# of SINGLE SITES:	2		
		MAX STAY:	14 days
		ELEVATION:	460 feet

6 Brazil Creek
Steelville • lat 37°59'13" lon 091°01'56"

DESCRIPTION: This CG is situated in oak and hickory forest with some pine on Brazil Creek. This CG accomodates horses and accesses the 24 mi. Berryman Loop Trail as well as the Ozark National Scenic Trail. Wildlife in this area includes infrequent black bears, bobcat, foxes, deer and turkeys. No drinking water.

GETTING THERE: From Steelville go E on state HWY 8 approx. 10 mi. to forest route 2265. Go E on 2265 approx. 10.5 mi. to Brazil Creek CG.

SINGLE RATE:	No fee	OPEN DATES:	Yearlong
# of SINGLE SITES:	8	MAX SPUR:	25 feet
		MAX STAY:	14 days
		ELEVATION:	1200 feet

7 Buffalo Creek
Doniphan • lat 36°41'21" lon 091°03'24"

DESCRIPTION: This CG rests in mixed hardwood and pine on Buffalo Creek. Creek gets low in summer so fishing is questionable. Wildlife includes coyotes, foxes, osprey, herons, turkeys, otters and armadillos. CG is busy holiday and weekends. Horse and hiking trails in area. No drinking water.

GETTING THERE: From Doniphan go W on US HWY 160 approx. 14 mi. to forest route 3145. Go N on 3145 approx. 2.5 mi. to Buffalo Creek CG.

SINGLE RATE:	Varies	OPEN DATES:	Yearlong
# of SINGLE SITES:	3	MAX SPUR:	20 feet
		MAX STAY:	14 days
		ELEVATION:	500 feet

8 Camp Ridge
Springfield • lat 36°54'37" lon 093°04'45"

DESCRIPTION: This ridgetop CG rests in an oak and hickory forest. Wildlife includes deer, wild turkeys, foxes, coyotes, and occasional black bears. Supplies available at Springfield. CG is busy holidays weekends. Campers may gather firewood. This CG offers OHV trail access. The Hercules Glades Wilderness is nearby. No drinking water.

GETTING THERE: From Springfield go S on US HWY 65 approx. 9 mi. to state HWY 14. Go E on 14 approx. 8.5 mi. state HWY 125. Go S on 125 approx. 7.5 mi. to state HWY H. Go SW on H approx. 1 mi. to Camp Ridge CG.

SINGLE RATE:	No fee	OPEN DATES:	Yearlong
# of SINGLE SITES:	8	MAX SPUR:	25 feet
		MAX STAY:	14 days
		ELEVATION:	1350 feet

9 Cobb Ridge
Springfiled • lat 36°53'31" lon 093°06'33"

DESCRIPTION: This CG rests in an oak and hickory forest near Bull and Barbers Creek. Wildlife in this area includes whitetailed deer, wild turkeys, foxes, coyotes, and the occasional black bears. CG is busy holidays and weekends. Campers may gather firewood. This CG is close to OHV trail access.

GETTING THERE: From Springfield go S on US HWY 65 approx. 9 mi. to state HWY 14. Go E on 14 approx. 8.5 mi. state HWY 125. Go S on 125 approx. 7.5 mi. to state HWY H. Go SW on H approx. 4 mi. to Cobb Ridge CG.

SINGLE RATE:	Varies	OPEN DATES:	Yearlong
# of SINGLE SITES:	19	MAX SPUR:	25 feet
		MAX STAY:	14 days
		ELEVATION:	1340 feet

10 Council Bluff
Potosi • lat 37°43'10" lon 090°54'37"

DESCRIPTION: This ridgetop CG rests in thick, oak and hickory forest with some pine near Council Bluff Lake. Fish for bass, crappie, sunfish and catfish. Wildlife in this area includes infrequent black bears, bobcat, foxes, deer and turkeys. Enjoy the beach, boat docks, or hiking trail around the lake.

GETTING THERE: From Potosi go SW on state HWY P approx. 14.5 mi. to state HWY DD. Go S on DD approx. 7.5 mi. to Council Bluff CG.

SINGLE RATE:	$8	OPEN DATES:	Yearlong
# of SINGLE SITES:	55	MAX SPUR:	60 feet
GROUP RATE:	$25	MAX STAY:	14 days
# of GROUP SITES:	4	ELEVATION:	1500 feet

 Campground has hosts   **Reservable sites**   **Accessible facilities**   **Fully developed**   **Semi-developed**   **Rustic facilities**

NOTE: Open dates listed are typical. Actual dates are dependent on conditions such as snow pack.

11 Deer Leap

Doniphan • lat 36°40'32" lon 090°53'07"

DESCRIPTION: This CG is located in mixed hardwood and pine on the Current River. Fish for catfish, bass, walley and perch. Wildlife in this area includes coyotes, foxes, osprey, herons, turkeys, otters and armadillos. CG is busy holiday and weekends. Horse and hiking trails in area. Campers may gather firewood.

GETTING THERE: From Doniphan go NW on state HWY Y approx. 6 mi. to Deer Leap CG.

SINGLE RATE:	Varies	OPEN DATES:	Yearlong
# of SINGLE SITES:	13	MAX SPUR:	30 feet
		MAX STAY:	14 days
		ELEVATION:	1285 feet

12 Denny Hollow
Greer • lat 36°47'02" lon 091°25'58"

DESCRIPTION: This dispersed CG is situated in mixed hardwood and pine on the Eleven Point National Scenic River. Fish for trout, catfish, bass, walley, and perch. Wildlife includes coyotes, foxes, osprey, herons, turkeys, otters and armadillos. Supplies available in Greer. Horse and hiking trails in area. No drinking water.

GETTING THERE: From Greer go W on state HWY 19 approx. 2 mi. to county route. Go W on county route approx. 3 mi. to boat ramp. Denny Hollow is a boat-in only CG located on the NE side of Eleven Point Lake.

SINGLE RATE:	Varies	OPEN DATES:	Yearlong
# of SINGLE SITES:	2		
		MAX STAY:	14 days
		ELEVATION:	595 feet

13 Dry Fork Recreation Area
Ashland • lat 38°45'30" lon 092°08'50"

DESCRIPTION: This CG is located in a oak and hickory hardwood forest. There are historic homesteads in area. Supplies available in Ashland. Wildlife in the area includes deer, turkeys, quail, and rabbits. Campers may gather dead and down firewood. Hike, bike and horseback trails adjacent to CG. Horses facilities on site.

GETTING THERE: From Ashland go E 8 mi. on route Y to county route 363. Go N 1 mi. on 363 to the junction of 363 and county route 361. Continue 1/2 mi. N to Dry Fork Rec. Area CG.

SINGLE RATE:	No fee	OPEN DATES:	Mar-Dec
# of SINGLE SITES:	8	MAX SPUR:	50 feet
GROUP RATE:	Donation	MAX STAY:	14 days
# of GROUP SITES:	1	ELEVATION:	800 feet

14 Float Camp
Doniphan • lat 36°40'03" lon 090°52'33"

DESCRIPTION: This CG is located in mixed hardwood and pine on the Current River. Fish for catfish, bass, walley and perch. Wildlife in this area includes coyotes, foxes, osprey, herons, turkeys, otters and armadillos. CG is busy holiday and weekends. Horse and hiking trails in area. No drinking water.

GETTING THERE: From Doniphan go NW on state HWY Y approx. 6 mi. to Float Camp CG.

SINGLE RATE:	Varies	OPEN DATES:	Yearlong
# of SINGLE SITES:	16	MAX SPUR:	30 feet
		MAX STAY:	14 days
		ELEVATION:	350 feet

15 Green Briar
Greer • lat 36°44'44" lon 091°13'53"

DESCRIPTION: This dispersed CG rests in mixed hardwood and pine on the Eleven Point National Scenic River. Fish for rainbow trout, catfish, bass, walley and perch. Wildlife includes coyotes, foxes, osprey, herons, otters and armadillos. Supplies available in Greer. Horse and hiking trails in area. No drinking water.

GETTING THERE: From Greer go N 4.5 mi. on state HWY 19 to forest route 3152. Go E 5.5 mi. on 3152 to forest route 3190. Go S 1.5 mi. on 3190 to the Turner Mill boat launch and boat-in 5.5 mi. to Green Briar CG.

SINGLE RATE:	Varies	OPEN DATES:	Yearlong
# of SINGLE SITES:	2		
		MAX STAY:	14 days
		ELEVATION:	500 feet

16 Greer Crossing

Winona • lat 36°47'37" lon 091°19'45"

DESCRIPTION: This CG is situated in mixed hardwood and pine on the Eleven Point National Scenic River. Fish for rainbow trout, catfish, bass, walley and perch. Wildlife includes coyotes, foxes, osprey, herons, turkeys, otters and armadillos. Trailhead leads to Greer Spring. Boat ramp on site.

GETTING THERE: From Winona go S on state HWY 19 approx. 15 mi. to Geer Crossing CG.

SINGLE RATE:	Varies	OPEN DATES:	Yearlong
# of SINGLE SITES:	19	MAX SPUR:	30 feet
		MAX STAY:	14 days
		ELEVATION:	630 feet

17 Hazel Creek
Potosi • lat 37°50'15" lon 091°01'00"

DESCRIPTION: This CG rests in oak and hickory forest with some pine on Hazel Creek. This CG accomodates horses and accesses the Ozark National Scenic Trail. Wildlife in this area includes infrequent black bears, bobcat, foxes, deer and turkeys. No drinking water. Campers may gather dead and down firewood.

GETTING THERE: From Potosi go SW on state HWY P approx. 14.5 mi. to state HWY C. Go NW on C approx. 4 mi. to state HWY Z. Go NW on Z approx. 2 mi. to Hazel Creek CG.

SINGLE RATE:	No fee	OPEN DATES:	Yearlong
# of SINGLE SITES:	3	MAX SPUR:	60 feet
		MAX STAY:	14 days
		ELEVATION:	1200 feet

18 Horseshoe Bend
Greer • lat 36°44'44" lon 091°13'53"

DESCRIPTION: This dispersed CG is located in mixed hardwood and pine on the Eleven Point National Scenic River. Fish for rainbow trout, catfish, bass, walley, and perch. Wildlife includes coyotes, foxes, osprey, herons, turkeys, otters, and armadillos. CG is busy holiday and weekends. Horse and hiking trails in area. No drinking water.

GETTING THERE: From Greer go N on state HWy 19 4.5 mi. to forest route 3152. Go E on 3152 5.5 mi. to forest route 3190. Go S on 3190 1.5 mi. to the Turner Mill boat launch. Horseshoe Bend CG is a boat-in only approx. 3.5 mi. downstream.

SINGLE RATE:	Varies	OPEN DATES:	Yearlong
# of SINGLE SITES:	6		
		MAX STAY:	14 days
		ELEVATION:	500 feet

19 Lane Spring
Rolla • lat 37°47'47" lon 091°50'12"

DESCRIPTION: This CG is located in oak, hickory, dogwood and persimmon on Little Piney River. Wildlife in this area includes deer, turkeys, coyotes, foxes, bald eagle, and small mammals. Campers may gather dead and down firewood. There is a hiking/horse trail (ride only when dry) and natural bridge in the area.

GETTING THERE: From Rolla go S on US HWY 63 approx. 5 mi. to Lane Spring CG.

SINGLE RATE:	Varies	OPEN DATES:	Yearlong
# of SINGLE SITES:	32	MAX SPUR:	20 feet
		MAX STAY:	14 days
		ELEVATION:	810 feet

20 Little Scotia
Salem • lat 37°31'46" lon 091°19'49"

DESCRIPTION: This CG is located in oak, hickory and pine on Little Scotia Pond. Fish and swim in the pond. Wildlife in this area includes coyotes, foxes, deer, turkeys and raptors. Campers may gather firewood. Supplies available in Salem. Enjoy mushroom picking or wildflower observation in this area.

GETTING THERE: From Salem go S 8 mi. on state HWY 19 to state HWY N. Go E 5 mi. on N to forest route 2222. Continue 8.5 mi. on 2222 to forest route 2340. Go W 1.5 mi. on 2340 to Little Scotia CG.

SINGLE RATE:	No fee	OPEN DATES:	Yearlong
# of SINGLE SITES:	14	MAX SPUR:	30 feet
		MAX STAY:	14 days
		ELEVATION:	1340 feet

 Campground has hosts   **Reservable sites**   **Accessible facilities**   **Fully developed**   **Semi-developed**   **Rustic facilities**

NOTE: Open dates listed are typical. Actual dates are dependent on conditions such as snow pack.

21 Loggers Lake
Salem • lat 37°23'24" lon 091°15'50"

DESCRIPTION: This CG is located in oak, hickory, and pine on LoggersLake. Fish for bass, sunfish and catfish. Wildlife in this area includes coyotes, foxes, deer, turkeys and raptors. There is an interpretive trail around the lake. CG is busy holidays and weekends. Campers may gather firewood.

GETTING THERE: From Salem go S on state HWY 19 approx. 22 mi. to state HWY CC. Go W on CC approx. 5.5 mi. to forest route 2221. Continue on 2221 approx. 3.5 mi. to Loggers Lake CG.

SINGLE RATE:	$8	OPEN DATES:	Yearlong
# of SINGLE SITES:	41	MAX SPUR:	30 feet
		MAX STAY:	14 days
		ELEVATION:	1100 feet

22 Marble Creek
Fredricktown • lat 37°27'04" lon 090°32'26"

DESCRIPTION: This CG is situated in oak and hickory forest with some pineon Marble Creek. Fish for perch and bass. This CG accesses the Ozark National Scenic Trail as well as the Marble Creek-Crane Lake Trail. Wildlife includes infrequent black bears, bobcats, foxes, deer and turkeys. No drinking water.

GETTING THERE: From Fredericktown go SE on state HWY E approx. 19 mi. to Marble Creek CG.

SINGLE RATE:	$8	OPEN DATES:	Yearlong
# of SINGLE SITES:	27	MAX SPUR:	40 feet
		MAX STAY:	14 days
		ELEVATION:	1200 feet

23 Markham Spring
Poplar Bluff • lat 36°58'54" lon 090°36'15"

DESCRIPTION: This CG is located in oak, willow, maple, and pine on Black River. Fish for crappie, bass, and catfish. Wildlife includes infrequent black bears, coyotes, foxes, deer, turkeys, herons and raptors. The Ozark National Scenic Trail is nearby. Campers may gather firewood.

GETTING THERE: From Poplar Bluff go N on US HWY 67 approx. 15 mi. to state HWY 49. Go NW on 49 approx. 10.5 mi. to Markham Spring CG.

SINGLE RATE:	$8	OPEN DATES:	Yearlong
# of SINGLE SITES:	41	MAX SPUR:	20 feet
GROUP RATE:	Varies	MAX STAY:	14 days
# of GROUP SITES:	3	ELEVATION:	400 feet

24 McCormack Lake
Winona • lat 36°49'18" lon 091°21'09"

DESCRIPTION: This CG rests in mixed hardwood and pine on McCormack Lake. Fish for catfish and bass. Wildlife includes coyotes, foxes, osprey, herons, turkeys, otters and armadillos. CG is busy holiday and weekends. Trailhead leads to an extensive trail system that includes the Ozark Trail. No drinking water.

GETTING THERE: From Winona go S on state HWY 19 approx. 12 mi. to forest route 3155. Go SW on 3155 approx. 1.5 mi. to McCormack Lake CG.

SINGLE RATE:	Varies	OPEN DATES:	Yearlong
# of SINGLE SITES:	8	MAX SPUR:	20 feet
		MAX STAY:	14 days
		ELEVATION:	600 feet

25 Mill Creek
Rolla • lat 37°02'10" lon 091°03'38"

DESCRIPTION: CG is in a mixed forest setting on Mill Creek. Fish or swim in the creek. Supplies available at Rolla. Numerous wildlife can be seen in the area. Campers may gather firewood. No designated trails nearby.

GETTING THERE: From Rolla go W on US HWY 44 approx. 7 mi. to state HWY T. Go S on T approx. 9 mi. to county route. Go NW on county route approx. 4 mi. to Mill Creek CG.

SINGLE RATE:	No fee	OPEN DATES:	Yearlong
# of SINGLE SITES:	6	MAX SPUR:	20 feet
		MAX STAY:	14 days
		ELEVATION:	600 feet

26 Morgan Spring
Doniphan • lat 36°33'46" lon 091°11'04"

DESCRIPTION: This dispersed CG rests in mixed hardwood and pine on the Eleven Point National Scenic River. Fish for rainbow trout, catfish, bass, walley, and perch. Wildlife includes coyotes, foxes, osprey, herons, turkeys, otters, and armadillos. CG is busy holiday and weekends. Horse and hiking trails in area. No drinking water.

GETTING THERE: From Doniphan go W on state HWY 142 approx. 21 mi. to The Narrows Access boat launch. Morgan Spring CG is a boat-in only CG located approx. 1 mi. upstream.

SINGLE RATE:	Varies	OPEN DATES:	Yearlong
# of SINGLE SITES:	2		
		MAX STAY:	14 days
		ELEVATION:	500 feet

27 North Fork
West Plains • lat 36°45'17" lon 092°09'09"

DESCRIPTION: This CG is located in oak and pine on the North Fork River. Wildlife in this area includes whitetailed deer, wild turkeys, foxes, coyotes and occasional black bears. CG is busy holiday weekends. Campers may gather firewood. This CG offers a trailhead that leads to Devils Backbone Wilderness.

GETTING THERE: From West Plains go W on state HWY CC approx. 16 mi. to North Fork CG.

SINGLE RATE:	Varies	OPEN DATES:	Yearlong
# of SINGLE SITES:	20	MAX SPUR:	25 feet
		MAX STAY:	14 days
		ELEVATION:	1300 feet

28 Paddy Creek
Rolla • lat 37°33'16" lon 092°02'28"

DESCRIPTION: This CG is located in hardwoods on Paddy Creek. Wildlife in this area includes deer, turkeys, coyotes, foxes, and bald eagles. Campers may gather dead and down firewood. This CG offers a boat ramp and an on site hiking/horse (ride only when dry) trail that leads to the Paddy Creek Wilderness. No drinking water.

GETTING THERE: From Rolla go S on US HWY 63 approx. 32 mi. to state HWY 32. Go NW on 32 approx. 4 mi. to state HWY N. Continue on N approx. 2 mi. to state HWY AF. Go W on AF approx. 8 mi. to Paddy Creek CG.

SINGLE RATE:	$15	OPEN DATES:	Yearlong
# of SINGLE SITES:	22	MAX SPUR:	20 feet
		MAX STAY:	14 days
		ELEVATION:	900 feet

29 Pine Ridge
Columbia • lat 38°45'35" lon 092°08'51"

DESCRIPTION: This CG is located in pine and red cedar on Big Dry Fork River. Enjoy fishing in area ponds. Visit Thomas S. Baskett Wildlife Research and Education Area. Hike or horseback ride (only when dry) the Cedar Creek Trail. This CG is a birdwatcher's delight. Campers may gather dead and down firewood.

GETTING THERE: From Columbia go S on US HWY 63 approx. 13 mi. to state HWY Y. Go E on Y approx. 6.5 mi. to Pine Ridge CG.

		OPEN DATES:	Yearlong
		MAX SPUR:	20 feet
GROUP RATE:	Donation	MAX STAY:	14 days
# of GROUP SITES:	3	ELEVATION:	800 feet

30 Pinewoods Lake
Poplar Bluff • lat 36°55'09" lon 090°46'22"

DESCRIPTION: This CG is located in oak, sycamore, and pine on Pinewoods Lake. Fish for crappie, bluegill, perch and catfish. Electric motorboats only. Wildlife includes infrequent black bears, coyotes, foxes, deer, turkeys and raptors. There is a barrier free fishing dock and trail. Campers may gather firewood.

GETTING THERE: From Poplar Bluff go NW on US HWY 67 approx. 8 mi. to US HWY 60. Go NW on 60 approx. 17.5 mi. to Pinewoods Lake CG.

SINGLE RATE:	$8	OPEN DATES:	Yearlong
# of SINGLE SITES:	15	MAX SPUR:	30 feet
		MAX STAY:	14 days
		ELEVATION:	795 feet

 Campground has hosts 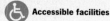 **Reservable sites**   **Accessible facilities**   **Fully developed**   **Semi-developed** **Rustic facilities**

NOTE: Open dates listed are typical. Actual dates are dependent on conditions such as snow pack.

31 Red Bluff
Steelville • lat 37°48'50" lon 091°10'09"

DESCRIPTION: This CG is located in a grassy area with larch on Huzzah Creek. Enjoy swimming or fishing for bass and perch. Wildlife in this area includes infrequent black bears, bobcat, foxes, deer and turkeys. Take a hike on this CG's loop trail. Supplies available at Steelville.

GETTING THERE: From Steelville go SE on state HWY 19 approx. 9 mi. to state HWY 49. Go SE on 49 approx. 5 mi. to state HWY V. Go E on V approx. 6.5 mi. to Red Bluff CG.

SINGLE RATE:	$8	OPEN DATES:	Yearlong
# of SINGLE SITES:	46	MAX SPUR:	40 feet
GROUP RATE:	$25	MAX STAY:	14 days
# of GROUP SITES:	3	ELEVATION:	810 feet

32 Silver Mines
Fredericktown • lat 37°33'43" lon 090°26'29"

DESCRIPTION: This CG rests in mixed hardwoods with some pine. Enjoy fishing or kayaking on the adjacent St. Francis River, Missouri's only whitewater. Wildlife includes infrequent black bears, bobcat, foxes, deer and turkeys. Take a hike on this CG's loop trail or access the Mill Stream Garden Area.

GETTING THERE: From Fredericktown go W on state HWY 72 approx. 6 mi. to state HWY D. Go SW on D approx. 3.5 mi. to Silver Mines CG.

SINGLE RATE:	$8	OPEN DATES:	Yearlong
# of SINGLE SITES:	80	MAX SPUR:	40 feet
GROUP RATE:	$25	MAX STAY:	14 days
# of GROUP SITES:	4	ELEVATION:	730 feet

33 Stinking Pond
Greer • lat 36°45'42" lon 091°15'24"

DESCRIPTION: This dispersed CG is situated in mixed hardwood and pine on the Eleven Point National Scenic River. Fish for rainbow trout, catfish, bass, walley and perch. Wildlife includes coyotes, foxes, osprey, herons, turkeys, otters and armadillos. CG is busy holiday and weekends. Horse and hiking trails in area. No drinking water.

GETTING THERE: From Greer go N 4.5 mi. on state HWY 19 to forest route 3152. Go E 5.5 mi. on 3152 to forest route 3190. Go S 1.5 mi. on 3190 to the Turner Mill boat launch. Boat-in 1.5 mi. to Stinking Pond CG.

SINGLE RATE:	Varies	OPEN DATES:	Yearlong
# of SINGLE SITES:	4		
		MAX STAY:	14 days
		ELEVATION:	492 feet

34 Sutton Bluff
Salem • lat 37°28'32" lon 091°00'23"

DESCRIPTION: This CG is located in oak, hickory and pine on West Fork Black River. Fish for crappie, bluegill, bass, sunfish, and catfish. Wildlife includes coyotes, foxes, deer, turkeys and raptors. There is a OHV trail system nearby as well as the Ozark National Scenic Trail. Campers may gather firewood.

GETTING THERE: From Salem go S 22 mi. on state HWY 19 to state HWY CC. Go W 5.5 mi. on CC to forest route 2221. Continue 10 mi. on 2221 to state HWY 72. Go E 19 mi. on 72 to forest route 2236. Go W 3 mi. on 2236 to Sutton Bluff CG.

SINGLE RATE:	$8	OPEN DATES:	Yearlong
# of SINGLE SITES:	35	MAX SPUR:	50 feet
		MAX STAY:	14 days
		ELEVATION:	1000 feet

35 Watercress Spring
Van Buren • lat 37°00'01" lon 091°01'10"

DESCRIPTION: This popular CG rests in mixed hardwood and pine on the Current River. Fish for catfish, bass, walley, and perch. Wildlife in this area includes coyotes, foxes, osprey, herons, turkeys, otters, and armadillos. CG is busy holiday and weekends. Horses and hiking trails in area. Campers may gather firewood.

GETTING THERE: Watercress Spring CG is located approx. 1/2 mi. N of Van Buren.

SINGLE RATE:	Varies	OPEN DATES:	Yearlong
# of SINGLE SITES:	17	MAX SPUR:	30 feet
		MAX STAY:	14 days
		ELEVATION:	560 feet

36 Whites Creek
Greer • lat 36°43'34" lon 091°12'41"

DESCRIPTION: This dispersed CG is located in mixed hardwood and pine on the Eleven Point National Scenic River. Fish for rainbow trout, catfish, bass, walley and perch. Wildlife includes coyotes, foxes, osprey, herons, turkeys, otters and armadillos. CG is busy holiday and weekends. Horse and hiking trails in area. No drinking water.

GETTING THERE: From Greer go N 4.5 mi. on state HWY 19 to forest route 3152. Go E 5.5 mi. on 3152 to forest route 3190. Go S 1.5 mi. on 3190 to the Turner Mill boat launch. Boat-in 5.5 mi. to Whites Creek CG.

SINGLE RATE:	Varies	OPEN DATES:	Yearlong
# of SINGLE SITES:	4		
		MAX STAY:	14 days
		ELEVATION:	500 feet

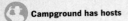 **Campground has hosts**   **Reservable sites**   **Accessible facilities**   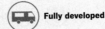 **Fully developed**   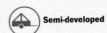 **Semi-developed**    **Rustic facilities**

NOTE: Open dates listed are typical. Actual dates are dependent on conditions such as snow pack.

Hunting & Fishing

Individual states manage fishing and wildlife resources on forest lands. A valid state fishing or hunting license is required to fish and hunt on a National Forest. It's your responsibility to know any special hunting or fishing regulations for the area you plan on participating

in these activities.

Jim Hughes Photo, USDA Forest Service

BEAVERHEAD-DEERLODGE NATIONAL FOREST

Straddling the Continental Divide, this national forest in Montana covers 3.32 million acres, and lies in eight southwest Montana counties.

The forest, founded in 1996 when the Forest Service merged the Beaverhead and Deerlodge National Forests, provides timber, minerals, and grazing lands. It also offers breath-taking scenery for a wide variety of recreational pursuits. The Continental Divide National Scenic Trail and Nez Perce Historic Trail pass through the forest. Georgetown Lake offers winter and summer recreation near Phillipsburg. At the ghost towns of Elkhorn and Coolidge, you can relive Montana's "boom and bust" past. Sheepshead Recreation Area, north of Butte, offers pleasant picnicking and lake fishing. For the angler seeking solitude, miles of blue-ribbon streams and high mountain lakes offer a real chance to "get a way from it all."

Winter enthusiasts find snowmobiling, cross-country skiing trails, as well as downhill skiing at Discovery, near Anaconda, and Maverick Mountain, near Dillon. Summertime affords chances to hike and drive primitive routes to high-mountain lakes or to drive more improved roads to places like Delmoe and Wade lakes.

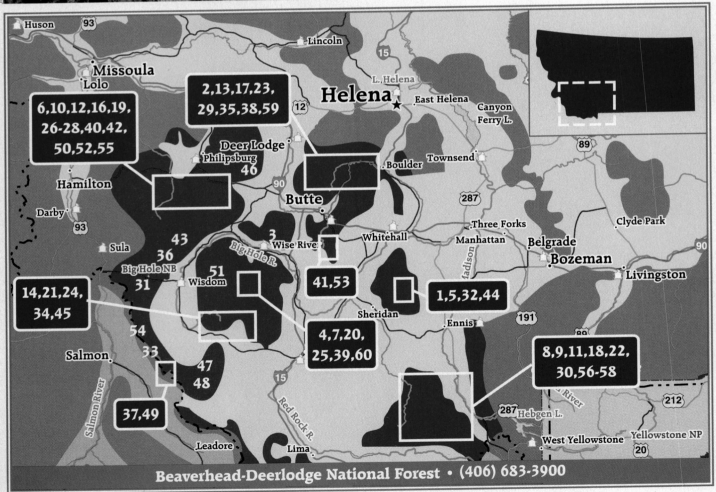

Beaverhead-Deerlodge National Forest • (406) 683-3900

1 Balanced Rock
Sheridan • lat 45°29'09" lon 112°00'57"

DESCRIPTION: This CG is situated in an open stand of douglas fir and pine. Fish for trout from Mill Creek nearby. Supplies at Sheridan. Deer, elk, moose, and bears can be seen in the surrounding area. Hunting when in season. Gather firewood locally. There are designated trails in the area. No drinking water on site.

GETTING THERE: From Sheridan go E on Mill Creek Road approx. 9 mi. to Balanced Rock CG.

SINGLE RATE:	No fee	OPEN DATES:	June-Oct
# of SINGLE SITES:	5	MAX SPUR:	25 feet
		MAX STAY:	14 days
		ELEVATION:	7200 feet

2 Basin Canyon
Basin • lat 46°18'37" lon 112°18'20"

DESCRIPTION: This CG is located near Basin Creek in a pleasant douglas fir stand. Cool days, cold nights. Fishing is fair on the Creek. Historic buildings and mines in the area. Supplies 15 mi. away at Boulder. Elk, deer, blue grouse and small wildlife in area. No firewood on site, bring your own. No local hiking.

GETTING THERE: From Basin go N on forest route 172 approx. 3.5 mi. to Basin Canyon CG.

SINGLE RATE:	No fee	OPEN DATES:	May-Sept
# of SINGLE SITES:	2	MAX SPUR:	16 feet
		MAX STAY:	16 days
		ELEVATION:	5400 feet

3 Beaver Dam
Butte • lat 45°53'01" lon 112°46'55"

DESCRIPTION: This CG is surrounded by lodgepole set on small stream nearby. Stream fishing at either of two creeks, each with beaver dams. Mild days, cold nights, noon rains are frequent. Supplies and groceries at Butte. Moose, deer, occasional bears, and small wildlife in area. Heavy weekend use.

GETTING THERE: From Butte go S on I-15/90 to exit 121 on I-15. Go S on I-15 approx. 9 mi. to Feeley exit 111 and route 96. Go W on 96 approx. 6 mi. to Beaver Dam CG.

SINGLE RATE:	$5	OPEN DATES:	May-Sept
# of SINGLE SITES:	15	MAX SPUR:	50 feet
		MAX STAY:	16 days
		ELEVATION:	6580 feet

4 Boulder Creek
Wise River • lat 45°40'00" lon 113°03'53"

DESCRIPTION: CG in a park-like setting above Wise River, with views of the river over steep timbered slopes. Mild days, cold nights. Expect summer rain. Fish for trout on Wise River. Historic ghost town and mine nearby. Supplies at Wise River or Butte. Deer, elk, and moose in area. Gather firewood locally.

GETTING THERE: From Wise River go S on primary forest route 73 (Pioneer Mountains Scenic Byway) approx. 12 mi. to Boulder Creek CG.

SINGLE RATE:	$8	OPEN DATES:	June-Sept
# of SINGLE SITES:	11	MAX SPUR:	24 feet
		MAX STAY:	16 days
		ELEVATION:	6420 feet

5 Branham Lakes
Sheridan • lat 45°31'02" lon 111°59'19"

DESCRIPTION: This CG is situated in an open stand of douglas fir and pine. Fish for trout nearby. Supplies available at Sheridan. Deer, elk, moose, and bears can be seen in surrounding area. Hunting when in season. Gather firewood locally. There are designated trails in the area. Drinkable water is avaible on site.

GETTING THERE: From Sheridan go E on mi.ll Creek Road approx. 21 mi. to Branham Lakes CG.

SINGLE RATE:	No fee	OPEN DATES:	July-Sept
# of SINGLE SITES:	6	MAX SPUR:	22 feet
		MAX STAY:	16 days
		ELEVATION:	8924 feet

6 Cable
Anaconda • lat 46°13'17" lon 113°14'45"

DESCRIPTION: Among lodgepole pine near North Fork of Flint Creek. Mild days, cold nights. Expect rains. Fish for trout on creek. Boat, fish, and ski on nearby Georgetown Lake. Some historic mine sites in lake area. Moderate use. Supplies at Georgetown Lake. Moose, elk, and deer in area. Firewood for sale.

GETTING THERE: From Georgetown Lake go N on forest route 65 approx. 2.7 mi. to county route 242. Go E on 242 approx. 0.2 mi. to Cable CG.

SINGLE RATE:	$8	OPEN DATES:	June-Nov
# of SINGLE SITES:	11	MAX SPUR:	22 feet
GROUP RATE:		MAX STAY:	14 days
		ELEVATION:	6500 feet

7 Canyon Creek
Dillon • lat 45°37'34" lon 112°56'29"

DESCRIPTION: CG set in a lodgepole pine forest with views of Canyon Creek. Fish for Brook and Cutthroat Trout from the creek. Supplies at Dillon. Watch for mountain goats on southern cliffs by CG. Deer, elk, moose, and squirrels in area. Lion Creek Trail, which leads to 6 different lakes, is nearby.

GETTING THERE: From Dillon go N on I-15 30 mi. to exit 93. Go W on Road 40 approx. 6.5 mi. to forest route 188. Go N on 188 approx. 7 mi. to forest route 7401. Go SW 7401 approx. 3.5 mi. to Canyon Creek CG.

SINGLE RATE:	No fee	OPEN DATES:	May-Sept
# of SINGLE SITES:	4	MAX SPUR:	12 feet
		MAX STAY:	14 days
		ELEVATION:	7360 feet

8 Cliff Point
West Yellowstone • lat 44°47'31" lon 111°33'40"

DESCRIPTION: CG in an open and park-like stand of douglas fir and pine. Fish for trout from Cliff Lake. Supplies at West Yellowstone. Deer, elk, moose, and bears can be seen in surrounding area. Gather firewood locally. There are designated trails in the area. Drinkable water available on site.

GETTING THERE: From West Yellowstone go N on US HWY 191 8 mi. to US HWY 287. Go W on 287 27 mi. to forest route 241. Go S on 241 3.5 mi. to forest route 572. Go W on 572 and follow signs to Cliff Point CG.

SINGLE RATE:	$8	OPEN DATES:	June-Sept
# of SINGLE SITES:	6	MAX SPUR:	16 feet
		MAX STAY:	16 days
		ELEVATION:	6900 feet

9 Clover Meadows
Ennis • lat 45°02'16" lon 111°50'05"

DESCRIPTION: This CG is in a high ridge setting of douglas fir and pine. Fish for trout nearby. Supplies are available at Ennis. Deer, elk, moose, and bears can be seen in the surrounding area. Campers may gather firewood locally. There are designated trails in the area. No drinking water on site.

GETTING THERE: From Ennis go S on US HWY 287 approx. 17 mi. to McAtee Bridge. Go W on Johnny Gulch Road (forest route 423) approx. 13 mi. to forest route 290. Go S on 290 approx. 1 mi. to Clover Meadows CG.

SINGLE RATE:	No fee	OPEN DATES:	July-Oct
# of SINGLE SITES:	1		
		MAX STAY:	14 days
		ELEVATION:	8482 feet

10 Copper Creek
Philipsburg • lat 46°03'58" lon 113°32'35"

DESCRIPTION: CG is adjacent to Copper Creek among lodgepole pine. Stream fish Copper and Rock Creeks. Noon rains common during summer. Supplies 25 mi. N. at Philipsburg. Moderate use. Gather firewood locally. Hike Middle Fork of Anaconda Pintler Wilderness 6 mi. S. Snow may affect dates.

GETTING THERE: From Philipsburg go S on state HWY 1 approx. 5 mi. to state HWY 38. Go SW on 38 approx. 9 mi. to forest route 5106. Go S on 5106 approx. 10 mi. to Copper Creek CG.

SINGLE RATE:	No fee	OPEN DATES:	May-Nov
# of SINGLE SITES:	7	MAX SPUR:	22 feet
		MAX STAY:	16 days
		ELEVATION:	5500 feet

 **Campground has hosts**   **Reservable sites** 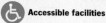 **Accessible facilities**   **Fully developed**   **Semi-developed**   **Rustic facilities**

NOTE: Open dates listed are typical. Actual dates are dependent on conditions such as snow pack.

11 Cottonwood Camp

Sheridan • lat 44°58'26" lon 111°58'20"

DESCRIPTION: CG in an open stand of Cottonwood. Fish for trout from Cottonwood Creek or Ruby River nearby. Supplies at Sheridan. Deer, elk, moose, and bears in area. Gather firewood locally. There are no designated trails in the area, venture off into forest to explore. No drinking water available on site.

GETTING THERE: From Sheridan go S on county route 248 approx. 3 mi. past Ruby Reservoir to county route 142. Go S on 142 (primary forest route 100) approx. 17 mi. to Cottonwood Camp CG.

SINGLE RATE:	No fee	OPEN DATES:	May-Nov
# of SINGLE SITES:	10	MAX STAY:	16 days
		ELEVATION:	6300 feet

16 East Fork

Anaconda • lat 46°08'06" lon 113°23'11"

DESCRIPTION: Near East Fork of Rock Creek among lodgepole pine. Expect noon rains during summer. Stream fish Rock Creek, boat or shore fish East Fork Reservoir nearby. Supplies at Philipsburg. Elk, moose, and deer in area. Gather firewood locally. 3 mi. to East Fork Trail Head of the Anaconda Pintler Wilderness.

GETTING THERE: From Philipsburg go S on state HWY 1 6.4 mi. to state HWY 38. Go W on 38 6 mi. to forest route 672. Go S on 672 5 mi. to forest route 9349. Go W on 9349 1 mi. to East Fork CG.

SINGLE RATE:	No fee	OPEN DATES:	May-Nov*
# of SINGLE SITES:	10	MAX SPUR:	22 feet
		MAX STAY:	16 days
		ELEVATION:	6000 feet

12 Crystal Creek
Philipsburg • lat 46°13'58" lon 113°44'42"

DESCRIPTION: Set among lodgepole pine. Expect mild days, cold nights with common noon rains. Stream fish nearby North Fork of Rock Creek. Supplies at Philipsburg. Moose, elk, and deer in area. Moderate use. Gather firewood locally. Hike nearby Crystal Creek trail. Prepare for heavy mosquitos in July and August.

GETTING THERE: From Philipsburg go S on state HWY 1 to state HWY 38. Go W on 38. Crystal Creek CG is located on state HWY 38 approx. 2 mi. E of Skalkaho Pass.

SINGLE RATE:	No fee	OPEN DATES:	July-Nov
# of SINGLE SITES:	1	MAX SPUR:	16 feet
		MAX STAY:	16 days
		ELEVATION:	7000 feet

17 Elder Creek
Boulder • lat 46°10'49" lon 112°11'04"

DESCRIPTION: CG is set in an open park like area. Fish for cutthroat on nearby Little Boulder River; catch and release only. Historic mining area. Supplies at Boulder. Elk, deer, grouse, and small wildlife in area. Moderate use. Gather firewood locally. No hiking in area. Most popular for picnicking.

GETTING THERE: From Boulder go S on forest route 86 approx. 7 mi. to Elder Creek CG.

SINGLE RATE:	No fee	OPEN DATES:	May-Sept
# of SINGLE SITES:	2		
		MAX STAY:	16 days
		ELEVATION:	5000 feet

13 Delmoe Lake

Butte • lat 45°59'06" lon 112°20'24"

DESCRIPTION: Set on Delmoe Lake shore among lodgepole pine. Lake is popular for large cutthroat fishing. Hot days, cool nights, expect afternoon rain. Supplies at Whitehall or Butte. Elk, deer, and blue grouse in area. Gather firewood locally. Heavy use. Popular for 200 mi. of 4X4 roads in the area.

GETTING THERE: From Butte go E on I-90 to exit 233 at Homestake Pass. Take forest route 222 approx. 8 mi. to forest route 9371. Go N on 9371 1/2 mi. to Delmoe Lake CG.

SINGLE RATE:	$6	OPEN DATES:	May-Sept
# of SINGLE SITES:	25	MAX SPUR:	32 feet
		MAX STAY:	16 days
		ELEVATION:	5200 feet

18 Elk Lake
Henrys Lake • lat 44°40'12" lon 111°34'50"

DESCRIPTION: This CG is situated in a wide open stand of douglas fir and pine. Fishing for trout from Elk Lake nearby. Wildlife in the area includes deer, elk, moose, and bears. Hunting when in season. Campers may gather firewood locally. There are designated trails in the area.

GETTING THERE: From Henrys Lake go W on Red Rock Pass Road approx. 16 mi. to forest route 8384. Go N on 8384 approx. 2 mi. to Elk Lake CG.

SINGLE RATE:	No fee	OPEN DATES:	July-Oct
# of SINGLE SITES:	1		
		MAX STAY:	14 days
		ELEVATION:	6880 feet

14 Dinner Station
Dillon • lat 45°25'42" lon 112°54'05"

DESCRIPTION: CG is located in pine near Birch Creek. Good fishing for brookies in creek. Busy on holidays and weekends in summer. Deer, elk and moose in area.

GETTING THERE: From Dillon go N on I-15 approx. 12 mi. to Birch Creek Road (Apex exit). Go W on Birch Creek Road approx. 11.5 mi. to Dinner Station CG.

SINGLE RATE:	No fee	OPEN DATES:	May-Sept
# of SINGLE SITES:	8	MAX SPUR:	16 feet
GROUP RATE:	Varies	MAX STAY:	16 days
# of GROUP SITES:	1	ELEVATION:	7200 feet

19 Flint Creek
Anaconda • lat 46°14'01" lon 113°17'58"

DESCRIPTION: CG set among logepole pine, adjacent to Flint Creek. Stream fish the creek. Expect rain during summer. Supplies and groceries can be found 8 mi. away at Philipsburg. Moose, elk, deer, and small wildlife frequent the area. Gather firewood locally. Snow may affect dates.

GETTING THERE: From Philipsburg go S on state HWY 1 approx. 7.7 mi. to Flint Creek CG.

SINGLE RATE:	No fee	OPEN DATES:	May-Nov
# of SINGLE SITES:	7	MAX SPUR:	16 feet
		MAX STAY:	16 days
		ELEVATION:	5500 feet

15 East Creek

Lima • lat 44°33'49" lon 112°39'35"

DESCRIPTION: This CG is situated among pine near East Creek. Fish in East Creek. Check fishing regulations for area. Wildlife in the area includes deer, elk, and moose. Hunting when in season. Gather firewood locally. RV facilities available. CG tends to be busy in the summer on weekends and holidays.

GETTING THERE: From Lima go W on forest route 179 approx. 7 mi. to forest route 70070. Go S on 70070 approx. 2.5 mi. to East Creek CG.

SINGLE RATE:	No fee	OPEN DATES:	May-Oct
# of SINGLE SITES:	4	MAX SPUR:	16 feet
		MAX STAY:	16 days
		ELEVATION:	6998 feet

20 Fourth of July

Wise River • lat 45°39'39" lon 113°03'53"

DESCRIPTION: In a lodgepole pine forest on the Wise River. Fish from the river. Supplies and groceries can be found in the town of Wise River. Deer, elk, and squirrels frequent the area. Full most holidays and weekends. No designated trails, just venture off into the forest for an enjoyable visit.

GETTING THERE: From Wise River go SW on primary forest route 73 (Pioneer Mountains Scenic Byway) approx. 11 mi. to Fourth of July CG.

SINGLE RATE:	$8	OPEN DATES:	June-Sept
# of SINGLE SITES:	5	MAX SPUR:	24 feet
		MAX STAY:	16 days
		ELEVATION:	6450 feet

 Campground has hosts   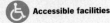 **Reservable sites**   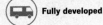 **Accessible facilities**   **Fully developed**   **Semi-developed**   **Rustic facilities**

NOTE: Open dates listed are typical. Actual dates are dependent on conditions such as snow pack.

21 Grasshopper
Dillon • lat 45°27'06" lon 113°07'08"

DESCRIPTION: This CG is situated among pine on Grasshopper Creek. Possible fishing on the creek. Wildlife in the area includes deer, elk, and moose. Hunting when in season. Campers may gather their firewood locally. CG tends to be busy on holidays and weekends in the summer.

GETTING THERE: From Dillon go S on I-15 approx. 4 mi. to state HWY 278. Go W on 278 approx. 27 mi. to forest route 73 (Pioneer Mountains Scenic Byway). Go N on 73 approx. 11.5 mi. to Grasshopper CG.

SINGLE RATE:	$8	OPEN DATES:	June-Sept
# of SINGLE SITES:	24	MAX SPUR:	16 feet
GROUP RATE:	Varies	MAX STAY:	16 days
# of GROUP SITES:	1	ELEVATION:	6900 feet

26 Lodgepole
Anaconda • lat 46°12'43" lon 113°16'21"

DESCRIPTION: CG across from Georgetown Lake among lodgepole pine. Boat, fish, and ski on Georgetown Lake. Expect rains during summer. Moderate use. Basic supplies nearby. Elk, moose, deer, and small wildlife. Firewood may be gathered or is sold by concessioniare. Hike nearby Lodgepole Trail. Snow may affect dates.

GETTING THERE: From Philipsburg go S on state HWY 1 approx. 11 mi. to the east shore or Georgetown Lake and Lodgepole CG.

SINGLE RATE:	$8	OPEN DATES:	May-Nov
# of SINGLE SITES:	31	MAX SPUR:	32 feet
		MAX STAY:	14 days
		ELEVATION:	6400 feet

22 Hilltop
West Yellowstone • lat 44°47'50" lon 111°33'35"

DESCRIPTION: CG is situated in an open stand of douglas fir and pine. Fish for trout from Wade and Cliff Lakes nearby. Supplies at West Yellowstone. Deer, elk, moose, and bears in the area. Campers may gather firewood. There are designated trails in the area. Drinking water available on site.

GETTING THERE: From West Yellowstone go N on US HWY 191 8 mi. to US HWY 287. Go W on 287 27 mi. to forest route 241. Go S on 241 approx. 3.5 mi. to forest route 572. Go W on 572 and follow signs to Hilltop CG.

SINGLE RATE:	$7	OPEN DATES:	June-Sept
# of SINGLE SITES:	18	MAX SPUR:	22 feet
		MAX STAY:	16 days
		ELEVATION:	6280 feet

27 Lower Seymour Lake
Wise River • lat 45°59'12" lon 113°11'00"

DESCRIPTION: CG is set in a dense stand of lodgepole pine close to Lower Seymour Lake and Seymour Creek. Brook trout fishing from lake or creek. Supplies can be found in the town of Wise River. Wildlife in the area includes deer, elk, moose, and squirrels. Hunting when in season. Seymour Creek Trail close to CG.

GETTING THERE: From Wise River go W on state HWY 43 approx. 11 mi. to county route 274. Go N on 274 approx. 4 mi. to primary forest route 934. Go NW on 934 approx. 8 mi. to Lower Seymour Lake CG.

SINGLE RATE:	No fee	OPEN DATES:	May-Sept
# of SINGLE SITES:	17	MAX SPUR:	16 feet
		MAX STAY:	16 days
		ELEVATION:	6750 feet

23 Ladysmith
Butte • lat 46°15'05" lon 112°24'10"

DESCRIPTION: This CG is situated in a lodgepole pine stand. Stream fish for trout on nearby Boulder River. Warm days, cool nights. Supplies 15 mi. away in Boulder. Elk, deer, grouse, and small wildlife in area. Mod-heavy use by hungting season. 4X4 access to surrounding roads. No drinking water.

GETTING THERE: From Butte go N on I-15 to exit 151. Go W on forest route 82 approx. 3.5 mi. to Ladysmith CG.

SINGLE RATE:	No fee	OPEN DATES:	May-Dec
# of SINGLE SITES:	6	MAX SPUR:	16 feet
		MAX STAY:	16 days
		ELEVATION:	5300 feet

28 Lower Warm Spring
Anaconda • lat 46°11'59" lon 113°10'00"

DESCRIPTION: Set in timber with thick underbrush in an area with small creek. CG is in creek bottom, making cool mornings, rain frequent. Fish nearby at Georgetown Lake. Grant Kohrs Nat'l Historic Site at Deer Lodge, an area rich in mining history. Deer, elk, moose, and big horn sheep in area. Bring your own firewood.

GETTING THERE: From Georgetown Lake go E on state HWY 1 approx. 5 mi. to forest route 170. Go N on 170 approx. 2 mi. to Lower Warm Spring CG.

SINGLE RATE:	No fee	OPEN DATES:	July-Sept
# of SINGLE SITES:	6	MAX SPUR:	36 feet
		MAX STAY:	16 days
		ELEVATION:	6300 feet

24 Little Joe
Wise River • lat 45°33'17" lon 113°05'26"

DESCRIPTION: This CG is in a lodgepole pine forest setting on the Wise River. Fish from the river for trout. Supplies at Wise River. Deer, elk, squirrels, and an occasional moose in the area. Gather firewood locally. No designated trails, just venture off into the forest to explore.

GETTING THERE: From Wise River go SW on primary forest route 73 (Pioneer Mountains Scenic Byway) approx. 20 mi. to Little Joe CG.

SINGLE RATE:	$7	OPEN DATES:	May-Sept
# of SINGLE SITES:	4	MAX SPUR:	16 feet
		MAX STAY:	16 days
		ELEVATION:	6800 feet

29 Lowland
Butte • lat 46°08'23" lon 112°30'13"

DESCRIPTION: Lowland CG is surrounded by lodgepole pine, with some sites overlooking a small meadow. Moose are common along the wet bottoms. Supplies and groceries can be found at Butte. Gather firewood locally. Good hunting area. Warm days, prepare for mosquitos during cool evenings.

GETTING THERE: From Butte go N on I-15 to Elk Park exit 138. Go W on Lowland road approx. 6 mi. to 9485 (Hail Columbia Road). Go on 9485 approx. 8 mi. to Lowland CG.

SINGLE RATE:	$5	OPEN DATES:	May-Sept
# of SINGLE SITES:	11	MAX SPUR:	22 feet
		MAX STAY:	16 days
		ELEVATION:	6600 feet

25 Lodgepole
Wise River • lat 45°38'55" lon 113°04'14"

DESCRIPTION: This CG is in a lodgepole and spruce forest setting on Wise River. Fish the river for trout. Supplies can be found in the town of Wise River. Gather firewood locally. Boulder Creek Trail and 4th of July Trail are close to CG. CG fills up early, usually from the 4th of July through August.

GETTING THERE: From Wise River go SW on primary forest route 73 (Pioneer Mountains Scenic Byway) approx. 13 mi. to Lodgepole CG.

SINGLE RATE:	$8	OPEN DATES:	May-Sept
# of SINGLE SITES:	10	MAX SPUR:	16 feet
		MAX STAY:	16 days
		ELEVATION:	6450 feet

30 Madison
Cameron • lat 44°53'13" lon 111°34'53"

DESCRIPTION: This CG is situated in an open stand of douglas fir and pine. Fish for trout from creeks and streams nearby. Supplies are available at Cameron. Deer, elk, moose, and bears in area. Hunting when in season. Campers may gather firewood. There are designated trails in the area.

GETTING THERE: From Cameron go S on US HWY 287 approx. 24 mi. to county route 8381. Go SW on 8381 approx. 1 mi. to Madison CG.

SINGLE RATE:	$8	OPEN DATES:	June-Sept
# of SINGLE SITES:	10	MAX SPUR:	22 feet
		MAX STAY:	16 days
		ELEVATION:	5960 feet

 Campground has hosts   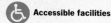 Reservable sites   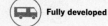 Accessible facilities

 Fully developed   Semi-developed   Rustic facilities

NOTE: Open dates listed are typical. Actual dates are dependent on conditions such as snow pack.

31 May Creek
Wisdom • lat 45°39'12" lon 113°46'45"

DESCRIPTION: CG set in a lodgepole forest with sparse underbrush. Views of a meadow, with May Creek flowing next to CG. Snow anytime during the year. Fish from the creek. Historical Big Hole National Battlefield nearby. Supplies at Wisdom. Elk, moose, deer, and bears in area. Gather firewood locally. Trails in area.

GETTING THERE: From Wisdom go W on state HWY 43 approx. 17 mi. to May Creek CG.

SINGLE RATE:	$5	OPEN DATES:	June-Sept
# of SINGLE SITES:	21	MAX SPUR:	32 feet
		MAX STAY:	16 days
		ELEVATION:	6300 feet

32 Mill Creek
Sheridan • lat 45°28'39" lon 112°04'01"

DESCRIPTION: This CG is situated in an open stand of douglas fir and pine. Fish for trout from Mill Creek nearby. Supplies are available at Sheridan. Deer, elk, moose, and bears can be seen in surrounding area. Gather firewood locally. There are designated trails in the area. Drinkable water available.

GETTING THERE: From Sheridan go E on mi.ll Creek Road approx. 6 mi. to mi.ll Creek CG.

SINGLE RATE:	No fee	OPEN DATES:	June-Oct
# of SINGLE SITES:	13	MAX SPUR:	22 feet
		MAX STAY:	16 days
		ELEVATION:	6500 feet

33 Miner Lake
Wisdom • lat 45°19'28" lon 113°34'38"

DESCRIPTION: CG in a lodgepole pine forest with views of Miner Lake and the Continental Divide. Snow can occur any day of the year. Fish on lake or Miner Creek. Historical Bannack, first territorial capital of Montana, 30 mi. away. Supplies at Jackson. Gather firewood locally. Many trails in area.

GETTING THERE: From Wisdom go S on state HWY 278 approx. 19 mi. to Jackson. Go W on county route 182 approx. 7 mi. to forest route 182. Go W on 182 approx. 3 mi. to Miner Lake CG.

SINGLE RATE:	$5	OPEN DATES:	June-Sept
# of SINGLE SITES:	18	MAX SPUR:	32 feet
		MAX STAY:	16 days
		ELEVATION:	7000 feet

34 Mono Creek
Wise River • lat 45°32'06" lon 113°04'41"

DESCRIPTION: This CG is situated in a lodgepole pine setting close to Wise River. Fish for brook and cutthroat trout from river. Supplies at Wise River. Deer, elk, moose, and squirrels in the area. Hunting when in season. Gather firewood locally. Jacobson Creek Trail is close to CG.

GETTING THERE: From Wise River go SW on primary forest route 73 (Pioneer Mountains Scenic Byway) approx. 21 mi. to forest route 2465. Go S on 2465 approx. 2 mi. to Mono Creek CG.

SINGLE RATE:	$7	OPEN DATES:	June-Sept
# of SINGLE SITES:	5	MAX SPUR:	16 feet
		MAX STAY:	16 days
		ELEVATION:	6895 feet

35 Mormon Gulch
Butte • lat 46°15'24" lon 112°21'42"

DESCRIPTION: CG among lodgepole stand with meadow openings. Warm days, cold nights. Stream fish for trout on nearby Boulder River. Supplies 16 mi. at Boulder. Elk, deer, grouse, and small wildlife in area. Moderate use turning heavy during fall hunting. Gather firewood locally. Heavy 4X4 access. No drinking water.

GETTING THERE: From Butte go N on I-15 to exit 151. Go W on forest route 82 approx. 1.5 mi. to Mormon Gulch CG.

SINGLE RATE:	No fee	OPEN DATES:	May-Dec
# of SINGLE SITES:	16	MAX SPUR:	16 feet
		MAX STAY:	16 days
		ELEVATION:	5300 feet

36 Mussigbrod
Wisdom • lat 45°47'23" lon 113°36'30"

DESCRIPTION: Peacefull CG in tall pine adjacent to Mussigbrod Lake. Fish for grayling and trout from lake. Supplies at Wisdom. Gather firewood locally. Many trails in area. Just before entrance to CG there is horse trailer parking, pull throughs and hitching rails. Bears and ticks could be a problem.

GETTING THERE: From Wisdom go W on state HWY 43 approx. 1.5 mi. to Lower North Fork Road. Go N on Lower North Fork 9 mi. to Mussigbrod Lake Road. Go W 10 mi. and follow signs to Mussigbrod Lake CG.

SINGLE RATE:	No fee	OPEN DATES:	June-Sept
# of SINGLE SITES:	10	MAX SPUR:	44 feet
		MAX STAY:	16 days
		ELEVATION:	6680 feet

37 North Van Houton
Jackson • lat 45°14'30" lon 113°29'00"

DESCRIPTION: CG set in lodgepole forest with views of Van Houton Lake and surrounding low hills. Fish from lake. Snow can occur in summer. Supplies at Wisdom. Rarely full. Nez Perce National Historical Trail next to CG. Nearby trails that access the Bitterroot Mountain Range. 4WD recommended.

GETTING THERE: From Jackson go S on state HWY 278 approx. 1 mi. to Skinner Meadows Road. Go S on Skinner Meadows approx. 10 mi. to North Van Houton CG.

SINGLE RATE:	No fee	OPEN DATES:	June-Sept
# of SINGLE SITES:	3	MAX SPUR:	15 feet
		MAX STAY:	16 days
		ELEVATION:	6700 feet

38 Orofino
Deer Lodge • lat 46°15'40" lon 112°36'38"

DESCRIPTION: This CG is situated in a douglas fir stand. Warm sunny days, cool nights. Grant Kohrs National Historic Site is nearby. Supplies and groceries can be found in Deer Lodge. Deer, elk, moose, occasional bears, and small wildlife in area. CG receives moderate use. Bring your own firewood.

GETTING THERE: From Deer Lodge go SE on forest route 82 approx. 9 mi. to Orofino CG.

SINGLE RATE:	No fee	OPEN DATES:	May-Sept
# of SINGLE SITES:	10	MAX SPUR:	22 feet
GROUP RATE:	$25	MAX STAY:	16 days
# of GROUP SITES:	1	ELEVATION:	6400 feet

39 Pettengill
Wise River • lat 45°40'30" lon 113°03'53"

DESCRIPTION: CG in a lodgepole pine forest setting close to Wise River. This CG is primarily used during winter for snowmobiling. Fishing in the Wise River and Pattengill Creek for trout. Supplies at Wise River. No designated trails, just venture off into the forest to explore.

GETTING THERE: From Wise River go SW on primary forest route 73 (Pioneer Mountains Scenic Byway) approx. 10 mi. to Pettengill CG.

SINGLE RATE:	$7	OPEN DATES:	May-Sept
# of SINGLE SITES:	3	MAX SPUR:	16 feet
		MAX STAY:	14 days
		ELEVATION:	6260 feet

40 Philipsburg Bay
Anaconda • lat 46°12'23" lon 113°17'24"

DESCRIPTION: Located among lodgepole pine on Georgetown Lake. Expect rain during summer. Fish, boat, and ski the lake. Basic supplies at nearby stores around lake. Moderate to heavy use. Elk, moose, and deer in area. Gather firewood or buy from concessionaire during summer. Snow may affect dates.

GETTING THERE: From Philipsburg go S on state HWY 1 approx. 10.6 mi. to Georgetown Lake Road #406. Go W on 406 approx. 1.7 mi. to Pilipsburg Bay CG.

SINGLE RATE:	$10	OPEN DATES:	May-Oct
# of SINGLE SITES:	69	MAX SPUR:	32 feet
		MAX STAY:	14 days
		ELEVATION:	6400 feet

 Campground has hosts   **Reservable sites**   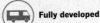 **Accessible facilities**   **Fully developed**   **Semi-developed**   **Rustic facilities**

NOTE: Open dates listed are typical. Actual dates are dependent on conditions such as snow pack.

41 Pigeon Creek
Butte • lat 45°48'03" lon 112°23'56"

DESCRIPTION: This CG is set in a thick spruce forest, Pigeon Creek runs through CG. Stream fish for trout. Mild days, cold nights. Historic mining area. Supplies and groceries at Whitehall or Butte. Elk, deer, grouse, and small wildlife. Light use. Gather firewood locally. Used as 4X4 access to forest.

GETTING THERE: From Butte go S on state HWY 2 to Toll Canyon. Go S on forest route 668 approx. 3.5 mi. to Pigeon Creek CG.

SINGLE RATE:	No fee	OPEN DATES:	May-Sept
# of SINGLE SITES:	8		
		MAX STAY:	16 days
		ELEVATION:	6150 feet

42 Piney
Anaconda • lat 46°11'46" lon 113°18'05"

DESCRIPTION: Situated among lodgepole pine adjacent to Georgetown Lake. Boating, fishing, and skiing on the lake. Mild days with rain are common all summer. Supplies can be found at several nearby stores. Elk, moose, and deer in area. Moderate use. Firewood sold in summer. Snow may affect dates.

GETTING THERE: From Philipsburg go S on state HWY 1 approx. 10. mi. to route 406 (Georgetown Lake Road). Go W on 406 approx. 2.5 mi. to Piney CG.

SINGLE RATE:	$10	OPEN DATES:	May-Sept
# of SINGLE SITES:	48	MAX SPUR:	32 feet
		MAX STAY:	14 days
		ELEVATION:	6400 feet

43 Pintler
Wisdom • lat 45°50'20" lon 113°26'08"

DESCRIPTION: CG situated in a rustic lodgepole pine setting with views of Pintler Creek and Pintler Lake. Fishing for trout in both creek and lake. Hunting when in season. No motorboats permitted on Pintler Lake. Supplies at Wisdom. Campers may gather firewood locally. Pintler Creek trail is nearby.

GETTING THERE: From Wisdom go W on state HWY 43 approx. 1.5 mi. to Lower North Fork Road. Go N on Lower North Fork Road approx. 17 mi. to forest route 185. Go N on 185 approx. 4.5 mi. to Pintler CG.

SINGLE RATE:	No fee	OPEN DATES:	May-Sept
# of SINGLE SITES:	2	MAX SPUR:	16 feet
		MAX STAY:	14 days
		ELEVATION:	6363 feet

44 Potosi
Harrison • lat 45°34'18" lon 111°54'47"

DESCRIPTION: This CG is in a timbered setting of douglas fir and pine. Fish for trout from Willow Creek nearby. Supplies are available at Harrison. Deer, elk, moose, and bears can be seen in the area. Gather firewood locally. There are designated trails in the area. Drinkable water available on site.

GETTING THERE: From Harrison go SW on Willow Creek Road to Pony. At Pony take Potosi Hot Springs Road approx. 8 mi. to Potosi CG.

SINGLE RATE:	No fee	OPEN DATES:	June-Sept
# of SINGLE SITES:	15	MAX SPUR:	32 feet
		MAX STAY:	16 days
		ELEVATION:	6248 feet

45 Price Creek
Dillon • lat 44°52'30" lon 112°25'47"

DESCRIPTION: CG is located in pine on Price Creek. Fishing for brook trout in creek. Deer, elk and moose in area. Busy on summer holidays and weekends.

GETTING THERE: From Dillon go S on I-15 3 mi. to HWY 278. Go W on 278 approx. 22 mi. to Pioneer Mtns Scenic Byway Rd 73. Go N on 73 approx. 16 mi. to forest route 2406. Go on 2406 1/4 mi. to Price Creek CG.

SINGLE RATE:	$8	OPEN DATES:	June-Sept
# of SINGLE SITES:	28	MAX SPUR:	30 feet
		MAX STAY:	16 days
		ELEVATION:	7000 feet

46 Racetrack
Deer Lodge • lat 46°16'52" lon 112°56'12"

DESCRIPTION: Shaded by large douglas firs on Racetrack Creek. Fish for cutthroat and brook trout. Grant Kohrs Nat'l Hist. Site and old prison with Town Car Collection nearby. Grocs. at Deer Lodge. Elk, moose, and bears in area. Bring own firewood. ATV, mountain biking, hiking, and horse trails.

GETTING THERE: From Warm Springs go N on I-90 to exit 195 (Racetrack). Go W on forest route 169 approx. 11 mi. to Racetrack CG.

SINGLE RATE:	$5	OPEN DATES:	May-Sept
# of SINGLE SITES:	12	MAX SPUR:	22 feet
		MAX STAY:	16 days
# of GROUP SITES:	1	ELEVATION:	5400 feet

47 Reservoir Lake
Dillon • lat 45°07'18" lon 113°27'12"

DESCRIPTION: This CG is situated among pine set on Reservior Lake. Good fishing in lake. Wildlife in the area includes deer, elk, and moose. Hunting when in season. Gather firewood locally. RV facilities are available. CG tends to be busy on weekends and holidays in the summer. Some trails in area.

GETTING THERE: From Clark Canyon Reservoir take county route 324 approx. 17 mi. to primary forest route 3909. Go W on 3909 to primary forest route 181. Go N on 181 approx. 14 mi. to Reservoir Lake CG.

SINGLE RATE:	No fee	OPEN DATES:	June-Sept
# of SINGLE SITES:	16	MAX SPUR:	16 feet
GROUP RATE:	Varies	MAX STAY:	14 days
# of GROUP SITES:	1	ELEVATION:	7000 feet

48 Sacajawea Memorial Camp
Dillon • lat 44°58'14" lon 113°26'35"

DESCRIPTION: CG is situated among pine in the location where Lewis and Clark once camped. LandC believed this to be the headwaters of the Missouri River-they were wrong. Wildlife in the area includes deer, elk, and moose. CG tends to be busy on holidays and weekends in the summer. Primitive camping.

GETTING THERE: From Clark Canyon Reservoir go W on county route 324 approx. 17 mi. to primary forest route 3909. Go W on 3909 approx. 13 mi. to Sacajawea Memorial Camp CG.

SINGLE RATE:	No fee	OPEN DATES:	June-Sept
		MAX STAY:	14 days
		ELEVATION:	7400 feet

49 South Van Houton
Jackson • lat 45°14'30" lon 113°29'00"

DESCRIPTION: CG in a lodgepole forest setting with views of Van Houton Lake and surrounding hills. Snow anytime during the year. Fish from lake. Nez Perce National Historical Trail goes past the CG. Supplies at Wisdom. CG is rarely full. Gather firewood locally. Numerous trails in the area. 4WD recomended.

GETTING THERE: From Jackson go S on state HWY 278 approx. 1 mi. to Skinner Meadows Road. Go S on Skinner Meadows approx. 10 mi. to South Van Houton CG.

SINGLE RATE:	No fee	OPEN DATES:	June-Sept
# of SINGLE SITES:	3	MAX SPUR:	20 feet
		MAX STAY:	16 days
		ELEVATION:	6700 feet

50 Spillway
Anaconda • lat 46°07'39" lon 113°22'57"

DESCRIPTION: Located in lodgepole pine near East Fork Reservoir. Boat and fish the reservoir. Expect rain during summer. Supplies 18 mi. away at Philisburg. Elk, moose, and deer frequent the area. Gather firewood locally. East Fork Trail Head for Anaconda Pintler Wilderness is 3 mi. away.

GETTING THERE: From Philipsburg go S on state HWY 1 6.4 mi. to state HWY 38. Go W on 38 6 mi. to forest route 672. Go S on 672 5.3 mi. to forest route 5141. Go S on 5141 1.2 mi. to Spillway CG.

SINGLE RATE:	No fee	OPEN DATES:	May-Nov
# of SINGLE SITES:	13	MAX SPUR:	22 feet
		MAX STAY:	16 days
		ELEVATION:	6000 feet

 Campground has hosts   Reservable sites   Accessible facilities   Fully developed   Semi-developed   Rustic facilities

NOTE: Open dates listed are typical. Actual dates are dependent on conditions such as snow pack.

51 Steel Creek
Wisdom • lat 45°35'59" lon 113°20'25"

DESCRIPTION: CG in a lodgepole forest setting with views of Steel Creek and surrounding hills. Snow anytime during the year. Fish from creek. Historical Big Hole National Battlefield nearby. Supplies at Wisdom. CG is rarely full. Campers may gather firewood locally. Many trails by CG.

GETTING THERE: From Wisdom go N on state HWY 43 approx. 1 mi. to Steel Creek Road. Go E on Steel Creek Road approx. 6 mi. to Steel Creek CG.

SINGLE RATE:	No fee	OPEN DATES:	June-Sept
# of SINGLE SITES:	9	MAX SPUR:	30 feet
		MAX STAY:	16 days
		ELEVATION:	6200 feet

52 Stony Creek
Philipsburg • lat 46°20'57" lon 113°36'24"

DESCRIPTION: CG situated on Stony Creek among lodgepole pine and spruce with willow underbrush. Stream fish Stony Creek and nearby Rock Creek. Supplies can be found in Philipsburg. Wildlife in the area includes elk, moose, deer, and bighorn sheep. Gather firewood locally. Receives moderate use.

GETTING THERE: From Philipsburg go N on state HWY 1 0.2 mi. to county route 348. Go W on 348 12.5 mi. to county route 102. Go W on 102 4.6 mi. to forest route 241. Go S on 241 0.1 mi. to Stony Creek CG.

SINGLE RATE:	No fee	OPEN DATES:	Apr-Nov
# of SINGLE SITES:	10	MAX SPUR:	32 feet
		MAX STAY:	16 days
		ELEVATION:	4500 feet

53 Toll Mountain
Butte • lat 45°50'53" lon 112°21'57"

DESCRIPTION: CG is situated among douglas fir and aspen. No fishing. Mild to cool days, cold nights. Supplies 10 mi. to Whitehall, or at Butte. Elk, deer, upland grouse, and small wildlife in area. Moderate use. Firewood may be gathered locally. No hiking in nearby vicinity. CG was reconstructed in 1995.

GETTING THERE: From Butte go S on state HWY 2 approx. 13 mi. to forest route 240. Go N on 240 following signs to Toll Mountain CG.

SINGLE RATE:	$5	OPEN DATES:	May-Sept
# of SINGLE SITES:	7	MAX SPUR:	32 feet
		MAX STAY:	16 days
		ELEVATION:	5200 feet

54 Twin Lakes
Wisdom • lat 45°24'40" lon 113°41'13"

DESCRIPTION: CG is in a pine forest on Twin Lakes. Fish Twin Lakes for trout, arctic grayling, and mountain whitefish. Boat ramp at CG. Historical Big Hole Natn'l Battlefield by Wisdom. Supplies at Wisdom. Trails in area are: Big Lake Creek Trail and access to Continental Divide National Scenic Trail.

GETTING THERE: From Wisdom go S on state HWY 278 7 mi. to county route 1290. Go W on 1209 approx. 8 mi. to forest route 945. Go S on 945 5 mi. to forest route 183. Go SW on 183 approx. 6 mi. to Twin Lakes CG.

SINGLE RATE:	$5	OPEN DATES:	June-Sept
# of SINGLE SITES:	18	MAX SPUR:	32 feet
		MAX STAY:	16 days
		ELEVATION:	7252 feet

55 Upper Spring Hill
Anaconda • lat 46°10'00" lon 113°10'00"

DESCRIPTION: CG set in a heavily timbered lodgepole pine site. Boat and shore fish George Town Lake. Historic mining towns of Anaconda, Philipsburg, and Butte nearby. Supplies 15 mi. away in Anaconda. Deer, elk, moose, and big horn sheep in area. Buy wood from host. Fills quickly, come early.

GETTING THERE: From Georgetown Lake go W on state HWY 1 approx. 5 mi. to Upper Spring Hill CG.

SINGLE RATE:	$8	OPEN DATES:	May-Sept
# of SINGLE SITES:	16	MAX SPUR:	22 feet
		MAX STAY:	14 days
		ELEVATION:	6400 feet

56 Wade Lake
West Yellowstone • lat 44°53'13" lon 111°34'53"

DESCRIPTION: CG is in a forested setting of douglas fir and pine. Fish for trout from Wade Lake nearby. Supplies are available at West Yellowstone. Deer, elk, moose, and bears in the area. Hunting when in season. Campers may gather firewood. There are designated trails in the area. No drinking water on site.

GETTING THERE: From West Yellowstone go N on US HWY 191 8 mi. to US HWY 287. Go W on 287 27 mi. to forest route 241. Go S on 241 3.5 mi. to forest route 572. Go W on 572 and follow signs to Wade Lake CG.

SINGLE RATE:	$8	OPEN DATES:	June-Sept
# of SINGLE SITES:	30	MAX SPUR:	24 feet
		MAX STAY:	16 days
		ELEVATION:	5960 feet

57 West Fork
Cameron • lat 44°53'13" lon 111°34'53"

DESCRIPTION: CG is situated in a wooded stand of douglas fir and pine. Fish for trout from the West Fork of Madison River nearby. Supplies at Cameron. Deer, elk, moose, and bears in the area. Campers may gather firewood locally. There are no designated trails in the area. Drinking water available on site.

GETTING THERE: From Cameron go S on US HWY 287 approx. 24 mi. to county route 8381. Go SW on 8381 approx. 1 mi. to West Fork CG.

SINGLE RATE:	$7	OPEN DATES:	June-Sept
# of SINGLE SITES:	7		
		MAX STAY:	16 days
		ELEVATION:	5880 feet

58 West Fork Rest Area
Cameron • lat 44°54'07" lon 111°35'33"

DESCRIPTION: CG is situated in an open stand of douglas fir and pine. Fish for trout from West Fork of the Madison River nearby. Supplies available at Cameron. Deer, elk, moose, and bears in the area. Gather firewood locally. There are designated trails in the area. No drinking water available on site.

GETTING THERE: From Cameron go S on US HWY 287 approx. 24 mi. to county route 8381. Go SW on 8381 West Fork Rest Area CG.

SINGLE RATE:	No fee	OPEN DATES:	July-Oct
# of SINGLE SITES:	1		
		MAX STAY:	16 days
		ELEVATION:	5870 feet

59 Whitehouse
Butte • lat 46°15'30" lon 112°28'45"

DESCRIPTION: In park like setting of fir and aspen on Boulder River. Hot days, cool nights, expect rain in August. Trout fish the river. Supplies 15 mi. away at Boulder. Elk, deer, and upland grouse. Mild use turning heavy during fall hunting. No firewood available. Popular for many miles of primitive roads for 4X4 use.

GETTING THERE: From Butte go N on I-15 to exit 151. Go W on forest route 82 approx. 7 mi. to Whitehouse CG.

SINGLE RATE:	No fee	OPEN DATES:	May-Dec
# of SINGLE SITES:	5	MAX SPUR:	22 feet
GROUP RATE:	Varies	MAX STAY:	16 days
		ELEVATION:	5400 feet

60 Willow
Wise River • lat 45°38'11" lon 113°04'35"

DESCRIPTION: This CG is situated in a dense forest of lodgepole pine and spruce, close to the Wise River. Fish for trout from the river. Wildlife in the area includes deer, elk, and moose. Hunting when in season. Supplies can be found in the town of Wise River. No designated trails in area.

GETTING THERE: From Wise River go SW on primary forest route 73 (Pioneer Mountains Scenic Byway) approx. 14 mi. to Willow CG.

SINGLE RATE:	$8	OPEN DATES:	June-Sept
# of SINGLE SITES:	6	MAX SPUR:	16 feet
		MAX STAY:	16 days
		ELEVATION:	6580 feet

 Campground has hosts   **Reservable sites**   **Accessible facilities**   **Fully developed**   **Semi-developed**   **Rustic facilities**

BITTERROOT NATIONAL FOREST

The Bitterroot National Forest encompasses 1.6 million-acres in southwest Montana and Idaho. Half of the forest is dedicated to the largest expanse of continuous pristine wilderness in the lower 48 states—the Selway, Bitterroot, Frank Church-River of No Return, and the Anaconda-Pintler.

To the west, drainages carved by glaciers, form 30 steep canyons that open into the valley floor. To the east, the Sapphire Range presents a gentler horizon. Elevation ranges from 3,200 feet at the north end of the Bitterroot Valley to Trapper Peak at 10,157 feet to the south.

The abundance of natural resources offers a wide range of opportunities for backcountry recreation, grazing, fishing, timber, and minerals. Hike and ride on more than 1,600 miles of trails, camp at 18 developed campgrounds, and raft and kayak on the area's many lakes and streams. In the winter enjoy snowmobiling and alpine and cross-country skiing.

The forest is also home to a variety of wildlife such as deer, elk, bighorn sheep, mountain goats, mountain lions, moose and black bears.

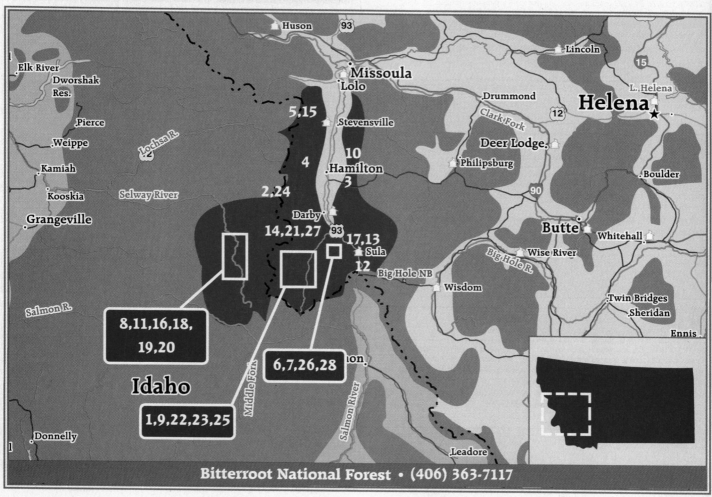

Bitterroot National Forest • (406) 363-7117

1 Alta
Darby • lat 45°37'27" lon 114°18'04"

DESCRIPTION: This CG is situated in a stand of old-growth ponderosa with a douglas fir understory with beautiful views of the West Fork River. OK trout fishing in the river. Campers may gather firewood locally. Occasionally some deer will pass through the area. CG is seldom full.

GETTING THERE: From Darby go S on US HWY 93 approx. 4 mi. to county route 473. Go S on 473 approx. 25 mi. to Alta CG.

SINGLE RATE:	$5	OPEN DATES:	Yearlong
# of SINGLE SITES:	15	MAX SPUR:	50 feet
		MAX STAY:	14 days
		ELEVATION:	4970 feet

2 Bear Creek Pass
Hamilton • lat 46°07'30" lon 114°30'00"

DESCRIPTION: This CG is situated among subalpine fir and lodgepole pine at Bear Creek Pass. Various small wildlife, deer, elk, and moose can be seen in the area around the CG. Gather firewood locally, or bring your own. CG is seldom full. Some trails area in the surrounding area.

GETTING THERE: From Hamilton go S on US HWY 93 approx. 9 mi. to county route 76. Go S on 76 approx. 2 mi. to forest route 429 and follow 429 approx. 16 mi. to Bear Creek Pass CG.

SINGLE RATE:	No fee	OPEN DATES:	July-Sept
# of SINGLE SITES:	6	MAX SPUR:	32 feet
		MAX STAY:	14 days
		ELEVATION:	6600 feet

3 Black Bear
Hamilton • lat 46°10'00" lon 113°55'00"

DESCRIPTION: This CG is situated among ponderosa pine and douglas fir along Skalkaho Creek. Fishing in creek. Wildlife in the area includes deer, elk, and moose. Hunting when in season. Gather firewood locally, or bring your own. CG tends to be busy on weekends in the summer. Some trails in area.

GETTING THERE: From Hamilton go E on county route 38 approx. 16 mi. to Black Bear CG.

SINGLE RATE:	No fee	OPEN DATES:	May-Sept
# of SINGLE SITES:	10	MAX SPUR:	18 feet
		MAX STAY:	14 days
		ELEVATION:	6000 feet

4 Blodgett Canyon
Hamilton • lat 46°18'00" lon 114°15'00"

DESCRIPTION: This CG is situated in mixed douglas fir and grand fir with some underbrush along Bloggett Creek. Fishing in creek. Wildlife in the area includes deer, elk, and moose. CG tends to be busy on weekends and holidays in the summer. Some trails are in the surrounding area.

GETTING THERE: From Hamilton go W on Blodgett Canyon Road approx. 4 mi. to Blodgett Canyon CG.

SINGLE RATE:	No fee	OPEN DATES:	Apr-Sept
# of SINGLE SITES:	6	MAX SPUR:	25 feet
		MAX STAY:	14 days
		ELEVATION:	4500 feet

5 Charles Waters Memorial
Stevensville • lat 46°34'00" lon 114°09'00"

DESCRIPTION: CG is located in ponderosa pine with grand fir and douglas fir along Bass Creek and adjacent to a large meadow. No, there are no bass in the creek. Full Weekends and holidays. Several trails in area including; Bass Creek Trail, Fitness Trail, and Nature Trail. Bears are occasionally a problem.

GETTING THERE: From Stevensville go N on US HWY 93 approx. 5 mi. to county route 20. Go W on 20 approx. 3 mi. to Charles Waters Memorial CG.

SINGLE RATE:	$7	OPEN DATES:	Apr-Sept
# of SINGLE SITES:	22	MAX SPUR:	35 feet
		MAX STAY:	14 days
		ELEVATION:	3300 feet

6 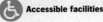 Crazy Creek
Darby • lat 45°48'00" lon 114°04'00"

DESCRIPTION: This CG is siuated among ponderosa pine and douglas fir on Warm Springs Creek. Fishing in creek. Wildlife in the area includes deer, elk, and moose. Hunting when in season. Gather firewood locally, or bring your own. CG is seldom busy. Some trails are in the surrounding area.

GETTING THERE: From Darby go S on US HWY 93 approx. 12 mi. to forest route 101D. Go S on 101D approx. 3.5 mi. to Crazy Creek CG.

SINGLE RATE:	$7	OPEN DATES:	May-Sept
# of SINGLE SITES:	7	MAX SPUR:	26 feet
		MAX STAY:	14 days
		ELEVATION:	5100 feet

7 Crazy Creek Horse Facility
Darby • lat 45°48'00" lon 114°04'00"

DESCRIPTION: This CG is situated among ponderosa pine and douglas fir on Warm Springs Creek. Fishing in creek. Wildlife in the area includes deer, elk, and moose. Hunting when in season. Gather firewood locally, or bring your own. CG is seldom busy. Some trails are in the surrounding area.

GETTING THERE: From Darby go S on US HWY 93 approx. 12 mi. to forest route 101D. Go S on 101D approx. 3.5 mi. to Crazy Creek Horse Facility CG.

SINGLE RATE:	$7	OPEN DATES:	May-Sept
# of SINGLE SITES:	12	MAX SPUR:	26 feet
		MAX STAY:	14 days
		ELEVATION:	5100 feet

8 Deep Creek
Darby • lat 45°42'00" lon 114°43'30"

DESCRIPTION: This CG is situated in a stand of old-growth ponderosa with a douglas fir understory on the Selway River. Excellent catch and release trout fishing. Gather firewood locally. Usually full September through November during the hunting season. Several hiking trails in the area.

GETTING THERE: From Darby go S on US HWY 93 approx. 4 mi. to county route 473. Go S on 473 approx. 12 mi. to primary forest route 468. Go W on 468 approx. 26 mi. to Deep Creek CG.

SINGLE RATE:	No fee	OPEN DATES:	Yearlong
# of SINGLE SITES:	3		
		MAX STAY:	14 days
		ELEVATION:	4870 feet

9 Fales Flat Group Camp
Darby • lat 45°44'22" lon 114°26'33"

DESCRIPTION: This CG is situated in a stand of lodgepole pine with some douglas fir on the Nez Perce Fork of the Bitterroot River. Some trout fishing on the river. Various small wildlife and deer in area. Gather firewood locally. CG tends to be busy on holidays. Adjacent to Sheephead trail head.

GETTING THERE: From Darby go S on US HWY 93 approx. 4 mi. to county route 473. Go S on 473 approx. 12 mi. to primary forest route 468. Go W on 468 approx. 8 mi. to Fales Flat Group Camp CG.

SINGLE RATE:	No fee	OPEN DATES:	Yearlong
# of SINGLE SITES:	12		
		MAX STAY:	14 days
		ELEVATION:	6300 feet

10 Gold Creek
Stevensville • lat 46°23'00" lon 113°55'00"

DESCRIPTION: This CG is situated among lodgepole pine with an understory of spruce. Set along Burnt Fork Creek. Fishing in creek, check regulations for the area. Various small wildlife and deer are in the area. Hunting when in season. CG receives light use. CG is adjacent to Gold Greek Trail.

GETTING THERE: From Stevensville go E on state HWY 372 to county route 27. Go S on 27 to Gold Creek CG.

SINGLE RATE:	No fee	OPEN DATES:	Apr-Sept
# of SINGLE SITES:	4	MAX SPUR:	25 feet
		MAX STAY:	14 days
		ELEVATION:	5000 feet

 Campground has hosts 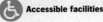 Reservable sites Accessible facilities Fully developed Semi-developed Rustic facilities

11 Indian Creek
Darby • lat 45°47'00" lon 114°46'00"

DESCRIPTION: This CG is situated in a stand of old-growth ponderosa pine on the Selway River. Check fishing regulations Various small wildlife and deer in the area. Gather firewood locally. Busy during the hunting season from September through the end of November. CG is adjacent to Indian Ridge Trailhead.

GETTING THERE: From Darby go S on US HWY 93 4 mi. to county route 473. Go S on 473 approx. 12 mi. to forest route 468. Go W on 468 30 mi. to forest route 6223. Go N on 6223 approx. 5 mi. to Indian Creek CG.

SINGLE RATE:	No fee	OPEN DATES:	Yearlong
# of SINGLE SITES:	8		
		MAX STAY:	14 days
		ELEVATION:	4700 feet

16 Magruder Crossing
Darby • lat 45°44'00" lon 114°46'00"

DESCRIPTION: This CG is situated in stand of logdepole pine and with an understory of douglas fir along Selway River. CG is set near some trailheads. Gather firewood locally. Various small wildlife and deer in the area. CG tends to fill up during the hunting season from September 1 through November 31.

GETTING THERE: From Darby go S on US HWY 93 approx. 4 mi. to county route 473. Go S on 473 approx. 12 mi. to primary forest route 468. Go W on 468 approx. 30 mi. to Magruder Crossing CG.

SINGLE RATE:	No fee	OPEN DATES:	Yearlong
# of SINGLE SITES:	6		
		MAX STAY:	14 days
		ELEVATION:	4750 feet

12 Indian Trees
Sula • lat 45°45'21" lon 113°57'12"

DESCRIPTION: This CG is situated among ponderosa pine. Deer, elk, moose, and various small wildlife can be seen in the surrounding area. Hunting when in season. Minimal supplies and groceries can be found approx. 4 mi. away in Sula. CG tends to be busy on holidays and weekends in the summer.

GETTING THERE: From Sula go S on US HWY 93 approx. 4 mi. to Indian Trees CG.

SINGLE RATE:	$9	OPEN DATES:	May-Sept
# of SINGLE SITES:	16	MAX SPUR:	50 feet
		MAX STAY:	14 days
		ELEVATION:	6800 feet

17 Martin Creek
Sula • lat 45°56'00" lon 113°40'00"

DESCRIPTION: This CG is situated in a ponderosa pine and douglas fir forest on Martin Creek. Good fising in creek. Summer weekends tend to be busy. Wildlife in the area includes deer, elk, and moose. Hunting when in season. Gather firewood locally or bring your own. Several trails are in the area.

GETTING THERE: From Sula go E on county route 101 approx. 16 mi. to Martin Creek CG.

SINGLE RATE:	$7	OPEN DATES:	May-Sept
# of SINGLE SITES:	7	MAX SPUR:	50 feet
		MAX STAY:	14 days
		ELEVATION:	6500 feet

13 Jennings
Sula • lat 45°53'00" lon 113°48'00"

DESCRIPTION: This CG is situated among ponderosa pine and douglas fir on the East Fork of the Bitterroot River. Fishing in river, check regulations for the area. Minimal supplies and groceries can be found in Sula. Wildlife in the area includes deer, elk, and moose. Hunting when in season. CG is seldom busy.

GETTING THERE: From Sula go E on county route 101 approx. 10 mi. to Jennings CG.

SINGLE RATE:	No fee	OPEN DATES:	May-Sept
# of SINGLE SITES:	4	MAX SPUR:	20 feet
		MAX STAY:	14 days
		ELEVATION:	5600 feet

18 Observation Point
Darby • lat 45°40'00" lon 114°49'00"

DESCRIPTION: This CG is situated among lodgepole pine with some subalpine fir on the Continental Divide. Gather firewood locally or bring your own. Various small wildlife, deer, and moose in the area. CG tends to fill up during the hunting season from September through November.

GETTING THERE: From Darby go S on US HWY 93 approx. 4 mi. to county route 473. Go S on 473 approx. 12 mi. to primary forest route 468. Go W on 468 approx. 38 mi. to Observation Point CG.

SINGLE RATE:	No fee	OPEN DATES:	Yearlong
# of SINGLE SITES:	4		
		MAX STAY:	14 days
		ELEVATION:	6800 feet

14 Lake Como Campground
Darby • lat 46°04'04" lon 114°14'55"

DESCRIPTION: This CG is situated among ponderosa pine and douglas fir on Lake Como. Fishing in lake. CG tends to be busy on weekends and holidays in the summer. Wildlife in the area includes deer, elk, and moose. Hunting when in season. Gather firewood locally. Several trails in area.

GETTING THERE: From Darby go N on US HWY 93 approx. 5 mi. to county route 82 (Rock Creek Road). Go W on 82 approx. 4 mi. to Lake Como Campground.

SINGLE RATE:	$12	OPEN DATES:	May-Sept
# of SINGLE SITES:	12	MAX SPUR:	50 feet
		MAX STAY:	14 days
		ELEVATION:	4245 feet

19 Paradise
Darby • lat 45°52'00" lon 114°46'00"

DESCRIPTION: This CG is located in a stand of old-growth ponderosa pine on Whitecap Creek at the end of the Selway River Road. Great fishing for trout. CG tends to fill up during the hunting season. Campers may gather their firewood locally. CG is adjacent to Whitecap Creek Trail.

GETTING THERE: From Darby go S on US HWY 93 approx. 4 mi. to county route 473. Go S on 473 12 mi. to forest route 468. Go W on 468 approx. 30 mi. to forest route 6223. Go N on 6223 approx. 11 mi. to Paradise CG.

SINGLE RATE:	No fee	OPEN DATES:	Yearlong
# of SINGLE SITES:	7		
		MAX STAY:	14 days
		ELEVATION:	4400 feet

15 Larry Creek Group Camp
Stevensville • lat 46°34'00" lon 114°07'30"

DESCRIPTION: This CG is situated among ponderosa pine with grand fir and douglas fir along Larry Creek and adjacent to a large meadow. Full Weekends and holidays. Several trails in area, including; Bass creek Trail, Fitness Trail, and Nature Trail. Occasional bear problems.

GETTING THERE: From Stevensville go N on US HWY 93 approx. 5 mi. to county route 20. Go W on 20 approx. 3 mi. to Charles Waters Memorial then N approx. 1 mi. to Larry Creek Group Camp CG.

SINGLE RATE:	$35	OPEN DATES:	Apr-Sept
# of SINGLE SITES:	3	MAX SPUR:	25 feet
		MAX STAY:	14 days
# of GROUP SITES:	1	ELEVATION:	3300 feet

20 Raven Creek
Darby • lat 45°46'00" lon 114°47'00"

DESCRIPTION: This CG is situated among lodgepole pine and douglas fir along the Selway river. Fishing on the river. Check fishing regulations. Low development level. Campers may gather their firewood locally. CG tends to fill up during the hunting season from September through November.

GETTING THERE: From Darby go S on US HWY 93 approx. 4 mi. to county route 473. Go S on 473 12 mi. to forest route 468. Go W on 468 30 mi. to forest route 6223. Go N on 6223 approx. 3 mi. to Raven Creek CG.

SINGLE RATE:	No fee	OPEN DATES:	Yearlong
# of SINGLE SITES:	2		
		MAX STAY:	14 days
		ELEVATION:	4725 feet

 Campground has hosts   Reservable sites   Accessible facilities   Fully developed   Semi-developed   Rustic facilities

NOTE: Open dates listed are typical. Actual dates are dependent on conditions such as snow pack.

21 Rock Creek Horse Camp
Darby • lat 46˚04'04" lon 114˚13'00"

DESCRIPTION: CG is situated among ponderosa pine and douglas fir on Como Lake. OK fishing in lake. Other CGs at Como lake fill on weekends and holidays but Rock Creek Horse camp seldom does. Wildlife in the area includes deer, elk, and moose. Hunting when in season. Several trails in area.

GETTING THERE: From Darby go N on US HWY 93 approx. 5 mi. to county route 82 (Rock Creek Road). Go W on 82 approx. 4 mi. to Lake Como and follow signs to Rock Creek Horse Camp CG.

SINGLE RATE:	$4	OPEN DATES:	May-Sept
# of SINGLE SITES:	11	MAX SPUR:	50 feet
		MAX STAY:	14 days
		ELEVATION:	4245 feet

22 Rombo Creek
Darby • lat 45˚46'00" lon 114˚17'00"

DESCRIPTION: This CG is located in a stand of old-growth ponderosa pine with an understory of douglas fir along Westfork River. Fishing in the river, check regulations. Gather firewood locally. CG tends to be busy on holidays and weekends in the summer. Usually full in mid July.

GETTING THERE: From Darby go S on US HWY 93 approx. 4 mi. to county route 473. Go S on 473 approx. 15 mi. to Rombo Creek CG.

SINGLE RATE:	$7	OPEN DATES:	May-Nov
# of SINGLE SITES:	15	MAX SPUR:	40 feet
		MAX STAY:	14 days
		ELEVATION:	4400 feet

23 Sam Billings Memorial
Darby • lat 45˚49'00" lon 114˚15'30"

DESCRIPTION: This CG is located in stand of old-growth ponderosa pine along Boulder Creek. Possible fishing in creek, check regulations. Wildlife in the area includes deer, elk, and moose. CG tends to fill up quickly on holidays and weekends in the summer. Adjacent to Boulder Creek Trailhead.

GETTING THERE: From Darby go S on US HWY 93 approx. 4 mi. to county route 473. Go S on 473 approx. 12 mi. to forest route 5731. Take 5731 approx. 1 mi. to Sam Billings Memorial CG.

SINGLE RATE:	No fee	OPEN DATES:	Yearlong
# of SINGLE SITES:	11	MAX SPUR:	30 feet
		MAX STAY:	14 days
		ELEVATION:	4200 feet

24 Schumaker
Hamilton • lat 46˚09'00" lon 114˚30'00"

DESCRIPTION: This CG is situated among subalpine fir and lodgepole pine on Twin Lakes Reservoir. Good fishing on reservoir. CG is seldom full. Wildlife in the area includes deer, elk, and moose. Gather firewood locally or bring your own. Some trails are in the surrounding area.

GETTING THERE: From Hamilton go S on US HWY 93 9 mi. to county route 76. Go S on 76 approx. 2 mi. to forest route 429 and follow 429 15 mi. to forest route 5605. Go N on 5605 approx. 2 mi. to Schumaker CG.

SINGLE RATE:	No fee	OPEN DATES:	July-Sept
# of SINGLE SITES:	5	MAX SPUR:	18 feet
		MAX STAY:	14 days
		ELEVATION:	6465 feet

25 Slate Creek
Darby • lat 45˚40'00" lon 114˚17'00"

DESCRIPTION: This CG is located in a stand of old-growth ponderosa pine along Slate Creek and across the HWY from Painted Rocks Lake. Fishing in creek and lake. Campers may gather their firewood locally. Various small wildlife and deer in the area. CG tends to fill up on holidays and weekends in the summer.

GETTING THERE: From Darby go S on US HWY 93 approx. 4 mi. to county route 473. Go S on 473 approx. 21 mi. to Slate Creek CG.

SINGLE RATE:	No fee	OPEN DATES:	Yearlong
# of SINGLE SITES:	9		
		MAX STAY:	14 days
		ELEVATION:	4726 feet

26 Spring Gulch
Darby • lat 45˚51'00" lon 114˚01'00"

DESCRIPTION: This CG is situated among ponderosa pine on the Main Bitterroot River. Good fishing on the river. Various small wildlife, deer, elk, and moose can be seen in the area around the CG. Tends to fill up quickly on weekends and holidays. Some trails are in the surrounding area.

GETTING THERE: From Darby go S on US HWY 93 approx. 13 mi. to Spring Gulch CG.

SINGLE RATE:	$11	OPEN DATES:	May-Sept
# of SINGLE SITES:	11	MAX SPUR:	50 feet
		MAX STAY:	14 days
		ELEVATION:	4475 feet

27 Upper Como Campground
Darby • lat 46˚04'04" lon 114˚14'30"

DESCRIPTION: This CG is situated among ponderosa pine and douglas fir on Como Lake. OK fishing on the lake. CG tends to be busy on weekends and holidays in the summer. Wildlife in the area includes deer, elk, and moose. Gather firewood locally. Several trails in the surrounding area.

GETTING THERE: From Darby go N on US HWY 93 approx. 5 mi. to county route 82 (Rock Creek Road). Go W on 82 approx. 4 mi. to Lake Como and follow signs to Upper Como Campground.

SINGLE RATE:	$7	OPEN DATES:	May-Sept
# of SINGLE SITES:	11	MAX SPUR:	16 feet
		MAX STAY:	14 days
		ELEVATION:	4245 feet

28 Warm Springs
Darby • lat 45˚48'00" lon 114˚02'00"

DESCRIPTION: This CG is situated among ponderosa pine and douglas fir on Warm Springs Creek. Fishing is alright in the creek. Various small wildlife, deer, elk, and moose can be seen in the area around the CG. Gather firewood locally, or bring your own. Some trails are in the surrounding area.

GETTING THERE: From Darby go S on US HWY 93 approx. 13 mi. to primary forest route 101D. Go S on 101D approx. 1 mi. to Warm Springs CG.

SINGLE RATE:	$8	OPEN DATES:	May-Sept
# of SINGLE SITES:	15	MAX SPUR:	26 feet
		MAX STAY:	14 days
		ELEVATION:	4500 feet

 Campground has hosts   **Reservable sites**   **Accessible facilities**   **Fully developed**    **Semi-developed**   **Rustic facilities**

NOTE: Open dates listed are typical. Actual dates are dependent on conditions such as snow pack.

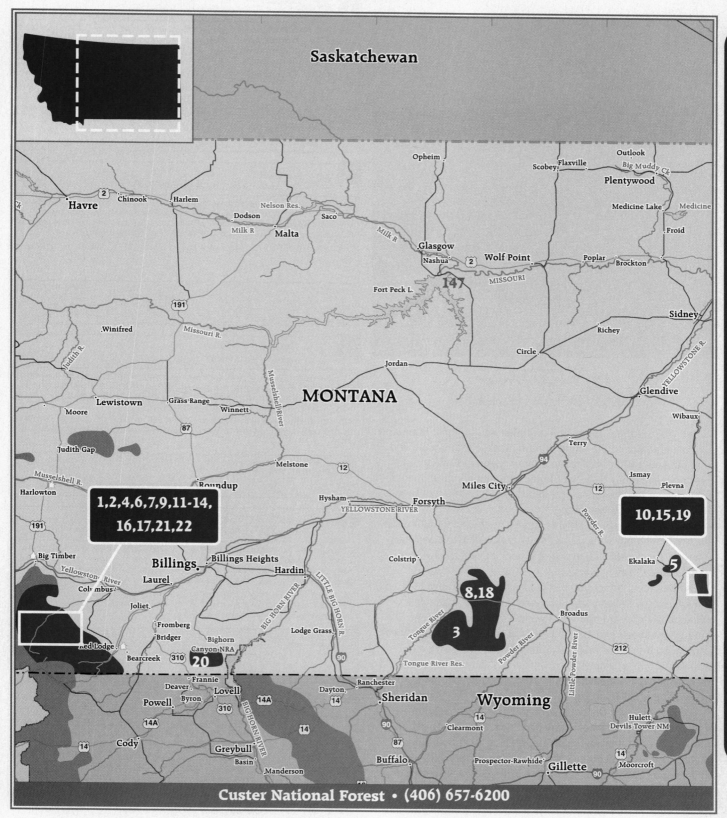

Saskatchewan

Plentywood

Havre · Chinook · Harlem

Outlook

Scobey · Flaxville · Big Muddy Ck

Medicine Lake · Medicine

Dodson · Saco · Froid

Nelson Res.

Milk R · Malta

Milk R

Glasgow · Wolf Point

Nashua

Poplar · Brockton

MISSOURI

Fort Peck L.

147

Sidney

Richey

Winifred

Missouri R.

Circle

Judith R.

Jordan

Glendive

Lewistown · Grass Range · Winnett

MONTANA

Wibaux

Moore

87

Terry

Judith Gap

Melstone

94

Ismay

Plevna

12

Harlowton

Musselshell R.

Roundup

Hysham · Forsyth

YELLOWSTONE RIVER

Miles City

12

Powder R.

1,2,4,6,7,9,11-14, 16,17,21,22

191

10,15,19

Big Timber

Yellowstone River

Billings · Billings Heights

Hardin

Colstrip

Ekalaka · **5**

Laurel

Columbus

Joliet

8,18

3

Broadus

212

Red Lodge · Bearcreek

Fromberg · Bridger

Bighorn Canyon NRA

20

310

BIG HORN RIVER

LITTLE BIG HORN R.

Lodge Grass

Tongue River

Tongue River Res.

Powder River

Little Powder River

Frannie

Deaver · Byron · Lovell

Dayton · Ranchester

Sheridan

Wyoming

Powell

14A

Hulett

Devils Tower NM

14A

310

BIG HORN RIVER

14

90

14

Clearmont

Moorcroft

14 · Cody

Greybull

Basin

Manderson

87 · Buffalo

Prospector-Rawhide

Gillette

90

Custer National Forest • (406) 657-6200

USFS Photo

CUSTER NATIONAL FOREST

The lands of the Custer National Forest and National Grasslands are scattered across 20 counties in Montana, North Dakota and South Dakota and are divided into three regions - The Ashland, Beartooth and Sioux districts. Elevations range from less than 1,000 feet in the Cheyenne Grasslands to the 12,799-foot Granite Peak, the highest in Montana.

The Ashland Ranger District is located in south central Montana and the topography varies from rolling grasslands, to steep rock outcrops. Rich in wildlife, this area is popular with trophy deer hunters, and turkey hunters.

The Beartooth Ranger District is located in Red Lodge Montana, and adjoins the Gallatin and Shoshone National Forests, and Yellowstone National Park. The area is also popular for deer, elk, and bighorn sheep hunters, as well as fishermen. For a spectacular view, take a scenic drive along the 10,947-foot Beartooth Highway. In winter, alpine skiers will enjoy skiing at Red Lodge Ski Resort while cross-country enthusiasts can take advantage of the area's touring trails.

The Sioux Ranger District is located in the southeast corner of Montana and the northwest corner of South Dakota. This area offers excellent antelope, mule deer, whitetail deer and turkey hunting. Ancient sand dunes covered with grasslands, rugged badlands, densely wooded forests, with carpets of alpine wildflowers all await the visitor to the easternmost portion of the northern region.

1 Basin
Red Lodge • lat 45°09'42" lon 109°23'31"

DESCRIPTION: CG set in a lodgepole pine forest on West Fork River. Fish for brook trout on river. Mountain lions, coyotes, deer, elk, moose, and raccoons in area. Bear regulations in effect. Fills weekends, holidays, and during Red Lodge events. Horse, hike, and mountain bike trails and roads available. Basin Lake trails nearby.

GETTING THERE: From Red Lodge go W on forest route 2071 approx. 7.5 mi. to Basin CG.

SINGLE RATE:	$9	OPEN DATES:	May-Sept*
# of SINGLE SITES:	28	MAX SPUR:	22 feet
		MAX STAY:	10 days
		ELEVATION:	6800 feet

2 Cascade
Red Lodge • lat 45°10'24" lon 109°27'05"

DESCRIPTION: CG in lodgepole pine forest on West Fork River. Fish for brook trout on river. Mountain lions, coyotes, deer, elk, moose, and raccoons. Bear regulations. in effect. Fills weekends, holidays, and during Red Lodge events. Horse, hike, and mountain bike trails and roads available. Access Absaroka-Beartooth Wilderness.

GETTING THERE: From Red Lodge go W on forest route 2071 approx. 11 mi. to Cascade CG.

SINGLE RATE:	$9	OPEN DATES:	May-Sept*
# of SINGLE SITES:	30	MAX SPUR:	22 feet
		MAX STAY:	10 days
		ELEVATION:	6800 feet

3 Cow Creek
Ashland • lat 45°18'37" lon 106°14'38"

DESCRIPTION: CG is set in pines scatterd in an open park like area. Hot summer days, cool mornings. Expect frequent noon rains. Limited supplies in Ashland, or Sheridan. Turkeys, mule deer, and small wildlife in area. Fills during hunting season. Prepare for ticks in spring, mosquitos in summer, and bees in fall.

GETTING THERE: From Ashland go E on US HWY 212 approx. 4 mi. to Otter Creek Road. Go S on Otter Creek Road approx. 19 mi. to Cow Creek Road and W 4 mi. to Cow Creek CG.

SINGLE RATE:	No fee	OPEN DATES:	Yearlong
# of SINGLE SITES:	5	MAX SPUR:	20 feet
		MAX STAY:	14 days
		ELEVATION:	3853 feet

4 East Rosebud
Absarokee • lat 45°11'57" lon 109°38'02"

DESCRIPTION: Set in pine and fir forest on E Rosebud Lake. Popular overnight stop for Cooke City travelers. Fish for brook trout. Deer, elk, moose, and black bears. Bear regulations. are in effect. Fills weekends and holidays. Beaten Path Trail near CG. Sylvan and Crow Lakes nearby, popular for golden trout fishing.

GETTING THERE: From Absarokee go S on state HWY 78 approx. 13 mi. to East Rosebud Creek Road. Go SW approx. 11 mi. to East Rosebud CG. Very rough road, not recommended for RV's and trailers.

SINGLE RATE:	$8	OPEN DATES:	May-Sept*
# of SINGLE SITES:	12	MAX SPUR:	20 feet
		MAX STAY:	10 days
		ELEVATION:	6340 feet

5 Ekalaka Park
Ekalaka • lat 45°47'54" lon 104°30'44"

DESCRIPTION: CG in open park-like setting in a hardwood draw. Sheltered by steep hills. Fishing on ponds only. Supplies in Ekalaka. Deer, bobcats, foxes, coyotes, and small wildlife in the area. CG tends to fill up during the fall hunting season. Gather firewood locally. Two-track trails.

GETTING THERE: From Ekalaka go S on state HWY 323 approx. 3 mi. to forest route 813. Go S on 813 approx. 5 mi. to Ekalaka CG.

SINGLE RATE:	No fee	OPEN DATES:	May-Nov
# of SINGLE SITES:	7		
		MAX STAY:	14 days
		ELEVATION:	3400 feet

 Campground has hosts 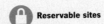 **Reservable sites** 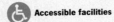 **Accessible facilities** **Fully developed** **Semi-developed** **Rustic facilities**

NOTE: Open dates listed are typical. Actual dates are dependent on conditions such as snow pack.

6 Emerald Lake
Absarokee • lat 45°15'14" lon 109°42'01"

DESCRIPTION: CG in pine and fir forest between West Rosebud and Emerald Lakes. Small dam and creek nearby. Brook and rainbow trout fishing on all. Mountain lions, coyotes, deer, elk, moose, raccoons, and black bears in area. Bear regulations. are in effect. Hiking trail nearby to Granite Peak, the highest point in MT.

GETTING THERE: From Absarokee go S on state HWY 78 approx. 3 mi. to state HWY 419. Go S on 419 approx. 4 mi. to state HWY 425. Go S on 425 approx. 17 mi. to Emerald Lake CG.

SINGLE RATE:	$8	OPEN DATES:	May-Sept*
# of SINGLE SITES:	21	MAX SPUR:	30 feet
		MAX STAY:	10 days
		ELEVATION:	6340 feet

11 Limber Pine
Red Lodge • lat 45°03'27" lon 109°24'43"

DESCRIPTION: CG in park-like fir and pine forest canyon at the base of Beartooth Pass. Fish for stocked rainbow trout on nearby Rock Creek. Heavy use, fills most days. Bear, deer, elk, and moose in the area. Bear regulations. in effect. Drive to nearby trailheads with access to the Absaroka-Beartooth Wilderness.

GETTING THERE: From Red Lodge go S on US HWY 212 approx. 12 mi. to Limber Pine CG.

SINGLE RATE:	$9	OPEN DATES:	May-Sept*
# of SINGLE SITES:	13	MAX SPUR:	35 feet
		MAX STAY:	10 days
		ELEVATION:	7200 feet

7 Greenough Lake
Red Lodge • lat 45°03'20" lon 109°24'47"

DESCRIPTION: In park-like fir and pine forest canyon at the base of Beartooth Pass. Fish for stocked rainbow trout on nearby Rock Creek. Heavy use, fills most days. Bear, deer, elk, moose, and small wildlife. Bear regulations. are in effect. Drive to nearby trailheads with access to the Absaroka-Beartooth Wilderness.

GETTING THERE: From Red Lodge go S on US HWY 212 approx. 12 mi. to Greenough Lake CG.

SINGLE RATE:	$9	OPEN DATES:	May-Sept*
# of SINGLE SITES:	18	MAX SPUR:	32 feet
		MAX STAY:	10 days
		ELEVATION:	7300 feet

12 M-K
Red Lodge • lat 45°02'18" lon 109°25'41"

DESCRIPTION: In pine and fir forest canyon at the base of Beartooth Pass. No drinking water, no services. Fish for stocked rainbow trout in nearby Rock Creek. Mountain lions, coyotes, elk, deer, moose, and bears in area. Bear regulations. in effect. Supplies in Red Lodge. Fills weekends and holidays. Drive to nearby trailheads.

GETTING THERE: From Red Lodge go S on US HWY 212 approx. 14 mi. to M-K CG.

SINGLE RATE:	No fee	OPEN DATES:	May-Sept
# of SINGLE SITES:	10	MAX SPUR:	22 feet
		MAX STAY:	10 days
		ELEVATION:	7400 feet

8 Holiday Springs
Ashland • lat 45°38'30" lon 105°59'00"

DESCRIPTION: CG is located among pines, area is open and park like. Expect hot days, and cool mornings; with noon rains. Limited supplies in Ashland. Mule deer, turkeys, and occasional black bears in the area. Moderate use. Prepare for ticks in spring, mosquitos in summer, and hornets and wasps in fall.

GETTING THERE: From Ashland go E on US HWY 212 approx. 6 mi. to East Fork Otter Creek Road then E approx. 9 mi. to Holiday Springs CG.

SINGLE RATE:	No fee	OPEN DATES:	Yearlong
# of SINGLE SITES:	3		
		MAX STAY:	14 days
		ELEVATION:	4123 feet

13 Palisades
Red Lodge • lat 45°10'18" lon 109°18'27"

DESCRIPTION: This CG is situated in a fir and pine forest along Willow Creek. No fish in the creek. No water and no services at CG. Rarely full, frequently used as overflow CG. Mountain lions, coyotes, deer, elk, moose, black bears, and raccoons in the area. Bear regulations are in effect. Drive to trailheads.

GETTING THERE: From Red Lodge go W on forest route 2071 approx. 1 mi. to forest route 3010. Go E on 3010 approx. 2 mi. to Palisades CG.

SINGLE RATE:	No fee	OPEN DATES:	May-Sept*
# of SINGLE SITES:	7	MAX SPUR:	22 feet
		MAX STAY:	10 days
		ELEVATION:	6396 feet

9 Jimmy Joe
Absarokee • lat 45°14'08" lon 109°35'59"

DESCRIPTION: Jimmy Joe CG was unfortunately burned during a forest fire in August, 1996. Still in the process of repair, this CG may not be open for the 2000 season. Check with the Beartooth Ranger District to be certain. There are no services, and no drinking water available on site.

GETTING THERE: From Absarokee go S on state HWY 78 approx. 13 mi. to East Rosebud Creek Road. Go SW on East Rosebud Creek Road approx. 7 mi. to Jimmy Joe CG.

SINGLE RATE:	No fee	OPEN DATES:	May-Sept
# of SINGLE SITES:	10	MAX SPUR:	20 feet
		MAX STAY:	10 days
		ELEVATION:	5560 feet

14 Parkside
Red Lodge • lat 45°03'43" lon 109°24'30"

DESCRIPTION: In park-like fir and pine forest canyon at the base of Beartooth Pass. Fish for stocked rainbow trout on Rock Creek. Heavy use, fills most days. Supplies in Red Lodge. Bears, deer, elk, and moose in area. Bear regulations. are in effect. Drive to nearby trailheads with access to the Absaroka-Beartooth Wilderness.

GETTING THERE: From Red Lodge go S on US HWY 212 approx. 12 mi. to Parkside CG.

SINGLE RATE:	$9	OPEN DATES:	May-Sept*
# of SINGLE SITES:	28	MAX SPUR:	32 feet
		MAX STAY:	10 days
		ELEVATION:	7300 feet

10 Lantis Spring
Camp Creek • lat 45°37'50" lon 104°10'35"

DESCRIPTION: CG was burned over in 1988 and is still in a recovery stage. Open, park like area with some aspen. Windy at times. Orginal homestead in 1930's, developed by CCCs in 1930. Deer, foxes, coyotes, bobcats, and rabbits in area. Fills in the hunting season. Gather firewood locally. Trails are two-tracks.

GETTING THERE: From Camp Creek, South Dakota go W on state HWY 20 (Tie Creek Road) approx. 3 mi. to forest route 117. Follow 117 approx. 10 mi. to Lantis Spring CG.

SINGLE RATE:	No fee	OPEN DATES:	May-Nov
# of SINGLE SITES:	5		
		MAX STAY:	14 days
		ELEVATION:	3500 feet

15 Picnic Spring
Buffalo • lat 45°52'45" lon 103°29'30"

DESCRIPTION: CG is situated a plateau of open grassy areas. Edge of site is lined with ponderosa pines. Supplies can be found in Buffalo. Deer, rabbits, foxes, coyotes, bobcats, squirrels, and various birds in the area. Moderate use, fills during the fall hunting season. Two track trails nearby.

GETTING THERE: From Buffalo go N on US HWY 85 approx. 22 mi. to Tufte Road. Go W 4 mi. and N 2 mi. to Picnic Spring CG.

SINGLE RATE:	No fee	OPEN DATES:	May-Nov
# of SINGLE SITES:	8		
		MAX STAY:	14 days
		ELEVATION:	3600 feet

  Campground has hosts Reservable sites Accessible facilities Fully developed Semi-developed Rustic facilities

16 Pine Grove
Absarokee • lat 45°16'42" lon 109°38'23"

DESCRIPTION: CG set in thick pine and fir trees at the base of a canyon. Mild days, cold nights. Nearby West Rosebud may be fished for brook trout. Mountain lions, elk, deer, moose, coyotes, and black bears in area. Bear regulations. are in effect. Supplies in Absarokee. Drive to trailheads. Prepare for mosquitos.

GETTING THERE: From Absarokee go S on state HWY 78 approx. 3 mi. to state HWY 419. Go S on 419 approx. 4 mi. to state HWY 425. Go S on 425 approx. 14 mi. to Pine Grove CG.

SINGLE RATE:	$8	OPEN DATES:	May-Sept*
# of SINGLE SITES:	46	MAX SPUR:	30 feet
		MAX STAY:	10 days
		ELEVATION:	5800 feet

17 Ratine
Red Lodge • lat 45°05'24" lon 109°19'23"

DESCRIPTION: A small site located on Rock Creek among pine and fir trees. Fish for brook and rainbow trout on the creek. Supplies in Red Lodge. Fills weekends and holidays. Mountain lions, coyotes, elk, deer, moose, and black bears in the area. Bear regulations. are in effect. Seven trailheads on site.

GETTING THERE: From Red Lodge go S on US HWY 212 approx. 4 mi. to forest route 2379. Go S on 2379 approx. 2.5 mi. to Ratine CG.

SINGLE RATE:	$9	OPEN DATES:	May-Sept*
# of SINGLE SITES:	7	MAX SPUR:	22 feet
		MAX STAY:	10 days
		ELEVATION:	6400 feet

18 Red Shale
Ashland • lat 45°34'09" lon 106°08'52"

DESCRIPTION: This CG is situated among pines. Expect warm to hot days, with cold nights and mornings. Limited supplies and groceries can be found in Ashland. Campers may gather their firewood locally. Prepare for ticks in spring, mosquitos in summer, and hornets and wasps in fall.

GETTING THERE: From Ashland go E on US HWY 212 approx. 6 mi. to Red Shale CG.

SINGLE RATE:	No fee	OPEN DATES:	Yearlong
# of SINGLE SITES:	16	MAX SPUR	40 feet
		MAX STAY:	14 days
		ELEVATION:	3100 feet

19 Reva Gap
Buffalo • lat 45°32'00" lon 103°10'30"

DESCRIPTION: CG situated in open areas with scattered ponderosa pines. Historic Battle of the Slim Buttes site nearby. Supplies can be found in buffalo. Deer, foxes, coyotes, rabbits, and various birds in the area. Moderate use, tends to fill up during the fall hunting season.

GETTING THERE: From Buffalo go S on US HWY 89 approx. 2 mi. to state HWY 20. Go E on 20 approx. 18 mi. to Reva Gap CG.

SINGLE RATE:	No fee	OPEN DATES:	May-Nov
# of SINGLE SITES:	8		
		MAX STAY:	14 days
		ELEVATION:	3500 feet

20 Sage Creek
Bridger • lat 45°12'52" lon 108°33'16"

DESCRIPTION: CG set in an open area surrounded by forest. No drinking water or services. Mild days, cold nights. Fish for brook trout in nearby Sage Creek. Rarely full. Mountain lions, elk, deer, moose, coyotes, and black bears in area. Bear regulations. are in effect. Basic supplies in Bridger. Drive to trailheads.

GETTING THERE: From Bridger go S on US HWY 310 to Pryor Mountain Road. Go E on Pryor Mountain Road approx. 20 mi. to Sage Creek CG.

SINGLE RATE:	No fee	OPEN DATES:	May-Sept*
# of SINGLE SITES:	12	MAX SPUR:	30 feet
		MAX STAY:	10 days
		ELEVATION:	5550 feet

21 Sheridan
Red Lodge • lat 45°06'05" lon 109°18'08"

DESCRIPTION: This CG is located on Rock Creek in a pine and fir forest. Fish for brook and rainbow trout on the creek. Supplies in Red Lodge. Fills weekends and holidays. Mountain lions, coyotes, elk, deer, moose, and black bears in the area. Bear regulations. are in effect. Seven trailheads on site.

GETTING THERE: From Red Lodge go S on US HWY 212 approx. 4 mi. to forest route 2374. Go S on 2374 approx. 1 mi. to Sheridan CG.

SINGLE RATE:	$9	OPEN DATES:	May-Sept*
# of SINGLE SITES:	8	MAX SPUR:	30 feet
		MAX STAY:	10 days
		ELEVATION:	6300 feet

22 Woodbine
Absarokee • lat 45°21'08" lon 109°53'44"

DESCRIPTION: CG is located at the end of the road in a thick pine and fir forest. Warm days, cold nights. Basic supplies are in Absarokee. Fills weekends and holidays. Mountain lions, elk, deer, moose, and occasional black bears in area. Bear regulations. are in effect. Multiple trails nearby including Woodbine Falls.

GETTING THERE: From Absarokee go S on state HWY 78 approx. 3 mi. to county route 419. Go W on 419 approx. 26 mi. to Woodbine CG.

SINGLE RATE:	$9	OPEN DATES:	May-Sept*
# of SINGLE SITES:	46	MAX SPUR:	32 feet
		MAX STAY:	10 days
		ELEVATION:	5240 feet

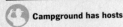 Campground has hosts   Reservable sites 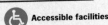 Accessible facilities  Fully developed 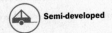 Semi-developed 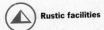 Rustic facilities

NOTE: Open dates listed are typical. Actual dates are dependent on conditions such as snow pack.

FLATHEAD NATIONAL FOREST

Located in northwestern Montana, the 2.3 million-acre Flathead National Forest lies adjacent to Glacier National Park and west of the Continental Divide. The Bob Marshall, Great Bear, and Mission Mountains Wildernesses comprise approximately 46 percent of the total land base.

Outdoor enthusiasts will discover an abundance of recreation opportunities. The forest's spectacular glaciated peaks and pristine alpine lakes beckon summer users to hike, camp and fish or spend the day huckleberry picking. The Flathead Wild and Scenic River and Swan River, dissect the beauty of the Mission, Swan, and Flathead Mountain ranges and are favorites of whitewater rafters.

With 34 developed campgrounds and picnic areas, the forest totals about 400 family units. Some have a daily use fee, while others are free. Additional developed sites include boat ramps, swimming areas, and trailhead facilities.

The forest also provides habitat for approximately 250 species of wildlife and 22 species of fish, including the threatened grizzly bear and endangered gray wolf.

USFS Photo

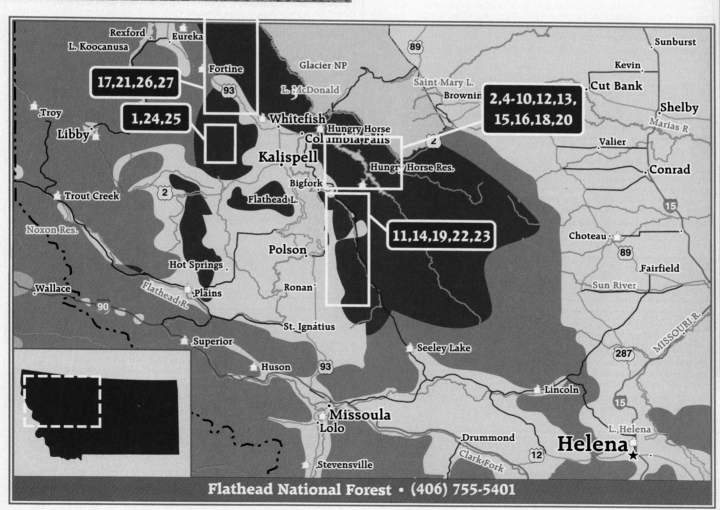

Flathead National Forest • (406) 755-5401

1 — Ashley Lake
Kalispell • lat 48°12'42" lon 114°34'06"

DESCRIPTION: In park like mature larch and fir forest on Ashley Lake. Fish perch, trout, and salmon in the lake. Boat launch 1 mi. away. Bears, deer, elk, bald eagles, loons, osprey, beavers, and various water fowl. Gather deadwood for fires. Supplies in Kalispell. Dispersed sites. Hiking within 30 miles.

GETTING THERE: From Kalispell go W on US HWY 2 14 mi. to forest route 679. Go N on 679 4 mi. to forest route 912. Go left on 912 and follow main road around lake 4 mi. to Ashley Lake CG. High clearance required.

SINGLE RATE:	No fee	OPEN DATES:	Yearlong*
# of SINGLE SITES:	5		
		MAX STAY:	14 days
		ELEVATION:	3960 feet

2 — Beaver Creek
Hungry Horse • lat 47°55'25" lon 113°22'16"

DESCRIPTION: CG is in a stand of mixed conifer with views of the Spotted Bear River. Fly fish for cutthroat trout in river. Supplies 65 mi. to Hungry Horse. CG can be busy during hunting season (Sept-Oct). Gather firewood. Numerous trails. CG is frequented by bears. Horse facilities. No running water.

GETTING THERE: From Hungry Horse go E on US HWY 2 approx. 1 mi. to primary forest route 38. Go S on 38 approx. 58 mi. to forest route 568. Go E on 568 approx. 8 mi. to Beaver Creek CG.

SINGLE RATE:	No fee	OPEN DATES:	May-Nov
# of SINGLE SITES:	6	MAX SPUR:	50 feet
		MAX STAY:	14 days
		ELEVATION:	3700 feet

3 — Big Creek
Columbia Falls • lat 48°36'02" lon 114°09'44"

DESCRIPTION: This CG is situated in an open stand of lodgepole pine with views of beautiful Glacier National Park. The North Fork of the Flathead River has good trout fishing and rafting opportunities, and runs adjacent to the CG. Several hiking and horse trails in the surrounding area. Boat ramp.

GETTING THERE: From Columbial Falls go N on HWY 486 approx. 17 mi. to Big Creek CG.

SINGLE RATE:	$8	OPEN DATES:	Yearlong
# of SINGLE SITES:	22	MAX SPUR:	35 feet
		MAX STAY:	14 days
		ELEVATION:	5500 feet
# of GROUP SITES:	1		

4 — Devil Creek
West Glacier • lat 48°15'05" lon 113°27'47"

DESCRIPTION: CG is located in a open, park-like stand of pine, fir, spruce, and some larch and is adjacent to Devil Creek. Fishing at nearby Bear Creek. Check fishing regs.. Various wildlife includes elk, deer, grizzly and black bears, and mountain lions. Devil Creek Trail on site leads to Great Bear Wilderness.

GETTING THERE: From West Glacier take US HWY 2 approx. 30 mi. to Devil Creek CG.

SINGLE RATE:	$10	OPEN DATES:	Yearlong
# of SINGLE SITES:	14		
		MAX STAY:	14 days
		ELEVATION:	3500 feet

5 — Devils Corkscrew
Hungry Horse • lat 48°06'35" lon 113°41'46"

DESCRIPTION: CG is located in a stand of pine, fir, spruce, and some larch. Views are of Hungry Horse Reservoir which offers excellent trout fishing opportunities. Check fishing regs.. Various wildlife includes elk, deer, grizzly and black bears, and mountain lions. Hiking and horse trails in area. Boat ramp on site.

GETTING THERE: From Hungry Horse go E on US HWY 2 approx. 1 mi. to primary forest route 38. Go S on 38 approx. 30 mi. to Devil's Corkscrew CG.

SINGLE RATE:	No fee	OPEN DATES:	Yearlong
# of SINGLE SITES:	4	MAX SPUR:	35 feet
		MAX STAY:	14 days
		ELEVATION:	3600 feet

6 — Elk Island
Hungry Horse • lat 48°13'00" lon 113°39'00"

DESCRIPTION: CG is located in a stand of lodgepole pine, douglas fir, spruce, and some larch. Views are of Hungry Horse Reservoir; which offers excellent trout fishing opportunities. Check fishing regs.. Various wildlife including elk, deer, grizzly bears, black bears, and mountain lions.

GETTING THERE: Elk Island CG is located on the N side of Elk Island in the Hungry Horse Reservoir and is accessible only by boat.

SINGLE RATE:	No fee	OPEN DATES:	Yearlong
# of SINGLE SITES:	7	MAX SPUR:	35 feet
		MAX STAY:	14 days
		ELEVATION:	3600 feet

7 — Emery Bay
Hungry Horse • lat 48°20'07" lon 113°56'52"

DESCRIPTION: CG is located in a dense stand of new growth lodgepole pine. Views are of Hungry Horse Reservoir which offers excellent trout fishing opportunities. Check fishing regs.. Wildlife includes elk, deer, grizzly bears, black bears, and mountain lions. Boat ramp. Various hiking/horse trails in area.

GETTING THERE: From Hungry Horse go E on US HWY 2 approx. 1 mi. to primary forest route 38. Go S on 38 approx. 5 mi. to Emery Bay CG.

SINGLE RATE:	$9	OPEN DATES:	Yearlong
# of SINGLE SITES:	26	MAX SPUR:	35 feet
GROUP RATE:	Varies	MAX STAY:	14 days
# of GROUP SITES:	1	ELEVATION:	3585 feet

8 — Fire Island
Hungry Horse • lat 48°17'40" lon 113°53'43"

DESCRIPTION: CG is located in a stand of lodgepole pine, douglas fir, spruce, and some larch. Views are of Hungry Horse Reservoir which offers excellent trout fishing opportunities. Check fishing regs.. Wildlife in the area includes elk, deer, grizzly bears, black bears, and mountain lions.

GETTING THERE: Fire Island CG is located on the N side of Fire Island in the Hungry Horse Reservoir and is accessible by boat only.

SINGLE RATE:	No fee	OPEN DATES:	Yearlong
# of SINGLE SITES:	4	MAX SPUR:	35 feet
		MAX STAY:	14 days
		ELEVATION:	3610 feet

9 — Graves Bay
Hungry Horse • lat 48°07'28" lon 113°46'51"

DESCRIPTION: CG is located in a stand of mixed conifer. Excellent trout fishing in Hungry Horse Reservoir and Graves Creek. Check fishing regs.. Various wildlife includes elk, deer, grizzly and black bears, and mountain lions. Hiking and horse trails on site lead to Graves Creek Falls and Jewel Basin.

GETTING THERE: From Hungry Horse go S on primary forest route 895 approx. 26 mi. to Graves Bay CG.

SINGLE RATE:	No fee	OPEN DATES:	Yearlong
# of SINGLE SITES:	10	MAX SPUR:	35 feet
		MAX STAY:	14 days
		ELEVATION:	3560 feet

10 — Handkerchief Lake
Hungry Horse • lat 48°08'37" lon 113°49'32"

DESCRIPTION: CG is walk-in only and is located in a stand of mixed conifer with views of Handkerchief Lake. Non-motorized boating and fishing for greyling on lake. Various wildlife includes elk, deer, grizzly and black bears, and mountain lions. Hiking and horse trail on site leads to Jewel Basin.

GETTING THERE: From Hungry Horse go S on primary forest route 895 approx. 26 mi. to Handkerchief Lake CG.

SINGLE RATE:	No fee	OPEN DATES:	Yearlong
# of SINGLE SITES:	9	MAX SPUR:	35 feet
		MAX STAY:	14 days
		ELEVATION:	3880 feet

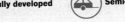

Campground has hosts **Reservable sites** **Accessible facilities** **Fully developed** **Semi-developed** **Rustic facilities**

NOTE: Open dates listed are typical. Actual dates are dependent on conditions such as snow pack.

11 Holland Lake
Condon • lat 47°27'10" lon 113°36'16"

DESCRIPTION: Set in mixed growth fir, cottonwood and pine. 2 loops, some views of Holland Lake. Fish for cutthroat. Deer, elk, moose, and black bears in area. Bear regulations are in effect. Busy holidays and weekends in Aug.. Hike to Holland Falls #416, mountain Bike on old roads. Horse access into Bob Marshall Wilderness.

GETTING THERE: From Condon go S on state HWY 83 approx. 6 mi. to forest route 44. Go E on 44 approx. 3 mi. to Holland Lake CG.

SINGLE RATE:	$10	OPEN DATES:	May-Sept*
# of SINGLE SITES:	40	MAX SPUR:	30 feet
		MAX STAY:	14 days
		ELEVATION:	4052 feet

12 Lakeview
Hungry Horse • lat 48°13'09" lon 113°48'16"

DESCRIPTION: This CG is located in a stand of lodgepole pine, douglas fir, spruce, and some larch. Views are of surrounding forest. Various wildlife includes elk, deer, grizzly and black bears, and mountain lions. Good fishing, hiking, and horseback riding opportunities in area.

GETTING THERE: From Hungry Horse go S on primary forest route 895 approx. 17 mi. to Lakeview CG.

SINGLE RATE:	No fee	OPEN DATES:	Yearlong
# of SINGLE SITES:	5	MAX SPUR:	35 feet
		MAX STAY:	14 days
		ELEVATION:	3615 feet

13 Lid Creek
Hungry Horse • lat 48°17'03" lon 113°54'23"

DESCRIPTION: CG is located in a stand of lodgepole pine, douglas fir, spruce, and some larch. Views are of Hungry Horse Reservoir; which offers excellent trout fishing opportunities. Check fishing regs.. Various wildlife includes elk, deer, grizzly and black bears, and mountain lions. Boat ramp.

GETTING THERE: From Hungry Horse go S on primary forest route 895 approx. 11 mi. to Lid Creek CG.

SINGLE RATE:	$7	OPEN DATES:	Yearlong
# of SINGLE SITES:	23	MAX SPUR:	35 feet
		MAX STAY:	14 days
		ELEVATION:	3615 feet

14 Lindbergh
Condon • lat 47°24'18" lon 113°43'26"

DESCRIPTION: Set in mixed growth fir, cottonwood and pine on Lindbergh Lake. Isolated, quiet CG with 5 walk-in sites. Fish cutthrout in the lake; boat ramp. Deer, elk, moose, and an occasional black bear. Bear regulations are in effect. Busy holidays and weekends in Aug. Approx. 6 mi. to TH for Mission Mountain Wilderness.

GETTING THERE: From Condon go S on state HWY 83 approx. 8 mi. to forest route 79. Go W on 79 approx. 4 mi. to Lindbergh CG.

SINGLE RATE:	No fee	OPEN DATES:	May-Sept*
# of SINGLE SITES:	9		
		MAX STAY:	14 days
		ELEVATION:	4360 feet

15 Lost Johnny Camp
Hungry Horse • lat 48°18'22" lon 113°58'08"

DESCRIPTION: CG is located in a stand of lodgepole pine, douglas fir, spruce, and some larch. Views are of Hungry Horse Reservoir which offers excellent trout fishing opportunities. Check fishing regs.. Various wildlife includes elk, deer, grizzly and black bears, and mountain lions. Hiking and horse trails in area.

GETTING THERE: From Hungry Horse go S on primary forest route 895 approx. 6 1/2 mi. to Lost Johnny Camp CG.

SINGLE RATE:	$9	OPEN DATES:	Yearlong
# of SINGLE SITES:	5	MAX SPUR:	57 feet
		MAX STAY:	14 days
		ELEVATION:	3600 feet

16 Lost Johnny Point
Hungry Horse • lat 48°18'37" lon 113°57'46"

DESCRIPTION: CG is located in a dense stand of mixed conifer. Views are of Hungry Horse Reservoir which offers excellent trout fishing opportunities. Check fishing regs.. Various wildlife includes elk, deer, grizzly and black bears, and mountain lions. Jimmy Ridge hiking/horse trail is on site. Boat ramp.

GETTING THERE: From Hungry Horse go S on primary forest route 895 approx. 7 mi. to Lost Johnny Point CG.

SINGLE RATE:	$9	OPEN DATES:	Yearlong
# of SINGLE SITES:	21	MAX SPUR:	35 feet
		MAX STAY:	14 days
		ELEVATION:	3600 feet

17 Moose Lake
Columbia Falls • lat 48°37'45" lon 114°22'30"

DESCRIPTION: CG is a short walk from the parking area and is situated in a mixed conifer grove of lodgepole pine and douglas fir. Meadow Lake is adjacent to CG with good fishing opportunities. Numerous wildlife including deer, elk, grizzly and black bear, and mountain lion. Hiking and horse trails on site.

GETTING THERE: From Columbia Falls go N on county route 486 17 mi. to forest route 316. Go W on 316 7 mi. to forest route 315. Go NW on 315 5 mi. to forest route 5207. Go E then N on 5207 5 mi. to Moose Lake CG.

SINGLE RATE:	No fee	OPEN DATES:	Yearlong
# of SINGLE SITES:	3	MAX SPUR:	30 feet
		MAX STAY:	14 days
		ELEVATION:	6500 feet

18 Murray Bay
Hungry Horse • lat 48°16'01" lon 113°48'45"

DESCRIPTION: CG is located in a stand of mixed conifer. Views are of Hungry Horse Reservoir which offers excellent trout fishing opportunities. Check fishing regulations Various wildlife includes elk, deer, grizzly and black bears, and mountain lions. Hiking/horse trails in area. Boat ramp.

GETTING THERE: From Hungry Horse go E on US HWY 2 approx. 1 mi. to primary forest route 38. Go S on 38 approx. 17 mi. to Murray Bay CG.

SINGLE RATE:	$7	OPEN DATES:	Yearlong
# of SINGLE SITES:	18	MAX SPUR:	35 feet
		MAX STAY:	14 days
		ELEVATION:	3600 feet

19 Owl Creek Packer Camp
Condon • lat 47°26'27" lon 113°36'18"

DESCRIPTION: Set in mixed growth fir, cottonwood, and pine. Primary use is overnight for those accessing the wilderness, not intended for long term use. Stock facilites, dispersed sites. No fishing, no drinking water. Deer, elk, moose, and black bears. Bear regulations are in effect. Fills in fall hunting season.

GETTING THERE: From Condon go S on state HWY 83 approx. 6 mi. to forest route 44. Go E on 44 approx. 4 mi. to Owl Creek Packer Camp CG.

SINGLE RATE:	No fee	OPEN DATES:	Yearlong*
# of SINGLE SITES:	5		
		MAX STAY:	14 days
		ELEVATION:	4080 feet

20 Peters Creek
Hungry Horse • lat 48°03'25" lon 113°38'31"

DESCRIPTION: CG is located in a dense stand of mixed conifer with views of Hungry Horse Reservoir. Shore fishing on site and boat landing nearby. Visit historic ranger station. Supplies 35 mi. to Hungry Horse. Elk, deer, and moose in area. Gather firewood locally. No drinking water.

GETTING THERE: From Hungry Horse go E on US HWY 2 approx. 1 mi. to primary forest route 38. Go S on 38 approx. 35 mi. to Peters Creek CG.

SINGLE RATE:	No fee	OPEN DATES:	May-Nov
# of SINGLE SITES:	6	MAX SPUR:	52 feet
		MAX STAY:	14 days
		ELEVATION:	3700 feet

 **Campground has hosts**   **Reservable sites**   **Accessible facilities**   **Fully developed**   **Semi-developed**   **Rustic facilities**

NOTE: Open dates listed are typical. Actual dates are dependent on conditions such as snow pack.

21 Red Meadow
Columbia Falls • lat 48°45'00" lon 114°33'30"

DESCRIPTION: CG is located in mixed conifer forest of lodgepole pine and douglas fir and is adjacent to Red Meadow Lake. Good fishing on lake with non-motorized boats. Numerous wildlife includes deer, elk, grizzly and black bear. Various hiking and horse trails in area.

GETTING THERE: From Columbia Falls go N on county route 486 approx. 30 mi. to forest route 1685. Go NW on 1685 approx. 5 mi. to forest route 115. Go W on 115 approx. 9 mi. to Red Meadow CG.

SINGLE RATE:	No fee	OPEN DATES:	Yearlong
# of SINGLE SITES:	6	MAX SPUR:	30 feet
		MAX STAY:	14 days
		ELEVATION:	6500 feet

22 Spotted Bear
Hungry Horse • lat 47°55'35" lon 113°31'36"

DESCRIPTION: CG is in an open stand of mixed conifer with river and mountain views. Good fly fishing for cutthroat trout and whitefish in the Spotted Bear and South Fork Flathead Rivers. Supplies 55 mi. to Hungry Horse. Busy holidays and weekends. Gather firewood locally. Trails nearby. Frequented by bears.

GETTING THERE: From Hungry Horse go E on US HWY 2 approx. 1 mi. to primary forest route 38. Go S on 38 approx. 58 mi. to Spotted Bear CG.

SINGLE RATE:	$8	OPEN DATES:	May-Nov
# of SINGLE SITES:	12	MAX SPUR:	52 feet
		MAX STAY:	14 days
		ELEVATION:	3738 feet

23 Swan Lake
Bigfork • lat 47°56'12" lon 113°51'02"

DESCRIPTION: Set in mixed growth fir, cottonwood and pine across the hwy from Swan Lake. Boat ramp nearby. Fish for cutthroat. Deer, elk, moose, and occasional black bears. Bear regulations are in effect. Busy holidays and weekends in Aug.. 5 mi. to hiking TH. Old roads for mountain bike use. Swim beach and picnic site.

GETTING THERE: From Big Fork go W on state HWY 209 approx. 4.5 mi. to state HWY 83. Go S on 83 approx. 9 mi. to Swan Lake CG.

SINGLE RATE:	$10	OPEN DATES:	May-Sept*
# of SINGLE SITES:	36	MAX SPUR:	40 feet
GROUP RATE:	Varies	MAX STAY:	14 days
# of GROUP SITES:	1	ELEVATION:	3078 feet

24 Sylvia Lake
Kalispell • lat 48°20'34" lon 114°49'08"

DESCRIPTION: In open area of thinned lodgepole pine on Sylvia Lake. Fish for cutthroat and grayling in lake. Supplies in Whitefish. Deer, moose, mountain lions, osprey, loons and waterfowl in area. Moderate use, full July 4. Gather deadwood for fires. Horse and hiking trails nearby.

GETTING THERE: From Kalispell go W on US HWY 2 18 mi. to primary forest route 538. Go N on 538 17 mi. to forest route 538B. Go N on 538B approx. 4 mi. to Sylvia Lake CG. Snowmobile access in winter.

SINGLE RATE:	No fee	OPEN DATES:	Yearlong*
# of SINGLE SITES:	2	MAX SPUR:	15 feet
		MAX STAY:	14 days
		ELEVATION:	4917 feet

25 Tally Lake
Whitefish • lat 48°24'50" lon 114°35'01"

DESCRIPTION: Set in open mature larch and fir forest over-looking deep Tally Lake. Fish for trout, pike, and salmon. Supplies in Whitefish. Black bears, deer, bald eagles, mountain lions, grouse, loons and waterfowl in area. Heavy use, fills July and Aug. Firewood sold on site. Horse/hiking trails nearby. Mosquitos.

GETTING THERE: From Whitefish go N on US HWY 93 approx. 5 mi. to Twin Bridges Road. Go S on Twin Bridges Road approx. 4 mi. to primary forest route 913. Go W on 913 approx. 7 mi. to Tally Lake CG.

SINGLE RATE:	$9	OPEN DATES:	Yearlong*
# of SINGLE SITES:	39	MAX SPUR:	35 feet
GROUP RATE:	$25	MAX STAY:	14 days
# of GROUP SITES:	1	ELEVATION:	4000 feet

26 Tuchuck
Columbia Falls • lat 48°55'22" lon 114°35'53"

DESCRIPTION: This CG is situated in a stand of lodgepole pine and has a small creek running adjacent to it. Views of the surrounding forest. Various wildlife in the area includes elk, deer, grizzly and black bears, and mountain lions. Hiking and horse trails on site.

GETTING THERE: From Columbial Falls go N on HWY 486 (turns into primary forest route 486) approx. 40 mi. to forest route 114. Go W on 114 approx. 11 mi. to Tuchuck CG.

SINGLE RATE:	No fee	OPEN DATES:	Yearlong
# of SINGLE SITES:	7	MAX SPUR:	35 feet
		MAX STAY:	14 days
		ELEVATION:	4645 feet

27 Upper Stillwater Lake
Whitefish • lat 48°35'13" lon 114°38'02"

DESCRIPTION: Set in mature conifer forest looking on Upper Stillwter Lake. Pike and cutthroat fishing on lake. Supplies in Whitefish. Resident packrats, deer, bald eagles, loons and waterfowl in area. Fills weekends. Gather firewood. Hiking on Finger Lake trail 1/2 mi. from CG. Mosquitos all summer.

GETTING THERE: From Whitefish go N on US HWY 93 approx. 22 mi. to Upper Stillwater Lake CG. High clearance required. Snowmobile access in winter.

SINGLE RATE:	No fee	OPEN DATES:	Yearlong*
# of SINGLE SITES:	2		
		MAX STAY:	14 days
		ELEVATION:	3200 feet

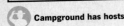 **Campground has hosts**   **Reservable sites** **Accessible facilities** 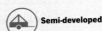 **Fully developed**  **Semi-developed** **Rustic facilities**

NOTE: Open dates listed are typical. Actual dates are dependent on conditions such as snow pack.

USFS Photo

GALLATIN NATIONAL FOREST

From its windswept snow covered mountain summits, among the highest and most spectacular in the state of Montana, to the internationally famous "Blue Ribbon" trout streams, adventures are unlimited on the 1.8 million acres of the Gallatin National Forest.

Created in 1907, the Gallatin National Forest is part of the Greater Yellowstone Area. The Shoshoni, Bannock and Crow tribes called this country home for 10,000 years. Here also, the famous mountain men, John Colter and Jim Bridger prepared the way for the first dude ranches, originally places where "easterners" were introduced to the Wild West and the wonders of the upper Yellowstone Country. Gold rushes, the railroads, ranching and timber production is all part of the Gallatin National Forest's colorful past...and present.

Whether you are running a challenging whitewater rapid, skiing a steep slope, biking along an old road, fishing a favorite pool or hunting in a hidden clearing, the Gallatin offers a wealth of both summer and winter recreation opportunities.

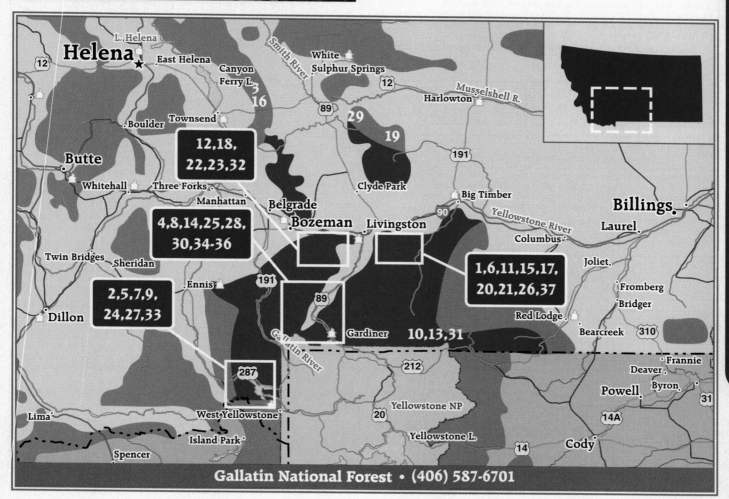

Gallatin National Forest • (406) 587-6701

1 Aspen Grove
Big Timber • lat 45°27'25" lon 110°11'47"

DESCRIPTION: This CG is located on Boulder River among pine and cottonwood. Fishing access on site. Accessible toilet. No firewood provided, gather locally or bring your own. Deer and small wildlife in the area. Supplies and groceries can be found in Big Timber. Bear regulations are in effect.

GETTING THERE: From Big Timber go S on US HWY 298 approx. 25 mi. to county route 212. Go S on 212 approx. 8.5 mi. to Aspen Grove CG.

SINGLE RATE:	No fee	OPEN DATES:	Yearlong*
# of SINGLE SITES:	8	MAX SPUR:	42 feet
		MAX STAY:	14 days
		ELEVATION:	5396 feet

6 Big Beaver
Big Timber • lat 45°28'30" lon 110°12'05"

DESCRIPTION: CG located among cottonwood trees and fir along the Main Boulder River. Fishing access to river on site. Supplies at Big Timber. No drinking water. No firewood provided, gather locally or bring your own. Pack it in, pack it out. Elk, deer, and occasional bears in area. Bear regulations are in effect.

GETTING THERE: From Big Timber go S on HWY 298 approx. 25 mi. to county route 212. Go S on 212 approx. 8 mi. to Big Beaver CG.

SINGLE RATE:	No fee	OPEN DATES:	Yearlong*
# of SINGLE SITES:	5	MAX SPUR:	42 feet
		MAX STAY:	14 days
		ELEVATION:	5200 feet

2 Bakers Hole
West Yellowstone • lat 44°42'15" lon 111°06'03"

DESCRIPTION: This CG is situated among tall pine trees on Madison River near Hebgen Lake. Great fishing on both the lake and the river. Large game frequent the area. Tent camping now allowed. Supplies at West Yellowstone. Buy firewood or gather locally. Airport nearby.

GETTING THERE: From West Yellowstone go N on US HWY 191 approx. 3 mi. to Bakers Hole CG.

SINGLE RATE:	$10.50	OPEN DATES:	May-Sept
# of SINGLE SITES:	72	MAX SPUR:	75 feet
		MAX STAY:	14 days
		ELEVATION:	6400 feet

7 Cabin Creek
West Yellowstone • lat 44°52'16" lon 110°20'26"

DESCRIPTION: In open park like area with great views of the Hebgen Dam area. Historic Earthquake memorial and Ghost Village nearby. Shore or boat fishing on Hebgen Lake. Mild days, cold nights. Buy or gather firewood. Supplies and groceries can be found in West Yellowstone. Bear regulations are in effect.

GETTING THERE: From West Yellowstone go N on US HWY 191 approx. 8 mi. to US HWY 287. Go W on 287 approx. 13 mi. to Cabin Creek CG.

SINGLE RATE:	$10.50	OPEN DATES:	May-Sept
# of SINGLE SITES:	15	MAX SPUR:	30 feet
		MAX STAY:	14 days
		ELEVATION:	6477 feet

3 Battle Ridge
Bozeman • lat 45°53'00" lon 110°52'52"

DESCRIPTION: This CG is located in a lodgepole pine and fir forest. No firewood provided, gather on site, or bring your own. No fishing from site. Supplies and groceries can be found in Bozeman. Large game and small wildlife in area. Bear regulations in effect. Hiking and horse trail nearby.

GETTING THERE: From Bozeman go E and N on state HWY 86 approx. 22 mi. to Battle Ridge CG.

SINGLE RATE:	No fee	OPEN DATES:	May-Sept
# of SINGLE SITES:	13	MAX SPUR:	32 feet
		MAX STAY:	14 days
		ELEVATION:	6000 feet

8 Canyon
Gardiner • lat 45°11'00" lon 110°53'00"

DESCRIPTION: Situated in high mountain area with Yankee Jim Recreational Area nearby. Boat access to fish Yankee Jim River. No services, no drinking water. Gather firewood locally. Supplies at Gardiner. Large game, mountain goats, and bears in the area. Bear regulations are in effect. Multiple hiking routes.

GETTING THERE: From Gardiner go N on US HWY 89 approx. 14 mi. to Canyon CG.

SINGLE RATE:	No fee	OPEN DATES:	Yearlong
# of SINGLE SITES:	12	MAX SPUR:	22 feet
		MAX STAY:	14 days
		ELEVATION:	6400 feet

4 Bear Creek
Gardiner • lat 45°06'00" lon 110°37'00"

DESCRIPTION: Rustic CG set in high mountains among tall pine. Sites are dispersed with no services and no drinking water. Gather or bring own firewood. Supplies at Gardiner or limited supplies at Jardine. Small creeks and hiking trails nearby. Bear regulations in effect. Moose, elk, and mountain goats in area.

GETTING THERE: From Gardiner go N on primary forest route 493 approx. 11 mi. to Bear Creek CG.

SINGLE RATE:	No fee	OPEN DATES:	June-Oct
		MAX SPUR:	34 feet
		MAX STAY:	14 days
		ELEVATION:	6400 feet

9 Cherry Creek
West Yellowstone • lat 44°44'47" lon 111°15'46"

DESCRIPTION: This CG is located in a pine and fir forest on Hebgen Lake. Dispersed sites. Good trout fishing on lake. Mild days, cold nights. Supplies available at West Yellowstone. No services, no drinking water. Gather firewood locally. Large game animals and bears frequent the area. Bear regulations are in effect.

GETTING THERE: From West Yellowstone go W on US HWY 20 approx. 8 mi. to Hebgen Lake Road. Go N on Hebgen Lake Rd approx. 6 mi. to Cherry Creek CG.

SINGLE RATE:	No fee	OPEN DATES:	May-Sept
		MAX STAY:	14 days
		ELEVATION:	6570 feet

5 Beaver Creek
West Yellowstone • lat 44°51'17" lon 111°22'44"

DESCRIPTION: CG is set in an open park-like area overlooking Quake Lake. Historic Earthquake Memorial and Ghost Village nearby. Mild days, cool nights. Fishing on Quake Lake or Hebgen Lake. Supplies can be found at West Yellowstone. Buy firewood or gather locally. Bear regulations are in effect.

GETTING THERE: From West Yellowstone go N on US HWY 191 approx. 8 mi. to US 287. Go W on 287 approx. 13 mi. to Beaver Creek CG.

SINGLE RATE:	$10.50	OPEN DATES:	May-Sept
# of SINGLE SITES:	64	MAX SPUR:	55 feet
		MAX STAY:	14 days
		ELEVATION:	6600 feet

10 Chief Joseph
Cooke City • lat 45°01'13" lon 109°52'28"

DESCRIPTION: CG located in high mountains among tall lodgepole pine and fir. Fishing at Kersey Lake aprox. 2 mi. away. Multiple hiking trails nearby. Go to Quaint Cooke City for limited supplies. Gather firewood locally. Elk, moose, mountain goats, and bears frequent the area. Bear regulations are in effect.

GETTING THERE: Chief Joseph CG is located 4 mi. E of Cooke City on US HWY 212.

SINGLE RATE:	$8	OPEN DATES:	July-Sept
# of SINGLE SITES:	6	MAX SPUR:	42 feet
		MAX STAY:	14 days
		ELEVATION:	8036 feet

 Campground has hosts   **Reservable sites**   **Accessible facilities**   **Fully developed**   **Semi-developed**   Rustic facilities

NOTE: Open dates listed are typical. Actual dates are dependent on conditions such as snow pack.

11 Chippy Park
Big Timber • lat 45˚26'13" lon 110˚11'21"

DESCRIPTION: Along the Main Boulder River set among cottonwood and fir stands. Fishing access to river nearby. Two accessible sites and toilets. Supplies at Big Timber. Drinking water May 25-Sept 30 only. No firewood, gather locally or bring own. Elk, deer, and bears in the area. Bear regulations are in effect.

GETTING THERE: From Big Timber go S on US HWY 298 approx. 25 mi. to county route 212. Go S on 212 approx. 8.5 mi. to Chippy Park CG.

SINGLE RATE:	No fee	OPEN DATES:	Yearlong*
# of SINGLE SITES:	7	MAX SPUR:	63 feet
		MAX STAY:	14 days
		ELEVATION:	5466 feet

12 Chisholm
Bozeman • lat 45˚28'23" lon 110˚57'20"

DESCRIPTION: Located on Hyalite Reservoir with beautiful views of the lake and mountains. Fishing access on site. Supplies at Bozeman. Firewood $4/bundle. Hiking trails nearby. Prepare for ticks and mosquitos until mid-summer. Bear regulations are in effect.

GETTING THERE: Chisholm CG is located 18 mi. S of Bozeman on Hyalite Canyon Road.

SINGLE RATE:	$9	OPEN DATES:	May-Sept
# of SINGLE SITES:	10	MAX SPUR:	60 feet
		MAX STAY:	14 days
		ELEVATION:	6715 feet

13 Colter
Cooke City • lat 45˚01'41" lon 109˚53'40"

DESCRIPTION: High mountain CG is situated among pine and fir stands. Cool days, cold nights. Snow is possible all year. Limited supplies at Cooke City. Fishing at Kersey Lake approx. 4 mi. away. Moose, elk, deer, mountain goats, and bears in the area. Bear regulations are in effect. Mosquitos all season.

GETTING THERE: From Cooke City go E on US HWY 212 approx. 2 mi. to Colter CG.

SINGLE RATE:	$8	OPEN DATES:	July-Sept*
# of SINGLE SITES:	23	MAX SPUR:	48 feet
		MAX STAY:	14 days
		ELEVATION:	8089 feet

14 Eagle Creek
Gardiner • lat 45˚02'47" lon 110˚40'40"

DESCRIPTION: Situated in high mountains among pine and fir stands on Eagle Creek. Cool days, cold nights. Snow is possible anytime of year. No services or drinking water. Gather firewood. Large game, mountain goats, and bears in area. Multiple hiking trails nearby. Bear regulations are in effect.

GETTING THERE: From Gardiner go N on primary forest route 493 approx. 3 mi. to Eagle Creek CG.

SINGLE RATE:	$6	OPEN DATES:	Yearlong
# of SINGLE SITES:	12	MAX SPUR:	48 feet
		MAX STAY:	14 days
		ELEVATION:	6500 feet

15 East Boulder
Big Timber • lat 45˚32'13" lon 110˚08'57"

DESCRIPTION: CG located on East Boulder River among cottonwood and fir stands. Fishing access to river nearby. Supplies at Big Timber. No drinking water. No firewood, gather locally or bring your own. Pack it in, pack it out. Not recommended for RVs. Elk, deer, and occasional bears in area. Bear regulations are in effect.

GETTING THERE: From Big Timber go S on US HWY 298 approx. 19 mi. to East Boulder Road. Go E on E Boulder Rd approx. 6 mi. to East Boulder CG.

SINGLE RATE:	No fee	OPEN DATES:	Yearlong*
# of SINGLE SITES:	2	MAX SPUR:	20 feet
		MAX STAY:	14 days
		ELEVATION:	5700 feet

16 Fairy Lake
Bozeman • lat 45˚54'31" lon 110˚57'39"

DESCRIPTION: CG is set in a beautiful scenic area with views of Sacagawea Peak. Fishing access to Fairy Lake on site. Deer, water fowl, and small wildlife can be seen in the area. Supplies at Bozeman. No firewood available. Pack it in, pack it out. Accessible toilets. Bear regulations are in effect.

GETTING THERE: From Bozeman go N on state HWY 86 approx. 22.5 mi. to forest route 74 (Fairy Lake Rd). Go W on 74 approx. 5 mi. to Fairy Lake CG.

SINGLE RATE:	No fee	OPEN DATES:	July-Sept
# of SINGLE SITES:	9	MAX SPUR:	32 feet
		MAX STAY:	14 days
		ELEVATION:	5000 feet

17 Falls Creek
Big Timber • lat 45˚29'25" lon 110˚13'04"

DESCRIPTION: CG situated among fir and cottonwood along the Main Boulder River. Fishing access to river nearby. No firewood, gather locally or bring your own. Drinking water May 25-Sept 30 only. Pack it in, pack it out. Deer, elk, and occasional bears can be found in the area. Bear regulations are in effect.

GETTING THERE: From Big Timber go S on US HWY 298 approx. 25 mi. to county route 212. Go S on 212 approx. 5 mi. to Falls Creek CG.

SINGLE RATE:	No fee	OPEN DATES:	Yearlong*
# of SINGLE SITES:	8	MAX SPUR:	40 feet
		MAX STAY:	14 days
		ELEVATION:	5210 feet

18 Greek Creek
Bozeman • lat 45˚22'52" lon 111˚10'39"

DESCRIPTION: CG is set in park like setting among pine and fir near Greek Creek. Fishing access, trash service, and accessible toilets. Firewood $4/bundle. 7 Accessible sites. Deer and small wildlife in area. Supplies at Bozeman. Prepare for ticks and mosquitos until mid-summer. Bear regulations are in effect.

GETTING THERE: From Bozeman go S on US HWY 191 approx. 31 mi. to Greek Creek CG.

SINGLE RATE:	$9	OPEN DATES:	May-Sept
# of SINGLE SITES:	14	MAX SPUR:	60 feet
		MAX STAY:	14 days
		ELEVATION:	5500 feet

19 Halfmoon
Big Timber • lat 46˚02'30" lon 110˚14'22"

DESCRIPTION: CG will close early summer 2000 for reconstruction. Please contact Big Timber RD (406) 932-5155 for info. Located near U Big Timber Falls and many hike-in fishing lakes. Drinking water May 25-Sept 30. No services. Supplies at Big Timber. Gather firewood. Bear regulations are in effect.

GETTING THERE: From Big Timber go N on US HWY 191 approx. 11 mi. to county route 25 (Big Timber Canyon Road). Go W on 25 approx. 12 mi. to Halfmoon CG.

SINGLE RATE:	No fee	OPEN DATES:	Yearlong*
# of SINGLE SITES:	8	MAX SPUR:	30 feet
		MAX STAY:	14 days
		ELEVATION:	5000 feet

20 Hells Canyon
Big Timber • lat 45˚21'42" lon 110˚12'52"

DESCRIPTION: CG is set among cottonwood and fir stands along the Main Boulder River. Fishing access to river nearby. No drinking water. No firewood, gather locally or bring your own. Pack it in, pack it out. Deer, elk, and bears in the area. Bear regulations are in effect. Ticks and mosquitos until mid-summer.

GETTING THERE: From Big Timber go S on US HWY 298 approx. 25 mi. to county road 212. Go S on 212 approx. 15.5 mi. to Hells Canyon CG.

SINGLE RATE:	No fee	OPEN DATES:	Yearlong*
# of SINGLE SITES:	11	MAX SPUR:	48 feet
		MAX STAY:	14 days
		ELEVATION:	6120 feet

 Campground has hosts   **Reservable sites**   **Accessible facilities**   **Fully developed**   **Semi-developed**   **Rustic facilities**

NOTE: Open dates listed are typical. Actual dates are dependent on conditions such as snow pack.

21 Hicks Park
Big Timber • lat 45°17'53" lon 110°14'21"

DESCRIPTION: This CG is situated among cottonwood and fir on the Main Boulder River. Fishing access on site. No firewood, gather locally or bring your own. Drinking water May 25-Sept 30 only. Deer and small wildlife in area. Bear regulations are in effect. Ticks and mosquitos in early season.

GETTING THERE: From Big Timber go S on US HWY 298 approx. 25 mi. to county route 212. Go S on 212 approx. 21 mi. to Hicks Park CG.

SINGLE RATE:	No fee	OPEN DATES:	Yearlong*
# of SINGLE SITES:	16	MAX SPUR:	51 feet
		MAX STAY:	14 days
		ELEVATION:	6350 feet

22 Hood Creek
Bozeman • lat 45°29'03" lon 110°58'01"

DESCRIPTION: In pine and fir forest on Hyalite Reservoir. Shore and boat fishing on reservoir. Two sites plus toilets are accessible. Gather firewood locally. Deer and small wildlife in area. Supplies at Bozeman. Prepare for ticks and mosquitos til mid-summer. Bear regulations in effect.

GETTING THERE: Hood Creek CG is 17 mi. S of Bozeman on Hyalite Canyon Road.

SINGLE RATE:	$9	OPEN DATES:	May-Sept
# of SINGLE SITES:	18	MAX SPUR:	50 feet
		MAX STAY:	14 days
		ELEVATION:	6715 feet

23 Langohr
Bozeman • lat 45°31'40" lon 111°00'57"

DESCRIPTION: This CG is set in a lodgepole pine forest on Hyalite Creek. Two accessible sites as well as toilets. CG complete with an accessible fishing trail and nature walk. Firewood is $4/bundle. Large game and small wildlife can be found in the area. Bear regulations are in effect.

GETTING THERE: From Bozeman go S on the Hyalite Canyon Road approx. 11 mi. to Langohr CG.

SINGLE RATE:	$9	OPEN DATES:	May-Sept
# of SINGLE SITES:	12	MAX SPUR:	32 feet
		MAX STAY:	14 days
		ELEVATION:	5800 feet

24 Lonesomehurst
West Yellowstone • lat 44°44'08" lon 111°13'50"

DESCRIPTION: This CG is set in a pine and fir forest on the South Fork Madison River. Boat access to fish Hebgen Lake or stream fish the river. Buy or gather firewood. Mild days, cold nights. Supplies are available at West Yellowstone. Large game and bears in the area. Bear regulations are in effect.

GETTING THERE: From West Yellowstone go W on US 20 approx. 8 mi. to Hebgen Lake Road. Go N on Hebgen Lake Road approx. 4 mi. to Lonesomehurst CG.

SINGLE RATE:	$10.50	OPEN DATES:	May-Sept
# of SINGLE SITES:	26	MAX SPUR:	30 feet
		MAX STAY:	14 days
		ELEVATION:	6500 feet

25 Moose Creek Flat
Bozeman • lat 45°21'19" lon 111°10'14"

DESCRIPTION: CG in a park like setting with fishing access to the Galatin River. Handicapped fishing access and accessible toilets available. Hiking and horse trail nearby. Firewood $4/bundle. Supplies at Bozeman. Bear regulations are in effect. Prepare for mosquitos and ticks until mid-summer.

GETTING THERE: From Bozeman go S on US HWY 191 approx. 32 mi. to Moose Creek Flat CG.

SINGLE RATE:	$9	OPEN DATES:	May-Sept
# of SINGLE SITES:	14	MAX SPUR:	60 feet
		MAX STAY:	14 days
		ELEVATION:	5800 feet

26 Pine Creek
Livingston • lat 45°29'52" lon 110°31'15"

DESCRIPTION: Newly renovated CG. Fishing creek nearby. Hiking trail to Pine Creek Falls on site. Some accessible facilities. Supplies available in Livingston. Bear regulations are in effect. Reduced services Oct-Nov. The road is narrow with steep, sharp curves; closed to vehicles Dec-May.

GETTING THERE: From Livingston go S on HWY 89 3 mi. to state route 540(at Carter's Bridge). Go S 7 mi. to forest route 202(Pine Cr Rd). Take 202 2.5 mi. to Luccock Park Rd. & Pine Creek CG.

SINGLE RATE:	$9	OPEN DATES:	May-Sept
# of SINGLE SITES:	26	MAX SPUR:	50 feet
		MAX STAY:	14 days
		ELEVATION:	5000 feet

27 Rainbow Point
West Yellowstone • lat 44°46'44" lon 111°10'45"

DESCRIPTION: CG is located in a forest on Grayling Arm of Hebgen Lake. Boat access to lake. Fishing OK. Mild days, cold nights. Buy or gather firewood locally. Supplies are available at West Yellowstone. Tent camping now allowed. Wildlife in the area includes elk, deer, and occasional mountain goats.

GETTING THERE: From West Yellowstone go N on US HWY 191 approx. 5 mi. to forest road 610. Go W on 610 approx. 3 mi. to forest road 6954. Go N on 6954 approx. 2 mi. to Rainbow Point CG.

SINGLE RATE:	$10.50	OPEN DATES:	May-Sept
# of SINGLE SITES:	66	MAX SPUR:	40 feet
		MAX STAY:	14 days
		ELEVATION:	6539 feet

28 Red Cliff
Bozeman • lat 45°10'11" lon 111°14'30"

DESCRIPTION: This CG is situated among lodgepole pine. Fishing access nearby. Accessible toilets. Firewood is $4/bundle. Electrical hookups for an additional $4 fee. Supplies and groceries can be found in Bozeman. Prepare for mosquitos and ticks until mid-summer.

GETTING THERE: From Bozeman go S on US HWY 191 approx. 48 mi. to Red Cliff CG.

SINGLE RATE:	$9	OPEN DATES:	May-Sept
# of SINGLE SITES:	68	MAX SPUR:	50 feet
		MAX STAY:	14 days
		ELEVATION:	5200 feet

29 Shields River
Livingston • lat 46°10'58" lon 110°24'12"

DESCRIPTION: This dispersed CG is in a fir and cottonwood forest setting with Shields River nearby. Fish or swim in the river. Supplies available in Livingston. Campers may gather firewood. Bear regulations are in effect.

GETTING THERE: From Livingston go N approx. 28 mi. on US HWY 89 to Wilsall and Shields River Road. Go NE approx. 24 mi. on Shields River Road to CG. Call ranger district for road conditions when wet.

SINGLE RATE:	No fee	OPEN DATES:	May-Sept
		MAX SPUR:	22 feet
		MAX STAY:	14 days
		ELEVATION:	6435 feet

30 Snowbank
Livingston • lat 45°17'17" lon 110°32'38"

DESCRIPTION: This CG is situated along Mill Creek. Fishing access available on site. Group sites must be reserved. Buy firewood on site or bring your own. Supplies and groceries are available at Livingston. Elk, deer, and occasional bears in the area. Bear regulations are in effect. Reduced services Oct-Nov.

GETTING THERE: From Livingston go S on US HWY 89 approx. 15 mi. to Mill Creek Road. Go E on Mill Creek Road approx. 12 mi. to Snowbank CG. Closed to vehicles Dec-May.

SINGLE RATE:	$9	OPEN DATES:	May-Sept
# of SINGLE SITES:	11	MAX SPUR:	35 feet
GROUP RATE:	Varies	MAX STAY:	14 days
# of GROUP SITES:	1	ELEVATION:	5755 feet

 Campground has hosts   🔒 **Reservable sites**   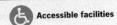 **Accessible facilities**   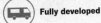 **Fully developed**   **Semi-developed**   **Rustic facilities**

NOTE: Open dates listed are typical. Actual dates are dependent on conditions such as snow pack.

31 Soda Butte
Cooke City • lat 45°01'27" lon 109°54'41"

DESCRIPTION: CG is located in lodgepole pine stand. Nearby Kersey Lake for fishing, pleasantly scenic. Snow stays late and comes early. Cool days, cold nights. Quaint Cooke City is nearby for limited supplies. Moose, bears, deer, and mountain goats in area. Bear regulations are in effect. Firewood may be gathered.

GETTING THERE: From Cooke City go E approx. 1 mi. on US HWY 212 to Soda Butte CG.

SINGLE RATE:	$8	OPEN DATES:	July-Sept
# of SINGLE SITES:	21	MAX SPUR:	48 feet
		MAX STAY:	14 days
		ELEVATION:	7807 feet

32 Spire Rock
Bozeman • lat 45°26'25" lon 111°11'31"

DESCRIPTION: CG is situated in a pine and fir forest with views of Garnet Mountain. Fishing access to Squaw Creek. Firewood $4/bundle. Supplies at Bozeman. No drinking water available on site. Multiple hiking and horse trails nearby. Prepare for ticks and mosquitos in early summer. Bear regulations in effect.

GETTING THERE: From Bozeman go S on US HWY 191 approx. 22 mi. to Squaw Creek Road. Go E on Squaw Creek Road approx. 3 mi. to Spire Rock CG.

SINGLE RATE:	$6	OPEN DATES:	May-Sept
# of SINGLE SITES:	16	MAX SPUR:	50 feet
GROUP RATE:	Varies	MAX STAY:	14 days
# of GROUP SITES:	1	ELEVATION:	5880 feet

33 Spring Creek
West Yellowstone • lat 44°47'05" lon 111°16'27"

DESCRIPTION: CG in a beautiful location on Hebgen Lake set in a pine and fir forest. Dispersed sites. Boat or shore fish the Lake. Mild days, cold nights. Supplies at West Yellowstone. No services, no drinking water. Gather firewood locally. Large game including bears frequent area. Bear regulations in effect.

GETTING THERE: From West Yellowstone go W on US HWY 20 approx. 8 mi. to Hebgen Lake Road. Go N on Hebgen L. Rd. approx. 10 mi. to Spring Creek CG.

SINGLE RATE:	No fee	OPEN DATES:	May-Sept
		MAX STAY:	14 days
		ELEVATION:	6540 feet

34 Swan Creek
Bozeman • lat 45°22'25" lon 111°09'07"

DESCRIPTION: This CG is situated in a thick lodgepole pine forest. Fishing access and swimming in area. Buy firewood for $4/bundle. Seven accessible sites. Supplies and groceries are available in Bozeman. Deer and large game can be found in the surrounding area. Bear regulations are in effect.

GETTING THERE: From Bozeman go S on US HWY 191 approx. 32 mi. to forest route 481. Go E on 481 approx. 1 mi. to Swan Creek CG.

SINGLE RATE:	$9	OPEN DATES:	May-Sept
# of SINGLE SITES:	11	MAX SPUR:	45 feet
		MAX STAY:	14 days
		ELEVATION:	5800 feet

35 Timber Camp
Gardiner • lat 45°06'30" lon 110°37'00"

DESCRIPTION: Located in high mountains among pine and fir on Upper Bear Creek. Stream fish the creek. Cool days, cold nights. Snow possible yearlong. No services, no drinking water. Gather firewood. Limited supplies at Jardine. Large game, and mountain goats. Bear regulations in effect. Mosquitos in early season.

GETTING THERE: From Gardiner go N on primary forest route 493 approx. 9 mi. to Timber Creek CG.

SINGLE RATE:	No fee	OPEN DATES:	June-Oct
		MAX SPUR:	48 feet
		MAX STAY:	14 days
		ELEVATION:	6200 feet

36 Tom Miner
Gardiner • lat 45°07'51" lon 111°03'42"

DESCRIPTION: CG set in the high mountains among tall pine and fir on Trail Creek. Mild days, cold nights. Snow is possible any time of year. Supplies are available at Gardiner. Gather firewood. Petrified Forest, hiking and fishing nearby. Bear regulations are in effect. Pack it in, pack it out.

GETTING THERE: From Gardiner go N on US HWY 89 approx. 19 mi. to county route 63 (Tom Miner Rd). Go SW on 63 approx. 12 mi. to Tom Miner CG.

SINGLE RATE:	$7	OPEN DATES:	May-Sept
# of SINGLE SITES:	16	MAX SPUR:	42 feet
		MAX STAY:	14 days
		ELEVATION:	7400 feet

37 West Boulder
Big Timber • lat 45°32'59" lon 110°18'37"

DESCRIPTION: CG situated among cottonwood and fir stands. Fishing access to Boulder River nearby. Supplies and groceries are available at Big Timber. No drinking water. No firewood, gather locally or bring your own. Deer and small wildlife in the area. Pack it in, pack it out. Bear regulations are in effect.

GETTING THERE: From Big Timber go S on US HWY 298 approx. 16 mi. to county route 35 (at McLeod). Go SW on 35 approx. 6.5 mi. to West Boulder Road. Go SW on W Boulder Rd approx. 8 mi. to West Boulder CG.

SINGLE RATE:	No fee	OPEN DATES:	Yearlong*
# of SINGLE SITES:	10	MAX SPUR:	60 feet
		MAX STAY:	14 days
		ELEVATION:	5705 feet

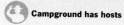 **Campground has hosts**   **Reservable sites** 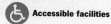 **Accessible facilities**   **Fully developed** 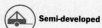 **Semi-developed**  **Rustic facilities**

NOTE: Open dates listed are typical. Actual dates are dependent on conditions such as snow pack.

USFS Photo

HELENA
NATIONAL FOREST

The Helena National Forest offers close to one million acres of diverse landscapes and wildland opportunities. Located in west central Montana, the Helena boasts some of the most vivid glimpses into the past of this historically rich area.

The forest is sprinkled with history from Native American inhabitants to early explorers and the booming days of gold mining. The natural beauty of the Helena National Forest provides a rather open atmosphere with many grassy parks interspersed amidst lodgepole pine and Douglas fir forests. Highlighting the forest, the Gates of the Mountains Wilderness, remains as impressive a sight as when Lewis and Clark described it on their journey.

The forest also provides outstanding opportunities for fishing the Blackfoot and Missouri rivers, hiking along the Continental Divide National Scenic Trail, and viewing magnificent big game in the 129,000-acre Elkhorn Wildlife Management Unit.

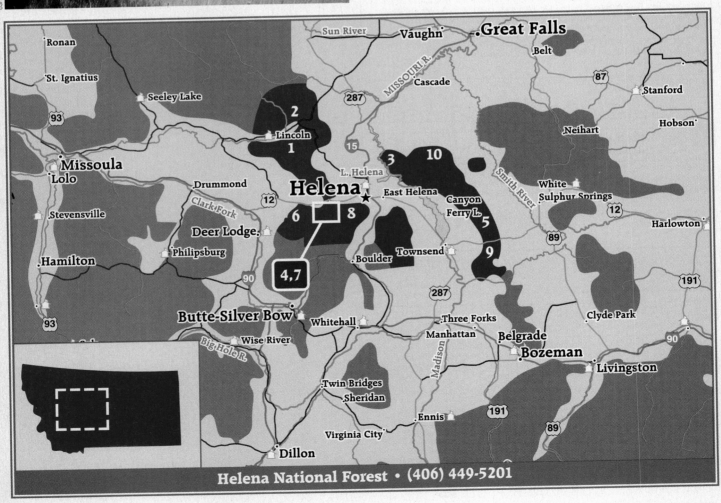

Helena National Forest • (406) 449-5201

1 Aspen Grove
Lincoln • lat 46°58'43" lon 112°31'50"

DESCRIPTION: This CG is situated in a mature stand of cottonwood mixed with pine on the Blackfoot River. Good fishing on river. Busy on holidays. Various wildlife in area includes deer, elk, and moose. Bears have been seen on occasion. CG is near the Continental Divide National Scenic Trail.

GETTING THERE: From Lincoln go E approx. 7 mi. on state HWY 200 to Aspen Grove CG.

SINGLE RATE:	$7	OPEN DATES:	May-Oct
# of SINGLE SITES:	25	MAX SPUR:	35 feet
		MAX STAY:	14 days
		ELEVATION:	4600 feet

6 Kading
Elliston • lat 46°25'49" lon 112°28'46"

DESCRIPTION: Kading CG is situated among beautiful ponderosa pine on the Little Blackfoot River. Check fishing regulations for the area. This CG tends to be busy on holidays. There are several trails in the surrounding area. Various wildlife in the area includes deer and elk, with an occasional bear or two.

GETTING THERE: From Elliston go E on US HWY 12 approx. 1 mi. to Road 5. Go S on Road 5 approx. 4 mi. to forest route 227. Go SW on 227 approx. 9 mi. to Kading CG.

SINGLE RATE:	No fee	OPEN DATES:	June-Sept
# of SINGLE SITES:	10	MAX SPUR:	25 feet
		MAX STAY:	14 days
		ELEVATION:	5800 feet

2 Copper Creek
Lincoln • lat 47°04'42" lon 112°37'07"

DESCRIPTION: Copper Creek CG is situated among lodgepole pine and spruce on Copper Creek. Good fishing on the creek. CG is almost always busy. Various wildlife in area includes deer, elk, moose, and occasional black and grizzly bears. Several trails area in the surrounding area.

GETTING THERE: From Lincoln go E on state HWY 200 approx. 6.5 mi. to forest route 330. Go NW on 330 approx. 8 mi. to Copper Creek CG.

SINGLE RATE:	$7	OPEN DATES:	May-Sept
# of SINGLE SITES:	20	MAX SPUR:	35 feet
		MAX STAY:	14 days
		ELEVATION:	4650 feet

7 Moose Creek
Helena • lat 46°31'31" lon 112°15'35"

DESCRIPTION: CG is located in lodgepole pine on Moose Creek. Check fishing regulations for the area. This CG tends to be busy on holidays. Supplies and groceries can be found approx. 14 mi. away at Helena. Various wildlife in the area includes deer and elk. Bears have been seen on occasion.

GETTING THERE: From Helena go W on US HWY 12 approx. 10 mi. to Rimi.ni Road. Go SW on Rimi.ni approx. 4 mi. to Moose Creek CG.

SINGLE RATE:	$5	OPEN DATES:	June-Sept
# of SINGLE SITES:	9	MAX SPUR:	20 feet
		MAX STAY:	14 days
		ELEVATION:	4856 feet

3 Coulter Creek
Helena • lat 46°51'30" lon 111°53'30"

DESCRIPTION: This CG is located in an open setting on the Missouri River. Hike or boat in access only. Check fishing regulations for area. Various wildlife in area includes deer and elk. Several trails in surrounding area. CG is situated near the Gates of the Mountains Wilderness Area.

GETTING THERE: From Helena go N on I-15 16 mi. to Gates of the Mountains interchange (exit 209). Go NW on county route 3 mi. to Upper Holter Lake. Go NW by boat 4 mi. to Coulter Creek CG.

SINGLE RATE:	No fee	OPEN DATES:	May-Sept
# of SINGLE SITES:	6		
		MAX STAY:	14 days
		ELEVATION:	3610 feet

8 Park Lake
Clancy • lat 46°26'32" lon 112°10'05"

DESCRIPTION: Park Lake CG os situated among conifer on Park Lake. Activities available include fishing on the lake, picnicking, and scenic hikes. CG tends to fill up quickly on weekends. Various wildlife in the area includes deer and elk. Bears have been seen in the area on occasion.

GETTING THERE: From Clancy go N on county route approx. 1 mi. to county route. Go W on county route approx. 8 mi. to forest route 4009. Go W on 4009 approx. 6 mi. to Park Lake CG.

SINGLE RATE:	$8	OPEN DATES:	June-Sept
# of SINGLE SITES:	22	MAX SPUR:	25 feet
		MAX STAY:	14 days
		ELEVATION:	6360 feet

4 Cromwell-Dixon
Helena • lat 46°33'17" lon 112°18'47"

DESCRIPTION: This CG is located in an open area set close to HWY 12. Various wildlife in area includes deer and elk. Bears have been seen on occasion. Several small trails in the surrounding area, and the CG is not far from the Continental Divide National Scenic Trail. CG is seldom full.

GETTING THERE: From Helena go W on US HWY 12 approx. 15 mi. to Cromwell-Dixon CG.

SINGLE RATE:	$6	OPEN DATES:	June-Sept
# of SINGLE SITES:	14	MAX SPUR:	20 feet
		MAX STAY:	14 days
		ELEVATION:	6260 feet

9 Skidway
Townsend • lat 46°21'16" lon 111°05'47"

DESCRIPTION: This CG is situated in aspen and douglas fir on the upper reaches of Deep Creek. Check fishing regulations for the area. CG is seldom full. Several trails in surrounding area. Various wildlife in area includes grouse, deer, and elk. Bears have been seen on occasion.

GETTING THERE: From Townsend go E on US HWY 12 approx. 23 mi. to forest route 4042. Go S on 4042 approx. 2 mi. to Skidway CG.

SINGLE RATE:	No fee	OPEN DATES:	May-Oct
# of SINGLE SITES:	18	MAX SPUR:	35 feet
		MAX STAY:	14 days
		ELEVATION:	6000 feet

5 Gipsy Lake
White Sulpher Springs • lat 46°30'12" lon 111°12'36"

DESCRIPTION: This CG is located in a spruce stand on Gipsy lake. Fair fishing for trout on the lake. Busy on holiday weekends. No drinking water available. Wildlife in area includes moose, deer, and elk. Several trails in surrounding area. Accessible facilities for camping and fishing.

GETTING THERE: From White Sulpher Springs go W on Birch Creek Road approx. 16 mi. to Gipsy Lake CG.

SINGLE RATE:	No fee	OPEN DATES:	May-Sept
# of SINGLE SITES:	5	MAX SPUR:	20 feet
		MAX STAY:	14 days
		ELEVATION:	6200 feet

10 Vigilante
Helena • lat 46°46'01" lon 111°38'59"

DESCRIPTION: Vigilante CG is situated among ponderosa pine on Trout Creek. Check fishing regulations for area. CG tends to be busy on holidays. Various wildlife in area includes deer, and elk. Bears have been spotted on occasion. Several trails in surrounding area.

GETTING THERE: From Helena go NE on state HWY 280 approx. 20 mi. to York-Trout Creek Road. Go NE on York-Trout Creek approx. 12 mi. to Vigilante CG.

SINGLE RATE:	$5	OPEN DATES:	May-Sept
# of SINGLE SITES:	22	MAX SPUR:	20 feet
		MAX STAY:	14 days
		ELEVATION:	4400 feet

 Campground has hosts   **Reservable sites**   **Accessible facilities**   **Fully developed**   **Semi-developed**   **Rustic facilities**

KOOTENAI NATIONAL FOREST

The Kootenai National Forest lies in the northwest corner of Montana. Its high craggy peaks, deep canyons and mixed conifer stretch from the Canadian border to the Clark Fork valley. Several U.S. and state highways allow easy access to some of Montana's scenic treasures: the Purcell Mountains, the Yaak River, Ross Creek Scenic Area Giant Cedars, Lake Koocanusa, and Libby Dam. Where roads stop, wilderness begins. The heart of the Kootenai is the Cabinet Mountain Wilderness, where majestic peaks tower over the surroundings.

Named for the Kootenai Indians who formerly occupied the area and still retain treaty rights, this 2.2 million-acre forest offers spectacular scenery and year-round recreation. Try the blue ribbon Kootenai River for fishing at its finest. Scale your way up Stone Hill, a popular rock climbing wall along Lake Koocanusa, which has challenging routes for both beginning and advanced climbers.

Lakes, streams and rivers offer fishing, boating and swimming opportunities. There are many developed campgrounds, for picnics or camping. And for those desiring solitude, small lakes and streams abound where only the rustle of the wind and the sound of rushing water await you.

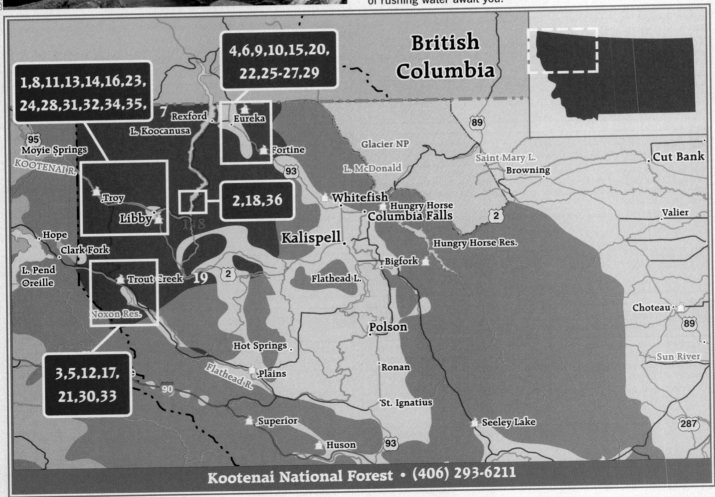

Kootenai National Forest • (406) 293-6211

1 Bad Medicine
Troy • lat 48°13'15" lon 115°51'18"

DESCRIPTION: CG is situated in a grove of fir, pine, and larch. Fish for trout, kokanee salmon, perch, and bass in adjacent Bull Lake. Check fishing regulations. Mountain lions, bears, coyotes, deer, elk, eagles, osprey, loons, and moose in area. Busy weekends and holidays. Hiking and horse trails in area.

GETTING THERE: From Troy go S on state HWY 56 approx. 21 mi. to Ross Creek Cedar Road. Go W on Ross Creek Cedar Road approx. 2 mi. to Bad Medicine CG.

SINGLE RATE:	$7	OPEN DATES:	Apr-Nov
# of SINGLE SITES:	17	MAX SPUR:	32 feet
		MAX STAY:	14 days
		ELEVATION:	2440 feet

2 Barron Creek
Libby • lat 48°31'30" lon 115°17'00"

DESCRIPTION: CG is located in an open meadow with some fir and pine. Great fishing for kokanee, camloops, and ling in adjacent, 90 mi. long, Lake Koocanusa. Visitor's center in area. Deer, bears, and mountain lions in area. Rarely full. Gather firewood locally. Hiking trails nearby. No drinking water.

GETTING THERE: From Libby go E on state HWY 37 approx. 12 mi. to forest route 228. Go N on 228 approx. 14 mi. to Barron Creek CG.

SINGLE RATE:	Varies	OPEN DATES:	Yearlong
# of SINGLE SITES:	15		
		MAX STAY:	14 days
		ELEVATION:	2500 feet

3 Big Eddy
Clark Fork • lat 48°03'30" lon 115°53'30"

DESCRIPTION: CG is located in ponderosa pine, larch and some cottonwood on the Cabinet Gorge Reservoir. Boat on the resevoir and fish for trout, perch, pike, and bass. Wildlife includes mountain lions, deer, elk, moose, bald eagles, grouse, and turkeys. Numerous trails in area. Boat ramp in area.

GETTING THERE: From Clark Fork go E on state HWY 200 approx. 14 mi. to Big Eddy CG.

SINGLE RATE:	No fee	OPEN DATES:	Yearlong
# of SINGLE SITES:	34	MAX SPUR:	40 feet
		MAX STAY:	14 days
		ELEVATION:	2200 feet

4 Big Therriault Lake
Eureka • lat 48°56'38" lon 114°53'22"

DESCRIPTION: CG is in larch, spruce, and fir on Big Therriault Lake. Boat fish for westslope cutthroat, and bull trout. Grizzly bears, black bears, mountain lions, wolves, coyotes, deer, elk, moose, wolverines, lynx, loons, osprey, and eagles in area. CG is busy in summer. Hiking/horse trails in area.

GETTING THERE: From Eureka go S on US HWY 93 approx. 8 mi. to forest route 114. Go N on 114 approx. 14 mi. to forest route 319. Follow 319 approx. 14 mi. to Big Therriault Lake CG.

SINGLE RATE:	$3	OPEN DATES:	Yearlong
# of SINGLE SITES:	10	MAX SPUR:	32 feet
		MAX STAY:	14 days
		ELEVATION:	5540 feet

5 Bull River
Clark Fork • lat 48°01'54" lon 115°50'37"

DESCRIPTION: CG is located in ponderosa pine, larch, and some cottonwood on the mouth of Bull River at Cabinet Gorge Reservoir. Boat and fish for trout, perch, pike, and bass. Mountain lions, deer, elk, moose, bald eagles, grouse, and turkeys in area. Numerous trails in area. Boat ramp on site.

GETTING THERE: From Clark Fork go E on state HWY 200 approx. 18 mi. to Bull River CG.

SINGLE RATE:	$7	OPEN DATES:	Apr-Nov
# of SINGLE SITES:	26	MAX SPUR:	32 feet
		MAX STAY:	14 days
		ELEVATION:	2200 feet

6 Camp 32
Rexford • lat 48°50'21" lon 115°10'15"

DESCRIPTION: This CG is situated among pine, aspen, birch, and larch along Pinkham Creek. Fish for small trout in creek. Wildlife in area includes black bears, mountain lions, coyotes, deer, moose, and raccoons. Gather firewood locally or bring your own. Busy weekends and holidays. Pinkham Falls Trail in area.

GETTING THERE: From Rexford go S on state HWY 37 7 mi. to forest route 7182. Go E on 7182 2.5 mi. to Camp 32 CG. Not recommended for trailers.

SINGLE RATE:	No fee	OPEN DATES:	Apr-Nov
# of SINGLE SITES:	1	MAX SPUR:	20 feet
		MAX STAY:	14 days
		ELEVATION:	3200 feet

7 Caribou
Yaak • lat 48°56'56" lon 115°30'08"

DESCRIPTION: CG is located in lodgepole pine at the confluence of Caribou Creek and the East Fork of the Yaak River. Fly fish for trout. mountain lions, coyotes, deer, elk, and moose in area. Busy weekends and holidays. Hiking and horse trails in area. CG may be frequented by bears. No drinking water.

GETTING THERE: From Yaak go E on primary forest route 92 approx. 17 mi. to Caribou CG.

SINGLE RATE:	No fee	OPEN DATES:	Apr-Nov
# of SINGLE SITES:	3	MAX SPUR:	32 feet
		MAX STAY:	14 days
		ELEVATION:	3600 feet

8 Dorr Skeels
Troy • lat 48°16'04" lon 115°51'15"

DESCRIPTION: CG is located in a conifer grove. Fish for trout, kokanee, perch, and bass in adjacent Bull Lake. Check fishing regulations. Mountain lions, coyotes, deer, elk, eagles, osprey, loons, and moose in area. Busy weekends and holidays. Hiking/horse trails in area. CG may be frequented by bears. No drinking water.

GETTING THERE: From Troy go S on state HWY 56 approx. 13 mi. to Dorr Skeels CG.

SINGLE RATE:	No fee	OPEN DATES:	Yearlong
# of SINGLE SITES:	7	MAX SPUR:	32 feet
		MAX STAY:	14 days
		ELEVATION:	2200 feet

9 Gateway Boat Camp
Rexford • lat 49°00'00" lon 115°09'40"

DESCRIPTION: In pine and larch on Lake Koocanusa. Fish for salmon, ling cod, trout, and dolly varden. Black bears, mountain lions, coyotes, deer, moose, elk, and raccoons in area. Busy weekends and holidays. Hiking, horse, and mountain biking trail on site leads to Swisher Lake. No drinking water. Open dates vary with water levels.

GETTING THERE: Gateway Boat Camp is accessed by boat, foot, or horseback only and is located on the E side of Lake Koocanusa just below the US and Canadian border.

SINGLE RATE:	No fee	OPEN DATES:	Varies
# of SINGLE SITES:	1		
		MAX STAY:	14 days
		ELEVATION:	2460 feet

10 Grave Creek
Eureka • lat 48°48'30" lon 114°53'00"

DESCRIPTION: CG is in larch, spruce, fir, aspen, and cottonwood on Grave Creek. Fish for kokanee, westslope cutthroat, rainbow, bull, and brook trout. Wildlife in area includes grizzly bears, black bears, mountain lions, wolves, coyotes, deer, elk, moose, and eagles. Hiking/horse trails in area. No drinking water.

GETTING THERE: From Eureka go S on US HWY 93 8 mi. to forest route 114. Go N on 114 approx. 2.5 mi. to Grave Creek CG. No trailers larger than 12 feet.

SINGLE RATE:	No fee	OPEN DATES:	Yearlong
# of SINGLE SITES:	4	MAX SPUR:	20 feet
		MAX STAY:	14 days
		ELEVATION:	3500 feet

 Campground has hosts   **Reservable sites**   **Accessible facilities**   **Fully developed**   **Semi-developed**   **Rustic facilities**

NOTE: Open dates listed are typical. Actual dates are dependent on conditions such as snow pack.

11 Howard Lake
Libby • lat 48°06'04" lon 115°31'45"

DESCRIPTION: CG is located in firs, larch, cedar, and hemlock next to Howard Lake. Fish for rainbow trout. Grizzly and black bears, mountain lions, coyotes, lynx, deer, elk, moose, osprey, and bald eagles in the area. Busy weekends and holidays. Several horse and hiking trails in nearby Cabinet Wilderness.

GETTING THERE: From Libby go S on US HWY 2 approx. 13 mi. to primary forest route 231 (West Fisher Road). Go NW on 231 approx. 13 mi. to Howard Lake CG. Road is narrow with sharp curves.

SINGLE RATE:	$5	OPEN DATES:	May-Oct
# of SINGLE SITES:	9	MAX SPUR:	20 feet
		MAX STAY:	14 days
		ELEVATION:	4100 feet

12 Jackpine Flats
Thompson Falls • lat 47°40'00" lon 115°37'55"

DESCRIPTION: CG is situated among lodgepole pine near Beaver Creek. Fish for cutthroat trout in creek. Wildlife in area includes mountain lions, deer, elk, moose, bald eagles, grouse, and turkeys. CG can be busy during the hunting season. Numerous hiking trails in area. No drinking water on site.

GETTING THERE: From Thompson Falls go NW on state HWY 200 approx. 10 mi. to primary forest route 251. Go W on 251 approx. 9 mi. to Jackpine Flats CG.

SINGLE RATE:	No fee	OPEN DATES:	Yearlong
# of SINGLE SITES:	2		
		MAX STAY:	14 days
		ELEVATION:	2800 feet

13 Kilbrennan Lake
Troy • lat 48°35'48" lon 115°53'14"

DESCRIPTION: CG is located in grove of fir and pine. Fish for trout, perch, and bullhead in adjacent Kilbrennan Lake. Wildlife includes mountain lions, coyotes, deer, elk, eagles, osprey, loons, and moose. Busy weekends and holidays. Hiking and horse trails in area. CG may be frequented by bears. No drinking water.

GETTING THERE: From Troy go N 4 mi. on US HWY 2 to primary forest route 176. Take 176 N 9 mi. to forest route 2394. Go S on 2394 2 mi. to Kilbrennan Lake CG.

SINGLE RATE:	No fee	OPEN DATES:	Apr-Nov
# of SINGLE SITES:	7	MAX SPUR:	32 feet
		MAX STAY:	14 days
		ELEVATION:	2900 feet

14 Lake Creek
Libby • lat 48°02'21" lon 115°29'20"

DESCRIPTION: CG is in an open grove of lodgepole pine next to Lake Creek. Wildlife in the area includes grizzly and black bears, mountain lions, coyotes, lynx, deer, elk, moose, osprey, and bald eagles. CG can be busy weekends and holidays. Several horse and hiking trails in nearby Cabinet Wilderness.

GETTING THERE: From Libby go S on US HWY 2 approx. 22 mi. to primary forest route 231 (West Fisher Road). Go W on 231 approx. 5 mi. to Lake Creek CG.

SINGLE RATE:	No fee	OPEN DATES:	Yearlong
# of SINGLE SITES:	4	MAX SPUR:	32 feet
		MAX STAY:	14 days
		ELEVATION:	3300 feet

15 Little Therriault
Eureka • lat 48°56'38" lon 114°53'22"

DESCRIPTION: CG set in larch, spruce, and fir on Little Therriault Lake. Fish for westslope cutthroat, and bull trout. Grizzly bears, black bears, mountain lions, wolves, coyotes, deer, elk, moose, wolverines, lynx, loons, osprey, and eagles in area. CG is busy in summer. Hiking/horse trails in area.

GETTING THERE: From Eureka go S on US HWY 93 8 mi. to forest route 114. Go N on 114 approx. 14 mi. to forest route 319. Follow 319 approx. 14 mi. to Little Therriault Lake CG.

SINGLE RATE:	$3	OPEN DATES:	Yearlong
# of SINGLE SITES:	6	MAX SPUR:	32 feet
		MAX STAY:	14 days
		ELEVATION:	5540 feet

16 Loon Lake
Libby • lat 48°35'53" lon 115°40'14"

DESCRIPTION: CG is located in fir, larch, and pine next to Loon Lake. Fish for bullhead and trout. Wildlife in the area includes bears, mountain lions, coyotes, lynx, deer, elk, moose, osprey, and bald eagles. Busy weekends and holidays. Several horse and hiking trails in nearby Cabinet Wilderness. No drinking water.

GETTING THERE: From Libby go N on primary forest route 68 for approx. 15 mi. to primary forest route 471. Go W on 471 approx. 2.5 mi. to Loon Lake CG.

SINGLE RATE:	No fee	OPEN DATES:	Yearlong
# of SINGLE SITES:	4	MAX SPUR:	20 feet
		MAX STAY:	14 days
		ELEVATION:	3790 feet

17 Marten Creek
Trout Creek • lat 47°52'48" lon 115°43'51"

DESCRIPTION: CG is located in douglas firs, larch, lodgepole pine, and ponderosa pine on the Noxon Reservoir. Trophy bass fishing. Wildlife includes mountain lions, deer, elk, moose, bald eagles, grouse, and turkeys. CG can be busy weekends and holidays. Swamp Creek Trail leads to the Cabinet Wilderness.

GETTING THERE: From Trout Creek go W on forest route 2229 approx. 8 mi. to Marten Creek CG.

SINGLE RATE:	No fee	OPEN DATES:	Yearlong
# of SINGLE SITES:	3	MAX SPUR:	32 feet
		MAX STAY:	14 days
		ELEVATION:	2200 feet

18 McGillivray
Libby • lat 48°29'20" lon 115°17'55"

DESCRIPTION: CG is located in a dense grove of fir, larch, and pine near Lake Koocanusa. Fish for ling, kokanee, and camloops. Bears, mountain lions, coyotes, lynx, deer, elk, moose, osprey, and bald eagles in area. Busy weekend holidays. Hiking trails, boat ramp, fish cleaning station, and pavillion on site.

GETTING THERE: From Libby go E on state HWY 37 approx. 12 mi. to forest route 228. Go N on 228 approx. 10 mi. to McGillivray CG.

SINGLE RATE:	$6	OPEN DATES:	May-Sept
# of SINGLE SITES:	50	MAX SPUR:	32 feet
GROUP RATE:	Varies	MAX STAY:	14 days
# of GROUP SITES:	2	ELEVATION:	2500 feet

19 McGregor Lake
Libby • lat 48°01'48" lon 114°53'54"

DESCRIPTION: CG will be closed for reconstruction this year. Please contact the Libby Ranger District at (406)293-7773 for an opening date. This CG is set among lodgepole pine on McGregor Lake. Fishing for mackinaw. Bears, mountain lions, coyotes, lynx, deer, elk, moose, osprey, and bald eagles in the area.

GETTING THERE: From Libby go S on US HWY 2 approx. 53 mi. to McGregor Lake CG.

SINGLE RATE:	$5	OPEN DATES:	Yearlong
# of SINGLE SITES:	18	MAX SPUR:	32 feet
		MAX STAY:	14 days
		ELEVATION:	4040 feet

20 North Dickey Lake
Fortine • lat 48°43'30" lon 114°50'00"

DESCRIPTION: CG is set in larch, spruce, and fir on North Dickey Lake. Boat fish for kokanee, Kamloops rainbow, and brook trout. Wildlife in area includes grizzly bears, black bears, mountain lions, wolves, coyotes, deer, elk, moose, loons, osprey, and eagles. CG is busy in summer. Hiking/horse trails in area.

GETTING THERE: From Fortine go S on US HWY 93 approx. 5 mi. to forest route 3785. Go S on 3785 for approx. 1/2 mi. to North Dickey Lake CG.

SINGLE RATE:	$7	OPEN DATES:	Yearlong
# of SINGLE SITES:	25	MAX SPUR:	50 feet
		MAX STAY:	14 days
		ELEVATION:	3110 feet

 Campground has hosts   **Reservable sites**   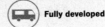 **Accessible facilities**   **Fully developed**   **Semi-developed**   **Rustic facilities**

NOTE: Open dates listed are typical. Actual dates are dependent on conditions such as snow pack.

21 North Shore
Trout Creek • lat 47°53'00" lon 115°38'00"

DESCRIPTION: CG is set among douglas firs, larch, lodgepole pine, and ponderosa pine on the Noxon Reservoir. Trophy bass fishing. Wildlife includes mountain lions, deer, elk, moose, bald eagles, grouse, and turkeys. CG is busy all summer. Swamp Creek Trail leads to the Cabinet Wilderness. Boat ramp on site.

GETTING THERE: From Trout Creek go NW on state HWY 200 approx. 3 mi. to North Shore CG.

SINGLE RATE:	$6	OPEN DATES:	Apr-Nov
# of SINGLE SITES:	13	MAX SPUR:	40 feet
		MAX STAY:	14 days
		ELEVATION:	2200 feet

26 Rock Lake
Eureka • lat 48°49'26" lon 115°00'33"

DESCRIPTION: CG is set in larch and fir on Rock Lake. Fish for rainbow trout. Grizzly bears, black bears, mountain lions, wolves, coyotes, deer, elk, moose, beavers, muskrats, loons, osprey, and eagles in area. Busy in summer. Hiking/horse trails. No drinking water. Facilities offered May 20-Oct 15.

GETTING THERE: From Eureka go S on forest route 688 for approx. 3 mi. to Rock Lake CG.

SINGLE RATE:	No fee	OPEN DATES:	Yearlong
# of SINGLE SITES:	5	MAX SPUR:	20 feet
		MAX STAY:	14 days
		ELEVATION:	3000 feet

22 Peck Gulch
Eureka • lat 48°43'29" lon 115°18'24"
 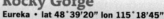

DESCRIPTION: CG is located in pine and larch on Lake Koocanusa. Fish for salmon, ling cod, trout, and dolly varden. Black bears, mountain lions, coyotes, deer, moose, elk, and raccoons in the area. Busy weekends and holidays. Hiking, horse, and mountain biking trail on site which leads to Swisher Lake.

GETTING THERE: From Eureka go approx. 1 mi. N on US HWY 93 to state HWY 37. Go W on 37 approx. 19 mi. to Peck Gulch CG.

SINGLE RATE:	$8	OPEN DATES:	Yearlong
# of SINGLE SITES:	75	MAX SPUR:	32 feet
		MAX STAY:	14 days
		ELEVATION:	2470 feet

27 Rocky Gorge
Eureka • lat 48°39'20" lon 115°18'45"

DESCRIPTION: CG is situated in pine and larch on Lake Koocanusa. Fish for salmon, ling, cod, trout, and dolly varden. Black bears, mountain lions, coyotes, deer, moose, elk, and raccoons in area. Busy weekends and holidays. Hiking, horse, and mountain biking trail on site. Facilities offered June 1-Sept 30.

GETTING THERE: From Eureka go approx. 1 mi. N on US HWY 93 to state HWY 37. Go W on 37 approx. 24 mi. to Rocky Gorge CG.

SINGLE RATE:	$8	OPEN DATES:	Yearlong
# of SINGLE SITES:	120	MAX SPUR:	32 feet
		MAX STAY:	14 days
		ELEVATION:	2470 feet

23 Pete Creek
Yaak • lat 48°49'51" lon 115°45'56"

DESCRIPTION: CG is located in grove of fir and pine at the confluence of Pete Creek and the Yaak River. Fish for brook and rainbow trout, and whitefish. Wildlife includes mountain lions, coyotes, deer, elk, and moose. Busy weekends and holidays. Hiking and horse trails in area. CG may be frequented by bears.

GETTING THERE: From Yaak go W on state HWY 508 approx. 2.5 mi. to Pete Creek CG.

SINGLE RATE:	$5	OPEN DATES:	Yearlong
# of SINGLE SITES:	12	MAX SPUR:	32 feet
		MAX STAY:	14 days
		ELEVATION:	3000 feet

28 Spar Lake
Troy • lat 48°16'11" lon 115°57'08"

DESCRIPTION: CG is located in an open grove of cedar and hemlock with lake views. Fish for trout, and kokanee salmon in adjacent Spar Lake. Wildlife includes mountain lions, coyotes, deer, elk, and moose. Busy weekends and holidays. Hiking and horse trails in area. CG may be frequented by bears.

GETTING THERE: From Troy go S on US HWY 2 approx. 3 mi. to primary forest route 384. Go S on 384 approx. 16 mi. to Spar Lake CG.

SINGLE RATE:	No fee	OPEN DATES:	May-Nov
# of SINGLE SITES:	8	MAX SPUR:	32 feet
		MAX STAY:	14 days
		ELEVATION:	4000 feet

24 Red Top
Yaak • lat 48°45'40" lon 115°55'05"

DESCRIPTION: CG is situated in douglas fir and ponderosa pine near Red Top Creek. Mountain lions, coyotes, deer, elk, and moose in area. Can be busy weekends and holidays. Trailhead on site leads to Red Top Mountain. Frequented by bears. No drinking water. Facilities offered May 20-Sept 30.

GETTING THERE: From Yaak go W on state HWY 508 approx. 12 mi. to Red Top CG.

SINGLE RATE:	No fee	OPEN DATES:	Yearlong
# of SINGLE SITES:	5	MAX SPUR:	32 feet
		MAX STAY:	14 days
		ELEVATION:	3000 feet

29 Swisher Lake
Eureka • lat 48°58'11" lon 115°07'57"

DESCRIPTION: CG is set in ponderosa pine on Swisher Lake. Fish for kamloops and rainbow trout. Black bears, mountain lions, coyotes, deer, moose, elk, and raccoons in area. Busy weekends and holidays. Hiking, horse, and mountain biking trail on site leads to Gateway Boat Camp. No drinking water. Walk-in sites only.

GETTING THERE: From Eureka go 1 mi. N on HWY 93 to HWY 37. Go W on 37 1 mi. to forest route 3440. Go N on 3440 3 mi. to forest route 3410. Go W on 3410 2 mi. to "T" intersection. Turn N to Swisher Lake CG.

SINGLE RATE:	No fee	OPEN DATES:	Yearlong
# of SINGLE SITES:	4		
		MAX STAY:	14 days
		ELEVATION:	2550 feet

25 Rexford Bench
Eureka • lat 48°54'08" lon 115°09'39"

DESCRIPTION: CG is located in fir and pine on Lake Koocanusa. Fish for salmon, ling cod, trout, and dolly varden. Wildlife in area includes black bears, mountain lions, coyotes, deer, moose, elk, and raccoons. Busy weekends and holidays. Hiking, horse, and mountain biking trail on site. Boat ramp.

GETTING THERE: From Eureka go approx. 1 mi. N on US HWY 93 to state HWY 37. Go W on 37 approx. 5 mi. to Rexforoute Bench CG.

SINGLE RATE:	$9	OPEN DATES:	May-Oct
# of SINGLE SITES:	54	MAX SPUR:	32 feet
		MAX STAY:	14 days
		ELEVATION:	2500 feet

30 Sylvan Lake
Libby • lat 47°54'57" lon 115°13'35"

DESCRIPTION: CG is set among large ponderosa pine and douglas firs on Sylvan Lake. Fish for cutthroat or canoe on the lake. Wildlife in the area includes grizzly and black bears, mountain lions, coyotes, lynx, deer, elk, moose, osprey, and bald eagles. Hiking trails in nearby Cabinet Wilderness. No drinking water.

GETTING THERE: From Libby go SE on US HWY 2 approx. 30 mi. to forest route 516 (Pleasant Valley Road). Go S on 516 approx. 7 mi. to forest route 7150. Go W on 7150 approx. 6 mi. to Sylvan Lake CG.

SINGLE RATE:	No fee	OPEN DATES:	May-Oct
# of SINGLE SITES:	5	MAX SPUR:	32 feet
		MAX STAY:	14 days
		ELEVATION:	3830 feet

 Campground has hosts   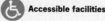 **Reservable sites**   **Accessible facilities**   **Fully developed**   **Semi-developed**   **Rustic facilities**

NOTE: Open dates listed are typical. Actual dates are dependent on conditions such as snow pack.

31 Timberlane

Libby • lat 48°29'23" lon 115°31'25"

DESCRIPTION: This CG is reservation only and is ideal for families and large groups. Set in spruce, larch, and fir near Pipe Creek. Fish for rainbow trout and swim in creek. Play volleyball and horseshoes in adjacent meadow. Bears, mountain lions, deer, moose, osprey, and eagles in the area. Hiking in area.

GETTING THERE: From Libby go N on primary forest route 68 for approx. 7 mi. to Timberlane CG.

SINGLE RATE:	$5	OPEN DATES:	June-Oct
# of SINGLE SITES:	11	MAX SPUR:	32 feet
		MAX STAY:	14 days
		ELEVATION:	2600 feet

36 Yarnell Island

Libby • lat 48°27'32" lon 115°17'43"

DESCRIPTION: CG is in fir and pine on two islands in Lake Koocanusa. Fish for ling, kokanee, and camloops. Bears, mountain lions, lynx, coyotes, deer, elk, moose, osprey, and bald eagles in area. Busy weekends and holidays. Horse and hiking trails in nearby Cabinet Wilderness. No drinking water. Open dates vary with water levels.

GETTING THERE: Yarnell Island CG is located on Yarnell Island in Lake Koocanusa approx. 3 mi. N of Libby Dam and is accessible only by boat.

SINGLE RATE:	No fee	OPEN DATES:	Varies
# of SINGLE SITES:	8	MAX STAY:	14 days
		ELEVATION:	2560 feet

32 Whitetail

Yaak • lat 48°49'40" lon 115°48'48"

DESCRIPTION: CG is located in grove of larch and douglas fir with forest and river views. Fish for trout and whitefish in adjacent Yaak River. Wildlife includes mountain lions, coyotes, deer, elk, and moose. Busy weekends and holidays. Hiking and horse trails in area. CG may be frequented by bears.

GETTING THERE: From Yaak go W on state HWY 508 approx. 5 mi. to Whitetail CG.

SINGLE RATE:	$5	OPEN DATES:	Yearlong
# of SINGLE SITES:	12	MAX SPUR:	32 feet
		MAX STAY:	14 days
		ELEVATION:	2910 feet

33 Willow Creek

Trout Creek • lat 47°52'20" lon 115°18'30"

DESCRIPTION: CG is set in larch and lodgepole pine at the confluence of Willow Creek and the Vermillion River. Fish for cutthroat and brook trout. CG can be busy during the hunting and berry-picking season. Many hiking trails in area. Wildlife in area includes mountain lions, deer, elk, moose, bald eagles, and grizzly bears.

GETTING THERE: From Trout Creek go NE on forest route 154 (Vermilion Road) approx. 19 mi. to Willow Creek CG. Large trailers not recommended.

SINGLE RATE:	No fee	OPEN DATES:	Yearlong
# of SINGLE SITES:	4	MAX SPUR:	20 feet
		MAX STAY:	14 days
		ELEVATION:	3600 feet

34 Yaak Falls

Troy • lat 48°38'55" lon 115°53'02"

DESCRIPTION: CG is located in fir, larch, and pine at confluence of the Yaak and Kootenai Rivers. Fish for cutthroat, rainbow, and brook trout. Wildlife includes mountain lions, coyotes, deer, elk, and moose. Frequented by bears. Busy weekends and holidays. Hiking and horse trails in area. No drinking water.

GETTING THERE: From Troy go N on US HWY 2 approx. 9 mi. to state HWY 508. Go N on 508 approx. 6 mi. to Yaak Falls CG.

SINGLE RATE:	No fee	OPEN DATES:	Yearlong
# of SINGLE SITES:	7	MAX SPUR:	32 feet
		MAX STAY:	14 days
		ELEVATION:	2400 feet

35 Yaak River

Troy • lat 48°33'37" lon 115°58'26"

DESCRIPTION: CG is located in fir, larch, and pine at the confluence of the Yaak and Kootenai Rivers. Fish for cutthroat, rainbow, and brook trout. Wildlife includes mountain lions, coyotes, deer, elk, and moose. CG may be frequented by bears. Busy weekends and holidays. Hiking and horse trails in area.

GETTING THERE: From Troy go N on US HWY 2 approx. 7 mi. to Yaak River CG.

SINGLE RATE:	$7	OPEN DATES:	Yearlong
# of SINGLE SITES:	44	MAX SPUR:	32 feet
		MAX STAY:	14 days
		ELEVATION:	1800 feet

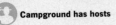 Campground has hosts   Reservable sites   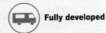 Accessible facilities   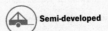 Fully developed   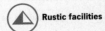 Semi-developed   Rustic facilities

NOTE: Open dates listed are typical. Actual dates are dependent on conditions such as snow pack.

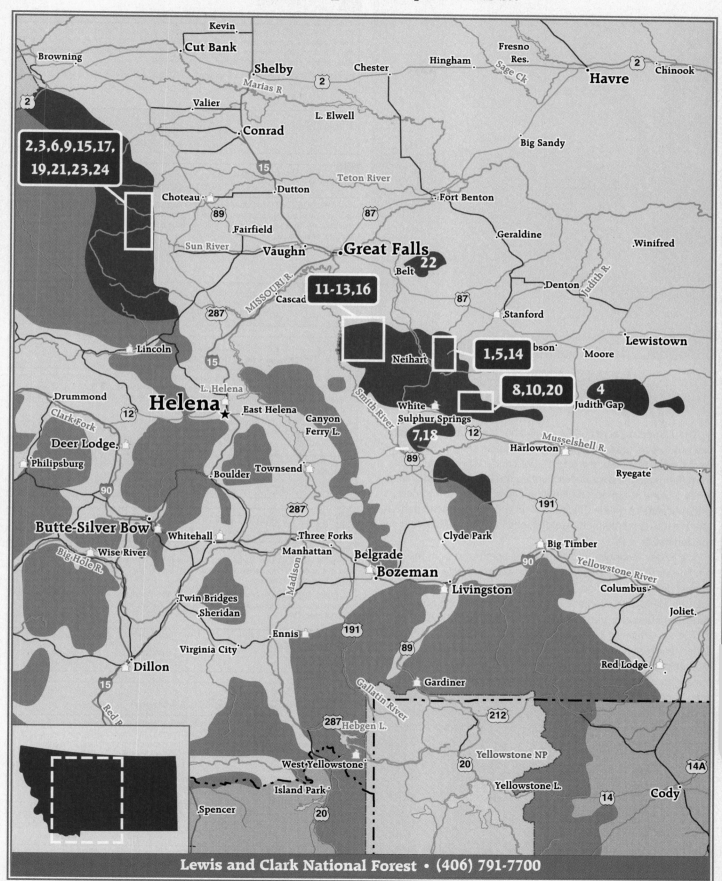

Kevin

Cut Bank

Browning

Shelby

Chester

Hingham

Fresno Res.

Sage Ck

Havre

Chinook

2

2

Valier

Marias R

L. Elwell

Big Sandy

Conrad

15

Teton River

Fort Benton

Choteau

89

Dutton

87

Geraldine

Winifred

Judith R.

2,3,6,9,15,17,
19,21,23,24

Fairfield

Sun River

Vaughn

Great Falls

Belt

22

Denton

87

Stanford

Cascade

11-13,16

Lewistown

Neihart

1,5,14

Moore

287

15

Lincoln

Smith River

8,10,20

4

Judith Gap

Drummond

Clark Fork

White
Sulphur Springs

Helena

East Helena

Canyon
Ferry L.

7,18

12

Musselshell R.

Harlowton

Deer Lodge

Boulder

Townsend

89

Ryegate

Philipsburg

12

287

191

Butte-Silver Bow

Whitehall

Three Forks

Clyde Park

Big Timber

Yellowstone River

Columbus

Big Hole R.

Wise River

Manhattan

Belgrade

90

Joliet

Twin Bridges

Bozeman

Livingston

Sheridan

191

Ennis

89

Red Lodge

Virginia City

Dillon

Gardiner

15

Red R

Gallatin River

212

287

Hebgen L.

Yellowstone NP

14A

West Yellowstone

20

Spencer

Island Park

Yellowstone L.

14

Cody

20

USFS Photo

LEWIS AND CLARK NATIONAL FOREST

The 1.8 million acres of the Lewis and Clark National Forest is like two forests scattered into seven mountain ranges. Situated in west central Montana, the forest's boundaries spread eastward from the rugged, mountainous Continental Divide onto the plains. When looking at a map, the forest appears as islands of forest within oceans of prairie. Because of its wide-ranging land pattern, the forest is separated into two divisions: the Rocky Mountain and the Jefferson.

The Rocky Mountain division extends southward from the southern border of Glacier National Park for approximately 100 miles. Almost half of the division, more than 380,000 acres, is part of the Bob Marshall Wilderness Complex. The remaining 390,000 acres are managed primarily for recreational opportunities.

The six remaining mountain ranges are spread across the Jefferson division of the forest. In comparison to the Rocky Mountains, where forest lands are contiguous to other national forests, these ranges spring from the surrounding expanses of wheat and ranch lands, creating a majestic rise in the flattened landscape. Mountain formations vary from the more dome-like, less obtrusive appearance of the Little Belts to the rocky spires of the Castle Mountains.

1 Aspen
Belt • lat 46°59'35" lon 110°46'03"

DESCRIPTION: CG is in an open canopy of aspen, fir, pine, and grass. Fishing in nearby Belt Creek. Hot summer days. Mining history throughout area. Supplies can be found 5 mi. in Neihart, White Sulphur Springs or Great Falls. Deer frequent the area. Gather firewood locally. Memorial Falls Trailhed is 5 mi. S of CG.

GETTING THERE: From Belt go S on US HWY 87/89 approx. 4 mi. to US HWY 89. Go S on 89 approx. 29 mi. to Aspen CG.

SINGLE RATE:	$6	OPEN DATES:	June-Oct
# of SINGLE SITES:	6	MAX SPUR:	63 feet
		MAX STAY:	14 days
		ELEVATION:	5129 feet

2 Benchmark
Augusta • lat 47°29'12" lon 112°52'49"

DESCRIPTION: This CG is situated on Wood Canyon Ford among conifer and aspen. CG is shady with cool temperatures. Pack it in, pack it out. Campers may gather their firewood locally. Supplies available at Augusta. Hike nearby Scapegoat Wilderness. Horse facilites available. Bears frequent the area.

GETTING THERE: From Augusta go W on forest road 235 approx. 30 mi. to Benchmark CG.

SINGLE RATE:	$5	OPEN DATES:	May-Nov
# of SINGLE SITES:	32		
		MAX STAY:	14 days
		ELEVATION:	5300 feet

3 Cave Mountain
Choteau • lat 47°53'34" lon 112°43'36"

DESCRIPTION: Located in the Front Range of the Rocky Mountains. Fish the North Fork of the Teton River. Shaded by aspen and fir with views of Sawtooth Range. Supplies at Choteau. Nature Conservancy and Montana Badlands nearby. Horse facilities. Middle Fork of the Teton trail head on site. Bears frequent area.

GETTING THERE: From Choteau go N on US HWY 89 approx. 5 mi. to forest route 144. Go W on 144 approx. 23 mi. to Cave Mountain CG.

SINGLE RATE:	$5	OPEN DATES:	May-Nov
# of SINGLE SITES:	14		
		MAX STAY:	14 days
		ELEVATION:	5200 feet

4 Crystal Lake
Lewistown • lat 46°47'40" lon 109°30'40"

DESCRIPTION: CG is situated in pine with thick underbrush. Short distance from Crystal Lake. Fly fishing on lake. Large open meadow in CG. Warmest temperatures in July. 35 mi. to supplies and groceries. Deer and mountain goats in area. Busy weekends and holidays. Several trails in area.

GETTING THERE: From Lewiston go W on US HWY 87 approx. 9 mi. to county route. Go S on county route approx. 16 mi. to forest road 275. Go S on 275 approx. 8.5 mi. to Crystal Lake CG.

SINGLE RATE:	$8	OPEN DATES:	June-Sept
# of SINGLE SITES:	28		
		MAX STAY:	14 days
		ELEVATION:	6040 feet

5 Dry Wolf
Stanford • lat 46°58'45" lon 110°31'03"

DESCRIPTION: CG is situated in pine with thick underbrush and grassy areas. Fishing on nearby Dry Wolf Creek. Frequently windy with moderate temperatures, weather can cool quickly. 30 mi. to supplies and groceries. Busy weekends and holidays. June-Aug are best. One trail on site. Facilities offered Mem. Day-Labor Day.

GETTING THERE: From Stanford go SW on county route approx. 17.5 mi. to forest route 251. Go SW on 251 approx. 6 mi. to Dry Wolf CG.

SINGLE RATE:	$5	OPEN DATES:	Yearlong
# of SINGLE SITES:	26		
		MAX STAY:	14 days
		ELEVATION:	5900 feet

 **Campground has hosts**   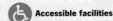 **Reservable sites**   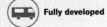 **Accessible facilities**   **Fully developed**   **Semi-developed**   **Rustic facilities**

NOTE: Open dates listed are typical. Actual dates are dependent on conditions such as snow pack.

6 Elko
Choteau • lat 47˚55'21" lon 112˚45'23"

DESCRIPTION: Located in timbered area with openings. Cool and shady CG. Stream fish for trout on nearby Teton River. groceries 31 mi. at Choteau. Bears, moose, elk, and deer in area. No drinking water. Firewood may be gathered, but scarce. Hiking, horse, snowmobile, and ATV trails. Parking lot on site. Bear regulations in effect.

GETTING THERE: From Choteau go N on US HWY 89 approx. 5 mi. to forest route 144. Go W on 144 approx. 25 mi. to Elko CG. Road plowed in winter.

SINGLE RATE:	No fee	OPEN DATES:	Yearlong
# of SINGLE SITES:	3	MAX SPUR:	18 feet
		MAX STAY:	14 days
		ELEVATION:	5720 feet

11 Jumping Creek
White Sulphur Springs • lat 46˚45'50" lon 110˚47'05"

DESCRIPTION: In a park-like setting with mixed sunny or shady sites. Expect strong storms and heat in mid-summer months. Trout fishing in Sheep Creek, which runs along CG. Supplies 19 mi. at White Sulphur Springs. Deer in area. Heavy use June-Aug.. Gather firewood locally. No water after Sept 15.

GETTING THERE: From White Sulphur Springs go E on US HWY 12 approx. 2.5 to US HWY 89. Go N on 89 approx. 19 mi. to Jumping Creek CG.

SINGLE RATE:	$6	OPEN DATES:	May-Nov
# of SINGLE SITES:	15	MAX SPUR:	68 feet
GROUP RATE:	$25	MAX STAY:	14 days
# of GROUP SITES:	1	ELEVATION:	5800 feet

7 Grasshopper Creek
White Sulphur Springs • lat 46˚32'14" lon 110˚44'17"

DESCRIPTION: Heavily forested hills surround the CG set among fir, aspen, and willows on Grasshopper Creek. Cool days, heavy shade. Stream fish for brook trout. groceries at White Sulphur Springs. Deer in area. Fills June-Aug. Several hiking, horse, and motor bike trails in area. Horse corrals available.

GETTING THERE: From White Sulphur Springs go E on US HWY 12 approx. 8 mi. to forest route 211. Go S on 211 approx. 4 mi. to Grasshopper Creek CG.

SINGLE RATE:	$6	OPEN DATES:	May-Nov
# of SINGLE SITES:	12	MAX SPUR:	55 feet
GROUP RATE:	Varies	MAX STAY:	14 days
# of GROUP SITES:	1	ELEVATION:	5700 feet

12 Kings Hill
White Sulpher Springs • lat 46˚50'30" lon 110˚41'46"

DESCRIPTION: This CG is situated among shady fir near historic CCC site and mining towns. Mild days, cold nights. Supplies can be found 30 mi. S at White Sulphur Springs. Deer and various small wildlife frequent the area. Campers may gather their firewood locally. No water after Sept 15.

GETTING THERE: From White Sulphur Springs go E on US HWY 12 approx. 2.5 mi. to US HWY 89. Go N on 89 approx. 28 mi. to Kings Hill CG.

SINGLE RATE:	$6	OPEN DATES:	June-Nov
# of SINGLE SITES:	16	MAX SPUR:	50 feet
GROUP RATE:	$25	MAX STAY:	14 days
# of GROUP SITES:	2	ELEVATION:	7400 feet

8 Hay Canyon
Hobson • lat 46˚47'54" lon 110˚17'58"

DESCRIPTION: This CG is situated in pine with underbrush and grassy areas. Across the road from the South Fork of Judith Creek. Frequently windy with moderate temperatures. Fishing on creek. Historic Judith Station nearby. 30 mi. to groceries and supplies. Gather firewood locally.

GETTING THERE: From Hobson go W on state HWY 239 approx. 12 mi. to county route. Go SW on county route approx. 12 mi. to forest route 487. Go SW on forest route 487 approx. 5 mi. to Hay Canyon CG.

SINGLE RATE:	No fee	OPEN DATES:	Yearlong
# of SINGLE SITES:	9		
		MAX STAY:	14 days
		ELEVATION:	5200 feet

13 Logging Creek
Belt • lat 47˚05'51" lon 111˚00'44"

DESCRIPTION: Grassy areas shaded by fir on Logging Creek. Trout fishing is catch and release only. Supplies 23 mi. N at Belt. Deer in area, bear have been seen on occasion. Hiking, horse, and motor bike trails. No water after Sept 15. Rocky, steep road with sharp curves, RVs and low clearance vehicles not recommended.

GETTING THERE: From Belt go S on HWY 89 11 mi. to Evans-Riceville Road. Go W 6 mi. to forest route 67. Go S on 67 4 mi. to forest route 839. Go SW on 839 2 mi. to Logging Creek CG.

SINGLE RATE:	$6	OPEN DATES:	May-Nov
# of SINGLE SITES:	26		
GROUP RATE:	$25	MAX STAY:	14 days
# of GROUP SITES:	1	ELEVATION:	4500 feet

9 Home Gulch
Augusta • lat 47˚36'52" lon 112˚43'01"

DESCRIPTION: This CG is located along the North Fork of the Sun River among aspen with cliff and river views. Fishing in the river. Shady, recieving moderate use. Supplies and groceries available at Augusta. Campers may gather their firewood locally. Bears frequent the area. No services after Labor Day.

GETTING THERE: From Augusta go NW on forest route 108 approx. 21 mi. to Home Gulch CG. Narrow road.

SINGLE RATE:	$5	OPEN DATES:	May-Nov
# of SINGLE SITES:	15		
		MAX STAY:	14 days
		ELEVATION:	4580 feet

14 Many Pine
Belt • lat 46˚53'56" lon 110˚41'14"

DESCRIPTION: Shady area among fir with mild days, cool nights. Trout fishing is catch and release only on Belt Creek which runs through CG. Historic mining towns nearby. Supplies 5 mi. N at Neihart. Deer frequent area. Gather firewood locally. Easy hike 2 mi. N to Memorial Falls. No water after Sept 15.

GETTING THERE: From Belt go S on US HWY 87/89 approx. 4 mi. to US HWY 89. Go S on 89 approx. 37 mi. to Many Pine CG.

SINGLE RATE:	$6	OPEN DATES:	May-Nov
# of SINGLE SITES:	23	MAX SPUR:	60 feet
GROUP RATE:	$25	MAX STAY:	14 days
# of GROUP SITES:	1	ELEVATION:	6040 feet

10 Indian Hill
Lewistown • lat 46˚48'53" lon 110˚17'03"

DESCRIPTION: CG is set in pine with underbrush and grassy areas. Across the road from the South Fork of Judith Creek. Frequently windy with moderate temps. Fishing on creek. 30 mi. to supplies and groceries. Various small wildlife in area, with occasional bears and deer. Busy holidays, best in July.

GETTING THERE: From Hobson go W on state HWY 239 approx. 12 mi. to county route. Go SW on county route approx. 12 mi. to forest route 487. Go SW on forest route 487 approx. 3 mi. to Indian Hill CG.

SINGLE RATE:	No fee	OPEN DATES:	Yearlong
# of SINGLE SITES:	7		
		MAX STAY:	14 days
		ELEVATION:	5900 feet

15 Mill Falls
Choteau • lat 47˚51'32" lon 112˚46'28"

DESCRIPTION: Heavily timbered site, shady and cool all summer. Views of Mill Falls. No drinking water. Supplies 34 mi. at Choteau. Bears, deer, and mtn. lions in area. Bring your own firewood. Horse and hiking trails into Bob Marshall Wilderness. Snowmobile trails outside wilderness areas. Bear regulations in effect.

GETTING THERE: From Choteau go N on US HWY 89 approx. 5 mi. to forest route 144. Go W on 144 approx. 16 mi. to forest route 109. Go S on 109 approx. 10 mi. to Mill Falls CG.

SINGLE RATE:	No fee	OPEN DATES:	Yearlong*
# of SINGLE SITES:	4	MAX SPUR:	20 feet
		MAX STAY:	14 days
		ELEVATION:	5760 feet

 Campground has hosts **Reservable sites** **Accessible facilities** **Fully developed** **Semi-developed** **Rustic facilities**

NOTE: Open dates listed are typical. Actual dates are dependent on conditions such as snow pack.

16 Moose Creek
White Sulpher Springs • lat 46°50'09" lon 110°52'27"

DESCRIPTION: This CG is set in an open area surrounded by heavily forested hills. Mild days with light use. Trout fishing is catch and release only on Moose Creek, which runs through the CG. Supplies and groceries can be found 16 mi. S on HWY 89. Deer frequent the area. Gather firewood on site.

GETTING THERE: From White Sulphur Springs go E on US HWY 12 2.5 mi. to US HWY 89. Go N on 89 16 mi. to forest route 119. Go W on 199 4 mi. to forest route 204. Go N on 204 3 mi. to Moose Creek.

SINGLE RATE:	$6	OPEN DATES:	June-Oct
# of SINGLE SITES:	5	MAX SPUR:	25 feet
GROUP RATE:	$25	MAX STAY:	14 days
		ELEVATION:	5600 feet

21 Summit
East Glacier • lat 48°19'11" lon 113°21'00"

DESCRIPTION: This CG is situated among fir with views of Summit Mountain. Warm to hot days in summer, with cool nights. CG recieves moderate use. Historic Memorial Square nearby. Wildlife in area includes deer, elk, bears, mountain lions, and moose. Firewood may be gathered on site.

GETTING THERE: From East Glacier Park go S on US HWY 2 approx. 10 mi. to Summit CG.

SINGLE RATE:	$8	OPEN DATES:	May-Oct
# of SINGLE SITES:	21		
		MAX STAY:	14 days
		ELEVATION:	5235 feet

17 Mortimer Gulch
Augusta • lat 47°36'37" lon 112°46'07"

DESCRIPTION: This CG is situated in a beautiful aspen and fir forest near Gibson Reservoir. Fish for trout on reservoir. Supplies and groceries in Augusta. CG recieves moderate use. Gather firewood locally. Wildlife in area includes elk, deer, bears, and moose. Hiking and horse trails nearby.

GETTING THERE: From Augusta go NW on forest route 108 approx. 26 mi. to Mortimer Gulch CG.

SINGLE RATE:	$6	OPEN DATES:	May-Nov
# of SINGLE SITES:	28	MAX SPUR:	20 feet
		MAX STAY:	14 days
		ELEVATION:	4910 feet

22 Thain Creek
Great Falls • lat 47°28'32" lon 110°35'00"

DESCRIPTION: CG is situated in pine with thick underbrush and grassy areas on the Thain and Briggs Creeks. Moderate temperatures, often windy with weather changing fast. Fly and bait fishing on creeks. 40 mi. to groceries. Busy holidays. July-Sept are best. Two trails on site.

GETTING THERE: From Great Falls go 6 mi. E on HWY 89 to HWY 228. Go 13 mi. E to E Highwood rt.. Go 8 mi. E to Burley Hill rt.. Go 3 mi. NE to FR121. Go 7 mi. E to FR8841, 1 mi. to Thain Creek CG.

SINGLE RATE:	$5	OPEN DATES:	Yearlong
# of SINGLE SITES:	16		
		MAX STAY:	14 days
		ELEVATION:	4700 feet

18 Richardson Creek
White Sulphur Springs • lat 46°32'14" lon 110°44'07"

DESCRIPTION: This CG is in a park-like setting with views of the surrounding mountains. Richardson Creek runs through the CG. Historical Castle Town is approx. 10 mi. E on forest route 112. Supplies are at White Sulphur Springs. Campers may gather dead and down firewood. Several trails are nearby.

GETTING THERE: From White Sulphur Springs go E on state HWY 12 approx. 7 mi. to forest route 211. Go approx. 4 mi. on 211 to the Y in road and go left for 1 mi. Follow road to Richardson Creek CG.

		OPEN DATES:	June-Oct
GROUP RATE:	No fee	MAX STAY:	14 days
# of GROUP SITES:	3	ELEVATION:	5700 feet

23 West Fork Teton
Choteau • lat 47°57'27" lon 112°48'08"

DESCRIPTION: Set in timber grove adjacent to Teton River. Views of Mt. Wright. Light stream trout fishing. Supplies at Choteau. Bears, elk, and deer in area. Bring your own firewood. Hiking, horse, ATV, and mtn. biking trails nearby. Bob Marshall Wilderness Access. Horse facilities nearby. Bear regs in effect.

GETTING THERE: From Choteau go N on US HWY 89 approx. 5 mi. to forest route 144. Go W on 144 approx. 33 mi. to West Fork Teton CG.

SINGLE RATE:	No fee	OPEN DATES:	Yearlong*
# of SINGLE SITES:	6	MAX SPUR:	30 feet
		MAX STAY:	14 days
		ELEVATION:	5800 feet

19 South Fork
Augusta • lat 47°30'07" lon 112°53'13"

DESCRIPTION: Set among lodgepole near the Sun River with views of the Bob Marshal Wilderness. groceries at Augusta. Deer, elk, black and grizzly bears in area. Gather firewood locally. Hiking, ATV, and horse trails. Access to the Bob Marshal Wilderness. Horse facilities nearby. Bear regulations in effect.

GETTING THERE: From Augusta go W on forest route 235 approx. 31 mi. to South Fork CG.

SINGLE RATE:	$6	OPEN DATES:	May-Nov
# of SINGLE SITES:	7	MAX SPUR:	30 feet
		MAX STAY:	14 days
		ELEVATION:	5320 feet

24 Wood Lake Camping
Augusta • lat 47°25'40" lon 112°47'34"

DESCRIPTION: Set in open park-like area adjacent to Wood Lake with views of lake and Crown Mountain. Canoeing and trout fishing on lake. Supplies at Augusta. Bears, deer, elk, and 7 Peregrin Falcons in area. Bring your own firewood. Hiking, horse, and mountain biking trails nearby. Bear regulations in effect.

GETTING THERE: From Augusta go W on forest route 235 approx. 25 mi. to Wood Lake Camping CG.

SINGLE RATE:	$5	OPEN DATES:	May-Nov
# of SINGLE SITES:	9	MAX SPUR:	30 feet
		MAX STAY:	14 days
		ELEVATION:	5880 feet

20 Spring Creek
White Sulpher Spgs • lat 46°35'11" lon 110°28'00"

DESCRIPTION: This CG is situated in cottonwood with underbrush. Set in a spring creek bottom. Moderate temperatures, often windy. Good fishing on nearby streams. 12 mi. to groceries and supplies. Various wildlife, bears frequent the area. Busy on holidays. Mid-June or July are best times. Trails in area.

GETTING THERE: From White Sulpher Springs go E on US HWY 12 approx. 24 mi. to forest route 274. Go N on 274 approx. 4 mi. to Spring Creek CG.

SINGLE RATE:	$5	OPEN DATES:	May-Dec
# of SINGLE SITES:	10		
		MAX STAY:	14 days
		ELEVATION:	5300 feet

 Campground has hosts 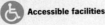 **Reservable sites**   **Accessible facilities**   **Fully developed**   **Semi-developed** **Rustic facilities**

NOTE: Open dates listed are typical. Actual dates are dependent on conditions such as snow pack.

LOLO NATIONAL FOREST

The Lolo National Forest surrounds the western Montana community of Missoula and is estimated to be the third largest forest in the northern region of the USDA Forest Service. Its 2.1 million acres of diverse and mountainous country extends into seven counties. The crest of the Bitterroot Mountains divides Montana from Idaho and serves as the forest's western boundary. The Continental Divide runs through the Scapegoat wilderness defining the forest's eastern boundary.

The forest provides recreation experiences in first-rate surroundings. You can travel along a forest trail or climb a challenging mountain peak. Several major tributaries to the Clark Fork River of the Columbia River Basin flow through the forest, offering some of the best fishing in the Rocky Mountains. The topography varies from remote, high alpine lakes to whitewater streams and from heavily forested ridges to smooth rolling meadows. A wide range of opportunities exists for everyone to enjoy.

R.E. Grossman Photo, USDA Forest service

Lolo National Forest • (406) 329-3750

1 Big Larch
Seeley Lake • lat 47°11'04" lon 113°29'30"

DESCRIPTION: CG is located in moderately dense conifer forest. Trout and pike fishing at adjacent Seeley Lake. 16 mi. to historic Lewis and Clark route. Supplies in Seeley Lake. Various water fowl including loons. Busy weekends. Gather firewood locally. Interpretive trail on site. Many hiking, horse, bike trails.

GETTING THERE: From Seeley Lake go N on state HWY 83 approx. 1 mi. to Big Larch CG.

SINGLE RATE:	$8	OPEN DATES:	Yearlong
# of SINGLE SITES:	48		
		MAX STAY:	14 days
		ELEVATION:	3993 feet

6 Clark Memorial
Thompson Falls • lat 47°37'56" lon 115°10'21"

DESCRIPTION: CG is located in an open grove of cottonwood and conifer with river views. Moderate weather and temperatures. Fly fishing on Thompson River. Supplies 11 mi. to Thompson Falls. Deer and moose in vicinity. Gather firewood locally. Several trails in area. Ticks in early season.

GETTING THERE: From Thompson Falls go E on state HWY 200 approx. 4.5 mi. to primary forest route 56. Go N on 56 approx. 6 mi. to Clark Memorial CG.

SINGLE RATE:	No fee	OPEN DATES:	May-Oct
# of SINGLE SITES:	4	MAX SPUR:	24 feet
		MAX STAY:	14 days
		ELEVATION:	2700 feet

2 Big Nelson
Lincoln • lat 47°04'15" lon 112°55'14"

DESCRIPTION: This CG is situated among douglas fir and larch on Coopers Lake. Fishing on lake. Various wildlife in the area includes bears, deer, and elk. Supplies and grocs. approx. 20 mi. to Lincoln. Campers may gather their firewood locally. Full on weekends and in July and August.

GETTING THERE: From Lincoln go W on state HWY 200 approx. 1 mi. to primary forest route 4106. Go N on 4106 approx. 19 mi. to Big Nelson CG.

SINGLE RATE:	No fee	OPEN DATES:	June-Sept
# of SINGLE SITES:	5		
		MAX STAY:	14 days
		ELEVATION:	4200 feet

7 Clearwater Crossing
Superior • lat 46°54'37" lon 114°47'50"

DESCRIPTION: CG is located in a lodgepole flat on the west fork of Fish Creek. Fly and spin fishing for cutthroats. Near Great Burn proposed wilderness. 25 mi. to Alberton, MT. for grocs.. Moose, deer, elk, and bears in area. Full on holidays. Several trails leave from CG. Horses accomodated.

GETTING THERE: From Superior go E on I-90 approx. 17 mi. (just past Tarkio). Exit 90 and go S on forest route 343 approx. 9 mi. to forest 7750. Go W on 7750 approx. 6 mi. to Clearwater Crossing CG.

SINGLE RATE:	No fee	OPEN DATES:	June-Nov
# of SINGLE SITES:	3		
		MAX STAY:	14 days
		ELEVATION:	3468 feet

3 Bitterroot Flat
Philipsburg • lat 46°28'09" lon 113°46'31"

DESCRIPTION: CG is in park-like grove of large ponderosa pine with mountain and creek views. Fly and float fishing in Rock Creek which is in sight of CG. Supplies 28 mi. to Philipsburg. Moose, deer and big horn sheep in vicinity. Busy summer weekends. Gather firewood locally. CG is frequented by black bears.

GETTING THERE: From Philipsburg go W on state HWY 348 approx. 13 mi. to primary forest route 102. Go N on 102 approx. 15 mi. to Bitterroot Flat CG. Not recommended for vehicles over 24 feet.

SINGLE RATE:	$5	OPEN DATES:	Yearlong
# of SINGLE SITES:	15	MAX SPUR:	30 feet
		MAX STAY:	14 days
		ELEVATION:	4300 feet

8 Copper King
Thompson Falls • lat 47°37'10" lon 115°11'13"

DESCRIPTION: CG is situated in an old growth forest. Moderate weather and temperatures. Fly fishing on Thompson River. Supplies and groceries 10 mi. to Thompson Falls. Deer, moose, and bighorn sheep in area. CG is rarely full. Campers may gather their firewood locally. Several trailheads in surrounding area.

GETTING THERE: From Thompson Falls go E on state HWY 200 approx. 4.5 mi. to primary forest route 56. Go N on 56 approx. 5 mi. to Copper King CG. Road not suitable for long trailers or RVs.

SINGLE RATE:	No fee	OPEN DATES:	June-Oct
# of SINGLE SITES:	4	MAX SPUR:	50 feet
		MAX STAY:	14 days
# of GROUP SITES:	1	ELEVATION:	2700 feet

4 Cabin City
St. Regis • lat 47°22'30" lon 115°15'00"

DESCRIPTION: CG is located in mixed lodgepole pine and larch on Twelvemile Creek. Fishing on creek is good. CG includes a pleasant self-guided nature trail. Deer, moose, and beaver dams in surrounding area. 5 miles to supplies and groceries in St. Regis. CG tends to be busy on holidays.

GETTING THERE: From St. Regis go W on Old Mullen Road approx. 10 mi. to primary forest route 352. Go N on 352 approx. 1/4 mi. to Cabin City CG.

SINGLE RATE:	$5	OPEN DATES:	May-Sept
# of SINGLE SITES:	24	MAX SPUR:	50 feet
		MAX STAY:	14 days
		ELEVATION:	3200 feet

9 Dalles
Bonita • lat 46°33'23" lon 113°42'35"

DESCRIPTION: CG is in partly open and partly dense grove of pine and larch with mountain and creek views. Fly and float fishing in Rock Creek which borders CG. Supplies 21 mi. to Clinton. Moose, deer, and big horn sheep. Busy weekends. Gather firewood locally. Hiking trail nearby. Frequented by bears.

GETTING THERE: From Bonita go S on primary forest route 102 approx. 14 mi. to Dalles CG.

SINGLE RATE:	$5	OPEN DATES:	Yearlong
# of SINGLE SITES:	10	MAX SPUR:	30 feet
		MAX STAY:	14 days
		ELEVATION:	4200 feet

5 Cascade
St. Regis • lat 47°18'10" lon 114°39'32"

DESCRIPTION: CG is situated in a dense grove of pine, fir, and larch. Moderate temperatures and weather. Float fishing nearby on Clark Fork River. Historical mine trail. Supplies 15 mi. to Plains. Bighorn sheep in spring and fall. Gather firewood locally. Trails nearby. Ticks in early season.

GETTING THERE: From St. Regis go N on state HWY 135 approx. 16 mi. to Cascade CG.

SINGLE RATE:	$6	OPEN DATES:	May-Oct
# of SINGLE SITES:	9	MAX SPUR:	50 feet
GROUP RATE:	$10	MAX STAY:	14 days
# of GROUP SITES:	1	ELEVATION:	3040 feet

10 Fishtrap Creek
Thompson Falls • lat 47°48'30" lon 115°08'30"

DESCRIPTION: CG is open and park-like in ponderosa and lodgepole pine with mountain and stream views. Moderate weather and temperatures. Fly fishing on Fishtrap Creek. Supplies 30 mi. to Thompson Falls. Deer and moose in surrounding area. Full on holidays. Campers may gather firewood locally.

GETTING THERE: From Thompson Falls go E on state HWY 200 approx. 4.5 mi. to primary forest route 56. Go N on 56 approx. 15 mi. to primary forest route 516. Go N on 516 approx. 10 mi. to Fishtrap Creek CG.

SINGLE RATE:	No fee	OPEN DATES:	Yearlong
# of SINGLE SITES:	4	MAX SPUR:	30 feet
		MAX STAY:	14 days
		ELEVATION:	4200 feet

 Campground has hosts   🔒 **Reservable sites**   **Accessible facilities**   **Fully developed**   **Semi-developed**   **Rustic facilities**

NOTE: Open dates listed are typical. Actual dates are dependent on conditions such as snow pack.

Page 362

11 Fishtrap Lake
Thompson Falls • lat 47˚52'07" lon 115˚11'42"

DESCRIPTION: CG is located in open stand of young larch above Fishtrap Lake. 36 mi. to Thompson Falls for groceries and supplies. Good trout fishing in lake. Deer common in area. Could be full on holidays and always nice in Fall. Nice trail around lake. Access road not recommended for trailers.

GETTING THERE: From Thompson Falls go E on state HWY 200 5 mi. to forest route 56. Go N on 56 15 mi. to forest route 516. Go N on 516 12 mi. to forest route 7553. Go W on 7553 3 mi. to Fishtrap Lake CG.

SINGLE RATE:	No fee	OPEN DATES:	June-Oct
# of SINGLE SITES:	11	MAX SPUR:	24 feet
		MAX STAY:	14 days
		ELEVATION:	4052 feet

12 Gold Rush
Thompson Falls • lat 47˚31'00" lon 115˚18'00"

DESCRIPTION: CG is situated in pine and fir in thick under brush on east-fork Dry Creek. Moderate weather and temperatures. Deer and various small wildlife. 10 mi. to Thompson Falls for groceries and supplies. CG is rarely full. Firewood can be gathered locally. Goldrush Trail # 562 begins in CG.

GETTING THERE: From Thompson Falls go S on primary forest route 352 approx. 8 mi. to Gold Rush CG.

SINGLE RATE:	No fee	OPEN DATES:	June-Oct
# of SINGLE SITES:	6	MAX SPUR:	50 feet
		MAX STAY:	14 days
		ELEVATION:	3000 feet

13 Grizzly
Bonita • lat 46˚34'21" lon 113˚39'35"

DESCRIPTION: CG is located in partly park-like and partly dense grove of pine and fir with mountain views. Fly fishing in Ranch Creek which flows through CG. Supplies 18 mi. to Clinton. Moose, deer, big horn sheep in area. Busy weekends. Gather firewood locally. Hiking/horse trails nearby. Frequented by bears.

GETTING THERE: From Bonita go S on primary forest route 102 approx. 11 mi. to forest route 4296. Go S on 4296 approx. 1 mi. to Grizzly CG.

SINGLE RATE:	$5	OPEN DATES:	Yearlong
# of SINGLE SITES:	9	MAX SPUR:	26 feet
		MAX STAY:	14 days
		ELEVATION:	4200 feet

14 Harrys Flat
Bonita • lat 46˚31'58" lon 113˚45'05"

DESCRIPTION: CG is located in partly park-like and partly dense trees with creek and forest views. Fly and float fishing in Rock Creek which runs along CG. Moose, deer, and big horn sheep in area. Gather firewood locally. Hiking and horse trails nearby. Frequented by bears.

GETTING THERE: From Bonita go S on primary forest route 102 approx. 17 mi. to Harrys Flat CG.

SINGLE RATE:	$5	OPEN DATES:	Yearlong
# of SINGLE SITES:	19	MAX SPUR:	30 feet
		MAX STAY:	14 days
		ELEVATION:	4300 feet

15 Kreis Pond
Alberton • lat 47˚06'00" lon 114˚25'30"

DESCRIPTION: CG is in ponderosa pine and douglas fir on Kreis Pond. Views of Ninemile valley. Damp and cool in spring and late fall, warm in summer. Several historical sites in area. 13 mi. to Alberton for grocs.. Deer, elk, and bears in area. Full weekends and holidays. Several marked trails in area.

GETTING THERE: From Alberton go E on US HWY 10 approx. 5 mi. to forest route 476. Go N on 476 4 mi. to forest route 456. Go N on 456 3 mi. to forest route 2176. Go S on 2176 approx. 2 mi. to Kreis Pond CG.

SINGLE RATE:	No fee	OPEN DATES:	Apr-Dec
# of SINGLE SITES:	8		
		MAX STAY:	14 days
		ELEVATION:	3600 feet

16   Lake Alva
Seeley Lake • lat 47˚18'27" lon 113˚34'31"

DESCRIPTION: Situated among fir with heavy underbrush. CG is near a trout fishing stream and lake. Supplies at Seeley Lake. Wildlife in area includes loons and other waterfowl. Firewood may be gathered locally. Several trails begin within 10 mi. of CG. Be aware that bears frequent this CG.

GETTING THERE: From Seeley Lake go N on state HWY 83 approx. 12 mi. to Lake Alva CG.

SINGLE RATE:	$8	OPEN DATES:	May-Sept
# of SINGLE SITES:	41		
GROUP RATE:	Varies	MAX STAY:	14 days
# of GROUP SITES:	2	ELEVATION:	4100 feet

17 Lake Elsina
Seeley Lake • lat 47˚14'30" lon 113˚42'00"

DESCRIPTION: CG is situated in a forest setting with beautiful mountain views on Lake Elsina. Trout fishing on Lake Elsina. Wildlife in area includes loons and other waterfowl. Firewood may be gathered locally. Supplies are 15 mi. away in the town of Seely Lake. 4WD recomended. Bears frequent CG area.

GETTING THERE: From Seeley Lake go N on state HWY 83 approx. 4 mi. to primary forest route 4349. Go W on 4349 approx. 7 mi. to forest route 465. Go W on 465 approx. 5 mi. to Lake Elsina CG.

SINGLE RATE:	No fee	OPEN DATES:	July-Sept
# of SINGLE SITES:	2		
		MAX STAY:	14 days
		ELEVATION:	6200 feet

18 Lake Inez
Seeley Lake • lat 47˚17'40" lon 113˚34'01"

DESCRIPTION: This CG is situated in a conifer forest setting with views of Lake Inez. Trout and Pike fishing are good on the lake. Wildlife in area includes loons and other waterfowl. Campers may gather their firewood locally. Supplies and groceries can be found 9 mi. from CG at Seely Lake.

GETTING THERE: From Seeley Lake go N on state HWY 83 approx. 9 mi. to Lake Inez CG.

SINGLE RATE:	No fee	OPEN DATES:	Yearlong*
# of SINGLE SITES:	4		
		MAX STAY:	14 days
		ELEVATION:	4100 feet

19   Lee Creek
Lolo • lat 46˚42'19" lon 114˚32'10"

DESCRIPTION: CG is in partly park-like stand of pine and partly dense spruce forest. Trout and fly fishing in nearby Lee and Lolo Creeks. Visit historical Lolo Pass. Supplies 2 mi. to Lolo Hot Springs. Moose and deer in area. Gather firewood locally. Interpretive trail on site. Frequented by bears.

GETTING THERE: From Lolo go W on US HWY 12 approx. 25 mi. to forest route 699. Go S on 699 approx. 1/4 mi. to Lee Creek CG.

SINGLE RATE:	$8	OPEN DATES:	May-Oct
# of SINGLE SITES:	21	MAX SPUR:	40 feet
		MAX STAY:	14 days
		ELEVATION:	4200 feet

20   Lewis and Clark
Lolo • lat 46˚46'30" lon 114˚22'58"

DESCRIPTION: CG is in a mix of open and dense larch, fir, and pine with mountain views. Fly fishing on Lolo Creek which borders CG. Supplies 7 mi. in historic Lolo Hot Springs. Moose and deer in area. Firewood available on site. Hiking trail near CG. Frequented by black bears.

GETTING THERE: From Lolo go W on US HWY 12 approx. 15 mi. to Lewis and Clark CG.

SINGLE RATE:	$8	OPEN DATES:	May-Oct
# of SINGLE SITES:	16	MAX SPUR:	30 feet
		MAX STAY:	14 days
		ELEVATION:	3800 feet

 Campground has hosts   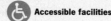 **Reservable sites**   **Accessible facilities**   **Fully developed**   **Semi-developed**   **Rustic facilities**

NOTE: Open dates listed are typical. Actual dates are dependent on conditions such as snow pack.

21 Monture Creek
Ovando • lat 47°07'24" lon 113°08'41"

DESCRIPTION: CG is set in a conifer forest with Monture Creek running beside it. Trout fishing off of creek. CG and trailheads are a portal to Bob Marshall Wilderness. Supplies are about 7 mi. away at Ovando. Campers may gather firewood. CG accomodates horses. Bears do frequent the area.

GETTING THERE: From Ovando go N on county route 89 approx. 7 mi. to Monture CG.

SINGLE RATE:	No fee	OPEN DATES:	June-Nov
# of SINGLE SITES:	6		
		MAX STAY:	14 days
		ELEVATION:	4200 feet

26 River Point
Seeley Lake • lat 47°11'14" lon 113°30'49"

DESCRIPTION: This CG is situated in a thick conifer forest with brush understory. Clearwater River and Seeley Lake next to CG. Fishing in river. Wildlife in area may include deer, moose, bears, and various waterfowl. Supplies are 3 mi. to Seeley Lake. Campers may gather and use firewood.

GETTING THERE: From Seeley Lake go W on primary forest route 77 approx. 2 1/2 mi. to River Point CG.

SINGLE RATE:	$8	OPEN DATES:	May-Sept
# of SINGLE SITES:	26	MAX SPUR:	30 feet
		MAX STAY:	14 days
		ELEVATION:	3933 feet

22 Norton
Bonita • lat 46°35'16" lon 113°40'04"

DESCRIPTION: CG is located in ponderosa pine forest with mountain views. Fly fishing in Rock Creek which is 1/4 mi. from CG. Visit the historic gold rush town of Quiggly. Moose, big horn sheep, and deer in area. Rarely full. Gather firewood locally. Hiking trails nearby. Frequented by black bears.

GETTING THERE: From Bonita go S on primary forest route 102 approx. 11 mi. to Norton CG.

SINGLE RATE:	$5	OPEN DATES:	Yearlong
# of SINGLE SITES:	13	MAX SPUR:	24 feet
		MAX STAY:	14 days
		ELEVATION:	3900 feet

27 Seeley Lake
Seeley Lake • lat 47°13'30" lon 113°31'04"

DESCRIPTION: CG is located in a huge old growth wester Larch with views of Seeley Lake. Supplies are 3 mi. at Seeley Lake. Campers may gather firewood locally or purchase in town. Wildlife in area may include deer, bears, waterfowl, and moose. The Seth Diamond Interpretive Trail is across the road from CG.

GETTING THERE: From Seeley Lake go W on primary forest route 77 approx. 3 mi. to Seeley Lake CG.

SINGLE RATE:	$9	OPEN DATES:	May-Sept
# of SINGLE SITES:	29	MAX SPUR:	30 feet
		MAX STAY:	14 days
		ELEVATION:	3993 feet

23 Old Alva
Seeley Lake • lat 47°18'27" lon 113°34'31"

DESCRIPTION: Set in a conifer forest with dense undergrowth and beautiful views of Lake Alva. Supplies are 10 mi. to Seely Lake. CG is near a trout fishing stream and lake. Wildlife in area includes loons and other waterfowl. Campers may gather firewood locally. Various hiking trails in area.

GETTING THERE: From Seeley Lake go N on state HWY 83 approx. 10 mi. to Old Alva CG.

SINGLE RATE:	No fee	OPEN DATES:	May-Oct*
# of SINGLE SITES:	8		
		MAX STAY:	14 days
		ELEVATION:	4200 feet

28 Siria
Philipsburg • lat 46°25'18" lon 113°42'54"

DESCRIPTION: CG is set in old growth pine forest w/ dense understory of fir. Mountain and open grassland views. Fly fishing in Rock Creek which runs along CG. Visit historic sites in area. Supplies in Philipsburg. Various wildlife. Gather firewood locally. Hiking/horse trails in area. Frequented by black bears.

GETTING THERE: From Philipsburg go W on state HWY 348 approx. 13 mi. to forest route 102. Go N on 102 approx. 10 mi. to Siria CG. CG road is very narrow and is not recommended for trailers or large RVs.

SINGLE RATE:	No fee	OPEN DATES:	Yearlong
# of SINGLE SITES:	4	MAX SPUR:	18 feet
		MAX STAY:	14 days
		ELEVATION:	4585 feet

24 Quartz Flat
Superior • lat 47°03'42" lon 114°46'58"

DESCRIPTION: CG is set in ponderosa pine within walking distance of the Clark Fork River. Fishing on river. Wildlife includes moose and deer. Waste disposal station available on site. Gas, groceries, and supplies available within 11 miles. Self-guided nature trail at CG.

GETTING THERE: From Superior go S on I-90 approx. 9 mi. to Quartz Flat CG.

SINGLE RATE:	$8	OPEN DATES:	May-Sept
# of SINGLE SITES:	50	MAX SPUR:	50 feet
		MAX STAY:	14 days
		ELEVATION:	2900 feet

29 Slowey
St. Regis • lat 47°14'22" lon 115°00'05"

DESCRIPTION: This CG is situated in ponderosa and lodgepole pine on the Clark Fork River. Carry-down boat ramp availble. Busy on holidays. Deer and various small wildlife in the vicinity. Gather firewood locally. Picnic area and playground available on site. Horse camp facilities.

GETTING THERE: From St. Regis go E on I-90 approx. 7 mi.. Exit onto Dry Creek Road (exit 43). Go approx. 3 mi. W on Dry Creek Road to Slowey CG. Located on Clark Fork River.

SINGLE RATE:	$7	OPEN DATES:	May-Sept
# of SINGLE SITES:	26	MAX SPUR:	50 feet
		MAX STAY:	14 days
		ELEVATION:	2800 feet

25 Rainy Lake
Seeley Lake • lat 47°20'17" lon 113°35'34"

DESCRIPTION: Set in a conifer forest with views of Swan Mountains and Rainy Lake. Trout fishing on Rainy Lake. Supplies are 12 mi. at Seely Lake. Campers may gather firewood locally. Wildlife in area includes waterfowl, deer, and bears. Bears can be a problem. Various hiking trails can be found in the area.

GETTING THERE: From Seeley Lake go N on state HWY 83 approx. 12 mi. to RainyLake CG.

SINGLE RATE:	No fee	OPEN DATES:	May-Oct*
# of SINGLE SITES:	6		
		MAX STAY:	14 days
		ELEVATION:	4200 feet

30 Trout Creek
Superior • lat 47°07'01" lon 114°52'04"

DESCRIPTION: CG is situated in mixed conifer forest on Trout Creek. Good fishing in creek. Busy on holidays. Groceries and supplies available within 7 miles in Superior. Campers may gather thier firewood locally. Deer and various small wildlife in area. Water and host available Memorial Day-Labor Day.

GETTING THERE: From Superior go S on primary forest route 250 approx. 6 mi. to Trout Creek CG.

SINGLE RATE:	$5	OPEN DATES:	Yearlong
# of SINGLE SITES:	12	MAX SPUR:	30 feet
		MAX STAY:	14 days
		ELEVATION:	2918 feet

 Campground has hosts 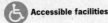 **Reservable sites** 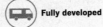 **Accessible facilities**   **Fully developed**   **Semi-developed** **Rustic facilities**

NOTE: Open dates listed are typical. Actual dates are dependent on conditions such as snow pack.

Good Creek
Flathead National Forest, Montana
Joel Stevenson Photo

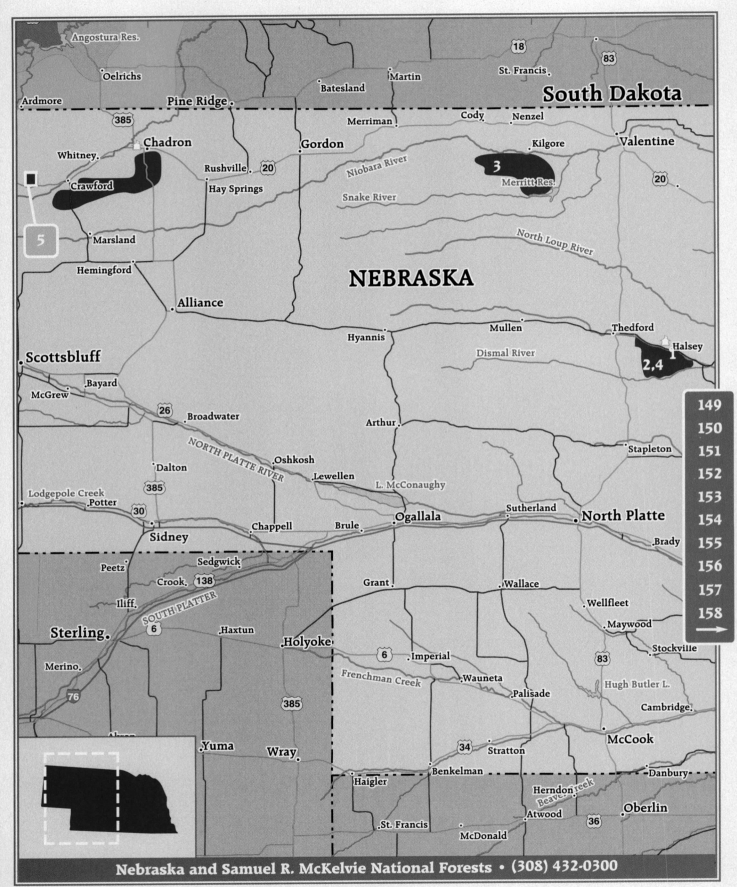

Angostura Res.

Oelrichs

Ardmore

Pine Ridge

Batesland

Martin

St. Francis

South Dakota

385

18

83

Whitney

Chadron

Merriman

Cody

Nenzel

Kilgore

Valentine

Rushville

20

Gordon

3

Hay Springs

Niobara River

Merritt Res.

20

Crawford

Snake River

5

Marsland

North Loup River

Hemingford

NEBRASKA

Alliance

Mullen

Thedford

Scottsbluff

Hyannis

Dismal River

Halsey

2,4

Bayard

McGrew

26

Broadwater

Arthur

Stapleton

NORTH PLATTE RIVER

Oshkosh

149

Dalton

Lewellen

L. McConaughy

150

Lodgepole Creek

385

Sutherland

North Platte

151

Potter

30

Chappell

Brule

Ogallala

Brady

152

Sidney

153

Peetz

Sedgwick

Grant

Wallace

154

Crook

138

Wellfleet

155

Iliff

SOUTH PLATTE

Maywood

156

Sterling

6

Haxtun

Holyoke

Stockville

157

Merino

6

Imperial

83

158

76

385

Frenchman Creek

Wauneta

Hugh Butler L.

→

Palisade

Cambridge

Yuma

Wray

34

Stratton

McCook

Benkelman

Danbury

Haigler

Herndon Creek

Beaver Creek

Oberlin

St. Francis

Atwood

36

McDonald

J. Schumacher Photo, USDA Forest Service

NEBRASKA AND SAMUEL R. MCKELVIE NATIONAL FOREST

This is a land of colorful contrasts from sandhills and flat, rolling prairies, to timbered hills, pine forests and spectacular rim rocks. The nearly 1.1 million acres are scattered across a large arc extending from central Nebraska west to the northern Panhandle, into southwestern South Dakota, and on east to the state's center. Representing a cross section of the northern Great Plains ecosystems are three national grasslands, the Buffalo Gap and Fort Pierre (pronounced "peer") in South Dakota, and the Oglala in Nebraska.

Outdoor recreation opportunities abound at the Bessey Recreation Comples. Broad, scenic vistas make any jaunt whether by car, on foot, or horseback, well worthwhile. The view from atop a butte can often be more expansive and scenic than from the beaten path. A swimming pool adds to the attractions of the area.

Rock hunters can find a variety of agates and rocks on the Oglala National Grassland. Hunting is the most popular activity, with mule deer, white-tail deer and pronghorn antelope the game animals preferred by hunters. Bird hunters can find turkey, sharp-tailed grouse and prairie chickens. Small streams in the Pine Ridge and Soldier Creek areas provide angling for rainbow, brook and brown trout. For a more primitive recreation experience, explore the Soldier Creek Managment Unit, a 10,000 acre area of native Ponderosa pine forest.

1 Bessey Recreation Complex
Thedford • lat 41°54'00" lon 100°17'50"

DESCRIPTION: CG is in trees with views of largest hand-planted forest in the US. Fish for trout on the Middle Loup River at CG. Historical Scott Fire Lookout nearby. Supplies at Halsey. Numerous birds. Busy holiday weekends. Firewood provided. Hiking trails nearby. Ticks in summer. Fish cleaning station and playground.

GETTING THERE: From Thedford go E on state HWY 2 approx. 15 mi. to Bessey Recreation Complex.

SINGLE RATE:	$12	OPEN DATES:	Yearlong
# of SINGLE SITES:	39	MAX SPUR:	30 feet
GROUP RATE:	$75	MAX STAY:	14 days
# of GROUP SITES:	1	ELEVATION:	2800 feet

2 Natick
Hasley • lat 41°52'30" lon 100°26'00"

DESCRIPTION: Among scattered timber stands and grasslands. Open views, great for sky watching, quiet. Fishing nearby. Historic CCC sites. Supplies at Halsey. Prairie birds, turkey, deer and antelopes. Full weekends and hunt seasons. No firewood. Hike, ATV, horse trails. Horse facilities. Ticks in summer.

GETTING THERE: From Hasley go W approx. 1.5 mi. to forest route 212 (forest entrance). Go W on 212 approx. 8 mi. to Natick CG.

SINGLE RATE:	$5	OPEN DATES:	Yearlong
# of SINGLE SITES:	5	MAX SPUR:	30 feet
		MAX STAY:	14 days
		ELEVATION:	2600 feet

3 Steer Creek
Nenzel • lat 42°41'22" lon 101°09'12"

DESCRIPTION: This CG is situated among ponderosa pine surrounded by grasslands with open views. Steer Creek next to CG. Trophy fishing in nearby reservoir. Supplies are available 15 mi. away. Full during hunting season. Firewood provided on site. Hiking trail at CG. Excellent stargazing.

GETTING THERE: From Nenzel go S on state HWY 97 approx. 9 mi. to Steer Creek CG.

SINGLE RATE:	$5	OPEN DATES:	Yearlong
# of SINGLE SITES:	23	MAX SPUR:	30 feet
		MAX STAY:	14 days
		ELEVATION:	3000 feet

4 Whitetail
Halsey • lat 41°47'46" lon 100°15'51"

DESCRIPTION: Among hardwoods and red cedar in park like open area. Overlooking the canoeing and tubing Dismal River (State Canoe Trail) and prairie. CCC built site nearby. Prairie birds, turkeys, deer, antelopes and coyotes in area. Bring your own firewood. ATV, horse trails. Horse facilities. Some poison ivy present.

GETTING THERE: From NE end of Halsey go W 1 mi. to state HWY 86B. Go E on 86B 2 mi. to forest route 203. Go E on 203 9 mi. to forest route 277. Go E on 277 3 mi. to Whitetail CG. Use caution on 203.

SINGLE RATE:	$5	OPEN DATES:	Yearlong
# of SINGLE SITES:	15	MAX SPUR:	30 feet
		MAX STAY:	14 days
		ELEVATION:	2695 feet

5 Toadstool Park
Crawford • lat 42°52'00" lon 103°34'00"

DESCRIPTION: CG is located in grass and native plants in classic badlands environment with hoodoos and other interesting rock formations. No natural shade but there are covered picnic tables. Supplies available at Crawford. Water available by hand pumps. Antelope, deer and rattle snakes in area. Interpretive trail through rock formations.

GETTING THERE: From Crawford go N on state HWY 2 approx. 4 mi. to forest route 904. Go W on 904 approx. 11 mi. to forest route 902. Go W on 902 approx. 1 mi. to Toadstool Park CG.

SINGLE RATE:	$5	OPEN DATES:	Yearlong
# of SINGLE SITES:	8	MAX SPUR:	35 feet
		MAX STAY:	14 days
		ELEVATION:	3500 feet

 Campground has hosts 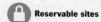 **Reservable sites** 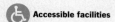 **Accessible facilities**   **Fully developed**   **Semi-developed**   **Rustic facilities**

NOTE: Open dates listed are typical. Actual dates are dependent on conditions such as snow pack.

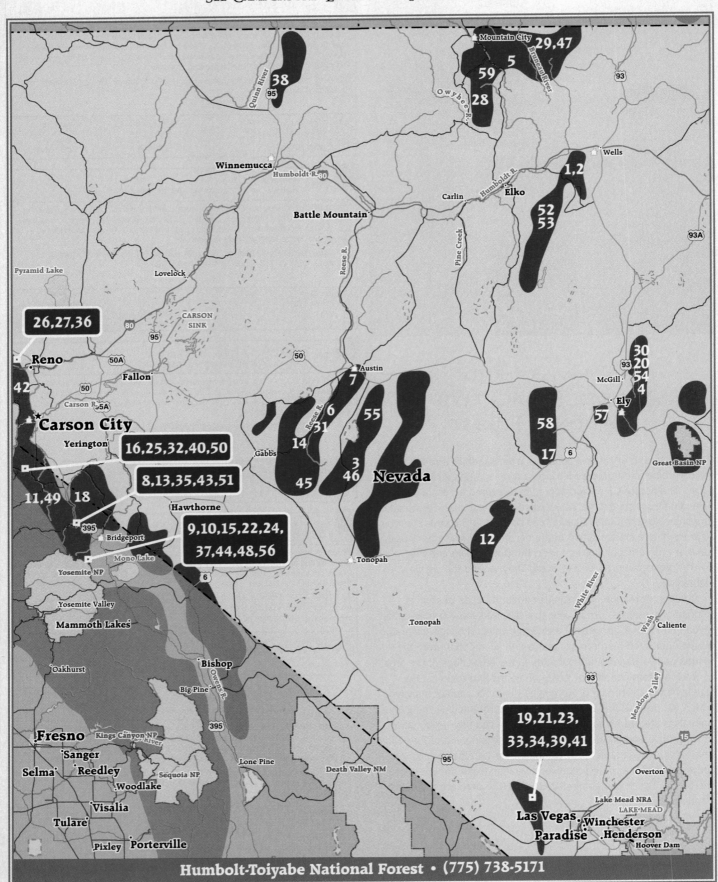

Scott Clemons Photo, USDA Forest Service

HUMBOLT-TOIYABE NATIONAL FOREST

The Humboldt-Toiyabe National Forest, the largest national forest outside the state of Alaska, sprawls from eastern California and western Nevada to the northeastern boundary of the state and on down to southern Nevada and takes in the higher elevations of some of Nevada's most spectacular mountain ranges. The name Nevada means "snow-capped" in Spanish. Thanks to its unique geographic history, Nevada has 26 mountain ranges, more than any other state in the nation.

In addition, the Humboldt-Toiyabe National Forest contains some of the most unique biological diversity in the nation. Many endemic plant and animal species (that is species found nowhere else in the world) are located here.

Great variations in climate, geology and topography, plants and wildlife, scenery and recreation blend together to provide nature lovers and outdoor recreationists a treasure trove of adventure.

Take a tour of the Lehman limestone caverns at Great Basin National Park. Soak in the soothing pools at Murphy Hot Springs. Picnic at the Levitt Falls Overlook or catch a glimpse of a herd of wild horses in the Ruby Mountains area. In winter, take advantage of the numerous cross-country and snowmobiling opportunities.

1 Angel Creek
Wells • lat 41°01'39" lon 115°02'58"

DESCRIPTION: CG in a tall aspen forest near Angel Lake. Good trout fishing at the lake. Supplies are 8 mi. away at Wells exit. Deer, antelope, and squirrels are common to the area. RV dump station at Flying J Truck Plaza at E Wells exit. Firewood for sale on site. Hiking and horseback riding trails in area.

GETTING THERE: From Wells go S on state HWY 231 approx. 7 mi. to forest route 500. Go S on 500 approx. .5 mi. to Angel Creek CG.

SINGLE RATE:	$6	OPEN DATES:	May-Nov
# of SINGLE SITES:	18	MAX SPUR:	35 feet
		MAX STAY:	14 days
		ELEVATION:	6800 feet

2 Angel Lake
Wells • lat 41°01'36" lon 115°05'01"

DESCRIPTION: This CG is sheltered by snowbank (dwarf) aspen near the shores of Angel Lake. Good fishing for trout in the lake. Supplies and RV disposal station at Flying J Truck Plaza (at the east Wells exit). Firewood is available for sale on site. Several hiking trails in the area.

GETTING THERE: From Wells go S on state HWY 231 approx. 7 mi. to forest route 231. Go S on 231 approx. 11 mi. to Angel Lake CG. Not recommended for trailers.

SINGLE RATE:	$12	OPEN DATES:	June-Sept
# of SINGLE SITES:	26	MAX SPUR:	35 feet
		MAX STAY:	14 days
		ELEVATION:	8500 feet

3 Barley
Tonopah • lat 38°39'17" lon 116°38'18"

DESCRIPTION: A remote and private CG in an open cottonwood forest setting. Supplies at Tonopah. Bighorn sheep, antelope, deer, rabbits, mountain lions and many birds can be seen from CG. Firewood may be gathered. This CG is a trailhead to the wilderness. Corrals for horses at CG.

GETTING THERE: From Tonopah go E on US HWY 6 approx. 5 mi. to state HWY 376. Go N on 376 approx. 11 mi. to state HWY 82 (Monitor Valley via Bellmont RD). Go NE on 82 approx. 39 mi. to Barley CG.

SINGLE RATE:	No fee	OPEN DATES:	Yearlong*
		MAX STAY:	14 days
		ELEVATION:	7834 feet

4 Berry Creek
Mcill • lat 39°20'57" lon 114°38'31"

DESCRIPTION: This primitive CG is in an open area of juniper. The sight and sounds of Berry Creek close to the CG makes for a relaxing stay. Supplies are available at Mcgill. Mule deer, coyotes, rabbits, birds, and squirrels are common to area. Many trails and old roads are nearby for hiking.

GETTING THERE: From Mcgill go N on US HWY 93 approx. 5 mi. to county route 1060. Go SE on 1060 approx. 11.5 mi. to county route 1067. Go E on 1067 approx. 5 mi. to Berry Creek CG.

SINGLE RATE:	No fee	OPEN DATES:	May-Sept
# of SINGLE SITES:	3		
		MAX STAY:	14 days
		ELEVATION:	8350 feet

5 Big Bend
Mountain City • lat 41°45'59" lon 115°41'57"

DESCRIPTION: This CG is situated among aspen trees. Historical Gold Creek Guard Station is located 2 mi. S of CG on forest route 056. The mining town site of Gold Creek is located 5 mi. S of Big Bend on county route 745. CG is popular with hunters. Fishing nearby. Supplies at Mountain City. Gather dead firewood.

GETTING THERE: From Mountain City go S on state HWY 225 approx. 4 mi. to forest route 930. Go E on 930 approx. 15.5 mi. to Big Bend CG.

SINGLE RATE:	$6	OPEN DATES:	June-Oct
# of SINGLE SITES:	15	MAX SPUR:	20 feet
		MAX STAY:	14 days
		ELEVATION:	6900 feet

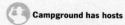 **Campground has hosts**   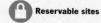 **Reservable sites**   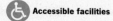 **Accessible facilities**   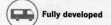 **Fully developed**   **Semi-developed**   **Rustic facilities**

NOTE: Open dates listed are typical. Actual dates are dependent on conditions such as snow pack.

6 Big Creek
Austin • lat 39°20'47" lon 117°08'10"

DESCRIPTION: This CG is situated among juniper and other mixed pine. Supplies are available at Austin. Watch for antelope, deer, mountain lions, bobcats, and small wildlife in the area. No designated trails are available for use; numerous roads and foot paths provide for limited hiking opportunities.

GETTING THERE: From Austin go W on US HWY 50 approx. 1.5 mi. to state HWY 722. Go W on 722 approx. .5 mi. to forest route 002. Go S on 002 approx. 12 mi. to Big Creek CG.

SINGLE RATE:	No fee	OPEN DATES:	May-Oct
# of SINGLE SITES:	6		
		MAX STAY:	14 days
		ELEVATION:	6900 feet

7 Bob Scott
Austin • lat 39°27'25" lon 116°59'43"

DESCRIPTION: This CG is situated among juniper and other mixed conifer. Supplies are available at Austin. Wildlife in the area includes deer, mountain lions, bobcats, and squirrels. No designated trails are available nearby.

GETTING THERE: Bob Scott CG is located approx. 6 mi. SE of Austin on US HWY 50.

SINGLE RATE:	No fee	OPEN DATES:	May-Oct
# of SINGLE SITES:	10	MAX SPUR:	10 feet
GROUP RATE:	$25	MAX STAY:	14 days
# of GROUP SITES:	1	ELEVATION:	7200 feet

8 Bootleg
Walker • lat 38°25'23" lon 119°26'58"

DESCRIPTION: Most of the sites in Bootleg are shaded by Jeffrey Pine trees. The West Walker River is located just on the other side of the road from the CG and offers great trout fishing. Check fishing regulations. Supplies at Walker. The Shingle Mill-Eastern Sierra Scenic Byway interpretive site is just N of the CG.

GETTING THERE: Bootleg CG is located approx. 7 mi. S of Walker on US HWY 395.

SINGLE RATE:	$10	OPEN DATES:	May-Sept
# of SINGLE SITES:	63	MAX SPUR:	20 feet
		MAX STAY:	14 days
		ELEVATION:	6600 feet

9 Buckeye
Bridgeport • lat 38°14'21" lon 119°20'38"

DESCRIPTION: CG rests among pine trees and sagebrush and is bordered by Buckeye Creek and Eagle Creek. A natural hot spring is at Buckeye Creek. Frequent afternoon t-showers. Trout fishing nearby. Hike the nearby Hoover Wilderness. Historic mining sites include Bodie State Historic Park. Firewood sold onsite.

GETTING THERE: From Bridgeport go NW on US HWY 395 approx. 4 mi. to forest route 017. Go SW on 017 approx. 5 mi. to Buckeye CG.

SINGLE RATE:	$9	OPEN DATES:	May-Oct
# of SINGLE SITES:	65	MAX SPUR:	40 feet
		MAX STAY:	14 days
		ELEVATION:	7000 feet

10 Buckeye Group
Bridgeport • lat 38°14'21" lon 119°20'38"

DESCRIPTION: This CG is located among large jeffrey pine trees and sagebrush. Bordered by Buckeye Creek and Eagle Creek. There are good fishing opportunities in both creeks. Hike the nearby Hoover Wilderness. Interpretive programs are provided at Robinson Creek CG, four miles away.

GETTING THERE: From Bridgeport go NW on US HWY 395 approx. 4 mi. to forest route 017. Go SW approx. 5 mi. to Buckeye Group CG. Road is narrow with sharp curves. Large vehicles should use caution.

		OPEN DATES:	May-Sept
		MAX SPUR:	40 feet
		MAX STAY:	14 days
GROUP RATE:	$40	ELEVATION:	7000 feet
# of GROUP SITES:	1		

11 Centerville Flats
Woodfords • lat 38°37'54" lon 119°43'12"

DESCRIPTION: This dispersed CG is located in a mixed conifer forest on the East Fork Carson River. Wildlife in the area includes black bears, deer, and birds. Enjoy a hike on the nearby Wolf Creek and High Trail/Carson River Trails that lead into the Carson-Iceberg Wilderness. Bring your own firewood.

GETTING THERE: From Woodford go S on state HWY 89 approx. 10 mi. to state HWY 4. Go S on 4 approx. 2.5 mi. to Centerville Flats CG.

SINGLE RATE:	No fee	OPEN DATES:	Apr-Sept
		MAX STAY:	16 days
		ELEVATION:	6000 feet

12 Cherry Creek
Sunnyside • lat 38°09'30" lon 115°37'30"

DESCRIPTION: Primitive CG in an open area of juniper with scenic canyon views. Cherry Creek nearby has access to the Quin Canyon Wilderness. Supplies located at Sunnyside. Mule deer, birds, coyotes, rabbits, and squirrels are common to area. Many trails and old roads are nearby for hiking.

GETTING THERE: Cherry Creek CG is located 42 mi. SW of Sunnside on the S end of Grant Range Wilderness.

SINGLE RATE:	No fee	OPEN DATES:	Apr-Oct
# of SINGLE SITES:	4		
		MAX STAY:	14 days
		ELEVATION:	6500 feet

13 Chris Flat
Walker • lat 38°23'41" lon 119°27'05"

DESCRIPTION: Chris Flat CG is not accessible at this time due to the destruction of HWY 395 during the New Year's flooding. The West Walker River flows through the CG and provides excellent fishing. Trout fishing can be done at the Walker River nearby. Check fishing regulations for the area.

GETTING THERE: Chris Flat CG is located approx. 9 mi. S of Walker on US HWY 395.

SINGLE RATE:	$10	OPEN DATES:	Apr-Nov
# of SINGLE SITES:	15	MAX SPUR:	20 feet
		MAX STAY:	14 days
		ELEVATION:	6600 feet

14 Columbine
Reese River • lat 38°53'59" lon 117°22'31"

DESCRIPTION: This CG is situated in a quaken aspen forest with Stewart Creek nearby. Fishing and playing at the creek. Supplies are available at Reese River. Deer and bears frequent the area. Campers may gather their firewood locally. Trailhead to Arc Dome Wilderness is nearby.

GETTING THERE: Columbine CG is located approx. 9 mi. SE of Reese River on forest route 119. 4WD is recommended.

SINGLE RATE:	No fee	OPEN DATES:	May-Oct
# of SINGLE SITES:	5		
		MAX STAY:	14 days
		ELEVATION:	9000 feet

15 Crags
Bridgeport • lat 38°10'30" lon 119°19'30"

DESCRIPTION: This CG is set among large jeffrey pine trees and sagebrush within the Twin Lakes Recreation Area. There is good fishing in Robinson Creek and Lower Twin Lake (both nearby). Interpretive programs and amphitheater are provided at Robinson Creek CG, one mile away. There is a boat ramp in the area.

GETTING THERE: Crags CG is located approx. 10 mi. SW of Bridgeport on county route 420 (forest route 018).

SINGLE RATE:	$10	OPEN DATES:	May-Oct*
# of SINGLE SITES:	27	MAX SPUR:	45 feet
GROUP RATE:	$60	MAX STAY:	14 days
# of GROUP SITES:	1	ELEVATION:	7000 feet

 Campground has hosts   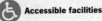 **Reservable sites**   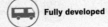 **Accessible facilities**   **Fully developed**   **Semi-developed**   **Rustic facilities**

NOTE: Open dates listed are typical. Actual dates are dependent on conditions such as snow pack.

16 Crystal Springs

Woodfords • lat 38°45'55" lon 119°50'42"

DESCRIPTION: This CG is situated in an open conifer forest. Popular activities include fishing, swimming, and boating (at Lake Tahoe). Enjoy a hike in the nearby Mokelumne Wilderness Area. Wildlife in the area includes deer and black bears. Supplies are available at Woodfords. Bring your own firewood.

GETTING THERE: Crystal Springs CG is located approx. 1 mi. W of Woodford on state HWY 88.

SINGLE RATE:	$9	**OPEN DATES:**	**Apr-Oct**
# of SINGLE SITES:	22	**MAX SPUR:**	**20 feet**
		MAX STAY:	**14 days**
		ELEVATION:	**6000 feet**

17 Currant Creek
Ely • lat 38°48'55" lon 115°21'10"

DESCRIPTION: Primitive CG set in an open area of juniper. The sight and sounds of Currant Creek close to the CG makes for a relaxing stay. Supplies located at Ely. Mule deer, coyotes, rabbits, birds, and squirrels are common to area. Many trails and old roads are nearby for hiking.

GETTING THERE: Currant Creek CG is located approx. 45 mi. SW of Ely on US HWY 6.

SINGLE RATE:	No fee	**OPEN DATES:**	**May-Sept**
# of SINGLE SITES:	7		
		MAX STAY:	**14 days**
		ELEVATION:	**6200 feet**

18 Desert Creek

Wellington • lat 38°37'17" lon 119°20'24"

DESCRIPTION: This CG is located in a mixed conifer forest near Desert Creek. There are fishing opportunities in the area but please check fishing regulations. Wildlife in the area includes deer and bears. There are numerous historic mining sites in the area. Supplies at Wellington. No drinking water on site.

GETTING THERE: From Wellington go SE on state HWY 338 approx. 3 mi. to forest route 027. Go S on 027 approx. 7 mi. to Desert Creek CG. 4WD required.

SINGLE RATE:	No fee	**OPEN DATES:**	**Apr-Oct**
# of SINGLE SITES:	13	**MAX SPUR:**	**20 feet**
		MAX STAY:	**14 days**
		ELEVATION:	**6300 feet**

19 Dolomite
Las Vegas • lat 36°18'27" lon 115°40'52"

DESCRIPTION: CG situated in an open pine forest leading up to a ridge. In the Spring Mountain National Recreation Area. Supplies at Las Vegas. Deer, chipmunks, and birds in area. Full on weekends. Firewood for sale on site. Hiking and biking on the Bristlecone Trail. CG may open late due to lingering snow.

GETTING THERE: From Las Vegas go NW on US HWY 95 approx. 29 mi. to state HWY 156. Go SW on 156 approx. 18 mi. to Dolomite CG. (Dolomite CG is located in Lee Canyon.)

SINGLE RATE:	$13	**OPEN DATES:**	**May-Oct**
# of SINGLE SITES:	30	**MAX SPUR:**	**40 feet**
		MAX STAY:	**14 days**
		ELEVATION:	**8500 feet**

20 East Creek

McGill • lat 39°29'49" lon 114°38'18"

DESCRIPTION: Primitive CG in an open area of juniper. The sight and sounds of East Creek close to the CG makes for a relaxing stay. Supplies located at Mcgill. Mule deer, coyotes, rabbits, birds, and squirrels are common to area. Many trails and old roads are nearby for hiking.

GETTING THERE: From McGill go N on US HWY 93 approx. 6 mi. to county road 1054. Go NE on 1054 approx. 4 mi. to county road 1056. Go E on 1056 approx. 3.5 mi. to East Creek CG.

SINGLE RATE:	No fee	**OPEN DATES:**	**June-Sept**
# of SINGLE SITES:	8		
		MAX STAY:	**14 days**
		ELEVATION:	**7300 feet**

21 Fletcher View

Las Vegas • lat 36°15'45" lon 115°37'01"

DESCRIPTION: This CG is situated in a pine forest located in the Spring Mountain National Recreation Area. Supplies are available at Las Vegas. Deer, chipmunks, and birds are common to the area. Full on weekends. Fletcher View Trail is nearby. CG may open late due to lingering snow.

GETTING THERE: From Las Vegas go NW on US HWY 95 approx. 6 mi. to state HWY 157. Go W on 157 approx. 17 mi. to Fletcher View CG. (Fletcher View CG is located in Kyle Canyon.)

SINGLE RATE:	$13	**OPEN DATES:**	**May-Oct**
# of SINGLE SITES:	12	**MAX SPUR:**	**25 feet**
		MAX STAY:	**14 days**
		ELEVATION:	**7000 feet**

22 Green Creek

Bridgeport • lat 38°06'39" lon 119°16'34"

DESCRIPTION: CG in a quiet primitive forest alongside of Green Creek. Green Lake and East or West Lakes are nearby. Excellent fishing from creek or lakes. Supplies are available at Bridgeport. Deer, bears, and birds are common to the area. Access point to the Hoover Wilderness. Horses allowed below CG.

GETTING THERE: From Bridgeport go S on US HWY 395 approx. 4.5 mi. to forest route 142. Go S on 142 approx. 8 mi. to Green Creek CG.

SINGLE RATE:	$8	**OPEN DATES:**	**May-Oct***
# of SINGLE SITES:	11	**MAX SPUR:**	**45 feet**
GROUP RATE:	Varies	**MAX STAY:**	**14 days**
# of GROUP SITES:	2	**ELEVATION:**	**7500 feet**

23 Hilltop

Las Vegas • lat 36°18'41" lon 115°36'22"

DESCRIPTION: This CG is situated in a juniper and pine forest located in the Spring Mountain National Recreation Area. Supplies at Las Vegas. Deer, chipmunks, and birds are common to the area. Full on weekends. Firewood for sale on site. No designated trails in the area. North Loop Trail is nearby.

GETTING THERE: From Las Vegas go NW on US HWY 95 approx. 29 mi. to state HWY 156. Go SW approx. 15 mi. to state HWY 158. Go SE approx. 4 mi. to Hilltop CG. Trailers over 25' long are not recommended.

SINGLE RATE:	Varies	**OPEN DATES:**	**May-Oct**
# of SINGLE SITES:	35	**MAX SPUR:**	**45 feet**
		MAX STAY:	**14 days**
		ELEVATION:	**8400 feet**

24 Honeymoon Flat
Bridgeport • lat 38°12'05" lon 119°19'12"

DESCRIPTION: CG in a primitive mountain setting of jeffrey pine and sagebrush next to Robinson Creek. Upper and Lower Twin Lakes are nearby. Great fishing and swimming in these lakes. Supplies at Bridgeport. Deer, bears, and birds are common to the area. Hiking trails nearby. Firewood for sale on site.

GETTING THERE: Honeymoon Flat CG is located approx. 7.5 mi. SW of Bridgeport on county route 420/forest route 018.

SINGLE RATE:	$9	**OPEN DATES:**	**Apr-Oct**
# of SINGLE SITES:	35	**MAX SPUR:**	**50 feet**
		MAX STAY:	**14 days**
		ELEVATION:	**7000 feet**

25 Hope Valley
Woodfords • lat 38°43'49" lon 119°55'41"

DESCRIPTION: This CG is situated in an open conifer forest. Popular activities include fishing, swimming, and boating (in Lake Tahoe). Enjoy a hike in the nearby Mokelumne Wilderness Area. Wildlife in the area includes deer and black bears. Supplies are available at Woodfords. Bring your own firewood

GETTING THERE: From Woodfords go W on state HWY 88 approx. 13 mi. to forest route 081. Go S on 081 approx. 2 mi. to Hope Valley CG.

SINGLE RATE:	$9	**OPEN DATES:**	**June-Sept**
# of SINGLE SITES:	20	**MAX SPUR:**	**20 feet**
GROUP RATE:	$16	**MAX STAY:**	**14 days**
# of GROUP SITES:	1	**ELEVATION:**	**7300 feet**

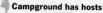 **Campground has hosts**   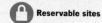 **Reservable sites**   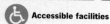 **Accessible facilities**   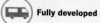 **Fully developed**    **Semi-developed**   **Rustic facilities**

NOTE: Open dates listed are typical. Actual dates are dependent on conditions such as snow pack.

26 Hunting Camp #2
Verdi • lat 39˚33'00" lon 120˚02'30"

DESCRIPTION: This CG is situated in an open conifer forest near a small spring. Accomodates large groups and has trailer parking sites. Visit the nearby Stampede Reservoir. Wildlife in this area includes deer and black bears. Supplies are available at Verdi. Bring your own firewood. Busy during hunting season.

GETTING THERE: Hunting Camp #2 is located approx. 3 mi. N of Verdi on forest route 046.

SINGLE RATE:	No fee	OPEN DATES:	Apr-Nov*
		MAX SPUR:	20 feet
		MAX STAY:	14 days
		ELEVATION:	6200 feet

27 Hunting Camp #4
Verdi • lat 39˚35'00" lon 120˚03'00"

DESCRIPTION: This CG is situated in an open conifer forest near a small spring. Accomodates large groups and has trailer parking sites. Visit the nearby Stampede Reservoir. Wildlife in this area includes deer and black bears. Supplies are available at Verdi. Bring your own firewood. Busy during hunting season.

GETTING THERE: Hunting Camp #4 CG is located approx. 6 mi. N of Verdi on forest route 046.

SINGLE RATE:	No fee	OPEN DATES:	Apr-Nov*
		MAX SPUR:	20 feet
		MAX STAY:	14 days
		ELEVATION:	6400 feet

28 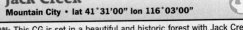 Jack Creek
Mountain City • lat 41˚31'00" lon 116˚03'00"

DESCRIPTION: This CG is set in a beautiful and historic forest with Jack Creek running along side. This creek as well as other streams and reservoirs in the area can be fished for trout, check regulations. This area is popular with hunters. Supplies are available at Mountain City. Gather downed firewood.

GETTING THERE: From Mountain City go S on state HWY 225 approx. 26 mi. to county route 732. Go W on 732 approx. 14 mi. to Jack Creek CG.

SINGLE RATE:	No fee	OPEN DATES:	May-Oct
# of SINGLE SITES:	6	MAX SPUR:	25 feet
		MAX STAY:	14 days
		ELEVATION:	6500 feet

29 Jarbidge
Jarbidge • lat 41˚51'48" lon 115˚25'42"

DESCRIPTION: Set in a primitive fir and cottonwood forest on Jarbridge River. Fish for trout in the river. Historical mining town of Jarbidge is only 1 mi. from CG. Supplies are available at Jarbidge. Deer, mountain lions, and birds are common to the area. Trailhead to Snow Slide Trail is approx. 1.5 mi. away.

GETTING THERE: Jarbidge CG is located approx. .5 mi. S of Jarbidge.

SINGLE RATE:	No fee	OPEN DATES:	May-Oct
# of SINGLE SITES:	3		
GROUP RATE:	No fee	MAX STAY:	14 days
# of GROUP SITES:	1	ELEVATION:	6300 feet

30 Kalamazoo
McGill • lat 39˚34'00" lon 114˚35'13"

DESCRIPTION: This primitive CG is situated in an open area of juniper. Supplies are available at Mcgill. Wildlife in the area includes mule deer, coyotes, rabbits, various birds, and squirrels. Hiking opportunities are available on the numerous trails and old roads in the surrounding area.

GETTING THERE: From Mcgill go N on US HWY 93 approx. 5 mi. to county route 1060. Go E on 1060 approx. 3.5 mi. to county route 1054. Go NE on 1054 approx. 9 mi. to Kalamazoo CG.

SINGLE RATE:	No fee	OPEN DATES:	June-Sept
# of SINGLE SITES:	5		
		MAX STAY:	14 days
		ELEVATION:	7000 feet

31 Kingston
Austin • lat 39˚13'34" lon 117˚08'30"

DESCRIPTION: This CG is situated among juniper and other mixed conifer on the shore Groves Lake. Fish for rainbow and brown trout in the lake. Non-motorized boats only. Supplies are available at Austin. Antelope, deer, mountain lions, and bobcats are common to the area. Toiyabe Crest Trail is nearby.

GETTING THERE: From Austin go W on US HWY 50 approx. 1.5 mi. to state HWY 722. Go W on 722 approx. .5 mi. to forest route 002. Go S on 002 approx. 24 mi. to Big Creek CG.

SINGLE RATE:	No fee	OPEN DATES:	May-Oct
# of SINGLE SITES:	11	MAX SPUR:	10 feet
GROUP RATE:	$25	MAX STAY:	14 days
# of GROUP SITES:	1	ELEVATION:	6800 feet

32 Kit Carson
Woodfords • lat 38˚46'35" lon 119˚53'48"

DESCRIPTION: This CG is situated in an open conifer forest near the West Fork Carson River. Offers trailer parking sites. Enjoy a hike in the nearby Mokelumne Wilderness. Wildlife in the area includes deer and black bears. Supplies are available at Woodfords. Bring your own firewood.

GETTING THERE: Kit Carson CG is located approx. 4 mi. W of Woodfords on state HWY 88.

SINGLE RATE:	$9	OPEN DATES:	May-Sept
# of SINGLE SITES:	12	MAX SPUR:	20 feet
		MAX STAY:	14 days
		ELEVATION:	6900 feet

33 Kyle Canyon
Las Vegas • lat 36˚15'46" lon 115˚36'21"

DESCRIPTION: CG located on a canyon floor, set between large pine tree covered slopes and Highway 157. CG parallels the creek bed. Fishing from creek. Open dates may vary due to lingering snow. Supplies can be found at Las Vegas. Firewood available from the CG manager. Numerous hiking trails in the area.

GETTING THERE: From Las Vegas go NW on US HWY 95 approx. 6 mi. to state HWY 157. Go W on 157 approx. 17 mi. to Kyle Canyon CG.

SINGLE RATE:	Varies	OPEN DATES:	May-Oct
# of SINGLE SITES:	19	MAX SPUR:	45 feet
GROUP RATE:	$55	MAX STAY:	14 days
# of GROUP SITES:	6	ELEVATION:	6900 feet

34 Kyle Canyon RV Camp
Las Vegas • lat 36˚15'49" lon 115˚36'58"

DESCRIPTION: This CG is situated in an open pine forest located in the Spring Mountain National Recreation Area. Supplies are available at Las Vegas. Deer, chipmunks, and birds are common to the area. Full on weekends. Firewood for sale on site. Fletcher View Trail is nearby. Maximum of 15 RV's at this CG.

GETTING THERE: From Las Vegas go NW on US HWY 95 approx. 6 mi. to state HWY 157. Go W on 157 approx. 17 mi. to Kyle Canyon RV Camp CG.

		OPEN DATES:	May-Oct
		MAX SPUR:	45 feet
GROUP RATE:	$55	MAX STAY:	14 days
# of GROUP SITES:	1	ELEVATION:	7000 feet

35 Leavitt Meadows
Walker • lat 38˚19'59" lon 119˚33'04"

DESCRIPTION: This CG is located in a mixed conifer forest on the West Walker River. There are trails leading from the day use parking area to nearby wilderness areas. Visit beautiful Silver Falls. Supplies are at Walker. Wildlife in the area includes deer, black bears, and birds. Busy weekend holidays.

GETTING THERE: From Walker go S on US HWY 395 approx. 12 mi. to state HWY 108. Go W on 108 approx. 7 mi. to Leavitt Meadows CG.

SINGLE RATE:	$9	OPEN DATES:	Apr-Nov
# of SINGLE SITES:	16	MAX SPUR:	20 feet
		MAX STAY:	14 days
		ELEVATION:	7000 feet

 Campground has hosts   **Reservable sites**   **Accessible facilities**   **Fully developed**   **Semi-developed**   **Rustic facilities**

NOTE: Open dates listed are typical. Actual dates are dependent on conditions such as snow pack.

36 Lookout
Verdi • lat 39°37'00" lon 120°03'30"

DESCRIPTION: This CG is situated in an open conifer forest near a small spring. Offers trailer parking sites. Enjoy a visit to the nearby Stampede Reservoir. Wildlife in the area includes deer and occasional black bears. Supplies are available at Verdi. Bring your own firewood.

GETTING THERE: Lookout CG is located approx. 7 mi. N of Verdi on forest route 046.

SINGLE RATE:	$5	OPEN DATES:	June-Sept
# of SINGLE SITES:	22	MAX SPUR:	20 feet
GROUP RATE:	$15	MAX STAY:	14 days
# of GROUP SITES:	1	ELEVATION:	6700 feet

37 Lower Twin Lakes
Bridgeport • lat 38°10'00" lon 119°19'00"

DESCRIPTION: In the Twin Lakes Recreation Area among pine trees and sagebrush. Robinson Creek flows through the CG with Lower Twin Lake nearby. Fish and swim in either place. Deer, bears, and birds in area. Boat ramp at CG. Firewood for sale on site. Interpretive programs and amphitheater at nearby Robinson Creek CG.

GETTING THERE: Lower Twin Lakes CG is located approx. 10 mi. SW of Bridgeport on county route 420/forest route 018.

SINGLE RATE:	$10	OPEN DATES:	May-Oct
# of SINGLE SITES:	15	MAX SPUR:	35 feet
		MAX STAY:	14 days
		ELEVATION:	7000 feet

38 Lye Creek
Paradise Valley • lat 41°41'30" lon 117°33'00"

DESCRIPTION: CG set among deeply wooded quaken aspen with Lye Creek running through. Fish for rainbow and brook trout from the creek. Supplies at Paradise Valley. Mule deer, bighorn sheep, squirrels, and birds in area. Full holidays and hunting season. No designated trails in the area. Use old roads for ATV's.

GETTING THERE: From Paradise Valley go N on State HWY 792 approx. 9 mi. to forest route 084. Continue N on 084 approx. 6 mi. to forest route 087. Go W on 087 approx. 2 mi. to Lye Creek CG.

SINGLE RATE:	Varies	OPEN DATES:	July-Oct
# of SINGLE SITES:	13	MAX SPUR:	20 feet
GROUP RATE:	$25	MAX STAY:	14 days
# of GROUP SITES:	1	ELEVATION:	7400 feet

39 Mahogany Grove Group
Las Vegas • lat 36°18'43" lon 115°36'58"

DESCRIPTION: This CG is situated in a juniper and pine forest located in the Spring Mountain National Recreation Area. Supplies are available at Las Vegas. Deer, chipmunks, and birds are common to the area. Full on weekends. Firewood for sale at Hilltop CG. No designated trails nearby.

GETTING THERE: From Las Vegas go NW on US HWY 95 approx. 29 mi. to state HWY 156. Go SW on 156 approx. 15 mi. to state HWY 158. Go SE on 158 approx. 4 mi. to Mahogany Grove Group CG.

		OPEN DATES:	May-Oct
		MAX SPUR:	99 feet
GROUP RATE:	$70	MAX STAY:	14 days
# of GROUP SITES:	2	ELEVATION:	8000 feet

40 Markleeville
Markleeville • lat 38°41'52" lon 119°46'23"

DESCRIPTION: This CG is situated in an open forest on Pleasant Valley Creek near the East Fork Carson River. Wildlife in the area includes deer, birds, and occasional black bears. Supplies are available in Markleeville. Enjoy a hike on the nearby Barney Riley Trail. Bring your own firewood.

GETTING THERE: Markleeville CG is located approx. 1 mi. E of Markleeville on state HWY 89.

SINGLE RATE:	$9	OPEN DATES:	Apr-Sept
# of SINGLE SITES:	10	MAX SPUR:	20 feet
		MAX STAY:	14 days
		ELEVATION:	5500 feet

41 McWilliams
Las Vegas • lat 36°18'33" lon 115°40'57"

DESCRIPTION: CG set in an open pine forest. Located in the Spring Mountain National Recreation Area. Supplies at Las Vegas. Deer, chipmunks, and birds are common to the area. Full on weekends. Firewood for sale on site. Hiking and biking on the Bristlecone Trail. CG may open late due to lingering snow.

GETTING THERE: From Las Vegas go NW on US HWY 95 approx. 29 mi. to state HWY 156. Go SW on 156 approx. 18 mi. to McWilliams CG. (McWilliams CG is located in Lee Canyon.)

SINGLE RATE:	Varies	OPEN DATES:	May-Oct
# of SINGLE SITES:	31	MAX SPUR:	25 feet
		MAX STAY:	14 days
# of GROUP SITES:	9	ELEVATION:	8500 feet

42 Mount Rose
Incline Village • lat 39°18'48" lon 119°53'29"

DESCRIPTION: This CG is set in an open conifer forest. BBQ and picnic tables are provided at each site. Popular activities include hiking, fishing, swimming, and boating (in Lake Tahoe). Access many trails from CG. Supplies at Incline Village. Bring your own firewood or purchase bundles on site.

GETTING THERE: Mount Rose CG is located approx. 7 mi. N of Incline Village on state HWY 27.

SINGLE RATE:	$9	OPEN DATES:	June-Sept
# of SINGLE SITES:	24	MAX SPUR:	50 feet
		MAX STAY:	14 days
		ELEVATION:	8900 feet

43 Obsidian
Walker • lat 38°17'52" lon 119°26'43"

DESCRIPTION: This CG is located in pine and sagebrush adjacent to the Little Walker River. There are fishing opportunities in the area but please check fishing regulations. Two nearby trails lead into the Hoover Wilderness. Supplies are available at Walker. No drinking water available on site.

GETTING THERE: From Walker go S on US HWY 395 approx. 13 mi. to forest route 066. Go S on 066 approx. 3.5 mi. to Obsidian CG.

SINGLE RATE:	$5	OPEN DATES:	June-Oct
# of SINGLE SITES:	14	MAX SPUR:	20 feet
		MAX STAY:	14 days
		ELEVATION:	7840 feet

44 Paha
Bridgeport • lat 38°10'11" lon 119°18'30"

DESCRIPTION: CG in a mountain setting of pine trees and sagebrush. Robinson Creek flows next to the CG with Lower Twin Lake nearby. Fish and swim in either place. Supplies at Bridgeport. Deer, bears, and birds are in the area. Hiking trails nearby. Interpretive programs and amphitheater at Robinson Creek CG.

GETTING THERE: Paha CG is located approx. 9.5 mi. SW of Bridgeport on county route 420/forest route 018.

SINGLE RATE:	$10	OPEN DATES:	May-Oct
# of SINGLE SITES:	22	MAX SPUR:	45 feet
		MAX STAY:	14 days
		ELEVATION:	7000 feet

45 Peavine
Carvers • lat 38°37'00" lon 117°19'00"

DESCRIPTION: CG in an open cottonwood forest with Peavine Stream running through. Fish in the stream. Supplies at Carvers. Bighorn sheep, deer, rabbits, mountain lions, and various birds reside in the area. Gather firewood locally. Toms Canyon Trail and Peavine Canyon Trail are nearby.

GETTING THERE: From Carvers go S on state HWY 376 approx. 20 mi. to forest route 020. Go W on 020 approx. 9 mi. to Peavine CG.

SINGLE RATE:	No fee	OPEN DATES:	Yearlong*
# of SINGLE SITES:	10	MAX SPUR:	26 feet
		MAX STAY:	14 days
		ELEVATION:	5500 feet

 Campground has hosts   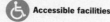 **Reservable sites**   **Accessible facilities**   **Fully developed**   **Semi-developed**   **Rustic facilities**

NOTE: Open dates listed are typical. Actual dates are dependent on conditions such as snow pack.

46 Pine Creek
Tonopah • lat 38°47'44" lon 116°50'58"

DESCRIPTION: A remote and private CG in an open cottonwood forest with Pine Creek running through. Fish in the creek. Supplies at Tonopah. Bighorn sheep, antelope, deer, rabbits, mountain lions, and many birds reside in the area. Gather firewood locally. Access the Alta Toquima Wilderness.

GETTING THERE: From Tonopah go E on US HWY 6 approx. 6 mi. to state HWY 376. Go N approx. 15 mi. to state HWY 82. Go NW approx. 44 mi. to forest route 009. Go W approx. 2.5 mi. to Pine Creek CG.

SINGLE RATE:	No fee	**OPEN DATES**	Yearlong*
# of SINGLE SITES:	24	**MAX SPUR:**	26 feet
		MAX STAY:	14 days
		ELEVATION:	6500 feet

51 Sonora Bridge
Walker • lat 38°21'55" lon 119°28'33"

DESCRIPTION: This CG is located in pine and sagebrush near Tule Lake and the West Walker River. There are fishing opportunities in the area but please check fishing regulations. Wildlife in this area includes deer, black bears, and birds. Hiking trails near this CG lead to the two nearby wilderness areas.

GETTING THERE: From Walker go S on US HWY 395 approx. 12 mi. to state HWY 108. Go W on 108 approx. 3 mi. to Sonora Bridge CG.

SINGLE RATE:	$9	**OPEN DATES**	May-Oct
# of SINGLE SITES:	23	**MAX SPUR:**	20 feet
		MAX STAY:	14 days
		ELEVATION:	6800 feet

47 Pine Creek
Jarbidge • lat 41°50'09" lon 115°25'31"

DESCRIPTION: CG set in a primative fir and cottonwood forest on Jarbridge River. Fish for trout in the river. Historical mining town of Jarbidge is only 1 mi. from CG. Supplies are at Jarbidge. Deer, mountain lions, and birds are common to the area. Trailhead to Snow Slide Trail is approx. 1.5 mi. away.

GETTING THERE: Pine Creek CG is located approx. 2 mi. S of Jarbidge on forest route 064.

SINGLE RATE:	No fee	**OPEN DATES:**	May-Oct*
# of SINGLE SITES:	4		
		MAX STAY:	14 days
		ELEVATION:	6600 feet

52 South Ruby
Elko • lat 40°10'30" lon 115°30'00"

DESCRIPTION: In a pine and juniper forest across the street from a wildlife refuge. Fish for trout and black bass. Deer and squirrels are common to the area. A fish cleaning and RV dump station are available across the road. Supplies 2 mi. S in Shanty Town. No designated trails in the area.

GETTING THERE: From Elko go S on state HWY 228 approx. 35 mi. to county route 718. Go SE on 718 approx. 13 mi. to county route 788. Go S on 788 approx. 9 mi. to South Ruby CG.

SINGLE RATE:	$6	**OPEN DATES**	May-Oct
# of SINGLE SITES:	35	**MAX SPUR:**	45 feet
		MAX STAY:	14 days
		ELEVATION:	6200 feet

48 Robinson Creek
Bridgeport • lat 38°11'10" lon 119°19'03"

DESCRIPTION: This CG is in large jeffrey pine and sagebrush with Robinson Creek flowing nearby. The Twin Lakes are also nearby. Good fishing opportunities at either place. Supplies at Bridgeport. Deer, bears, and birds in area. Trails nearby to the Hoover Wilderness. Interpretive programs and amphitheater on site.

GETTING THERE: Robinson Creek CG is located approx. 9 mi. SW of Bridgeport on county route 420/forest route 018.

SINGLE RATE:	$10	**OPEN DATES**	May-Oct
# of SINGLE SITES:	54	**MAX SPUR:**	40 feet
		MAX STAY:	14 days
		ELEVATION:	7000 feet

53 Thomas Canyon
Elko • lat 40°39'00" lon 115°24'13"

DESCRIPTION: This CG is surrounded by cottonwood and aspen trees with Lamoille Creek runing through. Fishing and playing in the creek. Supplies can be found 9 mi. away. Deer, elk, and birds can be seen in the surrounding area. Campers may gather thier firewood locally. Many trails are in the area.

GETTING THERE: From Elko go S on state HWY 228 approx. 6 mi. to state HWY 227. Go SE on 227 approx. 12 mi. to forest route 660. Go S on 660 approx. 7 mi. to Thomas Canyon CG.

SINGLE RATE:	$12	**OPEN DATES**	May-Sept
# of SINGLE SITES:	40	**MAX SPUR:**	45 feet
		MAX STAY:	14 days
		ELEVATION:	7600 feet

49 Silver Creek
Woodfords • lat 38°35'18" lon 119°47'06"

DESCRIPTION: This CG is located in an open forest near Silver Creek. Wildlife in the area includes deer, black bears, and birds. Enjoy a hike on the nearby trail which leads to Noble Lake and the Pacific Crest National Scenic Trail. Supplies are available in Woodfords. Bring your own firewood.

GETTING THERE: From Woodfords go S on state HWY 89 approx. 10 mi. to state HWY 4. Go S on 4 approx. 2.5 mi. to primary forest route 35. Go SW on 35 approx. 4 mi. to Silver Creek CG.

SINGLE RATE:	$9	**OPEN DATES**	June-Sept
# of SINGLE SITES:	22	**MAX SPUR:**	20 feet
		MAX STAY:	14 days
		ELEVATION:	6800 feet

54 Timber Creek
McGill • lat 39°24'04" lon 114°37'51"

DESCRIPTION: This CG rests in a forest of tall fir trees with beautiful canyon scenery. Timber Creek runs through the CG. Supplies are available at Mcgill. Mule deer, coyotes, rabbits, birds, and squirrels are common to area. Numerous hiking trails and old roads in the area for recreation.

GETTING THERE: From Mcgill go N on US HWY 93 approx. 5 mi. to county route 1060. Go SE on 1060 approx. 9.5 mi. to county route 1062. Go E on 1062 approx. 3.5 mi. to Timber Creek CG.

SINGLE RATE:	No fee	**OPEN DATES**	June-Sept
# of SINGLE SITES:	10		
		MAX STAY:	14 days
		ELEVATION:	8800 feet

50 Snowshoe Springs
Woodfords • lat 38°46'40" lon 119°53'06"

DESCRIPTION: This CG is situated in an open forest along side of the West Fork Carson River. Wildlife in the area includes deer, black bears, and birds. Bring your own firewood. Supplies are available at Woodfords. Enjoy a hike into Horsetheif Canyon on the adjacent trail.

GETTING THERE: Snowshoe Springs CG is located approx. 4 mi. W of Woodfords on state HWY 88.

SINGLE RATE:	$9	**OPEN DATES**	May-Sept
# of SINGLE SITES:	13	**MAX SPUR:**	20 feet
		MAX STAY:	14 days
		ELEVATION:	6600 feet

55 Toquima Caves
Austin • lat 39°11'30" lon 116°49'00"

DESCRIPTION: This CG is situated in a stand of juniper set in a mixed conifer forest. Investigate the Toquima Caves; only .25 mi. away. Enjoy spelunking in these natural caverns. Supplies are available at Austin. Watch for antelope, deer, mountain lions, bobcats, and small wildlife in the area.

GETTING THERE: From Austin go S on US HWY 50 approx. 11 mi. To state HWY 1. Go SE on 1 approx. 16 mi. to Toquima Caves CG.

SINGLE RATE:	No fee	**OPEN DATES**	May-Oct
# of SINGLE SITES:	4		
		MAX STAY:	14 days
		ELEVATION:	7880 feet

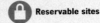 Campground has hosts   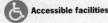 Reservable sites   Accessible facilities   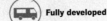 Fully developed   Semi-developed   Rustic facilities

NOTE: Open dates listed are typical. Actual dates are dependent on conditions such as snow pack.

Page 374

56 Trumbull Lake

Bridgeport • lat 38°03'02" lon 119°15'26"

DESCRIPTION: CG in a lodgepole pine forest with views of the Hoover Wilderness Area. Trumbull Lake is nearby for fishing and swimming. Deer and bears in area. Trails lead to the Hoover Wilderness and Yosemite National Park. Firewood sold on site. Interpretive activities occur at the Bridgeport Ranger Station.

GETTING THERE: From Bridgeport go S on US HWY 395 approx. 13 mi. to forest route 021. Go SW on 021 approx. 5 mi. to Trumbull Lake CG.

SINGLE RATE:	$9	OPEN DATES:	June-Oct
# of SINGLE SITES:	45	MAX SPUR:	82 feet
		MAX STAY:	14 days
		ELEVATION:	9500 feet

57 Ward Mountain

Ely • lat 39°12'43" lon 114°58'02"

DESCRIPTION: This CG is situated in an open area of juniper. CG is most developed site in the district. Supplies are available at Ely. Mule deer, coyotes, rabbits, birds, and squirrels are common to area. A major trail system is accessible from the CG, as well as several multi-use old roads.

GETTING THERE: From Ely go W on US HWY 50 approx. 1.5 mi. to US HWY 6. Go SW on 6 approx. 6 mi. to Ward Mountain CG.

# of SINGLE SITES:	27	OPEN DATES:	June-Sept
		MAX STAY:	14 days
		ELEVATION:	7200 feet

58 White River

Ely • lat 38°56'38" lon 115°20'25"

DESCRIPTION: A primitive CG set in an open area of juniper. Supplies are available at Ely. Wildlife in the area includes mule deer, coyotes, rabbits, various birds, and squirrels. Hiking opportunities are available on the numerous trails and old roads that can be found in the surrounding area.

GETTING THERE: From Ely go SW on US HWY 6 approx. 37 mi. to county route 1163. Go W on 1163 approx. 9 mi. to White River CG.

# of SINGLE SITES:	8	OPEN DATES:	June-Sept
		MAX STAY:	14 days
		ELEVATION:	7000 feet

59 Wildhorse Crossing

Mountain City • lat 41°43'00" lon 115°53'30"

DESCRIPTION: CG is adjacent to the Owyhee River. River can be fished for trout, check regulations. Wild Horse Crossing was an important meeting and trading ground for the Shoshone. Traditional brush shade shelters have been constructed in CG. Supplies are available at Mountain City. Trails nearby.

GETTING THERE: Wildhorse Crossing CG is located approx. 10 mi. S of Mountain City on state HWY 225.

SINGLE RATE:	$6	OPEN DATES:	June-Oct
# of SINGLE SITES:	22	MAX SPUR:	40 feet
		MAX STAY:	14 days
		ELEVATION:	5900 feet

  Campground has hosts   **Reservable sites**   **Accessible facilities**   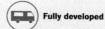 **Fully developed**   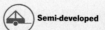 **Semi-developed**    **Rustic facilities**

NOTE: Open dates listed are typical. Actual dates are dependent on conditions such as snow pack.

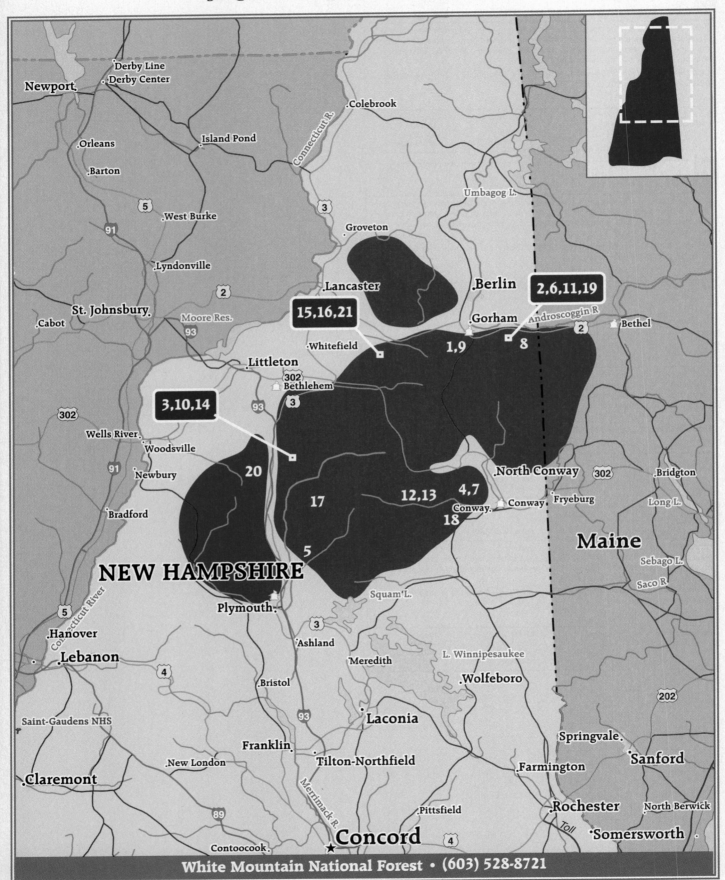

Newport

Derby Line
Derby Center

Colebrook

Orleans

Island Pond

Barton

5

West Burke

91

Connecticut R.

3

Groveton

Lyndonville

2

Umbagog L.

St. Johnsbury.

Moore Res.

Lancaster

Berlin

Cabot

93

Whitefield

15,16,21

2,6,11,19

Gorham

1,9

Androscoggin R.

8

Bethel

2

Littleton

302

Bethlehem

3,10,14

302

93

3

Wells River

Woodsville

North Conway

302

Bridgton

Newbury

20

Long L.

91

17

12,13

4,7

Bradford

Conway

18

Conway

Fryeburg

NEW HAMPSHIRE

5

Maine

Sebago L.

Squam'L.

Saco R

Plymouth.

Connecticut River

5

Ashland

3

Hanover

Meredith

L. Winnipesaukee

Lebanon

4

Bristol

Wolfeboro

202

Saint-Gaudens NHS

Springvale.

93

Laconia

Franklin

Sanford

New London

Tilton-Northfield

Farmington

Claremont

Merrimack R.

Rochester

North Berwick

89

Pittsfield

Toll

Somersworth

Concord

4

Contoocook

USFS Photo

WHITE MOUNTAIN NATIONAL FOREST

At nearly 800,000 acres, the forest covers a landscape ranging from hardwood forests (which give spectacular fall foliage) to the largest alpine area east of the Rocky Mountains and south of Canada. Spanning northern New Hampshire and southwestern Maine, the White Mountain has plenty of space just to sit back and relax.

The White Mountain provides a year-ground playground for outdoor enthusiasts. Some 1,200 miles of trails exist for groups of all experience levels, from the most expert mountain climber to the family out for an easy afternoon jaunt. Elevation varies from 500 feet to 6,288 feet at the top of Mount Washington, the highest peak east of the Mississippi. There are also five designated wilderness areas within the forest which offer backpackers more remote areas to explore.

In November, the forest becomes a winter wonderland for snowmobilers and skiers. Six downhill ski areas are located partially or totally in the forest and miles of touring trails and backcountry are available to nordic skiers.

The forest provides vital habitat for a number of wildlife including 184 species of birds, black bears, frogs, turtles, snakes and other mammals.

1 Barnes Field
Gorham • lat 44°20'20" lon 071°13'07"

DESCRIPTION: This CG features large, open sites located at the confluence of Peabody River and Bear Spring Brook. The CG provides one of the few winter camping opportunities in the Mt. Washington Valley. Enjoy fishing for trout and salmon in rivers and streams but please check fishing regulations.

GETTING THERE: From Gorham go S on state HWY 16 approx. 2 mi. to forest route 2. Go E on 2 approx. 1/4 mi. to Barnes Field CG.

SINGLE RATE:	$15	OPEN DATES:	Yearlong
# of SINGLE SITES:	3	MAX SPUR:	40 feet
GROUP RATE:	Varies	MAX STAY:	14 days
# of GROUP SITES:	9	ELEVATION:	1255 feet

2 Basin
Fryeburg • lat 44°16'05" lon 071°01'20"

DESCRIPTION: This CG rests in northern hardwoods on Basin Brook. Fish or boat in adjacent Basin Pond. Wildlife in this area includes black bear and moose. Supplies are in Fryeburg. Enjoy a hike in nearby Caribou Speckled Mountain Wilderness. There are snowmobile trails and a scenic overlook near this CG.

GETTING THERE: From Fryeburg go N approx. 15 mi. on state route 113 to Basin CG.

SINGLE RATE:	$14	OPEN DATES:	May-Oct
# of SINGLE SITES:	21	MAX SPUR:	35 feet
		MAX STAY:	14 days
		ELEVATION:	690 feet

3 Big Rock
Lincoln • lat 44°02'55" lon 071°33'40"

DESCRIPTION: This CG is located in northern hardwoods on the Hancock Branch of the Pemigewasset River. Fish for trout and salmon in this area's rivers and streams but please check fishing regulations. Enjoy a drive on scenic Kancamagus HWY. Wildlife in this area includes black bear and moose.

GETTING THERE: Big Rock CG is located approx. 6 mi. E of Lincoln.

SINGLE RATE:	$14	OPEN DATES:	Yearlong
# of SINGLE SITES:	28	MAX SPUR:	40 feet
		MAX STAY:	14 days
		ELEVATION:	2500 feet

4 Blackberry Crossing
Conway • lat 43°59'45" lon 071°13'31"

DESCRIPTION: This CG is rests in northern hardwoods on the Swift River. Fish for trout and salmon but please check fishing regulations. A barrier free fishing pier is nearby. Visit historic Albany Covered Bridge, CCC Camp and scenic Lower Falls. Enjoy a drive on the scenic Kancamagus HWY. Wildlife includes bear and moose.

GETTING THERE: From Conway go W approx. 6 mi. to Blackberry Crossing CG.

SINGLE RATE:	$14	OPEN DATES:	Yearlong
# of SINGLE SITES:	26	MAX SPUR:	35 feet
		MAX STAY:	14 days
		ELEVATION:	975 feet

5 Campton
Plymouth • lat 43°52'22" lon 071°37'42"

DESCRIPTION: This CG is located in northern hardwoods on Campton Pond. Fish for trout and salmon in this area's rivers and streams but please check fishing regulations. Wildlife in this area includes black bear and moose. Nature programs are available on Saturday nights. Hiking trails are nearby.

GETTING THERE: From Plymouth go N on state HWY 93 approx. 5.5 mi. to state HWY 49. Go NE on 49 approx. 2 mi. to Campton CG.

SINGLE RATE:	$16	OPEN DATES:	Apr-Oct
# of SINGLE SITES:	55	MAX SPUR:	30 feet
GROUP RATE:	Varies	MAX STAY:	14 days
# of GROUP SITES:	3	ELEVATION:	660 feet

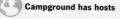 **Campground has hosts**   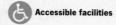 **Reservable sites**   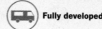 **Accessible facilities**   **Fully developed**   **Semi-developed**   **Rustic facilities**

NOTE: Open dates listed are typical. Actual dates are dependent on conditions such as snow pack.

6 Cold River
Fryeburg • lat 44°15'54" lon 071°00'49"

DESCRIPTION: This CG is rests in northern hardwoods on the Cold River. Fish or boat in nearby Basin Pond. Wildlife in this area includes black bear and moose. Supplies in Fryeburg. Enjoy a hike in nearby Caribou Speckled Mountain Wilderness. There are snow-mobile trails and a scenic overlook near this CG.

GETTING THERE: From Fryeburg go N on state HWY 113 approx. 15 mi. to Cold River CG.

SINGLE RATE:	$12	OPEN DATES:	May-Oct
# of SINGLE SITES:	14	MAX SPUR:	35 feet
		MAX STAY:	14 days
		ELEVATION:	700 feet

11 Hastings
Gilead • lat 44°21'08" lon 070°59'04"

DESCRIPTION: This CG is surrounded by trees and mountains near Evans Brook. Enjoy fishing for trout and salmon in this area's rivers and streams but please check fishing regulations. Wildlife includes black bear, moose, reptiles and small mammals. Campers may gather firewood. Hike and bike trails in area.

GETTING THERE: From Gilead go S approx. 3 mi. on route 2 to Hastings CG.

SINGLE RATE:	$12	OPEN DATES:	May-Oct
# of SINGLE SITES:	24	MAX SPUR:	35 feet
		MAX STAY:	14 days
		ELEVATION:	855 feet

7 Covered Bridge
Conway • lat 44°00'15" lon 071°13'59"

DESCRIPTION: This CG rests in northern hardwoods on the Swift River. Fish for trout and salmon but please check fishing regulations. There is a barrier free fishing pier nearby. Visit historic Albany Covered Bridge and scenic Lower Falls. Enjoy a drive on the scenic Kancamagus HWY. Wildlife includes bear and moose.

GETTING THERE: From Conway go W on Kancamagus HWY approx. 6 mi. to Covered Bridge CG.

SINGLE RATE:	$14	OPEN DATES:	May-Oct
# of SINGLE SITES:	49	MAX SPUR:	30 feet
		MAX STAY:	14 days
		ELEVATION:	865 feet

12 Jigger Johnson
Conway • lat 44°00'00" lon 071°17'30"

DESCRIPTION: This CG is located in northern hardwoods on the Swift River. Fish for trout and salmon but please check fishing regulations. There are several cross country ski and hiking trails in the vicinity. Wildlife includes black bear and moose. Visit scenic waterfalls and historic Russell-Colbath Homestead in this area.

GETTING THERE: From Conway go W on Kancamagus HWY (forest route 60) approx. 12.5 mi. to Jigger Johnson CG.

SINGLE RATE:	$15	OPEN DATES:	May-Oct
# of SINGLE SITES:	17	MAX SPUR:	35 feet
		MAX STAY:	14 days
		ELEVATION:	900 feet

8 Crocker Pond
Bethel • lat 44°18'37" lon 070°49'26"

DESCRIPTION: This CG is nestled among pine and hard wood trees on the eastern shore of Crocker Pond. This quiet, secluded CG offers fishing and boating. Please check fishing regulations. There is also a snowmobile trail that runs past the CG and a hiking trail to Round Pond. Wildlife includes moose and bear.

GETTING THERE: From Bethel go S on state route 5 approx. 4 mi. to forest route 7. Go SW on 7 approx. 2 mi. to forest route 18. Go S on 18 approx. 1 mi. to Crocker Pond CG.

SINGLE RATE:	$12	OPEN DATES:	May-Oct
# of SINGLE SITES:	7	MAX SPUR:	20 feet
		MAX STAY:	14 days
		ELEVATION:	840 feet

13 Passaconaway
Conway • lat 44°00'00" lon 071°22'00"

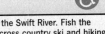

DESCRIPTION: This CG is located in northern hardwoods on the Swift River. Fish the river, but please check fishing regulations. There are several cross country ski and hiking trails in the vicinity. Wildlife includes black bear and moose. Visit scenic waterfalls and historic Russell-Colbath Homestead in this area.

GETTING THERE: From Conway go W on Kancamagus HWY (forest route 60) approx. 15 mi. to Passaconaway CG.

SINGLE RATE:	$14	OPEN DATES:	May-Oct
# of SINGLE SITES:	33	MAX SPUR:	35 feet
		MAX STAY:	14 days
		ELEVATION:	900 feet

9 Dolly Copp
Gorham • lat 44°19'57" lon 071°13'08"

DESCRIPTION: This CG features large, open sites located on the Peabody River. Interpretive programs are provided on summer weekends. Enjoy fishing for trout and salmon in this area's rivers and streams but please check fishing regulations. Enjoy a nearby self-guided auto tour of the area.

GETTING THERE: Dolly Copp CG is located approx. 6 mi. S of Gorham on route 16.

SINGLE RATE:	$15	OPEN DATES:	May-Oct
# of SINGLE SITES:	176	MAX SPUR:	45 feet
		MAX STAY:	14 days
		ELEVATION:	1255 feet

14 Russell Pond
Lincoln • lat 44°00'43" lon 071°39'04"

DESCRIPTION: This CG is located in northern hardwoods on Russell Pond. Fishing opportunities are excellent. This CG offers Saturday night nature programs, a barrier free dock, boat ramp and amphitheater. Wildlife in this area includes black bear and moose. Campers may gather dead and down firewood.

GETTING THERE: From Lincoln go S on I-93 approx. 3.5 mi. to forest route 30. Go E on 30 approx. 2 mi. go forest route 90. Go N on 90 approx. 2 mi. to Russell Pond CG.

SINGLE RATE:	$16	OPEN DATES:	May-Oct
# of SINGLE SITES:	86	MAX SPUR:	40 feet
		MAX STAY:	14 days
		ELEVATION:	2000 feet

10 Hancock
Lincoln • lat 44°03'52" lon 071°35'39"

DESCRIPTION: This CG is situated in northern hardwoods on the East Branch of Pemigewasset River. Fish for trout and salmon in this area's streams and rivers but please check fishing regulations. Enjoy a drive on the scenic Kancamagus HWY. Wildlife in this area includes black bear and moose.

GETTING THERE: From Lincoln go E on state route 112 approx. 3.5 mi. to Hancock CG.

SINGLE RATE:	Varies	OPEN DATES:	Yearlong
# of SINGLE SITES:	56	MAX SPUR:	40 feet
		MAX STAY:	14 days
		ELEVATION:	2400 feet

15 Sugarloaf 1
Bethlehem • lat 44°16'00" lon 071°30'30"

DESCRIPTION: This rustic CG is surrounded by trees and mountains near the Wild Ammonoosuc River. Enjoy fishing for trout and salmon area's rivers and streams but please check fishing regulations. Wildlife includes black bear, moose, reptiles and small mammals. Hiking and biking trails in area. Gather dead and down firewood.

GETTING THERE: From Bethlehem go E on state HWY 10 approx. 9 mi. to forest route 16. Go S on 16 approx. 1/2 mi. to Sugarloaf 1 CG.

SINGLE RATE:	$14	OPEN DATES:	May-Oct
# of SINGLE SITES:	29	MAX SPUR:	35 feet
		MAX STAY:	14 days
		ELEVATION:	2400 feet

 Campground has hosts 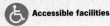 Reservable sites Accessible facilities   Fully developed   Semi-developed Rustic facilities

16 Sugarloaf 2
Bethlehem • lat 44°16'00" lon 071°30'30"

DESCRIPTION: This rustic CG is surrounded by trees and mountains near the Wild Ammonoosuc River. Enjoy fishing for trout and salmon area's rivers and streams but please check fishing regulations. Wildlife includes black bear, moose, reptiles and small mammals. Campers may gather firewood. Hike and bike trails in area.

GETTING THERE: From Bethlehem go E on state HWY 10 approx. 9 mi. to forest route 16. Go S on 16 approx. 1/2 mi. to Sugarloaf 2 CG.

SINGLE RATE:	$14	OPEN DATES:	May-Dec
# of SINGLE SITES:	32	MAX SPUR:	35 feet
		MAX STAY:	14 days
		ELEVATION:	2400 feet

21 Zealand
Bethlehem • lat 44°15'52" lon 071°29'44"

DESCRIPTION: This CG is surrounded by trees and mountains near the Wild Ammonoosuc and Zealand Rivers. Enjoy fishing from the rivers and streams but please check fishing regulations. Wildlife includes black bear, moose, reptiles and small mammals. Campers may gather firewood. Hike and bike trails in area.

GETTING THERE: From Bethlehem go E on HWY 302/10 approx. 9 mi. to Zealand CG.

SINGLE RATE:	$14	OPEN DATES:	May-Oct
# of SINGLE SITES:	11	MAX SPUR:	25 feet
		MAX STAY:	14 days
		ELEVATION:	2400 feet

17 Waterville
Campton • lat 43°56'33" lon 071°30'35"

DESCRIPTION: This CG is situated in a northern hardwood forest on the Mad River. Supplies available in Campton. Hike or horseback ride into nearby Sandwich Range Wilderness. This CG also offers a winter sports area and mountain biking. Wildlife in this area includes black bear and moose. Campers may gather firewood.

GETTING THERE: From Campton go NE on state route 49 approx. 11 mi. to Waterville CG.

SINGLE RATE:	$14	OPEN DATES:	May-Oct
# of SINGLE SITES:	27	MAX SPUR:	30 feet
		MAX STAY:	14 days
		ELEVATION:	1450 feet

18 White Ledge
Conway • lat 43°57'17" lon 071°12'52"

DESCRIPTION: This CG is surrounded by trees and is located near the Mt. Chocorua Scenic Area. Fish for trout and salmon in this area's rivers and streams but please check fishing regulations. A grassy play area and picnic shelter are on site. Wildlife includes bear and moose. Hike to White Ledge from this CG.

GETTING THERE: From Conway go S on route 16 approx. 5 mi. to White Ledge CG.

SINGLE RATE:	$12	OPEN DATES:	May-Dec
# of SINGLE SITES:	28	MAX SPUR:	35 feet
		MAX STAY:	14 days
		ELEVATION:	729 feet

19 Wild River
Gilead • lat 44°18'20" lon 071°03'50"

DESCRIPTION: This CG is surrounded by trees and mountains on the Wild River. Enjoy fishing for trout and salmon in this area's rivers and streams but please check fishing regulations. Wildlife includes black bear, moose, reptiles and small mammals. Campers may gather firewood. Hike and bike trails in area.

GETTING THERE: From Gilead go S on route 113 approx. 3 mi. to forest route 12. Go SW on 12 approx. 5 mi. to Wild River CG.

SINGLE RATE:	$12	OPEN DATES:	May-Oct
# of SINGLE SITES:	12	MAX SPUR:	40 feet
		MAX STAY:	14 days
		ELEVATION:	2500 feet

20 Wildwood
Lincoln • lat 44°04'33" lon 071°47'38"

DESCRIPTION: This CG is surrounded by trees and mountains on the Wild Ammonoosuc River. Enjoy fishing for trout and salmon in this area's rivers and streams but please check fishing regulations. Wildlife includes black bear, moose, reptiles and small mammals. Campers may gather firewood. Hiking and biking trails in area.

GETTING THERE: From Lincoln go W on state route 112 approx. 7 mi. to Wildwood CG.

SINGLE RATE:	$14	OPEN DATES:	May-Dec
# of SINGLE SITES:	26	MAX SPUR:	25 feet
		MAX STAY:	14 days
		ELEVATION:	1360 feet

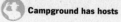 Campground has hosts   Reservable sites 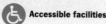 Accessible facilities 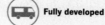 Fully developed  Semi-developed  Rustic facilities

NOTE: Open dates listed are typical. Actual dates are dependent on conditions such as snow pack.

CARSON NATIONAL FOREST

Some of the finest mountain scenery in the Southwest is found in the 1.5 million acres covered by The Carson National Forest, one of five national forests in New Mexico.

The Carson offers unlimited recreational opportunities in any season. The magnificent mountain scenery and cool summer temperatures lure vacationers to enjoy the peace and quiet, for fishing, hunting, camping, and hiking. There are 330 miles of trails and opportunities abound for horseback riding, mountain biking, and 4-wheel drive exploring. Some of the finest alpine downhill skiing in the U.S. is found within the forest at Taos Ski Valley, Red River and Sipapu ski areas.

There are many established campgrounds available, some with drinking water and toilets and some without. The Carson has 400 miles of sparkling clean mountain streams and numerous lakes, many stocked with native trout by the New Mexico Department of Game and Fish.

Big game animals such as mule deer, elk, antelope, black bear, mountain lion, and bighorn sheep roam the Carson. Forest personnel work closely with the state Game and Fish Department to provide the best wildlife habitat possible.

USFS Photo

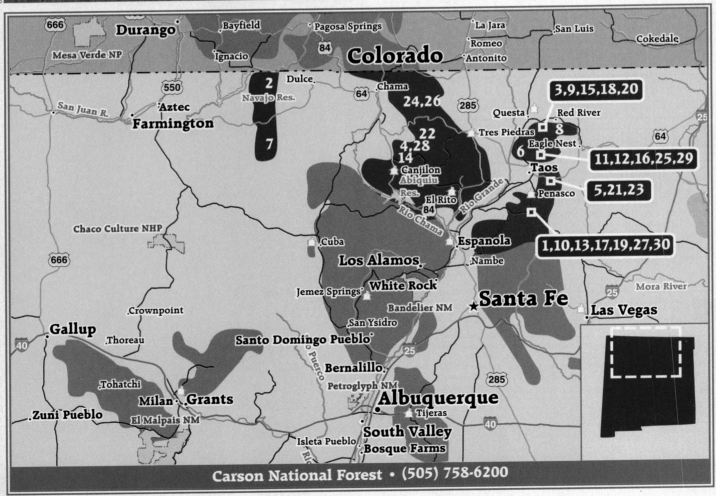

Carson National Forest • (505) 758-6200

1 Agua Piedra
Vadito • lat 36°08'07" lon 105°31'43"

DESCRIPTION: CG is located in mixed conifer along the Rio Pueblo River. Fish for cut-throat, rainbow, brown, and brook trout. Black bears, mountan lions, bobcats, coyotes, deer, elk, and bald eagles in area. Busy June - August. Hiking, horse, mountain biking, and ATV trails in area. No drinking water.

GETTING THERE: From Vadito go E on state HWY 75 approx. 3 mi. to state HWY 518. Go E on 518 approx. 6 mi. to Agua Piedra CG.

SINGLE RATE:	No fee	OPEN DATES:	May-Oct
# of SINGLE SITES:	40	MAX SPUR:	32 feet
		MAX STAY:	14 days
		ELEVATION:	8100 feet

2 Buzzard Park
Dulce • lat 36°52'53" lon 107°12'59"

DESCRIPTION: This CG is situated among ponderosa pine and oakbrush. No drinking water available on site. Supplies can be found in Dulce. Wildlife in the area indcludes deer, elk, bears, turkeys, and wild horses. CG tends to fill up quickly during the fall hunting season. Few hiking trails in area.

GETTING THERE: From Dulce go approx. 19 mi. W on US HWY 64 to forest route 310. Go N on 310 approx. 13 mi. to Buzzard Park CG.

SINGLE RATE:	No fee	OPEN DATES:	May-Nov
# of SINGLE SITES:	4	MAX SPUR:	32 feet
		MAX STAY:	14 days
		ELEVATION:	7300 feet

3 Cabresto Lake
Questa • lat 36°44'48" lon 105°29'55"

DESCRIPTION: CG is located in douglas fir and ponderosa pine with mountain views. Adjacent Cabresto Reservoir has good trout fishing. Black bears, mountain lions, coyotes, deer, hawks, and golden eagles in area. CG is busy weekends and holidays. Hike in adjacent Latir Peak Wilderness. No drinking water.

GETTING THERE: From Questa go N on state HWY 563 approx. 2 mi. to forest route 134. Go E on 134 approx. 3 mi. to forest route 134A. Go N on 134A approx. 1.5 mi. to Cabresto Lake CG. Not suitable for trailers. High clearance vehicles only.

SINGLE RATE:	No fee	OPEN DATES:	May-Sept
# of SINGLE SITES:	9		
		MAX STAY:	14 days
		ELEVATION:	9500 feet

4 Canjilon Lakes
Canjilon • lat 36°33'25" lon 106°19'45"

DESCRIPTION: This CG is in a park-like setting. Small lakes throughout the CG complete with rainbow, german brown, and cutthroat trout. Check fishing regulations. Historical Canjilon Mountain Lookout nearby. Supplies are 7 mi. from CG. Campers may gather their firewood locally. Trails in area.

GETTING THERE: From Canjilon go NE on forest route 559 approx. 7 mi. to forest route 129. Go N on 129 approx. 4 mi. to Canjilon Lakes CG.

SINGLE RATE:	Varies	OPEN DATES:	May-Sept
# of SINGLE SITES:	51	MAX SPUR:	16 feet
		MAX STAY:	14 days
		ELEVATION:	9900 feet

5 Capulin
Taos • lat 36°22'15" lon 105°28'57"

DESCRIPTION: CG is located in willow and cottonwood along the Rio Don Fernando River. Fish for cutthroat, rainbow, brown, and brook trout. Wildlife includes black bears, mountain lions, bobcats, coyotes, deer, elk, and bald eagles. Busy June through August. Numerous hiking, horse, mountain biking, and ATV trails in area.

GETTING THERE: Capulin CG is located approx. 6.5 mi. E of Taos on US HWY 64.

SINGLE RATE:	Varies	OPEN DATES:	May-Oct
# of SINGLE SITES:	11	MAX SPUR:	16 feet
		MAX STAY:	14 days
		ELEVATION:	8000 feet

6 Cebolla Mesa
Questa • lat 36°37'28" lon 105°41'06"

DESCRIPTION: CG is located in pinons and junipers with mountain views. On site trail-head leads to nearby (400 ft.) Rio Grande which has good cutthroat trout fishing. Black bears, mountain lions, coyotes, deer, hawks, bald and golden eagles, and various water-fowl in area. Busy weekends and holidays. No drinking water.

GETTING THERE: From Questa go S on state HWY 522 approx. 4 mi. to forest route 9. Go W on 9 approx. 3 mi. to Cebolla Mesa CG. Road slick when wet.

SINGLE RATE:	No fee	OPEN DATES:	May-Sept
# of SINGLE SITES:	5	MAX SPUR:	32 feet
		MAX STAY:	14 days
		ELEVATION:	7300 feet

7 Cedar Springs
Dulce • lat 36°39'30" lon 107°15'00"

DESCRIPTION: This CG is situated among ponderosa pine and oakbrush. Supplies can be found in Dulce. CG tends to fill up quickly during the fall hunting season. No drinking water available on site. Wildlife in the area consists primarily of deer, bears, elk, and turkeys. Few hiking trails in the area.

GETTING THERE: From Dulce go W on state HWY 64 approx. 19 mi. to forest route 357. Go S on 357 approx. 11 mi. to Cedar Springs CG.

SINGLE RATE:	No fee	OPEN DATES:	May-Nov
# of SINGLE SITES:	4	MAX SPUR:	32 feet
		MAX STAY:	14 days
		ELEVATION:	7300 feet

8 Cimarron
Amalia • lat 36°46'10" lon 105°12'16"

DESCRIPTION: This CG is situated among douglas fir and ponderosa pine with mountain views. Wildlife includes black bears, mountain lions, coyotes, deer, hawks, and golden eagles. CG is busy weekends and holidays. Set in an open area with numerous hiking opportunities. Historical sites in area.

GETTING THERE: From Amalia go S on forest route 1950 approx. 16 mi. to forest route 1910. Go S on 1910 approx. 1 mi. to Cimarron CG.

SINGLE RATE:	$10	OPEN DATES:	May-Nov
# of SINGLE SITES:	32	MAX SPUR:	32 feet
		MAX STAY:	14 days
		ELEVATION:	9400 feet

9 Columbine
Questa • lat 36°40'45" lon 105°30'54"

DESCRIPTION: CG is in douglas fir, spruce, and ponderosa pine with mountain views. Columbine Creek runs near this CG with good rainbow and brown trout fishing. Black bears, mountain lions, coyotes, deer, hawks, and golden eagles. CG is busy weekends and holidays. On site trailhead leads to Columbine drainage.

GETTING THERE: Columbine CG is located approx. 6 mi. E of Questa on state HWY 38.

SINGLE RATE:	$10	OPEN DATES:	May-Oct
# of SINGLE SITES:	27	MAX SPUR:	40 feet
		MAX STAY:	14 days
		ELEVATION:	7900 feet

10 Comales
Vadito • lat 36°09'36" lon 105°35'45"

DESCRIPTION: CG is located in mixed conifer along the Rio Pueblo River. Fish for cut-throat, rainbow, brown, and brook trout. Black bears, mountain lions, bobcats, coyotes, deer, elk, and bald eagles frequent area. Busy June-August. Hiking, horse, mountain biking, and ATV trails in area. No drinking water.

GETTING THERE: From Vadito go E on state HWY 75 approx. 3 mi. to state HWY 518. Go E on 518 approx. 3 mi. to Comales CG.

SINGLE RATE:	Varies	OPEN DATES:	May-Oct
# of SINGLE SITES:	2	MAX SPUR:	16 feet
		MAX STAY:	14 days
		ELEVATION:	7800 feet

 Campground has hosts   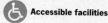 **Reservable sites**   **Accessible facilities**   **Fully developed**   **Semi-developed**   Rustic facilities

NOTE: Open dates listed are typical. Actual dates are dependent on conditions such as snow pack.

11 Cuchillo
Taos • lat 36°33'35" lon 105°31'58"

DESCRIPTION: CG is located in douglas fir and ponderosa pine with mountain views. Adjacent Rio Hondo has good trout fishing. Wildlife includes black bears, mountain lions, coyotes, deer, hawks, and golden eagles. CG is busy weekends and holidays. Several multi-use trails in area. No drinking water.

GETTING THERE: Cuchillo CG is located approx. 12 mi. N of Taos on state HWY 230.

SINGLE RATE:	No fee	OPEN DATES:	May-Oct
# of SINGLE SITES:	3	MAX SPUR:	16 feet
		MAX STAY:	14 days
		ELEVATION:	8600 feet

16 Fawn Lakes
Questa • lat 36°42'21" lon 105°27'22"

DESCRIPTION: CG is located in douglas fir, spruce, and ponderosa pine with mountain views. Nearby Fawn Lakes has good trout fishing and a barrier free fishing dock. Wildlife includes black bears, mountain lions, coyotes, deer, hawks, and golden eagles. Busy weekends and holidays. Several multi-use trails in area.

GETTING THERE: Fawn Lakes CG is located approx. 10 mi. E of Questa on state HWY 38.

SINGLE RATE:	$10	OPEN DATES:	May-Oct
# of SINGLE SITES:	21	MAX SPUR:	36 feet
		MAX STAY:	14 days
		ELEVATION:	8500 feet

12 Cuchillo del Medio
Taos • lat 36°33'35" lon 105°31'58"

DESCRIPTION: CG is located in douglas fir and ponderosa pine with mountain views. Adjacent Rio Hondo has good trout fishing. Wildlife includes black bears, mountain lions, coyotes, deer, hawks, and golden eagles. CG is busy weekends and holidays. Several multi-use trails in area. No drinking water.

GETTING THERE: Cuchillo del Medio CG is located approx. 11 mi. N of Taos on state HWY 230.

SINGLE RATE:	$10	OPEN DATES:	May-Sept
# of SINGLE SITES:	3	MAX SPUR:	16 feet
		MAX STAY:	14 days
		ELEVATION:	7800 feet

17 Flechado
Vadito • lat 36°08'52" lon 105°32'35"

DESCRIPTION: CG is located in mixed conifer along the Rio Pueblo River. Fish for cutthroat, rainbow, brown, and brook trout. Black bears, mountain lions, bobcats, coyotes, deer, elk, and bald eagles in area. Busy June-Aug.. Numerous hiking, horse, mountain biking, and ATV trails in area. No drinking water.

GETTING THERE: From Vadito go E on state HWY 75 approx. 3 mi. to state HWY 518. Go E on 518 approx. 5 mi. to Flechado CG.

SINGLE RATE:	No fee	OPEN DATES:	May-Sept
# of SINGLE SITES:	8	MAX SPUR:	16 feet
		MAX STAY:	14 days
		ELEVATION:	8400 feet

13 Duran Canyon
Vadio • lat 36°08'02" lon 105°28'36"

DESCRIPTION: CG is located in mixed conifer with canyon views. Fish for cutthroat, rainbow, brown, and brook trout in adjacent Rio La Junta River. Black bears, mountain lions, bobcats, coyotes, deer, elk, and bald eagles. Busy June-August. Numerous hiking, horse, mountain biking, and ATV trails in area.

GETTING THERE: From Vadito go E on state HWY 75 approx. 3 mi. to state HWY 518. Go E on 518 approx. 7 mi. to forest route 76. Go E on 76 approx. 2 mi. to Duran Canyon CG.

SINGLE RATE:	Varies	OPEN DATES:	May-Oct
# of SINGLE SITES:	12	MAX SPUR:	22 feet
		MAX STAY:	14 days
		ELEVATION:	9000 feet

18 Goat Hill
Questa • lat 36°41'00" lon 150°32'30"

DESCRIPTION: CG is set among douglas fir, spruce, and ponderosa pine with mountain views. Nearby Red River has good rainbow and brown trout fishing. Wildlife includes black bears, mountain lions, coyotes, deer, hawks, and golden eagles. Busy weekends and holidays. Several multi-use trails in area. No drinking water.

GETTING THERE: Goat Hill CG is located approx. 4 mi. of Questa on state HWY 38.

SINGLE RATE:	No fee	OPEN DATES:	May-Sept
# of SINGLE SITES:	3	MAX SPUR:	32 feet
		MAX STAY:	14 days
		ELEVATION:	7500 feet

14 El Rito
Las Placitas • lat 36°24'07" lon 106°15'14"

DESCRIPTION: This CG is situated on the banks of El Rito Creek, among ponderosa pine and oak trees. Descent fishing for rainbow trout on the creek. Check for local fishing regulations. Deer, elk, bears, and various birds can be seen in the area. CG tends to be busy on holiday weekends.

GETTING THERE: From Las Placitas go approx. 8 mi. N on forest route 559 to El Rito CG.

SINGLE RATE:	No fee	OPEN DATES:	Apr-Oct
# of SINGLE SITES:	11	MAX SPUR:	22 feet
		MAX STAY:	14 days
		ELEVATION:	7600 feet

19 Hodges
Camino Real • lat 36°06'30" lon 105°38'00"

DESCRIPTION: CG is located in willow and cottonwood along the Santa Barbara River. Fish for cutthroat and rainbow trout. Wildlife includes black bears, mountain lions, bobcats, coyotes, deer, elk, and bald eagles. Busy June-August. Numerous hiking, horse, mountain biking, and ATV trails in area. No drinking water.

GETTING THERE: Hodges CG is located approx. 4 mi. SE of Camino Real on forest route 116.

SINGLE RATE:	Varies	OPEN DATES:	May-Oct
# of SINGLE SITES:	8	MAX SPUR:	22 feet
		MAX STAY:	14 days
		ELEVATION:	8200 feet

15 Elephant Rock
Questa • lat 36°42'20" lon 105°27'04"

DESCRIPTION: CG is located in douglas fir, spruce, and ponderosa pine with mountain views. Adjacent Red River has good rainbow and brown trout fishing. Wildlife includes black bears, mountain lions, coyotes, deer, hawks, and golden eagles. CG is busy weekends and holidays. Several multi-use trails in area.

GETTING THERE: Elephant Rock CG is located approx. 11 mi. E of Questa on state HWY 38.

SINGLE RATE:	$10	OPEN DATES:	May-Oct
# of SINGLE SITES:	18	MAX SPUR:	36 feet
		MAX STAY:	14 days
		ELEVATION:	8300 feet

20 Junebug
Questa • lat 36°42'28" lon 105°26'03"

DESCRIPTION: CG is located in douglas fir, spruce, and ponderosa pine with mountain views. Adjacent Red River has good rainbow and brown trout fishing. Wildlife includes black bears, mountain lions, coyotes, deer, hawks, and golden eagles. CG is busy weekends and holidays. Several multi-use trails in area.

GETTING THERE: Junebug CG is located approx. 12 mi. E of Questa on state HWY 38.

SINGLE RATE:	$10	OPEN DATES:	May-Oct
# of SINGLE SITES:	17	MAX SPUR:	36 feet
		MAX STAY:	14 days
		ELEVATION:	8500 feet

 Campground has hosts   Reservable sites   Accessible facilities   Fully developed   Semi-developed   Rustic facilities

NOTE: Open dates listed are typical. Actual dates are dependent on conditions such as snow pack.

Page 382

21 La Sombra
Taos • lat 36°22'09" lon 105°28'22"

DESCRIPTION: CG is located in willow and cottonwood along Rio Don Fernando River. Fish for cutthroat, rainbow, brown, and brook trout. Wildlife includes black bears, mountain lions, bobcats, coyotes, deer, elk, and bald eagles. Busy June-August. Hiking, horse, mountain biking, and ATV trails in area with trailhead on site.

GETTING THERE: La Sombra CG is located approx. 7 mi. E of Taos on US HWY 64.

SINGLE RATE:	Varies	OPEN DATES:	May-Oct
# of SINGLE SITES:	13	MAX SPUR:	16 feet
		MAX STAY:	14 days
		ELEVATION:	7800 feet

26 McCrystal
Amalia • lat 36°46'37" lon 105°06'48"

DESCRIPTION: CG is located in douglas fir and ponderosa pine with mountain views. Wildlife includes black bears, mountain lions, coyotes, deer, hawks, and golden eagles. Busy weekends and holidays. CG is situated in an open area with lots of hiking opportunities. Historical sites in area. No drinking water.

GETTING THERE: McCrystal CG is located approx. 24 mi. E of Amalia on forest route 1950.

SINGLE RATE:	$10	OPEN DATES:	May-Nov
# of SINGLE SITES:	60	MAX SPUR:	32 feet
		MAX STAY:	14 days
		ELEVATION:	8100 feet

22 Lagunitas
Tres Piedras • lat 36°53'11" lon 106°19'12"

DESCRIPTION: CG is located in fir, spruce, and aspen. Float or bank fish for trout in adjacent Lagunita Lakes. Black bears, mountain lions, coyotes, bobcats, deer, elk, hawks, and eagles frequent area. Busy weekends and holidays. CG is located at the edge of the Cruces Basin Wilderness Area. No drinking water.

GETTING THERE: From Tres Piedras go N on US HWY 285 approx. 11 mi. to forest route 87. Go W on 87 approx. 25 mi. to Lagunitas CG.

SINGLE RATE:	No fee	OPEN DATES:	June-Oct
# of SINGLE SITES:	12	MAX SPUR:	16 feet
		MAX STAY:	14 days
		ELEVATION:	10400 feet

27 Santa Barbara
Camino Real • lat 36°05'08" lon 105°36'30"

DESCRIPTION: CG is located in willow and cottonwood along the Santa Barbara River. Fish for cutthroat and rainbow trout. Black bears, mountain lions, bobcats, coyotes, deer, elk, and bald eagles in area. Trailhead on site accesses the Pecos Wilderness Area. CG under construction, check with ranger district.

GETTING THERE: Santa Barbara CG is located approx. 7 mi. SE of Camino Real on forest route 116.

SINGLE RATE:	Varies	OPEN DATES:	May-Oct
# of SINGLE SITES:	22	MAX SPUR:	32 feet
		MAX STAY:	14 days
		ELEVATION:	8900 feet

23 Las Petacas
Taos • lat 36°22'54" lon 105°31'17"

DESCRIPTION: CG is located in willow and cottonwood along Rio Don Fernando River. Fish for cutthroat, rainbow, brown, and brook trout. Black bears, mountain lions, bobcats, coyotes, deer, elk, and bald eagles in area. Busy June-Aug.. Numerous hiking, horse, mountain biking, and ATV trails in area. No drinking water.

GETTING THERE: Las Petacas CG is located approx. 4 mi. E of Taos on US HWY 64.

SINGLE RATE:	Varies	OPEN DATES:	May-Nov
# of SINGLE SITES:	9	MAX SPUR:	16 feet
		MAX STAY:	14 days
		ELEVATION:	7400 feet

28 Trout Lakes
Cebolla • lat 36°36'32" lon 106°22'55"

DESCRIPTION: CG set in mixed conifer and aspen with moderate vegetation. Small lakes throughout CG complete with rainbow, german brown, and cutthroat trout. Check fishing regulations. Supplies are 11 mi. from CG. Gather firewood locally. Trails on Canjilon Mountain. Roads within CG are in ruff condition.

GETTING THERE: From Cebolla go N on forest route 125 approx. 11 mi. to Trout Lakes CG. Road is very slick when wet and is impossible when snowfall begins in late Sept. 4WD recomended.

SINGLE RATE:	No fee	OPEN DATES:	May-Sept
# of SINGLE SITES:	12	MAX SPUR:	16 feet
		MAX STAY:	14 days
		ELEVATION:	9300 feet

24 Los Pinos
Tres Piedras • lat 36°57'19" lon 106°10'40"

DESCRIPTION: CG is located in willow and narrowleaf cottonwood in a steep, narrow canyon. Fish for trout in adjacent Rio de los Pinos River. Check fishing regulations. Black bears, mountain lions, coyotes, bobcats, deer, elk, hawks, and eagles frequent area. Busy weekends and holidays. Hiking along river. No drinking water.

GETTING THERE: From Tres Piedras go N on US HWY 285 approx. 11 mi. to forest route 87. Go W on 87 approx. 21 mi. to forest route 87A. Go N on 87A approx. 8 mi. to Los Pinos CG.

SINGLE RATE:	No fee	OPEN DATES:	May-Sept
# of SINGLE SITES:	5	MAX SPUR:	16 feet
		MAX STAY:	14 days
		ELEVATION:	8000 feet

29 Twining
Taos • lat 36°35'45" lon 105°27'00"

DESCRIPTION: CG is located in douglas fir and ponderosa pine with mountain views. Adjacent Rio Hondo has good trout fishing. Wildlife includes black bears, mountain lions, coyotes, deer, hawks, and golden eagles. CG is busy weekends and holidays. On site trailhead leads to Wheeler Peak (highest in New Mexico).

GETTING THERE: Twining CG is located approx. 11 mi. N of Taos on state HWY 230.

SINGLE RATE:	No fee	OPEN DATES:	May-Sept
# of SINGLE SITES:	4	MAX SPUR:	16 feet
		MAX STAY:	14 days
		ELEVATION:	9300 feet

25 Lower Hondo
Taos • lat 36°32'50" lon 105°32'56"

DESCRIPTION: CG is located in douglas fir and ponderosa pine with mountain views. Adjacent Rio Hondo has good trout fishing. Wildlife includes black bears, mountain lions, coyotes, deer, hawks, and golden eagles. CG is busy weekends and holidays. Several multi-use trails in area. No drinking water.

GETTING THERE: Lower Hondo CG is located approx. 10 mi. N of Taos on state HWY 230.

SINGLE RATE:	No fee	OPEN DATES:	May-Sept
# of SINGLE SITES:	4	MAX SPUR:	16 feet
		MAX STAY:	14 days
		ELEVATION:	7700 feet

30 Upper La Junta
Vadito • lat 36°08'52" lon 105°27'17"

DESCRIPTION: CG is located in mixed conifer with canyon views. Fish for cutthroat, rainbow, brown, and brook trout in adjacent Rio La Junta River. Wildlife includes black bears, mountain lions, bobcats, coyotes, deer, elk, and bald eagles. Busy June-August. Hiking, horse, mountain biking, and ATV trails in area.

GETTING THERE: From Vadito go E on state HWY 75 approx. 3 mi. to state HWY 518. Go E on 518 approx. 7 mi. to forest route 76. Go E on 76 approx. 5 mi. to Upper La Junta CG.

SINGLE RATE:	Varies	OPEN DATES:	May-Sept
# of SINGLE SITES:	8	MAX SPUR:	16 feet
		MAX STAY:	14 days
		ELEVATION:	9400 feet

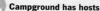 Campground has hosts   Reservable sites   Accessible facilities   Fully developed   Semi-developed   Rustic facilities

NOTE: Open dates listed are typical. Actual dates are dependent on conditions such as snow pack.

USFS Photo

CIBOLA NATIONAL FOREST

The Cibola National Forest is 1.6 million acres in size with an elevation that ranges from 5,000 feet to 11,301 feet. The Cibola includes national grasslands in northeastern New Mexico, western Oklahoma, and northwestern Texas.

The forest offers year-round recreational opportunities. The climate varies with elevation, from desert through high juniper, pine, and spruce and-fir forests. Summer nights are cool and cold above 8,000 feet and visitors can expect frequent afternoon showers in July and August.

The Cibola provides great hunting for deer, elk, antelope, and turkeys. Anglers will find fishing access at Bluewater and McGaffey Lakes in the Zuni Mountains; Skipout, Spring Creek, and Dead Indian Lakes in Oklahoma; and Lake Marvin and Lake McClellan in Texas.

Some of the Cibola's spectacular scenery is just a drive away. Capillia Peak (9,375') is accessible by car, Sandia Crest (10,678') is accessible by car, aerial tramway and trail, and Mount Taylor (11,301') has a good road to within a mile of the top.

Winter enthusiasts will enjoy skiing at the Sandia Peak Ski Area in the Sandia Mountains. Other visitor attractions include the nearby Indian Pueblos, prehistoric ruins, ice caves, and lava flows.

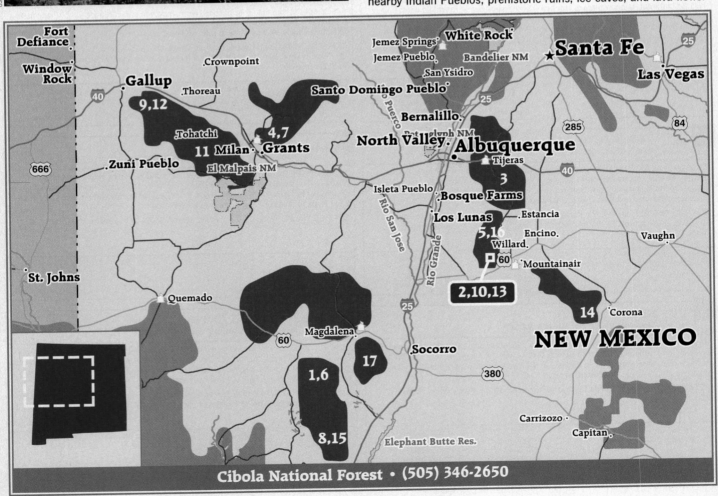

Cibola National Forest • (505) 346-2650

1 Bear Trap
Magdalena • lat 37˚53'00" lon 107˚30'00"

DESCRIPTION: CG is located in a semi open grove of mixed conifer with canyon views. There is a small, seasonal stream running near the CG. Wildlife includes black bears, mountain lions, bobcats, coyotes, deer, elk, turkeys, quails, bald eagles, and hawks. Several multi-use trails in area. No drinking water available.

GETTING THERE: From Magdalena go W on US HWY 60 approx. 12 mi. to state HWY 52 (forest route 549). Go S on 549 approx. 15 mi. to Bear Trap CG. High clearance vehicles only.

SINGLE RATE:	No fee	OPEN DATES:	May-Sept
# of SINGLE SITES:	4	MAX SPUR:	20 feet
		MAX STAY:	14 days
		ELEVATION:	8000 feet

2 Capilla
Manzano • lat 34˚41'53" lon 106˚24'04"

DESCRIPTION: CG is located in open area with bordering fir and oak. Views of Estnacia Valley. Wildlife includes black bears, mountain lions, coyotes, deer, bighorn sheep, and bobcats. This is a major fly-way for raptors. Hiking and horse trails in nearby Manzano Wilderness Area.

GETTING THERE: From Manzano go NW on forest route 245 approx. 9 mi. to Capilla CG. Rough road.

SINGLE RATE:	Varies	OPEN DATES:	May-Sept
# of SINGLE SITES:	8	MAX SPUR:	16 feet
		MAX STAY:	14 days
		ELEVATION:	9600 feet

3 Cedro Peak
Tijeras • lat 35˚02'51" lon 106˚21'07"

DESCRIPTION: This group CG is reservation only. The CG is located in pinon, juniper, and pine with views of Cedro Peak. Wildlife in the area includes black bears, mountain lions, deer, and raptors. This CG can be busy holiday weekends. There are hiking, horse, mountain biking, and ATV trails in the area.

GETTING THERE: From Tijeras go S on state HWY 337 approx. 5 mi. to forest route 542. Go N on 542 approx. 2 mi. to Cedro Peak CG. Not suitable for trailers.

		OPEN DATES:	May-Oct
GROUP RATE:	Varies	MAX STAY:	14 days
# of GROUP SITES:	2	ELEVATION:	7400 feet

4 Coal Mine
Grants • lat 35˚14'01" lon 107˚42'03"

DESCRIPTION: CG is located in pinon, juniper, and pine with views of Mount Taylor. Black bears, mountain lions, bobcats, coyotes, deer, elk, hawks, eagles, and porqupines. Busy weekends and holidays. Hiking, horse, mountain biking, and ATV trails in area. There is an interpretive trail on site.

GETTING THERE: From Grants go NE on Lobo Canyon Road (state HWY 547) approx. 9 mi. to Coal Mine CG.

SINGLE RATE:	$5	OPEN DATES:	May-Sept
# of SINGLE SITES:	17	MAX SPUR:	25 feet
		MAX STAY:	14 days
		ELEVATION:	7200 feet

5 Fourth of July
Tajique • lat 34˚47'34" lon 106˚22'57"

DESCRIPTION: CG is located in park-like stand of huge ponderosa pine, mixed conifer, juniper, and pinon. Canyon views. Small, seasonal spring in area. Wildlife includes black bears, mountain lions, coyotes, deer, bighorn sheep, and bobcats. Hiking and horse trails in nearby Manzano Wilderness Area.

GETTING THERE: From Tajique go W on forest route 55 approx. 7 mi. to Fourth of July CG. Not suitable for trailers.

SINGLE RATE:	$5	OPEN DATES:	Apr-Oct
# of SINGLE SITES:	25	MAX SPUR:	15 feet
		MAX STAY:	14 days
		ELEVATION:	7400 feet

6 Hughes Mill
Magdalena • lat 33˚51'26" lon 107˚32'23"

DESCRIPTION: CG is located in semi open grove of mixed conifer on a canyon. Wildlife in the area includes black bears, mountain lions, bobcats, coyotes, deer, elk, turkeys, quails, bald eagles, and hawks. Several multi-use trails in area. CG is close to two wilderness areas. No drinking water available.

GETTING THERE: From Magdalena go W on US HWY 60 approx. 12 mi. to state HWY 52 (forest route 549). Go S on 549 approx. 18 mi. to Hughes Mill CG. High clearance vehicles only.

SINGLE RATE:	No fee	OPEN DATES:	May-Oct
# of SINGLE SITES:	2	MAX SPUR:	20 feet
		MAX STAY:	14 days
		ELEVATION:	8000 feet

7 Lobo Canyon
Grants • lat 35˚12'00" lon 107˚43'00"

DESCRIPTION: CG is located in pinon, juniper, and pine with views of Mount Taylor. Wildlife in the area includes black bears, mountain lions, bobcats, coyotes, deer, elk, hawks, eagles, and porcupines. CG can be busy weekends and holidays. Hiking, horse, mountain biking, and ATV trails in area.

GETTING THERE: From Grants go NE on Lobo Canyon Road (state HWY 547) approx. 7 mi. to forest route 193. Go S on 193 approx. 2 mi. to Lobo Canyon CG. Not suitable for trailers.

SINGLE RATE:	Varies	OPEN DATES:	May-Sept
		MAX STAY:	14 days
		ELEVATION:	7400 feet

8 Luna Park
Monticello • lat 33˚29'45" lon 107˚24'53"

DESCRIPTION: CG is located in semi open grove of pinon and juniper with views of the surrounding hills. Wildlife in the area includes black bears, mountain lions, bobcats, coyotes, deer, elk, turkeys, quails, bald eagles, and hawks. Several multi-use trails in area. CG is close to two wilderness areas. No drinking water available.

GETTING THERE: From Monticello go N on forest route 139 approx. 5 mi. to forest route 225. Go N on 225 approx. 4 mi. to Luna Park CG. High clearance vehicles only.

SINGLE RATE:	No fee	OPEN DATES:	Mar-Nov
# of SINGLE SITES:	3	MAX SPUR:	20 feet
		MAX STAY:	14 days
		ELEVATION:	7400 feet

9 McGaffey
Fort Wingate • lat 35˚22'03" lon 108˚31'17"

DESCRIPTION: CG is located in ponderosa pine with red rock views. Fish for rainbow trout and sunfish in McGaffey lake; adjacent to CG. Wildlife in the area includes black bears, mountain lions, bobcats, coyotes, deer, elk, hawks, eagles, and porqupines. Many trails in area. There is an interpretive trail on site.

GETTING THERE: From Fort Wingate go S on state HWY 400 approx. 8 mi. to McGaffey CG.

SINGLE RATE:	Varies	OPEN DATES:	May-Oct
# of SINGLE SITES:	29	MAX SPUR:	25 feet
GROUP RATE:	Varies	MAX STAY:	14 days
# of GROUP SITES:	3	ELEVATION:	8000 feet

10 New Canyon
Manzano • lat 34˚40'14" lon 106˚24'32"

DESCRIPTION: CG is located in a steep-sided canyon with ponderosa pine, fir, and oak. A small, seasonal tributary runs near this CG. A small lake in Manzano offers trout fishing. Wildlife includes black bears, mountain lions, coyotes, deer, bighorn sheep, and bobcats. Hiking/horse trails in adjacent Manzano Wilderness Area.

GETTING THERE: From Manzano go NW on forest route 245 approx. 5 mi. to New Canyon CG. Road is narrow and rough with sharp curves. Not recommended for trailers.

SINGLE RATE:	Varies	OPEN DATES:	Yearlong
# of SINGLE SITES:	10	MAX SPUR:	22 feet
		MAX STAY:	14 days
		ELEVATION:	7800 feet

 Campground has hosts    **Reservable sites**   **Accessible facilities**   **Fully developed**   **Semi-developed**   **Rustic facilities**

NOTE: Open dates listed are typical. Actual dates are dependent on conditions such as snow pack.

11 Ojo Redondo
Grants • lat 35˚09'32" lon 108˚06'31"

DESCRIPTION: CG is located in mixed conifer with views of Mount Taylor. Wildlife in the area includes black bears, mountain lions, bobcats, coyotes, deer, elk, hawks, eagles, and porcupines. CG can be busy weekends and holidays. Hiking, horse, mountain biking, and ATV trails in area. No drinking water available.

GETTING THERE: From Grants go W on forest route 49 approx. 10 mi. to forest route 480. Go N on 480 approx. 9 mi. to Ojo Redondo CG.

SINGLE RATE:	No fee	OPEN DATES:	May-Nov
# of SINGLE SITES:	19	MAX SPUR:	25 feet
		MAX STAY:	14 days
		ELEVATION:	8900 feet

12 Quaking Aspen
Fort Wingate • lat 35˚24'20" lon 108˚32'23"

DESCRIPTION: CG is located in ponderosa pine with views of Mount Taylor. Wildlife in the area includes black bears, mountain lions, bobcats, coyotes, deer, elk, hawks, eagles, and porcupines. CG can be busy weekends and holidays. Hiking, horse, mountain biking, and ATV trails in area.

GETTING THERE: From Fort Wingate go S on state HWY 400 approx. 5 mi. to Quaking Aspen CG.

SINGLE RATE:	$5	OPEN DATES:	May-Sept
# of SINGLE SITES:	20	MAX SPUR:	25 feet
		MAX STAY:	14 days
		ELEVATION:	7600 feet

13 Red Canyon
Manzano • lat 34˚37'16" lon 106˚24'33"

DESCRIPTION: CG is in a canyon with pinon, juniper, fir, and pine. Canon Colorado Creek (seasonal) is a short walk from this CG. Wildlife includes black bears, mountain lions, coyotes, deer, bighorn sheep, and bobcats. On site trailhead leads to Manzano Wilderness. Camping with horses welcome. Songbird watchers delight!

GETTING THERE: From Manzano go S on forest route 253 approx. 5 mi. to Red Canyon CG.

SINGLE RATE:	Varies	OPEN DATES:	May-Sept
# of SINGLE SITES:	52	MAX SPUR:	22 feet
		MAX STAY:	14 days
		ELEVATION:	7600 feet

14 Red Cloud
Corona • lat 34˚12'37" lon 105˚45'19"

DESCRIPTION: This quiet, remote CG is located in a canyon surrounded by ponderosa pine. Supplies may be purchased in Corona. Wildlife includes black bears, mountain lions, coyotes, deer, bighorn sheep, antelope, and bobcats. CG tends to be busy during the hunting season (late fall).

GETTING THERE: From Corona go S on US HWY 54 approx. 9 mi. to forest route 99. Go NW on 99 approx. 8.5 mi. to Red Cloud CG. Road is narrow with sharp curves. Not recommended for trailers.

SINGLE RATE:	Varies	OPEN DATES:	Apr-Oct
# of SINGLE SITES:	5	MAX SPUR:	22 feet
		MAX STAY:	14 days
		ELEVATION:	7600 feet

15 Springtime
Monticello • lat 33˚34'31" lon 107˚24'14"

DESCRIPTION: CG is located under a thick canopy of mixed conifer in Springtime Canyon. There is a small seasonal stream near CG. Wildlife includes black bears, mountain lions, bobcats, coyotes, deer, elk, turkeys, bald eagles, and hawks. On site trailhead leads to Apache-Kid Wilderness. No drinking water.

GETTING THERE: From Monticello go N on forest route 139 5 mi. to forest route 225. Go N 11 mi. to forest route 225A. Go N 1 mi. to Springtime CG. High clearance vehicles only. Not suitable for trailers.

SINGLE RATE:	No fee	OPEN DATES:	Mar-Nov
# of SINGLE SITES:	6	MAX SPUR:	15 feet
		MAX STAY:	14 days
		ELEVATION:	7000 feet

16 Tajique
Tajique • lat 34˚45'57" lon 106˚19'38"

DESCRIPTION: CG is located in an open area with huge ponderosa pine and willow. Views are of adjacent Tajique Creek. Fish for rainbow trout. Sites are walk-in only. Wildlife includes black bears, mountain lions, coyotes, deer, bighorn sheep, and bobcats. Hiking and horse trails in nearby Manzano Wilderness Area.

GETTING THERE: From Tajique go W on forest route 55 approx. 3 mi. to Tajique CG. Road is narrow with sharp curves. Not suitable for trailers.

SINGLE RATE:	Varies	OPEN DATES:	Yearlong
# of SINGLE SITES:	5	MAX SPUR:	20 feet
		MAX STAY:	14 days
		ELEVATION:	6800 feet

17 Water Canyon
Magdalena • lat 34˚01'27" lon 107˚07'47"

DESCRIPTION: CG is located in a grove of mixed conifer, oak, pinon, and juniper on Water Canyon. A small seasonal stream runs near CG. Wildlife includes black bears, mountain lions, bobcats, coyotes, deer, elk, turkeys, bald eagles, and hawks. Lightening observatory on site. Hiking trails nearby. No drinking water.

GETTING THERE: From Magdalena go E on US HWY 60 approx. 10 mi. to forest route 235. Go S on 235 approx. 4 mi. to Water Canyon CG.

SINGLE RATE:	No fee	OPEN DATES:	Mar-Nov
# of SINGLE SITES:	16	MAX SPUR:	20 feet
		MAX STAY:	14 days
# of GROUP SITES:	1	ELEVATION:	6800 feet

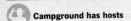 **Campground has hosts**   **Reservable sites**   **Accessible facilities**   **Fully developed**   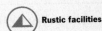 **Semi-developed**   **Rustic facilities**

NOTE: Open dates listed are typical. Actual dates are dependent on conditions such as snow pack.

USFS Photo

GILA
NATIONAL FOREST

Popular theory says that the Gila National Forest derived its name from a Spanish contraction of Hah-quah-sa-eel, a Yuma Indian word meaning "running water which is salty". The forest, tucked away in southwestern New Mexico, is a paradise for those seeking solitude and escape from modern society's busy lifestyle.

The Gila's beauty is in its diversity of rugged mountains, deep canyons, meadows, and semi-desert country. Elevations range from 4,200 to 10,900 feet and cover four of the six life zones. Ocotillo and cactus are found in the lower elevations, and juniper, pine, aspen, and spruce and fir forests are plentiful in the high mountains.

Another unique beauty of the Gila National Forest is its wilderness areas, which offer hiking, horseback riding and other recreational opportunities.

The Gila has a rich history replete with Indians, explorers, ranchers, prospectors and miners. Apache Chiefs Mangas Coloradas and Geronimo as well as Aldo Leopold, a conservationist, ecologist and author of the Sand County Almanac, are but a few of the personalities from the past that have left their mark in the Gila.

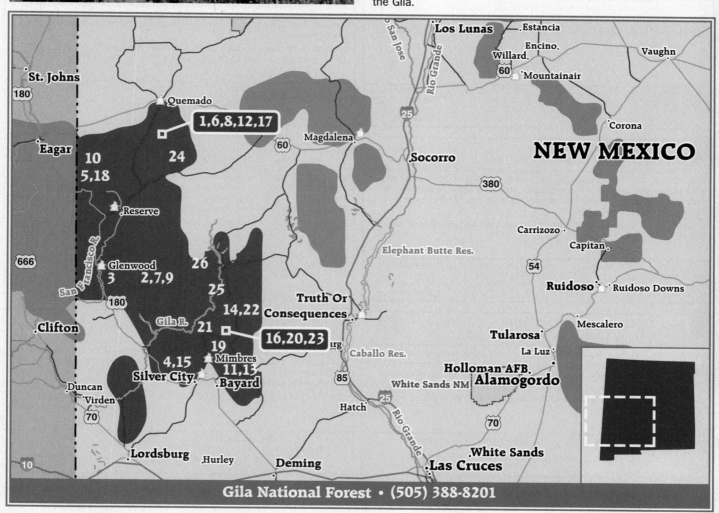

GILA NATIONAL FOREST • NEW MEXICO • LOCATOR MAP

1 Armijo
Quemado • lat 34°40'26" lon 107°55'44"

DESCRIPTION: CG set in a dispersed pine forest next to Armijo Springs. Lake Quemado is 10 mi. away for fishing. Sawmill Canyon is close by for great wildlife viewing. Elk, deer, and turkeys are frequently seen. Supplies at Quemado. No designated trails in this area, just venture off to explore. Gather firewood locally.

GETTING THERE: From Quemado go S on state HWY 32 approx. 18 mi. to forest route 854. Go S on 854 approx. 3 mi. to Armijo CG.

SINGLE RATE: # of SINGLE SITES:	No fee 4	OPEN DATES: MAX SPUR: MAX STAY: ELEVATION:	Apr-Nov 35 feet 30 days 7800 feet

6 Cove
Quemado • lat 34°06'11" lon 108°29'39"

DESCRIPTION: In a cottonwood and pine forest setting on Quemado Lake. This CG is used as an overflow for all the CG's in the lake area. Boat ramp at CG. Fish from the lake for trout. Deer, elk and turkey can be found in area. Supplies at Quemado. Firewood found locally.

GETTING THERE: From Quemado go S on state HWY 32 approx. 15 mi. to state HWY 103. Go E on 103 approx. 6 mi. to Cove CG.

SINGLE RATE:	Varies	OPEN DATES: MAX STAY: ELEVATION:	May-Oct 14 days 8000 feet

2 Ben Lilly
Alma • lat 33°23'50" lon 108°35'32"

DESCRIPTION: This CG is situated in a pine, spruce, and fir forest on the banks of Willow Creek. Fishing in creek. Please check for local fishing regulations. Deer frequent the area. CG tends to be busy on holiday weekends. Numerous trailheads can be found in the area, offering excellent hiking opportunities.

GETTING THERE: From Alma go E on state HWY 159 approx. 23 mi. to forest route 507. Go W on 507 approx. 2 mi. to Ben Lilly CG. Primitive road.

SINGLE RATE: # of SINGLE SITES:	No fee 6	OPEN DATES: MAX SPUR: MAX STAY: ELEVATION:	Apr-Nov 17 feet 14 days 8100 feet

7 Dipping Vat
Alma • lat 33°26'00" lon 108°30'00"

DESCRIPTION: This CG is situated among ponderosa pine within walking distance of Snow Lake. Fishing in lake, please check for local regulations. Deer, elk, and bald eagles can occasionally be seen in the area. CG tends to be busy on holiday weekends. Several trails can be found in the area.

GETTING THERE: From Alma go E on state HWY 159 approx. 24 mi. to forest route 28. Go N on 28 approx. 3 mi. to forest route 142. Go E on 142 approx. 7 mi. to Dipping Vat CG.

SINGLE RATE: # of SINGLE SITES:	$5 40	OPEN DATES: MAX SPUR: MAX STAY: ELEVATION:	Apr-Nov 40 feet 14 days 7300 feet

3 Bighorn
Glenwood • lat 33°19'00" lon 108°53'00"

DESCRIPTION: This CG is situated in a juniper and pinon forest. Deer, elk, javelinas, and turkeys reside in the area. CG tends to be busy on holiday weekends.

GETTING THERE: Big Horn CG is located approx. 1 mi. N of Glenwood on US HWY 180.

SINGLE RATE: # of SINGLE SITES:	No fee 7	OPEN DATES: MAX SPUR: MAX STAY: ELEVATION:	Yearlong 17 feet 14 days 5000 feet

8 El Caso
Quemado • lat 34°06'11" lon 108°29'39"

DESCRIPTION: This CG is in a cottonwood and pine forest on Quemado Lake. Fishing for stocked rainbow trout from lake. Electric motors allowed only. Supplies are available at Quemado. Trail system to upper end of the lake for excellent wildlife observation. Gather downed firewood.

GETTING THERE: From Quemado go S on state HWY 32 approx. 15 mi. to state HWY 103. Go E on 103 approx. 6 mi. to El Caso CG.

SINGLE RATE: # of SINGLE SITES:	No fee 18	OPEN DATES: MAX STAY: ELEVATION:	Apr-Nov 14 days 7800 feet

4 Cherry Creek
Silver City • lat 32°54'51" lon 108°13'25"

DESCRIPTION: This CG is situated in a pine forest on the banks of Cherry Creek. Wildlife in the area consists primarily of deer, chipmunks, and an occasional bear or two. CG tends to be busy on holiday weekends. Various trails in the area offer numerous hiking and mountain biking opportunities.

GETTING THERE: Cherry Creek CG is located approx. 9 mi. N of Silver City on state HWY 15.

SINGLE RATE: # of SINGLE SITES:	No fee 12	OPEN DATES: MAX SPUR: MAX STAY: ELEVATION:	Apr-Nov 17 feet 30 days 7400 feet

9 Gilita
Alma • lat 33°24'00" lon 108°34'00"

DESCRIPTION: This CG is situated in a pine, spruce, and fir forest on the banks of Willow Creek. Fishing in creek, please check for local fishing regulations. Deer frequent the area. CG tends to be busy on holiday weekends. Several trailheads are accessible in the area, offering many hiking opportunities.

GETTING THERE: From Alma go E on state HWY 159 approx. 24 mi. to Gilita CG.

SINGLE RATE: # of SINGLE SITES:	No fee 6	OPEN DATES: MAX SPUR: MAX STAY: ELEVATION:	Apr-Nov 17 feet 14 days 8100 feet

5 Cottonwood Canyon
Luna • lat 33°37'08" lon 108°53'36"

DESCRIPTION: This CG is situated in a dense pine forest; set in a canyon. Watch for deer, elk, javelinas, turkeys, and small wildlife in the vicinity. Receives moderate use, picking up on holiday weekends in the summer. Numerous roads and trails in the area offer hiking opportunities.

GETTING THERE: Cottonwood Canyon CG is located approx. 20 mi. S of Luna on US HWY 180.

SINGLE RATE: # of SINGLE SITES:	No fee 2	OPEN DATES: MAX STAY: ELEVATION:	Yearlong 30 days 6000 feet

10 Head of the Ditch
Luna • lat 33°49'00" lon 109°00'00"

DESCRIPTION: This CG offers large undesignated sites. Views of the San Fransico River running through the middle of CG. The river is good for wading and playing in. Supplies are available at Luna. Deer, elk, and turkeys can sometimes be seen at CG. No designated trails nearby. Gather firewood locally.

GETTING THERE: Head of the Ditch CG is located approx. 2 mi. W of Luna on US HWY 180.

SINGLE RATE: # of SINGLE SITES:	No fee 6	OPEN DATES: MAX STAY: ELEVATION:	Apr-Nov 30 days 7100 feet

 Campground has hosts   **Reservable sites**   **Accessible facilities**   **Fully developed**   **Semi-developed**   **Rustic facilities**

11 Iron Creek

Kingston • lat 32˚54'32" lon 107˚48'19"

DESCRIPTION: This CG is situated in a mixed pine forest on the banks of Iron Creek. Fish and swim in the creek. Check for local regulations. Supplies are available at Kingston. CG receives heavy use on holidays and weekends during the summer. Numerous trails can be found nearby.

GETTING THERE: From Kingston go W on state HWY 152 approx. 10 mi. to Iron Creek CG.

SINGLE RATE:	No fee	OPEN DATES:	Apr-Nov
# of SINGLE SITES:	15	MAX SPUR:	17 feet
		MAX STAY:	30 days
		ELEVATION:	7300 feet

16 Mesa

Silver City • lat 33˚02'01" lon 108˚09'30"

DESCRIPTION: A primitive CG in a ponderosa pine forest setting just above Lake Roberts. Fish for trout out of the lake. Elk, deer, turkey and bear frequent the area. Supplies at Silver City. Campers may gather firewood. Trails to the lake begin at CG. The Gila Cliff Dwellings National Monument is nearby.

GETTING THERE: Mesa CG is located approx. 26 mi. N of Silver City on state HWY 35.

SINGLE RATE:	$7	OPEN DATES:	May-Sept
# of SINGLE SITES:	14	MAX SPUR:	20 feet
		MAX STAY:	7 days
		ELEVATION:	6100 feet

12 Juniper

Quemado • lat 34˚08'00" lon 108˚29'00"

DESCRIPTION: This CG is situated in a cottonwood and pine forest on a bench above Quemado Lake. Fishing for trout from the lake. Supplies are available in Quemado. Deer, elk, and turkeys can sometimes be seen around the lake. Gather firewood locally. Trails are accessible at several areas around the lake.

GETTING THERE: From Quemado go S on state HWY 32 approx. 15 mi. to state HWY 103. Go E on 103 approx. 5 mi. to Juniper CG.

SINGLE RATE:	Varies	OPEN DATES:	May-Sept
# of SINGLE SITES:	18	MAX SPUR:	40 feet
		MAX STAY:	14 days
		ELEVATION:	8000 feet

17 Pinon

Quemado • lat 34˚08'00" lon 108˚29'00"

DESCRIPTION: CG set in a dense cottonwood and pine forest on a bench above Quemado Lake. Fishing for trout from the lake. Supplies in Quemado. Deer, elk, and turkeys can be seen around the lake. Gather firewood locally. Trails are accessible at several areas around the lake. Group sites by reservation only.

GETTING THERE: From Quemado go S on state HWY 32 approx. 15 mi. to state HWY 103. Go E on 103 approx. 4.5 mi. to Pinon CG.

SINGLE RATE:	Varies	OPEN DATES:	May-Sept
# of SINGLE SITES:	23	MAX SPUR:	40 feet
GROUP RATE:	Varies	MAX STAY:	14 days
# of GROUP SITES:	2	ELEVATION:	8000 feet

13 Kingston

Kingston • lat 32˚55'06" lon 107˚42'00"

DESCRIPTION: In a dense stand of ponderosa pine with views of Middle Percha Creek. No fishing in the creek, just wade in it and enjoy the view. Deer, bear and elk can be seen from the CG. Supplies available in Kingston. Campers may gather firewood. No designated trails near CG, just take short hikes around the CG area.

GETTING THERE: Kingston CG is located on the E edge of Kingston on state HWY 152.

SINGLE RATE:	No fee	OPEN DATES:	Yearlong
# of SINGLE SITES:	2		
		MAX STAY:	30 days
		ELEVATION:	6100 feet

18 Pueblo Park
Luna • lat 33˚35'35" lon 108˚57'39"

DESCRIPTION: This CG is situated in a pine forest on the banks of Pueblo Creek. Wildlife in the area consists primarily of deer, elk, javelinas, and turkeys. CG tends to be busy on holiday weekends. Some trails are accessible near the CG, offering numerous hiking and mountain biking opportunities.

GETTING THERE: From Luna go S on US HWY 180 approx. 19 mi. to forest route 232. Go W on 232 approx. 6 mi. to Pueblo Park CG.

SINGLE RATE:	No fee	OPEN DATES:	Yearlong
# of SINGLE SITES:	6		
		MAX STAY:	30 days
		ELEVATION:	7000 feet

14 Lower Black Canyon
Silver City • lat 33˚10'57" lon 108˚02'03"

DESCRIPTION: This primitive CG as in a ponderosa pine forest setting on Black Canyon Creek. Fish for trout or swim in the creek. Supplies avialable in Silver City. Elk, deer, turkey and bear frequent the area. System trails begin at CG, #72 is a 13 mi. hike. No water at this CG.

GETTING THERE: From Silver City go N on state HWY 35 approx. 33 mi. to forest route 150. Go N on 150 approx. 19 mi. to Lower Black Canyon CG. Primitive road.

SINGLE RATE:	No fee	OPEN DATES:	Apr-Nov
# of SINGLE SITES:	3	MAX SPUR:	17 feet
		MAX STAY:	30 days
		ELEVATION:	6900 feet

19 Rocky Canyon
Silver City • lat 33˚06'00" lon 108˚00'45"

DESCRIPTION: This primitive CG is in a ponderosa pine and oak forest setting. Elk, deer, turkey and bear frequent the area. Supplies available at Silver City. Campers may gather firewood. Trails to the lake begin at CG. Drinking water at this CG. This is the coldest CG in the forest.

GETTING THERE: From Silver City go N on state HWY 35 approx. 33 mi. to forest route 150. Go N on 150 approx. 11 mi. to Rocky Canyon CG. Primitive road.

SINGLE RATE:	No fee	OPEN DATES:	Apr-Nov
# of SINGLE SITES:	2	MAX SPUR:	17 feet
		MAX STAY:	30 days
		ELEVATION:	7300 feet

15 McMillan
Silver City • lat 32˚55'26" lon 108˚12'47"

DESCRIPTION: CG is located in a pine forest setting on Cherry Creek. Fish or swim in the creek. Supplies available in Silver City. CG can get busy on weekends and holidays in summer. Deer and chipmunks can be seen in the area. Campers may gather firewood. No designated trails in the area.

GETTING THERE: McMillan CG is located approx. 10 mi. N of Silver City on state HWY 35.

SINGLE RATE:	No fee	OPEN DATES:	Apr-Oct
# of SINGLE SITES:	2		
		MAX STAY:	30 days
		ELEVATION:	7400 feet

20 Sapillo
Silver City • lat 33˚00'00" lon 108˚07'30"

DESCRIPTION: A primitive CG in a ponderosa pine forest near Lake Roberts. Fish for trout in the lake. Elk, deer, turkeys, and bears frequent the area. Supplies are available at Silver City. Campers may gather firewood locally. Trails are in the area. Gila Cliff Dwellings National Monument nearby.

GETTING THERE: Sapillo CG is located approx. 29 mi. N of Silver City on state HWY 35.

		OPEN DATES:	Yearlong
GROUP RATE:	No fee	MAX STAY:	14 days
# of GROUP SITES:	10	ELEVATION:	6100 feet

 Campground has hosts   **Reservable sites**   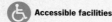 **Accessible facilities**    **Fully developed**   **Semi-developed**   **Rustic facilities**

NOTE: Open dates listed are typical. Actual dates are dependent on conditions such as snow pack.

21 Scorpion
Silver City • lat 33°13'51" lon 108°15'38"

DESCRIPTION: This primitive CG is in a ponderosa pine forest setting. Elk, deer, turkeys and bears frequent the area. Supplies available at Silver City. Campers may gather firewood. Trails in the area. This CG has drinking water and corrals for horses.

GETTING THERE: From Silver City go N on state HWY 35 approx. 22 mi. to state HWY 15. Go N on 15 approx. 16 mi. to Scorpion CG.

SINGLE RATE:	No fee	OPEN DATES:	Yearlong
# of SINGLE SITES:	10	MAX SPUR:	17 feet
		MAX STAY:	7 days
		ELEVATION:	5700 feet

22 Upper Black Canyon
Silver City • lat 33°11'07" lon 108°01'57"

DESCRIPTION: This primitive CG is in a ponderosa pine forest setting on Black Canyon Creek. Fish for trout or swim in the creek. Supplies available at Silver City. Elk, deer, turkeys and bears frequent the area. System trails begin at CG, #72 is a 13 mi. hike. No water at this CG.

GETTING THERE: From Silver City go N on state HWY 35 approx. 33 mi. to forest route 150. Go N on 150 approx. 19 mi. to Upper Black Canyon CG.

SINGLE RATE:	No fee	OPEN DATES:	Apr-Nov
# of SINGLE SITES:	2	MAX SPUR:	22 feet
		MAX STAY:	30 days
		ELEVATION:	6900 feet

23 Upper End
Silver City • lat 33°01'40" lon 108°09'05"

DESCRIPTION: This primitive CG is in a ponderosa pine forest setting just above Lake Roberts. Fish for trout in the lake. Elk, deer, turkeys and bears in the area. Supplies at Silver City. Gather firewood. Pergatory trail, a circular 2 mi. trail starts at CG. The Gila Cliff Dwellings National Monument are nearby.

GETTING THERE: Upper End CG is located approx. 27 mi. N of Silver City on state HWY 35.

SINGLE RATE:	$7	OPEN DATES:	May-Dec
# of SINGLE SITES:	11	MAX SPUR:	20 feet
		MAX STAY:	7 days
		ELEVATION:	6000 feet

24 Valle Tio Vinces
Quemado • lat 34°02'00" lon 108°21'30"

DESCRIPTION: CG is used as a horse camp and sits on the Continental Divide Trail. In tall ponderosa pine with two 9ft circular water troughs. Each trough has four separate corrals surrounding them.

GETTING THERE: From Quemado go approx. 9 mi. to forest route 214. Go E on 214 approx. 23 mi. to Valle Tio Vinces CG.

		OPEN DATES:	Yearlong*
GROUP RATE:	No fee	MAX STAY:	14 days
		ELEVATION:	8000 feet

25 Willow Creek
Alma • lat 33°23'50" lon 108°35'32"

DESCRIPTION: CG is located in pine, spruce and fir on Willow Creek. Fishing in Creek. Deer in area. Busy on holidaay weekends. Several trailheads in area.

GETTING THERE: From Alma go E on state HWY 159 approx. 23 mi. to forest route 507. Go W on 507 approx. 2 mi. to Willow Creek CG. Primitive road.

SINGLE RATE:	No fee	OPEN DATES:	Apr-Nov
# of SINGLE SITES:	6	MAX SPUR:	17 feet
		MAX STAY:	14 days
		ELEVATION:	8100 feet

26 Wolf Hollow
Truth or Consequences • lat 33°25'00" lon 108°13'00"

DESCRIPTION: A primitive CG in an open, dry, desert ground covered area. No water nearby. In the mornings you can see herds of elk near CG. Deer and bears are also seen nearby. CG is never full. Horse and hiking trails are nearby. CG has horse corrals.

GETTING THERE: From Truth or Consequences take I-25 to HWY 52. Go W on 52 to HWY 59. Go W on 59 past Beaverhead to Wolf Hollow CG.

SINGLE RATE:	No fee	OPEN DATES:	Yearlong
# of SINGLE SITES:	3	MAX STAY:	14 days
		ELEVATION:	8300 feet

 Campground has hosts   Reservable sites   Accessible facilities   Fully developed   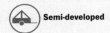 Semi-developed    Rustic facilities

NOTE: Open dates listed are typical. Actual dates are dependent on conditions such as snow pack.

USFS Photo

LINCOLN NATIONAL FOREST

The Lincoln National Forest is located in south central New Mexico. The forest covers over 1.1 million acres stretching north from Texas past the Capitan Mountains.

Higher elevations offer mountain meadows, mixtures of pine, fir, aspen, oak, and other vibrant landscapes broken by the brilliance of wildflowers, blossoming plants, and trees that change with the season. Two wilderness areas exist on the forest ranging in elevations from 4,000 to 11,500 feet, which pass through five different life zones from desert to sub-alpine forest. Wildlife, consisting of mule deer, turkeys, elk and black bears are plentiful, however, fishing opportunities are limited.

In the summer enjoy sightseeing, wildlife watching, picnicking, camping, hiking, hunting, fishing, mountain biking, horseback riding, or motorcycling. The mountains also provide winter sports opportunities not found elsewhere in the area. Tubing, snowmobiling and cross-county skiing activities are quite popular. Two downhill ski areas are partially located on the forest.

Travelers will find spectacular views of sunsets across the desert as well as breathtaking views of the Tularosa Basin and White Sands National Monument from the Sunspot Scenic Byway.

LINCOLN NATIONAL FOREST • NEW MEXICO • LOCATOR MAP

Lincoln National Forest • (505) 434-7200

1 Apache
Cloudcroft • lat 32˚58'00" lon 105˚43'42"

DESCRIPTION: In a dense forest mixture of douglas fir, pine and aspen. Warm, sunny days with cool nights. Thunderstorms happen often during July and August. No drinking water at CG. Supplies available at Cloudcroft. Black bears, deer and elk can be seen from the CG. CG is full most weekends. Small nature trail circles CG.

GETTING THERE: From Cloudcroft go N on forest route 244 approx. 2 mi. to forest route 24. Go S on 24 approx. 1 mi. to Apache CG.

SINGLE RATE:	Varies	OPEN DATES:	May-Oct
# of SINGLE SITES:	26	MAX SPUR:	32 feet
		MAX STAY:	14 days
		ELEVATION:	8900 feet

2 Aspen Group
Cloudcroft • lat 32˚56'30" lon 105˚45'00"

DESCRIPTION: In a forest mixture of douglas fir, pine and aspen. Warm, sunny days with cool nights. Thunderstorms often happen during July and August. No drinking water at CG. Supplies available at Cloudcroft. Black bears, deer and elk can be seen from the CG. CG is full most weekends.

GETTING THERE: Aspen Group CG is located approx. 1 mi. S of Cloudcroft on forest route 24B.

		OPEN DATES:	May-Oct
		MAX SPUR:	35 feet
GROUP RATE:	$50	MAX STAY:	14 days
# of GROUP SITES:	1	ELEVATION:	8800 feet

3 Black Bears Group
Cloudcroft • lat 32˚57'00" lon 105˚45'00"

DESCRIPTION: In a park-like setting of mixed conifer and an open meadow. Warm, sunny days with cool nights. Thunderstorms in July and August. No drinking water available at CG. Supplies available at Cloudcroft. Black bears, deer and elk can be seen from the CG. CG is full most weekends. Trails close to CG.

GETTING THERE: Black Bears Group CG is located approx. 1 mi. S of Cloudcroft on forest route 24B.

		OPEN DATES:	May-Oct
		MAX SPUR:	35 feet
GROUP RATE:	$50	MAX STAY:	14 days
# of GROUP SITES:	1	ELEVATION:	8800 feet

4 Cedar Creek Group
Ruidoso • lat 33˚21'28" lon 105˚40'55"

DESCRIPTION: This CG is in a pine forest setting with a scrub oak understory. Cedar Creek is nearby for fishing and swimming opportunities. Bears, elk and deer can be seen from the CG. Supplies available at Ruidoso. Campers may gather firewood. An informal trail system is nearby or follow old roads for great adventures.

GETTING THERE: Cedar Creek Group CG is located approx. 1 mi. N of Ruidoso on forest route 88.

		OPEN DATES:	May-Sept
		MAX SPUR:	35 feet
GROUP RATE:	Varies	MAX STAY:	14 days
# of GROUP SITES:	3	ELEVATION:	6900 feet

5 Deerhead
Cloudcroft • lat 32˚56'37" lon 105˚44'45"

DESCRIPTION: In a open park-like setting of douglas fir, pine and aspen. Warm, sunny days with cool nights. Thunderstorms often happen during July and August. Drinkable water available. Supplies available at Cloudcroft. Black bears, deer and elk can be seen from the CG. Rim Trail close to CG.

GETTING THERE: Deerhead CG is located approx. 1 mi. S of Cloudcroft on state HWY 130.

SINGLE RATE:	Varies	OPEN DATES:	May-Sept
# of SINGLE SITES:	35	MAX SPUR:	20 feet
		MAX STAY:	14 days
		ELEVATION:	8700 feet

6 James Canyon
Mayhill • lat 32˚54'16" lon 105˚30'15"

DESCRIPTION: In a open, park-like setting of douglas fir, pine and aspen. Warm, sunny days with cool nights. Thunderstorms often happen during July and August. No drinking water available at CG. Supplies can be found at Cloudcroft. Black bears, deer and elk can be seen from the CG.

GETTING THERE: From Mayhill go W on US HWY 82 approx. 2.5 mi. to James Canyon CG.

SINGLE RATE:	No fee	OPEN DATES:	Yearlong
# of SINGLE SITES:	5	MAX SPUR:	16 feet
		MAX STAY:	14 days
		ELEVATION:	6800 feet

7 Lower Fir Group
Cloudcroft • lat 32˚58'10" lon 105˚43'48"

DESCRIPTION: In an open park-like setting of douglas fir, pine and aspen. Warm, sunny days with cool nights. Thunderstorms often during July and August. Drinkable water available. Supplies at Cloudcroft. Black bears, deer and elk can be seen from the CG. Trails are nearby.

GETTING THERE: From Cloudcroft go N on state HWY 244 approx. 1 mi. to Lower Fir Group CG.

		OPEN DATES:	May-Oct
		MAX SPUR:	16 feet
GROUP RATE:	Varies	MAX STAY:	14 days
# of GROUP SITES:	1	ELEVATION:	8800 feet

8 Monjeau
Alto • lat 32˚25'55" lon 105˚43'46"

DESCRIPTION: CG is in an oak, fir and a pine forest setting on a high elevation rocky knob with majestic views. Historical rock CCC lookout stands nearby. Supplies available at Alto. Bears, deer, elk and turkeys can be seen near the CG area. Campers may gather firewood. There is a trail system nearby.

GETTING THERE: From Alto go W on state HWY 532 approx. 1 mi. to forest route 117. Go N on 117 approx. 4 mi. to Monjeau CG.

SINGLE RATE:	No fee	OPEN DATES:	May-Nov
# of SINGLE SITES:	4	MAX SPUR:	16 feet
		MAX STAY:	14 days
		ELEVATION:	9500 feet

9 Oak Grove
Alto • lat 33˚23'30" lon 105˚45'00"

DESCRIPTION: CG is in an oak, pine and fir forest setting with views of the mountain range adjacent to CG. A stream runs nearby with fishing and swimming opporunities. Supplies available at Alto. Bears, deer, elk and turkeys can be seen near the CG. Campers may gather firewood. Trail within 4 mi. of the CG.

GETTING THERE: Oak Grove CG is located approx. 4 mi. W of Alto on state HWY 532.

SINGLE RATE:	Varies	OPEN DATES:	May-Sept
# of SINGLE SITES:	30	MAX SPUR:	18 feet
		MAX STAY:	14 days
		ELEVATION:	8400 feet

10 Pines
Cloudcroft • lat 32˚57'00" lon 105˚44'00"

DESCRIPTION: In a dense forest mixture of douglas fir, pine and aspen. Warm, sunny days with cool nights. Thunderstorms often happen during July and August. Drinkable water available. Black bears, deer and elk can be seen from the CG. Trails close to CG.

GETTING THERE: Pines CG is located approx. 1 mi. N of Cloudcroft on state HWY 244.

SINGLE RATE:	Varies	OPEN DATES:	May-Oct
# of SINGLE SITES:	48	MAX SPUR:	16 feet
		MAX STAY:	14 days
		ELEVATION:	8800 feet

 Campground has hosts   **Reservable sites**   **Accessible facilities**   **Fully developed**   **Semi-developed**   **Rustic facilities**

NOTE: Open dates listed are typical. Actual dates are dependent on conditions such as snow pack.

11 Saddle
Cloudcroft • lat 32°58'13" lon 105°43'30"

DESCRIPTION: In a dense forest mixture of douglas fir, pine and aspen. Warm, sunny days with cool nights. Thunderstorms often during July and August. Drinkable water available. Supplies available at Cloudcroft. Black bears, deer and elk can be seen from the CG. CG is full most weekends. Small nature trail circles CG.

GETTING THERE: From Cloudcroft go N on forest route 244 approx. 2 mi. to forest route 24. Go S on 24 approx. 1/2 mi. to Saddle CG.

SINGLE RATE:	Varies	OPEN DATES:	May-Oct
# of SINGLE SITES:	17	MAX SPUR:	32 feet
		MAX STAY:	14 days
		ELEVATION:	9000 feet

12 Silver
Cloudcroft • lat 32°58'24" lon 105°43'29"

DESCRIPTION: In a dense forest mixture of douglas fir, pine and aspen. Warm, sunny days with cool nights. Thunderstorms often happen during July and August. Drinkable water available. Supplies can be purchased in Cloudcroft. Black bears, deer and elk can be seen from the CG. Trails close to CG.

GETTING THERE: From Cloudcroft go N on forest route 244 approx. 2 mi. to forest route 24. Go S on 24 approx. 3 mi. to Silver CG.

SINGLE RATE:	Varies	OPEN DATES:	May-Oct
# of SINGLE SITES:	32	MAX SPUR:	32 feet
		MAX STAY:	14 days
		ELEVATION:	9000 feet

13 Silver Overflow
Cloudcroft • lat 32°58'24" lon 105°43'29"

DESCRIPTION: In a dense forest mixture of douglas fir, pine and aspen. Warm, sunny days with cool nights. Thunderstorms often happen during July and August. Drinkable water available. Supplies can be purchased in Cloudcroft. Black bears, deer and elk can be seen from the CG. RV dump station and ampitheater at CG.

GETTING THERE: From Cloudcroft go N on forest route 244 approx. 2 mi. to forest route 24. Go S on 24 approx. 3 mi. to Silver Overflow CG.

SINGLE RATE:	Varies	OPEN DATES:	May-Oct
# of SINGLE SITES:	52	MAX SPUR:	32 feet
		MAX STAY:	14 days
		ELEVATION:	9000 feet

14 Skyline
Alto • lat 33°25'12" lon 105°44'02"

DESCRIPTION: In an oak, fir and a pine forest setting on a high elevation rocky knob with views of White Mountain Wilderness. Historical rock CCC lookout is nearby. Supplies available at Alto. Bears, deer, elk and turkeys can be seen near the CG area. Campers may gather firewood. A trail system is nearby.

GETTING THERE: Skyline CG is located approx. 3 mi. W of Alto on state HWY 532.

SINGLE RATE:	No fee	OPEN DATES:	May-Nov
# of SINGLE SITES:	17	MAX SPUR:	16 feet
		MAX STAY:	14 days
		ELEVATION:	9000 feet

15 Sleepygrass
Cloudcroft • lat 32°56'56" lon 105°43'08"

DESCRIPTION: In an open park-like setting of douglas fir, pine and aspen. Warm, sunny days with cool nights. Thunderstorms often happen during July and August. Drinkable water available. Supplies can be purchased in Cloudcroft. Black bears, deer and elk can be seen from the CG. Trails close to CG.

GETTING THERE: From Cloudcroft go S on state HWY 130 approx. 1 mi. to forest route 24B. Go E on 24B approx. 1.5 mi. to Sleepygrass CG.

SINGLE RATE:	$8	OPEN DATES:	May-Oct
# of SINGLE SITES:	45	MAX SPUR:	16 feet
		MAX STAY:	14 days
		ELEVATION:	8800 feet

16 Slide Group
Cloudcroft • lat 32°56'00" lon 105°45'15"

DESCRIPTION: In a dense forest mixture of douglas fir, pine and aspen. Warm, sunny days with cool nights. Thunderstorms often happen during July and August. No drinkable water available. Supplies available at Cloudcroft. Black bears, deer and elk can be seen from the CG. Trails nearby.

GETTING THERE: From Cloudcroft go S on state HWY 130 approx. 2 mi. to forest route 105. Go W on 105 approx. 1/2 mi. to Slide Group CG.

GROUP RATE:	Varies	OPEN DATES:	May-Oct
# of GROUP SITES:	1	MAX SPUR:	16 feet
		MAX STAY:	14 days
		ELEVATION:	8700 feet

17 South Fork
Angus • lat 33°26'00" lon 105°45'00"

DESCRIPTION: In a mixed conifer setting by Southfork stream. Fish the stream, but mostly great for relaxing, swimming and playing in the water. Bonito Lake nearby for trout fishing. Bears, deer, elk and turkeys seen by CG. Campers may gather downed firewood. A trailhead leads from CG to White Mountain Wilderness.

GETTING THERE: South Fork CG is located approx. 6 mi. W of Angus on forest route 107.

SINGLE RATE:	$10	OPEN DATES:	May-Sept
# of SINGLE SITES:	60	MAX SPUR:	22 feet
		MAX STAY:	14 days
		ELEVATION:	7500 feet

18 Three Rivers
Three Rivers • lat 33°24'04" lon 105°53'04"

DESCRIPTION: CG sits at the foothills of White Mountain Wilderness Area in a park-like setting. Open grass meadow within CG area. Three Rivers Stream is adjacent to the CG. Fish from the stream. Bears, elk, deer and turkeys can be seen by CG. Three Rivers Trailhead starts at CG. Campers may gather downed firewood.

GETTING THERE: From Three Rivers go E on forest route 579 approx. 15 mi. to Three Rivers CG.

SINGLE RATE:	Varies	OPEN DATES:	Yearlong
# of SINGLE SITES:	14	MAX SPUR:	16 feet
GROUP RATE:	Varies	MAX STAY:	14 days
# of GROUP SITES:	2	ELEVATION:	6400 feet

19 Upper Fir Group
Cloudcroft • lat 32°58'10" lon 105°43'48"

DESCRIPTION: In an open park-like setting of douglas fir, pine and aspen. Warm, sunny days with cool nights. Thunderstorms often happen during July and August. Drinkable water available. Supplies available at Cloudcroft. Black bears, deer and elk can be seen from the CG. Trails can be found in the area.

GETTING THERE: Fir Group CG is located approx. 1 mi. N of Cloudcroft off of state HWY 244.

GROUP RATE:	Varies	OPEN DATES:	May-Oct
# of GROUP SITES:	1	MAX SPUR:	16 feet
		MAX STAY:	14 days
		ELEVATION:	8800 feet

 Campground has hosts   Reservable sites   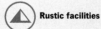 Accessible facilities   Fully developed   Semi-developed   Rustic facilities

NOTE: Open dates listed are typical. Actual dates are dependent on conditions such as snow pack.

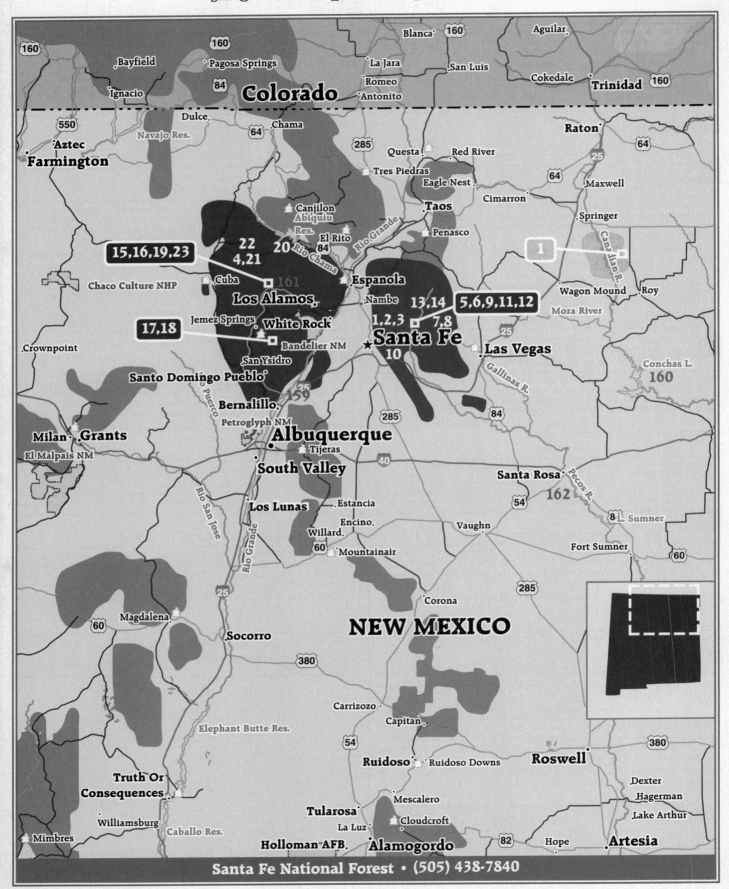

160

Bayfield

Pagosa Springs

160

Blanca

160

Aguilar

La Jara

San Luis

Cokedale

Trinidad

160

Ignacio

Colorado

Romeo

Antonito

550

Dulce

84

Chama

64

Raton

64

Aztec

Navajo Res.

285

Questa

Red River

25

64

Farmington

Tres Piedras

Eagle Nest

Maxwell

Canjilon

Abiquiu
Res.

Taos

Cimarron

64

Springer

15,16,19,23

22

4,21

20

Rio Chama

El Rito

84

Rio Grande

Penasco

Canadian R.

1

Chaco Culture NHP

Cuba

161

Espanola

Nambe

13,14

5,6,9,11,12

Wagon Mound

Roy

Los Alamos

1,2,3

7,8

Mora River

17,18

Jemez Springs

White Rock

Santa Fe

Crownpoint

Bandelier NM

10

Las Vegas

25

Conchas L.

San Ysidro

Gallinas R.

160

Santo Domingo Pueblo

Rio Puerco

159

Bernalillo

Petroglyph NM

285

84

Milan

Grants

El Malpais NM

Albuquerque

Tijeras

South Valley

40

Santa Rosa

Pecos R.

Rio San Jose

54

162

8 L. Sumner

Los Lunas

Estancia

Encino

Vaughn

Rio Grande

Willard

60

Fort Sumner

60

Mountainair

25

285

Corona

Magdalena

NEW MEXICO

60

Socorro

380

Carrizozo

Capitan

380

Elephant Butte Res.

54

Roswell

**Truth Or
Consequences**

Ruidoso

Ruidoso Downs

Dexter

Hagerman

Williamsburg

Caballo Res.

Mescalero

Lake Arthur

Tularosa

Cloudcroft

Mimbres

La Luz

82

Hope

Artesia

Holloman AFB

Alamogordo

USFS Photo

SANTA FE NATIONAL FOREST

Some of the finest mountain scenery in the Southwest is found in the 1.6 million acres covered by the Santa Fe National Forest. Established in 1915, the forest is dominated by the Sangre de Cristo and Jemez mountain ranges and consists of four wilderness areas.

The Chama River Wilderness, created in 1978, includes a 6-mile segment of the Chama River. River water levels vary due to the El Vado Lake dam upstream, which makes this area a favorite for river runners.

The Dome Wilderness provides a continuous expanse of primitive canyonland environments with elevations ranging from 5,800 feet to 8,200. When exploring this area, special care should be taken not to disturb the many prehistoric ruins scattered throughout the area.

A high plateau of rolling mountaintops with areas of dense spruce and mountain meadows–this is the 41,132-acre San Pedro Parks Wilderness, created in 1931. Fishermen rarely leave the small high streams empty-handed and the beauty of the 10,000-foot-high "peaks" is a satisfying reward to the hiker or rider.

The Pecos Wilderness, designated in 1933, lies at the southern end of the majestic Sangre de Cristo Mountains. It includes some of the most beautiful and scenic country in New Mexico. Excellent fishing and hunting, magnificent scenery, and quiet solitude attract many visitors. Many lakes, more than 150 miles of streams, a 100-foot waterfall, and innumerable springs are in the area.

1 Aspen Basin
Santa Fe • lat 35˚47'45" lon 105˚48'04"

DESCRIPTION: CG set in a high elevation of spruce and fir. Campsite are fairly open, receiving low use. The Rio El Medio River runs through the CG. Although this is a small stream, some fishing may be done. Major trailhead to the Pecos Wilderness. Deer, elk, and occasional mountain lions can be seen around CG.

GETTING THERE: Aspen Basin CG is located approx. 16 mi. NE of Santa Fe on the Hyde Park Road (state HWY 475). Not suitable for trailers.

SINGLE RATE:	No fee	OPEN DATES:	Yearlong
		MAX STAY:	14 days
		ELEVATION:	10300 feet

2 Big Tesuque
Santa Fe • lat 35˚46'09" lon 105˚48'01"

DESCRIPTION: This CG is situated in an aspen and pine forest with Tesuque Creek close by. Good trout fishing from the creek. Check for local fishing regulations. Supplies are available at Santa Fe. Deer, elk, birds, and occasional mountain lions can be seen in the area. Nice hiking trails can be found nearby.

GETTING THERE: Big Tesuque CG is located approx. 12 mi. NE of Santa Fe on the Hyde Park Road (state HWY 475). Not suitable for trailers.

SINGLE RATE:	No fee	OPEN DATES:	May-Oct
		MAX STAY:	14 days
		ELEVATION:	9700 feet

3 Black Canyon
Santa Fe • lat 35˚43'36" lon 105˚50'07"

DESCRIPTION: CG is situated in a mixed conifer, pine, and fir forest. There is a good mix of sun and shade. The rainy season lasts July through August. Temperatures often cool considerably in the evenings. Supplies are available at Santa Fe. Pecos Wilderness Trailhead is 8 mi. away. Dump station at nearby state park.

GETTING THERE: Black Canyon CG is located approx. 7.5 mi. NE of Santa Fe on Hyde Park Road (state HWY 475).

SINGLE RATE:	$9	OPEN DATES:	May-Oct
# of SINGLE SITES:	43	MAX SPUR:	40 feet
		MAX STAY:	14 days
		ELEVATION:	8400 feet

4 Clear Creek
Cuba • lat 35˚59'48" lon 106˚49'33"

DESCRIPTION: Under forest canopy of pine and fir with open meadows to the South. Hot days with frequent noon T-storms. Fly fish Clearcreek. old homesteads and RR beds in area. Supplies 8 mi.. Elk, deer, turkeys, raccoons, and occasional bears. Gather firewood locally. Hike various trails including San Pedro Wilderness.

GETTING THERE: From Cuba go E on state HWY 126 approx. 12 mi. to Clear Creek CG.

SINGLE RATE:	$5	OPEN DATES:	May-Oct
# of SINGLE SITES:	12	MAX SPUR:	16 feet
GROUP RATE:	$30	MAX STAY:	14 days
# of GROUP SITES:	1	ELEVATION:	8500 feet

5 Cow Creek
Pecos • lat 35˚39'39" lon 105˚38'12"

DESCRIPTION: In a mixed forest of fir, spruce, and pine. CG sits on Cow Creek which offers great rainbow and brown trout fishing. Supplies at Pecos. Deer, bears, mountain lions, elk, and bobcats frequent the area. Gather firewood locally. The Skyline Trail passes by the CG along with a trail to the Osha Area.

GETTING THERE: From Pecos go E on county route B44A 2 mi. to forest route 86. Go N 6 mi. to forest route 92. Go N 3 mi. to Cow Creek CG. Not suitable for trailers. Possible road access problems. Contact ranger.

GROUP RATE:	$50	OPEN DATES:	May-Oct
		MAX SPUR:	99 feet
# of GROUP SITES:	1	MAX STAY:	14 days
		ELEVATION:	8200 feet

 Campground has hosts   Reservable sites   Accessible facilities   Fully developed   Semi-developed   Rustic facilities

NOTE: Open dates listed are typical. Actual dates are dependent on conditions such as snow pack.

6 — Cowles
Pecos • lat 35˚48'43" lon 105˚39'43"

DESCRIPTION: In a mixed forest of fir, oak and pine near Winsor Creek. Fish for rainbow and brown trout from the creek. The Pecos River and stocked ponds are great for trout too. Supplies at Pecos. Deer, bears, mountain lions, elk and birds are common to the area. Campers may gather firewood. Trails to Pecos Wilderness from CG.

GETTING THERE: From Pecos go N on HWY 63 approx. 20 mi. to Cowles CG.

SINGLE RATE:	$6	OPEN DATES:	May-Nov
# of SINGLE SITES:	9	MAX SPUR:	28 feet
		MAX STAY:	14 days
		ELEVATION:	8165 feet

11 — Holy Ghost
Pecos • lat 35˚46'21" lon 105˚42'01"

DESCRIPTION: CG in a mixed forest of fir, oak, and pine near Holy Ghost Creek. Fish for rainbow and brown trout from the creek. Supplies are available at Pecos. Deer, bears, mountain lions, elk, turkeys, bobcats, and birds are common to the area. Gater firewood locally. Trails to Holy Ghost and Spirit Lake.

GETTING THERE: From Pecos go N on state HWY 63 approx. 13 mi. to forest route 122. Go N on 122 approx. 3 mi. to Holy Ghost CG.

SINGLE RATE:	$8	OPEN DATES:	May-Oct
# of SINGLE SITES:	25	MAX SPUR:	32 feet
		MAX STAY:	14 days
		ELEVATION:	8100 feet

7 — E.V. Long
Las Vegas • lat 35˚43'00" lon 105˚23'00"

DESCRIPTION: CG in a mixed forest of fir, oak, and pine near Gillinas Creek. Fish for rainbow and brown trout from the creek. Supplies at Las Vegas. Deer, bears, mountain lions, elk, turkeys, bobcats and birds are common to the area. Gather firewood locally. Trails to Johnson Mesa are within 2 mi. of CG.

GETTING THERE: E.V. Long CG is located approx. 16.5 mi. NW of Las Vegas on state HWY 65.

SINGLE RATE:	$8	OPEN DATES:	May-Oct
# of SINGLE SITES:	21	MAX SPUR:	16 feet
		MAX STAY:	14 days
		ELEVATION:	7500 feet

12 — Holy Ghost Group
Pecos • lat 35˚46'21" lon 105˚42'01"

DESCRIPTION: This CG is set in a mixed forest of fir, oak, and pine near Holy Ghost Creek. Fish for rainbow and brown trout from the creek. Supplies at Pecos. Deer, bears, mountain lions, elk, turkeys, bobcats, and birds are common to the area. Gather firewood locally. Trails to Holy Ghost and Spirit Lake.

GETTING THERE: From Pecos go N on state HWY 63 approx. 13 mi. to forest route 122. Go N on 122 approx. 3 mi. to Holy Ghost Group CG.

		OPEN DATES:	May-Nov
GROUP RATE:	$45	MAX STAY:	14 days
# of GROUP SITES:	1	ELEVATION:	8100 feet

8 — El Porvenir
Las Vegas • lat 35˚42'37" lon 105˚24'42"

DESCRIPTION: CG in a mixed forest of fir, oak, and pine near El Porvenir Creek. Fish for rainbow and brown trout from the creek. Supplies at Las Vegas. Deer, bears, mountain lions, elk, turkeys, bobcats, and birds are common to the area. Gather firewood locally. Trails to Hermits Peak and Hollanger close to CG.

GETTING THERE: From Las Vegas go NW on state HWY 65 approx. 16 mi. to El Porvenir CG.

SINGLE RATE:	$8	OPEN DATES:	May-Oct
# of SINGLE SITES:	14	MAX SPUR:	32 feet
		MAX STAY:	14 days
		ELEVATION:	7600 feet

13 — Iron Gate
Pecos • lat 35˚50'43" lon 105˚37'27"

DESCRIPTION: Primative CG in a mixed forest of fir, oak, and pine. Supplies are available at Pecos. Deer, bears, mountain lions, elk, turkeys, bobcats, and birds are common to the area. Gather firewood locally. Trails going into Pecos Wilderness from CG. 4 corrals are located on site.

GETTING THERE: From Pecos go N on state HWY 63 approx. 17 mi. to forest route 223. Go N on 223 approx. 4 mi. to Iron Gate CG.

SINGLE RATE:	$4	OPEN DATES:	May-Oct
# of SINGLE SITES:	6	MAX SPUR:	16 feet
		MAX STAY:	14 days
		ELEVATION:	9400 feet

9 — Field Tract
Pecos • lat 35˚41'12" lon 105˚41'33"

DESCRIPTION: CG in a mixed forest of fir, oak, and pine near Pecos River. Fish for rainbow and brown trout in the river. Supplies at Pecos. Deer, bears, mountain lions, elk, turkeys, bobcats, and birds are common to the area. Gather firewood locally. No designated trails in area. Private lands surround this CG.

GETTING THERE: Field Tract CG is located approx. 9 mi. N of Pecos on state HWY 63.

SINGLE RATE:	$8	OPEN DATES:	May-Oct
# of SINGLE SITES:	14	MAX SPUR:	22 feet
		MAX STAY:	14 days
		ELEVATION:	7400 feet

14 — Jacks Creek
Pecos • lat 35˚50'52" lon 105˚28'58"

DESCRIPTION: CG in a mixed forest with Pecos River nearby. Fish for trout in the river or nearby stocked ponds. Supplies at Pecos. Deer, bears, elk, turkeys, and birds are common to the area. Gather firewood. Upper camping for tents and trailers and lower camping for equestrian use with 5 corrals. Trails from lower area.

GETTING THERE: From Pecos go N on state HWY 63 approx. 20 mi. to Jacks Creek CG.

SINGLE RATE:	$10	OPEN DATES:	May-Oct
# of SINGLE SITES:	46	MAX SPUR:	40 feet
GROUP RATE:	$50	MAX STAY:	14 days
# of GROUP SITES:	2	ELEVATION:	8900 feet

10 — Glorieta
Pecos • lat 37˚32'00" lon 105˚48'00"

DESCRIPTION: This CG offers dispersed camping in a mixed forest of fir, oak, and pine. Supplies are available at Pecos. Deer, bears, mountain lions, elk, turkeys, bobcats, and birds are common to the area. CG is close to an old lookout. Gather firewood locally. Trail to Apache Canyon is close to CG.

GETTING THERE: From Pecos go W on state HWY 50 approx. 3.5 mi. to county route 63A. Go N on 63A and then forest route 375 approx. 12 mi. to Glorieta CG. Not suitable for trailers. Primitive road.

SINGLE RATE:	No fee	OPEN DATES:	May-Oct
		MAX STAY:	14 days
		ELEVATION:	10200 feet

15 — Jemez Falls
Jemez Springs • lat 35˚48'47" lon 106˚36'17"

DESCRIPTION: In a dense, tall pine forest with views of Redondo Peak. East Fork River surrounds the CG. Fish for trout from the river. Supplies at Jemez Springs. Deer, elk, and turkeys may be seen from the CG. Hike approx. 100 ft. to Jemez Falls. Trails to McCully Warm Springs close to CG. Gather firewood locally.

GETTING THERE: From Jemez Springs go N on forest route 135 approx. 11 mi. to forest route 133. Go W on 133 approx. 2 mi. to Jemez Falls CG.

SINGLE RATE:	$9	OPEN DATES:	May-Oct
# of SINGLE SITES:	47	MAX SPUR:	22 feet
		MAX STAY:	14 days
		ELEVATION:	7900 feet

 Campground has hosts   **Reservable sites**   **Accessible facilities**   **Fully developed**   **Semi-developed**   **Rustic facilities**

NOTE: Open dates listed are typical. Actual dates are dependent on conditions such as snow pack.

16 Las Conchas
Los Alamos • lat 35°48'53" lon 106°31'27"

DESCRIPTION: This CG is situated among mountain blue spruce on the East Fork River. Fish for native brown trout from the river. Supplies are available at Los Alamos. Deer, elk, bears, and turkeys can be seen on occasion. Gather firewood locally. Walk along side the river to explore.

GETTING THERE: From Los Alamos go SW on state HWY 4 approx. 19 mi. to Las Conchas CG. Not suitable for trailers.

SINGLE RATE:	No fee	OPEN DATES:	May-Oct
# of SINGLE SITES:	11		
		MAX STAY:	14 days
		ELEVATION:	8400 feet

17 Paliza
Ponderosa • lat 35°41'50" lon 106°38'01"

DESCRIPTION: This CG is set in a stand of huge ponderosa pine on Paliza Creek. Fish for native small brown trout from the creek. Supplies are available at Ponderosa. Deer, bears, turkeys, and coyotes in the area. Gather firewood locally. Trails can be found nearby. No OHVs allowed.

GETTING THERE: From Ponderosa go NE on forest route 10 approx. 5 mi. to Paliza CG.

SINGLE RATE:	$8	OPEN DATES:	May-Oct
# of SINGLE SITES:	21	MAX SPUR:	35 feet
		MAX STAY:	14 days
		ELEVATION:	7500 feet

18 Paliza Group
Ponderosa • lat 35°41'50" lon 106°38'01"

DESCRIPTION: This CG is situated in a juniper and pine forest with Paliza Creek running nearby. Fishing and playing in creek. Supplies are available at Ponderosa. Deer, elk, and bears can be seen on occasion. Gather firewood locally. Trails in the area. There are no OHVs allowed.

GETTING THERE: From Ponderosa go NE on forest route 10 approx. 5 mi. to Paliza Group CG.

		OPEN DATES:	May-Oct
		MAX SPUR:	35 feet
GROUP RATE:	Varies	MAX STAY:	14 days
# of GROUP SITES:	2	ELEVATION:	7500 feet

19 Redondo
Jemez Springs • lat 35°51'48" lon 106°37'32"

DESCRIPTION: CG set in a ponderosa pine forest near Fenton Lake. Fish for trout from the lake. Supplies at Jemez Springs. Firewood may be available for sale at CG. Trails nearby for nature walks and wildlife viewing. An overlook of the Jamez Valley is .25 mi. from CG. OHVs and ATVs are not allowed.

GETTING THERE: From Jemez Springs go N and E on state HWY 4 approx. 11 mi. to Redondo CG.

SINGLE RATE:	$8	OPEN DATES:	May-Oct
# of SINGLE SITES:	60	MAX SPUR:	22 feet
		MAX STAY:	14 days
		ELEVATION:	8100 feet

20 Rio Chama
Ghost Ranch • lat 36°20'00" lon 106°38'00"

DESCRIPTION: This CG is located in a Sonoran Desert environment with river cottonwoods and mesquite along the Rio Chama. OK fishing in the river. Good bird watching opportunities. Fills quickly on summer weekends. Popular rafting and kayaking area. Ojitos Trail runs through CG along the river.

GETTING THERE: From Ghost Ranch go N on state HWY 84 approx. 1 mi. to forest route 151. Go SW on 151 approx. 11 mi. to Rio Chama CG. Primitive road.

SINGLE RATE:	No fee	OPEN DATES:	May-Sept
# of SINGLE SITES:	18	MAX SPUR:	16 feet
		MAX STAY:	14 days
		ELEVATION:	6400 feet

21 Rio Las Vacas
Cuba • lat 35°59'49" lon 106°48'22"

DESCRIPTION: CG in a grassy park like area with pine and fir. Hot summers with frequent noon t-showers. Fly fish Rio de Las Vacas. Supplies 10 mi. away in Cuba. Elk, deer, raccoons, turkeys, and occasional bears in area. Fills holidays. Summer - early fall is most pleasant. Gather firewood. Hike Vacas Trail 6 mi. from CG.

GETTING THERE: From Cuba go E on state HWY 126 approx. 13 mi. to Rio Las Vacas CG.

SINGLE RATE:	$5	OPEN DATES:	May-Oct
# of SINGLE SITES:	15	MAX SPUR:	16 feet
		MAX STAY:	14 days
		ELEVATION:	8200 feet

22 Rio Puerco
Coyote • lat 36°06'02" lon 106°43'23"

DESCRIPTION: This CG is situated among mixed conifer on the Rio Puerco. Fishing in creek. Please check for local fishing regulations. Wildlife in the area includes beavers, hawks, and elk. Busy on weekends in the summer. Near trailhead for the San Pedro Peaks Wilderness Area.

GETTING THERE: From Coyote go W on state HWY 96 approx. 4.5 mi. to forest route 172. Go S on 172 approx. 4 mi. to forest route 103. Go S on 103 approx. 6 mi. to Rio Puerco CG. Not suitable for trailers.

SINGLE RATE:	No fee	OPEN DATES:	May-Oct
		MAX STAY:	14 days
		ELEVATION:	8200 feet

23 San Antonio
Jemez Springs • lat 35°53'13" lon 106°38'44"

DESCRIPTION: This CG is situated among tall pine trees on the banks of the Rio San Antonio River. Trout fishing is a popular activity from the river. Please check for local fishing regulations. CG is within one hour drive of the Los Alamos Science Museum. Few hiking trails in the area.

GETTING THERE: From Jemez Springs go N on state HWY 4 approx. 9 mi. to state HWY 126. Go W on 126 approx. 2 mi. to San Antonio CG.

SINGLE RATE:	$8	OPEN DATES:	May-Oct
# of SINGLE SITES:	11	MAX SPUR:	25 feet
		MAX STAY:	14 days
		ELEVATION:	7800 feet

1 Mills Canyon
Roy • lat 36°03'00" lon 104°22'35"

DESCRIPTION: CG is located in grass in a deep canyon with high walls and views of the Canadian River. Fish for channel catfish in river. Access road is primitive and RV's are discouraged from attempting the trip. Supplies available in Roy. Wild turkey, mountain lion, deer, bear, ducks and other small wildlife in area.

GETTING THERE: From Roy go N on state HWY 39 for 10 mi. to Mills. Go W on forest route 600 approx. 9 mi. to Mills Canyon CG. Primitive Road!

SINGLE RATE:	No fee	OPEN DATES:	Yearlong
# of SINGLE SITES:	5	MAX SPUR:	10 feet
		MAX STAY:	14 days
		ELEVATION:	5700 feet

 Campground has hosts   🔒 **Reservable sites**   ♿ **Accessible facilities**   **Fully developed**    **Semi-developed**   🏕 **Rustic facilities**

NOTE: Open dates listed are typical. Actual dates are dependent on conditions such as snow pack.

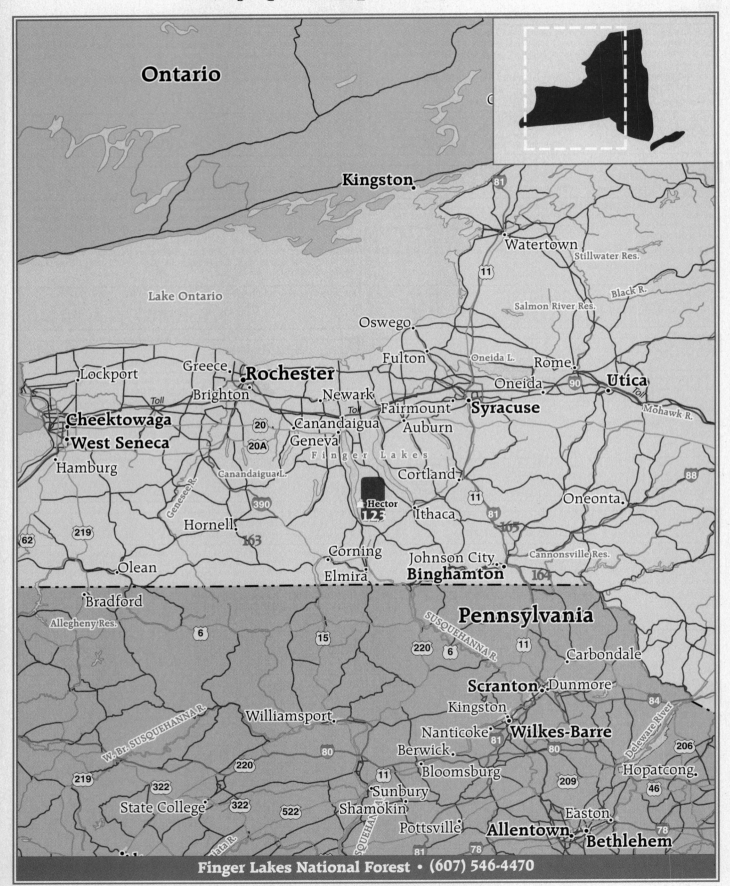

Ontario

Kingston

Lake Ontario

Watertown

Stillwater Res.

Salmon River Res.

Black R.

Oswego

Fulton

Oneida L.

Rome

Utica

Mohawk R.

Lockport

Greece

Rochester

Brighton

Newark

Fairmount

Oneida

Syracuse

Cheektowaga

Canandaigua

Auburn

West Seneca

Geneva

Finger Lakes

Hamburg

Canandaigua L.

Cortland

Oneonta

Hector

Ithaca

Hornell

Johnson City

Corning

Binghamton

Olean

Elmira

Cannonsville Res.

Bradford

Pennsylvania

Allegheny Res.

Susquehanna R.

Carbondale

Scranton

Dunmore

Kingston

Williamsport

Wilkes-Barre

W. Br. Susquehanna R.

Nanticoke

Berwick

Delaware River

Bloomsburg

Hopatcong

Sunbury

State College

Shamokin

Easton

Pottsville

Allentown

Bethlehem

Finger Lakes National Forest • (607) 546-4470

USFS Photo

FINGER LAKES NATIONAL FOREST

The 16,032-acre Finger Lakes National Forest lies on a ridge between Seneca and Cayuga lakes, in the beautiful Finger Lakes region of New York state. Rochester, Syracuse and Binghamton are all within a two-hour drive from the forest.

The forest has over 30 miles of interconnecting trails that traverse gorges, ravines, pastures, and woodlands. The 12-mile Interloken National Recreation Trail, beckons hikers, cross-country skiers, horseback riders and snowmobilers with beautiful vistas and breathtaking scenery. Whether you want to get away for the weekend or stay for two weeks, the forest offers three campgrounds and numerous undeveloped sites to pitch a tent or park a camper. Come explore and enjoy its history, natural beauty and many resources. The Finger Lakes National Forest provides plenty of "room to roam," with few restrictions on recreation use. Miles of roads which wind along ridgetops and open pastures allow the visitor to see the forest by car. Blueberry picking is a popular activity and five acres next to the Blueberry Patch Campground are managed for blueberry production. Apples, raspberries, and other fruits are also abundant throughout the forest. Woods, pastures, scrublands and many ponds provide excellent opportunities for hunting and fishing. A wide variety of birds, wildflowers and other creatures await discovery by the observant forest visitor, so bring your camera.

1 — Backbone
Logan • lat 42˚29'04" lon 076˚48'22"

DESCRIPTION: An equestrian CG in maple and pine forest with the corral adjacent to the camping sites and 7 main sites for horse trailers. Nearby watering pond. Services from May-Oct. Area is closed for resource protection off season. Supplies in Logan. Deer, small wildlife and occasional black bears. Horse riding trails nearby.

GETTING THERE: From Logan go E on Picnic Area Road approx. 1 mi. to Backbone CG.

SINGLE RATE:	No fee	OPEN DATES:	May-Oct
# of SINGLE SITES:	7	MAX SPUR:	35 feet
		MAX STAY:	14 days
		ELEVATION:	1690 feet

2 — Blueberry Patch
Logan • lat 42˚29'02" lon 076˚47'54"

DESCRIPTION: Popular CG along Picnic Area Road adjacent to a large blueberry patch. Services provided May-Oct, hike-in and no services off season. Supplies in Logan. Fish pond 1/2 mi. away, stocked with trout, bass, pumpkin seed and bluegill. Deer, small wildlife and occasional black bears in area.

GETTING THERE: From Logan go E on Picnic Area Road approx. 1.5 mi. to Blueberry Patch CG. Recommended for small trailers and tents.

SINGLE RATE:	$5	OPEN DATES:	May-Oct
# of SINGLE SITES:	9	MAX SPUR:	20 feet
		MAX STAY:	14 days
		ELEVATION:	1806 feet

3 — Potomac Group
Reynoldsville • lat 42˚29'24" lon 076˚47'17"

DESCRIPTION: Full services May-Oct. CG is intended for groups of 10-40 persons, by reservation only. Among maple and pine forest with a pond nearby. Supplies in Reynoldsville. Deer, small wildlife and occasional black bears in area. No nearby trails. Ballard Pond, 2 mi. N, is barrier free. Access to mountain bike routes.

GETTING THERE: From Reynoldsville go N on forest route 9C approx. 2 mi. to Potomac Group CG. Hike in only, approx. 200 yds from parking area.

		OPEN DATES:	May-Oct
GROUP RATE:	Varies	MAX STAY:	14 days
# of GROUP SITES:	1	ELEVATION:	1821 feet

 Campground has hosts   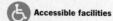 Reservable sites   Accessible facilities   Fully developed   Semi-developed   Rustic facilities

NOTE: Open dates listed are typical. Actual dates are dependent on conditions such as snow pack.

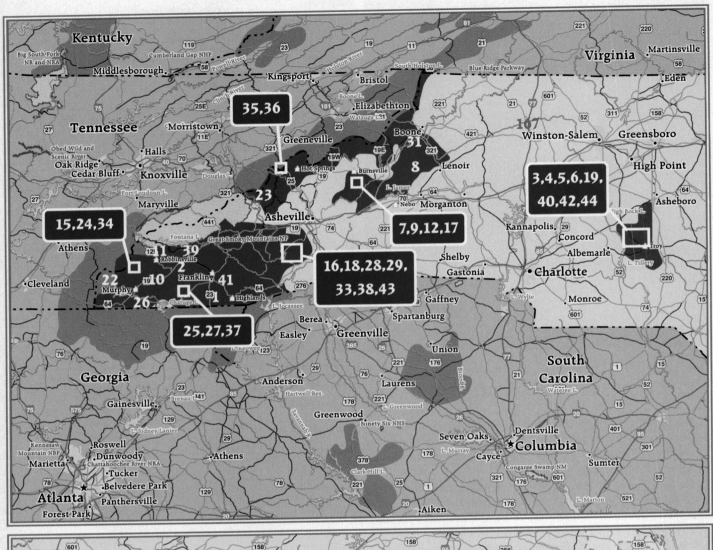

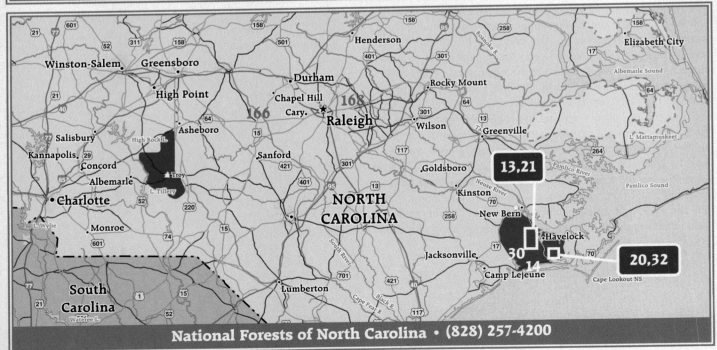

National Forests of North Carolina • (828) 257-4200

USFS Photo

NATIONAL FORESTS OF NORTH CAROLINA

The forests of North Carolina include the Croatan, the Nantahala, the Pisgah, and the Uwharrie National Forest.

Forty miles of streams and 4,300 acres of lakes exist on the Croatan. Anglers can enjoy both saltwater and freshwater fishing. Hike the Cedar Tideland Trail to see the marshland estuary or walk the Island Creek Forest to observe a stand of virgin hardwood trees.

The Nantahala offers mountain climbing, hiking, and world-class whitewater rafting. Visitors can enjoy a hike on the Appalachian Trail, a system that runs from Maine to Georgia.

A popular activity on the Pisgah is whitewater rafting on the Nolichucky and French Broad rivers. Hikers and horseback riders have miles of trails to explore including those in the Linville Gorge Wilderness.

The Uwharrie offers experienced trekkers an escape to the Birkhead Mountains Wilderness. Camp, hike, horseback ride, fish or boat at Badin Lake Recreation Area or hike the 20-mile Uwharrie National Recreation Trail.

1 Ammons Branch
Highlands • lat 35°00'00" lon 831°40'0"

DESCRIPTION: This tent only CG is situated in semi-open pine and hardwood forest. Frequent afternoon t-showers. Trout fishing at nearby wild and scenic Chattooga River. Visit historic Ellicott Rock. Supplies 5 mi. at Highlands. Wildlife includes black bears, small game and songbirds. Busy holidays. Gather firewood locally.

GETTING THERE: From Highlands go S on Horse Cove Road approx. 4.5 mi. to Bull Pen Road. Go West on Bull Pen Road approx. 1/2 mi. to Ammons Branch CG. Road is narrow with sharp curves. Large vehicles should use caution.

SINGLE RATE:	No fee	OPEN DATES:	Yearlong
# of SINGLE SITES:	4		
		MAX STAY:	14 days
		ELEVATION:	3100 feet

2 Appletree
Andrews • lat 35°14'00" lon 083°38'00"

DESCRIPTION: In a mixed forest setting near a creek. Fish and swim in the creek or go to nearby Nantahala Lake. Supplies available in Andrews. Numerous wildlife can be seen in the area. Campers may gather firewood. Many trails in the area. Reservations required.

GETTING THERE: From Andrews go SE on state HWY 1505 approx. 15 mi. to Appletree CG.

		OPEN DATES:	Apr-Oct
		MAX SPUR:	99 feet
GROUP RATE:	Varies	MAX STAY:	14 days
# of GROUP SITES:	4	ELEVATION:	3400 feet

3 Arrowhead
Troy • lat 35°26'30" lon 080°05'00"

DESCRIPTION: CG is located in a mature, open grove of oak, hickory, and pine. Very hot in summer. Fish for bass, catfish and panfish in nearby Badin Lake. Wildlife includes deer, turkeys, raccoons, and songbirds. Busy holidays and weekends. Gather firewood locally. Many multi-use trails nearby.

GETTING THERE: From Troy go NW on state HWY 109 8.5 mi. to forest route 576. Go W on 576 3 mi. to forest route 597. Go N on 597 1 mi. to Arrowhead CG. Large vehicles should use caution.

SINGLE RATE:	Varies	OPEN DATES:	Yearlong
# of SINGLE SITES:	50	MAX SPUR:	65 feet
		MAX STAY:	14 days
		ELEVATION:	600 feet

4 Badin Group Camp
Troy • lat 35°27'01" lon 080°04'18"

DESCRIPTION: In nice wooded oak and pine forest looking over an open green area. Hot summers, colder winter days. Boat fish for bass and catfish on nearby Badin Lake. Deer, turkeys, raccoons and songbirds in area. Fills holidays. Gather firewood. Horse, hike, ATV and Mountain bike trails nearby. Ticks and chiggers in spring.

GETTING THERE: From Troy go NW on state HWY 109 approx. 8.5 mi. to forest route 576. Go W on 576 approx. 3 mi. to forest route 597. Go N on 597 approx. 2 mi. to Badin Group CG.

		OPEN DATES:	Yearlong
GROUP RATE:	$40	MAX STAY:	14 days
# of GROUP SITES:	3	ELEVATION:	545 feet

5 Badin Horse Camp
Troy • lat 35°26'54" lon 080°04'44"

DESCRIPTION: In open grassy field surrounded by oak and pine woods. Hot summer, colder winters. Boat fish for bass and catfish on nearby Badin Lake. Supplies 2 mi. Deer, turkeys, raccoons and songbirds in area. Fills holidays and spring/fall weekends. Gather firewood. Horse trail system adjacent to CG. Ticks and chiggers spring-fall.

GETTING THERE: From Troy go NW on state HWY 109 approx. 8.5 mi. to forest route 576. Go W on 576 approx. 1/2 mi. to turnoff route for Badin and Canebrake Horse Camps. Go N on turnoff route approx. 1 mi. to CG.

		OPEN DATES:	Yearlong
GROUP RATE:	$5	MAX STAY:	14 days
# of GROUP SITES:	1	ELEVATION:	535 feet

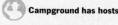 **Campground has hosts**   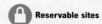 **Reservable sites**    **Accessible facilities**   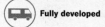 **Fully developed**   **Semi-developed**   **Rustic facilities**

NOTE: Open dates listed are typical. Actual dates are dependent on conditions such as snow pack.

6 Badin Lake
Troy • lat 35°26'54" lon 080°04'44"

DESCRIPTION: Overlooking lake and woods in an oak and pine forest. Hot summer, colder winter, great spring and fall. Boat fish for bass, catfish on Badin Lake. Supplies 5 mi. Deer, turkeys, raccoons in area. Full holidays. Gather firewood. Horse, hike, ATV and Mountain bike trails nearby. Ticks and chiggers spring-fall.

GETTING THERE: From Troy go NW on state HWY 109 approx. 8.5 mi. to forest route 576. Go W on 576 approx. 3 mi. to forest route 597. Go N on 597 approx. 2 mi. to Badin Lake CG.

SINGLE RATE:	$8	OPEN DATES:	Yearlong
# of SINGLE SITES:	41	MAX SPUR:	60 feet
		MAX STAY:	14 days
		ELEVATION:	535 feet

7 Black Mountain
Burnsville • lat 35°45'10" lon 082°13'17"

DESCRIPTION: This CG rests in hemlock, oak, and poplar along the South Toe River. Spring and fall are cool. Fly fish the river, catch and release only. Supplies approx. 5 mi. from CG. Wildlife includes black bears, deer, foxes, and owls. Firewood sold on site. Hike Mt. Mitchell. CG fills on weekends.

GETTING THERE: From Burnsville go E on US HWY 19 approx. 5 mi. to state HWY 80. Go W on 80 approx. 12 mi. to forest route 472. Go W on 472 approx. 3 mi. to Black Mountain CG.

SINGLE RATE:	$13	OPEN DATES:	Apr-Oct
# of SINGLE SITES:	46	MAX SPUR:	28 feet
		MAX STAY:	14 days
		ELEVATION:	3020 feet

8 Boone Fork
Lenoir • lat 36°00'02" lon 081°36'52"

DESCRIPTION: In a pine, oak forest with views of Raccoons Creek. Trout fishing at pond located along the entrance road to CG. Supplies at Lenoir. Firewood may be gathered. A trail system is available out of the CG.

GETTING THERE: From Lenoir go W on state HWY 90 approx. 7 mi. to state route 1368. Go E on 1368 for 3 mi. to forest route 2055. Go E on 2055 approx. 2 mi. to Boone Fork CG.

SINGLE RATE:	$3	OPEN DATES:	Apr-Dec
# of SINGLE SITES:	15		
GROUP RATE:	$20	MAX STAY:	14 days
# of GROUP SITES:	1	ELEVATION:	1350 feet

9 Briar Bottom Group
Asheville • lat 35°44'58" lon 082°13'33"

DESCRIPTION: In an open park-like setting of mixed hardwoods on the South Toe River. Fly fish, catch and release only in the river. Supplies are approx. 3 mi. from the CG. Deer and small wildlife are common to the area. Many hiking trails nearby.

GETTING THERE: From Asheville go N on US HWY 19 approx. 18 mi. to Black Briar CG.

SINGLE RATE:	$13	OPEN DATES:	Apr-Oct
# of SINGLE SITES:	45	MAX SPUR:	34 feet
GROUP RATE:	$50	MAX STAY:	14 days
# of GROUP SITES:	6	ELEVATION:	3030 feet

10 Bristol Horse Camp
Hayesville • lat 35°06'16" lon 083°49'08"

DESCRIPTION: Located in small open field surrounded by trees on Fires Creek. Fires Creek is a high quality trout fishing stream. Supplies approx. 10 mi. Deer, bears and small wildlife in area. Light use, rarely full. Gather firewood locally. Numerous hiking and horse trails in general area.

GETTING THERE: From Hayesville go NE approx. 3 mi. on state HWY 1307 to state HWY 1300. Go W approx. 6 mi. on 1300 to Bristol Horse Camp CG.

SINGLE RATE:	$6	OPEN DATES:	Yearlong
# of SINGLE SITES:	9	MAX SPUR:	99 feet
		MAX STAY:	14 days
		ELEVATION:	2500 feet

11 Cable Cove
Robinsville • lat 35°25'58" lon 083°45'08"

DESCRIPTION: An open parklike setting on small stream. Warm days, cool nights. Boat ramp 1/4 mi. on Fontana Lake. Fish stream or lake for trout, bass, walleye. Black bears and wild Russian boars in area. Yellow Cr. Mountain trail and Appalachian Trail access near Fontana Dam. Tsali Mountain bike trails 15 mi. E.

GETTING THERE: From Robinsville go NE on state HWY 143 approx. 7 mi. to state HWY 28. Go W on 28 approx. 6.5 mi. to forest route 520. Go N on 520 approx. 1 mi. to Cable Cove CG.

SINGLE RATE:	$8	OPEN DATES:	Apr-Oct
# of SINGLE SITES:	26	MAX SPUR:	20 feet
		MAX STAY:	14 days
		ELEVATION:	1840 feet

12 Carolina Hemlocks
Burnsville • lat 35°48'16" lon 082°12'16"

DESCRIPTION: In a mixed hardwood setting with views of the forest and the South Toe River. Fish for trout on the river. Supplies located approx. 1/2 mi. from CG. Deer and small wildlife are common to the area. Full on weekends during July-Aug. Hiking trails nearby.

GETTING THERE: From Burnsville go E on US HWY 19 approx. 5 mi. to state HWY 80. Go S on 80 approx. 9 mi. to Carolina Hemlocks CG.

SINGLE RATE:	$12	OPEN DATES:	Apr-Nov
# of SINGLE SITES:	32	MAX SPUR:	34 feet
		MAX STAY:	14 days
		ELEVATION:	3200 feet

13 Catfish Lake
Maysville • lat 34°55'58" lon 077°06'17"

DESCRIPTION: This dispersed CG is located on Catfish Lake. CG offers a boat ramp, fishing and canoeing opportunities. There are no facilities at this CG. Wildlife in the area includes deer, black bears, turkeys, osprey and alligators. View unusual plants such as the carnivorous Venus Fly Trap.

GETTING THERE: From Maysville go SE on state HWY 58 approx. 2 mi. to Catfish Lake Road. Go E on Catfish Lake Road approx. 7 mi. to forest route 158. Go NW on 158 approx. 2 mi. to Catfish Lake CG.

SINGLE RATE:	No fee	OPEN DATES:	Yearlong
		MAX STAY:	14 days
		ELEVATION:	25 feet

14 Cedar Point
Bogue • lat 34°41'36" lon 077°04'57"

DESCRIPTION: CG is on the fringe of the intercoastal water way. In mixed pine, oak and cedar with thick underbrush with views of Swansboro Inlet and Bogue Sound. Fish and boat in the Whiteoak River. Supplies are approx. 1/2 mi. away. Firewood may be gathered. The Tidelands Trail is nearby.

GETTING THERE: Cedar Point CG is approx. 1 mi. W of Bogue on state HWY 24.

SINGLE RATE:	$15	OPEN DATES:	Yearlong
# of SINGLE SITES:	40	MAX SPUR:	80 feet
		MAX STAY:	14 days
		ELEVATION:	11 feet

15 Cheoah Point
Robbinsville • lat 35°22'30" lon 083°52'30"

DESCRIPTION: Set among hardwood and white pine forest on peninsula of Lake Santetlah. Warm days. Bass and trout fish on lake. Historic Junaluska Grave nearby. Supplies in Robbinsville. Moderate use, fills holidays. Hike Wauchecha Bald trail or 10 mi. drive to Joyce Kilmer Memorial Forest.

GETTING THERE: From Robbinsville go NW on US HWY 129 approx. 8 mi. to Cheoah Point CG. Follow signs.

SINGLE RATE:	$8	OPEN DATES:	Mar-Nov
# of SINGLE SITES:	26	MAX SPUR:	20 feet
		MAX STAY:	14 days
		ELEVATION:	2000 feet

 Campground has hosts   **Reservable sites**   **Accessible facilities**   **Fully developed**   **Semi-developed**   **Rustic facilities**

NOTE: Open dates listed are typical. Actual dates are dependent on conditions such as snow pack.

16 Cove Creek

Brevard • lat 35°17'17" lon 082°48'59"

DESCRIPTION: In a mixed hardwood forest setting on Cove Creek. Fish for rainbow, brook and brown trout and swim on the creek. Supplies available at Brevard. Deer, bobcats, foxes, owls and raccoons are common in the area. Campers may gather firewood. The Caney Bottom Loop Trail is nearby.

GETTING THERE: From Brevard go N on state HWY 64 approx. 1 mi. to US HWY 276. Go NW on 276 approx. 1.5 mi. to forest route 475. Go W on 475 approx. 1.5 mi. to Cove Creek CG.

		OPEN DATES:	Yearlong
GROUP RATE:	$70	MAX STAY:	14 days
# of GROUP SITES:	2	ELEVATION:	2881 feet

17 Curtis Creek

Old Fort • lat 35°41'39" lon 082°11'38"

DESCRIPTION: In a pine/hardwood cove along Curtis Creek. Fish for trout out of creek. Supplies at Old Fort. Campers may gather firewood. Hiking trails nearby. Dispersed tent camping only.

GETTING THERE: From Old Fort go E on US HWY 70 for 1.7 mi. to forest route 482. Go NW on 482 approx. 3 mi. to Curtis Creek CG.

SINGLE RATE:	No fee	OPEN DATES:	Apr-Dec
		MAX STAY:	14 days
		ELEVATION:	2045 feet

18 Davidson River

Brevard • lat 35°17'13" lon 082°44'04"

DESCRIPTION: In a rich hardwood forest setting with great views of wildflowers. Davidson River borders CG and has great trout fishing. Historical Cradle of Forestry in America is 10 mi. from CG. Supplies are approx. 2 mi. Numerous wildlife in the area. Amphitheater is located at CG. No designated trails in the area.

GETTING THERE: From Brevard go NE on US HWY 64 approx. 3.5 mi. to US HWY 276. Go W on 276 approx. 1.5 mi. to Davison River CG.

SINGLE RATE:	Varies	OPEN DATES:	Yearlong
# of SINGLE SITES:	161	MAX SPUR:	30 feet
		MAX STAY:	14 days
		ELEVATION:	2180 feet

19 East Morris Mountain

Troy • lat 35°26'23" lon 079°57'32"

DESCRIPTION: Set in oak and pine forest. Hot summer days, mild to cold winters. No nearby fishing. Deer, turkeys, raccoons and songbirds in area. Moderate use, fall is a good time to visit. Gather firewood. No immediate trails. Ticks and chiggers a problem spring-fall. Numerous dispersed primitive sites. No water.

GETTING THERE: From Troy go NW on State HWY 109 approx. 2.5 mi. to state route 1134. Go N on 1134 approx. 4 mi. to East Morris Mountain Hunt Camp.

SINGLE RATE:	No fee	OPEN DATES:	Oct-Jan
# of SINGLE SITES:	1		
GROUP RATE:	No fee	MAX STAY:	14 days
		ELEVATION:	830 feet

20 Fishers Landing

New Bern • lat 35°00'02" lon 076°58'31"

DESCRIPTION: This tent only CG offers views of the Neuse River. Fish for flounder, ocean and fresh water fish, and marlin from the river. Several Civil War battle sites and forts are within 1/2 hour of CG. Supplies are 4 mi. away. Look for the rare Red Cocaded Woodpecker. Campers may gather dead and down firewood.

GETTING THERE: From New Bern go SE on US HWY 70 approx. 6 mi. to forest route 141 (at Riverdale). Go E on 141 approx. 1/2 mi. to Fishers Landing CG.

SINGLE RATE:	No fee	OPEN DATES:	Yearlong
# of SINGLE SITES:	9		
		MAX STAY:	14 days
		ELEVATION:	25 feet

21 Great Lake

Maysville • lat 34°51'34" lon 007°03'09"

DESCRIPTION: This dispersed CG is situated on Great Lake. This CG offers a boat ramp, fishing and canoeing opportunities. There are no facilities at this CG. Wildlife in the area includes deer, black bears, turkeys, osprey and alligators. View unusual plants such as the carnivorous Venus' Fly Trap.

GETTING THERE: From Maysville go SE on state HWY 58 approx. 7 mi. to Great Lake Road (state route 1100). Go E on Great Lake Road approx. 7 mi. to Great Lake CG.

SINGLE RATE:	No fee	OPEN DATES:	Yearlong
		MAX STAY:	14 days
		ELEVATION:	40 feet

22 Hanging Dog

Murphy • lat 35°06'31" lon 084°04'45"

DESCRIPTION: Set in mixture of pine and hardwoods on Hiwassee Lake. Boat or bank fish the lake for a variety of species. Supplies available in Murphy. Moderate use, full most holiday weekends. Gather firewood locally. Hiking and mountain biking trails available on site. Primitive facilities off season.

GETTING THERE: From Murphy go NW on state HWY 1326 approx. 4 mi. to forest route 652. Go S on 652 approx 1 mi. to Hanging Dog CG.

SINGLE RATE:	$8	OPEN DATES:	Apr-Oct
# of SINGLE SITES:	67	MAX SPUR:	46 feet
		MAX STAY:	14 days
		ELEVATION:	1680 feet

23 Harmon Den Horse Camp

Asheville • lat 35°44'28" lon 082°59'01"

DESCRIPTION: In a mixed hardwood forest setting. Fish for trout from Cold Spring Creek nearby. Supplies available at Asheville. Numerous wildlife can be seen in the area. Campers may gather firewood. CG has horse stalls, water troughs and hitching posts. Horse and hiking trails leave from CG and a trail network is in the area.

GETTING THERE: From Asheville go NW on state HWY 40 approx. 32 mi. to forest route 148. Go NE on 148 approx. 3 mi. to Harmon Den Horse Camp CG.

SINGLE RATE:	$15	OPEN DATES:	May-Oct
# of SINGLE SITES:	10	MAX SPUR:	30 feet
		MAX STAY:	14 days
		ELEVATION:	3745 feet

24 Horse Cove

Robbinsville • lat 35°21'53" lon 083°55'12"

DESCRIPTION: Beautiful setting among white pine, on Santeetlah Cr. Hot humid summers, cool winters. Supplies in Robbinsville. Bears and wild boars in area occasionally. Moderate use, fills holidays. Gather firewood or buy in town. Trails in nearby JK-Slickrock Wilderness and barrier free trail.

GETTING THERE: From Robbinsville/Milltown go S on state route 1127 approx. 18 mi. to Horse Cove CG.

SINGLE RATE:	$8	OPEN DATES:	Apr-Oct
# of SINGLE SITES:	18	MAX SPUR:	20 feet
		MAX STAY:	14 days
		ELEVATION:	2111 feet

25 Hurricane Creek

Franklin • lat 35°03'00" lon 083°30'00"

DESCRIPTION: In a mixed forest setting with the Nantahala River nearby. Fish and swim in the river. Supplies available at Franklin. Many animals can be seen in the area. Campers may gather firewood. Hiking loop trail is in the area.

GETTING THERE: From Franklin go SW on US HWY 64 approx. 12 mi. to state HWY 1448. Go SE on 1448 approx. 3 mi. to forest route 67. Go S on 67 approx. 7 mi. to Huricane Creek CG.

SINGLE RATE:	$4	OPEN DATES:	Mar-Jan
		MAX STAY:	14 days
		ELEVATION:	3400 feet

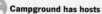 **Campground has hosts**    **Reservable sites**   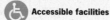 **Accessible facilities**   **Fully developed**   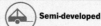 **Semi-developed**   **Rustic facilities**

NOTE: Open dates listed are typical. Actual dates are dependent on conditions such as snow pack.

26 Jackrabbit Mountain
Hayesville • lat 35°00'38" lon 083°46'00"

DESCRIPTION: In a park like setting on peninsula of Lake Chatuge. Views of lake all around. Frequent wind off the lake. Fish for a variety of species. Limited supplies 1/2 mi. Moderate-heavy use, full most holidays and weekends. Campers may gather firewood; may be scarce. Hiking trails on site.

GETTING THERE: From Hayesville go E on US HWY 64 approx. 5 mi. to state HWY 175. Go S on 175 approx. 2.5 mi. to turnoff (right) for Jackrabbit Mountain CG. CG is approx. 1 mi. W on this route.

SINGLE RATE:	$12	OPEN DATES:	May-Oct
# of SINGLE SITES:	101	MAX SPUR:	42 feet
		MAX STAY:	14 days
		ELEVATION:	1961 feet

31 Mortimer
Lenoir • lat 35°59'55" lon 081°46'11"

DESCRIPTION: In a pine/hardwood cove along creek. Thorps creek nearby for trout fishing. Supplies at Lenoir. Small game near CG. Campers may gather firewood. Many trails in the area. No water.

GETTING THERE: From Lenoir go W on state HWY 90 approx. 3 mi. to state route 1337. Go SW on 1337 approx. 2 mi. to state route 1328. Go NW on 1328 approx. 4.5 mi. to Mortimer CG.

SINGLE RATE:	$4	OPEN DATES:	Apr-Oct
# of SINGLE SITES:	23	MAX STAY:	14 days
		ELEVATION:	1490 feet

27 Kimsey Creek
Franklin • lat 35°04'28" lon 083°31'54"

DESCRIPTION: In a mixed forest setting on Kimsey Creek. Fish and swim in the creek. Supplies available at Franklin. Many animals can be seen in the area. Campers may gather firewood. Hiking loop trail nearby. This is a group CG.

GETTING THERE: From Franklin go SW on US HWY 64 approx. 12 mi. to state HWY 1884. Go E on 1884 approx. 3 mi. to forest route 67. Go SE on 67 approx. 5 mi. to Kimsey Creek CG.

		OPEN DATES:	Apr-Oct
		MAX SPUR:	99 feet
GROUP RATE:	$40	MAX STAY:	14 days
# of GROUP SITES:	3	ELEVATION:	3409 feet

32 Neuse River
Pine Grove • lat 34°59'05" lon 076°57'02"

DESCRIPTION: In open pine ridges to low open swamps with views of the Neuse River. Fish for Flounder, ocean and fresh fish and marlin from the Neuse River. Several Civil war battle sites and forts are within 1/2 hour of the CG. Supplies are 2 mi. away. Look for the Red Cocaded Woodpecker. Firewood may be gathered.

GETTING THERE: From Pine Grove go N on US HWY 70 approx. 2.5 mi. to forest route 1107. Go NE on 110 approx. 1.5 mi. to Neuse River CG.

SINGLE RATE:	Varies	OPEN DATES:	Yearlong
# of SINGLE SITES:	40	MAX SPUR:	70 feet
		MAX STAY:	14 days
		ELEVATION:	25 feet

28 Kuykendall
Brevard • lat 35°13'12" lon 082°46'42"

DESCRIPTION: This tents only CG is in a mixed hardwood forest setting. Fish for rainbow, brook and brown trout from the nearby streams. Supplies available at Brevard. Deer, bobcats, foxes, owls and raccoons are common in the area. Campers may gather firewood. The Artload Trail is nearby. Hitching post at the CG.

GETTING THERE: From Brevard go SW on US HWY 64 approx. 4 mi. to forest route 471. Go NW on 471 approx. 1 mi. to Kuykendall CG.

		OPEN DATES:	Yearlong
GROUP RATE:	$70	MAX STAY:	14 days
# of GROUP SITES:	1	ELEVATION:	2365 feet

33 North Mills River
Asheville • lat 35°24'26" lon 082°38'45"

DESCRIPTION: In a mixed hardwood forest setting on North Mills River. Fish for rainbow, brook and brown trout from the river. Supplies available at Asheville. Deer, bobcats, foxes, owls and raccoons are common in the area. Campers may gather firewood. The Trace Ridge Trail is nearby.

GETTING THERE: From Asheville go S on state HWY 191 for 13.5 mi. to state route 1345. Go W on 1345 approx. 5 mi. to North Mills River CG.

SINGLE RATE:	$8	OPEN DATES:	Apr-Oct
# of SINGLE SITES:	28	MAX STAY:	14 days
		ELEVATION:	2750 feet

29 Lake Powhatan
Asheville • lat 35°28'54" lon 082°37'48"

DESCRIPTION: In a mixed hardwood forest setting on Lake Powhatan. Fish for rainbow, brook and brown trout and swim in the lake. Supplies available at Asheville. Deer, bobcats, foxes, owls and raccoons are common in the area. Campers may gather firewood. Many trails in the nearby.

GETTING THERE: From Asheville go S on state HWY 191 approx. 4 mi. to forest route 806. Go E on 806 approx. 3.5 mi. to Lake Powhatan CG.

SINGLE RATE:	$14	OPEN DATES:	Apr-Oct
# of SINGLE SITES:	98	MAX SPUR:	28 feet
		MAX STAY:	14 days
		ELEVATION:	2240 feet

34 Rattler Ford
Franklin • lat 35°21'32" lon 083°54'59"

DESCRIPTION: Beautiful setting of group sites in both trees and open area on Santeetlah Cr. Supplies 15 mi. Occasional black bears and russian boars. Fills holidays. Adjacent to 60+ mi. of JK-Slickrock Wilderness withthe 2 mi. Joyce kilmer Nat'l Recreation trail through virgin yellow poplar and hemlocks.

GETTING THERE: From Robbinsville/Milltown go S on state route 1127 approx. 13 mi. to Rattler Ford CG.

		OPEN DATES:	Apr-Oct
GROUP RATE:	$25	MAX STAY:	14 days
# of GROUP SITES:	4	ELEVATION:	2103 feet

30 Long Point
Maysville • lat 34°47'00" lon 077°11'00"

DESCRIPTION: This dispersed CG is located on the White Oak River. There is a boat ramp nearby at Haywood Landing. Enjoy fishing and canoeing. There are no facilities at this CG. Wildlife in the area includes deer, black bears, osprey and alligators. View unusual plants such as the carnivorous Venus Fly Trap.

GETTING THERE: From Maysville go SE on state HWY 58 approx. 6 mi. to forest route 120 (Long Point Road). Go SW on 120 approx. 2 mi. to Long Point CG.

SINGLE RATE:	No fee	OPEN DATES:	Yearlong
		MAX STAY:	14 days
		ELEVATION:	5 feet

35 Rocky Bluff
Hot Springs • lat 35°51'41" lon 082°50'37"

DESCRIPTION: CG sits among a mixed forest setting near Spring Creek. Excellent trout fishing in the creek. Supplies available at Hot Springs. An old cemetery lies within the CG, this is all that is left of a farmstead that was located here. Many animals can be seen in the area. Trails in the area.

GETTING THERE: Rocky Bluff CG is approx. 2 mi. S of Hot Springs on state HWY 209.

SINGLE RATE:	$8	OPEN DATES:	May-Oct
# of SINGLE SITES:	30	MAX SPUR:	30 feet
		MAX STAY:	14 days
		ELEVATION:	1845 feet

 Campground has hosts   **Reservable sites**   **Accessible facilities**   **Fully developed**   Semi-developed   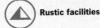 **Rustic facilities**

36 Silvermine Group
Hot Springs • lat 35°52'30" lon 082°48'30"

DESCRIPTION: CG sits among a mixed forest setting. Excellent trout fishing from nearby Silvermine Creek and French Broad River. Rafting and canoeing nearby. Supplies available at Hot Springs. Many animals can be seen in the area. Campers may gather firewood. Apalachian Trail is nearby. Reservation only.

GETTING THERE: Silvermine Group CG is located on the S side of Hot Springs, NC.

SINGLE RATE:		OPEN DATES:	May-Oct
		MAX SPUR:	30 feet
GROUP RATE:	Varies	MAX STAY:	14 days
# of GROUP SITES:	1	ELEVATION:	1400 feet

37 Standing Indian
Franklin • lat 35°04'43" lon 083°31'55"

DESCRIPTION: This hike-in, tent only CG is in a mixed forest setting on the Nantahala River. Fish and swim in the river. Supplies available at Franklin. Many animals can be seen in the area. Campers may gather firewood. Hiking loop trail nearby the CG.

GETTING THERE: From Franklin go SW on US HWY 64 approx. 12 mi. to state HWY 1448. Go SE on 1448 approx. 3 mi. to forest route 67 approx. 5 mi. to Standing Indian CG. A short hike to CG area.

SINGLE RATE:	$10	OPEN DATES:	Mar-Dec
# of SINGLE SITES:	84		
		MAX STAY:	14 days
		ELEVATION:	3395 feet

38 Sunburst
Waynesville • lat 35°22'12" lon 082°56'25"

DESCRIPTION: In a mixed hardwood forest setting on the East Fork of the Pigeon River. Fish for rainbow, brook and brown trout in the river. Supplies available at Waynesville. Deer, bobcats, foxes, owls and raccoons are common in the area. Campers may gather firewood. No designated trails in the area.

GETTING THERE: From Waynesville go E on US HWY 276 approx. 7 mi. to state HWY 215. Go S on 215 for 8 mi. to Sunburst CG.

SINGLE RATE:	$7	OPEN DATES:	Apr-Oct
# of SINGLE SITES:	14		
		MAX STAY:	14 days
		ELEVATION:	3240 feet

39 Tsali
Bryson City • lat 35°24'30" lon 083°35'19"

DESCRIPTION: In yellow pine park like setting on small tributary of Fontana Lake. Boat fish the lake for bass, trout and walleye. Hot days and cool nights. Supplies 7 mi. Whitetail deer, black bears in area. Fills weekends. Buy firewood from host. 4 trails (40 mi. total) of Tsali Mountain Biking area nearby.

GETTING THERE: From Bryson City go SW on US HWY 19 approx. 7 mi. to state route 28. Go W on 28 approx. 3 mi. to forest route 2550. Go N on 2550 approx. 1 mi. to Tsali CG.

SINGLE RATE:	Varies	OPEN DATES:	Mar-Nov
# of SINGLE SITES:	42	MAX SPUR:	20 feet
		MAX STAY:	14 days
		ELEVATION:	1873 feet

40 Uwharrie Hunt Camp
Troy • lat 35°25'45" lon 080°01'19"

DESCRIPTION: Tent camp in open park-like oak and pine woods. Hot summers, mild to cold winters. No nearby fishing. Supplies 2 mi. Deer, turkeys, raccoons and songbirds. Fills holidays. Spring and fall area nice times. Gather firewood. Horse, hike, ATV and mountain bike trails nearby. Ticks and chiggers spring-fall.

GETTING THERE: From Troy go NW on state HWY 109 approx. 8 mi. to Reservation Road. Turn left onto Reservation Road then go 1/2 mi. to Uwharrie Hunt Camp.

SINGLE RATE:	$5	OPEN DATES:	Yearlong
# of SINGLE SITES:	8		
		MAX STAY:	14 days
		ELEVATION:	320 feet

41 Vanhook Glade
Highlands • lat 35°04'38" lon 083°14'54"

DESCRIPTION: CG is located in semi-open hardwood and pine forest. Frequent afternoon t-showers. Trout fish in nearby Cullasaja River. Visit historic McCall Cabin. Supplies 4 mi. at Highlands. Wildlife includes black bears, small game and songbirds. Firewood sold on site. Many hiking trails in area.

GETTING THERE: Vanhook Glade CG is approx. 4 mi. NW of Highlands on US 64 West. Road is narrow with sharp curves. Large vehicles should use caution.

SINGLE RATE:	$10	OPEN DATES:	Apr-Oct*
# of SINGLE SITES:	20	MAX SPUR:	30 feet
		MAX STAY:	14 days
		ELEVATION:	3240 feet

42 West Morris Mountain
Troy • lat 35°25'46" lon 079°59'41"

DESCRIPTION: In stand of towering pines withwooded views. Hot summers, mild spring/fall, cold to mild winter. No nearby fishing. Deer, turkeys, raccoons and songbirds in area. Gather firewood. Supplies 1 mi. Hiking trail spur accesses Uwharrie Nat'l Recreation Tail. Ticks and chiggers spring-fall.

GETTING THERE: From Troy go NW on state HWY 109 approx. 6 mi. to state route 1150. Go N on 1150 approx. 1 mi. to West Morris Mountain. Camp.

SINGLE RATE:	$5	OPEN DATES:	Yearlong
# of SINGLE SITES:	14	MAX SPUR:	60 feet
		MAX STAY:	14 days
		ELEVATION:	450 feet

43 White Pines
Brevard • lat 35°17'31" lon 082°44'19"

DESCRIPTION: This tents only CG is in a mixed hardwood forest setting on Avery Creek. Fish for rainbow, brook and brown trout from the creek. Supplies available at Brevard. Deer, bobcats, foxes, owls and raccoons are common in the area. Campers may gather firewood. The Avery Creek Trail is nearby. Hitching post at the CG.

GETTING THERE: From Brevard go N on US HWY 64 approx. 2 mi. to US HWY 276. Go NW on 276 approx. 1 mi. to White Pines CG.

		OPEN DATES:	Yearlong
GROUP RATE:	$30	MAX STAY:	14 days
# of GROUP SITES:	2	ELEVATION:	2400 feet

44 Yates Place
Troy • lat 35°21'52" lon 079°59'20"

DESCRIPTION: In pine and oak forest withwooded views. Mild spring/fall, hot summer, mild to cold winters. Dispersed sites. No nearby fishing. Supplies 5 mi. Deer, turkeys, raccoons. Fills deer hunt season. Gather firewood. Hiking spur trail connects to Uwharrie Nat'l Recreation Trail. Ticks and chiggers spring-fall.

GETTING THERE: From Troy go W on state HWY 109 approx. 3 mi. to state route 1134. Go S on 1134 approx. 1.5 mi. to state route 1146. Go W on 1146 approx. 1.5 mi. to Yates Place Camp.

SINGLE RATE:	$5	OPEN DATES:	Yearlong
		MAX STAY:	14 days
		ELEVATION:	760 feet

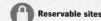 Campground has hosts   Reservable sites   Accessible facilities   Fully developed   Semi-developed   Rustic facilities

NOTE: Open dates listed are typical. Actual dates are dependent on conditions such as snow pack.

Dakota Prairie Grasslands

Stretching over 1,259,000 acres, the Dakota Prairie National Grasslands of North and South Dakota offer visitors the opportunity to view a variety of wildlife including elk, antelope, bighorn sheep, coyotes, sharptail grouse, eagles, and prairie dogs. Recreational opportunities include hiking, camping, horseback riding, photography, canoeing, fishing, hunting, and backpacking. These national grasslands are not solid blocks of the National Forest System lands. Instead, they are intermingled with other federal, state, and privately owned lands. This mixed ownership pattern contributes to the uniqueness of each grassland. For example, the tall grass prairie of the Sheyenne National Grasslands is a significant contrast to the stark badlands found in the Little Missouri National Grasslands. Resources also vary from paleontological and archeological digs, oil and gas production, cattle grazing, and recreation. The Dakota Prairie National Grasslands are a treasure of natural science. Plants and animals, rocks and minerals, water resources and even the air have been studied in this unique outdoor laboratory.

Dakota Prairie National Grasslands • (701) 250-4443

1 Buffalo Gap
Medora • lat 46˚55'00" lon 103˚39'00"

DESCRIPTION: CG is located in tall cottonwood in a coulee east of Theodore Roosevelt National Park. Nearby fishing ponds are being revamped. Supplies available in Medora. Antelope, deer, raptors and prairie dogs are common to the area. Busy all summer with national park overflow.

GETTING THERE: Buffalo Gap CG is located approx. 8 mi. W of Medora on the north side of Interstate 94.

SINGLE RATE:	$8	OPEN DATES:	May-Sept
# of SINGLE SITES:	37	MAX SPUR:	30 feet
		MAX STAY:	14 days
# of GROUP SITES:	1	ELEVATION:	2500 feet

2 Burning Coal Vein
Medora • lat 46˚35'00" lon 103˚27'00"

DESCRIPTION: This privitive CG is located in a ponderosa pine forest setting. Supplies available in Medora. Antelope, deer, prairie dogs and raptors are common to the area. A coal vein is nearby that used to be on fire. Many animals can be seen in the area.

GETTING THERE: From Medora go S on forest route 3 approx. 25 mi. to forest route 772. Go E on 772 appro. 2 mi. to Burning Coal Vein CG.

SINGLE RATE:	No fee	OPEN DATES:	Yearlong
# of SINGLE SITES:	5	MAX SPUR:	30 feet
		MAX STAY:	14 days
# of GROUP SITES:	1	ELEVATION:	2480 feet

3 CCC
Watford City • lat 47˚35'00" lon 103˚16'00"

DESCRIPTION: CG is located in open rolling setting on the Little Missouri River. Fish and swim in the river. Supplies available at Watford City. Deer, bighorn sheep and small animals are common to the area. Drinking water available. Hiking trail in area.

GETTING THERE: From Watford City go S on US HWY 85 approx. 15 mi. to Little Missouri River. Cross river and go W on forest route 842 1 mi. to CCC CG.

SINGLE RATE:	$6	OPEN DATES:	Yearlong
# of SINGLE SITES:	3	MAX SPUR:	40 feet
		MAX STAY:	14 days
		ELEVATION:	1980 feet

4 Sather
Watford City • lat 47˚40'00" lon 103˚49'00"

DESCRIPTION: CG is located in open rolling country on Sather Lake. This lake is a popular fishing area and good for swimming also. Supplies available at Watford City. No drinking water. Antelope can be seen in the area.

GETTING THERE: From Watford City go W on US HWY 85 approx. 17 mi. to state HWY 68. Go S and then W on 68 approx. 17 mi. to Sather CG.

SINGLE RATE:	No fee	OPEN DATES:	Yearlong
# of SINGLE SITES:	8	MAX SPUR:	15 feet
		MAX STAY:	14 days
		ELEVATION:	2261 feet

5 Summit
Watford City • lat 47˚32'30" lon 103˚14'50"

DESCRIPTION: CG is located in open rolling country. Supplies available at Watford City. Deer, bighorn sheep and small camp animals are common to the area. Campers may gather dead and downed firewood. No drinking water available in CG.

GETTING THERE: From Watford City go S on US HWY 85 approximately 19 mi. to Summit CG.

SINGLE RATE:	No fee	OPEN DATES:	Yearlong
# of SINGLE SITES:	5	MAX SPUR:	10 feet
		MAX STAY:	14 days
		ELEVATION:	2649 feet

 Campground has hosts   🔒 **Reservable sites**   **Accessible facilities**   **Fully developed**   **Semi-developed**   ▲ **Rustic facilities**

NOTE: Open dates listed are typical. Actual dates are dependent on conditions such as snow pack.

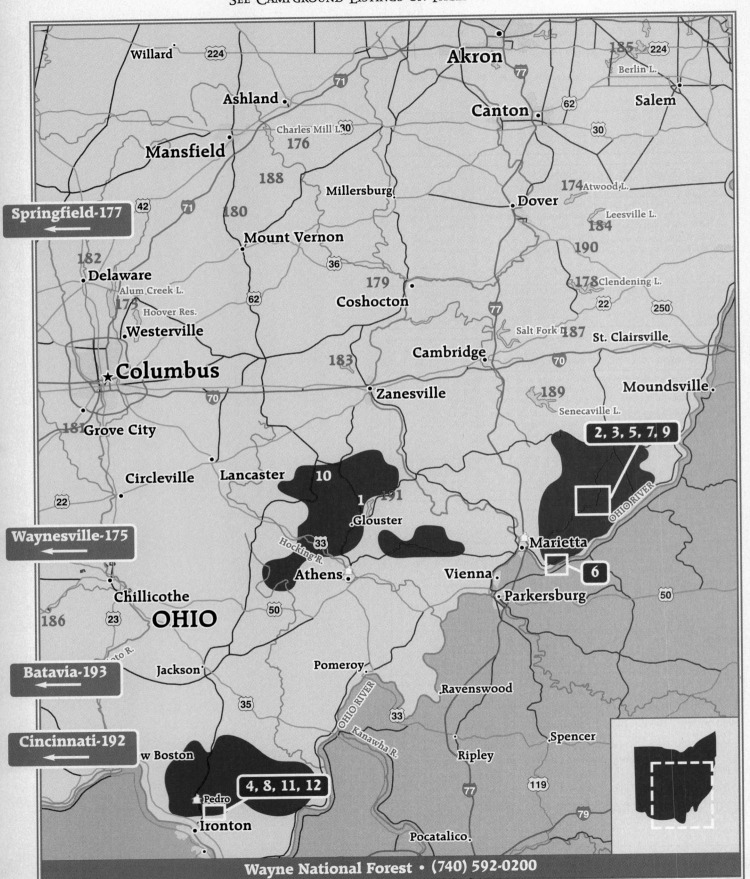

Willard

224

Ashland

Charles Mill L. 30

176

188

180

Springfield-177

42

71

182

Delaware

Alum Creek L.

173

Hoover Res.

Westerville

70

Columbus

181

Grove City

22

Circleville

22

186

23

Batavia-193

35

Cincinnati-192

w Boston

Pedro

Ironton

4, 8, 11, 12

Mansfield

Millersburg

Mount Vernon

36

62

Coshocton

183

Zanesville

70

Lancaster

10

1

191

Glouster

33

Hocking R.

Athens

50

OHIO

Jackson

35

Pomeroy

Ohio River

Kanawha R.

33

Pocatalico

71

Akron

77

Canton

62

30

Dover

174 Atwood L.

Leesville L.

184

190

178 Clendening L.

22

250

Salt Fork 187

St. Clairsville

70

189

Senecaville L.

2, 3, 5, 7, 9

Ohio River

Marietta

6

Vienna

Parkersburg

50

Ravenswood

Spencer

Ripley

77

119

79

185

224

Berlin L.

Salem

Moundsville

Waynesville-175

Chillicothe

USFS Photo

WAYNE NATIONAL FOREST

Nestled in the Appalachian foothills, the Wayne has many unique and interesting areas waiting to be found. You'll see remnants of our heritage, such as cabins and vintage oil wells. You'll also experience the natural beauty of wildflowers, rock formations, and abundant wildlife.

Recreation opportunities on the forest attract a record number of visitors each year. Leith Run Recreation Area is popular with boaters and fishermen alike because of the easy access to the Ohio River. The Little Muskingum and Hocking rivers, as well as Symmes Creek, offer opportunities for seasonal float trips through the forest. Miles of trails invite hikers, equestrians and mountain bikers while streams and rivers offer opportunities to catch bass, panfish and catfish. The mix of open land and forest provides a wide variety of wildlife habitats for animals such as white-tailed deer, gray foxes, turkeys and ruffed grouse.

Southeastern Ohio is rich in history. Mounds and prehistoric earthworks from the Adena and Hopewell cultures are still found on the forest. Cemeteries and historic buildings offer visitors a glimpse into the past. Vesuvius Furnace, Ring Mill House, the Shawnee Fire Tower and several rock shelters are interpreted for the public.

In addition, the Covered Bridge Scenic Byway showcases one of Ohio's most beautiful stretches of highway. Historic barns and covered bridges dot the landscape along the route.

1 Burr Oak Cove
Athens • lat 39°32'59" lon 082°03'38"

DESCRIPTION: A small, densely wooded CG on Burr Oak Reservoir. Fish for trout from the reservoir. Supplies located in Athens. Numerous wildlife can be found in the area. Campers may gather firewood. Buckeye Trail nearby or hike on the trail surrounding the reservoir. No drinking water at this CG.

GETTING THERE: From Athens go N on HWY 13 approx. 17 mi. to turnoff. Go E approx. 1/2 mi. to Burr Oak Cove CG.

SINGLE RATE:	$5	OPEN DATES:	May-Dec
# of SINGLE SITES:	19	MAX SPUR:	30 feet
		MAX STAY:	14 days
		ELEVATION:	900 feet

2 Haught Run
Marietta • lat 39°31'55" lon 081°13'35"

DESCRIPTION: A small CG in a mixture of hardwood and pine on the banks of the Little Muskingum River. Fish for bass and catfish from the river. A canoe access point is located at the CG. Supplies available at Marietta. Campers may gather firewood. CG is a trailhead for the North Country Trail.

GETTING THERE: From Marietta go NE on state HWY 26 approx. 15 mi. to Haught Run CG.

SINGLE RATE:	No fee	OPEN DATES:	Yearlong
# of SINGLE SITES:	4		
		MAX STAY:	14 days
		ELEVATION:	700 feet

3 Hune Bridge
Marietta • lat 39°30'35" lon 081°15'03"

DESCRIPTION: In a mix of pine and hardwoods just below the Hune Covered Bridge on the banks of the Little Muskingum River. Fish for bass and catfish in the river. CG is a canoe access point and trailhead to Haught Run. Supplies available at Marietta. Campers may gather firewood. Deer, foxes and squirrels are common in the area.

GETTING THERE: From Marietta go NE on state HWY 26 approx. 12 mi. to Hune Bridge CG.

SINGLE RATE:	No fee	OPEN DATES:	Yearlong
# of SINGLE SITES:	3		
		MAX STAY:	14 days
		ELEVATION:	655 feet

4 Iron Ridge
Ironton • lat 38°36'55" lon 082°37'50"

DESCRIPTION: In a hardwood and pine setting on Lake Vesuvius. Fish for panfish, catfish and bass from the lake. Boat ramp at the CG. Supplies available at Ironton. Deer, foxes, woodchucks and squirrels are common. Amphitheater, RV dump station and wildlife viewing area at CG. Interpretive and other trails nearby.

GETTING THERE: From Ironton go N on E state route 93 approximately 6.5 miles to Iron Ridge CG.

SINGLE RATE:	$12	OPEN DATES:	May-Sept
# of SINGLE SITES:	24	MAX SPUR:	40 feet
		MAX STAY:	14 days
		ELEVATION:	900 feet

5 Lamping Homestead
Marietta • lat 39°37'49" lon 081°11'13"

DESCRIPTION: This walk-in, tent only CG is in a hardwood and pine forest setting on a 2-acre pond. Pond is stocked with bluegill, bass, and catfish. This CG was the former homestead of the Lamping family. Supplies available at Marietta. Campers may gather firewood. There are 2 loop trails for hiking, one is 3.5 mi. and the other is 1.5 mi.

GETTING THERE: From Marietta go NE on state HWY 26 approx. 35 mi. to state route 537. Go on state route 537 approx. 2 mi. to Lamping Homestead CG.

SINGLE RATE:	No fee	OPEN DATES:	Yearlong
# of SINGLE SITES:	6		
		MAX STAY:	14 days
		ELEVATION:	770 feet

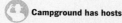 Campground has hosts   Reservable sites   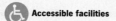 Accessible facilities   Fully developed   Semi-developed   Rustic facilities

NOTE: Open dates listed are typical. Actual dates are dependent on conditions such as snow pack.

6 Lane Farm
Marietta • lat 39°25'59" lon 081°21'44"

DESCRIPTION: A small CG in a mixture of hardwood and pine on the banks of the Little Muskingum River. Fish for bass and catfish from the river. A canoe access point is located at the CG. Supplies available at Marietta. Campers may gather firewood. CG is a trailhead for the North Country Trail.

GETTING THERE: From Marietta go NE on state HWY 26 approx. 4 mi. to Lane Farm CG.

SINGLE RATE:	No fee	OPEN DATES:	Yearlong
# of SINGLE SITES:	4		
		MAX STAY:	14 days
		ELEVATION:	650 feet

7 Leith Run
St. Marys • lat 39°26'38" lon 081°09'01"

DESCRIPTION: In a mixture of hardwoods and pine on the banks of the Ohio River. Fish for bass, catfish and panfish in the river. Boat ramp at CG for boats and canoes. Supplies available at Marietta. Campers may gather firewood. RV dump station at CG. Wildlife viewing area nearby. Hiking trails close to CG.

GETTING THERE: From Marietta go N on state HWY 7 approx. 7 mi. to Leith Run CG.

SINGLE RATE:	$18	OPEN DATES:	Apr-Oct
# of SINGLE SITES:	18	MAX SPUR:	28 feet
		MAX STAY:	14 days
		ELEVATION:	650 feet

8 Oak Hill
Ironton • lat 38°36'55" lon 082°37'50"

DESCRIPTION: In a hardwood and pine setting on Lake Vesuvius. Fish for panfish, catfish and bass in the lake. Boat ramp at the CG. Supplies available at Ironton. Deer, foxes, woodchucks and squirrels are common. Amphitheater, RV dump station and wildlife viewing area at CG. Interpretive and other trails nearby.

GETTING THERE: From Ironton go N on E state route 93 approximately 6.5 miles to Oak Hill CG.

SINGLE RATE:	$10	OPEN DATES:	Apr-Oct
# of SINGLE SITES:	41	MAX SPUR:	40 feet
GROUP RATE:		MAX STAY:	14 days
		ELEVATION:	900 feet

9 Ring Mill
Poulton • lat 39°36'27" lon 081°07'17"

DESCRIPTION: In a hardwood and pine forest setting on the banks of the Little Muskingum River. Fish for catfish and bass from the river. Canoe access at the CG. CG was once the site of an historical mill and farmstead. Supplies at Marietta. Deer, opossum, squirrels and foxes are common to the area. This is a trailhead for the North Country Trail.

GETTING THERE: From Marietta go N on county route 68 approx. 32 mi. to state route 26. Ring Mill CG is approx. 3 mi. off of 26.

SINGLE RATE:	No fee	OPEN DATES:	Yearlong
# of SINGLE SITES:	3		
		MAX STAY:	14 days
		ELEVATION:	700 feet

10 Stone Church Horse Trail
Shawnee • lat 39°36'17" lon 082°12'42"

DESCRIPTION: This CG rests in mixed hardwoods and conifer on Monday River. This CG is ideal for horse trail riders. The CG is a trailhead for the North Country Buckeye Trail. A daily permit is required for trail riding. Wildlife in this area includes deer, foxes, opossums, and neotropical migratory birds.

GETTING THERE: From Shawnee go NW on state HWY 155 approx. 3 mi. to Stone Church Horse Trail CG.

SINGLE RATE:	$5	OPEN DATES:	Apr-Dec
# of SINGLE SITES:	4	MAX SPUR:	30 feet
		MAX STAY:	14 days
		ELEVATION:	900 feet

11 Two Points Group
Ironton • lat 38°36'55" lon 823°75'0"

DESCRIPTION: In a hardwood and pine setting on Lake Vesuvius. Fish for panfish, catfish and bass from the lake. Boat ramp at the CG. Supplies available at Ironton. Deer, foxes, woodchucks and squirrels are common. Amphitheater, RV dump station and wildlife viewing area, interpretive and other trails in the area.

GETTING THERE: From Ironton go N on E state route 93 approximately 6.5 miles to Two Points Group CG.

		OPEN DATES:	May-Sept
		MAX SPUR:	40 feet
GROUP RATE:	Varies	MAX STAY:	14 days
# of GROUP SITES:	2	ELEVATION:	900 feet

12 Vesuvius Recreation Area
Ironton • lat 38°36'55" lon 082°37'50"

DESCRIPTION: In a hardwood and pine setting on Lake Vesuvius. Fish for panfish, catfish and bass from the lake. Boat ramp at the CG. Supplies available at Ironton. Deer, foxes, woodchucks and squirrels are common. Amphitheater, RV dump station and wildlife viewing area at CG. Interpretive and other trails nearby.

GETTING THERE: From Ironton go N on E state route 93 approximately 6.5 miles to Lake Vesuvius Reacreation Area CG.

SINGLE RATE:	Varies	OPEN DATES:	Yearlong
# of SINGLE SITES:	66	MAX SPUR:	40 feet
GROUP RATE:	Varies	MAX STAY:	14 days
# of GROUP SITES:	2	ELEVATION:	900 feet

 Campground has hosts   **Reserved sites**   **Accessible facilities**   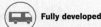 **Fully developed**    **Semi-developed**    **Rustic facilities**

NOTE: Open dates listed are typical. Actual dates are dependent on conditions such as snow pack.

THE ATV OF CHOICE WHEN YOU DON'T HAVE A PIT CREW STANDING BY.

Richard Childress runs the very best out on the track and it's made him a championship-winning NASCAR team owner. But when he's out hunting, only a Kawasaki ATV will do. There's loads of power under the hood. And with MacPherson Strut Independent Front Suspension, the rockiest trail can feel like a straightaway. Just call 1-877-KAWI-ATV or visit www.kawasaki.com for a Kawasaki ATV of your own. You don't have to be a legend from the track, but you'll quickly become one off of it.

USFS Photo

BLACK KETTLE/McCLELLAN CREEK NATIONAL GRASSLAND

For many years, farming proved successful on many small family farms that dotted the Black Kettle and McClellan Creek National Grasslands. But by the mid-1930s, the years of cropping with poor agricultural practices, combined with prolonged drought and strong winds, left the land denuded. The successful restoration of these lands has greatly benefited resident bird and mammal populations. Visitors can view white-tailed deer, turkeys, quail, raccoons, opossums, muskrats, rabbits, squirrels, bobcats, coyotes, and beavers. The non-game bird population is both numerous and varied. The five lakes McClellan, Marvin, Dead Indian, Skipout, and Spring Creek offer a variety of recreation opportunities. Camping, picnicking, and fishing can all be enjoyed at these areas. Some of the National Grassland units, excluding the five lakes, are not accessible by public road. Private land must be crossed in some instances and permission from the landowners should be requested.

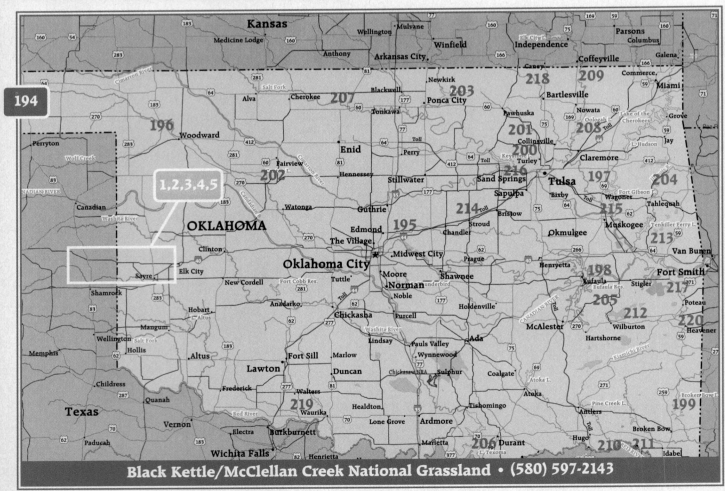

Black Kettle/McClellan Creek National Grassland • (580) 597-2143

1 Black Kettle Recreation Area
Cheyenne • lat 35˚44'00" lon 994˚10'0"

DESCRIPTION: CG is located mostly in cottonwood on Dead Indian Reservoir. Fish for catfish, largemouth bass and crappie in lake. Supplies available in Cheyenne. Deer, turkeys, quail and other small animals can be seen in the area. Trails can be found in the area. Busy in spring and in fall.

GETTING THERE: From Cheyenne go N on US HWY 287 approx. 10 mi. to Black Kettle Recreation Area CG.

SINGLE RATE:	No fee	OPEN DATES:	Yearlong
# of SINGLE SITES:	12	MAX SPUR:	45 feet
		MAX STAY:	14 days
		ELEVATION:	2100 feet

2 Lake Marvin
Canadian • lat 35˚52'50" lon 100˚10'30"

DESCRIPTION: CG is located mostly in cottonwood on Lake Marvin. Fish for catfish, largemouth bass and crappie in lake. Supplies available in Canadian. Deer, turkeys, quail and other small animals are common to the area. Trails in area. Busy in spring and in fall.

GETTING THERE: From Canadian go E on county route 2266 approx. 14 mi. to Lake Marvin CG.

SINGLE RATE:	Varies	OPEN DATES:	Yearlong
# of SINGLE SITES:	22	MAX SPUR:	45 feet
		MAX STAY:	14 days
		ELEVATION:	2000 feet

3 Lake McClellan
McLean • lat 35˚13'00" lon 100˚49'00"

DESCRIPTION: CG is located mostly in cottonwoods on Lake McClellan. Fish for catfish, largemouth bass and crappie in lake. Supplies available in McLean. Deer, turkeys, quail and other small animals are common to the area. Many trails in area including an 8 mi. motorcycle trail. Busy in spring and summer.

GETTING THERE: From McLean go W on I-40 approx. 16 mi. to the Lake McClellan exit. Go N following signs to Lake McClellan CG.

SINGLE RATE:	Varies	OPEN DATES:	Yearlong
# of SINGLE SITES:	60	MAX SPUR:	50 feet
		MAX STAY:	14 days
		ELEVATION:	3500 feet

4 Skipout
Cheyenne • lat 35˚38'00" lon 995˚23'0"

DESCRIPTION: CG is located partly in cottonwood and partly in the open on Skipout lake. Fishing for catfish and largemouth bass in lake. Supplies available at Cheyenne. Deer, turkeys, quail and other small animals in area. There is a 2 mi. trail around lake. Busy in spring and in fall for hunts.

GETTING THERE: From Cheyenne go W on state HWY 47 approx. 11 mi. to forest route 703. Go N on 703 approx. 1 mi. to Skipout CG.

SINGLE RATE:	No fee	OPEN DATES:	Yearlong
# of SINGLE SITES:	12	MAX SPUR:	45 feet
		MAX STAY:	14 days
		ELEVATION:	2100 feet

5 Spring Creek
Cheyenne • lat 36˚46'00" lon 995˚13'0"

DESCRIPTION: CG is located mostly in cottonwood on Spring Creek reservoir. Fishing for catfish, largemouth bass and crappie in lake. Supplies available in Cheyenne. Deer, turkeys, quail and other small animals can be seen in the area. Busy in spring and in fall.

GETTING THERE: From Cheyenne go N on US HWY 283 approx. 9 mi. to Spring Creek CG.

SINGLE RATE:	No fee	OPEN DATES:	Yearlong
# of SINGLE SITES:	9	MAX SPUR:	45 feet
		MAX STAY:	14 days
		ELEVATION:	2300 feet

 Campground has hosts   **Reservable sites**   **Accessible facilities**   **Fully developed**    **Semi-developed**   **Rustic facilities**

NOTE: Open dates listed are typical. Actual dates are dependent on conditions such as snow pack.

USFS Photo

DESCHUTES
NATIONAL FOREST

The Deschutes National Forest encompasses more than 1.6 million acres extending 100 miles along the east side of the Cascade Mountains. The forest is a scenic backdrop of volcanic mountains and alpine forests, dense evergreen forests, mountain lakes, caves, desert areas, and alpine meadows. Elevations range from 1,950 feet at Lake Billy Chinook to 10,358 feet on South Sister.

A wide range of recreation opportunities exist. The value of the forest as a place to play and enjoy has been reflected by the creation or expansion of the five wilderness areas, the six national wild and scenic rivers, the Oregon Cascade Recreation Area, the Metolius Conservation Area, and the Newberry National Volcanic Monument. Today, more than eight million people visit the forest annually to camp, fish, and hike. The forest also includes three of Oregon's five highest peaks to challenge mountain climbers. More than 150 lakes and 500 miles of streams are found here for anglers and boaters to enjoy.

From the Cascade Mountains on its western border to the high desert country east of Bend, from the old growth ponderosa pine forests along the Metolius River to Crescent and Odell Lakes in the south, the Deschutes is a true four season vacationland.

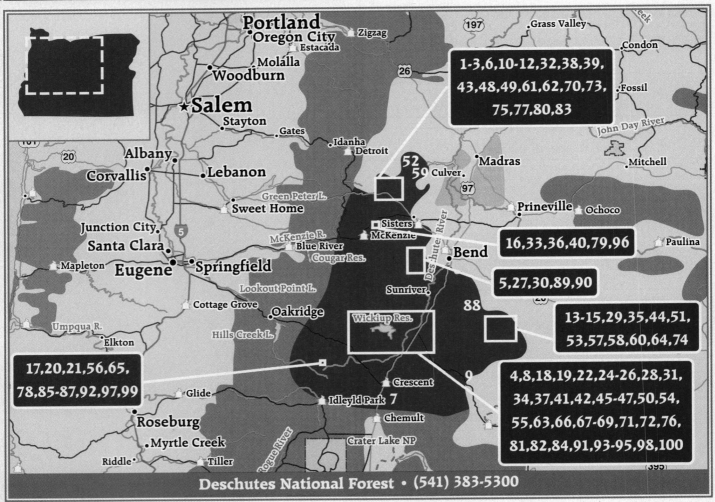

Deschutes National Forest • (541) 383-5300

1 — Abbot Creek
Sisters • lat 44˚32'45" lon 121˚40'19"

DESCRIPTION: This quiet, secluded CG offers tent sites only and is adjacent to Abbot Creek among mixed conifer. There is excellent trout fishing in the area but please check the fishing regulations Wildlife in this area includes black bears, coyotes, deer, and elk. Hike nearby Head of Jack Creek nature trail. No drinking water.

GETTING THERE: From Sisters go NW on HWY 20 approx. 12.4 mi. to primary forest route 12. Go NE on 12 approx. 9.9 mi. to Abbot Creek CG.

SINGLE RATE:	No fee	OPEN DATES:	Apr-Oct
# of SINGLE SITES:	4	MAX STAY:	14 days
		ELEVATION:	3050 feet

2 — Allen Springs
Sisters • lat 44˚32'30" lon 121˚37'30"

DESCRIPTION: This CG is located in mixed conifer on the Metolius River. Enjoy fly fishing for trout and swimming in the river. Wildlife in this area includes black bears, coyotes, deer, and elk. Hike nearby Head of Jack Creek nature trail. Supplies 5 mi. at Camp Sherman. CG is busy weekends and holidays.

GETTING THERE: From Sisters go NW on HWY 20 approx. 9 mi. to primary forest route 14. Go N on 14 approx. 11 mi. to Allen Springs CG.

SINGLE RATE:	$12	OPEN DATES:	Apr-Oct
# of SINGLE SITES:	13	MAX STAY:	14 days
		ELEVATION:	2750 feet

3 — Allingham
Sisters • lat 44˚28'20" lon 121˚38'05"

DESCRIPTION: This CG is located in mixed conifer on the Metolius River. Enjoy fly fishing for trout and swimming in the river. Wildlife in this area includes black bears, coyotes, deer, and elk. Hike nearby Head of Jack Creek nature trail. Supplies 1 mi. at Camp Sherman. CG is busy weekends and holidays.

GETTING THERE: From Sisters go NW on State HWY approx. 9.5 mi. to primary forest route 14. Go N on 14 approx. 6 mi. to forest route 1419. Go N on 1419 for 1 mi. to Allingham CG.

SINGLE RATE:	$12	OPEN DATES:	May-Sept
# of SINGLE SITES:	10	MAX STAY:	14 days
		ELEVATION:	2900 feet

4 — Big River
Bend • lat 43˚49'01" lon 121˚29'48"

DESCRIPTION: This CG is located on the Deschutes River with bank or small boat trout fishing; boat ramp on site. Supplies at Thousand Trails, 5 mi. E. or Sunriver, 10 mi. Moderate use. Great overnight stop. Gather firewood locally. Wildlife in this area includes mountain lions, black bears, coyotes, deer, and elk.

GETTING THERE: From Bend go S on US HWY 97 approx. 17 mi. to forest route 42. On 42 go W 8 mi. to Big River CG.

SINGLE RATE:	$5	OPEN DATES:	Apr-Oct
# of SINGLE SITES:	11	MAX SPUR:	30 feet
		MAX STAY:	14 days
		ELEVATION:	4150 feet

5 — Black Pine Springs
Sisters • lat 44˚11'47" lon 121˚36'56"

DESCRIPTION: This CG is located in mixed conifer at Black Pine Spring. There are excellent fly fishing opportunities in the area. Wildlife includes black bears, mountain lions, coyotes, deer and elk. CG is busy weekends and holidays. A nearby hiking trail leads to Three Sisters Wilderness. No drinking water.

GETTING THERE: From Sisters go S on primary forest route 16 approx. 8 mi. to Black Pine Springs CG.

SINGLE RATE:	No fee	OPEN DATES:	June-Sept
# of SINGLE SITES:	4	MAX STAY:	14 days
		ELEVATION:	4350 feet

6 — Blue Bay
Sisters • lat 44˚25'15" lon 121˚44'00"

DESCRIPTION: This CG rests in white fir, douglas fir, and ponderosa pine on Suttle Lake. Popular activities include water sports and fishing (fish cleaning station on site). Wildlife includes black bears, mountain lions, coyotes, deer and elk. CG is busy weekends and holidays. Hike in nearby Mt. Jefferson Wilderness.

GETTING THERE: From Sisters go NW on state HWY 20 approx. 13 mi. to forest route 2070. Go W of 2070 approx. 1 mi. to Blue Bay CG.

SINGLE RATE:	$12	OPEN DATES:	Apr-Sept
# of SINGLE SITES:	25	MAX SPUR:	40 feet
		MAX STAY:	14 days
		ELEVATION:	3450 feet

7 — Boundary Springs
Crescent • lat 43˚23'09" lon 121˚37'37"

DESCRIPTION: The busiest time at this dispersed CG is during hunting season. There are small creeks nearby. Campers may gather firewood locally. Supplies at Crescent. There are no tables, garbage service, or drinking water at this CG. Visit the nearby Oregon Cascades Recreation Area and Diamond Peak Wilderness.

GETTING THERE: From Crescent go S on US HWY 97 approx. 2 mi. to forest route 9768 600. Go E on 9768 600 approx. 1 mi. to Boundary Springs CG.

SINGLE RATE:	No fee	OPEN DATES:	Apr-Nov*
# of SINGLE SITES:	4	MAX STAY:	14 days
		ELEVATION:	4500 feet

8 — Bull Bend
Bend • lat 43˚43'32" lon 121˚37'37"

DESCRIPTION: This CG is located on the Deschutes River among ponderosa pines. Enjoy trout fishing in river. Supplies at Lapine. This CG has moderate use. Gather firewood locally. Visit adjacent Pringle Falls Research Natural Area. Wildlife in this area includes mountain lions, black bears, coyotes, deer, and elk.

GETTING THERE: From Bend go S on US HWY 97 approx. 26.5 mi. to forest route 43 (Wickiup Jct). Go W on 43 approx. 8 mi. to forest route 4370. Go S on 4370 approx. 1.5 mi. to Bull Bend CG.

SINGLE RATE:	$5	OPEN DATES:	Apr-Oct
# of SINGLE SITES:	12	MAX SPUR:	40 feet
		MAX STAY:	14 days
		ELEVATION:	4300 feet

9 — Cabin Lake
Bend • lat 43˚29'41" lon 121˚03'26"

DESCRIPTION: This CG is located among sage and lodge pole pines in high desert plains. Hot summer days. Historic Fort Rock State Park is nearby. Supplies at Lapine or 50 mi. away. Small wildlife and bird watching in vicinity. Light use area, spring and fall are the best times to visit. Visit nearby South Ice Cave.

GETTING THERE: From Bend go S on US HWY 97 approx. 29.5 mi. to forest route 22. Go E on 22 approx. 26.5 mi to forest route 18. Go S on 18 approx. 6 mi. to Cabin Lake CG.

SINGLE RATE:	No fee	OPEN DATES:	Apr-Nov
# of SINGLE SITES:	14	MAX SPUR:	40 feet
		MAX STAY:	14 days
		ELEVATION:	4550 feet

10 — Camp Sherman
Sisters • lat 44˚27'50" lon 121˚38'17"

DESCRIPTION: This CG is situated in mixed conifer on the Metolius River. Enjoy fly fishing for trout but please check fishing regulations Wildlife includes black bears, mountain lions, coyotes, deer and elk. CG is busy weekends and holidays. This CG offers a picnic shelter. Supplies 1/2 mi. at Camp Sherman. No drinking water.

GETTING THERE: From Sisters go NW on state HWY 20 approx. 10 mi. to forest route 14. Go N on 14 approx. 6 mi. to forest route 1419. Go N on 1419 approx. 1/2 mi. to Camp Sherman CG.

SINGLE RATE:	$12	OPEN DATES:	Apr-Oct
# of SINGLE SITES:	15	MAX STAY:	14 days
		ELEVATION:	2950 feet

 Campground has hosts **Reservable sites** **Accessible facilities** **Fully developed** **Semi-developed** **Rustic facilities**

NOTE: Open dates listed are typical. Actual dates are dependent on conditions such as snow pack.

11 Candle Creek
Sisters • lat 44˚34'31" lon 121˚37'09"

DESCRIPTION: This CG rests in mixed conifer at the confluence of Candle Creek and Metolius River. There are excellent fly fishing opportunities in the river but please check fishing regs. Wildlife includes black bears, mountain lions, coyotes, deer and elk. Busy weekends and holidays. Hiking trails in the area. No drinking water.

GETTING THERE: From Sisters go NW on state HWY 20 approx. 12 mi. to forest route 12. Go N on 12 approx. 12 mi. to forest route 1200/980. Go E on 1200/980 approx. 1.5 mi. to Candle Creek CG.

SINGLE RATE:	No fee	OPEN DATES:	Apr-Oct
# of SINGLE SITES:	4		
		MAX STAY:	14 days
		ELEVATION:	2600 feet

16 Cold Springs
Sisters • lat 42˚50'25" lon 122˚08'40"

DESCRIPTION: This CG is located in mixed conifer on Trout Creek. There are excellent fly fishing opportunities in the area but please check fishing regs. Black bears, mountain lions, coyotes, deer and elk. CG is busy weekends and holidays. A hiking trail runs along CG leading to other area CGs. No drinking water.

GETTING THERE: From Sisters go W on state HWY 242 approx. 4 mi. to Cold Springs CG.

SINGLE RATE:	$10	OPEN DATES:	Apr-Sept
# of SINGLE SITES:	23		
		MAX STAY:	14 days
		ELEVATION:	3400 feet

12 Canyon Creek
Sisters • lat 44˚21'36" lon 120˚22'08"

DESCRIPTION: This CG is located in mixed conifer at the confluence of Canyon Creek and Metolius River. Enjoy fly fishing for trout in the river but please check fishing regs. Black bears, deer and elk. CG is busy weekends and holidays. A nearby hiking trail leads to Mt. Jefferson Wilderness. No drinking water.

GETTING THERE: From Sisters go NW on state HWY 20 10 mi. to forest route 14. Go N on 14 2.5 mi. to forest route 1419. Go N on 1419 2 mi. to forest route 1420. Continue N on 1420 3.5 mi. to Canyon Creek CG.

SINGLE RATE:	No fee	OPEN DATES:	Apr-Sept
# of SINGLE SITES:	4		
		MAX STAY:	14 days
		ELEVATION:	2900 feet

17 Contorta Point
Crescent • lat 43˚27'45" lon 122˚00'30"

DESCRIPTION: CG is located in park-like stand of pine with lake and mountain views. Good fishing on adjacent Crescent Lake. Supplies 10 mi. at Crescent Lake Junction. Wildlife includes bald eagles. Busy weekends and holidays. Gather firewood locally. Multi-use trails in area. No drinking water.

GETTING THERE: From Crescent go W on primary forest route 61 approx. 12.2 mi. to state HWY 58. Go N on 58 3.5 mi. to forest route 60. Go SW on 60 approx. 10 mi. to Contorta Point CG.

SINGLE RATE:	No fee	OPEN DATES:	May-Oct*
# of SINGLE SITES:	15		
		MAX STAY:	14 days
		ELEVATION:	4850 feet

13 Chief Paulina
Bend • lat 43˚42'22" lon 121˚15'14"

DESCRIPTION: Lodge pole pine setting along Deschutes River, within Newberry Nat'l Volcanic Monument. Boat fish East and Paulina Lakes for trout and kokanee, fish river for trout. Supplies at Lapine. Firewood sold or gathered. Horse, hike and mountain bike trails nearby, horse facilities. Visit adjacent Pringle Falls Research Natural Area.

GETTING THERE: From Bend go S on US HWY 97 approx. 23.5 mi. to forest route 21. Go E on 21 approx. 14 mi. to Chief Paulina CG.

SINGLE RATE:	$12	OPEN DATES:	May-Oct
# of SINGLE SITES:	14	MAX SPUR:	40 feet
		MAX STAY:	14 days
		ELEVATION:	6400 feet

18 Cow Meadow
Bend • lat 43˚49'00" lon 121˚45'00"

DESCRIPTION: This CG located on the shore of Crane Prairie Reservoir. There is a boat launch for smaller boats at CG. Supplies at Bend. Campers may gather firewood. Hot summer days. Wildlife in this area includes black bears, mountain lions, coyotes, deer, and elk. CG may be busy weekends and holidays.

GETTING THERE: From Bend go SW on state HWY 46 (Cascades Lakes HWY) approx. 44.7 mi. to primary forest route 40. Go E on 40 approx. .5 mi. to forest route 4000/970. Go S on 4000/970 approx. 2 mi. to Cow Meadow CG.

SINGLE RATE:	$5	OPEN DATES:	May-Oct
# of SINGLE SITES:	21	MAX SPUR:	30 feet
		MAX STAY:	14 days
		ELEVATION:	4550 feet

14 China Hat
Bend • lat 43˚39'30" lon 121˚02'09"

DESCRIPTION: This CG is situated in ponderosa and lodge pole pine. Supplies 65 mi. to Bend. Campers may gather firewood locally. CG is located near the East Fort Rock OHV trail system. CG is also located adjacent to China Hat Guard Station. Wildlife in this area includes bears, mountain lions, coyotes, and deer.

GETTING THERE: From Bend go S on US HWY 97 approx. 29.5 mi. to forest route 22. Go E on 22 approx. 26.5 mi. to forest route 18. Go N on 18 approx. 6 mi. to China Hat CG.

SINGLE RATE:	No fee	OPEN DATES:	Apr-Nov
# of SINGLE SITES:	14	MAX SPUR:	30 feet
		MAX STAY:	14 days
		ELEVATION:	5100 feet

19 Crane Prairie
Bend • lat 43˚47'53" lon 121˚45'27"

DESCRIPTION: This CG located on the shore of Crane Prairie Reservoir. There is a boat launch and fish cleaning station at the CG. Supplies at Bend. Campers may gather firewood. Hot summer days. Wildlife in this area includes black bears, mountain lions, coyotes, deer, and elk. CG may be busy weekends and holidays.

GETTING THERE: From Bend go S on US HWY 97 for 26.8 mi. to forest route 43 (Wickiup Jct.). Go W on 43 for 11 mi. to forest route 42. Go W on 42 for 5.4 mi. to forest route 4270. Go N on 4270 for 4.2 mi. to Crane Prairie CG.

SINGLE RATE:	Varies	OPEN DATES:	Apr-Oct
# of SINGLE SITES:	146	MAX SPUR:	30 feet
		MAX STAY:	14 days
		ELEVATION:	4450 feet

15 Cinder Hill
Bend • lat 43˚44'05" lon 121˚11'39"

DESCRIPTION: This CG is situated within Newberry National Volcanic Monument. Boat fish East Lake and Paulina Lake for trout and kokanee. Supplies at Lapine. Firewood sold by High Lakes or may be gathered. Horse, hike and mountain bike trails nearby. CG may be frequented by bears. Boat ramp on site.

GETTING THERE: From Bend go S on US HWY 97 for 23.5 mi. to forest route 21. Go E on 21 for 17.6 mi. to forest route 2100 700. Go N on 2100 700 for 1/2 mi. to Cinder Hill CG.

SINGLE RATE:	Varies	OPEN DATES:	May-Oct
# of SINGLE SITES:	110	MAX SPUR:	45 feet
		MAX STAY:	14 days
		ELEVATION:	6400 feet

20 Crescent Creek
Crescent • lat 43˚29'50" lon 121˚50'24"

DESCRIPTION: CG is located in ponderosa pine, willow, and aspen along Crescent Creek. Good whitefish and trout fishing in Crescent Creek but be sure to check fishing regulations. Supplies 9 mi. to Crescent. Busy during hunting season. Gather firewood locally.

GETTING THERE: From Crescent go W on county route 61 approx. 8.7 mi. to Crescent Creek CG.

SINGLE RATE:	$8	OPEN DATES:	Apr-Oct*
# of SINGLE SITES:	10	MAX SPUR:	40 feet
		MAX STAY:	14 days
		ELEVATION:	4500 feet

 Campground has hosts   Reservable sites   Accessible facilities   Fully developed   Semi-developed   Rustic facilities

NOTE: Open dates listed are typical. Actual dates are dependent on conditions such as snow pack.

21 Crescent Lake
Crescent • lat 43°30'04" lon 121°58'27"

DESCRIPTION: CG is located in pine, fir, willow, and ash with some undergrowth. Lake and mountain views. Good fishing on adjacent Crescent Lake. Supplies 3 mi. to town of Crescent. Various wildlife includes bald eagles. Busy holidays. Firewood on site. Hiking and horse trails lead to Diamond Peak Wilderness. Boat ramp.

GETTING THERE: From Crescent go W on county route 61 approx. 12 mi. to state HWY 58. Go N on 58 approx. 3.5 mi. to forest route 60. Go W on 60 approx. 2.5 mi. to Crescent Lake CG.

SINGLE RATE:	Varies	OPEN DATES:	May-Oct*
# of SINGLE SITES:	47	MAX SPUR:	55 feet
		MAX STAY:	14 days
		ELEVATION:	4850 feet

22 Cultus Corral
Bend • lat 43°49'20" lon 121°48'00"

DESCRIPTION: This CG is located near the Cultus River, Crane Prairie Reservoir, and Cultus Lake. Enjoy boating and fishing on Crane Prairie Reservoir. This CG offers horse stalls and access to hiking and horse trails. Wildlife in this area includes black bears, mountain lions, coyotes, deer, and elk.

GETTING THERE: From Bend go SW on state HWY 46 (Cascade Lakes HWY) approx. 44.7 mi. to forest route 4630. Go W on 4630 approx. .5 mi. to Cultus Corral CG.

SINGLE RATE:	$5	OPEN DATES:	May-Oct
# of SINGLE SITES:	11	MAX SPUR:	30 feet
		MAX STAY:	14 days
		ELEVATION:	4550 feet

23 Cultus Lake
Bend • lat 43°50'10" lon 121°49'57"

DESCRIPTION: This CG is located on the shore of Cultus Lake. This CG offers a boat ramp, fishing, hiking and wind surfing opportunities. Hot summer days. Wildlife in this area includes black bears, mountain lions, coyotes, deer, and elk. CG may be busy weekends and holidays. Supplies in Bend.

GETTING THERE: From Bend go SW on state HWY 46 (Cascade Lakes HWY) approx. 46 mi. to forest route 4635. Go W on 4635 approx. 2 mi. to Cultus Lake CG.

SINGLE RATE:	$10	OPEN DATES:	May-Sept
# of SINGLE SITES:	55	MAX SPUR:	30 feet
		MAX STAY:	14 days
		ELEVATION:	4700 feet

24 Cultus North Shore
Bend • lat 43°50'10" lon 121°49'57"

DESCRIPTION: This boat or hike-in CG is located on the shore of Cultus Lake. There is an amphitheater, hiking, and fishing nearby. Hot summer days. Wildlife in this area includes black bears, mountain lions, coyotes, deer, and elk. CG may be busy weekends and holidays. Supplies in Bend.

GETTING THERE: From Bend go SW on state HWY 46 (Cascade Lakes HWY) 46 mi. to forest route 4635. Go W on 4635 for 2 mi. to trailhead. Cultus North Shore CG is approx. 2 mi. hike-in, or boat across.

SINGLE RATE:	$5	OPEN DATES:	May-Sept
# of SINGLE SITES:	15		
		MAX STAY:	14 days
		ELEVATION:	4700 feet

25 Deschutes Bridge
Bend • lat 40°52'30" lon 121°46'30"

DESCRIPTION: This CG is situated on the Deschutes River. Popular activities include fishing and bird watching. Hot summer days. Supplies in Bend. Campers may gather firewood. Wildlife in this area includes black bears, mountain lions, coyotes, deer, and elk. There are hiking trails in the nearby Three Sisters Wilderness.

GETTING THERE: From Bend go SW on state HWY 46 (Cascade Lakes HWY) 41 mi. to Deschutes Bridge CG.

SINGLE RATE:	$5	OPEN DATES:	May-Oct
# of SINGLE SITES:	12	MAX SPUR:	30 feet
		MAX STAY:	14 days
		ELEVATION:	4650 feet

26 Devils Lake
Bend • lat 44°02'04" lon 121°45'51"

DESCRIPTION: This CG is situated on the shore of Devils Lake, walk-in tent only sites. There is a $3 parking fee. The CG trailhead leads into the adjacent Three Sisters Wilderness. Supplies in Bend. Hot summer days. Wildlife in this area includes black bears, mountain lions, coyotes, deer, and elk.

GETTING THERE: From Bend go W on state HWY 46 (Cascade Lakes HWY) 28.7 mi. to Devils Lake CG.

SINGLE RATE:	No fee	OPEN DATES:	June-Oct
# of SINGLE SITES:	9		
		MAX STAY:	14 days
		ELEVATION:	5450 feet

27 Driftwood
Sisters • lat 44°06'06" lon 121°37'56"

DESCRIPTION: This CG rests in mixed conifer on Three Creek Lake. Enjoy fishing for trout in the lake. Wildlife in the area includes black bears, mountain lions, coyotes, deer, and elk. CG is busy weekends and holidays. A nearby trail leads to Three Sisters Wilderness. No drinking water.

GETTING THERE: From Sisters go S on primary forest route 16 approx. 16.5 mi. to Driftwood CG.

SINGLE RATE:	$6	OPEN DATES:	July-Sept
# of SINGLE SITES:	17		
		MAX STAY:	14 days
		ELEVATION:	6600 feet

28 East Davis Lake
Crescent • lat 43°35'19" lon 121°51'07"

DESCRIPTION: CG is located in lodge pole pine with good screening undergrowth at many sites. Lake and mountain views. Good fly fishing on adjacent Odell Creek and Davis Lake. Supplies 16 mi. to Crescent. Various wildlife including bald eagles. Busy holidays. Firewood on site. Barrier free trail on site.

GETTING THERE: From Crescent go W on county route 61 approx. 9 mi. to state HWY 46. Go N on 46 approx. 8 mi. to forest route 4600 850. Go W on 4600 850 approx. 2.5 mi. to East Davis Lake CG.

SINGLE RATE:	$8	OPEN DATES:	Apr-Oct*
# of SINGLE SITES:	33	MAX SPUR:	60 feet
		MAX STAY:	14 days
		ELEVATION:	4400 feet

29 East Lake
Bend • lat 43°43'03" lon 121°12'37"

DESCRIPTION: This CG is situated within Newberry National Volcanic Monument. Visit the nearby obsidian flow. Boat fish East Lake and Paulina Lake for trout and kokanee. Supplies at Lapine. Firewood sold or may be gathered. Horse, hike and mountain bike trails nearby. CG may be frequented by bears.

GETTING THERE: From Bend go S on US HWY 97 approx. 23.5 mi. to forest route 21. Go E on 21 approx. 16.5 mi. to East Lake CG.

SINGLE RATE:	Varies	OPEN DATES:	May-Oct
# of SINGLE SITES:	29	MAX SPUR:	45 feet
		MAX STAY:	14 days
		ELEVATION:	6400 feet

30 Elk Lake
Bend • lat 43°58'44" lon 121°48'29"

DESCRIPTION: This CG is located on the shore of Elk Lake. There is a boat ramp on site. Fishing, swimming, hiking, and sailing are popular activities. Hot summer days. Supplies in Bend. Wildlife in this area includes black bears, mountain lions, coyotes, deer, and elk.

GETTING THERE: From Bend go SW on state HWY 46 (Cascade Lakes HWY) 33.1 mi. to the N end of Elk Lake and Elk Lake CG.

SINGLE RATE:	$10	OPEN DATES:	June-Sept
# of SINGLE SITES:	23	MAX SPUR:	30 feet
		MAX STAY:	14 days
		ELEVATION:	4900 feet

 Campground has hosts   **Reservable sites**   **Accessible facilities**   **Fully developed**   **Semi-developed**   **Rustic facilities**

NOTE: Open dates listed are typical. Actual dates are dependent on conditions such as snow pack.

31 Fall River
Bend • lat 43°46'22" lon 121°37'08"

DESCRIPTION: This CG is adjacent to the Fall River. Enjoy fly fishing on this river. The Pringle Falls Research Natural Area is nearby. Summer days are hot. Supplies at Bend. Wildlife in this area includes black bears, mountain lions, coyotes, deer, and elk.

GETTING THERE: From Bend go S on US HWY 97 17.3 mi. to forest route 42. Go SW on 42 12.2 mi. to Fall River CG

SINGLE RATE:	$5	OPEN DATES:	Apr-Oct
# of SINGLE SITES:	10	MAX SPUR:	30 feet
		MAX STAY:	14 days
		ELEVATION:	4300 feet

32 Gorge
Sisters • lat 44°48'40" lon 123°46'35"

DESCRIPTION: This CG rests in mixed conifer on the Metolius River. There are excellent fly fishing opportunities in river. Wildlife in the area includes black bears, mountain lions, coyotes, deer and elk. CG is busy weekends and holidays. Supplies available at Camp Sherman.

GETTING THERE: From Sisters go NW on state HWY 20 approx. 9.5 mi. to primary forest route 14. Go N on 14 approx. 6 mi. to forest route 1419. Go N on 1419 approx. 2 mi. to Gorge CG.

SINGLE RATE:	$12	OPEN DATES:	May-Sept
# of SINGLE SITES:	18		
		MAX STAY:	14 days
		ELEVATION:	2900 feet

33 Graham Corral
Sisters • lat 44°20'42" lon 121°38'29"

DESCRIPTION: This horse camp rests in mixed conifer and offers corrals. Excellent fly fishing opportunities in the area but please check fishing regulations Wildlife in the area includes black bears, mountain lions, coyotes, deer and elk. A hike/horse trail runs along the CG that leads to area lakes and CGs.

GETTING THERE: From Sisters go W on state HWY 242 approx. 4 mi. to forest route 1012. Go NW on 1012 approx. 5 mi. to forest route 300. Go NW on 300 approx. 1/2 mi. to Graham Corral CG.

SINGLE RATE:	$8	OPEN DATES:	May-Oct
# of SINGLE SITES:	13		
		MAX STAY:	14 days
		ELEVATION:	3400 feet

34 Gull Point
Bend • lat 43°42'17" lon 121°45'42"

DESCRIPTION: This CG is situated on the shore of Wickiup Reservoir. There is a RV dump station and boat ramp on site. Fishing is the popular activity here. Summer days are hot. Supplies at Bend. Wildlife in this area includes black bears, mountain lions, coyotes, deer, and elk.

GETTING THERE: From Bend go S on US HWY 97 approx. 27 mi. to forest route 43. Go W on 43 approx. 11 mi. to forest route 42. Go W on 42 approx. 5 mi. to forest route 4260. Go S on 4260 approx. 3 mi. to Gull Point CG.

SINGLE RATE:	Varies	OPEN DATES:	Apr-Oct
# of SINGLE SITES:	79	MAX SPUR:	30 feet
GROUP RATE:	Varies	MAX STAY:	14 days
# of GROUP SITES:	2	ELEVATION:	4350 feet

35 Hot Springs
Bend • lat 43°43'03" lon 121°11'59"

DESCRIPTION: This CG is in a lodge pole pine stand within Newberry National Volcanic Monument. Boat fish East and Paulina Lakes for trout and kokanee. Supplies at Lapine. Firewood may be gathered. Horse, hike and mountain bike trails nearby. CG may be frequented by bears. Enjoy excellent bird watching opportunities.

GETTING THERE: From Bend go S on US HWY 97 approx. 23.5 mi. to forest route 21. Go E on 21 approx. 17 mi. to Hot Springs CG.

SINGLE RATE:	$7	OPEN DATES:	July-Sept
# of SINGLE SITES:	52	MAX SPUR:	30 feet
		MAX STAY:	14 days
		ELEVATION:	6400 feet

36 Indian Ford
Sisters • lat 44°21'29" lon 121°36'35"

DESCRIPTION: This CG is situated in mixed conifer on Indian Ford. Excellent fly fishing opportunities in the area but please check fishing regulations Wildlife in this area includes black bears, mountain lions, coyotes, deer and elk. CG is busy weekends and holidays. A hiking trail runs along the CG and leads to area lakes and CGs.

GETTING THERE: From Sisters go NW approx. 5.5 mi. on state HWY 20 to Indian Ford CG.

SINGLE RATE:	$10	OPEN DATES:	May-Sept
# of SINGLE SITES:	25		
		MAX STAY:	14 days
		ELEVATION:	2700 feet

37 Irish and Taylor
Bend • lat 43°48'35" lon 121°57'30"

DESCRIPTION: This tent only CG is located near Irish Lake and Taylor Lake. The Pacific Crest Trail runs adjacent to this CG. Enjoy a hike to the many, small lakes in adjacent Three Sisters Wilderness. Wildlife in this area includes black bears, mountain lions, coyotes, elk, and deer. No drinking water. 4WD required.

GETTING THERE: From Bend go 46 mi. SW on state HWY 46 to forest route 4635. Go W on 4635 .5 mi to forest route 4630. Go S on 4630 1.5 mi. to forest route 4636. Go W on 4636 6.4 mi. to Irish and Taylor CG.

SINGLE RATE:	No fee	OPEN DATES:	June-Oct
# of SINGLE SITES:	6		
		MAX STAY:	14 days
		ELEVATION:	5550 feet

38 Jack Creek
Sisters • lat 44°29'13" lon 121°41'44"

DESCRIPTION: This CG is located in mixed conifer on Jack Creek. There are excellent fly fishing opportunities in the area but please check fishing regulations Wildlife in this area includes black bears, mountain lions, coyotes, deer and elk. CG is busy weekends and holidays. A nearby hiking trail leads to area lakes and CGs.

GETTING THERE: From Sisters go NW on state HWY 20 approx. 12.5 mi. to primary forest route 12. Go N on 12 approx. 4.5 mi. to forest route 1230. Go N on 1230 approx. 1/2 mi. to Jack Creek CG.

SINGLE RATE:	No fee	OPEN DATES:	Apr-Oct
# of SINGLE SITES:	11		
		MAX STAY:	14 days
		ELEVATION:	3100 feet

39 Jack Lake
Sisters • lat 44°29'31" lon 121°47'37"

DESCRIPTION: This tent only CG is located near Jack Lake and offers horse facilities. Excellent fishing opportunities in the area but please check fishing regs. Wildlife includes black bears, deer and elk. Busy weekends and holidays. An on site hiking/horse trail leads into Mt. Jefferson Wilderness. No drinking water.

GETTING THERE: From Sisters go NW on state HWY 20 12 mi. to forest route 12. Go N on 12 4.5 mi. to forest route 1230. Go N on 1230 1.5 mi. to forest route 1234. Go W on 1234 6 mi. to Jack Lake CG.

SINGLE RATE:	No fee	OPEN DATES:	May-Oct
# of SINGLE SITES:	2		
		MAX STAY:	14 days
		ELEVATION:	5150 feet

40 Lava Camp Lake
Sisters • lat 44°15'41" lon 121°47'04"

DESCRIPTION: This CG is located near McKenzie Pass which offers panoramic views from Mt. Hood to the Three Sisters. There are also impressive views of volcanic activity. An interpretive trail is on site. Wildlife in this area includes black bears, deer and elk. CG is busy weekends and holidays.

GETTING THERE: From Sisters go W on state HWY 242 approx. 14.5 mi. to Lava Camp Lake CG.

SINGLE RATE:	No fee	OPEN DATES:	May-Oct
# of SINGLE SITES:	10		
		MAX STAY:	14 days
		ELEVATION:	5300 feet

 Campground has hosts   **Reservable sites**   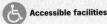 **Accessible facilities**   **Fully developed**   **Semi-developed**   **Rustic facilities**

NOTE: Open dates listed are typical. Actual dates are dependent on conditions such as snow pack.

41 Lava Flow
Crescent • lat 43°37'23" lon 121°49'11"

DESCRIPTION: CG is in park-like stand of ponderosa pine with lake and lava formation views. Fly fishing on adjacent Davis Lake. Supplies 17 mi. to Crescent. Various wildlife including bald eagles and waterfowl. Gather firewood locally. No water.

GETTING THERE: From Crescent go W on county route 61 approx. 9 mi. to state HWY 46. Go N on 46 approx. 8 mi. to forest route 4600/850. Go N on 4600/850 approx. 2 mi. to Lava Flow CG.

SINGLE RATE:	No fee	OPEN DATES:	Sept-Dec
# of SINGLE SITES:	12		
		MAX STAY:	14 days
		ELEVATION:	4200 feet

46 Little Fawn
Bend • lat 43°57'49" lon 121°47'47"

DESCRIPTION: This CG is located on the shore of Elk Lake. There is a boat ramp on site. Fishing, swimming, hiking, sailing, and wind surfing are popular activities. Hot summer days. Wildlife in this area includes black bears, mountain lions, coyotes, deer, and elk. Groups of up to 60 persons.

GETTING THERE: From Bend go SW on state HWY 46 (Cascade Lakes HWY) approx. 35.5 mi. to forest route 4625. Go E on 4625 approx. 1.5 mi. to Little Fawn CG.

SINGLE RATE:	$8	OPEN DATES:	June-Sept
# of SINGLE SITES:	20	MAX SPUR:	55 feet
GROUP RATE:	$70	MAX STAY:	14 days
# of GROUP SITES:	12	ELEVATION:	4900 feet

42 Lava Lake
Bend • lat 43°54'53" lon 121°45'57"

DESCRIPTION: This CG is situated on the shore of Lava Lake. There is a boat launch and fish cleaning station on site. Fishing and hiking are popular activities. This CG's trailhead leads to the adjacent Three Sisters Wilderness. Wildlife in this area includes black bears, mountain lions, coyotes, deer, and elk.

GETTING THERE: From Bend go SW on state HWY 46 approx. 38.5 mi. to forest route 4600/500. Go E on 4600/500 approx. 1 mi. to Lava Lake CG.

SINGLE RATE:	$10	OPEN DATES:	Apr-Oct
# of SINGLE SITES:	43	MAX SPUR:	30 feet
		MAX STAY:	14 days
		ELEVATION:	4750 feet

47 Little Lava Lake
Bend • lat 43°54'37" lon 121°45'38"

DESCRIPTION: This CG is situated on the shore of Little Lava Lake. There is a boat launch on site. Fishing and hiking are popular activities. This CG's trailhead leads to the adjacent Three Sisters Wilderness. Wildlife in this area includes black bears, mountain lions, coyotes, deer, and elk.

GETTING THERE: From Bend go SW on state HWY 46 approx. 38.5 mi. to forest route 4600/500. Go E on 4600/500 approx. .5 mi. to forest route 4600/520. Go E on 4600/520 approx. 1/2 mi. to Little Lava Lake CG.

SINGLE RATE:	$5	OPEN DATES:	Apr-Oct
# of SINGLE SITES:	10	MAX SPUR:	30 feet
		MAX STAY:	14 days
		ELEVATION:	4750 feet

43 Link Creek
Sisters • lat 44°25'00" lon 121°45'15"

DESCRIPTION: This CG is in a mixed pine and fir forest setting on Suttle Lake. Enjoy fishing for trout and swimming in the lake. Boat ramp and fish cleaning station located on the lake. Supplies available at Sisters. Deer, birds and squirrels are common to the area. Campers may gather firewood.

GETTING THERE: From Sisters go NW on state HWY 20 approx. 13 mi. to forest route 2070. Go W on 2070 approx. 2.5 mi. to Link Creek CG.

SINGLE RATE:	Varies	OPEN DATES:	Apr-Sept
# of SINGLE SITES:	33	MAX SPUR:	60 feet
		MAX STAY:	14 days
		ELEVATION:	3450 feet

48 Lower Bridge
Sisters • lat 44°33'25" lon 121°37'12"

DESCRIPTION: This CG is located in mixed conifer on the Metolius River. There are excellent fly fishing opportunities in the river but please check fishing regulations Supplies available at Camp Sherman. Wildlife in this area includes black bears, mountain lions, coyotes, deer and elk. CG is busy weekends and holidays.

GETTING THERE: From Sisters go NW on state HWY 20 approx. 9.5 mi. to primary forest route 14. Go N on 14 approx. approx. 13.5 mi. to Lower Bridge CG.

SINGLE RATE:	$10	OPEN DATES:	Apr-Oct
# of SINGLE SITES:	12		
		MAX STAY:	14 days
		ELEVATION:	2700 feet

44 Little Crater
Bend • lat 43°42'46" lon 121°14'31"

DESCRIPTION: This CG rests within Newberry National Volcanic Monument. Boat fish East and Paulina Lakes for trout and kokanee. Supplies at Lapine. Firewood sold or may be gathered. Horse, hike and mountain bike trails nearby. CG may be frequented by bears.

GETTING THERE: From Bend go S on US HWY 97 approx. 23.5 mi. to forest route 21. Go E on 21 approx. 14.5 mi. to forest route 2100/570. Go N on 2100/570 approx. .5 mi. to Little Crater CG.

SINGLE RATE:	$14	OPEN DATES:	May-Oct
# of SINGLE SITES:	50	MAX SPUR:	40 feet
		MAX STAY:	14 days
		ELEVATION:	6350 feet

49 Lower Canyon Creek
Sisters • lat 44°30'00" lon 121°30'00"

DESCRIPTION: This tent only CG is located in mixed conifer on the Metolius River. There are excellent fly fishing opportunities in the river but please check fishing regulations Wildlife in this area includes black bears, mountain lions, coyotes, deer and elk. CG is busy weekends and holidays. No drinking water.

GETTING THERE: From Sisters go NW 9.5 mi. on state HWY 20 to forest route 14. Go N 3 mi. on 14 to forest route 1419. Go N 2.5 mi. on 1419 to 1420. Go N 3 mi. on 1420 to forest route 400. Go E 1/2 mi. on 400 to Lower Canyon Creek CG.

SINGLE RATE:	No fee	OPEN DATES:	Yearlong
# of SINGLE SITES:	5		
		MAX STAY:	14 days
		ELEVATION:	2000 feet

45 Little Cultus Lake
Bend • lat 43°48'03" lon 121°51'53"

DESCRIPTION: This CG is situated on the shore of Little Cultus Lake. There is a boat launch on site. Fishing and hiking are popular activities. Enjoy a hike in the nearby Three Sisters Wilderness. Wildlife in this area includes black bears, mountain lions, coyotes, deer, and elk.

GETTING THERE: From Bend go SW on state HWY 46 approx. 46 mi. to forest route 4635. Go W on 4635 approx. .5 mi. to forest route 4630. Go S on 4630 approx. 1.5 mi. to forest route 4636. Go W on 4636 approx. 1 mi. to Little Cultus Lake CG.

SINGLE RATE:	$5	OPEN DATES:	May-Oct
# of SINGLE SITES:	10	MAX SPUR:	30 feet
		MAX STAY:	14 days
		ELEVATION:	4800 feet

50 Mallard Marsh
Bend • lat 43°57'49" lon 121°46'54"

DESCRIPTION: This CG is located on the shore of Hosmer Lake. Fly fishing and hiking are popular activities. Hot summer days. Supplies in Bend. Wildlife in this area includes black bears, mountain lions, coyotes, deer, and elk. Enjoy a hike in the nearby Three Sisters Wilderness.

GETTING THERE: From Bend go SW on state HWY 46 (Cascade Lakes HWY) approx. 35.5 mi. to forest route 4625. Go E on 4625 approx. 1.3 mi. to Mallard Marsh CG.

SINGLE RATE:	$5	OPEN DATES:	May-Oct
# of SINGLE SITES:	15	MAX SPUR:	30 feet
		MAX STAY:	14 days
		ELEVATION:	5000 feet

 Campground has hosts **Reservable sites** **Accessible facilities** **Fully developed** **Semi-developed** **Rustic facilities**

NOTE: Open dates listed are typical. Actual dates are dependent on conditions such as snow pack.

51 McKay Crossing
Bend • lat 43°43'00" lon 121°22'40"

DESCRIPTION: This CG is located among pine in the Newberry National Volcanic Monument. Paulina Creek runs adjacent to the CG. Supplies at Lapine. Firewood sold by High Lakes or may be gathered locally. Horse, hike and mountain bike uphill on nearby Peter Skene Ogden Trail which runs along the Creek.

GETTING THERE: From Bend go S on US HWY 97 approx. 23.5 mi. to forest route 21. Go E on 21 approx. 3.5 mi. to forest route 2120. Go E on 2120 approx. 2.5 mi. to McKay Crossing CG.

SINGLE RATE:	$5	OPEN DATES:	Apr-Sept
# of SINGLE SITES:	10	MAX SPUR:	30 feet
		MAX STAY:	14 days
		ELEVATION:	4750 feet

52 Monty
Sisters • lat 44°37'32" lon 121°28'55"

DESCRIPTION: This CG is located in mixed conifer on the Metolius River. There are excellent fly fishing opportunities in the river but please check fishing regulations Wildlife in this area includes black bears, mountain lions, coyotes, deer and elk. CG is busy weekends and holidays. Visit nearby Lake Billy Chinook. No drinking water.

GETTING THERE: From Sisters go NW on state HWY 20 approx. 5.5 mi. to forest route 11. Go N on 11 approx. 21 mi. to forest route 1170. Go E on 1170 approx. 5 mi. to forest route 64. Go N on 64 approx. 7 mi. to Monty CG.

SINGLE RATE:	$6	OPEN DATES:	May-Sept
# of SINGLE SITES:	20		
		MAX STAY:	14 days
		ELEVATION:	2000 feet

53 Newberry Group
Bend • lat 43°42'22" lon 121°15'26"

DESCRIPTION: This CG rests within Newberry National Volcanic Monument, among fir and lodge pole pine on Paulina Lake. Boat ramp to fish trout and kokanee on lake. Supplies at resort 2 mi. Firewood sold or may be gathered. Horse, hike and bike trails are nearby. CG may be frequented by bears.

GETTING THERE: From Bend go S on US HWY 97 approx. 23.5 mi. to forest route 21. Go E on 21 approx. 14 mi. to Newberry Group CG.

SINGLE RATE:	Varies	OPEN DATES:	June-Sept
# of SINGLE SITES:	3	MAX SPUR:	40 feet
GROUP RATE:	Varies	MAX STAY:	14 days
# of GROUP SITES:	3	ELEVATION:	6350 feet

54 North Davis Creek
Bend • lat 43°40'35" lon 121°49'17"

DESCRIPTION: This CG is located on Wickiup Reservoir among lodge pole pine. There is a boat ramp to fish reservoir for trout and kokanee. Supplies at resort 10 mi. away. Summer days are hot. Gather firewood locally. Wildlife in this area includes black bears, mountain lions, coyotes, deer and elk.

GETTING THERE: From Bend go SW on state HWY 46 (Cascade Lakes HWY) approx. 56.2 mi. to North Davis Creek CG.

SINGLE RATE:	$8	OPEN DATES:	Apr-Sept
# of SINGLE SITES:	17	MAX SPUR:	30 feet
		MAX STAY:	14 days
		ELEVATION:	4350 feet

55 North Twin
Bend • lat 43°43'58" lon 121°45'50"

DESCRIPTION: This CG is situated on the shore of North Twin Lake among pine stands. Fish from bank or boat for trout. Supplies 2 mi. at resort or 10 mi. at Lapine. Moderate use in summer. Campers may gather firewood locally. Hiking and mountain biking trails nearby. Wildlife includes black bears, mountain lions, deer and elk.

GETTING THERE: From Bend go S on US HWY 97 for 26.5 mi. to primary forest route 43. Go W on 43 approx. 11 mi. to forest route 42. Go W on 42 approx. 4.5 mi. to forest route 4260. Go S on 4260 approx. 1/2 mi. to North Twin CG.

SINGLE RATE:	$5	OPEN DATES:	Apr-Oct
# of SINGLE SITES:	10	MAX SPUR:	40 feet
		MAX STAY:	14 days
		ELEVATION:	4350 feet

56 Odell Creek
Crescent • lat 43°33'04" lon 121°57'41"

DESCRIPTION: CG is located in large trees with screening undergrowth. Lake and mountain views. Can be windy due to Odell Lake frontage (good fishing). Supplies 3 mi. to Crescent. Bald eagles. Busy holidays. Gather firewood locally. Horse and hiking trails lead to Diamond Peak Wilderness. Interpretive hike on site.

GETTING THERE: From Crescent go W on county route 61 approx. 12 mi. to state HWY 58. Go N on 58 approx. 5.5 mi. to Odell Creek CG.

SINGLE RATE:	$5	OPEN DATES:	Apr-Oct*
# of SINGLE SITES:	22	MAX SPUR:	30 feet
		MAX STAY:	14 days
		ELEVATION:	4800 feet

57 Ogden Group
Bend • lat 43°43'39" lon 121°25'17"

DESCRIPTION: This CG is located among pine in the Newberry National Volcanic Monument. Paulina Creek runs adjacent to the CG. Supplies at Lapine. Firewood sold or may be gathered locally. Horse, hike and mountain bike uphill on nearby Peter Skene Ogden Trail which runs along the Creek.

GETTING THERE: From Bend go S on US HWY 97 approx. 23.5 mi. to primary forest route 21. Go E on 21 approx. 2.5 mi. to Ogden Group CG.

		MAX SPUR:	30 feet
		MAX STAY:	14 days
GROUP RATE:	$60	ELEVATION:	4300 feet
# of GROUP SITES:	3	OPEN DATES:	May-Oct

58 Paulina Lake
Bend • lat 43°42'43" lon 121°16'26"

DESCRIPTION: Among pine and fir on Paulina Lake where trout and kokanee may be fished. Located within historic Newberry Nat'l Volcanic Monument. Supplies at adjacent resort or 5 mi. Moderate use. Firewood sold or may be gathered. Horse, bike and hike trails nearby. CG is frequented by deer and bears.

GETTING THERE: From Bend go S on US HWY 97 for 23.5 mi. to forest route 21. Go E on 21 for 12.9 mi. to Paulina Lake CG.

SINGLE RATE:	Varies	OPEN DATES:	May-Oct
# of SINGLE SITES:	69	MAX SPUR:	45 feet
		MAX STAY:	14 days
		ELEVATION:	6350 feet

59 Perry South
Sisters • lat 44°35'05" lon 121°27'20"

DESCRIPTION: This CG rests in mixed conifer on the Metolius Arm of Lake Billy Chinook. CG offers excellent fishing opportunities and a fish cleaning station. Please be sure to check fishing regs. Wildlife in this area includes black bears, mountain lions, coyotes, deer and elk. CG is busy weekends and holidays. No drinking water.

GETTING THERE: From Sisters go NW on state HWY 20 approx. 5.5 mi. to forest route 11. Go N on 11 approx. 21 mi. to forest route 1170. Go E on 1170 approx. 5 mi. to forest route 64. Go NW on 64 approx. 2.5 mi. to Perry South CG.

SINGLE RATE:	$12	OPEN DATES:	May-Sept
# of SINGLE SITES:	63		
		MAX STAY:	14 days
		ELEVATION:	2000 feet

60 Pine Mountain
Bend • lat 43°47'29" lon 120°56'37"

DESCRIPTION: This CG is located on Pine Mountain with beautiful views. There are a few small streams nearby. Enjoy a visit to the Pine Mountain Observatory, a University of Oregon Astronomical Observatory with three telescopes. Summer days are hot. Campers may gather firewood. Supplies in Bend.

GETTING THERE: From Bend go E on US HWY 20 for 25.1 mi. to forest route 2017. Go S on 2017 for 7.7 mi. to Pine Mountain CG (at top of mountain).

SINGLE RATE:	No fee	OPEN DATES:	Apr-Nov
# of SINGLE SITES:	3	MAX SPUR:	30 feet
		MAX STAY:	14 days
		ELEVATION:	6250 feet

 Campground has hosts   **Reservable sites**   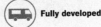 **Accessible facilities**   **Fully developed**   **Semi-developed**   **Rustic facilities**

NOTE: Open dates listed are typical. Actual dates are dependent on conditions such as snow pack.

61 Pine Rest
Sisters • lat 44°28'45" lon 121°38'07"

DESCRIPTION: This tent only CG rests in mixed conifer on the Metolius River. There are excellent fly fishing opportunities in the river but please check fishing regs. Wildlife in this area includes black bears, mountain lions, coyotes, deer and elk. CG is busy weekends and holidays. There is a covered picnic shelter on site.

GETTING THERE: From Sisters go NW on state HWY 20 approx. 6 mi. to forest route 14. On 14 go N approx. 1 mi. to forest route 1419. On 1419 go approx. .5 mi. to Pine Rest CG.

SINGLE RATE:	$12	OPEN DATES:	Apr-Oct
# of SINGLE SITES:	8		
		MAX STAY:	14 days
		ELEVATION:	2900 feet

66 Pringle Falls
Bend • lat 43°44'53" lon 121°36'07"

DESCRIPTION: This CG is located on the Deschutes River among ponderosa pines. Enjoy trout fishing in river. Supplies at Lapine. Gather firewood locally. Visit adjacent Pringle Falls Research Natural Area. Wildlife in this area includes mountain lions, black bears, coyotes, deer, and elk. No drinking water.

GETTING THERE: From Bend go S on US HWY 97 approx. 26.5 mi. to primary forest route 43. Go W on 43 approx. 7.5 mi. to forest route 4330/500. Go N on 4330/500 approx. 1 mi. to Pringle Falls CG.

SINGLE RATE:	$5	OPEN DATES:	Apr-Oct
# of SINGLE SITES:	6	MAX SPUR:	30 feet
		MAX STAY:	14 days
		ELEVATION:	4200 feet

 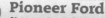

62 Pioneer Ford
Sisters • lat 44°33'10" lon 121°37'22"

DESCRIPTION: This CG is located in mixed conifer on the Metolius River. There are excellent fly fishing opportunities in the river but please check fishing regs. Wildlife in this area includes black bears, mountain lions, coyotes, deer and elk. CG is busy weekends and holidays. There is a picnic shelter on site.

GETTING THERE: From Sisters go NW on state HWY 20 approx. 9.6 mi. to forest route 14. Go N on 14 approx. 12.5 mi. to Pioneer Ford CG.

SINGLE RATE:	$12	OPEN DATES:	Apr-Oct
# of SINGLE SITES:	20		
		MAX STAY:	14 days
		ELEVATION:	2750 feet

67 Quinn Meadow Horse
Bend • lat 43°59'49" lon 121°47'08"

DESCRIPTION: This CG is located at the confluence of Quinn and Sink Creeks. The CG is surrounded by large meadows and trees and accesses the Three Sisters Wilderness. Enjoy the hiking and horse trail system there. Wildlife in this area includes black bears, coyotes, deer, and elk. There are horse stalls on site.

GETTING THERE: From Bend go SW on state HWY 46 (Cascade Lakes HWY) approx. 31.2 mi. to Quinn Meadow Horse Camp.

SINGLE RATE:	Varies	OPEN DATES:	June-Sept
# of SINGLE SITES:	24	MAX SPUR:	99 feet
		MAX STAY:	14 days
		ELEVATION:	5100 feet

63 Point
Bend • lat 43°58'00" lon 121°48'26"

DESCRIPTION: This CG is located on the shore of Elk Lake. There is a boat ramp on site. Fishing, swimming, hiking, and sailing are popular activities. Hot summer days. Supplies in Bend. Wildlife in this area includes black bears, mountain lions, coyotes, deer, and elk.

GETTING THERE: From Bend go SW on state HWY 46 (Cascade Lakes HWY) approx. 34 mi. to Point CG.

SINGLE RATE:	$10	OPEN DATES:	June-Oct
# of SINGLE SITES:	9	MAX SPUR:	30 feet
		MAX STAY:	14 days
		ELEVATION:	4900 feet

68 Quinn River
Bend • lat 43°47'07" lon 121°50'07"

DESCRIPTION: This CG located on the shore of Crane Prairie Reservoir. There is a boat launch at the CG. Supplies at Bend. Campers may gather firewood. Hot summer days. Wildlife in this area includes black bears, mountain lions, coyotes, deer, and elk. CG may be busy weekends and holidays. Hiking trails in area.

GETTING THERE: From Bend go SW on state HWY 46 (Cascade Lakes HWY) 48 mi. to Quinn River CG.

SINGLE RATE:	$9	OPEN DATES:	Apr-Sept
# of SINGLE SITES:	41	MAX SPUR:	30 feet
		MAX STAY:	14 days
		ELEVATION:	4450 feet

64 Prairie
Bend • lat 43°43'31" lon 121°25'23"

DESCRIPTION: This CG is located among pine in the Newberry National Volcanic Monument. Paulina Creek runs adjacent to the CG. Supplies at Lapine. Firewood sold or may be gathered locally. Horse, hike and mountain bike uphill on nearby Peter Skene Ogden Trail which runs along the creek.

GETTING THERE: From Bend go S on US HWY 97 approx. 23.5 mi. to primary forest route 21. Go E on 21 approx. 3 mi. to Prairie CG.

SINGLE RATE:	$10	OPEN DATES:	Apr-Oct
# of SINGLE SITES:	16	MAX SPUR:	30 feet
		MAX STAY:	14 days
		ELEVATION:	4300 feet

69 Reservoir
Bend • lat 43°40'20" lon 121°46'10"

DESCRIPTION: This CG is situated on the shore of Wickiup Reservoir. There is a boat ramp on site. Fishing is the popular activity here. Summer days are hot. Supplies at Bend. Wildlife in this area includes black bears, mountain lions, coyotes, deer, and elk.

GETTING THERE: From Bend go SW on state HWY 46 (Cascade Lakes HWY) approx. 57.5 mi. to forest route 44. Go E on 44 approx. 1.5 mi. to Reservoir CG.

SINGLE RATE:	$5	OPEN DATES:	Apr-Sept
# of SINGLE SITES:	28	MAX SPUR:	30 feet
		MAX STAY:	14 days
		ELEVATION:	4350 feet

65 Princess Creek
Crescent • lat 43°35'12" lon 122°00'34"

DESCRIPTION: CG is located in spruce, fire, and pine with screening undergrowth. Mountain and lake views. Good fishing on adjacent Odell Lake. Supplies 7 mi. to Crescent Lake Junction. Various wildlife including bald eagles. Busy holidays. Gather firewood locally. Lakeshore trail on site. Boat ramp.

GETTING THERE: From Crescent go W on county route 61 approx. 12 mi. to state HWY 58. Go W on 58 approx. 9 mi. to Princess Creek CG.

SINGLE RATE:	Varies	OPEN DATES:	May-Oct*
# of SINGLE SITES:	46	MAX SPUR:	45 feet
		MAX STAY:	14 days
		ELEVATION:	4800 feet

70 Riverside
Sisters • lat 44°26'00" lon 121°37'00"

DESCRIPTION: This walk-in tent only CG is in mixed conifer on the Metolius River. There are excellent fly fishing opportunities in the river but please check fishing regs. Wildlife in this area includes black bears, deer and elk. CG is busy weekends and holidays. Supplies 2 mi. at Camp Sherman. No drinking water.

GETTING THERE: From Sisters go NW on state HWY 20 approx. 9.6 mi. to forest route 14. Go N on 14 4.4 mi. to Riverside CG.

SINGLE RATE:	$8	OPEN DATES:	May-Sept
# of SINGLE SITES:	19		
		MAX STAY:	14 days
		ELEVATION:	3000 feet

 Campground has hosts   **Reservable sites**   **Accessible facilities**   **Fully developed**   **Semi-developed**   **Rustic facilities**

NOTE: Open dates listed are typical. Actual dates are dependent on conditions such as snow pack.

71 Rock Creek
Bend • lat 43°46'07" lon 121°49'59"

DESCRIPTION: This CG located on the shore of Crane Prairie Reservoir. There is a boat launch and fish cleaning station at the CG. Supplies at Bend. Campers may gather firewood. Hot summer days. Wildlife in this area includes black bears, mountain lions, coyotes, deer, and elk. CG may be busy weekends and holidays.

GETTING THERE: From Bend go SW on state HWY 46 (Cascade Lakes HWY) approx. 49.5 mi. to Rock Creek CG.

SINGLE RATE:	$10	OPEN DATES:	Apr-Oct
# of SINGLE SITES:	31	MAX SPUR:	30 feet
		MAX STAY:	14 days
		ELEVATION:	4450 feet

72 Rosland
Bend • lat 43°42'13" lon 121°30'05"

DESCRIPTION: This CG is located in an open area of pine, manzanita and grasses on Little Deschutes River. Trout fishing on the river. Deer and good bird watching. Rarely full, used by locals and as overflow site. Gather firewood locally. Mountain bike on roads, walk or hike fishing trails. Few ticks and bugs.

GETTING THERE: From Bend go S on US HWY 97 for 26.8 mi. to primary forest route 43 (at Wickiup Jct.). Go W on 43 for 1.5 mi. to Rosland CG.

SINGLE RATE:	$7	OPEN DATES:	Apr-Nov
# of SINGLE SITES:	11	MAX SPUR:	40 feet
		MAX STAY:	14 days
		ELEVATION:	4200 feet

73 Round Lake
Sisters • lat 44°25'00" lon 121°46'00"

DESCRIPTION: This CG is located in mixed conifer on Round Lake. There are excellent fishing opportunities in the area but please check fishing regs. Wildlife in this area includes black bears, deer and elk. CG is busy weekends and holidays. An on-site trail leads into the Mount Jefferson Wilderness. No drinking water.

GETTING THERE: From Sisters go NW on state HWY 20 for 12.4 mi. to forest route 12. Go N on 12 for 1 mi to forest route 1210. Go W on 1210 for 5.5 mi. to Round Lake CG.

SINGLE RATE:	Varies	OPEN DATES:	May-Oct
# of SINGLE SITES:	5	MAX SPUR:	15 feet
		MAX STAY:	14 days
		ELEVATION:	4300 feet

74 Sand Spring
Bend • lat 43°42'29" lon 120°50'48"

DESCRIPTION: This CG is near Sand Spring. Visit nearby Lavacicle Cave Geological Area. The cave is gated, please check with the Lava Land Visitor Center in Bend before entering the area. Enjoy a drive to nearby Pine Mountain Observatory. Wildlife includes black bears, coyotes, and deer. No drinking water.

GETTING THERE: From Bend go E on US HWY 20 approx. 21 mi. to primary forest route 23. Go SE on 23 approx. 18.8 mi. to Sand Spring CG.

SINGLE RATE:	No fee	OPEN DATES:	Apr-Nov
# of SINGLE SITES:	3	MAX SPUR:	30 feet
		MAX STAY:	14 days
		ELEVATION:	4950 feet

75 Scout Lake
Sisters • lat 44°24'40" lon 121°44'46"

DESCRIPTION: CG is in a mixed conifer setting on Scout Lake. Enjoy fishing for trout or swimming in the lake. Supplies 7 mi. at Camp Sherman. Wildlife in this area includes black bears, mountain lions, coyotes, deer and elk. CG is busy weekends and holidays. An on-site hiking trail leads to this area's scenic lakes.

GETTING THERE: From Sisters go NW on state HWY 20 13.2 mi. to forest route 2070. Go W on 2070 for 1.3 mi. to forest route 2066. Go S on 2066 approx. 0.8 mi. to Scout Lake CG.

SINGLE RATE:	Varies	OPEN DATES:	Apr-Sept
# of SINGLE SITES:	10	MAX SPUR:	40 feet
GROUP RATE:	Varies	MAX STAY:	14 days
# of GROUP SITES:	1	ELEVATION:	3700 feet

76 Sheep Bridge
Bend • lat 43°43'56" lon 121°47'09"

DESCRIPTION: This CG is situated between Crane Prairie and Wickiup Reservoirs on the Deschutes River. Enjoy fishing and boating on the reservoirs. Wildlife in this area includes black bears, mountain lions, coyotes, deer and elk. Summer days are hot. Campers may gather firewood. Supplies in Bend. Boat launch on site.

GETTING THERE: From Bend go S on US HWY 97 26.5 mi. to primary forest route 43. Go W on 43 11 mi. to forest route 42. Go W on 42 approx. 4.5 mi. to forest route 4260. Go S on 4260 .5 mi. to Sheep Bridge CG.

SINGLE RATE:	$5	OPEN DATES:	Apr-Oct
# of SINGLE SITES:	18	MAX SPUR:	30 feet
		MAX STAY:	14 days
		ELEVATION:	4350 feet

77 Sheep Spring
Sisters • lat 44°31'24" lon 121°41'55"

DESCRIPTION: This CG is located near Roaring Spring and is reservations only. CG offers 40 box stalls (4 per site), and creek water for livestock. Hike or horseback ride the Metolius-Windigo and Beaver Valley trails. Wildlife in this area includes black bears, coyotes, deer and elk. Supplies 7 mi. at Camp Sherman.

GETTING THERE: From Sisters go NW on state HWY 20 approx. 12 mi. to forest route 12. Go N on 12 approx. 7 mi. to forest route 1260. Go W on 1260 approx. 1 mi. to forest route 1260/200. Go N on 1260/200 approx. 1 mi. to Sheep Spring CG.

SINGLE RATE:	$10	OPEN DATES:	May-Oct
# of SINGLE SITES:	10		
		MAX STAY:	14 days
		ELEVATION:	3200 feet

78 Simax Group
Crescent • lat 43°29'13" lon 121°57'26"

DESCRIPTION: CG is in pine and fir with lake views. Good fishing on adjacent Crescent Lake. Supplies 4 mi. to Crescent Lake Junction. Various wildlife including bald eagles. Busy holidays. Gather firewood locally. Horse, hiking, and mountain biking trail along shoreline. Short walk to beach access.

GETTING THERE: From Crescent go W on county route 61 12 mi. to state HWY 58. Go N on 58 3.5 mi. to forest route 60. Go W on 60 2 mi. to forest route 6005. Go S on 6005 approx. 1 mi. to Simax Group CG.

		OPEN DATES:	May-Sept*
		MAX SPUR:	40 feet
GROUP RATE:	Varies	MAX STAY:	14 days
# of GROUP SITES:	3	ELEVATION:	4850 feet

79 Sisters Cow Camp
Sisters • lat 43°48'49" lon 121°46'31"

DESCRIPTION: This CG is situated in mixed conifer and offers corrals and water for horses. Excellent fly fishing opportunities in the area but please check fishing regs. Wildlife includes black bears, coyotes, deer and elk. Busy weekends and holidays. An on site hiking/horse trail leads to area lakes and CGs. No drinking water.

GETTING THERE: From Sisters go W on state HWY 242 1.2 mi. to forest route 15. Go SW on 15 approx. 3 mi. to forest route 100. Go SE on 100 1/8 mi. to Sisters Cow Camp CG.

SINGLE RATE:	No fee	OPEN DATES:	May-Oct
# of SINGLE SITES:	5		
		MAX STAY:	14 days
		ELEVATION:	3400 feet

80 Smiling River
Sisters • lat 44°28'30" lon 121°38'00"

DESCRIPTION: This CG is located in mixed conifer on the Metolius River. There are excellent fishing opportunities in the river but please check fishing regs. Wildlife in this area includes black bears, mountain lions, coyotes, deer and elk. CG is busy weekends and holidays. Supplies 1.5 mi. at Camp Sherman.

GETTING THERE: From Sisters go NW on state HWY 20 approx. 9.5 mi. to forest route 14. Go N on 14 approx. 6 mi. to forest route 1419. Go N on 1419 approx. 1 mi. to Smiling River CG.

SINGLE RATE:	$12	OPEN DATES:	May-Oct
# of SINGLE SITES:	38		
		MAX STAY:	14 days
		ELEVATION:	2900 feet

 Campground has hosts   **Reservable sites**   Accessible facilities   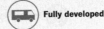 **Fully developed**   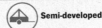 **Semi-developed**   **Rustic facilities**

NOTE: Open dates listed are typical. Actual dates are dependent on conditions such as snow pack.

81 Soda Creek
Bend • lat 44°01'33" lon 121°43'27"

DESCRIPTION: This CG is situated among pine and fir on Soda Creek. Enjoy beautiful views of the Three Sisters and Sparks Lake. Fly fish or canoe on Sparks Lake. Visit historic Elk Lake Visitor Center. Supplies at Lava Lakes 10 mi. away. Deer and birds frequent area. Gather firewood. Hike Three Sisters Wilderness.

GETTING THERE: From Bend go W on state HWY 46 (Cascade Lakes HWY) approx. 26.2 mi. to Soda Creek CG.

SINGLE RATE:	No fee	OPEN DATES:	June-Oct
# of SINGLE SITES:	10	MAX SPUR:	30 feet
		MAX STAY:	14 days
		ELEVATION:	5450 feet

82 South
Bend • lat 43°57'38" lon 121°47'13"

DESCRIPTION: This CG rests among a stand of lodge pole pine and fir on Hosmer Lake. There are majestic views of Mt. Bachelor. Fly fish for Atlantic Salmon and trout (no motors on lake). Supplies at resort 6 mi. away. Campers may gather firewood. Summer days are hot. This CG may be frequented by black bears.

GETTING THERE: From Bend go SW on state HWY 46 (Cascade Lakes HWY) 35.5 mi. to forest route 4625. Go E on 4625 for 1.2 mi. to South CG.

SINGLE RATE:	$5	OPEN DATES:	May-Oct
# of SINGLE SITES:	23	MAX SPUR:	30 feet
		MAX STAY:	14 days
		ELEVATION:	5000 feet

83 South Shore
Sisters • lat 44°25'00" lon 121°45'00"

DESCRIPTION: In a mixed forest setting on Suttle Lake. Fish for trout or swim in the lake. A boat ramp and fish cleaning station. Supplies available at Sisters. Deer, birds and squirrels are common in the area. Campers may gather firewood. Hiking trails in the area.

GETTING THERE: From Sisters go NW on US HWY 20 approx. 13 mi. to forest route 2070. Go W on 2070 approx. 1.5 mi. to South Shore CG.

SINGLE RATE:	$12	OPEN DATES:	Apr-Sept
# of SINGLE SITES:	39	MAX SPUR:	45 feet
		MAX STAY:	14 days
		ELEVATION:	3450 feet

84 South Twin
Bend • lat 43°44'05" lon 121°46'08"

DESCRIPTION: This CG is located on South Twin Lake near Wickiup Reservoir. There is a boat launch for small boats with no motors on site. Enjoy fishing in the lake and reservoir. Summer days are hot. Supplies at nearby resort or at Bend. Wildlife includes black bears, mountain lions, coyotes, deer, and elk.

GETTING THERE: From Bend go S on US HWY 97 26.5 mi. to primary forest route 43. Go W on 43 11 mi. to forest route 42. Go W on 42 4.5 mi. to forest route 4260. Go S on 4260 approx. 2 mi. to South Twin CG.

SINGLE RATE:	$12	OPEN DATES:	Apr-Oct
# of SINGLE SITES:	24	MAX SPUR:	30 feet
		MAX STAY:	14 days
		ELEVATION:	4350 feet

85 Spring
Crescent • lat 43°27'30" lon 122°01'00"

DESCRIPTION: CG is located in park-like grove of pine and aspen. Lake and mountain views. Good fishing on adjacent Crescent Lake. Supplies 10 mi. to Crescent Lake Jct. Bald eagles. Busy holidays. Firewood on site. Horse, hiking, and mountain biking trails in area. Boat ramp. Saturday night campfire talks.

GETTING THERE: From Crescent go W on county route 61 approx. 12 mi. to state HWY 58. Go N on 58 approx. 3.5 mi. to forest route 60. Go W on 60 approx. 8 mi. to Spring CG.

SINGLE RATE:	Varies	OPEN DATES:	May-Oct*
# of SINGLE SITES:	68	MAX SPUR:	50 feet
		MAX STAY:	14 days
		ELEVATION:	4850 feet

86 Summit Lake
Crescent • lat 43°27'47" lon 122°07'56"

DESCRIPTION: CG is located in pine/hemlock with lake views. Good fishing and canoeing on adjacent Summit Lake. Supplies 15 mi. to Crescent Lake Jct. Gather firewood. Numerous horse, hiking and mountain biking trails in area access recreation and wilderness areas. Bring mosquito repellent. Native boat launch. No water.

GETTING THERE: From Crescent go W on county route 61 12 mi. to state Hwy 58. Go N on 58 3.5 mi. to forest route 60. Go W on 60 7 mi. to forest route 6010. Go W on 6010 6.5 mi. to Summit Lake CG.

SINGLE RATE:	No fee	OPEN DATES:	July-Oct*
# of SINGLE SITES:	3	MAX STAY:	14 days
		ELEVATION:	5600 feet

87 Sunset Cove
Crescent • lat 43°33'45" lon 121°57'46"

DESCRIPTION: On Odell Lake, fully accessible boat ramp and jetty, fish cleaning station fishing, swimming, boating, wind surfing. Supplies in Crescent. Hiking nearby.

GETTING THERE: From Crescent go W on county route 61 approx. 12 mi. to state HWY 58. Go NW on 58 approx. 6 mi. to Sunset Cove CG.

SINGLE RATE:	$10	OPEN DATES:	May-Oct*
# of SINGLE SITES:	21	MAX SPUR:	50 feet
		MAX STAY:	14 days
		ELEVATION:	4800 feet

88 Swamp Wells
Bend • lat 43°51'30" lon 121°13'30"

DESCRIPTION: This CG is located on Swamp Wells Butte. Supplies in Bend. Firewood may be gathered locally. Horse, hike and mountain bike on the Swamp Wells Trails which start here. Enjoy a visit to the nearby Arnold, Wind, Skeleton, and Boyd Caves. No drinking water. Wildlife in this area includes bears, mountain lions, and deer.

GETTING THERE: From Bend go S on US HWY 97 for 4 mi. to forest route 18. Go SE on 18 for 5.4 mi. to forest route 1810. Go S on 1810 for 5.8 mi. to forest route 1816. Go SE on 1816 for 3 mi. to Swamp Wells CG.

SINGLE RATE:	No fee	OPEN DATES:	Apr-Nov
# of SINGLE SITES:	6	MAX SPUR:	30 feet
		MAX STAY:	14 days
		ELEVATION:	5400 feet

89 Three Creek Lake
Sisters • lat 44°05'45" lon 121°37'25"

DESCRIPTION: This CG is located in mixed conifer on Three Creek Lake. There are excellent fishing opportunities in the area but please check fishing regs. Wildlife in this area includes black bears, deer and elk. CG is busy weekends and holidays. An on-site trail leads to the Three Sisters Wilderness. No drinking water.

GETTING THERE: From Sisters go S on forest route 16 approx. 17 mi. to Three Creek Lake CG.

SINGLE RATE:	$6	OPEN DATES:	July-Sept
# of SINGLE SITES:	10	MAX STAY:	14 days
		ELEVATION:	6600 feet

90 Three Creek Meadow
Sisters • lat 44°06'55" lon 121°37'25"

DESCRIPTION: This CG is located in mixed conifer north of Three Creek Lake. The meadow is a very sensitive area with no camping allowed. This CG offers 36 box stalls for stock animals. Hike or horseback ride to adjacent Three Sisters Wilderness. Please use water trough for stock. No drinking water.

GETTING THERE: From Sisters go S on forest route 16 approx. 15 mi. to Three Creek Meadow CG.

SINGLE RATE:	$6	OPEN DATES:	June-Sept
# of SINGLE SITES:	11	MAX STAY:	14 days
		ELEVATION:	6350 feet

 Campground has hosts   **Reservable sites**   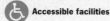 **Accessible facilities**   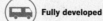 **Fully developed**   **Semi-developed**   **Rustic facilities**

NOTE: Open dates listed are typical. Actual dates are dependent on conditions such as snow pack.

91 Todd Lake
Bend • lat 44°01'45" lon 121°41'15"

DESCRIPTION: This walk-in only CG requires a 1/2 mi. hike to access sites. There is a $3/day vehicle parking pass required. A nearby trail leads into the Three Sisters Wilderness and to Soda Creek. Summer days are hot. Supplies in Bend. Wildlife in this area includes black bears, mountain lions, coyotes, deer, and elk.

GETTING THERE: From Bend go W on state HWY 46 (Cascade Lakes HWY) approx. 24 mi. to forest route 4600/370. Go N on 4600/370 for 1/2 mi. to Todd Lake CG.

SINGLE RATE:	No fee	OPEN DATES:	July-Oct
# of SINGLE SITES:	11	MAX SPUR:	30 feet
		MAX STAY:	14 days
		ELEVATION:	6200 feet

92 Trapper Creek
Crescent • lat 43°34'48" lon 122°02'40"

DESCRIPTION: CG is in spruce, hemlock and pine with dense undergrowth of huckleberries which may attract bears in fall. Views of Odell Lake. Good boat fishing on Odell Lake. Basic supplies on site. Bald eagles. Busy holidays and weekends. Horse and hiking trails lead to wilderness area.

GETTING THERE: From Crescent go W on county route 61 approx. 12 mi. to state HWY 58. Go NW on 58 approx. 10.5 mi. to forest route 5810. Go S on 5810 approx. 2 mi. to Trapper Creek CG.

SINGLE RATE:	Varies	OPEN DATES:	June-Oct*
# of SINGLE SITES:	32	MAX SPUR:	45 feet
		MAX STAY:	14 days
		ELEVATION:	4800 feet

93 West Cultus Lake
Bend • lat 43°50'20" lon 121°53'20"

DESCRIPTION: This tent camping only CG requires a $5/day parking pass. The CG is located on the shore of Cultus Lake. This CG offers, fishing, water skiing, hiking and wind surfing opportunities. Hot summer days. Black bears, mountain lions, coyotes, deer, and elk in area. CG may be busy weekends and holidays.

GETTING THERE: From Bend go SW on state HWY 46 approx. 46 mi. to forest route 4635. Go W on 4635 approx. 2 mi. to trailhead. West Cultus Lake CG is accessible by boat or hike-in approx. 4 mi. only.

SINGLE RATE:	No fee	OPEN DATES:	May-Sept
# of SINGLE SITES:	12		
		MAX STAY:	14 days
		ELEVATION:	4700 feet

94 West Davis Lake
Crescent • lat 43°35'34" lon 121°51'15"

DESCRIPTION: CG is located in lodge pole pine with some screening undergrowth and some grassy areas. Lake, creek, and mountain views. Fly fishing only on adjacent Davis Lake and Odell creek. Supplies 17 mi. to Crescent. Bald eagles. Gather firewood locally. Barrier free trail on site. Native boat launch.

GETTING THERE: From Crescent go W on county route 61 9 mi. to state HWY 46. Go N on 46 4 mi to forest route 4660. Go W on 4660 approx. 3 mi. to forest route 4669. Go N on 4669 2 mi. to West Davis Lake CG.

SINGLE RATE:	$8	OPEN DATES:	Apr-Oct*
# of SINGLE SITES:	25	MAX SPUR:	60 feet
		MAX STAY:	14 days
		ELEVATION:	4400 feet

95 West South Twin
Bend • lat 45°04'45" lon 117°03'14"

DESCRIPTION: This CG is located on the shore of Wickiup Reservoir. There is a boat launch on site. Enjoy fishing and boating in the reservoir. Supplies at nearby resort or in Bend. Summer days are hot. Wildlife in this area includes black bears, mountain lions, coyotes, deer, and elk.

GETTING THERE: From Bend go S on US HWY 97 26.5 mi. to primary forest route 43. Go W on 43 11 mi. to forest route 42. Go W on 42 4.5 mi. to forest route 4260. Go S on 4260 approx. 2 mi. to West South Twin CG.

SINGLE RATE:	$10	OPEN DATES:	Apr-Oct
# of SINGLE SITES:	24	MAX SPUR:	30 feet
		MAX STAY:	14 days
		ELEVATION:	4350 feet

96 Whispering Pine
Sisters • lat 44°06'55" lon 121°37'25"

DESCRIPTION: This CG is located in mixed conifer on Trout Creek. CG offers 36 box stalls (4 per site). Wildlife in the area include black bears, mountain lions, coyotes, deer and elk. Enjoy a hike or horseback ride in the nearby Three Sisters Wilderness. No drinking water.

GETTING THERE: From Sisters go W on state HWY 242 approx. 6 mi. to forest route 1018. Go S on 1018 approx. 4 mi. to Whispering Pine CG.

SINGLE RATE:	$8	OPEN DATES:	May-Oct
# of SINGLE SITES:	9		
		MAX STAY:	14 days
		ELEVATION:	4400 feet

97   Whitefish
Crescent • lat 43°28'20" lon 122°01'50"

DESCRIPTION: CG is designated for horse camping only with horse facilities on site. Campers are required to clean up and bag all animal waste. CG is located in dense pine grove with Whitefish Creek and Crescent Lake nearby. Busy holidays. Gather firewood locally. Horse/hiking trails on site access wilderness area.

GETTING THERE: From Crescent go W on county route 61 approx. 12 mi. to state HWY 58. Go N on 58 approx. 3.5 mi. to forest route 60. Go W on 60 approx. 7 mi. to Whitefish CG.

SINGLE RATE:	Varies	OPEN DATES:	May-Oct*
# of SINGLE SITES:	17	MAX SPUR:	65 feet
		MAX STAY:	14 days
		ELEVATION:	4850 feet

98 Wickiup Butte
Bend • lat 43°40'24" lon 121°41'03"

DESCRIPTION: This CG is situated on the shore of Wickiup Reservoir. Fishing is the popular activity here. Summer days are hot. Supplies at Bend. Wildlife in this area includes black bears, mountain lions, coyotes, deer, and elk.

GETTING THERE: From Bend go S on US HWY 97 26.5 mi. to primary forest route 43. Go W on 43 10.5 mi. to forest route 4380. Go S on 4380 3.5 mi. to forest route 4260. Go E on 4260 3 mi. to Wickiup Butte CG.

SINGLE RATE:	$5	OPEN DATES:	Apr-Sept
# of SINGLE SITES:	8	MAX SPUR:	30 feet
		MAX STAY:	14 days
		ELEVATION:	4350 feet

99 Windy
Crescent • lat 43°03'39" lon 122°58'05"

DESCRIPTION: CG is located in a stand of lodge pole pine with lake views. Good boat fishing in adjacent Crescent Lake. Supplies 7 mi. to Crescent Lake Junction. Bald eagles. Gather firewood locally. Horse and hiking trails in area. No water or permanent toilet. Campers must provide one toilet for every group of 20.

GETTING THERE: From Crescent go W on county route 61 approx. 12 mi. to state HWY 58. Go N on 58 approx. 3.5 mi. to FS 60. Go W on 60 approx. 7.5 mi. to Windy CG.

		OPEN DATES:	May-Oct*
GROUP RATE:	Varies	MAX STAY:	14 days
# of GROUP SITES:	1	ELEVATION:	4850 feet

100 Wyeth
Bend • lat 45°41'20" lon 121°46'12"

DESCRIPTION: This CG is located on the Deschutes River in ponderosa pines. Enjoy trout fishing. Supplies at Lapine. Horse facilities on site. Gather firewood locally. Visit adjacent Pringle Falls Natural Area. Wildlife includes mountain lions, black bears, coyotes, deer, and elk. Horse facilities.

GETTING THERE: From Bend go S on US HWY 97 approx. 26.5 mi. to primary forest route 43. Go W on 43 approx. 8 mi. to forest route 4370. Go S on 4370 approx. .5 mi. to Wyeth CG.

SINGLE RATE:	$5	OPEN DATES:	Apr-Oct
# of SINGLE SITES:	3	MAX SPUR:	30 feet
		MAX STAY:	14 days
		ELEVATION:	4250 feet

 Campground has hosts   **Reservable sites**   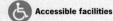 **Accessible facilities**    **Fully developed**   **Semi-developed**   **Rustic facilities**

NOTE: Open dates listed are typical. Actual dates are dependent on conditions such as snow pack.

USFS Photo

FREMONT NATIONAL FOREST

The Fremont National Forest was named for Captain John C. Fremont, an early explorer who traveled through this area in 1843 with Kit Carsen. The forest includes over a million acres of land located in south-central Oregon east of the Cascade Mountains.

Popular activities include fishing, hunting, backpacking, cross-country and downhill skiing, camping, and leisure driving. The Chewaucan, Sycan, and Sprague rivers are the forest's major rivers and many small lakes and reservoirs are popular fishing and camping areas.

Game animals most often hunted include mule deer, Rocky Mountain elk, and pronghorn antelope. Several varieties of trout inhabit forest lakes and streams, and a few lakes also support warm-water fish, such as largemouth bass. The forest also supports small populations of black bears, mountain lions, and bobcats.

The Gearhart Mountain Wilderness, totaling 22,823 acres, is the forest's only wilderness. Its dominant feature is Gearhart Mountain which is 8,380 feet at the summit. On a clear day visitors can see the distant Steens Mountain to the east, and to the west, the Cascade peaks, from Mt. Lassen in California north to the Three Sisters.

FREMONT NATIONAL FOREST • OREGON • LOCATOR MAP

Fremont National Forest • (541) 974-2151

1. Alder Springs
Silver Lake • lat 42°57'30" lon 121°08'30"

DESCRIPTION: Rustic camping with forest views. No drinking water. Historic tiered water troughs, made from dug out logs in area. Campers may gather firewood. Deer and small wildlife in area. Pack it in/pack it out. No nearby trailheads. Check with district office for fire restrictions.

GETTING THERE: From Silver Lake go S on county route 4-11 approx. 5.5 mi. to primary forest route 27. Go S on 27 approx. 8.5 mi. to forest route 021. Go W on 021 approx. 1.5 mi. to Alder Springs CG.

SINGLE RATE:	No fee	OPEN DATES:	June-Nov
# of SINGLE SITES	3	MAX SPUR:	18 feet
		MAX STAY:	14 days
		ELEVATION:	5020 feet

2. Antler
Silver Lake • lat 42°57'30" lon 121°14'00"

DESCRIPTION: A semi-primitive, secluded setting with spectacular views of Three Sisters, Mounts Thielson, Shasta and Bachelor. Gather firewood. Multiple horse/hike trails in the area. Corrals and hitch rails. mountain bike trails/roads nearby. No drinking water Nov-May. Pack it in/pack it out. Check with district office for fire restrictions.

GETTING THERE: From Silver Lake go S on route 4-11 5.5 mi. to forest route(fr) 27. Go S on 27 6 mi. to fr 041. Go SW on 041 4 mi. to fr 3038. Go NW on 3038 1 mi. to fr 035. Go W on 035 1 mi. to fr 036. Go W on 036 1.5 mi. to Antler CG.

SINGLE RATE:	No fee	OPEN DATES:	May-Nov
# of SINGLE SITES	5	MAX SPUR:	28 feet
		MAX STAY:	14 days
		ELEVATION:	6400 feet

3. Bunyard Crossing
Silver Creek • lat 43°03'30" lon 121°04'30"

DESCRIPTION: Rustic sites near Silver Creek. Fish for trout in creek. No drinking water. Good bird watching and wildlife viewing. Gather firewood. Hiking trails close to CG. Check at district office for fire restrictions.

GETTING THERE: From Silver Lake go S on primary forest route 28 approx. 6 mi. to forest route 2917. Go W on 2917 approx. 1.5 mi. to Bunyard Crossing CG. Please do not park on grassy meadow alongside creek.

SINGLE RATE:	No fee	OPEN DATES:	May-Nov
# of SINGLE SITES	3		
		MAX STAY:	14 days
		ELEVATION:	4600 feet

4. Campbell Lake
Paisley • lat 42°33'41" lon 120°45'14"

DESCRIPTION: CG is lodgepole pine setting with views of Dead Horse Lake. Fishing for stocked rainbow trout in the lake. Boat launch (elec. motors). Supplies can be found in Paisley approx. 33 mi. Campers may gather firewood nearby. Numerous trails are close to CG. Some pull thru sites. Pack it in/pack it out.

GETTING THERE: From Paisley go SW on primary forest route 33 1.5 mi. to forest route 3315. Go SW on 3315 20 mi. to primary forest route 28. Go S on 28 3 mi. to forest route 033. Go SW on 033 1.5 mi. to Campbell Lake CG.

SINGLE RATE:	No fee	OPEN DATES:	July-Oct
# of SINGLE SITES	21	MAX SPUR:	18 feet
		MAX STAY:	14 days
		ELEVATION:	7195 feet

5. Can Springs
Lakeview • lat 42°22'51" lon 120°10'04"

DESCRIPTION: On edge of high desert among large ponderosa pine. Historic Fort Warner nearby. Supplies available at Lakeview. Deer & waterfowl frequent area. Gather firewood locally. Hiking on Swale trailhead accessing Fremont National Recreational Trail 2 mi. Expect mosquitos all season.

GETTING THERE: From Lakeview go N on US HWY 395 approx. 3 mi. to state HWY 140. Go W on state HWY 140 approx. 8 mi. to forest route 3615. Go N on 3615 approx. 12 mi. to forest route 3720. Go NW on 3720 approx. 4 mi. to Can Springs CG.

SINGLE RATE:	No fee	OPEN DATES:	June-Oct
# of SINGLE SITES	3		
		MAX STAY:	14 days
		ELEVATION:	6300 feet

6. Chewaucan Crossing
Paisley • lat 42°36'30" lon 120°36'00"

DESCRIPTION: In pine setting along Chewaucan River with fishing access. Rainbow and brook trout. No drinking water. Gather firewood locally. Pack it in/pack it out. Supplies in Paisley. Birdwatching plus deer and small wildlife in area. Access Fremont National Recreation Trail is 8 miles away.

GETTING THERE: From Paisley go S on primary forest route 33 approx. 8 mi. to Chewaucan CG.

SINGLE RATE:	No fee	OPEN DATES:	Apr-Oct*
# of SINGLE SITES	5	MAX SPUR:	20 feet
		MAX STAY:	14 days
		ELEVATION:	4800 feet

7. Corral Creek
Bly • lat 42°27'22" lon 120°47'00"

DESCRIPTION: A tent CG set in lodgepole pine with horse stalls. Fishing nearby. Pack it in/pack it out. No drinking water. Gather firewood. Horse or hike into Gearhart Wilderness. Deer, mountain lion, small wildlife and birdwatching.

GETTING THERE: From Bly go E on state HWY 140 approx. 1.5 mi. to forest route 3411. Go N on 3411 approx. 1/2 mi. to primary forest route 34. Go E on 34 approx. 14.5 mi. to Corral Creek CG.

SINGLE RATE:	No fee	OPEN DATES:	May-Oct
# of SINGLE SITES	6		
		MAX STAY:	14 days
		ELEVATION:	6000 feet

8. Cottonwood Recreation Area
Lakeview • lat 42°16'00" lon 120°30'00"

DESCRIPTION: This CG is located in an open, mixed conifer forest with mountain views. Mornings tend to be cool. There is good trout fishing on a nearby lake. Supplies are available at Lakeview. Busy holiday week-ends. Firewood on site. Trails nearby. Horse corrals.

GETTING THERE: From Lakeview go W on state HWY 140 approx. 24 mi. to forest route 3870. Go N on 3870 approx. 8 mi. to Cottonwood Recreation Area CG.

SINGLE RATE:	No fee	OPEN DATES:	June-Oct
# of SINGLE SITES	21	MAX SPUR:	18 feet
		MAX STAY:	14 days
# of GROUP SITES	1	ELEVATION:	6150 feet

9. Dairy Point
Lakeview • lat 42°28'07" lon 120°38'25"

DESCRIPTION: This moderate use CG is set on a trout fishing stream. Fish and swim in the stream. Suitable for large groups. Horseshoe pits located in CG. Supplies available at Lakeview. Gather firewood or bring own. Deer and small animals in area. Birdwatching and springtime flowers.

GETTING THERE: From Lakeview go W 3 mi. on HWY 140 to county road 2-16. Go right 5 mi. on county road 2-16 to county route 2-16A. Turn left 2 mi. on 2-16A and go to forest route 28. Go 19 mi. on 28 to Dairy Point CG.

SINGLE RATE:	No fee	OPEN DATES:	May-Oct
# of SINGLE SITES	4	MAX SPUR:	18 feet
		MAX STAY:	14 days
		ELEVATION:	5200 feet

10. Deadhorse Creek
Bly • lat 42°28'30" lon 120°42'30"

DESCRIPTION: CG is in a forest setting alongside Dairy Creek where you can fish for stocked trout. Campers may bring or gather firewood. Water available at nearby Clear Springs. Supplies in Bly. Pack it in/pack it out. Deer and small animals to watch along with birds.

GETTING THERE: From Bly go E on state HWY 140 1.5 mi. to primary forest route 34. Go NE on 34 19.5 mi. to forest route 3428. Go SE on 3428 1.5 to forest route 047. Go E on 047 1 mi. to Deadhorse Creek CG.

SINGLE RATE:	No fee	OPEN DATES:	Apr-Oct
# of SINGLE SITES	4	MAX SPUR:	18 feet
		MAX STAY:	14 days
		ELEVATION:	5400 feet

 Campground has hosts   Reservable sites   Accessible facilities   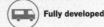 Fully developed   Semi-developed   Rustic facilities

NOTE: Open dates listed are typical. Actual dates are dependent on conditions such as snow pack.

11 Deadhorse Lake
Paisley • lat 42°33'30" lon 120°46'30"

DESCRIPTION: On high mountain lake with grassy, pebbly beaches. Fish for stocked rainbow in lake. Boat launch (elec. motors, 5 mph limit) and day use area. Bring or gather own firewood. Hike loop trails to Deadhorse Rim and Campbell Lake. Deadhorse Rim, Lee Thomas and Dead Cow Trails are nearby. Fills holidays.

GETTING THERE: From Paisley go SW on forest route 3315 approx. 18 mi. to primary forest route 28. Go S on 28 approx. 2 mi. to forest route 033. Go SW on 033 approx. 3 mi. to Deadhorse Lake CG.

SINGLE RATE:	No fee	OPEN DATES:	July-Oct
# of SINGLE SITES:	9	MAX SPUR:	18 feet
GROUP RATE:	No fee	MAX STAY:	14 days
# of GROUP SITES:	7	ELEVATION:	7372 feet

12 Deep Creek
Lakeview • lat 42°03'27" lon 120°10'27"

DESCRIPTION: This CG is set among large ponderosa pines and cottonwoods. Trout fish in the banks of nearby Deep Creek. Supplies are at Lakeview or Adel. Gather dead and down firewood locally. Deer and upland waterfowl frequent this area. This CG becomes busy in fall during hunting season.

GETTING THERE: From Lakeview go E on state HWY 140 approx. 7 mi. to forest route 3915. Go S on 3915 approx. 15 mi. to forest route 4015. Go W on 4015 approx. 1 mi. to Deep Creek CG.

SINGLE RATE:	No fee	OPEN DATES:	June-Oct
# of SINGLE SITES:	4	MAX SPUR:	18 feet
		MAX STAY:	14 days
		ELEVATION:	5600 feet

13 Deming Creek
Bly • lat 42°28'00" lon 120°53'00"

DESCRIPTION: Dispersed campsites in lodgepole pine forest. Trout fishing nearby. Gather firewood locally. Deer and small wildlife in area. The Gearhart Mountain Wilderness Trail System is nearby.

GETTING THERE: From Bly go E on HWY 140 1 mi. to Campbell Road. Turn left and go .5 mi. to forest route(fr) 34. Go 4 mi. on 34 and turn left onto fr 335. Go 2 mi. on 335 to fr 018. Go 2.7 mi. on 018 to Deming Creek CG.

SINGLE RATE:	No fee	OPEN DATES:	June-Oct
# of SINGLE SITES:	3		
		MAX STAY:	14 days
		ELEVATION:	5500 feet

14 Dismal Creek
Lakeview • lat 42°03'30" lon 120°09'30"

DESCRIPTION: CG is in a relaxing park-like setting with ponderosa pine and cottonwood. Good trout fishing in Dismal Creek which is adjacent to campsites. Gather firewood locally. Supplies in Lakeview. Numerous trails nearby.

GETTING THERE: From Lakeview go N on state HWY 140 approx. 11 mi. to forest route 3915. Go S on 3915 approx. 14 mi. to Dismal Creek CG.

SINGLE RATE:	No fee	OPEN DATES:	June-Oct
# of SINGLE SITES:	3	MAX SPUR:	18 feet
		MAX STAY:	14 days
		ELEVATION:	5600 feet

15 Dog Lake
Lakeview • lat 42°04'59" lon 120°42'16"

DESCRIPTION: CG is located in a large stand of ponderosa pine with lake and forested mountain views. Great bass, trout and perch fishing on adjacent Dog Lake. Supplies is available at Lakeview. Bird watcher's delight. Campers may gather firewood locally. No designated trails in the area.

GETTING THERE: From Lakeview go W on state HWY 140 approx. 10 mi. to county route 1-13. Go S on 1-13 approx. 4 mi. to Dog Lake Road (county route 1-11D). Go W on Dog Lake Road approx. 16 mi. to Dog Lake CG.

SINGLE RATE:	No fee	OPEN DATES:	June-Oct
# of SINGLE SITES:	12	MAX SPUR:	18 feet
		MAX STAY:	14 days
		ELEVATION:	5100 feet

16 Drews Creek
Lakeview • lat 42°07'10" lon 120°34'49"

DESCRIPTION: A popular CG in lodgepole pine setting. Fish, swim and water ski at Drew Reservoir. Horseshoe pits and softball area. Gather firewood locally. Supplies in Lakeview. Deer, small wildlife and various bird species in area. Bike path.

GETTING THERE: From Lakeview go W on state HWY 140 10 mi. to county route 1-13. Go S on 1-13 4 mi. to county route 1-11D. Go W on 1-11D 4 mi. to forest route 4017. Continue W on 4017 for 2 mi. to Drews Creek CG.

SINGLE RATE:	No fee	OPEN DATES:	June-Oct
# of SINGLE SITES:	5	MAX SPUR:	18 feet
		MAX STAY:	14 days
		ELEVATION:	4900 feet

17 East Bay
Silver Lake • lat 42°56'30" lon 121°03'55"

DESCRIPTION: In forest setting, a popular fishing and boating area. Boat ramp and fishing pier. Swimming and boating (10 mph speed limit). Gather firewood off site. Garbage service. Birdwatching and wildlife viewing (deer and small animals). Hiking trails nearby.

GETTING THERE: From Silver Lake go S on primary forest route 28 approx. 12.5 mi. to forest route 014. Go W on 014 approx. 2.5 mi. to East Bay CG.

SINGLE RATE:	$8	OPEN DATES:	May-Nov
# of SINGLE SITES:	17	MAX SPUR:	28 feet
		MAX STAY:	14 days
		ELEVATION:	4960 feet

18 Farm Well
Silver Lake • lat 43°02'30" lon 121°58'30"

DESCRIPTION: Rustic camp sites in forested setting. Gather firewood off site. Five mile trail leads to the top of Hager Mountain plus access to Fremont National Recreation Trail provide hiking, horseback riding, mountain bike riding use. Check with district office for fire restrictions.

GETTING THERE: From Silver Lake go W on primary forest route 28 approx. 6 mi. to forest route 2916. Go E on 2916 approx. 5 mi. to Farm Well CG.

SINGLE RATE:	No fee	OPEN DATES:	May-Nov
# of SINGLE SITES:	2		
		MAX STAY:	14 days
		ELEVATION:	5050 feet

19 Hanan/Coffeepot Springs
Paisley • lat 42°40'04" lon 120°38'00"

DESCRIPTION: Rustic campsites. Historical Hanan Trail is nearby, with trails open to hikers, horseback riders and mountain bike riders. Gather or bring own firewood. Deer and small animals in area. Birdwatching and wildflowers for photography buffs. Hanna Trail system access.

GETTING THERE: From Paisley go SW on primary forest route 33 approx. 1 mi. to forest route 3315. Go SW on 3315 approx. 13 mi. to Hanan/Coffeepot Springs CG.

SINGLE RATE:	No fee	OPEN DATES:	June-Oct
# of SINGLE SITES:	2	MAX SPUR:	30 feet
		MAX STAY:	14 days
		ELEVATION:	6820 feet

20 Hanan/Sycan Trailhead
Paisley • lat 42°39'00" lon 120°46'30"

DESCRIPTION: Rustic campsites. Historical Hanan Trail is nearby, with trails open to hikers, horseback riders and mountain bike riders. Gather or bring own firewood. Deer and small animals in area. Birdwatching and wildflowers for photography buffs. Hanan Trail system access.

GETTING THERE: From Paisley go SW on primary forest route 33 approx. 1 mi. to forest route 3315. Go SW on 3315 approx. 16 mi. to primary forest route 28. Go N on 28 approx. 6 mi. to Hanan/Sycan Trailhead CG.

SINGLE RATE:	No fee	OPEN DATES:	June-Oct
# of SINGLE SITES:	3	MAX SPUR:	40 feet
		MAX STAY:	14 days
		ELEVATION:	6300 feet

  Campground has hosts   Reservable sites   Accessible facilities   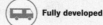 Fully developed   Semi-developed   Rustic facilities

NOTE: Open dates listed are typical. Actual dates are dependent on conditions such as snow pack.

21 Happy
Paisley • lat 42°28'34" lon 120°41'00"

DESCRIPTION: CG sits along Dairy Creek. Stream fishing for stocked rainbow trout in creek. Historical CCC picnic shelters built in the 1930's at CG. Gather or bring own firewood. Some pull through sites. Drinking water at Clear Springs. Horseshoe pits. Birdwatching, deer and small wildlife viewing in area.

GETTING THERE: From Paisley go SW on primary forest route 33 approx. 21 mi. to forest route 047. Go NW on 047 approx. 2.5 mi. to Happy CG.

SINGLE RATE:	No fee	OPEN DATES:	May-Oct
# of SINGLE SITES:	9	MAX SPUR:	25 feet
		MAX STAY:	14 days
		ELEVATION:	5289 feet

26 Lofton Reservoir
Bly • lat 42°15'48" lon 120°48'55"

DESCRIPTION: In lodgepole pine setting. Boat (electric motors only) fishing on lake. Barrier free fishing dock. Swimming, birdwatching and picnicking. Pack it in/pack it out. Gather firewood locally. Deer and small wildlife in area. Grey water dump. No nearby trailheads.

GETTING THERE: From Bly go SE on state HWY 140 approx. 12 mi. to forest route 3715. Go S on 3715 approx. 8 mi. to Lofton Reservoir CG.

SINGLE RATE:	No fee	OPEN DATES:	May-Oct
# of SINGLE SITES:	26	MAX SPUR:	28 feet
		MAX STAY:	14 days
		ELEVATION:	6180 feet

22 Holbrook Reservoir
Bly • lat 42°15'59" lon 120°51'09"

DESCRIPTION: CG is in a quiet forest setting that is a popular fishing area. Boats with electric motors only on lake, 5 mph speed limit. Boat ramp on site. Swim in lake. No drinking water. Campers may gather firewood nearby. Deer and small wildlife in area. Pack it in/pack it out. No trails close by.

GETTING THERE: From Bly go SE on state HWY 140 approx. 12.5 mi. to forest route 3715. Go S on 3715 approx. 5 mi. to forest route 3817. Go SW on 3817 approx. 1 mi. to Holbrook Reservoir CG.

SINGLE RATE:	No fee	OPEN DATES:	May-Oct
# of SINGLE SITES:	1	MAX SPUR:	20 feet
		MAX STAY:	14 days
		ELEVATION:	5400 feet

27 Lower Buck Crossing
Silver Lake • lat 43°04'00" lon 121°15'30"

DESCRIPTION: Rustic camping with forest views. No drinking water. Campers may gather firewood nearby. Fishing nearby. Wildflowers in spring and early summer. Deer and small wildlife viewing. No nearby trailheads.

GETTING THERE: From Silver Lake go NW on state HWY 31 1 mi. to county route 4-10. Go W on 4-10 10.5 mi. to forest route 2804. Go S on 2804 5 mi. to Lower Buck Crossing CG. Please keep vehicles 200' from creek's edge.

SINGLE RATE:	No fee	OPEN DATES:	May-Nov
# of SINGLE SITES:	5		
		MAX STAY:	14 days
		ELEVATION:	5000 feet

23 Horseglade Trailhead
Bly • lat 42°37'30" lon 121°05'30"

DESCRIPTION: In lodgepole pine setting. Fishing nearby. No drinking water. Pack it in/pack it out. Gather firewood locally. Deer and small wildlife in area. Birdwatching and wildflowers. Rails to Trails offers access to Five Mile Creek for bikers, hikers and horse use.

GETTING THERE: From Bly go W approx. 3.5 mi. to the Ivory Pine county road. Go NE on Ivory Pine for approx. 12 mi. to forest route 27. Go W on 27 approx. 1.5 mi. to Horseglade Trailhead CG.

SINGLE RATE:	No fee	OPEN DATES:	June-Oct*
# of SINGLE SITES:	2	MAX SPUR:	30 feet
		MAX STAY:	14 days
		ELEVATION:	5080 feet

28 Marster Spring
Paisley • lat 42°37'30" lon 120°36'00"

DESCRIPTION: On Chewaucan River in treed setting. Fish for rainbow and brook trout on the river. Beavers are active nearby. Birdwatching, wildflowers, deer and small wildlife. Campers may gather firewood for camp use. Chewaucan Crossing Trailhead access and other trails nearby. Fills frequently.

GETTING THERE: From Paisley go S on primary forest route 33 approximately 7.5 miles to Marster Springs CG.

SINGLE RATE:	No fee	OPEN DATES:	May-Oct
# of SINGLE SITES:	11	MAX SPUR:	30 feet
		MAX STAY:	14 days
		ELEVATION:	4845 feet

24 Jones Crossing
Paisley • lat 42°36'00" lon 120°35'30"

DESCRIPTION: CG is in a open forest setting with open meadow along the Chewaucan River. Fish for rainbow and brook trout. Campers may gather firewood nearby. No drinking water. Birdwatching and wildflowers in area. Deer and small wildlife. Pack it in/pack it out.

GETTING THERE: From Paisley go S on primary forest route 33 approx. 8.5 mi. to Jones Crossing CG.

SINGLE RATE:	No fee	OPEN DATES:	Apr-Oct
# of SINGLE SITES:	3	MAX SPUR:	30 feet
		MAX STAY:	14 days
		ELEVATION:	4810 feet

29 Mud Creek
Lakeview • lat 42°16'55" lon 120°12'14"

DESCRIPTION: CG is secluded in stands of lodgepole pine. Mud Creek is adjacent to campsites. Excellent trout fishing in Mud Creek. Busy holidays. Gather firewood locally. Crane Mountain National Recreation Trail is nearby.

GETTING THERE: From Lakeview go N on US HWY 395 approx. 5 mi. to state HWY 140. Go E on state HWY 140 approx. 8 mi. to forest route 3615. Go N on 3615 approx. 7 mi. to Mud Creek CG.

SINGLE RATE:	No fee	OPEN DATES:	June-Oct
# of SINGLE SITES:	7	MAX SPUR:	18 feet
		MAX STAY:	14 days
		ELEVATION:	6600 feet

25 Lee Thomas
Paisley • lat 42°35'25" lon 120°50'16"

DESCRIPTION: CG is a low use camp in a park-like setting. North Fork of Sprague Wild and Scenic River is next to CG with stream fishing for stocked rainbow trout. Bring or gather own firewood. Deadhorse Rim Trailhead close to CG. Mosquitos may be a problem early in season. Pack it in/pack it out.

GETTING THERE: From Paisley go SW on primary forest route 33 approx. 1.5 mi. to forest route 3315. Go SW on 3315 approx. 19 mi. to forest route 3411. Go W on 3411 approx. 4 mi. to Lee Thomas CG.

SINGLE RATE:	No fee	OPEN DATES:	June-Oct
# of SINGLE SITES:	8	MAX SPUR:	18 feet
		MAX STAY:	14 days
		ELEVATION:	6306 feet

30 Overton Reservoir
Lakeview • lat 42°22'30" lon 120°14'30"

DESCRIPTION: CG is in a forest setting of ponderosa pine and white fir. CG has a quiet pond stocked with trout. Supplies in Lakeview. Gather firewood locally. Deer, small animals, birdwatching and abundant wildflowers in area. Pack it in/pack it out.

GETTING THERE: From Lakeview go N on US HWY 395 5 mi. to state HWY 140. Go E on 140 8 mi. to forest route(fr) 3615. Go N on 3615 13 mi. to fr 3624. Go W on 3624 2 mi. to fr 011. Go N on 011 1/2 mi. to Overton Reservoir CG. 4WD needed.

SINGLE RATE:	No fee	OPEN DATES:	June-Oct
# of SINGLE SITES:	2	MAX SPUR:	18 feet
		MAX STAY:	14 days
		ELEVATION:	6600 feet

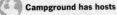 Campground has hosts   Reservable sites   Accessible facilities   Fully developed   Semi-developed   Rustic facilities

NOTE: Open dates listed are typical. Actual dates are dependent on conditions such as snow pack.

31 Pikes Crossing
Paisley • lat 42˚41'53" lon 120˚55'55"

DESCRIPTION: In a quiet and secluded setting adjacent to Paradise Creek and the Sycan Wild and Scenic River. Stream fishing for native trout. No drinking water. Campers may gather firewood nearby. Deer, birds and wildflowers in area. Fills during fall hunt season. Pack it in/pack it out.

GETTING THERE: From Paisley go W on forest route(fr) 33 mi. to fr 3315. Go W on 3315 5 mi. to fr 3360. Go W on 360 11 mi. to fr 29. Go SW on 29 8.5 mi. to fr 28. Go NW on 28 4.5 mi. to fr 30. Go SW on 30 3.5 mi. to Pikes Crossing CG.

SINGLE RATE:	No fee	OPEN DATES:	May-Oct
# of SINGLE SITES:	6	MAX SPUR:	18 feet
		MAX STAY:	14 days
		ELEVATION:	5760 feet

32 Rock Creek
Paisley • lat 42˚46'00" lon 120˚50'00"

DESCRIPTION: Quiet and secluded CG adjacent to the Sycan Wild and Scenic River. Stream fishing for native trout. Supplies are at Paisley approx. 24 mi. Fills during fall hunting season. Campers may gather firewood. No drinking water. Birdwatching, wildflowers, deer and small wildlife nearby. CG is close to the Hanan trail.

GETTING THERE: From Paisley go W on forest route(fr) 33 1 mi. to fr 3315. Go W on 3315 5 mi. to fr 3360. Go W on 3360 11 mi. to fr 29. Go SW on 29 8.5 mi. to fr 011. Go W on 011 .5 mi. to Rock Creek CG.

SINGLE RATE:	No fee	OPEN DATES:	May-Oct
# of SINGLE SITES:	6	MAX SPUR:	18 feet
		MAX STAY:	14 days
		ELEVATION:	5760 feet

33 Sandhill Crossing
Paisley • lat 42˚35'00" lon 120˚52'30"

DESCRIPTION: A low use camp in a park-like setting along the North Fork of Sprague Wild and Scenic River. Stream fish for stocked trout. Gather firewood nearby. Birdwatching, deer and small wildlife in area. Access to Gearhart Wilderness Trails not far. Mosquitos may be a problem early in the season. Fills for fall hunting season.

GETTING THERE: From Paisley go SW on primary forest route 33 approx. 1.5 mi. to forest route 3315. Go SW on 3315 approx. 19 mi. to forest route 3411. Go W on 3411 approx. 7 mi. to Sandhill Crossing CG.

SINGLE RATE:	No fee	OPEN DATES:	June-Oct
# of SINGLE SITES:	5	MAX SPUR:	18 feet
		MAX STAY:	14 days
		ELEVATION:	6306 feet

34 Silver Creek Marsh
Silver Lake • lat 43˚01'30" lon 121˚07'30"

DESCRIPTION: A popular site for fishing along Silver Creek. Horse corrals and 5 hitching rails. Gather firewood off site. Birdwatching, wading in area. Deer and small wildlife. Trailhead for the Fremont National Recreation Trail for horse, hiking and mountain bike use. Pack it in/pack it out.

GETTING THERE: From Silver Lake go W on HWY 31 for 1/4 mi. to county route 4-11. Go S on 4-11 approx. 5.5 mi. to forest road 27. Go S on 27 approx. 10 mi. to Silver Creek Marsh CG.

SINGLE RATE:	No fee	OPEN DATES:	May-Nov
# of SINGLE SITES:	14	MAX SPUR:	18 feet
		MAX STAY:	14 days
		ELEVATION:	4900 feet

35 Slide Lake
Paisley • lat 42˚42'00" lon 120˚43'30"

DESCRIPTION: Quiet, secluded CG with sites at trailhead and at the lake. Fish for trout in lake. No drinking water. Gather firewood nearby. Birdwatch, wildflowers and deer are in area. Many trails, including Slide Lake which has geological interest, close to CG.

GETTING THERE: From Paisley go .5 mi. N on state HWY 31 to forest route 3315. Continue on 3315 for approx. 6 mi. to forest route 3360. Go N on 3360 approx. 9 mi. to Slide Lake CG/trailhead sign on the W side of the road.

SINGLE RATE:	No fee	OPEN DATES:	May-Oct
# of SINGLE SITES:	3	MAX SPUR:	18 feet
		MAX STAY:	14 days
		ELEVATION:	5980 feet

36 Thompson Reservoir
Silver Lake • lat 42˚57'35" lon 121˚05'28"

DESCRIPTION: CG is in a forest setting on the reservoir. Boat fishing for trout (motors allowed, 10 mph speed limit). Swimming, birdwatching are popular. Deer and small wildlife in area. Gather firewood off site. Hiking trails nearby.

GETTING THERE: From Silver Lake go S on county route 4-11 approx. 5.5 mi. to primary forest route 27. Go S on 27 approx. 8.5 mi. to forest route 021. Go E on 021 approx. 1 mi. to Thompson Reservoir CG.

SINGLE RATE:	No fee	OPEN DATES:	May-Nov
# of SINGLE SITES:	19	MAX SPUR:	18 feet
		MAX STAY:	14 days
		ELEVATION:	5000 feet

37 Trapper Spring
Silver Lake • lat 44˚58'29" lon 121˚47'26"

DESCRIPTION: Relaxing, rustic camp sites. No drinking water. No fishing in vicinity. Wildflower viewing in spring and early summer. Deer and small wildlife in area. Gather firewood locally. Hiking trails nearby. Pack it in/pack it out.

GETTING THERE: From Silver Lake go N on state HWY 31 1 mi. to county route 4-10. Go W on 4-10 10 mi. to forest route 2780. Go N on 2780 3 mi. to forest route 2516. Go NW on 2516 10.5 mi. to Trapper Springs CG.

SINGLE RATE:	No fee	OPEN DATES:	May-Oct
# of SINGLE SITES:	2		
		MAX STAY:	14 days
		ELEVATION:	6400 feet

38 Twin Springs
Lakeview • lat 42˚09'30" lon 120˚13'30"

DESCRIPTION: Quiet camp in a forest setting of ponderosa pine, white fir, and aspen. There is also a running spring on site. Supplies in Lakeview. Gather firewood locally. Deer, small animals, birds for wildlife viewing in area. Crane Mountain National Recreation Trail is nearby. Pack it in/pack it out.

GETTING THERE: From Lakeview go N on US HWY 395 approx. 5 mi. to state HWY 140. Go E on 140 approx. 8 mi. to forest route 3910. Go S on 3910 approx. 5 mi. to Twin Springs CG.

SINGLE RATE:	No fee	OPEN DATES:	June-Oct
# of SINGLE SITES:	3	MAX SPUR:	18 feet
		MAX STAY:	14 days
		ELEVATION:	6300 feet

39 Upper Buck Creek
Silver Lake • lat 43˚04'00" lon 121˚15'00"

DESCRIPTION: Rustic camping with forest views. No drinking water. Fish for trout nearby. Campers may gather firewood locally. Wildflowers and birdwatching available in season. Deer and small wildlife in area. Check with district office for fire restrictions. Pack it in/pack it out.

GETTING THERE: From Silver Lake go N on state HWY 31 1 mi. to county route 4-10. Go W on 4-10 11.5 mi. to forest route 2804. Go S on 2804 2 mi. to forest route 013. Go E on 013 1.5 mi. to Upper Buck Creek CG.

SINGLE RATE:	No fee	OPEN DATES:	May-Nov
# of SINGLE SITES:	6		
		MAX STAY:	14 days
		ELEVATION:	5100 feet

40 Upper Jones
Paisley • lat 42˚36'30" lon 120˚36'30"

DESCRIPTION: CG is along the Chewaucan River with fishing access, for rainbow and brook trout. No drinking water. Gather firewood nearby. Birdwatching, wildflowers and wildlife in area. No nearby trailheads. Unmarked campsites are in the trees, off to the left, along the river.

GETTING THERE: From Paisley go 1/2 mi. N on state HWY 31. Turn left on Mill Street, which becomes forest route 33 at the "Y" junction. Stay to the left and continue on forest route 33 for 9.5 mi. to Upper Jones CG.

SINGLE RATE:	No fee	OPEN DATES:	Apr-Oct
# of SINGLE SITES:	2	MAX SPUR:	18 feet
		MAX STAY:	14 days
		ELEVATION:	4810 feet

 Campground has hosts   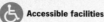 Reservable sites   Accessible facilities   Fully developed   Semi-developed   Rustic facilities

NOTE: Open dates listed are typical. Actual dates are dependent on conditions such as snow pack.

41 Willow Creek
Lakeview • lat 42°05'35" lon 120°12'06"

DESCRIPTION: CG is in secluded grove of pine and aspen with creek, forest, and meadow views. Trout fishing in adjacent Willow Creek. Supplies in Lakeview. Gather firewood locally. Mule deer and numerous birds in area. Busy holiday weekends. Hiking and OHV trails in area with access to Crane Mountain National Recreation Trail.

GETTING THERE: From Lakeview go E on state HWY 140 approx. 7 mi. to forest route 3915. Go S on 3915 approx. 9 mi. to forest route 4011. Go W on 4011 approx. 1 mi. to Willow Creek CG.

SINGLE RATE:	No fee	OPEN DATES:	June-Oct
# of SINGLE SITES:	8	MAX SPUR:	18 feet
		MAX STAY:	14 days
		ELEVATION:	5800 feet

Visitor Maps

Forest Visitor Maps are available at Regional, Forest and Ranger District offices as well as the many visitor centers located in recreation areas around the country. There is usually a fee for these maps.

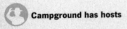 **Campground has hosts**   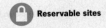 **Reservable sites**   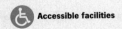 **Accessible facilities**   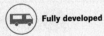 **Fully developed**   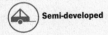 **Semi-developed**    **Rustic facilities**

USFS Photo

MALHEUR NATIONAL FOREST

Established in 1908, the 1.4 million acre Malheur National Forest is located in the Blue Mountains of eastern Oregon. The diverse and beautiful scenery of the forest includes high desert grasslands, lush evergreen forests and the hidden gems of alpine lakes and meadows.

The forest takes its name from the Malheur River named by an early French trapper whose supplies were stolen. Native Americans roamed the lands for thousands of years until explorers, fur trappers, and miners discovered the area.

More than 240 miles of trails which lead through high mountain terrain to river canyons await hikers of all abilities. Lakes and streams provide great fishing for cold water game fish, primarily rainbow trout. Bird-watching is popular with over 200 species on the forest. Elk and mule deer are a big attraction for hunters as well as black bear, bighorn sheep and blue and ruffed grouse.

Backcountry enthusiasts will enjoy the 81,000 acre Strawberry Mountain and Monument Rock wildernesses. In the winter, the Blue Mountains' gentle open terrain and miles of snow-covered forest roads are ideal for nordic skiing and snowmobiling.

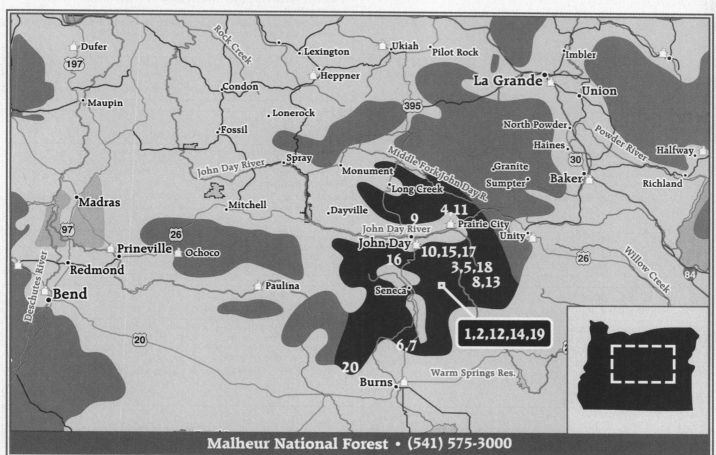

Malheur National Forest • (541) 575-3000

1 Big Creek
John Day • lat 44˚11'00" lon 118˚36'53"

DESCRIPTION: In an open pine forest setting on Big Creek. Fish for trout in the creek. Supplies at John Day. Deer, elk, antelope and birds are common to the area. Campers may gather firewood locally. Trails are with in 1\4 mi. of the CG. A bike trail leads from the CG.

GETTING THERE: From John Day go S on US HWY 395 approx. 9 mi. to county route 65. Go S on 65 approx. 13 mi. to forest route 16. Go E on 16 approx. 7 mi. to Big Creek CG.

SINGLE RATE:	$5	OPEN DATES:	May-Oct
# of SINGLE SITES:	14	MAX SPUR:	28 feet
		MAX STAY:	14 days
		ELEVATION:	5100 feet

6 Idlewild
Burns • lat 43˚47'59" lon 118˚59'20"

DESCRIPTION: In a pine forest setting on a small creek. Fish for trout and swim in the creek. Supplies available at Burns. Deer, bears, mountain lions and birds are common to the area. Campers may gather firewood locally. No designated trails in the area. Near Big Game Winter Range.

GETTING THERE: Idlewild CG is located approx. 15 mi. N of Burns on US HWY 398.

SINGLE RATE:	$6	OPEN DATES:	May-Oct
# of SINGLE SITES:	24	MAX SPUR:	28 feet
		MAX STAY:	14 days
		ELEVATION:	5300 feet

2 Canyon Meadows
John Day • lat 44˚14'25" lon 118˚46'29"

DESCRIPTION: In a mixed forest setting on Canyon Creek with Canyon Meadows Lake nearby. Fish for trout and swim in the creek or lake. Supplies available at Seneca. Deer, bears and birds are common to the area. Campers may gather firewood locally. Trails in the area.

GETTING THERE: From John Day go S on US HWY 395 9 mi. to county route 65. S on 65 9 mi. to forest route 1520. NE on 1520 4 mi. to Canyon Meadows CG.

SINGLE RATE:	No fee	OPEN DATES:	May-Oct
# of SINGLE SITES:	18	MAX SPUR:	28 feet
		MAX STAY:	14 days
		ELEVATION:	5100 feet

7 Jouquin Miller
Burns • lat 43˚51'00" lon 118˚57'00"

DESCRIPTION: This CG sets in a mixed pine forest setting. Campers may purchase supplies at Burns. Numerous wildlife can be viewed in the area. Campers may gather firewood. A horse trail that begins on site leads through the forest. Horse corrals and water are offered at this CG.

GETTING THERE: From Burns go N approx. 21 mi. off state HWY 395 to Jouquin Miller CG.

SINGLE RATE:	No fee	OPEN DATES:	Yearlong*
# of SINGLE SITES:	18	MAX SPUR:	30 feet
		MAX STAY:	14 days
		ELEVATION:	5300 feet

3 Crescent
Prairie City • lat 44˚16'55" lon 118˚32'39"

DESCRIPTION: In a pine and fir forest setting on John Day River. Fish for trout and swim in the river. Supplies available at Prairie City. Deer and birds are common to the area. Campers may gather firewood locally. No designated trails nearby. No drinking water.

GETTING THERE: From Prairie City go S on county route 62 approx. 15 mi. to Crescent CG.

SINGLE RATE:	No fee	OPEN DATES:	May-Oct
# of SINGLE SITES:	4	MAX SPUR:	28 feet
		MAX STAY:	14 days
		ELEVATION:	5200 feet

8 Little Crane
Prairie City • lat 44˚11'42" lon 118˚24'35"

DESCRIPTION: In a lodge pole pine forest setting on Little Crane Creek. Fish for trout and swim in creek. Supplies available at Prairie City. Deer, bears and birds are common to the area. Campers may gather firewood locally. No designated trails in the area. No drinking water.

GETTING THERE: From Prairie City go E and S on county route 61 approx. 7 mi. to forest route 13. Go E and S on 13 approx. 21 mi. to Little Crane CG.

SINGLE RATE:	No fee	OPEN DATES:	May-Oct
# of SINGLE SITES:	5	MAX SPUR:	28 feet
		MAX STAY:	14 days
		ELEVATION:	5500 feet

4 Dixie
Dixie Summit • lat 44˚32'21" lon 118˚35'16"

DESCRIPTION: In a mixed forest setting with a creek nearby. Supplies available at Prairie City. Deer, bears and birds are common to the area. Campers may gather firewood locally. Historical Sumpter Valley Railway. Sumpter Valley Trailhead is nearby along with Sumpter Valley Ski Bowl.

GETTING THERE: Dixie CG is located at Dixie Summit on US HWY 26.

SINGLE RATE:	$5	OPEN DATES:	May-Oct
# of SINGLE SITES:	20	MAX SPUR:	28 feet
		MAX STAY:	14 days
		ELEVATION:	5000 feet

9 Magone
Prairie City • lat 44˚33'10" lon 118˚54'30"

DESCRIPTION: Located in an open pine forest setting on Magone Lake. Fish for trout, bass or swim in the lake. Boat ramp at CG. Supplies available at Prairie City. Campers may gather firewood locally. Magone Lake Trail and the Magone Slide Trail begins at the CG. Wild flower viewing everywhere.

GETTING THERE: From Prairie City go W on US HWY 26 3 mi. to county route 18. N on 18 approx. 11 mi. to forest route 3620. S on 3620 approx. 1.5 mi. to forest route 3618. W on 3618 approx. 1.5 mi. to Magone CG.

SINGLE RATE:	$10	OPEN DATES:	May-Oct
# of SINGLE SITES:	23	MAX SPUR:	28 feet
GROUP RATE:	$10	MAX STAY:	14 days
# of GROUP SITES:	1	ELEVATION:	5000 feet

5 Elk Creek
Prairie City • lat 44˚14'43" lon 118˚23'50"

DESCRIPTION: In a lodge pole pine forest setting on Elk Creek. Fish for trout in the creek. Supplies available at Prairie City. Deer, bears and birds are common to the area. Campers may gather firewood locally. No designated trails nearby. No drinking water.

GETTING THERE: From Prairie City go E and S on county route 61 approx. 7 mi. to forest route 13. Go E and S on 13 approx. 16 mi. to Elk Creek CG.

SINGLE RATE:	No fee	OPEN DATES:	May-Oct
# of SINGLE SITES:	5	MAX SPUR:	28 feet
		MAX STAY:	14 days
		ELEVATION:	5000 feet

10 McNaughton
Prairie City • lat 44˚20'50" lon 118˚39'10"

DESCRIPTION: In fir and spruce on Strawberry Creek. Fish for trout in the creek. Supplies available at Prairie City. Deer, cougar and birds are common to the area. Campers may gather firewood locally. Trail nearby. Pick wild strawberries and huckleberries around CG. No drinking water.

GETTING THERE: From Prairie City go S on county route 60 approx. 8 mi. to McNaughton CG.

SINGLE RATE:	No fee	OPEN DATES:	May-Oct
# of SINGLE SITES:	4	MAX SPUR:	28 feet
		MAX STAY:	14 days
		ELEVATION:	4900 feet

 Campground has hosts　　 **Reservable sites**　　 **Accessible facilities**　　 **Fully developed**　　 **Semi-developed**　　△ **Rustic facilities**

NOTE: Open dates listed are typical. Actual dates are dependent on conditions such as snow pack.

11 Middle Fork
Bates • lat 44°37'48" lon 118°36'15"

DESCRIPTION: In mixed forest setting on the South Fork John Day River. Fish for trout and swim in the River. Supplies available at Bates. Deer, bears, mountain lions and birds are common to the area. Big game winter range nearby. Campers may gather firewood locally. Historical Sumpter Valley Railway. No drinking water.

GETTING THERE: From Bates go NW on county route 20 approx. 6 mi. to Middle Fork CG.

SINGLE RATE:	$5	OPEN DATES:	May-Oct
# of SINGLE SITES:	10	MAX SPUR:	28 feet
		MAX STAY:	14 days
		ELEVATION:	4100 feet

12 Murray
John Day • lat 44°12'45" lon 118°38'14"

DESCRIPTION: In a lodge pole pine forest setting on Lake Creek. Fish for trout and swim in the creek. Supplies available at John Day. Deer, bears and birds are common to the area. Campers may gather firewood locally. Trails with in 1/2 mi. of CG.

GETTING THERE: From John Day go S on US HWY 395 9 mi. to county route 65. Go S on 65 13 mi. to forest route 16. Go E on 16 5 mi. to the Murray CG Road (follow signs). Go N approx. 2 mi. to Murray CG.

SINGLE RATE:	No fee	OPEN DATES:	May-Oct
# of SINGLE SITES:	6	MAX SPUR:	28 feet
		MAX STAY:	14 days
		ELEVATION:	5200 feet

13 North Fork Malheur
Prairie City • lat 44°12'31" lon 118°22'53"

DESCRIPTION: This walk-in CG rests in lodge pole pine setting on the North Fork Malheur River (wild and scenic river). Fish for trout and swim in the river. Supplies available at Prairie City. Deer, bears and birds are common to the area. Campers may gather firewood locally. Trails with in 1/4 mi. of CG. No drinking water.

GETTING THERE: From Prairie City go E and S on county route 61 approx. 7 mi. to forest route 13. Go E and S on 13 approx. 16 mi. to forest route 1675. Go S on 1675 approx. 2 mi. to North Fork Malheur CG.

SINGLE RATE:	No fee	OPEN DATES:	May-Oct
# of SINGLE SITES:	5		
		MAX STAY:	14 days
		ELEVATION:	4700 feet

14 Parish Cabin
John Day • lat 44°10'48" lon 118°45'52"

DESCRIPTION: In a mixed conifer forest setting on a small creek. Fish for trout and swim in the creek. Supplies available at Seneca. Deer, bears and birds are common to the area. Starr Ridge Trailhead is with in 3 mi. of CG. Campers may gather firewood locally

GETTING THERE: From John Day go S on US HWY 395 9 mi. to county route 65. S on 65 13 mi. to Parish Cabin CG.

SINGLE RATE:	$6	OPEN DATES:	May-Oct
# of SINGLE SITES:	20	MAX SPUR:	28 feet
		MAX STAY:	14 days
		ELEVATION:	4900 feet

15 Slide Creek
Prairie City • lat 44°20'32" lon 118°39'30"

DESCRIPTION: In a spruce, larch and white fir forest setting on Slide Creek. Fish for trout and swim in the creek. Supplies available at Prairie City. Deer, bears and birds are common to the area. Campers may gather firewood locally. Wilderness Trail approx. 4.3 mi. long starts at CG. No drinking water.

GETTING THERE: From Prairie City go S on county route 60 approx. 9 mi. to Slide Creek CG.

SINGLE RATE:	No fee	OPEN DATES:	May-Oct
# of SINGLE SITES:	3		
		MAX STAY:	14 days
		ELEVATION:	4900 feet

16 Starr
John Day • lat 44°15'33" lon 119°01'01"

DESCRIPTION: In a mixed conifer forest setting on Starr Creek. Fish for trout or swim in the creek. Supplies available at John Day. Deer, bears and birds are common in the area. Campers may gather firewood locally. Starr Ridge Trailhead is nearby along with Starr Bowl Winter Sports Area.

GETTING THERE: Starr CG is located approx. 15 mi. S of John Day on US HWY 395.

SINGLE RATE:	$4	OPEN DATES:	May-Oct
# of SINGLE SITES:	8	MAX SPUR:	28 feet
		MAX STAY:	14 days
		ELEVATION:	5100 feet

17 Strawberry
Prairie City • lat 44°19'10" lon 118°40'26"

DESCRIPTION: In spruce and white fir on Strawberry Creek. Fish for trout and swim in the creek. Supplies available at Prairie City. Deer, bears and birds common to area. Campers may gather firewood locally. Wilderness trails start at the CG. No drinking water. Pick wild strawberries and huckleberries in area.

GETTING THERE: From Prairie City go S on county route 60 approx. 10 mi. to Strawberry CG.

SINGLE RATE:	$6	OPEN DATES:	May-Oct
# of SINGLE SITES:	11	MAX SPUR:	28 feet
		MAX STAY:	14 days
		ELEVATION:	5700 feet

18 Trout Farm
Prairie City • lat 44°18'23" lon 118°33'11"

DESCRIPTION: In a white fir and spruce forest setting next to the John Day River. Fish for trout in the river or stocked pond by the CG. Supplies available at Prairie City. Deer, bears and birds are common to the area. Campers gather firewood locally. Trail around pond starts at CG. No drinking water.

GETTING THERE: From Prairie City go S on county route 62 approx. 13 mi. to Trout Farm CG

SINGLE RATE:	$6	OPEN DATES:	May-Oct
# of SINGLE SITES:	9	MAX SPUR:	28 feet
		MAX STAY:	14 days
		ELEVATION:	4900 feet

19 Wickiup
Seneca • lat 44°13'00" lon 118°51'05"

DESCRIPTION: In a mixed conifer forest setting with views of Table Mountain. Wickiup Creek nearby for fishing and swimming. Supplies at John Day. Deer, bears and birds are common to the area. CG is located next to a big game range-no motor vehicles allowed. Gather firewood locally. Historic sites in area.

GETTING THERE: From John Day go S on US HWY 395 9 mi. to county route 65. S on 65 8 mi. to Wickiup CG.

SINGLE RATE:	No fee	OPEN DATES:	May-Oct
# of SINGLE SITES:	9		
		MAX STAY:	14 days
		ELEVATION:	4900 feet

20 Yellowjacket
Burns • lat 43°52'38" lon 119°16'19"

DESCRIPTION: In a pine forest setting with views of Yellowjacket Lake nearby. Fish for trout, swim or boat in the lake. Supplies at Burns. Deer, bears, mountain lions and birds are common to the area. Campers may gather firewood locally. Turner Cabin is nearby. No designated trails in the area.

GETTING THERE: From Burns go N on county route 127 to the forest boundary. Continue on forest route 47 approx. 6 mi. to forest route 37. E on 37 2 mi. to forest route 3745. S on 3745 1 mi. to Yellowjacket Cg.

SINGLE RATE:	No fee	OPEN DATES:	May-Oct
# of SINGLE SITES:	20	MAX SPUR:	28 feet
		MAX STAY:	14 days
		ELEVATION:	4800 feet

 Campground has hosts   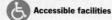 Reservable sites   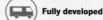 Accessible facilities   Fully developed   Semi-developed   Rustic facilities

NOTE: Open dates listed are typical. Actual dates are dependent on conditions such as snow pack.

MOUNT HOOD NATIONAL FOREST

Located 20 miles east of the city of Portland, Oregon and the northern Willamette River valley, the Mt. Hood extends south from the strikingly beautiful Columbia River Gorge across more than 60 miles of forested mountains, lakes and streams to Olallie Scenic Area, a high lake basin under the slopes of Mt. Jefferson.

Mt. Hood is a dormant or "sleeping" volcano which rises 11,235 above sea level. It's the highest mountain in Oregon and the fourth highest in the string of Cascade Mountain Range volcanoes that stretch from British Columbia to Northern California. Mt. Hood is also the second most climbed mountain in the world, second only to Japan's holy Mt. Fujiyama.

Some popular destinations that offer rewarding visits are Timberline Lodge, built in 1937 high on Mt. Hood, Lost Lake, Trillium Lake, Timothy Lake, Rock Creek Reservoir and portions of the Old Oregon Trail, including Barlow Road. There are 189,200 acres of designated wilderness and over 1200 miles of hiking trails, all providing a primitive recreation experience. Mount Hood boasts five ski areas. Timberline Lodge Ski Area has the only year-round ski season in North America, closed for only two weeks in late September.

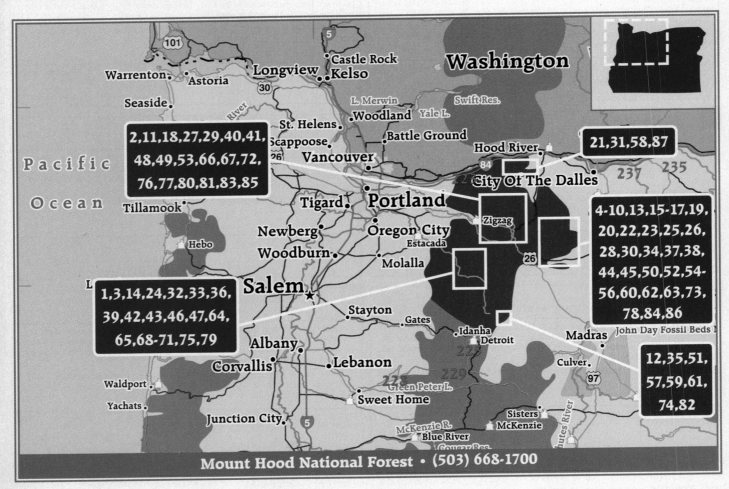

1 Alder Flat
Estacada • lat 45°05'02" lon 122°03'23"

DESCRIPTION: Set in pine forest on the Clackamas River. Expect rain in summer, nicer in July and Aug. Trout and steelhead fishing in the Clackamas River. Supplies available at Estacada. Deer, and small wildlife can be seen in the area. CG is full weekends and holidays. Fall visits are best. Campers may gather firewood.

GETTING THERE: Alder Flat CG is located approx. 20 mi. SE of Estacada on state HWY 224.

SINGLE RATE:	No fee	OPEN DATES:	May-Sept
# of SINGLE SITES:	6	MAX SPUR:	10 feet
		MAX STAY:	14 days
		ELEVATION:	1300 feet

2 Alpine
Government Camp • lat 45°19'12" lon 121°42'18"

DESCRIPTION: CG is located in fir on the Timberline road. Nice views of Mount Hood. Deer and elk can be seen in the area. Supplies available at Government Camp. Expect rain and sometimes snow in summers.

GETTING THERE: From Government Camp go E approx. 1/2 mi. on US HWY 26 to forest route 2645 (Timberline Road). Go N on 2645 approx. 3 mi. to Alpine CG.

SINGLE RATE:	$8	OPEN DATES:	June-Sept
# of SINGLE SITES:	16	MAX SPUR:	15 feet
		MAX STAY:	14 days
		ELEVATION:	5400 feet

3 Armstrong
Estacada • lat 45°09'45" lon 122°09'10"

DESCRIPTION: CG sits on the Clackamas River among pine and fir. Expect rainy days. Trout and steelhead fishing on river. Supplies available at Estacada. Deer and small wildlife are common in the area. Campers may gather firewood. CG is full weekends and holidays.

GETTING THERE: Armstrong CG is located approx. 13 mi. SE of Estacada on state HWY 224.

SINGLE RATE:	$12	OPEN DATES:	Apr-Sept
# of SINGLE SITES:	12	MAX SPUR:	16 feet
		MAX STAY:	14 days
		ELEVATION:	900 feet

4 Badger Lake
Wamic • lat 45°18'13" lon 121°33'26"

DESCRIPTION: Located among fir and pine on Badger Lake. Expect mild days, cool nights and possible rain. Non-motorized boats only on lake. Trout fishing in the lake and on Badger Creek. Moderate use, heavier on weekends. Supplies available at Wamic. Deer and small wildlife in area.

GETTING THERE: From Wamic go W approx. 13.5 mi. on primary forest route 48 to forest route 4860. Go N on 4860 approx. 7.5 mi. to forest route 140. Go N on 140 approx. 3.5 mi. to Badger Lake CG.

SINGLE RATE:	No fee	OPEN DATES:	July-Oct
# of SINGLE SITES:	4	MAX SPUR:	20 feet
		MAX STAY:	14 days
		ELEVATION:	4400 feet

5 Barlow Creek
Government Camp • lat 45°14'07" lon 121°37'36"

DESCRIPTION: CG is located in fir on Barlow Creek. Deer and elk are common in the area. Cool weather can be expected in summer. Go to Government Camp for supplies. Campers may gather firewood locally.

GETTING THERE: From Government Camp go E 3 mi. on US HWY 26 to state HWY 35. Go E 4 mi. on 35 to primary forest route 48 (White River road). Go S 8 mi. on 48 to forest route 43. Go W 1 mi. on 43 to forest route 220. Go N 1.5 mi. on 220 to Barlow Creek CG.

SINGLE RATE:	No fee	OPEN DATES:	Yearlong*
# of SINGLE SITES:	3	MAX SPUR:	10 feet
		MAX STAY:	14 days
		ELEVATION:	3100 feet

6 Barlow Crossing
Government Camp • lat 45°13'01" lon 121°36'47"

DESCRIPTION: CG is located in fir at the historic site of Barlow Road crossing the White River. Deer and elk are common to the area. Cool weather can be expected in summer. Go to Government Camp for supplies. Campers may gather firewood locally.

GETTING THERE: From Government Camp go E 3 mi. on US HWY 26 to state HWY 35. Go E 4 mi. on 35 approx. to primary forest route 48 (White River Road). Go S 8 mi. on 48 to forest route 43. Go W 1 mi. on 43 to Barlow Crossing CG.

SINGLE RATE:	No fee	OPEN DATES:	Yearlong*
# of SINGLE SITES:	6	MAX SPUR:	10 feet
		MAX STAY:	14 days
		ELEVATION:	3100 feet

7 Bears Springs
Pine Grove • lat 45°07'00" lon 121°31'45"

DESCRIPTION: Located among fir and pine on Inidan Creek. Expect mild days, cool nights and possible rain. Trout fish and swim in the creek. Moderate use, heavier on weekends. Supplies available at Pine Grove. Deer and small wildlife are common to the area.

GETTING THERE: Bears Springs CG is located approx. 7.5 mi. W of Pine Grove on state HWY 216.

SINGLE RATE:	$10	OPEN DATES:	May-Oct
# of SINGLE SITES:	21	MAX SPUR:	32 feet
		MAX STAY:	14 days
		ELEVATION:	3200 feet

8 Bonney Crossing
Wamic • lat 45°15'22" lon 121°23'22"

DESCRIPTION: Set among pine with underbrush on Badger Creek. Trout fish and swim in the creek. Supplies available at Wamic. Deer and small wildlife frequent the area. Moderate use execept holidays, fall is nice. Hike and horse trails into Badger Cr. Wilderness.

GETTING THERE: From Wimac go W approx. 5 mi. on primary forest route 48 to forest route 4810. Go NW on 4810 approx. 2 mi. to forest route 4811. Go N on 4811 approx. 1.5 mi. to forest route 2710. Go E on 2710 approx. 2 mi. to Bonney Crossing CG.

SINGLE RATE:	$3	OPEN DATES:	May-Oct
# of SINGLE SITES:	8	MAX SPUR:	16 feet
		MAX STAY:	14 days
		ELEVATION:	2200 feet

9 Bonney Meadow
Wamic • lat 45°15'55" lon 121°34'54"

DESCRIPTION: CG is located in the pine on Bonney Creek. Fish for trout and swim in the creek. Supplies available at Wamic. Deer and small wildlife are common in area. Campers may gather firewood. Mosquitos early in season. Hiking trails nearby.

GETTING THERE: From Wamic go W approx. 15 mi. on primary forest route 48 to forest route 4880. Go N on 4880 approx. 1.5 mi. to forest route 4881. Go W on 4881 approx. 2 mi. to forest route 4891. Go N on 4891 approx. 4.5 mi. to Bonney Meadows CG. 4WD recommended.

SINGLE RATE:	No fee	OPEN DATES:	July-Oct
# of SINGLE SITES:	6	MAX SPUR:	16 feet
		MAX STAY:	14 days
		ELEVATION:	4800 feet

10 Boulder Lake
Wamic • lat 45°15'28" lon 121°34'02"

DESCRIPTION: CG is located in pine with underbrush on Boulder Lake. Fish for trout and swim in the lake. Supplies available at Wamic. Deer frequent the area. Light use, fall is a good time to visit. Hiking nearby. Prepare for mosquitos through June.

GETTING THERE: From Wamic go W 15 mi. on primary forest route 48 to forest route 4880. Go N 1.5 mi. on 4880 to forest route 4881. Go W 1.5 mi. on 4881 to forest route 120. Go N 1.5 mi. on 120 to forest route 122. Go N 2 mi. on 122 to Boulder Lake CG.

SINGLE RATE:	No fee	OPEN DATES:	June-Oct
# of SINGLE SITES:	10		
		MAX STAY:	14 days
		ELEVATION:	4560 feet

 Campground has hosts   **Reservable sites**   **Accessible facilities**   **Fully developed**   **Semi-developed**   **Rustic facilities**

NOTE: Open dates listed are typical. Actual dates are dependent on conditions such as snow pack.

11 Camp Creek
Brightwood • lat 45˚18'11" lon 121˚51'53"

DESCRIPTION: Campground is located in fir and pine on Camp Creek. Fish for trout and steelhead in creek and the nearby Zigzag River. Supplies available in Brightwood. Expect rain in the summer, cool days. Campers may gather firewood locally.

GETTING THERE: From Brightwood go SE approx. 8 mi. on US HWY 26 to Camp Creek CG.

SINGLE RATE:	Varies	OPEN DATES:	Apr-Sept
# of SINGLE SITES:	25	MAX SPUR:	22 feet
		MAX STAY:	14 days
		ELEVATION:	2200 feet

12 Camp Ten
Mill City • lat 44˚48'12" lon 121˚47'16"

DESCRIPTION: CG is located in a pine and fir forest setting on Olallie Lake. Fish for trout and swim in the lake. Supplies available at Mill City or limited supplies at Olallie Lake Lodge. Deer and small wildlife are common to the area. Campers may gather firewood. No designated trails nearby.

GETTING THERE: From Mill City go E approx. 16.5 mi. on state HWY 22 to primary forest route 46. Go NE on 46 approx. 16.5 mi. to forest route 4690. Go SE on 4690 approx. 7 mi. to forest route 4220. Go S on 4220 approx. 6 mi. to Camp Ten CG.

SINGLE RATE:	$6	OPEN DATES:	May-Sept
# of SINGLE SITES:	10	MAX SPUR:	16 feet
		MAX STAY:	14 days
		ELEVATION:	5000 feet

13 Camp Windy
Wamic • lat 45˚17'20" lon 121˚34'56"

DESCRIPTION: Located in a park-like setting of pine and fir with underbrush. Supplies are available at Wamic. Campers may gather firewood. Numerous animals can be seen in the area. Hiking trail #458 is nearby.

GETTING THERE: From Wamic go E approx. 13.5 mi. on primary forest route 48 to forest route 4860. Go N on 4860 approx. 9 mi. to Camp Windy CG. 4WD is recomended.

SINGLE RATE:	No fee	OPEN DATES:	July-Oct
# of SINGLE SITES:	3	MAX SPUR:	10 feet
		MAX STAY:	14 days
		ELEVATION:	5200 feet

14 Carter Bridge
Estacada • lat 45˚10'05" lon 122˚09'30"

DESCRIPTION: Set in a pine and fir forest on the Clackamas River. Frequent summer rains. Fish for trout and steelhead in Clackamas River. Supplies available at Estacada. Campers may gather firewood locally.

GETTING THERE: Carter Bridge CG is located approx. 12 mi. SE of Estacada on state HWY 224.

SINGLE RATE:	$10	OPEN DATES:	Apr-Sept
# of SINGLE SITES:	15	MAX SPUR:	28 feet
		MAX STAY:	14 days
		ELEVATION:	900 feet

15 Clackamas Lake
Government Camp • lat 45˚05'45" lon 121˚44'50"

DESCRIPTION: Campground is located in fir and pine on Clackamas Lake. Deer, elk and small campground animals in area. 18 mi. to Government Camp for supplies. Cool in summer with some rain. Gather firewood locally.

GETTING THERE: From Government Camp go E and S on US HWY 26 approx. 10 mi. to primary forest route 42. Go S on 42 approx. 7.5 mi. to forest route 4270. Go E on 4270 approx. .5 mi. to Clackamas Lake CG.

SINGLE RATE:	$12	OPEN DATES:	May-Sept
# of SINGLE SITES:	46	MAX SPUR:	32 feet
		MAX STAY:	14 days
		ELEVATION:	3400 feet

16 Clear Creek Crossing
Pine Grove • lat 45˚08'42" lon 121˚34'40"

DESCRIPTION: Located in pine and fir with little underbrush with Clear Creek running next to CG. Fish and swim in the creek. Supplies available at Pine Grove. Numerous wildlife can be seen in the area. Campers may gather firewood. No designated trails in the area.

GETTING THERE: From Pine Grove go W on state HWY 216 approx. 8.5 mi. to forest route 2130. Go NW on 2130 approx. 2 mi. to Clear Creek Crossing CG. 4WD is recomended.

SINGLE RATE:	No fee	OPEN DATES:	May-Oct
# of SINGLE SITES:	7	MAX SPUR:	16 feet
		MAX STAY:	14 days
		ELEVATION:	3600 feet

17 Clear Lake
Government Camp • lat 45˚10'52" lon 121˚41'47"

DESCRIPTION: CG is located in pine and fir on Clear Lake. Fish for trout and swim in lake. Nice in summer but expect some cool weather and some rain. Supplies available at Government Camp. Busy on holidays and weekends. Campers may gather firewood locally.

GETTING THERE: From Government Camp go E and S on US HWY 26 approx. 9 mi. to forest route 2630. Go S on 2630 approx. 1 mi. to forest route 220. Go S on 220 approx. 1.5 mi. to Clear Lake CG.

SINGLE RATE:	$12	OPEN DATES:	Yearlong*
# of SINGLE SITES:	28	MAX SPUR:	32 feet
		MAX STAY:	14 days
		ELEVATION:	3600 feet

18 Cloud Cap Saddle
Parkdale • lat 45˚24'08" lon 121˚39'15"

DESCRIPTION: CG is located in fir high on the flank of Mount Hood on Cooper Spur. Popular area to begin climbs of Mout Hood. Supplies available in Parkdale. Expect cool weather and some rain.

GETTING THERE: From Parkdale go S on state HWY 35 approx. 8 mi. to forest route 3510. Go NW on 3510 approx. 1.5 mi. to forest route 3512. Go SW on 3512 approx. 7 mi. to Cloud Cap Saddle CG.

SINGLE RATE:	No fee	OPEN DATES:	Yearlong*
# of SINGLE SITES:	3	MAX SPUR:	10 feet
		MAX STAY:	14 days
		ELEVATION:	5900 feet

19 Cove
Government Camp • lat 45˚09'25" lon 121˚46'25"

DESCRIPTION: This walk-in CG is located in fir and pine on the W shore of Timothy Lake. Fish and swim in the lake. Deer, elk and small animals are common in the the area. Supplies available in Government Camp. Cool in summer with some rain. Campers may gather firewood locally.

GETTING THERE: From Government Camp go E and S on US HWY 26 approx. 10 mi. to primary forest route 42. Go S on 42 approx. 7 mi. to primary forest route 57. Go W on 57 approx. 4 mi. to forest route 5890. Go E on 5890 approx. 1.5 mi. to Cove CG.

SINGLE RATE:	$8	OPEN DATES:	May-Sept
# of SINGLE SITES:	10		
		MAX STAY:	14 days
		ELEVATION:	3200 feet

20 Devil's Half Acre
Government Camp • lat 45˚16'27" lon 121˚40'43"

DESCRIPTION: CG is located in fir and pine on upper Barlow Creek on the historic Barlow Road. Deer and elk are common in the area. Supplies available at Government Camp. Expect cool weather and rain in summers. Campers may gather firewood locally.

GETTING THERE: From Government Camp go E on US HWY 26 approx. 3 mi. to state HWY 35. Go E on 35 approx. 2 mi. to forest route 3530. Go S on 3530 approx. 1 mi. to Devil's Half Acre CG.

SINGLE RATE:	No fee	OPEN DATES:	Yearlong*
# of SINGLE SITES:	2	MAX SPUR:	10 feet
		MAX STAY:	14 days
		ELEVATION:	3600 feet

 Campground has hosts   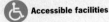 **Reservable sites**   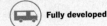 **Accessible facilities**   **Fully developed**   **Semi-developed**   **Rustic facilities**

NOTE: Open dates listed are typical. Actual dates are dependent on conditions such as snow pack.

21  Eagle Creek
Cascade Locks • lat 45°38'00" lon 121°54'00"

DESCRIPTION: This CG is located in a dense forest of fir, hemlock and cedar. It sits on a bluff above the Eagle Creek Fish Hatchery. Deer, bears and various birds of prey are common in the area. Visit Cascade Locks (approximately 2 miles away) for supplies and milkshakes.

GETTING THERE: Eagle creek CG is located east of Cascade Locks at Eagle Creek.

SINGLE RATE:	$10	**OPEN DATES:**	**May-Sept**
# of SINGLE SITES:	20	**MAX SPUR:**	**22 feet**
		MAX STAY:	**14 days**
		ELEVATION:	**400 feet**

22 Eightmile Crossing
Dufur • lat 45°24'23" lon 121°27'20"

DESCRIPTION: Located in pine with some underbrush with Eightmail Creek running nearby. Trout fish in the nearby Eightmile Creek. Supplies avaialble at Dufur. Campers may gather firewood.

GETTING THERE: From Dufur go W on primary forest route 44 approx. 15.5 mi. to forest route 4430. Go N on 4430 approx. 1/2 mi. to Eightmile Crossing CG.

SINGLE RATE:	No fee	**OPEN DATES:**	**May-Oct**
# of SINGLE SITES:	21	**MAX SPUR:**	**30 feet**
		MAX STAY:	**14 days**
		ELEVATION:	**4200 feet**

23 Fifteenmile
Dufur • lat 45°22'43" lon 121°25'15"

DESCRIPTION: Located in a pine and fir forest setting with Fifteenmile Creek nearby. Fish for trout and swim in Fifteenmile Creek. Supplies are available at Dufur. Numerous wildlife can be seen in the area.

GETTING THERE: From Dufur go W approx. 17 mi. on primary forest route 44 to forest route 4420. Go S on 4420 approx. 2 mi. to forest route 2730. Continue S on 2730 approx. 2 mi. to Fifteenmile CG.

SINGLE RATE:	No fee	**OPEN DATES:**	**June-Oct**
# of SINGLE SITES:	3	**MAX SPUR:**	**16 feet**
		MAX STAY:	**14 days**
		ELEVATION:	**4000 feet**

24 Fish Creek
Estacada • lat 45°09'34" lon 122°09'08"

DESCRIPTION: CG is located in pine and fir on the Clackamas River and Fish Creek. Trout and steelhead fishing in the creek and river. Supplies available at Estacada. Deer, and small wildlife can be seen in the area. Full weekends and holidays. Fall visits are best. Gather firewood locally.

GETTING THERE: From Estacada go SE on state HWY 224 approx. 13 mi. to primary forest route 54. Go S on 54 approx. 1/2 mi. to Fish Creek Cg.

SINGLE RATE:	$12	**OPEN DATES:**	**Apr-Sept**
# of SINGLE SITES:	24	**MAX SPUR:**	**16 feet**
		MAX STAY:	**14 days**
		ELEVATION:	**900 feet**

25 Forest Creek
Wamic • lat 45°10'50" lon 121°31'20"

DESCRIPTION: CG is located among pine and fir on Forest Creek. Fish and swim in the creek. Warm days, cool nights, expect rain in summer. Supplies available at Wamic. Deer and small wildlife are common to the area. Campers may gather firewood locally.

GETTING THERE: From Wamic go W on primary forest route 48 approx. 16 mi. to forest route 4885. Go S on 4885 approx. 1 mi. to Forest Creek CG.

SINGLE RATE:	No fee	**OPEN DATES:**	**May-Oct**
# of SINGLE SITES:	8	**MAX SPUR:**	**16 feet**
		MAX STAY:	**14 days**
		ELEVATION:	**3000 feet**

26 Frog Lake
Government Camp • lat 45°13'21" lon 121°41'33"

DESCRIPTION: CG is located in fir and pine on Frog Lake. Fish for trout and swim in the lake. Non-motorized boats only on lake. Deer and elk are common to the area. Expect cool weather and some rain in summer. Supplies available at Government Camp. Campers may gather forewood locally.

GETTING THERE: From Government Camp go SE on US HWY 26 approx. 7 mi. to Frog Lake CG.

SINGLE RATE:	$12	**OPEN DATES:**	**Yearlong***
# of SINGLE SITES:	33	**MAX SPUR:**	**22 feet**
		MAX STAY:	**14 days**
		ELEVATION:	**3800 feet**

27 Gibson Prairie Horse Camp
Hood River • lat 45°29'07" lon 121°31'12"

DESCRIPTION: Campground is set in a fir and pine forest setting on Upper Mill Creek. Fish and swim in the creek. Deer and elk are common to the area. Supplies available at Hood River. Nice weather in summer. Busy on weekends and holidays. Campers may gather firewood locally.

GETTING THERE: From Hood River go S on state HWY 35 approx. 7.5 mi. to primary forest route 17. Go SE on 17 approx. 8 mi. to Gibson Prairie Horse CG.

SINGLE RATE:	$8	**OPEN DATES:**	**Yearlong***
# of SINGLE SITES:	7	**MAX SPUR:**	**24 feet**
		MAX STAY:	**14 days**
		ELEVATION:	**1000 feet**

28 Gone Creek
Government Camp • lat 45°06'56" lon 121°46'11"

DESCRIPTION: Campground is located in fir and pine on the south shore of Timothy Lake. Deer, elk and small campground animals in area. 21 mi. to Government Camp for supplies. Cool in summer with some rain. Gather firewood locally.

GETTING THERE: From Government Camp go E and S on US HWY 26 approx. 10 mi. to primary forest route 42. Go S on 42 approx. 7 mi. to primary forest route 57. Go W on 57 approx. 3 mi. to Hoodview CG.

SINGLE RATE:	Varies	**OPEN DATES:**	**May-Oct**
# of SINGLE SITES:	50	**MAX SPUR:**	**32 feet**
		MAX STAY:	**14 days**
		ELEVATION:	**3200 feet**

29 Green Canyon
Zigzag • lat 45°18'30" lon 121°56'00"

DESCRIPTION: Campground is located in fir and cedar on the Salmon River. Trout and steelhead fishing in river. Cool weather common in summer. 4 mi. to Zigzag for supplies. Gather firewood locally.

GETTING THERE: From Zigzag go S on forest route 2618(Salmon River Road)approximately 4 mi. to Green canyon CG.

SINGLE RATE:	Varies	**OPEN DATES:**	**Apr-Oct**
# of SINGLE SITES:	15	**MAX SPUR:**	**22 feet**
		MAX STAY:	**14 days**
		ELEVATION:	**1350 feet**

30 Grindstone
Government Camp • lat 45°15'00" lon 121°38'00"

DESCRIPTION: CG is located in fir on Barlow Creek. Deer and elk in area. Cool weather can be expected in summer. Go to Government Camp for supplies, 18 mi. Gather firewood locally.

GETTING THERE: From Government Camp go E on US HWY 26 3 mi. to State HWY 35. Go E on 35 approx. 4 mi. to primary forest route 48(White River road). Go S on 48 8 mi. to forest route 43. Go W on 43 approx. 1 mi. to forest dirt route 220. Go N on 220 approx. 3.5 mi. to Barlow Creek CG.

SINGLE RATE:	No fee	**OPEN DATES:**	**Yearlong***
# of SINGLE SITES:	3	**MAX SPUR:**	**10 feet**
		MAX STAY:	**14 days**
		ELEVATION:	**3150 feet**

 Campground has hosts   **Reservable sites**    **Accessible facilities**   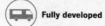 **Fully developed**   **Semi-developed**   **Rustic facilities**

NOTE: Open dates listed are typical. Actual dates are dependent on conditions such as snow pack.

MOUNT HOOD NATIONAL FOREST • OREGON • 21 — 30

31 Herman Creek Horse Camp
Cascade Locks • lat 45°39'00" lon 121°47'00"

DESCRIPTION: Campground is located in fir, cedar and hemlock in the Columbia River Gorge National Scenic Area. Deer, elk, bears and various birds of prey in area. 2 mi. to Cascade Locks for supplies. Gather firewood locally. Horse facilities available.

GETTING THERE: Herman Creek Horse Camp is located 2 mi. east of Cascade Locks just off I-84.

SINGLE RATE:	$8	OPEN DATES:	Yearlong
# of SINGLE SITES:	7	MAX SPUR:	24 feet
		MAX STAY:	14 days
		ELEVATION:	1000 feet

36 Indian Henry
Estacada • lat 45°06'30" lon 122°04'28"

DESCRIPTION: Set in pine forest on the Clackamas River. Expect rain in summer, nicer in July and Aug. Trout and steelhead fishing in the Clackamas River. Supplies at Estacada. Deer, and small wildlife. Fills weekends and holidays. Fall visits are best. Gather firewood locally.

GETTING THERE: Indian Henry CG is located approx. 18 mi. SE of Estacada on state HWY 224.

SINGLE RATE:	$12	OPEN DATES:	May-Sept
# of SINGLE SITES:	86	MAX SPUR:	22 feet
		MAX STAY:	14 days
		ELEVATION:	1250 feet

32 Hideaway Lake
Estacada • lat 45°07'25" lon 121°58'00"

DESCRIPTION: Campground is located in the pine on Hideaway Lake. Fish for trout and swim in the lake. Deer, elk and small animals can be seen in the area. Supplies available in Estacada. Expect rain in summer. Campers may gather firewood.

GETTING THERE: From Estacada go SE on state HWY 24 approx. 21 mi. to primary forest route 57. Go E on 57 approx. 6 mi. to primary forest route 58. Go N on 58 approx. 3 mi. to forest route 5830. Go NW on 5830 approx. 5.5 mi. to Hideaway Lake CG.

SINGLE RATE:	$10	OPEN DATES:	May-Sept
# of SINGLE SITES:	9	MAX SPUR:	16 feet
		MAX STAY:	14 days
		ELEVATION:	4500 feet

37 Joe Graham Horse Camp
Government Camp • lat 45°06'01" lon 121°44'45"

DESCRIPTION: Campground is located in fir and pine on Clackamas Lake. Deer, elk and small campground animals in area. Supplies available at Government Camp. Cool in summer with some rain. Gather firewood locally.

GETTING THERE: From Government Camp go E and S on US HWY 26 approx. 10 mi. to primary forest route 42. Go S on 42 approx. 7 mi. to Joe Graham Horse CG.

SINGLE RATE:	$12	OPEN DATES:	Apr-Sept
# of SINGLE SITES:	14	MAX SPUR:	28 feet
		MAX STAY:	14 days
		ELEVATION:	3350 feet

33 Highrock Springs
Estacada • lat 45°10'30" lon 121°53'30"

DESCRIPTION: Campground is located in a pine and fir forest setting at Highrock Springs. Deer, elk and small animals are common to the area. Supplies available at Estacada. Expect rain in summer. Campers may gather Firewood locally.

GETTING THERE: From Estacada go SE on state HWY 24 aprox. 21 mi. to primary forest route 57. Go E on 57 aprox. 6 mi. to primary forest route 58. Go N on 58 aprox. 6 mi. to forest route. Go W on forest route aprox. 1 mi. to Highrock Springs CG.

SINGLE RATE:	No fee	OPEN DATES:	May-Sept
# of SINGLE SITES:	6	MAX SPUR:	10 feet
		MAX STAY:	14 days
		ELEVATION:	5200 feet

38 Keeps Mill
Wamic • lat 45°09'17" lon 121°31'07"

DESCRIPTION: CG is in a pine and fir forest setting on Clear Creek. Fish for trout and swim in the creek. Expect warm days, cool mornings and rain may be possible. Historic Keeps Mill nearby. Supplies available at Wamic. Deer, marmots and small wildlife are common to the area. Gather firewood locally.

GETTING THERE: From Wamic go W on primary forest route 48 approx. 16 mi. to forest route 4885. Go S on 4885 approx. 3.5 mi. to Keeps Mill CG.

SINGLE RATE:	No fee	OPEN DATES:	May-Oct
# of SINGLE SITES:	5	MAX SPUR:	10 feet
		MAX STAY:	14 days
		ELEVATION:	2600 feet

34 Hoodview
Government Camp • lat 45°20'10" lon 122°49'00"

DESCRIPTION: Campground is located in a fir and pine forest setting on the south shore of Timothy Lake. Fish and swim in the lake. Deer, elk and small animals are common to the area. Supplies available at Government Camp. Cool in summer with some rain. Gather firewood locally.

GETTING THERE: From Government Camp go E and S on US HWY 26 approx. 10 mi. to primary forest route 42. Go S on 42 approx. 7 mi. to primary forest route 57. Go W on 57 approx. 3 mi. to Hoodview CG.

SINGLE RATE:	Varies	OPEN DATES:	May-Sept
# of SINGLE SITES:	43	MAX SPUR:	32 feet
		MAX STAY:	14 days
		ELEVATION:	3200 feet

39 Kingfisher
Estacada • lat 44°58'35" lon 122°05'30"

DESCRIPTION: Set in pine forest on Hot Springs Fork Creek. Expect rain in summer, nicer in July and Aug. Trout fishing in the creek. Close to Bagby Hot Springs. Supplies at Estacada. Deer, and small wildlife. Fills weekends and holidays. Fall visits are best. Gather firewood locally.

GETTING THERE: From Estacada go SE 18 mi. on state HWY 224 to primary forest route 46. Continue 6.5 mi. SE on 46 to primary forest route 63. Continue 3 mi. SE on 63 to primary forest route 70. Continue 1.5 mi. SE on 70 to Kingfisher CG.

SINGLE RATE:	$12	OPEN DATES:	May-Sept
# of SINGLE SITES:	23	MAX SPUR:	16 feet
		MAX STAY:	14 days
		ELEVATION:	1250 feet

35 Horseshoe Lake
Mill City • lat 44°46'48" lon 121°47'05"

DESCRIPTION: Campground is located in pine at Horseshoe Lake. Deer and elk in area. Trout fishing in the numerous lakes in the area. Some supplies available at the lodge at Olallie Lake. Gather firewood locally.

GETTING THERE: From Mill City go E approx. 16.5 mi. on state HWY 22 to primary forest route 46. Go NE on 46 approx. 16.5 mi. to forest route 4690. Go SE on 4690 approx. 7 mi. to forest route 4220. Go S on 4220 approx. 7.5 mi. to Horseshoe Lake CG.

SINGLE RATE:	$6	OPEN DATES:	May-Sept
# of SINGLE SITES:	6	MAX SPUR:	10 feet
		MAX STAY:	14 days
		ELEVATION:	5200 feet

40 Kinnikinnick
Parkdale • lat 45°26'30" lon 121°39'00"

DESCRIPTION: Campground is in a pine and fir forest setting on Laurance Lake. Fish and swim in the lake. Deer, bears and elk are common in the area. Supplies available in Parkdale. Nice weather, but expect some rain, you are in Oregon. Gather firewood locally.

GETTING THERE: From Parkdale go S on forest route 2840 approx. 6 mi. to Kinnikinnick CG.

SINGLE RATE:	$10	OPEN DATES:	Yearlong*
# of SINGLE SITES:	20	MAX SPUR:	16 feet
		MAX STAY:	14 days
		ELEVATION:	3000 feet

 Campground has hosts   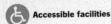 **Reservable sites**   **Accessible facilities**   **Fully developed**   **Semi-developed**   **Rustic facilities**

NOTE: Open dates listed are typical. Actual dates are dependent on conditions such as snow pack.

Page 438

41 Knebal Springs
The Dalles • lat 45°26'04" lon 121°28'39"

DESCRIPTION: CG is located in pine on Knebel Springs on the Middle Fork of Fivemile Creek. Deer, elk and bears are common in the area. Supplies available at The Dalles. Cool mornings and some rain in summer. Campers may gather firewood.

GETTING THERE: Knebal Springs CG is located approx. 18 mi. SW of The Dalles on forest route 1720.

SINGLE RATE:	No fee	OPEN DATES:	May-Oct
# of SINGLE SITES:	8	MAX SPUR:	22 feet
		MAX STAY:	14 days
		ELEVATION:	4000 feet

42 Lake Harriet
Estacada • lat 45°04'25" lon 121°57'25"

DESCRIPTION: Set in pine forest on the Oak Grove Fork Clackamas River. Expect rain in summer, nicer in July and Aug. Trout fishing in the River. Supplies available at Estacada. Deer and small wildlife can be seen nearby. Fall visits are best. Campers may gather firewood locally.

GETTING THERE: From Estacada go SE on state HWY 224 approx. 20.5 mi. to forest route 4630. Go E on 4630 approx. 4.5 mi. to Lake Harriet CG.

SINGLE RATE:	$12	OPEN DATES:	Apr-Sept
# of SINGLE SITES:	13	MAX SPUR:	30 feet
		MAX STAY:	14 days
		ELEVATION:	2000 feet

43 Lazy Bend
Estacada • lat 45°11'28" lon 122°12'23"

DESCRIPTION: Set in pine forest on the Clackamas River. Expect rain in summer, nicer in July and Aug. Trout and steelhead fishing in the River. Supplies available at Estacada. Deer and small wildlife can be seen nearby. Fall visits are best. Campers may gather firewood locally.

GETTING THERE: Lazy Bend CG is located approx. 9 mi. SE of Estacada on state HWY 224.

SINGLE RATE:	$12	OPEN DATES:	Apr-Sept
# of SINGLE SITES:	21	MAX SPUR:	16 feet
		MAX STAY:	14 days
		ELEVATION:	800 feet

44 Little Badger
Tygh Valley • lat 45°16'55" lon 121°20'50"

DESCRIPTION: On Little Badger Creek among pine and oak trees. Warm summers with some rain. Fish for trout or swim in the creek. Supplies available at Tygh Valley. Deer and small wildlife in area. Moderate use, fall is best time to visit. Campers may gather firewood locally.

GETTING THERE: Little Badger CG is located approx. 8.5 mi. NW of Tygh Valley on primary forest route 27.

SINGLE RATE:	No fee	OPEN DATES:	May-Oct
# of SINGLE SITES:	3	MAX SPUR:	16 feet
		MAX STAY:	14 days
		ELEVATION:	2700 feet

45 Little Crater Lake
Government Camp • lat 45°08'52" lon 121°44'47"

DESCRIPTION: CG is located in fir at the Little Crater Lake Geological Area. Deer and elk can be seen in the area. Trout fishing in nearby Timothy Lake. Supplies available at Government Camp. Cool days in summer, expect some rain. Campers may gather firewood locally.

GETTING THERE: From Government Camp go E and S on US HWY 26 approx. 10 mi. to primary forest route 42. Go S on 42 approx. 4.5 mi. to primary forest route 58. Go NW on 58 approx. 1.5 mi. to Little Crater Lake CG.

SINGLE RATE:	$12	OPEN DATES:	May-Sept
# of SINGLE SITES:	16	MAX SPUR:	22 feet
		MAX STAY:	14 days
		ELEVATION:	3200 feet

46 Little Fan Creek
Estacada • lat 44°59'31" lon 122°03'43"

DESCRIPTION: Campground is located in pine on the Collawash River. Deer and small animals can be seen in the area. Fishing for trout and steelhead in river. Supplies available in Estacada. Expect rain in summer. Campers may gather firewood locally.

GETTING THERE: From Estacada go SE 18 mi. on state HWY 224 to primary forest route 46. Continue SE 6.5 mi. on 46 to primary forest route 63. Continue on SE 3 mi. on 63 Little Fan Creek CG.

SINGLE RATE:	$10	OPEN DATES:	May-Sept
# of SINGLE SITES:	3	MAX SPUR:	15 feet
		MAX STAY:	14 days
		ELEVATION:	1500 feet

47 Lockaby
Estacada • lat 45°09'57" lon 122°09'07"

DESCRIPTION: On Clackamas River in a pine and fir forest setting. Expect rainy days. Fish for trout and steelhead or swim in the River. Supplies at Estacada, 13 mi. NW. Deer and small wildlife in area. Campers may gather firewood locally. CG fills weekends and holidays.

GETTING THERE: From Estacada go SE on state HWY 224 approx. 13 mi. to Lockaby CG.

SINGLE RATE:	$12	OPEN DATES:	Apr-Sept
# of SINGLE SITES:	30	MAX SPUR:	16 feet
		MAX STAY:	14 days
		ELEVATION:	900 feet

48 Lost Creek
Zigzag • lat 45°23'00" lon 121°44'00"

DESCRIPTION: Campground is located in fir and cedar on Lost Creek. Trout fishing in creek. Deer and elk in area. 7 mi. to Zigzag for supplies. Rain in summers, cool days. Gather firewood locally.

GETTING THERE: From Zigzag go NE on primary forest route 18 5 mi. to forest route 1825. E on 1825 2 mi. to Lost Creek CG.

SINGLE RATE:	Varies	OPEN DATES:	May-Sept
# of SINGLE SITES:	16	MAX SPUR:	22 feet
		MAX STAY:	14 days
		ELEVATION:	2600 feet

49 Lost Lake
Dee • lat 45°29'47" lon 121°49'03"

DESCRIPTION: Campground is located in fir on Lost Lake. Deer and elk in area. Fish for trout in lake. Some supplies can be purchased in store at Lost Lake Resort. Campers may gather firewood locally. No designated trails in the area.

GETTING THERE: From Dee go SW approx. 11 mi. on primary forest route 13 to forest route 1340. Go S on 1340 approx. 1/2 mi. to Lost Lake CG.

SINGLE RATE:	Varies	OPEN DATES:	Yearlong*
# of SINGLE SITES:	125	MAX SPUR:	32 feet
		MAX STAY:	14 days
		ELEVATION:	3200 feet

50 Lower Crossing
Dufur • lat 45°25'00" lon 121°26'00"

DESCRIPTION: Set among pine and fir on Eightmile Creek. Fish for trout and swim in the creek. Warm days with cool mornings. Deer and small wildlife are common in the area. Moderate use, fall is best time to visit. Campers may gather firewood locally.

GETTING THERE: From Dufur go W on primary forest route 44 approx. 15 mi. to forest route 4440. Go N on 4440 approx. 1 mi. to Lower Crossing CG.

SINGLE RATE:	No fee	OPEN DATES:	May-Oct
# of SINGLE SITES:	3	MAX SPUR:	16 feet
		MAX STAY:	14 days
		ELEVATION:	3800 feet

 Campground has hosts   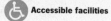 Reservable sites   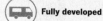 Accessible facilities   Fully developed   Semi-developed   Rustic facilities

NOTE: Open dates listed are typical. Actual dates are dependent on conditions such as snow pack.

51 Lower Lake
Mill City • lat 44°49'23" lon 121°47'47"

DESCRIPTION: Campground is located in a pine and fir forest setting on Lower Lake in the Olallie Lake Scenic Area. Deer and elk are common in the area. Some supplies can be purchased at the lodge at Olallie Lake. Expect rain in summer but otherwise nice. Campers may gather firewood locally.

GETTING THERE: From Mill City go E approx. 16.5 mi. on state HWY 22 to primary forest route 46. Go NE on 46 approx. 16.5 mi. to forest route 4690. Go SE on 4690 approx. 7 mi. to forest route 4220. Go S approx. 4 mi. on 4220 to Lower Lake CG.

SINGLE RATE:	$6	OPEN DATES:	May-Sept
# of SINGLE SITES:	8	MAX SPUR:	15 feet
		MAX STAY:	14 days
		ELEVATION:	4600 feet

52 McCubbins Gulch
Pine Grove • lat 45°06'56" lon 121°28'55"

DESCRIPTION: In a pine and fir forest setting. Expect warm summers with cool mornings. Supplies are available at Pine Grove. Deer, many bird species and small wildlife are common in the area. This is a light use area. Campers may gather firewood locally.

GETTING THERE: From Pine Grove go W on state HWY 216 approx. 7 mi. to forest route 2110. Go E on 2110 approx. 2 mi. to McCubbins Gulch CG.

SINGLE RATE:	No fee	OPEN DATES:	May-Oct
# of SINGLE SITES:	5	MAX SPUR:	25 feet
		MAX STAY:	14 days
		ELEVATION:	3000 feet

53 McNeil
Zigzag • lat 45°23'30" lon 121°52'00"

DESCRIPTION: CG is located in fir and pine forest setting on the Sandy River. Trout and steelhead fishing in river. Deer and elk in area. Supplies available in Zigzag. Expect cool weather and rain in summers. Campers may gather firewood locally.

GETTING THERE: From Zigzag go NE on primary forest route 18 approx. 5 mi. to McNeil CG.

SINGLE RATE:	$10	OPEN DATES:	Apr-Sept
# of SINGLE SITES:	34	MAX SPUR:	22 feet
		MAX STAY:	14 days
		ELEVATION:	2040 feet

54 Meditation Point
Government Camp • lat 45°07'39" lon 121°47'36"

DESCRIPTION: CG is a walk-in site located in fir and pine on the north shore of Timothy Lake. Fish and swim in the lake. Deer, elk and small animals can be seen in the area. Supplies available in Government Camp. Cool in summer with some rain. Gather firewood locally.

GETTING THERE: From Government Camp go E on US HWY 26 10 mi. to primary forest route 42. Go S on 42 approx. 7 mi. to primary forest route 57. Go W on 57 approx. 4 mi. to forest route 5890. Go E on 5890 approx. 1.5 mi. to Meditation Point CG.

SINGLE RATE:	No fee	OPEN DATES:	May-Sept
# of SINGLE SITES:	5		
		MAX STAY:	14 days
		ELEVATION:	3200 feet

55 North Arm
Government Camp • lat 45°09'30" lon 121°46'30"

DESCRIPTION: CG is a walk-in site located in fir and pine on the north shore of Timothy Lake. Deer, elk and small campground animals can be seen in the area. Supplies available at Government Camp. Cool in summer with some rain. Campers may gather firewood locally.

GETTING THERE: From Government Camp go E and S on US HWY 26 approx. 10 mi. to primary forest route 42. Go S on 42 approx. 7 mi. to primary forest route 57. Go W on 57 approx. 4 mi. to forest route 5890. Go E on 5890 approx. 3 mi. to North Arm CG.

SINGLE RATE:	$8	OPEN DATES:	May-Sept
# of SINGLE SITES:	8		
		MAX STAY:	14 days
		ELEVATION:	3200 feet

56 Oak Fork
Government Camp • lat 45°06'55" lon 121°46'10"

DESCRIPTION: CG is located in fir and pine on the SE shore of Timothy Lake. Deer, elk and small campground animals in area. 21 mi. to Government Camp for supplies. Cool in summer with some rain. Gather firewood locally.

GETTING THERE: From Government Camp go E and S on US HWY 26 approx. 10 mi. to primary forest route 42. Go S on 42 approx. 7 mi. to primary forest route 57. Go W on 57 approx. 2 mi. to Oakfork CG.

SINGLE RATE:	Varies	OPEN DATES:	May-Oct
# of SINGLE SITES:	47	MAX SPUR:	32 feet
		MAX STAY:	14 days
		ELEVATION:	3200 feet

57 Olallie Meadows
Mill City • lat 44°01'36" lon 122°02'22"

DESCRIPTION: CG is located in fir and pine on Olallie Creek north of the Olallie Lake Scenic Area. Trout fishing in numerous small lakes in area. Deer and elk in area. Some supplies are available at the lodge at Olallie Lake. Gather firewood locally.

GETTING THERE: From Mill City go E approx. 16.5 mi. on state HWY 22 to primary forest route 46. Go NE on 46 approx. 16.5 mi. to forest route 4690. Go SE on 4690 approx. 7 mi. to forest route 4220. Go S approx. 1 mi. on 4220 to Olallie Meadow CG.

SINGLE RATE:	$6	OPEN DATES:	May-Sept
# of SINGLE SITES:	7	MAX SPUR:	16 feet
		MAX STAY:	14 days
		ELEVATION:	4500 feet

58 Overlook
Cascade Locks • lat 45°38'00" lon 121°54'00"

DESCRIPTION: CG is available for groups by reservation only. It is located between the Columbia River and I-84 in Fir, cedar and hemlock. Deer and various birds of prey in area. 2 mi. to Cascade Locks for supplies.

GETTING THERE: Overlook CG is located west of Cascade Locks at Eagle Creek just between I-84 and the Columbia River.

GROUP RATE:	$80	OPEN DATES:	May-Sept
# of GROUP SITES:	1	MAX SPUR:	40 feet
		MAX STAY:	14 days
		ELEVATION:	400 feet

59 Paul Dennis
Mill City • lat 44°48'40" lon 121°47'10"

DESCRIPTION: CG is located in fir and pine on the N end of Olallie Lake in the Olallie Lake Scenic Area. Fish for trout or swim in any of the numerous small lakes in area. Deer and elk are common to the area. Some supplies are available at the lodge at Olallie Lake. Campers may gather firewood locally.

GETTING THERE: From Mill City go E approx. 16.5 mi. on state HWY 22 to primary forest route 46. Go NE on 46 approx. 16.5 mi. to forest route 4690. Go SE on 4690 approx. 7 mi. to forest route 4220. Go S approx. 5 mi. on 4220 to Paul Dennis CG.

SINGLE RATE:	$9	OPEN DATES:	May-Sept
# of SINGLE SITES:	17	MAX SPUR:	16 feet
		MAX STAY:	14 days
		ELEVATION:	5000 feet

60 Pebble Ford
Dufur • lat 45°24'01" lon 121°27'46"

DESCRIPTION: Thick pine and fir forest fronting Eightmile Creek. Stream fish for trout in the creek. Supplies available at Dufur. Deer and small wildlife frequent area. Moderate use, heaviest on holidays and weekends. Campers may gather firewood locally.

GETTING THERE: Pebble Ford CG is located approx. 16 mi. W of Dufur on primary forest route 44.

SINGLE RATE:	No fee	OPEN DATES:	May-Oct
# of SINGLE SITES:	3	MAX SPUR:	16 feet
		MAX STAY:	14 days
		ELEVATION:	4200 feet

Campground has hosts   **Reservable sites**   **Accessible facilities**   **Fully developed**   **Semi-developed**   **Rustic facilities**

NOTE: Open dates listed are typical. Actual dates are dependent on conditions such as snow pack.

61 Peninsula
Mill City • lat 44°48'30" lon 121°47'30"

DESCRIPTION: CG is located in fir and pine on the S end of Olallie Lake in the Olallie Lake Scenic Area. Fish for trout and swim in any of the numerous small lakes in area. Deer and elk can be seen in the area. Some supplies are available at the lodge at Olallie Lake. Campers may gather firewood locally.

GETTING THERE: From Mill City go E approx. 16.5 mi. on state HWY 22 to primary forest route 46. Go NE on 46 approx. 16.5 mi. to forest route 4690. Go SE on 4690 approx. 7 mi. to forest route 4220. Go S approx. 6 mi. on 4220 to Peninsula CG.

SINGLE RATE:	Varies	OPEN DATES:	May-Sept
# of SINGLE SITES:	35	MAX SPUR:	24 feet
		MAX STAY:	14 days
		ELEVATION:	4900 feet

62 Pine Point
Government Camp • lat 45°06'45" lon 121°48'20"

DESCRIPTION: CG is located in fir and pine on the SW shore of Timothy Lake. Deer, elk and small animals are common to the area. Supplies available at Government Camp. Cool in summer with some rain. Campers may gather firewood locally.

GETTING THERE: From Government Camp go E and S on US HWY 26 approx. 10 mi. to primary forest route 42. Go S on 42 approx. 7 mi. to primary forest route 57. Go W on 57 approx. 3.5 mi. to Pine Point CG.

SINGLE RATE:	Varies	OPEN DATES:	May-Sept
# of SINGLE SITES:	25	MAX SPUR:	32 feet
		MAX STAY:	14 days
		ELEVATION:	3200 feet

63 Post Camp
Wamic • lat 45°12'57" lon 121°31'07"

DESCRIPTION: Set among pine and fir forest. Expect warm summer days, cool mornings. No fishing on site. Supplies available in Wamic. Deer, birds and small wildlife are common in the area. Moderate use, busy during holidays. Fall is best time to visit.

GETTING THERE: From Wamic go W approx. 13.5 mi. on primary forest route 48 to forest route 4860. Go N on 4860 approx. 2 mi. to Post Camp CG.

SINGLE RATE:	No fee	OPEN DATES:	May-Oct
# of SINGLE SITES:	4	MAX SPUR:	16 feet
		MAX STAY:	14 days
		ELEVATION:	4600 feet

64 Raab
Estacada • lat 45°01'20" lon 122°04'10"

DESCRIPTION: Set in pine forest on the Collawash River. Expect rain in summer, nicer in July and Aug. Trout and steelhead fishing in the Clackamas and Collawash Rivers. Supplies available at Estacada. Deer and small wildlife can be seen in the area. Fills weekends and holidays. Campers may gather firewood locally.

GETTING THERE: From Estacada go SE on state HWY 224 approx. 18 mi. to primary forest route 46. Go SE on 46 approx. 7.5 mi. to primary forest route 63. Go S on 63 approx. 1 mi. to Raab CG.

SINGLE RATE:	$10	OPEN DATES:	May-Sept
# of SINGLE SITES:	27	MAX SPUR:	22 feet
		MAX STAY:	14 days
		ELEVATION:	1500 feet

65 Rainbow
Estacada • lat 43°51'53" lon 119°25'03"

DESCRIPTION: Set in pine forest on the Clackamas River. Expect rain in summer, nicer in July and Aug. Trout and steelhead fishing in the Clackamas River. Supplies available at Estacada. Deer and small wildlife can be seen in the area. Fall visits are best. Gather firewood locally.

GETTING THERE: From Estacada go SE on state HWY 224 approx. 18 mi. to primary forest route 46. Go SE on 46 approx. 3 mi. to Rainbow CG.

SINGLE RATE:	$10	OPEN DATES:	Apr-Sept
# of SINGLE SITES:	17	MAX SPUR:	16 feet
		MAX STAY:	14 days
		ELEVATION:	1400 feet

66 Rainy Lake
Dee • lat 45°37'37" lon 121°45'27"

DESCRIPTION: CG is located in a pine and fir forest setting on Rainy Lake. Fish for trout and swim in the lake. Deer and elk can be seen in the area. Supplies available in Dee. Campers may gather firewood locally.

GETTING THERE: Rainy Lake CG is located 12 mi. W of Dee on forest route 2820.

SINGLE RATE:	No fee	OPEN DATES:	Yearlong*
# of SINGLE SITES:	4		
		MAX STAY:	14 days
		ELEVATION:	4100 feet

67 Riley Horse Camp
Zigzag • lat 45°23'00" lon 121°51'30"

DESCRIPTION: CG is located in a fir and pine forest setting on the Sandy River. Deer, elk and birds are common to the area. Fish for trout and steelhead or swim in the river. Supplies available in Zigzag. Cool weather in summer is common. Campers may gather firewood locally.

GETTING THERE: From Zigzag go NE on primary forest route 18 approx. 5 mi. to Riley CG.

SINGLE RATE:	$12	OPEN DATES:	Apr-Sept
# of SINGLE SITES:	14	MAX SPUR:	16 feet
		MAX STAY:	14 days
		ELEVATION:	2100 feet

68 Ripplebrook
Estacada • lat 45°04'45" lon 122°02'30"

DESCRIPTION: Set in a pine forest setting on the Oak Grove Fork Clackamas River. Fish for trout and steelhead or swim in the Clackamas River. Supplies available at Estacada. Deer and small wildlife can be seen in the area. Fall visits are best. Campers may gather firewood locally.

GETTING THERE: From Estacada go SE on state HWY 224 approx. 18 mi. to primary forest route 46. Go SE on 46 approx. 3 mi. to Ripplebrook CG.

SINGLE RATE:	$10	OPEN DATES:	May-Sept
# of SINGLE SITES:	13	MAX SPUR:	16 feet
		MAX STAY:	14 days
		ELEVATION:	1500 feet

69 River Ford
Estacada • lat 45°02'00" lon 122°03'00"

DESCRIPTION: Set in pine forest on the Clackamas River. Expect rain in summer, nicer in July and Aug. Trout and steelhead fishing in the Clackamas River. Supplies available in Estacada. Deer and small wildlife can be seen in the area. Fall visits are best. Campers may gather firewood locally.

GETTING THERE: From Estacada go SE on state HWY 224 approx. 18 mi. to primary forest route 46. Go SE on 46 approx. 6.5 mi. to River Ford CG.

SINGLE RATE:	$10	OPEN DATES:	May-Sept
# of SINGLE SITES:	10	MAX SPUR:	20 feet
		MAX STAY:	14 days
		ELEVATION:	1500 feet

70 Riverside
Estacada • lat 45°03'00" lon 122°04'00"

DESCRIPTION: Set in pine forest on the Clackamas River. Expect rain in summer, nicer in July and Aug. Trout and steelhead fishing in the Clackamas River. Supplies available in Estacada. Deer can be seen in the area. Fall visits are best. Campers may gather firewood locally.

GETTING THERE: From Estacada go SE on state HWY 224 approx. 18 mi. to primary forest route 46. Go SE on 46 approx. 6 mi. to Riverside CG.

SINGLE RATE:	$12	OPEN DATES:	May-Sept
# of SINGLE SITES:	16	MAX SPUR:	22 feet
		MAX STAY:	14 days
		ELEVATION:	1400 feet

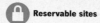 Campground has hosts 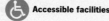 Reservable sites   Accessible facilities   Fully developed   Semi-developed Rustic facilities

NOTE: Open dates listed are typical. Actual dates are dependent on conditions such as snow pack.

71 Roaring River
Estacada • lat 45°09'30" lon 122°06'47"

DESCRIPTION: CG is located in pine forest on the Clackamas River. Expect rain in summer, nicer in July and Aug. Trout and steelhead fishing in the Clackamas River. Supplies available in Estacada. Deer are common in the area. Fall visits are best. Campers may gather firewood locally.

GETTING THERE: Roaring River CG is located approx. 15 mi. SE of Estacada on state HWY 224.

SINGLE RATE:	$12	OPEN DATES:	May-Sept
# of SINGLE SITES:	19	MAX SPUR:	16 feet
		MAX STAY:	14 days
		ELEVATION:	1000 feet

72 Robinhood
Hood River • lat 45°20'27" lon 121°34'12"

DESCRIPTION: CG is located on East Fork Hood River in fir and pine. Fish for steelhead and trout in the river. Deer and elk are common to the area. Campers may gather firewood locally. Good weather, but expect some rain.

GETTING THERE: Robinhood CG is located approx. 25 mi. S of Hood River on state HWY 35.

SINGLE RATE:	Varies	OPEN DATES:	Yearlong*
# of SINGLE SITES:	24	MAX SPUR:	18 feet
		MAX STAY:	14 days
		ELEVATION:	3500 feet

73 Rock Creek Reservoir
Wamic • lat 45°03'15" lon 121°22'50"

DESCRIPTION: In a thick pine and fir forest on Rock Creek Reservoir. Days are warm all summer. Fish for trout and bass in Rock Creek Reservoir. Deer, ducks and small bird are common to the area. Moderate use, heaviest on weekends and holidays. Campers may gather firewood locally.

GETTING THERE: Rock Creek Reservoir CG is located approx. 5 mi. W of Wamic on primary forest route 48.

SINGLE RATE:	$12	OPEN DATES:	May-Oct
# of SINGLE SITES:	33	MAX SPUR:	18 feet
		MAX STAY:	14 days
		ELEVATION:	2200 feet

74 Round Lake
Detroit • lat 44°52'35" lon 121°58'04"

DESCRIPTION: CG is located in a pine and fir forest setting on Round Lake just south of the Sugar Pine Botanical Area. Fish and swim in the lake. Supplies available in Detroit. Deer and elk are common to the area. Campers may gather Firewood locally

GETTING THERE: From Detroit go NE on primary forest route 46 approx. 4 mi. to forest route 4696. Go NE on 4696 approx. 2 mi. to forest route 4698. Go NE on 4698 approx. 5 mi. to forest route 6370. Go NE on 6370 approx. 5.5 mi. to Round Lake CG.

SINGLE RATE:	No fee	OPEN DATES:	May-Sept
# of SINGLE SITES:	6	MAX SPUR:	15 feet
		MAX STAY:	14 days
		ELEVATION:	3500 feet

75 Shellrock Creek
Estacada • lat 45°05'05" lon 121°55'21"

DESCRIPTION: CG is in a pine forest setting on Shellrock Creek. Expect rain in summer, nicer in July and Aug. Trout and steelhead fishing in the creek and the Oak Grove Fork Clackamas River. Supplies available at Estacada. Deer can be seen in the area. Campers may gather firewood locally.

GETTING THERE: From Estacada go SE on state HWY 224 approx. 18 mi. to primary forest route 46. Go SE on 46 approx. 3 mi. to primary forest route 57. Go E on 57 approx. 6 mi. to primary forest route 58. Go N on 58 approx. 1 mi. to Shellrock Creek CG.

SINGLE RATE:	$10	OPEN DATES:	May-Sept
# of SINGLE SITES:	8	MAX SPUR:	16 feet
		MAX STAY:	14 days
		ELEVATION:	2200 feet

76 Sherwood
Hood River • lat 45°23'41" lon 121°34'12"

DESCRIPTION: CG is located on the East Fork Hood River in a fir and pine forest setting. Fish for steelhead and trout or swim in the river. Deer and elk are common to the area. Campers may gather firewood locally. Good weather, but expect some rain.

GETTING THERE: Sherwood CG is located approx. 26.5 mi. S of Hood River on state HWY 35.

SINGLE RATE:	$10	OPEN DATES:	Yearlong*
# of SINGLE SITES:	14	MAX SPUR:	16 feet
		MAX STAY:	14 days
		ELEVATION:	3000 feet

77 Still Creek
Government Camp • lat 45°17'44" lon 121°44'10"

DESCRIPTION: CG is located in fir forest setting on Still Creek. Trout fishing in creek. Deer and elk are common to the area. Supplies available at Government Camp. Cool weather common in summers, expect rain. Campers may gather firewood locally.

GETTING THERE: From Government Camp go E approx. 1 mi. on US HWY 26 to forest route 2650. Go S on 2650 approx. 1 mi. to Still Creek CG.

SINGLE RATE:	$12	OPEN DATES:	June-Sept
# of SINGLE SITES:	27	MAX SPUR:	16 feet
		MAX STAY:	14 days
		ELEVATION:	3600 feet

78 Summit Lake
Government Camp • lat 45°01'55" lon 121°47'20"

DESCRIPTION: CG is located in pine and fir on Summit Lake. Fish for trout or swim in the lake. Deer, elk and bears are common to the area. Supplies available at Government Camp. Campers may gather firewood locally.

GETTING THERE: From Government Camp go E and S on US HWY 26 approx. 10 mi. to primary forest route 42. Go S on 42 approx. 11 mi. to forest route. Go W 1/2 mi. to Summit Lake CG.

SINGLE RATE:	$8	OPEN DATES:	May-Sept
# of SINGLE SITES:	5		
		MAX STAY:	14 days
		ELEVATION:	4200 feet

79 Sunstrip
Estacada • lat 45°09'10" lon 122°06'30"

DESCRIPTION: Set in pine forest on the Clackamas River. Expect rain in summer, nicer in July and Aug. Trout and steelhead fishing in the Clackamas River. Supplies in Estacada. Deer can be seen in the area. Fall visits are best. Campers may gather firewood locally.

GETTING THERE: Sunset CG is located approx. 15.5 mi. SE of Estacada on state HWY 224.

SINGLE RATE:	$12	OPEN DATES:	Apr-Sept
# of SINGLE SITES:	9	MAX SPUR:	18 feet
		MAX STAY:	14 days
		ELEVATION:	1000 feet

80 Tilly Jane
Hood River • lat 45°23'58" lon 121°38'47"

DESCRIPTION: CG is situated in fir and pine on Tilly Jane Creek. Deer and elk are common to the area. Cool weather is common in summer, expect some rain. Supplies available at Hood River. Campers may gather firewood.

GETTING THERE: From Hood River go S on state HWY 35 approx. 20 mi. to forest route 3510. Go NW on 3510 approx. 1.5 mi. to forest route 3512. Go SW on 3512 approx. 7 mi. to Tilly Jane CG.

SINGLE RATE:	No fee	OPEN DATES:	Yearlong*
# of SINGLE SITES:	14	MAX SPUR:	10 feet
		MAX STAY:	14 days
		ELEVATION:	5000 feet

 Campground has hosts　　 Reservable sites　　 Accessible facilities　　 Fully developed　　 Semi-developed　　 Rustic facilities

NOTE: Open dates listed are typical. Actual dates are dependent on conditions such as snow pack.

81 Tollgate

Rhododendron • lat 45°19'30" lon 121°55'00"

DESCRIPTION: CG is located in fir and willow on the Zigzag River at the historic western terminus of the Barlow Road. Fishing for trout and steelhead in river. Supplies available in Rhododendron. Deer and raccoons are common to the area. Cool weather in summer. Gather firewood locally.

GETTING THERE: Tollgate CG is located 1/2 mi. SE of Rhododendron on US HWY 26.

SINGLE RATE:	Varies	OPEN DATES:	Apr-Sept
# of SINGLE SITES:	15	MAX SPUR:	16 feet
		MAX STAY:	14 days
		ELEVATION:	1700 feet

82 Triangle Lake Equestrian Camp

Mill City • lat 45°21'25" lon 121°41'20"

DESCRIPTION: CG is located in pine and fir on Triangle Lake just north of the Olallie Lake Scenic Area. Fish and swim in the lake. Deer and elk are common to the area. Supplies can be obtained at the lodge at Olallie Lake. Campers may gather firewood locally.

GETTING THERE: From Mill City go 16.5 mi. on state HWY 22 to primary forest route 46. Go NE on 46 approx. 16.5 mi. to forest route 4690. Go SE on 4690 approx. 7 mi. to forest route 4220. Go S approx. 2 mi. on 4220 to Triangle Lake Equestrian CG.

SINGLE RATE:	No fee	OPEN DATES:	May-Sept
# of SINGLE SITES:	8	MAX SPUR:	30 feet
		MAX STAY:	14 days
		ELEVATION:	4560 feet

83 Trillium Lake

Government Camp • lat 45°16'13" lon 121°44'05"

DESCRIPTION: CG is located in fir on Trillium Lake and is featured on the cover of the Pacific Western edition of Our National Forests magazine. Fish for trout in lake. 4 mi. to Government Camp for supplies. Campers may gather firewood locally.

GETTING THERE: From Government Camp go E on US HWY 26 approximately 1 mi. to forest route 2650. Go S on 2650 approx. 2.5 mi. to Trillium Lake CG.

SINGLE RATE:	Varies	OPEN DATES:	May-Oct
# of SINGLE SITES:	57	MAX SPUR:	40 feet
		MAX STAY:	14 days
		ELEVATION:	3600 feet

84 Underhill Site

Dufur • lat 45°23'50" lon 121°25'15"

DESCRIPTION: Set in a pine and fir forest. Warm summer days, cool mornings. No fishing nearby. Most supplies available at Dufurt. Deer, birds and small wildlife frequent area. Moderate use, heaviest on weekends and holidays. Firewood available to gather nearby.

GETTING THERE: Underhill Site CG is located approx. 13.5 mi. W of Dufur on primary forest route 44.

SINGLE RATE:	No fee	OPEN DATES:	May-Oct
# of SINGLE SITES:	2	MAX SPUR:	10 feet
		MAX STAY:	14 days
		ELEVATION:	3500 feet

85 Wahtum
Dee • lat 45°34'47" lon 121°47'43"

DESCRIPTION: CG is located in fir and pine on Wahtum Lake. Fish for trout in lake. Deer and elk are common in the area. Supplies available at Dee. Nice weather in summer, but expect some rain. Campers may gather firewood locally.

GETTING THERE: From Dee SW on primary forest route 13 approx. 6 mi. to forest route 1310. Go W on 1310 approx. 6 mi. to Wahtum Lake CG.

SINGLE RATE:	No fee	OPEN DATES:	Yearlong*
# of SINGLE SITES:	5	MAX SPUR:	10 feet
		MAX STAY:	14 days
		ELEVATION:	3900 feet

86 White River Station
Wamic • lat 45°11'54" lon 121°35'54"

DESCRIPTION: Nestled in a beautiful pine and fir forest setting on the White River. Stream fish for trout on the White River. Most supplies available at Government Camp. Deer, small wildlife frequent area. Light use, anytime is good to visit. Campers may gather firewood locally.

GETTING THERE: From Wimac go W on primary forest route 48 approx. 19 mi. to primary forest route 43. Go W on 43 approx. 1 mi. to forest route 3530. Go S on 3530 approx. 1 mi. to White River Station CG.

SINGLE RATE:	No fee	OPEN DATES:	May-Oct
# of SINGLE SITES:	5	MAX SPUR:	32 feet
		MAX STAY:	14 days
		ELEVATION:	3000 feet

87 Wyeth
Cascade Locks • lat 45°39'00" lon 121°46'00"

DESCRIPTION: This CG is situated in a grove of fir on Gorton Creek. The CG rests at the start of the Cascade "rain shadow". It is drier than other CGs in the Columbia River Gorge. The Columbia River Gorge offers excellent wind-surfing adventures. Visit Cascade Locks which is approx. 6 mi. away for supplies.

GETTING THERE: Wyeth CG is located 6 mi. E of Cascade Locks just off I-84.

SINGLE RATE:	$10	OPEN DATES:	May-Sept
# of SINGLE SITES:	17	MAX SPUR:	32 feet
		MAX STAY:	14 days
		ELEVATION:	400 feet

 Campground has hosts Reservable sites Accessible facilities   Fully developed  Semi-developed  Rustic facilities

NOTE: Open dates listed are typical. Actual dates are dependent on conditions such as snow pack.

USFS Photo

OCHOCO NATIONAL FOREST

The Ochoco National Forest sits in the geographic center of Oregon. Established in 1911, the forest encompasses about 848,000 acres of vast natural resources, scenic grandeur, and tremendous recreation opportunities. People are drawn to the Ochoco for its majestic ponderosa pine stands, picturesque rim-rock vantage points, deep canyons, abundant wildlife and plentiful sunshine.

The canyons and rocks hold clues to those who once inhabited the Ochoco. Heritage sites are rich and varied with ancient Indian villages, campsites, sacred grounds, old historic wagon roads, mines, cabins, and lookouts.

The Ochoco, with a total of 5003 miles of forest roads and 50 miles of trails outside the wilderness, provides challenging biking and hiking through scenic terrain. Four wilderness areas invite visitors to backpack, camp and hike. For water lovers, there are six reservoirs either bordering or located within the boundaries of the forest, while 100 miles of streams on the north slopes of the forest provide excellent fishing for rainbow trout. Four scenic rivers flow through spectacular rugged, basalt canyons framed by ponderosa pine and douglas fir trees.

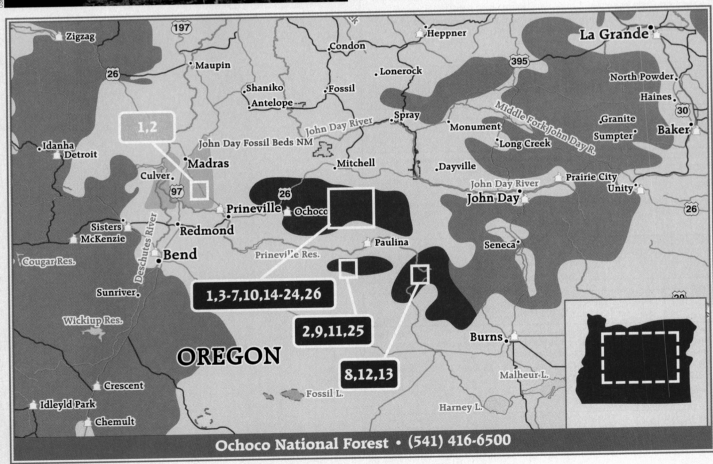

Ochoco National Forest • (541) 416-6500

1 Allen Creek
Ochoco Ranger Station • lat 44°23'40" lon 120°10'20"

DESCRIPTION: Located in Ponderosa Pine and open meadow setting on Allen Creek. Trout fish the creek. Gather firewood except in timber sale areas. Elk, deer, wild horses, antelopes, black bears and cougars in area. Horse facilities with 5 corrals. Horse, hike and mountain bike trails nearby.

GETTING THERE: From Ochoco RS go NE on forest route 22 approx. 19 mi. to Allen Creek CG.

SINGLE RATE:	No fee	OPEN DATES:	May-Oct*
# of SINGLE SITES:	5	MAX SPUR:	24 feet
		MAX STAY:	14 days
		ELEVATION:	4200 feet

2 Antelopes Flat Reservoir
Prineville • lat 44°00'17" lon 120°23'3"

DESCRIPTION: High desert pine and juniper setting. Dry, warm to hot days in summer. Fishing for trout, boating, swimming in the nearby lake. Gather firewood except for timber sale areas. Deer, elk, antelopes, black bears and cougars in area. No nearby trails.

GETTING THERE: From Prineville go SE on state HWY 380 approx. 26 mi. to forest route 17. Go S on 17 approx. 12 mi. to Antelopes Reservoir CG.

SINGLE RATE:	$8	OPEN DATES:	Apr-Oct*
# of SINGLE SITES:	24	MAX SPUR:	30 feet
		MAX STAY:	14 days
		ELEVATION:	4600 feet

3 Barn House
Mitchell • lat 44°28'25" lon 119°56'0"

DESCRIPTION: In a Ponderosa Pine forest setting on Mac Creek. Gather firewood except for timber sale areas. Deer, elk, antelopes, black bears and cougars in area. Trail from Barn House Springs to Fry Springs.

GETTING THERE: From Mitchell Go E on US HWY 26 approx. 11 mi. to forest route 12. Go S on 12 approx. 4 mi. to Barnhouse CG.

SINGLE RATE:	No fee	OPEN DATES:	May-Sept
# of SINGLE SITES:	6	MAX SPUR:	20 feet
		MAX STAY:	14 days
		ELEVATION:	5117 feet

4 Big Springs
Ochoco Ranger Station • lat 44°19'56" lon 119°59'2"

DESCRIPTION: In Ponderosa Pine forest on Big Springs Creek. No drinking water. Gather firewood except for timber sale areas. Deer, elk, antelopes, black bears and cougars in area.

GETTING THERE: From Ochoco RS go E on forest route 42 approx. 21 mi. to forest route 4270. N on 4270 3 mi. to Big Springs CG.

SINGLE RATE:	No fee	OPEN DATES:	May-Sept
# of SINGLE SITES:	6	MAX SPUR:	20 feet
		MAX STAY:	14 days
		ELEVATION:	5015 feet

5 Biggs Spring
Ochoco Ranger Station • lat 44°16'20" lon 120°15'30"

DESCRIPTION: In a meadow area surrounded by Ponderosa Pine on Biggs Spring Creek. No drinking water. Fish for trout on creek. Gather firewood except for timber sale areas. Deer, elk, wild horse, antelopes, black bears and cougars in area. Horse, hike and mountain. bike trails nearby.

GETTING THERE: From Ochoco RS go E on forest route 42 approx. 10 mi. to forest route 4215. Go S on 4215 approx. 4 mi. to Biggs Spring CG.

SINGLE RATE:	No fee	OPEN DATES:	May-Sept
# of SINGLE SITES:	3	MAX SPUR:	24 feet
		MAX STAY:	14 days
		ELEVATION:	4800 feet

6 Cottonwood
Mitchell • lat 44°23'16" lon 119°51'14"

DESCRIPTION: Located in Ponderosa Pine trees. No drinking water. Gather firewood except for timber sale areas. Deer, elk, antelopes, black bears and cougars in area.

GETTING THERE: From Mitchell Go E on US HWY 26 approx. 11 mi. to forest route 12. S on 12 approx. 13 mi. to Cottonwood CG.

SINGLE RATE:	No fee	OPEN DATES:	May-Sept
# of SINGLE SITES:	6	MAX SPUR:	20 feet
		MAX STAY:	14 days
		ELEVATION:	5700 feet

7 Deep Creek
Ochoco Ranger Station • lat 44°19'41" lon 120°04'34"

DESCRIPTION: In Ponderosa Pine on Deep Creek. No drinking water. Fish for trout on creek. Gather firewood except for timber sale areas. Deer, elk, wild horses, antelopes, black bears and cougars in area. Horse, hike and mountain. bike trails nearby.

GETTING THERE: From Ochoco RS go E on forest route 42 approx. 18 mi. to Deep Creek CG.

SINGLE RATE:	No fee	OPEN DATES:	May-Sept
# of SINGLE SITES:	6	MAX SPUR:	24 feet
		MAX STAY:	14 days
		ELEVATION:	4600 feet

8 Delintment Lake
Burns • lat 43°53'24" lon 119°37'24"

DESCRIPTION: A forest of large ponderosa pine and a large blue lake provide a beautiful campground setting. Lake is stocked with trout. Elk, deer, black bears in area. Trails nearby.

GETTING THERE: From Burns go N on county route 127 12 mi. to forest route 41. W and N on 41 31.5 mi. to Delintment Lake CG.

SINGLE RATE:	$8	OPEN DATES:	May-Sept
# of SINGLE SITES:	29	MAX SPUR:	24 feet
		MAX STAY:	14 days
		ELEVATION:	5600 feet

9 Double Cabin
Prineville • lat 44°01'50" lon 120°19'15"

DESCRIPTION: Set in Ponderosa Pine forest on Double Cabin Creek. No drinking water. Near Double Cabin Pond for trout fishing. Gather firewood except for timber sale areas. Deer, elk, antelopes, black bears and cougars in area. Trail leads around the pond.

GETTING THERE: From Prineville go E on state HWY 380 approx. 38 mi. to forest route 16. Go S on 16 approx. 11 mi. to Double Cabin CG.

SINGLE RATE:	No fee	OPEN DATES:	May-Sept
# of SINGLE SITES:	5	MAX SPUR:	20 feet
		MAX STAY:	14 days
		ELEVATION:	5200 feet

10 Dry Creek Horse Camp
Prineville • lat 44°24'00" lon 120°39'00"

DESCRIPTION: Nestled in a Ponderosa Pine forest setting. No drinking water. Gather firewood except for timber sale areas. Deer, elk, antelopes, black bears and cougars in area. 18 corrals in CG. Horse and hike trail (Gitty-up-go Trail) closed for 2000-2003 seasons for timber harvest. Contact Ranger District for info.

GETTING THERE: From Prineville go E on HWY 26 approx. 9 mi. to Mill Creek road. Go N approx. 5 mi. to forest route 3370. Go W and N on 3370 approx. 2.5 mi to Dry Creek CG. Road Not Suitable for large RV's.

SINGLE RATE:	No fee	OPEN DATES:	Apr-Nov
# of SINGLE SITES:	5	MAX SPUR:	20 feet
		MAX STAY:	14 days
		ELEVATION:	3900 feet

 Campground has hosts   **Reservable sites**   **Accessible facilities**   **Fully developed**   **Semi-developed**   **Rustic facilities**

NOTE: Open dates listed are typical. Actual dates are dependent on conditions such as snow pack.

11 Elkhorn
Prineville • lat 44°04'00" lon 121°17'00"

DESCRIPTION: Nestled in Ponderosa Pine near Drake Creek. Gather firewood except for timber sale areas. Deer, elk, antelopes, black bears and cougars in area. 18 corrals in CG. Horse and hike trail (Gitty-up-go Trail) closed for 2000-2003 seasons for timber harvest. Contact Ranger District for info.

GETTING THERE: From Prineville go E on state HWY 380 approx. 29 mi. to forest route 16. Go S on 16 approx. 4 mi. to Elkhorn CG.

SINGLE RATE:	No fee	OPEN DATES:	May-Sept
# of SINGLE SITES:	4	MAX SPUR:	24 feet
		MAX STAY:	14 days
		ELEVATION:	4500 feet

16 Ochoco Divide
Prineville • lat 44°30'01" lon 120°23'05"

DESCRIPTION: CG is located in an old growth ponderosa pine stand. No nearby fishing. Gather firewood except for timber sale areas. Deer, elk, wild horse, antelopes, black bears and cougars in area. Horse, hike, mountain. bike trails nearby.

GETTING THERE: Ochoco Divide CG is located approx. 30 mi. E of Prineville on US HWY 26.

SINGLE RATE:	$8	OPEN DATES:	May-Oct
# of SINGLE SITES:	28	MAX SPUR:	24 feet
		MAX STAY:	14 days
		ELEVATION:	4700 feet

12 Emigrant
Burns • lat 43°51'01" lon 119°24'35"

DESCRIPTION: CG is in a forest setting along Emigrant Creek. Good fishing for fly fishermen. Other activities to pursue in the area include wildlife viewing and hiking on developed trails.

GETTING THERE: From Burns go N on county route 127 to forest route 43. Go W on 43 approx. 10 mi. to forest route 4340. Go W on 4340 approx. 1/2 mi. to Emigrant CG.

SINGLE RATE:	$5	OPEN DATES:	May-Sept
# of SINGLE SITES:	and	MAX SPUR:	24 feet
		MAX STAY:	14 days
		ELEVATION:	5100 feet

17 Ochoco Forest Camp
Ochoco RS • lat 44°24'00" lon 120°25'10"

DESCRIPTION: CG is located along Ochoco Creek in a lush setting of ponderosa pine and aspen. Fish in the creek for small rainbow trout. Gather firewood except for timber sale areas. Deer, elk, wild horse, antelopes, black bears and cougars in area. Horse and hike trails include Lookout Mountain. Nat'l Recreation Trail.

GETTING THERE: Ochoco CG is located at the Ochoco Ranger Station on county route 23.

SINGLE RATE:	$8	OPEN DATES:	May-Oct
# of SINGLE SITES:	6	MAX SPUR:	24 feet
GROUP RATE:	Varies	MAX STAY:	14 days
# of GROUP SITES:	1	ELEVATION:	4000 feet

13 Falls
Burns • lat 43°51'00" lon 119°24'35"

DESCRIPTION: CG offers a quiet, relaxing opportunity in a fairly undeveloped setting. Large old ponderosa pine grace the campground and a small stream, Emigrant Creek, is nearby. Activities available include hiking, stream fishing, and wildlife viewing.

GETTING THERE: From Burns go N on county route 127 to forest route 43. W on 43 8 mi. to Emigrant CG.

SINGLE RATE:	$6	OPEN DATES:	May-Sept
# of SINGLE SITES:	6	MAX SPUR:	24 feet
		MAX STAY:	14 days
		ELEVATION:	5000 feet

18 Scotts
Mitchell • lat 44°25'29" lon 120°08'37"

DESCRIPTION: A secluded, quiet site in Ponderosa Pine forest. No drinking water. Gather firewood except for timber sale areas. Deer, elk, wild horse, antelopes, black bears and cougars in area. Horse, hike and mountain. bike trails nearby.

GETTING THERE: From Mitchell go S on county route 8 to forest route 22. Continue on 22 approx. 6 mi. to Scotts CG.

SINGLE RATE:	No fee	OPEN DATES:	May-Oct
# of SINGLE SITES:	3	MAX SPUR:	20 feet
		MAX STAY:	14 days
		ELEVATION:	5398 feet

14 Frazier
Paulina • lat 44°13'16" lon 119°34'34"

DESCRIPTION: Situated on Frazier Creek among tall Ponderosa Pine. No drinking water. Gather firewood except for timber sale areas. Deer, elk, antelopes, black bears and cougars in area.

GETTING THERE: From Paulina go E on county route 112 3.5 mi. to county route 113. Go E on 113 2 mi. to Puitt Rd. Go E on 135 to forest route 58. Go E on 58 5 mi. to forest route 500. Go N on 500 2 mi. to Frazier CG.

SINGLE RATE:	No fee	OPEN DATES:	May-Sept
# of SINGLE SITES:	5	MAX SPUR:	20 feet
		MAX STAY:	14 days
		ELEVATION:	4590 feet

19 Sugar Creek
Paulina • lat 44°14'02" lon 119°48'1"

DESCRIPTION: Near an old growth stand of pine on Sugar Cr. and Reservoir. Fish for trout or swim in lake. Some areas may be closed seasonally due to Bald Eagles nesting. Gather firewood except for timber sale areas. Deer, elk, antelopes, black bears and cougars in area. Hiking trails nearby.

GETTING THERE: From Paulina go E on 112 approx. 3.5 mi. to county route 113. Go E and N on 113 approx. and mi. to forest route 58. Go N on 58 approx. approx. 2.5 mi. to Sugar Creek CG.

SINGLE RATE:	$8	OPEN DATES:	May-Sept
# of SINGLE SITES:	20	MAX SPUR:	24 feet
		MAX STAY:	14 days
		ELEVATION:	4000 feet

15 Mud Springs
Paulina • lat 44°18'08" lon 119°38'45"

DESCRIPTION: Located near Mud Reservoir among tall Ponderosa Pine. No drinking water. Gather firewood except for timber sale areas. Deer, elk, antelopes, black bears and cougars in area. Trail access to Black Canyon Wilderness.

GETTING THERE: From Paulina go E on county route 112 3.5 mi. to county route 113. Go E on 113 and mi. to forest route 58. Continue on 58 11 mi. to forest route 5840. Go N on 5840 and mi. to Mud Springs CG.

SINGLE RATE:	No fee	OPEN DATES:	June-Sept
# of SINGLE SITES:	4	MAX SPUR:	20 feet
		MAX STAY:	14 days
		ELEVATION:	4975 feet

20 Walton Lake
Ochoco RS • lat 44°26'00" lon 120°20'08"

DESCRIPTION: A beautiful site in Ponderosa Pine forest near Walton Lake. Fish for trout on lake. Boat launch. Headwaters for Ochoco Creek. Fills most weekends. Gather firewood except for timber sale areas. Deer, elk, wild horse, antelopes, black bears and cougars in area. Access to Round Mountain. Trail System.

GETTING THERE: From Ochoco RS go NE on forest route 22 approx. and mi. to Walton Lake CG.

SINGLE RATE:	$8	OPEN DATES:	Apr-Oct*
# of SINGLE SITES:	30	MAX SPUR:	24 feet
GROUP RATE:	Varies	MAX STAY:	14 days
# of GROUP SITES:	1	ELEVATION:	5000 feet

 Campground has hosts   **Reservable sites**   **Accessible facilities**   **Fully developed**   **Semi-developed**   **Rustic facilities**

NOTE: Open dates listed are typical. Actual dates are dependent on conditions such as snow pack.

21 Whistler
Prineville • lat 44°29'34" lon 120°29'03"

DESCRIPTION: A primitive site in ponderosa pine. No drinking water. A rock hounding area and Lucky Strike Mine (open to the public) in area. Gather firewood except for timber sale areas. Deer, elk, antelopes, black bears, cougars and small wildlife. Horse, hike Wildcat mountain. Trail to access Mill Creek Wilderness.

GETTING THERE: From Prineville go N on McKay Creek road to forest boundary. Continue on forest route 27 approx. 16 mi. to Whistler CG.

SINGLE RATE:	No fee	OPEN DATES:	June-Sept
# of SINGLE SITES:	2	MAX SPUR:	24 feet
		MAX STAY:	14 days
		ELEVATION:	5560 feet

22 White Rock
Prineville • lat 44°25'25" lon 120°32'35"

DESCRIPTION: Set among tall ponderosa pine. No fishing in vicinity. Gather firewood except for timber sale areas. Deer, elk, wild horse, antelopes, black bears and cougars in area. Horse, hike access to Mill Creek Wilderness.

GETTING THERE: From Prineville go E on US HWY 26 approx. 19 mi. to forest route 3350. W on 3350 4 mi. to forest route 300. N on 300 2 mi. to White Rock CG.

SINGLE RATE:	No fee	OPEN DATES:	June-Sept
# of SINGLE SITES:	5	MAX SPUR:	20 feet
		MAX STAY:	14 days
		ELEVATION:	4500 feet

23 Wildcat
Prineville • lat 44°26'00" lon 120°35'00"

DESCRIPTION: This quiet, cool, forested site on E. Fork Miller Creek provides an escape from the intense desert heat in the summer months. No nearby fishing. Deer, elk, antelopes, black bears, cougars and birds in area. Gather firewood outside timber sale areas. Access Mill Creek Wilderness via Twin Pillars Trail.

GETTING THERE: From Prineville go E on US HWY 26 and mi. to Mill Creek Rd. N approx. 10 mi. to Wildcat CG.

SINGLE RATE:	$8	OPEN DATES:	May-Sept
# of SINGLE SITES:	17	MAX SPUR:	24 feet
		MAX STAY:	14 days
		ELEVATION:	3700 feet

24 Wildwood
Ochoco Ranger Station • lat 44°29'03" lon 120°20'13"

DESCRIPTION: Located in Ponderosa Pine forest, a secluded CG enjoyed for its relaxing environment. No nearby fishing or trails. Gather firewood except for timber sale areas. Deer, elk, wild horse, antelopes, black bears and cougars in area.

GETTING THERE: From Ochoco RS go NE on forest route 22 approx. 4 mi. to forest route 2210. N on 2210 4 mi. to Wildwood CG.

SINGLE RATE:	No fee	OPEN DATES:	June-Sept
# of SINGLE SITES:	5	MAX SPUR:	24 feet
		MAX STAY:	14 days
		ELEVATION:	4800 feet

25 Wiley Flat
Prineville • lat 44°02'36" lon 120°18'25"

DESCRIPTION: A nice setting of pine and meadow on Wiley Creek. Primitive camping, no drinking water. No nearby fishing. Gather firewood outside timber sale areas. Elk, deer, antelopes, black bears, cougars and small wildlife. No trails in vicinity.

GETTING THERE: From Prineville go E on state HWY 380 approx. 29 mi. to forest route 16. S on 16 approx. 10 mi. to Wiley Flat CG.

SINGLE RATE:	No fee	OPEN DATES:	May-Sept
# of SINGLE SITES:	5	MAX SPUR:	24 feet
		MAX STAY:	14 days
		ELEVATION:	5000 feet

26 Wolf Creek
Paulina • lat 44°15'11" lon 119°49'2"

DESCRIPTION: Located in old growth ponderosa pine forest near Sugar Creek Reservoir. Trout fishing in lake. No drinking water. Gather firewood except for timber sale areas. Deer, elk, antelopes, black bears and cougars in area.

GETTING THERE: From Paulina go E on county route 112 3.5 mi. to county route 113. N on 113 6.5 mi. to forest route 42. N on 42 2 mi. to Wolf Creek CG.

SINGLE RATE:	Varies	OPEN DATES:	May-Sept
# of SINGLE SITES:	12	MAX SPUR:	24 feet
		MAX STAY:	14 days
		ELEVATION:	4100 feet

1 Haystack West
Madras • lat 44°29'38" lon 121°08'24"

DESCRIPTION: An open, dispersed site on the Haystack Reservoir. No drinking water available. Fish for trout and crappie or boat, sailboat, or swim on the lake. Boat ramp available near CG. Deer and small wildlife can be seen in the area. Bring your own firewood.

GETTING THERE: From Madras go S on US HWY 97 approx. 8 mi to county route 96. Go E on 96 approx. 4 mi. to Forest Route 9605. Go NW on 9605 approx. 1/2 mi. to Haystack Reservoir.

SINGLE RATE:	No fee	OPEN DATES:	Yearlong
# of SINGLE SITES:	40		
		MAX STAY:	14 days
		ELEVATION:	2880 feet

2 Skull Hallow
Madras • lat 44°23'47" lon 144°23'47"

DESCRIPTION: In open area with dispersed sites. Primarily used as overflow from Smith Rock State Park for the climbers. No fishing or trails in vicinity. Deer and small wildlife can be seen in the area. Bring or gather firewood.

GETTING THERE: From Madras go S on US HWY 26 approx. 12 mi. to Forest Route 7960. Go S on 7960 approx. 3 mi. to Forest Route 5710. Go W on 5710 approx. 1/8 mi. to Skull Hollow CG.

SINGLE RATE:	No fee	OPEN DATES:	Yearlong
# of SINGLE SITES:	40	MAX SPUR:	20 feet
		MAX STAY:	14 days
		ELEVATION:	2880 feet

 Campground has hosts   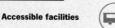 **Reservable sites**   **Accessible facilities**    **Fully developed**   **Semi-developed**   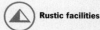 **Rustic facilities**

NOTE: Open dates listed are typical. Actual dates are dependent on conditions such as snow pack.

USFS Photo

ROGUE RIVER NATIONAL FOREST

The 630,000-acre Rogue River National Forest is composed of two separate units of land, each with its own diverse terrain and vegetation. On the west, the Forest includes the headwaters of the Applegate River, within the ancient and complex geology of the Siskiyou Mountains. This is a country of narrow canyons and high, steep ridges. The variety of environments includes open oak wood-lands, dense conifer forests, and barren, rocky ridgetops.

To the east, the Forest contains the upper reaches of the Rogue River, located along the slopes of the younger, volcanic Cascade Range. The southern Cascades have several deep canyons, such as the Middle Fork of the Rogue and the South Fork of Little Butte Creek. The area's extensive forest of douglas fir, ponderosa pine and other conifer is enlivened by occasional meadows, lakes and meandering streams.

A wide variety of recreation opportunities are available in the Rogue River National Forest, including fishing, swimming, hiking and skiing. The Forest contains approximately 400 miles of trails for hiking, mountain biking and horseback riding. The Pacific Crest National Scenic Trail runs the entire length of the Forest.

Rogue River National Forest • (541) 858-2200

1 Abbott Creek
Cascade Gorge • lat 42°52'53" lon 122°30'21"

DESCRIPTION: In old growth fir setting with the Rogue River approx. 1 mi. from CG. Fish, raft and swim in river. Warm-hot summers. Deer and elk are common in the area. Campers may gather own firewood. Supplies available in Prospect. Rogue River Trail within 1 mi.

GETTING THERE: From Cascade Gorge go NE on state HWY 62 approx. 10.5 mi. to primary forest route 68. Go NW on 68 approx. 4.5 mi. to Abbott Creek CG.

SINGLE RATE:	$8	OPEN DATES:	Yearlong*
# of SINGLE SITES:	25	MAX SPUR:	22 feet
		MAX STAY:	14 days
		ELEVATION:	3100 feet

2 Beaver Dam
Butte Falls • lat 42°18'30" lon 122°21'45"

DESCRIPTION: In semi-old growth forest on willow lined creek. Shady camp, cool mornings. Fish creek for trout or boat fish in any of 3 lakes in 10 mi. area. CCC built shelter and guard station nearby. Deer can be seen in the area. Limited supplies at Fish L resort. Gather firewood. Hike and mountain bike trails nearby.

GETTING THERE: From Butte Falls go SE on county route 821 approx. 15.5 mi. to primary forest route 37. Go S on 37 approx. 6.5 mi. to Beaver Dam CG.

SINGLE RATE:	No fee	OPEN DATES:	May-Nov
# of SINGLE SITES:	4	MAX SPUR:	16 feet
		MAX STAY:	14 days
		ELEVATION:	4600 feet

3 Beaver Sulphur
Jacksonville • lat 42°06'39" lon 123°01'58"

DESCRIPTION: Quiet "old-style" CG in douglas fir, alder and maple next to Beaver Creek. Fly fish for various fish species from the Applegate. Recreational mining on site. McKee covered bridge and historical trail nearby. Supplies available in Ruch. Campers may gather firewood. Deer, raptors, wildcats and bears can be seen in the area.

GETTING THERE: From Jacksonville go SW on county route 859 approx. 12.5 mi. to primary forest route 20. Go E on 20 approx. 3 mi. to Beaver Sulphur CG.

SINGLE RATE:	$4	OPEN DATES:	May-Nov
# of SINGLE SITES:	10	MAX SPUR:	12 feet
		MAX STAY:	14 days
		ELEVATION:	2100 feet

4 Big Ben
Prospect • lat 42°38'15" lon 122°19'15"

DESCRIPTION: In old growth fir forest near the Rogue River. Fishing for a variety of species on river. Rafting is popular. Supplies available in Prospect. Campers may gather firewood locally. Deer, raptors and small wildlife are common to the area. Hiking in area.

GETTING THERE: Big Ben CG is located approx. 15.5 mi. SE of Prospect on primary forest route 37

SINGLE RATE:	No fee	OPEN DATES:	Yearlong
# of SINGLE SITES:	2		
		MAX STAY:	14 days
		ELEVATION:	4000 feet

5 Carberry
Jacksonville • lat 42°01'30" lon 123°09'55"

DESCRIPTION: This tent only CG is located along Carberry Creek at end of Applegate Lake. Fish the lake for multiple species. Gather firewood locally. Supplies available in Jacksonville. Deer, osprey, bald eagle, bears and wildcats are common to the area. Drive to trailheads to access Red Buttes Wilderness.

GETTING THERE: From Jacksonville go SW on state HWY 238 approx. 6.5 mi. to US HWY 859. Go S on 859 approx. 19 mi. to Carberry CG.

SINGLE RATE:	$8	OPEN DATES:	Apr-Sept
# of SINGLE SITES:	10		
		MAX STAY:	14 days
		ELEVATION:	2000 feet

6 Copper
Jacksonville • lat 42°01'37" lon 123°08'51"

DESCRIPTION: In an old growth forest of fir and hardwoods at the end of Applegate Lake. Fish for a variety of species in the lake. Swimming and boat launch nearby. Gather firewood locally. Supplies available in Jacksonville. Deer, bald eagle, bears and wildcats can be seen in the area. The Red Buttes Wilderness is nearby.

GETTING THERE: From Jacksonville go SW on state HWY 238 approx. 6.5 mi. to US HWY 859. Go S on 859 approx. 24 mi. to Copper CG.

SINGLE RATE:	No fee	OPEN DATES:	Apr-Sept
# of SINGLE SITES:	3	MAX SPUR:	32 feet
		MAX STAY:	14 days
		ELEVATION:	2000 feet

7 Daley Creek
Butte Falls • lat 42°18'30" lon 122°21'45"

DESCRIPTION: Rustic, shady CG in a fir and pine forest near Daley Creek. Fish for rainbow or brook trout in creek and 4 lakes in area. CCC built shelter and cabin in vicinity. Supplies available at Fish Lake Resort. Deer can be seen in the area. Gather firewood. Numerous horse, hike and mountain bike trails nearby.

GETTING THERE: From Butte Falls go SE on county route 821 approx. 15.5 mi. to primary forest route 37. Go S on 37 approx. 6 mi. to Daley Creek CG.

SINGLE RATE:	No fee	OPEN DATES:	May-Nov
# of SINGLE SITES:	6	MAX SPUR:	18 feet
		MAX STAY:	14 days
		ELEVATION:	4600 feet

8 Doe Point
Butte Falls • lat 42°23'35" lon 122°19'25"

DESCRIPTION: In a park-like setting of fir and pine situated on Fish Lake. Fish for rainbow and brook trout up to 60 lbs. CCC picnic shelter at lake. Supplies at the Fish Lake Resort nearby. Osprey, bald eagle and deer can be seen in area. Campers may gather or buy firewood. RV dump station nearby. Many trails in area.

GETTING THERE: From Butte Falls go SE on county route 821 approx. 15.5 mi. to state HWY 140. Go E on 140 approx. 2 mi. to Doe Point CG.

SINGLE RATE:	$12	OPEN DATES:	May-Oct
# of SINGLE SITES:	30	MAX SPUR:	32 feet
		MAX STAY:	14 days
		ELEVATION:	4600 feet

9 Farewell Bend
Cascade Gorge • lat 42°55'11" lon 122°25'55"

DESCRIPTION: A popular site in old growth fir forest with good Rogue River access. Fishing and rafting on river. Deer and elk are common in the area. Supplies available at Cascade Gorge. Campers may gather firewood. Rogue River Trail access near Natural Bridge CG nearby.

GETTING THERE: From Cascade Gorge go NE on state HWY 62 approx. 13.5 mi. to Farewell Bend CG.

SINGLE RATE:	$12	OPEN DATES:	Yearlong*
# of SINGLE SITES:	61	MAX SPUR:	30 feet
		MAX STAY:	14 days
		ELEVATION:	3400 feet

10 Fish Lake
Butte Falls • lat 42°23'43" lon 122°19'12"

DESCRIPTION: In a semi old growth fir and pine forest setting situated on Fish Lake. Fish for rainbow and brook trout, up to 60 lbs. Supplies are located at Fish Lake Resort nearby. Osprey, Bald Eagles and Deer can be seen in the area. Campers may gather firewood. Many trails in the area. RV dump station nearby. Boat ramp at CG.

GETTING THERE: From Butte Falls go SE on county route 821 approx. 15.5 mi. to state HWY 140. Go E on 140 approx. 2.5 mi. to Fish Lake CG.

SINGLE RATE:	$12	OPEN DATES:	May-Oct
# of SINGLE SITES:	19	MAX SPUR:	32 feet
		MAX STAY:	14 days
		ELEVATION:	4600 feet

 Campground has hosts   Reservable sites   Accessible facilities   Fully developed   Semi-developed   Rustic facilities

NOTE: Open dates listed are typical. Actual dates are dependent on conditions such as snow pack.

ROGUE RIVER NATIONAL FOREST • OREGON • 1 — 10

11 Flumet Flat
Jacksonville • lat 42°07'03" lon 123°05'13"

DESCRIPTION: Located near Applegate River in a forested setting. Fish for steelhead and other species on river. Supplies available in Jacksonville. Campers may gather firewood locally. Deer, osprey, bald eagle, bears and wildcats can be seen in the area. Group camping by reservation only.

GETTING THERE: From Jacksonville go SW on state HWY 238 approx. 6.5 mi. to US HWY 859. Go S on 859 approx. 5.5 mi. to Flumet Flat CG.

SINGLE RATE:	$8	OPEN DATES:	Apr-Sept
# of SINGLE SITES:	27	MAX SPUR:	24 feet
		MAX STAY:	14 days
		ELEVATION:	1700 feet

12 Fourbit Ford
Butte Falls • lat 42°30'03" lon 122°24'15"

DESCRIPTION: CG is a quiet place near Willow Lake in an old growth fir forest. Fish for a variety of species on lake. Supplies available at Butte Falls. Campers may gather firewood locally. Deer, raptors and small wildlife are common in the area. Hiking in area.

GETTING THERE: From Butte Falls go SE on county route 821 approx. 8 mi. to forest route 3065. Go NE on 3065 approx. 2 mi. to Fourbit Ford CG.

SINGLE RATE:	Varies	OPEN DATES:	Yearlong*
# of SINGLE SITES:	7	MAX SPUR:	16 feet
		MAX STAY:	14 days
		ELEVATION:	3200 feet

13 French Gulch
Jacksonville • lat 42°02'55" lon 123°06'00"

DESCRIPTION: Walk-in sites set in an old growth pine and hardwood forest on Grench Gulch Creek. Fish or swim in the creek. Campers may gather firewood locally. Supplies available in Jacksonville. Deer, osprey, bald eagle, bears and wildcats are common in the area. Trails for hiking and mountain biking nearby.

GETTING THERE: From Jacksonville go S 6.5 mi. on state HWY 238 to US HWY 859. Go S on 859 approx. 10.5 mi. to forest route 1075. Go W on 1075 approx. 1 mi. to French Gulch CG.

SINGLE RATE:	$8	OPEN DATES:	Apr-Sept
# of SINGLE SITES:	9		
		MAX STAY:	14 days
		ELEVATION:	2000 feet

14 Hamaker
Cascade Gorge • lat 43°03'26" lon 122°19'21"

DESCRIPTION: On the upper stretch of Rogue River in old growth fir forest. Warm to hot summer days. Fishing and rafting on river. Supplies available at Cascade Gorge. Gather own firewood. Elk, deer, raptors and small wildlife in are common to the area. Rogue River trail and other hiking trails nearby.

GETTING THERE: From Cascade Gorge go NE 21 mi. on state HWY 62 to forest route 6530. Go NE 6 mi. on 6530 to forest route 800. Go N 4 mi. on 800 to forest route 6530. Go W 1/2 mi. on 6530 to forest route 900. Go S 1 mi. on 900 to Hamaker CG.

SINGLE RATE:	$8	OPEN DATES:	Yearlong*
# of SINGLE SITES:	10	MAX SPUR:	22 feet
		MAX STAY:	14 days
		ELEVATION:	4000 feet

15 Harr Point
Jacksonville • lat 42°02'01" lon 123°06'36"

DESCRIPTION: A semi-primitive tent site on the E shore of Applegate Lake accessible by boat and trail only. Fish and swim in the lake. No drinking water. Campers may gather firewood. Supplies available in Jacksonville. Watch for deer, ospreys, bald eagles, bears, and wildcats in the area. Many trails nearby.

GETTING THERE: From Jacksonville go S 6.5 mi. on state HWY 238 to US HWY 859. Go S 15 mi. (traveling across the dam). Go 3 mi. S to forest route 100. 1/2 mi. on 100 to Squaw Arm Parking Area. Hike W 1.25 mi. on Payette Trail to Harr Point CG.

SINGLE RATE:	No fee	OPEN DATES:	May-Sept
# of SINGLE SITES:	5		
		MAX STAY:	14 days
		ELEVATION:	2000 feet

16 Hart-tish
Jacksonville • lat 42°03'10" lon 123°07'39"

DESCRIPTION: CG has several acres of beautifully groomed lawn sloping down to the water's edge. Views across the lake to the peaks of the majestic Red Butte Wilderness. Boat ramp at the CG. Fishing (there is a fish cleaning station on-site) and swimming at lake. Supplies available at Jacksonville. Trails in area.

GETTING THERE: From Jacksonville go SW on state HWY 238 approx. 6.5 mi. to US HWY 859. Go S on 859 approx. 11.5 mi. to Hart-tish CG.

SINGLE RATE:	Varies	OPEN DATES:	Apr-Sept
# of SINGLE SITES:	10	MAX SPUR:	32 feet
		MAX STAY:	14 days
		ELEVATION:	2000 feet

17 Huckleberry Mountain
Cascade Gorge • lat 42°52'38" lon 122°20'11"

DESCRIPTION: In an old growth fir forest with several nearby creeks. Quiet and more secluded than most sites. Fish and swim in the creeks. Supplies available at Cascade Gorge. Elk, deer and small wildlife are common in the area. Campers may gather firewood. Hiking opportunities nearby.

GETTING THERE: From Cascade Gorge go N on state HWY 62 approx. 10.5 mi. to primary forest route 60. Go E on 60 approx. 2 mi. to forest route 6050. Go NE on 6050 approx. 11 mi. to Huckleberry Mountain CG.

SINGLE RATE:	No fee	OPEN DATES:	Yearlong*
# of SINGLE SITES:	25	MAX SPUR:	16 feet
		MAX STAY:	14 days
		ELEVATION:	5400 feet

18 Imnaha
Prospect • lat 42°42'10" lon 122°20'00"

DESCRIPTION: This tent only site among fir and hardwood trees. Near the Ranger Station, Imnaha Springs and several small creeks. Structures constructed by the CCC in the 1930s nearby. Gather firewood locally. Deer, raptors and small wildlife are common to the area. Hiking in area.

GETTING THERE: Imnaha CG is located approx. 11 mi. SE of Prospect on primary forest route 37.

SINGLE RATE:	No fee	OPEN DATES:	Yearlong
# of SINGLE SITES:	4	MAX SPUR:	16 feet
		MAX STAY:	14 days
		ELEVATION:	3800 feet

19 Jackson
Jacksonville • lat 42°06'00" lon 123°04'00"

DESCRIPTION: Along the Applegate River set among fir and hardwood forest. Fish for a variety of species in the river. Supplies available in Jacksonville. Campers may gather firewood locally. Deer, osprey, bald eagle, bears and wildcats can be seen in the area. Hiking trails can be found nearby.

GETTING THERE: From Jacksonville go SW on state HWY 238 approx. 6.5 mi. to US HWY 859. Go S on 859 approx. 5.5 mi. to Jackson CG. Tight corners on road; not recommended for trailers and RVs.

SINGLE RATE:	Varies	OPEN DATES:	Apr-Sept
# of SINGLE SITES:	12	MAX SPUR:	24 feet
		MAX STAY:	14 days
		ELEVATION:	1700 feet

20 Latgawa Cove
Jacksonville • lat 42°02'51" lon 123°06'46"

DESCRIPTION: A primitive CG set on Applegate Lake; situated in a mixed forest. No drinking water or services. Supplies available in Jacksonville. Campers may gather firewood. Watch for deer, ospreys, bald eagles, bears, and wildcats in the area. Fish on the lake. Numerous hiking trails nearby.

GETTING THERE: From Jacksonville go S 6.5 mi. on state HWY 238 to US HWY 859. Go S 15 mi. (traveling across the dam). Go E on county route 959 2 mi. to Latgawa Cove CG.

SINGLE RATE:	No fee	OPEN DATES:	Yearlong
# of SINGLE SITES:	5		
		MAX STAY:	14 days
		ELEVATION:	2000 feet

 Campground has hosts   **Reservable sites**   **Accessible facilities**    **Fully developed**   **Semi-developed**   **Rustic facilities**

21 Mill Creek
Prospect • lat 42˚47'44" lon 122˚28'00"

DESCRIPTION: Set in old growth douglas fir stand overlooking Mill Creek. Trout fish and swim in the creek. Union Creek Historic District is approx. 9 mi. from CG. Supplies available at Prospect. Deer and elk are common to the area. Campers may gather firewood. Mosquitoes till mid-summer.

GETTING THERE: From Prospect go E on state HWY 62 approx. 2.0 mi. to forest route 030. Go NE on 030 approx. 1 mi. to Mill Creek CG.

SINGLE RATE:	No fee	OPEN DATES:	Apr-Nov
# of SINGLE SITES:	8	MAX SPUR:	27 feet
		MAX STAY:	14 days
		ELEVATION:	2800 feet

22 Mt. Ashland
Ashland • lat 42˚04'31" lon 122˚42'38"

DESCRIPTION: An open site set in semi-old growth. Expect cool days September-June. Travel 18 mi. to Emigrant Lake for trout fishing. Supplies in Asland. Watch for deer and raptors in the area. Rarely full. Wildflowers abundant July-August. Gather firewood. Pacific Crest Trail passes nearby for horse and hike use.

GETTING THERE: From Ashland go S on I-5 9 mi. to Mt. Ashland ski resort and go 1 mi. past parking area on road 20 to Mt. Ashland CG. Not recommended for large RVs.

SINGLE RATE:	No fee	OPEN DATES:	June-Nov
# of SINGLE SITES:	8	MAX SPUR:	18 feet
		MAX STAY:	14 days
		ELEVATION:	6600 feet

23 Natural Bridge
Cascade Gorge • lat 42˚53'23" lon 122˚27'46"

DESCRIPTION: Located along the scenic Upper Rogue River in old growth fir forest. Warm to hot summer days. Fishing and rafting on river. Supplies available at Cascade Gorge. Campers may gather own firewood. Deer, elk, raptors and small wildlife in area. The Rogue River Trail and Natural Bridge interpretive trail is near by.

GETTING THERE: From Cascade Gorge go NE on state HWY 62 approx. 13.5 mi. to Natural Bridge CG.

SINGLE RATE:	No fee	OPEN DATES:	Yearlong*
# of SINGLE SITES:	17	MAX SPUR:	30 feet
		MAX STAY:	14 days
		ELEVATION:	3200 feet

24 North Fork
Butte Falls • lat 42˚22'42" lon 122˚21'33"

DESCRIPTION: In a semi-old growth setting of fir and pine on the North Fork of Little Butte Creek. Fish for rainbow trout on the creek. Historical Big Elk FS cabin 3 mi. from CG (ask host). Supplies available at Fish Lake Resort. Campers may gather firewood. Many trails in the area. Enjoy huckleberries in Aug.

GETTING THERE: From Butte Falls go SE on county route 821 approx. 15.5 mi. to primary forest route 37. Go S on 37 approx. 1 mi. to North Fork CG.

SINGLE RATE:	No fee	OPEN DATES:	Apr-Nov
# of SINGLE SITES:	9	MAX SPUR:	24 feet
		MAX STAY:	14 days
		ELEVATION:	4600 feet

25 Parker Meadows
Prospect • lat 42˚35'58" lon 122˚19'35"

DESCRIPTION: In old growth fir forest near Parker Creek. Rogue River is approx. 1/4 mi. from the CG. Fish and raft from the river. Campers may gather firewood locally. Deer, raptors and small wildlife are common to the area. Hiking trails can be found nearby.

GETTING THERE: Parker Meadows CG is located approx. 22.5 mi. SE of Prospect on primary forest route 37.

SINGLE RATE:	$3	OPEN DATES:	Yearlong
# of SINGLE SITES:	8	MAX SPUR:	16 feet
		MAX STAY:	14 days
		ELEVATION:	5000 feet

26 River Bridge
Prospect • lat 42˚49'20" lon 122˚29'33"

DESCRIPTION: CG sits in an old growth douglas fir stand adjacent to the Upper Rogue River. Bait or fly fishing for rainbow trout. Historical Union Creek District is approx. 6 mi. E of CG. Supplies are at Prospect. Campers may gather firewood. The Upper Rogue River National Rec. Trail passes the CG.

GETTING THERE: From Prospect go E on state HWY 62 approx. 4.5 mi. to forest route 6210. Go W on 6210 approx. 1 mi. to River Bridge CG.

SINGLE RATE:	No fee	OPEN DATES:	Apr-Nov
# of SINGLE SITES:	6	MAX SPUR:	25 feet
		MAX STAY:	14 days
		ELEVATION:	2900 feet

27 Snowshoe
Butte Falls • lat 42˚32'03" lon 122˚21'22"

DESCRIPTION: In old growth forest on edge of Big Butte Springs Watershed. No drinking water available at CG. Campers may gather firewood locally. Deer, raptors and small wildlife in area. Hiking trails in area.

GETTING THERE: From Butte Falls go SE on county route 821 approx. 8 mi. to forest route 3065. Go NE on 3065 approx. 5 mi. to Snowshoe CG.

SINGLE RATE:	No fee	OPEN DATES:	Yearlong
# of SINGLE SITES:	5		
		MAX STAY:	14 days
		ELEVATION:	4000 feet

28 South Fork
Prospect • lat 42˚39'30" lon 122˚20'30"

DESCRIPTION: Set in tall old growth fir forest setting with Rogue River nearby. Fish and swim in the river. Fishing for a variety of species. Gather firewood locally. Deer, raptors and small wildlife in area. Hiking in area.

GETTING THERE: From Prospect go SE on primary forest route 37 approx. 14 mi. to primary forest route 34. Go W on 34 approx. 1 mi. to South Fork CG.

SINGLE RATE:	Varies	OPEN DATES:	Yearlong
# of SINGLE SITES:	6	MAX SPUR:	16 feet
		MAX STAY:	14 days
		ELEVATION:	4000 feet

29 Squaw Lakes
Jacksonville • lat 42˚02'10" lon 123˚01'15"

DESCRIPTION: This walk-in, tent only CG is in a fir and hardwood forest setting. Boat, swim and fish on the lake. Campers may gather firewood locally. Supplies in Jacksonville. Deer, osprey, bald eagle, bears and wildcats can be seen in the area. Trails for hiking and mountain biking in area. Reservation only.

GETTING THERE: From Jacksonville go SW on state HWY 238 approx. 6.5 mi. to US HWY 859. Go S on 859 approx. 10.5 mi. to forest route 1075. Go W on 1075 approx. 5 mi. to Squaw Lakes CG.

SINGLE RATE:	$10	OPEN DATES:	May-Sept
# of SINGLE SITES:	17		
		MAX STAY:	14 days
		ELEVATION:	3000 feet

30 Stringtown
Jacksonville • lat 42˚02'10" lon 123˚06'00"

DESCRIPTION: Located in old growth forest on a small stream at end of Applegate Lake arm. Some walk-in sites. Fish for a variety of species. Gather firewood locally. Supplies in Jacksonville. Deer, osprey, bald eagle, bears and wildcats are common in the area. Hiking trails nearby.

GETTING THERE: From Jacksonville go S 6.5 mi. on state HWY 238 to US HWY 859. Go S 15 mi. on 859(traveling across the dam). Continue 3 mi. to forest route 100. Continue 1/2 mi. on 100 to Stringtown CG.

SINGLE RATE:	No fee	OPEN DATES:	Yearlong
# of SINGLE SITES:	6		
		MAX STAY:	14 days
		ELEVATION:	2000 feet

 Campground has hosts   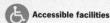 Reservable sites   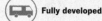 Accessible facilities   Fully developed   Semi-developed   Rustic facilities

NOTE: Open dates listed are typical. Actual dates are dependent on conditions such as snow pack.

31 Tipsu Tyee
Jacksonville • lat 42°02'06" lon 123°07'24"

DESCRIPTION: This tent only site is set on Applegate Lake and is accessible by boat or hike-in only. Fish the lake. Supplies available in Jacksonville. No drinking water or services. Campers may gather firewood. Watch for deer, ospreys, bald eagles, bears, and wildcats in the area. Hiking trails nearby.

GETTING THERE: From Jacksonville go S 6.5 mi. on HWY 238 to HWY 859. Go S 15 mi. on 859 (traveling across the dam). 3 mi. to forest route 100. 1/2 mi. to Squaw Arm Parking Area. Hike W 1.25 mi. on Payette Trail to Tipsu Tyee CG.

SINGLE RATE:	No fee	OPEN DATES:	May-Sept
# of SINGLE SITES:	5		
		MAX STAY:	14 days
		ELEVATION:	2000 feet

32 Union Creek
Cascade Gorge • lat 42°54'40" lon 122°27'02"

DESCRIPTION: A popular site with good Rogue River access. Warm to hot summer days. Fishing and rafting on river. Supplies available at Cascade Gorge. Campers may gather own firewood. Deer, elk, raptors and small wildlife are common in the area. Rogue River trail is nearby.

GETTING THERE: From Cascade Gorge go NE on state HWY 62 approx. 12.5 mi. to Union Creek CG.

SINGLE RATE:	$10	OPEN DATES:	Yearlong*
# of SINGLE SITES:	78	MAX SPUR:	25 feet
		MAX STAY:	14 days
		ELEVATION:	3200 feet

33 Watkins
Jacksonville • lat 42°01'30" lon 123°09'15"

DESCRIPTION: This tent only CG is located on Applegate Lake. Fish the lake for a variety of species. Supplies are available in Jacksonville. Campers may gather firewood locally. Deer, osprey, bald eagle, bears and wildcats are common to the area. Trails in area for hiking and mountain biking.

GETTING THERE: From Jacksonville go SW on state HWY 238 approx. 6.5 mi. to US HWY 859. Go S on 859 approx. 20 mi. to Watkins CG.

SINGLE RATE:	Varies	OPEN DATES:	Apr-Sept
# of SINGLE SITES:	14		
		MAX STAY:	14 days
		ELEVATION:	2100 feet

34 Whiskey Spring
Butte Falls • lat 42°30'00" lon 122°25'30"

DESCRIPTION: A quiet CG in an old growth fir forest a short drive from Willow Lake. Fish for a variety of species in the lake. Supplies available at Butte Falls. Campers may gather firewood locally. Deer, raptors and small wildlife can be seen in the area. Hiking trails are nearby.

GETTING THERE: From Butte Falls go SE on county route 821 approx. 8.5 mi. to forest route 3065. Go NE on 3065 approx. 1 mi. to Whiskey Springs CG.

SINGLE RATE:	$8	OPEN DATES:	Yearlong*
# of SINGLE SITES:	36	MAX SPUR:	22 feet
		MAX STAY:	14 days
		ELEVATION:	3200 feet

35 Willow Prairie Horse Camp
Butte Falls • lat 42°24'26" lon 122°23'28"

DESCRIPTION: A beautiful meadow nestled in tall timber just SW of Mt. McLaughlin. Adjacent is a wetlands with a beaver swamp and large ponds. Supplies available at Butte Falls. Deer, elk, sand hill cranes, geese and ducks can be seen in the area. Gather firewood locally. Corrals at each site. Horse trails from the CG.

GETTING THERE: From Butte Falls go SE on county route 821 approx. 14 mi. to forest route 3738. Go W on 3738 approx. 1.5 mi. to Willow Prairie Horse Camp.

SINGLE RATE:	$6	OPEN DATES:	May-Sept
# of SINGLE SITES:	10	MAX SPUR:	22 feet
		MAX STAY:	14 days
		ELEVATION:	4400 feet

36 Wrangle
Jacksonville • lat 42°03'03" lon 122°51'24"

DESCRIPTION: A tent site near Wrangle Gap and Glade Creek set in a fir and hardwood forest. Picnic tables, a rustic shelter and a cabin built by the CCC in the 1930's. Campers may gather firewood locally. Deer, osprey, bald eagle, bears and wildcats can be seen in the area. Hiking trails nearby.

GETTING THERE: From Jacksonville go S on state HWY 238 approx. 6.5 mi. to US HWY 859. Go S on 859 approx. 8.5 mi. to forest route 20. Go E on 20 approx. 18 mi. to Wrangle Gap and forest route 2030. Go N on 2030 approx. 1 mi. to Wrangle CG.

SINGLE RATE:	No fee	OPEN DATES:	June-Oct*
# of SINGLE SITES:	5		
		MAX STAY:	14 days
		ELEVATION:	6400 feet

 Campground has hosts   🔒 **Reservable sites**   **Accessible facilities**   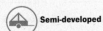 **Fully developed**    **Semi-developed**   **Rustic facilities**

Lee Webb Photo, USDA Forest Service

SISKIYOU NATIONAL FOREST

The 1.2 million acre Siskiyou National Forest is located in the Klamath Mountains and the Coast Ranges of southwestern Oregon with a small segment of the Forest extending into Northwestern California and the Siskiyou Mountain Range.

The Siskiyou National Forest embodies the most complex soils, geology, landscape, and plant communities in the Pacific Northwest. World-class rivers, biological diversity, fisheries, and complex watersheds rank the Siskiyou high in the Nation as an outstanding resource.

The Siskiyou National Forest has some of the most diverse flora in the country. During his studies here in 1950, Dr. Robert Whittaker found that only the Great Smokey Mountains rival the Siskiyou in plant diversity. The old and complex geology, the global position and transverse orientation of the Siskiyou Mountain Range across the Forest region are responsible for creating this myriad of species.

SISKIYOU NATIONAL FOREST • OREGON • LOCATOR MAP

Siskiyou National Forest • (541) 471-6724

1. Bearcamp Pasture
Grants Pass • lat 42˚37'28" lon 123˚49'32"

DESCRIPTION: Primitive camping in a pine forest setting and high elevation meadows. This camp is primarily used by hunters. Supplies at Grants Pass. Deer, bears and birds are common to the area. Campers may gather firewood. No designated trails in the area. No drinking water.

GETTING THERE: From Grants Pass go NW on county route 2400 approx. 17 mi. to primary forest route 23. Go W on 23 approx. 19 mi. to Bearcamp Pasture CG. RV's not recommended.

SINGLE RATE:	No fee	OPEN DATES:	May-Sept
# of SINGLE SITES:	1	MAX STAY:	14 days
		ELEVATION:	3600 feet

6. Butler Bar
Port Orford • lat 42˚43'35" lon 124˚16'15"

DESCRIPTION: Primitive camping in a pine forest setting on the Wild and Scenic Elk River. Fish for trout or swim in the river. Supplies available at Port Orford. Deer, bears and birds are common to the area. This CG is light to moderate use area. Many trails nearby. No RV's at this CG.

GETTING THERE: From Port Orford go N 1.5 mi. on US HWY 101 to forest route 5325 (county route 208). Go E on 5325 approx. 22 mi. to Butler Bar CG. NO RV'S at this CG.

SINGLE RATE:	No fee	OPEN DATES:	Yearlong
# of SINGLE SITES:	7	MAX SPUR:	30 feet
		MAX STAY:	14 days
		ELEVATION:	250 feet

2. Big Pine
Grants Pass • lat 42˚26'00" lon 123˚40'00"

DESCRIPTION: Rustic camp in a beautiful old-growth pine stand on Meyers Creek. Fish or swim in the creek. The world's tallest Ponderosa Pine tree near CG. Supplies available at Grants Pass. Deer, bears and birds are common to the area. Interpretive trails starting from the CG area. Campers may gather firewood.

GETTING THERE: From Grants Pass go N on I-5 2 mi. to county route 2400. Go NW on 2400 for approx. 12 mi. to primary forest route 25. Go SW n 25 approx. 12 mi. to Big Pine CG.

SINGLE RATE:	$5	OPEN DATES:	May-Oct
# of SINGLE SITES:	13	MAX SPUR:	30 feet
		MAX STAY:	14 days
		ELEVATION:	2300 feet

7. Cave Creek
Cave Junction • lat 42˚07'05" lon 123˚26'05"

DESCRIPTION: In a douglas fir and cedar forest setting on Cave Creek. Fish for trout and swim from creek. Supplies available at Cave Junction. Deer, bears and birds are common to the area. Campers may gather firewood. Trail to the Oregon Caves National Monument starts at CG.

GETTING THERE: From Cave Junction go E 16 mi. on state HWY 46 to Cave Creek CG.

SINGLE RATE:	$13	OPEN DATES:	May-Sept
# of SINGLE SITES:	18	MAX SPUR:	16 feet
		MAX STAY:	14 days
		ELEVATION:	2800 feet

3. Bolan Lake
O'Brien • lat 42˚01'24" lon 123˚27'22"

DESCRIPTION: In a fir forest setting on Bolan Lake. Fish for trout from stocked lake, only non-motorized boats are allowed on the lake. Supplies at O'Brien. Deer, bears, mountain lions and birds are common to the area. Campers may gather firewood. Bolan lookout trail starts at CG and is approx. 1.5 mi. long. No water.

GETTING THERE: From O'Brien go E on county route 5560 and 55. Go E on 5560 for 6 mi. to forest route 48. Go NE on 48 for 7 mi. to forest route 4812. Go E on 4812 for 4 mi. to Bolan Lake CG.

SINGLE RATE:	No fee	OPEN DATES:	June-Sept
# of SINGLE SITES:	12	MAX SPUR:	16 feet
		MAX STAY:	14 days
		ELEVATION:	5400 feet

8. Daphne Grove
Powers • lat 42˚44'11" lon 124˚03'10"

DESCRIPTION: In a pine forest setting on the South Fork Coquille River with Nature viewing and scenic area nearby. Fish for trout and swim in the river. Supplies available at Powers. Deer, bears and birds are common to the area. CG is a moderate to heavy use area. Campers may gather firewood. No trails in area.

GETTING THERE: From Powers go S 15 mi. to forest route 33 to Daphne Grove CG.

SINGLE RATE:	$8	OPEN DATES:	Yearlong
# of SINGLE SITES:	14	MAX SPUR:	30 feet
GROUP RATE:	Varies	MAX STAY:	14 days
# of GROUP SITES:	1	ELEVATION:	850 feet

4. Briggs Creek
Grants Pass • lat 42˚22'40" lon 123˚48'07"

DESCRIPTION: In a mixed conifer forest setting on Briggs Creek. Fish for trout and swim in the creek. Supplies at Grants Pass. Deer, bears and birds are common to the area. Campers may gather firewood. CG is a trailhead to the wilderness. No drinking water.

GETTING THERE: From Grants Pass go N on I-5 2 mi to county route 2400. Go W on 2400 approx. 12 mi. to primary forest route 25. Go SW on 25 approx. 9 mi. to Briggs Creek CG. RV's not recommended.

SINGLE RATE:	No fee	OPEN DATES:	May-Sept
# of SINGLE SITES:	2	MAX STAY:	14 days
		ELEVATION:	900 feet

9. Eden Valley
Powers • lat 42˚48'33" lon 123˚53'23"

DESCRIPTION: In a fir and cedar forest setting with the headwaters of South Fork of the Coquille River nearby. Supplies available at Powers. Deer, elk, bears, mountain lions, bobcats and birds are common in the area. Campers may gather firewood. No designated trails in the area. No Restrooms. No drinking water.

GETTING THERE: From Powers go S on primary forest route 33 for 12 mi. to forest route 3348. Go NE on 3348 approx. 11 mi. to Eden Valley CG.

SINGLE RATE:	No fee	OPEN DATES:	May-Sept
# of SINGLE SITES:	11	MAX SPUR:	24 feet
		MAX STAY:	14 days
		ELEVATION:	2100 feet

5. Buck Creek
Powers • lat 45˚43'10" lon 118˚11'05"

DESCRIPTION: Recently refurbished CG in an old growth timber setting near the Rogue River. Fish for trout and swim in the river. Supplies at Powers. Deer, bears and birds are in the area. Light to moderate use area. On the Powers to Glendale Bike Route. Panther Ridge Trail nearby. No Restrooms. No drinking water.

GETTING THERE: From Powers go S on primary forest route 33 (county route 90) approx. 12 mi. to forest route 3348. Go NE on 3348 approx. 6 mi. to Buck Creek CG.

SINGLE RATE:	No fee	OPEN DATES:	Yearlong
# of SINGLE SITES:	2	MAX SPUR:	26 feet
		MAX STAY:	14 days
		ELEVATION:	2400 feet

10. Elko
Gold Beach • lat 42˚23'20" lon 124˚13'41"

DESCRIPTION: Dispersed sites among a thick fir forest with low brush. Warm days, cool nights, frequent wind. Supplies available in Gold Beach. Deer, lizards, birds and small wildlife. CG is rarely full. Campers may gather firewood. Secluded quiet CG. No drinking water.

GETTING THERE: From Gold Beach go E on county route 635 approx. 5 mi. to forest route 635. Go E on 3680 approx. 6 mi. to forest route 1503. Go E on 1503 approx. 2 mi. to Elko CG.

SINGLE RATE:	No fee	OPEN DATES:	May-Nov
# of SINGLE SITES:	3	MAX STAY:	14 days
		ELEVATION:	3020 feet

 Campground has hosts　　 **Reservable sites**　　 **Accessible facilities**　　 **Fully developed**　　 **Semi-developed**　　 **Rustic facilities**

NOTE: Open dates listed are typical. Actual dates are dependent on conditions such as snow pack.

11 Foster Bar
Illahe • lat 42˚38'04" lon 124˚03'03"

DESCRIPTION: In a dense forest setting on the Rogue River. Hot, dry summers, frequently over 100'. Fish for salmon and steelhead on the river. Historical Big Bend Native American site nearby. Deer, bears and birds are common in the area. Campers may gather firewood. Upper Rogue River Trail with in 1 mi. of CG.

GETTING THERE: Foster Bar CG is located 1/2 mi. N of Illahe, 5 mi. N of Agness.

SINGLE RATE:	No fee	OPEN DATES:	May-Sept
# of SINGLE SITES:	12	MAX SPUR:	30 feet
		MAX STAY:	14 days
		ELEVATION:	200 feet

16 Laird Lake
Gold Beach • lat 42˚42'05" lon 124˚12'00"

DESCRIPTION: A primitive CG in a pine forest setting on the Elk River. Fish for trout or swim on the river. Supplies available at Gold Beach. Deer, bears, squirrels and birds are common to the area. Campers may gather firewood. CG is a light to moderate use area. No designated trails in the area. NO WATER.

GETTING THERE: From Gold Beach go NE on primary forest route 33 (county route 595) approx. 33 mi. to forest route 5325. Go NW on 5325 approx. 8 mi. to Laird Lake CG.

SINGLE RATE:	No fee	OPEN DATES:	Yearlong
# of SINGLE SITES:	4	MAX SPUR:	30 feet
		MAX STAY:	14 days
		ELEVATION:	1600 feet

12 Game Lake
Gold Beach • lat 42˚25'59" lon 124˚05'09"

DESCRIPTION: Dispersed tent CG in forested setting adjacent to Game Lake with views of meadow nearby. Moderate use, fills holidays and weekends. Supplies 1.5 hrs away. Deer and small wildlife. Campers may gather firewood. Access to Pupps Camp Trail and Kalmiopsis Wilderness nearby. No drinking water.

GETTING THERE: From Gold Beach go SE on county route 635 approx. 4 mi. to forest route 3680. Go E on 3680 approx. 21 mi. to Game Lake CG.

SINGLE RATE:	No fee	OPEN DATES:	May-Nov
# of SINGLE SITES:	3		
		MAX STAY:	14 days
		ELEVATION:	3800 feet

17 Little Redwood
Brookings • lat 42˚09'15" lon 124˚08'40"

DESCRIPTION: Is a moderate use CG, in a forest setting on the Wild and Scenic Chetco River with scenic views. Fish for trout or swim in the river. Supplies available at Brookings. Deer, bears and birds are common to the area. Hike and bike trails in the area. Campers may gather firewood.

GETTING THERE: From Brookings go NE on county route 784 approx. 7 mi. to forest route 1376. Go NE on 1376 approx. 3 mi. to Little Redwood CG.

SINGLE RATE:	$8	OPEN DATES:	May-Oct
# of SINGLE SITES:	12	MAX SPUR:	20 feet
		MAX STAY:	14 days
		ELEVATION:	200 feet

13 Grayback
Cave Junction • lat 42˚08'28" lon 123˚27'23"

DESCRIPTION: In a old growth douglas fir and cedar forest on Grayback Creek. Fish for trout and swim in creek. Supplies available at Cave Junction. Deer, bears and birds in area. Campers may gather firewood. Trail to the Oregon Caves National Monument starts at CG. Grayback interpretive trail starts at CG.

GETTING THERE: Grayback CG is located 12 mi. E of Cave Junction on state HWY 46.

SINGLE RATE:	$13	OPEN DATES:	May-Sept
# of SINGLE SITES:	35	MAX SPUR:	35 feet
		MAX STAY:	14 days
		ELEVATION:	1700 feet

18 Lobster Creek
Gold Beach • lat 42˚30'30" lon 124˚17'00"

DESCRIPTION: In forest with low brush set on a large gravel bar fronting the Rogue River. No drinking water. Salmon and steelhead fish from boat or river bank. Supplies 25 min. drive. Deer and small wildlife. Light use, fills holiday weekends. Buy firewood from hosts. Boat ramp on the Rogue River, Shrader Old Growth Trail.

GETTING THERE: Lobster Creek CG is located approx. 9 mi. E of Gold Beach on forest route 33.

SINGLE RATE:	$5	OPEN DATES:	Yearlong
# of SINGLE SITES:	6	MAX SPUR:	20 feet
		MAX STAY:	14 days
		ELEVATION:	100 feet

14 Illahe
Gold Beach • lat 42˚37'45" lon 124˚03'25"

DESCRIPTION: In an open park like setting approx. 1/2 mi. from Rogue River. Fly or bank fish for salmon and steelhead in the river. Bears, deer and small wildlife are common in the area. Fills weekends, early summer, early fall cools off. Buy firewood from host. Poison oak is abundant.

GETTING THERE: From Gold Beach go NE 26 mi. on primary forest route 33 to county route 375. Go N on 375 approx. 2 mi. to Illahe CG.

SINGLE RATE:	$5	OPEN DATES:	Yearlong
# of SINGLE SITES:	14	MAX SPUR:	20 feet
GROUP RATE:	Varies	MAX STAY:	14 days
# of GROUP SITES:	1	ELEVATION:	900 feet

19 Lockhart
Powers • lat 42˚46'00" lon 124˚00'00"

DESCRIPTION: Small primitive tent only CG in a pine forest setting. Fish for trout in nearby creeks. Supplies are available at Powers. This CG is in a moderate use area. Deer, bears, squirrels and birds are common to the area. Campers gather firewood. On the Powers to Glendale Bike Route. No drinking water.

GETTING THERE: From Powers go S on primary forest route 33 (county route 90) approx. 12 mi. to forest route 3348. Go NE on 3348 approx. 3.5 mi. to Lockhart CG. No RV's.

SINGLE RATE:	No fee	OPEN DATES:	Yearlong
# of SINGLE SITES:	1		
		MAX STAY:	14 days
		ELEVATION:	1800 feet

15 Island
Powers • lat 42˚44'00" lon 124˚03'00"

DESCRIPTION: In a pine forest setting along the South Fork of the Coquille River. Fish for trout or swim in the river. Supplies available at Powers. Deer, bears and birds are common to the area. CG is a light to moderate use area. Campers may gather firewood. Hiking trails nearby. No RV's. No water.

GETTING THERE: From Powers go S on forest route 3300 approx. 12 mi. to Island CG.

SINGLE RATE:	$6	OPEN DATES:	Yearlong
# of SINGLE SITES:	5	MAX SPUR:	16 feet
		MAX STAY:	14 days
		ELEVATION:	950 feet

20 Ludlum
Brookings • lat 42˚02'09" lon 124˚06'29"

DESCRIPTION: In a mixed hardwood forest setting adjacent to Wheeler Creek and the Winchuck River, just minutes from ocean beaches. Fish for trout and swim in the creek or river. Supplies at Brookings. Deer, bears and birds are common in the area. Gather firewood. No trails. 30 min. drive to the Redwoods of N CA.

GETTING THERE: From Brookings go S approx. 3 mi. on US HWY 101 to forest route 1107 (county route 896). Go E on 1107 approx. 6 mi. to forest route 1108. Go N on 1107 approx. 1 mi. to Ludlum House CG.

SINGLE RATE:	$10	OPEN DATES:	Yearlong
# of SINGLE SITES:	7	MAX SPUR:	35 feet
GROUP RATE:	Varies	MAX STAY:	14 days
# of GROUP SITES:	1	ELEVATION:	100 feet

 Campground has hosts   **Reservable sites**   **Accessible facilities**   **Fully developed** **Semi-developed**   **Rustic facilities**

NOTE: Open dates listed are typical. Actual dates are dependent on conditions such as snow pack.

21 Myers Camp
Grants Pass • lat 42°28'30" lon 123°40'30"

DESCRIPTION: Rustic camp in a beautiful old-growth pine stand on Meyers Creek. Fish for trout or swim in the creek. Supplies available at Grants Pass. Deer, bears and birds are common to the area. Campers may gather firewood. Trails are within a mile of the CG. No water.

GETTING THERE: From Grants Pass go N on I-5 for 2 mi. to county route 2400 approx. 12 mi. to primary forest route 25. Go SW on 25 approx. 7 mi. to Myers Camp CG. RV's not recommended.

SINGLE RATE:	No fee	OPEN DATES:	May-Sept
# of SINGLE SITES:	1		
		MAX STAY:	14 days
		ELEVATION:	2300 feet

26 Quosatana
Gold Beach • lat 42°29'55" lon 124°13'57"

DESCRIPTION: Open park like setting on Wild and Scenic Rogue River. Boat (ramp available) or shore fish for salmon and steelhead in river. Deer, birds and small wildlife are common to area. Barrier free trail to Myrtle Wood Grove. Fish cleaning station at CG. Ask camp host about firewood. Bears frequent the CG.

GETTING THERE: From Gold Beach go E approx. 13 mi. on primary forest route 33 (county route 595) to Quosatana CG.

SINGLE RATE:	$8	OPEN DATES:	Yearlong
# of SINGLE SITES:	43	MAX SPUR:	20 feet
GROUP RATE:	Varies	MAX STAY:	14 days
# of GROUP SITES:	2	ELEVATION:	120 feet

22 Myrtle Grove
Powers • lat 42°47'09" lon 124°01'27"

DESCRIPTION: Primitive camping in a pine forest setting along the South Fork Coquille River. Fish for trout or swim in the river. Supplies at Powers. Deer, bears are common to the area. CG is a light to moderate use area. Campers may gather firewood. CG sits along the Powers to Glendale Bike Route. NO WATER.

GETTING THERE: Myrtle Grove CG is located 8 mi. S of Powers on forest route 33. NO RV's, TENT CAMPING ONLY.

SINGLE RATE:	No fee	OPEN DATES:	Yearlong
# of SINGLE SITES:	5		
		MAX STAY:	14 days
		ELEVATION:	650 feet

27 Rock Creek
Powers • lat 42°42'29" lon 124°03'28"

DESCRIPTION: Tent only CG in a mixed forest setting next to Rock Creek. Fish for trout or swim at creek or Azalea Lake approx. 1 mi. S of CG. Deer, bears and birds are common to the area. CG is a light to moderate use area. Campers may gather firewood. Azalea Lake Trail is just S of CG. No water.

GETTING THERE: From Powers go S 19 mi. on primary forest route 13 to forest route 3348-080. Go S on 3348-080 1/4 mi. to Rock Creek CG. NO RV'S HERE.

SINGLE RATE:	No fee	OPEN DATES:	June-Sept
# of SINGLE SITES:	7		
		MAX STAY:	14 days
		ELEVATION:	1400 feet

23 Oak Flat
Gold Beach • lat 42°31'00" lon 124°03'30"

DESCRIPTION: Dispersed sites sit above gravel bar of the Illinois River in a mixed forest setting. Hot, dry summers. Supplies 2 hour drive. Bears, deer and small wildlife are common in the area. Campers may gather firewood. Illinois River Trail is nearby. Horse corrals in CG. Prepare for mosquitoes and flies all summer.

GETTING THERE: From Gold Beach go E on county route 545 approx. 22.5 mi. to county route 450. Go S on 450 approx. 3 mi. to Oak Flat CG. RV'S NOT RECOMMENDED

SINGLE RATE:	No fee	OPEN DATES:	May-Nov
# of SINGLE SITES:	10		
		MAX STAY:	14 days
		ELEVATION:	300 feet

28 Sam Brown
Grants Pass • lat 42°26'30" lon 123°41'11"

DESCRIPTION: In a pine forest setting next to Briggs Creek with views of nearby meadow. Fish in the creek. Supplies available at Grants Pass. Deer, elk and birds are common to the area. Sam Brown meadow is a good spot to view elk. Trails in the area. Accessible solar showers and an amphitheatre at CG.

GETTING THERE: From Grants Pass go N on I-5 approx. 2 mi. to county route 2400. Go W on 2400 approx. 12 mi. to primary forest route 25. Go SW on 25 approx. 9 mi. to Sam Brown CG.

SINGLE RATE:	$5	OPEN DATES:	May-Oct
# of SINGLE SITES:	36	MAX SPUR:	30 feet
		MAX STAY:	14 days
		ELEVATION:	2000 feet

24 Peacock
Powers • lat 42°44'30" lon 124°00'00"

DESCRIPTION: Small tent only campground in a mixed forest setting. Supplies available at Powers. This CG is a light to moderate use area. Deer, bears, squirrels and birds are common to the area. Campers may gather firewood. CG is on the Powers to Glendale Bike Route. No RV's. NO WATER.

GETTING THERE: From Powers go S on primary forest route 33 (county route 90) approx. 12 mi. to forest route 3348. Go NE on 3348 approx. 2.5 mi. to Peacock CG. No RV's.

SINGLE RATE:	No fee	OPEN DATES:	Yearlong
# of SINGLE SITES:	1		
		MAX STAY:	14 days
		ELEVATION:	2140 feet

29 Sam Brown Horse Camp
Grants Pass • lat 42°26'30" lon 123°41'11"

DESCRIPTION: In a pine forest setting next to Briggs Creek with a nearby meadow. Only horse camp on the RD and is adjacent to Sam Brown CG. Fish from the creek. Supplies available at Grant's Pass. Deer, elk and birds are common to the area. View elk at Sam Brown meadow. Gather firewood. Several trails in the area.

GETTING THERE: From Grants Pass go N on I5 2 mi to county route 2400. Go W on 2400 approx. 12 mi. to primary forest route 25. Go SW on 25 approx. 9 mi. to Sam Brown Horse Camp CG.

SINGLE RATE:	$5	OPEN DATES:	May-Oct
# of SINGLE SITES:	7	MAX SPUR:	30 feet
		MAX STAY:	14 days
		ELEVATION:	2000 feet

25 Pioneer
Powers • lat 42°48'25" lon 123°55'33"

DESCRIPTION: A tent only CG in a mixed forest setting along the Powers to Glendale Bike Route. Supplies available at Powers. Deer, bears, squirrels and birds are common to the area. CG is in a light to moderate use area. Campers may gather firewood. No water.

GETTING THERE: From Powers go S on primary forest route 33 (county route 90) approx. 12 mi. to forest route 3348. Go NE on 3348 approx. 7.5 mi. to Pioneer CG. NO RV'S.

SINGLE RATE:	No fee	OPEN DATES:	Yearlong
# of SINGLE SITES:	1		
		MAX STAY:	14 days
		ELEVATION:	2240 feet

30 Secret Creek
Grants Pass • lat 42°25'19" lon 123°41'17"

DESCRIPTION: Primitive camp with moderate use located in a pine forest setting next to Secret Creek. Fish for trout or swim in the creek. Supplies available at Grants Pass. Deer, bears and birds are common to the area. Campers may gather firewood. Trails are in the area.

GETTING THERE: From Grants Pass go N on I-5 2 mi to county route 2400. Go W on 2400 approx. 12 mi. to primary forest route 25. Go SW on 25 approx. 11 mi. to Secret Creek CG. RV's not recommended.

SINGLE RATE:	$2	OPEN DATES:	Apr-Oct
# of SINGLE SITES:	4		
		MAX STAY:	14 days
		ELEVATION:	2000 feet

 Campground has hosts   **Reservable sites**   **Accessible facilities**   **Fully developed**   **Semi-developed**   **Rustic facilities**

NOTE: Open dates listed are typical. Actual dates are dependent on conditions such as snow pack.

31 Sixmile

Selma • lat 42˚18'00" lon 123˚44'00"

DESCRIPTION: A primitive CG in a mixed conifer setting on the Illinois River. Fish for trout and swim in the river. Supplies available at Selma. Deer, bears and birds are common to the area. Osprey can be seen on the river feeding. Campers may gather firewood. No designated trails in the area.

GETTING THERE: From Selma go S on US HWY 199 to forest route 5240. Go NW on 4250-016 approx. 7 mi. to Sixmile CG. RV's not recommended.

SINGLE RATE:	No fee	OPEN DATES:	May-Sept
# of SINGLE SITES:	3		
		MAX STAY:	14 days
		ELEVATION:	1200 feet

32 Spalding Pond

Grants Pass • lat 42˚20'48" lon 123˚42'09"

DESCRIPTION: Primitive camping in a pine forest setting near historic mill site. Fish in pond stocked with rainbow trout. Supplies available at Grants Pass. Deer, bears and birds are common to the area. CG has moderate to heavy use. Accessible trail and fish platforms near CG.

GETTING THERE: From Grants Pass go N on I-5 2 mi. to county route 2400. Go W on 2400 12 mi. to primary forest route 25. Go SW on 25 approx. 3 mi. to Spalding Pond CG. Not recommended for RV's.

SINGLE RATE:	$5	OPEN DATES:	May-Oct
# of SINGLE SITES:	5		
		MAX STAY:	14 days
		ELEVATION:	3400 feet

33 Squaw Lake

Powers • lat 42˚43'50" lon 124˚00'20"

DESCRIPTION: In a mixed forest mountain lake setting on Squaw Lake. Fish for trout and swim in the lake. Supplies available at Powers. Deer, bears and birds are common to the area. CG is a moderate to heavy use area. Campers may gather firewood. Near Coquille River Falls NRA. Hiking trails in the area.

GETTING THERE: From Powers go S on primary forest route 33 (county route 90) approx. 12 mi. to forest route 3348-080. Go NE on 3348-080 approx. 3 mi. to Squaw Lake CG.

SINGLE RATE:	No fee	OPEN DATES:	Yearlong
# of SINGLE SITES:	6	MAX SPUR:	24 feet
		MAX STAY:	14 days
		ELEVATION:	2000 feet

34 Store Gulch

Selma • lat 42˚17'53" lon 123˚45'05"

DESCRIPTION: In a douglas fir forest setting with access to the Illinois River. Fish for trout and swim in the river. Supplies available at Selma. Deer, bears and birds are common to the area. Campers may gather firewood. There is a 1/3 mi. trail from the CG to the river.

GETTING THERE: From Selma go S on US HWY 199 to forest route 5240. Go NW on 4250-016 approx. 8 mi. to Store Gulch CG.

SINGLE RATE:	No fee	OPEN DATES:	May-Sept
# of SINGLE SITES:	2		
		MAX STAY:	14 days
		ELEVATION:	1200 feet

35 Sunshine Bar
Port Orford • lat 42˚43'30" lon 124˚18'30"

DESCRIPTION: In a pine forest setting located on the Wild and Scenic Elk River. Fish for trout and swim in the river. Supplies available at Port Orford. Deer, bears and birds are common to the area. CG is a light to moderate use area. Campers may gather firewood. No designated trails in the area. No water.

GETTING THERE: From Port Orford go N approx. 1.5 mi. on US HWY 101 to forest route 5325 (county route 208). Go E on 5325 approx. 19 mi. to Sunshine Bar CG.

SINGLE RATE:	No fee	OPEN DATES:	Yearlong
# of SINGLE SITES:	6	MAX SPUR:	24 feet
		MAX STAY:	14 days
		ELEVATION:	500 feet

36 Tin Can
Grants Pass • lat 42˚30'40" lon 123˚37'00"

DESCRIPTION: Primitive tent camp in a pine forest setting next to Taylor Creek. Nice cool spot to escape the summer heat. Fish for trout or swim in creek. Supplies available at Grants Pass. Deer, bears and birds are common in the area. Access to Taylor Creek trail from the campground.

GETTING THERE: From Grants Pass go N on I-5 for 2 mi. to county route 2400 approx. 12 mi. to primary forest route 25. Go SW on 25 approx. 3.5 mi. to Tin Can CG.

SINGLE RATE:	$2	OPEN DATES:	Yearlong
# of SINGLE SITES:	3		
		MAX STAY:	14 days
		ELEVATION:	1500 feet

37 Wildhorse
Gold Beach • lat 42˚27'39" lon 124˚09'44"

DESCRIPTION: Dispersed sites in a mixed forest setting with views of the meadow nearby. Mild warm days in summer. Supplies 1.5 hour drive. Deer, squirrels and birds are common to the area. CG is rarely full. Campers may gather firewood. No drinking water.

GETTING THERE: From Gold Beach go NE on primary forest route 33 (county route 595) approx. 15 mi. to forest route 3318. Go SE on 3318 approx. 3.5 mi. to Wildhorse CG.

SINGLE RATE:	No fee	OPEN DATES:	May-Nov
		MAX STAY:	14 days
		ELEVATION:	3505 feet

38 Winchuck
Brookings • lat 42˚01'13" lon 124˚06'24"

DESCRIPTION: Moderate use CG in a forest setting adjacent to the scenic Winchuck River. Swim or fish in river. CG is located just min. from ocean beaches and a 30 min. drive to the Redwoods of northern California. Supplies at Brookings. Campers may gather firewood. Many trails in the area.

GETTING THERE: From Brookings go S approx. 3 mi. on US HWY 101 to forest route 1107 (county route 896). Go E on 1107 approx. 6 mi. to forest route 1108. Go N on 1107 approx. 1 mi. to Winchuck CG.

SINGLE RATE:	$8	OPEN DATES:	May-Oct
# of SINGLE SITES:	15	MAX SPUR:	30 feet
GROUP RATE:	$30	MAX STAY:	14 days
# of GROUP SITES:	1	ELEVATION:	20 feet

39 Wooden Rock Creek
Powers • lat 42˚43'00" lon 124˚01'00"

DESCRIPTION: In a fir and cedar forest setting with the junction of Wooden Rock Creek and the South Fork Coquille River nearby. Supplies available at Powers. Deer, elk, bears, mountain lions, bobcats and birds are common in the area. Campers may gather firewood. No designated trails in the area. No Restrooms. No water.

GETTING THERE: From Powers go SE approx. 28 mi. on forest route 3300 then forest route 3348 to Wooden Rock Creek CG.

SINGLE RATE:	No fee	OPEN DATES:	Yearlong
# of SINGLE SITES:	1		
		MAX STAY:	14 days
		ELEVATION:	2240 feet

 Campground has hosts   🔒 **Reservable sites**   ♿ **Accessible facilities**   **Fully developed**   **Semi-developed**   **Rustic facilities**

NOTE: Open dates listed are typical. Actual dates are dependent on conditions such as snow pack.

Tom Iraci Photo, USDA Forest Service

SIUSLAW NATIONAL FOREST

The Siuslaw National Forest was established in 1908 and covers over 620,000 acres. The Siuslaw encompasses one of the most productive and diverse landscapes in the world,from fertile soils, which support tall stands of douglas fir, western hemlock and Sitka spruce forests laced with miles of rivers and streams, to miles of open sand dunes.

For thousands of years, the lands of the Suislaw National Forest have been home to diverse cultures and people. American Indian shell middens along the coast date back 8000 years. Other sites along the coast and within the forest indicate that different American Indian groups have long occupied these lands. Remnants from the more recent past can also be seen on the Siuslaw. You can view structures built by the Civilian Conservation Corps during the 1930s at several locations.

Points of interest scattered throughout the forest include Mary's Peak, Cape Perpetua Scenic Area, Kentucky Falls, Niagara Falls, and Cummins Creek, Drift Creek, and Rock Creek Wilderness areas.

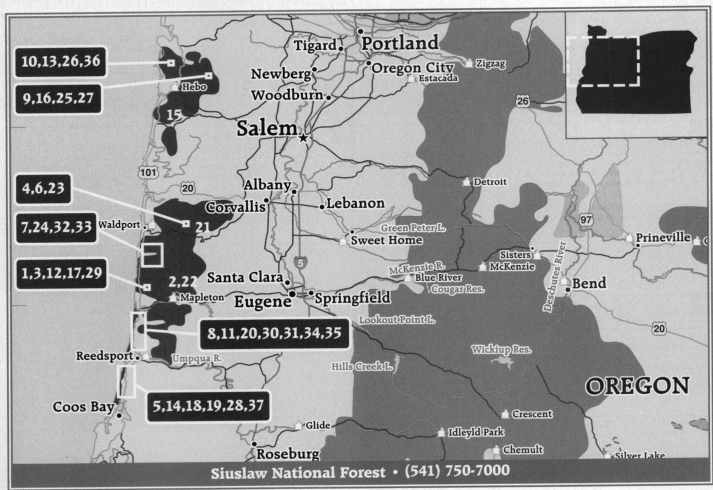

Siuslaw National Forest • (541) 750-7000

1 Alder Dune
Florence • lat 44°04'00" lon 124°05'00"

DESCRIPTION: CG is located in pine and cedar adjacent to Alder and Dune Lakes. Good fishing in the lakes. Supplies available in Florence. Campers may gather firewood. Numerous hiking trails in area. Beach located at CG.

GETTING THERE: Alder Dune CG is located approx. 4.5 mi. N of Florence on US HWY 101.

SINGLE RATE:	$12	OPEN DATES:	May-Sept
# of SINGLE SITES:	39	MAX SPUR:	80 feet
		MAX STAY:	14 days
		ELEVATION:	10 feet

2 Archie Knowles
Mapleton • lat 44°01'15" lon 123°48'20"

DESCRIPTION: CG is located in pine grove along Knowles Creek. Good fishing from the creek. Deer can often be seen in the area. Supplies available in Mapleton. Campers may gather firewood. Many hiking trails in the area.

GETTING THERE: Archie Knowles CG is located approx. 3 mi. E of Mapleton on state HWY 126.

SINGLE RATE:	$10	OPEN DATES:	May-Sept
# of SINGLE SITES:	9	MAX SPUR:	40 feet
		MAX STAY:	14 days
		ELEVATION:	100 feet

3 Baker Beach
Florence • lat 44°04'47" lon 124°07'10"

DESCRIPTION: CG is located in forested area with trail access to ocean. Visit nearby Lily Lake. Limited horse facilities. No water. Popular beachcombing area. Supplies six miles to Florence.

GETTING THERE: From Florence go N on US HWY 101 approximately 5.5 miles to Baker Beach CG.

SINGLE RATE:	$10	OPEN DATES:	Yearlong
# of SINGLE SITES:	5	MAX SPUR:	99 feet
		MAX STAY:	14 days
		ELEVATION:	30 feet

4 Blackberry
Waldport • lat 44°22'25" lon 123°50'05"

DESCRIPTION: CG is located in douglas fir, cedar and alder on the Alsea River. Good fishing for salmon and steelhead from the river. Supplies available at Waldport. Boat launch at the CG. Deer, elk and bears are common in the area. Busy all summer long.

GETTING THERE: Blackberry CG is located approx. 13 mi. E of Waldport on state HWY 34.

SINGLE RATE:	$9	OPEN DATES:	Apr-Oct
# of SINGLE SITES:	32	MAX SPUR:	25 feet
		MAX STAY:	14 days
		ELEVATION:	60 feet

5 Bluebill
North Bend • lat 43°27'00" lon 124°15'40"

DESCRIPTION: CG is located on Bluebill Lake in spruce and pine. Fish for trout in the area lakes. Supplies available at North Bend for Groceries and supplies. Deer and birds in area. 1 mi. Bluebill Loop Trail is adjacent to Campground.

GETTING THERE: From North Bend go N on US HWY 101 approx. 2 mi. to county route 1098. Go W on 1098 approx. 2 mi. to Bluebill CG.

SINGLE RATE:	$13	OPEN DATES:	May-Oct
# of SINGLE SITES:	18	MAX SPUR:	30 feet
		MAX STAY:	14 days
		ELEVATION:	22 feet

6 Canal Creek
Westwood Village • lat 44°22'08" lon 123°55'39"

DESCRIPTION: CG is located in douglas fir, blackberries and salmonberries on Canal Creek. Fish and swim in the creek. Supplies available at Westwood Village. Deer, elk and bears are common in the area. Campers may gather firewood. Many trails in the area.

GETTING THERE: From Westwood Village go S on forest route 3462 approx. 3 mi. to Canal Creek CG.

SINGLE RATE:	$6	OPEN DATES:	Apr-Oct
# of SINGLE SITES:	11	MAX SPUR:	20 feet
GROUP RATE:	$50	MAX STAY:	14 days
# of GROUP SITES:	1	ELEVATION:	250 feet

7 Cape Perpetua
Yachats • lat 44°16'52" lon 124°06'14"

DESCRIPTION: CG is located in spruce and douglas fir overlooking the Pacific Ocean. Supplies available at Yachats. Deer, elk and bears can be seen in the area. Nice viewpoint to watch whales or the sunset. Trail leading to Cape Perpetua Interpretive Center and the beach.

GETTING THERE: from Yachats go S on US HWY 101 approx. 4 mi. to forest route 55. Go E on 55 approx. 1/2 mi. to Cape Perpetua CG.

SINGLE RATE:	$14	OPEN DATES:	May-Sept
# of SINGLE SITES:	38	MAX SPUR:	40 feet
		MAX STAY:	14 days
		ELEVATION:	80 feet

8 Carter Lake
Florence • lat 43°51'24" lon 124°08'46"

DESCRIPTION: CG is located in spruce on Carter Lake. Good shore fishing for stocked trout yearlong. Supplies available at Florence. Campers may gather firewood. The 1.5 mi. Carter Dunes Trail is adjacent to the CG.

GETTING THERE: From Florence go S on US HWY 101 approx. 9 mi. to Carter Lake CG.

SINGLE RATE:	$13	OPEN DATES:	Apr-Sept
# of SINGLE SITES:	23	MAX SPUR:	35 feet
		MAX STAY:	14 days
		ELEVATION:	40 feet

9 Castle Rock
Hebo • lat 45°10'45" lon 123°49'05"

DESCRIPTION: CG is located inland in a forested environment on Three Rivers. Good fishing in area. Deer and elk are common in the area. Supplies available in Hebo. Campers may gather firewood.

GETTING THERE: Castle Rock CG is located approx. 5 mi. S of Hebo on state HWY 22.

SINGLE RATE:	No fee	OPEN DATES:	Yearlong
# of SINGLE SITES:	4	MAX SPUR:	18 feet
		MAX STAY:	14 days
		ELEVATION:	270 feet

10 Derrick Road
Sandlake • lat 45°18'00" lon 123°57'00"

DESCRIPTION: CG is a dispersed camping area in the Sandlake Recreation Area and is a popular ATV recreation spot due to sand dune access. Special permits may be required on holidays. Please contact Hebo Ranger District at (503) 392-3161. Horses not allowed. Waste dump station.

GETTING THERE: From Sandlake go W and S on forest route 1131 2 mi. to Derrick Road CG.

SINGLE RATE:	No fee	OPEN DATES:	Yearlong
		MAX STAY:	14 days
		ELEVATION:	10 feet

 Campground has hosts   **Reservable sites**   **Accessible facilities**   **Fully developed**   **Semi-developed**   **Rustic facilities**

NOTE: Open dates listed are typical. Actual dates are dependent on conditions such as snow pack.

11 Driftwood II
Florence • lat 43°53'01" lon 124°08'35"

DESCRIPTION: CG is located in spruce close to ocean beaches. Supplies available at Dunes City. Deer and shorebirds can be seen in the area. Popular dune buggying area.

GETTING THERE: From Florence go S on US HWY 101 approx. 7 mi. to the Siltcoos river road. W 1 mi. to Driftwood II CG.

SINGLE RATE:	$13	OPEN DATES:	Yearlong
# of SINGLE SITES:	69	MAX SPUR:	50 feet
		MAX STAY:	14 days
		ELEVATION:	35 feet

16 Hebo Lake
Hebo • lat 45°13'50" lon 123°47'50"

DESCRIPTION: CG is located in fir and cedar and has good fishing at the adjacent Hebo Lake. Visit historical Pioneer-Indian trail and camp. A 1933 CCC picnic shelter sets on site. Various hiking trails including barrier free trail around lake are nearby.

GETTING THERE: Hebo Lake CG is located approx. 4.5 mi. E of Hebo on forest route 1400.

SINGLE RATE:	$6	OPEN DATES:	Apr-Oct
# of SINGLE SITES:	15	MAX SPUR:	18 feet
		MAX STAY:	14 days
		ELEVATION:	1600 feet

12 Dry Creek
Florence • lat 44°06'30" lon 124°03'30"

DESCRIPTION: CG is located in pine and cedar. Popular horseback riding area. Deer and elk in area. 17 mi. to Florence for supplies.

GETTING THERE: From Florence go N on US HWY 101 approx. 11 mi. to forest route 58. Go W on 58 4 mi. to forest route 789. Go S on 789 2 mi. to Dry Creek CG.

SINGLE RATE:	No fee	OPEN DATES:	Yearlong
# of SINGLE SITES:	5	MAX SPUR:	99 feet
		MAX STAY:	14 days
		ELEVATION:	1000 feet

17 Horse Creek
Florence • lat 44°07'00" lon 124°07'30"

DESCRIPTION: CG is located in fir and cedar on Horse Creek. Popular horseback riding area. 14 mi. to Florence for supplies. Deer and elk in area.

GETTING THERE: From Florence go N on US HWY 101 approx. 11 mi. to forest route 58. Go E on 58 3 mi. to Horse Creek CG.

SINGLE RATE:	No fee	OPEN DATES:	Yearlong
# of SINGLE SITES:	10	MAX SPUR:	99 feet
		MAX STAY:	14 days
		ELEVATION:	600 feet

13 East Dunes
Sandlake • lat 45°17'45" lon 123°56'00"

DESCRIPTION: CG is in the Sandlake Recreation Area and is a popular ATV recreation spot due to sand dune access. Special permits may be required on holidays. Please contact Hebo Ranger District at (503) 392-3161. Horses not allowed. Waste dump station.

GETTING THERE: From Sandlake go W and S on forest route 1131 approx. 2 mi. to East Dunes CG.

SINGLE RATE:	$6	OPEN DATES:	Yearlong
# of SINGLE SITES:	100	MAX SPUR:	30 feet
		MAX STAY:	14 days
		ELEVATION:	50 feet

18 Horsfall
North Bend • lat 43°27'25" lon 124°14'52"

DESCRIPTION: CG is located in spruce and pine on the south end of Horsefall Lake. Close to ocean beaches. Supplies available at North Bend. Coin operated showers in campground. Popular OHV area.

GETTING THERE: From North Bend go N on US HWY 101 approx. 2 mi. to county route 1098. Go W on 1098 approx. 4 mi. to Horsefall CG.

SINGLE RATE:	$13	OPEN DATES:	Yearlong
# of SINGLE SITES:	69	MAX SPUR:	50 feet
		MAX STAY:	14 days
		ELEVATION:	21 feet

14 Eel Creek
Lakeside • lat 43°34'59" lon 124°11'05"

DESCRIPTION: Campground is located in spruce not far from the beach. Groceries and supplies are available in Lakeside. Deer and small critters in area. 3 mi. long Umpqua Dunes Trail is adjacent to campground.

GETTING THERE: Eel Creek CG is located on the N end of Lakeside on US HWY 101.

SINGLE RATE:	$13	OPEN DATES:	Yearlong
# of SINGLE SITES:	52	MAX SPUR:	35 feet
		MAX STAY:	14 days
		ELEVATION:	20 feet

19 Horsfall Beach Parking Area
North Bend • lat 43°27'25" lon 124°14'52"

DESCRIPTION: CG is located in spruce and pine west of Horsefall Lake on the beach. Fish and swim in the lake. Popular dune buggying area. Supplies available at North Bend. No designated trails in the area.

GETTING THERE: From North Bend go N on US HWY 101 approx. 2 mi. to county route 1098. Go W on 1098 approx. 2 mi. to Horsefall Beach parking area.

SINGLE RATE:	$12	OPEN DATES:	Yearlong
# of SINGLE SITES:	34	MAX SPUR:	50 feet
		MAX STAY:	14 days
		ELEVATION:	21 feet

15 George R. Vogel
Neskowin • lat 45°03'00" lon 123°53'00"

DESCRIPTION: CG is located in fir and cedar along Neskowin Creek. Fishing in creek. No water. Must furnish own portable toilet. Pack-in/pack-out. Deer and elk in area.

GETTING THERE: From Neskowin go S on Old HWY 101 approximately 5 miles to George R. Vogel CG.

		OPEN DATES:	Yearlong
		MAX SPUR:	75 feet
GROUP RATE:	$50	MAX STAY:	14 days
# of GROUP SITES:	1	ELEVATION:	350 feet

20 Lagoon
Florence • lat 43°52'51" lon 124°08'21"

DESCRIPTION: CG is located in spruce on the Siltcoos River. Good fishing in river. Supplies available at Dunes City. An accessible trail loop is adjacent to CG. CG is close to beach.

GETTING THERE: From Florence go S on US HWY 101 approx. 7 mi. to Siltcoos River Road. Go W on road approx. 1/2 mi. to Lagoon CG.

SINGLE RATE:	$13	OPEN DATES:	Yearlong
# of SINGLE SITES:	39	MAX SPUR:	35 feet
		MAX STAY:	14 days
		ELEVATION:	40 feet

 Campground has hosts   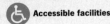 **Reservable sites**   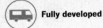 **Accessible facilities**   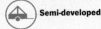 **Fully developed**   **Semi-developed**   **Rustic facilities**

NOTE: Open dates listed are typical. Actual dates are dependent on conditions such as snow pack.

21 Mary's Peak
Philomath • lat 44°30'34" lon 123°33'18"

DESCRIPTION: CG is located near stands of noble fir, shasta fir, douglas fir, cedar and alpine meadows with panoramic mountain views. Supplies available at Philomath. Many animals can be seen in the area. Numerous hiking and mountain biking trails in area.

GETTING THERE: From Philomath go SW on state HWY 34 approx. 9 mi. to Mary's Wayside (just E of Alsea summit). Go N on primary forest route 30 approx. 8 mi. to Mary's Peak CG.

SINGLE RATE:	$7	OPEN DATES:	May-Oct
# of SINGLE SITES:	6	MAX SPUR:	18 feet
		MAX STAY:	14 days
		ELEVATION:	3550 feet

22 North Fork Siuslaw
Minerva • lat 44°06'08" lon 123°56'10"

DESCRIPTION: CG is in a park-like grove of pine along the North Fork Siuslaw River. Good fishing from the river. CG is located on a historical homestead site. Supplies available at Minerva. Great trails nearby including trails through old growth forest.

GETTING THERE: North Fork Siuslaw CG is located approx. 3 mi. N of Minerva on county route 5084. Not recommended for larger RVs.

SINGLE RATE:	$5	OPEN DATES:	May-Oct*
# of SINGLE SITES:	6	MAX SPUR:	15 feet
		MAX STAY:	14 days
		ELEVATION:	150 feet

23 Riveredge Group
Waldport • lat 44°22'37" lon 123°47'59"

DESCRIPTION: CG is located in douglas fir, alder and lots of blackberries on the Alsea River. Fishing in river for salmon and steelhead. Supplies available at Waldport. Deer, elk and bears are common to the area. CG stays busy all summer.

GETTING THERE: Riveredge CG is located approx. 17 mi. E of Waldport on state HWY 34.

		OPEN DATES:	May-Oct
		MAX SPUR:	50 feet
GROUP RATE:	$50	MAX STAY:	14 days
# of GROUP SITES:	1	ELEVATION:	120 feet

24 Rock Creek
Searose Beach • lat 44°10'00" lon 124°06'50"

DESCRIPTION: CG is located in spruce and douglas fir across HWY 101 from the beach. Supplies available at Searose Beach. Deer, elk and bears are common to the area. Trails into the adjacent Rock Creek Wilderness Area.

GETTING THERE: Rock Creek CG is located approx. 3 mi. S of Searose Beach on US HWY 101.

SINGLE RATE:	$12	OPEN DATES:	May-Sept
# of SINGLE SITES:	15	MAX SPUR:	40 feet
		MAX STAY:	14 days
		ELEVATION:	40 feet

25 Rocky Bend
Blaine • lat 45°14'22" lon 123°36'17"

DESCRIPTION: CG is located in fir and cedar on the Nestucca River. Good salmon and steelhead fishing (seasonal) on the river. No drinking water. Supplies available in Blaine. Many animals can be seen in the area. Campers may gather firewood. Pack-in/pack-out.

GETTING THERE: From Blaine go S on primary forest route 85 approx. 7 mi. to Rocky Bend CG.

SINGLE RATE:	No fee	OPEN DATES:	Yearlong
# of SINGLE SITES:	6	MAX SPUR:	16 feet
		MAX STAY:	14 days
		ELEVATION:	500 feet

26 Sandbeach
Sandlake • lat 45°17'07" lon 123°57'20"

DESCRIPTION: CG is in the Sandlake Recreation Area and is a popular ATV recreation spot due to sand dune access. Special permits may be required on holidays. Please contact Hebo Ranger District at (503) 392-3161. Horses not allowed. Waste dump station.

GETTING THERE: From Sandlake go W and S on forest route 1131 approx. 3 mi. to Sandbeach CG.

SINGLE RATE:	$12	OPEN DATES:	Mar-Oct
# of SINGLE SITES:	101	MAX SPUR:	99 feet
		MAX STAY:	14 days
		ELEVATION:	10 feet

27 South Lake
Hebo • lat 45°12'15" lon 123°43'15"

DESCRIPTION: This primitive CG is located in fir forest setting on South Lake. Fish and swim from the lake. Supplies available in Hebo. Deer and elk are common in the area. Campers may gather firewood.

GETTING THERE: From Hebo go E on forest route 1400 approx. 11 mi. to forest route 1428. Go S on 1428 approx. 1 mi. to South Lake CG.

SINGLE RATE:	No fee	OPEN DATES:	Yearlong
		MAX SPUR:	16 feet
		MAX STAY:	14 days
		ELEVATION:	2360 feet

28 Spinreel
Lakeside • lat 43°34'09" lon 124°12'10"

DESCRIPTION: CG is located in spruce on Tenmile Creek. Good fishing for trout and Steelhead in creek. 1 mi. to Lakeside for groceries and supplies.

GETTING THERE: Spinreel CG is located 2 mi. S of Lakeside on US HWY 101.

SINGLE RATE:	$13	OPEN DATES:	Yearlong
# of SINGLE SITES:	36	MAX SPUR:	40 feet
		MAX STAY:	14 days
		ELEVATION:	15 feet

29 Sutton
Florence • lat 44°03'20" lon 124°06'30"

DESCRIPTION: CG is located in forested area with good fishing at nearby lake. Various activities including hiking, biking and amphitheater presentations. Visit on-site Darlingtonia Trail to see insect eating plant, and barrier free Holman Vista for views of Sutton Creek.

GETTING THERE: From Florence go N on US HWY 101 approximately 4 miles to Sutton CG.

SINGLE RATE:	Varies	OPEN DATES:	Yearlong
# of SINGLE SITES:	101	MAX SPUR:	60 feet
		MAX STAY:	14 days
# of GROUP SITES:	2	ELEVATION:	40 feet

30 Tahkenitch
Gardiner • lat 43°47'47" lon 124°08'51"

DESCRIPTION: CG is located in spruce on Tahkenitch Lake. Good fishing for trout and an occasional bass. Supplies available at Gardiner. A 2 mi. long Tahkenitch Dunes Trail is adjacent to CG. Near ocean beaches.

GETTING THERE: Tahkenitch CG is located approx. 6 mi. N of Gardiner on US HWY 101.

SINGLE RATE:	$13	OPEN DATES:	Yearlong
# of SINGLE SITES:	34	MAX SPUR:	30 feet
		MAX STAY:	14 days
		ELEVATION:	40 feet

 Campground has hosts    Reservable sites   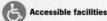 Accessible facilities   Fully developed   Semi-developed   Rustic facilities

NOTE: Open dates listed are typical. Actual dates are dependent on conditions such as snow pack.

31 Tahkenitch Landing
Gardiner • lat 43°48'04" lon 124°08'50"

DESCRIPTION: CG is located in spruce on Tahkenitch Lake. Good fishing for trout and an occasional bass. Supplies available in Gardiner. A 2 mi. long Tahkenitch Dunes Trail is adjacent to the CG. Near ocean beaches. Boat ramp and docks on lake.

GETTING THERE: Tahkenitch Landing CG is located approx. 6 mi. N of Gardiner on US HWY 101.

SINGLE RATE:	$12	OPEN DATES:	Yearlong
# of SINGLE SITES:	27	MAX SPUR:	30 feet
		MAX STAY:	14 days
		ELEVATION:	40 feet

32 Ten Mile
Searose Beach • lat 44°12'50" lon 124°00'28"

DESCRIPTION: Dispersed CG in douglas fir on Ten Mile Creek. Supplies are available in Searose Beach. Deer, elk and bears are just some of the wildlife that can be seen in the area. Campers may gather firewood. Many trails are in the area.

GETTING THERE: From Searose Beach go E on county route 5210 approx. 6 mi. to Ten Mile CG.

SINGLE RATE:	No fee	OPEN DATES:	Yearlong
# of SINGLE SITES:	5		
		MAX STAY:	14 days
		ELEVATION:	377 feet

33 Tillicum Beach
Yachats • lat 44°21'56" lon 124°05'29"

DESCRIPTION: CG is located in spruce on the beach. Enjoy fishing or swimming in the water. Supplies available at Yachats. Deer, elk and bears are just some of the animals that can be seen in the area. This CG is always busy, and is a popular beachcombing area.

GETTING THERE: Tillicum Beach CG is located approx. 3 mi. N of Yachats on US HWY 101.

SINGLE RATE:	$14	OPEN DATES:	Yearlong
# of SINGLE SITES:	59	MAX SPUR:	40 feet
		MAX STAY:	14 days
		ELEVATION:	20 feet

34 Tyee
Florence • lat 43°52'55" lon 124°07'18"

DESCRIPTION: This popular camping area is located in conifers on the Siltcoos River at the outlet of Siltcoos Lake. Good fishing in lake yearlong. Supplies available at Dunes City. Numerous wildlife can be seen in the area. No designated trails in the area.

GETTING THERE: Tyee CG is located approx. 6 mi. S of Florence on US HWY 101.

SINGLE RATE:	$13	OPEN DATES:	Apr-Oct
# of SINGLE SITES:	16	MAX SPUR:	30 feet
		MAX STAY:	14 days
		ELEVATION:	60 feet

35 Waxmyrtle
Florence • lat 43°52'32" lon 124°08'35"

DESCRIPTION: CG is located in spruce on the Siltcoos River. Fish for salmon, steelhead, trout and bass in the river. Supplies are available in Dunes City. Numerous animals can be seen in the area. Waxmyrtle Trail is a 1.5 mi. trail and is adjacent to CG.

GETTING THERE: From Florence go S on US HWY 101 approx. 7 mi. to Siltcoos River road. W 1/2 mi. to Waxmyrtle CG.

SINGLE RATE:	$13	OPEN DATES:	May-Oct
# of SINGLE SITES:	54	MAX SPUR:	35 feet
		MAX STAY:	14 days
		ELEVATION:	20 feet

36 West Winds
Sandlake • lat 45°18'00" lon 123°57'00"

DESCRIPTION: CG is in the Sandlake Recreation Area and is a popular ATV recreation spot due to sand dune access. Special permits may be required on holidays. Please contact Hebo Ranger District at (503) 392-3161. Horses not allowed. Waste dump station.

GETTING THERE: From Sandlake go W and S on forest route 1131 approx. 2 mi. to West Winds CG.

SINGLE RATE:	$6	OPEN DATES:	Yearlong
# of SINGLE SITES:	40	MAX SPUR:	30 feet
		MAX STAY:	14 days
		ELEVATION:	10 feet

37 Wild Mare
North Bend • lat 43°26'00" lon 124°16'00"

DESCRIPTION: CG is located in a spruce and pine forest setting not far from the ocean beaches. This is a horse camp with single and double corrals. Supplies are available at North Bend. No designated trails in the area.

GETTING THERE: From North Bend go N on US HWY 101 approx. 2 mi. to county route 1098. Go W on 1098 approx. 3 mi. to Wild Mare CG.

SINGLE RATE:	$12	OPEN DATES:	Yearlong
# of SINGLE SITES:	12	MAX SPUR:	50 feet
		MAX STAY:	14 days
		ELEVATION:	75 feet

 Campground has hosts 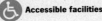 **Reservable sites** **Accessible facilities**   **Fully developed**  **Semi-developed** **Rustic facilities**

USFS Photo

UMATILLA NATIONAL FOREST

The Umatilla National Forest, located in the Blue Mountains of northeast Oregon and southeast Washington, covers 1.4 million acres. The Forest has some mountainous terrain, but most of the Forest consists of v-shaped valleys separated by narrow ridges or plateaus.

The landscape also includes heavily timbered slopes, grassland ridges and benches, and bold basalt outcroppings. Elevations range from 1,600 to 8,000 feet above sea level. Changes in weather are common, but summers are generally warm and dry with cool evenings.

Umatilla is an Indian word meaning "water rippling over sand." Explorers Lewis and Clark passed this way in 1805, and Marcus and Narcissa Whitman crossed the Forest in 1836 to establish a mission near Walla Walla, Washington. Thousands of emigrants followed the Oregon Trail westward, and many remained in Blue Mountain country.

A wide variety of recreation opportunities are available on the Umatilla National Forest. Three classified wilderness and three national Wild and Scenic Rivers add their assets to the forest recreation treasures.

UMATILLA NATIONAL FOREST • OREGON • LOCATOR MAP

Umatilla National Forest • (541) 278-3716

1 Alder Thicket
Pomeroy • lat 46˚15'32" lon 117˚33'57"

DESCRIPTION: This tent only CG is located in a mixed pine forest setting near Alder Thicket Springs. Supplies available at Pomeroy. No drinking water available at CG. Deer, elk, turkeys, mountain lions, bears and birds are common to the area. Campers may gather firewood. Hiking trails in the area.

GETTING THERE: From Pomeroy go S approx. 16.5 mi. on forest route 40 to forest route 4016. Go W on 4016 approx. 1 mi. to Alder Thicket CG.

SINGLE RATE:	No fee	OPEN DATES:	Yearlong*
# of SINGLE SITES:	5		
		MAX STAY:	14 days
		ELEVATION:	5100 feet

2 Bears Wallow
Ukiah • lat 45˚15'48" lon 118˚45'10"

DESCRIPTION: CG offers a pleasant experience among mixed pine adjacent to Bears Wallow Creek. Fish for trout and swim in the creek. Supplies are available at Ukiah. Wildlife includes deer, elk, mountain lions, and black bears. A 1/4-mile barrier free interpretive trail is nearby. No drinking water. Gather firewood locally.

GETTING THERE: Bears Wallow CG is located approx. 10 mi. NE of Ukiah on state HWY 244.

SINGLE RATE:	$5	OPEN DATES:	Yearlong*
# of SINGLE SITES:	6	MAX SPUR:	20 feet
		MAX STAY:	14 days
		ELEVATION:	3900 feet

3 Big Springs
Pomeroy • lat 46˚12'30" lon 117˚33'30"

DESCRIPTION: In a mixed conifer setting on Big Spring. Fish and swim in the spring. Supplies available at Pomeroy. Deer, elk, mountain lions, bears, birds and squirrels are common in the area. Campers may gather firewood. Hunting and hiking opportunities are in close proximity to the campground.

GETTING THERE: Located 26 miles south of Pomeroy, Washington on Forest Road #4225.

SINGLE RATE:	No fee	OPEN DATES:	Yearlong*
# of SINGLE SITES:	8	MAX SPUR:	40 feet
		MAX STAY:	14 days
		ELEVATION:	5000 feet

4 Bull Prairie
Heppner • lat 44˚57'00" lon 119˚38'00"

DESCRIPTION: This CG is set in mixed conifer on Bull Prairie Lake, a beautiful 24-acre lake. Fishing, non-motorized boating, hunting, and hiking are popular activities. Wildlife includes elk, deer, and black bears. CG is busy holidays. Firewood sold on site. Enjoy beautiful views at historic Ant Hill.

GETTING THERE: Bull Prairie CG is located approx. 36 mi. S of Heppner on forest route 2039.

SINGLE RATE:	$12	OPEN DATES:	Yearlong*
# of SINGLE SITES:	27	MAX SPUR:	30 feet
		MAX STAY:	14 days
		ELEVATION:	4000 feet

5 Fairview
Heppner • lat 44˚57'00" lon 119˚40'00"

DESCRIPTION: This CG is located in mixed conifer at Fairview Spring. Excellent mountain biking, hunting and fishing opportunities are in close proximity. Wildlife in the area includes deer, elk, and black bears. CG can be busy on holidays. Visit historic Ant Hill for beautiful views. No drinking water.

GETTING THERE: Located 34 miles south of Heppner, Oregon on State HWY 207.

SINGLE RATE:	No fee	OPEN DATES:	Yearlong*
# of SINGLE SITES:	5	MAX SPUR:	30 feet
		MAX STAY:	14 days
		ELEVATION:	4300 feet

6 Forest Boundary
Pomeroy • lat 46˚18'00" lon 117˚33'00"

DESCRIPTION: This tent only CG is located in a mixed pine forest setting. Supplies available at Pomeroy. No drinking water available at CG. Deer, elk, turkeys, mountain lions, bears and birds are common to the area. Campers may gather firewood. Hiking trails in the area.

GETTING THERE: Forest Boundary CG is located approx. 14.5 mi. S of Pomeroy on forest route 40.

SINGLE RATE:	No fee	OPEN DATES:	Yearlong*
# of SINGLE SITES:	5	MAX SPUR:	40 feet
		MAX STAY:	14 days
		ELEVATION:	4450 feet

7 Four Corners
Ukiah • lat 45˚10'43" lon 118˚36'21"

DESCRIPTION: This CG is located in mixed pine at the confluence of Camas Creek and Rancheria Creek. Enjoy fishing for trout in the creeks. A winter recreation area is close by. Wildlife in this area includes deer, elk, mountain lions, and black bears. No drinking water on site.

GETTING THERE: Four Corners CG is located approx. 19 mi. E of Ukiah on state HWY 244.

SINGLE RATE:	No fee	OPEN DATES:	Yearlong*
# of SINGLE SITES:	2	MAX SPUR:	20 feet
GROUP RATE:	No fee	MAX STAY:	14 days
# of GROUP SITES:	1	ELEVATION:	4200 feet

8 Frazier
Ukiah • lat 45˚09'35" lon 118˚38'20"

DESCRIPTION: This CG rests in mixed pine on Frazier Creek. Enjoy fishing for trout in the creek. The CG offers access to an OHV trail system, Lehman Hot Springs, a winter recreation area, and covered picnic shelter. Wildlife in this area includes deer, elk, mountain lions, and black bears. No drinking water.

GETTING THERE: From Ukiah go E approx. 16 mi. on state HWY 244 to forest route 5226. Go S on 5226 approx. 1 mi. to Frazier CG.

SINGLE RATE:	$5	OPEN DATES:	Yearlong*
# of SINGLE SITES:	32	MAX SPUR:	50 feet
		MAX STAY:	14 days
		ELEVATION:	4300 feet

9 Godman
Baileysburg • lat 46˚06'01" lon 117˚47'09"

DESCRIPTION: In a mixed conifer setting near Baker Pond with great sunsets. Fish and swim the pond. Campers may gather firewood. The Godman Trailhead provides easy access into the Wenah-Tucannon Wilderness. CG has horse facilities with hitching rails and troughs. No drinking water.

GETTING THERE: From Baileysburg go S on county route 9115 approx. 18 mi. to forest route 46. Go NE on 46 approx. 7 mi. to Godman CG.

SINGLE RATE:	No fee	OPEN DATES:	Yearlong*
# of SINGLE SITES:	8		
		MAX STAY:	14 days
		ELEVATION:	5750 feet

10 Jubilee Lake
Looking Glass • lat 45˚49'45" lon 117˚57'55"

DESCRIPTION: The largest and most popular CG on the forest. Is nestled among the trees on Jubilee Lake. Fish, swim and boat in the lake. Supplies available at Looking Glass. Numerous animals can be seen in the area. Jubilee Lake National Recreation Trail offers a pleasant 2.8 mile stroll around the lake.

GETTING THERE: From Looking Glass go NE on county route 42 approx. 1.5 mi. to primary forest route 63. Go NW on 63 approx. 12.5 mi. to Jubilee Lake CG.

SINGLE RATE:	$14	OPEN DATES:	Yearlong*
# of SINGLE SITES:	50	MAX SPUR:	36 feet
		MAX STAY:	14 days
		ELEVATION:	4800 feet

 Campground has hosts   **Reservable sites**   **Accessible facilities**   **Fully developed**   **Semi-developed**   **Rustic facilities**

NOTE: Open dates listed are typical. Actual dates are dependent on conditions such as snow pack.

11 Lady Bug
Pomeroy • lat 46˚11'30" lon 117˚42'23"

DESCRIPTION: In a mixed conifer setting with no drinking water available. Supplies are located at Pomeroy. Deer, elk, mountain lions, bears, birds and squirrels are common to the area. Campers may gather firewood. This CG is in close proximity of the Wenaha-Tucannon Wilderness.

GETTING THERE: From Pomeroy go S approx. 46 mi. on forest route 4713 to Lady Bug CG. High clearance required.

SINGLE RATE: # of SINGLE SITES:	No fee 7	OPEN DATES: MAX STAY: ELEVATION:	Yearlong* 14 days 3300 feet

12 Lane Creek
Ukiah • lat 45˚11'23" lon 118˚45'54"

DESCRIPTION: This CG is situated in mixed conifer on Lane Creek. Enjoy fishing for trout in the creek. Supplies are available at Ukiah. Wildlife includes deer, elk, mountain lions, and black bears. A 1/4-mile barrier free interpretive trail is at nearby Bears Wallow CG. No drinking water. Gather firewood locally.

GETTING THERE: Lane Creek CG is located approx. 10 mi. E of Ukiah on state HWY 244.

SINGLE RATE: # of SINGLE SITES:	$5 4	OPEN DATES: MAX SPUR: MAX STAY: ELEVATION:	Yearlong* 20 feet 14 days 3850 feet

13 Misery Spring
Pomeroy • lat 46˚07'15" lon 117˚28'57"

DESCRIPTION: In a mixed conifer setting with panoramic views from Ray Ridge into the Wenaha-Tucannon Wilderness. No drinking water. Supplies available at Pomeroy. Deer, elk, bears, mountain lions and birds are common to the area. Campers may gather firewood. Many hiking and hunting opportunities are available.

GETTING THERE: Misery Springs CG is located approx. 27 mi. S of Pomeroy on forest route 4030.

SINGLE RATE: # of SINGLE SITES:	No fee 5	OPEN DATES: MAX STAY: ELEVATION:	Yearlong* 14 days 6200 feet

14 Mottet
Tollgate • lat 45˚52'05" lon 117˚57'37"

DESCRIPTION: This primitive CG is in a mixed conifer setting with great views of the surrounding forest. Supplies available at Tollgate. Numerous animals can be seen in the area. Campers may gather firewood. No designated trails nearby.

GETTING THERE: From Tollgate go NE on primary forest route 64 approx. 3 mi. to forest route 6403. Go N on 6403 approx. 8 mi. to Mottet CG.

SINGLE RATE: # of SINGLE SITES:	Varies 7	OPEN DATES: MAX SPUR: MAX STAY: ELEVATION:	Yearlong* 25 feet 14 days 5200 feet

15 North Fork John Day
Ukiah • lat 44˚54'51" lon 118˚24'03"

DESCRIPTION: This CG sits along the Wild and Scenic North Fork John Day River. Enjoy fishing for salmon and trout. Horse handling facilities are available at the adjacent trailhead. Wildlife includes deer, elk, mountain lions, and black bears. Enjoy a drive along the Blue Mountain Scenic Byway. No drinking water.

GETTING THERE: North Fork John Day CG is located approx. 36 mi. SE of Ukiah on primary forest route 52.

SINGLE RATE: # of SINGLE SITES:	$5 8	OPEN DATES: MAX SPUR: MAX STAY: ELEVATION:	Yearlong* 20 feet 14 days 5200 feet

16 Olive Lake
Dale • lat 44˚47'44" lon 118˚35'46"

DESCRIPTION: This CG is nestled among mixed conifer on Olive Lake. High in the Blue Mountains, the lake covers 160 surface acres and offers fishing for trout and kokanee. Visit the historic powerhouse and mining town nearby. Wildlife includes deer, elk, mountain lions, and black bears. No drinking water.

GETTING THERE: Olive Lake CG is located approx. 26 mi. SE of Dale on primary forest route 10.

SINGLE RATE: # of SINGLE SITES:	$5 24	OPEN DATES: MAX SPUR: MAX STAY: ELEVATION:	Yearlong* 20 feet 14 days 6000 feet

17 Panjab
Pomeroy • lat 46˚12'18" lon 117˚42'23"

DESCRIPTION: In a mixed conifer setting on Panjab Creek. Fish and swim in the creek. Supplies available at Pomeroy. Deer, elk, mountain lions, bears, birds and squirrels are common to the area. Campers may gather firewood. You can enjoy Hiking and bicycling on nearby trails.

GETTING THERE: From Pomeroy go S on forest route 4713 approx. 46 mi. to Panjab CG.

SINGLE RATE: # of SINGLE SITES:	No fee 2	OPEN DATES: MAX STAY: ELEVATION:	Yearlong* 14 days 3300 feet

18 Pataha
Pomeroy • lat 46˚17'31" lon 117˚30'52"

DESCRIPTION: In a mixed conifer setting on Pataha Creek. Fish or swim in the creek. The creek is stocked each spring with fish. Supplies available at Pomeroy. Deer, elk, mountain lions, bears, birds and squirrels are common to the area. Campers may gather firewood. Many trails in the area.

GETTING THERE: From Pomeroy go S on primary forest route 40 approx. 17 mi. to forest route 4016. Go E on 4016 approx. 3.5 mi. to Pataha CG.

SINGLE RATE: # of SINGLE SITES:	No fee 3	OPEN DATES: MAX STAY: ELEVATION:	Yearlong* 14 days 4500 feet

19 Penland Lake
Ukiah • lat 45˚07'15" lon 119˚18'54"

DESCRIPTION: This CG is nestled in mixed conifer beside scenic Penland Lake. Fish in non-motorized boats for trout. Wildlife includes deer, elk, and black bears. This CG offers excellent picnic, paddling, and hiking adventures. Try a hike to scenic Potamus Point to view the lava flows. No drinking water.

GETTING THERE: From Ukiah go W on forest route 53 19 mi. to forest route 5321. Go S on 5321 3 mi. to forest route 2103. Go W on 2103 1.5 mi. to forest route 030. Go N on 030 1/2 mi. to CG.

SINGLE RATE: # of SINGLE SITES:	No fee 5	OPEN DATES: MAX STAY: ELEVATION:	Yearlong* 14 days 4950 feet

20 Spruce Springs
Pomeroy • lat 46˚10'43" lon 117˚32'33"

DESCRIPTION: In a mixed conifer forest setting with no drinking water available. Panoramic views of the Tucannon drainage and Wenaha-Tucannon Wilderness. Supplies available at Pomeroy. Deer, elk, turkeys, mountain lions and bears are common to the area. Many hiking opportunities available in the area.

GETTING THERE: Located 15 miles south of Pomeroy, Washington on Forest Road #40.

SINGLE RATE: # of SINGLE SITES:	No fee 3	OPEN DATES: MAX STAY: ELEVATION:	Yearlong* 14 days 5600 feet

Umatilla National Forest • Oregon • 11 — 20

 Campground has hosts   Reservable sites   Accessible facilities   Fully developed   Semi-developed Rustic facilities

NOTE: Open dates listed are typical. Actual dates are dependent on conditions such as snow pack.

21 Squaw Spring
Tollgate • lat 45°55'41" lon 117°56'18"

DESCRIPTION: This primitive CG is in a mixed forest setting on Squaw Spring. Fish or swim in the spring. Supplies available in Tollgate. Deer, elk, mountain lions, bears and birds are common in the area. Campers may gather firewood. No designated trails in the area. No drinking water.

GETTING THERE: From Tollgate go NE on primary forest route 64 approx. 3 mi. to forest route 6403. Go N on 6403 approx. 13.5 mi. to Squaw Spring CG.

SINGLE RATE:	No fee	OPEN DATES:	Yearlong*
# of SINGLE SITES:	12		
		MAX STAY:	14 days
		ELEVATION:	5600 feet

26 Umatilla Forks
Gibbon • lat 45°43'37" lon 118°11'07"

DESCRIPTION: In a mixed conifer setting situated between the South Fork and the North Fork of the Umatilla River. Fish and swim in river. Supplies at Gibbon. Numerous animals can be seen in the area. Hiking in the North Fork Umatilla Wilderness is popular from early spring to late fall.

GETTING THERE: Umatilla Forks CG is located approx. 8.5 mi. E of Gibbon on primary forest route 32.

SINGLE RATE:	$8	OPEN DATES:	Yearlong*
# of SINGLE SITES:	15	MAX SPUR:	25 feet
		MAX STAY:	14 days
		ELEVATION:	2400 feet

22 Target Meadows
Tollgate • lat 45°48'25" lon 118°04'42"

DESCRIPTION: In an open, park-like setting around a meadow. Supplies available in Tollgate. Deer, elk, mountain lions, bears and birds are common in the area. Campers may gather firewood. Burnt Cabin Trailhead and trail leads down to the South Fork Walla Walla River Trail.

GETTING THERE: Target Meadows CG is located approx. 2 mi. N of Tollgate on forest route 6401.

SINGLE RATE:	$10	OPEN DATES:	Yearlong*
# of SINGLE SITES:	20	MAX SPUR:	28 feet
		MAX STAY:	14 days
		ELEVATION:	4800 feet

27 Wickiup
Pomeroy • lat 46°08'11" lon 117°26'12"

DESCRIPTION: In a mixed conifer setting with no drinking water available. Supplies available at Pomeroy. Deer, elk, bears, mountain lions, turkeys and birds are common to the area. Campers may gather firewood. No desinated trails in the area.

GETTING THERE: Located 34 mi. S of Pomeroy on forest route 40 and 44.

SINGLE RATE:	No fee	OPEN DATES:	Yearlong*
# of SINGLE SITES:	5		
		MAX STAY:	14 days
		ELEVATION:	5960 feet

23 Teal Spring
Pomeroy • lat 46°11'24" lon 117°34'17"

DESCRIPTION: This is a small scenic CG in a mixed conifer setting offering a spectacular view of the Tucannon drainage and the Wenaha-Tucannon Wilderness. No drinking water available. Supplies available at Pomeroy. Deer, elk, bears, mountain lions and birds are common to the area. Day hike opportunities are available nearby.

GETTING THERE: Teal Springs CG is located approx. 23 mi. S of Pomeroy on forest route 40.

SINGLE RATE:	No fee	OPEN DATES:	Yearlong*
# of SINGLE SITES:	5	MAX SPUR:	40 feet
		MAX STAY:	14 days
		ELEVATION:	5700 feet

28 Winom Creek
Ukiah • lat 45°02'07" lon 118°37'30"

DESCRIPTION: This CG is located in mixed conifer on Winom Creek. Enjoy fishing for trout in the creek. Wildlife includes deer, elk, mountain. lions and black bears. There is a trail that leads to the North Fork John Day Wilderness nearby. Enjoy a drive on the scenic Blue Mountain. Scenic Byway. No drinking water.

GETTING THERE: Winom CG is located approx. 20 mi. SE of Ukiah on primary forest route 52.

SINGLE RATE:	No fee	OPEN DATES:	Yearlong*
# of SINGLE SITES:	5	MAX SPUR:	20 feet
		MAX STAY:	14 days
		ELEVATION:	5000 feet

24 Tollbridge
Dale • lat 44°59'50" lon 118°56'03"

DESCRIPTION: This CG rests in mixed hardwoods and conifer at the confluence of Desolation Creek and North Fork John Day River. Enjoy fishing for salmon and trout in the river. Visit the nearby Bridge Creek State Wildlife Area. Local wildlife includes deer, elk, mountain lions, and black bears.

GETTING THERE: Tollbridge CG is located approx. 1 mi. E of Dale on primary forest route 55.

SINGLE RATE:	Varies	OPEN DATES:	Yearlong*
# of SINGLE SITES:	7	MAX SPUR:	20 feet
		MAX STAY:	14 days
		ELEVATION:	3800 feet

29 Woodland
Tollgate • lat 45°43'59" lon 118°01'47"

DESCRIPTION: CG is in a nice, green open forest area with no drinking water available. Supplies available at Tollgate. Deer, elk, mountain lions, turkeys and birds are common in the area. Campers may gather firewood. Mountain biking and hiking are just a few of the favorite activities.

GETTING THERE: Woodland CG is located approx. 4 mi. S of Tollgate on state HWY 204.

SINGLE RATE:	$5	OPEN DATES:	Yearlong*
# of SINGLE SITES:	7		
		MAX STAY:	14 days
		ELEVATION:	5200 feet

25 Tucannon
Pomeroy • lat 46°14'36" lon 117°41'17"

DESCRIPTION: This popular CG is in a mixed conifer setting along the Tucannon River. There are several ponds in the area that are stocked with trout. Supplies available at Pomeroy. Deer, elk, bears, mountain lions and birds are common to the area. No designated hiking trails in the area. No drinking water available.

GETTING THERE: Tucannon CG is located approx. 20 mi. S of Pomeroy on primary forest route 47.

SINGLE RATE:	No fee	OPEN DATES:	Yearlong*
# of SINGLE SITES:	15	MAX SPUR:	40 feet
		MAX STAY:	14 days
		ELEVATION:	2600 feet

30 Woodward
Tollgate • lat 45°46'40" lon 118°05'55"

DESCRIPTION: Nestled in the trees, near Langdon Lake, this popular CG has a hiking trail and a view of Langdon Lake. (Please note, Langdon Lake is a private lake and campers do not have access to the lake.) Supplies available at Tollgate. Many animals are in the area. Campers may gather firewood.

GETTING THERE: Woodward CG is located just S of Tollgate.

SINGLE RATE:	$10	OPEN DATES:	Yearlong*
# of SINGLE SITES:	18	MAX SPUR:	32 feet
		MAX STAY:	14 days
		ELEVATION:	4950 feet

 Campground has hosts   Reservable sites   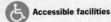 Accessible facilities   Fully developed   Semi-developed   Rustic facilities

NOTE: Open dates listed are typical. Actual dates are dependent on conditions such as snow pack.

UMPQUA NATIONAL FOREST

The nearly one million acre Umpqua National Forest is located on the western slopes of the Cascades in southwest Oregon and encompasses a diverse area of rugged peaks, high rolling meadows, sparkling rivers and lakes, and deep canyons. They produce a wealth of water resources, timber, forage, minerals, wildlife, and outdoor recreation opportunities.

Many theories exist as to the meaning of *Umpqua*-most have something to do with water. The most accepted definition is "thunder water", or more specifically, the noise water makes when it rushes through canyons and gorges and over rocks. *Umpqua* was the Indian name used to refer to the locality of the Umpqua River, and the Umpqua Indian Tribes of the area were named after the Umpqua.

The Umpqua has approximately 500 miles of "summer" trails and 225 miles of "winter" trails. Rafting, canoeing, and fishing are available on the North Umpqua Wild and Scenic River. The Boulder Creek, Mt. Thielsen, and Rogue-Umpqua Divide Wilderness Areas all offer visitors distinctive back country experiences.

UMPQUA NATIONAL FOREST • OREGON • LOCATOR MAP

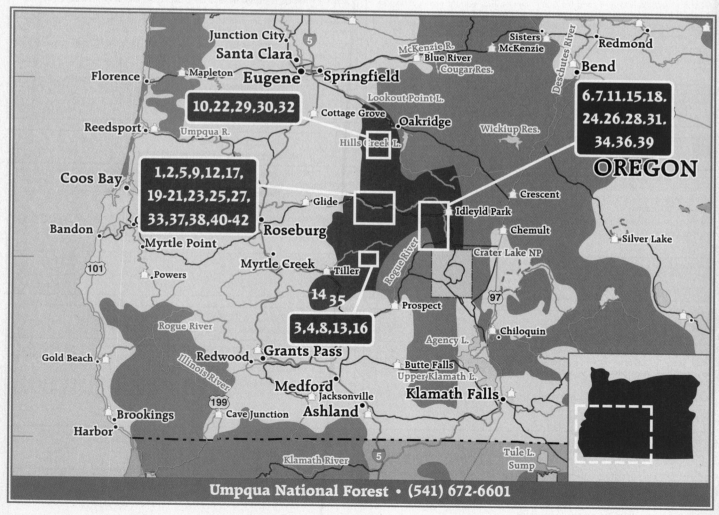

Umpqua National Forest • (541) 672-6601

1 Apple Creek
Roseburg • lat 43°18'19" lon 122°40'24"

DESCRIPTION: This CG is located a short walk away from the North Umpqua River and offers easy access to fishing (fly angling only). Supplies available at Roseburg. Hiking on the Calf and Panther segments of the North Umpqua National Recreation Trail #1414 nearby. Whitewater boating on the river.

GETTING THERE: Apple Creek CG is located approx. 34 mi. E of Roseburg on state HWY 138.

SINGLE RATE:	$5	MAX SPUR:	22 feet
# of SINGLE SITES:	8	MAX STAY:	14 days
		ELEVATION:	1365 feet
		OPEN DATES:	May-Oct

6 Broken Arrow

Roseburg • lat 43°08'05" lon 122°08'35"

DESCRIPTION: CG is set in a lodge pole pine forest, at the south end of Diamond Lake. CG has picturesque views of both Mount Bailey and Mount Thielsen. Numerous hiking trails close by. Lake fishing for Rainbow trout. Supplies can be purchased at the full service resort nearby. RV dump station at CG.

GETTING THERE: From Roseburg go E approx. 80 mi. on state HWY 138 to forest route 4795. Go S on 4795 approx. 4 mi. to Broken Arrow CG.

SINGLE RATE:	Varies	OPEN DATES:	May-Oct*
# of SINGLE SITES:	147	MAX SPUR:	35 feet
GROUP RATE:	Varies	MAX STAY:	14 days
# of GROUP SITES:	4	ELEVATION:	5190 feet

2 Bogus Creek
Roseburg • lat 43°19'30" lon 122°47'50"

DESCRIPTION: CG is located along the scenic North Umpqua River, with access to steelhead fishing, rafting and sightseeing. This site is a major launching point for whitewater boaters. Fall Creek Falls and Job's Garden Geological Area are located within 3 miles. Many trails in area. Grey water waste sump near CG.

GETTING THERE: Bogus Creek CG is located approx. 34.5 mi. E of Roseburg on state HWY 138.

SINGLE RATE:	$7	OPEN DATES:	May-Oct
# of SINGLE SITES:	15	MAX SPUR:	35 feet
		MAX STAY:	14 days
		ELEVATION:	1100 feet

7 Bunker Hill
Prospect • lat 43°19'13" lon 122°11'10"

DESCRIPTION: CG clings to the NW shore of Lemolo Reservoir beneath the heavily wooded Bunker Hill. The lake contains trout. Supplies at a full service resort nearby. Bald eagles soar above the CG in the lodge pole pine forest. Hiking trails nearby.

GETTING THERE: From Prospect go N on state HWY 230 approx. 35 mi. to state HWY 138. Go N on 138 approx. 10 mi. to forest route 2610. Go N on 2610 approx. 5.5 mi. to forest route 2612. Go S on 2612 approx. 1 mi. to Bunker Hill CG.

SINGLE RATE:	$5	OPEN DATES:	May-Oct*
# of SINGLE SITES:	8		
		MAX STAY:	14 days
		ELEVATION:	4150 feet

3 Boulder Creek
Tiller • lat 43°03'15" lon 122°46'35"

DESCRIPTION: CG is located along the South Umpqua River near the mouth of Boulder Creek. The campsites offer shade and seclusion in a setting of mixed age conifer. This is a reduced service level CG. Please gather firewood only from dead and down litter to avoid damaging vegetation and leave a clean camp for the next visitor.

GETTING THERE: Boulder Creek CG is located approx. 14 mi. E of Tiller on primary forest route 28.

SINGLE RATE:	No fee	OPEN DATES:	May-Oct
# of SINGLE SITES:	8	MAX SPUR:	45 feet
		MAX STAY:	14 days
		ELEVATION:	1400 feet

8 Camp Comfort

Tiller • lat 43°06'22" lon 122°35'33"

DESCRIPTION: CG is shaded by large old growth cedar and fir and is located near the upper South Umpqua River. Fish and swim in the river. A restored Civilian Conservation Corps shelter is part of one campsite. Supplies available in Tiller. Campers may gather firewood locally. Hiking trails nearby.

GETTING THERE: Camp Comfort CG is located approx. 26 mi. E of Tiller on county route 46/primary forest route 28.

SINGLE RATE:	No fee	OPEN DATES:	May-Oct
# of SINGLE SITES:	5	MAX SPUR:	45 feet
		MAX STAY:	14 days
		ELEVATION:	2033 feet

4 Boulder Creek Annex
Tiller • lat 43°03'15" lon 122°46'35"

DESCRIPTION: CG is in a shaded area of mixed conifer set along Boulder Creek. A short trail at the north end of the CG leads upstream to a pool in Boulder Creek. Campers may gather firewood locally. Trailer use is not recommended due to short parking spurs and lack of a turnaround.

GETTING THERE: Boulder Creek Annex CG is located approx. 14 mi. E of Tiller on primary forest route 28.

SINGLE RATE:	No fee	OPEN DATES:	May-Oct
# of SINGLE SITES:	4	MAX SPUR:	25 feet
		MAX STAY:	14 days
		ELEVATION:	1400 feet

9 Canton Creek
Roseburg • lat 43°21'00" lon 122°43'40"

DESCRIPTION: Located on Steamboat Creek a quarter mile from its confluence with the North Umpqua River, this site offers ready access to popular fishing holes on the North Umpqua, which is restricted to fly angling only. (Steamboat Creek is closed to fishing). Grey water waste sump at CG. Hiking trails in the area.

GETTING THERE: From Roseburg go E on state HWY 138 approx. 39 mi. to Steamboat Creek Road 38. Go NE on 38 approx. 1/4 mi. to Canton Creek CG.

SINGLE RATE:	$7	OPEN DATES:	May-Oct
# of SINGLE SITES:	5	MAX SPUR:	22 feet
		MAX STAY:	14 days
		ELEVATION:	1195 feet

5 Boulder Flat
Roseburg • lat 43°18'20" lon 122°31'30"

DESCRIPTION: Scenery viewed from the site is outstanding and trout fishing can be quite good. The CG is adjacent to a major launching point for whitewater boaters and the Boulder Creek Wilderness. Supplies available at Roseburg. Grey water waste sump at CG. Many hiking trails in the area.

GETTING THERE: Boulder Flat CG is located approx. 52 mi. E of Roseburg on state HWY 138.

SINGLE RATE:	$5	OPEN DATES:	May-Oct
# of SINGLE SITES:	11	MAX SPUR:	35 feet
		MAX STAY:	14 days
		ELEVATION:	1600 feet

10 Cedar Creek
Cottage Grove • lat 43°40'12" lon 122°42'17"

DESCRIPTION: CG is in an open stand of old-growth douglas fir and adjacent to Brice Creek. Fish and swim in the creek. Supplies available in Cottage Grove. Recreational gold panning is allowed. Campers may gather firewood. Many trails in the area.

GETTING THERE: From Cottage Grove take exit 174 on I-5, to county route 2400. Go E on 2400 approx. 16.5 mi. to county route 2470. Go SE on 2470 approx. 4 mi. to Cedar Creek CG.

SINGLE RATE:	No fee	OPEN DATES:	Yearlong
# of SINGLE SITES:	8	MAX SPUR:	16 feet
		MAX STAY:	14 days
		ELEVATION:	1520 feet

 Campground has hosts　 **Reservable sites**　 **Accessible facilities**　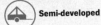 **Fully developed**　 **Semi-developed**　**Rustic facilities**

11 Clearwater Falls
Roseburg • lat 43°14'55" lon 122°13'48"

DESCRIPTION: CG is located along the Rogue-Umpqua Scenic Byway corridor. Here the Clearwater River dances through old growth douglas fir forest painting a picture in bright, moist greens and froths of white. Supplies at a full service resort nearby. Trails nearby.

GETTING THERE: Clearwater CG is located approx. 70 mi. E of Roseburg on state HWY 138.

SINGLE RATE:	$5	OPEN DATES:	June-Oct*
# of SINGLE SITES:	12	MAX SPUR:	25 feet
		MAX STAY:	14 days
		ELEVATION:	4100 feet

12 Coolwater
Roseburg • lat 43°13'30" lon 122°52'30"

DESCRIPTION: CG is in a forest setting along Little River with access to fishing. Supplies available at Roseburg. Some scenic hiking trails in the area include Overhang Trail #1509, Grotto Falls Trail #1503, Wolf Creek Nature Trail #1508, and Wolf Creek Falls Trail.

GETTING THERE: From Roseburg go E approx. 16.5 mi. on state HWY 138 to county route 17C. Go SE on 17C approx. 15.5 mi. to Coolwater CG.

SINGLE RATE:	$5	OPEN DATES:	May-Oct
# of SINGLE SITES:	7	MAX SPUR:	24 feet
		MAX STAY:	14 days
		ELEVATION:	1300 feet

13 Cover
Tiller • lat 42°58'37" lon 122°41'16"

DESCRIPTION: CG is shaded by a stand of mixed age douglas fir trees located in the Jackson Creek corridor, a tributary of the South Umpqua River. Fish and swim in the river. Supplies available at Tiller. Campers may gather firewood locally. Grey water sump at the CG.

GETTING THERE: Cover Camp CG is located approx. 13 mi. E of Tiller on county route 46/primary forest route 29.

SINGLE RATE:	No fee	OPEN DATES:	May-Oct
# of SINGLE SITES:	7	MAX SPUR:	45 feet
		MAX STAY:	14 days
		ELEVATION:	1700 feet

14 Devils Flat
Canyonville • lat 42°49'04" lon 123°01'30"

DESCRIPTION: CG is located on Cow Creek. Across the road from the campground is the old Devil's Flat Guard Station. A 1915 era Ranger Cabin and horse barn are located there. The Cow Creek Falls Trail and the Devil's Flat Trail begin at the Guard Station. Campers may gather firewood locally.

GETTING THERE: From Canyonville go S approx. 11 mi. on I-5 to county route 36. Go E on 36 approx. 17 mi. to Devil's Flat CG.

SINGLE RATE:	No fee	OPEN DATES:	Yearlong
# of SINGLE SITES:	3		
		MAX STAY:	14 days
		ELEVATION:	2200 feet

15 Diamond Lake
Roseburg • lat 43°09'40" lon 122°08'00"

DESCRIPTION: Meandering along most of the east shore of mile high Diamond Lake. Supplies at a full service resort nearby. RV dump station. Amphitheater and information gatehouse at CG. There are two boat ramps and a fish cleaning station located at CG.

GETTING THERE: From Roseburg go E approx. 80 mi. on state HWY 138 to forest route 4795. Go S on 4795 approx. 2.5 mi. to Diamond Lake CG.

SINGLE RATE:	$10	OPEN DATES:	May-Oct*
# of SINGLE SITES:	238	MAX SPUR:	35 feet
		MAX STAY:	14 days
		ELEVATION:	5190 feet

16 Dumont Creek
Tiller • lat 43°02'10" lon 122°48'30"

DESCRIPTION: CG is shaded by a mixed stand of douglas fir and is located on the South Umpqua River just above the mouth of Dumont Creek. Fish and swim in the river. Supplies available at Tiller. A short trail from the CG leads to a small beach on the river. Campers may gather firewood locally.

GETTING THERE: Dumont Creek CG is located approx. 11 mi. E of Tiller on county route 46/primary forest route 28.

SINGLE RATE:	No fee	OPEN DATES:	May-Oct
# of SINGLE SITES:	5	MAX SPUR:	45 feet
		MAX STAY:	14 days
		ELEVATION:	1300 feet

17 Eagle Rock
Roseburg • lat 43°17'45" lon 122°33'10"

DESCRIPTION: CG offers easy access to the North Umpqua River and scenic vistas of some outstanding rock formations. Eagle Rock, for which the CG is named, and Rattlesnake Rock tower are above the CG. The site is adjacent to Boulder Creek Wilderness. Grey water waste sump at CG. Many hiking trails in the area.

GETTING THERE: Eagle Rock CG is located approx. 51 mi. E of Roseburg on state HWY 138.

SINGLE RATE:	$7	OPEN DATES:	May-Sept
# of SINGLE SITES:	25	MAX SPUR:	30 feet
		MAX STAY:	14 days
		ELEVATION:	1676 feet

18 East Lemolo
Roseburg • lat 43°18'47" lon 122°09'55"

DESCRIPTION: CG is in a lodge pole pine forest along the SE shore of Lemolo Reservoir, this informal camp is a favorite with fishermen and sandpipers. Lake contains a variety of fish for troll or fly fishing. Hiking trails nearby. Supplies at the full service resort nearby. RV dump station close by.

GETTING THERE: From Roseburg go E on state HWY 138 approx. 72 mi. to forest route 2610. Go N on 2610 approx. 3 mi. to forest route 2614. Go E on 2614 approx. 1.5 mi. to East Lemolo CG.

SINGLE RATE:	$5	OPEN DATES:	May-Oct*
# of SINGLE SITES:	10	MAX SPUR:	22 feet
		MAX STAY:	14 days
		ELEVATION:	4150 feet

19 Emile Shelter
Roseburg • lat 43°14'27" lon 122°47'08"

DESCRIPTION: Among douglas and shasta red fir and brush meadows. Forest views from sites. No fishing in vicinity. Supplies available at Roseburg. Deer, elk, mountain lions and small wildlife. Black bears frequent area. Light use, rarely full. No designated hiking trails nearby.

GETTING THERE: From Roseburg go E approx. 16.5 mi. on state HWY 138 to county route 17C. Go SE on 17C approx. 15.5 mi. to forest route 2703. Go E on 2703 approx. 7 mi. to Emile Shelter CG. Parking spots are tight.

SINGLE RATE:	No fee	OPEN DATES:	Yearlong
# of SINGLE SITES:	1	MAX SPUR:	20 feet
		MAX STAY:	14 days
		ELEVATION:	4000 feet

20 Hemlock Lake
Roseburg • lat 43°11'30" lon 122°42'10"

DESCRIPTION: Hemlock Lake, a 28 acre man-made reservoir. There is a boat ramp at Hemlock Meadows. Hiking trails in the area include a one-mile loop trail around the lake and Yellow Jacket Loop Trail passes through high elevation timber and alpine meadows abundant with wildflowers in the spring.

GETTING THERE: From Roseburg go E approx. 16.5 mi. on state HWY 138 to county route 17C. Go SE on 17C approx. 32 mi. to Hemlock Lake CG.

SINGLE RATE:	$5	OPEN DATES:	June-Oct
# of SINGLE SITES:	13	MAX SPUR:	35 feet
		MAX STAY:	14 days
		ELEVATION:	4400 feet

 Campground has hosts   **Reservable sites**   **Accessible facilities**   **Fully developed**   **Semi-developed**   **Rustic facilities**

NOTE: Open dates listed are typical. Actual dates are dependent on conditions such as snow pack.

21 Hemlock Meadows
Roseburg • lat 43°11'20" lon 122°41'44"

DESCRIPTION: Hemlock Lake, a 28 acre man-made reservoir. Boating is allowed but no motors. Scenic hiking trails in the area include a one-mile loop around Hemlock Lake and the 5 mile Yellow Jacket Loop Trail passes through high elevation timber and alpine meadows abundant with wildflowers in the spring.

GETTING THERE: From Roseburg go E approx. 16.5 mi. on state HWY 138 to county route 17C. Go SE on 17C approx. 32.5 mi. to Hemlock Meadows CG.

		OPEN DATES:	June-Oct
		MAX SPUR:	35 feet
		MAX STAY:	14 days
GROUP RATE:	No fee	ELEVATION:	4400 feet
# of GROUP SITES:	1		

22 Hobo Camp
Cottage Grove • lat 43°38'50" lon 122°40'00"

DESCRIPTION: This CG is situated along the banks of Brice Creek. Fish and swim in the creek. Please check for local fishing regulations. Supplies available at Cottage Grove. A short trail leads to a beautiful pool in Brice Creek. Hiking trails in the area. Recreational gold panning is allowed.

GETTING THERE: From Cottage Grove Exit 174 on I-5. Go E on forest route 2400 approx. 19 mi. to forest route 2149. Go SE on 2149 approx. 7.5 mi. to Hobo Camp CG.

		OPEN DATES:	May-Sept
SINGLE RATE:	No fee	MAX SPUR:	16 feet
# of SINGLE SITES:	2	MAX STAY:	14 days
		ELEVATION:	1800 feet

23 Horseshoe Bend
Roseburg • lat 43°17'20" lon 122°37'35"

DESCRIPTION: CG is situated on a bench adjacent to the river and is shaded by an open stand of old growth douglas fir and sugar pine. A major launching point for whitewater boating is located near the entrance gate. Supplies available at Roseburg. Grey water waste sump at CG.

GETTING THERE: From Roseburg go E approx. 46 mi. to forest route 4750. Follow signs to Horseshoe Bend CG.

		OPEN DATES:	May-Sept
SINGLE RATE:	$10	MAX SPUR:	35 feet
# of SINGLE SITES:	22	MAX STAY:	14 days
GROUP RATE:	Varies	ELEVATION:	1300 feet
# of GROUP SITES:	9		

24 Inlet
Roseburg • lat 43°18'43" lon 122°08'57"

DESCRIPTION: CG is hidden in the deep, green, quiet forest where the North Umpqua River rushes into Lemolo Reservoir. The lake contains a variety of fish that can be taken on troll or fly fishing. Supplies can be found at the full service resort near the CG. Many hiking trails nearby.

GETTING THERE: From Roseburg go E approx. 72 mi. on state HWY 138 to forest route 2610. Go N on 2610 approx. 3 mi. to forest route 2614. Go NE on 2614 approx. 2.5 mi. to Inlet CG.

		OPEN DATES:	May-Oct*
SINGLE RATE:	$5	MAX SPUR:	25 feet
# of SINGLE SITES:	14	MAX STAY:	14 days
		ELEVATION:	4160 feet

25 Island
Roseburg • lat 42°31'25" lon 122°14'10"

DESCRIPTION: CG is located along the scenic North Umpqua River. It offers access to steelhead fishing (fly angling only), rafting, sightseeing, and hiking. Supplies available at Roseburg. Numerous wildlife can be seen in the area. Grey water waste sump at CG.

GETTING THERE: Island CG is located approx. 30 mi. E of Roseburg on state HWY 138.

		OPEN DATES:	May-Oct
SINGLE RATE:	$5	MAX SPUR:	24 feet
# of SINGLE SITES:	7	MAX STAY:	14 days
		ELEVATION:	1189 feet

26 Kelsay Valley
Roseburg • lat 43°19'10" lon 122°05'42"

DESCRIPTION: The North Umpqua River rushes through a lush high Cascade meadow. This CG is designed to accommodate equestrian use as well as standard camping. Serves as the trailhead to many trails in the area. Supplies and dump station at the full service resort near CG.

GETTING THERE: From Roseburg go E approx. 72 mi. on state HWY 138 to forest route 2610. Go N on 2610 approx. 3 mi. to forest route 2614. Go NE on 2614 approx. 2.5 mi. to forest route 2612. Go E on 2612 approx. 2 mi. to Kelsay Valley CG.

		OPEN DATES:	May-Sept*
SINGLE RATE:	$5	MAX SPUR:	20 feet
# of SINGLE SITES:	16	MAX STAY:	14 days
		ELEVATION:	4170 feet

27  Lake In The Woods
Roseburg • lat 43°13'00" lon 122°43'40"

DESCRIPTION: CG is a 4 acre man-made lake that is 8' at its deepest point. There are nearby hiking trails to scenic waterfalls (Hemlock Falls Trail #1520 and Yakso Falls Trail #1519). The trail cabin located on the site was built in 1907. Supplies available at Roseburg.

GETTING THERE: From Roseburg go E approx. 16.5 mi. to county route 17C. Go SE on 17C approx. 20 mi. to forest route 27. Continue on 27 approx. 7 mi. to Lake In The Woods CG.

		OPEN DATES:	May-Oct
SINGLE RATE:	$7	MAX SPUR:	35 feet
# of SINGLE SITES:	11	MAX STAY:	14 days
		ELEVATION:	3200 feet

28 Lemolo Two Forebay
Roseburg • lat 43°17'40" lon 122°24'05"

DESCRIPTION: In wooded douglas fir area. Fishing on nearby reservoir by shore or boat for german brown and rainbow trout. Boat ramp (non-motorized only). Limited supplies in Dry Creek or go to Roseburg. Gather own firewood locally.

GETTING THERE: From Roseburg go E approx. 60 mi. on state HWY 138 to primary forest route 34. Go N on 34 approx. 4 mi. to forest route 100/3402. Go approx. 1 mi. to Lemolo Two CG.

		OPEN DATES:	Yearlong*
SINGLE RATE:	No fee		
# of SINGLE SITES:	6	MAX STAY:	14 days
		ELEVATION:	3210 feet

29 Lund Park
Cottage Grove • lat 43°39'04" lon 122°40'32"

DESCRIPTION: Lund Park is situated along a river terrace above the picturesque Brice Creek. Fish and swim in the creek. Supplies available in Cottage Grove. Lund Park was once a stopover place for miners traveling from Cottage Grove to the Bohemia mining area. Recreational gold panning is permitted.

GETTING THERE: From Cottage Grove take exit 174 on I-5, to county route 2400. Go E on 2400 approx. 16.5 mi. to county route 2470. Go SE on 2470 approx. 7 mi. to Lund Park CG.

		OPEN DATES:	May-Sept
SINGLE RATE:	No fee	MAX SPUR:	16 feet
# of SINGLE SITES:	2	MAX STAY:	14 days
		ELEVATION:	1700 feet

30 Mineral
Cottage Grove • lat 43°34'58" lon 122°42'45"

DESCRIPTION: CG is a small dispersed camp situated along Sharps Creek at the base of the historic Hardscrabble Grade. Mineral was once a stopover place for miners before starting up the long steep grade to the Bohemia Mining Area. Fish and swim in nearby creek. Supplies available at Cottage Grove. Hiking trails nearby.

GETTING THERE: From Cottage Grove take exit 174 on I-5, to county route 2400. Go E on 2400 approx. 13 mi. to county route 2460. Go S on 2460 approx. 12 mi. to Mineral CG.

		OPEN DATES:	May-Sept
SINGLE RATE:	No fee		
# of SINGLE SITES:	2	MAX STAY:	14 days
		ELEVATION:	1800 feet

 Campground has hosts   **Reservable sites**   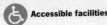 **Accessible facilities**   **Fully developed**   **Semi-developed**   **Rustic facilities**

NOTE: Open dates listed are typical. Actual dates are dependent on conditions such as snow pack.

31 Poole Creek
Roseburg • lat 43°18'46" lon 122°11'50"

DESCRIPTION: CG lies in lodge pole pine, mountain hemlock, and shasta red fir forest, on the W shore of Lemolo Lake. Lake contains a variety of fish that can be be trolled or by fly fishing. Hiking trails nearby. Supplies and dump station at the full service resort nearby.

GETTING THERE: From Roseburg go E on state HWY 138 approx. 72 mi. to forest route 2610. Go N on 2610 approx. 4 mi. Poole Creek CG.

SINGLE RATE:	$9	OPEN DATES:	May-Oct*
# of SINGLE SITES:	59	MAX SPUR:	35 feet
GROUP RATE:	$45	MAX STAY:	14 days
# of GROUP SITES:	1	ELEVATION:	4150 feet

36 Toketee Lake
Roseburg • lat 43°16'40" lon 122°24'10"

DESCRIPTION: In a mixed forest setting. Supplies are available 13.5 mi. away at Dry Creek. The North Umpqua River pauses at Toketee reservoir providing a secure home for a wide variety of wildlife. Here beaver and otter make their homes. Lake hosts a good population trout. Toketee Falls trail is 1.5 mi. S of the CG.

GETTING THERE: From Roseburg go E approx. 60 mi. on state HWY 138 to primary forest route 34. Go N on 34 (turn left at bottom of hill and cross a concrete bridge on the right.) approx. 1.5 mi. to Toketee Lake CG.

SINGLE RATE:	$5	OPEN DATES:	Yearlong*
# of SINGLE SITES:	33	MAX SPUR:	30 feet
		MAX STAY:	14 days
		ELEVATION:	3600 feet

32 Rujada
Cottage Grove • lat 43°42'22" lon 122°44'36"

DESCRIPTION: CG is situated on a river terrace above Layng Creek and offers several shaded, secluded camp spots. Fish and swim in nearby creek. Supplies available in Cottage Grove. Swordfern Trail follows along Layng Creek and back through a beautiful forest environment with a lush sword fern under story. Dump station available.

GETTING THERE: From Cottage Grove take exit 174 on I-5, to county route 2400. Go E approx. 19 mi. to Road #17 (2143). Go NE on 2143 approx. 2 mi. to Rujada CG.

SINGLE RATE:	$4	OPEN DATES:	May-Sept
# of SINGLE SITES:	10	MAX SPUR:	22 feet
		MAX STAY:	14 days
		ELEVATION:	1200 feet

37 Twin Lakes
Roseburg • lat 43°14'00" lon 122°35'00"

DESCRIPTION: This dispersed, hike-in only CG is located in an open park like setting of douglas fir and shasta red fir. Wonderful views of Willow Flat Reservoir can be seen from this CG. Fish and swim in the reservoir. Deer, elk, mountain lions are common in the area. Campers may gather firewood. Horse, hike trails nearby.

GETTING THERE: From Roseburg go E approx. 51.5 mi. on state HWY 138 to forest route 4770. Go S on 4770 approx. 5 mi. to Twin Lakes Trailhead. Hike-in only.

SINGLE RATE:	No fee	OPEN DATES:	Yearlong
		MAX STAY:	14 days
		ELEVATION:	6481 feet

33 Steamboat Falls
Roseburg • lat 43°22'30" lon 122°38'30"

DESCRIPTION: This CG offers some excellent scenery. Although Steamboat Creek is closed to all fishing, summer visitors often see large steelhead trout attempting to jump the falls during their spawning runs. Many hiking trails in the area.

GETTING THERE: From Roseburg go E on state HWY 138 approx. 39 mi. to Steamboat Creek Road 38. Go NE on 38 to Road 3810 and turn right. Cross the bridge, stay to the left, and continue on 3810 for 1 mi. to Steamboat Falls CG.

SINGLE RATE:	$5	OPEN DATES:	June-Dec
# of SINGLE SITES:	10	MAX SPUR:	24 feet
		MAX STAY:	14 days
		ELEVATION:	1400 feet

38 White Creek
Roseburg • lat 43°13'40" lon 122°52'05"

DESCRIPTION: This CG has a sandy beach on Little River with shallow water. Fish and swim in the river. Supplies available at Roseburg. Hiking on Grotto Falls Trail #1503 and Overhang Trail #1509, where there is a scenic cliff with various kinds of vegetation.

GETTING THERE: From Roseburg go E approx. 16.5 mi. on state HWY 138 to county route 17C. Go SE on 17C approx. 17 mi. to White Creek CG.

SINGLE RATE:	$5	OPEN DATES:	May-Sept
# of SINGLE SITES:	4		
		MAX STAY:	14 days
		ELEVATION:	1600 feet

34 Thielsen View
Roseburg • lat 43°10'10" lon 122°10'00"

DESCRIPTION: This CG takes its name from the view of the unforgettable peak of Mount Thielsen and sits on the shore of Diamond Lake. Lake fishing for Rainbow trout. Supplies at the full service resort close by. Numerous hiking trails nearby. An amphitheater and a visitor information center located at CG.

GETTING THERE: From Roseburg go E approx. 80 mi. on state HWY 138 to forest route 4795. Go W on 4795 approx. 3 mi. to Thielsen View CG.

SINGLE RATE:	$9	OPEN DATES:	May-Oct*
# of SINGLE SITES:	60	MAX SPUR:	35 feet
		MAX STAY:	14 days
		ELEVATION:	5190 feet

39 Whitehorse Falls
Roseburg • lat 43°14'50" lon 122°18'25"

DESCRIPTION: CG is beneath a sheltering canopy of old growth douglas fir with the Clearwater River tumbling into a tranquil pool. Fish and swim in the river. Supplies and dump station at the full service resort nearby. Many trails in the area.

GETTING THERE: Whitehorse Falls CG is located approx. 67 mi. E of Roseburg on state HWY 138.

SINGLE RATE:	$5	OPEN DATES:	June-Oct*
# of SINGLE SITES:	5	MAX SPUR:	25 feet
		MAX STAY:	14 days
		ELEVATION:	3790 feet

35 Threehorn
Tiller • lat 42°48'30" lon 122°52'00"

DESCRIPTION: CG is a higher elevation CG and is shaded by an open stand of large pine and fir. Supplies available at Tiller. CG is located near the Rogue-Umpqua divide off of the scenic road between Tiller and Trail. Campers may gather firewood locally.

GETTING THERE: Threehorn CG is located approx. 13 mi. S of Tiller on county route 1.

SINGLE RATE:	No fee	OPEN DATES:	Yearlong
# of SINGLE SITES:	5	MAX SPUR:	35 feet
		MAX STAY:	14 days
		ELEVATION:	2600 feet

40 Williams Creek
Roseburg • lat 43°20'20" lon 122°46'00"

DESCRIPTION: This site offers rustic campsites with wooden tables with access to the North Umpqua River for sightseeing and steelhead fishing and to the Williams Creek fish passage. Upstream from the campsites is a secluded pool. Supplies available at Roseburg. Numerous wildlife can be seen in the area.

GETTING THERE: Williams Creek CG is located approx. 37 mi. E of Roseburg on Highway 138. NOT RECOMMENDED FOR TRAILERS.

SINGLE RATE:	No fee	OPEN DATES:	June-Sept
# of SINGLE SITES:	3		
		MAX STAY:	14 days
		ELEVATION:	1100 feet

 Campground has hosts   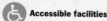 **Reservable sites**   **Accessible facilities**   **Fully developed**   **Semi-developed**   **Rustic facilities**

NOTE: Open dates listed are typical. Actual dates are dependent on conditions such as snow pack.

41 Willow Flat
Roseburg • lat 43°16'00" lon 122°46'30"

DESCRIPTION: In open park like area of douglas and shasta red fir. Views of Willow Flat Reservoir. Boat fishing for eastern Brook trout on reservoir. Supplies available at Roseburg. Deer, elk, mountain. lions and small wildlife. Occasional black bears in area. No designated hiking trails nearby.

GETTING THERE: From Roseburg go E on state HWY 138 approx. 34.5 mi. to forest route 4711. Go S on 4711 approx. 4.5 to forest route 600. Go E on 600 approx. 1.5 mi. to Willow Flat CG.

SINGLE RATE:	No fee	OPEN DATES:	Yearlong
		MAX SPUR:	45 feet
		MAX STAY:	14 days
		ELEVATION:	4000 feet

42 Wolf Creek
Roseburg • lat 43°14'20" lon 122°55'55"

DESCRIPTION: CG is located along Little River and provides access to fishing and swimming. Supplies available at Roseburg. The CG provides easy access to Nature Trail #1508. Abundant wildflowers can be seen in the spring. Grey water waste sumps in CG area. Many hiking trails in the area.

GETTING THERE: From Roseburg go E approx. 16.5 mi. on state HWY 138 to county route 17C. Go SE on 17C approx. 12 mi. to Wolf Creek CG.

SINGLE RATE:	$7	OPEN DATES:	May-Sept
# of SINGLE SITES:	8	MAX SPUR:	30 feet
GROUP RATE:	$70	MAX STAY:	14 days
# of GROUP SITES:	3	ELEVATION:	1100 feet

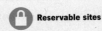 Campground has hosts   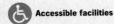 Reservable sites   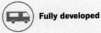 Accessible facilities   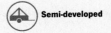 Fully developed   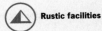 Semi-developed   Rustic facilities

NOTE: Open dates listed are typical. Actual dates are dependent on conditions such as snow pack.

WALLOWA-WHITMAN NATIONAL FOREST

The diversity begins with its landscapes, where elevations range from 800 feet on the Snake River to nearly 10,000 feet in the Eagle Cap Wilderness. The Wallowa-Whitman's varied forests are managed as sustainable ecosystems providing clean water, wildlife habitat and valuable forest products. And for things to do and places to be the Wallowa-Whitman National forest is the setting for a variety of year-round recreation.

In winter you can enjoy downhill and cross-country skiing and snowmobiling at many areas of the forest.

Hells Canyon is beautiful in the springtime. You'll want to enjoy the 800 miles of hiking trails, white water boating, and colorful wildflowers located on the Hells Canyon NRA.

You can spend your summers fishing and swimming in the Forest's many lakes, rivers, streams and reservoirs; or backpacking along its varied hiking trails on the forest.

Brilliant fall colors will delight you as you drive the National Scenic Byways, and the several hundred miles of roads maintained for passenger car travel.

WALLOWA-WHITMAN NATIONAL FOREST • OREGON • LOCATOR MAP

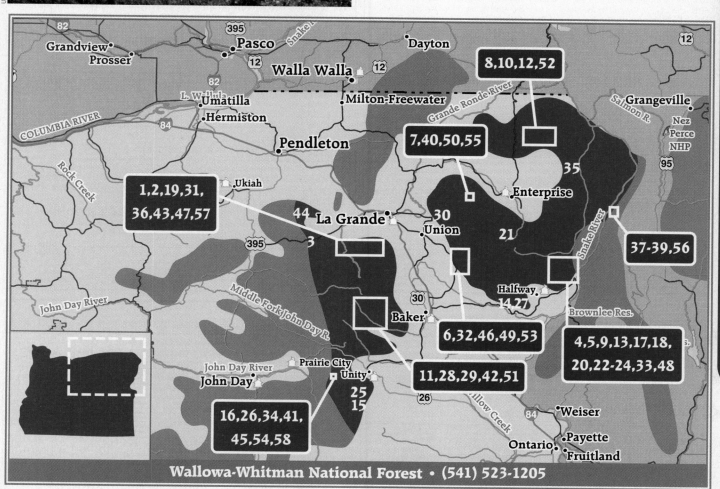

Wallowa-Whitman National Forest • (541) 523-1205

1 Anthony Creek
North Powder • lat 45°00'47" lon 118°03'32"

DESCRIPTION: Located among fir & pine forest on Anthony Cr. Fish the creek for trout. Warm days, cool nights. Gather firewood locally. Deer, elk, wildcats and small wildlife in area. Moderate use. Mountain. bike on roads. Trail to Anthony Butte. Snow may affect opening dates.

GETTING THERE: From North Powder go W on state HWY 237 approx. 6.5 mi. to county route 102. Go NW on 102 approx. 3.5 mi. to forest route 7312. Go W on 7312 approx. 1.5 mi. to Anthony Creek CG.

SINGLE RATE:	$8	OPEN DATES:	June-Sept*
# of SINGLE SITES:	4	MAX SPUR:	18 feet
		MAX STAY:	14 days
		ELEVATION:	4000 feet

2 Anthony Lakes
North Powder • lat 44°56'30" lon 118°13'30"

DESCRIPTION: This CG is in a fir and pine forest setting on Anthony Lake. Fish and swim in the lake. Warm days with cool nights. Deer, elk, wildcats and small wildlife in area. Gather firewood locally. Mountain bike on nearby roads. Mountain climbing opportunities in the area. Trail to Anthony Butte nearby.

GETTING THERE: From North Powder go W on state HWY 237 approx. 3 mi. to county route 1146. Go SW on 1146 approx. 14.5 mi. to Anthony Lakes CG.

SINGLE RATE:	$8	OPEN DATES:	June-Sept*
# of SINGLE SITES:	37	MAX SPUR:	25 feet
		MAX STAY:	14 days
		ELEVATION:	7100 feet

3 Birdtrack Springs
La Grande • lat 45°12'00" lon 118°30'00"

DESCRIPTION: Situated in pine and fir forest. Warm days, cold nights. Moderate use. Fishing in vicinity. Gather firewood locally. Deer, elk, wildcats and small wildlife in area. Hiking trailheads nearby. Snow may affect dates.

GETTING THERE: 20 mi. W of La Grande (1-84, Hwy. 244)

SINGLE RATE:	$8	OPEN DATES:	May-Sept*
# of SINGLE SITES:	16	MAX SPUR:	20 feet
		MAX STAY:	14 days
		ELEVATION:	3400 feet

4 Black Lake
Bears • lat 45°25'40" lon 117°16'45"

DESCRIPTION: A tent camp located in pine and fir forest on a high mountain. lake. Trout fish the lake. Warm days, cold nights. Light use. Gather firewood locally. Deer, elk, wildcats and small wildlife in area. Hiking trails and access to Hells Canyon Wilderness nearby. Snow may affect dates.

GETTING THERE: From Bears go NE approx. 4.5 mi. on forest route 105 to forest route 112. Go NE on 112 approx. 11.5 to Black Lake CG. Not for RVs.

SINGLE RATE:	No fee	OPEN DATES:	June-Sept
# of SINGLE SITES:	4		
		MAX STAY:	14 days
		ELEVATION:	7200 feet

5 Blackhorse
Joseph • lat 45°09'45" lon 116°52'25"

DESCRIPTION: Located in pine and fir forest on the Imnaha River. Trout fish. Warm days, cold nights. No drinking water. Light use. Gather firewood locally. Deer, elk, wildcats and small wildlife in area. Hiking trails nearby. Snow may affect dates.

GETTING THERE: From Joseph go E on county route 350 approx. 6.5 mi. to primary forest route 39. Go SE on 39 approx. 23 mi. to Blackhorse CG.

SINGLE RATE:	$5	OPEN DATES:	May-Sept
# of SINGLE SITES:	16	MAX SPUR:	18 feet
		MAX STAY:	14 days
		ELEVATION:	4000 feet

6 Boulder Park
Union • lat 45°03'30" lon 117°25'25"

DESCRIPTION: Situated in pine and fir forest. Warm to hot days, cold nights. No drinking water. Horse corrals and ramp. Moderate use. Gather firewood locally. Deer, elk, wildcats and small wildlife in area. Horse and hiking trails nearby. Snow may affect dates.

GETTING THERE: From Union go SE on HWY 203 approx. 15 mi. to forest route 77 (Eagle Cr Rd). Go E on 77 approx. 16 mi. to forest route 7755. Go N on 7755 approx. 4 mi. to Boulder Park CG.

SINGLE RATE:	No fee	OPEN DATES:	May-Sept
# of SINGLE SITES:	10		
		MAX STAY:	14 days
		ELEVATION:	3900 feet

7 Boundary
Wallowa • lat 45°28'22" lon 117°33'23"

DESCRIPTION: A tent site situated in high pine and fir forest. No drinking water. warm to hot days, cold nights. Light use. Gather firewood locally. Deer, elk, wildcats and small wildlife in area. Bears Creek Trailhead.

GETTING THERE: From Wallowa go S on forest route 8250 approx. 6 mi. to forest route 040. Go S on 040 approx. 1 mi. to Boundary CG.

SINGLE RATE:	No fee	OPEN DATES:	May-Sept
# of SINGLE SITES:	8		
		MAX STAY:	14 days
		ELEVATION:	3600 feet

8 Buckhorn
Enterprise • lat 45°45'21" lon 116°50'07"

DESCRIPTION: A tent camp located in pine and fir forest in Hells Canyon Recreation Area. Great mountain views. Warm days, cold nights. No drinking water. Light use. Gather firewood locally. Deer, elk, wildcats and small wildlife in area. Hiking nearby. Snow may affect dates.

GETTING THERE: From Enterprise go NE on primary forest route 46 approx. 42 mi. to forest route 780. Go E on 780 approx. 1/2 mi. to Buckhorn CG.

SINGLE RATE:	No fee	OPEN DATES:	June-Sept
# of SINGLE SITES:	6		
		MAX STAY:	14 days
		ELEVATION:	5200 feet

9 Coverdale
Joseph • lat 45°06'30" lon 116°55'20"

DESCRIPTION: Open tent sites located in pine and fir forest on Imnaha River. Trout fish the river. Warm to hot days, cold nights. No drinking water. Moderate use. Gather firewood locally. Deer, elk, wildcats and small wildlife in area. Hiking trails nearby. Snow may affect dates.

GETTING THERE: From Joseph go E on state HWY 350 approx. 6.5 mi. to primary forest route 39. Go S on 39 approx. 24 mi. to forest route 3960. Go W on 3960 approx. 3.5 mi. to Coverdale CG.

SINGLE RATE:	No fee	OPEN DATES:	June-Sept
# of SINGLE SITES:	11	MAX SPUR:	18 feet
		MAX STAY:	14 days
		ELEVATION:	4300 feet

10 Coyote
Enterprise • lat 45°50'00" lon 117°07'30"

DESCRIPTION: In tall fir and pine forest near Coyote Springs. No drinking water. warm to hot days, cold nights. Light use. Gather firewood locally. Deer, elk, wildcats and small wildlife in area. Trails nearby. Snow may affect dates.

GETTING THERE: From Enterprise go N on state HWY 3 approx. 14 mi. to primary forest route 46. Go NE on 46 approx. 23 mi. to Coyote CG.

SINGLE RATE:	No fee	OPEN DATES:	June-Sept*
# of SINGLE SITES:	29	MAX SPUR:	18 feet
		MAX STAY:	14 days
		ELEVATION:	4800 feet

 Campground has hosts   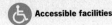 Reservable sites   Accessible facilities   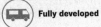 Fully developed   Semi-developed   Rustic facilities

NOTE: Open dates listed are typical. Actual dates are dependent on conditions such as snow pack.

11 Deer Creek
Baker City • lat 44°44'52" lon 118°06'22"

DESCRIPTION: In pine and fir forest near Deer Creek and Baboon Creek. No drinking water. Fishing for trout on creeks. Warm days, cool nights. Gather firewood locally. Deer, elk, wildcats and small wildlife in area. Light use. Trails and access to Baker city Watershed nearby. Snow may affect dates.

GETTING THERE: From Baker City go SW approx. 18.5 mi. on state HWY 7 to county route 656. Go N on 656 approx. 3.5 mi. to forest route 6530. Go E on 6530 approx. 1/2 mi. to Deer Creek CG.

SINGLE RATE:	No fee	OPEN DATES:	June-Sept*
# of SINGLE SITES:	6	MAX SPUR:	18 feet
		MAX STAY:	14 days
		ELEVATION:	4600 feet

12 Dougherty
Enterprise • lat 45°51'09" lon 117°01'56"

DESCRIPTION: Located in pine and fir forest. Warm to hot days, cold nights. No drinking water. Light use. Gather firewood locally. Deer, elk, wildcats and small wildlife in area. Berry picking. Hiking nearby. Snow may affect dates.

GETTING THERE: From Enterprise go N on state HWY 3 approx. 14 mi. to primary forest route 46. Go NE on 46 approx. 28.5 mi. to Dougherty CG.

SINGLE RATE:	No fee	OPEN DATES:	June-Sept
# of SINGLE SITES:	12	MAX SPUR:	18 feet
		MAX STAY:	14 days
		ELEVATION:	5100 feet

13 Duck Lake
Halfway • lat 45°05'41" lon 116°59'47"

DESCRIPTION: A tent camp located in pine and fir forest on a small mountain. lake. Trout fish the lake. Warm days, cold nights. No drinking water. Light use. Gather firewood locally. Deer, elk, wildcats and small wildlife in area. Hiking trails nearby. Snow may affect dates.

GETTING THERE: From Halfway go NE on forest route 66 approx. 23 mi. to forest route. Go N on forest route to Duck Lake CG.

SINGLE RATE:	No fee	OPEN DATES:	June-Sept
# of SINGLE SITES:	2	MAX SPUR:	18 feet
		MAX STAY:	14 days
		ELEVATION:	5200 feet

14 Eagle Forks
Newbridge • lat 44°53'30" lon 117°15'40"

DESCRIPTION: Situated in pine and fir forest on Recreation and Scenic Eagle River. Fish the river for trout species. warm to hot days, cold nights. Light use. Gather firewood locally. Deer, elk, wildcats and small wildlife in area. Multiple trails, including in river canyon. Snow may affect dates.

GETTING THERE: Eagle Forks CG is located approx. 6.5 mi NW of Newbridge on forest route 7735.

SINGLE RATE:	No fee	OPEN DATES:	May-Sept
# of SINGLE SITES:	7	MAX SPUR:	18 feet
		MAX STAY:	14 days
		ELEVATION:	3000 feet

15 Eldorado Group
Unity • lat 44°20'04" lon 118°07'20"

DESCRIPTION: Group tent sites situated in pine and fir forest on King Cr. No drinking water. Fish for trout. Warm days, cold nights. Moderate use. Gather firewood locally. Deer, elk, wildcats and small wildlife in area. Trails nearby. Snow may affect dates.

GETTING THERE: From Unity go SE on US HWY 26 approx. 10 mi. to primary forest route 16. Go SW on 16 approx. 2 mi. to Eldorado CG.

GROUP RATE:	No fee	OPEN DATES:	June-Sept*
# of GROUP SITES:	1	MAX STAY:	14 days
		ELEVATION:	4400 feet

16 Elk Creek Group
Unity • lat 44°24'03" lon 118°19'41"

DESCRIPTION: Group tent sites situated in pine and fir forest on Elk Cr. near the Burnt River. No drinking water. Fish for trout species. Warm days, cold nights. Moderate use. Gather firewood locally. Deer, elk, wildcats and small wildlife in area. Hike/horse/OHV trails nearby. Snow may affect dates.

GETTING THERE: From Unity go W on county route 600 approx. 8 mi. to forest route 6005. Go S on 6005 approx. 1/2 mi. to Elk Creek CG.

GROUP RATE:	No fee	OPEN DATES:	June-Sept*
# of GROUP SITES:	1	MAX STAY:	14 days
		ELEVATION:	4500 feet

17 Evergreen
Joseph • lat 45°06'45" lon 116°59'40"

DESCRIPTION: A dispersed site located in pine and fir forest. Trout fish in vicinity. Warm days, cold nights. No drinking water. Moderate use. South Peacock Mine nearby. Gather firewood locally. Deer, elk, wildcats and small wildlife in area. Hiking trails nearby. Snow may affect dates.

GETTING THERE: From Joseph go E on state HWY 350 approx. 6.5 mi. to primary forest route 39. Go S on 39 approx. 24 mi. to forest route 3960. Go W on 3960 approx. 6.5 mi. to Evergreen CG.

SINGLE RATE:	No fee	OPEN DATES:	June-Sept
# of SINGLE SITES:	15	MAX STAY:	14 days
		ELEVATION:	4500 feet

18 Fish Lake
Halfway • lat 45°03'02" lon 117°05'40"

DESCRIPTION: Situated in pine and fir forest on Fish Lake. Fish for trout species. Boat and swim on lake; launch nearby. warm to hot days, cold nights. Moderate use. Gather firewood locally. Deer, elk, wildcats and small wildlife in area. Multiple trails in area. Snow may affect dates.

GETTING THERE: Fish Lake CG is located approx. 15 mi. N of Halfway on forest route 66.

SINGLE RATE:	$5	OPEN DATES:	June-Sept*
# of SINGLE SITES:	15	MAX SPUR:	18 feet
		MAX STAY:	14 days
		ELEVATION:	6600 feet

19 Grande Ronde Lake
North Powder • lat 44°58'32" lon 118°14'33"

DESCRIPTION: Situated in high pine and fir forest on Grande Ronde Lake with open meadow leading to lake. Mild days, cold nights. Swimming, row boats in summer. CROSS-COUNTRY ski, snowmobile in winter. Gather firewood locally. Deer, elk, wildcats and small wildlife in area. Trail to Aurelia Mine. Snow may affect dates.

GETTING THERE: From North Powder go W on state HWY 237 approx. 3 mi. to county route 1146. Go SW on 1146 approx. 14.5 mi. to Grande Ronde Lake CG.

SINGLE RATE:	$8	OPEN DATES:	June-Sept*
# of SINGLE SITES:	8	MAX SPUR:	18 feet
		MAX STAY:	14 days
		ELEVATION:	6800 feet

20 Hidden
Joseph • lat 45°06'50" lon 116°58'45"

DESCRIPTION: Dispersed camping located in pine, tamarack and fir forest on Imnaha River. Trout fish the river. Warm days, cold nights. No drinking water. Light use. Gather firewood locally. Deer, elk, wildcats, bears and small wildlife in area. Hiking trails nearby. Snow may affect dates.

GETTING THERE: From Joseph go E on state HWY 350 approx. 6.5 mi. to primary forest route 39. Go S on 39 approx. 24 mi. to forest route 3960. Go W on 3960 approx. 6 mi. to Hidden CG.

SINGLE RATE:	No fee	OPEN DATES:	
# of SINGLE SITES:	13	MAX STAY:	14 days
		ELEVATION:	4400 feet

 Campground has hosts   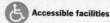 Reservable sites   Accessible facilities   Fully developed   Semi-developed   Rustic facilities

NOTE: Open dates listed are typical. Actual dates are dependent on conditions such as snow pack.

21 Hurricane Creek

Joseph • lat 45°19'48" lon 117°17'55"

DESCRIPTION: Situated in pine and fir forest on Hurricane Creek. No drinking water. Fish the river for trout species. warm to hot days, cold nights. Moderate use. Gather firewood locally. Deer, elk, wildcats and small wildlife in area. Hike Hurricane Creek Trail all the way to Eagle River. Snow may affect dates.

GETTING THERE: Hurricane Creek CG is located approx. 3.5 mi. W of Joseph on forest route 8205.

SINGLE RATE:	**No fee**	**OPEN DATES:**	**June-Sept***
# of SINGLE SITES:	**8**	**MAX SPUR:**	**18 feet**
		MAX STAY:	**14 days**
		ELEVATION:	**5000 feet**

22 Indian Crossing

Joseph • lat 45°06'48" lon 117°00'45"

DESCRIPTION: Horse camping in pine and fir forest on Imnaha River. Horse ramp, some pull thru sites. Trout fish the river. Warm days, cold nights. No drinking water. Moderate use. Gather firewood locally. Deer, elk, wildcats, bears and small wildlife in area. Horse and hiking trails nearby. Snow may affect dates.

GETTING THERE: From Joseph go E on state HWY 350 approx. 6.5 mi. to primary forest route 39. Go S on 39 approx. 24 mi. to forest route 3960. Go W on 3960 approx. 8 mi. to Indian Crossing CG.

SINGLE RATE:	**$5**	**OPEN DATES:**	**May-Sept**
# of SINGLE SITES:	**14**	**MAX SPUR:**	**30 feet**
		MAX STAY:	**14 days**
		ELEVATION:	**4400 feet**

23 Lake Fork

Joseph • lat 45°00'30" lon 116°54'40"

DESCRIPTION: Located in pine, tamarack and fir forest. Trout fish nearby. Warm to hot days, cold nights. No drinking water. Light use. Gather firewood locally. Deer, elk, wildcats, bears and small wildlife in area. Trails nearby. Snow may affect dates.

GETTING THERE: From Joseph go E on state HWY 350 approx. 6.5 mi. to primary forest route 39. Go S on 39 approx. 36 mi. to Lake Fork CG.

SINGLE RATE:	**$5**	**OPEN DATES:**	**May-Sept**
# of SINGLE SITES:	**10**	**MAX SPUR:**	**18 feet**
		MAX STAY:	**14 days**
		ELEVATION:	**3200 feet**

24 Lick Creek
Joseph • lat 45°09'30" lon 117°02'00"

DESCRIPTION: In open pine and fir setting. Warm days, cold nights. No drinking water. Fishing in area. Moderate use. Gather firewood locally. Deer, elk, wildcats, bears and small wildlife in area. Hiking in vicinity. Snow may affect dates.

GETTING THERE: From Joseph go E on state HWY 350 approx. 6.5 mi. to primary forest route 39. Go S on 39 approx. 13 mi. to Lick Creek CG.

SINGLE RATE:	**No fee**	**OPEN DATES:**	**May-Sept**
# of SINGLE SITES:	**12**	**MAX SPUR:**	**18 feet**
		MAX STAY:	**14 days**
		ELEVATION:	**5400 feet**

25 Long Creek Group
Unity • lat 44°21'25" lon 118°09'37"

DESCRIPTION: Group tent sites situated in pine and fir forest on the banks of Long Creek. No drinking water on site. Fish for trout on the creek. Expect warm days with cold nights. Moderate use. Gather firewood. Watch for deer, elk, and wildcats, in the area. Trails nearby. Snow may affect dates.

GETTING THERE: From Unity go S on forest route 1680 approx. 10 mi. to Long Creek Group CG.

		OPEN DATES:	**May-Sept**
GROUP RATE:	**No fee**	**MAX STAY:**	**14 days**
# of GROUP SITES:	**1**	**ELEVATION:**	**4480 feet**

26 Mammoth Spring Group
Unity • lat 44°24'12" lon 118°20'07"

DESCRIPTION: Group tent sites situated in pine and fir forest on Chance Cr. No drinking water. Fish for trout species. Warm days, cold nights. Moderate use. Gather firewood locally. Deer, elk, wildcats and small wildlife in area. Trails nearby. Snow may affect dates.

GETTING THERE: From Unity go W on county route 600 approx. 9 mi. to Mammoth Springs CG.

		OPEN DATES:	**June-Sept***
GROUP RATE:	**No fee**	**MAX STAY:**	**14 days**
# of GROUP SITES:	**1**	**ELEVATION:**	**4500 feet**

27 McBride
Carson • lat 44°56'06" lon 117°13'14"

DESCRIPTION: Situated in tall pine and fir forest on Brooks Ditch. No drinking water. Fish for trout species. warm to hot days, cold nights. Light use. Gather firewood locally. Deer, elk, wildcats and small wildlife in area. Trails in area. Snow may affect dates.

GETTING THERE: From Carson go W on forest route 7710 approx. 3.5 mi. to forest route 77. Go NW on 77 approx. 1 mi. to McBride CG.

SINGLE RATE:	**No fee**	**OPEN DATES:**	**June-Sept***
# of SINGLE SITES:	**11**	**MAX SPUR:**	**18 feet**
		MAX STAY:	**14 days**
		ELEVATION:	**4800 feet**

28 McCully Forks
Sumpter • lat 44°46'02" lon 118°14'46"

DESCRIPTION: Situated in high pine and fir forest at the mouth of Bears Canyon. Mild days, cold nights. Fish nearby creeks for trout. Moderate use. Gather firewood locally. Deer, elk, wildcats and small wildlife in area. Old roads serve as trails. Snow may affect dates.

GETTING THERE: McCully Forks CG is located approx. 3 mi. NW of Sumpter on county route 410.

SINGLE RATE:	**No fee**	**OPEN DATES:**	**June-Sept***
# of SINGLE SITES:	**6**	**MAX SPUR:**	**18 feet**
		MAX STAY:	**14 days**
		ELEVATION:	**4600 feet**

29 Millers Lane
Sumpter • lat 44°39'30" lon 118°03'00"

DESCRIPTION: Situated in high pine and fir forest near Phillips Lake. Boat or shore fish for trout. Boat launch at SW Shore. Swim or canoe lake. Mild days, cold nights. Light use. Gather firewood locally. Deer, elk, wildcats and small wildlife in area. Trail from SW Shore around lake past Union Creek. Snow may affect dates.

GETTING THERE: From Sumpter go SE on county route 410 approx. 6 mi. to county route 667. Go S on 667 approx. 4 mi. to Miller Lane CG.

SINGLE RATE:	**No fee**	**OPEN DATES:**	**June-Sept***
# of SINGLE SITES:	**7**	**MAX SPUR:**	**18 feet**
		MAX STAY:	**14 days**
		ELEVATION:	**4100 feet**

30 Moss Springs
Cove • lat 45°16'31" lon 117°40'41"

DESCRIPTION: A horse camp situated in pine and fir forest. Warm to hot days, cold nights. No drinking water. Horse corrals and ramp. Moderate use. Gather firewood locally. Deer, elk, wildcats and small wildlife in area. Horse and hiking trails nearby. Snow may affect dates.

GETTING THERE: Moss Springs CG is located approx. 7 mi. E of Cove on forest route 6220. Steep road.

SINGLE RATE:	**$8**	**OPEN DATES:**	**June-Sept***
# of SINGLE SITES:	**11**	**MAX SPUR:**	**30 feet**
		MAX STAY:	**14 days**
		ELEVATION:	**5400 feet**

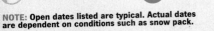 **Campground has hosts**   **Reservable sites**   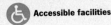 **Accessible facilities**   **Fully developed**   **Semi-developed**   **Rustic facilities**

NOTE: Open dates listed are typical. Actual dates are dependent on conditions such as snow pack.

31 Mud Lake
North Powder • lat 44°57'55" lon 118°13'56"

DESCRIPTION: Situated in high pine and fir forest on a small lake with some open meadow sites. Fish for trout species here and Anthony Lakes. Mild days, cold nights. Light use. Gather firewood locally. Deer, elk, wildcats and small wildlife in area. Hiking trails in vicinity. Snow may affect dates.

GETTING THERE: From North Powder go W on state HWY 237 approx. 3 mi. to county route 1146. Go SW on 1146 approx. 15 mi. to Mud Lake CG.

SINGLE RATE:	$8	OPEN DATES:	June-Sept*
# of SINGLE SITES:	8	MAX SPUR:	18 feet
		MAX STAY:	14 days
		ELEVATION:	7100 feet

32 North Fork Catherine Creek
Union • lat 45°08'56" lon 117°36'59"

DESCRIPTION: Situated in pine and fir forest on creek. Fish for trout species. warm to hot days, cold nights. Moderate use. Gather firewood locally. Deer, elk, wildcats and small wildlife in area. Trails nearby. Snow may affect dates.

GETTING THERE: From Union go SE on state HWY 203 approx. 12.5 mi. to forest route 7785. Go NE on 7785 approx. 5 mi. to North Fork Catherine Creek CG.

SINGLE RATE:	No fee	OPEN DATES:	June-Sept*
# of SINGLE SITES:	6	MAX SPUR:	18 feet
		MAX STAY:	14 days
		ELEVATION:	4400 feet

33 Ollokot
Joseph • lat 45°09'08" lon 116°52'33"

DESCRIPTION: Open sites located in pine and fir forest with mountain views. Trout fishing in area. Warm days, cold nights. No drinking water. Heavy use. Gather firewood locally. Berry picking. Deer, elk, wildcats, bears and small wildlife in area. Hiking trails nearby. Snow may affect dates.

GETTING THERE: From Joseph go E on state HWY 350 approx. 6.5 mi. to primary forest route 39. Go S on 39 approx. 24 mi. to Ollokot CG.

SINGLE RATE:	$5	OPEN DATES:	June-Sept
# of SINGLE SITES:	12	MAX SPUR:	18 feet
		MAX STAY:	14 days
		ELEVATION:	4000 feet

34 Oregon
Unity • lat 44°32'49" lon 118°20'27"

DESCRIPTION: Situated in pine and fir forest. Warm days, cold nights. Moderate use. Gather firewood locally. Deer, elk, wildcats and small wildlife in area. Hiking and OHV trails nearby. Snow may affect dates.

GETTING THERE: Oregon CG is located approx. 11 mi. NW of Unity on US HWY 26.

SINGLE RATE:	$5	OPEN DATES:	June-Sept*
# of SINGLE SITES:	11	MAX SPUR:	18 feet
		MAX STAY:	14 days
		ELEVATION:	4800 feet

35 Pittsburg Landing
White Bird • lat 45°37'30" lon 116°29'30"

DESCRIPTION: Located in pine and fir forest on Snake River, a wild and scenic river. Rafting and fishing on river. Warm to hot days, cold nights. Moderate use. Gather firewood locally. Deer, elk, wildcats and small wildlife in area. Hiking trails nearby. Snow may affect dates.

GETTING THERE: Pittsburg Landing CG is located approx. 13 mi. SW of White Bird on county route 493.

SINGLE RATE:	No fee	OPEN DATES:	May-Sept
# of SINGLE SITES:	35	MAX SPUR:	18 feet
		MAX STAY:	14 days
		ELEVATION:	1230 feet

36 River
Perry • lat 45°08'07" lon 118°21'55"

DESCRIPTION: Situated in pine and fir forest. Warm to hot days, cold nights. Horse corrals and ramp. Moderate use. Gather firewood locally. Deer, elk, wildcats and small wildlife in area. Hiking trails nearby. Snow may affect dates.

GETTING THERE: From Perry go SW on state HWY 244 approx. 13 mi. to primary forest route 51. Go S on 51 approx. 9 mi. to River CG.

SINGLE RATE:	$5	OPEN DATES:	June-Sept*
# of SINGLE SITES:	6	MAX SPUR:	18 feet
		MAX STAY:	14 days
		ELEVATION:	3800 feet

37 Sacajawea
Enterprise • lat 45°26'35" lon 116°39'50"

DESCRIPTION: Tent sites located in pine, tamarack and fir forest on edge of Hells Canyon Wilderness. Superb views. Warm days, cold nights. No drinking water. Moderate use. Gather firewood locally. Deer, elk, wildcats, bears and small wildlife in area. Hiking trails nearby. Snow may affect dates.

GETTING THERE: From Enterprise go SE on HWY 82 6.5 mi. to state route 350. Go N on 350 19 mi. to forest route 4240 (Hat Point Rd). Go SW on 4240 17 mi. to forest route 315. Go W on 315 2 mi. to Sacajawea CG.

SINGLE RATE:	No fee	OPEN DATES:	June-Sept
# of SINGLE SITES:	3		
		MAX STAY:	14 days
		ELEVATION:	6982 feet

38 Saddle Creek
Imnaha • lat 45°24'06" lon 116°43'22"

DESCRIPTION: Located in pine and fir forest. Great scenic mountain. views. Warm days, cold nights. No drinking water. Moderate use. Gather firewood locally. Deer, elk, wildcats and small wildlife in area. Hiking trails and access to Hells Canyon Wilderness nearby. Snow may affect dates.

GETTING THERE: Saddle Creek CG is located approx. 18 mi. S of Imnaha on forest route 4240. Steep road, not recommended for trailers or RVs.

SINGLE RATE:	No fee	OPEN DATES:	June-Sept
# of SINGLE SITES:	7	MAX SPUR:	18 feet
		MAX STAY:	14 days
		ELEVATION:	6800 feet

39 Seven Devils
Wisdom • lat 45°19'30" lon 116°31'00"

DESCRIPTION: A tent camp located in pine and fir forest. Warm days, cold nights. No drinking water. Moderate use. Gather firewood locally. Deer, elk, wildcats and small wildlife in area. Hiking trails and access to Hells Canyon Wilderness nearby. Snow may affect dates.

GETTING THERE: Seven Devils CG is located approx. 10.5 mi SW of Wisdom on forest route 517.

SINGLE RATE:	No fee	OPEN DATES:	June-Sept
# of SINGLE SITES:	7		
		MAX STAY:	14 days
		ELEVATION:	7200 feet

40 Shady
Lostine • lat 45°15'27" lon 117°22'58"

DESCRIPTION: Situated in pine and fir forest on Lostine River. No drinking water. Fish the river for trout species. warm to hot days, cold nights. Moderate use. Gather firewood locally. Deer, elk, wildcats and small wildlife in area. Trails in river canyon, trailhead nearby. Snow may affect dates.

GETTING THERE: Shady CG is located approx. 16 mi. S of Lostine on forest route 8210.

SINGLE RATE:	No fee	OPEN DATES:	June-Sept*
# of SINGLE SITES:	12	MAX SPUR:	18 feet
		MAX STAY:	14 days
		ELEVATION:	5400 feet

 Campground has hosts   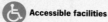 **Reservable sites**   **Accessible facilities**   **Fully developed**   **Semi-developed**   **Rustic facilities**

NOTE: Open dates listed are typical. Actual dates are dependent on conditions such as snow pack.

41 South Fork

Unity • lat 44°24'13" lon 118°18'20"

DESCRIPTION: Situated in pine and fir forest. Warm days, cold nights. Moderate use. Gather firewood locally. Deer, elk, wildcats and small wildlife in area. Hiking trails nearby. Snow may affect dates.

GETTING THERE: From Unity go W on county route 600 approx. 7 mi. to South Fork CG.

SINGLE RATE:	No fee	OPEN DATES:	June-Sept*
# of SINGLE SITES:	24	MAX SPUR:	22 feet
		MAX STAY:	14 days
		ELEVATION:	4400 feet

42 Southwest Shore

Sumpter • lat 44°40'33" lon 118°05'07"

DESCRIPTION: Situated in high pine and fir forest on Phillips Lake. Boat or shore fish for trout species. Boat launch at SW Shore. Swim or canoe in lake. Mild days, cold nights. Light use. Gather firewood locally. Deer, elk, wildcats and small wildlife in area. No drinking water. Snow may affect dates.

GETTING THERE: From Sumpter go SE on county route 410 approx. 6 mi. to county route 667. Go S on 667 approx. 3.5 mi. to Southwest Shore CG.

SINGLE RATE:	No fee	OPEN DATES:	June-Sept*
# of SINGLE SITES:	18	MAX SPUR:	18 feet
		MAX STAY:	14 days
		ELEVATION:	4100 feet

43 Spool Cart

La Grande • lat 45°12'15" lon 118°23'40"

DESCRIPTION: Situated in pine, cottonwood and fir forest. Warm to hot days, cold nights. No drinking water. Fish for trout nearby. Moderate use. Gather firewood locally. Deer, elk, wildcats and small wildlife in area. Hiking trails nearby. Snow may affect dates.

GETTING THERE: From La Grande go W on I-84 approx. 6 mi. to county route 244. Go SW on 244 approx. 9 mi. to primary forest route 51. Go S on 51 approx. 4.5 mi. to Spool Cart CG.

SINGLE RATE:	$8	OPEN DATES:	May-Sept
# of SINGLE SITES:	16	MAX SPUR:	22 feet
		MAX STAY:	14 days
		ELEVATION:	3500 feet

44 Spring Creek

La Grande • lat 45°18'30" lon 118°22'30"

DESCRIPTION: Situated in pine and fir forest. Warm to hot days, cold nights. No drinking water. Horse corrals and ramp. Moderate use. Gather firewood locally. Deer, elk, wildcats and small wildlife in area. Horse and hiking trails, including an interpretive trail nearby. Snow may affect dates.

GETTING THERE: From La Grande go NW on I-84 approx. 9 mi. to forest route 21. Go S on 21 approx. 6 mi. to Spring Creek CG.

SINGLE RATE:	$5	OPEN DATES:	May-Sept
# of SINGLE SITES:	14	MAX SPUR:	22 feet
		MAX STAY:	14 days
		ELEVATION:	3500 feet

45 Stevens Creek Group

Unity • lat 44°24'02" lon 118°19'12"

DESCRIPTION: Group camping situated in pine and fir forest. Warm days, cold nights. Moderate use. Gather firewood locally. Deer, elk, wildcats and small wildlife in area. Hiking and OHV trails nearby. Snow may affect dates. No drinking water.

GETTING THERE: From Unity go W on county route 600 approx. 8 mi. to Stevens Creek CG.

		OPEN DATES:	June-Sept*
		MAX SPUR:	18 feet
GROUP RATE:	No fee	MAX STAY:	14 days
# of GROUP SITES:	1	ELEVATION:	4400 feet

46 Tamarack

Union • lat 45°01'12" lon 117°27'10"

DESCRIPTION: Situated in pine and fir forest on Eagle River. Fish the river for trout species. warm to hot days, cold nights. Moderate use. Gather firewood locally. Deer, elk, wildcats and small wildlife in area. Trails in river canyon. Snow may affect dates.

GETTING THERE: From Union go SE on HWY 203 approx. 15 mi. to forest route 77 (Eagle Cr Rd). Go E on 77 approx. 16 mi. to forest route 7755. Go N on 7755 approx. 4 mi. to Tamarack CG.

SINGLE RATE:	No fee	OPEN DATES:	June-Sept*
# of SINGLE SITES:	24	MAX SPUR:	18 feet
		MAX STAY:	14 days
		ELEVATION:	4600 feet

47 Time and a Half

Perry • lat 45°09'34" lon 118°22'45"

DESCRIPTION: On Grande Ronde River in pine and fir forest. Warm to hot days, cold nights. No drinking water. Moderate use. Gather firewood locally. Deer, elk, wildcats and small wildlife in area. Hiking nearby. Snow may affect dates.

GETTING THERE: From Perry go SW on state HWY 244 approx. 13 mi. to primary forest route 51. Go S on 51 approx. 7.5 mi. to Time And A Half CG.

SINGLE RATE:	No fee	OPEN DATES:	May-Sept
# of SINGLE SITES:	5	MAX SPUR:	18 feet
		MAX STAY:	14 days
		ELEVATION:	3700 feet

48 Twin Lakes

Halfway • lat 45°04'45" lon 117°03'14"

DESCRIPTION: A tent site situated in pine and fir forest on the lake. No drinking water. Fish for trout species, dock on site. Warm days, cold nights. Light use. Gather firewood locally. Deer, elk, wildcats and small wildlife in area. Trails nearby. Snow may affect dates.

GETTING THERE: Twin Lakes CG is located approx. 19 mi. N of Halfway on forest route 66.

SINGLE RATE:	No fee	OPEN DATES:	June-Sept*
# of SINGLE SITES:	6		
		MAX STAY:	14 days
		ELEVATION:	6500 feet

49 Two Color

Carson • lat 45°02'15" lon 117°26'40"

DESCRIPTION: Situated in pine and fir forest on Eagle Creek, a Wild and Recreation River. Warm to hot days, cold nights. Fish for trout in creek. Moderate use. Gather firewood locally. Deer, elk, wildcats and small wildlife in area. Hiking trails nearby. Snow may affect dates.

GETTING THERE: From Union go SE on HWY 203 approx. 15 mi. to forest route 77 (Eagle Cr Rd). Go E on 77 approx. 16 mi. to forest route 7755. Go N on 7755 approx. 1/2 mi. to Two Color CG.

SINGLE RATE:	No fee	OPEN DATES:	June-Sept*
# of SINGLE SITES:	14	MAX SPUR:	18 feet
		MAX STAY:	14 days
		ELEVATION:	4800 feet

50 Two Pan

Enterprise • lat 45°14'47" lon 117°22'25"

DESCRIPTION: Situated in pine and fir forest at road's end on the Lostine River. Horse trailer parking. Fishing in river. Warm days, cold nights. No drinking water. Moderate use. Gather firewood locally. Deer, elk, wildcats and small wildlife in area. Horse and hiking trails. Snow may affect dates.

GETTING THERE: From Enterprise go NW on HWY 82 approx. 8 mi. to forest route 8210 (Lostine River Road). Go S on 8210 approx. 17 mi. to Two Pan CG.

SINGLE RATE:	No fee	OPEN DATES:	June-Sept
# of SINGLE SITES:	8	MAX SPUR:	28 feet
		MAX STAY:	14 days
		ELEVATION:	5600 feet

 Campground has hosts   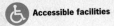 **Reservable sites**   **Accessible facilities**   **Fully developed**   **Semi-developed**   **Rustic facilities**

NOTE: Open dates listed are typical. Actual dates are dependent on conditions such as snow pack.

51 Union Creek
Baker City • lat 44°41'18" lon 118°01'31"

DESCRIPTION: Situated in high pine and fir forest near Phillips Lake. Boat or shore fish for trout species. Boat launch at SW Shore. Swim or canoe lake. Mild days, cold nights. Heavy use. Gather firewood locally. Deer, elk, wildcats and small wildlife in area. Snow may affect dates.

GETTING THERE: Union Creek CG is located approx. 18 mi. SW of Baker City on state HWY 7.

SINGLE RATE: # of SINGLE SITES:	Varies 70	OPEN DATES: MAX SPUR: MAX STAY: ELEVATION:	June-Sept* 18 feet 14 days 4100 feet

52 Vigne
Enterprise • lat 45°44'44" lon 117°01'15"

DESCRIPTION: Situated in pine and fir forest near Ellis Canyon. No drinking water. Fish the river for trout species. warm to hot days, cold nights. Light use. Gather firewood locally. Deer, elk, wildcats and small wildlife in area. Trails nearby. Snow may affect dates.

GETTING THERE: From Enterprise go N on state HWY 3 approx. 13 mi. to primary forest route 46. Go NE on 46 approx. 11.5 mi. to forest route 4625. Go E on 4625 approx. 10 mi. to Vigne CG.

SINGLE RATE: # of SINGLE SITES:	No fee 7	OPEN DATES: MAX SPUR: MAX STAY: ELEVATION:	June-Sept* 18 feet 14 days 3500 feet

53 West Eagle Meadow
Union • lat 45°04'55" lon 117°28'45"

DESCRIPTION: A tenting horse camp in a pine and fir forest. Fishing nearby. Warm to hot days, cold nights. No drinking water. Horse corrals and ramp. Moderate use. Gather firewood locally. Deer, elk, wildcats and small wildlife in area. Horse and hiking trails nearby. Snow may affect dates.

GETTING THERE: From Union go SE on HWY 203 approx. 15 mi. to forest route 77 (Eagle Cr Rd). Go E on 77 approx. 12 mi. to West Eagle Meadow CG.

SINGLE RATE: # of SINGLE SITES:	No fee 24	OPEN DATES: MAX STAY: ELEVATION:	June-Sept* 14 days 5200 feet

54 Wetmore
Unity • lat 44°31'29" lon 118°18'08"

DESCRIPTION: Situated in pine and fir forest. Warm days, cold nights. Moderate use. Gather firewood locally. Deer, elk, wildcats and small wildlife in area. Hiking and OHV trails nearby. Barrier free trail to Yellow Pine. Snow may affect dates.

GETTING THERE: Wetmore CG is located approx. 9 mi. NW of Unity on US HWY 26.

SINGLE RATE: # of SINGLE SITES:	$8 16	OPEN DATES: MAX SPUR: MAX STAY: ELEVATION:	June-Sept* 18 feet 14 days 4300 feet

55 Williamson
Lostine • lat 45°20'33" lon 117°24'44"

DESCRIPTION: Situated in pine and fir forest on Lostine River. No drinking water. Fish the river for trout species. warm to hot days, cold nights. Moderate use. Gather firewood locally. Deer, elk, wildcats and small wildlife in area. Trails in river canyon. Snow may affect dates.

GETTING THERE: Williamson CG is located approx. 10 mi. S of Lostine on forest route 8210.

SINGLE RATE: # of SINGLE SITES:	No fee 9	OPEN DATES: MAX SPUR: MAX STAY: ELEVATION:	June-Sept* 18 feet 14 days 4900 feet

56 Windy Saddle
Wisdom • lat 45°21'30" lon 116°31'00"

DESCRIPTION: A horse tent camp located in pine and fir forest. Horse ramp. Warm days, cold nights. No drinking water. Light use. Gather firewood locally. Deer, elk, wildcats and small wildlife in area. Hiking trails and access to Hells Canyon Wilderness nearby. Snow may affect dates.

GETTING THERE: Windy Saddle CG is located approx. 12 mi. SW of Wisdom on forest route 517.

SINGLE RATE: # of SINGLE SITES:	No fee 4	OPEN DATES: MAX STAY: ELEVATION:	June-Sept 14 days 7200 feet

57 Woodley
Perry • lat 45°04'12" lon 118°18'43"

DESCRIPTION: Located in pine and fir forest near Grande Ronde River. Fishing for trout. Warm to hot days, cold nights. Moderate use. Gather firewood locally. Deer, elk, wildcats and small wildlife in area. Hiking trails nearby. Snow may affect dates.

GETTING THERE: From Perry go SW on state HWY 244 approx. 13 mi. to primary forest route 51. Go S on 51 approx. 11 mi. to forest route 5125. Go SE on 5125 approx. 5.5 mi. to Woodley CG.

SINGLE RATE: # of SINGLE SITES:	No fee 7	OPEN DATES: MAX SPUR: MAX STAY: ELEVATION:	May-Sept 18 feet 14 days 4500 feet

58 Yellow Pine
Unity • lat 44°31'48" lon 118°18'38"

DESCRIPTION: Situated in pine and fir forest. Warm days, cold nights. Moderate use. Gather firewood locally. Deer, elk, wildcats and small wildlife in area. Hiking and OHV trails nearby. Barrier free trail to Wetmore. Snow may affect dates.

GETTING THERE: Yellow Pine CG is located approx. 10 mi. NW of Unity on US HWY 26.

SINGLE RATE: # of SINGLE SITES:	$8 21	OPEN DATES: MAX SPUR: MAX STAY: ELEVATION:	June-Sept* 18 feet 14 days 4400 feet

WALLOWA-WHITMAN NATIONAL FOREST • OREGON • 51 — 58

 Campground has hosts Reservable sites Accessible facilities  Fully developed  Semi-developed Rustic facilities

NOTE: Open dates listed are typical. Actual dates are dependent on conditions such as snow pack.

USFS Photo

WILLAMETTE NATIONAL FOREST

Seven major volcanic peaks exist within the Willamette National Forest's boundary, more than in any other Forest in the Northwest: Mt. Jefferson, Three Fingered Jack, Mt. Washington, Three Sisters, and Diamond Peak. Four of the seven wildernesses on the Willamette Forest owe their existence to the diverse and pristine nature of the lands surrounding them. Recreation opportunities are abundant, as long as the activities are "light on the land" and consistent with the Wilderness Act.

Developed campgrounds, trails, Scenic Byways, and ski resorts are only a few of the facilities available for use. Outdoor recreation activities not associated with developed facilities are limited only by one's imagination.

The Willamette Forest's rivers, streams and lakes are perhaps the most important features for recreationists. Most activities occur not far from its outstanding bodies of water. The clarity and quality of water and the scenic environs in which it occurs greatly enhance visitors' experiences. Virtually all of the featured trails, roads, developed campgrounds, and viewpoints are associated with outstanding rivers, streams or lakes.

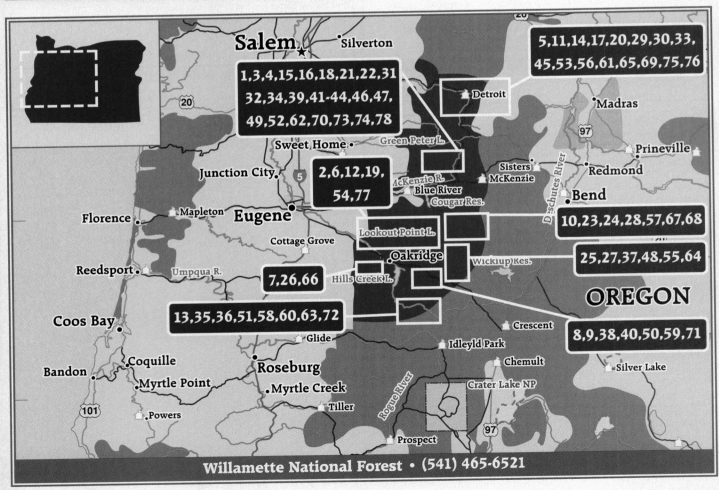

Willamette National Forest • (541) 465-6521

1 Alder Springs
Belknap Springs • lat 44°41'05" lon 118°12'46"

DESCRIPTION: This tent only CG is located in mixed conifer. Nearby Linton Lake offers fly fishing. Supplies are available at McKenzie Bridge. Bring firewood. Dee Wright Observatory and Craig Monument are nearby. Deer and elk are a common sight in the area. There is access nearby to Linton Lake Trail, a moderate 1.5 mi. hike.

GETTING THERE: Alder Springs CG is located approx. 13.5 SE of McKenzie Bridge on state HWY 242 (Santiam Pass/McKenzie Pass Nat'l Scenic Byway). Road is narrow with sharp curves.

SINGLE RATE:	No fee	OPEN DATES:	May-Sept
# of SINGLE SITES:	6		
		MAX STAY:	14 days
		ELEVATION:	3600 feet

2 Bed Rock
Unity • lat 43°58'30" lon 122°33'30"

DESCRIPTION: On Fall Creek in a douglas fir forest setting. Fish and swim in the creek. Supplies in Lowell or Springfield. Deer, elk and small wildlife can be seen in the area. Heavy use all summer. Buy or gather firewood. Fall Creek trailhead on site for hiking.

GETTING THERE: From Unity go E on county route 6204 approx. 6.5 mi. to primary forest route 18. Go E on 18 approx. 9 mi. to Bedrock CG.

SINGLE RATE:	$9	OPEN DATES:	May-Sept
# of SINGLE SITES:	19	MAX SPUR:	20 feet
		MAX STAY:	14 days
		ELEVATION:	1000 feet

3 Big Lake
Cascadia • lat 44°22'30" lon 121°52'30"

DESCRIPTION: In a mixed forest setting adjacent to Big Lake with views of Mt. Washington. Good fishing from this lake, which is stocked with 4 species annually. Boat ramp at lake. Supplies available in Cascadia. Campers may gather firewood. Many trails for hiking and ATV in the area. Mosquitoes in June.

GETTING THERE: From Cascadia go E on US HWY 20 approx. 34 mi. to forest route 2690. Go S on 2690 approx. 3 mi. to Big Lake CG.

SINGLE RATE:	$12	OPEN DATES:	June-Sept
# of SINGLE SITES:	49	MAX SPUR:	35 feet
		MAX STAY:	14 days
		ELEVATION:	4650 feet

4 Big Lake West
Cascadia • lat 44°22'30" lon 121°52'30"

DESCRIPTION: This primitive CG is in a pine and fir forest setting on Big Lake West. Fish for trout from the lake. Boat launch at lake. Supplies available in Cascadia. Wildlife in the area include deer, elk and birds. Campers should bring their own firewood. Hiking trailheads to Mt. Washington Wilderness and Patjens Lake nearby.

GETTING THERE: From Cascadia go E on US HWY 20 approx. 34 mi. to forest route 2690. Go S on 2690 approx. 3 mi. to Big Lake West CG.

SINGLE RATE:	$12	OPEN DATES:	May-Oct*
# of SINGLE SITES:	11		
		MAX STAY:	14 days
		ELEVATION:	4650 feet

5 Big Meadows Horse Camp
Marion Forks • lat 44°28'30" lon 122°58'30"

DESCRIPTION: In a fir forest near the N. Santiam River with trout fishing. T-storms frequent all summer. CG has 4-stall corral, loading ramp and stock water trough. Gather firewood. Supplies in Detroit. Deer, bears, cougars, coyotes frequent area. Many hiking trails and access to Mt. Jefferson Wilderness.

GETTING THERE: From Marion Forks go S on state HWY 22 approx. 8.5 mi. to forest route 2267. Go E on 2267 approx. 1 mi. to Big Meadows Horse Camp.

SINGLE RATE:	$9	OPEN DATES:	June-Oct*
# of SINGLE SITES:	9	MAX SPUR:	85 feet
		MAX STAY:	14 days
		ELEVATION:	3600 feet

6 Big Pool
Unity • lat 43°58'00" lon 122°35'50"

DESCRIPTION: In an open area with douglas fir on Fall Creek. Fish and swim in the creek. Supplies available in Lowell or Springfield. Fills weekends July-Aug. Campers may gather firewood. Deer and small wildlife are common in the area. Hike nearby Fall Creek Nat'l Rec Trail or Johnny Creek Nature Trail.

GETTING THERE: From Unity go E on county route 6204 approx. 6.5 mi. to primary forest route 18. Go E on 18 approx. 4.5 mi. to Big Pool CG.

SINGLE RATE:	$7	OPEN DATES:	May-Sept
# of SINGLE SITES:	5	MAX SPUR:	14 feet
		MAX STAY:	14 days
		ELEVATION:	1000 feet

7 Black Canyon
Oakridge • lat 44°22'36" lon 119°43'11"

DESCRIPTION: In old growth douglas fir forest overlooking Middle Fork of the Willamette River. Fish for trout and swim in the river. Boat ramp at CG. Supplies available in Oakridge. Elk herds frequent area. Firewood for sale. Nature trail on site. Mountain bike trails approx. 5.5 mi. from CG.

GETTING THERE: Black Canyon CG is located approx. 7 mi. NW of Oakridge on state HWY 58.

SINGLE RATE:	$12	OPEN DATES:	Apr-Sept
# of SINGLE SITES:	72	MAX SPUR:	44 feet
		MAX STAY:	14 days
		ELEVATION:	1000 feet

8 Blair Lake
Oakridge • lat 43°50'10" lon 122°14'25"

DESCRIPTION: This tent only CG is located in a beautiful alpine setting on the edge of Blair Lake. Fish for stocked brook and rainbow trout (non-motorized boats only). Known for wildflowers and huckleberries. Supplies available in Oakridge. Campers may gather firewood. Hiking and mountain biking trails nearby.

GETTING THERE: From Oakridge go NE on primary forest route 24 approx. 8 mi. to forest route 1934. Go N on 1934 approx. 6 mi. to forest route 733. Go SE on 733 approx. 1 mi. to Blair Lake CG.

SINGLE RATE:	$6	OPEN DATES:	June-Oct*
# of SINGLE SITES:	7		
		MAX STAY:	14 days
		ELEVATION:	4800 feet

9 Blue Pool
Oakridge • lat 43°42'33" lon 122°17'51"

DESCRIPTION: In old growth forest on Salt Creek. Fishing (artificial bait) and swimming are popular. McCredie Hot Springs is approx. 1/2 mi. from CG. Caution very hot at times. CG is full most weekends. Firewood for sale at CG. Supplies available in Oakridge. Several trails nearby.

GETTING THERE: Blue Pool CG is located approx. 8 mi. SE of Oakridge on state HWY 58.

SINGLE RATE:	$10	OPEN DATES:	May-Sept
# of SINGLE SITES:	25	MAX SPUR:	20 feet
		MAX STAY:	14 days
		ELEVATION:	1900 feet

10 Box Canyon Horse Camp
Oakridge • lat 43°54'00" lon 122°05'00"

DESCRIPTION: Groves of conifer and scattered tranquil meadows make an appealing setting for both hikers and pack saddle enthusiasts. CG is being developed to provide convenient access for equestrians to both wilderness and undeveloped roadless areas W of the Cascade Crest. Corrals at CG.

GETTING THERE: Box Canyon Horse Camp is located approx. 27 mi. NE of Oakridge on primary forest route 19.

SINGLE RATE:	No fee	OPEN DATES:	Apr-Nov*
# of SINGLE SITES:	14	MAX SPUR:	30 feet
		MAX STAY:	14 days
		ELEVATION:	3600 feet

 Campground has hosts   **Reservable sites**   **Accessible facilities**   **Fully developed**   **Semi-developed**   **Rustic facilities**

NOTE: Open dates listed are typical. Actual dates are dependent on conditions such as snow pack.

11 Breitenbush

Breitenbush Hot Springs • lat 44˚46'52" lon 121˚59'20"

DESCRIPTION: In old growth fir, cedar and hemlock forest on Breitenbush River. Warm-hot days, noon t-storms common. Fly fishing for trout on river. Supplies in Detroit. Deer, and small wildlife. Moderate use. Buy firewood in Detroit or gather deadwood. Hiking trailhead for S Breitenbush Gorge is nearby.

GETTING THERE: Breitenbush CG is located approx. 1 mi. W of Breitenbush Hot Springs on primary forest route 46.

SINGLE RATE:	$8	OPEN DATES:	Yearlong*
# of SINGLE SITES:	29	MAX SPUR:	70 feet
		MAX STAY:	14 days
		ELEVATION:	2100 feet

16 Cougars Crossing

Blue River • lat 44˚00'00" lon 122˚08'00"

DESCRIPTION: CG set in a mixed forest with open sites on Cougars Reservoir. Boat, fish, and swim in the reservoir. Supplies available at Blue River. Watch for deer, elk, and birds. Campers may gather firewood. Hike French Pete Trail which is within 3 mi. of CG. Mosquitos and ticks are thick in early spring.

GETTING THERE: From Blue River go E approx. 3.5 mi. on Hwy 126 to forest route 19 (Aufderheide Drive). Go S on 19 approx. 13 mi. to Cougars Crossing CG.

SINGLE RATE:	$5	OPEN DATES:	Yearlong*
# of SINGLE SITES:	12		
		MAX STAY:	14 days
		ELEVATION:	1700 feet

12 Broken Bowl

Unity • lat 43˚57'44" lon 122˚36'34"

DESCRIPTION: CG is in a douglas fir forest setting on Fall Creek. Fish and swim in the creek. Supplies available in Lowell or Springfild. CG is full most summer weekends. Firewood is sold at the CG. Hike Fall Creek National Recreation Trail or the Johnny Creek Nature Trail both within a few miles of the CG.

GETTING THERE: From Unity go NE on county route 6204 approx. 6.5 mi. to primary forest route 18. Go E on 18 approx. 4 mi. to Broken Bowl CG.

SINGLE RATE:	$9	OPEN DATES:	Apr-Sept
# of SINGLE SITES:	16	MAX SPUR:	20 feet
		MAX STAY:	14 days
		ELEVATION:	1000 feet

17 Cove Creek

Detroit • lat 44˚42'30" lon 122˚08'00"

DESCRIPTION: This CG is situated among mixed conifer on Detroit Reservoir. Enjoy fishing in the reservoir or Santiam River. Summer afternoons may bring t-showers. The South Breitenbush Gorge Trail is nearby. Bring your own firewood. Watch for deer, elk, mountain lions, bobcats, bears, and coyotes in the area.

GETTING THERE: From Detroit go E on state Hwy 22 approx. 2.5 mi. to Blowout Road #10. Proceed W on Blowout Road to Cove Creek CG.

SINGLE RATE:	$16	OPEN DATES:	Apr-Sept
# of SINGLE SITES:	63	MAX SPUR:	30 feet
GROUP RATE:	$120	MAX STAY:	14 days
# of GROUP SITES:	1	ELEVATION:	1600 feet

13 Campers Flat

Oakridge • lat 43˚30'04" lon 122˚24'44"

DESCRIPTION: In open area w/Douglas firs on Middle Fork of Willamette River. Hot days. Fish (artificial bait) the river. Historic Central Oregon Military Wagon road. Supplies in Oakridge. Deer, elk, coyotes in area. Fills holiday weekends, July-Aug and hunt season. Gather firewood. ATV, mountain biking and hiking nearby.

GETTING THERE: Campers Flat CG is located approx. 23 mi. S of Oakridge on primary forest route 21.

SINGLE RATE:	$8	OPEN DATES:	Apr-Nov
# of SINGLE SITES:	5	MAX SPUR:	18 feet
		MAX STAY:	14 days
		ELEVATION:	2000 feet

18 Delta

Rainbow • lat 44˚09'50" lon 122˚16'50"

DESCRIPTION: CG is in a mixed conifer and hardwood setting with oregon grapes and ferns. Sites have vegetation separating them, making them private. Catch and release trout on Delta Creek and Blue River. Supplies available at Rainbow. Deer, beavers, elk and birds are common to the area. Firewood for sale at CG. Delta Nature Trail nearby.

GETTING THERE: Delta CG is located approx. 2 mi. W of Rainbow on state HWY 126.

SINGLE RATE:	$12	OPEN DATES:	May-Sept
# of SINGLE SITES:	38	MAX SPUR:	36 feet
		MAX STAY:	14 days
		ELEVATION:	1200 feet

14 Cleator Bend

Breitenbush Hot Springs • lat 44˚46'40" lon 121˚59'54"

DESCRIPTION: This CG is located in mixed conifer on Breitenbush River. Enjoy fishing in the river. Summer afternoons may bring t-showers. South Breitenbush Gorge Trail is located approx. 3 mi. from CG. Campers should bring their own firewood. Wildlife includes deer, elk, mountain lions, bobcats, bears and coyotes.

GETTING THERE: Cleator Bend CG is located approx. 1.5 mi. W of Breitenbush Hot Springs on primary forest route 46.

SINGLE RATE:	$8	OPEN DATES:	May-Sept
# of SINGLE SITES:	9	MAX SPUR:	16 feet
		MAX STAY:	14 days
		ELEVATION:	2200 feet

19 Dolly Varden

Lowell • lat 43˚57'50" lon 122˚36'56"

DESCRIPTION: This tent only CG is located on Fall Creek. Fish and swim in the creek. Supplies are available in Lowell. CG is full most weekends, especially in July and August, and holidays. Campers may gather firewood. Hike Fall Creek National Recreation Trail which begins at CG.

GETTING THERE: From Unity go NE on county route 6204 approx. 6.5 mi. to primary forest route 18. Go E on 18 approx. 3.5 mi. to Dolly Varden CG.

SINGLE RATE:	$7	OPEN DATES:	May-Sept
# of SINGLE SITES:	5		
		MAX STAY:	14 days
		ELEVATION:	1000 feet

15 Cold Water Cove

Upper Soda • lat 44˚21'50" lon 121˚59'20"

DESCRIPTION: In an old growth douglas fir forest setting adjacent to Clear Lake. Fish from the lake. No motor boats in this lake. Supplies available at Clear Lake Resort. Deer, elk and small wildlife are common to the area. Campers should bring their own firewood or purchase at the CG. Many trails in the area.

GETTING THERE: From Upper Soda go E on US HWY 20 approx. 17 mi. to state HWY 126. Go S on 126 approx. 3.5 mi. to Coldwater Cove CG.

SINGLE RATE:	$12	OPEN DATES:	May-Oct
# of SINGLE SITES:	35	MAX SPUR:	40 feet
		MAX STAY:	14 days
		ELEVATION:	3500 feet

20 Elk Lake

Detroit • lat 44˚49'14" lon 122˚07'37"

DESCRIPTION: This tent only CG is situated on Elk Lake with a large meadow nearby. Wildflowers are a beautiful sight in the meadow. Fishing and boating are activities that one can do while at Elk Lake. The Bull of the Woods Wilderness is nearby and accessible from Elk Lake. Campers should bring their own firewood.

GETTING THERE: From Detroit go NE 5 mi. on primary forest route 46 to forest route 4696. Go N 1 mi. on 4696 to forest route 4697. Go NW 3.5 mi. on 4697 to forest route. Go W 2 mi. on forest route to Elk Lake CG.

SINGLE RATE:	No fee	OPEN DATES:	June-Oct
# of SINGLE SITES:	12		
		MAX STAY:	14 days
		ELEVATION:	4000 feet

 Campground has hosts   **Reservable sites**   **Accessible facilities**   **Fully developed**   **Semi-developed**   **Rustic facilities**

NOTE: Open dates listed are typical. Actual dates are dependent on conditions such as snow pack.

Page 482

21 **Fernview**
Upper Soda • lat 44°24'09" lon 122°17'55"

DESCRIPTION: CG is perched high above a scenic portion of the South Santiam River which makes for a beautiful view. The Rooster Rock Trailhead across Hwy 20 is a portal to the Menagerie Wilderness. Supplies available at Upper Soda. The Old Santiam Wagon Road runs through the back of the CG.

GETTING THERE: Fernview CG is located approx. 1 mi. W of Upper Soda on US HWY 20.

SINGLE RATE:	$8	OPEN DATES:	May-Sept
# of SINGLE SITES:	11	MAX SPUR:	22 feet
		MAX STAY:	14 days
		ELEVATION:	1300 feet

22 **Fish Lake**
Upper Soda • lat 44°24'15" lon 122°00'12"

DESCRIPTION: A Forest Service Guard Station is located nearby with an interpretive display describing the area. No firewood available. Supplies available at Upper Soda. No designated trails in the area.

GETTING THERE: From Upper Soda go E on US HWY 20 approx. 17 mi. to state HWY 126. Go S on 126 approx. 1.5 mi. to Fish Lake CG.

SINGLE RATE:	$6	OPEN DATES:	May-Sept
# of SINGLE SITES:	8		
		MAX STAY:	14 days
		ELEVATION:	3200 feet

23 **French Pete**
Oakridge • lat 44°02'30" lon 122°12'27"

DESCRIPTION: CG is in a thick canopy of conifer and hardwoods with little underbrush. Cool in summer. CG is located at the confluence of French Pete Creek and the South Fork of the McKenzie River. Catch and release fishing only. Supplies available in Rainbow. Firewood is available on site. Trailhead on site.

GETTING THERE: French Pete CG is located approx. 40 mi. NE of Oakridge on primary forest route 19.

SINGLE RATE:	$12	OPEN DATES:	May-Sept
# of SINGLE SITES:	17	MAX SPUR:	30 feet
		MAX STAY:	14 days
		ELEVATION:	1800 feet

24 **Frissell Crossing**
Oakridge • lat 43°57'25" lon 122°05'02"

DESCRIPTION: Originally constructed in 1934 by the Civilian Conservation Corp. In an open fir, hemlock and hardwood forest with views of the McKenzie River. Fish for rainbow trout, catch and release only for bull trout. Supplies approx. 31 mi. from CG. Deer, elk and varied birds. Firewood for sale by concessionaire. Many trails nearby.

GETTING THERE: From Oakridge go NE approx. 30.5 mi. on primary forest route 19 to forest route 1964. Go E on 1964 approx. 1/2 mi. to Frissell Crossing CG.

SINGLE RATE:	Varies	OPEN DATES:	May-Sept
# of SINGLE SITES:	12	MAX SPUR:	36 feet
		MAX STAY:	14 days
		ELEVATION:	2600 feet

25 **Gold Lake**
Oakridge • lat 43°37'49" lon 122°03'53"

DESCRIPTION: This primitive CG is located in a mixed forest setting on Golden Lake. Fish, boat and swim in the lake. Boat ramp at the CG. A primitive log shelter built by the Civilian Conservation Corps (CCC) is located at the CG. Supplies at Oakridge. Deer, elk and other smaller wildlife can be seen in the area. Trails nearby.

GETTING THERE: From Oakridge go SE on state HWY 58 approx. 22 mi. to forest route 500. Go N on 500 approx. 2.5 mi. to Gold Lake CG.

SINGLE RATE:	$10	OPEN DATES:	June-Oct*
# of SINGLE SITES:	25	MAX SPUR:	24 feet
		MAX STAY:	14 days
		ELEVATION:	4800 feet

26 **Hampton**
Oakridge • lat 43°48'55" lon 122°35'40"

DESCRIPTION: Located on Lookout Point Reservoir in douglas fir forest with views of Middle Fork of Willamette River. Adjacent to well used railroad line for train fans. Boating, fishing, swimming and water skiing on the reservoir. Rafting access to Middle Fork. Supplies in Oakridge. Gather firewood. Mountain bike trails nearby.

GETTING THERE: Hampton CG is located approx. 8 mi. NW of Oakridge on state HWY 58.

SINGLE RATE:	$8	OPEN DATES:	Apr-Sept
# of SINGLE SITES:	4	MAX SPUR:	36 feet
		MAX STAY:	14 days
		ELEVATION:	1000 feet

27 **Harralson Horse Camp**
Oakridge • lat 43°45'55" lon 121°59'33"

DESCRIPTION: Located in alpine forest. Supplies available in Oakridge. Deer, elk and small wildlife are common to the area. Horse facilities at CG. Full Labor Day and opening of hunt season. Gather firewood locally. Horse trails nearby, including Waldo Lake Wilderness. Mosquitoes are thick till July-Aug.

GETTING THERE: From Oakridge go SE on state HWY 58 approx. 20 mi. to forest route 5897. Go NE on 5897 approx. 10 mi. to Harralson Horse Camp.

SINGLE RATE:	No fee	OPEN DATES:	July-Sept
# of SINGLE SITES:	5		
		MAX STAY:	14 days
		ELEVATION:	5600 feet

28 **Homestead**
Oakridge • lat 43°29'19" lon 122°31'24"

DESCRIPTION: In a fir, hemlock and cedar forest with views of the McKenzie River. Fish for rainbow trout in the river, and catch and release only for bull trout. Supplies at Homestead. Deer, elk and many birds can be seen in the area. Campers may gather firewood. Rebel Rock Trail is approx. 3 mi. from CG.

GETTING THERE: Homestead CG is located approx. 34 mi. NE of Oakridge on primary forest route 19.

SINGLE RATE:	No fee	OPEN DATES:	Yearlong*
# of SINGLE SITES:	7	MAX SPUR:	32 feet
		MAX STAY:	14 days
		ELEVATION:	2200 feet

29 **Hoover**
Detroit • lat 44°37'20" lon 122°12'50"

DESCRIPTION: This CG is located in mixed conifer on Detroit Reservoir. There is a boat launch and a fishing pier on site. Summer afternoons may bring t-showers. CG offers an amphitheater, interpretive trail, and barrier free trails with viewing platforms. Wildlife includes bears, mountain lions, bobcats, and coyotes.

GETTING THERE: Hoover CG is located approx. 2 mi. SE of Detroit on state HWY 22.

SINGLE RATE:	$12	OPEN DATES:	Apr-Sept
# of SINGLE SITES:	37	MAX SPUR:	30 feet
GROUP RATE:	$120	MAX STAY:	14 days
# of GROUP SITES:	1	ELEVATION:	1600 feet

30 **Hoover Group Camp**
Detroit • lat 44°37'20" lon 122°12'50"

DESCRIPTION: In a mixed forest setting. Fish, swim and boat nearby. Boat launch close to CG. Compacted rock/dirt access routes. Supplies available at Detroit. Nature trail and an amphitheater program at CG.

GETTING THERE: Hoover Group CG is located approx. 2 mi. SE of Detroit on state HWY 22.

		OPEN DATES:	Yearlong
		MAX SPUR:	30 feet
GROUP RATE:	$120	MAX STAY:	14 days
# of GROUP SITES:	1	ELEVATION:	1600 feet

NOTE: Open dates listed are typical. Actual dates are dependent on conditions such as snow pack.

WILLAMETTE NATIONAL FOREST • OREGON • 21 — 30

31 Horse Creek
Rainbow • lat 44°09'44" lon 122°09'12"

DESCRIPTION: In a mixed forest setting on Horse Creek. Fish for trout and swim in the creek. Supplies available at McKenzie Bridge. Deer, squirrels and birds are common to the area. Campers may gather firewood. McKenzie River and Olallie trails nearby.

GETTING THERE: From Rainbow go E on state HWY 126 approx. 4 mi. to forest route 2638. Go S on 2638 approx. 2 mi. to Horse Creek CG.

		OPEN DATES:	Yearlong
		MAX SPUR:	35 feet
GROUP RATE:	Varies	MAX STAY:	14 days
# of GROUP SITES:	1	ELEVATION:	1400 feet

32 House Rock
Upper Soda • lat 44°23'37" lon 122°14'38"

DESCRIPTION: CG is located at the confluence of Sheep Creek and the South Santiam River in an old growth grove. Supplies available in Upper Soda. The House Rock Trail starts in the day use area and continues for 0.8 mi. returning to the day use area. The trail uses a portion of the historic Old Santiam Wagon Road.

GETTING THERE: From Upper Soda go SE on US HWY 20 approx. 2 mi. to forest route 2044. Go S on 2044 approx. 1/2 mi. to House Rock CG.

		OPEN DATES:	May-Sept
SINGLE RATE:	$8	MAX SPUR:	22 feet
# of SINGLE SITES:	16	MAX STAY:	14 days
		ELEVATION:	1800 feet

33 Humbug
Detroit • lat 44°46'15" lon 122°04'35"

DESCRIPTION: This CG is located in a mixed conifer setting on the Breitenbush River. Enjoy fishing in the river. Campers should bring firewood. Enjoy a walk through an old-growth forest along the river. May-July, the rhododendrons are in bloom. Wildlife includes black bears, mountain lions, bobcats, coyotes, and deer.

GETTING THERE: Humbug CG is located approx. 4.5 mi. NE of Detroit on primary forest route 46.

		OPEN DATES:	Apr-Sept
SINGLE RATE:	$8	MAX SPUR:	30 feet
# of SINGLE SITES:	21	MAX STAY:	14 days
		ELEVATION:	1800 feet

34 Ice Cap
Upper Soda • lat 44°20'35" lon 122°00'02"

DESCRIPTION: In a mixed forest setting on a "bench" above the McKenzie River and Carmen Reservoir. Fish in the river or reservoir. Non-motorized boats only allowed on reservoir. Supplies available at Upper Soda. Hike to nearby Koosah and Sahalie Falls. Mosquitoes in June.

GETTING THERE: From Upper Soda go E on US HWY 20 approx. 17 mi. to state HWY 126. Go S on 126 approx. 5.5 mi. to Ice Cap CG.

		OPEN DATES:	May-Sept
SINGLE RATE:	$10	MAX SPUR:	30 feet
# of SINGLE SITES:	22	MAX STAY:	14 days
		ELEVATION:	3000 feet

35 Indigo Lake Hike-In
Oakridge • lat 43°23'00" lon 122°07'00"

DESCRIPTION: This primitive, tent only CG is in an alpine forest on the shores of Indigo Lake. Fish and swim in the lake. A large escarpment on the S side of lake provides outstanding views. Deer and elk can be seen in the area. Campers may gather firewood. Numerous hiking trails in the area. Mosquitos heavy.

GETTING THERE: From Oakridge go E 2mi. on state HWY 58 to Kitson Springs Road. Go 1/2 mi. to forest route 21. Go 32 mi. to forest route 2154. Go 10 mi. to Indigo Lake Hike-In CG. Follow signs to CG.

		OPEN DATES:	June-Oct*
SINGLE RATE:	No fee		
# of SINGLE SITES:	5	MAX STAY:	14 days
		ELEVATION:	5900 feet

36 Indigo Spring
Oakridge • lat 43°29'52" lon 122°15'48"

DESCRIPTION: This tent only CG is set in a semi-open stand of old growth douglas fir on Indigo Creek. Enjoy sounds of springs. Oregon Central Military Wagon Road and Rigdon Meadows are nearby. Supplies available in Oakridge. Campers may gather firewood. Hiking access to Middle Fork Trail in area.

GETTING THERE: Indigo Springs CG is located approx. 30.5 mi. S of Oakridge on primary forest route 21.

		OPEN DATES:	Apr-Oct*
SINGLE RATE:	No fee		
# of SINGLE SITES:	3	MAX STAY:	14 days
		ELEVATION:	6000 feet

37 Islet Point
Oakridge • lat 43°45'04" lon 122°00'30"

DESCRIPTION: In alpine forest on Waldo Lake, one of the purest lakes in the world with wonderful sandy beaches. Expect afternoon winds, offering a cool break from the summer sun. Poor fishing in this lake. Supplies available in Oakridge. Deer and elk can be seen in the area. May trails available.

GETTING THERE: From Oakridge go SE on state HWY 58 approx. 20 mi. to forest route 5897. Go NE on 5897 approx. 9 mi. to Islet Point CG.

		OPEN DATES:	July-Sept
SINGLE RATE:	$10	MAX SPUR:	30 feet
# of SINGLE SITES:	55	MAX STAY:	14 days
		ELEVATION:	2800 feet

38 Kiahanie
Oakridge • lat 43°53'08" lon 122°15'17"

DESCRIPTION: The CG itself is rarely crowded, providing a quiet, peaceful setting. Among enormous douglas fir trees alongside the North Fork of Middle Fork of the Willamette, a Wild and Scenic River. Fly fish, catch and release only, for native fish. Campers may gather firewood nearby. Several trails nearby.

GETTING THERE: Kiananie CG is located approx. 16 mi. NE of Oakridge on primary forest route 19.

		OPEN DATES:	May-Sept
SINGLE RATE:	$8	MAX SPUR:	24 feet
# of SINGLE SITES:	19	MAX STAY:	14 days
		ELEVATION:	2200 feet

39 Lakes End
Upper Soda • lat 44°15'00" lon 122°02'45"

DESCRIPTION: This tent only CG is located in mixed conifer at the northern tip of Smith Reservoir. There are excellent fishing opportunities in the area but please check fishing regulations. Supplies available at Upper Soda. Visit the nearby Wildcat Mountain Research Natural Area and Mount Washington Wilderness. No drinking water.

GETTING THERE: From Upper Soda go E on US HWY 20 approx. 17 mi. to state HWY 126. Go S on 126 approx. 10 mi. to forest route. Go N on forest route to the boat launch for Smith Reservoir. Boat in only.

		OPEN DATES:	Apr-Oct
SINGLE RATE:	No fee		
# of SINGLE SITES:	17	MAX STAY:	14 days
		ELEVATION:	3000 feet

40 Larison Cove Canoe-In
Oakridge • lat 43°41'18" lon 122°27'10"

DESCRIPTION: This tent only CG is situated in a douglas fir forest on the south side of Hills Creek Reservoir. Fish and swim in Reservoir. Supplies available at Oakridge. Receives light use. Larison Creek Trail is located on the opposite side of the cove. Poison oak grows in the area.

GETTING THERE: From Oakridge go E 2 mi. on HWY 58 to Kitson Springs RD. Continue on RD 1/2 mi. to forest route 21. Continue 3 mi. on 21 to forest route 2106. CANOE ACCESS ONLY to Larison Cove Canoe-In CG.

		OPEN DATES:	Apr-Sept
SINGLE RATE:	No fee		
# of SINGLE SITES:	4	MAX STAY:	14 days
		ELEVATION:	1600 feet

 Campground has hosts   **Reservable sites**   **Accessible facilities**   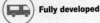 **Fully developed**   **Semi-developed**   **Rustic facilities**

NOTE: Open dates listed are typical. Actual dates are dependent on conditions such as snow pack.

41 Limberlost
Belknap Springs • lat 44°10'28" lon 122°03'07"

DESCRIPTION: This secluded, minimum use CG is in a mixed forest setting. Supplies available at Belknap Springs. Numerous animals can be seen in the area. No cut firewood provided. No designated trails in the area.

GETTING THERE: From McKenzie Bridge go E approx. 3 mi. to HWY 242. Go approx. 1/2 mi. on 242 to Limberlost CG.

SINGLE RATE:	$6	OPEN DATES:	Apr-Oct
# of SINGLE SITES:	12	MAX SPUR:	16 feet
		MAX STAY:	14 days
		ELEVATION:	1800 feet

42 Longbow Organization Camp
Cascadia • lat 44°25'00" lon 122°22'00"

DESCRIPTION: CG is in a forest setting with shelters for kitchen and dining area. Fishing and hiking opportunities are located near the old Santiam Wagon Road. Supplies available in Cascadia. There is an elk pasture nearby, visible in early May. Amphitheater that seats 75 in CG.

GETTING THERE: Longbow Organization Camp is located approx. 6 mi. E of Cascadia on US HWY 20.

		OPEN DATES:	May-Sept
GROUP RATE:	$65	MAX STAY:	14 days
# of GROUP SITES:	6	ELEVATION:	1200 feet

43 Lookout
Blue River • lat 45°12'46" lon 122°03'59"

DESCRIPTION: CG is situated in an open, park-like setting with views of Blue River Reservoir. Sites bordered by mixed conifer. Good trout fishing. Supplies available at Blue River. Watch for deer and elk. Campers may gather firewood locally. Hiking trails nearby. Boat ramp provided.

GETTING THERE: From Blue River go E on HWY 126 approx. 2 mi. to forest route 15. Proceed 3 mi. on 15 to Lookout CG.

SINGLE RATE:	$4	OPEN DATES:	Apr-Sept
# of SINGLE SITES:	55	MAX SPUR:	40 feet
		MAX STAY:	14 days
		ELEVATION:	1360 feet

44 Lost Prairie
Upper Soda • lat 44°24'30" lon 122°04'00"

DESCRIPTION: CG is located along Hackleman Creek in a forest of spruce and douglas fir. Supplies are available in Upper Soda. Nearby are many trailheads. The Old Santiam Wagon Road came through the CG and parts of it may still be hiked.

GETTING THERE: Lost Prairie CG is located approx. 13.5 mi. E of Upper Soda on US HWY 20.

SINGLE RATE:	$8	OPEN DATES:	May-Sept
# of SINGLE SITES:	4	MAX SPUR:	24 feet
		MAX STAY:	14 days
		ELEVATION:	3200 feet

45 Marion Forks
Marion Forks • lat 44°36'35" lon 121°56'42"

DESCRIPTION: This CG rests in mixed conifer on Marion Creek. Enjoy fishing from Marion Creek and the North Santiam River. Close by is a state run fish hatchery. The trailhead to Independence Rock and the Mount Jefferson Wilderness is nearby off of forest route 2255. Wildlife includes bears and mountain lions.

GETTING THERE: Marion Forks CG is located approx. 1/2 mi. S of Marion Forks on state HWY 20.

SINGLE RATE:	$8	OPEN DATES:	May-Sept
# of SINGLE SITES:	15	MAX SPUR:	24 feet
		MAX STAY:	14 days
		ELEVATION:	2500 feet

46 McKenzie Bridge
Rainbow • lat 44°10'30" lon 122°10'30"

DESCRIPTION: CG is situated in old growth douglas fir setting along the McKenzie River. Fish for trout in the river. Boat ramp provided in CG area. Basic supplies in McKenzie Bridge. Deer, squirrel and birds are common to the area. Campers may gather firewood. Hiking, biking and sight-seeing trails are nearby.

GETTING THERE: McKenzie Bridge CG is located approx. 3.5 mi. E of Rainbow on state HWY 126.

SINGLE RATE:	$10	OPEN DATES:	May-Sept
# of SINGLE SITES:	20	MAX SPUR:	30 feet
		MAX STAY:	14 days
		ELEVATION:	1300 feet

47 Mona
Blue River • lat 44°12'35" lon 122°15'55"

DESCRIPTION: The CG is situated in a dense conifer forest setting. CG is on the Blue River Reservoir and surrounded by steep slopes. Fish for rainbow trout in reservoir. Supplies available in Blue river. Wildlife includes deer, elk, and songbirds. Firewood sold on site. Wash water disposal site and boat ramp.

GETTING THERE: From Blue River go E on Hwy 126 approx. 3.5 mi. to forest route 15. Go NE on 15 approx. 3 miles to Mona CG.

SINGLE RATE:	$12	OPEN DATES:	Apr-Sept
# of SINGLE SITES:	23	MAX SPUR:	36 feet
		MAX STAY:	14 days
		ELEVATION:	1360 feet

48 North Waldo
Oakridge • lat 43°45'30" lon 122°00'10"

DESCRIPTION: Most popular CG on Waldo Lake, set in an alpine forest. Steady lake breezes offer good sailing. Amphitheater programs and boat launch at CG. The lake is very pure making fishing more challenging. Buy firewood at CG. Deer and elk can be seen in the area. Many wilderness trails start at CG. Mosquitoes July-early Aug.

GETTING THERE: From Oakridge go SE on state HWY 58 approx. 20 mi. to forest route 5897. Go NE on 5897 approx. 9.5 mi. to North Waldo CG.

SINGLE RATE:	$10	OPEN DATES:	July-Sept*
# of SINGLE SITES:	58	MAX SPUR:	30 feet
		MAX STAY:	14 days
		ELEVATION:	5400 feet

49 Olallie
Upper Soda • lat 44°15'25" lon 122°02'20"

DESCRIPTION: This CG is located in mixed conifer on the McKenzie River. There is a boat ramp on site. There are excellent fishing opportunities in the area but please check fishing regulations. Enjoy a hike in the nearby Mount Washington Wilderness. Bring your own firewood. Wildlife includes mountain lions and bears.

GETTING THERE: From Upper Soda go E on US HWY 20 approx. 17 mi. to state HWY 126. Go S on 126 approx. 12 mi. to Olallie CG.

SINGLE RATE:	$8	OPEN DATES:	Apr-Sept
# of SINGLE SITES:	17	MAX SPUR:	35 feet
		MAX STAY:	14 days
		ELEVATION:	2000 feet

50   Opal Lake
Oakridge • lat 43°25'23" lon 122°07'20"

DESCRIPTION: This single unit, tent only CG is situated in a beautiful alpine forest on the edge of Opal Lake. A place ideal for those who seek solitude. Huckleberries are abundant giving visitors a quick snack. Fish for native brook trout in Opal Lake. Please check for local regulations.

GETTING THERE: From Oakridge go E on state HWY 58 2 mi. to Kitson Springs Road. Continue on RD approx. 1/2 mi. to forest route 21. Follow 21 32 mi. to forest route 2154. Continue on 2154 9 mi. to Opal Lake CG.

SINGLE RATE:	No fee	OPEN DATES:	July-Oct*
# of SINGLE SITES:	1		
		MAX STAY:	14 days
		ELEVATION:	5450 feet

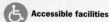 Campground has hosts   Reservable sites   Accessible facilities   Fully developed   Semi-developed   Rustic facilities

NOTE: Open dates listed are typical. Actual dates are dependent on conditions such as snow pack.

51 Packard Creek
Oakridge • lat 43°40'00" lon 122°25'50"

DESCRIPTION: In douglas fir forest with abundant poison oak. CG is on a large flat along Hills Creek Reservoir. Beach for swimming and skiing on lake. Boat fish several species. Deer and geese frequent the area. Buy firewood at the CG. Many trails with in 2 mi. of CG. Yellow jackets are common in hot days of Aug.

GETTING THERE: Packard Creek CG is located approx. 9.5 mi. S of Oakridge on primary forest route 21.

SINGLE RATE:	Varies	OPEN DATES:	Apr-Sept
# of SINGLE SITES:	33	MAX SPUR:	28 feet
		MAX STAY:	14 days
# of GROUP SITES:	1	ELEVATION:	1600 feet

52 Paradise
Belknap Springs • lat 44°11'00" lon 122°06'30"

DESCRIPTION: CG is situated along the McKenzie River in old growth douglas fir setting. Fish the river for trout. Boat ramp provided. Supplies available at Belknap Springs. Campers may gather firewood. Hiking and mountain biking trails nearby.

GETTING THERE: Paradise CG is located approx. 2 mi. W of Belknap Springs on state HWY 126.

SINGLE RATE:	$12	OPEN DATES:	Apr-Oct
# of SINGLE SITES:	64	MAX SPUR:	40 feet
		MAX STAY:	14 days
		ELEVATION:	1600 feet

53 Piety Island
Detroit • lat 44°43'15" lon 122°09'45"

DESCRIPTION: This tent only CG is located on Piety Island in the middle of Detroit Reservoir. Enjoy fishing and boating on the reservoir. The CG is busiest in spring and summer. This CG offers no drinking water or garbage service. Campers may gather dead and down firewood.

GETTING THERE: From Detroit go W on state HWY 22 approx. 3 mi. to boat launch. Piety Island CG is on the SE shore of Piety Island. Boat access only.

SINGLE RATE:	No fee	OPEN DATES:	Yearlong
# of SINGLE SITES:	12		
		MAX STAY:	14 days
		ELEVATION:	1600 feet

54 Puma
Unity • lat 43°58'43" lon 122°30'51"

DESCRIPTION: Located in a douglas fir forest on Fall Creek. Fish and swim in the creek. Supplies available in Lowell. Buy firewood from host. Deer and small wildlife are common to the area. Fall Creek National Recreation Trail is nearby.

GETTING THERE: From Unity go NE on county route 6204 approx. 6.5 mi. to primary forest route 18. Go E on 18 approx. 10 mi. to Puma Creek CG.

SINGLE RATE:	$9	OPEN DATES:	May-Sept
# of SINGLE SITES:	11	MAX SPUR:	20 feet
		MAX STAY:	14 days
		ELEVATION:	1000 feet

55 Rhododendron Island
Oakridge • lat 43°43'07" lon 122°03'15"

DESCRIPTION: This boat-in, small island near the W shore of Lookout Point Reservoir, is covered with rhododendrons as its name indicates. Supplies available at Oakridge. Numerous animals can be seen in the area. Campers may gather firewood. No designated trails in the area. It is an easy paddle from Shadow Bay.

GETTING THERE: From Oakridge go E on state HWY 58 25 mi. to the forest route 5897. Follow 5897 approx. 6.5 mi. to the Shadow Bay turnoff. Follow signs to the Shadow Bay Boat Ramp. Proceed by boat, about 1 1/2 miles NE, to Rhododendron Island.

SINGLE RATE:	No fee	OPEN DATES:	July-Sept
		MAX STAY:	14 days
		ELEVATION:	5420 feet

56 Riverside
Marion Forks • lat 44°38'30" lon 121°56'37"

DESCRIPTION: This CG is situated in mixed conifer on the Santiam River. Enjoy fishing for trout in this river. Summer afternoons may bring t-showers. Wildlife in this area includes black bears, mountain lions, bobcats and coyotes. Try a hike in the nearby Mount Jefferson Wilderness. Campers should bring firewood.

GETTING THERE: Riverside CG is located approx. 2 mi. N of Marion Forks on state HWY 22.

SINGLE RATE:	$8	OPEN DATES:	May-Sept
# of SINGLE SITES:	37	MAX SPUR:	24 feet
		MAX STAY:	14 days
		ELEVATION:	2400 feet

57 Roaring River Group Camp
Oakridge • lat 43°57'00" lon 122°05'00"

DESCRIPTION: In a douglas fir, white fir and hemlock setting with views of Roaring River Creek. Fish for rainbow trout from the creek. Supplies available at Oakridge. Elk, deer and birds can be seen from the CG area. Campers may gather firewood. Many trails nearby.

GETTING THERE: Roaring River Group Camp is located approx. 30 mi. NE of Oakridge on primary forest route 19.

		OPEN DATES:	May-Oct*
		MAX SPUR:	14 feet
GROUP RATE:	$30	MAX STAY:	14 days
# of GROUP SITES:	1	ELEVATION:	2600 feet

58 Sacandaga
Oakridge • lat 43°29'47" lon 122°19'42"

DESCRIPTION: Located in a fir forest along Middle Fork of the Willamette River where a segment of historic Oregon Central Military Wagon Road can be seen. Supplies available in Oakridge. Deer graze Rigdon Meadow nearby frequently. Camper may gather firewood. Short scenic hike or the Middle Fork Trail is nearby.

GETTING THERE: Sacandaga CG is located approx. 27 mi. S of Oakridge on primary forest route 21.

SINGLE RATE:	$6	OPEN DATES:	Apr-Oct
# of SINGLE SITES:	17	MAX SPUR:	24 feet
		MAX STAY:	14 days
		ELEVATION:	2400 feet

59 Salmon Creek Falls
Oakridge • lat 43°45'46" lon 122°22'23"

DESCRIPTION: Located in a lush, cool, old growth forest along Salmon Creek. The rocky gorge-like area creates two small beautiful waterfalls with deep pools of clear blue-green waters. CG is full most weekends and weekends July-Aug. Buy firewood at the CG. Supplies available in Oakridge. Bike and hike trails nearby.

GETTING THERE: Salmon Creek Falls CG is located approx. 4 mi. NE of Oakridge on primary forest route 24.

SINGLE RATE:	Varies	OPEN DATES:	Apr-Oct
# of SINGLE SITES:	15	MAX SPUR:	20 feet
		MAX STAY:	14 days
		ELEVATION:	1500 feet

60 Sand Prairie
Oakridge • lat 43°36'05" lon 122°27'05"

DESCRIPTION: CG is in a douglas fir and ponderosa pine forest setting. Access to The Middle Fork of the Willamette River at CG. Fish for rainbow and cutthroat trout from river. Supplies available at Oakridge. Deer and elk are often seen inside the CG. Firewood for sale. The Middle Fork Trail begins at S end of the CG.

GETTING THERE: Sand Prairie CG is located approx. 15.5 mi. S of Oakridge on primary forest route 21.

SINGLE RATE:	$10	OPEN DATES:	May-Sept
# of SINGLE SITES:	21	MAX SPUR:	28 feet
		MAX STAY:	14 days
		ELEVATION:	1600 feet

 Campground has hosts　　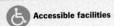 **Reservable sites**　　 **Accessible facilities**　　 **Fully developed**　　 **Semi-developed**　　 **Rustic facilities**

NOTE: Open dates listed are typical. Actual dates are dependent on conditions such as snow pack.

61 Santiam Flats
Detroit • lat 44°41'00" lon 122°06'00"

DESCRIPTION: This dispersed CG is set among mixed conifer on Detroit Reservoir. Enjoy fishing in the reservoir or Santiam River. Summer afternoons may bring t-showers. No drinking water on site. Bring your own firewood. Watch for deer, elk, mountain lions, bobcats, bears, and coyotes in the area.

GETTING THERE: Santiam Flats CG is located approx. 2 mi. E of Detroit on state HWY 22.

SINGLE RATE:	$5	OPEN DATES:	Apr-Sept
		MAX STAY:	14 days
		ELEVATION:	1600 feet

62 Scott Lake
McKenzie Bridge • lat 44°13'00" lon 121°53'00"

DESCRIPTION: This tent only CG is situated in mixed conifer on Scott Lake. There are excellent fishing opportunities in the area but please check fishing regulations. Access to Mount Washington Wilderness is in close proximity. July brings mosquitoes. Campers should bring their own firewood.

GETTING THERE: From McKenzie Bridge go E approx. 4 mi. on state HWY 126 to state HWY 242. Go SE on 242 approx. 13.5 mi. to Scott Lake CG.

SINGLE RATE:	No fee	OPEN DATES:	July-Oct
# of SINGLE SITES:	20		
		MAX STAY:	14 days
		ELEVATION:	4000 feet

63 Secret
Oakridge • lat 42°25'19" lon 123°41'17"

DESCRIPTION: A small CG beside the Middle Fork of the Willamette River. The tree cover is scant, but there is adequate vegetation to buffer the campsites from forest route 21. Fishing in the Middle Fork is fair. Supplies available at Oakridge. CG is full most of August. September is a good time to visit. Trails in the area.

GETTING THERE: Secret CG is located approx. 21.5 mi. S of Oakridge on primary forest route 21.

SINGLE RATE:	$6	OPEN DATES:	Apr-Oct
# of SINGLE SITES:	6	MAX SPUR:	24 feet
		MAX STAY:	14 days
		ELEVATION:	2000 feet

64 Shadow Bay
Oakridge • lat 43°41'35" lon 122°02'30"

DESCRIPTION: CG is located in an alpine forest on a large bay at the S end of Waldo Lake. Views of South Sister can be seen from CG. Supplies at Crescent Lake Junction. Elk and deer visit CG. CG is rarely full. Campers may gather firewood. Shore Line and Waldo Lake Trails are close by. Mosquitoes can be a problem until mid-August.

GETTING THERE: From Oakridge go SE on state HWY 58 approx. 20 mi. to forest route 5897. Go NE on 5897 approx. 5 mi. to forest route. Go W on forest route approx. 1.5 mi. to Shadow Bay CG.

SINGLE RATE:	Varies	OPEN DATES:	July-Sept*
# of SINGLE SITES:	92	MAX SPUR:	24 feet
		MAX STAY:	14 days
		ELEVATION:	5400 feet

65 Shady Cove
Elkhorn Woods • lat 44°50'30" lon 122°18'05"

DESCRIPTION: This CG is located in mixed conifer on the Little North Santiam River. There are excellent fishing opportunities in this area but please check fishing regulations. This CG offers no drinking water. Summer afternoons may bring t-showers. Wildlife in this area includes bears, mountain lions, bobcats, and deer.

GETTING THERE: From Elkhorn Woods go NE on county route approx. 4.5 mi. to forest route 2207. Go SE on 2207 approx. 1 mi. to Shady Cove CG.

SINGLE RATE:	$5	OPEN DATES:	Yearlong
# of SINGLE SITES:	13	MAX SPUR:	16 feet
		MAX STAY:	14 days
		ELEVATION:	1600 feet

66 Shady Dell
Oakridge • lat 43°47'16" lon 122°32'26"

DESCRIPTION: This low use group site is located in a mixed forest setting on the Willamette River. Fish or swim in the river. Supplies available at Oakridge. Many animals can be seen in the area. Campers may gather firewood. No designated trails in the area.

GETTING THERE: Shady Dell CG is located approx. 5 mi. NW of Oakridge on state HWY 58.

		OPEN DATES:	May-Sept
		MAX SPUR:	22 feet
GROUP RATE:	$40	MAX STAY:	14 days
# of GROUP SITES:	1	ELEVATION:	1000 feet

67 Skookum Creek
Oakridge • lat 43°01'11" lon 122°40'12"

DESCRIPTION: CG is located on Skookum Creek in a mixed forest setting. Fish in the creek. Supplies available at Oakridge. Many types of animals are in the area. Campers may gather firewood. The Erma Bell Lakes Trail starts here and is a portal into the Three Sisters Wilderness Area.

GETTING THERE: From Oakridge go NE on primary forest route 19 approx. 27 mi. to forest route 1957. Go SE on 1957 approx. 3.5 mi. to Skookum Creek CG.

SINGLE RATE:	$5	OPEN DATES:	May-Sept*
# of SINGLE SITES:	8		
		MAX STAY:	14 days
		ELEVATION:	4500 feet

68 Slide Creek
Rainbow • lat 44°04'30" lon 122°13'25"

DESCRIPTION: CG, boat ramp and swim area are dwarfed by steep slopes of mixed conifer and located on the E side of Cougars Reservoir. Trout fish the reservoir all year. Wildlife that can be seen in the area includes deer, elk, mountain lions and a variety of birds. Firewood for sale on site. Hiking trails nearby.

GETTING THERE: From Rainbow go S on primary forest route 19 approx. 8 mi. to forest route. Go N on forest route approx. 1.5 mi. to Slide Creek CG.

SINGLE RATE:	$12	OPEN DATES:	May-Sept
# of SINGLE SITES:	16	MAX SPUR:	40 feet
		MAX STAY:	14 days
		ELEVATION:	1700 feet

69 Southshore
Detroit • lat 44°42'20" lon 122°10'30"

DESCRIPTION: This CG is located in mixed conifer on Detroit Reservoir. Enjoy fishing and boating in the reservoir. Campers should bring their own firewood. Summer afternoons may bring thunder showers. Wildlife in this area includes black bears, mountain lions, bobcats, coyotes, and deer.

GETTING THERE: From Detroit go SE approx. 3.5 mi. on state HWY 22 to primary forest route 10. Go NW on 10 approx. 4 mi. to Southshore CG.

SINGLE RATE:	$12	OPEN DATES:	Apr-Sept
# of SINGLE SITES:	30	MAX SPUR:	30 feet
		MAX STAY:	14 days
		ELEVATION:	1600 feet

70 Sunnyside
Blue River • lat 44°00'00" lon 122°08'00"

DESCRIPTION: This CG is situated in a fir and maple forest with views of Cougars Reservoir. Fish for trout on the reservoir. Supplies available at Blue River. Campers may gather firewood. Watch for deer, elk, and various birds in the area. French Pete Trailhead is approx. 2 mi. away from CG.

GETTING THERE: From Blue River go E on state HWY 126 approx. 3.5 mi. to forest route 19. Go S on 19 approx. 13 mi. to Sunnyside CG.

SINGLE RATE:	$5	OPEN DATES:	Apr-Sept
# of SINGLE SITES:	13		
		MAX STAY:	14 days
		ELEVATION:	1700 feet

 Campground has hosts   **Reservable sites**   **Accessible facilities**   **Fully developed**   **Semi-developed**   **Rustic facilities**

NOTE: Open dates listed are typical. Actual dates are dependent on conditions such as snow pack.

71 Taylor Burn Forest Camp
Oakridge • lat 43°48'48" lon 122°01'54"

DESCRIPTION: This primitive camp requires patience to get to, but the outstanding alpine beauty is well worth the drive. Supplies are available at Oakridge. Numerous wildlife can be seen in the area. Campers may gather firewood. This camp serves as a trailhead to many wilderness trails. June-Aug brings mosquitoes.

GETTING THERE: From Oakridge go E 25 mi. on HWY 58 to forest route 5897. Follow 5897 11 mi. to forest route 5898. Continue on 5898, 1 mi. to forest route 514. Follow 514, 7 mi. to Taylor Burn Forest Camp. 4WD recomended

SINGLE RATE:	No fee	OPEN DATES:	July-Sept*
# of SINGLE SITES:	6		
		MAX STAY:	14 days
		ELEVATION:	5200 feet

72 Timpanogas Lake
Oakridge • lat 43°24'43" lon 122°06'42"

DESCRIPTION: CG is located in a high elevation, mixed forest setting on Timpanogas Lake with excellent views of Diamond Peak. Fish from the lake (non-motorized boating) for cutthroat and brook trout. Supplies available at Oakridge. Campers may gather firewood. Many hike, bike and horseback riding trails are in the area.

GETTING THERE: Timpanogas CG is located approx. 40.5 mi. SE of Oakridge on primary forest route 21.

SINGLE RATE:	Varies	OPEN DATES:	July-Sept*
# of SINGLE SITES:	10	MAX SPUR:	24 feet
		MAX STAY:	14 days
		ELEVATION:	5300 feet

73 Trail Bridge
Upper Soda • lat 44°16'45" lon 122°03'00"

DESCRIPTION: This CG is located in mixed conifer on the McKenzie River. There are excellent fishing opportunities in the area but please check fishing regulations. Access to the McKenzie River National Recreation Trail is in close proximity. There is a gravel boat launch on site.

GETTING THERE: From Upper Soda go E on US HWY 20 approx. 17 mi. to state HWY 126. Go S on 126 approx. 10 mi. to Trail Bridge CG.

SINGLE RATE:	$6	OPEN DATES:	Apr-Sept
# of SINGLE SITES:	26	MAX SPUR:	45 feet
		MAX STAY:	14 days
		ELEVATION:	2000 feet

74 Trout Creek
Upper Soda • lat 44°23'49" lon 122°21'08"

DESCRIPTION: CG is located in douglas fir and maple forest. The Menagerie Wilderness is accessible from the Trout Creek Trailhead located directly across Hwy 20. Due west is the historic Long Ranch that is now an Elk Refuge. Nearby is the Old Santiam Wagon Road. Fishing nearby.

GETTING THERE: Trout Creek CG is located approx. 3.5 mi. W of Upper Soda on US HWY 20.

SINGLE RATE:	$8	OPEN DATES:	May-Oct
# of SINGLE SITES:	24	MAX SPUR:	24 feet
		MAX STAY:	14 days
		ELEVATION:	1300 feet

75 Upper Arm
Detroit • lat 44°44'50" lon 122°08'29"

DESCRIPTION: This dispersed CG is located in mixed conifer on Breitenbush River. Enjoy fishing or boating in nearby Detroit Reservoir. Summer afternoons may bring thunder showers. Wildlife includes black bears, mountain lions, bobcats, coyotes, and deer. Enjoy a walk under old growth trees near the river.

GETTING THERE: Upper Arm CG is located approx. 1 mi. NE of Detroit on primary forest route 46.

SINGLE RATE:	No fee	OPEN DATES:	Yearlong
		MAX STAY:	14 days
		ELEVATION:	1600 feet

76 Whispering Falls
Detroit • lat 44°41'17" lon 122°00'28"

DESCRIPTION: This CG is located in mixed conifer on North Santiam River. Enjoy fishing for trout. Summer afternoons may bring thunder showers. Wildlife includes black bears, mountain lions, bobcats, coyotes, and deer. Campers should bring firewood. There is a waterfall located across the river from the campground.

GETTING THERE: Whispering Falls CG is located approx. 7.5 mi. SE of Detroit on state HWY 22.

SINGLE RATE:	$10	OPEN DATES:	Apr-Sept
# of SINGLE SITES:	16	MAX SPUR:	30 feet
		MAX STAY:	14 days
		ELEVATION:	2000 feet

77 Winberry
Unity • lat 43°54'03" lon 122°36'52"

DESCRIPTION: In a mixed forest setting on Winberry Creek. Fish and swim in the creek. Supplies available at Unity. Numerous animals can be found in the area. Campers may gather firewood. CG is a trailhead to many hiking trails in the area.

GETTING THERE: From Unity go SE approx. 4 mi. on county route 6245 to forest route 1802. Go SE on 1802 approx. 4.5 mi. to Winberry CG.

SINGLE RATE:	Varies	OPEN DATES:	May-Sept
# of SINGLE SITES:	7	MAX SPUR:	14 feet
		MAX STAY:	14 days
		ELEVATION:	1000 feet

78   Yukwah
Upper Soda • lat 44°25'00" lon 122°20'30"

DESCRIPTION: Yukwah CG is located in a second growth douglas fir on the banks of the South Santiam River. Fish and swim in the river. Supplies available in Upper Soda. The Menagerie Wilderness is to the north. Trails in the area.

GETTING THERE: Yukwah CG is located approx. 3 mi. W of Upper Soda on US HWY 20.

SINGLE RATE:	$8	OPEN DATES:	May-Oct
# of SINGLE SITES:	19	MAX SPUR:	28 feet
		MAX STAY:	14 days
		ELEVATION:	1300 feet

 Campground has hosts   **Reservable sites**   **Accessible facilities**   **Fully developed**    **Semi-developed**    **Rustic facilities**

NOTE: Open dates listed are typical. Actual dates are dependent on conditions such as snow pack.

USFS Photo

WINEMA
NATIONAL FOREST

The 1.1 million acre Winema National Forest lies on the eastern slopes of the Cascade Mountain Range in South Central Oregon. The Forest is located in the heart of "Klamath Country" which is known for its blue skies and year-round sunshine.

The Winema National Forest borders Crater Lake National Park near the crest of the Cascades and stretches eastward into the Klamath River Basin. Near the floor of the Basin the Forest gives way to vast marshes and meadows associated with Upper Klamath Lake and the Williamson River. To the north and east, extensive stands of ponderosa and lodgepole pine grow on deep pumice and ash. The pumice and ash blanketed the area during the eruption of Mt. Mazama (now called Crater Lake) nearly 7,000 years ago.

The Winema National Forest is named for a heroine of the Modoc War of 1872. Wi-ne-ma served as an interpreter and peace-maker between U.S. Troops and the Modoc Indians, saving many lives.

A wide array of recreation opportunities are available, ranging from the solitude of hiking a Wilderness trail to family activities in a social, developed setting at Lake of the Woods or Miller Lake.

Winema National Forest • (541) 883-6714

1 Aspen Point
Klamath Falls • lat 42°23'05" lon 122°12'45"

DESCRIPTION: In an old growth forest with view of Lake of the Woods and Cascade Mountains. Fish for trout and bass from shore or boat. Supplies .5 mi. at store. Mild weather. Deer and small wildlife. Firewood may be gathered or purchased. Hike Brown Mountain and Mountain Lakes Wilderness. Mosquitos in early season.

GETTING THERE: From Klamath Falls go NW on HWY 140 approx. 33 mi. to forest route 3704. Go S on 3704 approx. 1.5 mi. to Aspen Point CG.

SINGLE RATE:	$12	OPEN DATES:	May-Sept
# of SINGLE SITES:	61		
		MAX STAY:	14 days
		ELEVATION:	4950 feet

6 Head of the River
Chiloquin • lat 42°43'54" lon 121°25'10"

DESCRIPTION: In a pine forest setting around springs. Fishing for trout in nearby Williamson River. Supplies in Chiloquin approximately 27 miles away. Campers may gather firewood. ATV and mountain bike trails nearby. Tent only camping.

GETTING THERE: From Chiloquin on county route 858 approx. 5 mi. to Williamson River Road. Continue on Williamson River Road approx. 20 mi. to Head of the River CG.

SINGLE RATE:	No fee	OPEN DATES:	June-Sept
# of SINGLE SITES:	5		
		MAX STAY:	14 days
		ELEVATION:	4200 feet

2 Chemult (Walt Haring)
Chemult • lat 43°13'30" lon 121°47'15"

DESCRIPTION: Close to Chemult in second growth lodgepole forest with views of Cascade Mountains. Cool all year with deep snow in winter. Fish and boat 12 mi. W on Miller Lake. Supplies 1mi. at Chemult. Deer, elk, small wildlife. Light use. Gather firewood locally. Hike and bike trails. Cross-country and snowmobile in winter. No water in winter.

GETTING THERE: From Chemult go NW on HWY 97 for 1/2 mi. to forest route 9772. Go W on 9772 for 1/2 mi. to Chemult CG.

SINGLE RATE:	No fee	OPEN DATES:	Yearlong
# of SINGLE SITES:	5		
		MAX STAY:	14 days
		ELEVATION:	4750 feet

7 Jackson Creek
Diamond Junction • lat 42°58'55" lon 121°27'25"

DESCRIPTION: Sits along a small, marshy creek in an old growth and second growth lodgepole and pine forest. Jackson Creek nearby. Supplies available at Sand Creek Store approximately 27 miles W. Campers may gather firewood. Yamsi Mountain trailhead is nearby.

GETTING THERE: From Diamond Junction go S on US HWY 97 approx. 15 mi. to primary forest route 76 (county route 676). Go NE on 76 approx. 22 mi. to primary forest route 49. Go E on 49 approx. 5 mi. to Jackson Creek CG.

SINGLE RATE:	No fee	OPEN DATES:	Yearlong*
# of SINGLE SITES:	12	MAX SPUR:	30 feet
		MAX STAY:	14 days
		ELEVATION:	4600 feet

3 Corral Spring
Chemult • lat 43°15'30" lon 121°48'00"

DESCRIPTION: Lodepole pine forest setting with meadow. Walker Rim and Cascade Mountains are visisble from CG. Supplies are 4 miles away at Chemult. Campers may gather firewood. Numerous trails nearby.

GETTING THERE: From Chemult go N on US HWY 97 approx. 2 mi. to forest route 9774. Go W on 9774 approx. 2.5 mi. to Corral Spring CG.

SINGLE RATE:	No fee	OPEN DATES:	June-Oct
# of SINGLE SITES:	6	MAX SPUR:	35 feet
		MAX STAY:	14 days
		ELEVATION:	4900 feet

8 Odessa
Odessa • lat 42°25'47" lon 122°03'34"

DESCRIPTION: Among pine and fir on Klamath Lake with views of Cascade Mountains. Hot by mid-summer. Boat trout fish on U. Klamath L. Supplies at nearby stores on HWY 140. Deer and small wildlife. Light use. Gather firewood locally. Expect midges and mosquitos. No drinking water. Snow may close area.

GETTING THERE: From Odessa go SE on state HWY 140 approx. 1/2 mi. to Odessa CG.

SINGLE RATE:	No fee	OPEN DATES:	Yearlong
# of SINGLE SITES:	5		
		MAX STAY:	14 days
		ELEVATION:	4100 feet

4 Digit Point
Chemult • lat 43°13'42" lon 121°57'52"

DESCRIPTION: Open pine and fir stand with views of Miller Lake and Cascade Mountains. Several species of trout and Kokanee salmon fishable at Miller Lake. Supplies are 12 miles away at Chemult. Campers may gather firewood. Numerous trails nearby. CG has boat ramp and fish cleaning station.

GETTING THERE: From Chemult go W on forest route 9772 approx. 12 mi. to Digit Point CG.

SINGLE RATE:	$9	OPEN DATES:	June-Sept
# of SINGLE SITES:	64	MAX SPUR:	35 feet
		MAX STAY:	14 days
		ELEVATION:	5675 feet

9 Scott Creek
Diamond Junction • lat 42°53'05" lon 121°55'25"

DESCRIPTION: CG is in a forest setting. Some fishing in nearby Scott Creek. Historic railroad logging area. Supplies 25 mi. N. Deer and small wildlife. Light use 'til fall, hunting brings moderate use. Gather firewood locally. Bike, hike and ATV roads. Prepare for mosquitos.

GETTING THERE: From Diamond Junction go S on US HWY 97 15 mi. to county route 3104. Go W on 3104 3.5 mi. to forest route 2308. Go W on 2308 2 mi. to forest route 060. Go N on 060 1.5 mi. to Scott Creek CG.

SINGLE RATE:	No fee	OPEN DATES:	Yearlong*
# of SINGLE SITES:	6	MAX SPUR:	25 feet
		MAX STAY:	14 days
		ELEVATION:	4640 feet

5 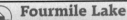 Fourmile Lake
Odessa • lat 42°27'20" lon 122°14'50"

DESCRIPTION: Among lodgepole pine with mountain views and boat or shore trout fishing on nearby lake. Supplies at store 7 mi. S. Deer and small wildlife are common. Light use. Gather firewood. Horse and hiking trails to Sky Lakes Wilderness. Mosquitos are ferocious June-Aug. No water after Labor Day.

GETTING THERE: From Odessa go NW on state HWY 140 approx. 9 mi. to forest route 3661. Go N on 3661 approx. 5 mi. to Fourmile Lake CG.

SINGLE RATE:	$9	OPEN DATES:	July-Sept
# of SINGLE SITES:	25		
		MAX STAY:	14 days
		ELEVATION:	5800 feet

10   Sunset
Odessa • lat 42°22'00" lon 122°12'20"

DESCRIPTION: Located in old-growth forest with view of lake and Cascade Mountains. Noon rains, mosquitoes in early summer. Shore or boat fish for bass and trout. Supplies at store 1 mi. Deer and small wildlife. Moderate use. Firewood may be gathered or bought. Hike Brown Mountain and Mountain Lakes Wilderness.

GETTING THERE: From Odessa go W on state HWY 140 approx. 9 mi. to forest route 3704. Go S on 3704 approx. 3.5 mi. to Sunset CG.

SINGLE RATE:	$12	OPEN DATES:	June-Sept
# of SINGLE SITES:	67		
		MAX STAY:	14 days
		ELEVATION:	4950 feet

 Campground has hosts   Reservable sites   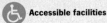 Accessible facilities   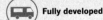 Fully developed   Semi-developed   Rustic facilities

NOTE: Open dates listed are typical. Actual dates are dependent on conditions such as snow pack.

11 **Williamson River**
Pine Ridge • lat 42°39'35" lon 121°50'55"

DESCRIPTION: Set in a ponderosa pine forest with views of the Williamson River. Fly fishing for rainbow trout in the river. Collier State Park logging museum is located 1 mi. W of CG. Supplies are 4 mi. at Chiloquin. Camper may gather firewood. Trails are nearby. CG has a fish cleaning station.

GETTING THERE: From Pine Ridge go N on US HWY 97 approx. 3 mi. to forest route 9730. Go NE on 9730 approx. 1.5 mi. to Williamson River CG.

SINGLE RATE:	$8	OPEN DATES:	June-Sept
# of SINGLE SITES:	10		
		MAX STAY:	14 days
		ELEVATION:	4200 feet

Mount St. Helens

In the 20 years since its eruption, an amazing recovery has taken place in an area that President Carter once called a "moonscape." Plants, animals and fish have recolonized the area and streams and ecosystems  have returned to life. If you would like to learn more about Mount St. Helens, visit these web sites: www.fs.fed.us/gpnf or www.vulcan.wr.usgs.gov.

 Campground has hosts   **Reservable sites**   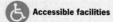 **Accessible facilities**   **Fully developed**   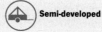 **Semi-developed**   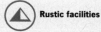 **Rustic facilities**

NOTE: Open dates listed are typical. Actual dates are dependent on conditions such as snow pack.

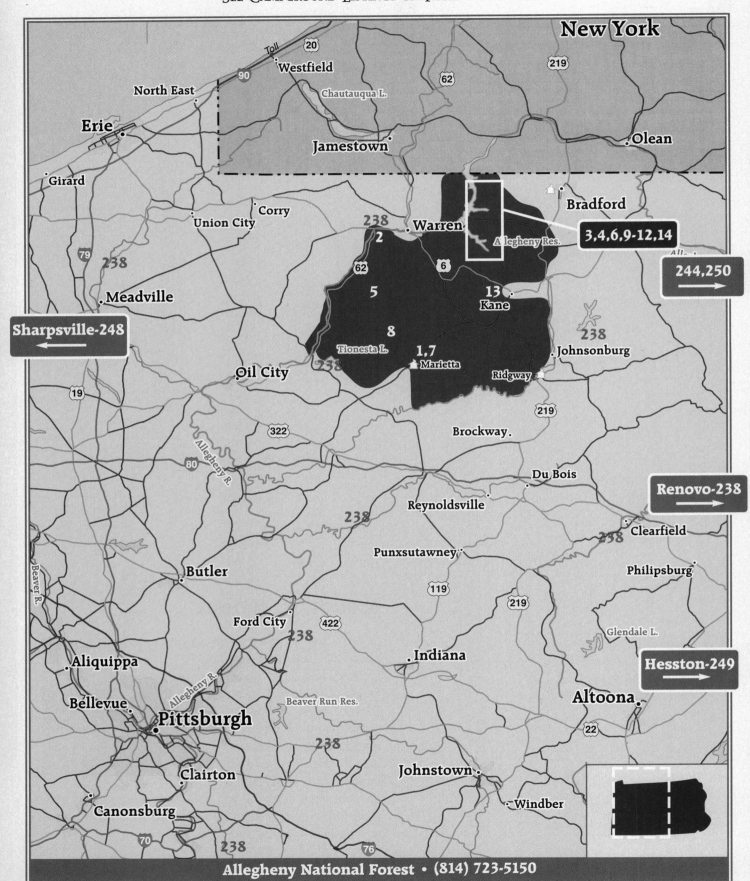

New York

Toll 20

Westfield

North East

Chautauqua L.

219

Erie

62

Girard

Jamestown

Olean

Corry

238

Bradford

Union City

Warren

2

3,4,6,9-12,14

Allegheny Res.

79

238

62

6

244,250

Meadville

5

13

Kane

Sharpsville-248

8

238

Tionesta L.

Johnsonburg

Oil City

238

1,7

Marietta

19

Ridgway

322

Brockway.

219

Allegheny R.

80

Du Bois

Renovo-238

Reynoldsville

Clearfield

238

238

Punxsutawney

Philipsburg

Butler

119

Ford City

422

238

219

Glendale L.

Aliquippa

Indiana

Hesston-249

Beaver R.

Allegheny R.

Bellevue

Beaver Run Res.

Altoona

PITTSBURGH

238

22

Clairton

Johnstown

Canonsburg

Windber

70

238

76

Robert Szaro Photo, USDA Forest Service

ALLEGHENY NATIONAL FOREST

The Allegheny National Forest is one of 15 national forests in the eastern United States and the only national forest in Pennsylvania. Located in the rugged plateau country of the northwestern part of the state, the Allegheny consists of over 513,000 acres. Many creeks and streams cut deeply into the plateau, creating a rolling and sometimes steep topography ranging from 1046 feet to 2263 feet above sea level.

Recreation opportunities abound in the Allegheny. One of the many features of the forest is the 27-mile long Allegheny Reservoir. You'll enjoy swimming, fishing, boating, water skiing, hiking and camping. To those who enjoy a leisurely scenic drive, dirt bikers, ATVers, mountain bikers and snowmobilers will love the loop trails that wind through the hills. Foot trails ranging from one-half mile interpretive trails to the 87-mile North Country National Scenic Trail traverse the terrain.

Several reservoirs and over 700 miles of streams offer outstanding fishing opportunities. Over 70 species of fish are present throughout the forest. The state record Northern Pike and walleye were taken from the Allegheny Reservoir.

The Allegheny is also home to more than 300 species of mammals which provides excellent opportunity for hunting or wildlife-viewing. The vast expanse of the Hickory Creek Wilderness and the unique Allegheny Islands Wilderness, (the smallest wilderness in the U.S.) offer great opportunities for primitive recreation.

---

1 **Beaver Meadows**
Marienville • lat 41°31'22" lon 079°06'24"

DESCRIPTION: In pine wood overstory on a manmade lake. Quiet refuge for blue herons, ducks, beavers and other wildlife. Fish from bank or boat for various species (no motors), or fish Salmon Creek nearby. Gather own firewood. Hike nearby trails. Historic tornado zone. WPA (1936) built dam.

GETTING THERE: From Marienville go N on forest road 128 (N Forest St) approx. 5 mi. to Beavers Meadows CG.

SINGLE RATE:	$9	OPEN DATES:	Apr-Dec
# of SINGLE SITES:	38		
		MAX STAY:	14 days
		ELEVATION:	1675 feet

2 **Buckaloons**
Warren • lat 41°50'19" lon 079°15'30"

DESCRIPTION: On Allegheny banks, the historic site of an Indian trading post and Indian village. Canoeing and boat launch. Dump station and 15 sites with electric hookups. Play area. Gather dead wood for fires. Supplies in Warren. Hike the one-mile Buckaloons Seneca Interpretive Trail.

GETTING THERE: From Warren go W on US HWY 6/62 approx. 3 mi. to Buckaloons CG.

SINGLE RATE:	$10	OPEN DATES:	May-Oct
# of SINGLE SITES:	51		
GROUP RATE:	$40	MAX STAY:	14 days
# of GROUP SITES:	1	ELEVATION:	1500 feet

3 **Dewdrop**
Kane • lat 41°49'55" lon 078°57'34"

DESCRIPTION: In the midst of a hardwood forest on the banks of Kinzua Bay, Allegheny Reservoir. Small boat launch, hot showers and dump station, play area. Gather own dead wood for fire. Some walk-in sites on water. Walk, hike nearby. Wildlife includes many bird species. Near Kinzua Beach and Bay.

GETTING THERE: From Kane go N on state route 321 approx. 6 mi. to Longhouse National Scenic Drive (LNSD). Go N on LNSD approx. 4 mi. to Dewdrop CG.

SINGLE RATE:	$14	OPEN DATES:	May-Sept
# of SINGLE SITES:	74		
		MAX STAY:	14 days
		ELEVATION:	1380 feet

4 **Handsome Lake**
Kane • lat 41°55'21" lon 078°55'49"

DESCRIPTION: A hike-in or boat-in area on the Allegheny Reservoir with fishing, skiing and boating. Parking fee. Gather firewood. No services, no water. Supplies in Kane.

GETTING THERE: From Kane go NW on state route 321 approx. 18 mi. to junction with 59. Continue NW on 321 approx. 8 mi. to Tracy Ridge CG. Hike SW approx. 4 mi. to Handsome Lake CG.

SINGLE RATE:	No fee	OPEN DATES:	Yearlong
# of SINGLE SITES:	8		
		MAX STAY:	14 days
		ELEVATION:	1380 feet

5 **Hearts Content**
Warren • lat 41°41'28" lon 079°15'35"

DESCRIPTION: A National Scenic Area in old growth forest. A National Natural Landmark site with 300-400 year old white pine, hemlock and beech trees. Built in 1936 by CCC's. Short barrier-free trail. Open play area. Wildlife viewing. Dump station. Supplies in Warren. Hiking access to Hickory Creek Wilderness.

GETTING THERE: Hearts Content CG is located just N of the town of Hearts Content.

SINGLE RATE:	$7	OPEN DATES:	May-Oct
# of SINGLE SITES:	26		
GROUP RATE:	$40	MAX STAY:	14 days
# of GROUP SITES:	1	ELEVATION:	1920 feet

 Campground has hosts   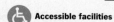 **Reservable sites**   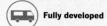 **Accessible facilities**   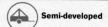 **Fully developed**   **Semi-developed**   ▲ **Rustic facilities**

NOTE: Open dates listed are typical. Actual dates are dependent on conditions such as snow pack.

6 Hooks Brook
Warren • lat 41°57'45" lon 078°56'30"

DESCRIPTION: Hike-in or boat-in sites only on west bank of Allegheny Reservoir with skiing, boating and fishing. Gather firewood locally. Moderate use. Wildlife opportunities. Supplies in Warren. Primitive camping, no services, no water.

GETTING THERE: From Warren go N on Allegheny Reservoir Scenic Drive approx. 10 mi. to Red Oak CG. From Red Oak CG hike in approx. 3 mi. to Hooks Brook CG.

SINGLE RATE:	No fee	OPEN DATES:	Yearlong
# of SINGLE SITES:	20		
		MAX STAY:	14 days
		ELEVATION:	1340 feet

11 Red Bridge
Kane • lat 41°46'45" lon 078°53'16"

DESCRIPTION: Among thin trees on shores of Allegheny Reservoir. Hot showers, dump station and playground. Gather dead wood for fires. Supplies in Kane. Historic CCC site. 1/4 mi. to North Country National Scenic Tril. Red Bridge Bank Fishing Area is handicap accessible.

GETTING THERE: From Kane go NW on state route 321 approx. 9 mi. to Red Bridge CG.

SINGLE RATE:	$14	OPEN DATES:	Apr-Dec
# of SINGLE SITES:	55		
		MAX STAY:	14 days
		ELEVATION:	1380 feet

7 Loleta
Marienville • lat 41°24'16" lon 079°04'47"

DESCRIPTION: On site of old mill town built by CCC's. Private sites, some with electricity. Bathhouse at beach has hot showers. Ampitheater, volleyball court. Fish and canoe Millstone Creek and Clarion River approx. 4 mi. S. Hike to scenic overlook of Millstone Valley. Limited services Sept 7-May 28.

GETTING THERE: From Marienville go S approx. 6 mi. on state route 27027 to Loleta CG.

SINGLE RATE:	Varies	OPEN DATES:	Apr-Dec
# of SINGLE SITES:	37	MAX SPUR:	50 feet
		MAX STAY:	14 days
		ELEVATION:	1400 feet

12 Tracy Ridge
Kane • lat 41°56'35" lon 078°52'40"

DESCRIPTION: On ridge set in thin trees on shores of Allegheny Reservoir. Hot showers, dump station and playground. 5/28-9/27 is full season. Limited services off season. Gather dead wood for fires. Tracy Ridge Hiking Trails system leads to reservoir and links up with North Country National Scenic Trail.

GETTING THERE: From Kane go NW on state route 321 approx. 18 mi. to junction with 59. Continue NW on 321 approx. 8 mi. to Tracy Ridge CG.

SINGLE RATE:	$7	OPEN DATES:	Apr-Dec
# of SINGLE SITES:	119		
GROUP RATE:	$45	MAX STAY:	14 days
# of GROUP SITES:	3	ELEVATION:	2225 feet

8 Minister Creek
Sheffield • lat 41°37'15" lon 079°09'13"

DESCRIPTION: Fish Minister or Tionesta Creeks for small trout. Excellent fishing and hunting as well as hiking nearby. Gather dead wood for fire. Hike Minister Creek Trail, a 6 mi. loop, which joins North Country National Scenic Trail.

GETTING THERE: From Mayburg go NE on state HWY 666 5 mi. to Minister. Minister Creek CG is located just north of town.

SINGLE RATE:	$7	OPEN DATES:	Apr-Dec
# of SINGLE SITES:	6		
		MAX STAY:	14 days
		ELEVATION:	1500 feet

13 Twin Lakes
Kane • lat 41°36'41" lon 078°45'20"

DESCRIPTION: Fish and swim in the lake. Hoffman Run, a CCC built dam, nearby. Multiple barrier-free areas and trails. Showers, beach house, fishing piers, playground and dump station. Gather firewood. Hiking access to Black Cherry National Recreation Interpretive Trail and Brush Hollow system. Group sites open 5/28 - 9/7.

GETTING THERE: From Kane go S on state route 321 8 miles to forest route 191. Go W on 191 approx. 2 miles to Twin Lakes CG. Trailer and RV height limit of 10' due to RR underpass.

SINGLE RATE:	$13	OPEN DATES:	Apr-Dec
# of SINGLE SITES:	50	MAX SPUR:	28 feet
GROUP RATE:	$45	MAX STAY:	14 days
# of GROUP SITES:	2	ELEVATION:	1900 feet

9 Morrison
Kane • lat 41°49'16" lon 078°55'44"

DESCRIPTION: Hike-in or boat-in site on east shore of Allegheny Reservoir (Kinzua Bay) with skiing, boating and fishing. Quiet with wildlife opportunites and hiking nearby. Gather own firewood. No services, no water.

GETTING THERE: From Warren go E on state HWY 59 approx. 6 mi. to forest route 454. Go W on 454 to parking area. Hike S approx. 2 mi. to Morrison CG.

SINGLE RATE:	No fee	OPEN DATES:	Yearlong
# of SINGLE SITES:	40		
		MAX STAY:	14 days
		ELEVATION:	1380 feet

14 Willow Bay
Bradford • lat 41°58'21" lon 078°55'04"

DESCRIPTION: Overlooking Willow Bay of Allegheny Reservoir in wooded and open area. Boat launch for skiing and fishing. Showers and dump station. Walks and hikes provide wildlife viewing. Access to North Country National Scenic Trail south of CG.

GETTING THERE: From Kane go S state route 321 8 miles to forest route 191. Go W on 191 approx. 2 mi. to Willow Bay CG.

SINGLE RATE:	$12	OPEN DATES:	May-Sept
# of SINGLE SITES:	68		
		MAX STAY:	14 days
		ELEVATION:	2006 feet

10 Pine Grove
Warren • lat 41°52'25" lon 078°56'44"

DESCRIPTION: Hike-in or boat-in to E shore of Allegheny Reservoir. Fee for parking. Ski, boat, fish or view wildlife. No services, no water. Gather own firewood.

GETTING THERE: From Warren go E on state HWY 59 approx. 10 mi. to forest route 146. Go NW on 147 approx. 2 mi. to Pine Grove CG.

SINGLE RATE:	No fee	OPEN DATES:	Yearlong
# of SINGLE SITES:	15		
		MAX STAY:	14 days
		ELEVATION:	1400 feet

Campground has hosts   **Reservable sites**   **Accessible facilities**    **Fully developed**   **Semi-developed**   **Rustic facilities**

INTRODUCING A SUPERIOR GAS GRILL FROM THE LEADING BRAND IN OUTDOOR COOKING.
It has a burner system so advanced, it outperforms the leading competition. A more evenly heated cooking surface creates fewer hot spots and less flare-ups for more consistent cooking and better meals. www.bbqhq.com

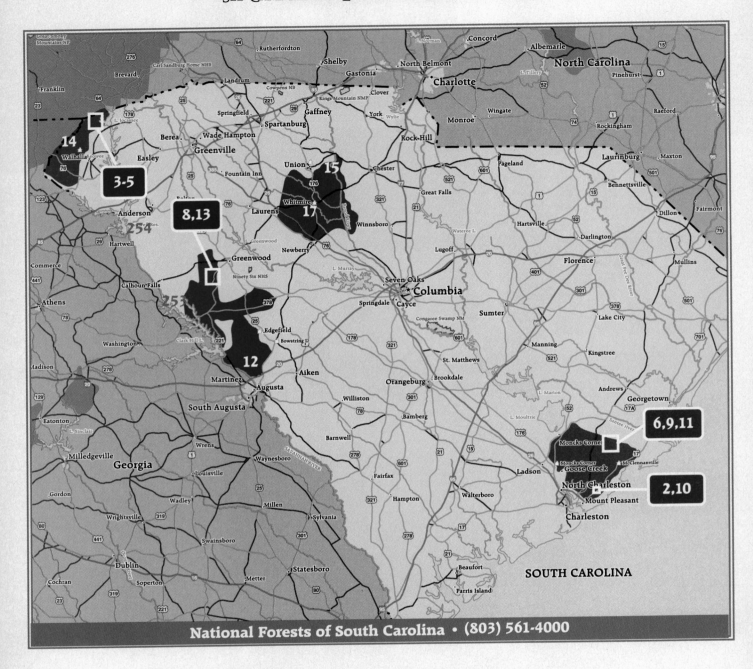

National Forests of South Carolina • (803) 561-4000

USFS Photo

NATIONAL FORESTS OF SOUTH CAROLINA

Mountain waterfalls, a challenging whitewater river, a forest thriving on old cotton fields, and another one recovering from the devastation of Hurricane Hugo—visitors to the Francis Marion and Sumter National Forests can see and experience all of these things—and much more.

Headquartered in the capital city of Columbia, both forests are managed for many uses, including watershed protection and improvement, habitat for wildlife and fish species and outdoor recreation.

The 360,000-acre Sumter National Forest was established in 1936. Named for Revolutionary War General Thomas Sumter, this national forest provides some of South Carolina's best hunting for deer and turkey, as well as for smaller species, including squirrels and rabbits. Lakes and streams offer good opportunities for bass, bream and bluegill fishing. The Chatooga Wild and Scenic River is a favorite of whitewater rafters and kayakers and miles of wilderness offer the trekker solitude.

The Francis Marion, named after another Revolutionary War general, provides excellent opportunities for hunting, fishing, hiking and camping. The Swamp Fox National Recreation Trail offers 20 miles of trails for hikers, bikers and horseback riders. The Francis Marion is a year-round paradise for anglers. Its rivers, ponds, and streams and the Intracoastal Waterway offer good fishing. Other points of interest within the forest are the Hampton Plantation and The Battery, an L-shaped Civil War fort, built to prevent Union gunboats from moving up the Santee River.

1 — Brick House
Whitmire • lat 34°26'51" lon 081°42'25"

DESCRIPTION: This CG is located in a mixed forest setting. Creeks and streams run nearby for fishing and swimming. Abundant wildlife populations provide some of the most desirable hunting areas in the upstate. Campers may gather firewood. The Buncombe Horse Trail is nearby. CG has horse stalls.

GETTING THERE: From Whitmire go SW on state HWY 66 approx. 6.5 mi. to forest route 358. Go S on 358 approx. 1/2 mi. to Brick House CG.

SINGLE RATE:	$5	OPEN DATES:	Yearlong
# of SINGLE SITES:	23	MAX SPUR:	36 feet
		MAX STAY:	14 days
		ELEVATION:	550 feet

2 — Buck Hall
Charleston • lat 33°02'15" lon 079°33'46"

DESCRIPTION: This CG is in an open, park-like area with some hardwoods. Spectacular views of the Cape Romain Nat'l Wildlife Refuge and the Atlantic Intracoastal Waterway. Fish for fresh and saltwater fish, shrimp, and crab. Interpretive sites and trails in area. RV dump station and boat ramp on site.

GETTING THERE: From Charleston go N on US HWY 17 approx. 30 mi. to Buck Hall Landing Road(forest route 242). Go E on Buck Hall Landing Road approx. 1 mi. to Buck Hall CG.

SINGLE RATE:	$15	OPEN DATES:	Yearlong
# of SINGLE SITES:	14		
		MAX STAY:	14 days
		ELEVATION:	10 feet

3 — Burrells Ford
Walhalla • lat 34°58'07" lon 083°07'08"

DESCRIPTION: This is a, hike-in tent only, primitive CG. CG lies in a mixed forest setting on the Chattooga River. Fish for Brown Trout or swim from the river. Supplies are available at Walhalla. Deer, bears, turkeys, squirrels and birds are common to the area. No designated trail in the CG area.

GETTING THERE: From Walhalla go N on state HWY 28 approx. 15.5 mi. to forest route 708. Go W on 708 approx. 2 mi. to Burrells Ford CG.

SINGLE RATE:	No fee	OPEN DATES:	Yearlong
		MAX STAY:	14 days
		ELEVATION:	2030 feet

4 — Cassidy Bridge Hunt Camp
Walhalla • lat 34°47'09" lon 083°12'37"

DESCRIPTION: This primitive camp is located in a wooded area along the banks of the Chauga River. The Chauga is a popular fishing stream. Supplies available at Walhalla. Numerous wildlife in the area. No designated trails close to CG. Watch out for usual dangers such as poisonous snakes and stinging insects.

GETTING THERE: From Walhalla go NW on state HWY 28 approx. 5.5 mi. to state HWY 193. Go W on 193 approx. 1.5 mi. to state HWY 290. Go SW on 290 approx. 4.5 mi. to Cassidy Bridge Hunt Camp.

		OPEN DATES:	Yearlong
GROUP RATE:	$30	MAX STAY:	14 days
# of GROUP SITES:	1	ELEVATION:	1230 feet

5 — Cherry Hill
Walhalla • lat 34°56'28" lon 083°05'07"

DESCRIPTION: CG is in a mixed forest setting with a small creek running nearby. This wilderness creek is a beautiful attraction for sight and sound. Deer, bears and birds are common to the area. Campers may gather firewood. The Foothills Trail runs close to the CG. RV dump station at CG.

GETTING THERE: From Walhalla go N on state HWY 28 approx. 14.5 mi. to Cherry Hill CG.

SINGLE RATE:	$10	OPEN DATES:	Apr-Oct*
# of SINGLE SITES:	29		
		MAX STAY:	14 days
		ELEVATION:	2320 feet

 Campground has hosts　 **Reservable sites**　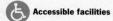 **Accessible facilities**　 **Fully developed**　 **Semi-developed**　 **Rustic facilities**

NOTE: Open dates listed are typical. Actual dates are dependent on conditions such as snow pack.

6 Elmwood
McClellanville • lat 33˚10'30" lon 079˚30'00"

DESCRIPTION: This CG is well shaded by hardwoods draped with spanish moss. Popular during deer and turkeys hunting season. Summers are hot. Visit nearby Hampton Plantation State Park and the Battery Warren Interpretive Trail. Campers may gather dead and down firewood. Supplies in McClellanville.

GETTING THERE: From McClellanville go NE on state HWY 9S approx. 5.5 mi. to state HWY 857-S (Rutledge Road). Go NW on 857-S approx. 3.5 mi. to forest route 211. Go N on 211 approx. 1/2 mi. to Elmwood CG.

SINGLE RATE:	No fee	OPEN DATES:	Yearlong
		MAX STAY:	14 days
		ELEVATION:	13 feet

7 Enoree Hunt Camps
Whitmire • lat ˚'" lon ˚'"

DESCRIPTION: There are numerous hunt camps in a deep forest setting located on the Enoree Ranger District. For more information on these camps, please contact: Enoree Ranger District office-(803) 637-5396.

GETTING THERE:

		OPEN DATES:	Yearlong*
GROUP RATE:		MAX STAY:	14 days

8 Fell Seasonal Camp
Greenwood • lat 34˚05'35" lon 082˚17'32"

DESCRIPTION: Situated in pine and hardwood, this primitive hunt camp has loop and linear sites with a centrally-located water source and pit toilets. The surrounding forest environment sustains abundant wildlife. Several stores are nearby. Trails in area. Water source for horses Ample parking for stock trailers

GETTING THERE: From Greenwood go S on state HWY 10 approx. 7.7 mi. to state HWY 47. Go W on 47 approx. 2.4 mi. to Fell Seasonal Camp.

SINGLE RATE:	$5	OPEN DATES:	Yearlong
		MAX STAY:	14 days
		ELEVATION:	550 feet

9 Guilliard Lake
Palmerville • lat 33˚17'11" lon 079˚37'13"

DESCRIPTION: This recreation area is on the bluff of an oxbow on the Santee River. CG is bordered by the Santee River floodplain forest. The recreation area offers a primitive boat landing, access to the 5-acre Guilliard Lake, and a nearby interpretive trail. Supplies 20 mi. at McClellanville. Summer days are hot.

GETTING THERE: From Palmerville go NE on forest route 150 (Guillard Lake Road) approx. 1.5 mi. to forest route 150-G. Go NE on 150-G approx. 2 mi. to Guiliard Lake CG. High clearance vehicles required.

SINGLE RATE:	No fee	OPEN DATES:	Yearlong
		MAX STAY:	14 days
		ELEVATION:	16 feet

10 Halfway Creek
Charleston • lat 33˚03'26" lon 079˚41'37"

DESCRIPTION: This dispersed CG rests in a stand of mixed loblolly and longleaf pine trees. Summers are hot and humid. Wildlife includes songbirds and foxes. Campers may gather dead and down firewood. Expect biting bugs/ticks in spring and summer. Water may not be potable, bring your purifier. Hike adjacent Palmetto Trail.

GETTING THERE: From Charleston go N on US HWY 17 15 mi. to state HWY 133S (Steed Creek Road). Go W on 133S approx. 5 mi. to forest route 200 (Halfway Creek Road). Go S on 200 1 mi. to Halfway Creek CG.

SINGLE RATE:	No fee	OPEN DATES:	Yearlong
		MAX STAY:	14 days
		ELEVATION:	50 feet

11 Honey Hill
Honey Hill • lat 33˚10'27" lon 079˚33'45"

DESCRIPTION: This primitive camping facility is located between McClellanville and Honey Hill. A short camp loop swings through an upland pine/oak forest and encircles a fire lookout tower which is no longer in use. Hiking and biking trails in area. Supplies 12 mi. at McClellanville. Summers are hot.

GETTING THERE: From Honey Hill go E on state HWY 45S (French Santee Road) 3 mi. to forest route 219. Go SW on 219 1/2 mi. to Honey Hill CG. Road is narrow with sharp curves. Large vehicles should use caution.

SINGLE RATE:	No fee	OPEN DATES:	Yearlong
		MAX STAY:	14 days
		ELEVATION:	28 feet

12 Lick Fork Lake
Edgefield • lat 33˚43'34" lon 082˚02'28"

DESCRIPTION: A heavily wooded CG on Lick Fork Lake. Fish for bass, bream and catfish from the lake. Boat ramp, for non-motorized boats, at CG. Deer, turkeys, raccoons and birds are common to the area. The Lick Fork Lake Hiking Trail originates at the swimming area and travels around the lake.

GETTING THERE: From Edgefield go S on state HWY 23 approx. 8.2 mi. to state HWY 230. Go S on 230 approx. 2 mi. to forest route 640. Go SE on 640 approx. 2.5 mi. to Lick Fork Lake CG.

SINGLE RATE:	$8	OPEN DATES:	Apr-Dec
# of SINGLE SITES:	10	MAX SPUR:	30 feet
		MAX STAY:	14 days
		ELEVATION:	400 feet

13 Parsons Mountain Lake
Abbeville • lat 34˚06'00" lon 082˚21'16"

DESCRIPTION: In a heavily-wooded setting on Parsons Mountain Lake. Fish for bass, bream and catfish from the lake. Boat ramp located at CG. Deer, turkeys, raccoons and birds are common to the area. Supplies available at Abbeville. A 1/2 mile interpretive trail originates at the swimming area.

GETTING THERE: From Abbeville go S on state HWY 28 approx. 2.1 mi. to state HWY 251. Go SE on 251 approx. 1.5 mi. to forest route 514. Go S on 514 approx. 1 mi. to Parson's Mountain Lake CG.

SINGLE RATE:	$8	OPEN DATES:	May-Oct
# of SINGLE SITES:	23	MAX SPUR:	30 feet
		MAX STAY:	14 days
		ELEVATION:	460 feet

14 Whetstone Horse Camp
Walhalla • lat 34˚50'00" lon 083˚09'00"

DESCRIPTION: In a mixed forest setting just off the Chatooga River. Fish for Brown Trout from the river. Deer, bears, turkeys and birds are common to the area. This CG is by reservation only. Busiest times are summer and fall. The Chattooga Trail is nearby. CG has hitching posts for horses.

GETTING THERE: From Walhalla go N 6 mi. on state HWY 28. Go left at Whetstone Road. Go straight at the four way stop. Pavement will end. A sign for Whetstone Horse Camp will be on the left about 3/4 mile down the gravel road.

SINGLE RATE:	$15	OPEN DATES:	Yearlong
# of SINGLE SITES:	20	MAX STAY:	14 days
		ELEVATION:	1680 feet

15 Woods Ferry Recreation Area
Lockhart • lat 34˚42'02" lon 081˚27'03"

DESCRIPTION: CG lies within a beautiful wooded flood plain, surrounded by a maturing hardwood forest. Broad River runs nearby with a boat launch and fishing on the river. Supplies available at Lockhart. Numerous wildlife in the area. Horse trail access nearby. Horse stalls located within CG area.

GETTING THERE: From Lockhart go S 3.5 mi. on state HWY 9 to state HWY 49. Go S 2 mi. on 49 to forest route 305. Go SW 3 mi. on 305 to forest route 305F. Go NW 1 mi. on 305F to forest route 309. Go N .5 mi. on 309 to Woods Ferry CG.

SINGLE RATE:	$7	OPEN DATES:	Yearlong
# of SINGLE SITES:	28	MAX SPUR:	28 feet
		MAX STAY:	14 days
		ELEVATION:	500 feet

 Campground has hosts   **Reservable sites**   **Accessible facilities**   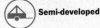 **Fully developed**   **Semi-developed**   **Rustic facilities**

NOTE: Open dates listed are typical. Actual dates are dependent on conditions such as snow pack.

Leaving No Trace: Camping Ethics

Use established Sites. Especially in popular back country.
Stay on good ground. More than 200 feet away from clean water. Respect delicate plant life and pick sites where you won't contribute to erosion.
Use a camping stove instead of a fire. If you must use a fire, collect dead wood and use only existing fire rings .
Return it to nature. leave no litter. Rocks, wood, should be put back where you found it. Erase all traces of fire. Scatter needles or brush over site.
Don't leave your Mark. Take a step back: Is there any thing else you can do to remove any trace of human use?

BLACK HILLS
NATIONAL FOREST

The Black Hills National Forest is located in western South Dakota and northeastern Wyoming. A million-acre island of forested mountains in a vast sea of grass, it rises as much as 4,000 feet above the surrounding prairies. Within its boundaries are rugged canyons, unique rock formations, tumbling streams, and quiet glades.

The name "Black Hills" comes from the Lakota words Paha Sapa, which mean "hills that are black." Indians, such as the Arapaho, Cheyenne, Kiowa and Lakota, came to the Black Hills to seek visions and to purify themselves. The Black Hills were also a sanctuary where tribes at war could meet in peace.

Visitors come to the Black Hills to find relief from the summer sun and winter winds of the plains. Shady campgrounds provide a place to rest after a long day of hiking and fishing. Harney Peak, at 7242 feet above sea level, is the highest point in the United States east of the Rockies. From the summit, one has a panoramic view of parts of South Dakota, Nebraska, Wyoming and Montana as well as the granite formations of the Black Elk Wilderness.

USFS Photo

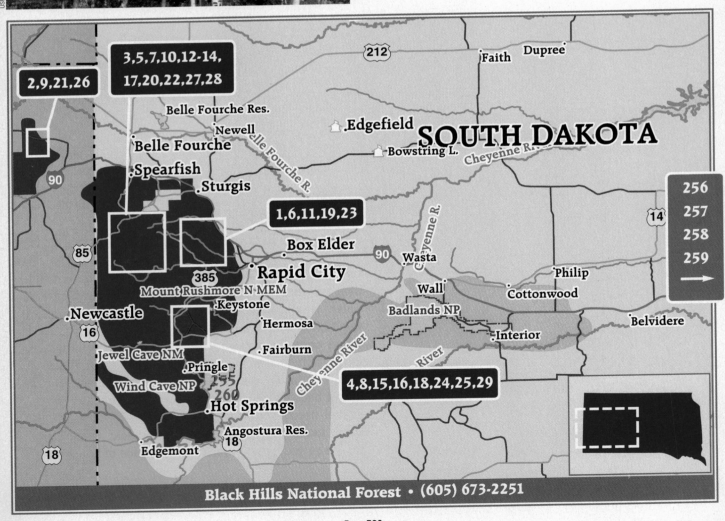

Black Hills National Forest • (605) 673-2251

1 Bear Gulch
Rapid City • lat 44°05'00" lon 103°30'30"

DESCRIPTION: CG is in ponderosa pine with scattered underbrush and is located on the shore of Pactola Reservoir (great fishing and views). Numerous historical sites in area. Supplies 6 mi. to Pactola Marina Store. Various wildlife includes bobcats and mountain lions. Gather firewood locally. Excellent trail opportunities.

GETTING THERE: Bear Gulch CG is located in the Pactola Reservoir Recreation Area off of US HWY 385 approx. 17 mi. W of Rapid City. Not recommended for large vehicles.

		OPEN DATES:	**May-Sept**
		MAX SPUR:	**50 feet**
GROUP RATE:	**$70**	**MAX STAY:**	**14 days**
# of GROUP SITES:	**1**	**ELEVATION:**	**4600 feet**

2 Bearlodge
Sundance • lat 44°39'17" lon 104°19'35"

DESCRIPTION: CG is located in a heavily forested area of ponderosa pine. Not far from Devils Tower, great for day visits. Beaver Springs is nearby. Fish for trout from creek. Historical Custer Expedition Trail nearby. Supplies at Aladdin. Gather firewood locally. Deer, elk, antelope, and turkeys in area.

GETTING THERE: From Sundance go N on I-90 approx. 10 mi. to state HWY 111. Go N on 111 approx. 8 mi. to state HWY 24. Go E on 24 approx. 8 mi. to Bearlodge CG.

SINGLE RATE:	**No fee**	**OPEN DATES:**	**Yearlong***
# of SINGLE SITES:	**8**	**MAX SPUR:**	**25 feet**
		MAX STAY:	**14 days**
		ELEVATION:	**4700 feet**

3 Beaver Creek
Newcastle • lat 44°04'31" lon 104°02'58"

DESCRIPTION: CG is located in an open meadow surrounded by spruce with forest views. Beaver Creek runs adjacent to CG (fishing for brook trout). Wildlife in area includes mule deer, mountain lions, and coyotes. Busy holidays. Short interpretive trail, cross country skiing, and hiking trails in area.

GETTING THERE: From Newcastle go N on US HWY 85 approx. 17 mi. to county route 811. E on 811 approx. 5 mi. to forest route 111. SE on 111 approx. 1 mi. to Beaver Creek CG.

SINGLE RATE:	**$8**	**OPEN DATES:**	**Yearlong***
# of SINGLE SITES:	**8**	**MAX SPUR:**	**45 feet**
		MAX STAY:	**14 days**
		ELEVATION:	**6500 feet**

4 Bismark Lake
Custer • lat 43°46'33" lon 103°30'35"

DESCRIPTION: CG is located in a forested area on Bismark Lake and is adjacent to the Norbeck Wildlife Preserve. Boat ramp and good fishing opportunities on lake (electric motors only). Deer and buffalo can be seen in the area. CG fills June-Aug. Supplies available in Custer. Gather firewood locally.

GETTING THERE: From Custer go E on US HWY 16 approx. 4.5 mi. to Bismark Lake CG.

SINGLE RATE:	**$14**	**OPEN DATES:**	**Yearlong**
# of SINGLE SITES:	**23**	**MAX SPUR:**	**55 feet**
		MAX STAY:	**14 days**
		ELEVATION:	**5300 feet**

5 Black Fox
Rochford • lat 44°08'44" lon 103°50'35"

DESCRIPTION: CG is in a park-like grove of spruce and pine with canyon views. Cool evenings. Great trout fishing at Rhodes Fork Creek which runs through CG. Visit numerous historical sites. Supplies 7 mi. to Rochford. Various wildlife including bobcats and mountain lions. Busy holidays. Gather firewood locally.

GETTING THERE: From Rochford go W on primary forest route 231 approx. 7 mi. to Black Fox CG.

SINGLE RATE:	**No fee**	**OPEN DATES:**	**Yearlong***
# of SINGLE SITES:	**9**	**MAX SPUR:**	**45 feet**
		MAX STAY:	**14 days**
		ELEVATION:	**5900 feet**

6 Boxelder Forks
Nemo • lat 44°11'52" lon 103°32'03"

DESCRIPTION: CG is located in a park-like grove of ponderosa pine and spruce with creek and forest views. Fly fishing in Boxelder Creek which flows through CG. Supplies available 2 mi. away in Nemo. Numerous wildlife. Busy late summer. Gather firewood locally. Centennial Trail nearby.

GETTING THERE: From Nemo go W on forest route 140 approx. 2 mi. to Boxelder Forks CG.

SINGLE RATE:	**$12**	**OPEN DATES:**	**Yearlong**
# of SINGLE SITES:	**14**	**MAX SPUR:**	**45 feet**
		MAX STAY:	**14 days**
		ELEVATION:	**4700 feet**

7 Castle Peak
Rochford • lat 44°04'43" lon 103°43'40"

DESCRIPTION: CG is in a park-like grove of spruce and pine with canyon views. Cool nights and cool days in summer. Great fly fishing for trout in Castle Creek which runs through CG. Visit many historical sites in area. Various wildlife including bobcats and mountain lions. Busy holiday weekends. Gather firewood locally.

GETTING THERE: From Rochford go S on primary forest route 306 approx. 3 mi. to forest route 181. S on 181 approx. 2.5 mi. to Castle Peak CG. 4WD recommended.

SINGLE RATE:	**No fee**	**OPEN DATES:**	**Yearlong***
# of SINGLE SITES:	**9**	**MAX SPUR:**	**45 feet**
		MAX STAY:	**14 days**
		ELEVATION:	**5300 feet**

8 Comanche Park
Custer • lat 43°44'06" lon 103°42'41"

DESCRIPTION: CG is located in a open stand of ponderosa pine. Warm days with cool nights. Weather may change quickly. Wildlife includes deer, mountain lions, and coyotes. Gather firewood locally. Custer State Park is close for a day visit. Jewel Cave National Monument is approx. 6 mi. west of CG.

GETTING THERE: From Custer go W on US HWY approx. 16 mi. to Comanche Park CG.

SINGLE RATE:	**$10**	**OPEN DATES:**	**Yearlong**
# of SINGLE SITES:	**34**	**MAX SPUR:**	**55 feet**
		MAX STAY:	**14 days**
		ELEVATION:	**5100 feet**

9 Cook Lake
Sundance • lat 44°35'30" lon 104°24'27"

DESCRIPTION: CG in an open and park-like setting of ponderosa pine, aspen, and oak with grassy meadows. Fish for trout and sun fish at Cook Lake and Beaver Creek nearby. Historical Devils Tower National Monument nearby. Supplies at Sundance. Deer, elk, turkeys, and beavers in area. Cliff Swallow Nature Trail by CG.

GETTING THERE: From Sundance go W on forest route 843 (Warren Peark turnoff). (Follow signs to Cook Lake Rec Area). Go W on 843 approx. 10 mi. to forest route 842. Go NW on 842 approx. 1.5 mi. to Cook Lake CG.

SINGLE RATE:	**Varies**	**OPEN DATES:**	**Yearlong***
# of SINGLE SITES:	**34**	**MAX SPUR:**	**45 feet**
		MAX STAY:	**14 days**
		ELEVATION:	**4400 feet**

10 Custer Trail
Hill City • lat 44°01'32" lon 103°47'50"

DESCRIPTION: CG is in forested area next to Reynolds Prairie with lake views. Cool in summer. Excellent fishing in adjacent Deerfield Lake. Visit numerous historical sites in area. Supplies on S shore of lake. Antelope, bobcats, and mountain lions in area. Seldom full. Gather firewood locally. Hiking trail on site.

GETTING THERE: Custer Trail CG is located in the Deerfield Lake Recreation Area approx. 11 mi. N of Hill City of off county route 308.

SINGLE RATE:	**Varies**	**OPEN DATES:**	**May-Sept***
# of SINGLE SITES:	**16**	**MAX SPUR:**	**50 feet**
		MAX STAY:	**14 days**
		ELEVATION:	**5900 feet**

 Campground has hosts   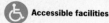 **Reservable sites**   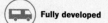 **Accessible facilities**   **Fully developed**   **Semi-developed**   **Rustic facilities**

NOTE: Open dates listed are typical. Actual dates are dependent on conditions such as snow pack.

11 Dalton Lake
Nemo • lat 44°14'00" lon 103°29'00"

DESCRIPTION: This CG is set in a pine and spruce forest with lake views. Thundershowers common. Trout fishing on adjacent Dalton Lake. Supplies can be found in Nemo. Busy holidays. Gather firewood locally. Motorized and non-motorized trails in area. CG is closed 2000 season for renovation.

GETTING THERE: From Nemo go N on primary forest route 26 approx. 3 mi. to forest route 224. Go E on 224 approx. 4 mi. to Dalton Lake CG. Not recommended for large vehicles.

SINGLE RATE:	$9	OPEN DATES:	Yearlong*
# of SINGLE SITES:	8	MAX SPUR:	45 feet
		MAX STAY:	14 days
		ELEVATION:	4400 feet

12 Ditch Creek
Hill City • lat 43°57'37" lon 103°50'29"

DESCRIPTION: CG is located in park-like grove of spruce with creek views. Cool in summer. Good fly fishing in Ditch Creek which runs through CG. Many historical sites in area. Supplies 7 mi. to local resort. Numerous wildlife including bobcats and mountain lions. Busy holidays. Gather firewood locally. Many trails in area.

GETTING THERE: From Hill City go NW on county route 308 approx. 17 mi. to forest route 291. Go S on 291 approx. 4 mi. to Ditch Creek CG.

SINGLE RATE:	$10	OPEN DATES:	Yearlong*
# of SINGLE SITES:	13	MAX SPUR:	50 feet
		MAX STAY:	14 days
		ELEVATION:	6200 feet

13 Dutchman
Hill City • lat 44°01'28" lon 103°46'56"

DESCRIPTION: CG is located in mature pine forest with screening undergrowth. Cool evenings and common afternoon t-showers. Good fishing on nearby Castle Creek and Deerfield Lake(boat launch). Numerous historical sites. Supplies 2 mi. to local resort. Bobcats and mountain lions. Gather firewood on site. Hiking trails nearby.

GETTING THERE: Dutchman CG is located in the Deerfield Lake Recreation Area approx. 14 mi. N of Hill City on primary forest route 17.

SINGLE RATE:	$12	OPEN DATES:	Yearlong
# of SINGLE SITES:	45	MAX SPUR:	50 feet
		MAX STAY:	14 days
		ELEVATION:	6100 feet

14 Hanna
Spearfish • lat 44°16'30" lon 103°50'58"

DESCRIPTION: This CG is situated in a mature fir forest on Little Spearfish Creek. Warm days, cool nights. Trout fish E Spearfish Creek. Limited supplies at Cheyenne Crossing. Deer and turkeys can be seen in the area. Firewood sold by FRM or may be gathered by campers. Short hiking loop nearby.

GETTING THERE: From Spearfish go S on HWY 14A (Nat'l Forest Scenic Byway) approx. 18 mi. to US HWY 85. Go S on 85 2 mi. to Hanna CG.

SINGLE RATE:	$10	OPEN DATES:	May-Nov
# of SINGLE SITES:	13	MAX SPUR:	55 feet
		MAX STAY:	14 days
		ELEVATION:	5600 feet

15 Horsethief Lake
Keystone • lat 43°53'00" lon 103°29'00"

DESCRIPTION: Located in mature pine forest with lake views. Common afternoon t-showers. Great fishing on adjacent Horsethief Lake. Numerous historical sites. Supplies in Keystone. Bobcats, mountain lions, and mountain goats. Busy all season. Buy or gather firewood. Black Elk Wilderness access and Centennial Trail nearby.

GETTING THERE: From Keystone go S on US HWY 16A approx. 2 mi. to state HWY 87 (Peter Norbeck Scenic Byway). Go W on 87 approx. 5 mi. to Horsethief Lake CG.

SINGLE RATE:	Varies	OPEN DATES:	May-Sept
# of SINGLE SITES:	36	MAX SPUR:	50 feet
		MAX STAY:	14 days
		ELEVATION:	5000 feet

16 Iron Creek Horse Camp
Custer • lat 43°49'47" lon 103°28'14"

DESCRIPTION: CG is located in an open stand of ponderosa pine and aspen. Iron Creek runs adjacent to CG and offers good trout fishing. Supplies in Custer. Wildlife includes deer, mountain goats, and beavers. Horse corrals. Numerous hiking, horse, and mountain bike trails in area. Custer State Park nearby.

GETTING THERE: Iron Creek Horse Camp CG is located on the Centennial Trail approx. 1 mi. N on state HWY 87. Access by horse or foot only.

SINGLE RATE:	$16	OPEN DATES:	May-Sept
# of SINGLE SITES:	9	MAX SPUR:	50 feet
		MAX STAY:	14 days
		ELEVATION:	5100 feet

17 Moon
New Castle • lat 43°56'47" lon 104°00'32"

DESCRIPTION: This CG is situated in an open, park-like stand of ponderosa pine with forest views. Numerous historical sites in area. Supplies are available in Newcastle. Wildlife includes deer, mountain lions, and coyotes. CG can be busy during hunting season. Numerous roads in area for ATV activities.

GETTING THERE: From New Castle go SE on US HWY 16 approx. 8 mi. to primary forest route 117. Go N on 117 approx. 15 mi. to Moon CG.

SINGLE RATE:	No fee	OPEN DATES:	Yearlong*
# of SINGLE SITES:	3	MAX SPUR:	30 feet
		MAX STAY:	14 days
		ELEVATION:	6400 feet

18 Oreville
Hill City • lat 43°52'29" lon 103°36'52"

DESCRIPTION: In park like setting with ponderosa pine. Warm days, cold nights, weather may change rapidly. Trout fish nearby Spring Creek. Numerous historical sites. Supplies in Hill City. Deer and coyotes in area. Busy CG, reservations encouraged. Buy or gather firewood. Mickelson Trail (Rails to Trails).

GETTING THERE: From Hill City go S on US HWY 16 approx. 7 mi. to Oreville CG.

SINGLE RATE:	$14	OPEN DATES:	May-Sept
# of SINGLE SITES:	24	MAX SPUR:	50 feet
		MAX STAY:	14 days
		ELEVATION:	5300 feet

19 Pactola
Rapid City • lat 44°03'58" lon 103°30'43"

DESCRIPTION: CG is located in ponderosa pine with scattered underbrush and views of Pactola Reservoir (great fishing). Visit numerous historical sites in area. Supplies 1/4 mi. to Pactola Reservoir store. Bobcats and mountain lions in area. Excellent trails. Busy holidays. Firewood on site. Boat ramp available.

GETTING THERE: Pactola CG is located on the Pactola Reservoir Recreation Area off of US HWY 385, approx. 14 mi. W of Rapid City.

SINGLE RATE:	Varies	OPEN DATES:	May-Sept
# of SINGLE SITES:	89	MAX SPUR:	50 feet
		MAX STAY:	14 days
		ELEVATION:	4700 feet

20 Redbank Spring
Newcastle • lat 43°59'45" lon 103°59'45"

DESCRIPTION: CG is located in an open stand of ponderosa pine. Views are of the surrounding forest. Redbank Spring and pond are on site. Historical sites in area. Supplies in Newcastle. Wildlife includes mule deer and coyotes. CG can be busy holiday weekends. No drinking water available on site.

GETTING THERE: From Newcastle go SE on US HWY 16 approx. 8 mi. to primary forest route 117. Go N on 117 approx. 19 mi. to forest route 294. Go E on 294 approx. 1 mi. to Redbank Spring CG.

SINGLE RATE:	No fee	OPEN DATES:	Yearlong*
# of SINGLE SITES:	4	MAX SPUR:	40 feet
		MAX STAY:	14 days
		ELEVATION:	6600 feet

 Campground has hosts   **Reservable sites**   **Accessible facilities**   **Fully developed**   **Semi-developed**   **Rustic facilities**

NOTE: Open dates listed are typical. Actual dates are dependent on conditions such as snow pack.

21 Reuter
Sundance • lat 44°26'43" lon 104°25'17"

DESCRIPTION: This CG is in an open ponderosa pine forest. Warm days with cool nights. Historical Devils Tower National Monument nearby. Gather firewood locally. Deer and small wildlife in area. Limited supplies in Sundance. Warren Peak Fire Lookout nearby. Carson Draw and Bearlodge Trail System nearby.

GETTING THERE: From Sundance go W on US HWY 14 approx. 2 mi. to primary forest route 838. Go N on 838 approx. 3.5 mi. to Reuter CG.

SINGLE RATE:	$8	OPEN DATES:	May-Sept*
# of SINGLE SITES:	24	MAX SPUR:	30 feet
		MAX STAY:	14 days
		ELEVATION:	4900 feet

22 Rod and Gun
Spearfish • lat 44°20'21" lon 103°57'50"

DESCRIPTION: CG set in an open canyon bottom with steep pine forested slopes. Views of limestone canyon walls & Little Spearfish Creek. Warm days, cool nights. Trout fish the creek. Limited supplies at Cheyenne Crossing. Deer, turkeys, and elk. Buy firewood or gather locally. Non-motorized use trails nearby.

GETTING THERE: From Spearfish go S on US HWY 14A (Spearfish Canyon Scenic Byway)13 mi. to FDR 222. Go W approx. 2 mi. to Rod and Gun CG. Although FDR 222 accomodates large vehicles, it has narrow segments.

SINGLE RATE:	$10	OPEN DATES:	Apr-Nov
# of SINGLE SITES:	7	MAX SPUR:	50 feet
		MAX STAY:	14 days
		ELEVATION:	5500 feet

23 Roubaix Lake
Lead • lat 44°11'55" lon 103°39'43"

DESCRIPTION: CG is located in a mature ponderosa pine forest with lake views. Thundershowers are common. Good trout fishing in adjacent Roubaix Lake. Visit historic mining areas. Supplies are 12 mi. away at Deadwood. Busy on holidays and weekends. Gather firewood locally. Hiking trails in area.

GETTING THERE: From Lead go S on US HWY 385 approx. 12 mi. to forest route 255. Go SW on 255 approx. 1 mi. to Roubaix Lake CG.

SINGLE RATE:	Varies	OPEN DATES:	Yearlong
# of SINGLE SITES:	56	MAX SPUR:	45 feet
		MAX STAY:	14 days
		ELEVATION:	5500 feet

24 Sheridan Lake Group Area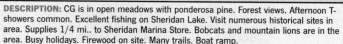
43°58'30" lon 103°30'00"

DESCRIPTION: CG is in open meadows with ponderosa pine. Forest views. Afternoon T-showers common. Excellent fishing on Sheridan Lake. Visit numerous historical sites in area. Supplies 1/4 mi.. to Sheridan Marina Store. Bobcats and mountain lions are in the area. Busy holidays. Firewood on site. Many trails. Boat ramp.

GETTING THERE: Sheridan Lake North Cove Group Area CG is located in the Sheridan Lake Recreation Area approx. 5 mi. NE of Hill City on US HWY 385.

		OPEN DATES:	May-Sept
		MAX SPUR:	60 feet
GROUP RATE:	Varies	MAX STAY:	14 days
# of GROUP SITES:	5	ELEVATION:	4600 feet

25 Sheridan Lake Southside
Hill City • lat 43°58'30" lon 103°27'00"

DESCRIPTION: CG is in pine forest with open, shaded, and lakeside sites. Cool evenings and afternoon t-showers common. Good fishing in adjacent Sheridan Lake. Many historical sites. Supplies 5 mi. away. Bobcats and mountain lions in the area. Busy holidays. Firewood on site. Trails at CG. Boat ramp and amphitheater.

GETTING THERE: Sheridan Lake Southside CG is located in the Sheridan Lake Recreation Area approx. 5 mi. NE of Hill City on US HWY 385.

SINGLE RATE:	Varies	OPEN DATES:	May-Sept
# of SINGLE SITES:	129	MAX SPUR:	60 feet
		MAX STAY:	14 days
		ELEVATION:	4600 feet

26 Sundance Trails
Sundance • lat 43°26'00" lon 104°20'30"

DESCRIPTION: CG in an open grass valley with views of tree covered mountains. Weather can change rapidly. Historical Custer Expedition Trail and Devils Tower National Monument nearby. Supplies at Sundance. Deer, elk, and antelope in area. Main trail head for the Bearlodge Trail System at CG. Corrals available.

GETTING THERE: Sundance Trails CG is located approx. 2.3 mi. NE of Sundance on Government Valley Road, off of US HWY 14.

SINGLE RATE:	$12	OPEN DATES:	May-Nov
# of SINGLE SITES:	10	MAX SPUR:	50 feet
		MAX STAY:	14 days
		ELEVATION:	4700 feet

27 Timon
Spearfish • lat 44°19'40" lon 103°59'19"

DESCRIPTION: CG is located in mature pine and spruce forest with canyon and creek views. Thundershowers are common. Trout fishing in adjacent Little Spearfish Creek. Supplies 9 mi. at Cheyenne Crossing. Various wildlife including elk. Busy holidays and weekends. Gather firewood locally. Numerous trails nearby.

GETTING THERE: From Spearfish go N on US HW 14A (Spearfish Canyon Scenic Byway) approx. 13 mi. to FDR 222. Go W on 222 approx. 4 mi. to Timon CG.

SINGLE RATE:	$10	OPEN DATES:	Apr-Nov
# of SINGLE SITES:	7	MAX SPUR:	60 feet
		MAX STAY:	14 days
		ELEVATION:	5600 feet

28 Whitetail
Hill City • lat 44°01'00" lon 103°47'50"

DESCRIPTION: CG is in pine and spruce on a wide ridge leading to Deerfield Lake. Good fishing. Cool evenings with afternoon thunderstorms are common. Numerous historical sites. Wildlife in the area includes bobcats and mountain lions. Busy holidays. Firewood available on site. Trails in area.

GETTING THERE: Whitetail CG is located in the Deerfield Lake Recreation Area approx. 16 mi. N of Hill City on county route 308.

SINGLE RATE:	$12	OPEN DATES:	Yearlong*
# of SINGLE SITES:	17	MAX SPUR:	50 feet
		MAX STAY:	14 days
		ELEVATION:	6000 feet

29 Willow Creek Horse Camp
Hill City • lat 43°54'11" lon 103°32'06"

DESCRIPTION: CG is in pine with open and shaded sites. Creek views. Good fishing on two adjacent creeks. Cool evening with common afternoon t-showers. Many historical sites. Supplies 8 mi. to Hill City. Bobcats and mountain lions. Busy all season. Gather firewood locally. Hiking trails in area. Horse facilities.

GETTING THERE: From Hill City go S on US HWY 16/385 approx. 5 mi. to US HWY 244. Go E on 244 approx. 3 mi. to Willow Creek CG.

		OPEN DATES:	Yearlong*
		MAX SPUR:	45 feet
GROUP RATE:	Varies	MAX STAY:	14 days
# of GROUP SITES:	8	ELEVATION:	5000 feet

 Campground has hosts    Reservable sites   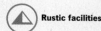 Accessible facilities   Fully developed   Semi-developed   Rustic facilities

NOTE: Open dates listed are typical. Actual dates are dependent on conditions such as snow pack.

BLACK HILLS NATIONAL FOREST • WYOMING • 21 — 29

CHEROKEE NATIONAL FOREST

USFS Photo

Tennessee's only national forest, the Cherokee, is separated into two parts by the Great Smoky Mountains National Park. The lands of the Cherokee are old and battle-scarred, marked by time and human influence.

The Cherokee's most famous mountains, the Appalachians, once had peaks higher than the Rocky Mountains. After many winters of bitter snows and cold winds and summer's warm, humid air wearing them down to their present heights, some peaks are still well above 5000 feet.

With more than 620,000 acres, the Cherokee provides stable habitat for more than a thousand species of plants and animals, clean water and outdoor recreation. The waters of the forest are as diverse as the surrounding landscape. Whether you're looking for the quiet pleasure of fly-fishing, slipping into a river's deep green pool on a sticky, hot summer day or plunging down a wild rapid on the Olympic River, there is something for you.

The Appalachian Trail, the longest continual footpath in the world, passes through the Cherokee. Another way to see the forest is by car. During spring, the East Tennessee hills are alive with hues of violet, purple, yellow and red. In autumn, the foliage is brilliant.

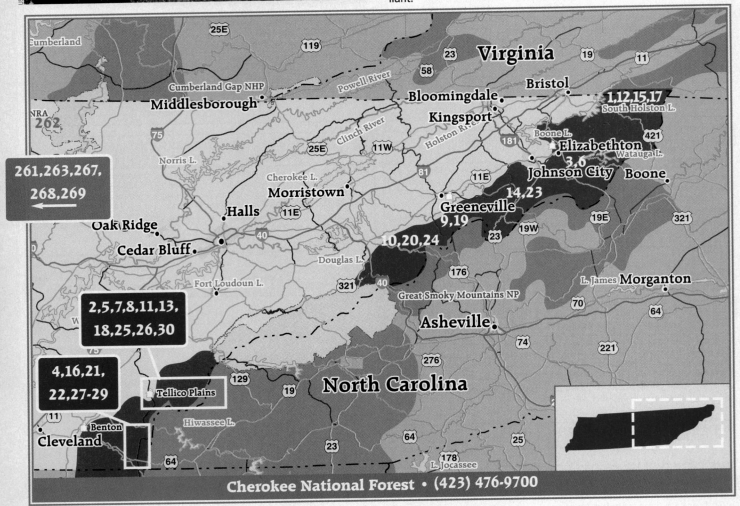

Cherokee National Forest • (423) 476-9700

1 Backbone Rock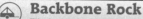

Elizabethton • lat 36˚35'40" lon 081˚48'52"

DESCRIPTION: This CG is located along Beaverdam Creek and gets its name from the spur of adjacent Holston Mountain. There is a nearby trail which connects with the Appalachian Trail as well as a 1/3 mi. loop to a narrow, scenic waterfall. There are two picnic shelters (built by the CCC). CG may be frequented by bears.

GETTING THERE: From Elizabethton go NE on state HWY 91 approx. 30 mi. to Backbone Rock CG.

SINGLE RATE:	Varies	OPEN DATES:	May-Dec
# of SINGLE SITES:	11	MAX SPUR:	30 feet
		MAX STAY:	7 days
		ELEVATION:	3500 feet

2 Big Oak Cove

Tellico Plains • lat 35˚16'20" lon 084˚05'12"

DESCRIPTION: This CG is located along the banks of Rough Ridge Creek, surrounded by dense forests and creeks. Fish and swim in the nearby creeks. Supplies available at Tellico plains. Deer, bears, turkeys and birds are common to the area.

GETTING THERE: From Tellico Plains go E on state route 165 approx. 2.5 mi. to forest route 210. Go SE on 210 approx. 13 mi. to Big Oak Cove CG.

SINGLE RATE:	$8	OPEN DATES:	Yearlong
# of SINGLE SITES:	6		
		MAX STAY:	7 days

3 Cardens Bluff

Elizabethton • lat 36˚18'33" lon 082˚07'03"

DESCRIPTION: This CG is situated on a peninsula on the southern shore of Watauga Lake. Enjoy fishing, boating, swimming and water skiing in this 6430 acre lake. There is a boat ramp and a shooting range nearby. Hike in the adjacent Pond Mountain Wilderness or on the Appalachian Trail.

GETTING THERE: From Elizabethton go SE on US HWY 19E/321 approx. 4 mi. to state HWY 67. Go E on 67 approx. 5 mi. to Cardens Bluff CG.

SINGLE RATE:	$10	OPEN DATES:	Apr-Oct
# of SINGLE SITES:	43	MAX SPUR:	30 feet
		MAX STAY:	7 days
		ELEVATION:	2060 feet

4 Chilhowee

Benton • lat 35˚09'01" lon 084˚36'20"

DESCRIPTION: This CG is located near a small pond just off of the Oswald Dome Road. Fish or swim in the pond. Supplies available at Benton. Enjoy a drive to the Oswald Lookout or on the Ocoee Scenic Byway. Enjoy a hike to the Rock Creek Gorge Scenic Area and Benton Falls. RV dump station on site.

GETTING THERE: From Benton go E on county HWY 100 approx. 2 mi. to forest route 77. Go NE on 77 approx. 1.5 mi. to turnoff for CG. Go E on turnoff approx. 1/4 mi. to Chilhowee CG.

SINGLE RATE:	$12	OPEN DATES:	Apr-Oct
# of SINGLE SITES:	88	MAX SPUR:	30 feet
		MAX STAY:	14 days
		ELEVATION:	1800 feet

5 Davis Branch

Tellico • lat 35˚16'00" lon 084˚06'30"

DESCRIPTION: This CG is located along the banks of Davis Creek, surrounded by dense forests and creeks. Fish and swim in the nearby creeks. Supplies available at Tellico plains. Deer, bears, turkeys and birds are common to the area.

GETTING THERE: From Tellico Plains go E on state HWY 165 approx. 2.5 mi. to forest route 210. Go SE on 210 approx. 12 mi. to Davis Branch CG.

SINGLE RATE:	$6	OPEN DATES:	Yearlong
		MAX STAY:	14 days

6 Dennis Cove

Elizabethton • lat 36˚15'24" lon 082˚06'43"

DESCRIPTION: This quiet, secluded CG is located alongside Laurel Fork Creek. Fish for rainbow trout in the creek but please check fishing regulations. Enjoy a hike on the on site trails which lead to the Appalachian Trail, Whiterock Lookout, Pond Mountain Wilderness, and Laurel Falls.

GETTING THERE: From Elizabethton go SE on US HWY 19E/321 approx. 3 mi. to state HWY 67. Go E on 67 approx. 1 mi. to county rte. 50. Go SE on 50 approx. 4 mi. to Dennis Cove CG. Road is steep and narrow.

SINGLE RATE:	$10	OPEN DATES:	May-Nov
# of SINGLE SITES:	15	MAX SPUR:	20 feet
		MAX STAY:	7 days
		ELEVATION:	2570 feet

7 Double Camp

Tellico Plains • lat 35˚25'08" lon 084˚05'20"

DESCRIPTION: This CG is located along the banks of Double Camp Creek, surrounded by dense forests and creeks. Fish and swim in the nearby creeks. Supplies available at Tellico plains. Deer, bears, turkeys and birds are common to the area.

GETTING THERE: From Tellico Plains go N on state HWY 360 approx. 7.5 mi. to county HWY 504. Go NE on 504 approx. 4.5 mi. to forest route 35-1. Go SE on 35-1 approx. 5.5 mi. to Double Camp CG.

SINGLE RATE:	Varies	OPEN DATES:	Yearlong
		MAX STAY:	14 days

8 Holly Flats

Tellico • lat 35˚17'05" lon 084˚10'45"

DESCRIPTION: This CG is located along the banks of the Upper Bald River, just south of the Bald River wilderness. Fish and swim in the nearby creeks. Supplies available at Tellico plains. Deer, bears, turkeys and birds are common to the area.

GETTING THERE: From Tellico go S on state HWY 68 approx. 1.5 mi. to state HWY 68. Go S on 68 approx. 4 mi. to county route 610/623. Go E on 610/623 approx. 6 mi. to Holly Flats CG.

SINGLE RATE:	$6	OPEN DATES:	Yearlong
		MAX STAY:	14 days

9 Horse Creek

Greenville • lat 36˚06'22" lon 082˚39'18"

DESCRIPTION: This CG is nestled in a hardwood cove on Horse Creek. Fish or swim in the creek. A rustic pavilion & swimming area were constructed by the CCC in the 1930s. There are several trails that lead into the Sampson Mountain Wilderness & Bald Mountain Ridge Scenic Area. CG is frequented by bears.

GETTING THERE: From Greenville go E on US 11E/411 approx. 2 mi. to state route 107. Go E on 107 approx. 5 mi. to county route 2519. Go S on 2519 approx. 3 mi. to Horse Creek CG.

SINGLE RATE:	$7	OPEN DATES:	May-Nov
# of SINGLE SITES:	15	MAX SPUR:	60 feet
		MAX STAY:	7 days
		ELEVATION:	1720 feet

10 Houston Valley

Greenville • lat 35˚57'45" lon 082˚56'45"

DESCRIPTION: This CG is situated at the confluence of Laurel Brook and a small stream. There is a covered picnic pavilion on site. The Bubbling Springs shooting range is nearby. Enjoy a hike on the adjacent trail that leads into the Meadow Creek Mountains. Visit the nearby Meadow Creek fire tower.

GETTING THERE: From Greenville go S on state HWY 107 approx. 16 mi. to Houston Valley CG.

SINGLE RATE:	$7	OPEN DATES:	Apr-Nov
# of SINGLE SITES:	8	MAX SPUR:	25 feet
		MAX STAY:	7 days
		ELEVATION:	1800 feet

 Campground has hosts   **Reservable sites**   **Accessible facilities**   **Fully developed**   **Semi-developed**   **Rustic facilities**

NOTE: Open dates listed are typical. Actual dates are dependent on conditions such as snow pack.

11 Indian Boundary
Tellico Plains • lat 35°24'08" lon 084°06'29"

DESCRIPTION: This CG is located along the east shore of Indian Boundary Lake, surrounded by dense forests and creeks. Fish and swim in the nearby creeks. Supplies available at Tellico plains. Deer, bears, turkeys and birds are common to the area.

GETTING THERE: From Tellico Plains go E on state HWY 165 approx. 10.5 mi. to forest route 345. Go NE on 345 approx. 2 mi. to Indian Boundary CG.

SINGLE RATE:	$10	OPEN DATES:	Apr-Sept
		MAX STAY:	14 days
		ELEVATION:	1920 feet

12 Jacobs Creek
Bristol • lat 36°33'59" lon 082°00'35"

DESCRIPTION: This CG is located on a peninsula on the eastern shore of South Holston Lake, a 7580 acre lake which supports fishing, boating, and water skiing. A public boat ramp is 1/2 mi. away. The Appalachian Trail, a shooting range, and an auto tour route are all nearby. There is a RV dump station on site.

GETTING THERE: From Bristol go SE on US HWY 421/state HWY 34 approx. 13 mi. to county route 32. Go N on 32 approx. 1 mi. to Jacobs Creek CG.

SINGLE RATE:	$12	OPEN DATES:	Apr-Oct
# of SINGLE SITES:	29	MAX SPUR:	40 feet
		MAX STAY:	7 days
		ELEVATION:	1820 feet

13 Jake Best
Tellico Plains • lat 35°26'45" lon 084°06'35"

DESCRIPTION: This CG is located along the banks of Jake Best Creek, surrounded by dense forests and creeks. Fish and swim in the nearby creeks. Supplies available at Tellico plains. Deer, bears, turkeys and birds are common to the area.

GETTING THERE: From Tellico Plains go N on state HWY 360 approx. 7.5 mi. to county HWY 504/506. Go NE on 504/506 approx. 4 mi. to forest route 35-1. Go S on 35-1 approx. 2.5 mi. to Jack Best CG.

SINGLE RATE:	Varies	OPEN DATES:	Yearlong
		MAX STAY:	14 days
		ELEVATION:	1040 feet

14 Limestone Cove
Erwin • lat 36°10'38" lon 082°17'46"

DESCRIPTION: This rustic CG is located at the confluence of North Indian Creek and Rocky Brook in beautiful Limestone Cove. Fish for trout in the creek. A fishing pier and loop trail access the creek. Hike the on site trail that leads into the Unaka Mountain Wilderness.

GETTING THERE: From Erwin go NE on state HWY 36 approx. 4 mi. to state HWY 107. Go E on 107 approx. 4 mi. to Limestone Cove CG.

SINGLE RATE:	$7	OPEN DATES:	May-Oct
# of SINGLE SITES:	18	MAX SPUR:	20 feet
		MAX STAY:	7 days
		ELEVATION:	2200 feet

15 Little Oak
Bristol • lat 36°31'18" lon 082°03'52"

DESCRIPTION: This CG is situated on a peninsula on the eastern shore of South Holston Lake. The CG is designated as a Watchable Wildlife Area with two interpretive trails. There is a short loop trail, boat ramp and RV dump station on site. An auto tour route and hiking trails are nearby.

GETTING THERE: From Bristol go SE on US HWY 421/state HWY 34 approx. 13 mi. to forest route 87. Go SW on 87 approx. 4.5 mi. to forest route 87G. Go W on 87G approx. 2 mi. to Little Oak CG.

SINGLE RATE:	$6	OPEN DATES:	Apr-Dec
# of SINGLE SITES:	72	MAX SPUR:	40 feet
		MAX STAY:	7 days
		ELEVATION:	1780 feet

16 Lost Creek
Ducktown • lat 35°09'43" lon 084°28'08"

DESCRIPTION: This isolated CG is located along the banks of Big Lost Creek, surrounded by dense forests and creeks. Fish and swim in the nearby creeks. Supplies available at Ducktown. Deer, bears, turkeys and birds are common to the area. The Smith Mountain Trail is nearby for a nice hike.

GETTING THERE: From Ducktown go W on state HWY 40 approx. 14 mi. to state HWY 30. Go N on 30 approx. 6 mi. to forest route 103. Go E on 103 approx. 4 mi. to Lost Creek CG.

SINGLE RATE:	$7	OPEN DATES:	Apr-Oct
# of SINGLE SITES:	15	MAX SPUR:	30 feet
		MAX STAY:	14 days
		ELEVATION:	1000 feet

17 Low Gap
Elizabethton • lat 36°26'25" lon 082°07'31"

DESCRIPTION: This rustic, tent only CG is located high in the Holston Mountain Range. Miller and Furnace brooks are nearby. A Forest Service fire lookout is approx. 5 mi. away at Holston Mountain. There is no drinking water on site. Campers may gather dead and down firewood.

GETTING THERE: From Elizabethton go NE on state HWY 91 approx. 10 mi. to forest route 56. Go NW on 56 approx. 3 mi. to forest route 202. Go W on 202 approx. 2.5 mi. to Low Gap CG. Road is steep and narrow.

SINGLE RATE:	No fee	OPEN DATES:	Apr-Dec
# of SINGLE SITES:	5	MAX SPUR:	20 feet
		MAX STAY:	7 days
		ELEVATION:	3920 feet

18 North River
Tellico Plains • lat 35°18'50" lon 084°07'33"

DESCRIPTION: This CG is located along the banks of the North River, surrounded by dense forests and creeks. Fish and swim in the river and nearby creeks. Supplies available at Tellico plains. Deer, bears, turkeys and birds are common to the area.

GETTING THERE: From Tellico Plains go E on state HWY 165 approx. 2.5 mi. to forest route 210. Go SE on 210 approx. 7 mi. to forest route 216. Go N on 216 approx. 1/2 mi. to North River CG.

SINGLE RATE:	$6	OPEN DATES:	Yearlong
		MAX STAY:	14 days

19 Old Forge
Tusculum • lat 36°05'27" lon 082°40'55"

DESCRIPTION: This small walk-in CG is situated in native flowering plants on Jennings Creek. This CG was originally a site for an iron forge. Enjoy a hike on the trails that lead from this CG to the Bald Mountain Ridge Scenic Area, the Appalachian Trail, and the Sampson Mountain Wilderness.

GETTING THERE: From Tusculum go E on state HWY 107 approx. 5 mi. to county route 2519. Go S on 2519 approx. 2 mi. to forest route 331. Go SW on 331 approx. 1.5 mi. to Old Forge CG.

SINGLE RATE:	$7	OPEN DATES:	May-Dec
# of SINGLE SITES:	10	MAX SPUR:	20 feet
		MAX STAY:	7 days
		ELEVATION:	1880 feet

20 Paint Creek
Greenville • lat 35°58'54" lon 082°51'50"

DESCRIPTION: This CG is situated among rhododendron, hemlock and laurel on Paint Creek. Enjoy fly fishing for trout in the creek. Numerous trails are nearby and include the Appalachian Trail. There are several scenic sites nearby that feature an overlook and waterfalls. CG may be frequented by bears.

GETTING THERE: From Greenville go S on state HWY 107 approx. 10 mi. to forest route 31. Go E then S on 31 approx. 1 mi. to Paint Creek CG. Road is narrow-sharp curves.

SINGLE RATE:	$14	OPEN DATES:	Apr-Dec
# of SINGLE SITES:	19	MAX SPUR:	60 feet
		MAX STAY:	7 days
		ELEVATION:	1600 feet

 Campground has hosts   **Reservable sites**   **Accessible facilities**   **Fully developed**   **Semi-developed**   **Rustic facilities**

NOTE: Open dates listed are typical. Actual dates are dependent on conditions such as snow pack.

21 Parksville Lake
Ducktown • lat 35˚06'56" lon 084˚34'28"

DESCRIPTION: This CG is located on Lake Ocoee with a boat ramp nearby. Enjoy fishing, swimming or whitewater rafting on the river. Supplies available at Ducktown. A nearby trail leads to the Rock Creek Gorge Scenic Area. Enjoy a drive on the Ocoee Scenic Byway. There is a shooting range close to this CG.

GETTING THERE: From Ducktown go W on state HWY 40 approx. 14 mi. to state WY 30. Go N on 30 approx. 1/2 mi. to Parksville Lake CG.

SINGLE RATE:	Varies	OPEN DATES:	Yearlong*
# of SINGLE SITES:	41	MAX SPUR:	30 feet
		MAX STAY:	14 days
		ELEVATION:	1500 feet

22 Quinn Springs
Benton • lat 35˚13'47" lon 084˚32'46"

DESCRIPTION: CG is situated in oaks and hickories adjacent to the Hiwassee River. Enjoy a meandering float down the river or follow the Fisherman's Trail along the river to many popular fishing holes. Supplies available at Benton. Deer, bears, turkeys and birds are common to the area. The Oswald Dome trail begins at the CG.

GETTING THERE: From Benton go N on US HWY 411 approx. 5.5 mi. to state HWY 30. Go E on 30 approx. 1 mi. to Quinn Springs CG.

SINGLE RATE:	$10	OPEN DATES:	Apr-Oct
# of SINGLE SITES:	24	MAX SPUR:	30 feet
		MAX STAY:	14 days
		ELEVATION:	800 feet

23 Rock Creek
Erwin • lat 36˚08'13" lon 082˚21'09"

DESCRIPTION: This CG is located on Rock Creek and offers a spring-fed swimming pool and bathhouse originally built by the CCC. Enjoy a drive on the Unaka Mountain Auto Tour Route. Hike the trails into the Stone Mountains, Unaka Mountain Scenic Area, and Unaka Wilderness. There is a RV dump station on site.

GETTING THERE: From Erwin go E on state HWY 395 approx. 2 mi. to Rock Creek CG.

SINGLE RATE:	Varies	OPEN DATES:	May-Oct
# of SINGLE SITES:	34	MAX SPUR:	40 feet
		MAX STAY:	7 days
		ELEVATION:	2327 feet

24 Round Mountain
Harmony Grove • lat 35˚50'18" lon 082˚57'21"

DESCRIPTION: This remote CG is located near the top of Round Mountain. It rests in rhododendrons and hardwoods on a small mountain stream. Campers may hike or drive the road up to Round Mountain Lookout. The Walnut Mountain Trail runs from the CG to the Appalachian Trail and offers spectacular views.

GETTING THERE: From Harmony Grove go S on state HWY 107 approx. 7 mi. to Round Mountain CG. Road is narrow with sharp curves.

SINGLE RATE:	$7	OPEN DATES:	May-Dec
# of SINGLE SITES:	14	MAX SPUR:	40 feet
		MAX STAY:	7 days
		ELEVATION:	3120 feet

25 Spivey Cove
Tellico Plains • lat 35˚18'12" lon 084˚06'58"

DESCRIPTION: This CG is located along the banks of the Tellico River, surrounded by dense forests and creeks. Fish and swim in the river and nearby creeks. Supplies available at Tellico plains.

GETTING THERE: From Tellico Plains go E on state route 165 approx. 2.5 mi. to forest route 210. Go E on 210 approx. 9 mi. to forest route 216 to Spivey Cove CG.

SINGLE RATE:	$6	OPEN DATES:	Apr-Sept
		MAX STAY:	14 days

26 State Line
Tellico Plains • lat 35˚15'40" lon 084˚04'55"

DESCRIPTION: This CG is located along the banks of the Tellico River, surrounded by dense forests and creeks. Fish and swim in the river and nearby creeks. Supplies available at Tellico plains. Deer, bears, turkeys and birds are common to the area.

GETTING THERE: From Tellico Plains go E on state route 165 approx. 2.5 mi. to forest route 210. Go E on 210 approx. 14 mi. to State Line CG.

SINGLE RATE:	$6	OPEN DATES:	Yearlong
		MAX STAY:	14 days

27 Sylco
Benton • lat 35˚01'37" lon 084˚36'05"

DESCRIPTION: This isolated, peaceful CG is in a nice forest setting just off of Sylco Creek. Fish and swim in the nearby creek. Supplies available at Benton. Campers may gather firewood. Enjoy a hike on the Blue Ridge Trail or in the nearby Big Frog and Cohutta Wilderness Areas. No drinking water on site.

GETTING THERE: From Benton go S on US HWY 411 approx. 6 mi. to Sloan Gap Rd. Go E on Sloan Gap approx. 5 mi. to forest route 55. Go SE on 55 approx. 6 mi. to Sylco CG.

SINGLE RATE:	No fee	OPEN DATES:	Yearlong
# of SINGLE SITES:	12	MAX SPUR:	20 feet
		MAX STAY:	14 days
		ELEVATION:	1100 feet

28 Thunder Rock
Ducktown • lat 35˚04'30" lon 084˚29'05"

DESCRIPTION: This CG is located on the Oconee River. Fish, raft and swim in the nearby river. There is a put-in point for rafting close to CG. There is a hiking trail that leads to the Little Frog Wilderness. There are also two trailheads in area–Thunder Rock Trail and Dry Pond Lead Trail.

GETTING THERE: From Ducktown go W on US HWY 64 approx. 6.5 mi. to Thunder Rock CG.

SINGLE RATE:	$10	OPEN DATES:	Yearlong
# of SINGLE SITES:	42	MAX SPUR:	20 feet
		MAX STAY:	14 days
		ELEVATION:	1400 feet

29 Tumbling Creek
McCaysville • lat 35˚01'00" lon 084˚28'00"

DESCRIPTION: This CG is situated on on Tumbling Creek near the Ocoee River. Fish or swim in the nearby creek and river. There are excellent whitewater opportunities (and an information center) on the Ocoee River. Supplies available at McCaysville. Enjoy a hike in the nearby Big Frog Wilderness.

GETTING THERE: From McCaysville go N on state HWY 68 approx. 1 mi. to county HWY 2326/A074. Go W on 2326/A074 approx. 5 mi. to forest route 221. Go NW on 221 approx. 2 mi. to Tumbling Creek CG.

SINGLE RATE:	No fee	OPEN DATES:	Yearlong
# of SINGLE SITES:	8	MAX SPUR:	20 feet
		MAX STAY:	14 days
		ELEVATION:	1480 feet

30 Young Branch Horse Camp
Tellico Plains • lat 35˚29'30" lon 084˚08'30"

DESCRIPTION: This CG is located along the banks of Chitico Creek, surrounded by dense forests and creeks. Fish and swim in the river and nearby creeks. Supplies available at Tellico plains. Deer, bears, turkeys and birds are common to the area. Reservation only.

GETTING THERE: From Tellico Plains go N on state HW 360 approx. 7.5 mi. to county HWY 504. Go E on 504 approx. 1.5 mi. to county HWY 506. Go N on 506 approx. 4 mi. to Young Branch Horse Camp CG.

SINGLE RATE:	$6	OPEN DATES:	May-Sept
		MAX STAY:	14 days

 Campground has hosts   **Reservable sites**   **Accessible facilities**   **Fully developed**   **Semi-developed**   ⚠ **Rustic facilities**

NOTE: Open dates listed are typical. Actual dates are dependent on conditions such as snow pack.

USFS Photo

NATIONAL FORESTS OF TEXAS

Come explore the Lone Star State. Relaxation and adventure await the visitor to the state's national forests. The Davy Crockett, Sam Houston, Angelina, and Sabine forests plus the Caddo-Lyndon B. Johnson National Grassland encompass approximately 675,000 acres of public land in eastern Texas.

There are 25 developed recreation areas, four hiking trails totaling 185 miles, five scenic areas, five wilderness areas, a canoe trail, off-road vehicle trails and 52 miles of horse trails.

The national forests and grasslands in Texas also provide excellent opportunities for bird watching and wildlife viewing. East Texas lies in the path of warblers, vireos, and other species of neotropical migrants, so spring migration can be great. The Davy Crockett and Sam Houston national forests are located where the pine forests of the southeastern United States join the blackland prairies of central Texas. The result is a marvelous mix of eastern and western species of birds and other wildlife found nowhere else in the state.

Other attractions include the Big Thicket National Preserve with its unique mixture of ecosystems and Lake Sam Rayburn, Toledo Bend Reservoir, and Lake Conroe are renowned for their scenic beauty and trophy black bass fishing.

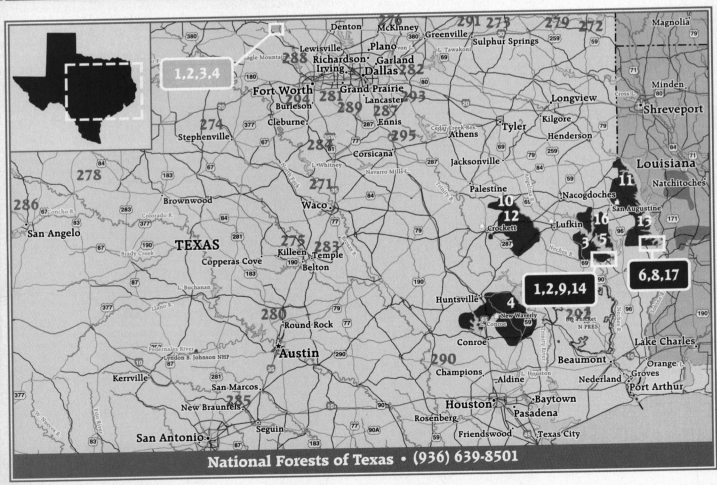

National Forests of Texas • (936) 639-8501

1 Bouton Lake
Zavalla • lat 31˚01'38" lon 094˚19'05"

DESCRIPTION: This primitive CG is in a hardwood and cypress forest setting on Bouton Lake. Fish for trout and swim in the lake. Supplies available at Zavalla. Numerous wildlife can be viewed in the area. Campers may gather firewood. The Sawmill Hiking Trail to Boykin Springs is nearby. No drinking water at CG.

GETTING THERE: From Zavalla go E on state HWY 63 approx. 7 mi. to forest route 303. Go S on 303 for 7 mi. to Bouton Lake CG.

SINGLE RATE:	No fee	OPEN DATES:	Yearlong*
# of SINGLE SITES:	7	MAX SPUR:	22 feet
		MAX STAY:	14 days
		ELEVATION:	115 feet

2 Boykin Springs
Zavalla • lat 31˚03'35" lon 094˚16'16"

DESCRIPTION: On Boykin Springs Lake in a natural forest setting. Fish or swim from the lake. Supplies available at Zavalla. Numerous wildlife can be seen in the area. Campers may gather firewood. The Sawmill Hiking Trail to Bouton Lake at the CG. RV dump station at CG.

GETTING THERE: From Zavalla go E on state HWY 63 for 11 mi. to forest route 313. Go S on 313 for 2.5 mi. to Boykin Spring CG.

SINGLE RATE:	$6	OPEN DATES:	Yearlong*
# of SINGLE SITES:	36	MAX SPUR:	24 feet
		MAX STAY:	14 days
		ELEVATION:	200 feet

3 Caney Creek
Zavalla • lat 31˚08'02" lon 094˚15'27"

DESCRIPTION: This rustic CG is located on the shores of Sam Rayburn Reservoir. Fish or swim in the reservoir. Supplies available at Zavalla. Many kinds of animals can be seen in the area. Campers may gather firewood. A self-guided 1/2 mi. trail starts at the CG. An amphitheater and RV dump station at CG.

GETTING THERE: From Zavalla go E on state HWY 63 approx. 5 mi. to FM 2743. Go E on 2743 approx. 4.5 mi. to forest route 336. Go NE on 336 for approx. 1 mi. to Caney Creek CG.

SINGLE RATE:	$6	OPEN DATES:	Yearlong*
# of SINGLE SITES:	123	MAX SPUR:	22 feet
		MAX STAY:	14 days
		ELEVATION:	191 feet

4 Double Lake
Coldspring • lat 30˚33'14" lon 095˚08'01"

DESCRIPTION: In a mixed forest setting on Double Lake. Fish from one of three piers on this lake, stocked with bass, bream and catfish. Boatramp at CG. A lakeside concession stand offers supplies. A 5-mile trail to the Big Creek Scenic Area, Lone Star Hiking Trail and an 8-mile mountain bike trail are all nearby.

GETTING THERE: From Coldspring go S on state HWY 150 approx. 1.5 mi. to Farm-to-Market 2025. Go S on 2025 approx. 1/2 mi. to forest route 210. Go E on 210 approx. 1 mi. to Double Lake CG.

SINGLE RATE:	Varies	OPEN DATES:	Yearlong
# of SINGLE SITES:	65	MAX SPUR:	40 feet
GROUP RATE:	$20	MAX STAY:	14 days
# of GROUP SITES:	9	ELEVATION:	291 feet

5 Harvey Creek
Broaddus • lat 31˚12'47" lon 094˚15'53"

DESCRIPTION: In a natural forest setting on the shores of Sam Rayburn Reservoir. Supplies available at Broaddus. Many species of wildlife can be seen in the area. Campers may gather firewood. No designated trails in the area. RV dump station is nearby. No drinking water

GETTING THERE: From Broaddus go S 1 mi. on state HWY 147 to FM 83. Go E on 83 approx. 3 mi. to FM 2390. Go S on 2390 approx. 6 mi. to Harvey Creek CG.

SINGLE RATE:	$2	OPEN DATES:	Yearlong*
# of SINGLE SITES:	22	MAX SPUR:	22 feet
		MAX STAY:	14 days
		ELEVATION:	232 feet

6 Indian Mounds
Hemphill • lat 31˚20'22" lon 093˚43'52"

DESCRIPTION: In a mixed forest setting on Toledo Bend Reservoir. Fish for bass, crappie and catfish in reservoir. Boat ramp at the CG. Supplies available at Hemphill. Deer, squirrels and birds are common to the area. RV dump station in CG. No designated trails in the area, there are a lot of old roads to hike on.

GETTING THERE: From Hemphill go E on state HWY 83 approx. 8 mi. to forest route 128-A. Go S on 128-A approx. 4 mi. to forest route 130. Go S on 130 approx. 1.5 mi. to Indian Mounds CG.

SINGLE RATE:	$4	OPEN DATES:	Mar-Oct
# of SINGLE SITES:	26	MAX SPUR:	30 feet
		MAX STAY:	14 days
		ELEVATION:	418 feet

7 Kellys Pond
Richards • lat 30˚30'32" lon 095˚39'33"

DESCRIPTION: This primitive, tent only CG has an open-air feeling with sparse vegetation consisting of southern pine and oak. Fishing is available in the three small ponds located directly S of camping area. Supplies at Richards. Deer and birds common to the area. The Lone Star Hiking Trail is located within a mile north of CG.

GETTING THERE: From Richards go E on Farm-to-Market 149 6.5 mi. to FM 1375. Go E on 1375 5 mi. to forest route 204. Go S on 204 1 mi. to forest route 271. Go W on 271 1.5 mi. to Kellys Pond CG. Park and hike in.

SINGLE RATE:	No fee	OPEN DATES:	Yearlong
# of SINGLE SITES:	8		
		MAX STAY:	14 days
		ELEVATION:	231 feet

8 Lakeview
Pineland • lat 31˚17'30" lon 093˚41'30"

DESCRIPTION: In a mixed forest setting on Toledo Bend Reservoir. Fish for bass, crappie and catfish in reservoir. Boat ramp nearby. Supplies available at Hemphill. Deer, squirrels and birds are common to the area. No designated trails in the area, there are a lot of old roads to hike on.

GETTING THERE: From Pineland go E on Farm-to-Market 2426 10 mi. to state HWY 87. Go S on 87 3 mi. to FM 2928. Go E on 2928 3.5 mi. to end of paved road; follow signs 4 mi. to Lakeview CG. Not recommended for large RV's.

SINGLE RATE:	$3	OPEN DATES:	Mar-Oct
# of SINGLE SITES:	10	MAX SPUR:	30 feet
		MAX STAY:	14 days
		ELEVATION:	180 feet

9 Letney
Zavalla • lat 31˚04'36" lon 094˚08'47"

DESCRIPTION: This primitive CG is located on the shores of Sam Rayburn Reservoir. Supplies available at Zavalla. Campers may gather firewood. This CG is popular with horseback riders because it is located near many trails. Reservation only.

GETTING THERE: From Zavalla go E on state HWY 63 approx. 10 mi. to forest route 347. Go E on 347 approx. 3.3 mi. to forest route 333. Go N on 333 approx. 1.5 mi. to Letney CG.

		OPEN DATES:	Yearlong*
		MAX SPUR:	22 feet
GROUP RATE:	Varies	MAX STAY:	14 days
		ELEVATION:	252 feet

10 Neches Bluff
Alto • lat 31˚34'00" lon 095˚09'51"

DESCRIPTION: A primitive CG in a hardwood forest setting on Neches River. Fish for trout or swim in the river. Supplies available at Alto. Deer, raccoons, bobats, birds and squirrels are common to the area. CG is a trailhead for the 4C Trail system.

GETTING THERE: From Alto go SW on state HWY 21 approx. 8 mi. to forest route 511. Go SE on 511 approx. 1 mi. to forest route 511-A. Go NE on 511-A approx. 1 mi. to Neches Bluff CG.

SINGLE RATE:	No fee	OPEN DATES:	Yearlong
		MAX STAY:	14 days
		ELEVATION:	361 feet

 Campground has hosts   **Reservable sites**   **Accessible facilities**   **Fully developed**   **Semi-developed**   **Rustic facilities**

NOTE: Open dates listed are typical. Actual dates are dependent on conditions such as snow pack.

11 Ragtown
Center • lat 31°40'53" lon 093°49'58"

DESCRIPTION: In a mixed forest setting nestled on a bluff overlooking Toledo Bend Reservoir. Fish for trout in reservoir. Supplies available at Center. Deer, squirrels and birds are common to the area. Campers may gather firewood. A one mi. trail takes you along the shore around the lake.

GETTING THERE: From Center go E on state HWY 87 approx. 11 mi. to Farm-to-Market 139. Go E on 139 approx. 6 mi. to FM 3184. Go E on 3184 approx. 4 mi. to Ragtown CG.

SINGLE RATE:	Varies	OPEN DATES:	Yearlong
# of SINGLE SITES:	25		
		MAX STAY:	14 days
		ELEVATION:	185 feet

12 Ratcliff Lake
Kennard • lat 31°23'03" lon 095°09'12"

DESCRIPTION: In a hardwood forest setting on Ratcliff Lake. Fish for trout or swim on the lake. Boat launch at the CG. Supplies available at Kennard. This is a historical CCC Camp. Deer, raccoons, bobcats, birds and squirrels are common to the area. CG is a trailhead for the 4C Trail system.

GETTING THERE: Ratcliff lake CG is located approx. 2.5 mi. NE of Kennard on state HWY 7.

SINGLE RATE:	Varies	OPEN DATES:	Yearlong
# of SINGLE SITES:	77	MAX SPUR:	28 feet
		MAX STAY:	14 days
		ELEVATION:	300 feet

13 Red Hills Lake
Milam • lat 31°28'27" lon 093°49'49"

DESCRIPTION: In a mixed forest setting on Red Hill Lake. Fish on the lake. Supplies available at Milam. Deer and birds are common in the area. RV dump station at CG. A 1/2 mi. trail to a historical CCC lookout tower on Chambers Hill.

GETTING THERE: From Milam go N on forest route 22 approx. 2.5 mi. to forest route 116. Go E on 116 approx. 1/2 mi. to Red Hills Lake CG.

SINGLE RATE:	$6	OPEN DATES:	Mar-Oct
# of SINGLE SITES:	28	MAX SPUR:	28 feet
GROUP RATE:	$30	MAX STAY:	14 days
# of GROUP SITES:	1	ELEVATION:	300 feet

14 Sandy Creek
Zavalla • lat 31°05'50" lon 094°12'10"

DESCRIPTION: In a natural forest setting on the shores of Sam Rayburn Reservoir with panoramic views of the lake. Fish or swim in the reservoir. Supplies available at Zavalla. Campers may gather firewood. Numerous wildlife in area. Hike along the shore of the reservoir.

GETTING THERE: From Zavalla go E on state HWY 63 approx. 17.5 mi. to forest route 333. Go N on 333 approx. 3 mi. to Sandy Creek CG.

SINGLE RATE:	$6	OPEN DATES:	Yearlong*
# of SINGLE SITES:	15	MAX SPUR:	22 feet
		MAX STAY:	14 days
		ELEVATION:	197 feet

15 Stubblefield
Richards • lat 30°33'28" lon 095°38'24"

DESCRIPTION: In a fairly open, mixed forest setting on Stubblefield Lake. Fishing on Stubblefield Lake bridge, Stubblefield Lake and Lake Conroe. Boat access at CG. Supplies at Richards. Campers may gather firewood. The Lone Star Hiking Trail near CG, and the Stubblefield Interpretive Trail is located nearby.

GETTING THERE: From Richards go E on Farm-to-Market 149 6.5 mi. to FM 1375. Go E on 1375 5 mi. to forest route 208. Go NW on 208 1 mi. to forest route 215. Go NE on 215 approx. 2 mi. to Stubblefield CG.

SINGLE RATE:	$9	OPEN DATES:	Yearlong
# of SINGLE SITES:	30	MAX SPUR:	20 feet
		MAX STAY:	14 days
		ELEVATION:	215 feet

16 Townsend
Broaddus • lat 31°20'59" lon 094°18'46"

DESCRIPTION: CG is located on Sam Rayburn Reservoir and offers a rustic and tranquil setting. Boat ramp at CG. Fish or swim in the reservoir. Supplies available at Broaddus. Campers may gather firewood. Many animals in the area. No designated trails in the area. RV dump station nearby.

GETTING THERE: From Broaddus go N on state HWY 147 for 1 mi. to FM 1277. Go W on 1277 for 4.5 mi. to FM 2923. Go W on 2923 for 1.5 mi. to Townsend CG.

SINGLE RATE:	$4	OPEN DATES:	Yearlong*
# of SINGLE SITES:	14	MAX SPUR:	22 feet
		MAX STAY:	14 days
		ELEVATION:	178 feet

17 Willow Oak
Hemphill • lat 33°16'15" lon 095°53'43"

DESCRIPTION: In a mixed forest setting on Toledo Bend Reservoir. Fish for bass, crappie and catfish in reservoir. Boat ramp at the CG. Supplies available at Hemphill. Deer, squirrels and birds are common to the area. RV dump station in CG. No designated trails in the area, there are a lot of old roads to hike on.

GETTING THERE: From Hemphill go S on state HWY 87 approx. 11 mi. to Willow Oak CG.

SINGLE RATE:	$4	OPEN DATES:	Yearlong
# of SINGLE SITES:	15	MAX SPUR:	30 feet
		MAX STAY:	14 days
		ELEVATION:	200 feet

1 Coffee Mill
Honey Grove • lat 33°40'00" lon 955°83'0"

DESCRIPTION: CG is located in mixed hardwoods on the north end of Coffee Mill Lake. Good fishing in lake for crappie, catfish and bass. Supplies available at Honey Grove. Deer, turkeys, hogs and small game can be seen in the area. Busy in fall during hunts. No designated trails in the area.

GETTING THERE: From Honey Grove go N on farm to market road 100 approx. 12 mi. to forest route 919. Go W on 919 approx. 4.5 mi. to the Coffee Mill CG entrance.

SINGLE RATE:	No fee	OPEN DATES:	Yearlong
# of SINGLE SITES:	15	MAX SPUR:	60 feet
		MAX STAY:	14 days
		ELEVATION:	520 feet

2 East Lake Davey Crockett
Honey Grove • lat 33°40'00" lon 955°54'5"

DESCRIPTION: CG is located in mixed hardwoods on the E side of Lake Davey Crockett. Good fishing in lake for crappie, catfish and bass. Supplies available in Honey Grove. Deer, turkeys, feral hogs and small game can be seen in the area. No camping spurs, just tent camp area. Popular horse trail in area.

GETTING THERE: From Honey Grove go N on farm to market road 100 approx. to forest route 919. Go W on 919 approx. 1.5 mi. to West Lake Davey Crockett CG.

SINGLE RATE:	No fee	OPEN DATES:	Yearlong
# of SINGLE SITES:	6	MAX SPUR:	10 feet
		MAX STAY:	14 days
		ELEVATION:	545 feet

3 West Lake Davey Crockett
Honey Grove • lat 33°40'00" lon 955°60'0"

DESCRIPTION: Campground is located in mixed hardwoods on Lake Davey Crockett. Good fishing in lake for crappie, catfish and bass. Supplies available at Honey Grove. Deer, turkeys, feral hogs and small game can be seen in the area. Busy in fall during hunts. No designated trails in the area.

GETTING THERE: From Honey Grove go N on farm to market road 100 for 12 approx. mi. to forest route 919. Go W on 919 approx. 1/2 mile to East Lake Davey Crockett CG.

SINGLE RATE:	$4	OPEN DATES:	Yearlong
# of SINGLE SITES:	12	MAX SPUR:	60 feet
		MAX STAY:	14 days
		ELEVATION:	545 feet

 Campground has hosts   **Reservable sites**   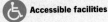 **Accessible facilities**   **Fully developed**   **Semi-developed**   **Rustic facilities**

NOTE: Open dates listed are typical. Actual dates are dependent on conditions such as snow pack.

4 Black Creek
Decatur • lat 33˚20'30" lon 973˚63'0"

DESCRIPTION: CG is located in mixed hardwoods on the north end of Coffee Mill Lake. Good fishing in lake for crappie, catfish and bass. Supplies available in Decatur. Deer, turkeys, feral hogs and small game can be seen in the area. No camping spurs, just camp along loop. Busy in fall during hunts.

GETTING THERE: From Decatur go N 3 mi. on Farm to Market 730 to Red Deer Road. Go N 5 mi. on RD to Claborn Road. Go W 3/4 mi. on RD to forest route 918. Go N 1 mi. on 918 to Black Creek Lake CG.

SINGLE RATE:	No fee	OPEN DATES:	Yearlong
# of SINGLE SITES:	6	MAX SPUR:	15 feet
		MAX STAY:	14 days
		ELEVATION:	1140 feet

Driving Off-Road

You can keep yourself informed of the latest travel regulations and physical conditions by picking up a forest travel map at your local ranger district office. Driving off designated roads and trails is illegal in many forests. Being a responsible user by obeying restrictions and prohibitions on use of vehicles will conserve our natural resources for future enjoyment.

 Campground has hosts   **Reservable sites**   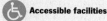 **Accessible facilities**   **Fully developed**   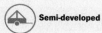 **Semi-developed**    **Rustic facilities**

NOTE: Open dates listed are typical. Actual dates are dependent on conditions such as snow pack.

ASHLEY NATIONAL FOREST

The Ashley National Forest comprises 1.3 million acres and is located in northeast Utah and southwest Wyoming. Forest landscape ranges from high desert country to high mountain areas and the elevation varies from a low of 6,000 feet to a high of 13,528 feet above sea level at the summit of Kings Peak.

Over 2.5 million visitors come to the forest each year to participate in outdoor activities, such as boating, fishing, camping, hiking, backpacking, and horseback riding.

Attractions include the Flaming Gorge National Recreation Area, a 91-mile reservoir famous for its record-producing fish, and the High Uintas Wilderness, which encompasses 460,000 acres and is the largest wilderness in Utah.

The Ashley is also one of the richest areas for wildlife-viewing and fossil-finding in the West. Ancient sand and limestone formations shape today's habitats. Elk and deer now walk over what was once an ancient sea, hawks and eagles fly over areas where dinosaurs walked, and fish swim among the remains of petrified forests. Dinosaur National Park and the rocks near Steinaker and Red Fleet State parks provide excellent areas for finding prehistoric bones.

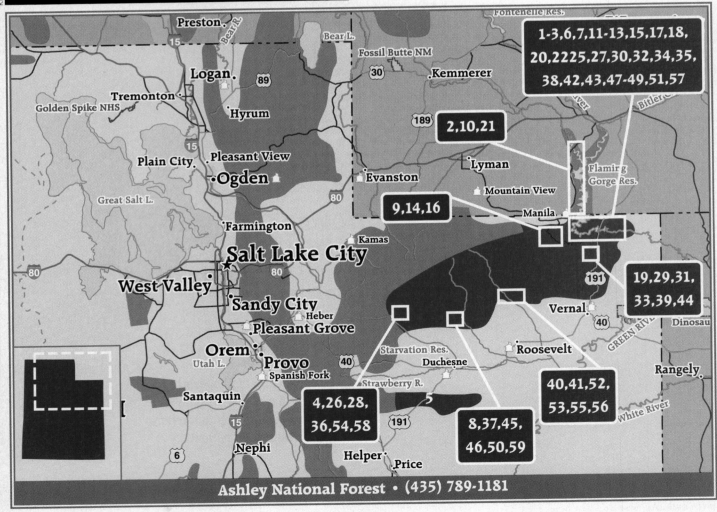

1. Antelope Flat
Dutch John • lat 40°57'58" lon 109°33'03"

DESCRIPTION: This CG is situated on sagebrush covered hills. Spectacular views of Flaming Gorge Reservoir. Hot days with cool nights. Supplies are available 10 mi. away in Dutch John. Antelope herds in area yearlong. Boat ramp at CG. There is a sanitation dump station nearby. Group maximum of 50/80.

GETTING THERE: From Dutch John go N on US HWY 191 approx. 4.5 mi. to forest route 145. Go W on 145 approx. 5 mi. to Antelope Flat CG.

SINGLE RATE:	$12	OPEN DATES:	May-Sept
# of SINGLE SITES:	46	MAX SPUR:	60 feet
GROUP RATE:	$65	MAX STAY:	14 days
# of GROUP SITES:	4	ELEVATION:	6060 feet

2. Anvil Draw
Manila • lat 41°04'30" lon 109°33'30"

DESCRIPTION: On Flaming Gorge Reservoir. No drinking water.

GETTING THERE: From Manila go NE on state HWY 530 approx. 8.5 mi. to forest route 001. Go E on 001 approx. 2.5 mi. to Anvil Draw CG.

SINGLE RATE:	No fee	OPEN DATES:	May-Sept
		MAX STAY:	14 days
		ELEVATION:	1840 feet

3. Arch Dam Overflow
Dutch John • lat 40°54'44" lon 109°24'30"

DESCRIPTION: This CG is situated in a park-like setting on the shores of Flaming Gorge Dam and access to the Green River within 1 mi. of CG. Please check for local fishing regulations. Supplies are available at Flaming Gorge Lodge nearby. Maximum group capacity of 60-75 people.

GETTING THERE: Arch Dam Overflow CG is located approx. 2 mi. S of Dutch John just W of US HWY 191.

SINGLE RATE:	$6	OPEN DATES:	May-Sept
		MAX SPUR:	40 feet
GROUP RATE:	$50	MAX STAY:	14 days
# of GROUP SITES:	4	ELEVATION:	6240 feet

4. Aspen
Hanna • lat 40°47'11" lon 111°02'10"

DESCRIPTION: This CG is situated among pine and aspen on the Duchesne River. Good fishing opportunities in the river, please check local regulations. Deer and elk are common to the area. CG tends to be busy on weekends and holidays. Supplies are available 11 mi. away in Tabiona.

GETTING THERE: From Hanna go N on state HWY 35 approx. 5 mi. to forest route 144. Go N on 144 approx. 3 mi. to Aspen Grove CG.

SINGLE RATE:	Varies	OPEN DATES:	May-Oct
# of SINGLE SITES:	32	MAX SPUR:	30 feet
		MAX STAY:	14 days
# of GROUP SITES:	1	ELEVATION:	6450 feet

5. Avintaquin
Duchesne • lat 39°53'03" lon 110°46'31"

DESCRIPTION: This CG is situated in a dense pine and spruce forest, set on a high mountain ridge. Watch for deer, small wildlife, and elk in the area. Various trails nearby. Supplies are available 33 mi. away in Duchesne. Receives moderate use, picking up on holiday weekends in the summer. No drinking water available.

GETTING THERE: From Duchesne go S on US HWY 191 approx. 32 mi. to forest route 147. Go W on 147 approx. 2 mi. to Avintaquin CG.

SINGLE RATE:	$5	OPEN DATES:	May-Oct
# of SINGLE SITES:	24	MAX SPUR:	20 feet
GROUP RATE:	$20	MAX STAY:	14 days
# of GROUP SITES:	1	ELEVATION:	8100 feet

6. Big Cottonwoods
Dutch John • lat 40°54'41" lon 109°15'57"

DESCRIPTION: This CG is situated among ponderosa pine trees on the B-section of the Green River. Watch for wildlife in the area such as deer, elk, and various birds. Supplies at Dutch John. Fish the Green River; please check for local fishing regulations. This CG is accessible only by boat or hike-in.

GETTING THERE: Big Cottonwoods CG is accessible only by boat and is located on the B section of the Green River approx. 1 mi. downstream from Little Hole.

SINGLE RATE:	$10	OPEN DATES:	Yearlong
		MAX STAY:	14 days
		ELEVATION:	5520 feet

7. Big Pine
Dutch John • lat 40°54'42" lon 109°15'57"

DESCRIPTION: This CG is situated among ponderosa pine on the B-section of the Green River. Fish the Green River; please check for local fishing regulations. Supplies at Dutch John. This CG is only accessible by boat or hike-in. Watch for wildlife in the area such as deer, elk, and various birds.

GETTING THERE: Big Pine CG is accessible only by boat and is located on the B section of the Green River approx. 3.5 mi. downstream from Little Hole.

SINGLE RATE:	$10	OPEN DATES:	Yearlong
		MAX STAY:	14 days
		ELEVATION:	5640 feet

8. Bridge
Mt. Home • lat 40°34'30" lon 110°19'30"

DESCRIPTION: This CG is situated in a pine and spruce forest on the banks of Yellowstone Creek. Good trout fishing in the creek, please check for local regulations. Supplies can be found 12 mi. away at Mountain Home. Various trails nearby. Watch for deer, elk, and small wildlife in the area.

GETTING THERE: From Mt. Home go N on the Moon Lake Road approx. 5 mi. to forest route 119. Go N on 119 approx. 5 mi. to forest route 124. Go N on 124 approx. 2 mi. to Bridge CG.

SINGLE RATE:	$9	OPEN DATES:	May-Oct
# of SINGLE SITES:	5	MAX SPUR:	20 feet
		MAX STAY:	14 days
		ELEVATION:	7100 feet

9. Browne Lake
Manila • lat 40°51'30" lon 109°47'30"

DESCRIPTION: This CG is situated among aspen and subalpine firs on Browne Lake. Good fishing opportunities in the lake. Wildlife in the area includes deer, elk, and various birds. CG is seldom busy. Limited supplies are available approx. 20 mi. away in Manila. No drinking water available on site.

GETTING THERE: From Manila go S on state HWY 44 approx. 11 mi. to forest route 221. Go W on 221 approx. 7 mi. to forest route 096. Go S on 096 approx. 2 mi. to Browne Lake CG.

SINGLE RATE:	$5	OPEN DATES:	May-Sept
# of SINGLE SITES:	8	MAX STAY:	14 days
		ELEVATION:	8100 feet

10. Buckboard Crossing
Green River • lat 41°14'49" lon 109°35'01"

DESCRIPTION: This CG is situated on flat terrain, adjacent to Buckboard Marina, set on Lake Flaming Gorge. Vegetation consists primarily of sagebrush and broadleaf trees. Firewood is scarce in the area, best to bring your own (charcoal is recommended). Supplies are available in Green River.

GETTING THERE: From Green River go S on state HWY 530 approx. 20 mi. to forest route 009. Go E on 009 approx. 1.5 mi. to Buckboard Crossing CG.

SINGLE RATE:	$13	OPEN DATES:	May-Oct
# of SINGLE SITES:	68	MAX SPUR:	45 feet
		MAX STAY:	14 days
		ELEVATION:	6010 feet

 Campground has hosts   **Reservable sites**   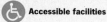 **Accessible facilities**    **Fully developed**   **Semi-developed**   **Rustic facilities**

NOTE: Open dates listed are typical. Actual dates are dependent on conditions such as snow pack.

11 Canyon Rim
Greendale Junction • lat 40°53'04" lon 109°32'46"

DESCRIPTION: This CG is situated among pine on a rim above Flaming Gorge Reservoir. Good fishing opportunities nearby, please check local fishing regulations. Wildlife in the area includes deer, elk, and various birds. Supplies are available approx. 2 mi. away at Red Canyon Lodge. Busy all summer.

GETTING THERE: From Greendale Junction on US HWY 191 go W on state HWY 44 approx. 3 mi. to forest route 095. Go N on 095 approx. 1.5 mi. to Canyon Rim CG.

SINGLE RATE:	$12	OPEN DATES:	May-Sept
# of SINGLE SITES:	18		
		MAX STAY:	14 days
		ELEVATION:	7418 feet

12 Carmel
Manila • lat 40°55'55" lon 109°44'04"

DESCRIPTION: No drinking water. On Sheep Creek.

GETTING THERE: From Manila go S on state HWY 44 approx. 6 mi. to forest route 218. Go W on 218 approx. 1/2 mi. to Carmel CG.

SINGLE RATE:	$6	OPEN DATES:	Yearlong
# of SINGLE SITES:	17		
		MAX STAY:	14 days
		ELEVATION:	6280 feet

13 Cedar Springs
Greendale • lat 40°54'32" lon 109°26'59"

DESCRIPTION: This CG is situated on the shores of Flaming Gorge Reservoir, and provides reservoir oriented recreation. Terrain is rolling and the temperatures tend to get hot. There is an RV sanitation dump station available nearby. Wildlife in the area includes deer, and elk. Showers are available at Deer Run CG.

GETTING THERE: From Greendale Junction go N on US HWY 191 approx. 6 mi. to forest route 183. Go N on 183 approx. 1 mi. to Cedar Springs CG.

SINGLE RATE:	$12	OPEN DATES:	May-Oct
# of SINGLE SITES:	21	MAX SPUR:	99 feet
		MAX STAY:	14 days
		ELEVATION:	6150 feet

14 Deep Creek
Manila • lat 40°51'19" lon 109°43'45"

DESCRIPTION: This CG is situated in a dense stand of conifer with spectacular meadow views. Wildlife in the area includes deer, elk, and various birds. Good trout fishing opportunities nearby, check local fishing regulations. Hiking, horse, and mountain bike trails in area. Visit historic Brush Creek Ranger Station.

GETTING THERE: From Manila go S on state HWY 4 approx. 11 mi. to forest route 221. Go W on 221 approx. 3 mi. to forest route 539. Go S on 539 approx. 4 mi. to Deep Creek CG.

SINGLE RATE:	$6	OPEN DATES:	May-Sept
# of SINGLE SITES:	17	MAX SPUR:	30 feet
		MAX STAY:	14 days
		ELEVATION:	7664 feet

15 Deer Run
Greendale • lat 40°54'22" lon 109°26'38"

DESCRIPTION: This CG is adjacent to Flaming Gorge Reservoir and provides reservoir oriented recreation. Terrain is rolling and temperatures tend to get quite hot. Vegetation includes pinyon pine trees. Showers are available on site. Flaming Gorge Dam and Visitor Center are within 2 miles of the CG.

GETTING THERE: Deer Run CG is located just W of US HWY 191 approx. 6 mi. N of Greendale Junction on fores route 183.

SINGLE RATE:	$14	OPEN DATES:	Apr-Oct
# of SINGLE SITES:	19	MAX SPUR:	86 feet
		MAX STAY:	14 days
		ELEVATION:	6200 feet

16 Dowd Springs
Manila • lat 40°52'55" lon 109°41'33"

DESCRIPTION: This CG is situated in a stand of conifer on Dowd Creek near Dowd Hole. Wildlife in the area includes deer, elk, and various birds. Good trout fishing opportunities nearby, check local fishing regulations. Hiking, horse, and mountain bike trails in area.

GETTING THERE: From Manila go S on state HWY 44 approx. 12 mi. to Dowd Springs CG.

SINGLE RATE:	Varies	OPEN DATES:	May-Sept
# of SINGLE SITES:	4		
		MAX STAY:	14 days
		ELEVATION:	7535 feet

17 Dripping Springs
Dutch John • lat 40°55'26" lon 109°21'05"

DESCRIPTION: CG vegetation consists primarily of pinyon pine and juniper trees. Activities include guided rafting trips on the Green River and fishing the Green River and Lake Flaming Gorge. Terrain is rolling and temperatures may be quite hot. Group capacity of 40/60. No fee, reduced services Oct-March.

GETTING THERE: Dripping Springs CG is located approx. 2 mi. E of Dutch John on the Little Hole Road.

SINGLE RATE:	$12	OPEN DATES:	Yearlong
# of SINGLE SITES:	21	MAX SPUR:	60 feet
GROUP RATE:	$65	MAX STAY:	14 days
# of GROUP SITES:	4	ELEVATION:	6160 feet

18 Dutch John Draw
Dutch John • lat 40°56'02" lon 109°26'00"

DESCRIPTION: This CG is situated on the shore of a scenic lake, no boat ramp available. Please check for local fishing regulations. Watch for various wildlife in the CG area. The gate to this CG is always kept locked; the key can be obtained from the host of Cedar Springs CG.

GETTING THERE: From Dutch John go S on US HWY 191 approx. 1/2 mi. to Dutch John Draw Road. Follow signs to Dutch John Draw CG. Large RV's are not recommended.

		OPEN DATES:	May-Sept
		MAX SPUR:	20 feet
GROUP RATE:	$50	MAX STAY:	14 days
# of GROUP SITES:	1	ELEVATION:	6040 feet

19 East Park
Vernal • lat 40°46'52" lon 109°33'10"

DESCRIPTION: This CG is situated among pine and aspen with grassy openings. Set on East Park reservoir, please check for local fishing regulations. Watch for wildlife in the area such as deer, elk, moose, and various birds. Supplies are available 30 mi. away at Vernal. No drinking water during the off season.

GETTING THERE: From Vernal go N on US HWY 191 approx. 20 mi. to forest route 18. Go W approx. 3.5 mi. to forest route 20. Go N on 20 approx. 5 mi. to forest route 22. Go N on 22 approx. 1 mi. to East Park CG.

SINGLE RATE:	$8	OPEN DATES:	June-Sept
# of SINGLE SITES:	21	MAX SPUR:	30 feet
		MAX STAY:	14 days
		ELEVATION:	9080 feet

20 Firefighters Memorial
Greendale • lat 40°53'00" lon 109°27'30"

DESCRIPTION: This CG is situated on flat terrain and the predominant vegetation is ponderosa pine. There are new tent pads in place. Popular activities include raft trips on the Green River, and guided fishing on the Green River and Flaming Gorge Reservoir. A sanitary dump station is available nearby.

GETTING THERE: Firefighters Memorial CG is located approx. 3 mi. N of Greendale Junction just E of US HWY 191.

SINGLE RATE:	$12	OPEN DATES:	May-Sept
# of SINGLE SITES:	94	MAX SPUR:	35 feet
		MAX STAY:	14 days
		ELEVATION:	6900 feet

 Campground has hosts   **Reservable sites**   **Accessible facilities**   **Fully developed**   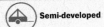 **Semi-developed**   **Rustic facilities**

NOTE: Open dates listed are typical. Actual dates are dependent on conditions such as snow pack.

21 Firehole Canyon
Green River • lat 41°21'02" lon 109°26'40"

DESCRIPTION: This CG is situated on the shores of Flaming Gorge Reservoir. Vegetation in the area consists primarily of sagebrush and broadleaf trees. Good fishing opportunities in the Reservoir. Please check local fishing regulations. Supplies are available 32 mi. away in Green River.

GETTING THERE: From Green River go E on I-80 approx. 8 mi. to US HWY 191. Go S on 191 approx. 14 mi. to forest route 106. Go W on 106 approx. 10 mi. to Firehole Canyon CG.

SINGLE RATE:	$12	OPEN DATES:	May-Oct
# of SINGLE SITES:	40		
GROUP RATE:		MAX STAY:	14 days
		ELEVATION:	6111 feet

22 Gooseneck
Manila • lat 40°53'20" lon 109°32'13"

DESCRIPTION: This CG is used as a boat camp. Situated among the junipers on Flaming Gorge Reservoir. Popular activites in the area include swimming, fishing, and boating. Wildlife in the area includes deer, elk, and various birds. Pack it in, pack it out. No drinking water available on site.

GETTING THERE: Gooseneck CG is located on Flaming Gorge Reservoir in Red Canyon and is accessible only by boat.

SINGLE RATE:	$5	OPEN DATES:	May-Sept
# of SINGLE SITES:	6		
		MAX STAY:	14 days
		ELEVATION:	6040 feet

23 Greendale East Group
Greendale • lat 40°52'59" lon 109°27'40"

DESCRIPTION: This CG is situated among ponderosa pine with open areas. Groceries may be purchased at Flaming Gorge Lodge across the road from CG. Wildlife in the area includes deer, elk, and various birds. CG tends to be busy on weekends and holidays in the summer. Groups only, maximum of 40 persons.

GETTING THERE: Greendale East CG is located approx. 2 mi. N of Greendale Junction just E of US HWY 191.

		OPEN DATES:	May-Sept
		MAX SPUR:	50 feet
GROUP RATE:	$50	MAX STAY:	14 days
# of GROUP SITES:	4	ELEVATION:	7000 feet

24 Greendale West
Greendale • lat 40°52'59" lon 109°27'40"

DESCRIPTION: This CG is situated among ponderosa pine and sagebrush. Supplies are available 2 mi. away at Flaming Gorge Lodge. Wildlife in the area includes deer, elk, and various birds.

GETTING THERE: Greendale West CG is located approx. 2 mi. N of Greendale Junction just W of US HWY 191. Just N of Flaming Gorge Lodge.

SINGLE RATE:	$12	OPEN DATES:	May-Sept
# of SINGLE SITES:	8		
GROUP RATE:		MAX STAY:	14 days
		ELEVATION:	7000 feet

25 Greens Lake
Greendale Junction • lat 40°52'24" lon 109°32'12"

DESCRIPTION: This CG is situated among pine on Greens Lake. Check fishing regulations for the local area. Wildlife in the area includes deer, elk, and various birds. Groceries can be purchased at Red Canyon Lodge adjacent to the CG. CG tends to be busy on weekends and holidays in the summer. Group maximum of 40.

GETTING THERE: From Greendale Junction on US HWY 191 go W on state HWY 44 approx. 3 mi. to forest route 095. Go N on 095 approx. 1 mi. to Greens Lake CG.

SINGLE RATE:	$12	OPEN DATES:	May-Sept
# of SINGLE SITES:	19		
GROUP RATE:	$50	MAX STAY:	14 days
# of GROUP SITES:	1	ELEVATION:	7460 feet

26 Hades
Hanna • lat 40°32'03" lon 110°52'22"

DESCRIPTION: This CG is situated among pine on the Duchesne River. Good fishing opportunities in the river, please check localy fishing regulations. Supplies are available 6 mi. away in Hanna. CG tends to be busy on weekends and holidays in the summer. Deer and elk are common to the area.

GETTING THERE: From Hanna go N on state HWY 35 approx. 5 mi. to forest route 144. Go N on 144 approx. 6 mi. to Hades CG.

SINGLE RATE:	$6	OPEN DATES:	May-Oct
# of SINGLE SITES:	17	MAX SPUR:	20 feet
		MAX STAY:	14 days
		ELEVATION:	6550 feet

27 Hideout Canyon Boat-In
Manila • lat 40°54'42" lon 109°38'25"

DESCRIPTION: This CG is situated on the shores of Flaming Gorge Reservoir. Possible fishing opportunities on the reservoir, please check for local regulations. Pack it in, pack it out. Maximum boat size permitted is 36 feet. Only one boat allowed per site. CG is accessible only by boat.

GETTING THERE: Hideout Canyon Boat-In CG is located in Flaming Gorge Reservoir in Hideout Draw and is accessible only by boat.

SINGLE RATE:	$18	OPEN DATES:	May-Sept
# of SINGLE SITES:	18		
		MAX STAY:	14 days
		ELEVATION:	6200 feet

28 Iron Mine
Hanna • lat 40°33'15" lon 110°53'12"

DESCRIPTION: This CG is situated among pine and aspen on the banks of the Duchesne River. Good fishing opportunities in the river. Mill Flat Trailhead is adjacent to CG for hiking access. Deer and elk are common to the area. CG tends to be busy on weekends and holidays during the summer.

GETTING THERE: From Hanna go N on state HWY 35 approx. 5 mi. to forest route 144. Go N on 144 approx. 8 mi. to Iron Mine CG.

SINGLE RATE:	$6	OPEN DATES:	May-Oct
# of SINGLE SITES:	27	MAX SPUR:	20 feet
GROUP RATE:	$25	MAX STAY:	14 days
# of GROUP SITES:	1	ELEVATION:	6600 feet

29 Iron Springs Group
Vernal • lat 40°42'07" lon 109°33'24"

DESCRIPTION: This CG is situated among pine and aspen with grassy openings, set on small stream. Fishing in lakes around the area. Supplies are available 25 mi. away at Vernal. Watch for wildlife in the area such as deer, elk, moose, and various birds. No services or drinking water available 9/16-5/14.

GETTING THERE: Iron Springs Group CG is located approx. 5 mi. W of US HWY 191 on the Redcloud Dryfork Scenic Loop.

		OPEN DATES:	May-Sept
		MAX SPUR:	45 feet
GROUP RATE:	$20	MAX STAY:	14 days
# of GROUP SITES:	2	ELEVATION:	8738 feet

30 Jarvies Canyon Boat-In
Manila • lat 40°55'47" lon 109°28'42"

DESCRIPTION: This CG is situated in a juniper and pinyon pine forest on the shores Flaming Gorge Reservoir. Fish from the reservoir, check for local regulations. Accessible only by boat. Wildlife in the area includes deer, elk, and various birds. No drinking water available on site. Pack it in, pack it out.

GETTING THERE: Jarvies Canyon Boat-In CG is located in Flaming Gorge Reservoir and is accessible only by boat.

SINGLE RATE:	No fee	OPEN DATES:	Yearlong
# of SINGLE SITES:	8		
		MAX STAY:	14 days
		ELEVATION:	6000 feet

 Campground has hosts   **Reservable sites**   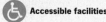 **Accessible facilities**   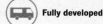 **Fully developed**   **Semi-developed**   **Rustic facilities**

NOTE: Open dates listed are typical. Actual dates are dependent on conditions such as snow pack.

31 Kaler Hollow
Vernal • lat 40°42'07" lon 109°35'47"

DESCRIPTION: This CG is situated among pine and aspen with grassy openings. Set on East Park reservoir, please check for local fishing regulations. Watch for wildlife in the area such as deer, elk, moose, and various birds. Supplies are available 29 mi. away at Vernal. No drinking water available on site.

GETTING THERE: Kaler Hollow CG is located approx. 9 mi. W of US HWY 191 on the Redcloud Dry Creek Loop.

SINGLE RATE:	No fee	OPEN DATES:	June-Sept
# of SINGLE SITES:	4	MAX SPUR:	20 feet
		MAX STAY:	14 days
		ELEVATION:	8600 feet

32 Kingfisher Island Boat-In
Manila • lat 40°56'26" lon 109°38'28"

DESCRIPTION: Accessible by boat located on the Reservoir. Fishing, swimming & boating. Pack it in, pack it out. No drinking water.

GETTING THERE: Kingfisher Island CG is located in Flaming Gorge Reservoir at the N end of Kingfisher Island and is accessible only by boat.

SINGLE RATE:	$6	OPEN DATES:	May-Sept
# of SINGLE SITES:	8		
		MAX STAY:	14 days
		ELEVATION:	6080 feet

33 Lodgepole
Vernal • lat 40°48'42" lon 109°27'56"

DESCRIPTION: This CG is situated among lodgepole pine and quaking aspen trees in a high desert setting. Firewood is available to be bought on site. Supplies are availalbe 6 mi. away at Flaming Gorge Lodge. Fishing opportunities at Lake Flaming Gorge. Watch for wildlife in the area such as deer, elk, moose, and various birds.

GETTING THERE: Lodgepole CG is located approx. 31 mi. N of Vernal on US HWY 191. Gated off season.

SINGLE RATE:	$12	OPEN DATES:	May-Sept
# of SINGLE SITES:	35	MAX SPUR:	45 feet
		MAX STAY:	14 days
		ELEVATION:	8080 feet

34 Lucerne Valley
Manila • lat 40°59'01" lon 109°35'24"

DESCRIPTION: This CG is set on flat terrain. The area is adjacent to Flaming Gorge Reservoir and good for large boats. A concrete boat ramp is adjacent to the marina and boat rentals are available. This is a trophy trout fishing area, please check local fishing regulations. Supplies are available in Manila.

GETTING THERE: From Manila go NE on state HWY 43 approx. 4 mi. to forest route 146. Go E on 146 approx. 4 mi. to Lucerne Valley CG.

SINGLE RATE:	$13	OPEN DATES:	Apr-Oct*
# of SINGLE SITES:	147	MAX SPUR:	35 feet
GROUP RATE:	$65	MAX STAY:	14 days
# of GROUP SITES:	4	ELEVATION:	6060 feet

35 Manns
Manila • lat 40°55'29" lon 109°42'26"

DESCRIPTION: This CG is situated among willow and open country on Sheep Creek. Limited supplies are available approx. 6 mi. away in Manila. Deer, small wildlife, and bighorn sheep are common to the area. CG tends to be busy on weekends and holidays. No drinking water available on site.

GETTING THERE: Mann CG is located approx. 6 mi. S of Manila on state HWY 44.

SINGLE RATE:	$6	OPEN DATES:	Yearlong
# of SINGLE SITES:	6		
		MAX STAY:	14 days
		ELEVATION:	6120 feet

36 Miners Gulch
Mt. Home • lat 40°32'01" lon 110°37'25"

DESCRIPTION: This CG is situated among aspen and pine accross the road from Rock Creek. Good fishing opportunities in the creek, please check local fishing regulations. Deer frequent the area. Supplies are available 16 mi. away in Mountain Home. Seldom busy. No drinking water available on site.

GETTING THERE: Miners Gulch CG is located approx. 16 mi. W of Mt. Home on the Rock Creek Road.

# of SINGLE SITES:	10	OPEN DATES:	May-Oct
GROUP RATE:	$25	MAX SPUR:	30 feet
# of GROUP SITES:	1	MAX STAY:	14 days
		ELEVATION:	6900 feet

37 Moon Lake
Mt. Home • lat 40°34'09" lon 110°30'34"

DESCRIPTION: This CG is situated among pine on the shores of Moon Lake. Deer and elk are common to the area. Busy all summer. Fishing in lake and many small streams in the area. Check regulations. Access point to High Uintas Wilderness Area. Supplies are 15 mi. away in Mountain Home. Group site reservations necessary.

GETTING THERE: Moon Lake CG is located approx. 15 mi. N of Mt. Home on Moon Lake Road.

SINGLE RATE:	$12	OPEN DATES:	May-Oct
# of SINGLE SITES:	56	MAX SPUR:	25 feet
GROUP RATE:	$50	MAX STAY:	14 days
# of GROUP SITES:	2	ELEVATION:	7500 feet

38 Mustang Ridge
Dutch John • lat 40°55'38" lon 109°26'21"

DESCRIPTION: This CG is situated in a high desert habitat with rolling terrain and scattered pinyon pine trees. Watch for various wildlife in the CG area. Temperatures in the area become hot in the summer months. Firewood is available to be bought on site. An amphitheater is available at the CG.

GETTING THERE: From Dutch John go N on US HWY 191 approx. 2 mi. to forest route 184. Go S on 184 approx. 2.5 mi. to Mustang Ridge CG.

SINGLE RATE:	$14	OPEN DATES:	May-Sept
# of SINGLE SITES:	72	MAX SPUR:	35 feet
		MAX STAY:	14 days
		ELEVATION:	6080 feet

39 Oaks Park
Vernal • lat 40°44'37" lon 109°37'23"

DESCRIPTION: This CG is situated among pine, spruce, and aspen with scattered open grassy areas. Set on Oaks Park Reservior, please check for fishing regulations. Watch for wildlife in the area such as deer and elk. Supplies are available 33 mi. away at Vernal. No drinking water availalbe 9/11-5/31.

GETTING THERE: From Vernal go N on US HWY 191 approx. 20 mi. to forest route 18. Go W on 18 approx. 13 mi. to forest route 25. Go N on 25 approx. 1 mi. to Oaks Park CG.

SINGLE RATE:	$5	OPEN DATES:	June-Sept
# of SINGLE SITES:	1	MAX SPUR:	20 feet
		MAX STAY:	14 days
		ELEVATION:	9280 feet

40 Paradise Park
Lapoint • lat 40°38'00" lon 109°53'00"

DESCRIPTION: CG is located in pine and aspen on Paradise Park Reservoir. Deer and elk in area. 35 mi. to Roosevelt for supplies.

GETTING THERE: From Lapoint go N on Deep Creek Road 14 mi. to forest boundary. Continue on forest route 104 approx. 10 mi. to Paradise Park CG.

SINGLE RATE:	$5	OPEN DATES:	May-Sept
		MAX SPUR:	20 feet
		MAX STAY:	14 days
		ELEVATION:	8000 feet

 Campground has hosts　　 **Reservable sites**　　 **Accessible facilities**　　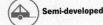 **Fully developed**　　 **Semi-developed**　　**Rustic facilities**

41 Pole Creek Lake
White Rocks • lat 40˚40'33" lon 110˚03'32"

DESCRIPTION: This CG is situated among pine and spruce on the shores of beautiful Pole Creek Lake. Deer, elk, and various small wildlife can be observed in the area. CG tends to be busy on holidays and weekends. Good fishing on the lake, please check local regulations. No drinking water available on site.

GETTING THERE: Pole Creek Lake CG is located approx. 2 mi. N of White Rocks on forest route 117.

SINGLE RATE:	$5	OPEN DATES:	July-Oct
# of SINGLE SITES:	18		
		MAX STAY:	14 days
		ELEVATION:	9500 feet

42 Red Canyon
Greendale Junction • lat 40˚53'21" lon 109˚33'29"

DESCRIPTION: This CG is situated in a pine stand, set on a rim over-looking Flaming Gorge Reservoir. Fish from the reservoir. Watch for deer, elk, and various birds in the area. Supplies are available approx. 2 mi. away at Red Canyon Lodge. CG receives moderate use, picking up through the summer season.

GETTING THERE: From Greendale Junction on US HWY 191 go W on state HWY 44 approx. 3 mi. to forest route 095. Go N on 095 approx. 2.5 mi. to Red Canyon CG.

SINGLE RATE:	$12	OPEN DATES:	May-Sept
# of SINGLE SITES:	8	MAX SPUR:	20 feet
		MAX STAY:	14 days
		ELEVATION:	7400 feet

43 Red Creek
Dutch John • lat 40˚54'03" lon 109˚15'04"

DESCRIPTION: This CG is situated among ponderosa pine on the B-section of the Green River. Fish the Green River; please check for local fishing regulations. Supplies at Dutch John. This CG is only accessible by boat or hike-in. Watch for wildlife in the area such as deer, elk, and various birds.

GETTING THERE: Red Creek CG is accessible only by boat and is located on the B section of the Green River approx. 4.5 mi. downstream from Little Hole.

SINGLE RATE:	$10	OPEN DATES:	Yearlong
		MAX STAY:	14 days
		ELEVATION:	5600 feet

44 Red Springs
Vernal • lat 40˚48'30" lon 109˚32'00"

DESCRIPTION: This CG is situated among lodgepole pine and quaking aspen trees in a high desert setting. Firewood is to be bought on site. Supplies are available 6 mi. away at Flaming Gorge Lodge. Watch for wildlife in the area such as deer, elk, moose, and various birds. CG is gated off after October 30 through the winter.

GETTING THERE: Red Springs CG is located approx. 30 mi. N or Vernal on US HWY 191.

SINGLE RATE:	$10	OPEN DATES:	May-Sept
# of SINGLE SITES:	12	MAX SPUR:	30 feet
		MAX STAY:	14 days
# of GROUP SITES:	1	ELEVATION:	8080 feet

45 Reservoir
Mt. Home • lat 40˚34'30" lon 110˚19'25"

DESCRIPTION: This CG is situated in a pine and spruce forest on the banks of Yellowstone Creek. Good fishing for small trout in the creek. Please check for local regulations. Various trails nearby. Supplies are available 14 mi. away in Mt. Home. Watch for deer, elk, and small wildlife in the area.

GETTING THERE: From Mt. Home go N on the Moonlake Road approx. 5 mi. to forest route 119. Go N on 119 approx. 5 mi. to forest route 124. Go N on 124 approx. 5 mi. to Reservoir CG.

SINGLE RATE:	$9	OPEN DATES:	May-Oct
# of SINGLE SITES:	5	MAX SPUR:	20 feet
		MAX STAY:	14 days
		ELEVATION:	7300 feet

46 Riverview
Mt. Home • lat 40˚35'25" lon 110˚20'08"

DESCRIPTION: This CG is situated among pine and willow along side of Yellowstone Creek. Good fishing for cutthroat trout in the creek. Supplies are available 15 mi. away in Mountain Home. Deer and elk are common to the area. Near trailhead for High Uintas Wilderness Area, with hiking opportunities.

GETTING THERE: From Mt. Home go N on the Moonlake Road approx. 5 mi. to forest route 119. Go N on 119 approx. 5 mi. to forest route 124. Go N on 124 approx. 7 mi. to Riverview CG.

SINGLE RATE:	$9	OPEN DATES:	May-Oct
# of SINGLE SITES:	19	MAX SPUR:	20 feet
		MAX STAY:	14 days
		ELEVATION:	7400 feet

47 Sheep Creek Bay
Manila • lat 40˚55'19" lon 109˚40'28"

DESCRIPTION: This CG is set on the shores of Sheep Creek Bay of the Flaming Gorge Reservoir, situated in the open country. Various multi-use trails nearby. A boat ramp is provided. Supplies are available approx. 8 mi. away in Manila. RV camping only, no tents.

GETTING THERE: From Manila go S on state HWY 44 approx. 7 mi. to forest route 092. Go N on 092 approx. 1/2 mi. to Sheep Creek Bay CG. RV camping only.

SINGLE RATE:	$6	OPEN DATES:	May-Sept
# of SINGLE SITES:	5		
		MAX STAY:	14 days
		ELEVATION:	6040 feet

48 Skull Creek
Greendale Junction • lat 40˚51'54" lon 109˚31'31"

DESCRIPTION: This CG is situated among ponderosa pine alongside of Skull Creek. Check local fishing regulations. Supplies may be purchased 4 mi. away at Flaming Gorge Lodge. Wildlife in the area includes deer, elk, and various birds. CG tends to be busy on weekends and holidays in the summer.

GETTING THERE: Skull Creek CG is located approx. 2 mi. W of Greendale Junction on state HWY 44.

SINGLE RATE:	$12	OPEN DATES:	May-Sept
# of SINGLE SITES:	17	MAX SPUR:	20 feet
		MAX STAY:	14 days
		ELEVATION:	7420 feet

49 Stateline Cove
Manila • lat 41˚00'00" lon 109˚36'30"

DESCRIPTION: CG is located on a large sandy beach with no designated campsites on Flaming Gorge Reservoir. Good fishing opportunities on the lake. Please check local fishing regulations. Deer are common to the area. Supplies are available 7 mi. away in Manila. No drinking water. Dispersed sites.

GETTING THERE: From Manila go NE on state HWY 43 approx. 4 mi. to forest route 146. Go E on 146 approx. 2.5 mi. to forest route 150. Go N on 150 approx. 1 mi. to Stateline Cove CG.

SINGLE RATE:	$7	OPEN DATES:	May-Sept
		MAX STAY:	14 days
		ELEVATION:	6200 feet

50 Swift Creek
Mt. Home • lat 40˚36'04" lon 110˚20'50"

DESCRIPTION: This CG is situated among pine at the confluence of Yellowstone Creek and Swift Creek. Good trout fishing in the creeks, check local fishing regulations. Deer and are common to the area. Supplies are available 17 mi. away in Mountain Home. Various trails in the area offer hiking opportunities.

GETTING THERE: From Mt. Home go N on the Moonlake Road approx. 5 mi. to forest route 119. Go N on 119 approx. 5 mi. to forest route 124. Go N on 124 approx. 8 mi. to Swift Creek CG.

SINGLE RATE:	$9	OPEN DATES:	May-Oct
# of SINGLE SITES:	11	MAX SPUR:	20 feet
		MAX STAY:	14 days
		ELEVATION:	7450 feet

 Campground has hosts   Reservable sites   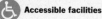 Accessible facilities   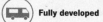 Fully developed   Semi-developed   Rustic facilities

NOTE: Open dates listed are typical. Actual dates are dependent on conditions such as snow pack.

51 Trails End
Dutch John • lat 40°54'41" lon 109°15'57"

DESCRIPTION: This CG is situated among ponderosa pine on the B-section of the Green River. Fish the Green River; please check for local fishing regulations. Supplies at Dutch John. This CG is only accessible by boat or hike-in. Watch for wildlife in the area such as deer, elk, and various birds.

GETTING THERE: Trails End CG is accessible only by boat and is located on the B section of the Green River approx. 3 mi. downstream from Little Hole.

SINGLE RATE:	$10	OPEN DATES:	Yearlong
		MAX STAY:	14 days
		ELEVATION:	5520 feet

52 Uinta Canyon
Neola • lat 40°37'24" lon 110°08'35"

DESCRIPTION: This CG is situated among pine on the Uinta River. Cutthroat trout fishing in creek. Supplies are available 14 mi. away in Roosevelt. Deer frequent the area. Not far from High Uintas Wilderness trailhead; for hiking. CG is busy weekends and holidays. No drinking water available on site.

GETTING THERE: Uinta Canyon CG is located approx. 14 mi. N of Neola on the Uinta River Road.

SINGLE RATE:	$9	OPEN DATES:	May-Oct
# of SINGLE SITES:	24	MAX SPUR:	30 feet
		MAX STAY:	14 days
		ELEVATION:	7000 feet

53 Uinta River Group
Neola • lat 40°37'24" lon 110°08'35"

DESCRIPTION: This CG is situated among pine and oakbrush on the Uinta River. Good trout fishing in river. Supplies are available 15 mi. away in Roosevelt. High Uintas wilderness trailhead is nearby for excellent hiking opportunities. Deer and elk frequent the area. No drinking water available on site.

GETTING THERE: Uinta CG is located approx. 14 mi. N of Neola on the Uinta River Road.

GROUP RATE:	$50	OPEN DATES:	May-Oct
# of GROUP SITES:	1	MAX SPUR:	30 feet
		MAX STAY:	14 days
		ELEVATION:	7100 feet

54 Upper Stillwater
Mt. Home • lat 40°33'38" lon 110°42'00"

DESCRIPTION: This CG is situated among pine adjacent to Rock Creek. Good fishing opportunities in the creek. Supplies are available 21 mi. away in Mountain Home. Deer and elk are common to the area. Upper Stillwater trail head is nearby. Busy on holidays in summer. Reservations necessary for group sites.

GETTING THERE: Upper Stillwater CG is located approx. 21 mi. W of Mt. Home on the Rock Creek Road.

SINGLE RATE:	$10	OPEN DATES:	May-Oct
# of SINGLE SITES:	18	MAX SPUR:	20 feet
GROUP RATE:	$30	MAX STAY:	14 days
# of GROUP SITES:	1	ELEVATION:	7100 feet

55 Wandin
Neola • lat 40°37'56" lon 110°09'12"

DESCRIPTION: This CG is situated among pine and spruce on the Uinta River. Good fishing for cutthroats in the river. Deer and elk are common in the area. Supplies are available 16 mi. away in Roosevelt. Trailhead for High Uintas Wilderness is located adjacent to CG for hiking. No drinking water available on site.

GETTING THERE: Wandin CG is located approx. 15 mi. N of Neola on the Uinta River Road.

SINGLE RATE:	$9	OPEN DATES:	May-Oct
# of SINGLE SITES:	6	MAX SPUR:	25 feet
		MAX STAY:	14 days
		ELEVATION:	7100 feet

56 Whiterocks
Whiterocks • lat 40°37'11" lon 109°56'30"

DESCRIPTION: This CG is situated among aspen and pine on the Whiterocks River. Possible fishing opportunities in creek, please check for local fishing regulations. Watch for wildlife in the area such as deer, elk, moose, squirrels, and various birds. Supplies are available in Duchesne.

GETTING THERE: Whiterocks CG is located approx. 10 mi. N of Whiterocks on forest route 117 (Farm Creek Road).

SINGLE RATE:	$8	OPEN DATES:	May-Sept
# of SINGLE SITES:	19	MAX SPUR:	20 feet
GROUP RATE:	Varies	MAX STAY:	14 days
# of GROUP SITES:	2	ELEVATION:	7320 feet

57 Willow
Manila • lat 40°55'34" lon 109°42'50"

DESCRIPTION: This CG is situated in a willow and cottonwood forest along the banks of Sheep Creek. Watch for deer, various small wildlife, and bighorn sheep in the surrounding area. Limited supplies are available approx. 6 mi. away in Manila. No drinking water available on site.

GETTING THERE: Willow CG is located approx. 6 mi. S of Manila on state HWY 44.

SINGLE RATE:	$6	OPEN DATES:	May-Sept
# of SINGLE SITES:	7		
		MAX STAY:	14 days
		ELEVATION:	6280 feet

58   Yellowpine
Mt. Home • lat 40°32'10" lon 110°38'10"

DESCRIPTION: CG is shadowed by large ponderosa pine trees, next to Rock Creek. Views of the bottom of the canyon. Running water, and flush restrooms are provided. Evenings are cool. Hiking trails nearby. Upper Stillwater Reservoir and Lower Stillwater Ponds are popular for fishing (short drive).

GETTING THERE: Yellowpine CG is located approx. 17 mi. W of Mt. Home on the Rock Creek Road.

SINGLE RATE:	$10	OPEN DATES:	May-Oct
# of SINGLE SITES:	29	MAX SPUR:	30 feet
GROUP RATE:	$30	MAX STAY:	14 days
# of GROUP SITES:	2	ELEVATION:	7000 feet

59 Yellowstone
Mt. Home • lat 40°32'31" lon 110°20'13"

DESCRIPTION: This CG is situated in a pine and spruce forest on the banks of Yellowstone Creek. Good trout fishing in the creek, please check for local regulations. Supplies can be found 12 mi. away at Mountain Home. Various trails nearby. Watch for deer, elk, and small wildlife in the area.

GETTING THERE: From Mountain Home go N on the Moonlake Road approx. 5 mi. to forest route 119. Go N on 119 approx. 5 mi. to forest route 124. Go N on 124 approx. 2 mi. to Yellowstone CG.

SINGLE RATE:	$9	OPEN DATES:	May-Oct
# of SINGLE SITES:	11	MAX SPUR:	25 feet
GROUP RATE:	$40	MAX STAY:	14 days
# of GROUP SITES:	1	ELEVATION:	7100 feet

 Campground has hosts   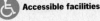 Reservable sites   Accessible facilities   Fully developed   Semi-developed    Rustic facilities

NOTE: Open dates listed are typical. Actual dates are dependent on conditions such as snow pack.

USFS Photo

DIXIE NATIONAL FOREST

The Dixie National Forest occupies almost two million acres and stretches for about 170 miles across southern Utah. It straddles the divide between the Great Basin and the Colorado River and has elevations which vary from 2,800 feet near St. George to 11,322 feet at Blue Bell Knoll on Boulder Mountain.

Three national parks and one national monument are adjacent to the forest. The red sandstone formations of Red Canyon rival those of Bryce Canyon National Park. Hells Backbone Bridge and the view into Death Hollow are breathtaking. From the top of Powell Point, it is possible to see for miles into three different states.

The terrain varies from gentle plateaus to rocky cliffs and furnishes habitat for many different wildlife species such as the cougar, bobcat, blue grouse, golden eagle, cottontail rabbit, wild turkey, antelope, and the Utah prairie dog.

Recreational opportunities on the forest are highly diversified. Visitors may enjoy camping, hunting, viewing scenery, hiking, horseback riding, and fishing. With 83,000 acres of wilderness, those seeking solitude can backpack or hike into the Pine Valley, Ashdown Gorge and Box-Death Hollow areas.

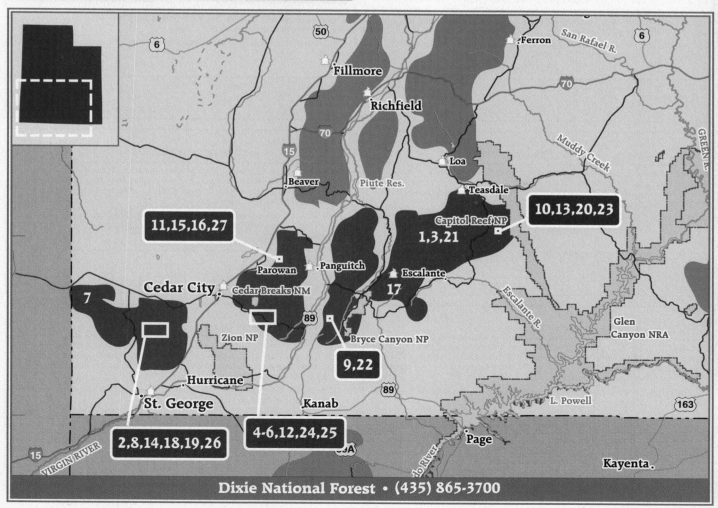

Dixie National Forest • (435) 865-3700

1 Barker Reservoir
Escalante • lat 37°55'06" lon 111°49'42"

DESCRIPTION: CG in a mixed conifer and aspen forest with multiple reservoirs in the area. Fish for rainbow and cutthroat trout in any of the reservoirs nearby. Supplies at Escalante. Deer, elk, turkeys, and bears in the area. Bear boxes are available for use. The Great Western Trail is nearby.

GETTING THERE: From Escalante go W on state HWY 12 approx. 4.5 mi. to forest route 149 (North Creek Road). Go N on 149 approx. 15 mi. to Barker Reservoir CG. Trailers not recommended.

SINGLE RATE:	$7	OPEN DATES:	June-Sept
# of SINGLE SITES:	29	MAX SPUR:	30 feet
GROUP RATE:	$50	MAX STAY:	14 days
# of GROUP SITES:	3	ELEVATION:	9560 feet

2 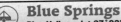 Blue Springs
Pine Valley • lat 37°22'16" lon 113°27'23"

DESCRIPTION: This CG is situated in a large ponderosa pine forest with views of Pine Valley Mountain. Fishing opportunities at Pine Valley Reservoir. Supplies are available at Pine Valley. Whipple Trailhead is close to CG for hiking, horseback riding, and wildlife observation.

GETTING THERE: Blue Springs CG is located approx. 3 mi. E of Pine Valley on forest route 35.

SINGLE RATE:	Varies	OPEN DATES:	May-Sept
# of SINGLE SITES:	17	MAX SPUR:	45 feet
		MAX STAY:	14 days
		ELEVATION:	6800 feet

3 Blue Spruce
Escalante • lat 37°58'22" lon 111°39'04"

DESCRIPTION: This CG is set on the banks of Pine Creek, situated in a blue spruce forest. CG offers pleasant temperatures and shade throughout the summer. River and stream fishing nearby. Supplies are available at Escalante. Box-Death Hollow Wilderness and The Great Western Trail are nearby.

GETTING THERE: From Escalante go N on forest route 153 (Hell's Backbone Road) approx. 17 mi. to forest route 145. Go N on 145 approx. 1/2 mi. to Blue Spruce CG.

SINGLE RATE:	$6	OPEN DATES:	May-Sept
# of SINGLE SITES:	6	MAX SPUR:	20 feet
		MAX STAY:	14 days
		ELEVATION:	7800 feet

4 Cedar Canyon
Cedar City • lat 37°35'30" lon 112°54'00"

DESCRIPTION: CG is in a forested setting, next to Crow Creek. Fish from creek. A kids' fishing pond is at county-owned Woods Ranch. Attractions nearby include Bryce Canyon NP and Cedar Breaks National Monument. Supplies at Cedar City. Trails nearby for hiking, biking, and horseback riding. Firewood is for sale on site.

GETTING THERE: Cedar Canyon CG is located approx. 13 mi. SE of Cedar City on state HWY 14.

SINGLE RATE:	$8	OPEN DATES:	May-Sept
# of SINGLE SITES:	19	MAX SPUR:	40 feet
GROUP RATE:	$40	MAX STAY:	14 days
# of GROUP SITES:	1	ELEVATION:	8100 feet

5 Deer Haven
Cedar City • lat 37°34'27" lon 112°54'35"

DESCRIPTION: This CG is shaded by an open stand of towering aspen trees. CG offers visitors solitude and breathtaking scenery including views of Cedar Breaks National Monument. The Virgin River Rim Trail near the CG. CG is for groups and is by reservation only. Group fire ring and amphitheater available.

GETTING THERE: From Cedar City go SE on state HWY 14 approx. 15 mi. to forest route 52. Go W on 52 approx. 2 mi. to Deer Haven CG.

		OPEN DATES:	June-Sept
		MAX SPUR:	99 feet
GROUP RATE:	$55	MAX STAY:	14 days
# of GROUP SITES:	1	ELEVATION:	8900 feet

6 Duck Creek
Duck Creek • lat 37°31'12" lon 112°41'50"

DESCRIPTION: This picturesque CG rests beneath a sheltering canopy of ponderosa pine and aspen which lies adjacent to Duck Creek Pond and Duck Creek. Great fishing from local pond and creeks. Supplies are available at Duck Creek Village. Excellent hiking, biking, and scenery in the vicinity.

GETTING THERE: Duck Creek CG is located approx. 2 mi. W of Duck Creek Village on state HWY 14.

SINGLE RATE:	$10	OPEN DATES:	May-Sept
# of SINGLE SITES:	94	MAX SPUR:	60 feet
GROUP RATE:	$55	MAX STAY:	14 days
# of GROUP SITES:	3	ELEVATION:	8600 feet

7 Honeycomb Rocks
Enterprise • lat 37°30'45" lon 113°50'45"

DESCRIPTION: This CG is situated in an open desert setting near Enterprise Reservoir. A boat ramp is available nearby. Fish from the Reservoir near CG. Campers may gather their firewood locally. Many hiking trails in the area for sight-seeing and wildlife viewing opportunities.

GETTING THERE: Honeycomb Rocks CG is located near Enterprise Reservoir. From Enterprise go W on state HWY 120 approx. 6.5 mi. to forest route 006. Go S on 006 approx. 5 mi. to Honeycomb Rocks CG.

SINGLE RATE:	$7	OPEN DATES:	May-Oct*
# of SINGLE SITES:	21	MAX SPUR:	25 feet
		MAX STAY:	14 days
		ELEVATION:	5700 feet

8 Juniper Park
Pine Valley • lat 37°22'32" lon 113°27'43"

DESCRIPTION: CG set among ponderosa pine with great views of Pine Valley Mountain. A stream is located near the CG. Fish at Pine Valley Reservoir. Trails nearby for hiking, sight-seeing, and wildlife viewing. There are showers and a cafe in the town of Pine Valley. Dump station located 5 mi. SW.

GETTING THERE: Juniper Park CG is located approx. 3 mi. E of Pine Valley on forest route 35.

SINGLE RATE:	Varies	OPEN DATES:	May-Oct*
# of SINGLE SITES:	23	MAX SPUR:	50 feet
		MAX STAY:	14 days
		ELEVATION:	6800 feet

9 King Creek
Tropic • lat 37°36'33" lon 112°15'35"

DESCRIPTION: CG is situated in ponderosa pine, adjacent to Tropic Reservoir and the East Fork of the Sevier River. Fishing on Reservoir and the River. Hiking and ATV trails adjacent to the CG. An amphitheater, volleyball court, and horseshoe pit located within CG. Trailer dump station is nearby.

GETTING THERE: Kings Creek CG is located on the W shore of Tropic Reservoir. From Tropic go NW on state HWY 12 approx. 10 mi. to forest route 87. Go S on 87 approx. 7 mi. to King Creek CG.

SINGLE RATE:	$8	OPEN DATES:	May-Oct*
# of SINGLE SITES:	37	MAX SPUR:	45 feet
GROUP RATE:	Varies	MAX STAY:	14 days
# of GROUP SITES:	1	ELEVATION:	8000 feet

10 Lower Bowns
Torrey • lat 38°06'30" lon 111°17'00"

DESCRIPTION: Primitive CG in an open setting close to Lower Bowns Reservoir. Reservoir is great for fishing rainbow and cutthroat trout. Supplies can be found in Torrey. No drinking water available on site. Elk, bears, and deer can be seen in the area. Many trails for hiking, sight-seeing, and viewing nature.

GETTING THERE: From Torrey go S on state HWY 12 approx. 22 mi. to forest route 186. Go E on 186 approx. 4 mi. to Lower Bowns CG.

SINGLE RATE:	$4	OPEN DATES:	Apr-Oct
# of SINGLE SITES:	4		
		MAX STAY:	14 days
		ELEVATION:	7400 feet

 Campground has hosts   **Reservable sites**   **Accessible facilities**   **Fully developed**   **Semi-developed**   **Rustic facilities**

NOTE: Open dates listed are typical. Actual dates are dependent on conditions such as snow pack.

11 Mammoth Springs
Panguitch Lake • lat 37°38'16" lon 112°40'15"

DESCRIPTION: This CG is in a mixed spruce and pine setting with Mamoth Creek running nearby. Fish from the creek for rainbow trout. Supplies are available at Panguitch Lake. Deer, elk, squirrels, and chipmunks in the area. Many trails nearby for hiking, sightseeing, and nature walks.

GETTING THERE: From Panguitch Lake go S on forest route 36 approx. 3.5 mi. to forest route 67. Go S on 67 approx. 2 mi. to Mammoth Springs CG.

SINGLE RATE:	No fee	OPEN DATES:	June-Sept
# of SINGLE SITES:	7		
		MAX STAY:	14 days
		ELEVATION:	8100 feet

12 Navajo Lake
Duck Creek Village • lat 37°31'14" lon 112°47'21"

DESCRIPTION: This CG is set on the shores of Navajo Lake. Great fishing from the lake. Supplies are available at nearby Navajo Lake Lodge. The Virgin River Rim Trail is accessible from the CG; it offers panoramic views of Zion National Park, the Kolob Plateau, and the Pine Valley Mountains.

GETTING THERE: From Duck Creek Village go W on state HWY 14 approx. 4 mi. to forest route 53 (Navajo Lake Road). Go W on 53 approx. 4.5 mi. to Navajo Lake CG.

SINGLE RATE:	$10	OPEN DATES:	May-Sept*
# of SINGLE SITES:	31	MAX SPUR:	24 feet
		MAX STAY:	14 days
		ELEVATION:	9200 feet

13 Oak Creek
Torrey • lat 38°05'19" lon 111°20'28"

DESCRIPTION: This small, secluded CG is in a ponderosa, aspen, and mixed conifer forest. A small creek runs through the lower portion. Trout fishing nearby in Lower Bowns Reservoir and Oak Creek Reservoir. Supplies at Torrey. Gather firewood. Trails in the area. Tents and small trailers are recommended.

GETTING THERE: Oak Creek CG is located approx. 24 mi. S of Torrey on state HWY 12. RVs over 25' are not advised.

SINGLE RATE:	$8	OPEN DATES:	May-Oct
# of SINGLE SITES:	8	MAX SPUR:	24 feet
		MAX STAY:	14 days
		ELEVATION:	8800 feet

14 Oak Grove
Leeds • lat 37°19'02" lon 113°27'09"

DESCRIPTION: This CG is in a timbered setting with views of the Pine Valley Mountains. Supplies are available in Leeds. Recreation opportunities include hiking, sight-seeing, and wildlife viewing. An interpretive trail is located near campsite #5. Campers may gather firewood locally.

GETTING THERE: From Leeds go NW on forest route 35 approx. 8 mi. to Oak Grove CG. Not recommended for large RVs due to access problems.

SINGLE RATE:	No fee	OPEN DATES:	June-Oct
# of SINGLE SITES:	6		
		MAX STAY:	14 days
		ELEVATION:	6800 feet

15 Panguitch Lake North
Panguitch • lat 37°42'08" lon 112°39'19"

DESCRIPTION: This CG offers visitors a slower, calm pace and cooler temperatures. Enjoy boating; lake fishing for rainbow, brown, and brook trout; fly fishing; mountain biking and hiking at Panguitch Lake. The lake is located 1/2 mi. from the CG. Supplies are available at the lake.

GETTING THERE: Panguitch Lake North CG is located approx. 19 mi. SW of Panguitch on forest route 35 at Panguitch Lake. Trailer dump station at CG.

SINGLE RATE:	$10	OPEN DATES:	June-Sept*
# of SINGLE SITES:	49	MAX SPUR:	99 feet
GROUP RATE:	$55	MAX STAY:	14 days
# of GROUP SITES:	2	ELEVATION:	8400 feet

16 Panguitch Lake South
Panguitch • lat 37°42'02" lon 112°39'18"

DESCRIPTION: CG offers visitors a slower pace and cooler temperatures. Enjoy boating; lake fishing for rainbow, brown, and brook trout; fly fishing; mountain biking and hiking at Panguitch Lake. The lake is located 1/2 mi. from the CG. Supplies are available at the lake. Trailer dump station 1/2 mi. away.

GETTING THERE: Panguitch Lake South CG is located approx. 19 mi. SW of Panguitch on forest route 35 at Panguitch Lake.

SINGLE RATE:	$8	OPEN DATES:	June-Sept
# of SINGLE SITES:	18	MAX SPUR:	45 feet
		MAX STAY:	14 days
		ELEVATION:	8400 feet

17 Pine Lake
Antimony • lat 37°44'38" lon 111°56'55"

DESCRIPTION: This CG is located in an open ponderosa pine and spruce forest. Pine Lake Reservoir lies to the SW. Fishing from the reservoir. Supplies are available at Antimony. Many trails in the area. The Great Western Trail accesses Powell Point Overlook, and Henderson Canyon Trails.

GETTING THERE: From Antimony go S on state HWY 22 approx. 26 mi. to forest route 132. Go SE on 132 approx. 6 mi. to Pine Lake CG.

SINGLE RATE:	$8	OPEN DATES:	June-Sept
# of SINGLE SITES:	33	MAX SPUR:	45 feet
GROUP RATE:	$40	MAX STAY:	14 days
# of GROUP SITES:	2	ELEVATION:	7700 feet

18 Pine Valley Equestrian
Pine Valley • lat 37°23'00" lon 113°29'30"

DESCRIPTION: CG is in a ponderosa pine, pinion and juniper forest with great views of Pine Valley Mountain Wilderness. Fish at Pine Valley Reservoir nearby. CG has horse stalls. Forsythe Canyon and Whipple Trailhead nearby for hiking. Supplies at Pine Valley. Gather firewood locally. Dump station 5 mi. SW on HWY 18.

GETTING THERE: Pine Valley Equestrian CG is located approx. 2 mi. E of Pine Valley on forest route 35.

SINGLE RATE:	Varies	OPEN DATES:	May-Sept
# of SINGLE SITES:	14	MAX SPUR:	45 feet
		MAX STAY:	14 days
		ELEVATION:	6800 feet

19 Pine
Pine Valley • lat 37°22'37" lon 113°27'37"

DESCRIPTION: This CG is in a setting of ponderosa pine, with views of the Pine Valley Mountains. A stream is located near the CG. Fishing at Pine Valley Reservoir. Trails nearby provide for hiking, sight-seeing, and wildlife viewing. There are showers and a cafe in the town of Pine Valley.

GETTING THERE: Pine CG is located approx. 3 mi. E of Pine Valley on forest route 35. Large RVs are not recommended because of the limited turn around space.

SINGLE RATE:	No fee	OPEN DATES:	May-Oct
# of SINGLE SITES:	13		
		MAX STAY:	14 days
		ELEVATION:	6800 feet

20 Pleasant Creek
Torrey • lat 38°06'03" lon 111°20'14"

DESCRIPTION: This is a favorite CG for campers. Set in a ponderosa pine and aspen forest. There is trout fishing nearby at Lower Bowns Reservoir and Lower Pleasant Creek. Supplies are available at Torrey. Campers may gather their firewood locally. Numerous trails can be found in the area.

GETTING THERE: Pleasant Creek CG is located approx. 22 mi. S of Torrey on state HWY 12. RVs over 25' long are not advised.

SINGLE RATE:	$8	OPEN DATES:	May-Oct
# of SINGLE SITES:	16	MAX SPUR:	24 feet
		MAX STAY:	14 days
		ELEVATION:	8700 feet

 Campground has hosts   Reservable sites   Accessible facilities   Fully developed   Semi-developed   Rustic facilities

NOTE: Open dates listed are typical. Actual dates are dependent on conditions such as snow pack.

21 Posy Lake
Escalante • lat 37°56'06" lon 111°41'36"

DESCRIPTION: This CG is in a forested setting of aspen on the hillside on the S side of Posy Lake. Good fishing from the Lake and the CG offers a fish cleaning station. Posy Lake Trail and Great Western Trail start close to the CG. Floating, rafting, and kayaking can be done on the lake.

GETTING THERE: From Escalante go N on forest route 153 (Hell's Backbone Road) approx. 12 mi. to forest route 154. Go N on 154 approx. 2 mi. to Posy Lake CG.

SINGLE RATE:	$7	OPEN DATES:	June-Sept
# of SINGLE SITES:	22	MAX SPUR:	20 feet
GROUP RATE:	$35	MAX STAY:	14 days
# of GROUP SITES:	1	ELEVATION:	8200 feet

22 Red Canyon
Panguitch • lat 37°44'34" lon 112°18'30"

DESCRIPTION: CG is situated in ponderosa pine surrounded by Pink Claron Limestone formations. Extensive hiking trails and many scenic overlooks in the Red Canyon area. ATV riding is not allowed in CG. Trailer dump station, volleyball court and horseshoe pit at CG. Red Canyon Visitors Center within walking distance.

GETTING THERE: From Panguitch go S on US HWY 89 approx. 7 mi. to state HWY 12 (to Bryce Canyon National Park). Go E on 12 approx. 3.5 mi. to Red Canyon CG.

SINGLE RATE:	$9	OPEN DATES:	May-Oct*
# of SINGLE SITES:	37	MAX SPUR:	45 feet
GROUP RATE:	Varies	MAX STAY:	14 days
# of GROUP SITES:	1	ELEVATION:	7400 feet

23 Single Tree
Torrey • lat 38°09'46" lon 111°19'47"

DESCRIPTION: CG is in a scenic ponderosa pine and aspen area with views of an open vista of Capital Reef. This is the largest CG in the area and has some sites that accommodate large RVs. Supplies are available at Torrey. Gather firewood locally. CG has trails to Single Tree Falls. Dump station at CG.

GETTING THERE: Single Tree CG is located approx. 15 mi. S of Torrey on state HWY 12.

SINGLE RATE:	$8	OPEN DATES:	May-Oct
# of SINGLE SITES:	26	MAX SPUR:	45 feet
GROUP RATE:	$35	MAX STAY:	14 days
# of GROUP SITES:	2	ELEVATION:	8600 feet

24 Spruces
Duck Creek Village • lat 37°31'04" lon 112°46'24"

DESCRIPTION: CG is on the shores of Navajo Lake, provides a spectacular setting for boating, camping, fishing, and photography. Supplies are available at nearby Navajo Lodge. Take advantage of several outstanding hiking and biking trails including the Virgin River Rim, and Cascade Falls trails.

GETTING THERE: From Duck Creek Village go W on state HWY 14 approx. 4 mi. to forest route 53 (Navajo Lake Road). Go W on 53 approx. 2 mi. to Spruces CG.

SINGLE RATE:	$10	OPEN DATES:	June-Sept*
# of SINGLE SITES:	28	MAX SPUR:	24 feet
		MAX STAY:	14 days
		ELEVATION:	9200 feet

25 Te-ah
Duck Creek • lat 37°32'03" lon 112°49'04"

DESCRIPTION: This CG is nestled in a pocket of aspen trees near Navajo Lake, which offers excellent fishing and boating opportunities. CG provides the perfect setting for wildlife observation and photography. Supplies are available at Navajo Lake Lodge nearby. Trails in the area.

GETTING THERE: From Duck Creek Village go W on state HWY 14 approx. 4 mi. to forest route 53 (Navajo Lake Road). Go W on 53 approx. 6 mi. to Te-ah CG.

SINGLE RATE:	$10	OPEN DATES:	June-Sept
# of SINGLE SITES:	42	MAX SPUR:	24 feet
		MAX STAY:	14 days
		ELEVATION:	9200 feet

26 Upper Pine Group
Pine Valley • lat 37°22'43" lon 113°28'15"

DESCRIPTION: CG is situated in large ponderosa pine and oak trees with great views of Pine Valley Mountain Wilderness. Fish at Pine Valley Reservoir, .5 mi. from CG. Popular activities include hiking, sight-seeing, wildlife viewing, and horseback riding. Supplies at Pine Valley. Dump station 5 mi. SW on HWY 18.

GETTING THERE: Upper Pine Group CG is located approx. 3 mi. E of Pine Valley on forest route 35.

		OPEN DATES:	May-Sept
		MAX SPUR:	40 feet
GROUP RATE:	$42	MAX STAY:	14 days
# of GROUP SITES:	1	ELEVATION:	6800 feet

27 White Bridge
Panguitch • lat 37°44'35" lon 112°35'12"

DESCRIPTION: This CG is situated on the banks of Panguitch Creek, with spectacular scenery. Panguitch Lake can be accessed 4 mi. away. Both lake and creek provide for excellent fishing. Supplies are available at Panguitch Lake. Explore the numerous hiking and mountain bike trails nearby.

GETTING THERE: White Bridge CG is located approx. 15.5 mi. SE of Panguitch on forest route 35 (Panguitch Lake Road).

SINGLE RATE:	$10	OPEN DATES:	June-Sept*
# of SINGLE SITES:	29	MAX SPUR:	45 feet
		MAX STAY:	14 days
		ELEVATION:	7900 feet

 Campground has hosts   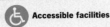 **Reservable sites**   **Accessible facilities**   **Fully developed**   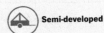 **Semi-developed**   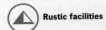 **Rustic facilities**

NOTE: Open dates listed are typical. Actual dates are dependent on conditions such as snow pack.

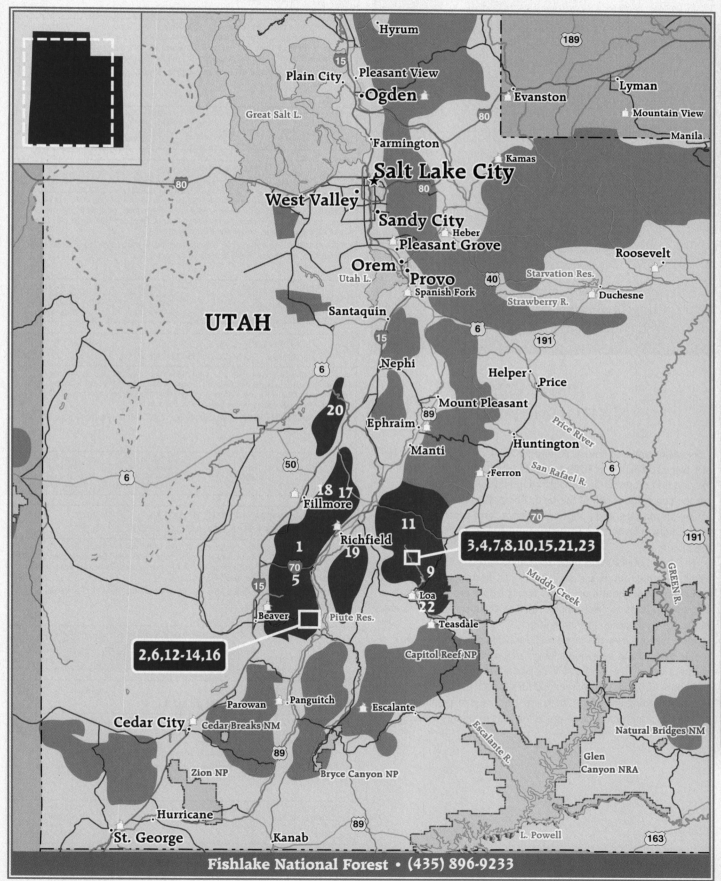

3,4,7,8,10,15,21,23

2,6,12-14,16

USFS Photo

FISHLAKE NATIONAL FOREST

Fishlake National Forest, named for the largest lake on the forest, was established in 1899 and occupies 1.4 million acres of plateau and mountain land. Vegetation is diverse; aspen and spruce cover about half of the land. Gambels oak and mountain brush, pinyon pine and juniper woodlands, and sagebrush-grasslands, along with some colorful rock outcrops and cliffs complete the picture.

The forest offers great opportunities to view scenery and wildlife. Campgrounds are available or just bring your equipment and camp throughout most of the forest. There are small streams and several lakes to "wet a hook" in. The enthusiast will also enjoy winter ice fishing and snowmobiling.

Most visitors view the forest while traveling by vehicle. Two scenic byways and several backways traverse the forest offering splendid vistas. The Pauite ATV Trail is a 260-mile loop with an additional 500 miles of marked side trails. Some visitors also enjoy horseback riding or hiking. There are 100 miles of groomed snowmobile trails and many open areas for your exploring pleasure.

---

1 Adelaide
Kanosh • lat 38˚45'13" lon 112˚21'49"

DESCRIPTION: CG in park like grassy area with oak and maple. Views of red rocks and mountains. Hot days. Fly or rod fish Corn Creek at CG. Historic Cove Fort is 20 mi. S. Supplies at Kanosh. Deer, elk, red foxes, bobcats, and rattlesnakes in area. Moderate use. Gather firewood nearby. ATV access to Pauite ATV Trail and others.

GETTING THERE: Adelaide CG is located approx. 5 mi. SE of Kanosh on forest route 106.

SINGLE RATE:	$8	OPEN DATES:	May-Oct
# of SINGLE SITES:	6	MAX SPUR:	20 feet
GROUP RATE:	$30	MAX STAY:	16 days
# of GROUP SITES:	1	ELEVATION:	5500 feet

---

2 Anderson Meadow
Beaver • lat 38˚12'30" lon 112˚25'30"

DESCRIPTION: Setting is spectacular mountain scenery overlooking Anderson Meadow Reservoir. Fly and bait fish Reservoir; no motors. Warm days, cold nights, may freeze. No water after Labor Day. Historic western sites in area. Deer and bald eagles. Mild use. Great fall colors. Hiking, horse, and ATV trails nearby.

GETTING THERE: From Beaver go E approx. 10 mi. on state HWY 153 to forest route 137. Go S on 137 approx. 8 mi. to Anderson Meadow CG.

SINGLE RATE:	$6	OPEN DATES:	June-Sept*
# of SINGLE SITES:	10	MAX SPUR:	30 feet
		MAX STAY:	14 days
		ELEVATION:	9400 feet

---

3 Bowery Creek
Fishlake • lat 38˚33'38" lon 111˚42'33"

DESCRIPTION: CG across HWY 25 from Fishlake with views of lake and Mytoge Mountain. Boat and shore fish for trout. Supplies less than 1/4 mi. away. Deer, moose, and marmots. Moderate use. Gather firewood. Hike interpretive Lakeshore Nat'l Rec. Trail and other trails. Mountain biking possible for the avid bikers.

GETTING THERE: Bowery CG is located approx. 2 mi. N of the Fishlake Lodge on state HWY 25.

SINGLE RATE:	$10	OPEN DATES:	May-Sept
# of SINGLE SITES:	30	MAX SPUR:	40 feet
GROUP RATE:	$20	MAX STAY:	10 days
# of GROUP SITES:	10	ELEVATION:	8800 feet

---

4 Bowery Group Area
Fishlake • lat 38˚33'43" lon 111˚42'22"

DESCRIPTION: Adjacent to W shore of Fish Lake with views of Mytoge Mountain. Boat and shore fish for perch, trout, and splake. Historic Lakeshore National Recreational Trail nearby. Supplies 1/2 mi. away. Deer, elk, and moose in area. Gather firewood locally. 0-50 persons $30, 51-100 persons $40.

GETTING THERE: Bowery Group Area CG is located approx. 2 mi. N of the Fishlake Lodge on state HWY 25.

		OPEN DATES:	May-Sept
		MAX SPUR:	40 feet
GROUP RATE:	Varies	MAX STAY:	10 days
# of GROUP SITES:	1	ELEVATION:	8800 feet

---

5 Castle Rock
Sevier • lat 38˚33'13" lon 112˚21'16"

DESCRIPTION: CG set among cottonwood, pinyon, and pine stands with spectacular rock formations and a small stream running through. Warm to hot days. Fish Piute reservoir (30 mi. S) for trout. Historic western sites in area. Great bird watching. Hiking, horse, mountain bike, and ATV trails. No horses in CG.

GETTING THERE: From Sevier go W on I-70 approx. 6 mi. to Freemont Indian State Park exit. Go S on forest route 478 approx. 1 mi. to Castle Rock CG.

SINGLE RATE:	$9	OPEN DATES:	Mar-Nov*
# of SINGLE SITES:	28	MAX SPUR:	30 feet
GROUP RATE:	Varies	MAX STAY:	14 days
# of GROUP SITES:	3	ELEVATION:	6200 feet

 Campground has hosts   🔒 **Reservable sites**   ♿ **Accessible facilities**   **Fully developed**   **Semi-developed**   △ **Rustic facilities**

6 City Creek
Junction • lat 38°16'10" lon 112°18'37"

DESCRIPTION: CG sits in basin among cottonwood, pine, and fir with North and South Forks of City Creek running through. Warm temperatures may turn cold quickly. Historic western sites nearby. Limited supplies in Junction. Light use. Gather firewood. Horse and hiking trails nearby. Restricted ATV roads.

GETTING THERE: City Creek CG is located approx. 5.5 mi. NW of Junction on state HWY 153.

SINGLE RATE:	No fee	OPEN DATES:	May-Oct*
# of SINGLE SITES:	7	MAX SPUR:	15 feet
GROUP RATE:		MAX STAY:	14 days
		ELEVATION:	7600 feet

7 Doctor Creek
Fishlake • lat 38°31'40" lon 111°44'42"

DESCRIPTION: This CG has views of Fish Lake, Mytoge Mountain and Coots Slough. Shore or boat fish for perch, trout, and splake. Historic Lakeshore Nat'l Recreational Trail nearby. Supplies 1/2 mi. away. Deer, elk, and moose in area. Receives moderate use. Gather firewood locally. Hiking trails nearby.

GETTING THERE: Doctor Creek CG is located approx. 2 mi. S of the Fishlake lodge on state HWY 25.

SINGLE RATE:	$10	OPEN DATES:	May-Sept
# of SINGLE SITES:	29	MAX SPUR:	40 feet
		MAX STAY:	10 days
		ELEVATION:	8800 feet

8 Doctor Creek Group Area
Fishlake • lat 38°31'45" lon 111°44'12"

DESCRIPTION: Open areas with covered tables and aspen; views of lake, Mytoge Mountain, and Coots Slough. Shore or boat fish 1/4 mi. N on Fish Lake. Hike historic Lakeshore Nat'l Rec. Trail, Fish Lake Basin, and other trails. Supplies 1/2 mi. away Deer, moose, elk, and marmots in area. Moderate use. Gather firewood locally.

GETTING THERE: Doctor Creek Group Area CG is located approx. 2 mi. S of the Fishlake lodge on state HWY 25.

		OPEN DATES:	May-Sept
		MAX SPUR:	40 feet
GROUP RATE:	Varies	MAX STAY:	10 days
# of GROUP SITES:	2	ELEVATION:	8800 feet

9 Elkhorn
Fremont • lat 38°27'50" lon 111°27'20"

DESCRIPTION: Views of Thousand Lake Mountain, set among spruce fir. Fly, shore, or small boat fish nearby Round Lake or Deep Creek Lake. Float tubing is popular. Supplies 25 mi. away at Loa. Moderate use. Gather firewood. Horseback riding and hiking on Great Western ATV, Neff's, or 1000 Lake Trails.

GETTING THERE: From Freemont go NE approx. 7 mi. on state HWY 72 to forest route 206. Go E on 206 approx. 7mi. To Elkhorn CG.

SINGLE RATE:	No fee	OPEN DATES:	June-Oct
# of SINGLE SITES:	6	MAX SPUR:	30 feet
GROUP RATE:	$20	MAX STAY:	14 days
# of GROUP SITES:	1	ELEVATION:	9300 feet

10 Frying Pan
Fishlake • lat 38°36'32" lon 111°40'44"

DESCRIPTION: CG set in sparse aspen stands with views of Mytoge Mountain. Stream and lake fishing nearby. Supplies 3 mi. away. Deer, elk, moose, and marmots in area. Moderte use. Gather firewood locally. Prepare for mosquitos all summer. Group fees: 1-25 $30; 26-50 $40; 51-75 $50; 76-100 $60.

GETTING THERE: Frying Pan CG is located approx. 8 mi. N of Fishlake Lodge on state HWY 25.

SINGLE RATE:	$8	OPEN DATES:	May-Sept
# of SINGLE SITES:	11	MAX SPUR:	40 feet
GROUP RATE:	Varies	MAX STAY:	14 days
# of GROUP SITES:	1	ELEVATION:	9000 feet

11 Gooseberry
Salina • lat 38°48'11" lon 111°41'11"

DESCRIPTION: This CG is situated in an open grove of aspen and pine with mountain views. Fish for trout in adjacent Gooseberry Creek. Black bear, mountain lions, wolves, coyotes, deer, elk, eagles, and goshawks in area. Busy all summer. There are several hiking, horse, mountain biking, and ATV trails in area.

GETTING THERE: From Salina go E on I-70 approx. 2 mi. to the Gooseberry Road. Go S on the Gooseberry Road approx. 9 mi. to Gooseberry CG.

SINGLE RATE:	$5	OPEN DATES:	May-Nov
# of SINGLE SITES:	6	MAX SPUR:	20 feet
		MAX STAY:	14 days
# of GROUP SITES:	1	ELEVATION:	7800 feet

12 Kents Lake
Beaver • lat 38°14'12" lon 112°27'33"

DESCRIPTION: CG set in aspen, fir, and pine stands with views of Birch Creek Mountain and Kents Lake. Mild days, cold nights, snow always possible. Fishing at lakes. Small boats and canoes on Kents Lake. Many historic western sites. Supplies in Beaver. Hiking and horse trail access, ATV roads with limitations.

GETTING THERE: From Beaver go E approx. 8 mi. on state HWY 153 to forest route 137. Go S on 137 approx. 3.5 mi. to Kents Lake CG. Tents only.

SINGLE RATE:	$8	OPEN DATES:	June-Sept
# of SINGLE SITES:	28	MAX SPUR:	60 feet
GROUP RATE:	$16	MAX STAY:	14 days
# of GROUP SITES:	2	ELEVATION:	8800 feet

13 Little Cottonwood
Beaver • lat 38°15'25" lon 112°32'35"

DESCRIPTION: This CG is set among pine, cottonwood, and aspen with views of Beaver Canyon rock cliffs. Beaver River nearby for fishing with accessible path. Mild to hot days. Many historic western sites in area. Supplies in Beaver. Moderate use. Buy firewood or gather locally. Trails 1/2 mi. W of CG.

GETTING THERE: Little Cottonwood is located approx. 6 mi. E of Beaver on state HWY 153. Paved or hardened surfaces in campsites.

SINGLE RATE:	$10	OPEN DATES:	May-Oct*
# of SINGLE SITES:	14	MAX SPUR:	40 feet
		MAX STAY:	14 days
		ELEVATION:	6500 feet

14 Little Reservoir
Beaver • lat 38°15'40" lon 112°29'19"

DESCRIPTION: Set among ponderosa pine, pinon, and choke cherries with reservoir views. Warm days, cold nights, noon rains. Fly or non-motorized boat fishing on the reservoir or Beaver River. Supplies are available in Beaver. Receives moderate use. Buy or gather firewood. Hiking, horse, and ATV trails nearby.

GETTING THERE: From Beaver go E approx. 10 mi. on state HWY 153 to forest route 137. Go S on 137 approx. 1 mi. to Little Reservoir CG.

SINGLE RATE:	$8	OPEN DATES:	June-Sept
# of SINGLE SITES:	8	MAX SPUR:	40 feet
		MAX STAY:	14 days
		ELEVATION:	7350 feet

15 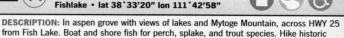 Mackinaw
Fishlake • lat 38°33'20" lon 111°42'58"

DESCRIPTION: In aspen grove with views of lakes and Mytoge Mountain, across HWY 25 from Fish Lake. Boat and shore fish for perch, splake, and trout species. Hike historic Lakeshore Nat'l Rec. Trail, Fish Lake Basin, and other trails. Supplies 1 mi. away. Deer, elk, and moose in area. Moderate use. Gather firewood locally.

GETTING THERE: Mackinaw CG is located approx. 1 mi. N of the Fishlake Lodge on state HWY 25.

SINGLE RATE:	$10	OPEN DATES:	May-Sept
# of SINGLE SITES:	66	MAX SPUR:	40 feet
GROUP RATE:	$20	MAX STAY:	10 days
# of GROUP SITES:	7	ELEVATION:	8800 feet

 Campground has hosts 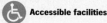 **Reservable sites** **Accessible facilities**   **Fully developed** **Semi-developed**   **Rustic facilities**

NOTE: Open dates listed are typical. Actual dates are dependent on conditions such as snow pack.

16 Mahogany Cove
Beaver • lat 38˚16'10" lon 112˚29'06"

DESCRIPTION: CG set in a grassy meadow with patches of mahogany, pinyons, and pine on a bench. Warm days with cool evenings; prepare for dropping temperatures. Fish nearby Beaver River. Many western history sites nearby. Supplies in Beaver. Light use, fall is spectacular. Many horse and hiking trails.

GETTING THERE: Mahogany Cove CG is located approx. 12 mi. E of Beaver on state HWY 153. Paved roads to CG.

SINGLE RATE:	$6	OPEN DATES:	May-Sept
# of SINGLE SITES:	7	MAX SPUR:	30 feet
		MAX STAY:	14 days
		ELEVATION:	7500 feet

21 Piute
Fishlake • lat 38˚37'19" lon 111˚38'53"

DESCRIPTION: CG in an open area on Johnson Valley Reservoir with views of Mytoge Mountain and the lake. Boat or shore fish for tiger muskie, perch, and rainbow trout. Supplies 5 mi. away. Deer, elk, moose, and pelicans. Gather firewood. Hike Tasha Creek trail, access to Lake Louise and Fish Lake Hightop. No drinking water.

GETTING THERE: From the Fishlake Lodge go N on state HWY 25 approx. 10 mi. to Piute CG.

SINGLE RATE:	$4	OPEN DATES:	May-Oct
# of SINGLE SITES:	48	MAX SPUR:	30 feet
		MAX STAY:	14 days
		ELEVATION:	8700 feet

17 Maple Grove
Scipio • lat 39˚00'55" lon 112˚05'20"

DESCRIPTION: On Ivie Creek among maple, oak, and pine with thick underbrush. Views of red rocks. Mild days with cold nights. Stream is stocked with rainbow trout for bank or fly fishing. Supplies 20 mi. away at Scipio. Gather firewood locally. Short hiking trails. Group pricing from $40 to $80, contact RD.

GETTING THERE: From Scipio go S on US HWY 50 approx. 15 mi. to Maple Grove route. Go W on Maple Grove route approx. 4 mi. to Maple Grove CG.

SINGLE RATE:	$8	OPEN DATES:	May-Oct
# of SINGLE SITES:	20	MAX SPUR:	20 feet
GROUP RATE:	Varies	MAX STAY:	16 days
# of GROUP SITES:	3	ELEVATION:	6400 feet

22 Sunglow
Bicknell • lat 38˚20'37" lon 111˚30'55"

DESCRIPTION: CG set in sparse stands of cottowood and pinyon juniper with a small stream running nearby. Views of Boulder Mountain and red rock formations. Supplies are available 1.5 miles away. Moderate use. Gather firewood locally or buy in Bicknell. Horseride or hike Durfey Canyon trail from CG.

GETTING THERE: From Bicknell go S approx. 0.5 mi. on state HWY 24 to forest route 143. Go E on 143 approx. 1 mi. to Sunglow CG.

SINGLE RATE:	$5	OPEN DATES:	Apr-Nov
# of SINGLE SITES:	6	MAX SPUR:	30 feet
GROUP RATE:	$20	MAX STAY:	14 days
# of GROUP SITES:	2	ELEVATION:	7500 feet

18 Maple Hollow
Holden • lat 39˚03'41" lon 112˚10'16"

DESCRIPTION: This CG is situated underneath a canopy of maple trees, set in a narrow canyon. Supplies are available at Holden. Receives moderate use in the summer season. Campers may gather their firewood. Numerous hiking and mountain bike trails can be found to the East. A small, low standard CG.

GETTING THERE: Maple Hollow CG is located approx. 6 mi. E of Holden on Maple Hollow route.

SINGLE RATE:	No fee	OPEN DATES:	May-Oct
# of SINGLE SITES:	10		
GROUP RATE:	$25	MAX STAY:	14 days
# of GROUP SITES:	1	ELEVATION:	6900 feet

23 Tasha Equestrain
Fishlake • lat 38˚37'25" lon 111˚39'58"

DESCRIPTION: Among spruce, fir, and aspen with views of Fish Lake Hightop. Stream fish nearby Tasha Creek or lake fish. Supplies 4 mi. awat. Deer, elk, moose, and marmots. Moderate use, heavy during hunting season. Gather firewood. Horse ride or hike Tasha Creek Trail. Prepare for mosquitos. Equestrant campers only.

GETTING THERE: From the Fishlake Lodge go N on state HWY 25 approx. 9 mi. to Rock Canyon Trailhead Road. Follow signs to Tasha Equestrain CG.

SINGLE RATE:	No fee	OPEN DATES:	May-Oct
# of SINGLE SITES:	10	MAX SPUR:	30 feet
		MAX STAY:	14 days
# of GROUP SITES:	1	ELEVATION:	9000 feet

19 Monrovian Park
Monroe • lat 38˚35'39" lon 112˚04'32"

DESCRIPTION: Dispersed sites rest in oak and cottowood in a ravine with cliff views. A small creek runs through this quiet, remote CG. Balck bears, mountain lions, wolves, coyotes, deer, elk, eagles, and goshawks in area. CG is busy all summer. There are many hiking and horse trails in the area.

GETTING THERE: Monrovian Park CG is located approx. 4 mi. S of Monroe on forest route 78.

SINGLE RATE:	No fee	OPEN DATES:	May-Oct
# of SINGLE SITES:	15	MAX SPUR:	20 feet
		MAX STAY:	14 days
# of GROUP SITES:	6	ELEVATION:	6300 feet

20 Oak Creek
Oak City • lat 39˚20'58" lon 112˚15'58"

DESCRIPTION: Semi-arid mountainous area located among scrub oak, pinyon juniper, cottowood, and maple on Oak Creek. Fly fish for small trout. Supplies at Oak City. Moderate use, quiet. Gather firewood locally. Some ATV and horse trails. Group site pricing from $30 to $302. Contact RD for information.

GETTING THERE: Oak Creek CG is located approx. 4 mi. E of Oak City on state HWY 135.

SINGLE RATE:	$8	OPEN DATES:	May-Oct
# of SINGLE SITES:	19	MAX SPUR:	20 feet
GROUP RATE:	Varies	MAX STAY:	16 days
# of GROUP SITES:	4	ELEVATION:	5900 feet

 Campground has hosts   **Reservable sites**   **Accessible facilities**   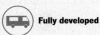 **Fully developed**    **Semi-developed**   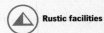 **Rustic facilities**

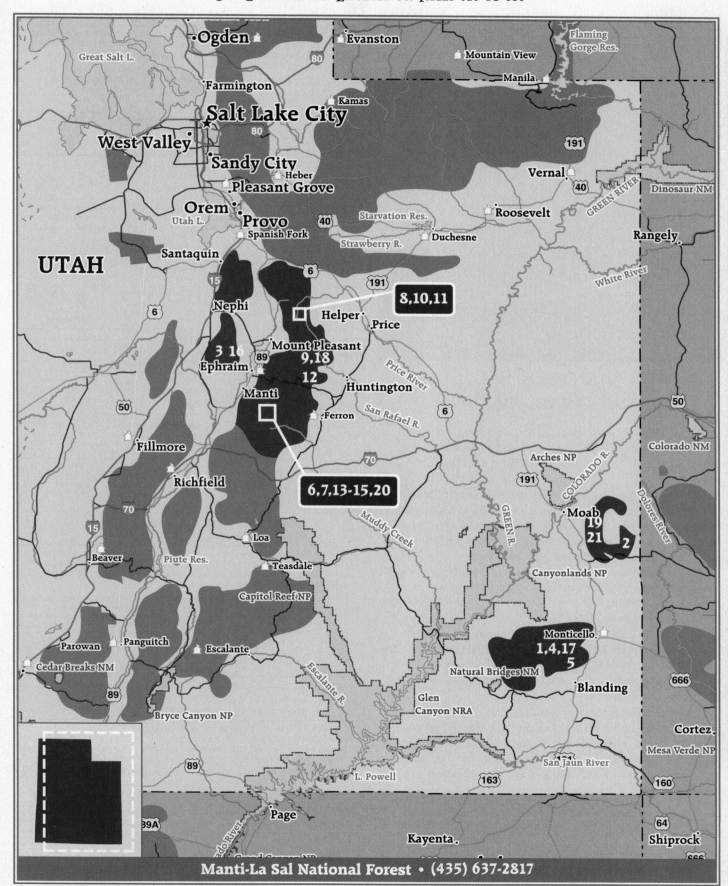

John Niebergall Photo

MANTI-LA SAL NATIONAL FOREST

The 1.3 million acre Manti-La Sal National Forest, located in southeastern Utah is divided into three separate land areas, the Manti Division, the La Sal Division at Moab, and the La Sal Division at Monticello.

The Manti Division is part of the remnant Wasatch Plateau exhibiting high elevation lakes, diverse vegetation and near vertical escarpments. The La Sal Division, mountain peaks, canyons, and forest adds climatic and scenic contrast to the hot red-rock landscape of Arches and Canyonlands National Parks.

The forest provides acres of recreation opportunity. Camping is available in more than 21 developed campgrounds as well as in more remote locations. Hundreds of miles of trails are found in the forest from open grassy slopes to deep spruce/fir groves. Peak-baggers can see vistas of the surrounding deserts and canyons while climbing the La Sals or Abajos to 12,000 feet and higher. Try your luck fishing for trout in mountain lakes, reservoirs, and streams. Huntington Creek is noted as one of the premiere fly-fishing streams in the state.

The Manti-La Sal is also rich in history. Scattered throughout the forest are ancient ruins and rock art left by the native cultures of the region. The sedimentary rocks carry evidence of life from ancient seas and lakes. Fossils range from petrified wood to large Ice Age mammals such as mastodons and the Columbian Mammoth.

1 Buckboard
Monticello • lat 37˚52'53" lon 109˚26'55"

DESCRIPTION: CG set in aspen, pine, and scrub oak. Birds, squirrels, chipmunks, deer, mountain lions, wild turkeys ,and black bears in area. County fair every August. Firewood available on site. Evening programs provided at the Edge of the Cedars Museum in Blanding. Trails into the Blue Mountain Area.

GETTING THERE: Buckboard CG is located approx. 6.5 mi. W of Monticello on forest route 105.

SINGLE RATE:	$7	OPEN DATES:	May-Sept
# of SINGLE SITES:	11	MAX SPUR:	25 feet
GROUP RATE:	Varies	MAX STAY:	16 days
# of GROUP SITES:	2	ELEVATION:	8900 feet

2 Buckeye
LaSal • lat 38˚26'30" lon 109˚03'30"

DESCRIPTION: CG set in spruce and pine trees on Buckeye Reservoir. Fish reservoir for trout. Hot days with cool nights. Expect quick weather changes. Supplies in LaSal. Drinking water available in summer only. Elk, deer, bear, and mountain lions in area. Nearby trails and roads to hike or bike.

GETTING THERE: From LaSal go N approx. 4 mi. on state HWY 46 to forest route 208. Go N on 208 approx. 19 mi. to Buckeye CG.

SINGLE RATE:	$5	OPEN DATES:	June-Sept
# of SINGLE SITES:	5	MAX SPUR:	30 feet
		MAX STAY:	14 days
		ELEVATION:	7600 feet

3 Chicken Creek
Levan • lat 39˚31'50" lon 111˚46'23"

DESCRIPTION: CG is located in park like area with open rangeland views. No fishing in vicinity. Warm to hot days. Supplies are available in Levan. Deer in spring and fall. Never fills. Gather firewood locally. No nearby hiking trails. Ticks in spring. Group fees $30 up to 50 persons, $40 up to 75 persons.

GETTING THERE: Chicken Creek CG is located approx. 6 mi. SE of Levan on forest route 101.

SINGLE RATE:	$5	OPEN DATES:	May-Oct
# of SINGLE SITES:	8	MAX SPUR:	30 feet
GROUP RATE:	Varies	MAX STAY:	16 days
# of GROUP SITES:	1	ELEVATION:	6200 feet

4 Dalton Springs
Monticello • lat 37˚52'26" lon 109˚25'56"

DESCRIPTION: CG set in aspen, pine, and scrub oak. Deer, mountain lions, wild turkeys, and black bears are common to the area. County fair every August. Firewood available at CG. Evening programs provided at the Edge of the Cedars Museum in Blanding. Nearby trails into the Blue Mountain Area.

GETTING THERE: Dalton Springs is located approx. 5 mi. W of Monticello on forest route 105.

SINGLE RATE:	Varies	OPEN DATES:	June-Sept
# of SINGLE SITES:	16	MAX SPUR:	32 feet
		MAX STAY:	14 days
		ELEVATION:	8400 feet

5 Devils Canyon
Blanding • lat 37˚44'20" lon 109˚24'22"

DESCRIPTION: CG set in pine and juniper on the road's edge. No nearby fishing. Firewood is limited. County fair in August. Evening programs are provided at Edge of the Cedars Museum in Blanding. Birds, squirrels, chipmunks, deer, and black bears in area. Self guided interpretive trail on site.

GETTING THERE: Devils Canyon CG is located approx. 9. mi. N of Blanding on US HWY 191.

SINGLE RATE:	$10	OPEN DATES:	May-Oct
# of SINGLE SITES:	32	MAX SPUR:	99 feet
		MAX STAY:	14 days
		ELEVATION:	7100 feet

 Campground has hosts　　 **Reservable sites**　　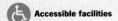 **Accessible facilities**　　 **Fully developed**　　 **Semi-developed**　　 **Rustic facilities**

NOTE: Open dates listed are typical. Actual dates are dependent on conditions such as snow pack.

6 Ferron Canyon
Ferron • lat 39°07'27" lon 111°15'38"

DESCRIPTION: This CG is situated among cottonwoods with limited views of the canyon. CG borders Ferron Creek with good fishing for cutthroat trout. Supplies are available 8 mi. away at Ferron. Campers may gather their firewood locally. Numerous trails can be found in the surrounding area.

GETTING THERE: Ferron Canyon CG is located approx. 8 mi. W of Ferron on forest route 22.

SINGLE RATE:	No fee	OPEN DATES:	May-Oct
# of SINGLE SITES:	4	MAX SPUR:	30 feet
GROUP RATE:	No fee	MAX STAY:	16 days
# of GROUP SITES:	1	ELEVATION:	6400 feet

7 Ferron Reservoir
Ferron • lat 39°08'17" lon 111°27'08"

DESCRIPTION: This CG is set on the shores of Ferron Reservoir, situated in an open park-like area with views of steep hillsides. The reservoir provides for excellent boat and lakeshore fishing. Check for local regulations. Campers may gather their firewood. Numerous trails can be found in the surrounding area.

GETTING THERE: Ferron Reservoir CG is located approx. 28 mi. W of Ferron on forest route 22.

SINGLE RATE:	$6	OPEN DATES:	June-Sept
# of SINGLE SITES:	29	MAX SPUR:	30 feet
GROUP RATE:	$30	MAX STAY:	16 days
# of GROUP SITES:	1	ELEVATION:	9500 feet

8 Flat Canyon
Fairview • lat 39°38'44" lon 111°15'34"

DESCRIPTION: A well shaded CG situated in a dense spruce, pine, and fir forest. Spectacular views of Boulger Canyon and Boulger Reservoir. Fish in lake for trout. Please check for local fishing regulations. Supplies are available at Fairview. Firewood may be scarce, best to bring your own.

GETTING THERE: Flat Canyon is located approx. 12 mi. E of Fairview on state HWY 31.

SINGLE RATE:	$8	OPEN DATES:	July-Sept
# of SINGLE SITES:	12	MAX SPUR:	25 feet
GROUP RATE:	$50	MAX STAY:	16 days
# of GROUP SITES:	1	ELEVATION:	8900 feet

9 Forks of Huntington
Huntington • lat 39°30'03" lon 111°09'34"

DESCRIPTION: CG is located along a stream amidst spruce trees. Views are limited to hillsides on each side of canyon. CG borders Left Fork of Huntington Creek with good stream fishing. Supplies are available at Huntington. Gather firewood locally. A few trails in the area. Tent camping preferred.

GETTING THERE: Forks of Huntington is located approx. 17.5 mi. NW of Huntington on state HWY 31.

SINGLE RATE:	$6	OPEN DATES:	June-Oct
# of SINGLE SITES:	5	MAX SPUR:	20 feet
GROUP RATE:	$40	MAX STAY:	16 days
# of GROUP SITES:	1	ELEVATION:	7700 feet

10 Gooseberry
Fairview • lat 39°41'15" lon 111°17'49"

DESCRIPTION: CG is in a primarily open area with some shade from aspen, spruce, and fir trees. Excellent views of Gooseberry Valley from CG. Good fishing from Gooseberry Reservoir for cutthroat and rainbow trout. Supplies are available at Fairview. Campers may gather their firewood locally.

GETTING THERE: From Fairview go E on state HWY 31 approx. 7 mi. to forest route 124. Go N on 124 approx. 2 mi. to Gooseberry CG.

SINGLE RATE:	$5	OPEN DATES:	June-Sept
# of SINGLE SITES:	9	MAX SPUR:	25 feet
GROUP RATE:	$40	MAX STAY:	14 days
# of GROUP SITES:	1	ELEVATION:	8600 feet

11 Gooseberry Reservoir
Fairview • lat 38°48'11" lon 111°41'11"

DESCRIPTION: Sunny open site on the reservoir. Warm days, cool nights. Fish small carry-in boats or shore fish for trout. Supplies in Fairview. Occasional waterfowl in area. Fills holidays. Bring your own firewood. No nearby hiking trails.

GETTING THERE: From Fairview go E on state HWY 31 approx. 7 mi. to forest route 124. Go N on 124 approx. 2 mi. to Gooseberry Reservoir CG.

SINGLE RATE:	$5	OPEN DATES:	June-Oct
# of SINGLE SITES:	16	MAX SPUR:	60 feet
GROUP RATE:		MAX STAY:	16 days
		ELEVATION:	8400 feet

12 Indian Creek
Orangeville • lat 39°26'34" lon 111°14'15"

DESCRIPTION: CG is situated in a grove of aspen with views of an open valley bordered by mountains in the distance. Indian Creek runs along the edge of the CG and Potters Pond is nearby. Supplies are available at Orangeville or Joes Valley nearby. Campers may gather their firewood.

GETTING THERE: From Orangeville go W on state HWY 29 approx. 7.5 mi. to forest route 40. Go N on 40 approx. 10 mi. to forest route 17. Go N on 17 approx. 1.5 mi. to Indian Creek CG.

SINGLE RATE:	$6	OPEN DATES:	June-Sept
# of SINGLE SITES:	7	MAX SPUR:	25 feet
GROUP RATE:	Varies	MAX STAY:	16 days
# of GROUP SITES:	5	ELEVATION:	8000 feet

13 Joes Valley
Orangeville • lat 39°18'02" lon 111°17'38"

DESCRIPTION: CG is in a desert setting of pine and sagebrush. Joes Valley Reservoir is nearby for boating or fishing. A fish cleaning station located on site. Supplies at Orangeville or nearby marina. There is a limited firewood supply, so it is best to bring your own. Many trails in the area.

GETTING THERE: Joes Valley CG is located approx. 17.5 mi. W of Orangeville on state HWY 29.

SINGLE RATE:	$8	OPEN DATES:	May-Oct
# of SINGLE SITES:	49	MAX SPUR:	40 feet
GROUP RATE:	$75	MAX STAY:	16 days
# of GROUP SITES:	1	ELEVATION:	7000 feet

14 Lake Hill
Ephraim • lat 39°19'37" lon 111°29'52"

DESCRIPTION: In aspen and fir forest on Lake Hill Reservoir. Cold mornings. Fly fish or small carry-in boat craft only. Black bear, mountain lion, elk, deer, golden eagle and goshawks in area. Fills holidays and during Mormon Miracle Pageant. Gather firewood locally. Hiking and ATV trails. Flies and mosquitos July-Aug.

GETTING THERE: From Ephraim go E on forest route 8 approximately 5 miles to Lake Hill CG.

SINGLE RATE:	$7	OPEN DATES:	June-Sept
# of SINGLE SITES:	11	MAX SPUR:	25 feet
GROUP RATE:	Varies	MAX STAY:	16 days
# of GROUP SITES:	2	ELEVATION:	8440 feet

15 Manti Community
Manti • lat 39°15'12" lon 111°32'25"

DESCRIPTION: CG is situated in a transition area between pinyon, juniper, spruce, and fir trees. Some areas shaded. Yearns Reservoir and Manti Creek nearby for fly or lakeshore fishing. Historical indian battle sight. Supplies at Manti. Gather firewood locally. Patton ATV trail system nearby.

GETTING THERE: Manti Community CG is located approx. 7 mi. E of Manti on forest route 45 in Manti Canyon.

SINGLE RATE:	$7	OPEN DATES:	June-Oct
# of SINGLE SITES:	9	MAX SPUR:	30 feet
GROUP RATE:	$40	MAX STAY:	16 days
# of GROUP SITES:	1	ELEVATION:	7400 feet

 Campground has hosts   **Reservable sites**   **Accessible facilities**   **Fully developed**   **Semi-developed**   **Rustic facilities**

NOTE: Open dates listed are typical. Actual dates are dependent on conditions such as snow pack.

16 **Maple Canyon**
Fountain Green • lat 39°33'25" lon 111°41'11"

DESCRIPTION: CG set in deep canyon among maple trees. Shady and cool on warm days. No fishing in vicinity. Supplies are 12 mi. away in Moroni. Fills weekends. Bring your own firewood. Several hiking trails through the rocky canyon. Popular rock-climbing site. Small sites, best suited for tent camping.

GETTING THERE: From Fountain Green go S on state HWY 31 approx. 5.5 mi. to Maple Canyon Road. Go W on Maple Canyon Road approx. 4 mi. to Maple Canyon CG. Tents or very small trailers recommended.

SINGLE RATE:	$5	OPEN DATES:	May-Oct
# of SINGLE SITES:	12	MAX SPUR:	35 feet
GROUP RATE:	$30	MAX STAY:	16 days
# of GROUP SITES:	1	ELEVATION:	6800 feet

17 **Nizhoni**
Blanding • lat 37°50'00" lon 109°31'00"

DESCRIPTION: This CG is situated in ponderosa pine. Visit historical Edge of Cedars Museum. Supplies in Blanding. Wildlife in this area includes the occasional black bear, deer, wild turkey, and numerous songbirds. Gather firewood locally.

GETTING THERE: From Blanding go NW on forest route 079 approximately 10 miles to Nizhoni CG.

SINGLE RATE:	$7	OPEN DATES:	May-Sept
# of SINGLE SITES:	20		
GROUP RATE:	Varies	MAX STAY:	16 days
# of GROUP SITES:	2	ELEVATION:	7000 feet

18 **Old Folks Flat**
Huntington • lat 39°32'20" lon 111°09'32"

DESCRIPTION: This CG is located in a park-like setting with views of Huntington Canyon. Huntington Creek runs nearby where fly and bait fishing are popular. Supplies are available at Huntington. Campers may gather their firewood locally. Castle Valley Ridge Trail system is in the area.

GETTING THERE: Old Folks Flat CG is located approx. 21 mi. NW of Huntington on state HWY 31.

SINGLE RATE:	$8	OPEN DATES:	June-Sept
# of SINGLE SITES:	5	MAX SPUR:	50 feet
GROUP RATE:	$50	MAX STAY:	16 days
# of GROUP SITES:	4	ELEVATION:	8100 feet

19 **Oowah**
Moab • lat 38°30'10" lon 109°16'18"

DESCRIPTION: This primitive CG is in a spruce and aspen forest near Buckeye Reservoir. Fish for trout on Buckeye and Oowah Reservoirs. No drinking water available on site. No services. Supplies are available in Moab. Access to horse, hiking, and mountain biking trails nearby.

GETTING THERE: From Moab go S on LaSal Mountian Loop Road approx. 19.5 mi. to forest route 76. Go N on 76 approx. 2.8 mi. to Oowah CG.

SINGLE RATE:	No fee	OPEN DATES:	June-Sept
# of SINGLE SITES:	6		
		MAX STAY:	16 days
		ELEVATION:	8800 feet

20 **Twelvemile Flat**
Mayfield • lat 39°07'30" lon 111°29'00"

DESCRIPTION: CG is in an open park-like setting of snglemann spruce. Small mountain lakes great for fishing are a short distance of CG. Historical Baldy Ranger Station nearby. Look for bears, elk, deer, eagles, and 3-toed woodpeckers in the area. Supplies are available at Mayfield. Gather firewood locally.

GETTING THERE: Twelvemile Flat CG is located approx. 12 mi. E of Mayfield on forest route 22.

SINGLE RATE:	$7	OPEN DATES:	July-Oct
# of SINGLE SITES:	16	MAX SPUR:	35 feet
GROUP RATE:	$40	MAX STAY:	16 days
# of GROUP SITES:	2	ELEVATION:	10200 feet

21 **Warner**
Moab • lat 38°31'08" lon 109°16'32"

DESCRIPTION: CG set on Warner lake in aspen trees. Hot summers, cooler in winter. Pleasant spring and fall days. T-storms come in quickly. Fish the lake. Supplies in Moab. Deer, elk, mountain lions, occasional bears, and small wildlife in area. Numerous hiking trails nearby. Area is known for mountain biking.

GETTING THERE: From Moab go S on 191 approx. 8 mi. to route 62 (La Sal Mountain Loop Road). Follow 62 approx. 21 mi. to route 63 (Warner Lake Rd). Go N on 63 approx. 5 mi. to Warner CG.

SINGLE RATE:	$7	OPEN DATES:	May-Sept
# of SINGLE SITES:	20	MAX SPUR:	25 feet
GROUP RATE:	$30	MAX STAY:	16 days
# of GROUP SITES:	1	ELEVATION:	9400 feet

 Campground has hosts   **Reservable sites**   **Accessible facilities** 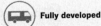 **Fully developed** 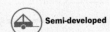 **Semi-developed**  **Rustic facilities**

USFS Photo

UINTA NATIONAL FOREST

The Uinta National Forest covers many steep canyons and high mountain peaks along the Wasatch Front. Around 950,000 acres in size, the Uinta ranges from high western desert at Vernon to lofty mountain peaks such as Mount Nebo and Mount Timpanogos.

The Uinta's scenic beauty offers unlimited recreational opportunities any season of the year. Whether you are a hiker, skier, camper, or horseback rider, the forest can provide the recreational experience you are seeking. There are 500 miles of trails crisscrossing the forest, including the Great Western Trail that enters the Uinta on the north at Sunset Peak and exits in the south at Tucker. Berry-picking, pine nut gathering, birding, fishing and hunting.

Other areas of interest include several scenic byways. The Nebo Scenic Loop Highway is a photographer's dream which offers 32 paved miles of rugged mountain beauty and several magnificent overlooks of the surrounding valleys. The Alpine Scenic Loop provides wonderful views of Mount Timpanogos which will remind you of the Swiss Alps, spectacular fall time foliage, and the Sundance Ski and Summer Resort.

UINTA NATIONAL FOREST • UTAH • LOCATOR MAP

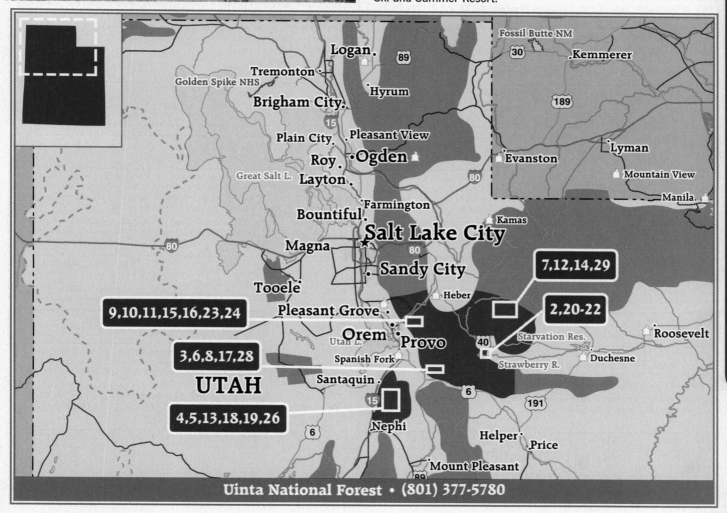

Uinta National Forest • (801) 377-5780

1 Altamont

Lehi • lat 40°26'00" lon 111°38'10"

DESCRIPTION: Aspen and fir on a stream. Views of Mount Timpanogos. Lake fish (no motors) Tibble Fork Reservoir. Historic mining area. Buy firewood or gather deadwood. Hike Great Western Trail. Biking trails. 100 person capacity, 25 vehicles. Key from host at Timpooneke CG. $3.00 per day fee demo entry fee.

GETTING THERE: From Lehi go N on I-15 3 mi. to state route 92. Go E 13 mi.to jct. w/forest route 144. Stay right (straight) for 3 mi. to Altamont CG (on left). Vehicles over 30 ft. not recommended.

		OPEN DATES:	June-Oct
		MAX SPUR:	30 feet
GROUP RATE:	$136	MAX STAY:	14 days
# of GROUP SITES:	1	ELEVATION:	7200 feet

6 Cherry

Springville • lat 40°10'12" lon 111°28'30"

DESCRIPTION: This CG is located in a forested canyon under cottonwood, oak, and maple. Enjoy brown and rainbow trout fishing in adjacent Hobble Creek. Wildlife includes infrequent bears, mountain lions, and coyotes as well as deer, elk, hawks, and eagles. Busy weekends and holidays. Interpretive trail on site.

GETTING THERE: Cherry CG is located approx. 7 mi. E of Springville on forest route 058.

SINGLE RATE:	$11	OPEN DATES:	Apr-Nov
# of SINGLE SITES:	14	MAX SPUR:	35 feet
GROUP RATE:	Varies	MAX STAY:	14 days
# of GROUP SITES:	4	ELEVATION:	5200 feet

2 Aspen Grove

Heber City • lat 40°47'11" lon 111°02'10"

DESCRIPTION: This CG is located in a mountainous area among in fir, maple, and cottonwood trees along side of Hobble Creek. Fish Hobble Creek or hike the nearby trails. Rental boat slips, rental boats, boat ramp and launch area, marina, and store are nearby. Fish cleaning station located at Aspen Boat Ramp.

GETTING THERE: From Heber City go SE on US HWY 40 approx. 33 mi. to forest route 090. Go S on 090 approx. 4 mi. to Aspen Grove CG.

SINGLE RATE:	$12	OPEN DATES:	May-Oct
# of SINGLE SITES:	60	MAX SPUR:	40 feet
		MAX STAY:	14 days
		ELEVATION:	7700 feet

7 Currant Creek

Heber City • lat 40°19'44" lon 111°04'08"

DESCRIPTION: This CG is set in a forest with views of a reservoir. Fish for cutthroat and rainbow trout. Supplies are at Currant Creek Lodge near CG. Firewood is scarce, best to bring your own. Trails nearby, please no ATV's in CG. Kids playground and boat ramp available. CG accomodates horses. Bears frequent the area.

GETTING THERE: From Heber City go E on US HWY 40 approx. 45 mi. to Current Creek Junction. Go 17 Mi. N on rough gravel road to Currant Creek CG.

SINGLE RATE:	$12	OPEN DATES:	June-Oct
# of SINGLE SITES:	94	MAX SPUR:	40 feet
GROUP RATE:	$50	MAX STAY:	14 days
# of GROUP SITES:	4	ELEVATION:	8000 feet

3 Balsam

Springville • lat 40°11'53" lon 111°24'06"

DESCRIPTION: This CG is set in fir, aspen, oak, and maple scattered in an open meadow. Enjoy brown and rainbow trout fishing in adjacent Hobble Creek. Wildlife includes infrequent bears, mountain lions, and coyotes as well as deer, elk, hawks, and eagles. Busy weekends and holidays. Hiking in area.

GETTING THERE: Balsam CG is located approx. 11.5 mi. E of Springville on forest route 058.

SINGLE RATE:	$11	OPEN DATES:	Apr-Nov
# of SINGLE SITES:	13	MAX SPUR:	25 feet
GROUP RATE:	$137	MAX STAY:	14 days
# of GROUP SITES:	1	ELEVATION:	6000 feet

8 Diamond

Spanish Fork • lat 40°04'27" lon 111°25'22"

DESCRIPTION: This CG is currently under construction. Please contact the Spanish Fork Ranger District at (801)798-3571 for opening date.

GETTING THERE: From Spanish Fork go S on state HWY 214 approx. 3 mi. to US HWY 89. Go S on US HWY 89 approx. 8 mi. to forest route 029. Go NE on 029 approx. 6.5 mi. to Diamond CG.

		OPEN DATES:	
		MAX STAY:	14 days
		ELEVATION:	5300 feet

4 Bear Canyon

Nephi • lat 39°47'16" lon 111°43'49"

DESCRIPTION: This walk-in CG rests in a creek canyon under cottonwood. Enjoy rainbow trout fishing in adjacent Salt Creek. Wildlife includes infrequent bears, mountain lions, and coyotes as well as deer, elk, hawks, and eagles. Busy weekends and holidays. Trailheads lead to Mount Nebo Wilderness and Nebo Scenic Byway.

GETTING THERE: From Nephi go E on state HWY 132 approx. 6 mi. to forest route 015. Go N on 015 approx. 7.5 mi. to Bear Canyon CG.

SINGLE RATE:	$7	OPEN DATES:	Apr-Oct
GROUP RATE:	Varies	MAX STAY:	14 days
# of GROUP SITES:	3	ELEVATION:	6200 feet

9 Granite Flat

Lehi • lat 40°29'23" lon 111°39'16"

DESCRIPTION: Park like fir and aspen on creek. Views of Lone Peak Wilderness and Box Elder Peak. Cool days, cold nights. Stream fish creek or lake fish Tibble Fork and Silver Lake Flat (no motors). Historic CCC site. Supplies 15 mi. away. Deer, elk, moose, skunks, and porcupines. Gather firewood. Horse and hiking trails nearby.

GETTING THERE: From Lehi go N on I-15 to exit 287 for state route 92. Go E 12.5 mi. to forest route 144. Go N 3 mi. past Tibble Fork Res., staying on pavement (curves left), go less than 1 mi. to Granite Flat CG.

SINGLE RATE:	Varies	OPEN DATES:	May-Oct
# of SINGLE SITES:	36	MAX SPUR:	30 feet
GROUP RATE:	Varies	MAX STAY:	14 days
# of GROUP SITES:	3	ELEVATION:	6800 feet

5 Blackhawk

Payson • lat 39°53'38" lon 111°37'39"

DESCRIPTION: CG is set in fir, aspen, oak, and maple scattered in an open meadow. Views of Skyline Drive area. Infrequent bears, mountain lions, and coyotes; as well as deer, elk, hawks, and eagles reside in the area. Trailhead leads to Payson Lakes CG and a larger hiking and horse trail system. Horse facilities.

GETTING THERE: From Payson go SE on forest route 015 approx. 15 mi. to forest route 175. Go S on 175 approx. 2 mi. to Blackhawk CG.

SINGLE RATE:	$11	OPEN DATES:	June-Oct
# of SINGLE SITES:	15	MAX SPUR:	35 feet
GROUP RATE:	Varies	MAX STAY:	14 days
# of GROUP SITES:	23	ELEVATION:	8000 feet

10 Hope

Orem • lat 40°18'07" lon 111°36'52"

DESCRIPTION: CG set among maple and box edler with views of Cascade Mountains. Cool days, cold nights. Nearby Provo River is a blue ribbon trout fishery. Supplies at Provo. Never full. Buy firewood on site or gather locally. ATV roads and hiking trails. Deer flies July-Sept. Vehicles over 30' not recommended.

GETTING THERE: From Orem go E on HWY 52 to Provo Canyon and HWY 180. Go NE on 189 approx. 2 mi. to forest route 199 (Squaw Peak turnoff). Go S on 199 approx. 3.5 mi. to Hope CG.

SINGLE RATE:	$7	OPEN DATES:	May-Oct
# of SINGLE SITES:	24	MAX SPUR:	35 feet
		MAX STAY:	14 days
		ELEVATION:	6600 feet

 Campground has hosts   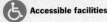 **Reservable sites**   **Accessible facilities**   **Fully developed**   Semi-developed   **Rustic facilities**

NOTE: Open dates listed are typical. Actual dates are dependent on conditions such as snow pack.

Page 532

11 Little Mill
Pleasant Grove • lat 40°26'58" lon 111°40'18"

DESCRIPTION: CG in an open area with cottonwood, box elder, and maple trees. Views of sheer cliff canyon walls. Cool canyon breezes in the mornings. Fish Tibble Fork Reservoir or American Fork River. Beware of dangerous spring runoff. Timpanogos Cave Nat'l Monument 2.5 mi. away. Buy firewood on site. Hiking trails.

GETTING THERE: From Pleasant Grove go N on state HWY 416 approx. 5.5 mi. state route 92. Go E on 92 approx. 4 mi. to Little Mill CG.

SINGLE RATE:	$11	OPEN DATES:	May-Oct
# of SINGLE SITES:	73	MAX SPUR:	30 feet
		MAX STAY:	14 days
		ELEVATION:	6000 feet

16 North Mill Group Site
Pleasant Grove • lat 40°26'56" lon 111°40'46"

DESCRIPTION: CG in an open area with cottonwood, box elder, and maple trees and views of sheer cliff canyon walls. Cool canyon breezes in the mornings. Fish Tibble Fork Reservoir or American Fork River. Beware of dangerous spring runoff. Timpanogos Cave Nat'l Monument 2.5 mi. Buy firewood on site. Hiking trails.

GETTING THERE: From Pleasant Grove go N on state HWY 416 5.5 mi. to state route 92. Go E 4 mi. to North Mill Group Site CG. Key for gate from host at Little Mill CG. $3.00 per day fee demo entry fee required.

GROUP RATE:	$136	OPEN DATES:	May-Oct
# of GROUP SITES:	1	MAX SPUR:	30 feet
		MAX STAY:	14 days
		ELEVATION:	6000 feet

12 Lodgepole
Heber City • lat 40°19'00" lon 111°15'40"

DESCRIPTION: This CG is situated in a mountainous area with pine and aspen trees. Popular activities include hiking, fishing, and boating, all available within 5 mi. of the CG. No firewood available on site, bring your own. Supplies can be found 1 mi. away, up HWY 40. No ATV's or OHV's allowed in CG.

GETTING THERE: From Heber City go SE on US HWY 40 approx. 17.5 mi. to forest route 113. Go W on 113 approx. 1 mi. to Lodgepole CG.

SINGLE RATE:	$12	OPEN DATES:	June-Oct
# of SINGLE SITES:	45	MAX SPUR:	70 feet
		MAX STAY:	14 days
		ELEVATION:	7800 feet

17   Palmyra
Spanish Fork • lat 40°04'16" lon 111°25'48"

DESCRIPTION: This CG is currently under construction. Please contact the Spanish Fork Ranger District at (801)798-3571 for open date.

GETTING THERE: From Spanish Fork go S on state HWY 214 approx. 3 mi. to US HWY 89. Go S on US HWY 89 approx. 8 mi. to forest route 029. Go NE on 029 approx. 6 mi. to Palmyra CG.

		OPEN DATES:	
		MAX STAY:	14 days
		ELEVATION:	5200 feet

13 Maple Bench
Payson • lat 39°57'49" lon 111°41'29"

DESCRIPTION: CG is set in maple with views of Utah Valley. Brown and rainbow trout fishing in nearby Peteenet Creek. Wildlife includes infrequent bears, mountain lions, and coyotes; as well as deer, elk, hawks, and eagles. Busy weekends and holidays. Trailhead leads to Maple Lake which offers fishing and hiking.

GETTING THERE: Maple Bench is located approx. 7.5 mi. SE of Payson on forest route 015.

SINGLE RATE:	$7	OPEN DATES:	May-Oct
# of SINGLE SITES:	10	MAX SPUR:	20 feet
		MAX STAY:	14 days
		ELEVATION:	5800 feet

18 Payson Lakes
Payson • lat 39°55'47" lon 111°38'32"

DESCRIPTION: This CG is set in fir and aspen with views of Mount Nebo. Rainbow trout fishing in adjacent Payson Lakes. Infrequent bears, mountain lions, and coyotes; as well as deer, elk, hawks, and eagles. Busy weekends and holidays. Trailhead leads to Blackhawk CG and a larger hiking trail system.

GETTING THERE: Payson Lakes CG is located approx. 12 mi. SE of Payson on forest route 015.

SINGLE RATE:	$11	OPEN DATES:	June-Oct
# of SINGLE SITES:	92	MAX SPUR:	35 feet
GROUP RATE:	Varies	MAX STAY:	14 days
# of GROUP SITES:	3	ELEVATION:	8000 feet

14 Mill Hollow
Heber City • lat 40°29'22" lon 111°06'12"

DESCRIPTION: This CG is in a forest setting of fir and lodgepole pines with views of Mill Hollow Reservoir. Fishing for rainbow and golden trout from reservoir. Supplies are 25 mi. away. Firewood available from the concessionaire. Hiking trails nearby. Horse flies may be a problem in the summer.

GETTING THERE: From Heber City go NE on US HWY 189 approx. 17 mi. to state HWY 35. Go SE on 35 approx. 12 mi. to forest route 054. Go S on 054 approx. 4 mi. to Mill Hollow CG.

SINGLE RATE:	$12	OPEN DATES:	June-Oct
# of SINGLE SITES:	28	MAX SPUR:	35 feet
		MAX STAY:	14 days
		ELEVATION:	8800 feet

19   Ponderosa
Nephi • lat 39°46'07" lon 111°42'49"

DESCRIPTION: This CG is set among ponderosa pines next to Salt Creek. Enjoy fishing for rainbow trout. Wildlife includes infrequent bears, mountain lions, and coyotes; as well as deer, elk, hawks, and eagles. CG is busy weekends and holidays. Hiking in area, 1/4 mi. to trailhead.

GETTING THERE: From Nephi go E on state HWY 132 approx. 6 mi. to forest route 015. Go N on 015 approx. 5 mi. to Ponderosa CG.

SINGLE RATE:	$11	OPEN DATES:	Apr-Oct
# of SINGLE SITES:	23	MAX SPUR:	25 feet
		MAX STAY:	14 days
		ELEVATION:	6200 feet

15 Mt. Timpanogos
Olmstead • lat 40°24'25" lon 111°36'09"

DESCRIPTION: Among cottonwood, spruce, and fir on small stream. Views of Mount Timpanogos Wilderness. Provo River is a blue ribbon trout fishery. Historic CCC site. Supplies at Provo or Orem. Deer, elk, and moose. Full weekends. Buy firewood from host or gather locally. Hike wilderness trails.

GETTING THERE: From Orem go E on state route 52 3.5 mi. to HWY 189. Go NE 8 mi. to state HWY 92 (Sundance turnoff). Go N on 92 approx. 5 mi. to Mt. Timpanogos CG. Vehicles over 30' not recommended.

SINGLE RATE:	$11	OPEN DATES:	June-Oct
# of SINGLE SITES:	27	MAX SPUR:	30 feet
		MAX STAY:	14 days
		ELEVATION:	6800 feet

20 Renegade Point
Heber City • lat 40°07'22" lon 111°09'11"

DESCRIPTION: This CG is situated in a park like area with spectacular views of Strawberry Reservoir. Boat, fly, and shore fishing are popular from the reservoir. Supplies are available approx. .5 mi. away. Hike Narrows Trail and other trails in the area. Horse flies may be a problem in the summer months

GETTING THERE: From Heber City go SE on US HWY 40 approx. 21 mi. to forest route 131. Go S on 131 approx. 13 mi. to Renegade Point CG.

SINGLE RATE:	$12	OPEN DATES:	May-Nov
# of SINGLE SITES:	62	MAX SPUR:	40 feet
		MAX STAY:	14 days
		ELEVATION:	7700 feet

 Campground has hosts   **Reservable sites**   **Accessible facilities**   **Fully developed**   **Semi-developed**   **Rustic facilities**

NOTE: Open dates listed are typical. Actual dates are dependent on conditions such as snow pack.

21 Soldier Creek
Heber City • lat 40°08'38" lon 111°02'46"

DESCRIPTION: This CG has panoramic views of Strawberry Reservoir and valley. Dump station and boat ramps provided. Marina and store are nearby. Popular activities include trout fishing, boating, water skiing, hiking, biking, and interpretive programs. Horse flies may be a problem.

GETTING THERE: From Heber City go SE on US HWY 40 approx. 30 mi. to forest route 480. Go S on 480 approx. 3 mi. to Soldier Creek CG.

SINGLE RATE:	$12	OPEN DATES:	May-Sept
# of SINGLE SITES:	166	MAX SPUR:	45 feet
		MAX STAY:	14 days
# of GROUP SITES:	3	ELEVATION:	7800 feet

26 Vernon Reservoir
Vernon • lat 39°59'30" lon 112°22'30"

DESCRIPTION: This CG rests in an open area with sagebrush. Views are of adjacent Vernon Reservoir and mountains. Enjoy fishing for brown trout with non-motorized boats. Wildlife in this area includes deer, coyote and several raptors. Bird watchers delight! Busy weekends and holidays.

GETTING THERE: From Vernon go S on forest route 005 approx. 8 mi. to Vernon Reservoir CG.

SINGLE RATE:	No fee	OPEN DATES:	Yearlong
# of SINGLE SITES:	10	MAX SPUR:	50 feet
		MAX STAY:	14 days
		ELEVATION:	5000 feet

22 Strawberry Bay
Heber City • lat 40°11'02" lon 111°09'45"

DESCRIPTION: This CG is situated in a sage brush setting with views of the Strawberry Reservoir and mountains. All types of fishing available. Supplies can be found 1 mi. away from CG. Firewood may be bought on site from concessionaire. Boat ramp and fish cleaning station available.

GETTING THERE: From Heber City go approx. 21 mi. SE on US HWY 40 to forest route 131. Go S on 131 approx. 4 mi. to forest route 452. Go SE on 452 approx. 1.5 mi. to Strawberry Bay CG.

SINGLE RATE:	Varies	OPEN DATES:	May-Nov
# of SINGLE SITES:	364	MAX SPUR:	40 feet
GROUP RATE:	Varies	MAX STAY:	40 days
# of GROUP SITES:	3	ELEVATION:	7600 feet

27 Whiting
Mapleton • lat 40°07'53" lon 111°31'37"

DESCRIPTION: This quiet, shady CG is nestled in a dense grove of cottonwood and maple along a drainage with spring runoff. Wildlife includes infrequent bears, mountain lions, and coyotes as well as deer, elk, hawks, and eagles. Trailhead leads to mountains and larger trail system. Horse facilities.

GETTING THERE: Whiting CG is located approx. 3 mi. E of Mapleton on forest route 025.

SINGLE RATE:	$11	OPEN DATES:	May-Oct
# of SINGLE SITES:	25	MAX SPUR:	35 feet
GROUP RATE:	Varies	MAX STAY:	14 days
# of GROUP SITES:	2	ELEVATION:	5400 feet

23 Theater-in-the-Pines
Olmstead • lat 40°24'18" lon 111°36'18"

DESCRIPTION: Among fir and aspen with mountain views. Frequent noon rains. Blue Ribbon trout fish Provo River. Historic CCC ampitheater. Supplies at Orem. Deer, moose, elk, and mountain goats. Moderate use. Firewood sold on site. Multiple hiking trails. Deer flies in Aug.. Key to gate with host of Mt. Timpanogos CG.

GETTING THERE: From N. Orem on I-15 take exit 275 (state route 52/800). Go E 3.5 mi. to state HWY 189. Go NE 7 mi. to state HWY 92 (Sundance turnoff). Go NW 4 mi. to Theater-in-the-Pines Group Site CG.

SINGLE RATE:	Varies	OPEN DATES:	June-Oct
		MAX SPUR:	30 feet
		MAX STAY:	14 days
# of GROUP SITES:	1	ELEVATION:	7000 feet

28 Wolf Creek
Heber City • lat 40°28'53" lon 111°01'55"

DESCRIPTION: This CG is situated in a thick fir forest, surrounded by scenic mountain views. Expect cool mornings with cold nights. Supplies are available 35 mi. away at Heber City. Wildlife in the area includes deer, elk, bears, fox, and moose. Firewood is scarce, best to bring your own.

GETTING THERE: From Heber City go NE on US HWY 189 approx. 17 mi. to state HWY 35. Go SE on 35 approx. 16 mi. to Wolf Creek CG.

		OPEN DATES:	July-Oct
		MAX SPUR:	40 feet
GROUP RATE:	Varies	MAX STAY:	14 days
# of GROUP SITES:	3	ELEVATION:	9400 feet

24 Timpooneke
Lehi • lat 40°25'54" lon 111°38'22"

DESCRIPTION: CG set in fir and aspen on a stream. Views of Mount Timpanogos Wilderness. Fish Tibble Fork Reservoir. Supplies 3 mi.. Deer, elk, and moose. Buy firewood from host or gather locally. Hiking, mountain bike, and horse wilderness trails. Deer flies in August. Vehicles over 30' not recommended.

GETTING THERE: From Lehi go N on I-15 to exit 287 for state route 92. Go E on 92 13 mi. up American Fork Canyon. Stay on 92 at Jct 2/144 for another 4 mi.. Turn right at T intersection to Timpooneke CG.

SINGLE RATE:	Varies	OPEN DATES:	June-Oct
# of SINGLE SITES:	32	MAX SPUR:	30 feet
		MAX STAY:	14 days
		ELEVATION:	7400 feet

25 Tinney Flat
Santaquin • lat 39°54'03" lon 111°43'38"

DESCRIPTION: This CG is located in a canyon with dramatic, unique rock formations under fir and cottonwood. Enjoy trout fishing in adjacent Santaquin Creek. Wildlife includes infrequent bears, mountain lions, and coyotes; as well as deer, elk, hawks, and eagles. Trailhead leads to Mount Nebo Wilderness.

GETTING THERE: Tinney Flat CG is located approx. 8 mi. SE of Santaquin on forest route 014.

SINGLE RATE:	$11	OPEN DATES:	June-Oct
# of SINGLE SITES:	7	MAX SPUR:	35 feet
GROUP RATE:	$66	MAX STAY:	14 days
# of GROUP SITES:	3	ELEVATION:	6200 feet

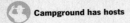 Campground has hosts   Reservable sites   Accessible facilities   Fully developed   Semi-developed   Rustic facilities

NOTE: Open dates listed are typical. Actual dates are dependent on conditions such as snow pack.

WASATCH-CACHE NATIONAL FOREST

Wasatch-Cache National Forest encompasses approximately two million acres and spans northern Utah and southwestern Wyoming. The forest name, Wasatch-Cache, pays tribute to two important groups whose survival and livelihood depended on the resources of the forests. Wasatch is a Ute Indian word meaning "high mountain pass". Cache is a legacy of the early fur trappers who dug caves in Cache Valley to store or "cache their furs so that they would be preserved until they could be traded.

The forest also holds important clues to the natural history of the area. The Jardine Juniper is 1500 years old and is reputed to be the oldest living tree in the Rocky Mountains. Evidence of ancient oceans, volcanoes, and glaciers can also be found throughout the forest.

With acres of trails, pristine mountain streams and spectacular scenery, the Wasatch-Cache provides the visitor with solitude and adventure. Skiers find the "greatest snow on earth" here. Fluffy dry powder falls for nearly five months a year, creating a winter paradise. There are several major ski resorts within the forest, including Alta, Snowbird, Brighton, Solitude, Snow Basin and Beaver Mountain.

USFS Photo

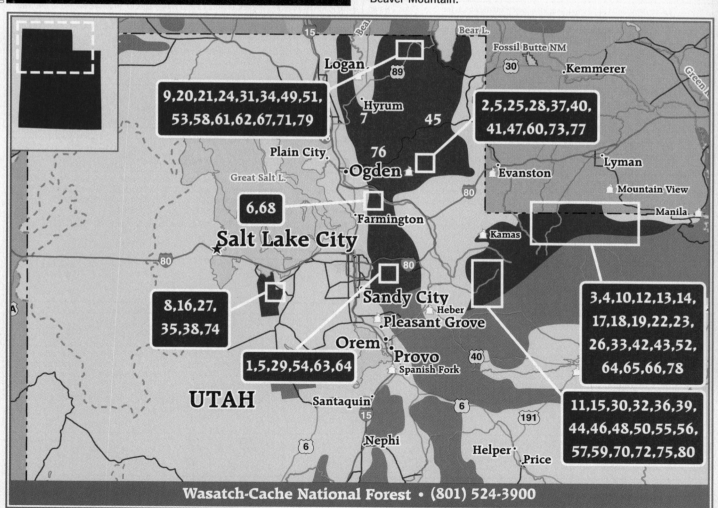

Wasatch-Cache National Forest • (801) 524-3900

1 Albion Basin
Sandy City • lat 40°34'36" lon 111°36'42"

DESCRIPTION: CG is located in mixed conifer with mountain peak views. Visit nearby Secret Lake. Mountain lions, coyotes, deer, moose, raptors, and Uinta ground squirrels. Bring your own firewood. Busy weekends and holidays. No pets allowed. On site interpretive trail. Abundance of beautiful wildflowers.

GETTING THERE: From Sandy City go E on state HWY 209 approx. 6 mi. to state HWY 210. Go E on 210 approx. 9 mi. to Albion Basin CG.

SINGLE RATE:	$10	OPEN DATES:	July-Sept
# of SINGLE SITES:	24	MAX SPUR:	18 feet
GROUP RATE:	Varies	MAX STAY:	7 days
# of GROUP SITES:	2	ELEVATION:	9500 feet

2 Anderson Cove
Ogden • lat 41°15'06" lon 111°47'23"

DESCRIPTION: CG rests in a grassy flat with exotic trees such as russian olives and locust. Enjoy crappie, bass, record-breaking tiger muskie fishing in adjacent Pineview Reservoir. Wildlife in this area includes the infrequent black bears and coyotes, deer, elk, moose, and raptors. Busy weekends and holidays.

GETTING THERE: From Ogden go E on state HWY 39 approx. 9.5 mi. to Anderson Cove CG.

SINGLE RATE:	$12	OPEN DATES:	May-Oct
# of SINGLE SITES:	74	MAX SPUR:	50 feet
GROUP RATE:	Varies	MAX STAY:	7 days
# of GROUP SITES:	2	ELEVATION:	5000 feet

3 Bear River
Evanston • lat 40°54'37" lon 110°49'46"

DESCRIPTION: This CG is located in lodgepole pine and aspen on the Bear River. Fly fish for trout in the river. Wildlife in the area includes black bears, mountain lions, deer, elk, moose, goshawks, and bald eagles. CG is busy holiday weekends in summer. Hike and horseback ride in nearby High Uinta Wilderness.

GETTING THERE: Bear River CG is located approx. 30 mi. S of Evanston on state HWY 150.

SINGLE RATE:	$9	OPEN DATES:	June-Oct
# of SINGLE SITES:	4	MAX SPUR:	35 feet
		MAX STAY:	14 days
		ELEVATION:	8300 feet

4 Beaver View
Kamas • lat 40°49'25" lon 110°51'44"

DESCRIPTION: This CG is located in lodgepole pine and aspen on the Hayden River. Fly fish for trout in the river. Wildlife in the area includes black bears, mountain lions, deer, elk, moose, goshawks, and bald eagle. CG is busy holiday weekends in the summer. Hike and horseback ride in nearby High Uinta Wilderness.

GETTING THERE: Beaver View CG is located approx. 41.5 mi. E of Kamas on state HWY 150.

SINGLE RATE:	$10	OPEN DATES:	June-Oct
# of SINGLE SITES:	8	MAX SPUR:	35 feet
		MAX STAY:	14 days
		ELEVATION:	9000 feet

5 Botts
Huntsville • lat 41°16'38" lon 111°39'22"

DESCRIPTION: CG is in cottonwood and willow on the South Fork of Ogden River. Enjoy trout fishing in river. Wildlife in this area includes the infrequent black bears and coyotes, deer, elk, moose, and raptors. CG is busy weekends and holidays. There is a fisherman's trail that runs along the river.

GETTING THERE: From Huntsville go E on state HWY 39 approx. 6.5 mi. to Botts CG.

SINGLE RATE:	$10	OPEN DATES:	May-Oct
# of SINGLE SITES:	8	MAX SPUR:	30 feet
		MAX STAY:	7 days
		ELEVATION:	5200 feet

6 Bountiful Peak
Bountiful • lat 40°58'47" lon 111°48'14"

DESCRIPTION: CG rests in mixed conifer with panoramic views of mountains and the Great Salt Lake. Mountain lions, coyotes, deer, moose, raptors, and Uinta ground squirrels. Busy weekends and holidays. No pets allowed. Max 100 persons at group site. Hiking, mountain biking, and horse trails. Bring firewood.

GETTING THERE: Bountiful Peak CG is located approx. 13 mi. from Bountiful on the Bountiful Peak route. Narrow road, RV's and trailers not recommended.

SINGLE RATE:	$8	OPEN DATES:	June-Oct
# of SINGLE SITES:	26		
GROUP RATE:	$100	MAX STAY:	7 days
# of GROUP SITES:	1	ELEVATION:	7500 feet

7 Box Elder
Brigham City • lat 41°29'32" lon 111°56'36"

DESCRIPTION: CG rests in box elder and hardwoods next to Box Elder Creek. Enjoy fishing at nearby Mantua Reservoir. Check fishing regulations. Wildlife in this area includes deer, elk, and numerous birds. CG tends to be busy weekends and holidays. Supplies are available in Brigham City.

GETTING THERE: From Brigham City go E on US HWY 89/91 approx. 4 mi. to forest route 084. Go S on 084 approx. .5 mi. to Box Elder CG.

SINGLE RATE:	$10	OPEN DATES:	May-Oct
# of SINGLE SITES:	26	MAX SPUR:	20 feet
		MAX STAY:	7 days
		ELEVATION:	5200 feet

8 Boy Scout
Grantsville • lat 40°29'39" lon 112°34'40"

DESCRIPTION: This remote CG is located in mixed conifer. Provides access to the nearby wilderness area. Wildlife includes mountain lions, coyotes, deer, moose, raptors, and Uinta ground squirrels. No pets allowed. Hiking, mountain biking, and horse trails in area. Bring your own firewood. No drinking water.

GETTING THERE: From Grantsville go S on Co 138 approx. 4.7 mi. to forest route 171. Go SW on 171 approx. 5.3 mi. to Boy Scout CG. No RVs or trailers.

SINGLE RATE:	$6	OPEN DATES:	May-Oct
# of SINGLE SITES:	5		
GROUP RATE:	Varies	MAX STAY:	7 days
# of GROUP SITES:	1	ELEVATION:	6320 feet

9 Bridger
Logan • lat 41°44'53" lon 111°44'04"

DESCRIPTION: CG is located in low elevation hardwoods such as willow, maple, and cottonwood. Enjoy trout fishing in adjacent Logan River. Check fishing regulations. Deer, elk, and numerous birds are common to the area. CG is busy weekends and holidays. Hike nearby riverside nature/interpretive trail.

GETTING THERE: Bridger CG is located approx. 6 mi. E of Logan on US HWY 89.

SINGLE RATE:	$10	OPEN DATES:	May-Oct
# of SINGLE SITES:	10	MAX SPUR:	20 feet
		MAX STAY:	7 days
		ELEVATION:	5100 feet

10 Bridger Lake
Mountain View • lat 40°57'57" lon 110°23'12"

DESCRIPTION: This CG is located in lodgepole pine and aspen with views of adjacent Bridger Lake. Enjoy fishing for trout. Wildlife in the area includes the infrequent black bears and mountain lions as weel as deer, elk, moose, and raptors. There are hiking and biking trails in the area. Boat ramp on site.

GETTING THERE: From Mountain View go S approx. 7 mi. on state HWY 410 to forest route 072. Go S on 072 approx. 15.4 mi. to forest route 126. Continue on 126 approx. .5 mi. to Bridger Lake CG.

SINGLE RATE:	$11	OPEN DATES:	June-Sept
# of SINGLE SITES:	32	MAX SPUR:	45 feet
		MAX STAY:	14 days
		ELEVATION:	9300 feet

 Campground has hosts   **Reservable sites**   **Accessible facilities** 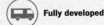 **Fully developed**   **Semi-developed**   **Rustic facilities**

NOTE: Open dates listed are typical. Actual dates are dependent on conditions such as snow pack.

Page 536

11   Butterfly Lake
Kamas • lat 40°43'20" lon 110°51'58"

DESCRIPTION: CG rests in an open grove of spruce next to Butterfly Lake. Enjoy fishing for rainbow, cutthroat, and albino trout. Wildlife in this area includes black bears, mountain lions, coyotes, deer, elk, moose, and raptors. Busy weekends and holidays. Nearby Highline Trail leads to the High Uinta Wilderness.

GETTING THERE: Butterfly Lake CG is located approx. 34 mi. E of Kamas on state HWY 150.

SINGLE RATE:	$10	OPEN DATES:	July-Sept
# of SINGLE SITES:	20	MAX SPUR:	35 feet
		MAX STAY:	14 days
		ELEVATION:	10360 feet

16   Cottonwood
Grantsville • lat 40°30'00" lon 112°33'30"

DESCRIPTION: This tent CG rests among mixed conifer. Wildlife in the area includes mountain lions, coyotes, deer, moose, raptors, and Uinta ground squirrels. CG is busy weekends and holidays. No pets allowed. Hiking and horse trails in area. Bring your own firewood. No drinking water available on site.

GETTING THERE: From Grantsville go S on Co 138 approx. 4.7 mi. to forest route 171. Go SW on 171 approx. 4 mi. to Cottonwood CG. Not recommended for RVs.

SINGLE RATE:	$6	OPEN DATES:	May-Oct
# of SINGLE SITES:	2		
		MAX STAY:	7 days
		ELEVATION:	6080 feet

12   China Meadows
Mountain View • lat 40°56'00" lon 110°24'30"

DESCRIPTION: This CG is located in lodgepole pine and aspen. Enjoy nearby China Lake. Wildlife in this area includes infrequent black bears and mountain lions as well as deer, elk, moose, and raptors. CG is busy weekends and holidays. Supplies in Mountain View. Several nearby hiking trails.

GETTING THERE: From Mountain View go S on state HWY 410 approx. 7 mi. to forest route 072. Go S on 072 approx. 18.5 mi. to China Meadows CG.

SINGLE RATE:	$7	OPEN DATES:	June-Oct
# of SINGLE SITES:	9	MAX SPUR:	20 feet
		MAX STAY:	14 days
		ELEVATION:	9500 feet

17   Deadhorse
Mountain View • lat 41°02'00" lon 110°22'00"

DESCRIPTION: This CG is located in lodgepole pine and aspen. Enjoy nearby springs and streams. Wildlife in this area includes the infrequent black bears and mountain lions; as well as deer, elk, moose, and raptors. CG is busy weekends and holidays. Supplies in Mountain View. CG offers an OHV trailhead.

GETTING THERE: From Mountain View go S approx. 7 mi. on state HWY 410 to forest route 072. Go S on 072 approx. 10.5 mi. to Deadhorse CG.

SINGLE RATE:	$4	OPEN DATES:	Yearlong
# of SINGLE SITES:	4	MAX SPUR:	20 feet
		MAX STAY:	14 days
		ELEVATION:	9000 feet

13   China Meadows Trailhead
Mountain View • lat 40°55'52" lon 110°24'07"

DESCRIPTION: This CG is located in lodgepole pine and aspen. Enjoy nearby China Lake. Wildlife in this area includes infrequent black bears and mountain lions as well as deer, elk, moose, and raptors. CG is busy weekends and holidays. Supplies in Mountain View. Several nearby hiking trails.

GETTING THERE: From Mountain View go S on state HWY 410 approx. 7 mi. to forest route 072. Go S on 072 approx. 18.5 mi. to China Meadows Trailhead CG.

SINGLE RATE:	No fee	OPEN DATES:	June-Oct
# of SINGLE SITES:	12	MAX SPUR:	20 feet
		MAX STAY:	14 days
		ELEVATION:	10000 feet

18   East Fork Bear River
Evanston • lat 40°54'42" lon 110°49'44"

DESCRIPTION: This CG is located in lodgepole pine and aspen on the Bear River. Fly fish for trout in the river. Wildlife in the area includes black bears, mountain lions, deer, elk, moose, goshawks, and bald eagles. CG is busy holiday weekends in summer. Hike and horseback ride in nearby High Uinta Wilderness.

GETTING THERE: East Fork Bear River CG is located approx. 29.5 mi. S of Evanston on state HWY 150.

SINGLE RATE:	$9	OPEN DATES:	June-Oct
# of SINGLE SITES:	8	MAX SPUR:	35 feet
		MAX STAY:	14 days
		ELEVATION:	8300 feet

14   Christmas Meadows
Evanston • lat 40°49'28" lon 110°48'05"

DESCRIPTION: This CG is a popular fly fishing and kayaking spot. Situated in lodgepole pine and aspen on the Stillwater River. There is an on-site trailhead which leads to small lakes and the Highline Trail. Wildlife in area includes bears, mountain lions, deer, elk, moose, goshawks, and bald eagles.

GETTING THERE: From Evanston go S approx. 32.5 mi. on state HWY 150 to forest route 057. Go SE on 057 approx. 3.5 mi. to Christmas Meadows CG.

SINGLE RATE:	$10	OPEN DATES:	June-Oct
# of SINGLE SITES:	11	MAX SPUR:	35 feet
		MAX STAY:	14 days
		ELEVATION:	8800 feet

19   East Fork Blacks Fork Trailhead
Evanston • lat 40°53'00" lon 110°32'24"

DESCRIPTION: This rustic CG is located in a grove of lodgepole pine and aspen. CG is an ideal place for horseback riding. Wildlife in the area includes black bears, mountain lions, deer, elk, moose, goshawks, and bald eagles. An on-site trailhead leads to the High Uinta Wilderness.

GETTING THERE: From Evanston go S approx. 30 mi. on state HWY 150 to forest route 058. Go E on 058 approx. 19 mi. to forest route 065. Go S on 065 approx. 4 mi. to East Fork Blacks Fork Trailhead CG.

SINGLE RATE:	No fee	OPEN DATES:	June-Oct
# of SINGLE SITES:	8	MAX SPUR:	35 feet
		MAX STAY:	14 days
		ELEVATION:	9300 feet

15   Cobble Rest
Kamas • lat 40°35'40" lon 110°58'29"

DESCRIPTION: CG is located in a park-like grove of pine with views of the Upper Provo River. Frequent thundershowers. Fishing for cutthroat and rainbow trout. Supplies at Kamas. Deer, moose, black bears, and mountain lions in area. CG full weekends. Several horse and hiking trails in area. Firewood sold on site.

GETTING THERE: Cobble Rest CG is located approx. 19.6 mi. E of Kamas on state HWY 150.

SINGLE RATE:	$11	OPEN DATES:	June-Sept
# of SINGLE SITES:	18	MAX SPUR:	30 feet
		MAX STAY:	14 days
		ELEVATION:	8280 feet

20   Friendship
Hyrum • lat 41°39'39" lon 111°39'52"

DESCRIPTION: This rustic CG is located in low elevation hardwoods near the Left Hand of Blacksmith River. Enjoy fishing for trout. Wildlife in this area includes deer, elk, and numerous birds. CG is busy weekends and holidays. Hiking trails within 1/2 mi. of CG. No drinking water available on site.

GETTING THERE: From Hyrum go E approx. 8.5 mi. E on state HWY 101 to forest route 245. Go NE on 245 approx. 4 mi. to Friendship CG.

SINGLE RATE:	$6	OPEN DATES:	May-Oct
# of SINGLE SITES:	6	MAX SPUR:	20 feet
		MAX STAY:	7 days
		ELEVATION:	5600 feet

 Campground has hosts   **Reservable sites**   **Accessible facilities**   **Fully developed**   **Semi-developed**   **Rustic facilities**

NOTE: Open dates listed are typical. Actual dates are dependent on conditions such as snow pack.

21 Guinavah-Malibu

Logan • lat 41°45'43" lon 111°41'55"

DESCRIPTION: CG is located in low elevation hardwoods such as willow, maple, and cottonwood. Enjoy trout fishing in adjacent Logan River. Check fishing regulations. Deer, elk, and numerous birds in the area. CG is busy weekends and holidays. Hike nearby riverside nature/interpretive trail.

GETTING THERE: Guinavah-Malibu CG is located approx. 8 mi. E of Logan on US HWY 89.

SINGLE RATE:	$12	OPEN DATES:	May-Oct
# of SINGLE SITES:	40	MAX SPUR:	20 feet
		MAX STAY:	7 days
		ELEVATION:	5200 feet

22 Hayden Fork

Evanston • lat 40°49'47" lon 110°51'10"

DESCRIPTION: This CG is located in lodgepole pine and aspen a short walk from the Hayden River. Fly fish for trout in the river. Wildlife in the area includes black bears, mountain lions, deer, elk, moose, goshawks, and bald eagles. CG is busy holiday weekends in the summer. Visit nearby High Uinta Wilderness.

GETTING THERE: Hayden Fork CG is located approx. 36.6 mi. S of Evanston on state HWY 150.

SINGLE RATE:	$9	OPEN DATES:	June-Oct
# of SINGLE SITES:	9	MAX SPUR:	35 feet
		MAX STAY:	14 days
		ELEVATION:	8900 feet

23 Henry's Fork

Mountain View • lat 40°55'00" lon 110°20'30"

DESCRIPTION: This CG is located in lodgepole pine and aspen. Enjoy Henry's Fork River. Wildlife includes the infrequent black bears and mountain lions; as well as deer, elk, moose, and raptors. CG is busy weekends and holidays. Supplies in Mountain View. Offers trail leading to Kings Peak. No drinking water on site.

GETTING THERE: From Mountian View go S approx. 7 mi. on state HWY 410 to forest route 072. Go S on 072 approx. 3.5 mi. to forest route 017. Continue SE on 017 approx. 9 mi. to Henry's Fork CG.

SINGLE RATE:	No fee	OPEN DATES:	June-Oct
# of SINGLE SITES:	7	MAX SPUR:	20 feet
		MAX STAY:	14 days
		ELEVATION:	9600 feet

24 High Creek

Richmond • lat 41°58'34" lon 111°44'02"

DESCRIPTION: This rustic CG is situated in hardwoods in a quiet, scenic canyon. Enjoy adjacent High Creek. CG provides access to nearby Mount Naomi Wilderness. Wildlife in this area includes deer, elk, and numerous birds. CG is busy weekends and holidays. Supplies are available in Richmond.

GETTING THERE: From Richmond go N on US HWY 91 approx. 3 mi. to forest route 048. Go E on 048 approx. 5 mi. to High Creek CG.

SINGLE RATE:	No fee	OPEN DATES:	June-Oct
# of SINGLE SITES:	2	MAX SPUR:	20 feet
		MAX STAY:	7 days
		ELEVATION:	5000 feet

25 Hobble

Huntsville • lat 41°16'27" lon 111°39'36"

DESCRIPTION: CG rests in cottonwood and willow on the South Fork of Ogden River. Enjoy trout fishing in river. Wildlife includes deer, elk, moose, raptors, and occasional black bears and coyotes. CG is busy weekends and holidays. There is a fisherman's trail that runs along the river. No drinking water.

GETTING THERE: From Huntsville go E on state HWY 39 approx. 6 mi. to Hobble CG.

SINGLE RATE:	$5	OPEN DATES:	May-Oct
# of SINGLE SITES:	4	MAX SPUR:	30 feet
		MAX STAY:	7 days
		ELEVATION:	5200 feet

26 Hoop Lake

Lonetree • lat 40°55'30" lon 110°07'26"

DESCRIPTION: This CG is located in lodgepole pine and aspen. Enjoy trout fishing in adjacent Hoop Lake. Wildlife in this area includes the infrequent black bears and mountain lions; as well as deer, elk, moose, and raptors. CG is busy weekends and holidays. Supplies in Lonetree. Several nearby hiking trails.

GETTING THERE: From Lonetree go approx. 1.8 mi. E on state HWY 414 to forest route 078. Go S on 078 approx. 10.5 mi. to Hoop Lake CG.

SINGLE RATE:	$8	OPEN DATES:	June-Oct
# of SINGLE SITES:	44	MAX SPUR:	20 feet
		MAX STAY:	14 days
		ELEVATION:	9500 feet

27 Intake

Grantsville • lat 40°29'52" lon 112°34'14"

DESCRIPTION: This tent CG rests among mixed conifer. Wildlife includes mountain lions, coyotes, deer, moose, raptors, and Uinta ground squirrels. CG is busy weekends and holidays. No pets allowed. Hiking, mountain biking, and horse trails in area. Bring your own firewood. No drinking water available.

GETTING THERE: From Grantsville go S on Co 138 approx. 4.7 mi. to forest route 171. Go SW on 171 approx. 5 mi. to Intake CG. No RVs.

SINGLE RATE:	$6	OPEN DATES:	May-Oct
# of SINGLE SITES:	4		
		MAX STAY:	7 days
		ELEVATION:	6320 feet

28 Jefferson Hunt

Huntsville • lat 41°14'56" lon 111°46'00"

DESCRIPTION: CG is situated in cottonwood on the South Fork of Ogden River. Crappie, bass, and record-breaking tiger muskie fishing in nearby Pineview Reservoir. Wildlife includes infrequent black bears and coyotes, deer, elk, moose, and raptors. CG is busy weekends and holidays. Several hiking trails in area.

GETTING THERE: From Huntsville go S on state HWY 39 approx. 2 mi. to Jefferson Hunt CG.

SINGLE RATE:	$9	OPEN DATES:	May-Oct
# of SINGLE SITES:	29	MAX SPUR:	30 feet
		MAX STAY:	7 days
		ELEVATION:	5000 feet

29 Jordan Pine

Park City • lat 40°38'47" lon 111°38'48"

DESCRIPTION: This CG is situated among mixed conifer near Silver Lake. There is a visitors center nearby. CG is reservation only with dispersed group sites. No pets allowed. Enjoy the on site trail which leads to Doughnut Falls. Maximum of 50-125 persons to group sites.

GETTING THERE: From Park City go S approx. 5 mi. on state HWY 224 to state HWY 190. Go W on 190 approx. 6.5 mi. to Jordan Pine CG. No RVs or trailers.

		OPEN DATES:	June-Sept
GROUP RATE:	Varies	MAX STAY:	7 days
# of GROUP SITES:	5	ELEVATION:	7200 feet

30 Ledgefork

Kamas • lat 40°44'28" lon 111°05'35"

DESCRIPTION: CG is located in ponderosa pine, douglas fir and aspen near Smith and Morehouse Reservoir. Enjoy fishing for trout. Supplies at Kamas. Deer, moose, black bears, and mountain lions in area. CG is busy holidays and weekends. Ledfork trailhead leads to "Lakes Country", a series of high alpine lakes.

GETTING THERE: From Kamas go N on state HWY 32 approx. 5.5 mi. to state HWY 213. Go NE on 213 approx. 12 mi. to forest route 33. Go S on 33 approx. 4 mi. to Ledgefork CG.

SINGLE RATE:	$12	OPEN DATES:	May-Sept
# of SINGLE SITES:	73	MAX SPUR:	45 feet
		MAX STAY:	14 days
		ELEVATION:	7750 feet

 Campground has hosts   **Reservable sites**   **Accessible facilities**   **Fully developed**   **Semi-developed**   **Rustic facilities**

NOTE: Open dates listed are typical. Actual dates are dependent on conditions such as snow pack.

31 Lewis M. Turner
Logan • lat 41˚53'06" lon 111˚34'19"

DESCRIPTION: This CG is located among pine, aspen, hardwoods, and some fir near Logan River. Enjoy fishing for trout but please check fishing regsulations. Deer, elk, moose, and numerous birds are common to the area. CG is busy weekends and holidays. Hike trail to nearby Red Banks CG. Supplies in Logan.

GETTING THERE: From Logan go approx. 21.5 mi. NE on US HWY 89 to forest route 003. Go W on 003 approx. .5 mi. to Lewis M. Turner CG.

SINGLE RATE:	$10	OPEN DATES:	June-Oct
# of SINGLE SITES:	10	MAX SPUR:	20 feet
		MAX STAY:	7 days
		ELEVATION:	5900 feet

36 Lost Creek
Kamas • lat 40˚41'00" lon 110˚55'30"

DESCRIPTION: This CG rests among ponderosa pine with mountain views. Enjoy trout fishing in adjacent Lost Lake. Deer, moose, black bears, and mountain lions reside in the area. CG is busy holidays and weekends. Hike the nearby Crystal Lake Trail. Supplies are available in Kamas. Bring your own firewood.

GETTING THERE: Lost Lake CG is located approx. 27.6 mi. E of Kamas on state HWY 150.

SINGLE RATE:	$11	OPEN DATES:	July-Sept
# of SINGLE SITES:	35	MAX SPUR:	40 feet
		MAX STAY:	14 days
		ELEVATION:	9940 feet

32 Lilly Lake
Kamas • lat 40˚40'51" lon 110˚56'16"

DESCRIPTION: This CG situated is among ponderosa pine with mountain views. Enjoy trout fishing with in adjacent Lilly Lake. Deer, moose, black bears, and mountain lions in area. CG is busy holidays and weekends. Hike the nearby Crystal Lake Trail. Supplies are available in Kamas. Bring your own firewood.

GETTING THERE: Lilly Lake CG is located approx. 27.4 mi. E of Kamas on state HWY 150.

SINGLE RATE:	$11	OPEN DATES:	July-Sept
# of SINGLE SITES:	14	MAX SPUR:	45 feet
		MAX STAY:	14 days
		ELEVATION:	9900 feet

37 Lower Meadows
Huntsville • lat 41˚17'15" lon 111˚39'08"

DESCRIPTION: CG sits in cottonwood and willow on the South Fork of Ogden River. Enjoy trout fishing in river. Wildlife in this area includes the infrequent black bears and coyotes, deer, elk, moose, and raptors. CG is busy weekends and holidays. There is a fisherman's trail that runs along the river.

GETTING THERE: From Huntsville go E on state HWY 39 approx. 8.5 mi. to Lower Meadows CG.

SINGLE RATE:	$10	OPEN DATES:	May-Oct
# of SINGLE SITES:	17	MAX SPUR:	30 feet
		MAX STAY:	7 days
		ELEVATION:	5200 feet

33 Little Lyman Lake
Evanston • lat 40˚56'05" lon 110˚36'48"

DESCRIPTION: This CG is located in lodgepole pine and aspen on Little Lyman Lake. Fish for pan-sized trout in lake. Wildlife in the area includes black bears, mountain lions, deer, elk, moose, goshawks, and bald eagles. CG is busy holiday weekends in summer. Hike and horseback ride in nearby High Uinta Wilderness.

GETTING THERE: From Evanston go S on state HWY 150 approx. 29.5 mi. to forest route 058. Go E on 058 approx. 17 mi. to Little Lyman Lake CG.

SINGLE RATE:	$7	OPEN DATES:	June-Oct
# of SINGLE SITES:	10	MAX SPUR:	35 feet
		MAX STAY:	14 days
		ELEVATION:	9300 feet

38 Lower Narrows
Grantsville • lat 40˚29'30" lon 112˚35'28"

DESCRIPTION: This CG rests among mixed conifer. Wildlife includes mountain lions, coyotes, deer, moose, raptors, and Uinta ground squirrels. CG is busy weekends and holidays. No pets allowed. Hiking, mountain biking, and horse trails in area. Bring your own firewood. No drinking water available.

GETTING THERE: From Grantsville go S on Co 138 approx. 4.7 mi. to forest route 171. Go SW on 171 approx. 5.9 mi. to Lower Narrows CG. No RVs.

SINGLE RATE:	$6	OPEN DATES:	May-Oct
# of SINGLE SITES:	5		
		MAX STAY:	7 days
		ELEVATION:	6800 feet

34 Lodge
Logan • lat 41˚46'43" lon 111˚37'16"

DESCRIPTION: CG is located in low elevation hardwoods such as willow, maple, and cottonwood. Enjoy trout fishing in nearby Right Hand Fork of Logan River. Check fishing regulations. Deer, elk, and numerous birds are common to the area. CG is busy weekends and holidays. Hike nearby interpretive trail.

GETTING THERE: From Logan go E aprox. 12 mi. on US HWY 89 to forest route 081. Go E on 081 approx. 1 mi. to Lodge CG.

SINGLE RATE:	$10	OPEN DATES:	May-Oct
# of SINGLE SITES:	10	MAX SPUR:	20 feet
		MAX STAY:	7 days
		ELEVATION:	5600 feet

39 Lower Provo River
Kamas • lat 40˚35'36" lon 111˚06'57"

DESCRIPTION: This CG sits in a grove of ponderosa pine and douglas fir. Enjoy rainbow and cutthroat trout fishing in nearby Lower Provo River. Deer, moose, black bears, and mountain lions in area. CG is busy holidays and weekends. Hike the nearby Scenic Byway Trail. Supplies in Kamas. Bring your own firewood.

GETTING THERE: From Kamas go E approx. 11 mi. on state HWY 150 to forest route 053. Go S on 053 approx. 1 mi. to Lower Provo River CG.

SINGLE RATE:	$10	OPEN DATES:	May-Oct
# of SINGLE SITES:	10	MAX SPUR:	40 feet
		MAX STAY:	14 days
		ELEVATION:	7400 feet

35 Loop
Grantsville • lat 40˚29'03" lon 112˚36'19"

DESCRIPTION: This quiet CG rests among mixed conifer. Wildlife includes mountain lions, coyotes, deer, moose, raptors, and Uinta ground squirrels. CG is busy weekends and holidays. No pets allowed. Hiking, mountain biking, and horse trails in area. Bring your own firewood. No drinking water available.

GETTING THERE: From Grantsville go S on Co 138 approx. 4.7 mi. to forest route 171. Go SW on 171 approx. 7.5 mi. to Loop CG. No RVs.

SINGLE RATE:	Varies	OPEN DATES:	May-Oct
# of SINGLE SITES:	9		
		MAX STAY:	7 days
		ELEVATION:	7400 feet

40 Magpie
Huntsville • lat 41˚16'14" lon 111˚39'55"

DESCRIPTION: This CG rests in cottonwood and willow on the South Fork of Ogden River. Enjoy trout fishing in river. Wildlife includes deer, elk, moose, raptors, and occasional black bears and coyotes. CG is busy weekends and holidays. There is a fisherman's trail that runs along the river.

GETTING THERE: From Huntsville go E on state HWY 39 approx. 5.5 mi. to Magpie CG.

SINGLE RATE:	$10	OPEN DATES:	May-Oct
# of SINGLE SITES:	17	MAX SPUR:	30 feet
		MAX STAY:	7 days
		ELEVATION:	5200 feet

 Campground has hosts   **Reservable sites**   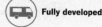 **Accessible facilities**   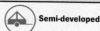 **Fully developed**   **Semi-developed**   **Rustic facilities**

NOTE: Open dates listed are typical. Actual dates are dependent on conditions such as snow pack.

41 Maple
Ogden • lat 41°13'37" lon 111°51'50"

DESCRIPTION: This rustic CG is in maple and aspen with spectacular views of surrounding mountains. Hike the on site trailhead leading to Wheeler Creek Trail. Wildlife includes infrequent black bears and coyotes, deer, elk, moose, and raptors. CG is busy weekends and holidays. No drinking water available.

GETTING THERE: From Ogden go W on state HWY 39 approx. 9.5 mi. to state HWY 226. Go SW on 226 approx. 7 mi. to forest route 122. Go N on 122 approx. 1.5 mi. to Maple CG.

SINGLE RATE:	No fee	OPEN DATES:	June-Oct
# of SINGLE SITES:	26	MAX SPUR:	30 feet
		MAX STAY:	7 days
		ELEVATION:	6200 feet

42 Marsh Lake
Mountain View • lat 40°57'06" lon 110°23'38"

DESCRIPTION: This CG is located in lodgepole pine and aspen on adjacent Marsh Lake. Enjoy trout fishing, hiking, mountain biking and OHV (outside of CG) opportunities. Wildlife in this area includes infrequent black bears and mountain lions, deer, elk, moose, and raptors. CG can be busy weekends and holidays.

GETTING THERE: From Mountain View go S approx. 7 mi. on state HWY 410 to US HWY 246. Go S on 246 approx. 8.2 mi. to forest route 072. Go S on 072 approx. 8.5 mi. to Marsh Lake CG.

SINGLE RATE:	$9	OPEN DATES:	June-Sept
# of SINGLE SITES:	38	MAX SPUR:	45 feet
		MAX STAY:	14 days
		ELEVATION:	9400 feet

43 Meeks Cabin
Evanston • lat 41°00'15" lon 110°35'30"

DESCRIPTION: This CG is located in lodgepole pine and aspen on Meeks Cabin Reservoir. Wildlife in the area includes black bears, mountain lions, deer, elk, moose, goshawks, and bald eagles. CG is seldom busy. Hiking and horseback riding opportunities in the nearby High Uinta Wilderness.

GETTING THERE: From Evanston go S approx. 30 mi. on state HWY 150 to forest route 058. Go E on 058 approx. 23 mi. to Meeks Cabin CG.

SINGLE RATE:	$8	OPEN DATES:	June-Oct
# of SINGLE SITES:	24	MAX SPUR:	35 feet
		MAX STAY:	14 days
		ELEVATION:	8700 feet

44 Mirror Lake
Kamas • lat 40°42'03" lon 110°53'01"

DESCRIPTION: CG is in an open grove of spruce and pine next to Mirror Lake. Enjoy fishing for rainbow, cutthroat, and albino trout. Black bears, mountain lions, coyotes, deer, elk, moose, and raptors. Busy weekends and holidays. Trailhead leads to the High Uinta Wilderness. Amphitheater and barrier free boardwalk.

GETTING THERE: From Kamas go approx. 31.8 mi. NE on state HWY 150 to forest route 104. Go E on 104 approx. 1 mi. to Mirror Lake CG.

SINGLE RATE:	$12	OPEN DATES:	July-Sept
# of SINGLE SITES:	80	MAX SPUR:	45 feet
		MAX STAY:	14 days
		ELEVATION:	10000 feet

45 Monte Cristo
Huntsville • lat 41°27'41" lon 111°29'49"

DESCRIPTION: This CG is in a grove of large spruce. Enjoy mountain vista views on the nearby scenic highway. Hike the on site trail to Sugar Pine Creek. Wildlife in this area includes the infrequent black bears and coyotes, deer, elk, moose, and raptors. CG is busy weekends and holidays.

GETTING THERE: From Huntsville go E on state HWY 39 approx. 28 mi. to Monte Cristo CG.

SINGLE RATE:	$9	OPEN DATES:	June-Sept
# of SINGLE SITES:	45	MAX SPUR:	30 feet
GROUP RATE:	Varies	MAX STAY:	7 days
# of GROUP SITES:	2	ELEVATION:	8400 feet

46 Moose Horn
Kamas • lat 40°42'00" lon 110°53'30"

DESCRIPTION: CG sits in an open grove of spruce and pine on Moose Horn Lake. Enjoy fishing for rainbow, cutthroat, and albino trout. Wildlife includes black bears, mountain lions, coyote, deer, elk, moose, and raptors. Busy weekends and holidays. Nearby trailhead leads to Fehr Lake, a scenic high alpine lake.

GETTING THERE: Moose Horn CG is located approx. 31 mi. E of Kamas on state HWY 150.

SINGLE RATE:	$10	OPEN DATES:	July-Sept
# of SINGLE SITES:	33	MAX SPUR:	75 feet
		MAX STAY:	14 days
		ELEVATION:	10400 feet

47 Perception Park
Huntsville • lat 41°17'05" lon 111°38'52"

DESCRIPTION: CG rests in cottonwood and willow on the South Fork of Ogden River. Enjoy trout fishing in river. Wildlife includes infrequent black bears and coyotes, deer, elk, moose, and raptors. CG is busy weekends and holidays. There is a barrier free fishing dock and trail that runs along the river.

GETTING THERE: From Huntsville go E on state HWY 39 approx. 7.5 mi. to Perception Park CG.

SINGLE RATE:	$11	OPEN DATES:	May-Oct
# of SINGLE SITES:	24	MAX SPUR:	30 feet
GROUP RATE:	Varies	MAX STAY:	7 days
# of GROUP SITES:	3	ELEVATION:	5200 feet

48 Pine Valley Group
Kamas • lat 40°35'54" lon 111°06'53"

DESCRIPTION: This CG rests in a grove of ponderosa pine and douglas fir. Enjoy rainbow and cutthroat trout fishing in nearby Lower Provo River. Deer, moose, black bears, and mountain lions in area. CG is busy holidays and weekends. Hike the nearby Scenic Byway Trail. Supplies in Kamas. Bring your own firewood.

GETTING THERE: Pine Valley Group CG is located approx. 11 mi. E of Kamas on state HWY 150.

		OPEN DATES:	June-Sept
GROUP RATE:	Varies	MAX STAY:	14 days
		ELEVATION:	7440 feet

49 Pioneer
Hyrum • lat 41°37'42" lon 111°41'33"

DESCRIPTION: CG rests in hardwoods on the Blacksmith Fork River. Enjoy fishing for trout but please check fishing regulations. Enjoy hiking in this area and driving the scenic backway. Wildlife in this area includes deer, elk, and numerous birds. CG is busy weekends and holidays. Supplies are available in Hyrum.

GETTING THERE: Pioneer CG is located approx. 9 mi. E of Hyrum on state HWY 101.

SINGLE RATE:	$10	OPEN DATES:	May-Oct
# of SINGLE SITES:	18	MAX SPUR:	20 feet
		MAX STAY:	7 days
		ELEVATION:	5600 feet

50 Ponderosa Group
Kamas • lat 40°38'00" lon 111°11'30"

DESCRIPTION: This CG rests in a grove of ponderosa pine and douglas fir. Enjoy rainbow and cutthroat trout fishing in nearby Lower Provo River. Deer, moose, black bears, and mountain lions in area. CG is busy holidays and weekends. Hike the nearby Yellow Pine Trail. Supplies in Kamas. Bring your own firewood.

GETTING THERE: Ponderosa Group CG is located approx. 5 mi. E of Kamas on state HWY 150.

		OPEN DATES:	May-Oct
GROUP RATE:	Varies	MAX STAY:	14 days
		ELEVATION:	7040 feet

 Campground has hosts 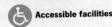 **Reservable sites**  **Accessible facilities**   **Fully developed**   **Semi-developed** **Rustic facilities**

NOTE: Open dates listed are typical. Actual dates are dependent on conditions such as snow pack.

51 Preston Valley
Logan • lat 41°46'00" lon 111°38'00"

DESCRIPTION: CG is located in low elevation hardwoods such as willow, maple, and cottonwood. Enjoy trout fishing in adjacent Logan River. Check fishing regs. Wildlife in this area includes deer, elk, and numerous birds. CG is busy weekends and holidays. Hike nearby riverside nature/interpretive trail.

GETTING THERE: From Logan go E on US HWY 89 approximately 10.5 miles to Preston Valley CG.

SINGLE RATE:	$10	OPEN DATES:	May-Oct
# of SINGLE SITES:	8	MAX SPUR:	20 feet
		MAX STAY:	7 days
		ELEVATION:	5500 feet

56 Shingle Creek
Kamas • lat 40°37'00" lon 111°07'58"

DESCRIPTION: This CG is in a grove of ponderosa pine and aspen. Enjoy nearby Beaver and Shingle Creeks. Deer, moose, black bears, and mountain lions in area. CG is busy holidays and weekends. Hike the nearby Scenic Byway Trail or ride the OHV trail which starts here. Supplies in Kamas. Bring your own firewood.

GETTING THERE: Shingle Creek CG is located approx. 9.5 mi. E of Kamas on state HWY 150.

SINGLE RATE:	$11	OPEN DATES:	May-Oct
# of SINGLE SITES:	21	MAX SPUR:	100 feet
		MAX STAY:	14 days
		ELEVATION:	7480 feet

52 Quarter Corner Lake
Mountain View • lat 40°57'30" lon 110°18'30"

DESCRIPTION: This CG is located in lodgepole pine and aspen. Enjoy nearby Quarter Corner Lake. Wildlife in this area includes infrequent black bears and mountain lions; as well as deer, elk, moose, and raptors. CG is busy weekends and holidays. Supplies in Mountain View. Several nearby hiking trails.

GETTING THERE: From Mountian View go S approx. 7 mi. on state HWY 410 to forest route 072. Go S on 072 approx. 3.5 mi. to forest route 017. Continue SE on 017 approx. 5.5 mi. to Quarter Corner Lake CG.

SINGLE RATE:	No fee	OPEN DATES:	June-Oct
# of SINGLE SITES:	3	MAX SPUR:	20 feet
		MAX STAY:	14 days
		ELEVATION:	9000 feet

57 Smith and Morehouse
Kamas • lat 40°45'44" lon 111°06'21"

DESCRIPTION: CG is located in ponderosa pine, douglas fir and aspen on Smith and Morehouse Reservoir. Enjoy fishing for trout. Supplies at Kamas. Deer, moose, black bears, and mountain lions in area. CG is busy holidays and weekends. Ledfork trailhead leads to "Lakes Country", a series of high alpine lakes.

GETTING THERE: From Kamas go N on state HWY 32 approx. 5.5 mi. to state HWY 213. Go NE on 213 approx. 12 mi. to forest route 33. Go S on 33 approx. 3 mi. to Smith and Morehouse CG.

SINGLE RATE:	$12	OPEN DATES:	May-Sept
# of SINGLE SITES:	34	MAX SPUR:	45 feet
		MAX STAY:	14 days
		ELEVATION:	7680 feet

53 Red Banks
Logan • lat 41°53'56" lon 111°33'51"

DESCRIPTION: This CG is located in pine, aspen, hardwoods, and some fir near Logan River. Enjoy fishing for trout but please check fishing regulations. Deer, elk, and numerous birds in area. CG is busy weekends and holidays. Hike trail to nearby Lewis M. Turner CG. Supplies are available in Logan.

GETTING THERE: Red Banks CG is located approx. 22.5 mi. NE of Logan on US HWY 89.

SINGLE RATE:	$10	OPEN DATES:	June-Oct
# of SINGLE SITES:	12	MAX SPUR:	20 feet
		MAX STAY:	7 days
		ELEVATION:	6500 feet

58 Smithfield Canyon
Smithfield • lat 41°50'15" lon 111°49'34"

DESCRIPTION: This CG rests among hardwoods with views of the adjacent Summit Creek. Provides access into the nearby Mount Naomi Wilderness. Watch for deer, elk, and numerous birds common to the area. CG is frequently busy on weekends and holidays. Supplies are available in Smithfield.

GETTING THERE: Smithfield Canyon CG is located approx. 5 mi. NE of Smithfield on forest route 049.

SINGLE RATE:	$10	OPEN DATES:	May-Oct
# of SINGLE SITES:	7	MAX SPUR:	20 feet
		MAX STAY:	7 days
		ELEVATION:	5500 feet

54 Redman
Park City • lat 40°37'00" lon 111°35'00"

DESCRIPTION: This CG rests among mixed conifer. Wildlife includes mountain lions, coyotes, deer, moose, raptors, and Uinta ground squirrels. Bring your own firewood. CG is busy weekends and holidays. No pets allowed. Enjoy hiking the on site trail which leads to Silver Lake. Maximum of 35-50 persons.

GETTING THERE: From Park City go S approx. 5 mi. on state HWY 224 to state HWY 190. Go W on 190 approx. 3.5 mi. to Redman CG.

SINGLE RATE:	Varies	OPEN DATES:	June-Sept
# of SINGLE SITES:	37	MAX SPUR:	30 feet
GROUP RATE:	Varies	MAX STAY:	7 days
# of GROUP SITES:	5	ELEVATION:	8300 feet

59 Soapstone
Kamas • lat 40°34'42" lon 111°01'33"

DESCRIPTION: CG is located in ponderosa pine and aspen near Provo River. Frequent thundershowers. Enjoy fishing for cutthroat and rainbow trout. Supplies at Kamas. Deer, moose, black bears, and mountain lions in area. CG is busy holidays and weekends. Several horse and hiking trails in area.

GETTING THERE: Soapstone CG is located approx. 16.3 mi. E of Kamas on state HWY 150.

SINGLE RATE:	$12	OPEN DATES:	June-Oct
# of SINGLE SITES:	34	MAX SPUR:	45 feet
		MAX STAY:	14 days
		ELEVATION:	7870 feet

55 Shady Dell
Kamas • lat 40°35'31" lon 111°00'43"

DESCRIPTION: CG is located in ponderosa pine and aspen near Upper Provo River. Frequent thundershowers. Enjoy fishing for cutthroat and rainbow trout. Supplies at Kamas. Deer, moose, black bears, and mountain lions in area. CG is busy holidays and weekends. Several horse and hiking trails in area.

GETTING THERE: Shady Dell CG is located approx. 17 mi. E of Kamas on state HWY 150.

SINGLE RATE:	$12	OPEN DATES:	June-Oct
# of SINGLE SITES:	20	MAX SPUR:	100 feet
		MAX STAY:	14 days
		ELEVATION:	8040 feet

60 South Fork
Huntsville • lat 41°16'55" lon 111°39'08"

DESCRIPTION: CG is set in cottonwood and willow on the South Fork of Ogden River. Enjoy trout fishing in river. Wildlife in this area includes infrequent black bears and coyotes, deer, elk, moose, and raptors. CG is busy weekends and holidays. There is a fisherman's trail that runs along the river.

GETTING THERE: South Fork CG is located approx. 7 mi. E of Huntsville on state HWY 39.

SINGLE RATE:	$10	OPEN DATES:	May-Oct
# of SINGLE SITES:	37	MAX SPUR:	30 feet
		MAX STAY:	7 days
		ELEVATION:	5200 feet

 Campground has hosts　　 **Reservable sites**　　 **Accessible facilities**　　 **Fully developed**　　 **Semi-developed**　　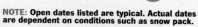 **Rustic facilities**

NOTE: Open dates listed are typical. Actual dates are dependent on conditions such as snow pack.

61 Spring
Hyrum • lat 41°39'30" lon 111°38'30"

DESCRIPTION: This rustic CG is located in low elevation hardwoods near the Left Hand of Blacksmith River. Enjoy fishing for trout. Wildlife in this area includes deer, elk, and numerous birds. CG is busy weekends and holidays. Hiking trails within 1/2 mi. of CG. No drinking water available on site.

GETTING THERE: From Hyrum go E approx. 8.5 mi. on state HWY 101 to forest route 245. Go NE on 245 approx. 5 mi. to Spring CG.

SINGLE RATE:	$6	OPEN DATES:	May-Oct
# of SINGLE SITES:	3	MAX SPUR:	20 feet
		MAX STAY:	7 days
		ELEVATION:	6000 feet

66 Sulpher
Kamas • lat 40°47'00" lon 110°52'30"

DESCRIPTION: CG situated in a mixed conifer and aspen forest. Watch for black bears, mountain lions, coyotes, deer, elk, moose, raptors, and small wildlife in the area. Supplies are available approx. 38.2 mi. away in Kamas. Numerous roads and trails in the area provide for hiking and biking opportunities.

GETTING THERE: Sulpher CG is located approx. 38.2 mi. E of Kamas on state HWY 150.

SINGLE RATE:	$10	OPEN DATES:	June-Oct
# of SINGLE SITES:	21	MAX SPUR:	35 feet
		MAX STAY:	14 days
		ELEVATION:	9100 feet

62 Spring Hollow
Logan • lat 41°45'12" lon 111°42'59"

DESCRIPTION: CG is located in low elevation hardwoods such as willow, maple, and cottonwood. Enjoy trout fishing in adjacent Logan River. Check fishing regulations. Deer, elk, moose, and many birds are common to the area. CG is busy weekends and holidays. Hike nearby riverside nature/interpretive trail.

GETTING THERE: Spring Hollow CG is located approx. 7 mi. E of Logan on US HWY 89.

SINGLE RATE:	$10	OPEN DATES:	May-Oct
# of SINGLE SITES:	12	MAX SPUR:	20 feet
		MAX STAY:	7 days
		ELEVATION:	5100 feet

67 Sunrise
Garden City • lat 41°55'12" lon 111°27'37"

DESCRIPTION: This CG is situated in lodgepole pine, fir, and spruce with beautiful views of Bear Lake Valley. Enjoy fishing for trout in nearby Bear Lake but please check fishing regulations. Deer, elk, and numerous birds are common to the area. Hike the nearby Limber Pine Nature Trail. Supplies in Garden City.

GETTING THERE: Sunrise CG is located approx. 8.5 mi. W of Garouteen City on US HWY 89.

SINGLE RATE:	$12	OPEN DATES:	June-Sept
# of SINGLE SITES:	27	MAX SPUR:	20 feet
		MAX STAY:	7 days
		ELEVATION:	7800 feet

63 Spruces
Salt Lake City • lat 40°38'30" lon 111°38'00"

DESCRIPTION: CG in a large open meadow. Volleyball, horseshoes, and an amphitheater. Trout fish at nearby Silver Lake which has a barrier free boardwalk. Mountain lions, coyotes, deer, moose, raptors, and Uinta ground squirrels. Fills weekends and holidays. No pets allowed. Winter use permit required. Bring firewood.

GETTING THERE: Spruces CG is located approx. 10 mi. E of Salt Lake up Big Cottonwood canyon.

SINGLE RATE:	Varies	OPEN DATES:	May-Oct
# of SINGLE SITES:	86		
GROUP RATE:	Varies	MAX STAY:	7 days
# of GROUP SITES:	3	ELEVATION:	7400 feet

68 Sunset
Bountiful • lat 41°00'13" lon 111°50'22"

DESCRIPTION: CG is situated among mixed conifer. Wildlife includes mountain lions, coyotes, deer, moose, raptors, and Uinta ground squirrels. CG is busy weekends and holidays. No pets allowed. Hiking, mountain biking, and horse trails in area. Bring your own firewood. Group site for smaller groups.

GETTING THERE: Sunset CG is located approx. 16 mi. on the Bountiful Peak route. Not recommended for RVs or trailers.

SINGLE RATE:	$6	OPEN DATES:	June-Oct
# of SINGLE SITES:	10		
GROUP RATE:	Varies	MAX STAY:	7 days
# of GROUP SITES:	1	ELEVATION:	6400 feet

64 State Line
Mountain View • lat 40°59'30" lon 110°23'00"

DESCRIPTION: This CG is located in lodgepole pine and aspen on adjacent Stateline Dam Lake. Enjoy trout fishing, hiking, and mountain biking opportunities. Wildlife in this area includes the infrequent black bears and mountain lions, deer, elk, moose, and raptors. Supplies in Mountain View. Firewood sold on site.

GETTING THERE: From Mountain View go S approx. 7 mi. on state HWY 410 to forest route 072. Go S on 072 approx. 14 mi. to State Line CG.

SINGLE RATE:	$10	OPEN DATES:	June-Sept
# of SINGLE SITES:	41	MAX SPUR:	45 feet
		MAX STAY:	14 days
		ELEVATION:	9200 feet

69 Tanner's Flat
Sandy City • lat 40°34'30" lon 111°42'00"

DESCRIPTION: CG rests in mixed conifer. Views of mountains and waterfalls. Enjoy nearby Secret Lake. Mountain lions, coyotes, deer, moose, raptors, and Uinta ground squirrels. Fills weekends and holidays. No pets allowed. On site interpretive trail. Mountain bike on area's trails. Maximum of 25-50 persons in group sites.

GETTING THERE: From Sandy City go E on state HWY 209 approx. 6 mi. to state HWY 210. Go E on 210 approx. 4 mi. to Tanner's Flat CG.

SINGLE RATE:	Varies	OPEN DATES:	May-Oct
# of SINGLE SITES:	36	MAX SPUR:	30 feet
GROUP RATE:	Varies	MAX STAY:	7 days
# of GROUP SITES:	3	ELEVATION:	7200 feet

65 Stillwater
Evanston • lat 40°52'07" lon 110°50'04"

DESCRIPTION: This CG is located in lodgepole pine and aspen at the confluence of the Stillwater and Hayden Rivers. Fly fish for trout in the rivers. Wildlife in the area includes black bears, mountain lions, deer, elk, moose, goshawks, and bald eagles. Busy holiday weekends in summer. Many hiking trails in area.

GETTING THERE: Stillwater CG is located approx. 33 mi. S of Evanston on state HWY 150.

SINGLE RATE:	$10	OPEN DATES:	June-Oct
# of SINGLE SITES:	21	MAX SPUR:	35 feet
		MAX STAY:	14 days
		ELEVATION:	8500 feet

70 Taylor Fork
Kamas • lat 40°37'00" lon 111°07'30"

DESCRIPTION: This CG rests in a grove of ponderosa pine and aspen. Enjoy nearby Beaver Creek. Deer, moose, black bears, and mountain lions in area. CG is busy holidays and weekends. Hike the nearby Scenic Byway Trail or ride the OHV trail which starts here. Supplies in Kamas. Bring your own firewood.

GETTING THERE: Taylor Fork CG is located approx. 9 mi. E of Kamas on state HWY 150.

SINGLE RATE:	$10	OPEN DATES:	May-Oct
# of SINGLE SITES:	11	MAX SPUR:	50 feet
		MAX STAY:	14 days
		ELEVATION:	7400 feet

 Campground has hosts   **Reservable sites**   **Accessible facilities**   **Fully developed**   **Semi-developed**   **Rustic facilities**

NOTE: Open dates listed are typical. Actual dates are dependent on conditions such as snow pack.

71 Tony Grove Lake
Logan • lat 41°53'25" lon 111°38'14"

DESCRIPTION: CG rests in fir, spruce, and some pine with high alpine lake views. Enjoy trout fishing in nearby Tony Grove Lake. Please check fishing regs.. Wildlife includes deer, elk, moose, and many birds. This CG is frequently full. There is a nature trail around the lake and there area numerous wildflowers.

GETTING THERE: From Logan go approx. 21.5 mi. NE on US HWY 89 to forest route 003. Go W on 003 approx. 5.5 mi. to Tony Grove Lake CG.

SINGLE RATE:	$12	OPEN DATES:	July-Sept
# of SINGLE SITES:	36	MAX SPUR:	20 feet
		MAX STAY:	7 days
		ELEVATION:	8100 feet

76 Willard Basin
Brigham City • lat 41°23'40" lon 111°58'28"

DESCRIPTION: This rustic CG is on the backside of Willard Peak in a dense forest. Enjoy adjacent Willard Lake. This CG is the terminus of Skyline Motorcycle Trail. Wildlife includes infrequent black bears and coyotes, deer, elk, moose, and raptors. CG is busy weekends and holidays. No drinking water.

GETTING THERE: From Brigham City go W on US HWY 91 approx. 3 mi. to forest route 084. Go S on 084 approx. 9 mi. to Willard Basin CG. Rough road, 4WD only.

OPEN DATES:	June-Oct
MAX STAY:	7 days
ELEVATION:	9000 feet

72 Trial Lake
Kamas • lat 40°40'54" lon 110°56'53"

DESCRIPTION: This CG sits in ponderosa pine with mountain views. Enjoy trout fishing with non-motorized boats in adjacent Trial Lake. Deer, moose, black bears, and mountain lions in area. CG is busy holidays and weekends. Hike the nearby Crystal Lake Trail. Supplies available in Kamas. Bring you own firewood.

GETTING THERE: From Kamas go E approx. 23.6 mi. on state HWY 150 to forest route 042. Go N on 042 approx. .5 mi. to Trial Lake CG.

SINGLE RATE:	$12	OPEN DATES:	July-Sept
# of SINGLE SITES:	60	MAX SPUR:	50 feet
		MAX STAY:	14 days
		ELEVATION:	9840 feet

77 Willow
Huntsville • lat 41°17'32" lon 111°37'59"

DESCRIPTION: CG sits in cottonwood and willow on the South Fork of Ogden River. Enjoy trout fishing in river. Wildlife in this area includes infrequent black bears and coyotes, deer, elk, moose, and raptors. CG is busy weekends and holidays. There is a fisherman's trail that runs along the river.

GETTING THERE: From Huntsville go E on state HWY 39 approx. 8 mi. to Willow CG.

SINGLE RATE:	$10	OPEN DATES:	May-Oct
# of SINGLE SITES:	13	MAX SPUR:	30 feet
		MAX STAY:	7 days
		ELEVATION:	5200 feet

73 Upper Meadows
Huntsville • lat 41°17'15" lon 111°39'08"

DESCRIPTION: CG rests in cottonwood and willow on the South Fork of Ogden River. Enjoy trout fishing in river. Wildlife in this area includes infrequent black bears and coyotes, deer, elk, moose, and raptors. CG is busy weekends and holidays. There is a fisherman's trail that runs along the river.

GETTING THERE: From Huntsville go E on state HWY 39 approx. 9 mi. to Upper Meadows CG.

SINGLE RATE:	$8	OPEN DATES:	May-Oct
# of SINGLE SITES:	8	MAX SPUR:	30 feet
		MAX STAY:	7 days
		ELEVATION:	5200 feet

78 Wolverine
Evanston • lat 40°50'49" lon 110°48'54"

DESCRIPTION: This rustic CG is located in a grove of lodgepole pine and aspen. This CG offers access to an OHV trail around Lily Lake. This is also a popular mountain biking area. Wildlife in the area includes black bears, mountain lions, deer, elk, moose, goshawks, and bald eagles.

GETTING THERE: From Evanston go S approx. 32.5 mi. on state HWY 150 to forest route 323. Go SE on 323 approx. 2 mi. to Wolverine CG.

SINGLE RATE:	No fee	OPEN DATES:	June-Oct
# of SINGLE SITES:	6	MAX SPUR:	35 feet
		MAX STAY:	14 days
		ELEVATION:	9000 feet

74 Upper Narrows
Grantsville • lat 40°29'30" lon 112°35'37"

DESCRIPTION: This CG rests among mixed conifer. Mountain lions, coyotes, deer, moose, raptors, and Uinta ground squirrels in area. Fills weekends and holidays. No pets allowed. Hike the on site trail leading to Desert Peak. Bring your own firewood. No drinking water. Maximum of 30-50 persons in group sites.

GETTING THERE: From Grantsville go S on Co 138 approx. 4.7 mi. to forest route 171. Go SW on 171 approx. 6.1 mi. to Upper Narrows CG. No RVs.

SINGLE RATE:	No fee	OPEN DATES:	May-Oct
# of SINGLE SITES:	8		
GROUP RATE:	Varies	MAX STAY:	7 days
# of GROUP SITES:	2	ELEVATION:	6900 feet

79 Wood Camp
Logan • lat 41°47'51" lon 111°38'39"

DESCRIPTION: CG is located in low elevation hardwoods. Enjoy trout fishing in adjacent Logan River. Check fishing regsulations. Wildlife in this area includes deer, elk, and numerous birds. CG is busy weekends and holidays. Hike on site trail to 1500 year old juniper tree. No drinking water available.

GETTING THERE: Wood Camp CG is located approx. 12.5 mi. NE of Logan on US HWY 89.

SINGLE RATE:	$10	OPEN DATES:	May-Oct
# of SINGLE SITES:	6	MAX SPUR:	20 feet
		MAX STAY:	7 days
		ELEVATION:	5600 feet

75 Washington Lake
Kamas • lat 41°03'30" lon 111°09'30"

DESCRIPTION: This new CG rests in ponderosa pine with mountain views. Enjoy trout fishing in adjacent Washington Lake. Deer, moose, black bears, and mountain lions in area. CG is busy holidays and weekends. Crystal Lake trailhead is nearby and there is a barrier free trail to the lake.

GETTING THERE: From Kamas go E approx. 23.6 mi. on state HWY 150 to forest route 041. Go N on 041 approx. .5 mi. to Washington Lake CG.

SINGLE RATE:	$12	OPEN DATES:	June-Sept
# of SINGLE SITES:	40		
GROUP RATE:	Varies	MAX STAY:	14 days
# of GROUP SITES:	5	ELEVATION:	10000 feet

80 Yellow Pine
Kamas • lat 40°37'51" lon 111°10'23"

DESCRIPTION: This CG sits in a dense grove of yellow and ponderosa pine. Enjoy nearby Yellow Pine Creek. Deer, moose, black bears, and mountain lions in area. CG is busy holidays and weekends. Hike the nearby Yellow Pine Trail which leads to Yellow Pine Lakes. Supplies available in Kamas. Bring your own firewood.

GETTING THERE: Yellow Pine CG is located approx. 6 mi. E of Kamas on state HWY 150.

SINGLE RATE:	$6	OPEN DATES:	May-Oct
# of SINGLE SITES:	33	MAX SPUR:	100 feet
		MAX STAY:	14 days
		ELEVATION:	7200 feet

 Campground has hosts   **Reservable sites**   **Accessible facilities**   **Fully developed**   **Semi-developed**   **Rustic facilities**

NOTE: Open dates listed are typical. Actual dates are dependent on conditions such as snow pack.

GREEN MOUNTAIN NATIONAL FOREST

The Green Mountain National Forest offers endless opportunities for people of all ages and abilities to get into the great outdoors. The most popular season is autumn when the mountains are ablaze with color. Summer offers camping, hiking, backpacking, fishing, and canoeing. The legendary Appalachian Trail and Long Trail run through the forest with a network of well-maintained shelters spaced a day's hike apart.

Whether you explore the forest by foot, car, wheelchair, horseback, or boat, you'll discover wildlife in its natural setting. Nearly 100 species of neotropical birds migrate here and the shy, reclusive black bear can be spotted occasionally. Other species that inhabit the forest are turkeys, white-tailed deer, small mammals and various songbirds.

The forest's scenic beauty along the backbone of Vermont's Green Mountains offers unlimited recreation opportunities any season of the year. Whether you are a hiker, skier, camper, fishing or hunting enthusiast, or wildlife watcher, the Green Mountain National Forest can provide the recreational experiences you are seeking.

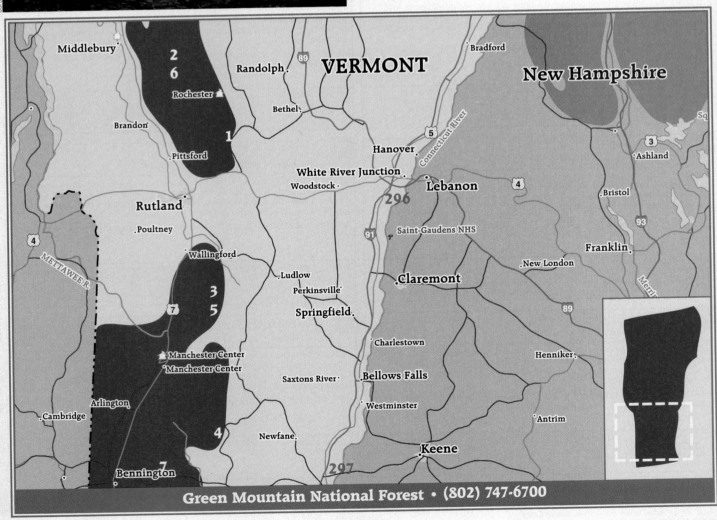

Green Mountain National Forest • (802) 747-6700

1 Chittenden Brook
Brandon • lat 43˚49'32" lon 072˚54'37"

DESCRIPTION: CG rests in pine and hardwoods on a lovely brook. Stream fish for trout. The wetland area may have beaver, tree swallows, deer and moose. Gather dead and down firewood locally. Supplies are in Brandon. Access to Long Trail (Appalachian Trail) is a short drive.

GETTING THERE: From Brandon go E on state HWY 73 approx. 7 mi. to forest route 45. Go S on 45 approx. 2.5 mi. to Chittenden Brook CG. Steep road limits trailers to less than 18 feet.

SINGLE RATE:	$5	OPEN DATES:	May-Sept
# of SINGLE SITES:	16	MAX SPUR:	18 feet
		MAX STAY:	14 days
		ELEVATION:	1763 feet

2 Falls of Lana
Forest Dale • lat 43˚54'33" lon 073˚03'35"

DESCRIPTION: This primitive CG is set in a pine and hardwood forest with views of the falls. Silver Lake is nearby with great fishing and swimming. Supplies available at Forest Dale. Deer, bears, moose and small wildlife can be seen in the area. Horse, hike and mountain bike trails are nearby.

GETTING THERE: From Forest Dale go E on state HWY 73 approx. 8 mi. to parking area. Hike Silver Lake Trail approx. 1/2 mi. to Falls of Lana CG.

SINGLE RATE:	No fee	OPEN DATES:	May-Sept
		MAX SPUR:	18 feet
		MAX STAY:	14 days
		ELEVATION:	940 feet

3 Greendale
Weston • lat 43˚21'03" lon 072˚49'20"

DESCRIPTION: Set among pine and maple in a remote area. Trout fishing can be done nearby. Supplies available in Weston. Deer, beavers, occasional black bears and moose are common to the area. CG is full most weekends and holidays. Campers may gather firewood. Access to Peru Peak Wilderness is nearby..

GETTING THERE: From Weston go N on state route 100 to forest route 18. Go NW on 18 approx. 2 mi. to Greendale CG.

SINGLE RATE:	$5	OPEN DATES:	May-Sept
# of SINGLE SITES:	11	MAX SPUR:	25 feet
		MAX STAY:	14 days
		ELEVATION:	1722 feet

4 Grout Pond
Arlington • lat 43˚02'44" lon 072˚57'15"

DESCRIPTION: In a mixed forest setting with Grout Pond nearby. Fish for various species from the pond. Electric motors allowed but discouraged. There are 12 mi. of trails that connect to a more extensive trail system accessing the wilderness at nearby Somerset Reservoir. Lye Brook Wilderness lies to the NW.

GETTING THERE: From Arlington go E on forest route 6 approx. 10 mi. to Grout Pond CG.

SINGLE RATE:	$5	OPEN DATES:	May-Sept
# of SINGLE SITES:	9	MAX SPUR:	25 feet
		MAX STAY:	14 days
		ELEVATION:	2326 feet

5 Hapgood Pond
Manchester • lat 43˚15'18" lon 072˚52'39"

DESCRIPTION: On a pond with swimming area and bath house. Canoes and small boats allowed on pond. Fishing pier available at CG. CG is an historic CCC camp and dam. Supplies available at Manchester. Campers may buy firewood at CG. Hiking trails nearby access Peru Wilderness. CG may be closed for 2000 season, please check with Ranger District.

GETTING THERE: From Manchester go E on state route 11 approx. 6 mi. to Hapgood Pond Road. Go N on Hapgood Pond Road approx. 2 mi. to Hapgood Pond CG.

SINGLE RATE:	$10	OPEN DATES:	May-Sept
# of SINGLE SITES:	28	MAX SPUR:	25 feet
		MAX STAY:	14 days
		ELEVATION:	1565 feet

6 Moosalamoo
Ripton • lat 43˚55'09" lon 073˚01'43"

DESCRIPTION: In pine and maple forest setting with Sugarhill Reservoir nearby. Fish and swim in the reservoir. Play field available for games and sports. Supplies available in Ripton. Trails lead visitors to active wildlife and bird watching. Wonderful berry picking– but be careful! Bears frequent area.

GETTING THERE: From Ripton go S state route 125 approx. 1 mi. to forest route 32 (Ripton-Goshen Road). Go S on 32 approx. 3.2 mi. to Moosalamoo CG.

SINGLE RATE:	$5	OPEN DATES:	May-Sept
# of SINGLE SITES:	19	MAX SPUR:	18 feet
GROUP RATE:	$5	MAX STAY:	14 days
# of GROUP SITES:	1	ELEVATION:	1562 feet

7 Red Mill Brook
Bennington • lat 42˚53'58" lon 073˚01'08"

DESCRIPTION: Set in pine and maple forest. Trout fishing nearby. Supplies available in Wilmington. Deer, small wildlife and occasional black bears or moose can be seen in the area. Full most weekends and holidays. Trails to active wildlife and bird watching. Access to George D. Aken Wilderness nearby.

GETTING THERE: From Bennington go E on Route 9 to Forest Route 274. Go N on 274 approx. 1 mi. to Red Mill Brook CG.

SINGLE RATE:	$5	OPEN DATES:	May-Sept
# of SINGLE SITES:	31	MAX SPUR:	25 feet
		MAX STAY:	14 days
		ELEVATION:	2190 feet

 Campground has hosts   **Reservable sites**   **Accessible facilities**   **Fully developed**   **Semi-developed**   **Rustic facilities**

NOTE: Open dates listed are typical. Actual dates are dependent on conditions such as snow pack.

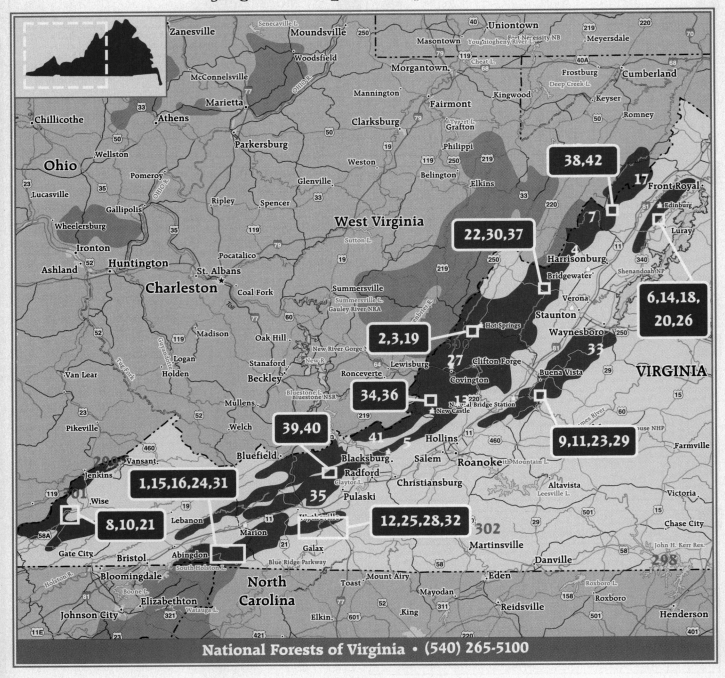

National Forests of Virginia • (540) 265-5100

USFS Photo

NATIONAL FORESTS OF VIRGINIA

With their mountains and valleys, woodlands and wildlife, the George Washington and Jefferson national forests offer a variety of outdoor recreation opportunities and provide a number of important resources for the surrounding area. The two forests extend over the Appalachian Mountains and contain nearly 1.8 million acres of public land in Virginia, West Virginia and Kentucky.

The forests provide habitat for a wide variety of species including several very rare species, sush as the water shrew and rock vole. Twenty-seven of the plant and animal species are listed as threatened or endangered. The lakes, ponds and reservoirs also support over 100 species of freshwater fish and mussels. The forests afford excellent opportunities for wildlife viewing, as well as hunting and fishing.

Recreation is a key resource. Hikers, bikers, picnickers and campers can pursue their interests surrounded by the natural beauty of the forests. Popular water sports include swimming and boating. Many visitors enjoy the forest scenery while driving over mountain and valley roads. Others explore the woods on horseback or with off-road vehicles. There are over 2,000 miles of hiking trails which vary in type of scenery and difficulty of terrain. The internationally famous Appalachian National Scenic Trail extends over 330 miles across the forests as it winds its way between Maine and Georgia. In addition, there are nine National Recreation trails totaling nearly 90 miles.

1. Beartree Recreation Area

Damascus • lat 36°41'05" lon 081°38'50"

DESCRIPTION: This secluded CG is nestled on a 5-acre, cold-water lake. Fish for small-mouth bass, sunfish, rainbow and brown trout in the lake. Swim at the sandy beach at CG. Many animals in the area. The Virginia Creeper Trail is nearby. Superb hiking trails in the nearby area.

GETTING THERE: From Damascus go E on US HWY 58 for 7 mi. to forest route 837. Go NE on 837 approx. 4 mi. to Beartree Family Camp CG.

SINGLE RATE:	Varies	OPEN DATES:	Apr-Dec
# of SINGLE SITES:	80	MAX SPUR:	75 feet
GROUP RATE:	Varies	MAX STAY:	14 days
# of GROUP SITES:	2	ELEVATION:	3400 feet

2. Blowing Springs
Covington • lat 38°04'08" lon 079°53'05"

DESCRIPTION: CG is ideally located for anglers and hunters. Back Creek, a stocked trout stream, flows adjacent to the CG and offers very good trout fishing. Supplies available at Covington. Many animals can be seen in the area. Arrive early if you want a campsite during the opening weekend of trout season.

GETTING THERE: From Covington go NE on US HWY 220 approx. 24 mi. to state HWY 39. Go W on 39 approx. 4 mi. to Blowing Springs CG.

SINGLE RATE:	$6	OPEN DATES:	May-Sept
# of SINGLE SITES:	23	MAX SPUR:	28 feet
		MAX STAY:	14 days
		ELEVATION:	1780 feet

3. Bolar Mountain
Warm Springs • lat 37°59'09" lon 079°58'17"

DESCRIPTION: CG is located on the NW shore of Lake Moomaw. Most of the campsites are located on a ridge above Lake Moomaw with some along or close to the lake shore. There is a camp store located at the Bolar Flat Marina for supplies. An amphitheater is available at the beach. No designated trails in the area.

GETTING THERE: From Warm Springs go W on state route 39 approx. 13 mi. to state route 600. Turn left onto 600 and go approx. 7 mi. to Bolar Mountain CG.

SINGLE RATE:	$16	OPEN DATES:	Apr-Nov
# of SINGLE SITES:	86	MAX SPUR:	75 feet
		MAX STAY:	21 days
		ELEVATION:	1600 feet

4. Brandywine Lake

Brandywine • lat 38°36'04" lon 079°12'18"

DESCRIPTION: CG is in a rustic setting with some open and shady private sites. Brandywine Lake is 10 acres in size and offers a sandy beach, swimming area, and changing rooms. The lake offers good fishing for stocked trout and is encircled by an angler's trail. Trailer dump station is available.

GETTING THERE: Brandwine CG is located approx. 2 mi. E of Brandywine on US HWY 33.

SINGLE RATE:	Varies	OPEN DATES:	May-Oct
# of SINGLE SITES:	30	MAX SPUR:	55 feet
		MAX STAY:	21 days
		ELEVATION:	1858 feet

5. Caldwell Fields
Blacksburg • lat 37°20'13" lon 080°19'33"

DESCRIPTION: In an oak and pine forest setting on Crag Creek. Fish for stocked trout from the creek. Supplies are available at Blacksburg. Deer, squirrels and birds are common to the area. Blue bird boxes are set up in CG. Campers may gather firewood. Many trails in the area.

GETTING THERE: From Blacksburg go NW on US HWY 460 approx. 9.5 mi. to county route 621. Go NE on 621 approx. 8 mi. to Caldwell Fields CG.

		OPEN DATES:	Yearlong
GROUP RATE:	Varies	MAX STAY:	14 days
# of GROUP SITES:	2	ELEVATION:	1702 feet

 Campground has hosts   Reservable sites   Accessible facilities   Fully developed   Semi-developed Rustic facilities

NOTE: Open dates listed are typical. Actual dates are dependent on conditions such as snow pack.

6 — Camp Roosevelt

Edinburg • lat 38°43'53" lon 078°31'01"

DESCRIPTION: This dispersed, canoe-in CG is located in a mixed hardwoods. Fish for trout and swim in Passage Creek. Supplies are located in Edinburg. Deer, bears, raccoons, turkeys, squirrels and oppossum are common in the area. Campers may gather dead and down firewood. Many trails nearby. RV dump station nearby.

GETTING THERE: From Edinburg go SE on state route 675 approx. 9 mi. to Camp Roosevelt CG.

SINGLE RATE:	$9	OPEN DATES:	May-Oct
# of SINGLE SITES:	10	MAX SPUR:	75 feet
		MAX STAY:	21 days
		ELEVATION:	1500 feet

7 — Camp Run
Broadway • lat 38°45'00" lon 079°08'30"

DESCRIPTION: This tent only CG is in a mixed hardwood forest setting. Fish in the nearby streams. Supplies located at Broadway. Many animals can be seen in the surrounding areas. Campers may gather firewood. No designated trails in the area.

GETTING THERE: From Broadway go W on state HWY 259 14 mi. to state HWY 820. Go W on 820 2 mi. to state HWY 826. Go SW on 826 approx. 6.5 mi. to county route 3/1. Go W on 3/1 approx. 3 mi. to Camp Run CG.

SINGLE RATE:	No fee	OPEN DATES:	Yearlong
		MAX STAY:	14 days
		ELEVATION:	1600 feet

8 — Cane Patch
Pound • lat 37°06'10" lon 082°40'43"

DESCRIPTION: CG is situated in a mature mixed woods. Some sites are adjacent to a creek and there is a basketball court and amphitheater. Fishing is available at North Fork of the Pound Reservoir by CG. Muskie, largemouth bass and catfish are available.

GETTING THERE: From Pound go W on state HWY 671 approximately 6.5 miles to Cane Patch CG.

SINGLE RATE:	$8	OPEN DATES:	May-Sept
# of SINGLE SITES:	25	MAX SPUR:	55 feet
		MAX STAY:	14 days
		ELEVATION:	1780 feet

9 — Cave Mountain Lake
Roanoke • lat 37°34'36" lon 079°32'10"

DESCRIPTION: CG is in a mixed forest setting on Cave Mountain Lake. Swim and explore the lake, no fishing or boating. Supplies located at Roanoke. CG area was built by the CCCs in the late thirty's. Some sites have stone terraces. Wildcat Mountain Trail & Panther Knob Nature Trail nearby. RV dump station nearby.

GETTING THERE: From Roanoke go NE on I-81 29.5 mi. to state route 130 (Natural Bridge exit). Go E on 130 3.2 mi. to state route 759. Go S on 759 for 3.2 mi. to state route 781. Go SW on 781 for 2.6 mi. to Cave Mountain Lake CG.

SINGLE RATE:	$10	OPEN DATES:	May-Nov
# of SINGLE SITES:	42	MAX SPUR:	35 feet
		MAX STAY:	14 days
		ELEVATION:	1100 feet

10 — Cave Springs
Big Stone Gap • lat 36°48'07" lon 082°55'20"

DESCRIPTION: CG is situated in a mixed hardwood forest. Swimming is actually in man-made, stream-fed pond. Hiking nearby at Little Stone Mountain Trail and Cave Overlook Trail. No fishing in area.

GETTING THERE: From Big Stone Gap go W on US 58A approximately 3.0 miles to state route 621. Turn right on state route 621 and go 6.7 miles to Cave Springs CG.

SINGLE RATE:	Varies	OPEN DATES:	May-Sept
# of SINGLE SITES:	40	MAX SPUR:	53 feet
		MAX STAY:	14 days
		ELEVATION:	1640 feet

11 — Colon Hollow Shelter
Roanoke • lat 37°32'37" lon 079°35'04"

DESCRIPTION: This tent only CG is in a mixed forest setting. Fishing for trout can be found nearby. Supplies are available at Roanoke. Numerous wildlife can be seen in the area. Campers may gather firewood. Many hiking opportunities are in the area.

GETTING THERE: From Roanoke go NE on US HWY I-81 approx. 22.5 mi. to state HWY 614. Go SE on 614 2.5 mi. to forest route 59. Go E on 59 approx. 2 mi. to Colon Hollow Shelter CG.

SINGLE RATE:	No fee	OPEN DATES:	Yearlong
		MAX STAY:	14 days
		ELEVATION:	1200 feet

12 — Comers Rock
Wytheville • lat 36°45'48" lon 081°13'25"

DESCRIPTION: In a mixed forest setting on Hale Lake. Fish for trout in this well-stocked lake. Supplies available at Wytheville. A small stone picnic shelter at CG. Iron Mountain Trail runs through CG. Other trails give access to Little Dry Run Wilderness.

GETTING THERE: From Wytheville go S on US HWY 21 approx. 16 mi. to forest route 57. Go W on 57 approx. 4 mi. to Comers Rock CG.

SINGLE RATE:	Varies	OPEN DATES:	Yearlong*
# of SINGLE SITES:	10		
GROUP RATE:		MAX STAY:	14 days
		ELEVATION:	3400 feet

13 — Craig Creek

New Castle • lat 37°36'47" lon 079°57'39"

DESCRIPTION: This primitive CG sits along side of Craig Creek. Fish and wade on the creek. Space at this CG for camping with horses. Supplies available at New Castle. Numerous wildlife can be seen in the area. Campers may gather dead and downed firewood. Many trails in the area.

GETTING THERE: From New Castle go NE on state route 615 approx. 11 mi. to state route 817. Go S on 817 approx. 1/2 mi. to Craig Creek CG.

SINGLE RATE:	No fee	OPEN DATES:	Yearlong
		MAX STAY:	14 days
		ELEVATION:	1080 feet

14 — Elizabeth Furnace
Strasburg • lat 38°55'44" lon 078°19'38"

DESCRIPTION: CG is very popular and attractive with Passage Creek meandering through it with lots of shade trees. Creek offers trout fishing. The historical iron furnace, known as "Elizabeth", dating back over 150 years is in the area. Several trails radiating from the area. CG offers an Amphitheater.

GETTING THERE: From Strasburg go E on state route 55 approx. 5 mi. to state route 678 (Waterlick). Go S on 678 approx. 5 mi. to Elizabeth Furnace CG.

SINGLE RATE:	$12	OPEN DATES:	Yearlong
# of SINGLE SITES:	30	MAX SPUR:	32 feet
GROUP RATE:	Varies	MAX STAY:	14 days
# of GROUP SITES:	3	ELEVATION:	2000 feet

15 — Fox Creek
Marion • lat 36°41'54" lon 081°30'15"

DESCRIPTION: This CG is used primarily as a horse camp located in a mixed forest setting with water nearby. Fish or swim nearby. Supplies are located in Marion. Numerous wildlife can be seen in the area. Campers may gather firewood. Many trails in the area. Horse facilities in this CG.

GETTING THERE: From Marion go S on stte HWY 14 approx. 16 mi. to state route 741. Go SW on 741 approx. 3 mi. to Fox Creek CG.

SINGLE RATE:	Varies	OPEN DATES:	Yearlong
		MAX STAY:	14 days
		ELEVATION:	3440 feet

 Campground has hosts   Reservable sites   Accessible facilities   Fully developed   Semi-developed   Rustic facilities

NOTE: Open dates listed are typical. Actual dates are dependent on conditions such as snow pack.

16 Grindstone

Marion • lat 36°41'13" lon 081°32'28"

DESCRIPTION: CG is situated in mature hardwoods and rhododendrons. There are trout streams in the area outside the CG. Hiking trails into high country and Mount Rogers. There is an amphitheater in CG. A three-foot deep mountain, stream-fed wading pool for the children. Dump station at CG.

GETTING THERE: From Marion go S on state HWY 16 approx. 16 mi. to state route 603 (@ Trout Dale). Go W on 603 approx. 10 mi. to Grindstone CG.

SINGLE RATE:	Varies	OPEN DATES:	May-Dec
# of SINGLE SITES:	100	MAX SPUR:	75 feet
		MAX STAY:	14 days
		ELEVATION:	3840 feet

21 High Knob
Norton • lat 36°53'15" lon 082°36'51"

DESCRIPTION: CG is located on a ridge in mature hardwoods, and was built by the Civilian Conservation Corps (CCC). Because of the difficult access and interior roads, CG is not RV friendly. A scenic hike is the High Knob Tower Trail. No fishing in area.

GETTING THERE: From Norton go S on state route 619 approx. 3.7 miles to campground sign (forest route 238). Turn left onto 238 and go 1.6 miles to another campground sign. Turn right at sign and go 1.7 miles to High Knob CG.

SINGLE RATE:	$8	OPEN DATES:	May-Sept
# of SINGLE SITES:	13	MAX SPUR:	42 feet
		MAX STAY:	14 days
		ELEVATION:	3520 feet

17 Hawk
Strasburg • lat 39°06'59" lon 078°29'57"

DESCRIPTION: This campground is located in a very serene, hardwood forest. Supplies located in Strasburg. Deer, bears, raccoons, turkeys, squirrels and birds are just some of the many wildlife to be seen in the area. Campers may gather firewood. Many trails nearby.

GETTING THERE: From Strasburg go NW 12 mi. on state HWY 55 to state route 16. Go W 1.5 mi. on 16 to state route 609. Go S 1 mi. on 609 to forest route 347. Go W 1 mi. on 347 to Hawk CG. RV's not recommended.

SINGLE RATE:	No fee	OPEN DATES:	Apr-Dec
# of SINGLE SITES:	13		
		MAX STAY:	21 days
		ELEVATION:	1200 feet

22 Hone Quarry
Dayton • lat 38°27'43" lon 079°08'10"

DESCRIPTION: CG is set in large hemlock along a mountain stream. Hone Quarry Lake is a mile west of the CG. Non-motorized boats and fishing are welcome. Supplies available at Dayton. Nearby trails offer loop hiking opportunities with excellent vistas. Waste station is about a mile from the CG.

GETTING THERE: From Dayton go W on state route 257 approx. 10.5 mi. to forest route 62. Go W on 62 approx. 3 miles to Hone Quarry CG.

SINGLE RATE:	$5	OPEN DATES:	Yearlong
# of SINGLE SITES:	10	MAX SPUR:	50 feet
		MAX STAY:	21 days
		ELEVATION:	1960 feet

18 Hazard Mill Canoe Camp
Luray • lat 38°49'53" lon 078°20'49"

DESCRIPTION: This dispersed, canoe-in CG is located in a mixed hardwood setting on the Shanandoah River. Fish and swim in the river. Supplies located in Luray. Deer, bears, raccoons, turkeys, squirrels and birds are just some of the many wildlife to be seen in the area. Campers may gather firewood. Many trails nearby.

GETTING THERE: From Luray go N on US HWY 340 approx. 13.5 mi. to forest route 236. Go W & S approx. 2 mi. to Hazard Mill Canoe Camp CG.

SINGLE RATE:	No fee	OPEN DATES:	Yearlong
		MAX STAY:	14 days
		ELEVATION:	750 feet

23 Hopper Creek
Roanoke • lat 37°33'37" lon 079°30'33"

DESCRIPTION: This tent only CG is in a mixed forest setting. Fishing for trout can be found nearby. Supplies are available at Roanoke. Numerous wildlife can be seen in the area. Campers may gather firewood. Many hiking opportunities are in the area.

GETTING THERE: From Roanoke go NE on I-81 29.5 mi. to state route 130 (Natural Bridge exit). Go E on 130 3.2 mi. to state route 759. Go S on 759 for 4 mi. to forest route 3105. Go S on 3105 1/4 mi. to Hopper Creek CG.

SINGLE RATE:	Varies	OPEN DATES:	Yearlong
		MAX STAY:	14 days
		ELEVATION:	1500 feet

19 Hidden Valley
Covington • lat 38°05'53" lon 079°49'22"

DESCRIPTION: This CG is located adjacent to the Jackson River in an open pastoral valley in the Allegheny mountains. Fish in this large clear stream with both native and stocked trout. Supplies available at Covington. Numerous wildlife can be seen in the area. No designated trails in the area.

GETTING THERE: From Covington go N 24 mi. to state route 39. Go W on 39 approx. 3 mi. to state route 621. Go N on 621 approx. 1 mi. to forest route 241. Go N on 241 approx. 1.5 mi. to Hidden Valley CG.

SINGLE RATE:	$6	OPEN DATES:	Mar-Nov
# of SINGLE SITES:	30	MAX SPUR:	64 feet
		MAX STAY:	14 days
		ELEVATION:	1805 feet

24 Hurricane
Marion • lat 36°43'21" lon 081°29'28"

DESCRIPTION: CG is located in mature mixed woods along Hurricane creek. Large grassy play area. CG is located near Highland Horse Trail, but has no facilities for horses. Hiking trails nearby. Hurricane and Comers Creeks run through the area, providing stocked trout fishing. Warm showers, flush toilets, drinking water.

GETTING THERE: From Marion go S on state HWY 16 approx. 15.5 mi. to state route 650. Go W on 650 approx. 2 mi. to Hurricane CG.

SINGLE RATE:	$10	OPEN DATES:	Apr-Oct
# of SINGLE SITES:	26	MAX SPUR:	96 feet
		MAX STAY:	14 days
		ELEVATION:	2800 feet

20 High Cliffs Canoe Camp
Luray • lat 38°46'29" lon 078°23'32"

DESCRIPTION: This dispersed, canoe-in CG is located in a mixed hardwood setting on the Shanandoah River. Fish and swim in the river. Supplies located in Luray. Deer, bears, raccoons, turkeys, squirrels and birds are just some of the many wildlife to be seen in the area. Campers may gather firewood. Many trails nearby.

GETTING THERE: From Luray go NW on state HWY 675 approx. 2 mi. to state HWY 684. Go NE on 684 approx. 10 mi. to High Cliff Canoe Camp.

SINGLE RATE:	No fee	OPEN DATES:	Yearlong
		MAX STAY:	14 days
		ELEVATION:	750 feet

25 Hussy Mountain Horse Camp
Wytheville • lat 36°46'17" lon 081°08'40"

DESCRIPTION: This horse camp is in a mixed forest setting with fishing and swimming nearby. Supplies are located at Wytheville. Many animals can be viewed in the area. Campers may gather firewood. Many hiking trails are located in the area.

GETTING THERE: From Wytheville go S on US HWY 21 approx. 14 mi. to forest route 14. Go E on 14 approx. 1 mi. to Hussy Mountain Horse Camp.

SINGLE RATE:	Varies	OPEN DATES:	Yearlong
		MAX STAY:	14 days
		ELEVATION:	2920 feet

 Campground has hosts   **Reservable sites** **Accessible facilities** 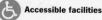 **Fully developed**   **Semi-developed**   **Rustic facilities**

NOTE: Open dates listed are typical. Actual dates are dependent on conditions such as snow pack.

26 — Little Fort
Detrick • lat 38°52'01" lon 078°26'37"

DESCRIPTION: In a mixed hardwood forest setting near Persmill Run. Fish and swim in the Run. Deer, raccoons, turkeys, bears, grouse, squirrels and birds are just some of the many animals that can be seen in the area. Supplies available at Detrick. An OHV trailhead starts at the CG.

GETTING THERE: From Detrick (E of Woodstock) go W on state route 678 (Fort Valley Rd.) approx. 1/2 mi. to state route 758. Turn right on 758 and go approx. 2.5 mi. to Little Fort CG.

SINGLE RATE:	No fee	OPEN DATES:	Yearlong
# of SINGLE SITES:	10	MAX STAY: ELEVATION:	21 days 1500 feet

31 — Raccoons Branch
Marion • lat 36°44'49" lon 081°25'31"

DESCRIPTION: CG is in a park-like setting with some sites adjacent to either Dickey Creek or Raccoons Branch. Fishing for trout in the area. Virginia Highlands Horse Trail passes nearby. This is a good CG to use as a home base for exploring the area and enjoying the fall colors. RV dump station.

GETTING THERE: From Marion go S on state HWY 16 approx. 10 mi. to Raccoons Branch CG.

SINGLE RATE:	$8	OPEN DATES:	Yearlong
# of SINGLE SITES:	20	MAX SPUR: MAX STAY: ELEVATION:	41 feet 14 days 2760 feet

27 — Morris Hill
Covington • lat 37°56'01" lon 079°58'19"

DESCRIPTION: CG is set on a wooded ridge at the S end of Lake Moomaw. Lake access trails nearby. Fish and swim in the lake. Boat ramp and RV dump station at the CG. Supplies available at Covington. Numerous animals can be seen in the area. No designated trails in the area.

GETTING THERE: From Covington go N 4 mi. on US HWY 220 to state 687. Go N 3 on 687 mi. to state 641. Go W 1 mi. on 641 to state 666. Go N 5 mi. on 666 to state 605. Turn right 2 mi. on 605 to Morris Hill CG.

SINGLE RATE:	$10	OPEN DATES:	Apr-Oct
# of SINGLE SITES:	55	MAX SPUR: MAX STAY: ELEVATION:	45 feet 14 days 2000 feet

32 — Raven Cliff
Wytheville • lat 36°50'12" lon 081°04'12"

DESCRIPTION: In a mixed pine forest setting on a ridge above Cripple Creek. A large meadow area is adjacent to CG. Fish for trout and bass or swim in the creek. Supplies located at Wytheville. Numerous animals can be seen in the area. Campers may gather firewood. Many trails in area.

GETTING THERE: From Wytheville go S on US HWY 21 approx. 13 mi. to state route 619. Go E on 619 approx. 8 mi. to Raven Cliff CG.

SINGLE RATE:	$5	OPEN DATES:	Yearlong
# of SINGLE SITES:	20	MAX SPUR: MAX STAY: ELEVATION:	64 feet 14 days 2350 feet

28 — New River
Ivanhoe • lat 36°48'00" lon 080°54'00"

DESCRIPTION: CG has little shade and most sites have a view of cliffs on opposite side of New River. Anglers and inner-tubers enjoy warm water recreation on the New River. Access to the New River Trail offers biking, horseback and hiking. A waste station is available about 1 mi. before CG.

GETTING THERE: From Ivanhoe go S on state HWY 94 approx. 4.5 mi. to state HWY 602. Go E on 602 approx. 3.5 mi. to state HWY 737. Go N on 737 approx. 2 mi. to New River CG.

SINGLE RATE:	$6	OPEN DATES:	Apr-Dec
# of SINGLE SITES:	21	MAX SPUR: MAX STAY: ELEVATION:	69 feet 14 days 2180 feet

33 — Sherando Lake
Waynesboro • lat 37°55'09" lon 079°00'48"

DESCRIPTION: CG lies with the scenic Blue Ridge Mountains and is one of the most popular recreation areas on the National Forest. Sherando Lake features swimming, camping, hiking, and fishing for stocked trout. CG has showers and a trailer dump station. Evening programs at the amphitheatre during the summer.

GETTING THERE: From Waynesboro go S on state HWY 624 5 mi. to state HWY 664. Go S on 664 approx. 3.5 mi. to forest route 91. Go W on 91 1 mi. to forest route 91B. Go W on 91B 1/2 mi. to Sherando Lake CG.

SINGLE RATE:	Varies	OPEN DATES:	Apr-Oct
# of SINGLE SITES:	65	MAX SPUR: MAX STAY: ELEVATION:	40 feet 14 days 1940 feet

29 — North Creek
Buchanan • lat 37°32'28" lon 079°35'05"

DESCRIPTION: CG is heavily wooded with hemlock and pine on the creek's edge. Some sites are adjacent to North Creek with rainbow and native trout fishing. Supplies available at Buchanan. Campers may gather firewood. Many trails in the area. Several sites built with stone terraces.

GETTING THERE: From Buchanan take I-81 N approx. 1/2 mi. to state HWY 614. Follow 614 approx. 2.5 mi. to forest route 59. Turn left onto 59 and go approx. 2.5 mi. to North Creek CG.

SINGLE RATE:	$5	OPEN DATES:	Yearlong
# of SINGLE SITES:	15	MAX SPUR: MAX STAY: ELEVATION:	57 feet 14 days 1200 feet

34 — Steel Bridge
New Castle • lat 37°36'03" lon 080°13'07"

DESCRIPTION: This rustic CG is adjacent to Shawvers Run Wilderness and Potts Creek (a stocked trout stream). Fish and swim in the creek. Supplies available at New Castle. Numerous wildlife in the area. Campers may gather firewood. Many trails in the area.

GETTING THERE: From New Castle go W on state HWY 311 approx. 13 mi. to state route 18. Go NE on 18 for 3.5 mi. to Steel Bridge CG.

SINGLE RATE:	No fee	OPEN DATES:	Yearlong
# of SINGLE SITES:	20	MAX SPUR: MAX STAY: ELEVATION:	20 feet 14 days 1740 feet

30 — North River
Bridgewater • lat 38°20'22" lon 079°12'27"

DESCRIPTION: CG is a remote site with tall pines surrounded by a creek on two sides. Fishing may be done at the creek. Supplies available at Bridgewater. The loop configuration of the CG makes it a good location for large families, scout outings, etc. During late summer and early fall, the campground is packed.

GETTING THERE: From Bridgewater go S on state route 747 approx. 12 mi. to forest route 95. Go W on 95 approx. 3.5 mi. to forest route 95B. Go E on 95B approx. 1 mi. to North River CG.

SINGLE RATE:	$5	OPEN DATES:	Mar-Nov
# of SINGLE SITES:	12	MAX SPUR: MAX STAY: ELEVATION:	99 feet 21 days 1840 feet

35 — Stony Fork
Wytheville • lat 37°00'32" lon 081°10'58"

DESCRIPTION: CG is located in a natural forest setting at the foot of Big Walker Mountain. The East Fork of Stony Fork Creek winds through the CG and provides trout fishing. A one mile nature trail takes campers through stands of pine and hardwoods. Supplies at Wytheville. Dump station on site.

GETTING THERE: From Wytheville go N on US HWY I-77 approx. 6 mi. to Exit 47 for state route 717. Go SW on 717 approx. 4 mi. to Stony Fork CG.

SINGLE RATE:	Varies	OPEN DATES:	Apr-Nov
# of SINGLE SITES:	50	MAX SPUR: MAX STAY: ELEVATION:	76 feet 14 days 2400 feet

---

 Campground has hosts   **Reservable sites**   **Accessible facilities**   **Fully developed**   **Semi-developed**   **Rustic facilities**

NOTE: Open dates listed are typical. Actual dates are dependent on conditions such as snow pack.

36 The Pines
New Castle • lat 37°36'18" lon 080°04'33"

DESCRIPTION: CG is located in a hardwood and pine forest on Barbours Creek. Fish for native trout in the creek. Supplies available at New Castle. Adjacent to CG is an area called "Horse Corral." There is a horse ramp and corral with a small area for trailers and dispersed camping. Some horse and hiking trails in area.

GETTING THERE: From New Castle go NE 2.5 mi. on state route 615 to state route 609. Go N 2 mi. on 609 to state route 611. Go W 3 mi. on 611 to state route 617. Go N 5.5 mi. on 617 to The Pines CG.

SINGLE RATE:	No fee	OPEN DATES:	Yearlong
# of SINGLE SITES:	14	MAX SPUR:	37 feet
GROUP RATE:	No fee	MAX STAY:	14 days
# of GROUP SITES:	4	ELEVATION:	1740 feet

37 Todd Lake
Bridgewater • lat 38°22'08" lon 079°12'48"

DESCRIPTION: CG is nestled between Trimble and Grindstone Mountains in a mixed forest setting on Todd Lake. The stream-fed lake features a sandy beach for swimming and fishing. Supplies available at Bridgewater. A trailer dump station is near the entrance. There are several nice hiking trails nearby.

GETTING THERE: From Bridgewater go S on state route 747 approx. 12 mi. to forest route 95. Go W on 95 approx. 3.5 mi. to forest route 95B. Go E on 95B approx. 1 mi. to Todd Lake CG.

SINGLE RATE:	Varies	OPEN DATES:	May-Oct
# of SINGLE SITES:	20	MAX SPUR:	70 feet
		MAX STAY:	21 days
		ELEVATION:	1960 feet

38 Trout Pond
Strasburg • lat 38°57'07" lon 078°43'58"

DESCRIPTION: This rustic looking CG is in a mixed forest setting on Trout Pond with views of surrounding mountains. Fish in this well stocked trout pond. Supplies available at Strasburg. Numerous animals can be seen in the area. There is a trail around the lake and other hiking trails nearby. RV dump station at CG.

GETTING THERE: From Strasburg go W 18 mi. on state 55 to state route 23/10. Go S 6 mi. on 23/10 to state route 259/5. Go S 6 mi. on 259/5 to forest route 500. Go S 1 mi. on 500 to Trout Pond CG.

SINGLE RATE:	Varies	OPEN DATES:	Apr-Dec
# of SINGLE SITES:	30	MAX SPUR:	64 feet
GROUP RATE:	Varies	MAX STAY:	21 days
# of GROUP SITES:	2	ELEVATION:	2030 feet

39 Walnut Flats
Pearisburg • lat 37°11'53" lon 080°53'10"

DESCRIPTION: This small remote CG is in a predominantly grassy area with several walnut and pine trees shading it. A small pond is next to the CG. Dismal Creek is a stocked trout stream and is nearby the CG. Campers may gather firewood. The Appalachian Trail and other hiking trails in the area.

GETTING THERE: From Pearisburg go S on state HWY 100 approx. 10 mi. to state route 42. Go SW on 42 10 mi. to state route 606. Go NW on 606 1 mi. to state route 201. Go NE on 201 for 2.5 mi. to Walnut Flats.

SINGLE RATE:	No fee	OPEN DATES:	Yearlong
# of SINGLE SITES:	6		
		MAX STAY:	14 days
		ELEVATION:	2460 feet

40 White Pine Horse Camp
Pearisburg • lat 37°11'35" lon 080°53'24"

DESCRIPTION: CG is a small, primitive camping area designed to accommodate horses and their riders. A stand of white pine shades the area. There are marked horse trails nearby. Adjacent to CG is Dismal Creek, a stocked trout stream. Loading ramp, hitching posts and central corral for horses.

GETTING THERE: From Pearisburg go S on state HWY 100 10 mi. to state route 42. Go SW on 42 10 mi. to state route 606. Go NW on 606 1 mi. to state route 201. Go NE on 201 for 1.7 mi. to White Pine Horse Camp CG.

SINGLE RATE:	No fee	OPEN DATES:	Yearlong
# of SINGLE SITES:	5	MAX SPUR:	99 feet
		MAX STAY:	14 days
		ELEVATION:	2340 feet

41 White Rocks
Pembroke • lat 37°25'24" lon 080°28'22"

DESCRIPTION: CG is wooded, with several open grassy fields. A nature trail, the Virginia's Walk is an easy 1.5 mi. loop that begins and ends in the CG. A wetland area has been established by a resident beaver colony. An excellent area for wildlife viewing. Native Trout streams are nearby. Waste dump station on site.

GETTING THERE: From Pembroke go E on US HWY 460 approx. 1.5 mi. to forest route 635. Go N on 635 approx. 15.5 mi. to forest route 645. Go E on 645 approx. 1.5 mi. to White Rocks CG.

SINGLE RATE:	$4	OPEN DATES:	Apr-Dec
# of SINGLE SITES:	47	MAX SPUR:	51 feet
		MAX STAY:	14 days
		ELEVATION:	2300 feet

42 Wolf Gap
Edinburg • lat 38°55'28" lon 078°41'21"

DESCRIPTION: This attractive tent only CG is in a mixed forest setting. Supplies available at Edinburg. Numerous animals can be seen in the area. Campers may gather dead and downed wood for firewood. Many hiking trails in the area. No drinking water.

GETTING THERE: From Edinburg go W on state HWY 675 approx. 9 mi. to state route 23/10. Go N on 23/10 approx. 2 mi. to Wolf Gap CG.

SINGLE RATE:	No fee	OPEN DATES:	Yearlong
# of SINGLE SITES:	10		
		MAX STAY:	21 days
		ELEVATION:	2100 feet

 **Campground has hosts**   **Reservable sites**   ♿ **Accessible facilities**   **Fully developed**   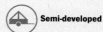 **Semi-developed**   **Rustic facilities**

NOTE: Open dates listed are typical. Actual dates are dependent on conditions such as snow pack.

COLVILLE NATIONAL FOREST

The Colville National Forest is located in the northeast corner of Washington and covers 1.9 million acres. The forest is a place of abundant pristine meadows and fragile landscapes first shaped 10,000 years ago by Ice Age glaciers. Over a million people relax and play in the Colville each year. In addition to camping and berry picking visitors can enjoy a variety of recreation activities.

The Sherman Pass Scenic Byway routes recreationists over Washington's highest maintained pass of 5,575 feet. The Byway offers interpretive sites and the remnants of a 20,000 acre forest fire. The Colville's lakes and streams teem with cutthroat, eastern brook and rainbow trout. There are several recreation sites and trailheads including a number of trails that are universally accessible. Other recreation opportunities include the beautiful Salmo-Priest Wilderness, historical interpretive sites, an environmental education lab, fossil beds and archaeological digs.

USFS Photo

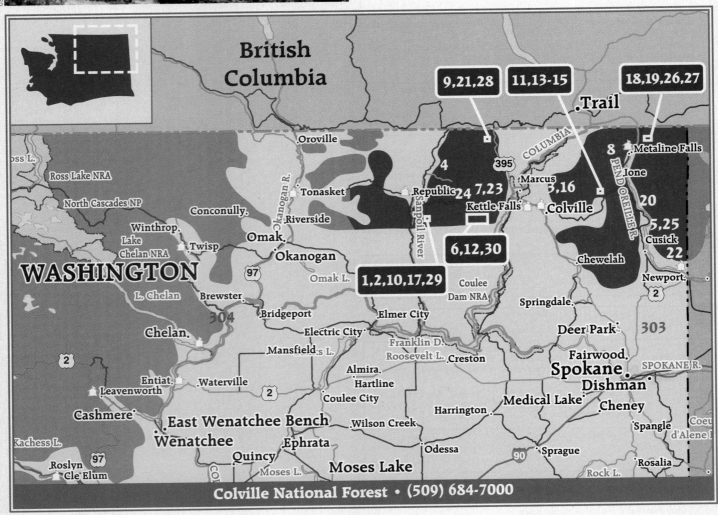

Colville National Forest • (509) 684-7000

1 10 Mile
Republic • lat 48°31'00" lon 118°44'00"

DESCRIPTION: In a park-like setting of conifer and hardwood on the San Poil River. Fish for trout and wade in the river. Supplies available at Republic. Deer, raccoons, bears, osprey, owls and squirrels are common to the area. Campers may gather firewood. Trailhead out of CG is 2.5 mi. long. No water.

GETTING THERE: From Republic go S on county route 21 approx. 10 mi. to Ten Mile CG.

SINGLE RATE:	$6	OPEN DATES:	May-Sept
# of SINGLE SITES:	9	MAX SPUR:	25 feet
		MAX STAY:	14 days
		ELEVATION:	3300 feet

2 13 Mile
Republic • lat 48°39'00" lon 118°44'00"

DESCRIPTION: In a conifer forest setting on San Poil River. Fish for trout and swim in the river. Supplies available at Republic. Deer, bears, raccoons, osprey, eagles and squirrels are common to the area. Camper may gather firewood. A 13-mi. trail leads out of the CG. NO WATER.

GETTING THERE: From Republic go S on county route 21 approx. 13 mi. to Thirteen mile CG.

SINGLE RATE:	No fee	OPEN DATES:	May-Sept
# of SINGLE SITES:	5	MAX SPUR:	25 feet
		MAX STAY:	14 days
		ELEVATION:	2080 feet

3 Big Meadow Lake
Ione • lat 48°44'00" lon 117°33'30"

DESCRIPTION: In a conifer forest setting on Big Meadow Lake. Fish for trout and swim in the lake. Supplies available at Wamic. Deer, elk, cougars, moose and birds are common to the area. This CG is considered a wildlife viewing area. Two small trails lead around the lake area.

GETTING THERE: From Ione go E on primary forest route 2714 approx. 2.5 mi. to primary forest route 2695. Go SE on 2695 approx. 5 mi. to Big Meadow Lake CG.

SINGLE RATE:	No fee	OPEN DATES:	Apr-Nov*
# of SINGLE SITES:	4	MAX SPUR:	10 feet
		MAX STAY:	14 days
		ELEVATION:	3400 feet

4 Boulder-Deer Creek
Curlew • lat 48°51'54" lon 118°23'40"

DESCRIPTION: In a subalpine forest setting with creek and spring adjacent to CG. Fish for trout and swim in the creek. Supplies available at Curlew. Deer, bears and birds are common in the area. Campers may gather firewood. Kettle Crest National Recreation Trail adjacent to the CG.

GETTING THERE: From Curlew go NE on county route 602 approx. 9 mi. to Boulder-Deer Creek CG.

SINGLE RATE:	No fee	OPEN DATES:	May-Sept
# of SINGLE SITES:	8	MAX SPUR:	99 feet
		MAX STAY:	14 days
		ELEVATION:	4640 feet

5 Browns Lake
Usk • lat 48°26'10" lon 117°11'43"

DESCRIPTION: CG is situated in cedar and western hemlock with sparse undergrowth. Fly fish for cutthroat on adjacent Browns Lake. Supplies 9 mi. at Usk. Moose and bears in area. There is a historical cabin on-site. Firewood can be bought at CG. Hiking trail on site.

GETTING THERE: From Usk go NE on county route 3389 approx. 5 mi. to forest route 5030. Go N on 5030 approx. 4 mi. to Browns Lake CG. Road is narrow with sharp curves. Large vehicles should use caution.

SINGLE RATE:	Varies	OPEN DATES:	May-Sept*
# of SINGLE SITES:	18	MAX SPUR:	24 feet
		MAX STAY:	14 days
		ELEVATION:	3400 feet

6 Canyon Creek
Republic • lat 48°34'47" lon 118°14'12"

DESCRIPTION: In an open park-like setting of pine, fir and larch on Canyon Creek. This creek is for looks, fish for trout from nearby Sherman Creek. Supplies at Republic. Bears, deer and squirrels are common to the area. Canyon Creek Trail starts from CG and is approx. 1 mi. in length. Huckleberries in CG.

GETTING THERE: From Republic go E approx. 27 mi. on state route 20 (Sherman Pass Nat'l Scenic Byway) to Canyon Creek CG.

SINGLE RATE:	No fee	OPEN DATES:	Yearlong*
# of SINGLE SITES:	12	MAX SPUR:	30 feet
		MAX STAY:	14 days
		ELEVATION:	2100 feet

7 Davis Lake
Boyds • lat 48°44'20" lon 118°13'40"

DESCRIPTION: In a mixed forest setting of pine, larch and fir on Davis Lake. Fish for cutthroat and rainbow trout from the lake. Boat launch at the CG. Supplies available at Boyds. Bears, deer and squirrels are common to the area. No designated trails in CG area. 4WD only.

GETTING THERE: From Boyds go W on county route 460 approx. 3 mi. to county route 465. Go N on 465 approx. 2 mi. to county route 480. Go W on 480 approx. 3 mi. to forest route 080. Go N on 080 approx. 3 mi. to Davis Lake CG.

SINGLE RATE:	No fee	OPEN DATES:	Yearlong*
# of SINGLE SITES:	4	MAX SPUR:	22 feet
		MAX STAY:	14 days
		ELEVATION:	4500 feet

8 Edgewater
Ione • lat 48°45'24" lon 117°24'27"

DESCRIPTION: In an open park-like setting of pine and fir on the Pend Oreille River. Fish for bass and trout from the river. Supplies at Ione. Deer, osprey, waterfowl and squirrels are common in the area. No designated trails in the area.

GETTING THERE: From Ione cross to the east side of the river on county route 9345 to county route 3669. Go N on 3669 2 mi. to Edgewater CG.

SINGLE RATE:	$10	OPEN DATES:	May-Sept
# of SINGLE SITES:	21	MAX SPUR:	28 feet
		MAX STAY:	14 days
		ELEVATION:	2000 feet

9 Elbow Lake
Northport • lat 48°27'53" lon 118°20'08"

DESCRIPTION: This dispersed CG is in a mixed forest setting. Supplies available at Northport. Numerous animals can be seen in the area. No designated trails in the area.

GETTING THERE: From Northport go NW on county route 4220 approx. 13 mi. to forest route 15. Go W on 15 approx. 3 mi. to Elbow Lake CG.

SINGLE RATE:	No fee	OPEN DATES:	Yearlong*
		MAX SPUR:	20 feet
		MAX STAY:	14 days
		ELEVATION:	2875 feet

10 Ferry Lake
Replubic • lat 48°31'24" lon 118°48'34"

DESCRIPTION: In a conifer forest setting on Ferry Lake. Fish for trout and swim in the lake. Non-motorized boats on lake only. Supplies available at Republic. Deer, bears, raccoons, squirrels and waterfowl are common in the area. Trail to the Lakes Area Mountain Bike Route near CG. NO WATER.

GETTING THERE: From Republic go S on county route 21 approx. 7 mi. to primary forest route 53. Go W and S on 53 approx. 7 mi. to Ferry Lake CG.

SINGLE RATE:	$6	OPEN DATES:	May-Sept
# of SINGLE SITES:	9	MAX SPUR:	25 feet
		MAX STAY:	14 days
		ELEVATION:	3300 feet

 Campground has hosts   **Reservable sites**   **Accessible facilities**   **Fully developed**   **Semi-developed** ▲ **Rustic facilities**

NOTE: Open dates listed are typical. Actual dates are dependent on conditions such as snow pack.

11 · Gillette
Ione • lat 48°36'44" lon 117°32'22"

DESCRIPTION: In a pine, fir and larch forest setting adjacent to Gillette Lake. Fish for trout and swim in the lake. Boat launch at lake. Supplies available at Ione. Deer, bears, raccoons, moose and birds are common to the area. The Little Pend Oreille ORV Trail is nearby. Amphitheater at adjacent CG.

GETTING THERE: From Ione go S on state route 31 for 3 mi. to state route 20. Go SW on 20 approx. 10 mi. to Gillette CG.

SINGLE RATE:	$10	OPEN DATES:	May-Oct*
# of SINGLE SITES:	30	MAX SPUR:	28 feet
		MAX STAY:	14 days
		ELEVATION:	3200 feet

16 · Little Twin Lakes
Colville • lat 48°34'32" lon 117°38'40"

DESCRIPTION: In a mixed fir and pine forest setting on Little Twin Lakes. Fish for trout and swim in the lake. Boat launch at lake. Supplies available at Colville. Deer, bears, elk, raccoons and birds are common to the area. No designated trails in the area.

GETTING THERE: From Colville Go E on state HWY 20 approx. 12 mi. to county route 4915. Go N on 4915 approx. 1.5 mi. to county route 4939. Go NE on 4939 to Little Twin Lakes CG.

SINGLE RATE:	No fee	OPEN DATES:	May-Sept
# of SINGLE SITES:	12	MAX SPUR:	20 feet
		MAX STAY:	14 days
		ELEVATION:	3700 feet

12 · Lake Ellen
Kettle Falls • lat 48°30'05" lon 118°14'56"

DESCRIPTION: In a mixed forest setting of pine, fir and larch on Lake Ellen. Fish for rainbow trout on the lake. Boat launch located at the CG. Supplies available at Kettle Falls. Deer, bears and squirrels are common to the area. No designated trails in the area.

GETTING THERE: From Kettle Falls go W on US HWY 395 to state HWY 20. Go S on 20 to county route 3. Go S on 3 approx. 5 mi. to county route 412. Go S on 412 approx. 4 mi. to Lake Ellen CG.

SINGLE RATE:	No fee	OPEN DATES:	Yearlong*
# of SINGLE SITES:	16	MAX SPUR:	22 feet
		MAX STAY:	14 days
		ELEVATION:	2200 feet

17 · Long Lake
Republic • lat 48°29'59" lon 118°48'36"

DESCRIPTION: In a conifer forest setting on Long Lake. Fly fish only for cutthroat trout on the lake. Boat ramp at lake, non-motorized boats only allowed on lake. Supplies available at Republic. Deer, bears, raccoons, squirrels and birds are common in the area. Long Lake Trail is adjacent to the CG.

GETTING THERE: From Republic go S on county route 21 approx. 7 mi. to primary forest route 53. Go W and S on 53 approx. 6 mi. to forest route 400. Go S on 400 approx. 2.5 mi. to Long Lake CG.

SINGLE RATE:	$8	OPEN DATES:	May-Sept
# of SINGLE SITES:	12	MAX SPUR:	25 feet
		MAX STAY:	14 days
		ELEVATION:	3250 feet

13 · Lake Gillette
Ione • lat 48°37'00" lon 117°33'00"

DESCRIPTION: In a pine, fir and larch forest setting on Gillette Lake. Fish for trout and swim in the lake. Boat launch at lake. Supplies available at Ione. Deer, bears, raccoons, moose and birds are common to the area. The Little Pend Oreille ORV Trail is nearby. Amphitheater at CG.

GETTING THERE: From Ione go S on state route 31 for 3 mi. to state route 20. Go SW on 20 approx. 10 mi. to Lake Gillette CG.

SINGLE RATE:	Varies	OPEN DATES:	May-Oct*
# of SINGLE SITES:	14	MAX SPUR:	28 feet
		MAX STAY:	14 days
		ELEVATION:	3200 feet

18 · Mill Pond
Metaline Falls • lat 48°51'14" lon 117°17'26"

DESCRIPTION: A nice quiet CG in a dense setting of fir, larch and pine on Mill Pond. Fish from pond or nearby Sulivan Creek. Supplies available at Metaline Falls. Bears, deer, elk, osprey and squirrels are common to the area. Trails lead from CG to the Mill Pond historic site and Elk Creek Trail nearby.

GETTING THERE: Mill Pond CG is located 4 mi. E of Metaline Falls on county route 9345.

SINGLE RATE:	$10	OPEN DATES:	May-Sept
# of SINGLE SITES:	10	MAX SPUR:	28 feet
		MAX STAY:	14 days
		ELEVATION:	2520 feet

14 · Lake Leo
Ione • lat 48°38'54" lon 117°29'55"

DESCRIPTION: In a pine and fir forest setting on Leo Lake. Fish for eastern trout and swim in the lake. Boat launch at lake. Supplies available at Ione. Deer, bears, raccoons, moose and birds are common to the area. Trails are in the area.

GETTING THERE: From Ione go S on state route 31 for 3 mi. to state route 20. Go SW on 20 approx. 6 mi. to Lake Leo CG.

SINGLE RATE:	$10	OPEN DATES:	May-Oct*
# of SINGLE SITES:	8	MAX SPUR:	20 feet
		MAX STAY:	14 days
		ELEVATION:	3200 feet

19 · Noisy Creek
Metaline Falls • lat 48°47'26" lon 117°17'00"

DESCRIPTION: Situated along the south shore of Sullivan Lake. Mountains surround the lake. a boat launch. Popular activities include fishing, swimming, hiking and boating.

GETTING THERE: From Metaline Falls go E on county route 9345 approx. 9 mi. to Noisy Creek CG.

SINGLE RATE:	$10	OPEN DATES:	May-Sept
# of SINGLE SITES:	19	MAX SPUR:	45 feet
		MAX STAY:	14 days
		ELEVATION:	2600 feet

15 · Lake Thomas
Ione • lat 48°37'26" lon 117°32'05"

DESCRIPTION: In a mixed forest setting on Lake Thomas. Fish for trout and swim in the lake. Boat launch at lake. Supplies available at Ione. Deer, bears, raccoons, moose and birds are common to the area. Trails are nearby.

GETTING THERE: From Ione go S on state route 31 for 3 mi. to state route 20. Go SW on 20 approx. 10 mi. to Lake Gillette CG. From Lake Gillette CG go E 3/4 mi. to Lake Thomas CG.

SINGLE RATE:	$10	OPEN DATES:	May-Sept*
# of SINGLE SITES:	16	MAX SPUR:	16 feet
		MAX STAY:	14 days
		ELEVATION:	3200 feet

20 · Panhandle
Usk • lat 48°30'21" lon 117°15'54"

DESCRIPTION: This newly remodeled CG in an open grove ponderosa pine and douglas fir setting on the bank of the Pend Oreille River. Boat ramp at CG. Enjoy fishing for perch, crappie, bass, rainbow and brown trout. Supplies available at Usk. Firewood is sold on site. Whitetail deer and black bears are common to the area.

GETTING THERE: From Usk go E on county route 3389 approx. 1 mi. to county route 9325. Go N on 9325 approx. 15 mi. to Panhandle CG.

SINGLE RATE:	Varies	OPEN DATES:	May-Sept*
# of SINGLE SITES:	13	MAX SPUR:	32 feet
		MAX STAY:	14 days
		ELEVATION:	2100 feet

 Campground has hosts   **Reservable sites**   Accessible facilities   **Fully developed**   **Semi-developed**   Rustic facilities

NOTE: Open dates listed are typical. Actual dates are dependent on conditions such as snow pack.

21 Pierre Lake
Orient • lat 48°54'15" lon 118°08'23"

DESCRIPTION: In a mixed forest setting of pine, fir and larch on Pierre Lake. Great fishing for many types of fish in this lake. Boat launch located at the CG. Supplies at Kettle Falls. Deer, bears and squirrels are common to the area. A lakeshore trail runs through CG and around the lake and is approx. 1 mi. long.

GETTING THERE: From Orient go E on county route 4134 approx. 2.5 mi. to county route 4013. Go N on 4013 approx. 3 mi. to Pierre Lake CG.

SINGLE RATE:	No fee	OPEN DATES:	Yearlong*
# of SINGLE SITES:	15	MAX SPUR:	24 feet
		MAX STAY:	14 days
		ELEVATION:	2100 feet

22 Pioneer Park
Newport • lat 48°12'00" lon 117°04'00"

DESCRIPTION: CG is located in mixed conifer with moderate undergrowth. Fish for various species in adjacent Pend Oreille River. This is a historic gathering place for the Kalispell Tribe. This CG is currently under construction. Please contact the Newport Ranger District at (509)447-3129 for open date.

GETTING THERE: Pioneer Park CG is located approx. 2 mi. N of Newport on county route 9305.

SINGLE RATE:	Varies	OPEN DATES:	May-Sept*
# of SINGLE SITES:	17	MAX SPUR:	32 feet
		MAX STAY:	14 days
		ELEVATION:	2100 feet

23 Renner Lake
Boyds • lat 48°47'00" lon 118°12'00"

DESCRIPTION: This walk-in, tent only CG is in a mixed forest setting of pine, fir and larch on Renner Lake. Great fishing on this stocked lake. Supplies are available at Boyds. Deer, bears and squirrels are common to the area. No designated trails in the area.

GETTING THERE: From Boyds go NW on county route 480 approx. 2 mi. to forest route 705. Go N on 705 approx. 3 mi. to Renner Lake CG.

SINGLE RATE:	No fee	OPEN DATES:	Yearlong*
		MAX STAY:	14 days
		ELEVATION:	2500 feet

24 Sherman Pass Overlook
Republic • lat 48°36'20" lon 118°27'44"

DESCRIPTION: In a mixed forest setting of pine, larch and fir. Supplies available at Republic. Deer, bears and squirrels area common to the area. Campers may gather firewood. A barrier free scenic overlook trail is nearby and only 3/8 of a mi. long.

GETTING THERE: From Republic go E on state HWY 20 (Sherman Pass National Scenic Byway) approx. 15 mi. to Sherman Pass Overlook CG.

SINGLE RATE:	No fee	OPEN DATES:	Yearlong*
# of SINGLE SITES:	10	MAX SPUR:	24 feet
		MAX STAY:	14 days
		ELEVATION:	5200 feet

25 South Skookum
Usk • lat 48°23'30" lon 117°10'59"

DESCRIPTION: This CG is situated in mixed conifer with a staffed lookout called South Baldy. Fish for cutthroat on adjacent South Skookum Lake which has a boat ramp & a barrier free fishing dock. Supplies in Usk. Whitetail deer, osprey, and black bears in area. Hiking trailhead and firewood on site.

GETTING THERE: From Usk go NE on county route 3389 approx. 8 mi. to South Skookum Lake CG. Road is narrow with sharp curves. Large Vehicles should use caution.

SINGLE RATE:	Varies	OPEN DATES:	May-Sept*
# of SINGLE SITES:	25	MAX SPUR:	32 feet
		MAX STAY:	14 days
		ELEVATION:	3500 feet

26 Sullivan Lake East
Metaline Falls • lat 48°50'24" lon 117°16'48"

DESCRIPTION: Campground is situated along the north shore of Sullivan Lake. Facilities provided include restrooms, a boat launch and a swimming area. There is a grassy airstrip adjacent to the campground. Popular activities include hiking, fishing, swimming, picnicking and piloting small aircraft.

GETTING THERE: From Metaline Falls go E on county route 9345 approx. 5 mi. to Sullivan Lake CG.

SINGLE RATE:	$10	OPEN DATES:	May-Sept
# of SINGLE SITES:	38	MAX SPUR:	45 feet
GROUP RATE:	$35	MAX STAY:	14 days
# of GROUP SITES:	1	ELEVATION:	2600 feet

27 Sullivan Lake West
Metaline Falls • lat 48°50'24" lon 117°16'48"

DESCRIPTION: CG is situated along the north shore of Sullivan Lake. Mountains surround the lake. Grassy airstrip is located adjacent to the campground. RV dump station is located within one mile. Popular activities include hiking, fishing, swimming, boating, picnicking and piloting small aircraft.

GETTING THERE: From Metaline Falls go E on county route 9345 approx. 5 mi. to Sullivan Lake CG.

SINGLE RATE:	$10	OPEN DATES:	May-Sept
# of SINGLE SITES:	7	MAX SPUR:	30 feet
		MAX STAY:	14 days
		ELEVATION:	2600 feet

28 Summit Lake
Orient • lat 48°57'28" lon 118°08'14"

DESCRIPTION: This dispersed CG is in a mixed forest setting on Summit Lake. Fish for Rainbow and Brook Trout from the lake. Boat launch at CG. Supplies available at Orient. Deer, bears and squirrels are common to the area. No designated trails in the area.

GETTING THERE: From Orient go E on county route 4134 approx. 2.5 mi. to county route 4013. Go N on 4013 approx. 5 mi. to forest route 045. Go N on 045 approx. 2.5 mi. to Summit Lake CG.

SINGLE RATE:	No fee	OPEN DATES:	Yearlong*
		MAX STAY:	14 days
		ELEVATION:	2500 feet

29 Swan Lake
Republic • lat 48°30'48" lon 118°50'02"

DESCRIPTION: In a conifer forest setting on Swan Lake. Fish for trout and in the lake. Boat ramp at lake for non-motorized boats only. Supplies available at Republic. Deer, bears, raccoons, squirrels and waterfowl are common in the area. Swan Lake Trail around lake and CG is a trailhead to Mountain Lakes Mountain Bike Route.

GETTING THERE: From Republic go S on county route 21 approx. 7 mi. to primary forest route 53. Go W approx. 3 mi. on 53 to forest route 5314. Go W and S on 5314 approx. 8 mi. to Swan Lake CG.

SINGLE RATE:	$8	OPEN DATES:	May-Sept
# of SINGLE SITES:	21	MAX SPUR:	99 feet
GROUP RATE:	$35	MAX STAY:	14 days
# of GROUP SITES:	1	ELEVATION:	3700 feet

30 Trout Lake
Republic • lat 48°37'29" lon 118°14'20"

DESCRIPTION: In a mixed forest setting on Trout Lake. Fish for rainbow trout in the lake. Boat launch at CG. Supplies available at Republic. Deer, bears and squirrels are common to the area. This CG is a trailhead for Hoodoo Canyon Trail, a non-motorized trail.

GETTING THERE: From Republic go E on state HWY 20 (Sherman Pass National Scenic Byway) approx. 27 mi. to forest route 020. Go N on 020 approx. 3.5 mi. to Trout Lake CG.

SINGLE RATE:	No fee	OPEN DATES:	Yearlong*
# of SINGLE SITES:	4	MAX STAY:	14 days
		ELEVATION:	3100 feet

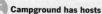 **Campground has hosts**   **Reservable sites**   **Accessible facilities**   **Fully developed**   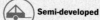 **Semi-developed**   **Rustic facilities**

NOTE: Open dates listed are typical. Actual dates are dependent on conditions such as snow pack.

USFS Photo

Gifford Pinchot National Forest

The Gifford Pinchot National Forest, located in southwest Washington is one of the oldest national forests in the United States. Established in 1949, the forest now contains 1.3 million acres and includes the 110,000-acre Mount St. Helens National Volcanic Monument.

Named after Gifford Pinchot, an active conservationist and the first chief of the Forest Service, the forest has something for everyone from solitude and scenic beauty to creative inspiration and outdoor activities. You can travel over 1,200 miles of trails of varying difficulty or bring your walking shoes or horse to discover the seven designated wilderness areas. Explore the lava tubes and caves on the Mount St. Helens National Volcanic Monument or if you're interested in canoeing, kayaking, rafting, and other forms of boating, you'll find them here. There are more than 20 species of fish in the 1,360 miles of streams and over 100 lakes in the Gifford Pinchot.

Climb the peaks of the forest for panoramic views of snow-capped mountains and spectacular wildflower displays. Make the journey to the crater rim of Mount St. Helens to experience the drama of an active volcano.

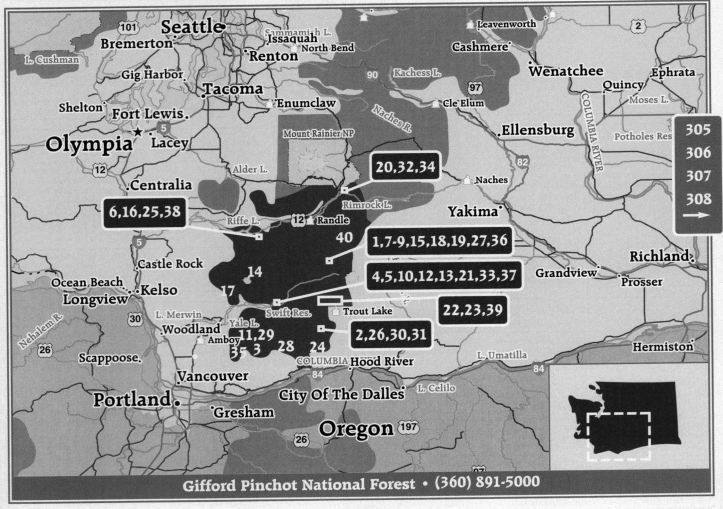

Gifford Pinchot National Forest • (360) 891-5000

1 Adams Fork
Randle • lat 46°20'22" lon 121°38'42"

DESCRIPTION: CG is located in tall, park-like grove of conifer with Adams Creek running adjacent to it. Supplies 17 mi. to Randle. Firewood sold on site. Motorcycle and ATV trails in nearby Blue Lake OHV area.

GETTING THERE: From Randle go SE on forest route 23 approx. 13. mi. to forest route 21. Go E on 21 approx. 4 mi. to Adams Fork CG.

SINGLE RATE:	$11	OPEN DATES:	May-Sept
# of SINGLE SITES:	21	MAX SPUR:	30 feet
GROUP RATE:	Varies	MAX STAY:	14 days
# of GROUP SITES:	3	ELEVATION:	2600 feet

2 Atkisson Group
Trout Lake • lat 45°75'00" lon 121°36'30"

DESCRIPTION: CG is located in tall grove of conifer with some underbrush, paved road. CG is a snow park in winter. Buy firewood from concessionaire. Great terrain for hiking and mountain biking. Berry picking in area. Large paved parking suitable for RVs. Max. group size 50 persons.

GETTING THERE: From Trout Lake go SW approx. 5 mi. on county route 141 to Atkisson Group CG.

		OPEN DATES:	May-Sept
GROUP RATE:	$59.18	MAX STAY:	14 days
# of GROUP SITES:	1	ELEVATION:	2800 feet

3 Beaver
Carson • lat 45°51'13" lon 121°57'14"

DESCRIPTION: CG is located in dense, mixed forest conifer and deciduous trees. CG is located next to Wind River. Berry picking in area. Supplies at Stabler Store, approx. 3 mi. Buy firewood from concessionaire. Grassy play area with swingset and horshoe pits.

GETTING THERE: From Carson go NW on state HWY 30 approximately 10miles to Beaver CG.

SINGLE RATE:	Varies	OPEN DATES:	May-Sept
# of SINGLE SITES:	24	MAX SPUR:	40 feet
GROUP RATE:	$64.56	MAX STAY:	14 days
# of GROUP SITES:	1	ELEVATION:	1100 feet

4 Berry Field Access
Trout Lake • lat 46°05'00" lon 121°48'00"

DESCRIPTION: Located in douglas fir forest with open huckleberry collecting areas nearby. Supplies in Trout Lake.

GETTING THERE: From Trout Lake go SW on county route 141, 5 mi. to primary forest route 24. Go W/NW on 24 approx. 17 mi. to primary forest route 30. Go W on 30 2.5 mi. to forest route 580. Go S on 580 to Berry Field Access CG.

SINGLE RATE:	No fee	OPEN DATES:	June-Oct
# of SINGLE SITES:	3	MAX SPUR:	30 feet
		MAX STAY:	14 days
		ELEVATION:	4400 feet

5 Big Creek
Ashford • lat 46°44'05" lon 121°58'02"

DESCRIPTION: CG is located in lush, dense conifer forest on Big Creek. Nearest supplies are 4.5 mi. to Ashland. CG can be busy on weekends and holidays. Firewood sold on site. Hiking, horse, and mountain biking trails in area including on-site Osborne Mountain trailhead. Visit Mount Rainier National Park for the day.

GETTING THERE: From Ashford go SE on primary forest route 52 4.5 miles to Big Creek CG.

SINGLE RATE:	Varies	OPEN DATES:	May-Sept
# of SINGLE SITES:	29	MAX SPUR:	22 feet
GROUP RATE:		MAX STAY:	14 days
		ELEVATION:	1800 feet

6 Blue Lake Creek
Randle • lat 46°24'14" lon 121°44'05"

DESCRIPTION: Set among conifer and fir forest with grassy undergrowth. Shady sites. Access to motorcycle trails in Blue Lake ORV system. OHV vehicles allowed in CG only to enter and exit trail system. Normally quiet with easy RV access.

GETTING THERE: From Randle go SE on forest route 23 approx. 11 mi. to Blue Lake Creek CG.

SINGLE RATE:	$10.50	OPEN DATES:	May-Sept
# of SINGLE SITES:	11	MAX SPUR:	30 feet
		MAX STAY:	14 days
		ELEVATION:	1900 feet

7 Cat Creek
Randle • lat 46°20'55" lon 121°37'25"

DESCRIPTION: A small CG located in lush shady conifer forest next to the Cispus River. Direct access to Blue Lake OHV trails system. Well defined sites, no room for RVs.

GETTING THERE: From Randle go SE on forest route 23 approx. 13. mi. to forest route 21. Go E on 21 approx.6 mi. to Cat Creek CG.

SINGLE RATE:	No fee	OPEN DATES:	May-Oct
# of SINGLE SITES:	5	MAX SPUR:	16 feet
		MAX STAY:	14 days
		ELEVATION:	3000 feet

8 Chain of Lakes
Trout Lake • lat 46°17'40" lon 121°35'35"

DESCRIPTION: CG is located in lush conifer forest close to a small, picturesque series of shallow lakes. Quiet boating. Supplies 24 mi. to Trout Lake. Horse, hiking, and OHV trail passes through the area. Purchase firewood at CG. Gravel road entrance for 5 mi. Large vehicles should take caution.

GETTING THERE: From Trout Lake go N on primary forest route 23 approx. 22 mi. to forest route 2329. Go N on 2329. 1 mi. to forest route 2329-022. Go NE on 2329-022 approx. 1 mi. to Chain of Lakes CG.

SINGLE RATE:	$9	OPEN DATES:	June-Sept
# of SINGLE SITES:	3	MAX SPUR:	16 feet
		MAX STAY:	14 days
		ELEVATION:	4400 feet

9 Council Lake
Northwoods • lat 46°15'48" lon 121°37'50"

DESCRIPTION: CG is in lush conifer forest next to Council Lake. An old road leads up to a spectacular cliff top view of the surrounding forest and Mount Adams. Good fishing on adjacent Council Lake. Hiking, horse, and OHV trail on site. Good berry picking in the fall.

GETTING THERE: From Northwoods go NE on primary forest route 90 approx. 25 mi. to forest route 2334. Go on 2334 approx. 2 mi. to Council Lake CG.

SINGLE RATE:	$9	OPEN DATES:	May-Sept*
# of SINGLE SITES:	9	MAX SPUR:	16 feet
		MAX STAY:	14 days
		ELEVATION:	4300 feet

10 Cultus Creek
Trout Lake • lat 46°02'50" lon 121°45'16"

DESCRIPTION: CG is located in a lush conifer forest. Popular camping during the fall huckleberry season. Basic supplies in Trout Lake. Gather dead wood for fires. Hiking and horse trails 33 and 108 start from the campground and access Indian Heaven Wilderness area.

GETTING THERE: From Trout Lake go SW on primary forest route 24 (county route 141) approx. 16 mi. to Cultus Creek CG.

SINGLE RATE:	$11	OPEN DATES:	May-Sept
# of SINGLE SITES:	51	MAX SPUR:	32 feet
		MAX STAY:	14 days
		ELEVATION:	4000 feet

 Campground has hosts　 **Reservable sites**　 **Accessible facilities**　 **Fully developed**　 **Semi-developed**　 **Rustic facilities**

NOTE: Open dates listed are typical. Actual dates are dependent on conditions such as snow pack.

11 Falls Creek Horse Camp
Trout Lake • lat 45˚57'59" lon 121˚50'40"

DESCRIPTION: This camp includes a loading ramp. Campgrounds and roads are unimproved. Supplies 23 mi. at Trout Lake or Carson. Gather dead and down wood for fires. Tight turning and small campsites. Trail 171 (hike and stock) access Indian Heaven Wilderness and Pacific Crest Trail 2000. Trail 57 (hike/stock/mtn bike) on site.

GETTING THERE: From Trout Lake go SW on primary forest route 24 (county route 141) approx. 7 mi. to forest route 60. Go W on 60 approx. 11 mi. to forest route 65. Go N on 65 approx. 5 mi. to Falls Creek Horse Camp.

SINGLE RATE:	No fee	OPEN DATES:	June-Oct
# of SINGLE SITES:	6	MAX SPUR:	20 feet
		MAX STAY:	14 days
		ELEVATION:	3500 feet

12 Forlorn Lakes
Trout Lake • lat 45˚57'28" lon 121˚45'19"

DESCRIPTION: CG is a series of small camping areas near small, isolated, picturesque lakes. CG is very popular and fills early in the week. Easy RV parking for some of the spots. Gather dead wood for fires. The picturesque lakes are shallow and are not usually fished. Good for very small watercraft.

GETTING THERE: From Trout Lake go SW on primary forest route 24 (county route 141) 7 mi. to forest route 60. Go SW on 60 4 mi. to forest route 6035. Go NW on 6035 2.5 mi. to Forlorn Lake CG.

SINGLE RATE:	No fee	OPEN DATES:	June-Oct
# of SINGLE SITES:	8	MAX SPUR:	18 feet
		MAX STAY:	14 days
		ELEVATION:	3600 feet

13 Goose Lake
Trout Lake • lat 45˚56'24" lon 121˚45'25"

DESCRIPTION: CG is in a lush comifer forest with Goose Lake access. Popular spot for fishing. Many walk in campsites on a hillside. Basic supplies in Trout Lake. Gather dead wood for fires.

GETTING THERE: From Trout Lake go SW on primary forest route 24 (county route 141) approx. 7 mi. to forest route 60. Go SW on 60 approx. 5.5 mi. to Goose Lake CG.

SINGLE RATE:	Varies	OPEN DATES:	June-Sept
# of SINGLE SITES:	14	MAX SPUR:	30 feet
		MAX STAY:	14 days
		ELEVATION:	3200 feet

14 Green River Horse Camp
Randle • lat 46˚20'00" lon 122˚05'30"

DESCRIPTION: CG is surrounded by blown down timber (from the Mt. St. Helens eruption) which has been salvaged and replanted. Drinking water is located 5 mi. N at Norway Pass trailhead (none on site). Water for stock should be carried by bucket from the Green River. There are trails and horse lines on site.

GETTING THERE: From Randle go S 10 mi. on primary forest route 25 to primary forest route 26. Go W 9 mi. to forest route 2612. Go W 1 mi. to Green River Horse Camp. Large vehicles should use caution.

SINGLE RATE:	No fee	OPEN DATES:	May-June*
# of SINGLE SITES:	8	MAX SPUR:	40 feet
		MAX STAY:	14 days
		ELEVATION:	2800 feet

15 Horseshoe Lake
Trout Lake • lat 46˚18'36" lon 121˚33'56"

DESCRIPTION: A popular CG located next to a picturesque high mountain lake. Poorly defined sites, some on lake. Excellent quiet boating. A horse and OHV trail runs partly around the lake. Access to CG is at least 12 mi. of gravel road.

GETTING THERE: From Trout Lake go N on forest route 23 approx. 23 mi. to forest route 2329. Go NE on 2329 approx. 7 mi. to forest route 2329-078. Go W on 2329-078 approx. 1 mi. to Horseshoe Lake CG.

SINGLE RATE:	No fee	OPEN DATES:	June-Oct
# of SINGLE SITES:	10	MAX SPUR:	16 feet
		MAX STAY:	14 days
		ELEVATION:	4200 feet

16 Iron Creek
Randle • lat 46˚25'51" lon 121˚59'06"

DESCRIPTION: CG is located in lush, old growth conifer forest along Iron Creek. Good fishing. Nice place to camp for those visiting the east side of Mount St. Helens. Supplies in Randle, 10 mi. Buy firewood on site. Creek side barrier free trail surrounds CG. Amphitheater on site.

GETTING THERE: From Randle go S on primary forest route 25 approx. 10 mi. to Iron Creek CG. Easy RV parking.

SINGLE RATE:	Varies	OPEN DATES:	May-Sept
# of SINGLE SITES:	98	MAX SPUR:	45 feet
GROUP RATE:		MAX STAY:	14 days
		ELEVATION:	1200 feet

17 Kalama Horse Camp
Cougar • lat 46˚08'36" lon 122˚19'28"

DESCRIPTION: CG is in a lush forest setting with a picnic area, horseshoe pit, loading/unloading ramp, staging area with stock water trough, hitch rails, mounting assist area, and lounging area. All sites have access to the loop trail from the stock holding area.

GETTING THERE: From Cougar go N on forest route 8100 approx. 6.5 mi. to Kalama Horse Camp/Trailhead.

SINGLE RATE:	No fee	OPEN DATES:	May-Nov
# of SINGLE SITES:	8	MAX SPUR:	100 feet
GROUP RATE:	No fee	MAX STAY:	14 days
# of GROUP SITES:	2	ELEVATION:	2000 feet

18 Keenes Horse Camp
Trout Lake • lat 46˚18'38" lon 121˚32'37"

DESCRIPTION: Located on Spring Creek, there is a loading ramp, corrals, a water trough, and vault toilets. Some units have tie stalls. Supplies in Trout Lake. Gather own dead firewood. Trails accessible from this area include Pacific Crest Trails.

GETTING THERE: From Trout Lake go N on primary forest route 23 approx. 23 mi. to forest route 2329. Go NE on 2329 approx. 9 mi. to Keenes Horse Camp.

SINGLE RATE:	No fee	OPEN DATES:	June-Oct
# of SINGLE SITES:	13	MAX SPUR:	40 feet
		MAX STAY:	14 days
		ELEVATION:	4300 feet

19 Killen Creek
Trout Lake • lat 46˚17'42" lon 121˚32'52"

DESCRIPTION: CG is located in lush pine forest next to Killen Creek. Gather dead and down firewood. Hiking, horse, and OHV trail with access to nearby wilderness area. Primarily used as base camp to access wilderness. Trail 113 provides access to Mount Adams Wilderness. Berry picking.

GETTING THERE: From Trout Lake go N on primary forest route 23 approx. 23 mi. to forest route 2329. Go NE on forest route 2329 approx. 7 mi. to Killen Creek CG.

SINGLE RATE:	No fee	OPEN DATES:	June-Oct
# of SINGLE SITES:	8	MAX SPUR:	22 feet
		MAX STAY:	14 days
		ELEVATION:	4400 feet

20 La Wis Wis
Packwood • lat 46˚40'26" lon 121˚35'12"

DESCRIPTION: CG is located in lush conifer forest near the Clear Fork Cowlitz and Ohanapecosh Rivers. Some walk-in sites on Ohanapecosh River. Good fishing in river. Supplies 6 mi. in Packwood. Firewood sold on site. Blue Hole and Purcell Falls hiking trailheads on site.

GETTING THERE: From Packwood go NE on US HWY 12 approximately 6 miles to La Wis Wis CG. Some sites are large enough for RVs (not over 24'). Signs indicate loops that are too small for RVs.

SINGLE RATE:	Varies	OPEN DATES:	May-Sept
# of SINGLE SITES:	117	MAX SPUR:	24 feet
GROUP RATE:	$25	MAX STAY:	14 days
# of GROUP SITES:	20	ELEVATION:	1400 feet

 Campground has hosts   **Reservable sites**   **Accessible facilities**   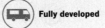 **Fully developed**   **Semi-developed**   **Rustic facilities**

NOTE: Open dates listed are typical. Actual dates are dependent on conditions such as snow pack.

21   Lower Falls Recreation Area
Northwoods • lat 46°09'18" lon 121°52'36"

DESCRIPTION: Paved CG sites among large fir tree on gently sloping ground. Accessible trails to picturesque falls. The trails go right along dangerous cliffs.

GETTING THERE: From Northwoods go NE on primary forest route 90 approx. 10 mi. to Lower Falls Recreation Area CG.

SINGLE RATE:	$12	OPEN DATES:	May-Sept
# of SINGLE SITES:	40	MAX SPUR:	60 feet
GROUP RATE:	$27	MAX STAY:	14 days
# of GROUP SITES:	1	ELEVATION:	1300 feet

22   Morrison Creek
Trout Lake • lat 46°07'46" lon 121°30'53"

DESCRIPTION: Several primitive camp sites are available. Tables, toilets, and fire rings are present. Basic supplies in Trout Lake. Gather dead wood for fires. Horse and hiking trails 16 and 73 access Mount Adams Wilderness.

GETTING THERE: From Trout Lake go N on forest route 17 2 mi. to forest route 80. Go N on 80 approx. 8 mi. to Morrison Creek CG. Access is rough and not recommended for trailers or motor homes.

SINGLE RATE:	No fee	OPEN DATES:	June-Oct
# of SINGLE SITES:	12	MAX SPUR:	20 feet
		MAX STAY:	14 days
		ELEVATION:	4600 feet

23   Morrison Creek Horse Camp
Trout Lake • lat 46°07'20" lon 121°31'00"

DESCRIPTION: Several primitive camp sites are available. Tables, toilets, and fire rings are present. Basic supplies in Trout Lake. Gather dead wood for fires. Horse and hiking trails 16 and 73 access Mount Adams Wilderness.

GETTING THERE: From Trout Lake go N on forest route 17 2 mi. to forest route 80. Go N on 80 approx. 8 mi. to Morrison Creek Horse Camp.

SINGLE RATE:	No fee	OPEN DATES:	June-Oct
# of SINGLE SITES:	12	MAX SPUR:	30 feet
		MAX STAY:	14 days
		ELEVATION:	4600 feet

24   Moss Creek
Willard • lat 45°47'50" lon 121°38'17"

DESCRIPTION: CG is in a lush forest setting by Moss Creek. Paved road to campground. Smaller campsites but useable by smaller RVs. Close to Columbia River Gorge. Buy firewood from concessionaire. Basic supplies in Willard.

GETTING THERE: From Willard go N on state HWY 86 1 mi. to Moss Creek CG.

SINGLE RATE:	$11	OPEN DATES:	June-Sept
# of SINGLE SITES:	18	MAX SPUR:	32 feet
		MAX STAY:	14 days
		ELEVATION:	1400 feet

25   North Fork
Randle • lat 46°27'07" lon 121°47'13"

DESCRIPTION: This is popular campground set in a lush forest setting along the North Fork Cispus River. Good fishing in river. Well defined camp spots. Easy RV parking. Campers may gather firewood. Deer, elk and bears in area. Go to Randle for supplies.

GETTING THERE: From Randle go SE on primary forest route 23 approx. 10 mi. to North Fork CG.

SINGLE RATE:	Varies	OPEN DATES:	May-Sept
# of SINGLE SITES:	33	MAX SPUR:	40 feet
GROUP RATE:	Varies	MAX STAY:	14 days
# of GROUP SITES:	3	ELEVATION:	1500 feet

26   Oklahoma
Willard • lat 45°52'17" lon 121°37'25"

DESCRIPTION: CG is in a lush forest setting with some open meadow space. Close to the Columbia River Gorge. Fishing on little White Salmon River. Easy RV parking.

GETTING THERE: From Willard go N on state HWY 86 approx. 8 mi. to forest route 181. Go W on 181 approx. 1/2 mi. to Oklahoma CG.

SINGLE RATE:	$11	OPEN DATES:	May-Sept
# of SINGLE SITES:	23	MAX SPUR:	25 feet
		MAX STAY:	14 days
		ELEVATION:	1700 feet

27   Olallie Lake
Trout Lake • lat 46°17'22" lon 121°37'05"

DESCRIPTION: CG is in a lush forest setting with several small sites and one larger area with room for RVs. CG is close to the lake shore with good fishing early in the season. There is a beautiful view of Mount Adams across the lake. Many trails nearby. Supplies 23 mi. to Trout Lake.

GETTING THERE: From Trout Lake go N on primary forest route 23 approx. 22 mi. to forest route 2329. Go N on 2329 1 mi. to forest route 2329-022. Go NE on 2329-022 approx. 1 mi. to forest route 5601. Go N on 5601 approx. 1/4 mi. to Olallie Lake CG.

SINGLE RATE:	$9.50	OPEN DATES:	June-Sept
# of SINGLE SITES:	5	MAX SPUR:	40 feet
		MAX STAY:	14 days
		ELEVATION:	3700 feet

28   Panther Creek
Carson • lat 45°49'14" lon 121°52'35"

DESCRIPTION: A lightly used CG in a lush deep forest, with nearby stream. Fishing in the stream. Horse facilities with loading ramp. Buy firewood from concessionaire. Supplies in Carson. Pacific Crest Trail 2000 passes along south edge of CG.

GETTING THERE: From Carson go N on state HWY 30 approx. 6 mi. to forest route 6517. Go E on 6517 approx. 2 mi. to Panther Creek CG.

SINGLE RATE:	Varies	OPEN DATES:	May-Sept
# of SINGLE SITES:	33	MAX SPUR:	40 feet
		MAX STAY:	14 days
# of GROUP SITES:	1	ELEVATION:	1000 feet

29   Paradise Creek
Carson • lat 45°56'56" lon 121°56'03"

DESCRIPTION: CG is heavily shaded by large evergreen trees near Wind River and Paradise Creek. Fishing in both river and creek. Generally light use. Supplies in Carson. Firewood sold on site. Lava Butte Trail 200 for hiking begins on site. Berry picking nearby.

GETTING THERE: From Carson go N on state HWY 30 approx. 17 mi. to Paradise Creek CG. Easy RV parking. Paved road to campground.

SINGLE RATE:	Varies	OPEN DATES:	May-Sept
# of SINGLE SITES:	42	MAX SPUR:	40 feet
		MAX STAY:	14 days
		ELEVATION:	1500 feet

30   Peterson Group Camp
Trout Lake • lat 45°58'07" lon 121°39'30"

DESCRIPTION: CG is a large group area in a lush forest setting. Popular camping during the fall huckleberry season. Easy RV parking. Trail to nearby ice cave. A stairway into the cave leads to cool ice formations (pun intended). Firewood sold by concessionaire.

GETTING THERE: From Trout Lake go SW on primary forest route 24 (county route 141) approx. 7 mi. to Peterson Group CG.

		OPEN DATES:	May-Sept
		MAX SPUR:	50 feet
		MAX STAY:	14 days
GROUP RATE:	$59.18	ELEVATION:	2800 feet
# of GROUP SITES:	1		

 Campground has hosts   **Reservable sites**   **Accessible facilities**   **Fully developed**   **Semi-developed**   **Rustic facilities**

NOTE: Open dates listed are typical. Actual dates are dependent on conditions such as snow pack.

31 Peterson Prairie

Trout Lake • lat 45°58'07" lon 121°39'30"

DESCRIPTION: CG is in a lush forest setting. Popular camping during the fall huckleberry season (August). The rest of the year, use is light. Graveled, level sites. Easy RV parking. Firewood sold by concessionaire. Trail to nearby ice cave. A stairway into the cave leads to cool ice formations.

GETTING THERE: From Trout Lake go SW on primary forest route 24 (county route 141) approx. 7 mi. to Peterson Prairie CG.

SINGLE RATE:	Varies	OPEN DATES:	May-Sept
# of SINGLE SITES:	29	MAX SPUR:	40 feet
GROUP RATE:	$26.75	MAX STAY:	14 days
# of GROUP SITES:	2	ELEVATION:	2800 feet

32 Soda Springs

Packwood • lat 46°42'12" lon 121°28'47"

DESCRIPTION: A small informal camping area in a lush conifer forest setting. Mainly serves as an access point to the William O. Douglas Wilderness.

GETTING THERE: From Packwood go N on USHWY 12 approx. 7 mi. to forest route 4510. Go NE on 4510 approx. 5 mi. to Soda Springs CG.

SINGLE RATE:	No fee	OPEN DATES:	June-Sept
# of SINGLE SITES:	6	MAX SPUR:	25 feet
		MAX STAY:	14 days
		ELEVATION:	3200 feet

33 South

Trout Lake • lat 46°06'43" lon 121°45'57"

DESCRIPTION: A small lightly used, out of the way campground. Access by a poor dirt road. Trails nearby. A busy campground during berry season. Several trails lead out of the campground.

GETTING THERE: From Trout Lake go SW on primary forest route 24 (county route 141) approx. 21 mi. to South CG.

SINGLE RATE:	No fee	OPEN DATES:	May-Sept
# of SINGLE SITES:	8	MAX SPUR:	18 feet
		MAX STAY:	14 days
		ELEVATION:	4000 feet

34 Summit Creek

Packwood • lat 46°42'38" lon 121°32'08"

DESCRIPTION: A small, informal CG located in mixed conifer forest above the Summit Creek. This CG cannot accommodate trailers but is suitable for tents or pickup campers. Supplies 9 mi. to Packwood. CG is on the way to Soda Springs and the William O. Douglas Wilderness.

GETTING THERE: From Packwood go N on USHWY 12 approx. 7 mi. to forest route 4510. Go NE on 4510 approx. 2 mi. to Summit Creek CG. Road is narrow with sharp curves. Not suitable for trailers or RVs.

SINGLE RATE:	No fee	OPEN DATES:	June-Sept
# of SINGLE SITES:	6	MAX SPUR:	20 feet
		MAX STAY:	14 days
		ELEVATION:	2200 feet

35 Sunset Falls

Yacolt • lat 45°49'08" lon 122°14'52"

DESCRIPTION: In a park-like forested setting at the edge of forest with views of Sunset Falls. East Fork Lewis River is near CG with good trout fishing. CG sits on a former CCC camp. Supplies approx. 9.5 mi. to Yacolt. CG full on holidays. Campers may gather firewood. Trails to Sunset Fall and Summit Springs nearby.

GETTING THERE: From Yacolt to SE on state HWY 12 9.5 miles to Sunset CG.

SINGLE RATE:	$11	OPEN DATES:	Yearlong*
# of SINGLE SITES:	18	MAX SPUR:	22 feet
		MAX STAY:	14 days
		ELEVATION:	1000 feet

36 Takhlakh Lake

Trout Lake • lat 46°16'42" lon 121°35'42"

DESCRIPTION: A very popular campground close to the shore of Takhlakh Lake with beautiful views of Mount Adams. Good fishing. Supplies 23 mi. to Trout Lake. Busy holiday weekends. Firewood sold on site. Barrier free trail (more difficult accessibility) around the lake. Other trails in the area.

GETTING THERE: From Trout Lake go N on primary forest route 23 approx. 22 mi. to Takhlakh Lake CG.

SINGLE RATE:	Varies	OPEN DATES:	June-Sept
# of SINGLE SITES:	54	MAX SPUR:	40 feet
		MAX STAY:	14 days
		ELEVATION:	4500 feet

37 Tillicum

Trout Lake • lat 46°07'24" lon 121°46'43"

DESCRIPTION: A lightly used campground during berry season. A few good camping spots, with numerous other poor ones. Several trails lead out of the campground. Paved road to campground.

GETTING THERE: From Trout Lake go SW on primary forest route 24 (county route 141) approx. 22 mi. to Tillicum CG.

SINGLE RATE:	No fee	OPEN DATES:	May-Sept
# of SINGLE SITES:	32	MAX SPUR:	18 feet
		MAX STAY:	14 days
		ELEVATION:	4300 feet

38 Tower Rock
Randle • lat 46°26'45" lon 121°51'57"

DESCRIPTION: CG is in a lush forest setting with easy access on paved roads. Located next to the Cispus River with good fishing. Easy RV camping. Conveniently located for those visiting the east side of Mount St. Helens. Small store and trout pond nearby.

GETTING THERE: From Randle go S on primary forest route 23 approx. 5.5 mi. to forest route 76. Go W on 76 approx. 1/2 mi. to Tower Rock CG.

SINGLE RATE:	Varies	OPEN DATES:	May-Sept
# of SINGLE SITES:	22	MAX SPUR:	40 feet
		MAX STAY:	14 days
		ELEVATION:	1100 feet

39 Trout Lake Creek
Trout Lake • lat 46°02'42" lon 121°35'45"

DESCRIPTION: A primitive campground located in fir equiped with toilets, table, and fire rings. Next to Trout Lake Creek. Fishing for trout in lake. Supplies at Trout Lake, approx. 4 mi. from CG. Camper may gather firewood.

GETTING THERE: From Trout Lake go NW on forest route 88 approximately 4 miles to Trout Lake Creek CG. Not recommended for trailers or motor homes.

SINGLE RATE:	No fee	OPEN DATES:	May-Oct
# of SINGLE SITES:	21	MAX SPUR:	28 feet
		MAX STAY:	14 days
		ELEVATION:	2200 feet

40 Walupt Lake

Packwood • lat 46°25'25" lon 121°28'21"

DESCRIPTION: CG is located in lush conifer forest and is adjacent to Walupt Lake. There is a boat ramp on site. Supplies are 21 mi. to Packwood. The Nannie Ridge Trail 98 and Walupt Lake Trail 101 both lead to the Goat Rocks Wilderness from the CG. Road is narrow with sharp curves. Large vehicles should take caution.

GETTING THERE: From Packwood go S on US HWY 12 for 2 mi. to primary forest route 21. Go SE on 21 approx. 15 mi. to forest route 2160. Go E on 2160 approx. 4 mi. to Walupt Lake CG.

SINGLE RATE:	Varies	OPEN DATES:	June-Sept
# of SINGLE SITES:	42	MAX SPUR:	40 feet
GROUP RATE:		MAX STAY:	14 days
		ELEVATION:	3900 feet

 Campground has hosts   **Reservable sites**   **Accessible facilities**   **Fully developed**   **Semi-developed**   **Rustic facilities**

NOTE: Open dates listed are typical. Actual dates are dependent on conditions such as snow pack.

MOUNT BAKER-SNOQUALMIE NATIONAL FOREST

The Mt. Baker-Snoqualmie National Forest in Washington extends over 140 miles along the western slopes of the Cascade Mountains from the Canadian border to the north boundary of Mt. Rainier National Park. Nearly five million people in or near the Puget Sound and Vancouver, B.C. metropolitan areas are within 70 miles west of the forest. In addition, four major mountain passes cross the Cascades through the Mt. Baker-Snoqualmie National Forest, making this one of the most visible national forests in the country.

Forest visitors will enjoy a wide range of year-round recreation opportunities which include 40 developed campgrounds, numerous picnic areas and scenic viewpoints. There are over 1,500 miles of trails including over 100 miles of the Pacific Crest National Scenic Trail. The forest also provides hundreds of accessible lakes, rivers and streams and ample opportunities for hunting and fishing, river rafting, bird-watching, mountain climbing, berry picking and general sightseeing. Eight wilderness areas, which comprise 720,000 acres, are great places to get away from the hustle and bustle of the city.

Mount Baker-Snoqualmie National Forest • (425) 775-9702

1 Beaver Creek
Granite Falls • lat 48°04'43" lon 121°31'31"

DESCRIPTION: This CG is located in mixed hardwood and conifer at the confluence of Beaver Creek and Stillaguamish River. Fish for trout. Popular activities include gold panning and visiting this area's ice caves. Visit historic Verlot Public Service Center or hike nearby Boulder River Wilderness. No drinking water.

GETTING THERE: From Granite Falls go E on Mountain Scenic Loop (primary forest route 20) approximately 24 miles to Beaver Creek CG.

		OPEN DATES:	May-Sept
		MAX SPUR:	30 feet
GROUP RATE:	$60	MAX STAY:	14 days
# of GROUP SITES:	1	ELEVATION:	1400 feet

6 Buck Creek
Darrington • lat 48°16'05" lon 121°19'50"

DESCRIPTION: This CG is located in old growth douglas fir on Buck Creek. Enjoy fishing for trout. Visit historic Suiattle Guard Station. Wildlife in this area includes black bears and deer. Gather firewood locally. Try a hike along the creek or into the Glacier Peak Wilderness. No drinking water.

GETTING THERE: From Darrington go N on state HWY 30 approx. 7 mi. to primary forest route 26. Go NE on 26 approx. 16 mi. to Buck Creek CG.

SINGLE RATE:	$8	OPEN DATES:	May-Sept
# of SINGLE SITES:	26	MAX SPUR:	60 feet
		MAX STAY:	14 days
		ELEVATION:	1200 feet

2 Beckler River
Mill River • lat 47°44'05" lon 121°19'52"

DESCRIPTION: Adjacent to the Beckler River in mixed alder and hemlock, mountain views. Trout fishing on Beckler River. Deer, black bears, cougars and small wildlife in area. Pets must be leashed. Bring your own firewood. Fills weekends and holidays. Hiking trail has been destroyed due to flooding. Drive to other trailheads.

GETTING THERE: From Mill River go E on US HWY 2 approx. 2.5 mi. to primary forest route 65. Go N on 65 approx. 2 mi. to Beckler River CG.

SINGLE RATE:	$12	OPEN DATES:	May-Sept
# of SINGLE SITES:	27	MAX SPUR:	40 feet
		MAX STAY:	14 days
		ELEVATION:	900 feet

7 Clear Creek
Darrington • lat 48°13'15" lon 121°34'16"

DESCRIPTION: This CG is along Clear Creek in old growth douglas fir. View the largest douglas fir tree on the district. Fish for trout and steelhead on Sauk River. Kayak and rafting popular; boat luanch available. Hike the Frog Leg Trail along Clear Creek which starts at CG. No drinking water.

GETTING THERE: From Darrington go SE on Mountain Scenic Loop (primary forest route 20) approximately 4 miles to Clear Creek CG.

SINGLE RATE:	$8	OPEN DATES:	May-Sept
# of SINGLE SITES:	13	MAX SPUR:	99 feet
		MAX STAY:	14 days
		ELEVATION:	500 feet

3 Bedal
Granite Falls • lat 48°05'48" lon 121°23'08"

DESCRIPTION: This CG rests in cedar, hemlock, and fir on North Fork Sauk River. Fish for trout and steelhead. A boat launch is provided to enjoy rafting on this river. Wildlife includes black bears and deer. Trails lead to Bedal and Sloan Peaks. Visit the dramatic North Fork Falls. No drinking water.

GETTING THERE: From Granite Falls go E on Mountain Scenic Loop (primary forest route 20) approximately 37 miles to Bedal CG.

SINGLE RATE:	$8	OPEN DATES:	May-Sept
# of SINGLE SITES:	18	MAX SPUR:	70 feet
		MAX STAY:	14 days
		ELEVATION:	1000 feet

8 Coal Creek Bar Group
Granite Falls • lat 48°04'44" lon 121°31'30"

DESCRIPTION: CG rests in a mixed hardwood and conifer forest at the confluence of Coal Creek and Stillaguamish River. Enjoy fishing for trout and steelhead. Popular activities include gold panning and the area's ice caves. Visit historic Verlot Public Service Center or hike Boulder River Wilderness. No drinking water.

GETTING THERE: From Granite Falls go E on Mountain Scenic Loop (primary forest route 20) approximately 23 miles to Coal Creek CG.

		OPEN DATES:	May-Sept
		MAX SPUR:	99 feet
GROUP RATE:	$60	MAX STAY:	14 days
# of GROUP SITES:	1	ELEVATION:	1100 feet

4 Boardman Creek
Granite Falls • lat 48°04'13" lon 121°40'33"

DESCRIPTION: CG rests in a mixed hardwood and conifer forest at the confluence of Boardman Creek and Stillaguamish River. Enjoy fishing for trout and steelhead. Popular activities include gold panning and this area's ice caves. Visit historic Verlot Public Service Center or hike Boulder River Wilderness. No drinking water.

GETTING THERE: From Granite Falls go E on Mountain Scenic Loop (primary forest route 20) approximately 18 miles to Boardman Creek CG.

SINGLE RATE:	$8	OPEN DATES:	May-Sept
# of SINGLE SITES:	8	MAX SPUR:	43 feet
		MAX STAY:	14 days
		ELEVATION:	1200 feet

9 Corral Pass
Greenwater • lat 47°00'46" lon 121°27'51"

DESCRIPTION: This tent only CG is located in mixed conifer on Small Creek. There is trailhead on-sitethat leads to Norse Peak Wilderness. Wildlife in this area includes bears, elk, coyotes, and raptors. Enjoy a drive to Crystal Mountain and ride the lift for a bird's eye view of Mount Rainier. No drinking water.

GETTING THERE: From Greenwater go S on primary forest route 72 (state HWY 410) approx. 13 mi. to forest route 7174. Go E on 7174 approx. 5 mi. to Corral Pass CG.

SINGLE RATE:	No fee	OPEN DATES:	May-Sept*
# of SINGLE SITES:	20		
		MAX STAY:	14 days
		ELEVATION:	4800 feet

5 Boulder Creek
Grassmere • lat 48°42'50" lon 121°41'25"

DESCRIPTION: This CG is on Boulder Creek near Baker Lake among mixed conifer. Trout fish in the lake but please check fishing regulations Hike on the nearby Shadow of Sentinals Nature Trail which is barrier free. Wildlife includes deer, elk, bald eagles and keep an eye out for black bears. No drinking water.

GETTING THERE: From Grassmere go N on the county road approx. 3 mi. to primary forest route 11. Go N on 11 approx. 10 mi. to Boulder Creek CG.

SINGLE RATE:	$8	OPEN DATES:	May-Oct
# of SINGLE SITES:	8	MAX SPUR:	30 feet
GROUP RATE:	$40	MAX STAY:	14 days
# of GROUP SITES:	1	ELEVATION:	700 feet

10 Denny Creek
North Bend • lat 47°25'15" lon 121°26'30"

DESCRIPTION: This CG is adjacent to the Snoqualmie River. Enjoy a hike on the Asahel Curtis Nature Trail. This trail runs through lush old-growth forest and crosses Humpback Creek. Wildlife includes winter wrens and pileated woodpecker. Firewood may be sold at campground. Supplies in North Bend.

GETTING THERE: From North Bend go SE on US HWY 90 approx. 20 mi. to Denny Creek CG.

SINGLE RATE:	Varies	OPEN DATES:	May-Oct
# of SINGLE SITES:	33	MAX SPUR:	35 feet
GROUP RATE:	$75	MAX STAY:	14 days
# of GROUP SITES:	1	ELEVATION:	2200 feet

 Campground has hosts   **Reservable sites**   **Accessible facilities**   **Fully developed** **Semi-developed**   **Rustic facilities**

NOTE: Open dates listed are typical. Actual dates are dependent on conditions such as snow pack.

11 ## Douglas Fir
Glacier • lat 48°54'10" lon 121°54'52"

DESCRIPTION: This CG is adjacent to the North Fork of the Nooksack River. Enjoy fishing for trout in the river. Hike to Heather Meadows, a scenic high alpine area. CG is busy weekends and holidays. Wildlife includes deer, elk, bald eagles, mountain goats and keep an eye out for black bears. Supplies in Glacier.

GETTING THERE: From Glacier go NE on state HWY 542 approximately 2.5 miles to Douglas Fir CG.

SINGLE RATE:	$12	OPEN DATES:	May-Sept
# of SINGLE SITES:	30	MAX SPUR:	60 feet
GROUP RATE:	$50	MAX STAY:	14 days
# of GROUP SITES:	1	ELEVATION:	1000 feet

16 ## Half Camp
Greenwater • lat 46°58'30" lon 121°28'00"

DESCRIPTION: This CG is ideal for campers with horses. CG rests in mixed conifer with a trail that leads to Goats Lake. Wildlife includes bears, elk, coyotes, and raptors. Enjoy a drive to Crystal Mountain and ride the lift for a bird's eye view of Mount Rainier. No drinking water. Horse trough and high lines on site.

GETTING THERE: From Greenwater go S on state HWY 410 approx. 15 mi. to forest route 7190. Go SE on 7190 approx. 5 mi. to Half Camp CG.

SINGLE RATE:	No fee	OPEN DATES:	May-Sept*
		MAX STAY:	14 days
		ELEVATION:	2800 feet

12 ## Esswine Group
Granite Falls • lat 48°06'00" lon 121°35'30"

DESCRIPTION: CG rests in a mixed hardwood and conifer forest on the Stillaguamish River. Enjoy fishing for trout and steelhead. Popular activities include gold panning and exploring this area's ice caves. Visit historic Verlot Public Service Center or hike Boulder River Wilderness. No drinking water.

GETTING THERE: From Granite Falls go E on Mountain Scenic Loop (primary forest route 20) approximately 15 miles to Esswine Group CG.

GROUP RATE:	$60	OPEN DATES:	May-Sept
# of GROUP SITES:	1	MAX SPUR:	75 feet
		MAX STAY:	14 days
		ELEVATION:	1100 feet

17 ## Horseshoe Cove
Grassmere • lat 48°40'19" lon 121°40'35"

DESCRIPTION: This CG is adjacent to Baker Lake among fir, hemlock, and cedar. Enjoy fishing for trout in the lake but please check fishing regulations Hike on the nearby Shadow of Sentinals Nature Trail which is barrier free. Wildlife in this area includes deer, elk, bald eagles and keep an eye out for black bears.

GETTING THERE: From Grassmere go N on primary forest route 11 approx. 11 mi. to forest route 1118. Go 3 mi. E on 1118 to Horseshoe Cove CG.

SINGLE RATE:	Varies	OPEN DATES:	May-Oct
# of SINGLE SITES:	9	MAX SPUR:	34 feet
GROUP RATE:	$75	MAX STAY:	14 days
# of GROUP SITES:	1	ELEVATION:	700 feet

13 ## Evans Creek ORV Area
Wilkeson • lat 46°56'00" lon 121°57'30"

DESCRIPTION: This CG is located in mixed conifer on Evans Creek. Wildlife in this area includes bears, elk, coyotes, and raptors. This CG is ideal for OHV use. There are almost forty miles of trails open to OHVs. A Trail Park Pass is required in the CG, parking areas, and on the trails. No drinking water.

GETTING THERE: From Wilkeson go SE on state HWY 165 (primary forest route 79) to Evans Creek ORV Area CG.

SINGLE RATE:	No fee	OPEN DATES:	May-Sept*
# of SINGLE SITES:	27	MAX SPUR:	26 feet
		MAX STAY:	14 days
		ELEVATION:	3000 feet

18 ## Maple Grove
Concrete • lat 48°41'10" lon 121°39'38"

DESCRIPTION: This CG is adjacent to Baker Lake among fir, hemlock, and cedar. Enjoy fishing for trout in the lake but please check fishing regulations Hike on the nearby Shadow of Sentinals Nature Trail which is barrier free. Wildlife includes deer, elk, bald eagles and keep an eye out for black bears. No drinking water.

GETTING THERE: From Concrete go N on county road approx. 10 mi. to forest route 1107. Go N on 1107 approx. 1/2 mi. to trailhead to Maple Grove CG. This CG is hike-in or boat access only.

SINGLE RATE:	No fee	OPEN DATES:	May-Sept
# of SINGLE SITES:	5		
		MAX STAY:	14 days
		ELEVATION:	700 feet

14 ## Excelsior Group
Seattle • lat 48°54'29" lon 121°49'18"

DESCRIPTION: This group CG is adjacent to the North Fork of the Nooksack River. Enjoy fishing for trout in the river. Supplies available in Seattle. Hike to Heather Meadows, a scenic high alpine area. CG is busy weekends and holidays. Wildlife includes deer, elk, bald eagles, mountain goats and keep an eye out for black bears.

GETTING THERE: From Seattle go N on I-5 to Bellingham. Take exit 255 off state HWY 542. Go past Glacier for 7 mi. CG is located on the North Fork of the Nooksack River.

GROUP RATE:	Varies	OPEN DATES:	May-Sept
# of GROUP SITES:	1	MAX SPUR:	30 feet
		MAX STAY:	14 days
		ELEVATION:	1300 feet

19 ## Marble Creek
Corkindale • lat 48°31'00" lon 121°16'00"

DESCRIPTION: This CG is at the confluence of Marble Creek and Cascade River. Enjoy fishing for trout in the river. Hike Glacier Peak Wilderness or visit North Cascades National Park. Busy weekends and holidays. Wildlife includes deer, elk, bald eagles, mountain goats and keep an eye out for black bears. No drinking water.

GETTING THERE: From Corkindale go NE on state HWY 20 approx. 3 mi. to county route. Go E on county route approx. 8 mi. to Marble Creek CG.

SINGLE RATE:	$7	OPEN DATES:	May-Sept
# of SINGLE SITES:	24	MAX SPUR:	30 feet
		MAX STAY:	14 days
		ELEVATION:	900 feet

15 ## Gold Basin
Granite Falls • lat 48°04'44" lon 121°44'08"

DESCRIPTION: CG rests in a mixed hardwood and conifer forest on the Stillaguamish River. Enjoy fishing for trout and steelhead. Popular activities include gold panning and this area's ice caves. Visit historic Verlot Public Service Center or hike Boulder River Wilderness. Supplies in Granite Falls. Showers provided.

GETTING THERE: From Granite Falls go E on Mountain Scenic Loop (primary forest route 20) approximately 13 miles to Gold Basin CG.

SINGLE RATE:	$12	OPEN DATES:	May-Oct
# of SINGLE SITES:	94	MAX SPUR:	45 feet
GROUP RATE:	Varies	MAX STAY:	14 days
# of GROUP SITES:	2	ELEVATION:	1200 feet

20 ## Marten Creek Group
Granite Falls • lat 48°04'18" lon 121°36'12"

DESCRIPTION: CG rests in a mixed hardwood and conifer forest at the confluence of Marten Creek and Stillaguamish River. Enjoy fishing for trout and steelhead. Popular activities include gold panning and this area's ice caves. Visit historic Verlot Public Service Center or hike Boulder River Wilderness. No drinking water.

GETTING THERE: From Granite Falls go E on Mountain Scenic Loop (primary forest route 20) approximately 20 miles to Martin Creek CG.

		OPEN DATES:	May-Sept
GROUP RATE:	$60	MAX SPUR:	75 feet
# of GROUP SITES:	1	MAX STAY:	14 days
		ELEVATION:	1100 feet

 Campground has hosts   Reservable sites   Accessible facilities   Fully developed Semi-developed   Rustic facilities

NOTE: Open dates listed are typical. Actual dates are dependent on conditions such as snow pack.

21 Miller River Group
Miller River • lat 47°41'29" lon 121°23'29"

DESCRIPTION: A group camp set among mixed fir, alder and hemlock on Miller River. Trout fish the river. No drinking water. Deer, black bears, cougars and small wildlife in area. Bring your own firewood. Fills weekends and holidays. Drive to trailheads.

GETTING THERE: From Miller River go S on county route 6410 approx. 3 mi. to Miller River Group CG.

		OPEN DATES:	May-Sept
		MAX SPUR:	30 feet
GROUP RATE:	Varies	MAX STAY:	14 days
# of GROUP SITES:	1	ELEVATION:	1000 feet

22 Mineral Park
Corkindale • lat 48°27'48" lon 121°09'50"

DESCRIPTION: This CG is on South Middle Fork Cascade River. Enjoy fishing for trout in the river. Hike in the Glacier Peak Wilderness or visit North Cascades National Park. Busy weekends and holidays. Wildlife includes deer, elk, bald eagles, mountain goats and keep an eye out for black bears. No drinking water.

GETTING THERE: From Corkindale go NE on primary route 20 (N Cascade Scenic HWY) approx. 3 mi. to the state fish hatchery. Go E on this county road approx. 15 mi. to Mineral Park CG.

SINGLE RATE:	No fee	OPEN DATES:	May-Sept
# of SINGLE SITES:	5	MAX SPUR:	30 feet
		MAX STAY:	14 days
		ELEVATION:	1400 feet

23 Money Creek
Miller River • lat 47°43'45" lon 121°24'25"

DESCRIPTION: CG is adjacent to the Skykomish River. Piped water throughout campground. Garbage service is available. Fish for trout on river. Train tracks run behind CG for those wishing to see a running train. Fills weekends. Gather or buy firewood on site. Drive to trailheads.

GETTING THERE: From Miller River go NW on forest route 6030 2 miles to Money Creek CG.

SINGLE RATE:	$12	OPEN DATES:	May-Oct
# of SINGLE SITES:	24	MAX SPUR:	30 feet
		MAX STAY:	14 days
		ELEVATION:	850 feet

24 Monte Cristo
Granite Falls • lat 47°59'14" lon 121°23'34"

DESCRIPTION: This tent only CG is set in hemlock on the South Fork Sauk River. Enjoy fishing for trout on the river. Wildlife in the area includes black bears, deer, and raptors. Visit the historic ghost town nearby or hike into the Henry M. Jackson Wilderness. No drinking water. Mountain biking nearby.

GETTING THERE: From Granite Falls go E on Mountain Scenic Loop (primary forest route 20) 30 mi. to forest route South 4710. Go S on 4710 approx. 4.5 mi. to Monte Cristo CG. Hike or bike in from parking area.

SINGLE RATE:	No fee	OPEN DATES:	May-Sept
# of SINGLE SITES:	8		
		MAX STAY:	14 days
		ELEVATION:	1000 feet

25 Mount Pilchuck
Granite Falls • lat 48°04'04" lon 121°48'45"

DESCRIPTION: This CG is a walk-in only that rests in a meadow. CG sits on the fringe of tree level subalpine fir with a small creek. Enjoy panoramic views of Puget Sound. Hike to historic Mt. Pilchuck Lookout. Gather firewood locally. Deer, bears and raptors are in area. Mountain. climbing and hiking in area. No drinking water.

GETTING THERE: Mount Pilchuckt CG is located approx. 12 mi. E of Granite Falls off of Mountain Scenic Loop (primary forest route 20). Follow signs.

SINGLE RATE:	No fee	OPEN DATES:	May-Sept
# of SINGLE SITES:	5	MAX SPUR:	75 feet
		MAX STAY:	14 days
		ELEVATION:	3000 feet

26 Panorama Point
Grassmere • lat 48°43'22" lon 121°40'10"

DESCRIPTION: This CG is on Baker Lake among fir, hemlock, and cedar. Enjoy fishing for trout in the lake but please check fishing regulations Hike on the nearby Shadow of Sentinals Nature Trail which is barrier free. Wildlife includes deer, elk, bald eagles and keep an eye out for black bears. No drinking water.

GETTING THERE: From Grassmere go N on primary route 11 approx. 15 mi. to Panorama Point CG.

SINGLE RATE:	$12	OPEN DATES:	May-Sept
# of SINGLE SITES:	16	MAX SPUR:	45 feet
		MAX STAY:	14 days
		ELEVATION:	700 feet

27 Park Creek
Grassmere • lat 48°44'06" lon 121°39'55"

DESCRIPTION: This CG is adjacent Baker Lake among fir, hemlock, and cedar. Enjoy fishing for trout in the river. Hike on the nearby Shadow of Sentinals Nature Trail which is barrier free. Wildlife includes deer, elk, bald eagles and keep an eye out for black bears. No drinking water.

GETTING THERE: From Grassmere go N on primary route 11 approx. 16 mi. to Park Creek CG.

SINGLE RATE:	$8	OPEN DATES:	May-Sept
# of SINGLE SITES:	12	MAX SPUR:	40 feet
		MAX STAY:	14 days
		ELEVATION:	700 feet

28 Red Bridge
Granite Falls • lat 48°04'20" lon 121°39'10"

DESCRIPTION: CG rests in a mixed hardwood and conifer forest on the Stillaguamish River. Enjoy fishing for trout and steelhead. Popular activities include gold panning and this area's ice caves. Visit historic Verlot Public Service Center or hike Boulder River Wilderness. Supplies in Granite Falls. No drinking water.

GETTING THERE: From Granite Falls go E on Mountain Scenic Loop (primary forest route 20) approximately 18 miles to Red Bridge CG.

SINGLE RATE:	$7	OPEN DATES:	May-Sept
# of SINGLE SITES:	16	MAX SPUR:	54 feet
		MAX STAY:	14 days
		ELEVATION:	1100 feet

29 San Juan
Gold Bar • lat 47°53'21" lon 121°21'55"

DESCRIPTION: On the North Fork Skykomish River in mixed fir, alder and hemlock forest. No drinking water. Deer, black bears, cougars and small wildlife in area. Fills weekends. Bring your own firewood. Drive to trailheads.

GETTING THERE: From Gold Bar go SE on US HWY 2 approx. 7 mi. to primary forest route 63. Go NE on 63 approx. 14 mi. to San Juan CG.

SINGLE RATE:	$7	OPEN DATES:	May-Oct
# of SINGLE SITES:	8		
		MAX STAY:	14 days
		ELEVATION:	1100 feet

30 Shannon Creek
Grassmere • lat 48°44'20" lon 121°35'54"

DESCRIPTION: This CG is adjacent to Baker Lake among fir, hemlock, and cedar. Enjoy fishing for trout in the lake but please check fishing regulations Hike on the nearby Shadow of Sentinals Nature Trail which is barrier free. Wildlife includes deer, elk, bald eagles and keep an eye out for black bears. No drinking water.

GETTING THERE: From Grassmere go N on primary route 11 approx. 20 mi. to Shannon Creek CG.

SINGLE RATE:	$12	OPEN DATES:	May-Sept
# of SINGLE SITES:	19	MAX SPUR:	26 feet
		MAX STAY:	14 days
		ELEVATION:	700 feet

 Campground has hosts 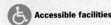 **Reservable sites** 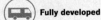 **Accessible facilities**   **Fully developed**   **Semi-developed**   **Rustic facilities**

NOTE: Open dates listed are typical. Actual dates are dependent on conditions such as snow pack.

31 Silver Fir
Glacier • lat 48°54'16" lon 121°42'03"

DESCRIPTION: This group CG is adjacent to the North Fork of the Nooksack River. Enjoy fishing for trout in the river. Hike to Heather Meadows, a scenic high alpine area. CG is busy weekends and holidays. Wildlife includes deer, elk, bald eagles, mountain goats and keep an eye out for black bears. Supplies in Glacier.

GETTING THERE: From Glacier go NE on state HWY 542 approximately 11 miles to Silver Fir CG.

SINGLE RATE:	$12	OPEN DATES:	May-Sept
# of SINGLE SITES:	21	MAX SPUR:	30 feet
GROUP RATE:	$50	MAX STAY:	14 days
# of GROUP SITES:	1	ELEVATION:	2000 feet

32 Silver Springs
Greenwater • lat 46°59'46" lon 121°31'52"

DESCRIPTION: This CG is situated in mixed conifer along the White River. This CG offers a picnic shelter, fishing, and hiking. Wildlife in this area includes bears, elk, coyotes, and raptors. Enjoy a drive to Crystal Mountain Ski Area and ride the lift for a bird's eye view of Mount Rainier. Firewood is sold on site.

GETTING THERE: From Greenwater go S on state HWY 410 approx. 14 mi. to Silver Springs CG.

SINGLE RATE:	$12	OPEN DATES:	May-Sept*
# of SINGLE SITES:	56	MAX SPUR:	40 feet
GROUP RATE:	$50	MAX STAY:	14 days
# of GROUP SITES:	1	ELEVATION:	2640 feet

33 Sulphur Creek
Darrington • lat 48°14'55" lon 121°11'36"

DESCRIPTION: This CG is situated in mixed conifer and hardwoods at the confluence of Sulpher Creek and Suittle River. Fish for trout. Hike an on-site trail to hot springs or the Suittle Trail, a major Glacier Peak Wilderness trailhead. Supplies in Darrington. Black bears and deer in area. No drinking water.

GETTING THERE: From Darrington go N on state HWY 30 approx. 7 mi. to primary forest route 26. Go NE on 26 approx. 23 mi. to Sulphur Creek CG.

SINGLE RATE:	$8	OPEN DATES:	May-Sept
# of SINGLE SITES:	20	MAX SPUR:	30 feet
		MAX STAY:	14 days
		ELEVATION:	2000 feet

34 The Dalles
Greenwater • lat 47°06'16" lon 121°34'36"

DESCRIPTION: This CG is situated in mixed conifer along the White River. Nearby nature trails lead to very large, old growth trees. Wildlife in this area includes bears, elk, coyotes, and raptors. Enjoy a drive to Crystal Mountain Ski Area and ride the lift for a bird's eye view of Mount Rainier. Firewood is sold on site.

GETTING THERE: From Greenwater go S on state HWY 410 approx. 8 mi. to The Dalles CG.

SINGLE RATE:	$12	OPEN DATES:	May-Sept*
# of SINGLE SITES:	46	MAX SPUR:	45 feet
GROUP RATE:	$50	MAX STAY:	14 days
# of GROUP SITES:	1	ELEVATION:	2140 feet

35 Tinkham
North Bend • lat 47°23'30" lon 121°33'30"

DESCRIPTION: This CG is adjacent to the Snoqualmie River. Enjoy a hike on the Asahel Curtis Nature Trail. This trail runs through lush old-growth forest and crosses Humpback Creek. Wildlife includes winter wrens and pileated woodpecker. Firewood may be sold at campground. Supplies in North Bend.

GETTING THERE: From North Bend go SE on US HWY 90 approx. 11 mi. to Tinkham CG.

SINGLE RATE:	$12	OPEN DATES:	May-Sept
# of SINGLE SITES:	47	MAX SPUR:	45 feet
		MAX STAY:	14 days
		ELEVATION:	1500 feet

36 Troublesome Creek
Gold Bar • lat 47°53'52" lon 121°24'09"

DESCRIPTION: At the North Fork Skykomish River confluence with Troublesome Creek in mixed fir, alder and hemlock forest. Deer, black bears, cougars and small wildlife in area. Fills weekends. Bring your own firewood. Drive to trailheads or use the nice 1 mile trail on-site.

GETTING THERE: From Gold Bar go SE on US HWY 2 approx. 7 mi. to primary forest route 63. Go NE on 63 approx. 12 mi. to Troublesome Creek CG.

SINGLE RATE:	$12	OPEN DATES:	May-Sept
# of SINGLE SITES:	30	MAX SPUR:	35 feet
		MAX STAY:	14 days
		ELEVATION:	980 feet

37 Tulalip Millsite Group
Granite Falls • lat 48°03'43" lon 121°37'52"

DESCRIPTION: CG rests in a mixed hardwood and conifer forest on the Stillaguamish River. Enjoy fishing for trout and steelhead. Popular activities include gold panning and this area's ice caves. Visit historic Verlot Public Service Center or hike Boulder River Wilderness. Supplies in Granite Falls. No drinking water.

GETTING THERE: From Granite Falls go E on Mountain Scenic Loop (primary forest route 20) approximately 19 miles to Tulalip Millsite Group CG.

		OPEN DATES:	May-Oct
		MAX SPUR:	45 feet
GROUP RATE:	$75	MAX STAY:	14 days
# of GROUP SITES:	1	ELEVATION:	1200 feet

38 Turlo
Granite Falls • lat 48°05'33" lon 121°47'02"

DESCRIPTION: CG rests in a mixed hardwood and conifer forest on the Stillaguamish River. Enjoy fishing for trout and steelhead. Popular activities include gold panning and this area's ice caves. Visit historic Verlot Public Service Center or hike Boulder River Wilderness. Supplies in Granite Falls.

GETTING THERE: From Granite Falls go E on Mountain Scenic Loop (primary forest route 20) approximately 11 miles to Turlo CG.

SINGLE RATE:	$12	OPEN DATES:	May-Sept
# of SINGLE SITES:	19	MAX SPUR:	40 feet
		MAX STAY:	14 days
		ELEVATION:	1200 feet

39 Verlot
Granite Falls • lat 48°05'24" lon 121°46'36"

DESCRIPTION: CG rests in a mixed hardwood and conifer forest on the Stillaguamish River. Enjoy fishing for trout and steelhead. Popular activities include gold panning and this area's ice caves. Visit historic Verlot Public Service Center or hike Boulder River Wilderness. Supplies in Granite Falls.

GETTING THERE: From Granite Falls go E on Mountain Scenic Loop (primary forest route 20) approximately 12 miles to Verlot CG.

SINGLE RATE:	$12	OPEN DATES:	May-Sept
# of SINGLE SITES:	26	MAX SPUR:	40 feet
		MAX STAY:	14 days
		ELEVATION:	1200 feet

40 Wiley Creek
Granite Falls • lat 48°04'26" lon 121°42'52"

DESCRIPTION: CG rests in a mixed hardwood and conifer forest on the Stillaguamish River. Enjoy fishing for trout and steelhead. Popular activities include gold panning and this area's ice caves. Visit historic Verlot Public Service Center or hike Boulder River Wilderness. Supplies in Granite Falls. No drinking water.

GETTING THERE: From Granite Falls go E on Mountain Scenic Loop (primary forest route 20) approximately 13 miles to Willey Creek CG.

		OPEN DATES:	May-Oct
		MAX SPUR:	45 feet
GROUP RATE:	$60	MAX STAY:	14 days
# of GROUP SITES:	1	ELEVATION:	1200 feet

 Campground has hosts   **Reservable sites**   **Accessible facilities**   **Fully developed**   **Semi-developed**   **Rustic facilities**

NOTE: Open dates listed are typical. Actual dates are dependent on conditions such as snow pack.

Okanogan National Forest

The Okanogan is located in north-central Washington and extends from the Canadian boundary south to the Methow-Chalan Divide. There are over a million acres of land ranging from craggy peaks to rolling meadows, rich old growth forest, and classic groves of ponderosa pine. Called the Sunny Okanogan, summers are hot and dry while the winters are famous for brilliant clear skies and plenty of snow.

The Okanaogan got its name from an Indian word meaning "rendezvous," applied to the section of the Okanogan Valley where the Indians of British Columbia and Washington often gathered for their annual potlatch.

The Okanogan is still a rendezvous for millions of visitors annually, offering plenty of outdoor activities. Two congressionally designated wilderness areas provide thousands of remote acres where visitors can find peace and solitude. The Okanogan offers miles of trails to explore by mountain bike, foot or horse, numerous pristine lakes to swim in, and scenic drives including the North Cascades Scenic Highway, the first national scenic highway in the nation. The forest is also a fisherman's paradise full of glacier-fed rivers and streams.

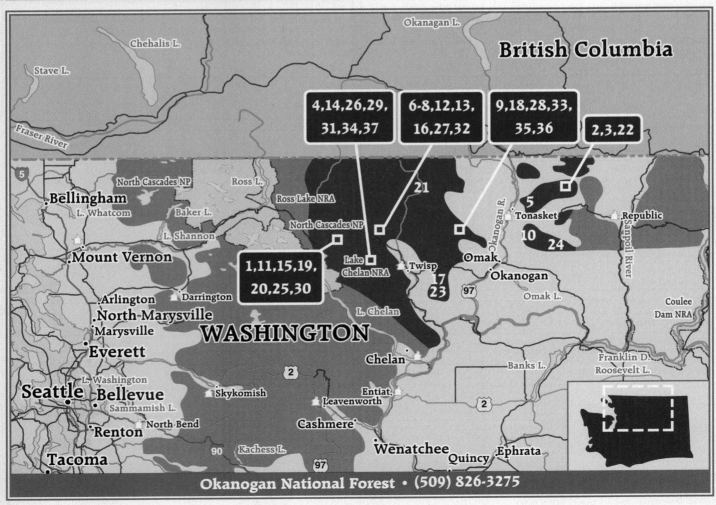

Okanogan National Forest • (509) 826-3275

1 Ballard
Mazama • lat 48°39'31" lon 120°32'36"

DESCRIPTION: In an old growth pine forest setting on the Methow River. Fish and swim in the river. Supplies available at Mazama. Deer, bears and birds are common to the area. Trail near CG leading to the Pasayten Wilderness.

GETTING THERE: Ballard CG is located approx. 9 mi. NW of Mazama on county route 1163 (forest route 5400).

SINGLE RATE:	Varies	OPEN DATES:	Apr-Nov
# of SINGLE SITES:	7	MAX SPUR:	22 feet
		MAX STAY:	5 days
		ELEVATION:	2521 feet

6 Buck Lake
Winthrop • lat 48°36'20" lon 120°12'04"

DESCRIPTION: In an old growth pine forest setting on the Buck Lake. Fish and swim in the lake. Boat ramp located at CG. Supplies available at Winthrop. Deer, bears and birds are common to the area. Campers may gather firewood. No designated trails nearby.

GETTING THERE: From Winthrop go N on county route 1213 approx. 7 mi. to primary forest route 51. Go N on 51 approx. 2 mi. to forest route 5130. Go NW on 5130 approx. 1/4 mi. to forest route 100. Go W on 100 approx. 2 mi. to Buck Lake CG.

SINGLE RATE:	Varies	OPEN DATES:	Apr-Nov
# of SINGLE SITES:	9	MAX SPUR:	16 feet
		MAX STAY:	14 days
		ELEVATION:	3250 feet

2 Beaver Lake
Wauconda • lat 48°51'00" lon 118°58'02"

DESCRIPTION: This CG is located in a mixed conifer setting on Beaver Lake. Enjoy fishing for trout and swimming in the lake. Supplies are available at Wauconda. Wildlife in this area includes deer, bears and birds. Campers may gather dead and down firewood. There is a trail nearby that leads to the Beth Lake area.

GETTING THERE: From Wauconda go SW on state HWY 20 approx. 3 mi. to county route 4953. Go N on 4953 approx. 12 mi. to Beaver Lake CG. Road is narrow with sharp curves. Large vehicles should use caution.

SINGLE RATE:	$6	OPEN DATES:	Yearlong
# of SINGLE SITES:	11	MAX SPUR:	22 feet
		MAX STAY:	14 days
		ELEVATION:	3000 feet

7 Camp 4
Winthrop • lat 48°42'55" lon 120°07'26"

DESCRIPTION: In an old growth pine forest setting on the Windy Creek. Fish and swim in the creek. Supplies available at Carlton. Deer, bears and birds are common to the area. Campers may gather firewood. No designated trails nearby. Tent only camping.

GETTING THERE: From Winthrop go N on county route 1213 approx. 6 mi. to primary forest route 51. Go N on 51 approx. 11 mi. to Camp 4 CG.

SINGLE RATE:	Varies	OPEN DATES:	Apr-Nov
# of SINGLE SITES:	5	MAX SPUR:	16 feet
		MAX STAY:	14 days
		ELEVATION:	2384 feet

3 Beth Lake
Wauconda • lat 48°51'25" lon 118°58'51"

DESCRIPTION: This CG is set in a mixed forest setting on Beth Lake. Fish for trout and swim in the lake. Boat ramp at the CG. Supplies available at Wauconda. Deer, bears and birds are common to the area. Campers may gather firewood. Trail nearby leads to Beaver Lake area. Visit nearby Big Tree Botanical Area.

GETTING THERE: From Wauconda go SW 3 mi. on state HWY 20 to county route 4953. Go N 12 mi. on 4953 to county route 9480. Go NW 1 mi. on 9480 to Beth Lake CG. Road is narrow with sharp curves. Large vehicles use caution.

SINGLE RATE:	$6	OPEN DATES:	Yearlong
# of SINGLE SITES:	15	MAX SPUR:	32 feet
		MAX STAY:	14 days
		ELEVATION:	2900 feet

8 Chewuch
Winthrop • lat 48°40'39" lon 120°07'43"

DESCRIPTION: In an old growth pine forest setting on the Windy Creek. Fish and swim in the creek. Supplies available at Winthrop. Deer, bears and birds are common to the area. Campers may gather firewood. No designated trails nearby. Tent only camping.

GETTING THERE: From Winthrop go N on county route 9137 approx. 6 mi. to forest route 5010. Go N on 5010 approx. 15 mi. to Chewuch CG.

SINGLE RATE:	Varies	OPEN DATES:	Apr-Nov
# of SINGLE SITES:	4	MAX SPUR:	16 feet
		MAX STAY:	14 days
		ELEVATION:	2278 feet

4 Blackpine Lake
Carlton • lat 48°18'49" lon 120°16'26"

DESCRIPTION: In an old growth pine forest setting on the Blackpine Lake. Fish and swim in the lake. Boat ramp located at CG. Supplies available at Carlton. Deer, bears and birds are common to the area. Campers may gather firewood. No designated trails nearby.

GETTING THERE: From Carlton go NW on county route 1049 approx. 1.5 mi. to primary forest route 43. Go NW on 43 approx. 11 mi. to Blackpine Lake CG.

SINGLE RATE:	Varies	OPEN DATES:	Apr-Nov
# of SINGLE SITES:	24	MAX SPUR:	22 feet
		MAX STAY:	14 days
		ELEVATION:	4200 feet

9 Cottonwood
Conconully • lat 48°35'15" lon 119°45'45"

DESCRIPTION: CG is in a mixed forest setting on Salmon Creek. Fish for trout and swim in the creek or in nearby Conconully Lake. Boat ramp at lake. Supplies available at Conconully. Deer, bears and birds are common to the area. Campers may gather firewood. Sunny Peak Mine and Wheeler Mine are both near the CG area.

GETTING THERE: Cottonwood CG is located approx. 2 mi. N of Conconully on county route 2361 (primary forest route 38).

SINGLE RATE:	$5	OPEN DATES:	Apr-Nov
# of SINGLE SITES:	4	MAX SPUR:	22 feet
		MAX STAY:	14 days
		ELEVATION:	2700 feet

5 Bonaparte Lake
Wauconda • lat 48°47'36" lon 119°03'36"

DESCRIPTION: This CG is set in a mixed conifer forest on Bonaparte Lake. Fish for trout and swim in the lake. Boat ramp at the CG. Supplies available at Wauconda. Deer, bears and birds are common to the area. Campers may gather firewood. There is a trail at South end of lake with views of Bonaparte Meadows.

GETTING THERE: From Wauconda go SW on state HWY 20 approx. 3 mi. to county route 4953 (primary forest route 32). Go N on 4953 approx. 6 mi. to Bonaparte Lake CG.

SINGLE RATE:	$8	OPEN DATES:	Yearlong
# of SINGLE SITES:	28	MAX SPUR:	32 feet
GROUP RATE:	Varies	MAX STAY:	14 days
# of GROUP SITES:	1	ELEVATION:	3600 feet

10 Crawfish Lake
Synarep • lat 48°29'02" lon 119°12'47"

DESCRIPTION: This CG is situated in a mixed conifer forest on Crawfish Lake with Lost Creek Meadow nearby. Enjoy fishing for trout and swimming in the lake. There is a boat ramp at the CG. Supplies are available at Synarep. Deer, bears and birds are common to the area. Campers may gather dead and down firewood.

GETTING THERE: From Synarep go SE on county route 9320 (primary forest route 30-100) approx. 7 mi. to Crawfish Lake CG.

SINGLE RATE:	No fee	OPEN DATES:	Apr-Nov
# of SINGLE SITES:	19	MAX SPUR:	32 feet
		MAX STAY:	14 days
		ELEVATION:	4500 feet

 Campground has hosts 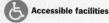 **Reservable sites**  **Accessible facilities**   **Fully developed**   **Semi-developed** **Rustic facilities**

NOTE: Open dates listed are typical. Actual dates are dependent on conditions such as snow pack.

11 Early Winters
Mazama • lat 48°35'50" lon 120°26'41"

DESCRIPTION: In an old growth pine forest setting on the Early Winters Creek. Fish and swim in the creek. Supplies available at Mazama. Deer, bears and birds are common to the area. Campers may gather firewood. No designated trails nearby.

GETTING THERE: Early Winters CG is located approx. 2 mi. W of Mazama off of state HWY 20.

SINGLE RATE:	Varies	OPEN DATES:	Apr-Nov
# of SINGLE SITES:	12	MAX SPUR:	16 feet
		MAX STAY:	5 days
		ELEVATION:	2160 feet

16 Honeymoon
Winthrop • lat 48°41'49" lon 120°15'49"

DESCRIPTION: In an old growth pine forest setting on Eightmile Creek with views of Eightmile Ridge. Fish and swim in the creek. Supplies available at Winthrop. Deer, bears and birds are common to the area. Campers may gather firewood. No designated trails nearby.

GETTING THERE: From Winthrop go N on county route 1213 approx. 7 mi. to primary forest route 51. Go N on 51 approx. 2 mi. to forest route 5130. Go NW on 5130 approx. 9 mi. to Honeymoon CG.

SINGLE RATE:	Varies	OPEN DATES:	Apr-Nov
# of SINGLE SITES:	6	MAX SPUR:	16 feet
		MAX STAY:	14 days
		ELEVATION:	3280 feet

12 Falls Creek
Winthrop • lat 48°38'05" lon 120°09'17"

DESCRIPTION: In an old growth pine forest setting on Falls Creek with views of Paul Mountain. Fish and swim in the creek. Supplies available at Winthrop. Deer, bears and birds are common to the area. Campers may gather firewood. No designated trails nearby. Tent only CG.

GETTING THERE: From Winthrop go N on county route 1213 approx. 6 mi. to primary forest route 51. Go N on 51 approx. 5 mi. to Falls Creek CG.

SINGLE RATE:	Varies	OPEN DATES:	Apr-Nov
# of SINGLE SITES:	6		
		MAX STAY:	14 days
		ELEVATION:	2100 feet

17 JR
Twisp • lat 48°23'22" lon 119°53'41"

DESCRIPTION: In an old growth pine forest setting on Frazer Creek with views of Little Buck Mountain nearby. Fish and swim from either creek. Supplies available at Twisp. Deer, bears and birds are common to the area. Campers may gather firewood. Loup Loup ski area is nearby.

GETTING THERE: From Twisp go NE on state HWY 20 approx. 10 mi. to JR CG.

SINGLE RATE:	Varies	OPEN DATES:	Apr-Nov
# of SINGLE SITES:	6	MAX SPUR:	16 feet
		MAX STAY:	14 days
		ELEVATION:	3900 feet

13 Flat
Winthrop • lat 48°36'54" lon 120°11'41"

DESCRIPTION: In an old growth pine forest setting on Eightmile Creek. Fish and swim in the creek. Supplies available at Winthrop. Deer, bears and birds are common to the area. Campers may gather firewood. No designated trails nearby. Tent only CG.

GETTING THERE: From Winthrop go N on county route 1213 approx. 7 mi. to primary forest route 51. Go N on 51 approx. 2 mi. to forest route 5130. Go NW on 5130 approx. 2 mi. to Flat CG.

SINGLE RATE:	Varies	OPEN DATES:	Apr-Nov
# of SINGLE SITES:	9		
		MAX STAY:	14 days
		ELEVATION:	2858 feet

18 Kerr
Conconully • lat 48°36'33" lon 119°47'07"

DESCRIPTION: Set in a mixed forest setting on Salmon Creek. Fish for trout and swim in the creek. Supplies available at Conconully. Deer, bears and birds are common to the area. Campers may gather firewood. No designated trails in the area.

GETTING THERE: From Conconully go NW on county route 2361 (primary forest route 38) approx. 3.5 mi. to Kerr CG.

SINGLE RATE:	$5	OPEN DATES:	Apr-Nov
# of SINGLE SITES:	13	MAX SPUR:	22 feet
		MAX STAY:	14 days
		ELEVATION:	3100 feet

14 Foggy Dew
Methow • lat 48°12'19" lon 120°11'27"

DESCRIPTION: In an old growth pine forest setting on Gold Creek and Foggy Dew Creek. Fish and swim in either creek. Supplies available at Methow. Deer, bears and birds are common to the area. Campers may gather firewood. No designated trails nearby. Tent only CG.

GETTING THERE: From Methow go NW on state HWY 153 approx. 3.5 mi. to county route 1034. Go W on 1034 approx. 1 mi. to forest route 4340. Go W on 4340 approx. 4 mi. to Foggy Dew CG.

SINGLE RATE:	Varies	OPEN DATES:	Apr-Nov
# of SINGLE SITES:	13		
		MAX STAY:	14 days
		ELEVATION:	2400 feet

19 Klipchuck
Mazama • lat 48°35'49" lon 120°30'44"

DESCRIPTION: In an old growth pine forest setting on Early Winters Creek. Fish and swim in the creek. Supplies available at Mazama. Deer, bears and birds are common to the area. Campers may gather firewood. There is a trail leading from CG area to the Driveway Butte.

GETTING THERE: From Mazama go W approx. 6 mi. on state HWY 20 to forest route 5310300. On 5310300 go NW approx. 1 mi. to Klipchuck CG.

SINGLE RATE:	Varies	OPEN DATES:	Apr-Nov
# of SINGLE SITES:	46	MAX SPUR:	32 feet
		MAX STAY:	5 days
		ELEVATION:	2920 feet

15 Harts Pass
Mazama • lat 48°43'14" lon 120°40'07"

DESCRIPTION: This dispersed, rustic horse camp is in an old growth pine forest setting. Supplies available at Mazama. Deer, bears and birds are common to the area. Campers may gather firewood. Many trails nearby. Near the Pacific Crest National Scenic Trail. Horse ramp at CG. No water at this CG.

GETTING THERE: From Mazama go NW on county route 1163 approx. 5 mi. to forest route 5400. Follow 5400 approx. 24 mi. to Harts Pass CG.

SINGLE RATE:	Varies	OPEN DATES:	Apr-Nov
# of SINGLE SITES:	5		
		MAX STAY:	14 days
		ELEVATION:	6198 feet

20 Lone Fir
Mazama • lat 48°34'48" lon 120°37'33"

DESCRIPTION: In an old growth pine forest setting on Early Winters Creek. Fish and swim in the creek. Supplies available at Mazama. Deer, bears and birds are common to the area. Campers may gather firewood. No designated trails nearby.

GETTING THERE: From Mazama go W on state HWY 20 approx. 12 mi. to Lone Fir CG.

SINGLE RATE:	Varies	OPEN DATES:	Apr-Nov
# of SINGLE SITES:	27	MAX SPUR:	22 feet
		MAX STAY:	5 days
		ELEVATION:	3640 feet

 Campground has hosts   **Reservable sites**   **Accessible facilities**   **Fully developed**   **Semi-developed**   **Rustic facilities**

NOTE: Open dates listed are typical. Actual dates are dependent on conditions such as snow pack.

21  Long Swamp
Loomis • lat 49°50'00" lon 119°56'30"

DESCRIPTION: Set in a mixed forest setting on Long Swamp. Fish for trout or swim at Long Swamp CG. Supplies available at Loomis. Deer, bears and birds are common to the area. Campers may gather firewood. Trails leading from CG to the Pasayten Wilderness. Horse ramps at the CG.

GETTING THERE: From Loomis go N on county route 9425 approx. 2 mi. to primary forest route 39. Go W on 39 approx. 19 mi. to Long Swamp CG.

SINGLE RATE:	Varies	OPEN DATES:	Apr-Nov
# of SINGLE SITES:	2		
		MAX STAY:	14 days
		ELEVATION:	5500 feet

22 Lost Lake
Chesaw • lat 48°51'08" lon 119°03'05"

DESCRIPTION: Set in a mixed forest setting on Lost Lake. Fish for trout and swim in the lake. Supplies available at Havillah. Deer, bears and birds are common to the area. Campers may gather firewood. Trail to Strawberry Mountain in the area. Big Tree Botanical Area nearby.

GETTING THERE: From Chesaw go S on county route 9480 approx. 2 mi. to county route 4887 (primary forest route 34). Go S on 4887 approx. 4.5 mi. to Lost Lake CG.

SINGLE RATE:	$8	OPEN DATES:	Apr-Nov
# of SINGLE SITES:	18	MAX SPUR:	22 feet
GROUP RATE:	Varies	MAX STAY:	14 days
# of GROUP SITES:	1	ELEVATION:	3800 feet

23 Loup Loup
Twisp • lat 48°23'45" lon 119°54'05"

DESCRIPTION: In an old growth pine forest setting with many creeks in the area. Fish and swim in the many creeks. Supplies available at Twisp. Deer, bears and birds are common to the area. Campers may gather firewood. Trails in the area for hiking. Ski area close by.

GETTING THERE: From Twisp go E on state HWY 20 approx. 10 mi. to primary forest route 42. Go N on 42 approx 1/2 mi. to Loup Loup CG.

SINGLE RATE:	Varies	OPEN DATES:	Apr-Nov
# of SINGLE SITES:	20	MAX SPUR:	22 feet
		MAX STAY:	14 days
		ELEVATION:	4460 feet

24 Lyman Lake
Tonasket • lat 48°32'00" lon 119°01'00"

DESCRIPTION: In a mixed forest setting on Lyman Lake. Fish for trout and swim in the lake. Supplies available at Tonasket. Numerous wildlife can be seen in the area. Campers may gather firewood. No designated trails.

GETTING THERE: From Tonasket go E on state HWY 20 to county route 9455. Go SE 13 mi. on 9455 to county route 3785. Go S 3 mi. on 3785 to forest route 500. Go W 1/2 mi. on 500 to Lyman Lake CG.

SINGLE RATE:	No fee	OPEN DATES:	Apr-Nov
# of SINGLE SITES:	4		
		MAX STAY:	14 days
		ELEVATION:	2900 feet

25 Meadows
Mazama • lat 48°42'39" lon 120°40'30"

DESCRIPTION: This tent only CG is in an old growth pine forest setting near a creek. Fish and swim in the nearby creek. Supplies available at Mazama. Deer, bears and birds are common to the area. Campers may gather firewood. The Pacific Crest National Scenic Trail which runs through the CG. No trailers at this CG.

GETTING THERE: From Mazama go N approx. 6 mi. to state HWY 5400. Go NW on 5400 approx. 21 mi. to forest route 500. Go S on 500 approx. 1.5 mi. to Meadows CG.

SINGLE RATE:	Varies	OPEN DATES:	Apr-Nov
# of SINGLE SITES:	14		
		MAX STAY:	5 days
		ELEVATION:	6200 feet

26 Mystery
Twisp • lat 48°24'08" lon 120°28'14"

DESCRIPTION: In an old growth pine forest setting on the Twisp River. Fish and swim in the river. Supplies available at Twisp. Deer, bears and birds are common to the area. Campers may gather firewood. Hiking trails near the CG area.

GETTING THERE: From Twisp go W on primary forest route 44 approx. 16 mi. to Mystery CG.

SINGLE RATE:	Varies	OPEN DATES:	Apr-Nov
# of SINGLE SITES:	21	MAX SPUR:	16 feet
		MAX STAY:	14 days
		ELEVATION:	2800 feet

27 Nice
Winthrop • lat 48°37'56" lon 120°13'13"

DESCRIPTION: This tent only CG is in an old growth pine forest setting on Eightmile Creek. Fish and swim in the creek. Supplies available at Winthrop. Deer, bears and birds are common to the area. Campers may gather firewood. Trails can be found in the area.

GETTING THERE: From Winthrop go N on county route 1213 approx. 7 mi. to primary forest route 51. Go N on 51 approx. 2 mi. to forest route 5130. Go NW on 5130 approx. 3 mi. to Nice CG.

SINGLE RATE:	Varies	OPEN DATES:	Apr-Nov
# of SINGLE SITES:	3	MAX SPUR:	16 feet
		MAX STAY:	14 days
		ELEVATION:	2738 feet

28 Oriole
Conconully • lat 48°35'39" lon 119°46'16"

DESCRIPTION: Set in a mixed forest setting on Salmon Creek. Fish for trout and swim in the creek. Supplies available at Conconully. Deer, bears and birds are common to the area. Campers may gather firewood. No designated trails in the area. Sunny Peak and Wheeler mines are in the area.

GETTING THERE: From Conconully go N on primary forest route 38 (county route 2361) approx. 3 mi. to forest route 38-026. Go left approx. 1 mi. to Oriole CG.

SINGLE RATE:	$5	OPEN DATES:	Apr-Nov
# of SINGLE SITES:	10	MAX SPUR:	22 feet
		MAX STAY:	14 days
		ELEVATION:	2900 feet

29 Poplar Flat
Twisp • lat 48°25'18" lon 120°29'51"

DESCRIPTION: In an old growth pine forest setting on Twisp River with views of the wilderness. Fish and swim in the river. Supplies available at Mazama. Deer, bears and birds are common to the area. Campers may gather firewood. There is a trail leading from CG area to the Driveway Butte.

GETTING THERE: From Twisp go W on primary forest route 44 approx. 18 mi. to Poplar Flat CG.

SINGLE RATE:	Varies	OPEN DATES:	Apr-Nov
# of SINGLE SITES:	15	MAX SPUR:	22 feet
		MAX STAY:	14 days
		ELEVATION:	2900 feet

30 River Bend
Mazama • lat 48°38'00" lon 120°33'00"

DESCRIPTION: In an old growth pine forest setting on Methow River. Fish or swim in the river. Supplies available at Mazama. Deer, bears and birds are common to the area. Campers may gather firewood. Trail leading from CG to the Pacific Crest National Scenic Trail.

GETTING THERE: River Bend CG is approx. 9 mi. NW of Mazama on county route 1163 (forest route 5400).

SINGLE RATE:	Varies	OPEN DATES:	Apr-Nov
# of SINGLE SITES:	5	MAX SPUR:	22 feet
		MAX STAY:	5 days
		ELEVATION:	2600 feet

 Campground has hosts   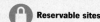 **Reservable sites**   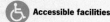 **Accessible facilities**   **Fully developed**   **Semi-developed**   **Rustic facilities**

NOTE: Open dates listed are typical. Actual dates are dependent on conditions such as snow pack.

31 Roads End
Twisp • lat 48°27'42" lon 120°34'27"

DESCRIPTION: This primitive CG is in an old growth pine forest setting on Twisp River. Fish and swim from the river. Supplies available at Twisp. Deer, bears and birds are common to the area. Campers may gather firewood. Trail leading from CG to the Pacific Crest National Scenic Trail.

GETTING THERE: From Twisp go W on primary forest route 44 approx. 23 mi. to South Creek CG.

SINGLE RATE:	Varies	OPEN DATES:	Apr-Nov
# of SINGLE SITES:	4	MAX STAY:	14 days
		ELEVATION:	3600 feet

32 Ruffed Grouse
Winthrop • lat 48°40'52" lon 120°15'26"

DESCRIPTION: In an old growth pine forest setting on Eightmile Creek with views of Eightmile Ridge. Fish or swim in the creek. Supplies available at Winthrop. Deer, bears and birds are common to the area. Campers may gather firewood. No designated trails nearby.

GETTING THERE: From Winthrop go N on county route 1213 approx. 7 mi. to primary forest route 51. Go N on 51 approx. 2 mi. to forest route 5130. Go NW on 5130 approx. 7.5 mi. to Ruffed Grouse CG.

SINGLE RATE:	Varies	OPEN DATES:	Apr-Nov
# of SINGLE SITES:	4	MAX SPUR:	14 feet
		MAX STAY:	14 days
		ELEVATION:	3120 feet

33 Salmon Meadows
Conconully • lat 48°39'33" lon 119°50'25"

DESCRIPTION: Set in a mixed forest setting on Mutton Creek. Fish for trout and swim in the creek. Supplies available at Conconully. Deer, bears and birds are common to the area. Campers may gather firewood. Trail from CG to nearby Tiffany springs, lake and meadow.

GETTING THERE: From Conconully go NW on primary forest route 38 (county route 2361) approx. 9 mi. to Salmon Meadows CG.

SINGLE RATE:	$5	OPEN DATES:	Apr-Nov
# of SINGLE SITES:	7	MAX SPUR:	22 feet
		MAX STAY:	14 days
		ELEVATION:	4480 feet

34 South Creek
Twisp • lat 48°26'17" lon 120°31'41"

DESCRIPTION: This CG is located on the Deschutes River among ponderosa pines. Enjoy trout fishing in river. Supplies at Lapine. This CG has moderate use. Gather firewood locally. Visit adjacent Pringle Falls Research Natural Area. Wildlife in this area includes mountain lion, black bears, coyote, deer, and elk.

GETTING THERE: From Twisp go W on primary forest route 44 approx. 20 mi. to South Creek CG.

SINGLE RATE:	Varies	OPEN DATES:	Apr-Nov
# of SINGLE SITES:	4	MAX SPUR:	16 feet
		MAX STAY:	14 days
		ELEVATION:	3100 feet

35 Sugarloaf
Conconully • lat 48°35'41" lon 119°41'47"

DESCRIPTION: Set in a mixed forest setting on north end of Sugarloaf Lake. Fish for trout and swim in the lake. Supplies available at Conconully. Deer, bears and birds are common to the area. Campers may gather firewood. No designated trails in the area.

GETTING THERE: From Conconully go NE on county route 4015 approx. 5 mi. to Sugarloaf CG.

SINGLE RATE:	$5	OPEN DATES:	Apr-Nov
# of SINGLE SITES:	4	MAX SPUR:	22 feet
		MAX STAY:	14 days
		ELEVATION:	2420 feet

36 Tiffany Springs
Winthrop • lat 48°42'03" lon 119°57'09"

DESCRIPTION: Set in a mixed forest setting within Tiffany Meadows. Fish for trout and swim in the lake. Supplies available at Winthrop. Deer, bears and birds are common to the area. Campers may gather firewood. Trail to Tiffany Lake from the CG.

GETTING THERE: From Winthrop go N on forest route 9137 approx. 7 mi. to primary forest route 37. Go NE on 37 approx. 11 mi. to primary forest route 39. Go N on 39 approx. 6 mi. to Tiffany Spring CG.

SINGLE RATE:	$5	OPEN DATES:	Apr-Nov
# of SINGLE SITES:	6	MAX SPUR:	16 feet
		MAX STAY:	14 days
		ELEVATION:	6770 feet

37 War Creek
Twisp • lat 48°22'04" lon 120°23'49"

DESCRIPTION: In an old growth pine forest setting on Twisp River. Fish and swim in the river. Supplies available at Twisp. Deer, bears and birds are common to the area. Campers may gather firewood. Horse ramp at the CG. Trail from CG to forest route 100, approx. 6 mi. in length.

GETTING THERE: From Twisp go W on primary forest route 44 approx. 12 mi. to War Creek CG.

SINGLE RATE:	Varies	OPEN DATES:	Apr-Nov
# of SINGLE SITES:	10	MAX SPUR:	22 feet
		MAX STAY:	14 days
		ELEVATION:	2400 feet

 Campground has hosts   **Reservable sites** **Accessible facilities**   **Fully developed**  **Semi-developed**  **Rustic facilities**

NOTE: Open dates listed are typical. Actual dates are dependent on conditions such as snow pack.

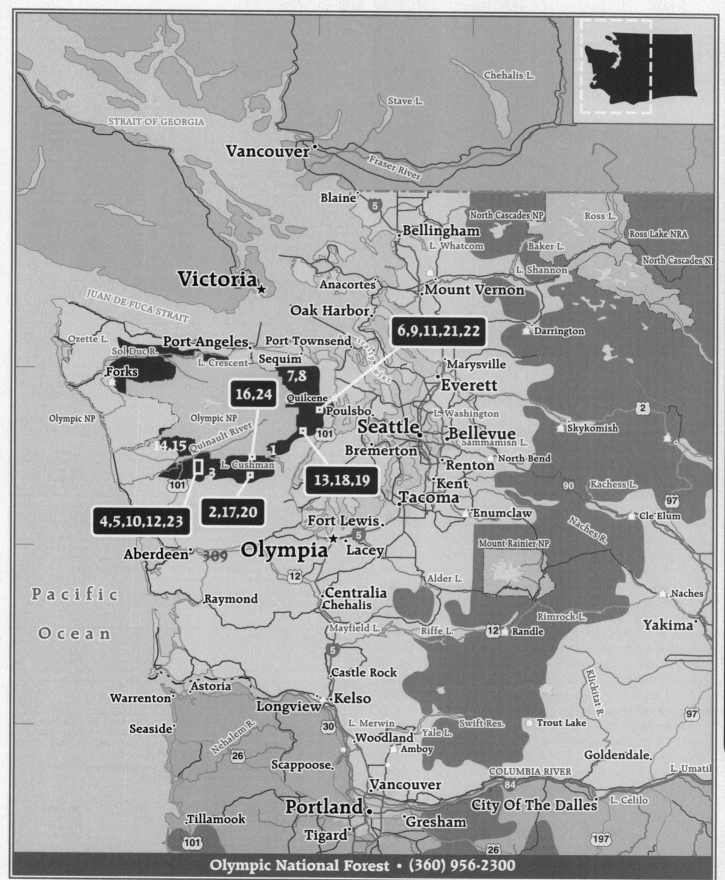

Olympic National Forest • Washington • Locator Map

USFS Photo

OLYMPIC NATIONAL FOREST

The Olympic National Forest is surrounded on three sides by saltwater and is noted for its marine climate, lush rain forests, Roosevelt elk and rugged, mountainous terrain.

The Olympic Mountains rise from sea level to 7,965 feet in the center of the Peninsula, while temperate rain forests cover the seaward slopes. Variations in elevation and moisture create a rich landscape which offers many opportunities for camping, picnicking, hiking, fishing, hunting, swimming, and boating. Special activities include clam digging, oyster picking, beachcombing, scuba diving, wildlife viewing and mountain climbing.

The forest offers over 200 miles of trails, half of which are at low elevations and can be enjoyed year-round. It also has five wilderness areas, totaling 88,265 acres and many lakes and streams on the Peninsula, as well as the surrounding bodies of salt water, offer outstanding fisheries. Anadromous fish (those that migrate to and from the ocean) include steelhead trout and Pacific salmon. Resident fish include cutthroat, Dolly Varden and rainbow trout. The beaches and estuaries offer a variety of shellfish including oysters, razor and steamer clams, and crab.

The Peninsula's Roosevelt elk population is the largest of its kind anywhere. Often weighing over 600 pounds, they are a major hunting and tourist attraction. A wide variety of other species are also found on the forest including coyotes, beavers, black bears, foxes, bats, otters, bobcats and snakes and lizards.

1 Big Creek
Hoodsport • lat 47°29'41" lon 123°12'34"

DESCRIPTION: This CG is located in mixed conifer on Big Creek and is close to Lake Cushman. There are fishing opportunities in the area but please check fishing regulations Wildlife in this area includes elk, deer, bobcats, mountain lions, river otters, eagles, and blue herons. There are hiking trails in the vicinity.

GETTING THERE: From Hoodsport go W and N on state HWY 119 approx. 8.5 mi. to Big Creek CG.

SINGLE RATE:	$10	OPEN DATES:	May-Sept*
# of SINGLE SITES:	25	MAX SPUR:	30 feet
		MAX STAY:	14 days
		ELEVATION:	950 feet

2 Brown Creek
Shelton • lat 47°24'30" lon 123°18'30"

DESCRIPTION: This CG is located in mixed conifer on Brown Creek. There is fishing in the area but please check fishing regulations Wildlife in this area includes elk, deer, bobcats, mountain lions, river otters, eagles, and blue herons. This CG is close to an interpretive trail and a horse trail which runs along a river.

GETTING THERE: From Shelton go N on US HWY 101 approx. 6 mi. to primary forest route 23. Go NW on 23 approx. 14 mi. to Brown Creek CG.

SINGLE RATE:	$5	OPEN DATES:	Yearlong
# of SINGLE SITES:	20	MAX SPUR:	21 feet
		MAX STAY:	14 days
		ELEVATION:	1300 feet

3 Campbell Tree Grove
Aberdeen • lat 47°28'53" lon 123°41'07"

DESCRIPTION: This CG rests in mixed conifer on the West Fork Humptulips River. There is a trail that runs from the CG along the river. Campers may also enjoy a hike in Colonel Bob Wilderness and Olympic Mountains National Park. Wildlife in this area includes black bears, mountain lions, elk, deer, and the Olympic marmots.

GETTING THERE: From Aberdeen go N on US HWY 101 approx. 25 mi. to primary forest route 22. Go N on 22 approx. 8 mi. to forest route 2204. Go N on 2204 approx. 13 mi. to Campbell Tree Grove CG.

SINGLE RATE:	No fee	OPEN DATES:	Yearlong
# of SINGLE SITES:	11	MAX SPUR:	16 feet
		MAX STAY:	14 days
		ELEVATION:	1035 feet

4 Chetwoot
Montesano • lat 47°24'30" lon 123°36'00"

DESCRIPTION: This hike-in only CG is located in mixed conifer on Wynoochee Lake. There are fishing opportunities in the area but please check fishing regulations Wildlife includes elk, deer, bobcats, mountain lions, river otters, eagles, and blue herons. There is a trail which runs along the lake. No drinking water.

GETTING THERE: From Montesano go N on the Wynoochee Road approx. 31 mi. to forest route 2294. Go N on 2294 approx. 2 mi. to Chetwoot CG.

SINGLE RATE:	No fee	OPEN DATES:	May-Sept*
# of SINGLE SITES:	8		
		MAX STAY:	14 days
		ELEVATION:	830 feet

5 Coho
Montesano • lat 47°23'30" lon 123°36'04"

DESCRIPTION: This CG is located in mixed conifer on Wynoochee Lake. There are fishing opportunities in the area but please check fishing regulations. Wildlife in the area includes elk, deer, bobcats, mountain lions, river otters, eagles, and blue herons. Popular activities include hiking, biking, swimming, and fishing.

GETTING THERE: From Montesano go N on the Wynoochee Road approx. 31 mi. to forest route 2294. Go N on 2294 approx. 1.5 mi. to Coho CG.

SINGLE RATE:	Varies	OPEN DATES:	May-Sept*
# of SINGLE SITES:	58	MAX SPUR:	36 feet
		MAX STAY:	14 days
		ELEVATION:	830 feet

 Campground has hosts   Reservable sites   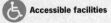 Accessible facilities   Fully developed   Semi-developed   Rustic facilities

6   Collins
Duckabush • lat 47˚40'00" lon 123˚01'00"

DESCRIPTION: This CG rests in mixed conifer on the Duckabush River. There are fishing opportunities in the area but please check fishing regulations Wildlife in this area includes elk, deer, bobcats, mountain lions, river otters, eagles, and blue herons. Hike the nearby Duckabush River trail or visit beautiful Murhut Falls.

GETTING THERE: From Duckabush go W on county route 2274 approximately 5 miles to Collins CG.

SINGLE RATE:	$10	OPEN DATES:	May-Sept*
# of SINGLE SITES:	16	MAX SPUR:	21 feet
		MAX STAY:	14 days
		ELEVATION:	400 feet

7   Dungeness Forks
Sequim • lat 47˚58'32" lon 123˚06'39"

DESCRIPTION: This tent only CG is situated in mixed conifer on the Dungeness River. There are fishing opportunities in the area but please check fishing regulations Wildlife includes elk, deer, bobcats, mountain lions, river otters, eagles, and blue herons. Enjoy a hike along the Wolf River to the Buckhorn Wilderness.

GETTING THERE: From Sequim go E on US HWY 101 approx. 1.5 mi. to Palo Alto route. Go S on Palo Alto approx. 8 mi. to forest route 2880. Go W on 2880 approx. 1 mi. to Dungeness Forks CG.

SINGLE RATE:	$5	OPEN DATES:	May-Sept*
# of SINGLE SITES:	10		
		MAX STAY:	14 days
		ELEVATION:	1000 feet

8   East Crossing
Sequim • lat 47˚57'24" lon 123˚06'17"

DESCRIPTION: This tent only CG is currently closed due to road access difficulties. Please contact Hood Canal Ranger District at (360) 765-2200 for open date.

GETTING THERE: From Sequim go E on US HWY 101 approx. 1.5 mi. to Palo Alto route. Go S on Palo Alto approx. 8 mi. to forest route 2880. Go S on 2880 approx. 3 mi. to East Crossing CG.

SINGLE RATE:	$8	OPEN DATES:	May-Sept*
# of SINGLE SITES:	10		
		MAX STAY:	14 days
		ELEVATION:	1000 feet

9   Elkhorn
Brinnon • lat 47˚44'00" lon 123˚06'00"

DESCRIPTION: This CG is located in mixed conifer on the Dosewallips River. There are fishing opportunities in the area but please check fishing regulations Wildlife in this area includes elk, deer, bobcats, mountain lions, river otters, eagles, and blue herons. Enjoy a hike on a nearby trail that leads to the Tunnel Creek Shelter.

GETTING THERE: From Brinnon go W on county route 2500 approx. 10 mi. to Elkhorn CG.

SINGLE RATE:	$10	OPEN DATES:	May-Sept*
# of SINGLE SITES:	20	MAX SPUR:	21 feet
		MAX STAY:	14 days
		ELEVATION:	1000 feet

10   Falls Creek
Humptulips • lat 47˚47'24" lon 122˚55'35"

DESCRIPTION: This CG is located in mixed conifer on Lake Quinalt. Be prepared for rapid weather changes. Wildlife in this area includes black bears, mountain lions, deer, and Olympic marmots. Visit the world's largest sitka spruce and western red cedar. Hike Colonel Bob Wilderness and Olympic Mountains National Park.

GETTING THERE: From Humptulips go N on US HWY 101 approx. 17 mi. to county route 3340. Go E on 3340 approx. 3 mi. to Falls Creek CG.

SINGLE RATE:	$10	OPEN DATES:	May-Sept*
# of SINGLE SITES:	30	MAX SPUR:	21 feet
		MAX STAY:	14 days
		ELEVATION:	450 feet

11   Falls View
Quilcene • lat 47˚47'00" lon 122˚54'00"

DESCRIPTION: This CG is located in mixed conifer on Big Quilcene River. There are fishing opportunities in the area but please check fishing regulations. Wildlife in this area includes, deer, elk, bobcats, eagles, blue herons, and river otters. Enjoy a visit to the Mount Walker Viewpoint.

GETTING THERE: From Quilcene go S on US HWY 101 3 mi. to Falls View CG.

SINGLE RATE:	$10	OPEN DATES:	May-Sept*
# of SINGLE SITES:	30	MAX SPUR:	21 feet
		MAX STAY:	14 days
		ELEVATION:	450 feet

12   Gatton Creek
Humptulips • lat 47˚28'26" lon 123˚50'07"

DESCRIPTION: This tent only CG is located in mixed conifer on Lake Quinalt. Prepare for rapid weather changes. Black bears, mountain lions, deer, and Olympic marmots are common. Visit the world's largest sitka spruce and western red cedar. Hike Colonel Bob Wilderness and Olympic Mountains National Park. No drinking water.

GETTING THERE: From Humptulips go N on US HWY 101 approx. 17 mi. to county route 3340. Go E on 3340 approx. 3.5 mi. to Gatton Creek CG.

SINGLE RATE:	$11	OPEN DATES:	Yearlong
# of SINGLE SITES:	15		
		MAX STAY:	14 days
		ELEVATION:	200 feet

13   Hamma Hamma
Eldon • lat 47˚35'00" lon 123˚07'30"

DESCRIPTION: This CG is situated in mixed conifer on the Hamma Hamma River. There are fishing opportunities in the area but please check fishing regulations Wildlife in this area includes elk, deer, bobcats, mountain lions, river otters, eagles, and blue herons. Hike the on-site interpretive trail.

GETTING THERE: From Eldon go N on US HWY 101 approx. 2 mi. to forest route 25. Go W on 25 approx. 6.5 mi. to Hamma Hamma CG.

SINGLE RATE:	$10	OPEN DATES:	May-Sept*
# of SINGLE SITES:	16	MAX SPUR:	21 feet
		MAX STAY:	14 days
		ELEVATION:	700 feet

14   Klahanie
Forks • lat 47˚57'49" lon 124˚18'15"

DESCRIPTION: This tent only CG is situated in mixed conifer on the South Sitkum River. Enjoy a visit to the nearby Sol Duc Hot Springs Resort and the High Rain Forest Visitor Center in the Olympic Mountains National Park. Wildlife in this area includes black bears, mountain lions, elk, and Olympic marmots. No drinking water.

GETTING THERE: From Forks go E on forest primary route 29 approximately 1.5 miles to Klahanie CG.

SINGLE RATE:	No fee	OPEN DATES:	Yearlong
# of SINGLE SITES:	15		
		MAX STAY:	14 days
		ELEVATION:	340 feet

15   Klahowya
Beaver • lat 48˚05'00" lon 124˚07'00"

DESCRIPTION: This CG is situated in a mixed conifer forest setting on the Sol Duc River. There are fishing opportunities in this area but please check fishing regulations. Be prepared for rapid weather changes. Wildlife in this area includes black bears, mountain lions, elk, deer, and Olympic Marmots.

GETTING THERE: From Beaver go E on US HWY 101 approximately 11 miles to Klahowya CG.

SINGLE RATE:	Varies	OPEN DATES:	Yearlong
# of SINGLE SITES:	55	MAX SPUR:	30 feet
		MAX STAY:	14 days
		ELEVATION:	350 feet

Campground has hosts   🔒 **Reservable sites**   **Accessible facilities**   **Fully developed**   **Semi-developed**   **Rustic facilities**

NOTE: Open dates listed are typical. Actual dates are dependent on conditions such as snow pack.

16 Laney
Sheldon • lat 47°29'00" lon 123°00'00"

DESCRIPTION: This tent only CG is located in mixed conifer on the South Fork Skokomish River. There is fishing in the area but please check fishing regulations Wildlife in this area includes elk, deer, bobcats, mountain lions, river otters, eagles, and blue herons. Enjoy a hike into the Olympic Mountains National Park. No facilities.

GETTING THERE: From Sheldon go N on US HWY 101 approx. 6 mi. to primary forest route 23. Go NW on 23 approx. 13 mi. to forest route 2353. Go NW on 2353 approx. 2 mi. to forest route 2355. Go NW on 2355 approx. 5 mi. to Laney CG.

SINGLE RATE:	No fee	OPEN DATES:	May-Sept*
# of SINGLE SITES:	10		
		MAX STAY:	14 days
		ELEVATION:	1300 feet

17 Le Bar Horse
Shelton • lat 47°25'30" lon 123°19'30"

DESCRIPTION: This CG is limited to campers with stock and is located in mixed conifer on Le Bar Creek. There is fishing in the area but please check fishing regulations Wildlife in this area includes elk, deer, bobcats, and blue herons. This CG is close to a nature trail and a horse trail. No drinking water.

GETTING THERE: From Shelton go N on US HWY 101 approx. 6 mi. to primary forest route 23. Go NW on 23 approx. 15 mi. to Le Bar Horse CG.

SINGLE RATE:	$5	OPEN DATES:	May-Sept*
# of SINGLE SITES:	13	MAX SPUR:	28 feet
		MAX STAY:	14 days
		ELEVATION:	605 feet

18 Lena Creek
Hoodsport • lat 47°35'55" lon 123°09'00"

DESCRIPTION: This CG rests in mixed conifer at the confluence of Lena Creek and the Hamma Hamma River. There is fishing in the area but please check fishing regulations Wildlife includes elk, deer, bobcats, mountain lions, river otters, eagles, and blue herons. Hike the on-site trail to Lena Lake and the Brothers Wilderness.

GETTING THERE: From Hoodsport go NE on US HWY 101 11 mi. to primary forest route 25. Go W on 25 approx. 6.5 mi. to Lena Creek CG.

SINGLE RATE:	$5	OPEN DATES:	May-Sept*
# of SINGLE SITES:	14	MAX SPUR:	21 feet
		MAX STAY:	14 days
		ELEVATION:	720 feet

19 Lena Lake
Hoodsport • lat 47°37'24" lon 123°09'21"

DESCRIPTION: This hike-in only CG is located in mixed conifer on Lena Lake. There is fishing in the area but please check fishing regulations Wildlife includes elk, deer, bobcats, mountain lions, river otters, eagles, and blue herons. Hike the on-site trail to Lena Creek and the Brothers Wilderness. No drinking water.

GETTING THERE: From Hoodsport go NE on US HWY 101 11 mi. to primary forest route 25. Go W on 25 approx. 9 mi. to Lena Lake CG.

SINGLE RATE:	No fee	OPEN DATES:	May-Sept*
# of SINGLE SITES:	35		
		MAX STAY:	14 days
		ELEVATION:	1800 feet

20 Oxbow
Shelton • lat 47°25'30" lon 123°19'30"

DESCRIPTION: This rustic, dispersed CG is set in mixed conifer on Brown Creek. There is fishing in the area but please check fishing regulations Wildlife in includes elk, deer, bobcats, and blue herons. This CG is close to a nature trail and a horse trail which runs along the Skokomish River. No drinking water.

GETTING THERE: From Shelton go N on US HWY 101 approx. 7 mi. to primary forest route 23. Go NW on 23 approx. 11.5 mi. to Oxbow CG.

SINGLE RATE:	No fee	OPEN DATES:	May-Sept*
# of SINGLE SITES:	30		
		MAX STAY:	14 days
		ELEVATION:	800 feet

21 Rainbow
Quilcene • lat 47°45'00" lon 122°60'00"

DESCRIPTION: This group only CG offers tent camping and reservations are required. The CG rests in mixed conifer at the confluence of Big Quilcene River and Elbo Creek. Enjoy fishing but please check fishing regulations Wildlife includes elk, deer, bobcats, river otters, eagles, and blue herons. No drinking water.

GETTING THERE: From Quilcene go S on US HWY 101 approx. 5 mi. to Rainbow CG.

GROUP RATE:	$25	OPEN DATES:	May-Sept*
# of GROUP SITES:	9	MAX STAY:	14 days
		ELEVATION:	450 feet

22 Seal Rock
Quilcene • lat 47°42'35" lon 122°53'17"

DESCRIPTION: This CG offers the only oyster beach in the national forests. It is located on Dabob Bay in Hood Canal and rests in mixed conifer. Enjoy fishing for shrimp or oysters but please check fishing regulations. Wildlife in the area includes sea birds, sea lions, and harbor seals. Nature trail on site.

GETTING THERE: From Quilcene go S on US HWY 101 approximately 10 miles to Seal Rock CG.

SINGLE RATE:	Varies	OPEN DATES:	May-Sept*
# of SINGLE SITES:	42	MAX SPUR:	21 feet
		MAX STAY:	14 days
		ELEVATION:	20 feet

23 Willaby Creek
Humptulips • lat 47°27'38" lon 123°51'36"

DESCRIPTION: This CG is located in mixed conifer on Lake Quinalt. Prepare for rapid weather changes. Black bears, mountain lions, deer, and Olympic marmots are common to the area. Visit the world's largest sitka spruce and western red cedar. Hike Colonel Bob Wilderness and Olympic Mountains National Park.

GETTING THERE: From Humptulips go N on US HWY 101 approx. 17 mi. to primary forest route 3340. Go NE on 3340 approx. 1 mi. to Willaby Creek CG.

SINGLE RATE:	$14	OPEN DATES:	Yearlong
# of SINGLE SITES:	34	MAX SPUR:	16 feet
		MAX STAY:	14 days
		ELEVATION:	400 feet

24 Wynoochee Falls
Montesano • lat 47°28'13" lon 123°31'24"

DESCRIPTION: This hike-in, tent only CG is located in mixed conifer on the Wynoochee River. There are fishing opportunities in the area but please check fishing regulations Wildlife in this area includes elk, deer, bobcats, mountain lions, river otters, eagles, and blue herons. No drinking water.

GETTING THERE: From Montesano go N on primary forest route 22 (Wynoochee route) approx. 28 mi. to forest route 2270. Go N on 2270 approx. 7 mi. to Wynoochee Falls CG. Mile hike in on the 2270 road.

SINGLE RATE:	No fee	OPEN DATES:	May-Sept*
# of SINGLE SITES:	12		
		MAX STAY:	14 days
		ELEVATION:	2500 feet

 Campground has hosts   🔒 Reservable sites   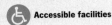 Accessible facilities   Fully developed    Semi-developed   Rustic facilities

NOTE: Open dates listed are typical. Actual dates are dependent on conditions such as snow pack.

British Columbia

1-3,5,16,28,29,35,38,39,
43,67,72,76,84,85,90,107

42,64,71,93,
103,108

21,37,47,56,60,61,
73,91,98,104,111

4,7,26,30,32,33,40,
41,44,45,48,51,66,69
70,80,83,87,92,97,99

Tonasket   Republic

Omak
Okanogan

WASHINGTON

Coulee
Dam NRA

Chehalis L.   Okanagan L.

Stave L.

Fraser River

Bellingham
L. Whatcom
North Cascades NP
Ross L.
Baker L.
L. Shannon
North
Cascades
NP

Lake
Chelan NRA

Twisp

Omak L.

Mount Vernon

6,9,13,17,25,27,
57,74,82,88,113

Everett

L. Chelan

Chelan

Banks L.

Franklin D.
Roosevelt L.

Sanpoil River

Okanogan R.

Seattle
L. Washington
Bellevue
Sammamisn L.
Skykomish
North Bend

2   105

Entiat
Leavenworth
Cashmere
Wenatchee

8,10,15,34,
36,53,55,86

Ephrata
Quincy
Moses L.

77

Kent
Tacoma
Enumclaw

90   Kachess L.

Cle Elum

59,62,68,100

Moses Lake

Othello

Mount Rainier NP

Naches R.

20   22

18,19,31,49,
54,75,95,106,
109,110,112

Alder L.

12   Randle

Rimrock L.

Naches

Ellensburg

82

11,52,81,96,
101,102

Yakima

COLUMBIA RIVER

Snake River

395

12,14,23,50,
65,78,79,94

24,46,58,
63,89

...andview

Richland

Pasco
Kennewick

L. Sacajawea

82

Merwin
Yale L.
Amboy
Battle Ground
Vancouver

Swift Res.

COLUMBIA
Goldendale
Hood River

L. Umatilla

Hermiston

L. Wallula   730

84

84

Portland

City Of The Dalles
Oregon

L. Celilo

Rock Creek

26   197

Wenatchee National Forest • Washington • Locator Map

USFS Photo

Wenatchee National Forest

The Wenatchee National Forest covers approximately 2.2 million acres. It stretches from upper Lake Chelan on the north to the Yakama Indian Reservation on the south.

The vegetation varies with the elevation, from the sagebrush and pine covered slopes at 2,000 feet, to higher elevation areas with alpine fir and mountain huckleberry, to the crest of the Cascade Mountain range at 8,000 feet and above where vegetation is sparse.

Approximately 40 percent of the Wenatchee is designated as Wilderness in seven Wilderness Areas: Lake Chelan-Sawtooth, Glacier Peak, Henry M. Jackson, Alpine Lakes, William O. Douglas, Norse Peak, and Goat Rocks. Here, foot travel is the only method of transportation allowed, and the land is managed in such a way as to preserve its natural, primitive condition. There are no developments or roads in Wilderness Areas.

The Wenatchee offers many recreation opportunities. Wenatchee National Forest campgrounds meet a variety of camping needs. Over 100 campgrounds and picnic sites provide room for a total of 13,000 people at any one time. There are approximately 5,000 miles of forest roads. In the winter, snow-covered roads are used for cross-country skiing, snowshoeing, and snowmobiling. Trail users will find about 2,500 miles of recreation trails available for hiking, horse use, trail biking, and mountain bike use. The winter months also bring opportunities for cross-country ski trips along developed, signed trail systems.

1 19 Mile
Plain • lat 48˚01'11" lon 120˚49'34"

DESCRIPTION: In a mixed forest setting on the Chiwawa River with views of the mountains. Fish or swim in the river. Supplies available at Ardenvoir. Deer, bears, squirrels and birds are common to the area. Campers may gather firewood. CG is adjacent to the Glacier Peak Wilderness with trails running to it.

GETTING THERE: From Plain go N on forest route 672 approx. 6 mi. to primary forest route 62. Go N on 62 approx. 17 mi. to 19 Mile CG.

SINGLE RATE:	$5	OPEN DATES:	Yearlong
# of SINGLE SITES:	4	MAX SPUR:	30 feet
		MAX STAY:	14 days
		ELEVATION:	2600 feet

2 Alder Creek Horse Camp
Plain • lat 47˚49'00" lon 120˚39'00"

DESCRIPTION: In a mixed conifer forest setting on Alder Creek. Fish on the nearby Chiwawa River. Supplies available in Plain. Wildlife in this area includes blackbears and deer. Campers may gather firewood. CG is busy on weekends and holidays. Hike and horseback trails begin at CG and go to Minnow Ridge.

GETTING THERE: From Plain go N on forest route 6100 approximately 7 miles to Alder Creek Horse Camp.

		OPEN DATES:	Yearlong
		MAX SPUR:	30 feet
GROUP RATE:	No fee	MAX STAY:	14 days
# of GROUP SITES:	1	ELEVATION:	2400 feet

3 Alpine Meadows
Plain • lat 48˚02'47" lon 120˚49'58"

DESCRIPTION: In a mixed conifer forest setting close to Willow Creek. Fish from the creek. Supplies available in Plain. Wildlife in this area includes black bears and deer. Campers may gather firewood. CG is busy on weekends and holidays. Hike in the nearby Glacier Peak Wilderness.

GETTING THERE: From Plain go N on forest route 672 approx. 6 mi. to primary forest route 62. Go N on 62 approx. 19 mi. to Alpine Meadows CG.

SINGLE RATE:	$5	OPEN DATES:	Yearlong
# of SINGLE SITES:	4	MAX SPUR:	20 feet
		MAX STAY:	14 days
		ELEVATION:	2600 feet

4 Antilon Lake
Manson • lat 47˚58'32" lon 120˚09'48"

DESCRIPTION: This tent only CG is in a mixed forest setting on Antilon Lake. Fish and swim in the lake. CG is near 4th of July Mountain. Supplies available in Manson. Numerous wildlife can be seen in the area. Campers may gather firewood. No designated trail near CG.

GETTING THERE: From Manson go N on county road 188 approx. 4 mi. to forest route 8200. Go N on 8200 approx. 2 mi. to Antilon Lake CG.

SINGLE RATE:	Varies	OPEN DATES:	Yearlong
		MAX STAY:	14 days
		ELEVATION:	2500 feet

5 Atkinson Flat
Plain • lat 47˚59'55" lon 120˚48'55"

DESCRIPTION: In a mixed conifer forest setting on the Chiwawa River. Fish in the river. Supplies can be purchased in Plain. Wildlife in this area includes black bears and deer. Campers may gather firewood. CG is busy on weekends and holidays. Hike in the nearby Glacier Peak Wilderness.

GETTING THERE: From Plain go N on forest route 672 approx. 6 mi. to primary forest route 62. Go N on 62 approx. 16 mi. to Atkinson Flat CG.

SINGLE RATE:	$5	OPEN DATES:	Yearlong
# of SINGLE SITES:	7	MAX SPUR:	30 feet
		MAX STAY:	14 days
		ELEVATION:	2550 feet

 Campground has hosts  **Reservable sites** 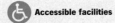 **Accessible facilities** **Fully developed** **Semi-developed** **Rustic facilities**

NOTE: Open dates listed are typical. Actual dates are dependent on conditions such as snow pack.

6 Beverly
Cle Elum • lat 47°22'42" lon 120°52'57"

DESCRIPTION: In a mixed forest setting adjacent to the North Fork of the Teanaway River. Fish and swim in the river. Supplies available at Cle Elum. Numerous wildlife can be seen in the area. Campers may gather firewood. A trail nearby follows Jackson Creek.

GETTING THERE: From Cle Elum go E approx. 6 mi. on state HWY 970 to county route 970. Go N on 970 approx. 13 mi. to forest route 9737. Go N on 9737 approx. 3.5 mi. to Beverly CG.

SINGLE RATE:	No fee	OPEN DATES:	May-Sept
# of SINGLE SITES:	16		
		MAX STAY:	14 days
		ELEVATION:	3100 feet

7 Big Creek
Chelan • lat 48°02'25" lon 120°25'34"

DESCRIPTION: This is a boat-in, tent only CG. The CG sits on the confluence of Big Creek and Lake Chelan. Boat, ski and fish in lake or creek. Supplies available at Chelan. Numerous wildlife includes mountain goats, deer, and bighorn sheep. Campers may gather dead and down firewood. Ferry rides available on Lake Chelan.

GETTING THERE: From Chelan go NW approximately 25 miles to Big Creek CG, on the south bank of Lake Chelan. Accessible by boat only.

SINGLE RATE:	No fee	OPEN DATES:	Yearlong
# of SINGLE SITES:	4		
		MAX STAY:	14 days
		ELEVATION:	1100 feet

8 Black Pine
Leavenworth • lat 47°36'34" lon 120°56'40"

DESCRIPTION: In a mixed forest setting on Black Pine Creek. Fish and swim in the creek. Supplies are available at Leavenworth. Deer, bears and birds are common to the area. Campers may gather firewood. This CG is a trailhead for hiking and horseback riding into the Alpine Lakes Wilderness. Stables at CG for horses.

GETTING THERE: From Leavonworth go SW on primary forest route 76 approx. 15 mi. to Black Pine CG.

SINGLE RATE:	$7	OPEN DATES:	Yearlong*
# of SINGLE SITES:	10	MAX SPUR:	99 feet
		MAX STAY:	14 days
		ELEVATION:	3000 feet

9 Boiling Lake
Twisp • lat 48°12'13" lon 120°21'05"

DESCRIPTION: This hike-in only CG is situated in a mixed forest on the shores of Boiling Lake. Fish and swim in the lake. Check for local regulations. Supplies available at Lake Chelan. Various wildlife can be seen in the area. Campers may gather firewood. Numerous trails in the area.

GETTING THERE: From Twisp go S 13.5 mi. on HWY 153 to county route 1034. Go W 1 mi. to FR4340. Go NW 5 mi. to FR300. Go W 4 mi. to Prince Creek Trail #1255. Hike #1255 to Boiling Lake CG.

SINGLE RATE:	No fee	OPEN DATES:	Yearlong
# of SINGLE SITES:	3		
		MAX STAY:	14 days
		ELEVATION:	6920 feet

10 Bridge Creek
Leavenworth • lat 47°33'50" lon 120°46'55"

DESCRIPTION: In a mixed forest setting on Bridge Creek. Fish and swim in the creek. Supplies available at Leavenworth. Numerous animals can be seen in the area. Bears viewing area nearby. Stables at the CG. No designated trails in the area.

GETTING THERE: From Leavenworth go SW on primary forest route 76 approx. 7 mi. to Bridge Creek CG.

SINGLE RATE:	$9	OPEN DATES:	Yearlong*
# of SINGLE SITES:	6	MAX SPUR:	15 feet
GROUP RATE:	$60	MAX STAY:	14 days
# of GROUP SITES:	1	ELEVATION:	1900 feet

11 Buck Meadows
Ellensburg • lat 47°04'30" lon 121°00'00"

DESCRIPTION: CG is located in pines along Manatash Creek. Activities include fishing, hiking, horseback riding, and motorcycle riding. Stock facilities. Water available.

GETTING THERE: From Ellensburg go W on primary forest route 31 approximately 24 miles to Buck Meadows CG.

SINGLE RATE:	No fee	OPEN DATES:	May-Sept
# of SINGLE SITES:	4		
		MAX STAY:	14 days
		ELEVATION:	4300 feet

12 Bumping Crossing
Naches • lat 46°52'46" lon 121°16'56"

DESCRIPTION: In a mixed forest setting on Bumping River. Fish and swim in the river. Supplies available at Naches. Numerous wildlife in the area. Campers may gather firewood. Several trails in area leading to the William O'Douglas Wilderness area.

GETTING THERE: From Naches go NW on state HWY 410 approx. 30 mi. to forest route 1800. Follow 1800 to Bumping Crossing CG.

SINGLE RATE:	No fee	OPEN DATES:	May-Oct
# of SINGLE SITES:	12	MAX SPUR:	30 feet
		MAX STAY:	14 days
		ELEVATION:	3200 feet

13 Cayuse Horse Camp
Lakedale • lat 47°23'59" lon 121°05'33"

DESCRIPTION: This developed horse camp is in a mixed forest setting near a river. Supplies available at Lakedale. Corrals and loading ramp located in CG. Campers may gather firewood. Many animals can be seen in the area. Many trails in the area. A maximum of 3 horses per campsite please.

GETTING THERE: From Lakedale go N on state HWY 903 approx. 10.5 mi. to road 903. Follow 903 to Cayuse Horse Camp CG.

SINGLE RATE:	$12	OPEN DATES:	May-Sept
# of SINGLE SITES:	15		
		MAX STAY:	14 days
		ELEVATION:	2400 feet

14 Cedar Springs
Naches • lat 46°58'17" lon 121°09'42"

DESCRIPTION: In a mixed forest setting on Bumping River. Fish and swim in the river. Supplies available at Naches. Numerous wildlife in the area. Campers may gather firewood. Several trails in area leading to the William O'Douglas Wilderness area.

GETTING THERE: From Naches go NW on state HWY 410 approx. 30 mi. to forest route 1800. Go SW on 1800 approx. 1/2 mi. to Cedar Springs CG.

SINGLE RATE:	Varies	OPEN DATES:	May-Oct
# of SINGLE SITES:	15	MAX SPUR:	22 feet
		MAX STAY:	14 days
		ELEVATION:	2800 feet

15 Chatter Creek
Leavenworth • lat 47°36'31" lon 120°53'04"

DESCRIPTION: In a mixed forest setting on Icicle Creek. Fish and swim in the creek. Supplies are available at Leavenworth. Deer, bears and birds are common to the area. Campers may gather firewood. This CG is a trailhead for hiking and horseback riding into the Alpine Lakes Wilderness.

GETTING THERE: From Leavenworth go SW on primary forest route 76 approx. 12 mi. to Chatter Creek CG.

SINGLE RATE:	$8	OPEN DATES:	Yearlong*
# of SINGLE SITES:	12	MAX SPUR:	22 feet
GROUP RATE:	$60	MAX STAY:	14 days
# of GROUP SITES:	1	ELEVATION:	2800 feet

 Campground has hosts   **Reservable sites**   **Accessible facilities**   **Fully developed**   **Semi-developed**   **Rustic facilities**

NOTE: Open dates listed are typical. Actual dates are dependent on conditions such as snow pack.

16 Chiwawa Horse Camp
Plain • lat 47°58'30" lon 120°46'00"

DESCRIPTION: In a mixed conifer forest setting near the Chiwawa River. Fish in the river. Supplies available in Plain. Wildlife in this area includes blackbears and deer. Campers may gather firewood. Trailhead from CG for hiking and horseback riding into the Glacier Peak Wilderness. Horse stable and information center at CG.

GETTING THERE: From Plain go N on forest route 672 approx. 6 mi. to primary forest route 62. On 62 go N approx. 15 mi. to Chiwawa Horse Camp.

SINGLE RATE:	$5	OPEN DATES:	Yearlong
# of SINGLE SITES:	21	MAX SPUR:	99 feet
		MAX STAY:	14 days
		ELEVATION:	2500 feet

17 Cle Elum River
Lakedale • lat 47°21'00" lon 121°06'12"

DESCRIPTION: The site is surrounded by mountains and a mixed conifer forest on Cle Elum River. The CG is adjacent to Lake Cle Elum. Fish and swim in the lake or river. Drinking water available at the group site. Supplies available at Lakedale. Many animals can be seen in the area. Many trails in the area. Winter sports area nearby.

GETTING THERE: From Lakedale go N on state HWY 903 approx. 8 mi. to Cle Elum River CG.

SINGLE RATE:	$10	OPEN DATES:	May-Sept
# of SINGLE SITES:	35	MAX SPUR:	40 feet
GROUP RATE:	$70	MAX STAY:	14 days
# of GROUP SITES:	1	ELEVATION:	2200 feet

18 Clear Lake North
Naches • lat 46°38'03" lon 121°15'59"

DESCRIPTION: In a mixed forest setting in between Clear Lake and Rim Rock Lake. Boat ramp nearby. Supplies available at Naches. Fish and swim in either of the lakes. Numerous wildlife in the area. Campers may gather firewood. Hike in the Goats Rocks Wilderness nearby. By reservation only.

GETTING THERE: From Naches go NW on US HWY 12 approx. 30 mi. to forest route 1200. Go SW on 1200 approx. 1.5 mi. to Clear Lake North CG.

SINGLE RATE:	$9	OPEN DATES:	May-Oct
# of SINGLE SITES:	34	MAX SPUR:	22 feet
		MAX STAY:	14 days
		ELEVATION:	3100 feet

19 Clear Lake South
Naches • lat 46°37'42" lon 121°15'59"

DESCRIPTION: In a mixed forest setting in between Clear Lake and Rim Rock Lake. Boat ramp nearby. Supplies available at Naches. Fish and swim in either of the lakes. Numerous wildlife in the area. Campers may gather firewood. Hike in the Goats Rocks Wilderness nearby. By reservation only.

GETTING THERE: From Naches go NW on US HWY 12 approx. 30 mi. to forest route 1200. Go SW on 1200 approx. 1.5 mi. to Clear Lake South CG.

SINGLE RATE:	$9	OPEN DATES:	May-Oct
# of SINGLE SITES:	23	MAX SPUR:	22 feet
		MAX STAY:	14 days
		ELEVATION:	3100 feet

20 Corral Creek
Chelan • lat 48°02'44" lon 120°26'16"

DESCRIPTION: This boat-in, tent only CG is in a mixed conifer setting on Lake Chelan. Fish and swim in the lake. This is a low level use CG. Supplies are available at Chelan. Numerous wildlife includes mountain goats, deer, and bighorn sheep. Take a ride on the ferry on the lake. Campers may gather firewood.

GETTING THERE: From Chelan go NW approximately 26 miles to Corral Creek CG, located on the south bank of Lake Chelan. Accessible by boat only.

SINGLE RATE:	No fee	OPEN DATES:	Yearlong
# of SINGLE SITES:	4		
		MAX STAY:	14 days
		ELEVATION:	1100 feet

21 Cottonwood
Ardenvoir • lat 48°01'00" lon 120°39'30"

DESCRIPTION: This CG is located in mixed conifers on the Entiat River. Enjoy fishing for trout on the river. Wildlife includes deer and blackbears. Supplies at Ardenvoir. CG is busy weekends and holidays. Drive to Shady Pass which offers beautiful mountain views or hike in nearby Glacier Peak Wilderness.

GETTING THERE: From Ardenvoir go NW on county route 371 (Entiat River Road) approx. 38 mi. to Cottonwood CG.

SINGLE RATE:	$8	OPEN DATES:	May-Oct*
# of SINGLE SITES:	25	MAX SPUR:	20 feet
		MAX STAY:	14 days
		ELEVATION:	3100 feet

22 Cottonwood
Nile • lat 46°54'26" lon 121°01'29"

DESCRIPTION: In a mixed forest setting on the Naches River. Fish for trout in the river. Supplies available at Nile. Numerous wildlife can be seen in the area. Campers may gather firewood. No designated trails in the area. A winter sports area is nearby.

GETTING THERE: From Nile go N on state HWY 410 approx. 7 mi. to Cottonwood CG.

SINGLE RATE:	Varies	OPEN DATES:	May-Oct
# of SINGLE SITES:	16	MAX SPUR:	22 feet
		MAX STAY:	14 days
		ELEVATION:	2300 feet

23 Cougar Flat
Naches • lat 46°54'58" lon 121°13'47"

DESCRIPTION: In a mixed forest setting on the Bumping River. Fish for trout in the river. Supplies available at Naches. Numerous wildlife in the area. Campers may gather firewood. Hike in the nearby William O'Douglas Wilderness.

GETTING THERE: From Naches go NW on state HWY 410 (US HWY 12) approx. 30 mi. to forest route 1800. Go SW on 1800 approx. 7 mi. to Cougar Flat CG.

SINGLE RATE:	Varies	OPEN DATES:	May-Oct
# of SINGLE SITES:	12	MAX SPUR:	20 feet
		MAX STAY:	14 days
		ELEVATION:	3100 feet

24 Crow Creek
Nile • lat 47°01'30" lon 121°08'00"

DESCRIPTION: In a mixed forest setting on the Naches River. Fish for trout in the river. Supplies available at Nile. Numerous wildlife in the area. Campers may gather firewood. This CG is a trailhead. A winter sports area is nearby.

GETTING THERE: From Nile go N on state HWY 410 approx. 26 mi. to primary forest route 19. Go N on 19 approx. 2.5 mi. to Crow Creek CG.

SINGLE RATE:	$5	OPEN DATES:	May-Oct
# of SINGLE SITES:	15	MAX SPUR:	30 feet
		MAX STAY:	14 days
		ELEVATION:	2900 feet

25 Crystal Springs
Cle Elum • lat 47°18'35" lon 121°18'45"

DESCRIPTION: In a mixed forest setting adjacent to the Yakima River. Fish and swim in the river. Supplies available at Cle Elum. Many animals can be seen in the area. Campers may gather firewood. Winter sports area nearby. Many trails in the area.

GETTING THERE: From Cle Elum go NW on US HWY 90 approx. 20 mi. to Crystal Springs CG.

SINGLE RATE:	$10	OPEN DATES:	Yearlong
# of SINGLE SITES:	25		
		MAX STAY:	14 days
		ELEVATION:	2400 feet

 Campground has hosts   **Reservable sites**   **Accessible facilities**   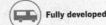 **Fully developed**    **Semi-developed**   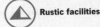 **Rustic facilities**

26 Cub Lake
Twisp • lat 48°11'53" lon 120°24'41"

DESCRIPTION: This hike-in only CG is situated in a mixed forest on the shores of Cub Lake. Fish and swim in the lake. Please check for local regulations. Supplies are available at Twisp. Numerous wildlife can be seen in the area. Campers may gather firewood. Several trails can be found nearby.

GETTING THERE: From Twisp go S 13.5 mi. on HWY 153 to county rte. 1034. Go W 1 mi. on 1034 to FR4340. Go NW 5 mi. on 4340 to FR300. Go W 4 mi. on 300 to Prince Creek Trail #1255. Hike #1255 to Cub Lake CG.

SINGLE RATE:	No fee	OPEN DATES:	Yearlong
# of SINGLE SITES:	3	MAX STAY:	14 days
		ELEVATION:	5200 feet

27 De Roux
Cle Elum • lat 47°25'04" lon 120°56'12"

DESCRIPTION: This tent only CG is in a mixed forest setting adjacent to the confluence of Teanaway River and Deroux Creek. Fish and swim in either creek or river. Supplies available at Cle Elum. Many animals can be seen in the area. Campers may gather firewood. Trails to the Alpine Lakes Wilderness area nearby.

GETTING THERE: From Cle Elum go E approx. 6 mi. on state HWY 970 to county route 970. Go N on 970 approx. 13 mi. to forest route 9737. Go N on 9737 approx. 7.5 mi. to De Roux CG.

SINGLE RATE:	No fee	OPEN DATES:	Yearlong*
# of SINGLE SITES:	3	MAX STAY:	14 days
		ELEVATION:	3840 feet

28 Deep Creek
Plain • lat 47°49'12" lon 120°37'58"

DESCRIPTION: In a mixed conifer forest setting on Deep Creek. Fish in nearby Chiwawa River. Supplies available in Plain. Wildlife in this area includes black bears and deer. Campers may gather firewood. Trail from CG continues on to other area CG's. Bike and motorcycle trails nearby.

GETTING THERE: From Plain go N on forest route 6100 approx. 4.5 mi. to Deep Creek CG.

SINGLE RATE:	No fee	OPEN DATES:	Yearlong
# of SINGLE SITES:	3	MAX SPUR:	30 feet
		MAX STAY:	14 days
		ELEVATION:	2400 feet

29 Deer
Plain • lat 47°48'00" lon 120°37'30"

DESCRIPTION: In a mixed conifer forest setting near Clear Creek. Fish from the creek. Supplies available in Plain. Wildlife in this area includes black bears and deer. Campers may gather firewood. Bike and motorcycle trail nearby.

GETTING THERE: From Plain go N on forest route 6100 approx. 6.5 mi. to forest route 6101. Go E on 6101 approx 3 mi. to Deer CG.

SINGLE RATE:	No fee	OPEN DATES:	Yearlong
# of SINGLE SITES:	3	MAX SPUR:	99 feet
		MAX STAY:	14 days
		ELEVATION:	3000 feet

30 Deer Point
Chelan • lat 48°01'35" lon 120°18'40"

DESCRIPTION: This boat-in, tent only CG is in a mixed conifer setting on Lake Chelan. Boat, swim and fish in this lake. There is a floating dock at the CG. Supplies available at Chelan. Numerous wildlife includes mountain goats, deer, and bighorn sheep. Campers may gather firewood. No designated trails from CG.

GETTING THERE: From Chelan go NW approximately 19 miles to Deer Point CG, located on the north bank of Lake Chelan. Accessible by boat only.

SINGLE RATE:	No fee	OPEN DATES:	Yearlong
# of SINGLE SITES:	5	MAX STAY:	14 days
		ELEVATION:	1100 feet

31 Dog Lake
Naches • lat 46°39'27" lon 121°21'31"

DESCRIPTION: In a mixed forest setting on the Dog Lake. Fish for trout in the lake. Supplies available at Naches. Numerous wildlife in the area. Campers may gather firewood. This CG is a trailhead to the nearby William O'Douglas Wilderness.

GETTING THERE: From Naches go NW on US HWY 12 approx. 35 mi. to Dog Lake CG.

SINGLE RATE:	$5	OPEN DATES:	May-Oct
# of SINGLE SITES:	11	MAX SPUR:	20 feet
		MAX STAY:	14 days
		ELEVATION:	3400 feet

32 Domke Falls
Chelan • lat 48°09'53" lon 120°32'33"

DESCRIPTION: This boat-in, tent only CG is situated in mixed conifers on Lake Chelan. Boat, swim and fish in this lake. There is a floating dock at the CG. Supplies are available at Chelan. Numerous wildlife includes mountain goats, deer, and bighorn sheep. Campers may gather firewood. No designated trails nearby.

GETTING THERE: From Chelan go NW approximately 35 miles to Domke Falls CG, located on the south bank of Lake Chelan. Accessible by boat only.

SINGLE RATE:	No fee	OPEN DATES:	Yearlong
# of SINGLE SITES:	4	MAX STAY:	14 days
		ELEVATION:	1100 feet

33 Domke Lake
Chelan • lat 48°10'52" lon 120°35'20"

DESCRIPTION: This hike-in, tent only CG is in a mixed forest setting on Lake Chelan. Boat, swim and fish in this lake. Supplies available at Chelan. Numerous wildlife can be viewed in this area. Campers may gather firewood. Trails in the area.

GETTING THERE: Domke Lake is approx. 37 mi. N of Chelan on Lake Chelan. By boat only to Refrigerator Harbor and hike-in approx. 1.5 mi. to Domke Lake CG.

SINGLE RATE:	No fee	OPEN DATES:	Yearlong
# of SINGLE SITES:	8	MAX STAY:	14 days
		ELEVATION:	2210 feet

34 Eightmile
Leavenworth • lat 47°33'02" lon 120°45'56"

DESCRIPTION: In a mixed forest setting on Icicle Creek. Fish and swim in the creek. Supplies are available at Leavenworth. Deer, bears and birds are common to the area. Campers may gather firewood. Hiking and horseback riding in the nearby Alpine Lakes Wilderness. Rock climbing nearby.

GETTING THERE: From Leavenworth go SW on primary forest route 76 approx. 6 mi. to Eightmile CG.

SINGLE RATE:	$9	OPEN DATES:	Yearlong*
# of SINGLE SITES:	45	MAX SPUR:	20 feet
GROUP RATE:	$60	MAX STAY:	14 days
# of GROUP SITES:	1	ELEVATION:	1800 feet

35 Finner Creek
Plain • lat 48°10'52" lon 120°35'20"

DESCRIPTION: In a mixed conifer setting on Finner Creek. Fish in nearby Chawawa River. Supplies available in Plain. Wildlife in this area includes blackbears and deer. Campers may gather firewood. Trailhead from CG for hiking and horseback riding to Scheafer Lake. Information center at the CG.

GETTING THERE: From Plain go N on forest route 6100 approx. 7 mi. to primary forest route 62 (6200). Go N on 62 approx. 12 mi. to Finner Creek CG.

SINGLE RATE:	$5	OPEN DATES:	Yearlong
# of SINGLE SITES:	3	MAX SPUR:	30 feet
		MAX STAY:	14 days
		ELEVATION:	2500 feet

 Campground has hosts   Reservable sites   Accessible facilities   Fully developed   Semi-developed   Rustic facilities

NOTE: Open dates listed are typical. Actual dates are dependent on conditions such as snow pack.

36 Fish Lake
Lakedale • lat 47°31'27" lon 121°04'18"

DESCRIPTION: In a mixed forest setting on Fish Lake. Fish and swim in the lake. Supplies available at Lakedale. Many animals can be seen in the area. Campers may gather firewood. Winter sports area nearby. CG is adjacent to the Alpine Lakes Wilderness Area.

GETTING THERE: From Lakedale go N on state HWY 903 approx. 10 mi. to forest route 4330. Go N on 4330 approx. 10 mi. to Fish Lake CG.

SINGLE RATE:	No fee	OPEN DATES:	May-Sept
# of SINGLE SITES:	15		
		MAX STAY:	14 days
		ELEVATION:	3400 feet

37 Fox Creek
Ardenvoir • lat 47°55'32" lon 120°30'35"

DESCRIPTION: This tent only CG is in an open, park-like setting of pine, fir, and cedar. Trout fishing in the Entiat River located next to CG. Historical Box Canyon Observation Point is nearby. Supplies available in Ardenvoir. Various wildlife in area. Campers may gather firewood. Many trails are nearby.

GETTING THERE: From Ardenvoir go N on primary forest route 51 (county route 371) approx. 16 mi. to Fox Creek CG.

SINGLE RATE:	$8	OPEN DATES:	May-Oct
# of SINGLE SITES:	16	MAX SPUR:	50 feet
		MAX STAY:	14 days
		ELEVATION:	2000 feet

38 Glacier View
Coles Corner • lat 47°49'28" lon 120°48'27"

DESCRIPTION: In a mixed conifer setting on Lake Wenatchee. Fish and swim in the lake. Supplies available in Coles Corner. Wildlife in this area includes blackbears and deer. Campers may gather firewood. Hiking trail and viewpoint area close to the CG. Boat ramp located on the lake near CG.

GETTING THERE: From Coles Corner go N on state HWY 207 approx. 3 mi. to county route 413. Go W on 413 approx. 3.5 mi. to forest route 6607. Go W on 6607 approx 1 mi. to Glacier View CG.

SINGLE RATE:	$9	OPEN DATES:	Yearlong
# of SINGLE SITES:	10	MAX SPUR:	20 feet
		MAX STAY:	14 days
		ELEVATION:	1900 feet

39 Goose Creek
Plain • lat 47°50'20" lon 120°38'48"

DESCRIPTION: In a mixed forest setting with views of Goose Creek. Fish in the nearby Chiwawa River. Supplies available at Plain. Deer, bears, squirrels and birds are common to the area. Information center located at the CG. Campers may gather firewood. Many trails in the area, one trail connects to area CG's.

GETTING THERE: From Plain go N on forest route 6100 approx. 6.5 mi. to Goose Creek CG.

SINGLE RATE:	$7	OPEN DATES:	Yearlong
# of SINGLE SITES:	29	MAX SPUR:	99 feet
		MAX STAY:	14 days
		ELEVATION:	2200 feet

40 Graham Harbor
Chelan • lat 48°04'55" lon 120°29'15"

DESCRIPTION: This boat-in, tent only CG rests in a mixed conifer setting on Lake Chelan off of Graham Harbor Creek. Fish for trout from the lake. Supplies available at Chelan. Numerous wildlife includes mountain goats, deer, and bighorn sheep. Campers may gather firewood. Enjoy a ferry ride on the lake.

GETTING THERE: Graham Harbor CG is located approx. 29 mi. NW of Chelan on the S bank of Lake Chelan. Accessible by boat only.

SINGLE RATE:	No fee	OPEN DATES:	Yearlong
# of SINGLE SITES:	5		
		MAX STAY:	14 days
		ELEVATION:	1100 feet

41 Graham Harbor Creek
Chelan • lat 48°05'02" lon 120°29'28"

DESCRIPTION: This boat-in, tent only CG is in a mixed conifer setting on Lake Chelan off of Graham Harbor Creek. Fish for trout in the lake. Supplies are available at Chelan. Numerous wildlife includes mountain goats, deer, and bighorn sheep. Campers may gather firewood. No designated trails nearby.

GETTING THERE: Graham Harbor CG is located approx. 29.5 mi. NW of Chelan on the S bank of Lake Chelan. Accessible by boat only.

SINGLE RATE:	No fee	OPEN DATES:	Yearlong
# of SINGLE SITES:	5		
		MAX STAY:	14 days
		ELEVATION:	1100 feet

42 Grasshopper Meadows
Coles Corner • lat 47°56'24" lon 120°55'26"

DESCRIPTION: In a mixed forest setting on White River. Fish for trout from the river. Supplies available at Coles Corner. Deer, bears, squirrels and birds are common to the area. Information center located at the CG. Campers may gather firewood. CG sits on the edge of the Glacier Peak Wilderness. Winter sports area nearby.

GETTING THERE: From Coles Corner go N on state HWY 207 approx. 9 mi. to state HWY 22. Go NW on 22 approx. 7 mi. to forest route 6400. Go N on 6400 approx. 2 mi. to Grasshopper Meadows CG.

SINGLE RATE:	No fee	OPEN DATES:	Yearlong
# of SINGLE SITES:	5	MAX SPUR:	30 feet
		MAX STAY:	14 days
		ELEVATION:	2050 feet

43 Grouse Creek
Plain • lat 47°53'50" lon 120°41'51"

DESCRIPTION: This group reservation only CG is in a mixed forest setting with views of Grouse Creek. Fish in the nearby Chiwawa River. Supplies available at Plain. Deer, bears, squirrels and birds are common to the area. Campers may gather firewood. Many trails in the area, one trail connects to area CG's.

GETTING THERE: From Plain go N on forest route 6100 approx. 7 mi. to forest route 62 (6200). Go N on 62 approx. 5 mi. to Grouse Creek CG.

		MAX SPUR:	99 feet
GROUP RATE:	Varies	OPEN DATES:	Yearlong
# of GROUP SITES:	3	MAX STAY:	14 days
		ELEVATION:	2400 feet

44 Grouse Mountain
Ardenvoir • lat 47°59'19" lon 120°18'30"

DESCRIPTION: This tent only CG is in a mixed forest setting near Lake Chelan. Fish for trout in the lake. Supplies available at Ardenvoir. Numerous wildlife can be seen in the area. Campers may gather firewood. No designated trails in the area. No drinking water. Busy during hunting season.

GETTING THERE: From Ardenvoir go N on primary forest route 51 (county route 371) approx. 17.5 mi. to forest route 5900. Go NE on 5900 approx. 16 mi. to Grouse Mountain CG.

SINGLE RATE:	No fee	OPEN DATES:	Yearlong
# of SINGLE SITES:	4		
		MAX STAY:	14 days
		ELEVATION:	4425 feet

45 Grouse Mountain Spring
Ardenvoir • lat 47°59'16" lon 120°18'34"

DESCRIPTION: This tent only CG is in a mixed forest setting near Lake Chelan. Fish for trout from the lake. Please check fishing regulations. Supplies available at Ardenvoir. Numerous wildlife can be seen in the area. Campers may gather firewood. No designated trails in the area.

GETTING THERE: From Ardenvoir go N on primary forest route 51 (county route 371) approx. 17.5 mi. to forest route 5900. Go NE on 5900 approx. 16 mi. to Grouse Mountain Spring CG.

SINGLE RATE:	No fee	OPEN DATES:	Yearlong
# of SINGLE SITES:	1		
		MAX STAY:	14 days
		ELEVATION:	4400 feet

 Campground has hosts   **Reservable sites**   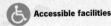 **Accessible facilities**   **Fully developed**   **Semi-developed**   **Rustic facilities**

NOTE: Open dates listed are typical. Actual dates are dependent on conditions such as snow pack.

46 — Halfway Flat
Nile • lat 46°59'02" lon 121°05'37"

DESCRIPTION: In a mixed forest setting on the Naches River. Fish for trout from the river. Supplies available at Nile. Numerous wildlife in the area. Campers may gather firewood. This CG is a trailhead to the nearby William O'Douglas Wilderness. There is a winter sports area nearby.

GETTING THERE: From Nile go N on state HWY 410 approx. 26 mi. to Halfway Flat CG.

SINGLE RATE:	$7	OPEN DATES:	May-Oct
# of SINGLE SITES:	9	MAX SPUR:	99 feet
		MAX STAY:	14 days
		ELEVATION:	2050 feet

47 — Handy Spring

Ardenvoir • lat 47°58'47" lon 120°24'40"

DESCRIPTION: This tent only CG is in a mixed forest setting on Handy Spring. Fish for trout from the lake. Supplies available at Ardenvoir. Numerous wildlife can be seen in the area. Campers may gather firewood. A trail leading to Ramona park is nearby. No drinking water available at CG.

GETTING THERE: From Ardenvoir go N on primary forest route 51 (county route 371) approx. 17.5 mi. to forest route 5900. Go NE on 5900 approx. 11 mi. to Handy Spring CG.

SINGLE RATE:	No fee	OPEN DATES:	Yearlong
# of SINGLE SITES:	1		
		MAX STAY:	14 days
		ELEVATION:	6300 feet

48 — Hatchery

Chelan • lat 48°10'23" lon 120°35'14"

DESCRIPTION: This hike-in, tent only CG is in a mixed forest setting on Domke Lake near Lake Chelan. Fish for trout, canoe and swim in either lake. Supplies available at Ardenvoir. Numerous wildlife can be seen in the area. Campers may gather firewood. No designated trails in the area.

GETTING THERE: Hatchery CG is approx. 37 mi. N of Chelan by boat or ferry to Refrigerator Harbor. Hike-in approx. 3 mi. to Hatchery CG.

SINGLE RATE:	No fee	OPEN DATES:	May-Sept
# of SINGLE SITES:	3		
		MAX STAY:	14 days
		ELEVATION:	2210 feet

49 — Hause Creek
Naches • lat 46°40'29" lon 121°04'42"

DESCRIPTION: In a mixed forest setting on the Tieton River. Fish for trout from the river. Supplies available at Naches. Numerous wildlife can be seen in the area. Campers may gather firewood. Winter sports area nearby. An information center is in the area.

GETTING THERE: From Naches go W on US HWY 12 approx. 21 mi. to Hause Creek CG.

SINGLE RATE:	Varies	OPEN DATES:	May-Oct
# of SINGLE SITES:	42	MAX SPUR:	30 feet
		MAX STAY:	14 days
		ELEVATION:	2500 feet

50 — Hells Crossing
Nile • lat 46°57'54" lon 121°15'55"

DESCRIPTION: In a mixed forest setting on the American River. Fish for trout from the river. Supplies available at Nile. Numerous wildlife in the area. Campers may gather firewood. This CG is a trailhead to the nearby William O'Douglas Wilderness.

GETTING THERE: From Nile go N on state HWY 410 approx. 34.5 mi. to Hells Crossing CG.

SINGLE RATE:	Varies	OPEN DATES:	May-Oct
# of SINGLE SITES:	18	MAX SPUR:	20 feet
		MAX STAY:	14 days
		ELEVATION:	3250 feet

51 — Holden Ballpark
Chelan • lat 48°12'02" lon 120°47'28"

DESCRIPTION: This hike-in/boat-in, tent only CG is in a mixed forest setting next to Railroad Creek. Fish and swim in the creek. Supplies are available at Holden. Numerous wildlife includes mountain goats, deer, and bighorn sheep. Trailhead access point to the Glacier Peak Wilderness Area.

GETTING THERE: From Chelan go 37 mi. N on Lake Chelan to Lucerne. Go W from Lucerne approx. 9 mi. on forest route 8301 to Holden Ballpark CG. There is a bus service from Lucerne to Holden.

SINGLE RATE:	No fee	OPEN DATES:	Yearlong
# of SINGLE SITES:	2		
		MAX STAY:	14 days
		ELEVATION:	3300 feet

52 — Ice Water
South Cle Elum • lat 47°06'46" lon 120°54'07"

DESCRIPTION: In a mixed forest setting on Ice Water Creek. Fish and swim in the creek. Supplies available at Cle Elum. Many animals can be seen in the area. Campers may gather firewood. Winter sports area nearby. CG is on the edge of Lt. Murray State Wildlife Area.

GETTING THERE: From Cle Elum go S on forest route 3350 approx. 8 mi. to Ice Water CG.

SINGLE RATE:	$8	OPEN DATES:	May-Sept
# of SINGLE SITES:	17		
		MAX STAY:	14 days
		ELEVATION:	2500 feet

53 — Ida Creek
Leavenworth • lat 47°36'28" lon 120°50'48"

DESCRIPTION: In a mixed forest setting at the confluence of Icicle and Ida Creek. Fish and swim in the creek. Supplies are available at Leavenworth. Deer, bears and birds are common to the area. Campers may gather firewood. Hiking and horseback riding in the nearby Alpine Lakes Wilderness.

GETTING THERE: From Leavenworth go SW on primary forest route 76 approx. 13 mi. to Ida Creek CG.

SINGLE RATE:	$8	OPEN DATES:	Yearlong*
# of SINGLE SITES:	10	MAX SPUR:	20 feet
		MAX STAY:	14 days
		ELEVATION:	2800 feet

54 — Indian Creek

Naches • lat 46°38'40" lon 121°14'28"

DESCRIPTION: In a mixed forest setting on the Rim Rock Lake. Fish for trout in the lake. Supplies available at Naches. Numerous wildlife in the area. Campers may gather firewood. There are many trails in the area. Point of interest nearby the CG area. Boat ramp at CG.

GETTING THERE: From Naches go W on US HWY 12 approx. 29 mi. to Indian Creek CG.

SINGLE RATE:	Varies	OPEN DATES:	May-Sept
# of SINGLE SITES:	39	MAX SPUR:	32 feet
		MAX STAY:	14 days
		ELEVATION:	3000 feet

55 — Johnny Creek
Leavenworth • lat 47°35'53" lon 120°48'56"

DESCRIPTION: In a mixed forest setting at the confluence of Icicle and Johnny Creek. Fish and swim in the creek. Supplies are available at Leavenworth. Deer, bears and birds are common to the area. Campers may gather firewood. Hiking and horseback riding in the nearby Alpine Lakes Wilderness. Rock climbing nearby.

GETTING THERE: From Leavenworth go SW on primary forest route 76 approx. 11.5 mi. to Johnny Creek CG.

SINGLE RATE:	Varies	OPEN DATES:	Yearlong*
# of SINGLE SITES:	65	MAX SPUR:	20 feet
		MAX STAY:	14 days
		ELEVATION:	2300 feet

 Campground has hosts   **Reservable sites**   **Accessible facilities**   **Fully developed**   **Semi-developed**   Rustic facilities

NOTE: Open dates listed are typical. Actual dates are dependent on conditions such as snow pack.

WENATCHEE NATIONAL FOREST • WASHINGTON • 46 — 55

56 Junior Point
Ardenvoir • lat 47°59'42" lon 120°23'59"

DESCRIPTION: This tent only CG is the site of an old fire lookout with great views. Supplies available at Ardenvoir. Numerous wildlife such as deer, elk, and mountain lions reside in the area. Campers may gather firewood. No designated trails in the area.

GETTING THERE: From Ardenvoir go N on primary forest route 51 (county route 371) approx. 17.5 mi. to forest route 5900. Go NE on 5900 approx. 12 mi. to Junior Point CG.

SINGLE RATE:	No fee	OPEN DATES:	Yearlong
# of SINGLE SITES:	5		
		MAX STAY:	14 days
		ELEVATION:	6600 feet

61 Lake Creek
Ardenvoir • lat 47°52'33" lon 121°00'44"

DESCRIPTION: In a mixed forest setting adjacent to the Little Wenatchee River. Fish or swim in the river. Supplies available at Ardenvoir. Deer, bears, squirrels and birds are common to the area. Campers may gather firewood. Many trails in the area leading to the Henry M Jackson Wilderness.

GETTING THERE: From Coles Corner go NW on state HWY 207 approx. 10 mi. to primary forest route 65. Go W on 65 approx. 10 mi. to Lake Creek CG.

SINGLE RATE:	No fee	OPEN DATES:	Yearlong
# of SINGLE SITES:	8	MAX SPUR:	99 feet
		MAX STAY:	14 days
		ELEVATION:	2300 feet

57 Kachess
Cle Elum • lat 47°21'18" lon 121°14'32"

DESCRIPTION: In a dense old-growth evergreen setting on Kachess Lake, surrounded by high mountains. Boat ramp located at the CG. Fish and swim from the lake. Supplies available at Cle Elum. Many animals can be seen in the area. Campers may gather firewood. A nature trail is within the CG and Rachel Lake Trail starts at CG.

GETTING THERE: From Cle Elum go NW on US HWY 90 approx. 18.5 mi. to primary forest route 49. Go NE on 49 approx. 4.5 mi. to Kachess CG.

SINGLE RATE:	$12	OPEN DATES:	May-Sept
# of SINGLE SITES:	183	MAX SPUR:	99 feet
GROUP RATE:	$60	MAX STAY:	14 days
# of GROUP SITES:	1	ELEVATION:	2300 feet

62 Lions Rock Springs
Ellensburg • lat 47°15'05" lon 120°34'57"

DESCRIPTION: This tent only CG is situated in a mixed forest setting on Lions Rock Springs. Supplies located at Ellensburg. Numerous animals can be viewed in the area. Campers may gather firewood. CG is a trailhead to many trails in the area. Point of interest nearby is A-Frame.

GETTING THERE: From Ellensburg go N on primary forest route 35 approx. 19 mi. to Lions Rock Springs CG.

SINGLE RATE:	No fee	OPEN DATES:	May-Sept
# of SINGLE SITES:	3		
		MAX STAY:	14 days
		ELEVATION:	6300 feet

58 Kaner Flat
Nile • lat 47°00'40" lon 121°07'44"

DESCRIPTION: In a mixed forest setting on the Little Naches River. Fish for trout in the river. Supplies available at Nile. Numerous wildlife frequent the area. Campers may gather firewood. The Horse Tail Falls and many trails can be found in the nearby area.

GETTING THERE: From Nile go N on state HWY 410 approx. 26 mi. to primary forest route 19. Go N on 19 approx. 2.5 mi. to Kaner Flat CG.

SINGLE RATE:	$9	OPEN DATES:	May-Oct
# of SINGLE SITES:	41	MAX SPUR:	30 feet
		MAX STAY:	14 days
		ELEVATION:	2678 feet

63 Little Naches
Nile • lat 46°59'23" lon 121°05'47"

DESCRIPTION: In a mixed forest setting on the Little Naches River. Fish for trout in the river. Supplies available at Nile. Numerous wildlife in the area. Campers may gather firewood. Many trails are in the area. The Horse Tail Falls is nearby.

GETTING THERE: From Nile go N on state HWY 410 approx. 26 mi. to primary forest route 19. Go N on 19 approx. 1/2 mi. to Little Naches CG.

SINGLE RATE:	Varies	OPEN DATES:	May-Oct
# of SINGLE SITES:	21	MAX SPUR:	32 feet
		MAX STAY:	14 days
		ELEVATION:	2562 feet

59 Ken Wilcox Horse Camp
Virden • lat 47°19'30" lon 120°31'00"

DESCRIPTION: In a mixed forest setting on Naneum Creek near Haney Meadow. Fish and swim int the creek. Supplies available in Virden. Many animals can be seen in the area. Stables at the CG. Campers may gather firewood. CG is a trailhead to many trails in the area. Point of interest nearby is Diamond Head.

GETTING THERE: From Virden go N on US HWY 97 approx. 13.5 mi. to forest route 9716. Go SE on 9716 approx. 3 mi. to Ken Wilcox Horse Camp CG.

SINGLE RATE:	No fee	OPEN DATES:	May-Sept
# of SINGLE SITES:	19	MAX SPUR:	99 feet
		MAX STAY:	14 days
		ELEVATION:	5500 feet

64 Little Wenatchee Ford
Coles Corner • lat 47°55'05" lon 121°05'09"

DESCRIPTION: In a mixed forest setting adjacent to the Little Wenatchee River. Fish or swim in the river. Supplies available at Coles Corner. Deer, bears, squirrels and birds are common to the area. Campers may gather firewood. Many trails in the area leading to the Henry M Jackson Wilderness. Stables at CG.

GETTING THERE: From Coles Corner go NW on state HWY 207 approx. 10 mi. to primary forest route 65. Go W on 65 approx. 15 mi. to Little Wenatchee Ford CG.

SINGLE RATE:	No fee	OPEN DATES:	Yearlong
# of SINGLE SITES:	3	MAX SPUR:	30 feet
		MAX STAY:	14 days
		ELEVATION:	2900 feet

60 Lake Creek
Ardenvoir • lat 47°56'13" lon 120°30'55"

DESCRIPTION: Open park-like setting of pines and firs alongside the Entiat River. Fish and swim in the river. Supplies are available at Coopers Store in Ardenvoir. Numerous wildlife can be seen in the area. Campers may gather firewood or purchase it at Coopers Store. Many trail nearby.

GETTING THERE: From Ardenvoir go N on primary forest route 51 (county route 371) approx. 17 mi. to Lake Creek CG.

SINGLE RATE:	$8	OPEN DATES:	May-Oct
# of SINGLE SITES:	18	MAX SPUR:	50 feet
		MAX STAY:	14 days
		ELEVATION:	2200 feet

65 Lodgepole
Nile • lat 46°55'01" lon 121°22'43"

DESCRIPTION: This CG is located in a mixed forest setting on the American River. Fish for trout in the river. Supplies available at Nile. Numerous wildlife in the area. Campers may gather firewood. Trails in the William O'Douglas Wilderness or the Norse Wilderness areas nearby.

GETTING THERE: From Nile go N on state HWY 410 approx. 41.5 mi. to Lodgepole CG.

SINGLE RATE:	Varies	OPEN DATES:	May-Oct
# of SINGLE SITES:	33	MAX SPUR:	20 feet
		MAX STAY:	14 days
		ELEVATION:	3500 feet

 Campground has hosts   Reservable sites   Accessible facilities   Fully developed   Semi-developed   Rustic facilities

NOTE: Open dates listed are typical. Actual dates are dependent on conditions such as snow pack.

66 Lucerne
Chelan • lat 48°12'06" lon 120°35'16"

DESCRIPTION: This boat-in, tent only CG is a stop off point for the Lake Chelan ferry. CG rests in a mixed conifer setting on the lake. Fish for trout in the lake. Supplies are available at Chelan. Numerous wildlife includes mountain goats, deer, and bighorn sheep. Hike the trail to Domke Mountain and Domke Lake Area.

GETTING THERE: Lucerne CG is located approx. 37 mi. NW of Chelan on the SW bank of Lake Chelan. Accessible by boat only.

SINGLE RATE:	No fee	OPEN DATES:	Yearlong
# of SINGLE SITES:	2	MAX STAY:	14 days
		ELEVATION:	1100 feet

67 Meadow Creek
Plain • lat 47°52'06" lon 120°41'34"

DESCRIPTION: In a mixed forest setting adjacent to the Chiwawa River. Fish, canoe, raft or swim in the river. Supplies available at Plain. Deer, bears, squirrels and birds are common to the area. Campers may gather firewood. Many trails in the area that access area CG's.

GETTING THERE: From Plain go N on primary forest route 62 (6100) approx. 10 mi. to Meadow Creek CG.

SINGLE RATE:	No fee	OPEN DATES:	Yearlong
# of SINGLE SITES:	4	MAX SPUR:	30 feet
		MAX STAY:	14 days
		ELEVATION:	2400 feet

68 Mineral Springs
Virden • lat 47°17'23" lon 120°41'57"

DESCRIPTION: In a mixed forest setting on the confluence of Medicine and Swauk Creeks. Fish and swim in the creeks. Supplies available at Virden. Many animals can be seen in the area. Campers may gather firewood. No designated trails in the area. Point of interest nearby is Red Top Mountian.

GETTING THERE: From Virden go N on US HWY 97 approx. 6 mi. to Mineral Springs CG.

SINGLE RATE:	$10	OPEN DATES:	May-Sept
# of SINGLE SITES:	12	MAX SPUR:	35 feet
GROUP RATE:	$50	MAX STAY:	14 days
# of GROUP SITES:	1	ELEVATION:	2700 feet

69 Mitchell Creek
Chelan • lat 47°58'14" lon 120°11'28"

DESCRIPTION: This boat-in, tent only CG is a popular picnic area on Mitchell Creek and Lake Chelan. Fish for trout in the creek or lake. Supplies available at Chelan. Numerous wildlife includes mountain goats, deer, and bighorn sheep. Campers may gather firewood. Enjoy a visit to the state wildlife areas nearby.

GETTING THERE: Mitchell Creek CG is located on the E bank of Lake Chelan approx. 15 mi. NW of Chelan. Accessible by boat only.

SINGLE RATE:	No fee	OPEN DATES:	Yearlong
# of SINGLE SITES:	7		
		MAX STAY:	14 days
		ELEVATION:	1100 feet

70 Moore Point
Chelan • lat 48°14'08" lon 120°36'53"

DESCRIPTION: This hike/boat-in, tent only CG is in a mixed forest setting on Fish Creek and Lake Chelan. Fish for trout in the lake. Supplies available at Chelan. Numerous wildlife can be seen in the area. Campers may gather firewood. Trail to Flick Creek to the north and Cascade Creek to the south.

GETTING THERE: Moore Point CG is located on the N Bank of Lake Chelan approx. 38 mi. NW from Chelan. Accessible by boat only.

SINGLE RATE:	No fee	OPEN DATES:	Yearlong
# of SINGLE SITES:	4		
		MAX STAY:	14 days
		ELEVATION:	1100 feet

71 Napeequa Crossing
Coles Corner • lat 47°55'05" lon 120°53'53"

DESCRIPTION: In a mixed forest setting on White River. Fish or swim in the river. Supplies available at Coles Corner. Deer, bears, squirrels and birds are common to the area. Campers may gather firewood. Trails into Twin Lakes in the Glacier Peak Wilderness.

GETTING THERE: From Coles Corner go N on state HWY 207 approx. 9 mi. to state HWY 22. Go NW on 22 approx. 7 mi. to Napeequa Crossing CG.

SINGLE RATE:	No fee	OPEN DATES:	Yearlong
# of SINGLE SITES:	5	MAX SPUR:	30 feet
		MAX STAY:	14 days
		ELEVATION:	2000 feet

72 Nason Creek
Coles Corner • lat 47°47'55" lon 120°42'47"

DESCRIPTION: In a mixed forest setting adjacent to the Lake Wenatchee. Fish or swim in the lake. Boat ramp nearby. Supplies available at Coles Corner. Deer, bears, squirrels and birds are common to the area. Campers may gather firewood. Many trails in the area. Winter sports area nearby.

GETTING THERE: From Coles Corner go N on state HWY 207 approx 3.5 mi. to Nason Creek CG.

SINGLE RATE:	$10	OPEN DATES:	Yearlong
# of SINGLE SITES:	73	MAX SPUR:	99 feet
		MAX STAY:	14 days
		ELEVATION:	1800 feet

73 North Fork
Ardenvoir • lat 47°59'21" lon 120°34'44"

DESCRIPTION: Open park-like setting of mixed pines with views of the Entiat River. Historical Entiat Falls is approx. 1/2 mi. away. Supplies are available at Coopers Store in Ardenvoir. Campers may gather firewood or purchase at Coopers Store. Numerous wildlife can be seen in the area.

GETTING THERE: From Ardenvoir go N on primary forest route 51 (county route 371) approx. 22 mi. to the North Fork CG.

SINGLE RATE:	$7	OPEN DATES:	May-Oct
# of SINGLE SITES:	8	MAX SPUR:	50 feet
		MAX STAY:	14 days
		ELEVATION:	2500 feet

74 Owhi
Lakedale • lat 48°13'18" lon 118°53'36"

DESCRIPTION: This walk-in, tent only CG is in a mixed forest setting on Cooper Lake. Boat and swim in the lake. Supplies available at Lakedale. Many animals can be seen in the area. Campers may gather firewood. Trail to Alpine Lakes Wilderness from the CG area.

GETTING THERE: From Lakedale go N on state HWY 903 approx. 8 mi. to primary forest route 46. Go N on 46 approx. 6.5 mi. to Owhi CG.

SINGLE RATE:	No fee	OPEN DATES:	Yearlong
# of SINGLE SITES:	23		
		MAX STAY:	14 days
		ELEVATION:	2800 feet

75 Peninsula
Naches • lat 46°38'12" lon 121°07'45"

DESCRIPTION: This dispersed CG is in a mixed forest setting on Rim Rock Lake. Fish for trout in the lake. A boat ramp is at the CG. Supplies available at Naches. Numerous wildlife can be seen in the area. Campers may gather firewood. Hike and bicycle trails in the area.

GETTING THERE: From Naches go W on US HWY 12 approx. 21 mi. to forest route 1200. Go SW on 1200 approx. 3 mi. to forest route 711. Go W on 711 approx 1 mi. to the Peninsula CG.

SINGLE RATE:	Varies	OPEN DATES:	May-Oct
		MAX STAY:	14 days
		ELEVATION:	3000 feet

 Campground has hosts   Reservable sites   Accessible facilities   Fully developed   Semi-developed   Rustic facilities

NOTE: Open dates listed are typical. Actual dates are dependent on conditions such as snow pack.

76 Phelps Creek
Plain • lat 48°04'11" lon 120°51'01"

DESCRIPTION: In a mixed forest setting on the Chiwawa River. Fish or swim in the river. Supplies available at Plain. Campers may gather firewood. Many animals can be seen in the area. Trail to Glaier Peak Wilderness leaves from the CG.

GETTING THERE: From Plain go N on forest route 672 approx. 6 mi. to primary forest route 62. Go N on 62 approx. 21 mi. to Phelps Creek CG.

SINGLE RATE:	$5	OPEN DATES:	Yearlong
# of SINGLE SITES:	7	MAX SPUR:	30 feet
		MAX STAY:	14 days
		ELEVATION:	2700 feet

77 Pine Flat
Ardenvoir • lat 47°45'30" lon 120°25'29"

DESCRIPTION: In a forest setting with views of Mad River. No fishing on the Mad River. Supplies are available at Coopers Store in Ardenvoir. Campers may gather firewood or purchase at Coopers Store. Numerous wildlife available in the area. No designated trails nearby.

GETTING THERE: Pine Flat CG is located approx. 4 mi. NW of Ardenvoir on forest route 5700.

SINGLE RATE:	$8	OPEN DATES:	Apr-Oct
# of SINGLE SITES:	7	MAX SPUR:	50 feet
GROUP RATE:	$60	MAX STAY:	14 days
# of GROUP SITES:	1	ELEVATION:	1600 feet

78 Pine Needle
Nile • lat 46°58'08" lon 121°12'31"

DESCRIPTION: This group CG rests in a mixed forest setting on the American River. The CG is reservation only. Fish for trout in the river. Supplies available at Nile. Numerous wildlife can be seen in the area. Campers may gather firewood. Trails nearby in the William O'Douglas Wilderness.

GETTING THERE: From Nile go N on state HWY 410 approx. 32 mi. to Pine Needle CG.

		OPEN DATES:	Yearlong*
		MAX SPUR:	40 feet
GROUP RATE:	Varies	MAX STAY:	14 days
# of GROUP SITES:	1	ELEVATION:	3250 feet

79 Pleasant Valley
Nile • lat 46°56'34" lon 121°19'27"

DESCRIPTION: In a mixed forest setting on the American River. Fish for trout in the river. Supplies available at Nile. Numerous wildlife in the area. Campers may gather firewood. Trail on the Kettle Creek in the William O'Douglas Wilderness. A winter sports area and Union Creek Falls are nearby.

GETTING THERE: From Nile go N on state HWY 410 approx. 38 mi. to Pleasant Valley CG.

SINGLE RATE:	Varies	OPEN DATES:	May-Oct
# of SINGLE SITES:	16	MAX SPUR:	32 feet
		MAX STAY:	14 days
		ELEVATION:	3300 feet

80 Prince Creek
Chelan • lat 48°08'46" lon 120°29'36"

DESCRIPTION: This boat-in, tent only CG is located in mixed conifers on Prince Creek and Lake Chelan. Fish for trout in the lake. Supplies are available at Chelan. Numerous wildlife in area includes mountain goats, deer, and bighorn sheep. Campers may gather firewood. Hiking trails lead into Lake Chelan Sawtooth Wilderness.

GETTING THERE: Prince Creek CG is located approx. 32 mi. NW of Chelan on the N bank of Lake Chelan. Accessible by boat only.

SINGLE RATE:	No fee	OPEN DATES:	Yearlong
# of SINGLE SITES:	6		
		MAX STAY:	14 days
		ELEVATION:	1100 feet

81 Quartz Mountain
Ellensburg • lat 47°04'24" lon 121°04'40"

DESCRIPTION: This tent only CG is situated in a mixed forest setting near the Manastash Creek. Supplies located at Ellensburg. Numerous animals can be viewed in the area. Campers may gather firewood. CG is a trailhead for trail that runs along the South Fork of the Manastash Creek.

GETTING THERE: From Ellensburg go W on primary forest route 31 approx. 21 mi. to forest route 3100. Go W on 3100 approx. 7 mi. to Quartz Mountain CG. 4WD recomended.

SINGLE RATE:	No fee	OPEN DATES:	May-Sept
# of SINGLE SITES:	3		
		MAX STAY:	14 days
		ELEVATION:	6200 feet

82 Red Mountain
Lakedale • lat 47°22'00" lon 121°06'05"

DESCRIPTION: This tent only CG is situated in a mixed forest setting on the Cle Elum River. Fish and swim in the river or nearby Cle Elum Lake. Supplies available at Lakedale. Campers may gather firewood. Trail runs along Sasse Ridge to Sasse Mountain from CG.

GETTING THERE: From Lakedale go N on 903 approx. 8 mi. to Red Mountain CG.

SINGLE RATE:	No fee	OPEN DATES:	May-Sept
# of SINGLE SITES:	9		
		MAX STAY:	14 days
		ELEVATION:	2200 feet

83 Refrigerator Harbor
Chelan • lat 48°12'06" lon 120°35'16"

DESCRIPTION: This boat-in, tent only CG is located in mixed conifer on Lake Chelan near Lucerne. Fish for trout in the lake. Supplies are available at Chelan. Numerous wildlife in area includes mountain goats, deer, and bighorn sheep. Campers may gather firewood. Hike the trail to Domke Mountain and Domke Lake area.

GETTING THERE: Refrigerator Harbor CG is located approx. 37 mi. NW of Chelan on the S bank of Lake Chelan. Accessible by boat only.

SINGLE RATE:	No fee	OPEN DATES:	Yearlong
# of SINGLE SITES:	4		
		MAX STAY:	14 days
		ELEVATION:	1100 feet

84 River Bend
Naches • lat 46°40'35" lon 121°04'12"

DESCRIPTION: In a mixed conifer forest setting on Finner Creek. Fish in nearby Chawawa River. Supplies available in Naches. Wildlife in this area includes blackbears and deer. Campers may gather firewood. Trails in the area that lead to Schaefer Lake.

GETTING THERE: From Naches go W on US HWY 12 approx. 20 mi. to River Bend CG.

SINGLE RATE:	$5	OPEN DATES:	Yearlong
# of SINGLE SITES:	6	MAX SPUR:	30 feet
		MAX STAY:	14 days
		ELEVATION:	2500 feet

85 Rock Creek
Plain • lat 47°58'12" lon 120°47'20"

DESCRIPTION: In a mixed conifer forest setting on Rock Creek. Fish in nearby Chawawa River. Supplies available in Naches. Wildlife in this area includes blackbears and deer. Campers may gather firewood. Trails in the area lead into the Schaefer Lake area.

GETTING THERE: From Plain go N on forest route 6100 approx. 7 mi. to primary forest route 62(6200). Go N on 62 approx. 14 mi. to Rock Creek CG.

SINGLE RATE:	$5	OPEN DATES:	Yearlong
# of SINGLE SITES:	4	MAX SPUR:	30 feet
		MAX STAY:	14 days
		ELEVATION:	2500 feet

 Campground has hosts   Reservable sites   Accessible facilities   Fully developed   Semi-developed   Rustic facilities

NOTE: Open dates listed are typical. Actual dates are dependent on conditions such as snow pack.

86 Rock Island
Leavenworth • lat 47°36'26" lon 120°55'00"

DESCRIPTION: In a mixed forest setting at the confluence of Icicle Creek. Fish and swim in the creek. Supplies are available at Leavenworth. Deer, bears and birds are common to the area. Campers may gather firewood. Trail onsight runs along Jack Creek into the Alpine Lakes Wilderness.

GETTING THERE: From Leavenworth go SW on primary forest route 76 approx. 17 mi. to Rock Island CG.

SINGLE RATE:	$8	OPEN DATES:	Yearlong*
# of SINGLE SITES:	22	MAX SPUR:	22 feet
		MAX STAY:	14 days
		ELEVATION:	2900 feet

87 Safety Harbor
Chelan • lat 48°02'56" lon 120°22'35"

DESCRIPTION: This boat-in, tent only CG is in a mixed conifer setting on Safety Harbor Creek and Lake Chelan. Fish for trout in the lake. Supplies available at Chelan. Numerous wildlife includes mountain goats, deer, and bighorn sheep. A hiking trail leads to Flick Creek (north) and Cascade Creek (south).

GETTING THERE: Safety Harbor CG is located approx. 24 mi. NW of Chelan on the N bank of Lake Chelan.

SINGLE RATE:	No fee	OPEN DATES:	Yearlong
# of SINGLE SITES:	2		
		MAX STAY:	14 days
		ELEVATION:	1100 feet

88 Salmon La Sac
Lakedale • lat 47°24'04" lon 121°05'56"

DESCRIPTION: In a mixed forest setting on the confluence of Cle Elum River and Salmon La Sac Creek. Fish or swim in either river or creek. Supplies available at Lakedale. Firewood is for sale at CG. Many animals can be seen in the area. Trails to the Alpine lakes Wilderness from CG.

GETTING THERE: From Lakedale go N on state HWY 903 approx. 10.5 mi. to Salmon La Sac CG.

SINGLE RATE:	$12	OPEN DATES:	May-Sept
# of SINGLE SITES:	127	MAX SPUR:	40 feet
		MAX STAY:	14 days
		ELEVATION:	2400 feet

89 Sawmill Flat
Naches • lat 46°58'30" lon 121°05'40"

DESCRIPTION: In a mixed forest setting on the Naches River. Fish for trout in the river. Supplies available at Niles. Numerous wildlife in the area. Campers may gather firewood. This CG is a trailhead to the nearby William O'Douglas Wilderness. There is a winter sports area nearby.

GETTING THERE: Off Hwy 410

SINGLE RATE:	Varies	OPEN DATES:	May-Oct
# of SINGLE SITES:	24	MAX SPUR:	24 feet
		MAX STAY:	14 days
		ELEVATION:	2500 feet

90 Schaefer Creek
Plain • lat 47°58'31" lon 120°48'07"

DESCRIPTION: In a mixed conifer forest setting near the Chiwawa River. Fish fin the river. Supplies available in Plain. Wildlife in this area includes blackbears and deer. Campers may gather firewood. Trailhead from CG for hiking and horseback riding into the Glacier Peak Wilderness.

GETTING THERE: From Plain go N on forest route 6100 approx. 7 mi. to primary forest route 62 (6200). Go N on 62 approx. 14.5 mi. to Schaefer Creek CG.

SINGLE RATE:	$5	OPEN DATES:	Yearlong
# of SINGLE SITES:	6	MAX SPUR:	30 feet
		MAX STAY:	14 days
		ELEVATION:	2500 feet

91 Silver Falls
Ardenvoir • lat 47°57'31" lon 120°32'10"

DESCRIPTION: This CG is located in mixed conifer at the confluence of Silver Creek and Entiat River. This CG offers a picnic shelter, barrier free interpretive site, fishing and hiking. Wildlife includes blackbears and deer. Supplies available in Ardenvoir. Visit the scenic Silver Falls nearby.

GETTING THERE: From Ardenvoir go N on primary forest route 51 (county route 371) approx. 19 mi. to Silver Falls CG.

SINGLE RATE:	$9	OPEN DATES:	May-Sept
# of SINGLE SITES:	31	MAX SPUR:	20 feet
GROUP RATE:	Varies	MAX STAY:	14 days
# of GROUP SITES:	1	ELEVATION:	2400 feet

92 Snowberry Bowl
Chelan • lat 47°57'00" lon 120°16'00"

DESCRIPTION: This tent only CG is situated in a mixed conifer forest a short distance away from Lake Chelan. Fish and swim in the lake. Supplies are available at Lake Chelan. Numerous wildlife includes mountain goats, deer, and bighorn sheep. Campers may gather firewood. Trails and snow park nearby.

GETTING THERE: From Chelan go W on US HWY 97 approx. 3 mi. to primary forest route 23. Go NW on 23 approx. 17 mi. to forest route 5900. Go SW on 5900 approx. 4 mi. to Snowberry Bowl CG.

SINGLE RATE:	$5	OPEN DATES:	Yearlong
# of SINGLE SITES:	3		
		MAX STAY:	14 days
		ELEVATION:	2000 feet

93 Soda Springs
Coles Corner • lat 46°54'30" lon 121°14'00"

DESCRIPTION: This tent only CG is in a mixed forest setting on Soda Creek. Fish and swim in the creek. Supplies available at Coles Corner. Many animals can be seen in the area. Campers may gather firewood. Hike in nearby Glacier Peak and Henry M. Jackson Wilderness Areas.

GETTING THERE: From Coles Corner go NW on state HWY 207 approx. 10.5 mi. to Soda Creek CG.

SINGLE RATE:	No fee	OPEN DATES:	Yearlong
# of SINGLE SITES:	5		
		MAX STAY:	14 days
		ELEVATION:	2000 feet

94 Soda Springs
Naches • lat 46°55'33" lon 121°12'47"

DESCRIPTION: In a mixed forest setting on the Bumping River. Fish for trout in the river. Supplies available at Nile. Numerous wildlife in the area. Campers may gather firewood. This CG is a trailhead to the nearby William O'Douglas Wilderness.

GETTING THERE: From Naches go NW on state HWY 410(US HWY 12) approx. 30 mi. to forest route 1800. Go SW on 1800 approx. 6 mi. to Soda Springs CG.

SINGLE RATE:	Varies	OPEN DATES:	May-Oct
# of SINGLE SITES:	26	MAX SPUR:	30 feet
		MAX STAY:	14 days
		ELEVATION:	3100 feet

95 South Fork
Naches • lat 46°37'16" lon 121°07'51"

DESCRIPTION: In a mixed forest setting near Rim Rock Lake. Fish for trout in the lake. Supplies available at Naches. Numerous wildlife in the area. Campers may gather firewood. There is a winter sports area nearby. By reservation only.

GETTING THERE: From Naches go W on US HWY 12 approx. 19 mi. to forest route 1200. Go SW on 1200 approx. 5 mi. to South Fork CG.

SINGLE RATE:	$7	OPEN DATES:	May-Oct
# of SINGLE SITES:	9	MAX SPUR:	20 feet
		MAX STAY:	14 days
		ELEVATION:	3000 feet

 Campground has hosts   **Reservable sites**   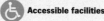 **Accessible facilities**   **Fully developed**   **Semi-developed**   **Rustic facilities**

NOTE: Open dates listed are typical. Actual dates are dependent on conditions such as snow pack.

96 South Fork Meadow
South Cle Elum • lat 47°05'46" lon 120°59'32"

DESCRIPTION: This tent only CG is situated in a mixed forest setting on South Fork Taneum Creek. Fish or swim in the creek. Supplies located at Cle Elum. Numerous animals can be viewed in the area. Campers may gather firewood. A trail runs along the Taneum Ridge.

GETTING THERE: From Cle Elum go S on forest route 3350 approx. 12.5 mi. to South Fork Meadow CG.

SINGLE RATE: # of SINGLE SITES:	No fee 3	OPEN DATES:	Yearlong
		MAX STAY:	14 days

97 South Navarre
Greens Landing • lat 48°06'26" lon 120°20'15"

DESCRIPTION: This tent only CG is in a mixed forest setting near Lake Chelan. Fish for trout in the lake. Supplies available at Greens Landing. Numerous wildlife can be seen in the area. Campers may gather firewood. Trail leads to Lake Chelan Sawtooth Wilderness. No drinking water.

GETTING THERE: From Greens Landing go NW on forest route 8200 approx. 29 mi. to South Navarre CG.

SINGLE RATE: # of SINGLE SITES:	No fee 4	OPEN DATES:	Yearlong
		MAX STAY: ELEVATION:	14 days 6475 feet

98 Spruce Grove
Ardenvoir • lat 48°00'17" lon 120°36'12"

DESCRIPTION: This tent only campground sits in mixed conifers on the Entiat River. Enjoy fishing for trout in the river. Wildlife in this area includes blackbears and deer. Supplies in Ardenvoir. CG is busy weekends and holidays. Campers may gather firewood. There are several multi-use trails in the area.

GETTING THERE: From Ardenvoir go N on primary forest route 51 (county route 371) approx. 25 mi. to Spruce Grove CG.

SINGLE RATE: # of SINGLE SITES:	$3 2	OPEN DATES:	May-Oct*
		MAX STAY: ELEVATION:	14 days 2900 feet

99 Stuart
Chelan • lat 48°10'52" lon 120°34'51"

DESCRIPTION: This hike/boat-in, tent only CG is in a mixed forest setting on Domke Lake. Fish for trout from the lake. Supplies available at Chelan. Numerous wildlife can be seen in the area. Campers may gather firewood. Trail to Domke Mountain.

GETTING THERE: From Chelan go approx. 37 mi. N by boat to Refrigerator Harbor. Hike-in approx. 3 mi. to Stuart CG.

SINGLE RATE: # of SINGLE SITES:	No fee 2	OPEN DATES:	Yearlong
		MAX STAY: ELEVATION:	14 days 2210 feet

100 Swauk
Virden • lat 47°19'42" lon 120°39'23"

DESCRIPTION: In a mixed forest setting on Swauk Creek. Fish and swim in the creek. Supplies located at Virden. Numerous animals can be viewed in the area. Campers may gather firewood. Winter sports and view point area nearby.

GETTING THERE: From Virden go N on US HWY 97 approx. 10 mi. to Swauk CG.

SINGLE RATE: # of SINGLE SITES:	$8 23	OPEN DATES:	May-Sept
		MAX STAY: ELEVATION:	14 days 3200 feet

101 Tamarack Spring
Ellensburg • lat 47°03'48" lon 120°53'46"

DESCRIPTION: This tent only CG is in a mixed forest setting near Tamarack Springs. Relax at the springs nearby. Supplies available at Ellensburg. CG borders the Lt. Murray State Wildlife Area where many types of wildlife can be seen. Campers may gather firewood. Stables available at CG. Many trails in the area.

GETTING THERE: From Ellensburg go W on primary forest route 31 approx. 21 mi. to forest route 3100. Go W on 3100 approx. 2 mi. to forest route 3120. Go E on 3120 approx. 4.5 mi. to Tamarack Spring CG.

SINGLE RATE: # of SINGLE SITES:	No fee 3	OPEN DATES:	May-Sept
		MAX STAY: ELEVATION:	14 days 4500 feet

102 Taneum
Cle Elum • lat 47°06'30" lon 120°51'23"

DESCRIPTION: This CG is in a mixed forest setting near Taneum Meadow on Taneum Creek. Fish and swim in the creek. Supplies available at Cle Elum. CG borders the Lt. Murray State Wildlife Area where many types of wildlife can be seen. Campers may gather firewood. Many trails in the area.

GETTING THERE: From Cle Elum go S on forest route 3350 approx. 10 mi. to Taneum CG.

SINGLE RATE: # of SINGLE SITES: GROUP RATE: # of GROUP SITES:	$10 13 $5 1	OPEN DATES: MAX STAY: ELEVATION:	May-Sept 14 days 2400 feet

103 Theseus Creek
Coles Corner • lat 47°52'22" lon 121°01'00"

DESCRIPTION: In a mixed forest setting on Theseus Creek. Fish in nearby Little Wenatchee River. Supplies available in Cole Corner. Numerous wildlife can be seen in the area. Campers may gather firewood. Hike in the nearby Henry M. Jackson Wilderness Area.

GETTING THERE: From Coles Corner go NW on state HWY 207 approx. 10 mi. to primary forest route 65. Go W on 65 approx. 10 mi. to Thesus Creek CG.

SINGLE RATE: # of SINGLE SITES:	No fee 3	OPEN DATES: MAX SPUR: MAX STAY: ELEVATION:	Yearlong 30 feet 14 days 2200 feet

104 Three Creek
Ardenvoir • lat 48°00'35" lon 120°36'55"

DESCRIPTION: This tent only CG sits in mixed conifers on the Entiat River. Enjoy fishing for trout in the river. Wildlife in this area include blackbears and deer. Supplies in Ardenvoir. CG is busy weekends and holidays. Campers may gather firewood. There are several multi-use trails in the area.

GETTING THERE: From Ardenvoir go N on primary forest route 51 (county route 371) approx. 25.5 mi. to Three Creek CG.

SINGLE RATE: # of SINGLE SITES:	$3 4	OPEN DATES:	May-Oct*
		MAX STAY: ELEVATION:	14 days 2900 feet

105 Tumwater
Leavenworth • lat 47°40'38" lon 120°43'55"

DESCRIPTION: In a mixed forest setting in Tumwater Canyon on the Wenatchee River. Fish and swim in the creek. Supplies are available at Leavenworth. Deer, bears and birds are common to the area. Campers may gather firewood. Hiking and horseback riding in the nearby Alpine Lakes Wilderness.

GETTING THERE: From Leavenworth go N on US HWY 2 approx. 8 mi. to Tumwater CG.

SINGLE RATE: # of SINGLE SITES: GROUP RATE: # of GROUP SITES:	$11 84 $80 1	OPEN DATES: MAX SPUR: MAX STAY: ELEVATION:	May-Oct 36 feet 14 days 2050 feet

 Campground has hosts   **Reservable sites**   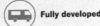 **Accessible facilities**   **Fully developed**   **Semi-developed**   **Rustic facilities**

NOTE: Open dates listed are typical. Actual dates are dependent on conditions such as snow pack.

106 White Pass Horse Camp
Naches • lat 46°38'40" lon 121°23'06"

DESCRIPTION: In a mixed forest setting on Leach Lake. Fish for trout in the lake. Supplies available at Naches. Numerous wildlife in the area. Campers may gather firewood. The Pacific Crest National Scenic Trail runs through CG. Horse stable and information center at the CG.

GETTING THERE: From Naches go NW on US HWY 12 approx. 36 mi. to White Pass Horse Camp CG.

SINGLE RATE:	$7	OPEN DATES:	May-Oct
# of SINGLE SITES:	16	MAX SPUR:	20 feet
		MAX STAY:	14 days
		ELEVATION:	4550 feet

107 White Pine
Coles Corner • lat 47°47'21" lon 120°52'13"

DESCRIPTION: In a mixed forest setting near several creeks. Fish or swim in the nearby creeks. The Cascade Meadows are nearby. Supplies available in Cole Corner. Numerous wildlife available in the area. Campers may gather firewood. Trail nearby to the Alpine Lookout.

GETTING THERE: From Coles Corner go W on forest route 7912 approx. 7 mi. to White Pine CG.

SINGLE RATE:	No fee	OPEN DATES:	Yearlong
# of SINGLE SITES:	5	MAX SPUR:	99 feet
		MAX STAY:	14 days
		ELEVATION:	1900 feet

108 White River Falls
Coles Corner • lat 47°57'11" lon 120°56'15"

DESCRIPTION: In a mixed forest setting on White River. Fish and swim in the River. Supplies available in Cole Corner. Numerous wildlife can be seen in the area. Campers may gather firewood. This CG is a trailhead into the Glacier Peak Wilderness Area.

GETTING THERE: From Coles Corner go N on state HWY 207 approx. 9 mi. to stae HWY 22. Go NW on 22 approx. 7 mi. to forest route 6400. Go N on 6400 approx. 3 mi. to White River Falls Meadows CG.

SINGLE RATE:	No fee	OPEN DATES:	Yearlong
# of SINGLE SITES:	5		
		MAX STAY:	14 days
		ELEVATION:	2100 feet

109 Wild Rose
Naches • lat 46°40'26" lon 121°02'32"

DESCRIPTION: In a mixed forest setting on the Tieton River. Fish for trout in the river. Supplies available at Naches. Numerous wildlife in the area. Campers may gather firewood. Many hiking trails in the area.

GETTING THERE: From Naches go SW on US HWY 12 approx. 18 mi. to Wild Rose CG.

SINGLE RATE:	No fee	OPEN DATES:	Yearlong*
# of SINGLE SITES:	8	MAX SPUR:	22 feet
		MAX STAY:	14 days
		ELEVATION:	2400 feet

110 Willows
Naches • lat 46°40'22" lon 121°02'19"

DESCRIPTION: In a mixed forest setting on the Tieton River. Fish for trout in the river. Supplies available at Naches. Numerous wildlife can be seen in the area. Campers may gather firewood. Many hiking trails in the area.

GETTING THERE: From Naches go SW on US HWY 12 approx. 18 mi. to Willows CG.

SINGLE RATE:	Varies	OPEN DATES:	May-Oct
# of SINGLE SITES:	16	MAX SPUR:	20 feet
		MAX STAY:	14 days
		ELEVATION:	2400 feet

111 Windy Camp
Ardenvoir • lat 47°53'58" lon 120°19'50"

DESCRIPTION: This tent only CG is in a mixed forest setting near First Creek. Fish for trout from the creek. Supplies are available at Ardenvoir. Numerous wildlife can be seen in the area. Campers may gather firewood. Point of interest within 1/2 mi. of CG.

GETTING THERE: From Ardenvoir go N approx. 1 mi. on county route 19 to forest route 5300 (county route 371). Go NE on 5300 approx. 6 mi. to forest route 8410. Go N on 8410 approx. 12 mi. to Windy Camp CG.

SINGLE RATE:	No fee	OPEN DATES:	Yearlong
# of SINGLE SITES:	2		
		MAX STAY:	14 days
		ELEVATION:	5900 feet

112 Windy Point
Naches • lat 46°41'35" lon 120°54'22"

DESCRIPTION: In a mixed forest setting on the Tieton River. Fish for trout in the river. Supplies available at Naches. Numerous wildlife in the area. Campers may gather firewood. Many hiking trails in the area.

GETTING THERE: From Naches go SW on US HWY 12 approx. 12 mi. to Windy Point CG.

SINGLE RATE:	Varies	OPEN DATES:	May-Oct
# of SINGLE SITES:	15	MAX SPUR:	22 feet
		MAX STAY:	14 days
		ELEVATION:	2000 feet

113 Wish Poosh
Lakedale • lat 47°16'48" lon 121°05'08"

DESCRIPTION: In a mixed forest setting on Cle Elum Lake. Fish and swim in the lake. Supplies available at Lakedale. Boat ramp at the CG. Many types of wildlife can be seen in the area. Campers may gather firewood. Trails from CG area connect to a larger system leading to the Alpine Lakes Wilderness.

GETTING THERE: From Lakedale go N on state HWY 903 approx. 2 mi. to Wish Poosh CG.

SINGLE RATE:	$12	OPEN DATES:	May-Sept
# of SINGLE SITES:	39		
		MAX STAY:	14 days
		ELEVATION:	2400 feet

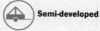 **Campground has hosts** **Reservable sites**  **Accessible facilities** **Fully developed** **Semi-developed** **Rustic facilities**

NOTE: Open dates listed are typical. Actual dates are dependent on conditions such as snow pack.

Page 587

WENATCHEE NATIONAL FOREST • WASHINGTON • 106 — 113

MONONGAHELA NATIONAL FOREST

Located in the highest mountains of east central West Virginia, the Monongahela National Park has much to offer visitors. Nearly 700 miles of marked trails invite you to take a hike, while the 43-mile long Highland Scenic Highway joins other roads to offer you a scenic drive. Spring wildflowers and bright autumn leaf colors, mountain streams and quiet woods all draw people into the forest.

The forest is noted for its rugged landscape with spectacular views, blueberry thickets, highland bogs, and open areas with exposed rocks. It's a prime place for recreation which can range from treks in the five wildernesses and mountain climbing to traditional developed site camping at Seneca Shadows and Lake Sherwood.

Hunting, trapping, fishing, and wildlife viewing are popular activities. The Monongahela also has 129 miles of warm water fishing and 576 miles of trout streams for anglers to try their luck. In addition, the forest provides habitat for nine federally listed endangered or threatened species and 50 other species of rare/sensitive plants and animals.

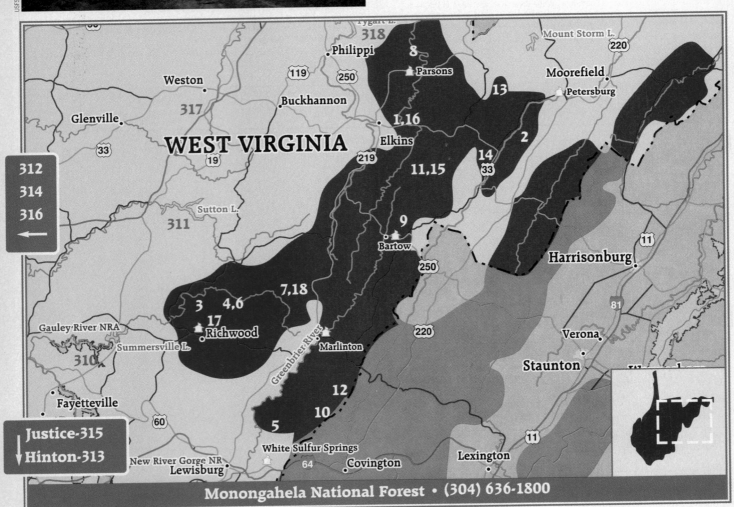

Monongahela National Forest • (304) 636-1800

1 Bear Heaven
Elkins • lat 38°55'45" lon 079°40'47"

DESCRIPTION: This tent only CG accesses the Otter Creek Wilderness trail system. There are unique rock outcroppings in this area. CG may be frequented by bears. Other wildlife in the area includes deer, foxes, and turkeys. Supplies in Elkins. Enjoy a scenic drive on the Stuart Memorial Drive.

GETTING THERE: From Elkins go E on US HWY 33 approx. 10 mi. to forest route 145. Go N on 145 approx. 1.5 mi. to Bears Heaven CG.

SINGLE RATE:	$5	OPEN DATES:	Yearlong
# of SINGLE SITES:	8		
		MAX STAY:	14 days
		ELEVATION:	3000 feet

2 Big Bend
Petersburg • lat 38°53'22" lon 079°14'23"

DESCRIPTION: This reservation only CG is situated on the South Branch of the Potomac River. Enjoy fishing in the river but please check fishing regulations. Boating and paddling are available but are limited to springtime periods of high water. A one mile loop trail is at the CG. Bird watch at Dolly Sods Scenic Area.

GETTING THERE: From Petersburg go S on US HWY 220 approx. 16 mi. to county route 2. Go W on 2 approx. 4 mi. to forest route 809. Go NW on 809 approx. 3.5 mi. to Big Bend CG.

SINGLE RATE:	Varies	OPEN DATES:	Apr-Dec
# of SINGLE SITES:	47	MAX SPUR:	20 feet
		MAX STAY:	14 days
		ELEVATION:	1600 feet

3 Big Rock
Richwood • lat 38°17'45" lon 080°31'27"

DESCRIPTION: This CG is located in mixed hardwoods on Cranberry River. There is a trail that runs along the lake. CG may be frequented by bears. Other wildlife includes deer, foxes and turkeys. Supplies in Richwood. Enjoy a drive on Highland Scenic HWY or drop by Cranberry Mountain Visitor Center.

GETTING THERE: From Richwood go N on forest route 76 approx. 5 mi. to Big Rock CG.

SINGLE RATE:	$6	OPEN DATES:	Mar-Dec
# of SINGLE SITES:	5	MAX SPUR:	40 feet
		MAX STAY:	14 days
		ELEVATION:	2158 feet

4 Bishop Knob
Richmond • lat 38°20'27" lon 080°29'20"

DESCRIPTION: This CG is centrally located on a ridgetop between the Cranberry and Williams Rivers. Fish for trout in the rivers. CG may be frequented by bears. Other wildlife includes deer, foxes and turkeys. Hiking trails nearby. Enjoy a drive on Highland Scenic HWY or drop by Cranberry Mountain Visitor Center.

GETTING THERE: From Richmond go N on forest route 76 approx. 5 mi. to forest route 81. Go N on 81 approx. 5.5 mi. to Bishop Knob CG.

SINGLE RATE:	$4	OPEN DATES:	Apr-Dec
# of SINGLE SITES:	61	MAX SPUR:	40 feet
		MAX STAY:	14 days
		ELEVATION:	3000 feet

5 Blue Bend
White Sulphur • lat 37°55'13" lon 080°16'16"

DESCRIPTION: This CG is located in mixed hardwoods on Anthony Creek. The CG offers swimming, fishing, an interpretive trail, and small picnic shelter. Group camping fees are charged 05/15-9/30 only. Campers may enjoy a hike to Round Mountain. Supplies in White Sulphur. CG can be busy weekends and holidays.

GETTING THERE: From White Sulphur go N on county route 36 approx. 8 mi. to county route 21. Go W on 21 approx. 1.5 mi. to Blue Bend CG.

SINGLE RATE:	$7	OPEN DATES:	Yearlong
# of SINGLE SITES:	22	MAX SPUR:	60 feet
GROUP RATE:	$25	MAX STAY:	14 days
# of GROUP SITES:	1	ELEVATION:	1960 feet

6 Cranberry
Richmond • lat 38°19'31" lon 080°26'31"

DESCRIPTION: This CG is situated in grassy, open bottomland on the Cranberry River. A nearby trail leads to the Cranberry Wilderness. CG fills in early summer. CG may be frequented by bears. Other wildlife includes deer, foxes and turkeys. Enjoy a drive on Highland Scenic HWY or drop by Cranberry Mtn. Visitor Center.

GETTING THERE: From Richmond go N on forest route 76 approx. 5 mi. to forest route 81. Go N on 81 approx. 8 mi. to Cranberry CG.

SINGLE RATE:	$8	OPEN DATES:	Yearlong
# of SINGLE SITES:	30	MAX SPUR:	40 feet
		MAX STAY:	14 days
		ELEVATION:	2500 feet

7 Day Run
Marlinton • lat 38°17'13" lon 080°12'57"

DESCRIPTION: This CG is situated in mixed hardwoods on the Williams River. Campers may hike along the west side of the river. Enjoy a drive on the Highlands Scenic HWY, or a visit to the Cranberry Mountain Visitor Center. Wildlife in this area includes black bears, turkeys, deer and foxes. Visit the Falls of Hills Creek.

GETTING THERE: From Marlinton go N on HWY 219/55 approx. 6 mi. to HWY 150 (Highland Scenic HWY). Go W on 150 approx. 7 mi. to forest route 98. Go S on 98 approx. 4 mi. to Day Run CG.

SINGLE RATE:	$6	OPEN DATES:	Mar-Dec
# of SINGLE SITES:	12	MAX SPUR:	30 feet
		MAX STAY:	14 days
		ELEVATION:	3119 feet

8 Horseshoe
Bretz • lat 39°10'25" lon 079°36'26"

DESCRIPTION: This CG is nestled in mixed hardwoods along Horseshoe Run. Fish for trout. There is a large open field nearby as well as several hiking trails. CG may be frequented by bears. Other wildlife in the area includes deer and turkeys. Visit Fernow Experimental Forest but follow restrictions and signs.

GETTING THERE: From Bretz go N on county route 1 approx. 6 mi. to county route 7. Go NE on 7 approx. 4.5 mi. to Horseshoe CG.

SINGLE RATE:	$10	OPEN DATES:	May-Dec
# of SINGLE SITES:	13	MAX SPUR:	50 feet
		MAX STAY:	14 days
		ELEVATION:	2500 feet

9 Island
Bartow • lat 38°34'49" lon 079°42'17"

DESCRIPTION: This tent only CG is a favorite among fisherman and is situated in mixed hardwoods. CG is adjacent to Long Run and the East Fork of the Greenbrier River. There is a trail that runs along the river. CG may be frequented by bears. Visit the Gaudineer Scenic Area, a virgin spruce forest. Area may flood.

GETTING THERE: Island CG is located approx. 5 mi. NE of Bartow on county route 28.

SINGLE RATE:	No fee	OPEN DATES:	Yearlong
# of SINGLE SITES:	6		
		MAX STAY:	14 days
		ELEVATION:	3000 feet

10 Lake Sherwood
White Sulphur • lat 38°00'24" lon 080°00'38"

DESCRIPTION: This CG is situated in mixed hardwoods on Lake Sherwood. This lake spans 165 acres and is the largest in the forest. The CG offers fishing, boating, a RV dump station, and amphitheater. There are evening programs throughout the summer. Supplies are in White Sulphur. There are hiking trails in the area.

GETTING THERE: From White Sulphur go N on state HWY 92 approx. 15 mi. to county route 14. Go E then N on 14 approx. 10 mi. to Lake Sherwood CG.

SINGLE RATE:	$12	OPEN DATES:	May-Sept
# of SINGLE SITES:	96	MAX SPUR:	40 feet
GROUP RATE:	$25	MAX STAY:	14 days
# of GROUP SITES:	1	ELEVATION:	2600 feet

 Campground has hosts   **Reservable sites**   **Accessible facilities**   **Fully developed**   **Semi-developed**   **Rustic facilities**

NOTE: Open dates listed are typical. Actual dates are dependent on conditions such as snow pack.

11 Laurel Fork
Glady • lat 38°44'25" lon 079°41'37"

DESCRIPTION: This CG is situated in mixed hardwoods next to Laurel Fork River. Visit the Gaudineer Scenic Area, a virgin spruce forest. Hike the many trails in Laurel Fork North and South Wilderness areas. Supplies in Glady. CG may be frequented by bears. Other wildlife includes deer, turkeys, foxes and coyotes. Area may flood.

GETTING THERE: From Glady go SE on county rte. 22 aprx. 3.5 mi. to forest rte. 422. Go E & S on 422 aprx. 2 mi. to forest rte. 14. Go S on 14 aprx. 1 mi. to forest rte. 423. Go S on 423 aprx. 2 mi. to CG.

SINGLE RATE:	No fee	OPEN DATES:	Yearlong
# of SINGLE SITES:	19	MAX SPUR:	45 feet
		MAX STAY:	14 days
		ELEVATION:	3102 feet

12 Pocahontas
White Sulphur • lat 38°06'07" lon 079°58'00"

DESCRIPTION: This CG is located in mixed hardwoods on Cochran Creek. Enjoy a hike from the CG along Two Lick Run which leads to High Top Lookout. Wildlife in this area includes black bears, turkeys and foxes. Supplies are in White Sulphur. Campers may gather dead and down firewood.

GETTING THERE: From White Sulphur go N on state HWY 92 approx. 27 mi. to Pocahontas CG.

SINGLE RATE:	$6	OPEN DATES:	Mar-Dec
# of SINGLE SITES:	9	MAX SPUR:	30 feet
		MAX STAY:	14 days
		ELEVATION:	2600 feet

13 Red Creek
Petersburg • lat 39°01'59" lon 079°18'57"

DESCRIPTION: This small CG sits on top of the Allegheny Plateau near Red Creek. Enjoy adjacent Dolly Sods Scenic Area which offers excellent birdwatching and unique plant communities. There are several trails to hike in this area. This CG is usually full on weekends. Supplies in Petersburg.

GETTING THERE: From Petersburg go W on state HWY 55/28 aprx. 9 mi. to county route 4. Go N on 4 aprx. 1 mi. to forest route 19. Go E and S on 19 aprx. 5 mi. to forest route 75. Go N on 75 aprx. 6 mi. to CG.

SINGLE RATE:	$8	OPEN DATES:	Apr-Dec
# of SINGLE SITES:	12	MAX SPUR:	20 feet
		MAX STAY:	14 days
		ELEVATION:	3887 feet

14 Seneca Shadows
Harman • lat 38°49'20" lon 079°23'14"

DESCRIPTION: This CG rests in mixed hardwoods with outstanding views of the 900 foot Seneca Rocks. A RV dump station and barrier free bathhouses are available. Enjoy fishing in the nearby North Fork River. CG may be frequented by bears. Other wildlife includes deer, foxes and turkeys. Hike the Seneca Rocks Trail.

GETTING THERE: From Harman go E on HWY 33/55 approx. 11 mi. to Seneca Rocks. Go S on 33 approx. 1 mi. to Seneca Shadows CG.

SINGLE RATE:	Varies	OPEN DATES:	Apr-Oct
# of SINGLE SITES:	81	MAX SPUR:	40 feet
GROUP RATE:	Varies	MAX STAY:	14 days
# of GROUP SITES:	3	ELEVATION:	1642 feet

15 Spruce Knob Lake
Durbin • lat 38°42'27" lon 079°35'17"

DESCRIPTION: This CG is located W of Spruce Knob, the highest point in West Virginia and is close to Spruce Knob Lake. Fish for trout on lake with electric motorboats only. There are several hiking trails in the area. CG may be frequented by bears. Other wildlife includes coyotes, foxes, deer and wild turkeys.

GETTING THERE: From Durbin go E on state HWY 28 approx. 13 mi. to forest route 112. Go N on 112 approx. 8.5 mi. to Spruce Knob Lake CG.

SINGLE RATE:	Varies	OPEN DATES:	Apr-Dec
# of SINGLE SITES:	42	MAX SPUR:	30 feet
		MAX STAY:	14 days
		ELEVATION:	3800 feet

16 Stuart
Elkins • lat 38°55'03" lon 079°46'16"

DESCRIPTION: This CG was originally built by the CCC and rests along the Shavers Fork River. Fish for trout in the river or hike the nearby interpretive trail. CG may be frequented by bears. Other wildlife in the area includes deer, foxes and turkeys. Visit Fernow Experimental Forest but follow restrictions and signs.

GETTING THERE: Stuart CG is located approx. 4 mi. E of Elkins on US HWY 33.

SINGLE RATE:	$15	OPEN DATES:	May-Oct
# of SINGLE SITES:	27	MAX SPUR:	50 feet
		MAX STAY:	14 days
		ELEVATION:	2200 feet

17 Summit Lake
Richwood • lat 38°14'54" lon 080°26'42"

DESCRIPTION: This CG is located in mixed hardwoods on Summit Lake. Fish for trout with electric motorboats only and no swimming. There is a trail that runs along the lake. CG may be frequented by bears. Other wildlife includes deer and turkeys. Enjoy a drive on Highland Scenic HWY or drop by Cranberry Mtn. Visitor Center.

GETTING THERE: From Richwood go NE on state route 39/55 approx. 6.5 mi. to county route 35/5. Go N on 35/5 approx. 2 mi. to Summit Lake CG.

SINGLE RATE:	$6	OPEN DATES:	Mar-Dec
# of SINGLE SITES:	33	MAX SPUR:	40 feet
		MAX STAY:	14 days
		ELEVATION:	3480 feet

18 Tea Creek
Marlinton • lat 38°20'29" lon 080°13'51"

DESCRIPTION: This CG rests in mixed hardwoods on Tea Creek. Enjoy a drive on the Highlands Scenic HWY, or a visit to the Cranberry Mountain Visitor Center. Wildlife in this area includes black bears, turkeys, deer and foxes. Hike from the CG along Tea Creek. Visit the beautiful Falls of Hills Creek.

GETTING THERE: From Marlinton go N on HWY 219/55 approx. 6 mi. to county route 150 (Highland Scenic HWY). Go W on 150 approx. 9 mi. to forest route 86. Go N on 86 approx. 1 mi. to Tea Creek CG.

SINGLE RATE:	$6	OPEN DATES:	Mar-Dec
# of SINGLE SITES:	29	MAX SPUR:	30 feet
		MAX STAY:	14 days
		ELEVATION:	2999 feet

 Campground has hosts   🔒 **Reservable sites**   **Accessible facilities**   **Fully developed**   **Semi-developed**   **Rustic facilities**

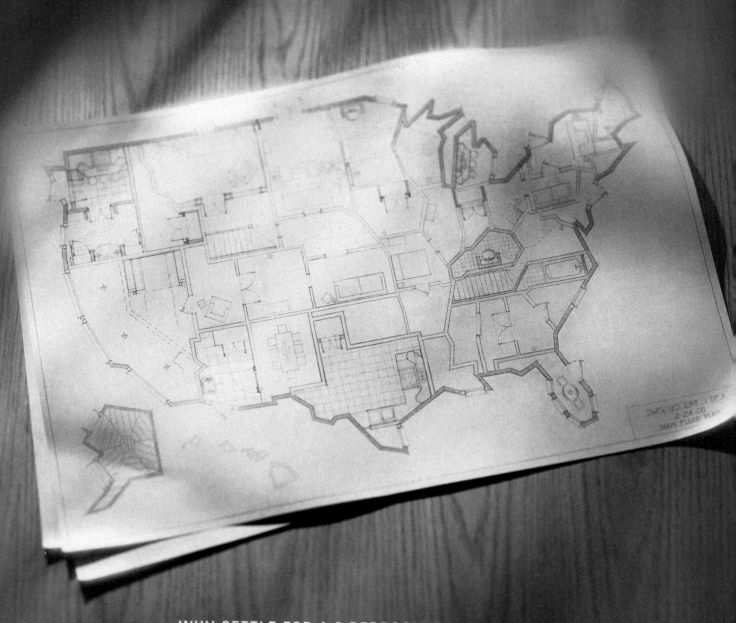

WHY SETTLE FOR A 3-BEDROOM RANCH WHEN

YOU CAN HAVE THIS BEAUTIFUL 50-ROOM HOME.

INSPIRED BY NATURE™

www.coleman.com Visit. Explore. Discover.

Chequamegon-Nicolet National Forest • (715) 762-2461

USFS Photo

CHEQUAMEGON-NICOLET NATIONAL FOREST

Located in Wisconsin's Northwoods, the Chequamegon and Nicolet National Forests span 1.5 million acres and offer a multitude of learning experiences and exciting recreational opportunities.

Both national forests were established by presidential proclamations in 1933, but that was not the beginning. The land, its wildlife, and its people were already there. The cultures, the traditions, and life of the past are very evident in Wisconsin's national forests that we know today.

The Chequamegon derives its name from the Chippewa Indians and means "place of shallow water" while the Nicolet was named for Jean Nicolet, the French explorer who discovered Wisconsin's shore in 1634. The area's many lakes, rivers, streams and unspoiled forest provide plenty of room to roam. In the summer, you will find the forests are ideal for hiking, biking, boating, waterskiing, picnicking, hunting. Camping is available in more developed campgrounds as well as places of relative solitude. With 175 miles of snowmobile routes and 75 miles of cross-country ski trails, the forests become the playground of winter sports enthusiasts.

The forests are also home to a variety of plants and animals and provide excellent wildlife viewing opportunities. Deer and black bears can be seen as well as red foxes, coyotes, otters, beavers and other small mammals. Anglers will find bass, perch, musky, walleye, trout, crappie, bluegill, and northern pike in the forests' lakes.

1 — Ada Lake

Wabeno • lat 45˚22'10" lon 088˚43'54"

DESCRIPTION: CG is located along Ada Lake which contains northern pike, bass, rainbow trout, and panfish. A sandy beach is on site. Various wildlife in area includes deer, black bears, grouse, and bald eagles. Hiking/horse trails in area. Can be busy holiday weekends. Boat landing for non-motorized boats.

GETTING THERE: From Wabeno go W on state HWY 52 approx. 5.5 mi. to forest route 2620. Go S on 2620 approx. 1.5 mi. to Ada Lake CG.

SINGLE RATE:	$10	OPEN DATES:	May-Oct
# of SINGLE SITES:	19	MAX SPUR:	36 feet
		MAX STAY:	14 days
		ELEVATION:	1550 feet

2 — Anvil Lake

Eagles River • lat 45˚56'12" lon 089˚03'38"

DESCRIPTION: This CG is located among 300-year old white pines. There is good walleye and trout fishing in adjacent Anvil Lake. A log shelter enhances the rustic setting of this CG. There are several hiking, mountain biking, horse and interpretive trails in this area. A boat ramp is on site.

GETTING THERE: From Eagles River go E on state HWY 70 approx. 7.5 mi. to Anvil Lake CG.

SINGLE RATE:	Varies	OPEN DATES:	May-Oct
# of SINGLE SITES:	18	MAX SPUR:	35 feet
		MAX STAY:	14 days
		ELEVATION:	1500 feet

3 — Bagley Rapids

Lakewood • lat 45˚09'32" lon 088˚27'57"

DESCRIPTION: This CG is located among pines on the Oconto River. Popular activities include trout fishing, berry picking, rafting, canoeing, and swimming. Various wildlife in the area includes deer, black bears, bald eagles, grouse, and hawks. Can be busy on weekends. Hiking and horse trails in the area.

GETTING THERE: Bagley Rapids CG is located approx. 12 mi. SE of Lakewood on state HWY 64.

SINGLE RATE:	$10	OPEN DATES:	Apr-Oct
# of SINGLE SITES:	30	MAX SPUR:	45 feet
		MAX STAY:	14 days
		ELEVATION:	1550 feet

4 — Bears Lake

Laona • lat 45˚30'40" lon 088˚31'54"

DESCRIPTION: CG is a quiet area with a wooded shore and ridge with views of the lake. Great fishing for bass and northern on Bears Lake. The nearby Peshtigo and Rat Rivers also offer good trout fishing. Several walk-in campsites are available. Wildlife includes deer, black bears, bald eagles, and grouse.

GETTING THERE: From Laona go SE on state HWY H approx. 5 mi. to forest route 2136. Go E on 2136 approx. 4 mi. to forest route 3770. Go S on 3770 approx. 1 mi. to Bears Lake CG.

SINGLE RATE:	$10	OPEN DATES:	May-Nov
# of SINGLE SITES:	27	MAX SPUR:	30 feet
		MAX STAY:	14 days
		ELEVATION:	1550 feet

5 — Beaver Lake

Mellen • lat 46˚18'07" lon 090˚53'49"

DESCRIPTION: This CG is located in red pine, maple, and birch on Beaver Lake. Fish for panfish, trout and catfish. Deer, elk, loon, bears, raccoonss, skunks and eagles are in the area. Enjoy the North Country Trail, nearby Marengo Semi-Primitive Non-motorized Area, St. Peter's Dome, and Morgan Falls.

GETTING THERE: From Mellen go W aprx. 8 mi. on county route GG to forest route 187 (Mineral Lake RD). Go N on 187 aprx. 3 mi. to forest route 198 (Pine Stump Corner). Go W on 198 aprx. 2 mi. to CG.

SINGLE RATE:	$8	OPEN DATES:	May-Oct
# of SINGLE SITES:	10	MAX SPUR:	30 feet
		MAX STAY:	14 days
		ELEVATION:	1400 feet

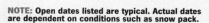 **Campground has hosts**   **Reservable sites**   **Accessible facilities**   **Fully developed**   **Semi-developed**   **Rustic facilities**

NOTE: Open dates listed are typical. Actual dates are dependent on conditions such as snow pack.

6 Big Joe
Cavour • lat 45°39'53" lon 088°39'08"

DESCRIPTION: This CG is located in a mixed hardwood forest setting along the Peshtigo River. Walk-in sites only (short walk). Wildlife in this area includes deer, grouse, bald eagles, and black bears. The CG can be busy holiday weekends. There are hiking and horse trails in the vicinity.

GETTING THERE: From Cavour go W on US HWY 8 approx. 1 mi. to state HWY 139. Go N on 139 approx. 1 mi. to Big Joe CG.

SINGLE RATE:	No fee	OPEN DATES:	Yearlong*
# of SINGLE SITES:	2		
		MAX STAY:	14 days
		ELEVATION:	1510 feet

11 Brule River
Iron River • lat 46°01'42" lon 088°47'48"

DESCRIPTION: CG is set in a beautiful balsam fir and red pine grove. Carry-in canoe access to the Brule River with good trout fishing. Wildlife includes deer, grouse, song birds, osprey, bald eagles, black bears and timber wolves. Several hiking, mountain biking, horse, and interpretive trails in area. Boat ramp.

GETTING THERE: Brule River CG is located approx. 7 mi. SW of Iron River on state HWY 73.

SINGLE RATE:	$8	OPEN DATES:	Apr-Sept
# of SINGLE SITES:	11	MAX SPUR:	35 feet
		MAX STAY:	14 days
		ELEVATION:	1500 feet

7 Birch Grove
Washburn • lat 46°41'14" lon 091°03'42"

DESCRIPTION: Nestled between East and West Twin Lakes in mixed hardwoods with lake views. Boat access for bass and pike fishing. Supplies in Washburn. Bears, deer, hawks, beaver and small wildlife in area. Valhalla trail for hiking, mountain biking, horse use. ATV activities nearby. Biting bugs in summer.

GETTING THERE: From Washburn go NW on county route C approx. 7.5 mi. to forest route 252. Go S on 252 approx. 3 mi. to forest route 435. Go E on 435 approx. 1/2 mi. to Birch Grove CG.

SINGLE RATE:	$9	OPEN DATES:	May-Oct
# of SINGLE SITES:	16	MAX SPUR:	35 feet
		MAX STAY:	14 days
		ELEVATION:	1150 feet

12 Chipmunk Rapids
Tipler • lat 45°53'32" lon 088°33'26"

DESCRIPTION: CG is located in mixed hardwoods and conifers. Trout fishing in nearby lakes. Wildlife includes deer, grouse, song birds, osprey, bald eagles, black bears and timber wolves. Several hiking, mountain biking, horse, interpretive trails in vicinity. Artesian well produces excellent drinking water. Boat ramp.

GETTING THERE: From Tipler go SE on forest route 2450 approx. 2 mi. to forest route 2156. Go SE on 2156 approx. 2.5 mi. to Chipmunk Rapids CG.

SINGLE RATE:	Varies	OPEN DATES:	Apr-Dec
# of SINGLE SITES:	6	MAX SPUR:	35 feet
		MAX STAY:	14 days
		ELEVATION:	1500 feet

8 Black Lake
Winter • lat 45°59'16" lon 090°55'47"

DESCRIPTION: Set among paper birch, red pine and spruce with 3 walk-in sites. Fish for muskie, bass, northern, pike and panfish in nearby Black Lake. Boat dock nearby. Wolves, coyotes, deer, elk, loon, herons, and eagles in area. CG is frequented by bears. There is a 4 mi. interpretive trail nearby.

GETTING THERE: From Winter go N 5 mi. on county route W to forest route 172. Go N 7 mi. on 172 to forest route 173. Go NE 1/2 mi. on 173 to forest route 1666. Go NE 1 mi. on 1666 to Black Lake CG.

SINGLE RATE:	$8	OPEN DATES:	May-Oct
# of SINGLE SITES:	29	MAX SPUR:	45 feet
		MAX STAY:	14 days
		ELEVATION:	1410 feet

13 Chippewa
Medford • lat 45°13'14" lon 090°42'14"

DESCRIPTION: In old growth northern hardwoods and many shady sites on the Chequamegon Waters Flowage. Boat ramp, fish for bass and panfish. RV dump stationon site. Store approx. 3 mi. away. Perkinstown trail is nearby for ATV, mountain biking and hiking. Biting bugs in June.

GETTING THERE: From Medford go N on state HWY 13 approx. 4 mi. to county route M. Go W on M approx. 24 mi. to forest route 1417. Go S on 1417 approx. 1 mi. to Chippewa CG.

SINGLE RATE:	$10	OPEN DATES:	May-Oct
# of SINGLE SITES:	78	MAX SPUR:	35 feet
GROUP RATE:	$18	MAX STAY:	14 days
# of GROUP SITES:	12	ELEVATION:	1200 feet

9 Boot Lake
Townsend • lat 45°16'07" lon 088°38'44"

DESCRIPTION: Enjoy fishing Boot Lake, nearby streams and the Wolves River for walleye, northern pike, bass, musky, panfish and trout. There are rafting and canoeing opportunities on the Wolves River. Busy in summer. Jones Spring non-motorized area is nearby and offers hiking, hunting, and cross-country skiing.

GETTING THERE: Boot Lake CG is located approx. 6 mi. SW of Townsend on state HWY T.

SINGLE RATE:	$12	OPEN DATES:	Apr-Nov
# of SINGLE SITES:	35	MAX SPUR:	30 feet
		MAX STAY:	14 days
		ELEVATION:	1550 feet

14 Day Lake
Mellen • lat 46°10'55" lon 090°54'15"

DESCRIPTION: Among paper birch, red and Jack pine on Day Lake (near many other lakes and streams). Boat launch, muskie fishing, barrier free pier, on site. Eagless, loon and deer in area. Supplies at Clam Lake. Mild to hot summer days. CAMBA mountain bike and Dead Horse ATV trails are nearby.

GETTING THERE: From Mellen go SW on county route GG approx. 17 mi. to Day Lake CG.

SINGLE RATE:	$10	OPEN DATES:	May-Oct
# of SINGLE SITES:	52	MAX SPUR:	45 feet
		MAX STAY:	14 days
		ELEVATION:	1450 feet

10 Boulder Lake
Markton • lat 45°08'25" lon 088°37'42"

DESCRIPTION: CG is located in mixed hardwoods on Boulder Lake. Good walley, pike, trout and bass fishing on Boulder Lake or nearby streams. Ice fishing is popular and the parking area is plowed in winter. The nearby Wolves River offers trout fishing, rafting and canoeing. Heavy use in summer.

GETTING THERE: Boulder Lake CG is located approx. 1.5 mi. N of Markton on forest route 2116.

SINGLE RATE:	$12	OPEN DATES:	Yearlong*
# of SINGLE SITES:	89	MAX SPUR:	45 feet
GROUP RATE:	Varies	MAX STAY:	14 days
# of GROUP SITES:	10	ELEVATION:	1550 feet

15 East Twin Lake
Mellen • lat 46°11'33" lon 090°51'32"

DESCRIPTION: Set among maple, birch and hemlock on the lake with a boat ramp and pier. Fish for bass, muskie and panfish. Supplies at Clam Lake, 2 mi. SW. Wildlife in area includes black bears, wolves, coyotes, elk, loons, herons, and eagless. North Country Nat'l Scenic Trail is nearby.

GETTING THERE: From Mellen go SW on county route GG approx. 15 mi. to forest route 190. Go E on 190 approx. 1 mi. to East Twin Lake CG.

SINGLE RATE:	$8	OPEN DATES:	May-Oct
# of SINGLE SITES:	10	MAX SPUR:	30 feet
		MAX STAY:	14 days
		ELEVATION:	1470 feet

 Campground has hosts   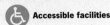 **Reservable sites**   **Accessible facilities**   **Fully developed**   **Semi-developed**   **Rustic facilities**

NOTE: Open dates listed are typical. Actual dates are dependent on conditions such as snow pack.

16 Eastwood
Westboro • lat 45°19'55" lon 090°26'41"

DESCRIPTION: Nestled along the hardwood shores of the Mondeaux Flowage with panoramic views. Shady in hot months. Supplies are in Westboro. Deer and small wildlife in area. Boat fish for panfish. Basic supplies are 1 mi. away. The Ice Age Nat'l Scenic trail is accessible on site.

GETTING THERE: From Westboro go W on county route D for 6.5 miles. Go S on forest route 104 for 1.5 miles to forest route 106. Go S on 106 approx. 1/2 mi. to Eastwood CG.

SINGLE RATE:	$10	OPEN DATES:	May-Oct
# of SINGLE SITES:	22	MAX SPUR:	40 feet
		MAX STAY:	14 days
		ELEVATION:	1200 feet

21 Kathryn Lake
Medford • lat 45°12'04" lon 090°37'13"

DESCRIPTION: CG is set in a northern hardwood forest near Kathryn Lake. Boat fish for panfish from the lake. Supplies are at a small store 1 mi. from the CG. Campers may gather firewood. Perkinstown trail passes near the CG. Mosquitoes and deer flies are in the area in May and June.

GETTING THERE: From Medford go N on state HWY 13 approx. 4 mi. to county route M. Go W on M approx. 15 mi. to forest route 121. Go S on 121 approx. 1/2 mi. to CG.

SINGLE RATE:	$10	OPEN DATES:	May-Oct
# of SINGLE SITES:	8	MAX SPUR:	30 feet
		MAX STAY:	14 days
		ELEVATION:	1490 feet

17 Emily Lake
Lac du Flambeau • lat 45°57'51" lon 090°00'52"

DESCRIPTION: CG is set among thick, tall, pines with a nearby boat landing. Fish Emily Lake for panfish. Gather firewood locally. CG can be busy holiday weekends. Expect warm to hot summer days. Deer and small wildlife frequent this area. Black flies are in the area until July.

GETTING THERE: From Lac du Flambeau go W on forest route 142 approx. 3.5 mi. to forest route 1178. Go N on 1178 approx. 1/2 mi. to Emily Lake CG.

SINGLE RATE:	$10	OPEN DATES:	May-Oct
# of SINGLE SITES:	11	MAX SPUR:	35 feet
		MAX STAY:	14 days
		ELEVATION:	1580 feet

22 Kentuck Lake
Alvin • lat 45°59'33" lon 088°58'49"

DESCRIPTION: CG is located in mixed hardwood and conifer forest. Walleye, musky, bass, crappies, and panfish are abundant in Kentuck Lake (named from early settlers from Kentucky). Wildlife includes deer, grouse, song birds, osprey, bald eagles, black bears and timber wolves. Several trails in area. Boat ramp.

GETTING THERE: From Alvin go S on state HWY 55 approx. 1 mi. to state HWY 70. Go W on 70 approx. 7.5 mi. to forest route 2181. Go S on 2181 approx. 2.5 mi. to Franklin Lake CG.

SINGLE RATE:	Varies	OPEN DATES:	Apr-Dec
# of SINGLE SITES:	31	MAX SPUR:	35 feet
		MAX STAY:	14 days
		ELEVATION:	1740 feet

18 Fanny Lake
Townsend • lat 45°15'58" lon 088°39'56"

DESCRIPTION: This CG is located in a rustic, mixed hardwood setting. There are walk-in sites only with no drinking water. Bass and panfish fishing is available on adjacent Fanny Lake (non-motorized boats only). Various wildlife in the area includes deer, black bears, grouse, hawks, and bald eagles.

GETTING THERE: From Townsend go SW on state HWY T approx. 6.5 mi. to forest route 2938. Go SW on 2938 approx. 1 mi. to Fanny Lake CG.

SINGLE RATE:	No fee	OPEN DATES:	Yearlong*
# of SINGLE SITES:	5		
		MAX STAY:	14 days
		ELEVATION:	1550 feet

23 Lac Vieux Desert
Land O Lakes • lat 46°08'09" lon 089°09'11"

DESCRIPTION: This CG rests at the headwaters of the Wisconsin River, home to the Chippewa (Ojibwa) Indians for centuries. Musky, walleye, bass, and northern fishing. Boat access and rustic resorts nearby. Wildlife includes deer, black bears, grouse, song birds, bald eagles. There are several trails in area.

GETTING THERE: From Land O Lakes go S on state HWY 32 approx. 2 mi. to county route E. Go E on E approx. 2.5 mi. to forest route 2205. Go N on 2205 approx. 1.5 mi. to Lac Vieux Desert CG.

SINGLE RATE:	$10	OPEN DATES:	Apr-Oct
# of SINGLE SITES:	31	MAX SPUR:	35 feet
		MAX STAY:	14 days
		ELEVATION:	1691 feet

19 Franklin Lake
Alvin • lat 45°53'55" lon 088°59'37"

DESCRIPTION: Historic stone and log structures mix with campsites in tall pines and hemlock. CG is on the lake with boating and fishing (walleye, bass, northern pike). Naturalist programs throughout summer. Wildlife in area includes deer, grouse, song birds, osprey, bald eagles, black bears and timber wolves. Boat ramp.

GETTING THERE: From Alvin go S on state HWY 55 approx. 1 mi. to state HWY 70. Go W on 70 approx. 7.5 mi. to forest route 2181. Go S on 2181 approx. 2.5 mi. to Franklin Lake CG.

SINGLE RATE:	Varies	OPEN DATES:	Apr-Oct
# of SINGLE SITES:	77	MAX SPUR:	35 feet
		MAX STAY:	14 days
		ELEVATION:	1700 feet

24 Lake Three
Mellen • lat 46°19'07" lon 090°51'22"

DESCRIPTION: Located in maple forest with lake views. Fish for bass and panfish in Lake Three and class 1 brook trout in a nearby stream. Black bears, wolves, deer, elk, loons, and herons. Nearby trails include North Country National Scenic Trail, Morgan Falls, and St. Peter's Dome.

GETTING THERE: From Mellen go W on county route GG approx. 7 mi. to forest route 187. Go NW on 187 approx. 3.5 mi. to Lake Three CG.

SINGLE RATE:	$8	OPEN DATES:	May-Oct
# of SINGLE SITES:	8	MAX SPUR:	30 feet
		MAX STAY:	14 days
		ELEVATION:	1420 feet

20 Horseshoe Lake
Washburn • lat 46°38'00" lon 091°08'30"

DESCRIPTION: In a shady pine and oak park setting near Horseshoe Lake. Fish and swim in Hoist Lake. Supplies available at Iron River or Washburn. Eagless, hawks, grouse and occasional black bearss can be seen in the area. Campers may gather own firewood. ATV trails and a 12 mi. horse trail network nearby.

GETTING THERE: From Washburn go SW on state HWY 26 13 mi. to forest route 236 (at Ino). Go N on 236 8 mi. to forest route 245. Go E on 245 3 mi. to Horseshoe Lake CG (watch for signs.) High clearance required.

SINGLE RATE:	$8	OPEN DATES:	May-Oct
# of SINGLE SITES:	11	MAX SPUR:	75 feet
		MAX STAY:	14 days
		ELEVATION:	1200 feet

25 Laura Lake
Armstrong Creek • lat 45°42'16" lon 088°30'28"

DESCRIPTION: CG is located in mixed hardwood and conifer forest. Good fishing for bass and northern pike in Laura Lake. Various wildlife includes bald eagles, song birds, deer, black bears, and timber wolves. CG can be busy holidays, weekends, and late summer. There are numerous trails nearby.

GETTING THERE: From Armstrong Creek go W on US HWY 8 approx. 2 mi. to forest route 2163. Go NW on 2163 approx. 3.5 mi. to Laura Lake CG.

SINGLE RATE:	$10	OPEN DATES:	May-Oct
# of SINGLE SITES:	42	MAX SPUR:	30 feet
		MAX STAY:	14 days
		ELEVATION:	1500 feet

 Campground has hosts   Reservable sites   Accessible facilities   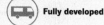 Fully developed   Semi-developed   Rustic facilities

NOTE: Open dates listed are typical. Actual dates are dependent on conditions such as snow pack.

26 Laurel Lake
Eagles River • lat 45°48'56" lon 089°06'33"

DESCRIPTION: CG is located in mixed hardwood and conifer forest. Good fishing for bass. Wildlife in area includes deer, grouse, song birds, osprey, bald eagles, black bears and timber wolves. CG can be busy holidays, weekends, and late summer. Several hiking, mountain biking, horse and interpretive trails in area. Boat ramp.

GETTING THERE: From Eagles River go S 8 mi. on US HWY 45 to state HWY 32. Go E 4.5 mi. on 32 to forest route 2178. Go N 4 mi. on 2178 to forest route 3742. Go S 4 mi. on 3742 to Laurel Lake CG.

SINGLE RATE:	$10	OPEN DATES:	Apr-Oct
# of SINGLE SITES:	12	MAX SPUR:	35 feet
		MAX STAY:	14 days
		ELEVATION:	1639 feet

31 Moose Lake
Hayward • lat 46°00'56" lon 091°01'19"

DESCRIPTION: This CG is located in hardwoods and pines on Moose Lake. Fish for muskie, walleye, bass, and panfish. Wildlife in the area includes black bears, wolves, coyotes, deer, elk, loon, herons, eagles, and hawk. CG can be busy weekends and holidays. Gather firewood locally.

GETTING THERE: From Hayward to E on state HWY 77 approx. 27 mi. to forest route 174. Go S on 174 approx. 6 mi. to forest route 1643. Go W on 1643 approx. 1.5 mi. to Moose lake CG.

SINGLE RATE:	$8	OPEN DATES:	May-Oct
# of SINGLE SITES:	15	MAX SPUR:	40 feet
		MAX STAY:	14 days
		ELEVATION:	1380 feet

27 Lauterman Lake
Florence • lat 45°54'49" lon 088°30'55"

DESCRIPTION: This CG is walk-in only. There is good fishing for northern pike in adjacent Lauderman Lake. Wildlife in the area includes deer, grouse, song birds, osprey, bald eagles, black bears and timber wolves. This CG can be busy holidays, weekends, and late summer. there are several trails in the area.

GETTING THERE: From Florence go W on state HWY 70 approx. 9.5 mi. to forest route 2553. Go S on 2553 approx. 2 mi. to Lauterman Lake CG.

SINGLE RATE:	No fee	OPEN DATES:	Yearlong
# of SINGLE SITES:	5		
		MAX STAY:	14 days
		ELEVATION:	1480 feet

32 Morgan Lake
Popple River • lat 45°46'20" lon 088°32'38"

DESCRIPTION: CG is located in mixed hardwood and conifer forest setting. Wildlife in area includes deer, grouse, song birds, osprey, bald eagles, black bears and timber wolves. There are several trails in the area. A boat ramp is on site. Only boats with electric motors are permitted on Morgan Lake.

GETTING THERE: From Popple River go N on state HWY 139 approx. 1 mi. to forest route 2161. Go E on 2161 approx. 7 mi. to Morgan Lake CG.

SINGLE RATE:	$8	OPEN DATES:	Apr-Oct
# of SINGLE SITES:	18	MAX SPUR:	35 feet
GROUP RATE:	$30	MAX STAY:	14 days
# of GROUP SITES:	1	ELEVATION:	1500 feet

28 Lost Lake
Florence • lat 45°53'02" lon 088°33'30"

DESCRIPTION: CG is amid aspen and sugar maple. A nearby 1 mi. interpretive trail leads to a stand of 150-year-old hemlock. Lost Lake is stocked with brown and rainbow trout, and smallmouth bass. No motorboats are permitted on Lost Lake. Eight Cabins are available for reservations.

GETTING THERE: From Florence go W on state HWY 70 approx. 13 mi. to forest route 2450. Go S on 2450 approx. 1 mi. to forest route 2156. Go SE on 2156 approx. 3 mi. to Lost Lake CG.

SINGLE RATE:	$10	OPEN DATES:	Apr-Oct
# of SINGLE SITES:	27	MAX SPUR:	35 feet
		MAX STAY:	14 days
		ELEVATION:	1500 feet

33 Namekagon Lake
Cable • lat 46°14'41" lon 091°05'11"

DESCRIPTION: This CG is situated in thick pines on the headwaters of the Namekagon River. Fish for northern pike, bass, muskie, and walleye. A boat ramp, fishing pier and the North Country National Scenic Trail are all nearby. Wildlife includes black bears, wolves, coyotes, elk, loon and herons.

GETTING THERE: From Cable go E on county route M approx. 11 mi. to state route D. Go N on D approx. 5.5 mi. to forest route 209. Go W on 209 approx. 1/2 mi. to Namekagon CG.

SINGLE RATE:	$10	OPEN DATES:	May-Nov
# of SINGLE SITES:	33	MAX SPUR:	45 feet
		MAX STAY:	14 days
		ELEVATION:	1400 feet

29 Luna-White Deer
Eagles River • lat 45°54'00" lon 088°57'43"

DESCRIPTION: CG is located in mixed hardwood and conifer forest. Good fishing for trout and bass on adjacent lakes. Numerous wildlife in area including loon and bald eagles. CG can be busy holidays, weekends, and late summer. Hiking trail around lakes as well as numerous multi-use trails in area. Boat ramp.

GETTING THERE: From Eagles River go E on state HWY 70 approx. 13 mi. to forest route 2176. Go S on 2176 approx. 5.5 mi. to forest route 2188. Go NW on 2188 approx. 1.5 mi. to Luna-White Deer CG.

SINGLE RATE:	Varies	OPEN DATES:	Apr-Oct
# of SINGLE SITES:	37	MAX SPUR:	35 feet
		MAX STAY:	14 days
		ELEVATION:	1500 feet

34 North Twin
Medford • lat 45°16'49" lon 090°26'40"

DESCRIPTION: This CG is set in a stand of paper birch trees with views of North Twin Lake. Fish for panfish from lake. Supplies are at Mondeaux Concession which is approx. 4 mi. away. Campers may gather dead and down firewood. The Ice Age National Scenic Trail is near the CG.

GETTING THERE: From Medford go N 4 mi. on HWY 13. Go W 7 mi. on county route M. Go N 6 mi. on county route E. Go E 1 mi. on forest route 102. Go S 1 mi. on forest route 566 to CG.

SINGLE RATE:	$10	OPEN DATES:	May-Oct
# of SINGLE SITES:	6	MAX SPUR:	30 feet
		MAX STAY:	14 days
		ELEVATION:	1470 feet

30 Mineral Lake
Mellen • lat 46°17'33" lon 090°49'54"

DESCRIPTION: This CG is located on Mineral Lake which offers muskie, bass, walleye, and panfish fishing. Eagless frequent this area. Other wildlife include black bears, wolves, coyotes, deer, elk, loon, herons, and hawk. CG can be busy weekends and holidays. Supplies are in Mellen.

GETTING THERE: Mineral Lake is approximately 10 mi.W of Mellen on county route GG.

SINGLE RATE:	$8	OPEN DATES:	May-Oct
# of SINGLE SITES:	11	MAX SPUR:	30 feet
		MAX STAY:	14 days
		ELEVATION:	1381 feet

35 Perch Lake
Florence • lat 45°56'04" lon 088°29'41"

DESCRIPTION: This CG is walk-in only. CG is located in mixed hardwood and conifer forest. Good bass fishing on adjacent Perch Lake. Wildlife in area includes deer, grouse, song birds, osprey, bald eagles, black bears and timber wolves. Several hiking, mountain biking, horse and interpretive trails in the area.

GETTING THERE: From Florence go W on state HWY 70 approx. 9 mi. to forest route 2150. Go N on 2150 approx. 1 mi. to Perch Lake CG.

SINGLE RATE:	No fee	OPEN DATES:	Yearlong
# of SINGLE SITES:	5		
		MAX STAY:	14 days
		ELEVATION:	1520 feet

 Campground has hosts   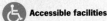 **Reservable sites**   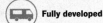 **Accessible facilities**   **Fully developed**   **Semi-developed**   **Rustic facilities**

NOTE: Open dates listed are typical. Actual dates are dependent on conditions such as snow pack.

36 Perch Lake
Drummond • lat 46°23'19" lon 091°16'09"

DESCRIPTION: Set in mixed conifer and hardwood forest on Perch Lake. Boat ramp to fish for trout, panfish, and bass. Supplies in Drummond. Deer, bears, beaver, ducks and small wildlife in area. Trails nearby for Rainbow Lake Wilderness and the North Country National Scenic Trail.

GETTING THERE: From Drummond go N on primary forest route 35 approx. 5.5 mi. to Perch Lake CG.

SINGLE RATE:	$9	OPEN DATES:	May-Oct
# of SINGLE SITES:	21	MAX SPUR:	35 feet
GROUP RATE:		MAX STAY:	14 days
		ELEVATION:	1220 feet

41 Smith Rapids
Fifield • lat 45°54'38" lon 090°10'20"

DESCRIPTION: Among tall pines on the South fork of the Flambeau River, Riley Creek runs past the CG. Historic Round Lake Logging Dam nearby. Horse facilities available. Supplies at Fifield. Black flies May-June. Smith Rapids Equestrian trail on site. ATV trail nearby.

GETTING THERE: From Fifield go E on state HWY 70 approx. 12.5 mi. to forest route 148. Go N on 148 approx. 2 mi. to Smith Rapids CG.

SINGLE RATE:	$10	OPEN DATES:	May-Oct
# of SINGLE SITES:	9	MAX SPUR:	35 feet
GROUP RATE:	$18	MAX STAY:	14 days
# of GROUP SITES:	4	ELEVATION:	1400 feet

37 Pine Lake
Hiles • lat 45°41'14" lon 088°59'06"

DESCRIPTION: CG is located in mixed hardwoods next to one of the largest lakes in the area. Pine Lake is reknown for northern pike, bass, walleye, and panfish fishing. Various wildlife in area includes deer, black bears, and bald eagles. CG can be busy holiday weekends. Hiking and horse trails in area.

GETTING THERE: From Hiles go W approx. 1/2 mi. to forest route 2185. Go S on 2185 approx. 2 mi. to Pine Lake CG.

SINGLE RATE:	$10	OPEN DATES:	May-Oct
# of SINGLE SITES:	12	MAX SPUR:	36 feet
		MAX STAY:	14 days
		ELEVATION:	1639 feet

42 Spearhead Point
Medford • lat 45°19'40" lon 090°26'41"

DESCRIPTION: This CG rests under a large canopy of northern hardwoods with panoramic views of Mondeaux Flowage. Enjoy boat fishing for panfish. Basic supplies 1 mi. at Mondeaux Concession. Deer and small wildlife in the area. Ice Age National Scenic Trail is nearby. Mosquitos and flies can be bothersome May to June.

GETTING THERE: From Medford go N 4 mi. on HWY 13 to county rte M. Go W 7 mi. on M to county rte E. Go E 8.5 mi. on E to forest rte 106. Go E 1/2 mi. on 106 to CG.

SINGLE RATE:	$10	OPEN DATES:	May-Oct
# of SINGLE SITES:	27	MAX SPUR:	35 feet
GROUP RATE:		MAX STAY:	14 days
		ELEVATION:	1400 feet

38 Richardson Lake
Wabeno • lat 45°26'30" lon 088°42'49"

DESCRIPTION: This CG is located in mixed hardwoods with views of Richardson Lake. Enjoy fishing for bass, northern pike, and panfish. Boat or canoe on the lake. Various wildlife in area includes deer, black bears, bald eagles, hawks, and grouse. The CG is busy holiday weekends. Hiking/horse trails in area.

GETTING THERE: From Wabeno go W on state HWY 32 approx. 2 mi. to state HWY 52. Go W on 52 approx. 3 mi. to Richardson Lake CG.

SINGLE RATE:	$10	OPEN DATES:	May-Nov
# of SINGLE SITES:	26	MAX SPUR:	36 feet
		MAX STAY:	14 days
		ELEVATION:	1550 feet

43 Spectacle Lake
Eagles River • lat 46°00'32" lon 089°00'35"

DESCRIPTION: CG is located in a mixed hardwood and conifer forest on Spectacle Lake. Good bass fishing. Wildlife in area includes deer, grouse, song birds, osprey, bald eagles, black bears and timber wolves. CG can be busy holidays, weekends, and late summer. A 2.5 mi. trail connects with Kentuck Lake CG. Boat ramp at CG.

GETTING THERE: From Eagles River go E on state HWY 70 approx. 10 mi. to forest route 2196. Go N on 2196 approx. 4 mi. to forest route 2572. Go E on 2572 approx. 1.5 mi. to Spectacle Lake CG.

SINGLE RATE:	Varies	OPEN DATES:	May-Sept
# of SINGLE SITES:	34	MAX SPUR:	35 feet
		MAX STAY:	14 days
		ELEVATION:	1500 feet

39 Sailor Lake
Fifield • lat 45°50'31" lon 090°16'36"

DESCRIPTION: In a northern hardwood forest setting with panoramic views of Sailor Lake. Fish for panfish in the lake. Supplies in Fifield, approx. 10 mi. from CG. Campers may gather firewood. Flambeau ATV trail is nearby. Mosquitoes and deer flies may be a problem in May and June.

GETTING THERE: From Fifield go SE approx. 11 mi. on state HWY 70 to forest route 139. Go S on 139 aprox. 3 mi. to Sailor Lake CG.

SINGLE RATE:	$10	OPEN DATES:	May-Oct
# of SINGLE SITES:	20	MAX SPUR:	35 feet
GROUP RATE:	$18	MAX STAY:	14 days
# of GROUP SITES:	3	ELEVATION:	1525 feet

44 Stevens Lake
Tipler • lat 45°55'27" lon 088°42'43"

DESCRIPTION: CG is located in a mixed stand of sugar maple and aspen with lake views. Fish for walleye, northern pike, and bass. Various wildlife including song birds, bald eagles, deer, black bears and timber wolves. Heavy use through fall hunting season. Numerous trails in area. Boat ramp at CG.

GETTING THERE: From Tipler go W on state HWY 70 approx. 2 mi. to forest route 2423. Go W on 2423 approx. 3 mi. to forest route 2424. Go S on 2424 approx. 1 mi. to Stevens Lake CG.

SINGLE RATE:	$10	OPEN DATES:	Apr-Dec
# of SINGLE SITES:	6	MAX SPUR:	35 feet
		MAX STAY:	14 days
		ELEVATION:	1500 feet

40 Sevenmile Lake
Three Lakes • lat 45°52'30" lon 089°04'00"

DESCRIPTION: CG is located on a ridge overlooking Sevenmile Lake. Mild days. Muskey, walleye, and bass fishing in the lake. Various wildlife including deer, bald eagles, osprey, and song birds can be seen in the area. Numerous mountain bike, hike, horse, and interpretive trails in area. Boat ramp at the CG.

GETTING THERE: From Three Lakes go E on state HWY 32 approx. 4.5 mi. to forest route 2178. Go N on 2178 approx. 5.5 mi. to forest route 2435. Go NE on 2435 approx. 2 mi. to Sevenmile Lake CG.

SINGLE RATE:	$10	OPEN DATES:	May-Sept
# of SINGLE SITES:	27	MAX SPUR:	35 feet
		MAX STAY:	14 days
		ELEVATION:	1600 feet

45 Stock Farm Bridge
Glidden • lat 46°02'48" lon 090°42'52"

DESCRIPTION: This secluded CG is located in red pine trees on the East Fork of the Chippewa River. Campers may gather dead and down firewood locally. There is a boat launch on site. This CG offers access to the Dead Horse Run ATV trail system. Wildlife in this area includes black bears, wolves, deer, loon and herons.

GETTING THERE: From Glidden go W 2 mi. on county route D to forest route 167. Go S 7.5 mi. on 167 to forest route 166. Go S 4 mi. on 166 to forest route 164. Go SE 3 mi. on 164 to CG.

SINGLE RATE:	$8	OPEN DATES:	May-Oct
# of SINGLE SITES:	8	MAX SPUR:	40 feet
		MAX STAY:	14 days
		ELEVATION:	1450 feet

 Campground has hosts   **Reservable sites**   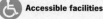 **Accessible facilities**   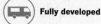 **Fully developed**   **Semi-developed**   **Rustic facilities**

NOTE: Open dates listed are typical. Actual dates are dependent on conditions such as snow pack.

46 Twin Lakes
Park Falls • lat 45°57'53" lon 090°04'19"

DESCRIPTION: This CG is set on Twin Lakes with views of the lake. Beach, boating and fishing for trout and panfish nearby. Gather firewood locally. Supplies at Park Falls. Deer and small wildlife frequent area. Historic Round Lake Logging Dam nearby. Lac du Flambeau approx. 10 mi. away. Mosquitos and flies May-June.

GETTING THERE: From Park Falls go E on state HWY 182 approx. 21 mi. to forest route 144. Go S on 144 approx. 5 mi. to forest route 142. Go E on 142 approx. 2 mi. to Twin Lakes CG.

SINGLE RATE:	$10	OPEN DATES:	May-Oct
# of SINGLE SITES:	16	MAX SPUR:	35 feet
GROUP RATE:	$18	MAX STAY:	14 days
# of GROUP SITES:	1	ELEVATION:	1580 feet

51 Windsor Dam
Tipler • lat 45°55'47" lon 088°51'38"

DESCRIPTION: Secluded CG located along the N branch of the cascading Pine River. Trout fishing and canoeing on river. Various wildlife including deer and grouse. CG can be busy holidays, weekends, and late summer. Several hiking, mountain biking, horse and interpretive trails in area.

GETTING THERE: From Tipler go NW on HWY 70 approx. 12 mi. to HWY 55. Go S on 55 approx. 1.5 mi. to forest route 2427. Go SW on 2427 approx. 2 mi. to forest route 2174. Go S on 2174 approx. 1/2 mi. to CG.

SINGLE RATE:	No fee	OPEN DATES:	Apr-Dec
# of SINGLE SITES:	8	MAX SPUR:	20 feet
		MAX STAY:	14 days
		ELEVATION:	1500 feet

47 Two Lakes
Cable • lat 46°17'32" lon 091°11'36"

DESCRIPTION: This CG offers shaded campsites under pines and hardwoods. There is a boat ramp and RV dump station on site. Fish for northern pike, walleye, bass and trout. Supplies are at Drummond. The North Country National Scenic Trail and Porcupine Lake Wilderness are nearby. Black flies can be bothersome in spring.

GETTING THERE: From Cable go N on state HWY 63 approx. 5 mi. to forest route 216. Go E on 216 approx. 2 mi. to forest route 214. Go S on 214 approx. 1/2 mi. to Two Lakes CG.

SINGLE RATE:	$8	OPEN DATES:	May-Oct
# of SINGLE SITES:	90	MAX SPUR:	50 feet
GROUP RATE:	$10	MAX STAY:	14 days
# of GROUP SITES:	4	ELEVATION:	1400 feet

48 Wabasso Lake
Lac du Flambeau • lat 45°58'24" lon 089°59'54"

DESCRIPTION: This CG offers beautiful primitive camping with walk or canoe-in sites. Gasoline powered boats are prohibited. Supplies are approx. 8 miles away. Deer, waterfowl and small wildlife are common. Gather dead and down firewood locally. Mosquitos and deer flies can be bothersome in May and June.

GETTING THERE: From Lac du Flambeau go W on forest route 142 approx. 3.5 mi. to forest route 1178. Go N on 1178 approx. 1 mi. to Wabasso Lake CG parking. Canoe or hike to CG.

SINGLE RATE:	$3	OPEN DATES:	May-Oct
# of SINGLE SITES:	3		
		MAX STAY:	14 days
		ELEVATION:	1600 feet

49   Wanoka Lake
Iron River • lat 46°32'36" lon 091°16'59"

DESCRIPTION: Among pine and hardwood, with carry-in boat access to Wanoka Lake. Enjoy fly fishing for trout. Supplies in Iron River. Bears, deer, and hawks are in the area. Moderate use. Gather or buy firewood. Mountain bike trails to Tri-County Corridor. ATV trails nearby. Black flies, ticks and mosquitos June-Aug.

GETTING THERE: From Iron River go E on US HWY 2 approx. 7 mi. to forest route 234. Go S on 234 approx. 1/2 mi. to Wanoka Lake CG.

SINGLE RATE:	$8	OPEN DATES:	May-Oct
# of SINGLE SITES:	20	MAX SPUR:	35 feet
		MAX STAY:	14 days
		ELEVATION:	1148 feet

50 West Point
Medford • lat 45°19'02" lon 090°26'11"

DESCRIPTION: On Mondeaux Flowage among tall pines, hemlock and hardwoods. Views of flowage. Boat fish for muskie, crappie and other species. Warm to hot days with black flies in spring. Gather dead and down firewood. Moderate to heavy use in summer. Deer and small wildlife in area. Ice Age Nat'l Scenic trail is nearby.

GETTING THERE: From Medford go N approx. 4 mi. on HWY 13 to county route M. Go W on M approx. 7 mi. to county route E. Go N on E approx. 8.5 mi. to forest route 1563. Go E on 1563 approx. 1 mi. to CG.

SINGLE RATE:	$10	OPEN DATES:	May-Oct
# of SINGLE SITES:	15	MAX SPUR:	35 feet
		MAX STAY:	14 days
		ELEVATION:	1400 feet

 Campground has hosts　　 **Reservable sites**　　 **Accessible facilities**　　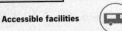 **Fully developed**　　 **Semi-developed**　　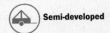 **Rustic facilities**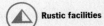

NOTE: Open dates listed are typical. Actual dates are dependent on conditions such as snow pack.

Gannett Peak Slope Wildflowers
Bridger-Teton National Forest, Wyoming
Brandon Goodin Photo

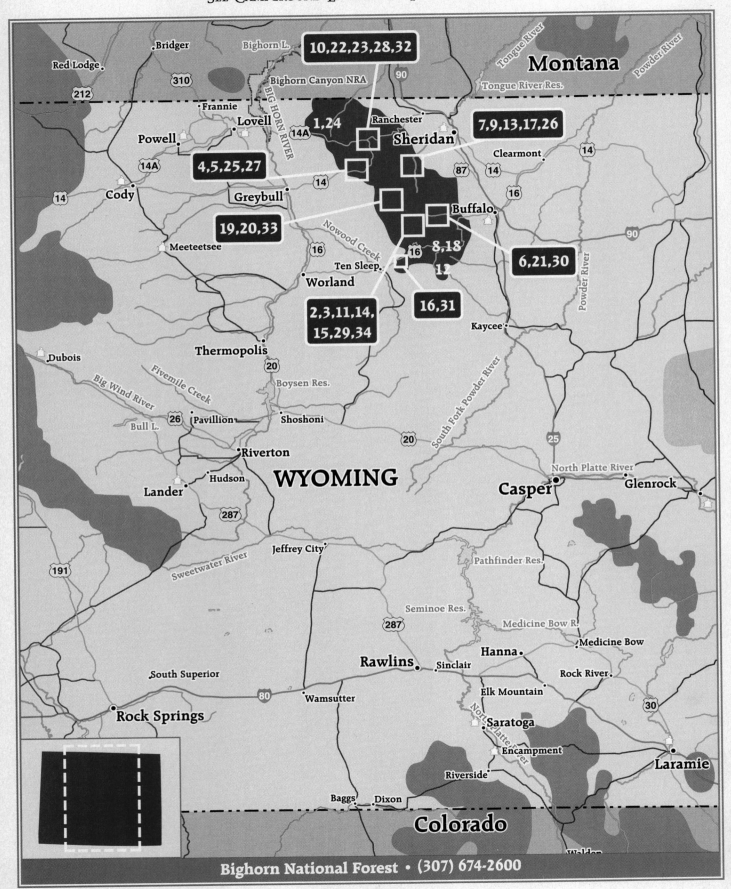

Montana

Red Lodge

Bridger

Bighorn L.

10,22,23,28,32

Bighorn Canyon NRA

Tongue River

Powder River

Tongue River Res.

212

310

Frannie

Lovell

1,24

Ranchester

Sheridan

7,9,13,17,26

Clearmont

14

Powell

14A

BIG HORN RIVER

14A

Cody

4,5,25,27

87

14

16

Greybull

14

19,20,33

Nowood Creek

Buffalo

14

Meeteetse

16

Ten Sleep

8,18

6,21,30

Powder River

90

Worland

16

12

2,3,11,14, 15,29,34

16,31

Kaycee

Dubois

Thermopolis

Big Wind River

Fivemile Creek

20

Boysen Res.

South Fork Powder River

26

Pavillion

Bull L.

Shoshoni

20

25

Riverton

North Platte River

Hudson

WYOMING

Casper

Glenrock

Lander

287

Jeffrey City

Sweetwater River

Pathfinder Res.

Seminoe Res.

Medicine Bow R.

287

Hanna

Medicine Bow

191

Rawlins

Sinclair

Rock River

South Superior

Elk Mountain

30

80

Wamsutter

North Platte River

Saratoga

Rock Springs

Encampment

Laramie

Riverside

Baggs

Dixon

Colorado

Walden

USFS Photo

BIGHORN NATIONAL FOREST

The Bighorn National Forest covers over one million acres with elevations ranging from 5,500 feet to 12,175 feet. The Big Horn River, flowing along the west side of the forest was first named by Native Americans after the great herds of bighorn sheep in the area. Lewis and Clark transferred the name to the mountain range in the early 1800s. The Bighorn provides a diverse landscape, from lush grasslands to alpine meadows, and rugged mountain tops to canyon lands and deserts.

The Bighorn offers many developed recreation sites including camping areas, scenic areas, hiking trails and spectacular canyons. Numerous area streams and lakes provide outstanding fishing for the angler. Large herds of deer and elk provide a multitude of photo opportunities and excellent hunting in season. The entire Cloud Peak Wilderness Area lies above 8,500 feet and has excellent hiking and horseback riding trails. This forest also features several geologic formations and interpretive signs explaining the many historic attractions.

1 Bald Mountain

Lovell • lat 44°48'21" lon 107°51'30"

DESCRIPTION: Island of timber looking across alpine meadows. Cold nights with weather changing quickly. Fishing in Porcupine Creek, 2 mi. N on FR 13. Medicine Wheel Nat'l Historic Landmark 1 mi. W. Limited supplies 20 mi. E or in Lovell. Elk, mule deer, and moose in area. Gather firewood. Hiking TH 12 mi. N.

GETTING THERE: Bald Mountain CG is located 33 mi. E of Lovell on US HWY 14A (Medicine Wheel Scenic Byway).

SINGLE RATE:	$10	OPEN DATES:	June-Sept*
# of SINGLE SITES:	15	MAX SPUR:	60 feet
		MAX STAY:	14 days
		ELEVATION:	9200 feet

2 Boulder Park

Ten Sleep • lat 44°09'48" lon 107°15'08"

DESCRIPTION: Situated in lodgepole stand near meadow. Stream fish nearby W. Ten Sleep Creek. Lake fish Meadowlark Lake. Lake Dam built by CCC. Supplies at Tensleep. Mule Deer and small wildlife. Fills July-Aug. Buy firewood or gather. Hiking access point to Cloud Peak Wilderness 7 mi. N. Heavy mosquitos.

GETTING THERE: From Ten Sleep go NE on US HWY 16 (Cloud Peak Skyway) approx. 16 mi. to Boulder Park CG.

SINGLE RATE:	$9	OPEN DATES:	May-Sept*
# of SINGLE SITES:	34	MAX SPUR:	50 feet
		MAX STAY:	30 days
		ELEVATION:	8000 feet

3 Bull Creek
Ten Sleep • lat 44°10'10" lon 107°12'45"

DESCRIPTION: In stand of lodgepole and spruce. Walk to fishing at Meadowlark Lake. Dam constructed by CCC's. Supplies at Tensleep. Mule Deer and small wildlife in area. Moderate use. Gather firewood locally. Shorter hiking trail nearby. Mosquitos common until mid-summer. No drinking water.

GETTING THERE: Bull Creek CG is located off of US HWY 16 (Cloud Peak Skyway) at Meadowlark Lake between Ten Sleep and Buffalo. CG not suitable for trailers or large RVs.

SINGLE RATE:	$7	OPEN DATES:	June-Sept*
# of SINGLE SITES:	10	MAX SPUR:	25 feet
		MAX STAY:	14 days
		ELEVATION:	8400 feet

4 Cabin Creek
Shell • lat 44°34'33" lon 107°32'50"

DESCRIPTION: Adjacent to US 16 in small stand of pine with views of Shell Cyn. Generally used by travelers overnight stop. Fish Shell Creek; no immediate fishing spots. Supplies in Shell or Greybull. Mule deer in area. Firewood is scarce, but may be gathered. Mosquitos in early summer.

GETTING THERE: From Shell go E on US HWY 14 (Big Horn Scenic Byway) approx. 16 mi. to Granite Creek CG (via forest route 17). Not recommended for large RVs.

SINGLE RATE:	$8	OPEN DATES:	May-Sept*
# of SINGLE SITES:	4	MAX SPUR:	30 feet
		MAX STAY:	14 days
		ELEVATION:	7400 feet

5 Cabin Creek Trailer Park

Shell • lat 44°34'12" lon 107°31'42"

DESCRIPTION: In open meadow surrounded by hills. Warm days, cold nights, frequent noon t-showers. Trout fish in nearby Shell Creek. Limited supplies in Shell or major community at Greybull, 31 mi. W. Mule deer in area. Moderate use. Buy or gather firewood. Primitive, no tables. Fee $105/30 days.

GETTING THERE: From Shell go E on US HWY 14 (Big Horn Scenic Byway) approx. 16 mi. to Cabin Creek CG (access via forest route 17).

SINGLE RATE:	$6	OPEN DATES:	May-Sept*
# of SINGLE SITES:	26	MAX SPUR:	50 feet
		MAX STAY:	30 days
		ELEVATION:	7600 feet

 Campground has hosts　　 **Reservable sites**　　 **Accessible facilities**　　 **Fully developed**　　 **Semi-developed**　　 **Rustic facilities**

NOTE: Open dates listed are typical. Actual dates are dependent on conditions such as snow pack.

6 Circle Park
Buffalo • lat 44°16'57" lon 106°59'21"

DESCRIPTION: Surrounding a meadow, most sites have trees and views of meadow where moose or deer may be seen. Warm days, rains frequent. Fish nearby streams or lake fish Tie Hack Reservoir. Supplies at Buffalo. Gather firewood locally. Major Wilderness (Cloud Peak) access 1/2 mi. Prepare for mosquitos until mid-summer.

GETTING THERE: From Buffalo go W on US HWY 16 (Cloud Peak Skyway) approx. 14 mi. to forest route 20. Go W on 20 approx. 2 mi. to Circle Park CG.

SINGLE RATE:	$9	OPEN DATES:	May-Sept*
# of SINGLE SITES:	10	MAX SPUR:	50 feet
		MAX STAY:	14 days
		ELEVATION:	8100 feet

11 Deer Park
Ten Sleep • lat 44°14'39" lon 107°13'27"

DESCRIPTION: CG set in lodgepole pine stand adjacent to small meadow and West Tensleep Creek. Mild days, frequent noon t-showers. Fish creek or West Tensleep Lake, 1 mi. N. Limited supplies 8 mi. S, or in Ten Sleep. Fills weekends and holidays. Gather firewood locally. Multiple hiking trails nearby.

GETTING THERE: From Ten Sleep go E on US HWY 16 (Cloud Peak Skyway) approx. 16 mi. to forest route 27. Follow 27 N approx. 6 mi. to Deer Park CG.

SINGLE RATE:	$8	OPEN DATES:	June-Sept*
# of SINGLE SITES:	7	MAX SPUR:	35 feet
		MAX STAY:	14 days
		ELEVATION:	8900 feet

7 Coffeen Park
Sheridan • lat 44°31'13" lon 107°14'33"

DESCRIPTION: In stand of pine adjacent to large meadow. Mild days, cold nights, noon t-showers possible. Fish nearby Park Reservoir or stream. Supplies in Sheridan. Mule Deer and small wildlife in area. CG serves as TH access to Cloud Peak Wilderness. Gather firewood. Tents recommended. No drinking water.

GETTING THERE: From Sheridan go S on state HWY 87 4 mi. to forest route 335. Go S on 335 12 mi. to forest route 26. Go W 8 mi. to forest route 293. Go S on 293 7 mi. to Coffeen Park CG. 4WD recommended.

SINGLE RATE:	No fee	OPEN DATES:	July-Sept*
# of SINGLE SITES:	5	MAX SPUR:	20 feet
		MAX STAY:	14 days
		ELEVATION:	8500 feet

12 Doyle
Buffalo • lat 44°05'00" lon 106°59'00"

DESCRIPTION: This CG is set among lodgepole pine stands surrounded by meadows. Warm days. Rains are possible anytime. Supplies at Buffalo. Mule deer in area. Moderate use. Gather firewood locally. No hiking nearby; ATV roads are available. No drinking water.

GETTING THERE: From Buffalo go W on US HWY 16 (Cloud Peak Skyway) approx. 24 mi. to county route 3. Go S on 3 approx. 6 mi. to forest route 514. Go E on 514 approx. 1 mi. to Doyle CG.

SINGLE RATE:	$6	OPEN DATES:	June-Sept*
# of SINGLE SITES:	19	MAX SPUR:	50 feet
		MAX STAY:	14 days
		ELEVATION:	8100 feet

8 Crazy Woman
Buffalo • lat 44°09'55" lon 106°55'14"

DESCRIPTION: Among lodgepole pine adjacent to Crazy Woman Cr. with views of open meadow and stream. Moose, mule deer frequent meadow. Warm days, cold nights. Supplies at Buffalo. Gather firewood locally; may be scarce. Hiking trails not accessed from this area. Mosquitos til mid-summer.

GETTING THERE: From Buffalo go W on US HWY 16 (Cloud Peak Skyway) approx. 23 mi. to Crazy Woman CG.

SINGLE RATE:	$9	OPEN DATES:	June-Sept*
# of SINGLE SITES:	6	MAX SPUR:	30 feet
		MAX STAY:	14 days
		ELEVATION:	7600 feet

13 East Fork
Sheridan • lat 44°35'44" lon 107°12'30"

DESCRIPTION: In pine and spruce with views of adjacent wetlands and meadows. Warm days, noon t-storms common. Short walk to fishing stream or Park Reservoir is 2 mi. S. Supplies in Sheridan. moose, deer in area. Fills weekends. Gather firewood. ATV use on forest roads. Mosquitos in early summer.

GETTING THERE: From Sheridan go S on state HWY 87 4 mi. to county route 335. Go S on 335 12 mi. to forest route 26. Go S on 26 8 mi. to forest route 298. Go on 298 approx. 1/2 mi. to East Fork CG.

SINGLE RATE:	$8	OPEN DATES:	July-Sept*
# of SINGLE SITES:	12	MAX SPUR:	50 feet
		MAX STAY:	14 days
		ELEVATION:	7600 feet

9 Cross Creek
Sheridan • lat 44°32'47" lon 107°12'54"

DESCRIPTION: Located in stand of lodgepole pine. Mild days, frequent noon t-storms. Fish at park Reservoir, N of CG. Supplies in Sheridan. Mule Deer and small wildlife. Mod use, filling holidays. Gather own firewood. Hiking trail access to Cloud Peak Wilderness at Coffeen Park, 2 mi. W. No drinking water.

GETTING THERE: From Sheridan go S on state HWY 87 4 mi. to county route 335. Go S 12 mi. to forest route 26. Go S 8 mi. to forest route 293. Go S 4 mi. to Cross Creek CG. High clearance, 4WD recommended.

SINGLE RATE:	No fee	OPEN DATES:	July-Sept*
# of SINGLE SITES:	3	MAX SPUR:	20 feet
		MAX STAY:	14 days
		ELEVATION:	8400 feet

14 Island Park
Ten Sleep • lat 44°12'19" lon 107°14'12"

DESCRIPTION: CG in a lodgepole pine stand adjacent to West Tensleep Creek. Noon t-showers frequent. Trout fish the creek. Limited supplies 5 mi. S or in Ten Sleep. Fills weekends and holidays. Gather firewood locally. Hike trails into wilderness approx. 4 mi. N. Mosquitos possible in early summer.

GETTING THERE: From Ten Sleep go E on US HWY 16 (Cloud Peak Skyway) approx. 16 mi. to forest route 27. Follow 27 N approx. 3 mi. to Island Park CG.

SINGLE RATE:	$8	OPEN DATES:	June-Sept*
# of SINGLE SITES:	10	MAX SPUR:	40 feet
		MAX STAY:	14 days
		ELEVATION:	8600 feet

10 Dead Swede
Dayton • lat 44°41'22" lon 107°26'43"

DESCRIPTION: in stand of lodgepole pine with views of S. Fork tongue River. Warm days, noon t-storms common. Trout fish river. Historic Tie Hacks Sites (RR logging). Limited supplies 9 mi. N or in Dayton. mule deer in area. Moderate use. Gather firewood. No hiking in immediate vicinity. Mosquitos in early summer.

GETTING THERE: From Dayton go W on US HWY 14 (Big Horn Scenic Byway) approx. 34 mi. to forest route 26. Go E on 26 approx. 4 mi. to Dead Swede CG.

SINGLE RATE:	$9	OPEN DATES:	June-Sept*
# of SINGLE SITES:	22	MAX SPUR:	45 feet
		MAX STAY:	14 days
		ELEVATION:	8400 feet

15   Lake View
Ten Sleep • lat 44°11'00" lon 107°12'45"

DESCRIPTION: In stand of pine overlooking Meadowlark Lake. Mild days, possible noon t-storms. Rainbow, brook, and cutthroat trout fishing in lake, boat ramp 1 mi.. Dam built by CCC's in 1930; interpretive signs. Limited supplies 2 mi. E or in Ten Sleep. Fills weekends and holidays. Gather firewood.

GETTING THERE: Lake View CG is located off of US HWY 16 (Cloud Peak Skyway) at Meadowlark Lake, 24 mi. E of Ten Sleep, WY.

SINGLE RATE:	$10	OPEN DATES:	June-Sept*
# of SINGLE SITES:	11	MAX SPUR:	45 feet
		MAX STAY:	14 days
		ELEVATION:	8300 feet

 Campground has hosts   **Reservable sites**   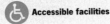 **Accessible facilities**   **Fully developed**   **Semi-developed**   **Rustic facilities**

NOTE: Open dates listed are typical. Actual dates are dependent on conditions such as snow pack.

16 Leigh Creek
Ten Sleep • lat 44°04'49" lon 107°18'48"

DESCRIPTION: CG on Tensleep Creek in cottonwood stand. Views of creek and canyon. Trout fish in creek. State fish hatchery nearby. Supplies in Ten Sleep. Mule deer and coyotes in area. Light use. Gather firewood, may be scarce. Bike and hike forest road, great views of canyon. Snow leaves early.

GETTING THERE: From Ten Sleep go E on US HWY 16 (Cloud Peak Skyway) approx. 8 mi. to Leigh Creek CG.

SINGLE RATE:	$9	OPEN DATES:	May-Sept*
# of SINGLE SITES:	11	MAX SPUR:	45 feet
		MAX STAY:	14 days
		ELEVATION:	5400 feet

17 Little Goose
Sheridan • lat 44°35'24" lon 107°02'27"

DESCRIPTION: Located in stand of lodgepole pine. Mild days, noon t-storms frequent. Stream fish adjacent creeks. Supplies in Sheridan. Mule deer and small wildlife in area. Light to moderate use. Gather firewood. No hiking in vicinity. ATV use on forest roads 7/1-9/12. Mosquitos until mid summer. No drinking water.

GETTING THERE: From Sheridan go S on state HWY 87 approx. 4 mi. to county route 335. Go SW on 335 approx. 9 mi. to forest route 314. Go S on 314 approx. 2.5 mi. to Little Goose CG. 4WD REQUIRED.

SINGLE RATE:	No fee	OPEN DATES:	July-Sept*
# of SINGLE SITES:	3	MAX SPUR:	20 feet
		MAX STAY:	14 days
		ELEVATION:	7000 feet

18 Lost Cabin
Buffalo • lat 44°08'51" lon 106°57'13"

DESCRIPTION: In grove of lodgepole pine. Warm days, possible rain in summer. No fishing in immediate area. Supplies at Buffalo, limited supplies at Pine Lodge, E 5 mi. Mule deer frequent roads and area. Light use. Gather firewood. Heavy mosquitos until mid-summer. Sites for larger trailers and pull-thru sites.

GETTING THERE: From Buffalo go W on US HWY 16 (Cloud Peak Skyway) approx. 26 mi. to Lost Cabin CG.

SINGLE RATE:	$9	OPEN DATES:	June-Sept*
# of SINGLE SITES:	19	MAX SPUR:	55 feet
		MAX STAY:	14 days
		ELEVATION:	8200 feet

19 Lower Paint Rock Lake
Shell • lat 44°23'44" lon 107°22'56"

DESCRIPTION: CG in stand of pine adjacent to Lower Paintrock Lake. Mild days, noon t-storms common. Short meadow walk to trout fishing on lake. Limited supplies in Shell or visit Greybull. Mule deer in area. Moderate use. Gather firewood. Hiking access to Cloud Peak Wilderness via adjacent trailhead.

GETTING THERE: From Shell go E on US HWY 14 (Bighorn Scenic Byway) 16 mi. to forest route 17. Go S 26 mi. to Paint Rock Lakes and Lower Paint Rock Lake CG. High clearance required. RD slippery in rain.

SINGLE RATE:	$8	OPEN DATES:	July-Sept*
# of SINGLE SITES:	4	MAX SPUR:	60 feet
		MAX STAY:	14 days
		ELEVATION:	9300 feet

20 Medicine Lodge Lake
Shell • lat 44°24'01" lon 107°23'07"

DESCRIPTION: Overlooking Upper Medicne Lodge Lake and meadows located in stand of pine. Mild days, noon t-storms common. Short walk to lake for trout fishing. Limited supplies in Shell or go to Greybull. Mule deer in area. Moderate use. Buy or gather firewood. Trails into Cloud Peak Wilderness 1 mi. S.

GETTING THERE: From Shell go E on US HWY 14 (Bighorn Scenic Byway) approx. 16 mi. to forest route 17. Go S on 17 approx. 26 mi. to Medicine Lodge Lake CG. High clearance recommended. Road slippery in rain.

SINGLE RATE:	$8	OPEN DATES:	July-Sept*
# of SINGLE SITES:	8	MAX SPUR:	55 feet
		MAX STAY:	14 days
		ELEVATION:	9300 feet

21 Middle Fork
Buffalo • lat 44°18'06" lon 106°57'04"

DESCRIPTION: CG is located in a canyon on Clear Creek in a lodgepole stand. Stream fish creek. Supplies in Buffalo or small store at nearby Pine lodge. Moose and deer frequent area. CG fills most evenings. Gather firewood. No immediate hiking trails. Hunter corrals, access to Cloud Peak Wilderness 5 mi. N.

GETTING THERE: From Buffalo go W on US HWY 16 (Cloud Peak Skyway) approx. 13 mi. to Middle Fork CG.

SINGLE RATE:	$10	OPEN DATES:	June-Sept*
# of SINGLE SITES:	10	MAX SPUR:	60 feet
		MAX STAY:	14 days
		ELEVATION:	7400 feet

22 North Tongue
Dayton • lat 44°46'48" lon 107°31'59"

DESCRIPTION: located in lodgepole stand adjacent to N. Fork of Tongue River. Warm days, t-storms common. Stream fish river for trout. Supplies 1 mi. S or in Dayton. Moose and mule deer frequent area. Mod use filling weekends and holidays. Gather firewood. Multiple hiking trails nearby. Mosquitos in early summer.

GETTING THERE: From Dayton go W on US HWY 14 (Big Horn Scenic Byway) approx. 29 mi. to forest route 15. Go approx. 1 mi. to North Tongue CG.

SINGLE RATE:	$9	OPEN DATES:	June-Sept*
# of SINGLE SITES:	12	MAX SPUR:	60 feet
		MAX STAY:	14 days
		ELEVATION:	7900 feet

23 Owen Creek
Dayton • lat 44°42'17" lon 107°29'59"

DESCRIPTION: In stand of pine adjacent to stream withviews of adjoining meadow. Warm days, noon t-storms in summer. Short walk to fish trout in Owen Creek. Limited supplies 5 mi. E or at Dayton. Moose and mule deer frequent area. Mod use, fills holiday weekends. Gather firewood, may be scarce. No hiking in nearby vicinity.

GETTING THERE: From Dayton go W on US HWY 14 (Big Horn Scenic Byway) approx. 34 mi. to Owen Creek CG.

SINGLE RATE:	$9	OPEN DATES:	June-Sept*
# of SINGLE SITES:	7	MAX SPUR:	60 feet
		MAX STAY:	14 days
		ELEVATION:	8400 feet

24 Porcupine
Lovell • lat 44°49'56" lon 107°51'12"

DESCRIPTION: Located in lodepole pine stand withviews of Procupine Cr and mtns. Noon t-showers possible. Fish for rainbow, brown and cutthroat on adjacent creek. Medicine Wheel Nat'l Historic Landmark 3 mi. Supplies in Lovell. Mule deer, elk, Moose in area. Fills weekends. Buy or gather firewood. Hike trails nearby.

GETTING THERE: From Lovell go E on US HWY 14A (Medicine Wheel Passage) approx. 36 mi. to forest route 13. Go N on 13 approx. 1.6 mi. to Porcupine CG.

SINGLE RATE:	$10	OPEN DATES:	June-Sept*
# of SINGLE SITES:	16	MAX SPUR:	60 feet
		MAX STAY:	14 days
		ELEVATION:	8900 feet

25 Ranger Creek
Shell • lat 44°35'30" lon 107°13'13"

DESCRIPTION: In stand of lodgepole pine and spruce withviews down Canyon and meadows. Noon t-showers frequent. Rainbow Brook trout fish adjacent Shell Cr. Limited suplies in Shell or go to Greybull, 31 mi. W. Mule Deer and small wildlife in area. Softball field. Gather own firewood. Hiking into Cloud Peak Wilderness.

GETTING THERE: From Shell go E on US HWY 14 (Big Horn Scenic Byway) aprox. 16 mi. to forest route 17. Go S on 17 approx. 2 mi. to Ranger Creek CG. Not recommended for larger RVs.

SINGLE RATE:	$9	OPEN DATES:	May-Sept*
# of SINGLE SITES:	10	MAX SPUR:	45 feet
GROUP RATE:	Varies	MAX STAY:	14 days
# of GROUP SITES:	1	ELEVATION:	7800 feet

 Campground has hosts   **Reservable sites**   **Accessible facilities**   **Fully developed**   **Semi-developed**   **Rustic facilities**

NOTE: Open dates listed are typical. Actual dates are dependent on conditions such as snow pack.

BIGHORN NATIONAL FOREST • WYOMING • 16 — 25

26 Ranger Creek
Sheridan • lat 44°32'46" lon 107°29'54"

DESCRIPTION: In lodgepole stand adjacent to Big Goose Ranger Station. Warm days, frequent noon t-storms. Trout fish nearby streams or Park Reservoir (3 mi. S). Supplies in Sheridan. Moose, mule deer in area. Mod use, fills holiday weekends. Gather firewood. ATV use common on adjoining forest roads.

GETTING THERE: From Sheridan go S on state HWY 87 4 mi. to county route 335. Go S 12 mi. to FR 26. Go S 9 mi. to Ranger Creek CG. US14 to FR 26 is an alternate route, 50 mi. longer, for autos and large RVs.

SINGLE RATE:	$8	OPEN DATES:	July-Sept*
# of SINGLE SITES:	11	MAX SPUR:	50 feet
		MAX STAY:	14 days
		ELEVATION:	7600 feet

27 Shell Creek
Shell • lat 44°33'01" lon 107°30'52"

DESCRIPTION: On Shell Creek in stand of lodgepole pine and aspen adjoining large meadow. Views of Upper Shell Cyn and meadows. Noon t-showers possible. Fish Rainbow and Brook trout in creek. Moderate use. Limited supplies in Shell or go to Greybull. Gather firewood. TH to access Cloud Peak Wilderness, 1 mi. W.

GETTING THERE: From Shell go E on US HWY 14 (Big Horn Scenic Byway) approx. 16 mi. to forest route 17. Go E on 17 approx. 1.2 mi. to Shell Creek CG.

SINGLE RATE:	$8	OPEN DATES:	May-Sept*
# of SINGLE SITES:	11	MAX SPUR:	55 feet
		MAX STAY:	14 days
		ELEVATION:	7500 feet

28  Sibley Lake
Dayton • lat 44°45'33" lon 107°26'19"

DESCRIPTION: On a small ridge above Sibley Lake in pine forest. Warm days, noon t-storms common. Fish for trout in lake, no motors. Dam built by CCC's. Supplies in Dayton. Mule deer in area. Heavy use, fills early in summer. Buy or gather firewood (scarce). Nature trail hike nearby. Some elec. hookups ($13).

GETTING THERE: From Dayton Go W on US HWY 14 (Big Horn Scenic Byway) approx. 25 mi. to Sibley Lake CG.

SINGLE RATE:	$10	OPEN DATES:	June-Sept*
# of SINGLE SITES:	25	MAX SPUR:	60 feet
		MAX STAY:	14 days
		ELEVATION:	8000 feet

29  Sitting Bull
Ten Sleep • lat 44°11'28" lon 107°12'43"

DESCRIPTION: This CG is looking across a large meadow in a stand of lodgepole pine. Warm days, noon t-storms common. Fish for trout 1 mi. S at Meadowlark Lake (boat dock on lake). Dam built by CCC's. Supplies in Ten Sleep. Mule deer in area. Fills weekends. Buy or gather firewood. Short nature trail nearby.

GETTING THERE: From Ten Sleep go NE on US HWY 16 (Cloud Peak Skyway) approx. 23 mi. to forest route 431. Go N approx. 1 mi. on 431 to Sitting Bull CG.

SINGLE RATE:	$10	OPEN DATES:	June-Sept*
# of SINGLE SITES:	43	MAX SPUR:	60 feet
		MAX STAY:	14 days
		ELEVATION:	8600 feet

30 South Fork
Buffalo • lat 44°16'38" lon 106°56'19"

DESCRIPTION: CG is bisected by the South Fork of Clear Creek, located in stand of lodgepole pine. Stream fish the creek for trout. Warm days, noon t-storms frequent. Limited supplies 2 mi. E or in Buffalo. Mule deer and moose in area. Fills by noon all summer. Buy or gather firewood. No hiking in vicinity.

GETTING THERE: From Buffalo go W on US HWY 16 (Cloud Peak Skyway) approx. 15 mi. to South Fork CG. Large trailers not recommended.

SINGLE RATE:	$10	OPEN DATES:	June-Sept*
# of SINGLE SITES:	15	MAX SPUR:	35 feet
		MAX STAY:	14 days
		ELEVATION:	7800 feet

31 Tensleep Creek
Ten Sleep • lat 44°05'00" lon 107°18'48"

DESCRIPTION: Set in a cottonwood stand on Tensleep Creek. Views of canyon. Warm to hot days. Trout fish in creek. State fish hatchery 1 mi. S. Supplies in Ten Sleep. Mule deer and coyotes in area. Moderate use. Gather firewood. Bike and hike on forest road 18. Limited traffic and excellent views of Tensleep Canyon.

GETTING THERE: From Ten Sleep go E on US HWY 16 (Cloud Peak Skyway) appros. 9 mi. to Tensleep Creek CG.

SINGLE RATE:	$9	OPEN DATES:	May-Sept*
# of SINGLE SITES:	5	MAX SPUR:	35 feet
		MAX STAY:	14 days
		ELEVATION:	5400 feet

32 Tie Flume
Dayton • lat 44°42'52" lon 107°26'59"

DESCRIPTION: In stand of pine forest adjacent to meadows with views of S. Fork of Tongue River. Warm days, noon t-storms common. Trout fish River from lower loop. Historic Tie Hack site (RR building period) 6 mi. Supplies 7 mi. E or in Dayton. Light use. Buy or gather firewood. Hiking trails nearby.

GETTING THERE: From Dayton go W on US HWY 14 (Big Horn Scenic Byway) approx. 34 mi. to forest route 26. Go E on 26 approx. 2 mi. to Tie Flume CG.

SINGLE RATE:	$9	OPEN DATES:	June-Sept*
# of SINGLE SITES:	25	MAX SPUR:	60 feet
		MAX STAY:	14 days
		ELEVATION:	8400 feet

33 Upper Paint Rock Lake
Shell • lat 44°24'12" lon 107°22'54"

DESCRIPTION: CG in a lodgepole pine stand. Mild days, noon t-storms possible. Trout fish Upper Paintrock Lake. Limited supplies in Shell or go to Greybull. Mule deer in area. Gather firewood. Trails into Cloud Peak Wilderness using Paintrock Lakes TH 1 mi. S. Access to Tepee Pole Flats and Clife Lakes area.

GETTING THERE: From Shell go E on US HWY 14 (Bighorn Scenic Byway) 16 mi. to forest route 17. Go S 26 mi. to Paint Rock Lakes and Upper Paint Rock Lake CG. High clearance required. RD slippery in rain.

SINGLE RATE:	$8	OPEN DATES:	July-Sept*
# of SINGLE SITES:	4	MAX SPUR:	60 feet
		MAX STAY:	14 days
		ELEVATION:	9300 feet

34 West Tensleep Lake
Ten Sleep • lat 44°15'50" lon 107°12'56"

DESCRIPTION: Located in stand of pine and fir with views of W. Tensleep Lake and Cloud Peak Wilderness with some sites on lake. Mild days, weather changes quickly with noon t-storms common. Limited supplies 10 mi. S or in Ten Sleep. Small wildlife and birds in area. Gather firewood. Major wilderness access adjacent to CG.

GETTING THERE: From Ten Sleep go E on US HWY 16 (Cloud Peak Skyway) approx. 16 mi. to forest route 27. Follow 27 N approx. 7 mi. to West Tensleep Lake CG.

SINGLE RATE:	$9	OPEN DATES:	June-Sept*
# of SINGLE SITES:	10	MAX SPUR:	40 feet
		MAX STAY:	14 days
		ELEVATION:	9100 feet

 Campground has hosts   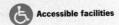 **Reservable sites**   **Accessible facilities**    **Fully developed**    **Semi-developed**   **Rustic facilities**

NOTE: Open dates listed are typical. Actual dates are dependent on conditions such as snow pack.

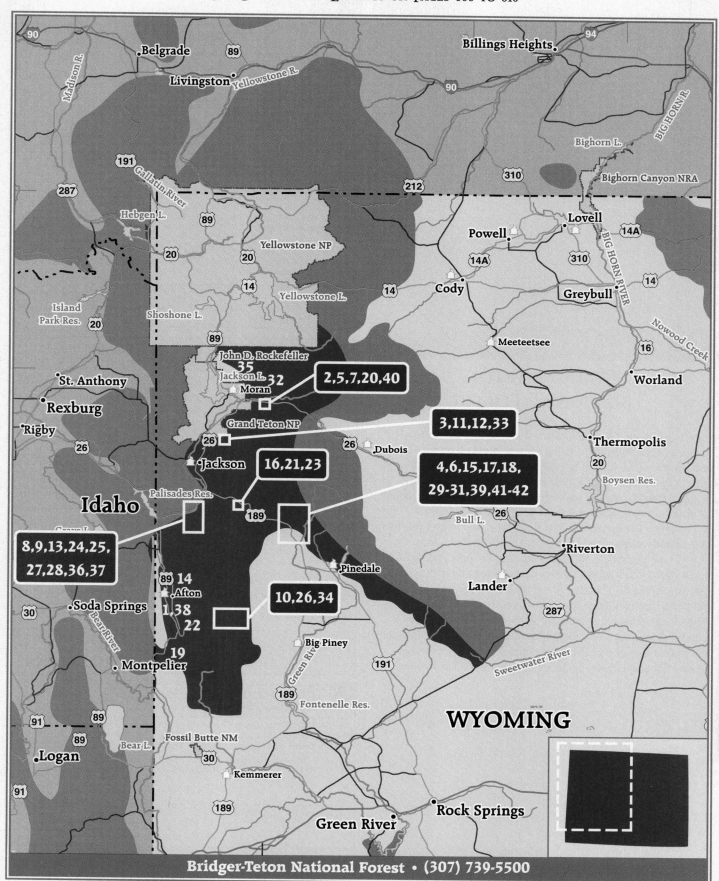

90

Belgrade

89

Livingston Yellowstone R.

Madison R.

191

Gallatin River

287

Hebgen L.

89

20

20

Yellowstone NP

14

Yellowstone L.

14

Island Park Res.

20

Shoshone L.

89

St. Anthony

John D. Rockefeller

35

Jackson L. 32

Moran

2,5,7,20,40

Rexburg

Rigby

26

Grand Teton NP

26

26 Dubois

3,11,12,33

Jackson

16,21,23

**4,6,15,17,18,
29-31,39,41-42**

Idaho

Palisades Res.

189

Bull L.

26

**8,9,13,24,25,
27,28,36,37**

Grays L.

89 14

Afton

1,38

22

Pinedale

10,26,34

30

Bear River

Soda Springs

19

Montpelier

Big Piney

Green River

191

91 89

189

Fontenelle Res.

WYOMING

89

Logan

Bear L.

Fossil Butte NM

30

91

Kemmerer

189

Green River

Rock Springs

Billings Heights

94

90

212

310

Bighorn L.

BIG HORN R.

Bighorn Canyon NRA

Lovell

14A

Powell

14A

BIG HORN RIVER

310

14

Cody

Greybull

Meeteetsee

Nowood Creek

16

Worland

Thermopolis

20

Boysen Res.

Riverton

Lander

287

Sweetwater River

USFS Photo

BRIDGER-TETON NATIONAL FOREST

With its 3.4 million acres, the Bridger-Teton National Forest in western Wyoming is the second largest National Forest outside Alaska. Included are more than 1.2 million acres of wilderness in the Bridger, Gros Ventre, and Teton Wildernesses. The Bridger-Teton is a land of varied recreational opportunities, beautiful vistas, and abundant wildlife. The Bridger-Teton National Forest is part of the Greater Yellowstone Ecosystem, the largest remaining area of undeveloped lands in the continental United States.

Recreationists will find a multitude of opportunities within the Bridger-Teton National Forest. Backpackers and rock climbers can explore the high country of the Bridger Wilderness. Fishermen will find a variety of sport fish in the many lakes and streams. Hunters can pursue the abundant game and off-road vehicle enthusiasts can explore hundreds of miles of non-wilderness roads and trails. Other opportunities for outdoor enthusiasts include floating the Snake River, mountain biking, and wildlife viewing.

1 Allred Flat

Afton • lat 42°29'17" lon 110°57'43"

DESCRIPTION: CG situated in a pine and fir forest on the banks of Little White Creek. Stream fish in creek for trout. Warm days with cold nights. Supplies in Afton. Gather firewood locally. Watch for moose, elk, deer, and bears in the area. Horse and hiking trails available in vicinity. Prepare for mosquitos in the evening.

GETTING THERE: From Afton go S on US HWY 89 approx. 19 mi. to Allred Flat CG.

SINGLE RATE:	$5	OPEN DATES:	May-Oct
# of SINGLE SITES:	32	MAX SPUR:	99 feet
GROUP RATE:	Varies	MAX STAY:	16 days
# of GROUP SITES:	2	ELEVATION:	6800 feet

2 Angles

Jackson • lat 43°50'30" lon 110°10'00"

DESCRIPTION: In thick forest of pine, aspen and fir. No services, no water. Mild days, cold nights. Supplies in Jackson. Gather firewood locally. Elk, deer, moose and bears in area. Bears boxes available. Trailhead for horse or hiking into Teton Wilderness. Horse corral.

GETTING THERE: From Jackson go N on US HWY 191 approx. 30 mi. to Moran Jct. Go E at the Jct on US HWY 26/287 approx. 16 mi. to forest route 30041. Go N on 30041 approx. 1/2 mi. to Angles CG.

SINGLE RATE:	$5	OPEN DATES:	June-Sept*
# of SINGLE SITES:	4		
		MAX STAY:	10 days
		ELEVATION:	7000 feet

3 Atherton Creek

Kelly • lat 43°38'13" lon 110°31'21"

DESCRIPTION: CG set in an open area overlooking the Gros Ventre River and a geologic slide. Trout fish river or Lower Slide Lake. Warm days with cold nights. Supplies in Jackson. Gather firewood locally. Watch for deer, elk, moose, and occasional bears. Hiking and horse trails nearby. Access into the Gros Ventre Wilderness.

GETTING THERE: Atherton Creek CG is located approx. 7.5 mi. E of Kelly on forest route 30400 (Gros Ventre Road).

SINGLE RATE:	$5	OPEN DATES:	June-Oct
# of SINGLE SITES:	13	MAX SPUR:	45 feet
		MAX STAY:	14 days
		ELEVATION:	7200 feet

4 Big Sandy

Boulder • lat 42°41'13" lon 109°16'16"

DESCRIPTION: A rustic CG in high mountain pine forest. No drinking water, no services. Rain common in June. Supplies 60 mi.. Elk, moose, deer, and bears in area. Gather firewood. Horse/hike access into Bridger Wilderness. Corrals on site. Nearest access from West side to Cirque of Towers. ATV use on forest roads.

GETTING THERE: From Boulder go SE on state HWY 353 15 mi. to county route. Continue SE 9 mi. to Emigrant Trail Road (Lander Cutoff). Go E 6.5 mi. to forest route 850. Go N 11 mi. to Big Sandy CG. Rough road.

SINGLE RATE:	$4	OPEN DATES:	June-Sept
# of SINGLE SITES:	12	MAX SPUR:	22 feet
		MAX STAY:	10 days
		ELEVATION:	9100 feet

5 Blackrock Bike Camp

Jackson • lat 43°50'00" lon 110°18'00"

DESCRIPTION: Off highway in stand of old growth pine and fir. Bike-in stopover only. Rustic, no services, no drinking water. Bears boxes. Mild days, cold nights. Supplies in Jackson. Gather local firewood. Moose, elk, deer and small wildlife. Bears country!

GETTING THERE: From Jackson go N on US HWY 191 approx. 30 mi. to US HWY 26/187. Go E on 26/187 approx. 11.5 mi. to Blackrock Bike Camp.

SINGLE RATE:	No fee	OPEN DATES:	June-Sept*
# of SINGLE SITES:	9		
		MAX STAY:	14 days
		ELEVATION:	7500 feet

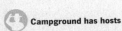 Campground has hosts   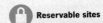 Reservable sites   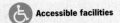 Accessible facilities   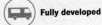 Fully developed   Semi-developed   Rustic facilities

NOTE: Open dates listed are typical. Actual dates are dependent on conditions such as snow pack.

6 · Boulder Lake

Boulder • lat 42˚51'20" lon 109˚37'13"

DESCRIPTION: Rustic CG set on the shore of Boulder Lake in a pine forest. Views of creek and lake. Mild days, cold nights. Trout and kokanee fishing. Supplies in Pinedale. Gather firewood. Moose, elk, deer, raptors, and bears in area. No services, no drinking water. Horse and hiking access into wilderness.

GETTING THERE: From Boulder go E on state HWY 353 approx. 2.5 mi. to forest route 780. Go N on 780 approx. 10 mi. to Boulder Lake CG. Rough road.

SINGLE RATE:	No fee	OPEN DATES:	June-Oct
# of SINGLE SITES:	20	MAX SPUR:	45 feet
		MAX STAY:	14 days
		ELEVATION:	7315 feet

7 · Box Creek

Moran • lat 44˚51'00" lon 110˚18'00"

DESCRIPTION: CG situated in a thick lodgepole pine forest. A popular hunting camp with horse corrals. No drinking water or services. Stream fish for trout on Box Creek. Warm days with cold nights. Deer, moose, elk, and grizzly bears in area. Gather firewood. Supplies in Jackson. Access into Teton Wilderness nearby.

GETTING THERE: From Moran go E on US HWY 26/287 approx. 4 mi. to forest route 30050. Go NE on 30050 approx. 8 mi. to Box Creek CG.

SINGLE RATE:	$5	OPEN DATES:	June-Sept
# of SINGLE SITES:	6		
		MAX STAY:	10 days
		ELEVATION:	7300 feet

8 · Bridge

Alpine • lat 43˚08'36" lon 110˚58'36"

DESCRIPTION: CG set on the banks of the Greys River, situated in an old growth pine and aspen forest. Blue ribbon trout fishing on river. No drinking water or services. Warm days with cold nights. Limited supplies in Alpine. Gather firewood. CG is at the beginning of long canyon with several hiking and horse trails nearby.

GETTING THERE: From Alpine go SE on forest route 10138 approx. 3 mi. to Bridge CG. Not suitable for trailers.

SINGLE RATE:	$3	OPEN DATES:	May-Oct
# of SINGLE SITES:	5	MAX SPUR:	36 feet
		MAX STAY:	16 days
		ELEVATION:	5600 feet

9 · Cabin Creek
Alpine • lat 43˚15'06" lon 110˚46'33"

DESCRIPTION: CG set on the banks of the Snake River. Canyon views. River is swift and high with spring runoff, making it well-known for rafting. Mild days with cold nights. Astoria Hot Springs are 4 mi. away. Supplies are available in Hoback or Jackson. Gather firewood locally. Hiking and horse trails nearby.

GETTING THERE: Cabin Creek CG is located approx. 19 mi. S of Jackson on US HWY 26/89.

SINGLE RATE:	$10	OPEN DATES:	May-Sept
# of SINGLE SITES:	10	MAX SPUR:	30 feet
		MAX STAY:	10 days
		ELEVATION:	5800 feet

10 · Cottonwood Lake

Afton • lat 42˚38'27" lon 110˚48'57"

DESCRIPTION: CG set on the shores on Cottonwood Lake in an old growth pine and aspen forest. Fishing and boating on lake. Warm days with cold nights. Supplies in Afton. Gather firewood locally. Watch for elk, moose, deer, and occasional bears in the area. Horse corrals available. Hiking and horse trail head nearby.

GETTING THERE: From Afton go S on US HWY 89 approx. 10 mi. to forest route 10208. Go E on 10208 approx. 5.5 mi. to Cottonwood Lake CG.

SINGLE RATE:	$5	OPEN DATES:	May-Oct
# of SINGLE SITES:	18	MAX SPUR:	75 feet
GROUP RATE:	Varies	MAX STAY:	16 days
# of GROUP SITES:	2	ELEVATION:	7000 feet

11 · Crystal Creek
Kelly • lat 43˚36'39" lon 110˚25'50"

DESCRIPTION: CG set among aspen on Crystal Creek. Views of colorful Gros Ventre Moutains. Stream fish for trout in creek or Soda Lake. Warm days, cold nights. Watch for elk, moose, deer, and occasional bears. Supplies in Jackson. Gather firewood locally. Hiking and horse trails access into Gros Ventre Wilderness.

GETTING THERE: Crystal Creek CG is located approx. 13 mi. E of Kelly on forest route 30400 (Gros Ventre Road).

SINGLE RATE:	$10	OPEN DATES:	June-Oct
# of SINGLE SITES:	6	MAX SPUR:	45 feet
		MAX STAY:	14 days
		ELEVATION:	7300 feet

12 · Curtis Canyon
Jackson • lat 43˚30'45" lon 110˚39'38"

DESCRIPTION: CG set in a park like area of pine and aspen. Spectacular views of Jackson Hole Valley. Warm days with cold nights. Gather firewood locally. Supplies in Jackson. Watch for elk, deer, and occasional bears. Mountain biking on roads. Hiking and horse access into Gros Ventre Wilderness nearby.

GETTING THERE: From Jackson go NE on Flat Creek Road approx. 6 mi. to forest route 30440. Continue on 30440 approx. 1 mi. to Curtis Canyon CG.

SINGLE RATE:	$10	OPEN DATES:	June-Sept
# of SINGLE SITES:	12	MAX SPUR:	45 feet
		MAX STAY:	10 days
		ELEVATION:	7600 feet

13 · East Table

Jackson • lat 43˚12'42" lon 110˚48'24"

DESCRIPTION: CG in a mixed conifer and cottonwood forest set in the Snake River Canyon. Mild days with cold nights. Fish the river upstream. Popular white water rafting (Class 3) launch spot. Astoria Hot Springs are 6 mi. away. Gather firewood. Supplies in Hoback or Jackson. Horse and hiking trails nearby.

GETTING THERE: East Table CG is located approx. 24 mi. S of Jackson on US HWY 26/89.

SINGLE RATE:	$15	OPEN DATES:	June-Sept
# of SINGLE SITES:	18	MAX SPUR:	30 feet
		MAX STAY:	10 days
		ELEVATION:	5800 feet

14 · Forest Park
Alpine • lat 42˚49'53" lon 110˚41'21"

DESCRIPTION: CG set on the banks of the Greys River among old growth lodgepole pine. Blue ribbon trout fishing on river. Warm days with cold nights. Weather changes quickly. Limited supplies in Alpine. Gather firewood locally. Watch for elk, deer, moose, and occasional bears in the area. Hiking and mountain bike trails.

GETTING THERE: Forest Park CG is located approx. 34 mi. SE of Alpine on forest route 10138.

SINGLE RATE:	$5	OPEN DATES:	May-Oct
# of SINGLE SITES:	13	MAX SPUR:	75 feet
		MAX STAY:	16 days
		ELEVATION:	7000 feet

15 · Fremont Lake

Pinedale • lat 42˚54'23" lon 109˚50'14"

DESCRIPTION: This CG is set on the shores of Fremont Lake, among pine and fir. Boat launch on site or shore fish for a variety of trout and kokanee. Mild days with cold nights. Supplies in Pinedale. Gather firewood locally. Fills holidays. Deer and moose reside in the in area. Mosquitos all summer.

GETTING THERE: From Pinedale go NE on county route approx. 3 mi. to forest route 741. N on 741 approx. 3 mi. to Fremont Lake CG.

SINGLE RATE:	$7	OPEN DATES:	May-Sept
# of SINGLE SITES:	53	MAX SPUR:	45 feet
		MAX STAY:	10 days
		ELEVATION:	7600 feet

 Campground has hosts   **Reservable sites**   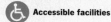 **Accessible facilities**   **Fully developed**   **Semi-developed**   **Rustic facilities**

NOTE: Open dates listed are typical. Actual dates are dependent on conditions such as snow pack.

16 Granite Creek
Bondurant • lat 43°21'32" lon 110°26'39"

DESCRIPTION: CG set among thick old growth pine on the banks of Granite Creek. Fish for trout. Granite Hot Springs swimming pool (fee area) built by CCCs is approx. 2 mi. away. Warm days with cold nights. Supplies in Jackson. Gather firewood locally. Horse and hiking trails access into Gros Ventre Wilderness nearby.

GETTING THERE: From Bondurant go W on US HWY 189/191 approx. 10 mi. to forest route 30500. Go NE on 30500 approx. 9 mi. to Granite Creek CG.

SINGLE RATE:	$12	OPEN DATES:	June-Sept
# of SINGLE SITES:	52	MAX SPUR:	45 feet
		MAX STAY:	14 days
		ELEVATION:	7100 feet

17 Green River Lake
Pinedale • lat 43°18'43" lon 109°51'35"

DESCRIPTION: CG set in a pine & fir forest. Short walk to Green River Lake for shore or boat trout fishing. Spectacular views of Square Top Mountain. Mild days with cold nights. Supplies in Pinedale. Moose, elk, deer, and occasional bears in area. Gather firewood locally. Horse and hiking access into Bridger Wilderness.

GETTING THERE: From Pinedale go W on US HWY 191 10 mi. to state HWY 352. Go N approx. 24 mi. to forest route 600. Go N 3 mi. to forest route 650. Go NE 15 mi. to Green River Lake CG. Rough road, slick when wet.

SINGLE RATE:	$7	OPEN DATES:	June-Sept
# of SINGLE SITES:	37	MAX SPUR:	30 feet
GROUP RATE:	$25	MAX STAY:	10 days
# of GROUP SITES:	3	ELEVATION:	8000 feet

18 Half Moon Lake
Pinedale • lat 42°55'54" lon 109°45'21"

DESCRIPTION: CG set on Half Moon Lake among old growth pine and fir. Mild days with cold nights. Shore or boat fishing for trout. Gather firewood locally. Supplies in Pinedale. Deer, elk, moose, raptors, and bears in area. Receives moderate use. Horse and hiking access to wilderness nearby. No drinking water.

GETTING THERE: From Pinedale go NE on county route approx. 3 mi. to forest route 740. N on 740 approx. 3 mi. to forest route 743. E on 743 approx. 2 mi. to Half Moon Bay CG.

SINGLE RATE:	$3	OPEN DATES:	June-Sept
# of SINGLE SITES:	18	MAX SPUR:	45 feet
		MAX STAY:	14 days
		ELEVATION:	7600 feet

19 Hams Fork
Cokeville • lat 42°15'03" lon 110°43'47"

DESCRIPTION: CG set in a pine and fir forest on the Ham's Fork. Stream fish for trout. Mild to hot days with cold nights. Supplies in Cokeville. Watch for moose, elk, deer, and occasional bears in the area. Fills during the fall hunting season. Gather firewood locally. Horse, mountain bike, and hiking trails nearby.

GETTING THERE: From Cokeville go N on state HWY 232 approx. 7 mi. to forest route 10069. Go NE on 10069 approx. 11 mi. to forest route 10062. Go E on 10062 approx. 2 mi. to Hams Fork CG.

SINGLE RATE:	$5	OPEN DATES:	May-Oct
# of SINGLE SITES:	13	MAX SPUR:	45 feet
		MAX STAY:	14 days
		ELEVATION:	8000 feet

20 Hatchet
Moran • lat 43°49'27" lon 110°21'10"

DESCRIPTION: CG set in a lodgepole pine forest with spectacular views of the Grand Tetons. Stream fish the Buffalo River in the spring. Supplies are available in Jackson. Gather firewood locally. Watch for elk, moose, deer, and grizzly bears. Bears resistant storage boxes. Access into Teton Wilderness nearby.

GETTING THERE: From Moran go E on US HWY 26/287 approx. 8 mi. to forest route 30160. Go SW on forest route 30160 approx. 1/2 mi. to Hatchet CG.

SINGLE RATE:	$10	OPEN DATES:	June-Sept
# of SINGLE SITES:	9		
		MAX STAY:	14 days
		ELEVATION:	8000 feet

21 Hoback
Jackson • lat 43°16'47" lon 110°35'37"

DESCRIPTION: CG set on the banks of the Hoback River in old growth pine and aspen. Scenic canyon setting. River is high and swift in spring, settling into good fishing by July 4. Mild days with cold nights. Limited supplies are available at Hoback Junction. Hiking trails available in Cliff Creek area (approx. 6 mi. E).

GETTING THERE: From Jackson go S on US HWY 89 approx. 13 mi. to Hoback Jct. and HWY 189/161. Go E on 189/161 approx. 12 mi. to Hoback CG.

SINGLE RATE:	$12	OPEN DATES:	June-Sept
# of SINGLE SITES:	14	MAX SPUR:	45 feet
		MAX STAY:	14 days
		ELEVATION:	6225 feet

22 Hobble Creek
Cokeville • lat 42°23'54" lon 110°46'56"

DESCRIPTION: CG set in a pine and fir forest on the banks of Hobble Creek. Stream fish for trout on creek or Lake Alice (1.5 mi.). Mild to hot days, cold nights. Supplies in Cokeville. Watch for moose, elk, deer, and occasional bears. Fills during the fall hunting season. Gather firewood locally. Horse and hiking trails nearby.

GETTING THERE: From Cokeville go N on state HWY 232 13 mi. to forest route 10062. NE 9 mi. to forest route 10066. Go N 5 mi. to forest route 10193. Go N 10 mi. to Hobble Creek CG. Roads not suitable for trailers.

SINGLE RATE:	$5	OPEN DATES:	July-Oct
# of SINGLE SITES:	18	MAX SPUR:	35 feet
		MAX STAY:	14 days
		ELEVATION:	7300 feet

23 Kozy
Jackson • lat 43°16'13" lon 110°30'47"

DESCRIPTION: This CG is situated in the Hoback River Canyon among tall pine. Views of river and canyon. River runs high and fast with spring runoff, settling down for good trout fishing by July 4. Popular kayaking river. Limited supplies at Hoback Junction or go to Jackson. Gather firewood locally. Hiking trails nearby.

GETTING THERE: From Jackson go S on US HWY 189/191 approx. 12 mi. to Hoback Jct. Go E at the Jct on HWY 189/191 approx. 12 mi. to Kozy CG.

SINGLE RATE:	$5	OPEN DATES:	June-Sept
# of SINGLE SITES:	8	MAX SPUR:	25 feet
		MAX STAY:	16 days
		ELEVATION:	6400 feet

24 Little Cottonwood Group
Jackson • lat 45°02'25" lon 108°48'01"

DESCRIPTION: Set among cottonwood on the Snake River with canyon views. Fishing upstream. White water rafting is popular. Astoria Hot Springs in canyon. Basic supplies in Hoback or go to Jackson. Moose, elk and deer in area. Fills quickly until fall. Gather firewood nearby. Horse and hiking trails nearby.

GETTING THERE: From Jackson go S on US HWY 89 approximately 30 miles to Little Cottonwood Group CG.

		OPEN DATES:	June-Sept
		MAX SPUR:	20 feet
GROUP RATE:	$60	MAX STAY:	10 days
# of GROUP SITES:	5	ELEVATION:	6500 feet

25 Lynx Creek
Alpine • lat 43°05'53" lon 110°50'44"

DESCRIPTION: CG set on the banks of the Greys River, situated in an old growth pine and aspen forest. Blue ribbon trout fishing on river. No drinking water or services. Warm days with cold nights. Weather changes quickly. Limited supplies in Alpine. Gather firewood. Numerous hiking and horse trails nearby.

GETTING THERE: Lynx Creek CG is located approx. 12.5 mi. SE of Alpine on forest route 10138.

SINGLE RATE:	$3	OPEN DATES:	May-Oct
# of SINGLE SITES:	14	MAX SPUR:	36 feet
		MAX STAY:	16 days
		ELEVATION:	6200 feet

 Campground has hosts   **Reservable sites**   **Accessible facilities**   **Fully developed**   **Semi-developed**   **Rustic facilities**

NOTE: Open dates listed are typical. Actual dates are dependent on conditions such as snow pack.

26 Middle Piney Lake
Big Piney • lat 42°36'10" lon 110°33'46"

DESCRIPTION: CG set on Middle Piney Lake among tall pine. Fishing for trout and boating on lake, electric motors permitted. Warm days with cold nights. Gather firewood locally. Supplies in Big Piney. Watch for deer, elk, moose, and occasional bears in area. Hiking trails nearby. Snow lingers late at this elevation.

GETTING THERE: From Big Piney go W on state HWY 350 (Middle Piney Road) approx. 22 mi. to forest route 10024. Go SW on 10024 approx. 3 mi. to Middle Piney Lake CG. Not recommended for trailers.

SINGLE RATE:	$5	OPEN DATES:	July-Sept*
# of SINGLE SITES:	5		
		MAX STAY:	16 days
		ELEVATION:	8600 feet

27 Moose Flat
Alpine • lat 42°58'20" lon 110°45'56"

DESCRIPTION: CG set on the banks of the Greys River among old growth lodgepole pine. Blue ribbon trout fishing on river. Warm days with cold nights. Weather changes quickly. Limited supplies in Alpine. Gather firewood locally. Watch for elk, deer, moose, and occasional bears in the area. Hiking trails nearby.

GETTING THERE: Moose Flat CG is located approx. 22 mi. SE of Alpine on forest route 10138.

SINGLE RATE:	$10	OPEN DATES:	May-Oct
# of SINGLE SITES:	10	MAX SPUR:	75 feet
		MAX STAY:	16 days
		ELEVATION:	6400 feet

28 Murphy Creek
Alpine • lat 43°04'20" lon 110°50'07"

DESCRIPTION: This CG is situated at confluence of Murphy Creek and Greys River. Blue ribbon trout fishing on river. No drinking water or services. Warm days with cold nights. Limited supplies in Alpine. Gather firewood locally. Various hiking, mountain bike, and horse trails available nearby.

GETTING THERE: Murphy Creek CG is located approx. 14 mi. SE of Alpine on forest route 10138.

SINGLE RATE:	$5	OPEN DATES:	May-Oct
# of SINGLE SITES:	12	MAX SPUR:	75 feet
		MAX STAY:	16 days
		ELEVATION:	6300 feet

29 Narrows
Pinedale • lat 43°05'30" lon 109°55'00"

DESCRIPTION: This CG is set at the end of a lake with beautiful views. Mild days with cold nights. Boat or shore fish for trout; launch spots nearby. Check local regulations. Supplies are available in Pinedale. Moose, deer, and occasional bears in area. Fills holidays. Firewood may be scarce. Access to Bridger Wilderness.

GETTING THERE: From Pinedale go NW on state HWY 191 approx. 4 mi. to state HWY 352. Go N on 352 approx. 13 mi. to forest route 730. E on 730 approx. 6 mi. to Narrows CG.

SINGLE RATE:	$6	OPEN DATES:	June-Sept
# of SINGLE SITES:	15	MAX SPUR:	30 feet
		MAX STAY:	10 days
		ELEVATION:	7800 feet

30 New Fork Lake
Pinedale • lat 43°04'59" lon 109°57'59"

DESCRIPTION: CG set at the end of a lake with beautiful views. Boat or shore fish for trout; launch spots nearby. Supplies in Pinedale. Moose, deer, and occasional bears in area. Light use. Gather firewood locally. Access to Bridger Wilderness. Mosquitos and flies in July.

GETTING THERE: From Pinedale go NW on state HWY 191 approx. 4 mi. to state HWY 352. Go N on 352 approx. 13 mi. to forest route 730. E on 730 approx. 4 mi. to New Fork Lake CG.

SINGLE RATE:	No fee	OPEN DATES:	June-Sept
# of SINGLE SITES:	15	MAX SPUR:	45 feet
GROUP RATE:	$25	MAX STAY:	10 days
# of GROUP SITES:	1	ELEVATION:	7800 feet

31 New Fork Lake Group
Pinedale • lat 43°04'59" lon 109°57'59"

DESCRIPTION: CG set at the end of a lake with beautiful views. Mild days with cold nights. Boat or shore fish for trout; launch spots nearby. Supplies in Pinedale. Moose, deer, and occasional bears in area. Light use. Gather firewood locally. Access to Bridger Wilderness. No drinking water on site.

GETTING THERE: From Pinedale go NW on state HWY 191 approx. 4 mi. to state HWY 352. Go N on 352 approx. 13 mi. to forest route 730. E on 730 approx. 4 mi. to New Fork Lake Group CG.

SINGLE RATE:	No fee	OPEN DATES:	June-Sept
		MAX SPUR:	45 feet
GROUP RATE:	$25	MAX STAY:	14 days
# of GROUP SITES:	3	ELEVATION:	7800 feet

32 Pacific Creek
Moran • lat 42°55'30" lon 110°26'00"

DESCRIPTION: CG set in a pine and aspen forest on the banks of Pacific Creek. Stream fish on creek. Warm days with cold nights. Supplies in Jackson. Gather firewood locally. Elk, deer, moose, and grizzly bears frequent the area. Bears resistant food boxes on site. Access into Teton Wilderness. CG accomodates horses.

GETTING THERE: From Moran go N on US HWY 89/287 approx. 1.5 mi. to Pacific Creek Road. Go NE on Pacific Creek Road approx. 8 mi. to Pacific Creek CG.

SINGLE RATE:	$5	OPEN DATES:	June-Sept
# of SINGLE SITES:	8		
		MAX STAY:	14 days
		ELEVATION:	7000 feet

33 Red Hills
Kelly • lat 43°36'41" lon 110°26'12"

DESCRIPTION: CG situated in a pine and aspen grove on Gros Ventre River with excellent views of the surrounding hills. Fish for trout in river. Warm days with cold nights. Supplies are available in Jackson. Watch for elk, moose, deer, and occasional bears in the area. Hiking and horse access into the Gros Ventre Wilderness.

GETTING THERE: Red Hills CG is located approx. 13 mi. E of Kelly on forest route 30400 (Gros Venture Road).

SINGLE RATE:	$10	OPEN DATES:	June-Oct
# of SINGLE SITES:	5	MAX SPUR:	45 feet
		MAX STAY:	14 days
		ELEVATION:	7300 feet

34 Sacajawea
Big Piney • lat 42°37'04" lon 110°31'53"

DESCRIPTION: This CG is situated in a lodgepole pine forest. Fish for trout on nearby Middle Piney Lake. Check for local regulations. Warm days with cold nights. Supplies are available in Big Piney. Gather firewood locally. Watch for deer, elk, moose, and occasional bears in the area. Hiking trails nearby.

GETTING THERE: From Big Piney go W on state HWY 350 (Middle Piney Road) approx. 22 mi. to forest route 10024. Go SW on 10024 approx. 1 mi. to Sacajawea CG. Road is narrow with sharp curves.

SINGLE RATE:	$5	OPEN DATES:	June-Sept*
# of SINGLE SITES:	24	MAX SPUR:	30 feet
		MAX STAY:	16 days
		ELEVATION:	8200 feet

35 Sheffield Creek
Jackson • lat 44°05'00" lon 110°38'00"

DESCRIPTION: CG was burned over in fires of 1988. New growth is mostly small trees and bushes. No services, no water. Stream fish in Sheffield Creek. Mild days, cold nights. Basic supplies at Flagg Ranch or go to Jackson. Moose, elk, deer and bears country. Hike or horse trail to Huckleberry Lookout. Horse corral.

GETTING THERE: From Jackson go N on US HWY 191/89/287 30 mi. to Moran Jct. and HWY 89/287. Continue N on 89/287 24 mi. to Sheffield Creek CG. Creek must be forded, caution is needed with trailers.

SINGLE RATE:	No fee	OPEN DATES:	June-Sept*
# of SINGLE SITES:	5	MAX SPUR:	30 feet
		MAX STAY:	14 days
		ELEVATION:	7000 feet

 Campground has hosts   **Reservable sites**    **Accessible facilities**   **Fully developed**   **Semi-developed**   **Rustic facilities**

NOTE: Open dates listed are typical. Actual dates are dependent on conditions such as snow pack.

36 Squaw Flat
Alpine • lat 43°08'00" lon 110°54'00"

DESCRIPTION: Set on Greys River in old growth pine and fir stands. Blue ribbon trout fishing on the River, very high and swift in spring. Basic supplies in Alpine. Dispersed sites. No services, no drinking water. Warm days, cold nights. Gather firewood. Moderate use, never full. Horse, hiking trails nearby.

GETTING THERE: From Alpine go S on Greys River Road approx. 4 mi. to Squaw Flat CG.

SINGLE RATE:	No fee	OPEN DATES:	June-Sept*
		MAX SPUR:	60 feet
		MAX STAY:	14 days
		ELEVATION:	6500 feet

37 Station Creek
Jackson • lat 43°12'16" lon 110°50'01"

DESCRIPTION: CG set among aspen, cottonwood, and fir on the banks of the Snake River. Views of canyon and river. Fish river upstream. Popular for white river rafting; boat launch on site. Supplies in Hoback or Jackson. Gather firewood locally. Fills quickly. Horse and hiking trails nearby.

GETTING THERE: Station Creek CG is located approx. 25 mi. S of Jackson on US HWY 26/89.

SINGLE RATE:	$15	OPEN DATES:	June-Sept
# of SINGLE SITES:	15	MAX SPUR:	30 feet
		MAX STAY:	10 days
		ELEVATION:	5800 feet

38 Swift Creek
Alpine • lat 42°43'30" lon 110°54'07"

DESCRIPTION: CG situated in an old growth pine forest on the banks of Swift Creek. Stream fish for trout on creek. Warm days with cold nights. Supplies in Afton. Gather firewood locally. Watch for elk, moose, deer, and occasional bears in the area. Periodic Springs trail is 3 mi. away. Access into Salt River Range Mountains.

GETTING THERE: From Afton go E on forest route 10211 approx. 1 mi. to Swift Creek CG.

SINGLE RATE:	$5	OPEN DATES:	May-Oct
# of SINGLE SITES:	11	MAX SPUR:	40 feet
GROUP RATE:	Varies	MAX STAY:	16 days
# of GROUP SITES:	1	ELEVATION:	6300 feet

39 Trails End
Pinedale • lat 43°00'44" lon 109°45'06"

DESCRIPTION: CG at the edge of a meadow, in a pine forest. Noon t-storms July-August. Receives heavy use. Corrals provided. Supplies in Pinedale. Moose, elk, deer, and bears in area. Gather firewood locally. Horse and hiking access into wilderness. No motor-vehicles. Prepare for mosquitos all season.

GETTING THERE: From Pinedale go NE on county route approx. 3 mi. to forest route 740. N on 740 approx. 10 mi. Trails End CG.

SINGLE RATE:	$7	OPEN DATES:	June-Sept
# of SINGLE SITES:	8	MAX SPUR:	45 feet
		MAX STAY:	10 days
		ELEVATION:	9100 feet

40 Turpin Meadow
Moran • lat 43°51'18" lon 110°15'44"

DESCRIPTION: CG set in a thick old growth lodgepole pine forest. Stream fishing available nearby. Warm days with cold nights. Weather changes quickly. Supplies in Jackson. Gather firewood locally. Watch for elk, moose, deer, and bears. Bears resistant food storage. Access into the Teton Wilderness trails.

GETTING THERE: From Moran go E on US HWY 26/287 approx. 4 mi. to forest route 30050. Go NE on forest route 30050 approx. 9.5 mi. to forest route 30065. Go N on 30065 approx. 1/2 mi. to Turpin Meadow CG.

SINGLE RATE:	$10	OPEN DATES:	June-Sept
# of SINGLE SITES:	18		
		MAX STAY:	10 days
		ELEVATION:	7300 feet

41 Upper Fremont Lake
Pinedale • lat 43°01'21" lon 109°46'29"

DESCRIPTION: Rustic CG set among old growth pine and fir off Fremont Lake. Trout fish on lake. Mild days with cold nights. Supplies in Pinedale. Gather firewood locally. Moose, elk, deer, raptors, and bears frequent area. Hiking access to Bridger Wilderness. Mosquitos all summer. No services or drinking water.

GETTING THERE: Upper Fremont Lake CG is located on the N shore of Fremont Lake (approx. 2 mi. NE of Pinedale) and is accessible only by boat.

SINGLE RATE:	No fee	OPEN DATES:	June-Sept
# of SINGLE SITES:	5	MAX SPUR:	45 feet
		MAX STAY:	14 days
		ELEVATION:	7600 feet

42 Whiskey Grove
Pinedale • lat 43°15'23" lon 110°01'30"

DESCRIPTION: CG is in a lodgepole pine and sagebrush setting on the Green River. Rain is common in June. Fishing on the Green River. Supplies in Pinedale. Moose and deer reside in the area. Gather firewood locally. Some trails nearby. Mosquitoes and flies are a problem in July. Bears are a problem on occasion.

GETTING THERE: From Pinedale go W on US HWY 191 approx. 10 mi. to state HWY 352. Go N approx. 24 mi. to forest route 600. Go N 3 mi. (across the Green River) to forest route 605. Go S .5 mi. to Whiskey Grove CG.

SINGLE RATE:	$4	OPEN DATES:	June-Sept
# of SINGLE SITES:	9	MAX SPUR:	45 feet
		MAX STAY:	14 days
		ELEVATION:	7600 feet

43 Willow Lake
Pinedale • lat 42°59'31" lon 109°54'00"

DESCRIPTION: CG on edge of glacier formed Willow Lake with views of mountains. Mild days, cold nights. Trout fish on lake; boat ramp. Supplies in Pinedale. Gather firewood. Deer, moose, elk, raptors, and bears in area. Light use. No services or drinking water on site. Horse and hiking access into wilderness at the far end of lake.

GETTING THERE: From Pinedale go N on Willow Lake Road approx. 9 mi. to forest route 751. Go W on 751 1 mi. to Willow Lake CG.

SINGLE RATE:	No fee	OPEN DATES:	June-Oct
# of SINGLE SITES:	6	MAX SPUR:	45 feet
		MAX STAY:	10 days
		ELEVATION:	7700 feet

 Campground has hosts   Reservable sites   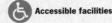 Accessible facilities   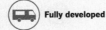 Fully developed    Semi-developed    Rustic facilities

NOTE: Open dates listed are typical. Actual dates are dependent on conditions such as snow pack.

USFS Photo

MEDICINE BOW-ROUTT NATIONAL FOREST

The Medicine Bow/Routt National Forests (MBR) and Thunder Basin National Grasslands (TBNG) encompass nearly three million acres from the north and eastern borders of Wyoming, south to the I-70 corridor that traverses north central Colorado. The forests provide a variety of uses and outdoor opportunities.

There are 13 designated wilderness areas on the forest, approximately 1360 developed sites, and eight mountain lakes with developed boating facilities. On the combined Medicine Bow/Routt National Forests, downhill skiing and winter sports are the most popular activities, followed by mechanized travel (including driving, boating, and bicycling), camping, hunting, and fishing.

The origin of the "Medicine Bow" is legendary. Native American tribes which inhabited southeastern Wyoming found mountain mahogany in one of the valleys, from which bows of exceptional quality were made. Friendly tribes assembled there annually to construct their weapons and hold ceremonial powwows for the cure of disease, which was known as "making medicine." Eventually settlers associated the terms "making medicine" and "making bows", and Medicine Bow resulted as the name of the locality.

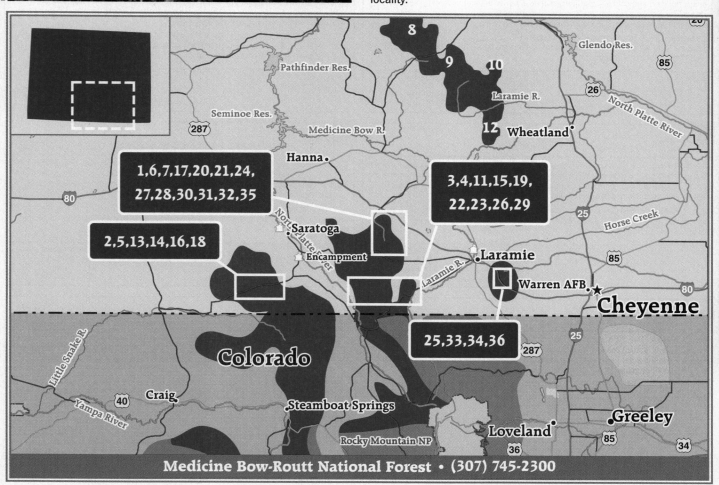

Medicine Bow-Routt National Forest • (307) 745-2300

MEDICINE BOW-ROUTT NATIONAL FOREST • WYOMING • LOCATOR MAP

1 Aspen
Centennial • lat 41°19'07" lon 106°09'36"

DESCRIPTION: Expect hot summer days with cold nights in this high plains desert location. Gather firewood (which may be scarce), or bring your own. Supplies and groceries can be found in Centennial. Fishing nearby. Hiking and mountain biking opportunities.

GETTING THERE: Aspen CG is located 2 mi. W of Centennial on state HWY 130 at the Libby Creek Recreation Area.

SINGLE RATE:	$10	OPEN DATES:	May-Sept
# of SINGLE SITES:	8	MAX SPUR:	22 feet
		MAX STAY:	14 days
		ELEVATION:	8600 feet

2 Battle Creek
Encampment • lat 41°05'36" lon 107°09'34"

DESCRIPTION: This CG is near Battle Creek set in open grassy meadow. Trout fish the creek. Historic Battle Townsite 10 mi. E. Supplies can be found 24 mi. away in Encampment. Elk and dear frequent the area. Moderate use turning heavier in fall hunting season. Horse, ATV, and bike riding in area. A remote and rustic CG.

GETTING THERE: From Encampment go W on state HWY 70 approx. 22 mi. to forest route 807. Go S on 807 2 mi. to Battle Creek CG. High clearance vehicle required.

SINGLE RATE:	No fee	OPEN DATES:	May-Oct
# of SINGLE SITES:	4	MAX SPUR:	16 feet
		MAX STAY:	14 days
		ELEVATION:	7800 feet

3 Bobbie Thompson
Laramie • lat 41°09'30" lon 106°15'00"

DESCRIPTION: This CG is located high in the Wyoming mountains. The high elevation brings hot days and cold nights. Campers may enjoy fishing and boating in the area. Please check fishing regulations. Supplies and groceries can be found in Laramie. Firewood may be scarce, it is best to bring your own.

GETTING THERE: From Laramie go W on state HWY 130 approx. 21 mi. to state HWY 11. S on 11 to Albany. Continue on primary forest route 500 2 mi. to forest route 542. W on 542 6 mi. to Bobbie Thompson CG.

SINGLE RATE:	$10	OPEN DATES:	June-Oct
# of SINGLE SITES:	18	MAX SPUR:	32 feet
		MAX STAY:	14 days
		ELEVATION:	8800 feet

4 Boswell Creek
Laramie • lat 40°01'24" lon 106°01'51"

DESCRIPTION: This CG is located high in the Wyoming mountains. With the higher elevation campers should expect hot days with cold nights. Fishing and boating is available in the area. Firewood may be scarce. Supplies and groceries can be found in Laramie. Hiking and mountain biking opportunities are nearby.

GETTING THERE: From Laramie go S on state HWY 230 to Woods Landing. Go S on state HWY 10 to Boswell Ranch, 1/2 mi. N of Colorado line. Go W on forest route 526 approx. 7 mi. to Boswell Creek CG.

SINGLE RATE:	$10	OPEN DATES:	June-Oct
# of SINGLE SITES:	9	MAX SPUR:	16 feet
		MAX STAY:	14 days
		ELEVATION:	8900 feet

5 Bottle Creek
Encampment • lat 41°10'38" lon 106°53'58"

DESCRIPTION: This CG is set in a conifer and aspen grove with spectacular overlook views. Historic Bottle Creek CCC Camp site. Supplies at Encampment, 6 mi. E. Elk, deer, and bears in the area. Large gathering during mid-July, otherwise moderate use. Host sells firewood, or gather own. Hiking trail in area.

GETTING THERE: From Encampment go W on state HWY 70 approx. 6 mi. to Bottle Creek CG.

SINGLE RATE:	$10	OPEN DATES:	May-Oct
# of SINGLE SITES:	16	MAX SPUR:	45 feet
		MAX STAY:	14 days
		ELEVATION:	8800 feet

6 Bow River
Arlington • lat 41°30'52" lon 106°22'15"

DESCRIPTION: This CG is located in dense stand of pine and aspen. Trout fishing in Bow River next to CG. Visit historic Brush Creek Ranger Station and Turpin Tie Hack Cabins. Supplies and groceries can be found 15 mi. away from CG at Elk Mountain. CG is generally quiet and peaceful.

GETTING THERE: From Arlington go S on forest route 111 approx. 6 mi. to forest route 120. Take 120 4 mi. W to forest route 101. W on 101 2 mi. to Bow River CG.

SINGLE RATE:	$7	OPEN DATES:	May-Oct
# of SINGLE SITES:	13	MAX SPUR:	32 feet
		MAX STAY:	14 days
		ELEVATION:	8600 feet

7 Brooklyn Lake
Centennial • lat 41°22'30" lon 106°15'00"

DESCRIPTION: This CG is situated on Brooklyn Lake with views of the lake. Campers may enjoy brook trout fishing in the lake. Please check fishing regulations. Expect warm to hot days with cold nights. Gather firewood locally. Supplies and groceries can be found in Centennial. Hiking trails nearby.

GETTING THERE: From Centennial go W on state HWY 130 approx. 8 mi. to forest route 317. N on 317 2 mi. to Brooklyn Lake CG.

SINGLE RATE:	$10	OPEN DATES:	July-Sept
# of SINGLE SITES:	19	MAX SPUR:	45 feet
		MAX STAY:	14 days
		ELEVATION:	10500 feet

8 Campbell Creek
Douglas • lat 42°27'18" lon 105°50'08"

DESCRIPTION: This CG is situated in a remote area at the western end of the Laramie Mountains. Road passes through scenic LaPrele Canyon. Mild to hot days with cold nights. Supplies are available at Douglas. Gather firewood locally. Fishing, hiking, mountain biking, and ATV use in LaPrele Cyn.

GETTING THERE: From Douglas go SW on HWY 94 (Esterbrook Rd) for 2 mi.. Turn right on Chalk Buttes Rd. Go 3 mi. to state HWY 91. Go S 25 mi. to county route 24. Go SW on 24 approx. 14 mi. to Campbell Creek CG.

SINGLE RATE:	$5	OPEN DATES:	June-Oct*
# of SINGLE SITES:	8	MAX SPUR:	22 feet
		MAX STAY:	14 days
		ELEVATION:	8200 feet

9 Curtis Gulch
Douglas • lat 42°24'27" lon 105°37'18"

DESCRIPTION: CG at the base of Laramie Peak surrounded by fir and pine. Mild to hot days with cold nights. Gather firewood locally. Supplies ae availble at Douglas. Deer and small wildlife in area. The Oregon and Mormon trails went through area. Trailhead to Laramie Peak and Friend Park Trail on site.

GETTING THERE: From Douglas go W on I-25 approx. 1 mi. to state HWY 91. Go S on 91 approx. 17 mi. to county route 16. Go S approx. 11 mi. to forest route 658. Go NE on 658 approx. 2 mi. to Curtis Gulch CG.

SINGLE RATE:	$15	OPEN DATES:	May-Oct
# of SINGLE SITES:	6	MAX SPUR:	22 feet
		MAX STAY:	14 days
		ELEVATION:	7400 feet

10 Esterbrook
Esterbrook • lat 42°25'27" lon 105°19'22"

DESCRIPTION: This CG is set in a park-like stand of ponderosa pine on a broad ridge north of Laramie Peak. Good trout fishing in vicinity. Supplies are available in Douglas. Campers may gather their firewood locally. Hiking trail on site is a good jumping-off point for recreating in the Laramie Peak unit.

GETTING THERE: From Douglas go S on HWY 94 (Esterbrook Rd) approx. 17 mi. to county route 5. Go S on 5 approx. 11 mi. to forest route 633. Go E on 633 approx. 3 mi. to Esterbrook CG.

SINGLE RATE:	$5	OPEN DATES:	May-Oct*
# of SINGLE SITES:	12	MAX SPUR:	22 feet
		MAX STAY:	14 days
		ELEVATION:	6300 feet

 Campground has hosts   **Reservable sites**   **Accessible facilities**   **Fully developed**   **Semi-developed**   **Rustic facilities**

NOTE: Open dates listed are typical. Actual dates are dependent on conditions such as snow pack.

11 French Creek
Encampment • lat 41°13'34" lon 106°28'52"

DESCRIPTION: CG in aspen with brushy undergrowth. Trout fishing in nearby French Creek. Expect rain in July. Historic CCC camp 10 mi. away. Supplies at Encampment or 16 mi. in Saratoga. Wildlife includes moose, elk, deer, mountain lions, and bears. Gather firewood. Horse and hiking trails nearby. ATV's may use roads.

GETTING THERE: French Creek CG is located approx. 16 mi. E of Encampment, on French Creek Road (county route 660).

SINGLE RATE:	$7	OPEN DATES:	June-Nov
# of SINGLE SITES:	11	MAX SPUR:	32 feet
		MAX STAY:	14 days
		ELEVATION:	8000 feet

16 Lakeview
Encampment • lat 41°01'30" lon 106°50'30"

DESCRIPTION: Among fir on Hog Park Reservoir with lake views. Boat dock and pier nearby. Stream fish Hog Park Creek below the dam. Supplies 30 mi. at Encampment. Deer, elk, and moose in area. Gather firewood or buy from the host. Horse, hiking, and mountain biking trails and ATV roads. Bears frequent the area.

GETTING THERE: From Encampment go SW on state HWY 70 approx. 7 mi. to forest route 550. Go S on 550 21 mi. to forest route 496. Go S on 496 2 mi. to Lakeview CG.

SINGLE RATE:	$10	OPEN DATES:	June-Oct
# of SINGLE SITES:	50	MAX SPUR:	70 feet
		MAX STAY:	14 days
		ELEVATION:	8400 feet

12 Friend Park
Esterbrook • lat 42°15'23" lon 105°29'06"

DESCRIPTION: CG set at the base of Laramie Peak in a grove of fir and pine with views of Friend Park. Laramie Peak at 10,200' is the highest peak in the Laramie Range. Oregon and Mormon Trails went through area. Wild turkeys and bighorn sheep in area. Rock climbing, hiking, mountain bike, and horse trails nearby.

GETTING THERE: From Douglas go S on HWY 94 (Esterbrook Rd) 17 mi. to county route 5. Go SW on 5 aprox. 15 mi. to forest route 671. Go SE on 671 2 mi. to forest route 661. Continue on 661 to Friend Park CG.

SINGLE RATE:	$5	OPEN DATES:	June-Oct
# of SINGLE SITES:	11	MAX SPUR:	22 feet
		MAX STAY:	14 days
		ELEVATION:	7500 feet

17   Lincoln Park
Saratoga • lat 41°22'19" lon 106°31'17"

DESCRIPTION: This CG is located in a park-like stand of fir. Trout fishing in nearby Brush Creek. Hiking, horse, mountain bike, and ATV trails in area. Visit historic Brush Creek Ranger Station. Supplies available at Saratoga, 24 mi. or stores 6 mi. away. Moose, elk, beavers, deer, marmots, and bears in the area.

GETTING THERE: From Saratoga go S and E on state HWY 130 approx. 19 mi. to forest route 100. Go N on 100 2 mi. to Lincoln Park CG.

SINGLE RATE:	$10	OPEN DATES:	May-Nov
# of SINGLE SITES:	12	MAX SPUR:	65 feet
		MAX STAY:	14 days
		ELEVATION:	7800 feet

13 Haskins Creek
Encampment • lat 41°09'07" lon 107°02'40"

DESCRIPTION: This is a shady and cool CG set among fir. Supplies and groceries can be found in Encampment 15 mi. east of the CG. Elk and deer frequent the area. CG is quiet, small and rarely fills. A nearby trailhead leads to Baby Lake and the Huston Park Wilderness. Campers should expect mosquitos all year.

GETTING THERE: From Encampmetnt go W on state HWY 70 approx. 15 mi. to Haskins Creek CG.

SINGLE RATE:	$7	OPEN DATES:	June-Oct
# of SINGLE SITES:	10	MAX SPUR:	20 feet
		MAX STAY:	14 days
		ELEVATION:	9000 feet

18 Lost Creek
Encampment • lat 41°08'30" lon 107°04'31"

DESCRIPTION: This CG has sites set in sunny, grassy spots or shaded spots on Lost Creek. Campers may enjoy fishing in the area but please check fishing regulations. Supplies can be found in Encampment. Elk and deer frequent the area. A nearby trailhead leads to Baby Lake and the Huston Park Wilderness.

GETTING THERE: From Encampment go W on state HWY 70 approx. 17 mi. to Lost Creek CG.

SINGLE RATE:	$7	OPEN DATES:	June-Oct
# of SINGLE SITES:	13	MAX SPUR:	22 feet
		MAX STAY:	14 days
		ELEVATION:	8800 feet

14 Jack Creek
Saratoga • lat 41°17'04" lon 107°07'12"

DESCRIPTION: This CG is situated on Jack Creek in park-like fir. Cool and shady area with trout fishing on Jack Creek. Supplies available at Saratoga 24 mi. E. Elk, deer, moose, and bears frequent the area. Nearby trailheads to Continental Divide National Scenic Trail (Deep Jack TH).

GETTING THERE: From Saratoga go W on county route 500 approx. 15 mi. to forest route 452. Go S on 452 8 mi. to Jack Creek CG.

SINGLE RATE:	$7	OPEN DATES:	May-Oct
# of SINGLE SITES:	16	MAX SPUR:	22 feet
		MAX STAY:	14 days
		ELEVATION:	8500 feet

19 Miller Lake
Laramie • lat 41°04'10" lon 106°09'19"

DESCRIPTION: This CG is located near Miller Lake. Campers can enjoy fishing in the area but please check fishing regulations. Expect warm to hot days with cold nights. Campers may gather their firewood locally. Supplies and groceries can be found in Laramie.

GETTING THERE: From Laramie go W on state HWY 230 approx. 29 mi. to forest route 512. Go N on 512 1 mi. to Miller Lake CG.

SINGLE RATE:	$10	OPEN DATES:	June-Oct
# of SINGLE SITES:	7	MAX SPUR:	22 feet
		MAX STAY:	14 days
		ELEVATION:	9100 feet

15 Lake Owen
Laramie • lat 41°08'44" lon 106°06'02"

DESCRIPTION: This CG is situated in a park-like grove of lodgepole pine and aspen with views of the Snowy Range. Campers may enjoy trout fishing from the shore or by boat on adjacent Lake Owen. Expect hot days with cold nights. Supplies and groceries can be found in Laramie.

GETTING THERE: From Laramie go SW on state HWY 230 to Jelm Post Office. Go N on county route 47 (Fox Creek Road) 5 mi. to forest route 517. Go W 2 mi. to forest route 540. S on 540 3 mi. to Lake Owen CG.

SINGLE RATE:	$10	OPEN DATES:	June-Nov
# of SINGLE SITES:	35	MAX SPUR:	35 feet
		MAX STAY:	14 days
		ELEVATION:	9000 feet

20   Nash Fork
Laramie • lat 41°20'55" lon 106°12'56"

DESCRIPTION: This CG is set in a grove of fir and spruce. Trout fishing in Nash Fork Creek which runs through the CG. Expect warm to hot days with cold nights. Supplies and groceries can be found in Laramie. Campers may gather their firewood locally. Numerous trails in vicinity.

GETTING THERE: From Laramie go W on state HWY 130 approx. 34 mi. to Nash Fork CG.

SINGLE RATE:	$10	OPEN DATES:	July-Sept
# of SINGLE SITES:	27	MAX SPUR:	22 feet
		MAX STAY:	14 days
		ELEVATION:	10200 feet

 Campground has hosts   **Reservable sites**   **Accessible facilities**   **Fully developed**   **Semi-developed**   **Rustic facilities**

NOTE: Open dates listed are typical. Actual dates are dependent on conditions such as snow pack.

21 North Fork
Centennial • lat 41°19'28" lon 106°09'22"

DESCRIPTION: This CG is situated in a grove of conifer. Trout fishing on the North Fork of the Little Laramie River nearby. Expect warm to hot days with cold nights. Supplies and groceries can be found in Centennial. Gather firewood locally. Hiking, mountain biking, and horse trails nearby.

GETTING THERE: From Centennial go W on state HWY 130 approx. 4 mi. to forest route 101. N on 101 2 mi. to North Fork CG.

SINGLE RATE:	$10	OPEN DATES:	June-Sept
# of SINGLE SITES:	60	MAX SPUR:	30 feet
		MAX STAY:	14 days
		ELEVATION:	8600 feet

26 Rob Roy
Laramie • lat 41°11'48" lon 106°15'54"

DESCRIPTION: This CG is situated in a park-like stand of pine with views of the Rob Roy Reservoir. Fish from shore or boat for trout in the reservoir. Please check fishing regulations. Motorized boats are allowed. Campers may gather their firewood locally. Supplies and groceries can be found in Laramie.

GETTING THERE: From Laramie go W on state HWY 130 121 mi. to state HWY 11. S on 11 to Albany. W on forest route 500 approx. 7 mi. to Rob Roy CG.

SINGLE RATE:	$10	OPEN DATES:	June-Oct
# of SINGLE SITES:	65	MAX SPUR:	35 feet
		MAX STAY:	14 days
		ELEVATION:	9500 feet

22 Pelton Creek
Laramie • lat 41°04'25" lon 106°18'15"

DESCRIPTION: This CG is situated in a park-like stand of lodgepole pine. There is trout fishing in Pelton Creek which runs along the CG. Expect warm to hot days with cold nights. Supplies and groceries can be found in Laramie. Gather firewood locally. Hiking and horse trails are nearby.

GETTING THERE: From Laramie go W on state HWY 230 to the Colorado state line. N on Pelton Creek Road (forest route 898) 8 mi. to Pelton Creek CG.

SINGLE RATE:	$10	OPEN DATES:	June-Oct
# of SINGLE SITES:	15	MAX SPUR:	16 feet
		MAX STAY:	14 days
		ELEVATION:	8100 feet

27   Ryan Park
Saratoga • lat 41°19'17" lon 106°30'30"

DESCRIPTION: This CG is situated among spruce and aspen. Historic site of former POW camp. Fish Barrett Creek or French Creek. Supplies and groceries can be found at stores 1 mi. away or in Saratoga 20 mi. Moose, bears, deer, and elk in area. Firewood available from host or to be gathered by campers.

GETTING THERE: From Saratoga go S and E on state HWY 130 approx. 21 mi. to Ryan Park CG.

SINGLE RATE:	$10	OPEN DATES:	May-Nov
# of SINGLE SITES:	49	MAX SPUR:	32 feet
GROUP RATE:	Varies	MAX STAY:	14 days
# of GROUP SITES:	1	ELEVATION:	8000 feet

23 Pike Pole/Pickaroon
Laramie • lat 41°15'07" lon 105°24'52"

DESCRIPTION: This CG has no services, and possibly no drinking water on site. Campers may enjoy fishing in the area but please check for fishing regulations. Firewood may be scarce, it is best to bring your own. Supplies and groceries are available in Laramie.

GETTING THERE: From Laramie go W on state HWY 230 29 mi. to forest route 512. N on 512 25 mi. to Pike Pole and Pickaroon CGs.

SINGLE RATE:	$10	OPEN DATES:	June-Oct
# of SINGLE SITES:	14	MAX SPUR:	16 feet
		MAX STAY:	14 days
		ELEVATION:	7800 feet

28 Silver Lake
Saratoga • lat 41°18'46" lon 106°21'32"

DESCRIPTION: This CG is set in a grove of fir, with trout fishing in nearby Silver Lake, Lake Marie, and Mirror Lake. Snow may linger on through the early summer. Expect mild days with cold nights. Hiking and mountain biking trails nearby. Historic CCC built CG toilets. Several trailheads nearby.

GETTING THERE: From Saratoga go S and E on state HWY 130 approx. 29 mi. to Silver Lake CG.

SINGLE RATE:	$10	OPEN DATES:	July-Oct
# of SINGLE SITES:	17	MAX SPUR:	32 feet
		MAX STAY:	14 days
		ELEVATION:	10400 feet

24 Pine
Centennial • lat 41°19'07" lon 106°09'36"

DESCRIPTION: This CG is located high in the Wyoming mountains near Libby Creek. Campers can enjoy fishing in the creek but please check fishing regulations. Campers may gather their firewood locally. Supplies and groceries can be found in Centennial. There are hiking trails nearby.

GETTING THERE: Pine CG is located 2 mi. W of Centennial on state HWY 130 at the Libby Creek Recreation Area.

SINGLE RATE:	$10	OPEN DATES:	May-Sept
# of SINGLE SITES:	6	MAX SPUR:	16 feet
		MAX STAY:	14 days
		ELEVATION:	8600 feet

29 Six Mile Gap
Encampment • lat 41°02'38" lon 106°23'36"

DESCRIPTION: Sites are mixed open and aspen with views of Platte River. Mild days, cool nights. Fishing on river. Supplies 24 mi. N at Encampment. Elk, deer, bighorn sheep, and bears in area. Moderate use in summer, used as launching area to float river in spring. Hunting camp in fall. Platte River Wilderness access nearby.

GETTING THERE: From Encampment go S on state HWY 230 approx. 20 mi. to forest route 492. Go E on 492 2 mi. to Six Mile Gap CG.

SINGLE RATE:	$10	OPEN DATES:	May-Oct
# of SINGLE SITES:	9	MAX SPUR:	70 feet
		MAX STAY:	14 days
		ELEVATION:	8000 feet

25 Pole Creek Group
Laramie • lat 41°15'07" lon 105°24'52"

DESCRIPTION: This CG is situated in a park-like stand of conifers and aspen. Set in a high plains desert area with interesting rock formations. Expect hot days with cold nights. Firewood may be scarce. Supplies can be found in Laramie. Hiking and mountain biking on roads and trails.

GETTING THERE: From Laramie go S and E on I-80 to state HWY 210. E on 210 approx. 2 mi. to Pole Creek Group CG road. Follow Signs.

SINGLE RATE:	Varies	OPEN DATES:	May-Oct
# of SINGLE SITES:	1	MAX SPUR:	20 feet
		MAX STAY:	14 days
		ELEVATION:	8300 feet

30 South Brush Creek
Saratoga • lat 41°21'37" lon 106°32'42"

DESCRIPTION: CG is located in among pine, fir, and aspen. Trout fishing in South Brush Creek which runs along CG. Mild days. Host sells firewood. Visit historic Brush Creek Ranger Station. Hiking, horse, ATV, and mountain biking trails are nearby. Expect mosquitos early in the season.

GETTING THERE: From Saratoga go SE on state HWY 130 approx. 19 mi. to forest route 100. Go E on 100 1/2 mi. to forest route 200. Go E on 200 2 mi. to South Brush Creek CG.

SINGLE RATE:	$10	OPEN DATES:	May-Nov
# of SINGLE SITES:	20	MAX SPUR:	32 feet
		MAX STAY:	14 days
		ELEVATION:	7900 feet

 Campground has hosts   **Reservable sites**   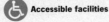 **Accessible facilities**   **Fully developed**   **Semi-developed**   **Rustic facilities**

NOTE: Open dates listed are typical. Actual dates are dependent on conditions such as snow pack.

31 Spruce
Centennial • lat 41°19'07" lon 106°09'36"

DESCRIPTION: This CG is a part of the Libby Creek Recreation area. Campers can enjoy fishing on Libby Creek but please check fishing regulations. Expect hot days with cold nights. Supplies and groceries can be found in Centennial. There are hiking trails nearby.

GETTING THERE: Spruce CG is located 2 mi. W of Centennial on state HWY 130 at the Libby Creek Recreation Area.

SINGLE RATE:	$10	OPEN DATES:	May-Sept
# of SINGLE SITES:	8	MAX SPUR:	16 feet
		MAX STAY:	14 days
		ELEVATION:	8600 feet

32 Sugarloaf
Centennial • lat 41°21'16" lon 106°17'43"

DESCRIPTION: This CG is located in a grove of spruce and fir with views of the Snowy Range. Trout fishing is available at nearby Lewis and Libby lakes. Supplies and groceries can be found in Centennial. Campers may gather firewood locally. There are numerous hiking trails in vicinity.

GETTING THERE: from Centennial go W on state HWY 130 approx. 11 mi. to Lewis Lake Road. N 1 mi. to Sugarloaf CG.

SINGLE RATE:	$10	OPEN DATES:	July-Sept
# of SINGLE SITES:	16	MAX SPUR:	22 feet
		MAX STAY:	14 days
		ELEVATION:	10700 feet

33 Tie City
Laramie • lat 41°15'11" lon 105°26'05"

DESCRIPTION: This CG is located partially in a dense stand of fir, spruce, and aspen; and partially in an open meadow. Supplies and groceries can be found in Laramie. Campers may gather dead and down firewood locally. There are numerous mountain biking trails nearby.

GETTING THERE: From Laramie go S and E on I-80 to state HWY 210. E on 210 approx. 2 mi. to Pole Creek Group CG road. Follow Signs to Tie City CG.

SINGLE RATE:	$10	OPEN DATES:	May-Oct
# of SINGLE SITES:	18	MAX SPUR:	32 feet
		MAX STAY:	14 days
		ELEVATION:	8600 feet

34 Vedauwoo
Laramie • lat 41°09'39" lon 105°22'05"

DESCRIPTION: CG is located in an area with granite rock boulders and formations. There are pine, spruce, aspen, and fir in the area. Set in a high plains desert. Firewood may be scarce. Supplies in Laramie. Hiking and mountain biking trails nearby. Formations are exciting to explore. No services available.

GETTING THERE: From Laramie go S and E on I-80 15 mi. to forest route 700. E on 700 2 mi. to Vedauwoo CG.

SINGLE RATE:	$10	OPEN DATES:	May-Oct
# of SINGLE SITES:	28	MAX SPUR:	32 feet
		MAX STAY:	14 days
		ELEVATION:	8200 feet

35 Willow
Centennial • lat 41°19'07" lon 106°09'36"

DESCRIPTION: This CG is a part of the Libby Creek Recreation area. There is good fishing on Libby Creek but please check fishing regulations. Campers should expect hot days with cold nights. Supplies and groceries can be found in Centennial. There are hiking trails in the area.

GETTING THERE: Willow CG is located 2 mi. W of Centennial on state HWY 130 at the Libby Creek Recreation Area.

SINGLE RATE:	$10	OPEN DATES:	May-Sept
# of SINGLE SITES:	16	MAX SPUR:	22 feet
		MAX STAY:	14 days
		ELEVATION:	8600 feet

36 Yellow Pine
Laramie • lat 41°15'20" lon 105°24'38"

DESCRIPTION: This CG is located in a park-like stand of conifir and aspen. Set in a high plains desert area with interesting rock formations. Expect hot days with cold nights. Firewood may be scarce. Supplies can be found in Laramie. Hiking and mountain biking on roads and trails are available.

GETTING THERE: From Laramie go S and E on I-80 to state HWY 210. E on 210 approx. 2 mi. to Pole Creek Group CG road. Follow Signs to Yellow Pine CG.

SINGLE RATE:	$10	OPEN DATES:	May-Sept
# of SINGLE SITES:	19	MAX SPUR:	32 feet
		MAX STAY:	14 days
		ELEVATION:	8400 feet

 Campground has hosts   🔒 **Reservable sites**   **Accessible facilities**   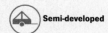 **Fully developed**    **Semi-developed**   ▲ **Rustic facilities**

NOTE: Open dates listed are typical. Actual dates are dependent on conditions such as snow pack.

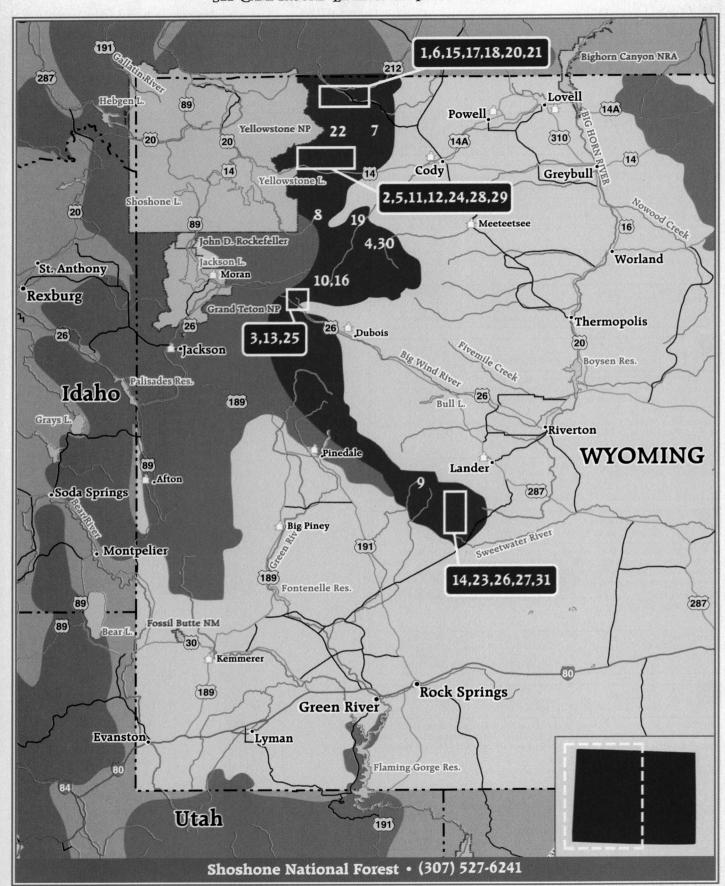

1,6,15,17,18,20,21

Bighorn Canyon NRA

212

Lovell

Powell

14A

Yellowstone NP

22   7

14A

Cody

Greybull

14

Yellowstone L.

2,5,11,12,24,28,29

Shoshone L.

Meeteetsee

Nowood Creek

8   19

4,30

Worland

John D. Rockefeller

Jackson L.

Moran

10,16

Grand Teton NP

26   Dubois

Big Wind River

Fivemile Creek

Thermopolis

3,13,25

St. Anthony

Rexburg

Jackson

Palisades Res.

Bull L.

Boysen Res.

Idaho

189

Riverton

Grays L.

Pinedale

WYOMING

9

Lander

287

Soda Springs

Afton

Big Piney

Montpelier

Green Riv

191

Sweetwater River

14,23,26,27,31

189

Fontenelle Res.

Fossil Butte NM

30

Kemmerer

80

Rock Springs

189

Green River

Evanston

Lyman

80

Flaming Gorge Res.

84

Utah

191

USFS Photo

SHOSHONE NATIONAL FOREST

With Yellowstone National Park on its western border, the Shoshone National Forest encompasses the area from the Montana state line south to Lander, Wyoming. The western boundary of the forest (south of Yellowstone) is the crest of the Continental Divide. Elevations on the Shoshone range from 4,600 feet at the mouth of the spectacular Clarks Fork Canyon to 13,804 feet atop Gannett Peak, Wyoming's highest.

The higher mountains are snow-clad most of the year. Approximately 58% of the Shoshone National Forest's 2.4 million acres are designated Wilderness Areas. Visitors can hike into the backcountry or drive through the North Fork of the Shoshone River Canyon or over the Beartooth Plateau. There are approximately 1700 miles of perennial streams that support some type of trout fishery. There are also many resorts and dude ranches within or near the forest that provide food, lodging, guide and outfitting services.

1 Beartooth Lake
Cooke City • lat 44°56'51" lon 109°35'07"

DESCRIPTION: This CG is situated next to Beartooth Lake which offers fly and boat fishing. Clay Butte Fire Lookout Tower is located nearby. Supplies and groceries are available 1 mi. away at the Top of the World Store. Numerous animals frequent the CG area. This CG may be frequented by bears.

GETTING THERE: From Cooke City go E on US HWY 212 approx. 17 mi. to Beartooth Lake CG. On the Beartooth Plateau.

SINGLE RATE:	$9	OPEN DATES:	July-Sept
# of SINGLE SITES:	20	MAX SPUR:	32 feet
		MAX STAY:	16 days
		ELEVATION:	9000 feet

2 Big Game
Cody • lat 44°27'43" lon 109°36'17"

DESCRIPTION: Among willow and cottonwood near volcanic cliffs and the Shoshone River. Views of high peaks of Absaroka Mountain Range. Noon rains June and July. Historic Phaska Teepee and Wapiti Ranger Station. Supplies 8 mi. E or in Cody. Gather firewood. Many trails nearby. Ticks until July. Frequented by bears.

GETTING THERE: Big Game CG is located approx. 27 mi. W of Cody, WY on US HWY 20 along the Shoshone River.

SINGLE RATE:	$9	OPEN DATES:	May-Sept
# of SINGLE SITES:	17	MAX SPUR:	32 feet
		MAX STAY:	16 days
		ELEVATION:	5900 feet

3 Brooks Lake
Dubois • lat 43°45'04" lon 110°00'15"

DESCRIPTION: Situated on Brooks Lake with excellent views of the Pinnacles. Shore or small boat fising on the Lake. Supplies at Dubois. Elk, deer, moose, and bears frequent the area. Fills early on weekends. Gather firewood locally. Horse and hiking trails are available. Ticks and mosquitos in late spring.

GETTING THERE: From Dubois go N on US HWY 26 approx. 22 mi. to forest route 515. Go N on 515 approx. 5 mi. to Brooks Lake CG.

SINGLE RATE:	$8	OPEN DATES:	June-Sept
# of SINGLE SITES:	13	MAX SPUR:	22 feet
		MAX STAY:	14 days
		ELEVATION:	9200 feet

4 Brown Mountain
Meeteetse • lat 43°56'07" lon 109°10'44"

DESCRIPTION: Park-like area in Wood River Corridor. Noon rains with cold mornings; snow possible by October. Trout fishing. 1900's mining town nearby (4X4 access). Supplies 9 mi. at Meeteetse. Deer, moose, sheep, and bears. Firewood gathered locally. Multiple trailheads nearby. Bears regulations are in effect.

GETTING THERE: From Meeteetse go SE on state HWY 290 to county route 4DT (Wood River Road). Go SW on 4DT, also known as FS route 200, approx. 24 mi. to Brown Mountain CG.

SINGLE RATE:	No fee	OPEN DATES:	May-Nov
# of SINGLE SITES:	7	MAX SPUR:	65 feet
		MAX STAY:	14 days
		ELEVATION:	7600 feet

5 Clearwater
Cody • lat 44°27'40" lon 109°40'06"

DESCRIPTION: Set in park-like area with open views of Absaroka Mountain peaks and volcanic cliffs on Shoshone River. Showers common until mid-July. Historic Pahaska Teepee and Wapiti Ranger Station. Supplies 9 mi E or at Cody. Gather firewood locally. Various trails nearby. Ticks until mid-July. Bears area.

GETTING THERE: Clearwater CG is located approx. 30 mi. W of Cody, WY on US HWY 20 along the Shoshone River.

SINGLE RATE:	$9	OPEN DATES:	May-Sept
# of SINGLE SITES:	32	MAX SPUR:	32 feet
GROUP RATE:	Varies	MAX STAY:	16 days
# of GROUP SITES:	2	ELEVATION:	6000 feet

 Campground has hosts　　 **Reservable sites**　　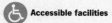 **Accessible facilities**　　 **Fully developed**　　 **Semi-developed**　　 **Rustic facilities**

NOTE: Open dates listed are typical. Actual dates are dependent on conditions such as snow pack.

Page 617

6 Crazy Creek
Cooke City • lat 45°56'33" lon 109°46'25"

DESCRIPTION: CG is an open area surrounded by lodgepole pine with the Clarks Fork River nearby. World class trout fly fishing. Old mining town of Cooke City. Supplies are 10 mi. away in Cooke City. Numerous wildlife in the area. Bears can sometimes be a problem. Many trails in area.

GETTING THERE: Crazy Creek CG is located approx. 8 mi. E of Cooke City, off of US HWY 212.

SINGLE RATE:	$9	OPEN DATES:	May-Oct
# of SINGLE SITES:	16	MAX SPUR:	32 feet
		MAX STAY:	16 days
		ELEVATION:	6920 feet

11 Eagle Creek
Cody • lat 44°28'18" lon 109°53'17"

DESCRIPTION: CG is in a park-like setting with little underbrush. Views of volcanic cliffs on the Absoraka Mountain Range. Trout fishing on Eagle Creek and North Fork of Shoshone River. Historical Pahaska Teepee nearby. Various wildlife in area. Camper may gather firewood. Bears may be a problem.

GETTING THERE: From Cody go 44.7 mi. W on HWY 14/16/20.

SINGLE RATE:	$9	OPEN DATES:	May-Sept
# of SINGLE SITES:	20	MAX SPUR:	22 feet
		MAX STAY:	14 days
		ELEVATION:	6500 feet

7 Dead Indian
Cody • lat 44°45'05" lon 109°25'12"

DESCRIPTION: This CG is situated in a park-like setting in a valley with views of the Clarks Fork Canyon area. Dead Indian Creek runs alongside the CG. Please check for fishing regulations. Chief Joseph trail is nearby. Supplies are 24 mi. away in Cody. Numerous wildlife in the area. Bears do frequent the area.

GETTING THERE: From Cody go N on state HWY 120 approx. 17 mi. to state HWY 296 (Chief Joseph Scenic Byway). Take 296 approx. 17 mi. to Dead Indian CG.

SINGLE RATE:	$7	OPEN DATES:	Yearlong
# of SINGLE SITES:	12	MAX SPUR:	32 feet
		MAX STAY:	16 days
		ELEVATION:	6034 feet

12 Elk Fork
Cody • lat 44°27'47" lon 109°37'43"

DESCRIPTION: Open area with views of Absaroka Mountain peaks and volcanic cliffs on Shoshone River. Showers common until mid-July. Historic Pahaska Teepee and Wapiti Ranger Station. Supplies 9 mi E or at Cody. Firewood gathered locally. Various trails nearby. Ticks until mid-July. Bears area. Fees mid-May to Sept.

GETTING THERE: From Cody go W on US HWY 20 approx. 28 mi. to Elk Fork CG.

SINGLE RATE:	$9	OPEN DATES:	Yearlong
# of SINGLE SITES:	13	MAX SPUR:	22 feet
		MAX STAY:	16 days
		ELEVATION:	6200 feet

8 Deer Creek
Cody • lat 44°09'31" lon 109°37'12"

DESCRIPTION: CG is in an open setting with views of the Absaroka Mountain peaks. Deer Creek and the South Fork of the Shoshone River are nearby with trout fishing. Historical Valle Ranch nearby. Supplies can be found 40 mi. away from CG. Various wildlife in area. Bears do frequaent area.

GETTING THERE: From Cody go SE on forest route 479 (South Fork Road) approx. 39 mi. to Deer Creek CG.

SINGLE RATE:	$9	OPEN DATES:	Yearlong
# of SINGLE SITES:	6	MAX SPUR:	16 feet
		MAX STAY:	16 days
		ELEVATION:	6400 feet

13 Falls
Dubois • lat 43°42'21" lon 109°57'55"

DESCRIPTION: This CG is in a forest with beatiful views of Breccia Cliffs. Set on a small stream. Stream fishing on site. Suplies at Dubois. Elk, deer, moose, and bears frequent area. Gather firewood. Short trail to picturesque waterfall in Brooks Lake Creek. Ticks and mosquitos in late spring.

GETTING THERE: From Dubois go NW on US HWY 26 approx. 23 mi. to Falls CG.

SINGLE RATE:	$8	OPEN DATES:	June-Oct
# of SINGLE SITES:	46	MAX SPUR:	32 feet
		MAX STAY:	14 days
		ELEVATION:	8000 feet

9 Dickinson Creek
Fort Washakie • lat 42°50'09" lon 109°03'25"

DESCRIPTION: Located in lodgepole pine with views of mountains. Quiet with spring wild flowers. Fish for small brook trout in nearby Dickinson Creek. Mountain lions, deer, elk, moose, and bears in area. Light use, fills Labor Day and fall hunting season. Horse, hike Bears Ears Wilderness. No drinking water.

GETTING THERE: From Fort Washakie go W then S on Moccasin Lake Road approx. 22 mi. to Dickinson Creek CG.

SINGLE RATE:	No fee	OPEN DATES:	July-Sept
# of SINGLE SITES:	15	MAX SPUR:	20 feet
		MAX STAY:	14 days
		ELEVATION:	9400 feet

14 Fiddlers Lake
Lander • lat 42°37'48" lon 108°52'54"

DESCRIPTION: This CG is in a lodgepole pine setting on lake with views of rock formations. Fish for rainbow and brook trout from lake. Deer, elk, moose, bears, and mountain lions in area. Fills quick during the fall hunting season. Christina Lake Trail is near CG. Barrier free boat dock at CG.

GETTING THERE: From South Pass on state HWY 28 take Louis Lake Road (primary forest route 300) approx. 13 mi. to Fiddlers Lake CG.

SINGLE RATE:	$6	OPEN DATES:	July-Sept
# of SINGLE SITES:	20	MAX SPUR:	24 feet
		MAX STAY:	14 days
		ELEVATION:	9400 feet

10 Double Cabin
Dubois • lat 43°48'18" lon 109°33'35"

DESCRIPTION: Located in pine forest near an open meadow amid towering cliffs. Cold mornings, cool days. Excellent fishing on nearby Wiggins Fork. Supplies at Dubois. Elk, deer, moose, and bears in area. Light use. Gather firewood. Hiking trails into Washakie Wilderness. Ticks and mosquitos in early spring.

GETTING THERE: From Dubois go N on Horse Creek Road (forest route 508) approx. 10 mi. to forest route 285. Go N on 285 approx. 11 mi. to Double Cabin CG.

SINGLE RATE:	$6	OPEN DATES:	June-Sept
# of SINGLE SITES:	15	MAX SPUR:	16 feet
		MAX STAY:	14 days
		ELEVATION:	8053 feet

15 Fox Creek
Cooke City • lat 44°58'44" lon 109°50'17"

DESCRIPTION: This CG is surrounded with dense vegetation. Clarks Fork River runs next to the CG. Fish for brook, cutthroat, and rainbow trout in the river. Please check fishing regulations. Numerous wildlife in the area. Historical Cooke City is 8 mi. away for supplies. CG may be frequented by bears.

GETTING THERE: From Cooke City go E on US HWY 212 approx. 4 mi. to Fox Creek CG.

SINGLE RATE:	$9	OPEN DATES:	June-Sept
# of SINGLE SITES:	27	MAX SPUR:	32 feet
		MAX STAY:	16 days
		ELEVATION:	7100 feet

 Campground has hosts   **Reservable sites**   **Accessible facilities**   **Fully developed**   **Semi-developed**   **Rustic facilities**

NOTE: Open dates listed are typical. Actual dates are dependent on conditions such as snow pack.

16 Horse Creek
Dubois • lat 44˚27'54" lon 109˚35'08"

DESCRIPTION: This CG is situated in forest setting with Horse Creek running along the CG. Stream fish the creek. Supplies and groceries can be found in Dubois. Elk, deer, moose, and bears frequent the area. Fills early on weekends. Gather firewood locally. Ticks and mosquitos in early spring.

GETTING THERE: From Dubois go N on Horse Creek Road (forest route 508) approx. 12 mi. to Horse Creek CG.

SINGLE RATE:	$6	OPEN DATES:	June-Sept
# of SINGLE SITES:	9	MAX SPUR:	16 feet
		MAX STAY:	14 days
		ELEVATION:	7500 feet

21 Lily Lake
Cooke City • lat 44˚56'51" lon 109˚42'41"

DESCRIPTION: Located on the lake in the pine with views of Pilot Index Peak and the Absaroka-Beartooth Wilderness. Supplies 6 mi. to Top-of-the-World Store. Great fishing in the lake. Crazy lakes trail is nearby. Gather firewood locally. Be prepared for bugs. Area is frequented by bears.

GETTING THERE: From Cooke go SE on US HWY 212 approx. 12 mi. to forest route 130. Go N on 130 approx. 1.5 mi. to forest route 189. Go E on 189 approx. 1/2 mi. to Lily Lake CG.

SINGLE RATE:	No fee	OPEN DATES:	May-Oct
# of SINGLE SITES:	8	MAX SPUR:	22 feet
		MAX STAY:	16 days
		ELEVATION:	7500 feet

17 Hunter Peak
Cooke City • lat 44˚53'03" lon 109˚39'08"

DESCRIPTION: This CG is situated in a park-like setting with lodgepole pine and open grassy areas. Campers may enjoy fly fishing on the Clarks Fork River but please check fishing regulations. Supplies are 22 mi. away at historical Cooke City. This CG may be frequented by bears.

GETTING THERE: From Cooke City go E on US HWY 212 approx. 11 mi. to state HWY 296 (Chief Joseph Scenic Byway). Take 296 approx. 5 mi. to Hunter Peak CG.

SINGLE RATE:	$9	OPEN DATES:	Yearlong
# of SINGLE SITES:	9	MAX SPUR:	32 feet
		MAX STAY:	16 days
		ELEVATION:	6500 feet

22 Little Sunlight
Cody • lat 44˚43'07" lon 109˚35'23"

DESCRIPTION: This CG is situated in an open setting of lodgepole pine. Sunlight Creek offers good fishing, and runs next to CG. Please check fishing regulations. Supplies and groceries are available 35 mi. away in Cody. There is various wildlife in the area including bears that frequent the CG area.

GETTING THERE: From Cody go N on state HWY 120 17 mi. to state HWY 296 (Chief Joseph Scenic Byway). Take 296 18 mi. to primary forest route 101 (Sunlight Basin Road). Take 101 10 mi. to Little Sunlight CG.

SINGLE RATE:	$9	OPEN DATES:	May-Nov
# of SINGLE SITES:	4	MAX SPUR:	32 feet
		MAX STAY:	16 days
		ELEVATION:	6900 feet

18 Island Lake
Cooke City • lat 44˚56'40" lon 109˚32'38"

DESCRIPTION: This CG offers campsites in a forested area with open areas close by. Expect afternoon thunder showers. Enjoy fishing for brook, cutthroat, and rainbow trout but please check fishing regulations. Supplies are 1 mi. away at the Top of the World Store. This CG may be frequented by bears.

GETTING THERE: Island Lake CG is located approx. 19 mi. E of Cooke City, MT on US HWY 212 on the Beartooth Plateau.

SINGLE RATE:	$9	OPEN DATES:	July-Sept
# of SINGLE SITES:	20	MAX SPUR:	32 feet
		MAX STAY:	16 days
		ELEVATION:	9518 feet

23 Louis Lake
Lander • lat 42˚35'39" lon 108˚50'45"

DESCRIPTION: CG set in a park-like pine area with views of lake. Fish in the lake for brook and rainbow trout. Boat launch at lake. Beach for swimming. Mountain lions, deer, elk, moose, and bears in area. Light use, fills Labor Day and fall hunting season. No nearby trails. Accessible floating dock coming soon.

GETTING THERE: From South Pass on state HWY 28 take Louis Lake Road (primary forest route 300) approx. 8 mi. to Louis Lake CG.

SINGLE RATE:	$6	OPEN DATES:	July-Sept
# of SINGLE SITES:	9	MAX SPUR:	30 feet
		MAX STAY:	14 days
		ELEVATION:	8550 feet

19 Jack Creek
Meeteetse • lat 44˚06'37" lon 109˚21'05"

DESCRIPTION: This CG is situated in a park-like grove of lodgepole pine. Campers may enjoy trout fishing in Jack Creek which runs next to CG. Please check fishing regulations. Historic Jack Creek Ranger Station nearby. Limited supplies at Meeteetse. Limited firewood on site. Jack Creek Trailhead nearby.

GETTING THERE: From Meeteetse go W on state HWY 290 approx. 11 mi. Continue on forest route 208 (through private land) approx. 17 mi. to Jack Creek CG. 4WD recommended.

SINGLE RATE:	No fee	OPEN DATES:	Yearlong*
# of SINGLE SITES:	7	MAX SPUR:	50 feet
GROUP RATE:	Donation	MAX STAY:	14 days
# of GROUP SITES:	4	ELEVATION:	7600 feet

24 Newton Creek
Cody • lat 44˚27'11" lon 109˚45'22"

DESCRIPTION: This CG is situated in a park-like setting of douglas fir and cottonwood. Views of volcanic cliff peaks. Newton Creek and North Fork of Shoshone River with trout fishing. Historical Wapiti Ranger Station is nearby. Supplies are 12 mi. away. Bears frequent area. East loop open yearlong.

GETTING THERE: Newton Creek CG is located approx. 34 mi. W of Cody on US HWY 20.

SINGLE RATE:	$9	OPEN DATES:	May-Sept
# of SINGLE SITES:	31	MAX SPUR:	35 feet
		MAX STAY:	16 days
		ELEVATION:	6300 feet

20 Lake Creek
Cooke City • lat 44˚55'16" lon 109˚42'16"

DESCRIPTION: This CG is situated in lodgepole pine and spruce. Lake Creek and the Clarks Fork River are nearby. Campers may enjoy fishing in the area but please check fishing regulations. There is numerous wildlife in the area. Supplies are 18 mi. away at historical Cooke City.

GETTING THERE: From Cooke City go E on US HWY 212 approx. 11 mi. to state HWY 296 (Chief Joseph Scenic Byway). Take 296 approx. 1 mi. to Lake Creek CG.

SINGLE RATE:	$9	OPEN DATES:	June-Sept
# of SINGLE SITES:	6	MAX SPUR:	22 feet
		MAX STAY:	16 days
		ELEVATION:	6900 feet

25 Pinnacles
Dubois • lat 43˚45'13" lon 109˚59'40"

DESCRIPTION: CG with beautiful views of the Pinnacles near Brooks Lake. Cold mornings and frequent noon thunderstorms. Boat fish the lake. Supplies in Dubois. Elk, deer, moose, and bears in the area. Fills up on weekends. Jade Lake, Upper Brooks Lake and Dunoir Trails nearby. Mosquitos in late spring.

GETTING THERE: From Dubois go N on US HWY 26 approx. 23 mi. to forest route 515. Go N on 515 approx. 5 mi. to Pinnacles CG.

SINGLE RATE:	$8	OPEN DATES:	June-Sept
# of SINGLE SITES:	21	MAX SPUR:	22 feet
		MAX STAY:	14 days
		ELEVATION:	9200 feet

 **Campground has hosts**   **Reservable sites**   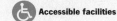 **Accessible facilities**   **Fully developed**   **Semi-developed**   **Rustic facilities**

NOTE: Open dates listed are typical. Actual dates are dependent on conditions such as snow pack.

26 Popo Agie
Lander • lat 42°36'00" lon 108°51'00"

DESCRIPTION: Set near the Little Popo Agie River in pine and fir forest with river views. Fish for brook trout in river. Black bears, mountain lions, deer, elk and moose in area. Horse, hike, mountain bike and ATV roads and trails in vicinity. No drinking water, no services. Light use, frequently used as overflow.

GETTING THERE: From Lander go SW on state HWY 131 approx. 7 mi. to forest route 300. Go S on 300 approx. 19 mi. to Popo Agie CG.

SINGLE RATE:	No fee	OPEN DATES:	July-Sept
# of SINGLE SITES:	4	MAX SPUR:	16 feet
		MAX STAY:	16 days
		ELEVATION:	8800 feet

31 Worthen Meadow
Lander • lat 42°42'05" lon 108°55'06"

DESCRIPTION: Located in lodgepole pine with view of mountains and Worthen Reservoir. Fish for cutthroat and brook trout on lake. Mountain. lions, deer, elk, moose and black bears in area. Moderate to heavy use, fills most weekends and fall hunt season. Horse, hike into wilderness. Mountain. bike and ATV (must be registered) on roads.

GETTING THERE: From Lander go S on state HWY 131 approx. 7.5 mi. to primary forest route 300 (Louis Lake Road). Take 300 approx. 8 mi. to Worthen Meadow CG.

SINGLE RATE:	$6	OPEN DATES:	July-Sept
# of SINGLE SITES:	28	MAX SPUR:	29 feet
		MAX STAY:	14 days
		ELEVATION:	8800 feet

27 Sinks Canyon
Lander • lat 42°44'14" lon 108°50'00"

DESCRIPTION: CG set in the canyon among juniper trees on the Popo Agie River. Popular climbers camp. Fish brook and cutthroat trout. Mountain lions, bighorn sheep, deer, elk, moose, and black bears in area. Moderate use, fills most summer weekends. Horse and hiking trails. Mountain biking and ATV roads.

GETTING THERE: From Lander go S on state HWY 131 approx. 6 mi. to Sinks Canyon CG.

SINGLE RATE:	$6	OPEN DATES:	June-Oct
# of SINGLE SITES:	9	MAX SPUR:	30 feet
		MAX STAY:	14 days
		ELEVATION:	6850 feet

28 Threemile
Cody • lat 44°29'47" lon 109°57'02"

DESCRIPTION: This CG is situated in a park-like setting with views of volcanic peaks. North Fork of Shoshone River is nearby with trout fishing. Historical Pahaska Teepee nearby. Various wildlife in the area. Supplies and groceries can be found 1 mi. away. Campers may gather their firewood locally.

GETTING THERE: Threemile CG is located approx. 45 mi. W of Cody on US HWY 20. CG is restricted to hard sided camping units only due to grizzly bears in area.

SINGLE RATE:	$9	OPEN DATES:	May-Sept
# of SINGLE SITES:	29	MAX SPUR:	45 feet
		MAX STAY:	16 days
		ELEVATION:	6800 feet

29 Wapiti
Cody • lat 44°27'58" lon 109°37'33"

DESCRIPTION: Open area with views of Absaroka Mountain peaks and volcanic cliffs on Sweetwater and Shoshone Rivers. Expect Showers until mid-July. Historic Pahaska Teepee and Wapiti Ranger Station. Supplies 9 mi E or at Cody. Gather firewood locally. Various trails nearby. Ticks until mid-July. Bears area. Fees in summer.

GETTING THERE: From Cody go W on US HWY 20 approx. 28 mi. to Wapiti CG.

SINGLE RATE:	$9	OPEN DATES:	Yearlong
# of SINGLE SITES:	41	MAX SPUR:	35 feet
		MAX STAY:	16 days
		ELEVATION:	6000 feet

30 Wood River
Meeteetse • lat 43°55'55" lon 109°07'53"

DESCRIPTION: CG is in a forest setting with the Wood River adjacent to CG. Trout fishing in Wood River. 1900's era mining town of Kirwin is approx. 11 mi. away. Limited supplies and groceries can be found in Meeteetse. Various wildlife. Camper may gather firewood outside of CG. Several trails in area.

GETTING THERE: From Meeteetse go SW on state HWY 290 to county route 4DT (Wood River Road). Go SW on 4DT, also known as forest route 200, approx. 22 mi. to Wood River CG.

SINGLE RATE:	No fee	OPEN DATES:	May-Nov
# of SINGLE SITES:	5	MAX SPUR:	30 feet
		MAX STAY:	14 days
		ELEVATION:	7300 feet

 Campground has hosts   **Reservable sites**   **Accessible facilities**   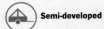 **Fully developed**   **Semi-developed**   **Rustic facilities**

NOTE: Open dates listed are typical. Actual dates are dependent on conditions such as snow pack.

Alabama

Tennessee-Tombigbee Waterway
1 • Cochrane • Map page 6
Aliceville • Alabama
DESCRIPTION: The Tenn-Tom Waterway is an outdoor enthusiast's paradise. From picnicking to fishing to camping, the Tenn-Tom has it all. The Cochran Campground has 60 sites with electric and water hookups. Additional amenities include convenient access to boat ramps, shower and laundry facilities, sanitary dump stations, fish cleaning stations, handicap accessible sites and facilities, playgrounds and multi-use courts.
GETTING THERE: From Aliceville, AL, take US 17 S 10 mi. Turn right at the sign for Cochrane Recreation Area (2 mi from Huyck Bridge). Follow the paved road 2 mi, campground on the left.

Black Warrior and Tombigbee Lakes
2 • Demopolis Lake • Map page 6
Demopolis • Alabama
DESCRIPTION: The Black Warrior and Tombigbee Rivers have been important commercial waterways since the earliest settlers moved inland and built homes along the riverbanks. Today historic sites, picturesque terrain, and abundant recreational opportunities welcome visitors year round to the 47 recreation areas on the six lakes that make up this 453-mile-long project.
GETTING THERE: From Demopolis, US 80 W 2 mi to Lock & Dam road to the Resource Manager's Office.

Gainesville Lake
3 • Gainesville Lake • Map page 6
Pickensville • Alabama
DESCRIPTION: Part of the Tennessee-Tombigbee Waterway. This 234-mile system of locks and dams forms a chain of 10 lakes reaching from the Tennessee River in the north to Demopolis, AL, in the south. The "Teen Tom," offering excellent fishing, hunting, and lakeside recreation, is a scenic short cut to the Gulf of Mexico.
GETTING THERE: From Pickensville, AL 14, S 1 mi to Tom Bevill Visitor Center.

Alabama River Lakes Woodruff
4 • Gunter Hill • Map page 6
Montgomery • Alabama
DESCRIPTION: Part of the Alabama River Lakes-the project consists of three lakes with campgrounds, primitive sites, day-use areas, and swimming beaches. There is something for everyone; historic sites, abundant fish and wildlife, and scenic bluffs.
GETTING THERE: From Montgomery, US 80 30 mi to Benton.

Black Warrior and Tombigbee Lakes
5 • Holt Lake • Map page 6
Tuscaloosa • Alabama
DESCRIPTION: The Black Warrior and Tombigbee Rivers have been important commercial waterways since the earliest settlers moved inland and built homes along the riverbanks. Today.historic sites, picturesque terrain, and abundant recreational opportunities welcome visitors year round to the 47 recreation areas on the six lakes that make up this 453-mile-long project.
GETTING THERE: From Tuscaloosa, 10 mi E on AL 216 to Peterson Asst. Resource Manager's Office.

Alabama River Lakes Claiborne
6 • Isaac Creek • Map page 6
Grove Hill • Alabama
DESCRIPTION: Part of the Alabama River Lakes-the project consists of three lakes with campgrounds, primitive sites, day-use areas, and swimming beaches. There is something for everyone; historic sites, abundant fish and wildlife, and scenic bluffs.
GETTING THERE: From Grove Hill, Hwy 84 E to 41 N to county road 17 to dam.

Tennessee-Tombigbee Waterway
7 • Pickensville • Map page 6
Pickensville • Alabama
DESCRIPTION: Pickensville Campground is located on the Tennessee-Tombigbee Waterway– an outdoor enthusiast's paradise. From picnicking to fishing to camping, the Tenn-Tom has it all. The Pickensville Campground offers 176 sites with electric and water hookups. Several sites have sewer hookups. Additional amenities include convenient access to boat ramps, shower and laundry facilities, sanitary dump stations, fish cleaning stations, handicap accessible sites and facilities, playgrounds and multi-use courts.
GETTING THERE: From Tuscaloosa, AL, take US 82 W to the JCT w/US 86. Turn left onto US 86 W to Pickensville, AL. Entrance road to the campground will be 2.5 mi from yellow caution light.

Alabama River Lakes Dannelly
8 • Six Mile Creek • Map page 6
Camden • Alabama
DESCRIPTION: Part of the Alabama River Lakes, the project consists of three lakes with campgrounds, primitive sites, day-use areas, and swimming beaches. There is something for everyone; historic sites, abundant fish and wildlife, and scenic bluffs.
GETTING THERE: From Camden, Hwy 28 W 9 mi to dam.

Black Warrior and Tombigbee Lakes
9 • Warrior Lake • Map page 6
Demopolis • Alabama
DESCRIPTION: The Black Warrior and Tombigbee Rivers have been important commercial waterways since the earliest settlers moved inland and built homes along the riverbanks. Today... historic sites, picturesque terrain, and abundant recreational opportunities welcome visitors year round to the 47 recreation areas on the six lakes that make up this 453-mile-long project.
GETTING THERE: From Demopolis, US 80 W 2 mi to Lock & Dam road to the Resource Manager's Office.

Alaska

Chena River Lakes
10 • Chena River Lakes • Map page 10
Fairbanks • Alaska
DESCRIPTION: Gently rolling slopes characterize the landscape of this area dotted with ponds, peat bogs, oxbow lakes and meandering streams. The varied plant life provides visual contrast. The clear waters of the rivers, ponds and lakes provide excellent fish habitat. RV dump station, boat ramp and visitor information center at CG.
GETTING THERE: From Fairbanks go E approx. 17 mi. on Richardson Hwy to Chena River Lakes CG.

Arizona

Alamo Lake
11 • Alamo Lake • Map page 33
Wenden • Arizona
DESCRIPTION: One of the best bass lakes in Arizona. The Bill Williams River Basin is of historical interest.
GETTING THERE: N of Wenden, off 1-10.

Arkansas

Robert S. Kerr Lake
12 • Applegate Cove • Map page 44
Fort Smith • Arkansas
DESCRIPTION: Scene of a capture by Confederate troops of an armed Union steamboat. The Oklahoma Historical Society is developing the area for public use.
GETTING THERE: From Fort Smith, AR, 22 mi W on 1-40, .8 mi S on US 59.

DeGray Lake
13 • Arlie Moore • Map page 44
Little Rock • Arkansas

DESCRIPTION: A relatively new lake with sophisticated public use facilities. The State park on the lake has a lodge, marina, golf course and campground.
GETTING THERE: From Little Rock, 55 mi S on I-30 to Caddo Valley, 2 mi N on US 67.

Millwood Lake
14 • Beards Bluff • Map page 44
Texarkana • Arkansas

DESCRIPTION: The campground is located on millwood lake which provides excellent fishing year round.
GETTING THERE: From Texarkana, 16 mi N on US 59-71, 9 mi E of Ashdown on AR 32.

Gillham Lake
15 • Big Coon Creek • Map page 44
DeQueen • Arkansas

DESCRIPTION: On the Cossatot River about 6 mi NE of Giliham, there is good hunting on 5,400 acres. Game includes whitetail deer, squirrel, cottontail and swamp rabbit, and bobwhite quail. Most waterfowl are found in the downstream flood plain.
GETTING THERE: From DeQueen, 15 mi N on US 71, 5 mi E to lake.

Lake Greeson
16 • Dam Area • Map page 44
Little Rock • Arkansas

DESCRIPTION: Chimney Rock, an outstanding geological formation, and a cinnabar mine nature trail are located at the project.
GETTING THERE: From Little Rock, 60 mi S on I-30 to AR 26, 37 mi W to Murfreesboro, 6 mi N on AR 27.

Greers Ferry Lake
17 • Dam Site • Map page 44
Little Rock • Arkansas

DESCRIPTION: A highly developed and popular recreation area. Sugar Loaf Nature Trail, on an island in the lake, has received many awards for scenic beauty.
GETTING THERE: From Little Rock, 15 mi N on US67-167, 50 mi N on AR 5.

Beaver Lake
18 • Dam Site • Map page 44
Fayetteville • Arkansas

DESCRIPTION: Located in the picturesque Ozark Mountains, Beaver Lake is noted for excellent fishing and hunting. There are caves and museums nearby.
GETTING THERE: From Fayetteville, 22 mi N on US 71, then E on US 62.

Ouachita-Black Rivers Navigation Project
19 • Felsenthal Lock & Dam • Map page 44
Huttig • Arkansas

DESCRIPTION: Felsenthal Lock & Dam Pool Project has 3 public access points to Ouachita River and Felsenthal National Wildlife Refuge with boating, fishing, camping, and day use. Pool extends from H.K. Thatcher Lock & Dam south to the Felsenthal Lock & Dam.
GETTING THERE: Located 5 mi NE of Huttig, AR on county road.

Dierks Lake
20 • Jefferson Ridge • Map page 44
Texarkana • Arkansas

DESCRIPTION: Campground is located on Dierks Lake near the Ouachita National Forest.
GETTING THERE: From Texarkana, 46 mi N on US 71, 11 mi E on US 70 to access road.

Bull Shoals Lake
21 • Lakeview • Map page 44
Little Rock • Arkansas

DESCRIPTION: A popular area with anglers for its lunker bass. Float trips and trout fishing are available on the White River nearby. State park borders lake.
GETTING THERE: From Little Rock, 135 mi N on US65, 50 mi. E on US 62 to Flippin, 4 mi N to lake. From Springfield, MO, S on US 65, then E on AR 14.

McClellan-Kerr Arkansas River Navigation System
22 • Lock & Dam 6 & 7 • Map page 44
Little Rock • Arkansas

DESCRIPTION: Part of the McClellan-Kerr Arkansas River Navigation System. Good boating, fishing, scenery and nearby historical sites along the river. Located on the eastern and western city limits of Little Rock, the recreation activities provided by these two pools attract many outdoor enthusiasts. The pools offer excellent fishing, especially in the old river cutoffs and the tail waters downstream of each dam.
GETTING THERE: Located on the eastern and western city limits of Little Rock.

DeQueen Lake
23 • Oak Grove • Map page 44
DeQueen • Arkansas

DESCRIPTION: DeQueen Lake is located on the Rolling Fork River about 4 mi NW of DeQueen. With 4,000 acres open to hunters, whitetail deer is the principal game. Other wildlife includes squirrel, cottontail and swamp rabbit, raccoon, bobwhite quail, and duck.
GETTING THERE: From DeQueen, 8 mi N on US 71.5 mi W to lake.

Blue Mountain Lake
24 • Outlet Area • Map page 44
Fort Smith • Arkansas

DESCRIPTION: In the Ouachita Mountains of western Arkansas. Excellent crappie fishing in the shadow of Mt. Magazine, the tallest mountain between the Rockies and the Allegheny Mountains.
GETTING THERE: From Fort Smith, 50 mi E on AR 10.

Nimrod Lake
25 • River Road • Map page 44
Hot Springs • Arkansas

DESCRIPTION: A hunting and fishing paradise, Nimrod offers largemouth bass, channel cat, crappie and bream. The project includes a duck hunting area, wildlife refuge, and goose sanctuary. Food and cover plots have been developed for quail.
GETTING THERE: From Hot Springs. 40 mi N on AR 7.

Lake Ouachita
26 • Stephens Park • Map page 44
Hot Springs • Arkansas

DESCRIPTION: High in the Ouachita Mountains near the resort spa of Hot Springs, the exceptionally clear water of Lake Ouachita is popular with skin divers.
GETTING THERE: From Hot Springs.13 mi W on AR 227.

Norfolk Lake
27 • Tecumseh • Map page 44
Little Rock • Arkansas

DESCRIPTION: Noted for good fishing, nearby attractions include caves, museums and golf courses.
GETTING THERE: From Little Rock, 135 mi N on US 65, 50 mi E on US62.

McClellan-Kerr Arkansas River
28 • Toad Suck • Map page 44
Russellville • Arkansas

DESCRIPTION: Part of the McClellan-Kerr Arkansas River Navigation System. Good boating, fishing, scenery and nearby historical sites along the river. Lying between the Ozark and Ouachita Mountains, the pools reach 48 miles up the Arkansas River from Conway to Russelville. This stretch of river provides excellent fishing and boating, with scenic views of the mountains and fertile farms along the riverbank.
GETTING THERE: Lying between the Ozark and Ouachita Mountains, the pools reach 48 miles up the Arkansas River from Conway to Russeliville.

California

New Hogan Lake
29 • Acorn • Map page 149
Stockton • California
DESCRIPTION: About an hour east of Stockton near historic gold rush towns of the California Mother Lode. This scenic setting in the Sierra Nevada foothills boasts exciting fishing, water-skiing, and hiking.
GETTING THERE: From Stockton, 35 mi E via CA 26.

Martis Creek Lake
30 • Alpine Meadow • Map page 156
Truckee • California
DESCRIPTION: Less than one hour west of Reno near world- famous Lake Tahoe, the Martis Creek area features exciting trout fishing in the lake and surrounding streams.
GETTING THERE: From Truckee, 5 mi SE on CA 267.

Black Butte Lake
31 • Buckhorn • Map page 99
Orland • California
DESCRIPTION: Situated at the northern end of the Central Valley, one hour south of Red Bluff. This quiet park, surrounded by beautiful, dark volcanic buttes, is well known for outstanding fishing and sailing.
GETTING THERE: From Orland, 10 mi W via Newville Road.

Lake Mendocino
32 • Che-Ka-Ka • Map page 99
Ukiah • California
DESCRIPTION: Two hours north of San Francisco near the world-renowned Redwood Country, this beautiful park is popular with local residents as well as visitors exploring the Northern California coast. Fishing, hiking, and boating are all available.
GETTING THERE: From Ukiah, 3 mi N on US 101, then E on Lake Mendocino Dr.

Eastman Lake
33 • Codorniz • Map page 138
Chowchilla • California
DESCRIPTION: Just one hour north of Fresno in the Sierra Nevada foothills. Rolling oak-covered hills provide a scenic and restful setting for fishing, boating, and hiking.
GETTING THERE: Located 25 mi E of Chowchilla at the N end of County Road 29.

Harry L Englebright Lake
34 • Englebright Lake/Boat-in • Map page 156
Marysville • California
DESCRIPTION: Only one hour north of Sacramento on the historic Yuba River. A grand and rugged canyon hides many small and inviting boat-access campsites. Boat Access Camping ONLY.
GETTING THERE: From Marysville, 20 mi E on CA 20.

Hensley Lake
35 • Hidden View • Map page 138
Madera • California
DESCRIPTION: Less than an hour drive north of Fresno in the foothills of the Sierra Nevada. As a gateway to Yosemite National Park and an excellent water- skiing and fishing lake, this park is always popular with visitors.
GETTING THERE: Located 17 mi NE of Madera on County Road 400.

Lake Kaweah
36 • Horse Creek • Map page 44
Visalia • California
DESCRIPTION: One hour SE of Fresno in the rugged foothills of the Sierra Nevada. High mountains provide an exciting background for fishing and boating at this popular park.
GETTING THERE: located on the main southern route into Sequoia-Kings Canyon National Park, From Visalia . 20 mi E on CA 198.

Stanislaus River Parks
37 • Horseshoe Road • Map page 149
Modesto • California
DESCRIPTION: Just a few minutes NE of Modesto in the Central Valley. Here, a serene series of small parks are located along the Stanislaus River, providing exciting fishing, rafting, and canoeing opportunities. Boat Access Camping Only.
GETTING THERE: Horseshoe Road CG is N of Modesto approx. 10 mi. on state HWY 99.

Lake Sonoma
38 • Liberty Glen • Map page 99
Healdsburg • California
DESCRIPTION: In the wine-growing region of Sonoma County. A picturesque lake with secluded vehicle and boat-in camping are available for the fishing and boating enthusiast.
GETTING THERE: From Healdsburg, 10 mi NW on Dry Creek Road.

Mojave River
39 • Mojave River Dam • Map page 50
Hesperia • California
DESCRIPTION: In the high desert wilderness at the foot of the San Bernardino Mountains. No permanent pool, but camping and equestrian facilities are available.
GETTING THERE: Near Hesperia, 15 mi E of 1-15 via CA 13R and 173.

Pine Flat Lake
40 • Pine Flat Recreation • Map page121
Fresno • California
DESCRIPTION: Less than an hour east of Fresno in the Sierra and Sequoia National Forests. The scenic and rugged Kings River Canyon is the location of this beautiful park where fishing, boating, and water-skiing are all available.
GETTING THERE: E of Fresno 32 mi via CA 180.

Prado Dam
41 • Prado Dam • Map page 50
Chino • California
DESCRIPTION: An oasis within one of the fastest growing areas of Southern California, the Prado Basin is home to the Olympic Shooting Facilities and Corona Airport (for small aircraft).
GETTING THERE: Located in the Chino-Corona area near CA 71, 83 and 91.

Success Lake
42 • Tule • Map page 121
Porterville • California
DESCRIPTION: At the southern end of the Central Valley, this scenic setting with the Sierra Nevada in the background provides great fishing and boating pleasure for the visitor.
GETTING THERE: From Porterville go E on state HWY 190 approx. 5 mi. to Tule CG.

Whittier Narrows Dam
43 • Whittier Narrows Dam • Map page 50
Whittier • California
DESCRIPTION: No permanent pool located in a highly developed industrial, agricultural, and residential area of Los Angeles County's San Gabriel Valley. Golfing and riding stables are among the attractions at this project.
GETTING THERE: On Pomona Freeway (CA 60) at Rosemead Blvd. (CA 19).

Colorado

Bear Creek Lake
44 • Bear Creek Lake • Map page 184
Denver • Colorado
DESCRIPTION: Fishing, boat launching facilities, camping, picnicking, game fields and winter sports are available.
GETTING THERE: Bear Creek Lake CG is located just W of Denver near Morrison, on state HWY 8.

Chatfield Lake
45 • Chatfield Lake • Map page 184
Denver • Colorado
DESCRIPTION: This lake features a heron and marsh bird observatory and sailboat harbor. Horseback riding and bicycling are available. Snowmobile riding, ice fishing, ice skating, ice boating, and cross-country skiing are popular during the winter months. RV dump station, boat launch and a visitor information center located in the CG.
GETTING THERE: Chatfield Lake CG is located off 1-25 directly S of Denver.

Cherry Creek Lake
46 • Cherry Creek Lake • Map page 184
Denver • Colorado
DESCRIPTION: Camping, picnicking, water skiing, a skeet range, model airplane airstrip, archery, rifle ranges, dog training areas, and a wildlife management section are a few of the amenities offered here. RV dump station, boat launch and a marina located in the CG.
GETTING THERE: Cherry Creek Lake CG is located on the SE fringe of Denver.

John Martin Dam
47 • Lake Hasty • Map page 184
Las Animas • Colorado
DESCRIPTION: Located near the outlet of James Martin Reservoir and next to the Arkansas River. A portion of the Santa Fe Trail is preserved for visitor viewing. Fish for bass and walleye from the reservoir. RV dump station and boat ramp located nearby.
GETTING THERE: From Las Animas go E approx. 15 mi. on US HWY 50 to county route 260 in Hasty. Go S on 260 approx. 2 mi. to Lake Hasty CG.

Trinidad Lake
48 • Trinidad Lake • Map page 184
Trinidad • Colorado
DESCRIPTION: This lake impounds the Purgatoire River in south-central Colorado. It provides 4,500 acres of water for recreation and flood control. RV dump station and a boat launch at the CG.
GETTING THERE: From Trinidad go W approx. 3 mi. on state HWY 12 to Trinidad Lake CG.

Florida

Lake Seminole
49 • East Bank • Map page 214
Tallahassee • Florida
DESCRIPTION: In a rural setting, the lake features rugged ravines, cypress ponds, lime sinks and hardwood and pine forests. Nationally known for its largemouth bass and wide variety of plant and animal life, this lake offers very good bird watching.
GETTING THERE: From Tallahassee, FL, 42 mi W on US 90 to Chattahoochee, FL, 1 mi N to dam.

Lake Ocklawaha
50 • Lake Ocklawaha • Map page 214
Palatka • Florida
DESCRIPTION: Located on the eastern end of the Cross Florida Barge Canal, offers four recreation areas, all with good fishing opportunities. This facility is scheduled to be turned over to the State of Florida in 1992.
GETTING THERE: From Palatka 10 mi SW on FL 19 and access roads.

Lake Okeechobee
51 • Moore Haven Lock • Map page 214
Miami • Florida
DESCRIPTION: Located at the center of Florida's heartland, Lake Okeechobee is Florida's largest lake and the second largest freshwater lake in the U.S. Ten Corps recreation areas are located along the 152-mile waterway, which offers excellent boating, bass fishing, and waterfowl hunting. Corps-managed boat-in camping areas are available at St. Lucie Lock and the W. P. Franklin Lock.
GETTING THERE: From Miami, 130 mi N on US 27 to Moore Haven.

Lake Okeechobee and Okeechobee Waterway
52 • Ortona Lock • Map page 214
Ft. Myers • Florida
DESCRIPTION: Located at the center of Florida's heartland, Lake Okeechobee is Florida's largest lake and the second largest freshwater lake in the U.S. Ten Corps recreation areas are located along the 152-mile waterway, which offers excellent boating, bass fishing, and waterfowl hunting. Corps-managed boat-in camping areas are available at St. Lucie Lock and the W. P. Franklin Lock.
GETTING THERE: From Ft. Myers, 33 mi E on FL 80, paved road to lock, 778

Lake Okeechobee and Waterway
53 • W.P. Franklin Lock • Map page 214
Ft. Myers • Florida
DESCRIPTION: Located at the center of Florida's heartland, Lake Okeechobee is Florida's largest lake and the second largest freshwater lake in the U.S. Ten Corps recreation areas are located along the 152-mile waterway, which offers excellent boating, bass fishing, and waterfowl hunting. Corps-managed boat-in camping areas are available at St. Lucie Lock and the W. P. Franklin Lock.
GETTING THERE: From Ft. Myers, 12 mi E off US 80

Georgia

Walter F. George Lake
54 • Cotton Hill • Map page 220
Albany • Georgia
DESCRIPTION: The area features Indian trails and mounds, battlegrounds, antebellum homes, and a restored village of the 1850's.
GETTING THERE: From Albany, 24 mi W on GA 62 to Leary, 36 mi W on GA 37 to Fort Gaines, 2 mi N on GA 39 to dam.

George W. Andrews Lake
55 • George W. Andrews Lake • Map page 220
Albany • Georgia
DESCRIPTION: Located in an area of historical and archeological significance, Indian trails and battlegrounds are well marked. This lake features a scenic waterfall.
GETTING THERE: From Albany, 60 mi W GA 62 to Hilton, follow signs to dam.

Carters Lake
56 • Harris Branch • Map page 220
Chatsworth • Georgia
DESCRIPTION: This small scenic lake is backed up by a 445-foot-high dam in the lower reaches of the Blue Ridge. There is a power plant with pumped storage operation.
GETTING THERE: From Chatsworth, 9 mi S on US 411.

J. Strom Thurmond Lake
57 • Modoc • Map page 220
Augusta • Georgia
DESCRIPTION: This is the largest Corps lake east of the Mississippi River. The adjacent area abounds with historical and geological sites. J. Strom Thurmond provides excellent striper and black bass fishing and its large wildlife management areas offer some of the south's best hunting and wildlife observation opportunities. The visitor center and public overlook are located at the Natural Resource Management Center.
GETTING THERE: From Augusta, GA, 20 mi N on GA 28 nr 104 tn GA 150.

Allatoona Lake
58 • Old HWY 41 #3 • Map page 220
Atlanta • Georgia
DESCRIPTION: Located in the foothills of the Blue Ridge Mountains, this is the oldest Corps lake in the southeastern U.S. Camping, hiking, marinas and cabins are available, and historic Civil War battlefields are nearby.
GETTING THERE: From Atlanta, 45 mi N on 1-75 to Exit 125, E on GA 20, S on GA 294 to the dam.

West Point Project
59 • R Shaefer Heard • Map page 220
Atlanta • Georgia
DESCRIPTION: Designed as a recreation demonstration project, this lake has fishing piers for the handicapped and other special features. Excellent camping, good fishing.
GETTING THERE: From Atlanta, I-RE ~S and US 29.

Lake Sidney Lanier
60 • Shoal Creek • Map page 220
Atlanta • Georgia
DESCRIPTION: The combination of recreation facilities, panoramic views, climate, and proximity to Atlanta has attracted more visitors to this large lake than to any other Corps project.
GETTING THERE: From Atlanta, 1-85 N to 1-985, take Exits 1 thru 7, W.

Idaho

Dworshak Dam and Reservoir
61 • Dent Acres • Map page 238
Lewiston • Idaho
DESCRIPTION: This CG is on the 54 mi. long Dworshak Lake and surrounded by forest. Fish for salmon, trout and bass as well as swim and ski from the lake. Boat ramp, marina, RV dump station, visitor information center and playground located at CG. Wildlife is abundant in this area. Many hiking trails in the area.
GETTING THERE: Dent Acres CG is located approx. 45 mi. E of Lewiston on US HWY 12.

Illinois

Andalusia Slough
62 • Andalusia Slough • Map page 276
Andalusia • Illinois
DESCRIPTION: CG has drinking water, picnic area and a boat launch but no electricity available.
GETTING THERE: Primitive camping and a launch ramp. Located 2 mi W of Andalusia on IL 92.

Bear Creek
63 • Bear Creek • Map page 276
Marceline • Illinois
DESCRIPTION: CG has electricity, drinking water, RV dump station, picnic area and a boat launch available.
GETTING THERE: From IL 96, 2 mi W on Rounty Rd. 2450 N. From Marceline, IL, 2 mi turn L, Y2mi turn R onto County Rd. 240ON 4 Y2mi, Y2mibeyond levee.

Mississippi River Pools 11-22
64 • Blanchard Island • Map page 276
Springfield • Illinois
DESCRIPTION: CG has electricity, showers, drinking water, RV dump station, picnic area and a boat launch available.
GETTING THERE: Turn right (S) 11/2 mi E of Muscatine Bridge onto County Rd. A, S 4 mi past Copper's Creek Bridge, R at Blanchard Island sign, W to the levee.

Mississippi River Pools 11-22
65 • Blanding Landing • Map page 276
Hanover • Illinois
DESCRIPTION: This campground is great for camping and day use. RV dump station, boat launch and a marina located in the CG.
GETTING THERE: Turn W of IL 84 on the first road N of Apple River Bridge in Hanover. Proceed approximately 8 mi NW on a county road to the first railroad crossing.

Mississippi River Pools 11-22
66 • Fisherman's Corner • Map page 276
Hampton • Illinois
DESCRIPTION: Campsites have electricity, drinking water, RV dump station, playground, amphitheater, bike trails,
GETTING THERE: Located 1 mi N of Hampton, IL on IL 84 adjacent to Lock and Dam 14.

Rend Lake
67 • North Sandusky Camping • Map page 276
Mt. Vernon • Illinois
DESCRIPTION: Water-oriented outdoor recreation opportunities including camping, picnicking, swimming, boating, fishing, and hunting. Well known for waterfowl hunting and wildlife viewing. An RV dump station, boat ramp, and playgrounds are located at the CG.
GETTING THERE: Located near Mt. Vernon, 15 mi S of junction of 1-64 and 1-57.

Lake Shelbyville
68 • Opossum Creek • Map page 276
Springfield • Illinois
DESCRIPTION: Sandy beaches, hiking trails, marinas, and popular lakeside campsites combined with the natural beauty of the area provide an ideal vacation spot. A resort offers rooms, convention facilities and a championship golf course.
GETTING THERE: 60 mi SE of Springfield just off IL 16 and 128.

Mississippi River Pools 11-22
69 • Park 'n' Fish • Map page 276
Hull • Illinois
DESCRIPTION: CG has electricity, drinking water, RV dump station and picnic area available.
GETTING THERE: From Hull, IL, 1/2 mi W on US 36, left 2 1/2 mi, right 3/4 mi on gravel road, left 2 mi on paved road.

Mississippi River Pools 11-22
70 • Thomson Causeway • Map page 276
Thomson • Illinois
DESCRIPTION: A well-developed camping and boating area. RV dump station, boat launch and a marina located in the CG. Bike and hiking trails located nearby. Playground located within the CG area.
GETTING THERE: Located adjacent to the west edge of Thomson.

Indiana

Brookville Lake
71 • Brookville Lake • Map page 280
Brookville • Indiana
DESCRIPTION: Sits on a 5,260-acre lake. CG has sites with or without electricity. RV dump station, day use area, boat ramp and marina available at the CG.
GETTING THERE: Located 1/2 mi NE of Brookville, on IN 101.

Cagles Mill Lake
72 • Cagles Mill Lake • Map page 280
Terre Haute • Indiana
DESCRIPTION: The lake features the largest waterfall in the state, a rock cut showing a number of geologic ages, native hardwood trees, a State park, and a nearby covered bridge. CG has sites with or without electricity. RV dump station, day use area, boat ramp and marina available at the CG.
GETTING THERE: From Terre Haute go approx. 30 mi. E on 1-70 to state HWY 243. Go S on 243 approx. 5 mi. to Cagles Mill Lake CG.

Cecil M. Hardin Lake
73 • Cecil M. Hardin Lake • Map page 280
Indianapolis • Indiana
DESCRIPTION: Fall forest colors are vivid in October when Parke County holds it nine day Covered Bridge Festival. 20 mi. from Turkey Run State Park. CG has sites with or without electricity. RV dump station, day use area, boat ramp and marina available at the CG.
GETTING THERE: From Indianapolis, 55 mi W on US 36.

Huntington Lake
74 • Huntington Lake • Map page 280
Huntington • Indiana
DESCRIPTION: A quiet recreation area on the Wabash River. Day use area, boat ramp and marina available at CG.
GETTING THERE: In north central Indiana, S of Huntington on IN 5.

Mississinewa Lake
75 • Mississinewa Lake • Map page 280
Peru • Indiana
DESCRIPTION: In an area rich in Indian history, the lake includes both State and Corps managed recreation areas. CG has sites with or without electricity. RV dump station, day use area, boat ramp and marina available at the CG.
GETTING THERE: From Peru, S on IN 21, E on IN 400, N on Rt.550.

Monroe Lake
76 • Monroe Lake • Map page 280
Bloomington • Indiana
DESCRIPTION: Indiana's largest lake, near the Indiana University campus, features a scenic stone-bluffed shoreline and wooded hills. CG has sites with or without electricity. RV dump station, day use area, boat ramp and marina available at the CG.
GETTING THERE: From IN 37, exit at Smithville Road or Harrodsburg exit, S of Bloomington; or E on IN 46, S on IN 446.

Patoka Lake
77 • Patoka Lake • Map page 280
Indianapolis • Indiana
DESCRIPTION: An 8,800 acre lake located within the Hoosier National Forest Purchase Area. CG has sites with or without electricity. RV dump station, day use area, boat ramp and marina available at the CG.
GETTING THERE: The major recreation area is W of the intersection of IN 64 and 145.

Salamonie Lake
78 • Salamonie Lake • Map page 280
Wabash • Indiana
DESCRIPTION: Attractions include Hanging Rock, 2 mi downstream from the dam, and Old Canal Locks at Lagro. CG has sites with or without electricity. RV dump station, day use area, visitor information center, boat ramp and marina available at the CG.
GETTING THERE: From Wabash, S on IN 15, E on IN 124, N on IN 105 to Lost Bridge recreation sites.

Iowa

Rathbun Lake
79 • Buck Creek • Map page 282
Des Moines • Iowa
DESCRIPTION: Over 1,000 campsites are available at this 11,000-acre lake in the rolling hills of southern Iowa. Excellent fishing, hunting, sailing, state fish hatchery, and floating restaurant are major attractions.
GETTING THERE: From Des Moines, 85 mi SE on IA 5.

Mississippi River Pools 11-22
80 • Bulger's Hollow • Map page 282
Clinton • Iowa
DESCRIPTION: Campsites, a boat ramp and picnic areas. RV dump station and a boat launch located in the CG.
GETTING THERE: Bulger's Hollow CG is located approx. 4 mi. N of Clinton on state HWY 67.

Saylorville Lake
81 • Cherry Glen • Map page 282
Des Moines • Iowa
DESCRIPTION: In the heart of Iowa, 14 recreational areas offer camping and a variety of other outdoor activities.
GETTING THERE: From Des Moines I-235 W to I-35 N to IA 141.

Mississippi River Pools 11-22
82 • Clark's Ferry • Map page 282
Montpelier • Iowa
DESCRIPTION: CG has electricity, showers, drinking water, RV dump station, picnic area and a boat launch available.
GETTING THERE: Located at the southern edge of Montpelier, IA. Turn off IA 22 at the sign.

Mississippi River Pools 11-22
83 • Ferry Landing • Map page 282
Oakville • Iowa
DESCRIPTION: Primitive camping and boat ramp. Boat launch and RV dump station located at the CG.
GETTING THERE: At the northern edge of Oakville. Follow the county road approximately 6 mi. N to the levee.

Lake Red Rock
84 • North Overlook Camp • Map page 282
Pella • Iowa
DESCRIPTION: North Overlook Campground is located on Lake Red Rock, Iowa's largest lake. Six major park developments offer camping and day-use activities. A State wildlife management area provides refuge and public hunting.
GETTING THERE: 4 mi SW of Pella on County Rd. TI 5.

Mississippi River Pools 11-22
85 • Pleasant Creek • Map page 282
Bellevue • Iowa
DESCRIPTION: This CG features an RV dump station and boat launch ramp.
GETTING THERE: Located 3Y2 mi. S of Bellevue, IA off IA 52.

Mississippi River Pools 11-22
86 • Shady Creek • Map page 282
Fairport • Iowa
DESCRIPTION: CG has electricity, showers, drinking water, RV dump station, picnic area and a boat launch available.
GETTING THERE: Located IY2 mi N of Fairport, Iowa. Turn off IA 22 at the sign.

Coralville Lake
87 • West Overlook Camp • Map page 282
Dubuque • Iowa
DESCRIPTION: Recreation opportunities are available at 5 Federal recreation developments and adjacent Lake MacBride State Park.
GETTING THERE: From I-80 take Dubuque Street (exit 244) N to Coralville Lake turn off.

Kansas

Melvern Lake
88 • Arrow Rock • Map page 282
Topeka • Kansas
DESCRIPTION: Located on the east edge of the Flint Hills region, Melvern features a 12 mile equestrian trail and 2 self guided nature trails.
GETTING THERE: From Topeka, 39 mi S on US 75. From Kansas City, 72 mi SW on I-35.

Clinton Lake
89 • Bloomington • Map page 282
Lawrence • Kansas
DESCRIPTION: Located close to Lawrence and the University of Kansas, the lake offers the Clinton Lake Historical Society Museum, a restored historic building in Bloomington Park.
GETTING THERE: From Lawrence, 4 mi W on Clinton Parkway.

Council Grove
90 • Canning Creek • Map page 282
Topeka • Kansas
DESCRIPTION: Named for the nearby town of Council Grove, where the Osage Indians signed a treaty to establish the Old Santa Fe Trail. Marker in town indicates place where the treaty was signed.
GETTING THERE: From Topeka, 30 mi S on KS Turnpike, W on US 56.

Pomona Lake
91 • Carbolyn • Map page 282
Topeka • Kansas
DESCRIPTION: Located near the Santa Fe Trail, this 4,000 acre lake features scenic beauty as well as an abundance of wildlife. Interpretive programs are presented at the Poweshieck Amphitheater.
GETTING THERE: From Topeka, 24 mi S on US 75, 7 mi E on KS 268.

Elk City Lake
92 • Card Creek • Map page 282
Independence • Kansas
DESCRIPTION: A precipitous rock bluff marks the north margin of the river for several miles above the dam site. The State of Kansas uses 11,680 acres of project lands for wildlife management and public hunting.
GETTING THERE: From Independence, 7 mi N on US 75, 4 mi W and 2 mi S on county road.

Pearson-Skubitz/Big Hill Lake
93 • Cherryvale Park • Map page 282
Independence • Kansas
DESCRIPTION: Located on Big Hill Creek in Labette County, this lake impounds 1,240 acres of water. It has three public use areas totaling 367 acres.
GETTING THERE: From Independence, 7 mi E on US 160, 4 mi N on KS 169. 5 mi E on county road.

Milford Lake
94 • Curtis Creek • Map page 282
Topeka • Kansas
DESCRIPTION: The Milford Conservation Education Center and Fish Hatchery are located below the dam.
GETTING THERE: From Topeka.63 mi W on I-70,5 mi N on US 77.

John Redmond Reservoir
95 • Dam site • Map page 282
Emporia • Kansas
DESCRIPTION: Sightseers will enjoy the Flint Hills Wildlife Refuge. Enjoy wandering old Indian grounds.
GETTING THERE: From Emporia, 27 mi E on I-35 11 mi. US 50, 25 mi S on US 75.

Fall River Lake
96 • Dam site • Map page 282
El Dorado • Kansas
DESCRIPTION: Flowers, birds and game enhance this project in rolling prairie country. The 10,900 acre Fall River Game Management Area is located here.
GETTING THERE: From El Dorado, 10 mi S on US 77, 46 mi E on KS 96.

El Dorado Lake
97 • El Dorado Lake • Map page 282
Wichita • Kansas
DESCRIPTION: An overlook provides unobstructed view of this 8,000-acre lake impounding the Walnut River in Butler County.
GETTING THERE: From Wichita, about 20 mi NE via I-35, then 6 mi E on KS 54, 1 mi N on KS 177.

Perry Lake
98 • Longview • Map page 282
Topeka • Kansas
DESCRIPTION: Hikers will enjoy the scenic beauty of the 30- mile National Recreation Trail which follows the eastern shoreline.
GETTING THERE: From Topeka 17 mi NE on US 24 to Perry.

Wilson Lake
99 • Lucas Park • Map page 282
Salina • Kansas
DESCRIPTION: One of the prettiest lakes in the State, Wilson features clear blue water and excellent striper fishing.
GETTING THERE: From Salina, 48 mi W on I-70, 7 mi N from the Wilson exit.

Marion Reservoir
100 • Marion Cove • Map page 282
Newton • Kansas
DESCRIPTION: Ruts of the old Santa Fe Trail and a few pioneer adobe houses may be seen in the area.
GETTING THERE: From Newton, 24 mi N on KS 15,12 mi E on US 56.

Kanopolis Lake
101 • Riverside Park • Map page 282
Salina • Kansas
DESCRIPTION: The nearby Fort Harker Museum at Kanopolis and the Rogers Art Gallery and Museum at Ellsworth portray the settlement of the American West. Kanopolis is also the home of Kansas' first State park. Early Indian rock carvings on Inscription Rock in Horse Thief Canyon offer an interesting glimpse into the past.
GETTING THERE: From Salina, 26 mi SE on KS 140, 10 mi S on KS 141.

Tuttle Creek Lake
102 • Stockdale • Map page 282
Topeka • Kansas
DESCRIPTION: Fort Riley, Kansas State University, and the Prairie Parkway are among the nearby attractions.
GETTING THERE: From Topeka, 45 mi W on I-70, 15 mi N on KS 177.

Toronto Lake
103 • Toronto Lake • Map page 282
El Dorado • Kansas
DESCRIPTION: Kansas' only granite outcrop is located here, at the scene of a short lived gold rush in 1887.
GETTING THERE: From El Dorado, 50 mi E on US 54, 9 mi S on KS 105.

Kentucky

Cave Run Lake
104 • Cave Run Lake • Map page 284
Huntington • Kentucky
DESCRIPTION: The Minor Clark Fish Hatchery, one of the largest in the United States, is located below the Corps-operated dam. The U.S. Forest Service manages the lake with varied recreational opportunities. CG has sites with or without electricity. RV dump station, day use area, boat ramp and marina available at the CG.
GETTING THERE: Located on KY 826 via US 60 from I-64.

Buckhorn Lake
105 • Dam Site • Map page 284
Hazard • Kentucky
DESCRIPTION: Beautiful, mountainous terrain in the heart of Kentucky coal country. CG has sites with or without electricity. RV dump station, day use area, boat ramp and marina available at the CG.
GETTING THERE: From Hazard, 9 mi N on KY 15, 20 mi E on KY 28.

Nolin River Lake
106 • Dog Creek • Map page 284
Brownsville • Kentucky
DESCRIPTION: Campground is located in a scenic area, rich in Americana.
GETTING THERE: From Brownsville, N 5 mi on KY 259, right on KY 728, follow signs.

Lake Barkley
107 • Eureka • Map page 284
Louisville • Kentucky
DESCRIPTION: Bordering TVA's Land Between the Lakes Recreation Area in the gently rolling hills of southwestern Kentucky and north central Tennessee, this lake offers excellent waterfowl hunting, good fishing, nature trails, a national battlefield, and a national waterfowl refuge.
GETTING THERE: From Louisville, KY, S on I-65 to Western Kentucky Parkway, 13 mi W on US 62 through Eddyville, KY, to dam.

Dewey Lake
108 • German Area • Map page 284
Prestonburg • Kentucky
DESCRIPTION: Wooded hills rise some 700 feet above the lake. A full range of facilities is at Jenny Wiley State Park. CG has sites without electricity. Day use area, visitor information center, boat ramp and marina available at the CG.
GETTING THERE: From Prestonburg, 6 mi N on US 23, 3 mi NE on KY 304.

Fish trap Lake
109 • Grapevine Area • Map page 284
Pikeville • Kentucky
DESCRIPTION: In rich coalfield country, steep mountains surround the project area. CG has sites without electricity. RV dump station, day use area, boat ramp and marina available at the CG.
GETTING THERE: From Pikeville,12 mi E on US 460, 2 mi E on KY 1789.

Grayson Lake
110 • Grayson Lake • Map page 284
Grayson • Kentucky
DESCRIPTION: Vertical rock cliffs rim the lake's 40 miles of shoreline. See the well preserved log cabin at the project and visit the caves at nearby Carter Caves State Park. CG has sites with or without electricity. RV dump station, day use area, boat ramp and marina available at the CG.
GETTING THERE: 7 mi S of Grayson on KY 7.

Lake Cumberland
111 • Kendall • Map page 284
Somerset • Kentucky
DESCRIPTION: This large, deepwater lake in southern Kentucky offers a variety of attractions and activities. Cumberland Falls, on the lake, is famous for its "moon bow" which can be seen on clear nights. Restored Mill Springs Mill is nearby. Canoeing opportunities on the Big South Fork and the Rock castle River.
GETTING THERE: From Somerset, KY,5 mi S off US 27 on Boat Dock Road.

Rough River Lake
112 • Laurel Branch • Map page 284
Louisville • Kentucky
DESCRIPTION: See the old mill, in continuous operation from 1823 to 1968, located at the Falls of Rough, near Rough River State Park.
GETTING THERE: From Louisville, W on US 60 to Harned. S 10 mi on KY 79.

Laurel River Lake
113 • Laurel River Lake • Map page 284
London • Kentucky
DESCRIPTION: Located in the heart of Daniel Boone National Forest, this lake has clear water and excellent largemouth and small mouth bass fishing. Recreational facilities include campgrounds, boat ramps, picnic areas, hiking trails, and more.
GETTING THERE: From London, KY, 20 mi W on KY 1193.

Carr Creek Lake
114 • Littcarr • Map page 284
Hazard • Kentucky
DESCRIPTION: A scenic 710-acre lake in the rugged eastern Kentucky mountains. CG has sites with or without electricity. RV dump station, day use area, boat ramp and marina available at the CG.
GETTING THERE: Located 14 mi E of Hazard on KY 15.

Green River Lake
115 • Smith Ridge • Map page 284
Louisville • Kentucky
DESCRIPTION: In the hills of central Kentucky. An interpretive center at the dam site acquaints the visitor with the geology, culture and history of the area. Tebbs Bend, a Civil War battlefield area, is nearby.
GETTING THERE: Located 90 mi SE of Louisville via I-65 and KY 61, 210 and 55.

Barren River Lake
116 • Tail water • Map page 284
Louisville • Kentucky
DESCRIPTION: A 10,000-acre lake in the slightly rolling, timbered countryside. CG has sites with or without electricity. RV dump station, day use area, boat ramp and marina available at the CG.
GETTING THERE: From Louisville, 95 mi S on I-65 to Cave City, 10 mi S on KY 90 to Glaspow,5 mi S on US 31 to KY 252,9 mi S to dam.

Louisiana

Bayou Bodcau Reservoir
117 • Tom Merrill Area • Map page 288
Shreveport • Louisiana
DESCRIPTION: There is no permanent pool at this flood control dam. However, Bossier Parish maintains Ivan Lake on 520 acres of reservoir lands. A major waterfowl and upland game management and hunting area is open to the public.
GETTING THERE: From Shreveport, 20 mi E on I-20, then N on LA 157 to Bellevue, 2 mi N on county road.

Maryland

Jennings Randolph Lake
118 • Robert W Craig CPGD
Cumberland • Maryland
DESCRIPTION: Situated in the scenic, rugged hills of the Maryland/West Virginia border.
GETTING THERE: From Cumberland, MD, S on US 220 t0 US 50, W to WV 42, N to WV 46 E. Follow project signs.

Massachusetts

Lake Denison Recreation Area
119 • Birch Hill Dam
Baldwinville • Massachusetts
DESCRIPTION: The Lake Denison Recreation Area, on an 82-acre natural lake, offers campground, swim beach, and picnic area. Reservoir lands are managed by the Commonwealth of Massachusetts for hunting, fishing, and snowmobile riding.
GETTING THERE: To Lake Dennison from MA 2, US 202 N 6 miles. Dam on MA 68 4 mi W of US 202.

Cape Cod Canal
120 • Cape Cod Canal
Boston • Massachusetts
DESCRIPTION: The gateway to Cape Cod, with many nearby shops, tourist attractions and recreation facilities. State and town-managed campgrounds are located at various points next to the Canal. Area is popular for bicycling and fishing.
GETTING THERE: Take I-195 from Providence, RI, or MA 3 from Boston.

Knightville Dam
121 • Knightville Dam
Westfield • Massachusetts
DESCRIPTION: The river and tributary streams offer excellent trout fishing and are surrounded by prime upland game habitat. A picnic area and seasonal visitor center are next to the dam. Streamside campground available for community groups by reservation. Trout and pheasant are stocked by the State, which manages a portion of the reservoir area.
GETTING THERE: From Westfield, W on US 20 to Huntington, right on MA 112 N to dam.

Tully Lake
122 • Tully
Athol • Massachusetts
DESCRIPTION: A small primitive camping area and boat ramp (10-hp limit for boats) on the 300-acre lake are managed by the State. Warm-water fishing opportunities. Two nearby waterfalls are popular with visitors-Doanes Falls on Lawrence Brook (accessible by car) and Spirit Falls on Spirit Brook (accessible by hiking).
GETTING THERE: From Athol, 3 mi N on MA 32.

Michigan

Lake Superior
123 • Lower Keewenaw • Map page 301
Chassell • Michigan
DESCRIPTION: This waterway entrance for Great Lakes shipping is used as a shortcut and refuge from storms on Lake Superior. Day use facilities.
GETTING THERE: From Chassell, 4 mi E on US 41.

Minnesota

Big Sandy Lake
124 • Big Sandy Lake • Map page 306
McGregor • Minnesota
DESCRIPTION: Is located at the outlet of Big Sandy Lake. This was the site of a trading post in the early 1800's. Grave stones mark an Indian burial mound. Campsites with electricity. RV dump station and boat ramps available at the CG.
GETTING THERE: From McGregor go N approx. 13 mi. on state HWY 65 to Big Sandy Lake CG.

Mississippi River Headwaters Lakes Project
125 • Cross Lake • Map page 306
Brainerd • Minnesota
DESCRIPTION: Located in the heart of Crow Wing State Forest, at the headwaters of the Whitefish Chain Lakes.
GETTING THERE: From Brainerd, E on US 210 approx. 8 mi N on MN 25, right on County Road 3, 18 mi N to Cross Lake.

Eau Galle Lake
126 • Eau Galle Lake • Map page 306
St. Paul • Minnesota
DESCRIPTION: Located in a scenic area with steep hills, valleys, bluffs, streams and lakes. Campsites with have electricity, drinking water, RV dump station, and a boat launch are in the CG area.
GETTING THERE: From St. Paul go approx. 40 mi. E on 1-94 to county route 29. Go S on 29 approx. 10 mi. to Eau Galle Lake CG.

Mississippi River Headwaters Lakes Project
127 • Gull Lake • Map page 306
Brainerd • Minnesota
DESCRIPTION: Located in the heart of Crow Wing State Forest, at the headwaters of the Whitefish Chain Lakes.
GETTING THERE: From Brainerd, 7 mi N on US 371, 2 mi W on County 125,1.5 mi W on County 105.

Leech Lake
128 • Leech Lake • Map page 306
Grand Rapids • Minnesota
DESCRIPTION: This is the largest resort lake in northern Minnesota. The CG offers wooded campsites with access to Leech Lake, a famous walleye and Musky fishery.
GETTING THERE: From Grand Rapids go W approx. 43 mi. on US HWY 2 and 8 to Leech Lake CG.

Pokegame Lake
129 • Pokegame Lake • Map page 306
Grand Rapids • Minnesota
DESCRIPTION: Features nature trail, scenic drives, and an abundance of wildlife. Nearby mining and paper mill tours are available.
GETTING THERE: From Grand Rapids go W approx. 2 mi. on US HWY 2 to Pokegame Lake CG.

Winnibigoshish Lake
130 • Winnibigoshish Lake • Map page 306
Deer River • Minnesota
DESCRIPTION: Indian burial grounds are found in the area. Campsites have electricity, drinking water, RV dump station and a boat launch available in the CG area.
GETTING THERE: From Deer River go approx. 1 mi. W on US HWY 2 to US HWY 46. Go approx. 12 mi. NW on 46 to county route 9. Go E approx. 2 mi. on 9 to Winnibigoshish Lake CG.

Mississippi

Tennessee-Tombigbee Waterway
131 • Aberdeen Lake • Map page 314
Columbus • Mississippi
DESCRIPTION: Part of the Tennessee-Tombigbee Waterway. This 234-mile system of locks and dams forms a chain of 10 lakes reaching from the Tennessee River in the north to Demopolis, AL, in the south. The "Teen Tom," offering excellent fishing, hunting, and lakeside recreation, is a scenic short cut to the Gulf of Mexico.
GETTING THERE: From Columbus, Hwy 82, W to Waterway Mannaement Center.

Tennessee-Tombigbee Waterway
132 • Bay Springs Lake • Map page 314
Dennis • Mississippi
DESCRIPTION: Part of the Tennessee-Tombigbee Waterway. This 234-mile system of locks and dams forms a chain of 10 lakes reaching from the Tennessee River in the north to Demopolis, AL, in the south. The "Teen Tom," offering excellent fishing, hunting, and lakeside recreation, is a scenic short cut to the Gulf of Mexico.
GETTING THERE: From Dennis, MS 4, W 5 mi to Bay Springs Visitor Center.

Tennessee-Tombigbee Waterway
133 • Canal Section Locks • Map page 314
Dennis • Mississippi
DESCRIPTION: Part of the Tennessee-Tombigbee Waterway. This 234-mile system of locks and dams forms a chain of 10 lakes reaching from the Tennessee River in the north to Demopolis, AL, in the south. The "Teen Tom," offering excellent fishing, hunting, and lakeside recreation, is a scenic short cut to the Gulf of Mexico.
GETTING THERE: Divide Section/Upper Canal Section-From Dennis, MS 4, W 5 mi to Bay Springs Visitor Center. Lower Canal Section-From Columbus, Hwy 82, W to Waterway Mannaement Center.

Okatibbee Lake
134 • Twiltley Branch • Map page 314
Meridian • Mississippi
DESCRIPTION: Irregular, wooded shoreline offers attractive recreation. A 5,000-acre managed hunting area is open to the public.
GETTING THERE: From Meridian, 7 mi N on MS 19.

Missouri

Harry S. Truman Dam & Reservoir
135 • Berry Bend • Map page 320
Kansas City • Missouri
DESCRIPTION: Located adjacent to the Lake of the Ozarks, Truman features excellent fishing, a regional visitor center and power plant exhibit area. Rugged hills, scenic bluffs, hardwood forest and prairie offer some of the best scenery in the State.
GETTING THERE: From Kansas City 19 mi S on US 71, 75 mi E on MO 7, to Warsaw, 1 mi N.

Carlyle Lake
136 • Boulder • Map page 320
St. Louis • Missouri
DESCRIPTION: Water-oriented outdoor recreation opportunities including camping, picnicking, swimming, boating, fishing, and hunting. Especially attractive to sailboaters. Illinois' largest lake. Boat launch, marina, RV dump station and visitor information center located at the CG.
GETTING THERE: 50 mi E of St. Louis, MO on US 50.

Stockton Lake
137 • Cedar Ridge • Map page 320
Springfield • Missouri
DESCRIPTION: A popular lake in the scenic Missouri Ozarks.
GETTING THERE: From Springfield, 29 mi N on MO 13, 22 mi W nn MO 32.

Pomme de Terre Lake
138 • Dam site • Map page 320
Springfield • Missouri
DESCRIPTION: Dam site was a (Union Electric) company town started in 1929 for the workers near the site of the Osage (Bagnell) Dam in Franklin T. Cool, clear spring waters make this lake the "Gem of the Ozarks."
GETTING THERE: From Springfield, 53 mi N on US 65, 5 mi W on US 54, 4 mi S on MO 254.

139 • Fenway Landing • Map page 320
Canton • Missouri
DESCRIPTION: A lightly developed area. CG has electricity, showers, drinking water, picnic area and a boat launch available.
GETTING THERE: Proceed 4Y2 mi N of Canton, MO on US 61, turn E at sign.

Table Rock Lake
140 • Indian Point • Map page 320
Springfield • Missouri
DESCRIPTION: A highly developed lake in the southern Ozark Mountain region. Nearby attractions include caves, museums, and resorts.
GETTING THERE: From Springfield, 45 mi S on US 65.

Little Blue River Lakes
141 • Little Blue River Lakes • Map page 320
Kansas City • Missouri
DESCRIPTION: Within the metropolitan area of Kansas City 2 lakes, Longview and Blue Springs, are operated by the Jackson County Department of Parks and Recreation.
GETTING THERE: Located between 1-70 and US 50 within the city limits of Grandview, Lee's Summit and Kansas City.

Long Branch Lake
142 • Long Branch Lake • Map page 320
Columbia • Missouri
DESCRIPTION: This lake offers beautiful shoreline vistas and abundant hunting and fishing opportunities. Long Branch State Park provides a variety of water-related recreation opportunities.
GETTING THERE: From Columbia, 59 mi N on US 63 to Macon, then 2 mi W on US 36.

Clearwater Lake
143 • Piedmont • Map page 320
Piedmont • Missouri
DESCRIPTION: Located near three State parks and several historical sites, such as Gads Hill, where the notorious Frank and Jesse James gang staged the world's second train robbery in 1874.
GETTING THERE: 5 mi W of Piedmont, or 100 mi S of St. Louis via US 67, then W on MO 34.

Clarence Cannon Dam-Mark Twain Lake
144 • Ray Behrens Rec Area • Map page 320
Hannibal • Missouri
DESCRIPTION: Offers a blend of picturesque natural resources and modern recreation facilities to suit everyone. Features the largest hydropower generating plant in Northeast Missouri.
GETTING THERE: Located 28 mi SW of historic Hannibal via US 61 to MO 19.

Wappapello Lake
145 • Redman Creek • Map page 320
St. Louis • Missouri
DESCRIPTION: The natural beauty of the Ozark Mountains is part of the universal appeal of the lake area. Sport fishing opportunities are excellent.
GETTING THERE: From St. Louis, 120 mi S on US 67 to Greenville then 20 mi SE on MO Rd D.

Smithville Lake
146 • Smithville Lake • Map page 320
Kansas City • Missouri
DESCRIPTION: Within 30 minutes of downtown Kansas City, this 7,190 acre lake offers a regional visitor center and an 18 hole golf course in addition to water related recreation activities.
GETTING THERE: From Kansas City, N on 1-29, 15 mi N on US 169, 2 mi E on MO Rd. DD.

Montana

Fort Peck Lake
147 • Downstream • Map page 337
Glasgow • Montana
DESCRIPTION: This dam was featured on the cover of the first issue of "Life" Magazine, in 1936. Buffalo, elk, deer, antelope and small game abound at this project in the Charles M. Russell National Wildlife Refuge. The largest known fossil beds in the world are found along a portion of the south shore.
GETTING THERE: From Glasgow go SE approx. 18 mi. on state HWY 24 to Downstream CG.

Lake Koocanusa
148 • Libby Dam • Map page 352
Libby • Montana
DESCRIPTION: In a National Forest in a wild and scenic section of northwest Montana. Forty eight miles of the 90-mi-long Lake Koocanusa is in Montana, and the remaining 42 miles extend into Canada. The Kootenai River below the Libby Dam is a blue ribbon fishery. RV dump station, boat launch and a marina located in the CG.
GETTING THERE: Libby Dam CG is located approx. 17 mi. N of Libby on state HWY 37.

Nebraska

Bluestem Lake
149 • Bluestem Lake • Map page 366
Sprague • Nebraska
DESCRIPTION: Part of the Salt Creek Valley Lake Project-ten small lakes near Lincoln. RV dump station, boat launch and a marina located in the CG.
GETTING THERE: Bluestem Lake CG is located near Sprague.

Salt Creek Valley Lake
150 • Branched Oak • Map page 366
Raymond • Nebraska
DESCRIPTION: Part of the Salt Creek Valley Lake Project-ten small lakes near Lincoln. RV dump station, boat launch and a marina located in the CG.
GETTING THERE: Branched Oak CG is located near Raymond.

Conestoga Lake
151 • Conestoga Lake • Map page 366
Emerald • Nebraska
DESCRIPTION: Part of the Salt Creek Valley Lake Project-ten small lakes near Lincoln. Boat launch located in the CG.
GETTING THERE: Conestoga Lake CG is located near Emerald.

Beech Fork Lake
152 • Glenn Cunningham Lake • Map page 366
Omaha • Nebraska
DESCRIPTION: Part of the Papio Creek Watershed Lake Project-four small lakes near Omaha. RV dump station, boat launch and a marina located in the CG.
GETTING THERE: Near 96th and 1-680.

Harlan County Lake
153 • Gremlin Cove • Map page 366
Lincoln • Nebraska
DESCRIPTION: Located in south-central Nebraska, this is the second largest lake in the state. It is well known for its excellent spring walleye fishing. RV dump station, boat launch and a marina located in the CG.
GETTING THERE: From Lincoln go SW approx. 14 mi. on 1-80 to US HWY 183. Go S on 183 approx. 41 mi. to Gremlin Cove CG.

Olive Creek Lake
154 • Olive Creek Lake • Map page 366
Kramer • Nebraska
DESCRIPTION: Part of the Salt Creek Valley Lake Project-ten small lakes near Lincoln.
GETTING THERE: Near Kramer.

Pawnee Lake
155 • Pawnee Lake • Map page 366
Emerald • Nebraska
DESCRIPTION: Part of the Salt Creek Valley Lake Project-ten small lakes near Lincoln. RV dump station, boat launch and a marina located in the CG.
GETTING THERE: Near Emerald.

Stage Coach Lake
156 • Stage Coach Lake • Map page 366
Hickman • Nebraska
DESCRIPTION: Part of the Salt Creek Valley Lake Project-ten small lakes near Lincoln. Boat launch located in the CG.
GETTING THERE: Near Hickman.

Wagon Train Lake
157 • Wagon Train Lake • Map page 366
Hickman • Nebraska
DESCRIPTION: Part of the Salt Creek Valley Lake Project-ten small lakes near Lincoln. RV dump station and a boat launch located in the CG.
GETTING THERE: Near Hickman.

Yankee Hill Lake
158 • Yankee Hill Lake • Map page 366
Denton • Nebraska
DESCRIPTION: Part of the Salt Creek Valley Lake Project-ten small lakes near Lincoln. Boat launch located in CG.
GETTING THERE: Near Denton.

New Mexico

Cochiti Lake
159 • Cochiti Area • Map page 394
Santa Fe • New Mexico
DESCRIPTION: On the Rio Grande about halfway between Santa Fe and Albuquerque, 14 mi from junction of NM 22 and 1-25 (US 85). Adjacent Indian land is closed to public.
GETTING THERE: On the Rio Grande about halfway between Santa Fe and Albuquerque, 14 mi from junction of NM 22 and 1-25 (US 85). Adjacent Indian land is closed to public.

Conchas Lake
160 • Conchas Lake • Map page 394
Tucumcari • New Mexico
DESCRIPTION: Petroglyphs indicate early cultures near here.
GETTING THERE: 34 mi NW of Tucumcari on NM 104.

Abiquiu Dam
161 • Riana • Map page 394
Espanola • New Mexico
DESCRIPTION: This 5,200-surface-acre reservoir offers some of the finest fishing in northern New Mexico. Reptile fossils 200 million years old have been found in the area. The area includes a fine panoramic view of the Cerro Pedernal from the dam.
GETTING THERE: From Espanola, 30 mi W on US 84, 2 mi S on NM 96.

Santa Rosa Lake
162 • Santa Rosa Lake • Map page 394
Santa Rosa • New Mexico
DESCRIPTION: The visitor center contains an interesting display on project area.
GETTING THERE: Impounds the Pecos River approximately 121 mi E of Albuquerque. Follow direction signs through city of Santa Rosa to lake.

New York

Almond Lake
163 • Almond Lake • Map page 398
Hornell • New York
DESCRIPTION: In the Finger Lake region, near the wineries at Hammondsport.
GETTING THERE: From Hornell, 2 mi S on NY 21.

East Sidney Lake
164 • East Sidney Lake • Map page 398
Binghamton • New York
DESCRIPTION: Located in rolling dairy country of New York. The annual canoe slalom is held downstream of dam during October.
GETTING THERE: From Binghamton, E on 1-88 to Unadilla, 5 miles E on NY 357 to park.

Whitney Point Lake
165 • Whitney Point Lake • Map page 398
Binghamton • New York
DESCRIPTION: In the hills of south central New York, the lake provides a productive sport fishery and excellent hunting for small game.
GETTING THERE: From Binghamton, 19 mi N on 1-81, 3 mi N on NY 26 to park.

North Carolina

B. Everett Jordan Reservoir
166 • B. Everett Jordan • Map page 400
Raleigh • North Carolina
DESCRIPTION: This 13,900-acre lake is located within a 45- minute drive from Raleigh and Durham. Boat launching, picnic, swim beach, and public marina facilities are available for public use. Recreation areas operated by agencies of the State of North Carolina.
GETTING THERE: From Raleigh, 30 mi S on US 1. From Sanford, 15 mi N on US 1.

W. Kerr Scott Dam and Reservoir
167 • Bandits Roost Park • Map page 400
Winston-Salem • North Carolina
DESCRIPTION: Located in the heart of scenic country, with Moravian and Cascade Falls in the immediate vicinity and the Blue Ridge Parkway 28 mi away. This area has many historical and cultural attractions. Day-use facilities and modern camp sites are available for public use.
GETTING THERE: From Winston-Salem, W on US 421 to Wilkesboro, then 5 mi W on NC 263.

Falls Lake
168 • Falls Lake • Map page 400
Durham • North Carolina
DESCRIPTION: This 12,500-acre lake is located within a 30- minute drive from Raleigh and Durham. Boat launching, public marina, swim beach and picnic facilities are available. Other recreation facilities are operated by the North Carolina State Parks.
GETTING THERE: From Durham, 25 mi E on NC 98.

North Dakota

Baldhill Dam/ Lake Ashtabula
169 • Ashtabula Lake • Map page 406
Valley City • North Dakota
DESCRIPTION: Nearby historic Sibley Trail was used by pioneers moving west. RV dump station, boat launch and a marina located in the CG.
GETTING THERE: From Valley City go NW approx. 11 mi. on River Road to Ashtabula Lake CG.

Bowman-Haley Lake
170 • Bowman-Haley Lake • Map page 406
Bowman • North Dakota
DESCRIPTION: Located on a former Sioux hunting ground of treeless slopes and plains.
GETTING THERE: From Bowman, 13 mi S on US 85,9 mi E and 2 mi on gravel county road.

Garrison Dam/Lake Sakakawea
171 • Downstream • Map page 406
Bismarck • North Dakota
DESCRIPTION: The Corps of Engineers' largest lake, and one of six built to control recurrent flooding on the Missouri River. Sites of early Indian culture and of trading and Army posts are located in the area. RV dump station, boat launch and a marina located in the CG.
GETTING THERE: From Bismarck go N approx. 70 mi. On US HWY 83 and state HWY 200.

Homme Lake
172 • Homme Lake • Map page 406
Grand Forks • North Dakota
DESCRIPTION: Visit the Memorial Gardens near this lake in northeast North Dakota.
GETTING THERE: From Grand Forks go N approx. 39 mi. on US HWY 81 to state HWY 17. Go W on 17 approx. 24 mi. to Homme Lake CG.

Ohio

Alum Creek Lake
173 • Alum Creek Lake • Map page 408
Columbus • Ohio
DESCRIPTION: Fort Cheshire, used by early settlers, was in this area.
GETTING THERE: Located 2 mi N of Columbus off US 23 on Lewis Center Rd.

Atwood Lake
174 • Atwood Lake • Map page 408
Dover • Ohio
DESCRIPTION: Atwood Lake Lodge, operated by the Muskingum Watershed Conservancy District, provides extensive recreation facilities, including pools and ski slopes.
GETTING THERE: From Dover, 7 mi N on OH 800, 9 mi E on OH 212.

Caesar Creek Lake
175 • Caesar Creek Lake • Map page 408
Waynesville • Ohio
DESCRIPTION: The regional visitor center for the Corps of Engineers is located at the dam. There is also a reconstructed pioneer village on the southeast side of the project.
GETTING THERE: Located just E of Waynesville, on OH 73.

Charles Mill Lake
176 • Charles Mill Lake • Map page 408
Lucas • Ohio
DESCRIPTION: Malabar Farm, home of Louis Bromfield, a Pulitzer prize winning novelist, is maintained near here by the state. In Mansfield, see the Kingwood Center formal gardens in bloom April-October.
GETTING THERE: From Lucas, 5 mi E on US 30, 4 mi S on OH 603.

Clarence J. Brown Reservoir
177 • Clarence J. Brown • Map page 408
Springfield • Ohio
DESCRIPTION: A 2,100-acre lake and Corps-operated visitors center. CG has sites with or without electricity. RV dump station, visitor information center, day use area, boat ramp and marina available at the CG.
GETTING THERE: Located outside Springfield city limits, just off OH 4.

Clendening Lake
178 • Clendening Lake • Map page 408
Uhrichsville • Ohio
DESCRIPTION: Retained in a natural setting with no commercial development except the marina. CG has sites with or without electricity. RV dump station, day use area, boat ramp and marina available at the CG.
GETTING THERE: From Uhrichsville, 15 mi S on OH 800.

Mohawk Dam
179 • Dam Site • Map page 408
Coshocton • Ohio
DESCRIPTION: There is no permanent pool but day-use and camping facilities are available along the river. Roscoe Village, a restored and historical canal town, is located near Coshocton.
GETTING THERE: From Coshocton, 13 mi W on US 36, 2 mi NW on OH 715.

North Branch of Kokosing Lake
180 • Dam site • Map page 408
Fredericktown • Ohio
DESCRIPTION: Campground is located on Kokosing Lake, a small, quiet fishing lake.
GETTING THERE: Located 1.5 mi from Fredericktown, just off OH 13.

Deer Creek Lake
181 • Deer Creek Lake • Map page 408
Columbus • Ohio
DESCRIPTION: The Pumpkin Show is held annually in October in nearby Circleville. Several prehistoric Indian sites are within the project area.
GETTING THERE: From Columbus, SW on I-71, SW on US 62, S on OH 207.

Delaware Lake
182 • Delaware Lake • Map page 408
Columbus • Ohio
DESCRIPTION: Delaware Lake offers Corps, state park, and state wildlife area recreational opportunities. CG has sites with or without electricity. RV dump station, day use area, boat ramp and marina available at the CG.
GETTING THERE: From Columbus. 35 mi N on US 23.

Dillon Lake
183 • Dillon Lake • Map page 408
Zanesville • Ohio
DESCRIPTION: Prehistoric Indian burial grounds have been identified in this area. CG has sites with or without electricity. RV dump station, day use area, boat ramp and marina available at the CG.
GETTING THERE: From Zanesville, 4 mi NW on OH 146.

Leesville Lake
184 • Leesville Lake • Map page 408
New Philadelphia • Ohio
DESCRIPTION: Campground is located on Leesville Lake, a popular camping spot for youth and church groups.
GETTING THERE: From New Philadelphia, 13 mi E on OH 39, 4 mi SE on OH 212.

Berlin Lake
185 • Mill Creek • Map page 408
Deerfield • Ohio
DESCRIPTION: A historic area with an old stagecoach station in Deerfield. John Brown was born near here.
GETTING THERE: From Deerfield, 2 mi E on OH 224.

Paint Creek Lake
186 • Paint Creek Lake • Map page 408
Chillicothe • Ohio
DESCRIPTION: Impressive, prehistoric Indian sites in the central Scioto River basin are in the vicinity of this lake.
GETTING THERE: Located 24 mi SW of Chillicothe, off US 50.

Piedmont Lake
187 • Piedmont Lake • Map page 408
Cambridge • Ohio
DESCRIPTION: Salt Fork Lodge and State Park are near this 2,700-acre lake.
GETTING THERE: From Cambridge, 24 mi NE on US 22.

Pleasant Hill Lake
188 • Pleasant Hill Lake • Map page 408
Lucas • Ohio
DESCRIPTION: Louis Bromfield's home, Malabar Farm, is maintained by the State Historical Society at upper end of reservoir. Mohican State Park is downstream of dam.
GETTING THERE: From Lucas, 6 mi S on OH 60, then SW on OH 95.

Senecaville Lake
189 • Senecaville Lake • Map page 408
Cambridge • Ohio
DESCRIPTION: One of the attractions is a Federal fish hatchery. Salt Fork Lodge and State Park are near the lake.
GETTING THERE: From Cambridge, 6 mi S on I-77,6 mi E on OH 313.

Tappan Lake
190 • Tappan Lake • Map page 408
Uhrichsville • Ohio
DESCRIPTION: Near a restored Indian village at Shoebrunn State Park and the outdoor historical drama, "Trumpet in the Land."
GETTING THERE: From Uhrichsville, 6 mi E on US 250.

Burr Oak Lake
191 • Tom Jenkins Dam • Map page 408
Athens • Ohio
DESCRIPTION: Within an hour's drive of the caves and cliffs of Hocking Hills State Park.
GETTING THERE: From Athens, 20 mi N on US 33 and OH 13.

Mill Creek Lake
192 • West Fork • Map page 408
Cincinnati • Ohio
DESCRIPTION: The project features Hamilton County Park District campgrounds and naturalist services.
GETTING THERE: Located in Cincinnati, W on I-275 to Winton Road, S to park.

William H. Harsha Lake
193 • William H. Harsha Lake • Map page 408
Batavia • Ohio
DESCRIPTION: A 2,160-acre lake made popular by Cincinnati boaters, also the site of two abandoned gold mines.
GETTING THERE: Located SE of Batavia just S of OH 32.

Oklahoma

Optima Lake
194 • Angler Point • Map page 412
Guymon • Oklahoma
DESCRIPTION: Located in an area once known as "No Man's Land" in the Oklahoma Panhandle, this lake is set in a scenic area of sand hills, rock outcroppings and rolling grasslands. Historical points of interest exist close to the lake.
GETTING THERE: From Guymon, 30 mi E on OK 3, 3 mi N on county road.

Arcadia Lake
195 • Arcadia Lake • Map page 412
Edmond • Oklahoma
DESCRIPTION: This lake impounds 1,820 acres of water on the Deep Fork River in central Oklahoma.
GETTING THERE: From Edmond,5 mi E on US 66.

Fort Supply Lake
196 • Beaver Point • Map page 412
Woodward • Oklahoma
DESCRIPTION: Some original buildings from Fort Supply, used as a base by Lt. Col. George Custer's 7th Cavalry, are located nearby.
GETTING THERE: From Woodward, 13 mi NW, US 270 and OK 3.

Newt Graham Lock & Dam 18
197 • Bluff Landing • Map page 412
Tulsa • Oklahoma
DESCRIPTION: The Port of Catoosa, terminal point of the McClellan-Kerr Arkansas River Navigation System, is nearby.
GETTING THERE: From Tulsa, 25 mi E on OK 33. 7 mi S on county road.

Webbers Falls Lock & Dam
198 • Brewers Bend • Map page 412
Muskogee • Oklahoma
DESCRIPTION: On the site of an important steamboat landing, the Falls were mentioned by General Zebulon Pike in his early (1806) explorations.
GETTING THERE: From Muskogee, 20 mi S on Muskogee Turnpike, 5 mi E on US 64, 2 mi N on OK 10.

Broken Bow Lake
199 • Broken Bow Lake • Map page 412
Broken Bow • Oklahoma
DESCRIPTION: The McCurtain County Wilderness Area at the lake's north end retains its primitive, natural beauty.
GETTING THERE: From Broken Bow, 7 mi N on US 259, 2 mi. E on OK 259-A.

Keystone Lake
200 • Brush Creek • Map page 412
Tulsa • Oklahoma
DESCRIPTION: Author Washington Irving noted Bear's Cove (formerly Bear's Glen) in his 1832 book, "A Tour of the Prairies."
GETTING THERE: From Tulsa, 19 mi W on Keystone Expressway (US 64).

Skiatook Lake
201 • Bull Creek • Map page 412
Tulsa • Oklahoma
DESCRIPTION: The Skiatook Dam is located 14 mi upstream of the confluence of Hominy and Bird Creeks. It forms a 10,500 acre impoundment.
GETTING THERE: About 20 mi NW of Tulsa via OK 11, then 5 mi N on OK 20.

Canton Lake
202 • Canadian • Map page 412
Fairview • Oklahoma
DESCRIPTION: Named for a pioneer Army post or "cantonment" at the halfway point between Forts Reno and Supply. Deactivated in 1882, the post also served as a Mennonite school for Indians.
GETTING THERE: From Fairview,13 mi S on OK 58,2 mi W on OK 58A.

Kaw Lake
203 • Coon Creek • Map page 412
Ponca City • Oklahoma
DESCRIPTION: On the Arkansas River in Kay and Osage Counties in Oklahoma and Crowley County in Kansas, this 17,000 acre lake offers camping and picnicking; 24,000 acres in both states are open to hunting and other activities. Game include: deer, turkey, quail, dove, waterfowl, rabbit and prairie chicken.
GETTING THERE: From Ponca City, 9.5 mi E on US 60, N on county road.

Fort Gibson Lake
204 • Dam Site • Map page 412
Fort Gibson • Oklahoma
DESCRIPTION: The Fort Gibson Stockade, a restored frontier fort is located near the lake. Fort Gibson is the oldest town in Oklahoma.
GETTING THERE: From Fort Gibson, 6 mi. N on OK. 80

Eufala Lake
205 • Dam Site South • Map page 412
McAlester • Oklahoma
DESCRIPTION: One of the largest Corps lakes. Outlaw Belle Starr lived near here in the turbulent days between the 1830's and the Civil War.
GETTING THERE: From McAlester,23 mi N on US 69,16 mi E on OK9.6 mi N on OK71.

Texoma Lake
206 • Damsite • Map page 412
Denison • Oklahoma
DESCRIPTION: The second most popular Corps lake in the country (after Lake Sidney Lanier, GA). Old Fort Washita is maintained as a museum by the Oklahoma Historical Society. A regional visitors center is planned for the lake.
GETTING THERE: From Denison, TX, 5 mi NW on TX 75A.

Great Salt Plains Lake
207 • Great Salt Plains Lake • Map page 412
Enid • Oklahoma
DESCRIPTION: Visit Great Salt Plains National Wildlife Refuge, one of the chain of refuge areas for ducks and geese on the Continental Central Flyway. Crystal digging is allowed Saturdays, Sundays and holidays from April 1 to Oct.15.
GETTING THERE: From Enid, 31 mi NW on US 64 to Jet, then 8 mi N on OK 38.

Oologah Lake
208 • Hawthorn Bluff • Map page 412
Tulsa • Oklahoma
DESCRIPTION: Will Rogers' home is nearby, restored as a State Park.
GETTING THERE: From Tulsa, 30 mi N on US 169, 3 mi E on OK 88.

Hulah Lake
209 • Hulah Lake • Map page 412
Bartlesville • Oklahoma
DESCRIPTION: Oil discoveries here made the Osage Indian tribe the wealthiest in America. Woolaroc Museum is nearby.
GETTING THERE: From Bartlesville,12 mi N on US 75,12 mi W on OK 10.

Hugo Lake
210 • Kiamichi Park • Map page 412
Hugo • Oklahoma
DESCRIPTION: The Oklahoma Department of Wildlife Conservation manages over 18,000 acres of land and water, which is open to hunting along with an additional 8,000 acres managed by the Corps. Wildlife around the lake includes waterfowl, bobwhite quail, dove, whitetail deer, mink, fox and beaver.
GETTING THERE: On the Kiamichi River, about 7 mi E of Hugo.

Pine Creek Lake
211 • Little River Park • Map page 412
Idabel • Oklahoma
DESCRIPTION: French trader Jean de la Harpe explored this area, later used by Choctaw Indians to establish small farmsteads.
GETTING THERE: From Idabel, 18 mi W on US 70 to Valliant, 2 mi N on OK 98, 7 mi N on county road.

Sardis Lake
212 • Potato Hills • Map page 412
McAlester • Oklahoma
DESCRIPTION: This lake provides 14,360 acres of surface water. It impounds Jackfork Creek, a tributary of the Kiamichi River in the foothills of the Ouachita Mountains of southeastern Oklahoma.
GETTING THERE: From McAlester, 36 mi SE on OK 1,15 mi S on OK 2.

Tenkiller Ferry Lake
213 • Strayhorn Landing • Map page 412
Muskogee • Oklahoma
DESCRIPTION: The area around this beautiful, clear lake is rich in history of the Cherokee Nation. A nearby point of interest is Tsa-La-Gi, an authentic recreation of a Cherokee Village of 1700's, where the Trail of Tears drama is presented.
GETTING THERE: From Muskogee, 21 mi SE on OK 10, 7 mi E on OK 10A.

Heyburn Lake
214 • Sunset Bay • Map page 412
Sapulpa • Oklahoma
DESCRIPTION: Located near Kellyville in the Sandstone Hills of the Osage Section central lowlands with good hunting and fishing.
GETTING THERE: From Sapulpa, 8 mi SW on US 66, 5 mi W on county road.

Chouteau Lock & Dam 17
215 • Tullahasee Loop • Map page 412
Muskogee • Oklahoma
DESCRIPTION: Named for Col. Auguste P. Chouteau, whose father built a shipyard on the river bank to build keelboats for the fur trade.
GETTING THERE: From Muskogee,7 mi N on US 69,3 mi SE on access road.

Birch Lake
216 • Twin Cove Point • Map page 412
Tulsa • Oklahoma
DESCRIPTION: This lake impounds about 1,137 acres of water on Birch Creek, a tributary of Bird Creek in Osage County.
GETTING THERE: From Tulsa, 35 mi NW on OK 11. To Burnsdall, 2 mi S on County Road.

W.D. Mayo Lock & Dam
217 • W.D. Mayo Lock & Dam • Map page 412
Fort Smith • Oklahoma
DESCRIPTION: Nearby Indian mounds date from 700- 1500 A. D.
GETTING THERE: From Fort Smith, AR, 12 mi W on AR 9, 4 mi N on county road.

Copan Lake
218 • Washington Cove • Map page 412
Bartlesville • Oklahoma
DESCRIPTION: About 43,000 acres of water is impounded behind this dam on the Little Caney River.
GETTING THERE: 15 mi N of Bartlesville via US 75.

Waurika Lake
219 • Wichita Ridge • Map page 412
Waurika • Oklahoma
DESCRIPTION: This lake impounds the waters of Beaver Creek. It forms a 10,100 acre lake.
GETTING THERE: About 6 mi NE of Waurika, on OK 5.

Wister Lake
220 • Wister Lake • Map page 412
Wister • Oklahoma
DESCRIPTION: Near the home of the famous Choctaw Light horsemen, who kept peace and order during the turbulent years of the last quarter of the 19th century.
GETTING THERE: From Wister, 2 mi E on US 270.

Oregon

Applegate Lake
221 • Applegate Lake • Map page 448
Medford • Oregon
DESCRIPTION: Nestled in the beautiful Applegate River Valley on the California-Oregon border near historic Jacksonville, OR. An RV dump station and boat ramp are located at the CG.
GETTING THERE: From Medford go approx. 23 mi SW on state HWY 238 and county road to Applegate Lake CG.

Blue River Lake
222 • Blue River Lake • Map page 448
Springfield • Oregon
DESCRIPTION: In the Willamette National Forest in the foothills of the Cascade Mountains. Supplies available at Springfield. Boat launch area located at the CG. Fish and swim in the lake.
GETTING THERE: From Springfield go E approx. 38 mi. on state HWY 126 to Blue River Lake CG.

Bonneville Dam
223 • Bonneville Dam • Map page 434
Portland • Oregon
DESCRIPTION: Rugged rock walls of the Columbia River Gorge rise to 2,000 feet above the lake. Visitors can experience first-hand the operation of two of the Nation's largest hydroelectric powerhouses and watch migrating fish traveling upstream at the underwater viewing rooms next to the fish ladders. RV dump station at CG.
GETTING THERE: From Portland go E approx. 40 mi. on 1-84 to Bonneville Dam and Lock CG.

Cougar Lake
224 • Cougar Lake • Map page 448
Eugene • Oregon
DESCRIPTION: A steep shoreline surrounds this scenic lake in the Willamette National Forest. Boat launch available at the CG. Boat, fish and swim from the lake. Supplies available at Eugene.
GETTING THERE: From Eugene go E approx. 42 mi. on state HWY 126.

Detroit Lake
225 • Detroit Lake • Map page 434
Salem • Oregon
DESCRIPTION: On the edge of the Cascade Mountains. Take a guided tour of the powerhouse. Boat launch at CG. Boat, swim or fish from the lake. Supplies available at Salem. RV dump station and visitor information center located at the CG.
GETTING THERE: From Salem go E approx. 45 mi. on state HWY 22 to Detroit Lake CG.

Fall Creek Lake
226 • Fall Creek Lake • Map page 448
Eugene • Oregon
DESCRIPTION: This attractive lake features extensive day-use facilities. Boat launch area at the CG.
GETTING THERE: From Eugene go SE approx. 25 mi. on state HWY 58 and Lowell-Jasper Rd to Fall Creek Lake CG.

Fern Ridge Lake
227 • Fern Ridge Lake • Map page 448
Eugene • Oregon
DESCRIPTION: State and county recreation areas supplement Corps facilities at this large lake in the Willamette Valley.
GETTING THERE: From Eugene go W approx. 12 mi. on state HWY 126 to Fern Ridge Lake CG.

Foster Lake
228 • Foster Lake • Map page 434
Sweet Home • Oregon
DESCRIPTION: A scenic mountain lake with good steelhead and trout fishing. Guided tour to powerhouse. RV dump station, visitor information center and boat launch area are available at the CG.
GETTING THERE: From Sweet Home go NE approx. 4 mi. on state HWY 20 to Foster Lake CG.

Green Peter Lake
229 • Green Peter Lake • Map page 434
Sweet Home • Oregon
DESCRIPTION: Nearby Green Peter Mountain was named by a pioneer with a vivid imagination, but the name stuck. The Quartzville section of the project is an historic gold mining area and a favorite with rock hounds.
GETTING THERE: From Sweet Home go NE approx. 10 mi. on state HWY 20 and the Quartzville Road to Green Peter Lake CG.

Hills Creek Lake
230 • Hills Creek Lake • Map page 448
Eugene • Oregon
DESCRIPTION: A scenic lake in a narrow canyon of the Willamette National Forest. Boat launch area at the CG. Supplies available at Eugene.
GETTING THERE: From Eugene go SE approx. 45 mi. on state HWY 58 to Hills Creek Lake CG.

McNary Lock and Dam/Lake Wallula
231 • Hoop Park • Map page 463
Umatilla • Oregon
DESCRIPTION: View migrating fish and tour powerhouse and navigation lock on the Columbia River. Sacajawea State Park is on one of the campsites of Lewis and Clark. Visit the Whitman Mission National Monument and Historic Site nearby. RV dump station, boat launch, marina and a visitor information center located in the CG.
GETTING THERE: From Umatilla go E approx. 2 mi. on state HWY 730 to Hoop Park CG.

Lookout Point Lake
232 • Lookout Point Lake • Map page 448
Eugene • Oregon
DESCRIPTION: Popular for catching cutthroat and rainbow trout. Self-guided tour of powerhouse.
GETTING THERE: From Eugene go SE approx. 22 mi. on state HWY 58 Lookout Point Lake CG.

Lost Creek Lake
233 • Lost Creek Lake • Map page 448
Medford • Oregon
DESCRIPTION: In the scenic Rogue River Valley, offering diversity of recreation opportunities en route to Crater Lake National Park. RV dump station, marina, boat launch area and visitor information center are located in the CG.
GETTING THERE: From Medford go NE approx. 30 mi. on state HWY 62 to Lost Creek Lake CG.

Cottage Grove Lake
234 • Pine Meadows • Map page 448
Cottage Grove • Oregon
DESCRIPTION: CG is in a mixed conifer setting on Cottage Grove Lake. Fish, boat or swim from the lake. Boat launch area at CG. Supplies are located in Cottage Grove. Numerous wildlife can be seen in the area. Campers may gather firewood. Many trails in the surrounding area. RV dump station at CG.
GETTING THERE: From Cottage Grove go S approx. 5 mi. on 1-5 and London Road to Pine Meadows CG.

John Day Lock and Dam/Lake Umatilla
235 • Plymouth Park • Map page 434
The Dalles • Oregon
DESCRIPTION: Offers excellent walleye fishing as well as chance to watch migrating fish and tour a working lock and powerhouse on the Columbia. RV dump station, marina and boat launch area at the CG.
GETTING THERE: From The Dalles go E approx. 25 mi. on 1-84 to Plymouth Park CG.

Dorena Lake
236 • Schwarz Park • Map page 448
Cottage Grove • Oregon
DESCRIPTION: CG is on Dorena Lake surrounded by a mixed conifer forest setting with views of the Cascade Mountains. Fish, boat and swim from the lake. Supplies available in Cottage Grove. Many animals can be seen in the area. A 12 mi. paved bike path is located nearby.
GETTING THERE: From Cottage Grove go E approx. 6 mi. on Row River Road to Schwarz Park CG.

Lake Celilo
237 • The Dalles Dam • Map page 434
The Dalles • Oregon
DESCRIPTION: Ancient Indian fishing, hunting and camping grounds are within the project area. During the summer season a train provides transportation for tourists around this large navigation and hydropower project on the Columbia. RV dump station, marina and boat launch available at the CG.
GETTING THERE: From The Dalles go E approx. 2 mi. on 1-84 to The Dalles Lock and Dam CG.

Pennsylvania

Alvin R Bush Dam
238 • Alvin R Bush Dam • Map page 492
Renovo • Pennsylvania
DESCRIPTION: Surrounded by high mountains in a wild, scenic area. Kettle Creek State Park provides the recreational facilities at this project.
GETTING THERE: From Renovo, 5 mi W on PA 120 to Westport, 8 mi N on unmarked state road.

Loyalhanna Lake
239 • Bush Area • Map page 492
Saltsburg • Pennsylvania
DESCRIPTION: Campground is located in an area of rugged, unspoiled scenery.
GETTING THERE: From Saltsburg, 3 mi. S on PA 981.

Crooked Creek Lake
240 • Crooked Creek • Map page 492
Kittanning • Pennsylvania
DESCRIPTION: A wide variety of recreational facilities can be found at the Corps-operated lake, including a large beach. There is good hunting in the area.
GETTING THERE: From Kittanning, 7 mi S on PA 66.

Curwensville Lake
241 • Curwensville Lake • Map page 492
Clearfield • Pennsylvania
DESCRIPTION: Day-use and overnight facilities are provided at this central Pennsylvania lake.
GETTING THERE: From Clearfield, W on PA 879 to Curwensville, 4 mi S on PA 453.

East Branch Clarion R. Lake
242 • East Branch • Map page 492
Johnsonburg • Pennsylvania
DESCRIPTION: Elk State Park is located at this lake in scenic western Pennsylvania.
GETTING THERE: 9 mi NE of Johnsonburg.

Foster J Sayers Dam
243 • Foster J Sayers Dam • Map page 492
Howard • Pennsylvania
DESCRIPTION: Bald Eagle State Park provides a marina, campground, picnic areas, and beach at this 1,730-acre lake. A historical village is under restoration.
GETTING THERE: From 1-80, exit 23, 10 mi N on PA 150.

Tioga-Hammond Lakes
244 • Ives Run • Map page 492
Tioga • Pennsylvania
DESCRIPTION: Twin lakes in north central Pennsylvania provide overnight and day use facilities in a scenic environment.
GETTING THERE: Near the Borough of Tioga, at the intersection of PA 287 and US 15.

Tionesta Lake
245 • Kelletville • Map page 492
Tionesta • Pennsylvania
DESCRIPTION: Located in the high hills of the Allegheny Mountains.
GETTING THERE: From Tionesta, 1.5 mi S on PA. 36.

Allegheny Reservoir
246 • Kinzua Dam • Map page 492
Warren • Pennsylvania
DESCRIPTION: The Allegheny National Forest and the Seneca Nation of Indians are highlights of this lake.
GETTING THERE: From Warren, 9 mi E on PA 59.

Mahoning Creek Lake
247 • Mahoning Creek Lake • Map page 492
New Bethlehem • Pennsylvania
DESCRIPTION: Another lake set in the rugged hills of western Pennsylvania. Hiking, hunting, and fishing are among its attractions.
GETTING THERE: Follow project signs south from New Bethlehem.

Shenango River Lake
248 • Shenango Rec. Area • Map page 492
Sharpsville • Pennsylvania
DESCRIPTION: The area features 8 archeological sites and 4 historical areas.
GETTING THERE: Follow project signs north from Sharpsville.

Raystown Lake
249 • Susquehannock • Map page 492
Hesston • Pennsylvania
DESCRIPTION: Here you will find boating, fishing, camping, hiking, swimming, and scenic beauty. This twisting lake, the largest entirely within Pennsylvania, extends 27 miles and covers 8,300 acres.
GETTING THERE: Park Headquarters is 2 mi E of PA 26 at Hesston.

Cowanesque Lake
250 • Tompkins • Map page 492
Lawrenceville • Pennsylvania
DESCRIPTION: This project provides a 1,085-acre lake with 17 miles of shoreline.
GETTING THERE: Located at Lawrenceville, near New York border, between County Route 58052 and PA 49, accessible from US 15.

Youghiogheny River Lake
251 • Tub Run Rec. Area • Map page 492
Confluence • Pennsylvania
DESCRIPTION: Releases from the dam allow some of the best whitewater canoeing in the East. Visit spectacular Ohiopyle Falls.
GETTING THERE: From Confluence, 1.5 mi S on PA 281.

Woodcock Creek Lake
252 • Woodcock Creek Lake • Map page 492
Meadville • Pennsylvania
DESCRIPTION: Provides a 333-acre summer pool with the largest recreation facility managed by Crawford County.
GETTING THERE: Located N of Meadville, off PA 86.

South Carolina

Russell Lake
253 • Richard B. Russell Lake • Map page 496
Calhoun • South Carolina
DESCRIPTION: Lying between J. Strom Thurmond Lake to the south and Hartwell Lake to the north, Russell is one of the finest fishing lakes in the Southeast, offering both cold and warm water fisheries. Russell Lake has two unique and informative visitor centers at the powerhouse and the Natural Resource Management Center.
GETTING THERE: Located 20 mi E of Elberton, GA, and 8 mi W of Calhoun, SC off US 72.

Hartwell Lake
254 • Watsadlers • Map page 496
• South Carolina
DESCRIPTION: This lake in the upstate region of Georgia and South Carolina has a reputation as an excellent location for all types of outdoor recreation activity. The area is rich in historical lore, and Clemson University adjoins the lake.
GETTING THERE: The Natural Resource Management Center is located 5 mi N of Hartwell, Ga. on US 29, or 100 mi E of Atlanta on 1-85. Several lake access areas are easily reached from the Hartwell, Anderson or Clemson exits on 1-85.

South Dakota

Cold Brook Lake
255 • Cold Brook • Map page 500
Hot Springs • South Dakota
DESCRIPTION: On the south fringe of the Black Hills. Visit nearby Mt. Rushmore, Custer State Park, and Wind Cave National Park.
GETTING THERE: About 1 mi. N of Hot Springs.

Oahe Dam Lake Oahe
256 • Downstream Area • Map page 500
Pierre • South Dakota
DESCRIPTION: A very large lake on the mainstream of the Missouri River. Rich in historic sites-fort, trading posts, and Lewis and Clark campsites. RV dump station, boat launch and a marina located in the CG.
GETTING THERE: From Pierre go N approx. 8 mi. on state HWY 1804.

Big Bend Dam/Lake Sharpe
257 • Left Tailrace • Map page 500
Sioux Falls • South Dakota
DESCRIPTION: One of six large lakes on the Missouri River. Area contains numerous village sites of early Indian culture. A visitor center contains exhibits and displays. RV dump station, boat launch and a marina located in the CG.
GETTING THERE: From Sioux Falls, W on I-90 to Chamberlain, then N on SD 50.

Gavins Point Dam/Lewis and Clark Lake
258 • Pierson Ranch Camp • Map page 500
Yankton • South Dakota
DESCRIPTION: This Missouri River lake provides a tree-covered shoreline characterized by picturesque chalky bluffs in the lower segment and an interesting view of the Missouri Valley in the upper reach. RV dump station, boat launch and a marina located in the CG.
GETTING THERE: From Yankton go W on state HWY 52.

Ft. Randall Dam/Lake Francis Case
259 • Randall Creek • Map page 500
Pickstown • South Dakota
DESCRIPTION: On the Missouri River, the area contains many historic and archeological sites. Numerous tributary streams and their embayment afford protected boating and fishing sites. RV dump station, boat launch and a marina located in the CG.
GETTING THERE: Near Pickstown on US HWY 18.

Cottonwood Springs Lake
260 • South Side • Map page 500
Hot Springs • South Dakota
DESCRIPTION: On the south fringe of the Black Hills. Visit nearby Mt. Rushmore, Custer State Park, and Wind Cave National Park.
GETTING THERE: About 1 mi. N of Hot Springs.

Tennessee

Old Hickory Lake
261 • Cages Bend • Map page 504
Nashville • Tennessee
DESCRIPTION: This extensively developed lake is located northeast of Nashville. Sailing and yachting are popular and numerous regattas are held on the lake. The Old Hickory Nature Trail, a part of the National Trails System, provides interesting features for all age groups.
GETTING THERE: From Nashville, N on 1-65 to Madison exit, E on TN 45 to the lake.

Dale Hollow Lake
262 • Dale Hollow Dam • Map page 504
Nashville • Tennessee
DESCRIPTION: Located in the Highland Rim section of northern Tennessee and southern Kentucky, Dale Hollow's crystalline waters are ideal for virtually all water sports, including scuba diving. House boaters also find a haven in the clear waters and secluded coves. A Federal fish hatchery and Standing Stone State Park are nearby.
GETTING THERE: From Nashville, 69 mi E on 1-40,17 mi N to TN 56,23 mi N on TN 53 to Celina, follow signs.

Cordell Hull Lake
263 • Defeated Creek Park • Map page 504
Nashville • Tennessee
DESCRIPTION: Located at the base of the Highland Rim of middle Tennessee, the lake boasts modern campgrounds and day use areas, opportunities for hunters and fishermen, and trails for hikers, backpackers, and horseback riders. Canoeing is excellent on the Roaring River section of the lake. There is excellent small game and deer hunting in season.
GETTING THERE: From Nashville, E on 1-40, N on TN 43 to Carthage.

Grenada Lake
264 • Grenada Landing A • Map page 314
Memphis • Tennessee
DESCRIPTION: Features include a Civil War redoubt, tennis courts, fitness trail and visitor center.
GETTING THERE: From Memphis, TN, 82 mi S on 1-55 to Grenada, 3 mi. E on MS 8.

Sardis Lake
265 • Hurricane Landing • Map page 314
Memphis • Tennessee
DESCRIPTION: Has a large swimming beach and beach house, and a State Park with swimming pool, recreation hall and cabins.
GETTING THERE: From Memphis, TN, 38 mi S on I-55 to Sardis, 7 mi E on MS 315.

Arkabutla Lake
266 • Kelly's Crossing • Map page 314
Memphis • Tennessee
DESCRIPTION: Known for its large crappie, this project offers camping, swimming, and excellent sailing. Special events include the Fall Arts and Crafts Fair.
GETTING THERE: From Memphis, TN,12 mi S on I-55 to Hernando, MS, then 13 mi W on Scenic Loop 304.

Cheatham Lake
267 • Lock A • Map page 504
Nashville • Tennessee
DESCRIPTION: This project passes through Middle Tennessee and features a 2,700-acre waterfowl refuge and game management area. The lake meanders through Nashville and past Opryland. Fort Nashboro and Riverfront Park overlook the lake in downtown Nashville. Excellent waterfowl hunting and lunker bass await the sportsman.
GETTING THERE: From Nashville, 32 mi W on TN 12.

Center Hill Lake
268 • Long Branch • Map page 504
Nashville • Tennessee
DESCRIPTION: Located in the Cumberland Mountains of middle Tennessee, this lake offers excellent small mouth bass, walleye, and white bass fishing. Deep, clear water provides recreationists a beautiful setting for nearly any activity. Fancher and Burgess Falls provide beautiful scenic views. Bluffs and steep, forested hillsides enrich the natural beauty of the lake.
GETTING THERE: From Nashville, 50 mi E on I-40 to Center Hill exit. 6 mi S on TN 141.

J. Percy Priest Lake
269 • Seven Points • Map page 504
Nashville • Tennessee
DESCRIPTION: Located near metropolitan Nashville, good fishing is enhanced by rockfish stocked by the Tennessee Wildlife Resources Agency, providing anglers with excellent opportunity. Multipurpose recreation areas dot the shoreline, offering good access and recreational enjoyment. A panoramic view of the lake can be enjoyed from the visitor center near the dam.
GETTING THERE: From Nashville, 5 mi E on I-40 to Stewarts Ferry Pike exit, right on Stewarts Ferry Pike, left on Bell Rd.

Enid Lake
270 • Wallace Creek • Map page 314
Memphis • Tennessee
DESCRIPTION: Just off I-55, this lake has a fishing pier for the handicapped below the dam and an equestrian trail in addition to its numerous campsites and day use facilities.
GETTING THERE: From Memphis, TN, 56 mi S on I-55.

Texas

Waco Lake
271 • Airport • Map page 508
Waco • Texas
DESCRIPTION: Points of interest include Cameron Park, fourth largest municipal park in the U.S., and the Nation's oldest suspension bridge (1870) still in operation.
GETTING THERE: From Waco, 4 mi NW on FM 3051, then left for 1.5 mi on local road.

Lake O' the Pines
272 • Brushy Creek • Map page 508
Jefferson • Texas
DESCRIPTION: Fishing is popular on this 19,780-acre lake.
GETTING THERE: From Jefferson, 4 mi W on TX 49, continue on FM 729 and 726.

Cooper Lake
273 • Cooper Lake • Map page 508
Cooper • Texas
DESCRIPTION: When complete, will impound the South Sulphur River in Delta and Hopkins Counties.
GETTING THERE: From Cooper, 5 mi E on FM 154, then 4 mi S on FM 19.

Proctor Lake
274 • Copperas Creek • Map page 508
Comanche • Texas
DESCRIPTION: Campground is located on Proctor Lake in the historic territory of the Comanche Indians.
GETTING THERE: From Comanche, 5 mi E on US 377,2 mi N on FM 2861.

Stillhouse Hollow Lake
275 • Dana Peak • Map page 508
Belton • Texas
DESCRIPTION: Visit Old Sommers Mill, built in 1866 and still in working order.
GETTING THERE: From Belton 5 mi SW on US 190, 4 mi left on FM 1670.

Lake Texoma
276 • Denison Dam • Map page 508
Denison • Texas
DESCRIPTION: The second most popular Corps lake in the country features Old Fort Washita, maintained as a museum by the Oklahoma Historical Society. A regional visitors center is planned for the lake.
GETTING THERE: From Denison, 5 mi NW on TX 75A.

Sam Rayburn Lake
277 • Ebenezer • Map page 508
Jasper • Texas
DESCRIPTION: A 114,000-acre lake in the Big Thicket country of Texas, with native flora including orchids, insect-eating plants and scores of animal species.
GETTING THERE: From Jasper, 15 mi NW on TX 63, then E on TX 255.

Hords Creek Lake
278 • Flatrock • Map page 508
Coleman • Texas
DESCRIPTION: Camp Colorado, a replica of a military outpost, may be seen in nearby Coleman.
GETTING THERE: From Coleman 8 mi W on FM 53, then 2 mi S on county road.

Wright Patman Lake
279 • Herron Creek • Map page 508
Texarkana • Texas
DESCRIPTION: One of the largest lakes in Texas. Nearby Texarkana offers a variety of recreation opportunities.
GETTING THERE: From Texarkana, 8 mi S on TX 59.

Lake Georgetown
280 • Jim Hogg • Map page 508
Georgetown • Texas
DESCRIPTION: The dam impounds the San Gabriel River in the Hill Country of central Texas.
GETTING THERE: Located 4 mi W of Georgetown via FM 2338, the lake is easily accessible from the Austin area.

Joe Pool Lake
281 • Joe Pool Lake • Map page 508
Dallas • Texas
DESCRIPTION: This lake forms a 7,470-acre impoundment on Mountain Creek.
GETTING THERE: Located SE of TX 360 and I-20. It is easily accessible from the Dallas-Fort Worth Metroplex.

Lavon Lake
282 • Lavonia • Map page 508
Wylie • Texas
DESCRIPTION: The Heard Natural Science Museum and Wildlife Sanctuary in nearby McKinney features natural history exhibits and nature trails.
GETTING THERE: From Wylie, 3 mi E on TX 78,1 mi N on county road.

Belton Lake
283 • Live Oak Ridge • Map page 508
Belton • Texas
DESCRIPTION: Historical sites include the old "Charter Oak" on the Leon River, just below the dam, and the Stage Coach Inn in nearby Salado.
GETTING THERE: From Belton, 3 mi N on TX 317,1 mi NW on FM 2271.

Whitney Lake
284 • Lofers Bend • Map page 508
Whitney • Texas
DESCRIPTION: See the reconstructed Fort Graham, traces of the Old Chisholm Trail, and the dinosaur tracks at nearby Glen Rose.
GETTING THERE: From Whitney, 5 mi SW on TX 22.

Canyon Lake
285 • North Park • Map page 508
New Braunfels • Texas
DESCRIPTION: Area settled by early German immigrants.
GETTING THERE: From New Braunfels,15 mi NW on FM 306.

O.C. Fisher Lake
286 • O.C. Fisher Lake • Map page 508
San Angelo • Texas
DESCRIPTION: Desert plants bloom in this semi-desert region. Turkey, deer and quail are hunted here.
GETTING THERE: Adjacent to the western city limits of San Angelo, off FM 853 and Mercedes Ave.

Navarro Mills Lake
287 • Oak • Map page 508
Corsicana • Texas
DESCRIPTION: Points of interest includes the ghost town of Dresden near Dawson.
GETTING THERE: From Corsicana, 20 mi SW on TX 31,1 mi N on FM 667.

Lewisville Lake
288 • Oakland • Map page 508
Lewisville • Texas
DESCRIPTION: A 540-acre park includes a golf course among its facilities.
GETTING THERE: Located .5 mi NE of downtown Lewisville. At Lewisville, E of 1-35E.

Ray Roberts Lake
289 • Ray Roberts Lake • Map page 508
Sanger • Texas
DESCRIPTION: When completed it will impound 29,350 acres of water on the Elm Fork of the Trinity River in Cooke, Denton and Grayson Counties in north Texas.
GETTING THERE: From Sanger, 5 mi E on FM 455.

Somerville Lake
290 • Rocky Creek • Map page 508
Somerville • Texas
DESCRIPTION: Nearby points of interest include Bluebonnet Trails, Independence Day Trek and Salt Grass Trek.
GETTING THERE: From Somerville, 1 mi W of TX 36.

Pat Mayse Lake
291 • Sanders Cove • Map page 508
Paris • Texas
DESCRIPTION: Visit nearby John C. Gambill Canada Goose Refuge.
GETTING THERE: From Paris, 15 mi N on US 271, 3 mi W on FM 906.

Town Bluff Dam/B.A. Steinhagen Lake
292 • Sandy Creek • Map page 508
Jasper • Texas
DESCRIPTION: Points of interest in this majestic "Big Thicket" region of Texas include 4 National Forests and an Indian Reservation.
GETTING THERE: From Jasper, 15 mi W on US 190, 3 mi S on FM 92.

Grapevine Lake
293 • Silver Lake • Map page 508
Grapevine • Texas
DESCRIPTION: Several large "theme" amusement parks in the vicinity provide varied family entertainment.
GETTING THERE: From Grapevine. 2 mi NE on TX 121.

Benbrook Lake
294 • South Holiday • Map page 508
Benbrook • Texas
DESCRIPTION: Nearby Fort Worth offers stock shows, indoor rodeo, and botanical gardens.
GETTING THERE: From Benbrook, 1 mi S on US 377, 2.5 mi E on county road.

Bardwell Lake
295 • Waxahachie Creek • Map page 508
Ennis • Texas
DESCRIPTION: Close to the Dallas-Fort Worth metropolitan areas.
GETTING THERE: From Ennis, 4.5 mi S on county paved road and TX 34.

Vermont

North Hartland Lake
296 • North Hartland Lake • Map page 544
White River Junction • Vermont
DESCRIPTION: At the upper end of the reservoir, the Ottaquechee River flows through sheer-faced 165- ft-deep Quechee Gorge, one of the outstanding natural spectacles in the state. An overlook area and state-managed campground are nearby. A park with small beach offers swimming, picnicking and boating at the 215- acre lake.
GETTING THERE: From White River Junction, 5 mi S on US 5.

Ball Mountain Lake
297 • Winhall Brook • Map page 544
Brattleboro • Vermont
DESCRIPTION: Winhall Brook Campground (seasonal) offers streamside campsites; modern restrooms with hot showers; trailer dump station and resident campground attendants. The river and 75-acre lake offer fishing, and reservoir lands are open for hunting.
GETTING THERE: From Brattleboro, N on VT 30 to Jamaica to dam. Campground is 5 mi N of dam, off VT 100.

Virginia

John H Kerr Reservoir
298 • Buffalo Park • Map page 546
Petersburg • Virginia
DESCRIPTION: This 50,000-acre lake, one of the largest manmade lakes in the East, is noted for its record striped bass and camping facilities. Camp areas are operated by the Corps, the States of Virginia and North Carolina, and private concessionaires.
GETTING THERE: From Petersburg, 70 mi SW via 1-85 or US 1, then west on US 58 or VA 4.

John W. Flannagan Reservoir
299 • Cranesnest • Map page 546
Haysi • Virginia
DESCRIPTION: Project lands adjoin Jefferson National Forest. Nearby Breaks Interstate Park contains massive geological features.
GETTING THERE: From Haysi, take VA 63, 614 and 739 (total 7 ml).

Lake Moomaw
300 • Gathright Dam • Map page 546
Covington • Virginia
DESCRIPTION: Situated within the George Washington National Forest, recreation facilities are managed by the US Forest Service.
GETTING THERE: From Covington, US 220 N to VA 687, follow project signs to dam site.

Pound Lake
301 • North Fork Pound Lake • Map page 546
Pound • Virginia
DESCRIPTION: A hikers' paradise, lying adjacent to the wooded hills of Jefferson National Forest.
GETTING THERE: From Pound, 1 mi SW on VA 630.

Philpott Lake
302 • Salthouse Branch • Map page 546
Roanoke • Virginia
DESCRIPTION: Nestled in the rugged foothills of the Blue Ridge, adjoining Fairy Stone State Park. Canoe to camp sites on Deer Island.
GETTING THERE: From Roanoke, S on US 220, W on VA 57. N on VA 904.

Washington

Albeni Falls Dam/Lake Pond Oreille
303 • Albeni Cove • Map page 552
Spokane • Washington
DESCRIPTION: Forests and mountains, clear water, sandy beaches and excellent trout fishing are a few of the many attractions of this large lake. RV dump station, boat ramp, marina and a visitor information center are available at the CG.
GETTING THERE: Albeni Cove CG is located approx. 50 mi. NE of Spokane on US HWY 2.

Rufus Woods Lake
304 • Chief Joseph Dam • Map page 552
Chelan • Washington
DESCRIPTION: A visitor center features a view within the world's largest straight line powerhouse as well as interpretive displays. Bridgeport State Park is adjacent to the project. RV dump station, marina and boat launch available at the CG.
GETTING THERE: From Chelan go N approx. 30 mi. on US HWY 7 to state HWY 17. Go E approx. 8 mi. on 17 to Chief Joseph Dam/Rufus Woods Lake CG..

Ice Harbor Lock and Dam/Lake Sacajawea
305 • Fishhook Park • Map page 556
Burbank • Washington
DESCRIPTION: CG is located on Lake Sacajawea near the Snake River. Boat ramp at the CG. Fish and swim from the lake. Camp on the historic Lewis and Clark route located in the CG. An RV dump station, marina, visitor information center and playground is located at the CG.
GETTING THERE: Fishhook Park CG is located approx. 8 mi. E of Burbank on state HWY 124.

Lake Bryan
306 • Little Goose • Map page 556
Starbuck • Washington
DESCRIPTION: Visitor facilities at the fish ladder provide an excellent opportunity to see Pacific salmon and steelhead trout en route from rearing grounds in the Pacific to spawning grounds in the headwaters of the Snake River. RV dump station, boat launch, marina and a visitor information center located in the CG.
GETTING THERE: From Starbuck go NE approx. 8 mi. to Little Goose Lock and Dam CG. (follow signs).

Snake River
307 • Lower Granite • Map page 556
Pomeroy • Washington
DESCRIPTION: A marina and launching ramps are available at this project on the Snake River. RV dump station, boat launch, marina and a visitor information center located in the CG.
GETTING THERE: From Pomeroy go NE approx. 20 mi. to Lower Granite Lock and Dam CG. (follow signs)

Lake West
308 • Lower Monumental • Map page 556
Kahlotus • Washington
DESCRIPTION: Interpretive displays and excellent facilities for viewing Pacific salmon and steelhead trout in route to their spawning grounds on the Snake River are located at the dam. RV dump station, boat launch, marina and a visitor information center located in the CG.
GETTING THERE: From Kahlotus go S approx. 6 mi. to Lower Monumental Lock and Dam CG.

Wynoochee Lake
309 • Wynoochee Lake • Map page 571
Montesano • Washington
DESCRIPTION: Located in a narrow canyon of the Wynoochee River, in the Olympic National Forest, with the Olympic Mountains as a backdrop. Boat launch located in the CG.
GETTING THERE: From Montesano go N approx. 38 mi. on county and forest routes to Wynoochee Lake CG.

West Virginia

Summersville Lake
310 • Battle Run • Map page 588
Mt. Nebo • West Virginia
DESCRIPTION: Noted for its spectacular cliffs and white water on the Gauley River. Near Carnifax Ferry Battlefield State Park, a Civil War battlefield.
GETTING THERE: On WV 129 at Mt.Nebo. 3 mi W of US19.

Sutton Lake
311 • Bee Run • Map page 588
Sutton • West Virginia
DESCRIPTION: With 45 mi of shoreline, this lake attracts fishing and boating enthusiasts. Located in the wooded hills of central West Virginia, 1 mi E of Sutton.
GETTING THERE: Located in the wooded hills of central West Virginia, 1 mi E of Sutton.

Beech Fork Lake
312 • Beech Fork Lake • Map page 588
Huntington • West Virginia
DESCRIPTION: Small lake nestled in the hills of West Virginia with boating and camping opportunities, and solar energy information center.
GETTING THERE: Located 7 mi S of Huntington, just off WV 152.

Bluestone Lake
313 • Bluestone Lake • Map page 588
Hinton • West Virginia
DESCRIPTION: Many artifacts remain from a large Indian town once located on project land.
GETTING THERE: Located at Hinton on WV 3 and 20.

East Lynn Lake
314 • East Fork Campground • Map page 588
Wayne • West Virginia
DESCRIPTION: A region important for natural gas, oil and coal. Wooded hills of 600 ft rise gently around the lake.
GETTING THERE: From Wayne, 12 mi SE on WV 37.

R.D. Bailey Lake
315 • Guyandotte Camp • Map page 588
Justice • West Virginia
DESCRIPTION: Beautiful lake in rugged terrain with visitor center overlooking the lake and many recreational opportunities.
GETTING THERE: Located near Justice, just off US 52.

Burnsville Lake
316 • Riffle Run Camp • Map page 588
Burnsville • West Virginia
DESCRIPTION: Numerous recreation opportunities include excellent hunting. A historical complex with a Civil War battle site is part of this project.
GETTING THERE: Easily accessible from 1-79 at the Burnsville exit.

Stonewall Jackson Lake
317 • Stonewall Jackson Lake • Map page 588
Weston • West Virginia
DESCRIPTION: Accessibility and modern facilities combined with the scenic beauty of the area make Stonewall Jackson Lake extremely attractive to recreationists. The State Park and recreation areas.
GETTING THERE: May be reached via 1-79 at Exit 96 (second Weston exit).

Tygart Lake
318 • Tygart Lake • Map page 588
Grafton • West Virginia
DESCRIPTION: The Tygart State Park supplements Corps facilities at this lake in the West Virginia mountains.
GETTING THERE: 3 mi S of Grafton on County Rd. 9.

Wisconsin

Mississippi River Pool #9
319 • Blackhawk Park • Map page 592
LaCrosse • Wisconsin
DESCRIPTION: Direct access to the main channel and some of the best fishing on the Upper Mississippi River at Pool 9, near La Crosse, WI. Several historical landmarks of the Blackhawk Wars are located near the park. RV dump station, boat launch and a marina located in the CG.
GETTING THERE: From La Crosse go S approx. 20 mi. on state HWY 35.

Mississippi River Pools 11-22
320 • Grant River • Map page 592
Potosi • Wisconsin
DESCRIPTION: A well-developed camping area with numerous conveniences. A boat ramp is located at the CG.
GETTING THERE: Turn E off state HWY 133 at the sign near the southern edge of Potosi, WI. Proceed 2 mi. and turn right on the first improved road.

Full state coverage in handy book form!

Great Maps Make Any Camping Trip Better!

Discover the most scenic trails, the hottest fishing spots, the most fascinating points of interest, and the back roads to get you anywhere you want to go. The **Coleman® Atlas & Gazetteer** series— unbeatable backcountry detail!

Get it all with the Atlas & Gazetteer

- **Topographic Detail**
- **Back Roads**
- **Boat Ramps**
- **Unique Natural Features**
- **Canoe Trips**
- **State and National Parks and Forests**
- **BLM and Other Public Lands**
- **Hiking Trailheads**
- **Points of Interest**

Available for all 50 states, where Coleman products are sold.

www.coleman.com ©2000 The Coleman Company, Inc. COLEMAN® is a registered trademark of The Coleman Company, Inc. used under license. Manufactured by DeLorme, Yarmouth, ME.

CAMPGROUND NOTES

CAMPGROUND NOTES

CAMPGROUND NOTES

CAMPGROUND NOTES

CAMPGROUND NOTES

CAMPGROUND NOTES

CAMPGROUND NOTES

CAMPGROUND NOTES

CAMPGROUND NOTES

CAMPGROUND NOTES

CAMPGROUND NOTES